Y0-CAX-983
WITHDRAWN

Cisco Networking Academy Program: Fundamentals of UNIX Companion Guide

Cisco Systems, Inc.

Cisco Networking Academy Program

Dan Myers

Jim Lorenz

Sponsored By:

Cisco Press

201 West 103rd Street

Indianapolis, Indiana 46290 USA

Cisco Networking Academy Program: Fundamentals of UNIX Companion Guide

Cisco Systems, Inc.
Cisco Networking Academy Program
Dan Myers
Jim Lorenz

Sponsored By Sun Microsystems, Inc.

Published by:
Cisco Press
201 West 103rd Street
Indianapolis, IN 46290 USA

Printed in the United States of America 1 2 3 4 5 6 7 8 9 0

First Printing December 2001

Library of Congress Cataloging-in-Publication Number: 2001091176

ISBN: 1-58713-044-0

Trademark Acknowledgments

All terms mentioned in this book that are known to be trademarks or service marks have been appropriately capitalized. Cisco Press or Cisco Systems, Inc., cannot attest to the accuracy of this information. Use of a term in this book should not be regarded as affecting the validity of any trademark or service mark.

Warning and Disclaimer

This book is designed to provide information about the fundamentals of UNIX. Every effort has been made to make this book as complete and as accurate as possible, but no warranty or fitness is implied.

The information is provided on an "as is" basis. The author, Cisco Press, and Cisco Systems, Inc., shall have neither liability nor responsibility to any person or entity with respect to any loss or damages arising from the information contained in this book or from the use of the discs or programs that may accompany it.

The opinions expressed in this book belong to the author and are not necessarily those of Cisco Systems, Inc.

Feedback Information

At Cisco Press, our goal is to create in-depth technical books of the highest quality and value. Each book is crafted with care and precision, undergoing rigorous development that involves the unique expertise of members from the professional technical community.

Readers' feedback is a natural continuation of this process. If you have any comments regarding how we could improve the quality of this book, or otherwise alter it to better suit your needs, you can contact us through e-mail at networkingacademy@ciscopress.com. Please make sure to include the book title and ISBN in your message.

We greatly appreciate your assistance.

Publisher	*John Wait*
Editor-in-Chief	*John Kane*
Executive Editor	*Carl Lindholm*
Cisco Systems Management	*Michael Hakkert* *Tom Geitner* *William Warren*
Production Manager	*Patrick Kanouse*
Senior Editor	*Sheri Cain*
Copy Editor	*Krista Hansing*
Technical Editor	*Mark Anderson*
Team Coordinator	*Sarah Kimberly*
Cover Designer	*Louisa Klucznik*
Interior Designer	*Steve Gifford*
Indexer	*Tim Wright*

About the Authors

Dan Myers, of Highlands Ranch, Colorado, is an international program manager for the Cisco Networking Academy Program. He is responsible for the worldwide implementation of courses sponsored by various computer and network vendors. Prior to joining Cisco, Dan was the curriculum and operations manager for the Sun Microsystems Academic Initiative Program that authorizes educational institutions to offer Solaris System Administration and Java Programming courses.

As a technical instructor for 15 years, Dan taught Solaris system administration, backup administration, Lotus Domino administration, and computer-aided design courses at vendor-authorized education centers and the University of Colorado. He earned his bachelor of science degree in Technology Education at Ohio State University and his Masters degree in Technology Education at Colorado State University. Dan was the Subject Matter Expert in the development of the Sun sponsored Fundamentals of UNIX course and has 15 years experience working with UNIX.

Jim Lorenz is a senior technical writer and curriculum developer for the Cisco Networking Academy Program. He has more than 20 years experience in information systems and has held various IT positions in several Fortune 500 companies, including Allied-Signal, Honeywell, and Motorola. He was also the manager of information technology and a UNIX system administrator for a division of Harcourt Brace publishing company. Jim has developed and taught computer and networking courses for both public and private institutions for more than 15 years. He is also the author of the Cisco Networking Academy Program Lab Companion manuals.

Jim is a Certified Novell Netware Engineer (CNE), a Microsoft Certified Trainer (MCT), and a Cisco Certified Network Academy Instructor (CCAI). Jim earned his bachelor's degree in computer information systems from Prescott College.

About the Contributor

Brad Johnson is a project manager for the Cisco Networking Academy Program. He has worked in the design and development of many courses offered through the CNAP. He has a bachelor of arts degree from Central Michigan University and a law degree from the University of Denver College of Law. Brad was the project manager in the design, development, and implementation of the Fundamentals of UNIX course.

Dedications

This book is dedicated to my wonderful wife, Jamie, and our kids, Daniel, Audrey, and Grace, who endured my late nights and weekends as I worked on its completion. I would also like to dedicate this book to my parents, Stephen and Margaret, who have always had an endless supply of encouragement and love.

—Dan Myers

This book is dedicated to the three most important people in my life: my wife, Mary, and my daughters, Jessica and Natasha. Thanks for your patience and support.

—Jim Lorenz

Acknowledgments

Many thanks to Brad Johnson, who coordinated the project, providing input, excellent support, and careful technical reviews of content at every step of the way. We worked to an aggressive schedule, and it would not have been possible without the dedication of Brad and the curriculum development support team.

Thanks to Vito Amato and Matthias Giessler from the Cisco Networking Academy Program for providing leadership and management support. Thanks also to the Cisco Press folks for their expertise and assistance in helping this book become a reality, and to Sun Educational Services, Worldwide Education and Research, and the Solaris Marketing Group for their vision and support for the course.

—Dan and Jim

Contents at a Glance

Contents

Foreword

Dear Colleague:

Chosen as the first outside vendor to join the Cisco Networking Academy Program, Sun Microsystems is proud to collaborate with Cisco Systems, Inc. to train students worldwide on the fundamentals of UNIX. Those with direct experience in the deployment and support of enterprise applications fully appreciate the importance of the operating system and computing hardware upon which those applications reside—in simple terms, the platform matters. Because Solaris is widely recognized as the premiere platform for creating and deploying mission-critical networked applications, Cisco and Sun have joined forces to provide the Fundamentals of UNIX course to the Cisco Networking Academy community worldwide.

We invite you to become part of the global Solaris community, built around the operating environment that received top marks from InfoWorld's UNIX survey (*InfoWorld*; 18.January 2001) and leapt ahead of the competition to be named the highest-rated UNIX operating system, according to the results of the D.H. Brown's *2001 UNIX Function Review*. To fully benefit from Sun's resources, you might want to check out the comprehensive list of Sun.com URLs provided on the tearcard in the back of this book.

Welcome to the world of UNIX operating environments and especially to Solaris, the leading UNIX operating environment.

Best regards,

Andy Ingram
Vice President Solaris Marketing
Solaris Software
Sun Microsystems, Inc.

Introduction

The Fundamentals of UNIX course and the accompanying Companion Guide and Lab Companion were developed as a cooperative effort between Cisco Systems and Sun Microsystems to provide an introduction to the UNIX operating system for end users and potential system administrators. The course is offered as part of the Cisco Networking Academy Program.

This course is complementary to the other Cisco networking courses, such as routing and switching, because it provides network operating system (NOS) exposure. Although it might be helpful, it is not necessary to have taken the Cisco networking courses before taking this one. Basic knowledge of UNIX will broaden the skills of the Cisco academy students to include a major network operating system. This course provides a strong foundation for those who want to move on to more advanced courses in UNIX system administration. You will become familiar with powerful UNIX command-line utilities as well as the graphical Common Desktop Environment (CDE). By successfully completing this course, you will be well on your way to becoming a power user, and you will feel comfortable with most varieties of UNIX, including Sun's own Solaris.

UNIX Careers

Knowledge of UNIX is quite valuable in the field of information technology (IT) today. Many of the world's most powerful computer networks and Internet sites are based on UNIX, and there is a tremendous demand for people with skills in UNIX system administration. UNIX is a world-class operating system that supports mission-critical applications. One inhibitor to the growth of UNIX is the lack of trained, qualified personnel who know and understand the UNIX environment. Knowledge of Cisco networking technology along with knowledge of the UNIX network operating system is a strong combination when seeking employment. UNIX system administrators, or sysadmins, are among the highest-paid IT professionals. To gain an appreciation of the demand for UNIX professionals and find out the types of UNIX job opportunities available, look at the job ads in any major newspaper or any job search site on the Internet.

The Goal of This Book

This book is designed to complement the Cisco Networking Academy Fundamentals of UNIX course sponsored by Sun Microsystems. It contains additional content to enhance the online materials, and it offers a variety of learning options. The book contains a hard-copy version of the online curriculum, with added content and supplemental materials to assist in studying.

The following is a summary of the additional features provided in this book to supplement the online curriculum:

- It contains all the information in the online content, providing additional information and going into greater depth on some topics.
- New commands are introduced and explained in this book.
- Each chapter has numerous tips on the use of commands and techniques for practical use.
- Additional real-world examples of UNIX concepts and applications are presented.
- Each chapter has a "Key Terms" section for focused study.
- A list of commands and utilities just introduced is found at the end of each chapter.
- Solaris for Intel download and dual-boot installation instructions are provided.
- The book contains reference guides with the following:
  - The class file system tree structure graphic.
  - UNIX commands quick reference listing all commands used in book/course. A list of commands and utilities is also found at the end of each chapter in which they are introduced.
  - UNIX-to-DOS commands quick reference chart.
  - Commonly used vi editor commands reference.

The book also contains referenced graphics on the inside-front and inside-back covers:

- The class file system tree structure
- UNIX command hierarchy

This Book's Audience

This book is intended for students enrolled in the Cisco Networking Academy Program Fundamentals of UNIX course. It also can be used as a standalone reference for anyone wanting to gain a good basic knowledge of the current UNIX and Sun Microsystems Solaris operating environment. It is introductory in nature and does not presume any previous knowledge of the UNIX operating system. Although it might be helpful, it is not necessary to have taken the Cisco networking courses before taking this one. Basic knowledge of UNIX will broaden the skills of the Cisco academy students to include a major network operating system. This course and text will provide a strong foundation for those who want to move on to more advanced UNIX system administration.

This Book's Features

Many of this book's features help facilitate a full understanding of the information covered in this book:

- **Chapter objectives**—At the beginning of each chapter is a list of objectives to be mastered by the end of the chapter. In addition, the list provides a reference to the concepts covered in the chapter, which can be used as an advanced organizer.
- **Figures, examples, and tables**—This book contains figures, examples, and tables that help explain theories, concepts, and commands; they reinforce concepts and help you visualize the content covered in the chapter. In addition, examples and tables provide such things as command summaries with descriptions, examples of screen outputs, and practical and theoretical information.
- **Chapter summaries**—At the end of each chapter is a summary of the concepts covered in the chapter; it provides a synopsis of each chapter and serves as a study aid.
- **"Check Your Understanding" questions**—The end of each chapter presents review questions that serve as an end-of-chapter assessment. In addition, the questions reinforce the concepts introduced in the chapter and help you test your understanding before you move on to new concepts.
- **Key terms**—In many chapters after the "Check Your Understanding" questions, a list of key terms provides you with a summary of the new terms covered in the chapter. These terms serve as a study aid. In addition, the key terms reinforce the concepts introduced in the chapter and help your understanding of the chapter material before you move on to new concepts. You can find the key terms highlighted in *blue* throughout the chapter where they are used in practice.

Skill Builder

Lab activities—Throughout this book, you see references to the lab activities found in the *Cisco Networking Academy Program: Fundamentals of UNIX Lab Companion*. These labs allow you to make a connection between theory and practice.

Skill Builder

e-Lab activities—Throughout this book, the e-Lab activities found on the accompanying CD-ROM are referenced.

Conventions Used in This Book

In this book, the following conventions are used:

- Key terms, defined at the end of each chapter and in the Glossary, appear in a *blue* color.
- All code examples appear in monospace type, and parts of code use the following conventions:
  - Commands and keywords are in a **bold** type.
  - Arguments, which are placeholders for values that the user inputs, appear in *italics*.
  - Square brackets ([ ]) indicate optional keywords or arguments.
  - Braces ({ }) indicate required choices.
  - Vertical bars (|) are used to separate required choices.

About the CD-ROM

The CD-ROM provided with this book contains all interactive media activities from the online curriculum.

This Book's Organization

This book is divided into 17 chapters, 8 appendixes, and a glossary.

Chapter 1, "The UNIX Computing Environment," presents the history and the main components and capabilities of the UNIX operating system. It reviews operating systems in general and compares UNIX to other operating systems in use today. This chapter also introduces Sun Microsystems' version of the UNIX operating system, known as the Solaris Operating Environment and commonly referred to as Solaris.

Chapter 2, "Accessing Your System and the Common Desktop Environment," discusses the requirements for user accounts and passwords, as well as the procedure for logging in and out of the system using both the command line and the Common Desktop Environment (CDE). The features, functions, and customization of the CDE graphical desktop also are covered.

Chapter 3, "CDE User Applications," presents several useful graphical applications that are included with the graphical CDE, including the Mail Tool for viewing and managing e-mail messages, the Calendar Manager for managing dates and appointments, Voice Notes and Text notes, the Address Manager, Calculator, and Clock.

Chapter 4, "Getting Help," introduces the various forms of help provided by the Solaris environment, including the graphical help available with the CDE; AnswerBook2, is an online version of the Solaris manuals; and command-line help known as manual or "man" pages. This chapter also reviews basic troubleshooting techniques and provides a DOS-to-UNIX cross-reference table for those with a DOS background.

Chapter 5, "Accessing Files and Directories," reinforces file system concepts covered earlier and also introduces the major concept of absolute and relative path names used to identify locations in the directory tree. In addition, commands used to navigate the file system and list the contents of directories are covered. Lastly, the chapter presents metacharacters as a way to manipulate groups of files and directories.

Chapter 6, "Basic Directory and File Management," presents how to create, view, and manipulate files and directories using both the UNIX command line and the CDE File Manager. Commands such as **cat**, **more**, **mkdir**, **touch**, **diff**, and **rm** are covered.

Chapter 7, "Advanced Directory and File Management," explores more advanced file- and directory-management tasks using the command-line interface and the CDE File Manager. Commands used to copy, link, move, and rename files and directories are covered. In addition, the concepts of pipelines and input/output redirection are introduced.

Chapter 8, "File and User Information Utilities," presents an overview of hard-drive technology, physical and logical disk partitions, and file systems. Additionally, file-processing commands used to locate files on a hard drive, search for strings of characters within files, and sort file contents are introduced. Finally, this chapter presents how to identify which users are logged on and how to switch to other user accounts.

Chapter 9, "Using Text Editors," presents an overview of two popular text editors available in UNIX: the vi editor and the CDE Windows-based text editor. In addition to presenting how to use these text editors to create and modify files, there is a discussion of why it is important to learn how to use a text editor from both a user and a system administrator perspective. Finally, there is a short discussion about other popular text editors and UNIX word processor programs.

Chapter 10, "File System Security," provides some guidelines for an overall security policy and then focuses on file system security. Specific attention is given to determining and modifying file and directory access permissions, including user, group, and other permissions. Changing permissions using two command-line methods and the CDE File Manager is covered.

Chapter 11, "UNIX Printing," discusses the various hardware and software elements that provide printing services in the UNIX environment. Both printing and print job management from the command line and CDE are presented.

Chapter 12, "Backing Up Data," discusses the important topic of backing up and restoring data. Focus is given to the most common network- and workstation-backup strategies and the built-in UNIX backup and restore utilities. There is also a discussion of third-party compression programs used in both UNIX and the PC world.

Chapter 13, "System Processes and Memory Management," presents the concept of foreground and background processes, demonstrating the power and flexibility of UNIX. Special attention is given to commands used to identify and manage system processes. At the end of the chapter is a short discussion on the concepts of physical memory, virtual memory, and swap files as they relate to process execution and system performance.

Chapter 14, "Basic Features of the Korn and C Shells," provides a more in-depth discussion of the shell program as the primary user interface and command interpreter on a UNIX system. Focus is given to the three built-in shells (Bourne, C, and Korn) and a brief introduction to other popular third-party shells. This chapter goes into greater detail about the unique features of each shell and provides information on how to become more efficient by using custom prompts, aliases, history, and re-execution of commands. Lastly, there is a discussion about local and global variables used to customize your work environment in preparation for Chapter 15.

Chapter 15, "Customizing Your Login Environment," builds upon the knowledge of shells from the previous chapter. This chapter covers how to automatically have shell features enabled and variables set at login by modifying specific initialization files. It discusses which initialization files get read during the login process for Bourne, C, and Korn shells, and it covers what is contained in each file, allowing for easy customization of the working environment.

Chapter 16, "Network Basics," provides an introduction to networking technologies and concepts. Presented in this chapter are the most common examples of networking architectures, protocols, and topologies, along with an explanation of the concept of client/server networking. The chapter also covers UNIX network commands and utilities such as **ping**, **telnet**, **rlogin**, and **ftp**. Additionally, this chapter contains a discussion of network naming services such as Domain Name Service (DNS) and Network Information Service (NIS). Lastly, there is an introduction to the distributed Network File System (NFS).

Chapter 17, "Career Guidance," provides information and resources for students who want to learn more about UNIX. It discusses careers in UNIX system administration, covers the process for obtaining certification in Solaris system administration, and concludes with an overview of the Sun Academic Initiative, a program that offers Solaris system administration courses from Sun Education to authorized educational institutions.

Appendix A, "Check Your Understanding Answer Key," provides the answers to the "Check Your Understanding" questions that you find at the end of each chapter.

Appendix B, "Master Command List," provides an alphabetized list of commands used in this book.

Appendix C, "vi Editor Quick Reference," provides a list of the most frequently used vi editor commands.

Appendix D, "Solaris for Intel Download and Installation Instructions," provides the download site for obtaining a free copy of Solaris for Intel for personal use. Tips for installing Solaris for Intel and Solaris for Intel support Web sites are also provided.

Appendix E, "mailx," provides information on how to use the UNIX mailx command-line mail program.

Appendix F, "e-Lab Activities Listing," lists all the activities on the accompanying CD-ROM.

Appendix G, "Hands-On Lab Listing," provides an outline of the lab activities that are referenced throughout this book. The full labs can be found in *Cisco Networking Academy Program: Fundamentals of UNIX Lab Companion*.

NOTE

Instructors: Support, information, downloads, and tools can be found at cisco.netacad.net.

Appendix H, "Web Site Resources," provides recommended sites for further study.

The Glossary defines the terms and abbreviations used in this book.

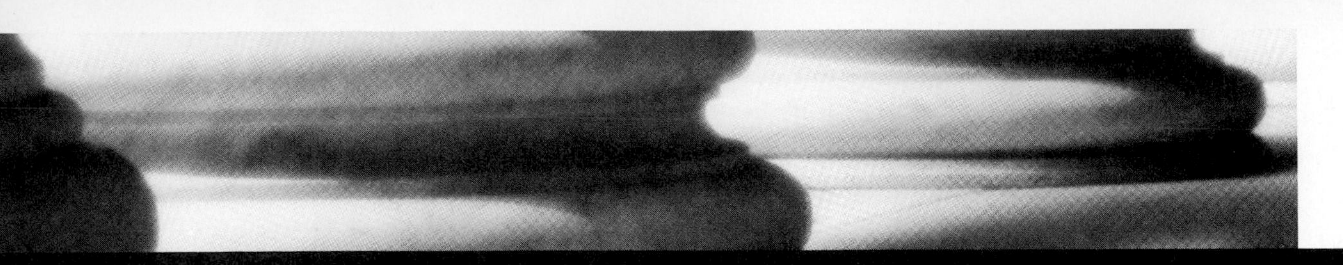

Objectives

After reading this chapter, you will be able to

- Describe the main components of a computer
- Identify and compare various computer operating systems
- Describe the features common to all versions of the UNIX operating system
- Describe the main components of the Solaris Operating Environment

Chapter 1

The UNIX Computing Environment

Introduction

In this chapter, you learn about the main components of a computer and the history, components, and capabilities of the UNIX operating system. You review operating systems in general and see how UNIX compares to other types of operating systems. This chapter also introduces the Sun Microsystems version of the UNIX operating system known as the *Solaris Operating Environment* (commonly referred to as Solaris).

The Main Components of a Computer

The four main components of a computer are the *random-access memory (RAM)*, the *central-processing unit (CPU)*, the *Input/Output (I/O)*, and the hard disk or other mass storage devices (see Figure 1-1).

CPU

The CPU is the computer logic microprocessor chip that executes (processes) instructions that are received from the primary computer memory (RAM). These instructions are stored in binary language.

RAM

RAM, in the form of microchips, is normally located on the motherboard or the memory board of the computer. It is the main computer memory, often referred to as *primary memory* or *working memory.* Primary memory is the part of memory in which the activity of the running system takes place. When you hear, "My system has 128 MB (megabytes) of memory," the speaker is talking about primary memory (RAM).

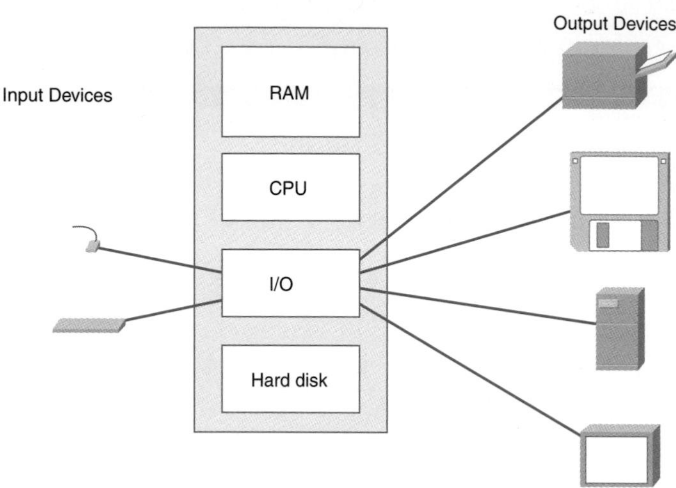

Figure 1-1 The main components of a computer.

Operating systems and software programs usually reside on the hard disk. When the computer is booted, an image or copy of the operating system is loaded into RAM. When a program is activated, an image or copy of that program is loaded into RAM. Images in RAM remain as long as they are needed. When these images are no longer required, they are overwritten by other images. If power is lost or the system is rebooted, images in RAM disappear.

I/O

The I/O portion of the computer accepts or reads input from a device (such as your keyboard) into memory, or it writes output from memory to a device. For example, the keyboard and the mouse are the primary user input devices; the monitor and the printer are the primary output devices. Disk drives and tape drives are considered both input and output because they can be read from as well as written to. A normal CD-ROM drive is an output device, but a CD-R (recordable) and CD-RW (read/write) are considered both input and output devices. A monitor also can be an input device if it has a touch screen.

Hard Disk (or Other Forms of Mass Storage)

The hard disk is a magnetic storage device in which information is stored. All files, including the operating system and applications or utilities, are stored on a hard disk. The contents of the hard disk are managed by the file system, which will be covered later. Forms of optical storage, such as CD-ROMs, DVDs, and CD-Rs, are becoming standard components on many new computers.

Overview of Computer Operating Systems

All computers require an operating system (OS) to manage their functions, regardless of the manufacturer and whether it is a microcomputer, midrange computer, or mainframe computer. OSs can be divided into two major categories: single user (desktop) and multiuser (network).

Desktop Operating Systems

Most desktop operating systems are single-user systems, which means that they can keep track of only what one user is doing at a time. DOS and Windows 3*x* are examples of single-user desktop operating systems because only the activities of one user can be managed or only one user can be logged in at a time. Windows 9*x*, NT Workstation, Windows 2000 Professional, and Mac OS have some networking capabilities for peer-to peer workgroup networking, but they are largely considered single-user desktop operating systems.

UNIX also can serve as a desktop operating system, but primarily for use with high-end workstations. Examples of these include engineering and scientific applications, which require dedicated high-performance computers. Specific applications that frequently run on UNIX workstations include computer-aided design (CAD), electronic circuit design, weather data analysis, computer graphics and animation, and medical equipment management.

Network Operating Systems

Network operating systems (NOS) usually are installed on a powerful server or central host systems on all but the smallest networks. The focus here is on server- (or host-) based NOSs. Most OSs, in general, are designed to work with a particular manufacturer's CPUs. Some can run on different manufacturers' CPUs, and some can support multiple CPUs of the same type. OSs and CPUs often are classified based on the number of bits they can manipulate. The more bits they can manipulate, the more powerful the CPU and the OS are. Early NOSs and CPUs were 16-bit. Most of today's NOSs and CPUs are 32-bit (with some being 64-bit). Examples of NOSs include UNIX, Windows NT/2000 Server, Novell NetWare, and various mainframe OSs (see Figure 1-2). Mainframe NOSs include Digital Equipment VMS, Hewlett-Packard MPE, IBM MVS, and several varieties of UNIX. Solaris or SunOS is the Sun Microsystems version of UNIX.

Although UNIX is used frequently as a workstation OS for high-performance applications, it is not generally considered an end-user desktop OS. It is most often used on servers as an NOS and is a popular one used with Internet Web servers.

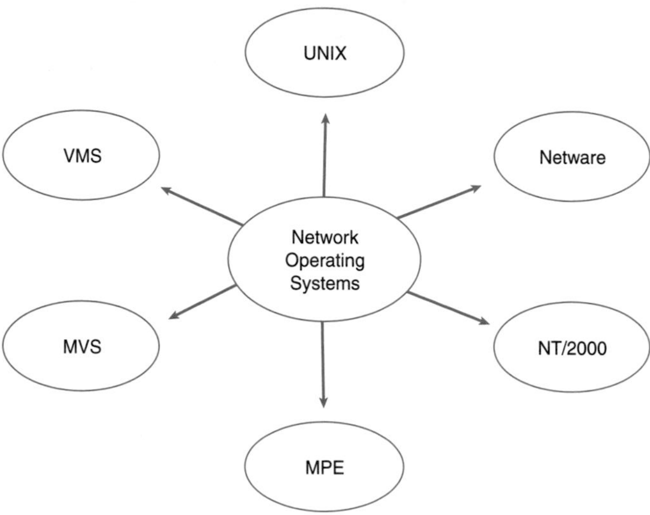

Figure 1-2
Network operating systems.

NOS Capabilities

UNIX and most other modern NOSs support advanced features, including the following:

- Multiuser capability
- Multitasking
- Distributed processing

Multiuser capability enables more than one user to access the same resources, thus providing support for many users simultaneously. The OS keeps track of each resource, such as CPU, RAM, hard disk, and printers, and allows them all to be shared. Each program or application that runs is referred to as a task or process. *Multitasking* enables the OS to keep track of several processes simultaneously, which allows more than one tool or application to be used at one time. *Distributed processing* enables the use of resources across the network. For example, a user might be sitting at a workstation and would be able to access files and applications on the hard disk of another computer or a printer located on a remote part of the network. See Figure 1-3.

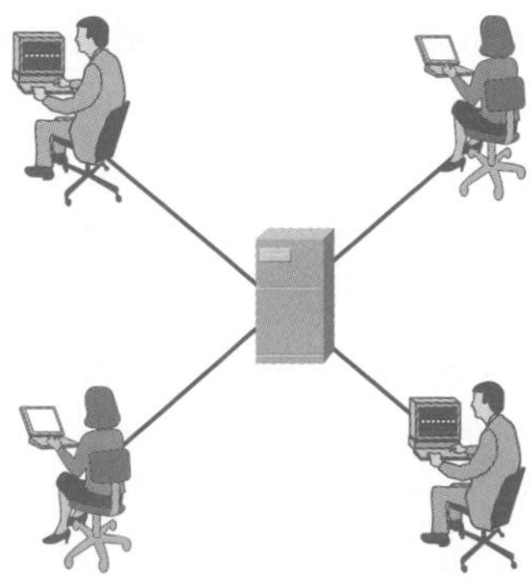

Figure 1-3
Distributed computing environment.

Overview of the UNIX Operating System

The UNIX operating system originally was developed at AT&T Bell Labs (with involvement from General Electric and the Massachusetts Institute of Technology) in the mid-1960s as a multiuser operating system called *Multics* (Multiplexed Information and Computing Service). Multics was an interactive operating system written for a specific General Electric computer that, after several years of development, proved to be expensive; Bell Labs thus withdrew from the project.

Ken Thompson, a Multics programmer at Bell Labs, wrote a space travel game for the GE computer before the Multics project lost its funding. With the help of another programmer, Dennis Ritchie, he rewrote the game to run on a Digital Equipment Corporation (DEC) PDP-7 computer that had a better graphics display. The DEC computer was great for running the space travel game, but it lacked a viable OS. In 1969, Thompson got the urge to develop his own OS. Originally, Thompson called the new OS that he had developed with a colleague UNICS (UNiplexed Information and Computing Service). The name was eventually changed to UNIX. The space travel game later was modified to run under UNIX.

UNIX was first written in *assembly language*, a primitive set of instructions that controls the computer's internal instructions, but it could run on only a specific computer. In 1971, Ritchie created the *C language*. In 1973, he and Thompson rewrote the UNIX system programs in C. Because C is a higher-level language, UNIX then could be moved (or ported) to another computer with far less programming effort. The decision to develop this portable operating system proved to be the key to the success of UNIX.

The early UNIX source code was made available to universities all over the country. Programmers at the University of California at Berkeley made significant modifications to the original source code and called it ***Berkeley Software Distribution (BSD)*** UNIX.

They sent this new version of the UNIX environment to other programmers around the country, who then added tools and code as they saw fit. Possibly the most important advance made to the software by the programmers at Berkeley was the addition of networking software, which allowed the OS to function in a local-area network (LAN). BSD UNIX became popular with computer manufacturers such as Hewlett-Packard, Digital Equipment Corporation, and Sun Microsystems.

The Sun Microsystems original version of UNIX, the Sun operating system (SunOS) was based on BSD UNIX Version 4.2. At that time, AT&T's version of the UNIX environment was known as System V (system 5). In 1988, Sun OS/BSD, AT&T System V Release 3, and XENIX (a version of UNIX developed by Microsoft for PCs with Intel processors) were combined into what became ***System V Release 4 (SVR4)***. This new generation of the OS was an effort to combine the best features of both BSD and AT&T UNIX, to create an industry standard for the OS. This enabled software to be developed for UNIX without consideration for whether it was System V or BSD 4.2. The new SVR4 became the basis for most of the current varieties of UNIX. The timeline shown in Figure 1-4 lists some of the major events in the evolution of the UNIX OS.

Figure 1-4
A brief history of UNIX.

A Brief History of UNIX

1969—Ken Thompson and Dennis Ritchie of AT&T Bell Laboratories start developing what was to become UNIX.
1973—UNIX was rewritten in C making it a portable operating system able to run on different computers.
1975—Version 6 distributed outside of Bell Labs. The first BSD version (1.x) was derived from V6.
1980—Microsoft introduces Xenix and 4.2 BSD becomes widely used.
1982—AT&T's UNIX System Group (USG) release System III, the first public release outside Bell Labs.
1984—University of California at Berkeley releases 4.2BSD, includes TCP/IP and much more.
1984—SVR2 System V Release 2 introduced. Approximately 100,000 UNIX installations around the world.
1986—4.3BSD released, including internet name server.
1987—System V Release 3 (SVR3) released. Approximately 750,000 UNIX installations around the world.
1988—UNIX System V Release 4 (SVR4) released, unifying System V, BSD and Xenix.
1991—UNIX System Laboratories (USL) becomes a company - majority-owned by AT&T. Linus Torvalds begins development of Linux.
1992—USL releases UNIX System V Release 4.2 (SVR4.2). Novell announces intent to acquire USL.
1993—4.4BSD the final release from Berkeley. Novell acquires USL.
1999—UNIX turns 30. Linux 2.2 kernel released.

UNIX Varieties

The two main versions of UNIX are System V (SVR4) and BSD. Currently, a number of varieties, or flavors, of UNIX exist. Most are similar because they are based on the industry standard SVR4. (The other varieties are based on BSD.) You can tell if you are working on a System V- or BSD-based version of UNIX by knowing which command you use to print. (You use **lp** for System V and **lpr** for BSD-based systems.) Or, you can tell by which command is used to determine what processes are running (**ps –ef** for System V and **ps –aux** for BSD). Other differences exist with system administration commands.

UNIX is now a trademarked name (owned by The Open Group, www.opengroup.org), so each vendor called its version of UNIX by a unique name. Sun's version of UNIX is called Solaris and it is the most widely used version in networking today. AT&T's version is referred to as UNIX. IBM's version is AIX, Hewlett-Packard's is HP-UX, and Digital Equipment's (now Compaq's) is called Ultrix. These varieties of UNIX are designed to run on the hardware and CPUs made by the manufacturer (IBM, HP, and so on). Solaris runs not only on Sun computers, but also on Intel-based machines. By learning any one of these UNIX varieties, it is fairly easy to move to one of the others.

The latest version of UNIX to emerge is called Linux. It was developed to run on the Intel microprocessor (even an 80386) from workstations to large servers. It has become popular among computer enthusiasts, those looking for an alternative to traditional PC operating systems, and companies looking for a stable, low-cost OS.

Linux originally was developed in 1992 by Linus Torvalds at the University of Helsinki, Finland, who posted it on the Internet and encouraged others to contribute to its development. Periodically, a group of developers review and test the latest contributions and release a stable version of the OS.

Linux is free under the GNU General Public License (www.gnu.org). However, you can go to a computer store and discover several companies that are bundling Linux along with other products (such as office-suite software, a graphical desktop, Web server software, and so on) for a fee.

Figure 1-5 shows some of the CPU manufacturers and the various UNIX versions and operating systems that they can run.

Benefits of UNIX

UNIX is an open standard, and although it varies somewhat from one manufacturer to another, it is basically still UNIX. Nearly all major computer manufacturers support some form of UNIX, a tribute to its importance as an operating system. It is one of the most powerful, flexible, and scalable OSs in the world.

Figure 1-5
UNIX varieties.

CPU Manufacturer	UNIX OS Version	Propriety
IBM	AIX	MVS, VM
Hewlett Packard	HP-UX	MPE
Digital Equipment (Compaq)	Tru64, Ultrix	VMS
Sun Microsystems	Solaris (SunOS)	
Intel	Solaris, Linux	NetWare, Win9*x*, NT, Win2000

In general, UNIX continues to advance its position as the "bulletproof" OS of choice for mission-critical applications. Mission-critical applications are those that are crucial to the operation of a business or other organization. UNIX is also tightly integrated with the Transmission Control Protocol/Internet Protocol (TCP/IP). TCP/IP basically grew out of UNIX because of the need for LAN and WAN communications. TCP/IP is the acknowledged standard protocol of the Internet and many private networks. All computers (workstations and servers) running the TCP/IP protocols are referred to as "hosts" and are given an IP address and a host name. The IP address is what allows the host to be uniquely identified on the Internet. If a local translation file or a name server is available, the computer can be referred to by its name, which then is translated to its IP address. The TCP/IP protocols, IP addresses, and name servers will be covered more in Chapter 16, "Network Basics."

The Sun Microsystems Solaris Operating Environment, with its core OS, SunOS, is a high-performance, versatile, 64-bit implementation of UNIX. Solaris runs on a wide variety of computers, from Intel-based personal computers to powerful mainframes and supercomputers. Solaris is currently the most widely used version of UNIX in the world for large networks and Internet Web sites. Sun is also the developer of the Write Once, Run Anywhere Java technology. The benefits of UNIX and Solaris, in particular, are summarized in Figure 1-6.

Figure 1-6
The benefits of UNIX.

Solaris UNIX Benefits

Industry Standards-Based Operating System

Powerful, Flexible, Scalable, and Secure

Supported by Various Equipment Manufacturers

Mature and Stable Operating System

Tightly Integrated with TCP/IP Protocols

Widely Used for Mission Critical Applications

The Solaris Operating Environment

The OS environment on Sun systems is called the *Solaris Operating Environment*. The Solaris environment consists of the SunOS 5.*x* operating system, the *Open Network Computing (ONC) protocols*, and a graphical user interface (GUI). SunOS 5.*x* is a multiuser, multitasking NOS that is based on the standard SVR4 UNIX operating system. ONC is a family of published networking protocols and distributed services that enables remote resource sharing, among other things. The Solaris environment supports three graphical interfaces: *Common Desktop Environment (CDE)*, *GNOME*, and *Open Windows* (see Figure 1-7). You are introduced to CDE in this book.

Figure 1-7 The Solaris operating environment.

Solaris Operating Environment Key Components

SunOS 5.*x* UNIX Operating System

Open Network Computing (ONC) Protocols

Graphical User Interface (CDE or Open Windows)

SunOS Operating System

SunOS is a set of programs that manages all computer operations. It also provides a link between the user and system resources, converting requests that come from the mouse or the keyboard into computer operations. Most OSs, including UNIX, have four main components: the *kernel*, the shell, the *file system*, and commands or utilities. The kernel manages the operation of the computer. The shell provides for interaction between the user and the computer. The file system provides a way to organize and manage the information on the computer's hard disk(s), and the commands are used to instruct the computer to perform tasks. These main components are summarized in Figure 1-8. Much of the following information applies to all varieties of UNIX, although some of the information is Solaris-specific.

Figure 1-8 Main OS components.

Main Operating System Components

Kernel—Manages the operation of the computer

Shell—Provides a user interface to the computer

File System—Organizes information on the computer

Commands—Instruct the computer to perform a task

The OS Kernel

The *kernel* is the core OS with the necessary basic capabilities to run the computer. The kernel is the closest to the CPU and hardware. It is an executable file that gets loaded when the computer boots and is conventionally named *unix* (System V-based systems) or *vmunix* (BSD-based system). Genunix is a platform-independent generic kernel file that is combined with a platform-specific kernel file called unix (such as for a SUN Ultra 5 computer) during the boot process. These combined two files create the static core kernel that initializes and controls the system. After the kernel loads, it performs the following functions (see Figure 1-9):

- Manages devices, memory, and processes
- Controls the functions (transmission of information) between the system programs (utilities) and the system hardware
- Manages functions such as swap space, daemons, and file systems:
  - *Swap space*—A reserved part of the hard disk for the kernel to use during processing. Portions of running programs can be "swapped out" of RAM to the hard disk and then brought back into RAM later, if needed. This swap space is actually on the hard disk, but it looks like additional memory or RAM and is sometimes called virtual memory.
  - *Daemons*—Programs or processes that perform a particular task or monitor disks and program execution. Daemons are special processes that begin after the OS loads. Daemons then wait for something to do in support of the OS. They can be started or stopped as necessary. An example is the printer daemon, lpsched (line printer scheduler). It starts when the system starts up and then waits in the background until someone needs to print something. Daemons in the UNIX world are similar to Services with Windows NT/2000 or Netware Loadable Modules (NLMs) with Novell NetWare.
  - **File Systems**—A hierarchy of directories, subdirectories, and files that organize and manage the information on hard disks. File systems can be either local or remote. Local file systems are located on the hard disk of your workstation. Remote file systems are located on another computer, which is usually a server.

Figure 1-9
The kernel functions.

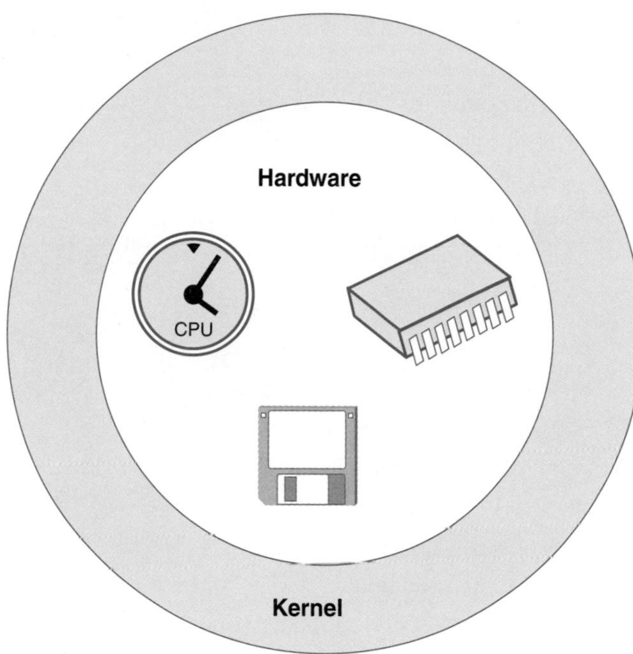

The Shell

A *shell* is an interface between the user and the kernel (see Figure 1-10). It acts as an interpreter or translator. In other words, the shell accepts commands issued by you, interprets these commands, and executes the appropriate programs. Shells can be command-line–driven or graphical. Three command-line shells are available in the Solaris UNIX environment. It is possible to initiate or switch between these shells when working on the computer. You can use the **ps** (process status) or **echo $SHELL** commands to see which shell you are using. The Solaris Operating Environment has six available shells that come with Solaris 8. The three primary command-line shells (available in all UNIX versions) are the ***Bourne shell***, the ***Korn shell***, and the ***C shell***. The other three shells, BASH, Z shell, and TC shell, have been gaining in popularity among UNIX users.

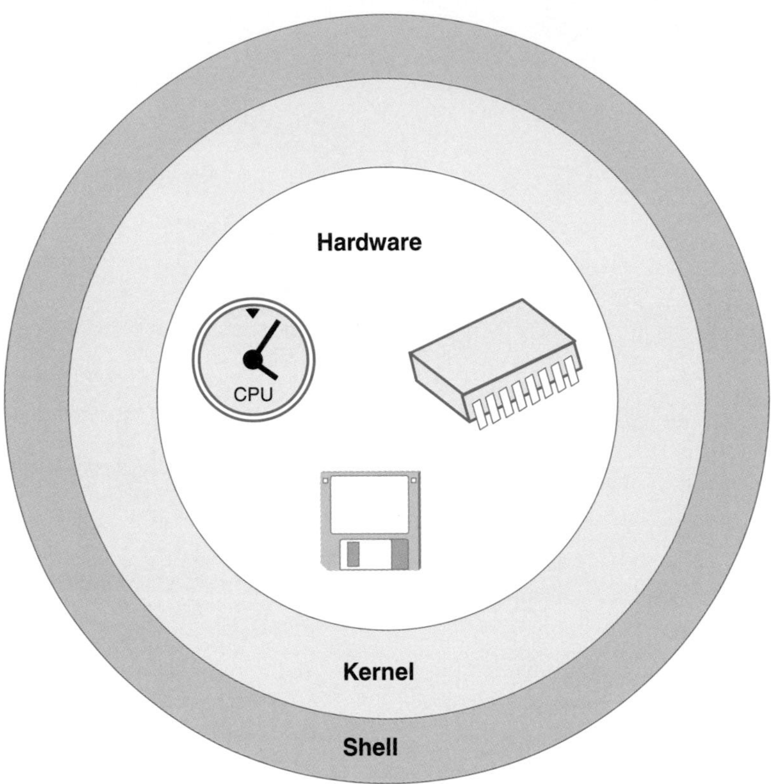

Figure 1-10
The shell functions.

- **Bourne shell** ($)—The Bourne shell (/bin/sh) was the original shell program for the UNIX. It is the default shell for the Solaris computing environment. Stephen Bourne developed the Bourne shell for the AT&T System V.2 UNIX environment. This shell does not have aliasing or history capabilities. System administrators mostly use it. The Bourne shell prompt is a dollar sign (**$**) which is similar to a DOS C:\> prompt.
- **Korn shell** ($)—The Korn shell (/bin/ksh) is a superset of the Bourne shell and was developed by Stephen Korn at Bell Labs. It has many of the Bourne shell features, plus added features such as aliasing and history. This is the most widely used shell and is the industry standard for system users. The Korn shell prompt is also a dollar sign ($).
- **C shell** (%)—The C shell (/bin/csh) is based on the C programming language. Similar to the Korn shell, it has additional features such as aliasing and history. The C shell was developed by Sun's Bill Joy and is still widely used today. The C shell prompt is a percent sign (%).

NOTE

Examples given in this book are based primarily on the Korn shell.

- **Others**—Other shell programs are available for UNIX systems. The more popular ones are the following:
  - — **Bash**—GNU (www.gnu.org). Bourne-Again Shell (bash) that has the feel of the Bourne and Korn shells that incorporates features from the C and Korn shells.
  - — **TC shell**—The TC shell (tcsh) is a popular variant of the C shell that supports command-line editing and command-line completion.
  - — **Z shell**—The Z shell closely resembles the Korn shell, but it has many other enhancements.

The File System

The file system provides a way to separate and keep track of the information on a hard disk. The Solaris operating environment file structure is a hierarchy of directories, subdirectories, and files that are grouped together for a specific purpose. The file system is integrated with the kernel to provide an organizational structure for your software and data (see Figure 1-11). The file structure subdivides hard disks to make them more manageable, and it enables users to locate files. Hard disks can be divided into file systems, directories, subdirectories, and files. The file system organizes your data similar to the way a file cabinet stores information. The file system is like the file cabinet, directories are like drawers, subdirectories are like folders, and files are like the pages in a folder.

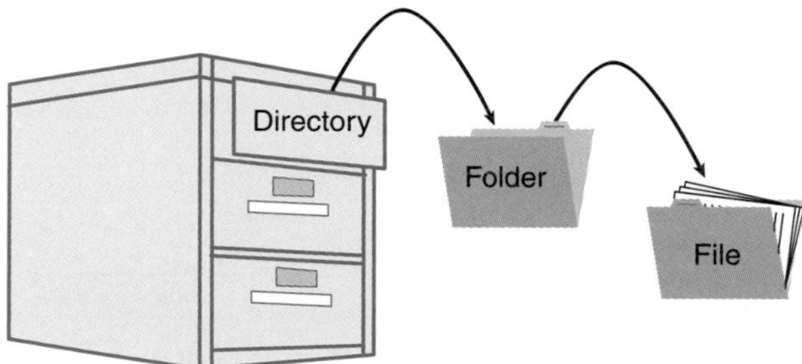

Figure 1-11
The organization of a file system.

A *directory* hierarchy looks like an inverted tree, with the root at the top (see Figure 1-12). The following is the hierarchy of the UNIX file system:

- **File system**—A group of directories that can be thought of as a separate tree structure. A hard disk can be divided into multiple separate file systems, which are similar to logical partitions in the Windows/DOS world (like drive C: or D:) or volumes, as with Novell NetWare. The file systems can be made available (mounted) or unavailable (unmounted) at the administrator's discretion. Each file system has its own directory structure and can be either local (on your computer) or remote (on another computer).

- **Directory**—A location for files and other subdirectories. The Solaris file system, or directory structure, enables you to create files and directories accessed through a hierarchy of directories. A directory is like a file drawer in a file cabinet. The highest directory in the directory structure of a file system is the root directory, which is designated as a single forward slash (/).
- *Subdirectory*—Any directory below another directory. For example, some of the subdirectories under the root (/) directory are /usr, /etc, and /kernel.
- *Files*—Files are contained in directories and subdirectories. They are the lowest level of the file system. There are usually thousands of files on a hard disk and there are several different types:
  - **Directories**—Directories are considered a type of file under the UNIX file system.
  - **Plain ASCII (American Standard Code for Information Interchange)**—These files are pure text files, with no special formatting characters in them.
  - **Application files**—These files are created by an application such as a word processor, spreadsheet, or database program.
  - **Executable programs**—These are UNIX utility commands and application programs.

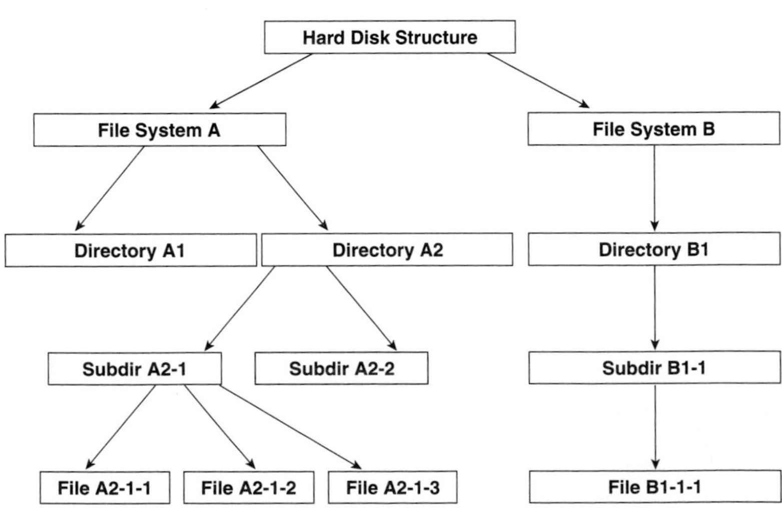

Figure 1-12
The file-system directory hierarchy.

Common Solaris Directories

The topmost directory in a file system is called the *root directory*. It is the starting point of the file-system hierarchy. The root directory (/) is required for the operating system to function, and it contains critical system files (such as the kernel). The following list contains some of the more important directories and their purposes. The slash in front of these directories indicates that they are actually subdirectories of the root directory (see Figure 1-13):

- **/bin (binary) directory**—Contains many of the UNIX commands.
- **/usr/bin (user) directory**—Contains executable commands, system administration utilities, and library routines.
- **/usr/ucb**—Contains commands originally developed under BSD. They exist because some users prefer the BSD version of a command to the System V version.
- **/opt (optional) directory**—Contains Sun's unbundled software applications and third-party applications.
- **/etc (etcetera) directory**—Contains system administration files, such as the passwd file. (Commonly referred to as et-cee for "etcetera.")
- **/export/home directory***—Contains the user home directories. Depending on how the system has been set up by the administrator, the home directories can instead be found in /home.
- **/dev (devices) directory**—Contains files that are pointers to device names. All devices in UNIX have standard filenames.
- **/kernel directory***—Contains the basic operating system files, such as the main UNIX kernel genunix.
- **/sbin (single user binaries)directory**—Contains essential executables used in the booting process and in system failure recovery. Also includes some system-administration utilities.
- **/tmp (temp) directory**—Contains temporary files placed by users. Occasionally, files in /tmp get deleted by an administrator or automatically are deleted as part of system startup.
- **/var (variable) directory**—Contains print spooling and mail system error messages.

NOTE

The directories indicated by a * are specific to Solaris.

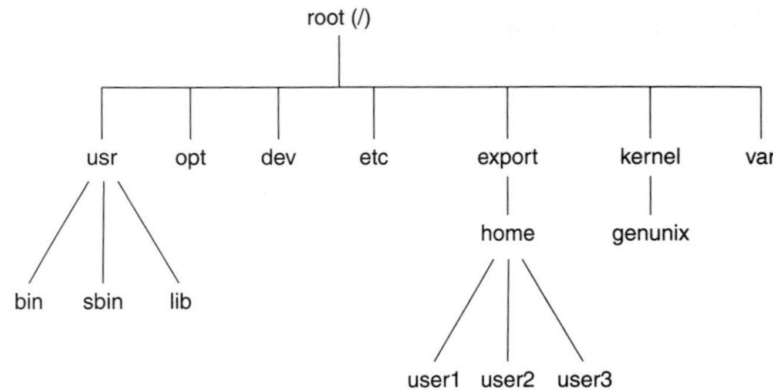

Figure 1-13
Common Solaris subdirectories.

Commands

The UNIX operating system comes with more than 350 commands and utility programs used for administration (adding new users, printers, disks, and so on), file maintenance (creating, editing, copying, deleting, printing, and so on), networking/communication, programming, and obtaining help.

Commands tell the shell what to do, such as list the contents of a directory or copy a file. Some commands are built into the shell program, such as change directory (**cd**) and **exit**, but most reside on the hard drive, typically in a directory named bin (which is short for binary code).

Graphical User Interface Options

All modern operating systems include a graphical user interface (GUI). A number of popular ones, including Microsoft Windows, UNIX CDE, and several others, will be covered.

Common Desktop Environment

Sun Microsystems was the first company to use a windowing environment in conjunction with the UNIX OS. In 1993, a consortium of UNIX platform vendors was formed to develop an integrated, standard, and consistent GUI desktop environment. The contributors included Hewlett-Packard, IBM, Novell, and Sun Microsystems, along with many other companies and members of the Open Software Foundation (OSF), X/Open, and the X Consortium. CDE is Motif-based, and users of other UNIX and personal computer (PC) desktops should be comfortable using CDE; many of the features are common to other desktop environments. The CDE offers the following for users:

- Provides a GUI between the user and the OS
- Includes built-in menus for users to select and run utilities and programs without using Solaris Environment commands

- Provides more than 300 utility programs and tools
- Enables users to control multiple documents or applications on the screen at the same time
- Controls activities in windows using both the mouse and the keyboard

Figure 1-14 represents some of the major programs and tools available with CDE, including Calendar, file management, e-mail, printer management, and notes. CDE is discussed in greater detail in subsequent chapters.

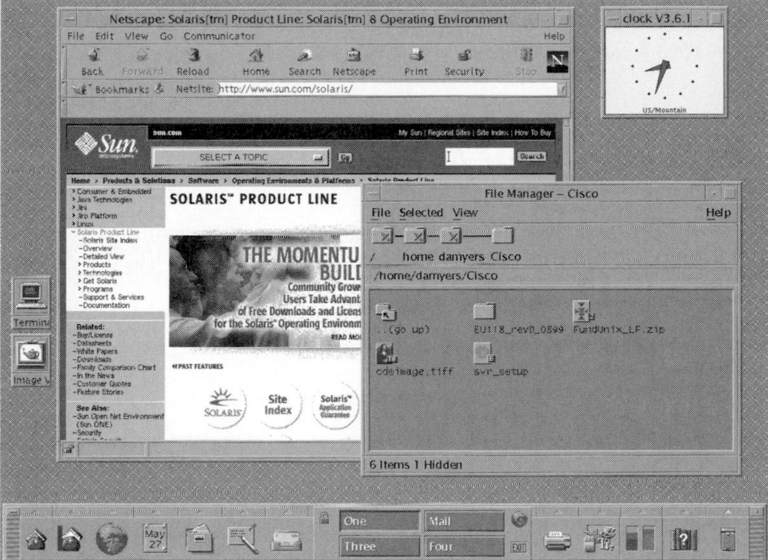

Figure 1-14
CDE graphical user interface.

GNOME

The latest windowing system to emerge in the UNIX world is the *GNU Network Object Model Environment (GNOME)*. GNOME is part of the GNU open source software project. GNOME has built an easy-to-use desktop environment for the user and a powerful application framework for the software developer, free of cost.

GNOME (http://gnome.org) is included in most BSD versions of UNIX and with the GNU/Linux distribution. GNOME also works with many other UNIX systems, including Solaris (www.sun.com/gnome).

With its intuitive user interface, GNOME combines advanced desktop organization and navigational features that enable easy access to information. It provides excellent usability, appearance, and personalization to match a user's unique working style. The GNOME v.1.4 Desktop key features include the following:

- Attractive, intuitive user interface
- Personalization capabilities
- Convenient front panel for rapid access to favorite programs
- Full suite of powerful applications
- Capability to run existing CDE and Java-based applications

Open Windows

Open Windows is Sun's original GUI developed for the Solaris environment (see Figure 1-15). It is similar to CDE, but it is proprietary and not well supported. The user has a choice when logging into a Solaris workstation to select either CDE or Open Windows.

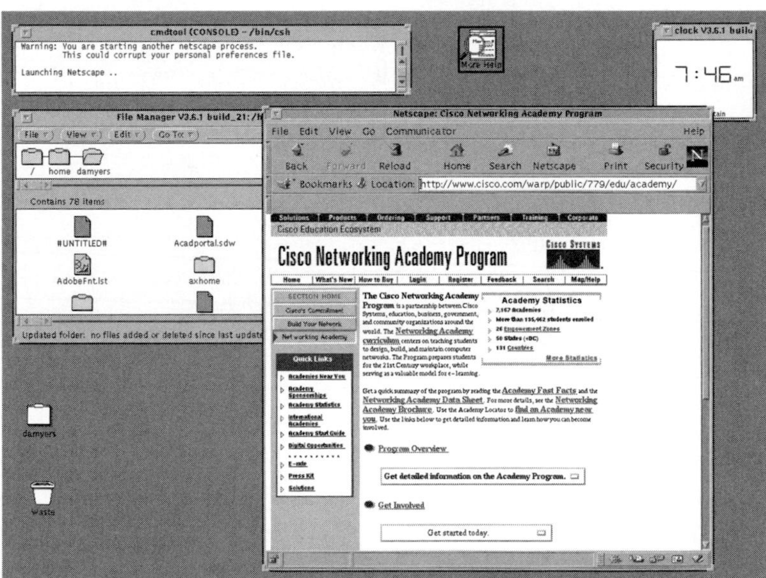

Figure 1-15
The Open Windows graphical user interface.

Skill Builder

Lab Activity 1.4.3

UNIX Computing Environment

This lab exercise reviews UNIX computing environment terminology and helps reinforce the concepts introduced in this chapter. You also can investigate the use of UNIX at your institution or another organization and research Web sites to see what organizations are using Solaris UNIX. Refer to the *Cisco Networking Academy Program: Fundamentals of UNIX Lab Companion.*

Summary

Now that you have completed this chapter, you should have an understanding of the following:

- The main components of a computer are RAM, CPU, I/O, and disk. They are controlled by the operating system.
- Most desktop operating systems are intended for use by a single user. Network operating systems such as UNIX usually are installed in servers that can support many users and large networks.
- UNIX originally was developed at Bell Labs, and significant improvements were made at UC Berkeley, including the addition of networking capabilities. The industry standard SVR4 lead to the development of several current varieties of UNIX, including Sun Microsystems Solaris.
- The key pieces of the Solaris Operating Environment are the SunOS, the Open Network Computing (ONC) protocols, and the CDE GUI.
- The main components of the SunOS are the kernel, the shell, the file system, and commands. The kernel manages hardware, daemons, swap space, and the file system. The shell is an interpreter that provides an interface between the kernel and the user. The file system manages and organizes and information on the hard disk. Commands dictate what action the shell is to take.

Check Your Understanding

1. All of the following are main components of a computer system *except*:
   - **A.** Memory
   - **B.** Hard disk
   - **C.** CPU
   - **D.** CD-ROM
2. Which type of computer does a network operating system normally running on, and how many users can it accommodate?
   - **A.** Server computer with a single user
   - **B.** Workstation computer with a single user
   - **C.** Server computer with multiple users
   - **D.** Workstation computer with multiple users
3. What industry-standard UNIX operating system became the basis for many of today's varieties of UNIX, including Solaris?
   - **A.** AT&T System 3
   - **B.** SVR4
   - **C.** BSD 4.2
   - **D.** SUVR7
4. Each of the following is a variety of UNIX *except*:
   - **A.** SunOS
   - **B.** Linux
   - **C.** HP-UX
   - **D.** Matrix
5. All of the following are characteristics of the UNIX operating system *except*:
   - **A.** Proprietary
   - **B.** Scalable
   - **C.** Secure
   - **D.** Support by many manufacturers

6. The SUN Operating Environment contains all the following *except*:
   A. SunOS 5.*x* operating system
   B. Open Network Computing (ONC) protocols
   C. Common Desktop Environment (CDE) GUI
   D. Network computing topology architecture
7. The main components of the SunOS UNIX operating system include the following:
   A. Swap space, daemons, and the file system
   B. Kernel, file system, and swap space
   C. Kernel, shell, and the file system
   D. Shell, daemons, and the kernel
8. The most commonly used shell with UNIX varieties is the:
   A. Korn shell
   B. Bourne shell
   C. Clam shell
   D. C Shell
9. What is the proper sequence of terms that define the UNIX hard disk hierarchical structure from top to bottom?
   A. File, subdirectory, directory, file system
   B. Hard disk, CD-ROM, floppy disk
   C. File system, file, subdirectory, directory
   D. File system, directory, subdirectory, file
10. All of the following are common directories in the Solaris file system *except*:
    A. /usr
    B. /export/home
    C. /kernel
    D. /shell

UNIX Command Summary

Ctrl d Indicates end of file or exit. Example:

```
$ bc
5280/3
1760
<Ctrl d>
$
```

Ctrl u Erases the entire command line.

echo Echos (displays) arguments. Example:

```
$ echo "hi mom"
hi mom

$ echo $SHELL
/bin/ksh
```

ps Prints information about active processes. Example:

```
-e, -f, -u
$ ps
```

Key Terms

Bourne shell The default shell for the Solaris computing environment. It does not have aliasing or history capabilities. The Bourne shell prompt is a dollar sign ($).

BSD (Berkeley Software Distribution) One of two main versions of UNIX that is not an industry standard but is still fairly widely used. Some varieties of UNIX, such as Linux, are based on BSD.

C shell A shell (/bin/csh) based on the C programming language. Like the Korn shell, it has additional features such as aliasing and history. The C shell was developed by Sun's Bill Joy and is still widely used today. The C shell prompt is a percent sign (%).

CDE (Common Desktop Environment) A standard and consistent GUI desktop developed by a consortium of UNIX platform vendors, including Hewlett-Packard, IBM, Novell, and Sun Microsystems, along with many other companies and members of the Open Software Foundation, X/Open, and the X Consortium. CDE is Motif-based.

CPU (central processing unit) The brains of the computer that performs calculations and data manipulation. Usually a microchip, the CPU moves from RAM to the CPU and back.

Daemon Programs or processes that perform a particular task or monitor disks and program execution. Daemons are special processes that begin after the OS loads. Daemons then wait for something to do in support of the OS. For instance, the lpsched daemon exists for the sole purpose of handling print jobs. When no printing is taking place on the system, the lpsched daemon is running but inactive. When a print job is submitted, this daemon becomes active until the job is finished.

Directory A location for files and other directories. The Solaris file system or directory structure enables you to create files and directories, which can be accessed through a hierarchy of directories.

Distributed processing Enables the use of resources across the network. For instance, a user might be sitting at a workstation and be able to access files and applications on the hard disk of another computer or a printer located on a remote part of the network.

File A named collection of related data stored on a disk.

File system A hierarchy of directories, subdirectories, and files that are usually organized or grouped together for a specific purpose.

GNOME (GNU Network Object Model) The latest windowing system to emerge in the UNIX world. GNOME is part of the GNU open source software project. GNOME has been developed as an easy-to-use desktop environment for the user and a powerful application framework for the software developer, free of cost.

I/O device Peripheral devices provide a means to get data into and out of a computers. Input devices include a keyboard, mouse, and scanner; output devices include a printer and a monitor.

Kernel The master program (core) of the UNIX operating system. It manages devices, memory, swap, processes, and daemons. The kernel also controls the functions between the system programs and the system hardware.

Korn shell A shell (/bin/ksh) that is a superset of the Bourne shell and that has many of the Bourne shell features, plus added features such as aliasing and history. This is the most widely used shell and is the industry standard for system users. The Korn shell prompt is also a dollar sign ($).

Multitasking A feature of the Solaris computing environment and UNIX that enables more than one tool or application to be used at a time. Multitasking enables the kernel to keep track of several processes simultaneously.

Multiuser A feature of UNIX that enables more than one user to access the same system resources.

NOS (network operating system) A group of programs that runs on servers and provides access to network resources for users.

ONC (Open Network Computing) protocols A family of published networking protocols and distributed services that enable remote resource sharing, among other things.

Open Windows Sun's original GUI developed for the Solaris environment. It is similar to CDE, but it is proprietary and not as well supported. The user has a choice when logging into a Solaris workstation to select either CDE or Open Windows.

RAM (random access memory) The microchips that make up the real memory of a computer. RAM is the working storage area of the computer where programs (sequence of instructions) and data related to the programs are stored while the program is running. When a program is running, it is copied off the hard disk into RAM, and space is allocated in RAM for the program to do its work.

Service A process that provides a service such as remote file access, remote login capability, or electronic mail transfer.

Shell An interface between the user and the kernel. It acts as an interpreter or translator. The shell accepts commands issued by the user, interprets what the user types, and requests execution of the programs specified. Execution is performed by the kernel.

Subdirectory Any directory below another directory. For example, the /usr directory is a subdirectory of the root (/) directory.

SVR4 (System Five Release Four) One of the two main versions of UNIX. Currently, a number of varieties or "flavors" of UNIX exist, and most are similar because they are based on the industry standard SVR4. System V is a version of the UNIX operating system developed by AT&T. Sun Solaris SunOS is based on SVR4.

Swap space A reserved part of the hard disk for the kernel to use during processing. Portions of running programs can be "swapped out" to the hard disk and then brought back in later, if needed. This swap space is actually on the hard disk, but it looks like additional memory or RAM; it sometimes is called virtual memory. Swap space is a raw slice or disk file that is set aside during system installation for the purpose of paging programs out to disk temporarily while they are not being used.

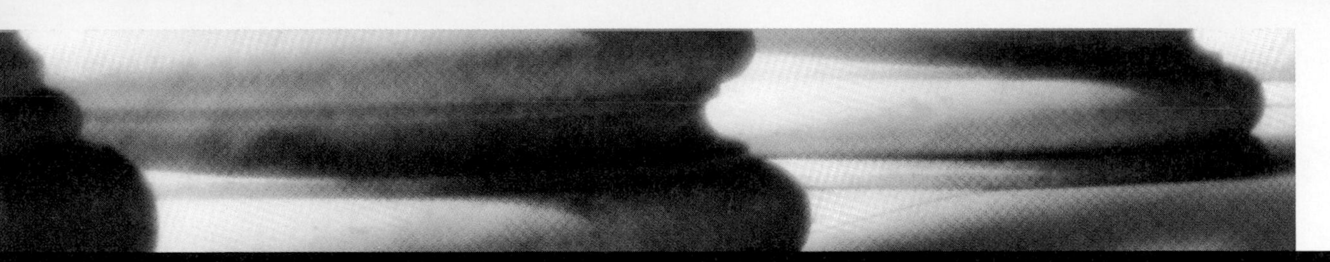

Objectives

After reading this chapter, you will be able to

- Describe different types of UNIX user accounts
- Use the Common Desktop Environment (CDE) windowing system
- Customize your workspace with Style Manager
- Work with subpanels to add and remove applications

Chapter 2

Accessing Your System and the Common Desktop Environment

Introduction

This chapter covers the requirements for user accounts and passwords, as well as the procedure for logging in and out of the system using both the command line and the Common Desktop Environment (CDE). You become familiar with the CDE and its basic features and functions. You also work with the Style Manager to customize your CDE workspace and work with subpanels.

User Accounts

Users must have an account to access resources on a UNIX system. User accounts identify a user to the system and are used to determine what activities a user can perform and what files a user can access.

Account Types

Two types of user accounts exist on a UNIX computer: the *root* (or *superuser*) account and regular user accounts. The root account is the system administration account and is set up automatically during the operating system installation process. It is the only account on the system when it is first installed. The root login account owns all system files and has access to all files. It is similar to the Administrator account with Windows NT/2000 and the Admin account with Novell NetWare.

The root account creates new users, manages file systems, installs software, and performs other high-level system administration tasks (see Figure 2-1). Because it is "all powerful," the root account should be used sparingly. Most UNIX superusers have a regular user account that they use on a daily basis and log in as root only to perform administrative tasks.

Figure 2-1
The functions of the root account.

- The superuser account
- Default account created during operating system installation
- Used for system administration

Regular user accounts are created and maintained by the system administrator when logged on as root. Every user who needs access to the system must have a user account to log in and use the computer. Regular users can run applications and customize their working environment. They also can create and modify files in their ***home directory*** (see Figure 2-2).

Figure 2-2
A regular user account.

- All other users
- Access to applications and printers
- Access to personal files

Login ID and Password Requirements

For users to log in, they must have a user account that includes a *login identification (ID)* and password. The login ID is the user's *public name*. Depending on the system administrator, login IDs are usually some combination of a user's first and last names. For example, user Bob Wood's login ID might be bobw, bwood, woodb, or bw2. The login ID must be unique on the system and is limited to eight alphanumeric characters (see Figure 2-3). It can be any combination of letters (lowercase only) and numbers. The administrator can add a comment with the user's full name when creating the user. The login ID, user's full name, and other information are stored in the password (/etc/passwd) file, which can be viewed by all users. A user's encrypted passwords are stored in the /etc/shadow file.

Figure 2-3
User account login ID requirements.

- Limited to eight alphanumeric characters
- Must be lowercase characters only
- Must be unique for this system
- Can contain numbers

The user's password protects the account from unauthorized access. In the Solaris computing environment, there are specific rules for creating passwords to help ensure system security.

A password must be no less than six and no more than eight characters in length, and must be different from the login ID. The first six characters of the password must contain at least two alphabetic characters and at least one numeric or special character, such as a dollar sign ($) or a semicolon (;). UNIX passwords also can contain spaces.

Passwords are case-sensitive, which means that they can be created with uppercase or lowercase letters and must be entered exactly the same way when logging in. The password ABc123 is different from the password ABC123, for example. When changing passwords, the new password must differ from the previous password by at least three characters. Passwords may contain spaces and special characters. As an example, the password a9$B7 c5 is perfectly valid. The length is between six and eight characters. It has upper and lowercase letters, numbers, a special character, and a space. Note that these password rules do not apply to the administrator (root or superuser) account. See Figure 2-4 for a list of password requirements that apply to regular user accounts.

Figure 2-4
User account password requirements.

- Must be six to eight characters in length
- Must contain at least two alphabetic characters (upper- or lowercase)
- Must contain at least one numeric or special character
- Must differ from the user's login ID
- Must differ from the previous password by three characters
- Can contain spaces and special characters
- Are case-sensitive (letters must be typed in as upper- or lowercase)

CDE Versus Command-Line Environment

Most UNIX systems provide two ways to log in: a graphical interface, such as CDE, and the standard character-based login that has been part of UNIX since it first was developed and before graphical interfaces existed.

CDE Login Manager

Most Solaris workstations have the graphical Common Desktop Environment (CDE) installed and will boot automatically to a graphical environment. Before logging into your account, CDE displays the graphical Login Manager screen shown in Figure 2-5.

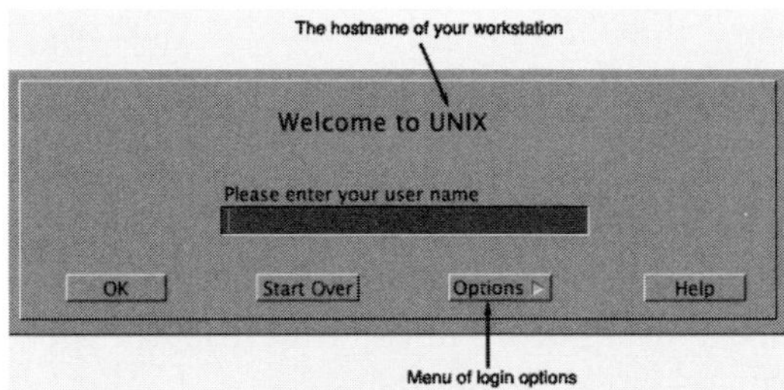

Figure 2-5
CDE Login Manager.

Four buttons are located at the bottom of the Login Manager screen:

- **OK**—Accepts the username and password as entered
- **Start Over**—Clears the username and password fields
- **Options**—Provides several choices for logging in
- **Help**—Provides assistance for using Login Manager

Logging in identifies you to the system. You can log in using the login screen shown, or you can log in at the command line. If you log in at the CDE Login Manager screen, you then enter the CDE graphical user interface (GUI) environment.

Options Button. The CDE Login Manager Options drop-down menu provides a set of choices for logging in. Five choices are available with the Options menu:

- **Language**—The Language option typically is set at installation and is not used often.
- **Session**—The Session option offers a choice of GUI desktop environments (CDE or Open Windows) and provides a fail-safe login option, which can be used for troubleshooting.
- **Remote Login**—Remote Login allows you to log into another Solaris machine, such as a server or another workstation on the network.
- **Command Line Login**—The Command Line Login option bypasses the GUI environment and goes directly to a console prompt; it stays at the command line.

- **Reset Login Screen**—The Reset Login Screen option restores all settings to their defaults.

Logging In Using the CDE Login Screen

The CDE login screen replaces the usual login prompt common in UNIX systems. The Login screen is the entry point into the system. If you do not have a login ID (or username) and password, you will not be able to access the system. Your username for the interactive e-Lab activities will be user2.

You must enter your login name in the appropriate boxed area and then press the Return key or left-click the OK button. If you log in incorrectly, you must repeat the procedure of entering your login name and password.

The Start Over button completely refreshes the screen and removes any typed entries. After you log into the CDE graphical desktop, you are presented with the front panel, which is your primary desktop-management tool.

> **TIP**
>
> If you make a mistake when entering either your login name or your password, you will be required to re-enter both pieces of information. You can press Ctrl+u (Ctrl key and a lowercase letter u, for "undo") to clear the screen, or you can left-click the Start Over button to return to the login display.

Exiting from CDE

Logging out prevents unauthorized users from gaining access to your files. You should log out anytime you will be away from your system for an extended period of time. To leave the CDE session and log out of the UNIX system, click the EXIT button on the *front panel.* It is not necessary to shut down the typical UNIX computer because these computers are designed to be left running. However, if you must shut down the system, always be sure to exit (log out) first. By default, you are asked to confirm that you want to log out. Confirmation is done by clicking the OK button or by pressing Return when the OK button is highlighted, as shown in Figure 2-6.

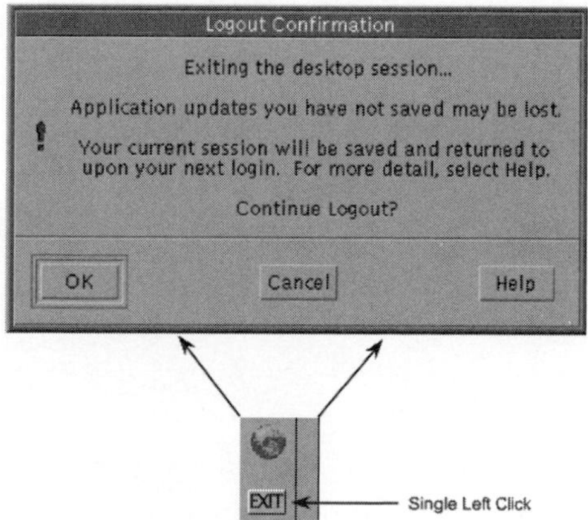

Figure 2-6
Exiting from CDE.

The current CDE session is saved automatically so that you can return to the same *workspace* windows at your next CDE session. However, any data contained in the current set of open windows will be lost. You must therefore save all data before exiting from your CDE session. It is possible to change the default activities of the Exit button so that confirmation is not required. This is discussed later, in the section "Customizing Your Workspace with Style Manager." Upon exiting the system, you return to the CDE Login Manager screen.

Logging In Using the Command Line

As an alternative to logging in with the CDE login screen, you can bypass the CDE graphical desktop and go directly to the command line. To log in from the command line, you will display the Options drop-down menu and select Command Line Login. You need to press Return fairly quickly, or the Login Manager will restart.

> **NOTE**
>
> Your password does not appear as you type it. By default, if you do not have a password, you automatically are prompted to create one during the initial login.

Enter your username at the console login and then your password at the password prompt.

Command-line login is quick because the CDE graphical desktop is not loaded. Use this option to do file management or troubleshooting from a shell prompt.

Logging In Using the Telnet Program

Another way to access the command line of a UNIX system is to use the *Telnet* program. The procedure for accessing a remote UNIX system depends on what Telnet program you use (UNIX **telnet** command, Windows Telnet, NCSA Telnet for Macintosh users, or a shareware Telnet program). To Telnet to another system, you must specify its IP address or host name. When connection is established with the remote host, you will be asked to enter a valid username and password. IP addresses and the UNIX Telnet program are covered in Chapter 16, "Network Basics." Figure 2-7 shows the connection screen when using the Windows Telnet program. After connection is established, another screen appears requesting a valid username and password.

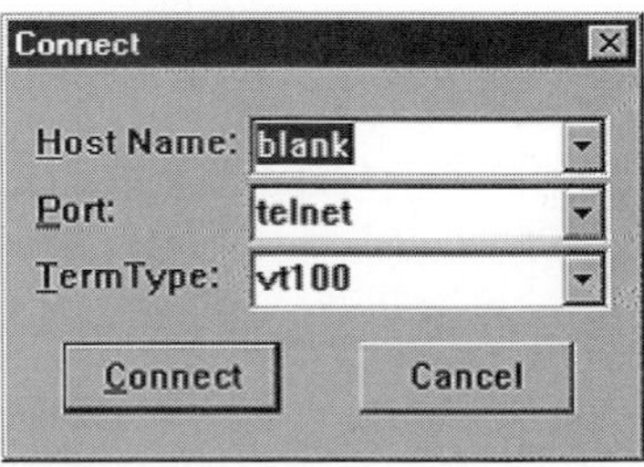

Figure 2-7
The Telnet Connect screen.

Exiting from the Command Line

To log out while at the command prompt, you simply type **exit** and press Enter. This exits you from the system and redisplays the console login prompt. If you do not log back in within 30 seconds, the CDE Login Manager screen is displayed again. Use the accompanying e-Lab activity to practice logging in and out as user2 using the command line.

Figure 2-8
The login process.

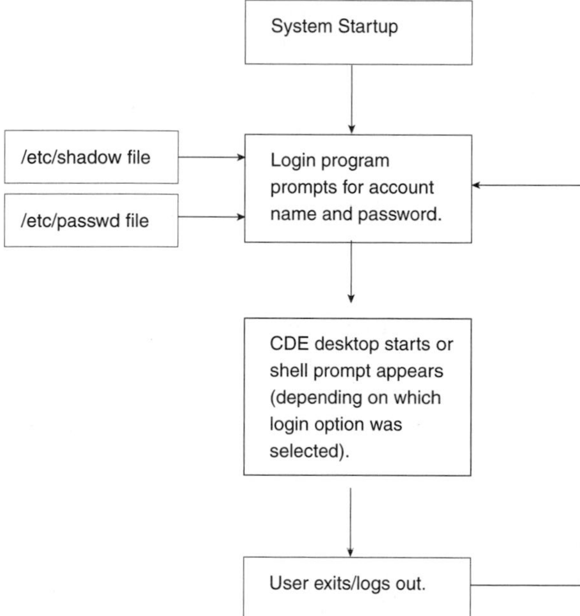
System Startup
/etc/shadow file
/etc/passwd file
Login program prompts for account name and password.
CDE desktop starts or shell prompt appears (depending on which login option was selected).
User exits/logs out.

The /etc/passwd File

The */etc/passwd file* contains the master list of user information and is consulted each time someone attempts to access the system. Each line in the passwd file represents a single user's account information and contains seven fields separated by a colon. Each entry has the following form:

> name : placeholder for password : UID : GID : user information : users home directory : shell program

Here's an example: mmouse:x:1100:10:Micky Mouse in sales:/home/mmouse:/bin/ksh

The meanings of the fields are as follows:

- **name**—Contains the username assigned to the user by the administrator. Usernames are typically some combination of a user's first and last names. If the

TIP

If the Backspace and Delete keys don't work after you Telnet to a remote UNIX system, look for an option in your Telnet program that allows you to define these keys. If your Telnet program does not allow you to define these keys, type the following at the shell prompt after you log in: stty erase. Next, press the Backspace key (this will enter a ^H) followed by Enter. This allows the Backspace key to work properly.

TIP

On most systems, you can use the Ctrl and d keys (Ctrl-d) to log out or exit a Terminal window. C shell users also can choose to use the logout command. Any other commands (such as bye) might be an alias set up by your administrator that runs the exit command and might not work on another UNIX system. Figure 2-8 shows the UNIX login process.

username entered on the login screen does not match any username listed in the /etc/passwd file, that user will not have access to the system.

- **placeholder for password**—Contains an **x** or an **!** (in some versions of UNIX), which tells the system to look for the encrypted password in the shadow password file (/etc/shadow). The shadow file is protected from all users except the root user, to prevent hackers from trying to crack user passwords.
- *UID*—Contains the unique user identification number assigned by the system administrator. Think of the UID as your Social Security number for system access. The UID is how you are known to the system. This number relates to the username and is used to determine ownership of files that the user creates and access to files and directories. The system administrator can assign the user ID, or the system will generate one automatically when a new user is created. The UID of the root user account is 0.

TIP

You can find out your UID number, username, GID number, and group name for your account by typing the **id** command at the command prompt.

- *GID*—Contains the user's primary group membership number. This number relates to a group (such as a set of users working on the same project) name that is used to determine group ownership of files that the user creates and access to files and directories. The system administrator assigns the group ID. For example, one group may be Finance for the accountants that access the system.
- **User information**—Typically contains the user's full name so that anybody viewing the /etc/passwd file can determine who is associated with a potentially cryptic username. This information also is used by mail systems and commands, such as **finger**, discussed later.
- **User's home directory**—Contains the absolute path name of the user home directory. When users log in, the system automatically places the users in their "home" directory (where their personal files are located).
- **Shell program**—Contains the path name to the program that UNIX uses as the command interpreter for the user when first logging in and when a Terminal window is opened.

Proper UNIX System Shutdown

UNIX systems are designed to be left running continuously and normally are shut down by an administrator (the root account password is required) to install a new release of the operating system, add hardware, or perform routine system maintenance.

If you must power off a UNIX system, it is important to shut down correctly. This is the case with most operating systems, and it allows all system changes recorded in RAM to be written to disk and facilitates an orderly shutdown of processes and file systems. It is similar to clicking Start/Shutdown with Windows 9*x* or NT/2000. Failure to do so can result in file corruption.

Using the **init** and **shutdown** commands are the primary ways to shut down a UNIX system. To accomplish this, see Figure 2-9 for the actual commands and use the following steps:

Step 1 Become a superuser.

Step 2 Shut down the system by using either the **init 0** or the **shutdown** commands.

Step 3 Power off at the type any key to continue prompt (Intel PC) or the OK prompt (Sun workstation).

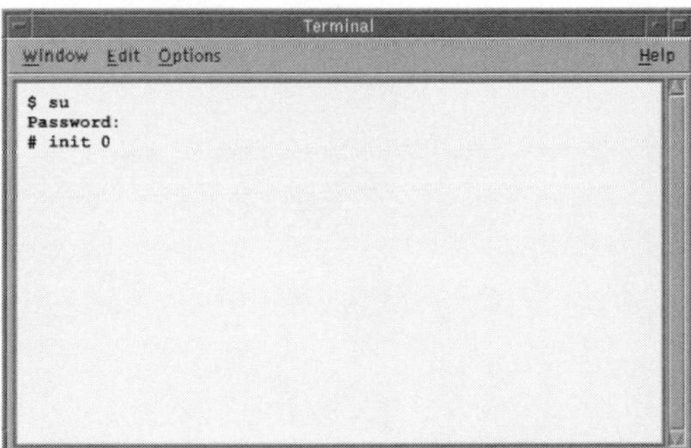
Terminal
Window Edit Options
Help
$ su
Password:
init 0

Figure 2-9
The proper system shutdown.

Skill Builder

e-Lab Activity 2.1

Using the CDE Login Screen

Work through the interactive e-Lab activity to practice logging in and out of a UNIX system using the Login Manager screen.

Skill Builder

e-Lab Activity 2.2

Using Command-Line Login

Work through the interactive e-Lab activity to practice logging in and out from a UNIX system command-line environment.

Changing Your Password

Changing your password frequently helps prevent unauthorized access to your system. The actual process of changing your password is the same whether you logged in through CDE or the command line. The password is changed at the command line, in either case.

If you are logged into a CDE session, you right-click the background to bring up the Workspace menu, click Tools, and open a Terminal window, as shown in Figure 2-10.

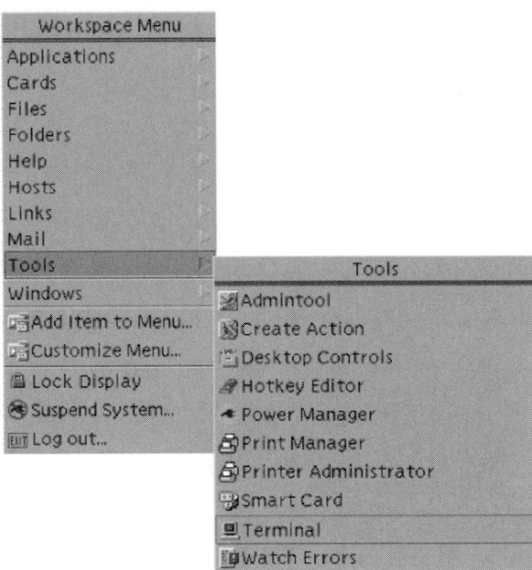

Figure 2-10
Opening a Terminal window.

NOTE

On some systems, the Terminal window can be found under the Windows Workspace menu option. If that is the case, click this instead of Applications to access a Terminal window.

The Terminal window gives you access to a command-line $ prompt. The dollar sign ($) represents a Korn or Bourne shell. You also might have a percent sign (%) for the C Shell or a number or pound sign (#), indicating that you are logged in as root. After you have a Terminal window open, type the **passwd** command after the system prompt and press Return. When prompted to enter the login password, type your current password and press Return. When prompted for a new password, type your new password and press Return. You then are prompted to retype your new password to confirm it. (This is required for verification of the new password by the system.) Use the accompanying e-Lab activity to practice changing the password for user2 using the command line in a Terminal window. Be sure to follow the rules for valid passwords previously covered. Remember that passwords are case-sensitive and can contain spaces and special characters.

The following is the series of prompts that results from the **passwd** command:

```
$ passwd
passwd: Changing password for user2
Enter login password: ABC 123
New password: abc 456
Re-enter new passwd: abc 456
$
```

NOTE

Your password will not appear on the screen as you type.

Password Aging

Password aging is a security feature that might or might not be implemented by the system administrator. Password aging options can include requiring a user to change the password after a certain number of days, setting an absolute expiration date when the account no can longer be accessed, and even locking the account after a certain number of days of inactivity.

TIP

If you are having problems accessing your account, contact the system administrator.

FORGOT YOUR PASSWORD?

If you forget your password, your only option is to contact your system administrator. The administrator will not be able to tell you what your password is, but he will be able to assign a new, temporary one. When you are given the new password, you should immediately use the **passwd** command to change the password to something that you will remember.

Skill Builder

e-Lab Activity 2.3

Changing Your Password in a Terminal Window

Work through the interactive e-Lab activity to enter the commands to change your login password.

Skill Builder

Lab Activity 2.1.5

Accessing Your System

In this lab, you review the requirements for UNIX login IDs and passwords. You practice logging in to a UNIX system using the CDE login screen. You then change your password, exit (or log out), and return to the CDE login screen. Refer to the *Cisco Networking Academy Program: Fundamentals of UNIX Lab Companion.*

Becoming Familiar with the Common Desktop Environment

This section discusses ways in which you can familiarize yourself with the CDE.

Workspace Buttons

When you log into a CDE session, four workspaces are available to you by default (see Figure 2-11). Each workspace is equivalent to a desktop environment. Surrounding the workspace buttons are the workstation lock icon, the "system busy" globe icon, and the EXIT icon.

Figure 2-11
The workspace buttons.

NOTE

In some locations, the function of the metakey differs. It might be necessary to use the Alt key or the spacebar with the arrow keys to perform the function described here.

You can independently set the characteristics of each workspace and add more workspaces (desktops), if needed. You can alternate among your workspaces by left-clicking the appropriate workspace button or by using the keyboard metakey (diamond) combined with the left or right arrow keys (Sun workstation only).

Multiple workspaces or virtual desktops can be useful. As an example, you could have one desktop arrangement for administrative tasks, one for applications and regular user tasks, one for special projects, and another for application development.

The Front Panel Arrangement

The front panel allows you to manage applications, files, and network services easily. The front panel has been organized to include icons for a Web browser, text notes, and a performance meter (see Figure 2-12). The *subpanels* contain cascading submenus for ease of navigation. Click an up-arrow button to open a subpanel; click an item in a subpanel to run it. The spinning globe above the Exit button indicates that the system is busy. When it is clicked, it becomes an "Action: Go" entry panel and prompts you for a uniform resource locator (URL), path name, host, e-mail address, and so forth to open (see Figure 2-13).

Front Panel Menu Button

At the top-left side of the front panel is the Front Panel window menu button. If this is selected, a menu of choices is displayed.

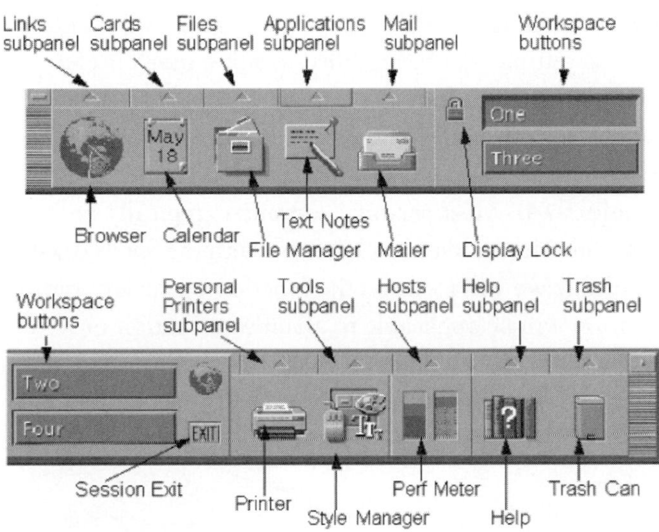

Figure 2-12 The front panel arrangement.

Figure 2-13 The Action button.

From this menu, it is possible to perform the following actions:

- Move the front panel to another location on the screen. (This also can be done by dragging the front panel to a new position by one of the move handles.)
- Minimize the front panel display.
- Lower the front panel display behind overlapping windows.
- Refresh the entire workspace display.
- Log out from the CDE session.

Using the Mouse and the Keyboard

The mouse and the keyboard are the primary input devices for most computers. You might be working with a Sun Solaris workstation or an Intel-based personal computer running the Solaris operating system. It is helpful to understand the differences between the Sun workstation version and the typical PC version of these two input devices.

The Mouse

A mouse is used with the CDE in a similar way as with other graphical user interfaces. The mouse settings can be modified to suit a user's preferences. When a setting has been modified, that setting can be stored into a user-specific file. This means that any personalized settings will be the default whenever a CDE session is initiated. The mouse used with a Sun workstation has three buttons, a left, middle, and right button (see Figure 2-14). Most personal computers typically have two buttons, a left and a right button. The middle mouse button with the Sun workstation is used primarily as a paste button. We will focus on the function of the left and right buttons so that this information will be applicable to a Sun workstation or a PC running Solaris for Intel.

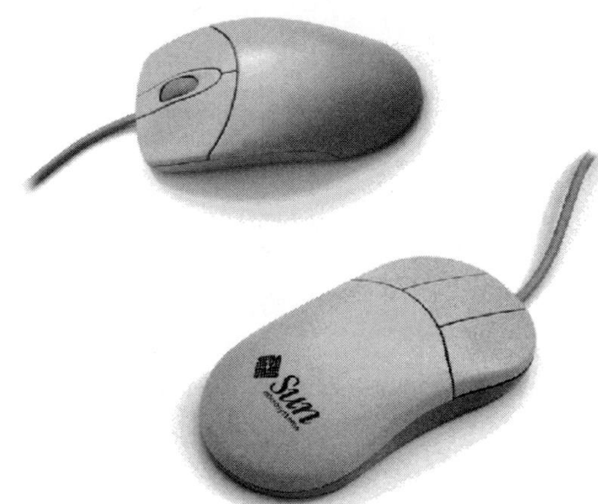

Figure 2-14 The Sun mouse versus the more standard mouse.

The Left Mouse Button

Most actions use the left mouse button, alternatively known as button 1 or the SELECT button. This button is used to make selections in any of the following ways:

- **Make a window active**—Click the left mouse button while the mouse pointer is in that window area.
- **Invoke a window menu**—Click the left mouse button while the mouse pointer is on the window's menu box area.
- **Select an option from the front panel**
- **Select a File or Folder icon**—You can do this while working with the File Manager.
- **Open an icon**—Double-click the left mouse button while the pointer is over the icon.

- **Highlight text to be selected**—Drag over the text area while the left mouse button is being pressed.

NOTE

For the purposes of this course, you will be instructed to left- or right-click to perform a specific action. This assumes the standard right-hand configuration of the buttons. These notes will instruct you when a double-click is required.

The Right Mouse Button

When the right mouse button, or the MENU button, is clicked or held down, a menu of choices appears. This is button 3 on a Sun workstation. The options available on the menu are determined by the position of the mouse pointer when the right button was pressed.

The Keyboard

This section contrasts the Sun workstation and PC keyboards.

PC Keyboard

It is useful to compare the two keyboards so that you can work with either one. As with the mouse, the Sun workstation keyboard and the PC keyboards differ somewhat (see Figure 2-15).

Figure 2-15
The Sun workstation and the PC keyboards.

A typical PC has a keyboard with 104 keys and 4 major sections or areas on the keyboard:

- Typewriter keys (letters, special characters, Ctrl, Shift, Alt, and others)
- Function keys (F1, F2, F3, and so on)
- Cursor-management keys (Insert, Home, End, arrow keys, and others)
- Numeric keypad

TIP

Use the Front key to bring a window currently behind another window to the front.

Use the Open key to open a minimized program residing on the desktop as an icon or to reduce an open window to an icon.

Use the Copy and Paste keys to paste long path names from one Terminal window to another.

Sun Workstation Keyboard

The Sun workstation keyboard is wider than the one for a typical PC. It has all the previously mentioned keys and a few more, for a total of 118. Most of the additional keys are in two additional sections of the keyboard. A section to the left of the keyboard provides 10 keys for window management and common functions such as cut, copy, and paste. A large Help key is in the top left corner of the keyboard. In the typewriter portion of the keyboard are two keys with diamonds on them, known as *metakeys*. These perform various functions, such as alternating between workspaces. Another section exists at the top right, which allows control of sound volume. Refer to Figure 2-15 for a comparison between the two keyboards.

Managing Windows

Most PC users are accustomed to working in a graphical environment with windows. The UNIX Common Desktop Environment (CDE) is very similar in its operation. The following are common tasks that are normally performed in a windowed environment.

Overlapping Windows

When an icon is selected from the front panel, a window opens on your workspace screen. Normally, windows on the workspace overlap each other, with the most recently opened window overlapping previously opened windows (see Figure 2-16).

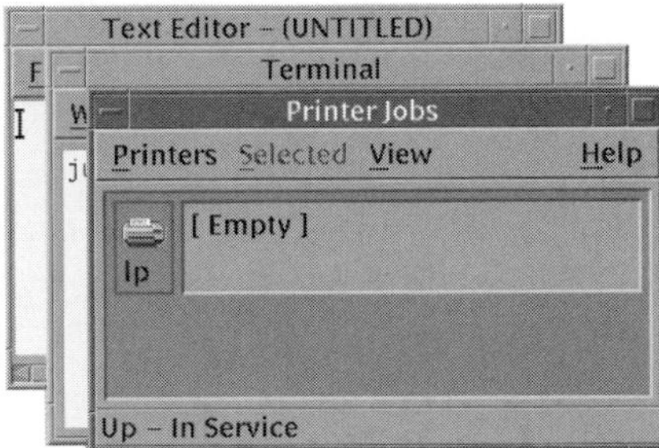

Figure 2-16
An example of overlapping windows.

NOTE

There is no alternative to raising a window to the front of a set of overlapping windows. When selected, a window automatically comes to the front of any overlapping windows in a CDE display. The Front key on a Sun workstation keyboard also brings a window to the front of the display (see Figure 2-18).

Lowering a Window

To choose the window menu, position the mouse pointer on the window title area and press the right mouse button. One option in the resulting menu is to lower the window. This option forces the window to the back of the overlapping windows on your screen display (see Figure 2-17).

The alternative keyboard action is to hold down the Alt key and press function key 3 (Alt-F3).

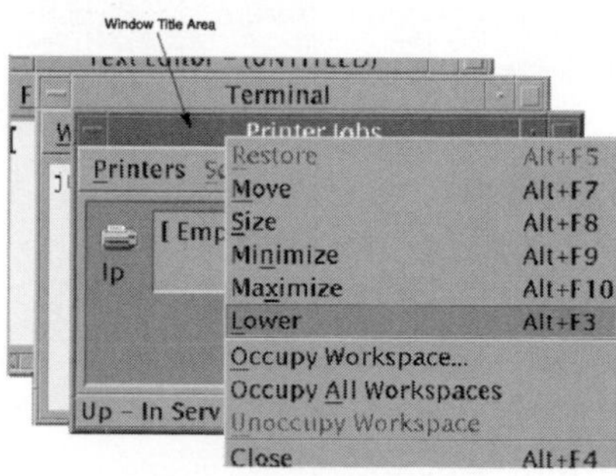

Figure 2-17
Lowering a window.

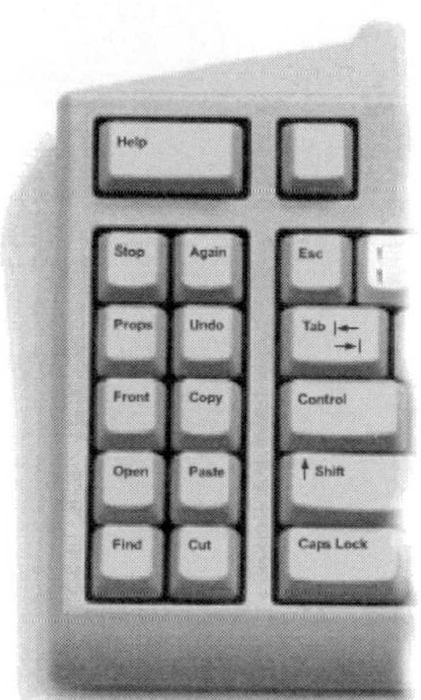

Figure 2-18
The Sun keyboard's edit keys.

Moving a Window

You can move a window in two ways. One way is to choose the Move option from the window menu, as shown in Figure 2-19. The mouse pointer changes from an arrow to a small cross. Drag the cross pointer to move the window. As the cross moves, an outline of the window is displayed on your screen. When the outline is in the desired position, click once with the left mouse button and the window will move there.

The other method is easier and uses the drag-and-drop technique, as shown in Figure 2-20. With this method, you place the mouse pointer over the window's title area, hold down the left mouse button, and drag the window to its new screen location. When the window is being moved, a pair of numbers is displayed on your screen. These are the x- and y-axis values, which show the new position of the window on your workspace display. The number on the left (385) represents the horizontal (X) position. The number on the right (231) represents the vertical (Y) position. (These numbers are useful to developers and programmers who want to have a window appear in the same position every time an application is invoked.)

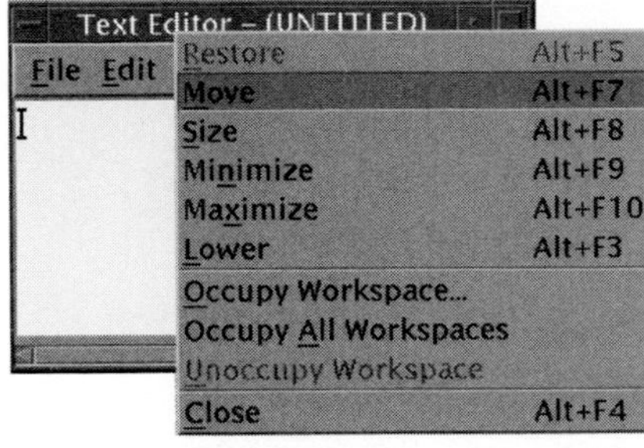

Figure 2-19
Moving a window by using the menu method.

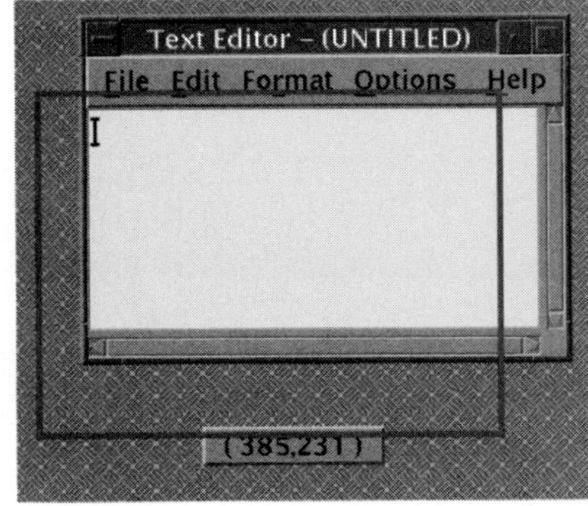

Figure 2-20
Moving a window by using the drag-and-drop method.

NOTE

When a window occupies all of the workspace display, no other windows can be seen (because they are covered up). To switch to another window, you must either lower the full-display window or reduce it to its previous size. You can use the F9 and F10 function keys with the Alt key as keyboard alternatives to using the mouse.

Minimizing and Restoring a Window

At the top-right side of the window is a Minimize button. Clicking this button converts the window into an icon (see Figure 2-21). The icon of a minimized window is placed at the left edge of the workspace display, by default. However, it can be moved to any desktop location by dragging the icon to the desired position. Only one click of the left button is required to change a window to an icon. To change the icon back into a window, you must double-click the icon with the left button. Clicking once on an icon invokes the window menu (see Figure 2-22). Selecting Restore then changes the icon back into a window.

Maximizing a Window

To make a window fill the entire workspace display, you must left-click the box button at the top-right side of the window. To reduce the full-display window to its previous window size, select the box button again. When the window is reduced to its previous size, it is placed in its previous display position on the workspace.

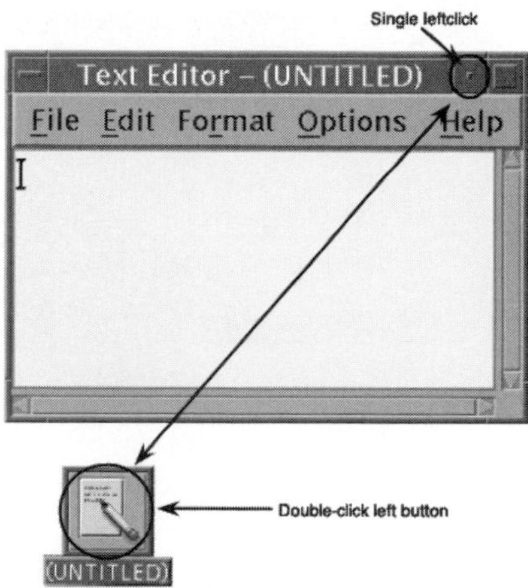

Figure 2-21
Minimizing a window

Restore	Alt+F5
Move	Alt+F7
Size	Alt+F8
Minimize	Alt+F9
Maximize	Alt+F10
Lower	Alt+F3
Occupy Workspace...	
Occupy All Workspaces	
Unoccupy Workspace	
Close	Alt+F4

Figure 2-22
Restoring a window.

The Minimize and Maximize buttons are shown in Figure 2-23, along with the window menu equivalents.

Closing a Window

To close a window, double-click with the left mouse button on the dash in the upper-left corner of the window (see Figure 2-24). Windows also can be closed by single-clicking with the left mouse button in the upper-left corner and then selecting the Close option from the menu that is displayed. If, by closing the window, unsaved data might be lost, UNIX will prompt you to save the information (see Figure 2-25). The keyboard alternative to close a window is Alt-F4. Most applications will request that you confirm the closure of a window that contains unsaved data.

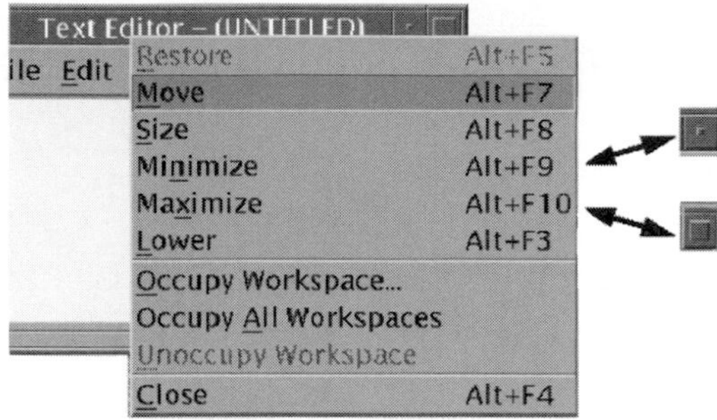

Figure 2-23
The Minimize and Maximize menus (with buttons).

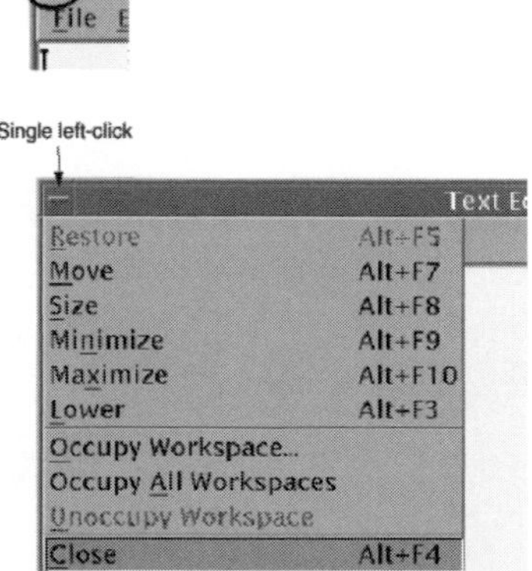

Figure 2-24
Closing a window.

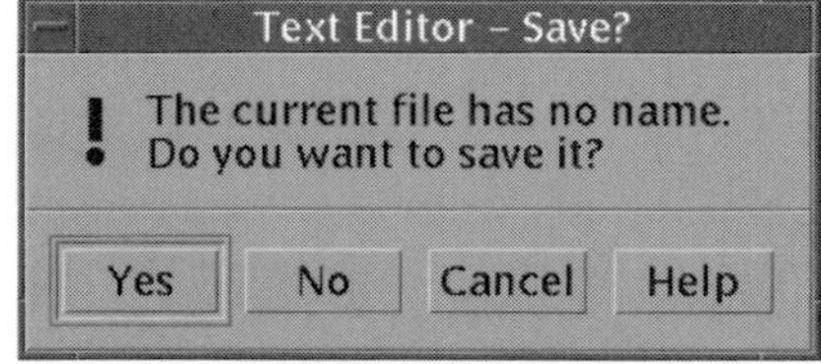

Figure 2-25
The UNIX prompt to save your information.

NOTE

If a user locks the display and forgets the password, the root user (super-user) can enter the root password to unlock the display. The *Style Manager*, discussed later, enables you to choose a screen-saver program while the display is locked.

Locking the Display

Left-clicking the Display Lock button on the front panel locks the screen. The backdrop will be blank, by default, and the Password Prompt box will be displayed for only a short time. To bring the password prompt back to the display, move the mouse or press a key on the keyboard. When the display has been locked, it can be unlocked only by entering the correct password for the user who locked the screen.

Workspace Buttons

As mentioned earlier, four workspaces are available when you start your first CDE session. You can create additional workspaces, each of which takes up the whole display area of the screen. If you click the right mouse button while the pointer is situated over the workspace buttons area, you get a menu of options (see Figure 2-26). One of these options is to add a workspace. A limited menu will appear if the pointer is positioned over the area between the workspace buttons instead of over the button itself. When a new workspace is added, it is given the name New.

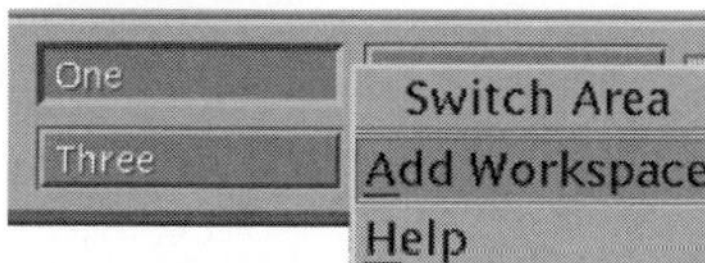

Figure 2-26
Adding a workspace.

You can change the name of a workspace by either of the following two methods:

- Choose the Workspace Buttons menu option Rename.
- Double-click the workspace name in the central area of the front panel display.

Be careful not to give the workspace a name that is too long to be fully displayed. If the name is too wide for the display, only the left-most characters will be displayed in the front panel display area.

Workspaces can be deleted from the front panel area by using the Workspace Buttons menu's Delete option.

Minimizing and Maximizing the Front Panel

Minimize the front panel by clicking the Minimize button at the top-right corner of the front panel window (see Figure 2-27). The resulting icon shows the name of the current workspace immediately below it. To restore the front panel display, double-click the Front Panel icon. If the icon is hidden behind another window, you can either lower the overlapping windows until you can see the Front Panel icon or keep pressing the Alt-Tab keys until the Front Panel icon is brought to the front of the overlapping windows displayed on your screen.

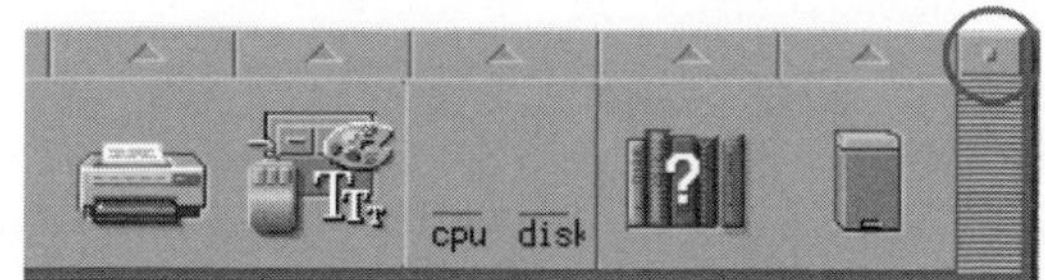

Figure 2-27
Minimizing the front panel.

The Workspace Menu

The Workspace menu provides easy mouse access to all your applications, tools, and files through cascading submenus (see Figure 2-28). To display the menu, move the pointer to the backdrop and then press the right mouse button.

NOTE

The Workspace menu on your system might look different than what's pictured in Figure 2-28.

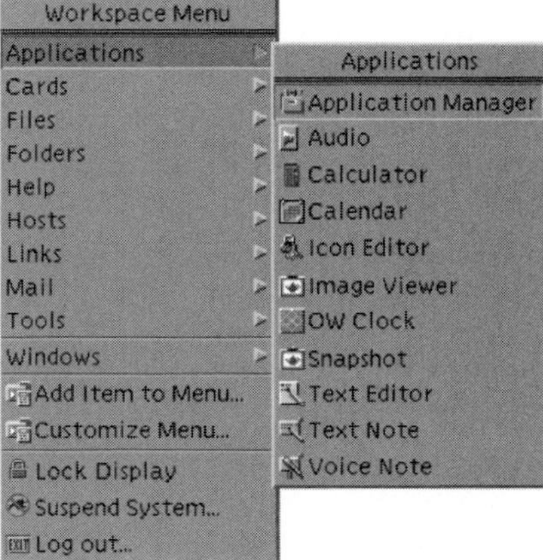

Figure 2-28 The Workspace menu.

Skill Builder

Lab Activity 2.2.7

Becoming Familiar with CDE

In this lab, you work with the standard UNIX graphical user interface (GUI) known as Common Desktop Environment (CDE). You become familiar with the front panel and use the mouse and keyboard to manage windows. You also practice locking the display, moving between workspaces, and using the Workspace menu. Refer to the *Cisco Networking Academy Program: Fundamentals of UNIX Lab Companion.*

Customizing Your Workspace with Style Manager

The Style Manager enables you to customize the following workspace attributes (see Figure 2-29):

- **Color**—Sets the color attributes of the windows and the workspace background
- **Font**—Sets the size of the font display (in points)

- **Backdrop**—Sets the workspace backdrop display
- **Keyboard**—Sets key-click and key-repeat characteristics
- **Mouse**—Sets mouse button positions, acceleration, and threshold values
- **Beep**—Sets the tone and duration of the beep
- **Screen**—Sets screen-blanking characteristics and background-lock programs
- **Window**—Sets the behavior controls for windows and icons
- **Startup**—Sets the logout and CDE session startup controls.

Figure 2-29
The Style Manager options.

Color

The color controls enable you to select a color system for the backdrop, window borders, window pane, and menu areas of the display (see Figure 2-30). Each is set to a color based on the palette chosen from the list. After you choose a palette, you can modify it to suit your needs by clicking Modify. Color changes will apply to all workspaces.

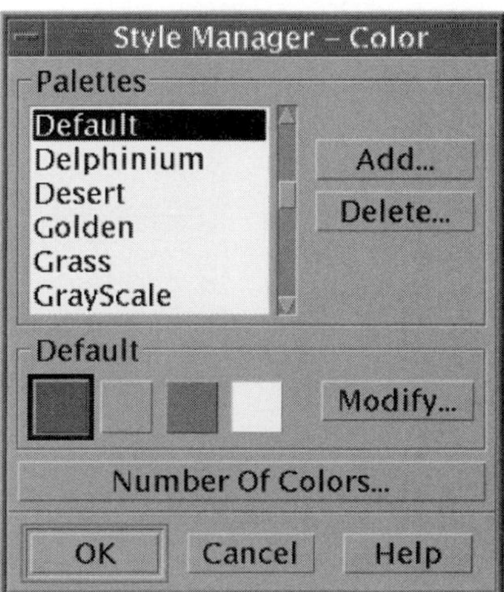

Figure 2-30
Style Manager: color.

Font

Changing the font size alters the display character size of the next and subsequent windows opened. The text size in the Help Viewer documents is not affected by changing font size.

Different font sets can be added to the list of Font Groups by clicking the Add button. The Attributes button enables you to choose alternate character sets. (See Figure 2-32.)

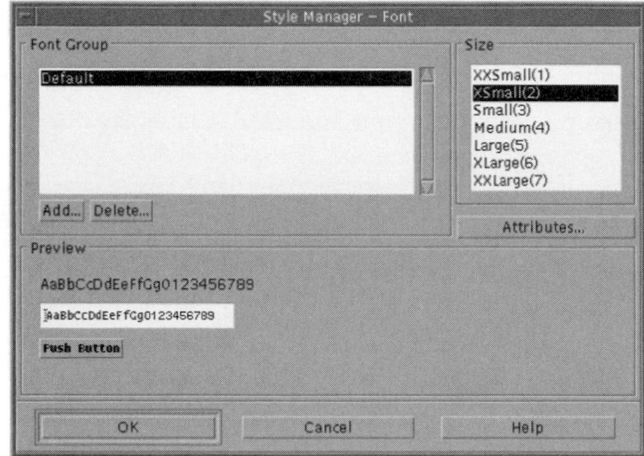

Figure 2-31
Style Manager: font.

Backdrop

The Backdrop choice enables you to change the background for the current workspace (see Figure 2-32). Color choices that you make also will affect the backdrop appearance. Each workspace can have a different backdrop applied to it.

Figure 2-32
Style Manger: backdrop.

Keyboard

The keyboard controls enable you to turn key repeating on and off. If you want to have the keys make a sound when they are pressed, you can adjust the click volume to be as loud as possible. If the value is set to 0, the key click is effectively turned off. If any changes have been made to the settings, selecting the Default button restores the values to those shown in Figure 2-33.

Figure 2-33
Style Manager: keyboard.

Mouse

Changing the handedness of the mouse reverses mouse buttons 1 and 3. Button 2 can be used to select text or objects (Adjust) or drag-and-drop objects (Transfer). If Adjust is selected, transfer actions (drag) will require the use of mouse button 1. The maxi mum time between clicks of a double-click can be adjusted. Changes to this will become effective with a new login session. Acceleration changes how fast the mouse pointer moves across the display. Threshold determines the distance in pixels that the pointer moves at slow speed before moving at the accelerated rate. (See Figure 2-34.)

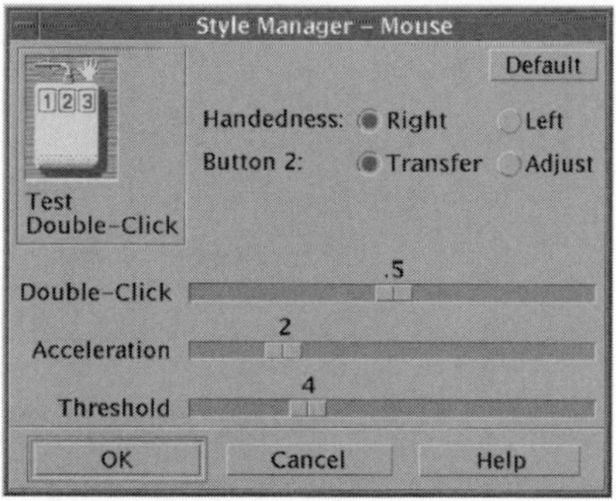

Figure 2-34
Style Manager: mouse.

Beep

The volume of the beep noise can be set to a value between 0 and 100. If set to 0, the beep noise effectively is turned off. Tone determines the pitch of the beep, from 82 to 9000 Hertz (Hz). The duration of the beep noise can be set to last up to 2.5 seconds. (See Figure 2-35.)

Figure 2-35
Style Manager: beep.

Screen

The Screen controls enable you to designate which screen-saver program will run when you lock your workstation display. You can designate a number of screen savers to run, in succession, and you have each of them run for a period between 0 and 120 minutes. You also can set the period of screen inactivity (in the example, 15 minutes) at which the screen saver will automatically be invoked. (See Figure 2-36.)

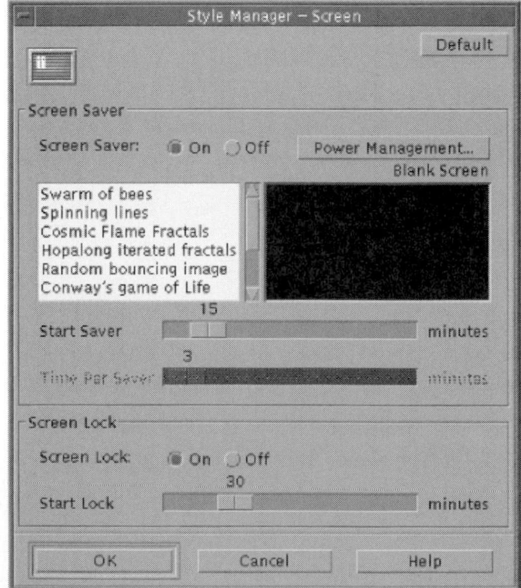

Figure 2-36
Style Manager: screen.

Window

The Window control allows you to designate how windows and icons can be manipulated. (See Figure 2-37.)

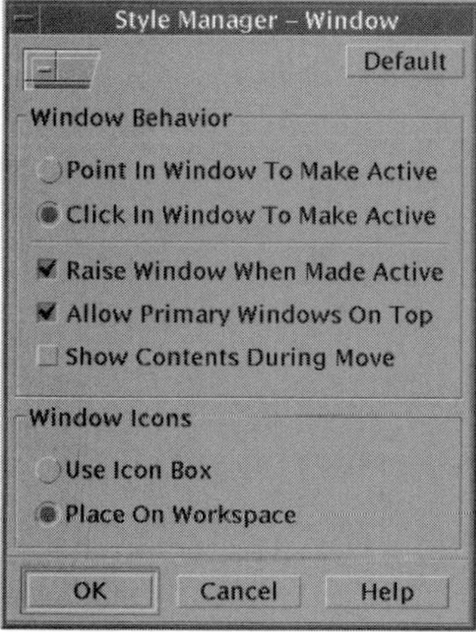

Figure 2-37
Style Manager: window.

Startup

Setting the home session saves the current work session windows as the default windows to open when the next home session is started. If you choose Set Home Session, this overrides any previously saved information. You can choose to return to either the session as it is when you log out (the current session) or your home session when you log back in. Turning off the Logout Confirmation Dialog option means that you automatically will be logged out when the Exit button is selected, without any further confirmation being requested. If the Logout Confirmation Dialog option is set to On, you will be asked to confirm that you do want to log out when you choose to exit. When you start your next work session, the data contained in any windows will either be gone or be set to default values. (See Figure 2-38.)

Working with Subpanels

This section discusses how you can work with subpanels to add and remove applications and icons.

Adding and Removing Applications with Subpanels

The subpanels, or pull-up menus, located on the front panel enable you to add desired applications for easier access (see Figure 2-39). It is easy to add and delete new action buttons for launching your most frequently used applications or scripts.

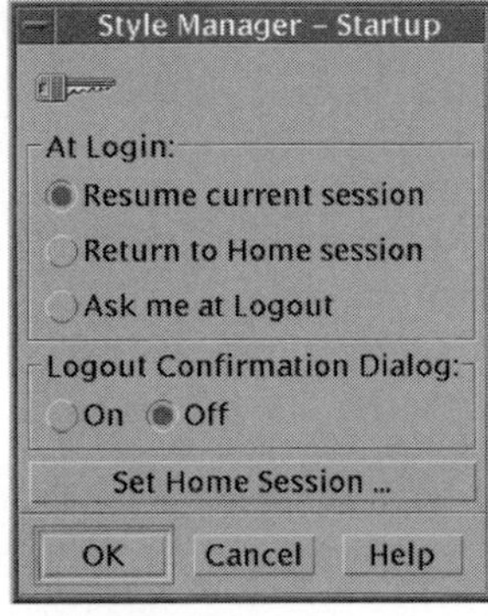

Figure 2-38
Style Manager: startup.

Figure 2-39
Working with subpanels.

Adding Applications Icons

You can add applications to the subpanel menu list by dragging the appropriate icon from the *Application Manager* window display and dropping it on the Install Icon area of the subpanel. Many frequently used applications can be found by clicking on the Applications icon on the Applications subpanel.

You can place the most frequently used icons on your front panel display by clicking the Promote to Front Panel choice in the menu of options. This speeds up access to the most commonly used programs and helps reduce the need to open subpanel lists.

Removing Applications Icons

To manipulate an icon on a subpanel or delete it from the subpanel, right-click the desired icon. This displays a menu of options relating to the icon (see Figure 2-40).

Subpanels can be "torn off" and placed on the workspace by using the same method that you use to move a window.

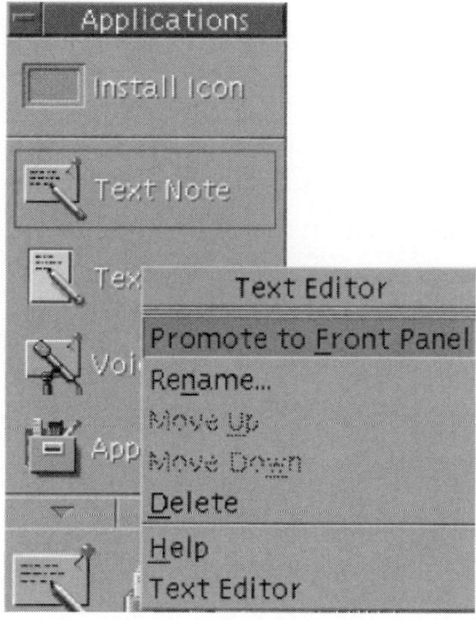

Figure 2-40
Adding and removing applications with subpanels.

Application Manager

The Application Manager window contains six folders. Open the desktop folders to see icons that can be added to a subpanel. This is achieved by dragging and dropping the desired icon on the Install Icon area of the subpanel. When the icon has been added to the subpanel, that application can be invoked from the subpanel itself. Icons also can be added to the front panel by right-clicking a blank area of the front panel and then clicking Add Icon.

> **NOTE**
>
> An application icon can be placed on the workspace display in the same way. The application is then available directly from the workspace. The System_Admin folder contains icons that are useful for system administrators. The OpenWindows folder contains icons that can be used to open OpenWindows programs while working in a CDE environment.

Skill Builder

Lab Activity 2.4.2

Customizing Your Workspace

In this lab, you work with CDE Style Manager, Application Manager, subpanel menus, front panel, and the desktop to customize your workspace environment. Refer to the *Cisco Networking Academy Program: Fundamentals of UNIX Lab Companion*.

Summary

Two types of accounts exist on a UNIX system. The root account has access to the entire system and can perform system-administration tasks such as creating new users, setting up printers, and installing software. All other users have a regular user account to access applications and personal files.

User accounts and passwords have specific rules that must be adhered to. These include minimum and maximum length and which characters they can contain. Users can change their passwords at the command line with the **passwd** command. Password rules do not apply to the root account.

You can log in via CDE, from the command line, or using a Telnet program with a valid username and password. You must log out or exit the system properly before shutting it off.

The front panel is the main user interface to the CDE desktop. You should be familiar with the front panel arrangement and should know the buttons and options available from it.

The mouse and keyboard on a Sun workstation are somewhat different than those of a typical PC. The Sun keyboard has extra keys, and the mouse has three buttons instead of two, as with the PC mouse. You should be familiar with the functions of the left and right mouse buttons.

The CDE environment allows you to manage your windows by changing their location, size, and position relative to other windows. CDE provides up to four workspaces, which are separate desktop environments. The front panel includes a button for locking your workstation and buttons for changing between workspaces.

You can use Style Manager to customize each of your workspaces by changing things such as colors, fonts, screen savers, mouse settings, and keyboard settings.

Subpanels are pull-up or pull-down menus that provide access to many desktop applications. You can add or remove icons or applications with subpanels.

Check Your Understanding

1. Which of the following is a characteristic of the root account?
   - **A.** It must have at least two numeric characters in the password.
   - **B.** It must be created after installation is complete.
   - **C.** Regular users have access to it.
   - **D.** It is used for system administration tasks.
2. User account names or login IDs must adhere to which one of these rules?
   - **A.** They cannot be less than eight characters in length.
   - **B.** They must be uppercase.
   - **C.** They must be unique for the system.
   - **D.** They must contain at least one numeric or special character.
3. A system user with the login ID of dsmith wants to change her password. Her current password is set to DBS-001. Which of the following would be an invalid password?
   - **A.** ABC$123
   - **B.** Dbs-002
   - **C.** Dbs-1
   - **D.** Dbs ABC
4. When logging in at the CDE Login Manager, the OPTIONS menu has several choices. Which of these would you use to log in when troubleshooting or having possible hardware problems?
   - **A.** Remote Login
   - **B.** Session
   - **C.** Command Line Login
   - **D.** Reset Login Screen
5. You are ready to shut down your system for the day and go home. You currently are logged in and running CDE. You should:
   - **A.** Click Start/Shutdown from the Start menu.
   - **B.** Type **QUIT** at the command line of the Terminal window.
   - **C.** Click the Exit button on the front panel.
   - **D.** Click the Logout button on the front panel.

6. You need to leave your workstation for a while, and you are working on several projects with multiple windows open. What should you do to prevent another user from getting into your workstation and seeing your work?

   A. Click the Lock icon on the front panel.

   B. Type suspend at the command line of a Terminal window.

   C. Click the SUSPEND button on the front panel.

   D. Type lock at the command line of a Terminal window.

7. If you perform several functions in your work, such as system administration and project management as well as application program development (you are very busy), which would be the best choice if you needed different desktop requirements for each function?

   A. Create a user account for each function, and create a custom desktop for each user.

   B. Define multiple desktops using the workspace buttons.

   C. Log in as root and create multiple desktop arrangements using the desktop-management function.

   D. Click the Style Manager button and select the desired workspace.

8. All of the following desktop characteristics can be changed using the Style Manager *except*:

   A. Screen resolution

   B. Startup session options

   C. Screen saver options

   D. Mouse settings

9. The Workspace menu provides mouse access to all your applications, tools, and files through cascading submenus. How is the Workspace menu activated?

   A. Double-click the World icon on the front panel.

   B. Right-click one of the workspace buttons.

   C. Left-click the backdrop.

   D. Right-click the backdrop.

10. To add an application to a subpanel, you will need to do which of the following?
    - **A.** Open a folder in Application Manager and drag one of the icons to the Install Icon option on the subpanel.
    - **B.** Click the Add Icon option in the front panel and select the desired subpanel from the list.
    - **C.** Select the icon from the front panel and drag it to the appropriate subpanel.
    - **D.** Right-click the icon and select Cut from the menu; then select the subpanel and click Paste.

UNIX Command Summary

init 0 Its primary role is to create processes from information stored in the file /etc/inittab. At any given time, the system is in one of eight possible run levels. A run level is a software configuration under which only a select group of processes exist. Run levels 0 and 6 are reserved states for shutting down and restarting the system. The **init** command can be run only by the root user.

passwd Changes login password and password attributes. Example:

```
$ passwd
passwd: Changing password for user2
Enter login password:  abc123
New password:  unix123
Re-enter new password:  unix123
passwd (SYSTEM): passwd successfully changed for user2
$
```

shutdown By default, **shutdown** brings the system to a state in which only the console has access to the operating system. This state is called single-user. **shutdown** can be run only by the root user. Example:

```
$ shutdown
```

stty Sets options for a terminal. Example:

```
$ stty erase ^H  sets the backspace key to erase one character to the left
```

Key Terms

/etc/passwd file File that contains the master list of user information and that is consulted each time someone attempts to access the system.

Application Manager The Application Manager window contains six folders containing icons that can be added to a subpanel.

Front panel The primary graphical access area for CDE that contains workspace buttons, pull-down/up menus, and other applications.

GID (group identifier) Contains the user's primary group membership number. This number relates to a group name that is used to determine group ownership of files that the user creates and access to files and directories.

Home directory The user's own directory, which is set up by the system administrator.

Login ID Your username or ID used to access a UNIX computer.

Password aging Can be used to force users to change their passwords at regular intervals.

Root The username of the superuser account on a UNIX system. The superuser is a privileged user with total system access. The terms *superuser* and *root* have the same meaning and are used interchangeably.

Style Manager A component of CDE that allows you to customize each of your workspaces by changing things such as colors, fonts, screen savers, mouse settings, and keyboard settings.

Subpanel Pull-up or pull-down menus on the CDE front panel that provide access to many desktop applications. You can add or remove icons or applications with subpanels.

Superuser Privileged user with total system access. The terms *superuser* and *root* have the same meaning and are used interchangeably.

Telnet A way to access a UNIX system remotely. To Telnet to another system, you must specify its IP address or host name.

UID (user identifier) Contains the unique user identification number assigned by the system administrator. This number relates to the username and is used to determine ownership of files that the user creates and access to files and directories. The UID of the root user account is 0.

Workspace When you log into a CDE session, four workspaces are available to you by default. Each workspace is equivalent to a desktop environment.

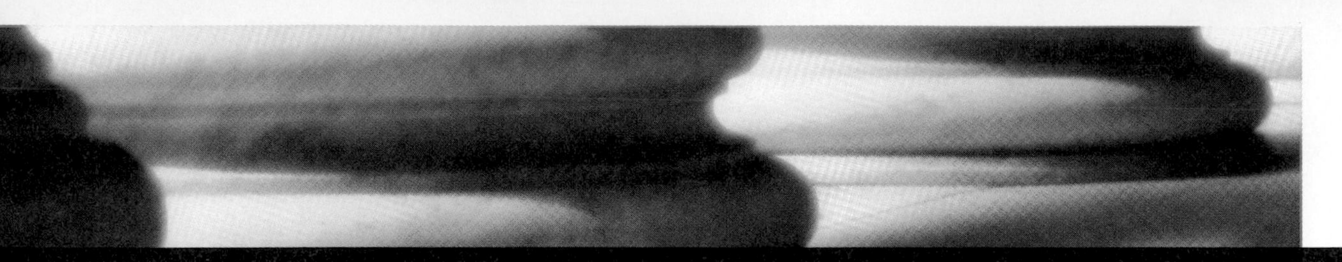

Objectives

After reading this chapter, you will be able to

- Use the Mail Tool
- Use Calendar Manager
- Use other built-in CDE applications

Chapter 3

CDE User Applications

Introduction

This chapter introduces you to several useful applications that are included with the graphical Common Desktop Environment (CDE). You will work with the Mail Tool to view and manage e-mail messages, and you will use the Calendar Manager to manage dates and appointments. CDE contains many other useful applications, such as Voice Notes and Text Notes, Address Manager, Audio, Icon Editor, Image Viewer, Snapshot, Calculator, and Clock. These applications and the use of a Terminal window in the CDE environment are covered in this chapter.

Using the Mail Tool

Mail Tool is a full-featured graphical e-mail–management program. The Mail Tool is an e-mail client that is a standard component of the Solaris CDE. With Mail Tool, you can perform all normal functions related to your e-mail. You can read mail and attachments, create new mail with attachments, and delete and manage your e-mail.

Mail Tool's features include spell-checking, message-drafting, and template capabilities. In addition, Mail Tool saves copies of outgoing messages, creates views for reading selected mail messages, supports aliases, and handles "out-of-office" or vacation automessages.

The Mail Icon

A Mail icon appears on the front panel of the CDE. You can click the Mail icon to start the Mail Tool program and read and work with your e-mail. When you receive a new e-mail, the icon changes slightly to alert you of new mail (see Figure 3-1).

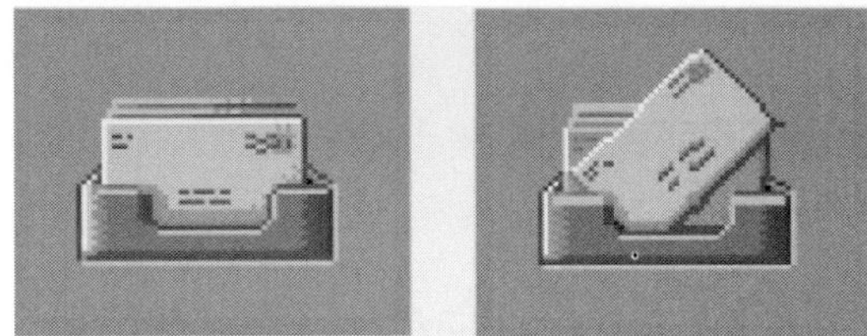

Figure 3-1
The Mail icons.

The Mail Window

By default, the Mail window is divided into two areas, as shown in Figure 3-2. The upper portion displays a list of the e-mail messages that have been received. The lower portion displays the text content of the currently highlighted message. This enables you to view each message's content by clicking once on an e-mail's subject line. Clicking the Control button between the upper and lower portions of the screen window and dragging it down or up can change the size of the message viewing area.

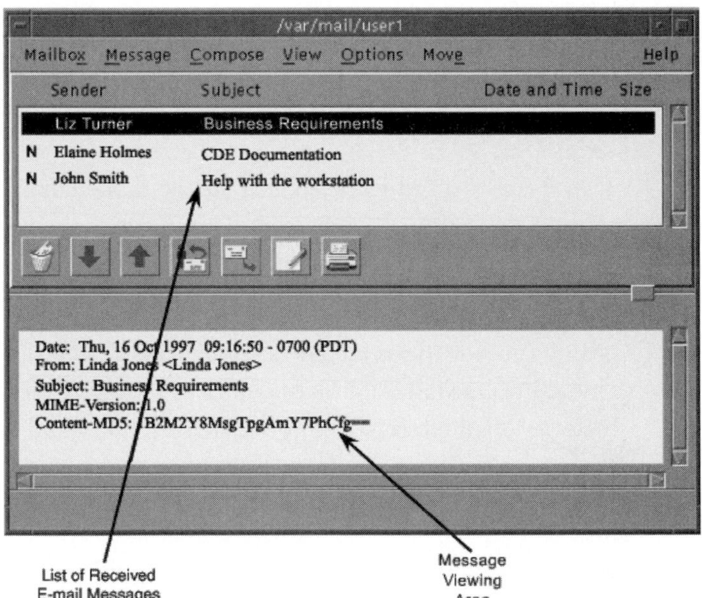

Figure 3-2
The Mail window.

New Messages

When you receive a new, unread message, the letter *N* appears to the left of the sender's name in the top portion of the Mail window (see Figure 3-3). After you open the new message, the *N* disappears to indicate that the message is no longer new.

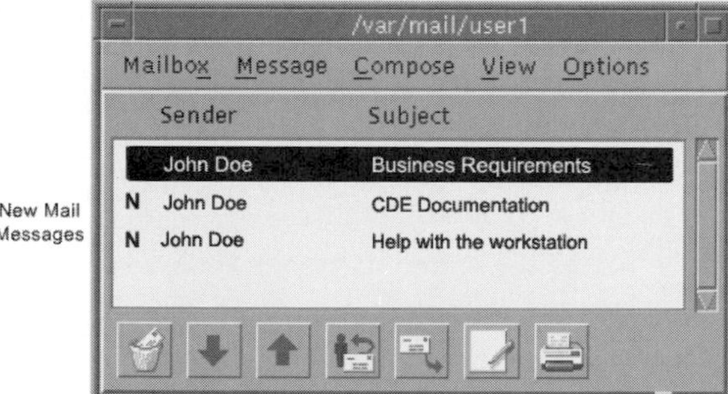

Figure 3-3
New e-mail messages.

Attached Files

When an e-mail message contains attached files, a diamond character is displayed after the new message indicator (the letter *N*). To read an attachment, double-click its icon at the bottom of the window (see Figure 3-4).

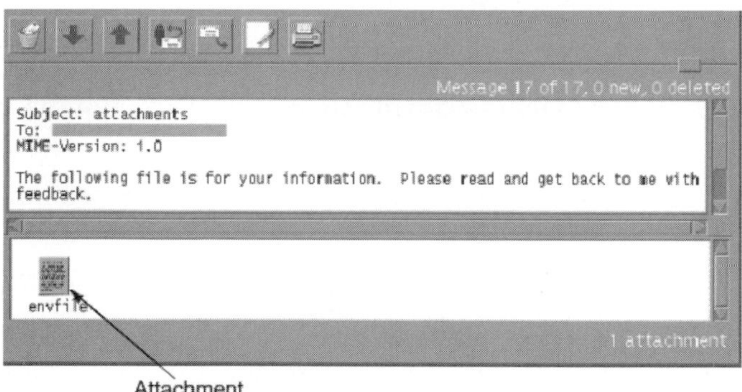

Figure 3-4
An e-mail with an attachment.

Composing New E-Mail Messages

You can compose a new mail message by clicking Compose, New Message from the main menu, as shown in Figure 3-5. A window appears where you can fill in the appropriate information. Make sure that the address you are sending the message to is complete. You can include more than one name, separated by commas, in the To: and CC: fields. After you create the message, click the Send button in the bottom-left corner of the pane to send the message to the addressee(s).

E-Mail Addressing

As with regular mail, you need to specify the address of the person(s) to whom you are sending the e-mail. If you are sending a message to someone whose computer is on the same local-area network (LAN) as yours, use the address username@hostname. For example, to mail a message to user05 on a computer named buckeye, enter user05@buckeye in the To: field.

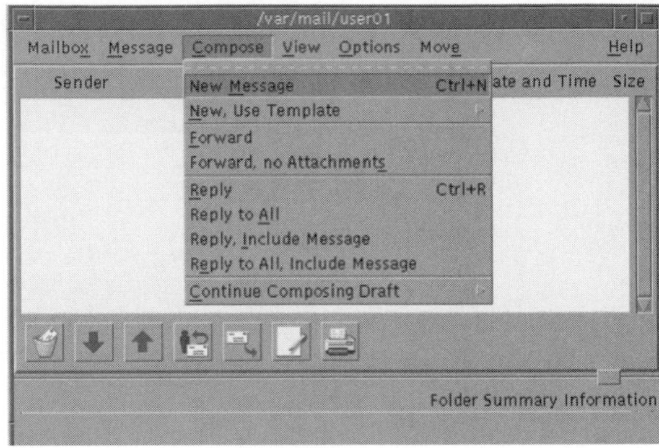

Figure 3-5
The New Message menu option.

If you send Internet mail (somebody outside your institution or company), you must address the e-mail using the following format:

danm@informance.com

Here's a breakdown of this format:

- *Username* (**danm**)—Usually some combination of the letters of a person's first and last name.
- **The "at" symbol** (@)—Separates the username from the rest of the e-mail address.
- *Domain name* (**Informance.com**)—A unique, registered name; usually a company or Internet service provider (ISP) name followed by a "dot" (.) and then a domain-name extension that determines the organization type. (For example, .com means a company in the commercial domain, .edu represents the education domain, .mil stands for military, and so on.)

TIP

You also can drag a file from the File Manager into the Attachment area in the bottom of the Compose window.

Adding Attachments

To attach a file to a message that you compose, click the Attachments option from the New Message screen menu, as shown in Figure 3-6. Click Add File, and a window appears from which you can choose the file that you want to attach.

Responding to Received Messages

To reply to a message that you received, open the Compose menu to see your options, as shown in Figure 3-7. You are given the choice of replying to the sender or replying to all recipients of the message. You also are given a choice of including the original message. Mail frequently is sent out in a mass mailing to many recipients who happen to be on a mail alias. Mail aliases are often large and general, so use the Reply to All option with caution. If you want to reply and include the message that you received, you can bypass the Compose menu and click the Reply, Include Message icon on the toolbar of the Mail Tool. After you choose a method of reply, a window appears so that you can type your response. By default, the original Subject text is used, preceded by Re:, and the To: entry automatically is set to the e-mail address of the original sender of the message.

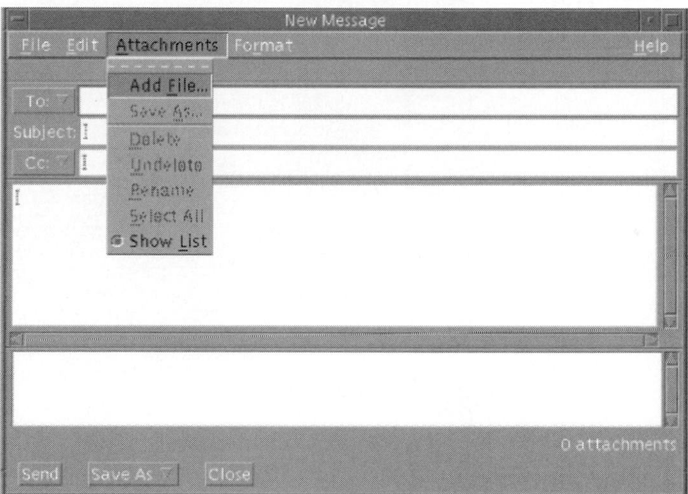

Figure 3-6
Add attachments to your e-mail by selecting Attachments, Add File.

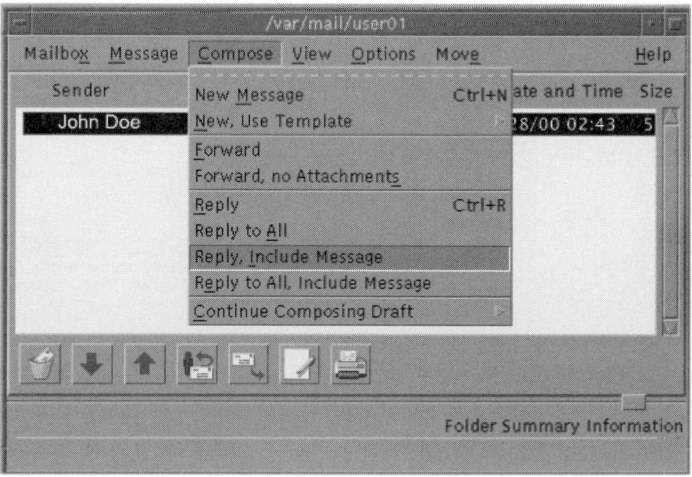

Figure 3-7
Mail reply options.

Deleting Mail Messages

To keep the list of received mail messages to a minimum (and to save disk space), you should periodically delete your e-mail messages. A number of delete options are shown in Figure 3-8. Choosing to delete the mail messages does not remove the mail. Instead, the messages are stored until you close the mail window. This gives you an opportunity to decide not to delete the message. You can force the mail program to delete any mail messages that previously were selected for deletion by clicking Mailbox and then Destroy Deleted Messages.

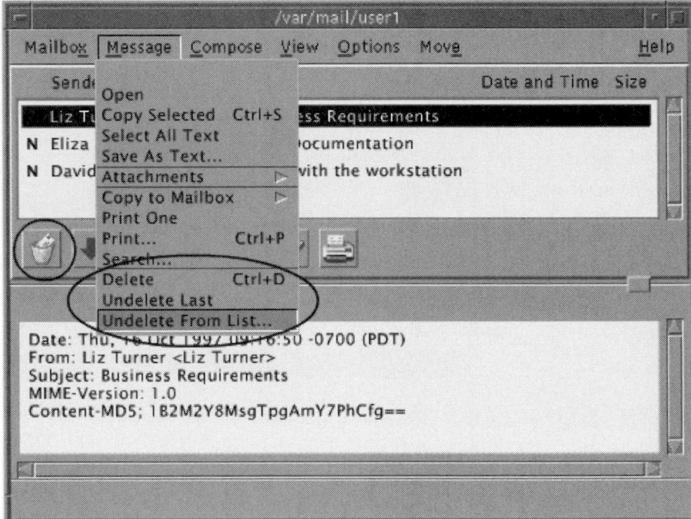

Figure 3-8
Mail delete options.

Undeleting Mail

While you continue to work with the mail program, you can view a list of the deleted mail messages and undelete one or more messages from the list (see Figure 3-9). When a message is undeleted, it reappears in the list of received mail messages.

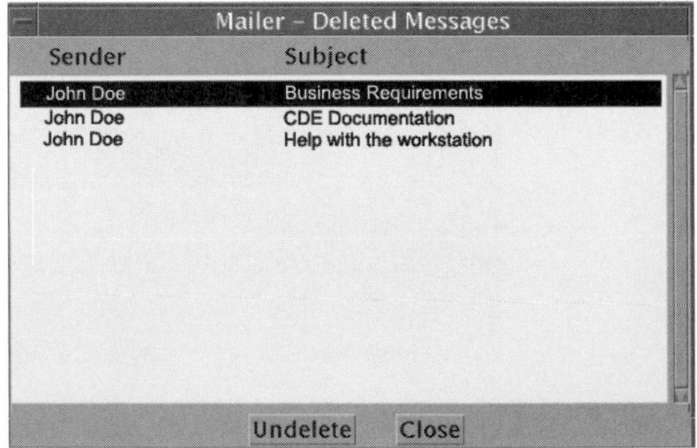

Figure 3-9
Deleted messages.

Mail Tool Options Menu

The Mail Tool Options menu enables you to create distribution lists and signatures, and it also gives you many other useful tools.

Alias Option

E-mail addresses can be difficult to remember. Mail Tool provides a tool that enables you to set up aliases for either a particular person or a group of people that you frequently send mail to. A mail alias is similar to a group or distribution list with other mail systems. This utility can be accessed by clicking Options and then Aliases, as shown in Figures 3-10 and 3-11. Choose a name for the alias, and enter the e-mail addresses of all users that you want to be part of the alias. A comma must separate the e-mail addresses. After an alias has been entered, click Add to place it in your list of aliases. When you finish creating aliases, click OK.

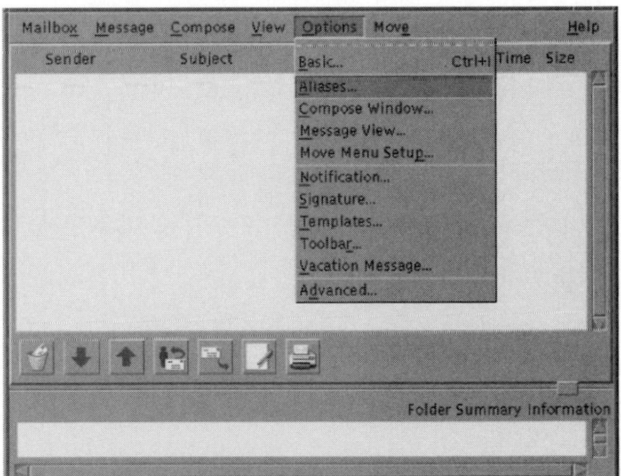

Figure 3-10 Mail Tool Options menu.

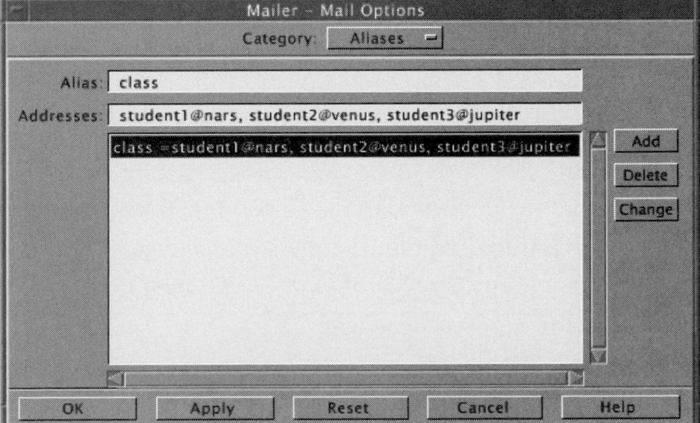

Figure 3-11 Mail Options: aliases.

Creating and Using a Signature

A signature is text that you can include with each mail message that you send. A typical signature includes your name, institution or company, phone number, e-mail address, and Web site. Signatures appear at the bottom of the message.

To create a signature, choose Signature from the Options menu, and then enter your signature text in the Signature text area.

To include your signature in a specific message (or all messages), choose Include Signature from the Format menu of the Compose window.

Other Customizable Options

Many other options can be customized with the different categories listed under the Options menu. Some of these include the following:

- Saving copies of mail that you send
- Specifying how often you would like the system to check for new mail
- Specifying how you would like to be notified of new mail
- Setting a vacation message to be sent in reply to messages when you are unavailable
- Creating a custom signature that can be attached to all outgoing e-mail

Creating Alternate Mailboxes

Messages that you receive can contain information that you might want to access at a later time. In the CDE Mail Tool, you can create multiple mailboxes for the purpose of storing mail for later retrieval and organization (see Figures 3-12 and 3-13). These mailboxes can be named to reflect the contents that you intend to store in them. After a new mailbox is created, you can use the Move menu to move received mail into it and save it for future reference, as shown in Figure 3-14.

Skill Builder

Lab Activity 3.1.6

Using CDE Mail Tool

In this lab, you work with the CDE Mail Tool, also known as Mailer. Mail Tool is a full-featured graphical e-mail–management program. Refer to the *Cisco Networking Academy Program: Fundamentals of UNIX Lab Companion.*

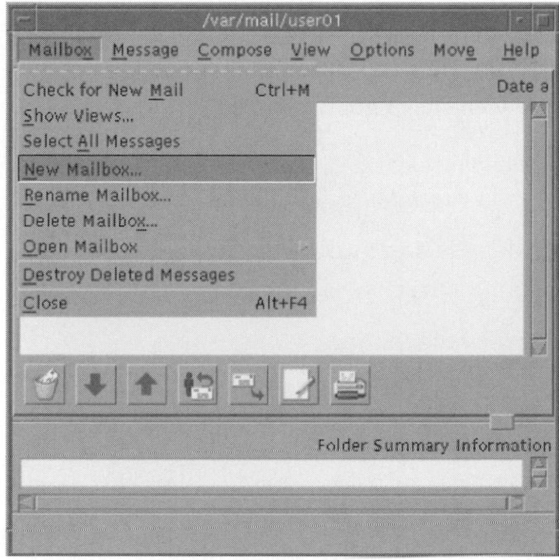

Figure 3-12
The Add Mailbox menu option.

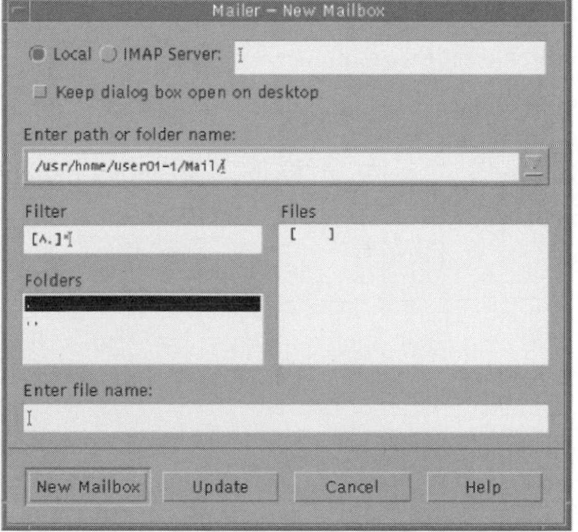

Figure 3-13
The Add Mailbox dialog box.

The Netscape Mail Alternative

The CDE Mailer program has many advantages. For example, it is integrated with other CDE tools and applications, aliases, vacation automessage capability, and so on. However, it also has the following disadvantages:

- It cannot attach multiple files simultaneously.
- It cannot choose addresses from a "pick list."

- It cannot create nested mailboxes easily; this must be done manually using the **mkdir** command.
- Some files can be too large to mail.

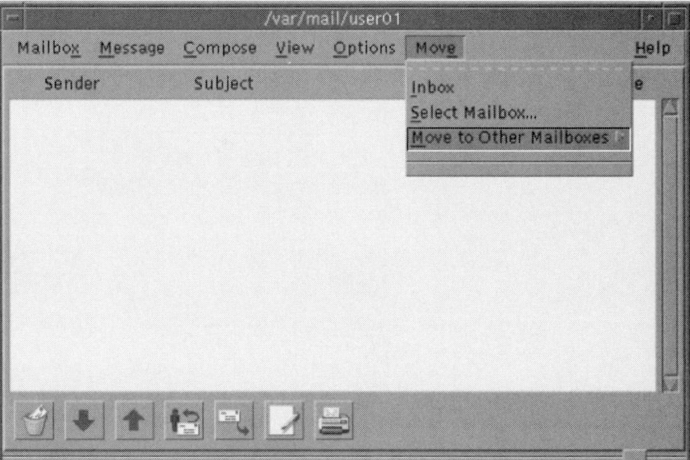

Figure 3-14
Move mail to a mailbox.

As an alternative, some users choose to set up and use the Netscape Mail program that is built into Netscape Communicator and loaded on your system along with the CDE. (Microsoft has not developed a UNIX version of Internet Explorer.) If you do not have Netscape Communicator on your system, you can download it for free from www.netscape.com/download. Figure 3-15 shows the Netscape Mail screen.

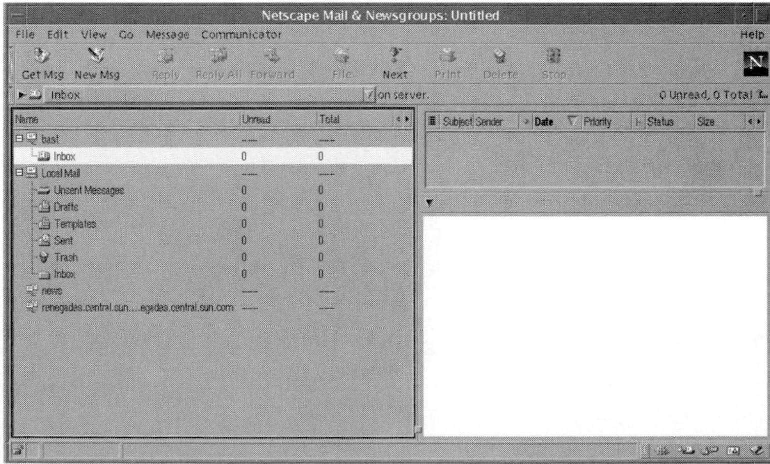

Figure 3-15
Netscape mail.

Non-Windows–Based Mail Programs

Sometimes you might find yourself on a UNIX system without the availability of a graphical interface because it was set up that way (user preference) or because you used the Telnet program to access the system. If you can't access the CDE mailer or Netscape mail, what can you do?

Fortunately, text-based and menu-based mail programs can be run from the command line. The two most popular programs are the following:

- *mailx* **(and the earlier, more basic mail program)**—This program comes with every version of UNIX and is an acceptable program for reading and sending mail. The *mailx* program basics are found in Appendix E, "mailx," and this program is worth learning for those times when you need a mail program but don't have access to CDE.
- *Pine*—This program is menu-based and easier to use than the mailx program. Pine was developed at the University of Washington and can be accessed by typing pine at the command prompt.

> **TIP**
>
> The mailx program was designed for sending text-only messages, not for sending programs, formatted application files, or image attachments. If you need to send a non-text attachment, you will need to use the **uuencode** command to convert the file to text for attaching and sending. If you are receiving an attachment using mailx, you will have to use the **uudecode** command on the detached file to use it. See the UNIX manual pages (man pages) for additional information. The use of man pages is covered in Chapter 4, "Getting Help."

Figure 3-16 displays Pine's main menu with the list of one-letter commands that can be chosen by either typing the letter or using the arrow keys and pressing Enter.

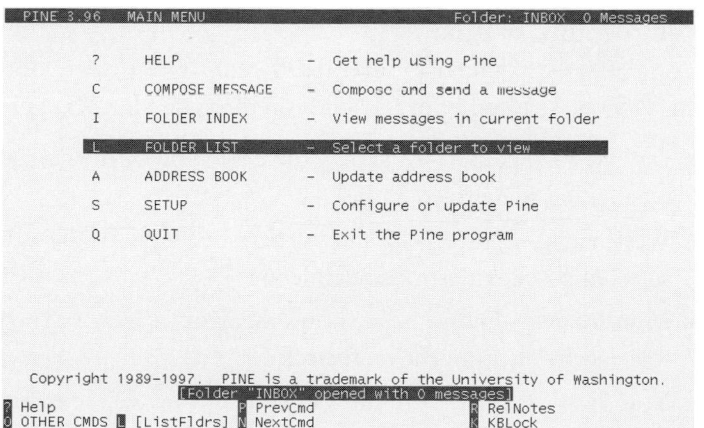

Figure 3-16
Pine main menu.

Using Calendar Manager

Calendar Manager is a full-featured graphical schedule and appointment management program. It is a standard component of the Solaris CDE. With Calendar Manager, you can perform all normal scheduling functions and share your calendar with others. You also can set meetings on other people's calendars.

Calendar Manager Window

To start Calendar Manager, click the Calendar icon on the CDE Front Panel. By default, the Calendar window displays a month view of your calendar. The view can be changed by clicking one of the four view icons at the top-right side of the Calendar Manager window, as shown in Figure 3-17.

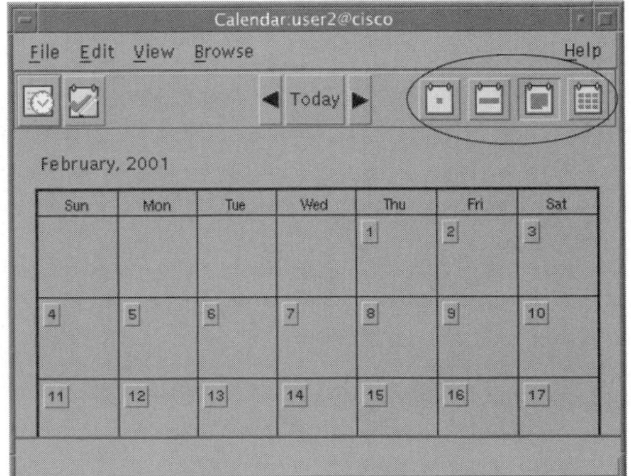

Figure 3-17 The Calendar Manager window.

Viewing Your Calendar

You can view the calendar in several different formats. Any of the following viewing formats can be selected with the icons on the Calendar Manger window:

- **Day view**—Figure 3-18 shows the Day view of the calendar. It can be selected by clicking the circled icon.
- **Week view**—Figure 3-19 shows the Week view of the calendar. It can be selected by clicking the circled icon.
- **Month view**—Figure 3-20 shows the Month view of the calendar. It can be selected by clicking the icon circled.
- **Year view**—Figure 3-21 shows the Year view of the calendar. It can be selected by clicking the icon circled.

Setting Calendar Options

By setting the calendar options, you can customize your calendar by adjusting the display, print, and date settings. You also can add appointments.

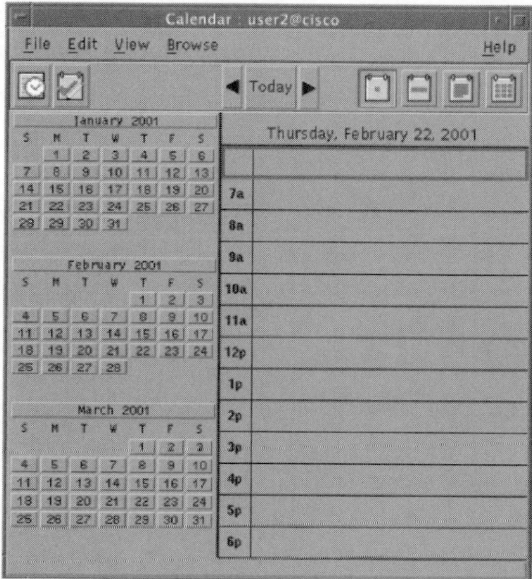

Figure 3-18
The calendar Day view.

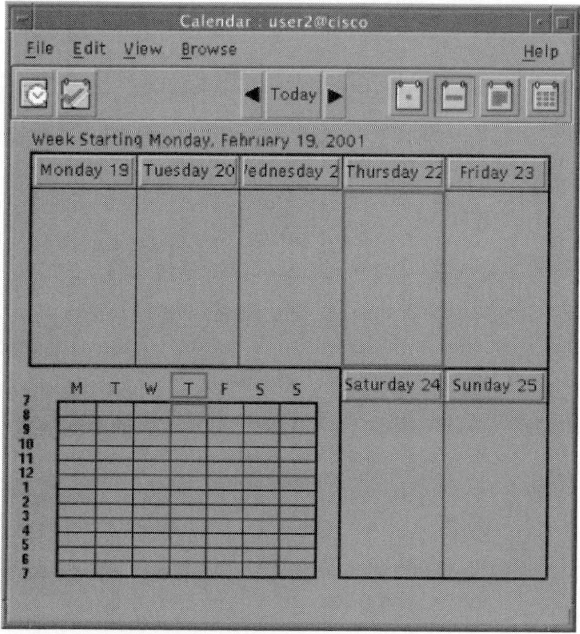

Figure 3-19
The calendar Week view.

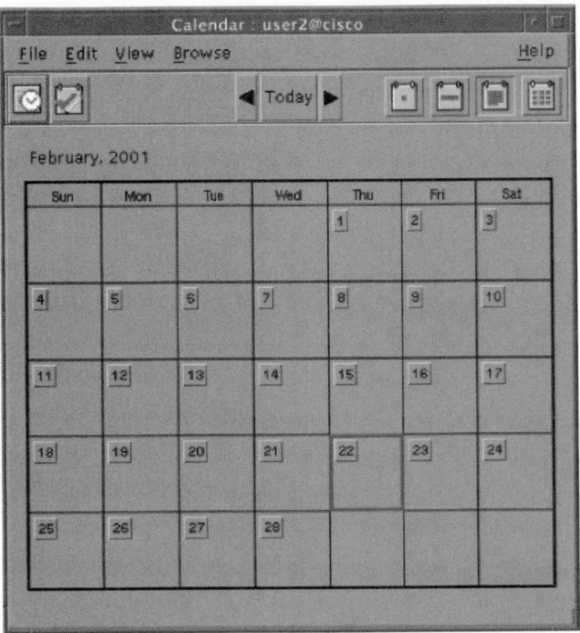

Figure 3-20
The calendar Month view.

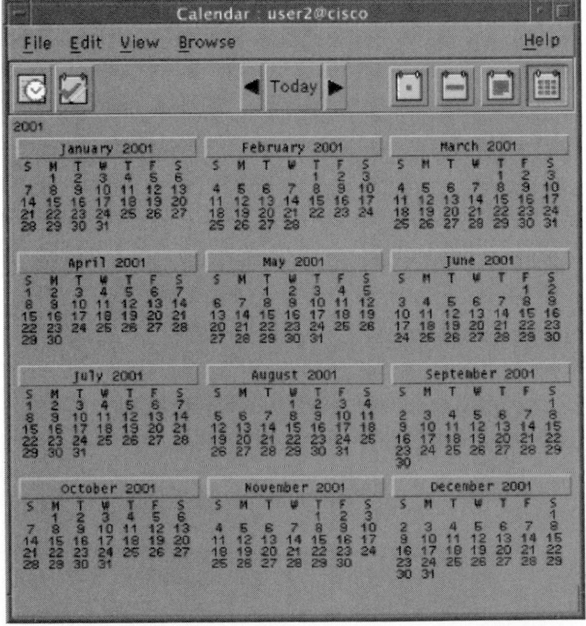

Figure 3-21
The calendar Year view.

Calendar Editor Defaults

The File, Options menu option displays the calendar Editor Defaults window by default (see Figure 3-22). In the Editor Defaults window, you can set the options to suit your personal preferences. After the values are modified, click either OK or Apply to save the updated details. Selecting the appropriate choice from the drop-down menu can set other Options settings, as shown in Figure 3-23.

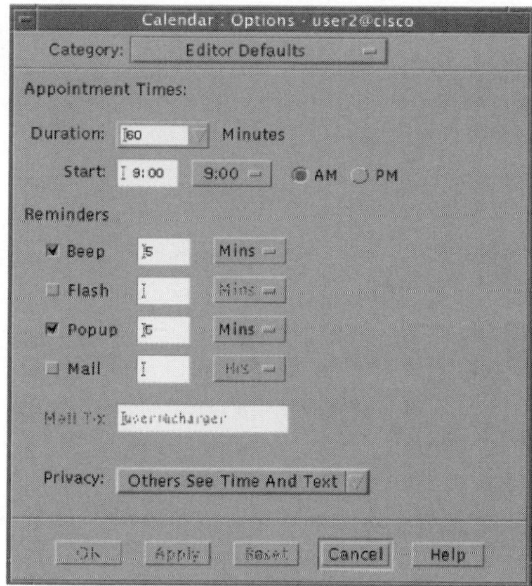

Figure 3-22 Editor Defaults window.

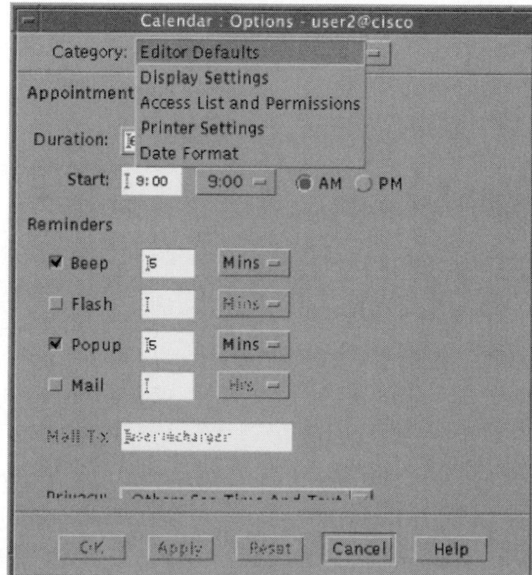

Figure 3-23 Other calendar options.

Display Settings

In Display Settings, you can do the following (see Figure 3-24):

- Set the time range for the working day
- Set the hour display as 12- or 24-hour
- Designate the default view for the Calendar Manager
- Designate the default calendar to view

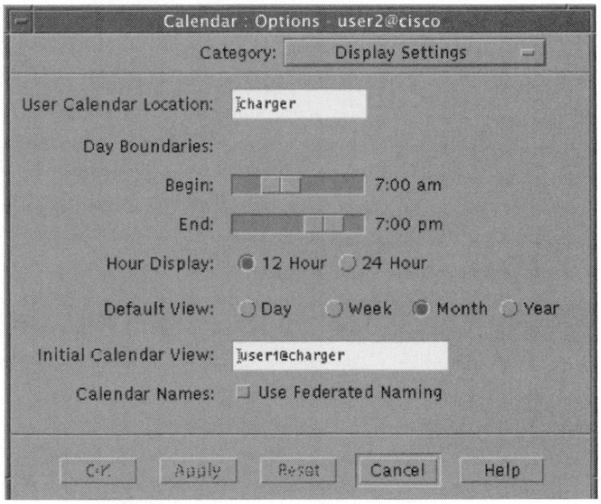

Figure 3-24
The display settings.

Printer Settings

The Printer Settings window enables you to set your personal options for the printing of calendar appointments (see Figure 3-25).

Date Format

The Date Format window enables you to set the format for date, display, and date entry (see Figure 3-26).

Working with Appointments

Appointments or things-to-do can be added to your calendar by clicking the appropriate icon at the top-left side of the window (see Figure 3-27).

Adding an Appointment

When you click the Appointment button, an Appointment Editor window is displayed (see Figure 3-28). Details that can be entered into this window include these:

- The date on which the appointment is to be made
- The start and end times of the appointment
- Details relating to the appointment (in the What box).

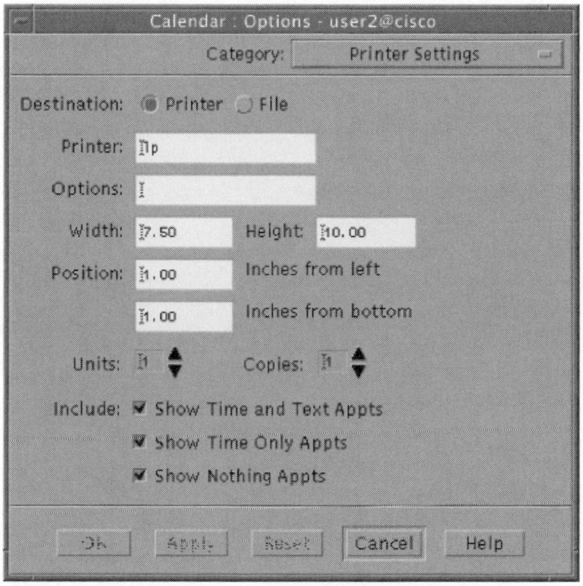

Figure 3-25
The printer settings.

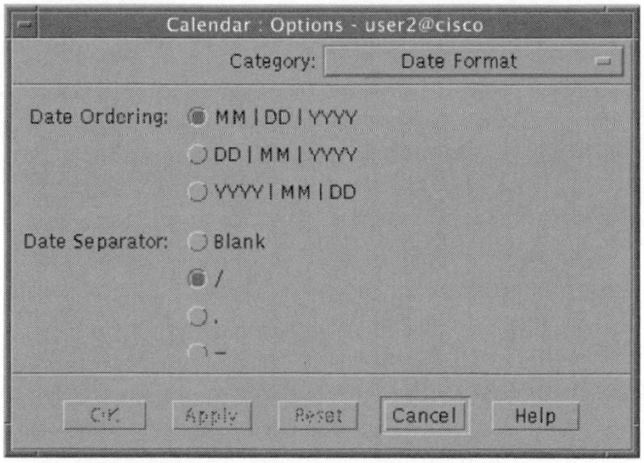

Figure 3-26
The date format.

After the appropriate details are selected or entered into the relevant window areas, click Insert to add that appointment. When an appointment has been inserted, it will be displayed in the Time What area at the right side of the window and on the appropriate day of your calendar. The Drag Appointment icon can be used to drag an "appointment by e-mail" onto your calendar.

Figure 3-27
The Appointment icons.

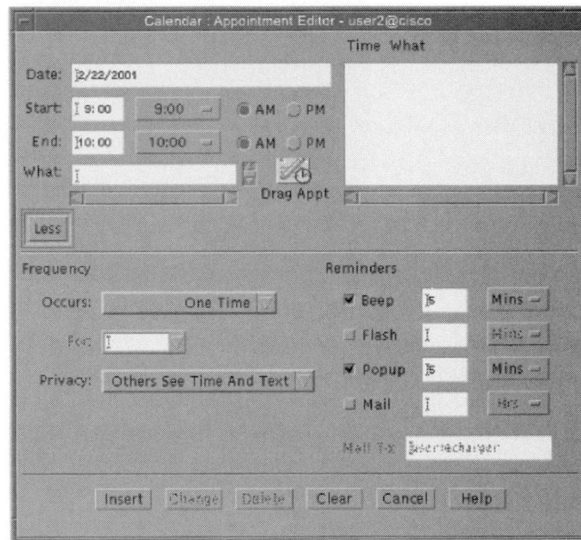

Figure 3-28
The Appointment Editor window.

NOTE

By default, you can add several appointments on the same day to start at the same time. The Calendar Manager does not warn you of conflicting appointments.

Setting Start and End Times Pick-and-point lists are provided to indicate the times that your appointments start and end. These lists can be selected by clicking the appropriate time box to the right of the start and end times.

Selecting a Date Regardless of the current view of the calendar, you can scroll forward and backward along a timescale associated with that view. After an appropriate date is visible on the display, you can open the Appointments Editor by double-clicking the area in the window associated with that day. If you are looking at the weekly view, click the area at the bottom left of the window, and then double-click in the hourly section to set an appointment for that time, as shown in Figure 3-29.

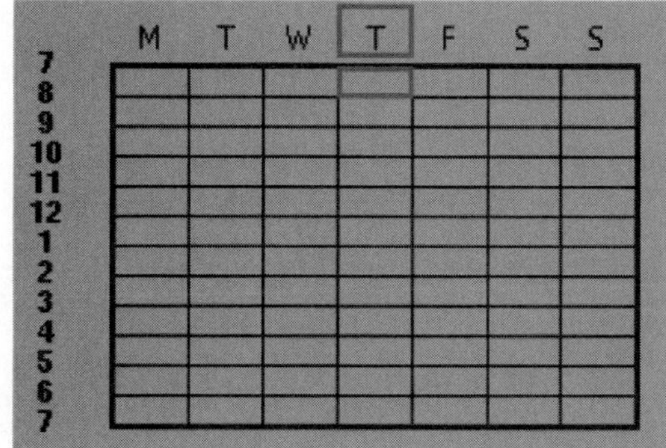

Figure 3-29
The weekly view's time scale.

Appointment Editor Options Additional options are available when adding an appointment (see Figure 3-30). By clicking More in the lower-left corner of the window, this display opens at the bottom of the Appointment Editor window. The following options are available:

- Frequency of the appointment
- Number of times that a frequent appointment is to be added to the calendar
- Privacy controls
- Appointment reminders
- Who to send e-mail to (when an appointment reminder is to be sent)

To close the additional options window area, click Less.

TIP

If someone sends you an e-mail with an Appointment icon, you can drag the icon to an *open* calendar window or to the Calendar control on the Front Panel, to add it to your calendar. The Appointment icon *cannot* be dropped on a minimized calendar.

Finding Appointments

The Find window enables you to search for text in the appointment entries (see Figure 3-31). You can specify the time period to search, giving a start and end date. After appointments are found, you can double-click the details (shown in the lower portion of the window) to view the actual appointment details.

Working with Other Users' Calendars

This section shows you how to work with the calendars of other users.

Setting Access to Your Calendar

In this window, you can set the access rights for the calendar (see Figure 3-32). You can designate who has the right to work with or view your calendar. By default, this is set to World, which means that everyone has access rights.

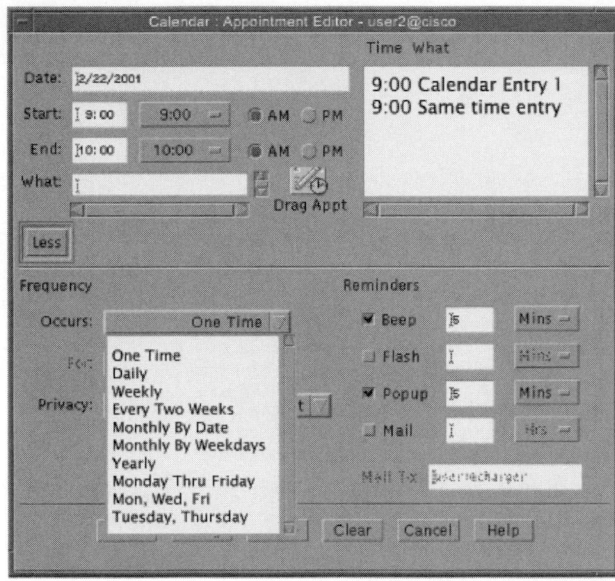

Figure 3-30 The Appointment Editor options.

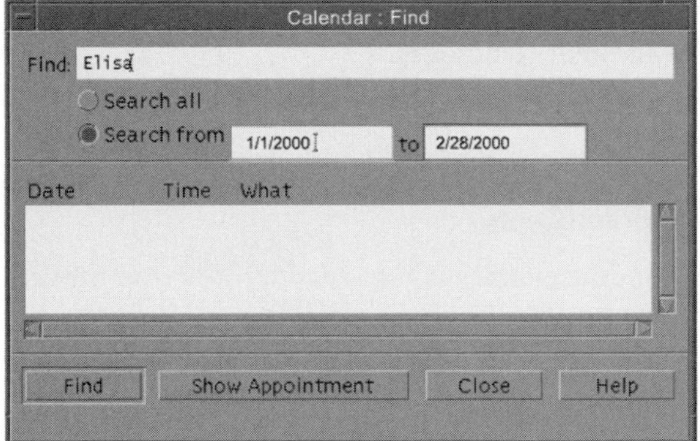

Figure 3-31 Finding appointments.

Browsing Other Calendars

If you want to check the appointments that have been made in another user's calendars, use the Browse, Show Other Calendar menu option (see Figure 3-33). With the correct permission settings to view other calendars, you can compare people's appointments to help arrange meetings that do not conflict with existing appointments. The Browse menu option also provides a menu editor for configuring the menu options that are used by the calendar window.

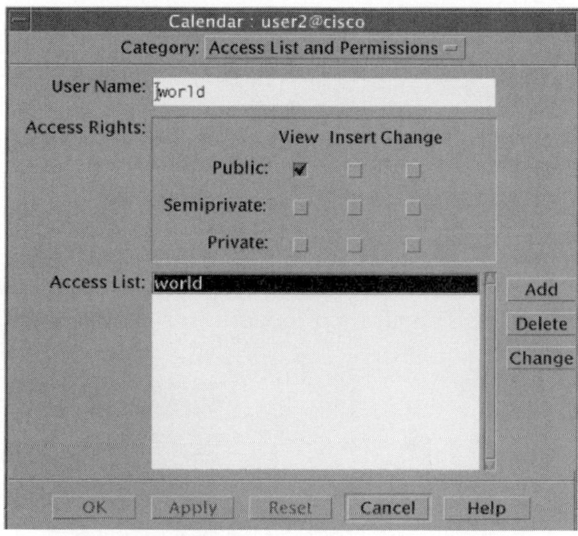

Figure 3-32
Access list and permissions.

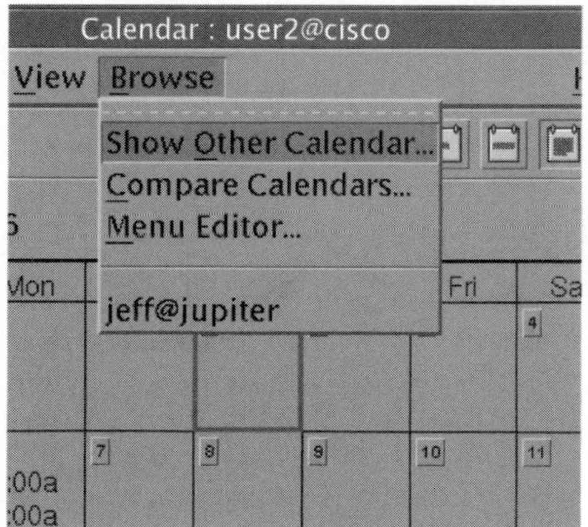

Figure 3-33
Show another person's calendar.

Skill Builder

Lab Activity 3.2.5

Using CDE Calendar Manager

In this lab, you work with CDE Calendar Manager. Calendar Manager is a full-featured graphical schedule- and appointment-management program. Refer to the *Cisco Networking Academy Program: Fundamentals of UNIX Lab Companion*.

Other Built-In Applications

CDE provides a number of other useful applications for managing notes and addresses, as well as tools for playing sounds, tools for viewing images, and a simple calculator.

Voice Notes

The Voice Notes application lets you personalize your mail messages. Select Voice Note from the Applications subpanel to record voice input (see Figure 3-34). Note that selecting Voice Note starts Audio in record mode. A microphone or voice input device is necessary for this application to work (see Figure 3-35).

Figure 3-34
The Voice Note subpanel.

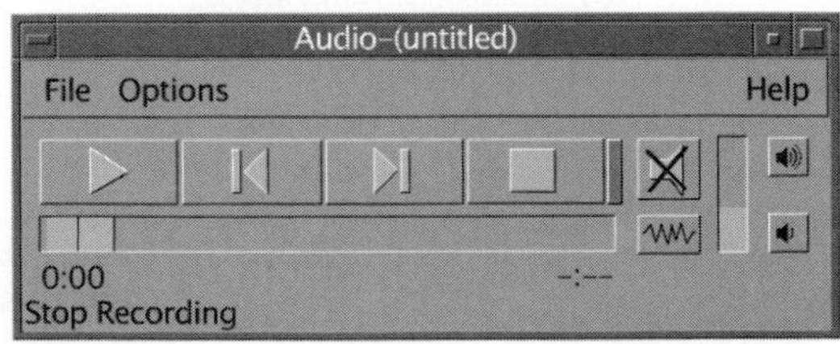

Figure 3-35
The Audio panel.

Text Notes

Text Notes enable you to create Post-It–style notes on your workspace. Select Text Note from the Applications subpanel to record text input. (See Figures 3-36 and 3-37.) The note then can be minimized and left on your workspace as a reminder. You can drag notes into mail messages as mail attachments.

Figure 3-36
The Text Note subpanel.

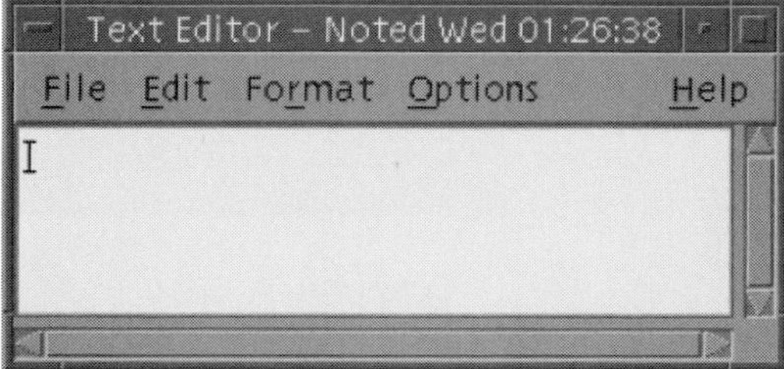

Figure 3-37
The text editor note.

Address Manager

Address Manager enables you to search corporate name databases and organize your contacts in electronic cards. You can schedule appointments, send e-mail, and dial telephone numbers from the electronic cards. You can access the Address Manager in one of two ways. First, you can right-click the desktop to bring up the Workspace menu and then select Cards/Address Manager, or you can access the Address Manager from the Front Panel/Cards subpanel. (See Figures 3-38 and 3-39.)

Figure 3-38
The Address Manager subpanel.

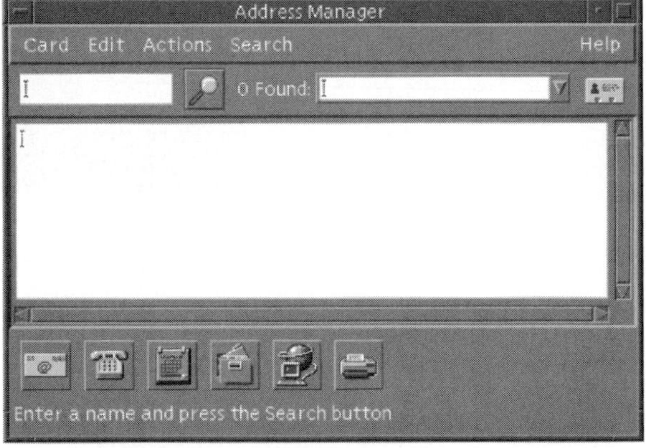

Figure 3-39
The Address Manager screen.

Audio

The Audio application provides a way to record and play sounds. A microphone is necessary to record sound files. Sound files can be played through the built-in speakers on a Sun workstation. Solaris for Intel systems must have a supported sound card and speakers. To activate the Audio application, right-click the desktop and choose Applications; then select Audio and Video (see Figure 3-40).

TIP

Sample sound files are on Solaris systems in the /usr/demo/SOUND/sounds directory.

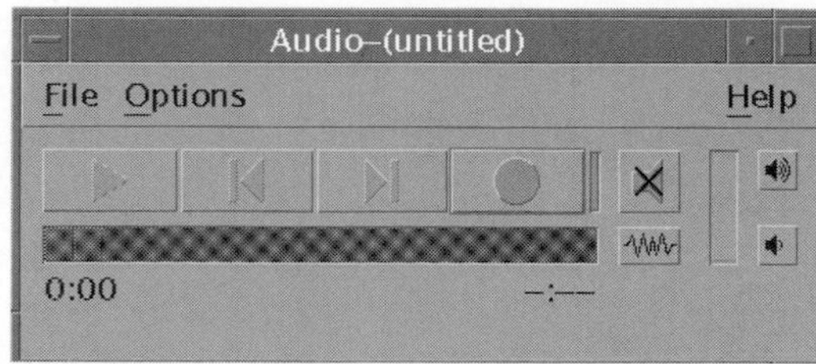

Figure 3-40
Audio applications.

Calculator

The Calculator provides an online tool for quick calculations. It includes a basic simple calculator function and a more sophisticated scientific calculator function. You can place the calculator on your desktop to have it available whenever you need it. To activate the calculator, right-click your desktop and select Calculator. (See Figures 3-41 and 3-42.)

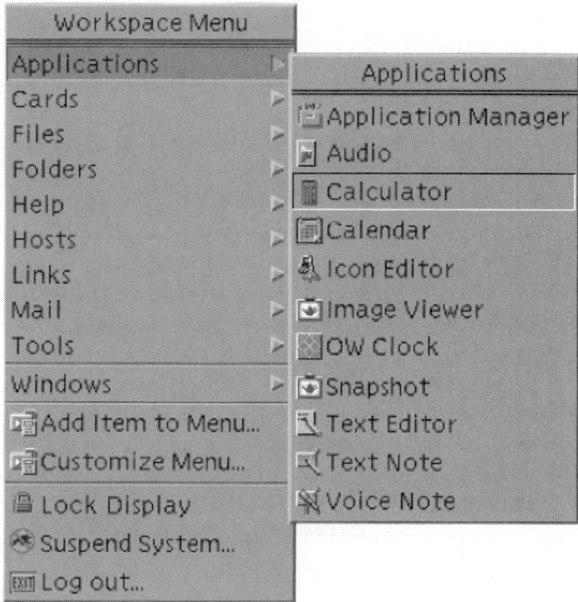

Figure 3-41
The calculator menu option.

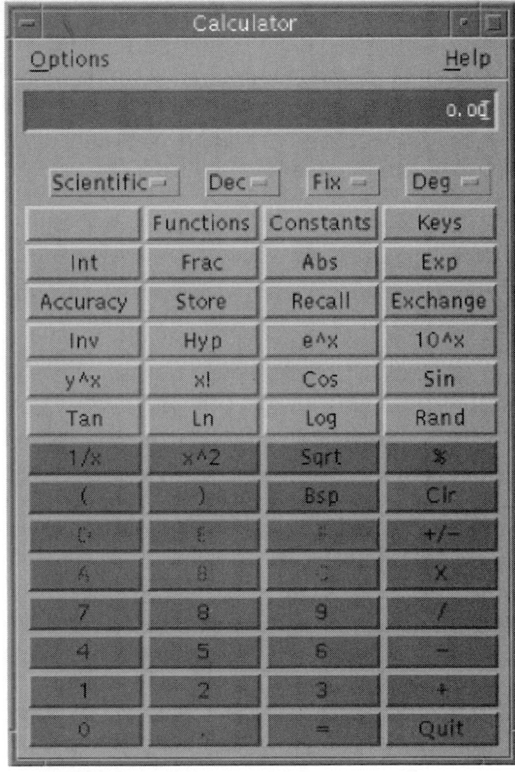

Figure 3-42
The calculator application.

TIP

Sample image files are on Solaris systems in the /usr/openwin/share/images directory.

NOTE

You must be logged in as root to change the date on a UNIX system. The Clock only views current time/date settings and can't be used to change them.

Icon Editor

The Icon Editor application is used to edit or create icon images associated with an application. To activate the Icon Editor, right-click the desktop and choose Applications, Icon Editor (see Figure 3-43).

Image Viewer

The Image Viewer application is used to view and manipulate graphics images. To activate the Image Viewer, right-click the desktop and choose Applications, Image Viewer (see Figure 3-44).

Clock

The Clock provides a graphical method of viewing the time, date, and time zone. To activate the Clock, right-click your desktop and choose Applications, OW Clock. (See Figures 3-45 and 3-46.)

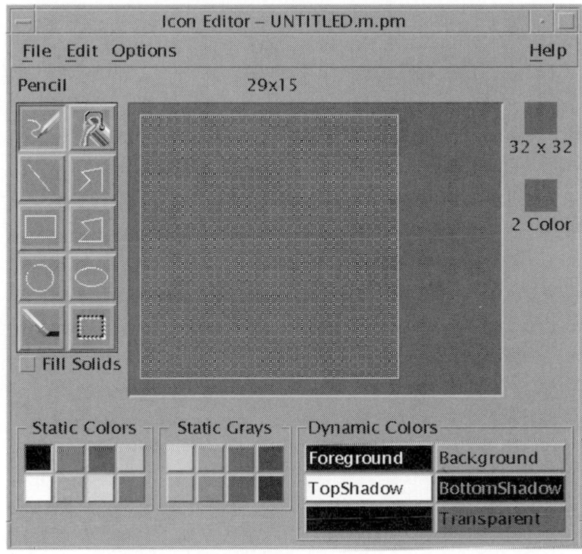

Figure 3-43
The Icon Editor application.

Figure 3-44
The Image Viewer application.

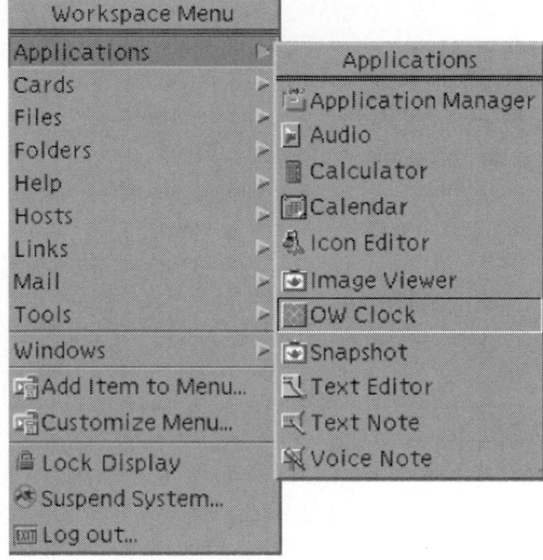

Figure 3-45
The Clock menu option.

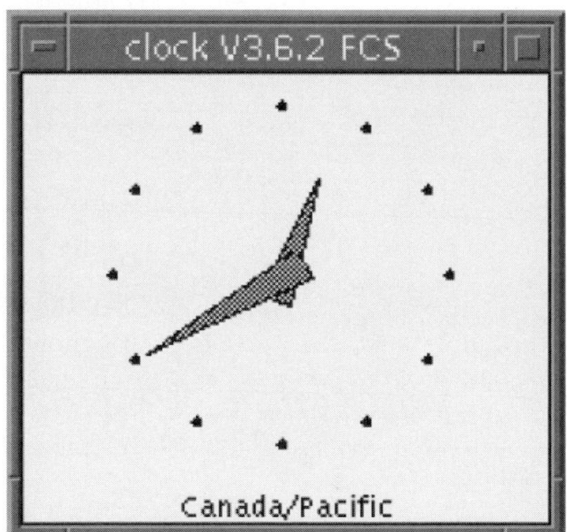

Figure 3-46
The Clock application.

Other Clock display properties include the following and can be changed by right-clicking the Clock and choosing Properties:

- A digital versus an analog display
- A 12-hour or 24-hour display
- An option to select whether seconds are displayed
- An option to select the time zone
- An option to set a stopwatch
- An option to set an alarm

Snapshot

The Snapshot application is used to capture screen images into a file to be later inserted into a document (see Figure 3-47). Most images for this course were created with the Snapshot application. Snapshot supports the popular graphic file formats. To activate the Snapshot, right-click the desktop and choose Applications; then select Snapshot.

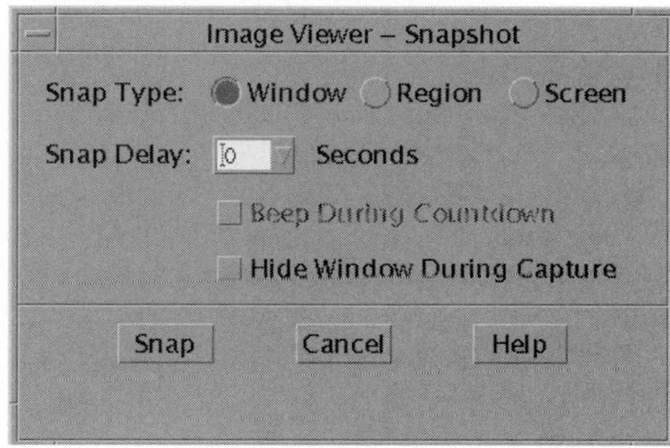

Figure 3-47 Editor Defaults window.

Terminal Windows

A Terminal window can be opened in the graphical environment to provide a command-line interface to the system, as shown in Figure 3-48. Multiple Terminal windows can be open at the same time. Each Terminal window represents a new shell and displays a shell prompt waiting for user input.

Anything you can do from the command line you can do from a Terminal window. You will be working in a Terminal window throughout much of this book as you learn various UNIX commands and their functions.

TIP

You can open an additional Terminal window anytime by entering the **dtterm&** (desktop terminal) command in an existing Terminal window. The ampersand (&) tells the shell program to run the **dtterm** command in the background and to return the shell prompt so that you can continue working in that Terminal window.

To close a Terminal window, type exit or press Ctrl-D.

Skill Builder

e-Lab Activity 3.1

Terminal Window Shell

In this e-Lab activity, you enter the UNIX **date** command. This activity demonstrates how a command is entered from the command line. The **date** command works similarly to the CDE Clock application that you learned previously.

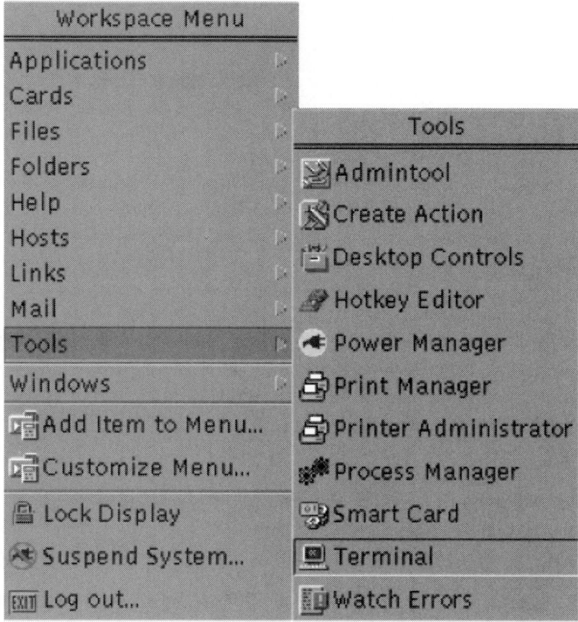

Figure 3-48 Opening the Terminal windows.

Skill Builder

Lab Activity 3.3.5

Other Built-In CDE Applications

In this lab, you work with several additional user applications that are included with the CDE. These include Voice and Text Notes, Address Manager, Calculator, and Clock. You learn how to open a Terminal window that gives you access to the UNIX command line. Refer to the *Cisco Networking Academy Program: Fundamentals of UNIX Lab Companion.*

Summary

Now that you have completed this chapter, you should have an understanding of the following:

The CDE is a standard graphical user interface for the UNIX platform that comes with several built-in productivity applications such as the Mail Tool and Calendar Manger. Several others also are included, such as Voice and Text Notes, Address Manager, Calculator, and Clock. You also have the capability of opening a Terminal window at any to access the command line.

The Mail Tool is a graphical e-mail application that can perform all normal e-mail functions. It allows you to view e-mail and attachments, compose new e-mail with attachments, and delete old messages. Received messages can be saved and managed by filing them in alternate mailboxes.

The Calendar Manager manages scheduling and appointments through the use of a powerful graphical interface that supports networking. You can view your calendar in several formats by clicking icons. You can add new appointments and find existing ones. Many options can be set with the calendar. Your calendar can be shared with others, and you can make appointments on other people's calendars if they have given you permission to do so.

Many other graphical applications are built into the CDE. The ones that this chapter focused on include Voice and Text Notes, Address Manager, Calculator, and Clock.

You can open a Terminal window from the CDE, which starts a new shell. You have a command line available in the Terminal window, which enables you to enter commands and run command-line utilities. Entering the **dtterm&** command opens another Terminal window.

Check Your Understanding

1. All of the following are graphical applications included with CDE *except*:
   - A. Mail Tool
   - B. Calendar Manager
   - C. Address Manager
   - D. Outlook
2. The Mail Tool is a basic command-line e-mail application that cannot accommodate attachments (True/False).
   - A. True
   - B. False
3. Marcia sends regular e-mail to the members of her project team and would like to be able to create a list under one name to avoid having to specify each name when she sends out memos. What is this called with Mail Tool?
   - A. Distlist
   - B. Alien
   - C. GroupName
   - D. Alias
4. All of the following are customizable options with Mail Tool *except*:
   - A. Specifying how often you would like the system to check for new mail
   - B. Specifying autoreturn for junk mail
   - C. Setting a vacation message to be sent in reply to messages when you are unavailable
   - D. Creating a custom signature that can be attached to all outgoing e-mail
5. The Calendar Manager allows users to change preferences, including View (day, week, and so on), Display Format, and Printer Settings (True/False).
   - A. True
   - B. False
6. All of the following are available with the Appointment Editor *except*:
   - A. Frequency of the appointment
   - B. Number of times that a frequent appointment is to be added to the calendar

C. Appointment priority

D. Appointment reminders

7. By default, everyone can see your calendar unless you limit access rights (True/False).

A. True

B. False

8. With Address Manager, you can do all of the following from the electronic cards *except*:

A. Schedule appointments

B. Send e-mail

C. Dial telephone numbers

D. Put someone on hold

9. Calculator and Clock have which characteristic in common?

A. They can be run only as command-line utilities.

B. They are installed as optional components.

C. They are graphical utilities that are part of the CDE.

D. They are display utilities only and cannot accept input.

10. Which of the following is true of a Terminal window?

A. Each terminal window starts in a new shell.

B. Terminal windows are initiated from within the CDE.

C. Terminal windows give you access to the command line.

D. All of the above.

UNIX Command Summary

mailx Interactive message processing system. Example:

```
$ mailx user2@cisco.com < dante.doc
```

uuencode Used to convert a binary file into an ASCII-encoded representation that can be sent using e-mail. The encoded file is an ordinary ASCII text file.

Key Terms

Calendar Manager A full-featured graphical schedule and appointment management program. It is a standard component of the Solaris CDE.

Domain name The company and type portion of an e-mail address, such as jiml@company.com, where company.com is the domain name.

Mail Tool A full-featured graphical e-mail–management program. It is an e-mail client that is a standard component of the Solaris CDE.

mailx The mailx (and the earlier, more basic mail) program comes with every version of UNIX and is an acceptable program for reading and sending mail. The mailx program basics are found in Appendix E and are worth learning for those times when you need a mail program but don't have access to the CDE.

Pine The Pine mail program is menu-based and is easier to use than the mailx program. Pine was developed at the University of Washington and can be accessed by typing **pine** at the command prompt.

Username The login name of a UNIX user that is part of the user's e-mail address, such as jiml@company.com, where jiml is the username.

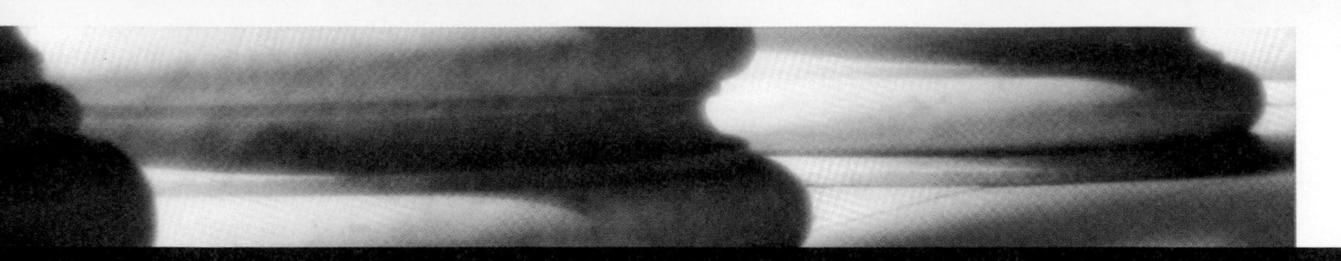

Objectives

After reading this chapter, you will be able to

- Use CDE help
- Reference AnswerBook2
- Use command-line help
- Perform basic UNIX workstation troubleshooting
- Compare DOS and UNIX commands

Chapter 4

Getting Help

Introduction

This chapter introduces various forms of help provided by the Solaris environment. It covers graphical help available with the Common Desktop Environment (CDE). CDE help includes many options, such as the Help Manager and Front Panel help. AnswerBook2, which is an online version of the Solaris manuals, is accessible through CDE as well. This chapter also works with command-line help known as *manual*, or *man*, pages. These pages provide character-based help with UNIX commands and utilities. This chapter also reviews some basic troubleshooting techniques and provides a DOS-to-UNIX cross-reference table for those who have a background in DOS.

Using CDE Help

A number of graphical help functions are built into the CDE. This section identifies the location of these and describes the type of help they can provide.

Using Help Viewer

The Help icon is situated at the right side of the front panel. Clicking the icon with the left mouse button opens up the Help subpanel, shown in Figure 4-1, with a number of help options. These are listed here with a brief description of the type of help that each one provides.

- *Help Manager*—The primary help tool for most situations
- **SunSolve Online**—Web-based online help from Sun Microsystems
- **Solaris Support**—Web-based Sun Microsystems Support contact information
- **Information**—Access to the Application Manager information readme files
- **Desktop Introduction**—Basic tutorial on using the desktop
- **Front Panel Help**—Help with the front panel icons and features

- **On Item Help**—Specific onscreen information about an item, available by selecting that item
- *AnswerBook2*—Solaris reference manuals in online format

Figure 4-1
The Help Manager subpanel.

The hypertext links, shown as underlined text or boxed graphics, can quickly move you to a related help page. Just click the appropriate area of text in the Help window.

The Backtrack button allows you to retrace the path that you followed through the help screens.

The Print button can be used to print a copy of a particular help topic.

Searching the Help Index

The index search enables you to see all volumes of help. To access the help index search, click the Index button while in the Help Viewer window to bring up the screen shown in Figure 4-2. These volumes are displayed as hyperlinks, which can be used to reference any help page. You also can search for specific help items based on a keyword search. The number to the left of the help index item is the number of subtopics available.

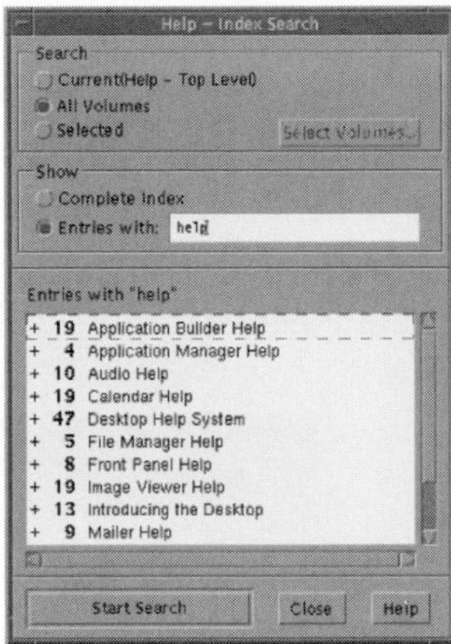

Figure 4-2
Help index search.

Using Item Help

The On Item Help icon is on the Help subpanel shown in the Figure 4-3. When this function is selected, the mouse pointer changes from an arrow pointer to a question mark with an arrowhead at its base. The pointer then can be positioned over a front panel icon to access the appropriate help page for that item, which will be displayed in a Help Viewer window. The mouse pointer reverts back to an arrow pointer at this time. The on-item help function works only on icons or within the Application Manager window.

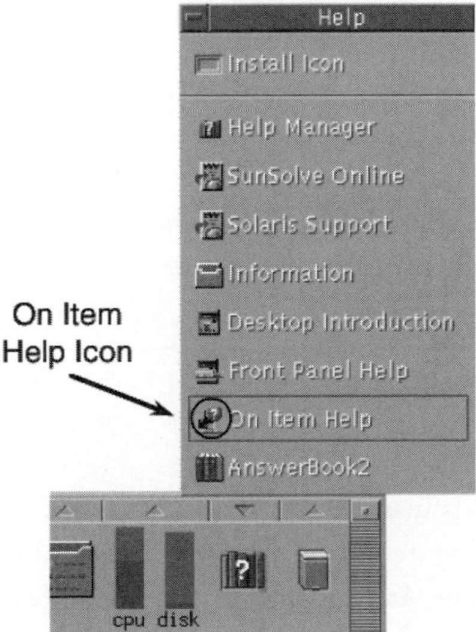

Figure 4-3
The on-item help function.

Other Ways to Access Help

Right-clicking any free space on the desktop displays the Workspace menu. From the Workspace menu, you can select the Help option from the Programs submenu. Clicking the Help icon on the *Terminal window* activates a drop-down help menu. After the Help Viewer is invoked, you can use it as described in the section, "Using Help Viewer." Most windows also have a Help menu option specific to the current application, as shown in Figure 4-4.

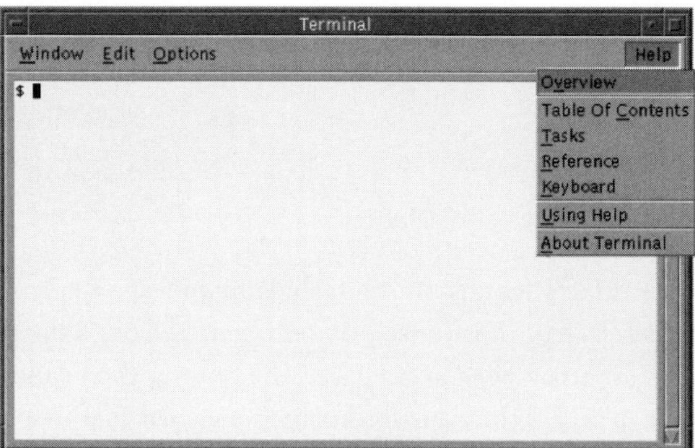

Figure 4-4
Application-specific help.

Skill Builder

Lab Activity 4.1.4

Using CDE Help

In this lab, you work with several help functions built into the CDE to assist users when performing CDE-related tasks. You use the main CDE help viewer and search the Help index for help on specific topics. You also can use the on-item help feature to discover what desktop icons are. Refer to the *Cisco Networking Academy Program: Fundamentals of UNIX Lab Companion.*

AnswerBook2

If AnswerBook2 is installed on your system or network server, you can see the icon that's shown in Figure 4-5 on the Help subpanel that you can use to access AnswerBook2. The AnswerBook2 system enables you to view an online version of printed Solaris manuals (including graphics). Several collections of online books contain a tremendous amount of information, including the following:

- Solaris 8 System Administrator Collection
- Solaris 8 User Collection
- Solaris 8 Software Developer Collection

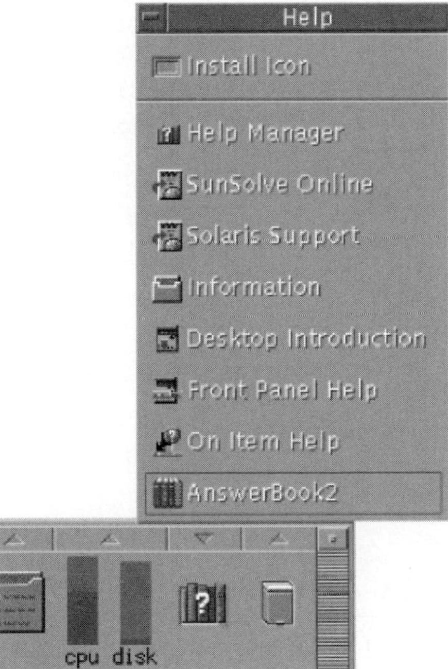

Figure 4-5
The Help subpanel menu.

As with the Help Viewer, hyperlinks can be used to skip to the relevant pages of the online manual. By default, AnswerBook2 uses the HotJava browser to display information. You can perform searches on parts of the AnswerBook2 or the entire collection. Figure 4-6 shows the initial AnswerBook2 screen.

Because of the amount of disk space the AnswerBook2 pages take, your system administrator might not have installed AnswerBook2 on the computer's hard disk. However, it is possible to access AnswerBook2 files from a CD-ROM or hard disk device connected to a remote host such as a server on your network.

If AnswerBook2 is accessible through your network, be aware that there will be a delay between requesting and displaying AnswerBook2 pages. The speed with which the pages are collected from the remote hard drive or CD-ROM device depends on network configuration and activity.

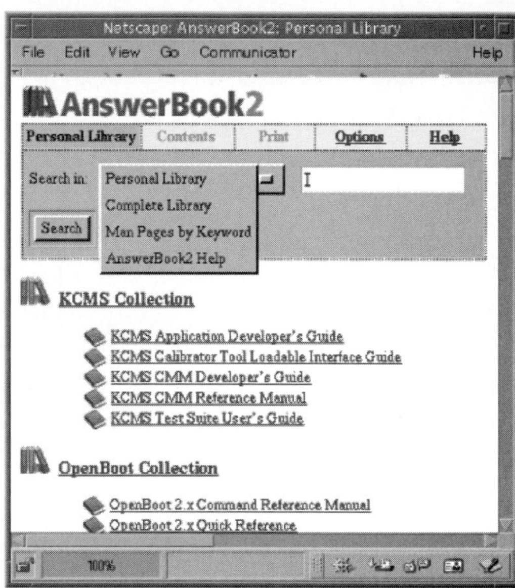

Figure 4-6 The initial AnswerBook2 screen.

Skill Builder

Lab Activity 4.2.1

Referencing AnswerBook2 Help

In this lab, you work with Sun Solaris AnswerBook2 and become familiar with the various collections of available online manuals. The AnswerBook2 system enables you to use your Web browser to view online versions of many of the printed Solaris manuals, including the graphics. Refer to the *Cisco Networking Academy Program: Fundamentals of UNIX Lab Companion.*

Command-Line Help

In addition to the graphical CDE help, you can get help on UNIX commands, system calls, file formats, and system maintenance using command-line help known as man pages.

Man Pages

The *UNIX Programmer's Manual* (also called *man pages*) describes what you need to know about the system's online commands, system calls, file formats, and system maintenance. The online man pages are part of the Solaris computing environment (and all other versions of *UNIX*) and are installed by default. Man pages are in the form of simple character-based screen displays and are not graphical.

To access the man pages, you need to be at a command prompt. You can log in at the command line or open a Terminal window in CDE and start with a command prompt such as the Korn shell ($). Man pages are helpful when you want to use a command or utility and you have forgotten the syntax or you need just some information about how to use it. The man pages provide information on how to enter the command, a description of its purpose, and what options or arguments are available. Some commands will not work with all three shells; the man pages tell which commands will work with which shells. They refer to the Bourne shell as (sh), the Korn shell as (ksh), and the C shell as (csh).

The man Command

The **man** command displays online man pages for any of the hundreds of UNIX commands that are available. You can get a listing of all the UNIX commands with a brief description of what they do by entering **man intro** at the command line. You even can display a man page on the **man** command itself by typing **man man.**

You can use the **man** command in several ways. The basic form is **man** ***name***, where *name* is the name of the command for which you want information. There are several handy options to the **man** command for performing keyword searches and displaying specific sections of the Programmer's Manual. Several different ways to use the **man** command are listed here, with a brief explanation of each one:

- **$ man** *name*—Provides help on a particular command, where *name* is the name of the command that you want to get help with, such as **ls**, **cat**, or **mkdir**.
- **$ man -k** *keyword*—Searches the man pages' table of contents for the specified keyword and displays a one-line summary for each entry. Figure 4-7 shows an example of the output from this command.

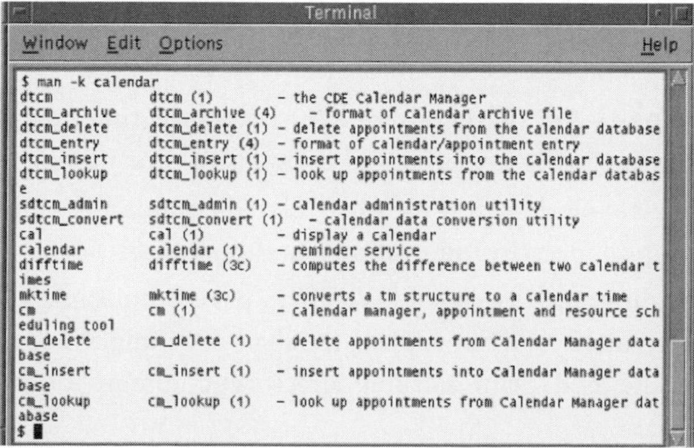
Terminal
Window Edit Options Help
$ man -k calendar
dtcm dtcm (1) - the CDE Calendar Manager
dtcm_archive dtcm_archive (4) - format of calendar archive file
dtcm_delete dtcm_delete (1) - delete appointments from the calendar database
dtcm_entry dtcm_entry (4) - format of calendar/appointment entry
dtcm_insert dtcm_insert (1) - insert appointments into the calendar database
dtcm_lookup dtcm_lookup (1) - look up appointments from the calendar databas
e
sdtcm_admin sdtcm_admin (1) - calendar administration utility
sdtcm_convert sdtcm_convert (1) - calendar data conversion utility
cal cal (1) - display a calendar
calendar calendar (1) - reminder service
difftime difftime (3c) - computes the difference between two calendar t
imes
mktime mktime (3c) - converts a tm structure to a calendar time
cm cm (1) - calendar manager, appointment and resource sch
eduling tool
cm_delete cm_delete (1) - delete appointments from Calendar Manager data
base
cm_insert cm_insert (1) - insert appointments into Calendar Manager data
base
cm_lookup cm_lookup (1) - look up appointments from Calendar Manager dat
abase
$

Figure 4-7
The **man –k** keyword.

- **$ man -s** *section name*—Displays a particular section of the man pages, which can include multiple commands. Figure 4-8 shows an example of the output from this command.

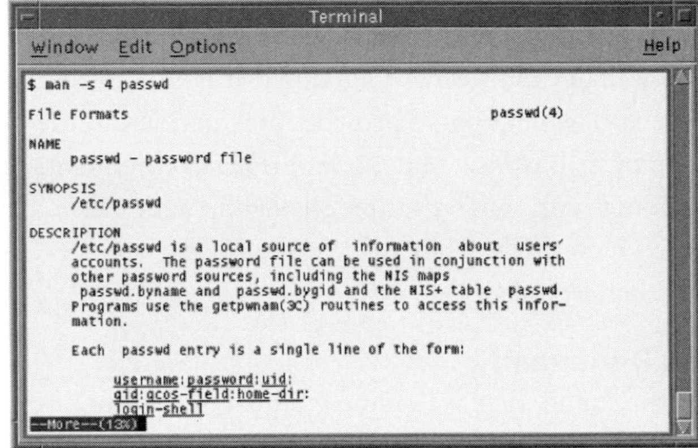

Figure 4-8
The **man –s** section name.

Working with Man Pages

Man pages are a quick and convenient way to check on UNIX command syntax while at a command prompt.

Man Page Headings

A number of different headings or informational areas are in a typical man page. The more common ones are the following:

- **name**—Contains the name of the command and other commands that may accomplish the same thing.
- **synopsis**—Shows the syntax of the command with any allowable options and arguments.
- **description**—Gives an overview of what the command does.
- **operands**—The target of the command or what the command will take effect on such as a directory or a file.
- **options**—Are switches that can change the function or effect of the command. They normally are preceded by a dash (–) or minus sign.
- **see also**—Refers you to other related commands and subjects, such as **name, synopsis, description, options**, and **operands.**

These headings are displayed in the man page output in all capital letters. Depending on the command and its purpose, the man page might not contain all headings. For example, the **pwd** (print working directory) command does not have an options or operands information heading because no options or operands can be used with the command. All commands will have at least a name, a synopsis, and a description.

A common UNIX command is **cd**, which allows you to change directories. The results of the man page for the **cd** command are shown in Figure 4-9. Note the different headings that previously were discussed. Some of the output has been omitted because the output from the **cd** man page is normally about nine pages long.

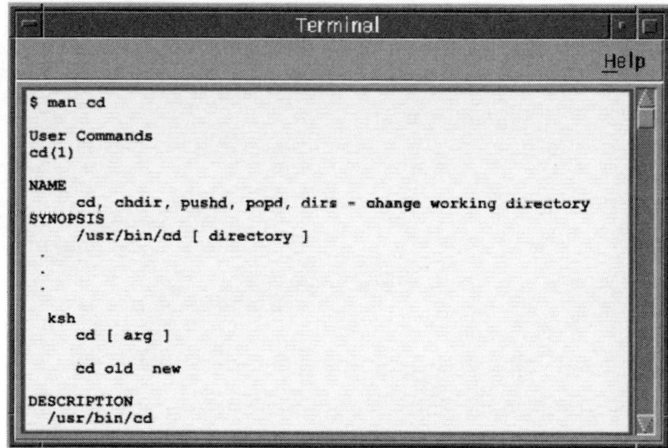

Figure 4-9
Man page output.

Scrolling in Man Pages

The output from some man pages can be as many as 10 to 20 screens of output. Several keys are helpful in moving around in the man utility after the pages for a specific command have been located. Use the keys shown in Figure 4-10 to control the scrolling capabilities while using the **man** command.

Figure 4-10
Scrolling the man pages.

Space bar	Scrolls one screen at a time
Return	Scrolls one line at a time
b	Back — Moves back one screen
f	Forward — Moves forward one screen
q	Quit — Exits the man command
/string	Search — Forwards for information
n	Next — Finds the next occurence of string
h	Help — Gives a description of all scrolling capabilities

Searching Man Pages by Section

As previously discussed, the SEE ALSO part at the bottom of a man page lists alternate references that pertain to the topic addressed. When these references are followed by a number other than 1 in parentheses, it indicates a section of the man pages that can be accessed using the **-s** option with the **man** command.

For example, executing $ **man passwd**, as shown in Figure 4-11, displays information on the **passwd** command and gives instructions on how to change a password. The SEE ALSO section of this man page reads in part as follows:

```
SEE ALSO
finger(1), login(1), nispasswd(1), crypt(3C), passwd(4)
```

Figure 4-11
Searching the man pages by section.

```
$ man passwd
...
... (Output Omitted)
...
SEE ALSO
finger(a), login(1), nispasswd(1),
crypt(3C), passwd(4)

$ man -s 4 passwd

$ man -s 3C crypt
```

Executing $ **man** -s 4 **passwd** displays information on the /etc/passwd file, and $ **man** -s 3C **crypt** displays information on password encryption. The other SEE ALSO items listed, finger and login, are related but do not have a separate section that can be searched.

Searching Man Pages by Keyword

NOTE

The keyword lookup for searching man pages is not enabled by default. To enable this feature, the system administrator must execute the following command as the root user:

```
# catman -w
```

The **-k** option for the **man** command also can be helpful. As an example, if you know that you are looking for a command that has to do with the calendar but you are not sure what commands are available, you can use the **-k** option to specify a keyword as a subject. Figure 4-12 shows the results of using the **-k** option with the **man** command when looking for commands related to the calendar..

Displaying Man Page Headers with whatis

Using the **whatis** command displays the header line from the manual section, as shown in Figure 4-13. The man page itself then can be displayed by using the **man** command. The **whatis** command can be helpful if you can remember the command name but forget what is does. You can use **whatis** to get a brief definition of the command. The example in the figure shows using **whatis** to find out what the **grep** command does (**grep** is covered later in the course).

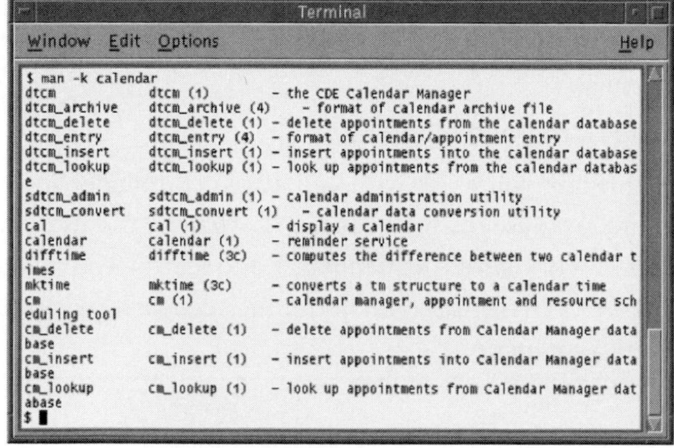

Terminal
Window Edit Options Help
$ man -k calendar
dtcm dtcm (1) - the CDE Calendar Manager
dtcm_archive dtcm_archive (4) - format of calendar archive file
dtcm_delete dtcm_delete (1) - delete appointments from the calendar database
dtcm_entry dtcm_entry (4) - format of calendar/appointment entry
dtcm_insert dtcm_insert (1) - insert appointments into the calendar database
dtcm_lookup dtcm_lookup (1) - look up appointments from the calendar databas
e
sdtcm_admin sdtcm_admin (1) - calendar administration utility
sdtcm_convert sdtcm_convert (1) - calendar data conversion utility
cal cal (1) - display a calendar
calendar calendar (1) - reminder service
difftime difftime (3c) - computes the difference between two calendar t
imes
mktime mktime (3c) - converts a tm structure to a calendar time
cm cm (1) - calendar manager, appointment and resource sch
eduling tool
cm_delete cm_delete (1) - delete appointments from Calendar Manager data
base
cm_insert cm_insert (1) - insert appointments into Calendar Manager data
base
cm_lookup cm_lookup (1) - look up appointments from Calendar Manager dat
abase
$

Figure 4-12 Searching man pages by keyword.

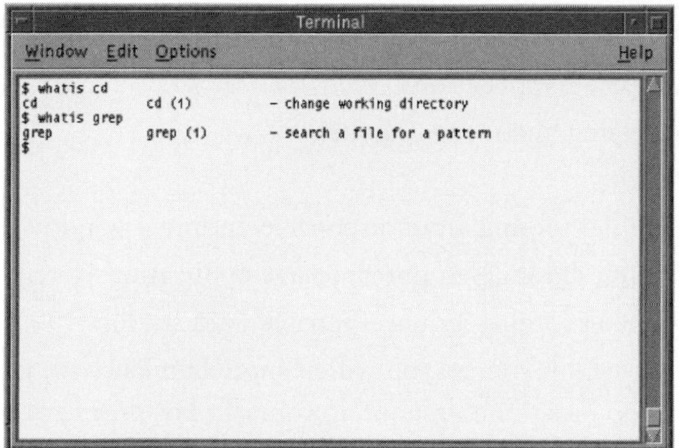

Figure 4-13 The **whatis** command.

SAVING MAN PAGES FOR FUTURE USE

You can save a man page to a text file for editing or e-mailing. Use the command **man** *command_name | col -b > filename*—for example, man intro | col -b > ~/unixcmnds. The intro command contains a list of all UNIX commands; the vertical bar, or pipe, (|) is covered in Chapter 7, "Advanced Directory and File Management"; col -b formats the man page output; the greater-than sign (>) means to send the output of the man command to a file; and ~/unixcmnds is the file (unixcmnds) that gets created in your home directory (~ represents your home directory).

TIP

You can print a man page by using the command **man** *command_name* | *lp* (or *lpr*). The line printer commands (**lp** and **lpr**) are covered in Chapter 11, "UNIX Printing."

Basic features of the shell program are covered throughout this course. Advanced shell features can be learned by issuing the **man** command for the shell program that you use. For example, **man ksh** prints the manual pages for the Korn shell. Replace **ksh** with **sh** for the Borne shell and **csh** for the C shell.

Skill Builder

Lab Activity 4.3.3

Using Command-Line Help

In this lab, you work with and access command-line help using the **man** command. You use the man pages to determine the use of various UNIX commands as you work with the man pages and learn to navigate through them. Refer to Lab 4.3.3 in the *Cisco Networking Academy Program: Fundamentals of UNIX Lab Companion.*

Troubleshooting

The most common issues people have with operating their UNIX workstation are the following:

- Accessing applications
- Accessing and managing files
- Printing
- Troubleshooting an unresponsive Terminal window
- Troubleshooting an unresponsive application
- Troubleshooting an unresponsive workstation

By the end of this course, you will be more familiar with your workstation and the ability to do basic troubleshooting yourself. For problems that you can't fix, you should contact your system administrator or service/help desk designated to help users with workstation problems.

If you do contact the company service/help desk, you probably will be asked for some information about your system before you are asked about your problem.

WORKSTATION INFORMATION

Information about your workstation (type, memory, OS release, and so on) can be viewed by choosing Hosts and then Workstation Info from the Workspace menu, as shown in Figure 4-14.

If CDE is not available, you can use the following commands to obtain system information:

- $ **hostname**—Displays the name of your workstation or host
- **$ uname –X**—Displays expanded system information, including the name of your workstation, the OS version, and more
- $ **arp <hostname>**—Displays the host name, IP address, and Ethernet address
- $ **domainname**—Displays the domain that the workstation is in (such as Corp.East.Sun.com)
- $ **prtconf | grep Memory**—Displays the amount of system memory

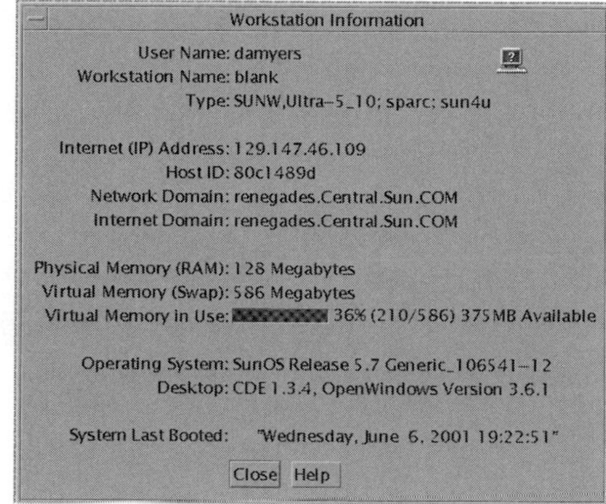

Figure 4-14 Workstation information.

To display messages from the network and to inform you of system errors that might be helpful in troubleshooting, open a Console window, as shown in Figure 4-15. A Console window looks like a Terminal window but should not used for entering commands. In addition, only one Console window should be open on the desktop if you choose to display messages at all. To open a Console window, right-click the desktop and choose Hosts; then select Terminal Console.

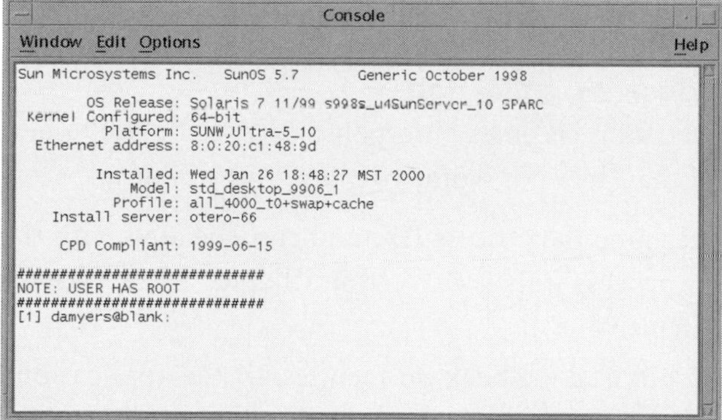

Figure 4-15 The terminal console.

Accessing Applications

Typically, applications are installed and maintained by the system administrator. If you are having difficulty starting an application, you should call the service/help desk. If you have questions regarding using an application that did not come up in a training class, you also should call the service/help desk.

Accessing and Managing Files

By the end of this course, you will have worked with files and directories enough that you should feel comfortable doing some basic troubleshooting on your own.

Printing

Most of your printing will be done from an application and is easy. Printing files and managing print jobs is covered in Chapter 11.

If a printer is down because of repairs or other reasons and you can't print, contact the service/help desk.

Unresponsive Terminal Window

If a Terminal window's prompt becomes unresponsive to keyboard entry, you might need to enable screen scroll, enter EOF (end of file), or interrupt the process.

To check an unresponsive terminal, follow these steps:

Step 1 Enable screen scroll by using Ctrl-Q. Sometimes a user turns off screen scrolling (by using Ctrl-S) and forgets to turn it back on. Therefore, the terminal appears locked.

Step 2 Interrupt the process by using Ctrl-C . This "cancels" the current task and should restore the shell prompt.

Step 3 Enter EOF (end of file) using Ctrl-D. You might be in the middle of a UNIX command that needs to be terminated by an EOF (bc, mail, mailx, and so on).

Step 4 Quit the window and start a new one.

Unresponsive Application

If an application becomes unresponsive, try to "close" the window by using the mouse. If that does not work, you have two options:

- Determine the process ID number associated with the application, and kill that process (this is covered in Chapter 13, "System Processes and Memory Management").
- Log out and log back in; then restart the application.

Unresponsive Workstation

If the window environment or the system in its entirety becomes unresponsive, you can perform a series of steps.

When attempting to unlock an unresponsive system, the first thing to do is to go to another system, do a remote login, and terminate the login shell program. The **rlogin,** **ps**, and **kill** commands are covered in more detail later in this curriculum.

If the previous procedure does not work, you must reboot your system using one of the following actions:

- The Stop-A keyboard sequence on a Sun workstation is used to abort and should be used only when the system is completely unresponsive to keyboard and mouse input for a period of minutes. The Stop-A sequence abruptly aborts and does not bring down the system cleanly. Stop-A brings down the system to a > (greater-than) prompt, where you can issue the **b** (boot) command to reboot.
- If the abort (Stop-A) does not work, your last resort is to power off the system, wait 10 seconds, and then power on the system.

NOTE

It's best to contact a system administrator or the help desk before you attempt this procedure.

DOS/UNIX Cross-Reference

Even though all the newer operating systems, including Microsoft Windows 9*x*, Millennium Edition (Me), Windows NT/2000 and Solaris have graphical user interfaces, they all still have a command prompt available. Knowledge of the command-line and command syntax for any operating system is still quite valuable in today's information technology world. Graphical user environments are nice, but sometimes the command line is all that is available for performing critical system tasks and troubleshooting. You might be at home, for example, and need to access your system at school or work. Bringing up a GUI over a modem would be extremely slow, so command-line access is a good option.

Command-line capabilities are generally more powerful and flexible than GUI interfaces, especially in the UNIX environment. In addition, system administrators frequently construct scripts (similar to batch files in *DOS*, NT, and other operating systems) containing commands to support end users, perform system administration functions, and automate routine tasks.

Some users who are new to the UNIX operating system might have a background in DOS that will make learning UNIX commands easier. Figure 4-16 lists some of the more common DOS commands and their UNIX equivalent. Because UNIX predates DOS, most DOS commands are based on those found in UNIX. In general, UNIX commands can do everything that DOS commands can do and more. For instance, the DOS **DIR** command lists the files in a directory. The UNIX **ls list** command does the same but has many more options available. There are also UNIX commands that DOS does not have an equivalent for, such as the **mv** (move) command. Figure 4-16 helps you transition from the DOS to the UNIX world. (This is not intended to be an exhaustive list of all the commands in either operating system. As usual, the 80/20 rule applies. You can do 80 percent of what you normally need to do on a daily basis with 20 percent of the tools or commands available.)

NOTE

All UNIX commands are lowercase, as shown in Figure 4-16.

Figure 4-16
The DOS/UNIX reference table.

DOS Command Abbreviated Version	UNIX Command	Function/Purpose
DIR	**ls**	Lists content of a directory.
CD (show current dir)	**pwd**	Prints (displays) working directory.
CD	**cd**	Changes working directory.
MD	**mkdir**	Makes directory under current directory.
RD	**rm**	Removes directories.
DEL (or ERASE)	**rm**	Removes files.
COPY	**cp**	Copies files.
TYPE	**cat**	Displays files (**cat** will also concentrate files).
REN	**mv**	Moves or renames files (DOS will not move files).
VER	**uname -rs**	Displays OS name and release number.
SORT	**sort**	Sorts files.
MORE	**more**	Displays file contents a screen at a time.
CLS	**clear**	Clears the screen.
DATE	**date**	Displays current date and time.
EDIT	**vi**	Invokes an ASCII text editor.
PRINT	**lp**	Prints a file.
HELP	**man**	Provides help on a command.

Summary

The Sun Solaris Operating Environment has many different forms of help available to users and administrators. With CDE help, you can use the Help Viewer window, search for a particular help topic, and use on-item help. Each CDE window and application also has a help option in the upper-right corner. The Help Viewer window can be accessed from the Workspace menu or the Help icon on the front panel.

AnswerBook2 is a powerful online searchable version of the Solaris manuals. Several book collections are presented, including information for administrators, users, and developers.

Command-line help is available in the form or man pages and can be displayed using the **man** command. Man pages cover nearly every UNIX command and provide a quick reference when you need to check the syntax or options available with a particular command. Several options are available with the **man** command, including keyword and section search capabilities. The **whatis** command can be used to refresh your memory as to what a command does by providing a brief definition and purpose of the command.

When problems occur, you can help to narrow the possibilities by following a s ystematic approach to identifying and correcting the problem. Contact a system administrator or the service/help desk for problems that you can't resolve.

Users who are familiar with DOS commands will have an easier time learning UNIX because many of the DOS commands were derived from UNIX. There are hundreds of UNIX commands, and they can be used to accomplish all the tasks that DOS users normally would need to do, but in a UNIX environment.

Check Your Understanding

1. All of the following are options on the CDE Help subpanel *except*:
   - **A.** Help Manager
   - **B.** Front Panel Help
   - **C.** Terminal Window Help
   - **D.** On Item Help
2. If it is installed, AnswerBook2 provides which of these capabilities or features?
   - **A.** Web-based search engine to access the Sun Web site
   - **B.** Help text on the Front panel
   - **C.** Hard-copy manuals for help with specific applications
   - **D.** Online searchable versions of the Solaris manuals
3. Command-line help is available using man pages. Which of the following is a valid variation of the **man** command?
   - **A.** **man** *page-number*
   - **B.** **man** *name*
   - **C.** **man** *keyword*
   - **D.** **man** *section name*
4. What command can be used to get a brief description of a UNIX command from the man pages?
   - **A.** **manb** *name*
   - **B.** **whatmean** *name*
   - **C.** **mandesc** *name*
   - **D.** **whatis** *name*
5. When troubleshooting an unresponsive Terminal window, what is the recommended sequence of keys to press to try to free up the Terminal window?
   - **A.** Ctrl–C, Ctrl–D, Ctrl-Q
   - **B.** Ctrl–D, Ctrl–Q, Ctrl-X
   - **C.** Ctrl–Q, Ctrl–C, Ctrl-D
   - **D.** Ctrl–X, Ctrl–Y, Ctrl-Z

6. Why is it important to know command-line commands and syntax?

   A. Sometimes the GUI will not be available and the command line is the only interface available to correct the problem.

   B. UNIX commands can be used to build scripts to automate system-administration tasks.

   C. Commands are frequently more powerful and flexible than their GUI counterparts.

   D. All of the above.

7. What is the Solaris UNIX command that will give a listing of files in a directory similar to the DOS **DIR** command?

   A. list

   B. dir

   C. ls

   D. files

8. Which of the following functions can be accomplished using the same command whether you are using DOS or UNIX?

   A. Display a listing of file in a directory

   B. Change directories

   C. Copy a file

   D. Delete a file

9. Which of the following answers show valid combinations of DOS and UNIX commands that are correctly paired to perform similar functions? (The DOS command is listed first for each answer.)

   A. **type** and **cat**

   B. **deldir** and **rd**

   C. **cls** and **clr**

   D. **copy** and **copy**

10. When attempting to unlock an unresponsive system, the first thing to do is:

    A. Go to another system and do a remote login and terminate the login shell program.

    B. Press the Stop-A keyboard sequence.

C. Turn off the system.

D. Press Ctrl-Alt-Del.

UNIX Command Summary

Ctrl-c Cancels the current activity. Example:

```
$ man intro <Ctrl c>
```

Ctrl-d Indicates the end of file or exit. Example:

```
$ bc
5280/3
1760
<Ctrl d>
$
```

Ctrl-q Resumes screen output. Example:

```
$ cat largfile <Ctrl s> <Ctrl q>
```

domainname Displays name of the current domain. Example:

```
$ domainname
elvis.central.Sun.com
```

hostname Displays name of current host system. Example:

```
$ hostname
buckeye
```

man Displays information from the reference manuals. It displays complete manual pages that you select by name, or one-line summaries if selected by keyword. Example:

```
-s, -k
$ man man
$ man cd
```

prtconf Prints system configuration information. Example:

```
$prtconf | grep Memory
Memory size: 128 Megabytes
```

uname Displays the name of the current system. Example:

```
-n

$ uname -n
buckeye
```

whatis Looks up a given command and displays the header line from the manual section. Example:

```
$ whatis cd
cd    cd (1)   -change working directory
```

Key Terms

AnswerBook2 System that enables you to view an online version of the printed Solaris manuals, including graphics.

Console The main input/output device that is used to access a system and display all system messages. This can be either a display monitor and keyboard or a shell window.

DOS An early single-user, single-tasking, character-based PC Disk Operating System developed by Microsoft and IBM.

Help Manager The primary CDE help tool for most situations available from the front panel.

Man pages Describe what you need to know about the system's online commands, system calls, file formats, and system maintenance. The online man pages are part of all versions of UNIX and are installed by default. Man pages are in the form of simple character-based screen displays and are not graphical. The **man** command is used to access man pages.

Terminal window A graphical window that can be opened within the CDE for access to the command line and UNIX commands. Multiple Terminal windows can be opened simultaneously. Terminal windows support scrolling and cut/copy/paste.

UNIX Multiuser, multitasking network operating system. Different computer manufacturers produce their own versions of UNIX.

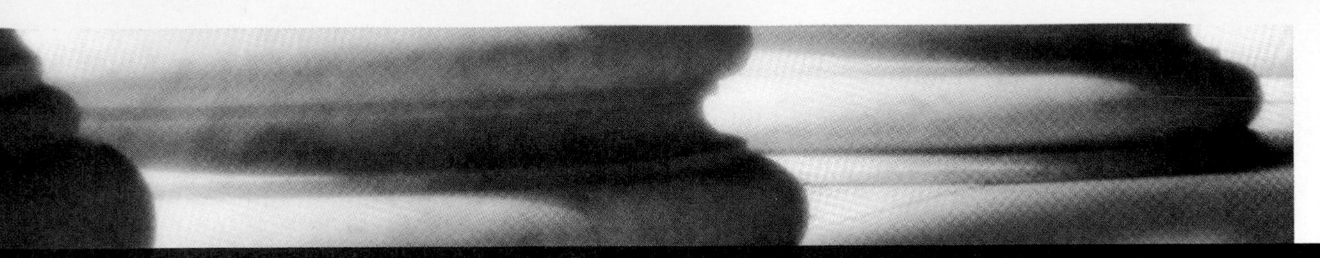

Objectives

After reading this chapter, you will be able to

- Understand and describe the structure of the UNIX file system
- Identify relative and absolute path names
- Navigate the directory structure
- List the contents of a directory
- Define the function of the parts of the directory listing
- Identify and use metacharacters

Chapter 5

Accessing Files and Directories

Introduction

This chapter reviews file system concepts covered earlier and introduces path names to identify locations of files and directories in the directory tree. You work with the **cd** command to change directories and navigate the file system. The use of the flexible **ls** command to list the contents of directories also is covered, as is the meaning of various types of directory listings. Metacharacters are introduced, and their role in file system navigation and directory listings is explored.

The File System

A *file system* is a hierarchy of directories, subdirectories, and files that organize and manage the information on hard disks. Knowing the directory structure of a file system and how to navigate the file system is essential to working with UNIX.

Sample User Directory Structure

Figure 5-1 shows a sample UNIX file system structure for a user. This is the *class file tree structure*, which you refer to throughout this chapter and again later in this book. This structure should exist in each student's home directory. Note that there are directories, subdirectories, and files in the structure. Directories and subdirectories have a folder icon, and files have a document icon. The exercises in this chapter and subsequent chapters use this directory structure.

The structure and names of directories within a user's home directory can vary considerably, depending on the user and his needs. For example, a user could have major directories named Projects, WPDocs, Finances, and Hobbies under the home directory. The names of the directories are determined by their purpose and what they contain.

Figure 5-1
The class file tree structure.

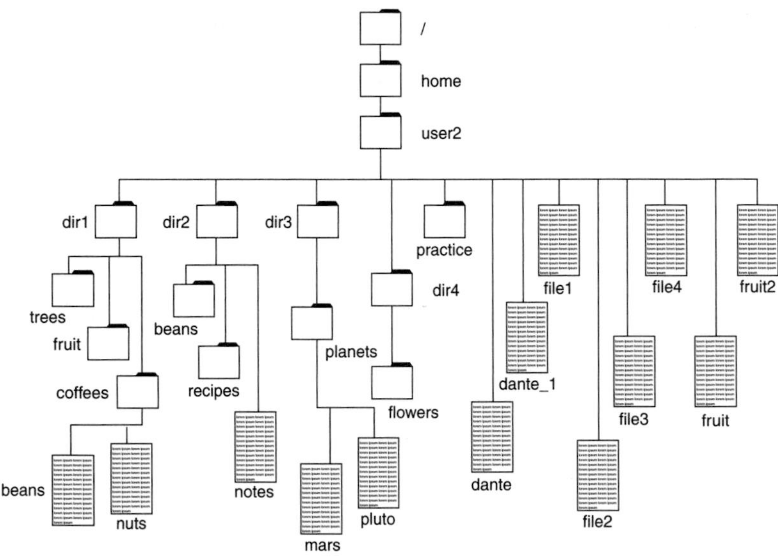

Function of Directories

UNIX file system and directories were introduced in Chapter 1, "The UNIX Computing Environment." Hard disks are divided into file systems and directories. These exist to group information into containers that categorize them. By organizing or grouping files into directories, applications and users can find their files when they need them. We will cover the creation of directories and naming conventions later in the course. Directories are created in one of four ways:

- **They are created by the operating system during installation**—Several standard Solaris directories are created when an operating system (OS) is first installed. In the UNIX environment, these include usr, dev, etc, export, kernel, and others, which are shown in Figure 5-2. They are used by the OS to store files critical to the operation of the computer, including the kernel itself.
- **They can be created by applications during installation**—When applications such as StarOffice are installed, directories are created automatically to give the application places to store installation files and for use by the application and users to store data files.
- **The system administrator can create them**—When creating user accounts on a workstation or server, the system administrator (sysadmin) can create a particular directory or set of directories, depending on user needs.
- **Users can create their own directories**—Users themselves can create directories, provided that they have proper permission. By default, users have permission

to create subdirectories and files under their home directories. Directory and file permissions are covered later in the course.

Figure 5-2 Common UNIX directories.

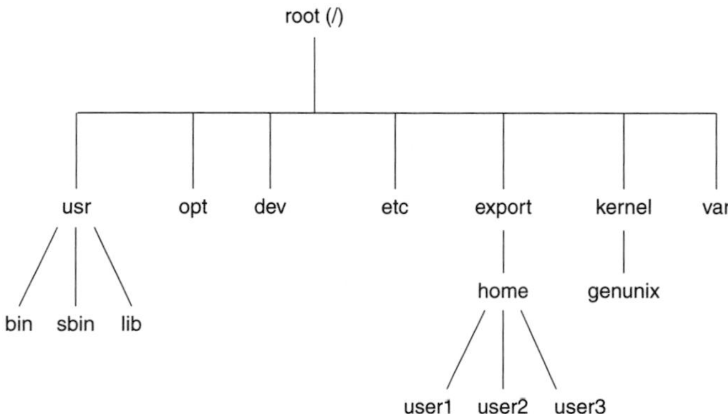

File System Structure

The structure of the file system is a *hierarchy* that looks like an inverted or upside-down tree with the root at the top. It is common for directories to have subdirectories. This is similar to having a file drawer called Projects (directory) containing folders in it with the names of individual projects (subdirectories). Directories can contain subdirectories and files. Subdirectories also can contain additional subdirectories and more files. All operating systems have some sort of directory structure to organize information on their hard disks. With some operating systems such as Windows and MacOS, directories are referred to as folders. With the UNIX file system, they are called directories but are used in the same manner.

Figure 5-3 shows a hierarchical directory structure as an inverted tree. A common hierarchical system or structure that you likely are familiar with is the family tree of your ancestors. The file system directory structure is similar to a family tree. With the exception of the *root directory*, each directory in the hierarchy has a *parent directory*, and most have *child directories*, which are referred to as subdirectories. The root directory is always at the top of the hierarchy and is designated as a forward slash (/). There can be only one root directory in a UNIX file system.

Each child directory is contained in a parent directory, as shown in Figure 5-4. This is similar to having a set of file folders, where each folder (directory) has a folder inside (subdirectory). The location of a file or directory in the tree can be specified by naming each directory that you have to go through to access it. A fully qualified filename or directory name also is known as an absolute path name, and it includes the names of all parent directories above it. For example, to determine the location of the notes document, you must name all folders above it.

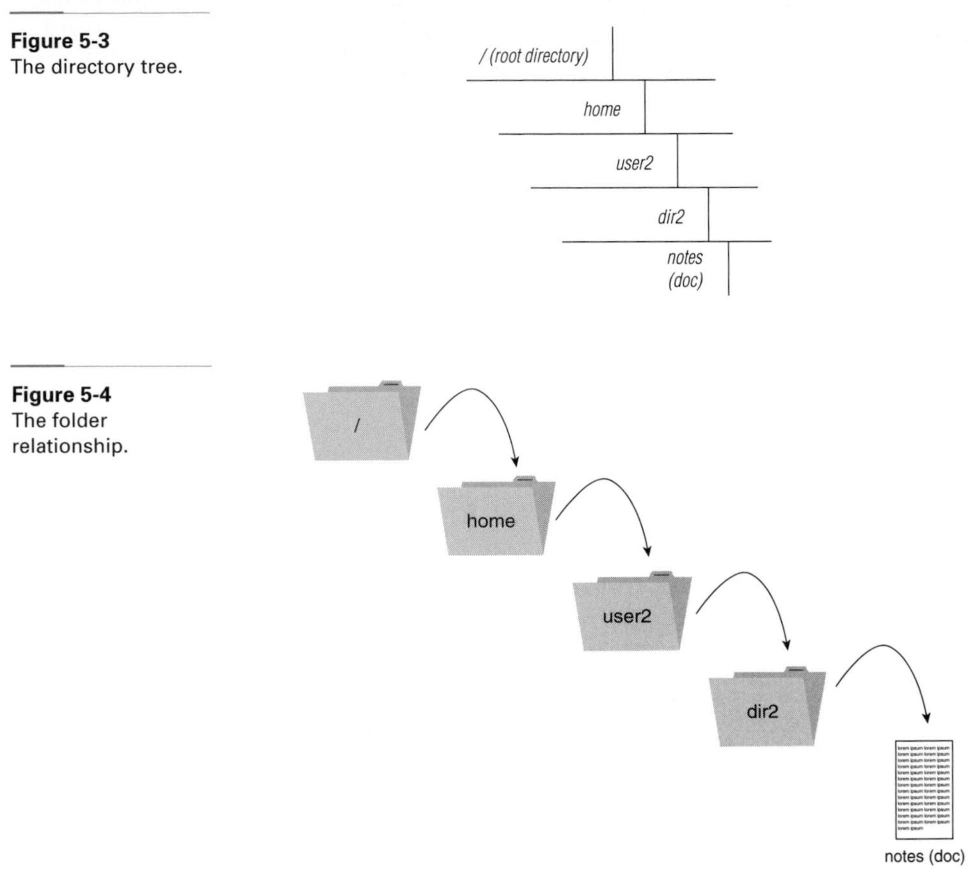

Figure 5-3
The directory tree.

Figure 5-4
The folder relationship.

Directory Paths

Understanding path names to directories and files is critical to understanding file systems and is fundamental to understanding UNIX or any other operating system.

Path Names

A path name uniquely identifies a particular file or directory by specifying its location. Path names are similar to a road map or a set of directions telling you how to get from one place in the directory hierarchy to another. For example, if you were giving someone from another country directions on how to get to you, you would have to specify where you live. The directories in a file system can be compared to a country, state, city, and so on. If the Earth were like a hard disk with a file system, we would consider it the root of the file system. If we wanted to identify the location of a guy named Brad to tell someone where he lives, we would specify the path name until we got to Brad. We would use a fully qualified path name so that there would be no doubt that we are talking about Brad of planet Earth, not some other planet (see Figure 5-5).

Figure 5-5
The solar system hierarchy.

Solar System Container	Solar System Location	Solar System Path Name	File System Term
Planet	Earth	/root	File System Root
Country	USA	/USA	Main Directory
State	Arizona	/USA/Arizona	Subdirectory
City	Phoenix	/USA/Arizona/Pheonix	Subdirectory
Address	Cactus	/USA/Arizona/Phoenix /Cactus	Subdirectory
Name	Brad	/USA/Arizona/Phoenix /Cactus/Brad	Filename

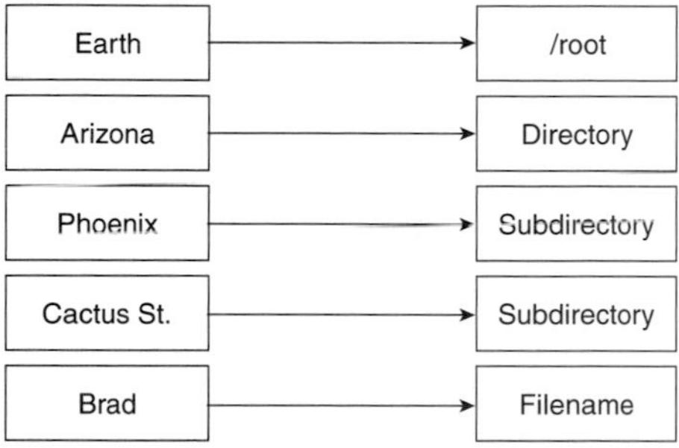

Figure 5-6 shows the hierarchical relationship between the root directory and the coffees subdirectory. The set of directories that you must go through from the root directory is the path name from the root directory through several intermediate subdirectories to the coffees subdirectory. Every file and directory in the file system has a path name.

NOTE

Depending on the setup of your system, users' home directories can be found in either /home or /export/home. If your home directory resides on your local system, it usually is found in /export/home. If it is on a server, it is usually in /home. For the purposes of this discussion, /home is used.

Path Components

Look at the individual components of the path to the /home/user2/dir1/coffees subdirectory, as shown in Figure 5-7. The slashes within the path name are ***delimiters*** between object names. The slashes act like separators. Object names can be directories, subdirectories, or files. DOS and Windows indicate directories using a backward slash (\), or backslash. The Backslash key is usually near the Backspace key on a keyboard.

All UNIX file systems use a forward slash (/) in path names. The forward slash is usually near the right Shift key on most keyboards. A slash (/) in the first position of any path name represents the root directory.

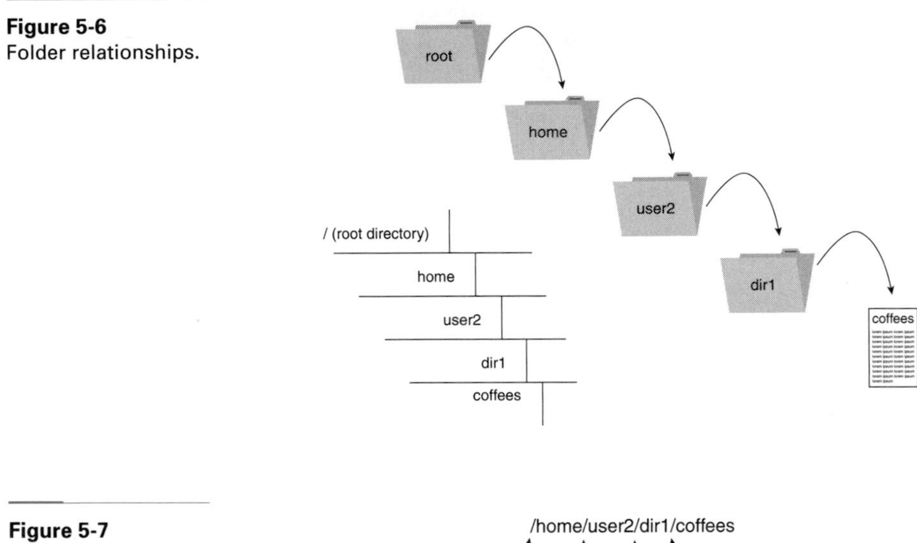

Figure 5-6
Folder relationships.

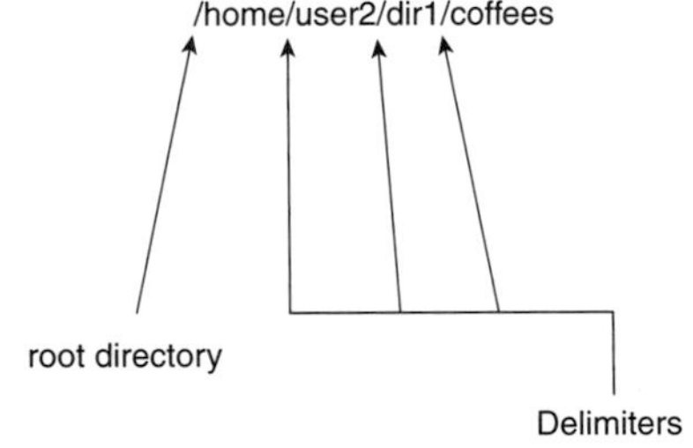

Figure 5-7
The path to coffees.

Types of Path Names

Path names specify the location of a directory or file in the directory structure (refer to Figure 5-1). To navigate the directory structure, it is necessary to have an understanding of path names. Two types of path names are used with UNIX and other operating systems, absolute and relative. Either method can be used at any time. An understanding of each is critical to understanding and navigating the file system.

Absolute Path Names An *absolute path name* specifies a file or directory in relation to the entire UNIX file hierarchy. The hierarchy begins at the / (root) directory. If you refer to a directory using its absolute path name, you can always be sure that you will get to the correct directory because you always have the common starting point of the root directory. Figure 5-8 shows some examples of absolute path names that have the following characteristics:

- They always start at the root (/) directory and list each directory along the path to the destination file (or directory).
- They always use a slash (/) between each directory name in the path to indicate different directories.

Figure 5-8
Examples of absolute path names.

- **Absolute pathname to the user2 directory**
  /home/user2
- **Absolute pathname to the dir1 directory**
  /home/user2/dir1
- **Absolute pathname to the coffees file**
  /home/user2/dir1/coffee

Relative Path Names A *relative path name* describes the location of a file or directory as it relates to the current directory (the directory you are currently in). If you are in a directory and you want to move down the directory tree, it is not necessary to type the absolute path name starting from the root directory (/). You can just type the path starting with the name of the next directory down in the directory structure. If a path name does not begin with a slash, it is a relative path name.

Relative path names are useful because they are usually shorter than absolute path names. To use relative path names, you must know what directory you are currently in because that is your starting point. The directory that you are in at any point can change, so you must know where you are in the directory tree or hierarchy. Absolute path names are usually longer than relative path names, but they are consistent because you always specify the path from the root, regardless of what directory you are currently in. Figure 5-9 shows some examples of relative path names.

Figure 5-9
Examples of relative path names.

If your current directory is /home:

- **Relative pathname to the user2 directory**
  user2
- **Relative pathname to the dir1 directory**
  user2/dir1
- **Relative pathname to the coffees file**
  user2/dir1/coffees

Skill Builder

e-Lab Activity 5.1

Path Names Exercise

Work through this interactive e-Lab activity to demonstrate your understanding of absolute and relative path names. Refer to the class file tree structure on the inside-front cover of this book. Enter the absolute or relative path name for the directory or file requested in the exercise. Be sure to use forward slashes, and note that all directory, subdirectory, and filenames are case-sensitive.

Navigating the File System

To navigate the file system, you must learn the command that displays your current directory location with in the file system and the command that is used to change to a different directory. First, however, you must know the proper syntax for using UNIX commands.

Command-Line Syntax

When logged in at the command line or when using a Terminal window, a shell prompt appears on the screen. For the Bourne and Korn shells, the shell prompt for a user is a dollar sign ($). For a C shell user, the prompt is a percent sign (%). At the shell prompt, you can type commands. Commands are instructions that tell the system to perform an action. Syntax refers to the structure of the command and specifies allowable options and *arguments*.

NOTE

Items in square brackets are optional, meaning that they are not always required.

The general format for UNIX commands is shown here:

```
$ command  [option(s)]  [argument(s)]
```

See Figure 5-10 for an explanation of each component.

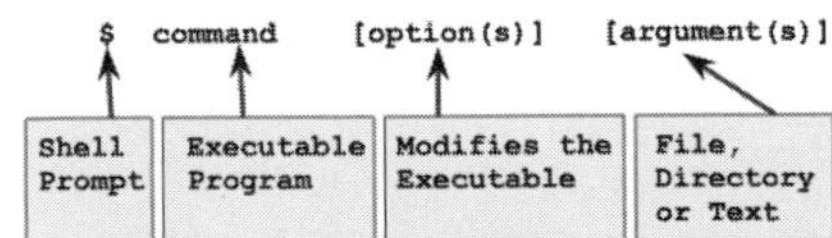

Command	Executable program (specifies what you want the system to do)
option(s)	Modifies the executable (specifies how you want the command run)
Argument	File or directory, including the pathname, or text. If a pathname is not specified for a file or directory argument, then the operating system will use the current directory.

Figure 5-10 Command-line syntax.

A space must be used as a delimiter between each part of the command entered. Up to 256 characters can be entered on a single command line, although this is not common. UNIX commands are always lowercase. Options are usually a single letter preceded by a hyphen (–), also called a dash or a minus sign. Multiple options can be combined using only one hyphen. The option might be uppercase or lowercase, depending on the command. Many commands do not require all three parts. Multiple commands can be entered on one line by separating them with a semicolon (;). Figure 5-11 summarizes the syntax rules for using UNIX commands. Figure 5-12 illustrates some examples of UNIX commands with and without options and arguments.

Figure 5-11
UNIX syntax rules.

- Space is used as a delimiter between command parts.
- Maximum of 256 characters on a single line.
- Commands are lowercase.
- Options can be upper- or lowercase.
- Options usually preceded by a hyphen.
- Multiple options can be used with one hyphen.
- Many commands do not require all three parts.
- Multiple commands can be entered on one line if separated by a semicolon (;).

Figure 5-12
UNIX command examples.

```
$ cal(Command only)
$ cal 1987(Command and argument)
$ date(Command only)
$ date -u(Command and option)
$ banner "hi there"(Command and argument)
$ ls  -F  dir1(Command, option and argument)
$ clear ; date(Command, ; seperator, command)
```

Skill Builder

Lab Activity 5.3.1

Basic Command-Line Syntax

In this lab, you work with various UNIX commands to develop an understanding of UNIX commands and syntax. Refer to the *Cisco Networking Academy Program: Fundamentals of UNIX Lab Companion.*

Displaying the Current Directory

Remembering which directory you currently are working in is often difficult. Use the **pwd** (print working directory) command to display the absolute path name of your current directory. The **pwd** command is used frequently to check the current location in the directory tree or hierarchy. When you know your location in the tree, you can move from one directory to another with the **cd** (change directory) command.

To determine the directory that you are currently in, which is known as your current directory, simply type **pwd** at the shell prompt and press Enter to execute the command. Note that the **pwd** command does not have any options or arguments. It simply tells you what directory you are in using the absolute path name, so there is no doubt. Assuming that you are currently in the /home/user2 directory, you get the following response from the **pwd** command:

```
$ pwd
/home/user2
```

Skill Builder

e-Lab Activity 5.2

Using the **pwd** Command

Work through this e-Lab activity to demonstrate your understanding of the **pwd** command. Refer to the class file tree structure on the inside-front cover of this book. Type what you think the result of the **pwd** command would be, depending on the directory you are currently in. Be sure to use forward slashes and note that all directory, subdirectory, and filenames are case-sensitive.

Changing Directories Using the cd Command

Files that you need to access often are stored in subdirectories below your home directory. Because of the way in which a UNIX file system is set up, it is often desirable to change directory locations. The **cd** (change directory) command is used to change to a new current directory. This command, like all UNIX commands, accepts both absolute and relative path names. Here's an example of the **cd** command:

```
cd  [directory_name]
```

You can move around in the directory hierarchy using the **cd** command along with an absolute or relative path name, as shown in the examples in Figure 5-13. In the first example, we use the **cd** command with an absolute path name. It does not make any difference where you currently are in the directory hierarchy because you are specifying to start at the root (/) directory. The second example uses the **cd** command with a relative path name. It assumes that you are currently in the /home directory, which you changed to in Example 1. If you were not in the /home directory, you would receive an error stating that the directory that you were trying to change to does not exist. The third example shows a feature of the **cd** command that allows you to quickly return to your home directory (example: /home/user2). Entering the **cd** command by itself (without specifying a path name) automatically places you in your home directory.

Figure 5-13
Using the **cd** command.

1. **Using cd with an absolute pathname:**

```
$ cd /home
```

2. **Using cd with a relative pathname:**

```
$ cd user2/dirl
```

3. **Use cd without a directory name returns you to your home directory:**

```
$ cd
```

Navigation Shortcuts with cd

Path name abbreviations are a form of shorthand when moving between or referring to directories. They can save keystrokes when used with the **cd** command. The shortcuts covered include the dot (.), which is basically a period; the dot/dot (..), or two periods; and the tilde (~), the wavy symbol usually found above the Tab key on most keyboards, representing your home directory. Directories always contain a link to their parent directory, which is designated by the dot/dot (..) and a link to themselves, which is the dot (.). The **ls -a** (list files, all) command, which will be covered in the next section, will show a dot (.) and a dot/dot (..) even if the directory is empty. These shortcuts can be useful when changing directories using the **cd** command and others.

NAVIGATION TIME SAVER

Another nice navigation time saver for Korn shell users is **cd** ~- (tilde followed by a dash). The ~- represents the full path to the previous directory visited. For example:

```
$pwd
/home/dano
$cd ..
$pwd
/home
$cd ~/docs
$pwd
```

```
/home/dano/docs
$cd ~-
$pwd
/home
```

Use **cd** ~username as a quick way to change directories to another user's home directory (if multiple home directories reside on the same system). For example, **cd** ~dano would change to the / home/dano directory.

NOTE

All directory names, subdirectory names, and filenames are case-sensitive.

You can use path name abbreviations or shortcuts with the **cd** command to move around the file structure. Figure 5-14 shows some examples for using the shortcuts with the **cd** command, assuming that your current working directory is /home/user2/ dir1.

Figure 5-14
Using the navigation shortcuts.

1. **Using the .. to change the parent directory:**
   $ cd ..
   $ pwd
   /home/user2
2. **Using the .. to move up two directory levels to root:**
   $ cd ../..
   $ pwd
   /
3. **Using the ~ to go to a directory under your home directory:**
   $ cd ~/practice
   $ pwd
   /home/user2/practice

Symbol	Meaning
. (dot)	Current (working) directory
.. (dot/dot)	Parent directory; the directory directly above the current directory
~ (tilde)	User's home directory (Korn and C shells)

Skill Builder

e-Lab Activity 5.3

Using the **pwd** and **cd** Commands

This e-Lab activity demonstrates your ability to use the **pwd** and **cd** commands. Refer to the class file tree structure on the inside-front cover of this book. Be sure to use lowercase command names and forward slashes.

Skill Builder

Lab Activity 5.3.3

Navigating the File System

In this lab, you work with the UNIX file system or directory tree that has been set up for the class. You learn how to determine your current location in the directory tree and how to change from one directory to another. Refer to the *Cisco Networking Academy Program: Fundamentals of UNIX Lab Companion.*

Listing Directory Contents

The only way to know what files and directories are available to work with is by displaying a list.

The ls Command

To determine the contents of a directory, use the **ls** (list) command. This command displays a listing of all files and directories within the current directory or specified directories. If no path name is given as an argument, **ls** displays the contents of the current directory. The **ls** command lists any subdirectories and files that are in the *current working directory* if a path name is specified. It also defaults to a wide listing display. Many options can be used with the **ls** command, which makes it one of the more flexible and useful UNIX commands.

Figure 5-15 shows some examples using the **ls** command with various options, assuming that your current directory is /home/user2. Refer to the class file tree structure while reviewing the examples. Example 1 is the basic **ls** command by itself, with no options or directory specified. It returns a listing of all directories and files in the current directory. Note that you cannot tell whether the listed item is a directory or a file

TIP

The output for the **ls** command is sorted alphabetically by default. However, because the operating system is case-sensitive, you might have files and directories that begin with lowercase letters, upper case and even a number (such as 2002_budget). The **ls** command displays those beginning with a number first and then displays uppercase letters next and then lowercase letters—for example: 123, 1abc, Abc Doc, abc doc.

ls [-option(s)] [pathname[s]]

unless the name indicates it. Example 2 specifies a relative path name dir1, which is a subdirectory of /home/users. Only files and directories in dir1 will be listed. Example 3 specifies an absolute path name of /var/mail, which is in another part of the directory tree. Only files and directories from /var/mail will be listed.

Figure 5-15
Using the **ls** command.

1. Using the basic **ls** command (from /home/user2)

```
$ ls
dante    dir1  dir3  file1  file3  practice
dante_1  dir2  dir4  file2  file4
```

2. Using the **ls** command with a relative pathname

```
$ ls dirl
coffees fruit     trees
```

3. Using the **ls** command with an absolute pathname

```
$ ls /var/mail
user1   user2  user3   user4   user5
```

Skill Builder

e-Lab Activity 5.4

The **ls** Command

In this e-Lab activity, you are logged in as user2, and your current working directory is /home/user2/dir1. Refer to the class file tree structure on the inside-front cover of this book. Type the commands that would accomplish the requested objectives. *Note:* Be sure to press Enter after each one. Click Step 1 to begin.

Displaying Hidden Files

Filenames that begin with a period (.) are called dot or hidden files. *Hidden files* frequently are used to customize a user's work environment. They are not shown by default because they are edited infrequently. The current directory link (.) and the parent directory link (..) are hidden are and are not displayed either because they begin with a dot. Using the **ls** command with the **-a** (all) option lists all files in a directory, including hidden (.) files. Note that the **-a** option is lowercase. The example shown in Figure 5-16 shows the result of the **ls -a** command while you're in your home directory (/home/user2).

NOTE

The current and parent directory links and the .kshrc file, which is a user-environment file, are normally hidden files.

Figure 5-16
Using the **ls –a** command.

```
            (Note files that start with a dot)
$ ls -a
.   .kshrc   dante1   dir2   dir4    file2   file4
..  dante    dir1     dir3   file1   file3   practice
```

Skill Builder

e-Lab Activity 5.5

Displaying Hidden Files

In this e-Lab activity, you are logged in as user2, and your current working directory is /home/user2. Refer to the class file tree structure on the inside-front cover of this book. Type the commands that would accomplish the requested objectives. *Note:* Be sure to press Enter after each one. Click Step 1 to begin.

TIP

To display a list of only the hidden files, use **$ls** .??*.

Displaying File Types

When using the **ls** command by itself, you can obtain a listing of directory contents, but you cannot tell which are files and which are directories. By using the **ls** command with the **-F** (file type) option, you can display a listing with a symbol to indicate the file type. The symbol (if present) is found at the end of the file or directory name. Note that the **-F** option is an uppercase *F.* Four UNIX file types exist: directory, executable, ASCII text file, and symbolic link, as shown in Figure 5-17. We focus on the first three in this course.

- **Directory**—A forward slash (/) after the name indicates that this is a directory (or subdirectory). A directory is considered a type of file with UNIX.
- *ASCII text file*—If there is no symbol after the name, this indicates a plain ASCII text file with no formatting characters. (ASCII is the American Standard Code for Information Interchange.) An ASCII text file is similar to a DOS text file.
- *Executable*—An asterisk (*) after the name indicates that this is a command, an application, or a script file that can be run or executed.
- *Symbolic link*—An at sign (@) after the name indicates a symbolic link, which is a way of giving a file an alternate name. Symbolic links allow a file to exist in more than one place, for convenience. Links are covered in Chapter 7, "Advanced Directory and File Management."

Figure 5-17 shows two examples using the **ls -F** command to see the file type; it assumes that you are in your home directory, /home/user2. The first example shows only files and directories. The second shows a symbolic link, an executable and a directory.

Figure 5-17
Using the **ls –F** command.

```
$ ls -F
dante      dir1/dir3/file1   file3   practice/
dante_1    dir2/dir4/file2   file4

$ ls -F /etc
cron@      asppp.cf* shadowuucp/
<output omitted>
```

Skill Builder

e-Lab Activity 5.6

Displaying File Types

In this e-Lab activity, you are logged in as user2, and your current working directory is /home/user2/dir2. Refer to the class file tree structure on the inside-front cover of this book. Type the commands that would accomplish the requested objectives. *Note:* Be sure to press Enter after each one. Click Step 1 to begin.

NOTE

The -l option uses a lowercase *l*.

Displaying a Long Listing

The previous versions of the **ls** command displayed only the names of directories and files in a wide format (across the screen). The **ls** command can be used with the **-l** (long) option to see more detailed information on each file or directory. The **ls -l** option also distinguishes between files and directories.

The **ls -l** command provides the file information shown in the Figures 5-18 and 5-19. By default, the **ls** command lists files in alphabetic order. Using the **-t** (time) option lists files with the most recently modified at the top of the list. To get a detailed (long) listing of files sorted by time (most recent at the top), use the **ls -lt** command.

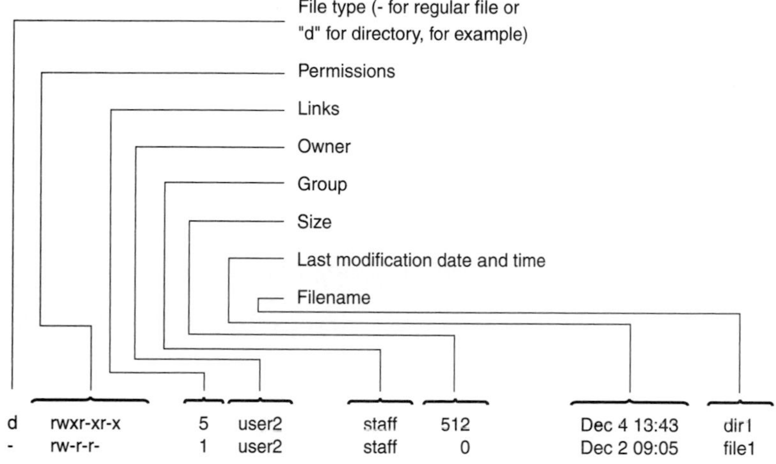
File type (- for regular file or "d" for directory, for example)
Permissions
Links
Owner
Group
Size
Last modification date and time
Filename
d rwxr-xr-x 5 user2 staff 512 Dec 4 13:43 dir1
- rw-r-r- 1 user2 staff 0 Dec 2 09:05 file1

Figure 5-18
Directory information.

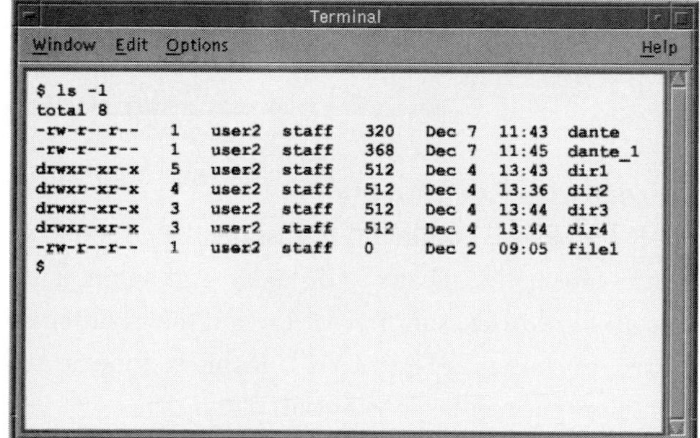
Terminal
Window Edit Options Help
$ ls -l
total 8
-rw-r--r-- 1 user2 staff 320 Dec 7 11:43 dante
-rw-r--r-- 1 user2 staff 368 Dec 7 11:45 dante_1
drwxr-xr-x 5 user2 staff 512 Dec 4 13:43 dir1
drwxr-xr-x 4 user2 staff 512 Dec 4 13:36 dir2
drwxr-xr-x 3 user2 staff 512 Dec 4 13:44 dir3
drwxr-xr-x 3 user2 staff 512 Dec 4 13:44 dir4
-rw-r--r-- 1 user2 staff 0 Dec 2 09:05 file1
$

Figure 5-19
Detailed information from the **ls –l** command.

Skill Builder

e-Lab Activity 5.7

Displaying a Long Listing

In this e-Lab activity, you are logged in as user2, and your current working directory is /home/user2/dir2. Refer to the class file tree structure on the inside-front cover of this book. Type the commands that would accomplish the requested objectives. *Note:* Be sure to press Enter after each one. Click Step 1 to begin.

Listing Individual Directories

Use the **ls -ld** command to display detailed information about a directory, but not its contents. This is useful when you want to see the permissions on a directory and not the information about its contents. (Permissions are discussed in detail Chapter 10, "File System Security.") As shown in Figure 5-20, the **ls -l** command lists detailed information on files and directories in dir1, while the **ls -ld** command lists detailed information only on dir1 itself.

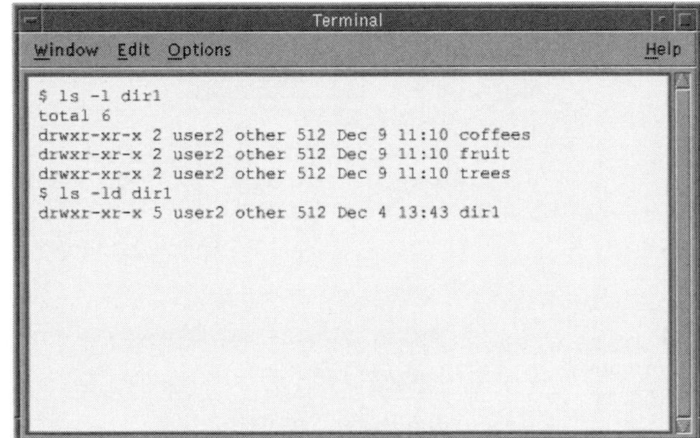

Figure 5-20
Using the **ls –l** and **ls –ld** commands.

Listing Directories Recursively

NOTE
The -R option uses an uppercase *R*.

Use the **ls -R** (recursive) command to display the contents of a directory and all of its subdirectories. Recursive means to do again and again. This option is useful if you want to see all directories, subdirectories, and their contents for a particular part of the directory tree, as shown in Figure 5-21. If this is done at a high level in the directory structure, the output can be substantial.

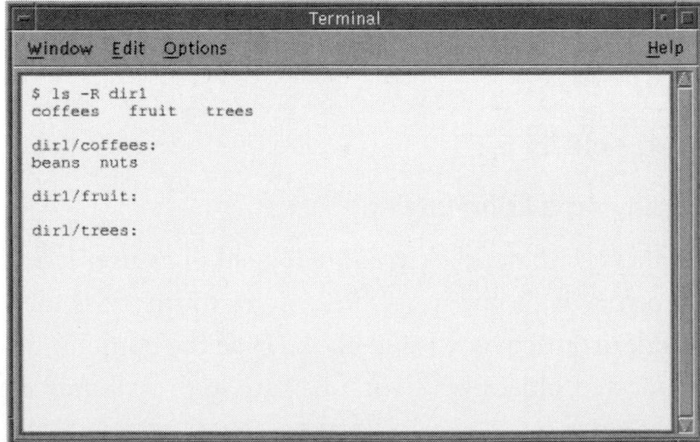

Figure 5-21
Listing directories recursively.

The **-R** option commonly is used with many UNIX commands to indicate a recursive action (although it is sometimes a lowercase *r*, depending on the command). *Recursive* generally refers to the contents of a directory and all of its subdirectories.

Skill Builder

Lab Activity 5.4.6

Listing Directory Information

In this lab, you use the **ls** command, which is used to determine the contents of a directory. Refer to the *Cisco Networking Academy Program: Fundamentals of UNIX Lab Companion*.

Identifying and Using Metacharacters

Metacharacters are keyboard characters with special meaning to the shell. They are a powerful feature of any shell. A general definition of a metacharacter is any keyboard character that is not alphanumeric. Metacharacters are used with many UNIX commands to provide greater flexibility.

Identifying Metacharacters

Some of the metacharacters used with UNIX are similar in function to those used with DOS. The asterisk (*) and the question mark (?) are metacharacters that also are known as wildcards and are used to work with groups of files efficiently. Figure 5-22 shows some of the more common metacharacters and gives a brief description of their primary function.

It is important *not* to use metacharacters when naming files and directories. The dot (.) and the underscore (_) are the only two nonalphanumeric characters that are not metacharacters. This is why you can use the dot (.) and the underscore (_) in filenames. A hyphen (–), even though it is a metacharacter (used to delineate options in a command line), also can be used in filenames.

Using Metacharacters

The asterisk (*), question mark (?), and square brackets ([ ]) are the three most often used metacharacters when manipulating groups of files.

Figure 5-22
Metacharacters.

Metacharacter	Description	Command Format	Example(s)
; (semicolon)	Enables you to enter multiple commands on a single command line.	command;command	date;cal;who
* (asterisk)	Represents any character or characters.	*	ls d*
? (question mark)	Matches any single character.	?	ls dir?
[ ] (square brackets)	Matches a set or range of characters for a single character position.	[range]	ls [b-f]* ls [bf]* ls [cab]* ls [A-z]*
;>, <, 2>, >> (angle brackets for redirection)	Redirects the output of a command to a file rather than to the screen. < - Redirects the input to a command from a file rather than from the keyboard. 2> - Redirects error from a command to a file rather than to the screen. >> - Appends the output of a command to an existing file.	command > file command < file command 2 > file command >> file	ls /etc > etc.listmailx user2@saturn < /etc/hostsDate 2> errorfilecat errorfilecal 1 1996 >> mon00cat mon00
| (pipe)	Takes the output of one command and passes it as input into the following command.	command | command	ls -l /etc | more
$	Default Korn and Bourne shell prompt variable indicator	N/A	$
%	Default C shell prompt variable indicator	N/A	%
~	Shortcut to home directory in C and Korn shells (Tilde)	~	cd ~
!	Command Re-execution	! n where n is the number of the command entered	!! Repeats the last Command in C Shell Used in conjunction with the history command to repeat an earlier command:!

Asterisk

The asterisk (*, also called splat or star) is a substitution symbol that represents zero or more characters, except the leading dot on a hidden file. The asterisk often is referred to as a wildcard character. The asterisk can be very helpful with many commands, such as **ls** (list), **cp** (copy), **rm** (remove), and **mv** (move). If there were a large number of files in a directory and you wanted to get a listing of only project files that start with "p1," you could use an example like the one shown in Figure 5-23. If you enter the **ls** command by itself, you will see all files in the current directory, as in Figure 5-24.

> **TIP**
>
> As a time saver, use the splat (*) with the **cd** command to change directories. For example, instead of typing **cd** */usr/openwin/share/images*, type **cd** */usr/open*/sh*/im**. Just make sure that no other directories start with the same few characters.

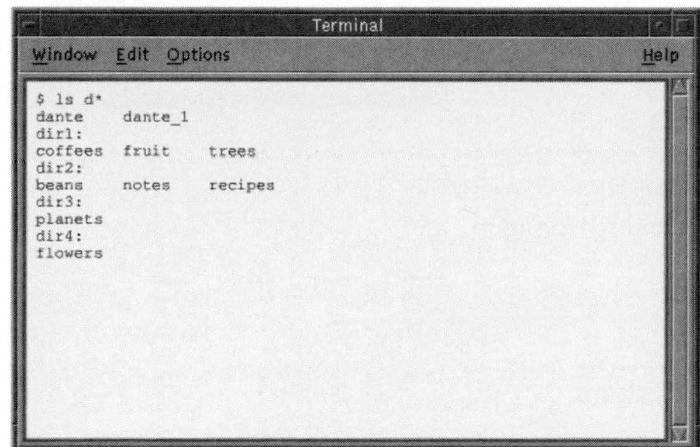

Figure 5-23
The **ls** command with the asterisk.

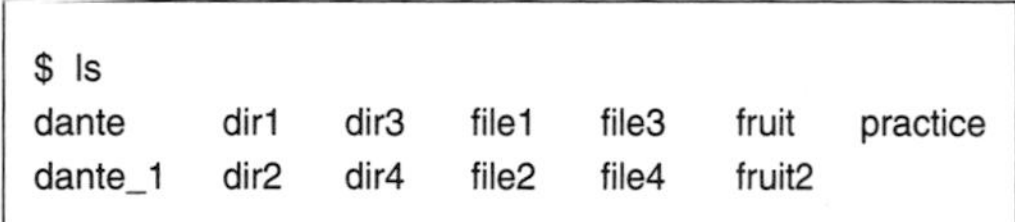

```
$ ls
dante     dir1  dir3  file1  file3  fruit   practice
dante_1   dir2  dir4  file2  file4  fruit2
```

Figure 5-24
Files within the current directory.

If you enter **ls d***, you will see all files that start with the letter *d*, plus all directories that start with *d*, followed by a colon, and then the directory contents.

Question Mark

The question mark (?) is a substitution character that matches any single character, except for the leading dot on a hidden file. The question mark also is referred to as a wildcard character. Figure 5-25 shows an example of the **ls** command using the question mark in the fourth position. This indicates that the file or directory name must start with the letters "dir," but any character can be in the fourth position and the filename cannot be more than four characters long.

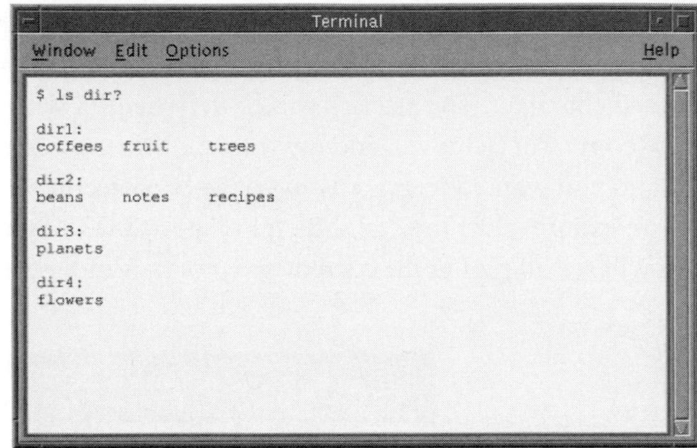

Figure 5-25
The **ls** command with the question mark.

TIP

To list files when you want to match one character *or* another, use the (x|y) format. For example, the command **$ls chap(2|4)** lists all files that begin with "chap" and have either a 2 or a 4 as the next character.

If no filename matches the wildcard character (whether * or ?), you receive the following error message:

```
$ ls z?
z?: No such file or directory
$
```

Square Brackets

Square brackets ([ ]) can be used to match a set or range of characters for a single character position in the file or directory name. The characters inside the brackets generally do not need to be in any order; for example, [abc] is the same as [cab]. However, if you are looking for a range of characters, they must be in proper order (for example, [a–z] or [3–9]). If you want to search for all alphabetic characters, whether lowercase or uppercase, use [A–z] for the pattern to match. You can use alphabetic or numeric characters for the search pattern.

Figure 5-26 shows two examples using square brackets along with the asterisk wildcard character. The first example defines a range and lists all files and directories that start with the lowercase letters *b* through *f*, with anything after that. The second example specifies that the first character must be either the letters *a* or *f*, and anything can come after that. Notice that only files starting with *f* are displayed in Example 2.

Semicolon

The semicolon (;) enables you to enter multiple commands on a single command line before pressing Enter. Entering multiple commands on one command line is an efficient way to accomplish a task. The semicolon also is referred to as the command separator. Figure 5-27 shows two examples using the semicolon to separate commands. In the first example, the **clear** command clears the screen, the **cd** command returns you to your home directory, and the **ls** command lists files in that directory. The second example displays the current date and time, and then displays the calendar for the current month.

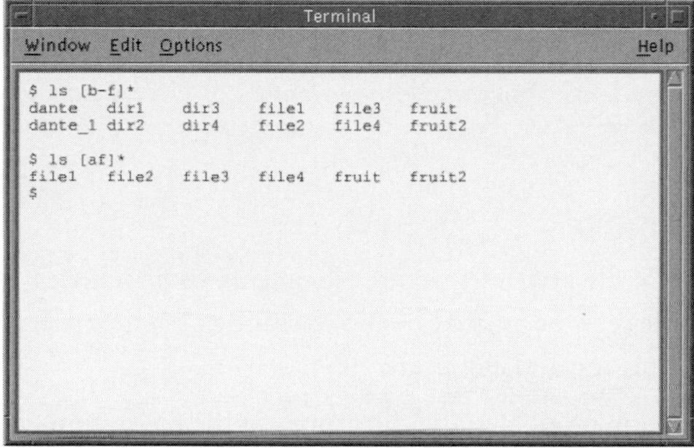

Figure 5-26 Using the **ls** command with square brackets.

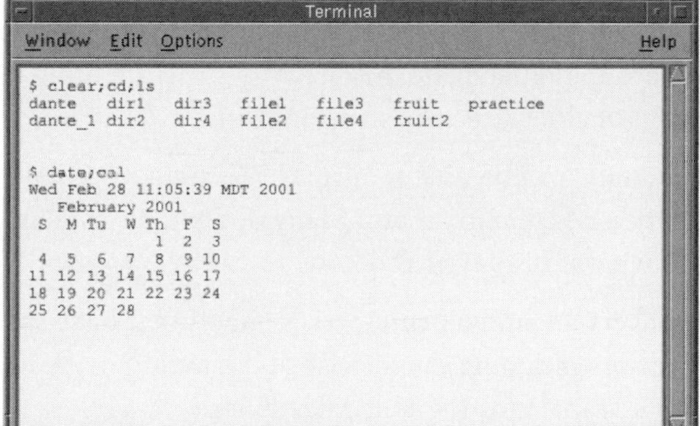

Figure 5-27 Using a semicolon to separate commands.

Skill Builder

e-Lab Activity 5.8

Using Metacharacters

In this e-Lab activity, you are logged in as user2, and your current working directory is /home/user2. Refer to the class file tree structure on the inside-front cover of this book. Type the commands that would accomplish the requested objectives. *Note:* Be sure to press Enter after each one. Click Step 1 to begin.

Skill Builder

Lab Activity 5.5.2

Directory Listings with Metacharacters

In this lab, you work with various metacharacters and use them with the **ls** command to refine your directory listings. Refer to the *Cisco Networking Academy Program: Fundamentals of UNIX Lab Companion.*

Summary

The UNIX file system structure is made up of directories, subdirectories, and files. Directories can be created by the operating system, applications programs, system administrators, and end users.

The location of all files and directories in the file system can be specified using an absolute or relative path name. Absolute path names always start with the root directory (/). Relative path names are specified based on where you are in the directory structure.

You can tell where you are in the directory structure using the **pwd** command, and you can move around or navigate the directory structure using the **cd** command. Shortcuts make navigating the directory structure easier.

The **ls** command can be used to display the contents of a directory, showing the files and subdirectories that are there. Many options are available with the **ls** command to determine what is displayed and how.

Metacharacters are nonalphanumeric symbols that have special meaning to the shell. Metacharacters including the asterisk and question mark wildcards can be used with many UNIX commands for added flexibility.

Check Your Understanding

1. Which of the following is incapable of creating directories?
   A. The operating system
   B. The system administrator
   C. The end user
   D. The directory daemon
2. What do absolute path names identify the location of?
   A. A directory or file based on the current directory
   B. A directory or file relative to the user's home directory
   C. A directory or file starting from the root
   D. A logical partition on the hard drive
3. If your current directory was /home/user2, what would be the relative path name to get to the trees directory under dir1?
   A. dir1/trees
   B. /home/user2/dir1/trees
   C. /user2/dir1/trees
   D. user2/dir1/trees
4. What are the three parts of the command syntax of most UNIX commands, in the proper sequence?
   A. Command argument option
   B. Option argument option
   C. Command option argument
   D. Argument option command
5. If you want to find out what your current directory is and then move from it to a subdirectory, what two commands would you use?
   A. twd, chdr
   B. pwd, cd
   C. ls, cd
   D. pwd, ls

6. Your current directory was /home/user2/dir1/coffees. You typed in the **cd** command to change directories and forgot to specify the directory that you want to change to. You type the **ls** command and get a listing of files and directories from your home directory. Why is this?
   A. The **cd** command requires an option and an argument, or you will get an error.
   B. You accidentally typed in your home directory name.
   C. The **cd** command without options or arguments takes you to your home directory.
   D. The operating system kernel was installed in your home directory.
7. Which form of the **ls** command will list the file type along with the filename?
   A. ls –T
   B. ls –f
   C. ls –F
   D. ls –FT
8. If you want to get a listing of all files in a subdirectory (including hidden files) and you want to see the details on each one (such as permission and file size), which command would you use?
   A. cd -ld
   B. ls -la
   C. ls -fa
   D. cd -fs
9. You have thousands of files in your projects directory, and you want to see only those that begin with the letters "prj," regardless of how long the filename is. Which command would accomplish this?
   A. cd prj
   B. ls prj
   C. ls prj*
   D. ls prj?

10. Your current directory is /home/user2/dir1, and you are logged in as user1. You would like to clear the screen first and then view all the files in your home directory. What series of commands could you type in on one command line to do this?

A. clear ; cd ; ls –la

B. cls ; cd home ; ls –ld

C. clear ; chdir ; ls –ld

D. cls ; cd ; ls -ta

UNIX Command Summary

cd The **cd** command changes the working directory of the current shell execution environment. Example:

```
$ cd
$ cd ..
$ cd /home/user2/dir1
$ cd ./dir1
```

ls For each file that is a directory, **ls** lists the contents of the directory; for each file that is an ordinary file, **ls** repeats its name and any other information requested. Example:

```
-a,-F,-l,-lt,-ld,-E
$ ls
dante   dir1   dir3
$ ls -l
-rwxr-xr-x  1  user2  staff  110 Apr 19  dante
drwxr-xr-x  5  user2  staff  110 Apr 19  dir1
drwxr-xr-x  4  user2  staff  110 Apr 19  dir3
```

pwd Writes an absolute path name of the current working directory to standard output. Example:

```
$ pwd
/home/user2/dir1
```

Key Terms

Absolute path name Specifies a file or directory in relation to the entire UNIX file hierarchy. The hierarchy begins at the / (root) directory. If a path name begins with a slash, it is an absolute path name.

Argument Used to specify how and on what the preceding command is to be performed.

ASCII file (American Standard Code for Information Interchange) A file with normal printable characters and no special control or formatting characters. Commonly referred to as a text file.

Current working directory The directory where you are currently located in the directory tree structure.

Delimiter A special character, often a slash or a space, used to separate one string of characters from another.

Executable file A file that can be executed by the system. An executable may contain command text, as in the case of a shell script, or binary instructions. Examples of executables include applications and programs.

Hidden files Files that have names beginning with a dot (.). Examples of a hidden file are .login and .profile.

Hierarchy Structure with parent and child relationships that resembles an upside-down tree. The UNIX file system and UNIX system processes are examples of hierarchical structures.

Metacharacters Keyboard characters with special meaning to the shell. A general definition of a metacharacter is any keyboard character that is not alphanumeric. Metacharacters are used with many UNIX commands to provide greater flexibility. Some of the metacharacters used with UNIX are similar in function to those used with DOS. The asterisk (*) and the question mark (?) are metacharacters that also are known as wildcards and that are used to work with groups of files efficiently.

Parent directory Directory that contains other directories. For example, the /usr directory is the parent directory of /usr/bin.

Relative path name Describes the location of a file or directory as it relates to the current directory (the directory that you are currently in). If a path name does not begin with a slash, it is a relative path name.

Root directory The top of the UNIX directory system. All other directories are subdirectories of the root (/) directory.

Symbolic link A link is a mechanism that allows several filenames to refer to a single file on disk. Symbolic (soft) links are pointer files that name another file elsewhere in the file system. Symbolic links may span physical devices because they point to a UNIX path name and not to an actual disk location.

Objectives

After reading this chapter, you will be able to

- Manage directories and files using the command line
- Manage directories and files using the graphical CDE File Manager

Chapter 6

Basic Directory and File Management

Introduction

In this chapter, you perform basic file- and directory-management tasks using the command-line interface as well as the CDE File Manager. The importance of learning command-line utilities is emphasized. We start with the command-line interface and work with a number of file information commands to discover the characteristics and contents of various file types. We cover the rules and procedure for creating files and directories and then discuss how to remove them. CDE File Manager is introduced, which is a utility that can perform many file- and directory-management functions through a graphical user interface.

Directory and File Management Using the Command Line

Although you can use the CDE interface for many file-management tasks, it is important to know how to use the UNIX command line and UNIX commands. In some cases, using the command line to issue commands is faster than CDE, but there are two main reasons for learning the command line:

- It gives you access to the many command options, providing more flexibility.
- It gives you the ability to perform file management on a remote system where a graphical interface is not available.

Command-Line Capabilities

Knowledge of file and directory management using commands is important in building a solid foundation for further study of the UNIX operating system. UNIX power users and system administrators must have a working knowledge of command-line capabilities and syntax. Many operating system management and device-configuration tasks require an understanding of UNIX commands, and, in some cases, the command line is the only tool available. Power users and administrators frequently create executable script files, which are useful tools for automating certain tasks such as backing up files or creating new user accounts. Script files are a series of UNIX commands and are similar to batch files used with other network operating systems.

Using Control Characters

Control characters are used to perform specific tasks, such as stopping and starting screen output and others. Most PC keyboards have two control keys, normally labeled Ctrl and found in the lower-left and lower-right corners of the keyboard. On a Sun workstation, one control key is in the lower left of the keyboard (labeled Control.) When displayed on the screen, the Ctrl key is represented by the caret (^) symbol.

To enter a control character sequence, hold down the Ctrl key and press the appropriate character on the keyboard. Ctrl-c is a common control character sequence and frequently is used to interrupt or cancel a program or process. The actual character in the shell appears as ^C, even though you press the Ctrl key and the c key at the same time. The following control characters can be used:

- **Ctrl-s**—Stops screen output. The Ctrl-s and Ctrl-q characters originally were needed by teletype operators and are rarely used today. You might use Ctrl-s when viewing a large file with the **cat** command (covered in the section "Displaying File Contents with **cat** and **more**," later in this chapter).
- **Ctrl-q**—Resumes screen output stopped by Ctrl-s and is not used frequently.
- **Ctrl-c**—Interrupts the current activity and frequently is used to abort processes or long display outputs resulting from the **man**, **cat**, or **ls** commands. If you do a man page on a command and want to stop the remaining display of the man output, you can press Ctrl-c to interrupt the output and return to a command prompt.
- **Ctrl-d**—Indicates the end of the file or exit. Ctrl-d is used to exit some UNIX utilities (bc, write, and several others), exit a Terminal window, and to log out of a terminal session or command-line login session. As a general rule, when you are stuck or if Ctrl-c does not work, try Ctrl-d. The following introduces the handy basic calculator (bc) to demonstrate how Ctrl-d is used to exit a UNIX utility program:

  $bc—Runs the basic calculator

  5280/3—Divides 5280 by 3. Also can use +, -, *, and ^ for exponents

  1760—Answer

TIP

Use Ctrl-c to restore the shell prompt if an unrecognized command (such as **$ls "**) is typed and the secondary prompt (>) in the Korn shell is received.

Press Ctrl-d to exit bc and return to the shell prompt.

$

- **Ctrl-u**—Erases the entire command line. This can be used as a quick way to erase a command line that you decided not to execute, or when you are logged into a remote system and the Backspace key does not work.
- **Ctrl-w**—Erases the last word on the command line. This can be used as a quick way to erase the last argument (such as a path name or filename) on the command line that you decided not to use or when you are logged into a remote system and the Backspace key does not work.
- **Ctrl-h**—Erases the last character on the command line. This primarily is used when you are logged into a remote system and the Backspace key does not work properly because the operator of that remote system has not configured the Backspace key to act like the Ctrl-h key.

TIP

Use Ctrl-u to ensure that you are starting with a fresh user ID and password entry when logging in. Because passwords cannot be seen when they are typed, use Ctrl-u to erase the password and start over when an incorrect character(s) has been typed.

TIP

When you use the Telnet program to log onto a remote system, the Backspace might not work. See the tip at the end of the section "Logging In Using the Telnet Program," in Chapter 2, "Accessing Your System and the Common Desktop Environment," for instructions on how to assign the Ctrl-h function to the Backspace key.

Skill Builder

e-Lab Activity 6.1

Using Control Characters

In this e-Lab activity, you execute a UNIX utility called basic calculator from a Terminal window. You use the Ctrl-d command to exit the utility.
Note: Be sure to press Enter after each one. Click Step 1 to begin.

Determining File Type

Knowing a file's type (text, program file, shell script, and so on) is important when a user is attempting to open or view a file. Determining the file type can help a user decide which program or command to use when working with the file.

The file Command

Many types of files are found on a UNIX system. The file type can be determined by using the **file** command:

```
file filename(s)
```

The output from this command most often is one of the following: text, executable, or data.

- **Text**—Examples include ASCII text (nonformatted text) or English text (text with punctuation characters), commands text, and executable shell scripts. This type of file can be read using the **cat** or **more** commands, which are discussed in this chapter, and can be edited using vi or another text editor.

- **Executable or binary**—Examples include 32-bit executable and extensible linking format (ELF) code files and other dynamically linked executables. This file type indicates that the file is a command or a program. The **strings** command, which is covered next, prints readable characters in this type of file.
- **Data**—Data files are those that are created by an application running on the system. In some cases, the type of file is indicated—for example, a FrameMaker document. When the application in which this file was created cannot be determined by the **file** command, the output simply indicates that it is a data file. The only way to read a data file is to determine which application created it and open the file with that application.

NOTE

For information on other file types, see the man pages.

Figure 6-1 shows several examples using the **file** command. The first example is a ***text file***. The second is a ***data file*** that must be read by FrameMaker. The third is the **cat** command file, which is an executable. In the first two examples, we change to the directory where the file is located first. In the third example, we specify the file using its absolute path name.

Figure 6-1
Using the **file** command.

Text File Example:
```
$ cd /home/user2
$ file dante
dante:     English text
```

Data File Example:
```
$ cd /home/user2/dir1/coffees
$ file beans
beans:     Frame Maker document
```

Executable File Example:
```
$ file /usr/bin/cat
/usr/bin/cat: ELF 32-bit MSB executable SPARC
Version 1, dynamically linked, stripped
```

The strings Command

The **strings** command can be used to print readable characters in an executable or binary file. Someone with a programming background can interpret the output produced by the **strings** command. The command is introduced here solely as a method for demonstrating the printable characters of an executable file. The **strings** command must be used to read an executable file such as /usr/bin/cat. In Figure 6-2, the **strings** command is followed by the filename of the command, including the absolute path name. The **strings** command also shows the usage syntax of the command in most cases.

Figure 6-2
Using the **strings** command.

```
$ strings /urs/bin/cat
SUNW_OST_OSCMD
usvtebn
usage:    cat [ -usvtebn ] [ - | file ]
cat:    Cannot stat stdout
cat:    cannot open %s
cat:    cannot stat %s
cat:    input/output files '%s' identical
cat:    close error
<some output omitted>
```

Skill Builder

e-Lab Activity 6.2

Using the **file** and **strings** Commands

In this e-Lab activity, you are logged in as user2, and your current working directory is /home/user2/dir2. Refer to the class file tree structure on the inside-front cover of this book. Type the commands that would accomplish the requested objectives. *Note:* Be sure to press Enter after each one. Click Step 1 to begin.

Displaying File Contents with cat and more

The **cat** and **more** commands are the two common commands used to view the contents of a text file.

Using the cat Command

The **cat** (short for "concatenate") command displays the contents of a text file on the screen. It often is used to display short text files such as script files (similar to batch files). Because **cat** flashes through the entire file rapidly without pausing, you should be prepared to either stop and start the scrolling with the Ctrl-s and Ctrl-q keys or use the **more** command (covered next). The **cat** command also can be used to *concatenate* (join) two or more files into one large file.

```
cat filename(s)
```

Figure 6-3 shows the use of the **cat** command to display the dante text file in the /home/user2 directory. If the file fills more than one screen, the data scrolls off the screen—unless you are using a scrolling window, such as a Terminal window, within

NOTE

The **cat** command is comparable to the **type** command in the DOS world.

the CDE environment. If you are using a Terminal window, you can scroll up or down using the scroll arrows.

Figure 6-3
Using the **cat** command.

```
$ cat dante
The Life and Times of Dante
by Dante Pocai

Mention "Alighieri" and few may know about whom you
are talking. Say "Date," instead, and the whole world
knows who you mean. For Dante Alighieri, like Raphael
.
.
.
$
```

Using the more Command

Use the **more** command to display the contents of a text file one screen at a time. If the information in a file is longer than one screen, the following message appears at the bottom of the screen, where *n* is the percentage of the file already displayed:

```
--More--(n%)
```

TIP

When viewing a file with the **more** command, you can drop into the visual (vi) text editor at the current line if you decide to edit the file (see Chapter 9, "Using Text Editors"). To use vi on a file that you are viewing with the **more** command, enter the letters **vi** when **-- more -- (NN%)** appears on the screen. *Note:* Only the files that cause the screen to scroll can be edited with vi while viewing the file with the **more** command.

The online manual pages use **more** for display purposes, so the scrolling keys in Figure 6-4 are the same ones used to display man pages. Using **cat** or **more** to read executable or binary files can cause a terminal or window to hang, and you would need to use Ctrl-c to restore the shell prompt.

```
more filename(s)
```

At the **--More--** prompt, you can use the keys in Figure 6-4 to control the scrolling capabilities.

Figure 6-4
more command scrolling keys.

Scrolling Keys	Purpose
Spacebar	Scrolls to the next screen.
Return	Scrolls one line at a time.
b	Moves back one screen.
f	Moves forward one screen.
h	Displays a Help menu of more features.
q	Quits and return to the shell prompt.
/string	Searches forward for string.
N	Finds next occurrence of string.

 **Skill Builder**

e-Lab Activity 6.3

Using **cat** and **more**

In this e-Lab activity, you are logged in as user2, and your current working directory is /home/user2. Refer to the class file tree structure on the inside-front cover of this book. Type the commands that would accomplish the requested objectives. *Note:* Be sure to press Enter after each one. Click Step 1 to begin.

Displaying File Contents with head and tail

System administrators frequently utilize the **head** and **tail** commands to quickly check portions of text files that they do not need to view in their entirety.

Using the head Command

The **head** command is used to display the first *n* lines of one or more text files. The first 10 lines are displayed by default if the **-n** option is omitted. The **head** command is useful when you want to check only the first few lines of a file, regardless of its length. Figure 6-5 uses the **head** command to display the first five lines of the /usr/dict/words file. In this example, the **head** command is used by itself, but it typically is used in a command line containing several commands in a pipeline. This is covered later in the course.

head [-n] *filename(s)*

Figure 6-5
Using the **head** command.

```
$ head -5 /usr/dict/words
1st
2nd
3rd
4th
5th
$
```

Using the tail Command

Use the **tail** command to display the last n lines of a text file. The last 10 lines are displayed by default if the **-n** option is omitted. The **tail** command is useful for checking the most recent entries in large log files. Backup utility programs frequently write their results to a log file showing which files were backed up and when. The final entries in a backup log file are usually the total number of files backed up and messages indicating whether the backup finished successfully. Backup logs can be quite large, and the **tail** command allows you to check the end result of the backup log without looking at the entire file.

Like the **head** command, the **tail** command can be used by itself, but it typically is used in a command line containing several commands in a pipeline. This will be covered later in the course.

tail [-n] *filename(s)*

or

tail [+n] *filename(s)*

The previous command format shows two options with the **tail** command: **-n** and **+n**. The **-n** option displays the last *n* lines of the file. The **+n** option allows you to start displaying lines from a specific point in a file. It starts at the *n*th line in the file and displays all lines from there to the end. The first example in Figure 6-6 shows the use of the **tail** command to see the last five lines of the /usr/dict/words file. The second example uses the +23 option to start at line 23 of the file and displays the remaining lines.

TIP

You can use wildcards to display the top (head) or bottom (tail) lines of multiple files. For example, **$head chap* | more** displays the top lines of all files that begin with chap.

Figure 6-6
Using the **tail** command.

```
$  tail -5 /usr/dict/words
zounds
z's
zucchini
Zurich
zygote
$

$  tail +23 /usr/dict/words
abase
abash
abate
...
Zurich
zygote
$
```

TIP

You can split a file into two separate files using either **head** or **tail** in conjunction with the greater-than (>) redirect symbol (see Chapter 7, "Advanced Directory and File Management"). For example, **$tail -25 us_states > bottom_25,** creates a new file named bottom_25, containing the last 25 lines of the us_states file.

Skill Builder

e-Lab Activity 6.4

Using **head** and **tail**

In this e-Lab activity, you are logged in as user2, and your current working directory is /home/user2. Refer to the class file tree structure on the inside-front cover of this book. Type the commands that accomplish the requested objectives. *Note:* Be sure to press Enter after each one. Click Step 1 to begin.

The wc Command

The **wc** (word count) command can be used to display line, word, byte, or character counts for a text file. This command is useful when trying to determine characteristics of a file or when comparing two files. Using **wc** without options gives a line, word, and byte count of the contents of the file. Using it with individual options allows you to determine which of these you would like to see. Figure 6-7 lists the options that are available with the **wc** command.

Figure 6-7
The **wc** command options.

Option	Function
-l	Counts lines.
-w	Counts words.
-c	Counts bytes.
-m	Counts characters.

Like the **head** and **tail** commands, **wc** can be used by itself, but it typically is used in a command line containing several commands in a pipeline when you want to count the output. This is covered later in the course.

`wc [options] filename(s)`

Figure 6-8 shows examples using the **wc** command. In the first example, the **wc** command by itself indicates that the file dante contains 33 lines, 223 words, and 1320 bytes. The second example shows only the line count.

Figure 6-8
Using the **wc** command.

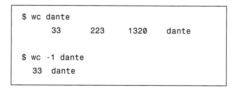

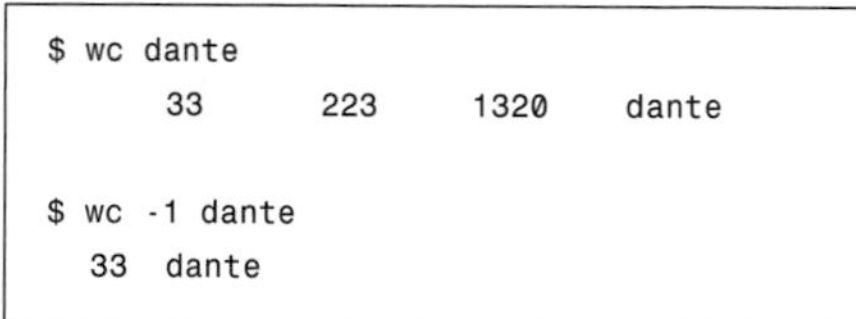

```
$ wc dante
      33       223      1320     dante

$ wc -l dante
  33  dante
```

Comparing Files

The **wc** command also can be used as a quick way to see if two files are different by comparing the number of characters, words, and lines. However, if you need to see the actual differences, use the **diff** command.

Using the diff Command

The **diff** (difference) command compares two **text** files and find differences between them. The **wc** command also can be used to compare files because it counts lines, words, and bytes. It is possible for two files to have the same line, word and byte counts but have different characters and words. The **diff** command can find the actual differences between the files. For example:

```
diff [option] file1 file2
```

The output of this command displays line-by-line differences between two text files. There are two options with the **diff** command: **-i** and **-c**.

- The **-i** option ignores the case of the letters; for example, *A* is equal to *a*.
- The **-c** option performs a detailed comparison and produces a listing of differences with three lines of context. With this option, the output begins with identification of the files involved and their creation dates.

Following a line of a dozen asterisks (*), the line numbers of file1 that are to be displayed are listed. The actual lines from file1 then are displayed, with a minus symbol (–) in front of the lines that are different from those in file2. The same display follows as it applies to file2, with a plus sign (+) for the lines that are different from those in file1. Figure 6-9 shows the contents of the individual fruit and fruit2 files using the **cat** command. Figure 6-10 shows the output from the comparison of the fruit and fruit2 files using **diff**.

TIP

Use the **cmp** (compare) command to quickly determine whether two files differ without displaying the differences. The **cmp** command displays no output if the files are identical, or it provides the character position and line number of the first occurrence of a difference.

Figure 6-9
The output of the **cat** command for fruit and fruit2.

```
$ cat fruit
lemon
orange
apple
banana
pear
mango
tomato
pomegranate
```

```
$ cat fruit2
lemon
orange
apple
banana
tomato
guava
pomegranate
```

Figure 6-10 Using the **diff** command.

```
$ diff -c fruit fruit2
*** fruit  Fri  May 8     11:32:49  1998
--- fruit2 Fri  May 8     14:55:21  1998
**********
***2,           8****
orange
apple
banana
-pear
-mango
tomato
pomegranate
***2,           8****
orange
apple
banana
tomato
+guava
+mango
pomegranate
```

Skill Builder

e-Lab Activity 6.5

Using **wc** and **diff**

In this e-Lab activity, you are logged in as user2, and your current working directory is /home/user2. Refer to the class file tree structure on the inside-front cover of this book. Type the commands that would accomplish the requested objectives. *Note:* Be sure to press Enter after each one. Click Step 1 to begin.

Skill Builder

Lab Activity 6.1.6

File Information Commands

In this lab, you work with various informational commands. These are important because they allow you to investigate and discover information about files. You use commands to help you determine what type a file is and what application created it. You also work with several commands that let you see the contents of text files and compare them. Refer to the *Cisco Networking Academy Program: Fundamentals of UNIX Lab Companion*.

File- and Directory-Naming Conventions

TIP

File or directory names beginning with a dot (.) are considered "hidden" and can be displayed only using the **ls -a** (all) option. "Dot" files typically are reserved for initialization or customization files (see Chapter 15, "Customizing Your Login Environment"). However, you can name a file that begins with a dot if you don't want it to show up when the **ls** command is used without the **–a** option. Think of this as a way to "hide" a file.

This section covers the creation of files and directories, so it is important to review the naming of UNIX files and directories before beginning. All operating systems have some basic guidelines or conventions that must be followed. The rules here apply to UNIX files and directories. See Figure 6-11 for a summary of the UNIX file- and directory-naming guidelines or conventions.

Figure 6-11
Summary of naming conventions for files and directories.

- Long file and directory names are not recommended although combined, they can be as long as 255 characters.
- Alphanumeric characters are recommended along with the non-alphanumeric characters of the dash (-) and underscore (_)
- Other non-alphanumeric metacharacters are allowed, but not recommended.
- Filenames normally contain one extension, but can have more than one.
- Directory names normally do not contain extensions but can.

- **Maximum length**—The maximum length of files and directories combined is 255 alphanumeric characters.
- **Nonalphanumeric characters (some alphanumeric characters are allowed)**—Underscores (_), hyphens (-), and periods (.) can be used multiple times in a file or directory name (for example, Feb.Reports.Sales). Although the shell will allow asterisks (*), ampersands (&), pipes (|), quotes (" "), and dollar signs ($) to be used in a filename, this is not recommended because these characters have special meaning to the shell.
- **Filename extensions**—Filenames can contain one or more extensions. Extensions usually are appended to files by an application. Extensions are usually one to three characters that are appended to the end of a filename and are preceded by a period (.). You might choose to use this convention when naming files, but it is not a necessary part of a filename.
- **Directory name extensions**—Directory names generally do not contain extensions, but there are no rules against it.

Creating Files

As with directories, files are created by administrators and users. Many applications also create files. Every time you create a new word-processing document or spreadsheet, you are creating a new file and should adhere to the file-naming conventions previously mentioned. You also must have adequate permissions for the directory in which you are working to create files.

You can create new, empty files by using the **touch** command. If you list these files using the **ls -l** command (long listing), you will see that they exist but are 0 bytes in length. Using the **touch** command, you can create one or multiple files simultaneously. Some applications require files to exist before they can be written. The **touch** command is useful for quickly creating files to experiment with and is used extensively with this course. You also can use the **touch** command to update the time and date that a file is accessed, which will reset the archive bit, making the file available for backup again. Absolute and relative path names can be specified when creating files or directories. Figure 6-12 shows the use of the **touch** command to create multiple files.

```
touch  filename(s)
```

NOTE

To help distinguish between files and directories, some UNIX administrators prefer their users to start filenames with lowercase letters and directory names with capital letters. They also might recommend including an uppercase letter D_ in the first position or including .dir on the end of directory names to distinguish them from filenames. If no convention is used to distinguish files from directories, you can always use the **ls -F** command line to visibly show which is which. The **ls –l** command, which shows a long listing, also indicates files and directories by the first character of the display.

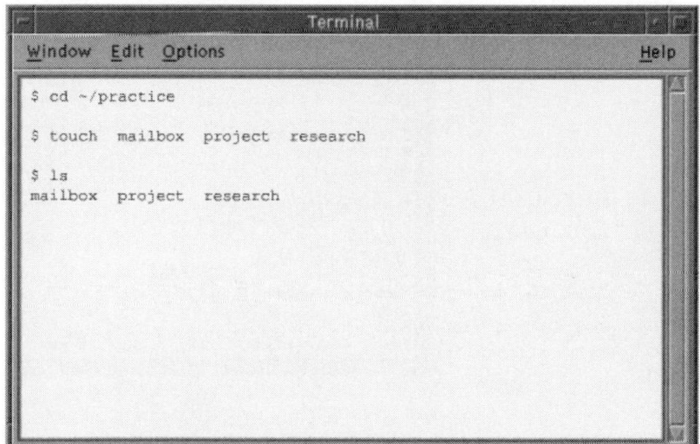
Terminal
Window Edit Options Help
$ cd ~/practice
$ touch mailbox project research
$ ls
mailbox project research

Figure 6-12
Using the **touch** command.

Creating Directories

The **mkdir** command creates directories or folders. Directories can contain other directories, which are referred to as subdirectories; they can contain files. This section deals with user-created directories, those created by a system administrator or a user. Directories can be created using either an absolute or a relative path name. You can specify more than one directory name on the same line to create more than one new directory.

You must have the appropriate permissions to create a directory. (Permissions are covered later in the course.) If you change to a directory in which you do not have the

NOTE

The **touch** command creates an empty file if the filename specified does not exist. Otherwise, the access/modification time of the existing file is updated.

correct permissions to create a new file or directory, you will receive an error message similar to this one:

```
$ mkdir /home/Olympic
mkdir: Failed to make directory "/home/Olympic"; Permission denied
```

Figure 6-13 starts with the **pwd** command to verify that you are in your home directory, and it shows several examples of using the basic **mkdir** command. Variations of the **ls** command are used to list the directories created. Using the **mkdir** command with the -p option, you can create multiple levels of directories, including all the directories in a path name, simultaneously. If you use the **-p** option and specify a directory in the path name that does not exist, it will be created.

```
mkdir [-p] directory_name directory_name
```

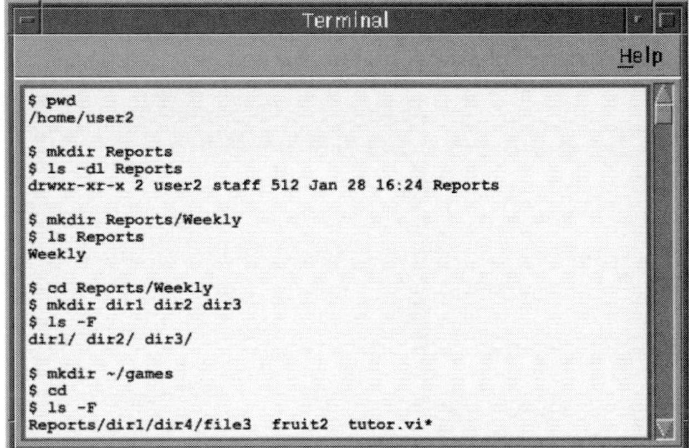

Figure 6-13
Using the **mkdir** command.

WARNING

When using wildcards with the **rm** command, you need to exercise caution. For example, accidentally typing the command line **$rm * budget*** instead of **$rm *budget*** could be disastrous. The first command would remove all (*) files in the current directory, including those that begin with budget. The second command removes all files that have "budget" in the filename.

Skill Builder

e-Lab Activity 6.6

Using **mkdir** and **touch**

In this e-Lab activity, you are logged in as user2, and your current working directory is /home/user2/dir4. Refer to the class file tree structure on the inside-front cover of this book. Type the commands that would accomplish the requested objectives. *Note:* Be sure to press Enter after each one. Click Step 1 to begin.

Removing Files and Directories

Files that are deleted from the command line on a UNIX system are permanently deleted and cannot be recovered. However, if you are using the File Manager in CDE, you have the capability to take a deleted file from the Trash Can and drag it back to a folder, thus "undeleting" it. CDE File Manager is covered later. The **rm** command is a versatile one that can be used to remove (delete) files or directories from the UNIX file system.

Removing Files

The **rm** command can remove a single file or multiple files. You can remove several files at once by specifying their names after the **rm** command, or you can use the asterisk (*) and question mark (?) metacharacters (wildcards).

Files that are deleted on a UNIX system are permanently deleted and cannot be recovered unless you are using the CDE graphical interface. As a safeguard, the **rm** command can be used with the **-i** (interactive) option, which prompts the user before removing files. Use the **rm -i** command as a precaution to avoid accidentally deleting files.

rm [-i] *filename(s)*

In the first example in Figure 6-14, the **cd** command is used to change to the letters subdirectory under your home directory, which you can see by the results of the **pwd** command. The **ls** command lists the files currently in the letters directory. The **touch** command is used to create an empty file named projection, which you can see in the next listing. The **rm** command then is used to delete the research and project2 files, and the **ls** command shows that they were removed. The second example uses the **–I**, or interactive, option with **rm** command to remove the projection file created earlier with the **touch** command.

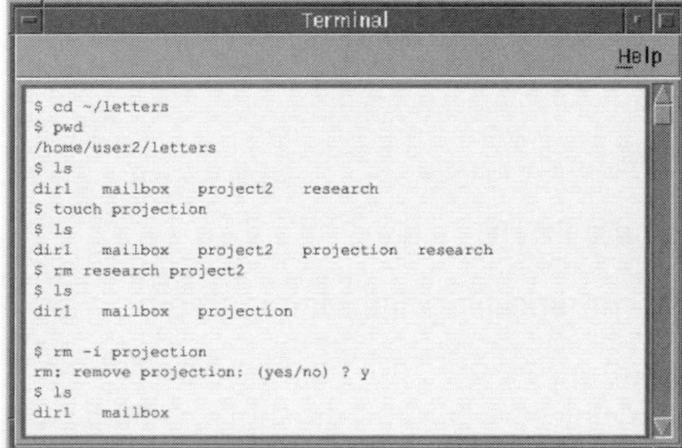

Figure 6-14
Removing files with the **rm** command.

> **TIP**
> Many systems are set up with an alias (see Chapter 14, "Basic Features of the Korn and C Shells") for the **rm** command. The alias is set up so that when the user uses the **rm** command, the **rm -i** command actually is executed. This ensures that a user is prompted before removing a file. To temporarily bypass the alias so that you are not prompted, enter a backslash before the command. For example, **$ \rm file1 fil2** executes the original **rm** command (not the alias) and removes the files file1 and file2 without being prompted.

Removing Directories

The **rm -r** (recursive) command is used to remove directories. It removes the directory being targeted, including all subdirectories and files in it. When the **rm** command is used with the **-r** option, it can remove a single directory (empty or not) or an entire section of the directory tree. Figure 6-15 shows examples of removing files and directories using the **rm** command.

```
rm -r [i] directory_name(s)
```

TIP

If the directory is empty, you can use either the **rm –r** command or the **rmdir** command. **rmdir** can be used only to remove empty directories.

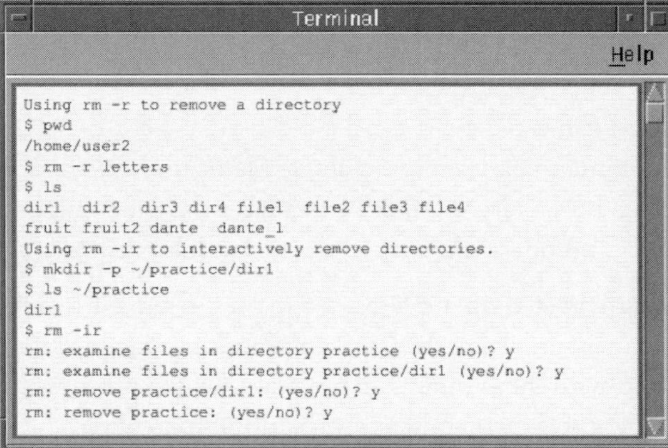

Terminal
Help
Using rm -r to remove a directory
$ pwd
/home/user2
$ rm -r letters
$ ls
dir1 dir2 dir3 dir4 file1 file2 file3 file4
fruit fruit2 dante dante_1
Using rm -ir to interactively remove directories.
$ mkdir -p ~/practice/dir1
$ ls ~/practice
dir1
$ rm -ir
rm: examine files in directory practice (yes/no)? y
rm: examine files in directory practice/dir1 (yes/no)? y
rm: remove practice/dir1: (yes/no)? y
rm: remove practice: (yes/no)? y

Figure 6-15 Removing directories with the **rm** command.

Skill Builder

e-Lab Activity 6.7

Using the **rm** Command

In this e-Lab activity, you are logged in as user2, and your current working directory is /home/user2/dir4. Refer to the class file tree structure on the inside-front cover of this book. Type the commands that would accomplish the requested objectives. *Note:* Be sure to press Enter after each one. Click Step 1 to begin.

Skill Builder

Lab Activity 6.1.10

Basic Command-Line File Management

In this lab, you work with file-management commands from the command line. The guidelines for file and directory naming, which are known as naming conventions, are reviewed. You create a simple directory structure and then create some files in those directories. You practice creating and removing both files and directories. Refer to the *Cisco Networking Academy Program: Fundamentals of UNIX Lab Companion.*

Using CDE File Manager

File Manager can be accessed from the front panel or by right-clicking the desktop, as shown in Figure 6-16. The CDE method of file and directory management allows you to do many of the same tasks that were performed earlier at the command line. The CDE provides a nice graphical interface to file management and executes most of the same commands that you used from the command line behind the scenes.

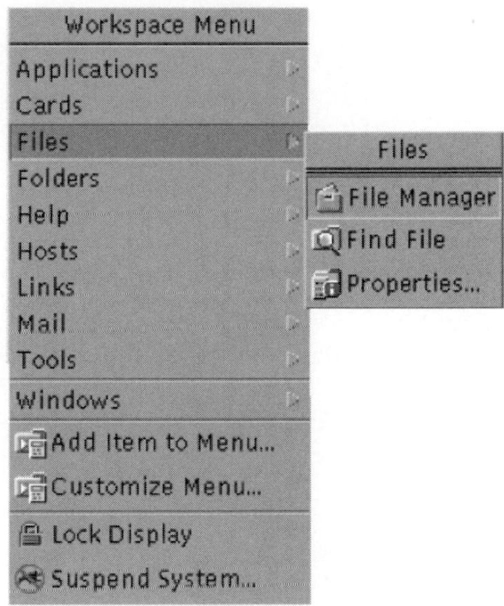

Figure 6-16 Accessing File Manager from the Workspace menu.

The File Manager, by default, opens a view of a folder that is the current directory (the term folder is used interchangeably with the terms directory and subdirectory). The initial screen displays the contents of the current folder, as shown in Figure 6-17. From that folder, you can change to other folders, both up and down in the hierarchy, to view each directory's contents. The path to the current folder always is displayed in the top area of the File Manager window, as shown in Figure 6-18.

File and Folder Icons

The File Manager enables you to graphically organize files into a hierarchical structure of folders (directories) and subfolders (subdirectories). Directories are displayed as folder icons. Files are displayed as appropriate icons, based on the type of file. File types are based on their function and the applications that created them. Examples of file types are shown in Figure 6-19 and include audio, binary, core, graphic, PostScript, and standard.

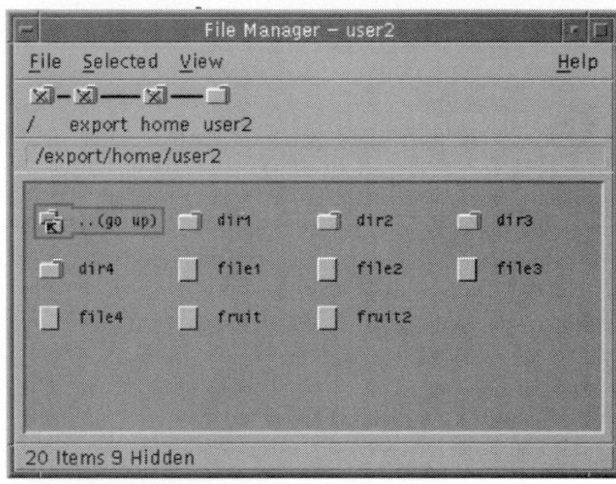

Figure 6-17
Contents of the current folder.

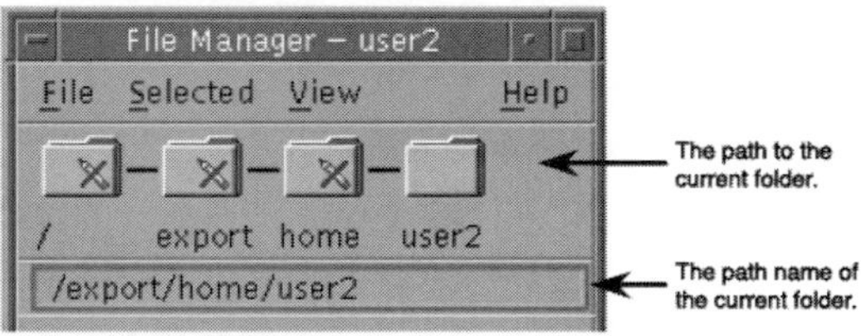

Figure 6-18
Path and path name of the current folder.

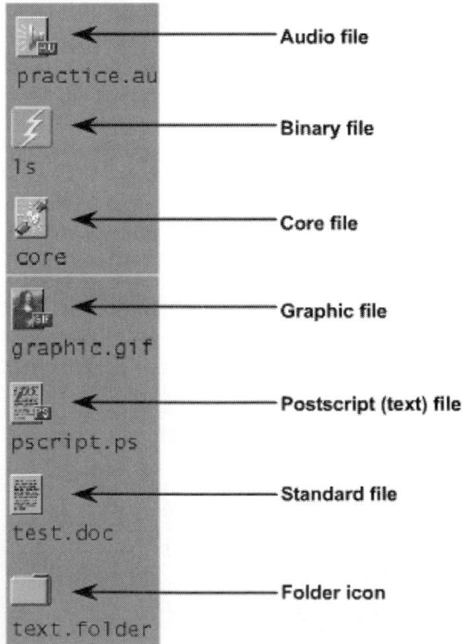

Figure 6-19
File and folder icons.

To help you identify files and directories more easily, the File Manager displays different icons depending on the content of the file. The most common file icon that you will see will be the standard file icon, shown in Figure 6-20. If a file is associated with a particular application, that application automatically starts when you double-click the icon.

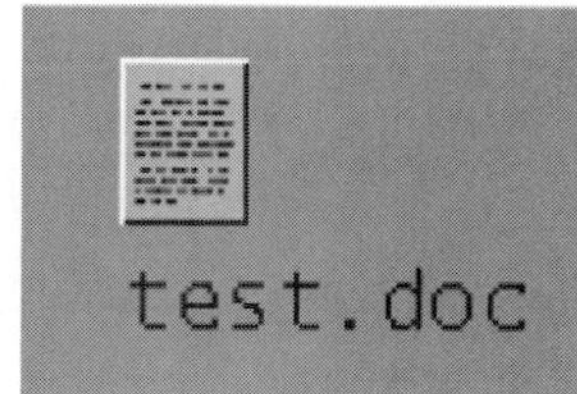

Figure 6-20
The standard file icon.

If you double-click a folder icon, the File Manager moves you into that directory and displays its contents. You can move down through the file system hierarchy only in this way. A special icon always is displayed in the upper-left corner of the File Manager display, as shown in Figure 6-21. Double-clicking this Go Up icon moves you to the next level up in the hierarchy.

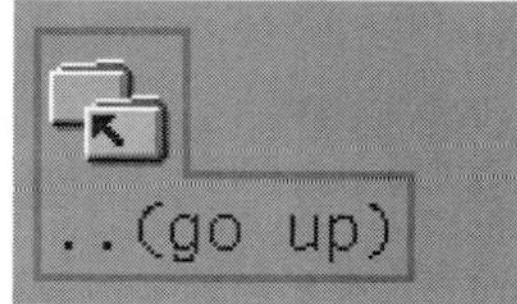

Figure 6-21
The Go Up icon.

File Menu Options

Click the File menu option from within File Manager to access options. The File menu options enable you to perform the tasks on the menu in Figure 6-22. These same tasks can be accomplished using the command line. The following is a listing of the File menu items, with a brief description of each:

- **New Folder**—You can create a new directory or subdirectory, but you must have adequate permission. (The command-line equivalent is **mkdir**.)
- **New File**—You can create new files in any directory where you have permission. (The command-line equivalent is **touch**.)
- **Go Home**—You can change to your home directory if your current folder is different from your home folder. (The command-line equivalent is **cd** or **cd~**.)
- **Go Up**—You can go up one level of folder in the directory tree or hierarchy. (The command-line equivalent is **cd ..**.)

- **Go To**—You can change to a specified directory. (The command-line equivalent is **cd dir_name**.)
- **Find**—You can locate files based on their name or content. (The command line equivalent is **find** *filename*, which is covered in Chapter 8, "File and User Information Utilities.")
- **Open Terminal**—You can opens a Terminal window with a shell prompt where you can enter UNIX commands.
- **Open Floppy**—You can access a floppy disk in the drive (DOS or UNIX).
- **Open CD-ROM**—You can access a CD-ROM in the drive.
- **Close**—You can close the File Manager window.

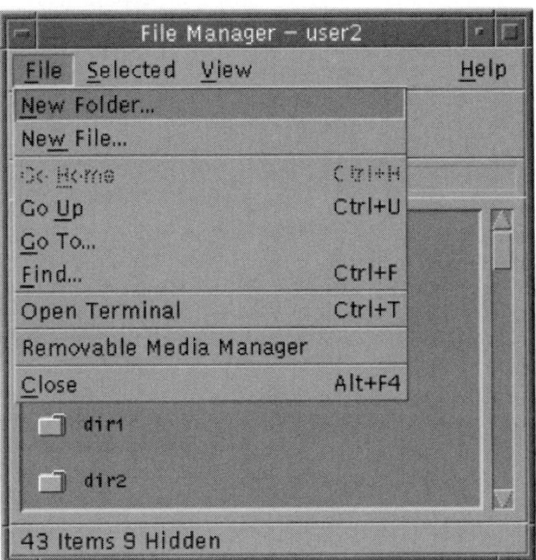

Figure 6-22
File Manager's File menu options.

Skill Builder

e-Lab Activity 6.8

Comparing File Manager to Command Line

For each of the following File Manager menu options, enter the command that accomplishes the same thing from the command line.

Creating New Folders and Files

The File Manger allows you to quickly and easily create folders and files as an alternative to using the **mkdir** command to create a new directory and the **touch** command to create a new, empty text file.

Creating New Folders

When the New Folder option is chosen, a separate window is displayed where you can enter the new folder name, as shown in Figure 6-23. Enter the name of the new folder or directory, and be sure to follow the directory-naming conventions covered earlier. After the name has been applied, you have the choice of left-clicking either OK or Apply.

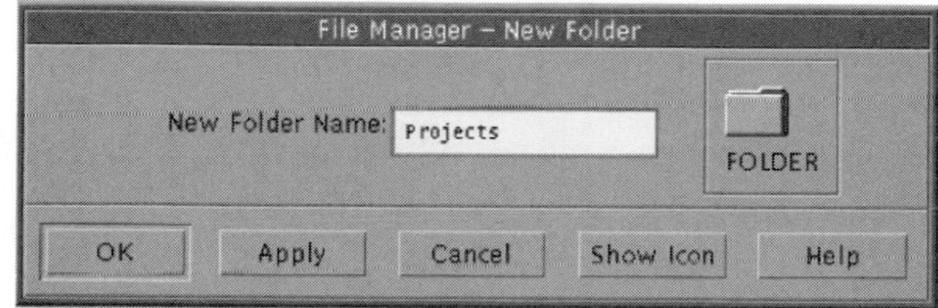

Figure 6-23
Creating a new folder.

Clicking OK adds the new folder with the name that you just typed and closes the New Folder window. Clicking Apply adds the new folder and keeps the New Folder window on the screen display, ready for you to type in the name of another new folder. Figure 6-24 shows the newly created Projects folder.

Figure 6-24
The new Projects folder.

NOTE

When you click Apply, the name is retained in the typing area of the New Folder window. You must remove the previous folder name using the Backspace key or the equivalent mouse action.

If you want to create several new directories, click Apply for all new folder names except the last. When the last folder name has been typed, click OK to close the New Folder window.

Creating New Files

As with the New Folder option, a New File window is displayed in which you must type the name of the file to be created, as shown in Figure 6-25. If you click OK, the file is created with the name that you typed, and the New File window closes. However, if you click Apply, the file is created and the New File window stays on the screen so that you can create another new file. By clicking Apply after each filename has been typed, you can add several new files from the same New File window. Figure 6-26 shows the newly created file.

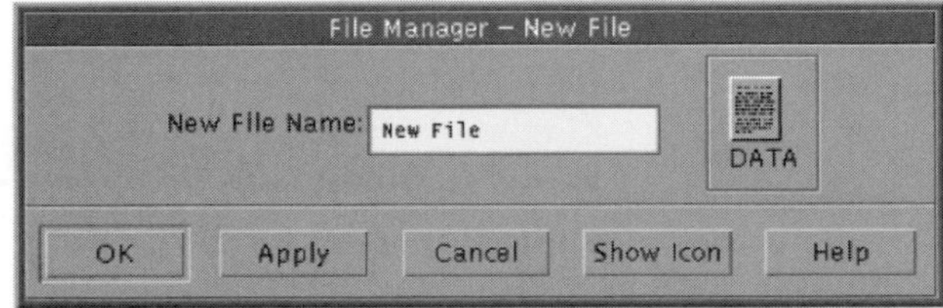

Figure 6-25
Creating a new file.

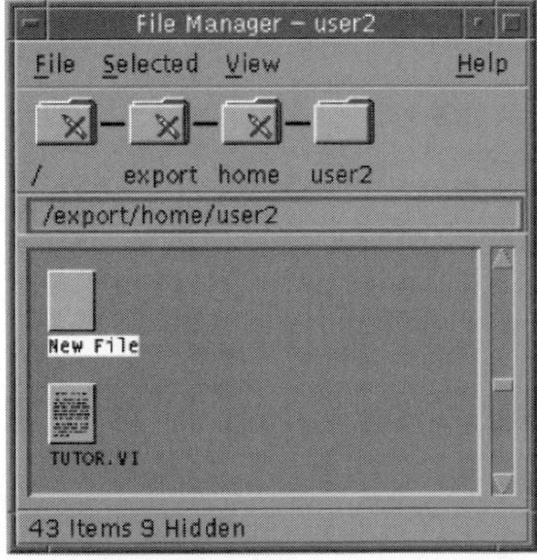

Figure 6-26
The newly created file.

If you attempt to create a folder or file with the same name as an existing folder or file, the File Manipulation Error window in Figure 6-27 alerts you. Click OK and then type an alternative name for the folder or file that is to be created.

Figure 6-27
The file manipulation error window.

Changing Folders

The Go To option on the File Manager's File menu enables you to specify which folder to change to by specifying a path name, as shown in Figure 6-28. Enter a valid path name into the appropriate entry box, and then click OK. If any permission controls prevent you from changing to the specified folder, you are notified with the window shown in Figure 6-29.

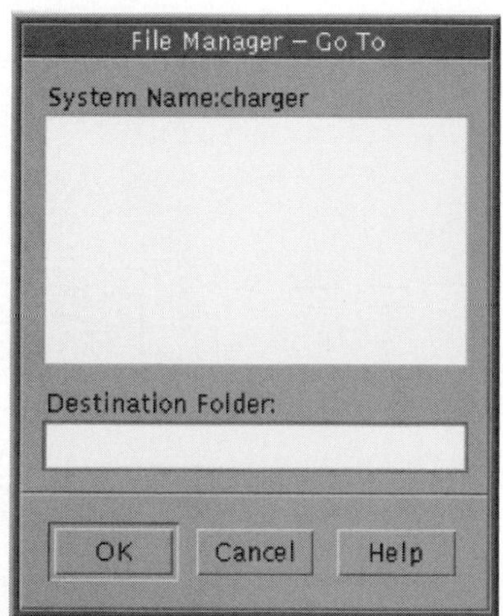

Figure 6-28
Changing folders.

Figure 6-29
The action error window.

Recovering Files

A benefit of File Manager over the command-line environment is its capability to recover deleted files. This is also known as the "undelete" function. If a file is deleted using File Manager, you can undelete it, provided that the file has not been overwritten. Within the CDE, any file or directory that is deleted is placed within the *Trash Can* using the Put in Trash option from the File Manager Selected menu (or by right-clicking the file and selecting Put in Trash). The Trash Can is accessed from the front panel, as shown in Figure 6-30, and the file to be recovered can be selected, as shown in Figure 6-31. The files within the Trash Can can be "undeleted" by selecting the Put Back option from the File menu, as shown in Figure 6-32. The Trash Can also allows you to shred the files or directories within the Trash Can, which permanently deletes the files.

Figure 6-30
Accessing the Trash Can.

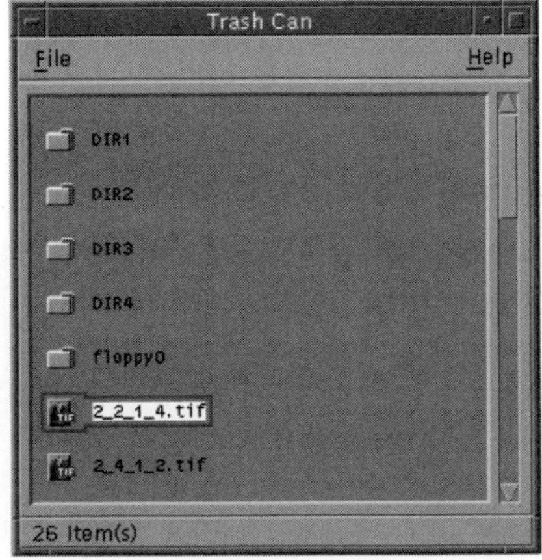

Figure 6-31
Selecting a file to put back.

Figure 6-32
Using the Put Back option.

Skill Builder

Lab Activity 6.2.6

Basic CDE File Manager

In this lab, you work with Common Desktop Environment (CDE) File Manager. The CDE method of file and directory management allows you to do many of the same tasks that were performed earlier at the command line. Refer to the *Cisco Networking Academy Program: Fundamentals of UNIX Lab Companion*.

Summary

Knowledge of UNIX commands provides a good foundation for understanding UNIX and is critical to success as a power user or system administrator.

Control characters such as Ctrl-c, Ctrl-d, and Ctrl-u are used in the UNIX environment to perform special functions such as interrupting command output, logging out, and clearing screen entries.

A number of file information commands are available. These include the **file, strings, cat, more, head, tail, wc**, and **diff** commands. They can be used to find out information about the type and characteristics of a file as well as its contents.

When creating new files and directories, you should adhere to the naming conventions. These are the basic rules for naming files and directories, which include length and recommended characters.

New directories are created using the **mkdir** command, and new files are created using the **touch** command. Files and directories can be removed or deleted using the **rm** command.

CDE File Manager is a graphical utility that you can use to perform many of the same functions as the file- and directory-management commands entered at the command line.

Check Your Understanding

1. You have displayed the man page for the **ls** command and have found what you were looking for. Which control key combination would you use to stop the screen output and return to the command prompt?

   A. Ctrl-s

   B. Ctrl-c

   C. Ctrl-d

   D. Ctrl-q

2. You have tried to use Ctrl-c to exit from the UNIX program that you are using, and it doesn't work. What other Ctrl key combination often works?

   A. Ctrl-s

   B. Ctrl-q

   C. Ctrl-x

   D. Ctrl-d

3. You would like to display the contents of a directory and be able to distinguish between files and directories. Which command accomplishes this?

   A. **ls –l**

   B. **ls –a**

   C. **ls –d**

   D. **ls**

4. You would like to see the first few lines of a text file. Which command could you use to do this?

   A. **cat**

   B. **head**

   C. **type**

   D. **quickview**

5. You have two copies of a text file that you were working on, but you are not sure that the two files are exactly the same. Which command would you use to ensure that they are the same?

   A. **wc**

   B. **filecomp**

C. **difffile**

D. **diff**

6. You are creating a new document using your word processor. When you save the file, what is a good convention or guideline to follow?

   A. Use the longest filename possible.

   B. Use metacharacters wherever possible, for uniqueness.

   C. Add multiple extensions to the file when you name it.

   D. Use alphanumeric characters with dashes and hyphens, if necessary.

7. Which of the following is a common directory-naming convention discussed in this chapter?

   A. abcxyz

   B. a1b2c3

   C. D_mydir

   D. mydir

8. You can create new files and directories using which of the following commands?

   A. **touch** and **mkdir**

   B. **new** and **crdir**

   C. **create** and **md**

   D. **file** and **mkdir**

9. If you want to remove a directory and all the subdirectories and files under it, which command should you use?

   A. **del –d** direname

   B. **erase** direname /r

   C. **rm –r** dirname

   D. **rmvdir** -all dirname

10. Which of the following must be done through a command-line utility rather than the CDE File Manager?

    A. Copy files to a different directory

    B. Change the permissions on a file

    C. Change the name of a file

    D. Compare two files for differences

UNIX Command Summary

bc Basic calculator command. Example:

```
$ bc
5280/3
1760
<Ctrl d>
$
```

cat Concatenate and display files. Example:

```
$ cat dante
The Life and Times of Dante
by Dante Pocai
Mention "Alighieri" and few may know about whom you are talking. Say "Dante,"
instead, and the whole world knows whom you mean. For Dante Alighieri, like Raphael
$
```

Ctrl c Cancels the current activity. Example:

```
$ man intro <Ctrl c>
```

Ctrl d Indicates the end of a file or exit. Example:

```
$ bc
5280/3
1760
<Ctrl d>
$
```

Ctrl q Resumes screen output. Example:

```
$ cat largfile <Ctrl s> <Ctrl q>
```

Ctrl s Stops screen output. Example:

```
$ cat largfile <Ctrl s>
```

Ctrl u Erases the entire command line.

Ctrl w Erases the last word on the command line.

diff Compares the contents of two files and writes to standard output a list of changes necessary to convert the first file into the second file. No output is produced if the files are identical. Example:

```
$ diff -c fruit fruit2
*** fruit Fri May 8 11:32:49 1998
--- fruit2 Fri May 8 14:55:21 1998
***********
***2, 8****
orange
apple
banana
-pear
-mango
tomato
```

```
pomegranate
---2, 8-----
orange
apple
banana
tomato
+guava
+mango
pomegranate
```

file Determines file type. Example:

```
$ file dante
dante:    English text

$ file beans
beans:    Frame Maker Document

$ file da* fi*
dante:      English Text
dante_1:    English Text
file1:      English Text
file2:      ascii text
files.jar:  java program
files.tar:  USTAR tar archive
```

head Displays the first few lines of files. Example:

```
$ head -5 /usr/dict/words
1st
2nd
3rd
4th
5th
$
```

mkdir Creates the named directories in mode 777 (possibly altered by the file mode creation mask umask(1)). Example:

```
$ mkdir Reports
$ ls -dl Reports
drwxr-xr-x 2 user2 staff 512 Jan 28 16:24 Reports

$ mkdir -p practice/dir1/admin
$ ls -R practice
practice:
dir1 mailbox project research
practice/dir1:
admin
practice/dir1/admin:
```

more A filter that displays the contents of a text file on the terminal, one screen at a time. It normally pauses after each full screen. Example:

```
$ cat dante | more
```

rm Removes directory entries. Example:

```
-i,-r
$ rm -r dir1
```

strings Finds printable strings in an object or binary file. Example:

```
$ strings /usr/bin/cat
SUNW_OST_OSCMD
usvtebn
usage: cat [ -usvtebn ] [-|file] ...
cat: Cannot stat stdout
cat: cannot open %s
cat: cannot stat %s
cat: input/output files '%s' identical
cat: close error
<some output omitted>
```

tail Displays the last few lines of files. Example:

```
$ tail -5 /usr/dict/words
zounds
z's
zucchini
Zurich
zygote
$
```

touch Sets the access and modification times of each file. The file is created if it does not already exist. Example:

```
$ cd ~/practice
$ touch mailbox project research
$ ls
mailbox project research
```

wc Reads one or more input files and, by default, writes the number of newline characters, words, and bytes contained in each input file to the standard output. Example:

```
$ wc dante
33 223 1320 dante
$ wc -l dante
33 dante
```

Key Terms

Concatenate To join the output of one or more files or commands.

Control character Used to perform specific tasks, such as stopping and starting screen output and aborting processes There are two control keys on most PC keyboards. They normally are labeled Ctrl and are found in the lower-left and lower-right corners of the keyboard. On a Sun workstation, one control key in the lower left of the keyboard that is labeled Control. When displayed on the screen, the Ctrl key is represented by the caret (^) symbol.

Data file A file created by a particular application such as a word processor or database. These files must be opened with the application that created them.

File Manager Can be accessed from the CDE front panel or by right-clicking the desktop. The CDE method of file and directory management allows you to do many of the same tasks that are performed at the command line. CDE provides a graphical interface to file management and executes most of the same commands used from the command line behind the scenes.

Text file A file made up of standard ASCII characters and no special formatting characters. Script files are text files.

Trash Can A temporary holding place for files that are deleted. Files can be placed in the Trash Can. They then can be permanently deleted by shredding them, or they can be put back (or "undeleted").

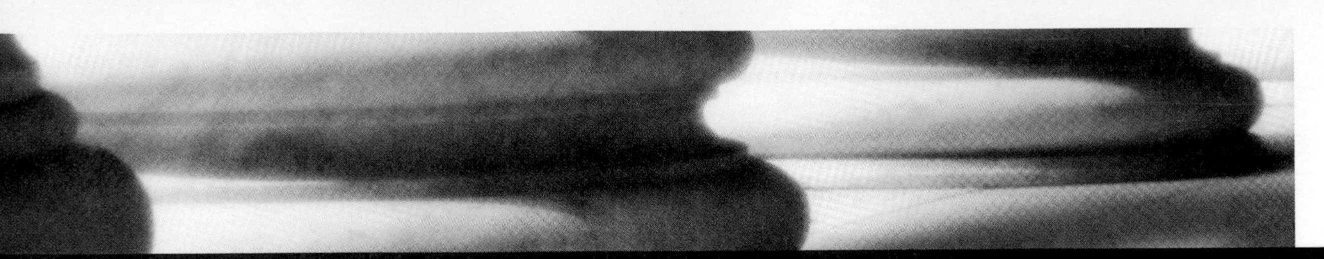

Objectives

After reading this chapter, you will be able to

- Perform advanced directory and file management using the command line
- Use the **cp** (copy) command to copy files and directories
- Create, remove, and rename links to files
- Use the **mv** (move) command to rename and move files and directories
- Redirect input/output to and from commands
- Pipe output from one command to another
- Perform advanced directory and file management using the Common Desktop Environment (CDE) File Manager

Chapter 7

Advanced Directory and File Management

Introduction

In this chapter, you work with some of the more advanced file- and directory-management tasks using the command-line interface as well as the CDE File Manager. You start with the command-line interface and work with the commands necessary to copy, link, move, and rename files and directories. You then learn about command *piping* and input/output *redirection*. You use the CDE File Manager to perform some of the same tasks that you accomplished earlier using the command line. Accessing the floppy disk is also discussed.

Copying Files Using the Command Line

The **cp** (copy) command copies files and directories. We focus on copying files in this section.

Copying files is a normal occurrence when working with the file system. A common use of the **cp** command is to make a backup of an existing file for safekeeping so that the original can be modified.

Files can be copied in two different ways:

- A new file can be created with a different name in the same directory.
- Files can be copied to a different location in the directory hierarchy with the same name or a different name. They also can be copied to a different disk, such as a floppy, or to a centralized server.

Two different ways exist of using the copy command with files, depending on your goal: copying files within a directory and copying them to another directory.

Copying Files Within a Directory

If you want to copy a file to create within the same directory a new file that has a different filename, use the format in Figure 7-1. This format copies from an existing filename (source_file) to a new filename (destination_file) in the same directory. This method of copying files can be thought of as copying from *old* to *new* in the same directory.

NOTE

You cannot have two files of the same name in one directory.

TIP

Most UNIX commands enable you to specify multiple source files. To specify more than one file, separate the filenames with a blank character space. For example, the command **cp Chap1 Chap2 book.dir** copies both Chap files to the book.dir directory.

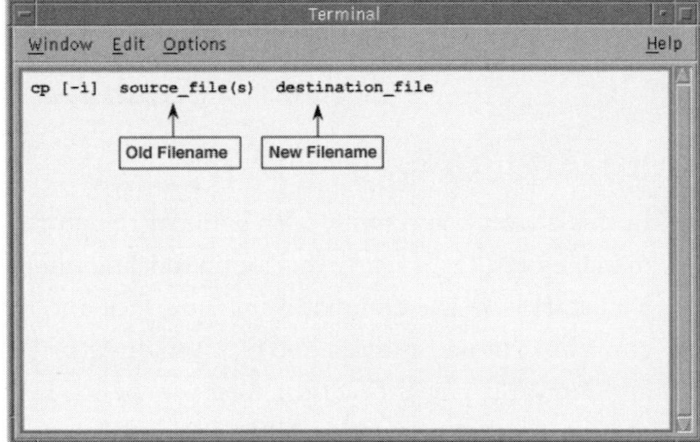
Terminal
Window Edit Options Help
cp [-i] source_file(s) destination_file
Old Filename
New Filename

Figure 7-1
Copy (**cp**) old file/new file.

Figure 7-2 illustrates copying a file within a directory. The file3 file is being copied to a new file named feathers that will reside in the same directory, as can be seen with the **ls** command.

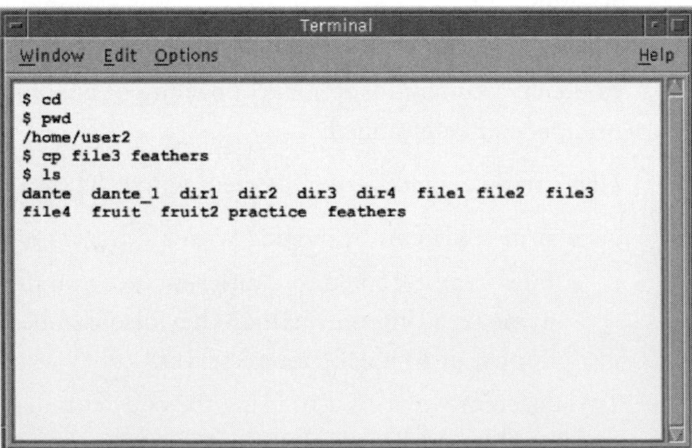
Terminal
Window Edit Options Help
$ cd
$ pwd
/home/user2
$ cp file3 feathers
$ ls
dante dante_1 dir1 dir2 dir3 dir4 file1 file2 file3
file4 fruit fruit2 practice feathers

Figure 7-2
Copying a file within a directory.

Copying Files to Another Directory

If you want to copy one or more files to another directory, use the format in Figure 7-3. This copies the existing file(s) (what you want to copy) to another directory in the directory structure (where you want to copy it to). When copying a file in this way, the file normally keeps its original name. You can add a slash and a filename after the destination directory to give the file a different name, if desired. This version can be thought of as copying *what* to *where*.

NOTE

If a file is copied and the name of the destination directory does not exist, a new file is created with that name; otherwise, the file is copied to the directory specified.

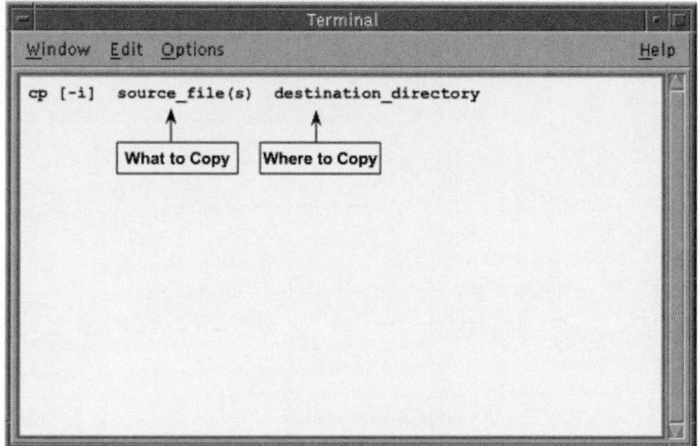

Figure 7-3
Copy (**cp**) what/where.

The **cp** command also can be used with metacharacters or wildcards, such as the asterisk (*) and question mark (?), to copy groups of files at the same time. Figure 7-4 shows how to copy several files using the format in Figure 7-3. The **cp** command assumes that the last entry (dir1) is a directory name and that the two previous entries (feathers and feathers_6) are files. Figure 7-4 also shows the use of the asterisk to copy the same files using an alternative command line.

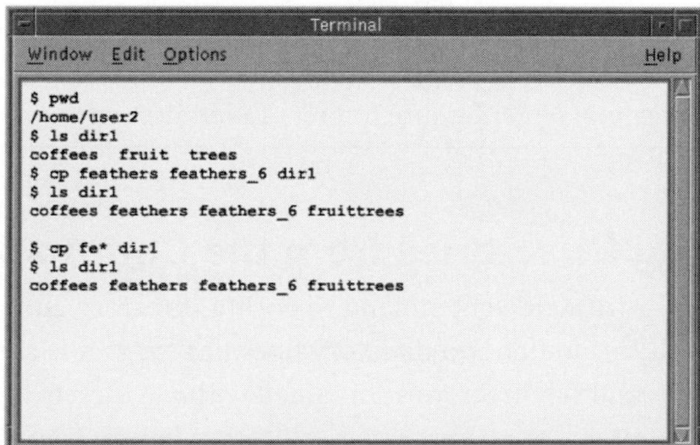

Figure 7-4
Copying files to another directory.

Preventing Overwriting of Files

If you copy a file and the target name already exists, you will *overwrite* or "clobber" the file, and you will not receive a warning. To prevent overwriting an existing file when copying, use the **cp -i** (interactive) option as a security measure. The **-i** option prompts you only if you are about to overwrite an existing file, and it gives you a choice. Answering y overwrites the file; answering **n** returns the shell prompt without copying. It is a good idea to get into the habit of using **cp -i** because it can prevent accidental mistakes. Figure 7-5 shows an example of the **cp -i** command.

TIP

You can create an alias for the **cp** command to ensure that you will always be prompted before accidentally copying over an existing file. See Chapter 14, "Basic Features of the Korn and C Shells," for details.

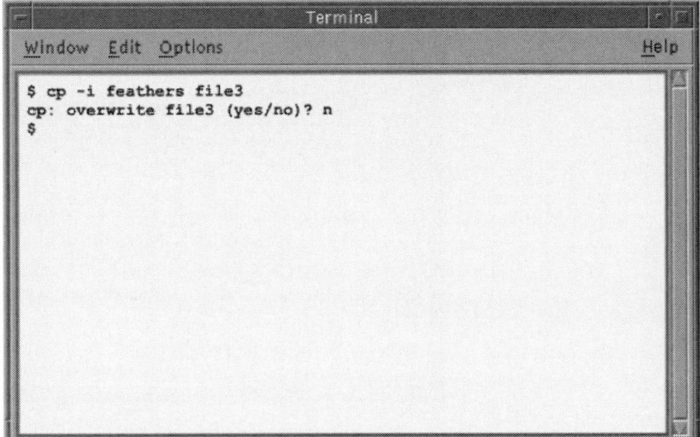

Figure 7-5
Copying files using the –**i** interactive option.

Skill Builder

e-Lab Activity 7.1

Copying Files

In this e-Lab activity, you are logged in as user2, and your current working directory is /home/user2/dir2. Refer to the class file tree structure on the inside-front cover of this book. Type the commands that would accomplish the requested objectives. *Note:* Be sure to press Enter after each one. Click Step 1 to begin.

Copying Directories from the Command Line

Use the **cp -r** (*recursive*) command to copy a directory and its contents to another directory. If the destination directory does not exist, it is created. Without the **-r** option, files and subdirectories contained within a directory are not copied. When used with the -i option, **cp** prompts for verification before overwriting an existing file.

```
cp -r[i] source_directory(s) destination_directory
```

Copying a Directory Within the Same Directory

The **cp -r** command can be used to copy a directory and all of its contents to a new directory in the current directory. You *must* use the **-r** option when copying directories. The first example in Figure 7-6 shows copying the dir3 directory to a new directory named ski.places without using the **-r** option, and it demonstrates the error that results. The error states that dir3 is a directory, indicating it cannot be copied without the –r option. The second example shows the proper use of the **cp -r** command to copy a directory. Notice that the dir3 directory is being copied to a new directory named ski.places, which has an extension of five characters. It is permissible to have multiple extensions of varying lengths with UNIX directory names.

Figure 7-6
Copying a directory within thc same directory.

```
Terminal
Window  Edit  Options                                      Help
$ cd
$ pwd
/home/user2
$ ls dir3
planets

$ cp dir3 ski.places
cp:  dir3: is a directory

$ cp -r dir3 ski.places
$ ls ski.places
planets
$
```

Copying a Directory to Another Directory

Figure 7-7 demonstrates how to copy a directory to another directory that is not in the current directory. In the first example, the planets directory is copied to dir1/constellation using a relative pathname. The .. (two dots) moves up one directory and then down to the dir1 directory. The second example copies two directories at the same time—dir1 and ski.places—to the absolute pathname of the /tmp directory.

Skill Builder

e-Lab Activity 7.2

Copying Directories

In this e-Lab activity, you are logged in as user2, and your current working directory is /home/user2/dir3. Refer to the class file tree structure on the inside-front cover of this book. Type the commands that would accomplish the requested objectives. *Note:* Be sure to press Enter after each one. Click Step 1 to begin.

Figure 7-7
Copying a directory to another directory.

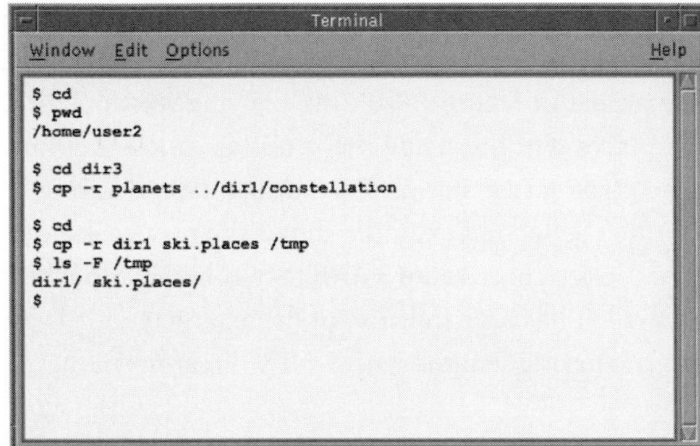

Terminal
Window Edit Options Help
$ cd
$ pwd
/home/user2
$ cd dir3
$ cp -r planets ../dir1/constellation
$ cd
$ cp -r dir1 ski.places /tmp
$ ls -F /tmp
dir1/ ski.places/
$

NOTE

You might be asking yourself when you should link and when you should copy. Link if you need to access the same file, such as a shared team project file, from multiple directories. Copy, rather than link, if users need to modify the file differently.

Skill Builder

Lab Activity 7.1.2

Copying Files and Directories

In this lab, you perform more advanced file- and directory-management tasks using the command-line interface and the **cp** (copy) command. Refer to the *Cisco Networking Academy Program: Fundamentals of UNIX Lab Companion.*

Linking Files

The **ln** (link) command is used to give a file an additional name so that you can access it from more than one directory (in the same file system or a different one) or by another name in the same directory. *Linking* can be useful if several users need to work on the same file from different locations without making a copy, or if they need to reference the file using a different (shorter) name. When you link a file to another file, the linked file is merely a name that references the actual file and, thus, saves disk space.

TIP

You also can link multiple files to the same directory. For example, **ln ~/book/chap* /home/brad** creates links for each chapter file and puts the new links in the /home/brad directory.

To link a file to another file in the same directory, use this format:

```
ln file1 newfilename
```

To link a file to another file in a different directory, use this format:

```
ln file1 directory/newfilename
```

Using the ls –l Command to See File Linkages

When a file is created, a link is established between the directory and the file. Thus, the link count for every file is at least 1. The link count is displayed in the second column of a long listing (**ls –l**). Each time a link is established with another file, the link count increases by 1. Figure 7-8 uses the **ls –l** (long listing) command to show the link count of two files after they were linked.

> **TIP**
>
> When a file is linked to another file in the same file system, it is called a *hard link*. A *soft link*, or *symbolic link*, occurs when you link a file across file systems and is accomplished using the **ln -s** command. For example, you might have a file in your home directory (in the /home file system) that is linked to the /docs/training/unix file residing in the /docs file system. File systems are covered in Chapter 8, "Files and User Information Utilities."

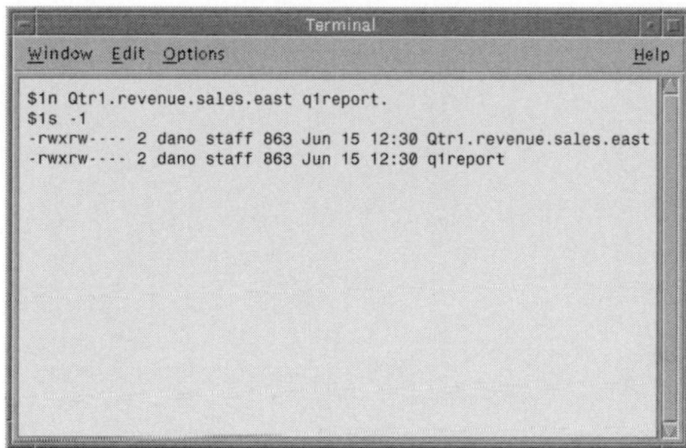

Terminal
Window Edit Options Help
$ln Qtr1.revenue.sales.east q1report.
$ls -l
-rwxrw---- 2 dano staff 863 Jun 15 12:30 Qtr1.revenue.sales.east
-rwxrw---- 2 dano staff 863 Jun 15 12:30 q1report

Figure 7-8
Using **ls –l** to check link count.

Removing and Renaming links

To remove a link, you use the same **rm** command used to remove a file. Using the **rm** command on a link removes the link but not the original source file. After a link is removed, the link count for the original file decreases by 1. Issuing the **rm** command on the original source file also removes the link that was created.

To rename a link, you use the same command used to rename any file. The **mv** (move) command, which is used to move or rename a UNIX file, is covered in the next section.

Renaming and Moving Files Using the Command Line

Files and directories can be renamed and moved using the same multipurpose **mv** (move) command. There is no renaming command in UNIX.

Renaming a File in the Current Directory

The command format in Figure 7-9 shows the syntax to rename a file in the same directory. This format changes the name of the source (the old filename) to a target filename (the new filename) in the same directory. This version can be thought of as moving from old to new in the same directory.

Figure 7-10 shows renaming a file using this format. Note that in Figure 7-9, the interactive option (**-i**) is also available with the **mv** command. The **mv -i** option prompts for confirmation whenever the move would overwrite an existing target file. An answer of **y** means that the move should proceed. Any keystroke other than y prevents **mv** from overwriting the target file. The **mv** command changes the name of the original file, whereas the **cp** command copies a file and gives it a new name, leaving the original file intact.

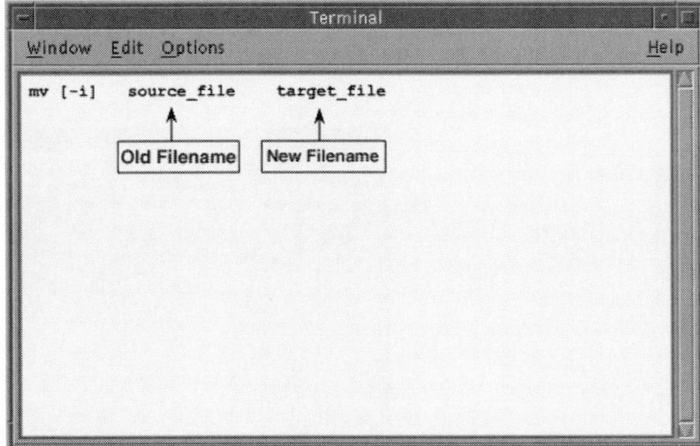

Figure 7-9
Move (**mv**) old file name/new filename.

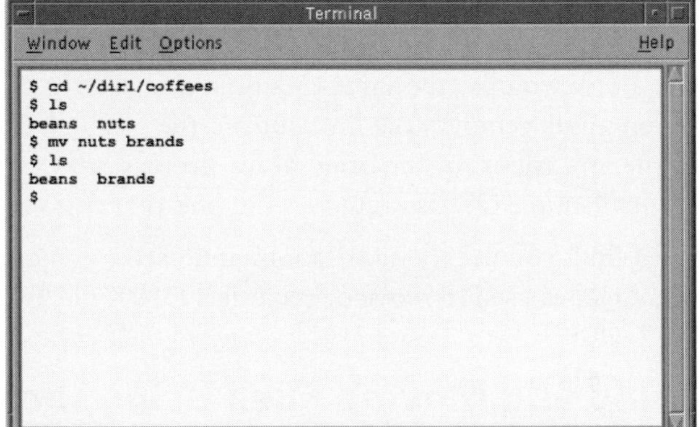

Figure 7-10
Renaming a file in the current directory.

Moving a File to Another Directory

If you want to move a file to a different directory, use the format in Figure 7-11. This format moves the source file(s) to a new target directory. You can add a slash and a filename after the destination directory to give the file a different name, if desired. It moves the source (what to move) to a target directory name (where to move). This version can be thought of as moving from *what* to *where* in the same directory.

Figure 7-12 shows moving a file to another directory using this format. The example shows moving the brands file from the coffees subdirectory to the home directory using the tilde (~) shortcut.

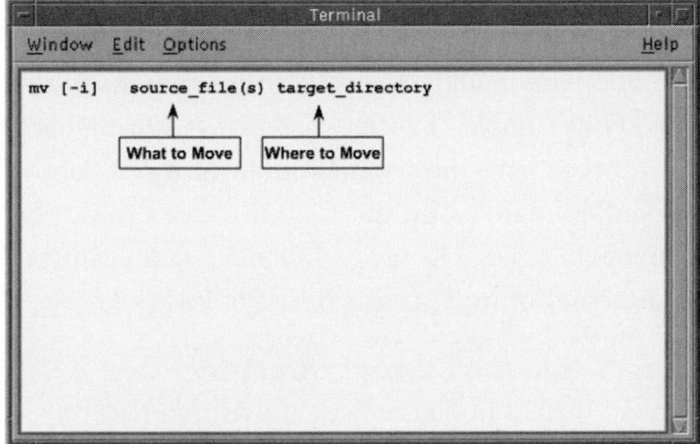

Figure 7-11
Move (**mv**) what to where.

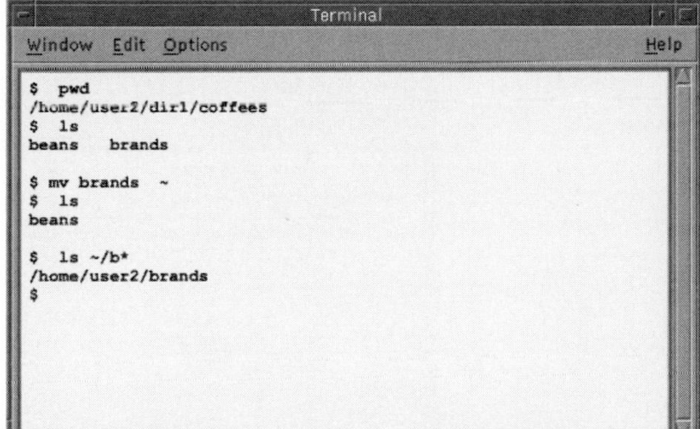

Figure 7-12
Moving a file to another directory.

Skill Builder

e-Lab Activity 7.3

Renaming and Moving Files

In this e-Lab activity, you are logged in as user2, and your current working directory is /home/user2/dir2. Refer to the class file tree structure on the inside-front cover of this book. Type the commands that would accomplish the requested objectives. *Note:* Be sure to press Enter after each one. Click Step 1 to begin.

Renaming and Moving Directories Using the Command Line

You can manipulate small portions or entire sections of the directory tree to manage file systems. For example, if a user currently is storing his personal files on his hard drive and wants to have the system administrator move them to a server so that they can be backed up more easily, the administrator can do this quickly and efficiently by using the **mv** command. The **mv** command is a multipurpose command that can rename a directory or move it to a different location.

Renaming Within the Current Directory

The command format in Figure 7-13 shows two different versions of the **mv** command, depending on your goal. As with files, the **mv** command has two basic formats used to rename and move directories. Figure 7-13 shows the format of moving an old name to a new name, which is used to rename directories within the current directory.

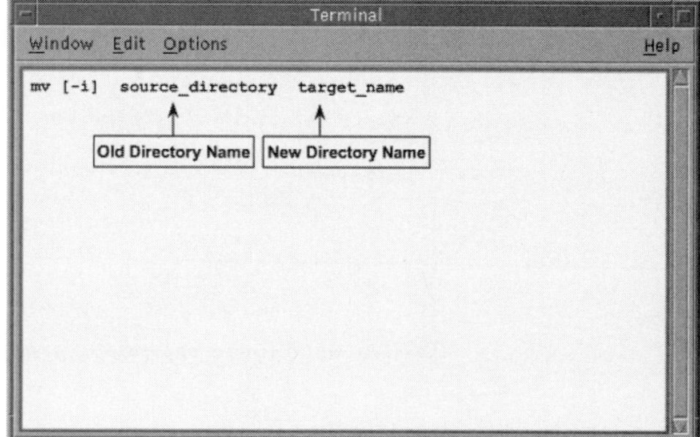

Figure 7-13
Move old name to new name.

Figure 7-14 demonstrates using the **mv** command to rename a directory within the current directory. In the example, the **cd** command changes to your home directory, and the **pwd** command verifies this. Next, the **mkdir** command is used to create the maildir directory using a relative path name. The **mv** command then is used to rename the maildir directory to monthly.

Renaming a File in a Noncurrent Directory

Figure 7-15 demonstrates how to use the **mv** command to rename a file in a noncurrent directory. Here the **mv** command is used to rename the project subdirectory in the practice directory to project2 using a relative path name.

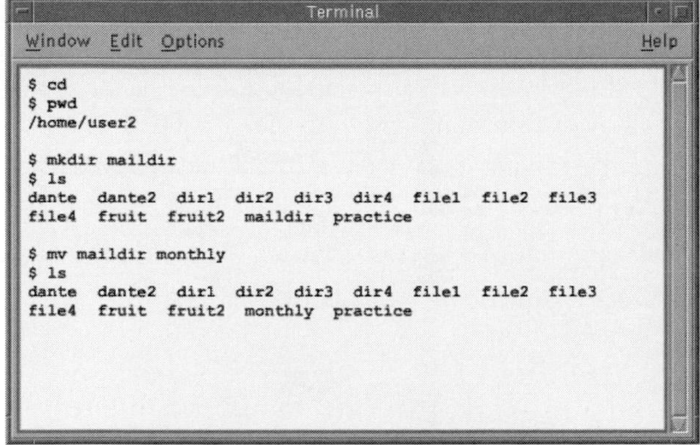

Terminal
Window Edit Options Help
$ cd
$ pwd
/home/user2
$ mv practice/project practice/project2
$ mkdir maildir
$ ls
dante dante2 dir1 dir2 dir3 dir4 file1 file2 file3
file4 fruit fruit2 maildir practice
$ mv maildir monthly
$ ls
dante dante2 dir1 dir2 dir3 dir4 file1 file2 file3
file4 fruit fruit2 monthly practice

Figure 7-14
Renaming within the current directory.

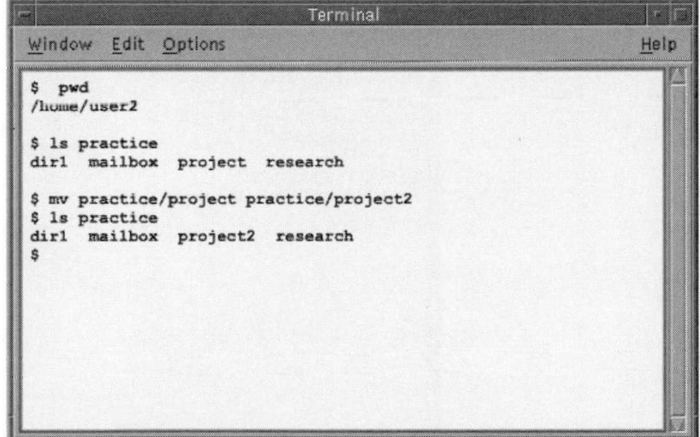

Figure 7-15
Renaming in a non-current directory.

Moving a Directory and Its Contents

Figure 7-16 shows the command format to move a directory and its contents to another directory or location in the directory tree. Figure 7-17 demonstrates using the **mv** command to move the practice directory from /home/user2 to the existing dir3 directory. When moving a directory this way, if the target location exists, the source directory is copied into the target location. If the location does not exist, the source directory is renamed.

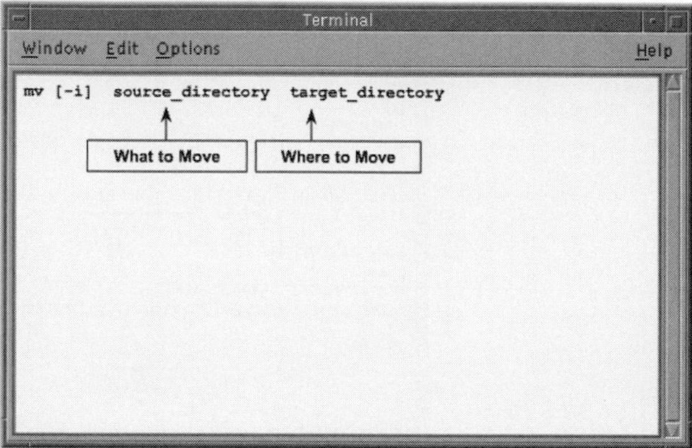

Figure 7-16
Move what to where.

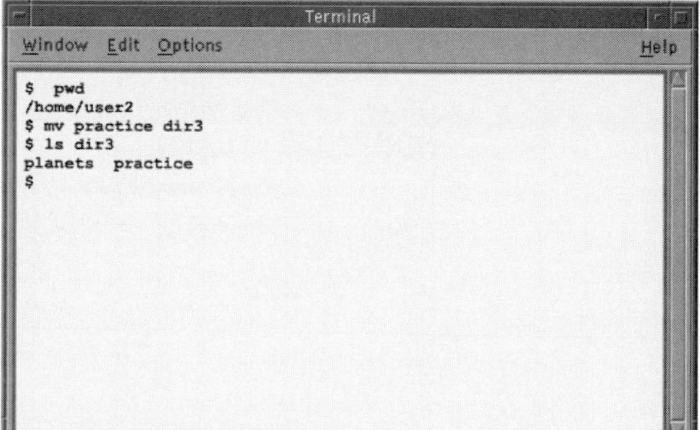

Figure 7-17
Moving a directory to another directory.

Skill Builder

e-Lab Activity 7.4

Renaming and Moving Directories

In this e-Lab activity, you are logged in as user2, and your current working directory is /home/user2/dir2. Refer to the class file tree structure on the inside-front cover of this book. Type the commands that would accomplish the requested objectives. *Note:* Be sure to press Enter after each one. Click Step 1 to begin.

Skill Builder

Lab Activity 7.1.4

Renaming and Moving Files and Directories

In this lab, you work with the versatile **mv** (move) command to rename and move files as well as directories. Refer to the *Cisco Networking Academy Program: Fundamentals of UNIX Lab Companion.*

Input/Output Redirection

All central processing unit (CPU) operations have input or output (I/O). The keyboard, for example, provides *standard input* (*stndin*), while the monitor displays *standard output* (*stndout*) and *standard error* (*stnderr*), as shown in Figure 7-18.

Figure 7-18
Input, CPU, and output.

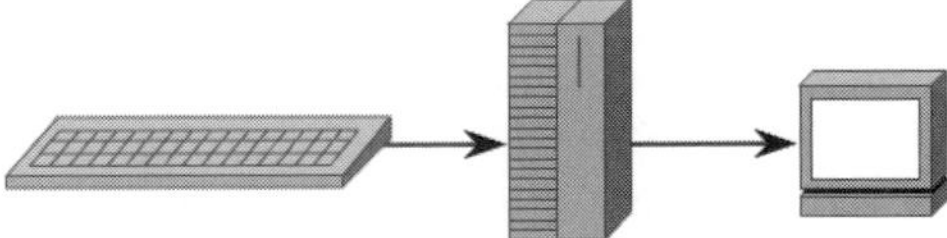

Every UNIX command has a source for standard input and a destination for standard output. For this chapter's purpose, input and output are defined with respect to a UNIX command. The input to a command normally comes from the keyboard, although it also can come from a file. The output from a command normally goes to the monitor or screen. Errors that might result from a command are another form of output and also are displayed on the screen. Figure 7-19 shows input to a command and the two types of output from it. Input is sending data to a command. Output is receiving data from a command. Errors are generated when a command is entered incorrectly.

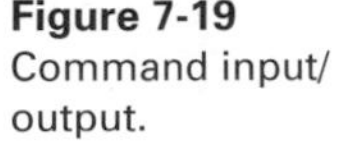

Figure 7-19
Command input/output.

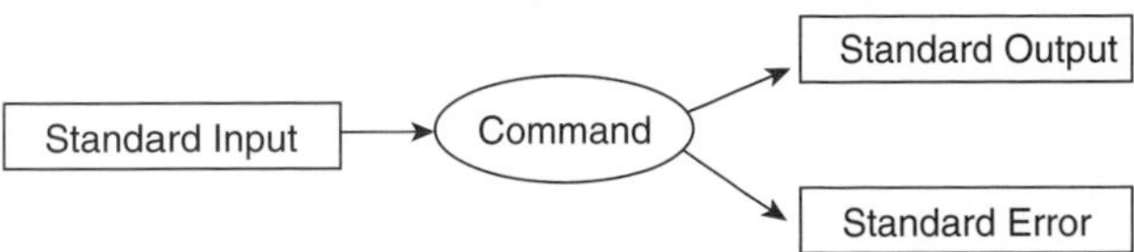

The UNIX computing environment enables command I/O to be controlled using redirection. This is useful when attempting to save the output of a command to a file for later viewing, sending the contents of a file as an e-mail message, or redirecting error messages to a file for use when debugging a program.

NOTE

Spaces between the command and a redirect symbol are optional.

Several metacharacters are used as redirection symbols. Output redirection uses the right angle bracket (>), which also is referred to as the greater-than symbol. Input redirection uses the left angle bracket (<), or less-than symbol. Error output redirection uses the right angle bracket, preceded by the number 2 (2>). The general format for using redirection is shown next. The File after the redirection symbol can be a text file or a device file. All devices in UNIX are defined by filenames. For instance, the screen or monitor device file is /dev/console. It is not necessary to specify this file because it is the default.

```
$ Command Redirection-Symbol File (text file or device file)
```

Redirecting Standard Input

Standard input is not often redirected, although it is possible to substitute a text file instead of the normal keyboard input. In Figure 7-20, note that the left angle bracket, or less-than symbol, which allows the command to receive input from whatever file, is present. The default input is the keyboard device.

Figure 7-20 illustrates redirection of input using the **mailx** command. In this case, the dante file is sent to the email address using the mailx program. The **mailx** command invokes the standard command-line mail program. (For more information on the mailx program, see Chapter 3, "CDE User Applications.")

```
command  <  file
```

(This command uses the file as input to the command.)

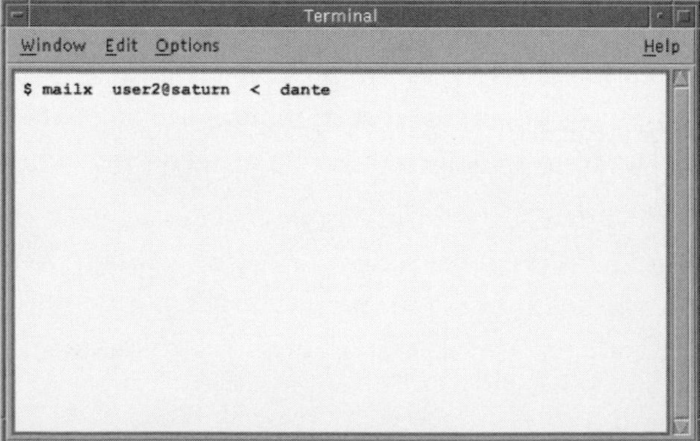

Figure 7-20 Redirecting standard input of a file to a command.

Redirecting Standard Output

Standard output is redirected much more frequently than standard input or standard error. Many commands, such as **ls, cat, head,** and **tail,** generate standard output to the screen, and it frequently is desirable to redirect this output to a file for future viewing or manipulation.

By substituting a filename, you can capture the output of a command rather than letting it go to the default monitor. As an example, if you wanted to get a listing of all files in a directory, you could redirect the output from the **ls** command, capturing it in a file that then could be edited using a word processor. The output from commands shown in this course was captured in this way.

Creating a New Output File

The right angle bracket (>) allows the command to send output to a file. Using the single right angle bracket creates a new file if the filename specified does not exist. If the filename exists, it will be overwritten.

```
command  >  file
```

(This command creates a new file or overwrites an existing one.)

The first example in Figure 7-21 illustrates redirection of the output of the **ls** command. The listing of the contents of the /etc directory would be captured in a file called etc.list, which would be placed in the current directory. The second example captures the calendar for October 2000 to a file named mon2000. The third example captures the calendar for January 2001 and appends it to the October calendar in the mon00 file.

The double right angle brackets (**>>**) can be used if you want to append (add to the end) to an existing file instead of overwriting it:

```
command  >>  file
```

(This command creates a new file or appends to an existing file.)

Redirecting Standard Error

Standard error is redirected when you want to capture the output of a command that might generate an error. It is useful when developing script files, and it normally is used by system administrators and programmers. Standard output usually is redirected to a text file, while standard errors are redirected to an error file to assist in troubleshooting if the script or program does not execute properly. To redirect standard error, use the right angle bracket with the number 2 in front of it (2>). Think of it as the second type of output from a command (optional). If a command executes with no problems, it will not generate an error.

```
command 2> file
```

(This creates new file or overwrites an existing one.)

TIP

To prevent the accidental overwriting of a file during redirection, you can use the noclobber shell feature. To enable noclobber in the Korn shell, enter at the command line **set -o noclobber**. To re-enable clobbering, use **set +o noclobber**. To enable/disable clobbering in the C shell, use the **% set noclobber** and **% unset noclobber** features.

You can override the noclobber feature by using the **>!** command. For example, **ls –l >! myfiles** would overwrite the existing myfiles file as if noclobber was disabled. The **>|** command accomplishes the same thing but uses the pipe symbol.

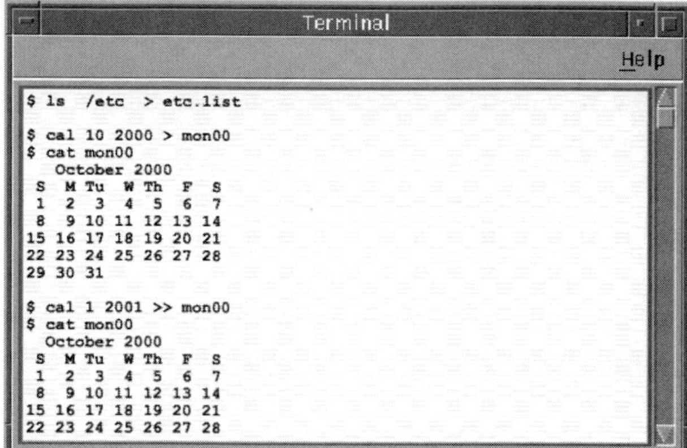

Figure 7-21 Redirecting standard output of a command to a file.

Figure 7-22 illustrates the use of 2> to create an error file. This example captures the error generated from the **ls** command because the directory specified does not exist.

Input/output redirection for standard input, standard output, and standard error is summarized in Figure 7-23.

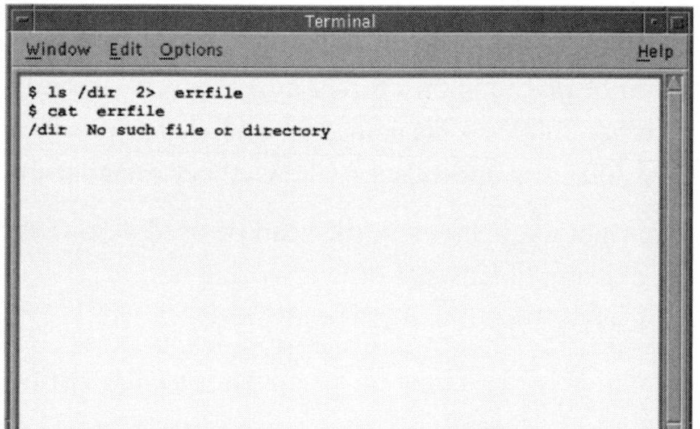

Figure 7-22 Redirecting standard error to a file.

Figure 7-23 Command input/output redirection summary.

Function	Logical Name	Normal File / Device	Command Format & Redirection Symbol Used
Input	**stndin**	Keyboard	Command < file
Output	**stndout**	Monitor	Command > file or command >> file
Error	**stnderr**	Monitor	Command 2> file

Skill Builder

e-Lab Activity 7.5

Input Output Redirection

In this e-Lab activity, you are logged in as user2, and your current working directory is /home/user2/dir2. Refer to the class file tree structure on the inside-front cover of this book. Type the commands that would accomplish the requested objectives. *Note:* Be sure to press Enter after each one. Click Step 1 to begin.

Command Piping

One of the most powerful metacharacters is the pipe (|). The pipe passes the standard output of one command as standard input into a following command. In effect, pipes enable you to build a miniature program. The pipe symbol sometimes is referred to as a double vertical bar, and it is found below the Backspace key. You *must* always have a command on each side of a pipe. Spaces between the commands and the pipe are optional. See Figure 7-24.

```
command  |  command
```

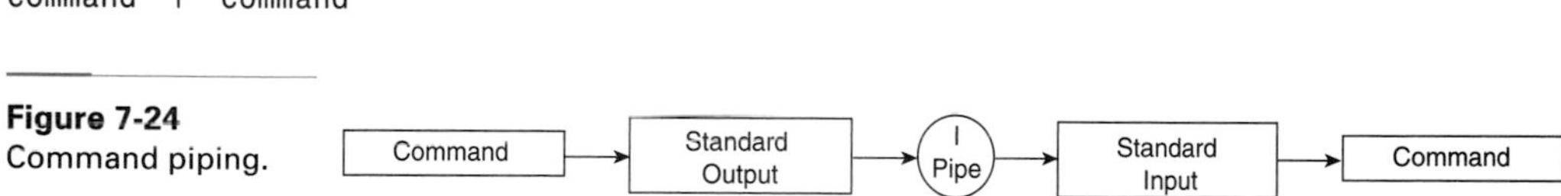

Figure 7-24
Command piping.

Displaying Command Output One Screen at a Time

One of the most common uses of the pipe metacharacter is to send the output of an **ls** command to the **more** command to enable you to see a long directory listing one screen at a time. The first example in Figure 7-25 shows this basic use of the pipe. The standard output from the **ls –l /etc** command to the left of the pipe becomes the standard input for the **more** command on the right side of the pipe.

The second example in Figure 7-25 is an example of multiple command piping to demonstrate how powerful piping can be. Several commands are introduced here that you will work with later in the course. In this example, the **ps -ef** command displays a detailed list of all processes running on the system, and that output is passed as input to the **grep** command, which searches for the string "brad" in all processes. The resulting output of the **grep** command is passed as input to the **sort** command, which sorts the output using the process ID (PID). The sorted output then becomes input to the **tail** command, which selects only the last 10 lines of output. That output then is sent to the default line printer (lp).

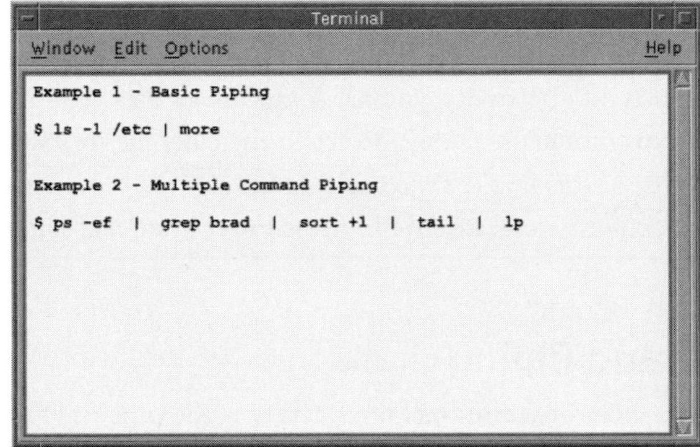

Figure 7-25
Command piping examples.

Choosing to Redirect or Pipe

Both redirecting and piping have their advantages. Redirecting is preferable if the data stored in the file will be of further use. If not, a pipeline is better because the commands will run simultaneously and the overhead of storing and retrieving data from the disk file is avoided. As many as 20 to 30 commands may be strung together in a pipeline.

Skill Builder

e-Lab Activity 7.6

Command Piping

In this e-Lab activity, you are logged in as user2, and your current working directory is /home/user2/dir2. Refer to the class file tree structure on the inside-front cover of this book. Type the commands that would accomplish the requested objectives. *Note:* Be sure to press Enter after each one. Click Step 1 to begin.

Skill Builder

Lab Activity 7.1.6

Redirection and Piping

In this lab, you use advanced UNIX commands to accomplish redirection and piping. Refer to the *Cisco Networking Academy Program: Fundamentals of UNIX Lab Companion.*

NOTE

You cannot move or copy file icons to the path icon display in the top part of the File Manager window display.

TIP

If you want to move or copy files to the parent directory of the current folder, you can drag and drop the file icon to the ("go up") icon.

Advanced Directory and File Management Using File Manager

As you saw in Chapter 6, "Basic Directory and File Management," File Manager can perform many basic file- and directory-navigation functions. File Manager also can perform more advanced functions, such as copying and moving files and directories. You can access File Manager by right-clicking the desktop to bring up your workspace menu. Click the File menu and then the File Manager utility.

TIP

To access the floppy without the CDE File Manager, you must insert the disk in the drive and type **volcheck** (volume check). This tells Solaris to check the floppy drive, determine the disk type, and then mount the floppy on the /floppy mount point. To use the floppy, change directories to /floppy/floppy0. You can list the contents of the floppy with the **ls** command, or you can copy files to the floppy using /floppy/floppy0 as the destination.

Moving Files Using Drag-and-Drop

You can move files by using the select and drag and drop technique. To move a file from one folder to another, position the mouse pointer over the file icon, hold down the left mouse button, and drag the icon to the appropriate folder icon.

When the file icon is positioned over the folder icon, release the mouse button and the file will be moved to that folder.

Copying Files Using Drag-and-Drop

You can copy files using the Control and select and drag and drop technique. If you press the Control key before the file icon has been selected and hold it down while the drag-and-drop process takes place, the file is copied rather than just moved to the other folder.

Copying Files to a Floppy Disk

You can copy files to a UNIX or DOS disk by first selecting Open Floppy from the File menu. The Open Floppy command tells Solaris to check the floppy drive for a disk, determine the disk type (UNIX or DOS), and then open a File Manager window for the floppy. Use the drag-and-drop procedure discussed in the previous paragraph for copying files to or from the floppy.

Menu Options

Three main menus are available in File Manager: File, Selected, and View. The File menu enables you to create new files and folders. The Selected menu enables you to manipulate certain files once selected. The View menu enables you to change the options for viewing files in File Manager.

The File and Selected Menus

As a quick review, Figure 7-26 shows the basic menu options available on the File menu within File Manager. Figure 7-27 shows the options available with the Selected menu.

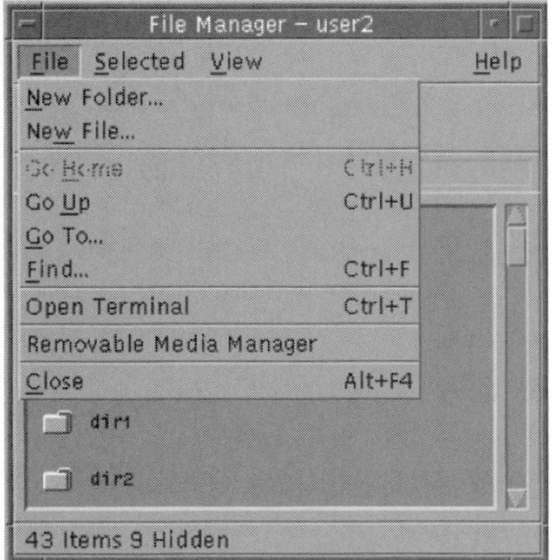

Figure 7-26
File Manager File options.

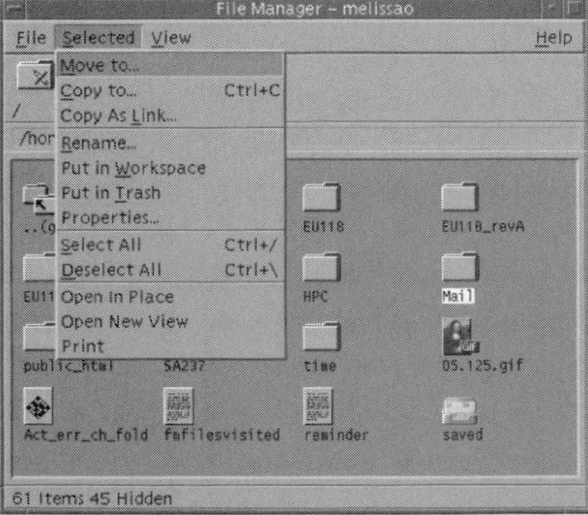

Figure 7-27
File Manager Selected options.

File and folder icons can be selected by clicking the left mouse button. When you have selected a file or folder, the File Manager Selected menu options enable you to perform a number of tasks. Table 7-1 is a brief explanation of the options on the Selected menu.

Table 7-1 File Manager—Selected Menu Options

Option	Description
Move to	Moves the selected object to another folder location.
Copy to	Copies the selected object to another folder location or to a different named folder or file.
Copy as Link	Links the folder or file to another folder or filename. (This option creates a symbolic link with the same name as the original file or folder.)
Rename	Allows changing the names of file and folders.
Put in Workspace	Places the object on the workspace area. This placement makes that object available whether or not you have a File Manager window open.
Put in Trash	Places the object in the Trash Can. An alternative to this option is to drag and drop the object over the Trash Can icon on the Front Panel display. *Note:* Files deleted in this way can be recovered using the Trash Can Control icon on the Front Panel. Files deleted from the command line with the **rm** command cannot be recovered.
Properties	Changes the permissions of a folder or file.
Select/Deselect All	Selects or deselects all objects in the current folder. Once selected, they can be moved, copied, or deleted as a complete group of objects.
Open	Opens a folder or file. This menu option is the same as double-clicking the object icon.
Print	Prints the file. This is the same as using drag-and-drop with the Print Manager icon on the Front Panel.

NOTE

Different options display in the Selected menu, depending on the type of file or folder selected.

View Menu Options

The View menu in Figure 7-28 enables you to customize your File Manager windows. A number of options are available in the View menu. Table 7-2 is a brief explanation of the options on the View menu.

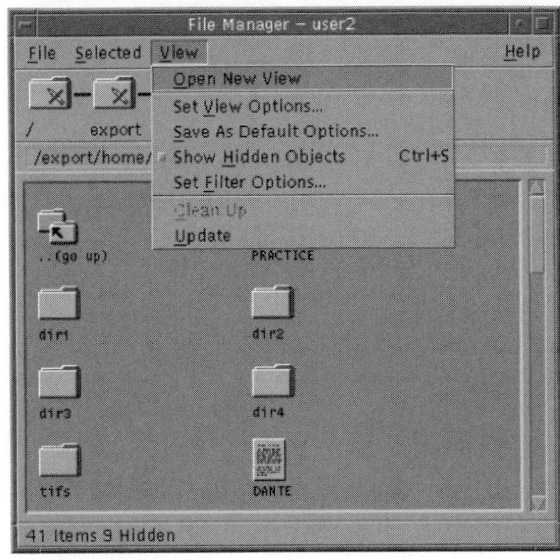

Figure 7-28
View menu options.

Table 7-2 File Manager—View Menu Options

Option	Description
Open New View	Clicking Open New View in the View menu opens another File Manager window. This facilitates moving files between different directory hierarchies.
Set View Options	Enables you to choose the way in which the File Manager information is displayed in the window. These are discussed in the section, "Set View Options Submenu."
Save Default Options	Allows these settings to be retained after File Manager has closed.
Show Hidden Objects	The File Manager window can be set to Show Hidden Objects, allowing viewing of all objects in a directory.
Set Filter Options	Enables you to decide what objects will be hidden objects if you choose not to have these objects displayed.
Update	Redraw the File Manager window screen. This is useful if objects have been hidden or moved during the current File Manager session.

Set View Options Submenu

The Options from this submenu item enable you to change the way File Manager displays the files and folders in its windows. You can change the ordering of the display by name, file type, date, or size. These options are shown in Figure 7-29 and can be modified at any time.

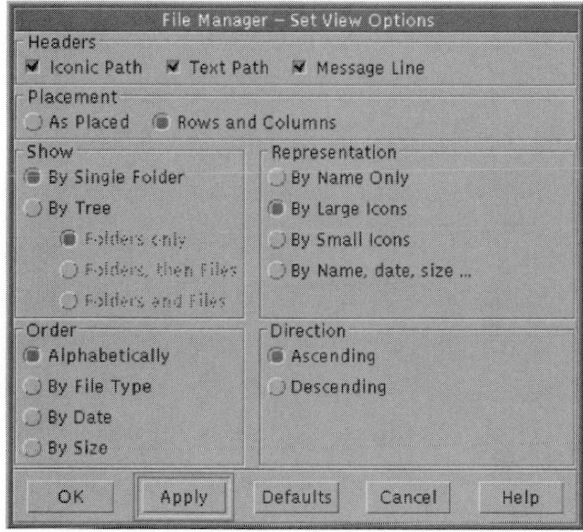

Figure 7-29
Set View options.

The Tree Display

The file system can be displayed by a single folder or as a hierarchical tree, as shown in Figure 7-30. By using the Tree display for your folders, it becomes easier to move around the file system hierarchy.

When a folder is double-clicked, another File Manager window automatically is invoked and the contents of the selected folder are displayed in the new File Manager window.

NOTE

For every folder selected, a new File Manager window will be invoked. Close the File Manager windows if you have finished working with the contents of the folder; otherwise, the performance of your workstation will begin to degrade.

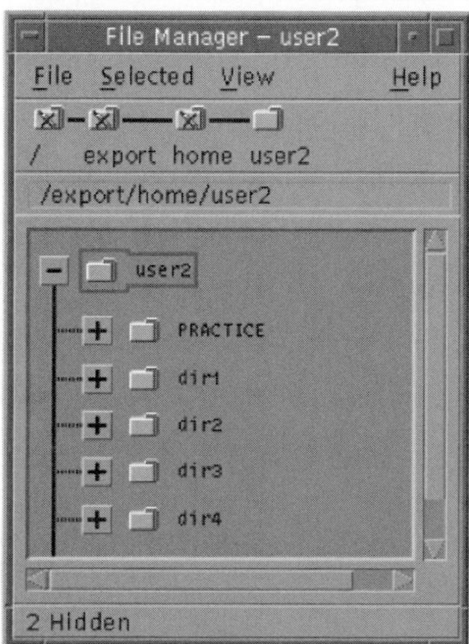

Figure 7-30
Tree display.

Skill Builder

Lab Activity 7.2.3

Advanced CDE File Manager

In this lab, you work with some of the more advanced features and functions of CDE File Manager. You perform additional file- and directory-management tasks, such as those that were performed earlier at the command line. Refer to the *Cisco Networking Academy Program: Fundamentals of UNIX Lab Companion.*

Summary

Now that you have completed this chapter, you should have a firm understanding of the following:

- The command-line interface provides several more advanced file- and directory-manipulation commands to enable you to manage the file system.
- Files and directories can be linked with the **ln** command, copied using the **cp** command, and moved and renamed using the **mv** command. When these commands are used with the **-i** or interactive option, you are prompted before files are overwritten.
- The workstation keyboard is the standard input device and the monitor or screen is the standard output device. UNIX commands can receive input (stndin) and produce output (stndout and stnderr). It is common to redirect output from the screen to a file to capture the results of a command such as **ls** or **cat** for future viewing or manipulating. The right angle bracket (>) is used to redirect command output.
- Command piping uses the output of one command as input to the next command, enabling you to create mini programs or custom commands. The pipe symbol (|) is used to separate commands to accomplish this.

- File Manager has several advanced capabilities for manipulating files and folders. These include moving (select+drag+drop) and copying (Control+select+drag+drop). The Selected menu allows files and folders to be preselected and then copied, moved, renamed, or put in the Trash Can. File and directory permissions also can be changed using the Properties option from the Selected menu.
- The File Manager View menu can be used to customize the way File Manager displays files and folders, which includes displaying the file system as a tree.

Check Your Understanding

1. Your current directory is /home/user2/dir2. If you want to copy the notes file from your current directory to the dir3 directory, which command would you use?
   - **A.** **copy notes /dir3**
   - **B.** **cp notes ../dir3**
   - **C.** **copy notes ../dir3**
   - **D.** **cp /notes dir3**
2. Your current directory is /home/user2. If you wants to copy the two files fruit and fruit2 to dir4, which command could you use?
   - **A.** **cp fruit fruit2 dir4**
   - **B.** **cp fruit? /dir4**
   - **C.** **cp fru* /dir4**
   - **D.** **cp f??????? dir4**
3. Your current directory is /home/user2/, and you need to copy the entire dir1 section of the directory tree to another location as a backup. The new directory will be named dir.bak *and will reside in the same directory as dir1*. Which command would you use?
   - **A.** **cp dir1 dir1.bak**
   - **B.** **cp dir1 ../dir1.bak**
   - **C.** **cp -r dir1 dir1.bak**
   - **D.** **cp -a dir1 dir1.bak**
4. If you want to move or copy a file to another location and be warned if you are going to accidentally overwrite an existing file, which option would you use with the **cp** or **mv** commands?
   - **A.** **–w**
   - **B.** **-i**
   - **C.** **-r**
   - **D.** **-F**
5. To rename a directory, you would use which command?
   - **A.** **mv**
   - **B.** **chdir**

C. ren

D. md

6. Redirection can be used to send the output of a command to a file instead of the screen. Which command format would accomplish this?

   A. Command > filename

   B. Command < filename

   C. Filename > command

   D. Command << filename

7. Redirection normally overwrites existing files. When using the Korn shell, what can you do to prevent this?

   A. Use the interactive option

   B. Set –o noclobber

   C. Use the right angle bracket

   D. Set overwrite to off

8. Command piping can be used to use the output of one command as input to another command. Which of the following would display a directory listing a screen at a time?

   A. ls –l | pause

   B. cat files > pause

   C. cat files | more

   D. ls –l | more

9. All of the following are valid ways to copy a file with UNIX *except*:

   A. Use the **cp** command from the command line.

   B. Use the File Manager Selected menu.

   C. Use the Control+select+drag+drop technique with File Manager.

   D. Use the **copy** command.

10. The tree display is available through which File Manager menu?

    A. The File menu

    B. The Selected menu

    C. The View menu

    D. The Options menu

UNIX Command Summary

> Redirects standard output. Example:

```
$ ls > myfiles
```

< Redirects standard input. Example:

```
$ mailx dano@buckeye < ski_listing
```

| Takes standard output of one command and passes it as standard input into a following command. Example:

```
$ ls -l | more
```

cp Copies files. Example:

```
-i, -r

$ cp ~/home/* /tmp

$ cp -i ~/home/user2/* /bkup

$ cp -ri ~/home/user2/* /bkup
```

ln Gives a file an additional name so you can access it from more than one directory. Example:

```
$ ln report  /HQ/reports/Jan02report
```

mv Moves files. Example:

```
-I

$ mv file1 file_april30

$ mv file1 /home/user2/bkup
```

noclobber Prevents the overwriting of files during redirection. Example:

```
$ set -o noclobber

$ cat fruit > fruit2
/bin/ksh: fruit2: file already exists
```

Key Terms

Linking The **ln** (link) command is used to give a file an additional name so that you can access it from more than one directory (in the same or different file system) or by another name in the same directory.

Overwrite If a file is copied and the target name already exists, you will overwrite or "clobber" the file and will not receive a warning. The **–i** (interactive) option can be used with the **cp** and **mv** commands so that you are warned when a file is about to be overwritten.

Piping The process of using the output of one command as input to the next command.

Recursive To do repetitively. The **cp -r** (recursive) command can be used to copy a directory and all of its contents to a new directory in the current directory. You *must* use the **–r** option when copying directories.

Redirection The process of redirecting the standard output from a command to another location, such as a file. If not redirected, the output normally goes to the screen.

Stnderr Any output that normally would result from an error in the execution of a command. Stnderr normally goes to the screen.

Stndin (Standard Input) Usually provided by the computer's keyboard, but can come from a file.

Stndout (Standard Output) The results of issuing a command. Stndout usually goes to the computer screen or monitor.

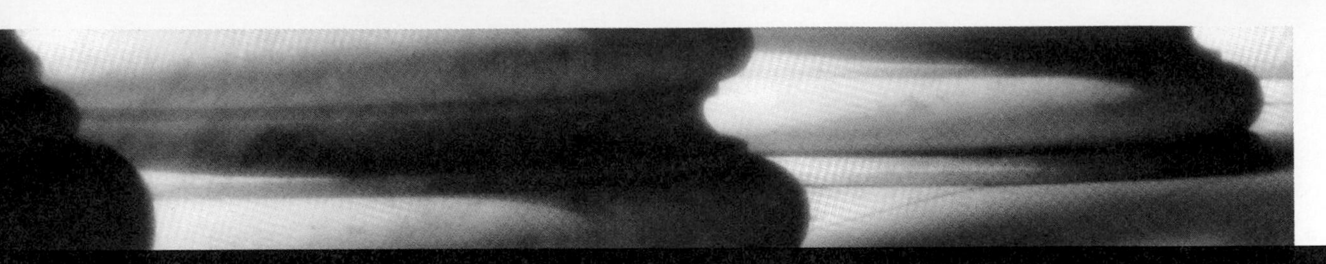

Objectives

After reading this chapter, you will be able to

- Describe hard disks, partitions, and file systems
- Display file system utilization and free space
- Search for files and directories using the **find** command
- Use the **grep** command to find character strings within files and command output
- Work with File Manager to locate files and directories
- Sort the contents of files and command output using the **sort** command
- Use commands such as **who** and **finger** to identify users who are logged on
- Assume the identity of another user using the **su** (switch user) command
- Determine your real and effective user ID using the **who am I**, **whoami**, and **id** commands

Chapter 8

File and User Information Utilities

Introduction

This chapter covers hard-drive technology, physical and logical disk partitions, and file systems in more detail than in previous chapters. You use file-processing commands to locate files on a hard drive, search for strings of characters within files, and sort file contents and command output. You also learn how to identify which users are logged on and how to determine your current login status when switching between user accounts.

Disk Technology Overview

A hard drive is the main permanent storage device for a computer. A drive consists of multiple platters (a rigid material with a magnetic coating that also accounts for the name "hard" drive) stacked on a common spindle that spins at various speeds. A series of read/write heads, one for each platter, travels across the disk surfaces as a single unit, as shown in Figure 8-1.

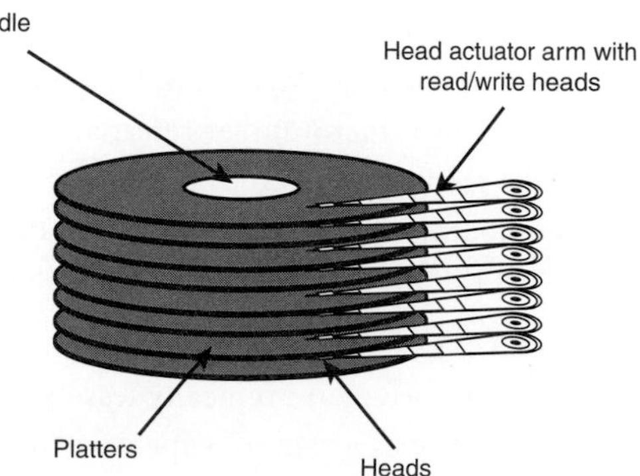

Figure 8-1 Hard-disk components.

Drives are assembled in a "clean room," where the environment is managed to allow the hard drive to be vacuum-sealed to protect the drive from contamination. After it is assembled, the platter surfaces are quality-checked for defects and are formatted with concentric tracks. Each track then is segmented into sectors. A sector is defined as 512 bytes (one block) in size.

The two prominent drive types today are *IDE/EIDE (Intelligent Drive Electronics or Enhanced IDE)* and *SCSI (Small Computer Systems Interface)*. With IDE drives, all drive activity is CPU-dependent and supports only two devices (two hard drives, or one hard drive and a CD-ROM drive). EIDE drives improve upon the IDE limitations by increasing speed (transfer rates) and offering the capability to support four devices. For most desktop systems, EIDE is more than adequate. However, for high-performance workstations and servers requiring support for more than four devices (multiple hard drives, CD-ROMs, tape drives, and so on), EIDE does not provide the best solution.

The big advantages of SCSI are device independence and fast data-transfer rates. Interfaces earlier than SCSI were not intelligent and were designed for specific devices. Thus, there was a hard-disk interface for a hard drive, a tape drive interface for a tape drive, and so on. With SCSI, a standard interface was defined for all devices so that only a single adapter (SCSI host adapter or interface card) was required. The other key advantage of SCSI over other disk interface technologies has been its capability to process multiple overlapped commands, allowing SCSI drives to fully overlap their read and write operations with other drives in the system. This allows different SCSI devices to be processing commands concurrently rather than serially, leading to high data-transfer rates. This design is considered a better design in a multiprocessing environment such as UNIX.

The current standard, SCSI-3, has data-transfer rates up to 40 MBps and supports up to 15 devices connected to a single SCSI host adapter. Each device has a unique user-selectable identifier or target number referred to as a SCSI ID. The higher the number is, the greater the priority is given to the device. Hard drives normally are assigned a lower target number because they are faster than other SCSI devices such as tape drives and CD-ROMs.

Today's PCs and UNIX-based workstations and servers can use either Enhanced IDE or SCSI drives. EIDE drives are typically less expensive and most often are found in workstations. SCSI drives are more expensive and usually offer higher performance capabilities. For these reasons, they are used most often in servers.

Partitions and File Systems

When the UNIX operating system first was developed, hard disks could store what is now considered a very small amount of data. When disks larger than 300 MB arrived on the market, the operating system could not address such a large amount of space. This necessitated the development of *logical partitions* of the hard drive to allow the kernel to access smaller, addressable parts of the drive.

Partitions can be either physical or logical. If a partition takes up the entire physical hard disk, then it is a physical partition. If the hard disk is divided into smaller sections, these are considered logical partitions. UNIX hard drives can be divided into as many as eight partitions or *slices*. Each partition is treated by the operating system as a logical, independent drive, similar to a drive letter in the PC world or a volume with Novell NetWare. Most hard disks in today's PCs are one physical partition, which is referred to as drive C:.

A PC hard disk also can be divided into smaller logical partitions, which in the DOS or Windows world is referred to as drive C:, drive D: and drive E:. In the UNIX world, these logical partitions are referred to as "slices" and are associated with a name (referred to as a mount point), such as / (root), /usr, and /home, as shown in Figure 8-2. A UNIX partition or slice is actually a cryptic-looking filename such as /dev/dsk/c0t3d0s0 (Solaris system). See the output of the **df** command in Figure 8-4 for a detailed explanation.

Today, with hard drives being sold with up to a *terabyte* (TB, or a million million bytes) or more of space on them, the kernel can access all available space. Despite this, the convention of partitioning a hard drive into logical partitions has persisted for various reasons. Partitioning allows an administrator to functionally organize data so that user files are on a different logical partition than the operating system, executables, or applications.

Before a disk partition can be used, a file system must be created to provide a structure for organizing and accessing data on the partition.

For example, a Solaris system may be configured to have the partitions and file systems shown in Table 8-1.

Table 8-1 **Solaris Partitions and File Systems**

Partition	File System	Description
0	Root	Contains standard UNIX system files, plus empty directories such as /home and /var that are used as *mount points* for other file systems.
1	Swap	Used for temporary memory storage. There is no file system created on the swap partition. Swap uses the partition in its "raw" state.
2	Entire disk	By backing up this partition, you back up all file systems.
3	Usr	Contains many user commands and utilities. Contents change very little, so there is no need to back up frequently.
4	Home	Contains a user's home directories. Having it as a separate file system allows for easy backup. Often home directories are located on a server and are mounted on /home of a workstation from over the network.
5	Unassigned	
6	Unassigned	
7	Unassigned	

* Note: Partitions on BSD systems are labeled using letters *a* to *h* instead of 0 to 7.

Figure 8-2 shows conceptually how these partitions are laid out on the hard drive.

One of the main advantages to partitioning is the ease with which daily backups can occur. Partitions on servers are usually shared and made available to network users by mounting them. This means that a network administrator can make them unavailable to users when desired for increased security. Logical partitioning also cuts down on seek time. If the disk is partitioned, when a user specifies a file to search for or a directory to change to, the name of the directory gives the kernel information about where the data is stored. This prevents the system from having to seek the information over the entire disk.

Other benefits of partitioning include security and reliability. For increased security, partitions on servers can be shared to the network, which means that a system administrator can make them unavailable for workstations to access when desired. Partitioning also makes a system more reliable. If a file system is corrupt, repair to the file system can happen while the remaining file systems are still accessible. For example, if the entire drive contains only the root file system and becomes corrupt, users would not be capable of accessing the system while file system repairs were being made.

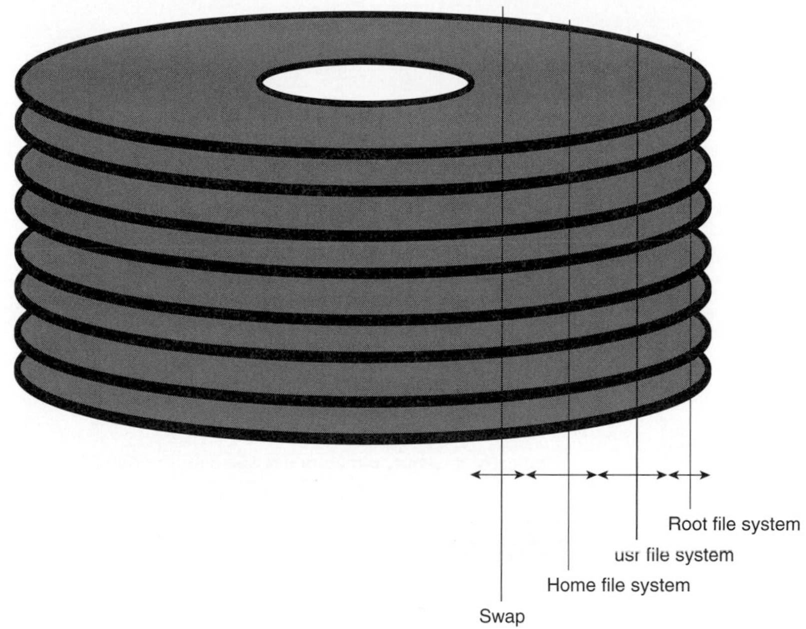

Figure 8-2
UNIX partitions on a hard drive.

Here are the characteristics and benefits of partitions:

- Subdivides a hard disk
- Functionally organizes data
- Facilitates daily backups
- Reduces data access time
- Provides security options
- Improves reliability
- Examples include / (root), /usr, and /home.

After file systems are created on disk partitions, all separate file systems are combined to form a single directory tree by attaching (mounting) the file system to an empty directory (mount point), as shown in Figure 8-3. This happens at boot time. When the system boots, the root file system automatically is mounted by the kernel and contains files, directories, and mount points (empty directories) for the other file systems. After the root file system is mounted, a file referred to as the *mount table* is read to determine what additional file systems are to be mounted and at what location (mount point). File systems can be manually mounted and unmounted anytime.

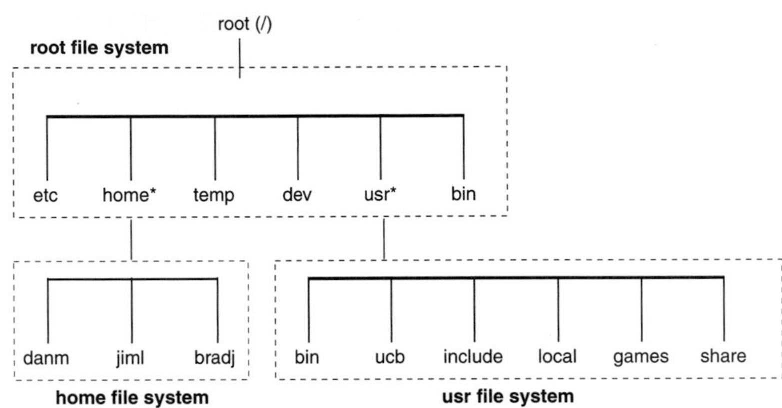

Figure 8-3 Directory tree with mounted file systems.

File System Statistics

File system statistics can be displayed using the **df** (disk free) command. System V–based systems list disk usage in 512-byte blocks (.5 K), by default, instead of 1024-byte blocks (1 K). Use **df -k** to display usage in kilobytes. Figure 8-4 displays the output of the **df –k** command.

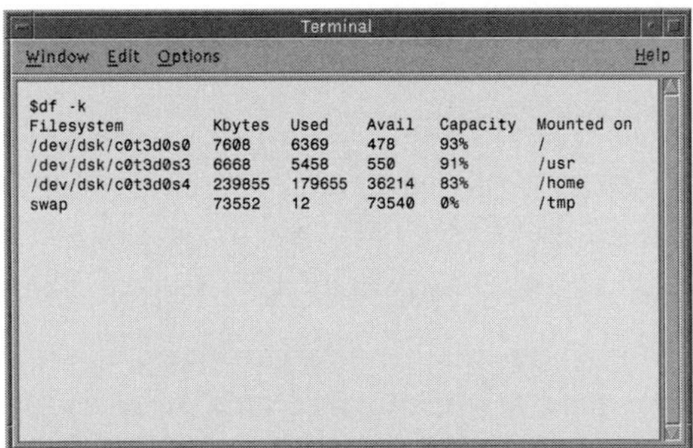

Figure 8-4 Using the **df** (disk free) command to check file systems.

The Filesystem column lists the device filename for the file system that gets created when the OS is installed or created manually by the system administrator. Each version of UNIX has a slightly different device file-naming convention. The output in Figure 8-4 is from a Solaris system and is interpreted as follows:

- **c0 (controller 0)**—The number of the disk controller or interface. 0 is the first controller.
- **t3 (target 3)**—The target number for the hard drive.

- **d0 (disk 0)**—The number of the disk installed. 0 is the first disk.
- **s0 (slice 0)**—The slice or partition number. 0 is the first slice.

The Kbytes column reports the size of the file system in kilobytes. The Used and Avail(able) columns report on the number of kilobytes that the file system is currently using and how much space remains available. The Capacity column allows you to quickly see how full a file system is. Some file systems remain rather static, so a capacity of more than 90 percent is not alarming. The Mounted On column is the ***mount point*** and typically indicates the file system name. The previous output shows that the capacity of the home file system is at 83 percent and has 36 MB (36,214,000) of available space remaining.

The **df** command shows capacity and availability from a file system level. The **du** command displays disk space used by files and subdirectories and is more frequently used by a user. The **du** command is similar to the DOS **DIR** command, which shows available disk space at the end of the listing. Output is displayed in 512-byte blocks (.5 K) by default. Use **du -k** to display usage in kilobytes (as in **$du –k** or **$du –k /usr**. The **–s** displays only the summary.

Finding Files in the File System

The **find** command is one of the most powerful and useful commands available to a UNIX environment user. This command can be used to find files based on specific criteria. When a file or group of files matching a search criterion is found, another command can be executed on the matching files.

The **find** command can be used for many purposes, including deleting, backing up, and printing files. The **find** command can be used to locate files on your local hard drive or on remote servers. Try to avoid using the **find** command on remote server file systems because it might place a heavy load on the CPU and hard disk of the server, which will decrease performance for other users.

When searching for files with the **find** command, try to start at the lowest point in the directory structure where you most likely will find them. The **find** command starts at the point in the directory hierarchy specified and searches all directories and subdirectories below that point. A search of your hard drive starting at the root can take a long time. When a file is found, it is listed with the starting directory and any subdirectories below it.

Path Options

The path in the syntax shown in Figure 8-5 indicates the directory where the search begins.

The path can be a tilde (~) representing your home directory, a dot (.) representing the current directory, an absolute or relative pathname, or even the root directory (see Figure 8-6).

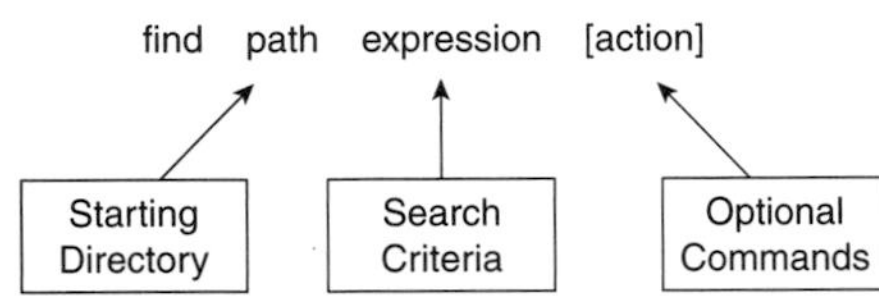

Figure 8-5
find command syntax.

Figure 8-6
Path options for the **find** command.

Path Entry	Function
~ (tilde)	Start looking in a home directory.
. (dot)	Start looking in current directory.
/etc	Start looking in absolute pathname.
dir2/beans	Start looking in relative pathname.
/ (root)	Start looking in the root directory.

Search Expression Options

The expression is one or more search criteria options that indicate what to look for. It is specified by one or more values. Basic find options include filename, type, and size. If more than one expression is specified, **find** treats the statement as an "and" request, and all listed expressions must be verified as true or present. The **-o** (or) option can be used between expressions to allow for an "or" type of criteria definition, which means that if any of the expressions is true, the file will be found. Many search expressions require a value to match, and, in some cases, metacharacters, or wildcards, may be used for the arguments. Examples of search expressions are shown in Figure 8-7. The expressions used with the **find** command evaluate as true or false.

NOTE

Some versions of UNIX require the -print action to see the output from the find command on the screen.

Action Options

The action at the end of the command is optional and can be used to execute various commands after the desired file(s) have been found. Figure 8-8 shows examples of actions that can be performed.

Figure 8-7
Search expressions for the **find** command.

Search Expressions	Meaning	Definition
name filename	Filename	Search for all files matching the specified filename. Metacharacters (such as * or ?) are acceptable but will be interpreted literally unless placed inside quotes.
type filetype	Type of File	Search for all files matching the specified filetype (d = directory).
mtime [+I-]n	Modified Time	Search for all files whose modification time either matches, is older than (+), or is newer than (-) n days.
atime [+I-]n	Access Time	Search for all files whose access time either matches, is older than (+), or is newer than (-) n days.
user loginid **-group groupid**	User ID and Group ID	Search for all files that match the ownership of **loginid** or group of **groupid**.
perm mode	Permissions	Search for all files that match the permission settings indicate (octal notation only).
size [+I-]n[c]		Search for all files whose size either matches, is larger than (+), or is smaller than (-) n. The n represents 512 byte blocks, or characters (bytes) if followed by a c.

Figure 8-8
Action options for the **find** command

-exec command {} \;	The exec option must be terminated by { } \; which allows find to apply the specified command to each file that it identifies from the search criteria.
-ok command {} \;	Interactive form of -exec. This option is used with commands that require input from the user; for example, rm -i.
-ls	Prints the current path name using the long listing format. This expression is most commonly used in conjunction with a redirection of output to a file in order for the listing to be examined at a later time.

Using the find Command

Figure 8-9 shows several examples using the **find** command.

A brief explanation of each example follows:

1. Specifies an absolute pathname to start in and finds files and directories with a particular name.
2. Specifies an absolute pathname to start in and finds filenames with a character string in a specific location using a metacharacter or wildcard. The quotes are necessary, or the **find** command will look for an asterisk in the first position.
3. Specifies the home directory (tilde ~) as a starting point. Finds a particular file by name and performs the action of deleting it.

NOTE

Core files are memory dumps created by a program ending abnormally.

4. Specifies a relative pathname as a starting point. Finds files that have a file type of directory (**d**).
5. Specifies the current directory (dot **.**) as a starting point. Finds files that have a modification date (**mtime**) of older than X numbers of days.
6. Specifies an absolute pathname to start in and finds files that are greater than a specified size.
7. Specifies the home directory (tilde ~) as a starting point. Finds files with a specific permission level (777 is open permissions and is covered later in the course). Redirects the output to a file for later viewing.
8. Specifies the current directory (dot **.**) as a starting point. Finds files that are owned by a particular user and lists them. Redirects listing output to a file for later viewing.

Figure 8-9 Using the **find** command.

```
1. Search for openwin starting at the /usr directory:
   $ find  /usr  -name  openwin
   /usr/openwin
   /usr/openwin/bin/openwin

2. Search for files ending in tif starting at the /usr directory:
   $ find  /usr  -name  '*tif'
   /usr/openwin/demo/kcms/images/tiff/ireland.tif
   /usr/openwin/demo/kcms/images/tiff/new_zealand.tif

3. Search for core files starting at the user's home directory and delete them:
   $ find  ~  -name  core  -exec  rm  {}  \;

4. Look for all files with a type of directory, starting at the current directory:
   $ find  dir3  -type d
   <find output omitted>

5. Look for all files, starting at the current directory, that have not been
   modified in the last 90 days:
   $ find  .  -mtime  +90
   <find output omitted>

6. Find files larger than 400 blocks (512-byte blocks) starting at /etc:
   $ find  /etc  -size  +400
   <find output omitted>

7. Find files with open permissions starting at the user's home directory:
   $ find  ~  -perm  777  >  holes

8. Find files owned by a specific user or group in the current directory hierarchy,
   lists them, and puts the listing in a file:
   $ find  ~  -user  bradj  =ls  >  bradj-userfiles
```

Skill Builder

e-Lab Activity 8.1

Finding Files

In this e-Lab activity, you are logged in as user2, and your current working directory is /home/user2. Refer to the class file tree structure on the inside-front cover of this book. Type the commands that would accomplish the requested objectives. *Note:* Be sure to press Enter after each one. Click Step 1 to begin.

Searching for Strings in Files and Command Output

Use the **grep** (global regular expression print) command to search a file or the output of a command for a specified text string. A *string* is one or more characters; it can be a character, a word, or a sentence. A string can include whitespace or punctuation, if enclosed in quotations. The **grep** command searches a file for a character string and prints all lines that contain that pattern to the screen. The **grep** command frequently is used as a filter with other commands. For instance, you can issue the **ps** (process status) command and look for all occurrences of a specific process. The **grep** command is case-sensitive. You must match the pattern with respect to uppercase and lowercase letters, unless you use the **-i** option, which ignores the case. The **-v** option searches for all lines that do not match the string specified.

Figure 8-10 shows the basic format of the **grep** command, and Figure 8-11 shows examples of how to search lines in a file or standard output.

Figure 8-10
The **grep** command.

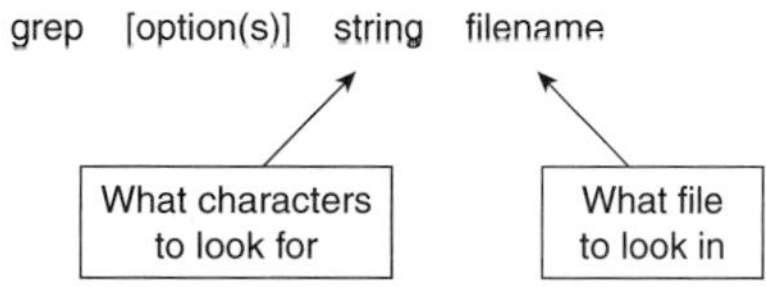

Figure 8-11
Using the **grep** command.

```
$ grep root /etc/passwd
root:x:0:1:Super-User:/:/sbin/sh

$ grep Raphael  ./* (or just * if the shell is set
up to look in your current directory)
./dante: Dante Alieghieri like Raphael ...
./dante: one Raphael, one Michelangelo ...

$ ls  -la ¦ grep  -i  'jun 11'
drwzr-zr-z   3   user1  staff  512  Jun  11  13:13  dir4
```

Note: If the date is a single numeral date, the grep string needs to have two spaces between the month and the numeral; for example, Jun 3

TIP

Displaying the line number containing the text string that you searched for can come in handy. For example, if you use **grep** with the –**n** option to print the line number(s) containing the text string that you searched for, you then can go into a text editor that supports line numbers (such as vi) and quickly go to the line and edit it.

In addition to searching for simple text strings, you can search for regular expressions. Regular expressions are special metacharacters and wildcards that help you search for different parts of files, such as the beginning or end of a line. Examples of some regular expressions are shown in Figure 8-12.

Figure 8-12 Common regular expressions used with the **grep** command.

Regular Expression	Function	Example	Result
. (dot)	Matches any character and can be used multiple times. Similar to using the ? with the **ls** command.	**grep chap.. file**	Displays all lines containing chap followed by two characters
* (asterisk)	Matches zero or more characters in the pattern.	**grep chap* file**	Displays all lines containing chap followed by any number of characters
\ (back slash)	Tells the shell to treat the special character after \ literally.	**grep dollar* file**	Displays all lines containing dollar*. The backslash tells the shell to literally look for a * instead of treating it like a wildcard.
^ (caret)	Match all lines beginning (^) with the pattern.	**grep ^Name file**	Displays all lines containing Name at the beginning of a line.
$	Match all lines ending ($) with the pattern.	**grep $800 file**	Displays all lines containing 800 at the end of a line.
[ ]	Matches one character in the pattern.	**Grep [64.128]MB file**	Displays all lines containing 64 MB or 128 MB.

Skill Builder

e-Lab Activity 8.2

Searching for Strings

In this e-Lab activity, you are logged in as user2, and your current working directory is /home/user2. Refer to the class file tree structure on the inside-front cover of this book. Type the commands that would accomplish the requested objectives. *Note:* Be sure to press Enter after each one. Click Step 1 to begin.

Finding Files Using CDE File Manager

The Find option on the File Manager File menu provides tools to locate files and directories based on various search criteria. File Manager Find can perform many of the functions of the **find** command as well as the **grep** command. The criteria can be either the name of a folder or file or, in the case of a file, the contents. Figure 8-13 shows the Find window.

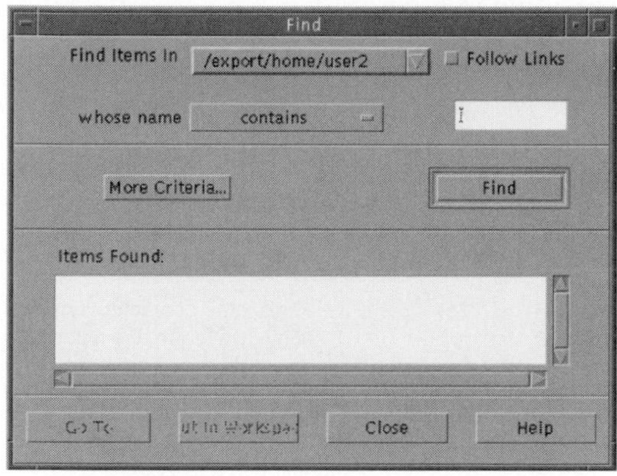

Figure 8-13
Finding files using CDE File Manager.

The Find Items In button displays a pull-down menu that allows you to select from various options, including the following:

- My Home Directory
- Floppy
- CD-ROM
- Other Host
- Other Folder

The Whose Name button allows you to select from three options:

- Contains
- Does Not Contain
- Equal To

The button labeled More Criteria gives you the option of finding files by the following criteria:

- Name (default)
- Content
- Size
- Date modified
- Owner
- Type
- Permissions

NOTE

If you start in the root of the file system (the / directory), the find operation might take a considerable amount of time to complete.

Wildcard characters can be used when specifying the name of the file to find. Some examples are shown in Figure 8-14.

Figure 8-14 Using wildcards to find files with File Manager.

Wildcard Example	Function
A*	Finds folder or filenames that start with an uppercase letter A.
s*	Finds folder or filenames that start with a lowercase letter s.
??a	Finds three-character folder or filenames where the last character in the name is a lowercase letter a.
[Aa]*	Finds folder or filenames that start with the letter a (either uppercase or lowercase).

Sorting Files and Command Output

The **sort** command provides a quick and easy way for operators to organize data in either numerical or alphabetical order. This command uses the ASCII character set as its sorting order, working from left to right on a character-by-character basis. By default, **sort** relies on whitespace to delimit the various fields within the data of a file. Some **sort** features include these:

- Performing multilevel sorting
- Performing field-specific sorting
- Accepting standard input
- Producing standard output

The following shows the syntax for the **sort** command:

```
sort  [options]  [input_filename]
```

Figure 8-15 shows the various options available with the **sort** command. These enable the operator to define the type of sort to perform, as well as the field on which to begin sorting. Figure 8-16 shows some basic examples using the **sort** command with a simple format. The **cat** command displays the unsorted contents of **fileA**. The first **sort** command produces an ASCII type of sort, beginning with the first character of each line. The second **sort** example is a numerical sort on the second field (**sort** skips one separator with the +1 syntax).

Figure 8-17 shows some more advanced options sorting on different fields within a file. The first example represents beginning a sort on some field other than the first and shows a numeric, reverse-order example. The **sort** command line would read as, "Do a reverse order, numeric sort on the fifth field of the data in the file list, and place the output into a file called num.list."

Figure 8-15
sort command options.

Option	Description
-n	Allows for a numeric sort. The n can be used alone with a dash or can follow a field reference.
(+I-)n	Begins (+) or ends (-) with the field following the nth separator. The default seperator is white space.
-r	Reverses the order of the sort. The r can be used alone with a dash or can follow a field reference.
-f	Folds uppercase and lowercase characters together (ignore case in sort order).
+nM	Sorts the first three characters of the field as abbreviated month names.
-d	Uses dictionary order. Only letters, digits, and white space are compared; all other symbols are ignored.
-o filename	Places any output into the file's name.

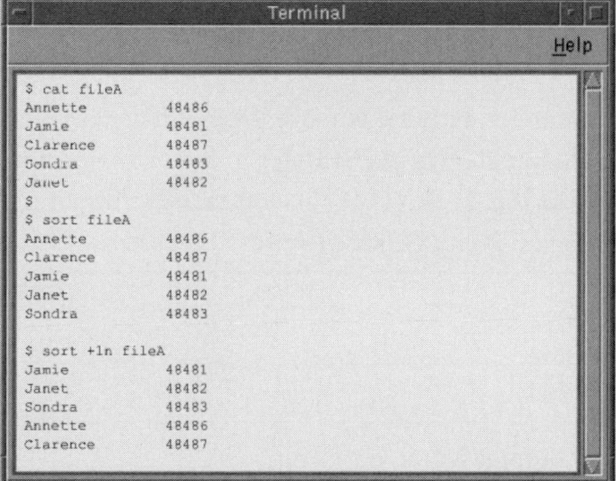

Figure 8-16
Using the basic **sort** command.

The second example represents a multilevel sort showing how the **M** option would work. This command would read as, "Do a month order sort beginning with the sixth field. Do a second-level sort in numeric order, begin on the seventh field (this will sort the numeric day of the month correctly), and name the output file update.list."

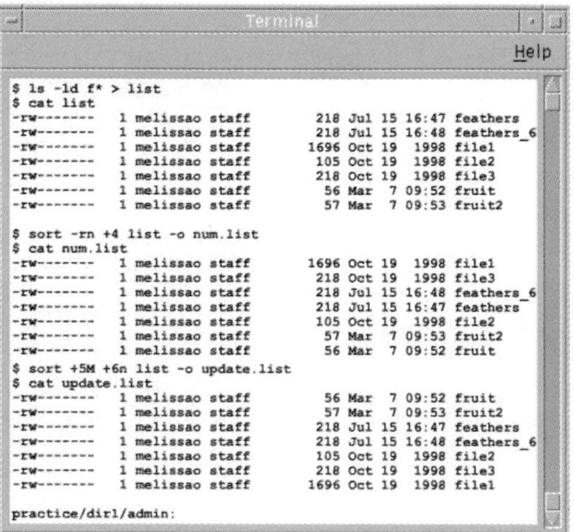

Figure 8-17
Sorting on different fields within a file.

Skill Builder

e-Lab Activity 8.3

Using the **sort** Command

In this e-Lab activity, you are logged in as user2, and your current working directory is /home/user2. Refer to the class file tree structure on the inside-front cover of this book. Type the commands that would accomplish the requested objectives. *Note:* Be sure to press Enter after each one. Click Step 1 to begin.

Skill Builder

Lab Activity 8.2.4

File-Processing Commands

In this lab, you use advanced UNIX commands to find files and specific strings contained in files. CDE File Manager also is used to locate files based on filename or file contents. Refer to the *Cisco Networking Academy Program: Fundamentals of UNIX Lab Companion.*

Identifying Users with the who and finger Commands

Two main commands display who is using your system: **who** and **finger**.

The **who** command displays information about all users currently logged onto the local system. This command lists the user's name, terminal, login time, elapsed time since the last activity on the terminal line, and the machine (host) name. Figure 8-18 shows some examples using the **who** command. The host name is the name of the computer the user is logged in from.

Figure 8-18
Using the **who** command.

Displaying users on the system:

```
$ who
user2 console May 24 10:17  (buckeye)
user3 pts/4   May 24 17:36  (wildcat)
$
```

Use the **who -H** option to print column headings above the regular output:

```
$ who -H
NAME   LINE     TIME
user2  console  May 24  10:17  (buckeye)
user3  pts/4    May 24  17:36  (wildcat)
$
```

Use the **who -q** option to display only the names and the numbers of users currently logged on:

```
$ who -q
user2 user3
# users=2
$
```

The **finger** command displays the same information as the **who** command, plus more specific user information such as the user's full name (from the /etc/password file), how long since the user has typed something (idle), and the host name, if logged in remotely.

When one or more username arguments are given (**finger mmouse dduck**), more detailed information is given for each username specified, whether that user is logged in or not. Figure 8-19 shows some examples using the **finger** command.

TIP

Use **finger** plus a specific user's address to find out about users on other local (**finger** jdoe@hal) or remote (**finger** jdoe@informance.com) systems. Many times when you **finger** a remote system, you might not get a response, or you might get a "connection refused" message.

Figure 8-19
Using the **finger** command.

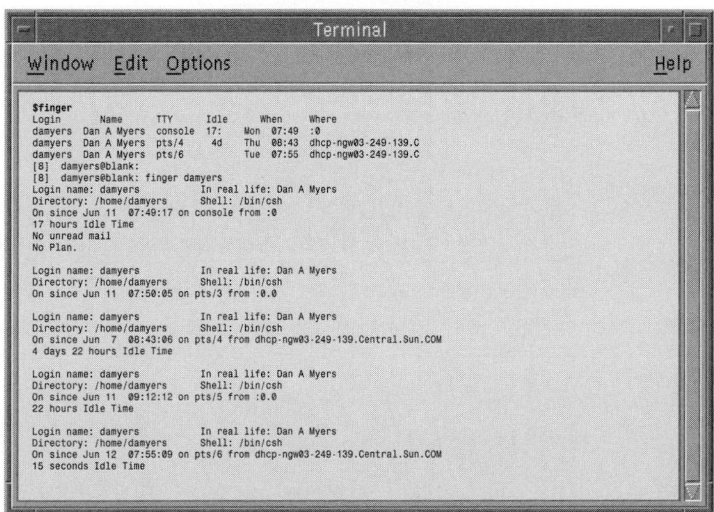

Switching to Another User Account

You can temporarily switch to another user account to access files and directories that belong to that user by using the **su** (switch user) command. You sometimes need to switch to another user account to modify files that the user owns or to do something on that user's behalf. Administrators typically utilize the **su** command when troubleshooting user problems or to test authorization and account behavior with certain applications. When switched to another user's account, you have access to the same files that the user has. The following shows the syntax for the **su** command:

```
su [-] username
```

To switch user IDs, you must supply the password of the user ID that you are switching to, unless you currently are logged in as root. When you switch to another user account, you become that user and have all access and privileges that the user has. To switch back to your previous user ID, type **exit**.

Figure 8-20 shows two examples of the **su** command. In the first example, **su** is used without options. When **su** is used without options, you do not change directory locations. Environmental settings customized for your user ID also remain in effect. To switch to another UID and have the system read the new user's initialization files, you must use a dash (–) between the command and the new user ID, as shown in the second example.

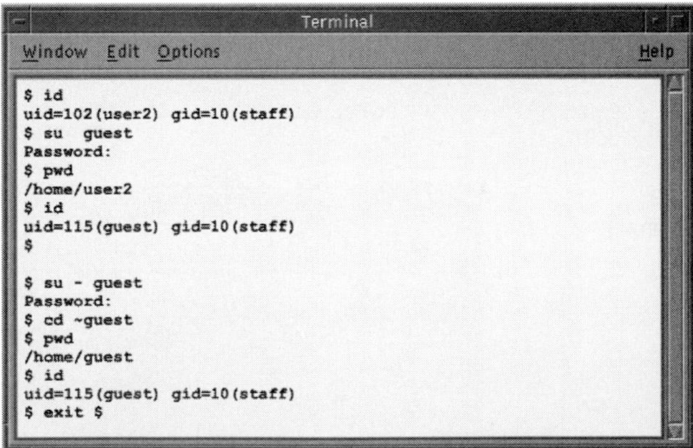

Figure 8-20
Switching users with the **su** command.

If **su** is used without specifying options or a user account to switch to, you switch to the superuser or root account. System administrators normally work under their regular user account and **su** to root when necessary to perform administrative tasks. As with switching to another user account, the root account requires knowledge of the root password before the system allows you to switch accounts.

User Account Information

The login ID that you use to initially log into a UNIX system is your *real user ID (RUID)*. While logged in, you can switch to another user's ID and become that user for a period of time to modify files that the user owns or to do something on that user's behalf. You have all the same characteristics and permissions of the account that you switched to; this is now your *effective user ID (EUID)*.

Figure 8-21 shows three commands that can be used to help determine your identity when working with different user accounts: **who am i**, **whoami**, and **id**. The **who am i** command shows your RUID. The **id** and **whoami** commands in Figure 8-22 show your EUID. The **id** command also can be used with the **-a** (all) option to show all groups that the effective user is a member of.

Figure 8-21
User ID commands.

Command	Function
who am i	The **who am i** command displays information about your real user ID (RUID). If you use the **su** command to switch from one UID to another, the **who am i** command displays your original login UID (RUID) and lists the terminal line, and then date and time logged on.
whoami	The **whoami** command displays only the login name of the real user.
id [option(s)]	The **id** command displays the username corresponding effective UID (EUID). Use the **id -a** command to identify the username, user ID, and all of the groups to which the user belongs. In this example, the user is identified as guest and belongs to the group's staff and sysadmin. The listing for gid identifies the user's primary group and the groups listing identifies all groups to which the user belongs.

Figure 8-22
Displaying RUID and EUID.

```
Displaying your current or effective UID.
$ id
uid=115 (guest)  gid=10 (staff)

Displaying you EUID with group information
$ id -a
uid=115 (guest)  gid=10 (staff)  groups=10 (staff)  14 (sysadmin)
```

```
Displaying your real UID with login information.
$ who am i
user2  console  May 24  10:17

Displaying your Real UID without login information
$ whoami
user2
```

Note: In this example, you are logged in as user2.

Skill Builder

e-Lab Activity 8.4

Identifying Users

In this e-Lab activity, you are logged in as user2, and your current working directory is /home/user2. Refer to the class file tree structure on the inside-front cover of this book. Type the commands that would accomplish the requested objectives. *Note:* Be sure to press Enter after each one. Click Step 1 to begin.

Skill Builder

Lab Activity 8.3.3

User Identification Commands

In this lab, you use advanced UNIX commands to determine your identity and the identity of other users logged onto a system. Refer to the *Cisco Networking Academy Program: Fundamentals of UNIX Lab Companion.*

Summary

Now that you have completed this chapter, you should have an understanding of the following:

- Hard drives consist of a multiple platters stacked on a common spindle that spin at various speeds.
- UNIX hard drives are divided into any number of sections, called partitions or slices, with a file system to provide a structure for organizing and accessing data on the partition.
- At boot time, all file systems are combined to form a single directory tree file structure by mounting file systems to an empty directory called a mount point.
- To display the amount of available space on a file system, use the disk free (**df –k**) command.
- A number of useful command-line utilities are available for processing files and discovering information about users on a UNIX system. The **find** command can be used to find files and folders on your local computer or on a remote computer such as a server. Files also can be located by searching for specific strings in their contents. The **grep** command can do this and can search for strings of characters in the output of other commands, such as **ls** and **ps**, when used with the pipe (|). The CDE File Manager File menu has a Find option that can perform some of the capabilities of the **find** command and the **grep** command using a graphical user interface.
- The contents of files and the output of commands can be sequenced using the **sort** command. The **sort** command has a number of options, including what field to start sorting, numeric or alpha sort, and reverse sorts.
- Several commands are available to discover information about logged-in user accounts. The **who** command can display all the users currently logged onto a particular machine. The **finger** command displays more detailed information about who is logged onto a local or remote machine. The **who am i** and the **whoami** commands display your RUID, and the **id** command displays your EUID if you have switched to another user's account. The **id** command also can be used to see what groups a user is a member of. The **su** (switch user) command allows you to temporarily assume another user's account for access to that user's files or for testing and troubleshooting purposes.

Check Your Understanding

1. Your current directory is /home/user2. You need to find all files that start with the letters "pr" in your projects subdirectory. Which command accomplishes this?
   - **A.** find projects -name 'pr*'
   - **B.** locate pr* in projects
   - **C.** find pr* -name projects
   - **D.** search projects –name pr*
2. How can you use the **find** command to locate only directories in your home folder?
   - **A.** Use the **–D** option.
   - **B.** Use the **–d** option.
   - **C.** Use the **–F** option.
   - **D.** Use the **–dir** option.
3. Your home directory on the server's hard disk is getting full, and you would like to see a list of some of the larger files to decide which ones to delete. Which command should you use to search for all files in your home folder that are larger (approximately) than one million bytes? (File size is specified in 512-byte blocks.)
   - **A.** **find** /home/user3 -size +2000
   - **B.** **search** /home/user3 > 2000
   - **C.** **find** /home/user3 -size +1000
   - **D.** **grep** /home/user3 - size +2000
4. You are looking for a text file that contains the word *resume*, and you forgot which folder you put it in. Which command would allow you to search for the file and show you where it is located?
   - **A.** **grep** home "resume"
   - **B.** **grep** ~/* resume
   - **C.** **grep** resume ./*
   - **D.** **grep** root resume ./*

5. If you want to get a listing of all files owned by user bsmith in the current directory, what command could you use to accomplish this?
   - A. **grep** RUID bsmith
   - B. **ps** –ef | grep bsmith
   - C. **ls** –l | grep bsmith
   - D. **ls** –a | grep bsmith
6. You want to see a listing of the files in your current directory that is sorted to show the largest files first. To obtain a directory listing in sequence by file size in reverse numeric order, which of these commands could you use?
   - A. **sort** | ls -l +4nr
   - B. **ls** –l | sort +4nr
   - C. **ps** –l | sort +4nr
   - D. **ls** –a | sort +4nr
7. In CDE File Manager, the File menu Find option allows you to search for files by filename as well as by the contents of the file (True/False).
   - A. True
   - B. False
8. You have switched from your login user account to another user's account so that you can access that user's files. Which of the following commands would tell you what your current EUID is?
   - A. **whoami**
   - B. **who am i**
   - C. **who**
   - D. **id**
9. To determine who is currently logged onto your system and see the output sorted by user ID, what command would you use?
   - A. **whoisloggedon | sort**
   - B. **who | sort**
   - C. **whois | sort**
   - D. **id | sort**

10. You were logged in as user2, and, when you switched to the user3 account, your home folder did not change to that of user3. What could be the problem?
    A. You did not actually switch to the user3 account.
    B. You specified the RUID option when switching.
    C. You need to be logged in as root to switch to another user's account.
    D. You did not specific the dash (–) option when switching accounts to invoke user3's environment.

UNIX Command Summary

df Displays the amount of disk space occupied by mounted or unmounted file systems, directories, or resources; the amount of available space; and how much of a file system's total capacity has been used. Example:

```
-k

$ df -k
```

du Reports the number of 512-byte blocks contained in all files and (recursively) directories within each directory and file specified. Example:

```
-k

$ du -k
```

find Recursively descends the directory hierarchy for each path, seeking files that match a Boolean expression. Example:

```
-o
$ find /home/user2 -name 'dir*'
/home/user2/dir2
/home/user2/dir3
```

finger Displays information about local and remote users. Example:

```
$ finger
damyers  Dan Myers  Console  Thu 19:07

$finger jdoe@hal
```

grep Searches a file for a pattern. Example:

```
-I

$ grep banana ./*
/home/user2/fruit: banana
/home/user2/fruit.tar:banana
/home/user2/fruit2: banana
/home/user2/fruit2.tar:banana
```

id Returns the user identity. Example:

```
-a

$ id
uid=1002(user2) gid=10(staff)

$ id -a
uid=1002(user2) gid=10(staff) groups=10(staff)
```

sort Sorts lines of all the named files together and writes the result on the standard output. Example:

```
$ sort file1
$ sort +1n file2
```

su Allows a user to become superuser or another user. Example:

```
username

$ su -student6
Password:
$
```

who Lists who is on the system. Example:

```
0H,-q
$ who
user2 console  Apr 30 12:37   (:0)
user2 pts/4    Apr 30 12:40   (:0.0)
$
```

whoami Displays the effective current username. Example:

```
$ whoami
user2
```

who am I Displays the effective current username. Example:

```
$ who am I
user2 pts/4    Apr 30 12:40   (:0.0)
```

Key Terms

EUID (effective user ID) If you switch to another user's ID, you have all the same characteristics and permissions of the account that you switched to; this is now your EUID. The **whoami** and **id** commands show your EUID.

IDE/EIDE (Intelligent Drive Electronics or Enhanced IDE) One of the two prominent drives types today. Used primarily in standard workstations and home computers. EIDE can support up to four devices (hard disk drives or CDs).

Logical device name Used by system administrators or users to access the disk (partitions) and tape devices for such tasks as mounting and backing up file systems. Logical device names are stored in the /dev/ directory in subdirectories. All logical device names are symbolic links to the physical device names in the /devices directory.

Mount point An empty directory in a file hierarchy at which a mounted file system is logically attached. The **mount** command logically attaches a file system, either local or remote, to the file system hierarchy.

Partition A smaller division or portion of a hard drive. UNIX hard drives can be divided into as many as eight partitions or "slices." Each partition is treated by the operating system as a logical, independent drive, similar to a drive letter in the PC world or a volume with Novell NetWare.

RUID (real user ID) The login ID that you use to initially log into a UNIX system. The **who am I** command shows your RUID.

SCSI (Small Computer Systems Interface) One of the two prominent drives types today. Used primarily in high-end workstations and servers. Can support up to 15 devices (hard disk drives, CDs, and tape drives).

Slice A logical subdivision of a physical disk drive. It is treated as an individual device.

String One or more characters. It can be a character (alphabetic or numeric), a word, or a sentence. A string can include whitespace or punctuation if enclosed in quotations.

Terabyte Approximately one trillion bytes or a billion kilobytes.

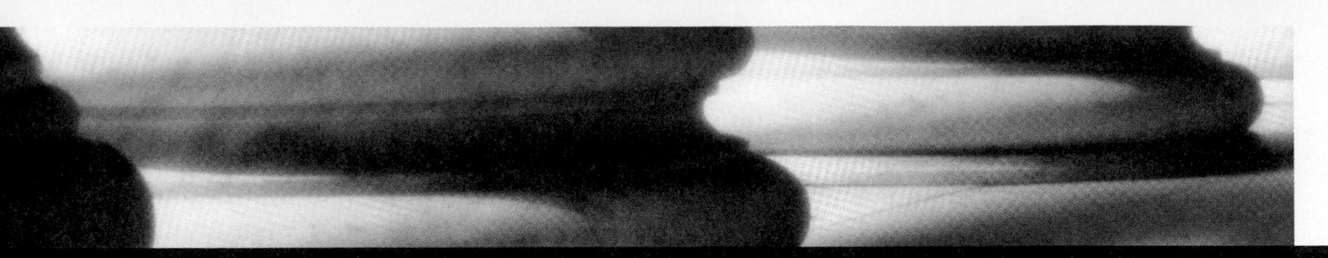

Objectives

After reading this chapter, you will be able to

- Use the vi text editor to create and modify text files
- Use the vedit version of vi to set show mode on
- Use the CDE Text Editor application to create and edit text files

Chapter 9

Using Text Editors

Introduction

This chapter covers the two main text editing tools that you will use in the UNIX environment: the *vi* (pronounced "vee eye" or "veye," as in the word *viable*) editor and the *CDE Text Editor*. These text editors primarily are used for creating and modifying files that customize your work environment (as discussed in Chapter 15, "Customizing Your Login Environment,"), writing script files to automate tasks, and editing HTML Web site files. System administrators use text editors to create and modify system files used for networking, security, application sharing, and so on. The vi editor has been a part of the UNIX operating system nearly since its inception in the early 1970s, and it is universally available with UNIX systems. vi is a very flexible and powerful editor with many options. These will be reviewed here with examples of their use. You will work with the vi editor and the CDE editor as part of this chapter. Finally, this chapter includes a short discussion about UNIX word processor programs. Appendix C, "vi Editor Quick Reference," is a vi editor reference guide for commonly used commands.

Introducing the vi Editor

The vi editor is an interactive editor that is used to create or modify ASCII (American Code for Information Interchange) text files. It is a character-based editor that is an integral part of all UNIX operating systems. The vi editor uses a screen display, but you cannot use the mouse to position the cursor. All editing with the vi editor is done within a memory buffer. Changes can be written to the disk or can be discarded. The vi editor works only with text files and does not have any formatting capabilities.

For users learning to become system administrators, it is important to know how to use vi. It is sometimes the only full-screen editor available to edit crucial system files. Examples of these include scripts and environment control files. Because the vi editor does not impart any special formatting characters, it also can be used to create programs for various programming languages. Skill in using vi also is needed if the windowing system is not available. The vi editor is a useful tool when working remotely on other UNIX workstations or servers. Administrators routinely remotely log in or Telnet to another UNIX computer to perform maintenance and troubleshooting tasks using vi. The availability and operation of vi is consistent across all UNIX platforms, and, thus, it is a tool that will always be available.

The vi Modes

There are three modes of operation in vi: command, entry, and last-line. Understanding the function of these three modes is the key to working with vi. All commands available with vi can be classified in one of the three modes. Figure 9-1 lists the modes and gives a brief description of each. Figure 9-2 shows how to switch modes and get from one mode to another.

Figure 9-1
Mode characteristics in vi.

Mode	Function/Characteristics
Command mode	Initial default mode for creating and editing files, cursor positioning, and modification of existing text. All commands are initiated from this mode. Pressing Esc from either of the other modes returns you to command mode.
Entry mode	Used for entry of new text. Entering an insert command such **i** (insert), **a** (append), and **o** (open new line) takes you from command mode to entry mode. Pressing Esc returns you to command mode. Entry commands are entered by themselves without pressing the Enter key.
Last-line mode	Used for saving your work and quitting vi. Type a colon (:) to get to this mode. Pressing the Enter key returns you to command mode.

Figure 9-2
Moving between vi modes.

From Mode	To Mode	Command/Keys
Command	Entry	**i** (input), **o** (open new line), **a** (append to existing line).
Entry	Command	Press Esc (Escape).
Command	Last-line	Colon (:).
Last-line	Command	Press Enter.
Entry	Last-line	Press Esc to return to Command mode, the enter a colon.
Last-line	Entry	Press Enter or Esc to return to command mode, then enter an insert command.

Command Mode

This is the initial mode for creating and editing files. When you start the vi editor and open a file, you are in command mode. In this mode, you can enter cursor-positioning commands to move around the file, and editing commands to perform functions and modifications of existing text. *Command mode* is the starting point for the other modes. You can change to *entry mode* or *last-line mode* from here. To move from entry mode to last-line mode or vice versa, you first must switch back to command mode. All commands are initiated from command mode. Figures 9-3 and 9-4 show the commands necessary to move from command mode to entry mode and then back to command mode. Figures 9-5 and 9-6 show the commands necessary to move from command mode to last-line mode and then back to command mode.

NOTE

Entry mode is also referred to as edit mode in Sun Solaris course documentation, and the Solaris 8 man pages refer to it as input mode.

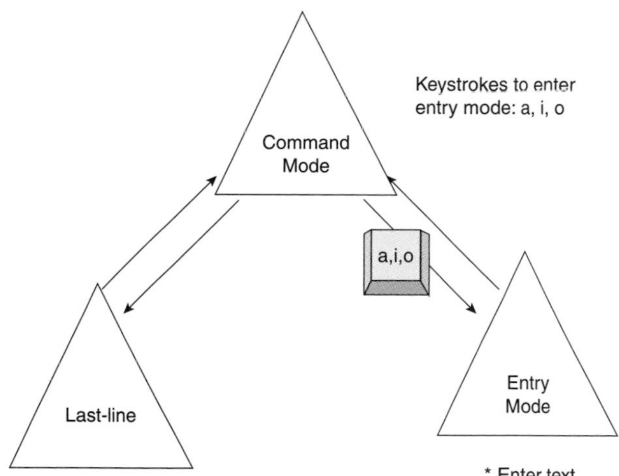

Figure 9-3
Moving from command mode to entry mode.

The Escape (Esc) key always puts you in command mode. Use the Escape key if you are not sure what mode you are in. When in doubt, press Esc to return to command mode before issuing any other commands. While in command mode, you can move your cursor around the text on the screen and perform advanced editing commands.

Entry Mode

You must be in entry mode (also known as input mode) to enter text. To enter text, you must type a vi insert command such as **i** (input), **o** (open new line), or **a** (append). This takes vi out of command mode and puts it into entry mode. In this mode, text will not be interpreted as editing commands. When you finish entering text in your file, press the Esc key to return to command mode.

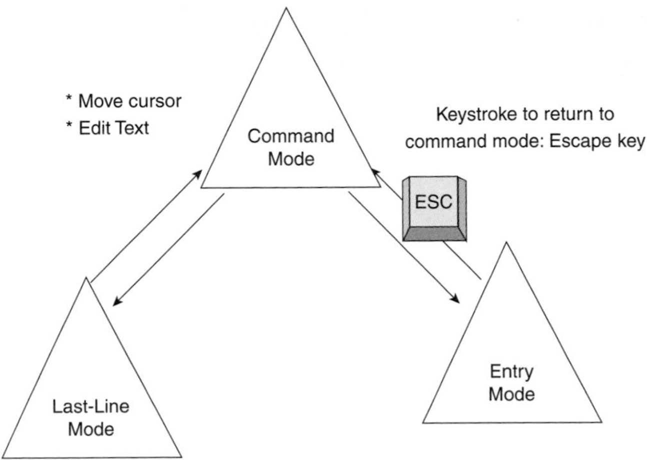

Figure 9-4
Moving from entry mode to command mode.

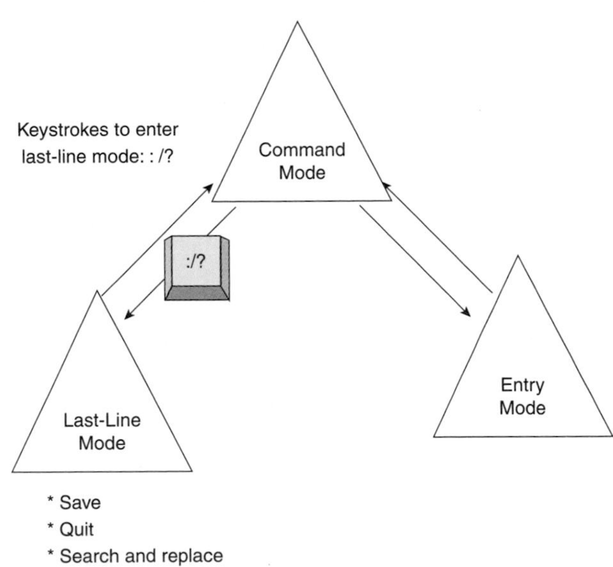

Figure 9-5
Moving from command mode to last-line mode.

Last-Line Mode

From command mode, you can type a colon (**:**), which places you at the bottom line of the screen. This is called last-line mode. The changes made to a document are kept in a memory buffer until they are written to the disk. From last-line mode, you can save your work periodically by writing it to disk while remaining in vi, or you can save and quit vi. You also can quit vi without saving the changes. Last-line mode also can be used to search for strings and to set preferences.

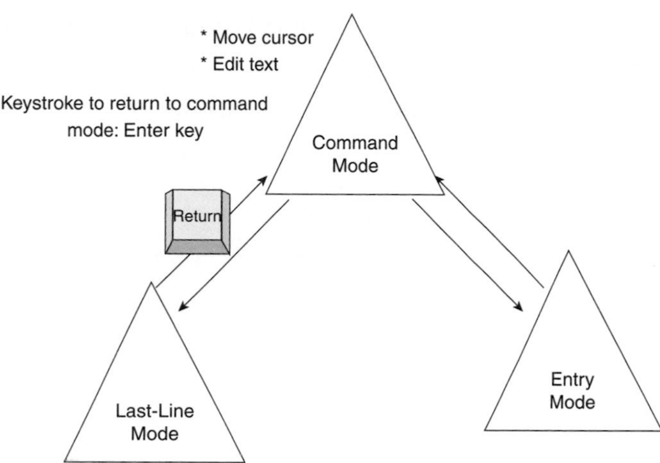

Figure 9-6 Moving from last-line mode to command mode.

Opening Files with vi

The vi editor is a UNIX text-editing application that is started from the command line. Whenever you start vi, you are opening a file. You can specify the file that you want to create or edit when you start vi, or you can open a new file to be named later. The following shows the basic syntax of the vi command:

```
vi [option(s)] [filename]
```

The most basic and common steps when using vi are (in this order):

1. Open a new file.
2. Input some text.
3. Save it to disk.
4. Exit vi.

Methods of Invoking vi

The vi editor can be invoked or started in one of two ways: using the **vi** command or the **vedit** command. vedit is a slightly modified version of vi that visually indicates the current mode.

- **vi filename**—Specifies the filename at the time vi is started. If the file exists, it is opened for editing. If the file does not exist, it is created. When you issue the **write** command in last-line mode, this file is updated.
- **vedit**—Starts the vi editor with showmode turned on. showmode displays the entry or input mode you are currently in (insert, append, or open) at the lower-right corner of the screen. If you are in command mode, nothing is displayed. If you are in last-line mode, your cursor usually is in the lower-left corner with a

colon displayed. You also can enable showmode after you have started vi by entering **set showmode** at the colon in last-line mode. Use vedit when possible so that you will know what mode you are in.

Figure 9-7 show examples of opening files using both vi and vedit.

Figure 9-7
Opening files with vi and vedit.

Command	Function
vi filename	Opens or creates a file.
vedit filename	Opens or creates a file with set show mode automatically enabled.

NOTE

Only the needed basic entry mode, command mode, and last-line mode commands are covered in this chapter.

Input Commands (Entry Mode)

After you start vi and specify a file to work with, you most often will use one of the input commands to add text to the file. These commands are entered from command mode and switch vi into entry mode. In entry mode, if you want to use one of the other entry mode commands shown, you first must press Esc to return to command mode.

TIP

When you are not sure where you are, press the Esc key, which always takes you back to command mode.

If you are working with vedit or have **set showmode** on, you will see the mode (append, insert, or open) shown in the lower-right corner of the screen. If no mode appears, you are not in one of the entry or input modes. The single-letter commands shown in Figure 9-8 are case-sensitive and are used to insert or append text.

Figure 9-8
Append, insert, and open commands.

Command	Function
a	Appends text after the cursor.
A (uppercase)	Appends text at the end of the line.
i	Inserts text before the cursor.
o	Opens a new line below the cursor.

Saving Files and Quitting vi (Last-Line Mode)

Several last-line mode commands are available for saving your work and exiting vi. You should save your work to disk periodically using the **:w** (write) command. This writes the file to disk and leaves you in vi. To save a copy of the file currently being edited to disk under a new name, use the **:w** command followed by a new filename. This is a good way to make a backup of the file. To save the file and quit, you can use either the **:wq** or the **ZZ** commands. If you accidentally made changes and want to discard them without saving, or you want to exit vi and ensure that you have not made any changes, use the **:q!** (quit) command. If you open a read-only file and want to modify it, you can save changes and overwrite the existing file with the **:wq!** (write-quit) command. If you want to discard all your changes since the last write (save) and re-edit the file, use the **:e!** command (erase changes and start again). Figure 9-9 shows the various save/exit options.

Figure 9-9
Save and quit commands.

Command	Function
:w	Write buffer (save changes and continue working in vi).
:w new_filename	Write buffer to new_filename.
:wq	Write buffer (save changes) and quit vi.
ZZ (uppercase)	Save changes and quit vi. Alternative to :wq.
:q!	Quit without saving changes.
:wq!	Write buffer (save changes) and quit vi (The ! will override read only permissions if you are the owner of the file).
e!	Discards your changes since your last save.

Positioning Commands (Command Mode)

Cursor-positioning commands are used in command mode when there is existing text and you want to move around the document. On most UNIX workstations, the cursor control keys can be used to position the cursor to begin editing. However, a number of additional shortcut keystrokes and key sequences are available that can be faster than using the cursor arrow keys. In addition, some dumb terminals do not support arrow keys, and cursor movement must be done using the other positioning methods. Figure 9-10 lists the vi editor's cursor-positioning commands, which are helpful when moving around the screen. The vi editor is case-sensitive, so be sure to use the specified case when using the positioning commands.

Editing Commands (Command and Last-Line Modes)

Many editing commands can be used to modify existing text in a file. These include commands for deleting, undoing, repeating, and changing text, as well as those for copying and pasting. The majority of these commands are entered while in command mode. Commands preceded by a colon indicate to the user that the command is to be entered while in last-line mode.

Figure 9-10
Basic cursor positioning commands.

Command	Function
j (or down arrow)	Moves down one line.
k (or up arrow)	Moves up one line.
h (or left arrow)	Moves back one character.
l (or right arrow)	Moves forward one character.
Space bar	Moves right (forward) one character.
w	Moves forward one word (including punctuation).
b	Moves back one word (including punctuation).
$	Moves to the end of the line.
0 (zero) or ^	Moves to the beginning of the line.
Return	Moves down to the beginning of the next line.

Deleting Text

To delete text, you must be in command mode. While in command mode, position the cursor to the desired location and use the options shown in Figure 9-11 to delete text. These commands are case-sensitive and are entered without the Enter key.

Figure 9-11
Basic text deletion commands.

Command	Function
x (lowercase)	Deletes character at the cursor.
dw	Deletes word (or part of word to right of cursor).
3dw	Deletes three words.
dd	Deletes line containing the cursor.
3dd	Deletes three lines.

Undoing, Repeating, and Changing Text

To change text or to cancel or repeat edit functions, use the commands shown in Figure 9-12. Many of these commands change you to insert mode until you press Esc.

Copying and Pasting Text

Often you can save time and keystrokes by copying existing text and placing it another place(s) in the file using the copy (yank) and paste (put) vi commands. To copy and paste text, use the following options in Figure 9-13.

Figure 9-12
Undo, repeat, and change commands.

Command	Function
cw	Changes word (or part of the word) at the cursor location to the end of the word. This command is a multistep operation: **1.** Position the cursor at the beginning of the word. **2.** Press cw. **3.** Type new word. **4.** Press Esc.
3cw	Changes three words.
r	Replaces character at cursor with one other character.
u	Undoes previous command.

Figure 9-13
Basic copy and paste commands.

Command	Function
yy	Yanks a copy of line to the clipboard.
p	Puts yanked or deleted line below current line.
P (uppercase)	Puts yanked or deleted line above current line.

More About the vi Editor

The vi editor is part of the ex (pronounced "ee x") family of editors. vi is a *screen-oriented* editor containing commands that enable you to move the cursor, add and delete text, and so on. With its own set of commands, ex is a *line-oriented* editor that can be used while in the vi editor. All the last-line mode commands (those that begin with :, ?, and /) discussed so far are actually ex editor commands.

The man pages for vi do not contain any descriptions of commands such as **:q**, **:w**, **:[line #]**, or **:set**. You must read the ex man pages (**man ex**) to learn more about the last-line mode commands.

Advanced Editing—Session-Customization Commands

The vi editor includes options for customizing your edit sessions. These are summarized in Figure 9-14, and they include displaying line numbers and displaying invisible characters such as tab and end-of-line characters. The ex editor **set** command is used from last-line mode to control these options.

NOTE

Both delete (**dw** and **dd** commands) and yank (**yy**) write to a buffer (memory). When yanking, deleting, and pasting, the put commands (**p** and **P**) insert the text differently depending on whether you are pasting words or lines.

TIP

To automatically have vi options enabled when you enter vi, create a file in your home directory called .exrc (ex editor run control). The set options are placed in this file, without the preceding colon, one command to a line. When the .exrc file exists, it is read by the system each time a vi session is opened. The **set nu** option shows line numbers and is used frequently when writing programs and script files. The line numbers are not part of the file.

You can enable vi as your command-line editor, which enables you to bring up previously entered commands and modify them. See the section "Editing the Command Line in the Korn Shell" in Chapter 14, "Basic Features of the Korn and C Shells," for details.

Figure 9-14
Edit session customizing commands.

Command	Function
:set nu	Shows line numbers.
:set nonu	Hides line numbers.
:set showmode	Displays current mode of operation (turned on automatically if the vedit command is used).
:set noshowmode	Turns off mode display.
:set	Displays all vi variables set.
:set all	Displays all possible vi variables and their current settings.

Advanced Editing and Searching

The commands in Figure 9-15 enable you to perform advanced editing such as finding lines or conducting search-and-replace functions. Note that the forward slash (**/**) and the question mark (**?**) search options are also last-line commands, but they do not require a colon first. The next (**n**) and next previous (**N**) commands can be used to find the next occurrence after the **/string** or **?string** commands found what you were looking for.

Figure 9-15
Basic editing search/replace commands.

Command	Function
G (uppercase)	Goes to last line of file.
:21	Goes to line 21.
/string	Searches forward for string.
?string	Searches backward for string.
n	Finds next occurrence of string.

Skill Builder

Lab Activity 9.1.8

Using the vi Editor

In this lab, you use a UNIX text-editing tool: the vi editor. This text editor primarily is used for creating and modifying files that customize your work environment and for writing script files to automate tasks. Refer to the *Cisco Networking Academy Program: Fundamentals of UNIX Lab Companion.*

Spell-Checking Text Files

Long before word processors became popular with a built-in spell checker, there was the UNIX **spell** command.

The **spell** command compares the words contained in the specified text file against a dictionary file and displays suspected words not found in the dictionary. When the misspelled words are identified, you use your favorite editor to search and replace the misspelled words.

If you will be using a text editor to create many text files that need spell-checking, you will be better off downloading the pico text editor (discussed in the next section) for its ease of use and built-in spell-checker. The following is the basic format of the **spell** command.

```
spell [-options] file
```

TIP

You can temporarily suspend the vi editor to check the spelling of a word by doing the following:

1. While in vi, type **:!spell**. (*Note:* You can run any UNIX command from vi using **:![command]**.)
2. Type the word in question, and then press Enter.
3. Press Ctrl-D. If the word is displayed, it is not in the dictionary. If nothing returns, the word is in the dictionary and is spelled correctly.
4. Hit Enter to continue.

Other Text Editors

Many non-Windows–based UNIX text editors are available. Most people learn vi because the vi editor and the older ed (editor) text editors are part of almost every UNIX system. Even though easy-to-use Windows-based text editors are available (the CDE Text Editor is covered next), it is nice to know at least the basics of vi in case you need to edit a file after accessing a remote system where no GUI environment is available. If you plan to become a system administrator, you might want to consider one of the other popular non-Windows–based editors such as emacs or pico.

The emacs Editor

The emacs (editor macros) editor is considered by many to be easier than vi because there are no modes. However, emacs commands are mostly a combination of the Control (Ctrl) key plus a letter (as in Ctrl-d to delete a character and Ctrl-XS to save), and they must be learned, as is the case with vi.

The most common version of emacs is the GNU emacs editor, available for free (www.gnu.org).

TIP

Several vi editors are available for DOS and Windows users. Search the Internet for "vi editor" to locate a download site.

The pico Editor

The pico editor comes with the Pine mail program (discussed in Chapter 3, "CDE User Applications") and, like Pine, also was developed at the University of Washington. Also like Pine, pico is an easy-to-use, menu-driven program. It is not as powerful as vi, but it is more than capable of handling most user editing needs. To obtain a free version of pico, search the Internet for "pico editor" and choose from any number of download sites.

Text Editor Alternative—Creating Small Text Files Using cat

Chapter 6, "Basic Directory and File Management," introduced the **cat** command as a way to view the contents of a file. The **cat** command is a multipurpose command that also can be used to create (not edit) small text files as an alternative to using a text editor. The steps necessary to create a file using the **cat** command are listed here. The file will be placed in the default directory unless a path is specified. The basic syntax of the cat command is shown here:

```
cat > filename
```

1. Type the lines of text, pressing Enter after each line. (After you press Enter to go to the next line, you can't move back.)
2. Press Enter after the last line.
3. Press Ctrl-d to save the file.

Using the CDE Text Editor

The CDE Text Editor is a full-screen graphical text editor that supports a mouse and can be used to edit files. It is equivalent to the Windows Notepad. As with vi, this editor does not put any special formatting characters into the file, and it is suitable for creating system environment and script files. To start the CDE Text Editor, click the Text Note subpanel (see Figure 9-16) from the Front Panel and open a Text Editor window. The default name for the file that opens will be UNTITLED, as shown in Figure 9-17.

You can type any text into the Text Editor window. If you want to insert characters into an area where you have already typed, position the pointer where you want to insert text and then click the left mouse button.

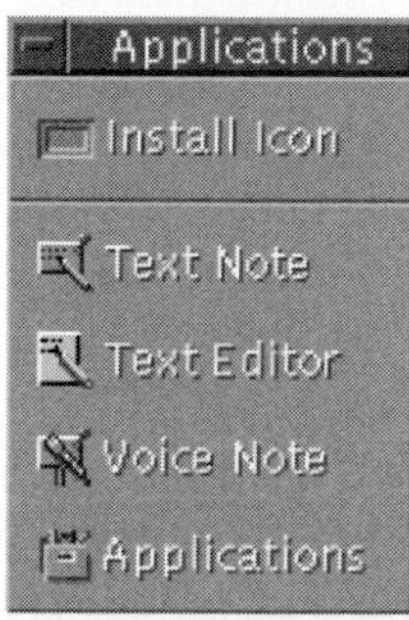

Figure 9-16
The text note sub-panel.

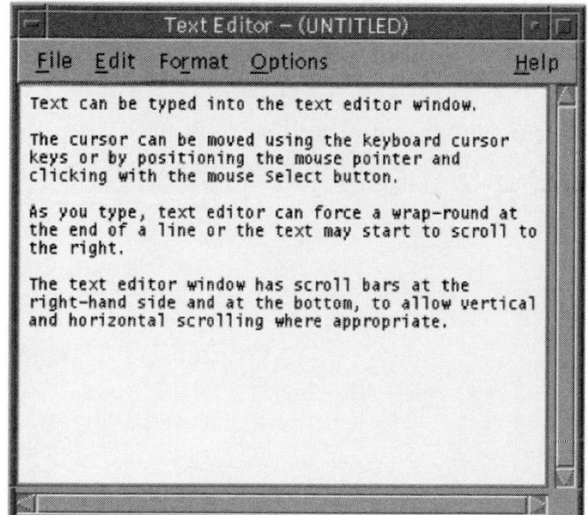

Figure 9-17
The Text Editor window.

By default, Text Editor is in insert mode. That is, when you type, the characters automatically are inserted into the text rather than overwriting any existing characters to the right of the pointer. You can change from insert to overwrite mode at any time while working with Text Editor by clicking the Options menu and selecting Overstrike.

Using File Options

The File Options menu shown in Figure 9-18 contains commands for creating new documents, saving your work, opening and closing documents, and printing. The following is a description of each command:

- **New**—Start a new Text Editor session in the same window, and discard any current text contents. If the current text has not been saved, you will be prompted to confirm saving or discarding it.

- **Open**—Open an existing text file in the current Text Editor window. You will be provided with a window displaying a list of filenames to choose from.
- **Include**—Include the contents of an existing (text) file. The contents of the included file will be inserted at the current cursor position.
- **Save**—Save the current text to the current filename. If you have altered the current text since the last time you saved it, the menu option will display as Save (Needed).
- **Save As**—Save the current Text Editor window contents under an alternative filename. This option automatically is chosen when you first use the Save menu option.
- **Print**—Print the current text.
- **Close**—Close the Text Editor window. If you have not saved the current text, you will be asked if you want to save your changes. If you click the No button, any text that has been added or changed since the last save will be lost.

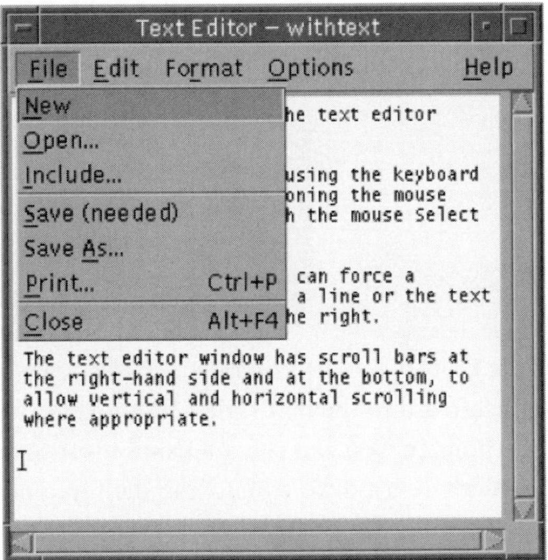

Figure 9-18
Using file options.

Editing Options

This section introduces you to many different editing options that you have available.

Edit Menu

The Edit menu shown in Figure 9-19 contains the standard options to manipulate text, such as Cut, Copy, and Paste. However, if no text is selected, the Cut and Copy options will not be available. The Find option enables you to find text or to find and change text. It is case-sensitive, so anything that you are searching for will be found only if it is an exact match. Similarly, any text can be changed to be exactly the same as the text that you typed in the change box, as shown in the example in Figure 9-20. If the text string cannot be found in the document, you will see the window in Figure 9-21.

Figure 9-19
Text Editor: the Edit menu.

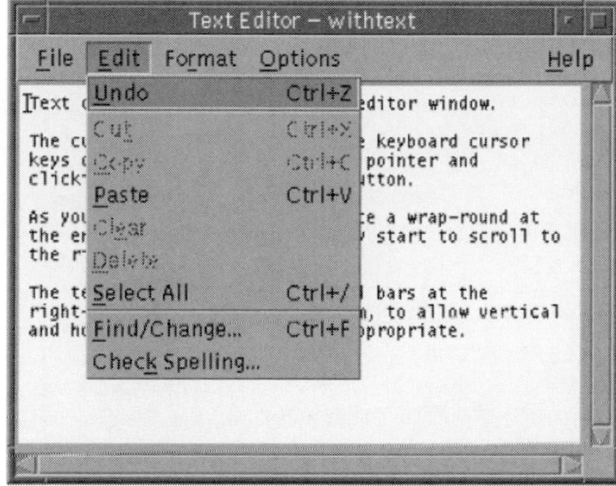

Figure 9-20
Text Editor: Find/Change.

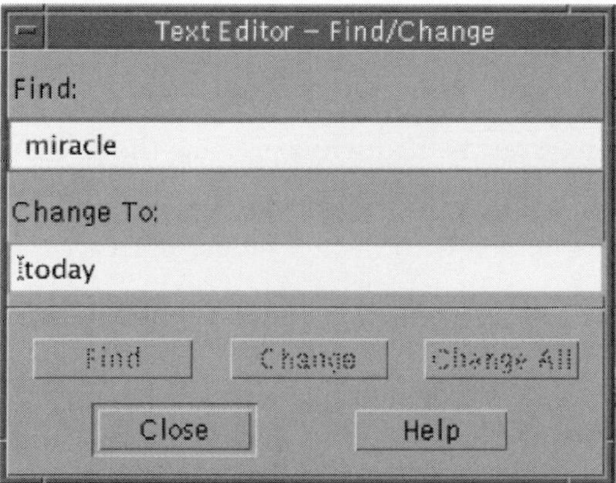

Figure 9-21
Search item not found.

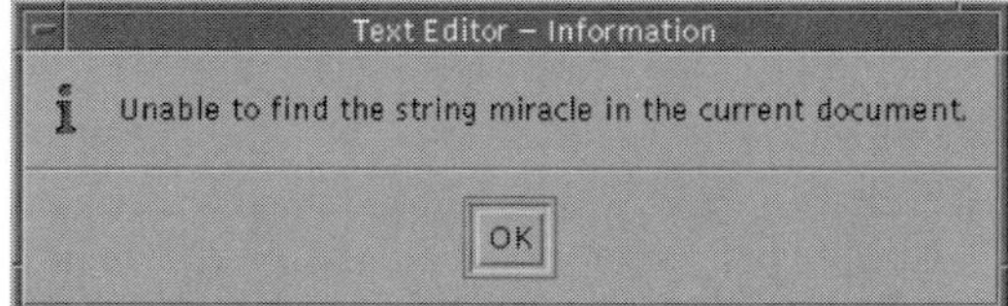

Editing Keys

The Sun workstation keyboard has a set of editing keys on the left side that can be used instead of the editing menu options. (See Figure 9-22.) By selecting text with the mouse, these keys can be used to copy, cut, and paste, among other things.

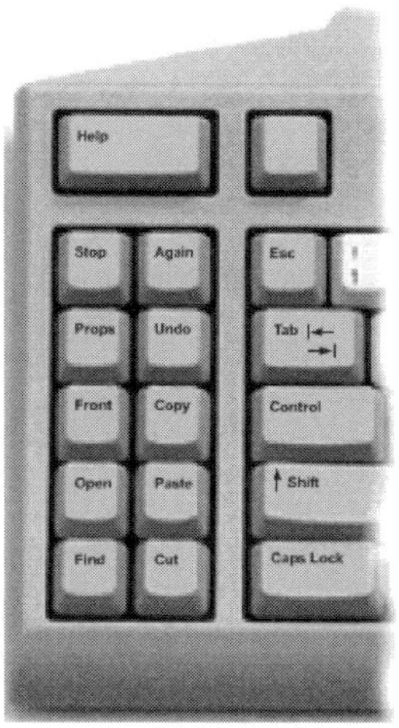

Figure 9-22
Sun keyboard editing keys.

Replacing Text

Text can be selected and replaced using any of the following four methods:

- Dragging over the text while pressing the left mouse button. This will highlight all of the text that the mouse pointer passes over.
- Double-clicking with the left mouse button on a word to highlight that word.
- Triple-clicking with the left mouse button to highlight the paragraph over which the mouse pointer is situated.
- Quadruple-clicking with the left mouse button to highlight all of the text in the current Text Editor file.

When text has been highlighted using any of these four methods, it will be replaced by whatever characters are next typed at the keyboard. Figure 9-23 shows selected text.

Instead of typing characters, you can cut, copy, or clear the highlighted text using the special keyboard keys or the options on the Text Editor Edit menu, as shown in Figure 9-24.

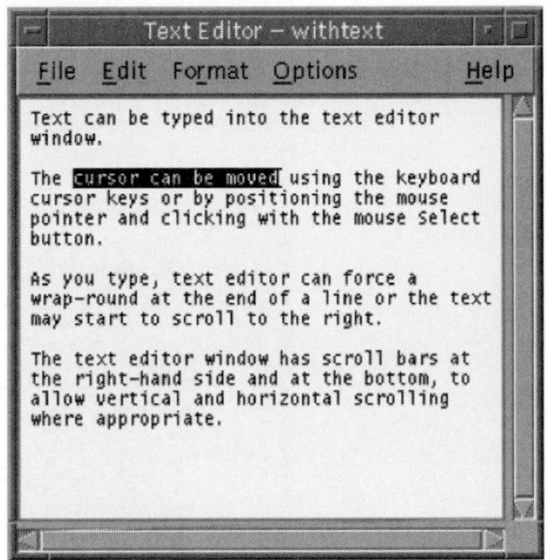

Figure 9-23
Selecting text to be replaced

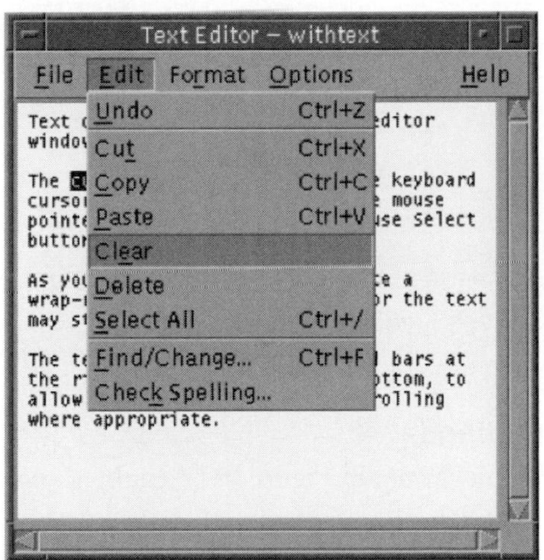

Figure 9-24
Replacing text with the edit menu options

TIP

On a Sun workstation, the Find key is used to quickly find text in a file or e-mail. To use this "quick find" feature, highlight one occurrence of the text that you want to search for (or type it at the top of the file and then highlight it) and then press the Find key. Press Find again to go to the next occurrence.

Format Menu Options

The Settings option under the Format menu, shown in Figures 9-25 and 9-26, will enable you to change margins and alignment of your text, either for a paragraph or for the entire document. When the settings have been defined, clicking the Format menu again gives a shortcut to changing settings for the current paragraph or the entire document (Paragraph or All).

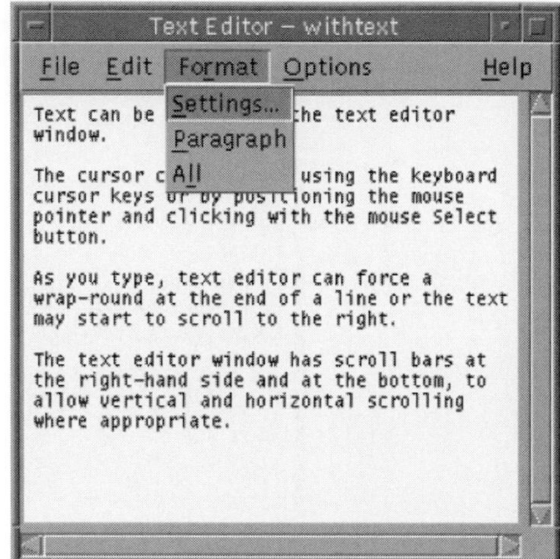

Figure 9-25
Format menu options.

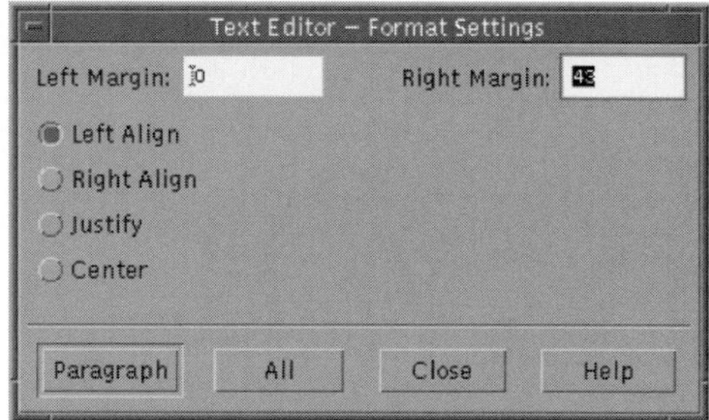

Figure 9-26
Format settings.

Text Editor Options

The Options menu shown in Figure 9-27 enables you to switch between insert and overstrike modes. The chosen mode affects any new text typed into an existing text area. The wrap-to-fit mode formats the text in the current Text Editor window by automatically wrapping or moving text to the next line when it reaches the edge of the window. The status line can be switched on or off, using the Status Line menu option. When the status line is on, it shows the current line number on which the cursor is situated and the total number of lines in the text, as shown in Figure 9-28. Finally, the Backup on Save option creates a backup file each time you save the contents of your Text Editor session.

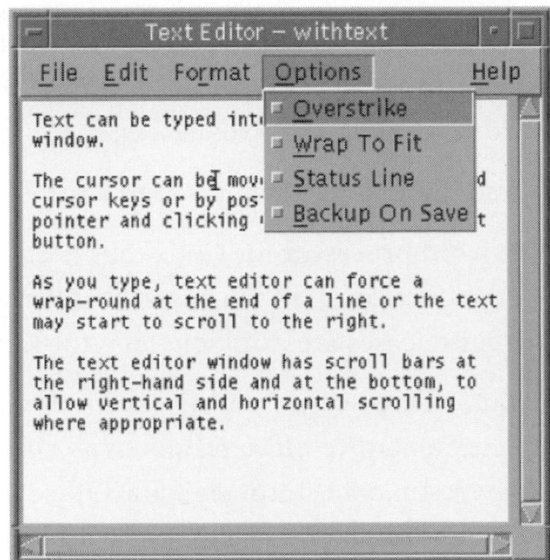

Figure 9-27
Text editor options.

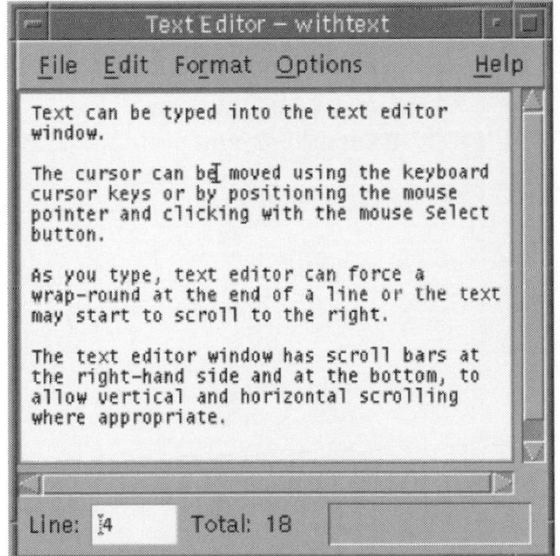

Figure 9-28
Status line option.

Skill Builder

Lab Activity 9.2.6

Using the CDE Text Editor

In this lab, you work with the Common Desktop Environment (CDE) Text Editor. Refer to the *Cisco Networking Academy Program: Fundamentals of UNIX Lab Companion*.

Word Processors

Word processors are different from text editors. Word processors are designed for creating documents that are easy to read. They include features for formatting text (bold, underline, and so on), embedding graphics and pictures, inserting tables, and flexible printing.

Several full-featured word-processing programs for UNIX also run on PCs.

The most popular word processor for UNIX has been WordPerfect, from Corel Corporation (www.wordperfect.com). In the past, WordPerfect has supported many UNIX varieties, but current releases are available only for Linux.

StarWriter from Sun Microsystem is a full-featured word processor program that is part of the complete StarOffice office productivity suite, which is available at no charge to users (www.sun.com/staroffice). StarOffice also includes spreadsheet, drawing, database, presentation, and scheduling programs. With StarOffice, users have the capability to access files created with Microsoft Office. StarOffice runs on Solaris, Microsoft Windows, and Linux, enabling users to access files across multiple platforms. Figure 9-29 shows the StarOffice desktop with the various applications available. Figure 9-30 shows the StarOffice Word Processor with a new open document.

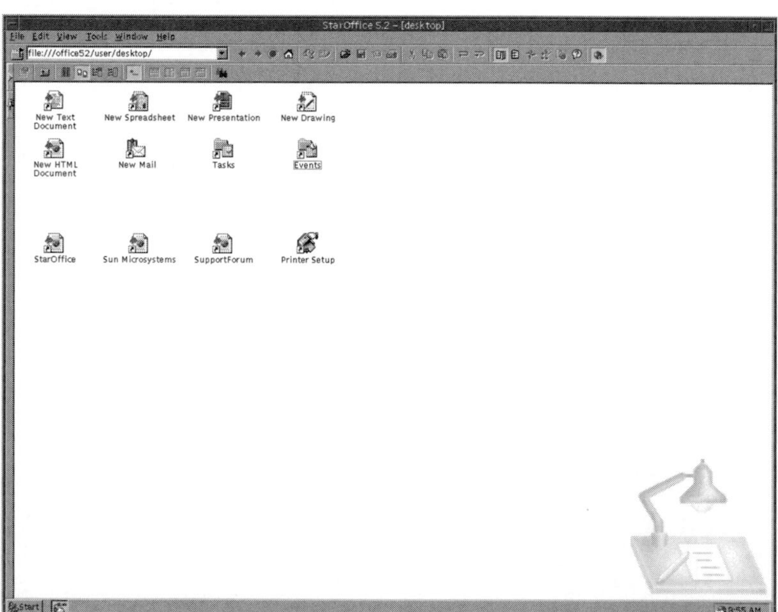

Figure 9-29
StarOffice applications.

TIP

To open a file created with a word processor in a text editor, save the file using the text or text-only file type. Doing so removes all formatting characters, pictures, tables, and so on, and saves only text.

Files created with a text editor can be opened with a word processor. However, word processor files cannot be opened with a text editor because word processor files contain formatting characters.

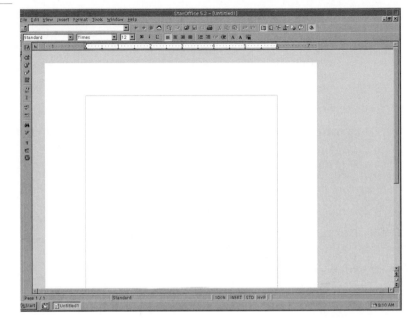

Figure 9-30
StarOffice word processor.

Summary

Now that you have completed this chapter, you should have an understanding of the following:

- The vi editor is a simple but powerful text editor that can be used to create system and script files. It is an integral part of all UNIX operating systems. Sometimes a graphical text editor will not be available, and vi might be your only available tool to perform administrative tasks and troubleshoot problems.
- The vi editor has three main modes of operation: command mode, entry mode, and last-line mode.
- Command mode is the starting point for the other modes and is used to edit existing text. All commands are entered from command mode. Pressing Esc always returns you to command mode. Entry (insert) mode is used for entering new text. Last-line mode primarily is used to save files and exit vi. Understanding the purpose of these modes and knowing how to switch between them is key to working with the vi editor. Numerous positioning, editing, and other commands also are available.
- In addition to vi, other non-Windows–based text editors can be downloaded for free and are considered easier to use. The two most popular editors are emacs and pico.

- The CDE Text Editor is a graphical editor that performs a similar function to vi. As with vi, you can create text files that do not have any formatting in them. These can be user environment configuration files, script files, program files, or notes. The CDE editor provides mouse support, making it easier to work with existing text.

Check Your Understanding

1. Which of the following characteristics is true of vi?
   - **A.** It is not a full-screen text editor.
   - **B.** It operates in three modes.
   - **C.** It can be used to edit both text and binary files.
   - **D.** It is available only with the Sun Solaris operating environment.
2. What are the modes vi uses to create, edit, and save files?
   - **A.** Command, entry, and last-line
   - **B.** Keyboard, monitor, and printer
   - **C.** Insert, delete, and edit
   - **D.** Command, edit, and last-line
3. When working with vi, it is important to remember that all commands are entered from command mode (True/False).
   - **A.** True
   - **B.** False
4. If you currently are inserting text in entry mode, what combination of keystrokes or commands will allow you to change to last-line mode?
   - **A.** Enter-Esc-Q
   - **B.** Esc-:
   - **C.** Esc-*-Enter
   - **D.** Enter-:
5. Which of the following can be used to change to entry mode and begin adding text?
   - **A.** i, o, a
   - **B.** d, q, w
   - **C.** :, /, ?
   - **D.** i, o, q

6. You have created a new file using vi and have inserted some text, and now you want to save it and quit. Which command should you use?

   A. quit

   B. :wq

   C. :!q

   D. :w

7. Which of these statements is true of the vedit utility?

   A. vedit has more modes than vi.

   B. vedit is used to open files in read-only mode.

   C. vi is used for text files, and vedit is used for word processing.

   D. vedit sets **showmode** to on automatically.

8. You have started editing a file using vi and have made some changes. You realize that you are working with the wrong file, and you want to exit vi without saving any changes to the file. Which command accomplishes this?

   A. :wq

   B. :qq

   C. :wq!

   D. :q!

9. Which of the following is true when comparing the CDE editor to the vi?

   A. The CDE Text Editor cannot be used to edit script files.

   B. The CDE Text Editor is a line editor, whereas vi is a full-screen editor.

   C. The CDE Text Editor is a graphical editor, whereas vi is a character-based editor.

   D. The CDE Text Editor is available from the command line.

10. When working with the CDE Text Editor, you can use the options on the File menu as well as the keyboard editing keys to cut, copy, and paste text (True/False).

    A. True

    B. False

UNIX Command Summary

spell Compares the words contained in the specified text file against a dictionary file and displays suspected words that are not found in the dictionary. Example:

```
$ spell memo
aint
partyiing
```

vedit Starts the vi editor with showmode turned on, which displays the current mode (entry or input) that you're in.

vi editor command mode Initial default mode for creating and editing files, cursor positioning, and modification of existing text. All commands are initiated from this mode. Pressing Esc from either of the other modes returns you to command mode.

vi editor entry mode Used for new text entry. Entering an insert command, such **i** (insert), **a** (append), and **o** (open new line) takes you from command mode to entry mode. Pressing Esc returns you to command mode. Entry commands are entered by themselves, without pressing the Enter key. Example:

```
a, i, o, A, I, O
```

vi editor last line mode Used to save your work and quit vi. Type a colon (:) to get into this mode. Pressing the Return key returns you to command mode.

```
:w, :wq, ZZ, :q!, :wq!
```

Key Terms

Command mode When using the vi editor, the command mode is the mode in which you can position the cursor and use edit commands to perform various actions. When you open a file with vi, you are in command mode. All commands are initiated from command mode.

Entry mode When using vi, the entry mode is the mode in which you can type text. To enter text, you must type a vi insert command such as **i**, **o**, or **a**. This takes vi out of command mode and puts it into entry mode. In this mode, text is not interpreted literally and becomes part of the document. When you finish entering text in your file, press the Escape key to return to command mode.

Last-line mode When using the vi editor, the last-line mode is the mode in which you can type advanced editing commands and perform searches. This mode is entered in a variety of ways (most commonly with a colon, a slash, or a question mark), all of which place you at the bottom of the screen.

Text Editor (CDE) A full-screen graphical text editor that supports a mouse and can be used to edit files. It is similar to the Windows Notepad. As with vi, this editor does not put any special formatting characters into the file, and it is suitable for creating system environment and script files.

vi An interactive editor that is used to create and modify ASCII (American Code for Information Interchange) text files. It is a character-based editor that is an integral part of all UNIX operating systems. The vi editor uses a screen display, but you cannot use the mouse to position the cursor.

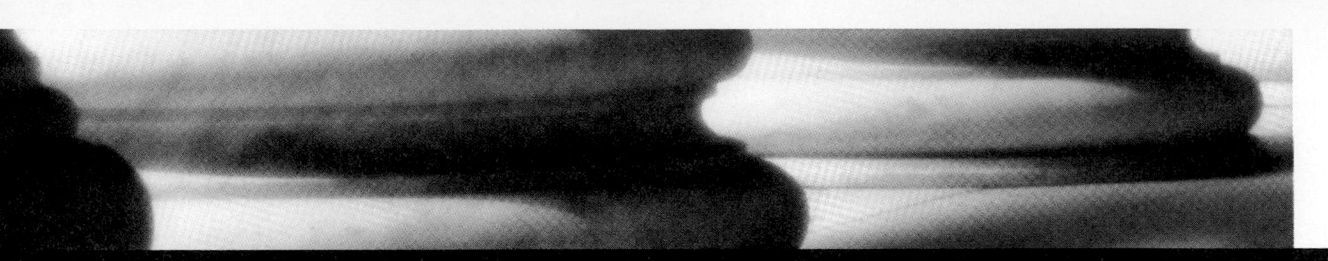

Objectives

After reading this chapter, you will be able to

- Describe the components of a good security policy
- Explain file system permissions
- Determine current file system permissions
- Change file and directory permissions from the command line
- Change file and directory permissions using the CDE File Manager

Chapter 10

File System Security

Introduction

All network operating systems have some means of controlling access to resources. The file system is a key resource on any workstation or server. Protecting that file system from unauthorized access and allowing access as needed are key components in a comprehensive security policy. This chapter provides some guidelines for an overall security policy and specific information about file system security. UNIX file system security concepts are introduced, and examples are provided showing how to apply them. You learn how to determine file and directory permissions, and you discover what types and categories of permission exist. You analyze the meaning of the various permission types as they relate to user and group access. You also work with directory and file permissions using the command line and CDE to determine and change file and directory permissions.

Security Policies

An organization's information is one of its most valuable assets. Network security is becoming increasingly important as networks become larger and more complex. Today's mobile and telecommuting users require access locally as well as from outside the network. Threats to an organization's resources can come from internal and external sources. Information theft and destruction as well as resource access denial are real concerns for users and system administrators. The overall goal of any information system is to ensure that information is accurate and available where and when needed. A comprehensive information systems security policy can help to ensure this. A number of components must interact in a comprehensive security policy. These components are shown in Figure 10-1 and are discussed in greater detail in the following sections.

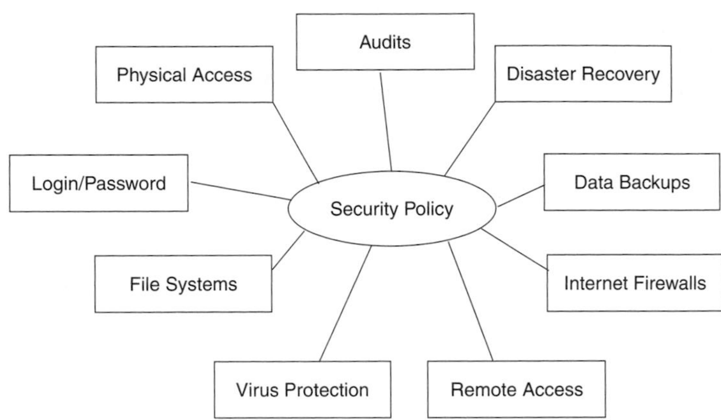

Figure 10-1
Security policy components.

Physical Access Security

The first line of defense locally to protect network equipment such as servers, switches, and routers is to keep them in a locked, climate-controlled, fire-protected environment. If equipment is not physically accessible to unauthorized personnel, there's less chance of accidental or intentional tampering.

Login/Password Security

Login and password security require that any user accessing a workstation or server have a valid login ID and password. As you saw in Chapter 2, "Accessing Your System and the Common Desktop Environment," UNIX has specific requirements for creating and changing passwords. The system administrator also can require that passwords be changed periodically. Setting screen savers that time out and activating your workstation lock are additional measures that enhance login and password security.

File Systems Security

A major component in any comprehensive security policy, file system security determines who can get to what data and what they can do with it. System administrators set up file system security based on users, *groups*, and *permissions*. Permissions are applied to files and directories in the file system to control access to these resources.

Virus Protection

Viruses can do tremendous damage to individual workstations and network servers. Many network operating systems and workstations require antivirus software for adequate protection. UNIX is susceptible to virus attacks like other operating systems, but most viruses are written for Windows-based systems because they can affect more systems faster. In addition, most virus creators are not familiar with the UNIX environment enough to know how to create a UNIX virus.

Remote Access Security

With increases in telecommuting, the network must allow legitimate users to access resources remotely while protecting those resources from unauthorized access. Access servers and remote access software provide this function.

Internet Firewalls

Organizations that provide their users with Internet access or that maintain Internet Web sites need protection from hackers. Various software and hardware firewall and user authentication solutions are available to help ensure that Web servers are available to provide services to legitimate users and stop the attacks of hackers.

Data Backups

A comprehensive security policy must include regular backups of important data to minimize downtime in the event of a security breach, loss of data, or a disaster such as fire or flood. Backup media, such as tapes, should be kept offsite in a climate-controlled, secure environment. Test restores of data should be performed periodically to ensure that data could be recovered from the backups in case it is needed.

Disaster Recovery Plan

A *disaster recovery plan* is a written plan that identifies critical data and documents by functional department within an organization. It describes protective measures and steps necessary to ensure that the organization can continue to operate and get back to business quickly, with minimal impact to customers in the event of a disaster.

Audits

Security audits must be performed periodically to ensure that the organization and its users are following the security policy and preparing adequately for disaster recovery. Security audit tools are also available for system administrators to analyze and detect security loopholes such as files with open permissions.

Standard UNIX Security Features

The primary function of system security is to deny access to unauthorized users. Keeping computer information secure is important to the user and the system administrator. By protecting their files and accounts from unauthorized use, users also are protecting their jobs and reputations. Standard UNIX environment security features include the following:

- User passwords that restrict access to the system
- File and directory protection with permissions
- Files that control remote logins and commands on individual workstations
- Other features that enable system administrators to check for security breaches

UNIX operating systems have two default levels of security. First, users must supply a login ID and password to access a UNIX workstation or server. Second, files and directories automatically are protected by permissions when they are created.

UNIX provides a special user account called *root* that has total access to the system. All permissions placed on files and directories can be overridden by the root user. This account's user is also called the *superuser.* The superuser account runs system administration commands and edits critical system files such as the password file. Individuals with root access often are referred to as *system administrators*.

Skill Builder

e-Lab Activity 10.1

Security Policy Exercise

In this drag-and-drop e-Lab activity, you drag the term on the left of the graphic to match the appropriate definition listed on the right.

File System Permissions

Permissions control who can do what to files and directories in the file system. Directory and file permissions can be determined using the **ls** (list) command with the **-l** (long) option, as shown in Figure 10-2. The **ls -l** command displays a long listing of the contents of a directory. If the **-a** (all) option is included, all files, including hidden files (those beginning with a dot), will be displayed. As previously discussed in Chapter 5, "Accessing Files and Directories," the long listing displays a separate line of output, which includes eight pieces of information for each file or directory. The permissions portion of the **ls -l** output is the focus of this chapter. Figure 10-3 shows the location of each component, and Figure 10-4 provides a brief definition of the components of the **ls -l** command output.

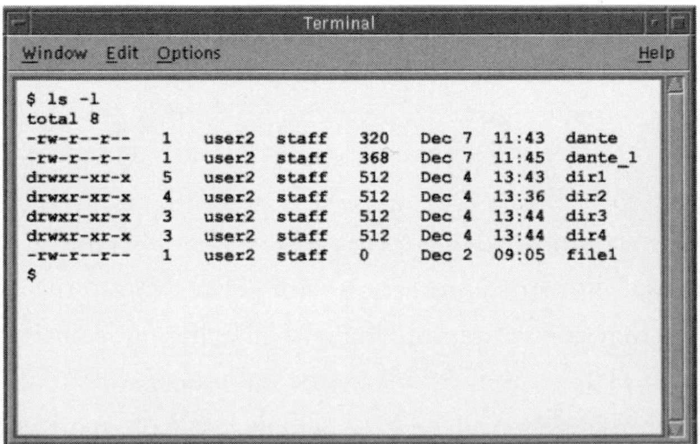
Terminal
Window Edit Options
Help
$ ls -l
total 8
-rw-r--r-- 1 user2 staff 320 Dec 7 11:43 dante
-rw-r--r-- 1 user2 staff 368 Dec 7 11:45 dante_1
drwxr-xr-x 5 user2 staff 512 Dec 4 13:43 dir1
drwxr-xr-x 4 user2 staff 512 Dec 4 13:36 dir2
drwxr-xr-x 3 user2 staff 512 Dec 4 13:44 dir3
drwxr-xr-x 3 user2 staff 512 Dec 4 13:44 dir4
-rw-r--r-- 1 user2 staff 0 Dec 2 09:05 file1
$

Figure 10-2 Detailed information from the **ls –l** command.

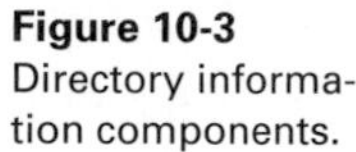

Figure 10-3
Directory information components.

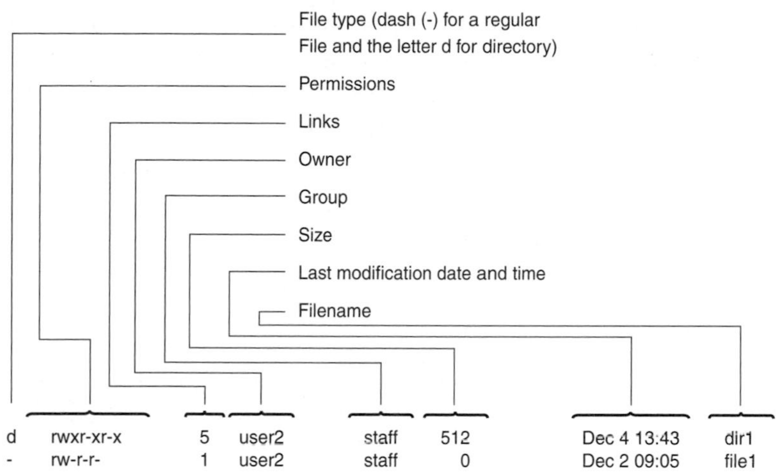

Figure 10-4
Directory component definitions

File Type	A dash (-) in the first position indicates a regular file. A d indicates directory.
Permissions	Three sets of permissions: User, Group, Others.
Links	Number of links that the file has to other files. Links are covered in Chapter 7.
Owner	User (login) ID of user who created the file or directory unless ownership was assigned.
Group	Primary group name that owner belongs to established by the system administrator.
Size	File size in bytes.
Modification Date/Time	Month, day, year (if not current year) and time the file was created or last modified.
Filename	File or directory name.

Permission Categories (Classes)

The first character of the display is not actually a part of the permissions. It indicates whether this is a file (-) or a directory (d). The next nine characters represent the permissions of the file or directory. These are divided into three sets of three permissions each. There is one set for each category or category of users: user, group, or other. The first set of three permissions are permissions of the user. The second set applies to the group that the user belongs to. The third set applies to all other users.

- **File type**—(Not part of permissions) Whether it is a directory or a file
- *Owner*—The user who created or owns the file or directory

- **Group**—Group of users defined by the system administrator
- **Others (public)**—All other users (other than user or group)

It is important to understand each of the categories or classes of users and how file and directory access permissions affect them. The categories and permissions associated with users determine who can access these resources and what they can do with them.

Figure 10-5 shows the **ls –l** listing for the .profile file. The first 10 characters of the display represent the file type and the permissions for the file. The dash in the first position indicates that this is a file. The user (user2) permissions are read and write (r w -), the group (staff) permissions are read (r - -), and the other (all other users) permissions are read (r - -).

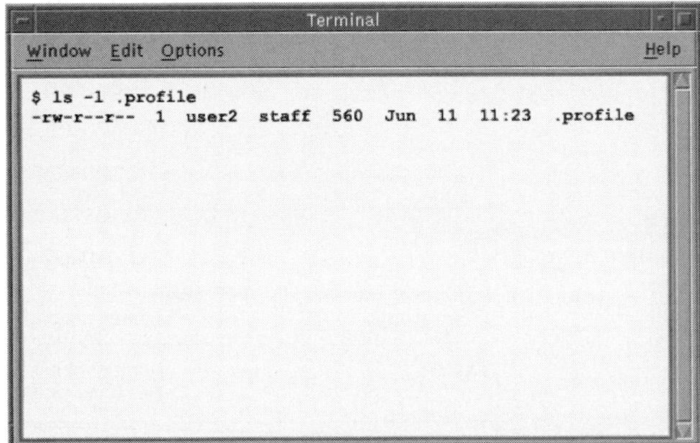
Terminal
Window Edit Options Help
$ ls -l .profile
-rw-r--r-- 1 user2 staff 560 Jun 11 11:23 .profile

Figure 10-5
Directory listing for the .profile file.

The following sections provides a more detailed explanation of the file type indicator and the three permission categories.

File Type

As previously mentioned, the first character is not a category, but it refers to the file type. An ordinary file is represented by a dash (-), and a directory is represented by a d. A dash anywhere else in a permission set indicates no permission. The interpretation of permissions is slightly different for files and directories.

User (Owner)

The next three characters are the user or owner permissions. They show the type of access that the owner of the file or directory has. When you create a new file or directory, you own it. The owner of the file .profile in Figure 10-5 is user2.

Group

The second set of three characters, called group permissions, identifies the permissions of the group that owns the file. A user group (system group) is a set of users with common file access needs. System administrators define system groups and determine which users belong to which groups. For example, a system administrator may establish an accounting group or a management group.

Users in the same group can access each other's files based on the group permissions. The group owner of the file .profile in Figure 10-5 is the group staff.

Others (Public)

The last set of characters, called others permissions, are the permissions that everyone else has. Others refers to anyone who is neither the file owner nor a member of the group that owns the file, but who has access to the system.

Applying Permission Based on Category

You own the files that you create, and the group association on these files is your primary group. Access is determined by the highest category to which you belong. The user or owner category has a higher priority than the group category, which, in turn, is higher than the other category. If you are the user (owner), even though you are a member of the group, only the user category of permissions applies. The permissions for others apply only to someone who is neither the owner of a file or directory nor a member of the group the owner belongs to. As an example, you are the owner of a file and you have read, write, and execute permissions. The group you belong to has permissions for read access, and others have no access. Because user permissions have a higher priority than group permissions, your permissions will be read, write, and execute, which are the permissions of the user (owner) category. If someone from your same group tries to access the file, that person will be able to only read it. Anyone else (other) will not be able to access the file at all.

Permission Types

Every file or directory has a set of permissions that determines who can do what with it. Permissions are represented by characters that control who may read, write, and execute the contents of a file or directory.

The set of permissions for each category of users (users, group, or other) consists of three possible permission types. These are used to control access to the file or directory with which the permissions are associated. The first position in each set is the read (r) permission, the second is write (w), and the third is execute (x). You might see a dash (-) in place of r, w, or x. This indicates that the permission (r, w, or x) where the dash is located is denied.

Figure 10-6 shows the permissions for the .profile file in the /home/user2 directory. This is a text file that usually is placed in the user's home directory by the system administrator. When the user logs in, this file is read, and the environment is tailored to the user's needs. This file can be read (viewed) and written to (modified) by the user.

The set of permissions for user access to this file is r w -. The presence of the r allows the owner to read the file, and the w allows the user to write to or modify the file. The absence of an x means that the user cannot execute the file because this is not an executable file. A dash is used in place of a permission that is not allowed. The group and other categories of users can read the file but cannot write to it or execute it.

NOTE

To copy (**cp**) a file from a directory or move (**mv**) a file into or out of a directory, you must have the execute (x) permission for the directory. You also must have the read permission for the file being copied or moved. Additionally, changing the permissions on a folder doesn't change the permissions for that folder's subfolders. To change permissions on a folder and all of its subfolders, the **-R** (recursive) command needs to be used.

By default, directories have read and execute permissions. Without these permissions, a user would be unable to access any of the content within the directory. Access problems sometimes can be traced back to a user accidentally or intentionally removing read and or execute permissions on a directory.

Figure 10-6 Permissions for the .profile file.

```
$ls -1 .profile
-rw-r--r--   1  user2  staff  582  Mar 16  15:07  .profile
```

Type	User	Group	Other
-	rw-	r--	r--

Figure 10-7 shows the permissions for the mkdir file in the /bin directory. This is an executable UNIX command file, which you have used previously to create new directories. Because all users need to be able to use the **mkdir** command, all three categories of users have the permission to read the file and to execute it. The set of permissions for user, group, and other access to this file is r - x. The presence of the r and x allows everyone (user, group, and other) to read and execute the file. The dash in place of the write permission prevents anyone from writing to or changing the file.

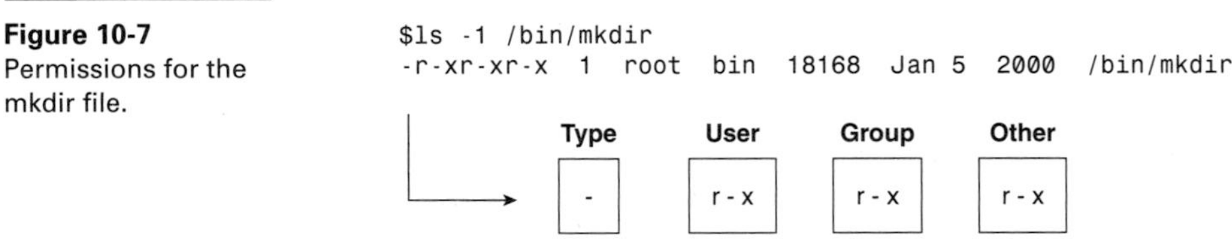

Figure 10-7 Permissions for the mkdir file.

Meaning of Permissions for Files and Directories

The meaning of the r, w, and x permissions vary depending on whether you are working with a file or a directory. Figure 10-8 shows the three possible permissions and the differences in their effect on files and directories. For a directory to be of any practical use, at least read and execute permissions must be set.

Figure 10-9 shows several examples of the different permissions for files and directories.

Figure 10-8
File and directory permissions.

Permission	Symbol	Plain File	Directory
Read	r	File can be displayed or copied (copied file takes on new owner). Can't move or remove a file with only read permission.	Contents can be listed with the **ls** command Must also have execute permission to use ls command options.
Write	w	File can be modified, moved, and removed (only if the directory it resides in has write permission).	Files can be added or deleted. Directory must also have execute permission.
Execute	x	File can be executed (shell script or executables).	Controls access to the directory. A user can **cd** to the directory and list the contents. Files can be moved or copied to the directory.
No permission	-	A dash indicates permission is denied.	A dash indicates permission is denied.

Figure 10-9
File and directory permissions.

Command	Permission
-rwx------	The file is read/write/execute for user only.
dr-xr-x---	The directory is read/execute for user and group.
-rwxr-xr-x	The file is read/write/execute for user, and read/execute for group and others.
drwxr-x--x	The directory is read/write/execute for user, read/execute for group, and execute for others.
-r-xr-xr-x	The file is read/execute for user, group, and others. Common for scripts and executables.

Determining File and Directory Access

All files and directories have a user identifier (UID) and group identifier (GID) number associated with them. The kernel uses these numbers to identify ownership of files rather than the user or group name familiar to the user.

The **ls -n** command displays the numeric UID and the GID, as shown in Figure 10-10. Note that, in the figure, the **-a** (all) option was included to see the .profile file that normally is hidden. Figure 10-10 also shows two other useful commands when working with UIDs and GIDs. As you will recall, the **id** command displays numeric and alphabetic UIDs and GIDs for your effective user identifier (EUID). The **groups** command displays all the groups you are a member of. Figure 10-10 shows examples using the **ls –an**, the **id**, and the **groups** commands.

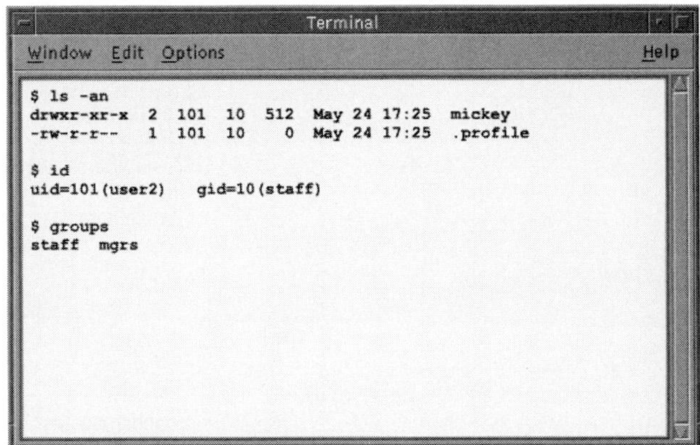
Terminal
Window Edit Options Help
$ ls -an
drwxr-xr-x 2 101 10 512 May 24 17:25 mickey
-rw-r-r-- 1 101 10 0 May 24 17:25 .profile
$ id
uid=101(user2) gid=10(staff)
$ groups
staff mgrs

Figure 10-10
Displaying the user identifier (UID) and group identifier (GID).

Process for Determining Permissions

Every system process is initiated by the operating system and also has a UID and GID, depending on who initiated the process. When a process (user) attempts to read, write to, or execute a file, the UID and GID of the process are compared to the UID of the file or directory and then to the GID. If neither matches, the other category of permissions is used. When a match is made, the permissions specified on the file or directory for that category of user (user, group, or other) are applied. The user ID and group ID of whoever is attempting to access a file or directory are compared to the allowable access list for the file or directory to determine whether the user should be permitted to perform the action.

The flowchart in Figure 10-11 illustrates the logic applied to determine whether a system process is allowed to access a file or directory. This flowchart is applied to a user attempting to perform an action such as viewing (**cat**) a file.

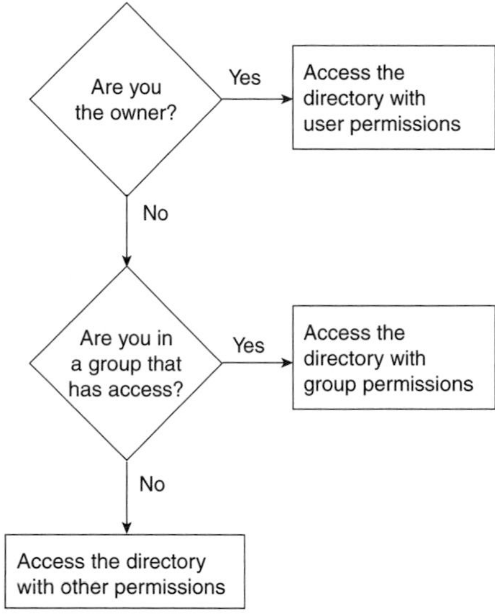

Figure 10-11
User attempting to view (**cat**) a file.

Default Permissions

When a user accesses the system, files and directories are protected by *default permissions*. These are put in place automatically when a file or directory is created. The default permissions for a new file are read/write for the user (owner) who created the file, and read for group and other. For directories, the default permissions are read/write/execute for the user and read/execute for group and other. Figure 10-12 shows the default permission for a new file created with the **touch** command and a new directory created with the **mkdir** command. The default size for a new directory is 512 bytes. A new empty file is 0 bytes.

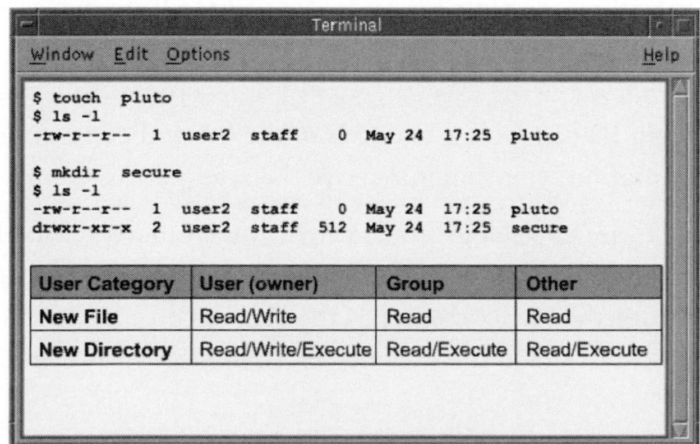

User Category	User (owner)	Group	Other
New File	Read/Write	Read	Read
New Directory	Read/Write/Execute	Read/Execute	Read/Execute

Figure 10-12
Default file and directory permissions.

Skill Builder

e-Lab Activity 10.2

Access Permission

In this e-Lab activity, you are logged in as user2, and your current working directory is /home/user2/dir2. Refer to the class file tree structure on the inside-front cover of this book. Type the commands that would accomplish the requested objectives. *Note:* Be sure to press Enter after each one. Click Step 1 to begin.

Skill Builder

Lab Activity 10.2.4

Determining File System Permissions

In this lab, you become familiar with file system permissions. You display permissions on files and directories, interpret the results, and evaluate the effect on various user categories. Refer to the *Cisco Networking Academy Program: Fundamentals of UNIX Lab Companion.*

Changing Permissions from the Command Line

File and directory permissions can be changed using the **chmod** (change mode) command or with the CDE File Manager. Normally, the default permissions for a file or directory will be adequate for most security needs. Sometimes you will want to change the permissions on a file or directory, though. By default, all files are created with permissions that allow the user category of others to read the file. This means that *anyone* with a login ID can see the contents of the file and copy it. For classified files and private information, you should remove the read permission from the others category.

Shell scripts are another example where you would want to change permissions. When you create a shell script file (or any file), the default permissions do not include execute, even for the owner/creator of the file. To run the shell script, you must change the permissions by adding the execute permission, as shown in the Figure 10-13.

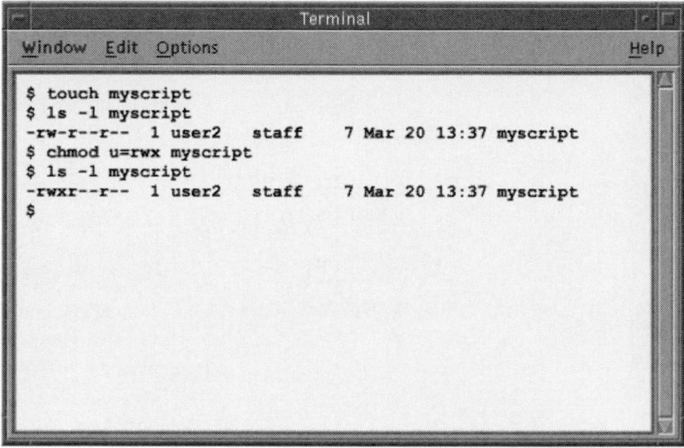

Terminal
Window Edit Options Help
$ touch myscript
$ ls -l myscript
-rw-r--r-- 1 user2 staff 7 Mar 20 13:37 myscript
$ chmod u=rwx myscript
$ ls -l myscript
-rwxr--r-- 1 user2 staff 7 Mar 20 13:37 myscript
$

Figure 10-13 Changing permissions.

The chmod Command

The **chmod** command is used by a file's owner (or superuser) to change file permissions. The two modes of operation with the **chmod** command are *symbolic (or relative)* and *octal* (or *absolute)*:

- *Symbolic mode*—Uses combinations of letters and symbols to add or remove permissions for selected categories of users. Symbolic mode also is referred to as relative mode.
- *Octal mode*—Uses octal numbers to represent file permissions and is used to set permissions for all three categories of users. Octal mode also is referred to as absolute or numeric mode.

Symbolic (Relative) Mode

When using symbolic mode to set permissions, you typically work with one category of users, although you can give all categories the same permissions simultaneously. The mode is referred to as relative because you are assigning or removing permissions relative to the ones that are already there. You can add one or more permissions to a specific category of users or take them away. The command format for symbolic mode is as follows:

```
chmod mode filename
```

The mode portion of the command format is made up of three parts, as explained here and shown in Figure 10-14:

- **Who**—Category of users you are working with (u, g, o, or a).
- **Op**—Operator or what you are going to do—for instance, set (=), remove (-), or give (+).

- **Permissions**—Permission(s) assigned—for instance, read (r), write (w), or execute (x).

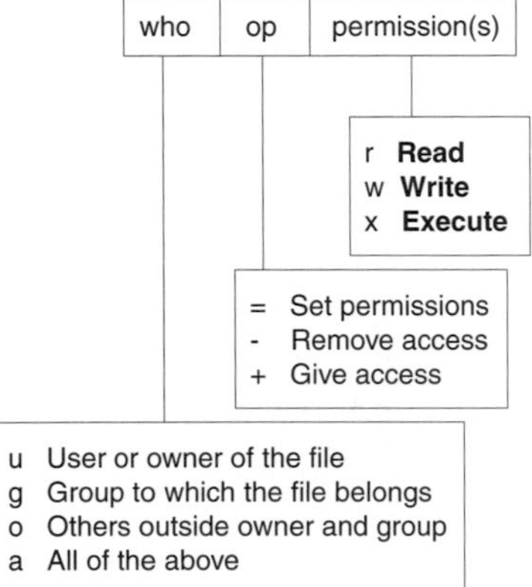

Figure 10-14 Symbolic mode parts.

Figure 10-15 shows several examples of assigning permissions using symbolic mode.

Figure 10-15 Changing permissions with symbolic mode.

Remove (deny) group read permission:

```
$ ls -1 dante
-rw-r--r--  1  user2  staff2  Jun 11  1:44  dante
$ chmod g-r dante
$ ls -1 dante
-rw-r--r--  1  user2  staff2  Jun 11  1:44  dante
```

Deny read permission to others:

```
$ chmod o-r dante
$ ls -1 dante
-rw-------  1  user2  staff2  Jun 11  1:44  dante
```

Add execute permission for owner, and read permission for group and others:

```
$ chmod u+x,go+r dante
$ ls -l dante
-rwxr--r--  1  user2  staff2  Jun 11  1:44  dante
```

Note: There is no space after u+x and before go+r, although there is a comma between them.

Set permissions to read and write for everyone:

```
$ chmod a=rw dante
$ ls -1 dante
-rw-rw-rw-  1  user2  staff2  Jun 11  1:44  dante
```

Skill Builder

e-Lab Activity 10.3

Changing Permission (Symbolic)

In this e-Lab activity, you are logged in as user2, and your current working directory is /home/user2/dir2. Refer to the class file tree structure on the inside-front cover of this book. Type the commands that would accomplish the requested objectives. *Note: Be* sure to press Enter after each one. Click Step 1 to begin.

Octal (Absolute) Mode

Octal mode provides a quick numeric means of changing permissions for all categories of users simultaneously, while still allowing each set of permissions to be different. This mode also is referred to as absolute because the permissions that you apply will explicitly replace the existing ones (even though they sometimes will be the same).

As previously discussed, there are three sets of permissions, one set for each category of users (user, group, and other). There are three possible permissions for each set (r, w, and x): Each set of permissions for a category of users can be assigned a numeric value (from 0 to 7), depending on which permissions are allowed. The mode is referred to as octal because there are eight possible values for each set of permissions.

By associating each of the three positions (permission types r, w, x) with a power of 2, each can be represented with a number. By adding the numbers, you can get a total that represents all three permissions for that category of user (user, group, and other). Figure 10-16 shows how this is accomplished using the first set of permissions (user) as an example (rwx). In this example, the user has read (r), write (w), and execute (x) permissions. If the permission is allowed, count the value in the total; if the permission is not allowed, then it is not counted.

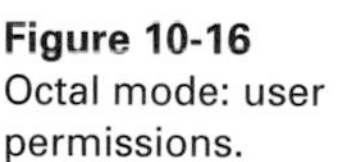

Figure 10-16
Octal mode: user permissions.

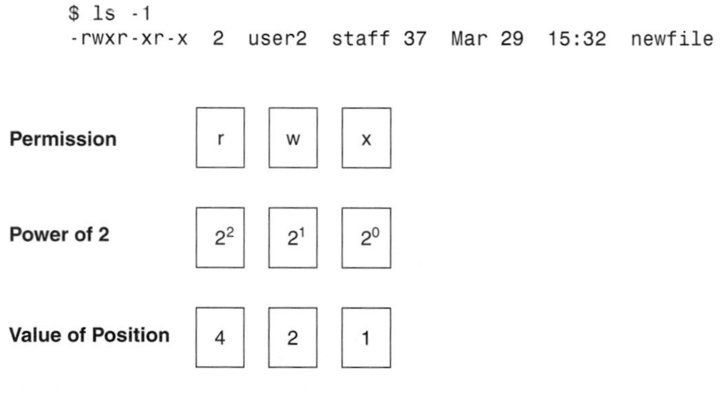

As shown in Figure 10-16, each set of three permissions can be represented by one number, from 0 to 7, by adding the values of the three positions. After adding the position values, associate/assign that value with the category of user (categories are user, group, and other). So, a 7 would be associated with the user category. Next, you could move on to group, add its values, assign that number to group, and finally move on to other and assign that number to other. When you have completed all three categories of users (user, group, and other), you will have a three-digit number representing the permissions for all three categories of users.

NOTE

When using octal mode with the **chmod** command, you must list all three numbers, one for each category: user, group, and others.

The command format for the octal method of changing permission is similar to that of the symbolic method. However, it is not necessary to specify the category of users because the position of each number represents the category. Figure 10-17 shows the value of each permission separately and the values of all possible sets or combinations of the three permissions. The octal mode is made up of three numbers, each of which is the sum of the three permissions for one of the user categories (user, group, and other). Octal values are combined to identify the octal mode that is used with the **chmod** command. The following shows the format for using the **chmod** command in octal mode with a file and then with a directory:

```
chmod octal_mode filename
```

or

```
chmod -R octal_mode directoryname
```

Figure 10-17
Octal values.

Octal Value	Permissions
4	Read
2	Write
1	Execute

Octal Value	Sum of Permission Category Values	Corresponding Permissions	Definition
7	4 + 2 + 1	r w x	Read, Write, and Execute
6	4 + 2 + 0	r w -	Read and Write
5	4 + 2 + 0	r - x	Read and Execute
4	4 + 0 + 0	r - -	Read only
3	0 + 2 + 1	- w x	Write and Execute
2	0 + 2 + 0	- w -	Write only
1	0 + 0 + 1	- - x	Execute only
0	0 + 0 + 0	- - -	No permissions

Some common examples of the combined octal values for all three categories are shown in Figure 10-18. The first octal value defines the user (owner) permissions, the second defines the group, and the last position defines others. Default permissions on files have an octal value of 644, and default permissions on directories have an octal value of 755. Most scripts and executable files have an octal value of 555.

Figure 10-18 Combined octal mode values and permissions.

Octal Value	Permissions	Notes
555	r-xr-xr-x	Standard permissions for executable UNIX commands such as **cat** and **pwd**.
644	rw-r--r--	Default permissions for file.
755	rwxr-xr-x	Default permissions for directories.
744	rwxr--r--	Typical permissions for user script file.
777	rwxrwxrwx	All permissions to everyone (open).

Figure 10-19 illustrates several examples using the **chmod** command to change permissions with octal mode. In the first example, the existing read and write (4 + 2 + 0 = 6) permissions are replaced by the read and execute permission (4 + 0 + 1 = 5). In the second example, the two number 7s represent all permissions for user and group (4 + 2 + 1), and the number 5 represents read and execute permissions for others (4 + 0 + 1), which remains unchanged. In the last example, the group permissions of read, write, and execute (4 + 2 + 1 = 7) are replaced with read and execute (4 + 1 = 5).

The –**R** option recursively changes permissions on directories and all files. This is a quick way to change the permissions on all subdirectories and files in a directory at once.

Figure 10-19 Changing permissions with octal (absolute) mode.

Give user, group, and others read and execute permissions:
```
$ ls -l dante
-rw-rw-rw-  1  user2  staff2  Jun 11   11:54  dante

$ chmod 555 dante
$ ls -l dante
-r-xr-xr-x  1  user2  staff2  Jun 11   11:54  dante
```

Change user and group permissions to include write access:
```
$ chmod 775 dante
$ ls -l dante
-rwxrwxr-x  1  user2  staff2  Jun 11   11:54  dante
```

Change group permission to read and execute:
```
$ chmod 755 dante
$ ls -l dante
-rwxr-xr-x  1  user2  staff2  Jun 11   11:54  dante
```

Skill Builder

e-Lab Activity 10.4

Octal Permission Conversion

In this e-Lab activity, you practice converting file permissions into octal mode.

TIP

The umask value applies to both files and directories. Users often calculate the umask for files without applying it to directories. In some cases, the umask is sufficient for files but is not desirable for directories. For example, a umask of 026 would result in file permissions of 640 and directory permissions of 751. A umask of 027 would result in the same file permissions (640) but directory permissions of 750, which would mean no execute permission for the directory. Refer to Figure 10-8 to realize the impact of having no execute permissions on a directory.

Skill Builder

e-Lab Activity 10.5

Changing Permissions (Octal)

In this e-Lab activity, you are logged in as user2, and your current working directory is /home/user2/dir2. Refer to the class file tree structure on the inside-front cover of this book. Type the commands that would accomplish the requested objectives. *Note:* Be sure to press Enter after each one. Click Step 1 to begin.

Skill Builder

Lab Activity 10.3.3

Changing Permissions from the Command Line

In this lab, you analyze and change UNIX file system security permissions using command-line utilities. Refer to the *Cisco Networking Academy Program: Fundamentals of UNIX Lab Companion*.

Changing Default Permissions with umask

As discussed earlier in this chapter, default permissions automatically are applied to new files (644) and directories (755). In most cases, the default permissions are adequate. In some cases, you might want to change the default permissions to create a group of files with different permissions. Your options are to create the files using default permissions and then changing permissions with the **chmod** command, or to use the **umask** command.

The **umask** command tells which permissions to withhold or "mask out" instead of specifying which permissions to grant, as you do with the **chmod** command. Execute (x) permissions are not considered when determining the umask, so you can't set the default permissions to include execute permissions for user protection.

The easy way to calculate the umask is to take 666 (rw-rw-rw-) for files and 777 (rwxrwxrwx) for directories, and subtract the desired new permission. For example, if the desired new permission for new files is 740, you would subtract 740 from 666 (omit negative numbers), resulting in a umask of 026. Put as a subtraction problem, it would look like this:

rw- rw- rw- (permissions start calculation with 666)

minus

rwx r-- --- (desired new file permissions 740)

equals

--- -w- rw- (calculated umask of 026)

Use the **umask** command to display and set the umask:

```
umask (displays current umask)
umask  umask_value (sets umask)
```

TIP

To return the umask to the original value, either use the **umask** command or log out and log back in again. The default umask on UNIX systems is 022.

Changes to the umask are lost when you log out of the system unless it is placed in the login initialization file (see Chapter 15 for more information).

Changing Ownership

When a file or directory is created, the owner (user) automatically is assigned. Only the owner (or superuser) of the file or directory can change the ownership using the **chown** (change owner) command.

When you change ownership of a file, you are no longer the owner and you may or may not be able to access the file even though it is in your directory. Because you are no longer the owner, group or other permissions will determine your access. The following shows the syntax for the **chown** command for a file and then for a directory:

```
chown new_owner filename
```

or

```
chown -R new_owner directoryname
```

Like the **chmod** command, the **–R** option recursively changes ownership on directories and all files. This is a quick way to change ownership on all files in a directory at once.

More on Groups

A user can belong to two types of groups:

- *Primary group*—Each user must belong to a primary group. A user's primary group is determined by the system administrator at the time the user account is created, and it is stored in the /etc/password file (see Chapter 2). The primary group is the group the operating system assigns to files and directories created by the user. The **chgrp** command (mentioned later) is used to change primary group ownership of a file.
- *Secondary groups*—Each user also can belong to between 8 and 16 secondary groups (depending on the version of UNIX), stored in the /etc/groups file.

TIP

If someone copies a file to your home directory, that person is still the owner. You can't use the **chown** command to make yourself the owner because only the owner can give up ownership. In most cases, there will be read permissions on the file allowing you to make a copy. When you copy a file, you are the owner of the file.

Some systems might be set up to prevent the use of the **chown** command for security reasons. If this is the case, contact your system administrator.

When a user logs on, that user obtains a primary group from the /etc/passwd file. Next, the /etc/groups file is scanned looking for the login name and any additional groups that the user belongs to. This enables a user to belong to several groups at the same time for file and directory access purposes.

Figure 10-20 shows how group membership is assigned when user2 logs on. In this example, the /etc/passwd file is read to determine the primary group (staff), and the /etc/groups file is read to determine that the user is also a member of the managers (mgrs) and the accounting (acctg) secondary groups. As a result, user2 will have permissions to any files and directories assigned to any of the three groups (primary or secondary).

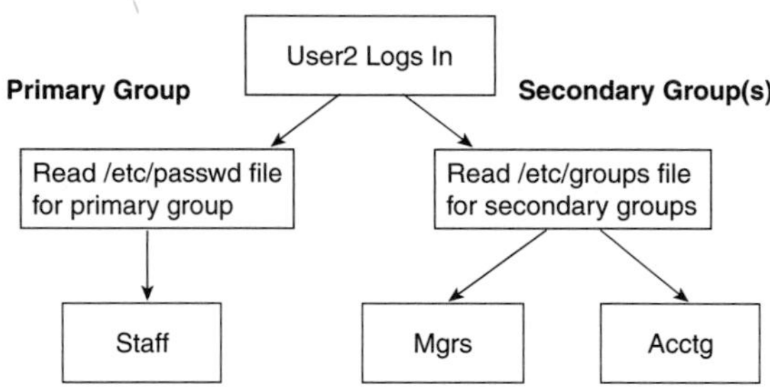
User2 Logs In
Primary Group
Secondary Group(s)
Read /etc/passwd file for primary group
Read /etc/groups file for secondary groups
Staff
Mgrs
Acctg
After logging in, User2 is a member of the staff primary group as well as the managers (mgrs) and accounting (acctg) secondary groups.

Figure 10-20
Primary and secondary groups.

UNIX HISTORY NOTE

Current group functionality came from BSD UNIX and was implemented in SVR4. When a user logged on prior to SVR4, that user could belong to only one group at a time—the primary group, by default. If a user needed to switch to another group temporarily, he used the **newgroup** command. A user could switch to only another group in which he was a member.

TIP

To determine your primary and secondary groups, use the **id –a** command (see Chapter 8, "Files and User Information Utilities") or the **groups** command.

Changing Group Ownership

When a file or directory is created, the user's primary group automatically is assigned. The owner (or superuser) can change the group that can access it using the **chgrp** (change group) command, as shown here:

```
chgrp new_group filename
```

or

```
chgrp -R new_group directoryname
```

Like the **chmod** command, the –**R** option recursively changes group ownership on directories and all files. This is a quick way to change the group ownership on all files in a directory at once.

Changing Permissions with File Manager

File Manager provides a graphical interface to view and change permissions for files and directories. You must have adequate permissions to change permissions.

Changing Properties

The CDE File Manager utility provides a graphical interface to the file system and can be used to view or change file and directory permissions. You can view and change the properties for a file or directory by selecting it from the File Manager window and then choosing Properties from the Selected menu (see Figure 10-21).

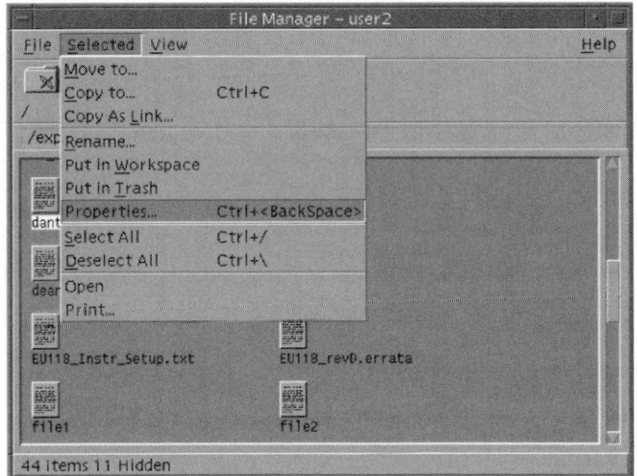

Figure 10-21
Properties from the Selected menu.

An alternate method is to right-click the file or directory and choose Properties from the menu displayed, as shown in Figure 10-22.

Figure 10-23 shows the Properties window for the dante file. Clicking the Information Category button enables you to view information about the file, such as file size and last modification date. Clicking the Permissions button enables you to view and change permissions. To change permissions for owner (user), group, or other, simply select the desired permission by clicking the check box. With this screen, you also can see the access control list for the file.

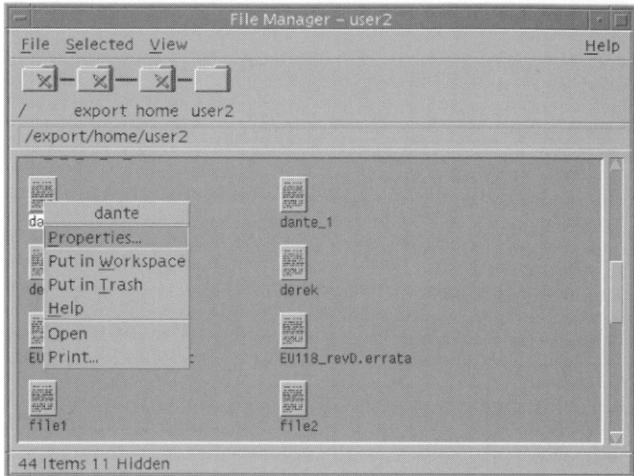

Figure 10-22
Properties by right-clicking.

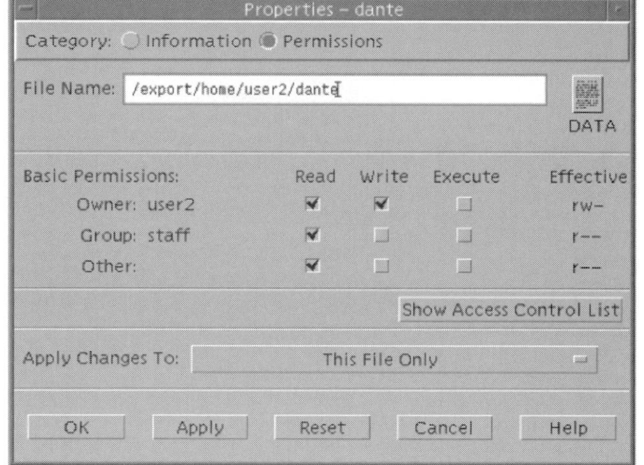

Figure 10-23
The Properties window.

When working with files, by clicking the Apply Changes To button, you have the option of applying the changes to the following:

- This file only
- All files in the parent folder
- All files in the parent folder and its subfolders

When working with directories, you have the options of applying changes to the following:

- This folder only
- This folder and its subfolders

Skill Builder

Lab Activity 10.4.1

Changing Permissions with File Manager

In this lab, you work with the Common Desktop Environment (CDE) File Manager to analyze and make changes to file system permissions. The CDE File Manager utility provides a graphical interface to the file system and can be used to view or change file and folder permissions. Refer to the *Cisco Networking Academy Program: Fundamentals of UNIX Lab Companion*.

Summary

Now that you have completed this chapter, you should have an understanding of the following:

- File system security is a key component of an overall network security policy. An overall network security policy should include the following:
  - — Physical equipment access security
  - — Login/password security
  - — File system security
  - — Virus protection
  - — Remote access security
  - — Internet firewall
  - — Data backups
  - — Disaster recovery plan
  - — Audits
- Files and directories are protected by access permissions. The **ls -l** (list long) command lists the permissions of a file or directory. These permissions are assigned to three user categories: user, group, and other. The user is the owner of the file or directory. Group is the primary group that the user belongs to, and other represents all other users.
- Three types of permissions can be applied to each file or folder, one set for each user category. These are read, write, and execute. Read protects a file but allows its contents to be viewed. Write allows the contents to be modified, and execute allows programs and shell scripts to be run. The meaning of permission types varies somewhat between file and directories.

- Permission can be changed from the command line by using the **chmod** (change mode) command. This command can be used in symbolic (relative) mode or octal (absolute) mode. Symbolic mode uses characters to represent the user category (u = user, g = group, o = other) and permission types (r = read, w = write, x = execute). Octal mode uses numbers from 0 through 7 to represent the permissions based on their total value of the permission for one of the three user categories.
- File and directory ownership can be changed using the **chown** command. Group ownership can be changed using the **chgrp** command.
- Users are always a member of a primary group defined by the system administrator. They also can be a member of other secondary groups.
- Permission also can be changed using the CDE File Manager utility. By selecting a file or directory and clicking Properties, you can view statistics for the file and view or change its permissions.

Check Your Understanding

1. File system security is part of an overall network security policy that includes other areas. Which of the following is another facet of the comprehensive security policy?
   - A. Weekly log rotation
   - B. Network performance review
   - C. Cable testing
   - D. Periodic audits
2. File- and directory-level security permissions are assigned to allow or disallow access by which objects?
   - A. User, superuser, and group
   - B. User, group, and other
   - C. Machine, group, and domain
   - D. User, team, and world
3. Each user category can be assigned three types of permissions to files and directories with the UNIX file system. When issuing the **ls –l** command, permissions are displayed in what order?
   - A. Read, write, and execute
   - B. Copy, modify, and delete
   - C. Execute, write, and read
   - D. View, change, and execute
4. For a user to be able to see the contents of a file and make changes to it, that user would need which permissions?
   - A. Read and change
   - B. Read and modify
   - C. Read and execute
   - D. Read and write
5. You have created a script file with the visual editor (vi), and when you try to run it, you are not successful. What could be the problem?
   - A. You do not have the run permission.
   - B. You do not have the execute permission.

C. You are not the owner of the file.

D. You must belong to the administrators group to run a script file.

6. A file has the following permissions: - r w x r - - r - -. Which of the following can the user category group do?

A. Execute the file

B. View the file

C. Change the file

D. Delete the file

7. Which set of permissions will allow the user to view, modify, and run a file, allow the group to view and modify the file, and allow others to view the file?

A. – r w – r w – r w -

B. d r w x r w – r w -

C. – r w x r w – r - -

D. – r - - r w – r w x

8. Using symbolic mode, which command would give group execute permission?

A. **chmod g+x filename**

B. **chmod u+e filename**

C. **chmod g-e filename**

D. **chmod o+e filename**

9. Which command would grant read, write, and execute permissions to a user, read and write permission to a group, and read permission to others?

A. **chmod 742 filename**

B. **chmod 764 filename**

C. **chmod 754 filename**

D. **chmod 731 filename**

10. File Manager can be used to set permission on files using which option from the Selected menu?

A. Attributes

B. Permissions

C. Rights

D. Properties

UNIX Command Summary

chgrp Changes the group association of a file. The group might be either a decimal group ID or a group name found in the group ID file /etc/group. Example:

```
-R

$ chgrp marketing chap15

$ chgrp -R engineering cad_dwgs.dir
```

chmod Changes file or directory permissions. Example:

To deny execute permission to everyone:

```
$ chmod a-x filename
```

To allow only read permission to everyone:

```
$ chmod 444 file1
```

To make a file readable and writeable by the group and others:

```
$ chmod go+rw file2
```

chown Changes the owner of a file. The owner might be either a decimal user ID or a login name found in the /etc/passwd file. Example:

```
-R

$ chown bradj chap15

$ chown -R jiml book.dir
```

groups Displays all the groups that a user is a member of. Example:

```
$ groups user1 user2
user1 : staff
user2 : staff
```

Key Terms

Default permissions The permissions that are assigned automatically when a new file or directory is created.

Group Identifies the users associated with a file. A user group is a set of users who have access to a common set of files. User groups are defined in the /etc/group file and are granted the same sets of permissions.

Mode The permissions that currently are set for a file or directory. The mode can be changed using the **chmod** command.

Octal (absolute) mode Method of setting permissions that uses numbers to represent file permissions and is used to set permissions for all three categories of users at the same time. Octal mode also is referred to as absolute or numeric mode.

Owner The user who creates a file or directory. A different user can be made the owner of a file or directory using the **chown** (change ownership) command.

Permission category Category or class of users: *User (owner):* The user who created or owns the file or directory. *Group:* Group of users defined by the system administrator. *Other (public):* All other users (other than user or group).

Permissions Attributes of a file or directory that specify who has read, write, or execute access.

Primary group Each user must belong to a primary group. A user's primary group is determined by the system administrator at the time the user account is created, and it is stored in the /etc/password file.

Secondary group Each user also can belong to between 8 and 16 secondary groups (depending on the version of UNIX), stored in the /etc/groups file.

Symbolic (relative) mode Method of setting permission that uses combinations of letters and symbols to add or remove permissions for selected categories of users. Symbolic mode also is referred to as relative mode.

Umask The system setting that determines what the default permissions will be for newly created files and directories. The umask can be changed using the **umask** command.

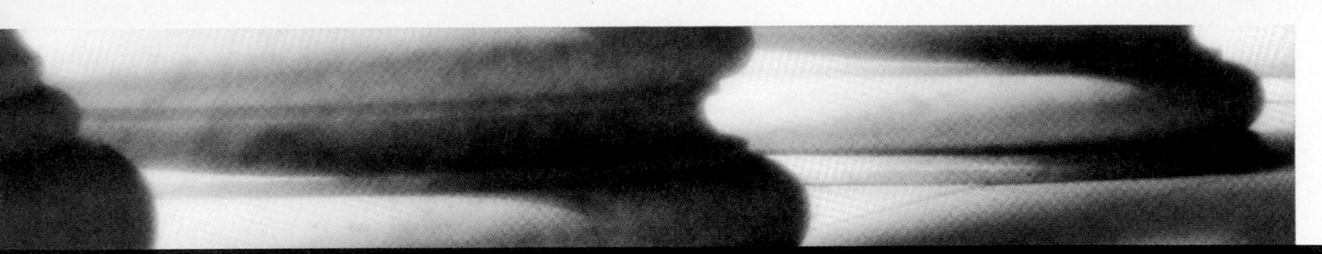

Objectives

After reading this chapter, you will be able to

- Describe the components of the UNIX printing environment
- Perform command-line printing using the **lp** command
- Manage print queues using the **lpstat** command
- Use the CDE Print Manager to print files and manage print queues

UNIX Printing

Introduction

Printing services are an essential component of any network operating system. UNIX provides local and remote printing capabilities. In this chapter, you learn about the various hardware and software elements that provide printing services in the UNIX environment. You work with several methods of printing, including printing from the command line and from File Manager. You learn how to determine the status and availability of network printers that you can print to. Monitoring the print queue status and managing print requests using UNIX commands and CDE Print Manager also are covered.

The UNIX Printing Environment

All network operating systems must provide users with the capability to print to local and remote *printers*. With the UNIX printing environment, users can have local printers attached to their workstations and also can print to remote network printers.

Three main components exist in the UNIX printing environment:

- **Printer**—A physical printing device. The printer can be attached to a workstation or network server using a parallel cable or, in some cases, a serial cable, as with plotters. Network printers have an Ethernet or other network interface card (NIC) built in, and they are very common in the business environment. These can be attached directly to a networking concentration device such as an Ethernet hub or switch. A cable such as Category 5 (CAT 5) unshielded twisted pair (UTP) typically is used. Printers can be reserved for use by a particular user or can be centralized to provide access for many users. In Figure 11-2, Local Printer1 and Network Printer3 are attached by parallel cables to computers. Network Printer2 is connected directly to the Ethernet switch via a cable, as are the computers themselves.

- **Printer name (queue)**—The name of a print queue associated with the physical printer. It is a logical name for the printer, which is assigned by the system administrator. This is the name that the users print to. A name such as hplaser1 describes a particular type of printer, and this is the first one installed. A name such as acctg1 might be used to refer to the first printer in the accounting department. A printer description also can be included when defining a printer to specify its location or other characteristics. A print queue is a directory on the hard disk of a ***print server***, which is the computer where print requests from users are stored.
- **Print server**—The computer that manages incoming print requests and releases them as the printer is ready. Print servers run the printer daemon lpsched, which manages print requests. The print queue is located on the hard disks of the print server. Print requests or print jobs are stored on the hard disk until they are printed, and then they are deleted or purged. A print server can be a workstation or a network server. Printers that are attached to a workstation typically use the workstation as the print server and keep the queue with its print requests locally. Printers that are attached to a network server or are attached directly to the network typically use a network server as the print server, and requests from many different users are processed centrally. Centralized print servers can handle multiple printers and queues.

The system administrator sets up the printing environment by installing printers and defining print queues and servers to support them. The system administrator manages the printing environment. The administrator can control the availability of printers, define default printers, and decide who can print to which printers. The administrator also can manage the print queue for each printer, which is the list of jobs waiting to be printed. Figures 11-1 and 11-2 show the process and major components for printing within the UNIX environment.

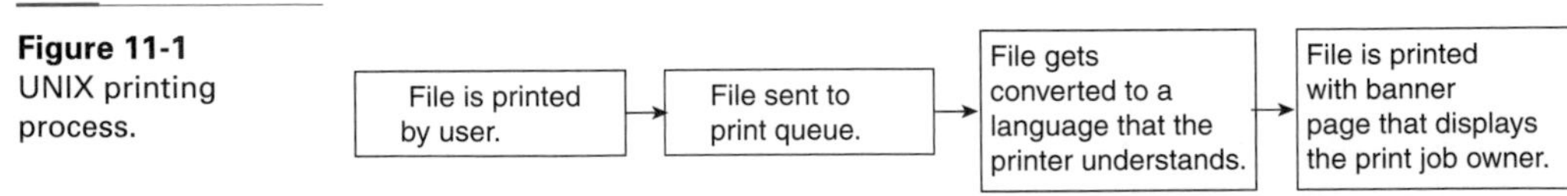

Figure 11-1 UNIX printing process.

Figure 11-2 UNIX printing environment components.

Printer	Physical printing device
Printer Name	Name of the print queue associated with the printer
Print Server	Workstation or server providing printing services

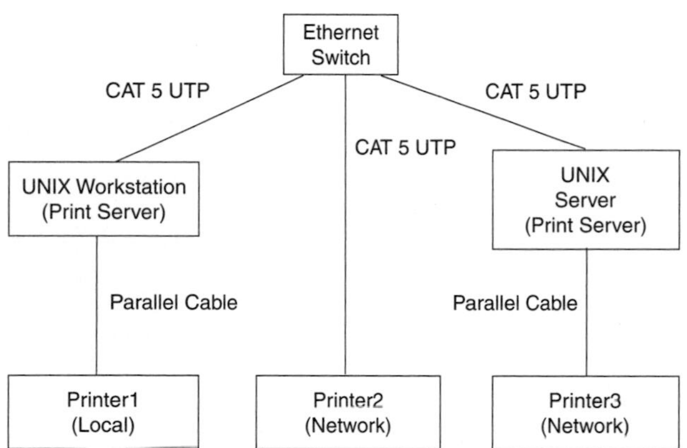

The Printing Process

When you send a print request to a printer, you actually are sending it to a print queue. The print queue is a special directory that is stored on the hard disk of your workstation or on a remote network server. All requests or print jobs go to the queue first. If the printer is available, the request is serviced immediately. If the printer is busy, the request is queued until the printer is available. Every printer, whether attached to a computer or attached directly to the network, must be serviced by a print queue that is located on a computer. Printers do not have hard disks or the capability to store print requests.

Figure 11-3 illustrates the process that a print request goes through to be printed. In this case, the user at the UNIX workstation is printing a document to network printer Printer2 whose print server is the UNIX server. The user's print request must first go through the Ethernet switch to the UNIX server's print queue. The UNIX server sends it back through the switch to the network-attached printer when the printer is ready for it. The user also could print to the local printer, if desired, in which case the user's workstation acts as the print server.

Command-Line Printing

Printing ASCII text or PostScript files can be done from the command line using the **lp** (line printer) print *spooler* command. Do not use this method to print data files (files created in applications such as FrameMaker or Sun's Star Office) or binary files. The function of the **lp** command is to queue data for printing. The Berkeley version of

UNIX uses a variation of the **lp** command known as **lpr print spooler.** The Solaris computing environment supports the **lp print spooler.** The syntax of the **lp** command is shown here. Figure 11-4 shows the options available for use with the **lp** command.

```
lp [ -options ] [ filename(s) ]
```

TIP

BSD UNIX and Linux systems use the **lpr** command. Solaris supports both **lp** and **lpr** (/usr/ucb/lpr) print commands. A comparison of System V and BSD print commands can be found in Table 11-1.

To receive a system-generated e-mail after the print job is complete, use the **lp -m** *[filename(s)]* command. This is useful if the print queue is full and you want to be notified only when the print job is available for pickup.

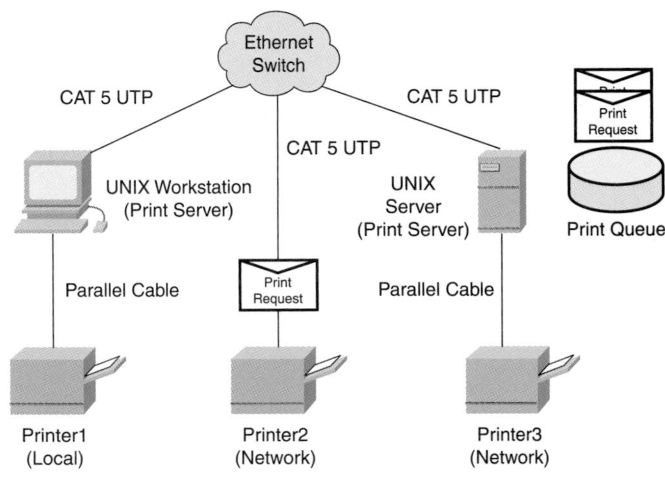

Figure 11-3 The print request process.

Table 11-1 System V and BSD/Linux Print Command Comparison

Function	System V	BSD/Linux
Print file1 to default printer	lp file1	lpr file1
Print file1 to the hplaser printer	lp –d hplaser file1	lpr -Phplaser file1
Print file1 with no banner page	lp -o nobanner file1	lpr -h file1
Print two copies of file1	lp –n 2 file1	lpr -#2 file1
Print file1 and notify by mail when finished	lp -m file1	lpr -m file1
Check the print queue	lpstat	lpq
Check the print queue of the hplaser printer	lpstat -d hplaser	lpq -Phplaser
Cancel a print job	cancel [job #]	lprm [job #]
Cancel all print jobs owned by you	cancel -u [username]	lprm -

Figure 11-4
Print spooler options with **lp**.

Option	Meaning	Purpose
-d	Destination	Specifies the desired printer. (If you are printing to your default printer, the -d option is not necessary).
-o nobanner	Option	Specifies that banner page is not to be printed.
-n	Number	Prints a specified number of copies.
-m	Mail	Sends mail message to user after job is complete.

Sending Files to a Printer

Figure 11-5 shows some examples using the **lp** command with various options to print files. The first example sends a file from the user's home directory (~) to the default printer, which is printer1. An administrator must set up the default printer in advance. The –7 after the printer name indicates that this is the seventh print job received since the printer came online. Although this example prints only one file, it is possible to send multiple files simultaneously to the printer, and wildcard metacharacters such as * and ? also can be used.

Figure 11-5
Using the **lp** command to print.

Print the file feathers in your home directory on the default printer:
```
$ lp ~/feahers
request id is printer-7 (1 file(s))
$
```

Use the **-d** option to specify another printer (if one is available):
```
$ lp -o nobanner ~/feathers
request id is printer 1-9 (1 file(s))
$
```

Use the **-m** option to send mail to a user:
```
$ lp -m dmyers@xyz.com ~/feathers
request is is printer 1-9 (1 file(s))
$
```

Use the **-n** option to specifies the number of copies:
```
$ lp -n 3 ~/feathers
request id is printer 1-9 (1 file(s))
$
```

Printing Banner Pages

By default, a sheet called a *banner page* is printed before every print job. A banner page identifies who submitted the print request, the print request ID, and when the request was printed. Banner pages make it easy to identify the owner of a print job, which is especially helpful when many users submit jobs to the same printer. Printing banner pages uses more paper and might not be necessary if a printer has only a few users or if a printer has special paper or forms where a banner page is undesirable.

To submit a print job without a banner page, use the following command:

```
lp -o nobanner filename(s)
```

Skill Builder

e-Lab Activity 11.1

Using the **lp** Command

In this e-Lab activity, you are logged in as user2, and your current working directory is /home/user2/dir2. Refer to the class file tree structure on the inside-front cover of this book. Type the commands that would accomplish the requested objectives. *Note:* Be sure to press Enter after each one. Click Step 1 to begin.

Locating Your Printout

The system administrator assigns a default printer for each user. The default printer name can be displayed with the **lpstat –d** command. However, that will tell you the name of the printer, but not the location of the printer. In small organizations, this is not a problem. In larger organizations, you might have to ask where the [printer name] printer is located so that you can pick up your print job.

Managing Printer Queues

As mentioned earlier, when you use the **lp** command to send a print request to a printer, you actually are sending it to a print queue. The *printer queue* is a special directory that is stored on the hard disk of your workstation or of a remote network server. Because printers do not have hard disks to store documents, all requests or print jobs must be spooled or go to the queue first. If the printer is available, the request is serviced immediately. If the printer is busy, the request is queued until the printer is available. On large networks with centralized printers, print queues can become quite large, with many print jobs waiting to be printed. An administrator can monitor and manage the print queues for multiple printers.

The **lpstat** (line printer status) command (**lpq** on BSD systems) displays the status of the printer queue. To see the print requests for a specific printer, use the basic form of the command, which specifies the *printer name* or queue to display. The basic command and an explanation of the output are shown in Figure 11-6. Figure 11-7 shows the options available with the **lpstat** command, and Figure 11-8 shows examples using the command.

Figure 11-6
lpstat command format.

```
lpstat  [ -options ]

$ lpstat staffp

staffp-2  user2  551  Dec 10  16:45
staffp-3  user3  632  Dec 10  16:47
```

Figure 11-7
Print queue options with **lpstat**.

Option	Meaning	Purpose
Printer name	Name of printer (queue)	Displays requests for a specific printer's queue.
-p	Printers	Displays status of all printers.
-o	Output (or Outstanding)	Displays status of all output or outstanding print requests sent to any printer.
-d	Default	Displays which printer is the system default.
-t	Tell All	Displays complete status information for all printers.
-s	Summary	Displays a status summary for all Printers configured on your system.
-a	Accepting	Displays which printers are accepting requests.

Print Process Management-Control Points

When a file gets printed, it is first placed in the queue, as discussed previously. When the current print job is finished, the print daemon sends the next request from the queue to the printer. Thus, two control points are available to the administrator to manage the print process: entering the queue and exiting the queue (see Figure 11-9).

Entering the Queue

The administrator usually rejects requests if the printer is to be removed or moved to another location. This stops the queue from accepting any new requests. Existing queued requests will continue printing as long as the printer is enabled. A good administrator will specify a reason for rejecting further requests, and the reason is displayed in the **lpstat – a, –p** or **-t** output. If the printer is accepting requests, the message "destination [printer name] accepting requests" is displayed.

Figure 11-8
Using **lpstat** to check print queue status.

Displaying the status of all of your default printer output requests:
```
$ lpstat
printer1-7    user2  391  Dec 10  16:30  on  printer1
printer1-12   user2  649  Dec 10  16:41  on  printer1
```

Displaying the status of all of your output requests (any printer):
```
$ lpstat -o
printer1-7    user2  391  Dec 10  16:30  on  printer1
staffp-2      user2  551  Dec 10  16:45  filtered
```

Displaying requests on a specific printer's queue:
```
$ lpstat staffp
staffp-2      user2  551  Dec 10  16:45
staffp-3      user2  632  Dec 10  16:47
```

Determining the status of all configured printers:
```
$ lpstat -s
scheduler is running
system default destination: printer1
system for printer1: venus
system for staffp: mars
printer1 accepting requests since Wed May 6 08:20:00 EST 1998
staffp accepting requests since Mon May 25 09:43 EST 1998
```

Determining which printers are configured on your system:
```
$ lpstat -s
scheduler is running
system default destination: printer1
system for printer1: venus
system for staffp: mars
```

Displaying which printers are accepting requests:
```
$ lpstat -a
scheduler is running
printer1 accepting requests since Thu Mar 22 15:57:02 PST 2001
staffp accepting requests since Mon May 25 09:43 PST 1998
```

TIP

Knowing how the print queue works will enable you to print smart. Before printing, check the queue of the destination printer for the following:

- Is the printer "accepting requests"?
- Is the printer "enabled"?
- Does the queue contain any (or few) requests?

If all of these conditions exist, then print to the printer. Otherwise, check the queue of other printers until you find one that can process your print request quickly. Then, using the **lp -d** command, print to that printer.

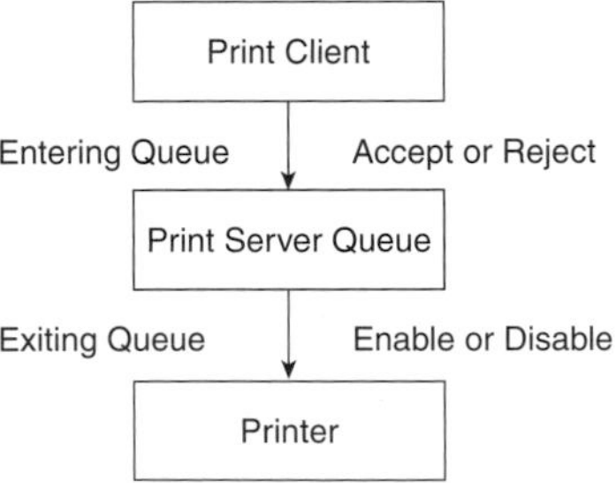

Figure 11-9
Print process control points.

Exiting the Queue

The administrator usually disables print requests when the printer needs to be taken offline for short-term maintenance. Even though print jobs in the queue are not being printed, the queue still is accepting requests and can become backed up. A good administrator specifies a reason for disabling a printer, and the reason is displayed in the **lpstat – a, –p** or **-t** output. If the printer is enabled and printing jobs in the queue, the message "printer [printer name] enabled" is displayed.

Canceling a Print Request

Sometimes you will want to remove a print request from the print queue. This can occur if you accidentally print the wrong document, especially if it is lengthy. You also might have to remove a request if you accidentally schedule a print request for something that you already printed out. In either case, if the print job is still in the print queue, you can cancel it before it prints.

You can cancel only those print requests that you have initiated. You cannot remove another user's print requests. Only the system administrator can cancel print jobs for other users. The **cancel** command (**lprm** on BSD systems) enables you to cancel print requests previously sent with the **lp** command. To do this, you must first use the **lpstat** command to identify the request ID. Figure 11-10 shows an example using the **lpstat** command to find the request ID and then the **cancel** command to delete the print request from the queue. If you cancel a print job, it does not affect the request ID numbers of the other jobs still in the queue. To cancel a print request, use the format shown here:

```
cancel request-ID
```

Figure 11-10 Canceling a print request.

Use the **lpstat** command to determine the request ID:

```
$ lpstat staffp
staffp-2   user2  551  Dec 10  16:45  on  staffp
staffp-3   user3  632  Dec 10  16:47  on  staffp
```

Use the **cancel** command to remove the print request on all printers:

```
$ cancel staffp-3
request "staffp-3" cancelled
$
```

Use the cancel -u username (login ID) to remove all requests owned by you:

```
$ cancel -u user2
request "staffp-2" cancelled
```

Skill Builder

e-Lab Activity 11.2

Using the **lpstat** and **cancel** Commands

In this e-Lab activity, you are logged in as user2, and your current working directory is /home/user2/dir2. Refer to the class file tree structure on the inside-front cover of this book. Type the commands that would accomplish the requested objectives. *Note:* Be sure to press Enter after each one. Click Step 1 to begin.

Skill Builder

Lab Activity 11.3.2

Command Line Printing

In this lab, you work with UNIX printing commands to send jobs to printers and manage print queues. Refer to the *Cisco Networking Academy Program: Fundamentals of UNIX Lab Companion.*

Using CDE Print Manager

Print Manager is a graphical tool for managing print queues, and it performs many of the same functions as the **lpstat** command. To activate Print Manager, click the Printer icon on the Front Panel. Figure 11-11 shows the Printer Jobs window, which displays a list of the current printers. Double-clicking the printer icon shows any outstanding print requests in the print queue, as shown in Figure 11-12. Only one printer icon is displayed in the Printer Jobs window. This represents the printer chosen by the user (which might or might not be the same as the system default printer).

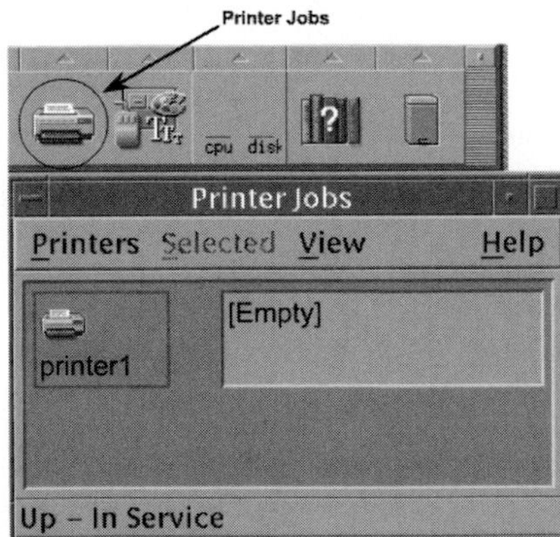

Figure 11-11
Printer jobs.

Viewing Printer Properties

When the printer icon is selected, you can display the properties of your default printer by choosing the Selected menu and then the Properties menu option. A window appears that provides details regarding that printer. You can change the label name associated with the printer using the Printer Properties window. In addition, if the printer has been disabled or there is a problem with the printer, this window will display information regarding the problem. (See Figure 11-13.)

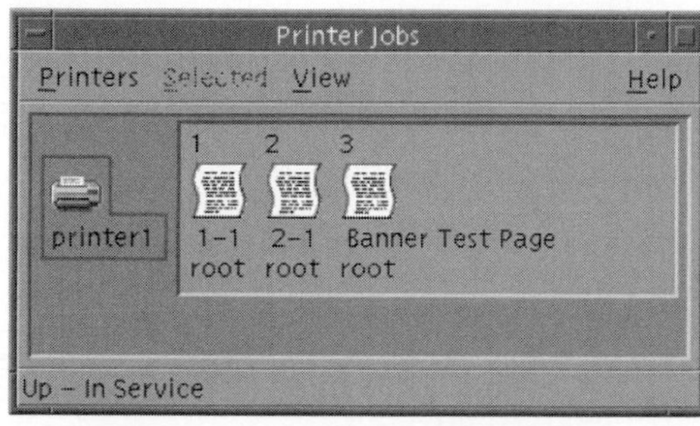

Figure 11-12 Outstanding print requests.

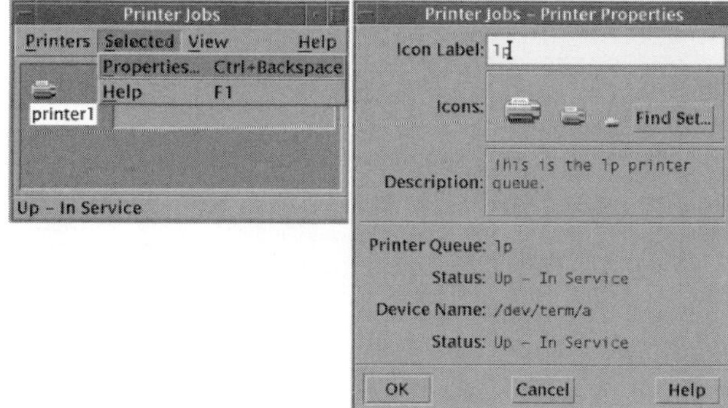

Figure 11-13 Viewing printer properties.

Setting Printer Job Options

From the View menu, select the Set Options menu choice, which enables you to configure how the print queue requests are displayed. See Figure 11-14. You also can set the time interval that the Print Manager uses to check the current print queue.

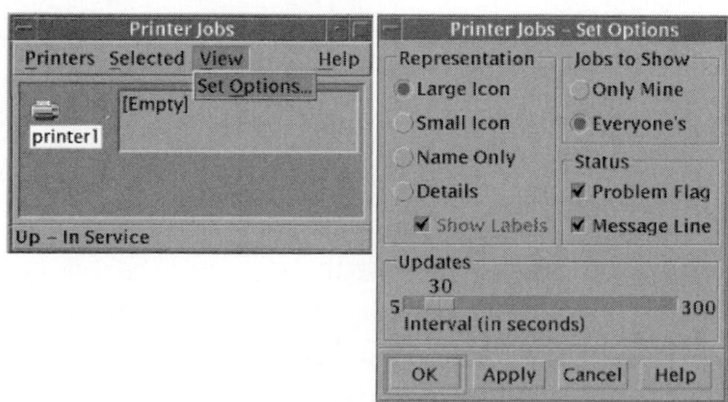

Figure 11-14 Setting printer job options.

Printing from the File Manager

You can print a file from the File Manager window by dragging and dropping it on the Print Manager icon or dropping the object directly into the Print Manager Printer Jobs window, as shown in Figure 11-15. After the file object has been dropped into the Print Jobs window, another window is displayed in which you can do the following:

- Designate an alternative printer to print the file
- Designate the number of copies of the file to be printed
- Set a banner title (which will be displayed in the Print Manager window alongside the print object)
- Select specific pages to print
- Designate which UNIX print command options should be used as an alternative to the default print command

After the Print button is selected, the file is sent to the appropriate printer queue.

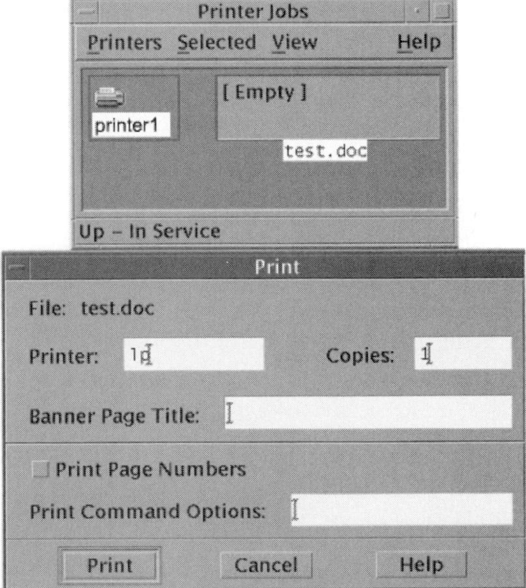

Figure 11-15 Printing from the File Manager.

Displaying the Banner Page Title

When a banner page title has been entered for a print request, that text is displayed in the Print Manager window. The name of the user who submitted the print request is displayed below the banner text. (See Figure 11-16.)

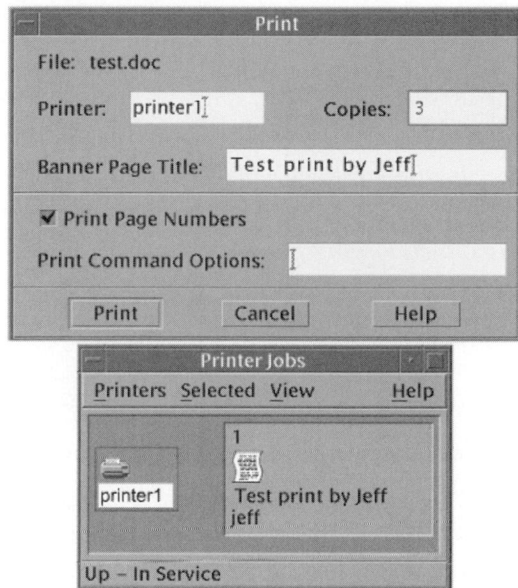

Figure 11-16 Displaying the banner page title.

Canceling a Print Request

To cancel a print request, you must first select the Print Manager display object corresponding to that print request. When the object has been selected, use the Selected menu's Cancel option. You are asked to confirm that you want to have the print request cancelled, as shown in Figure 11-17. Again, you can cancel only your own print requests. If you attempt to cancel another user's print job from the Print Manager, the print job will reappear in the printer queue.

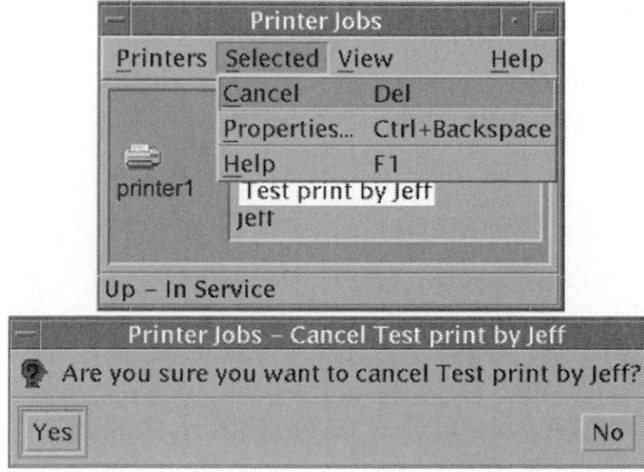

Figure 11-17 Canceling a print request.

Skill Builder

Lab Activity 11.4.3

Using the CDE Print Manager

In this lab, you work with the Common Desktop Environment (CDE) Print Manager and File Manager to control your printing environment. Refer to the *Cisco Networking Academy Program: Fundamentals of UNIX Lab Companion.*

Summary

Now that you have completed this chapter, you should understand the following:

- Printing to local and remote printers is an essential function in a work environment. There are three main components in the UNIX printing environment: the printer (physical device), the printer name (print queue), and the print server (the computer that managers the print queue). The system administrator sets up the printing environment by installing printers and defining print queues and servers to support them. Printers can be attached to workstations, servers, or directly to a network hub or switch. The administrator sets up and manages the printing environment.
- When a user prints a document, a print request is generated. This request passes through the network to the print server that manages the print queue for the printer name that the user selected. The print server stores the documents on its hard drive temporarily and then forwards them to the physical printer when it becomes available.
- Understanding the print queue enables you to print smart by knowing whether the printer is accepting requests, is enabled, and has few print jobs in the queue.
- Files can be printed using the **lp** command from the command line or with the CDE File Manager. A number of options are available, including printer selection, banner output, and number of copies. With the File Manager, documents can be dragged with the mouse to the printer icon or Print Manager window to print them.
- Print requests residing in print queues can be viewed and managed using the **lpstat** command or with the CDE Print Manager. Users can see their outstanding requests in the queue and can remove them using the **cancel** command or with the graphical Print Manager utility. A user can cancel only his print jobs.

Check Your Understanding

1. The UNIX printing environment is made up of three main components. Which of the following is *not* one of these components?
   - **A.** Printer
   - **B.** Printer name
   - **C.** Print server
   - **D.** Printer hub
2. The user sends print requests to a logical printer name that is also known as which of the following?
   - **A.** Queue
   - **B.** Server
   - **C.** Switch
   - **D.** pname
3. Printers in a UNIX network can be attached to a workstation, server, or a switch.
   - **A.** True
   - **B.** False
4. Which command syntax would send a copy of the projstat document from you current directory to the default printer named hp3?
   - **A.** **lp -l hp3 projstat**
   - **B.** **print projstat**
   - **C.** **lp –o projstat hp3**
   - **D.** **lp projstat**
5. Which command syntax would send two copies of the projstat document to a printer named staff2, which is not your default printer?
   - **A.** **lp -n 2 -d staff2 projstat**
   - **B.** **lp -c 2 staff2 projstat**
   - **C.** **lp -n 2 projstat staff2**
   - **D.** **lp projstat c=2 d=staff2**

6. To print a document from the File Manager, you can click and drag it to the Print Jobs window in the Print Manager, or you can drag it to the printer icon on the front panel.
   A. True
   B. False
7. Which command syntax allows you to see an outstanding print request for a document named projstat document in the print queue for the printer named acctg2?
   A. **lpstat acctg2**
   B. **lpstat –d acctg2 projstat**
   C. **lpstat projstat d=acctg2**
   D. **lpstat projstat acctg2**
8. Which command syntax would allow you to see the status of all your outstanding output print requests?
   A. **lpstat -o**
   B. **lpstat –d**
   C. **lpstat -t**
   D. **lpstat -a**
9. Which command syntax displays a status summary for all printers configured on your system?
   A. **lpstat -s**
   B. **lpstat –d**
   C. **lpstat -t**
   D. **lpstat -a**
10. You just sent a print request to printer staff2. You realized that you have printed the wrong document and that it is also quite large. You do not want to tie up the printer and waste paper. What steps should you follow to remove this request from the queue using the command line?
    A. Use the **lp** command to determine the request ID, and then use the **cancel** command to remove the request from the queue.
    B. Use the **lpstat** command to determine the request ID, and then use the **cancel** command to remove the request from the queue.

C. Use the **lpstat** command to determine the document name, and then use the **cancel** command to remove the request from the queue.

D. Use the **lpstat** command to determine the document name, and then use the **remove** command to remove the request from the queue.

UNIX Command Summary

lp Submits print requests to a destination. Example:

```
-d, -o, -n, -m

$ lp ~/fruit2
request id is printer1-203 (1 file(s))
```

lpstat Displays information about the current status of the LP print service to standard output. Example:

```
$ lpstat printer1
printer1-106  root    587 Mar 22 16:06 on printer1
printer1-107  user2    85 Mar 22 16:10 on printer1
$
```

Key Terms

Print job number In the lp system, a number that automatically is assigned to each print request, known as a job.

Print Manager A graphical tool for managing print queues. It performs many of the same functions as the **lpstat** command. To activate the Print Manager, click the Printer icon on the Front Panel.

Printer A physical printing device. The printer may be attached to a workstation or network server, or it may contain a network interface card (NIC) and be attached directly to the network.

Printer name The name of a print queue associated with the physical printer. It is a logical name for the printer, which is assigned by the system administrator. This is the name that the users print to.

Printer queue A directory located in the hard disks of the print server. Print requests or print jobs are stored on the hard disk until they are printed, and then they are deleted or purged.

Print server The computer that manages incoming print requests and releases them as the printer is ready. Print servers run the printer daemon **lpsched**, which manages print requests. A print server can be a workstation or a network server.

Spool To spool items is to place them in a queue, each waiting its turn for some action, such as printing.

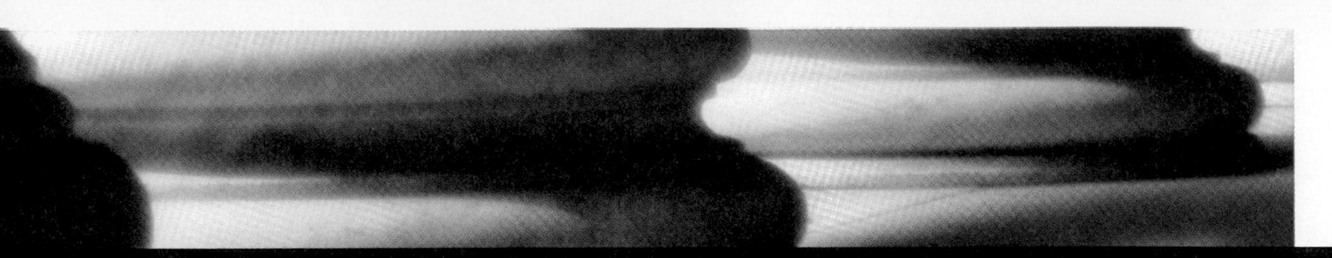

Objectives

After reading this chapter, you will be able to

- Describe the requirements and strategies for network backups
- Compare and contrast different backup methods and media
- Back up and restore files using the UNIX tar utility
- Use **compress** and **uncompress** to manage file space
- Use the **jar** command to perform backup and compression
- Describe the use of third-party backup programs
- Use the CDE graphical tools to back up, compress, and restore files

Chapter 12

Backing Up Data

Introduction

This chapter deals with one of the most important areas of network security and support: backing up and restoring data. *Backups* are another key component in a comprehensive security plan. This chapter covers the most common network and workstation backup strategies and then introduces the built-in UNIX backup utilities.

To back up or easily transfer files via e-mail, ftp, or another method, you need to be able to package and restore the files easily. In this chapter, you work with the tape archive (tar) and Java archive (jar) utilities to perform backups of data as well as restore data from backups. This chapter also covers the UNIX file compression utility and the use of the File Manager to perform basic backup tasks. In addition, specific instructions for backing up and restoring your home directory using tar and the **compress** command are included. Finally, the popular third-party compression programs gzip and zip are introduced.

The Importance of Backups

Good backups are critical to the health of a network. The value of a good backup system is most appreciated when it is needed in an emergency. When a system is down and data becomes unavailable, people cannot get their work done and companies cannot do business.

A well-managed network includes regular backups performed by a system administrator. Network administrators who do not have good backups or who are unable to *restore* data quickly might lose their jobs because of it. Having a good backup system and a tested restoration process can save an organization millions of dollars and thousands of hours in lost productivity.

Causes for Lost or Corrupted Data

Data can be lost or corrupted from a number of causes, as summarized in Figure 12-1 and discussed in the following sections.

Figure 12-1
Causes of data loss and corruption.

- Hard disk failure
- File corruption
- Malicious destruction
- Disasters
- Accidental deletion/overwrites

Hard Disk Failure

Disk drives (floppies, hard disks, and CDs) are the most likely components in a computer to fail because they are electromechanical devices (containing electrical and mechanical components) with moving parts that wear. Most other components in a computer, such as the CPU and RAM, are electronic with no moving parts.

When a hard drive fails, some or all of the data on the drive can be damaged or can become inaccessible. This is why fault-tolerant disk systems such as *Redundant Array of Independent Disks—Level 5 (RAID 5)* were developed for network servers. RAID 5 combines three or more drives as a group so that if one fails, the others take over. The bad drive can be replaced with no loss of service to the users. Another fault-tolerant technique, *RAID 1*, or mirroring, uses two drives, with the second drive storing the same data as the first. If one of the drives fails, the other takes over. A more robust version of RAID 1 that uses dual drive controllers as well as dual drives is known as *duplexing*. Fault-tolerant disk systems are the first line of defense in a solid backup strategy.

File Corruption

File corruption can occur as the result many things, including improper system shutdown, magnetic fields (from motors and other electrical devices) near the data, or an area of the disk going bad. In any case, the data becomes inaccessible. A good backup system will allow the administrator to find and recover a specific file or group of files that might be lost because of correction.

Malicious Destruction

Files also can be lost because of intentional destruction of data. File deletion can result from disgruntled employees, virus attacks, or hackers who can remotely access a system. Damage can vary from deletion of one or two files to the loss of all data on a hard drive.

Most virus attacks come from the Internet, and firewalls can help in some cases. Fortunately, not many viruses can infect UNIX systems, but this is not the case with most other network operating systems and desktop operating systems. For non-UNIX operating systems, virus-protection software can be installed to help detect and remove viruses before they can do damage. Firewalls also can help to prevent destruction of data from remote access hackers by detecting and blocking the attacks. Proper file permissions provide good protection in the case of a disgruntled employee deleting data. No amount of preventive measures can provide complete protection, and the best defense is having good backups of important data.

Disasters

Disasters such as fires and floods can destroy computers, data centers, and entire buildings. Chapter 10, "File System Security," discussed the importance of a disaster recovery plan. If a fire were to destroy a place of business, how would the company recover? How much would it cost per day or per hour to not be capable of doing business?

Backups are a big part of a disaster recovery plan. To get systems back up and running quickly, it is important to have good-quality, current backups of critical data. The backups also should contain copies of operating system and applications software so that they can be reinstalled, and these copies should be stored offsite at a nearby location.

Accidental Deletion/Overwrite

It is not uncommon for a user to accidentally delete a file. Files deleted from the command line cannot be recovered, except from a backup. If the file cannot be recovered from a backup, it might need to be recreated, causing lost productivity. Files deleted using the CDE File Manager can be recovered from the Trash Can.

Work also can be lost because of accidental overwrites. This occurs when a user makes a copy of a file and then makes substantial changes to it. The user then opens the original file and saves it over the one with changes. It is also possible to overwrite files when copying them from one location to another where the file already exists. When this occurs, the only way to recover the original file is from data backups.

Backup Methods

Several different backup types or methods can be compared, based on how long the backup takes and how easy it is to restore data. The three most common types of backups are full, incremental, and differential backups. All the methods discussed here assume that backups of critical user data to a tape drive occur daily. Alternatives to tape backup media are discussed later in the chapter. The operating system and applications software are not typically backed up because they can be reinstalled from the original media.

It is common to have a set of 5 to 7 daily tapes, 4 or 5 weekly tapes, and 12 monthly tapes. The daily tapes can be overwritten each week. The weekly tapes can be overwritten each month, and the monthly tapes usually are kept and are not overwritten. Weekly and monthly tapes should be kept offsite.

If the volume of data to be backed up requires multiple tapes, it might be necessary to install a larger-capacity tape drive or a tape-changing system. If not, it will be necessary for someone to be there when the first tape finishes and put in the next tape. Backup methods performed by organizations vary. However, all organizations take a number of factors into account when determining which method to utilize:

- The criticality of the data
- The amount of data to be backed up
- The time window available to do backups
- Funds available for a backup system

Loss of data can be just as damaging for a small business as for a large corporation. The backup system is not the place to cut costs. Figure 12-2 compares the three different backup methods, and Figure 12-3 shows the relationships between quantities of data backed up each day.

Figure 12-2 Comparison of backup methods.

Backup Method	Total Time to Backup	Ease of Restore	Number of Tapes Required to Restore if Hard Drive Fails on Friday Morning
Full	Longest	Simplest	1
Incremental	Shortest	Most Complicated	5
Differential	Moderate	Moderate	2

Full Backup

With *full backup*, all critical data is backed up daily. Every night after close of business, all data is backed up, whether it has changed or not. This method takes the longest and could require multiple tapes, depending on the amount of data. A larger-capacity drive or tape-changing system might be required if data volumes get too large.

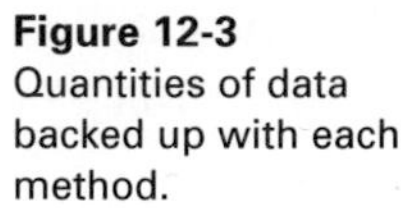

Figure 12-3 Quantities of data backed up with each method.

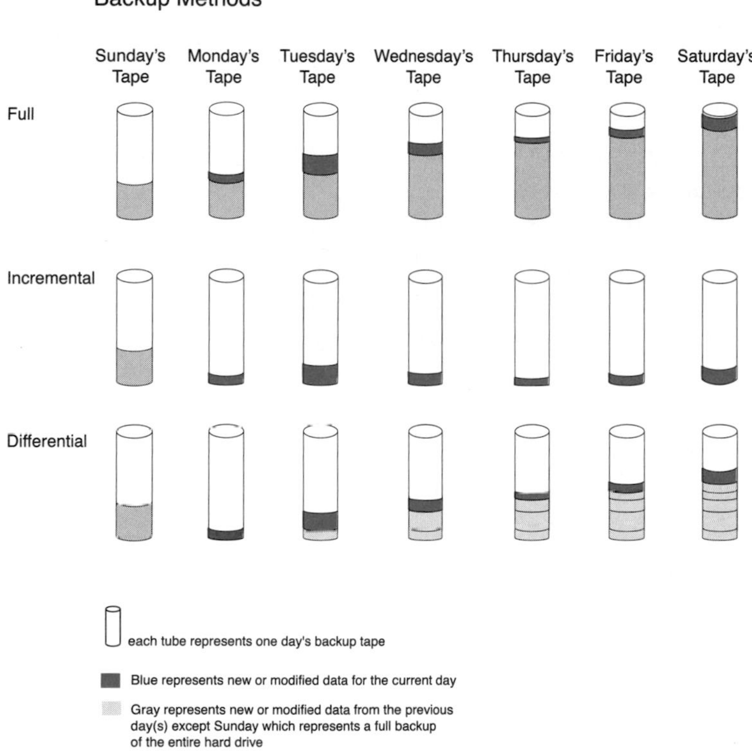

If an organization has a large volume of data or a short window of time to back it up, the full backup method might not work. However, it is the surest method because all data is backed up every day to one or more tapes. A full backup also can make it easier to find and restore data because it is usually all on one tape or a set of tapes for a given day. For purposes of comparison to the other methods, this chapter assumes that you can do a full backup on one tape.

Incremental Backup

With *incremental backup*, data is backed up in increments. All critical data is backed up once a week on a particular day (for example, Sunday in the evening). Each day after that, only the changes are backed up. The next backup on Monday will back up only new files or those that have changed since Sunday night. Tuesday's backup will back up only the new and changed files since Monday's backup. Wednesday's backup will get only the new and changed file since Tuesday's, and so on, until you get back to Sunday and then do another full backup. The Sunday night full backup creates the baseline backup and might take a significant amount of time, but the successive incremental backups on the weekdays will take much less time. The amount of data and the time that it takes to back up on each weekday varies depending on the number of new and changed files, but the time will be relatively small compared to the full backup.

With the incremental backup, each tape has a piece of the whole backup. As a result, the overall time required to back up the data is significantly less than doing a full backup each day. The disadvantage of the incremental backup is the number of tapes that it might require to rebuild the data. If a hard drive fails on Monday morning, the Sunday night backup tape will be the only tape needed to restore the data. However, if the drive fails on Friday morning, it will require Sunday's full backup tape plus Monday through Thursday's incremental backup tapes to fully restore the data. This means that you must successfully read and restore data from five tapes, any of which could have a problem. This results in a more complicated and time-consuming restoration process. Because incremental backups back up only a portion of the data each day to multiple tapes, a failure of any of the tapes will result in a corrupt backup. In other words, if you need five tapes to do the restore, the entire backup will be bad if any one of them cannot be read.

Differential Backup

With *differential backup*, you still do a full backup once a week (on Sunday). On Monday, back up anything that has changed since Sunday. On Tuesday, also back up anything that has changed since Sunday. On Wednesday, again, back up anything that has changed since Sunday, and so on. Monday's backup might not take much time because you are backing up only one day's worth of data (same as incremental), but every day after that the backup will take longer. On Saturday night, everything that has changed since last Sunday, which is six days' worth of data, is backed up.

The differential backup is a compromise between a full backup and an incremental backup. It takes less time than a full backup because you are not backing up all the data every night, but it takes more time than an incremental backup. If a hard drive fails and you need to restore all the data, it will take only two tapes. As an example, if the hard drive fails on Friday morning, you will need only the Sunday baseline tape and the Thursday night tape because the one from Thursday night's backup includes everything from Sunday night through Thursday night. This makes restoration a little easier than the incremental backup, but not as simple as the full backup.

Data Restoration Issues

All the backup methods discussed allows all critical data to be restored in the event of loss. The capability to restore data quickly is the true test of a good backup system. It is not enough to do nightly backups and not actually practice the restoration process.

Users typically are not required to back up their own files. This is the job of the network administrator or network support staff. The network support staff not only must do regular backups but also must test the backups periodically to verify that they are good and that they can restore data from them.

Backups should be checked regularly by conducting "test restores" to verify that the tapes are good and that the staff can perform the necessary steps to restore data under a variety of conditions. The time to verify the restore process is not when the hard drive fails and workers are wandering around with nothing to do and the boss is looking over your shoulder asking why it is taking so long.

To adequately test your capability to recover from data lost, the network support staff should be able to accomplish the following restoration tasks, which are summarized in Figure 12-4:

- **Restore a file**—Thousands of files typically are backed up in any organization. If a user accidentally deletes or overwrites a file, an administrator should be able to find that file on the backup tapes and restore it to the user's home directory on a server or on the workstation.
- **Restore a directory**—If a directory is damaged, an administrator should be able to restore the entire directory structure, with all subdirectories and files intact.
- **Restore a file system**—If necessary, an administrator should be able to restore an entire file system.
- **Restore a hard drive**—In the event of a total failure of a hard drive, an administrator should be able to re-create the contents of the original drive, including the operating system, applications software, and data, if applicable.

Figure 12-4
Restore capabilities.

- Restore a file
- Restore a directory
- Restore a file system
- Restore a hard drive

Magnetic Tape Backup Media

A number of different media options exist for backing up your data. They range from very low-capacity floppy disks to very high-capacity tape drives.

Streaming magnetic tape is the most common *media* for backing up large amounts of data. Tape drives are sequential recording devices, which means that the data is laid down in a stream of bits from one end to the other as the tape passes the magnetic read/write heads.

To locate a specific file on a tape, it must be rewound or advanced to the location where the file was recorded. This can take several minutes, depending on the speed of the drive and where the file is located. In spite of this, modern tape drives will continue to be widely used because they are efficient, they are cost-effective, and they serve as a proven backup solution.

Today's new technology tape drives are small and very fast, and they have very large recording capacities. The cost per megabyte for tape backup is the lowest of any recording media. A single tape about the size of a videocassette can record more than 100 GB (gigabytes, or billion bytes) of data with *compression*. Autoloader systems with multiple tapes can exceed that significantly.

Magnetic and Optical Disks

Although tape traditionally has been the media of choice, new forms of backup media are starting to become popular, including optical CD recordable (CD-R) disks and CD re-writeable (CD-RW) optical disks. Various forms of magnetic media, such as removable hard drives and Jaz and Zip disks, are also becoming more common. Most of these backup media are not intended to back up large volumes of data, but they are a flexible alternative that is very fast, and they can be treated as another disk drive on the computer.

Disk drives, whether magnetic or optical, have one characteristic in common: They are random-access devices. Instead of advancing or rewinding, as with tape, they can seek and find the desired file in a fraction of a second. This makes them flexible for backing up relatively small amounts of data (usually less than 1 or 2 GB). Writeable CD changers can handle very large amounts of data with maximum flexibility; however, they are relatively expensive. Figure 12-5 shows the variety of backup media available, and Figure 12-6 lists them in order of capacity.

Figure 12-5
Backup media.

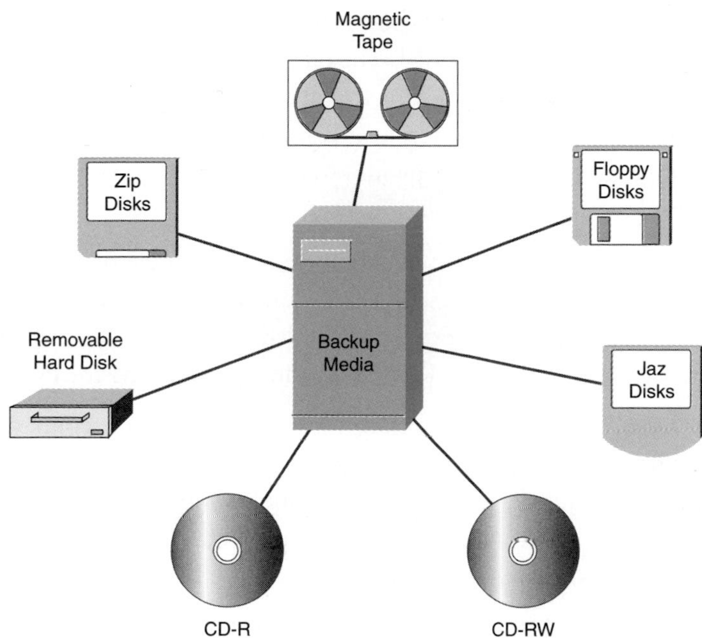

Figure 12-6
Comparison of backup media.

Backup Media	Media Type	Access Method	Capacity
Streaming Tape	Magnetic Tape	Sequential	High
Removable Hard Drives	Magnetic Disk	Direct Access	Med–high
Jaz Disk	Magnetic Disk	Direct Access	Low—medium
CD-R (CD Recordable)	Optical Disk	Direct Access	Low—medium
CD-RW (CD Read/Write)	Optical Disk		Low—medium
Zip Disk	Magnetic Disk	Direct Access	Low
Floppy Disk	Magnetic Disk	Direct Access	Very Low

Backing Up Files with tar

The UNIX operating system has several integrated utilities that allow multiple files to be backed up and compressed. The **tar** (tape archive) command enables you to back up single or multiple files in a directory hierarchy. The **tar** command is standard with all versions of the UNIX operating system. Although it originally was developed for use with tape drives, **tar** can copy files to other locations on the hard disk or to a floppy disk and other removable media.

The **tar** command can create an archive from a single file, but it primarily is used to combine multiple files, such as the contents of a directory, into a single file and then extract them later, if they are needed. By itself, it does not compress the files as it bundles them, like the PKZIP and WinZip programs for PCs.

The most frequently used options available with the **tar** command are **c, t,** and **x.** It is not necessary (but accepted) to precede these with a dash (-), as with other UNIX command options. The command syntax is shown here. Refer to Figure 12-7 for an example with an explanation of the syntax. Figure 12-8 shows the functions (letters and modifiers) that are used with the **tar** command.

```
tar function [modifier] [output file] filename(s)|directory(s)
```

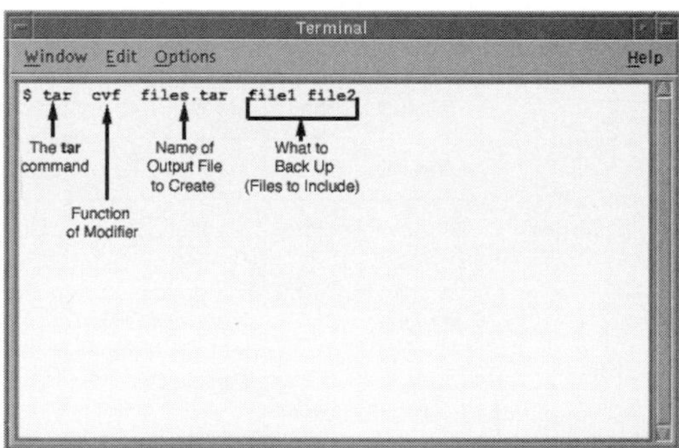

Figure 12-7 Command format example.

NOTE

When specifying the name of the output file to be created, be sure to specify a .tar extension so that tar files can easily be distinguished from others.

tar Functions

tar functions are one-letter characters used to create a tar file, view the contents of a tar file, or extract files from a tar file. These functions are summarized here:

- **c (create)**—Used to archive one or more files or directories to create an archive file.
- **t (table of contents)**—Used to see a table of contents of the tar file. This is a listing of the files that were combined to make the one tar file.
- **x (extract)**—Used to extract the file(s) from the archive and separate them into multiple files again. The tar file still exists after this is done.

Figure 12-8
tar command function letters.

Function Letter (Lowercase)	Meaning	Function Performed
c	Create (or combine)	Creates a new tar file.
t	Table of Contents	Lists the table of contents of the tar file.
x	Extract files	Extracts the specified files from the tar file.

Modifier Letter (Lowercase)	Meaning	Function Modified
f	Filename	Specifies the tar file to be created as either a file on the hard disk (/tmp/file.tar), or a device file for an output device (/dev/xxx) like a floppy disk, optical drive or tape drive.
v	Verbose	Executes in verbose mode.

Function Modifiers

tar function modifiers are one-letter characters used in conjunction with a function character when creating, viewing, or extracting from a tar file. The two most common function modifiers are summarized here:

- **f (file)**—Allows you to specify a tar file to create (**c**), extract from (**x**), or see the table of contents of (**t**).
- **v (verbose)**—Executes the command in verbose mode, which enables you to see the detailed results of the **tar** command as they occur.

Figure 12-9 illustrates some examples using the **tar** command. These are explained in greater detail in the Table 12-1.

Table 12-1 tar Command Examples

Modifier	Meaning	Function Modifier
f	Filename	Specifies the tar file to be created as either a file on the hard disk (/tmp/file.tar) or a device file for an output device (/dev/xxx) such as a floppy disk (/vol/dev/aliases/floppy0 in Solaris), optical drive, or tape drive (/dev/rmt0 in Solaris).
v	Verbose (view)	Execute in verbose mode. This mode allows you to view what the tar command is doing as it is copying, displaying the table of contents, or extracting to or from the backup file or device. This option normally is used with the c, t, and x tar options.

Figure 12-9
Using **tar** to create archives.

```
Archives the user2 directory to tape:
$ cd /home
$ tar cv user2
a user2/file1 2k
a user2/fruit2 1k
... (output omitted)
$

Archives the dir2 directory to a subdirectory for backup:
$ cd
$ tar cvf /home/user2/backup/dir2.tar dir2
a dir2/  0K
a dir2/beans/  0K
a dir2/recipes/  0K
a dir2/notes  2K

Archives selected files to hard drive:
$ cd
$ tar cvf files.tar file1 file2 file3
a file1  1K
a file2  1K
a file3  1K

View the table of contents of the archive file:
$ cd
$ tar tvf files.tar
-rw-r-r--   1002/10  512  mar 28  5:53  2001  file1
-rw-r-r--   1002/10  512  mar 28  5:53  2001  file2
-rw-r-r--   1002/10  512  mar 28  5:53  2001  file3

Archive selected files to floppy disk:
$ cd
$ tar cvf /dev/rdiskette file1 file2 file3
-rw-r-r--   1002/10  512  mar 28  5:53  2001  file1
-rw-r-r--   1002/10  512  mar 28  5:53  2001  file2
-rw-r-r--   1002/10  512  mar 28  5:53  2001  file3
```

- **Example 1**—Archives all files in the user1 directory to tape. If no filename (f) option is specified, the default output device is tape (/dev/rmt/0—Raw magnetic tape 0 is the first tape drive on a Solaris system. Device filenames vary between UNIX flavors).
- **Example 2**—Archives all files and subdirectories in the dir2 to a tar file called dir2.tar, and places it in the /home/user2/backup directory. If you refer to the class file tree, you will see that beans and recipes are subdirectories, whereas notes is a file. Any files in subdirectories also will be included in the resulting tar file.
- **Example 3**—Combines several files to create an archive file called files.tar in the default directory of the hard drive (usually your home directory).
- **Example 4**—Views the table of contents of the tar file in verbose mode, which displays the detail of the files including permission and size.
- **Example 5**—Archives three files to the floppy disk for backup.

TIP

To append another file(s) to an existing archive, use the –**r** option. For example, **$tar rvf files.tar newfile** adds (appends) the newfile to the existing files.tar archive file.

Skill Builder

e-Lab Activity 12.1

Archiving Files with **tar**

In this e-Lab activity, you are logged in as user2, and your current working directory is /home/user2. Refer to the class file tree structure on the inside-front cover of this book. Type the commands that would accomplish the requested objectives. *Note:* Be sure to press Enter after each one. Click Step 1 to begin.

Compressing Files

It is frequently useful to archive files that have not been used for a while and then compress them so they take up less disk space. It is also a good idea to compress files before transferring them to another UNIX user (that has the **uncompress** command) to save time. Any file, including those archives created with **tar**, can be compressed. Compression is a valuable tool because it reduces the amount of disk space that files occupy, while still keeping them readily available.

The **compress** command is used to compress files and is included with all versions of the UNIX operating system. The compress utility uses a special format to reduce the size of the file anywhere from 20 percent to 80 percent, depending on the type of file. If the compress utility determines that the file cannot be compressed or that there will be no reduction in file size, the file will remain unchanged. See Figure 12-10.

Figure 12-10
Compressing files.

```
List the files to determine the current file size:
$ ls -l bin.file
-rw-r--r--  1  user2  staff  57380  Mar 22  09:17  bin.file

Compress the file:
$ compress -v bin.file
bin.file: Compression: 53.81% -- replaced with bin.file.Z

List the files again to see the compressed size:
$ ls -l bin.file.Z
-rw-r--r--  1  user2  staff  26500  Mar 22  09:17  bin.file

Change to your home directory (/home/user2):
$ cd

Compress all files in the current directory beginning with da:
$ compress -v da
dante: Compression: 32.12% -- replaced with dante.Z
dante_1: Compression: 17.66% -- replaced with dante_1.Z
```

When files are compressed with the **compress** command, the existing file is replaced using the same name but with a .Z suffix appended. Note that this is an uppercase letter Z. Figure 12-10 shows an example of the **compress** command with the verbose (**-v**) option. This shows the name of the input (bin.file) and output files (bin.file.Z) and the amount of compression achieved. Use the **ls -l** (list long) command before compressing a file to see its original size in bytes, and then again afterward to see the compressed size. Multiple files can be compressed simultaneously, and wildcard metacharacters are supported. Compressed files are considered binary and can't be viewed with the **cat** or **more** commands.

```
compress option file1 file2
```

Uncompressing Files

The corresponding command used to reverse the effects of the **compress** command is **uncompress.** Files cannot be used in their compressed form, so it is necessary to use the **uncompress** command to restore them to their original size. The **uncompress** command is a UNIX utility and can be used only to uncompress files compressed with the UNIX compress command. Figure 12-11 shows an example of the **uncompress** command with the **v** (verbose) option. This allows you to see the results of uncompressed process.

NOTE

It is not necessary to specify the .Z extension with the uncompress command. This command can uncompress multiple files and support the use of wildcard metacharacters such as ? and *.

TIP

To view the contents of a compressed file without actually uncompressing it, use the **–c** option. For example, to view the contents of the june02bkup.tar.Z compress file, use the following command: **$uncompress –c** june02bkup.tar.Z | more.

Figure 12-11
Uncompressing files.

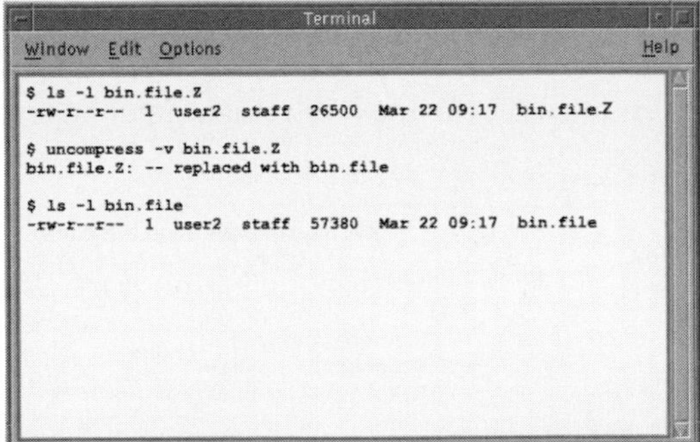

Skill Builder

e-Lab Activity 12.2

Compressing and Uncompressing Files

In this e-Lab activity, you are logged in as user2, and your current working directory is /home/user2. Refer to the class file tree structure on the inside-front cover of this book. Type the commands that would accomplish the requested objectives. *Note:* Be sure to press Enter after each one. Click Step 1 to begin.

Backing Up and Compressing the Home Directory

Because most work is done in a user's home directory, system administrators often schedule these directories for backup on a nightly basis. If the system administrator is not backing up your home directory, it is good practice to perform a regular nightly backup of changing data.

This section describes the process used to archive your home directory files to a tar file and then compress it. Figures 12-12 through 12-15 summarize the steps necessary to accomplish this. The section following this one describes how to restore the files that were backed up and compressed.

Figure 12-12
Backing up and compressing the home directory: Step 1.

Create the tar file. This example creates a tar file named home.tar in the /tmp directory combining all file in the user1 directory using a relative path name:

```
$ cd /export/home

$ tar cvf /tmp/home.tar user1
```

Figure 12-13
Backing up and compressing the home directory: Step 2.

Display the table of contents. The t option lets you see a list of files that were archived into the home.tar file:

```
$ tar tvf /tmp/home.tar
```

Figure 12-14
Backing up and compressing the home directory: Step 3.

Compress the tar file. To save space on the disk where the tar file is stored, it is compressed using the compress command. Notice the new name of the tar file: home.tar.Z.

```
$ compress -v /tmp/home.tar

/tmp/home.tar: Compression: 80.85%
--replaced with /tmp/home.tar.Z
```

Figure 12-15
Backing up and compressing the home directory: Step 4.

Back up the compressed file to the default tape drive. Change the directory to /tmp and use the tar command to copy the compressed tar file to the default tape drive.

$ cd/tmp

$ tar cv home.tar.Z

Restoring Files

This section describes the process of restoring the compressed tar file of your home directory that previously was created. Just as **tar** can combine files to a single archive file, it can be used to restore them. To restore files in your home directory, perform the following steps:

1. **Make a new directory and change to it.** In the home directory, make a new directory and change to it to prevent overwriting files. This will create a separate directory to temporarily hold the restored archived file.
```
$ cd
$ mkdir newhome
$ cd newhome
```
2. **Extract the home directory from tape.** The **x** option extracts the previously tarred file from tape to your current directory (/home/newhome), and the **v** (verbose) option lets you see the activity as the file is copied. Because no file is specified, home.tar.Z, which is the only file on the tape, will be copied to the current directory.
```
$ tar xv
```
3. **Uncompress the compressed tar file.** After the file has been copied from tape to the newhome directory, you can uncompress the home.tar file.
```
$ uncompress home.tar.Z
```
4. **Extract the tar file.** After the file is copied from tape to the newhome directory, you can extract the individual files from the home.tar file.
```
$ tar xvf home.tar
```
5. **Move files as needed.** The files in your newhome directory now can be moved to replace those in your real home directory.

Skill Builder

e-Lab Activity 12.3

Extracting Files with the **tar** Command

In this e-Lab activity, you are logged in as user2, and your current working directory is /home/user2. Refer to the class file tree structure on the inside-front cover of this book. Type the commands that would accomplish the requested objectives. *Note:* Be sure to press Enter after each one. Click Step 1 to begin.

Combining Backup and Compression with the jar Command

The **jar** (Java archive) command is similar to the **tar** command, but it compresses the resulting file in the same step. It is a Java application that combines multiple files into a single jar (Java archive) file. It is also a general-purpose archiving and compression tool, based on ZIP and the ZLIB compression format.

The **jar** command originally was created for Java programmers to download multiple files with one request, rather than having to issue a download request for each separate file. The **jar** command is standard with the Solaris operating system, but it is available on any system that has Java virtual machine (JVM) installed. The syntax for the **jar** command is almost identical to the syntax for the **tar** command. Figure 12-16 shows the options available with the **jar** command.

Figure 12-16
The **jar** command options.

Option	Function
c	Creates a new jar file.
t	Lists the table of contents of the jar file.
x	Extracts the specified files from the jar file.
f	Specifies the jar file (/tmp/file.jar) or tape drive (/dev/rmt/x) if other than default.
v	Executes in verbose mode.

It is not necessary to use a hyphen (–) before options when issuing the **jar** command. Figure 12-17 provides an example of the use of the **jar** command to archive and compress all directories and files in the /home/user2 directory.

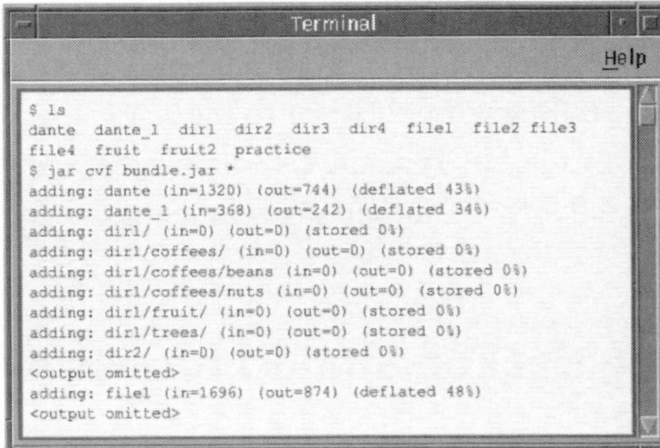

Figure 12-17 Archiving and compressing with **jar**.

Skill Builder

e-Lab Activity 12.4

Archiving and Compressing Files with **jar**

In this e-Lab activity, you are logged in as user2, and your current working directory is /home/user2. Refer to the class file tree structure on the inside-front cover of this book. Type the commands that would accomplish the requested objectives. *Note:* Be sure to press Enter after each one. Click Step 1 to begin.

Skill Builder

Lab Activity 12.4.1

Command Line Archive Tools

In this lab, you work with the tape archive (tar) and Java archive (jar) utilities to perform backups of data, as well as restore data from backups. We will cover the UNIX file compression utility, and you will use the **tar** and **compress** commands to back up and restore your home directory. Refer to the *Cisco Networking Academy Program: Fundamentals of UNIX Lab Companion.*

Third-Party Compression Programs

Many third-party compression programs are available for UNIX. This section is a summary of the most popular ones that can be downloaded and used as an alternative to those that come with UNIX.

The GNU Compression Commands

GNU is an operating system similar to UNIX that includes source code that can be copied, modified, and redistributed. The GNU project was started by a group known as the Free Software Foundation (FSF). Portions of the following text are excerpted from the GNU Project Web site, www.gnu.org:

> The GNU Project was launched in 1984 to develop a complete UNIX-like operating system which is free software: the GNU system. (GNU is a recursive acronym for "GNU's Not Unix"; it is pronounced "guh-NEW.") (A gnu is a large African antelope with a head like an ox.) Variants of the GNU operating system, which use the kernel Linux, are now widely used; though these systems are often referred to as "Linux," they are more accurately called GNU/Linux systems.

GNU provides several commands that can supplement the **tar** and **jar** commands. **gzip**, **gunzip**, and **gzcat** are available in most flavors of UNIX. If not, they can be downloaded from www.gzip.org.

gzip and **gunzip** work the same way as **compress** and **uncompress**. **gzip** typically produces a smaller file than **compress** and adds a .gz extension instead of .Z. An advantage of **gunzip** is that it can uncompress files created with **compress** and several other compression programs.

Figure 12-18 shows an example of using the **gzip** commands.

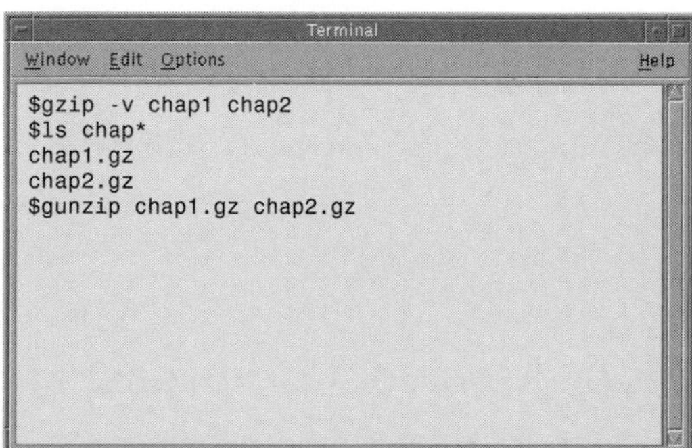
Terminal
Window Edit Options
Help
$gzip -v chap1 chap2
$ls chap*
chap1.gz
chap2.gz
$gunzip chap1.gz chap2.gz

Figure 12-18
Using the **gzip** commands.

NOTE

If the version of UNIX that you are using does not have the **zip** command, do an Internet search to locate a download site. Use the UNIX **zip** command if you will be exchanging files with a PC user.

zip and unzip Commands

Due to the popularity of the PKZIP and WinZip programs used in the DOS and Windows worlds, there are now UNIX versions that work in the same way and can read files zipped on a PC.

The **zip** command is similar to the **jar** command and is capable of compressing multiple files into a single zip file. The **unzip** command is used to uncompress a file created with zip. Figure 12-19 shows an example of using the **zip** and **unzip** commands.

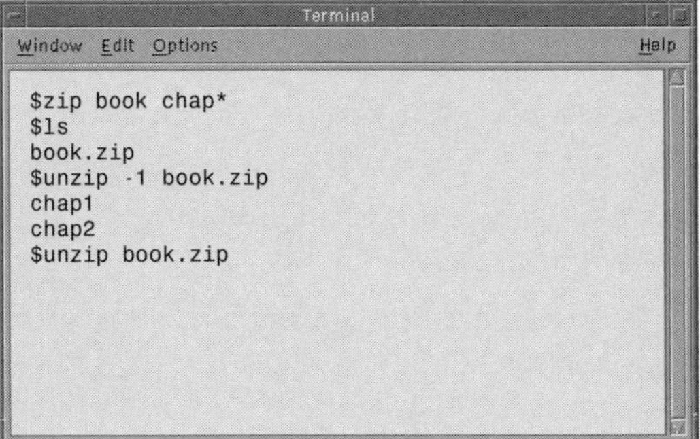
Terminal
Window Edit Options Help
$zip book chap*
$ls
book.zip
$unzip -1 book.zip
chap1
chap2
$unzip book.zip

Figure 12-19
Using the **zip** and **unzip** commands.

Third-Party Dedicated GUI Backup Tools

A number of third-party vendors have created dedicated backup application packages for use with the UNIX file system that utilize a graphical interface. Most mission-critical servers utilize one of these for regular backups. They typically provide more advanced features with greater flexibility in scheduling and managing backups and restores. See Figure 12-20.

Figure 12-20
Features of dedicated backup applications.

- Designed specifically to work with various backup media
- More flexibility with scheduling of backups
- Graphical user interface
- Drag and drop capabilities for backup and restore

Using CDE to Archive, Compress, and Restore

The Files subpanel on the Front Panel in conjunction with File Manager can be used to archive and compress files, creating the same results as using the **tar, compress**, and **uncompress** commands.

Archiving a File

Click the File subpanel from the CDE Front Panel, and then select the Archive menu option, as shown in Figure 12-21. The Archive window, shown in Figure 12-22, will open to allow you to enter the following information:

- **Folder for archive**—The folder where the archive (tar) file will be placed. The default is your home folder (for example, /home/user2).
- **Name for archive**—The name that you want to give the archive file.
- **File or folder to archive**—The name of a folder, file, or group of files to be combined into an archive. You can use wildcard metacharacters such as ? and *.

Figure 12-21
Archive menu option.

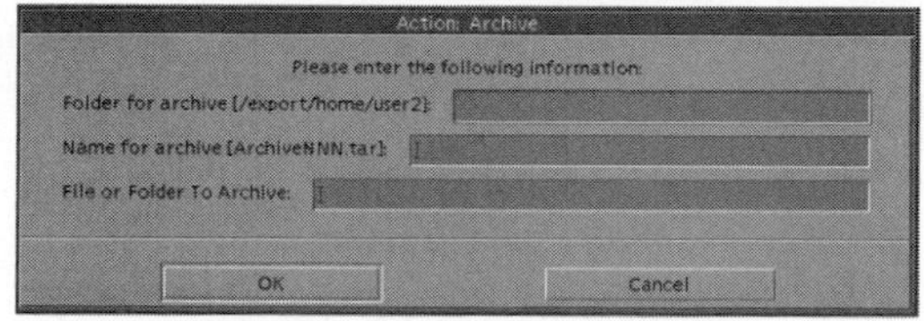

Figure 12-22
Archive window.

Restoring an Archive

Open File Manager and navigate to the folder where the archive file was placed (the default is your home directory). Select the archive (it should have a .tar extension), and either use the Selected menu or right-click the mouse to get to the Archive Unpack option. (See Figure 12-23.) If the original file exists in the directory where the archive is unpacked, it will be overwritten by the unpacked version.

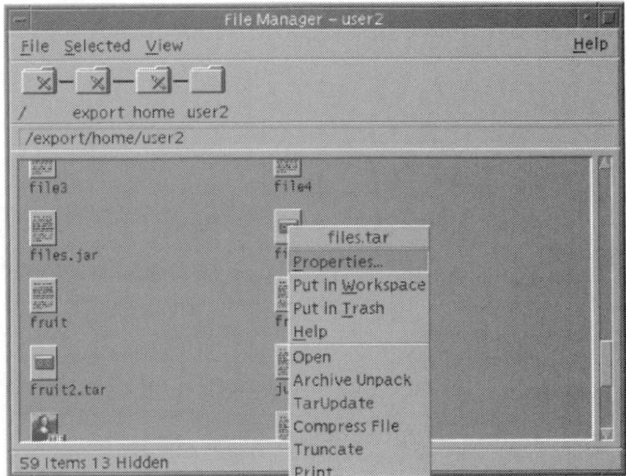

Figure 12-23
Archive unpack.

Compressing a File

Click the File subpanel from the CDE Front Panel, and then select the Compress File menu option, as shown in Figure 12-24. The Compress window, shown in Figure 12-25, will open to allow you to enter the name of the file to compress. The compressed file will be renamed with a .Z extension, and it will reside in whatever directory it was in before the compress (the default is the home directory).

Uncompressing a File

Open File Manager and navigate to the folder where the compressed file was placed (the default is your home directory). Select the compressed file (it should have a .Z extension), and either use the Selected menu or right-click the mouse to get to the Uncompress File option, as shown in Figure 12-26. The file will be uncompressed and renamed back to its original name, with the .Z extension removed.

Figure 12-24
Compress file menu options.

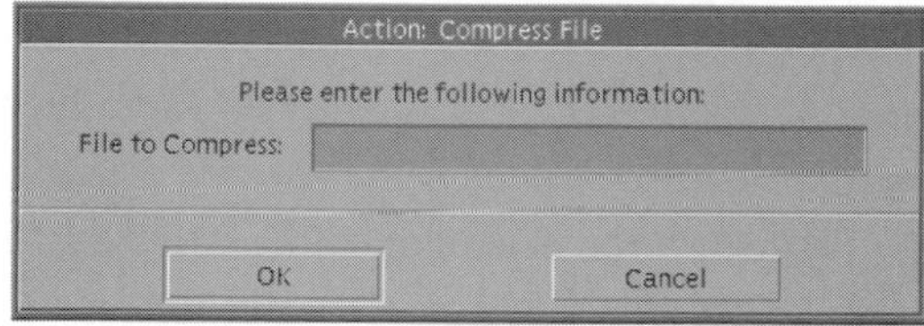

Figure 12-25
Compress window.

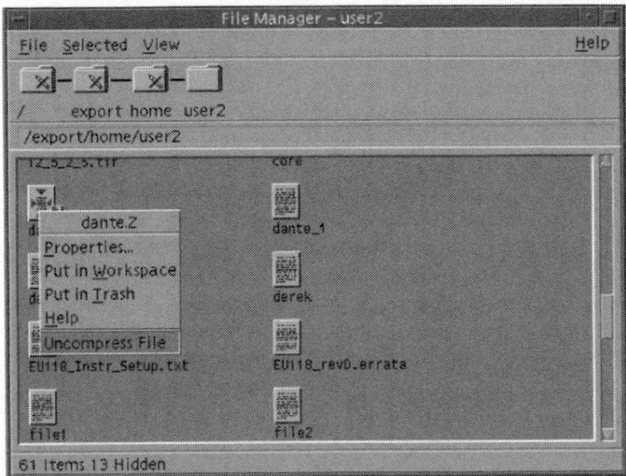

Figure 12-26
Uncompress a file.

Skill Builder

Lab Activity 12.5.2

CDE Archive Tools

In this lab, you work with the Common Desktop Environment (CDE) utilities to back up, compress, and restore files and folders. The Files subpanel on the Front Panel, in conjunction with File Manager, can be used to archive, compress, and restore files creating the same results as using the **tar**, **compress**, and **uncompress** commands. Refer to the *Cisco Networking Academy Program: Fundamentals of UNIX Lab Companion.*

Summary

Now that you have completed this chapter, you should have an understanding of the following:

- Backing up data is one of the most important functions that a network administrator can perform. Data can become lost or corrupted for a variety of reasons. The most important thing is to have good backups available to restore the lost data quickly and accurately.
- Three basic backup strategies exist: full, incremental, and differential backups. Full backups take the longest but are the easiest to restore. Incremental backups take less time but are harder to restore because more tapes are involved. Differential backups are a compromise, taking less time than a full backup and being easier to restore than an incremental backup.

- Magnetic tape traditionally has been the primary backup media because of its high capacity and relatively low cost. Recently, some newer technologies such as removable drives, Jaz disks, and writeable CDs have begun to replace tape drives for backing up quantities of data of less than 1 GB.
- The UNIX operating system has several command-line backup utilities available, the including **tar** (tape archive), **jar** (Java archive), and **compress/uncompress** commands. The **tar** command combines multiple files into an archive file but does not compress them. The **tar** command can be used to archive and extract files. The **compress** command is used to reduce the disk space taken up by a file. The **uncompress** command expands files back to their original size so that you can work with the file. The **jar** command combines the capabilities of the **tar** and **compress** commands, and simultaneously can archive and compress files. When they are extracted, they are automatically uncompressed.
- Several other UNIX compression programs are available for free. The **gzip** and **gunzip** commands are used to compress and uncompress files. **gzip** creates a smaller file than **compress**.
- The **zip** and **unzip** commands work the same way as the PKZIP commands on a PC, and they should be used if exchanging files with a PC user.
- CDE has some graphical tools to archive and compress files, which are available from the Files subpanel on the Front Panel. The CDE File Manager can be used to extract and uncompress files.

Check Your Understanding

1. Backups are important to the health of a network and to an organization's capability to recover lost data. Which of the following is *not* cause for data loss or corruption?
   A. Hard disk failure
   B. Deletion
   C. Disasters
   D. CPU failure
2. Company ABC processes information from 6:00 a.m. to 10:00 p.m. every day. As a result, the network administrator has limited time to do backups. Which backup method most likely will take the least time on a daily basis?
   A. Full backup
   B. Incremental backup
   C. Differential backup
   D. Sequential backup
3. Company XYZ has ample time to do backups every night, and the volume of data will fit on a single 40-GB tape. Which backup method would make the restoration process simpler?
   A. Full backup
   B. Incremental backup
   C. Differential backup
   D. Sequential backup
4. To be adequately prepared for data loss, the network administration staff should practice doing restores. Which of the following would they not be expected to be capable of recovering from?
   A. Accidental overwrite of a file
   B. Loss of a directory
   C. Complete hard drive failure
   D. Moving a file to another directory
5. Which of the following backup methods or media is in the proper order from *least* storage capacity to the MOST storage capacity?
   A. Tape, CD-R, floppy
   B. Floppy, CD-R, tape

C. Jaz, tape, floppy

D. Tape, floppy, Jaz

6. You want to archive some project files to a file called projfiles.tar and put them in a backup folder, but you do not want to compress them. The filenames all begin with prj. Which UNIX command would accomplish this?

   A. **tar cvf projfiles.tar prj***

   B. **jar cvf projfiles.tar prj***

   C. **tar cv projfiles.tar prj?**

   D. **tar xvf projfiles.tar prj***

7. You previously archived some files from your home directory into a tar archive named hist.tar. You accidentally deleted one of them, and now you want to restore that file from the archive. You have newer versions of the others, and you want to be sure that you do not overwrite them. Which of the following would not be a step in the process to accomplish this?

   A. Create a temporary directory and move the hist.tar to it.

   B. Compress the hist.tar file.

   C. Use the **tar** command to extract the files.

   D. Copy or move the desired file to your home directory.

8. Your hard disk is filling up, and you would like to reclaim some space. You do not want to delete any of your files, and you want them to be readily available. Which UNIX command(s) could be used to accomplish this?

   A. **compress**

   B. **tar**

   C. **jar**

   D. Both **compress** and **jar** will reclaim space

9. To simultaneously archive and compress the big1, large2, and gigantic3 files, which UNIX command should you use?

   A. **tar cvf bigfiles.tar big1 large2 gigantic3**

   B. **jar xvf bigfiles.tar big1 large2 gigantic3tar**

   C. **jar cvf bigfiles.tar big1 large2 gigantic3**

   D. **compress tar cvf bigfiles.tar big1 large2 gigantic3jar**

10. CDE includes some graphical utilities to assist with archiving, compressing, and restoring files. What are these?
    A. File Manager and Application Manager
    B. File subpanel menu and File Manager
    C. File Archive subpanel and Application Manager
    D. Archive Restore Manager and Compression Manager

UNIX Command Summary

compress Attempts to reduce the size of the named files. Example:

```
-v, -f
$ compress -vf file
file: compression 37% -- replaced with file.Z
```

gunzip Uncompresses files created with the **gzip** command. Example:

```
$ gunzip chap1.gz chap2.gz
```

gzcat Enables you to read a gzipped file without uncompressing it. Example:

```
$ gzcat bookfile
chap1
chap2
```

gzip A compression utility (short for "GNU zip") designed to be a replacement for **compress**. Its main advantages over **compress** are much better compression and freedom from patented algorithms. The GNU Project uses it as the standard compression program for its system. Example:

```
-v

$ gzip -v chap1 chap2
$ ls chap*
chap1.gz
chap.gz
```

jar Combines **backup** and **compress** into one tool. Example:

```
-c,-t,-x, -f, -v

$ jar cvf bundle.jar *
adding 0.au
adding 1.au
adding 2.au
adding 3.au
$
```

tar Archives and extracts files to and from a single file called a tar file. Example:

```
c, t, x, f, v
$ tar cvf backup.tar /home/user2/*
```

uncompress Returns a previously compressed file to its original size. Example:

```
-v
$ uncompress -vf file.Z
```

unzip Uncompresses files created with the **zip** command. Example:

```
$ unzip bookfile.zip
$ls
chap1 chap2 chap3
```

zip A compression utility designed to be compatible with the PC zip utility. Example:

```
$ zip bookfile chap*

$ls

book.zip
```

Key Terms

Backup A copy of file system data that is stored separately from the disk drive on which the data resides.

Compression Removing redundant characters and space from a file to reduce its size. Programs such as zip, PKZIP, WinZip, and the UNIX **compress** command can be used to compress files.

Differential backup A full backup is still done once a week. Each day after, all changed data from the full backup is backed up again. The amount of data being backup up increases each day until the next full backup. A differential backup is a compromise because it takes less time than a full backup and might be easier to restore than an incremental.

Full backup All selected data is backed up daily, whether it has changed or not. This method takes the longest time and might require multiple tapes, depending on the amount of data. It is the safest and easiest to restore.

GNU An operating system similar to UNIX that includes source code that can be copied, modified, and redistributed. The GNU project was started by a group known as the Free Software Foundation (FSF).

Incremental backup Data is backed up in increments. A full backup is performed once a week on a particular day (such as Sunday in the evening). Each day after the full backup, only the changes (new and modified files) are backed up. An incremental backup takes the least amount of time, but it is potentially more difficult to restore because it generally requires more tapes.

Media Various types of storage media for data, including magnetic tape, fixed and removable magnetic disks, and recordable optical media such as CD-R and CD-RW.

RAID 1 (Redundant Array of Independent Disks—Level 1) RAID 1, or mirroring, uses two drives, with the second drive storing the same data as the first. If one of the drives fails, the other will take over. A more robust version of RAID 1, which uses dual drive controllers as well as dual drives, is known as duplexing.

RAID 5 (Redundant Array of Independent Disks) (Level 5) Combines three or more drives as a group so that if one fails, the others take over. The bad drive can be replaced with no loss of service to the users.

Restore To bring data back from tape or other backup media and replace the corrupted or lost data on the original disks.

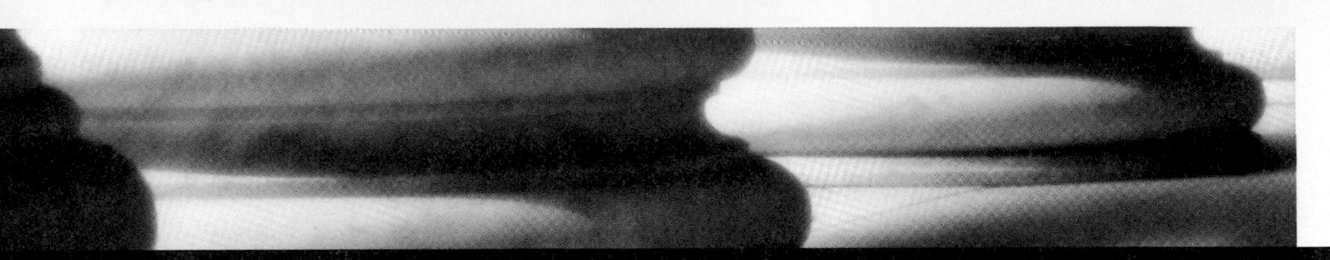

Objectives

After reading this chapter, you will be able to

- Describe the different types of UNIX system processes
- Display system processes for yourself and other users
- Interpret the information displayed for system processes
- Identify process hierarchy (parent and child) process relationships
- Terminate system processes
- Manage foreground and background processes
- Understand the concepts of physical memory, virtual memory, and swap files

Chapter 13

System Processes and Memory Management

Introduction

An understanding of processes is critical to understanding the inner workings of the UNIX operating system. This chapter introduces UNIX processes and process management. All program execution and tasks performed on a UNIX system are accomplished with processes that are managed by the operating system kernel.

In this chapter, you learn how to determine which processes currently are running and how to interpret the process information displayed with the **ps** (process status) command. You will be able to identify parent and child processes, as well as terminate unwanted or unresponsive processes. In addition, you learn the difference between foreground and background processes and how to manage them. The concepts of virtual memory and physical memory, swap files, and paging are also introduced.

UNIX System Processes

All operating systems have some means of managing tasks. The UNIX network operating system manages tasks using *processes*.

Processes can be initiated either by the operating system or by users. The majority of tasks performed in the UNIX environment start a process. A process can start or *spawn* a subprocess, thus creating a process hierarchy or tree similar to the file system structure with parent/child relationships. For example, when you use vi to edit a file, or when you are sending a file to the printer with the **lp** command, a process is spawned. However, some simple commands, such as **cd**, are executed by the shell itself and do not create a separate process. Each program that you run creates a process, which is assigned a unique *process identification number (PID)*. The PID is used by the system to identify and track the process until it is completed.

The operating system (OS) kernel manages the initiation and termination of all processes. Every process requires system resources, such as central processing unit (CPU) time and random access memory (RAM) space to work in. The OS allocates these system resources to each process when it starts and deallocates them when the process ends. The first two processes started when a UNIX system is booted are sched (scheduler) and init (initialization), which manage other processes. Figure 13-1 shows the relationships between the OS kernel, the CPU, RAM, and processes.

Figure 13-1
Kernel allocation for processes.

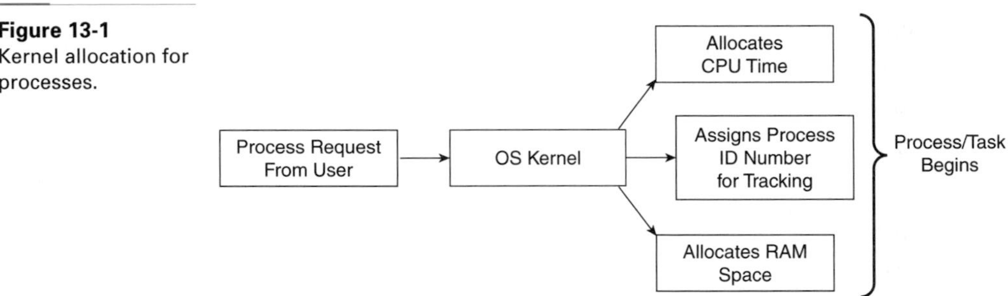

Types of Processes

Several different types of UNIX processes exist, as discussed in the next several sections and summarized in Figure 13-2.

Figure 13-2
Types of UNIX processes.

Daemon—Processes started by the UNIX kernel

Parent—The process that spawned another

Child—The process spawned by the parent

Orphan—Result of parent process terminating before child returns

Zombie (or defunct)—Child process that does not return to the parent

Daemon

Daemons are processes that are started by the UNIX kernel and that exist for a specific purpose. For instance, the lpsched daemon exists for the sole purpose of handling print jobs. When no printing is taking place on the system, the lpsched daemon is running but inactive. When a print job is submitted, this daemon becomes active until the job is finished. The dtlogin daemon provides the CDE login screen at the beginning of a user's session and again after the user exits the CDE File Manager. UNIX daemons are similar to services in Windows NT/2000 and NetWare Loadable Modules (NLMs) with Novell NetWare.

Parent

A process that spawns another process is referred to as its *parent*. Following system bootup, a process called the init daemon is invoked. Every process except init has a *parent process*. The init daemon is always process 1. The init process is at the top of the process hierarchy and is responsible for spawning many system processes. The dtlogin daemon is spawned by init and, therefore, is referred to as the *parent process* of the dtlogin daemon.

Child

A process that is spawned by another process is referred to as a *child process*. When a user is working in a Terminal window in the CDE, that terminal's PID is the parent process ID (PPID) of any commands issued in the terminal. These commands are child processes of the terminal process. The parent process receives and displays the output from the child process and then "kills" the process. When you issue a command from the shell, the shell spawns a child process and waits for it to execute. When it is finished, control returns to the parent shell.

Orphan

If a command is issued in a Terminal window and the window is closed before the command returns output, that process becomes an *orphan*. The system passes the *orphan process* to init, which is the master system process, and init then becomes the parent process and terminates the child process.

Zombie (or Defunct)

Occasionally, a child process does not return to the parent process with its output. This process becomes "lost" in the system. The only resource that this process uses is a slot in the process table; it cannot be stopped in a conventional manner. This type of process is called a *zombie* or *defunct* process. The only way to kill a defunct process is to reboot the system.

Displaying Processes with the ps Command

The **ps** (process status) command is used to list the processes currently running on the system. This normally is done if a process is taking too long or appears to have stopped, as indicated by a Terminal window not responding or "hanging." By listing the processes, you can see the name of the command or program that initiated the process, plus any child processes that it might have spawned. By executing the **ps** command more than once, you can see if a process is still running by looking at the *time* for the process, which is the amount of CPU time that the process is using. If the amount of time does not increase, then the process might have stopped. You can use the **ps** command to check the PID of the process and then “kill” the process if it is taking too long or has stopped.

The output of the **ps** command will display the PID number and the command or program associated with it. The PID number normally is used to terminate a process. The following show the syntax for the **ps** command:

```
ps [-options]
```

As shown in Figure 13-3, there are three main options with the **ps** command: **-e** (every process), **-f** (full listing), and **-u** (user). The column information displayed for these various commands is defined in Figure 13-6.

Figure 13-3
ps command options.

Option	Meaning	Function
ps	No Options	Displays information for current user processes in current shell or terminal window.
ps -e	Every	Displays information about every process on the system.
ps -f	Full	Generates a full listing with all available information on each process.
ps -u userid	User	Displays all processes for a particular user.

- **ps**—The **ps** command by itself displays PID, TTY (terminal type), TIME (CPU time), and CMD (command that initiated the process) for only your processes running in the current shell. If you open a Terminal window under the CDE File Manager, you will not see any of the other processes that you have initiated.
- **ps -e**—The **ps** command with the **-e** (every) option displays PID, TTY, TIME, and CMD for all processes running on the system.
- **ps -f**—The **ps** command with the **-f** (full) option shows a listing of all information (UID, PID, PPID, C, STIME, TTY, TIME, and CMD), but only for those processes running under the current shell or Terminal window.
- **ps -u**—The **ps** command with the **-u** (user ID) option displays PID, TTY TIME, and CMD for every process running on the system for a particular user.

Figure 13-4 shows the output of the basic **ps** command with no options. Multiple options can be used with most commands, and the **ps -ef** command combines the –e and –f options. The **ps –ef** command shows every process on the system and all information available in a full listing. Because of the number of processes usually running on a system, it is useful to pipe the **ps -ef** command to **more** so that the output can be read a page at a time, as shown in the example in Figure 13-5. (Note that root initiated the /etc/init daemon as process 1. User aster with PID 1292 is running a Korn shell (**-ksh**) process from the console. User rose with PID 1400 is running a clock program under Open Windows).

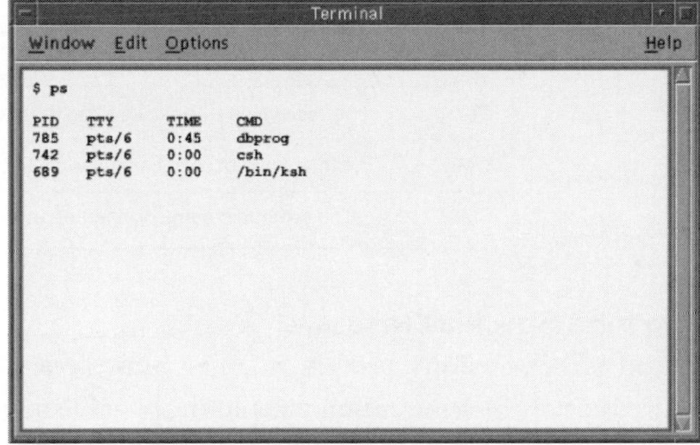

Figure 13-4 Displaying a listing of your processes with **ps**.

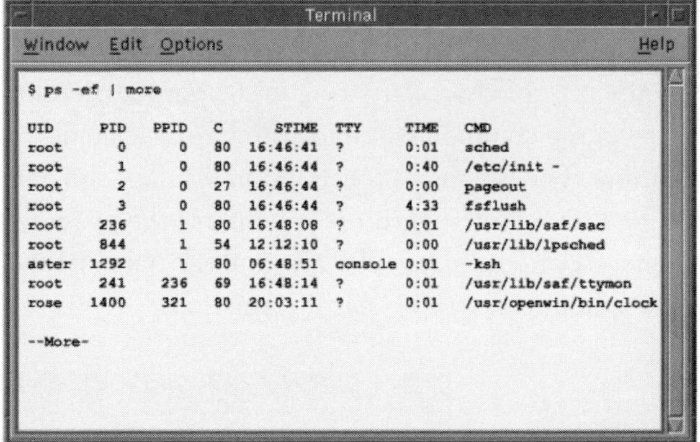

Figure 13-5 Displaying a full listing of all processes with **ps –ef**.

Figure 13-6 describes the column headings from the **ps -ef** command. The controlling terminal for system daemons appears as a question mark (?). The word **<defunct>** appears in the CMD column if a process is a zombie or defunct process. (*Note:* The CPU time might be a bit higher for a defunct process than for other processes.)

NOTE

The equivalent process status command on a BSD system **is ps –aux**.

Figure 13-6
Column heading for the **ps –ef** display.

Value	Description
UTD	The user ID of the user that initiated the process.
PID	The process identification number of the process. PID kills a process.
PPID	The parent process identification number of the process.
C	The priority of the process.
STIME	Start time of the process.
TTY	Terminal type—The controlling terminal for the process.
TIME	The amount of CPU time used by the process.
CMD	The command name or daemon (name of the program executed).

Searching for a Specific Process

As mentioned earlier, to stop a process, you first must determine the PID. On most systems, hundreds of processes are running, and the **ps -ef** listing can be quite long. If you know the name of the executable program that started the process, you can find the PID faster. By piping the output of the **ps** command through **grep**, you can search for the specific process that you want to terminate and determine the correct PID. As you recall from Chapter 8, "Files and User Information Utilities," the **grep** command can search for any type of character string in the output of another command. Specific to Solaris is the **pgrep** command used to search for a specific process by name rather than by PID number. The **-l** (long output) option displays the names of the processes associated with the PID found. Figure 13-7 compares the **ps -e** command using **grep** with **pgrep -l**. The **-e** option displays the PID and the name of the initiating command, which allows **grep** to search on this information.

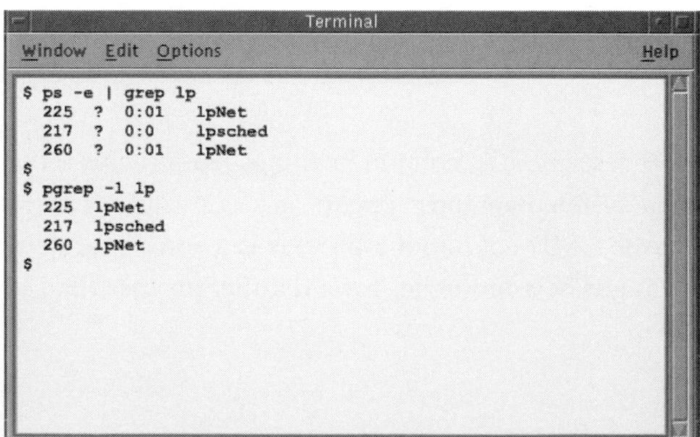

Figure 13-7
Piping **ps** output to **grep** and **pgrep**.

Skill Builder

e-Lab Activity 13.1

Displaying System Processes

In this e-Lab activity, you are logged in as user2, and your current working directory is /home/user2. Refer to the class file tree structure on the inside-front cover of this book. Type the commands that would accomplish the requested objectives. *Note:* Be sure to press Enter after each one. Click Step 1 to begin.

Terminating Processes

The **ps -ef** command displays a full listing of every process, including the PID and its PPID. When trying to terminate a program or release a hung Terminal window, it might not be enough to kill the PID that is associated with the unresponsive application. It might be necessary to kill the parent of that process and, on rare occasions, even the parent of the parent. It is important to look at a PID and PPID to be able to trace from the child up the hierarchy to the parent processes that spawned them.

To do this, you first must identify the PID of the lowest-level unresponsive process. Normally, you would try to kill that process's PID. If this does not stop the process, you might need to kill its parent. Killing a parent process will kill all child processes spawned by it. Therefore, it is quicker to kill a parent process rather than killing several child processes.

Figure 13-8 shows three processes and the relationships among them. In this figure, the first process was started when the user opened a Terminal window from the CDE File Manager, which spawned the user to open a Terminal window for the default Korn shell (ksh). From there, the user opened a C Shell with the **csh** command. Next, he ran a program called sleep 500&, which suspended execution for 500 seconds. (The ampersand [&] tells the shell to run the command in the background and return the shell prompt so that the user can continue working.)

NOTE

The **sleep** command frequently is used in shell scripts to cause the machine to pause for a specified number of seconds before continuing on to the next command. It is used in this example only for purposes of illustration.

The **ps -f** command in Figure 13-10 is used to see only those processes initiated from the current Terminal window. The sleep process has a PID of 785, and its PPID is 742, which is the PID of the C Shell (csh). If you terminate PID 742, you also will terminate 785. If you terminate the PID of the Korn shell (ksh), which is 689, you will terminate all processes.

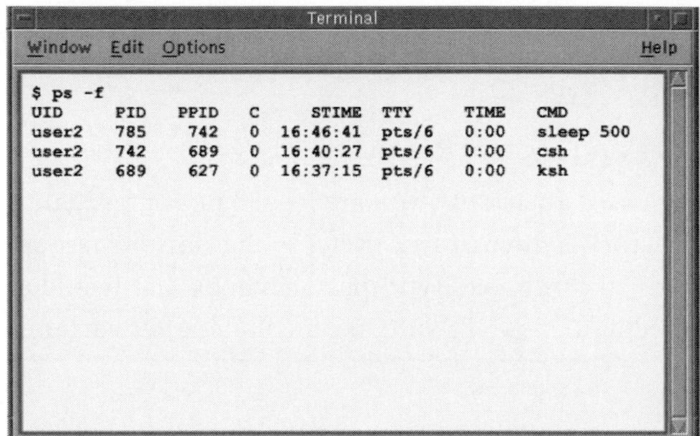
Terminal
Window Edit Options Help
$ ps -f
UID PID PPID C STIME TTY TIME CMD
user2 785 742 0 16:46:41 pts/6 0:00 sleep 500
user2 742 689 0 16:40:27 pts/6 0:00 csh
user2 689 627 0 16:37:15 pts/6 0:00 ksh

Figure 13-8
Parent and child process relationships.

Signals

Currently, 30 to 40 *signals* are defined in UNIX, depending on the implementation. Each signal is associated with a number and a name. Signals are used to terminate, suspend, and continue processes. Information on the different signals can be found by using the following **man** command:

```
$ man -s 5 signal or man signal
```

Using Ctrl-c sometimes can terminate a process that is not responding. This sends an interrupt (INT) signal to the process, terminating it and any child processes that it might have spawned.

The kill Command

The **kill** command provides a direct way to terminate unwanted command processes. It is useful when you want to stop a command that takes a long time to run, or when you need to terminate a process that you cannot quit in the normal way. Specifying their PIDs normally kills processes. *Background processes* (those submitted using the ampersand) also are assigned a job ID. You can kill background processes by using either the **process id** or the **job id** command. To view all jobs running in the background and their job IDs, you use the **jobs** command. The number returned in brackets is the job ID number. The syntax of the **kill** command is shown here:

```
kill [-signal] process-id or %job-id
```

To terminate a process with the **kill** command, you type **ps** to find out the PID(s) for the process(es); then you type **kill** followed by the PID(s). If you use the **kill** command without specifying a signal, signal 15 (SIGTERM) is sent to the process with the specified PID number. This is referred to as a *soft kill* and usually causes the process to terminate. It is best to use a soft kill on a process, if possible, because it closes files properly and terminates the process(es) gracefully.

If you need to forcibly terminate a process, you can append the -9 option to the **kill** command. This option is referred to as a *sure kill* and is necessary for killing shells that will not respond to any other signal to terminate. The following syntax shows the **kill** command with the –9 or sure kill option:

```
$ kill -9 PID#
```

> **NOTE**
>
> For processes other than shells, use the **kill -9** (SIGKILL) command as a last resort because it is an abrupt method and does not allow for proper process termination.

Finding and Terminating a Process by User

The **ps** command can be used with the **-u** (user) option to find processes for a specific user. You might find processes for users by their login name or UID number. A user can terminate only his own processes, but the superuser can terminate any process running on the system. If multiple windows are open on a user's desktop, the output of the **ps** command will show pts/# under the TTY heading for every window open.

A pseudoterminal (pts) is the device name given to windows and remote login sessions. Each window the user opens after logging in gets a new pts#. Figure 13-9 shows the results of the **ps -u** command for user2 and uses the **kill** command to terminate the find process, which is PID 12932. The syntax for the **ps –u** command is shown here:

```
ps -u login-ID or UID
```

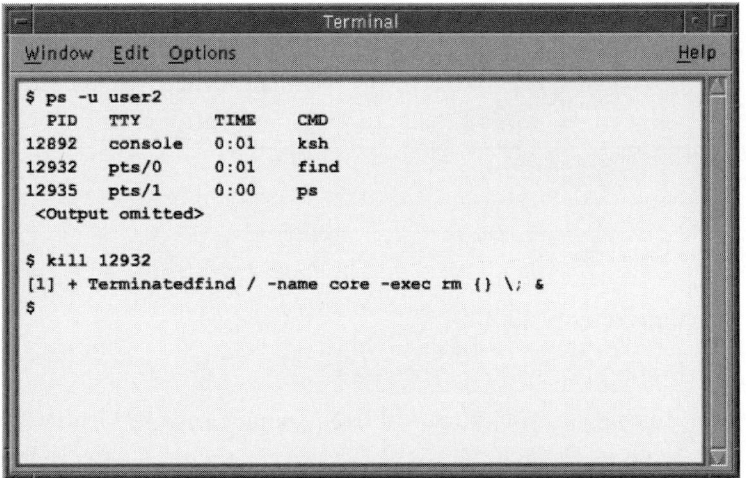

Terminal
Window Edit Options Help
$ ps -u user2
PID TTY TIME CMD
12892 console 0:01 ksh
12932 pts/0 0:01 find
12935 pts/1 0:00 ps
<Output omitted>
$ kill 12932
[1] + Terminatedfind / -name core -exec rm {} \; &
$

Figure 13-9 Finding and terminating processes for a user.

The pkill Command

The **pkill** command is specific to Solaris and works exactly like the **pgrep** command, except that it terminates the process by matching the command name (CMD) of the process(es) and sends a kill signal. Figure 13-10 shows using the **pkill** command to kill a process by its name: sleep. The syntax of the **pkill** command is shown here:

```
$ pkill CMD name
```

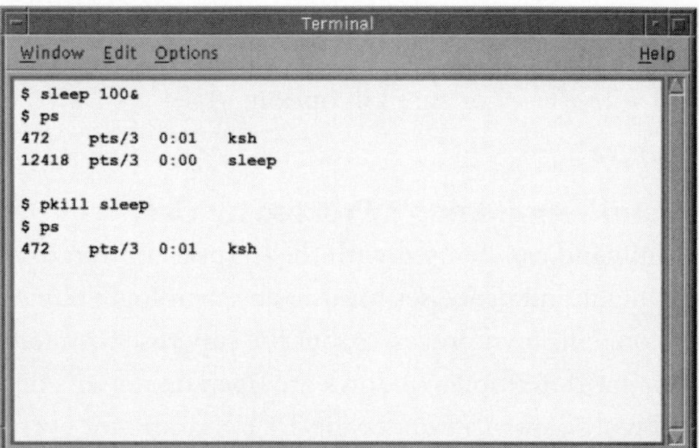
Terminal
Window Edit Options Help
$ sleep 100&
$ ps
472 pts/3 0:01 ksh
12418 pts/3 0:00 sleep
$ pkill sleep
$ ps
472 pts/3 0:01 ksh

Figure 13-10 Terminating a process with **pkill**.

Skill Builder

e-Lab Activity 13.2

Terminating Processes

In this e-Lab activity, you are logged in as user2, and your current working directory is /home/user2. Refer to the class file tree structure on the inside-front cover of this book. Type the commands that would accomplish the requested objectives. *Note:* Be sure to press Enter after each one. Click Step 1 to begin.

Skill Builder

Lab Activity 13.3.2

Managing System Processes

In this lab, you work with UNIX commands to identify system processes and control them. Refer to the *Cisco Networking Academy Program: Fundamentals of UNIX Lab Companion.*

Foreground and Background Processes

UNIX is a multitasking OS with the capability to work on many different tasks at the same time. Even as you work in a Terminal window or access your Internet browser in the foreground, the system is running many processes (programs and daemons) in the background, enabling the system to properly function.

Foreground Processing

Typically, the communication between the user and the shell happens interactively, one task at a time. For example, when you enter a command in a Terminal window, the shell processes the command and displays the output. You must wait until the shell completes the task before requesting another task. This is considered *foreground processing*.

Background Processes

Although UNIX is a multitasking operating system, running processes in the foreground can limit the execution of commands and programs to a serial process in which they run one after another and unnecessarily tie up a Terminal window. If programs are to run simultaneously, they must either run from a different Terminal window or run in the background.

You can run a process in the background by adding an ampersand (&) to the end of the command line. Background processes run concurrently with other system processes and shell programs. You might want to run processes in the background because they are time-consuming (that is, sorting a large file or searching the file system for a file), or you might want to start a program and be able to continue interacting with the shell. For example, if you started Netscape from a Terminal window by typing **netscape** at the command prompt, Netscape would start but the Terminal window would appear "locked." That is because the Terminal window shell is the parent process of the Netscape program running in the foreground. As soon as Netscape is exited, the shell prompt returns. If you type **netscape&**, Netscape would start as a background task and the shell prompt would return to the Terminal window, allowing you to continue working.

Controlling Foreground and Background Jobs

Job control gives you the capability to place a job (process) currently running in the foreground into the background because it is taking longer than expected and you need the shell prompt to work on something else.

Job control also enables you to manage background jobs by moving them to the foreground, suspending or terminating them. For example, suppose that you used the Windows Telnet program to log into your school's computer and began downloading a file using the **ftp** command (see Chapter 16, "Network Basics") when you realized that you were just sitting there waiting for it to finish. Why not suspend (pause) the job and then place it in the background so that you can continue to work from a shell prompt?

After a period of time, you might decide to bring the download job back to the foreground to check on the progress.

Figure 13-11 lists the commands that enable you to manage jobs.

Figure 13-11
Controlling foreground and background.

Command	Meaning
Ctrl-z or stop %job#n	Suspends (not terminates) the foreground process.
jobs	Displays all background jobs.
bg %job#n	Places job# in the background and restores the shell prompt.
fg %job#n	Places job# in the foreground.
Ctrl-c	Cancels the current foreground job.
kill %job#n	Terminates job#.

TIP

When you log off, your background processes are terminated. Use the **nohup** (no hang up) command to enable a background job to complete even after you log off. For example, the command line **$nohup sort customerids > custfile &** followed by you logging off allows the sort to continue. After logging back on, you could view the custfile for the results of the **sort** command.

Figure 13-12 shows a sequence of starting a job in the background (sleep 500 counts 500 seconds and then continues—it frequently is used in shell scripts), displaying the job number, moving to the foreground, suspending, moving back to the background, and finally terminating it. Note that the number in the square brackets ([x]) is the job number. The job preceded by a plus sign (+) is the *current job* and can be manipulated with **fg** (foreground) or **bg** (background) without specifying the job number.

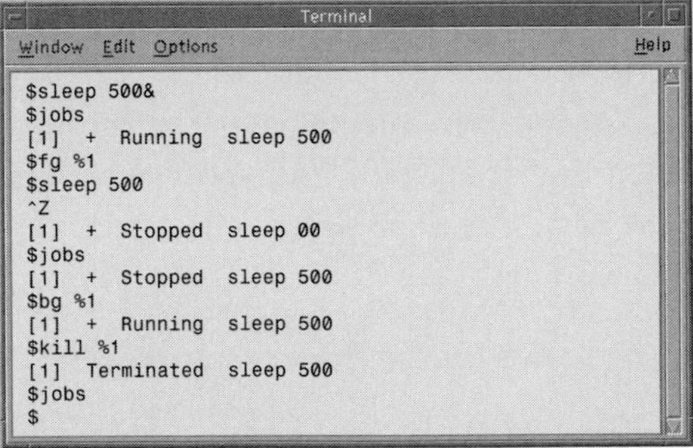

Terminal
Window Edit Options Help
$sleep 500&
$jobs
[1] + Running sleep 500
$fg %1
$sleep 500
^Z
[1] + Stopped sleep 00
$jobs
[1] + Stopped sleep 500
$bg %1
[1] + Running sleep 500
$kill %1
[1] Terminated sleep 500
$jobs
$

Figure 13-12
Foreground and background jobs.

Process Scheduling

The multitasking capability of UNIX is not limited to running processes only in the present. UNIX contains programs that enable you to schedule programs to run one time only at a specified time using the **at** command, and to schedule repeated operations using the **crontab** command (not covered in this book).

The **at** command enables you to run programs, commands, or shell scripts at some future date and time. For example, imagine that you would like to e-mail a friend the contents of a file on January 1 at exactly 12:01. Or, to be considerate, you schedule the **find** command to search the entire hard drive for a missing file to run at 3:00 a.m., when user activity is low.

To schedule a one-time job using the **at** command, perform these steps:

1. Enter the **at** command followed by a time specification, where the time specification could be:

   $at 10:30am today, $at midnight, $at 12:01 1 Jan 2002, and so on.

   (See the man page for many more examples.)

2. At the **at** prompt (**at>**), enter the first command to run at the specified time, and then press Enter.

3. Enter the next command to run, followed by Enter (or press Ctrl-D, if finished).

   An *at job number* is assigned to track the **at** job. Use the **atq** command to view the **at** job queue. Use the **atrm** [**at job#**] command to remove a scheduled job.

> **TIP**
>
> To run a script file at a specified time, use the command **$at [time spec] [script file name]**. For example, **$at midnight whoison** would run the whoison shell script that runs the **who** command to see what users are accessing the system at midnight and then would redirect the output to a file to be viewed in the morning.

Memory Management: Physical Memory and Swap Space

To handle multiple tasks simultaneously, computers must memory manage memory efficiently. This is accomplished through the use of physical memory management and *virtual memory* or swap space management.

Physical Memory

All computers have *physical* or *system memory* microchips. This most often is referred to as random access memory (RAM). This *physical memory* is controlled directly by the processor in conjunction with the memory management unit (MMU). RAM is the working storage area of the computer where programs (sequences of instructions) and data related to the programs are stored while the program is running. When a program is running, it is copied off the hard disk into RAM, and space is allocated in RAM for the program to do its work.

RAM is empty when the system first starts up. The UNIX operating system kernel is the first thing to load into RAM. Other critical system programs such as init and lpsched then are loaded. As mentioned earlier, the OS kernel manages all other programs or processes by assigning CPU time and RAM space to them.

Virtual Memory

Many processes are held simultaneously in RAM, so it is possible to use it up. If a new process needs to be placed in RAM, the pageout process selects pages of a process that are not currently in use and sends them temporarily out to swap space on the disk. The selection of pages is made based on a "not recently used" algorithm. *Swap space* is a raw slice or disk file that is set aside during system installation for this purpose. Processes remain in RAM while they are active. The swapping process uses swap space on the disk, which is limited.

The combination of RAM plus swap space constitutes *virtual memory*, which is the maximum space that processes can use. Virtual memory has a much shorter access time than accessing something on the formatted areas of the disk. Because the kernel manages the swapping process, it cannot be swapped. In Figure 13-13, the kernel is swapping programs in and out of the swap space on the hard disk.

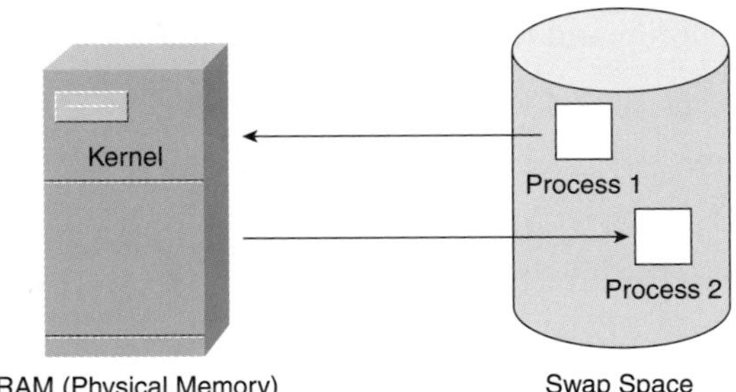

Figure 13-13
Kernel and swap space.

Paging

A program on a Sun workstation can address up to 4 GB of memory. A system typically is equipped with some number of megabytes of RAM. During its execution, a process is placed in RAM (divided into pages) and is swapped page by page in and out of RAM. This process of swapping pages in and out of RAM is also called *paging*. Swapping or paging rarely takes place on systems with very large amounts of RAM.

Summary

Now that you have completed this chapter, you should have an understanding of the following:

- UNIX initiates, manages, and terminates programs using system processes. When a program such as the **sort** command or the vi editor starts, the operating system kernel assigns it a unique process identification number (PID). The kernel also allocates CPU time and RAM space for the program to run. UNIX processes are hierarchical, similar to the UNIX file system. Every process has a parent process except the init process, which is process 1.

- Five types of system processes exist on a UNIX system:
  - **Daemon**—A process started by the UNIX kernel
  - **Parent**—A process that spawns another process
  - **Child**—The process spawned by the parent
  - **Orphan**—The result of a parent process terminating before the child returns
  - **Zombie**—A child process that does not return to the parent
- The **ps** command is used to display processes and has several options. The command **ps -ef** displays every process with full information.
  - **-e**—Every process
  - **-f**—A full listing of information
  - **-u**—User processes
- The output of the **ps** command can be piped to the **more** command to see one screen at a time, or to the **grep** command to search for specific strings such as program names.
- UNIX is a multitasking operating system capable of running jobs in the foreground and the background.
- Placing a job in the background is accomplished using the & (ampersand). Several commands can be used to manage background jobs, including **jobs, stop, fg, bg,** and **kill.**
- Jobs don't always have to run in the present; they can be scheduled at a later date and time using the **at** command.
- Long-running or unresponsive processes can be terminated using the **kill** command while specifying the PID of the process. Most processes can be terminated with the basic **kill PID#** command, also called a soft kill. Killing a shell process requires the **kill -9 PID#** command, also called a sure kill.
- Computers have physical memory, which is known as random access memory (RAM). During installation, the UNIX operating system sets aside an area on the hard disk called swap space. As programs are executed, they are copied from the hard disk into system RAM and divide into pages. To make the best use of RAM, portions of programs that have not been used recently are paged out to the swap area of the hard disk. This allows more programs to fit into RAM. If pages that are on the hard disk are needed, they can be paged back into RAM. The combination of physical RAM and the swap space on the hard disk is known as virtual memory.

Check Your Understanding

1. The majority of tasks performed on a UNIX system create a process with a unique:
   A. UID
   B. PID
   C. PPID
   D. EUID
2. The operating system manages processes and allocates resources to each process, which include:
   A. RAM and ROM
   B. ROM and hard disk
   C. CPU and RAM
   D. CPU and ROM
3. Which type of system process is started by the kernel and performs system support services?
   A. Zombie
   B. Daemon
   C. Wizard
   D. Warlock
4. A user opens a Terminal window and displays the processes using the **ps –ef** command. Process A has a PID of 234 and a PPID of 223. Process B has a PID of 241 and a PPID of 234. What conclusion can be drawn from this?
   A. Process A is the parent of process B.
   B. Process A is an orphan, and process B is a zombie.
   C. Process B is a daemon, and process A is a wizard.
   D. Process B is the parent of process A.
5. If you want to see only your own processes in the current shell, which version of the process status command should you use?
   A. ps –ef
   B. ps -e
   C. ps
   D. ps –u

6. The **ps –ef** command displays full information on every system task. What does the TIME column mean?
   A. The time that the process started
   B. The time that the user logged on
   C. The amount of CPU time that the process has used
   D. The amount of RAM time that the process has used
7. To search for all process IDs that have to do with the wizbang program, which command would accomplish this?
   A. **ps -f -s wizbang**
   B. **ps -e | more wizbang**
   C. **ps -e grep | wizbang**
   D. **ps –e | grep wizbang**
8. You are working in a Terminal window where you recently ran a program. The program seems to be taking a long time to finish, and you would like to end it. You check the process status and see that its PID is 1234 and that the time is not changing. Which command would you try first to terminate the program while closing files properly?
   A. **kill 1234**
   B. **kill PID 1234**
   C. **kill -9 1234**
   D. **kill -9 PID 1234**
9. You are working in a Terminal window where you recently ran a program. You killed the program using its PID, but your Terminal window is unresponsive and you cannot enter any commands. Which option would provide a sure kill and terminate that shell process?
   A. Open a new Terminal window.
   B. Check the PID of the TTY for the unresponsive Terminal window.
   C. Kill the unresponsive Terminal window with a **–9** option.
   D. Kill the unresponsive Terminal window with a **-15** option.
10. Which of the following is *not* true of virtual memory?
   A. It is a combination of RAM and swap space.
   B. It allows more programs to be run simultaneously.

C. It uses paging to move portions of programs in and out of RAM.

D. It makes programs run faster.

UNIX Command Summary

& Runs job/process in the background and restores the shell prompt. Example:

```
$ Netscape&
```

at Executes specified commands (read from standard input) or script file at a later time that you specify. Example:

```
$ at 10:30am whoson
```

bg Places a job in the background. Example:

```
$ bg %3
```

Ctrl-Z Suspends the foreground process. Example:

```
$ sleep 500&
[1] 453
$ jobs
[1] Running sleep 500
$fg %1
$ sleep 500
^Z
[1] Stopped sleep 500
```

fg Places a job in the foreground. Example:

```
$ sleep 500&
[1] 453
$ jobs
[1] Running sleep 500
$fg %1
$ sleep 500
```

jobs Lists all jobs running in the shell. Example:

```
$ jobs
[1] Running find ~ -name memo1
```

kill Sends a signal to the process or processes specified by each PID operand. Example:

```
-9

$ kill -9 100 -165
$ kill -s kill 100 -165
```

pgrep Examines the active processes on the system and reports the process IDs of the processes whose attributes match the criteria specified on the command line. Example:

```
Obtain the process ID of sendmail:
$ pgrep -x -u root sendmail
283
```

pkill Searches for the process to kill. Example:

Terminate the most recently created xterm:

```
$ pkill -n xterm
```

ps Prints information about active processes. Example:

```
-e, -f, -u
$ ps
```

sleep Suspends execution for at least the integral number of seconds specified in the time operand. Example:

```
$ sleep 60&
```

Key Terms

Background job number In the C shell or Korn shell, a job number is assigned to commands (jobs) executed in the background. Several commands are used to manage background jobs, including **jobs, stop, fg, bg** and **kill.**

Background process You can run a process in the background by adding an ampersand (&) to the end of the command line. Background processes run concurrently with other system processes and shell programs. You might want to run processes in the background because they are time-consuming (such as sorting a large file or searching the file system for a file), or you might want to start a program and be able to continue interacting with the shell.

Child process A process that is spawned by another process. When a user is working in a Terminal window in CDE, that terminal's PID is the *parent process ID* (PPID) of any commands issued in the terminal.

Foreground process The process that is currently in control of the cursor or mouse. Usually in the front window.

Orphan process If a command is issued in a Terminal window and the window is closed before the command returns output, that process becomes an orphan.

Paging The process of moving memory pages between physical memory and the swap space on the disk.

Parent process A process that spawns another process. Following system bootup, a process called the init daemon is invoked. Every process except init has a parent process.

Physical memory All computers have physical or system memory microchips. This most often is referred to as random access memory (RAM). This memory is controlled directly by the processor in conjunction with the memory management unit (MMU).

PID Each program run on a UNIX system creates a process, which is assigned a unique *process identification number* (PID). The PID is used by the system to identify and track the process until it has completed.

Process A unit of work or task on a UNIX system that is manager by the kernel. Each process is assigned CPU time, RAM, and a process ID (PID) until it completes.

Process scheduling The capability to run a process at a predetermined time. The **at** command and the **crontab** command can be used to schedule UNIX jobs or processes.

Signals Currently 30 to 40 signals are defined in UNIX, depending on the implementation. Each signal is associated with a number and a name. Signals are used to terminate, suspend, and continue processes. The **kill –9** command uses a signal 9 to terminate a shell.

Spawn A Process can start or spawn a subprocess, thus creating a process hierarchy or tree similar to the file system structure with parent/child relationships.

Virtual memory The swapping process uses swap space on the disk, which is limited. The combination of RAM plus swap space constitutes virtual memory, which is the maximum space that processes can use.

Zombie process Occasionally, a child process does not return to the parent process with its output. This process becomes “lost” in the system.

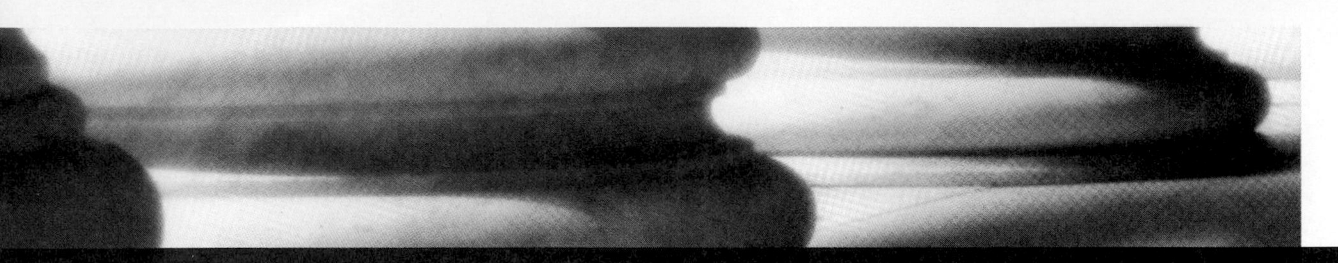

Objectives

After reading this chapter, you will be able to

- Compare and contrast the most common UNIX shells
- Describe the features of the Korn and C shells
- Create custom prompts and aliases with the Korn and C shells
- Use history and re-execute commands with the Korn and C shells
- Work with local and global variables

Chapter 14

Basic Features of the Korn and C Shells

Introduction

The *shell* is the primary user interface to a UNIX system. The concept of the shell was introduced in Chapter 1, "The UNIX Computing Environment," along with other key UNIX operating system components: the kernel and the file system. The UNIX environment provides support for many built-in (Bourne, C, Korn) and third-party shells. This chapter provides a brief review of the function of the shell and focuses on two of the most widely used shells today: the Korn shell and the C shell. It goes into greater detail about the unique features of each shell, and it provides information on how to become more efficient by using custom prompts, aliases, history, and re-execution of commands. Finally, there is a discussion about local and global variables used to customize your work environment.

Review of the Shell

A *shell* is an interface between the user and the kernel. It acts as an interpreter or translator. In other words, the shell accepts commands issued by you, interprets these commands, and executes the appropriate programs.

Shells can be command-line–driven or graphical. Also, shells are interchangeable, making it possible to initiate or switch between them at any time to use certain features not available in other shells.

The shell is the first program to run when you log onto the system. In addition to its primary role as a command interpreter, the shell program has numerous features and built-in commands that make interacting with the system and completing tasks easy. A lot of the shell features already have been addressed in this book.

- **Wildcard matching**—(See Chapter 5, "Accessing Files and Directories.") Special characters reserved for specifying a pattern to select one or more files as a group for processing. For example, **$lp chap***.
- **Input/output redirection**—Special characters reserved for redirecting input and output (>, >> and <). For example, **$who > userlog**. (See Chapter 7, "Advanced Directory and File Management.")
- **Pipes**—(See Chapter 7.) Used to connect one or more simple commands to perform more complex operations. For example, **$who | sort | lp**.
- **Background processing**—(See Chapter 13, "System Processes and Memory Management.") Enables programs and commands to run in the background while the user continues to interact with the shell to complete other tasks. For example, **$sort largefile &**.
- **Programming language (advanced topic)**—Programming features used to create shell scripts that perform complex operations. For example, a shell script was written to set up all the user accounts, create home directories, and copy lab files into each user's home directory for the Fundamentals of UNIX class.

This chapter focuses on the Korn (ksh) and C (csh) shells, the two most widely used shells for end users. You can use the **ps** (process status) command to see which shell you are using.

The Korn Shell in Brief

Developed by Stephen Korn at Bell Labs, the Korn shell is a superset of the Bourne shell. The Bourne shell was the original shell program for the UNIX environment, and it is the default shell for the Solaris computing environment. Developed by Stephen Bourne for the AT&T System V.2 UNIX environment, this shell does not have aliasing, history, or command-line editing capabilities, and it is used primarily by system administrators. The Bourne shell prompt is a dollar sign ($), which is similar to a DOS C:> prompt.

The Korn shell has many of the Bourne shell features, plus added features such as aliasing, history, and command-line editing. The Korn shell is the most widely used shell and is the industry standard for system users. The Korn shell prompt is also a dollar sign ($).

NOTE

Examples given in this course are based primarily on the Korn shell.

The C Shell in Brief

The C shell is based on the C programming language. Like the Korn shell, it has additional features over the Bourne shell, such as aliasing and history. The C shell was developed by Bill Joy of Sun Microsystems and is still widely used today. The C shell prompt is a percent sign (%).

> **NOTE**
> Both the Korn and the C shells are discussed in greater detail in the following sections. Korn shell features are discussed first.

Additional Korn Shell Features

In addition to the features listed previously and addressed earlier, the Korn shell has other features that make interacting with it easier and faster:

- **Command aliasing**—Provides a shortcut method for entering commands by enabling you to assign a definition to an alias name—for example, creating an alias named **ll** that executes the **ls –l** command.
- **Command history and command-line editing**—Allows you to build and reference a history of commands that can be recalled without having to retype them—for example, repeating the last command line that began with **vi**. Command-line editing allows you to recall a previous command line and make changes.
- **Shell variables**—Serve as predefined and user-defined variables for writing shell scripts and customizing your work environment—for example, modifying a predefined shell variable to change your prompt from **$** to **UNIX$**.

Each feature is discussed in greater detail in the following sections.

Korn Shell Aliases

An *alias* is a way to give a command a different name for use in the shell. Aliases provide an excellent way to improve efficiency and productivity when using shell commands. When set from the command line, aliases are activated only for the shell in which they are created. Adding aliases to the .kshrc file (covered in Chapter 15, "Customizing Your Login Environment") activates them upon login or whenever a new window or shell is opened. The following shows the basic syntax of the **alias** command used to create an alias:

> **NOTE**
> There is a space after the alias command and the **alias** name. There are no spaces before or after the equals sign (=).

```
alias aliasname=value
```

There are several reasons to use aliases:

- **To substitute a short command for a long one**—You can reduce the number of keystrokes for commonly used long commands by creating an alias for the command.
- **To create a single command for a series of commands**—You can string together several commands and assign them one short alias name, to reduce keystrokes.
- **To create alternate forms of existing commands**—Some commands, such as **rm** (remove files and directories) and **cp** (copy files), can be dangerous. If you are not careful, you accidentally could overwrite an important file. An alias allows

you to change the meaning of these commands to include the **-i** option so that they prompt a user before overwriting a file or directory.

NOTE

Use single quotes for commands with options, spaces, or other special characters.

Figure 14-1 shows some examples creating aliases. Examples 1 and 2 in the figure show how to substitute a short command for a long one, Example 3 shows how to create a single command for a series of commands, and Example 4 shows how to create alternate forms of existing commands.

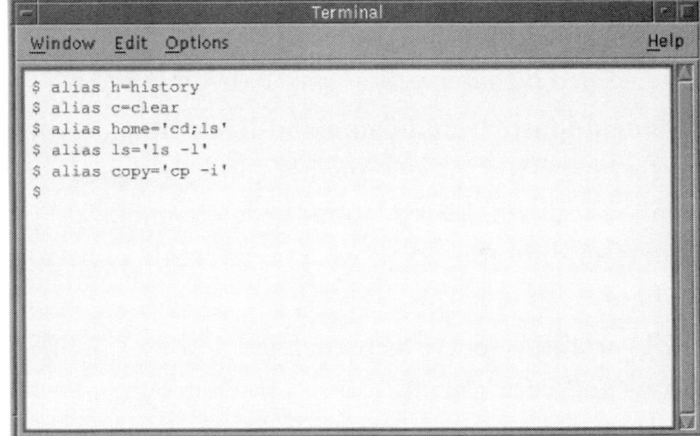
Terminal
Window Edit Options Help
$ alias h=history
$ alias c=clear
$ alias home='cd;ls'
$ alias ls='ls -l'
$ alias copy='cp -i'
$

Figure 14-1
Creating aliases.

Displaying Korn Shell Aliases

To display aliases, use the **alias** command with no argument. Figure 14-2 shows using the **alias** command to display all aliases set for the current session. Some aliases are predefined as part of the Korn shell.

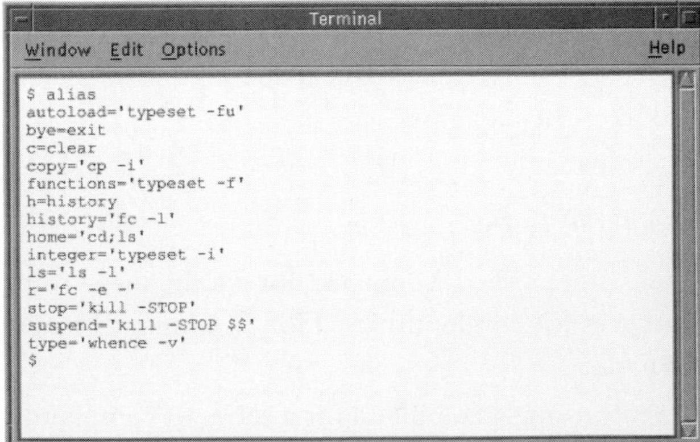
Terminal
Window Edit Options Help
$ alias
autoload='typeset -fu'
bye=exit
c=clear
copy='cp -i'
functions='typeset -f'
h=history
history='fc -l'
home='cd;ls'
integer='typeset -i'
ls='ls -l'
r='fc -e -'
stop='kill -STOP'
suspend='kill -STOP $$'
type='whence -v'
$

Figure 14-2
Displaying all aliases set for the current session.

Removing an Alias in the Current Shell

You can unset a previously defined alias with the **unalias** command. Figure 14-3 shows using the **unalias** command to unset the bye alias, which no longer will appear in the alias listing. You also can temporarily bypass an alias. To bypass the alias and use the original version of a command, use a backslash, as shown in Figure 14-3. The following shows the basic syntax of the **unalias** command used to remove an alias:

```
unalias  aliasname
```

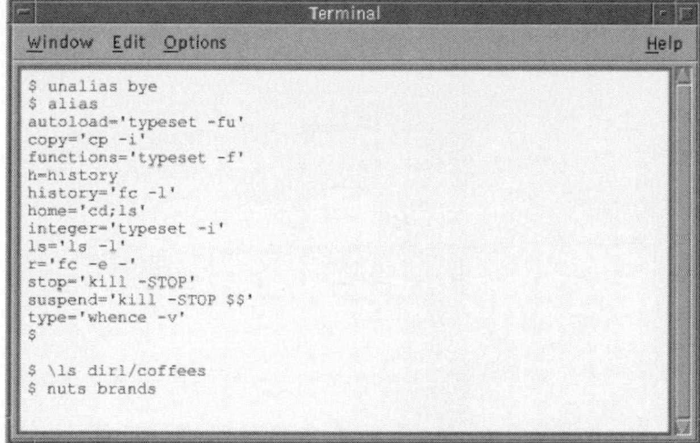
Terminal
Window Edit Options Help
$ unalias bye
$ alias
autoload='typeset -fu'
copy='cp -i'
functions='typeset -f'
h=history
history='fc -l'
home='cd;ls'
integer='typeset -i'
ls='ls -l'
r='fc -e -'
stop='kill -STOP'
suspend='kill -STOP $$'
type='whence -v'
$
$ \ls dirl/coffees
$ nuts brands

Figure 14-3 Unsetting a previously defined alias.

Skill Builder

e-Lab Activity 14.1

Using Korn Shell Aliases

In this e-Lab activity, you are logged in as user2, and your current working directory is /home/user2. Refer to the class file tree structure on the inside-front cover of this book. Type the commands that would accomplish the requested objectives. *Note*: Be sure to press Enter after each one. Click Step 1 to begin.

The history Command in the Korn Shell

The **history** command records commands typed in the Korn shell. In the Korn shell, **history** automatically is set up when the user first enters the shell. Whenever the user types in a command, this function records it on a history list. The history list is stored in the user's home directory in a file named ~/.sh_history. By default, the Korn shell keeps a record of the last 128 commands entered, but it displays only the last 16 commands, by default. The following shows the basic syntax of the history command:

```
history  [options]
```

Specifying a number preceded by a dash as an option displays that number of lines. Specifying a number without a dash shows the history lines from that number to the last command entered. Figure 14-4 shows the listing from the history command. In the first example, using the history command by itself, the last 16 commands are displayed. The second example displays only the last three commands because the -3 option was used.

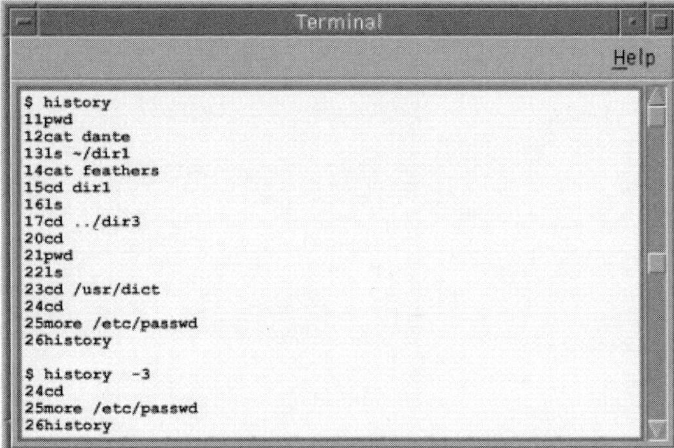

Figure 14-4
Displaying history.

Re-Executing Commands in the Korn Shell

The **r** (repeat) command is one of many predefined aliases in the Korn shell. This enables the user to re-execute commands from the history list. The following shows the basic syntax of the **r** command:

```
r [argument(s)]
```

The argument passed to the **r** command is the history line number of a particular command, or a letter indicating the most recent command in the history list that started with that letter. In Figure 14-5, the first example shows the **r** command by itself, which repeats the last command entered (pwd). This is similar to the F3 key in DOS. The second example uses the **history** command to see the commands from the 27th command onward and then uses the r command to repeat the 27th command. Example 3 repeats the last command that started with the letter *p*.

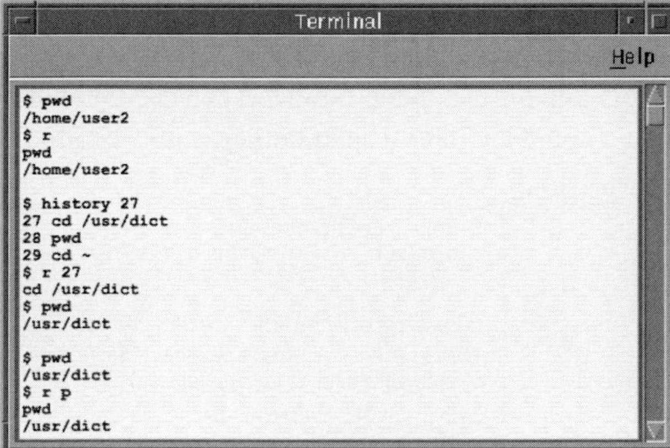

Terminal
Help
$ pwd
/home/user2
$ r
pwd
/home/user2
$ history 27
27 cd /usr/dict
28 pwd
29 cd ~
$ r 27
cd /usr/dict
$ pwd
/usr/dict
$ pwd
/usr/dict
$ r p
pwd
/usr/dict

Figure 14-5
Using the **r** (repeat) command.

Skill Builder

e-Lab Activity 14.2

Re-Executing Commands in the Korn Shell

In this e-Lab activity, you are logged in as user2, and your current working directory is /home/user2. Refer to the class file tree structure on the inside-front cover of this book. Type the commands that would accomplish the requested objectives. Note: Be sure to press Enter after each one. Click Step 1 to begin.

Editing the Command Line in the Korn Shell

The in-line edit mode enables you to edit a previous command on the current command line. Use vi commands to move and edit the previous command line. When enabled from the command line, the command-line editing feature is activated only for the shell in which it was set. Adding command-line editing to the .kshrc file (covered in Chapter 15) enables it upon login or whenever a new window or shell is opened. The following shows the basic syntax of the set command used to enable command-line editing:

```
set [- +] o vi
```

Using **set -o vi** turns on command-line editing, while **set +o vi** turns it off. When the editing has been turned on, pressing the Esc key activates the in-line editor. You then have access to vi commands.

In Figure 14-6, the use of the **more** command generates an error because there was a misspelling of words. Next, the **set -o vi** command is used to turn on vi editing, and the

NOTE

The arrow keys cannot be used to reposition the cursor during in-line editing.

k key then is used to repeat the previous command so that it can be corrected. In this example, the user edited the command to change *worfs* to *words*. The **k** key moves up through the command list, and the **j** key moves down. A way to remember these is, **k** is for "kick up" and **j** is for "jump down." The vi commands shown in the figure can be used to edit a command line. The Enter key is pressed after all changes are made.

Figure 14-6
Editing the command line.

```
$ more /usr/dict/worfs
/usr/dict/worfs: No such file or directory


$ set -o vi
(Press the Esc key and then the k key until the desired command
displays then edit appropriately.)


$ more /usr/dict/words
```

vi Command	Meaning
k	Moves backward through history list.
j	Moves forward through history list.
l	Moves to the right one character.
h	Moves to the left one character.
r	Replaces one character.
cw	Changes word.
x	Deletes one character.

Skill Builder

e-Lab Activity 14.3

Command-Line Editing in the Korn Shell

In this e-Lab activity, you are logged in as user2, and your current working directory is /home/user2. Refer to the class file tree structure on the inside-front cover of this book. Type the commands that would accomplish the requested objectives. Note: Be sure to press Enter after each one. Click Step 1 to begin.

Custom Prompts with the Korn Shell

The default prompt for the Korn shell is the dollar sign ($). The user can customize his own shell prompt to his liking using the predefined PS1 (prompt string 1) shell prompt variable (PS1=$). A variable is an informational placeholder used when customizing the shell. Shell variables are discussed in more detail at the end of this chapter.

The PS1 variable can include a wide range of expressions, such as character strings, commands, or other variables. Figure 14-7 shows several different ways the standard PS1 prompt ($) can be customized. The variable PS1 is a shell variable. Any change in the variable setting remains until the shell is exited or until a subshell is opened. To make the customized prompt available from one session to the next, place the PS1 variable in the .kshrc file (covered in Chapter 15). The following shows the basic syntax used to customize the Korn shell prompt:

```
PS1=value
```

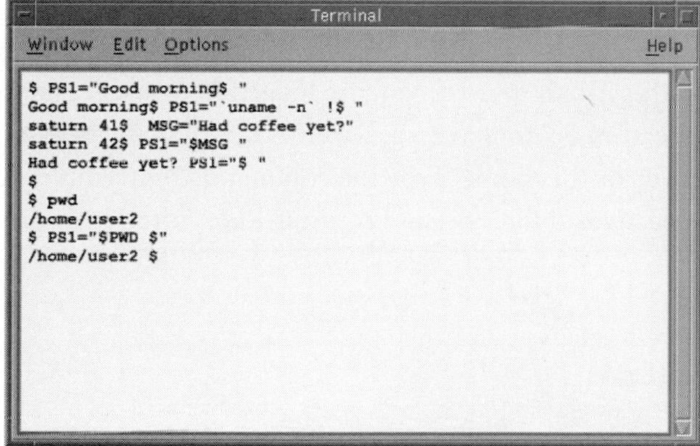

Figure 14-7 Customizing your Korn shell prompt.

The following are several customized prompts that include examples of text or output of a command. Note that, by convention (not required), they all end in a dollar sign ($), representing the Korn shell.

- **$ PS1="Good morning$ "**—The first example assigns the prompt to a character string. The prompt is changed from the conventional $ to a greeting (Good morning), with the $ at the end. The double quotes are necessary because of the space (metacharacter) between good and morning. Single quotes also tell the shell to display a metacharacter literally, and they also could have been used in this case. Double quotes have an additional function, as discussed next.
- **Good morning$ PS1="'uname -n' !$ "**—This example demonstrates using a command (uname -n) with the history line number (!) for a unique prompt. This command causes the prompt to show the name of the host on which you are working (saturn 41). The back quotes (') are used to substitute the output of the uname command instead of interpreting it literally. Double quotes surround the entire string.

- **saturn 41? PS1="$ "**—This example sets the prompt back to the original Korn shell dollar sign ($) prompt. Single or double quotes are necessary because of the space metacharacter.
- **$ PS1="$PWD $"**—In this example, the prompt is customized to reflect the current working directory. Double quotes surround the string and allow expansion of the $PWD variable, which always keeps track of the current working directory. Single quotes do not allow for variable expansion and would not work in this case

NOTE

The previous examples use various quoting characters recognized by the shell to do something different. Quoting is an important feature used with many different commands. For example, Chapter 8, "Files and User Information Utilities," introduced the **grep** command to look for a string of characters inside a file. It was noted that the string could include whitespace or punctuation if enclosed in quotations (as in **grep "howdy doody" file1**). As in the previous PS1 examples, the quotes are necessary because of the space metacharacter between "howdy" and "doody".

Quotes are used anytime you want the shell to interpret any metacharacter (*,?,>,|, and so on) literally, not just spaces. For example, if you wanted to print in large letters ***HELLO*** to the screen using the **banner** command, you would need to put ***HELLO*** in quotes to make sure that the shell does not try to interpret the * as a wildcard.

Skill Builder

e-Lab Activity 14.4

Customizing Your Korn Shell Prompt

In this e-Lab activity, you are logged in as user2, and your current working directory is /home/user2. Refer to the class file tree structure on the inside-front cover of this book. Type the commands that would accomplish the requested objectives. Note: Be sure to press Enter after each one. Click Step 1 to begin.

Skill Builder

Lab Activity 14.2.5

Korn Shell Features

In this lab, you work with UNIX commands to identify system processes and control them. Refer to the Cisco Networking Academy Program: Fundamentals of UNIX Lab Companion.

Additional C Shell Features

The C shell is the other widely used shell, and it is similar to the Korn shell. It has many of the same features, but it implements them slightly differently. The following sections cover corresponding C shell features that make interacting with it easier and faster:

- **Command aliasing**—Using, displaying, and removing aliases is the same as in the Korn shell. Creating aliases in the C shell uses a slightly different syntax.
- **Command history and command-line substitution**—The history feature is the same as the Korn shell, but re-executing previous commands is slightly

different. There is no command-line editing feature in the C shell. Instead, this shell has a command-line substitution feature.

- **Shell variables**—Like the Korn shell, the C shell has predefined and user-defined variables for writing shell scripts and customizing your work environment. Some of the variable names are the same. Setting variables is different than in the Korn shell.

Each feature is discussed in greater detail in the following sections.

C Shell Aliases

Command aliases are also available in the C shell. As explained previously, an alias is a way to give a command a different name for use in the shell. Aliases provide an excellent way to improve efficiency when using shell commands. When set from the command line, aliases are activated only for the shell in which they are created. Add aliases to your .cshrc file to activate them upon login or whenever a new window or shell is opened. The function of an alias within the C shell is the same as that of the Korn shell.

The reasons for using C shell aliases are identical to those for using Korn shell aliases. The commands used are identical, except that the C shell does not use an equals sign. Figure 14-8 shows some examples of the **alias** command and an example of the **unalias** command used to remove an alias.

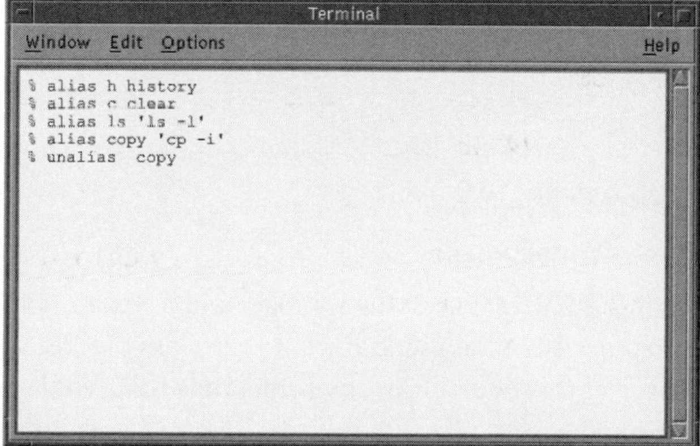
Terminal
Window Edit Options Help
% alias h history
% alias c clear
% alias ls 'ls -l'
% alias copy 'cp -i'
% unalias copy

Figure 14-8 Creating and removing aliases.

The command format used to create aliases is similar to that of the Korn shell, except that the C shell does not use the equals sign between the alias name and the command(s) for the alias:

```
alias  aliasname  value
```

Removing an Alias in the Current Shell

You can unset a previously defined alias with the **unalias** command. Figure 14-8 shows using the **unalias** command to unset the copy alias, which no longer will appear in the alias listing. As with the Korn shell, you can temporarily bypass an alias and use the original version of a command by using a backslash. The following shows the basic syntax of the **unalias** command used to remove an alias:

```
unalias  alias_name
```

Displaying C Shell Aliases

To display aliases, use the **alias** command with no argument. Figure 14-9 shows using the alias command to display all aliases set for the current session. Some aliases are predefined as part of the C shell.

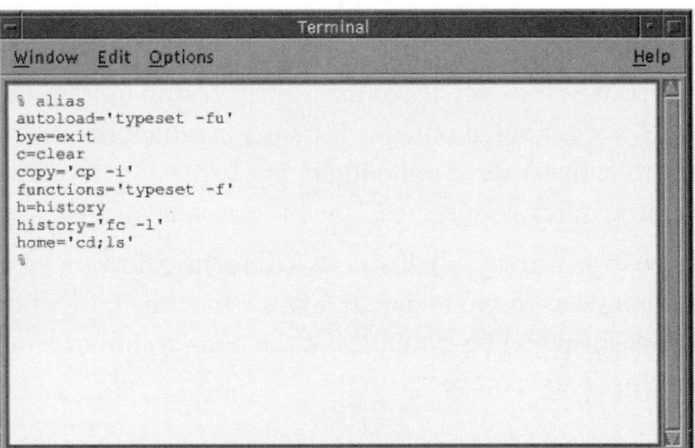
Terminal
Window Edit Options Help
% alias
autoload='typeset -fu'
bye=exit
c=clear
copy='cp -i'
functions='typeset -f'
h=history
history='fc -l'
home='cd;ls'
%

Figure 14-9 Displaying all aliases set for the current session.

Skill Builder

e-Lab Activity 14.6

Using C Shell Aliases

In this e-Lab activity, you are logged in as user2, and your current working directory is /home/user2. Refer to the class file tree structure on the inside-front cover of this book. Type the commands that would accomplish the requested objectives. Note: Be sure to press Enter after each one. Click Step 1 to begin.

The history Command in the C Shell

The **history** variable saves and prints the current command and history list number to the screen. The history list keeps a record of the exact command lines that you enter, in the order that you enter them. Unlike the Korn shell, the C shell does not automatically have the history variable set. You must set the history variable (history list) before the **history** command can be executed. You can set **history** to a specific number to display that number of previous commands to the screen, as shown here:

```
set  history=n
```

In the first example in Figure 14-10, the last five command lines are displayed from the history list after setting history to 5 and then typing the **history** command. After you have set the history variable, the history list is created from that point on. Any commands entered before executing the set history command are not part of the history list. Any commands typed after setting the history variable are added to the history list, as shown in the second example, and are displayed each time you type the history command. To stop capturing history, use the unset history command.

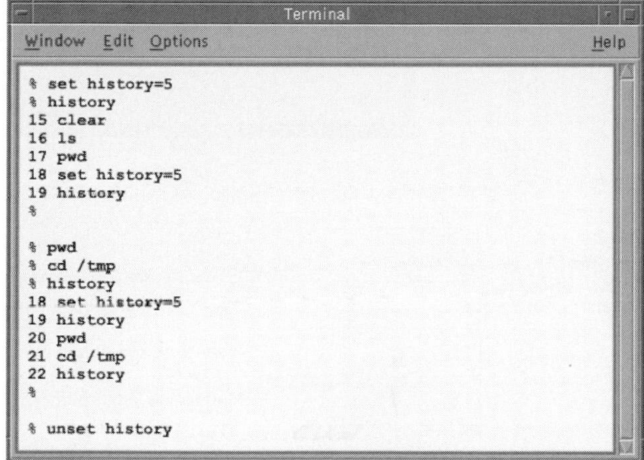

Figure 14-10 Using the **history** command.

Re-executing Commands in the C Shell

Like the Korn shell, the C shell offers additional features for repeating and editing previously entered command lines. Figure 14-11 shows an example using the history command-line number 32 from the previous history file output (cd home/user2/practice). Figure 14-12 shows options available with the history command. The Bourne shell does not offer these features for editing previously entered commands.

Figure 14-13 shows how to re-execute commands with the history options in the C shell.

The following are detailed explanations of the examples in Figure 14-13.

- !!—Use the double exclamation marks (!!) to execute the most recent command exactly as it was executed previously. If you entered the **lpstat** command, sent some print jobs from other Terminal windows, and want to enter the **lpstat** command again from the original Terminal window, type **!!** at the shell prompt to execute **lpstat** the second time, as shown in the first example in Figure 14-14.
- !*—Use the exclamation mark (!) and asterisk (*) to repeat all arguments of the previous command, as shown in the second example in Figure 14-14.

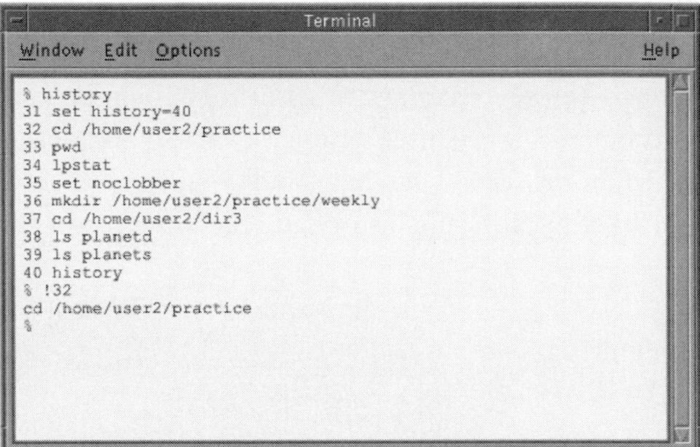

Figure 14-11
Re-executing commands.

Figure 14-12
history options.

Feature	Function
!!	Executes the previous command.
! *	Repeats all arguments from the previous command.
! $	Repeats the last argument from the previous command.
! number	Executes command number from the history list.
! n : p	Views command n from the history list without executing it.

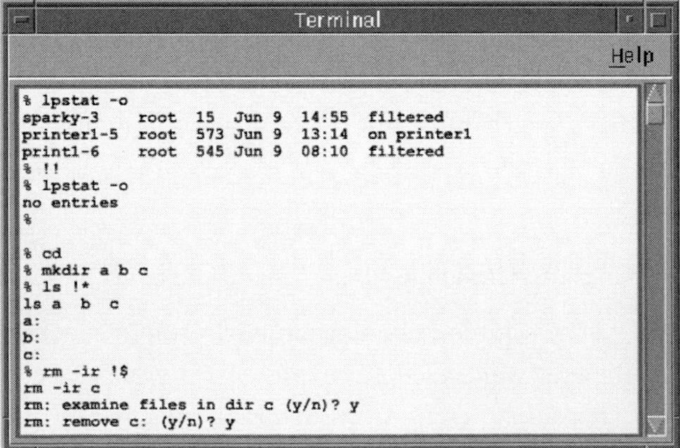

Figure 14-13
Re-executing commands with the **history** options.

- **!$**—Use the exclamation mark (!) and the dollar sign ($) to repeat the last argument of the previous command, as shown in Examples 3 and 4 in Figure 14-14.
- **!number**—Use the exclamation mark (!) followed by a command number to repeat a specific command from the command list, as shown in Example 5 in Figure 14-14.
- **!n:p**—With this option, you can see a previous command but not execute it. This is useful for editing the command, which is covered later in this chapter.

Figure 14-14
Making corrections to the command line.

```
% lp -d ztaffp feathers
UX:lp: Error:ztaffp: unknown printer
% ^z^s
lp -d staffp feathers
request id is staffp-5 ( 1 file )
%

% !37
cd /home/user2/dir3
% !38:p
ls planetd
% ^d^s
ls planets
mars moon pluto
```

Skill Builder

e-Lab Activity 14.7

C Shell History and Re-Execution

In this e-Lab activity, you are logged in as user2, and your current working directory is /home/user2. Refer to the class file tree structure on the inside-front cover of this book. Type the commands that would accomplish the requested objectives. *Note*: Be sure to press Enter after each one. Click Step 1 to begin.

Command-Line Substitution with the C Shell

Unlike the Korn shell, the C shell does not have a command-line editing feature where you can recall a previously executed command line, modify it using vi editor keystrokes, and then execute it. Instead, the C shell has a command-line substitution feature that enables you to make changes to only the last command by replacing an old string with a new string and then executing it. The syntax is shown here:

```
^old_string^new_string
```

Each string can be any length. The caret (^) symbols tell **history** to locate the first occurrence of the letter(s) old_string in the previous command, substitute the letter(s) new_string for it, and execute the modified command. There are no spaces between the carets and strings.

The first example in Figure 14-15 replaces the *z* in the previous command with an *s*.

The second example combines history and command-line substitution to recall and change a previous command. The **:p** is used to view command number 38 first without executing it. Then the ***d*** is replaced with an *s*.

Skill Builder

e-Lab Activity 14.8

C Shell Command-Line Substitution

In this e-Lab activity, you are logged in as user2, and your current working directory is /home/user2. Refer to the class file tree structure on the inside-front cover of this book. Type the commands that would accomplish the requested objectives. *Note:* Be sure to press Enter after each one. Click Step 1 to begin.

Custom Prompts in the C Shell

NOTE

There are no spaces on either side of the equals sign (=).

The default prompt for the C shell is the percent sign (%). As with the Korn shell, the user can customize his own shell prompt to his liking. The Korn shell uses the PS1 variable, whereas the C shell uses the **set prompt** command. A wide range of expressions, such as character strings, commands, or other variables, can be used. The following shows the basic syntax used to customize the C shell prompt:

```
set  prompt=value
```

Figure 14-15 shows several different ways to customize the standard prompt (**%**). Any change in the prompt setting remains until the shell is exited or until a sub shell is opened. To make the customized prompt available from one session to the next, place the **set prompt** command in the .cshrc (C shell run control) file (covered in Chapter 15).

The following list covers several customized prompts that include examples of text or output of a command. Note that, by convention (not required), they all end in a percent sign (%), representing the C shell.

- **% set prompt="Get started %"**—This form of the command sets the prompt to a fixed string.
- **% set prompt="Hello, 'hostname'%"**—The prompt is set to a fixed string (**Hello**) followed by a shell variable host name that places the name of the computer in the prompt.
- **Hello venus% set prompt="%"**—This sets the prompt back to the default C shell prompt of %.

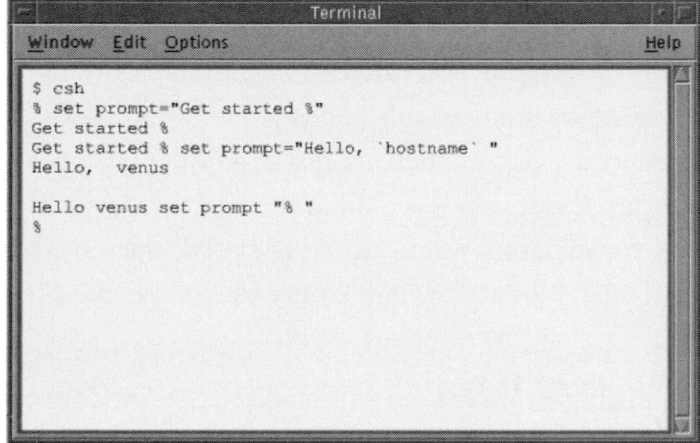
Terminal
Window Edit Options Help
$ csh
% set prompt="Get started %"
Get started %
Get started % set prompt="Hello, `hostname` "
Hello, venus

Hello venus set prompt "% "
%

Figure 14-15 Customizing your C shell prompt.

Skill Builder

e-Lab Activity 14.5

Customizing Your C Shell Prompt

In this e-Lab activity, you are logged in as user2, and your current working directory is /home/user2. Refer to the class file tree structure on the inside-front cover of this book. Type the commands that would accomplish the requested objectives. *Note*: Be sure to press Enter after each one. Click Step 1 to begin.

Shell Variables

Two categories of variables are used by all UNIX shells:

- **Local (*shell*) variables**—Variables that are available only for the current shell session
- **Environment (*global*) variables**—Variables that are available to all shell sessions

Regardless of category type, a *variable* is a placeholder for information to be used by the system or user. Predefined variables for UNIX users include information for the default terminal prompt (PS1) and the default printer (LPDEST).

NOTE

This section covers setting and unsetting Bourne and Korn shell and environment variables. See the man pages on csh for C shell variables.

Overview

When you first login to the host, you are placed in a predefined shell. If you type **sh** (Bourne shell), **ksh** (Korn shell), or **csh** (C shell) on the command line, a subshell is created. This process can be repeated to create additional shells. To change to the previous shell, type **exit**.

Shell variables (local and global) can be either user-defined or built-in, and they can be customized by the user or predefined by the system.

Initially, when a variable is created, it is available only in that shell. This is referred to as a *local variable*. If a new subshell is created (manually or by the system), the variables created in the parent shell are not available. However, the parent shell is still running, and when the subshell is exited, the variables will be available again. When the shell where the variables were created is exited, the variables of that shell are terminated. Local variables are available only to the specific shell where they are created.

NOTE

See the man pages on **ksh**, **csh**, and **sh** for more on shell variables.

To make a local variable available in all subshells, it must be exported, either by adding it to an initialization file, as will be discussed in Chapter 15, or by exporting it on the command line (discussed later in this chapter).

Setting Local Shell Variables

By convention, the Bourne and Korn shells use capital letters for shell variable names—for example, PS1="MyPrompt$". The **unset** command removes the variable from the current shell and subshells, but it rarely is done. The following shows the basic syntax used to set and unset shell variables:

```
VARIABLE=value
unset  VARIABLE
```

Displaying Shell Variable Values

To display the value of a single variable, use the **echo** command. For example, **echo $PS1** would return "MyPrompt$". The dollar sign ($) metacharacter preceding a variable tells the shell to use the value of the variable, not the name of the variable. Because this is a local variable, if a new subshell is opened, the customized PS1 variable would not be available.

To display all variables in the local shell and their values, type the **set** command, as shown in Figure 14-16.

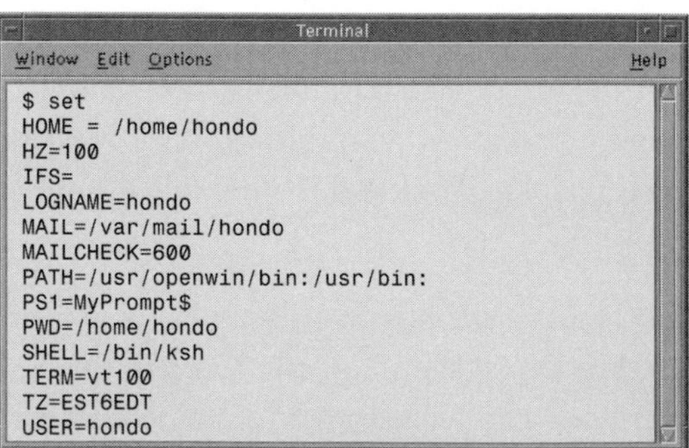
Terminal
Window Edit Options Help
$ set
HOME = /home/hondo
HZ=100
IFS=
LOGNAME=hondo
MAIL=/var/mail/hondo
MAILCHECK=600
PATH=/usr/openwin/bin:/usr/bin:
PS1=MyPrompt$
PWD=/home/hondo
SHELL=/bin/ksh
TERM=vt100
TZ=EST6EDT
USER=hondo

Figure 14-16 Displaying shell variables by using the **set** command.

Environment Variables

Environment variables are variables available to all shells (including subshells), not just the local shell. To make a variable known to a subshell, it must be exported with the **export** command. For example, in Figure 14-16, note that the PS1 variable is set to MyPrompt$. MyPrompt$ will appear in that shell only. If you were to start a subshell by typing **ksh** and pressing Enter, the prompt in the new shell would display the default $ prompt, not MyPrompt$. The reason for this is that when the PS1 variable was set, it was set for use in that shell only. If, after the PS1 variable was set, it was exported (**$export PS1**) all subshells inherit the value. Think of an environmental variable as something valuable that a parent (current shell) is passing down to the child (subshell).

Behind the scenes, UNIX automatically creates subshells to complete a task, and it is important that the environment set up in the parent shell is passed to any child subshells. The following shows the basic syntax used to create an environmental variable:

```
VARIABLE=value ; export  VARIABLE
```

or

```
export  VARIABLE=value
```

or

```
export  VARIABLE (if variable is already defined)
```

For example, to set your default printer to xerox1, you would do the following:

```
$ LPDEST=xerox1; export LPDEST
$ echo $LPDEST
xerox1
```

To have line numbers automatically turned on when starting vi, you could set the ex initialization variable (EXINIT) and then export it:

```
$ EXINIT='set showmode'; export EXINIT
$ echo $EXINIT
set showmode
```

UNIX provides several important predefined environment variables, such as HOME, LOGNAME, SHELL, and PATH. These variables have been defined by the shell to have a specific function, and they are available to the login shell and all subshells.

Variables can set up to be exported automatically upon log-in by modifying the initialization files, discussed in Chapter 15.

Exporting variables in an initialization file enables the variables to be used by the system, processes, scripts, users, and all shells. Exporting variables at the command line makes the variables available to the current shell and all its child processes. A variable set in a subshell and exported will be available to any shells opened afterward, but it will not be available to the parent shell.

Displaying Environment Variables

Environment variables and their values can be displayed by typing the export command by itself:

```
export  Or  env
```

Summary

Now that you have completed this chapter, you should have an understanding of the following:

- The UNIX shell is a key component of the UNIX operating system. The shell is the interface between the user and the kernel. Three commonly used shells exist: the Bourne shell, the Korn shell, and the C shell. This chapter focused on the Korn and C shells, which have more features than the Bourne and are the most popular for regular users.
- The default prompt for the Korn shell is the dollar sign (**$**) (same as Bourne shell). The default prompt for the C shell is the percent sign (%). Both Korn and C shell users can customize their prompts. The Korn shell sets the PS1 variable, and the C shell uses the **set prompt** command.
- Both Korn and C shells support aliasing and history, although their command syntax varies somewhat. Aliases allow the user to create new command names and associate them with existing commands to increase productivity. The **history** command allows the user to reuse previous commands to avoid having to type them in again.
- The Korn shell provides command-line editing by allowing the user to use vi editor commands to modify previous command lines. The C shell allows the user to make command-line substitutions for simple changes, but it does not have a command-line editing feature like the Korn shell does.
- Variables are placeholders for information. You can change many predefined variables to customize your work environment, such as using PS1 to change the prompt.
- Variables are either local (available only in the current shell) or global (exported to all subshells). To set a variable, use the format **VARIABLE=value**. To make it available to all subshells, export it with the **export** command. To display the value of an individual variable, use the **echo $VARIABLE** command. Use the **set** command to display a list of local variables, and use the **export** command to display a list of all environment variables.

Check Your Understanding

1. What is the primary purpose of the UNIX shell?
   - A. An interface to the kernel
   - B. Security for the operating system
   - C. Process control for the kernel
   - D. An interface to the partition
2. The UNIX environment supports which operating system shells?
   - A. Bourne
   - B. Korn
   - C. C
   - D. All of the above
3. The Korn shell uses the Bourne shell as a basis for its features. Which of the following added features does the Korn shell support that the Bourne shell does not?
   - A. Aliasing
   - B. History
   - C. Command-line editing
   - D. All of the above
4. Which command would be used to customize a Korn shell prompt to include an absolute path to the current directory?
   - A. **$ PS1="$CWD $"**
   - B. **$ PS1="$PWD $"**
   - C. **$ PS1="$DIR $"**
   - D. **$ PS1="PG $"**
5. Which command would be used to customize a C shell prompt to include the name of the computer?
   - A. **% set prompt="'hostname' %"**
   - B. **% set prompt="'computer' %"**
   - C. **% set prompt="'uname -n' %"**
   - D. **% set prompt="'machine' %"**

6. Aliases can help improve user productivity at the command line by reducing keystrokes. Which of the following cannot be accomplished using aliases?
   A. Substitute a short command for a long one
   B. Create a single command for a series of commands
   C. Create alternate forms of existing commands
   D. Change a command
7. You want to create a Korn shell alias called h, which will execute the **history** command when typed. What is the proper command syntax to accomplish this?
   A. **h=history**
   B. **alias h=history**
   C. **trans h=history**
   D. **alias h history**
8. In the Korn shell, history is automatically set up as a default when the user first enters the shell. In the C shell, it is necessary to activate a variable for this feature using which command?
   A. **% set hist=n**
   B. **% set hist on**
   C. **% set history=n**
   D. **% history on**
9. To re-execute the 38th command in a Korn shell history list, which command format would accomplish this?
   A. $ r38
   B. $!38
   C. $ *38
   D. $ h38
10. How would you turn on command-line editing with the Korn shell?
    A. editor=vi
    B. cledit –o vi
    C. set +o vi
    D. set -o vi

UNIX Command Summary

!! Re-executes the last command in C shell. Example:

```
$ !!
```

!$ Repeats the last argument from the previous command in C shell. Example:

```
$ !$
```

!* Repeats all arguments of the previous command in C shell. Example:

```
$ !*
```

!number Repeats a specific number command from the C shell history file. Example:

```
170 pwd
171 ls
172 cd ~
$ !171
```

alias **alias** and **unalias** utilities create or remove a pseudonym or shorthand term for a command or series of commands. Example:

Change copy (cp) to include a confirmation prompt before overwriting a file:

```
alias cp="cp -i"
```

csh Starts a C shell subshell.

echo Echoes (displays) arguments. Example:

```
$ echo "hi mom"
hi mom

$ echo $SHELL
/bin/ksh
```

exit Leaves the current terminal window or current shell and returns to the previous one. Also used to log out of the login shell.

export Displays all environmental variables available to all shells. Example:

```
$ export
FRAME=/opt/fm/
HOME=/home/hondo
PS1=MyPrompt$
SHELL=/bin/ksh
TERM=vt100
```

history Lists or edits and re-executes commands previously entered into an interactive shell. Example:

```
$ history
339 man grep
340 pwd
341 grep banana ./*
342 history
$ r 340
```

```
pwd
/home/user2
$
```

ksh Starts a Korn shell subshell.

logout Used to exit the login shell for a C shell user. Example:

```
logout
```

PS1 A variable that can be changed by the user to alter the appearance of the default shell prompt. Example:

```
$ PS1="new prompt$ "
$ PS1="$PWD $ "
```

r Repeats a command from the history list. Example:

```
170 pwd
171 ls
172 cd ~
$ r 170
```

set Displays all variables in the local shell. Example:

```
$ set
HOME=/home/hondo
PS1=MyPrompt$
SHELL=/bin/ksh
```

set + o vi Turns on command-line editing.

set - o vi Turns off command-line editing.

set prompt Sets the default shell prompt in a C shell. Example:

```
% set prompt="hello %"
```

sh Starts a Borne shell subshell.

unalias The **alias** and **unalias** utilities create or remove a pseudonym or shorthand term for a command or series of commands. Example:

```
$ alias cp="cp -i"
$ unalias cp
```

unset history Turns off history tracking.

Key Terms

Environment variable A system-recognized name tag that is defined to hold various values. Environment variables are system-defined or user-defined variables that provide information about the operating environment to the shell. For instance, the PS1 (prompt string one) variable contains whatever your prompt is currently set to.

Global variable Variables that are available to all shell sessions.

Local variable Variables that are available only for the current shell session.

Objectives

After reading this chapter, you will be able to

- Describe the function and contents of initialization files
- Compare and contrast system-wide and user-specific initialization files
- Describe login and the processing sequence of initialization files
- Customize the Korn shell login environment
- Identify the CDE customization file

Chapter 15

Customizing Your Login Environment

Introduction

In Chapter 14, "Basic Features of the Korn and C Shells," you covered how to set variables (PS1 and HISTORY) to customize your environment and create aliases. These and other features automatically can be made available after login by modifying specific initialization files. This chapter shows you how to work with various initialization files to make these changes take effect each time you log in. System-wide and user-specific initialization files and variables will be covered in more detail. You will work with Korn and C shell customization as well as Common Desktop Environment (CDE) customization.

Features of Initialization Files

Initialization files contain a series of commands and variable settings that are executed when a shell is started. These files customize the environment for the system and the user. These files are not executable, but they are read by the shell when the user logs in to customize the environment.

Two levels of initialization files exist. The first level is *system-wide*. System-wide initialization files are maintained by a system administrator and reside in the /etc directory. The second level is *user-specific* initialization files that reside in a user's home directory. The system-wide initialization files are read first, and the user-specific files are read next. See Figure 15-1.

In Chapter 14, we introduced a variable as a placeholder for information used for customizing the shell, such as PS1 for customizing your Korn shell prompt. Variables also contain information required by other processes so that they function properly and either are available to only the current shell (*local variable*) or are recognized in any shell or subshell (*global* or *environment variable*).

Figure 15-1
User-specific initialization files.

Shell	System Wide (Read First)	User Specific (Read Second)
Bourne	1. /etc/profile	2. $HOME/.profile
Korn	1. /etc/profile	2. $HOME/.profile (ENV=$HOME/.kshrc;export ENV) 3. $HOME/.kshrc
C	1. /etc/.login	2. $HOME/.login 3. $HOME/.cshrc 4. $HOME/.logout

Variables are predefined (and typically global) and set automatically when you log in, or they are set by the user. When a predefined global variable such as one of those in Figure 15-2 is placed in one of the system-wide initialization files, it is recognized in any shell or subshell. Users can customize many of these variables for their own environments by placing them in the initialization files in their home directories. To make the customizations available to all subsequent shells, the variable must be exported. Each shell uses variables common to all shells and others that are shell-specific.

Figure 15-2
Common variables set by the shell at login.

Variable	Meaning
Home	The directory that cd changes to when no argument is supplied on the command line.
Logname	Sets the login name of the user.
Path	A list of directories to be searched when the shell needs to find a command to be executed.
Shell	The name of the login shell (/bin/sh, /bin/ksh or /bin/csh).

Unlike variables, commands (like aliases) cannot be exported (made available to all subshells). If commands are to be available in a subshell, they must be placed in a secondary initialization file that is read each time a subshell is opened.

Figure 15-3 shows the location of these system-wide and user-specific files in the directory structure. The Korn shell user has two files: *.profile* and .kshrc (Korn shell run control) in the home directory. The C shell user can have three files: *.login*, .cshrc (C shell run control), and *.logout*. These are discussed later.

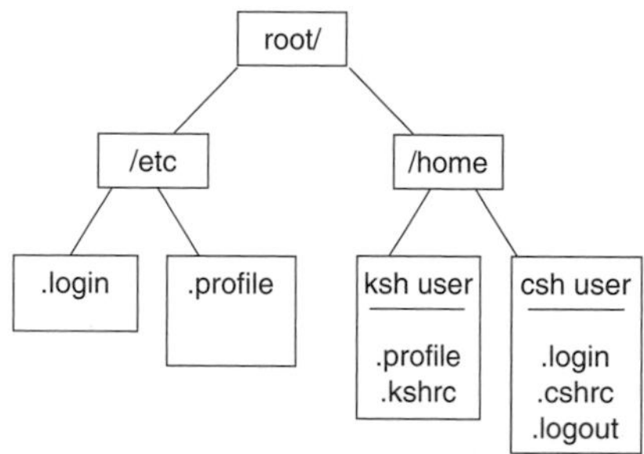

Figure 15-3
Initialization files in the tree structure.

System-Wide Initialization Files for Bourne and Korn Shell Users

The primary system-wide initialization file for Bourne and Korn shell users is the .profile file, which resides in the /etc directory. The */etc/profile file* is created by default when the operating system is installed, and it can be edited and customized by a system administrator. When a Bourne or Korn shell user logs in, the system reads the /etc/profile file first, and then it reads the user's .profile file and, for Korn shell users, the *.kshrc file*. This means that the user's preferences for variable settings can override the default settings set and can be maintained by a system administrator in the /etc/profile file. The /etc/profile file performs the following functions:

- **Exports environment variables**—The file makes environment variables available to subshells, such as LOGNAME for login name.
- **Exports PATH for default command path**—The default path is a list of directories where the shell will look when a command is executed. Exporting it makes the list of directories available to all shells and subshells.
- **Sets TERM variable default terminal type**—This defines the screen and keyboard characteristics of your workstation.
- **Displays contents of /etc/motd file**—The message of the day file is used by the system administrator to display greetings or news, or to provide system information.
- **Sets default file-creation permissions**—The file sets a umask value that determines the default permissions when a new file or directory is created. The **umask** command is covered in Chapter 10, "File System Security."
- **Checks for mail**—The file checks mail and will print a mail message upon login.

User-Specific Initialization Files

After the system-wide initialization file that sets system-wide defaults is read, the user initialization files for the appropriate shell are read. The user initialization files provide great flexibility to the user for customizing the environment. Login initialization and customization can be accomplished using the system-wide file /etc/profile by itself or in combination with the user-specific initialization files. Depending on the network administration policies, many custom settings can be placed in the /etc/profile file. This would set them automatically for all users, and no user-specific initialization files would be needed. Because users do not have permission to modify the /etc/profile file, this also would prevent the users from modifying the login initialization settings.

The user initialization files can be set up as templates by the system administrator and then can be modified by the user. The user-specific initialization file(s) are stored in the home directory of the user. Depending on network administration policy, user-specific initialization files can perform all or part of the following:

- **Set default prompt**—Determines what the prompt looks like when the user initially logs in or opens a new Terminal window. The default prompt for a Bourne and Korn shell user is a dollar sign ($). Customizing the prompt is covered in Chapter 14.
- **Define default printer**—Provides access to the local printer.
- **Set default permissions**—Sets **umask** for new files and directories.
- **Set default terminal type**—Used by vi and other tools.
- **Set new mail location**—Tells the shell where to look for new mail.
- **Set noclobber**—Prevents overwriting of files during redirection.
- **Set command path**—Defines directories to look in for executable files.
- **Define custom commands**—Defines user command aliases, as described in Chapter 14.

Korn Shell Customization

As part of creating a user account, the system administrator chooses the login shell. The login shell determines which initialization files are read during login. The Bourne shell uses only the .profile file to set the user's environment, and this is read only once at login. The Korn shell uses two user-specific environment files to set the user's environment:

- **~/.profile**—Typically contains one-time-only commands and variable definitions
- **~/.kshrc**—Typically contains aliases, turns on shell features, and sets the custom prompt

The .profile File

If a Korn shell user wants to customize the environment, that user needs to create or modify the .profile file and then must export the ENV variable, as shown here:

```
ENV=$HOME/.kshrc;  export  ENV
```

The ENV variable defines the path to the .kshrc (Korn shell run control) file. This variable can be added anywhere in the .profile file to inform the system that the .kshrc file exists and is to be read each time a Korn shell is started.

The previous command sets the environment variable to point to the .kshrc file in the home directory. HOME is a variable that is defined by the system to be the absolute path to the user's login directory. Preceding the HOME variable with the dollar sign ($) metacharacter enables the system to use the value of HOME in the specified location. When the ENV variable is placed in the .profile file and is read by other shells (such as the Bourne shell), it does not act as a pointer to the .kshrc file. This variable has no meaning outside the Korn shell. Figure 15-4 shows a sample .profile file.

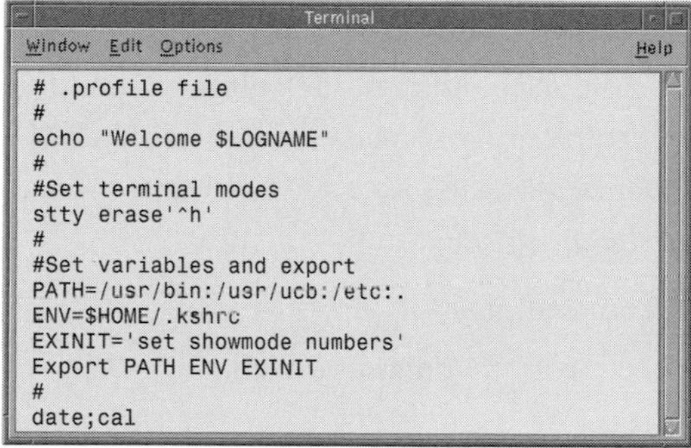

Figure 15-4
Contents of a sample .profile file.

Each element within the sample .profile file in Figure 15-4 is explained as follows:

- **# .profile file**—The pound sign (#) indicates a comment line that which is not acted upon when the file is read. Anything after a # on a line is considered a comment and ignored by the shell.
- **echo "Welcome $LOGNAME"**—The **echo** command displays "Welcome [user name]". The double quotes tell the shell to display any text and the value of any variables ($LOGNAME, in this case).
- **stty erase '^h'**—The Backspace (erase) key function is set to move one character to the left. You have to do this only if you will be logging on remotely using a Telnet program such as Windows Telnet.
- **PATH=/usr/bin:/usr/ucb:/etc:**—The PATH variable is used by the shell to locate commands in directories in the order specified by the PATH statement.

The dot (.) in the PATH variable enables the system to search the current working directory for commands.

- **ENV=$ HOME/.kshrc**—The ENV (environment) variable defines the Korn shell–specific startup file to read. Normally this is .kshrc, but it doesn't have to be. The .kshrc file is discussed in the next section.
- **EXINIT='set showmode numbers'**—The EXINIT (ex initialization) variable holds vi/ex editor preferences to be set automatically by vi at startup (see Chapter 9, "Using Text Editors," for other preferences).
- **LPDEST=colorlaser1**—The LPDEST (line printer destination) variable is used to set the default printer. If set, the LPDEST variable overrides the default printer set in the /etc/profile system file.
- **export PATH ENV EXINIT**—This exports the PATH, ENV, and EXINIT variables, making them available to all shells and subshells.
- **date;cal**—This displays the output of the **date** command, followed by the calendar of the current month.

The .kshrc File

Korn shell–specific commands and features should be placed in the .kshrc file. The .kshrc file automatically is read each time a new shell (such as a new Terminal window) or subshell is started, so there is nothing to export. The contents of the .kshrc file typically include the following:

- A customized prompt
- Custom variables
- Aliases

Figure 15-5 shows a sample .kshrc file.

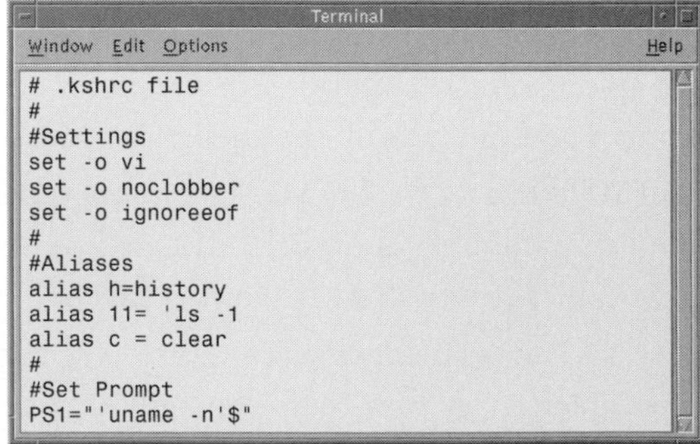

Terminal
Window Edit Options Help
.kshrc file
#
#Settings
set -o vi
set -o noclobber
set -o ignoreeof
#
#Aliases
alias h=history
alias 11= 'ls -1
alias c = clear
#
#Set Prompt
PS1="'uname -n'$"

Figure 15-5
Contents of a sample .kshrc file.

Each element within the sample .kshrc file in Figure 15-5 is explained as follows:

- **Set –o vi**—Informs the shell which editor's editing capabilities to use with command-line editing (see Chapter 14).
- **Set –o noclobber**—Turns on the **noclobber** option, preventing accidental overwriting or "clobbering" of an existing files when using redirection (see Chapter 7, "Advanced Directory and File Management").
- **Set –o ignoreeof**—Turns on the **ignore end of file** option, preventing a user from accidentally logging off by typing Ctrl-D. This is for users with a single-screen command-line login, such as a user who logged in using a Telnet program.
- **Aliases**—Defines personal aliases for the history command (**h**) and the long listing command (**ll**), and clears the screen or Terminal window (**c**) (see Chapter 14).
- **PS1="`uname –n`$ "**—Defines a custom shell prompt (see Chapter 14).

Korn Shell Login Process

As a review, Figure 15-6 illustrates what happens when a Korn shell user logs into a UNIX system. When any user logs into the system, the system /etc/profile file is always read first. The Korn shell user's .profile file in the home directory is read next. Then, if the ENV variable in the .profile file is assigned and exported, the .kshrc file is read. The .profile file is read only once, while the .kshrc file is read every time a new Korn shell is started. Remember, the tilde (~) indicates the user's home directory.

To have the system reread the .kshrc or .profile files after changes have been made (for example, after a new alias has been added to .kshrc), the user either can log out and log back in or can type the following from the command line:

```
$ . ~/.kshrc
$ . ~/.profile
```

NOTE

Rereading an initialization file only updates the current shell environment.

Skill Builder

e-Lab Activity 15.1

Customizing the Korn Shell

In this e-Lab activity, you are logged in as user2, and your current working directory is /home/user2. Refer to the class file tree structure on the inside-front cover of this book. Type the commands that would accomplish the requested objectives. *Note:* Be sure to press Enter after each one. Click Step 1 to begin.

Figure 15-6 Korn shell login process.

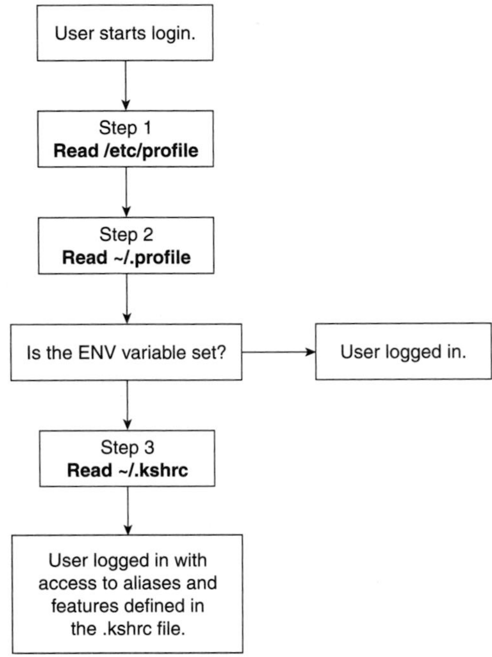

Skill Builder

Lab Activity 15.2.1

Customizing the Korn Shell

In this lab, you work with UNIX initialization files to customize your Korn shell login environment and tailor various options to your needs. Refer to the *Cisco Networking Academy Program: Fundamentals of UNIX Lab Companion.*

C Shell Customization

The primary system-wide initialization file for C shell users is the .login file, which resides in the /etc directory along with the profile file used by Bourne and Korn shell users. The /etc/.login file is created by default when the operating system is installed, and it can be edited and customized by a system administrator. When a C shell user logs in, the system reads the /etc/.login file first, the user's **~/.login** file next, and finally the *~/.cshrc file*. This means that the user's preferences for variable settings can override the default settings set and can be maintained by a system administrator in the /etc/.login file.

The two user-specific initialization files for a C shell user contain the following:

- **.login**—Typically contains one-time-only commands and variable definitions
- **.cshrc**—Typically contains aliases, turns on shell features, and sets the custom prompt

Both files are located in the user's home directory. The .login file is read only when a user logs in to the system, whereas the .cshrc (C shell run control) file is automatically read each time a new subshell is started. There is no ENV variable to set, like in the Korn shell. As with the Korn shell, similar entries can be made in the **.cshrc** file using C shell prompt and alias syntax (see Chapter 14). To have the system reread the .login or .cshrc file after changes have been made (i.e., a new alias has been added to .cshrc), the user can either log out and log back in, or type the following from the command line:

```
% source ~/.login
% source ~/.cshrc
```

Figure 15-7 shows the login sequence for a typical C shell user.

NOTE

Rereading an initialization file only updates the current shell environment.

NOTE

A .log out file is available for C shell users that allows for customization after the user logs out. Clear the screen and print "Bye," for instance.

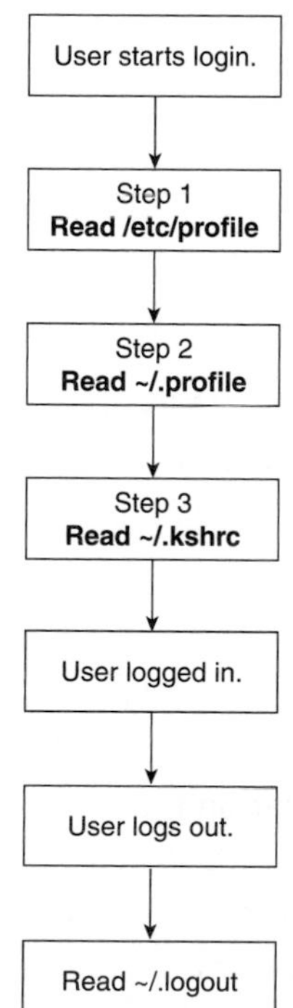
User starts login.
Step 1
Read /etc/profile
Step 2
Read ~/.profile
Step 3
Read ~/.kshrc
User logged in.
User logs out.
Read ~/.logout

Figure 15-7 C shell login sequence.

The CDE Initialization File

For users of the graphical CDE File Manager, another initialization file, called *.dtprofile* (desktop profile), resides in the user's home directory and determines settings for the CDE. This file is standard system-wide and is created in a user's home directory the first time that the user logs into the CDE. In versions of CDE shipped with Solaris 2.6 and later, the .dtprofile file causes the system to read a Korn shell user's .kshrc file each time a Terminal window is opened within CDE and to read the .profile and .kshrc files each time a console window is opened. Both initialization files also are read when CDE initially starts up.

Summary

Now that you have completed this chapter, you should have an understanding of the following:

- When a user logs into a UNIX system, several initialization files are read and processed. These files contain settings for variables that customize the user's environment. Two types of initialization files exist: system-wide and user-specific. The etc/profile file is the system-wide initialization file that affects all Bourne and Korn shell users. The /etc/.login file is the system-wide initialization file affecting C shell users. Both files are created when the operating system is installed, and both can be edited and customized by a system administrator. The /etc/profile file can perform the following:
  - — Exports environment variables
  - — Exports PATH for the default command path
  - — Sets the TERM variable default terminal type
  - — Displays the contents of the /etc/motd file
  - — Sets default file-creation permissions
  - — Checks for mail
- The Korn shell uses two additional user-specific initialization files that are kept in the user's home directory: .profile and .kshrc (Korn shell run control). The C shell potentially uses three user-specific files: .login, .cshrc (C shell run control) and .log out. These user-specific files are read after /etc/profile to provide additional customization for the user's environment. They can perform some or all of the following:
  - — Set the default prompt
  - — Define the default printer
  - — Set default permissions

- — Set the default terminal
- — Set the new mail location
- — Set **noclobber**
- — Set the command path
- — Define custom commands

- CDE users have a special file called .dtprofile (desktop profile) that is read to provide settings for the graphical desktop and windowing environment.

Check Your Understanding

1. What is the purpose of initialization files?
   - **A.** Define and set variables to customize the users login environment
   - **B.** Define the user's default shell and computer name
   - **C.** Create scripts that are executed at login
   - **D.** Define user permissions to files and folders in the file system
2. The initialization files are found in what two directories?
   - **A.** The /login and user's home directories
   - **B.** The /etc and user's home directories
   - **C.** The /etc and system administrator's directories
   - **D.** The /system and /user directories
3. What is the name of the system-wide initialization file used by Bourne and Korn shell users?
   - **A.** profile
   - **B.** .profile
   - **C.** login
   - **D.** .login
4. The system-wide initialization file provides settings that apply to all users. Which of the following is *not* a function of the system-wide initialization file?
   - **A.** Exports environment variables
   - **B.** Sets TERM variable default terminal type
   - **C.** Displays the contents of the /etc/motd file
   - **D.** Defines the default shell for all users
5. What are the names of the two user-specific files for Korn shell users?
   - **A.** profile and .kshrc
   - **B.** .profile and .kshrc
   - **C.** .login and .kshrc
   - **D.** .cshrc and .kshrc

6. What are the names of the three user-specific files for C shell users?
   A. login, cshrc, and logout
   B. .profile, .cshrc, and .kshrc
   C. .login, .cshrc and .logout
   D. .profile, .login and .logout
7. The contents of the .kshrc file typically includes all of the following *except*:
   A. CDE preferences
   B. Customized prompt
   C. Custom variables
   D. Aliases
8. What is the correct sequence of files read when a Korn shell user logs in?
   A. .login, .cshrc, .logout
   B. profile, .profile, .cshrc
   C. profile, .profile, .kshrc
   D. .login, .profile, .kshrc
9. Which of the following is *not* true of the CDE initialization file?
   A. It is called .dtprofile.
   B. It is copied to the user's home directory at login.
   C. It reads user-specific files when a Terminal window is opened.
   D. It is called .cdeprofile.
10. Brad is a Korn shell user. He created an alias called h to display the history file. He added the alias to his .kshrc file. When he logged in again, he tried to use the alias and got the error: /bin/ksh: h: not found. What could be the problem?
    A. He should have put the alias in the .cshrc file.
    B. He did not define and export the ENV variable in his .profile file.
    C. He did not export the .kshrc variable from his .login file.
    D. The alias should have been in the /etc/profile file.

UNIX Command Summary

. (dot) Used to re-execute a Korn shell initialization file after changes are made. Example:

```
$ .  .kshrc
```

ENV Variable used in conjunction with personalizing the login environment. Example:

```
ENV=$HOME/.kshrc; export ENV
```

source Used to re-execute a C shell initialization file after changes are made. Example:

```
$ source .cshrc
```

Key Terms

.cshrc file C shell run control file. User-specific initialization file stored in the home directory that typically contains aliases, turns on shell features, and sets the custom prompt. Read for C shell users.

.dtprofile Desktop profile file. User-specific initialization file that resides in the user's home directory and determines settings for the CDE. This file is standard system-wide and is created in a user's home directory the first time the user logs into the CDE.

.kshrc file Korn shell run control file. User-specific initialization file stored in the home directory that typically contains aliases, turns on shell features, and sets the custom prompt. Read for Korn shell users.

.login User-specific initialization file stored in the home directory that contains one-time-only commands and variable definitions. Read for C shell users.

.logout file File available for C shell users that allows for customization after the user logs out. Clear the screen and print "Bye," for example. Read for C shell users.

.profile file User-specific initialization file stored in the home directory that contains one-time-only commands and variable definitions. Read for both Bourne and Korn shell users.

/etc/profile file The primary system-wide initialization file for Bourne and Korn shell users is located in the /etc directory. The profile file is created by default when the operating system is installed, and it can be edited and customized by a system administrator. When a Bourne or Korn shell user logs in, the system reads the /etc/profile file first.

/etc/.login The primary system-wide initialization file for C shell users is located in the /etc directory. The .login file is created by default when the operating system is installed, and it can be edited and customized by a system administrator. When a C shell user logs in, the system reads the /etc/.login file first.

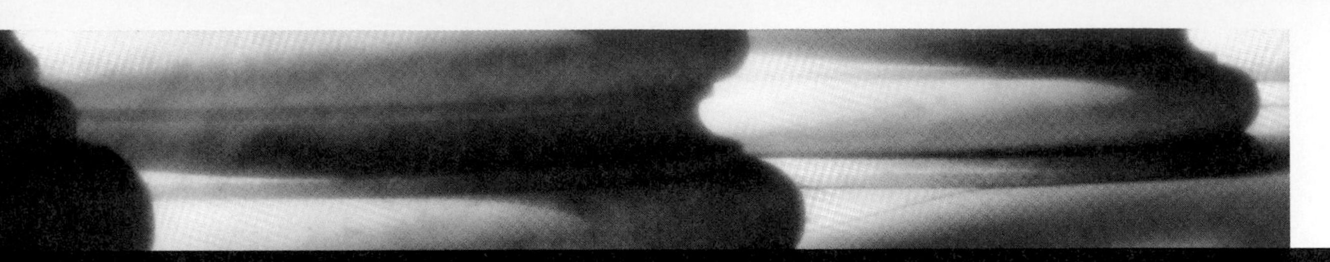

Objectives

After reading this chapter, you will be able to

- Describe the characteristics of LANs
- Describe the characteristics of WANs
- Name the most common LAN and WAN technologies
- Compare and contrast shared Ethernet and switched Ethernet
- Explain the differences among network architectures, topologies, and protocols
- Work with key TCP/IP networking commands such as **ping** and **telnet**
- Explain the concepts and give examples of naming services
- Describe the characteristics and benefits of the Network File System (NFS)

Chapter 16

Network Basics

Introduction

This chapter provides an introduction to networking technologies and concepts. You learn about the most common networking architectures, protocols, and topologies, as well as the concept of client/server networking. You work with UNIX network commands and utilities such as **ping** (packet internet groper), **telnet** (terminal emulator), **rlogin** (remote login), and **ftp** (file transfer protocol). The Domain Name Service (DNS), the Network Information System (NIS+), and the Network File System (NFS) also are covered.

Local-Area Networks

Networks can be divided into two basic categories: *local-area networks (LANs)* and *wide-area networks (WANs)*. LANs are made up of groups of computers (nodes) that have simultaneous access to common high-bandwidth media. Media can be copper wire, fiber-optic cable, or even air, as with wireless LANs. *Bandwidth* is the data-carrying capacity of the media and LAN technology being used. Each node or computer (in most cases) gains access to the network media through a network interface card (NIC), which is installed in the computer.

These nodes are connected in a relatively confined geographical location in which the distance between nodes is normally less than 500 feet, or approximately 150 meters. Most LANs cover a small area, usually less than 10,000 square feet, or approximately 1000 square meters. Distances between nodes can be greater than 1 mile and still be considered a LAN, but this is uncommon. A *node* is an endpoint on the network and can be a workstation, a *server*, or a printer. LANs can have as few as two computers or as many as thousands. They can occupy a single room or can span multiple buildings, as with a campus environment.

LANs provide high-speed communications among all interconnected nodes or devices. This allows users to share network resources such as documents, databases, applications, printers, and *Internet* connections. High-speed communication is defined here as 10 Mbps (10 million bits per second) or faster. Current LAN technologies support speeds of more than 1 Gbps (gigabits per second, or 1000 million bits per second).

Physical cabling, such as copper or fiber optic, usually interconnects LANs. However, in recent years wireless LANs have become more common. All cabling, conduit, and interconnected network equipment such as hubs and switches typically are owned by the organization that uses the LAN. Examples of LAN technologies or architectures include Ethernet, Token Ring, and Fiber Distributed Data Interface (FDDI).

Figure 16-1 shows a LAN with nodes interconnected by a multiport switch in a *star topology*, which is very common in today's LAN network designs. Topologies are covered later in this chapter. Multiport switches can be interconnected, allowing a large number of workstations to be on the same LAN. Routers, on the other hand, can be used to divide the LAN into multiple segments for improved performance and security.

Figure 16-1
LAN.

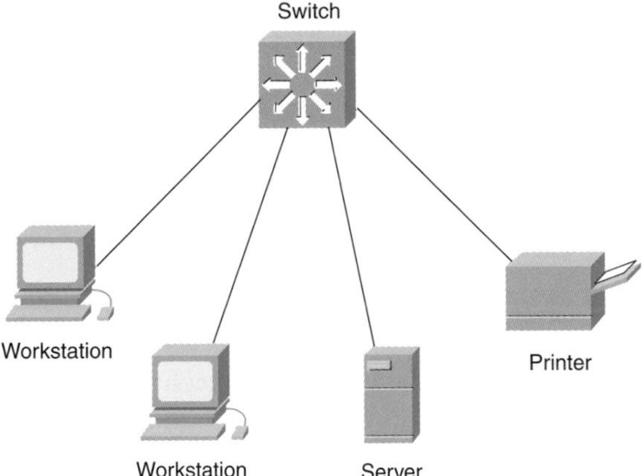

Wide-Area Networks

Organizations with multiple LANs in different geographical locations use WAN technologies to interconnect them. When the distance between LANs becomes too great, a WAN is needed. For instance, an organization might have three locations—Phoenix, Arizona; Denver, Colorado; and Raleigh, North Carolina. It is not realistic or cost-effective for the organization to own all the cabling and equipment needed to interconnect these locations, so a WAN connection is needed. The WAN's links or communication lines between locations can be dedicated leased lines, as with T1, or they can be shared using a packet-switched link such as Frame Relay. These links are leased from a service provider such as the phone company and are not owned by the organization whose LANs are interconnected. WANs can be worldwide, spanning thousands of miles.

Virtually every organization of any size today has a connection to the Internet. In its simplest form, a WAN is created when a company connects its LAN to an Internet service provider (ISP). There might be 100 or more users on the LAN but there is only one WAN link to the ISP's network. Although a single LAN with an Internet connection is technically a WAN, the term more often is used to describe the links between two or more of an organization's LANs.

Many WAN technologies can connect LANs, but the link usually is provided by a leased T1 (Trunk 1) connection or a fraction of a T1. A T1 connection provides 1.544 Mbps of bandwidth, which is considered a relatively low-speed connection (compared to LANs), but it is usually adequate for Internet access or interconnecting multiple sites. The two most common WAN connection technologies are dedicated T1 or shared Frame Relay. Others include Integrated Services Digital Network (ISDN) and Asynchronous Transfer Mode (ATM).

In most cases, there is only one WAN link between locations, but it is possible to have more than one WAN link for redundancy or increased performance. For instance, if there are three locations, WAN links can be set up between each of the LANs (three links), as shown in Figure 16-2. This creates multiple paths in case one of the links goes down.

Figure 16-2
WAN.

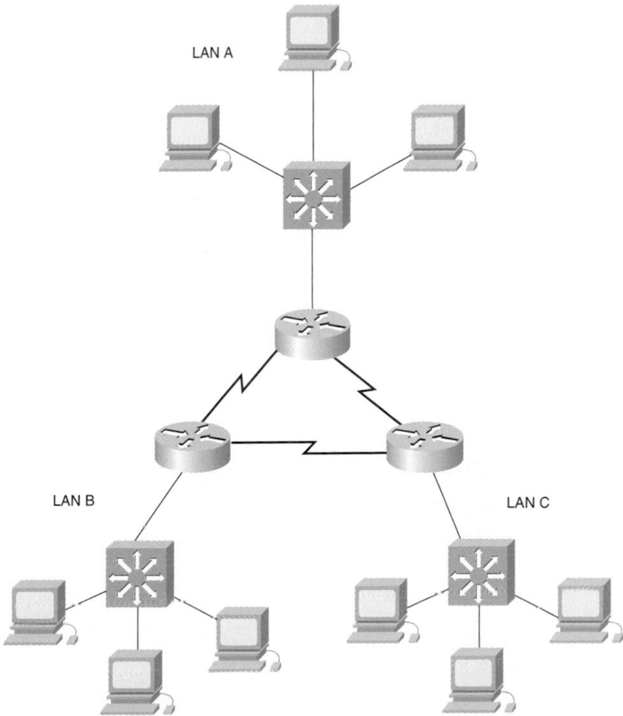

Whether connecting to the Internet or connecting multiple corporate LANs, a networking device called a *router* is required. For an organization to connect to the Internet, a single router is needed. If an organization wants to connect multiple sites across a WAN link, a router is needed at each location.

LAN Architecture Elements

Three primary LAN architectures or technologies are in use today: *Ethernet*, *Token Ring*, and *Fiber Distributed Data Interface (FDDI)*. Of these, Ethernet is by far the most common. It is estimated that more than 90 percent of installed networks use some form of Ethernet. The Institute of Electronic and Electrical Engineers (IEEE) 802.3 committee developed the current standards on Ethernet. The IEEE 802.5 committee developed standards for Token Ring, and The American National Standards Associations (ANSI) is responsible for FDDI standards. The LAN architecture is relatively independent of the network operating system. As a result, most network operating systems, including Windows NT/2000, Novell NetWare, and UNIX, can utilize various underlying architectures.

All LAN and WAN architectures or technologies are comprised of five major design elements. When building a network, you must consider all of these factors. For instance, if you are designing an Ethernet network, you must acquire Ethernet components and follow the requirements and specifications of the Ethernet standards. Major design elements for any network architectures or technologies include these:

- **Topologies supported**—*Topology* is the layout or arrangement of network components. Some architectures support more than one topology. Examples of topologies include a bus, a star, a ring, and a mesh. These topologies are discussed later in this chapter.
- **Cabling specifications**—These specifications include cable types, connectors, patch panels, wall plates, electrical/optical characteristics, and maximum distances allowed.
- **NIC design**—The design of the NIC includes electrical characteristics, physical connectors, transmit and receive electronics, and hardware addressing.
- **Interconnecting devices**—These are concentration or aggregation devices and usually include hubs, switches, multistation access units, and routers.
- **Access method**—Technique used to allow multiple users to share the network.

Because of its prevalence Ethernet and its current implementations are the focus of this chapter.

Shared Ethernet

Shared Ethernet or standard Ethernet is a bus-based network in which all workstations can try to send packets simultaneously. Early versions of Ethernet used a single coaxial cable known as a *linear bus*. Workstations tapped into the bus to gain access. Ethernet networks today are almost exclusively star-based designs in which the bus has been compressed into a small concentrator known as a *hub* or *switch*. These shared-Ethernet star networks typically use unshielded twisted-pair (UTP) Category 5 cabling that supports speeds up to 100 Mbps.

Because only one packet could be on the wire at a time, earlier versions of Ethernet used the *carrier sense multiple access collision detect (CSMA/CD)* method of access, which allowed many workstations to share the wire. *Carrier sense* means the workstation (NIC) is sensing or listening to the carrier (the wire or media) to see if there is any traffic. *Multiple access* means that more than one computer might be trying to send data simultaneously. *Collision detect* means that if there is a collision, the computers will detect it and retransmit. Every NIC has a transmit and receive circuit so that it can not only send data, but also receive data, listen for traffic, and detect collisions. In a shared Ethernet network, the NIC is either transmitting or receiving but cannot do both at the same time. This is referred to as *half-duplex communication*.

The disadvantage to early Ethernet and CSMA/CD was that, with many workstations creating traffic, a lot of collisions and significant slowdowns in network performance occurred. The early versions of shared Ethernet ran at 10 Mbps, so actual throughput might be only 5 Mbps with collisions taken into account. If there were 10 workstations connected to the bus or hub, they had to share 10 Mbps of bandwidth, resulting in a 10-node collision domain. Figure 16-3 shows a shared Ethernet LAN with packets from two nodes colliding on the linear bus. If there were 20 nodes, the size of the collision domain would be 20 nodes, and so on.

Figure 16-3
Shared Ethernet technology with *bus topology*.

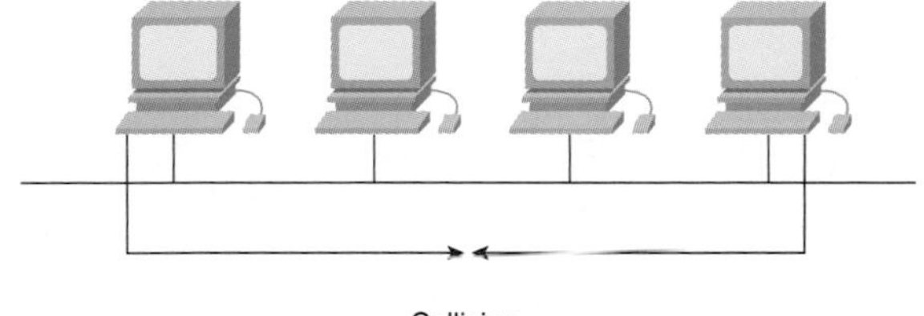

As network applications began to require more speed, a 100-Mbps version of Ethernet was introduced, known as *Fast Ethernet*. This helped to alleviate congestion, but although the speed was 10 times faster, it was still shared Ethernet and there were still collisions to deal with.

Switched Ethernet

The most modern implementations of Ethernet use switching technology, which replaces the traditional shared hub with a switch. A *switch* creates a direct internal connection between any two nodes attached to it when they need to communicate, which effectively eliminates collisions. With 10-Mbps shared Ethernet, a hub with 24 ports creates a collision domain of 24 nodes. All 24 workstations or servers are competing for a share of the 10 Mbps of total bandwidth. If you replace the 24-port hub with a 24-port 10-Mbps switch, you provide a full 10 Mbps of bandwidth between any *two* nodes. The size of the collision domain with a switch is always two nodes, regardless of the number of ports.

With a shared Ethernet hub, only one data packet can be on the cable at a time. A switch can handle multiple packets simultaneously, so multiple workstations can communicate with each other at the same time. Traditional shared Ethernet hubs also can be connected to a switch to reduce the size of collision domains. Ethernet switches are compatible with Ethernet hubs.

The first Ethernet switches were 10 Mbps, but because they did not have to contend with collisions, they provided a dedicated 10 Mbps between any two nodes that needed to communicate. This was a vast improvement over the shared collision domain approach.

By using switching technology, this bandwidth can be increased to 20 Mbps with *full-duplex* transmission. Because the receive circuit of the NIC does not have to listen for collisions, the NIC can transmit and receive at the same time. This results in a full 20 Mbps of dedicated bandwidth to a workstation or server.

Switched Ethernet has become increasingly popular in recent years and is the dominant LAN technology being implemented today. Ethernet switches and NICs are available in 10 Mbps, 100 Mbps (*Fast Ethernet*), and 1000 Mbps (*Gigabit Ethernet*) speeds. Because these are switched technologies, using full-duplex data transmission if the NICs in the workstations and servers can support it can double all these numbers. Figure 16-4 shows the use of a switch to connect workstations.

Figure 16-4 Benefits of switching.

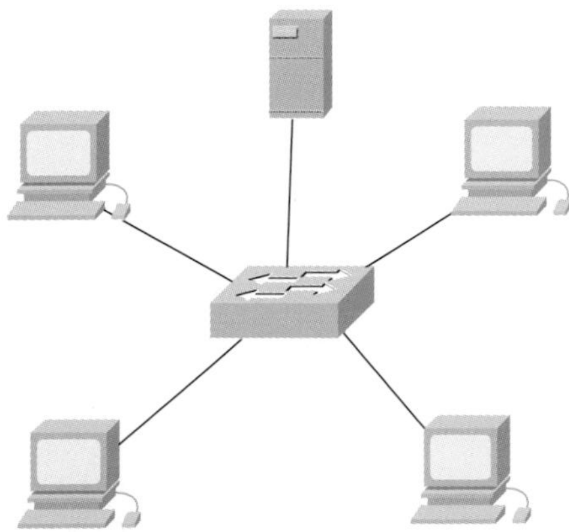

- Number of collisions reduced
- Simultaneous multiple communications
- High-speed uplinks
- Improved network response
- Increased user productivity

Token Ring

Token Ring originally was developed by IBM and then became IEEE standard 802.5. The Token Ring network architecture uses the ring topology and a token to provide access for workstations. The token passes around the ring; when a workstation has the token, it can place data on the ring. Token Ring commonly is implemented as a star with a central concentration device known as a multistation access unit (MAU); technically, it is a star-wired ring. On a true ring, if a cable to a workstation failed, the entire ring would cease to function. With the ring concentrated into the MAU, the cable to a workstation can be broken and the MAU will bridge the ring to keep it up and running. Token Ring speeds are either 4 or 16 Mbps. Figure 16-5 shows a *ring topology*.

FDDI

Pronounced "fiddi," FDDI is an ANSI standard and was developed primarily as a backbone technology to interconnect LANs in a campus environment. It runs over fiber-optic cable and can span many miles. FDDI uses two rings, one primary and one for backup. It transmits data at 100 Mbps using the token-passing access method.

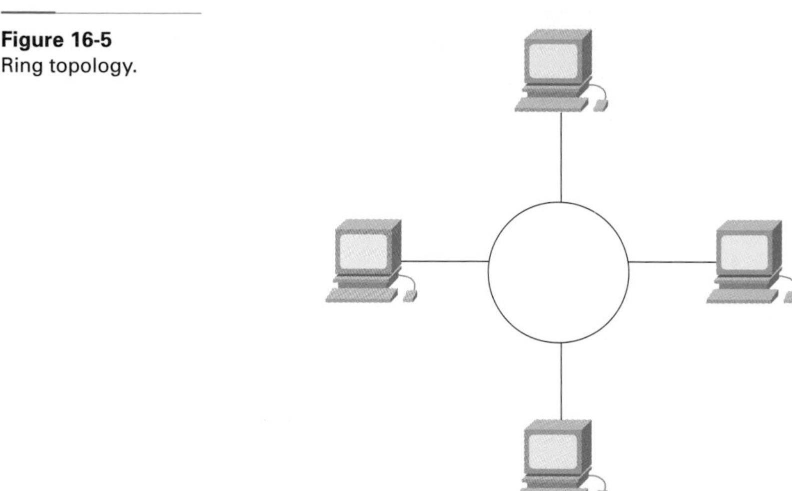
Figure 16-5
Ring topology.

Network Topologies

As previously mentioned, a topology is the physical way that the components in a network are arranged or laid out. Four primary topologies exist.

Bus

Early Ethernet LANs used a bus topology. A *bus* is a cable (coaxial) that is run through an area, and workstations and servers tap into the cable to get access to the network. The bus is a single length of cable that is terminated at each end. As such, the bus design was prone to problems because a break anywhere in the bus could bring down the entire network. Although there are still many bus-based networks in service, new installation almost always uses the extended star topology. Figure 16-6 shows an example of a bus topology.

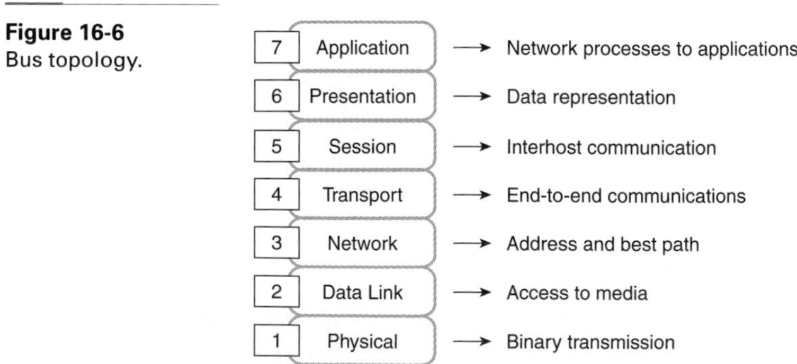

Figure 16-6
Bus topology.

Star

The star topology is the most common and is the one used with Ethernet hubs and switches. The hub or switch is the center of the star, and cables radiate out to nodes like spokes on a wheel. The biggest advantage of the star over the bus is that if a cabling connection to any node fails, it does not affect the others. Two or more switches can be connected using backbone cable (usually fiber-optic cable), which creates an extended star. The extended star is the most common topology used in today's networks. Extended stars also are used to create WANs. See Figure 16-7.

Figure 16-7
Extended star topology.

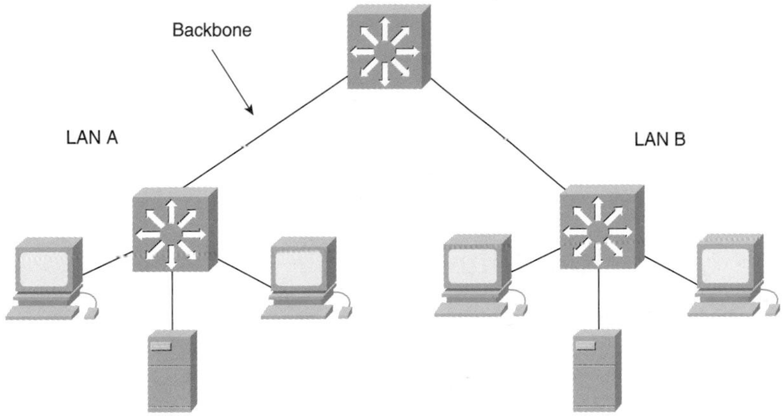

Backbone
LAN A
LAN B

Ring

The Token Ring and FDDI network architectures use the ring topology. Token Ring commonly is implemented as a star with a central concentration device MAU and is technically a star ring. FDDI is a true ring used primarily to interconnect other types of LANs. FDDI is actually a dual ring, with one acting as the primary and one a as backup in case the primary fails.

The ring topology also is found in WANs. FDDI can be used to create a WAN, although this is not commonly done. Another widely used WAN technology that is based on the ring topology is the Synchronous Optical Network (SONET). SONET also uses dual rings for redundancy. Refer to Figure 16-5 for an example of a ring topology.

Mesh

The mesh is typically a WAN topology used to interconnect multiple LANs for redundancy of communications paths. Meshes also can be used in LANs to provide redundant links between routers and switches. With a *full mesh*, each site has a link to every other site. With a *partial mesh*, each site has a link to more than one site, but not to every site.

Routers typically interconnect sites. Figure 16-8 shows a partial *mesh topology* between LANs at four different locations or sites. Note that every site is not directly connected to every other site, but every site has at least two connections to other sites, to provide redundancy if one of the WAN links goes down. This partial mesh uses four links among three sites so that every site has an alternate route to get to another site if a WAN link goes down. The minimum number of links would be three: LANs B, C, and D could all link back to LAN A, which would create a star topology. The full mesh would require the maximum of six links.

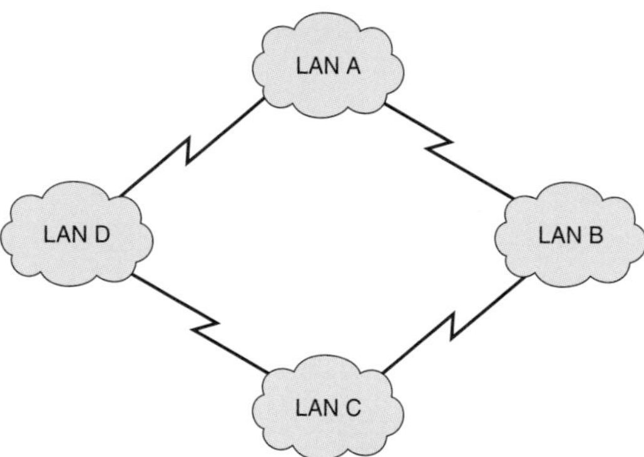

Figure 16-8
Partial mesh topology.

Network Protocols and the OSI Model

When two nodes on a network want to communicate, they must use networking protocols. Many types of networking protocols exist. This section focuses on the OSI model and some of the more common networking protocols.

The OSI Model

The *OSI model* was developed by the International Organization for Standardization (ISO) to describe the functions that occur as two nodes on a network communicate. OSI is short for "Open System Interconnection" and is an internationally recognized, structured, and standardized architecture for network design. The seven-layer OSI reference model (or just OSI model) is one of the most useful tools that we have for analyzing and comparing various technologies and networking products from different vendors. The model or "protocol stack" itself rarely is adhered to completely by any one vendor, but it serves as a frame of reference for everyone to compare to.

The OSI model helps to define the process of communication between two devices or nodes on a network. Various protocols operate at each layer to pass the data from one device or node to another. These "nodes" can be user devices such as workstations and servers, or network devices such as routers and switches. The important thing to realize is that the OSI model does not really come into play unless you want to communicate over a network between two devices. If you open a local document file on your hard disk with a word processor on your standalone PC at home, the OSI model is not involved. If you open a file from your workstation, which is actually in your home folder on a network server in another building, the OSI model is involved. When your word processor attempts to open the file on the server, network communication must take place from the user's level down through the protocol stack on your workstation and out the NIC on your computer, through the network media (cable) to the server and up its protocol stack to retrieve the file.

By splitting the process of communicating from one device to another over a network into smaller digestible chunks, you can study it more easily. We also provide a structured blueprint from which network equipment engineers can create their products and create modular network designs. Thus, the OSI model facilitates communication and education relating to networks as well as the development of networking products and services.

Figure 16-9 shows the seven layers of the OSI model, with a brief description of the function of each layer. These are divided into two main groups: the applications layers and the data flow layers, as shown in Figures 16-10 and 16-11. All the layers are discussed in greater detail in the following list.

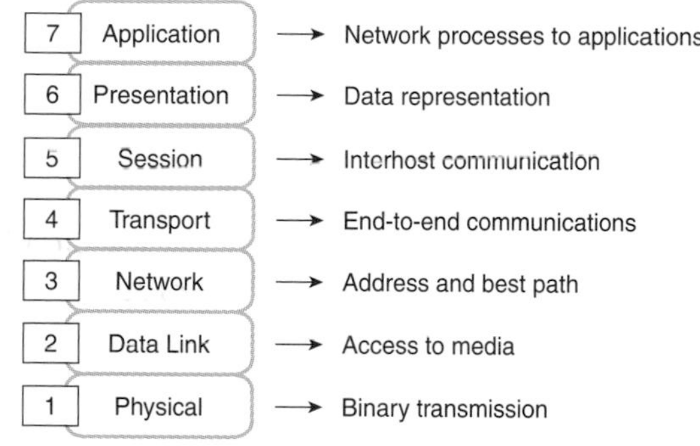

Figure 16-9
OSI layer functions.

- **Application layer (Layer 7)**—Network processes to applications. This layer provides network communication services to user applications for file transfers, WWW access, e-mail, and remote terminal access. For example, a word-processing application is serviced by file-transfer services at this layer.
- **Presentation layer (Layer 6)**—Data representation. This layer provides translation for character sets, data compression, encryption, and support for various file types (graphics, video, sound).
- **Session layer (Layer 5)**—Interhost communications. This layer keeps track of which application is doing what and where. It establishes, manages, and terminates the relationships among multiple applications such as a client and server.

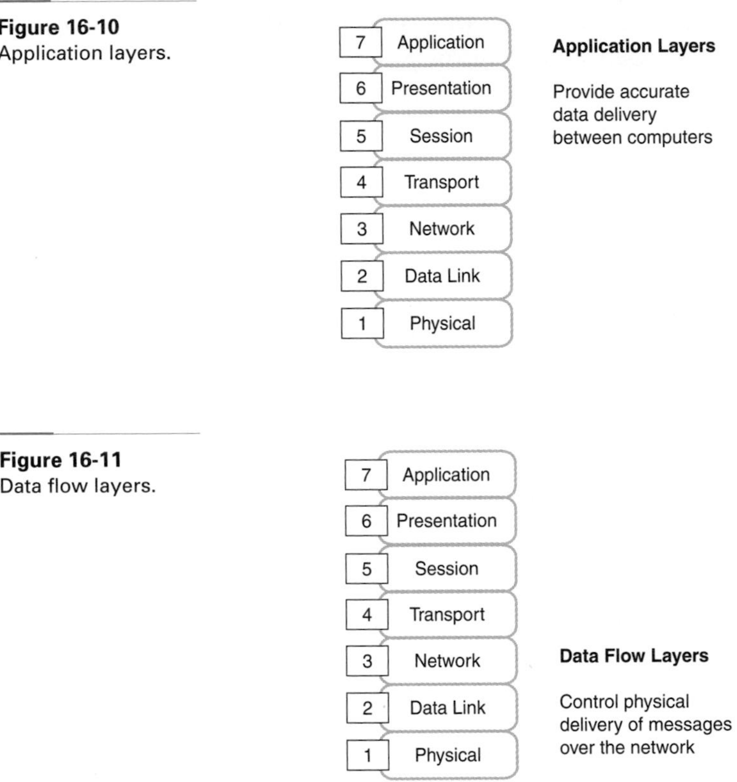

Figure 16-10
Application layers.

Figure 16-11
Data flow layers.

It also acts as a funnel to the lower four layers. This layer establishes, maintains, and manages sessions between applications.

- **Transport layer (Layer 4)**—End-to-end connections. This is the shipping department of the OSI model. Packages can be shipped via guaranteed or non-guaranteed services. This layer segments information into smaller packets for processing by the network layer, and it segments and reassembles data into a data stream. The transport layer has the potential to guarantee a connection and offer reliable transport.
- **Network layer (Layer 3)**—Addressing and best-path selection. Packets are addressed and directed through an internetwork (between networks) at this layer. This layer determines the best way to move data from one place to another. The router operates at this layer. The network layer uses logical addressing schemes that can be managed by an administrator. The Internet Protocol (IP), IPX, and AppleTalk are examples of addressing schemes.
- **Data link layer (Layer 2)**—Access to media. These are the shipping methods and drivers of the shipping vehicles (truck, train, boat, plane), and they

determine how they get onto the pathways. This layer provides physical transmission across the medium. It handles error notification, network topology, and flow control. This layer uses Media Access Control (MAC) addresses, which also are referred to as physical or hardware addresses.

- **Physical layer** (Layer 1)—Binary transmission. The physical cabling and connections (wired and wireless) that make up the pathways for electricity, light, and radio waves (the highways, railways, shipping lanes, and airways) are governed by this layer. The physical layer provides the electrical, mechanical, procedural, and functional means for activating and maintaining the physical link between systems. This layer uses such physical media as twisted-pair, coaxial, and fiber-optic cable.

Skill Builder

e-Lab Activity 16.1

OSI Layer Exercise

In this drag-and-drop e-Lab activity, you drag the term on the left of the graphic to match the appropriate definition listed on the right.

The TCP/IP Protocol

TCP/IP is not a single protocol, but a suite comprised of a number of protocols operating at most of the layers of the OSI model. The Defense Advance Research Projects Agency (DARPA) originally developed TCP/IP to interconnect defense department computer networks across the country to form a fault-tolerant network. It was adopted and further developed as the standard networking communications component of the UNIX operating system.

Many networking protocols have come and gone over the years. Proprietary protocols rapidly are losing ground in favor of open protocols such as TCP/IP. Proprietary protocols include Novell's IPX and Apple Computer's AppleTalk. In fact, current versions of both Novell's and Apple's network operating systems support TCP/IP as a primary protocol. TCP/IP is an open standard and is the only protocol that is supported by every major operating system and nearly every networking equipment vendor. Virtually every computer manufactured in the world today, from laptops to the largest mainframes, can communicate using the TCP/IP protocol.

TCP/IP originally was developed as a WAN protocol but recently has become a required LAN protocol because most PCs on LANs need access to the Internet. With some LANs, TCP/IP runs along with other protocols such as IPX and AppleTalk;

however, it is becoming increasingly common to build LANs using only the TCP/IP protocol.

TCP/IP is the language of the Internet, which is the largest international network in the world, with millions of nodes. The Internet is a packet-switched network that uses the Internet Protocol (IP) to identify and encapsulate its packets. TCP/IP is the *de facto* UNIX standard and is the most widely used protocol suite in the world. Nearly every network equipment manufacturer has developed or is developing products that support TCP/IP.

The name TCP/IP is a combination of the two most important protocols in the suite: Transmission Control Protocol (TCP) and Internet Protocol (IP). TCP is one of the Layer 4 transport protocols in the suite, and IP is the Layer 3 routing protocol in the suite. TCP provides connection-oriented services to ensure that all packets reach their destinations. Most Internet communication such as HTTP use TCP as their transport mechanism.

UDP is the other Layer 4 protocol that provides connectionless services and can be used when delivery does not need to be guaranteed and for real-time applications such as voice and video transmission. Whether TCP or UDP, all packets ride over the Internet on IP. All computers (*hosts*) such as workstations and servers that want to communicate over the Internet must have an IP address and must run the TCP/IP protocol. As a result, TCP/IP is fast becoming the protocol of choice for LANs and WANs.

TCP/IP is a *routed*, or *routable*, protocol. A host IP address has in it both the network's address and the address of the host on that network. This provides a way for one host to send packets to a host on another network while allowing each packet to be directed from the source host to a destination host, sometimes through many routers along the way.

Any computer running the TCP/IP protocol is considered to be a *host*. A host is uniquely identified on the Internet by a 32-bit IP address. This address is divided into four sets of 8 bits each, which are referred to as *octets*. In addition to an IP address, TCP/IP computers are given a host name, such as www.sun.com. Most TCP/IP networks allow a user to refer to the user-friendly host name when browsing the Internet, and a network naming service such as *Domain Name System (DNS)* or *Network Information Server (NIS)* translates the host name into an IP address. Figure 16-12 shows two hosts, each having a host name and an IP address. Figure 16-13 shows two hosts communicating over the Internet using TCP/IP. Figures 16-14 and 16-15 compare the OSI model to the TCP/IP protocol stack.

Figure 16-12
Name server translates host name to IP address.

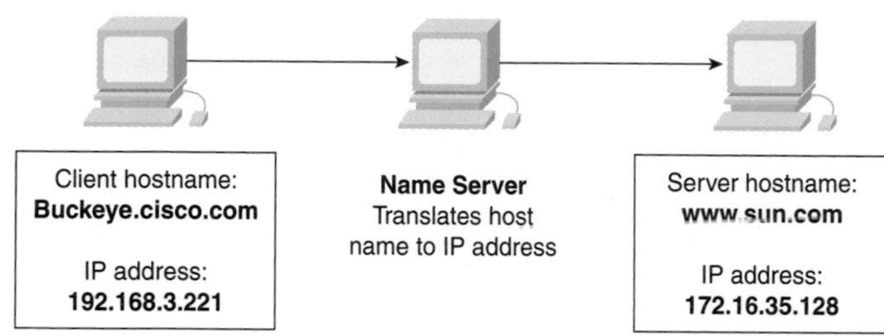

Figure 16-13
Introduction to TCP/IP.

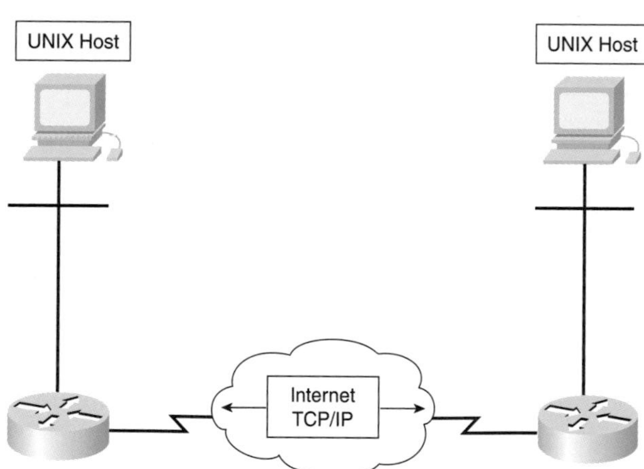

Figure 16-14
Comparing TCP/IP with OSI.

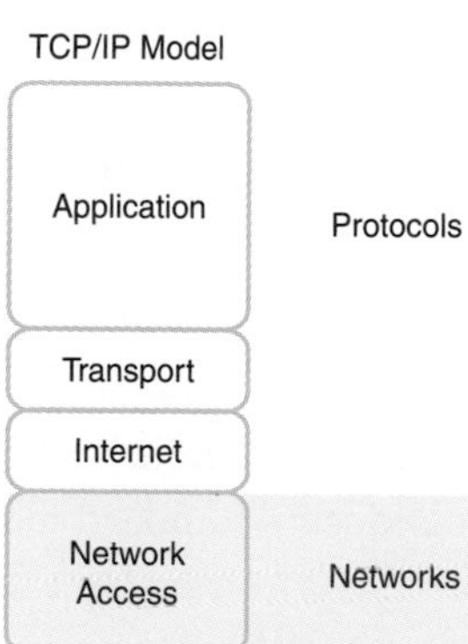

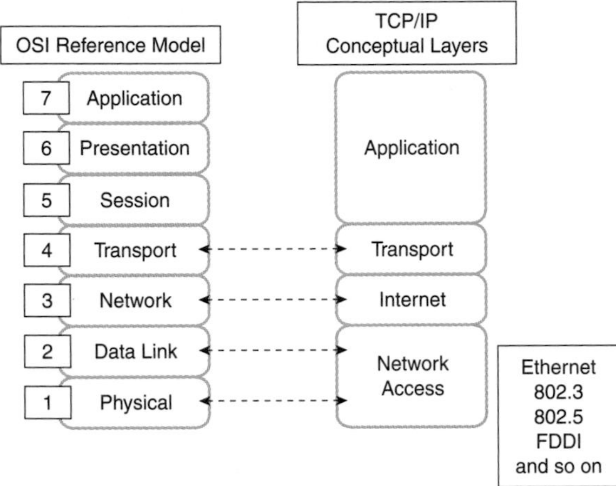

Figure 16-15
TCP/IP protocol stack.

Client/Server Computing

The *client/server* computing model distributes processing over multiple computers. *Distributed processing* enables access to remote systems for the purpose of sharing information and network resources. In a client/server environment, the client and server share or distribute processing responsibilities. Computers on a network can be referred to as a host, a server, or a client.

- **Host**—A *host* is a computer system on a UNIX network. Any UNIX computer running TCP/IP (workstation or server) is considered a host computer. The *local host* is the machine on which the user currently is working. A *remote host* is a system that is being accessed by a user from another system.
- **Server**—A *server* provides resources to one or more clients by means of a network. Servers provide services in a UNIX environment by running daemons. Examples of daemons include Printer, FTP, and Telnet.
- **Client**—A *client* is a machine that uses the services from one or more servers on a network. Your computer can be a printer client, an FTP client, and a Telnet client simultaneously.

A simple example of a client/server relationship is an FTP session. *FTP*, or the *File Transfer Protocol*, is a basic industry-standard method of transferring a file from one computer to another. For the client to transfer a file, the server must be running the FTP daemon or service. In this case, the client requests the file to be transferred and the server provides the file.

The Internet is also a good example of a distributed processing client/server computing relationship. The *client* or *front end* typically handles user presentation functions such as screen formatting, input forms, and data editing. This is done with a browser such as Netscape or Internet Explorer. The *server* or *back end* handles the client's requests for Web pages and provides HTTP or WWW services.

Another example of a client/server relationship is a database server and a data entry or query client in a LAN. The client or front end might be running an application written in the C or Java language, and the server or back end could be running Oracle or other database-management software. In this case, the client also would handle formatting and presentation tasks for the user. The server would store the database itself and retrieve the data for the user.

In a typical file server environment, the client might have to retrieve large portions of the database files to process them locally, which can cause excess network traffic. With the client/server model, the client presents a request to the server, and the server database "engine" might process 100,000 records and pass only a few back to the client to satisfy the request. Servers are typically much more powerful than client computers and are better suited to processing large amounts of data. With client/server computing, the large database is stored and the processing takes place on the powerful server. The client has to deal with only creating the query, and a relatively small amount of data or results might be passed across the network. This satisfies the client's query and results in less usage of bandwidth. Figure 16-16 shows an example of client/server computing. Note that the workstation and server normally would be connected in LAN by a hub or switch.

Figure 16-16 Client/server environment.

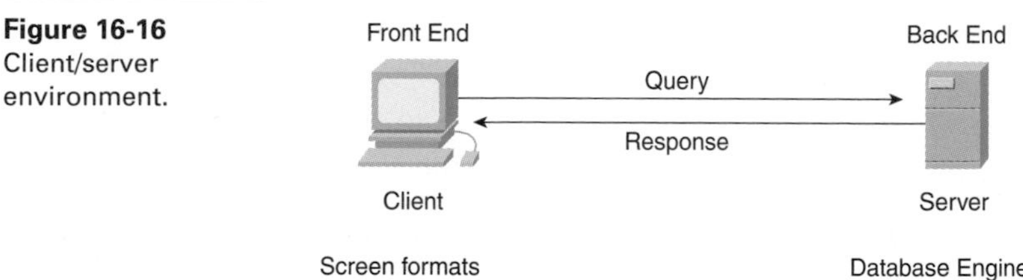

Network Commands

As UNIX computer networks began to develop, commands and utilities were added to facilitate working with programs and files residing on other computers on the network and transferring files. These commands were either specific to UNIX (such as **rlogin** and **rcp**) or common to TCP/IP (such as **ping**, **telnet**, and **ftp**). This section describes the most common and most useful of the UNIX and TCP/IP network commands.

The Ping Utility

Ping (Packet Internet Groper) is a useful utility that is part of the basic TCP/IP protocols package and is standard with every UNIX system. A computer that is running the TCP/IP protocol stack can make use of the **ping** command.

Ping is a good low-level troubleshooting tool. The **ping** command tests basic connectivity between TCP/IP hosts by sending an Internet Control Message Protocol (ICMP) echo request to another computer or "host" on a TCP/IP network. If there is a reply from the destination host, there is a good connection between them. Ping uses IP datagrams to pass connection information, so a ping will test from the physical layer (Layer 1) of the OSI model up through the network layer (Layer 3). If you are incapable of running an application on a remote host, you can ping it as a basic connectivity test. If you do not get a response, the problem might not be with the application; instead, the host or the network link might be down.

NOTE

To use the **ping** command in Solaris, you might need to specify the full path name of /usr/sbin/ping.

Any network operating system that is running the TCP/IP protocol can send and respond to **ping**. You can **ping** the name of a host computer if you have a naming service running such as DNS or if you have entered the host name and IP address in your /etc/inet/hosts file. If not, you can directly **ping** the IP address of the host, which is preferred because it is a more basic test of connectivity. Figure 16-17 shows an example using the **ping** command.

TIP

A handy troubleshooting option to the **ping** command allows for the continuous sending of packets. This saves the hassle of repeatedly having to type the **ping** command to see if a system is "alive." In Solaris, use the command **ping –s** [hostname or IP address].

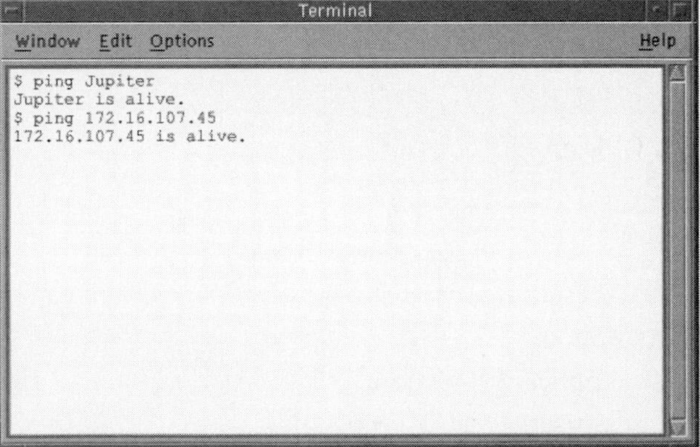

Figure 16-17
The **ping** command.

Skill Builder

e-Lab Activity 16.2

Using the **ping** Command

In this e-Lab activity, you are logged in as user2, and your current working directory is /home/user2. Refer to the class file tree structure on the inside-front cover of this book. Type the commands that would accomplish the requested objectives. *Note:* Be sure to press Enter after each one. Click Step 1 to begin.

The Telnet Utility

Another very useful TCP/IP utility is Telnet, which is standard on most operating systems. Telnet is a client/server terminal emulation program that allows you to connect to another system. The Telnet server simulates a terminal to authorize a user or Telnet client to connect to a remote system and work in that environment. When you Telnet to another host, you are prompted for a username and password. After a session is established from your Telnet client, you can enter commands as if you were entering them directly on the server console. You can Telnet to several different hosts and have multiple Telnet sessions open simultaneously.

All operating systems that support TCP/IP provide at least a Telnet client. Not all operating systems provide a Telnet server or daemon; however, UNIX provides both. In addition to connecting to other hosts, Telnet can be used to connect to and manage network devices such as switches and routers. These devices are actually microcomputers with a CPU and RAM, but they do not have a keyboard or monitor. Telnet allows you to use your computer's keyboard and monitor to remotely access and administer these devices.

Telnet is another good network troubleshooting tool. It is a nongraphical communications utility that can be used to check the upper layers of the OSI model. It runs at Layer 7, the application layer. If you are having trouble executing another, perhaps graphical, client/server application, you can try to Telnet to the host or server to verify that the TCP/IP protocol stack is functioning correctly. Remember, not all network operating systems support the Telnet server function. For instance, you can Telnet from a Windows 9*x* or NT/2000 workstation to a UNIX server, but you cannot Telnet to the Windows workstation. The Windows operating system includes a Telnet client but not a Telnet daemon or server. As long as the host operating system is running a Telnet daemon, you can Telnet to it.

NOTE

The procedure for Telnetting to another system depends on the Telnet program that you use. For example, you could use the UNIX telnet command, the Windows Telnet program, NCSA Telnet for Macintosh users, or a shareware Telnet program. Each is slightly different.

You can Telnet to the name of a host computer if you have a naming service running such as DNS or if you have entered the host name and IP address in your /etc/inet/hosts file. If not, you can Telnet the IP address of the host. When using Telnet, you can do the following:

- Open a session on a remote machine
- Alternate between the remote session and the local session
- Access machines that do not run under the UNIX environment

Figure 16-18 shows an example of using Telnet to connect to a remote system called beach. Notice that the host name beach is converted to an IP address using name-to-IP-address resolution. You also could Telnet directly to the IP address of the host if you knew it. Figure 16-19 shows alternating between the remote session and a local session.

TIP

If the Backspace and Delete keys don't work after you telnet to a remote UNIX system, look for an option in your Telnet program that allows you to define these keys. If your Telnet program does not allow you to define these keys, type **stty erase** at the shell prompt after you log in, and then hit the Backspace key (this will enter a ^H), followed by Enter. This will allow the Backspace key to work properly. To keep from having do this procedure each time you Telnet to the system, place **stty erase '^h'** somewhere in the .profile file. See Chapter 15, "Customizing Your Login Environment," for more details.

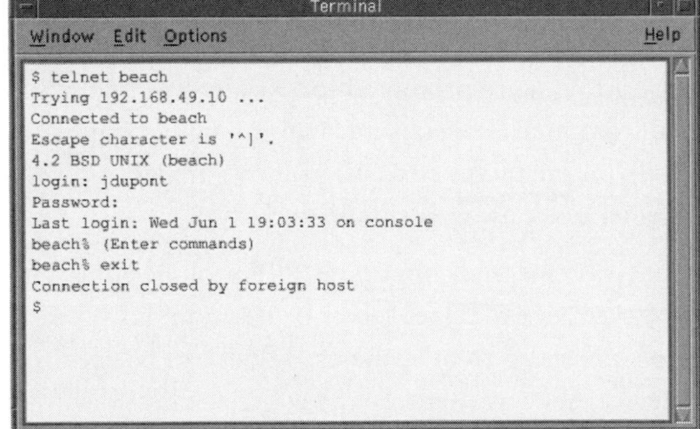

Figure 16-18
Using the Telnet utility.

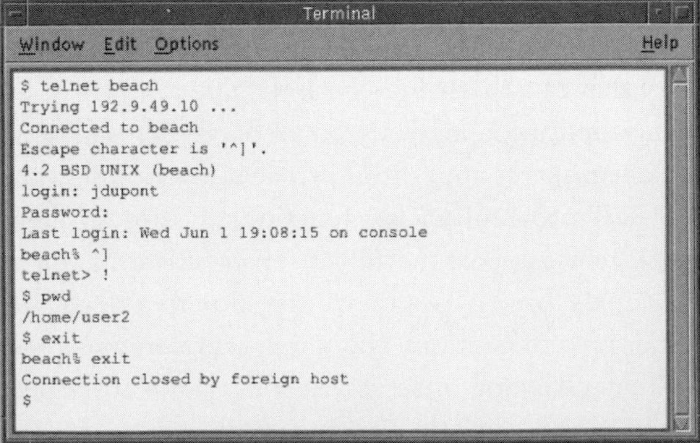

Figure 16-19
Using Telnet to alternate between sessions.

Skill Builder

e-Lab Activity 16.3

Using Telnet

In this e-Lab activity, you are logged in as user2, and your current working directory is /home/user2. Refer to the class file tree structure on the inside-front cover of this book. Type the commands that would accomplish the requested objectives. *Note:* Be sure to press Enter after each one. Click Step 1 to begin.

The rlogin Command

Use the **rlogin** command to establish a remote login session on another UNIX workstation. Remotely logging into a workstation is helpful under the following circumstances:

- To access information on another workstation that is not available otherwise
- To access your workstation remotely to read mail
- To kill a process that has caused your workstation to hang

Figure 16-20 lists some functions that can be performed with **rlogin**. Figure 16-21 shows how to log into another host under your current user ID.

Figure 16-20 Functions performed with **rlogin**.

- Login remotely to a server to run applications
- Login remotely to your workstation to kill process
- Access information on another workstation that is not available otherwise
- Access your workstation remotely to read mail

Specifying a Different Login ID

Use the -l option to specify a different login ID for the remote login session. The system administrator can set up a guest account so that users can remotely log onto a server. Figure 16-22 shows how to log in remotely as another user. The syntax for the **rlogin** command is as follows:

```
rlogin hostname -l username
```

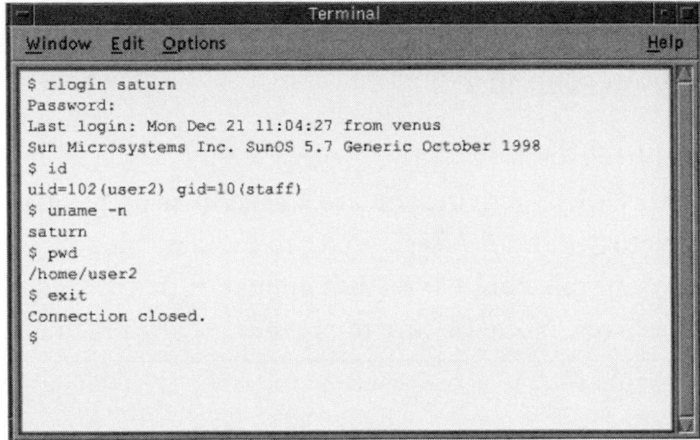
Terminal
Window Edit Options Help
$ rlogin saturn
Password:
Last login: Mon Dec 21 11:04:27 from venus
Sun Microsystems Inc. SunOS 5.7 Generic October 1998
$ id
uid=102(user2) gid=10(staff)
$ uname -n
saturn
$ pwd
/home/user2
$ exit
Connection closed.
$

Figure 16-21
Remotely logging into another host.

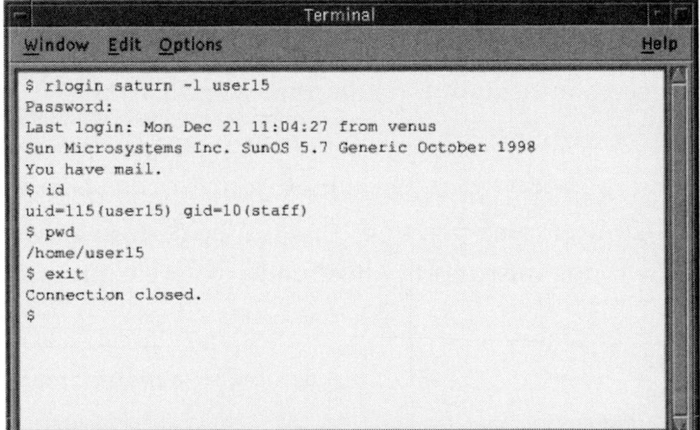
Terminal
Window Edit Options Help
$ rlogin saturn -l user15
Password:
Last login: Mon Dec 21 11:04:27 from venus
Sun Microsystems Inc. SunOS 5.7 Generic October 1998
You have mail.
$ id
uid=115(user15) gid=10(staff)
$ pwd
/home/user15
$ exit
Connection closed.
$

Figure 16-22
Logging in remotely as another user.

Before attempting to remotely log into another host (system) as a different user, be sure that you have an account on the desired remote host. Check with your system administrator if you do not have an account on the remote host. You will need to know this information:

- Host name or IP address
- Login ID
- Password of the new account

Terminating a Local Process from a Remote Machine

When your system is not responding and you do not want to reboot, you might be able to kill a process on your system remotely by logging onto another machine and using the **rlogin** command to access your system. After successfully killing the process that caused your system to not respond, the **exit** command ends your **rlogin** session. Figure 16-23 shows an example of terminating a process from a remote machine.

Figure 16-23
Terminating a process from a remote machine.

```
$ rlogin hostname
Password:
Last login: Tue Jun 8 17:40:30 from venus
Sun Microsystems Inc. SunOS 5.7 Generic October 1998
You have mail.
$ ps -e
PID     TTY       TIME  CMD
10153  console  0:03  cm
12892  console  0:01  sh
217term  /a0:0 /usr/lib/lpsched
14490pts  /20:03  maker3ol
12932pts  /00:01  /bin/sh
13162pts  /70:08  admintool
10138console  0:04  clock
10159console  7:29  mailtool
10140pts  /10:05  cmdtool
10151console  12:42  xnews
10614pts  /10:27  cmdtool
10109console  0:00  xinit
$ kill 14490
```

Using rlogin and pkill to Recover from a "Hung" CDE Session

When your workstation does not appear to be responding to mouse or keyboard input, the odds are that the problem stems from within your CDE session instead of the underlying operating system itself. In such cases, you can use another workstation to access your workstation via **rlogin** (or **telnet**) and then use the **pkill** command to terminate the corrupted CDE session, all without rebooting your workstation.

Figure 16-24 shows how to use **rlogin** and **pkill** to recover from a hung CDE session. If you know your default shell, use the first example of **pkill**. If you do not know your default shell, use the second example of **pkill**, which determines and terminates all instances of your login shell for you. Either variant returns you to the **dtlogin** screen, enabling you to start a new CDE session.

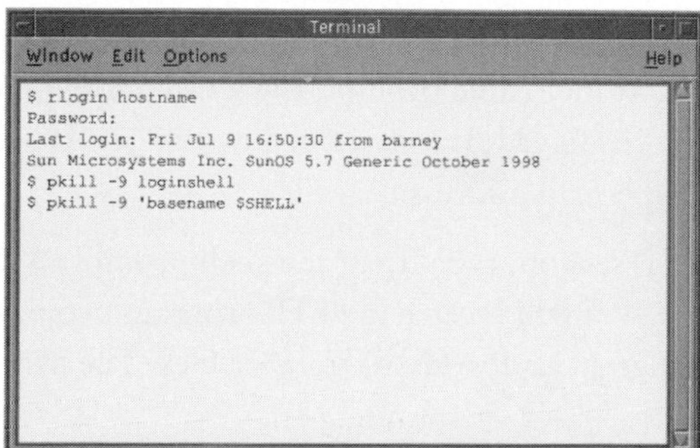
Terminal
Window Edit Options
Help
$ rlogin hostname
Password:
Last login: Fri Jul 9 16:50:30 from barney
Sun Microsystems Inc. SunOS 5.7 Generic October 1998
$ pkill -9 loginshell
$ pkill -9 'basename $SHELL'

Figure 16-24
Using **rlogin** to recover from a hung CDE session.

Skill Builder

e-Lab Activity 16.4

Using rlogin

In this e-Lab activity, you are logged in as user2, and your current working directory is /home/user2. Refer to the class file tree structure on the inside-front cover of this book. Type the commands that would accomplish the requested objectives. *Note:* Be sure to press Enter after each one. Click Step 1 to begin.

TIP

It is important to know the type of file(s) that you are transferring ("ftp-ing") so that you can set the appropriate transfer mode. If you are transferring a non-ASCII file, you must set the transfer mode from the default ASCII to binary. This is accomplished by typing **bin** at the ftp prompt (**ftp>bin [Enter]**). Transferring a non-ASCII file in ASCII transfer mode renders the file useless. Transferring text files in binary mode could result in a scrambled file.

The ftp Command

The File Transfer Protocol (FTP) application is part of the TCP/IP protocol suite and is standard with most operating systems. It can be used to transfer files using ASCII or binary mode between systems using similar or dissimilar operating systems. This provides a basic means of transferring files from one file format to another. For instance, a UNIX file normally would be unreadable by a Windows operating system. Because both operating systems support FTP, the file is converted from one file format to another as it is transferred.

An ASCII file is an ordinary text file with no formatting characters—for example, a file created with vi in UNIX or Notepad in Windows. A binary file is any other type of file (such as a file from a word processor, a program file, a zip file, and so on). When transferring ASCII text files between two different operating systems (UNIX to Windows, or vice versa), the default ASCII transfer mode saves the file in a format that makes the file readable by the different OSs.

Most computers running servers with sites set up for downloading files sometimes provide an *anonymous ftp* account so that users can pull files off the server. For this kind of an account, at the Name prompt, the word *anonymous* is entered instead of accepting the default displayed. If a password is required for the anonymous account, it usually is your full e-mail address.

TIP

Type asc or ascii to switch back to ASCII transfer mode from binary mode.

To start an FTP session, type **ftp** at the shell prompt. After supplying an account name and password, you will receive the FTP program prompt (**ftp>**) indicating that you are in the FTP program and ready to transfer files. The syntax for the **ftp** command is shown here:

```
ftp hostname or ftp [ip address]
```

After you successfully use **ftp** to access a remote site, some familiar file and directory access commands such as **cd** and **ls** are available. To view a list of FTP available commands, enter the ? at the **ftp>** prompt. If permissions are set by the site's system administrator for a user to see the contents of a directory, the **ls** command displays files in that directory. If permissions are set so that a user does not have access to the files, when the **ls** command is entered, a prompt is returned in response. As on your local system, **cd** will change directories on the remote system. If it is necessary for you to change directories on your own system in the middle of the ftp session, the **lcd** (local change directory) command can be used. To end an FTP session, type **bye** at the prompt.

> **TIP**
> The File Transfer Protocol supports approximately 50 UNIX and FTP commands. Refer to the man pages on the **ftp** command for a complete list.

In addition to the previous commands, the others that you will use often are **put**, **mput**, **get**, and **mget**. The **put** command is used to transfer a file to the remote host. The **mput** (multiple put) command allows you to transfer more than one file at a time by specifying a space-delimited list of files. Wildcards are accepted. The **get** and **mget** commands are used to transfer one or more file from a remote host to your system.

Figure 16-25 shows an example using the **ftp** command to transfer (get) two files (hosts and /tmp/hosts) in binary mode from another host. In this case, we are initiating an FTP session to the host name **venus**. As with **ping** and **telnet**, you can FTP directly to the host's IP address.

> **TIP**
> Use the **cd** and **lcd** commands mentioned previously to change to the desired directory before transferring files. Files are put into the current directory on the remote system, and files that you get are placed in the current directory on your system.

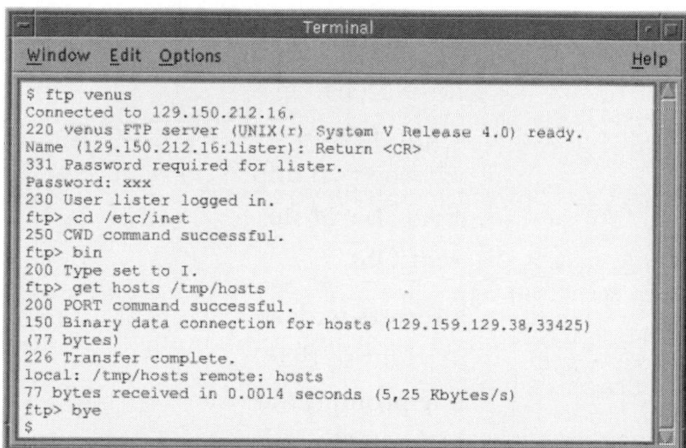
Terminal
Window Edit Options
Help
$ ftp venus
Connected to 129.150.212.16.
220 venus FTP server (UNIX(r) System V Release 4.0) ready.
Name (129.150.212.16:lister): Return <CR>
331 Password required for lister.
Password: xxx
230 User lister logged in.
ftp> cd /etc/inet
250 CWD command successful.
ftp> bin
200 Type set to I.
ftp> get hosts /tmp/hosts
200 PORT command successful.
150 Binary data connection for hosts (129.159.129.38,33425)
(77 bytes)
226 Transfer complete.
local: /tmp/hosts remote: hosts
77 bytes received in 0.0014 seconds (5,25 Kbytes/s)
ftp> bye
$

Figure 16-25 Retrieving a file from another host using FTP.

Skill Builder

e-Lab Activity 16.5

Using FTP

In this e-Lab activity, you are logged in as user2, and your current working directory is /home/user2. Refer to the class file tree structure on the inside-front cover of this book. Type the commands that would accomplish the requested objectives. *Note:* Be sure to press Enter after each one. Click Step 1 to begin.

Skill Builder

Lab Activity 16.4.4

Using Network Commands

In this lab, you work with UNIX and Transmission Control Protocol/Internet Protocol (TCP/IP) networking commands. Refer to the *Cisco Networking Academy Program: Fundamentals of UNIX Lab Companion.*

The rcp Command

The **rcp** (remote copy) command is another command from the *r* (remote) family of commands. Like **rlogin**, the **rcp** command is a UNIX (not a TCP/IP) command for use between UNIX systems. The **rcp** command works in much the same way the **cp** (copy) command does and is used to "get" and "put" (to borrow FTP terms) files and directories to and from a remote UNIX system. The syntax for the **rcp** command is shown here:

```
rcp source_file hostname:destination_file  ("put")
rcp hostname:source_file destination_file  ("get")
```

For example, to copy the memo file to the /tmp directory on the host buckeye, use this command:

```
$rcp  memo  buckeye:/tmp
```

To copy ("get") the budget file from dano's home directory on buckeye to the current directory, use this command:

```
$rcp buckeye:~dano/budget  . (dot)
```

To remotely copy the chapters directory to the /book directory on the host production1, use this command:

```
$rcp -r ~/chapters  production1:/book
```

Naming Services and Host Name Resolution

Name services store information in a central place that users, workstations, and applications must have to communicate across the network. These services include the following:

- Host names and addresses
- Usernames
- Passwords

Without a central name service, each workstation would have to maintain its own copy of this information. Name service information may be stored in files, maps, or database tables. Centrally locating this data makes it easier to administer large networks.

The goal of a naming service is to allow centralization of network administration. The administration of a group of machines grows in complexity with the number of machines and users to manage. Thus, decentralized administration is conceivable for two or three machines, but it becomes more complex if the number exceeds that limit. For example, imagine a group of five machines. If all the users have to be able to log in as themselves on each machine, the administrator must duplicate the /etc/passwd on every machine. Although putting this in place initially is possible, maintenance becomes difficult. In effect, each modification of one element of the password file makes it necessary to reproduce the change on each machine. The problem that is raised by the /etc/password file is exponentially increased by necessary changes to many other administrative files, such as the groups and hosts files.

Centralized Administration

It is advisable for administrators to set up networks with a centralized administration that distributes a database to all the machines known by the distributed administration. This database can be centralized on one server, which provides the administrative services. The group of machines using the database on the server is called a *domain*. This centralized administration uses a naming service as the framework for the domain(s). The Domain Name System (DNS) and Network Information Service (NIS) are two naming services that can be set up for use in the UNIX networked environment. *NIS+* is another naming service developed by Sun Microsystems for Solaris. Each naming service is discussed in greater detail in the following sections.

DNS

The Domain Name System (DNS) is the name service provided by the Internet for TCP/IP networks. It was developed so that workstations and servers on the network could be identified with common names instead of Internet addresses. DNS performs resolution or translation of host name to Internet (IP) address between hosts within your local administrative domain and across domain boundaries.

For instance, when you start your *browser* and type in a Web site such as cisco.netacad.net or www.sun.com, a DNS server within your domain or at your ISP tries to translate the Internet domain name to an IP address. If it cannot, it requests help from other DNS servers on the Internet. If none of the DNS servers can translate the name that you entered, you will get an error from your browser. In the example of www.sun.com, the name of the Web server (www) in the sun.com domain would be translated to an IP address such as 172.16.133.89. It is only because of the DNS server that you can enter www.sun.com and have it translated to the IP address of the Web site that you want to go to. If the DNS server is down or unavailable, you will not be able to connect to the desired Web site using the domain name. If you know the IP address of the server, though, you could enter it and connect. Without an IP address, your request would never make it to the Web server at Sun Microsystems.

The collection of networked workstations that use DNS is referred to as the *DNS namespace*. The DNS namespace can be divided into a hierarchy of domains. A DNS domain is simply a group of workstations. Each domain is supported by two or more name servers: a principal server and one or more secondary servers.

Host/etc Files

The original host-based UNIX naming system was developed for standalone UNIX machines and then was adapted for network use. Many older UNIX operating systems and machines still use this system, but it is not well suited for large, complex networks. With this system, name resolution is performed on each machine and requires that a static */etc/hosts file* be created on each machine to translate host names to IP addresses. The addition of a new machine to the network means updating the /etc/hosts file on every machine on the network.

Likewise, if all the users have to be able to log in as themselves on each machine, the administrator must duplicate the /etc/passwd on every machine. This method of constantly updating the etc files on each machine on the network can take up an enormous amount of time with a medium or larger network.

NIS

The Network Information Service (NIS) was developed by Sun Microsystems and has a slightly different focus than DNS. Whereas DNS focuses on making communication simpler by using host and domain names instead of numerical IP addresses, NIS focuses on making network administration more manageable by providing centralized control over a variety of network information. NIS stores information about workstation names and IP addresses, users, the network itself, and network services. This collection of network information is referred to as the *NIS namespace*.

NIS namespace information is stored in NIS maps. NIS maps were designed to replace UNIX /etc files, as well as other configuration files, so they store much more than names and addresses. As a result, the NIS namespace has a large set of maps.

NIS uses a client/server arrangement similar to that of DNS. Replicated NIS servers provide services to NIS clients. The principal servers are called *master servers*, and, for reliability, they have *backup servers*, or *slave servers*. Both master and slave servers use the NIS information retrieval software, and both store NIS maps. The following list summarizes the characteristics of NIS:

- Provides centralized administration of network information for users, workstations, applications, and so on
- Runs on top of TCP/IP
- Stable and widely used by all UNIX vendors and many non-UNIX operating systems
- Easy to implement
- Works well in small, flat domains (for example, acme.com)
- No security features

NIS+

The Network Information Service Plus (NIS+) is similar to NIS, but with many more features. NIS+ is not an extension of NIS.

NIS+ enables you to store information about workstation addresses, security information, mail information, Ethernet interfaces, and network services in central locations where all workstations on a network can have access to it. This configuration of network information is referred to as the *NIS+ namespace*.

The NIS+ namespace is hierarchical and is similar in structure to the UNIX directory file system. The hierarchical structure allows an NIS+ namespace to be configured to conform to the logical hierarchy of an organization. The namespace's layout of information is unrelated to its physical arrangement. Thus, an NIS+ namespace can be divided into multiple domains that can be administered autonomously. Clients may have access to information in other domains, in addition to their own, if they have the appropriate permissions.

NIS+ uses a client/server model to store and control access to the information contained in an NIS+ namespace. Each domain is supported by a set of servers. The principal server is called the *master server*, and the backup servers are called *replicas*. The network information is stored in 16 standard NIS+ tables in an internal NIS+ database. Both master and replica servers run NIS+ server software, and both maintain copies of NIS+ tables. Changes made to the NIS+ data on the master server incrementally are propagated automatically to the replicas.

NIS+ includes a sophisticated security system to protect the structure of the namespace and its information. It uses authentication and authorization to verify whether a client's request for information should be fulfilled. *Authentication* determines whether the information requester is a valid user on the network. *Authorization* determines whether a particular user is allowed to have or modify the information requested. The following list summarizes the characteristics of NIS+:

- Sun's newest naming service for Solaris
- Enhanced security features
- Difficult to configure
- Scales well for large hierarchical domains (for example, sun.com, sales.sun.com, and so on)

The Network File System

The *Network File System (NFS)* is Sun's distributed computing file system. It is a network service that allows users to transparently access files and directories located on another disk on the network. NFS has become adopted as the industry-standard networked file system for most UNIX vendors.

NFS provides users with several benefits:

- Centralized files
  - Multiple computers can use same files. Because the files reside on one or more computers and shared to the network, others can access them.
  - This is useful with login directories or common data files. It is easier for an administrator to back up a home file system containing many users' home directories residing on one system instead of individual workstations.
- Common software
  - Systems can share software programs. It is easier to install and upgrade a network version of programs on one server than to install the program on each individual workstation.
- Files that appear to be local
  - Accessing files is transparent to the user. Users might start an application or change to a directory residing on another computer on the network and not

even know it. The automounter feature makes this happen behind the scenes.

— Shared files typically are made available at bootup (automounted) or on the fly.

Summary

Now that you have completed this chapter, you should have an understanding of the following:

- Networks are groups of interconnected computers. LANs and WANs are two basic categories of networks. If computers are relatively close together and the networking equipment and cabling are owned by the organization, this is a LAN. WANs are created by interconnecting two or more geographically separate LANs. The links interconnecting the LANs are not typically owned by the organization. Routers generally are used to connect LANs to WANs.
- The computers and networking equipment on both LANs and WANs are connected using various types of media, including copper cable, fiber-optic cable, and various forms of wireless communications.
- Ethernet is the most common LAN architecture or technology. Other LAN technologies include Token Ring and FDDI. Switched Ethernet using an extended star topology is the dominant LAN technology being deployed today. Examples of WAN technologies include T1, Frame Relay, ISDN, and ATM.
- The most popular data communications protocol is TCP/IP, which is actually a suite of protocols. The Internet and many LANs and WANs use the TCP/IP protocol. Several utilities are part of the TCP/IP protocol suite, including **ping**, **telnet**, **rlogin**, and **ftp**.
- The **ping** command is a low-level troubleshooting tool. The **telnet** command can be used to take over the console of a remote host. The **rlogin** command is used to log in and run programs on another computer. The File Transfer Protocol is a very useful utility that can be used to transfer file between computers with dissimilar operating systems. The **rcp** command is used to copy file and directories between UNIX computers.
- A client/server architecture is a popular computing model used with the Internet. It is used to distribute or share processing loads when performing tasks. The server or back end runs software such as a daemon to provide services for client requests.

- Sun developed NIS, NIS+, and NFS. NIS and NIS+ simplify network administration by providing a centralized database for user account authorization. NFS provides for distributed processing by allowing a file system on a remote computer to appear as part of the local hosts file system.

Check Your Understanding

1. Which of the following are characteristics of LANs?
   - A. Multiple geographical locations
   - B. Links typically owned by a service provider
   - C. Single confined geographical area
   - D. Low-speed connections
2. Which of the following are characteristics of WANs?
   - A. Multiple geographical locations
   - B. Links typically owned by the organization
   - C. Single confined geographical area
   - D. Low-speed connections
3. What is the most common LAN architecture or technology?
   - A. Token Ring
   - B. FDDI
   - C. Ethernet
   - D. Arcnet
4. Switched Ethernet provides which of the following?
   - A. Dedicated point-to-point bandwidth between two nodes
   - B. Large collision domains
   - C. Shared bandwidth with half-duplex communication
   - D. Client/server processing
5. The most common and scalable LAN topology is:
   - A. Ring
   - B. Extended star
   - C. Mesh
   - D. Bus

6. Which of the following is true regarding TCP/IP?
   A. It is an Internet standard.
   B. It is a protocol suite made up of many protocols.
   C. It is used with LANs and WANs.
   D. All of the above.
7. A client/server architecture provides which of the following?
   A. Distributed processing
   B. Centralized processing
   C. User authentication
   D. Security processing
8. Three troubleshooting utilities that are part of TCP/IP and UNIX are:
   A. **ping**, **telnet**, and **rlogin**
   B. **telnet**, **ping**, and FTP
   C. **rlogin**, **ping**, and **mkdir**
   D. TCP, IP, and UDP
9. Which of the following is true of the FTP utility?
   A. It can transfer files between two computers.
   B. It use the **get** and **put** subcommands.
   C. Files are converted from one file system to another on differing operating systems.
   D. All of the above.
10. Two network-management features developed by Sun Microsystems are:
    A. INS+ and FNS
    B. TCP and IP
    C. NFS and NIS+
    D. LAN and WAN

UNIX Command Summary

ftp The File Transfer Protocol (FTP) application is part of the TCP/IP protocol suite and is standard with the UNIX operating system. It can be used to transfer files using

ASCII or binary mode between systems using similar or dissimilar operating systems. Example:

```
$ ftp venus
Connected to 129.150.212.16.
220 venus FTP server (UNIX(r) System V Release 4.0) ready.
Name (129.150.212.16:lister): Return <CR>
331 Password required for lister.
Password: xxx
230 User lister logged in.
ftp> cd /etc/inet
250 CWD command successful.
ftp> bin
200 Type set to I.
ftp> get hosts /tmp/hosts
200 PORT command successful.
150 Binary data connection for hosts (129.159.129.38,33425)
(77 bytes)
226 Transfer complete.
local: /tmp/hosts remote: hosts
77 bytes received in 0.0014 seconds (5,25 Kbytes/s)
ftp> bye
ftp> get hosts /tmp/hosts
200 PORT command successful.
150 Binary data connection for hosts (129.159.129.38,33425)
(77 bytes)
226 Transfer complete.
local: /tmp/hosts remote: hosts
77 bytes received in 0.0014 seconds (5,25 Kbytes/s)
ftp> bye
```

ping Tests basic connectivity between TCP/IP hosts by sending an Internet Control Message Protocol (ICMP) echo request to another computer or "host" on a TCP/IP network. If there is a reply from the destination host, there is a good connection between them. Example:

```
-s

$ ping jupiter
jupiter is alive
$ ping 192.13.145.10
192.13.145.10 is alive
```

rcp Copies to or from one UNIX system to another. Example:

```
$ rcp big10schedule spartan:/tmp

$ rcp buckeye:~dano/budget  .
```

rlogin Use the **rlogin** command to establish a remote login session on another workstation. Example:

```
$ rlogin saturn
Password:
Last login: Mon Dec 21 11:04:27 from venus
Sun Microsystems Inc. SunOS 5.7 Generic October 1998
$
```

telnet Another good network troubleshooting tool. Telnet is a nongraphical communications utility that can be used to check the upper layers of the OSI model. Example:

```
$ telnet beach
Trying 192.168.49.10 ...
Connected to beach
Escape character is '^]'.
4.2 BSD UNIX (beach)
login: jdupont
Password:
Last login: Wed Jun 1 19:03:33 on console
beach% (Enter commands)
beach% exit
Connection closed by foreign host
$
```

Key Terms

/etc/hosts file With /etc/hosts name resolution, each machine requires that a static /etc/hosts file be created to translate host names to IP addresses.

1000Base-T 1000-Mbps baseband Gigabit Ethernet specification using twisted-pair (copper) or fiber-optic cable. 1000Base-T, which is part of the IEEE 802.3*z* specification, has a distance limit of from 100 to 2000 meters per segment, depending on the type of cable.

100Base-FX 100-Mbps baseband Fast Ethernet specification using fiber-optic cable. 100Base-FX, which is part of the IEEE 802.3u specification, has a distance limit of from 400 to 2000 meters per segment, depending on whether it is shared or switched and the type of fiber used. Commonly used for LAN backbones.

100Base-TX 100-Mbps baseband Fast Ethernet specification using twisted-pair (copper) cable. 100Base-TX, which is part of the IEEE 802.3u specification, has a distance limit of from 100 meters per segment. Commonly used for workstation and server connections.

10Base-2 10-Mbps baseband Ethernet specification using 50-ohm thin (RG-58) coaxial cable. 10Base-2, which is part of the IEEE 802.3 specification, has a distance limit of 185 meters per segment.

10Base-5 10-Mbps baseband Ethernet specification using standard (thick) 50-ohm baseband coaxial cable. 10Base-5, which is part of the IEEE 802.3 baseband physical layer specification, has a distance limit of 500 meters per segment.

10Base-F 10-Mbps baseband Ethernet specification that refers to the 10Base-FB, 10Base-FL, and 10Base-FP standards for Ethernet over fiber-optic cabling.

10Base-T 10-Mbps baseband Ethernet specification using two pairs of twisted-pair cabling (Category 3, 4, or 5): one pair for transmitting data and the other for receiving data. 10Base-T, which is part of the IEEE 802.3 specification, has a distance limit of approximately 100 meters per segment.

Anonymous FTP A site that is set up for general use and that does not require an account to obtain files. The word *anonymous* is the username, and the user's e-mail address is the password.

Browser A graphical program that allows convenient access to the World Wide Web (WWW). The first browser was Mosaic. Some browsers are Netscape Navigator, Microsoft Internet Explorer, and HotJava.

Bus topology Early Ethernet LANs used a bus topology. A bus is a cable (coaxial) that is run through an area, and workstations and servers tap into the cable to get access to the network. The bus is a single length of cable that is terminated at each end.

Client A machine that uses the services from one or more servers on a network. Your computer can be a printer client, an FTP client, and a Telnet client simultaneously.

Client/server Computing model that distributes processing over multiple computers. This enables access to remote systems for the purpose of sharing information and network resources. In a client/server environment, the client and server share or distribute processing responsibilities. Computers on a network can be referred to as a host, a server, or a client.

CSMA/CD (carrier sense multiple access collision detect) Access method used by Ethernet to allow more than one user to share the network.

DNS (Domain Name System) The name service provided by the Internet for TCP/IP networks. It was developed so that workstations and servers on the network could be identified with common names instead of Internet addresses. DNS performs resolution or translation of host name to Internet (IP) address between hosts within your local administrative domain and across domain boundaries.

Domain The name assigned to a group of systems on a local network that share administrative files. The domain name is required for the network information service database to work properly.

Ethernet Popular LAN architecture or technology based on IEEE 802.3 standards. Used in most modern networks, Ethernet uses the CSMA/CD access method. It is a broadcast network, which means that all the workstations on the network receive all transmissions. Ethernet has evolved from speeds of 10 Mbps speeds to 100 Mbps (Fast Ethernet) and now to 1000 Mbps (Gigabit Ethernet).

Ethernet address The physical address of an individual Ethernet controller board. It is called the hardware address or Media Access Control (MAC) address. The Ethernet address of every Sun workstation is unique and is coded into a chip on the motherboard.

Fast Ethernet Ethernet based on speeds of 100 Mbps. 100Base-TX and 100Base-FX are two versions. Fast Ethernet can be shared or switched.

FDDI (Fiber Distributed Data Interface) Pronounced "fiddi." An ANSI standard that was developed primarily as a backbone technology to interconnect LANs in a campus environment. It runs over fiber-optic cable and can span many miles. FDDI uses two rings, one primary and one for backup. It transmits data at 100 Mbps using the token-passing access method.

Full-duplex Communication method in which the nodes can send and receive simultaneously. Examples include the telephone and switched Ethernet.

Gigabit Ethernet Newest version of Ethernet running at 1 billion bps. IEEE standard is 1000Base-T. It is becoming more common as a backbone for LANs and for high-speed servers and storage devices.

Half-duplex Communication method in which the nodes can only send or receive but cannot do both simultaneously. Examples include walky-talkies and shared Ethernet.

Host A computer system on a UNIX network. Any UNIX (or other OS) computer running TCP/IP (workstation or server) is considered a host computer. The *local host* is the machine on which the user is currently working. A *remote host* is a system that is being accessed by a user from another system.

Internet The largest network in the world. It consists of a large national backbone network that contains the Military Network (MILNET), the National Science Foundation Network (NSFNET), the European Laboratory for Particle Physics (CREN), and a myriad of regional and local campus networks all over the world. To be able to log on the Internet the user must have Internet Protocol (IP) connectivity; that is, the user be capable of communicating with other systems by using **telnet** or **ping**. Networks with only e-mail connectivity are not classified as being on the Internet.

LAN (local-area network) Made up of groups of computers (nodes) that have simultaneous access to common high-bandwidth media.

Mesh topology The mesh is typically a WAN topology used to interconnect multiple LANs for redundancy of communications paths. This topology also can be used in LANs to provide redundant links between routers and switches. With a full mesh, each site has a link to every other site. With a partial mesh, each site has a link to more than one site, but not to every site.

Name service Provides a means of identifying and locating resources (traditionally host names and Internet protocol [IP] addresses) available to a network. The default name service product available in the Solaris 2.x environment is NIS+.

Namespace A collection of machines using a network information service such as domain name service (DNS) (yp), NIS, or NIS+, all sharing a common name.

NFS (Network File System) Sun's distributed computing file system. It is a network service that allows users to transparently access files and directories located on another disk on the network. NFS has become adopted as the industry-standard networked file system for most UNIX vendors.

NIS (Network Information Service) Focuses on making network administration more manageable by providing centralized control over a variety of network information. NIS stores information about workstation names and IP addresses, users, the network itself, and network services. This collection of network information is referred to as the NIS namespace.

NIS+ Enables you to store information about workstation addresses, security information, mail information, Ethernet interfaces, and network services in central locations where all workstations on a network can have access to it. This configuration of network information is referred to as the NIS+ namespace.

OSI model Developed by the International Organization for Standardization (ISO) to describe the functions that occur as two nodes on a network communicate. OSI is short for "Open System Interconnection" and is an internationally recognized, structured, and standardized architecture for network design. The seven-layer OSI reference model, or just OSI model, is one of the most useful tools we have for analyzing and comparing various technologies and networking products from different vendors.

Ring topology The Token Ring and Fiber Distributed Data Interface (FDDI) network architectures use the ring topology. Token Ring commonly is implemented as a star with a central concentration device known as a multistation access unit (MAU); technically, it is a star ring.

Server Provides resources to one or more clients by means of a network. Servers provide services in an UNIX environment by running daemons. Examples of daemons include Printer, FTP, and Telnet.

Shared Ethernet The original version of Ethernet using a linear bus and (more recently) hubs, in which only one node could have a packet on the network at a time. Shared Ethernet uses half-duplex technology, in which a workstation can be transmitting or receiving but cannot do both at the same time. It is prone to collisions and performance degradation due to excessive traffic.

Star topology The most common topology, and the one used with Ethernet hubs and switches. The hub or switch is the center of the star, and cables radiate out to nodes like spokes on a wheel. If more than one hub or switch is interconnected, it becomes an extended star topology.

Switched Ethernet Newer version of Ethernet using switches to provide full-duplex transmission and dedicated bandwidth to each node on the network. Nodes can send and receive multiple packets simultaneously.

TCP/IP The Defense Advance Research Projects Agency (DARPA) originally developed TCP/IP to interconnect defense department computer networks across the country to form a fault-tolerant network. It was adopted and further developed as the standard networking communications component of the UNIX operating system.

Token Ring Originally was developed by IBM and then became IEEE standard 802.5. The Token Ring network architecture uses the ring topology and a token to provide access for workstations. Token Ring uses the token-passing access method. Token Ring speeds are 4 and 16 Mbps.

Topology The layout or arrangement of network components. Some architectures support more than one topology. Examples of topologies include a bus, a star, a ring, and a mesh.

WAN (wide-area network) Connections between multiple LANs in different geographical locations.

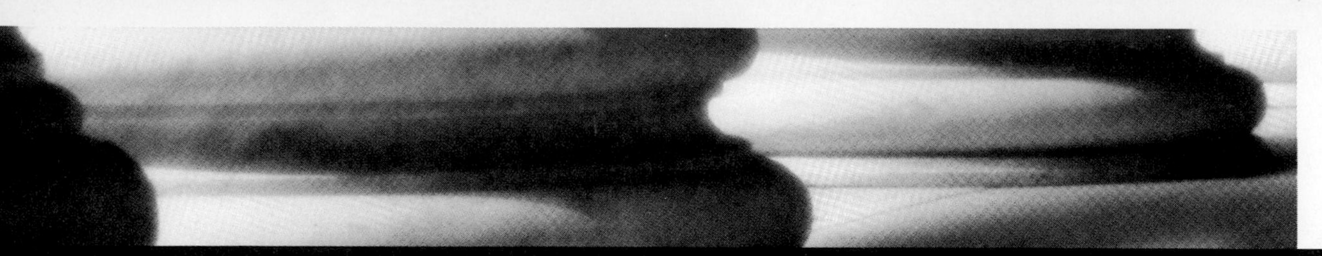

Objectives

After reading this chapter, you will be able to

- Understand the role and responsibilities of a UNIX system administrator
- Appreciate career opportunities as a UNIX system administrator
- Describe the Sun certification path for system administrators
- Describe the Sun Academic Initiative

Chapter 17

Career Guidance

Introduction

This chapter provides information and resources for students who want to learn more about UNIX. It covers careers in UNIX system administration and the process of obtaining certification in Solaris system administration. It concludes with an overview of the Sun Academic Initiative, a program that offers Solaris system administration courses from Sun Education to authorized educational institutions.

What's Next?

The Fundamentals of UNIX course was designed to give you a strong understanding and foundation of the UNIX network operating system. Now that you have completed the course, what's next? Plenty! The UNIX OS has evolved into a powerful, robust operating system that you can spend a lifetime learning. As a user, you can continue to learn more about the UNIX world from a variety of sources, including Web sites, newsgroups, user groups, and, of course, books. However, if you really enjoy working with UNIX, the next step might be a career in system administration.

Careers in UNIX System Administration

Job-placement sites (monster.com, dice.com, and others) illustrate that plenty of jobs are available for UNIX system administrators. So, what is a system administrator?

System administration is a broad topic, which can make it difficult to define. Generally, a *system administrator* is someone who sets up UNIX systems (workstations and servers) on a network and handles day-to-day tasks for maintaining a large number of systems. These tasks can include creating and maintaining user accounts, installing software, ensuring system security, backing up data, and solving computer and network problems.

In large organizations, system administrators often have specialized roles. Some administrators focus entirely on creating and maintaining user accounts. Others focus on system security, and others spend their time ensuring that data is successfully backed up in case of a system failure or disaster.

The sidebar "Careers in System Administration" is reprinted from an article of the same title written by Barbara Dijker for the *Dr. Dobb's Journal*, Fall 1999. The sidebar discusses the following topics:

- Careers in system administration
- Specialties and career-advancement paths
- Market areas and industries
- Market demands and trends
- Salaries and salary trends
- Consulting and contracting versus direct employment
- Job requirements
- Training and education

CAREERS IN SYSTEM ADMINISTRATION

Dr. Dobb's Journal Fall 1999

The Future Looks Bright for Problem Solvers

By Barbara Dijker

What are system administrators? In general, sysadmins are those people we complain to when our computer systems aren't working the way we expect. If they can make everything right, then they must be system administrators. Therefore, a system administrator is someone who solves problems in computer and network systems operations.

The problem set in computing and network operations generally includes all those system tasks users might want to offload—specification, evaluation, installation, configuration, integration, maintenance, data-integrity management, upgrade management, automation, security management, performance analysis, failure analysis, failure mitigation, recovery design, recovery implementation, testing, and more. In reality, the definition of system administration is usually a subset of all those tasks specific to the organization doing the hiring. For example, some organizations have a separate staff of network administrators to handle network administration, while in other organizations system administrators manage both computers and network infrastructure. Other organizations have separate staff dedicated to security administration. Some organizations allow users a high degree of self-administration that makes the system administrator's job focus more on the integration and systemic issues.

Specialties and Career Advancement Paths

Because system administration is so broad, room exists for specialization. Examples of where you can specialize are security, data encryption, networks, heterogeneous integration, specific operating systems or platforms (Sun, NT, or Linux), specific subsystems (file sharing, mail, or naming systems), specific applications (supercomputing), and (more recently) Web-server administration. Web-server administrators specialize in the operational issues specific to Web servers, usually in the area of performance, security, reliability, and redundancy.

System administration is often thought of as a job in the trenches. However, good system administrators, through experience, hone unique problem solving skills, people skills, organizational skills, and a keen sense of the big picture and potential implications of change. These skills are invaluable for someone interested in a management track that can lead up the chain all the way to corporate information technology director and even chief technical officer.

Because system administrators seem to enjoy the challenge of actually fixing problems, career advancement often tends to stay on a more technical track. System administrators have plenty of responsibility for the operational integrity of the systems they administer, so the lure of responsibility for staff or budgets is less appealing. Advancement technically can be toward:

- Consulting, which often provides the ability to select work or truly focus on a specialty.
- Back-line, away from the "front-line" of interruptions to the more challenging problems.
- Specialties, focused and more detailed work, more available in larger organizations.

Large organizations may provide pre-defined advancement from the front-line of basic user support or "help-desk" through multiple levels of system administration toward the back-line of elite troubleshooters. Some companies even have a "special forces" team of system administrators to swoop in and fix really tough problems.

Market Areas and Industries

Every organization that has computing systems needs someone to perform system administration tasks. While every such site may have that need, solving it does not always involve hiring a full-time system administrator. When the load of system administration tasks is low, they are usually delegated to an existing staff person whose primary responsibility is something else. Interestingly, this is often the genesis of a system administrator. That person finds he enjoys the system administration tasks more than his other work.

The affect of this on the market for system administrators is that you can find a job in system administration in any industry in any market sector. Small, growing, and changing organizations feed the free-lance consulting and contract system administrator markets. Other organizations feed the consulting and contract pools with experienced system administrators who are looking for a change. In short, system administrators work for everything from churches and hospitals to multinational and Fortune 500 companies.

Market Demands and Trends

Some people have long predicted that the need for system administration would die out like dinosaurs as computers and applications become more automated and sophisticated and solved their own problems. The opposite is actually the case. As computers and applications have become more sophisticated, they've created different problems from those they may have solved.

continues

For example, ubiquitous computer networks have solved many problems in transport of information and resource sharing. However, for each problem solved, networking has introduced at least a dozen in the areas of security and data integrity. As problems crop up, system administrators have to figure out what to do about them to allow users to continue the "real" work.

There has never been a market glut of systems administrators. In fact, there are probably five jobs available for every existing sysadmin today. In fact, most experienced system administrators find they are doing the work of five people. Demand has out-paced supply for at least the last six years.

Of course, this is mostly subjective information. There are at least two problems with clearly quantifying trends in the system administrator job market. The first problem is that most system administrators have a job title that has nothing to do with system administration—a member of technical staff, systems programmer, systems analyst, and so on. According to studies conducted by the Systems Administrators' Guild (SAGE; http://www .usenix.org/sage/jobs/salary_survey/index.html), fewer than half of all system administrators are given title recognition for it. The second problem is that market analysts don't usually track system administrator as a unique job title because of the first problem. Any surveys of system administrators are based on self-identification, not job title.

Salaries and Salary Trends

As you would expect with increasing demand and shortage of qualified applicants, salaries for system administrators are attractive and competitive. According to SAGE studies, the average salary for all system administrators—regardless of experience, industry, or geography—was approximately $62,000 in 1998. System administrators with 1–2 years of experience on average earned $47,000, while those with 10 or more years of experience earned more than $70,000. About five percent of all sysadmins earned over $100,000 in 1998. As with most jobs, salaries are higher in the commercial sector than they are in education, government, and other organizations. Salaries are also higher in parts of the country where there is more demand and higher costs of living, such as California and New England.

Salary increases for system administrators tend to be larger than those in other jobs, usually to keep someone from leaving for greener pastures. The increase in average salary from 1997 to 1998 was 6 percent. Salary disparities between men and women are significantly less in system administration than other fields. In fact, the 1998 survey referenced here indicates women made about 15 percent more than men. However, that could be attributed to more men coming into the field than women. System administration tends to attract more women than other technical and computing fields. Sixteen percent of system administrators are women.

Note: Latest survey results from SAGE can be viewed by going to http://www.usenix.org/sage/jobs/salary_survey/salary_survey.html.

Consulting and Contracting Versus Direct Employment

Because of the large demand for system administrators, there is also a large market for "on-demand" system administrators through contract employment or consulting. Some system administrators prefer consulting or contracting because it provides greater variety and flexibility.

System administrators who are independent consultants tend to be specialists and make significantly more money than those who work for a firm and are contracted out. (For more information, see the SANS Salary Survey, http://www.sans .org/newlook/publications/1998salarysurvey.htm). As with most other computing contract employment, those who work for contract firms tend to make slightly more money than those who are directly employed. In this respect, system administration is similar to other technical fields. The only difference may be that due to significant demands for system administrators, making a go of it as an independent may be more readily lucrative than in other fields. There are plenty of opportunities regardless of which employment structure is most attractive.

Job Requirements

Becoming a system administrator is relatively straightforward. Anyone curious to explore a challenge while possessing a reasonably solid background in computing fundamentals may find himself or herself drafted anyway. Due to demand, organizations are also more likely to consider offering entry-level positions with training than in other computing fields.

Gaining a background in computing fundamentals is pretty easy. A degree in computer science isn't required, just a basic understanding of how computers, operating systems, and applications work and interact; logic; binary numbers; a little electronics; and some common sense. The most important traits of a new system administrator are the abilities to find and digest information, solve problems, develop creative strategies, and recognize and work within one's own limits. System administrators who have formal education and a degree tend to be preferred and sometimes required for jobs. However, that's not necessarily because the education is particularly relevant to the job; it's more because it is evidence of follow through and perseverance. Many practicing system administrators hold degrees in technical fields other than computer science, such as physics.

System administrators solve problems daily. The problems change every day and there is no step-by-step guide for solving them. So a system administrator has to be able to think on his/her feet, learn about the aspects of the problem, find the cause, find a fix, and then implement one that actually works within the constraints of the situation. Sysadmins are usually working on production systems, because it is expensive to duplicate a system purely for the system administrator's benefit. Consequently, it is imperative that a system administrator knows when he/she is in over his/her head—and how not to create more problems. Other than that, it's all about experience and system-specific—UNIX, NT, applications—training.

Training and Education

There is no widely accepted formal curriculum for system administration. Unfortunately, you can't go to the local university and sign up for a degree program in system administration.

Still, there are plenty of education and training opportunities for system administrators, including commercial education programs, university continuing education, vendor-specific courses, conference and seminar tutorials, and self-education through books. Commercial technical training companies, such as Technology Exchange Company (http://www.technologyexchange.com/) and Global Knowledge Network (http://www.globalknowledge .com/), also provide system-administration courses. Major platform vendors (Sun, Microsoft, Novell, and the like) provide system-administration training as well.

Nonetheless, universities are starting to develop system-administration curricula. The University of Indiana, for instance, offers an independent study program in system administration called

continues

"UNIX System Administration Independent Learning" (USAIL; http://www.uwsg.indiana.edu/usail/). The System Administrators' Guild (SAGE; http://www.usenix.org/sage/) provides publications, conferences, and tutorial programs on system administration. The number of books on system administration increases all the time. There are currently about 75 books in print on various aspects of system administration. Two books stand out as required reading for UNIX system administrators: *UNIX System Administration Handbook*, by Nemeth, Hein, Snyder, and Seabass (http://www.admin.com/); and *Essential System Administration*, by Frisch (http://www.ora.com/catalog/esa2/).

Furthermore, there are certification programs for system administration. Most existing certification programs are vendor-specific; such as Solaris and/or NT administration, for instance. The Linux Professional Institute (http://www.lpi.org/) is developing certification for Linux professionals, who are essentially system administrators. SAGE is conducting an occupational analysis of system administration to begin the process of the only platform-independent system administration certification program.

Conclusion

The profession of system administration and programs for system administrators are growing all the time. In part, to meet this demand, SAGE is currently conducting a pilot program in mentoring and plans to have an established mentoring program next year. Furthermore, companies such as Sun are creating new multifaceted programs to spawn and encourage new system administrators. Why? Because system administration is a career that is in high demand—with no let-up in sight.

Resources

There are plenty of resources for the system administrator beyond the man pages. The following list shows many popular resources that are worth visiting if you are interested in system administration:

- Web Sites
  - **Usenix (Sage)**—www.usenix.org/sage
  - **UNIX Guru Universe**—www.ugu.com
  - **Stokely Consulting**—www.stokely.com
  - **Sun Microsystems, Inc. (System Administration Site)**—www.sun.com/bigadmin
- Newsgroups
  - comp.unix.admin
  - comp.os.linux.admin
  - comp.unix.solaris

- Magazines and Professional Journals
  - **Server/Workstation Expert**—www.swexpert.com
- User Groups
  - **Usenix (Sage)**—www.usenix.org/sage/locals/sage-localgroups.html
- Books
  - **Fatbrain Computer Books (search for UNIX administration)**—www.fatbrain.com

Sun Solaris Certification Path for System Administrators

The Solaris Operating Environment is the foundation on which some of the world's leading companies are built. Offering unparalleled reliability, availability, security, and scalability, Solaris systems meet today's demands while anticipating tomorrow's innovation.

Sun's Solaris 8 operating environment certification tests are rigorous and include real-world scenarios. Certification also prepares you to stand up to today's challenging systems issues. Figure 17-1 shows the current Sun courses and the sequence in which they are to be taken for Sun certification.

And, like all other certifications from Sun, they can exponentially expand your professional opportunities. Sun offers the following professional certification for the Solaris Operating Environment:

- Sun Certified System Administrator for Solaris
- Sun Certified Network Administrator for Solaris

NOTE

For further information on certification for the Solaris Operating Environment, visit http://suned.sun.com/HQ/certification.

The Sun Academic Initiative

The Sun Academic Initiative (SAI) is designed to give students the skills needed to fast-track their careers in today's hottest job market (see Figure 17-2). The course paths and learning tools included in the Sun Academic Initiative help prepare students for certifications in the Java programming language and the Solaris Operating Environment. Either industry-recognized certification will go a long way in making you stand above the competitive noise when marketing yourself to potential employers.

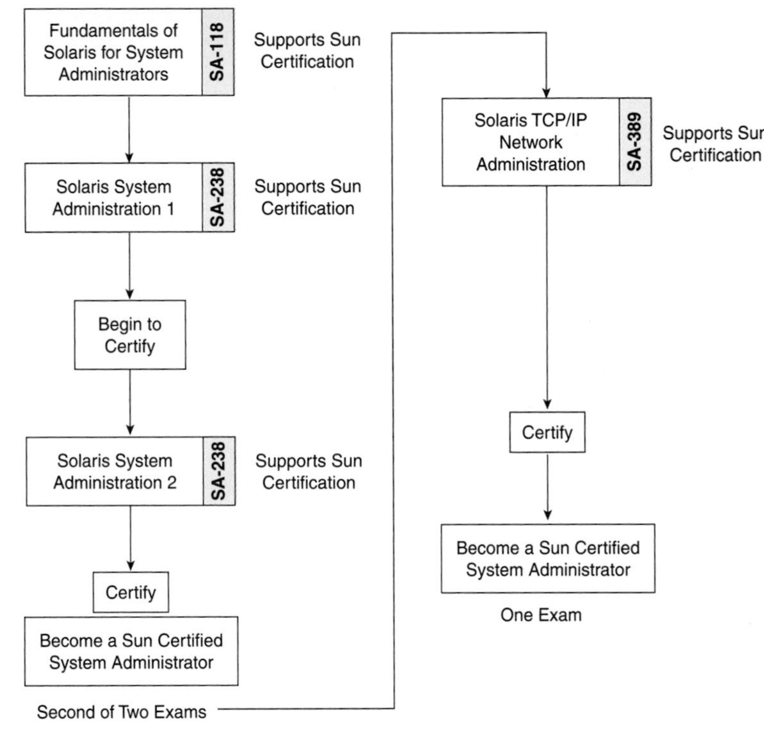

Figure 17-1 Solaris certification path.

Figure 17-2 Sun Academic Initiative.

The Academic Initiative offers the following courses to students whose school is an Authorized Sun Education Center.

Java Education Track:

- **Java Programming Language for Nonprogrammers**—This course provides first-time programmers an excellent choice for learning programming using the Java programming language. This course helps students understand the significance of the Java programming language. With this knowledge, students will develop programming skills in the areas of object-orientated and Java technology. By the end of class, students will be able to create simple programs using Java technology ("Java programs") and will be able to read and edit Java technology source code.

- **Migrating to Object-Oriented Programming with Java Technology**—This course provides students with the necessary concepts and skills to move to Java technology. This course teaches basic object-oriented concepts and object-oriented analysis and design as they relate to Java technology, as well as introductory Java programming language constructs.
- **Java Programming Language**—This course teaches students the syntax of the Java programming language, object-oriented programming with the Java programming language, creating graphical user interfaces (GUI), using exceptions, handling file input/output (I/O), using threads, and networking. Programmers familiar with object-oriented concepts can learn how to develop Java application. The course uses the Java 2 Software Development Kit (SDK).

Solaris Education Track:

- **Fundamentals of Solaris System Administration**—This course covers most topics in this Fundamentals of UNIX course, plus several system administration topics that include an introduction to shell programming, **sed** and **awk** commands, and so on.
- **Shell Programming**—This course provides students with the knowledge to read, write, and debug C shell scripts. Students are taught how to develop simple scripts to automate frequently executed sequences of commands, and how to use conditional logic, user interaction, loops, and menus to enhance the productivity and effectiveness of the user.
- **Solaris System Administration I**—The Solaris 8 Operating Environment System Administration I course provides students with the necessary knowledge and skills to perform essential system administration tasks in the Solaris 8 Operating Environment. Instructional topics include standalone Solaris installation, file system management, backup procedures, process control, security measures, user administration, printing services, and device management.
- **Solaris System Administration II**—The Solaris 8 Operating Environment System Administration II course provides students with the skills necessary to administer Sun systems running the Solaris 8 Operating Environment in a network environment. Students are taught how to maintain Sun systems, configure and troubleshoot the Network File System (NFS), and configure the Network Information System (NIS) environment.

NOTE

For further information on the Sun Academic Initiative, visit http://sun.com/academic.

Summary

The Fundamentals of UNIX course was designed to give you a good basic understanding of the UNIX network operating system. The UNIX OS has evolved into a powerful, robust operating system that you can spend a lifetime learning. As a user, you can continue to learn more about the UNIX world from a variety of sources, including Web sites, newsgroups, user groups, and, of course, books.

Appendix A

Check Your Understanding Answer Key

This appendix contains the answers to the "Check Your Understanding" questions at the end of each chapter.

Chapter 1

1. D.
2. C.
3. B.
4. D.
5. A.
6. D.
7. C.
8. A.
9. D.
10. D.

Chapter 2

1. D.
2. C.
3. C.
4. B.

5. C.
6. A.
7. B.
8. A.
9. D.
10. A.

Chapter 3

1. D.
2. B.
3. D.
4. B.
5. A.
6. C.
7. A.
8. D.
9. C.
10. D.

Chapter 4

1. C.
2. D.
3. B.
4. D.
5. C.
6. D.
7. C.
8. B.
9. A.
10. A.

Chapter 5

1. D.
2. C.
3. A.
4. C.
5. B.
6. C.
7. C.
8. B.
9. C.
10. A.

Chapter 6

1. B.
2. D.
3. A.
4. B.
5. D.
6. D.
7. C.
8. A.
9. C.
10. D.

Chapter 7

1. B.
2. A.
3. C.
4. B.
5. A.

6. A.
7. B.
8. D.
9. D.
10. C.

Chapter 8

1. A.
2. B.
3. A.
4. C.
5. C.
6. B.
7. A.
8. D.
9. B.
10. D.

Chapter 9

1. B.
2. A.
3. A.
4. B.
5. A.
6. B.
7. D.
8. D.
9. C.
10. B.

Chapter 10

1. D.
2. B.
3. A.
4. D.
5. B.
6. B.
7. C.
8. A.
9. B.
10. D.

Chapter 11

1. D.
2. A.
3. A.
4. D.
5. A.
6. A.
7. A.
8. A.
9. A.
10. B.

Chapter 12

1. D.
2. B.
3. A.
4. D.
5. B.

6. A.
7. B.
8. D.
9. C.
10. B.

Chapter 13

1. B.
2. C.
3. B.
4. A.
5. C.
6. C.
7. D.
8. A.
9. C.
10. D.

Chapter 14

1. A.
2. D.
3. D.
4. B.
5. A.
6. D.
7. B.
8. C.
9. A.
10. D.

Chapter 15

1. A.
2. B.
3. A.
4. D.
5. B.
6. C.
7. A.
8. C.
9. D.
10. B.

Chapter 16

1. C.
2. A.
3. C.
4. A.
5. B.
6. D.
7. A.
8. A.
9. D.
10. C.

Appendix B

Master Command List

This appendix is a compilation of all the commands and symbols used in this book, along with a brief description of their purpose and an example of their use. The list is alphabetical, starting with special characters, and it can be used as a quick reference. You also can go to the chapter indicated, which is where the command is introduced, to get more detailed information. The first line in some of the examples lists the most frequently used options of the command before giving examples.

<table>
<tr><th>Command</th><th>Description</th><th>Example</th><th>Chapter Reference</th></tr>
<tr><td>. (dot)</td><td>Used to re-execute a Korn shell initialization file after changes are made.</td><td><code>$ . .kshrc</code></td><td>15</td></tr>
<tr><td>&</td><td>Runs job/process in the background and restores the shell prompt.</td><td><code>$ Netscape&</code></td><td>13</td></tr>
<tr><td>></td><td>Redirects standard output.</td><td><code>$ ls > myfiles</code></td><td>7</td></tr>
<tr><td><</td><td>Redirects standard input.</td><td><code>$ mailx dano@buckeye < ski_listing</code></td><td>7</td></tr>
<tr><td>*
?
[]</td><td>Metacharacters commonly referred to as wildcards that manipulate groups of files.</td><td></td><td>5</td></tr>
<tr><td>|</td><td>Passes standard output of one command as standard input into a following command.</td><td><code>$ ls -l | more</code></td><td>7</td></tr>
<tr><td>!!</td><td>Re-executes the last command in C shell.</td><td><code>$!!</code></td><td>14</td></tr>
</table>

continues

Command	Description	Example	Chapter Reference
!$	Repeats the last argument from the previous command in C shell.	`$ !$`	14
!*	Repeats all arguments of the previous command in C shell.	`$ !*`	14

!number	Repeats a specific number command from the C shell history file.	`170 pwd`
		`171 ls`
		`172 cd ~`
		`$ !171`
			14

alias	**alias** and **unalias** utilities create or remove a pseudonym or shorthand term for a command or series of commands.	Change copy (**cp**) to include a confirmation prompt before overwriting a file: `alias cp="cp -i"`	14

arp	Displays the hostname, IP address, and Ethernet address of the system.	`$ arp buckeye`
		`buckeye`
		`(127.134.45.109)`
		`8:0:20:c2:43:9d`
			4

at	Executes specified commands (read from standard input) or script file at a later time that you specify.	`$ at 10:30am whoson`	13

bc	Basic calculator command.	`$ bc`
		`5280/3`
		`1760`
		`<Ctrl d>`
		`$`
			6

bg	Places a job in the background.	`$ bg %3`	13

cal	Writes a Gregorian calendar to standard output.	`$ cal`
		`$ cal 2000`
		`$ cal 9 2005`
			4

cancel	Cancels print requests.	`$ cancel printer1-203`
		`request "printer1-`
		`203" cancelled`
		`$ cancel -u`
		`<username>`
			13

Command	Description	Example	Chapter Reference

cat	Concatenates (combines) and displays files.	`$ cat dante`
		`The Life and Times of Dante`
		`by Dante Pocai`
		`Mention "Alighieri"`
		`and few may know about`
		`whom you are talking.`
		`Say "Dante," instead,`
		`and the whole world`
		`knows whom you mean.`
		`For Dante Alighieri,`
		`like Raphael`
		`$`
			6

cd	Change the working directory of the current shell execution environment.	`$ cd`
		`$ cd ..`
		`$ cd /home/user2/dir1`
		`$ cd ./dir1`
			5

chgrp	Used to change the group association of a file. The group may be either a decimal group ID or a group name found in the group ID file /etc/group.	`-R`
		
		`$ chgrp marketing chap15`
		
		`$ chgrp -R engineering cad_dwgs.dir`
			10

chmod	Changes file or directory permissions.	Deny execute permission to everyone:
		`$ chmod a-x filename`
		
		Allow only read permission to everyone:
		`$ chmod 444 file1`
		
		Make a file readable and writeable by the group and others:
		`$ chmod go+rw file2`
			10

chown	Changes the owner of a file. The owner can be either a decimal user ID or a login name found in the /etc/passwd file.	`-R`
		
		`$ chown bradj chap15`
		
		`$ chown -R jiml book.dir`
			10

compress	Attempts to reduce the size of the named files.	`-v, -f`
		`$ compress -vf file`
		`file: compression 37% -- replaced with file.Z`
			12

continues

Command	Description	Example	Chapter Reference

cp	Copies files.	`-i, -r`
		
		`$ cp ~/home/* /tmp`
		`$ cp -i ~/home/user2/`
		`* /bkup`
		
		`$ cp -ri ~/home/`
		`user2/* /bkup`
			7

csh	Starts a C shell subshell.		14
Ctrl-C	Cancels the current activity.	`$ man intro <Ctrl c>`	4, 6

Ctrl-D	Indicates the end of the file or exits.	`$ bc`
		`5280/3`
		`1760`
		`<Ctrl d>`
		`$`
			1, 4, 6

Ctrl-Q	Resumes screen output.	`$ cat largfile <Ctrl` `s> <Ctrl q>`	4, 6
Ctrl-S	Stops screen output.	`$ cat largfile <Ctrl` `s>`	6
Ctrl-U	Erases the entire command line.		1, 6
Ctrl-W	Erases the last word on the command line.		6

Ctrl-Z	Suspends the foreground process.	`$ sleep 500&`
		`[1] 453`
		`$ jobs`
		`[1] Running sleep 500`
		`$fg %1`
		`$ sleep 500`
		`^Z`
		`[1] Stopped sleep 500`
			13

df	Displays the amount of disk space occupied by mounted or unmounted file systems, directories, or resources; the amount of available space; and how much of a file system's total capacity has been used.	`-k`
		
		`$ df -k`
			8

Command	Description	Example	Chapter Reference

diff	Compares the contents of two files and write to standard output a list of changes necessary to convert the first file into the second file. No output is produced if the files are identical.	`$ diff -c fruit fruit2`
		`*** fruit Fri May 8 11:32:49 1998`
		`--- fruit2 Fri May 8 14:55:21 1998`
		`***********`
		`***2, 8****`
		`orange`
		`apple`
		`banana`
		`-pear`
		`-mango`
		`tomato`
		`pomegranate`
		`---2, 8-----`
		`orange`
		`apple`
		`banana`
		`tomato`
		`+guava`
		`+mango`
		`pomegranate`
			6

domain-name	Displays the name of the current domain.	`$ domainname` `elvis.central.Sun.com`	4

du	Reports the number of 512-byte blocks contained in all files and (recursively) directories within each directory and file specified.	`-k`
		
		`$ du -k`
			8

echo	Echoes (displays) arguments.	`$ echo "hi mom"`
		`hi mom`
		
		`$ echo $SHELL`
		`/bin/ksh`
			1, 14

ENV	Variable used in conjunction with personalizing the login environment.	`ENV=$HOME/.kshrc;` `export ENV`	15
exit	Leaves the current terminal window or current shell and returns to the previous one. Also used to log out of the login shell.		14

export	Displays all environmental variables available to all shells.	`$ export`
		`FRAME=/opt/fm/`
		`HOME=/home/hondo`
		`PS1=MyPrompt$`
		`SHELL=/bin/ksh`
		`TERM=vt100`
			14

continues

Command	Description	Example	Chapter Reference

fg	Places a job in the foreground.	`$ sleep 500&`
		`[1] 453`
		`$ jobs`
		`[1] Running sleep 500`
		`$fg %1`
		`$ sleep 500`
			13

file	Determines the file type.	`$ file dante`
		`dante:    English text`
		
		`$ file beans`
		`beans:    Frame Maker Document`
		
		`$ file da* fi*`
		`dante:      English Text`
		`dante_1:    English Text`
		`file1:      English Text`
		`file2:      ascii text`
		`files.jar:  java program`
		`files.tar:  USTAR tar archive`
			6

find	Recursively descends the directory hierarchy for each path, seeking files that match a Boolean expression.	`-o`
		`$ find /home/user2 -name 'dir*'`
		`/home/user2/dir2`
		`/home/user2/dir3`
			8

finger	Displays information about local and remote users.	`$ finger`
		`damyers  Dan Myers Console  Thu 19:07`
		
		`$finger jdoe@hal`
			8

Command	Description	Example	Chapter Reference

ftp	Part of the TCP/IP protocol suite and is standard with the UNIX operating system. The application can be used to transfer files using ASCII or binary mode between systems using similar or dissimilar operating systems.	`$ ftp venus`
		`Connected to`
		`129.150.212.16.`
		`220 venus FTP server`
		`(UNIX(r) System V`
		`Release 4.0) ready.`
		`Name`
		`(129.150.212.16:liste`
		`r): Return <CR>`
		`331 Password required`
		`for lister.`
		`Password: xxx`
		`230 User lister`
		`logged in.`
		`ftp> cd /etc/inet`
		`250 CWD command`
		`successful.`
		`ftp> bin`
		`200 Type set to I.`
		`ftp> get hosts /tmp/`
		`hosts`
		`200 PORT command`
		`successful.`
		`150 Binary data`
		`connection for hosts`
		`(129.159.129.38,33425`
		`)`
		`(77 bytes)`
		`226 Transfer`
		`complete.`
		`local: /tmp/hosts`
		`remote: hosts`
		`77 bytes received in`
		`0.0014 seconds (5,25`
		`Kbytes/s)`
		`ftp> bye`
			16

grep	Searches a file for a pattern.	`-i`
		
		`$ grep banana ./*`
		`/home/user2/fruit:`
		`banana`
		`/home/user2/`
		`fruit.tar:banana`
		`/home/user2/fruit2:`
		`banana`
		`/home/user2/`
		`fruit2.tar:banana`
			8

groups	Displays all the groups that a user is a member of.	`$ groups user1 user2`
		`user1 : staff`
		`user2 : staff`
			10

continues

Command	Description	Example	Chapter Reference
gunzip	Uncompresses files created with the **gzip** command.	`$ gunzip chap1.gz chap2.gz`	12

gzcat	Enables you to read a gzipped file without uncompressing it.	`$ gzcat bookfile`
		`chap1`
		`chap2`
			12

gzip	A compression utility (short for "GNU zip") designed to be a replacement for **compress**. Its main advantages over **compress** are much better compression and freedom from patented algorithms. The GNU Project uses it as the standard compression program for its system.	`-v`
		
		`$ gzip -v chap1 chap2`
		`$ ls chap*`
		`chap1.gz`
		`chap.gz`
			12

head	Displays the first few lines of files.	`$ head -5 /usr/dict/words`
		`1st`
		`2nd`
		`3rd`
		`4th`
		`5th`
		`$`
			6

history	Lists or edits and re-executes commands previously entered into an interactive shell.	`$ history`
		`339 man grep`
		`340 pwd`
		`341 grep banana ./*`
		`342 history`
		`$ r 340`
		`pwd`
		`/home/user2`
		`$`
			14

hostname	Displays the name of the current host system.	`$ hostname` `buckeye`	4

id	Returns the user identity.	`-a`
		
		`$ id`
		`uid=1002(user2) gid=10(staff)`
		
		`$ id -a`
		`uid=1002(user2) gid=10(staff) groups=10(staff)`
			8

Command	Description	Example	Chapter Reference
init 0	Has a primary role to create processes from information stored in the file /etc/inittab. At any given time, the system is in one of eight possible run levels. A run level is a software configuration under which only a selected group of processes exists. Run levels 0, 5, 6 are reserved states for shutting down the system. **init** can be run only by the root user.	`init 0`	2

jar	Combines **backup** and **compress** into one tool.	`c,-t,-x, -f, -v`
		
		`$ jar cvf bundle.jar *`
		`adding 0.au`
		`adding 1.au`
		`adding 2.au`
		`adding 3.au`
		`$`
			12

jobs	Lists all jobs running in the shell.	`$ jobs`
		`[1] Running find ~ -`
		`name memo1`
			13

kill	Sends a signal to the process or processes specified by each PID operand.	`-9`
		
		`$ kill -9 100 -165`
		`$ kill -s kill 100 -`
		`165`
			13

ksh	Starts a Korn shell subshell.		14
ln	Short for "link." Gives a file an additional name so that you can access it from more than one directory.	`$ ln report /HQ/` `reports/Jan02report`	7
logout	Used to exit the login shell for a C shell user.	`logout`	14

lp	Submits print requests to a destination.	`-d, -o, -n, -m`
		
		`$ lp ~/fruit2`
		`request id is`
		`printer1-203 (1`
		`file(s))`
			11

continues

Command	Description	Example	Chapter Reference

lpstat	Displays information about the current status of the LP print service to standard output.	`$ lpstat printer1`
		`printer1-106 root 587 Mar 22 16:06 on printer1`
		`printer1-107 user2 85 Mar 22 16:10 on printer1`
		`$`
			11

ls	For each file that is a directory, lists the contents of the directory; for each file that is an ordinary file, repeats its name and any other information requested.	`-a,-F,-l,-lt,-ld,-E`
		`$ ls`
		`dante dir1 dir3`
		`$ ls -l`
		`-rwxr-xr-x 1 user2 staff 110 Apr 19 dante`
		`drwxr-xr-x 5 user2 staff 110 Apr 19 dir1`
		`drwxr-xr-x 4 user2 staff 110 Apr 19 dir3`
			5

mailx	Interactive message-processing system.	`$ mailx user2@cisco.com < dante.doc`	3

man	Displays information from the reference manuals. It displays complete manual pages that you select by name, or one-line summaries if selected by keyword.	`-s, -k`
		`$ man man`
		`$ man cd`
			4

mkdir	Creates the named directories using current permissions (default is 755) as established with the file creation mask (unmask).	`$ mkdir Reports`
		`$ ls -dl Reports`
		`drwxr-xr-x 2 user2 staff 512 Jan 28 16:24 Reports`
		
		`$ mkdir -p practice/dir1/admin`
		`$ ls -R practice`
		`practice:`
		`dir1 mailbox project research`
		`practice/dir1:`
		`admin`
		`practice/dir1/admin:`
			6

Command	Description	Example	Chapter Reference
more	Acts as a filter that displays the contents of a text file on the terminal, one screen at a time. It normally pauses after each full screen.	`$ cat dante I more`	6

mv	Moves and renames files and directories.	`-i`
		
		`$ mv file1 file_april30`
		
		`$ mv file1 /home/user2/bkup`
			7

noclobber	Prevents the overwriting of files during redirection.	`$ set -o noclobber`
		`$ cat fruit > fruit2`
		`/bin/ksh: fruit2: file already exists`
			7

passwd	Changes login password and password attributes.	`$ passwd`
		`passwd: Changing password for user2`
		`Enter login password: abc123`
		`New password: unix123`
		`Re-enter new password: unix123`
		`passwd (SYSTEM): passwd successfully changed for user2`
		`$`
			2

pgrep	Examines the active processes on the system and reports the process IDs of the processes whose attributes match the criteria specified on the command line.	`Obtain the process ID of sendmail:`
		`$ pgrep -x -u root sendmail`
		`283`
			13

ping	Tests basic connectivity between TCP/IP hosts by sending an Internet Control Message Protocol (ICMP) echo request to another computer or "host" on a TCP/IP network. If there is a reply from the destination host, then there is a good connection between them.	`-s`
		
		`$ ping jupiter`
		`jupiter is alive`
		`$ ping 192.13.145.10`
		`192.13.145.10 is alive`
			16

continues

Command	Description	Example	Chapter Reference
pkill	Searches for the process to kill.	Terminate the most recently created xterm: `$ pkill -n xterm`	13
Prtconf	Prints system configuration information.	`$prtconf | grep Memory` `Memory size: 128 Megabytes`	4
ps	Prints information about active processes.	`-e, -f, -u` `$ ps`	1, 13
PS1	A variable that can be changed by the user to alter the appearance of the default shell prompt.	`$ PS1="new prompt$ "` `$ PS1="$PWD $ "`	14
pwd	Writes an absolute path name of the current working directory to standard output.	`$ pwd` `/home/user2/dir1`	5

r	A Korn shell command repeats a command from the history list.	`170 pwd`
		`171 ls`
		`172 cd ~`
		`$ r 170`
			14

rcp	Copies to or from one UNIX system to another.	`$ rcp big10schedule spartan:/tmp`
		
		`$ rcp buckeye:~dano/budget .`
			16

rlogin	Establishes a remote login session on another workstation.	`$ rlogin saturn`
		`Password:`
		`Last login: Mon Dec 21 11:04:27 from venus`
		`Sun Microsystems Inc. SunOS 5.7 Generic October 1998`
		`$`
			16

rm	Removes directory and file entries.	`-i,-r` `$ rm -r dir1`	6

set	Displays all variables in the local shell.	`$ set`
		`HOME=/home/hondo`
		`PS1=MyPrompt$`
		`SHELL=/bin/ksh`
			14

set + o vi	Turns on command-line editing.		14
set - o vi	Turns off command-line editing.		14

Command	Description	Example	Chapter Reference
set prompt	Sets the default shell prompt in a C shell.	`% set prompt="hello %"`	14
sh	Starts a Borne shell subshell.		14
shutdown	By default, brings the system to a state in which only the console has access to the operating system. This state is called single-user. **shutdown** can be run only by the root user.	`$ shutdown`	2
sleep	Suspends execution for at least the integral number of seconds specified in the time operand.	`$ sleep 60&`	13
sort	Sorts lines of all the named files together, and writes the result in the standard output.	`$ sort file1` `$ sort +1n file2`	8
source	Re-executes a C shell initialization file after changes are made.	`$ source .cshrc`	15

spell	Compares the words contained in the specified text file against a dictionary file, and displays suspected words not found in the dictionary.	`$ spell memo`
		`aint`
		`partyiing`
			9

strings	Finds printable strings in an object or binary file.	`$ strings /usr/bin/cat`
		`SUNW_OST_OSCMD`
		`usvtebn`
		`usage: cat [ -usvtebn ] [-lfile] ...`
		`cat: Cannot stat stdout`
		`cat: cannot open %s`
		`cat: cannot stat %s`
		`cat: input/output files '%s' identical`
		`cat: close error`
		`<some output omitted>`
			6

stty	Sets options for a terminal.	`$ stty erase ^H` sets the backspace key to erase one character to the left	2

continues

Command	Description	Example	Chapter Reference

su	Switches users. Allows a user to become a superuser or another user.	`- username`
		
		`$ su - student6`
		`Password:`
		`$`
			8

tail	Displays the last few lines of files.	`$ tail -5 /usr/dict/`
		`words`
		`zounds`
		`z's`
		`zucchini`
		`Zurich`
		`zygote`
		`$`
			6

tar	Archives and extracts files to and from a single file called a tar file.	`c, t, x, f, v`
		`$ tar cvf backup.tar /`
		`home/user2/*`
			12

telnet	Another good network troubleshooting tool. It is a nongraphical communications utility that can be used to check the upper layers of the OSI model. Telnet allows you to take over the console of another host or network device.	`$ telnet beach`
		`Trying 192.168.49.10`
		`...`
		`Connected to beach`
		`Escape character is`
		`'^]'`
		`.`
		`4.2 BSD UNIX (beach)`
		`login: jdupont`
		`Password:`
		`Last login: Wed Jun 1`
		`19:03:33 on console`
		`beach% (Enter`
		`commands)`
		`beach% exit`
		`Connection closed by`
		`foreign host`
		`$`
			16

touch	Sets the access and modification times of each file. The file is created if it does not already exist.	`$ cd ~/practice`
		`$ touch mailbox`
		`project research`
		`$ ls`
		`mailbox project`
		`research`
			6

unalias	The **alias** and **unalias** utilities create or remove a pseudonym or shorthand term for a command or series of commands.	`$ alias cp="cp -i"` `$ unalias cp`	14

Command	Description	Example	Chapter Reference

uname	Displays the name of the current system.	`-n`
		
		`$ uname -n`
		`buckeye`
			4

uncom-press	Returns a previously com-pressed file to its original size.	`-v` `$ uncompress -vf file.Z`	12
unset his-tory	Turns off history tracking.		14

unzip	Uncompresses files created with the **zip** command.	`$ unzip bookfile.zip`
		`$ls`
		`chap1 chap2 chap3`
			12

uuencode	Used to convert a binary file into an ASCII-encoded represen-tation that can be sent using e-mail. The encoded file is an ordinary ASCII text file.		3
vedit	Starts the vi editor with show-mode turned on, which displays the current mode that you're in.		
vi	Invokes the visual text editor.	`vi filename`	9
vi editor Command Mode	Initial default mode for creating and editing files, positioning the cursor, and modifying existing text. All commands are initiated from this mode. Pressing Esc from either of the other modes will return you to command mode.		9
vi editor Entry Mode	Used for entry of new text. Entering an insert command such as **i** (insert), **a** (append), and **o** (open new line) will take you from command mode to entry mode. Pressing escape (Esc) returns you to command mode. Entry commands are entered by themselves without pressing the Enter key.	`-a, -i, -o, -A, -I, -O`	9

continues

Command	Description	Example	Chapter Reference
vi editor Last Line Mode	Used for saving your work and quitting vi. Type a colon (:) to get to this mode. Pressing the Enter key returns you to command mode.	`:w, :wq, ZZ, :q!, :wq!`	9

wc	Reads one or more input files and, by default, writes the number of lines, characters, words, and bytes contained in each input file to the standard output.	`$ wc dante`
		`33 223 1320 dante`
		`$ wc -l dante`
		`33 dante`
			6

whatis	Looks up a given command and displays the header line from the manual section.	`$ whatis cd`
		`cd    cd (1)    -`
		`change working`
		`directory`
			4

who	Lists who is logged on to the system.	`-H,-q`
		`$ who`
		`user2 console  Apr 30`
		`12:37   (:0)`
		`user2 pts/4    Apr 30`
		`12:40   (:0.0)`
		`$`
			8

whoami	Displays the effective current username.	`$ whoami` `user2`	8

who am i	Displays the effective original username specified at login, not the current user you might have switched to.	`$ who am I`
		`user2 pts/4    Apr 30`
		`12:40   (:0.0)`
			8

zip	A compression utility designed to be compatible with the PC zip utility.	`$ zip bookfile chap*`
		`$ls`
		`book.zip`
			12

Appendix C

vi Editor Quick Reference

The vi editor is a powerful command-line editor that has many commands. This appendix contains the basic commands that you must know, followed by additional commands that make working with vi easier and faster if you use the editor often.

To edit an existing file or create a new file, use either of the following commands:

```
vi filename
```

or

```
vedit filename
```

The Three Modes of vi

The three modes of the vi editor are

- **Entry**—Used to type text
- **Command**—Used to move the cursor and modify text
- **Last line**—Used to save the file, quit vi, and search for text

NOTE

Press Esc to move from insert mode to command mode. Command mode is the default mode when entering vi.

Basic vi Commands That You Must Know—Don't Leave Home Without Them

vi Command	Function
i	Inserts new text.
Esc	Puts you in command mode, where you can edit text and mover the cursor.
j (jump down)	Moves the cursor down one line (same as the down arrow).
k (kick up)	Moves the cursor up one line (same as the up arrow).
G	Goes to the last line in the file.
:*n*	Goes to line number *n*.
a	Appends text to the right of the cursor.
A	Appends text to the end of the current line.
o	Opens a new line below the cursor and leaves you in input mode.
x	Deletes the character that the cursor is on (**3x** deletes three characters).
u	Undoes the last operation.
dw	Deletes the word that the cursor is on (**3dw** deletes three words).
cw	Changes the word. Press **cw**, type the new word, and press Esc.
r	Replaces the current character with a new character.
dd	Deletes the current line (**3dd** deletes three lines).
dd then **p**	Deletes and pastes. Same as cut and paste.
yy then **p**	Yanks and pastes. Same as copy and paste.
/ *<search string>*	Searches for the search string specified. Press N to find the next occurrence.
Shift-ZZ or **:wq!**	Saves (writes) the file to disk and exits vi. Must use **:wq!** for admin files.
:q!	Quits vi without saving any changes.

Other vi Commands That Are Nice to Know

The following are additional vi commands categorized by command type that make working in vi easier.

Insert Text Commands

These commands are used while you're in entry mode.

Command	Function
i	Inserts text to the left of the cursor
I	Inserts text at the beginning of a line
a	Appends text to the right of the cursor
A	Appends text at the end of a line
o	Opens a new line below the cursor
O	Inserts a new line above the cursor

Other Handy Cursor-Movement Commands

These commands are used while you're in command mode.

Command	Function
left arrow or **h**	Moves left
right arrow or **l**	Moves right
$	Moves the cursor to the end of the line
0 (zero)	Moves the cursor to the beginning of the line
w	Moves the cursor to the beginning of the next word
b	Moves the cursor backward to the previous word

Save Commands

These commands are used during the saving process.

Command	Function
Shift-ZZ or **:x** or **:wq!**	Saves the file to disk and exits vi
:q!	Exits without saving changes
:w	Writes changes and saves what you have done so far

Other Handy Commands

These commands are used while you're in command mode.

Command	Function
U	Undoes all changes that you have made to the current line.
R	Replaces multiple characters from the current cursor location onward. This is like a word processor "type over" mode.

Appendix D

Solaris for Intel Download and Installation Instructions

The Solaris License Program for PC's & Desktops program offers educators, students, and researchers free Solaris for just the cost of media and shipping and handling. Or, it can be downloaded for free. The main program site is located at www.sun.com/products-n-solutions/edu/solaris/index.html.

Free Solaris Binary License Program

Go to www.sun.com/software/solaris/binaries/get.html to either order a copy of the Solaris Operating Environment Media Kit (for either Intel or Sun SPARC Platforms) or to download Solaris free.

The Solaris 8 Media Kit is available for purchase for $75 from and contains all the CD-ROMs needed for a successful Solaris installation, plus a CD with useful Solaris applications.

Downloading Free Solaris

Given the size of the download (800 MB), we strongly recommend that this option be considered only by those with a fast connection (T1, DSL, cable modem, or faster). All others should consider obtaining the Solaris media kit.

Here is what you need to download Solaris:

- High-speed Internet connection
- CD writer
- Minimum of three recordable or rewriteable CDs

NOTE

Before ordering a media kit or downloading, check the Hardware Compatibility List for Solaris 8 support (http://soldc.sun.com/support/drivers/hcl or http://docs.sun.com). Some hardware might not be supported. In particular, the video cards need to be checked.

To download Solaris, follow these steps:

1. Review the system requirements for information about hardware compatibility and drivers.
2. Select the appropriate version of the Solaris 8 Operating Environment for your hardware platform (at the bottom of the page).
3. Complete the customer registration (SIGN ON).
4. Complete the license registration (SURVEY). After registration is successful, you'll receive e-mail notification of your registered license(s).
5. Download the CD images of the Solaris 8 software. At a minimum, you need three CD images: the installation CD and two software CDs (800 MB total).
6. The remaining three CD images are not necessary to perform a successful installation. They contain additional translations of the software (languages CD, 363 MB) and online documentation in 10 languages (documentation CD, English and Asian, 243 MB, and documentation CD, English and other European languages, 329 MB). All these documents are posted at http://docs.sun.com.
7. Extract the CD images using unzip software. We recommend that you use the most up-to-date versions you can find. We have successfully used WinZip 8.0, PKZIP 4.0, and Netzip Classic 7.5.1. The result will be a file with the same name as the file you downloaded, but without the .zip extension. Each file is a CD image that might be up to 650 MB in size; make sure that you have sufficient space on your hard drive before you start the unzip process.
8. Create a CD from these images using your favorite CD-creation software. Depending on the software package you use, you might have to rename the file first to give it an extension that the software recognizes as a CD image. For example, if you use Easy CD Creator, add the extension .iso to the filename. Next, from the File Menu in the program, select Create CD from CD Image. Then select that image file. If you use Nero burning rom, also use a .iso extension. *Note:* This has been verified only using Adaptec's EZ-CD Creator. When attempting to burn this software using Nero 5.0, we were unsuccessful.
9. Using the CDs that you just created, install the Solaris 8 Operating Environment on your computer. (Make sure that it meets the system requirements referenced in Step 1.) To ensure a successful installation, we strongly recommend that you read the Solaris 8 Installation Documentation first.

Dual Boot Installation Instructions Using Windows 98 and Windows 2000

Solaris for Intel installation instructions also are provided with the media kit if purchased), with the free Solaris download, or from Sun at http://docs.sun.com.

Dual Boot Installation of Solaris 8 and Windows 98

This guide assumes that Win98 is already installed on the computer. Before you start, you should know the computer's hard drive size. You will need this later when figuring the percentage of that hard drive to allocate to each OS. The approximate minimum space required for operating systems, common applications, and storage of files are as follows: Win98—400 MB; Solaris 8—2 GB.

This procedure consists of three sections:

1. Delete existing partitions and create the Solaris partition at the beginning of the disk.
2. Install Win98 into unallocated space.
3. Install Solaris 8 into the Solaris partition.

The Solaris OS must have its swap slice and OS installed on the *first* partition of the computer disk; therefore, you must start the Solaris installation first. However, because you want the Solaris Boot Manager to be active upon every reboot, you must finish installing Solaris 8 after Win98. This will allow the user to boot into Win98 by choosing the appropriate partition, or the computer will boot into Solaris by default. You have to do this because Win98 does not have a boot manager.

Partition Configuration

This section follows the preliminary steps to install the Solaris OS to get to the Solaris fdisk application:

1. Insert the Solaris 8/Intel Installation CD. Shut down the computer and power back on.
2. The computer boots from the Solaris CD into the Solaris Device Configuration Assistant screen. Select F2 to perform a full scan of the system.
3. The Bus Enumeration screen and Scanning Devices screen lead into the Identified Devices screen. Select F2 to continue.
4. The Loading Drivers screen is replaced by the Boot Solaris screen. Use the arrow keys to place an X in the box next to CD. This tells the computer where to boot the Solaris kernel. Then select F2 to continue.
5. The next screen is the Starting Solaris Webstart Installation page. The computer reboots.

6. The Solaris Web Start 3.0 installer window comes next. You are asked to select the language that you want to use.
7. The next option is to create a Solaris fdisk. Answer (y)es.
8. The Solaris fdisk menu now appears. At this point, delete the existing partition(s). You then need to create one partition of at least 2 GB for Solaris. The installer asks for either the size of the partition, in blocks, or the percentage of the disk to be used. Allow this partition to become the active partition.
9. Select (4) Exit and update the disk *without* creating a partition for Win98—later you will let the Win98 setup CD claim this unused space for its installation.
10. Accept the default swap size of 512 MB.
11. Allow the swap slice to start at the beginning of the disk.
12. Confirm the disk slice and size, and start the cylinder. All information will be erased.
13. The installer then copies miniroot to local disk- and platform-specific files. This should take about 8 to 10 minutes.
14. Remove the boot media and press Enter to reboot.
15. After rebooting, do *not* continue with Solaris 8 installation. Instead, insert the Win98 setup CD and restart the computer.

Windows 98 Installation

This section installs the Windows 98 operating system:

1. Allow the Win98 installer to configure unallocated disk space.

   Do not use large disk support.
2. Win98 Setup will restart the computer and format drive C.
3. Continue through the menu-driven Win98 installation until complete. This takes approximately 40 to 60 minutes, depending on the components installed.

Installation of Solaris 8 for Intel

This section completes the installation of Solaris 8 for Intel:

1. Reinsert the Solaris 8/Intel Installation CD. Shut down Windows and restart the computer.
2. The computer boots from the Solaris CD into the Solaris Device Configuration Assistant screen. Select F2 to perform a full scan of your system.
3. The Bus Enumeration screen and Scanning Devices screen lead into the Identified Devices screen. Select F2 to continue.

4. The Loading Drivers screen is replaced by the Boot Solaris screen. Use the arrow keys to place an X in the box next to CD. This tells the computer where to boot the Solaris kernel. Then select F2 to continue.
5. The next screen is the Starting Solaris Webstart Installation page. The computer reboots.
6. The Solaris Web Start 3.0 installer window comes next. You are asked to select the language that you want to use.
7. Installer searches the system's hard disks for a location to place the Solaris installer software. Confirm the formatting of /dev/dsk/c0d0.
8. Accept the default swap size of 512 MB.
9. Allow the swap slice to start at the beginning of the disk.
10. Confirm the disk slice and size, and start the cylinder. All information will be erased.
11. The installer then copies miniroot and platform-specific files. This should take about 8 to 10 minutes.
12. Remove the boot media and press Enter to reboot.

    Upon rebooting, the boot menu displays the partitions that are configured on the computer. The X86 BOOT partition should be the active one. Let the computer boot into that partition to finish the installation of Solaris 8 software.
13. The Solaris Installation Program screen proceeds to kdmconfig screens to test device configuration, mouse operation, and color display.
14. A series of menu screens guide you through network and system settings.
15. The next screen prompts you for the Solaris 8 Software 1 of 2 CD.
16. When prompted, select Default Install. The software installation process will take approximately 40 minutes for CD 1, approximately 30 minutes for CD 2, and approximately 15 minutes for the Solaris 8 Documentation European CD.
17. Reboot the computer. Allow the computer to boot into the default Solaris, which completes the installation.

Dual boot installation of Solaris 8 and Win98 is now complete. At every reboot, the Solaris Boot Manager allows the user to boot into Win98 by choosing that partition (usually option 3), or the computer will boot into Solaris by default.

Dual Boot Installation of Solaris 8 and Windows 2000

This guide assumes that a Windows OS is already installed on the computer. Before you start, you should know the computer's hard drive size. You will need this later when figuring the percentage of that hard drive to allocate to each OS. The approximate minimum space required for operating systems, common applications, and storage of files is as follows: Win2000—1.5 GB; Solaris 8—2 GB.

This procedure consists of three sections:

- Delete existing partitions and create Solaris partition.
- Install Solaris 8 into the Solaris partition—Solaris *must* be in the first partition.
- Install Win2000 into unallocated space.

Partition Configuration

This section follows the steps to install the Solaris OS:

1. Insert the Solaris 8/Intel Installation CD. Shut down the computer and power back on.
2. The computer will boot from the Solaris CD into the Solaris Device Configuration Assistant screen. Select F2 to perform a full scan of the system.
3. The Bus Enumeration screen and Scanning Devices screen lead into the Identified Devices screen. Select F2 to continue.
4. The Loading Drivers screen is replaced by the Boot Solaris screen. Use the arrow keys to place an X in the box next to CD. This tells the computer where to boot the Solaris kernel. Then select F2 to continue.
5. The next screen is the Starting Solaris Webstart Installation page. The computer reboots.
6. The Solaris Web Start 3.0 installer window comes next. You are asked to select the language that you want to use.
7. The next option is to create a Solaris fdisk. Answer (y)es.
8. The Solaris fdisk menu now appears. At this point, delete the existing partition(s). You then need to create one partition of at least 2 GB for Solaris. The installer asks for either the size of the partition, in blocks, or the percentage of the disk to be used. Allow this partition to become the active partition.
9. Select (4) Exit, and update the disk *without* creating a partition for Win2000. Later, you will let the Win2000 setup CD claim this unused space for its installation.
10. Accept the default swap size of 512 MB.
11. Allow the swap slice to start at the beginning of the disk.
12. Confirm the disk slice and size, and start the cylinder. All the information will be erased.

13. The installer then copies miniroot and platform-specific files. This should take about 8 to 10 minutes.
14. Remove the boot media and press Enter to reboot.

    Upon rebooting, the boot menu displays the partitions that are configured on the computer. The X86 BOOT partition should be the active one. Let the computer boot into that partition to finish the installation of Solaris 8 software.

    The Solaris Installation Program screen will proceed to kdmconfig screens to test device configuration, mouse operation, and color display.
15. A series of menu screens guides you through network and system settings.

    The next screen prompts you for the Solaris 8 Software 1 of 2 CD.
16. When prompted, select Default Install. The software installation process takes approximately 40 minutes for CD 1, approximately 30 minutes for CD 2, and approximately 15 minutes for the Solaris 8 Documentation European CD.
17. Reboot the computer. Allow the computer to boot into the default Solaris, which completes the installation.

Windows 2000 Installation

This section installs the Windows 2000 operating system:

1. Allow the Win2000 installer to configure unallocated disk space.

   Do not use large disk support.
2. Win2000 Setup restarts the computer and formats drive C.
3. Continue through the menu-driven Win2000 installation until complete. This takes approximately 40 to 60, minutes depending on the components installed.

The computer now boots by default into Windows 2000. Use the Disk Management utility to make the SOLARISBOOT partition active.

1. Right-click the My Computer icon.
2. Select Manage.
3. Expand the Storage heading, and then select Disk Management.
4. Select the SOLARISBOOT partition (should be about 10 MB in size).
5. In the top menu, select Action.
6. Expand All Tasks.
7. Select Mark Partition Active (if this option is grayed out, it means that this is already the active partition).

Dual boot installation of Solaris 8 and Win2000 is now complete. At every reboot, the Solaris Boot Manager will allow the user to boot into Win2000 by choosing that partition (usually option 3), or the computer will boot into Solaris by default.

Appendix E

mailx

This appendix introduces the mailx command-line mail program and it covers tasks related to the following:

- Sending mail from the command line using the mailx program
- Reading and printing messages
- Creating and using a mail alias

Introduction to mailx

The UNIX operating environment provides a program called mailx for sending and receiving electronic mail (e-mail). The mailx program provides facilities for reading, writing, sending, receiving, saving, and deleting messages from the command line.

The mailx program (utility) is not window-based; therefore, it can be run in either a window environment or from any terminal.

Command-Line Mail

Use the mailx program from the command-line in these situations:

- When you are using a command-line login shell
- When you are using a terminal
- When you remotely log into your workstation to read your mail

Here's the command format:

```
mailx
mailx username@hostname
```

Each user has a mailbox file in which to receive mail. By default, this mailbox is located in /var/mail/username, where username is your login ID.

The mailx program notifies you when you receive mail and places the mail in your mailbox. After you read your mail, mailx automatically places these letters in a storage file called mbox, which is located in your home directory.

Reading a Mail Message

To read your mail messages, invoke the mailx program. If you do not have mail, the mailx program indicates that to you.

```
$   mailx
No mail for user2
$
```

However, if you do have mail, mailx notifies you each time you log in with the messages "You have mail" or "You have new mail."

NOTE

The question mark (?) is the mail prompt.

To access your mail, you must enter the **mailx** command at the command line:

```
$   mailx
mailx version 5.0 Thu Aug 5 10:36:57 PDT 1999 type ? for help.
"/var/mail/user2": 2 messages 2 new
>N     1 user3      Mon May 14 14:4416/334     About lunch!
 N     2 user4      Mon May 14 14:5314/326     Your lunch
?
```

When you have a large number of letters in your mailbox, the displayed list might not show all of your mail headers. If this is the case, type one of the following options:

- **z+**—Displays the next screenful of mail headers
- **z-**—Displays the previous screenful of mail headers
- **h**—Redisplays the list of mail headers at any time

Saving a Mail Message

To save a current message, type the following:

```
? s  filename
```

This saves the message in the specified file in your home directory. A saved message can be read using the **cat** or **more** commands, or can be edited using vi, the CDE Text Editor, or any editor your system uses.

To save a noncurrent message, type the following:

```
? s  <message number>  filename
```

Reading a Specific Message

Reading mail messages is the most basic function of any mail program. The following illustrates how you use the mailx program to display all new mail message headers and view message 2:

```
$ mailx
mailx version 5.0 Thu Aug 5 10:36:57 PDT 1999 Type? for help.
"/var/mail/user2": 2 messages 2 new
>N  1  user3Mon May 14 14:4416/334About lunch!
 N  2  user4Mon May 14 14:5314/326Your lunch
? 2
Message 2:
From user4@jupiter Mon Aug 2 14:53 PST 1999
Date: Mon, 2 Aug 1999 14:53:31 PST
From: user4@jupiter
To: user2@venus
Subject: Your lunch
Hi user2!
I heard you are going out to lunch.
Mind if I join you?

user4
?
```

Mail Headers

The output from the **mailx** command is called the *mail header*. The mail header displays the following:

- The version of the program
- A question mark (?) for help with mail
- The location of the mail box (for example, /var/mail/username) where your mail messages are saved
- The status of the mailbox:
  - The total number of messages in the mailbox
  - The number of new messages
  - The status (new or read) for each message
  - The number of each message in the order it was received
  - The sender (user and machine name)
  - The time and date that the message was sent
  - The size of the message (the number of lines and number of characters in the message)
  - The subject of the message
- When a new message is received, or if an old message was not read, one of the following characters shown in Table E-1 appears next to the applicable message.

Table E-1 Message Classification Characters

Character	Message
N	Indicates a new message
U	Indicates a message that was received earlier but that was not read before quitting the mailx program previously
R	Indicates a new message that was read during the current invocation of mailx
O	Indicates a message that was read previously and that is saved in the current mailbox
>	Indicates the current message
?	Indicates which message number or, if typed by user, listing of options to look for

The following code is the mail message headers for two new messages, as indicated by the N character in the first column.

```
$   mailx
mailx version 5.0 Thu Aug 5 10:36:57 PDT 1999 type ? for help.
"/var/mail/user2": 2 messages 2 new
>N  1 user3 Mon May 14 14:4416/334About lunch!
 N  2 user4 Mon May 14 14:5314/326Your lunch
?
```

To read the first mail message, press Return at the mail prompt (?). The first (or current) message appears on your screen.

Press Return to read any subsequent messages.

Sending a Mail Message

To send mail, follow these steps:

Step 1 Specify username@hostname as an argument to the **mailx** command.

Step 2 Enter the subject of your mail and press Return.

Step 3 Enter the text of your message, and press the . (period) key or Ctrl-D (to transmit message) on a line by itself to signal the end of the message.

For example:

NOTE

EOT is an acronym for "end of transmission."

```
$   mailx user3@cisco
Subject: lunch!
Hi there!
Do you have any plans for lunch today?
If not, would you care to join me?
user2
. (Type a dot [.] and press Return)
EOT
$
```

Sending a File Using Mail

Use the **mailx** command and standard input redirection to send someone a file—for example:

```
$   mailx user3@saturn < dante
$
```

Using the previous command with the -s option allows you to include a subject line:

```
$   mailx -s "myfile" user3@saturn < dante
$
```

NOTE

When writing mail messages, remember to press Return at the end of each line. There is no automatic line wrap with mail.

Creating a Mail Alias

A mail alias is a group of usernames (login IDs) in a single file. Use mail aliases when you want to send the same message to a group of users. A mail alias is also called a distribution list.

```
mailx aliasname
```

Use an editor to add mail aliases to your .mailrc file, which is located in your home (or login) directory. The .mailrc file is used to store *private* mail aliases and variables relating to the mail program. Your system administrator can set up public mail aliases, available for any user on the system to use, in the /etc/aliases file.

You can use any editor to create or add mail aliases to the .mailrc file. Create one mail alias per line, and then save the changes—for example:

```
$ cd
$ vi .mailrc
alias class user3@saturn user4@jupiter user5@earth
~
~
~
".mailrc" [newfile]
:wq

$   mailx class
Subject: test!

This is a test of my newly created alias

user2
.
EOT
```

NOTE

A piece of e-mail is not a single file. A piece of e-mail is made into pages, which are appended into one file. By default, the storage area for all mail messages is /var/mail/*username*.

Canceling a Mail Message

Press Ctrl-C to cancel a mail message:

```
$ mailx user3@saturn
Subject: lunch!
Do you have any plans . . . (press Ctrl-C)
^C
(Interrupt -- one more to kill letter)
(press Ctrl-C)
```

> **NOTE**
> Each line of text within your message can be up to 256 characters long. When you exceed this limitation, your screen freezes. If this occurs, press Ctrl-C to abort your message.

```
^C "/home/user2/dead.letter" 3/29
$
```

If you cancel a message, it is saved in your home directory under the name dead.letter. Either remove this file or save the text under another name for later transmission.

Deleting and Undeleting a Mail Message

Use the **d** (delete) command within mailx to delete mail messages:

```
d [ number...range ]
```

Table E-2 lists several examples of deleting and undeleting messages either one at a time or multiple messages at once.

Table E-2 Examples of Deleting/Undeleting Messages

To Do This...	Use This Command
To delete the current message	? **d**
To delete a noncurrent message	? **d** *number*
To delete several messages at a time	? **d 1 3 5**
To delete a range of messages	? **d 1-5**
To undelete mail messages	? **u** *number* ? **u** *number number...* ? **u** *number-number*

> **NOTE**
> You can undelete messages only until you quit mailx.

Replying to a Mail Message

Use the **r** command within mailx to reply to the current message—for example:

```
$ mailx
mailx version 5.0 Thu Aug 5 10:36:57 PDT 1999 Type? for help.
"/var/mail/user2": 2 messages 2 new
>N 1     user3     Mon Aug 2 14:44     16/334     About lunch!
 N 2      user4     Mon Aug 2 14:53     14/326     Your lunch
? 1
Message 1:
From user3@saturn Mon Aug 2 14:44 PST 1999
Date: Mon, 2 Aug 1999 14:45:31 PST
From: user3@saturn
To: user2@venus
Subject: About lunch!

I have no plans for lunch and would be happy
to join you.

user3

? r
To: user3@saturn
Subject: Re: About lunch!
```

```
Great! Let's meet in the lobby after class.

user2
.
EOT
?
```

To reply to a noncurrent message, type the following:

```
? r number
```

Your reply will be sent to the sender of the message.

To reply to the sender and everyone who received the current message, type this:

```
? R
```

To reply to the sender and everyone who received a noncurrent message, type this:

```
? R number
```

WARNING

Be careful about using R to reply if you are sending any confidential information. Mail messages frequently are sent to large groups of people that you might not want receiving the contents of your reply.

Printing a Mail Message

Use the **lp** command with the pipe (|) symbol to print a mail message within mailx:

```
? |number lp
```

The following mail message is printed to the default printer. However, you can specify a destination printer by using the **lp -d** *printername* option.

Here's how you would send message number 1 to the default printer after first reading it:

```
? 1
Message 1:
From user3@saturn Mon Aug 2 14:44 PST 1999
Date: Mon, 2 Aug 1999 14:45:21 PST
From: user3@saturn
To: user2@venus
Subject: About lunch!

I have no plans for lunch, and would be happy
to join you.

user 3

? |1 lp
Pipe to: "lp"
request id is printer1-9 (standard input)
"lp" 16/334
?
```

Quitting Mail

Use the **q** (quit) command to save changes and exit mailx. Read and unread messages are automatically stored.

If you exit using **q**, unread messages remain in /var/mail/*username*. By default, read messages are stored in the mbox file in your home directory.

Use the **x** command to exit mailx without saving changes.

It is good practice to save messages that contain important information in a separate file and to clean out your mailbox on a regular basis because it can grow too large.

To access messages stored in your mailbox file, type the following:

```
$ mailx -f
mailx version 5.0 Thu Aug 5 10:36:57 PDT 1999 Type? for help.
"/export/home/user2/mbox": 5 messages
>0     1     user1     Mon Aug 14 09:08     15/342     News
 0    2     user5     Mon Aug 14 10:25     90/555     Meeting
 0     3     user3     Mon Aug 14 10:52     33/912     Project
 0     4     user1     Mon Aug 14 11:58     45/215     Deadline
 0     5     user4     Mon Aug 14 12:02     16/347     Interview
 0     6     user3     Mon Aug 14 14:45     16/334     About lunch!
 0     7     user4     Mon Aug 14 14:53     14/326     Your lunch
?
```

Using Tilde Commands

NOTE

If you want to include a literal tilde character in a letter, type two tildes in succession. Only one tilde is displayed.

While composing a letter, you can use tilde (~) commands to perform a variety of functions:

```
~ single character [string]
```

Table E-3 lists some of the more useful tilde commands.

Table E-3 Tilde Commands and Functions

Command	Function
~!	Escapes to a shell command.
~.	Simulates pressing Ctrl-D to mark the end of a file.
~?	Lists a summary of tilde commands.
~b *username*	Adds username(s) to the blind carbon copies (Bcc:) list.
~c *username*	Adds username(s) to the carbon copies (Cc:) list.
~f *number*	Forwards the specified letter. This is valid only when sending a message while reading mail.
~h	Prompts for header lines: Subject, To, Cc, and Bcc.
~r *filename*	Reads in the text from the specified file.
~t *name*	Adds the specified name(s) to the To list.
~p	Prints the message being entered to the screen.

Table E-3 Tilde Commands and Functions

Command	Function
~s *string*	Changes the subject line to a string.
~t *name*	Adds the specified name(s) to the To list.
~m *number*	Inserts text from the specified letter into the current letter. This is valid only when sending a message while reading mail.

The following code demonstrates the use of some of the tilde commands to make a change to the Subject line (~s string) and to refresh and print the message being entered to the screen (**~p**):

```
$ mailx all_staff_alias

Subject: Meeting Today
There will be a staff meeting at 3:00 p.m. today
~s Staff meeting 3:00 p.m. Today
in the large conference room.

Please be prompt.
~p
----------

Message contains:
To: all_staff_alias
Subject: Staff Meeting 3:00 p.m. Today

There will be a staff meeting at 3:00 p.m. today
in the large conference room.

Please be prompt.
(continue)
.
EOT
```

Summary

The UNIX operating environment provides a program called mailx for sending and receiving e-mail. The mailx program provides facilities for reading, writing, sending, receiving, saving, and deleting messages from the command line.

The **mailx** command is a full-featured UNIX utility that allows a user to access mail under these conditions:

- When using a command-line login shell
- When using a terminal
- When remotely logging into a workstation to read mail

To send mail within the mailx program, you must do the following:

- Specify username@hostname as an argument to the **mailx** command.
- Enter the subject of your mail and press Return.
- Enter the text of your message, and press the . (period) key or Ctrl-D (to transmit message) on a line by itself to signal the end of the message.

Appendix F

e-Lab Activities Listing

This is a master listing of all interactive e-Lab activities in the online curriculum to assist the student and instructor in planning classroom and study time effectively. The activity number and title are provided, as is a brief description of the activity, the estimated difficulty rating (1 = easy and 3 = more difficult), and the approximate time required to complete the activity. These activities are referenced in this textbook at the appropriate place where they should be performed. They are on the CD that accompanies this book.

Number	Title	Description	Diffi-culty	Estimated Time	Type
2.1	Logging In and Out with the CDE Login Screen	In this activity, you log into the Common Desktop Environment (CDE) of a UNIX workstation.	1	5	Activity
2.2	Logging In and Out from the Command Line	In this activity, you log into the command-line environment of a UNIX workstation.	2	5	Activity
2.3	Changing Password in a Terminal Window	In this activity, you enter the commands to change your login password.	1	5	Terminal
3.1	Terminal Window Shell	In this activity, you enter the UNIX **date** command. This activity demonstrates how a command is entered from the command line.	1	5	Terminal

continues

NOTE

Your username for the interactive e-Lab activities is user2. For the e-Lab activities, you are assigned a username by the instructor that should be in the form of user99, where user is lowercase and 99 represents a number such as 01, 02, 14, and so on.

Number	Title	Description	Difficulty	Estimated Time	Type
5.1	Path Names Exercise	In this activity, you demonstrate your understanding of absolute and relative path names.	1	10	Q&A
5.2	Using the **pwd** Command	In this activity, you demonstrate your understanding of the **pwd** command.	1	5	Q&A
5.3	Using the **pwd** and **cd** Commands	In this activity, you demonstrate your ability to use the **pwd** and **cd** commands.	2	10	Terminal
5.4	Using the **ls** Command	In this activity, you demonstrate your ability to use the **ls** command to view the contents of the files within your directory structure.	1	5	Terminal
5.5	Displaying Hidden Files	In this activity, you demonstrate your ability to use the **ls -a** command to view the contents of the hidden files within your directory structure.	1	5	Terminal/ Q&A
5.6	Displaying File Types	In this activity, you demonstrate your ability to use the **ls -F** command to view the types of files that reside within your directory structure.	1	5	Terminal
5.7	Displaying a Long Listing	In this activity, you demonstrate your ability to use the **ls -l** command to view a long listing of the files that reside within your directory structure.	1	5	Terminal/ Q&A

Number	Title	Description	Difficulty	Estimated Time	Type
5.8	Using Metacharacters	In this activity, you demonstrate your ability to use metacharacters with the **ls** command to view files that reside within your directory structure.	2	10	Terminal
6.1	Control Characters	In this activity, you use a control character to halt operation of a common Terminal window utility.	1	5	Terminal
6.2	Using the **strings** Command	In this activity, you use the **strings** command to view readable characters from within an executable file.	1	5	Terminal
6.3	Using **cat** and More	In this activity, you demonstrate your ability to use the **cat** and other commands properly.	1	5	Terminal
6.4	Using **head** and **tail**	In this activity, you demonstrate your ability to use the **head** and **tail** commands properly.	1	5	Terminal
6.5	Using **wc** and **diff**	In this activity, you demonstrate your ability to use the **wc** and **diff** commands properly.	1	5	Terminal
6.6	Using **mkdir** and **touch**	In this activity, you demonstrate your ability to use the **mkdir** and **touch** commands properly.	2	5	Terminal

continues

Number	Title	Description	Difficulty	Estimated Time	Type
6.7	Removing Directories with the **rm** Command	In this activity, you demonstrate your ability to remove files and directories from your system.	2	5	Terminal
6.8	Comparing File Manager to Command Line	In this activity, you demonstrate your ability to perform common File Manager functions from within the command-line environment.	1	5	Q&A
7.1	Copying Files	In this activity, you demonstrate your ability to copy files between and within directories.	3	10	Terminal
7.2	Copying Directories	In this activity, you demonstrate your ability to copy directories.	2	5	Terminal
7.3	Renaming and Moving Files	In this activity, you demonstrate your ability to rename and move files.	2	10	Terminal
7.4	Renaming and Moving Directories	In this activity, you demonstrate your ability to rename and move directories.	2	10	Terminal
7.5	Input/Output Redirection	In this activity, you demonstrate your ability to create a file through redirection and then view the contents of that file.	2	5	Terminal
7.6	Command Piping	In this activity, you demonstrate your ability to pipe multiple commands together on one command line.	2	5	Terminal/ Q&A

Number	Title	Description	Difficulty	Estimated Time	Type
8.1	Finding Files	In this activity, you demonstrate your ability to find files within the file directory structure.	3	10	Terminal
8.2	Searching for Strings	In this activity, you demonstrate your ability to search for strings within files using the **grep** command.	2	10	Terminal
8.3	Using the **sort** Command	In this activity, you demonstrate your ability to use the **sort** command.	2	5	Terminal
8.4	Identifying users	In this activity, you demonstrate your ability to use the commands that will differentiate between the real user ID and the effective user ID.	1	5	Terminal
10.1	Security Policy—Match Game	In this activity, you demonstrate your understanding of the key components of a sound security policy.	2	5	Drag and Drop
10.2	Determining File and Directory Access Permissions	In this activity, you demonstrate your understanding of permission groups.	2	5	Terminal/ Q&A
10.3	Changing Permissions With Symbolic (Relative) Mode	In this activity, you demonstrate your ability to change file and directory permissions using symbolic (relative) mode.	2	10	Terminal

continues

Number	Title	Description	Difficulty	Estimated Time	Type
10.4	Octal Permission Conversion	In this activity, you practice converting a symbolic permission code into a corresponding octal mode value.	1	5	Q&A
10.5	Changing Permissions with Octal (Absolute) Mode	In this activity, you demonstrate your ability to change file and directory permissions using octal (absolute) mode.	3	15	Terminal
11.1	Using the **lp** Command	In this activity, you demonstrate your ability to send items to the print manager from the command line.	1	5	Terminal
11.2	Using the **lpstat** and **cancel** Commands	In this activity, you demonstrate your ability to view and delete items from the print queue.	2	10	Terminal
12.1	Archiving Files with **tar**	In this activity, you demonstrate your ability to archive files with the **tar** command.	3	10	Terminal
12.2	Compressing and Uncompressing Files	In this activity, you demonstrate your ability to compress and uncompress files.	2	5	Terminal
12.3	Extracting Files with **tar**	In this activity, you demonstrate your ability to extract files with the **tar** command.	3	5	Terminal
12.4	Archiving and Compressing Files with **jar**	In this activity, you demonstrate your ability to archive and compress files with the **jar** command.	2	5	Terminal

Number	Title	Description	Difficulty	Estimated Time	Type
13.1	Displaying System Processes	In this activity, you demonstrate your ability to find and list system processes.	1	5	Terminal
13.2	Terminating Processes	In this activity, you demonstrate your ability to terminate system processes.	2	5	Terminal
14.1	Using Korn Shell Aliases	In this activity, you demonstrate your ability to create and use command aliases.	2	10	Terminal
14.2	Using the **r** (Repeat) Command	In this activity, you demonstrate your ability to re-execute commands in the Korn shell.	1	5	Terminal
14.3	Korn Shell Command-Line Editing	In this activity, you demonstrate your ability to set and use command-line editing with the Korn shell.	2	5	Terminal
14.4	Customizing a Korn Shell Prompt	In this activity, you demonstrate your ability to customize your Terminal window prompt within your Korn shell environment.	3	10	Terminal
14.5	Customizing Your C Shell Prompt	In this activity, you demonstrate your ability to change the terminal prompt in a C shell window.	2	5	Terminal
14.6	Using C Shell Aliases	In this activity, you demonstrate your ability to create and use command aliases.	1	5	Terminal

continues

14.7	C Shell History and Re-execution	In this activity, you demonstrate your ability to set up and then re-execute previously executed commands.	2	5	Terminal
14.8	C Shell Command-Line Substitution	In this activity, you demonstrate your ability to edit previously entered commands.	2	5	Terminal
15.1	Customizing the Korn Shell	In this activity, you demonstrate your ability to customize your Korn shell environment.	3	10	Terminal
16.1	OSI Layer Exercise	In this activity, you demonstrate your understanding of the key components of the OSI layers.	2	10	Drag and drop
16.2	Using the **ping** Command	In this activity, you demonstrate your ability to use the **ping** command.	1	5	Terminal
16.3	Using **telnet**	In this activity, you demonstrate your ability to **telnet**.	1	5	Terminal
16.4	Using **rlogin**	In this activity, you demonstrate your ability to **rlogin**.	1	5	Terminal
16.5	Using **ftp**	In this activity, you demonstrate your ability to use the **ftp** command.	1	5	Terminal

Appendix G

Hands-On Lab Listing

This appendix contains a brief description of the lab activities that are referenced throughout this book. These activities can be found in *Cisco Networking Academy Program: Fundamentals of UNIX Lab Companion*. The estimated difficulty rating is described as 1 being easy and 3 being the most difficult.

Lab Number	Title	Brief Description	Difficulty	Estimated Time
1.4.3	UNIX Computing Environment	This lab helps reinforce the UNIX computing environment terminology and concepts introduced in Chapter 1, "The UNIX Computing Environment." You investigate the use of UNIX at your institution.	2	30
2.1.5	Accessing Your System	In this lab, you review the requirements for UNIX login IDs and passwords. You practice logging into a UNIX system using the CDE login screen.	2	30
2.2.7	Becoming Familiar with CDE	In this lab, you work with the standard UNIX graphical user interface (GUI) known as Common Desktop Environment (CDE).	1	30
2.4.2	Customizing Your Workspace	In this lab, you work with the CDE Style Manager, the Application Manager, subpanel menus, the front panel, and the desktop to customize your workspace environment.	2	30
3.1.6	Using CDE Mail Tool	In this lab, you work with the CDE Mail Tool, also known as Mailer.	1	30

continues

Lab Number	Title	Brief Description	Difficulty	Estimated Time
3.2.5	Using CDE Calendar Manager	In this lab, you work with the CDE Calendar Manager.	1	30
3.3.5	Other Built-in CDE Applications	In this lab, you work with several additional user applications that are included with the Common Desktop Environment (CDE). You also work with a Terminal window to get access to the command line.	2	30
4.1.4	Using CDE Help	In this lab, you work with several help functions built into CDE to assist users when performing CDE-related tasks.	1	30
4.2.1	Referencing AnswerBook2 Help	In this lab, you work with Sun Solaris AnswerBook2 and become familiar with the various collections of online manuals available.	1	30
4.3.3	Using Command-Line Help	In this lab, you work with the command-line help in the form of UNIX man pages.	2	30
5.3.1	Basic Command-Line Syntax	In this lab, you work with various UNIX commands to develop an understanding of UNIX commands and syntax.	1	30
5.3.3	Navigating the File System	In this lab, you work with the UNIX file system or directory tree that has been set up for the class.	2	20
5.4.6	Listing Directory Information	In this lab, you use the **ls** command, which is used to determine the contents of a directory.	2	30
5.5.2	Directory Listings with Metacharacters	In this lab, you work with various metacharacters and use them with the **ls** command to refine your directory listings.	3	30
6.1.6	File Information Commands	In this lab, you work with various commands to discover information about files.	2	30

Lab Number	Title	Brief Description	Difficulty	Estimated Time
6.1.10	Basic Command-Line File Management	In this lab, you work with file-management commands from the command line. You also review naming conventions.	2	30
6.2.6	Basic CDE File Manager	In this lab, you work with the Common Desktop Environment (CDE) File Manager.	2	30
7.1.2	Copying Files and Directories	In this lab, you perform more advanced file- and directory-management tasks using the command-line interface and the **cp** (copy) command.	3	45
7.1.4	Renaming and Moving Files and Directories	In this lab, you work with the versatile **mv** (move) command to rename and move files as well as directories.	3	45
7.1.6	I/O Redirection and Piping	In this lab, you use advanced UNIX commands to accomplish redirection and piping.	3	45
7.2.3	Advanced CDE File Manager	In this lab, you work with some of the more advanced file-management features of the Common Desktop Environment (CDE) File Manager.	2	30
8.2.4	File-Processing Commands	In this lab, you use advanced UNIX commands to find files and specific strings contained in files.	3	45
8.3.3	User Identification Commands	In this lab, you use advanced UNIX commands to determine your identity and the identity of other users logged onto a system.	3	45
9.1.8	Using the vi Editor	In this lab, you use a common text-editing tool in the UNIX environment: the vi editor.	3	45
9.2.6	Using the CDE Editor	In this lab, you work with the Common Desktop Environment (CDE) text editor.	2	30

continues

Lab Number	Title	Brief Description	Difficulty	Estimated Time
10.2.4	Determining File System Permissions	In this lab, you become familiar with file system permissions.	3	30
10.3.3	Changing Permissions from the Command Line	In this lab, you analyze and change UNIX file system security permissions using command-line utilities.	3	45
10.4.1	Changing Permissions with File Manager	In this lab, you work with the Common Desktop Environment (CDE) File Manager to analyze and make changes to file system permissions.	2	30
11.3.2	Command-Line Printing	In this lab, you work with UNIX printing commands to send jobs to printers and manage print queues.	2	30
11.4.3	Using CDE Print Manager	In this lab, you work with the Common Desktop Environment (CDE) Print Manager and File Manager to control your printing environment.	1	30
12.4.1	Command-Line Archive Tools	In this lab, you work with the built-in UNIX utilities to back up (or archive), compress, and restore data.	3	45
12.5.2	CDE Archive Tools	In this lab, you work with the Common Desktop Environment (CDE) utilities that allow you to back up, compress, and restore files and folders.	2	20
13.3.2	Managing System Processes	In this lab, you work with UNIX commands to identify system processes and control them. The UNIX network operating system manages tasks using processes.	3	50
14.2.5	Korn Shell Features	In this lab, you work with UNIX the Korn shell to understand its features and capabilities. The shell is the primary user interface to a UNIX system.	2	45

Lab Number	Title	Brief Description	Difficulty	Estimated Time
15.2.1	Customizing the Korn Shell	In this lab, you work with UNIX initialization files to customize your Korn shell login environment and tailor various options to your needs.	3	45
16.4.4	Networking Commands	In this lab, you work with UNIX and Transmission Control Protocol/ Internet Protocol (TCP/IP) networking commands.	2	45

Appendix H

Web Site Resources

Additional Web Resources

The following Sun and independent sites contain more information and resources regarding the Solaris for Intel Operating Environment.

Sun Microsystems Sites

- **Sun Solaris 8 Installation Guide**—http://docs.sun.com/
- **Solaris Intel Spotlight**—This is the Sun Web site for downloading Solaris for Intel or for ordering the Solaris for Intel CD media: www.sun.com/software/intel/
- **Solaris Freeware**—www.sunfreeware.com/
- **The Solaris Developers Connection—Discussion Forums** —http://forum.sun.com
- **Sun's BigAdmin site**—Sun's one-stop location for system administrators: www.sun.com/bigadmin

Independent Sites

- **College Resource and Instructor Support Program (CRISP)**—http://snap.nlc.dcccd.edu/
- **Solaris on Intel FAQ site**—http://sun.drydog.com/faq
- **Solaris for Intel information site**—www.execpc.com/~keithp/bdlogsol.htm
- **Solaris for Intel mailing list**—www.egroups.com/group/solarisonintel

Glossary

Common UNIX System Files

.cshrc file C shell run control file. User-specific initialization file stored in the home directory that typically contains aliases, turns on shell features, and sets the custom prompt. Read for C shell users.

.dtprofile Desktop profile file. User-specific initialization file that resides in the user's home directory and determines settings for the CDE. This file is standard system-wide and is created in a user's home directory the first time that the user logs into the CDE.

.kshrc file Korn shell run control file. User-specific initialization file stored in the home directory that typically contains aliases, turns on shell features, and sets the custom prompt. Read for Korn shell users.

.login User-specific initialization file stored in the home directory that contains one-time-only commands and variable definitions. Read for C shell users.

.logout file File available for C shell users that allows for customization after the user logs out. Clears the screen and prints "Bye," for example. Read for C shell users.

.profile file User-specific initialization file stored in the home directory that contains one-time-only commands and variable definitions. Read for both Bourne and Korn shell users.

/etc/hosts file With /etc/hosts name resolution, each machine requires that a static /etc/hosts file be created to translate host names to IP addresses.

/etc/passwd file File that contains the master list of user information and is consulted each time someone attempts to access the system.

/etc/profile file The primary system-wide initialization file located in the /etc directory. The profile file is created by default when the operating system is installed, and it can be edited and customized by a system administrator. When a Bourne, Korn, or C shell user logs in, the system reads the /etc/profile file first.

Numeric Terms

1000Base-T 1000-Mbps baseband Gigabit Ethernet specification using twisted-pair (copper) or fiber-optic cable. 1000Base-T, which is part of the IEEE 802.3z specification, has a distance limit of from 100 to 2000 meters per segment, depending on the type of cable. Commonly used for campus backbones.

100Base-FX 100-Mbps baseband Fast Ethernet specification using fiber-optic cable. 100Base-FX, which is part of the IEEE 802.3u specification, has a distance limit of from 400 to 2000 meters per segment, depending on whether it is shared or switched and the type of fiber used. Commonly used for LAN backbones.

100Base-TX 100-Mbps baseband Fast Ethernet specification using twisted-pair (copper) cable. 100Base-TX, which is part of the IEEE 802.3u specification, has a distance limit of from 100 meters per segment. Commonly used for workstation and server connections.

10Base-2 10-Mbps baseband Ethernet specification using 50-ohm thin (RG-58) coaxial cable. 10Base-2, which is part of the IEEE 802.3 specification, has a distance limit of 185 meters per segment.

10Base-5 10-Mbps baseband Ethernet specification using standard (thick) 50-ohm baseband coaxial cable. 10Base-5, which is part of the IEEE 802.3 baseband physical layer specification, has a distance limit of 500 meters per segment.

10Base-F 10-Mbps baseband Ethernet specification that refers to the 10Base-FB, 10Base-FL, and 10Base-FP standards for Ethernet over fiber-optic cabling.

10Base-T 10-Mbps baseband Ethernet specification using two pairs of twisted-pair cabling (Category 3, 4, or 5): one pair for transmitting data and the other for receiving data. 10Base-T, which is part of the IEEE 802.3 specification, has a distance limit of approximately 100 meters per segment.

A

Absolute path name Specifies a file or directory in relation to the entire UNIX file hierarchy. The hierarchy begins at the / (root) directory. If a path name begins with a slash, it is an absolute path name.

Admintool Administration Tool, a system-administration utility run under the root account with a graphical interface that enables administrators to maintain system database files, printers, serial ports, user accounts, and hosts.

Anonymous FTP Anonymous File Transfer Protocol (FTP), a site that is set up for general use and does not require an account to obtain files. The word *anonymous* is the username, and the user's e-mail address is the password.

AnswerBook2 System that enables you to view an online version of the printed Solaris manuals, including graphics.

Application Manager The Application Manager window contains six folders containing icons that can be added to a subpanel.

Argument Used to specify how and on what the preceding command is to be performed.

ASCII file American Standard Code for Information Interchange. A file with normal printable characters and no special control or formatting characters. Commonly referred to as a text file.

B

Background job number In the C shell or Korn shell, a job number is assigned to commands (jobs) executed in the background. Several commands are used to manage background jobs, including **jobs, stop, fg, bg** and **kill.**

Background process You can run a process in the background by adding an ampersand (&) to the end of the command line. Background processes run concurrently with other system processes and shell programs. You might want to run processes in the background because they are time-consuming (such as when sorting a large file or searching the file system for a file) or because you want to start a program and be able to continue interacting with the shell.

Backup A copy of file system data that is stored separately from the disk drive on which the data resides.

Bourne shell The default shell for the Solaris computing environment. It does not have aliasing or history capabilities. The Bourne shell prompt is a dollar sign ($).

Browser A graphical program that allows convenient access to the World Wide Web (WWW). The first browser was Mosaic. Some browsers are Netscape Navigator, Microsoft Internet Explorer, and HotJava.

BSD (Berkeley Software Distribution) One of two main versions of UNIX that is not an industry standard but is still fairly widely used. Some varieties of UNIX such as Linux are based on BSD.

Bus topology Early Ethernet LANs used a bus topology. A bus is a cable (coaxial) that is run through an area, and workstations and servers tap into the cable to get access to the network. The bus is a single length of cable that is terminated at each end.

C

C shell Based on the C programming language. Like the Korn shell, the C shell (/bin/csh) has additional features such as aliasing and history. The C shell was developed by Sun's Bill Joy and is still widely used today. The C shell prompt is a percent sign (%).

Calendar Manager A full-featured graphical schedule and appointment-management program. It is a standard component of the Solaris CDE.

CDE (Common Desktop Environment) A standard and consistent graphical user interface desktop developed by a consortium of UNIX platform vendors, including Hewlett-Packard, IBM, Novell, and Sun Microsystems, along with many other companies and members of the Open Software Foundation (OSF), X/Open, and the X Consortium. CDE is Motif-based.

Child process A process spawned by another process. When a user is working in a Terminal window in CDE, that terminal's PID is the parent process ID (PPID) of any commands issued in the terminal.

Client A machine that uses the services from one or more servers on a network. Your computer can be a printer client, an FTP client, and a Telnet client simultaneously.

Client/server Computing model that distributes processing over multiple computers. This enables access to remote systems for the purpose of sharing information and network resources. In a client/server environment, the client and server share or distribute processing responsibilities. Computers on a network can be referred to as host, server, or client.

Command mode When using the vi editor, the command mode is the mode in which you can position the cursor and use edit commands to perform various actions. When you open a file with vi, you are in command mode. All commands are initiated from command mode.

Compression Removing redundant characters and space from a file to reduce its size. Programs such as zip, pkzip, and winzip, and the UNIX **compress** command can be used to compress files.

Concatenate To join the output of one or more files or commands.

Console The main input/output device that is used to access a system and display all system messages. This can be either a display monitor and keyboard or a shell window.

Control character Character that performs specific tasks such as stopping and starting screen output and aborting processes. There are two control keys on most PC keyboards. They are normally labeled Ctrl and found in the lower-left and lower-right corners of the keyboard. On a Sun workstation, there is one control key in the lower left of the keyboard, labeled Control. When displayed on the screen, the Control key is represented by the caret (^) symbol.

CPU (central processing unit) The brains of the computer that performs calculations and data manipulation. Usually a microchip, data moves from RAM to the CPU and back.

CSMA/CD (carrier sense multiple access collision detect) Access method used by Ethernet to allow more than one user to share the network.

Current working directory The directory where you are currently located in the directory tree structure.

D

Daemon Programs or processes that perform a particular task or monitor disks and program execution. Daemons are special processes that begin after the OS loads. Daemons then wait for something to do in support of the OS. For instance, the lpsched daemon exists for the sole purpose of handling print jobs. When no printing is taking place on the system, the lpsched daemon is running but inactive. When a print job is submitted, this daemon becomes active until the job is finished.

Data file A file created by a particular application, such as a word processor or database. These files must be opened with the application that created them.

Default permissions The permissions that are assigned automatically when a new file or directory is created.

Delimiter A special character, often a slash or a space, used to separate one string of characters from another.

Differential backup Backup method in which a full backup is done once a week and each day afterward, all changed data from the full backup is backed up again. The amount of data being backed up increases each day until the next full backup. Differential backup is a compromise because it takes less time than a full backup and is potentially easier to restore than an incremental backup.

Directory A location for files and other directories. The Solaris file system or directory structure enables you to create files and directories that can be accessed through a hierarchy of directories.

Distributed processing Enables the use of resources across the network. For instance, a user might be sitting at a workstation and be able to access files and applications on the hard disk of another computer or a printer located on a remote part of the network.

DNS (Domain Name System) The name service provided by the Internet for TCP/IP networks. It was developed so that workstations and servers on the network could be identified with common names instead of Internet addresses. DNS performs resolution or translation of host name to Internet (IP) address between hosts within your local administrative domain and across domain boundaries.

Domain The name assigned to a group of systems on a local network that share administrative files. The domain name is required for the network information service database to work properly.

Domain name The company and type portion of an e-mail address such as jiml@company.com, where company.com is the domain name.

DOS An early single-user, single-tasking, character-based PC Disk Operating System developed by Microsoft and IBM.

E

Entry mode When using vi, the mode in which you can type text. To enter text, you must type a vi insert command such as **i**, **o**, or **a**. This takes vi out of command mode and puts it into entry mode. In this mode, text is not interpreted literally and becomes part of the document. When you finish entering text in your file, press the Esc key to return to command mode.

Environment variable A system-recognized name tag that is defined to hold various values. Environment variables are system-defined or user-defined variables that provide information about the operating environment to the shell. For instance, the PS1 (prompt string one) variable contains whatever your prompt is currently set to.

Ethernet Popular LAN architecture or technology based on IEEE 802.3 standards. Used in most modern networks, Ethernet uses the CSMA/CD access method. It is a broadcast network, which means that all the workstations on the network receive all transmissions. Ethernet has evolved from speeds of 10 Mbps to 100 Mbps (Fast Ethernet) and now to 1000 Mbps (Gigabit Ethernet).

Ethernet address The physical address of an individual Ethernet controller board. It is called the hardware address or Media Access Control (MAC) address. The Ethernet address of every Sun workstation is unique and coded into a chip on the motherboard.

EUID (effective user ID) If you switch to another user's ID, you will have all the same characteristics and permissions of the account that you switched to; this is now your EUID. The **whoami** and **id** commands show your EUID.

Executable file A file that can be executed by the system. An executable may contain command text, as in the case of a shell script, or binary instructions. Examples of executables include applications and programs.

F

Fast Ethernet Ethernet based on 100-Mbps speeds. 100Base-TX and 100Base-FX are two versions. Fast Ethernet can be shared or switched.

FDDI (Fiber Distributed Data Interface) Pronounced "fiddi." An ANSI standard that was developed primarily as a backbone technology to interconnect LANs in a campus environment. It runs over fiber-optic cable and can span many miles. FDDI uses two rings, one primary and one for backup. It transmits data at 100 Mbps using the token-passing access method.

File A named collection of related data stored on a disk.

File Manager Can be accessed from the CDE front panel or by right-clicking the desktop. The CDE method of file and directory management allows you to do many of the same tasks that are performed at the command line. CDE provides a graphical interface to file management and executes most of the same commands used from the command line behind the scenes.

File system A hierarchy of directories, subdirectories, and files that usually are organized or grouped for a specific purpose.

Foreground process The process that is currently in control of the cursor or mouse. Usually in the front window.

Front panel The primary graphical access area for CDE, which contains workspace buttons, pull-down/up menus, and other applications.

Full backup Backup method in which all selected data is backed up daily, whether it has changed or not. This method takes the longest and might require multiple tapes, depending on the amount of data. It is the safest and easiest to restore.

Full-duplex Communication method in which the nodes can send and receive simultaneously. Examples include the telephone and switched Ethernet.

G

GID (group identifier) Contains the user's primary group membership number. This number relates to a group name that is used to determine group ownership of files that the user creates and access to files and directories.

Gigabit Ethernet Newest version of Ethernet, running at 1 billion bps. The IEEE standard is 1000Base-T. It is becoming more common as a backbone for LANs and for high-speed servers and storage devices.

Global variable Variables that are available to all shell sessions.

GNOME (GNU Network Object Model) The latest windowing system to emerge in the UNIX world. GNOME is part of the GNU open source software project. GNOME has been developed as a free, easy-to-use desktop environment for the user and a powerful application framework for the software developer.

GNU GNU is an operating system similar to UNIX that includes source code that can be copied, modified, and redistributed. The GNU project was started by a group known as the Free Software Foundation (FSF).

Group Identifies the users associated with a file. A user group is a set of users who have access to a common set of files. User groups are defined in the /etc/group file and are granted the same sets of permissions.

H

Half-duplex Communication method in which the nodes can only send or receive but cannot do both simultaneously. Examples include walky-talkies and shared Ethernet.

Help Manager The Primary CDE help tool for most situations, available from the front panel.

Hidden files Files that have names beginning with a dot (.). Examples of a hidden file are .login and .profile .

Hierarchy Structure with parent and child relationships that resembles an upside-down tree. The UNIX file system and UNIX system processes are examples of hierarchical structures.

Home directory The user's own directory, which is set up by the system administrator.

Host A computer system on a UNIX network. Any UNIX (or other OS) computer running TCP/IP (workstation or server) is considered a host computer. The local host is the machine on which the user currently is working. A remote host is a system that is being accessed by a user from another system.

I

I/O device (input/output) Peripheral devices provide a means to get data into and out of a computers. Input devices include a keyboard, a mouse, and a scanner; output devices include a printer and a monitor.

IDE/EIDE (Intelligent Drive Electronics, or Enhanced IDE) One of the two prominent drives types today. Used primarily in standard workstations and home computers. EIDE can support up to four devices (hard-disk drives or CDs).

Incremental backup Backup method in which data is backed up in increments. A full backup is performed once a week on a particular day (for example, Sunday in the evening). Each day after the full backup, only the changes (new and modified files) are backed up. An incremental backup takes the least amount time but is potentially more difficult to restore because it generally requires more tapes.

Internet The largest network in the world. It consists of a large national backbone network that contains the Military Network (MILNET), the National Science Foundation Network (NSFNET), the European Laboratory for Particle Physics (CREN), and a myriad of regional and local campus networks all over the world. To be able to log onto the Internet the user must have Internet Protocol (IP) connectivity; that is, the user must be capable of communicating with other systems by using **telnet** or **ping**. (Networks with only e-mail connectivity are not classified as being on the Internet.)

K

Kernel The master program (core) of the UNIX operating system. It manages devices, memory, swap, processes, and daemons. The kernel also controls the functions between the system programs and the system hardware.

Korn shell A superset of the Bourne shell. The Korn shell (/bin/ksh) has many of the Bourne shell features, plus added features such as aliasing and history. This is the most widely used shell and is the industry standard for system users. The Korn shell prompt is also a dollar sign ($).

L

LAN (local-area network) Made up of groups of computers (nodes) that have simultaneous access to common high-bandwidth media.

Last-line mode When using the vi editor, the mode in which you can type advanced editing commands and perform searches. This mode is entered in a variety of ways (most commonly with a colon, a slash, or a question mark), all of which place you at the bottom of the screen.

Linking The **ln** command is used to give a file an additional name so that you can access it from more than one directory (in the same or different file system) or by another name in the same directory.

Local variable Variables available only for the current shell session.

Logical device name Used by system administrators or users to access the disk (partitions) and tape devices for such tasks as mounting and backing up file systems. Logical device names are stored in the /dev directory in subdirectories. All logical device names are symbolic links to the physical device names in the /devices directory.

Login ID Username or ID used to access a UNIX computer.

M

Mail Tool A full-featured graphical e-mail-management program. It is an e-mail client that is a standard component of the Solaris CDE.

mailx The mailx (and the earlier, more basic mail) program comes with every version of UNIX and is an acceptable program for reading and sending mail. The mailx program basics are found in Appendix E, "mailx," and it is worth learning for those times when you need a mail program but don't have access to CDE.

Man pages Pages describing what you need to know about the system's online commands, system calls, file formats, and system maintenance. The online man pages are part of all versions of UNIX and are installed by default. Man pages are in the form of simple character-based screen displays and are not graphical. The **man** command is used to access man pages.

Media Various types of storage media for data, including magnetic tape, fixed and removable magnetic disks, and recordable optical media such as CD-R and CD-RW.

Mesh topology Typically a WAN topology used to interconnect multiple LANs for redundancy of communications paths. They also can be used in LANs to provide redundant links between routers and switches. With a full mesh, each site has a link to every other site. With a partial mesh, each site has a link to more than one site, but not to every site.

Metacharacters Keyboard characters with special meaning to the shell. A general definition of a metacharacter is any keyboard character that is not alphanumeric. Metacharacters are used with many UNIX commands to provide greater flexibility. Some of the metacharacters used with UNIX are similar in function to those used with DOS. The asterisk (*) and the question mark (?) are metacharacters that also are known as wildcards and are used to work with groups of files efficiently.

Mode The permissions that currently are set for a file or directory. The mode can be changed using the **chmod** command.

Mount point An empty directory in a file hierarchy at which a mounted file system is logically attached. The **mount** command logically attaches a file system, either local or remote, to the file system hierarchy.

Multitasking A feature of the Solaris computing environment and UNIX that enables more than one tool or application to be used at a time. Multitasking enables the kernel to keep track of several processes simultaneously.

Multiuser A feature of UNIX that enables more than one user to access the same system resources.

N

Name service Provides a means of identifying and locating resources (traditionally host names and Internet Protocol [IP] addresses) available to a network. The default name service product available in the Solaris environment is NIS+.

Namespace A collection of machines using a network information service such as Domain Name Service (DNS) (yp), NIS, or NIS+, all sharing a common name.

NFS (Network File System) Sun's distributed computing file system. It is a network service that allows users to transparently access files and directories located on another disk on the network. NFS has become adopted as the industry-standard networked file system for most UNIX vendors.

NIS (Network Information Service) Focuses on making network administration more manageable by providing centralized control over a variety of network information. NIS stores information about workstation names and IP addresses, users, the network itself, and network services. This collection of network information is referred to as the NIS namespace.

NIS+ Enables you to store information about workstation addresses, security information, mail information, Ethernet interfaces, and network services in central locations where all workstations on a network can have access to it. This configuration of network information is referred to as the NIS+ namespace.

NOS (network operating system) A group of programs that runs on servers and provides access to network resources for users.

O

Octal (absolute) mode Method of setting permissions that uses numbers to represent file permissions and that is used to set permissions for all three categories of users at the same time. Octal mode also is referred to as absolute or numeric mode.

ONC (Open Network Computing) protocols A family of published networking protocols and distributed services that enable remote resource sharing, among other things.

Open Windows Sun's original graphical user interface developed for the Solaris environment. It is similar to CDE but is proprietary and not as well supported. The user has a choice when logging into a Solaris workstation to select either CDE or Open Windows.

Orphan process If a command is issued in a Terminal window and the window is closed before the command returns output, that process becomes an orphan.

OSI model Developed by the International Organization for Standardization (ISO) to describe the functions that occur as two nodes on a network communicate. OSI is short for "Open Systems Interconnection" and is an internationally recognized, structured, and standardized architecture for network design. The seven-layer OSI reference model, or just OSI model, is one of the most useful tools we have for analyzing and comparing various technologies and networking products from different vendors.

Overwrite If a file is copied and the target name already exists, you will overwrite or "clobber" the file and will not receive a warning. The **–I** (interactive) option can be used with the **cp** and the **mv** commands so that the user is warned when a file is about to be overwritten.

Owner The user who creates a file or directory. A different user can be made the owner of a file or directory using the **chown** (change ownership) command.

P

Paging The process of moving memory pages between physical memory and the swap space on the disk.

Parent directory A directory that contains other directories. For example, the /usr directory is the parent directory of /usr/bin.

Parent process A process that spawns another process. Following system bootup, a process called the init daemon is invoked. Every process except init has a parent process.

Partition A smaller division or portion of a hard drive. UNIX hard drives can be divided into as many as eight partitions, or slices. Each partition is treated by the operating system as a logical, independent drive, similar to a drive letter in the PC world or a volume with Novell NetWare.

Password aging Can be used to force users to change their password at regular intervals.

Permission category Category or class of users: The user (owner) is the user who created or owns the file or directory. The group is a group of users defined by the system administrator. Other (public) refers to all other users (other than the user or group).

Permissions Attributes of a file or directory that specify who has read, write, or execute access.

Physical memory All computers have physical, or system, memory microchips. This is most often referred to as random-access memory (RAM). This memory is controlled directly by the processor in conjunction with the memory management unit (MMU).

PID (process identification number) Each program run on a UNIX system creates a process, which is assigned a unique PID. The PID is used by the system to identify and track the process until it has completed.

Pine Mail program that is menu-based and easier to use than the mailx program. Pine was developed at the University of Washington and can be accessed by typing pine at the command prompt.

Piping The process of using the output of one command as input to the next command.

Primary group Each user must belong to a primary group. A user's primary group is determined by the system administrator at the time the user account is created; it is stored in the /etc/password file.

Print job number In the lp system, a number that is automatically assigned to each print request, known as a job.

Print Manager A graphical tool for managing print queues. It performs many of the same functions as the **lpstat** command. To activate Print Manager, click the Printer icon on the front panel.

Printer A physical printing device. The printer can be attached to a workstation or network server or can contain a network interface card (NIC) and be directly attached to the network.

Printer name The name of a print queue associated with the physical printer. It is a logical name for the printer, which is assigned by the system administrator. This is the name that the users print to.

Printer queue A directory located on the hard disks of the print server. Print requests or print jobs are stored on the hard disk until they are printed; then they are deleted or purged.

Printer server The computer that manages incoming print requests and releases them as the printer is ready. Print servers run the printer daemon lpsched, which manages print requests. A print server can be a workstation or a network server.

Process A unit of work or task on a UNIX system that is managed by the kernel. Each process is assigned CPU time, RAM, and a process ID (PID) until it completes.

Process scheduling The capability to run a process at a predetermined time. The **at** command and the **crontab** command can be used to schedule UNIX jobs or processes.

PROM (programmable read-only memory) A chip containing permanent, nonvolatile memory and a limited set of commands used to test the system and start the boot process.

R

RAID 1 (Redundant Array of Independent Disks—Level 1) RAID 1, or mirroring, uses two drives, with the second drive storing the same data as the first. If one of the drives fails, the other takes over. A more robust version of RAID 1 that uses dual drive controllers as well as dual drives is known as duplexing.

RAID 5 (Redundant Array of Independent Disks—Level 5) Combines three or more drives as a group so that if one fails, the others take over. The bad drive can be replaced with no loss of service to the users.

RAM (random-access memory) The microchips that make up the real memory of a computer. RAM is the working storage area of the computer where programs (sequence of instructions) and data related to the programs are stored while the program is running. When a program is running, it is copied off the hard disk into RAM, and space is allocated in RAM for the program to do its work.

Recursive To do repetitively. The **cp -r** (recursive) command can be used to copy a directory and all its contents to a new directory in the current directory. You must use the **–r** option when copying directories.

Redirection The process of taking the standard output from a command and directing it to another location such as a file. If not redirected, the output normally goes to the screen.

Relative path name Describes the location of a file or directory as it relates to the current directory (the directory you are currently in). If a path name does not begin with a slash, it is a relative path name.

Restore To bring data back from tape or other backup media and replace the corrupted or lost data on the disk.

Ring topology Topology used by the Token Ring and Fiber Distributed Data Interface (FDDI) network architectures. Token Ring commonly is implemented as a star with a central concentration device known as a multistation access unit (MAU); it is technically a star ring.

Root The username of the superuser account on a UNIX system. The superuser is a privileged user with total system access. The terms *superuser* and *root* have the same meaning and are used interchangeably.

Root directory The top of the UNIX directory system. All other directories are subdirectories of the root (/) directory.

RUID (real user ID) The login ID that you use to initially log into a UNIX system is your RUID. The **who am I** command shows your RUID.

S

SCSI (Small Computer Systems Interface) One of the two prominent drive types today. It is used primarily in high-end workstations and servers, and it can support up to 15 devices (hard disk drives, CDs, tape drives).

Secondary group Each user also can belong to between 8 and 16 secondary groups (depending on the version of UNIX) stored in the /etc/groups file.

Server Provides resources to one or more clients by means of a network. Servers provide services in an UNIX environment by running daemons. Examples of daemons include Printer, FTP, and Telnet.

Service A process that provides a service such as remote file access, remote login capability, or electronic mail transfer.

Shared Ethernet The original version of Ethernet using a linear bus and (more recently) hubs in which only one node could have a packet on the network at a time. Shared Ethernet uses half-duplex technology, in which a workstation can be transmitting or receiving but cannot do both at the same time. It is prone to collisions and performance degradation due to excessive traffic.

Shell An interface between the user and the kernel. It acts as an interpreter or translator. The shell accepts commands issued by the user, interprets what the user types, and requests execution of the programs specified. Execution is performed by the kernel.

Signals Currently, 30 to 40 signals are defined in UNIX, depending on the implementation. Each signal is associated with a number and a name. Signals are used to terminate, suspend, and continue processes. The **kill –9** command uses a signal 9 to terminate a shell.

Slice A logical subdivision of a physical disk drive. It is treated as an individual device.

Spawn A Process can start or spawn a subprocess, thus creating a process hierarchy or tree similar to the file system structure with parent/child relationships.

Spool To place items in a queue, each waiting its turn for some action, such as printing.

Star topology The most common topology, and the one used with Ethernet hubs and switches. The hub or switch is the center of the star, and cables radiate out to nodes like spokes on a wheel. If more than one hub or switch is interconnected, it becomes an extended star topology.

Stnderr Any output that normally would result from an error in the execution of a command. Stnderr normally goes to the screen.

Stndin (standard input) Usually provided by the computer's keyboard but can come from a file.

Stndout (standard output) The results of issuing a command. Stndout usually goes to the computer screen or monitor, but can go to a file.

String One or more characters; it can be a character (alphabetic or numeric), a word, or a sentence. A string can include whitespace or punctuation if enclosed in quotations.

Style Manager A component of CDE that enables you to customize each of your workspaces by changing things such as colors, fonts, screen savers, mouse settings, and keyboard settings.

Subdirectory Any directory below another directory. For example, the /usr directory is a subdirectory of the root (/) directory.

Subpanel Pull-up or drop-down menus on the CDE front panel that provide access to many desktop applications. You can add or remove icons or applications with subpanels.

Superuser A privileged user with total system access. The terms *superuser* and *root* have the same meaning and are used interchangeably.

SVR4 (System Five Release Four) One of the two main versions of UNIX. There are currently a number of varieties or "flavors" of UNIX, and most are similar because they are based on the industry-standard SVR4. System V is a version of the UNIX operating system developed by AT&T. Sun Solaris SunOS is based on SVR4.

Swap space A reserved part of the hard disk for the kernel to use during processing. Portions of running programs can be "swapped out" to the hard disk and then brought back in later, if needed. This swap space is actually on the hard disk, but it looks like additional memory or RAM and is sometimes called virtual memory. Swap space is a raw slice or disk file that is set aside during system installation for the purpose of paging programs out to disk temporarily while they are not being used.

Switched Ethernet Newer version of Ethernet using switches to provide full-duplex transmission and dedicated bandwidth to each node on the network. Nodes can send and receive multiple packets simultaneously.

Symbolic (relative) mode Method of setting permission that uses combinations of letters and symbols to add or remove permissions for selected categories of users. Symbolic mode also is referred to as relative mode.

Symbolic link A mechanism that allows several filenames to refer to a single file on disk. Symbolic (soft) links are pointer files that name another file elsewhere in the file system. Symbolic links may span physical devices because they point to a UNIX path name and not to an actual disk location.

T

TCP/IP The Defense Advance Research Projects Agency (DARPA) originally developed TCP/IP to interconnect defense department computer networks across the country to form a fault-tolerant network. It was adopted and further developed as the standard networking communications component of the UNIX operating system.

Telnet A way to access a UNIX system remotely. To Telnet to another system, you must specify its IP address or host name.

Terabyte Approximately one trillion bytes or a billion kilobytes.

Terminal window A graphical window that can be opened within CDE for access to the command line and UNIX commands. Multiple Terminal windows can be opened simultaneously. Terminal windows support scrolling and cut/copy/paste.

Text Editor (CDE) A full-screen graphical text editor that supports a mouse and can be used to edit files. It is similar to the Windows Notepad. As with vi, this editor does not put any special formatting characters into the file and is suitable for creating system environment and script files.

Text file A file that is made up of standard ASCII characters and no special formatting characters. Script files are text files.

Token Ring Architecture that was originally developed by IBM and that then became IEEE standard 802.5. The Token Ring network architecture uses the ring topology and a token to provide access for workstations. Token Ring uses the token-passing access method. Token Ring speeds are 4 Mbps and 16 Mbps.

Topology The layout or arrangement of network components. Some architectures support more than one topology. Examples of topologies include a bus, a star, a ring, and a mesh.

Trash can A temporary holding place for files that are deleted. Files can be placed in the Trash Can. They can then be permanently deleted by shredding them, or they can be put back or "undeleted."

U

UID (user identifier) Contains the unique user identification number assigned by the system administrator. This number relates to the username and is used to determine ownership of files that the user creates and access to files and directories. The UID of the root user account is 0.

Umask The system setting that determines what the default permissions will be for newly created files and directories. The umask can be changed using the **umask** command.

UNIX Multiuser, multitasking network operating system used by several major computer manufacturers.

Username The login name of a UNIX user that is part of the user's e-mail address, such as jiml@company.com, where jiml is the username.

V

vedit Starts the vi editor with showmode turned on, which displays the current mode (entry or input) that you're in.

vi (visual display) An interactive editor that is used to create or modify American Code for Information Interchange (ASCII) text files. It is a character-based editor that is an integral part of all UNIX operating systems. The vi editor uses a screen display, but you cannot use the mouse to position the cursor.

Virtual memory The swapping process uses swap space on the disk, which is limited. The combination of RAM plus swap space constitutes virtual memory, which is the maximum space that processes can use.

W

WAN (wide-area network) Connections between multiple LANs in different geographical locations.

Workspace When you log into a CDE session, four workspaces are available to you by default. Each workspace is equivalent to a desktop environment.

X

X Terminal Allows a user simultaneous access to several different applications and resources in a multivendor environment through implementation of X Windows.

X Windows Distributed, network-transparent, device-independent, multitasking windowing and graphics system originally developed by MIT for communication between X Terminals and UNIX workstations.

Zombie process Occasionally, a child process does not return to the parent process with its output. This process becomes "lost" in the system.

Index

Symbols

Numerics

A

B

C

D

J

K

M

N

O

P

Q

R

S

T

U

V

W

X-Z

Solaris™ 8 Operating Environment

Resources for Developers, System Administrators, and Educators

www.sun.com/solaris/

Welcome to Solaris!

Sun makes it easy for developers, systems administrators, and students to get started with the Free Solaris™ Binary License Program. Now you can use the Solaris™ 8 Operating Environment at home, work, or school without paying a license fee. You can use Solaris on an unlimited number of computers with a capacity of eight or fewer CPUs. Free downloads are available (you must have a fast Internet connection, such as DSL or a cable modem, and the ability to create CDs) or you might want to purchase a Solaris Media Kit. The SPARC™ platform edition is available for $75 and includes the StarOffice suite of office-productivity tools, Netscape browser, Forte tools, Java, and dozens of other freeware tools. The Intel® platform edition costs $45, but does not include the iPlanet tools. For full information on what comes with each edition, visit **www.sun.com/software/solaris/binaries/package.html**.

Useful Sun.com Sites

Solaris 8 Operating Environment (www.sun.com/solaris)—Learn everything you need to know about the Solaris platform, with links to datasheets, white papers, guided tours, press releases, family comparison chart, customer success stories, documentation, and more.

Sun Open Net Environment (Sun ONE) (www.sun.com/sunone)—Find out about the Sun ONE framework for developing Web services based on the Solaris 8 platform.

Free Solaris 8 Binary License Program (www.sun.com/solaris/binaries)—Download Solaris 8 binaries here. Or, for the cost of media and shipping, order the Solaris 8 Media Kit (SPARC or Intel Platform Edition).

Solaris 8 Operating Environment (Intel Architecture Edition) (www.sun.com/intel)—Links to information and resources including hardware compatibility lists, drivers, FAQs, support, forums, and documentation for the Intel platform.

User Communities

BigAdmin™ Portal (www.sun.com/bigadmin)—Sun's one-stop location for system administrators. Tap into the community through discussion forums, newsgroups, scripts, and FAQs. Plus, find up-to-date information on software updates, patches, downloads, and services.

Solaris Developer Connection™ Program (http://soldc.sun.com)—Free community forums, technical articles, certification programs, and much more.

Solaris™ 8 Operating Environment

Resources for Developers, System Administrators, and Educators

www.sun.com/solaris/

Java Developer Connection™ Program (http://developer.java.sun.com/developer)—A central place for developers to learn about the latest Java™ technologies. Access to downloads, tutorials, technical articles, book excerpts, and more.

Support

Support, Training, and Consulting Services (www.sun.com/service)—Links to the online service center as well as complete information about Sun's wide range of consulting, training, and support programs.

Sun SupportForum™ Site (http://supportforum.sun.com)—Free support through user discussion forums, documentation, and downloads, as well as links to valuable resources and tools.

U.S. Sun Store—http://store.sun.com

21. $\displaystyle\int \sqrt{a^2+x^2}\,dx = \frac{x}{2}\sqrt{a^2+x^2}+\frac{a^2}{2}\sinh^{-1}\frac{x}{a}+C$

22. $\displaystyle\int x^2\sqrt{a^2+x^2}\,dx = \frac{x(a^2+2x^2)\sqrt{a^2+x^2}}{8}-\frac{a^4}{8}\sinh^{-1}\frac{x}{a}+C$

23. $\displaystyle\int \frac{\sqrt{a^2+x^2}}{x}\,dx = \sqrt{a^2+x^2}-a\sinh^{-1}\left|\frac{a}{x}\right|+C$

24. $\displaystyle\int \frac{\sqrt{a^2+x^2}}{x^2}\,dx = \sinh^{-1}\frac{x}{a}-\frac{\sqrt{a^2+x^2}}{x}+C$

25. $\displaystyle\int \frac{x^2}{\sqrt{a^2+x^2}}\,dx = -\frac{a^2}{2}\sinh^{-1}\frac{x}{a}+\frac{x\sqrt{a^2+x^2}}{2}+C$

26. $\displaystyle\int \frac{dx}{x\sqrt{a^2+x^2}} = -\frac{1}{a}\ln\left|\frac{a+\sqrt{a^2+x^2}}{x}\right|+C$

27. $\displaystyle\int \frac{dx}{x^2\sqrt{a^2+x^2}} = -\frac{\sqrt{a^2+x^2}}{a^2x}+C$

28. $\displaystyle\int \frac{dx}{\sqrt{a^2-x^2}} = \sin^{-1}\frac{x}{a}+C$

29. $\displaystyle\int \sqrt{a^2-x^2}\,dx = \frac{x}{2}\sqrt{a^2-x^2}+\frac{a^2}{2}\sin^{-1}\frac{x}{a}+C$

30. $\displaystyle\int x^2\sqrt{a^2-x^2}\,dx = \frac{a^4}{8}\sin^{-1}\frac{x}{a}-\frac{1}{8}x\sqrt{a^2-x^2}\,(a^2-2x^2)+C$

31. $\displaystyle\int \frac{\sqrt{a^2-x^2}}{x}\,dx = \sqrt{a^2-x^2}-a\ln\left|\frac{a+\sqrt{a^2-x^2}}{x}\right|+C$

32. $\displaystyle\int \frac{\sqrt{a^2-x^2}}{x^2}\,dx = -\sin^{-1}\frac{x}{a}-\frac{\sqrt{a^2-x^2}}{x}+C$

33. $\displaystyle\int \frac{x^2}{\sqrt{a^2-x^2}}\,dx = \frac{a^2}{2}\sin^{-1}\frac{x}{a}-\frac{1}{2}x\sqrt{a^2-x^2}+C$

34. $\displaystyle\int \frac{dx}{x\sqrt{a^2-x^2}} = -\frac{1}{a}\ln\left|\frac{a+\sqrt{a^2-x^2}}{x}\right|+C$

35. $\displaystyle\int \frac{dx}{x^2\sqrt{a^2-x^2}} = -\frac{\sqrt{a^2-x^2}}{a^2x}+C$

36. $\displaystyle\int \frac{dx}{\sqrt{x^2-a^2}} = \cosh^{-1}\frac{x}{a}+C = \ln\left|x+\sqrt{x^2-a^2}\right|+C$

37. $\displaystyle\int \sqrt{x^2-a^2}\,dx = \frac{x}{2}\sqrt{x^2-a^2}-\frac{a^2}{2}\cosh^{-1}\frac{x}{a}+C$

38. $\displaystyle\int (\sqrt{x^2-a^2})^n\,dx = \frac{x(\sqrt{x^2-a^2})^n}{n+1}-\frac{na^2}{n+1}\int(\sqrt{x^2-a^2})^{n-2}\,dx, \qquad n\neq -1$

39. $\displaystyle\int \frac{dx}{(\sqrt{x^2-a^2})^n} = \frac{x(\sqrt{x^2-a^2})^{2-n}}{(2-n)a^2}-\frac{n-3}{(n-2)a^2}\int\frac{dx}{(\sqrt{x^2-a^2})^{n-2}}, \qquad n\neq 2$

40. $\displaystyle\int x(\sqrt{x^2-a^2})^n\,dx = \frac{(\sqrt{x^2-a^2})^{n+2}}{n+2}+C, \qquad n\neq -2$

41. $\displaystyle\int x^2\sqrt{x^2-a^2}\,dx = \frac{x}{8}(2x^2-a^2)\sqrt{x^2-a^2}-\frac{a^4}{8}\cosh^{-1}\frac{x}{a}+C$

42. $\displaystyle\int \frac{\sqrt{x^2-a^2}}{x}\,dx = \sqrt{x^2-a^2}-a\sec^{-1}\left|\frac{x}{a}\right|+C$

43. $\displaystyle\int \frac{\sqrt{x^2-a^2}}{x^2}\,dx = \cosh^{-1}\frac{x}{a}-\frac{\sqrt{x^2-a^2}}{x}+C$

Continued overleaf.

44. $\displaystyle\int \frac{x^2}{\sqrt{x^2 - a^2}}\,dx = \frac{a^2}{2}\cosh^{-1}\frac{x}{a} + \frac{x}{2}\sqrt{x^2 - a^2} + C$

45. $\displaystyle\int \frac{dx}{x\sqrt{x^2 - a^2}} = \frac{1}{a}\sec^{-1}\left|\frac{x}{a}\right| + C = \frac{1}{a}\cos^{-1}\left|\frac{a}{x}\right| + C$

46. $\displaystyle\int \frac{dx}{x^2\sqrt{x^2 - a^2}} = \frac{\sqrt{x^2 - a^2}}{a^2x} + C$

47. $\displaystyle\int \frac{dx}{\sqrt{2ax - x^2}} = \sin^{-1}\left(\frac{x - a}{a}\right) + C$

48. $\displaystyle\int \sqrt{2ax - x^2}\,dx = \frac{x - a}{2}\sqrt{2ax - x^2} + \frac{a^2}{2}\sin^{-1}\left(\frac{x - a}{a}\right) + C$

49. $\displaystyle\int (\sqrt{2ax - x^2})^n\,dx = \frac{(x - a)(\sqrt{2ax - x^2})^n}{n + 1} + \frac{na^2}{n + 1}\int (\sqrt{2ax - x^2})^{n-2}\,dx,$

50. $\displaystyle\int \frac{dx}{(\sqrt{2ax - x^2})^n} = \frac{(x - a)(\sqrt{2ax - x^2})^{2-n}}{(n - 2)a^2} + \frac{(n - 3)}{(n - 2)a^2}\int \frac{dx}{(\sqrt{2ax - x^2})^{n-2}}$

51. $\displaystyle\int x\sqrt{2ax - x^2}\,dx = \frac{(x + a)(2x - 3a)\sqrt{2ax - x^2}}{6} + \frac{a^3}{2}\sin^{-1}\frac{x - a}{a} + C$

52. $\displaystyle\int \frac{\sqrt{2ax - x^2}}{x}\,dx = \sqrt{2ax - x^2} + a\sin^{-1}\frac{x - a}{a} + C$

53. $\displaystyle\int \frac{\sqrt{2ax - x^2}}{x^2}\,dx = -2\sqrt{\frac{2a - x}{x}} - \sin^{-1}\left(\frac{x - a}{a}\right) + C$

54. $\displaystyle\int \frac{x\,dx}{\sqrt{2ax - x^2}} = a\sin^{-1}\frac{x - a}{a} - \sqrt{2ax - x^2} + C$

55. $\displaystyle\int \frac{dx}{x\sqrt{2ax - x^2}} = -\frac{1}{a}\sqrt{\frac{2a - x}{x}} + C$

56. $\displaystyle\int \sin ax\,dx = -\frac{1}{a}\cos ax + C$

57. $\displaystyle\int \cos ax\,dx = \frac{1}{a}\sin ax + C$

58. $\displaystyle\int \sin^2 ax\,dx = \frac{x}{2} - \frac{\sin 2ax}{4a} + C$

59. $\displaystyle\int \cos^2 ax\,dx = \frac{x}{2} + \frac{\sin 2ax}{4a} + C$

60. $\displaystyle\int \sin^n ax\,dx = \frac{-\sin^{n-1} ax\cos ax}{na} + \frac{n - 1}{n}\int \sin^{n-2} ax\,dx$

61. $\displaystyle\int \cos^n ax\,dx = \frac{\cos^{n-1} ax\sin ax}{na} + \frac{n - 1}{n}\int \cos^{n-2} ax\,dx$

62. (a) $\displaystyle\int \sin ax\cos bx\,dx = -\frac{\cos(a + b)x}{2(a + b)} - \frac{\cos(a - b)x}{2(a - b)} + C, \qquad a^2 \neq b^2$

(b) $\displaystyle\int \sin ax\sin bx\,dx = \frac{\sin(a - b)x}{2(a - b)} - \frac{\sin(a + b)x}{2(a + b)}, \qquad a^2 \neq b^2$

(c) $\displaystyle\int \cos ax\cos bx\,dx = \frac{\sin(a - b)x}{2(a - b)} + \frac{\sin(a + b)x}{2(a + b)}, \qquad a^2 \neq b^2$

63. $\displaystyle\int \sin ax\cos ax\,dx = -\frac{\cos 2ax}{4a} + C$

64. $\displaystyle\int \sin^n ax\cos ax\,dx = \frac{\sin^{n+1} ax}{(n + 1)a} + C, \qquad n \neq -1$

This table is continued on the endpapers at the back.

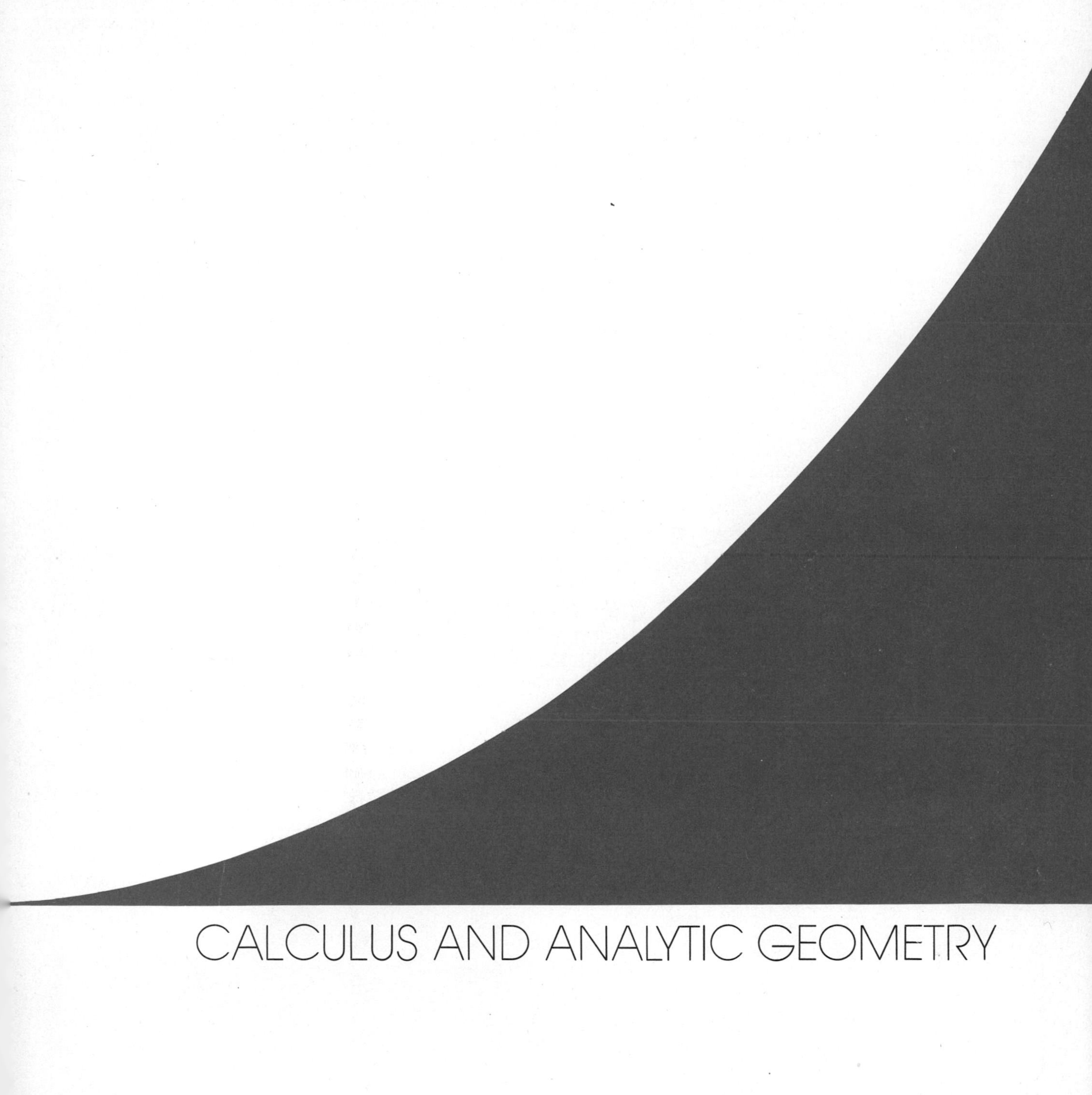

CALCULUS AND ANALYTIC GEOMETRY

GEORGE B. THOMAS, JR.
MASSACHUSETTS INSTITUTE OF TECHNOLOGY
ROSS L. FINNEY
MASSACHUSETTS INSTITUTE OF TECHNOLOGY

FIFTH EDITION

CALCULUS AND ANALYTIC GEOMETRY

ADDISON-WESLEY PUBLISHING COMPANY

READING, MASSACHUSETTS • MENLO PARK, CALIFORNIA • LONDON • AMSTERDAM • DON MILLS, ONTARIO • SYDNEY

Sponsoring editor: Stephen H. Quigley
Production editor: Mary Cafarella
Designer: Jean King
Illustrator: Richard Morton
Cover design: Marshall Henrichs

Fifth printing, June 1981

 Printed in the United States of America. Published simultaneously in Canada. Library of Congress Catalog Card No. 78-55832.

ISBN 0-201-07540-7
ABCDEFGHIJ-DO-8987654321

PREFACE

The *Fifth Edition* has been adapted primarily from the *Alternate Edition,* but in addition to some new applications of calculus to engineering and the physical sciences, the present book contains a variety of interesting professional applications of calculus to business, economics, and the life sciences. The chapter on infinite series (Chapter 16) has been completely rewritten, and now contains twice the number of examples and exercises. Sequences are treated first, and separately from series, and more attention is paid to estimation. A chapter on vector analysis (Chapter 15), including line and surface integrals, Green's theorem, Stokes's theorem, and the Divergence Theorem, has been added. A section on Lagrange multipliers is included in Chapter 13 (Partial Differentiation). The presentation of vectors (Chapters 11 and 12) has been reorganized, and now the treatment of vector geometry precedes the treatment of vector functions and their derivatives. The book also incorporates some hand-held calculator exercises. More art has been included, and the art has been captioned throughout.

At the request of many users, we have moved several topics toward the front of the book. Trigonometric functions are introduced briefly in Chapter 1, and the review of trigonometry and the presentation of differentiation of sines and cosines that used to be in Chapter 4 now appear in Chapter 2. L'Hôpital's rule is presented in Chapter 3, and Newton's method has been moved to Chapter 2. Simpson's rule is now included with the trapezoidal rule in Chapter 4.

The level of rigor is about the same as in earlier editions of the Thomas books. For example, we do not prove that a function that is continuous on a closed and bounded interval has a maximum on the interval, but we state that theorem and use it in proving the Mean Value Theorem.

The first three chapters deal with the definition of, formulas for, and applications of derivatives of functions of one variable. Chapters 4 and 5 are on integration, with applications. Among the new applications are: estimating cardiac output, calculating light output from flashbulbs, determining the average daily inventory of a business, and using Delesse's rule to analyze tissue composition.

Chapter 6 deals with the derivatives of the remaining trigonometric functions, and with the logarithmic and exponential functions. If one wished to include some of the material on hyperbolic functions immediately after Chapter 6, then the material on methods of integration in Chapter 7 could be expanded to include the integration formulas XXVII′ to XXXII′ from Article 9–5. Otherwise, it is possible to skip Chapter 9 if one also omits subsequent problems that involve hyperbolic functions.

Chapter 8 (Plane Analytic Geometry) and Chapter 10 (Polar Coordinates) treat properties of the conic sections, cardioids, and other standard topics, including areas and arc length.

Chapters 11 and 12 introduce coordinates in space, vector algebra, parametric equations, and motion on a space curve. Chapter 12 concludes with a derivation of Kepler's second law of planetary motion in a central force field.

The remaining chapters include partial differentiation, multiple integration, vector analysis, infinite series, complex numbers and functions, differential equations, an appendix on matrices and determinants (useful in its own right and for the formal expansion of a third-order determinant used in Article 11–7), assorted formulas from elementary mathematics, and brief tables of sines, cosines, tangents, exponential functions, and natural logarithms. The endpapers of the book contain a brief table of integrals for convenient reference.

Answers for most of the problems are given and are keyed to the text by page, as well as by problem number, article, and chapter. The answers that are new to this edition were provided by Paul H. Siegel and Daniel W. Litwhiler. We are grateful to them for this valuable help, and we continue to be grateful to our friends and colleagues who contributed solutions and problems to earlier editions.

Many students, colleagues, and friends have given us the benefit of their criticism and suggestions. We would especially like to mention the valuable contributions of Carl W. R. de Boor, Fred A. Franklin, William A. Ferguson, Solomon Garfunkel, Andrew D. Jorgensen, William Ted Martin, Arthur P. Mattuck, Eric Reissner, J. Barkley Rosser, Oliver G. Selfridge, Donald R. Sherbert, Norton Starr, William U. Walton, and Felicia de May Weitzel. But even with the addition of the reviewers mentioned separately, this list is far from complete. To each and every person who has at any time contributed helpful suggestions, comments, or criticisms, whether or not we have been able to incorporate these into the book, we say "Thank you very much."

It is a pleasure to acknowledge the superb assistance in illustration, editing, design, and composition that the staff of Addison-Wesley Publishing Company has given to the preparation of this edition. The senior author also acknowledges with gratitude the special talent and productivity beyond his expectation that his co-author has brought to this new edition.

The text is available in one complete volume, which can be covered in three or four semesters, depending on the pace, or as two separate parts. The first part treats functions of one variable, analytic geometry in two dimensions, and infinite series (Chapters 1 through 10, and Chapter

16). It also contains the appendix on matrices and determinants. The second part begins with Chapter 11 on vectors and parametric equations, and contains all subsequent chapters, including Chapter 16, and the appendix on matrices and determinants. Both parts include answers.

Any errors that may appear are the responsibility of the authors. We will appreciate having these brought to our attention.

G. B. T., Jr.

October 1978 R. L. F.

ACKNOWLEDGMENTS

The authors would like to thank the following reviewers for the quality of their attention and for their many thoughtful suggestions.

Kenneth C. Abernethy	Virginia Military Institute
Fred G. Brauer	University of Wisconsin at Madison
William R. Fuller	Purdue University
Douglas Hall	Michigan State University
Roger B. Hooper	University of Maine
William Perry	Texas A & M University
David Rearick	University of Colorado
Virginia Skinner Dwann Veroda	El Camino College
Robert D. Stalley	Oregon State University
G. Wayne Sullivan	Volunteer State Community College

AVAILABLE SUPPLEMENTS

The following supplementary materials are available for use by students:

Pocket Calculator Supplement for Calculus	J. Barkley Rosser and Carl W. R. de Boor (University of Wisconsin at Madison)
Self-Study Manual	Maurice D. Weir (Naval Postgraduate School)
Student Supplement	Gurcharan S. Gill (Brigham Young University)

CONTENTS

5 APPLICATIONS OF THE DEFINITE INTEGRAL 227

6 TRANSCENDENTAL FUNCTIONS 289

7 METHODS OF INTEGRATION 331

8 PLANE ANALYTIC GEOMETRY 387

9 HYPERBOLIC FUNCTIONS 439

10 POLAR COORDINATES 459

THE RATE OF CHANGE OF A FUNCTION

1-1 INTRODUCTION

Calculus is the mathematics of change and motion. Where there is motion or growth, where forces are at work producing acceleration, calculus is the right mathematical tool. This was true in the beginnings of the subject, and it is true today. Calculus is used to predict the orbits of earth satellites; to design inertial navigation systems, cyclotrons, and radar systems; to explore problems of space travel; to test scientific theories about ocean currents and the dynamics of the atmosphere; and to model economic, social, and psychological behavior. Calculus is used increasingly to model problems in the fields of business, biology, medicine, animal husbandry, and political science. Of course, a scientist needs a great deal more than mathematical competence, and needs more mathematics than calculus. But calculus is a tool of great importance and usefulness and is a prerequisite for further study in nearly all branches of higher mathematics.

One of the great mathematicians of the twentieth century, John von Neumann (1903–57), wrote: "The calculus was the first achievement of modern mathematics, and it is difficult to overestimate its importance. I think it defines more unequivocally than anything else the inception of modern mathematics; and the system of mathematical analysis, which is its logical development, still constitutes the greatest technical advance in exact thinking."*

Calculus provides methods for solving two large classes of problems. The first of these involves finding the rate at which a variable quantity is changing. When a body travels in a straight line, its distance from its starting point changes with time and we may ask *how fast* it is moving at any given instant. *Differential calculus* is the branch of calculus that treats such problems.

On the other hand, if we are given the *velocity* of a moving body at every instant of time, we may seek to find the distance it has moved as a function of time. This second type of problem, that of finding a function when its rate of change is known, belongs to the domain of *integral calculus*.

Modern science and engineering use both branches of calculus to express physical laws in precise mathematical terms, and to study the consequences of those laws. It was with calculus that Sir Isaac Newton (1642–1727) was able to explain the motion of the planets about the sun as a consequence of the physical assumption known today as the law of gravitational attraction. Kepler (1571–1630) spent some twenty years studying observational data and using empirical methods to discover the three laws now known as Kepler's laws:

a) Each planet traces an orbit about the sun which is an ellipse with the sun at one focus.

b) The line joining the planet and the sun sweeps over equal areas in equal intervals of time.

c) The squares of the periods of revolution of the planets about the sun are proportional to the cubes of their mean distances from the sun.

---

* World of Mathematics, Vol. 4, "The Mathematician," by John von Neumann, pp. 2053–2063.

With the calculus as the main mathematical tool, all three of these laws can be derived from Newton's laws of gravitation and motion.

German mathematician and philosopher Gottfried Wilhelm Leibniz (1646–1716) independently developed a large part of the calculus. His notation has been widely adopted in preference to Newton's.

Analytic geometry, which forms a third division of the subject matter of this book, was the creation of several mathematicians.* Two French mathematicians, René Descartes (1596–1650) and Pierre de Fermat (1601–1665), are the chief inventors of analytic geometry as we now know it. The idea of locating a point in the plane by means of its directed distances from two perpendicular axes is Descartes', and his name is commemorated in the terminology "Cartesian coordinates." We discuss coordinates in Article 1–2. The distinguishing characteristic of analytic geometry is that it uses algebraic methods and equations to gain information about geometric problems. Conversely, it lets us portray algebraic equations as geometric curves, and thus bring the tools of geometry to bear on algebraic problems. Most of the theory of calculus can be presented in geometrical terms, and calculus and analytic geometry may be profitably united and studied as a whole.

1–2 COORDINATES

The connection between algebra and geometry in analytic geometry is made by setting up a one-to-one correspondence between the points of a plane and ordered pairs of numbers (x, y). There are many ways to establish such a correspondence. The one most commonly used is the one described here.

A line in the plane, extending indefinitely to the left and to the right, is chosen, defined to be horizontal, and called the *x-axis* or *axis of abscissas*. (See Fig. 1–1.) A point of origin O on this line and a unit of length are then chosen. The axis is scaled off in terms of this unit. The number zero is attached to O, the number $+a$ is attached to the point which is a units to the right of O, and the number $-a$ is attached to the point located symmetrically to the left of O. This establishes a one-to-one correspondence between the points of the x-axis and the set of all *real numbers* (numbers which may be represented by terminating or nonterminating decimals).

Now through O take a second, vertical line in the plane, extending indefinitely up and down. This line is to be the *y-axis*, or *axis of ordinates*. The unit of length used to represent $+1$ on the y-axis need not be the one used to represent $+1$ on the x-axis. The y-axis is scaled off in terms of the unit of length adopted for it, with the positive number $+b$ attached to the point b units above O and the negative number $-b$ attached to the point located symmetrically b units below O.

We are now ready to assign number pairs to points. If a line perpendicular to the x-axis is drawn through the point marked a, and another line is

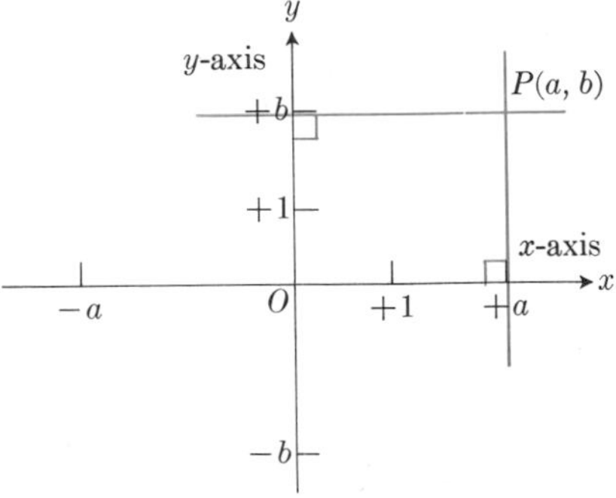

1–1 The line perpendicular to the x-axis at a and the line perpendicular to the y-axis at b cross at $P(a, b)$.

* See *World of Mathematics*, Vol. 1, "Commentary on Descartes and Analytical Geometry," pp. 235–37. Also the article "The Invention of Analytic Geometry," by Carl B. Boyer, *Scientific American*, January, 1949.

drawn perpendicular to the y-axis at b, their point of intersection is labeled $P(a, b)$. The number a is the *x-coordinate* of P, and the number b is the *y-coordinate* of P. The pair (a, b) is called the *coordinate pair* of the point P. Note that (a, b) is an *ordered pair*; we list the x-coordinate first and the y-coordinate second.

To be sure that none of the points in the plane has been missed, we can start with any point P and draw lines through it perpendicular to the two axes. If these perpendiculars cross the x- and y-axes at a and b, then P has already been assigned the coordinate pair (a, b).

Points can never be assigned more than one coordinate pair; when we drop perpendiculars from $P(a, b)$ to the axes the perpendiculars must meet the axes at a and b. Only one perpendicular can be drawn from a point to a line.

The two axes divide the plane into four quadrants, called the first quadrant, second quadrant, and so on, as in Fig. 1–2.

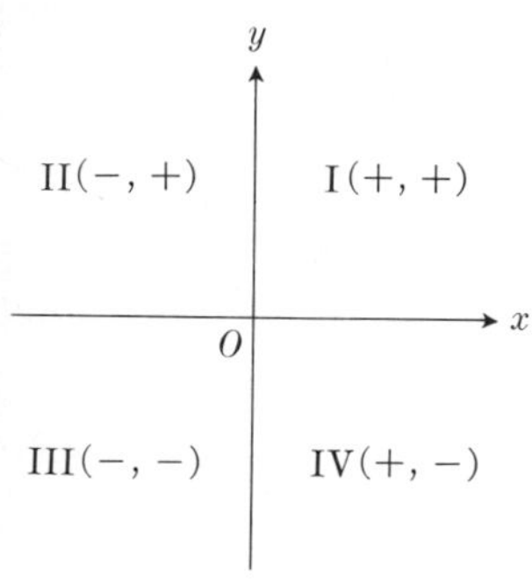

1–2 The four quadrants.

There are times when there is no physical relation between the units used to measure x and y. For example, if y is the maximum number of minutes that a diver can stay at a depth of x meters without having to stop to decompress on the way up, then the "1" on the x-axis stands for one meter, while the "1" on the y-axis stands for one minute. Clearly, there is no need to mark the two 1's the same number of millimeters, or whatever, from the origin.

In surveying, on the other hand, one foot measured north-and-south should be the same as one foot measured east-and-west. For this reason, it is usually assumed in trigonometry that the units of length on the two axes are the same. We make this assumption in analytic geometry also.

In this book, if coordinates of points are given without any physical units attached, it is to be assumed that the scales on the two axes are the same. In particular, this assumption is made wherever our work involves angles between lines or lengths of line segments that are not parallel to the axes.

PROBLEMS

In each of the following problems (1–12), first draw a pair of coordinate axes. Then plot the given point $P(a, b)$ and plot:

a) The point Q such that PQ is perpendicular to the x-axis and is bisected by it. Give the coordinates of Q. (P and Q are symmetric with respect to the x-axis.)

b) The point R such that PR is perpendicular to and is bisected by the y-axis. Give the coordinates of R. (P and R are symmetric with respect to the y-axis.)

c) The point S such that PS is bisected by the origin. Give the coordinates of S. (P and S are symmetric with respect to the origin.)

d) The point T such that PT is perpendicular to and is bisected by the 45° line L through the origin bisecting the first quadrant and the third. Give the coordinates of T, assuming equal units on the axes. (P and T are symmetric with respect to L.)

1. $(1, -2)$ **2.** $(2, -1)$ **3.** $(-2, 2)$
4. $(-2, 1)$ **5.** $(0, 1)$ **6.** $(1, 0)$
7. $(-2, 0)$ **8.** $(0, -3)$ **9.** $(-1, -3)$
10. $(\sqrt{2}, -\sqrt{2})$ **11.** $(-\pi, -\pi)$ **12.** $(-1.5, 2.3)$

13. If $P = P(x, y)$, then the coordinates of the point Q described in (a) above can be expressed in terms of x and y as $(x, -y)$. Express the coordinates of R, S, and T in terms of x and y.

In Problems 14–17, take the units of length on the two axes to be equal.

14. A line is drawn through the point (0, 0) and the point (1, 1). What acute angle does it make with the positive x-axis? Sketch.

15. There are three parallelograms with vertices at $(-1, 1)$, (2, 0), and (2, 3). Sketch them and give the coordinate pairs of the missing vertices.

16. A circle in quadrant II is tangent to both axes. It touches the y-axis at (0, 3).

a) At what point does it meet the x-axis? Sketch.

b) What are the coordinates of the center of the circle?

17. The line through the points (1, 1) and (2, 0) cuts the y-axis at the point $(0, b)$. Find b by using similar triangles.

1–3 INCREMENTS

If a particle starts at a point $P_1(x_1, y_1)$ and goes to a new position $P_2(x_2, y_2)$, we say that its coordinates have changed by increments Δx (read *delta x*) and Δy (read *delta y*). For example, if the particle moves from $A(1, -2)$ to $B(6, 7)$, as in Fig. 1–3, then these increments are

$$\Delta x = 5, \qquad \Delta y = 9.$$

Observe that the *increment* in a coordinate is the *net change*, given by

$$\Delta x = (x \text{ of terminal point}) - (x \text{ of initial point})$$

and

$$\Delta y = (y \text{ of terminal point}) - (y \text{ of initial point}).$$

The positions the particle occupies between its initial and terminal locations do not affect these net changes.

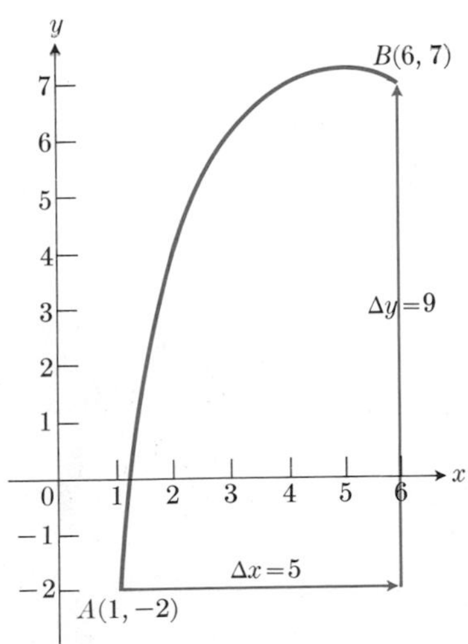

1–3 When a particle moves from one point to another, Δx and Δy are computed from the coordinates of the initial and terminal positions:

$$\Delta x = 6 - 1 = 5, \qquad \Delta y = 7 - (-2) = 9.$$

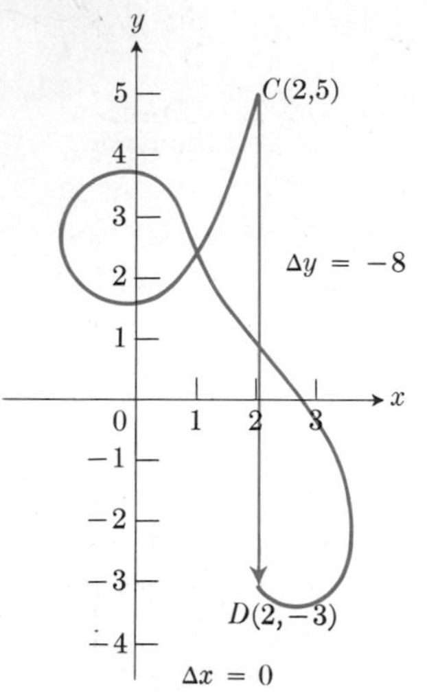

1–4 The net change in the x-coordinate in moving from $C(2, 5)$ to $D(2, -3)$ is zero.

If the initial position of a particle is $P_1(x_1, y_1)$ and its terminal position is $P_2(x_2, y_2)$, then we compute the increments Δx and Δy by the formulas

$$\Delta x = x_2 - x_1, \qquad \Delta y = y_2 - y_1.$$

Either increment can be any real number: positive, negative, or zero. The increments from $C(2, 5)$ to $D(2, -3)$ in Fig. 1–4, for example, are

$$\Delta x = 2 - 2 = 0, \qquad \Delta y = -3 - 5 = -8.$$

The net change in x from C to D is zero. The y-coordinate decreases by 8 as we move from C to D.

If the same unit of measurement is used on both coordinate axes, we can express all distances in the plane in terms of this common unit. We use the Pythagorean theorem, as shown in Fig. 1–5. The distance d between two points $P_1(x_1, y_1)$ and $P_2(x_2, y_2)$ is the length of the hypotenuse. It can be computed as:

$$d = \sqrt{(\Delta x)^2 + (\Delta y)^2} = \sqrt{(x_2 - x_1)^2 + (y_2 - y_1)^2}.$$

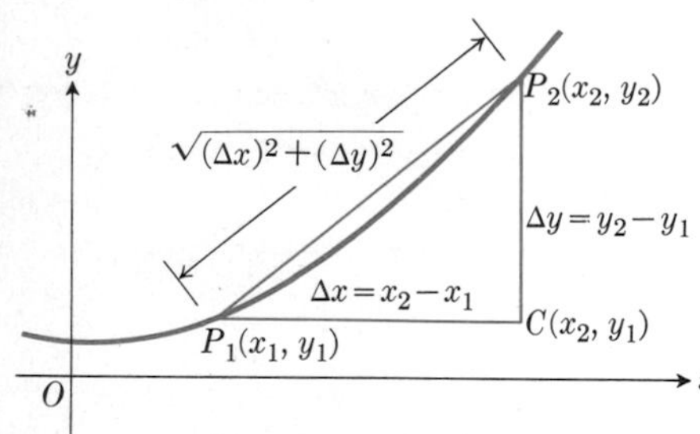

1–5 Distance is calculated with the Pythagorean theorem.

EXAMPLE 1. If a particle starts from $P_1(-1, 2)$ and goes straight to $P_2(2, -2)$, then its x-coordinate changes by

$$\Delta x = x_2 - x_1 = 2 - (-1) = 3.$$

Its y-coordinate changes by

$$\Delta y = y_2 - y_1 = -2 - 2 = -4.$$

The distance between P_1 and P_2 is

$$d = \sqrt{(\Delta x)^2 + (\Delta y)^2} = \sqrt{(3)^2 + (-4)^2} = \sqrt{9 + 16} = 5.$$

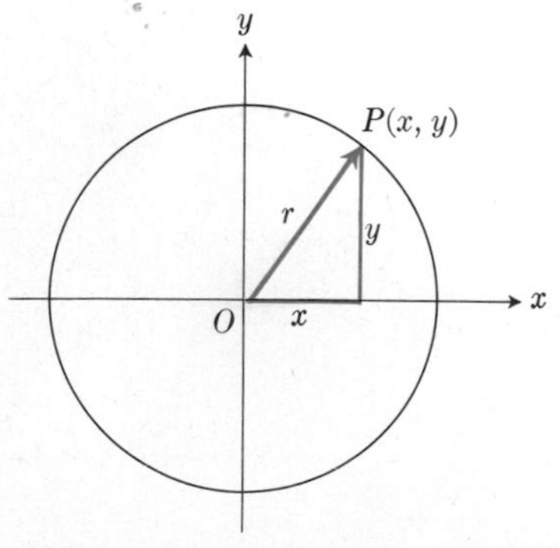

1–6 $x^2 + y^2 = r^2$, for points on the circle of radius r centered at (0, 0).

EXAMPLE 2. The set of all points whose distance from the origin is a positive number r is a circle whose radius is r and whose center is the origin. The coordinates of any point $P(x, y)$ on this circle satisfy the equation

$$\sqrt{(x - 0)^2 + (y - 0)^2} = r,$$

or

$$\sqrt{x^2 + y^2} = r,$$

or

$$x^2 + y^2 = r^2.$$

(See Fig. 1–6.)

PROBLEMS

In Problems 1 through 6, a particle moves in the plane from A to B. Point C is to be found at the intersection of the horizontal line through A and the vertical line through B. Sketch, and find

a) the coordinates of C **b)** Δx **c)** Δy

d) the length of AB under the assumption that the x-axis and y-axis have the same units.

1. $A(-1, 1)$, $B(1, 2)$ **2.** $A(1, 2)$, $B(-1, -1)$

3. $A(-3, 2)$, $B(-1, -2)$ **4.** $A(-1, -2)$, $B(-3, 2)$

5. $A(-3, 1)$, $B(-8, 1)$ **6.** $A(0, 4)$, $B(0, -2)$

In Problems 7 through 10, write an equation that must be satisfied by the coordinates of a point $P(x, y)$ if P is to lie on the circle of radius 5 whose center is at the given point. It may help to sketch the circle first.

7. $(0, 0)$ **8.** $(5, 0)$ **9.** $(-3, 4)$ **10.** (h, k)

11. If a particle starts at $A(-2, 3)$ and its coordinates change by increments $\Delta x = 5$, $\Delta y = -6$, what will its new position be?

12. The coordinates of a particle change by $\Delta x = 5$ and $\Delta y = 6$ in moving from $A(x, y)$ to $B(3, -3)$. Find x and y.

13. Find the starting position of a particle whose terminal position is $B(u, v)$ after its coordinates have changed by increments $\Delta x = h$, and $\Delta y = k$.

14. A particle moves from the point $A(-2, 5)$ to the y-axis in such a way that $\Delta y = 3\Delta x$. What are its new coordinates?

15. A particle moves along the parabola $y = x^2$ from the point $A(1, 1)$ to the point $B(x, y)$. Sketch the parabola and show that

$$\frac{\Delta y}{\Delta x} = x + 1 \quad \text{if } \Delta x \neq 0.$$

1–4 SLOPE OF A STRAIGHT LINE

Lines in the coordinate plane rise or fall at a steady rate as we move along them from left to right, unless, of course, they are horizontal or vertical. Horizontal lines do not rise or fall at all, and on a vertical line one cannot move from left to right. The rate of rise or fall as we move from left to right along a line is called the *slope* of the line. We measure slopes in such a way that rising lines have positive slopes, falling lines have negative slopes, and horizontal lines slope 0. Vertical lines are not assigned any slope.

To begin, let L be a line in the plane that is not parallel to the y-axis, and let $P_1(x_1, y_1)$ and $P_2(x_2, y_2)$ be any two distinct points on L (see Fig. 1–7). As we move along L from P_1 to P_2, the increment $\Delta y = y_2 - y_1$ is called the *rise* from P_1 to P_2. The increment $\Delta x = x_2 - x_1$ is called the *run* from P_1 to P_2. Since L is not vertical, $\Delta x \neq 0$, and we define the *slope* of L to be

$$\frac{\text{rise}}{\text{run}} = \frac{\Delta y}{\Delta x} = \frac{y_2 - y_1}{x_2 - x_1} = m. \tag{1}$$

It is traditional to use the letter m to denote slope.

Figure 1–7 shows both Δx and Δy to be positive, but either one, or both, could be negative, depending on the inclination of L and on the choice of P_1 and P_2. However, the ratio $\Delta y/\Delta x$ of these two quantities does not depend on how we choose P_1 and P_2 from L. It depends only on the inclination of L. There are two reasons for this:

1. When we choose the two points P_1 and P_2 from L it does not matter which we call P_1 and which we call P_2. If we interchange the labels P_1 and

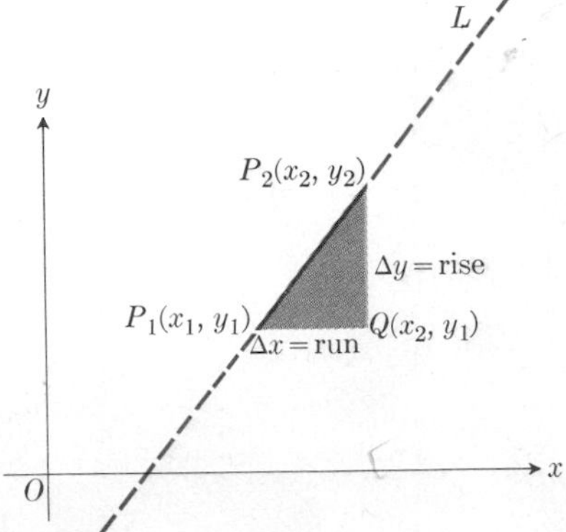

1–7 The slope of this line is $\Delta y/\Delta x = m$.

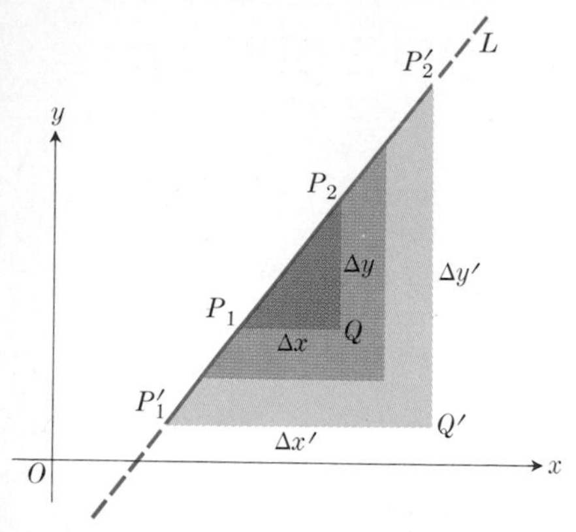

1–8 $\Delta y/\Delta x = \Delta y'/\Delta x'$ because the ratios of corresponding sides of similar triangles are equal.

P_2 the number we calculate as m is the same as before, because

$$\frac{y_1 - y_2}{x_1 - x_2} = \frac{y_2 - y_1}{x_2 - x_1}. \tag{2}$$

2. If we start with any other two points from L, say $P_1'(x_1', y_1')$ and $P_2'(x_2', y_2')$, the number m' we get for the slope is the same as m. Why? Because the triangles P_1QP_2 and $P_1'Q'P_2'$ in Fig. 1–8 are similar. Thus,

$$m' = \frac{\Delta y'}{\Delta x'} = \frac{\Delta y}{\Delta x} = m. \tag{3}$$

EXAMPLE 1. The slope of the line through the points $P_1(1, 2)$ and $P_2(3, 8)$ in Fig. 1–9 is

$$m = \frac{8-2}{3-1} = 3.$$

If we take P_2 first and P_1 second, we obtain

$$m = \frac{2-8}{1-3} = \frac{-6}{-2} = 3,$$

the same as before.

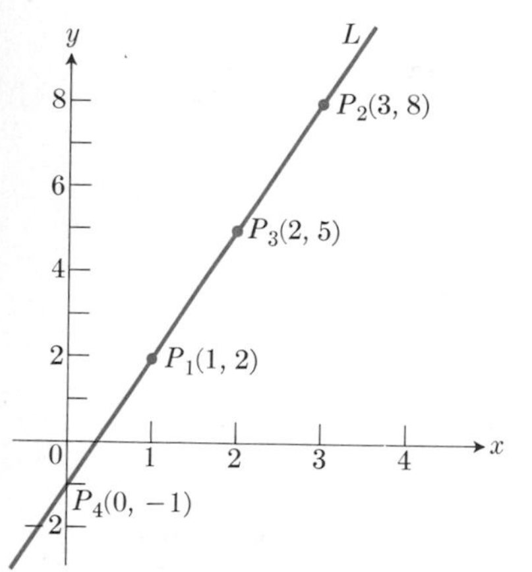

1–9 $\Delta y = 3\,\Delta x$ for every change of position on this line.

REMARK. If we multiply both sides of the equation $\Delta y/\Delta x = m$ by Δx, we obtain

$$\Delta y = m\,\Delta x. \tag{4}$$

This means that as a particle moves along L, the change in y is proportional to the change in x. The slope m is the proportionality factor. The slope is the rate of rise per unit of run. To compute the amount of rise, multiply the slope by the amount of run.

EXAMPLE 2. If (x, y) and $(x + \Delta x, y + \Delta y)$ are any two points on the line L in Fig. 1–9, then

$$\Delta y = 3\,\Delta x.$$

Starting from $P_1(1, 2)$, if we increase x by 1 unit we increase y by 3 units, bringing us to the point $P_3(2, 5)$. Or, if we decrease x by 1 unit, we *decrease* y by 3 units, taking us to $P_4(0, -1)$.

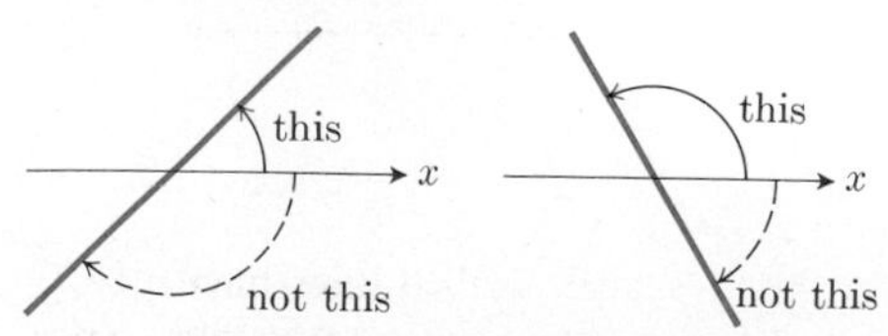

1–10 Angles of inclination.

The *angle of inclination* of a line that crosses the x-axis is the smallest positive angle that the line makes with the positively directed x-axis (Fig. 1–10). (Positive angles are measured counterclockwise.) The angle of inclination of a line that does not cross the x-axis is 0. Thus, angles of inclination may have any measure from 0° up to but not including 180°.

Slopes and angles of inclination are related in the following way. The slope of a nonvertical line is the tangent of its angle of inclination:

$$m = \tan \phi. \tag{5}$$

(See Fig. 1–11.)

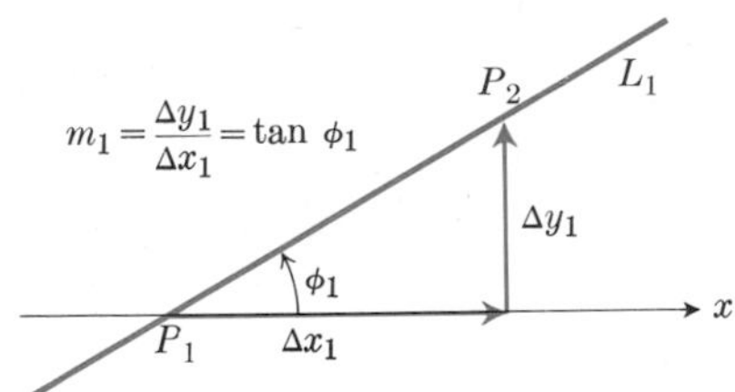

Both Δx_1 and Δy_1 are positive, so m_1 is positive.

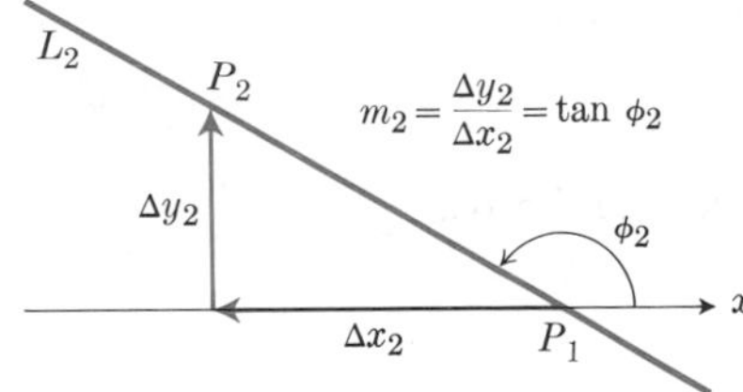

Here, Δx_2 is negative but Δy_2 is positive. Therefore, m_2 is negative.

1–11 In each picture m is $\tan \phi$.

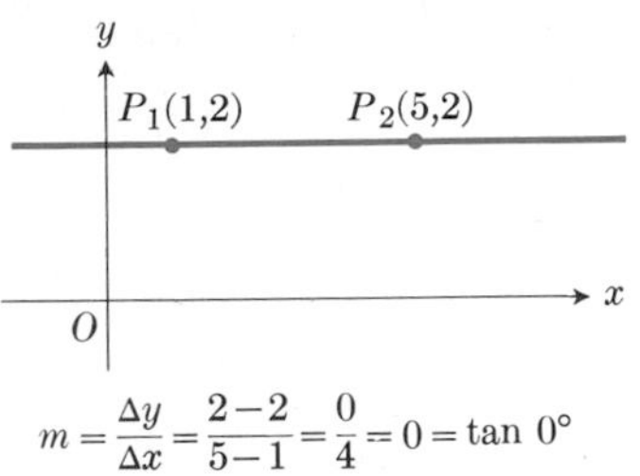

Figure 1–12

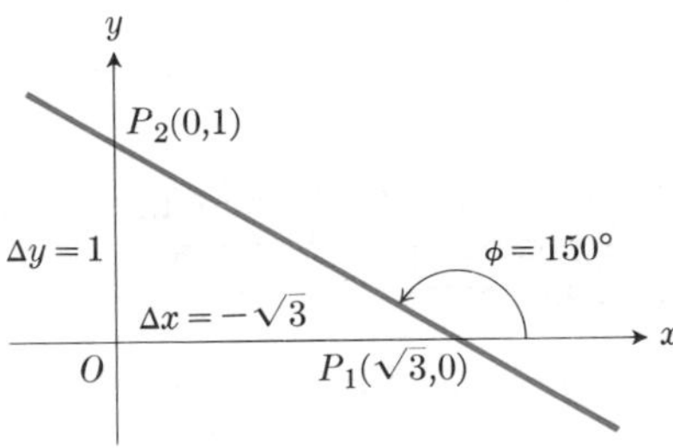

Figure 1–13

EXAMPLE 3. Figures 1–12 and 1–13 give numerical examples of Eq. (5).

Lines whose inclination angles are near 90° have slopes that are numerically very large.

$$\phi_1 = 89°59' \qquad m_1 = \tan \phi_1 \approx 3437.7$$

$$\phi_2 = 90°01' \qquad m_2 = \tan \phi_2 \approx -3437.7$$

In fact we can make the slope numerically larger than any preassigned number N by taking ϕ still closer to 90°. This point is sometimes summarized by saying that "a vertical line has infinite slope," or "the slope of a line becomes infinite as its angle of inclination approaches 90°." But, strictly speaking, we do not assign *any* real number to be the slope of a *vertical* line.

The symbol ∞ is used to represent "infinity." However, we do not use this symbol in arithmetic in the ordinary way. Infinity is not a real number. We used the phrase "becomes infinite" in the preceding paragraph only as a way to say "outgrows every preassigned real number."

Parallel lines have equal angles of inclination. Hence, in general, they have equal slopes (Fig. 1–14). The only exception is when the parallel lines are vertical, for then they have no slope at all (Fig. 1–15). [*Caution.* This does not mean that they have zero slope.]

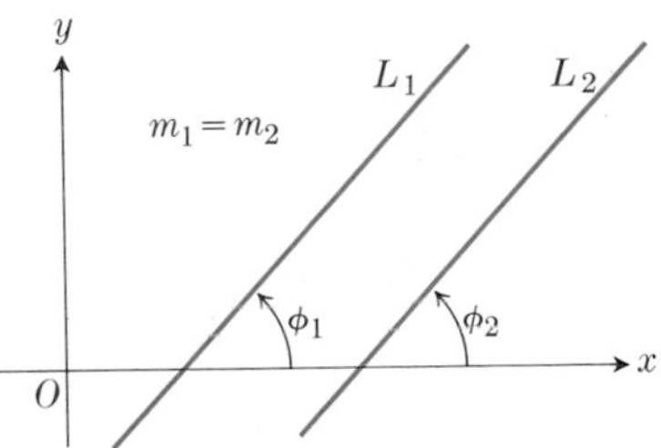

1–14 When parallel lines are not vertical, they have the same slope, $\tan \phi$.

Two lines that have equal slopes $m_1 = \tan \phi_1$ and $m_2 = \tan \phi_2$ also have equal angles of inclination. The reason is this: If

$$\tan \phi_1 = \tan \phi_2 \tag{6}$$

and

$$0 \le \phi_1 < 180°, \qquad 0 \le \phi_2 < 180°, \tag{7}$$

then $\phi_1 = \phi_2$.

When two nonvertical lines are *perpendicular*, their slopes m_1 and m_2 are related by the equation

$$m_1 = -\frac{1}{m_2} \qquad \text{or} \qquad m_1 m_2 = -1. \tag{8}$$

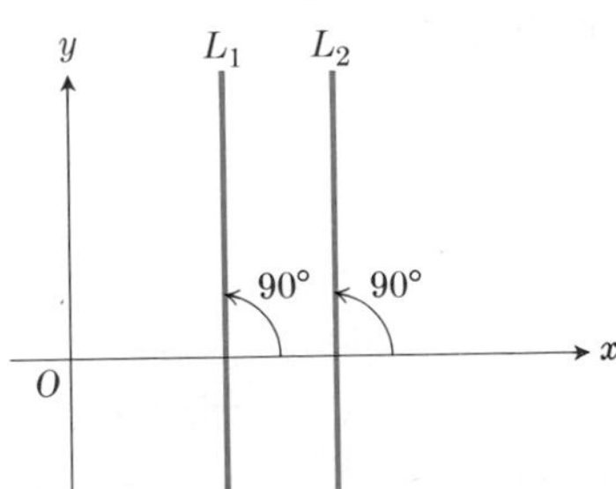

1–15 Parallel vertical lines have equal angles of inclination, but no slope. Note that $\tan \phi$ is not defined when $\phi = 90°$.

To see why, note that the angles of inclination of the lines differ by 90°, so that

$$\phi_2 = 90° + \phi_1,$$

as shown in Fig. 1–16. (If not, just renumber the lines.) This lets us write m_2 as

$$m_2 = \tan \phi_2 = \tan (90° + \phi_1) = -\cot \phi_1 = -\frac{1}{\tan \phi_1} = -\frac{1}{m_1}.$$

The argument can be reversed to show that two lines whose slopes satisfy Eq. (8) have angles of inclination that differ by 90°.

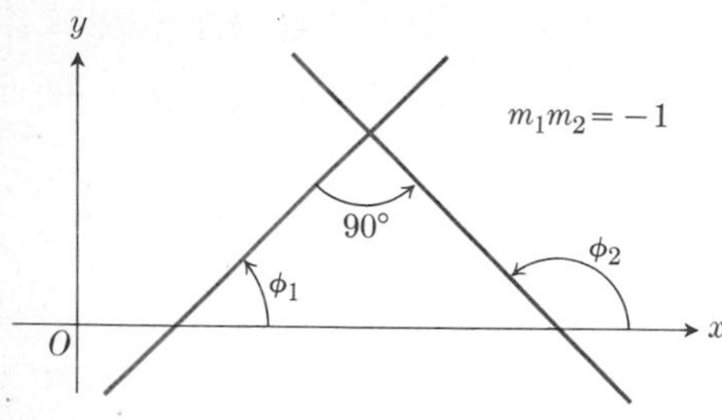

1–16 The exterior angle theorem of geometry says that $\phi_2 = 90° + \phi_1$ in this figure. This in turn means that $m_1m_2 = -1$, as explained in the text.

PROBLEMS

Plot the given points A and B, and find the slope (if any) of the line determined by them. Find the slope of a line perpendicular to AB, in each case.

1. $A(1, -2), B(2, 1)$ **2.** $A(-2, -1), B(1, -2)$

3. $A(1, 0), B(0, 1)$ **4.** $A(-1, 0), B(1, 0)$

5. $A(2, 3), B(-1, 3)$ **6.** $A(1, 2), B(1, -3)$

7. $A(0, 0), B(-2, -4)$ **8.** $A(\frac{1}{2}, 0), B(0, -\frac{1}{3})$

9. $A(0, 0), B(x, y)$ $(x \neq 0, y \neq 0)$

10. $A(0, 0), B(x, 0)$ $(x \neq 0)$

11. $A(0, 0), B(0, y)$ $(y \neq 0)$

12. $A(a, 0), B(0, b)$ $(a \neq 0, b \neq 0)$

In Problems 13–16, plot the points A, B, C, and D. Then determine whether or not $ABCD$ is a parallelogram. Say which parallelograms are rectangles.

13. $A(0, 1), B(1, 2), C(2, 1), D(1, 0)$

14. $A(-2, 2), B(1, 3), C(2, 0), D(-1, -1)$

15. $A(-1, -2), B(2, -1), C(2, 1), D(1, 0)$

16. $A(-1, 0), B(0, -1), C(2, 0), D(0, 2)$

Answer the next two questions by measuring slopes in Fig. 1–17.

17. Find the rate of change of temperature in degrees per inch for:

a) gypsum wall board **b)** fiberglass insulation

c) wood sheathing

18. Which of the materials just listed is the best insulator? the poorest? Explain.

19. The line through the origin and $P(x, y)$ has slope $+2$, and the line through $(-1, 0)$ and $P(x, y)$ has slope $+1$. Find x and y.

20. Sketch the line L that passes through the origin with slope $-\frac{1}{2}$. Show that if $P(x, y)$ lies on L, then $y = -(x/2)$.

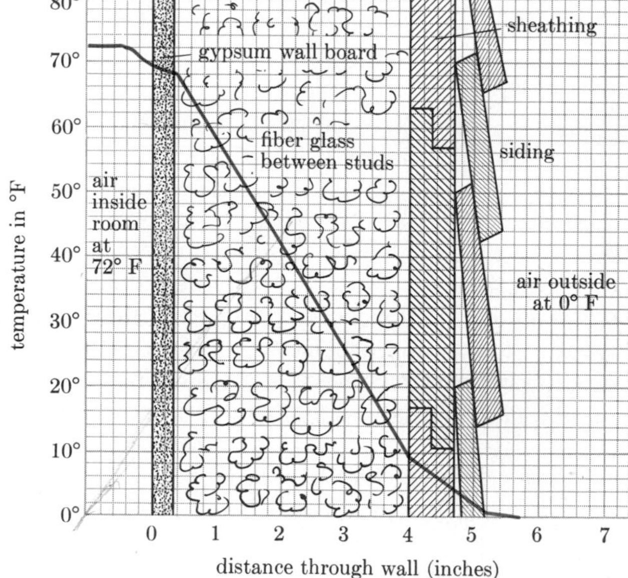

1–17 Temperature gradients in a wall. (*Source: Differentiation*, by W. U. Walton *et al.*, Project CALC, Education Development Center, Inc., Newton, Mass. (1975); p. 25.)

In Problems 21–23, use slopes to determine whether the given points are collinear (lie on a common straight line).

21. $A(1, 0), B(0, 1), C(2, -1)$

22. $A(-2, 1), B(0, 5), C(-1, 2)$

23. $A(-2, 1), B(-1, 1), C(1, 5), D(2, 7)$

24. Let $P_1(x_1, y_1)$ and $P_2(x_2, y_2)$ be two points. Find the coordinates of the midpoint of the segment P_1P_2.

EQUATIONS OF STRAIGHT LINES

We continue the development of analytic geometry in this article by finding equations for lines in the coordinate plane. An *equation for a line* is an equation that is satisfied by the coordinates of the points that lie on the line and is not satisfied by the coordinates of the points that lie elsewhere. Lines that have slopes and lines that do not have slopes will be treated separately.

We start with a line L that is perpendicular to the x-axis at $(x_1, 0)$. Every point on L has its first coordinate equal to x_1. Its second coordinate can be any number. In other words, the coordinates of the points (x, y) that lie on L all satisfy the equation

$$x = x_1. \tag{1}$$

(See Fig. 1–18.) To check that $x = x_1$ is an equation for L, it remains to show that the points of the plane that are not on L have first coordinates different from x_1. They all do, because the perpendiculars from these points to the x-axis do not cross the axis at x_1.

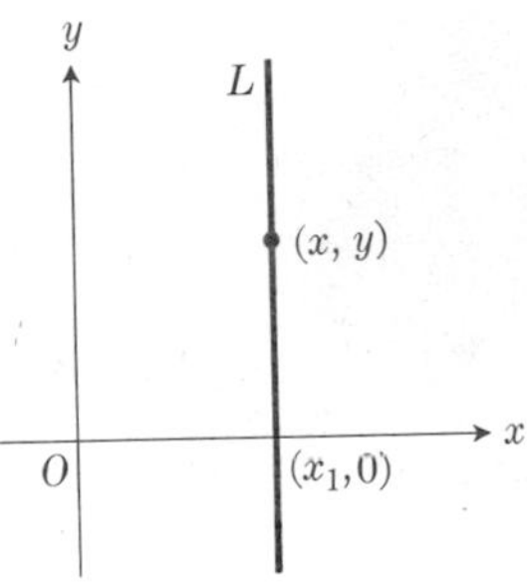

1–18 $x = x_1$ is an equation for the vertical line through the point $(x_1, 0)$.

To write an equation for a line L that is not vertical, we may start with its slope m, together with the coordinates of a point $P_1(x_1, y_1)$ on L. If $P(x, y)$ is any other point of L, then we can write the slope of L as

$$\frac{y - y_1}{x - x_1} = m, \tag{2}$$

or

$$y - y_1 = m(x - x_1). \tag{3}$$

(See Fig. 1–19.) If $P(x, y)$ coincides with $P_1(x_1, y_1)$ then its coordinates still satisfy Eq. (3). Thus the coordinates of all the points that lie on L satisfy Eq. (3). If $P(x, y)$ is a point not on L, then the slope of PP_1 is different from m. This means that the coordinates x and y of P do not satisfy Eq. (2), and therefore do not satisfy Eq. (3). It follows that Eq. (3) is an equation for L.

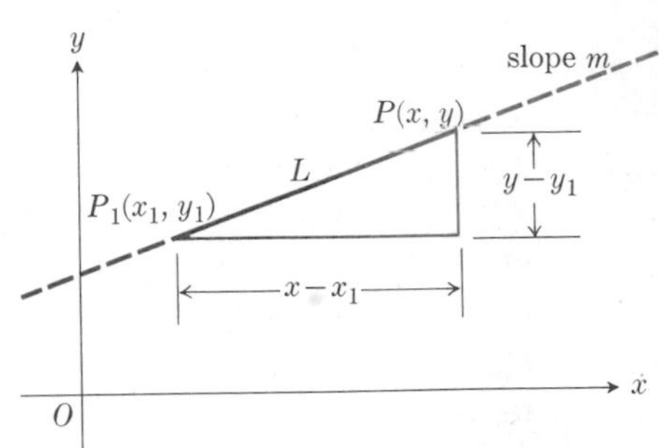

1–19 L is the line through $P_1(x_1, y_1)$ whose slope is m. A point $P(x, y)$ lies on L if and only if $P = P_1$ or slope $PP_1 = m$.

EXAMPLE 1. Write an equation for the line through $(-2, -1)$ and $(3, 4)$.

Solution. The slope of the line is

$$\frac{4 - (-1)}{3 - (-2)} = \frac{5}{5} = 1.$$

Either of the given points $(-2, -1)$ or $(3, 4)$ will serve as the point (x_1, y_1) in Eq. (3), as shown below:

Using (3, 4) we obtain	Using (−2, −1) we obtain
$y - 4 = 1 \cdot (x - 3)$,	$y - (-1) = 1 \cdot (x - (-2))$,
$y - 4 = x - 3$	$y + 1 = x + 2$,
$y = x + 1$.	$y = x + 1$.

We get the same equation no matter which point we use. The line is shown in Fig. 1–20.

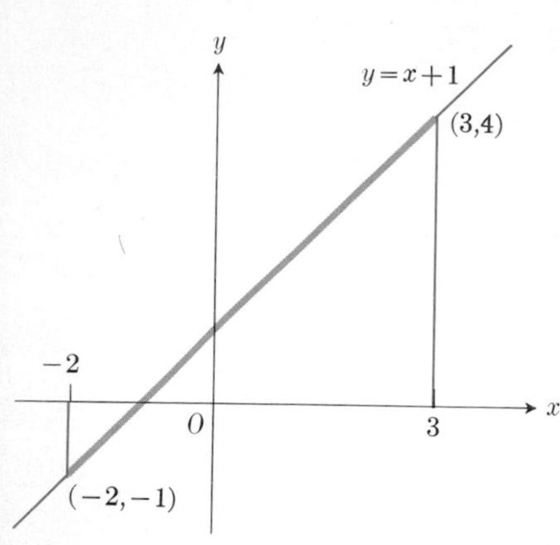

1–20 The line $y = x + 1$. The segment corresponding to $-2 \leq x \leq 3$ is shaded.

Equation (3) is called the *point–slope* form of the equation of the line, since it gives the equation in terms of one point $P_1(x_1, y_1)$ on the line and the slope m. The three numbers x_1, y_1, and m are constants, while x and y are variables. By a *variable* we mean a symbol, such as x, which may take any value in some set of numbers. In Eq. (3), x may take any real value whatever. As x varies continuously from a negative value $-N$ to a positive value $+M$, the corresponding point $P(x, y)$ traces an unbroken portion of the line from left to right.

When we solve Eq. (3) for y we find that

$$y = mx + b, \tag{4}$$

where m is the slope of the line and b is $y_1 - mx_1$, which is a constant. In fact, $(0, b)$ is the point where the line crosses the y-axis (Fig. 1–21). The number b is called the *y-intercept* of the line, and Eq. (4) is called the *slope–intercept equation* of the line.

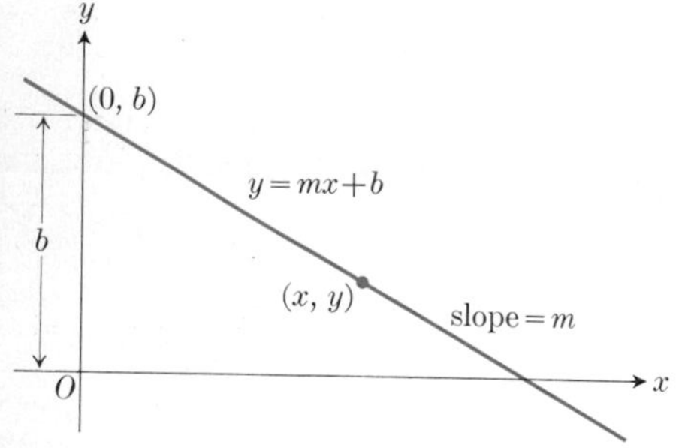

1–21 The line $y = mx + b$ has slope m and y-intercept b.

EXAMPLE 2. The slope–intercept equation of the line

$$y - 7 = 5(x + 4)$$

is

$$y = 5x + 27.$$

The slope is $m = 5$ and the intercept is $b = 27$.

For a horizontal line, the equation $y = mx + b$ reduces to $y = 0 \cdot x + b$, or

$$y = b.$$

EXAMPLE 3. The equation $y = -5$ is the slope–intercept equation of the line that passes through $(0, -5)$ with slope $m = 0$.

More generally, an equation

$$Ax + By + C = 0, \tag{5}$$

where A, B, and C are constants with at least one of A and B different from zero, represents a *straight line.*

$$\text{If } B = 0, \quad \text{then } Ax + C = 0 \quad \text{and } x = -\frac{C}{A},$$

and the line is a vertical line, as in Eq. (1). On the other hand,

$$\text{if } B \neq 0, \quad \text{then } y = -\frac{A}{B}x - \frac{C}{B},$$

and this represents a straight line with

$$m = -\frac{A}{B}, \qquad b = -\frac{C}{B}.$$

An equation like (5) that contains only first powers of x and y is said to be "linear in x and in y." Thus we may summarize our discussion by saying

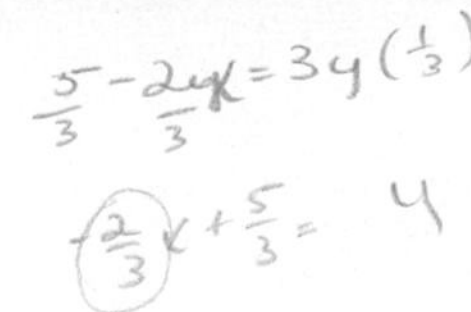

that every straight line in the plane is represented by a linear equation and, conversely, every linear equation represents a straight line.

EXAMPLE 4. Find the slope of the line $2x + 3y = 5$.

Solution. By solving $2x + 3y = 5$ for y, we obtain the slope–intercept form $y = -\frac{2}{3}x + \frac{5}{3}$. The slope is $m = -\frac{2}{3}$.

Lines that cross both axes have nonzero slopes, and, if they do not pass through the origin, so that $b \neq 0$, dividing both sides of $y = mx + b$ by b leads to an equation of the form

$$\frac{x}{a} + \frac{y}{b} = 1, \tag{6}$$

where $a = -b/m$. When $x = 0$, Eq. (6) simplifies to $y = b$, the y-intercept. When $y = 0$, Eq. (6) simplifies to $x = a$, the x-intercept. We call Eq. (6) the *two-intercept equation* of the line.

EXAMPLE 5. The line through $(-3, 0)$ and $(0, 4)$ has x-intercept $a = -3$ and y-intercept $b = 4$. The two-intercept equation of the line is

$$\frac{x}{-3} + \frac{y}{4} = 1.$$

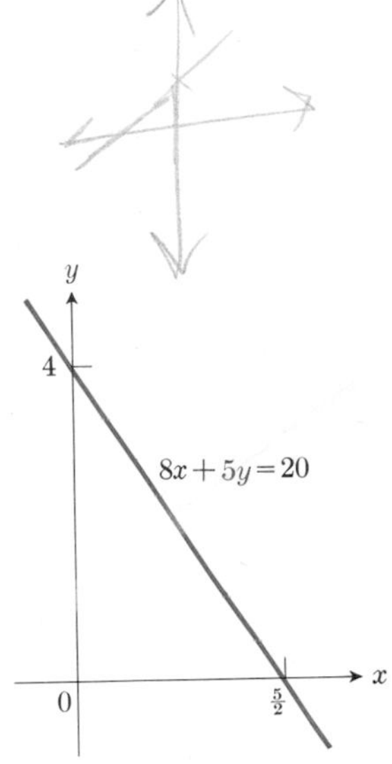

1–22 To draw this graph, the intercepts were located first.

A quick way to graph a line that crosses both axes is this: Find the intercepts, mark them on the axes, and sketch the line through the marked points.

EXAMPLE 6. Graph the line $8x + 5y = 20$.

Solution. Find the x-intercept: Set $y = 0$ in the equation to obtain $8x = 20$, or $x = \frac{5}{2}$. Find the y-intercept: Set $x = 0$ in the equation to obtain $5y = 20$, or $y = 4$. Then mark the intercepts on a pair of axes and sketch the line (Fig. 1–22).

EXAMPLE 7. (*Demand*) The demand for a product, x (number of units sold), and the price p per unit of the product are sometimes related by a linear equation of the form

$$\frac{x}{x_0} + \frac{p}{p_0} = 1, \tag{7}$$

where x_0 and p_0 are constants. The equation is the *demand law* for the product. The graph of the equation, in this case the line in Fig. 1–23, is called the *demand curve*.

The quantities x and p are never negative in their economic context. Therefore, only the points from $(x_0, 0)$ to $(0, p_0)$ on the graph of Eq. (7) have coordinates with economic meaning. The intercepts x_0 and p_0 can have the following interpretations. The demand x_0 is the demand for a "free" product,

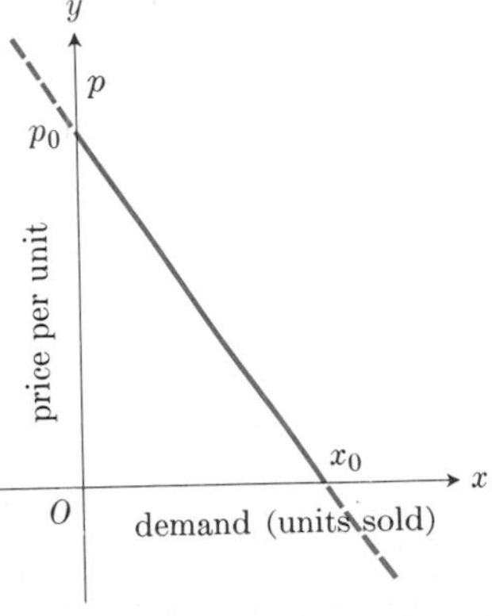

1–23 The graph of a demand law shows how consumer demand responds to different prices of a product.

because it corresponds to $p = 0$. The demand disappears at the price p_0. (See Problem 19.)

Table 1–1 summarizes the representative equations for straight lines, including vertical and horizontal lines.

Table 1–1 Equations of lines

$Ax + By + C = 0$	Linear equation (general form)
$y - y_1 = m(x - x_1)$	Point–slope equation
$y = mx + b$	Slope–intercept equation
$\frac{x}{a} + \frac{y}{b} = 1$	Two-intercept equation
$x = a$	Vertical line
$y = b$	Horizontal line

PROBLEMS

In each of the following problems (1 through 10), plot the given pair of points and find an equation for the line determined by them.

1. (0, 0), (2, 3) **2.** (1, 1), (2, 1)
3. (1, 1), (1, 2) **4.** (−2, 1), (2, −2)
5. (−2, 0), (−2, −2) **6.** (1, 3), (3, 1)
7. $(a, 0), (0, b)$ $(a \neq 0, b \neq 0)$
8. (0, 0), (1, 0) **9.** (0, 0), (0, 1)
10. (2, −1), (−2, 3)

In each of the following problems (11 through 18), find the slope and intercepts of the line. Then graph the line.

11. $y = 3x + 5$ **12.** $2y = 3x + 5$
13. $x + y = 2$ **14.** $2x - y = 4$
15. $x - 2y = 4$ **16.** $3x + 4y = 12$
17. $4x - 3y = 12$ **18.** $x = 2y - 5$

19. The demand law $x + 6p = 20$ gives the relation between the wholesale price p of coffee (dollars per pound) and the number of pounds x consumed per person in the United States from 1960 through 1974.* [See Example 7.]

a) Write the law in two-intercept form and sketch the demand curve.

b) At what price does the demand law predict that the demand for coffee will disappear? What would the consumption be if coffee were free?

c) In 1974, U.S. coffee consumption was 12.8 pounds per person. What was the wholesale price?

d) What consumption does the law predict for a wholesale price of \$1.30 per pound? (This was the U.S. consumption at that price in 1975.)

20. Find the line that passes through the point (1, 2) and is parallel to the line $x + 2y = 3$.

21. a) Find the line L through $A(-2, 2)$ and perpendicular to the line

$$L': 2x + y = 4.$$

b) Find the point B where the lines L and L' of part (a) intersect.

c) Using the result of part (b), find the distance from the point A to the line L' of part (a).

22. Find the line through (1, 4) and having angle of inclination $\phi = 60°$.

23. Find the angle of inclination of the line $2x + y = 4$.

24. The pressure p experienced by a diver under water is proportional to the depth d. In sea water the pressure at $d = 100$ meters is approximately 10.42 atmospheres.

a) Write an equation for p in terms of d.

b) What is the pressure 50 meters below the surface?

25. A ray of light comes in along the line $x + y = 1$ above the x-axis and reflects off the x-axis. Write an equation for its new path.

26. The carbon steel used in railroad track expands when heated. For the temperatures normally encountered in use, the length ℓ of a piece of track is related to the temperature t by a linear equation. To express ℓ in terms of t, two mea-

---

* Based on U.S. Department of Commerce figures. See *The U.S. Fact Book*, an unabridged edition of *The Statistical Abstract of the United States*, Grosset and Dunlap, Publishers, New York (1977), pp. 95 and 437.

surements are taken:

$$\ell_1 = 35 \text{ ft}, \qquad t_1 = 65°\text{F}$$

$$\ell_2 = 35.16 \text{ ft}, \qquad t_2 = 135°\text{F}$$

Write a linear equation for ℓ and t.

27. The perpendicular distance ON between the origin and the line L is p, and ON makes an angle α with the positive x-axis. Show that L has equation $x \cos \alpha + y \sin \alpha = p$.

28. If A, B, C, C' are constants, and not both A and B are zero, show that (a) the lines

$$Ax + By + C = 0, \qquad Ax + By + C' = 0,$$

either coincide or are parallel, and that (b) the lines

$$Ax + By + C = 0, \qquad Bx - Ay + C' = 0,$$

are perpendicular.

1–6 FUNCTIONS AND GRAPHS

We begin this article by describing sets of values that are typical of those taken on by variables in calculus.

Intervals

The set of values that a variable x may take on is called the *domain* of x. The domains of the variables in many applications of calculus are intervals like those shown in Fig. 1–24. An *open* interval is the set of all real numbers that lie *strictly between* two fixed numbers a and b:

In symbols			In words
$a < x < b$	or	(a, b)	"The open interval a b"

Closed intervals contain both endpoints:

In symbols			In words
$a \le x \le b$	or	$[a, b]$	"The closed interval a b"

Half-open intervals contain one but not both endpoints:

In symbols			In words
$a \le x < b$	or	$[a, b)$	"The interval a less than or equal to x less than b"
$a < x \le b$	or	$(a, b]$	"The interval a less than x less than or equal to b"

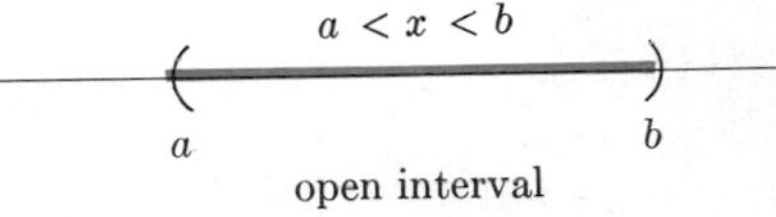

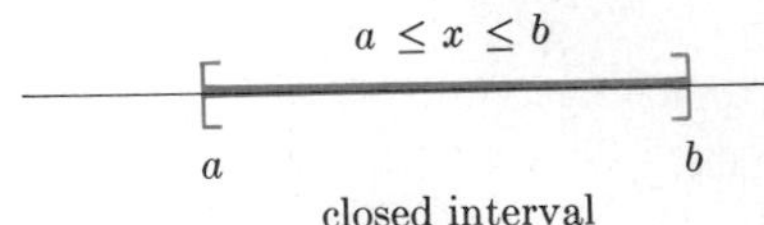

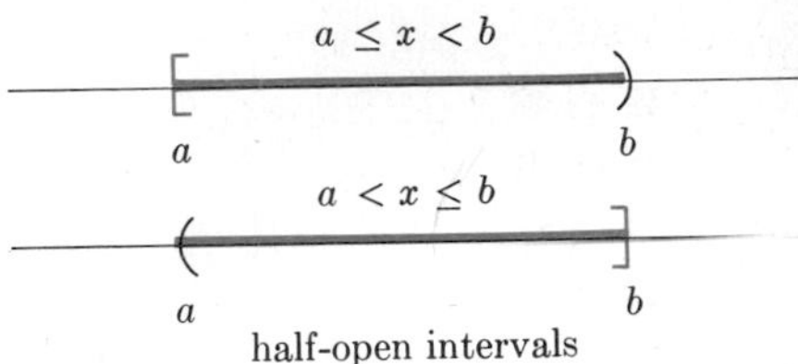

Figure 1–24

EXAMPLE 1. If both x and y are to be real variables in the expression

$$y = \sqrt{1 - x^2},$$

then x^2 must not be greater than 1, because the square root of a negative number is not a real number. The appropriate domain for x is the closed interval $-1 \le x \le 1$.

EXAMPLE 2. If x and y are to be real variables in the expression

$$y = \frac{1}{\sqrt{1 - x^2}},$$

then x must be further restricted to the open interval $-1 < x < 1$ because $1/0$ is not a number.

EXAMPLE 3. If x and y are to be real variables and

$$y = \sqrt{\frac{1}{x} - 1},$$

then $(1/x) - 1 \geq 0$ or $(1/x) \geq 1$. That is, x must be positive and less than or equal to 1. Therefore, the largest possible domain for x is the half-open interval $0 < x \leq 1$.

The domains of variables are sometimes unbounded sets, like the set of real numbers, or the set of nonnegative numbers, or the set of numbers less than 3. We can describe these sets with inequalities too, as in the next example.

EXAMPLE 4

Equation	Largest possible domain if x and y are to be real variables
$y = x^2$	$-\infty < x < \infty$
$y = \sqrt{x}$	$0 \leq x$
$y = \dfrac{1}{\sqrt{3 - x}}$	$x < 3$

Sets like these are sometimes called "infinite" intervals.

Some domains are unions of intervals.

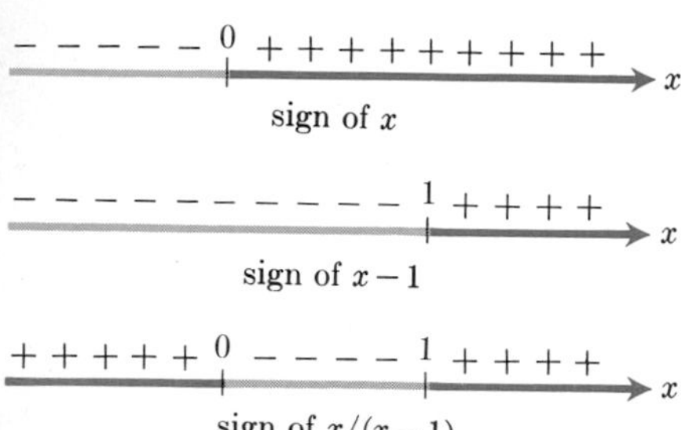

EXAMPLE 5. The value of $y = \sqrt{x/(x-1)}$ is real if x takes on any value in the union of the infinite intervals $x \leq 0$ and $x > 1$, as we shall now show.

The fraction under the square-root sign is zero when $x = 0$, and it is undefined when $x = 1$. An easy way to determine the sign of the fraction for the other values of x is shown at the left.

Functions

In calculus we are interested in how variables are related. We want to know, for example, how the distance an object travels is related to its speed; or how the concentration of a medicine in the bloodstream is related to the length of time between doses; or how the number of rabbits in an arctic predator–prey food chain depends on the number of foxes. There is an especially important kind of relation between two variables that we call a *function*. The key idea of a function is that as soon as we choose a value for the first variable, the corresponding value of the second variable is then determined. In other words, a function pairs the values of the variables together in such a way that each value of the first variable is paired with *exactly one* value of the second variable.

Definition. *A function is a set of ordered pairs of numbers (x, y) with the following property: To each value of the first variable (x) there corresponds a unique value of the second variable (y).*

EXAMPLE 6. Let the domain of x be the set $\{0, 1, 2, 3, 4\}$. Assign to each value of x the number $y = x^2$. The function so defined is the set of pairs

$$\{(0, 0), \quad (1, 1), \quad (2, 4), \quad (3, 9), \quad (4, 16)\}.$$

EXAMPLE 7. Let the domain of x be the closed interval $-2 \le x \le 2$. Assign to each value of x the number $y = x^2$. The set of ordered pairs (x, y) such that $-2 \le x \le 2$ and $y = x^2$ is a function. We can also describe the function with set-builder notation:

$$\{(x, y) \mid -2 \le x \le 2, \ y = x^2\}. \qquad (1)$$

The outside braces denote "set," (x, y) denotes the typical element of the set, and the vertical bar is read "such that." The statement after the bar is the condition or rule the typical element must satisfy to qualify for membership in the set. We often use this notation when the elements in a set are too numerous to list individually. The basic idea is still present: When a value is assigned to the first variable x, the corresponding value of the second variable y is then determined. In this case, $y = x^2$. If x is $\frac{1}{3}$, then $y = \frac{1}{9}$. The pair $(\frac{1}{3}, \frac{1}{9})$ belongs to the function.

The next example shows how to describe functions without set-builder notation. Every function is determined by two things: (1) *the domain* of the first variable x and (2) *the rule* or condition that the pairs (x, y) must satisfy to belong to the function. We can therefore describe a function completely by giving its domain and rule.

EXAMPLE 8

Function	Name
The function whose domain is the set $-2 \le x \le 2$ and that pairs with each value of x the number $y = x^2$.	The function $y = x^2, \quad -2 \le x \le 2$
The function that pairs with each value of x different from 2 the number $x/(x - 2)$.	The function $y = \dfrac{x}{x-2}, \quad x \ne 2$

Graphs

The set of points in the plane whose coordinate pairs are also the ordered pairs of a function is called the *graph* of the function. The next example shows how to sketch such a graph. The process of sketching the graph of a function is called *graphing* the function.

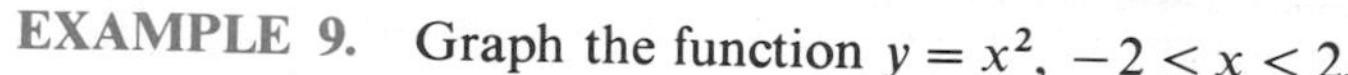

EXAMPLE 9. Graph the function $y = x^2$, $-2 \leq x \leq 2$.

Solution. To graph a function we carry out three steps.

1. Make a table of pairs from the function, as in Table 1–2.

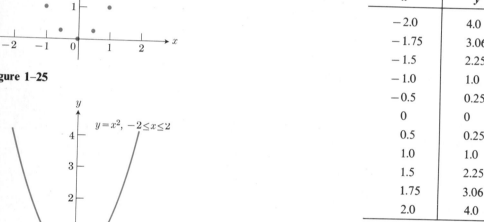

Table 1–2.

x	y
−2.0	4.0
−1.75	3.06
−1.5	2.25
−1.0	1.0
−0.5	0.25
0	0
0.5	0.25
1.0	1.0
1.5	2.25
1.75	3.06
2.0	4.0

2. Plot enough of the corresponding points to learn the shape of the graph. Add more pairs to the table if necessary (Fig. 1–25).

3. Complete the sketch by connecting the points (Fig. 1–26).

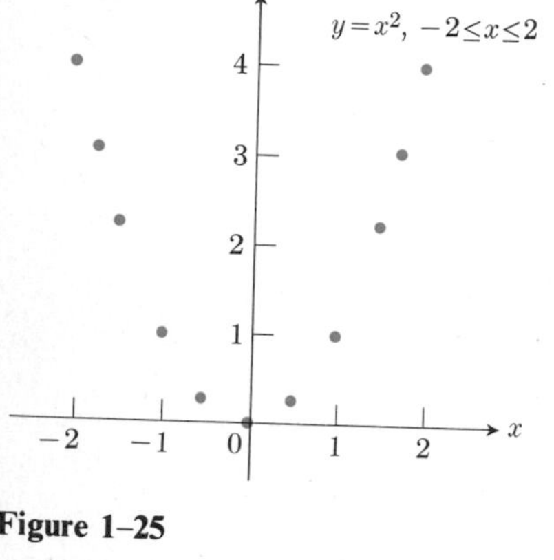

Figure 1–25

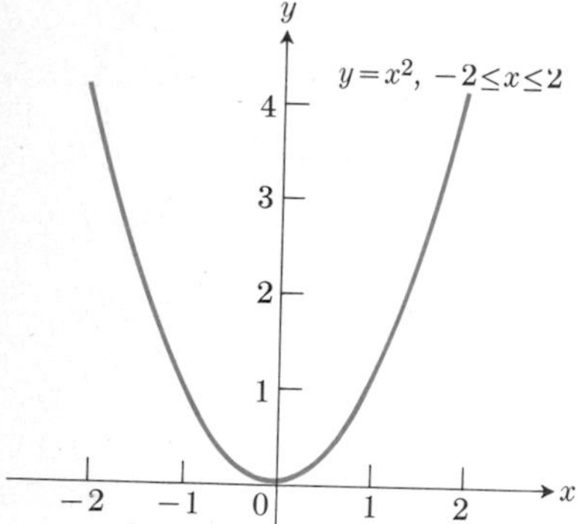

Figure 1–26

Here is some more terminology associated with functions. The variable x which generates the first of the two numbers in the ordered pairs (x, y) of a function is called the *independent variable* or *argument* of the function. The second variable y is called the *dependent variable*. The y-value that corresponds to a particular x-value is called the *image* of that x-value. We say that the function *maps* the x-value to its image. The domain of the independent variable x is called the *domain* of the function. The set of values taken on by the dependent variable y is the *range* of the function. The range is the image of the domain.

EXAMPLE 10. *The function* $y = 1/x$, $x \neq 0$. The domain of this function is the set of all real numbers different from 0. The image of each number in the domain is the reciprocal of the number. The pairs of the function all have the form $(x, 1/x)$. Table 1–3 shows some of the pairs. The range of the function is also the set of all numbers different from 0. Because the domain and range are infinite we cannot show the entire graph. We sketch just enough to show the behavior of the function. We refer to the sketch as the graph of the function, even though it is incomplete. It is conventional to do that (Fig. 1–27).

Table 1–3. Values of $y = 1/x$ for selected values of x

x	$\pm\frac{1}{10}$	$\pm\frac{1}{3}$	$\pm\sqrt{2}$	± 2
$y = \dfrac{1}{x}$	± 10	± 3	$\pm\dfrac{1}{\sqrt{2}}$	$\pm\frac{1}{2}$

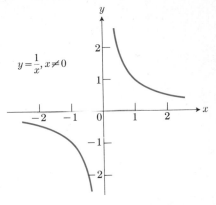

1–27 The graph of $y = 1/x$, $x \neq 0$.

EXAMPLE 11. *The function* $y = \sqrt{x}$, $x \geq 0$. This function maps every nonnegative number x to the number $\sqrt{x}$.

Pairs:	$(x, \sqrt{x})$	Graph:	Fig. 1–28
Domain:	$x \geq 0$	Range:	$y \geq 0$

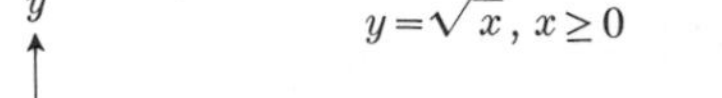

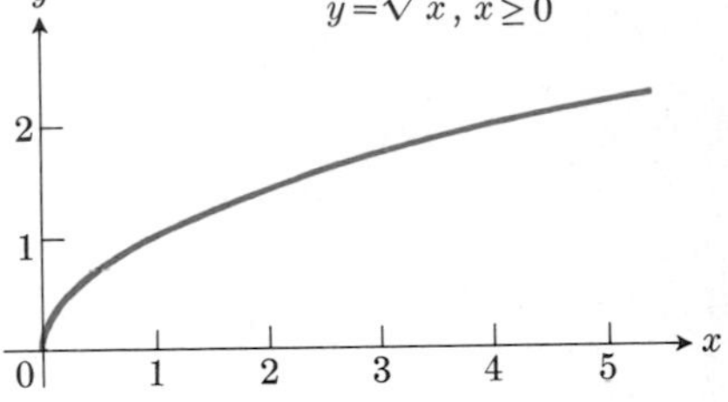

1–28 The graph of $y = \sqrt{x}$, $x \geq 0$.

Obsidian dating has led to estimates of glacial events as old as 179,000 years, well beyond the reliable 40,000-year range of carbon-14 dating. Obsidian (volcanic glass) absorbs water from the atmosphere, which seeps into the glass to form a layer called a *hydration* layer that can be seen under a microscope. The depth of the layer beneath a given surface (with some variation) is proportional to the square root of the time elapsed since the surface was created. Thus, measuring the depths of hydration layers in artifacts and stones allows us to estimate the dates of past events, like the shaping of a prehistoric axe or the chipping of a pebble by a glacier. A typical formula relating a layer's depth d to elapsed time t is

$$d = \sqrt{5t}\ \mu\text{m (millionths of a meter)},$$

where t is measured in thousands of years. The layer is $\sqrt{5} \approx 2.24\ \mu$m thick after 1000 years, $\sqrt{10} \approx 3.16\ \mu$m thick after 2000 years, and so on. For more about this relatively recent dating technique, read Friedman and Trembour, "Obsidian: The Dating Stone," *American Scientist*, Jan.–Feb., 1978, pp. 44–51.

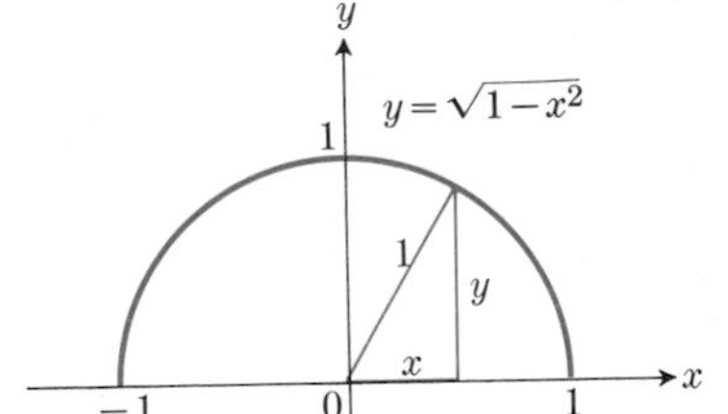

1–29 The graph of $y = \sqrt{1 - x^2}$, $-1 \leq x \leq 1$.

EXAMPLE 12. *The function* $y = \sqrt{1 - x^2}$, $-1 \leq x \leq 1$.

Pairs:	$(x, \sqrt{1 - x^2})$	Graph:	The semicircle shown in Fig. 1–29.
Domain:	$-1 \leq x \leq 1$	Range:	$0 \leq y \leq 1$

EXAMPLE 13. *The function* $y = 1/\sqrt{3 - x}$, $x < 3$.

Pairs:	$(x, 1/\sqrt{3 - x})$	Graph:	Fig. 1–30.
Domain:	The set of real numbers less than 3 (see Table 1–4).	Range:	$y > 0$

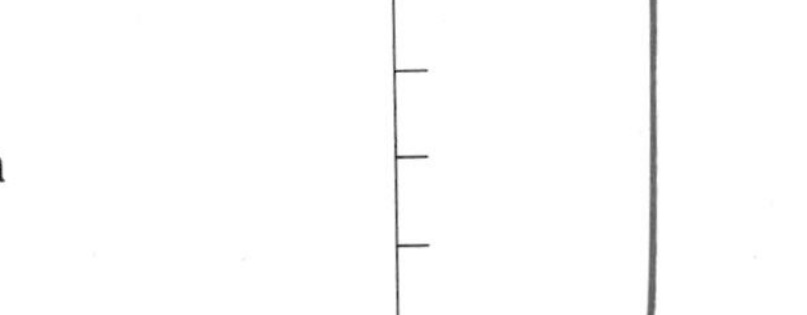
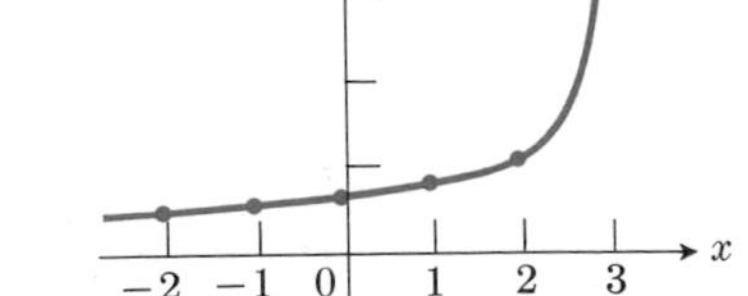

1–30 The graph of $y = 1/\sqrt{3 - x}$, $x < 3$.

Table 1–4. Values of $y = 1/\sqrt{3-x}$ for selected values of x

x	-2	-1	0	1	2	2.9
y	0.45	0.50	0.58	0.71	1.00	3.16

We always keep two restrictions in mind when we define functions. First, we **never divide by zero.** When we see $y = x/(x-2)$, we must think "$x \neq 2$." We must do so even if this restriction is not stated explicitly. Second, we deal with real-valued functions exclusively. We must restrict our domains when we have square roots, or fourth roots, or other even roots. If $y = \sqrt{1-x^2}$, we should think "x^2 must not be greater than 1. The domain must not extend beyond the interval $-1 \leq x \leq 1$."

EXAMPLE 14. *The absolute value function,* $y = |x|$. This function assigns to each number x the nonnegative number $\sqrt{x^2}$. We call this number the *absolute value* of x. The symbol for the absolute value of x is $|x|$:

$$|x| = \sqrt{x^2} = \begin{cases} x, & \text{if } x \geq 0, \\ -x, & \text{if } x < 0. \end{cases}$$

The absolute value function maps every positive number to itself. It maps every negative number to its negative, which is the corresponding positive number. Thus, $|x|$ is never negative. The absolute value function works like an electric current rectifier that converts either positive or negative current to positive current.

Pairs:	$(x, \|x\|)$	Graph:	Fig. 1–31
Domain:	$-\infty < x < \infty$	Range:	$y \geq 0$

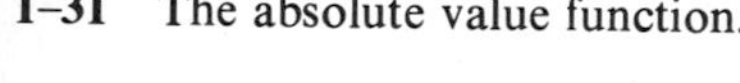

1–31 The absolute value function.

Absolute Value

The absolute value function of Example 14 has an important geometric interpretation. The number $|x|$ measures the distance between the origin 0 and the point that represents x on the scale of real numbers. It does so regardless of whether x is positive or negative. (See Fig. 1–32.)

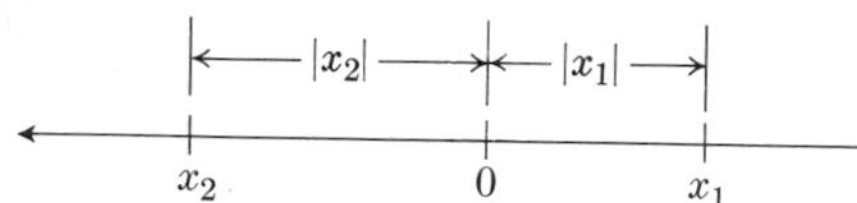

1–32 The absolute value of a number is its distance from 0.

EXAMPLE 15. A number x that lies between -1 and $+1$ is less than one unit away from zero. That is, $|x| < 1$. Conversely, if $|x| < 1$, then x lies between -1 and $+1$. For this reason we often write $|x| < 1$ as a shorthand way of describing the interval $-1 < x < 1$ (Fig. 1–33).

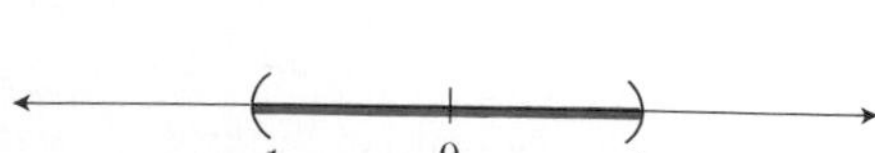

1–33 The domain $|x| < 1$.

EXAMPLE 16. Describe the domain $|x| \geq 1$ without absolute values. Sketch the domain.

Solution. $|x| \geq 1$ means that the distance between x and the origin is one unit or more. That is, either $x \leq -1$ or $x \geq 1$. The domain is the union of the intervals sketched in Fig. 1–34.

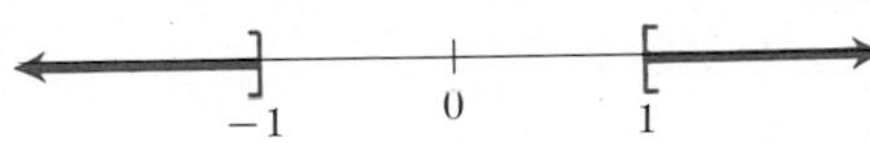

1–34 The domain $|x| \geq 1$.

The equality

$$|ab| = |a|\,|b| \tag{2}$$

holds for all real numbers a and b. The steps from left to right are

$$|ab| = \sqrt{(ab)^2} = \sqrt{a^2 b^2} = \sqrt{a^2}\sqrt{b^2} = |a|\,|b|.$$

The *triangle inequality*

$$|a + b| \leq |a| + |b| \tag{3}$$

is true for all real numbers a and b. If the numbers a and b have the same sign, then $|a + b| = |a| + |b|$. If they have opposite signs, then $|a + b| < |a| + |b|$.

When we subtract one of the numbers a and b from the other, the sign of the result depends on which way we subtract. But $a - b$ and $b - a$ differ from each other only in sign. That is,

$$|a - b| = |b - a|. \tag{4}$$

The number $|a - b| = |b - a|$ measures the distance between a and b on the real number line.

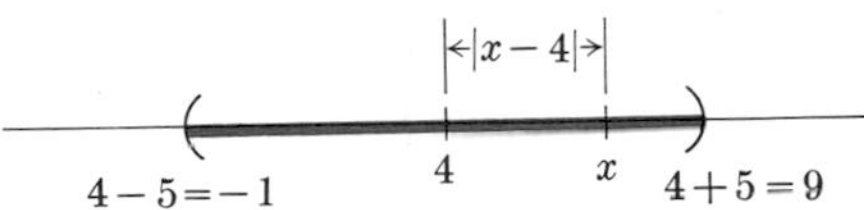

1–35 $|x - 4| < 5$ and $-1 < x < 9$ both describe the open interval $(-1, 9)$.

EXAMPLE 17. Describe the domain $|x - 4| < 5$ without absolute values.

Solution **1.** $|x - 4| < 5$ says the distance between x and 4 is less than 5. This lets x vary between $4 - 5 = -1$ and $4 + 5 = 9$. The domain is the interval $-1 < x < 9$. See Fig. 1–35.

Solution **2.** $|x - 4| < 5$ says $(x - 4)$ lies between -5 and $+5$, or

$$-5 < x - 4 < 5.$$

To find out what this inequality says about x, as opposed to $x - 4$, we can add 4 to each quantity in the inequality. The addition preserves the inequality, and shows that $-1 < x < 9$. Moreover, these algebraic steps are reversible.

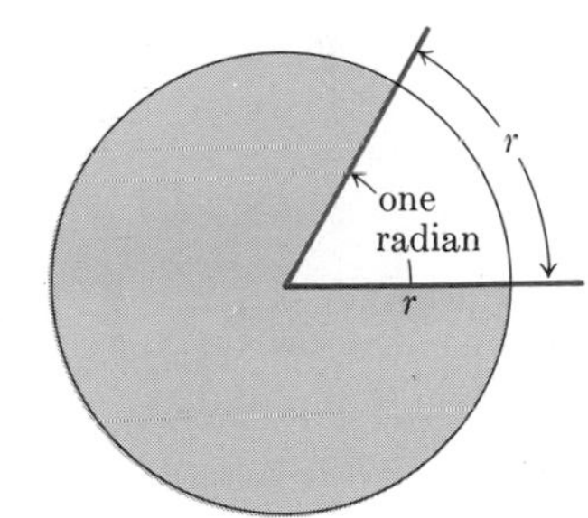

Figure 1–36

Radian Measure

The measure of an angle at the center of a circle that is subtended by an arc of the circle one radius long is said to be one *radian* (Fig. 1–36). More generally, the number of radians in an angle that is subtended by an arc s units long is

$$\theta = \frac{s}{r}. \tag{5}$$

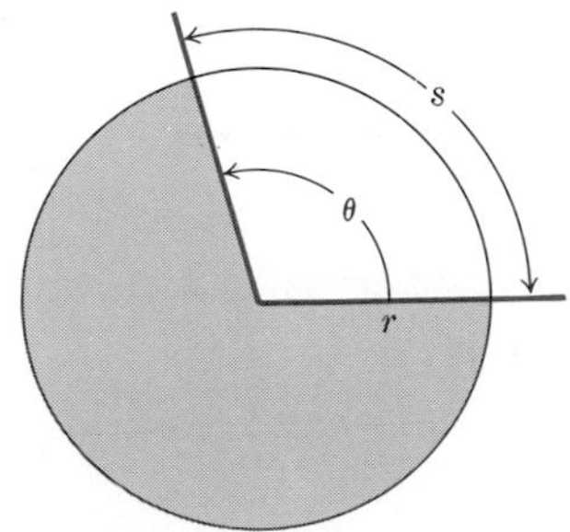

1–37 $\theta = (s/r)$ radians.

(See Fig. 1–37.) To see how radians correspond to degrees we can look at a semicircle. The length of the semicircle is π radii. Therefore a 180° angle has

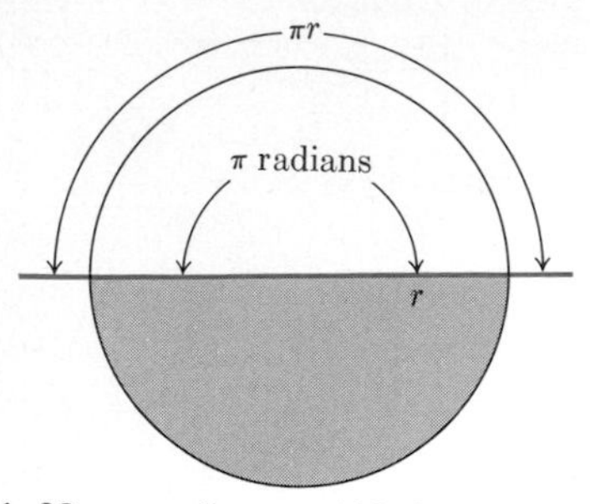

1–38 π radians = 180 degrees.

a measure of π radians (Fig. 1–38). An angle of 1° then measures $\pi/180 \approx 0.01745$ radians, or about two hundredths of a radian. One radian measures $180/\pi \approx 57.3$ degrees. As with degree measure, counterclockwise rotations have positive radian measures and clockwise rotations have negative radian measures (Fig. 1–39).

A radian is normally too large a unit to be convenient in the daily practice of navigation and civil engineering, but radians play a special role in the calculus of trigonometric functions, as we shall see in Article 2–10. We therefore include radian measure in the tables of values of the functions sin θ, cos θ, and tan θ in the following example.

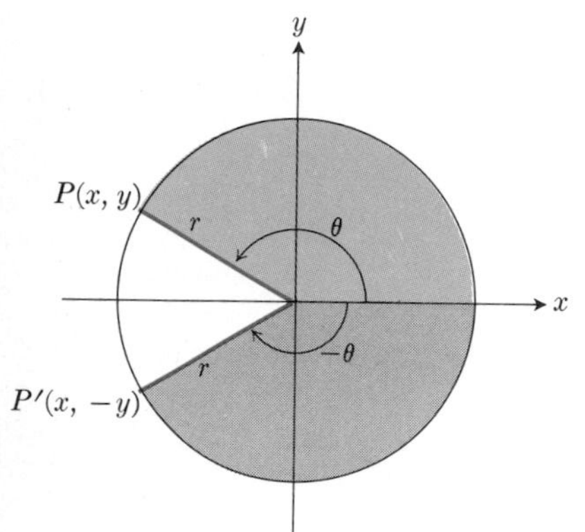

1–39 Angles of opposite sign.

EXAMPLE 18. *The sine, cosine and tangent functions.* When an angle of measure θ is placed in standard position at the center of a circle of radius r as in Fig. 1–40, then

$$\sin \theta = \frac{y}{r}, \qquad \cos \theta = \frac{x}{r}, \qquad \tan \theta = \frac{y}{x}. \tag{6}$$

Note that $\tan \theta = y/x$ is not defined for values of θ for which $x = 0$. In radian measure this means that $\pi/2, 3\pi/2, \ldots, -\pi/2, -3\pi/2, \ldots$ are excluded from the domain of the tangent function.

Table 1–5. Values of sin θ, cos θ, and tan θ for selected values of θ

Degrees	−180	−135	−90	−45	0	45	90	135	180
θ (radians)	$-\pi$	$-\frac{3\pi}{4}$	$-\frac{\pi}{2}$	$-\frac{\pi}{4}$	0	$\frac{\pi}{4}$	$\frac{\pi}{2}$	$\frac{3\pi}{4}$	π
sin θ	0	−0.71	−1	−0.71	0	0.71	1	0.71	0
cos θ	−1	−0.71	0	0.71	1	0.71	0	−0.71	−1
tan θ	0	1		−1	0	1		−1	0

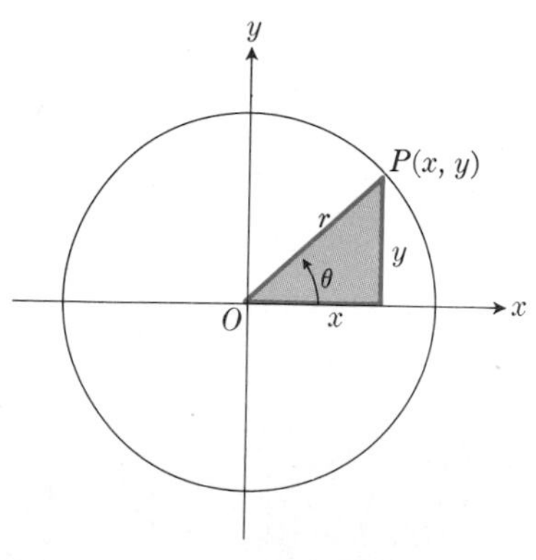

1–40 Angle θ in standard position.

In Table 1–5,

$$\tan \theta = \frac{\sin \theta}{\cos \theta}, \qquad \text{except when } \cos \theta = 0,$$

which can also be seen by dividing the formulas at the beginning of the example. Note also that the values of the sine, cosine, and tangent repeat. This regular repetition, or *periodicity*, can be seen even more clearly in the graphs in Fig. 1–41. The values of the sine and cosine repeat every 2π units. The values of the tangent repeat every π units. In symbols, we write

$$\sin(\theta + 2\pi) = \sin \theta; \qquad \cos(\theta + 2\pi) = \cos \theta; \qquad \tan(\theta + \pi) = \tan \theta. \tag{7}$$

Functional Notation

We often name functions with a single letter like f. This lets us use the simple notation $f(x)$, read "f of x," for the number y that corresponds to x. The number $f(x)$ is called *the value of f at x*, or *the image of x under f*. If f is the function that squares each number in its domain, then the rule that defines f is $f(x) = x^2$. This gives us another name for the function: "the function $f(x) = x^2$."

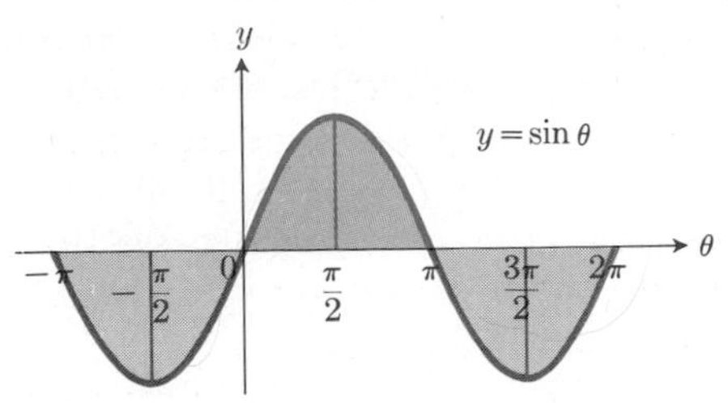

a) Domain: $-\infty < \theta < \infty$
Range: $-1 \le y \le 1$

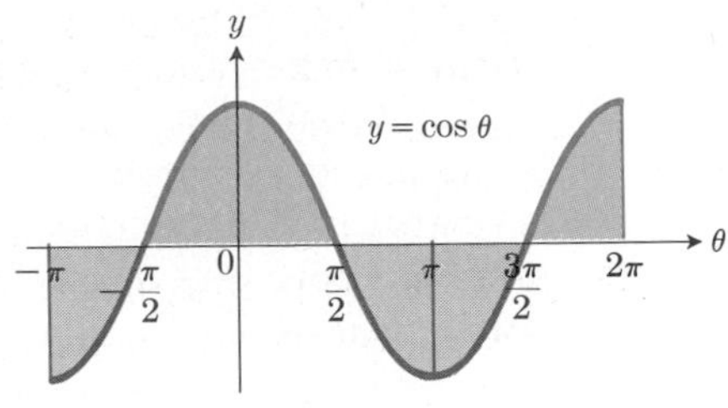

b) Domain: $-\infty < \theta < \infty$
Range: $-1 \le y \le 1$

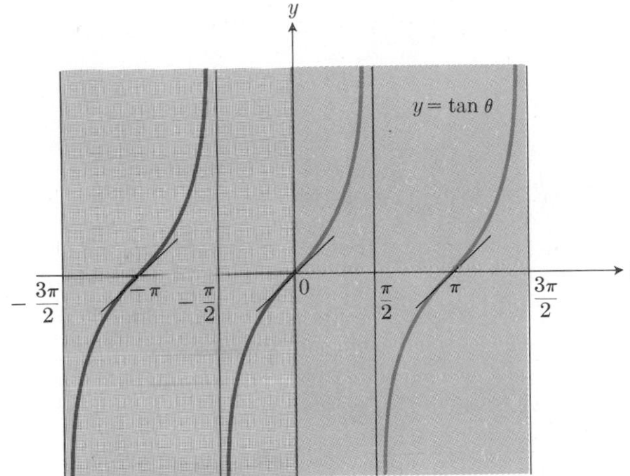

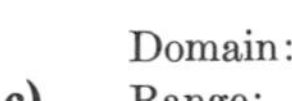

c) Domain: All real numbers except odd integer multiples of $\pi/2$.
Range: $-\infty < y < \infty$

1–41 Graphs of the sine, cosine, and tangent functions.

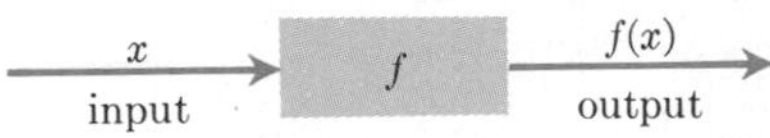

1–42 Diagram for the function f.

EXAMPLE 19. If $f(x) = (2 - x)/(1 + x)$, then the value of f at $x = -5$ is

$$f(-5) = \frac{2 - (-5)}{1 + (-5)} = \frac{7}{-4} = -\frac{7}{4}.$$

Functions are like Machines

It is sometimes useful to think of a function as a machine with an input x and output $y = f(x)$. (See Fig. 1–42.) The machine may be offered any real number as input, but the first thing it asks is "Are you in my domain?" If the answer is "No", the machine politely flashes a signal that says, "Sorry, I can't accept you." But if the answer is "Yes", then the machine proceeds to calculate the value of $f(x)$ and displays the answer, or prints it out. In this way, a table of pairs (x, y) such that $y = f(x)$ is produced.

EXAMPLE 20. The machine shown in Fig. 1–43 calculates values of the function $y = 1/\sqrt{3 - x}$. Table 1–4 in Example 13 is a table of input–output pairs (x, y) from this machine.

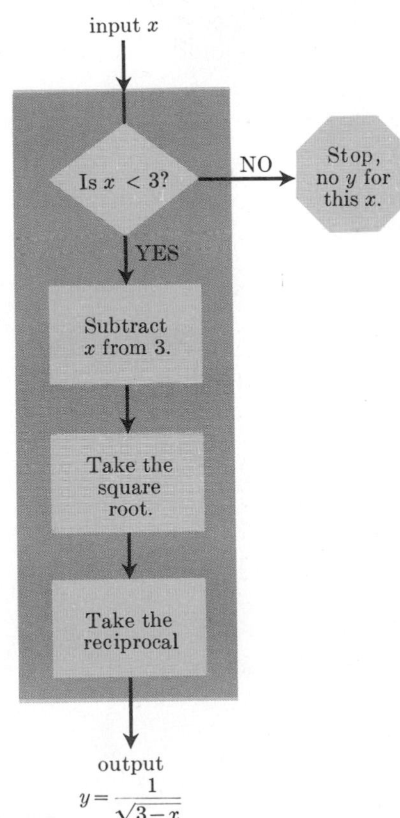

1–43 Diagram for the function $y = 1/\sqrt{3 - x}$.

Composition

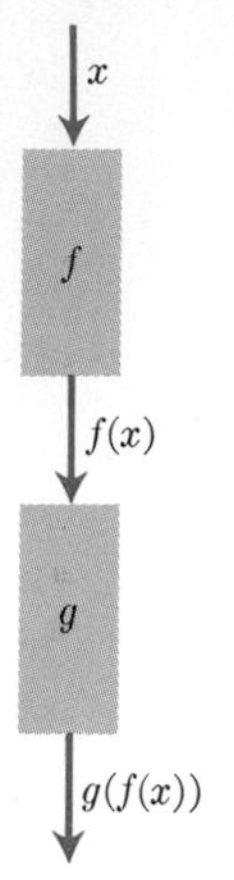

1–44 Two functions can be composed when the range of the first lies in the domain of the second.

Think of making a new function machine by hooking two machines together so that the outputs of the first are the inputs of the second. The new machine is the *composite* of the ones of which it is made, and its output function is *composed* of the functions of the two machines. If the first machine is f, and the second is g, as in Fig. 1–44, then the output of the composite that corresponds to the input x is $g(f(x))$, read "g of f of x."

EXAMPLE 21. If $f(x) = \sin x$ and $g(x) = -(x/2)$, then $g(f(x)) = -(\sin x)/2$.

EXAMPLE 22. If $f(x) = x^2$ and $g(x) = x - 7$, find a formula for $g(f(x))$. Then find $g(f(2))$.

Solution

$$g(f(x)) = f(x) - 7 = x^2 - 7;$$
$$g(f(2)) = f(2) - 7 = 2^2 - 7 = -3.$$

The order in which functions are composed can affect the result. Watch what happens when we compose the functions of Example 22 in the reverse order, first g, then f.

EXAMPLE 23. If $f(x) = x^2$ and $g(x) = x - 7$, find a formula for $f(g(x))$. Then find $f(g(2))$.

Solution

$$f(g(x)) = (g(x))^2 = (x - 7)^2,$$
$$f(g(2)) = (2 - 7)^2 = 25.$$

The functions $g(f(x)) = x^2 - 7$ and $f(g(x)) = (x - 7)^2$ are not the same. In fact, the only value of x for which their values are equal is $x = 4$. We can check this by solving the equation $x^2 - 7 = (x - 7)^2$ for x:

$$x^2 - 7 = x^2 - 14x + 49,$$
$$14x = 56,$$
$$x = 4.$$

Functions of More than One Independent Variable

The values of some functions are calculated from the values of more than one independent variable.

EXAMPLE 24. *Economic order quantity* (EOQ). Items that are sold regularly by a retail store have to be reordered when they begin to run low. The question that always arises is how many of the items, radios, shoes, or what have you, to reorder. To answer this question, a store manager has to think about two kinds of costs. There are the costs of holding the items between the time they arrive and the time they are sold—costs of insurance and storage space, and of capital tied up. There is also a setup cost incurred each time an order is placed, associated with secretarial time and communications. If we assume that the setup cost is the same for each order, no matter how large or small, then the problem of determining the size of an order comes down to the following. Large orders have a low setup cost per item, but a high holding cost. Small orders have a high setup cost per item, but a low holding cost. How can one find an order quantity Q that strikes an economical balance between the cost of ordering and the cost of holding inventory?

One of the simplest estimates for Q is given by the formula

$$Q = \sqrt{\frac{2KM}{h}}, \tag{8}$$

where

$K =$ the setup cost (fixed cost of placing an order),

$M =$ number of items sold per week,

$h =$ holding cost for each item per week.

For example, if $K = \$2.00$, $M = 20$ radios per week, and $h = \$0.05$, then $Q = 40$ radios. The most economical quantity to order is 40 radios. Since weekly sales are 20 radios, this means placing an order every two weeks.

As you can see, the formula for Q ignores a number of real factors that may influence a store manager's decision. Shipping charges may vary with order size, for instance, or prices may be about to change. Nevertheless, the formula is accurate enough in many cases to be of practical importance. We will show how the formula is derived in Article 3–6. (For more information, see *Principles of Operations Research*, Second Edition, by Harvey M. Wagner. Prentice-Hall, Inc., 1975, p. 18.)

EXAMPLE 25. (From "Concorde Sonic Booms as an Atmospheric Probe," N. K. Balachandran, W. L. Donn, and D. H. Rind, *Science*, 1 July 1977; Vol. 197, p. 47.)

The distance y at which the grazing (farthest) ray of sound from an atmospheric source hits the surface of the earth is a function of

$T =$ surface temperature (in degrees Kelvin),

$h =$ elevation (in km) of the source (for example, the Concorde),

$d =$ vertical temperature gradient (in degrees Kelvin per km).

The formula for y is

$$y = 2(Th/d)^{1/2}. \tag{9}$$

Evaluated for $T = 296°\text{K}$, $h = 13$ km, and $d = 6°$ K/km, the formula yields $y = 50.65$ km.

To calculate the distance at which the Concorde's sonic boom is heard in the preceding example, we need to know the values of the earth's surface temperature T, the plane's elevation h, and the vertical temperature gradient d. But these values are all that we need to know. As soon as they are known, the value of y is determined. The set of all ordered 4-tuples (T, h, d, y) with

$$y = 2(Th/d)^{1/2}, \qquad T \geq 0, \qquad h \geq 0, \qquad d \geq 0, \tag{10}$$

is a function of the three variables T, h, and d. The physical meanings of the variables keep their values from being negative.

The *domain* of the function $y = 2(Th/d)^{1/2}$ is the set of all ordered triples (T, h, d) with T, h, and d nonnegative. The *range* is the set of numbers $y \geq 0$. The variables T, h, and d are *independent* in the sense that the values assigned to any one variable need not depend on the others. The variable y is the *dependent* variable of the function. Its value is fixed by T, h, and d.

We say that y is a function of T, h, and d. This statement leaves out a lot of detail, but it still says two things:

1. T, h, and d can be assigned values independently;
2. Giving T, h, and d determines y.

More generally, suppose that some quantity y is determined by n other quantities $x_1, x_2, x_3, \ldots, x_n$. Then the set of all ordered $(n+1)$-tuples $(x_1, x_2, x_3, \ldots, x_n, y)$ obtained by substituting values of $x_1, x_2, x_3, \ldots, x_n$ along with the value of y that corresponds to them, is a function. The domain of the function is the set of allowable n-tuples $(x_1, x_2, x_3, \ldots, x_n)$. The range is the set of corresponding y-values. If values can be assigned independently to each of the x's, we call them independent variables and say that y is a function of the n x's. We write

$$y = f(x_1, x_2, x_3, \ldots, x_n). \tag{11}$$

The Greatest Integer Function

Most of the information about functions in this book will come from graphs and equations. However, any rule that gives a value y for each value of x expresses y as a function of x. Here is an example of a function that is determined by a verbal statement.

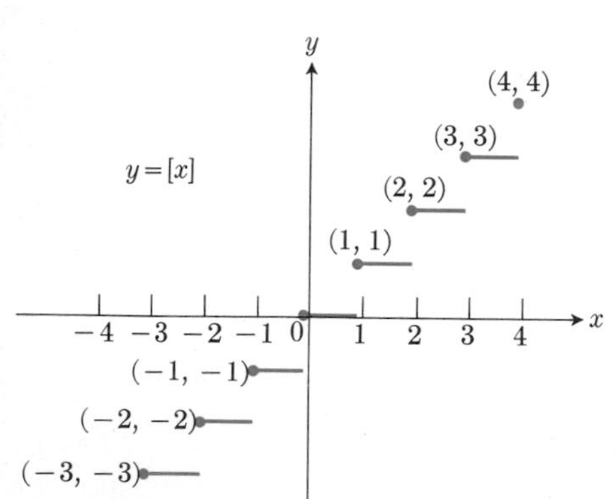

1–45 For each number x, the number $y = [x]$ is the greatest integer less than or equal to x.

EXAMPLE 26. *The greatest integer function* $y = [x]$. For each real number x, the value of this function is the largest integer less than or equal to x. The symbol for this integer is $[x]$, read "the greatest integer in x." Some sample values are

$$[1.9] = 1, \qquad [2] = 2, \qquad \text{and} \qquad [3.4] = 3.$$

If x is negative, $[x]$ may have a larger absolute value than x does:

$$[-2.7] = -3, \qquad [-0.5] = -1.$$

The range of $y = [x]$ is the set of integers. Figure 1–45 shows the graph.

The greatest integer function is an example of a *step function*. Phenomena that we can model with step functions are:

1. The price of postage for first-class mail, as a function of weight.
2. The output of a blinking light, as a function of time.
3. The number displayed by a meter or machine that gives digital outputs, as a function of time.

Step functions exhibit points of *discontinuity*, where they suddenly jump from one value to another without taking on any of the intermediate values. In Fig. 1–45, the greatest integer in x jumps from 1 when $x < 2$ to 2 at $x = 2$, without taking on any of the intervening values.

PROBLEMS

Find the largest possible domain of x and the corresponding range of y for each function in Problems 1–6.

1. $y = \sqrt{x + 4}$ **2.** $y = \sqrt{1 - \sqrt{x}}$

3. $y = \dfrac{x^2}{x^2 + 1}$ **4.** $y = \sqrt{\dfrac{x}{x + 1}}$

5. $y = x - \dfrac{1}{x}$ **6.** $y = (\sqrt{x})^2$

In Problems 7–9, graph each function. Use a calculator, if one is available, to calculate the function values.

7. $y = \sqrt{9 - x^2}$ **8.** $y = \dfrac{1}{x^2}, \quad -2 \leq x \leq 2, x \neq 0$

9. $y = \sqrt{x + 1}, \quad -1 \leq x \leq 3$

10. Which of the graphs in Fig. 1–46 could be the graph of $y = x^2 - 1$? Why?

a) b)

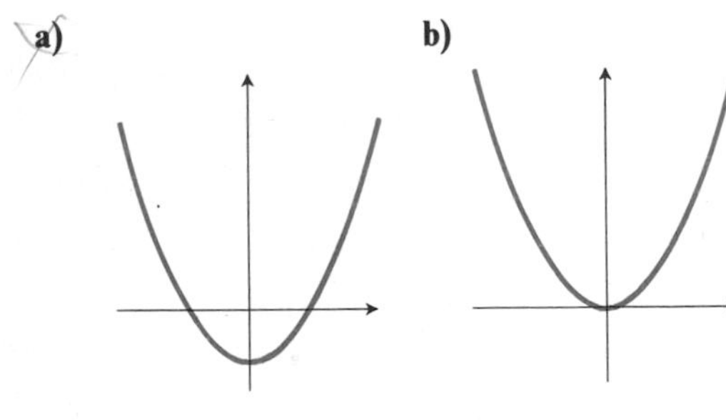

c) d)

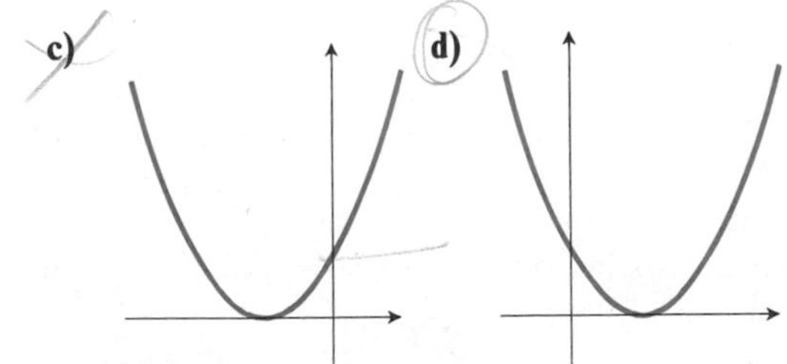

Figure 1–46

11. Which of the graphs in Fig. 1–46 could be the graph of $y = (x - 1)^2$? Why?

12. By solving $x^2 + y^2 = 1$ for y, replace the equation by an equivalent system of two equations each of which determines y as a function of x. Graph these two equations. [*Hint*. See Example 12.]

13. Make a table of values with $x = 0, \frac{1}{2}, 1, \frac{3}{2}$, and 2, and sketch the graph of the function

$$y = \begin{cases} x, & \text{when } 0 \leq x \leq 1 \\ 2 - x, & \text{when } 1 \leq x \leq 2. \end{cases}$$

In Problems 14–17, describe the domain of x without the use of absolute values.

14. $|x| < 2$ **15.** $|x| \geq 2$

16. $|x - 1| \leq 5$ **17.** $\left|\dfrac{x}{2} - 1\right| \leq 1$

In Problems 18–20, use absolute values to describe the domain of x.

18. $-8 \leq x \leq 8$ **19.** $-3 < x < 5$ **20.** $-5 < x < -1$

21. When does $|1 - x|$ equal $1 - x$, and when does it equal $x - 1$?

Graph the functions in Problems 22 and 23.

22. $y = |4 - x^2|, \; -3 \leq x \leq 3$

23. $y = |x| + x, \; -2 \leq x \leq 2$

Convert the following degree measures to radian measure.

24. 45° **25.** −60° **26.** 90°

27. 120° **28.** −30° **29.** −135°

Convert the following radian measures to degree measure.

30. $\dfrac{\pi}{3}$ **31.** $-\dfrac{\pi}{6}$ **32.** $\dfrac{\pi}{4}$

33. $\dfrac{2\pi}{3}$ **34.** $\dfrac{3\pi}{2}$ **35.** $-\dfrac{\pi}{2}$

A function f is an *even* function of x if $f(-x) = f(x)$ for every value of x, and *odd* if $f(-x) = -f(x)$ instead. The function $f(x) = x^2$ is even, because $(-x)^2$ always equals x^2. The function $f(x) = x^3$ is odd, because $(-x)^3 = -x^3$. Which of the functions in Problems 36–43 are even functions of x, and which are odd?

36. x **37.** $|x|$ **38.** x^4

39. $\sin x$ **40.** $\cos x$ **41.** $\tan x$

42. If $f(x) = 1/x$, find $f(2)$, $f(x+2)$, and $(f(x+2) - f(2))/2$.

43. If $F(t) = 4t - 3$, find $(F(t+h) - F(t))/h$.

Copy and complete the following table.

	$f(x)$	$g(x)$	$g(f(x))$
44.	$x - 7$	$\sqrt{x}$	
45.	$x + 2$	$3x$	
46.	$x^2 + 2x + 1$		$\lvert x + 1 \rvert$
47.		$\sqrt{x - 5}$	$\sqrt{x^2 - 5}$

48. The hydration layer in an obsidian axe is found to be 10 μm thick. Use the formula, $d = \sqrt{5t}$, following Example 11, to estimate how many years ago the axe was shaped.

49. During the summer, Martin Enterprises sells 50 lawnmowers a week. The setup cost for each order of mowers is \$4.50, and the holding cost for each mower is \$1.05 a week. What is the company's economic order quantity? (See Example 24.)

50. If weekly sales double, by what factor does this increase the economic order quantity, Q, of Example 24? By what factor do weekly sales have to increase for Q to double?

51. As a Concorde pilot preparing to land near Washington, D.C., you plan to slow the Concorde to subsonic speeds far enough away so that no one in the city will hear the sonic boom. You will be flying at an altitude of 16 km when you break the sound barrier, and the temperature gradient in the Washington area is 7°K/km. How close to Washington can you break the sound barrier under these circumstances? (See Example 25.) Use $T = 296$°K.

52. For nonnegative numbers, $[x]$ is the integer part of the decimal form of x. What is the corresponding description of $[x]$ when $x < 0$?

Graph the functions in Problems 53 and 54. The number $[x]$ is the greatest integer in x.

53. $y = x - [x], \quad -3 \le x \le 3$

54. $y = \left[\dfrac{x}{2}\right], \quad -3 \le x \le 3$

1–7 SLOPE OF A CURVE

In this article we shall define what we mean by the *slope of a curve* at a point P on the curve. We start with the slope of a secant line through P and a nearby point.

In Fig. 1–47, $P(x_1, y_1)$ is any point on the curve $y = f(x)$. Let $Q(x_2, y_2)$ be another point on the curve, with $\Delta x = x_2 - x_1 \neq 0$. Then the slope of the secant line joining the points P and Q is

$$m_{\text{sec}} = \text{slope of } PQ = \frac{y_2 - y_1}{x_2 - x_1} = \frac{\Delta y}{\Delta x}. \tag{1}$$

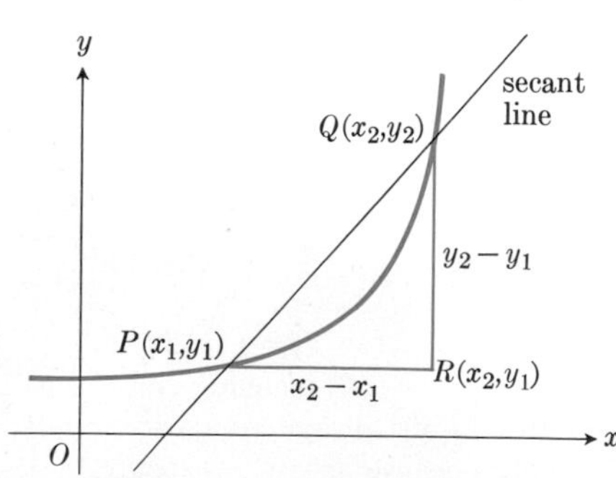

1–47 In many cases the slope $(y_2 - y_1)/(x_2 - x_1)$ of the secant line will approach a constant limiting value as Q moves toward P along the curve.

Suppose now we hold P fixed and move Q along the curve toward P. As we do so, the slope of the secant line PQ will probably vary. But it may happen (and does for most curves encountered in practice) that as Q moves closer and closer to P along the curve, the slope of the secant line varies by smaller and smaller amounts and, in fact, approaches a constant limiting value. When this happens, as it does in the following example, we call this limiting value the *slope of the tangent to the curve at* P, or more briefly, *the slope of the curve at* P. In Fig. 1–47, Q approaches P from the right. But in attempting to compute the limiting value of the slope of the secant line, we must allow Q to approach P from the left as well.

EXAMPLE 1. Find the slope of the curve

$$y = x^3 - 3x + 3 \tag{2}$$

at the point $P(x_1, y_1)$.

Solution. Since $P(x_1, y_1)$ is a point on the curve, its coordinates satisfy the equation

$$y_1 = x_1^3 - 3x_1 + 3. \tag{3a}$$

If $Q(x_2, y_2)$ is a second point on the curve, and if

$$\Delta x = x_2 - x_1, \qquad \Delta y = y_2 - y_1,$$

then

$$x_2 = x_1 + \Delta x, \qquad y_2 = y_1 + \Delta y$$

must also satisfy Eq. (2). That is,

$$\begin{aligned} y_1 + \Delta y &= (x_1 + \Delta x)^3 - 3(x_1 + \Delta x) + 3 \\ &= x_1^3 + 3x_1^2\,\Delta x + 3x_1(\Delta x)^2 + (\Delta x)^3 - 3x_1 - 3\,\Delta x + 3. \end{aligned} \tag{3b}$$

When we subtract Eq. (3a) from Eq. (3b), we obtain

$$\Delta y = 3x_1^2\,\Delta x + 3x_1(\Delta x)^2 + (\Delta x)^3 - 3\,\Delta x. \tag{4}$$

We find the slope of the secant line PQ by dividing both sides of Eq. (4) by Δx. (For this, we need $\Delta x \neq 0$, which is why we never let Q coincide with P.) The result is

$$m_{\text{sec}} = \frac{\Delta y}{\Delta x} = 3x_1^2 + 3x_1\,\Delta x + (\Delta x)^2 - 3. \tag{5}$$

Now comes the most important step! When Q approaches P along the curve, Δx and Δy both approach zero. Thus the slope of PQ will be the ratio of two small numbers. This information alone is not helpful, since the ratio of two small numbers may be practically anything. But we have further information here, since we also know from Eq. (5) that

$$m_{\text{sec}} = (3x_1^2 - 3) + (3x_1 + \Delta x)\,\Delta x.$$

The right side of this equation is the sum of two terms, one of which,

$$3x_1^2 - 3,$$

remains constant as Δx approaches zero, while the other,

$$(3x_1 + \Delta x)\,\Delta x,$$

becomes smaller and, in fact, itself approaches zero as Δx does. We summarize this by saying that

the limit of m_{sec} as Δx approaches zero is $3x_1^2 - 3$.

By definition, this limit is the slope of the tangent to the curve, or the slope of the curve at the point (x_1, y_1). Since (x_1, y_1) might have been *any* point on the curve of Eq. (2), we may delete the subscript 1 and say that

$$m = 3x^2 - 3 \tag{6}$$

gives the slope at any point $P(x, y)$ on the curve.

We can use the slope formula for a curve to learn more about its shape than we would discover without this information.

a)

x	y	m
-2	1	9
-1	5	0
0	3	-3
1	1	0
2	5	9

EXAMPLE 2. From the slope formula $m = 3x^2 - 3$ for the curve $y = x^3 - 3x + 3$ in Example 1, we can see that $m = 0$ when $x = \pm 1$. We also see that the slope is negative for x between -1 and $+1$, and that elsewhere it is positive. If we substitute values of x between -2 and $+2$, say, into Eq. (2) to find y, and into Eq. (6) to find m, we obtain the table of values shown in Fig. 1–48(a). When the points from this table are plotted, and a tangent is drawn at each point, we obtain Fig. 1–48(b). With the aid of this tangent frame we can now draw a good picture of the curve (Fig. 1–48(c)).

b)

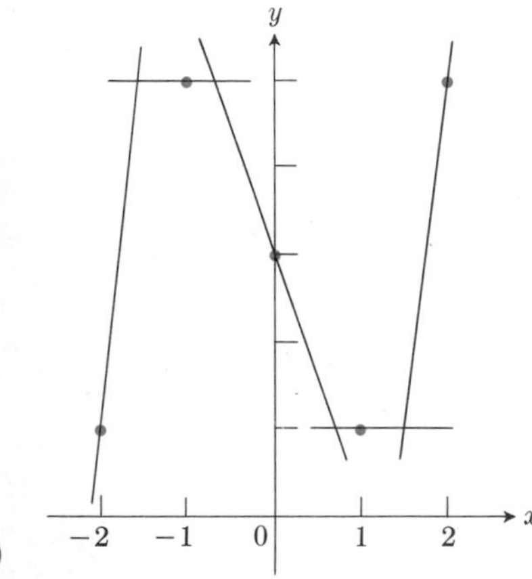

c)

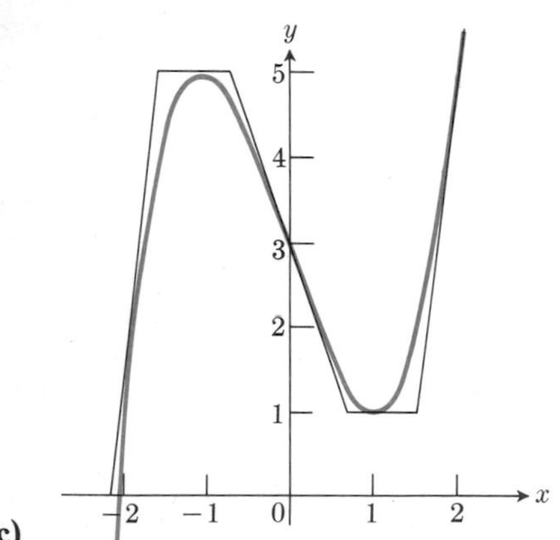

Figure 1–48

REMARK. We sometimes think of the slope of a secant line as an average rate of change, as in the next example.

EXAMPLE 3. Biologists are interested in average growth rates of populations. The graph in Fig. 1–49 shows how the number of *Drosophila* flies grew in a controlled experiment during a fifty-day interval. The graph was made by counting the flies at regular intervals, plotting a point for each count, and drawing a smooth curve through the plotted points. The slope $\Delta p/\Delta t$ of the secant line PQ in the figure is about nine flies per day. It was computed from the coordinates of P and Q in the following way:

$$\frac{\Delta p}{\Delta t} = \frac{(340 - 150)(\text{flies})}{(45 - 23)(\text{days})} = \frac{190(\text{flies})}{22(\text{days})} \simeq 9 \text{ flies/day}.$$

This is the average rate of change in the number of flies in the twenty-two day interval from $t = 23$ to $t = 45$.

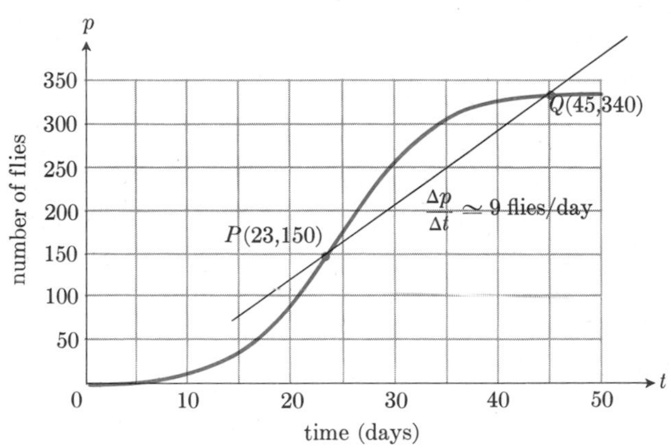

1–49 Growth of a *Drosophila* population in a controlled experiment. (*Source:* A. J. Lotka, *Elements of Mathematical Biology.* Dover, New York (1956); p. 69.)

PROBLEMS

Use the method illustrated in Example 1 to find the slope of each of the following curves at a point (x, y) on the curve. Use the equation of the curve and the equation you get for its slope to make a table of values, as in Example 2. Include in your table all points where the curve has a horizontal tangent. Sketch the curve, making use of all the information in your table of values.

1. $y = x^2 - 2x - 3$

2. $y = 2x^2 - x - 1$

3. $y = 4 - x^2$

4. $y = x^2 - 4x$

5. $y = x^2 - 4x + 4$

6. $y = x^2 + 4x + 4$

7. $y = 6 + x - x^2$

8. $y = 6 + 5x - x^2$

9. $y = x^2 + 3x + 2$

10. $y = 2 - x - x^2$

11. $y = 2x^3 + 3x^2 - 12x + 7$

12. $y = x^3 - 3x$

13. $y = x^3 - 12x$

14. $y = x^2(4x + 3) + 1$

15. $y = x^3 - 3x^2 + 4$

16. From Fig. 1–49, estimate the increase that took place in the *Drosophila* population during the twenty-third day.

1–8 DERIVATIVE OF A FUNCTION

We now show how to find the slope of the curve defined by the equation $y = f(x)$. Let $P(x_1, y_1)$ be a fixed point on the curve. The subscript 1 is used to emphasize that x_1 and y_1 are to be held constant throughout the following discussion. If $Q(x_1 + \Delta x, y_1 + \Delta y)$ is another point on the curve, then

$$y_1 + \Delta y = f(x_1 + \Delta x),$$

and from this we subtract

$$y_1 = f(x_1)$$

to obtain

$$\Delta y = f(x_1 + \Delta x) - f(x_1).$$

(See Fig. 1–50.) Then the slope of the secant line PQ is

$$m_{\text{sec}} = \frac{\Delta y}{\Delta x} = \frac{f(x_1 + \Delta x) - f(x_1)}{\Delta x}. \tag{1}$$

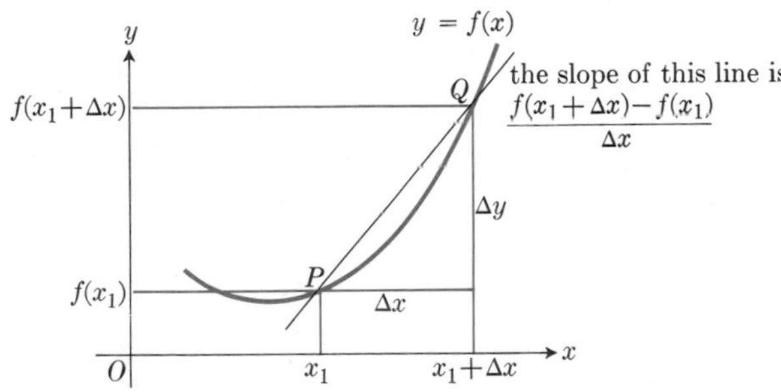

Figure 1–50

The division in Eq. (1) can only be *indicated* when we are talking about a general function $f(x)$, but for any specific equation such as $f(x) = x^3 - 3x + 3$ in Eq. (2) of Article 1–7, this division of Δy by Δx is actually to be carried out *before* we do the next operation, as we did in going from Eq. (4) to Eq. (5) in Article 1–7.

Having performed the division indicated in Eq. (1), we now investigate what happens when we hold x_1 fixed and take Δx to be smaller and smaller, approaching zero. If m_{sec} approaches a constant value, we call this value its *limit* and define this to be the *slope* $m_{\tan}$ *of the tangent to the curve at* $P(x_1, y_1)$. The mathematical symbols which summarize this discussion are

$$m_{\tan} = \lim_{Q \to P} m_{\text{sec}} = \lim_{\Delta x \to 0} \frac{\Delta y}{\Delta x} = \lim_{\Delta x \to 0} \frac{f(x_1 + \Delta x) - f(x_1)}{\Delta x}. \tag{2}$$

The symbol "lim" with "$\Delta x \to 0$" written beneath it is read "the limit, as Δx approaches zero, of ..."

It is customary to indicate that the limit in Eq. (2) (when it exists) is related to the original function f at the point x_1, by writing it as $f'(x_1)$ (read "f-prime at x_1"). Thus $f'(x_1)$ is *defined* by

$$f'(x_1) = \lim_{\Delta x \to 0} \frac{f(x_1 + \Delta x) - f(x_1)}{\Delta x}. \tag{3}$$

The indicated limit may exist for some values of x_1 and fail to exist for other values. (We shall discuss this situation in more detail below.) At each point x_1 where the limit does exist, the function f is said to have a *derivative* (or to be *differentiable*) and the number $f'(x_1)$ is said to be the derivative of f at x_1.

The process of finding the derivative of a function is the fundamental operation of differential calculus. In fact, we may now define *differential calculus* to be that branch of mathematics which deals with the following two general problems.

PROBLEM I. Given a function f, determine those values of x (in the domain of f) at which the function possesses a derivative.

PROBLEM II. Given a function f and an x at which the derivative exists, find $f'(x)$.

EXAMPLE 1. In Article 1–7 we found that the result of applying the operations on the right side of Eq. (3) to the function

$$f(x) = x^3 - 3x + 3 \tag{4}$$

for any x_1, was $3x_1^2 - 3$. That is, the function f in Eq. (4) possesses a derivative whose value at *any* x_1 is

$$f'(x_1) = 3x_1^2 - 3. \tag{5}$$

Thus the answer to Problem I above is: "The function f of Eq. (4) possesses a derivative at every x in the domain $-\infty < x < +\infty$." The answer to Problem II is given by Eq. (5).

Now for most of the functions considered in this book, it will turn out that the answer to Problem I is that the derivative exists at all but a few values of x; that is, the places where the derivative fails to exist will be exceptional. Then the x_1 in Eq. (3) may be *any* of the nonexceptional values of x. Therefore, we might as well write x instead of x_1 in Eq. (3) if we remember that

x is to be held constant, while Δx varies and approaches zero

in the calculation of the derivative

$$f'(x) = \lim_{\Delta x \to 0} \frac{f(x + \Delta x) - f(x)}{\Delta x}. \tag{6}$$

With this understanding, we shall henceforth omit the subscript 1 in talking about the derivative and shall use Eq. (6) to define the derivative of f, with respect to x, at any x in its domain for which the limit exists.

The Derived Function

Let x be a number in the domain of the function f. If the limit indicated in Eq. (6) exists, then it provides a rule for associating a number $f'(x)$ with the number x. The set of all pairs of numbers $(x, f'(x))$ that can be formed by this process is called the *derived function* f'. The *domain* of f' is a subset of the domain of f. It contains all numbers x in the domain of f at which the limit in

(6) exists, but does not contain those exceptional values where the derivative fails to exist. The derived function f' is also called the *derivative* of f.

EXAMPLE 2. For every value of x, the derivative of the function $f(x) = mx + b$ is the slope m.

STEP 1. Write out $f(x + \Delta x)$ and $f(x)$:

$$f(x + \Delta x) = m(x + \Delta x) + b$$
$$= mx + m\,\Delta x + b,$$
$$f(x) = mx + b.$$

STEP 2. Subtract $f(x)$ from $f(x + \Delta x)$:

$$f(x + \Delta x) - f(x) = m\,\Delta x.$$

STEP 3. Divide by Δx:

$$\frac{f(x + \Delta x) - f(x)}{\Delta x} = \frac{m\,\Delta x}{\Delta x} = m.$$

STEP 4. Calculate the limit as Δx approaches zero:

$$f'(x) = \lim_{\Delta x \to 0} \frac{f(x + \Delta x) - f(x)}{\Delta x} = m.$$

The derivative $f'(x)$ is defined at every value of x. It has the constant value m, the slope of the line.

In the next example, the domain of the derived function is not the domain of the function itself.

EXAMPLE 3. The absolute-value function

$$f(x) = |x|$$

has a derivative at every point except the origin. As shown in Fig. 1–51, the derivative of f is $+1$ when x is positive and -1 when x is negative. To see that f has no derivative at $x = 0$, note that a secant line through the origin and some other point Q on the graph has slope $+1$ if the point is to the right, and slope -1 if the point is to the left. Therefore, there is no unique number that is the limit of the slopes of these secants as Q approaches the origin.

The domain of the derivative of $f(x) = |x|$ consists of all real numbers $x \neq 0$. The range consists of the two numbers -1 and $+1$. We summarize this by writing

$$f'(x) = \begin{cases} -1 & \text{if } x < 0, \\ +1 & \text{if } x > 0. \end{cases}$$

(See Problem 21.)

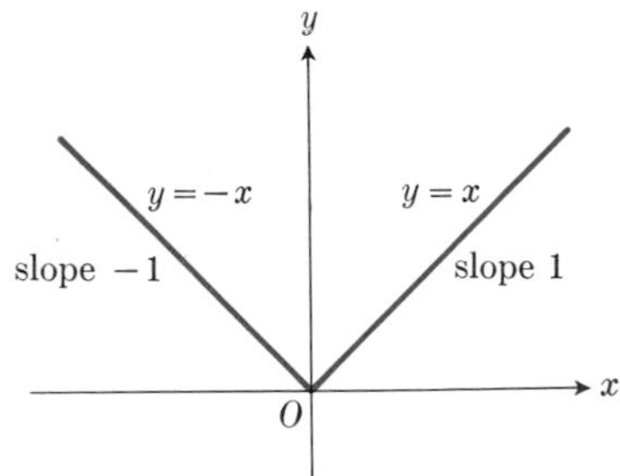

1–51 The graph of $y = |x|$.

Another way to see why $f(x) = |x|$ has no derivative at $x = 0$ is to write down the difference quotient of Eq. (6) for this function at $x = 0$, namely

$$\frac{f(x + \Delta x) - f(x)}{\Delta x} = \frac{|0 + \Delta x| - |0|}{\Delta x} = \frac{|\Delta x|}{\Delta x}.$$

The limit of this quotient as $\Delta x \to 0$ is $+1$ for positive values of Δx and -1 for negative values of Δx. For the limit in Eq. (6) to exist, we would have to arrive at the same number for both positive and negative values of Δx.

NOTATIONS. In addition to $f'(x)$, various notations are used to denote the derivative of $y = f(x)$ with respect to x. The ones most commonly used are

$$y', \qquad \frac{dy}{dx}, \qquad \text{and} \qquad D_x y.$$

The last two of these may be interpreted as

$$\frac{dy}{dx} = \frac{d}{dx}(y),$$

where d/dx stands for the operation "derivative with respect to x of" the expression that follows it, and

$$D_x y = D_x(y)$$

with D_x meaning the same thing as d/dx, namely, "derivative with respect to x of" the expression that follows it.

EXAMPLE 4. Find $f'(x)$ for the function

$$f(x) = x^2 + \frac{1}{x}, \qquad x \neq 0.$$

Solution. We carry out the operations indicated on the right side of Eq. (6) in the following order:

1. Write out $f(x + \Delta x)$ and $f(x)$:

$$f(x + \Delta x) = (x + \Delta x)^2 + \frac{1}{x + \Delta x}$$

$$= x^2 + 2x\,\Delta x + (\Delta x)^2 + \frac{1}{x + \Delta x},$$

$$f(x) = x^2 + \frac{1}{x}.$$

2. Subtract $f(x)$ from $f(x + \Delta x)$:

$$f(x + \Delta x) - f(x) = 2x\,\Delta x + (\Delta x)^2 + \frac{1}{x + \Delta x} - \frac{1}{x}$$

$$= 2x\,\Delta x + (\Delta x)^2 + \frac{x - (x + \Delta x)}{x(x + \Delta x)}$$

$$= \Delta x\left(2x + \Delta x - \frac{1}{x(x + \Delta x)}\right).$$

3. Divide by Δx:

$$\frac{f(x + \Delta x) - f(x)}{\Delta x} = 2x + \Delta x - \frac{1}{x(x + \Delta x)}.$$

4. Calculate the limit as Δx approaches zero:

$$f'(x) = \lim_{\Delta x \to 0} \frac{f(x+\Delta x) - f(x)}{\Delta x}$$

$$= \lim_{\Delta x \to 0} \left(2x + \Delta x - \frac{1}{x(x+\Delta x)}\right) \tag{a}$$

$$= 2x + 0 - \frac{1}{x(x+0)} \tag{b}$$

$$= 2x - \frac{1}{x^2}.$$

In a later article we shall discuss the validity of the various limit operations involved in going from (a) to (b) in Step 4. If we anticipate these results, we may say that, *after* the division by Δx has been carried out and the expression has been reduced to a form that does not involve division by zero when Δx is set equal to zero, the limit as Δx *approaches* zero does exist and may be found by replacing Δx by 0 in this reduced form.

The replacement of Δx by a single letter makes the expressions that come up when we calculate derivatives somewhat easier to read and write. If we replace Δx by h in Eq. (6) we get

$$f'(x) = \lim_{h \to 0} \frac{f(x+h) - f(x)}{h}. \tag{7}$$

The next example shows the use of h in place of Δx. It also shows what to do when the steps we would normally follow to calculate a derivative lead to division by 0 when Δx, now h, approaches 0.

EXAMPLE 5. Find dy/dx if $y = \sqrt{x}$ and $x > 0$.

Solution. With $f(x) = \sqrt{x}$ and $f(x+h) = \sqrt{x+h}$, we form the quotient

$$\frac{f(x+h) - f(x)}{h} = \frac{\sqrt{x+h} - \sqrt{x}}{h}. \tag{a}$$

Unfortunately, this will involve division by 0 if we replace h by 0. We therefore look for an equivalent expression in which this difficulty does not arise. If we attempt to rationalize the numerator in (a), we find

$$\frac{\sqrt{x+h} - \sqrt{x}}{h} = \frac{\sqrt{x+h} - \sqrt{x}}{h} \cdot \frac{\sqrt{x+h} + \sqrt{x}}{\sqrt{x+h} + \sqrt{x}}$$

$$= \frac{(x+h) - x}{h(\sqrt{x+h} + \sqrt{x})} = \frac{1}{\sqrt{x+h} + \sqrt{x}}.$$

When we let h approach 0 now, we learn that

$$\frac{dy}{dx} = \lim_{h \to 0} \frac{1}{\sqrt{x+h} + \sqrt{x}} = \frac{1}{\sqrt{x+0} + \sqrt{x}} = \frac{1}{2\sqrt{x}}.$$

EXAMPLE 6. Find the slope of the curve $y = \sqrt{x}$ at $x = 4$, and write an equation for the tangent to the curve at $x = 4$.

Solution. The slope we seek is the value of the derivative of $y = \sqrt{x}$ at $x = 4$. According to Example 5, this is the value of $1/(2\sqrt{x})$ at $x = 4$, or $\frac{1}{4}$.

The tangent to the curve $y = \sqrt{x}$ at $x = 4$ is the line through the point (4, 2) whose slope is the slope of the curve at (4, 2), or $m = \frac{1}{4}$. The point-slope equation of this line is

$$(y - 2) = \tfrac{1}{4}(x - 4),$$

which simplifies to

$$y = \tfrac{1}{4}x + 1.$$

EXAMPLE 7. The graphs in Fig. 1–52(a) show the number of rabbits and foxes in a small arctic population. They are plotted as functions of time for 200 days. The number of rabbits increases at first, as the rabbits reproduce. But the foxes prey on the rabbits, and as the number of foxes increases, the rabbit population levels off and then drops.

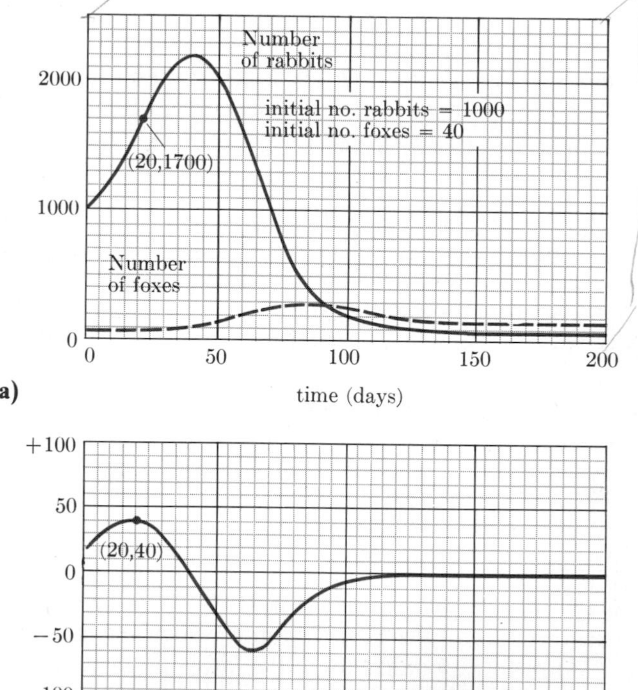

1–52 Rabbits and foxes in an arctic predator–prey food chain. (*Source: Differentiation*, by W. U. Walton *et al.*, Project CALC, Education Development Center, 1975, p. 86.)

The graph in Fig. 1–52(b) is the graph of the derivative of the rabbit population. It was made by estimating the slope of the population curve at frequent intervals. These estimates were plotted as values of the derivative, and a smooth curve was drawn through them. For example, the slope of the rabbit population curve at $t = 20$ is about 40. Figure 1–53 shows how this value was estimated. Accordingly, (20, 40) was plotted as a point on the graph of the derivative. In other words, the slope at the point (20, 1700) on the upper curve is the ordinate of the point (20, 40) on the lower curve.

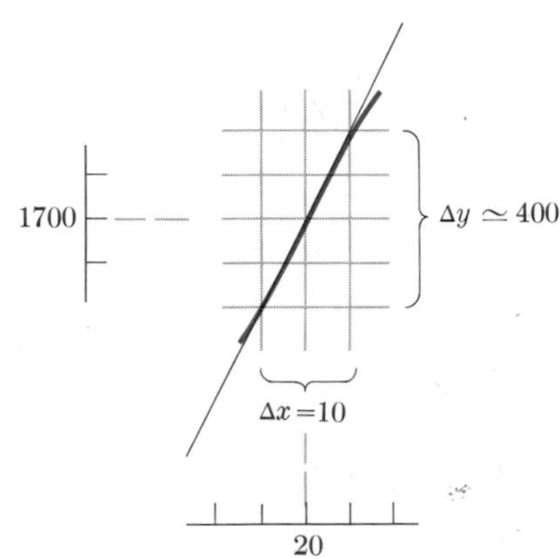

1–53 Enlarged view of rabbit-population curve near the day $x = 20$. The ratio $\Delta y/\Delta x = 40$ is a good estimate of the slope of the curve at the point (20, 1700) because the short segment of the curve is so close to being straight.

Note that the time when the rabbit population is dropping fastest is not when the fox population is largest. It occurs before the fox population peaks, about when the fox population is growing most rapidly. Rates of increase and decrease, and more generally the interpretation of derivatives as rates of change, are the subject of the next article.

PROBLEMS

For each of the functions f in Problems 1–20, find the derivative $f'(x)$, by means of the definition in Eq. (6) or Eq. (7). Then find the slope of the tangent to the curve $y = f(x)$ at $x = 3$, and write an equation for the tangent line.

1. $f(x) = x^2$ **2.** $f(x) = x^3$

3. $f(x) = 2x + 3$ **4.** $f(x) = x^2 - x + 1$

5. $f(x) = \dfrac{1}{x}$ **6.** $f(x) = \dfrac{1}{x^2}$

7. $f(x) = \dfrac{1}{2x + 1}$ **8.** $f(x) = \dfrac{x}{x + 1}$

9. $f(x) = 2x^2 - x + 5$ **10.** $f(x) = x^3 - 12x + 11$

11. $f(x) = x^4$

12. $f(x) = ax^2 + bx + c$ (a, b, c constants)

13. $f(x) = x - \dfrac{1}{x}$ **14.** $f(x) = ax + \dfrac{b}{x}$ (a, b constants)

15. $f(x) = \sqrt{2x}$ **16.** $f(x) = \sqrt{x + 1}$

17. $f(x) = \sqrt{2x + 3}$ **18.** $f(x) = \dfrac{1}{\sqrt{x}}$

19. $f(x) = \dfrac{1}{\sqrt{2x + 3}}$ **20.** $f(x) = \sqrt{x^2 + 1}$

21. Graph the derivative of $f(x) = |x|$ (Example 3). Then graph the function $y = |x|/x$, $x \neq 0$. What can you conclude?

22. What is the value of the derivative of the rabbit population in Example 7 when the number of rabbits is largest? smallest?

23. What is the size of the rabbit population in Example 7 when its derivative is largest? smallest?

24. Use the graphical technique described in Example 7 to sketch the graph of the derivative of the *Drosophila* population shown in Fig. 1–49.

1–9 VELOCITY AND RATES

When a body moves in a straight line, it is customary to represent the line of motion by a coordinate axis. We select a reference point 0 on the line as origin, adopt a positive direction and a unit of distance on the line, and then describe the motion by an equation which gives the coordinate of the body as a function of the time t that has elapsed since the start of the motion.

EXAMPLE 1. The equation of motion for a freely falling body is

$$s = \tfrac{1}{2}gt^2, \tag{1}$$

where g is the acceleration due to gravity and is approximately 32 (ft/sec^2), and s is the distance in feet that the body has fallen in t seconds from the start when it was at rest. (See Fig. 1–54.)

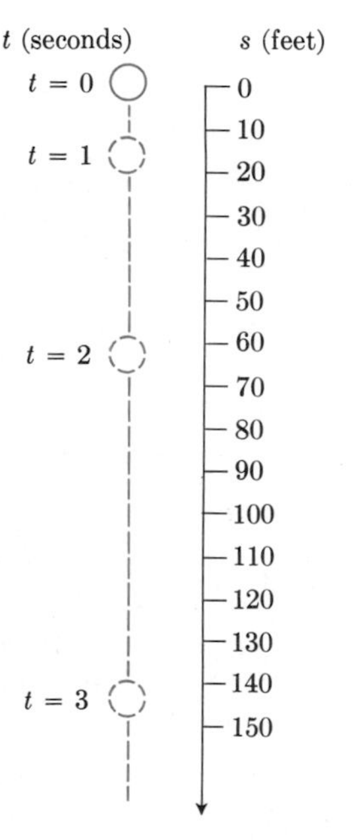

1–54 Distance fallen by a 3-cm ball bearing released at $t = 0$ seconds.

More generally, suppose the law of motion is given by a function f,

$$s = f(t), \tag{2}$$

and that we are required to find the *velocity* of the body at some instant of time t. First of all, how shall we *define* the instantaneous velocity of a moving body?

If we assume that *distance* and *time* are the fundamental physical quantities that we can measure, we may be led to reason as follows. At time t, the body is in the position

$$s = f(t), \tag{3}$$

and at time $t + \Delta t$ the body is in the position

$$s + \Delta s = f(t + \Delta t). \tag{4}$$

Hence during the interval of time from t to $t + \Delta t$, the body has undergone a displacement

$$\Delta s = f(t + \Delta t) - f(t). \tag{5}$$

The quantities in Eqs. (3), (4), and (5) are all physical quantities that can be measured (by clocks and tapelines, say).

We now define the *average velocity* of the moving body to be Δs divided by Δt:

$$v_{\text{av}} = \frac{\Delta s}{\Delta t} = \frac{f(t + \Delta t) - f(t)}{\Delta t}. \tag{6}$$

For example, a sprinter who runs 100 meters in 10 seconds has an average velocity of

$$v_{\text{av}} = \frac{\Delta s}{\Delta t} = \frac{100 \text{ m}}{10 \text{ sec}} = 10 \text{ m/sec}.$$

To obtain the *instantaneous velocity* of the moving body at time t, we take its average velocity over shorter and shorter intervals of time Δt. Then the instantaneous velocity, or what we call the *velocity at time t*, is the limit of the average velocities as Δt approaches zero:

$$v = \lim_{\Delta t \to 0} v_{\text{av}} = \lim_{\Delta t \to 0} \frac{\Delta s}{\Delta t} = \lim_{\Delta t \to 0} \frac{f(t + \Delta t) - f(t)}{\Delta t}. \tag{7}$$

Note that Eq. (7) defines v to be the derivative of $s = f(t)$ with respect to t:

$$v = \frac{ds}{dt} = f'(t). \tag{8}$$

EXAMPLE 2. Find the velocity of the freely falling body in Example 1.

Solution. The equation of motion in Example 1 is

$$s = \tfrac{1}{2}gt^2.$$

We apply the method of the previous article to find the derivative of s with respect to t. The result is

$$v = \frac{ds}{dt} = gt.$$

In general, when we graph $s = f(t)$ as a function of t, the average and instantaneous velocities both have geometric interpretations. The average velocity is the slope of a secant line (Fig. 1–55). The instantaneous velocity at time t is the slope of the tangent to the graph at the point $(t, f(t))$. (See Fig. 1–56.) The latter interpretation is sometimes used to estimate the velocity when our information about a motion is given by a graph instead of by an equation.

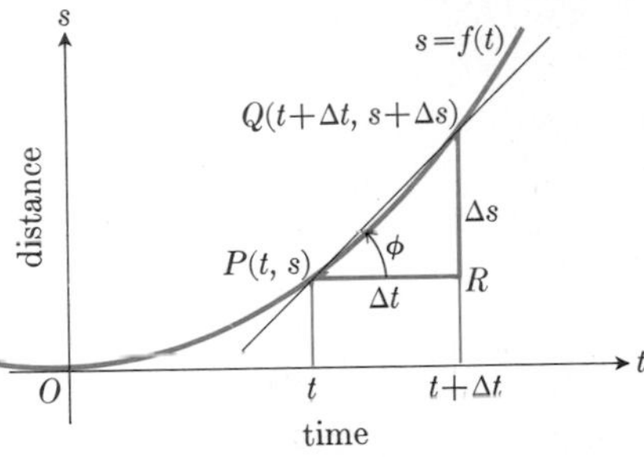

1–55 Distance vs. time for a moving body. The slope $\Delta s/\Delta t$ of the secant line PQ is the average velocity of the body over the interval from t to $(t + \Delta t)$.

EXAMPLE 3. In the graph of Fig. 1–56, s represents the coordinate of some point of a bicycle being ridden along a straight road. At $t = 8$, the tangent line appears to be rising at the rate of 40 s-units in an interval of two t-units; that is, the velocity at time $t = 8$ is apparently

$$\frac{40 \text{ (ft)}}{2 \text{ (sec)}} = 20 \text{ (ft/sec)}.$$

We say the velocity is "apparently" 20 ft/sec because we cannot be sure that we have accurately constructed the tangent to the curve. Indeed, an accurate construction would require that we know the derivative $f'(t)$ exactly at $t = 8$, and this is the very thing we are trying to estimate. On the other hand, we can make a fair approximation to the tangent line by inspection, and this is what we have done in the graph.

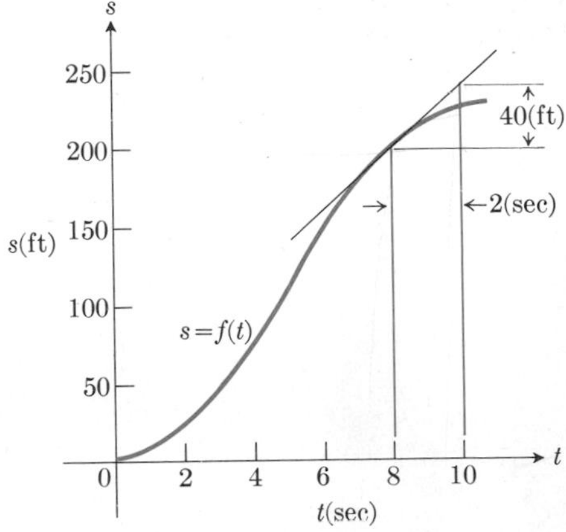

1–56 The motion of a bicyclist. The slope $m = 20$ ft/sec of the tangent line at $t = 8$ is the velocity at that instant. It is the limit of average velocities taken over shorter and shorter intervals.

There are many other applications of the notion of average rate and instantaneous rate.

EXAMPLE 4. The quantity of water Q (gal) in a reservoir at time t (min) is a function of t. Water may flow into or out of the reservoir. As it does so, suppose that Q changes by an amount ΔQ from time t to time $(t + \Delta t)$. Then the average and instantaneous rates of change of Q with respect to t are:

$$\text{Average rate:} \quad \frac{\Delta Q}{\Delta t} \text{ (gal/min)}$$

$$\text{Instantaneous rate:} \quad \frac{dQ}{dt} = \lim_{\Delta x \to 0} \frac{\Delta Q}{\Delta t} \text{ (gal/min).}$$

EXAMPLE 5. (*Marginal analysis*) Economists often call the derivative of a function the *marginal value* of the function. Suppose, for example, that a company produces x tons of steel per week at a total cost of $y = f(x)$ dollars. This total cost includes such items as a portion of the cost of building and maintaining the company's steel mills, salaries of executives, taxes, office maintenance, cost of raw materials, labor, etc. Suppose that to produce $x + \Delta x$ tons of steel weekly would cost $y + \Delta y$ dollars. The increase in cost per unit increase in output would be $\Delta y/\Delta x$. The limit of this ratio, as Δx tends to zero, is called the *marginal cost*. In other words, if the total cost is y for weekly output x, then the marginal cost is the derivative of y with respect to x. It gives the rate of increase of cost per unit increase of output from the level x. (See Problem 18.)

To sell x tons of steel per week, the company prices its steel at $P = F(x)$ dollars per ton. The company's *revenue* is then the product $xP = xF(x)$. Its *marginal revenue* is the derivative of xP with respect to x, or the rate of change of revenue per unit increase in production. The company's profit, T, is the difference between revenue and cost:

$$T = xP - y.$$

In Chapter 3 we shall see how the company should adjust production to achieve maximum profit. The adjustment involves the *marginal profit*, dT/dx, which is the rate of increase of profit per unit increase of production. (For a further discussion of applications to economics, see Chapter 3 of William J. Baumol's *Economic Theory and Operations Research, Fourth Edition*, Prentice-Hall, Inc., 1977.)

Every derivative may be interpreted as the instantaneous rate of change of one variable per unit change in another. Thus, if the function defined by $y = f(x)$ has a derivative

$$f'(x) = \lim_{\Delta x \to 0} \frac{\Delta y}{\Delta x} = \lim_{\Delta x \to 0} \frac{f(x + \Delta x) - f(x)}{\Delta x},$$

we may interpret $\Delta y/\Delta x$ as *average rate of change* and

$$f'(x) = \lim_{\Delta x \to 0} \frac{\Delta y}{\Delta x}$$

as *instantaneous rate of change* of y with respect to x. Such a rate tells us the amount of change that would be produced in y by a change of one unit in x, provided the rate of change remained constant.

The average rate of change of y per unit change in x, $\Delta y/\Delta x$, when multiplied by the number of units of change in x, Δx, gives the actual change in y:

$$\Delta y = \frac{\Delta y}{\Delta x}\Delta x.$$

The instantaneous rate of change of y per unit change in x, $f'(x)$, multiplied by the number of units change in x, Δx, gives the change that would be produced in y if the point (x, y) were to move along the *tangent line* instead of moving along the curve; that is,

$$\Delta y_{\tan} = f'(x)\,\Delta x.$$

(See Fig. 1–57.)

One reason calculus is important is that it enables us to find quantitatively how a change in one of two related variables affects the other variable.

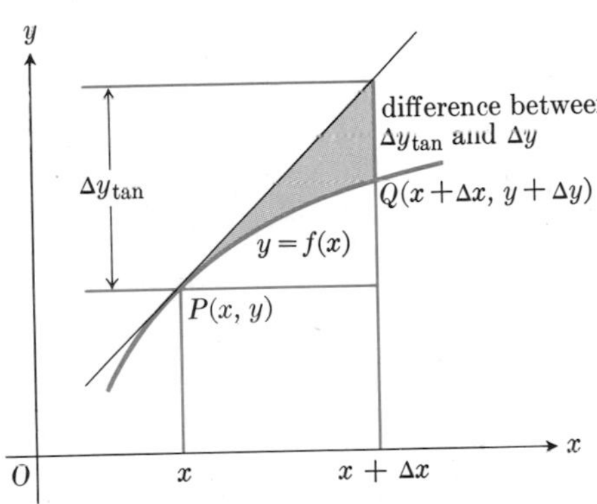

1–57 If f has a derivative at x, the difference between $\Delta y_{\tan} = f'(x)\,\Delta x$ and Δy will be small when Δx is small.

PROBLEMS

1. If a, b, c are constants and

$$f(t) = at^2 + bt + c,$$

show that

$$f'(t) = \lim_{\Delta t \to 0} \frac{f(t + \Delta t) - f(t)}{\Delta t} = 2at + b.$$

In Problems 2 through 10, the law of motion gives s as a function of t. Apply the *result* found in Problem 1 above to write the velocity, $v = ds/dt$, by inspection.

2. $s = 2t^2 + 5t - 3$

3. $s = \frac{1}{2}gt^2 + v_0 t + s_0$ $(g, v_0, s_0$ constants)

4. $s = 4t + 3$

5. $s = t^2 - 3t + 2$

6. $s = 4 - 2t - t^2$

7. $s = (2t + 3)^2$

8. $s = (2 - t)^2$

9. $s = 3 - 2t^2$

10. $s = 64t - 16t^2$

11. The following data give the coordinates s of a moving body for various values of t. Plot s versus t on coordinate paper and sketch a smooth curve through the given points. Assuming that this smooth curve represents the motion of the body, estimate the velocity (a) at $t = 1.0$, (b) at $t = 2.5$, (c) at $t = 2.0$.

s (in ft)	10	38	58	70	74	70	58	38	10
t (in sec)	0	0.5	1.0	1.5	2.0	2.5	3.0	3.5	4.0

12.* When a certain chemical reaction was allowed to run for t minutes, it produced the amounts of substance $A(t)$ shown in the following table.

t (min)	10	15	20	25	30	35	40
$A(t)$ (moles)	26.5	36.5	44.8	52.1	57.1	61.3	64.4

a) Find the average rate of the reaction for the interval from $t = 20$ to $t = 30$.

b) Plot the data points from the table, draw a smooth curve through them, and estimate the instantaneous rate of the reaction at $t = 25$.

When a model rocket is launched, the propellant burns for a few seconds, accelerating the rocket upwards. After burnout, the rocket coasts upward for a while, then begins a period of free fall back to the ground. A small explosive charge pops out a parachute shortly after the rocket starts down. The parachute slows the rocket's fall enough to keep it from breaking when it lands. Figure 1–58 shows velocity data from the flight of a model rocket. Use the data to answer the questions in Problems 13–17.

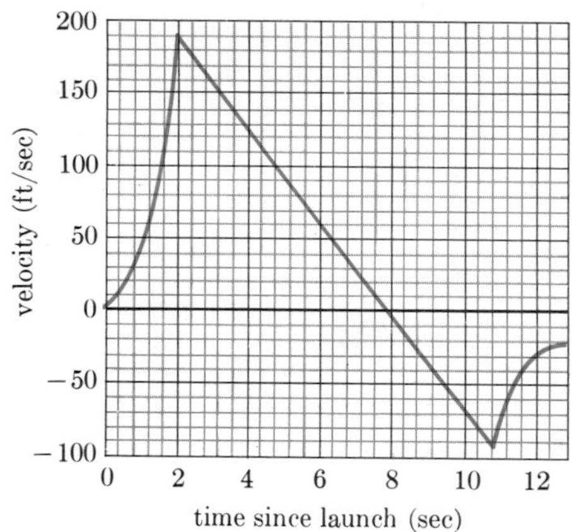

1–58 Velocity of a model rocket.

13. How fast was the rocket climbing when the engine stopped?

* Data from *Some Mathematical Models in Biology*, Revised Edition, R. M. Thrall, J. A. Mortimer, K. R. Rebman, R. F. Baum, Eds., December, 1967, PB-202 364, p. 72; distributed by N.T.I.S., U.S. Department of Commerce.

14. For how many seconds did the engine burn?

15. When did the rocket reach its highest point? What was its velocity then?

16. When did the parachute pop out? How fast was the rocket falling then?

17. How long did the rocket fall before the parachute popped out?

18. Suppose that the dollar cost of producing x washing machines is $f(x) = 2000 + 100x - 0.1x^2$.

a) Find the average cost of producing 100 washing machines.

b) Find the marginal cost for 100 washing machines.

c) Show that the marginal cost for 100 washing machines is approximately the cost of producing one more washing machine after the first 100 have been made, by (i) computing the cost directly, (ii) interpreting Fig. 1–57 drawn for $f(x) = 2000 + 100x - 0.1x^2$, with $x = 100$ and $\Delta x = 1$.

19. When a bactericide was added to a nutrient broth in which bacteria were growing, the bacteria population continued to grow for a while, but then stopped growing and began to decline. The size of the population at time t (hours) was $b(t) = 10^6 + 10^4 t - 10^3 t^2$. Use the result of Problem 1 to find the growth rates at

a) $t = 0$, **b)** $t = 5$, and **c)** $t = 10$ hours.

d) About how long did it take to kill all the bacteria?

20. A swimming pool is to be drained for cleaning. If Q represents the number of gallons of water in the pool t minutes after the pool has started to drain, and $Q = 200(30 - t)^2$, how fast is the water running out at the end of 10 minutes? What is the *average* rate at which the water flows out during the first 10 minutes?

21. **a)** If the radius of a circle changes from r to $(r + \Delta r)$, what is the average rate of change of the area of the circle with respect to the radius?

b) Find the instantaneous rate of change of the area with respect to the radius.

22. The volume V (ft³) of a sphere of radius r (ft) is $V = \frac{4}{3}\pi r^3$. Find the rate of change of V with respect to r.

23. The radius r and altitude h of a certain cone are equal at all times. Find the rate of change of the volume $V = \frac{1}{3}\pi r^2 h$ with respect to h.

PROPERTIES OF LIMITS

In this article we look more carefully at what it means to say that something "approaches a limit." The limits we are most concerned with are the ones that come up in the calculation of the derivative

$$f'(x) = \lim_{\Delta x \to 0} \frac{f(x + \Delta x) - f(x)}{\Delta x} \tag{1}$$

of the function $y = f(x)$. In the next chapter we shall develop rules that will let us calculate the derivatives of a wide variety of functions without having to apply Eq. (1) directly each time, as we have had to do so far. But these rules still rest upon this defining equation, for they are themselves derived from it.

Let us return to the function

$$f(x) = x^3 - 3x + 3 \tag{2}$$

investigated in Article 1–7. By algebra we find that

$$\frac{f(x + \Delta x) - f(x)}{\Delta x} = 3x^2 - 3 + 3x\,\Delta x + (\Delta x)^2. \tag{3}$$

The notion of limit has not entered so far. But now we say "hold x fixed and make Δx approach 0." That is, Δx is to vary in Eq. (3) while x is held constant. What is the domain of the variable Δx in this equation? The answer is first that Δx must be such that the function in (2) is defined at $(x + \Delta x)$. That is, $f(x + \Delta x)$ must make sense. In the present case this places no restriction on Δx, since Eq. (2) defines f for the domain of all real numbers. But there is also the second restriction that Δx *must be different from zero*, because we cannot divide by zero. Thus we reach a crucial point. We want to know what happens in Eq. (3) when Δx is taken nearer and nearer to zero, but we cannot take $\Delta x = 0$.

We get past this point by making two observations. First, Eq. (3) holds for every value of Δx different from zero, no matter how small. Second, for each fixed value of x we can make the right side of Eq. (3) as nearly equal to

$$L(x) = 3x^2 - 3 \tag{4}$$

as we wish, provided we don't wish for exact equality, by taking Δx sufficiently close to zero. Let us write $F(x, \Delta x)$ for the right side of Eq. (3) to acknowledge that it depends on both x and Δx. That is,

$$F(x, \Delta x) = 3x^2 - 3 + 3x\,\Delta x + (\Delta x)^2. \tag{5}$$

Then our second observation is what we mean when we say that for each x the limit of $F(x, \Delta x)$, as Δx approaches zero, is $L(x)$. We illustrate this idea and develop a more formal statement of it in the course of the next example.

EXAMPLE 1. Suppose that we are manufacturers of the product $F(x, \Delta x)$ in Eq. (5), which, if we could achieve perfection, would be the $L(x)$ of Eq. (4). A buyer comes to us to place an order. The buyer is particular, but does not expect perfection. To satisfy the buyer, we need only produce an $F(x, \Delta x)$ that differs from perfection by an amount less than a certain tolerance limit, which the buyer will specify. In other words, we can sell our $F(x, \Delta x)$ if we can guarantee that it lies between

$$L(x) - \epsilon \quad \text{and} \quad L(x) + \epsilon, \tag{6}$$

where ϵ (epsilon) is a positive number representing the prescribed tolerance limit. For instance, we might contract to grind a shaft to a diameter of 3 ± 10^{-5} inches. The ideal diameter is $L(x) = 3$ in. The tolerance limit is $\epsilon = 10^{-5}$ in. The diameter of the shaft we produce is $F(x, \Delta x)$. We can sell our work provided $F(x, \Delta x)$ lies between $L(x) - 10^{-5}$ and $L(x) + 10^{-5}$ inches.

Now, the way we improve the quality of our product $F(x, \Delta x)$ is to make Δx small. In other words, the amount of imperfection,

$$F(x, \Delta x) - L(x) = 3x\,\Delta x + (\Delta x)^2 \tag{7}$$

is brought between $-\epsilon$ and $+\epsilon$,

$$-\epsilon < 3x\,\Delta x + (\Delta x)^2 < +\epsilon, \tag{8a}$$

by making Δx close to zero. By taking pains, we can make Δx as close to zero (either positive or negative) as we wish. Therefore we can always satisfy the most exacting customer.

Here is the order of events. The customer first places an order and specifies an $\epsilon > 0$. Then, for any fixed x, we satisfy the inequalities in (8a) by taking Δx close enough to zero. That is, given the ϵ, there is a positive number δ (Greek letter "delta"), which may be very small, such that (8a) is satisfied when we take Δx so small that $-\delta < \Delta x < \delta$, $\Delta x \neq 0$.

How do we find a δ that will work for the given ϵ?

The inequalities in (8a) are the same as

$$|3x\,\Delta x + (\Delta x)^2| < \epsilon. \tag{8b}$$

Can we solve (8b) for Δx, in terms of ϵ and x? *Yes*, if we use a bit of strategy! That $(\Delta x)^2$ in (8b) makes the mathematics harder than it has to be. We do not, in fact, have to find the *complete* solution set for (8b): We need only be sure we make $|\Delta x|$ small enough to win. We can take advantage of the fact that powers like $(\Delta x)^2$, $(\Delta x)^3$, and so on are smaller in absolute value than the first power $|\Delta x|$, whenever $|\Delta x| < 1$. Since we plan to make $|\Delta x|$ small anyway, we start by making it less than one. So our first step in "solving" (8b) is to make

i) $$0 < |\Delta x| < 1,$$

and to observe that (i) implies

ii) $$|(\Delta x)|^2 < |\Delta x|.$$

The next step is to apply the triangle inequality $|a + b| \leq |a| + |b|$ to the left side of (8b), and get

iii) $$|3x\,\Delta x + (\Delta x)^2| \leq |3x\,\Delta x| + |(\Delta x)^2|.$$

Combining (i) through (iii), we get

$$\begin{aligned} |3x\,\Delta x + (\Delta x)^2| &\leq |3x\,\Delta x| + |(\Delta x)^2| \\ &< |3x|\,|\Delta x| + |\Delta x| = (|3x| + 1)|\Delta x|. \end{aligned} \tag{8c}$$

From this we see that any $|\Delta x|$ that is both less than 1 and small enough to make

$$(|3x| + 1)|\Delta x| < \epsilon \tag{8d}$$

will satisfy (8b). To find such a Δx, we divide both sides of (8d) by $(|3x| + 1)$:

$$|\Delta x| < \frac{\epsilon}{|3x| + 1}. \tag{8e}$$

For specific numerical values of ϵ and x we can satisfy (8b) if we let δ be the smaller of the two numbers

$$1 \quad \text{and} \quad \frac{\epsilon}{|3x| + 1},$$

and then require that $0 < |\Delta x| < \delta$.

What we have just shown, for the particular functions $L(x)$ and $F(x, \Delta x)$ given by Eqs. (4) and (5), is this: *Given any number x and any positive number ϵ, there exists a positive number δ such that*

$$|F(x, \Delta x) - L(x)| < \epsilon$$

for all Δx with

$$0 < |\Delta x| < \delta.$$

Because there is such a positive number δ for *each* possible tolerance specification ϵ, we say that $L(x)$ is the *limit* of $F(x, \Delta x)$ as Δx approaches zero.

REMARK 1. In the foregoing example, if we were interested only in values of x for which $-4 \le x \le 4$, say, then $|3x| + 1 \le 12 + 1 = 13$. In such a situation, for any positive number ϵ, the number $\delta = \min\{1, \epsilon/13\}$ would always be a sufficiently small positive number to guarantee fulfillment of our contract.

REMARK 2. We sometimes have to impose a further restriction $|\Delta x| \le h$ on Δx to keep $(x + \Delta x)$ within the domain of f. (This eventuality is taken into account in the first sentence of the definition below.) If $f(x) = \sqrt{9 - x^2}$, then

$$F(x, \Delta x) = \frac{\sqrt{9 - (x + \Delta x)^2} - \sqrt{9 - x^2}}{\Delta x},$$

and we need to require

$$|x + \Delta x| \le 3 \quad \textit{as well as} \quad |x| \le 3 \quad \textit{and} \quad \Delta x \ne 0.$$

For $x = 2.7$, for example, we could take $h = 0.3$ to guarantee $|x + \Delta x| \le 3$ when $|\Delta x| \le h$.

These preliminary remarks should now enable us to understand the following definition of a limit.

Definition. *Let $F(x, \Delta x)$ be defined for some fixed value of x and for all values of Δx (different from zero) in some interval $-h < \Delta x < +h$, that is, for $-h < \Delta x < 0$ and for $0 < \Delta x < +h$. Let there be a number $L(x)$ (which may depend upon x), such that, to any positive number ϵ, there corresponds a positive number δ, $0 < \delta < h$, having the property that $F(x, \Delta x)$ differs from $L(x)$ by less than ϵ for every $|\Delta x|$ that is different from zero and less than δ. That is, if*

$$0 < |\Delta x| < \delta, \tag{9a}$$

then

$$|F(x, \Delta x) - L(x)| < \epsilon. \tag{9b}$$

We then say that $L(x)$ *is the limit of* $F(x, \Delta x)$ *as* Δx *approaches zero, and abbreviate this by writing*

$$L(x) = \lim_{\Delta x \to 0} F(x, \Delta x). \tag{10}$$

The notation in the definition above is complicated by the fact that the function $F(x, \Delta x)$ depends upon both x and Δx, although only Δx varies during the limit process. If we ignore the x completely and use another letter, say t instead of Δx, to stand for the variable, we obtain a simpler definition of limit, as follows.

Definition. *A function F, which is defined on the domain*

$$t_1 < t < c \quad \text{and} \quad c < t < t_2,$$

is said to approach the limit L as t approaches c, and we write

$$\lim_{t \to c} F(t) = L$$

if, given any positive number ϵ*, there is a positive number* δ *such that the values of F are within* ϵ *of L for all t within* δ *of c,* $t \neq c$*:*

$$|F(t) - L| < \epsilon \quad \text{when} \quad 0 < |t - c| < \delta.$$

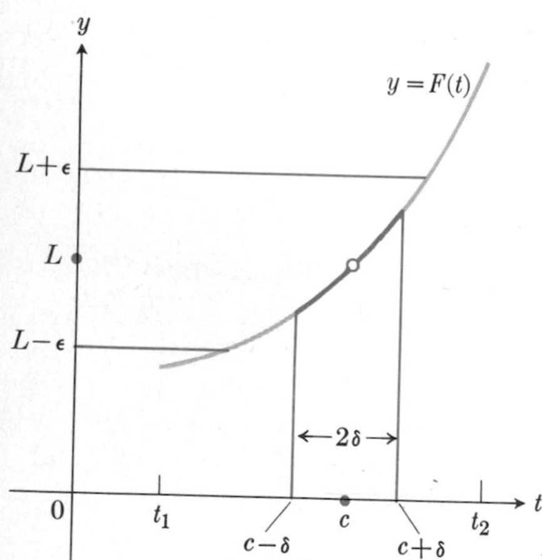

1–59 $F(t)$ can be kept between $L - \epsilon$ and $L + \epsilon$ by keeping t between $c - \delta$ and $c + \delta$.

Note that saying "$F(t)$ approaches L" is the same as saying "$F(t) - L$ approaches zero." Also, there is no best value of δ. If one value of δ works for a given ϵ, then every positive number *smaller* than that δ will work, too. (See Fig. 1–59.)

The function F may or may not be defined at $t = c$. We shall illustrate the definition by several examples.

Sometimes, the function F is defined at c and the limit as t approaches c is just $F(c)$. This is the situation when $F(t)$ is a polynomial function of t.

EXAMPLE 2. Show that the limit of $F(t) = t^2$, as t approaches 3, is $L = 9$.

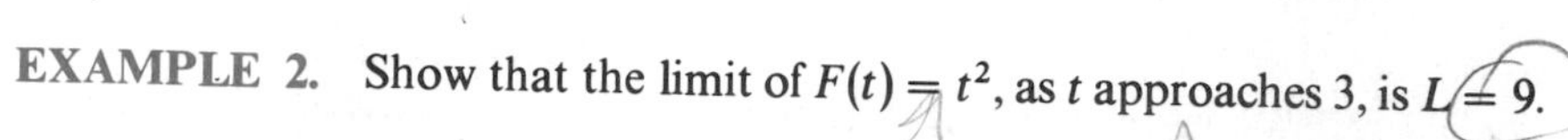

Solution. What we have to show is this: For any positive number ϵ there is a positive number δ such that

$$|t^2 - 9| < \epsilon \quad \text{when} \quad 0 < |t - 3| < \delta.$$

Note that

$$|t^2 - 9| = |(t + 3)(t - 3)| = |t + 3|\,|t - 3|$$

is the product of a factor $|t + 3|$ that is near 6 and a factor $|t - 3|$ that is near 0 when t is near 3. If we first require t to stay within, say, 0.5 of 3, then

$$2.5 < t < 3.5 \quad \text{and} \quad 5.5 < t + 3 < 6.5.$$

As a result,

$$|t^2 - 9| < 6.5|t - 3|.$$

Now

$$6.5|t - 3| < \epsilon \qquad \text{provided} \quad |t - 3| < \frac{\epsilon}{6.5}.$$

Therefore, if $\delta = \min\{0.5, \epsilon/6.5\}$ then

$$|t^2 - 9| < \epsilon \qquad \text{when} \quad 0 < |t - 3| < \delta.$$

(See Fig. 1–60.)

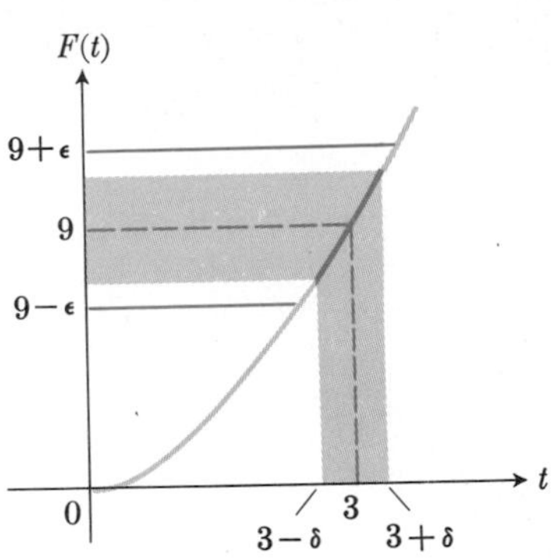

1–60 $F(t) = t^2$ lies between $9 - \epsilon$ and $9 + \epsilon$ for every $t \neq 3$ between $3 - \delta$ and $3 + \delta$.

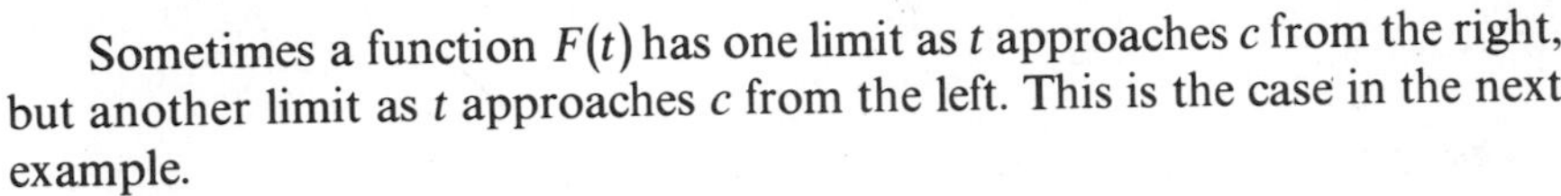

Sometimes a function $F(t)$ has one limit as t approaches c from the right, but another limit as t approaches c from the left. This is the case in the next example.

EXAMPLE 3. Investigate the limit of the function F defined by

$$F(t) = [t], \text{ the greatest integer in } t,$$

as t approaches 3. (See Fig. 1–61.)

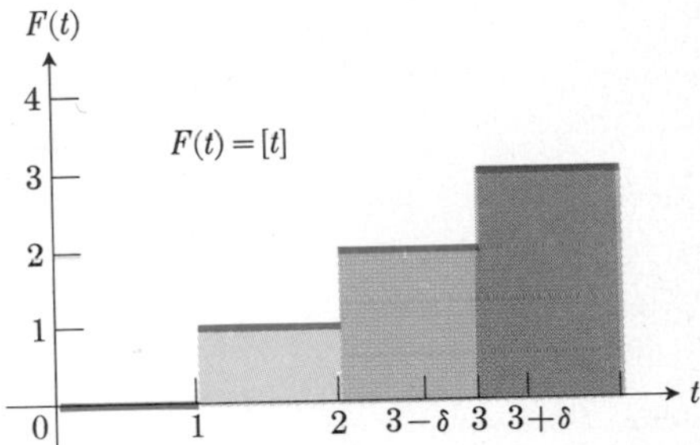

1–61 At each integer the greatest integer function has different right- and lefthand limits.

Solution. Our first guess might be that the required limit is $L = 3$, since certainly the functional values of $F(t) = [t]$ are close to 3 when t is equal to or slightly *greater* than 3. But when t is slightly *less* than 3, say $t = 2.9999$, then $[t] = 2$. That is, if δ is any positive number less than unity, $0 < \delta < 1$, then

$$[t] = 2 \qquad \text{if} \quad 3 - \delta < t < 3,$$

while

$$[t] = 3 \qquad \text{if} \quad 3 < t < 3 + \delta.$$

Hence, if we are challenged with a small positive ϵ, for example $\epsilon = 0.01$, we cannot find a $\delta > 0$ that makes

$$|[t] - 3| < \epsilon \qquad \text{for} \quad 0 < |t - 3| < \delta.$$

In fact, no number L will work as the limit in this case. When t is near 3, *some* of the functional values of $[t]$ are 2 while others are 3. Hence the functional values are not all close to any one number L. Therefore,

$$\lim_{t \to 3} [t] \text{ does not exist.}$$

The so-called "right- and lefthand limits" do, however, exist. As the names imply, the righthand limit L^+ is a number such that the functional values of $F(t)$ are close to L^+ when t is slightly greater than 3 (that is, to the right of 3), and the lefthand limit L^- is a number such that $F(t)$ is close to L^- when t is slightly less than 3. In our example,

$$L^+ = \lim_{t \to 3^+} [t] = 3, \qquad L^- = \lim_{t \to 3^-} [t] = 2.$$

The notation $t \to 3^+$ may be read "t approaches 3 from above" (or "from the right," or "through values larger than 3") with an analogous meaning for $t \to 3^-$.

Sometimes a function $F(t)$ has neither a right- nor a lefthand limit as t approaches c.

EXAMPLE 4. The function F, $F(t) = \sin(1/t)$, $t \neq 0$, has no limit as $t \to 0$. This is a consequence of the fact that in every neighborhood of $t = 0$ the function F takes all values between -1 and $+1$. Hence there is no single number L such that the functional values $F(t)$ are *all* close to L when t is close to zero. These remarks apply even when we restrict t to positive values or to negative values. In other words, this function does not even have a righthand limit or a lefthand limit as t approaches zero. (See Fig. 1–62.)

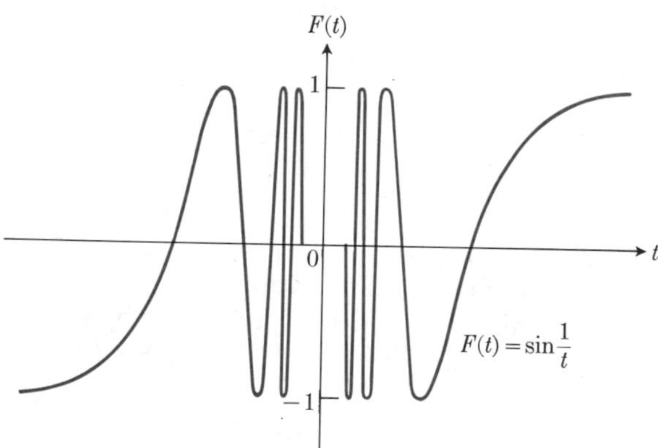

1–62 The function $F(t) = \sin(1/t)$, $t \neq 0$, has neither a right- nor a lefthand limit as t approaches 0.

Sometimes a function $F(t)$ has a limit as $t \to c$ even though the function is not defined at $t = c$. We shall describe such a function in Example 6, but first we state a theorem that gives us information we can use to treat the example easily. The theorem presents four fundamental properties of limits.

***Theorem* 1.** *If $L_1 = \lim_{t\to c} F_1(t)$ and $L_2 = \lim_{t\to c} F_2(t)$ both exist and are finite, then*

i) $\lim [F_1(t) + F_2(t)] = \lim F_1(t) + \lim F_2(t) = L_1 + L_2$,

ii) $\lim [kF_1(t)] = k \lim F_1(t) = kL_1$ $\quad$ (*k any number*),

iii) $\lim [F_1(t) \cdot F_2(t)] = \lim F_1(t) \cdot \lim F_2(t) = L_1 L_2$,

iv) $\lim \dfrac{F_1(t)}{F_2(t)} = \dfrac{\lim F_1(t)}{\lim F_2(t)} = \dfrac{L_1}{L_2}, \quad \text{if} \quad L_2 \neq 0,$

it being understood that all of the limits are to be taken as $t \to c$.

The formal proof of Theorem 1 is given in Article 1–11. You may wish to postpone the details until then. Informally, we can paraphrase the theorem in terms that make it highly reasonable: When t is close to c, $F_1(t)$ is close to L_1 and $F_2(t)$ is close to L_2. Then we naturally think that $F_1(t) + F_2(t)$ is close to $L_1 + L_2$, $kF_1(t)$ is close to kL_1, $F_1(t) \cdot F_2(t)$ is close to $L_1 L_2$, and $F_1(t)/F_2(t)$ is close to L_1/L_2 if L_2 is not zero. We use these ideas when we calculate sums, products, or quotients in which we approximate irrational numbers like π or $\sqrt{3}$ with rational numbers like 3.14159 or 1.732. What keeps this discussion from being a proof is that the word "close" is not precise. The phrases "arbitrarily close to" and "sufficiently close to" might improve things a bit, but the full ϵ and δ treatment of Article 1–11 is the clincher.

The limits must be *finite* in this theorem, and (iv) applies only if the denominator does not tend to zero.

We should add a word about the meaning to be attached to such statements as: "When t approaches zero, $1/t$ approaches infinity" or, in symbols,

$$\lim_{t \to 0} \frac{1}{t} = \infty.$$

(See Fig. 1–63.) The specific meaning of the expression

$$\lim_{t \to c} F(t) = \infty$$

is: "For any M, however large it may be, there is an $h > 0$ such that $|F(t)| > M$ for all t satisfying $0 < |t - c| < h$." Note that this allows $F(t)$ to be either negative or positive, and requires only that the *numerical* or *absolute* value of $F(t)$ can be made indefinitely large by taking t sufficiently close to c. If we may replace $|F(t)| > M$ by $F(t) > M$ in the statement above, we say $\lim F(t) = +\infty$, and if we may replace $|F(t)| > M$ by $F(t) < -M$, we say $\lim F(t) = -\infty$. Thus

$$\lim_{t \to 0} \frac{1}{t} = \infty, \qquad \lim_{t \to 0} \frac{1}{|t|} = +\infty, \qquad \lim_{t \to 0} -\frac{1}{t^2} = -\infty. \tag{11}$$

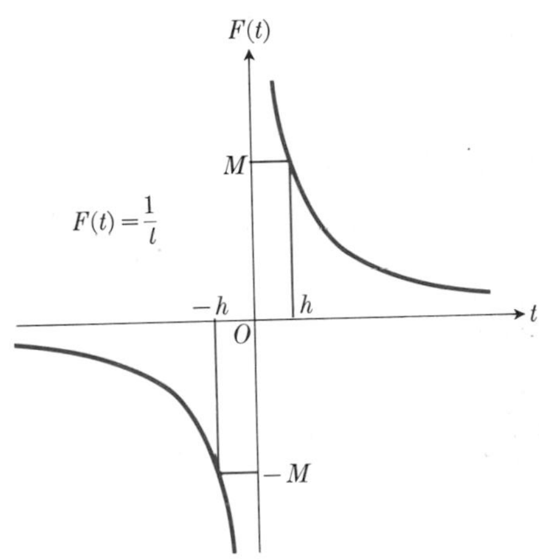

1–63 $\lim_{t \to 0^+} (1/t) = +\infty$ and $\lim_{t \to 0^-} (1/t) = -\infty$.

When speaking of infinity as the limit of a function f, we do not mean that the difference between $f(t)$ and infinity becomes small, but rather that $f(t)$ is numerically large when t is near c.

The great virtue of Theorem 1 is this: Once we notice that, for the function $F(t) = t$,

$$\lim_{t \to c} t = c, \tag{12}$$

and that, for the constant function $F(t) = k$ (the function whose value is the constant k for every t),

$$\lim_{t \to c} k = k, \tag{13}$$

then we immediately have

$$\lim_{t \to c} t^2 = c^2, \qquad \text{(from (iii))}$$

$$\lim_{t \to c} t^2 - 5 = c^2 - 5, \qquad \text{(from (i))}$$

$$\lim_{t \to c} 4t^2 = 4c^2, \qquad \text{(from (ii))}$$

and, if $c \neq 0$,

$$\lim_{t \to c} \frac{t^2 - 5}{4t^2} = \frac{c^2 - 5}{4c^2} \qquad \text{(from (iv))}.$$

In short, if $f(t)$ and $g(t)$ are any polynomials in t whatsoever, then

$$\lim_{t \to c} \frac{f(t)}{g(t)} = \frac{f(c)}{g(c)}, \qquad \text{provided } g(c) \neq 0. \tag{14}$$

(See Problems 1–6 of Article 1–11.)

EXAMPLE 5. Find

$$\lim_{t \to 2} \frac{t^2 + 2t + 4}{t + 2}.$$

Solution. The function whose limit we are to find is the quotient of two polynomials. The denominator, $t + 2$, is not zero when $t = 2$. Therefore, by Eq. (14),

$$\lim_{t \to 2} \frac{t^2 + 2t + 4}{t + 2} = \frac{(2)^2 + 2 \cdot 2 + 4}{2 + 2} = 3.$$

The condition $L_2 \neq 0$ in part (iv) of Theorem 1 means, of course, that limits like the ones required in the determination of instantaneous velocity and the slope of a curve, that have *both* L_1 and L_2 equal to zero, cannot be evaluated by the direct use of (iv). The next example shows how we can sometimes get around this problem. The key is to replace the offending quotient $f(t)/g(t)$ by an expression that (1) has the same values as the quotient for all values of t near c, and therefore the same limit as $t \to c$ (if there is one), and (2) whose limit as $t \to c$ is found by evaluating the expression at $t = c$. Fortunately, to do all this is often easier than it sounds.

EXAMPLE 6. Does the function

$$F(t) = \frac{t^3 - 8}{t^2 - 4}$$

have a limit as t approaches 2? If so, what is it?

Solution. Both the numerator and the denominator of $F(t)$ approach 0 as $t \to 2$. However, if we factor the numerator and denominator, we find that

$$\frac{t^3 - 8}{t^2 - 4} = \frac{(t - 2)(t^2 + 2t + 4)}{(t - 2)(t + 2)}$$

Therefore, for all values of t different from 2, $(t - 2)/(t - 2) = 1$ and

$$\frac{t^3 - 8}{t^2 - 4} = \frac{t^2 + 2t + 4}{t + 2}.$$

Hence,

$$\lim_{t \to 2} \frac{t^3 - 8}{t^2 - 4} = \lim_{t \to 2} \frac{t^2 + 2t + 4}{t + 2} = 3.$$

The function $F(t)$ does have a limit as $t \to 2$, and that limit is 3.

(1–10)

The two basic steps in evaluating the limit of the quotient $F(t)$ as t approached 2 were: (1) divide the numerator and denominator by a common factor, and (2) evaluate the simplified expression at $t = 2$.

We conclude this article with a theorem that will be used repeatedly in our later work. The theorem is often called the "sandwich theorem."

***Theorem* 2** (The Sandwich Theorem). *Suppose $f(t) \le g(t) \le h(t)$ for all values of t near c. Furthermore, suppose that the function values $f(t)$ and $h(t)$ approach a common limit L as t approaches c. Then $g(t)$ also approaches L as limit when t approaches c.*

Proof. By hypothesis, to any positive number ϵ there corresponds a positive number δ such that both $f(t)$ and $h(t)$ lie between $L - \epsilon$ and $L + \epsilon$ when t is within δ units of c, and $t \neq c$; that is,

$$L - \epsilon < f(t) < L + \epsilon, \qquad L - \epsilon < h(t) < L + \epsilon$$

when

$$0 < |t - c| < \delta.$$

But this also implies

$$L - \epsilon < f(t) \le g(t) \le h(t) < L + \epsilon$$

or

$$L - \epsilon < g(t) < L + \epsilon.$$

In other words,

$$|g(t) - L| < \epsilon \qquad \text{when} \quad 0 < |t - c| < \delta.$$

This establishes the conclusion,

$$\lim_{t \to c} g(t) = L. \qquad \text{Q.E.D.}$$

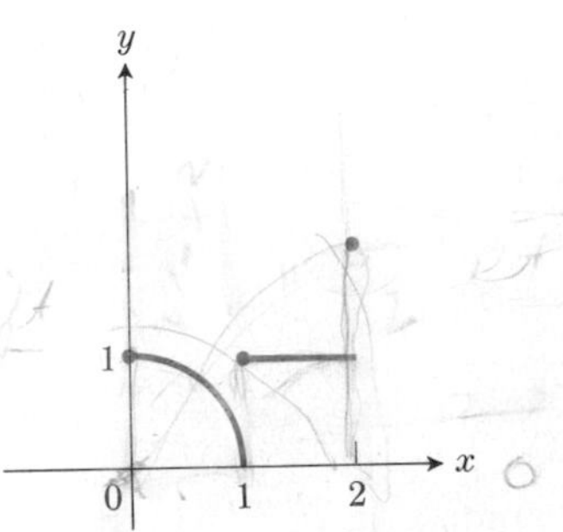

1–64 To define a function like the one graphed here, different formulas may be used for different parts of the domain.

PROBLEMS

Evaluate the limits indicated in Problems 1–8.

1. $\displaystyle\lim_{t \to 2} \frac{t+3}{t+2}$

2. $\displaystyle\lim_{x \to 1} \frac{x^2 - 1}{x - 1}$

3. $\displaystyle\lim_{y \to 2} \frac{y^2 + 5y + 6}{y + 2}$

4. $\displaystyle\lim_{y \to 2} \frac{y^2 - 5y + 6}{y - 2}$

5. $\displaystyle\lim_{x \to -3} \frac{x^2 + 4x + 3}{x + 3}$

6. $\displaystyle\lim_{x \to 1} \frac{2x - 1}{8x^3 - 1}$

7. $\displaystyle\lim_{t \to \infty} \frac{t+1}{t^2 + 1}$ [Set $t = 1/h$, simplify, and let $h \to 0$.]

8. $\displaystyle\lim_{t \to \infty} \frac{t^2 - 2t + 3}{2t^2 + 5t - 3}$

9. The values of the function graphed in Fig. 1–64 are given by:

$$f(x) = \begin{cases} \sqrt{1 - x^2}, & \text{if } 0 \le x < 1, \\ 1, & \text{if } 1 \le x < 2, \\ 2, & \text{if } x = 2. \end{cases}$$

a) At what points c in the domain of f does $\lim_{x \to c} f(x)$ exist?

b) At what points does only the lefthand limit exist?

c) Only the righthand limit?

10. Suppose that the function f is defined by

$$f(x) = \begin{cases} x & \text{if } -1 \le x < 0, \text{ or } 0 < x \le 1, \\ 1 & \text{if } x = 0, \\ 0 & \text{if } x < -1, \text{ or } x > 1. \end{cases}$$

Graph f, and repeat parts (a), (b), and (c) of Problem 9.

11. The attempt to find a derivative for $f(x) = |x|$ at $x = 0$ leads to the consideration of $\lim (|\Delta x|/\Delta x)$. Find $\lim_{\Delta x \to 0^+} (|\Delta x|/\Delta x)$ and $\lim_{\Delta x \to 0^-} (|\Delta x|/\Delta x)$ and conclude that $|x|$ has no derivative at 0.

12. Find some neighborhood of $t = 3$, that is, a domain $0 < |t - 3| < \delta$, such that, when t is restricted to this domain, the difference between $t^2 + t$ and 12 will be numerically smaller than (a) $\frac{1}{10}$, (b) $\frac{1}{100}$, (c) ϵ, where ϵ may be any positive number. [See Example 2.]

13. As $x \to 0^+$, the functions $1/x$, $1/x^2$, $1/\sqrt{x}$ all become infinite. Which one increases most rapidly and which one least rapidly?

14. Find $\lim_{x \to 1} [(x^n - 1)/(x - 1)]$, n a positive integer. Compare your result with the limit in Problem 2.

It is sometimes easy to guess the value of a limit once it is known to exist. Ignoring the question of whether the limits in Problems 15 and 16 exist (they do, and are finite), use a calculator to guess their value. First take $\Delta x = 0.1, 0.01, 0.001, \ldots$, continuing until you are ready to guess the right-hand limit. Then test your guess by using $\Delta x = -0.1, -0.01, \ldots$

15. (*Calculator*) $\displaystyle\lim_{\Delta x \to 0} \frac{\sqrt{4 + \Delta x} - 2}{\Delta x}$

16. (*Calculator*) $\displaystyle\lim_{\Delta x \to 0} \frac{\sin \Delta x}{\Delta x}$

[Use radian measure. Also see Fig. 1–65.]

17. (*Calculator*) To estimate the value of the derivative of $f(x) = \sqrt{9 - x^2}$ at $x = 0$, first write $F(x, \Delta x)$ from *Remark 2* with $x = 0$. Then proceed as in Problems 15 and 16.

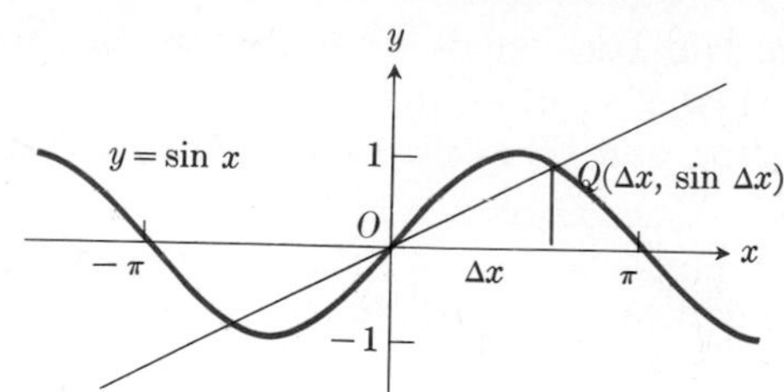

1–65 The slope of the secant OQ is $(\sin \Delta x)/\Delta x$.

18. (*Calculator*) Example 4 shows that the function $F(t) = \sin(1/t)$, $t \neq 0$, has no limit as $t \to 0$. However, the function $F(t) = t \cdot \sin(1/t)$, $t \neq 0$, does have a limit as $t \to 0$. Use a calculator to collect numerical evidence for this.

19. Each of the limits in Problems 15 and 16 is the derivative of a function at $x = 0$. Find the function in each case.

In Problems 20 and 21, each limit is the derivative of a function at some point. Find the function and the point.

20. $\displaystyle\lim_{h \to 0} \frac{(1 + h)^2 - 1}{h}$

21. $\displaystyle\lim_{h \to 0} \frac{|-1 + h| - |-1|}{h}$

22. The inequality

$$1 - \frac{t^2}{6} < \frac{\sin t}{t} < 1$$

holds when t is measured in radians and $|t| < 1$. Use this inequality and Theorems 1 and 2 to find $\lim_{t \to 0} (\sin t)/t$.

*1–11 A PROOF OF THE LIMIT THEOREM

We now prove Theorem 1 of Article 1–10. In all four parts of the theorem we assume that $F_1(t)$ and $F_2(t)$ have finite limits L_1 and L_2 as t approaches c:

$$\lim F_1(t) = L_1, \qquad \lim F_2(t) = L_2. \tag{1}$$

i) $\lim [F_1(t) + F_2(t)] = L_1 + L_2$

To prove that the sum, $F_1(t) + F_2(t)$, has the limit $L_1 + L_2$, as t approaches c we must show that:

To any positive number ϵ, there corresponds a positive number δ such that

$$|F_1(t) + F_2(t) - (L_1 + L_2)| < \epsilon \quad \textit{whenever} \quad 0 < |t - c| < \delta. \tag{2a}$$

To this end, let ϵ be an arbitrary positive number. Then $\epsilon/2$ is also a positive number and, because $F_1(t)$ has L_1 as limit, there is a positive number δ_1 such that

$$|F_1(t) - L_1| < \frac{\epsilon}{2} \quad \text{when} \quad 0 < |t - c| < \delta_1. \tag{2b}$$

Likewise, there is a positive number δ_2 such that

$$|F_2(t) - L_2| < \frac{\epsilon}{2} \quad \text{when} \quad 0 < |t - c| < \delta_2. \tag{2c}$$

Now let $\delta = \min\{\delta_1, \delta_2\}$. Then δ is a positive number, and whenever $0 < |t - c| < \delta$, we have

$$\begin{aligned}|F_1(t) + F_2(t) - (L_1 + L_2)| &= |F_1(t) - L_1 + F_2(t) - L_2| \\ &\leq |F_1(t) - L_1| + |F_2(t) - L_2| \\ &< \frac{\epsilon}{2} + \frac{\epsilon}{2} = \epsilon.\end{aligned}$$

This establishes part (i) of the theorem, because we have shown that the condition required by (2a) is met.

ii) $\lim\,[kF_1(t)] = kL_1$

For the second part of the theorem, let k be any number and suppose that ϵ is an arbitrary positive number. Then $\epsilon/(1 + |k|)$ is positive, and, because $F_1(t)$ has L_1 as its limit when t approaches c, there is a positive number δ such that

$$|F_1(t) - L_1| < \frac{\epsilon}{1 + |k|} \quad \text{when} \quad 0 < |t - c| < \delta. \tag{3a}$$

If we multiply both sides of the first inequality (3a) by $|k|$, and use the fact that $|k|/(1 + |k|)$ is less than 1, we see that

$$|kF_1(t) - kL_1| = |k| \cdot |F_1(t) - L_1| < \epsilon \quad \text{when} \quad 0 < |t - c| < \delta. \tag{3b}$$

This establishes part (ii) of the theorem.

iii) $\lim\,[F_1(t) \cdot F_2(t)] = L_1 \cdot L_2$

Let ϵ be an arbitrary positive number, and write

$$F_1(t) = L_1 + (F_1(t) - L_1), \qquad F_2(t) = L_2 + (F_2(t) - L_2).$$

When we multiply these expressions and subtract $L_1 L_2$, we get

$$\begin{aligned}F_1(t) \cdot F_2(t) - L_1 L_2 &= L_1(F_2(t) - L_2) + L_2(F_1(t) - L_1) \\ &\quad + (F_1(t) - L_1) \cdot (F_2(t) - L_2).\end{aligned} \tag{4a}$$

The numbers $\sqrt{\epsilon/3}$, $\epsilon/[3(1 + |L_1|)]$, and $\epsilon/[3(1 + |L_2|)]$ are all positive, and, because $F_1(t)$ has limit L_1 and $F_2(t)$ has limit L_2, there are positive numbers δ_1, δ_2, δ_3, and δ_4 such that

$$\begin{aligned}|F_1(t) - L_1| &< \sqrt{\epsilon/3} && \text{when} \quad 0 < |t - c| < \delta_1, \\ |F_2(t) - L_2| &< \sqrt{\epsilon/3} && \text{when} \quad 0 < |t - c| < \delta_2, \\ |F_1(t) - L_1| &< \epsilon/[3(1 + |L_2|)] && \text{when} \quad 0 < |t - c| < \delta_3, \\ |F_2(t) - L_2| &< \epsilon/[3(1 + |L_1|)] && \text{when} \quad 0 < |t - c| < \delta_4.\end{aligned}$$

We now let δ be the minimum of the four positive numbers $\delta_1, \delta_2, \delta_3, \delta_4$. Then δ is a positive number and, by taking absolute values in Eq. (4a) and applying the triangle inequality, we get

$$\begin{aligned}|F_1(t)F_2(t) - L_1L_2| &\le |L_1|\cdot|F_2(t) - L_2| + |L_2|\cdot|F_1(t) - L_1| \\ &\quad + |F_1(t) - L_1|\cdot|F_2(t) - L_2| \\ &< \frac{\epsilon}{3} + \frac{\epsilon}{3} + \frac{\epsilon}{3} = \epsilon \quad \text{when} \quad 0 < |t - c| < \delta. \qquad \textbf{(4b)}\end{aligned}$$

This completes the proof of the third part of the theorem.

iv) $\lim \dfrac{F_1(t)}{F_2(t)} = \dfrac{L_1}{L_2}$ **if** $L_2 \neq 0$

Since L_2 is not zero, $|L_2|$ is a positive number and, because $F_2(t)$ has L_2 as limit when t approaches c, we know that there is a positive number δ_1 such that

$$|F_2(t) - L_2| < \frac{|L_2|}{2} \quad \text{when} \quad 0 < |t - c| < \delta_1. \qquad \textbf{(5a)}$$

Now, for any numbers A and B, it can be shown that

$$|A| - |B| \le |A - B| \quad \text{and} \quad |B| - |A| \le |A - B|,$$

from which it follows that

$$||A| - |B|| \le |A - B|. \qquad \textbf{(5b)}$$

Taking $A = F_2(t)$ and $B = L_2$ in (5b), we can deduce from (5a) that

$$-\tfrac{1}{2}|L_2| < |F_2(t)| - |L_2| < \tfrac{1}{2}|L_2| \quad \text{when} \quad 0 < |t - c| < \delta_1.$$

By adding $|L_2|$ to the three terms of the foregoing inequality we get

$$\tfrac{1}{2}|L_2| < |F_2(t)| < \tfrac{3}{2}|L_2|,$$

from which it follows that

$$\left|\frac{1}{F_2(t)} - \frac{1}{L_2}\right| = \left|\frac{L_2 - F_2(t)}{L_2F_2(t)}\right| \le \frac{2}{|L_2|^2}|L_2 - F_2(t)| \qquad \textbf{(5c)}$$

when $0 < |t - c| < \delta_1$. All that we have done so far is to show that the difference between the reciprocals of $F_2(t)$ and L_2, at the left side of the inequality, is no greater in absolute value than a constant times $|L_2 - F_2(t)|$, when t is close enough to c. The fact that L_2 is the limit of $F_2(t)$ has not yet been used with full force. But now let ϵ be an arbitrary positive number. Then $\frac{1}{2}|L_2|^2\epsilon$ is also a positive number and there is a positive number δ_2 such that

$$|L_2 - F_2(t)| < \frac{\epsilon}{2}|L_2|^2 \quad \text{when} \quad 0 < |t - c| < \delta_2. \qquad \textbf{(5d)}$$

We now let $\delta = \min\{\delta_1, \delta_2\}$ and have a positive number δ such that the inequalities in (5c) and (5d) combine to produce the result

$$\left|\frac{1}{F_2(t)} - \frac{1}{L_2}\right| < \epsilon \quad \text{when} \quad 0 < |t - c| < \delta.$$

What we have just shown is that

If $\lim F_2(t) = L_2$ *as t approaches c, and* $L_2 \neq 0$, *then*

$$\lim \frac{1}{F_2(t)} = \frac{1}{L_2}.$$

Having already proved the product law, we get the final quotient law by applying the product law to $F_1(t)$ and $1/F_2(t)$ as follows:

$$\lim \frac{F_1(t)}{F_2(t)} = \lim \left[F_1(t) \cdot \frac{1}{F_2(t)}\right] = [\lim F_1(t)] \cdot \left[\lim \frac{1}{F_2(t)}\right] = L_1 \cdot \frac{1}{L_2}.$$

PROBLEMS

1. Prove:

a) $\lim_{t \to c} t = c$ **b)** $\lim_{t \to c} k = k$, k a constant

2. If $F_1(t)$, $F_2(t)$, and $F_3(t)$ have limits L_1, L_2, and L_3, respectively, as t approaches c, prove that their sum has limit $L_1 + L_2 + L_3$. Generalize the result to the sum of any finite number of functions.

3. If n is any positive integer greater than 1, and $F_1(t)$, $F_2(t)$, ..., $F_n(t)$ have the finite limits L_1, L_2, ..., L_n, respectively, as t approaches c, prove that the product of the n functions has limit $L_1 \cdot L_2 \cdot \cdots \cdot L_n$. [Use part (iii) of Theorem 1, and induction on n.]

4. Use the results of Problems 1(a) and 3 to deduce that

$$\lim_{t \to c} t^n = c^n \quad \text{for any positive integer } n.$$

5. Use Theorem 1 and the results of Problems 1, 2, and 4 to prove that $\lim_{t \to c} f(t) = f(c)$ for any polynomial function

$$f(t) = a_0 t^n + a_1 t^{n-1} + \cdots + a_n.$$

6. Use Theorem 1 and the result of Problem 5 to prove that if $f(t)$ and $g(t)$ are polynomials, and if $g(c) \neq 0$, then

$$\lim_{t \to c} \frac{f(t)}{g(t)} = \frac{f(c)}{g(c)}.$$

REVIEW QUESTIONS AND EXERCISES

1. Define what is meant by the *slope* of a straight line. How would you find the slope of a straight line from its graph? From its equation?

2. In Fig. 1–66, the lines L_1, L_2, and L_3 have slopes m_1, m_2, m_3, respectively. Which slope is algebraically least? Greatest? Write the three slopes in order of increasing size with the symbols for "less than" or "greater than" correctly inserted between them.

3. Describe the family of lines $y - y_1 = m(x - x_1)$:

a) If (x_1, y_1) is fixed and different lines are drawn for different values of m;

b) If m and x_1 are fixed and different lines are drawn for different values of y_1.

4. Define *function*. What is the *domain* of a function? What is its *range*?

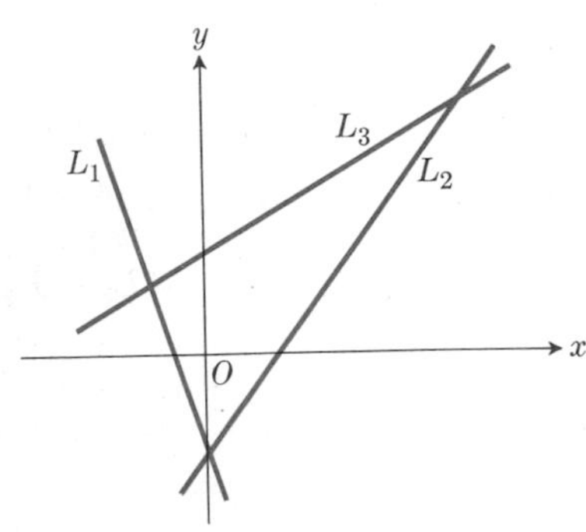

1–66 Lines L_1, L_2, L_3 have slopes m_1, m_2, m_3, respectively.

5. The domain of a certain function is the set $0 \le x \le 2$. The range of the function is the single number $y = 1$.

a) Sketch and describe the graph of the function.

b) Write an expression for the function.

c) If we interchange the axes in part (a), does the new graph so obtained represent a function? Explain.

6. Give an example of a step function different from those mentioned in the text.

7. Write a rule of the form $y = f(x)$ for the function f that is the composite of $y = |x - 10|$ followed by $y = \sqrt{1 - x}$. Find the largest possible domain of f and the corresponding range of y.

8. ***Definition.*** *A rational number is one that can be expressed in the form p/q, where p and q are integers with no common divisor greater than one, and $q > 0$. A real number that is not rational is called irrational.*

With these definitions in mind, plot a few points on the graph of the function that maps the rational number p/q (reduced to lowest terms as above) into $1/q$, and maps each irrational number into zero. This function has been described as the "ruler function" because of the resemblance of its graph to the markings on an ordinary ruler showing inches, half-inches, quarters, eighths, and sixteenths by lines of different lengths. The edge of the ruler corresponds to the x-axis. Do you see why this terminology is rather appropriate?

9. Is it appropriate to define a *tangent line* to a curve C at a point P on C as a line that has just the one point P in common with C? Illustrate your discussion with graphs.

10. Define, carefully, the concept of *slope of a tangent* to a curve at a point on the curve.

11. Define the concept of *average velocity*; of *instantaneous velocity*.

12. What more general concept includes both the concept of slope of the tangent to a curve and the concept of instantaneous velocity?

13. Define the derivative of a function at a point in its domain. Illustrate your definition by applying it to the function f defined by $f(x) = x^2$, at $x = 2$.

14. A function f, whose domain is the set of all real numbers, has the property that $f(x + h) = f(x) \cdot f(h)$ for all x and h; and $f(0) \ne 0$.

a) Show that $f(0) = 1$. [*Hint.* Let $h = x = 0$.]

b) If f has a derivative at 0, show that f has a derivative at every real number x, and that

$$f'(x) = f(x) \cdot f'(0).$$

15. Give an example of a function, defined for all real x, that fails to have a derivative (a) at some point, (b) at several points, (c) at infinitely many points.

16. Suppose F is a function whose values are all less than or equal to some constant M; $F(t) \le M$. Prove: If $\lim_{t \to c} F(t) = L$, then $L \le M$. [*Suggestion.* An indirect proof may be used to show that $L > M$ is false. For, if $L > M$, we may take $\frac{1}{2}(L - M)$ as a positive number ϵ, apply the definition of limit, and arrive at a contradiction.]

17. Let $f(x) = mx + b$. Prove that, for any positive number ϵ, the number $\delta = \epsilon/(1 + |m|)$ is a positive number such that

$$|f(x) - f(c)| < \epsilon \quad \text{when} \quad |x - c| < \delta.$$

What conclusion can you now draw about the limit of $f(x)$ as x approaches c?

18. Suppose that $\lim_{t \to c} F(t) = -7$ and $\lim_{t \to c} G(t) = 0$. Find the limit as t approaches c of each of the following functions.

a) $F^2(t)$ **b)** $3 \cdot F(t)$ **c)** $F(t) \cdot G(t)$ **d)** $\dfrac{F(t)}{G(t) + 7}$

MISCELLANEOUS PROBLEMS

1. a) Plot the points $A(8, 1)$, $B(2, 10)$, $C(-4, 6)$, $D(2, -3)$, $E(4\frac{2}{3}, 6)$.

b) Find the slopes of the lines AB, BC, CD, DA, CE, BD.

c) Do four of the five points A, B, C, D, E form a parallelogram? (Why?)

d) Do three of the five points lie on a common straight line? (Why?)

e) Does the origin (0, 0) lie on a straight line through two of the five points? (Why?)

f) Find equations of the lines AB, CD, AD, CE, BD.

g) Find the coordinates of the points in which the lines AB, CD, AD, CE, BD intersect the x- and y-axes.

2. Given the straight line $2y - 3x = 4$ and the point $(1, -3)$.

a) Find the equation of the straight line through the given point and perpendicular to the given line.

b) Find the distance between the given point and the given line.

3. Plot the three points $A(6, 4)$, $B(4, -3)$, and $C(-2, 3)$.

a) Is triangle ABC a right triangle? Why?

b) Is it isosceles? Why?

c) Does the origin lie inside, outside, or on the boundary of the triangle? Why?

d) If C is replaced by a point $C'(-2, y)$ such that angle $C'BA$ is a right angle, find y, the ordinate of C'.

4. Find the equations of the straight lines passing through the origin which are tangent to the circle of center (2, 1) and radius 2.

5. Let $P_1(x_1, y_1)$ and $P_2(x_2, y_2)$ be any two points. Find the coordinates of the midpoint of the line segment P_1P_2.

6. The x- and y-intercepts of a line L are respectively a and b. Show that an equation of L is $(x/a) + (y/b) = 1$.

7. Given the line L: $ax + by + c = 0$. Find (a) its slope, (b) its y-intercept, (c) its x-intercept, (d) the line through the origin perpendicular to L.

8. Show that the distance between a point $P(x_1, y_1)$ and a line $ax + by + c = 0$ is equal to

$$\frac{|ax_1 + by_1 + c|}{\sqrt{a^2 + b^2}}.$$

(There are neat solutions of this problem in Vol. 59, 1952, of the *American Mathematical Monthly*, pp. 242 and 248.)

9. How many circles can you find that are tangent to the three lines

$$L_1:\ x + y = 1;$$

$$L_2:\ y = x + 1;$$

$$L_3:\ x - 3y = 1?$$

Give the center and radius of at least one such circle. You may use the result of Problem 8.

10. Find, in terms of b, b', and m, the perpendicular distance between the parallel lines $y = mx + b$ and $y = mx + b'$.

11. Given the two lines

$$L_1:\ a_1x + b_1y + c_1 = 0; \qquad L_2:\ a_2x + b_2y + c_2 = 0.$$

If k is a constant, describe the set of points whose coordinates satisfy the equation

$$(a_1x + b_1y + c_1) + k(a_2x + b_2y + c_2) = 0.$$

12. Determine the coordinates of the point on the straight line $y = 3x + 1$ that is equidistant from $(0, 0)$ and $(-3, 4)$.

13. Find an equation of a straight line that is perpendicular to $5x - y = 1$ and is such that the area of the triangle formed by the x-axis, the y-axis, and the straight line is equal to 5.

14. Given the equation $y = (x^2 + 2)/(x^2 - 1)$. Express x in terms of y and determine the values of y for which x is real.

15. Express the area A and the circumference C of a circle as functions of the radius r. Express A as a function of C.

16. In each of the following functions, what is the largest domain of x and the corresponding range of y?

a) $y = \dfrac{1}{1 + x}$ **b)** $y = \dfrac{1}{1 + x^2}$

c) $y = \dfrac{1}{1 + \sqrt{x}}$

17. Without the use of the absolute-value symbol, describe the domain of x for which $|x + 1| < 4$.

18. If $y = 2x + |2 - x|$, express x in terms of y.

19. For what range of values of y does the equation $y = x + |2 - x|$ determine x as a single-valued function of y? Solve for x in terms of y on this set of values.

20. If $y = x + (1/x)$, express x in terms of y and determine the values of y for which x is real.

21. a) If $f(x) = x^2 + 2x - 3$, find $f(-2)$; $f(-1)$; $f(x_1)$; $f(x_1 + \Delta x)$.

b) If $f(x) = x - (1/x)$, show that $f(1/x) = -f(x) = f(-x)$.

22. Sketch the graph of each of the following equations:

a) $y = |x - 2| + 2$ **b)** $y = x^2 - 1$

c) Find the point on the curve in part (b) where the tangent to the curve makes an angle of 45° with the positive x-axis.

23. Sketch a graph of the function $y = |x + 2| + x$ for the domain $-5 \leq x \leq 2$. What is the range?

24. Show that the expression

$$M(a, b) = \frac{(a + b)}{2} + \frac{|a - b|}{2}$$

is equal to a when $a \geq b$ and is equal to b when $b \geq a$. In other words, $M(a, b)$ gives the larger of the two numbers a and b. Find a similar expression, $m(a, b)$, which gives the smaller of the two numbers.

25. For each of the following expressions $f(x)$, sketch first the graph of $y = f(x)$, then the graph of $y = |f(x)|$, and finally the graph of $y = f(x)/2 + |f(x)|/2$.

a) $f(x) = (x - 2)(x + 1)$ **b)** $f(x) = x^2$

c) $f(x) = -x^2$ **d)** $f(x) = 4 - x^2$

26. *Lagrange interpolation formula.* Let (x_1, y_1), (x_2, y_2), ..., (x_n, y_n) be n points in the plane, no two of them having the same abscissas. Find a polynomial, $f(x)$, of degree $(n - 1)$, which takes the value y_1 at x_1, y_2 at x_2, ..., y_n at x_n; that is, $f(x_i) = y_i$ $(i = 1, 2, \ldots, n)$. [*Hint:*

$$f(x) = y_1\phi_1(x) + y_2\phi_2(x) + \cdots + y_n\phi_n(x),$$

where $\phi_k(x)$ is a polynomial that is zero at x_i $(i \neq k)$ and $\phi_k(x_k) = 1$.]

27. Let $f(x) = ax + b$ and $g(x) = cx + d$. What condition must be satisfied by the constants a, b, c, and d in order that $f(g(x))$ and $g(f(x))$ shall be identical?

28. Let $f(x) = (ax + b)/(cx + d)$. If $d = -a$, show that $f(f(x)) = x$, identically.

29. If $f(x) = x/(x - 1)$, find (a) $f(1/x)$, (b) $f(-x)$, (c) $f(f(x))$, (d) $f(1/f(x))$.

30. Using the definition of the derivative, find $f'(x)$ if $f(x)$ is

a) $(x - 1)/(x + 1)$ **b)** $x^{3/2}$ **c)** $x^{1/3}$

31. Use the definition of the derivative to find:

a) $f'(x)$ if $f(x) = x^2 - 3x - 4$,

b) $\dfrac{dy}{dx}$ if $y = \dfrac{1}{3x} + 2x$,

c) $f'(t)$ if $f(t) = \sqrt{t - 4}$.

32. a) By the Δ-method, find the slope of the curve $y = 2x^3 + 2$ at the point (1, 4). (b) At which point of the curve in (a) is the tangent to the curve parallel to the x-axis? Sketch the curve.

33. If $f(x) = 2x/(x - 1)$, find (a) $f(0)$, $f(-1)$, $f(1/x)$; (b) $\Delta f(x)/\Delta x$; (c) $f'(x)$, using the result of part (b).

34. Given $y = 180x - 16x^2$. Using the method of Article 1–7, find the slope of the curve at the point (x_1, y_1). Sketch the curve. At what point does the curve have a horizontal tangent?

35. Find the velocity $v = ds/dt$ if the distance a particle moves in time t is given by $s = 180t - 16t^2$. When does the velocity vanish?

36. If a ball is thrown straight up with a velocity of 32 ft/sec, its height after t sec is given by the equation $s = 32t - 16t^2$. At what instant will the ball be at its highest point, and how high will it rise?

37. If the pressure P and volume V of a certain gas are related by the formula $P = 1/V$, find (a) the average rate of change of P with respect to V, (b) the rate of change of P with respect to V at the instant when $V = 2$.

38. The volume V (in^3) of water remaining in a leaking pail after t sec is $V = 2000 - 40t + 0.2t^2$. How fast is the volume decreasing when $t = 30$?

39. Given $(x - 1)/(2x^2 - 7x + 5) = f(x)$. Find (a) the limit of $f(x)$ as $x \to \infty$, (b) the limit of $f(x)$ as $x \to 1$, (c) $f(-1/x)$, $f(0)$, $1/f(x)$.

40. Compute the coordinates of the point of intersection of the straight lines $3x + 5y = 1$ and $(2 + c)x + 5c^2y = 1$, and determine the limiting position of this point as c tends to 1.

41. Find (a) $\lim_{n\to\infty} (\sqrt{n^2 + 1} - n)$,

(b) $\lim_{n\to\infty} (\sqrt{n^2 + n} - n)$.

42. Given $\epsilon > 0$, find $\delta > 0$ such that $\sqrt{t^2 - 1} < \epsilon$ when $0 < |t - 1| < \delta$.

43. Given $\epsilon > 0$, find M such that

$$\left| \frac{t^2 + t}{t^2 - 1} - 1 \right| < \epsilon$$

when $t > M$.

44. Show that $\lim_{t\to 0} t \sin (1/t)$ exists and is zero, even though $\sin (1/t)$ has no limit as t approaches zero.

45. Prove that if $f(t)$ is bounded (that is, $|f(t)| < M$ for some constant M) and $g(t)$ approaches zero as t approaches a, then $\lim_{t\to a} f(t)g(t) = 0$.

46. Prove that if $f(t)$ has a finite limit as t approaches a, then there exist numbers m, M, and $h > 0$ such that $m < f(t) < M$ if $0 < |t - a| < h$.

47. *Properties of inequalities.* If a and b are any two real numbers, we say a is less than b and write $a < b$ if (and only if) $b - a$ is positive. If $a < b$ we also say that b is greater than a $(b > a)$. Prove the following properties of inequalities:

a) If $a < b$, then $a + c < b + c$ and $a - c < b - c$ for any real number c.

b) If $a < b$ and $c < d$, then $a + c < b + d$. Is it also true that $a - c < b - d$? If so, prove it; if not, give a counterexample.

c) If a and b are both positive (or both negative) and $a < b$, then $1/b < 1/a$.

d) If $a < 0 < b$, then $1/a < 0 < 1/b$.

e) If $a < b$ and $c > 0$, then $ac < bc$.

f) If $a < b$ and $c < 0$, then $bc < ac$.

48. *Properties of absolute values.*

a) Prove that $|a| < |b|$ if, and only if, $a^2 < b^2$.

b) Prove that $|a + b| \le |a| + |b|$.

c) Prove that $|a - b| \ge ||a| - |b||$.

d) Prove, by mathematical induction, that

$$|a_1 + a_2 + \cdots + a_n| \le |a_1| + |a_2| + \cdots + |a_n|.$$

e) Using the result from part (d), prove that

$$|a_1 + a_2 + \cdots + a_n| \ge |a_1| - |a_2| - \cdots - |a_n|.$$

49. Graph $|x| + |y| = 1$. [*Hint.* For each quadrant write an equivalent equation without absolute values.]

50. Graph $y = \sqrt{|x|}$, $-4 \le x \le 4$. Compare your graph with Fig. 1–28.

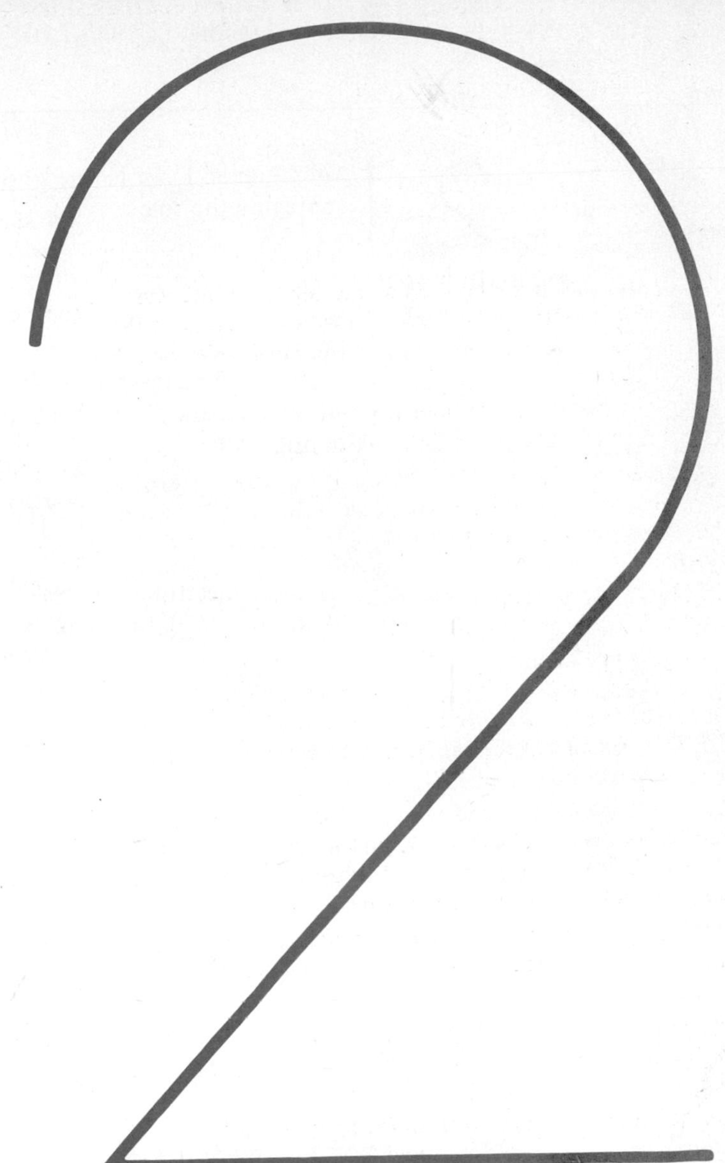

FORMAL DIFFERENTIATION

2–1 INTRODUCTION

In Chapter 1, we learned how to find the rate of change of a function by applying the rule

$$\text{Rate of change of } y \text{ with respect to } x = \lim \frac{\Delta y}{\Delta x}, \tag{1}$$

at any point where the limit $(\Delta y/\Delta x)$ exists. We also saw that this rate of change can be interpreted as the slope of the graph of the function $y = f(x)$. If we want the slope at just one point, say $x = x_1$, $y = y_1$, we can calculate numerically

$$\text{Slope at } P_1(x_1, y_1) = \lim_{h \to 0} \frac{f(x_1 + h) - f(x_1)}{h}. \tag{2}$$

With an electronic calculator and a formula for $f(x)$ that can be evaluated with the calculator, we choose some sequence of values of h, like 0.1, 0.01, 0.001, 0.0001, and so on. With x_1 held fixed, we calculate successive values of the quotient

$$\frac{\Delta y}{\Delta x} = \frac{f(x_1 + h) - f(x_1)}{h}, \tag{3}$$

and from these we deduce what we think the limit would be, if there were a limit. But this does not tell us that the limit exists; and even if it does exist, we may not be able to find its value with sufficient accuracy by straight numerical work.

In addition to the numerical method of finding slope, we were able to go at the job algebraically in some instances. The result of the algebra was a formula that gave useful information about the graph of the function. But each new equation $y = f(x)$ led to heavy algebra if we used the Δ-process of Eq. (1) every time. In one of the exercises, we saw that we could take a general second-degree equation $y = ax^2 + bx + c$, where a, b, and c are constants, apply the Δ-process to this, and get a general formula for the derivative (the slope), $dy/dx = 2ax + b$. Here we have a very simple way of going directly from the equation of the curve to its slope formula, if the equation is a quadratic expression in x. The obvious question to ask is whether there are other simple rules that we can use for general cubic equations, or polynomials of higher degree. The purpose of this chapter is to provide an affirmative answer, and to go beyond that to other types of functions as well. We shall develop a set of easy rules that make it possible to write down the derived function for any polynomial and some other functions as well. The use of these rules is called formal differentiation. When we find the derivative of a function, whether by use of the Δ-process or a standard formula, we say that we differentiate the function. In calculus, the verb "differentiate" means "find the derivative of." Applications of the derivative will be taken up in more detail in Chapter 3. In Chapter 4 we take up the opposite question: Can you find a function $f(x)$ whose derivative is equal to a given expression? That process is called formal integration, or antidifferentiation.

As we go on, we shall learn how to differentiate and integrate the trigonometric functions, logarithmic and exponential functions, and combinations of such functions. We shall also learn some of the many applications of these calculus operations. Theory and applications are interwoven.

2–2 POLYNOMIAL FUNCTIONS AND THEIR DERIVATIVES

A single term of the form cx^n, where c is a constant and n is zero or a positive integer, is called a *monomial* in x. A function that is the sum of a finite number of monomial terms is called a *polynomial* in x. For example,

$$f(x) = x^3 - 5x + 7, \qquad g(x) = (x^2 + 3)^3, \qquad h(x) = 4x, \qquad \phi(x) = 5$$

are polynomials in x, and

$$s(t) = \tfrac{1}{2}gt^2, \qquad v(t) = v_0 + gt$$

are polynomials in t.

We shall now derive some formulas that will enable us to find the derivatives of polynomial functions very easily. In every case we derive the formula from the basic definition:

Let $y = f(x)$ define a function f. If the limit

$$\frac{dy}{dx} = \lim_{\Delta x \to 0} \frac{\Delta y}{\Delta x}, \tag{1a}$$

meaning

$$f'(x) = \lim_{\Delta x \to 0} \frac{f(x + \Delta x) - f(x)}{\Delta x}, \tag{1b}$$

exists and is finite, we call this limit the derivative of y with respect to x and say that f is differentiable at x.

Rule 1. *The derivative of a constant is zero.*

The geometric meaning of this result is that the graph of the equation $y = c$ is everywhere parallel to the x-axis (Fig. 2–1). To prove it analytically, let

$$y = f(x) = c,$$

where c is a constant. Then

$$\Delta y = f(x + \Delta x) - f(x) = c - c = 0.$$

Dividing by Δx gives

$$\frac{\Delta y}{\Delta x} = \frac{0}{\Delta x} = 0$$

and

$$\frac{dy}{dx} = \lim_{\Delta x \to 0} \frac{\Delta y}{\Delta x} = 0.$$

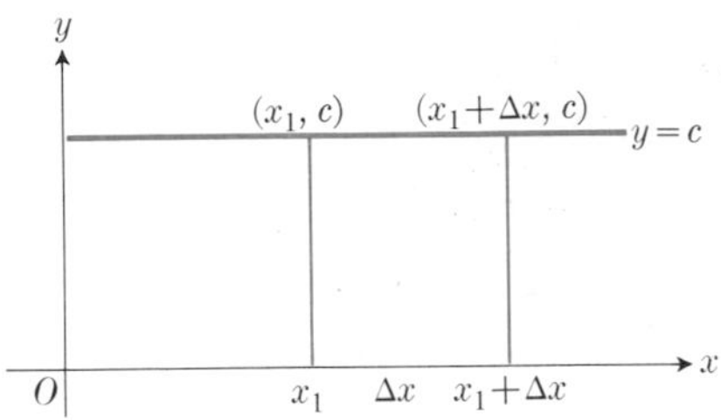

2–1 The slope of the graph of y = constant is zero.

Rule 2. *The derivative, with respect to x, of x^n is nx^{n-1} when n is any positive integer.*

To prove this result, we let

$$y = f(x) = x^n,$$

where n may be any positive integer. Then, by the binomial theorem,

$$y + \Delta y = f(x + \Delta x) = (x + \Delta x)^n$$

$$= \begin{cases} x + \Delta x & \text{if } n = 1, \\ x^2 + 2x\,\Delta x + (\Delta x)^2 & \text{if } n = 2, \\ x^3 + 3x^2\,\Delta x + 3x\,(\Delta x)^2 + (\Delta x)^3 & \text{if } n = 3, \\ x^n + nx^{n-1}\,\Delta x + (\text{terms in } x \text{ and } \Delta x)\cdot(\Delta x)^2 & \text{if } n > 3. \end{cases}$$

From this we subtract $y = x^n$ and obtain

$$\Delta y = \begin{cases} \Delta x & \text{if } n = 1, \\ 2x\,\Delta x + (\Delta x)^2 & \text{if } n = 2, \\ 3x^2\,\Delta x + (3x + \Delta x)\cdot(\Delta x)^2 & \text{if } n = 3, \\ nx^{n-1}\,\Delta x + (\text{terms in } x \text{ and } \Delta x)\cdot(\Delta x)^2 & \text{if } n > 3. \end{cases}$$

Dividing by Δx, we find next that

$$\frac{\Delta y}{\Delta x} = \begin{cases} 1 & \text{if } n = 1, \\ 2x + \Delta x & \text{if } n = 2, \\ 3x^2 + (3x + \Delta x)\cdot\Delta x & \text{if } n = 3, \\ nx^{n-1} + (\text{terms in } x \text{ and } \Delta x)\cdot\Delta x & \text{if } n > 3. \end{cases}$$

Finally, we let Δx approach zero and find

$$\frac{dy}{dx} = \lim_{\Delta x \to 0} \frac{\Delta y}{\Delta x} = \begin{cases} 1 & \text{if } n = 1, \\ 2x & \text{if } n = 2, \\ 3x^2 & \text{if } n = 3, \\ nx^{n-1} & \text{if } n > 3. \end{cases}$$

In particular, the case $n = 1$ tells us that

$$\frac{dx}{dx} = 1.$$

Since the results for $n = 1, 2, 3$ are simply special cases of the general result, we have

$$\frac{dy}{dx} = nx^{n-1} \quad \text{if} \quad y = x^n \text{ and } n = \text{any positive integer.} \qquad \textbf{(2)}$$

EXAMPLE 1. If $y = x^5$, then $dy/dx = 5x^4$.

Rule 3. *If $u = f(x)$ is a differentiable function of x and c is a constant, then*

$$\frac{d(cu)}{dx} = c\frac{du}{dx}. \tag{3}$$

Proof. Let

$$y = cu, \tag{4a}$$

where

$$u = f(x).$$

Then if x is replaced by $x + \Delta x$, we have

$$y + \Delta y = c(u + \Delta u), \tag{4b}$$

where

$$u + \Delta u = f(x + \Delta x).$$

Subtracting (4a) from (4b), we obtain

$$\Delta y = c\,\Delta u$$

and dividing this by Δx, we have

$$\frac{\Delta y}{\Delta x} = c\frac{\Delta u}{\Delta x}. \tag{4c}$$

Since u has a derivative

$$\lim_{\Delta x \to 0} \frac{\Delta u}{\Delta x} = \frac{du}{dx}$$

and

$$\frac{dy}{dx} = \lim_{\Delta x \to 0} \frac{\Delta y}{\Delta x} = \lim_{\Delta x \to 0} c\frac{\Delta u}{\Delta x} = c\frac{du}{dx}.$$

Since $y = cu$, this is the same as

$$\frac{d(cu)}{dx} = c\frac{du}{dx},$$

which we wished to show.

EXAMPLE 2. $d(7x^5)/dx = 7 \cdot 5x^4 = 35x^4$. Geometrically this says that if we stretch the graph of $y = x^5$ in the y-direction by multiplying each ordinate by 7, then we multiply each slope by 7 also (Fig. 2–2).

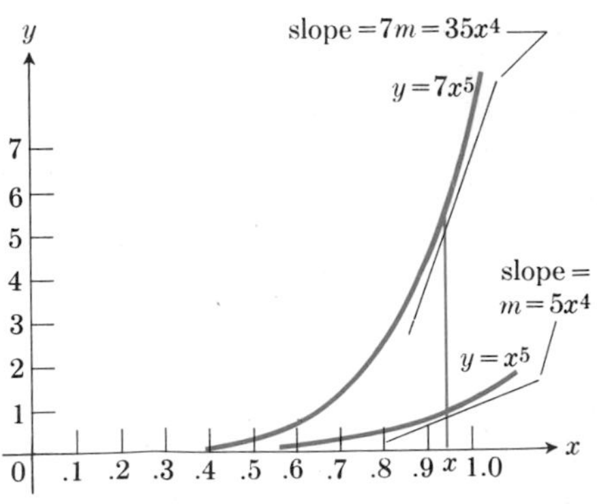

2–2 Graphs of $y = x^5$ and the stretched curve $y = 7x^5$. Multiplying the ordinates by 7 multiplies all the slopes by 7.

In general, if c is a constant and n is a positive integer, Eqs. (2) and (3) together tell us that

$$\frac{d(cx^n)}{dx} = cnx^{n-1}. \tag{5}$$

$\frac{d(ct^2)}{dt} = c2t$ $2ct$

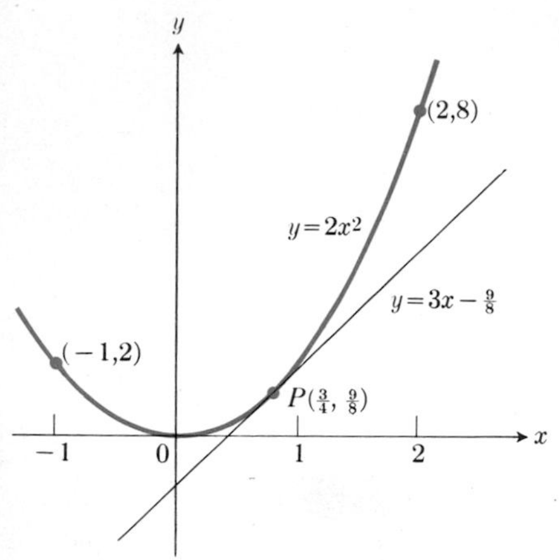

2–3 The line $y = 3x + c$ is tangent to the curve $y = 2x^2$ at $P(0.75, 1.125)$ if $c = -\frac{9}{8} = -1.125$.

EXAMPLE 3. Find the value of the constant c if the line $y = 3x + c$ is tangent to the curve $y = 2x^2$. Also find the point of tangency.

Solution. The slope of the line $y = 3x + c$ is $m = 3$. The slope of the curve at $P(x, y)$ is $dy/dx = 4x$. If P is a point of tangency, the two slopes are equal:

$$\text{At } P(x, y), \qquad m = 3 = 4x, \qquad \text{or} \qquad x = \tfrac{3}{4}.$$

Then $y = 2(\frac{3}{4})^2 = \frac{18}{16} = \frac{9}{8}$ must also equal $3x + c = 3(\frac{3}{4}) + c$. Therefore,

$$\tfrac{9}{4} + c = \tfrac{9}{8} \qquad \text{and} \qquad c = \tfrac{9}{8} - \tfrac{9}{4} = -\tfrac{9}{8}.$$

The point of tangency is

$$P(x, y) = P(\tfrac{3}{4}, \tfrac{9}{8}) = P(0.75, 1.125).$$

(See Fig. 2–3.)

Rule 4. *The derivative of the sum of a finite number of differentiable functions is the sum of their derivatives.*

To prove this, we first consider the sum of two terms,

$$y = u + v,$$

where we suppose that u and v are differentiable functions of x. When x is replaced by $x + \Delta x$, the new values of the variables will satisfy the equation

$$y + \Delta y = (u + \Delta u) + (v + \Delta v).$$

We subtract

$$y = u + v$$

from this and obtain

$$\Delta y = \Delta u + \Delta v,$$

and hence

$$\frac{\Delta y}{\Delta x} = \frac{\Delta u}{\Delta x} + \frac{\Delta v}{\Delta x}.$$

When Δx approaches zero, we get

$$\frac{dy}{dx} = \lim_{\Delta x \to 0} \frac{\Delta y}{\Delta x} = \lim_{\Delta x \to 0} \left(\frac{\Delta u}{\Delta x} + \frac{\Delta v}{\Delta x}\right) = \lim_{\Delta x \to 0} \frac{\Delta u}{\Delta x} + \lim_{\Delta x \to 0} \frac{\Delta v}{\Delta x} = \frac{du}{dx} + \frac{dv}{dx}.$$

Therefore,

$$\frac{d(u + v)}{dx} = \frac{du}{dx} + \frac{dv}{dx}.$$

This equation says that the derivative of the sum of two terms is the sum of their derivatives.

We may proceed by induction to establish the result for the sum of any finite number of terms. For example, if

$$y = u_1 + u_2 + u_3,$$

where u_1, u_2, and u_3 are differentiable functions of x, then we may take

$$u = u_1 + u_2, \qquad v = u_3,$$

and apply the result already established for the sum of two terms, namely,

$$\frac{dy}{dx} = \frac{d(u_1 + u_2)}{dx} + \frac{du_3}{dx}.$$

Since the first term is again a sum of two terms, we have

$$\frac{d(u_1 + u_2)}{dx} = \frac{du_1}{dx} + \frac{du_2}{dx},$$

so that

$$\frac{d(u_1 + u_2 + u_3)}{dx} = \frac{du_1}{dx} + \frac{du_2}{dx} + \frac{du_3}{dx}.$$

Finally, if it has been established for some integer n that

$$\frac{d(u_1 + u_2 + \cdots + u_n)}{dx} = \frac{du_1}{dx} + \frac{du_2}{dx} + \cdots + \frac{du_n}{dx},$$

and we let

$$y = u + v,$$

with

$$u = u_1 + u_2 + \cdots + u_n,$$

$$v = u_{n+1},$$

then we find in the same way as above that

$$\frac{d(u_1 + u_2 + \cdots + u_{n+1})}{dx} = \frac{du_1}{dx} + \frac{du_2}{dx} + \cdots + \frac{du_{n+1}}{dx}.$$

This enables us to conclude that if the theorem is true for a sum of n terms it is also true for a sum of $(n + 1)$ terms; and since it is already established for the sum of two terms, we conclude that it is true for the sum of any finite number of terms.

EXAMPLE 4. Find dy/dx if $y = x^3 + 7x^2 - 5x + 4$.

Solution. We find the derivatives of the separate terms and add the results:

$$\begin{aligned}\frac{dy}{dx} &= \frac{d(x^3)}{dx} + \frac{d(7x^2)}{dx} + \frac{d(-5x)}{dx} + \frac{d(4)}{dx}\\ &= 3x^2 + 14x - 5x^0 + 0\\ &= 3x^2 + 14x - 5.\end{aligned}$$

Second Derivatives

The derivative

$$y' = \frac{dy}{dx}$$

is the first derivative of y with respect to x, and its derivative

$$y'' = \frac{dy'}{dx} = \frac{d}{dx}\left(\frac{dy}{dx}\right)$$

is called the *second derivative of y with respect to x*. The operation of taking the derivative of a function twice in succession is denoted by

$$\frac{d}{dx}\left(\frac{d}{dx}\cdots\right), \qquad \text{or} \qquad \frac{d^2}{dx^2}(\ldots).$$

In this notation, we write the second derivative of y with respect to x as

$$\frac{d^2y}{dx^2}.$$

More generally, the result of differentiating a function $y = f(x)$ n times in succession is denoted by $y^{(n)}$, $f^{(n)}(x)$, or d^ny/dx^n.

EXAMPLE 5. For example, if $y = x^3 - 3x^2 + 2$, then

$$y' = \frac{dy}{dx} = 3x^2 - 6x, \qquad y''' = \frac{d^3y}{dx^3} = 6,$$

$$y'' = \frac{d^2y}{dx^2} = 6x - 6, \qquad y^{(iv)} = \frac{d^4y}{dx^4} = 0.$$

In mechanics, if $s = f(t)$ gives the position of a moving body at time t, then

The first derivative ds/dt gives the *velocity*, and

The second derivative d^2s/dt^2 gives the *acceleration*

of the body at time t.

EXAMPLE 6. A body moves in a straight line according to the law of motion

$$s = t^3 - 4t^2 - 3t.$$

Find its acceleration at each instant when the velocity is zero.

Solution. The velocity v and acceleration a are

$$v = \frac{ds}{dt} = 3t^2 - 8t - 3, \qquad a = \frac{dv}{dt} = 6t - 8.$$

The velocity is zero when

$$3t^2 - 8t - 3 = (3t + 1)(t - 3) = 0,$$

that is, when

$$t = -\tfrac{1}{3} \qquad \text{or} \qquad t = 3.$$

The corresponding values of the acceleration are

$$t = -\tfrac{1}{3}, \quad a = -10; \qquad t = 3, \quad a = 10.$$

PROBLEMS

In Problems 1–5, s represents the position of a moving body at time t. Find the velocity $v = ds/dt$ and the acceleration $a = dv/dt = d^2s/dt^2$.

1. $s = t^2 - 4t + 3$
2. $s = 2t^3 - 5t^2 + 4t - 3$
3. $s = gt^2/2 + v_0t + s_0$; (g, v_0, s_0 constants)
4. $s = 3 + 4t - t^2$
5. $s = (2t + 3)^2$

Find $y' = dy/dx$ and $y'' = dy'/dx$ in Problems 6–15.

6. $y = x^4 - 7x^3 + 2x^2 + 5$
7. $y = 5x^3 - 3x^5$
8. $y = 4x^2 - 8x + 1$
9. $y = \dfrac{x^4}{4} - \dfrac{x^3}{3} + \dfrac{x^2}{2} - x + 3$
10. $y = 2x^4 - 4x^2 - 8$
11. $12y = 6x^4 - 18x^2 - 12x$
12. $y = 3x^7 - 7x^3 + 21x^2$
13. $y = x^2(x^3 - 1)$
14. $y = (x - 2)(x + 3)$
15. $y = (3x - 1)(2x + 5)$

16. A particle projected vertically upward with a speed of 160 ft/sec reaches an elevation $s = 160t - 16t^2$ at the end of t seconds. (a) How high does it rise? (b) How fast is it traveling when it reaches an elevation of 256 feet going up and again when it reaches this elevation coming down?

17. Find the line tangent to the curve $y = 2x^2 + 4x - 3$ at the point (1, 3).

18. Find the lines tangent to the curve $y = x^3 + x$, where the slope is equal to 4. What is the smallest value the slope of this curve can ever have and where on the curve does the slope equal this smallest value?

19. Find the points on the curve $y = 2x^3 - 3x^2 - 12x + 20$, where the tangent is parallel to the x-axis.

20. Suppose that you have plotted the point $P(x, x^2)$ on the graph of $y = x^2$. To construct the tangent to the graph at P, locate the point $T(x/2, 0)$ on the x-axis and draw the line through T and P. Show that this construction is correct.

21. The tangent to the curve $y = x^n$ at $P(x_1, y_1)$ intersects the x-axis at $T(t, 0)$. Express t in terms of n and x_1, then show how the result can be used to construct the tangent at P.

22. Find the x- and y-intercepts of the line L that is tangent to the curve $y = x^3$ at $A(-2, -8)$.

23. A line L is drawn tangent to the curve $y = x^3 - x$ at the point $A(-1, 0)$. Where else does this line intersect the curve?

24. (*Curvature*) It is shown later in this book that one can define a number that represents the curvature of $y = f(x)$ at $P(x, y)$. The formula is

$$\text{Curvature} = y''/(1 + (y')^2)^{3/2},$$

where $y' = dy/dx$ and y'' is the second derivative. Use this formula to find the curvature of $y = x^2$:

a) at the origin, **b)** at (1, 1), and **c)** as $x \to \infty$.

25. Find the values of the constants a, b, and c if the curve $y = ax^2 + bx + c$ is to pass through the point (1, 2) and is to be tangent to the line $y = x$ at the origin.

26. Find the constants a, b, and c so that the two curves $y = x^2 + ax + b$ and $y = cx - x^2$ shall be tangent to each other at the point (1, 0).

27. Find the constant c if the curve $y = x^2 + c$ is to be tangent to the line $y = x$.

2–3 RATIONAL FUNCTIONS AND THEIR DERIVATIVES

In the preceding article we learned how to find the derivative of a polynomial very quickly by using certain simple formulas. First we found the derivative of a monomial in x,

$$\frac{d}{dx}(cx^n) = cnx^{n-1},$$

and then we proved that the derivative of the sum of a finite number of such terms is the sum of their derivatives.

In this article we shall derive formulas for finding the derivative with respect to x of

Products:	$y = uv$,
Quotients:	$y = u/v$,
Powers:	$y = u^n$,

when u and v are any differentiable functions of x. For the present, this will mean that u and v may be polynomials in x, for example. But after we learn to differentiate functions like $\sin x$ and $\log x$, the same basic formulas will apply to combinations of these as well.

The product of two polynomials in x is again a polynomial in x; hence if u and v are polynomials the product uv is also a polynomial. Similarly, if n is a positive integer and u is a polynomial, then u^n is again a polynomial. For example, if

$$u = x^2 + 1, \quad v = x^3 + 3, \qquad \text{then} \qquad uv = x^5 + x^3 + 3x^2 + 3,$$

and if

$$u = x^2 + 1, \quad n = 2, \qquad \text{then} \qquad u^n = x^4 + 2x^2 + 1.$$

But the ratio u/v of two polynomials in x is generally not a polynomial. Such a function is called a *rational* function of x, where the word *ratio* is the key to the real meaning of the word rational.

Rule 5. *The derivative of the product*

$$y = uv$$

of two differentiable functions of x is given by

$$\frac{d(uv)}{dx} = u\frac{dv}{dx} + v\frac{du}{dx}. \tag{1}$$

To prove this result, we let

$$y = uv,$$

where u and v are differentiable functions of x. Let Δx be an increment in x, and let the corresponding increments in y, u, v be denoted by Δy, Δu, Δv. These increments may be either positive, negative, or zero, but $\Delta x \neq 0$. Then

$$\begin{aligned} y + \Delta y &= (u + \Delta u)(v + \Delta v) \\ &= uv + u\,\Delta v + v\,\Delta u + \Delta u\,\Delta v. \end{aligned}$$

When we subtract from this the equation

$$y = uv,$$

we obtain

$$\Delta y = u\,\Delta v + v\,\Delta u + \Delta u\,\Delta v.$$

Next we divide by Δx,

$$\frac{\Delta y}{\Delta x} = u\frac{\Delta v}{\Delta x} + v\frac{\Delta u}{\Delta x} + \Delta u\frac{\Delta v}{\Delta x}.$$

Finally, when Δx approaches zero, so will Δu, since

$$\lim \Delta u = \lim\left(\frac{\Delta u}{\Delta x}\Delta x\right) = \lim \frac{\Delta u}{\Delta x}\lim \Delta x = \frac{du}{dx}\cdot 0.$$

Thus,

$$\lim \frac{\Delta y}{\Delta x} = \lim \left(u\frac{\Delta v}{\Delta x} + v\frac{\Delta u}{\Delta x} + \Delta u\frac{\Delta v}{\Delta x} \right)$$

$$= \lim u\frac{\Delta v}{\Delta x} + \lim v\frac{\Delta u}{\Delta x} + \lim \Delta u\frac{\Delta v}{\Delta x}$$

$$= \lim u \lim \frac{\Delta v}{\Delta x} + \lim v \lim \frac{\Delta u}{\Delta x} + \lim \Delta u \lim \frac{\Delta v}{\Delta x}$$

$$= u\frac{dv}{dx} + v\frac{du}{dx} + 0 \cdot \frac{dv}{dx}.$$

That is,

$$\frac{dy}{dx} = u\frac{dv}{dx} + v\frac{du}{dx},$$

which establishes (1).

EXAMPLE 1. Economists often use the expression "rate of growth" in relative rather than absolute terms. For example, in a given industry, let $u = f(t)$ be the size of the labor force at time t. (This function will be treated as though it were differentiable even though it is an integer-valued step function. We approximate the step function by a smooth curve.) Let $v = g(t)$ be the average production per person in the labor force at time t. Then the total production is $y = uv$. If the labor force is growing at the rate of 4 percent annually and the production per worker is growing at the rate of 5 percent per year, find the rate of growth of the total production, y.

Solution. We are given these data:

$$y = uv, \qquad \frac{du}{dt} = 0.04u, \qquad \frac{dv}{dt} = 0.05v.$$

By the rule for the derivative of a product, we have

$$\frac{dy}{dt} = u\frac{dv}{dt} + v\frac{du}{dt} = u(0.05v) + v(0.04u) = 0.09uv = 0.09y.$$

From the result $dy/dt = 0.009y$ we deduce that the total production is increasing at the rate of 9 percent annually. All of the rates are instantaneous rates, valid at some instant of time t.

Note that the derivative of a product is *not* the product of the derivatives. Instead, we add together two terms $u(dv/dx)$ and $v(du/dx)$. In the first of these we leave u untouched and differentiate v, and in the second we differentiate u and leave v alone. In fact, it is possible to extend the formula, by the method of mathematical induction, to show that the derivative of a product

$$y = u_1 u_2 \ldots u_n$$

of a finite number of differentiable functions is given by

$$\frac{d}{dx}(u_1 u_2 \cdots u_n) = \frac{du_1}{dx} \cdot u_2 \cdots u_n + u_1 \frac{du_2}{dx} \cdots u_n + \cdots + u_1 u_2 \cdots u_{n-1} \frac{du_n}{dx}, \tag{2}$$

where the right side of the equation consists of the sum of the n terms obtained by multiplying the derivative of each one of the factors by the other $(n - 1)$ factors undifferentiated.

Rule 6. *At a point where $v \neq 0$, the derivative of the quotient*

$$y = \frac{u}{v}$$

of two differentiable functions u and v is given by

$$\frac{d}{dx}\left(\frac{u}{v}\right) = \frac{v \dfrac{du}{dx} - u \dfrac{dv}{dx}}{v^2}. \tag{3}$$

To prove this, consider a point $x = c$ where $v \neq 0$ and where u and v are differentiable. Let x be given an increment Δx and let Δy, Δu, Δv be the corresponding increments in y, u, v. Then, as $\Delta x \to 0$,

$$\lim (v + \Delta v) = \lim v + \lim \Delta v$$

while

$$\lim \Delta v = \lim \frac{\Delta v}{\Delta x} \cdot \Delta x = \frac{dv}{dx} \cdot 0 = 0.$$

Therefore the value of $v + \Delta v$ is close to the value of v when $x + \Delta x$ is close to c, that is, when Δx is near zero. In particular, since $v \neq 0$ at $x = c$, it follows that $v + \Delta v \neq 0$ when Δx is *near* zero, say when $0 < |\Delta x| < h$. Let Δx be so restricted. Then $v + \Delta v \neq 0$ and

$$y + \Delta y = \frac{u + \Delta u}{v + \Delta v}.$$

From this we subtract

$$y = \frac{u}{v}$$

and obtain

$$\begin{aligned} \Delta y &= \frac{u + \Delta u}{v + \Delta v} - \frac{u}{v} \\ &= \frac{(vu + v\,\Delta u) - (uv + u\,\Delta v)}{v(v + \Delta v)} \\ &= \frac{v\,\Delta u - u\,\Delta v}{v(v + \Delta v)}. \end{aligned}$$

We divide this by Δx and have

$$\frac{\Delta y}{\Delta x} = \frac{v \dfrac{\Delta u}{\Delta x} - u \dfrac{\Delta v}{\Delta x}}{v(v + \Delta v)}.$$

When Δx approaches zero,

$$\lim \frac{\Delta u}{\Delta x} = \frac{du}{dx},$$

$$\lim \frac{\Delta v}{\Delta x} = \frac{dv}{dx},$$

and

$$\lim v(v + \Delta v) = \lim v \lim (v + \Delta v) = v^2 \neq 0.$$

Therefore,

$$\frac{dy}{dx} = \lim \frac{\Delta y}{\Delta x} = \frac{\lim \left(v \frac{\Delta u}{\Delta x} - u \frac{\Delta v}{\Delta x} \right)}{\lim v(v + \Delta v)} = \frac{v \frac{du}{dx} - u \frac{dv}{dx}}{v^2},$$

which establishes Eq. (3).

EXAMPLE 2. $y = (x^2 + 1)/(x^2 - 1)$, $x^2 \neq 1$. We apply Rule 6 for the derivative of a fraction, and have

$$\frac{dy}{dx} = \frac{(x^2 - 1) \cdot 2x - (x^2 + 1) \cdot 2x}{(x^2 - 1)^2}$$

$$= \frac{-4x}{(x^2 - 1)^2}.$$

Rule 7. *If $u = g(x)$ is a differentiable function of x and n is a positive integer, then*

$$\frac{d}{dx}(u^n) = nu^{n-1} \frac{du}{dx}. \tag{4}$$

For $n = 1$, we interpret Eq. (4) as

$$\frac{d}{dx}(u) = u^0 \frac{du}{dx} = \frac{du}{dx}$$

which is certainly true provided $u \neq 0$. When $u = 0$, we would get 0^0, which is an indeterminate expression but which we shall interpret as being 1 to be consistent. For n greater than or equal to 2, we let

$$y = u^n,$$

where u and n satisfy the hypotheses, give x an increment Δx, and call the increments of y and u, Δy and Δu. Then

$$y + \Delta y = (u + \Delta u)^n$$

$$= u^n + nu^{n-1} \Delta u + \frac{n(n-1)}{2} u^{n-2} (\Delta u)^2 + \cdots + (\Delta u)^n.$$

From this we subtract the original equation and obtain

$$\Delta y = nu^{n-1} \Delta u + (\text{terms in } u \text{ and } \Delta u)(\Delta u)^2.$$

Next, we divide by Δx:

$$\frac{\Delta y}{\Delta x} = nu^{n-1} \frac{\Delta u}{\Delta x} + (\text{terms in } u \text{ and } \Delta u) \frac{(\Delta u)^2}{\Delta x}.$$

Now when Δx approaches zero,

$$\lim \frac{\Delta u}{\Delta x} = \frac{du}{dx}$$

by the definition of the derivative, while

$$\lim \frac{(\Delta u)^2}{\Delta x} = \lim \left(\frac{\Delta u}{\Delta x} \Delta u \right) = \lim \frac{\Delta u}{\Delta x} \lim \Delta u = \frac{du}{dx} \cdot 0 = 0.$$

Hence,

$$\begin{aligned} \lim \frac{\Delta y}{\Delta x} &= \lim \left[nu^{n-1} \frac{\Delta u}{\Delta x} + (\cdots) \frac{(\Delta u)^2}{\Delta x} \right] \\ &= \lim nu^{n-1} \frac{\Delta u}{\Delta x} + \lim (\cdots) \frac{(\Delta u)^2}{\Delta x} \\ &= nu^{n-1} \frac{du}{dx} + 0; \end{aligned}$$

that is,

$$\frac{dy}{dx} = nu^{n-1} \frac{du}{dx},$$

which establishes Eq. (4).

EXAMPLE 3. $y = (x^2 + 1)^3(x^3 - 1)^2$. We could, of course, expand everything here and write y as a polynomial in x, but this is not necessary. Instead, we first use Eq. (1) for the derivative of a product:

$$\frac{dy}{dx} = (x^2 + 1)^3 \frac{d}{dx}(x^3 - 1)^2 + (x^3 - 1)^2 \frac{d}{dx}(x^2 + 1)^3.$$

Then we evaluate the remaining derivatives by Eq. (4):

$$\begin{aligned} \frac{d}{dx}(x^3 - 1)^2 &= 2(x^3 - 1) \frac{d}{dx}(x^3 - 1) \\ &= 2(x^3 - 1) \cdot 3x^2 = 6x^2(x^3 - 1), \end{aligned}$$

and

$$\begin{aligned} \frac{d}{dx}(x^2 + 1)^3 &= 3(x^2 + 1)^2 \frac{d}{dx}(x^2 + 1) \\ &= 3(x^2 + 1)^2 \cdot 2x = 6x(x^2 + 1)^2. \end{aligned}$$

We substitute these into the earlier equation and have

$$\begin{aligned} \frac{dy}{dx} &= (x^2 + 1)^3 6x^2(x^3 - 1) + (x^3 - 1)^2 6x(x^2 + 1)^2 \\ &= 6x(x^2 + 1)^2(x^3 - 1)[x(x^2 + 1) + (x^3 - 1)] \\ &= 6x(x^2 + 1)^2(x^3 - 1)(2x^3 + x - 1). \end{aligned}$$

EXAMPLE 4. Write the polynomial

$$f(x) = x^3 - 2x + 3 \tag{5}$$

in the form

$$f(x) = C_0 + C_1(x-2) + C_2(x-2)^2 + C_3(x-2)^3, \tag{6}$$

where C_0, C_1, C_2, and C_3 are constants.

Solution. We differentiate both expressions for $f(x)$ three times, and substitute $x = 2$ to get

$$f(x) = C_0 + C_1(x-2) + C_2(x-2)^2 + C_3(x-2)^3, \qquad f(2) = C_0;$$

$$f'(x) = C_1 + 2C_2(x-2) + 3C_3(x-2)^2, \qquad f'(2) = C_1;$$

$$f''(x) = 2C_2 + 6C_3(x-2), \qquad f''(2) = 2C_2;$$

$$f'''(x) = 6C_3, \qquad f'''(2) = 6C_3;$$

and

$$f(x) = x^3 - 2x + 3, \qquad f(2) = 8 - 4 + 3 = 7;$$
$$f'(x) = 3x^2 - 2, \qquad f'(2) = 12 - 2 = 10;$$
$$f''(x) = 6x, \qquad f''(2) = 12;$$
$$f'''(x) = 6, \qquad f'''(2) = 6.$$

This gives two expressions for the value of each derivative of f at $x = 2$. Equating them, we find

$$C_0 = f(2) = 7, \quad C_1 = f'(2) = 10, \quad C_2 = \tfrac{1}{2}f''(2) = 6, \quad C_3 = \tfrac{1}{6}f'''(2) = 1.$$

Therefore,

$$f(x) = x^3 - 2x + 3 = 7 + 10(x-2) + 6(x-2)^2 + (x-2)^3.$$

The first way of writing $f(x)$ is less informative than the second way if we are especially interested in the way $f(x)$ varies for values of x near 2. One of the ways calculus is used is to make approximations. Two things are important in making an approximation: First, the form of the approximation, and second, the size of the error. For the present example we can say that, when x is near 2, the successive powers of $(x - 2)$ are small, and

$f(x) \approx 7$, with an error about $10(x-2)$

$f(x) \approx 7 + 10(x-2)$, with an error about $6(x-2)^2$

$f(x) \approx 7 + 10(x-2) + 6(x-2)^2$, with an error exactly $(x-2)^3$

$f(x) = 7 + 10(x-2) + 6(x-2)^2 + (x-2)^3$, with no error.

Figure 2–4 shows the first two of these approximations to $f(x)$.

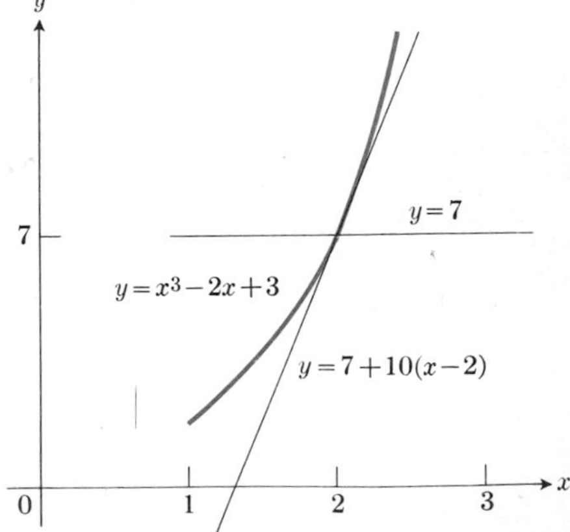

2–4 Graph of $y = x^3 - 2x + 3$ near $x = 2$ with horizontal and tangent line approximations.

Rule 8. *At a point where $u = g(x)$ is differentiable and different from zero, the derivative of*

$$y = u^n$$

is given by

$$\frac{d(u^n)}{dx} = nu^{n-1}\frac{du}{dx} \tag{7}$$

if n is a negative integer.

Rule 8 is the extension of Eq. (4) to the case where n is a *negative integer*. To prove it, we combine the results in Eqs. (3) and (4) as follows. Let

$$y = u^{-m} = \frac{1}{u^m},$$

where $-m$ is a negative integer, so that m is a positive integer. Then, using (3) for the derivative of a quotient, we have

$$\frac{dy}{dx} = \frac{d\left(\frac{1}{u^m}\right)}{dx} = \frac{u^m\frac{d(1)}{dx} - 1\frac{d(u^m)}{dx}}{(u^m)^2} \tag{8}$$

at any point where u is differentiable and different from zero. Now the various derivatives on the right side of (8) can be evaluated by formulas already proved, namely,

$$\frac{d(1)}{dx} = 0,$$

since 1 is a constant, and

$$\frac{d(u^m)}{dx} = mu^{m-1}\frac{du}{dx},$$

since m is a *positive integer*. Therefore,

$$\frac{dy}{dx} = \frac{u^m \cdot 0 - 1 \cdot mu^{m-1}\frac{du}{dx}}{u^{2m}} = -mu^{-m-1}\frac{du}{dx}.$$

If $-m$ is replaced by its equivalent value n, this equation reduces to Eq. (7).

EXAMPLE 5. $y = x^2 + 1/x^2$, $x \neq 0$. We may write

$$y = x^2 + x^{-2}.$$

Then

$$\begin{aligned}\frac{dy}{dx} &= 2x^{2-1}\frac{dx}{dx} + (-2)x^{-2-1}\frac{dx}{dx}\\ &= 2x - 2x^{-3}.\end{aligned}$$

PROBLEMS

Find dy/dx in each of the following problems (1 through 8).

1. $y = x^3/3 - x^2/2 + x - 1$ **2.** $y = (x-1)^3(x+2)^4$

3. $y = (x^2+1)^5$ **4.** $y = (x^3 - 3x)^4$

5. $y = (x+1)^2(x^2+1)^{-3}$ **6.** $y = \dfrac{2x+1}{x^2-1}$

7. $y = \dfrac{2x+5}{3x-2}$ **8.** $y = \left(\dfrac{x+1}{x-1}\right)^2$

Find ds/dt in each of the following problems (9 through 15).

9. $s = \dfrac{t}{t^2+1}$ **10.** $s = (2t+3)^3$

11. $s = (t^2 - t)^{-2}$ **12.** $s = t^2(t+1)^{-1}$

13. $s = \dfrac{2t}{3t^2+1}$ **14.** $s = (t + t^{-1})^2$

15. $s = (t^2 + 3t)^3$

16. With the book closed, state and prove the formula for the derivative of the product of two differentiable functions u and v.

17. With the book closed, state and prove the formula for the derivative of the quotient u/v of two differentiable functions u and v.

18. With the book closed, state and prove the formula for the derivative with respect to x of u^n, where n is a positive integer and u is a differentiable function of x.

19. In Example 1, suppose that the labor force u is decreasing at the rate of 2 percent per year while the productivity per person is increasing at the rate of 3 percent per year. Is the total productivity increasing or decreasing, and at what rate?

20. In Example 4, $f(x) = x^3 - 2x + 3$ was claimed to be equal to $7 + 10(x-2) + 6(x-2)^2 + (x-2)^3$. Expand the terms in this latter expression, using the binomial theorem, and thus show that the two expressions are identical.

21. Suppose that the function $f(x) = x^3 - 2x + 3$ of Example 4 is put into the form $f(x) = a_0 + a_1(x-1) + a_2(x-1)^2 + a_3(x-1)^3$, where a_0, a_1, a_2, and a_3 are constants. Determine these constants in terms of $f(1)$, $f'(1)$, $f''(1)$, and $f'''(1)$. If the linear expression $L_1(x) = a_0 + a_1(x-1)$ is used to approximate $f(x)$ for values of x near 1, about how large is the error? What is the limit of

$$\frac{f(x) - L_1(x)}{(x-1)^2}$$

as x approaches 1?

2–4

INVERSE FUNCTIONS AND THEIR DERIVATIVES

Let us begin with an example.

EXAMPLE 1. What is the inverse of the function $f(x) = x^3$ and what is its derivative?

Solution. We look at the graph of $y = x^3$, shown in Fig. 2–5, and also at the graph of $x = y^3$ or $y = x^{1/3}$. The function $f(x) = x^3$ corresponds to a mapping from any real number to its cube. The inverse function should take that output and map it back to the original x. The function that does this is $g(x) = x^{1/3}$. Thus,

$$g(f(x)) = (f(x))^{1/3} = (x^3)^{1/3} = x,$$

and also, in the opposite order,

$$f(g(x)) = (g(x))^3 = (x^{1/3})^3 = x.$$

The composite of f with g or of g with f is the *identity mapping* $y = x$ (Fig. 2–6).

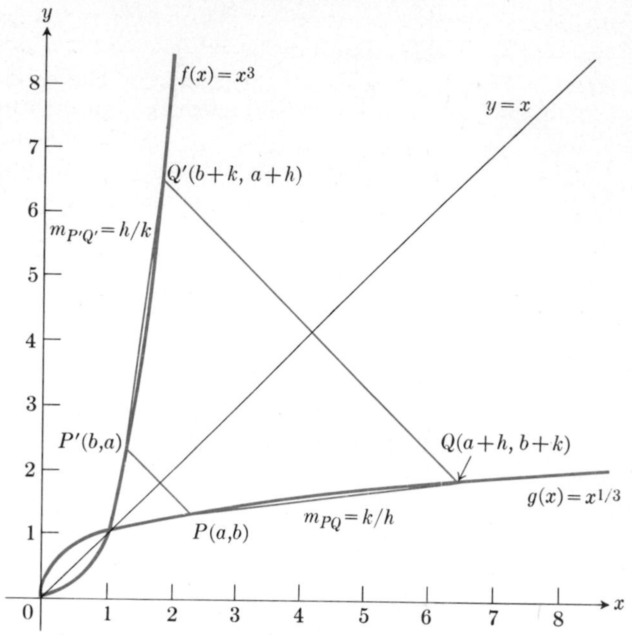

2-5 Graphs of the inverse functions $f(x) = x^3$ for $0 \le x \le 2$ and $g(x) = x^{1/3}$ for $0 \le x \le 8$. Each curve is the mirror image of the other with respect to the line $y = x$. Both curves should be reflected into the third quadrant for negative x.

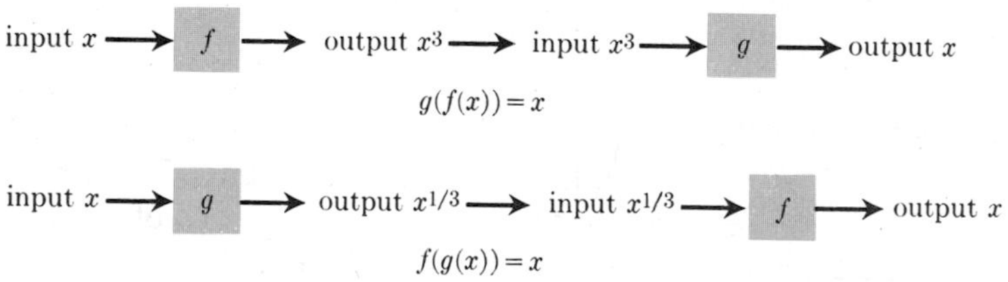

2-6 The composite of $f(x) = x^3$ and $g(x) = x^{1/3}$ in both orders is the identity function: $f(g(x)) = g(f(x)) = x$; f is the inverse of g and g is the inverse of f.

Next, we look at the slopes of the two curves in Fig. 2-5. If we want the derivative of $g(x)$ at $x = a$, we can start with the slope of a secant line PQ through $P(a, b)$ where $b = a^{1/3}$ and $Q(a + h,\ b + k)$ where $b + k = (a + h)^{1/3}$. The slope of PQ is $m_{PQ} = \text{rise/run} = k/h$. The slope of the tangent at P is the limit of m_{PQ} as h approaches zero:

$$m_{\tan P} = \lim_{h \to 0} m_{PQ} = \lim_{h \to 0} \frac{(a + h)^{1/3} - a^{1/3}}{h}. \tag{1}$$

We could rationalize the numerator in the last expression in Eq. (1) by multiplying the numerator and denominator by $(a + h)^{2/3} + (a + h)^{1/3}a^{1/3} + a^{2/3}$. But we prefer to go about the task in a geometric way that can be extended to any two inverse functions. The point $P'(b, a)$ is on the graph of $f(x) = x^3$ because $b^3 = a$. Likewise, the point $Q'(b + k, a + h)$ is on the graph of f. The slope of the secant line through these two points P' and Q' is

$$m_{P'Q'} = \text{rise/run} = h/k = 1/m_{PQ}. \tag{2}$$

When Q approaches P on the g curve, its mirror image Q' approaches P' on the f curve, and vice versa. The slopes of the two secant lines approach the respective slopes of the tangents. For the secant lines, the product of the slopes is 1. The same relation must hold for the limits: The slope of the tangent to one curve is the reciprocal of the slope of the tangent to the other, at mirror-imaged points P and P', provided that neither tangent slope is zero. We have a fast way to find the slope of the curve $f(x) = x^3$ at $x = b$; just take the formal derivative and put $x = b$:

$$f'(x) = 3x^2, \qquad \text{so} \quad m_{\tan P'} = f'(b) = 3b^2. \tag{3}$$

Therefore, if $b \neq 0$, we also have a formula for the slope of the curve $g(x) = x^{1/3}$ at $x = a = b^3$:

$$g'(a) = g'(b^3) = \frac{1}{3b^2} = \frac{1}{3a^{2/3}} = \tfrac{1}{3}a^{-2/3}. \tag{4}$$

To summarize:

The derivative of $g(x) = x^{1/3}$ *at* $x = a$ *is*

$$g'(a) = \tfrac{1}{3}a^{-2/3} \qquad \textit{for any } a \neq 0. \tag{5}$$

Or, in terms of x, for any $x \neq 0$, the function $g(x) = x^{1/3}$ is differentiable and its derivative is $\frac{1}{3}x^{-2/3}$.

We have just shown that, for all $x \neq 0$, the derivative of x^n is nx^{n-1} when $n = \frac{1}{3}$. The same argument will apply to x^n for $n = \frac{1}{5}, \frac{1}{7}, \frac{1}{9}$, and so on. And if we keep $x > 0$, so that even roots of x are defined, then the argument will also apply to x^n for $n = \frac{1}{2}, \frac{1}{4}, \frac{1}{6}, \ldots$. We take $n = 1/m$, where m is a positive integer, and consider the two functions $f(x) = x^m$ and $g(x) = x^{1/m}$. Each is the inverse of the other (on suitably restricted domains). Their graphs are mirror images of one another in the line $y = x$. The slope of the tangent to one curve at $P(a, b)$ is the reciprocal of the slope of the other at $P'(b, a)$, provided a and b are both different from zero. That is,

If $a^{1/m} = b \neq 0$, and $f(x) = x^m$, $g(x) = x^{1/m}$, *then*

$$g'(a) = \frac{1}{f'(b)} = \frac{1}{mb^{m-1}} = \frac{1}{m}b^{1-m} = \frac{1}{m}(a^{1/m})^{1-m} = \frac{1}{m}a^{(1/m)-1}. \tag{6}$$

In more familiar notation, with $n = 1/m$, we have:

Rule 9. *If* $g(x) = x^n$ *with* $n = 1/m$, *where* m *is a positive integer, then* $g'(x) = nx^{n-1}$ *for any* $x \neq 0$ *if* m *is odd, or for any* $x > 0$ *if* m *is even.*

EXAMPLE 2

a) When $x \neq 0$,

$$\frac{d}{dx}(x^{1/5}) = \tfrac{1}{5}x^{-4/5}.$$

b) When $x > 0$,

$$\frac{d}{dx}(x^{1/2}) = \tfrac{1}{2}x^{-1/2}.$$

REMARK. We can extend Rule 9 to any rational n in the following way.

If n is any rational number, then there are integers p and q, with q positive, such that $n = p/q$. We put $g(x) = x^n = (x^{1/q})^p = u^p$ with $u = x^{1/q}$. Then, by applying Rules 7 (or 8) and 9, we get

$$\begin{aligned} g'(x) &= pu^{p-1}\frac{du}{dx} = pu^{p-1}(1/q)x^{(1/q)-1} \\ &= p(x^{1/q})^{p-1}(1/q)x^{(1/q)-1} \\ &= \frac{p}{q}(x)^{(p/q)-(1/q)+(1/q)-1} = nx^{n-1}. \end{aligned}$$

In writing this we assume that, for any given p and q, the domain of x is restricted to avoid division by zero and to avoid even roots of negative numbers.

Let us return now to the two graphs in Fig. 2–5. The mirror-image relations that are shown there apply to any two inverse functions. Hence the slopes of their tangents at corresponding mirrored points are reciprocals, provided neither is zero. We state the result as Rule 10.

Rule 10. *Let $f(x)$ and $g(x)$ be inverse functions on suitably restricted domains. If $g(a) = b$ and $f(b) = a$, then $g'(a) = 1/f'(b)$ provided the derivatives are defined and $f'(b)g'(a) \neq 0$.*

REMARK. A function defined by a formula $y = f(x)$ may fail to have a unique inverse. But if it does, we can attempt to find a formula for the inverse function g by interchanging the letters x and y in the original equation and then solving for y. We may not always be able to solve conveniently for y but, when we can, the resulting equation will express the inverse we seek in terms of x.

EXAMPLE 3. Find the inverse of the function $f(x) = x^3 + 1$.

Solution. In the original formula, $y = x^3 + 1$, we interchange the letters x and y and get $x = y^3 + 1$. We then solve for y to get

$$y^3 = x - 1 \qquad \text{or} \qquad y = (x-1)^{1/3}.$$

The inverse function is expressed in terms of x by the formula

$$g(x) = (x-1)^{1/3}.$$

Formally, we have

$$f(g(x)) = ((x-1)^{1/3})^3 + 1 = x \qquad \text{and} \qquad g(f(x)) = ((x^3+1)-1)^{1/3} = x.$$

EXAMPLE 4. Find the inverse of the function $f(x) = 1/x$, for $x \neq 0$.

Solution. In the original equation $y = 1/x$, interchange the letters x and y and get $x = 1/y$. When we solve this for y we get $y = 1/x$. In this example, $g(x) = 1/x$ is the inverse of $f(x) = 1/x$. That is, f is its own inverse. Formally, we have $f(f(x)) = 1/f(x) = 1/(1/x) = x$.

EXAMPLE 5. Find the inverse of $f(x) = x^2$ on the domain $x \geq 0$.

Solution. In the equation $y = x^2$, interchange x and y and get $x = y^2$. Solve for y to get $y = \pm\sqrt{x}$. Choose the positive square root, $y = \sqrt{x}$, because it is the one whose graph is the mirror image of the graph of f on the domain $x \geq 0$. Thus, the inverse of $f(x) = x^2$ on the domain $x \geq 0$ is $g(x) = \sqrt{x}$. Formally, when $x \geq 0$, we have $\sqrt{x^2} = x$ and $(\sqrt{x})^2 = x$.

PROBLEMS

1. Find the inverse of the function $f(x) = 2x + 3$. Verify that Rule 10 applies to the function f and its inverse function g.

2. Use Rule 10 to find the derivative of the function $g(x) = (x - 1)^{1/3}$ in Example 3.

3. Sketch the curve $y = 1/x$ and observe that it is symmetric about the line $y = x$. What is the slope of the curve at $P(a, 1/a)$? What is its slope at the point $P'(1/a, a)$? Do these slopes satisfy Rule 10?

4. If $b = a^{2/3}$, find db/da. What restrictions, if any, should be put on the domain of a?

5. Find the x- and y-intercepts of the line L that is tangent to the curve $y = x^{1/2}$ at $x = 4$.

6. The function

$$f(x) = x^{1/2} + x^{-1/2}$$

is to be approximated near $x = 4$ by a quadratic function

$$Q(x) = C_0 + C_1(x - 4) + C_2(x - 4)^2$$

by choosing coefficients C_0, C_1, and C_2 in such a way that $f(4) = Q(4)$, $f'(4) = Q'(4)$, and $f''(4) = Q''(4)$. Find the coefficients. Use the result to estimate the difference between $f(x)$ and the tangent-line approximation $L(x) = C_0 + C_1(x - 4)$, and compare this estimate of error with the actual error at $x = 4.41 - (2.1)^2$. (We use "error" to mean $f(x) - L(x)$.)

7. a) Sketch graphs of $y = x^3$ and $y = x^{1/3}$ for $-2 \leq x \leq 2$, and sketch the lines tangent to them at $(1, 1)$ and $(-1, -1)$.

b) Which of these functions fails to have a derivative at one value of x, and what is that x? What is the slope of the other curve at that x? What lines are tangent to the curves at that x?

2–5 IMPLICIT RELATIONS AND THEIR DERIVATIVES

The functions we have dealt with so far have been of the form $y = f(x)$, which express y explicitly in terms of x. Quite often, however, we encounter equations like

$$x^2 + y^2 = 1, \qquad xy = 1,$$
$$y^2 = x, \qquad x^2 + xy + y^2 = 3,$$

which do not give y explicitly in terms of x. Nevertheless each of the equations listed defines a relation between y and x. When a definite number from some domain is substituted for x, the resulting equation determines one or more values of y to be associated with the given value of x. We therefore say that the equation determines y as one or more *implicit functions* of x. The domain of x is usually restricted to make y real.

It happens that each of the equations given above can be solved to give y explicitly in terms of x, but such is not the case for

$$x^5 + 4xy^3 - 3y^5 = 2.$$

Nevertheless, it is possible to calculate dy/dx from such an equation by the method known as *implicit differentiation*. In this method we simply treat y as an unknown but differentiable function of x and apply the rules for finding derivatives of u^n, uv, u/v, etc., which we have already developed. (For a discussion of the validity of the assumption that the equation does define y as one or more differentiable functions of x, we must refer the reader to more advanced textbooks, such as Olmsted, *Advanced Calculus*, Appleton-Century-Crofts, 1961, p. 289.)

EXAMPLE 1. Find dy/dx if $x^5 + 4xy^3 - 3y^5 = 2$.

Solution. We simply differentiate both sides of the given equation with respect to x. Thus,

$$\frac{d}{dx}(x^5) + \frac{d}{dx}(4xy^3) - \frac{d}{dx}(3y^5) = \frac{d}{dx}(2),$$

or

$$5x^4 + 4\left(x\frac{d(y^3)}{dx} + y^3\frac{dx}{dx}\right) - 15y^4\frac{dy}{dx} = 0,$$

$$5x^4 + 4\left(3xy^2\frac{dy}{dx} + y^3\right) - 15y^4\frac{dy}{dx} = 0,$$

$$(12xy^2 - 15y^4)\frac{dy}{dx} = -(5x^4 + 4y^3).$$

Finally, at all points where

$$12xy^2 - 15y^4 \neq 0,$$

we have

$$\frac{dy}{dx} = \frac{5x^4 + 4y^3}{15y^4 - 12xy^2}.$$

Note that the rule

$$\frac{d}{dx}u^n = nu^{n-1}\frac{du}{dx}$$

becomes

$$\frac{dy^5}{dx} = 5y^4\frac{dy}{dx}$$

when applied to y^5.

The result of applying this method to any of the equations listed above will be to give an expression for dy/dx in terms of both x and y. This is no real handicap since, if we want the slope of the tangent to a curve at a point (x_1, y_1), for instance, we need merely substitute x_1 for x and y_1 for y in the final expression for dy/dx.

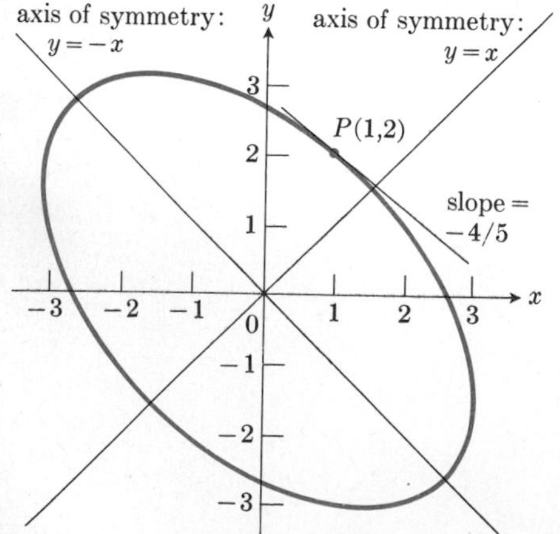

2–7 Graph of $x^2 + xy + y^2 = 7$ with slope of tangent at $P(1, 2)$: $(dy/dx)_{(1,2)} = -\frac{4}{5}$.

EXAMPLE 2. Find the slope of the tangent to the curve $x^2 + xy + y^2 = 7$ at the point (1, 2). (See Fig. 2–7.)

Solution. We differentiate both sides of the equation with respect to x, noting that xy is a product, uv, and that y^2 has the form u^n, while 7 is a constant. Thus

$$2x\frac{dx}{dx} + \left(x\frac{dy}{dx} + y\frac{dx}{dx}\right) + 2y\frac{dy}{dx} = 0,$$

$$(x + 2y)\frac{dy}{dx} = -(2x + y),$$

and wherever $x + 2y \neq 0$, we have

$$\frac{dy}{dx} = -\frac{2x + y}{x + 2y}.$$

In particular, at (1, 2) we have

$$\left(\frac{dy}{dx}\right)_{(1,2)} = -\frac{4}{5}.$$

Note that at those points where $2x + y = 0$, the slope is zero and the tangent is parallel to the x-axis. Where $x + 2y = 0$, the tangent is parallel to the y-axis: At these points we cannot solve for dy/dx but we can solve for dx/dy and it is zero.

The method of implicit differentiation enables us to show also that:

Rule 11. *If u is a differentiable function of x and*

$$y = u^{p/q},$$

where p and q are integers with $q > 0$, *then*

$$\frac{dy}{dx} = \frac{p}{q}u^{(p/q)-1}\frac{du}{dx} \tag{1}$$

provided $u \neq 0$ *if* $p/q < 1$.

This is the familiar rule for the derivative of u^n, but extended to the case where $n = p/q$ is any rational number.

Restrictions on x

The domain of x in Rule 11 is assumed to be restricted to values for which $u^{p/q}$ and $u^{(p/q)-1}$ are both defined as real numbers. For example, if $u = 1 - x^2$ and $p/q = \frac{1}{2}$, then, in order for

$$y = u^{1/2} = (1 - x^2)^{1/2}$$

to be real, we must have $x^2 \leq 1$. Any larger value of x^2 would make $1 - x^2$ negative. Also, in order for

$$\frac{dy}{dx} = \frac{1}{2}(1 - x^2)^{-1/2}(-2x) = \frac{-x}{\sqrt{1 - x^2}}$$

to be defined as a real number, we need to impose the added restriction that $x^2 \neq 1$, which corresponds to $u \neq 0$, thus avoiding division by zero. Therefore, in applying Eq. (1) to $u = 1 - x^2$ with $p/q = \frac{1}{2}$, we assume that x lies in the interval $-1 < x < 1$.

To establish Rule 11, let

$$y = u^{p/q},$$

which means that

$$y^q = u^p.$$

Then, differentiating both sides of the equation implicitly and using the familiar formulas for the derivatives of y^q and u^p (since p and q are integers, these formulas are valid), we obtain

$$qy^{q-1}\frac{dy}{dx} = pu^{p-1}\frac{du}{dx}.$$

Hence if $y \neq 0$, we have

$$\frac{dy}{dx} = \frac{pu^{p-1}}{qy^{q-1}}\frac{du}{dx}.$$

But

$$y^{q-1} = (u^{p/q})^{q-1} = u^{p-(p/q)},$$

so that

$$\frac{dy}{dx} = \frac{p}{q}\frac{u^{p-1}}{u^{p-(p/q)}}\frac{du}{dx} = \frac{p}{q}u^{(p/q)-1}\frac{du}{dx}.$$

This establishes Eq. (1).

REMARK. The restriction $y \neq 0$ is the same as the restriction $u \neq 0$ but was made without reference to whether p/q was or was not less than one. The restriction is certainly not needed if $p/q = 1$, since then we simply have $y = u$ and

$$\frac{dy}{dx} = \frac{du}{dx}.$$

The case

$$y = x^{3/2}$$

is typical of the case

$$y = u^{p/q}, \qquad p/q > 1,$$

and we shall show that for this case the slope of the curve is 0 at $x = 0$. We may work directly with the definition of the tangent to the curve at (0, 0) as the limiting position of a secant line through (0, 0) and a second point $P_1(x_1, y_1)$ on the curve as P_1 approaches the origin (Fig. 2–8). Then the slope of OP_1 is

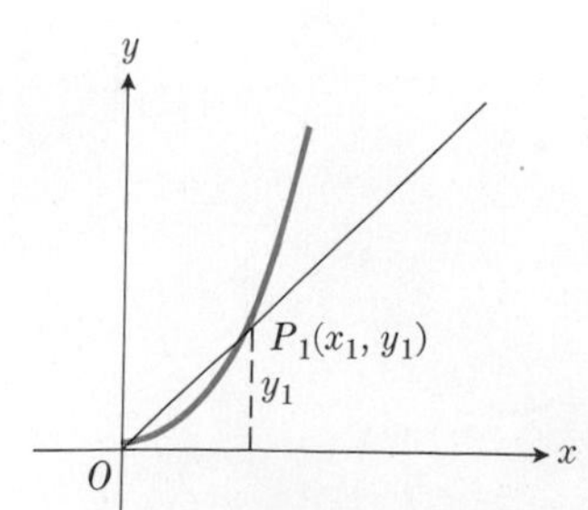

2–8 Graph of $y = x^{3/2}$. Slope at $x = 0$ is $\lim m_{OP_1} = 0$.

$$m = \frac{\text{rise}}{\text{run}} = \frac{y_1 - 0}{x_1 - 0} = \frac{x_1^{3/2}}{x_1} = x_1^{1/2}.$$

Now as P_1 approaches O, we have

$$m_0 = \lim_{x_1 \to 0} m = \lim_{x_1 \to 0} x_1^{1/2} = 0;$$

that is, the slope of the tangent to the curve at O is zero. If we use the formula just derived, we obtain

$$y = x^{3/2}, \qquad \frac{dy}{dx} = \frac{3}{2}x^{1/2},$$

and at $x = 0$ this also equals zero.

In the strictest sense, this function has no derivative at $x = 0$, since the function does not exist to the left of the origin. This means that only the righthand limit,

$$\lim_{\Delta x \to 0+} \frac{f(x + \Delta x) - f(x)}{\Delta x},$$

can be calculated at $x = 0$. Nevertheless, it is customary to say that the curve in Fig. 2–8 has a horizontal tangent at the origin, since the only secant lines that can be drawn from $O(0, 0)$ to points P on the curve tend to a unique limiting position as P approaches O along the curve.

PROBLEMS

In Problems 1–23, find dy/dx.

1. $x^2 + y^2 = 1$ **2.** $y^2 = \dfrac{x - 1}{x + 1}$

3. $x^2 + xy = 2$ **4.** $x^2y + xy^2 = 6$

5. $y^2 = x^3$ **6.** $x^{2/3} + y^{2/3} = 1$

7. $x^{1/2} + y^{1/2} = 1$ **8.** $x^3 - xy + y^3 = 1$

9. $x^2 = \dfrac{x - y}{x + y}$ **10.** $y = \dfrac{x}{\sqrt{x^2 + 1}}$

11. $y = x\sqrt{x^2 + 1}$ **12.** $y^2 = x^2 + \dfrac{1}{x^2}$

13. $2xy + y^2 = x + y$ **14.** $y = \sqrt{x} + \sqrt[3]{x} + \sqrt[4]{x}$

15. $y^2 = \dfrac{x^2 - 1}{x^2 + 1}$ **16.** $(x + y)^3 + (x - y)^3 = x^4 + y^4$

17. $(3x + 7)^5 = 2y^3$ **18.** $y = (x + 5)^4(x^2 - 2)^3$

19. $\dfrac{1}{y} + \dfrac{1}{x} = 1$ **20.** $y = (x^2 + 5x)^3$

21. $y^2 = x^2 - x$ **22.** $x^2y^2 = x^2 + y^2$

23. $y = \dfrac{\sqrt[3]{x^2 + 3}}{x}$

24. a) By differentiating the equation $x^2 - y^2 = 1$ implicitly, show that $dy/dx = x/y$.

b) By differentiating both sides of the equation $dy/dx = x/y$ implicitly, show that

$$\frac{d^2y}{dx^2} = \frac{y - x\left(\dfrac{dy}{dx}\right)}{y^2} = \frac{y - \dfrac{x^2}{y}}{y^2} = \frac{y^2 - x^2}{y^3},$$

or, since $y^2 - x^2 = -1$ from the original equation,

$$\frac{d^2y}{dx^2} = \frac{-1}{y^3}.$$

Use the method outlined in Problem 24 to find dy/dx and d^2y/dx^2 in each of the following problems (25 through 28).

25. $x^2 + y^2 = 1$ **26.** $x^3 + y^3 = 1$

27. $x^{2/3} + y^{2/3} = 1$ **28.** $xy + y^2 = 1$

29. A particle of mass m moves along the x-axis. The velocity $v = dx/dt$ and position x satisfy the equation

$$m(v^2 - v_0^2) = k(x_0^2 - x^2),$$

where k, v_0, and x_0 are constants. Show, by implicitly differentiating this equation with respect to t, that whenever $v \neq 0$,

$$m\frac{dv}{dt} = -kx.$$

Find the lines that are respectively *tangent* and *normal* to the following curves at the points indicated as P_0. (A line is said to be *normal* to a curve at a point P_0 if it is perpendicular to the tangent at P_0.)

30. $x^2 + xy - y^2 = 1$, $P_0(2, 3)$

31. $x^2 + y^2 = 25$, $P_0(3, -4)$

32. $x^2y^2 = 9$, $P_0(-1, 3)$

33. $\dfrac{x - y}{x - 2y} = 2$, $P_0(3, 1)$

34. $(y - x)^2 = 2x + 4$, $P_0(6, 2)$

35. Find the two points where the curve $x^2 + xy + y^2 = 7$

crosses the x-axis, and show that the tangents to the curve at these points are parallel. What is the common slope of these tangents?

36. Find points on the curve $x^2 + xy + y^2 = 7$ (a) where the tangent is parallel to the x-axis; (b) where the tangent is parallel to the y-axis. (In the latter case, dy/dx is not defined, but dx/dy is. What value does dx/dy have at these points?)

37. Use the quadratic equation formula to solve $x^2 + xy + y^2 - 7 = 0$ for y in terms of x. Then find dy/dx at $P(1, 2)$ directly from an expression of the form $y = f(x)$.

2–6 THE INCREMENT OF A FUNCTION

In this article we estimate the change produced in a function $y = f(x)$ when x changes by a small amount Δx. To be precise, let us focus our attention on a portion of the graph of $y = f(x)$ in the neighborhood of a point $P(x, y)$ where the function is differentiable. Then, if $Q(x + \Delta x, y + \Delta y)$ is a second point on the curve, with $\Delta x \neq 0$, we know that

$$\text{The slope of the secant line } PQ = \frac{\Delta y}{\Delta x}$$

approaches the limiting value

$$\frac{dy}{dx} = f'(x)$$

as Δx approaches zero. Therefore, the difference

$$\epsilon = \frac{\Delta y}{\Delta x} - \frac{dy}{dx} \tag{1}$$

is small when $|\Delta x|$ is small.

Now, saying that

$$\lim_{\Delta x \to 0} \frac{\Delta y}{\Delta x} = \frac{dy}{dx} = f'(x) \tag{2}$$

is equivalent to saying that

$$\lim_{\Delta x \to 0} \epsilon = 0. \tag{3}$$

In other words, we may deduce from Eqs. (1), (2), and (3) that

$$\frac{\Delta y}{\Delta x} = \frac{dy}{dx} + \epsilon, \tag{4a}$$

where

$$\epsilon \to 0 \quad \text{as} \quad \Delta x \to 0. \tag{4b}$$

If we multiply both sides of (4a) by Δx, we also have

$$\Delta y = \frac{dy}{dx} \Delta x + \epsilon \, \Delta x. \tag{4c}$$

Although Eq. (4c) was derived with $\Delta x \neq 0$, it is still a true equation even when $\Delta x = 0$. In fact, if we define ϵ by Eq. (1) when $\Delta x \neq 0$, and take $\epsilon = 0$ when $\Delta x = 0$, then Eqs. (4b, c) hold whether $\Delta x = 0$ or not.

Figure 2–9 shows that the first term on the right side of Eq. (4c) is equal to the change $\Delta y_{\tan}$ that would be produced in y by a change Δx along the tangent line. This is called the *principal part* of Δy since, for small values of Δx, it usually is large in comparison with the second term, $\epsilon\,\Delta x$.

The significance of Eqs. (4b, c) is that

$$\Delta y = \Delta y_{\tan} + \epsilon\,\Delta x = \text{change in } y \text{ along the curve}$$

and

$$\Delta y_{\tan} = \frac{dy}{dx}\Delta x = \text{change in } y \text{ along the tangent line}$$

differ by an amount

$$\epsilon\,\Delta x,$$

which tends to zero more rapidly than Δx does when Δx approaches zero.

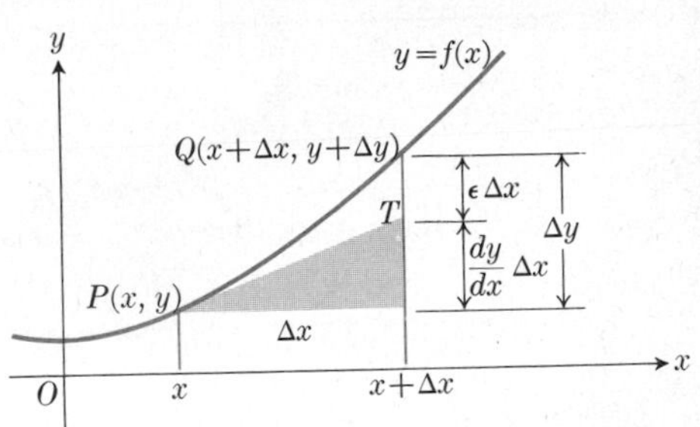

2–9 The increment Δy given by $\Delta y = f(x+\Delta x) - f(x) = (dy/dx)\,\Delta x + \epsilon \cdot \Delta x$.

EXAMPLE. (See Fig. 2–10.) The area enclosed by a circle of radius r is $A = \pi r^2$. If the radius is increased to $r + h$, find the increase in A and compare with Eqs. (4b) and (4c).

Solution. $\Delta A = \pi(r+h)^2 - \pi r^2 = 2\pi rh + \pi h^2$. This has the form

$$\Delta A = \frac{dA}{dr}\Delta r + \epsilon(\Delta r)$$

with

$$\frac{dA}{dr} = 2\pi r, \qquad \Delta r = h, \qquad \text{and} \qquad \epsilon = \pi\,\Delta r = \pi h.$$

Geometrically, $2\pi rh$ is the product of the circumference of the original circle and the change in radius $\Delta r = h$. When h is small, this accounts for nearly all of the change in the area. The remaining bit, πh^2, is the product of two numbers, $\epsilon = \pi h$ and $\Delta r = h$, which are both small when h is small.

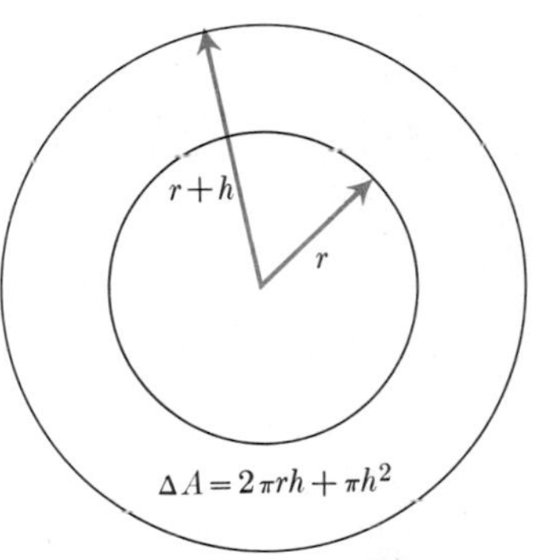

2–10 The area between the circles is $\Delta A = \pi(r+h)^2 - \pi r^2$.

PROBLEMS

For each of the following functions, find (a) Δy; (b) the principal part of Δy, namely, $\Delta y_{\tan} = (dy/dx)\Delta x$; and (c) the difference, $\Delta y - \Delta y_{\tan}$.

1. $y = x^2 + 2x$

2. $y = 2x^2 + 4x - 3$

3. $y = x^3 - x$

4. $y = x^4$

5. $y = x^{-1}$

For each of the following functions $y = f(x)$, *estimate* $y + \Delta y = f(x + \Delta x)$ by calculating y plus the principal part of Δy for the given data.

6. $y = \sqrt{x}, \quad x = 4, \quad \Delta x = 0.5$

7. $y = \sqrt[3]{x}, \quad x = 8, \quad \Delta x = -0.5$

8. $y = x^{-1}, \quad x = 2, \quad \Delta x = 0.1$

9. $y = \sqrt{x^2 + 9}, \quad x = -4, \quad \Delta x = -0.2$

10. $y = \dfrac{x}{x+1}, \quad x = 1, \quad \Delta x = 0.3$

11. The volume $y = x^3$ of a cube of edge x increases by an amount Δy when x increases by an amount Δx. Show that Δy may be represented geometrically as the sum of the volumes of:

a) three slabs of dimensions x by x by Δx,
b) three bars of dimensions x by Δx by Δx,
c) one cube of dimensions Δx by Δx by Δx.

Illustrate by a sketch.

2–7 NEWTON'S METHOD FOR SOLVING EQUATIONS

We know simple formulas for solving linear and quadratic equations. There are somewhat more complicated formulas for cubic and quartic equations. At one time it was hoped that similar formulas might be found for quintic and higher-degree equations, but a young Norwegian mathematician, Niels Henrik Abel (August 5, 1802–April 6, 1829), showed that no formulas like these are possible for quintic or higher-order equations.

There are, however, several numerical techniques for solving equations. One of these is the Newton or, as it is more accurately named, the Newton–Raphson method, which we discuss in this article. If you have access to a computer or a programmable calculator, you can easily write a program to do the arithmetic. If not, you can still see how it can be done. The method is:

1. Guess a first approximation to a root of the equation $f(x) = 0$. A graph of $y = f(x)$ will help.

2. Use the first approximation to get a second, the second to get a third, and so on. To go from the nth approximation x_n to the next approximation x_{n+1}, use the formula

$$x_{n+1} = x_n - \frac{f(x_n)}{f'(x_n)} \tag{1}$$

where $f'(x_n)$ is the derivative of f at x_n. We first show how the method works, and then go to the theory behind it.

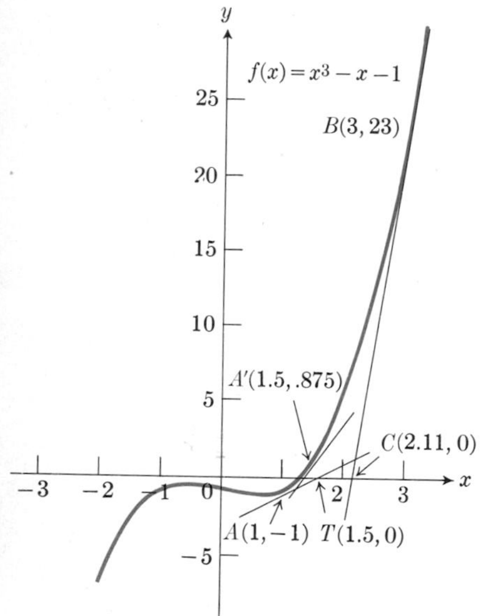

2–11 Newton's method for finding a root of $f(x) = 0$ uses the tangent to approximate the curve.

EXAMPLE. Use the procedure described above to find where the graph of $y = x^3$ intersects the line $y = x + 1$.

Solution. The curve and line cross when $x^3 = x + 1$. We put this equation into the form $f(x) = 0$ with

$$f(x) = x^3 - x - 1.$$

Then $f'(x) = 3x^2 - 1$. A brief table of values of $f(x)$, $f'(x)$, and $x - f(x)/f'(x)$ was used to construct the graph shown in Fig. 2–11. The curve crosses the x-axis at a root of the equation $f(x) = 0$. We have taken $x_1 = 1$ as our first approximation. We then used Eq. (1) repeatedly to get x_2, x_3, and so on, as shown in Table 2–1.

Table 2–1. Approximate data for Fig. 2–11.

n	x_n	$f(x_n)$	$f'(x_n)$	$x_{n+1} = x_n - \frac{f(x_n)}{f'(x_n)}$
1	1	−1	2	1.5
2	1.5	0.875	5.75	1.347826087
3	1.347826087	0.100682174	4.449905482	1.325200399
4	1.325200399	0.002058363	4.268468293	1.324718174
5	1.324718174	0.000000925	4.264634722	1.324717957
6	1.324717957	-5×10^{-10}	4.264632997	1.324717957

At $n = 6$ we come to the result $x_6 = x_5 = 1.324717957$. When $x_{n+1} = x_n$, Eq. (1) shows that $f(x_n) = 0$. Hence we have found a solution of $f(x) = 0$ to nine decimals, or so it appears. (Our calculator shows only ten figures, and we cannot guarantee the accuracy of the ninth decimal, though we believe it to be correct as given.)

What is the theory behind the method? It is this: We use the tangent to approximate the graph of $y = f(x)$ near the point $P(x_n, y_n)$, where $y_n = f(x_n)$ is small, and we let x_{n+1} be the value of x where that tangent line crosses the x-axis. (We assume that the slope $f'(x_n)$ of the tangent is not zero.) The equation of the tangent is

$$y - y_n = f'(x_n)(x - x_n). \tag{2}$$

We put $y_n = f(x_n)$ and $y = 0$ into Eq. (2) and solve for x:

$$x - x_n = \frac{-f(x_n)}{f'(x_n)},$$

or, as in Eq. (1),

$$x = x_n - \frac{f(x_n)}{f'(x_n)}.$$

REMARK 1. The method doesn't work if $f'(x_n) = 0$. In that case, choose a new starting place. Of course, it may happen that $f(x) = 0$ and $f'(x) = 0$ have a common root. To detect whether that is so, we could first find the solutions of $f'(x) = 0$, and then check the value of $f(x)$ at such places.

In the example, we started at the point $A(1, -1)$ in Fig. 2–11. The tangent at A crosses the x-axis at $T(1.5, 0)$. We take $x_2 = 1.5$, $y_2 = f(x_2) = 0.875$, and approximate the graph near $A'(1.5, 0.875)$ by the line tangent to the curve at A'. That tangent crosses the x-axis at $x_3 = 1.347\ldots$. Each successive approximation becomes the input for the right side of Eq. (1) to get the next approximation. It is clear from Eq. (1) that $x_{n+1} = x_n$ implies that $f(x_n) = 0$, and conversely. Therefore, if the process stops with $x_{n+1} = x_n$, as in the example, we have a zero of $f(x)$.

REMARK 2. In Fig. 2–11 we have also indicated that the process might have started at the point $B(3, 23)$ on the curve, with $x_1 = 3$. Point B is quite far from the x-axis, but the tangent at B crosses the x-axis at $C(2.11\ldots, 0)$, so that x_2 is still an improvement over x_1. If we take $x_1 = 3$ and use Eq. (1) repeatedly as before, with $f(x) = x^3 - x - 1$ and $f'(x) = 3x^2 - 1$, we confirm the nine-place solution $x_7 = x_6 = 1.324717957$ in seven steps.

The curve in Fig. 2–11 has a high turning point at $x = -1/\sqrt{3}$ and a low turning point at $x = +1/\sqrt{3}$. We would not expect good results from Newton's method if we were to start with x_1 between these points, but we can start any place between A and B and get the answer. It would not be very clever to do so, but we could even begin far to the right of B, for example with $x_1 = 10$. It takes a bit longer, but the process still converges to the same answer as before.

REMARK 3. Newton's method does not always converge. For instance, if

$$f(x) = \begin{cases} \sqrt{x - r} & \text{for } x \geq r, \\ -\sqrt{r - x} & \text{for } x \leq r, \end{cases} \tag{3}$$

the graph will be like that shown in Fig. 2–12. If we begin with $x_1 = r - h$, we get $x_2 = r + h$, and successive approximations go back and forth between these two values. No amount of iteration will bring us any closer to the root r than our first guess.

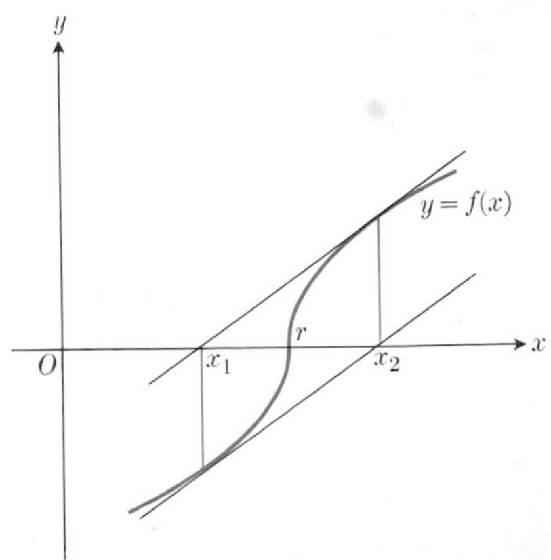

2–12 Graph of a function for which Newton's method fails to converge.

PROBLEMS

Sketch the graph of $y = f(x)$ in each of the following problems (1 through 6). Show that $f(a)$ and $f(b)$ have opposite signs and use Newton's method to estimate the root of the equation $f(x) = 0$ between a and b. One might use $x_1 = (a + b)/2$ as first approximation.

1. $f(x) = x^2 + x - 1, \quad a = 0, \quad b = 1$
2. $f(x) = x^3 + x - 1, \quad a = 0, \quad b = 1$
3. $f(x) = x^4 + x - 3, \quad a = 1, \quad b = 2$
4. $f(x) = x^4 - 2, \quad a = 1, \quad b = 2$
5. $f(x) = 2 - x^4, \quad a = -1, \quad b = -2$
6. $f(x) = \sqrt{2x + 1} - \sqrt{x + 4}, \quad a = 2, \quad b = 4$

7. Suppose our first guess is lucky, in the sense that x_1 is a root of $f(x) = 0$. What happens to x_2 and later approximations?

8. To find $x = \sqrt[q]{a}$, we apply Newton's method to $f(x) = x^q - a$. Here we assume that a is a positive real number and q is a positive integer. Show that x_2 is a "weighted average" of x_1 and a/x_1^{q-1}, and find the coefficients m_1, m_2 such that

$$x_2 = m_1 x_1 + m_2 \left(\frac{a}{x_1^{q-1}}\right), \qquad m_1 > 0, \quad m_2 > 0, \quad m_1 + m_2 = 1.$$

What conclusion would you reach if x_1 and a/x_1^{q-1} were equal? What would be the value of x_2 in that case? (You may also wish to read the article by J. P. Ballantine, "An averaging method of extracting roots," *American Mathematical Monthly*, **63**, 1956, pp. 249–252, where more efficient ways of averaging are discussed. *Also see* J. S. Frame, "The solution of equations by continued fractions," *Ibid.*, **60**, 1953, pp. 293–305.)

9. Show that Newton's method applied to $f(x)$ in Eq. (3) leads to $x_2 = r + h$ if $x_1 = r - h$, and to $x_2 = r - h$ if $x_1 = r + h$, where $h > 0$. Interpret the result geometrically.

10. (See Remark 3.) Is it possible that successive approximations actually get "worse," in that x_{n+1} is farther away from the root r than x_n is? Can you find such a "pathological" example? [*Hint.* Try cube roots in place of square roots in Eq. (3).]

2–8 COMPOSITE FUNCTIONS AND THEIR DERIVATIVES: THE CHAIN RULE

We have already seen that, if u is a differentiable function of x, and $y = u^n$, then

$$\frac{dy}{dx} = nu^{n-1}\frac{du}{dx} \tag{1}$$

for n a rational number. This is a special case of a more general rule. One part of Eq. (1) is

$$nu^{n-1} = \frac{dy}{du},$$

so that the equation can also be written in the form

$$\frac{dy}{dx} = \frac{dy}{du}\cdot\frac{du}{dx}, \tag{2}$$

and the latter form is known as the chain rule for the derivative of a composite function.

Rule 12. The Chain Rule for the Derivative of a Composite Function. *If y is a differentiable function of u and u is a differentiable function of x, then y is a differentiable function of x and*

$$\frac{dy}{dx} = \frac{dy}{du}\cdot\frac{du}{dx}. \tag{3}$$

Before we prove this rule, let us look at a particular example.

EXAMPLE 1. For oscillations of small amplitude, the relation between the period T and the length L of a simple pendulum may be approximated by the equation

$$T = 2\pi\sqrt{\frac{L}{g}}, \tag{4}$$

where $g = 980$ cm/sec^2 is the acceleration due to gravity. When the temperature θ changes, the length L either increases or decreases at a rate that is proportional to L:

$$\frac{dL}{d\theta} = kL, \tag{5}$$

where k is a proportionality constant. What is the rate of change of the period with respect to temperature?

Solution. We assume that g is constant and then

$$T = \left(\frac{2\pi}{\sqrt{g}}\right)L^{1/2}$$

is a function of L. We don't need an explicit formula for the relation between L and θ in order to apply Rule 12, which, for this example takes the form

$$\frac{dT}{d\theta} = \frac{dT}{dL}\cdot\frac{dL}{d\theta} = \left(\frac{2\pi}{\sqrt{g}}\right)\tfrac{1}{2}L^{-1/2}\frac{dL}{d\theta}$$
$$= \left(\frac{2\pi}{\sqrt{g}}\right)\tfrac{1}{2}L^{-1/2}(kL) = \left(\frac{k}{2}\right)\left(2\pi\sqrt{\frac{L}{g}}\right) = \left(\frac{k}{2}\right)T.$$

Thus the rate of change of the period is proportional to the period, with proportionality factor $k/2$.

If θ changes by a small increment $\Delta\theta$, then L and T change by increments

$$\Delta L \approx \Delta L_{\tan} = kL\,\Delta\theta \quad \text{and} \quad \Delta T \approx \Delta T_{\tan} = \frac{kT\,\Delta\theta}{2}.$$

Thus,

$$\frac{\Delta T}{T} \approx \frac{1}{2}\frac{\Delta L}{L}.$$

A temperature change that gives a 0.002-percent change in L results in approximately a 0.001-percent change in the period T.

The idea behind the chain rule is this: If $y = f(u)$ is differentiable at $u = u_0$, then an increment Δu produces an increment Δy such that

$$\Delta y = f'(u_0)\,\Delta u + \epsilon_1\,\Delta u, \tag{6a}$$

and if $u = g(x)$ is differentiable at $x = x_0$, then an increment Δx produces an increment Δu such that

$$\Delta u = g'(x_0)\,\Delta x + \epsilon_2\,\Delta x, \tag{6b}$$

where

ϵ_1 approaches zero when Δu does,

and

ϵ_2 approaches zero when Δx does.

Combining Eqs. (6a) and (6b) gives

$$\Delta y = [f'(u_0) + \epsilon_1][g'(x_0) + \epsilon_2]\,\Delta x.$$

Dividing through by Δx, we get

$$\frac{\Delta y}{\Delta x} = f'(u_0)g'(x_0)$$

$$+ \text{ (terms in } \epsilon_1 \text{ and } \epsilon_2 \text{ that go to zero when } \Delta x \text{ and } \Delta u \text{ do)}.$$

As Δx approaches zero, so does Δu, and we get

$$\lim \frac{\Delta y}{\Delta x} = f'(u_0)g'(x_0),$$

which is the same as

$$\left(\frac{dy}{dx}\right)_{x_0} = \left(\frac{dy}{du}\right)_{u_0}\left(\frac{du}{dx}\right)_{x_0}.$$

EXAMPLE 2. *Snowball melting.* How long does it take a snowball to melt?

Discussion. We start with a mathematical model. Let us assume that the snowball is, approximately, a sphere of radius r and volume $V = (\frac{4}{3})\pi r^3$. (Of course the snowball is not a perfect sphere, but we can apply mathematics only to a mathematical model of the situation, and we choose one that seems reasonable and is not too complex.) In the same way, we choose some hypothesis about the rate at which the volume of the snowball is changing. One model is to assume that the volume decreases at a rate that is proportional to the surface area: In mathematical terms,

$$\frac{dV}{dt} = -k(4\pi r^2).$$

We tacitly assume that k, the proportionality factor, is a constant. (It probably depends upon several things, like the relative humidity of the surrounding air, the air temperature, the incidence of sunlight or its absence, to name a few.) Finally, we need at least one more bit of information: How long has it taken for the snowball to melt some specific percent? We have nothing to guide us unless we make one or more observations, but let us now assume a particular set of conditions in which the snowball melted $\frac{1}{4}$ of its volume in two hours. (You could use letters instead of these precise numbers: say n percent in h hours. Then your answer would be in terms of n and h.) Now to work. Mathematically, we have the following problem.

Given:

$$V = \tfrac{4}{3}\pi r^3 \quad \text{and} \quad \frac{dV}{dt} = -k(4\pi r^2),$$

and $V = V_0$ when $t = 0$, and $V = \frac{3}{4}V_0$ when $t = 2$ hr.

To find: The value of t when $V = 0$.

We apply the chain rule to differentiate $V = (\frac{4}{3})\pi r^3$ with respect to t:

$$\frac{dV}{dt} = \frac{4}{3}\pi(3r^2)\frac{dr}{dt} = 4\pi r^2\frac{dr}{dt}.$$

We set this equal to the given rate, $-k(4\pi r^2)$, and divide by $4\pi r^2$ to get

$$\frac{dr}{dt} = -k.$$

The radius is changing at a *constant rate.*

How long does it take for the radius to go from its initial value

$$r_0 = \left(\frac{3V_0}{4\pi}\right)^{1/3}$$

to $r = 0$? In two hours, r decreases from r_0 to

$$r_2 = \left(\frac{9V_0}{16\pi}\right)^{1/3},$$

because V has decreased to $3V_0/4$. Dividing the second of these equations by the first, we get

$$\frac{r_2}{r_0} = \left(\frac{3}{4}\right)^{1/3} = c \approx 0.91.$$

Thus, $r_2 = cr_0$, where $c \approx 0.91$. Since dr/dt is a constant, $-k$, the constant rate at which r is changing is equal to

$$k = \frac{r_0 - r_2}{2} = \frac{(1-c)r_0}{2}.$$

The time it takes the snowball to melt is

$$\frac{r_0}{k} = \frac{2}{(1-c)} \approx 21.87 \text{ hr}.$$

If $\frac{1}{4}$ of the volume melts in two hours, it takes nearly 20 hours for the rest of it to melt.

REMARK 1. If we were natural scientists who were really interested in testing our model, we could collect some data and compare them with the results of the mathematics. One practical application may lie in analyzing the proposal to tow large icebergs from polar waters to offshore locations near Southern California to provide fresh water from the melting ice. As a first approximation, we might assume that the iceberg is a large cube, or a pyramid, or a sphere.

Parametric Equations

In many applications a curve traced by a moving particle can be described by expressing the coordinates x and y of a point $P(x, y)$ on the curve as functions of a third variable, say the time t, for a specified domain of that variable. The equations

$$x = f(t), \qquad y = g(t),$$

which express x and y in terms of t, are then called *parametric equations*, and the variable t is called a *parameter*.

EXAMPLE 3. Sketch the path traced by the point $P(x, y)$ if

$$x = t + \frac{1}{t}, \qquad y = t - \frac{1}{t} \tag{7}$$

for each positive real number t.

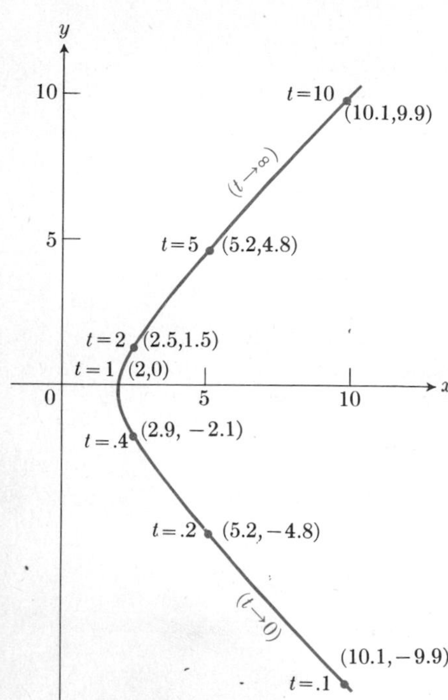

2–13 Graph of $x = t + (1/t)$, $y = t - (1/t)$, $t > 0$. (Part shown is for $0.1 \le t \le 10$.)

Solution. We make a brief table of values, plot the points, and draw a smooth curve through them (Fig. 2–13). From Table 2–2, or from Eqs. (7), we see that, if t is replaced by $1/t$, the value of x is unchanged and only the sign of y changes. Thus the graph is symmetric with respect to the x-axis. For large values of t, the difference between x and y is small:

$$x - y = \frac{2}{t}, \tag{8a}$$

and if we add the two equations in (7) we get

$$x + y = 2t. \tag{8b}$$

It is now easy to eliminate t between Eqs. (8a) and (8b) by multiplication:

$$(x - y)(x + y) = x^2 - y^2 = 4. \tag{9}$$

The coordinates of all the points described by the parametric equations (7) satisfy Eq. (9), but the converse is not true because Eq. (9) does not require x to be positive. Figure 2–13 shows the part of the graph that corresponds to $0.1 \le t \le 10$. For smaller positive values of t, the curve extends downward and to the right, approaching the line $y = -x$. As t tends to $+\infty$, the curve extends up and to the right and approaches the line $y = x$. If we want the slope at any point on the curve, other than at $t = 1$ where the tangent is vertical, we use the chain rule in the form

$$\frac{dy}{dx} = \frac{dy/dt}{dx/dt} = \frac{1 + t^{-2}}{1 - t^{-2}} = \frac{t^2 + 1}{t^2 - 1}. \tag{10}$$

For example, when $t = 5$, $x = 5.2$, $y = 4.8$, and $dy/dx = 26/24$. The line tangent to the graph at this point is

$$y - 4.8 = \tfrac{13}{12}(x - 5.2).$$

Table 2–2. Values of $x = t + (1/t)$ and $y = t - (1/t)$ for selected values of t

t	$1/t$	x	y
0.1	10.0	10.1	−9.9
0.2	5.0	5.2	−4.8
0.4	2.5	2.9	−2.1
1.0	1.0	2.0	0.0
2.0	0.5	2.5	1.5
5.0	0.2	5.2	4.8
10.0	0.1	10.1	9.9

REMARK 2. In the foregoing example, we can also find dy/dx by differentiating Eq. (9) implicitly:

$$2x - 2y\frac{dy}{dx} = 0, \qquad \frac{dy}{dx} = \frac{x}{y} = \frac{t + t^{-1}}{t - t^{-1}} = \frac{t^2 + 1}{t^2 - 1}.$$

We get a result that is equivalent to Eq. (10). We expect the same result, because the chain rule works that way. The derivative dy/dx does not exist at $t = 1$, where $dx/dt = 0$ and $y = 0$.

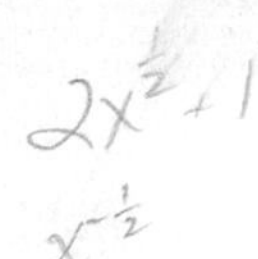

PROBLEMS

In Problems 1–4, each pair of equations represents a curve in parametric form. In each case, find the equation of the curve in the form $y = F(x)$ by eliminating t, then calculate dy/dt, dy/dx, and dx/dt, and verify that they satisfy the chain rule, Eq. (3). (See Example 3.)

1. $x = 3t + 1, \quad y = t^2$
2. $x = t^2, \quad y = t^3$
3. $x = \dfrac{t}{1 - t}, \quad y = t^2$
4. $x = \dfrac{t}{1 + t}, \quad y = \dfrac{t^2}{1 + t}$
5. If a point traces the circle $x^2 + y^2 = 25$ and if $dx/dt = 4$ when the point reaches (3, 4), find dy/dt there.

In each of the following problems (6 through 10), find dy/dx, (a) by using the chain rule, and also (b) by first expressing y directly in terms of x, and then differentiating.

6. $y = u^2 + 3u - 7; \quad u = 2x + 1$
7. $y = \dfrac{u^2}{u^2 + 1}; \quad u = \sqrt{2x + 1}$
8. $y = z^{2/3}; \quad z = x^2 + 1$
9. $y = w^2 - w^{-1}; \quad w = 3x$
10. $y = 2v^3 + \dfrac{2}{v^3}; \quad v = (3x + 2)^{2/3}$

2-9 BRIEF REVIEW OF TRIGONOMETRY

Many natural phenomena are periodic; that is, they repeat after definite periods of time. Such phenomena are most readily studied with trigonometric functions, particularly sines and cosines. Our object in this article and the next is to apply the operations of the calculus to these functions, but before we do, we shall review some of their properties.

When an angle of measure θ is placed in standard position at the center of a circle of radius r, as in Fig. 2–14, the trigonometric functions of θ are defined by the equations

$$\sin\theta = \frac{y}{r}, \qquad \cos\theta = \frac{x}{r}, \qquad \tan\theta = \frac{y}{x},$$
$$\csc\theta = \frac{r}{y}, \qquad \sec\theta = \frac{r}{x}, \qquad \cot\theta = \frac{x}{y}. \tag{1}$$

Observe that $\tan\theta$ and $\sec\theta$ are not defined for values of θ for which $x = 0$. In radian measure, this means that $\pi/2, 3\pi/2, \ldots, -\pi/2, -3\pi/2, \ldots$ are excluded from the domains of the tangent and the secant functions. Similarly, $\cot\theta$ and $\csc\theta$ are not defined for values of θ corresponding to $y = 0$: that is, for $\theta = 0, \pi, 2\pi, \ldots, -\pi, -2\pi, \ldots$. For those values of θ where the functions are defined, it follows from Eqs. (1) that

$$\csc\theta = \frac{1}{\sin\theta}, \qquad \sec\theta = \frac{1}{\cos\theta}, \qquad \cot\theta = \frac{1}{\tan\theta}.$$

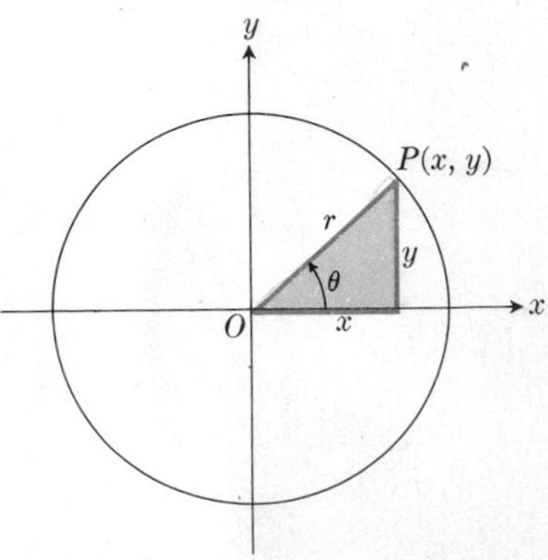

2–14 Angle θ in standard position.

Since, by the theorem of Pythagoras, we have

$$x^2 + y^2 = r^2,$$

it follows that

$$\cos^2 \theta + \sin^2 \theta = 1. \tag{2}$$

It is also useful to express the coordinates of $P(x, y)$ in terms of r and θ as follows:

$$\begin{aligned} x &= r \cos \theta, \\ y &= r \sin \theta. \end{aligned} \tag{3}$$

When $\theta = 0$ in Fig. 2–14, we have $y = 0$ and $x = r$; hence, from the definitions (1), we obtain

$$\sin 0 = 0, \qquad \cos 0 = 1.$$

Similarly, for a right angle, $\theta = \pi/2$, we have $x = 0$, $y = r$; hence

$$\sin \frac{\pi}{2} = 1, \qquad \cos \frac{\pi}{2} = 0.$$

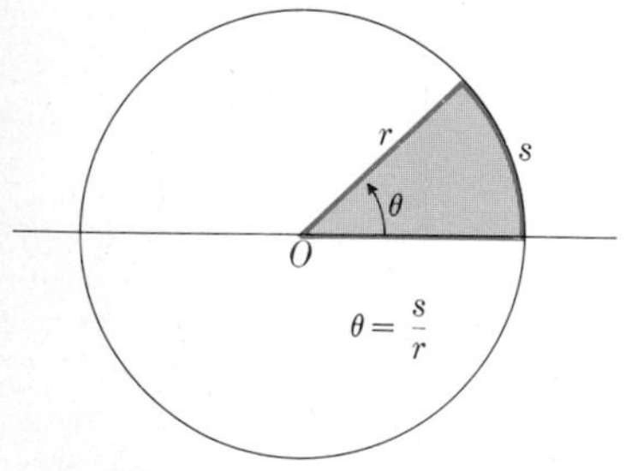

2–15 In radian measure, $\theta = s/r$.

Radian Measure

As defined in Article 1–6, the number of radians θ in the angle in Fig. 2–15 is the number of "radius units" contained in the arc s subtended by the central angle θ; that is,

$$\theta \text{ (in radians)} = \frac{s}{r}. \tag{4a}$$

This also implies that

$$s = r\theta \qquad (\theta \text{ in radians}). \tag{4b}$$

Another useful interpretation of radian measure is easy to get if we take $r = 1$ in (4b). Then the central angle θ, in radians, is just equal to the arc s subtended by θ. We may imagine the circumference of the circle marked off with a scale from which we may read θ. We think of a number scale, like the y-axis shifted one unit to the right, as having been wrapped around the circle. The unit on this number scale is the same as the unit radius. We put the zero of the scale at the place where the initial ray crosses the circle, and then we wrap the positive end of the scale around the circle in the counterclockwise direction, and wrap the negative end around in the opposite direction (see Fig. 2–16). Then θ can be read from this curved s-"axis."

Two points on the s-axis that are exactly 2π units apart will map onto the same point on the unit circle when the wrapping is carried out. For example, if $P_1(x_1, y_1)$ is the point to which an arc of length s_1 reaches, then arcs of length $s_1 + 2\pi$, $s_1 + 4\pi$, and so on, will reach exactly the same point after going completely around the circle one, or two, or more, times. Similarly P_1 will be the image of points on the negative s-axis at $s_1 - 2\pi$, $s_1 - 4\pi$, and so on. Thus, from the wrapped s-axis, we could read

$$\theta_1 = s_1,$$

or

$$\theta_1 + 2\pi, \quad \theta_1 + 4\pi, \quad \ldots, \quad \theta_1 - 2\pi, \quad \theta_1 - 4\pi, \quad \ldots.$$

A unit of arc length $s = 1$ radius subtends a central angle of $57°18'$ (approximately); so

$$1 \text{ radian} \approx 57°18'. \tag{5}$$

We find this, and other relations between degree measure and radian measure, by using the fact that the full circumference has arc length $s = 2\pi r$ and central angle 360°. Therefore

$$360° = 2\pi \text{ radians,} \tag{6a}$$

$$180° = \pi \text{ radians} = 3.14159\ldots \text{ radians,} \tag{6b}$$

$$\left(\frac{360}{2\pi}\right)^\circ = 1 \text{ radian} \approx 57°17'44.8'', \tag{6c}$$

$$1° = \frac{2\pi}{360} = \frac{\pi}{180} \approx 0.01745 \text{ radians.} \tag{6d}$$

It should be emphasized, however, that the radian measure of an angle is dimensionless, since r and s in Eqs. (4a, b) both represent lengths measured in identical units, for instance feet, inches, centimeters, or light-years. Thus $\theta = 2.7$ is to be interpreted as a pure number. The sine and cosine of 2.7 are the ordinate and abscissa, respectively, of the point $P(x, y)$ on a circle of radius r at the end of an arc of length 2.7 radii. For practical purposes we would convert 2.7 radians to $2.7(360/2\pi)$ degrees and say

$$\sin 2.7 = \sin\left[2.7\left(\frac{360}{2\pi}\right)^\circ\right] \approx \sin\,[154°41'55'']$$

$$\approx 0.42738.$$

(See Article 1–6 for a short table of angles, their radian measures, and their sines and cosines.)

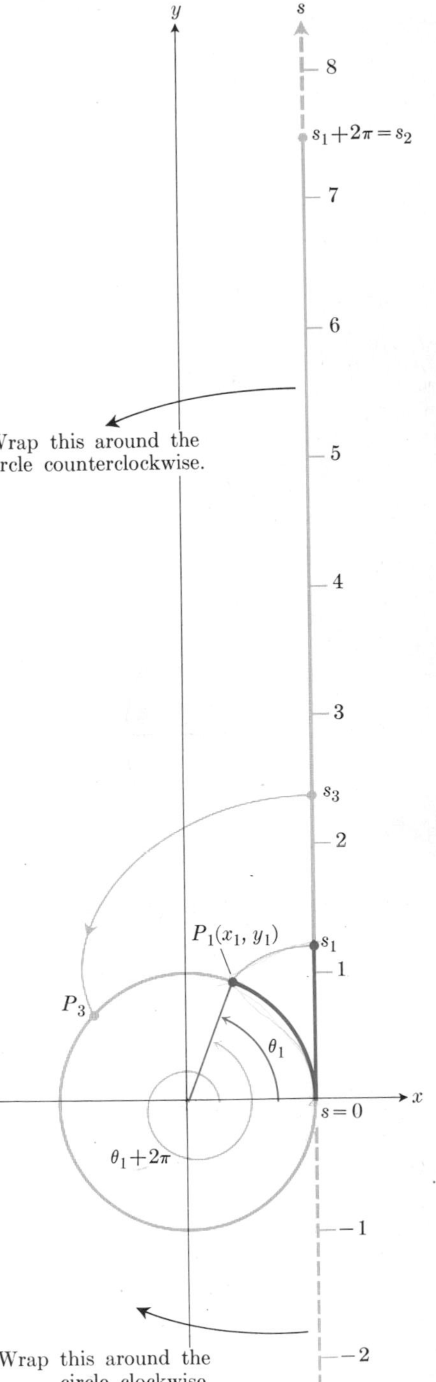

2–16 The curved s-"axis" wrapped around the unit circle.

Periodicity

The mapping from the real numbers s onto points $P(x, y)$ on the unit circle by the wrapping process described above and illustrated in Fig. 2–16 defines the coordinates as functions of s because Eqs. (1) apply, with $\theta = s$ and $r = 1$:

$$x = \cos\theta = \cos s, \qquad y = \sin\theta = \sin s.$$

Because $s + 2\pi$ maps onto the same point that s does, it follows that

$$\cos(\theta + 2\pi) = \cos\theta,$$
$$\sin(\theta + 2\pi) = \sin\theta. \tag{7}$$

Equations (7) are *identities*; that is, they are true for all real numbers θ. These identities would be true for $\theta' = \theta + 2\pi$:

$$\cos\theta' = \cos(\theta' - 2\pi) \quad \text{and} \quad \sin\theta' = \sin(\theta' - 2\pi). \tag{8}$$

Equations (7) and (8) say that 2π can be added to or subtracted from the domain variable of the sine or cosine functions with no change in the function values. The same process could be repeated any number of times. Consequently

$$\cos(\theta + 2n\pi) = \cos\theta, \qquad \sin(\theta + 2n\pi) = \sin\theta, \qquad n = 0, \pm 1, \pm 2, \ldots. \tag{9}$$

Figure 2–17(a, b) shows graphs of the curves

$$y = \sin x \qquad \text{and} \qquad y = \cos x.$$

The portion of each curve between 0 and 2π is repeated endlessly to the left and to the right. We also note that the cosine curve is the same as the sine curve shifted to the left an amount $\pi/2$.

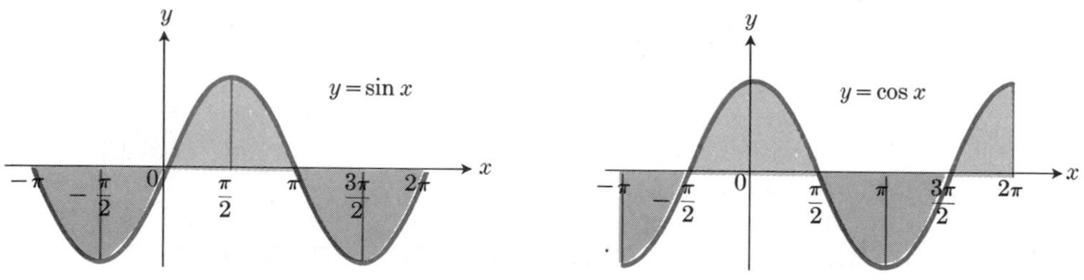

2–17 The value of the sine at x is the value of the cosine at $(x - \pi/2)$. That is, $\sin x = \cos(x - \pi/2)$.

EXAMPLE.* The builders of the Trans-Alaska Pipeline used insulated pads to keep the heat from the hot oil in the pipeline from melting the permanently frozen soil beneath. To design the pads, it was necessary to take into account the variation in temperature throughout the year. The variation was represented in the calculations by a *general sine function* of the form

$$f(x) = A \sin\left[\frac{2\pi}{B}(x - C)\right] + D,$$

where $|A|$ is the *amplitude*, $|B|$ is the *period*, C is the *horizontal shift*, and D is the *vertical shift* (Fig. 2–18). Figure 2–19 shows how such a function can be used to represent temperature data. The data points in the figure are plots of the mean air temperature for Fairbanks, Alaska, based on records of the National Weather Service from 1941 to 1970. The sine function that is used to fit the data is

$$f(x) = 37 \sin\left[\frac{2\pi}{365}(x - 101)\right] + 25,$$

where f is temperature in degrees fahrenheit, and x is the number of the day counting from the beginning of the year.

The fit is remarkably good.

* From "Is the curve of temperature variation a sine curve?" by B. M. Lando and C. A. Lando. *The Mathematics Teacher*, September 1977, **7**, 6, pages 534–537.

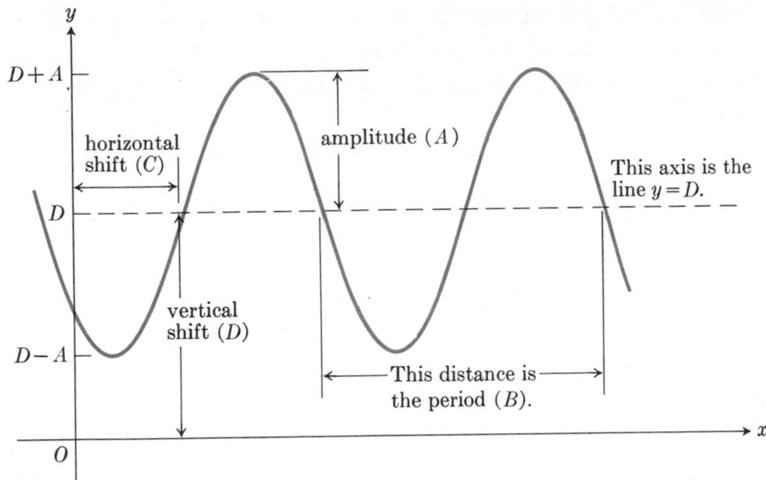

2–18 The general sine curve $y = A \sin[(2\pi/B)(x - C)] + D$, shown for A, B, C and D positive.

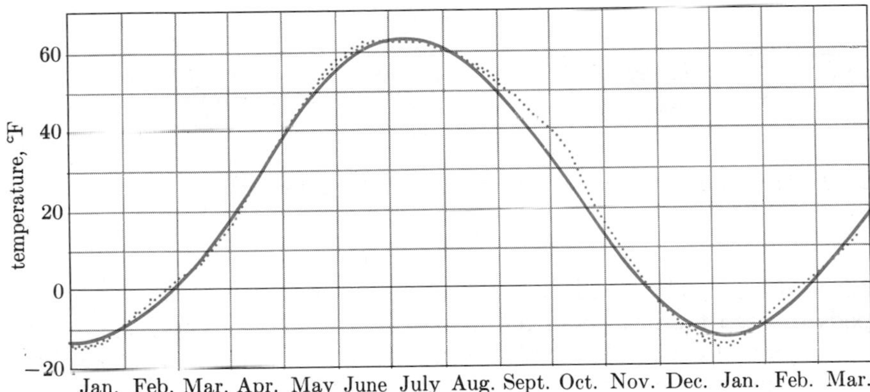

2–19 Normal mean air temperatures at Fairbanks, Alaska, plotted as data points. The approximating sine function is

$$f(x) = 37 \sin\left[\frac{2\pi}{365}(x - 101)\right] + 25.$$

(From "Is the curve of temperature variation a sine curve?" by B. M. Lando and C. A. Lando. *The Mathematics Teacher*, September 1977, **7**, 6; Fig. 2, p. 535.)

More Trigonometric Identities

Figure 2–20 shows two angles of opposite sign but of equal magnitude. By symmetry, the points $P(x, y)$ and $P'(x, -y)$, where the rays of the two angles θ and $-\theta$ intersect the circle, have equal abscissas, and ordinates that differ only in sign. Hence we have

$$\sin(-\theta) = -\frac{y}{r} = -\sin\theta, \quad \textbf{(10a)}$$

$$\cos(-\theta) = \frac{x}{r} = \cos\theta. \quad \textbf{(10b)}$$

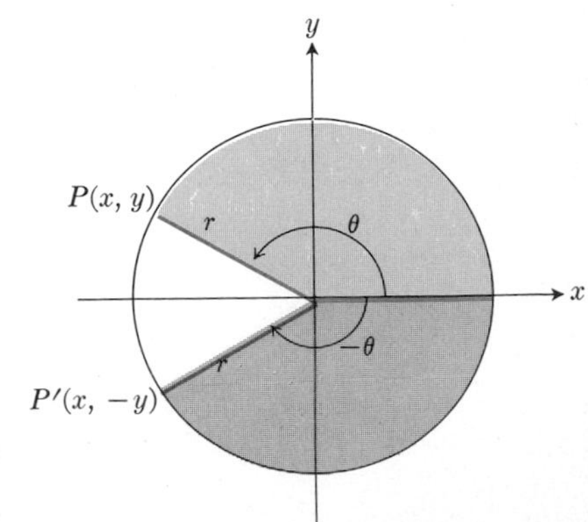

2–20 Angles of opposite sign.

In particular,

$$\sin\left(-\frac{\pi}{2}\right) = -\sin\frac{\pi}{2} = -1,$$

$$\cos\left(-\frac{\pi}{2}\right) = \cos\frac{\pi}{2} = 0.$$

It will be helpful, for reasons which will soon be made apparent, to review the formulas

$$\sin(A + B) = \sin A \cos B + \cos A \sin B, \tag{11a}$$

$$\cos(A + B) = \cos A \cos B - \sin A \sin B, \tag{11b}$$

together with two formulas obtained from these by replacing B by $-B$ and recalling that

$$\sin(-B) = -\sin B, \qquad \cos(-B) = \cos B, \tag{11c}$$

namely,

$$\sin(A - B) = \sin A \cos B - \cos A \sin B, \tag{11d}$$

$$\cos(A - B) = \cos A \cos B + \sin A \sin B. \tag{11e}$$

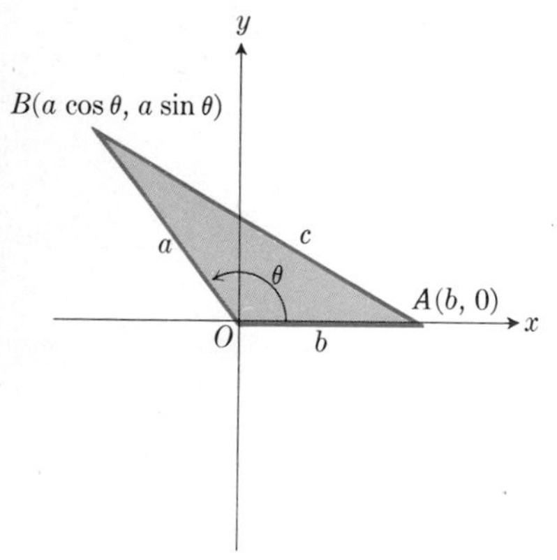

2–21 To derive the law of cosines, compute the distance between A and B, and square.

Equation (11e) may be established for all angles A and B by two applications of the formula for the distance between two points:

$$d = \sqrt{(x_2 - x_1)^2 + (y_2 - y_1)^2}.$$

The first application gives the law of cosines. The second then yields the identity (11e). The other formulas (11a, b, d) can be derived from (11e) as shown below.

Law of cosines. In Fig. 2–21 triangle OAB has been placed with O at the origin and A on the x-axis at $A(b, 0)$. The third vertex B has coordinates

$$x = a \cos\theta, \qquad y = a \sin\theta,$$

as given by Eq. (3) with $r = a$. The angle AOB has measure θ. By the formula for the distance between two points,

The square of the distance c between A and B is:

$$c^2 = (a\cos\theta - b)^2 + (a\sin\theta)^2 = a^2(\cos^2\theta + \sin^2\theta) + b^2 - 2ab\cos\theta,$$

or

$$c^2 = a^2 + b^2 - 2ab\cos\theta. \tag{12}$$

Equation (12) is called the *law of cosines*. In words, it says: "The square of any side of a triangle is equal to the sum of the squares of the other two sides minus twice the product of those two sides and the cosine of the angle between them." When the angle θ is a right angle, its cosine is zero, and Eq. (12) reduces to the theorem of Pythagoras. Equation (12) holds for a general angle θ, since it is based solely on the distance formula and on Eqs. (3) for the coordinates of a point. The same equation works with the exterior angle $(2\pi - \theta)$, or the opposite of $(2\pi - \theta)$, in place of θ, because

$$\cos(2\pi - \theta) = \cos(\theta - 2\pi) = \cos\theta.$$

It is still a valid formula when B is on the x-axis and $\theta = \pi$ or $\theta = 0$, as we can easily verify if we remember that $\cos 0 = 1$ and $\cos \pi = -1$. In these special cases, the right side of Eq. (12) becomes $(a - b)^2$ or $(a + b)^2$.

Addition formulas. Equation (11e) follows from the law of cosines applied to the triangle OPQ in Fig. 2–22. We take $OP = OQ = r = 1$. Then the coordinates of P are

$$x_P = \cos A, \qquad y_P = \sin A$$

and of Q,

$$x_Q = \cos B, \qquad y_Q = \sin B.$$

Hence the square of the distance between P and Q is

$$\begin{aligned}(PQ)^2 &= (x_Q - x_P)^2 + (y_Q - y_P)^2\\ &= (x_Q^2 + y_Q^2) + (x_P^2 + y_P^2) - 2(x_Q x_P + y_Q y_P)\\ &= 2 - 2(\cos A \cos B + \sin A \sin B).\end{aligned}$$

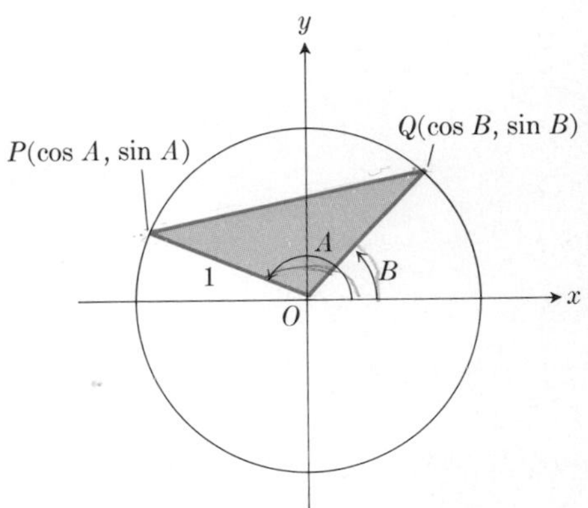

2–22 Diagram for $\cos(A - B)$.

But angle $QOP = A - B$, and the law of cosines gives

$$(PQ)^2 = (OP)^2 + (OQ)^2 - 2(OP)(OQ)\cos(A - B) = 2 - 2\cos(A - B).$$

When we equate these two expressions for $(PQ)^2$, we obtain

$$\cos(A - B) = \cos A \cos B + \sin A \sin B.$$

We now deduce Eqs. (11a, b, d) from Eq. (11e). We shall also need the results

$$\begin{aligned}&\sin 0 = 0, \qquad \sin(\pi/2) = 1, \qquad \sin(-\pi/2) = -1,\\ &\cos 0 = 1, \qquad \cos(\pi/2) = 0, \qquad \cos(-\pi/2) = 0.\end{aligned} \tag{13}$$

1. In Eq. (11e), we put $A = \pi/2$ and use Eqs. (13) to get

$$\cos\left(\frac{\pi}{2} - B\right) = \sin B. \tag{14a}$$

In this equation, if we replace B by $\pi/2 - B$ and $\pi/2 - B$ by $\pi/2 - (\pi/2 - B)$, we get

$$\cos B = \sin\left(\frac{\pi}{2} - B\right). \tag{14b}$$

Equations (14a, b) express the familiar results that the sine and cosine of an angle are the cosine and sine, respectively, of the complementary angle.

2. We next put $B = -\pi/2$ in Eq. (11e) and use Eq. (13) to get

$$\cos\left(A + \frac{\pi}{2}\right) = -\sin A. \tag{14c}$$

3. We can get the formula for cos $(A + B)$ from Eq. (11e) by substituting $-B$ for B everywhere:

$$\begin{aligned}\cos(A+B) &= \cos[A-(-B)]\\ &= \cos A\cos(-B)+\sin A\sin(-B)\\ &= \cos A\cos B-\sin A\sin B, \qquad \textbf{(11b)}\end{aligned}$$

where the final equality uses Eqs. (11c), established earlier.

4. To derive formulas for sin $(A \pm B)$, we use the identity Eq. (14a) with B replaced by

$$A + B \qquad \text{or} \qquad A - B.$$

Thus we have

$$\begin{aligned}\sin(A+B) &= \cos[\pi/2-(A+B)]\\ &= \cos(\pi/2-A-B)\\ &= \cos(\pi/2-A)\cos B+\sin(\pi/2-A)\sin B\\ &= \sin A\cos B+\cos A\sin B. \qquad \textbf{(11a)}\end{aligned}$$

Equation (11d) follows from this if we replace B by $-B$.

These are the key results of analytic trigonometry, and all have been derived simply from the distance formula and the definitions of sine and cosine. The most important formulas to remember are the following:

$$\sin(A+B) = \sin A\cos B+\cos A\sin B, \qquad \textbf{(11a)}$$

$$\cos(A+B) = \cos A\cos B-\sin A\sin B, \qquad \textbf{(11b)}$$

$$\sin(-B) = -\sin B, \qquad \cos(-B) = \cos B. \qquad \textbf{(11c)}$$

If we let

$$\alpha = A + B \qquad \text{and} \qquad \beta = A - B,$$

so that

$$A = \tfrac{1}{2}(\alpha+\beta), \qquad B = \tfrac{1}{2}(\alpha-\beta),$$

and subtract Eq. (11d) from Eq. (11a), we obtain the further useful identity

$$\sin\alpha - \sin\beta = 2\cos\frac{\alpha+\beta}{2}\sin\frac{\alpha-\beta}{2}. \qquad \textbf{(15)}$$

PROBLEMS

In Problems 1 through 9, sketch the graph of the given equation.

1. $y = 2\sin x$

2. $y = 5\sin 2x$

3. $y = \sin 2\pi x$

4. $y = 2\cos 3x$

5. $y = \tan\dfrac{x}{3}$

6. $y = \sin x + \cos x$

7. $y = \sin x - \cos x$

8. $y = \sin(x - 1)$

9. $y = \cos[2\pi(x + 1)]$

10. Find the (a) amplitude, (b) period, (c) horizontal shift, and (d) vertical shift of the general sine function

$$f(x) = 37\sin\left[\frac{2\pi}{365}(x-101)\right] + 25.$$

11. Use the equation in Problem 10 to approximate the answers to the following questions about the temperatures in Fairbanks, Alaska, shown in Fig. 2–19. Assume that the year has 365 days.

a) What is the highest mean daily temperature shown?

b) What is the lowest mean daily temperature shown?

c) What is the average of the highest and lowest mean daily temperatures shown? Why is this average the vertical shift of the function?

12. Show that the area of a sector of a circle having central angle θ and radius r is $\frac{1}{2}r^2\theta$, if θ is measured in radians.

13. Let $A(r, 0)$ be the point where the positive x-axis cuts a circle of radius r, center at the origin O. Let $P(r\cos\theta, r\sin\theta)$ be a point on the circle in the first quadrant, with angle $AOP = \theta$ radians. Let AT be tangent to the circle at A and suppose it intersects the line OP at T. By considering the areas of triangle AOP, sector AOP, and triangle AOT, prove the following inequality:

$$\sin\theta < \theta < \tan\theta \quad \text{if} \quad 0 < \theta < \pi/2.$$

14. In Eq. (11e) take $B = A$. Does the result agree with something else you know?

15. In Eq. (11d) take $B = A$. Does the result agree with something you already know?

16. Derive a formula for $\tan(A - B)$ from Eqs. (11d, e).

17. Derive a formula for $\tan(A + B)$ from Eqs. (11a, b).

18. Express all of the trigonometric functions of a general angle θ in terms of $\sin\theta$ and $\cos\theta$.

19. A function $f(\theta)$ is said to be

an even function of θ if $f(-\theta) = f(\theta)$,

an odd function of θ if $f(-\theta) = -f(\theta)$.

Which of the six trigonometric functions are even, and which are odd?

20. Derive formulas for $\cos 2A$ and $\sin 2A$ from Eqs. (11a, b).

21. Let P and Q be points on a circle with radius $r = 1$, center at the origin O, and such that OP makes an angle $-B$ with the positive x-axis, OQ an angle A. Use the law of cosines to derive a formula for $\cos(A + B)$ directly from this configuration.

(*Problems 22–27 require a calculator.*) Try out the following identities for various values of θ.

22. $\sin(-\theta) = -\sin\theta$ **23.** $\cos(-\theta) = \cos\theta$

24. $\cos\theta = \sin\left(\frac{\pi}{2} - \theta\right)$ **25.** $\sin\theta = \cos\left(\frac{\pi}{2} - \theta\right)$

The equations in Problems 26 and 27 hold for some values of θ but not for others. Experiment with values of θ until you think you know for which values of θ they hold.

26. $\sin\frac{\theta}{2} = \sqrt{\frac{1 - \cos\theta}{2}}$ **27.** $\cos\frac{\theta}{2} = \sqrt{\frac{1 + \cos\theta}{2}}$

2–10 DIFFERENTIATION OF SINES AND COSINES

We shall now apply the operations of the calculus to the sine and cosine functions. We need the result given by the following theorem.

Theorem. *If θ is measured in radians, then*

$$\lim_{\theta\to 0}\frac{\sin\theta}{\theta} = 1. \tag{1}$$

Proof. First we shall suppose that θ is a small positive angle at the center of a circle of radius $r = 1$ (Fig. 2–23). In the figure, OP and OQ are sides of the angle, PT is tangent to the circle at P and intersects the side OQ at T. We observe that

$$\text{Area } \triangle OPQ < \text{Area sector } OPQ < \text{Area } \triangle OPT. \tag{2}$$

These areas may be expressed in terms of θ as follows:

$$\text{Area } \triangle OPQ = \tfrac{1}{2}\overline{OP}\cdot\overline{OQ}\cdot\sin\theta = \tfrac{1}{2}\sin\theta, \tag{3a}$$

$$\text{Area sector } OPQ = \tfrac{1}{2}r^2\theta = \tfrac{1}{2}\theta, \tag{3b}$$

$$\text{Area } \triangle OPT = \tfrac{1}{2}\overline{OP}\cdot\overline{PT} = \tfrac{1}{2}\tan\theta. \tag{3c}$$

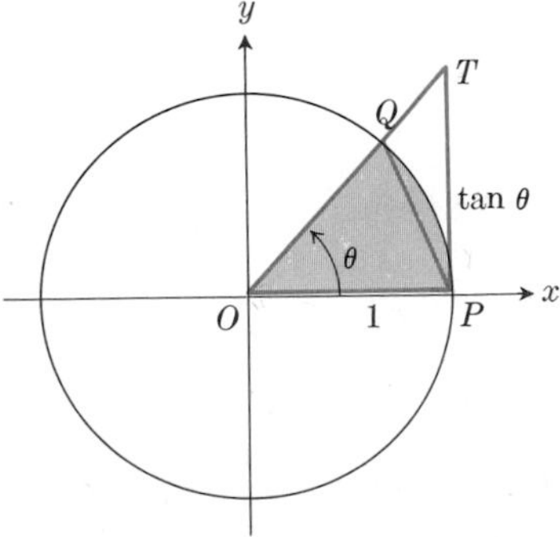

2–23 Area $\triangle OPQ <$ area sector $OPQ <$ area $\triangle OPT$.

We substitute from Eqs. (3a, b, c) into (2) and obtain

$$\tfrac{1}{2}\sin\theta < \tfrac{1}{2}\theta < \tfrac{1}{2}\tan\theta, \qquad \text{when} \quad 0 < \theta < \frac{\pi}{2}. \tag{4}$$

Since $\sin\theta$ is positive in (4), the inequality signs will go the same way if we divide all three terms by $\frac{1}{2}\sin\theta$. Therefore,

$$1 < \frac{\theta}{\sin\theta} < \frac{1}{\cos\theta}, \qquad \text{when} \quad 0 < \theta < \frac{\pi}{2}. \tag{5a}$$

We next take reciprocals in (5a), which requires that we reverse the inequality signs:

$$1 > \frac{\sin\theta}{\theta} > \cos\theta, \qquad \text{when} \quad 0 < \theta < \frac{\pi}{2}. \tag{5b}$$

This quickly brings us to our goal. Since $\cos\theta$ approaches 1 as θ approaches zero, the Sandwich Theorem (Theorem 2, Article 1–10) tells us that

$$\lim_{\theta\to 0} \frac{\sin\theta}{\theta} = 1.$$

The geometrical argument leading to Eq. (1) is based on the assumption that θ is positive, but the same limit is obtained if θ approaches zero through negative values. For if $\theta = -\alpha$ and α is positive, then when α approaches zero, we have

$$\frac{\sin\theta}{\theta} = \frac{\sin(-\alpha)}{-\alpha} = \frac{-\sin\alpha}{-\alpha} = \frac{\sin\alpha}{\alpha} \to 1.$$

This concludes the proof.

If θ were not measured in radians but in degrees, the limit that we would obtain in place of Eq. (1) would be

$$\lim_{\theta\to 0} \frac{\sin\theta^\circ}{\theta} = \frac{\pi}{180}. \tag{6}$$

It is to avoid the factor $\pi/180$ in this equation that we use radian measure in all calculus operations with trigonometric functions.

Table 2–3 shows $\sin\theta$ and $(\sin\theta)/\theta$ for a few selected values of θ near zero. To get the effect of $(\sin\theta)/\theta$ approaching 1, we read the last column upward from the bottom.

Table 2–3

Degrees	θ (radians)	$\sin\theta$	$\frac{\sin\theta}{\theta}$
0°	0	0	Undefined
1°	0.017453	0.017452	0.99994
2°	0.034907	0.034899	0.9998
5°	0.08727	0.08716	0.9987
10°	0.17453	0.17365	0.995

Derivative of sin *u*

We now consider a function defined by

$$y = \sin u$$

and calculate the derivative from the definition

$$\frac{dy}{du} = \lim_{\Delta u \to 0} \frac{\Delta y}{\Delta u}.$$

Let u be given an increment Δu and y a corresponding increment Δy. Then

$$y + \Delta y = \sin (u + \Delta u),$$

and hence

$$\Delta y = \sin (u + \Delta u) - \sin u \quad \textbf{(a)}$$

$$= 2 \cos \left(u + \frac{\Delta u}{2}\right) \sin \frac{\Delta u}{2}, \quad \textbf{(b)}$$

where we have used Eq. (15) of Article 2–9, with $\alpha = u + \Delta u$ and $\beta = u$, in going from (a) to (b). If we divide (b) by Δu, we have

$$\frac{\Delta y}{\Delta u} = 2 \cos \left(u + \frac{\Delta u}{2}\right) \frac{\sin (\Delta u/2)}{\Delta u}$$

$$= \cos \left(u + \frac{\Delta u}{2}\right) \frac{\sin (\Delta u/2)}{\Delta u/2},$$

$$= \cos (u + \theta) \frac{\sin \theta}{\theta},$$

where $\theta = \Delta u/2$. We now let θ approach zero and make use of Eq. (1), and obtain

$$\lim_{\Delta u \to 0} \frac{\Delta y}{\Delta u} = \lim_{\theta \to 0} \left[\cos (u + \theta) \frac{\sin \theta}{\theta}\right] = \cos u.$$

But since $y = \sin u$, this means that

$$\frac{dy}{du} = \frac{d (\sin u)}{du} = \cos u.$$

If u is a differentiable function of x, we may apply the chain rule

$$\frac{dy}{dx} = \frac{dy}{du} \frac{du}{dx}$$

to this, with the result that we obtain

$$\frac{d (\sin u)}{dx} = \cos u \cdot \frac{du}{dx}. \quad (7)$$

Thus to find the derivative of the sine of a function, we take the cosine of the same function and multiply it by the derivative of the function.

EXAMPLE 1. If

$$y = \sin 2x,$$

then

$$\frac{dy}{dx} = \cos 2x \cdot \frac{d(2x)}{dx} = 2 \cos 2x.$$

Derivative of cos *u*

To obtain a formula for the derivative of cos u, we make use of the identities

$$\cos u = \sin\left(\frac{\pi}{2} - u\right), \qquad \sin u = \cos\left(\frac{\pi}{2} - u\right).$$

Thus

$$\frac{d\,(\cos u)}{dx} = \frac{d \sin\,[(\pi/2) - u]}{dx}$$

$$= \cos\left(\frac{\pi}{2} - u\right)\frac{d[(\pi/2) - u]}{dx}$$

$$= \sin u \cdot -\frac{du}{dx},$$

or

$$\frac{d\,(\cos u)}{dx} = -\sin u \frac{du}{dx}. \qquad \textbf{(8)}$$

This equation tells us that the derivative of the cosine of a function is minus the sine of the same function, times the derivative of the function.

EXAMPLE 2. Let

$$y = \cos\,(x^2).$$

Then

$$\frac{dy}{dx} = -\sin\,(x^2)\frac{d(x^2)}{dx} = -2x \sin\,(x^2).$$

The formulas (7) and (8) may be combined with the formulas given previously, as in the following examples.

EXAMPLE 3. Find dy/dx if

$$y = \sin^2\,(3x).$$

Solution. Let

$$y = \sin^2\,(3x) = u^2, \qquad u = \sin 3x.$$

Then,

$$\frac{dy}{dx} = 2u\frac{du}{dx} = 2 \sin 3x \frac{d(\sin 3x)}{dx}$$

$$= 2 \sin 3x \cdot \cos 3x \frac{d(3x)}{dx}$$

$$= 6 \sin 3x \cos 3x$$

$$= 3 \sin 6x.$$

EXAMPLE 4. Find dy/dx if

$$y = \sec^2 5x = (\cos 5x)^{-2}.$$

Solution. We apply the formula for the derivative of a function to a power,

$$\frac{d(u^n)}{dx} = nu^{n-1}\frac{du}{dx}.$$

We then have

$$\frac{dy}{dx} = -2(\cos 5x)^{-3}\frac{d(\cos 5x)}{dx}$$

$$= (-2 \sec^3 5x)\left(-\sin 5x \frac{d(5x)}{dx}\right)$$

$$= +10 \sec^3 5x \sin 5x.$$

EXAMPLE 5. Find the velocity and acceleration of a particle moving in a circle of radius r with constant angular velocity $\omega = d\theta/dt > 0$.

Solution (See Fig. 2–24a). If the position of the particle at time t is $P(x, y)$, then

$$x = r \cos \theta, \qquad y = r \sin \theta, \tag{9a}$$

and it is given that the angular velocity

$$\frac{d\theta}{dt} = \omega \tag{9b}$$

is constant. The velocity (Fig. 2–24b) is a vector $\mathbf{v}$ with components

$$v_x = \frac{dx}{dt} = \frac{dx}{d\theta}\frac{d\theta}{dt}, \qquad v_y = \frac{dy}{dt} = \frac{dy}{d\theta}\frac{d\theta}{dt} \tag{9c}$$

parallel to the x- and y-axes respectively. Also, the acceleration (Fig. 2–24c) is a vector $\mathbf{a}$ with components

$$a_x = \frac{dv_x}{dt}, \qquad a_y = \frac{dv_y}{dt} \tag{9d}$$

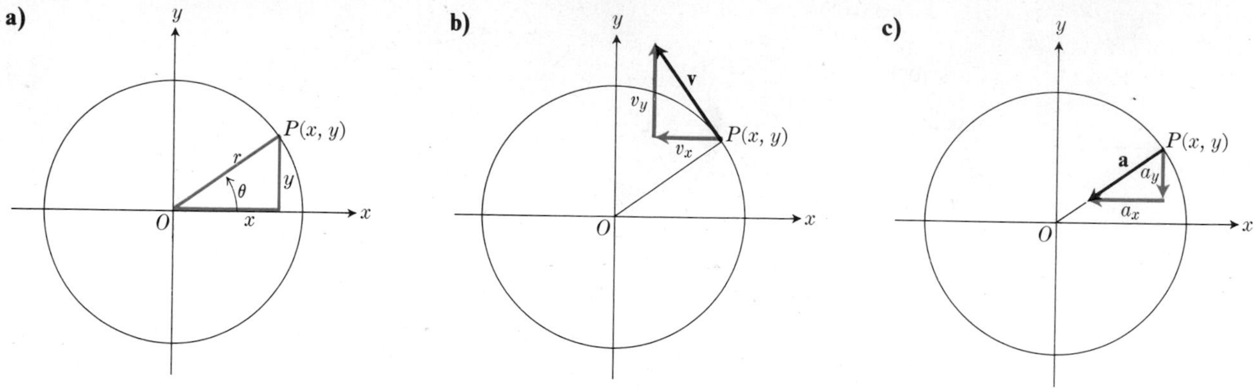

2–24 The velocity and acceleration vectors of a particle moving counterclockwise around a circle at a constant angular velocity.

parallel to the coordinate axes. From (9a) and (9b), we find

$$v_x = \frac{dx}{dt} = -r \sin \theta \frac{d\theta}{dt} = -\omega r \sin \theta = -\omega y,$$
$$v_y = \frac{dy}{dt} = r \cos \theta \frac{d\theta}{dt} = \omega r \cos \theta = \omega x, \tag{9e}$$

and from these we find in turn

$$a_x = \frac{dv_x}{dt} = -\omega \frac{dy}{dt} = -\omega^2 x,$$
$$a_y = \frac{dv_y}{dt} = \omega \frac{dx}{dt} = -\omega^2 y. \tag{9f}$$

The velocity vector has both magnitude and direction. Its magnitude is

$$\sqrt{v_x^2 + v_y^2} = \sqrt{\omega^2 y^2 + \omega^2 x^2} = \omega\sqrt{y^2 + x^2} = \omega r,$$

which is the angular velocity ω times the radius of the circle. Its direction is specified, except for sense, by its slope, which is given by

$$\frac{v_y}{v_x} = \frac{dy/dt}{dx/dt} = \frac{dy}{dx},$$

which is the same as the slope of the tangent to the curve at P. In Fig. 2–24(b), the sense is seen graphically to be in the counterclockwise direction, since from (9e) the x-component has a sign opposite to the sign of y because ω is positive.

Similarly, the acceleration vector has magnitude

$$\sqrt{a_x^2 + a_y^2} = \omega^2\sqrt{x^2 + y^2} = \omega^2 r,$$

and its direction will be opposite to that of the vector from O to P, since the latter has components x and y, while (9f) shows that the acceleration has its corresponding components just $(-\omega^2)$ times these; that is,

$$\text{The acceleration vector } \mathbf{a} = -\omega^2(\mathbf{OP}).$$

This shows that the acceleration is toward the center of the circle at each instant and has a constant magnitude $\omega^2 r$.

To summarize: If a particle moves in a circle of radius r with constant angular velocity $\omega > 0$, then its velocity vector is tangent to the circle and has magnitude ωr, while its acceleration vector points toward the center of the circle and has magnitude $\omega^2 r$. Hence (by Newton's second law) the force needed to keep a particle of mass m moving at constant speed ωr in a circle of radius r is $m\omega^2 r$, directed toward the center of the circle.

PROBLEMS

Evaluate limits 1–22 by making use of Eq. (1) together with appropriate trigonometric identities and theorems on limits.

1. $\lim_{\theta \to 0} \frac{\tan \theta}{\theta}$

2. $\lim_{\theta \to \pi} \frac{\sin \theta}{\pi - \theta}$ [*Hint.* Let $x = \pi - \theta$.]

3. $\lim_{\theta \to 0} \frac{\sin 2\theta}{\theta}$

4. $\lim_{x \to 0} \frac{\sin x}{3x}$

5. $\lim_{t \to 0} \frac{t}{\sin t}$

6. $\lim_{x \to 0} \frac{x}{\sin 3x}$

7. $\lim_{x \to 0} \frac{\sin 5x}{\sin 3x}$

8. $\lim_{x \to 0} \tan 2x \csc 4x$

9. $\lim_{\theta \to 0} \frac{\sin^2 \theta}{\theta}$

10. $\lim_{\theta \to 0} \frac{1 - \cos \theta}{\theta}$ [*Hint.* If $|\theta| < \pi$, then $1 - \cos \theta = \frac{\sin^2 \theta}{1 + \cos \theta}$.]

11. $\lim_{\theta \to 0} \frac{1 - \cos \theta}{\theta^2}$

12. $\lim_{y \to 0} \frac{\tan 2y}{3y}$

13. $\lim_{u \to 0} \frac{3u}{\sin 5u}$

14. $\lim_{x \to \infty} x \sin \frac{1}{x}$ [*Hint.* Let $1/x = u$.]

15. $\lim_{y \to \infty} 2y \tan \frac{\pi}{y}$

16. $\lim_{x \to \pi/2} \frac{2x - \pi}{\cos x}$

17. $\lim_{\theta \to 0} \theta \cot 2\theta$

18. $\lim_{x \to 0} \frac{x^2 + 2x}{\sin 2x}$

19. $\lim_{x \to 0} \frac{\sin 2x}{2x^2 + x}$

20. $\lim_{h \to 0} \frac{\sin (a + h) - \sin a}{h}$

21. $\lim_{h \to 0} \frac{\cos (a + h) - \cos a}{h}$

22. $\lim_{h \to 2} \frac{\cos (\pi/h)}{h - 2}$

In Problems 23 through 40, find dy/dx.

23. $y = \sin (3x + 4)$

24. $y = x \sin x$

25. $y = \frac{\sin x}{x}$

26. $y = \cos 5x$

27. $y = x^2 \sin 3x$

28. $y = \sqrt{2 + \cos 2x}$

29. $y = \sin^2 x + \cos^2 x$

30. $y = \frac{2}{\cos 3x}$

31. $y = 3 \sin 2x - 4 \cos 2x$

32. $y = 3 \cos^2 2x - 3 \sin^2 2x$

33. $y = 2 \sin x \cos x$

34. $y = \frac{1}{\sin x}$

35. $y = \cos^2 3x$

36. $y = \cot x$

37. $y = \sin^2 x^2$

38. $y = \cos (\sin \sqrt{x^2 + 1})$

39. $x \sin 2y = y \cos 2x$

40. $y^2 = \sin^4 2x + \cos^4 2x$

41. Find an equation of the tangent to the curve $y = \sin mx$ at $x = 0$.

42. A particle moves on the curve

$$x = a \cos \omega t, \qquad y = b \sin \omega t,$$

where a, b, and ω are constants. Show that the acceleration components are

$$a_x = -\omega^2 x \quad \text{and} \quad a_y = -\omega^2 y.$$

2–11 CONTINUITY

Before we take up further applications of differentiation in Chapter 3, it is desirable to discuss the *continuity* of a function. We shall see that continuity is even more basic than differentiability.

Definition. *A function f which is defined in some neighborhood of c is said to be continuous at c provided*

a) *the function has a definite finite value $f(c)$ at c, and*

b) *as x approaches c, $f(x)$ approaches $f(c)$ as limit:*

$$\lim_{x \to c} f(x) = f(c).$$

If a function is continuous at all points of an interval $a \leq x \leq b$ (or $a < x < b$, etc.), then it is said to be continuous on, or in, that interval.

EXAMPLE 1. As an example of a continuous function, let us investigate

$$f(x) = x^2$$

at some fixed value $x = c$. Certainly

$$f(c) = c^2$$

at $x = c$. Furthermore, the difference

$$f(x) - f(c) = x^2 - c^2 = (x - c)(x + c)$$

approaches zero as a limit when $x - c$ approaches zero, since as $x \to c$ we have

$$\begin{aligned} \lim\,[f(x) - f(c)] &= \lim\,(x - c)\,\lim\,(x + c) \\ &= 0 \cdot 2c = 0. \end{aligned}$$

Thus, both requirements of the definition are satisfied. Therefore, $f(x) = x^2$ is continuous at *any* $x = c$; that is, it is continuous for all x, $-\infty < x < +\infty$.

The graph of a function that is continuous on an interval $a \leq x \leq b$ is an unbroken curve over that interval. This fact is of practical importance in using curves to represent functions. It makes it possible to sketch a curve by constructing a table of values (x, y), plotting relatively few points from this table, and then sketching a continuous (i.e., unbroken) curve through these points. For example, to graph $y = x^2$, we first make a short table of values:

x	0	± 0.5	± 1	± 2
y	0	0.25	1	4

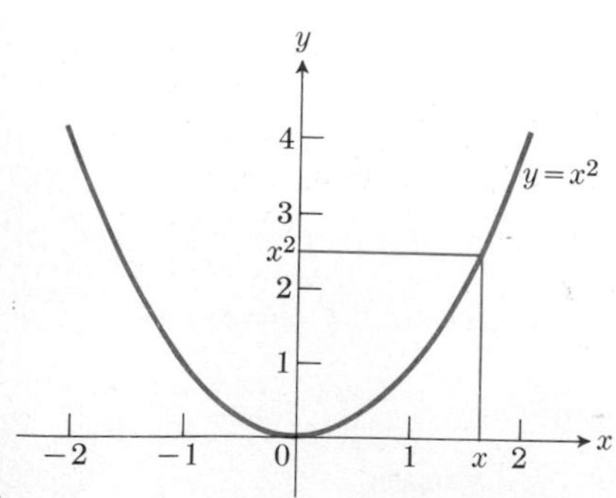

2–25 The graph of $y = x^2$ is a continuous curve. It can be used to read $x^2 = 2.6$ when $x = 1.6$.

then plot these points and draw a continuous curve through them, as shown in Fig. 2–25. Then we might go one step further and use the curve itself to find the value of x^2 corresponding to an x different from those used in making the table of values. For example, in Fig. 2–25, $x = 1.6$ is indicated on the x-scale and the corresponding reading on the y-scale gives $x^2 \approx 2.6$. Of course, the graph probably won't give *exact* values except at those points that have been plotted exactly. But it will give values that are *near* the exact values, if the calculated points aren't spread too far apart.

A function that is not continuous at a point $x = c$ is said to be *discontinuous* or to have a *discontinuity* at $x = c$.

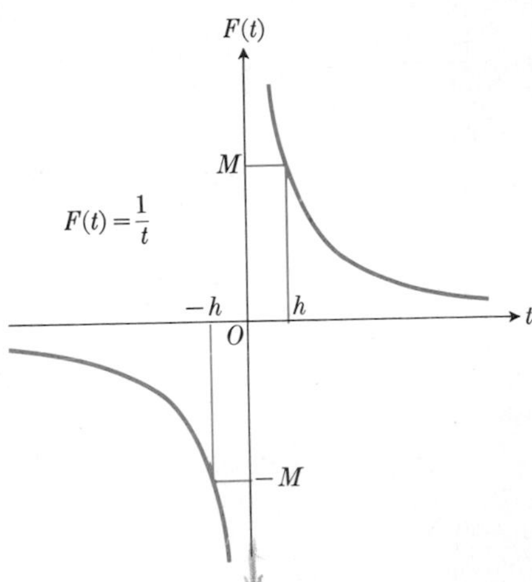

2–26 The function $F(t) = 1/t$ is not continuous at $t = 0$, but is continuous elsewhere.

EXAMPLE 2. The function $F(t) = 1/t$ is discontinuous at $t = 0$ because it violates both requirements (a) and (b) (see Fig. 2–26). This function has an infinite discontinuity at $t = 0$.

Removable Discontinuity

A function may have a discontinuity at a point c because the function is not defined at c, or because the limit of $f(x)$ as x approaches c differs from $f(c)$, or because the limit may not exist. One simple type, called a *removable discontinuity*, is illustrated in the next example: The function has a limit as x approaches $c = 0$, but the formula defining the function has no meaning at 0. We remove the discontinuity by defining the function by its original formula for $x \neq 0$ and by the actual limit as its value at $x = 0$.

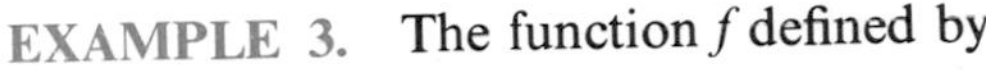

EXAMPLE 3. The function f defined by

$$f(x) = \frac{\sin x}{x} \quad \text{for} \quad x \neq 0$$

has a removable discontinuity at $x = 0$. The formula is not valid when $x = 0$, but

$$\lim_{x \to 0} \frac{\sin x}{x} = 1.$$

We therefore extend the domain of f to include the origin by defining its value there to be $f(0) = 1$ (Fig. 2–27). Strictly speaking, when we change the domain we should change the name of the function. But mathematicians often don't make that distinction in a situation of this type, and use the same letter to name the function, saying, let

$$f(x) = \begin{cases} \dfrac{\sin x}{x} & \text{when } x \neq 0, \\ 1 & \text{when } x = 0. \end{cases}$$

By so defining the value of f at 0, we have made f continuous there, since we now have $f(0) = \lim f(x)$ as x approaches zero.

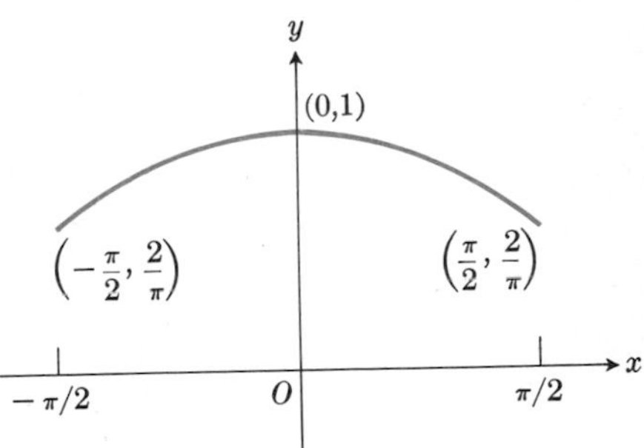

2–27 The graph of $f(x) = (\sin x)/x$ for $-\pi/2 \leq x \leq \pi/2$, $x \neq 0$, does not include the point (0, 1) because the formula $(\sin x)/x$ is not valid for $x = 0$. But we have removed the discontinuity from the graph by defining $f(0) = 1$. When we have filled in the missing point in this way we get a continuous curve.

Nonremovable Discontinuity

The discontinuity at $x = 0$ in the foregoing example could be removed because f had a limit, namely 1, as x approached zero. On the other hand, if

$$g(x) = \frac{|x|}{x} \quad \text{for} \quad x \neq 0,$$

then there is a discontinuity of g at 0 that cannot be removed. When x is

the limit is the value as the function approaches zero. when you plug numbers approaching 0 into $g(x) = \frac{|x|}{x}$ you get a left + right hand limit and therefore since there is not limit, the function is discontinuous

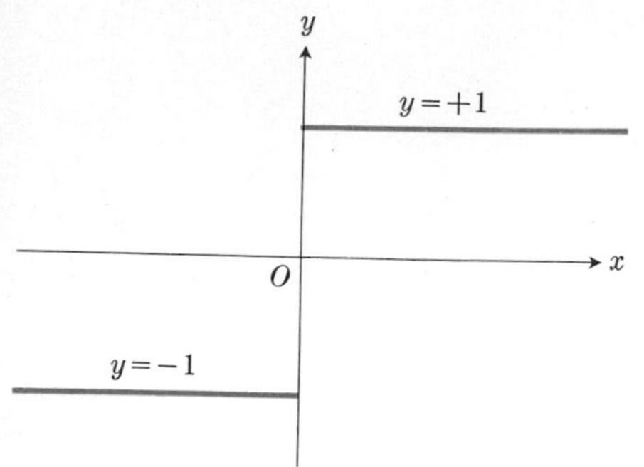

2–28 The graph of $g(x) = |x|/x$ for $x \neq 0$ cannot be made continuous because the righthand limit and the lefthand limit of $g(x)$ as x approaches zero are not equal.

negative, $g(x) = -1$, and when x is positive, $g(x) = +1$ (Fig. 2–28). Therefore, $g(x)$ does not approach a limit as x approaches zero: Its limit as x approaches zero from the left is -1 and its limit as x approaches zero from the right is $+1$. If we assign the value 0 to $g(0)$, the resulting function is the *signum function* (or *sign function*) of x:

$$\operatorname{sgn} x = \begin{cases} +1 & \text{if } x \text{ is positive,} \\ 0 & \text{if } x = 0, \\ -1 & \text{if } x \text{ is negative.} \end{cases}$$

The signum function is defined for all x, but it is not continuous at $x = 0$. It is continuous for $x \neq 0$.

With these examples before us, the question arises as to how, in practice, we can tell whether or not a given function is continuous. When we sketch its graph, should we be sure to sketch a connected, unbroken curve, as for the graph of $y = x^2$, or must we be careful *not* to connect all of the points as, for example, in the case $y = 1/x$, where points in the third quadrant must not be connected with points in the first quadrant?

Since we have studied differentiation, the following theorem, which says that every function that has a derivative at a point is also continuous at that point, enables us to conclude that:

a) Every polynomial

$$f(x) = ax^n + bx^{n-1} + \cdots + px + q$$

is continuous for all x, $-\infty < x < +\infty$, and

b) Every rational function

$$f(x) = \frac{F(x)}{G(x)},$$

$F(x)$ and $G(x)$ being polynomials, is continuous for all x where the denominator $G(x)$ is not zero.

c) The functions $\sin u$ and $\cos u$ are differentiable, and therefore are continuous, wherever $u = f(x)$ is a differentiable function of x.

Thus, for example, the graphs of

$$y = x^3, \qquad y = 2x^2 - x + 3, \qquad y = \frac{x^2 - 1}{x^2 + 1}, \qquad y = \sin 2x$$

are continuous, connected curves over the domain $-\infty < x < +\infty$.

On the other hand, the graph of

$$y = \frac{x^2 + 1}{x^3 - 4x} \tag{1}$$

goes shooting off toward $\pm\infty$ as x approaches one of the three values

$$x = -2, \qquad x = 0, \qquad x = +2,$$

where the denominator vanishes. But, over the intervals $-\infty < x < -2$, $-2 < x < 0$, $0 < x < 2$, and $2 < x < +\infty$, the graph consists of separate continuous curves, since the denominator does not vanish in any of these intervals. (See Fig. 2–29.)

Let us now state and prove the theorem we mentioned above.

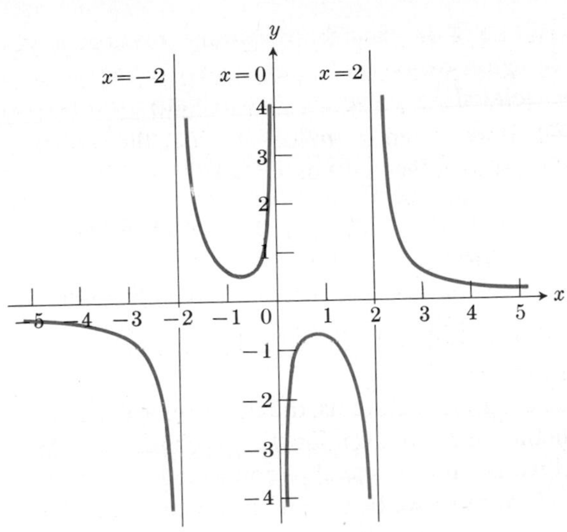

2–29 The function $f(x) = (x^2 + 1)/(x^3 - 4x)$ has infinite discontinuities where $x^3 - 4x = 0$. Elsewhere the function is continuous. The graph is symmetric with respect to the origin.

Theorem 1. *If the function f has a finite derivative*

$$f'(c) = \lim_{\Delta x \to 0} \frac{f(c + \Delta x) - f(c)}{\Delta x} \tag{2}$$

at $x = c$, then f is continuous at $x = c$.

Proof. For the limit in (2) to exist, it is necessary that $f(c)$ and $f(c + \Delta x)$ both exist, at least for all Δx near zero. We change the notation slightly by writing x in place of $c + \Delta x$. Then

$$x = c + \Delta x$$

is near c when

$$\Delta x = x - c$$

is near zero. Equation (2) now may be written in the form

$$f'(c) = \lim_{x \to c} \frac{f(x) - f(c)}{x - c}.$$

Suppose then that $f'(c)$ exists and is finite. We want to prove that $f(x) - f(c)$ tends to zero as $x \to c$. This follows at once from

$$\begin{aligned} \lim_{x \to c} [f(x) - f(c)] &= \lim_{x \to c} \left[(x - c)\frac{f(x) - f(c)}{x - c}\right] \\ &= \lim_{x \to c} (x - c) \cdot \lim_{x \to c} \frac{f(x) - f(c)}{x - c} \\ &= 0 \cdot f'(c) = 0. \end{aligned}$$

Q.E.D.

We have just shown that differentiability implies continuity. The converse, however, is not true.

EXAMPLE 4. The function $f(x) = |x|$ is continuous at $x = 0$, but does not have a derivative there. (See Fig. 2–30; also, Example 3, Article 1–8.)

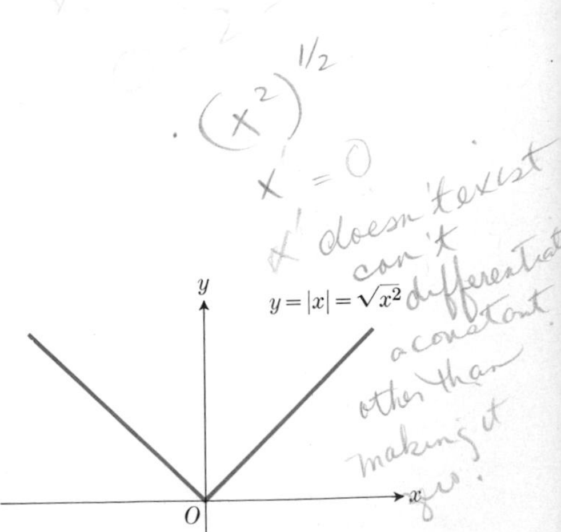

2–30 The absolute value function is continuous everywhere but has no derivative at zero.

Until the middle of the nineteenth century it was generally believed that a continuous function would have a derivative at most places, even though there might be isolated points where the derivative did not exist, as at $x = 0$ in our example. However, the German mathematicians Riemann (1826–1866) and Weierstrass (1815–1897) gave examples of functions that are continuous but that fail to have derivatives anywhere. (For a readable account of this, see *World of Mathematics*, Vol. 3, p. 1963.)

We conclude this chapter with some theorems which we shall state without proofs. Some of these theorems follow rather simply from the corresponding theorems on limits. Others require, for rigorous proofs, a deeper study of the properties of the real number system than we are able to make at this time.

Theorem 2. *Suppose f and g are two functions that are continuous at $x = c$. Then the functions F_1, F_2, F_3 defined by*

$$F_1(x) = f(x) + g(x),$$

$$F_2(x) = kf(x), \qquad k \text{ any number},$$

$$F_3(x) = f(x) \cdot g(x)$$

are also continuous at $x = c$. Furthermore, if $g(c)$ is not zero, then

$$F_4(x) = \frac{f(x)}{g(x)}$$

is also continuous at $x = c$.

Theorem 2 says that the sum, product, and quotient of two continuous functions are continuous except where the denominator in a quotient would be zero. The product $kf(x)$ for k = a constant is really a special case, because the function $g(x) = k$ is continuous everywhere.

The next three theorems describe properties of any function f that is continuous on a bounded closed interval $a \leq x \leq b$. Theorems 3 and 4 together guarantee that the image of such an interval under a continuous mapping f either is a single point (if f is constant) or, is a closed bounded interval $m \leq f(x) \leq M$, where m and M are the least and greatest values of $f(x)$ for x in the interval. We shall have more appreciation for these results as we see how they are used.

Theorem 3 (Existence of maximum and minimum values). *Suppose that $f(x)$ is continuous for all x in the closed interval $[a, b]$. Then f has a minimum value m and a maximum value M on $[a, b]$. That is, there are numbers α and β in $[a, b]$ such that $f(\alpha) = m$, $f(\beta) = M$, and*

$$m \leq f(x) \leq M \qquad \text{for all } x \text{ in } [a, b].$$

Figure 2–31 illustrates that (α, m) is the lowest point, and (β, M) is the highest point of the graph of the function f over the interval $a \leq x \leq b$.

Theorem 4 (The Intermediate Value Theorem). *If $f(x)$ is continuous on the closed interval $[a, b]$ and N is any number between $f(a)$ and $f(b)$, then there is at least one number c between a and b such that $f(c) = N$.*

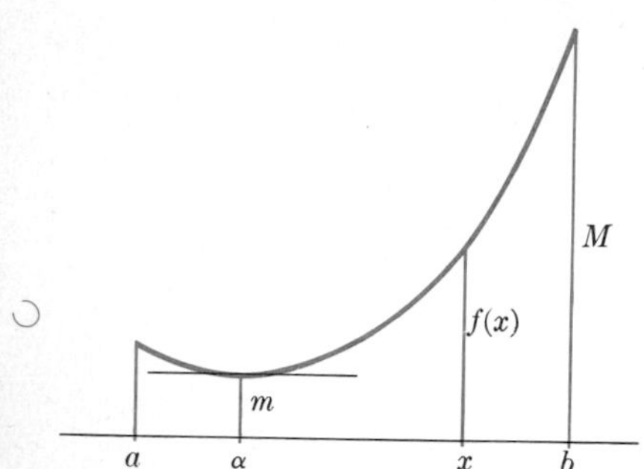

Minimum m at inner point α of interval; maximum M at endpoint b.

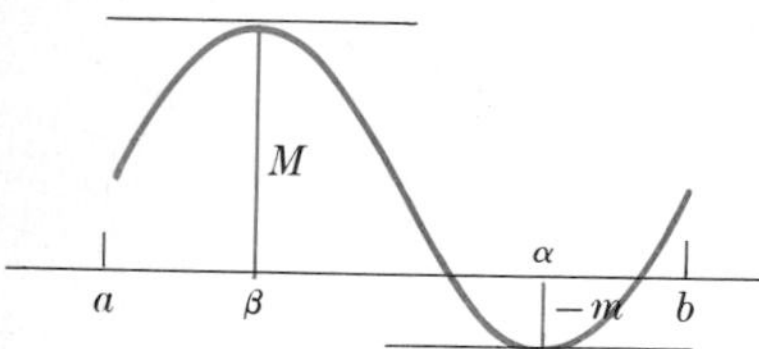

Minimum and maximum at inner points.

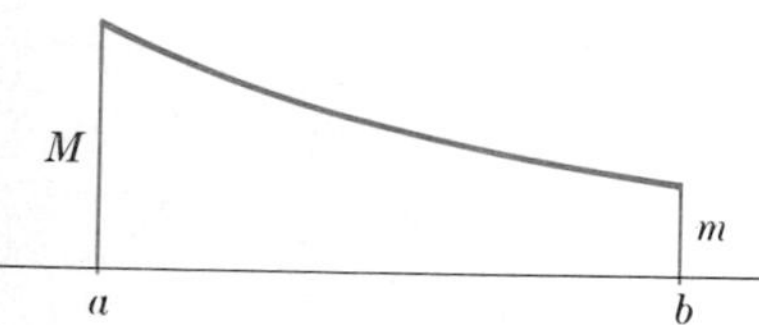

Maximum and minimum at endpoints of $[a,b]$.

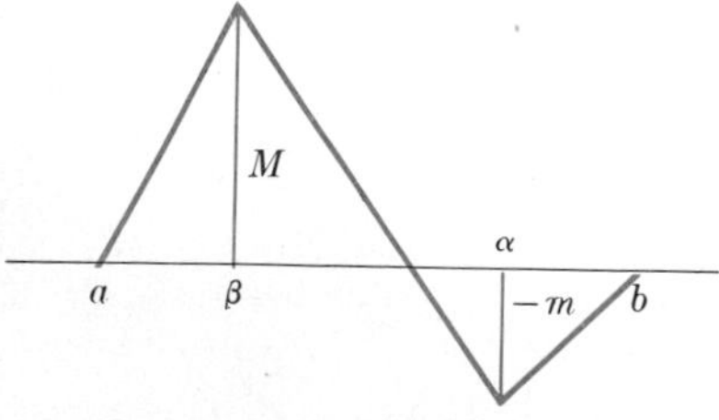

Minimum and maximum at interior points α and β where the slope is not zero. This function is continuous on $[a,b]$ but is not differentiable at α and β.

2–31 A continuous function over the domain $a \leq x \leq b$ has a minimum and a maximum (low point and high point).

The theorem gets its name, the Intermediate Value Theorem, from the fact that the continuous function $f(x)$ takes on all values between $f(a)$ and $f(b)$ as x varies from a to b. In particular, if f is negative at $x = a$ and positive at $x = b$, then f takes on the value $N = 0$ at some point c between a and b. Thus, the theorem guarantees that there is a solution of the equation $f(x) = 0$ somewhere in the interval (a, b); or, in geometric terms, that the graph of f crosses the x-axis somewhere between a and b. This guarantee is the basis of the approximation technique illustrated in the next example.

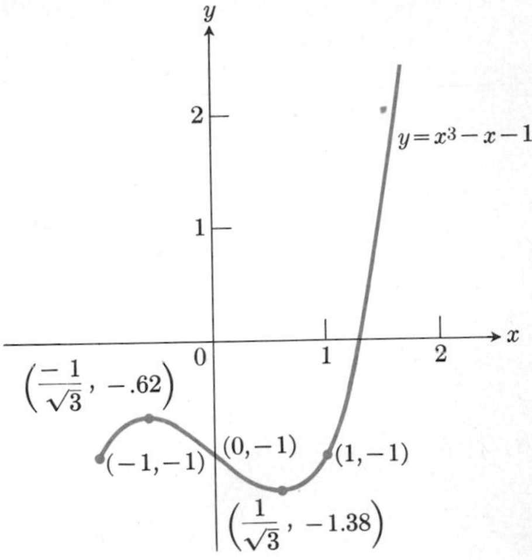

2–32 The graph of $f(x) = x^3 - x - 1$ crosses the x-axis between $x = 1.3$ and $x = 1.4$. (The slope is zero at $x = \pm 1/\sqrt{3}$.)

EXAMPLE 5. Find a real number x that is one less than its cube.

Solution. We want $x = x^3 - 1$, or $x^3 - x - 1 = 0$. Let $f(x) = x^3 - x - 1$. A part of the graph of $y = f(x)$ is shown in Fig. 2–32. We have plotted enough points to find that $f(1.3) = -0.10$ and $f(1.4) = +0.34$ so the curve must cross the x-axis between $x = 1.3$ and $x = 1.4$. With a calculator it is easy to compute values of $f(x)$ for $x = 1.31$, 1.32, 1.33, and so on, until we locate an interval of length 0.01 in which a zero of $f(x)$ lies. In fact, one gets $f(1.32) \approx -0.02$ and $f(1.33) \approx +0.02$, so a solution of $f(x) = 0$ lies between 1.32 and 1.33. The process can be continued, using 1.321, 1.322, 1.323, and so on. Or we can use linear interpolation, or Newton's method. The latter is very good in this example and gives, as the solution of $f(x) = 0$, the answer 1.324717957 (see Example in Article 2–7).

Epsilons and Deltas and Uniform Continuity

We know that the function $f(x) = x^2$ is everywhere differentiable, so we also know that it is continuous at every $x = c$. Thus the limit of x^2 as x approaches c is c^2, and we can make the difference between $f(x) = x^2$ and $f(c) = c^2$ as small as we please by keeping x sufficiently close to c. The precise way to say that is:

For every real number c and every positive number ϵ there exists a positive number δ such that

$$|f(x) - f(c)| < \epsilon \quad \text{whenever} \quad |x - c| < \delta.$$

Figure 2–33 illustrates these ideas for two possible values of c, namely $c = \sqrt{0.5} = 0.707$ and $c = 2.5$, and with $\epsilon = 0.25$. These numbers were chosen solely for the purpose of showing exactly how one might find deltas for given c's and a given positive epsilon. Focus your attention for a moment on one of the two values of c, say $c = \sqrt{0.5}$. Look at c^2 on the y-axis, and go up a distance ϵ and down the same distance. Now look at that part of the graph that is between the lines $y = c^2 + \epsilon$ and $y = c^2 - \epsilon$. It runs from $x = c - \delta_1 = \sqrt{c^2 - \epsilon}$ to $x = c + \delta_2 = \sqrt{c^2 + \epsilon}$.

In this example, $c^2 = 0.5$ and $\epsilon = 0.25$, so $c^2 - \epsilon = 0.25$ and $c^2 + \epsilon = 0.75$. Therefore, to four decimal places, we have

$$c = \sqrt{0.5} = 0.7071, \qquad c - \delta_1 = \sqrt{0.25} = 0.5000,$$

$$c + \delta_2 = \sqrt{0.75} = 0.8660, \qquad \delta_1 = 0.2071, \qquad \delta_2 = 0.1589.$$

We don't have to produce the "best" value of δ but we can see that our curve will stay between $y = c^2 - \epsilon$ and $y = c^2 + \epsilon$ in the neighborhood

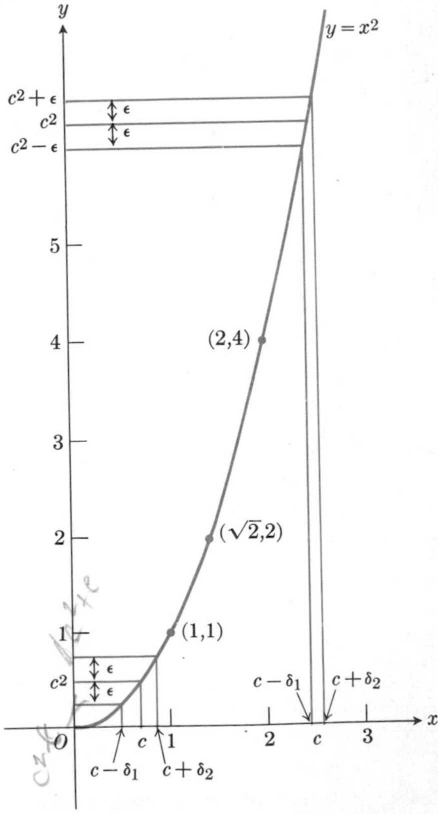

2–33 Graph of $y = x^2$.

$(c - \delta, c + \delta)$ if δ is any number that is positive and less than or equal to the minimum of δ_1 and δ_2. Thus, we can take $\delta = 0.1588$, or 0.15, or 0.01, or 0.0001. Each of these is a positive number that is small enough to guarantee that $f(x)$ stays within the interval $(c^2 - \epsilon, c^2 + \epsilon)$ when x stays in the interval $(c - \delta, c + \delta)$, for $c = \sqrt{0.5}$ and $\epsilon = 0.25$. A different value of c with the same value of epsilon would probably call for a different delta. Also, a different value of epsilon for the same c, or a different c, would probably call for a different delta. For $c = 2.5$ and $\epsilon = 0.25$, one must choose δ less than or equal to the minimum of $\delta_1 = 0.0505$ and $\delta_2 = 0.0495$. The curve is much steeper in the neighborhood of $c = 2.5$ than it is near $c = \sqrt{0.5}$, and this means that we must keep x much closer to $c = 2.5$ if we want $f(x)$ to stay close to $f(c)$.

Continuing to study the function $f(x) = x^2$, observe that we can factor $f(x) - f(c)$ as follows:

$$f(x) - f(c) = x^2 - c^2 = (x - c)(x + c).$$

By keeping x close to c, we make the first factor, $x - c$, as small as we please, and the second factor gets close to $2c$. If we restrict the domain of f to the closed interval $[-3, +5]$, say, then we can be sure that the factor $(x + c)$ will be no greater than $5 + 5 = 10$:

If x and c are in $[-3, +5]$, then

$$|x + c| \leq 10 \quad \text{and} \quad |f(x) - f(c)| \leq 10|x - c|,$$

and we can guarantee

$$|f(x) - f(c)| < \epsilon \quad \text{when} \quad |x - c| < \delta,$$

provided that δ is any positive number not greater than $\epsilon/10$.

If ϵ is any positive number, then

$$10|x - c| < \epsilon \quad \text{if} \quad |x - c| < \frac{\epsilon}{10}.$$

Therefore, $\delta = \epsilon/10$ will be small enough to work for every value of c in the domain $[-3, +5]$. When a function has the property that, for each positive ϵ, there exists a positive δ such that

$$|f(x) - f(c)| < \epsilon \quad \text{when } x \text{ and } c \text{ are in } D \text{ and } |x - c| < \delta,$$

we say that $f(x)$ is *uniformly continuous on D*.

EXAMPLE 6. Functions that are uniformly continuous on their domains:

1. $f(x) = k$, where k is any real number, and D is the set of all real numbers. For any positive number ϵ we can take $\delta = 1$, because

$$|f(x) - f(c)| = |k - k| = 0 \quad \text{for all } x \text{ and } c \text{ in } D.$$

2. $f(x) = 5x + 3$ and D is the set of all real numbers. For any positive number ϵ we can take $\delta = \epsilon/5$ and have

$$|f(x) - f(c)| = |5(x - c)| < \epsilon \quad \text{when } |x - c| < \frac{\epsilon}{5}.$$

3. $f(x) = \sin x$ and D is the set of all real numbers. For any positive number ϵ we can take $\delta = \epsilon$ because

$$|\sin x - \sin c| = \left|2 \sin\left(\frac{x-c}{2}\right)\cos\left(\frac{x+c}{2}\right)\right|$$

$$\leq \left|2\left(\frac{x-c}{2}\right)\cdot 1\right|$$

$$= |x - c| < \epsilon \quad \text{if} \quad |x - c| < \delta = \epsilon.$$

If the trigonometry here is not familiar, you can see intuitively why the result is true by thinking of the slope of the chord from the point $(c, \sin c)$ to the point $(x, \sin x)$. That slope is not greater than the slope of the sine curve at its steepest, which is -1 or $+1$. Therefore,

$$\left|\frac{(\sin x - \sin c)}{(x - c)}\right| \leq 1, \quad \text{so} \quad |\sin x - \sin c| \leq |x - c|.$$

EXAMPLE 7. Functions that are continuous but not uniformly continuous on their domains:

1. $f(x) = 1/x$ and the domain D is the set of all real numbers $x \neq 0$. If c is very small, and x is near c, then

$$|f(x) - f(c)| = \left|\frac{1}{x} - \frac{1}{c}\right| = \left|\frac{x-c}{xc}\right| \approx \frac{1}{c^2}|x - c|.$$

To make this less than a preassigned positive ϵ when $|x - c| < \delta$, we would need to take $\delta \approx c^2\epsilon$. The smaller the value of c, the smaller must be our δ. No δ that depends upon ϵ alone will work for all c's $\neq 0$.

2. $f(x) = \sin(1/x)$ for $x \neq 0$. This curve gets very steep near $x = 0$ and, although we could find a δ for given ϵ and c, we have to take δ smaller and smaller if c is near zero. That is, δ depends upon c as well as ϵ, and therefore the function is not uniformly continuous on the domain given. On the other hand, if we were to change the domain to the set of all x greater than 0.001, say, then, for a given positive number ϵ, we could in fact find a δ that works for the "steepest" part of the graph over this domain, and that same value of δ would work for the entire domain.

The following theorem tells us that every function that is continuous at each point of a closed bounded interval $[a, b]$ is uniformly continuous on the interval. We do not prove the theorem in this book,* but we use it later.

Theorem 5. *A function f that is continuous for all x in the closed bounded interval $a \leq x \leq b$ is uniformly continuous there.* That is, *for each positive number ϵ, there is a positive number δ such that*

$$|f(x) - f(x')| < \epsilon \quad \text{when} \quad a \leq x,\ x' \leq b, \text{ and } |x - x'| < \delta.$$

* For a proof see, for example, *Elementary Calculus from an Advanced Viewpoint* by Moulton, Thomas, and Zelinka, Addison-Wesley Publishing Co., 1967, or *Continuity*, by G. B. Thomas, Jr., Addison-Wesley Publishing Co., 1965 (pp. 35–36).

The following physical interpretation of continuity may help you to understand the difference between the notion of "continuous at every point of an interval" on the one hand and "uniformly continuous in an interval" on the other. We recall that a function is continuous at $x = c$ if $f(c)$ exists and $f(x) \to f(c)$ as $x \to c$. This means that if we are challenged with a positive "tolerance limit" ϵ and required to make

$$|f(x) - f(c)| < \epsilon \tag{3}$$

for *all* x sufficiently close to c, we can produce a positive number δ such that condition (3) is met whenever

$$|x - c| < \delta. \tag{4}$$

Let us translate this into physical terms.

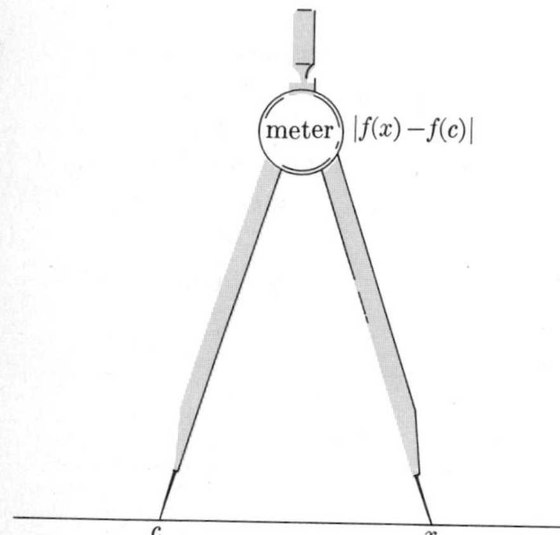

Figure 2–34

Suppose that we have a pair of dividers (Fig. 2–34) with a meter that reads $|f(x) - f(c)|$ when the points touch x and c. Suppose now we hold one prong of the dividers at c and move the other prong around near c, either to the left of c or to its right. Suppose that to *each* positive number ϵ we are able to assign a band of width 2δ around c,

$$c - \delta < x < c + \delta,$$

such that whenever the second prong is inside this band the meter reading is less than ϵ. Then the function is, by our definition, continuous at c.

Now the "bandwidth" 2δ will in general depend upon ϵ. That is, the smaller the tolerance limit ϵ that is required, the more narrowly must we restrict the range of x around c. Furthermore, the "bandwidth" 2δ will also, in general, depend upon c. That is, for a given function $f(x)$,

$$\delta = \delta(c, \epsilon).$$

But it may happen that there is a positive number $k = k(\epsilon)$ that depends upon ϵ alone such that if x and x' are any two points in the domain of f and

$$|x - x'| < k(\epsilon),$$

then

$$|f(x) - f(x')| < \epsilon.$$

In other words, if the two prongs of the dividers are spread apart any distance less than $k(\epsilon)$ and the dividers are placed so that they touch any two points x and x' in the domain of f, the meter reads less than ϵ. This exemplifies uniform continuity. Theorem 5 says that, when the domain of f is a closed bounded interval, the continuity of f at each point of the domain guarantees uniform continuity.

To summarize these remarks we may say that:

a) *ordinary continuity* at a point c means that the bandwidth depends not only upon the tolerance ϵ but also upon c, whereas

b) *uniform continuity* means that with any positive ϵ we may associate *one* bandwidth that works for *all* points in the domain.

PROBLEMS

1. (a) Prove that the function $f(x) = x^3$ is continuous at $x = c$ for any real c. (b) If $c = 5$, and ϵ is a preassigned positive number, find δ such that

$$|x^3 - 5^3| < \epsilon \quad \text{when} \quad |x - 5| < \delta.$$

2. For what values of x is each of the following functions discontinuous?

a) $f(x) = \dfrac{x}{x+1}$ b) $f(x) = \dfrac{x+1}{x^2 - 4x + 3}$.

3. Is the function f defined by the rule

$$f(x) = \begin{cases} \dfrac{x^2 - 1}{x - 1}, & \text{when } x \neq 1, \\ 2, & \text{when } x = 1, \end{cases}$$

continuous or discontinuous at $x = 1$? Prove your result.

4. The function $f(x) = |x|$ is continuous at $x = 0$. Given a positive number ϵ, how large may δ be in order that $|f(x) - 0| < \epsilon$ when $|x - 0| < \delta$?

5. What is the maximum of $f(x) = |x|$ for $-1 \leq x \leq 1$? What is the minimum? Sketch.

6. Does the function $f(x) = x^2$ have a maximum for $0 < x < 1$? Does it have a minimum? Give reasons for your answers.

7. A continuous function $y = f(x)$ is known to be negative at $x = 0$ and positive at $x = 1$. Why is it true that the equation $f(x) = 0$ has at least one root between $x = 0$ and $x = 1$? Illustrate with a sketch.

8. Is the function $f(x) = \sqrt[3]{x}$ continuous at $x = 0$? Is it differentiable there? Give reasons for your answers.

9. *Prove the following theorem.* Let f be continuous and positive at $x = c$. Prove that there is some interval around $x = c$, say $c - \delta < x < c + \delta$, throughout which $f(x)$ remains positive. [*Hint.* In the definition of continuity, Eqs. (3) and (4), take $\epsilon = \frac{1}{2}f(c)$.] Illustrate with a sketch.

10. For $x \neq 2$, the function $f(x)$ is equal to $(x^2 + 3x - 10)/(x - 2)$. What value should be assigned to $f(2)$ to make $f(x)$ continuous at $x = 2$?

2–12 DIFFERENTIALS

We have used both y' and dy/dx to denote the derivative of y with respect to x. Can some useful meaning be given to the symbols dy, called the *differential* of y, and dx separately? The answer is *yes*, and we do so as follows.

Definitions. *If x is the independent variable and $y = F(x)$ has a derivative at x_0, we define dx to be an independent variable with domain $(-\infty, +\infty)$ and define dy to be*

$$dy = F'(x_0)\, dx. \tag{1}$$

If $F(x)$ has a derivative at each point x in some domain D, then dy is a function of two independent variables x and dx: $dy = F'(x)\, dx$. Geometrically, we often think of dx as a certain number of units of change in the x-direction, and dy then is the corresponding number of units of change in the y-direction along the tangent to the graph of the function (Fig. 2–35).

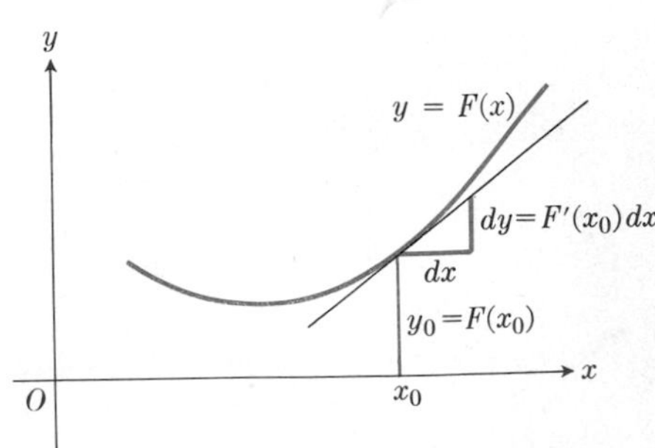

2–35 Geometric interpretations of the differentials dx and dy for a function $y = F(x)$.

If $dx = 0$ in Eq. (1), then $dy = 0$. If $dx \neq 0$, then we can divide both sides of Eq. (1) by dx and have

$$F'(x_0) = \frac{\text{The differential of } y}{\text{The differential of } x}. \tag{2}$$

There is nothing profound about Eq. (2); it just means that our notations $F'(x)$ and dy/dx are compatible.

If $x = f(t)$ and $y = g(t)$ are functions of t that are differentiable at t_0, the differential of t is a new independent variable, dt. The differentials of x and y

are, by definition,

$$dx = f'(t_0)\,dt \qquad \text{and} \qquad dy = g'(t_0)\,dt. \tag{3}$$

Once again, if $dt \neq 0$ and $f'(t_0) \neq 0$, we can divide and write

$$\frac{dy}{dx} = \frac{\text{Differential of } y}{\text{Differential of } x} = \frac{g'(t_0)\,dt}{f'(t_0)\,dt} = \frac{g'(t_0)}{f'(t_0)}$$

$$= \frac{\text{Derivative of } y \text{ with respect to } t}{\text{Derivative of } x \text{ with respect to } t}. \tag{4}$$

Equation (4) is the same as the chain rule. It says that the derivative of y with respect to x is the quotient of the differentials dy and dx when both dy and dx are functions of t and dt, as well as when y is a function of x.

EXAMPLE 1. Use differentials to find approximately how much the function $y = x^{2/3}$ changes when x decreases from $x_0 = 8$ to 7.8.

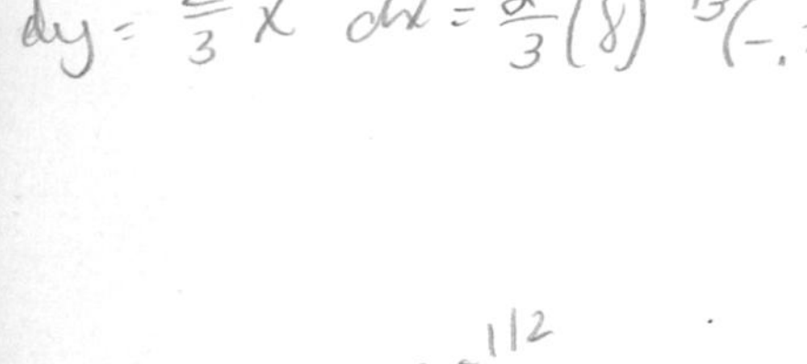

Solution. Take $x = x_0 = 8$, $dx = -0.2$, and

$$dy = \frac{2}{3}x^{-1/3}\,dx = \frac{2}{3}\left(\frac{1}{2}\right)(-0.2) = \frac{-0.2}{3} \approx -0.0667.$$

This is the tangent-line approximation to the actual change $7.8^{2/3} - 8^{2/3} \approx -0.0669$.

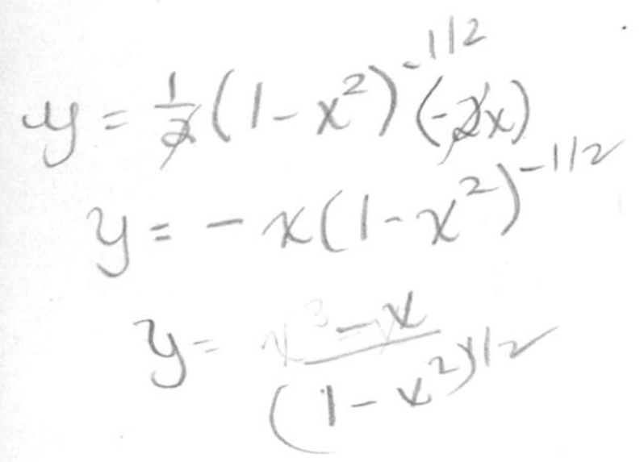

EXAMPLE 2. If $x = \cos t$, $y = \sin t$, and $0 < t < \pi$, find: (a) dx and dy, and (b) dy/dx. Compare your answer in (b) to the derivative of $y = (1 - x^2)^{1/2}$.

Solution

a) $dx = -\sin t\,dt, \quad dy = \cos t\,dt.$

b) $\dfrac{dy}{dx} = \dfrac{\cos t\,dt}{-\sin t\,dt} = \dfrac{x}{-y} = -x/(1 - x^2)^{1/2}.$

From $y = f(x) = (1 - x^2)^{1/2}$ we calculate directly,

$$f'(x) = \tfrac{1}{2}(1 - x^2)^{-1/2}(-2x) = -x/(1 - x^2)^{1/2},$$

which agrees with the result in (b) above.

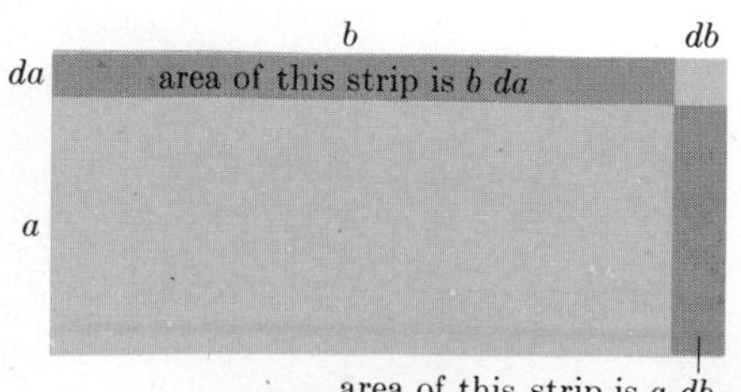

2–36 If b is greater than a and $da = db$, then $b\,da$ is greater than $a\,db$: The product ab is more sensitive to small changes in the smaller factor.

We often use letters a, b, c and others at the start of the alphabet to denote constants, and x, y, z and other letters at the end of the alphabet for variables. But that is not a hard-and-fast rule. The next example illustrates a situation where a and b are used as variables.

EXAMPLE 3. The dimensions of a rectangle are a cm and b cm. How do small changes in a and b affect the area $A = ab$?

Solution. We can use differentials to estimate small changes. (See Fig.

2–36.) The rule for the differential of a product gives

$$dA = a\,db + b\,da.$$

If b is the length of the longer side of the rectangle, and if da and db are assumed to be equal, then the term $b\,da$ is greater than $a\,db$: A change da in the shorter side makes more of a contribution to dA than does an equal change in the longer side.

Second Derivative

The second derivative of y with respect to x is the result obtained from y by doing twice in succession the operation "differentiate with respect to x"; that is,

$$\frac{d^2y}{dx^2} = \frac{d}{dx}\left[\frac{d}{dx}(y)\right].$$

It is also possible to define a second differential, d^2y, in such a way that the second derivative of y with respect to x is equal to d^2y divided by $(dx)^2$. However, things get rather complicated in the case of parametric equations

$$x = f(t), \qquad y = F(x) = F[f(t)] = g(t).$$

In such cases, it is simplest to calculate second and higher order derivatives by using such rules as

$$\frac{dy}{dx} = y' = \frac{dy/dt}{dx/dt},$$

$$\frac{d^2y}{dx^2} = y'' = \frac{dy'}{dx} = \frac{dy'/dt}{dx/dt}.$$

The second of these equations says that, to find the second derivative of y with respect to x, we

1. Express $y' = dy/dx$ in terms of t.
2. Differentiate y' with respect to t.
3. Divide the result by dx/dt.

EXAMPLE 4. Find d^2y/dx^2 if $x = t - t^2$ and $y = t - t^3$.

Solution

$$y' = \frac{dy}{dx} = \frac{dy/dt}{dx/dt} = \frac{1 - 3t^2}{1 - 2t},$$

$$\frac{d^2y}{dx^2} = \frac{dy'/dt}{dx/dt} = \frac{\dfrac{d}{dt}\left[\dfrac{1 - 3t^2}{1 - 2t}\right]}{(1 - 2t)}$$

$$= \frac{(1 - 2t)\cdot(-6t) - (1 - 3t^2)\cdot(-2)}{(1 - 2t)^3}$$

$$= \frac{2 - 6t + 6t^2}{(1 - 2t)^3}.$$

2–13 FORMULAS FOR DIFFERENTIATION REPEATED IN THE NOTATION OF DIFFERENTIALS

Earlier in this chapter we derived formulas for the derivatives listed below on the left. By multiplying each one by dx we now obtain the corresponding formulas for differentials.

Derivatives	Differentials
I. $\dfrac{dc}{dx} = 0$	I′. $dc = 0$
II. $\dfrac{d(cu)}{dx} = c\dfrac{du}{dx}$	II′. $d(cu) = c\,du$
III. $\dfrac{d(u+v)}{dx} = \dfrac{du}{dx} + \dfrac{dv}{dx}$	III′. $d(u+v) = du + dv$
IV. $\dfrac{d(uv)}{dx} = u\dfrac{dv}{dx} + v\dfrac{du}{dx}$	IV′. $d(uv) = u\,dv + v\,du$
V. $\dfrac{d\left(\dfrac{u}{v}\right)}{dx} = \dfrac{v\dfrac{du}{dx} - u\dfrac{dv}{dx}}{v^2}$	V′. $d\left(\dfrac{u}{v}\right) = \dfrac{v\,du - u\,dv}{v^2}$
VI. $\dfrac{du^n}{dx} = nu^{n-1}\dfrac{du}{dx}$	VI′. $d(u^n) = nu^{n-1}\,du$
VIa. $\dfrac{dcx^n}{dx} = cnx^{n-1}$	VI′a. $d(cx^n) = cnx^{n-1}\,dx$
VII. $\dfrac{d\sin u}{dx} = \cos u\dfrac{du}{dx}$	VII′. $d(\sin u) = \cos u\,du$
VIII. $\dfrac{d\cos u}{dx} = -\sin u\dfrac{du}{dx}$	VIII′. $d(\cos u) = -\sin u\,du$

We collect these formulas primarily for future reference. Any problem involving differentials, say that of finding dy when y is a given function of x, may be handled either

a) by finding the derivative dy/dx and then multiplying by dx, or
b) by direct use of formulas I′–VIII′.

EXAMPLE. Find the differentials of:

a) $\sin(2x)$ **b)** $\cos^2(3x)$ **c)** $\dfrac{x}{x^2+1}$

Solutions

a) $d\sin(2x) = \cos(2x)\,d(2x) = 2\cos(2x)\,dx.$

b) $$d \cos^2 (3x) = 2 \cos (3x)\, d \cos (3x)$$
$$= 2 \cos (3x) \cdot (-\sin 3x)\, d(3x)$$
$$= -6 \sin 3x \cos 3x\, dx$$
$$= -3 \sin (6x)\, dx.$$

c) $$d \frac{x}{x^2+1} = \frac{(x^2+1)\, dx - x\, d(x^2+1)}{(x^2+1)^2}$$
$$= \frac{(x^2+1)\, dx - x(2x\, dx)}{(x^2+1)^2}$$
$$= \frac{(1-x^2)\, dx}{(x^2+1)^2}.$$

It should be noted that a *differential* on the left side of an equation, say dy, also calls for a *differential*, usually dx, on the right side of the equation. Thus we never have $dy = 3x^2$, but instead $dy = 3x^2\, dx$.

The term "differentiate" means either to find the derivative or to find the differential, and either operation is referred to as "differentiation."

PROBLEMS

In each of the following problems (1 through 8), find dy.

1. $y = x^3 - 3x^2 + 5x - 7$ **2.** $y^2 = (3x^2 + 1)^{3/2}$

3. $xy^2 + x^2y = 4$ **4.** $y = \dfrac{2x}{1+x^2}$

5. $y = x\sqrt{1-x^2}$ **6.** $y = \dfrac{x+1}{x^2-2x+4}$

7. $y = \dfrac{(1-x)^3}{2-3x}$ **8.** $y = \dfrac{1+x-x^2}{1-x}$

Use differentials to obtain reasonable approximations to the following:

9. $\sqrt{145}$ **10.** $(2.1)^3$

11. $\sqrt[4]{17}$ **12.** $\sqrt[3]{0.126}$

13. $(8.01)^{4/3} + (8.01)^2 - \dfrac{1}{\sqrt[3]{8.01}}$

Given the following functions $x = f(t)$, $y = g(t)$.

a) Express dx and dy in terms of t and dt.

b) Use the results of **(a)** to find, at the point for which $t = 2$, the slope of the curve traced by the point (x, y).

c) Use the results of **(b)** to find an equation of the line tangent to the curve at the point for which $t = 2$.

14. $x = t + \dfrac{1}{t}$, $y = t - \dfrac{1}{t}$

15. $x = \sqrt{2t^2 + 1}$, $y = (2t + 1)^2$

16. $x = t\sqrt{2t + 5}$, $y = (4t)^{1/3}$

17. $x = \dfrac{t-1}{t+1}$, $y = \dfrac{t+1}{t-1}$ **18.** $x = \dfrac{1}{t^2}$, $y = \sqrt{t^2 + 12}$

19. Find d^2y/dx^2 from the parametric equations in Problem 14.

20. Find d^2y/dx^2 from the parametric equations in Problem 17.

21. Given the parametric equations $x = f(t)$, $y = g(t)$. Show that

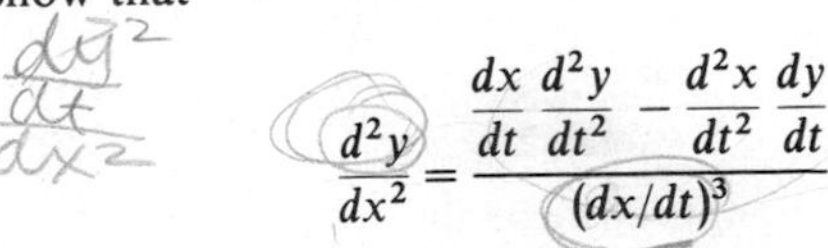

$$\frac{d^2y}{dx^2} = \frac{\dfrac{dx}{dt}\dfrac{d^2y}{dt^2} - \dfrac{d^2x}{dt^2}\dfrac{dy}{dt}}{(dx/dt)^3}.$$

22. If $A = ab$ and da and db are small changes in a and b, show that

$$\frac{dA}{A} = \frac{da}{a} + \frac{db}{b}.$$

Interpret the result in terms of percentage changes: If a changes by m percent and b changes by n percent, by what percent (approximately) does ab change? (Assume that m and n are small.)

REVIEW QUESTIONS AND EXERCISES

1. Using the definition of the derivative, deduce the formula for the derivative of a product uv of two differentiable functions.

2. In the formula for the derivative of uv, let $v = u$, and thereby deduce a formula for the derivative of u^2. Repeat the process, with $v = u^2$, and get a formula for the derivative of u^3. Extend the result, by the method of mathematical induction, to deduce the formula for the derivative of u^n for every positive integer n.

3. Explain how the three formulas

a) $\dfrac{d(x^n)}{dx} = nx^{n-1}$,

b) $\dfrac{d(cu)}{dx} = c\dfrac{du}{dx}$,

c) $\dfrac{d(u+v)}{dx} = \dfrac{du}{dx} + \dfrac{dv}{dx}$

are sufficient to differentiate any polynomial.

4. What formula do we need, in addition to the three listed in Problem 3 above, in order to differentiate rational functions?

5. Does the derivative of a polynomial function exist at every point of its domain? What is the largest domain the function can have? Does the derivative of a rational function exist at every point in its domain? What real numbers, if any, must be excluded from the domain of a rational function?

6. *Definition of algebraic function.* Let $y = f(x)$ define a function of x such that every pair of numbers (x, y) belonging to f satisfy an irreducible equation of the form

$$P_0(x)y^n + P_1(x)y^{n-1} + \cdots + P_{n-1}(x)y + P_n(x) = 0 \quad (\alpha)$$

for some positive integer n, with coefficients $P_0(x), \ldots, P_n(x)$ polynomials in x, and $P_0(x)$ not identically zero. Then f is said to be an *algebraic function*. What technique of this chapter can be used to find the derivative of an algebraic function if the polynomial coefficients $P_0(x), \ldots, P_n(x)$ in its defining equation (α) are given?

7. Show that the function f defined by $f(x) = x^{2/3}$ is an algebraic function by finding an appropriate equation of the type (α) in the definition in Problem 6 above. On what domain of values of x is this function defined? Where is it continuous? Where is it differentiable?

8. Show that every rational function is algebraic. Do you think the converse is also true? Explain.

9. It can be shown (though not very easily) that sums, quotients, products, powers, and roots of algebraic functions are algebraic functions. Thus

$$f(x) = x\sqrt{3x^2+1} + \frac{5x^{4/3}}{3x+2}, \qquad x \neq -\frac{2}{3},$$

defines an algebraic function. Find its derivative. What formulas of this chapter are used in finding derivatives of functions like this one?

10. Show that $y = |x|$ satisfies the equation $y^2 - x^2 = 0$. Is the absolute value function algebraic? What is its derivative? Where does the derivative exist? Where is the absolute value function continuous?

11. Develop the formula for $\cos(A - B)$ from the law of cosines.

12. Write expressions for $\sin(A + B)$ and $\sin(A - B)$. Set $\alpha = A + B$, $\beta = A - B$, and develop a formula for $\sin\alpha - \sin\beta$.

13. Under what assumptions is it true that

$$\lim\,((\sin\theta)/\theta) = 1?$$

Prove the result.

14. Write expressions for $\cos(A + B)$ and $\cos(A - B)$. Set $\alpha = A + B$, $\beta = A - B$, and develop a formula for $\cos\alpha - \cos\beta$. Use the result to develop a formula for the derivative of $\cos x$, from the definition

$$\frac{d(\cos x)}{dx} = \lim_{\Delta x \to 0} \frac{\cos(x + \Delta x) - \cos x}{\Delta x}.$$

15. Let A_n be the area bounded by a regular n-sided polygon inscribed in a circle of radius r. Show that $A_n = (n/2)r^2 \sin(2\pi/n)$. Find $\lim A_n$ as $n \to \infty$. Does the result agree with what you know about the area of a circle?

16. Define differentials. If $y = f(x)$ defines a differentiable function, how are dy and dx related? Give geometrical interpretations of dx and dy.

17. State the chain rule for derivatives. Prove it, with the book closed.

18. Show how the chain rule is used to prove that the derivative of y with respect to x is the ratio of dy to dx when x and y are both differentiable functions of t, and $dx \neq 0$.

19. Give an example of a function that is defined and bounded on $0 \le t \le 1$, continuous in the open interval $0 < t < 1$, and discontinuous at $t = 0$.

20. State and prove a theorem about the relationship between continuity and differentiability of a function, at a point in its domain.

21. Read the article "The Lever of Mahomet," by R. Courant and H. Robbins, and the accompanying "Commentary on Continuity," by J. R. Newman, in *World of Mathematics*, Vol. 4, pp. 2410–2413.

MISCELLANEOUS PROBLEMS

Find dy/dx in each of the following problems (1 through 33).

1. $y = \dfrac{x}{\sqrt{x^2 - 4}}$ **2.** $x^2 + xy + y^2 - 5x = 2$

3. $xy + y^2 = 1$ **4.** $x^3 + 4xy - 3y^3 = 2$

5. $x^2y + xy^2 = 6$ **6.** $y = (x + 1)^2(x^2 + 2x)^{-2}$

7. $y = \cos(1 - 2x)$ **8.** $y = \dfrac{\cos x}{\sin x}$

9. $y = \dfrac{x}{x + 1}$ **10.** $y = \sqrt{2x + 1}$

11. $y = x^2\sqrt{x^2 - a^2}$ **12.** $y = \dfrac{2x + 1}{2x - 1}$

13. $y = \dfrac{x^2}{1 - x^2}$ **14.** $y = (x^2 + x + 1)^3$

15. $y = \sec^2(5x)$ **16.** $y^3 = \sin^3 x + \cos^3 x$

17. $y = \dfrac{(2x^2 + 5x)^{3/2}}{3}$ **18.** $y = \dfrac{3}{(2x^2 + 5x)^{3/2}}$

19. $xy^2 + \sqrt{xy} = 2$ **20.** $x^2 - y^2 = xy$

21. $x^{2/3} + y^{2/3} = a^{2/3}$ **22.** $x^{1/2} + y^{1/2} = a^{1/2}$

23. $xy = 1$ **24.** $\sqrt{xy} = 1$

25. $(x + 2y)^2 + 2xy^2 = 6$ **26.** $y = \sqrt{\dfrac{1 - x}{1 + x^2}}$

27. $y^2 = \dfrac{x}{x + 1}$ **28.** $x^2y + xy^2 = 6(x^2 + y^2)$

29. $xy + 2x + 3y = 1$ **30.** $y = u^2 - 1, \quad x = u^2 + 1$

31. $y = \sqrt{2t + t^2}, \quad t = 2x + 3$

32. $x = \dfrac{t}{1 + t^2}, \quad y = 1 + t^2$

33. $t = \dfrac{x}{1 + x^2}, \quad y = x^2 + t^2$

34. Find the slope of $y = x/(x^2 + 1)$ at the origin. Write the equation of the tangent line at the origin.

35. Write the equation of the tangent at (2, 2) to the curve

$$x^2 - 2xy + y^2 + 2x + y - 6 = 0.$$

36. Determine the constant c such that the straight line joining the points (0, 3) and (5, −2) is tangent to the curve $y = c/(x + 1)$.

37. What is the slope of the curve $y = 2x^2 - 6x + 3$ at the point on the curve where $x = 2$? What is the equation of the tangent line to the curve at this point?

38. Find the points on the curve $y = 2x^3 - 3x^2 - 12x + 20$ where the tangent is parallel to the x-axis.

39. Find the derivatives of the following functions:

a) $y = (x^2 + 2x)^5$; **b)** $f(t) = \sqrt{3t^2 - 2t}$;

c) $f(r) = \sqrt{r^2 + 5} + \sqrt{r^2 - 5}$;

d) $f(x) = \dfrac{x^2 - 1}{x^2 + 1}$.

40. Find the equation of the tangent to the curve $y = 2/\sqrt{x - 1}$ at the point on the curve where $x = 10$.

41. Write the equation of the straight line passing through the point (2, 1) and normal to the curve $x^2 = 4y$.

42. Use the definition of the derivative to find dy/dx for $y = \sqrt{2x + 3}$ and then check the result by finding the same derivative by the power formula.

43. Find the value of

$$\lim_{\Delta x \to 0} \frac{[2 - 3(x + \Delta x)]^2 - [2 - 3x]^2}{\Delta x}$$

and specify the function $f(x)$ of which this is the derivative.

44. Find the slope of the curve $x^2y + xy^2 = 6$ at the point (1, 2).

45. A cylindrical can of height 6 (in.) and radius r (in.) has volume $V = 6\pi r^2$ (in.^{3}). What is the difference between ΔV and its principal part as r varies? What is the geometric significance of the principal part?

46. If a hemispherical bowl of radius 10 in. is filled with water to a depth of x in., the volume of water is given by $v = \pi[10 - (x/3)]x^2$. Find the rate of increase of the volume per inch increase of the depth.

47. A bus will hold 60 people. If the number x of persons per trip who use the bus is related to the fare charged (p nickels), by the law $p = [3 - (x/40)]^2$, write the function expressing the total revenue per trip received by the bus company. What is the number x_1 of people per trip that will make the marginal revenue equal to zero? What is the corresponding fare?

48. Prove Eq. (2), Article 2–3, by mathematical induction.

49. Given $y = x - x^2$, find the rate of change of y^2 with respect to x^2 (expressed in terms of x).

50. If $x = 3t + 1$ and $y = t^2 + t$, find dy/dt, dx/dt, and dy/dx. Eliminate t to obtain y as a function of x, and then determine dy/dx directly. Do the results check?

51. A particle projected vertically upward with a speed of a ft/sec reaches an elevation $s = at - 16t^2$ ft at the end of t sec. What must the initial velocity be in order for the particle to travel 49 ft upward before it starts coming back down?

52. Find the rate of change of $\sqrt{x^2+16}$ with respect to $x/(x-1)$ at $x = 3$.

53. The circle $(x-h)^2 + (y-k)^2 = r^2$, center at (h, k), radius $= r$ (see Article 8–4), is tangent to the curve $y = x^2 + 1$ at the point $(1, 2)$. (a) Find the locus of the point (h, k). (b) If, also, the circle and the curve have the same second derivative at $(1, 2)$, find h, k, and r. Sketch the curve and the circle.

54. If $y = x^2 + 1$ and $u = \sqrt{x^2+1}$, find dy/du.

55. If $x = y^2 + y$ and $u = (x^2+x)^{3/2}$, find dy/du.

56. If $f'(x) = \sqrt{3x^2-1}$ and $y = f(x^2)$, find dy/dx.

57. If $f'(x) = \sin(x^2)$ and $y = f((2x-1)/(x+1))$, find dy/dx.

58. Given $y = 3\sin 2x$ and $x = u^2 + \pi$, find the value of dy/du when $u = 0$.

59. If $0 < x < \pi/2$, prove that $x > \sin x > 2x/\pi$.

60. If $y = x\sqrt{2x-3}$, find d^2y/dx^2.

61. Find the value of d^2y/dx^2 in the equation $y^3 + y = x$ at the point $(2, 1)$.

62. If $x = t - t^2$, $y = t - t^3$, find the values of dy/dx and d^2y/dx^2 at $t = 1$.

63. Prove Leibniz's rule:

a) $$\frac{d^2(uv)}{dx^2} = \frac{d^2u}{dx^2}\cdot v + 2\frac{du}{dx}\frac{dv}{dx} + u\frac{d^2v}{dx^2},$$

b) $$\frac{d^3(uv)}{dx^3} = \frac{d^3u}{dx^3}\cdot v + 3\frac{d^2u}{dx^2}\frac{dv}{dx} + 3\frac{du}{dx}\frac{d^2v}{dx^2} + u\frac{d^3v}{dx^3},$$

c) $$\frac{d^n(uv)}{dx^n} =$$

$$\frac{d^nu}{dx^n}\cdot v + n\frac{d^{n-1}u}{dx^{n-1}}\frac{dv}{dx} + \cdots$$

$$+ \frac{n(n-1)\cdots(n-k+1)}{k!}\frac{d^{n-k}u}{dx^{n-k}}\frac{d^kv}{dx^k} + \cdots + u\frac{d^nv}{dx^n}.$$

The terms on the right side of this equation may be obtained from the terms in the binomial expansion $(a+b)^n$ by replacing $a^{n-k}b^k$ by $(d^{n-k}u/dx^{n-k})\cdot(d^kv/dx^k)$ for $k = 0, 1, 2, \ldots, n$, and interpreting d^0u/dx^0 as being u itself.

64. Find d^3y/dx^3 in each of the following cases:

a) $y = \sqrt{2x-1}$ **b)** $y = \dfrac{1}{3x+2}$

c) $y = ax^3 + bx^2 + cx + d$.

65. If $f(x) = (x-a)^n g(x)$, where $g(x)$ is a polynomial and $g(a) \neq 0$, show that $f(a) = 0 = f'(a) = \cdots = f^{(n-1)}(a)$; but $f^{(n)}(a) = n!\,g(a) \neq 0$.

66. If $y = 2x^2 - 3x + 5$, find Δy for $x = 3$ and $\Delta x = 0.1$. Approximate Δy by finding its principal part.

67. (a) Show that the perimeter P_n of an n-sided regular polygon inscribed in a circle of radius r is $P_n = 2nr\sin(\pi/n)$. (b) Find the limit of P_n as $n \to \infty$. Is the answer consistent with what you know about the circumference of a circle?

68. Find dy/dx and d^2y/dx^2 if $x = \cos 3t$ and $y = \sin^2 3t$.

69. To compute the height h of a lamppost, the length a of the shadow of a six-foot pole is measured. The pole is 20 ft from the lamppost. If $a = 15$ ft, with a possible error of less than one inch, find the height of the lamppost and estimate the possible error in height.

70. Find the differential dy in each of the following cases:

a) $y = x^2/(1+x)$ **b)** $x^2 - y^2 = 1$ **c)** $xy + y^2 = 1$.

71. Suppose a function f satisfies the following two conditions for all x and y:

a) $f(x+y) = f(x)\cdot f(y)$;

b) $f(x) = 1 + xg(x)$, where $\lim_{x\to 0} g(x) = 1$.

Prove that (a) the derivative $f'(x)$ exists, (b) $f'(x) = f(x)$.

72. Let $f(x) = x^2 + 1$. Given $\epsilon > 0$, find $\delta > 0$ such that $|f(x_1) - f(x_2)| < \epsilon$ whenever $|x_1 - x_2| < \delta$ and x_1, x_2 both lie in the closed interval $-2 \le x \le 2$. State precisely what this means concerning the continuity of this function.

73. Given a function $f(x)$, defined for all real x, and a positive constant c such that $|f(x+h) - f(x)| \le ch^2$ for all real h. Prove that (a) $f(x)$ is uniformly continuous, (b) $f'(x) = 0$ for all x.

74. A function $f(x)$ is said to satisfy a Lipschitz condition of order m on the closed interval $a \le x \le b$ if there is a constant C such that

$$|f(x_2) - f(x_1)| \le C|x_2 - x_1|^m$$

for all values of x_1, x_2 on $[a, b]$. Prove that a function which satisfies a Lipschitz condition of order $m > 0$ on $[a, b]$ is uniformly continuous there.

75. Suppose $[a, b]$ is the interval $[-1, 1]$ and $f(x) = \sqrt{1-x^2}$. Find appropriate values of C and of m to satisfy the conditions in Problem 74. [*Hint.* Show that if $y_2 > y_1 > 0$ and $y_2 - y_1 = h$, then $|\sqrt{y_2} - \sqrt{y_1}| \le \sqrt{h}$.]

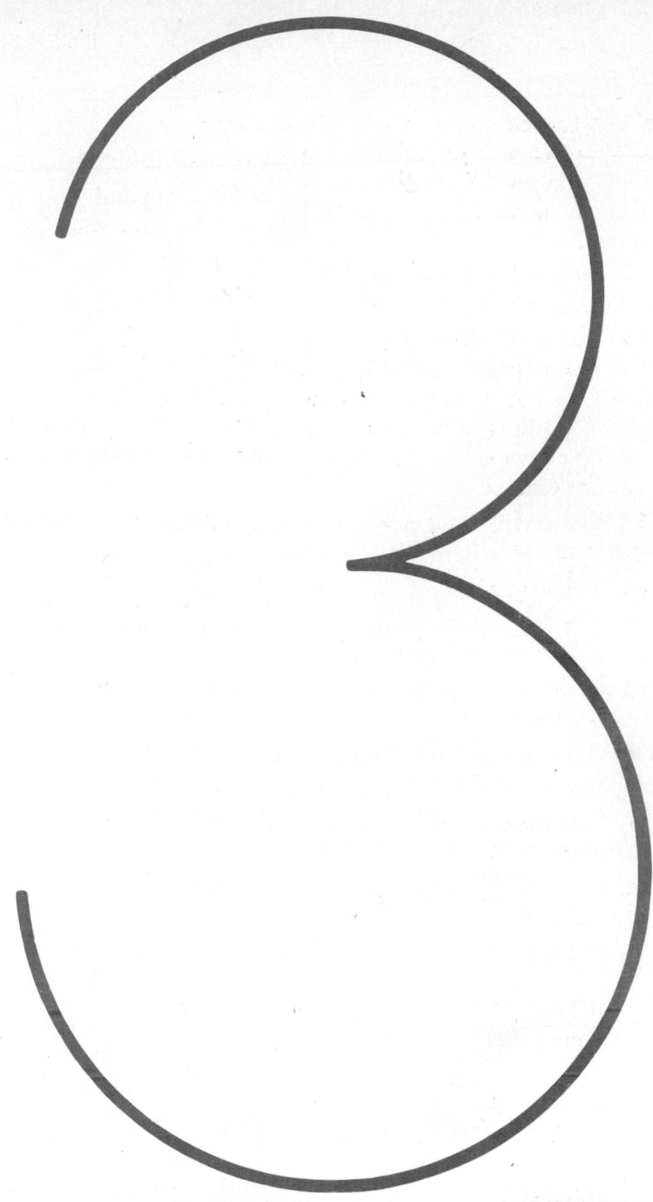

APPLICATIONS

3–1 SIGN OF THE FIRST DERIVATIVE. APPLICATION TO CURVE SKETCHING

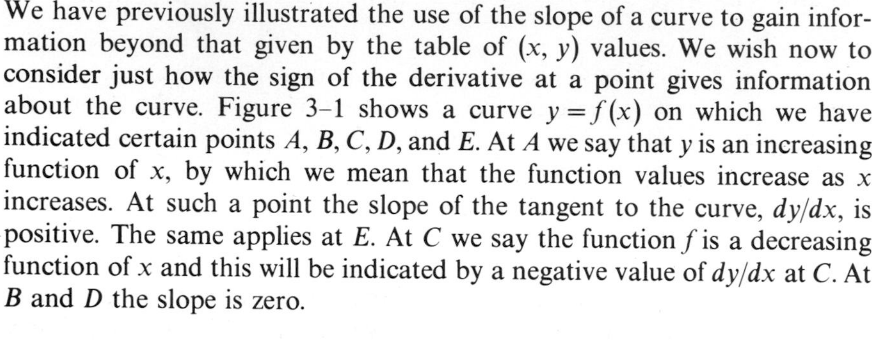

We have previously illustrated the use of the slope of a curve to gain information beyond that given by the table of (x, y) values. We wish now to consider just how the sign of the derivative at a point gives information about the curve. Figure 3–1 shows a curve $y = f(x)$ on which we have indicated certain points A, B, C, D, and E. At A we say that y is an increasing function of x, by which we mean that the function values increase as x increases. At such a point the slope of the tangent to the curve, dy/dx, is positive. The same applies at E. At C we say the function f is a decreasing function of x and this will be indicated by a negative value of dy/dx at C. At B and D the slope is zero.

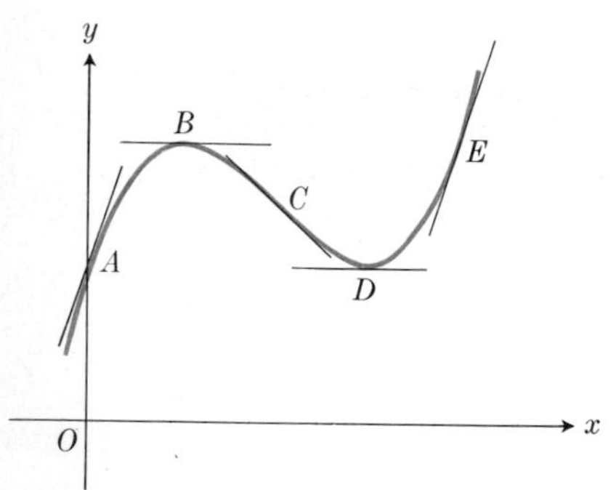

3–1 Tangents to a curve $y = f(x)$. The derivative dy/dx is positive at A and E, negative at C, and zero at B and D.

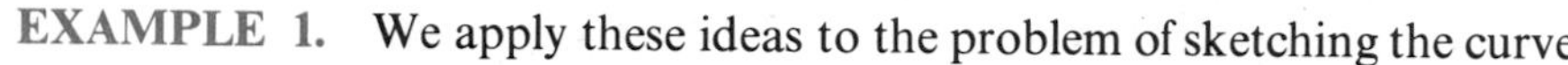

EXAMPLE 1. We apply these ideas to the problem of sketching the curve

$$y = \tfrac{1}{3}x^3 - 2x^2 + 3x + 2.$$

The slope at (x, y) is

$$\frac{dy}{dx} = x^2 - 4x + 3 = (x - 1)(x - 3).$$

To determine where dy/dx is positive and where it is negative, we first determine where it is zero:

$$\frac{dy}{dx} = 0 \quad \text{when} \quad x = 1 \quad \text{or} \quad x = 3,$$

since these points will mark the transition from positive to negative or from negative to positive slopes. The sign of dy/dx depends upon the signs of the two factors $(x - 1)$ and $(x - 3)$. Since the sign of $(x - 1)$ is negative when x is to the left of 1 and positive to the right, we have the pattern of signs indicated in Fig. 3–2(a). Similarly, the sign of $(x - 3)$ is shown in Fig. 3–2(b), and the sign of the product $dy/dx = (x - 1)(x - 3)$ is shown in Fig. 3–2(c). We can get a rough idea of the shape of the curve just from this pattern of signs of its slope, if we sketch a curve which is rising, falling, and rising again for $x < 1$, $1 < x < 3$, and $x > 3$, respectively (Fig. 3–3).

To get a more accurate curve, we would construct a table for some range of values extending, say, from $x = 0$ to $x = 4$, which includes the transition points between rising and falling portions of the curve (Fig. 3–4).

The terms "rising" and "falling," or "increasing" and "decreasing," are always taken to apply to the behavior of the curve as the point that is tracing

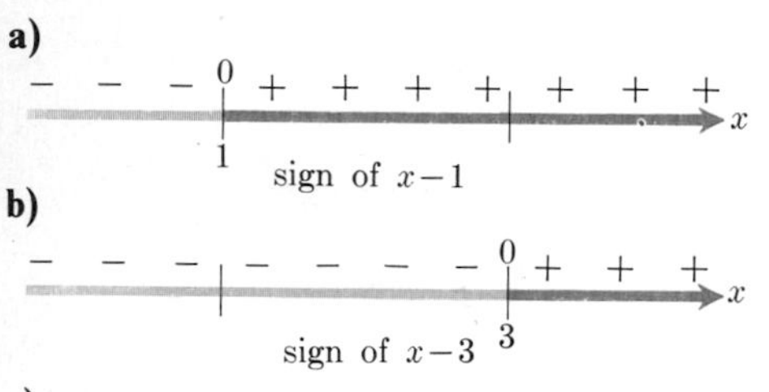

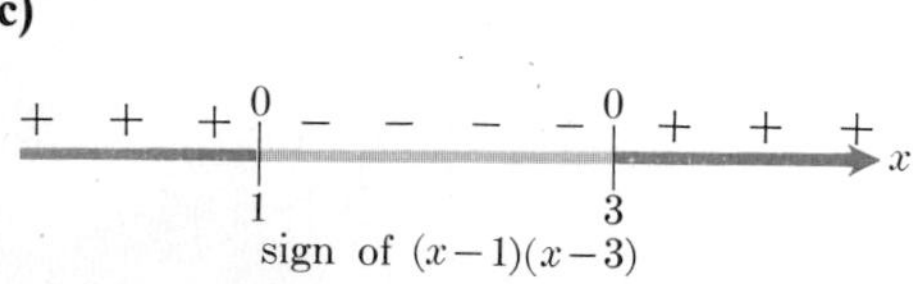

3–2 The sign pattern of the product $(x - 1)(x - 3)$.

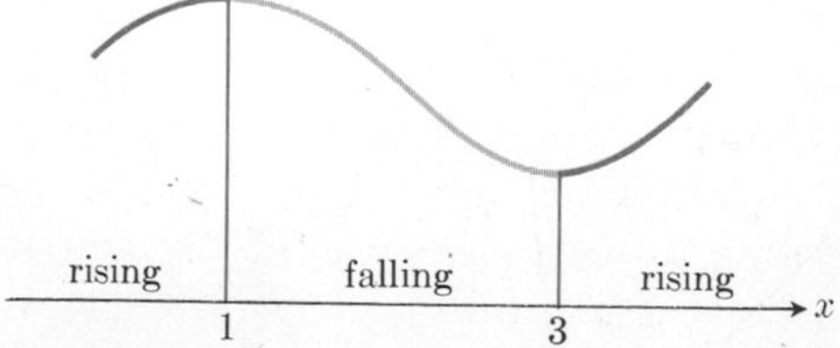

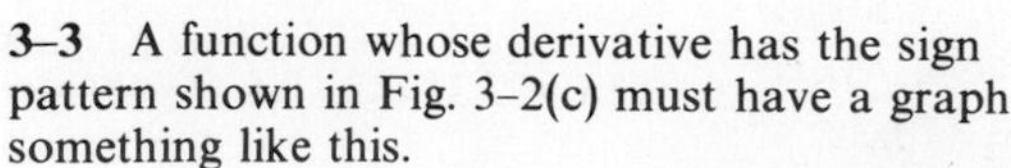

3–3 A function whose derivative has the sign pattern shown in Fig. 3–2(c) must have a graph something like this.

it moves from left to right or, in other words, relative to its behavior as x increases. The same concepts apply to functions that vary with time.

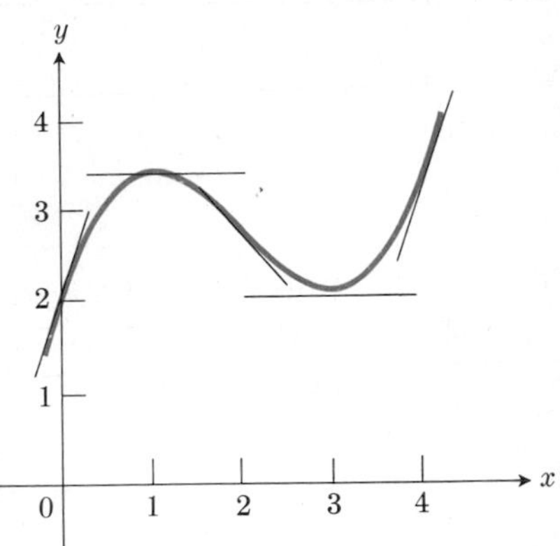

3–4 This graph of $y = \frac{1}{3}x^3 - 2x^2 + 3x + 2$ combines the general information about shape from Fig. 3–3 with a selection of plotted points and slopes.

EXAMPLE 2. Figure 3–5 shows a rope running through a pulley at P, bearing a weight W at one end. The other end is held in a worker's hand M at a distance of 5 feet above the ground as the worker walks straight away from the pulley at the rate of 6 ft/sec. If x represents the distance in feet of the worker's hand away from the vertical line PW, and t represents time, then x is an increasing function of t. We are given the rate at which x changes with t, namely, 6 ft/sec. This would be stated in mathematical terms by saying $dx/dt = +6$ ft/sec. On the other hand, if the worker were to walk *toward* the line PW at the rate of 6 ft/sec, we would have $dx/dt = -6$ ft/sec, because x would then be a decreasing function of t.

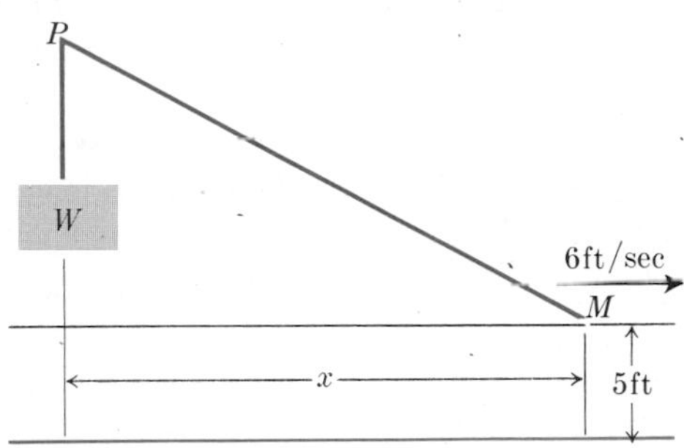

3–5 If the worker at M moves to the right at the speed shown, then $dx/dt = 6$ ft/sec.

PROBLEMS

In each of the following exercises, determine dy/dx and find the sets of values of x where the graph of y versus x is rising (as x moves to the right) and where it is falling. Sketch each curve, showing in particular the points of transition between falling and rising portions of the curve.

1. $y = x^2 - x + 1$

2. $y = \dfrac{x^3}{3} - \dfrac{x^2}{2} - 2x + \dfrac{1}{3}$

3. $y = 2x^3 - 3x^2 + 3$

4. $y = x^3 - 27x + 36$

5. $y = x^4 - 8x^2 + 16$

6. $y = \dfrac{1}{x}$

7. $y = \sin x$

8. $y = \tan x$

9. $y = x|x|$

3–2 RELATED RATES

In this article we look at problems that ask for the rate at which some quantity changes. In each case this rate is a derivative that has to be computed from the rate at which some other quantity is known to change. To find it, we write an equation that relates the first quantity to the second. We then differentiate both sides of the equation to express the derivative we seek in terms of the derivative we know.

EXAMPLE 1. Suppose that the pulley in Example 2 at the end of Article 3–1 is 25 ft above the ground, the rope is 45 ft long, and the worker is walking away from the pulley at the rate of 6 ft/sec. How fast is the weight being raised at the instant when the distance x is 15 ft?

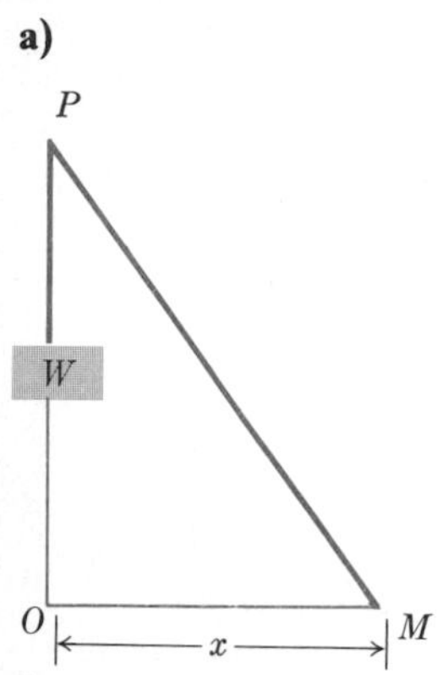

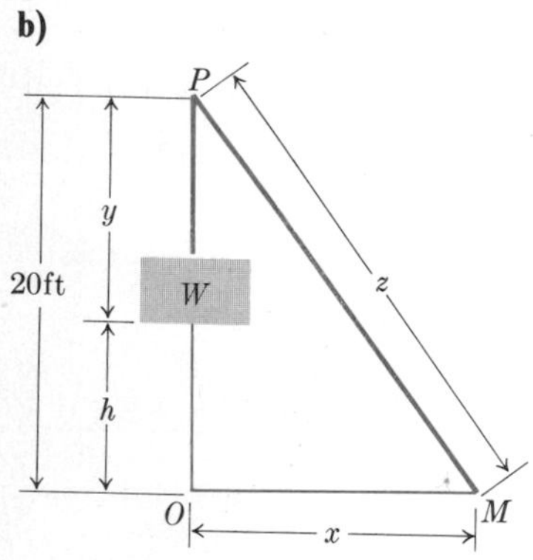

3–6 A typical sketch for a related rate problem shows the situation for any time t, not just for the time in question. The reason for this is that certain distances in the figure vary (here, x, y, z, and h) and it is important to treat them as variables and not as constants.

Solution. To help visualize the problem, we draw and label a preliminary sketch, Fig. 3–6(a). In the figure, M represents the worker's hand, P the pulley, and OM the horizontal line from the worker's hand to a point directly beneath the pulley. The angle at O is a right angle.

The quantities that are changing in the figure are the distance from M to O, the height of the weight above O, the distance from the weight to P, and the length of rope from P to M. The quantities that remain constant are the height of P above O (20 ft, because O is 5 ft above the ground), the total length of the rope (45 ft), and the rate at which the worker walks (6 ft/sec).

The quantity we are asked to find is a rate. If we let h be the height of the weight W above O, and denote time by t, then we can write this rate as dh/dt. We have been asked to find the value of dh/dt when $x = 15$ ft.

We label the other changing dimensions in the sketch (Fig. 3–6(b)), and write down any numerical information we have about them. We choose y, say, for the distance from P to the bottom of the weight, and z for the length of the rope from P to M. These variables, as well as h and x, are to be considered to be functions of t. We have been told that $dx/dt = 6$ ft/sec.

We now write equations to express the relationships that are to hold between the variables at all values of t under consideration:

$$\begin{aligned} y + z &= 45 \text{ (The total length of the rope is 45 ft)} \\ h + y &= 20 \text{ (P is 20 ft above O)} \\ 20^2 + x^2 &= z^2 \text{ (The angle at O is a right angle).} \end{aligned} \tag{1}$$

If these equations are differentiated with respect to t, the new equations so obtained will tell how the derivatives of the variables are related to each other. From this information we can express dh/dt in terms of x and dx/dt.

Actually, it will save time and effort if we first obtain a single equation relating the variable x (whose rate is given) and the variable h (whose rate is wanted) before we take derivatives. Using the equations in (1), we find successively:

$$z = 45 - y, \qquad y = 20 - h,$$

$$z = 45 - (20 - h) = (25 + h), \qquad 20^2 + x^2 = z^2 = (25 + h)^2,$$

that is,

$$20^2 + x^2 = (25 + h)^2.$$

This last equation relates the variables x and h for all values of t under consideration. Both sides of this equation are functions of t, and the equality says they represent the same function of t. Thus when we differentiate both sides of the equation with respect to t, we will have another equation:

$$\frac{d}{dt}(20^2 + x^2) = \frac{d}{dt}(25 + h)^2, \qquad 0 + 2x\frac{dx}{dt} = 2(25 + h)\frac{dh}{dt}.$$

This may be solved for the rate we want, namely,

$$\frac{dh}{dt} = \frac{x}{25 + h}\frac{dx}{dt}. \tag{2}$$

Now at the given instant, we have

$$x = 15, \qquad \frac{dx}{dt} = 6,$$

and we find h at this instant from the equation

$$20^2 + 15^2 = (25 + h)^2: \qquad 25 + h = 25, \qquad h = 0.$$

When we substitute these values in Eq. (2), we obtain

$$\frac{dh}{dt} = \frac{15}{25 + 0}\cdot 6 = \frac{18}{5} = 3\tfrac{3}{5} \text{ ft/sec}$$

as the rate at which the weight is being raised at the instant in question.

The problem in Example 1 is called a problem in related rates. It is typical of such problems that:

a) certain variables are related in a definite way for all values of t under consideration;

b) the values of some or all of these variables and the rates of change of some of them are given at some particular instant; and

c) it is required to find the rate of change of one or more of them at this instant.

The variables may then all be considered to be functions of time, and if the equations that relate them for all values of t are differentiated with respect to t, the new equations so obtained will tell how their rates of change are related. From this information it should be possible to answer the question posed by the problem.

A strategy for solving such problems is this:*

1. *Visualize the problem.* Make a sketch. Note which quantities change, and which stay the same.

2. *Write down what you are asked to find* (in Example 1, a rate). Express it in terms of a variable (dh/dt). Show the variable in the sketch (the h in Fig. 3–6(b)).

3. *Identify the other variables in the problem.* Write down any numerical information that is given about them. Show them in the sketch.

4. *Write equations that relate the variables.*

5. *Use substitution and differentiation* to get a single equation that expresses the desired quantity in terms of the quantities whose values are known.

We carried out these steps in Example 1, and we do so again in Example 2.

---

* See *The Solving of Word Problems in Beginning Calculus, A Strategic Approach*, by Peter Ross, Group in Science and Mathematics Education (SESAME), University of California, Berkeley, May, 1977.

EXAMPLE 2. A ladder 26 ft long leans against a vertical wall. The foot of the ladder is being drawn away from the wall at the rate of 4 ft/sec. How fast is the top of the ladder sliding down the wall at the instant when the foot of the ladder is 10 ft from the wall?

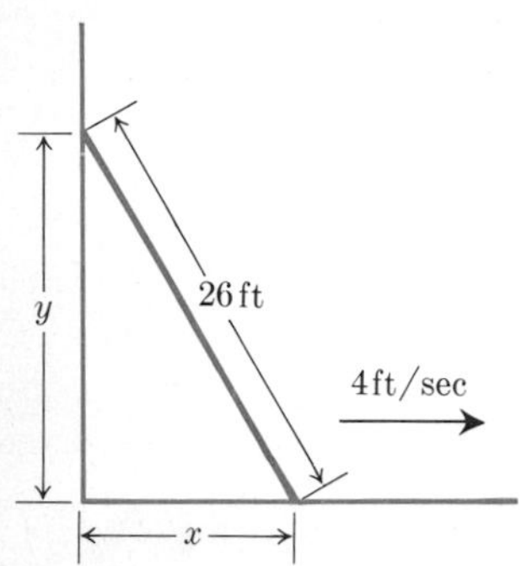

3–7 x increases and y decreases when the foot of the ladder slides away from the wall.

Solution. Figure 3–7 shows the ladder against the wall. The quantities that change are the height of the top of the ladder above the ground and the distance of the base of the ladder from the wall. The quantities that remain constant are the length of the ladder and the rate at which the base moves away from the wall.

We are asked to find a rate. If y denotes the height of the top of the ladder above the ground in feet and t denotes time measured in seconds, then the rate we seek is dy/dt. What is the value of dy/dt when the base of the ladder is 10 ft from the wall?

Denote the distance of the base of the ladder from the wall by x. Then $dx/dt = 4$ ft/sec.

The variables x and y are related by the equation $x^2 + y^2 = 26^2$. To express dy/dt in terms of dx/dt, we differentiate both sides of the equation with respect to t, and get

$$2x\frac{dx}{dt} + 2y\frac{dy}{dt} = 0.$$

Hence

$$\frac{dy}{dt} = \frac{-x}{y}\frac{dx}{dt}.$$

When $x = 10$, $y = 24$, $dx/dt = 4$, this leads to $dy/dt = -\frac{5}{3}$. That is, y is *decreasing* (the top of the ladder is moving *down*) at the rate of $\frac{5}{3}$ ft/sec.

In the next example we combine Steps 1 and 3 of the strategy.

EXAMPLE 3. Water runs into the conical tank shown in Fig. 3–8 at the constant rate of 2 ft^3 per minute. How fast is the water level rising when the water is 6 ft deep?

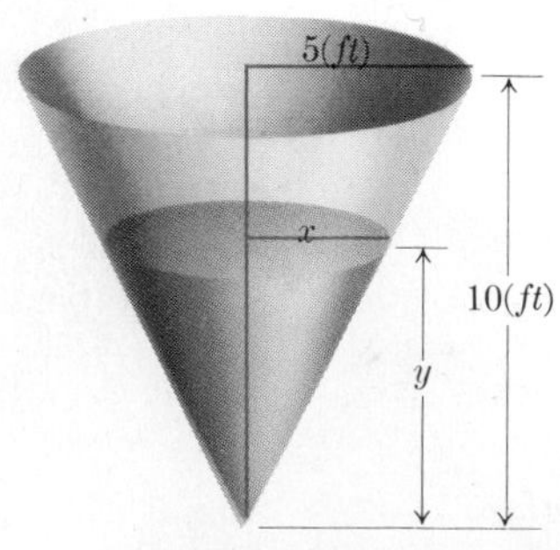

3–8 To show that the water level is changing in this conical tank, the depth of the water is denoted by a variable, y. The rate at which the level changes is then dy/dt.

Solution. The quantities that are changing in the problem are:

$v =$ the volume (ft^3) of water in the tank at time t (min),

$x =$ the radius (ft) of the surface of the water at time t,

$y =$ the depth (ft) of water in the tank at time t.

The quantities that remain the same are the dimensions of the tank and the rate

$$\frac{dv}{dt} = 2 \text{ ft}^3/\text{min}$$

at which the tank fills.

We are asked to find the rate dy/dt at the instant when $y = 6$.

The relationship between the volume of water v and depth y is expressed by the equation

$$v = \tfrac{1}{3}\pi x^2 y.$$

But this involves the additional variable x as well as v and y. However, we may eliminate x since, by similar triangles, we have

$$\frac{x}{y} = \frac{5}{10} \qquad \text{or} \qquad x = \tfrac{1}{2}y.$$

Therefore

$$v = \tfrac{1}{12}\pi y^3,$$

and when we differentiate this with respect to t, we have

$$\frac{dv}{dt} = \frac{1}{4}\pi y^2 \frac{dy}{dt}.$$

Hence

$$\frac{dy}{dt} = \frac{4}{\pi y^2}\frac{dv}{dt},$$

and when

$$\frac{dv}{dt} = 2 \qquad \text{and} \qquad y = 6,$$

this gives

$$\frac{dy}{dt} = \frac{4 \cdot 2}{\pi \cdot 36} = \frac{2}{9\pi} \approx 0.071 \text{ ft/min}.$$

PROBLEMS

1. Let A be the area of a circle of radius r. How is dA/dt related to dr/dt?

2. Let V be the volume of a sphere of radius r. How is dV/dt related to dr/dt?

3. Sand falls onto a conical pile at the rate of 10 ft^3/min. The radius of the base of the pile is always equal to one-half of its altitude. How fast is the altitude of the pile increasing when it is 5 ft deep?

4. Suppose that a raindrop is a perfect sphere. Assume that, through condensation, the raindrop accumulates moisture at a rate proportional to its surface area. Show that the radius increases at a constant rate.

5. Point A moves along the x-axis at the constant rate of a ft/sec while point B moves along the y-axis at the constant rate of b ft/sec. Find how fast the distance between them is changing when A is at the point $(x, 0)$ and B is at the point $(0, y)$.

6. A spherical balloon is inflated with gas at the rate of 100 ft^3/min. Assuming that the gas pressure remains constant, how fast is the radius of the balloon increasing at the instant when the radius is 3 ft?

7. A boat is pulled in to a dock by means of a rope with one end attached to the bow of the boat, the other end passing through a ring attached to the dock at a point 4 ft higher than the bow of the boat. If the rope is pulled in at the rate of 2 ft/sec, how fast is the boat approaching the dock when 10 ft of rope are out?

8. A balloon is 200 ft off the ground and rising vertically at the constant rate of 15 ft/sec. An automobile passes beneath it traveling along a straight road at the constant rate of 45 mi/hr = 66 ft/sec. How fast is the distance between them changing one second later?

9. Water is withdrawn from a conical reservoir 8 ft in diameter and 10 ft deep (vertex down) at the constant rate of 5 ft^3/min. How fast is the water level falling when the depth of water in the reservoir is 6 ft?

10. A particle moves around the circle $x^2 + y^2 = 1$ with an x-velocity component $dx/dt = y$. Find dy/dt. Does the particle travel in the clockwise or counterclockwise direction around the circle?

11. A man 6 ft tall walks at the rate of 5 ft/sec toward a street light that is 16 ft above the ground. At what rate is the tip of his shadow moving? At what rate is the length of his shadow changing when he is 10 ft from the base of the light?

12. When air changes volume adiabatically (without any heat being added to it), the pressure p and the volume v satisfy the relationship $pv^{1.4}$ = constant. At a certain instant the pressure is 50 lb/in^2 and the volume is 32 in^3 and is decreasing at the rate of 4 in^3/sec. How rapidly is the pressure changing at this instant?

13. A light is at the top of a pole 50 ft high. A ball is dropped from the same height from a point 30 ft away from the light. How fast is the shadow of the ball moving along the ground $\frac{1}{2}$ sec later? (Assume the ball falls a distance $s = 16t^2$ ft in t seconds.)

14. A girl flies a kite at a height of 300 ft, the wind carrying the kite horizontally away from her at a rate of 25 ft/sec. How fast must she pay out the string when the kite is 500 ft away from her?

15. A spherical iron ball 8 in. in diameter is coated with a layer of ice of uniform thickness. If the ice melts at the rate of 10 in^3 per minute, how fast is the thickness of the ice decreasing when it is 2 in. thick? How fast is the outer surface area of ice decreasing?

16. Two ships A and B are sailing away from the point O along routes such that the angle $AOB = 120°$. How fast is the distance between them changing if, at a certain instant, $OA = 8$ mi, $OB = 6$ mi, ship A is sailing at the rate of 20 mi/hr, and ship B at the rate of 30 mi/hr? [*Hint.* Use the law of cosines.]

3–3 SIGNIFICANCE OF THE SIGN OF THE SECOND DERIVATIVE

We have already seen how we may use the information given by dy/dx about the slope of the tangent to a curve to help in sketching it. We recall that in an interval where dy/dx is positive, the curve is rising to the right, while if dy/dx is negative the curve is falling to the right. Also it is evident that the regions of rise and fall are usually separated by high or low points where dy/dx is zero and the tangent is horizontal. However, it is possible for dy/dx to be zero at points that are neither high nor low points of the curve.

EXAMPLE 1. If

$$y = (x - 2)^3 + 1,$$

then

$$\frac{dy}{dx} = 3(x - 2)^2,$$

and although

$$\frac{dy}{dx} = 0 \quad \text{at} \quad x = 2,$$

for all values of x other than 2, the slope is positive and y is an increasing function of x (Fig. 3–9).

3–9 The point (2, 1) where $dy/dx = 0$ is neither a high point nor a low point of the curve.

The regions of rise and fall may also be separated by points where the derivative fails to exist.

EXAMPLE 2. If $y = x^{2/3}$, then

$$\frac{dy}{dx} = \frac{2}{3}x^{-1/3} = \frac{2}{3\sqrt[3]{x}}$$

is positive when x is positive, and negative when x is negative. At the transition point $x = 0$, dy/dx does not exist, but $dx/dy = \frac{3}{2}x^{1/3}$ is zero, which means that the tangent to the curve at (0, 0) is vertical instead of horizontal (Fig. 3–10).

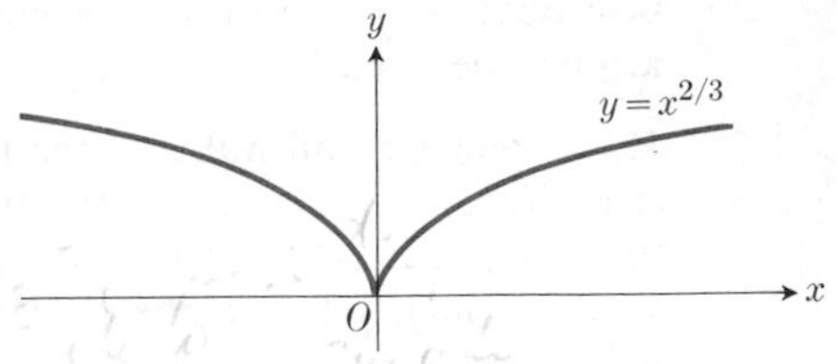

3–10 Here the regions of rise and fall are separated by a point where the derivative does not exist.

Next we shall see that when the second derivative is not zero its sign tells whether the graph of $y = f(x)$ is concave upward (y'' positive) or downward (y'' negative).

Consider, for example, the curve in Fig. 3–11(a). The first and second derivatives are represented by the curves in Fig. 3–11(b) and (c). The arc ABC of the y-curve is concave upward; CDE is concave downward; EF is again concave upward. To focus attention, let us consider a section near A on arc ABC. Here y' is negative and the y-curve slopes downward to the right. But as we travel through A, moving from left to right, we find the slope becomes less negative. That is, y' is an *increasing* function of x. Therefore the y'-curve slopes upward at A'. Hence its own slope, which is y'', is positive there. The same kind of argument applies at all points along the arc ABC; namely, y' is an increasing function of x, so its derivative (that is, y'') is positive. This is indicated by drawing the arc $A''B''C''$ of the y''-curve above the x-axis.

Similarly, where the y-curve is concave downward (along CDE), the y'-curve is falling, so its slope y'' is negative.

The direction of concavity is, therefore,

upward if the second derivative is *positive*,

downward if the second derivative is *negative*.

In the first case we could also say the curve is cupped so as to "hold water"; in the second case it would "spill water." Another way to think of concave upward is that locally the curve lies *above* its tangents. Near the points of a region where a curve is concave downward, the curve lies *below* its tangents.

a)

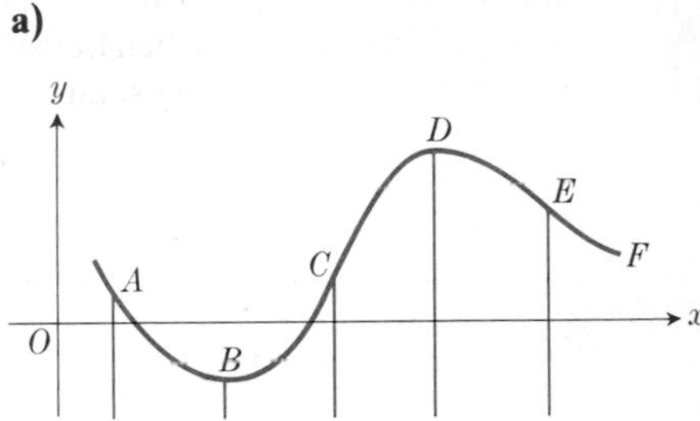

b)

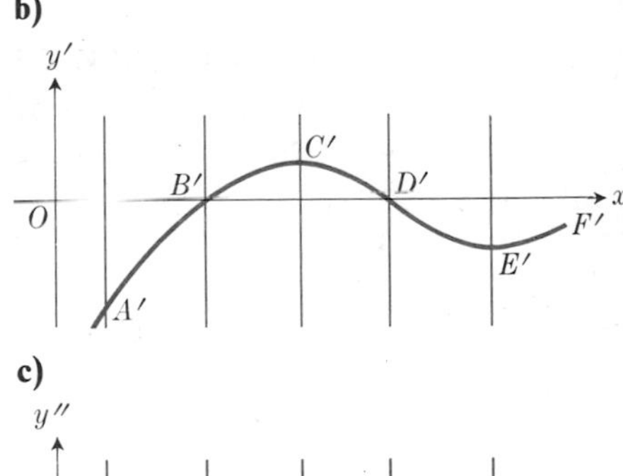

c)

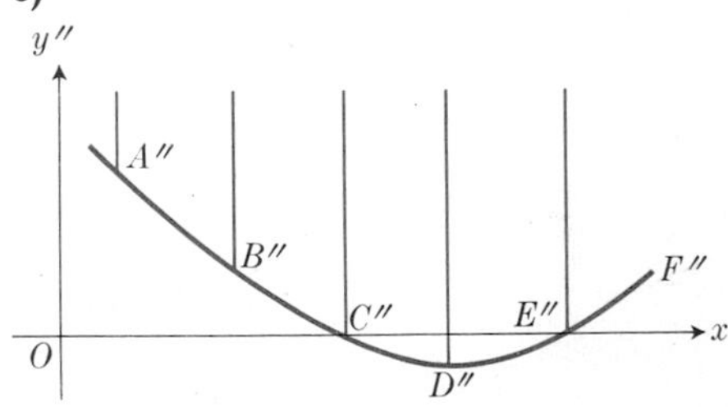

3–11 Compare the graph of the function in (a) with the graphs of its first and second derivatives in (b) and (c).

Points of inflection. A point where the curve changes its concavity from downward to upward or vice versa is called a *point of inflection.* Inflection points occur at C and E in Fig. 3–11(a), and are characterized by a change in the sign of d^2y/dx^2. Such a change of sign may occur where

a) $d^2y/dx^2 = 0$, or

b) d^2y/dx^2 fails to exist (for example, it may become infinite at such a point).

EXAMPLE 3. Figure 3–11 shows case (a). Case (b) is shown in Fig. 3–12, where the curve is

$$y = x^{1/3},$$

from which we find

$$y' = \tfrac{1}{3}x^{-(2/3)},$$

$$y'' = -\tfrac{2}{9}x^{-(5/3)},$$

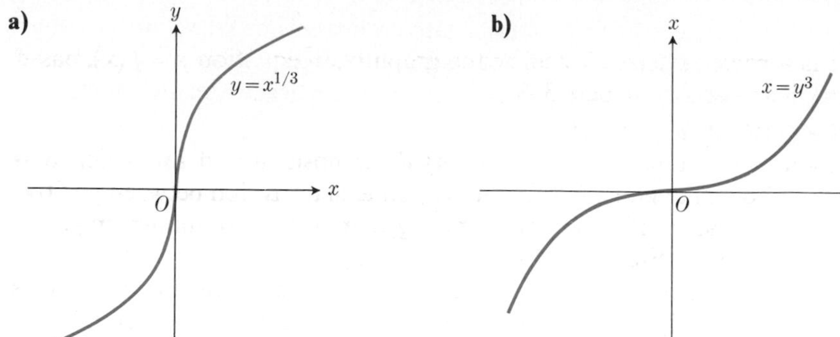

3–12 (a) The graph of $y = x^{1/3}$ shows that a point where y'' fails to exist can be a point of inflection. (b) The same function graphed with the y-axis horizontal and the x-axis vertical.

so that both y' and y'' become infinite when x approaches zero. On the other hand,

$$y' = \frac{1}{3x^{2/3}} = \frac{1}{3y^2}$$

is always positive for both positive and negative values of x, so the curve is always rising and has a vertical tangent at (0, 0). Also,

$$y'' = -\frac{2}{9}\left(\frac{1}{\sqrt[3]{x}}\right)^5 = \frac{-2}{9y^5}$$

is positive (the curve "holds water") when x is negative, and is negative (the curve "spills water") when x is positive, so that (0, 0) is a point of inflection.

REMARK. Another way to discuss Example 3 is to write the equation $y = x^{1/3}$ in the form $x = y^3$, and then

$$\frac{dx}{dy} = 3y^2, \qquad \frac{d^2x}{dy^2} = 6y,$$

so that we have

$$\frac{dx}{dy} = 0 \quad \text{and} \quad \frac{d^2x}{dy^2} = 0$$

at (0, 0). It is clear that dx/dy is positive for all y different from zero and d^2x/dy^2 has the same sign as y and therefore changes its sign at $y = 0$. If we interchange the x- and y-axes so as to take the x-axis to be vertical and the y-axis to be horizontal, the curve will be as shown in Fig. 3–12(b).

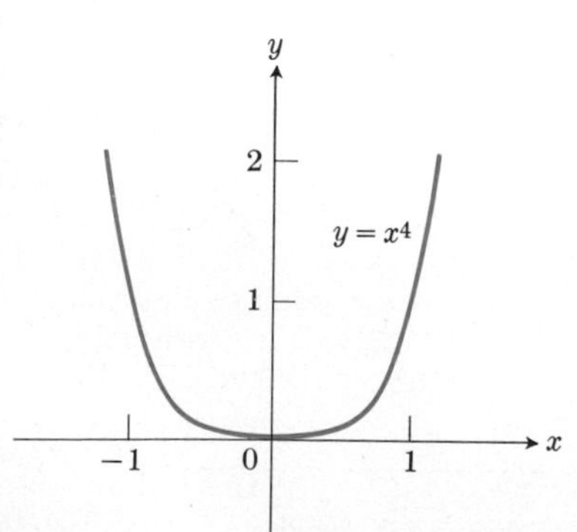

3–13 The graph of $y = x^4$ has no inflection point at the origin even though $y''(0) = 0$.

WARNING. The condition $y'' = 0$ by itself is not enough to guarantee a point of inflection. The graph of $y = x^4$ (Fig. 3–13) is concave upward at $x = 0$ even though the value of $y'' = 12x^2$ is 0 when $x = 0$.

3–4 CURVE PLOTTING

Here is a procedure for sketching the graph of an equation $y = f(x)$, based on the discussion in Article 3–3.

A. Calculate dy/dx and d^2y/dx^2.

B. Find the values of x for which dy/dx is positive and for which it is negative. Calculate y and d^2y/dx^2 at the points of transition between positive and negative values of dy/dx. These may give maximum or minimum points on the curve. (See Figs. 3–4, 3–10, and 3–11a.)

C. Find the values of x for which d^2y/dx^2 is positive and for which it is negative. Calculate y and dy/dx at the points of transition between positive and negative values of d^2y/dx^2. These may give points of inflection of the curve. (See Figs. 3–11 and 3–12.)

D. Plot a few additional points. In particular, points which lie between the transition points already determined or points which lie to the left or to the right of all of them will ordinarily be useful. The nature of the curve for large values of $|x|$ should also be indicated.

E. Sketch a smooth curve through the points found above, unless there are discontinuities in the curve or its slope. Have the curve pass through its points rising or falling as indicated by the sign of dy/dx, and concave upward or downward as indicated by the sign of d^2y/dx^2.

We shall now apply this procedure to a few examples.

EXAMPLE 1. (See Fig. 3–14b.) Graph the function

$$y = \tfrac{1}{6}(x^3 - 6x^2 + 9x + 6).$$

Solution. We take the five steps listed above.

A.
$$\frac{dy}{dx} = \frac{1}{6}(3x^2 - 12x + 9) = \frac{1}{2}(x^2 - 4x + 3),$$

$$\frac{d^2y}{dx^2} = \frac{1}{2}(2x - 4) = x - 2.$$

a)

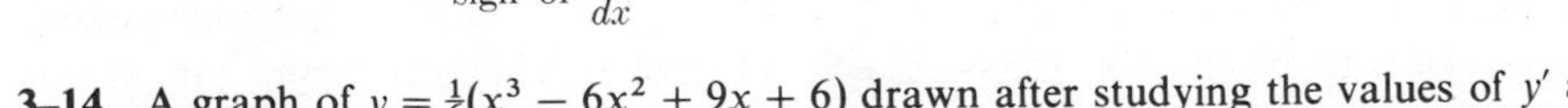

b)

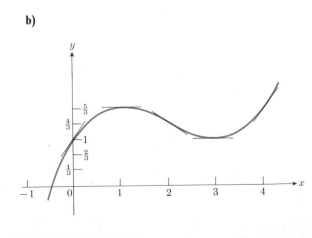

3–14 A graph of $y = \frac{1}{6}(x^3 - 6x^2 + 9x + 6)$ drawn after studying the values of y' and y''.

B. When factored,

$$\frac{dy}{dx} = \frac{1}{2}(x-1)(x-3),$$

and the two factors change their signs at $x = 1$ and $x = 3$. (See Fig. 3–14a.) When $x = 1$, $d^2y/dx^2 = -1$ and when $x = 3$, $d^2y/dx^2 = 1$. We enter the information in Table 3–1.
C. It is readily seen that $d^2y/dx^2 = x - 2$ is negative to the left of $x = 2$ and is positive to the right of $x = 2$, so that an inflection point occurs at $x = 2$.
D. We calculate y, y', and y'' at a few additional points to get general information about the curve.
E. A fairly good sketch of the curve can now be made (Fig. 3–14(b)) by using the information in the table.

Table 3–1

x	y	y'	y''	Conclusions
-1	$-\frac{5}{3}$	$+$	$-$	Rising; concave down
0	1	$+\frac{3}{2}$	$-$	Rising; concave down
1	$\frac{5}{3}$	0	$-$	"Spills water"; max.
2	$\frac{4}{3}$	$-\frac{1}{2}$	0	Falling; point of inflection
3	1	0	$+$	"Holds water"; min.
4	$\frac{5}{3}$	$+\frac{3}{2}$	$+$	Rising; concave up

EXAMPLE 2. (See Fig. 3–15b.)

$$y = x + \frac{1}{x} = x + x^{-1}.$$

Solution

$$\frac{dy}{dx} = 1 - x^{-2} = 1 - \frac{1}{x^2} = \frac{x^2 - 1}{x^2},$$

$$\frac{d^2y}{dx^2} = 2x^{-3} = \frac{2}{x^3}.$$

The sign of dy/dx will be the same as the sign of $x^2 - 1 = (x-1)(x+1)$. (See Fig. 3–15a.) But when x is near zero, $|y|$ will be large and y, dy/dx, d^2y/dx^2 all become infinite as x approaches zero. This curve is discontinuous at $x = 0$. Also, for large values of x, the $1/x$ term becomes small and $y \approx x$. In fact,

$$\text{when } |x| \text{ is small,} \quad y \approx \frac{1}{x},$$

$$\text{when } |x| \text{ is large,} \quad y \approx x,$$

so that it is helpful to sketch (as can quickly be done) the curves

$$y_1 = \frac{1}{x}, \qquad y_2 = x,$$

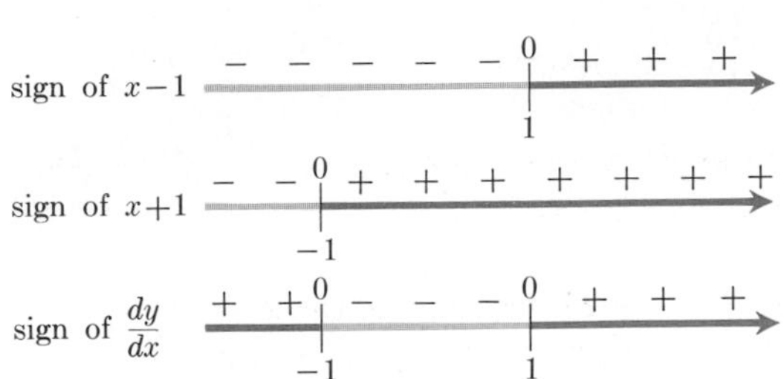

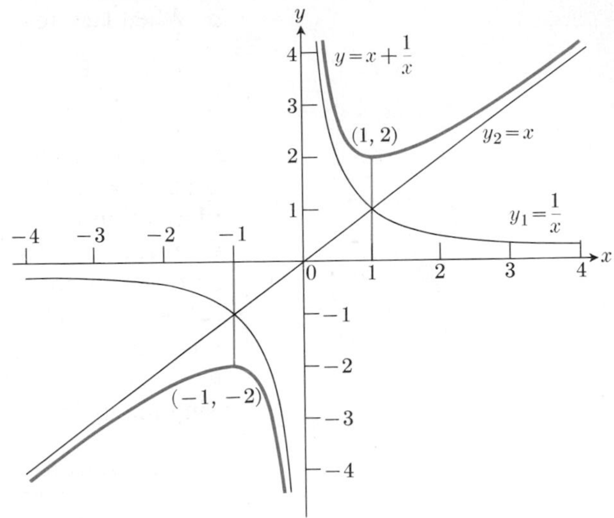

3–15 The graph of $y = x + (1/x)$, from the data in Example 2. The ordinate of each point on the graph is the sum of the ordinates x and $1/x$.

as well as

$$y = x + \frac{1}{x} = y_1 + y_2.$$

Actually, replacing x by $-x$ merely changes the sign of y, so that it would suffice to sketch the portion of the curve in the first quadrant and then reflect the result with respect to the origin to get the portion in the third quadrant (Fig. 3–15b). (See Table 3–2.)

Table 3–2. Data for Fig. 3–15(b).

x	y_1	y_2	y	y'	y''	Conclusions
-4	$-\frac{1}{4}$	-4	$-\frac{17}{4}$	+	−	Rising; concave down
-2	$-\frac{1}{2}$	-2	$-\frac{5}{2}$	+	−	Rising; concave down
-1	-1	-1	-2	0	-2	"Spills water"; max.
$-\frac{1}{2}$	-2	$-\frac{1}{2}$	$-\frac{5}{2}$	−	−	Falling; concave down
$-\frac{1}{4}$	-4	$-\frac{1}{4}$	$-\frac{17}{4}$	−	−	Falling; concave down
$+\frac{1}{4}$	4	$\frac{1}{4}$	$\frac{17}{4}$	−	+	Falling; concave up
$\frac{1}{2}$	2	$\frac{1}{2}$	$\frac{5}{2}$	−	+	Falling; concave up
1	1	1	2	0	$+2$	"Holds water"; min.
2	$\frac{1}{2}$	2	$\frac{5}{2}$	+	+	Rising; concave up
4	$\frac{1}{4}$	4	$\frac{17}{4}$	+	+	Rising; concave up

PROBLEMS

In each of the following problems (1 through 6), find intervals of values of x for which the curve is (a) rising, (b) falling, (c) concave upward, (d) concave downward. Sketch the curves, showing the high turning points M, low turning points m, and points of inflection I.

1. $y = x^2 - 4x + 3$
2. $y = \dfrac{x}{x+1}$
3. $y = 4 + 3x - x^3$
4. $y = \dfrac{x^3}{3} - \dfrac{x^2}{2} - 6x$
5. $y = x + \dfrac{4}{x}$
6. $y = \cos x$

7. Sketch a smooth curve $y = f(x)$ illustrating

$$f(1) = 0,$$
$$f'(x) < 0 \quad \text{for} \quad x < 1,$$
$$f'(x) > 0 \quad \text{for} \quad x > 1.$$

8. Sketch a smooth curve $y = f(x)$ illustrating

$$f(1) = 0,$$
$$f''(x) < 0 \quad \text{for} \quad x < 1,$$
$$f''(x) > 0 \quad \text{for} \quad x > 1.$$

Sketch each of the following curves (9 through 14), indicating high and low turning points and points of inflection.

9. $y = 6 - 2x - x^2$ **10.** $y = 2x^2 - 4x + 3$
11. $y = 12 - 12x + x^3$ **12.** $y = x^3 - 3x^2 + 2$
13. $y = -x^4$ **14.** $y = x^4 - 32x + 48$

For the following curves (15 through 18), find vertical tangents and sketch the curves.

15. $x = y^3 + 3y^2 + 3y + 2$ **16.** $x = y^3 + 3y^2 - 9y - 11$

17. $x = y^4 - 2y^2 + 2$ **18.** $x = y^2 + \dfrac{2}{y}$

19. Sketch a continuous curve $y = f(x)$ having the following characteristics:

$$f(-2) = 8, \qquad f'(2) = f'(-2) = 0,$$
$$f(0) = 4, \qquad f'(x) < 0 \quad \text{for} \quad |x| < 2,$$
$$f(2) = 0, \qquad f''(x) < 0 \quad \text{for} \quad x < 0,$$
$$f'(x) > 0 \quad \text{for} \quad |x| > 2, \qquad f''(x) > 0 \quad \text{for} \quad x > 0.$$

20. Sketch a continuous curve $y = f(x)$ having

$$f'(x) > 0 \quad \text{for} \quad x < 2, \qquad f'(x) < 0 \quad \text{for} \quad x > 2,$$

a) if $f'(x)$ is continuous at $x = 2$,
b) if $f'(x) \to 1$ as $x \to 2-$ and $f'(x) \to -1$ as $x \to 2+$,
c) if $f'(x) = 1$ for all $x < 2$ and $f'(x) = -1$ for all $x > 2$.

21. Sketch a continuous curve $y = f(x)$ for $x > 0$ if

$$f(1) = 0 \quad \text{and} \quad f'(x) = 1/x \quad \text{for all} \quad x > 0.$$

Is such a curve necessarily concave upward or concave downward?

22. Show that the sum of any positive real number and its reciprocal is at least 2.

23. Sketch the curve

$$y = 2x^3 + 2x^2 - 2x - 1$$

after locating its maximum, minimum, and inflection points. Then answer the following questions from your graph:

a) How many times and approximately where does the curve cross the x-axis?
b) How many times and approximately where would the curve cross the x-axis if $+3$ were added to all the y-values?
c) How many times and approximately where would the curve cross the x-axis if -3 were added to all the y-values?

24. Show that the curve

$$y = x + \sin x$$

has no maximum or minimum points even though it does have points where dy/dx is zero. Sketch the curve.

3–5 MAXIMA AND MINIMA. THEORY

A function f is said to have a relative, or local, *maximum* at $x = a$ if

$$f(a) \geq f(a + h)$$

for all positive and negative values of h sufficiently near zero. For a local *minimum* at $x = b$,

$$f(b) \leq f(b + h)$$

for values of h close to zero. The word *relative* or *local* is used to distinguish such a point from an *absolute* maximum or minimum that would occur if we could say, for example,

$$f(a) \geq f(x)$$

for all x and not just for all x close to a. The function

$$f(x) = x + \frac{1}{x}$$

(Fig. 3–15(b)) has a *relative* minimum at $x = 1$, because

$$x + \frac{1}{x} \geq 2$$

for all values of x close to 1. But certainly when x is negative, the inequality is no longer satisfied. Indeed, the function has a relative maximum at $x = -1$. It has no absolute maximum or absolute minimum.

Figure 3–16 shows the graph of a function $y = f(x)$ defined only for the domain $0 \leq x \leq L$. This function has a relative minimum at $x = c$ which is also an absolute minimum. It also has relative maxima at $x = 0$ and $x = L$, and an absolute maximum at $x = L$.

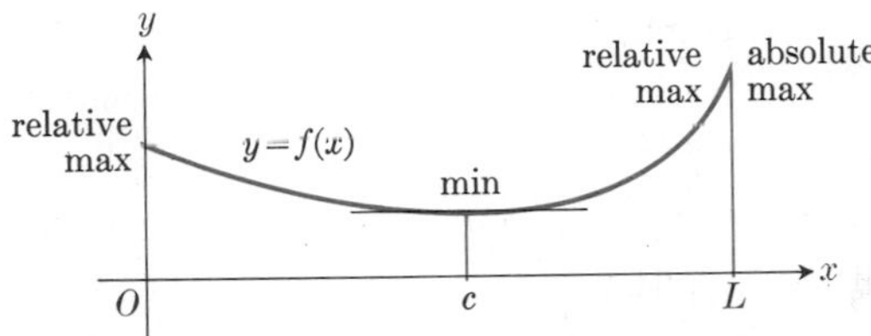

3–16 A relative maximum occurs at each endpoint. The one at $x = L$ is also the absolute maximum.

We have encountered relative maxima and minima in sketching curves and have observed that they occur at transition points between rising and falling portions of a curve. At such transition points we have also observed that dy/dx is usually zero, but may in exceptional cases become infinite (Fig. 3–10). We shall now prove the following theorem.

Theorem. *Let the function f be defined for $a \leq x \leq b$. Suppose that f has a relative maximum or minimum at an interior point $x = c$ of the interval (i.e., $a < c < b$). If the derivative $f'(x)$ exists as a finite number at $x = c$, then*

$$f'(c) = 0.$$

Proof. We shall give the proof for the case of a relative minimum at $x = c$; namely,

$$f(c) \leq f(c + h)$$

for all h close to zero (that is, when $c + h$ is close to c). By hypothesis,

$$f'(c) = \lim_{h \to 0} \frac{f(c + h) - f(c)}{h}$$

exists as a definite number which we want to prove is zero. In the ratio whose limit is $f'(c)$, when h is small, we have

$$\frac{f(c+h)-f(c)}{h} \geq 0 \qquad \text{if} \quad h>0$$

and

$$\frac{f(c+h)-f(c)}{h} \leq 0 \qquad \text{if} \quad h<0,$$

because in both cases the numerator either is positive or is zero. Hence if we let $h \to 0$ through positive values, we have

$$f'(c) \geq 0$$

from the first case; but if we let $h \to 0$ through negative values, we also have

$$f'(c) \leq 0$$

from the second case. Since the derivative is assumed to exist, we must have the same limit in both cases, so

$$0 \leq f'(c) \leq 0,$$

and the only way this can happen is to have

$$f'(c) = 0. \qquad \text{Q.E.D.}$$

The proof in case of a relative maximum at $x = c$ is similar.

CAUTION. Be careful not to read into the theorem more than it says. It says that $f' = 0$ at every interior point where f has a relative maximum or minimum and f' exists. It does not say what happens if a maximum or minimum occurs

a) at a point c where the derivative fails to exist, or
b) at an endpoint of the interval of definition of the function.

Neither does it say that the function necessarily does have a maximum or minimum at every place where the derivative is zero.

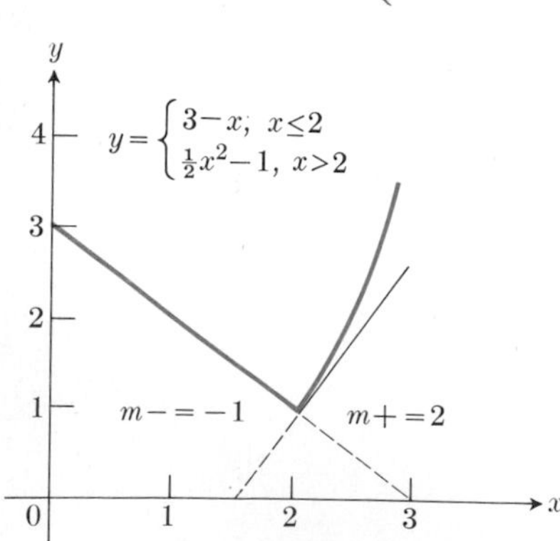

3–17 A function can have a minimum value at a point where its derivative does not exist. One way this can happen is shown in Fig. 3–10, where the tangent to the curve is vertical at $x = 0$. Another way is shown here, where the right and left tangents are different.

In Fig. 3–17, the graph represents the continuous function defined by

$$y = f(x) = \begin{cases} 3 - x & \text{for} \quad x \leq 2, \\ \frac{1}{2}x^2 - 1 & \text{for} \quad x > 2. \end{cases}$$

The slope is

$$\frac{dy}{dx} = \frac{d(3-x)}{dx} = -1 \quad \text{for} \quad x < 2,$$

$$\frac{dy}{dx} = \frac{d(\frac{1}{2}x^2 - 1)}{dx} = x \quad \text{for} \quad x > 2.$$

At the point $x = 2$, the lefthand tangent has slope $m- = -1$ and the righthand tangent has slope $m+ = 2$. Clearly, the curve is falling before $x = 2$ and rising after $x = 2$, and has a minimum at $x = 2$, $y = 1$. The derivative at $x = 2$ does not exist because $m+ \neq m-$. This shows that a minimum may occur where the derivative is not zero: where it doesn't even exist.

It is also easy to see from the proof of the theorem that when a maximum or minimum occurs at the *end* of a curve which exists only over a limited interval, the derivative need not vanish at such a point. For example, if the point $x = c$ is at the left end of such a curve, then in the limit in Eq. (2) it is not possible to take h to be negative, because $f(c + h)$ with h negative does not exist in this case. Strictly speaking, $f'(c)$ does not exist in these circumstances, although there may be a righthand tangent at one end of the curve and a lefthand tangent at the other end (Fig. 3–16).

The point (0, 0) on the curve $y = x^3$ is an example of a point where a curve has zero slope without having either a maximum or a minimum there.

It is customary to refer to a point on a curve $y = f(x)$ at which $f'(x) = 0$ as a *stationary point* on the curve. Values of x that satisfy the equation $f'(x) = 0$ are also called *critical values*. In other words, a critical value of x is a value at which the curve $y = f(x)$ has a stationary point.

Conclusion. If f is continuous on the closed interval $a \leq x \leq b$, then Theorem 3 of Article 2–11 tells us that f has both a maximum and a minimum value somewhere on the interval. The theorem of this article now tells us where to look for them. Every point where f has a maximum or a minimum must be one of the following:

1. an endpoint of the interval, or
2. a point where f' does not exist, or
3. an interior point where $f' = 0$.

We need to investigate only these three classes of points to find the extreme values of f. The next article shows how we do this.

3–6 MAXIMA AND MINIMA. PROBLEMS

The differential calculus is a powerful tool for solving problems that call for minimizing or maximizing a function. We shall illustrate how this is done in several instances, and then summarize the technique in a list of specific rules.

EXAMPLE 1. Find two positive numbers whose sum is 20 and whose product is as large as possible.

Solution. If one of the numbers is x, then the other is $(20 - x)$, and their product is

$$y = x(20 - x) = 20x - x^2.$$

Therefore,

$$\frac{dy}{dx} = 20 - 2x = 2(10 - x),$$

which is

positive	when $x < 10$,
negative	when $x > 10$,
zero	when $x = 10$.

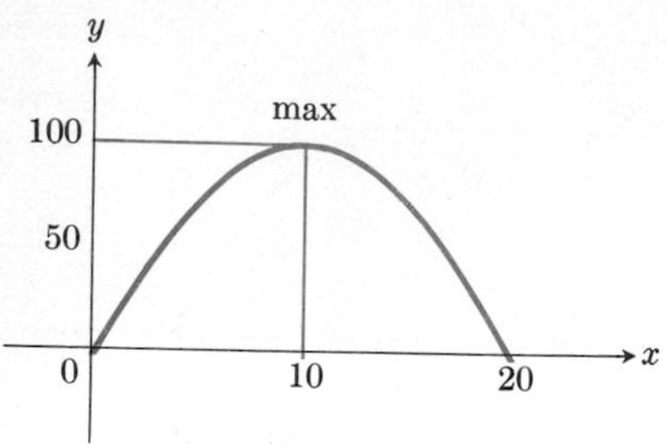

3–18(a) The product $y = x(20 - x)$ reaches a maximum value of 100 when $x = 10$.

Furthermore,

$$\frac{d^2y}{dx^2} = -2$$

is always negative. Thus the graph of y is concave downward at every point. Therefore, y has an absolute maximum at $x = 10$. The two numbers are $x = 10$ and $20 - x = 10$. (See Fig. 3–18a.)

With the same mathematical analysis that we used in Example 1, we can study the rate of the chemical reaction in the next example.

EXAMPLE 2. *Autocatalytic reactions.* A catalyst for a chemical reaction is a substance that controls the rate of the reaction without undergoing any permanent change in itself. An autocatalytic reaction is one whose product is a catalyst for its own formation. Such a reaction may proceed slowly at first if the amount of catalyst present is small, and slowly again at the end when most of the original substance is used up. But in between, when both the substance and its product are abundant, the reaction may proceed at a faster rate.

In some cases it is reasonable to assume that the rate v of the reaction is proportional both to the amount of the original substance present and to the amount of product. That is,

$$v = kx(a - x) = kax - kx^2, \tag{1}$$

where

$x =$ the amount of product,

$a =$ the amount of substance at the beginning,

$k =$ a positive constant.

At what value of x does the rate v have a maximum? What is the maximum value of v?

Solution. From Eq. (1) we find that

$$\frac{dv}{dx} = ka - 2kx = k(a - 2x),$$

which is

$$\text{positive} \quad \text{when } x < \frac{a}{2},$$

$$\text{negative} \quad \text{when } x > \frac{a}{2},$$

$$\text{zero} \quad \text{when } x = \frac{a}{2}.$$

Furthermore,

$$\frac{d^2v}{dx^2} = -2k$$

is always negative, because k is positive. Thus the graph of v is concave downward at every point. Therefore, v has a maximum value at $x = a/2$, that is, when the original substance is half used up. When $x = a/2$,

$$v = k\frac{a}{2}\left(\frac{a}{2}\right) = \frac{ka^2}{4}.$$

Note that the value $x = a/2$ does not depend on the rate constant k. (A graph of v appears in Fig. 3–18b.)

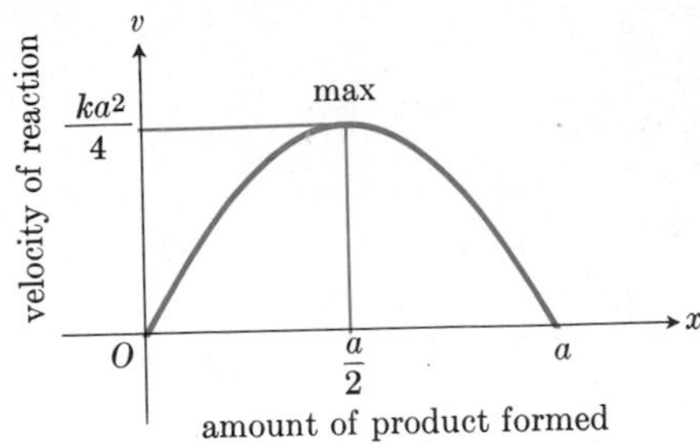

3–18(b) The chemical reaction modeled in Example 2 runs at its fastest ($v = ka^2/4$) when half of the product is formed ($x = a/2$).

EXAMPLE 3. A square sheet of tin a inches on a side is to be used to make an open-top box by cutting a small square of tin from each corner and bending up the sides. How large a square should be cut from each corner in order that the box shall have as large a volume as possible?

Solution. We first draw a figure to illustrate the problem (Fig. 3–19). In the figure, the side of the square cut from each corner is taken to be x inches and the volume of the box in cubic inches is then given by

$$y = x(a - 2x)^2, \qquad 0 \le x \le a/2. \tag{2}$$

The restrictions placed on x in (2) are clearly those imposed by the fact that one can neither cut a negative amount of material from a corner, nor can one cut away an amount which is more than the total amount present. It is also evident that $y = 0$ when $x = 0$ or when $x = a/2$, so that the maximum volume y must occur at some value of x between 0 and $a/2$. The function in (2) possesses a derivative at every such point, and hence

when y is a maximum, dy/dx must be zero.

From (2), we find

$$y = a^2x - 4ax^2 + 4x^3,$$
$$\frac{dy}{dx} = a^2 - 8ax + 12x^2$$
$$= (a - 2x)(a - 6x),$$

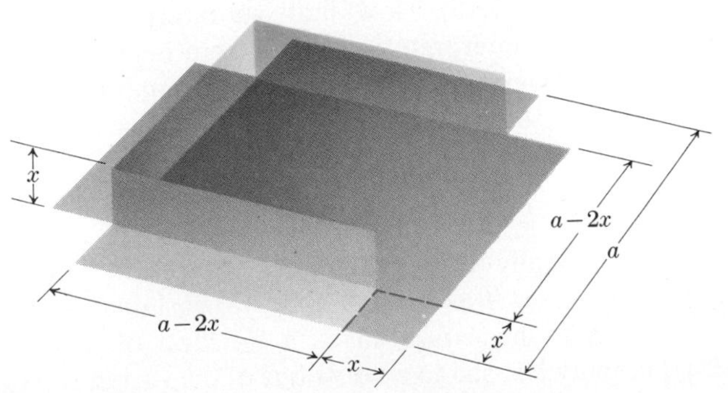

3–19 To make an open box, squares are cut from the corners of a square sheet of tin and the sides are bent up. What value of x gives the largest volume?

so that

$$\frac{dy}{dx} = 0 \qquad \text{when} \quad x = \frac{a}{2} \quad \text{or} \quad \frac{a}{6}.$$

We gain additional information about the shape of the curve representing (2) from

$$\frac{d^2y}{dx^2} = 24x - 8a = 24\left(x - \frac{a}{3}\right),$$

which shows that the curve is

$$\text{concave downward} \quad \text{for } x < \frac{a}{3},$$

$$\text{concave upward} \quad \text{for } x > \frac{a}{3}.$$

In particular,

$$\begin{aligned} &\text{at} \quad x = \frac{a}{6}: \quad \frac{dy}{dx} = 0, \quad \frac{d^2y}{dx^2} = -4a, \\ &\text{at} \quad x = \frac{a}{2}: \quad \frac{dy}{dx} = 0, \quad \frac{d^2y}{dx^2} = +4a. \end{aligned} \tag{3}$$

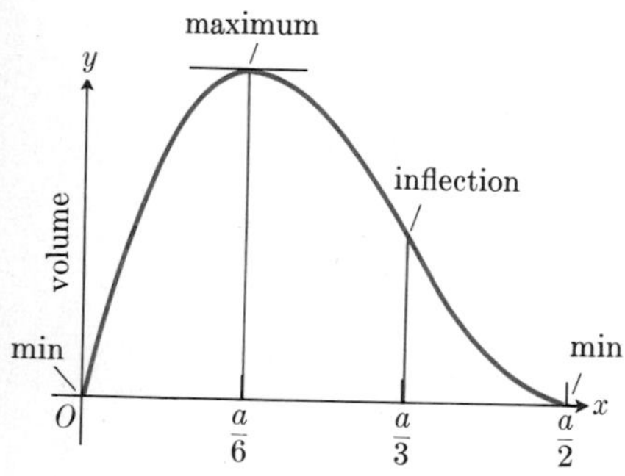

3–20 The volume of the box in Fig. 3–19 graphed as a function of x.

From (3) we see that if we were to draw the graph of the curve (2) it would "spill water" at $x = (a/6)$ and this is the only point between $x = 0$ and $x = (a/2)$ where a relative maximum of the volume y may occur (Fig. 3–20). Each corner square should thus have dimensions $a/6$ by $a/6$ to produce a box of maximum volume.

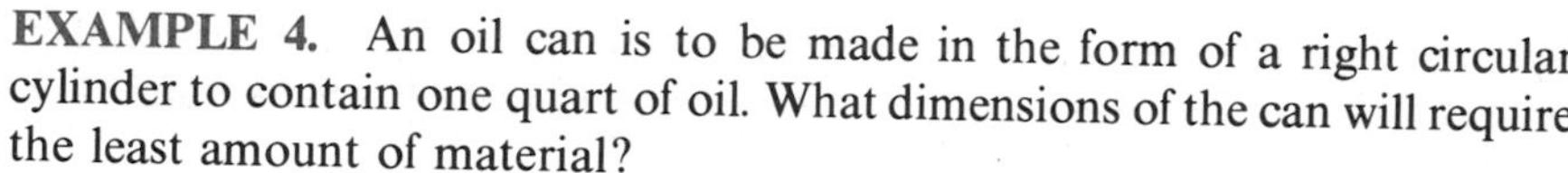

EXAMPLE 4. An oil can is to be made in the form of a right circular cylinder to contain one quart of oil. What dimensions of the can will require the least amount of material?

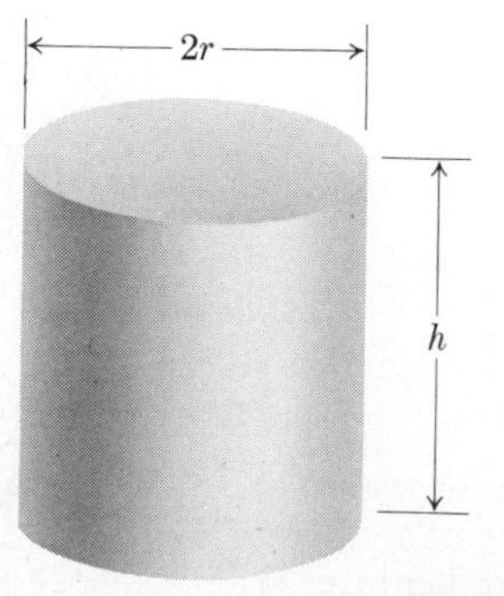

3–21 This one-quart can can be made from the least material when $h = 2r$.

Solution. Again we start with a figure (Fig. 3–21). Clearly, the requirement that the can hold a quart of oil is the same as

$$V = \pi r^2 h = a^3, \tag{4a}$$

if the radius r and altitude h are in inches and a^3 is the number of cubic inches in a quart ($a^3 = 57.75$). How shall we interpret the phrase "least material"? A reasonable interpretation arises from neglecting the thickness of the material and the waste due to the manufacturing process. Then we ask for dimensions r and h that make the total surface area

$$A = 2\pi r^2 + 2\pi rh \tag{4b}$$

as small as possible while still satisfying (4a).

We are not quite ready to apply the methods used in Examples 1 and 2, because Eq. (4b) expresses A as a function of *two* variables, r and h, and our methods call for A to be expressed as a function of just *one* variable. However, Eq. (4a) may be used to express one of the variables r or h in terms of the other; in fact, we find

$$h = \frac{a^3}{\pi r^2} \tag{4c}$$

or

$$r = \sqrt{\frac{a^3}{\pi h}}. \tag{4d}$$

The division in (4c) and (4d) is legitimate because neither r nor h can be zero, and only the positive square root is used in (4d) because the radius r can never be negative. If we substitute from (4c) into (4b), we have

$$A = 2\pi r^2 + \frac{2a^3}{r}, \qquad 0 < r < \infty, \tag{4e}$$

and now we may apply our previous methods. A minimum of A can occur only at a point where

$$\frac{dA}{dr} = 4\pi r - 2a^3 r^{-2} \tag{4f}$$

is zero, that is, where

$$4\pi r = \frac{2a^3}{r^2}, \qquad r = \frac{a}{\sqrt[3]{2\pi}}. \tag{4g}$$

At such a value of r, we shall have

$$\frac{d^2A}{dr^2} = 4\pi + 4a^3 r^{-3} = 12\pi > 0,$$

so the curve representing A as a function of r has $dA/dr = 0$ and d^2A/dr^2 positive ("holds water") at $r = a/\sqrt[3]{2\pi}$, which must therefore produce a relative minimum. Since the second derivative is *always positive* for $0 < r < \infty$, the curve is concave upward everywhere, and there can be no other relative minimum, so we have also found the absolute minimum. From (4g) and (4c), we find

$$r = \frac{a}{\sqrt[3]{2\pi}} = \sqrt[3]{\frac{V}{2\pi}}, \qquad h = \frac{2a}{\sqrt[3]{2\pi}} = 2\sqrt[3]{\frac{V}{2\pi}}$$

as the dimensions of the can of volume V having minimum surface area. Note that the height of the can is equal to its diameter. Figure 3–22 shows a curve representing A as a function of r as given by (4e).

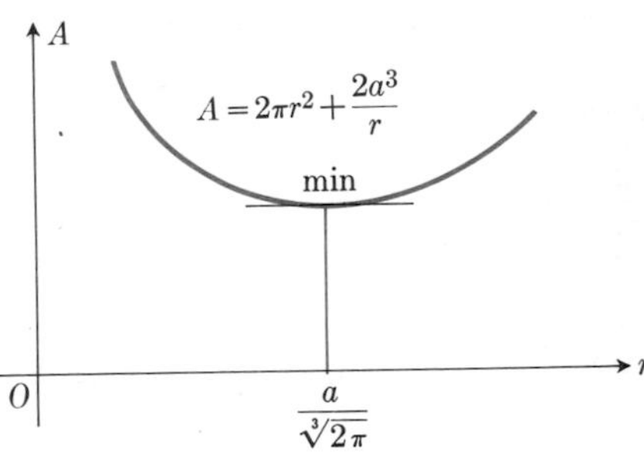

3–22 A graph of $A = 2\pi r^2 + (2a^3/r)$.

Some problems about maxima and minima have no solution. The next example discusses one such problem.

EXAMPLE 5. A wire of length L is to be cut into two pieces, one of which is bent to form a circle and the other to form a square. How should the wire be cut if the sum of the areas enclosed by the two pieces is to be a maximum?

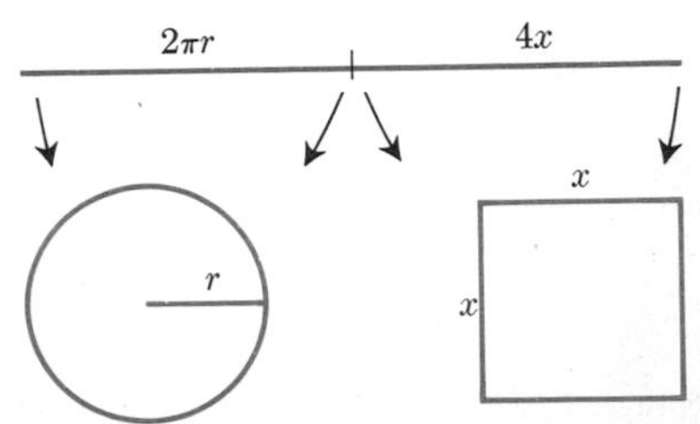

3–23 A circle and a square made from a wire $2\pi r + 4x$ units long. How large an area can they enclose together?

In the notation of Fig. 3–23, the sum of the areas is

$$A = \pi r^2 + x^2, \tag{5a}$$

where r and x must satisfy the equation

$$L = 2\pi r + 4x. \tag{5b}$$

We could solve (5b) for x in terms of r, but instead we shall differentiate both (5a) and (5b), treating A and x as functions of r for $0 \le 2\pi r \le L$. Then

$$\frac{dA}{dr} = 2\pi r + 2x\frac{dx}{dr}, \tag{5c}$$

and

$$\frac{dL}{dr} = 2\pi + 4\frac{dx}{dr} = 0, \qquad \frac{dx}{dr} = -\frac{\pi}{2}, \tag{5d}$$

where dL/dr is zero because L is a constant. If we substitute dx/dr from (5d) into (5c), we get

$$\frac{dA}{dr} = \pi(2r - x) \tag{5e}$$

and, for future reference, we note that

$$\frac{d^2A}{dr^2} = \pi\left(2 - \frac{dx}{dr}\right) = \pi\left(2 + \frac{\pi}{2}\right) \tag{5f}$$

is a positive constant, so that the curve which represents A as a function of r is always concave upward (Fig. 3–24).

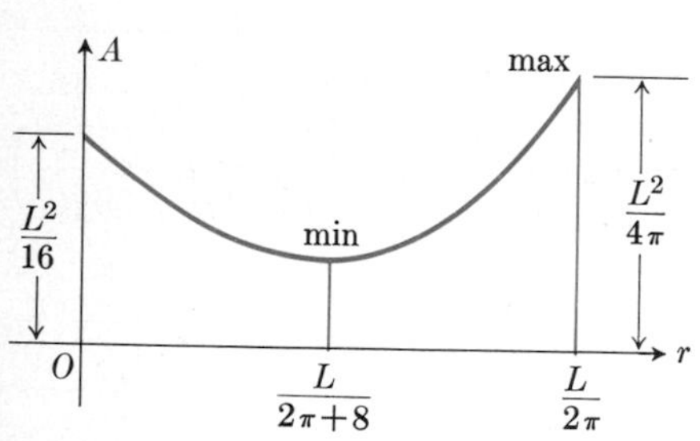

3–24 The sum of the areas in Fig. 3–23 graphed as a function of r.

Now

$$\frac{dA}{dr} = 0 \quad \text{when} \quad x = 2r,$$

and when we substitute $x = 2r$ into (5b),

$$L = 2\pi r + 4(2r) = (2\pi + 8)r,$$

we have

$$\frac{dA}{dr} = 0 \quad \text{when} \quad r = \frac{L}{2\pi + 8}, \quad x = \frac{L}{\pi + 4}.$$

But the fact that the second derivative is positive means that this value of r gives a *minimum* for A. The problem asks for the *maximum* of A.

Since r is limited to

$$0 \le r \le \frac{L}{2\pi},$$

we examine the values of A at the ends of this interval. When

$$r = 0: \qquad x = \frac{L}{4}, \quad A = \tfrac{1}{16}L^2,$$

and when

$$r = \frac{L}{2\pi}: \qquad x = 0, \quad A = \frac{1}{4\pi}L^2.$$

At the minimum,

$$r = \frac{1}{2}\frac{L}{\pi + 4}, \qquad x = \frac{L}{\pi + 4}, \qquad A = \frac{1}{4\pi + 16}L^2.$$

Using these values to make a rough sketch of A as a function of r (Fig. 3–24), we can readily see that the maximum value of A occurs when $r = L/2\pi$, which means that the wire should not be cut at all, but all of it should be bent into the circle for maximum total area. Or, if we adopt the point of view that the wire *must* be cut, then there is no answer to the problem. For no matter how little of it is used for the square, we could always get a larger total area by using still less of it for the square.

EXAMPLE 6. *Snell's law.* Fermat's principle in optics states that light travels from a point A to a point B along that path for which the time of travel is a minimum. Let us find the path that a ray of light will follow in going from a point A in a medium where the velocity of light is c_1 to a point B in a second medium where the velocity of light is c_2, when both points lie in the xy-plane and the x-axis separates the two media, as shown in Fig. 3–25.

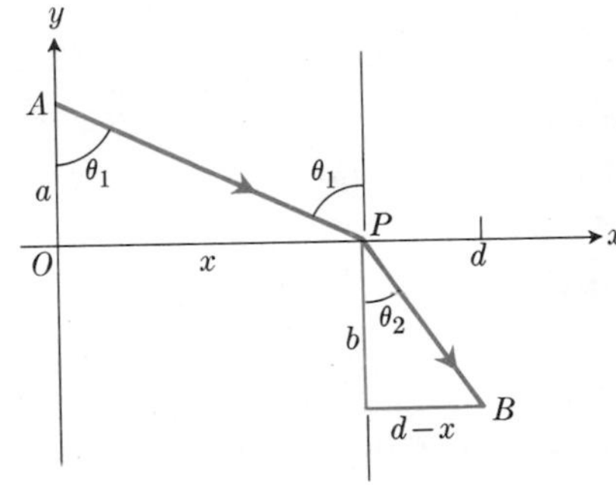

3–25 A light ray is refracted (deflected from its path) when it passes from one medium to another. θ_1 is the angle of incidence. θ_2 is the angle of refraction.

Solution. In either medium, where the velocity of light remains constant, the light ray will follow a straight path, since then "shortest time" and "shortest distance" amount to the same thing. Hence the path will consist of a straight line segment from A to P in the first medium and another line segment PB in the second medium. The time required for the light to travel from A to P is

$$t_1 = \frac{\sqrt{a^2 + x^2}}{c_1},$$

and from P to B the time required is

$$t_2 = \frac{\sqrt{b^2 + (d - x)^2}}{c_2}.$$

We therefore seek to minimize

$$t = t_1 + t_2 = \frac{\sqrt{a^2 + x^2}}{c_1} + \frac{\sqrt{b^2 + (d - x)^2}}{c_2}. \tag{6a}$$

We find

$$\frac{dt}{dx} = \frac{x}{c_1\sqrt{a^2 + x^2}} - \frac{(d - x)}{c_2\sqrt{b^2 + (d - x)^2}} \tag{6b}$$

or

$$\frac{dt}{dx} = \frac{\sin \theta_1}{c_1} - \frac{\sin \theta_2}{c_2}, \tag{6c}$$

if we make use of the angles θ_1 and θ_2 in the figure.

If we restrict x to the interval $0 \le x \le d$, then t has a negative derivative at $x = 0$ and a positive derivative at $x = d$, while at the value of x, say x_c, for which

$$\frac{\sin \theta_1}{c_1} = \frac{\sin \theta_2}{c_2}, \tag{6d}$$

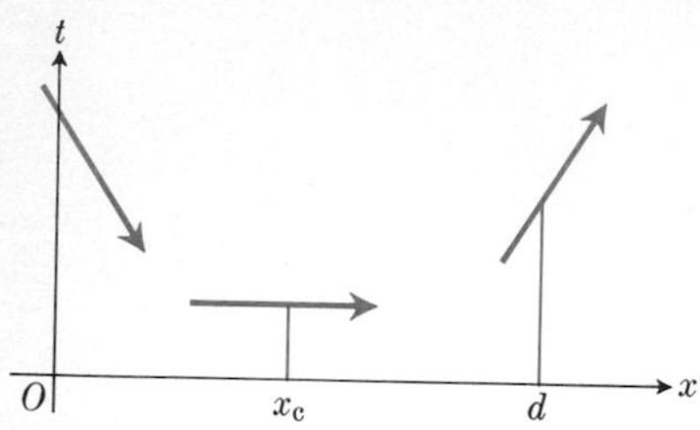

3–26 These tangents to the graph of Eq. (6a) suggest that t has a minimum at $x = x_c$.

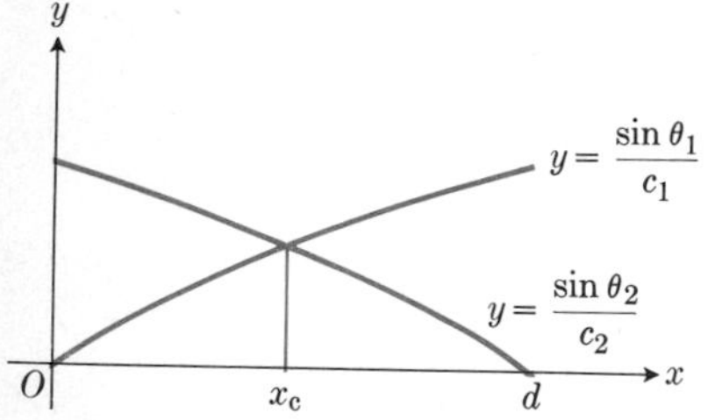

3–27 At $x = x_c$, $(\sin\theta_1)/c_1 = (\sin\theta_2)/c_2$.

dt/dx is zero. Figure 3–26 indicates the directions of the tangents to the curve giving t as a function of x, at these three points, and suggests that t will indeed be a minimum at $x = x_c$. If we want further information on this point, by referring to Fig. 3–25 we see that a decrease in x will cause P to move to the left, making θ_1 smaller, and hence also $\sin\theta_1$ smaller, but will have the opposite effect on θ_2 and $\sin\theta_2$. Figure 3–27 shows that since $(\sin\theta_1)/c_1$ is an increasing function of x which is zero at $x = 0$, while $(\sin\theta_2)/c_2$ is a decreasing function of x which is zero at $x = d$, the two curves can cross at only one point, $x = x_c$, between 0 and d. To the right of x_c, the curve for $(\sin\theta_1)/c_1$ is above the curve for $(\sin\theta_2)/c_2$, but these roles are reversed to the left of x_c, so that

$$\frac{dt}{dx} = \frac{\sin\theta_1}{c_1} - \frac{\sin\theta_2}{c_2} \begin{cases} \text{is negative for } x < x_c, \\ \text{is zero for } x = x_c, \\ \text{is positive for } x > x_c, \end{cases}$$

and the minimum of t does indeed occur at $x = x_c$.

Instead of determining this value of x explicitly, it is customary to characterize the path followed by the ray of light by leaving the equation for $dt/dx = 0$ in the form (6d), which is known as the *law of refraction* or Snell's law. [See Sears, Zemansky, Young, *University Physics*, Fifth edition (1976), Chap. 38.]

REMARK. The following argument can be applied to many problems in which we are trying to find an extreme value, say a maximum, of a function. Suppose that we know that:

1. We can restrict our search to a closed interval I;
2. The function is continuous and differentiable everywhere (we might know this from a formula for the function, or from physical considerations); and
3. The function does not attain a maximum at either endpoint of I.

Then we know that the function has at least one maximum at an interior point of I, at which the derivative must be zero. Therefore, if we find that the derivative of the function is zero at only one interior point of I, then this point is where the function takes on its maximum. A similar argument applies to a search for a minimum value.

EXAMPLE 7. A manufacturing company can sell x items per week at a price $P = 200 - 0.01x$ cents, and it costs $y = 50x + 20{,}000$ cents to make x items. What is the most profitable number to make?

Solution. The total weekly revenue from x items is

$$xP = 200x - 0.01x^2.$$

The profit T is revenue minus cost:

$$T = xP - y = (200x - 0.01x^2) - (50x + 20{,}000)$$
$$= 150x - 0.01x^2 - 20{,}000.$$

For very large values of x, say beyond a million, T is negative. Therefore, T takes on its maximum value somewhere in the interval $0 \le x \le 10^6$. The

STRATEGY FOR FINDING MAXIMA AND MINIMA

First. When possible, draw a figure to illustrate the problem and label those parts that are important in the problem. Constants and variables should be clearly distinguished.

Second. Write an equation for the quantity that is to be a maximum or a minimum. If this quantity is denoted by y, it is desirable to express it in terms of a single independent variable x. This may require some algebraic manipulation to make use of auxiliary conditions of the problem.

Third. If $y = f(x)$ is the quantity to be a maximum or a minimum, find those values of x for which

$$\frac{dy}{dx} = f'(x) = 0.$$

Fourth. Test each value of x for which $f'(x) = 0$ to determine whether it provides a maximum or minimum or neither. The usual tests are:

a) If $\frac{d^2y}{dx^2}$ is positive when $\frac{dy}{dx} = 0$, y is a minimum.

If $\frac{d^2y}{dx^2}$ is negative when $\frac{dy}{dx} = 0$, y is a maximum.

If $\frac{d^2y}{dx^2} = 0$ when $\frac{dy}{dx} = 0$, the test fails.

b) If

$$\frac{dy}{dx} \text{ is } \begin{cases} \text{positive for } x < x_c, \\ \text{zero for } x = x_c, \\ \text{negative for } x > x_c, \end{cases}$$

then a maximum occurs at x_c. But if dy/dx changes from negative to zero to positive as x advances through x_c, there is a minimum. If dy/dx does not change its sign, neither a maximum nor a minimum need occur.

Fifth. If the derivative fails to exist at some point, examine this point as possible maximum or minimum. (See Fig. 3–17.)

Sixth. If the function $y = f(x)$ is defined for only a limited range of values $a \leq x \leq b$, examine $x = a$ and $x = b$ for possible extreme values of y. (See Fig. 3–24.)

formula for T shows that T is differentiable at every x, and obviously T does not take on its maximum at either endpoint, 0 or 10^6. The derivative

$$\frac{dT}{dx} = 150 - 0.02x$$

is zero only when

$$x = 7500.$$

Therefore, $x = 7500$ is the production level for maximum profit.

To solve the problem in Example 7 it would have been as effective to calculate the second derivative $d^2T/dx^2 = -0.02$ and conclude that T has a relative maximum at $x = 7500$. A quick look at the domain of x or the graph of T is all that would then be needed to show that the maximum was absolute. The virtue of the argument that we gave instead is that it can apply to a function whose second derivative is nonexistent or difficult to compute.

As a last example, we derive the order-quantity formula of Example 24 in Article 1–6.

EXAMPLE 8. *Economic Order Quantity* (continued from Article 1–6). As described in Article 1–6, the most economical quantity of merchandise for a retailer to order when supplies run low is

$$Q = \sqrt{\frac{2KM}{h}},$$

where K is the setup cost (fixed cost of placing an order), M is the number of items sold each week (assumed to be a constant), and h is the weekly holding cost for each item. This quantity, it was said, strikes an economical balance between the costs of ordering and holding inventory. To see why this is so, we first derive a formula for the average cost per week of ordering, paying for, and holding merchandise. We then find a value of Q that minimizes this average cost.

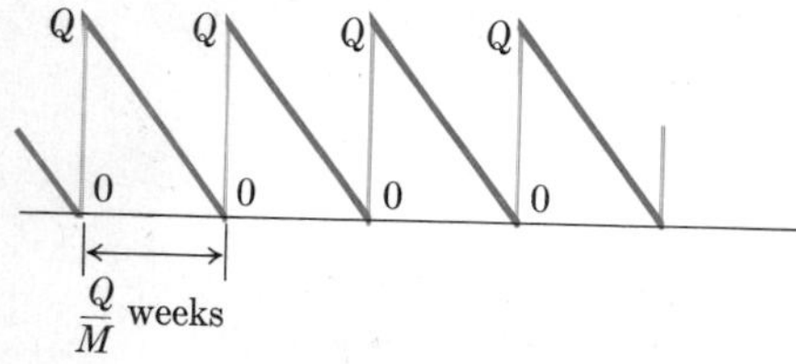

3–28 Graph of a store's inventory level. M is the weekly demand. Q is the quantity reordered.

We assume that we reorder the same number Q of items each time, and that the supply arrives just when the inventory level at the store falls to zero. Thus, a newly arrived quantity Q takes Q/M weeks to deplete, and the graph of the number of items on hand looks like Fig. 3–28. The average cost per week of carrying the merchandise in question is the sum of three quantities:

1. $K(M/Q)$, the average setup cost per week (the setup cost K divided by the number of weeks Q/M);

2. cM, the average purchase cost per week (c is the purchase cost of one item);

3. $h(Q/2)$, the average holding cost per week ($Q/2$ is the average level of inventory, as you can see from Fig. 3–28).

Thus the average cost per week is given by the formula

$$A(Q) = \frac{KM}{Q} + cM + \frac{hQ}{2}.$$

What values of Q, if any, minimize $A(Q)$?

We find that

$$\frac{dA}{dQ} = -\frac{KM}{Q^2} + \frac{h}{2},$$

which equals zero when

$$Q = \sqrt{\frac{2KM}{h}}.$$

(The negative square root is not a possible value for Q.) The second derivative,

$$\frac{d^2A}{dQ^2} = \frac{2KM}{Q^3},$$

is positive, so that A has a relative minimum at $Q = \sqrt{2KM/h}$. There are no endpoints to worry about because A is defined for all $Q > 0$, and A is differentiable for all $Q > 0$. Hence the minimum is absolute. Incidentally, the graph of A is like the right branch of the graph of $y = x + (1/x)$ in Fig. 3–15.

PROBLEMS

1. Show that the rectangle that has maximum area for a given perimeter is a square.

2. Find the dimensions of the rectangle of greatest area that can be inscribed in a semicircle of radius r.

3. Find the area of the largest rectangle with lower base on the x-axis and upper vertices on the curve $y = 12 - x^2$.

4. An open rectangular box is to be made from a piece of cardboard 8 in. wide and 15 in. long by cutting a square from each corner and bending up the sides. Find the dimensions of the box of largest volume.

5. One side of an open field is bounded by a straight river. How would you put a fence around the other three sides of a rectangular plot in order to enclose as great an area as possible with a given length of fence?

6. An open storage bin with square base and vertical sides is to be constructed from a given amount of material. Determine its dimensions if its volume is a maximum. Neglect the thickness of the material and waste in construction.

7. A box with square base and open top is to hold 32 in^3. Find the dimensions that require the least amount of material. Neglect the thickness of the material and waste in construction.

8. A variable line through the point (1, 2) intersects the x-axis at $A(a, 0)$ and the y-axis at $B(0, b)$. Find the area of the triangle AOB of least area if both a and b are positive.

9. A poster is to contain 50 in^2 of printed matter with margins of 4 in. each at top and bottom and 2 in. at each side. Find the overall dimensions if the total area of the poster is a minimum.

10. A right triangle of given hypotenuse is rotated about one of its legs to generate a right circular cone. Find the cone of greatest volume.

11. It costs a manufacturer c dollars each to manufacture and distribute a certain item. If the items sell at x dollars each, the number sold is given by $n = a/(x - c) + b(100 - x)$, where a and b are certain positive constants. What selling price will bring a maximum profit?

12. A cantilever beam of length L has one end built into a wall, while the other end is simply supported. If the beam weighs w lb per unit length, its deflection y at distance x from the built-in end satisfies the equation

$$48EIy = w(2x^4 - 5Lx^3 + 3L^2x^2),$$

where E and I are constants depending upon the material of the beam and the shape of its cross section. How far from the built-in end does the maximum deflection occur?

13. Determine the constant a in order that the function

$$f(x) = x^2 + \frac{a}{x}$$

may have (a) a relative minimum at $x = 2$, (b) a relative minimum at $x = -3$, (c) a point of inflection at $x = 1$. (d) Show that the function cannot have a relative maximum for any value of a.

14. Determine the constants a and b in order that the function

$$f(x) = x^3 + ax^2 + bx + c$$

may have (a) a relative maximum at $x = -1$ and a relative minimum at $x = 3$, (b) a relative minimum at $x = 4$ and a point of inflection at $x = 1$.

15. A wire of length L is cut into two pieces, one being bent to form a square and the other to form an equilateral triangle. How should the wire be cut (a) if the sum of the two areas is a minimum, (b) if the sum of the areas is a maximum?

16. Find the points on the curve $5x^2 - 6xy + 5y^2 = 4$ that are nearest the origin.

17. Find the point on the curve $y = \sqrt{x}$ nearest the point $(c, 0)$, (a) if $c \geq \frac{1}{2}$, (b) if $c < \frac{1}{2}$.

18. Find the volume of the largest right circular cone that can be inscribed in a sphere of radius r.

19. Find the volume of the largest right circular cylinder that can be inscribed in a sphere of radius r.

20. Show that the volume of the largest right circular cylinder that can be inscribed in a given right circular cone is $\frac{4}{9}$ the volume of the cone.

21. The strength of a rectangular beam is proportional to the product of its width and the square of its depth. Find the dimensions of the strongest beam that can be cut from a circular cylindrical log of radius r.

22. The stiffness of a rectangular beam is proportional to the product of its breadth and the cube of its depth. Find the stiffest beam that can be cut from a log of given diameter.

23. The intensity of illumination at any point is proportional to the product of the strength of the light source and the inverse of the square of the distance from the source. If two sources of relative strengths a and b are a distance c apart, at what point on the line joining them will the intensity be a minimum? Assume the intensity at any point is the sum of intensities from the two sources.

24. A window is in the form of a rectangle surmounted by a semicircle. If the rectangle is of clear glass while the semicircle is of colored glass which transmits only half as much light per square foot as clear glass does, and the total perimeter is fixed, find the proportions of the window that will admit the most light.

25. Right circular cylindrical tin cans are to be manufactured to contain a given volume. There is no waste involved in cutting the tin that goes into the vertical sides of the can, but each end piece is to be cut from a square and the corners of the square wasted. Find the ratio of height to diameter for the most economical cans.

26. A silo is to be made in the form of a cylinder surmounted by a hemisphere. The cost of construction per square foot of surface area is twice as great for the hemisphere as for the cylinder. Determine the dimensions to be used if the volume is fixed and the cost of construction is to be a minimum. Neglect the thickness of the silo and waste in construction.

27. If the sum of the areas of a cube and a sphere is constant, what is the ratio of an edge of the cube to the diameter of the sphere when (a) the sum of their volumes is a minimum, (b) the sum of their volumes is a maximum?

* 28. Two towns, located on the same side of a straight river, agree to construct a pumping station and filtering plant at the river's edge, to be used jointly to supply the towns with water. If the distances of the two towns from the river are a and b and the distance between them is c, show that the sum of the lengths of the pipe lines joining them to the pumping station is at least as great as $\sqrt{c^2 + 4ab}$.

* 29. Light from a source A is reflected to a point B by a plane mirror. If the time required for the light to travel from A to the mirror and then to B is a minimum, show that the angle of incidence is equal to the angle of reflection.

30. Show that a manufacturer's profit is maximized (or minimized) at a level of production where the marginal revenue equals the marginal cost.

31. Suppose the government imposes a tax of ten cents, for each item sold, on the product of Example 7, but other features are unchanged. To maximize the company's profits, how much of the tax should the company absorb and how much should be passed on to the customer? Why? Compare the profits before and after the tax.

32. Shipping costs are likely to depend on order size, and it might be more realistic in modeling the inventory problem of Example 8 to assume that the setup cost is not a constant. Suppose instead that the setup cost is $K + pQ$, the sum of a constant and a multiple of Q. What is the most economical quantity to order now?

33. The reaction of the body to a drug is sometimes represented by the function

$$R(D) = D^2\left(\frac{C}{2} - \frac{D}{3}\right),$$

where $C =$ the maximum amount of the drug that could be given, $D =$ the amount given $(0 \leq D \leq C)$, and $R =$ a measure of the strength of the reaction (e.g., blood pressure measured in millimeters of mercury). The derivative $R'(D)$ is used as a measure of the sensitivity of the body to the drug. At the point where $R'(D)$ has a maximum, there is the greatest change in R for a small change in D. Show that this point is $D = C/2$, and that

$$R(C) = 2R\left(\frac{C}{2}\right).$$

[From *Some Mathematical Models in Biology*, p. 221.]

---

* You may prefer to do these problems without calculus.

34. When we cough, the trachea (windpipe) can be observed to contract in a way that increases the velocity of the air going out. This naturally raises the questions of how much it should contract to maximize the velocity, and whether it really contracts that much. Under reasonable assumptions about the elasticity of the tracheal wall, and about how the air flow is slowed near the wall by friction, the overall flow velocity v can be modeled by the equation

$$v = c(r - r_0)r^2 \ \frac{\text{cm}}{\text{sec}}, \qquad \frac{r_0}{2} \le r \le r_0,$$

where r_0 is the rest radius of the trachea in centimeters, and $c < 0$ is a constant that depends on the length of the trachea.

Show that v has a maximum when $r = \frac{2}{3}r_0$, that is, when the trachea is about 33 percent contracted. The remarkable fact is that x-ray photographs confirm that the trachea contracts just about this much during a cough. (For more information, see *The Human Cough*, Philip Tuchinsky, UMAP Project, Education Development Center, Newton, MA, 1978.)

35. Find all maxima and minima of $y = \sin x + \cos x$. Sketch.

3–7 ROLLE'S THEOREM

There is strong geometrical evidence to support the belief that between two points where a smooth curve $y = f(x)$ crosses the x-axis there must be at least one point where it has a horizontal tangent (Fig. 3–29a). But such is not the case if the curve has a corner, as in Fig. 3–29(b), where the derivative fails to exist. More precisely, we have the following theorem.

Rolle's Theorem.* *Let the function f be defined and continuous on the closed interval $a \le x \le b$ and differentiable in the open interval $a < x < b$. Furthermore, let*

$$f(a) = f(b) = 0.$$

Then there is at least one number c between a and b where $f'(x)$ is zero; i.e.,

$$f'(c) = 0 \qquad \text{for some } c, \qquad a < c < b.$$

Proof. Either $f(x)$ is identically equal to zero for all x, $a \le x \le b$, or else $f(x)$ is different from zero for some values of x in this interval. In the former case, $f'(x)$ is also identically zero and the theorem is true for this case.

But if $f(x)$ is not zero everywhere between a and b, then either it is positive some place, or negative some place, or both. In any case, the function will then have a maximum positive value or a minimum negative value, or both. That is, it has an extreme value at a point c where $f(c)$ is negative (in the case of a minimum) or $f(c)$ is positive (in the case of a maximum). In either case, c is neither a nor b, since

$$f(a) = f(b) = 0, \qquad f(c) \ne 0.$$

Therefore c is between a and b and the theorem of Article 3–5 applies, showing that the derivative must be zero at $x = c$:

$$f'(c) = 0 \qquad \text{for some } c, \qquad a < c < b. \qquad \text{Q.E.D.}$$

There may be more than one place between a and b where the derivative is zero. In Fig. 3–29(a), for example, dy/dx is zero at c_1 and at c_2 and they both lie between $a = -2$ and $b = +2$.

a)

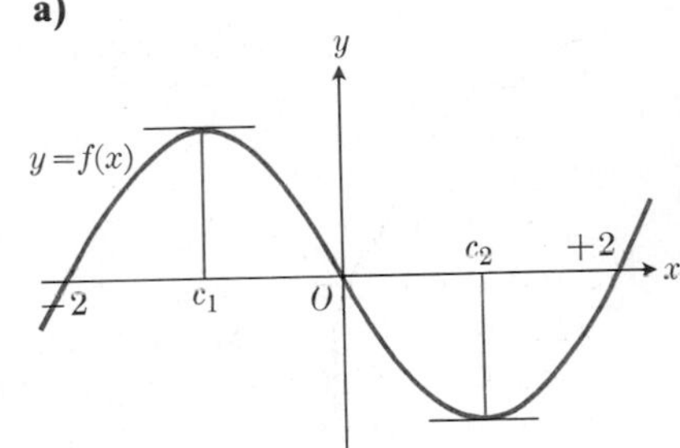

b)

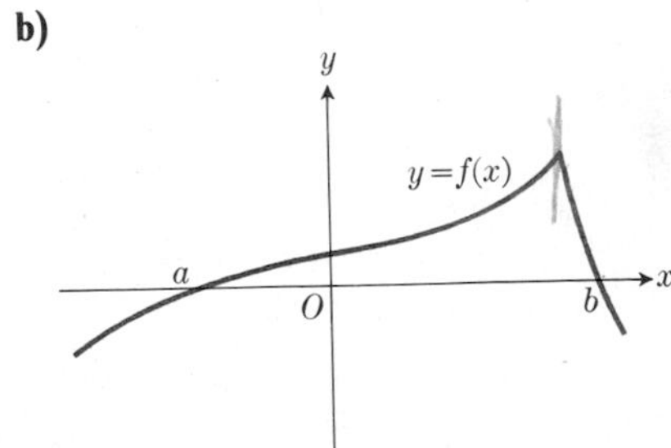

3–29 The functions graphed in (a) and (b) are both continuous. Graph (b), however, has no horizontal tangent between the two points where it crosses the x-axis. This could not have happened if $y = f(x)$ had been differentiable at every point between $x = a$ and $x = b$. The proof of Rolle's theorem explains why.

* Published in 1691 in *Méthode pour Résoudre les Egalités* by the French mathematician Michel Rolle. See *Source Book in Mathematics* by D. E. Smith, p. 253.

EXAMPLE 1. The polynomial

$$y = x^3 - 4x = f(x)$$

is continuous and differentiable for all x, $-\infty < x < +\infty$. If we take

$$a = -2, \qquad b = +2,$$

the hypotheses of Rolle's Theorem are satisfied, since

$$f(-2) = f(+2) = 0.$$

Thus

$$f'(x) = 3x^2 - 4$$

must be zero at least once between -2 and $+2$. In fact, we find

$$3x^2 - 4 = 0$$

at

$$x = c_1 = -\frac{2\sqrt{3}}{3} \quad \text{and} \quad x = c_2 = +\frac{2\sqrt{3}}{3}.$$

Rolle's Theorem may be combined with the Intermediate Value Theorem of Article 2–11 to obtain a criterion for isolating the real solutions of an equation $f(x) = 0$. Suppose that a and b are two real numbers such that

a) $f(x)$ and its first derivative $f'(x)$ are continuous for $a \leq x \leq b$,

b) $f(a)$ and $f(b)$ have opposite signs,

c) $f'(x)$ is different from zero for all values of x between a and b.

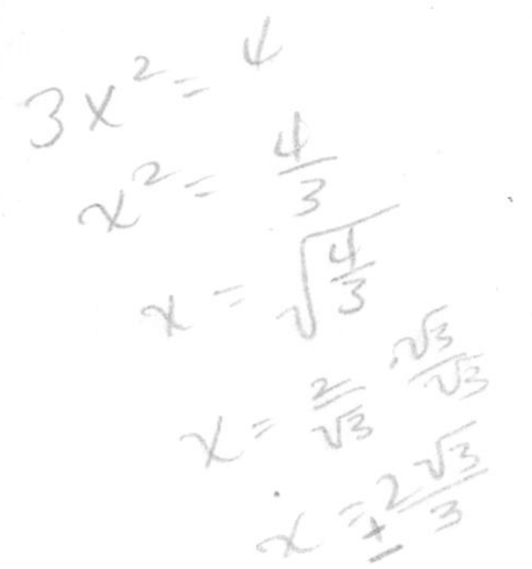

Then there is one and only one solution of the equation $f(x) = 0$ between a and b. This solution is called a *zero* of the function f. It is also called a *root* of the equation $f(x) = 0$.

EXAMPLE 2. Show that the equation

$$x^3 + 3x + 1 = 0$$

has exactly one real root.

Solution. Let

$$f(x) = x^3 + 3x + 1.$$

Then the derivative

$$f'(x) = 3x^2 + 3$$

is never zero (because it is always positive). Now, if there were even two points $x = a$ and $x = b$ where $f(x)$ was zero, Rolle's Theorem would guarantee the existence of a point $x = c$ where f' was zero. Therefore, f has no more than one zero. It does in fact have one zero, because the Intermediate Value Theorem tells us that the graph of $y = f(x)$ crosses the x-axis somewhere between $x = -1$ (where $y = -3$) and $x = 0$ (where $y = 1$). (See Fig. 3–30.)

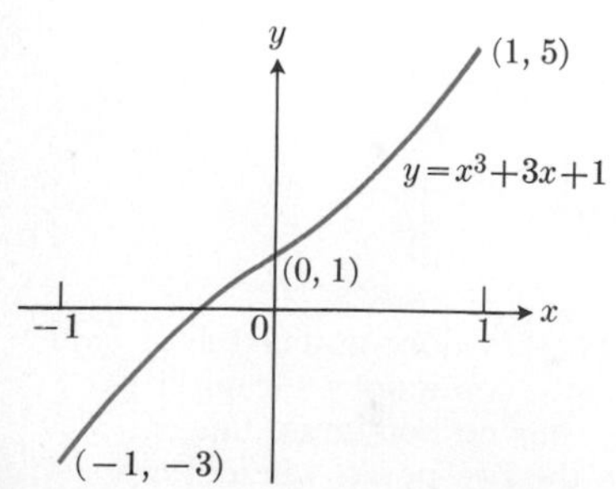

3–30 The only real root of the polynomial $y = x^3 + 3x + 1$ is the one shown here between -1 and 0.

PROBLEMS

Without trying to solve the equations exactly, show that the equation $f(x) = 0$ has one and only one real root between the given pair of numbers for each of the following functions $f(x)$.

1. $x^4 + 3x + 1$, $\quad a = -2$, $\quad b = -1$
2. $x^4 + 2x^3 - 2$, $\quad a = 0$, $\quad b = 1$
3. $2x^3 - 3x^2 - 12x - 6$, $\quad a = -1$, $\quad b = 0$
4. Let $f(x)$, together with its first two derivatives $f'(x)$ and $f''(x)$, be continuous for $a \le x \le b$. Suppose the curve $y = f(x)$ intersects the x-axis in at least three different places between a and b inclusive. Use Rolle's Theorem to show that the equation $f''(x) = 0$ has at least one real root between a and b. Generalize this result.
5. Use Rolle's Theorem to prove that between every two zeros of the polynomial $x^n + a_{n-1}x^{n-1} + \cdots + a_1x + a_0$ there lies a zero of the polynomial

$$nx^{n-1} + (n-1)a_{n-1}x^{n-2} + \cdots + a_1.$$

6. The function

$$y = f(x) = \begin{cases} x & \text{if } 0 \le x < 1, \\ 0 & \text{if } x = 1, \end{cases}$$

is zero at $x = 0$ and at $x = 1$. Its derivative, $y' = 1$, is different from zero at every point between 0 and 1. Why doesn't that contradict Rolle's Theorem?

3–8 THE MEAN VALUE THEOREM

In this article we shall prove the Mean Value Theorem, which is a generalization of Rolle's Theorem. Again we shall be concerned with a function $y = f(x)$ that is continuous for $a \le x \le b$ and has a nonvertical tangent at each point between $A[a, f(a)]$ and $B[b, f(b)]$. (See Fig. 3–31.) The tangent may be vertical at one or both of the endpoints A and B. For example, the function might be

$$f(x) = \sqrt{a^2 - x^2}, \qquad -a \le x \le a,$$

which represents a semicircle that fulfills the requirements above.

DISCUSSION. Geometrically, the Mean Value Theorem states that if the function $y = f(x)$ is continuous for $a \le x \le b$ and has a derivative at each value of x for $a < x < b$, then there is at least one point c between a and b where the tangent to the curve will be parallel to the chord through the two points $A[a, f(a)]$ and $B[b, f(b)]$. This is intuitively plausible, for if we consider displacing the chord AB in Fig. 3–31 upward, keeping it parallel to AB, there will be a transition between positions where it cuts the curve in two nearby points and where it will fail to touch the curve, and the transition will take place at a point C where the line will be tangent to this curve. This transition will occur where the vertical distance between the chord AB and the curve is a maximum. The analytic proof of the Mean Value Theorem has its key idea in this last statement.

The Mean Value Theorem. *Let $y = f(x)$ be continuous for $a \le x \le b$, and possess a derivative at each x for $a < x < b$. Then there is at least one number c between a and b such that*

$$f(b) - f(a) = f'(c)(b - a).$$

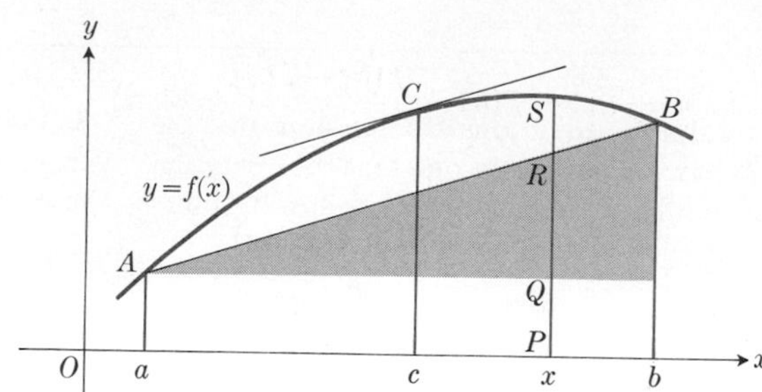

3–31 If $y = f(x)$ is differentiable on (a, b) and continuous on $[a, b]$, then the length RS is a function of x that is differentiable on (a, b) and continuous on $[a, b]$. In fact, RS satisfies all the requirements of Rolle's Theorem because it is zero at $x = a$ and $x = b$. Therefore, its derivative is zero at some value c of x between a and b. When we translate this observation into a statement about the function f, we obtain one of the most useful theorems of calculus.

Proof of the Mean Value Theorem. The vertical distance between the chord and the curve is measured by RS in Fig. 3–31 and

$$RS = PS - PR.$$

Now PS is simply the ordinate y on the curve $y = f(x)$, so that

$$PS = f(x).$$

On the other hand, PR is the ordinate on the chord AB and may be found by using the equation

$$y - f(a) = m(x - a),$$

which is the equation of the straight line AB through the point $A[a, f(a)]$ with slope

$$m = \frac{f(b) - f(a)}{b - a}.$$

That is, the ordinate y of the point R on the line AB is

$$y = PR = f(a) + \frac{f(b) - f(a)}{b - a}(x - a).$$

Hence

$$RS = f(x) - f(a) - \frac{f(b) - f(a)}{b - a}(x - a) \tag{1}$$

measures the vertical displacement from the chord AB to the curve $y = f(x)$ for any x between a and b.

It will simplify the discussion somewhat to change the notation on the left side of Eq. (1) and replace RS by $F(x)$.

That is,

$$F(x) = f(x) - f(a) - \frac{f(b) - f(a)}{b - a}(x - a). \tag{2}$$

Then

$$F(a) = f(a) - f(a) - \frac{f(b) - f(a)}{b - a}(a - a) = 0$$

and

$$F(b) = f(b) - f(a) - \frac{f(b) - f(a)}{b - a}(b - a) = 0,$$

so that this function $F(x)$ is zero at both $x = a$ and $x = b$. But since $f(x)$ and $x - a$ in Eq. (2) are continuous for $a \leq x \leq b$ and differentiable for $a < x < b$, and the other expressions on the right side of the equation are constants, the function $F(x)$ satisfies all the hypotheses of Rolle's Theorem. Therefore its derivative must be zero at some place between a and b; that is,

$$F'(c) = 0 \qquad \text{for some } c, \qquad a < c < b. \tag{3a}$$

If we take the derivative of both sides of (2), we get

$$F'(x) = f'(x) - \frac{f(b) - f(a)}{b - a} \cdot \frac{d(x - a)}{dx}$$

and the result (3a) is equivalent to stating

$$f'(c) = \frac{f(b) - f(a)}{b - a} \tag{3b}$$

or

$$f(b) - f(a) = f'(c)(b - a) \qquad \text{for some } c, \qquad a < c < b, \tag{4}$$

which is what we wished to prove.

We note that (3b) states that the slope $f'(c)$ of the curve at $C[c, f(c)]$ is the same as the slope $[f(b) - f(a)]/(b - a)$ of the chord joining the point $A[a, f(a)]$ and $B[b, f(b)]$; this is a form that is easily recalled.

When we are presented with a specific function f and specific values of a and b, we find the value or values of c that are guaranteed by the Mean Value Theorem by solving Eq. (4).

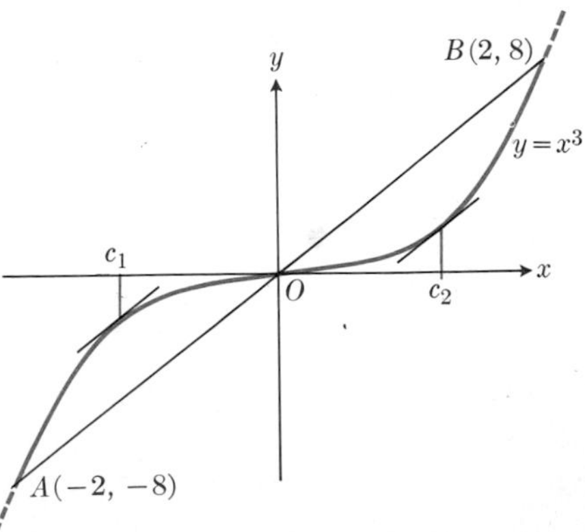

3–32 At $c = \pm\frac{2}{3}\sqrt{3}$, the tangents to the curve are parallel to the chord AB.

EXAMPLE 1. (See Fig. 3–32.) Let $f(x) = x^3$, $a = -2$, and $b = +2$. Then

$$f'(x) = 3x^2, \qquad f'(c) = 3c^2,$$

$$f(b) = 2^3 = 8, \qquad f(a) = (-2)^3 = -8,$$

$$\frac{f(b) - f(a)}{b - a} = \frac{8 - (-8)}{2 - (-2)} = \frac{16}{4} = 4,$$

so that

$$f'(c) = \frac{f(b) - f(a)}{b - a}$$

becomes

$$3c^2 = 4, \qquad c = \pm\tfrac{2}{3}\sqrt{3}.$$

There are thus two values of c, namely,

$$c_1 = -\tfrac{2}{3}\sqrt{3}, \qquad c_2 = +\tfrac{2}{3}\sqrt{3},$$

between $a = -2$ and $b = +2$, where the tangent to the curve $y = x^3$ is parallel to the chord through the points $(-2, -8)$ and $(+2, +8)$.

EXAMPLE 2. (See Fig. 3–33.) Let $f(x) = x^{2/3}$, $a = -8$, $b = +8$. Then

$$f'(x) = \frac{2}{3}x^{-1/3} = \frac{2}{3\sqrt[3]{x}}$$

exists everywhere between a and b *except* at $x = 0$. We find that

$$\frac{f(b) - f(a)}{b - a} = \frac{(8)^{2/3} - (-8)^{2/3}}{8 - (-8)} = \frac{4 - 4}{16} = 0,$$

and

$$f'(c) = \frac{2}{3\sqrt[3]{c}}$$

is not zero for any finite value of c. The result (3b) need not hold, and does not hold, in this case due to the failure of the derivative to exist at a point, namely $x = 0$, between $a = -8$ and $b = +8$. Note, however, that the curve $y = x^{2/3}$ does have a tangent at $x = 0$ (it is vertical) and therefore has a tangent everywhere between a and b.

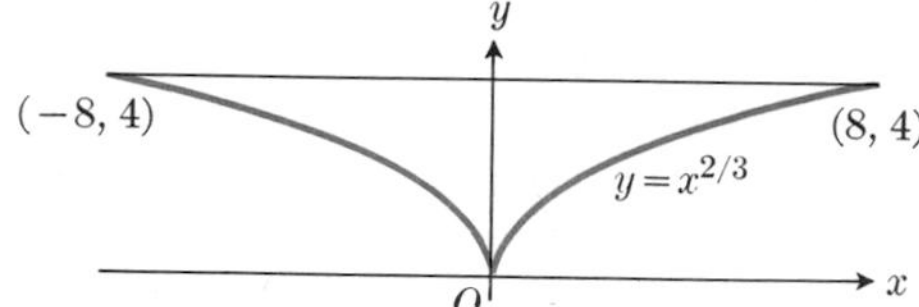

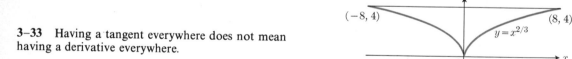

3–33 Having a tangent everywhere does not mean having a derivative everywhere.

REMARK. The Mean Value Theorem has the following interesting interpretation when applied to an equation of motion $s = f(t)$. Let $\Delta s = f(b) - f(a)$ be the change in s corresponding to $\Delta t = b - a$; then the right side of Eq. (3b) is

$$\frac{\Delta s}{\Delta t} = \frac{f(b) - f(a)}{b - a} = \text{Average velocity from } t = a \text{ to } t = b. \tag{5}$$

The equation then tells us that there is an instant $t = c$ between a and b at which the instantaneous velocity $f'(c)$ is equal to the average velocity. The theorem may therefore be paraphrased as follows: If a motorist makes a trip in which the *average* velocity is 30 mi/hr, then at least once during the trip the speedometer must also have registered precisely 30 mi/hr.

Corollary 1. *If a function F has a derivative that is equal to zero for all values of x in an interval $a < x < b$,*

$$F'(x) \equiv 0, \qquad a < x < b, \tag{6a}$$

then the function is constant throughout the interval:

$$F(x) \equiv \text{constant}, \qquad a < x < b. \tag{6b}$$

Proof. Suppose (6a) is satisfied. Let x_1 and x_2 be any two points in the interval with $a < x_1 < x_2 < b$. Then, since the function is differentiable for $x_1 \le x \le x_2$, it is also continuous in the same closed interval. Hence the Mean Value Theorem applies. That is, there is at least one number c, $x_1 < c < x_2$, such that

$$F(x_1) - F(x_2) = F'(c)(x_1 - x_2).$$

But $F'(c)$ is zero by hypothesis. Therefore

$$F(x_1) = F(x_2).$$

That is, the value of the function at any point x_1 is the same as its value at any other point x_2, for all x_1, x_2 in the interval (a, b). This is what is meant by Eq. (6b). Q.E.D.

Corollary 2. *If F_1 and F_2 are two functions each of which has its derivative equal to $f(x)$ for $a < x < b$, that is,*

$$\frac{dF_1(x)}{dx} = \frac{dF_2(x)}{dx} = f(x), \qquad a < x < b,$$

then

$$F_1(x) - F_2(x) \equiv \text{constant}, \qquad a < x < b.$$

Proof. Apply Corollary 1, above, to the function $F(x) = F_1(x) - F_2(x)$.

PROBLEMS

In each of the following problems (1 through 5), a, b, and c refer to the equation $f(b) - f(a) = (b - a)f'(c)$, which expresses the Mean Value Theorem. Given $f(x)$, a, and b, find c.

1. $f(x) = x^2 + 2x - 1$; $a = 0$, $b = 1$.

2. $f(x) = x^3$; $a = 0$, $b = 3$.

3. $f(x) = x^{2/3}$; $a = 0$, $b = 1$.

4. $f(x) = x + \dfrac{1}{x}$; $a = \frac{1}{2}$, $b = 2$.

5. $f(x) = \sqrt{x - 1}$; $a = 1$, $b = 3$.

6. Suppose you know that $f(x)$ is differentiable and that $f'(x)$ always has a value between -1 and $+1$. Show that

$$|f(x) - f(a)| \le |x - a|.$$

7. The Mean Value Theorem gives the equation

$$f(b) = f(a) + (b - a)f'(c),$$

c between a and b. When all terms on the right side of this equation are known, the equation determines $f(b)$ for us. Usually, however, $f'(c)$ is not known unless $f(b)$ is known. But when b is near a, then c will also be near a, and the approximation

$$f'(c) \approx f'(a)$$

leads to the approximation

$$f(b) \approx f(a) + (b - a)f'(a).$$

Using this approximation, calculate

a) $\sqrt{10}$ by taking $f(x) = \sqrt{x}$, $a = 9$, $b = 10$;
b) $(2.003)^2$ by taking $f(x) = x^2$, $a = 2$, $b = 2.003$;
c) $1/99$ by taking $f(x) = 1/x$, $a = 100$, $b = 99$.

8. Let $P_1(x_1, y_1)$ and $P_2(x_2, y_2)$ be any two points on the parabola

$$y = ax^2 + bx + c,$$

and let $P_3(x_3, y_3)$ be the point on the arc P_1P_2 where the tangent is parallel to the chord P_1P_2. Show that $x_3 = (x_1 + x_2)/2$.

9. Use the Mean Value Theorem to prove that $|\sin b - \sin a| \leq |b - a|$.

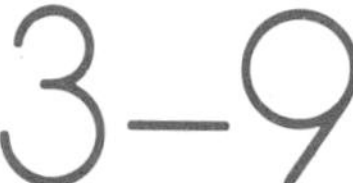

INDETERMINATE FORMS AND L'HÔPITAL'S RULE

As an application of the Mean Value Theorem, we develop a rule that will significantly extend our ability to calculate limits. The rule is named after Guillaume François Antoine de l'Hôpital (1661–1704), Marquis de St. Mesme, a French nobleman who wrote the first calculus text.

1. The Indeterminate Form 0/0

We sometimes wish to know the value of

$$\lim_{x \to a} \frac{f(x)}{g(x)} \tag{1}$$

at a point a where the functions $f(x)$ and $g(x)$ both vanish. However, if we substitute $x = a$ in the numerator and denominator of the fraction, we are led to the meaningless expression 0/0.

EXAMPLE 1. Both x and $\sin x$ are zero at $x = 0$, so we cannot just put $x = 0$ in the numerator and denominator if we want to find the limit

$$\lim_{x \to 0} \frac{\sin x}{x},$$

which we know (from earlier investigations) is one. This is also the derivative of $\sin x$ at $x = 0$. Indeed, the derivative

$$f'(a) = \lim_{x \to a} \frac{f(x) - f(a)}{x - a}$$

was our first example of the indeterminate form 0/0, since both the numerator and the denominator of the fraction $(f(x) - f(a))/(x - a)$ approach zero when x approaches a.

The key to a rule that will let us deal with indeterminate forms in many cases is a mean value theorem of Augustin L. Cauchy (1789–1857). It involves two functions instead of one.

Theorem 1. Cauchy's Mean Value Theorem. *Suppose that the functions $f(x)$ and $g(x)$ are continuous for $a \leq x \leq b$ and differentiable for $a < x < b$, and* *that* $g'(x) \neq 0$ *for* $a < x < b$. *Then there exists a number c between a and b such that*

$$\frac{f'(c)}{g'(c)} = \frac{f(b) - f(a)}{g(b) - g(a)}. \tag{2}$$

Proof. We apply the Mean Value Theorem of Article 3–8 twice. First we use it to show that $g(b) \neq g(a)$. For if $g(b)$ did equal $g(a)$, then the Mean-Value Theorem would apply to g, to give

$$g'(c) = \frac{g(b) - g(a)}{b - a} = 0$$

for some c between a and b. But this cannot happen because $g'(x) \neq 0$ for $a < x < b$.

We next apply the Mean Value Theorem to the function

$$F(x) = f(x) - f(a) - \frac{f(b) - f(a)}{g(b) - g(a)}[g(x) - g(a)]. \tag{3}$$

This function is continuous and differentiable where f and g are, and $F(b) = F(a) = 0$. Therefore there is a number c between a and b for which $F'(c) = 0$. In terms of f and g this says

$$F'(c) = f'(c) - \frac{f(b) - f(a)}{g(b) - g(a)}[g'(c)] = 0, \tag{4}$$

or

$$\frac{f'(c)}{g'(c)} = \frac{f(b) - f(a)}{g(b) - g(a)},$$

which is what we wished to prove.

REMARK. The auxiliary function in Eq. (3) has a geometric interpretation similar to the interpretation of the auxiliary function F that appears in the proof of the Mean Value Theorem in Article 3–8. We rewrite Eq. (3) in terms of a parameter t, so that

$$F(t) = f(t) - f(a) - \frac{f(b) - f(a)}{g(b) - g(a)}[g(t) - g(a)]. \tag{3'}$$

Then $F(t)$ is the vertical difference RS between the ordinate $y = f(t)$ on the graph of the parametric equations $x = g(t)$, $y = f(t)$ at S, and the chord through the points A (where $t = a$) and B (where $t = b$). (See Fig. 3–34.) For

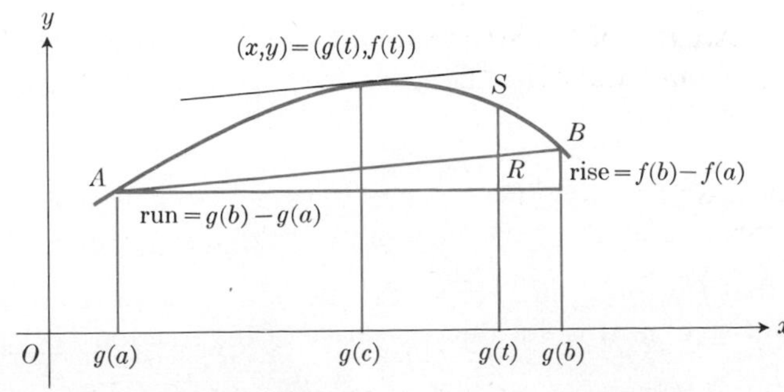

3–34 At $t = c$, the slope of the tangent to the parametric curve is the slope of chord AB.

some value $t = c$ between a and b, the tangent to the curve is parallel to the chord. Using the parametric equations, this says that

$$\left.\frac{dy}{dx}\right|_{t=c} = \left.\frac{f'(t)}{g'(t)}\right|_{t=c} = \frac{f'(c)}{g'(c)} = \frac{f(b)-f(a)}{g(b)-g(a)}.$$

We can now prove l'Hôpital's rule.

Theorem 2. l'Hôpital's Rule. *Suppose that the functions $f(x)$ and $g(x)$ are both zero at some point x_0, that is, $f(x_0) = g(x_0) = 0$, and that f and g are both differentiable at every point except possibly x_0 of an open interval $a < x < b$ that contains x_0. Suppose also that $g'(x) \neq 0$ for every $x \neq x_0$ in (a, b). Then*

$$\lim_{x\to x_0} \frac{f(x)}{g(x)} = \lim_{x\to x_0} \frac{f'(x)}{g'(x)}, \tag{5}$$

provided $f'(x)/g'(x)$ has a limit as x approaches x_0.

Proof. We first establish Eq. (5) for the case $x \to x_{0+}$. The method needs almost no change to apply to $x \to x_{0-}$, and the combination of these two cases establishes the result.

Suppose that x lies to the right of x_0. Then $g'(x) \neq 0$ and we can apply Cauchy's Mean Value Theorem to the closed interval from x_0 to x. This produces a number c between x_0 and x such that

$$\frac{f'(c)}{g'(c)} = \frac{f(x)-f(x_0)}{g(x)-g(x_0)}. \tag{6}$$

But $f(x_0) = g(x_0) = 0$, so that

$$\frac{f'(c)}{g'(c)} = \frac{f(x)}{g(x)}. \tag{7}$$

As x approaches x_0, c approaches x_0, because it lies between x and x_0. Therefore,

$$\lim_{x\to x_0^+} \frac{f(x)}{g(x)} = \lim_{c\to x_0^+} \frac{f'(c)}{g'(c)} = \lim_{x\to x_0^+} \frac{f'(x)}{g'(x)}.$$

This establishes l'Hôpital's rule for the case where x approaches x_0 from above. The case where x approaches x_0 from below is proved by applying Cauchy's Mean Value Theorem to the closed interval $[x, x_0]$, $x < x_0$.

We apply l'Hôpital's rule first to compute a limit we already know.

EXAMPLE 2

$$\lim_{x\to 0} \frac{\sin x}{x} \qquad \left[\frac{0}{0}\right]$$

$$= \lim_{x\to 0} \frac{\cos x}{1} = 1.$$

Notice that $f'(x)/g'(x)$ in l'Hôpital's rule is the derivative of f divided by the derivative of g. It is *not* the derivative of the fraction $f(x)/g(x)$.

It may happen that, in applying l'Hôpital's rule, we find that $f'(x_0) = g'(x_0) = 0$. When this happens, we may apply l'Hôpital's rule again, provided $f'(x)$ and $g'(x)$ are differentiable for $a < x < b$, except perhaps at $x = x_0$, and $g''(x) \neq 0$ near x_0.

EXAMPLE 3

$$\lim_{x\to 0} \frac{\sqrt{1+x} - 1 - (x/2)}{x^2} \qquad \left[\frac{0}{0}\right]$$

$$= \lim_{x\to 0} \frac{\frac{1}{2}(1+x)^{-1/2} - \frac{1}{2}}{2x} \qquad \left[\text{still } \frac{0}{0}\right]$$

$$= \lim_{x\to 0} \frac{-\frac{1}{4}(1+x)^{-3/2}}{2} = -\frac{1}{8}.$$

In practice, the functions we deal with in this book satisfy the hypotheses of l'Hôpital's rule. We apply the method by proceeding to differentiate the numerator and denominator separately so long as we still get the form 0/0 at $x = x_0$. As soon as one or the other of these derivatives is different from zero at $x = x_0$, we stop differentiating; *l'Hôpital's rule does not apply when either the numerator or the denominator has a finite nonzero limit.*

EXAMPLE 4

$$\lim_{x\to 0} \frac{1 - \cos x}{x + x^2} \qquad \left[\frac{0}{0}\right]$$

$$= \lim_{x\to 0} \frac{\sin x}{1 + 2x} = 0.$$

If we continue to differentiate in an attempt to apply l'Hôpital's rule once more, we get

$$\lim_{x\to 0} \frac{1 - \cos x}{x + x^2} = \lim_{x\to 0} \frac{\sin x}{1 + 2x} = \lim_{x\to 0} \frac{\cos x}{2} = \frac{1}{2},$$

which is wrong.

It may happen that one of the derivatives is zero at $x = x_0$ and the other is not. Then the limit of the fraction is either zero, as in Example 4, or infinity, as in the next example.

EXAMPLE 5

$$\lim_{x\to 0} \frac{\sin x}{x^2} \qquad \left[\frac{0}{0}\right]$$

$$= \lim_{x\to 0} \frac{\cos x}{2x} = \infty.$$

---

2. The Indeterminate Forms ∞/∞ and $\infty \cdot 0$

In more advanced textbooks it is proved that if $f(t) \to \infty$ and $g(t) \to \infty$ as $t \to a$, then

$$\lim_{t\to a} \frac{f(t)}{g(t)} = \lim_{t\to a} \frac{f'(t)}{g'(t)},$$

provided the limit on the right exists.* This simply says that l'Hôpital's rule applies to the indeterminate form ∞/∞ as well as to the form 0/0. The form $\infty \cdot 0$ must be reduced to one or the other of these two. In the notation $t \to a$, a may either be finite or infinite.

EXAMPLE 6. Find the limit

$$\lim_{t\to\infty} \frac{t^2 + t}{2t^2 + 1}.$$

Solution. This assumes the form ∞/∞ as $t \to \infty$.

a) We apply l'Hôpital's rule and have

$$\lim_{t\to\infty} \frac{t^2 + t}{2t^2 + 1} = \lim_{t\to\infty} \frac{2t + 1}{4t} \left[\text{still} = \frac{\infty}{\infty}\right] = \lim_{t\to\infty} \frac{2}{4} = \frac{1}{2}.$$

b) Note that this could also have been evaluated by writing $t = 1/h$ and letting $h \to 0$:

$$\lim_{t\to\infty} \frac{t^2 + t}{2t^2 + 1} = \lim_{h\to 0} \frac{\dfrac{1}{h^2} + \dfrac{1}{h}}{\dfrac{2}{h^2} + 1} = \lim_{h\to 0} \frac{1 + h}{2 + h^2} = \frac{1}{2}.$$

c) Another way is to divide both the numerator and denominator by t^2 (the highest power of t that occurs in either numerator or denominator) and observe that $1/t$ and $1/t^2$ approach zero as t increases without bound:

$$\lim_{t\to\infty} \frac{t^2 + t}{2t^2 + 1} = \lim_{t\to\infty} \frac{1 + \dfrac{1}{t}}{2 + \dfrac{1}{t^2}} = \frac{1 + 0}{2 + 0} = \frac{1}{2}.$$

This is actually the same as the method given above in (b).

---

3. The Indeterminate Form $\infty - \infty$

The differences $n - n = 0$, $n - n^2 = n(1 - n)$, and $n^2 - n = n(n - 1)$ behave entirely differently as $n \to \infty$. They all become formally $\infty - \infty$ and illustrate why such an expression is called an indeterminate form.

It may be possible, by preliminary algebraic manipulations, to reduce an expression $F(x) - G(x)$ that becomes $\infty - \infty$ as x approaches x_0 to a form

* There is also a proof of l'Hôpital's rule for both forms 0/0 and ∞/∞ in the article "L'Hôpital's Rule," by A. E. Taylor, *American Mathematical Monthly*, 59, 20–24 (1952).

$f(x)/g(x)$ that becomes $0/0$ or ∞/∞. While l'Hôpital's rule does not apply directly to the original expression $F(x) - G(x)$, it does apply to the algebraically equivalent form $f(x)/g(x)$.

EXAMPLE 7. Find

$$\lim_{x\to 0}\left(\frac{1}{\sin x} - \frac{1}{x}\right).$$

Solution. If $x \to 0^+$, then $\sin x \to 0^+$ and $1/\sin x \to +\infty$, while $1/x \to +\infty$. The expression $(1/\sin x) - (1/x)$ formally becomes $+\infty - (+\infty)$, which is indeterminate. On the other hand, if $x \to 0^-$, then $1/\sin x \to -\infty$ and $1/x \to -\infty$, so that $(1/\sin x) - (1/x)$ becomes $-\infty + \infty$, which is also indeterminate. But we may also write

$$\frac{1}{\sin x} - \frac{1}{x} = \frac{x - \sin x}{x \sin x}$$

and apply l'Hôpital's rule to the expression on the right. Thus,

$$\lim_{x\to 0}\left(\frac{1}{\sin x} - \frac{1}{x}\right) = \lim_{x\to 0}\frac{x - \sin x}{x \sin x} \qquad \left[\frac{0}{0}\right]$$

$$= \lim_{x\to 0}\frac{1 - \cos x}{\sin x + x\cos x} \qquad \left[\text{still } \frac{0}{0}\right]$$

$$= \lim_{x\to 0}\frac{\sin x}{2\cos x - x\sin x} = 0.$$

PROBLEMS

Find the limits in Problems 1 through 18.

1. $\lim_{x\to 2}\dfrac{x-2}{x^2-4}$
2. $\lim_{t\to\infty}\dfrac{6t+5}{3t-8}$
3. $\lim_{x\to\infty}\dfrac{5x^2-3x}{7x^2+1}$
4. $\lim_{x\to 1}\dfrac{x^3-1}{4x^3-x-3}$
5. $\lim_{t\to 0}\dfrac{\sin t^2}{t}$
6. $\lim_{x\to\pi/2}\dfrac{2x-\pi}{\cos x}$
7. $\lim_{x\to 0}\dfrac{\sin 5x}{x}$
8. $\lim_{t\to 0}\dfrac{\cos t - 1}{t^2}$
9. $\lim_{\theta\to\pi}\dfrac{\sin\theta}{\pi-\theta}$
10. $\lim_{x\to\pi/2}\dfrac{1-\sin x}{1+\cos 2x}$
11. $\lim_{x\to 2}\dfrac{\sqrt{x^2+5}-3}{x^2-4}$
12. $\lim_{x\to 0}\dfrac{\sqrt{a(a+x)}-a}{x}$, $a>0$
13. $\lim_{t\to 0}\dfrac{10\sin t - t}{t^3}$
14. $\lim_{x\to 0}\dfrac{x(\cos x - 1)}{\sin x - x}$
15. $\lim_{h\to 0}\dfrac{\sin(a+h)-\sin a}{h}$
16. $\lim_{r\to 1}\dfrac{a(r^n-1)}{r-1}$, n a positive integer
17. $\lim_{x\to 0+}\left(\dfrac{1}{x}-\dfrac{1}{\sqrt{x}}\right)$
18. $\lim_{x\to\infty}\left(x-\sqrt{x^2+x}\right)$
19. Which is correct, (a) or (b)? Explain.

    a) $\lim_{x\to 3}\dfrac{x-3}{x^2-3} = \lim_{x\to 3}\dfrac{1}{2x} = \dfrac{1}{6}.$

    b) $\lim_{x\to 3}\dfrac{x-3}{x^2-3} = \dfrac{0}{6} = 0.$

In Problems 20–22, find all values of c that satisfy Eq. (2), the conclusion of Cauchy's Mean Value Theorem, for the given functions and interval.

20. $f(x)=x$, $g(x)=x^2$, $(a,b)=(-2,0)$
21. $f(x)=x$, $g(x)=x^2$, (a,b) arbitrary
22. $f(x)=x^3/3-4x$, $g(x)=x^2$, $(a,b)=(0,3)$

3–10 EXTENSION OF THE MEAN VALUE THEOREM

In Article 3–8 we established the existence of a number c, between a and b, such that

$$f(b) - f(a) = f'(c)(b - a), \tag{1}$$

under suitable hypotheses on the function f. If the number c is replaced by a on the right side of Eq. (1), the equality must be changed to an approximation, which turns out to be the approximation we obtain by using the line tangent to the curve at $(a, f(a))$ to approximate the curve $y = f(x)$ at $x = b$. When b is close to a, we expect the approximation to be quite good. The following theorem tells us that if the function has a second derivative, as well as a first, then the difference between the tangent approximation and the function itself is proportional to $(b - a)^2$.

Extended Mean Value Theorem (Special case). *Let $f(x)$ and its first derivative $f'(x)$ be continuous on the closed interval $a \le x \le b$, and suppose its second derivative $f''(x)$ exists in the open interval $a < x < b$. Then there is a number c_2 between a and b such that*

$$f(b) = f(a) + f'(a)(b - a) + \tfrac{1}{2}f''(c_2)(b - a)^2. \tag{2}$$

Proof. Let K be the number defined by the equation

$$f(b) = f(a) + f'(a)(b - a) + K(b - a)^2. \tag{3}$$

Consider the function $F(x)$ that we get by replacing b by x in Eq. (3) and subtracting the right side from the left:

$$F(x) = f(x) - f(a) - f'(a)(x - a) - K(x - a)^2. \tag{4}$$

Then, by substitution in (4), we find

$$F(a) = 0.$$

Also, from (3), we have

$$F(b) = 0.$$

Moreover, F and its first derivative are continuous on $a \le x \le b$, and

$$F'(x) = f'(x) - f'(a) - 2K(x - a). \tag{5}$$

Therefore, F satisfies the hypotheses of Rolle's Theorem, so there is a number c_1 between a and b such that

$$F'(c_1) = 0,$$

and, by substitution in (5), we also have

$$F'(a) = 0.$$

The derived function F' satisfies Rolle's Theorem on the interval $a \le x \le c_1$. Hence there is a number c_2 between a and c_1 such that

$$F''(c_2) = 0.$$

We differentiate (5) and get

$$F''(x) = f''(x) - 2K. \tag{6}$$

If we put $x = c_2$ in (6), set the result equal to zero, and solve for K, we have

$$K = \tfrac{1}{2}f''(c_2).$$

When this is substituted into Eq. (3), we have Eq. (2). Q.E.D.

By a similar method, it is easy to prove the more general Extended Mean Value Theorem.

Extended Mean Value Theorem (General case). *Let $f(x)$ and its first $n-1$ derivatives $f'(x), f''(x), \ldots, f^{(n-1)}(x)$ be continuous on the closed interval $a \le x \le b$, and suppose the nth derivative $f^{(n)}(x)$ exists at least in the open interval $a < x < b$. Then there is a number c_n between a and b such that*

$$\begin{aligned} f(b) = f(a) &+ f'(a)(b-a) + \tfrac{1}{2}f''(a)(b-a)^2 \\ &+ \tfrac{1}{6}f'''(a)(b-a)^3 + \cdots \\ &+ \frac{1}{(n-1)!}f^{(n-1)}(a)(b-a)^{n-1} \\ &+ \frac{1}{n!}f^{(n)}(c_n)(b-a)^n. \end{aligned} \tag{7}$$

REMARK. The law of formation of the terms on the right side of Eq. (7) may be discovered by continuing a term at a time from $n = 1$ to $n = 2$ (as we have done), then to $n = 3$, and so on. Equation (7) is the basis of a powerful general method for evaluating a large class of functions that have derivatives of all orders. The proof of the general case of thc Mean Value Theorem is left as an exercise. (See Problem 74 at the end of this chapter.)

PROBLEMS

1. Prove the special case $n = 3$ of the Extended Mean Value Theorem, Eq. (7).

2. Prove the case $n = 4$ of the Extended Mean Value Theorem, Eq. (7).

3. Verify the validity of the Extended Mean Value Theorem for each of the following polynomials, for the given values of a and n:

a) $f(x) = 3x^2 + 2x + 4$; $a = 1$, $n = 2$.
b) $f(x) = x^3 + 5x - 7$; $a = 1$, $n = 3$.

4. Using the Extended Mean Value Theorem, prove that a polynomial $f(x)$ of degree n may be written, precisely, in the form:

$$f(x) = f(a) + f'(a)(x-a) + \frac{f''(a)}{2}(x-a)^2 + \cdots + \frac{f^{(n)}(a)}{n!}(x-a)^n.$$

5. Use the Extended Mean Value Theorem for $n = 2$, Eq. (2), to prove the following: Let $f(x)$ be continuous and have continuous first and second derivatives. Suppose that $f'(a) = 0$. Then $f(x)$ has:

a) a relative maximum at a if its second derivative is less than or equal to zero throughout some neighborhood of a,

b) a relative minimum at a if its second derivative is greater than or equal to zero throughout some neighborhood of a.

(A "neighborhood" of a is an open interval centered at a, that is, an interval of the form $a - h < x < a + h$ for some positive h.)

*3–11 APPLICATIONS OF THE MEAN VALUE THEOREM TO CURVE TRACING

The discussion of the signs of dy/dx and d^2y/dx^2 in Articles 3–1 and 3–3 can be made more rigorous by applying the Mean Value Theorems to prove the following results.

Theorem 1. First derivative test for rise and fall. *Let $y = f(x)$ be continuous in the closed interval $a \leq x \leq b$ and differentiable in the open interval $a < x < b$. Then,*

if dy/dx is positive for $a < x < b$, the curve $y = f(x)$ steadily rises,

if dy/dx is negative for $a < x < b$, the curve $y = f(x)$ steadily falls

as x increases from a to b.

Proof. (We urge you to make your own sketch to illustrate the following statements.) Let x_1 and x_2 be any two points in the closed interval (a, b) with x_1 to the left of x_2; that is,

$$a \leq x_1 < x_2 \leq b.$$

Then by the Mean Value Theorem, there is a number c between x_1 and x_2 such that

$$f(x_2) - f(x_1) = f'(c) \cdot (x_2 - x_1).$$

Since $x_2 - x_1$ is positive, the sign of the right side of this equation is the same as the sign of the derivative $f'(c)$. Therefore

$$y_2 = f(x_2) \quad \text{is greater than } y_1 = f(x_1) \quad \text{if } f'(c) \text{ is positive,}$$

and

$$y_2 = f(x_2) \quad \text{is less than } y_1 = f(x_1) \quad \text{if } f'(c) \text{ is negative.}$$

In other words, when dy/dx is positive, the point $P_2(x_2, y_2)$ is to the right of and above the point $P_1(x_1, y_1)$ and when dy/dx is negative, the point $P_2(x_2, y_2)$ is to the right of and below the point $P_1(x_1, y_1)$, as the theorem asserts.

Q.E.D.

Second Derivative Test for Maxima and Minima

In Article 3–6 we found that we can sometimes tell a relative maximum from a minimum of a function by the sign of the second derivative at a point where the first derivative is zero. When the second derivative is also zero at the same point, the test fails. But we may use the second derivative, even when it is zero at the point a where $f'(a) = 0$, provided there is some *interval* $a - h < x < a + h$, containing a, where the second derivative does not change its sign. Theorem 2 explains this procedure.

Theorem 2. Second derivative test for maxima and minima. *Let f be continuous and twice differentiable in some open interval containing a, and suppose*

* This section may be omitted without loss of continuity. The results are not used in later chapters.

that the first derivative is zero at a:

$$f'(a) = 0. \tag{1}$$

Then $f(x)$ has a relative maximum at $x = a$ if its second derivative $f''(x)$ is negative or zero for all x in some interval $a - h < x < a + h$, and has a relative minimum if $f''(x)$ is positive or zero there.

Proof. Let h be a number such that $f''(x)$ exists for $a - h < x < a + h$. Let b be any number between $a - h$ and $a + h$. By the Extended Mean Value Theorem for $n = 2$, we know that there is a number c between a and b such that

$$f(b) - f(a) = f'(a)(b - a) + \tfrac{1}{2}f''(c)(b - a)^2.$$

This reduces to

$$f(b) - f(a) = \tfrac{1}{2}f''(c)(b - a)^2, \tag{2}$$

in view of the hypothesis (1). The right side of Eq. (2) has the same sign as $f''(c)$. If the second derivative is negative or zero throughout $a - h < x < a + h$, then $f(b) - f(a) \leq 0$ and $f(b) \leq f(a)$; hence f has a relative maximum at a. If the second derivative is positive or zero throughout $a - h < x < a + h$, then $f(b) \geq f(a)$ and f has a relative minimum at a. Q.E.D.

EXAMPLE 1. The function

$$f(x) = x^4 - 4x^3 + 6x^2 - 4x + 4$$

is differentiable any number of times for all values of x. Its first two derivatives are

$$f'(x) = 4x^3 - 12x^2 + 12x - 4 = 4(x - 1)^3,$$

$$f''(x) = 12x^2 - 24x + 12 = 12(x - 1)^2.$$

The first derivative is zero at $x = 1$. So is the second derivative. But the second derivative is positive everywhere else, so the function has a minimum at $x = 1$.

Curves Concave Upward or Downward

By using the Extended Mean Value Theorem for $n = 2$, we can now give an analytic proof of the results in Article 3–3 on the direction of concavity of a curve.

Theorem 3. Second derivative test for concavity. *Let $y = f(x)$ be continuous together with its first derivative $y' = f'(x)$ in the closed interval $a \leq x \leq b$. Let the second derivative $y'' = f''(x)$ exist at least over the open interval $a < x < b$. Then the curve $y = f(x)$ is*

concave upward if $f''(x)$ is positive,

and

concave downward if $f''(x)$ is negative,

for $a < x < b$.

REMARK. To prove Theorem 3 we need a more precise formulation of what the phrases "concave upward" and "concave downward" mean. A portion of

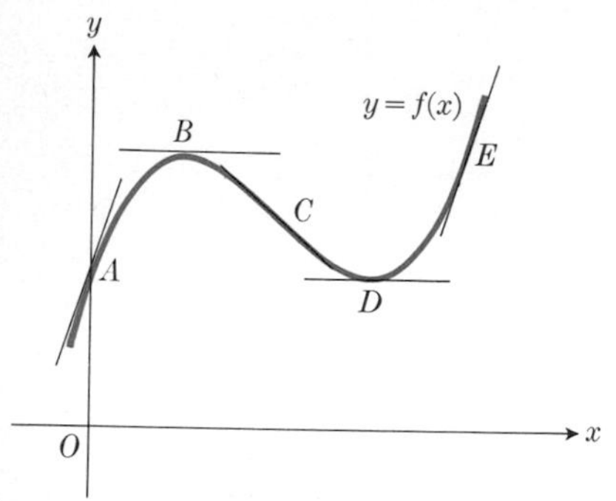

3–35 The second derivative $f''(x)$ is negative between A and C, zero at C, and positive between C and E.

a curve is *concave upward* if the chord PQ lies above the arc PQ for all pairs of points P and Q on it, as it would in the region CDE in Fig. 3–35. Similarly, it is *concave downward* when each chord lies below its arc, as it would in the region ABC in the figure.

Proof of Theorem 3. In Fig. 3–36(a), $P_1(x_1, y_1)$ and $P_2(x_2, y_2)$ represent two points on the curve $y = f(x)$ with $a \leq x_1 < x_2 \leq b$. The point P_L is on the chord P_1P_2. Its abscissa x lies between x_1 and x_2. By similar triangles, we have

$$\frac{y_L - y_1}{h_1} = \frac{y_2 - y_L}{h_2} \qquad \text{or} \qquad y_L = \frac{h_1 y_2 + h_2 y_1}{h_1 + h_2}.$$

Suppose now that $P(x, y)$ is the point of abscissa x on the curve $y = f(x)$. Then we know that:

$$\begin{aligned} &P \text{ lies above the chord} && \text{if } y > y_L, \\ &P \text{ lies on the chord} && \text{if } y = y_L, \\ &P \text{ lies below the chord} && \text{if } y < y_L. \end{aligned}$$

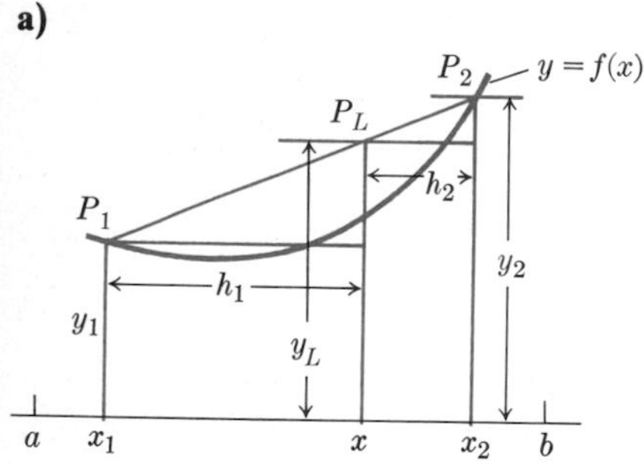

To be specific, let us consider the case where the second derivative $f''(x)$ is positive for $a < x < b$. By the Extended Mean Value Theorem with $n = 2$, we have:

$$f(x_1) - f(x) = f'(x)(x_1 - x) + \tfrac{1}{2}f''(c)(x_1 - x)^2, \tag{3a}$$

$$f(x_2) - f(x) = f'(x)(x_2 - x) + \tfrac{1}{2}f''(e)(x_2 - x)^2 \tag{3b}$$

for some numbers c, between x_1 and x, and e, between x and x_2 (Fig. 3–36b). We multiply (3a) by $x_2 - x = h_2$ and (3b) by $x - x_1 = h_1$ and add, thereby eliminating the terms in $f'(x)$. We obtain

$$h_2[f(x_1) - f(x)] + h_1[f(x_2) - f(x)] = \tfrac{1}{2}[h_2 f''(c)h_1^2 + h_1 f''(e)h_2^2]. \tag{4}$$

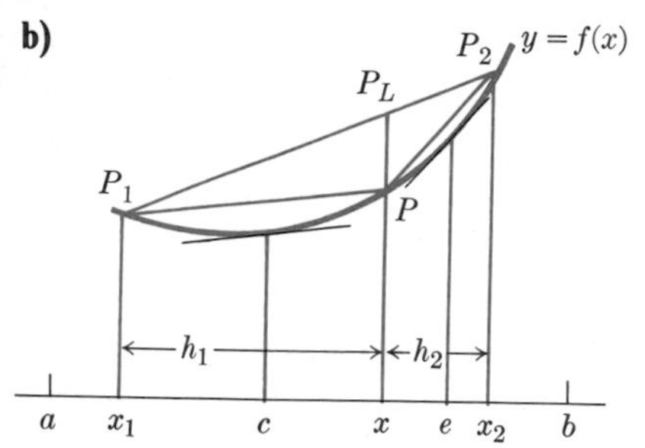

3–36 The portion of the curve $y = f(x)$ shown here is concave upward. Each chord lies above its arc.

If f'' is positive throughout the interval (a, b), all terms on the right side of (4) are positive and we have

$$h_2 f(x_1) + h_1 f(x_2) - (h_1 + h_2)f(x) > 0$$

or

$$\frac{h_2 f(x_1) + h_1 f(x_2)}{h_1 + h_2} > f(x) \tag{5}$$

or

$$\frac{h_1 y_2 + h_2 y_1}{h_1 + h_2} > y.$$

The expression on the left side of this inequality is the ordinate y_L of the point P_L on the chord P_1P_2. Since y is less than y_L, the point $P(x, y)$ is below the chord. Since this is true for any position of the points P_1 and P_2, provided only that $a \leq x_1 < x_2 \leq b$, and for any intermediate point P of abscissa x between x_1 and x_2, it follows that the curve is concave upward in this case, that is, when the second derivative is positive for $a < x < b$.

In case the second derivative is negative over $a < x < b$, the inequalities above are reversed, and we find that

$$y_L < y \qquad \text{when} \quad f''(x) \text{ is negative.}$$

That is, the curve-point $P(x, y)$ is above the chord-point $P_L(x, y_L)$. This means that the curve is concave downward when the second derivative is negative. Q.E.D.

REVIEW QUESTIONS AND EXERCISES

1. Discuss the significance of the signs of the first and second derivatives. Sketch a small portion of a curve, illustrating how it looks near a point where:

a) both y' and y'' are positive;
b) $y' > 0$, $y'' < 0$; **c)** $y' < 0$, $y'' > 0$;
d) $y' < 0$, $y'' < 0$.

2. Define *point of inflection*. How do you find points of inflection from an equation of a curve?

3. How do you locate local maximum and minimum points of a curve? Discuss exceptional points, such as endpoints and points where the derivative fails to exist, in addition to the nonexceptional type. Illustrate with graphs.

4. Let n be a positive integer. For which values of n does the curve $y = x^n$ have (a) a local minimum at the origin, (b) a point of inflection at the origin?

5. Outline a general method for solving "related rates" problems.

6. Outline a general method for solving "max-min" problems.

7. What are the hypotheses of Rolle's theorem? What is the conclusion?

8. Is the converse of Rolle's theorem true?

9. With the book closed, state and prove the Mean Value Theorem. What is its geometrical interpretation?

10. We know that if $F(x) = x^2$, then $F'(x) = 2x$. If someone knows a function G such that $G'(x) = 2x$ but $G(x) \neq x^2$, what can be said about the difference $G(2) - G(1)$? Explain.

11. Describe a method of finding

$$\lim_{x \to a} f(x)/g(x) \text{ if } f(a) = g(a) = 0.$$

Illustrate with an example.

12. Read the article "Mathematics in warfare" by F. W. Lanchester, *World of Mathematics*, **4**, pp. 2138–2157, as a discussion of a practical problem in "related rates."

MISCELLANEOUS PROBLEMS

In each of the following problems (1 through 14) find y' and y''. Determine in each case the sets of values of x for which:

a) y is increasing (as x increases),
b) y is decreasing (as x increases),
c) the graph is concave upward,
d) the graph is concave downward.

Also sketch the graph in each case, indicating *high* and *low* turning points and points of inflection.

1. $y = 9x - x^2$ **2.** $y = x^3 - 5x^2 + 3x$
3. $y = 4x^3 - x^4$ **4.** $y = 4x + x^{-1}$
5. $y = x^2 + 4x^{-1}$ **6.** $y = x + 4x^{-2}$
7. $y = 5 - x^{2/3}$ **8.** $y = \dfrac{x-1}{x+1}$
9. $y = x - \dfrac{4}{x}$ **10.** $y = x^4 - 2x^2$
11. $y = \dfrac{x^2}{ax+b}$; $a > 0$, $b > 0$ **12.** $y = 2x^3 - 9x^2 + 12x$
13. $y = (x-1)(x+1)^2$ **14.** $y = x^2 - \frac{1}{6}x^3$

15. The slope of a curve at any point (x, y) is given by the equation

$$\frac{dy}{dx} = 6(x-1)(x-2)^2(x-3)^3(x-4)^4.$$

a) For what value (or values) of x is y a maximum? Why?
b) For what value (or values) of x is y a minimum? Why?

16. A particle moves along the x-axis with velocity $v = dx/dt = f(x)$. Show that its acceleration is $f(x)f'(x)$.

17. A meteorite entering the earth's atmosphere has velocity inversely proportional to $\sqrt{s}$ when at distance s from the center of the earth. Show that its acceleration is inversely proportional to s^2.

18. If the velocity of a falling body is $k\sqrt{s}$ at the instant when the body has fallen a distance s, find its acceleration.

19. The volume of a cube is increasing at a rate of 300 in^3/min at the instant when the edge is 20 in. Find the rate at which the edge is changing.

20. Sand falling at the rate of 3 ft^3/min forms a conical pile whose radius always equals twice the height. Find the rate at which the height is changing at the instant when the height is 10 ft.

21. The volume of a sphere is decreasing at the rate of 12π ft^3/min. Find the rates at which the radius and the surface area are changing at the instant when the radius is 20 ft. Also find approximately how much the radius and surface area may be expected to change in the following 6 sec.

22. At a certain instant airplane A is flying a level course at 500 mi/hr. At the same time, airplane B is straight above airplane A and flying at the rate of 700 mi/hr on a course that intercepts A's course at a point C that is 4 mi from B and 2 mi from A. (a) At the instant in question, how fast is the distance between the airplanes decreasing? (b) What is the minimum distance between the airplanes, if they continue on the present courses at constant speed?

23. A point moves along the curve $y^2 = x^3$ in such a way that its distance from the origin increases at the constant rate of 2 units per second. Find dx/dt at $(2, 2\sqrt{2})$.

24. Refer to the triangle in Fig. 3–7. How fast is its area changing when $x = 17\sqrt{2}$?

25. Suppose the cone in Fig. 3–8 has a small opening at the vertex through which the water escapes at the rate of $0.08\sqrt{y}$ ft^3/min when its depth is y. Water is also running into the cone at a constant rate of c ft^3/min. When the depth is $6\frac{1}{4}$ ft, the depth of the water is observed to be increasing at the rate of 0.02 ft/min. Under these conditions, will the tank fill? Give a reason for your answer.

26. A particle projected vertically upward from the surface of the earth with initial velocity v_0 has velocity $\sqrt{v_0^2 - 2gR[1 - (R/s)]}$ when it reaches a distance $s \geq R$ from the *center* of the earth. Here R is the radius of the earth. Show that the acceleration is inversely proportional to s^2.

27. Given a triangle ABC. Let D and E be points on the sides AB and AC, respectively, such that DE is parallel to BC. Let the distance between BC and DE equal x. Show that the derivative, with respect to x, of the area $BCED$ is equal to the length of DE.

28. Points A and B move along the x- and y-axes, respectively, in such a way that the perpendicular distance r (inches) from the origin to AB remains constant. How fast is OA changing, and is it increasing or decreasing, when $OB = 2r$ and B is moving toward O at the rate of $0.3r$ in/sec?

29. Ships A and B start from O at the same time. Ship A travels due east at a rate of 15 mi/hr. Ship B travels in a straight course making an angle of 60° with the path of ship A at a rate of 20 mi/hr. How fast are they separating at the end of 2 hr?

30. Water is being poured into an inverted conical tank (vertex down) at the rate of 2 ft^3/min. How fast is the water level rising when the depth of the water is 5 ft? The radius of the base of the cone is 3 ft and the altitude is 10 ft.

31. Divide 20 into two parts (not necessarily integers) such that the product of one part with the square of the other shall be a maximum.

32. Find the largest value of $f(x) = 4x^3 - 8x^2 + 5x$ for $0 \leq x \leq 2$. Give reasons for your answer.

33. Find two *positive* numbers whose sum is 36 and whose product is as large as possible. Can the problem be solved if the product is to be as small as possible?

34. Determine the coefficients a, b, c, d so that the curve whose equation is $y = ax^3 + bx^2 + cx + d$ has a maximum at $(-1, 10)$ and an inflection point at $(1, -6)$.

35. Find that number which most exceeds its square.

36. The perimeter p and area A of a circular sector ("piece of pie") of radius r and arc length s are given by $p = 2r + s$; $A = \frac{1}{2}rs$. If the perimeter is 100 ft, what value of r will produce a maximum area?

37. If a ball is thrown vertically upward with a velocity of 32 ft/sec, its height after t sec is given by the equation $s = 32t - 16t^2$. At what instant will the ball be at its highest point, and how high will it rise?

38. A right circular cone has altitude 12 ft and radius of base 6 ft. A cone is inscribed with its vertex at the center of the base of the given cone and its base parallel to the base of the given cone. Find the dimensions of the cone of maximum volume that can be so inscribed.

39. An oil can is to be made in the form of a right circular cylinder to contain 16π in^3. What dimensions of the can will require the least amount of material?

40. An isosceles triangle is drawn with its vertex at the origin, its base parallel to and above the x-axis and the vertices of its base on the curve $12y = 36 - x^2$. Determine the area of the largest such triangle.

41. A tire manufacturer is able to make x (hundred) grade A tires and y (hundred) grade B tires per day, where $y = (40 - 10x)/(5 - x)$, with $0 \leq x \leq 4$. If the profit on each grade A tire is twice the profit on a grade B tire, what is the most profitable number of grade A tires per day to make?

42. Find the points on the curve $x^2 - y^2 = 1$ that are nearest the point $P(a, 0)$ in case (a) $a = 4$, (b) $a = 2$, (c) $a = \sqrt{2}$.

43. A motorist, stranded in a desert 5 mi from a point A, which is the nearest point on a long straight road, wishes to get to a point B on the road. If the car can travel at 15 mi/hr on the desert and 39 mi/hr on the road, find the point where it must meet the road to get to B in the shortest possible time if (a) B is 5 mi from A, (b) B is 10 mi from A, (c) B is 1 mi from A.

44. Points A and B are ends of a diameter of a circle and C is a point on the circumference. Which of the following statements about triangle ABC is (or are) true?

a) The area is a maximum when the triangle is isosceles.
b) The area is a minimum when the triangle is isosceles.
c) The perimeter is a maximum when the triangle is isosceles.
d) The perimeter is a minimum when the triangle is isosceles.

45. The base and the perimeter of a triangle are fixed. Determine the remaining two sides if the area is to be a maximum.

46. The base b and the area k of a triangle are fixed. Determine the base angles if the angle at the vertex opposite b is to be a maximum.

47. A line is drawn through a fixed point (a, b) to meet the axes Ox, Oy in P and Q. Show that the minimum values of PQ, $OP + OQ$, and $OP \cdot OQ$ are, respectively,

$$(a^{2/3} + b^{2/3})^{3/2}, \qquad (\sqrt{a} + \sqrt{b})^2, \qquad \text{and} \qquad 4ab.$$

48. Find the smallest value of the constant m if $mx - 1 + (1/x)$ is to be greater than or equal to zero for all positive values of x.

49. Let s be the distance between the fixed point $P_1(x_1, y_1)$ and a point $P(x, y)$ on the line

$$L: \quad ax + by + c = 0.$$

Using calculus methods, (a) show that s^2 is a minimum when P_1P is perpendicular to L, and (b) show that the minimum distance is

$$|ax_1 + by_1 + c|/\sqrt{a^2 + b^2}.$$

50. A playing field is to be built in the shape of a rectangle plus a semicircular area at each end. A 400-m race track is to form the perimeter of the field. Find the dimensions of the field if the rectangular part is to have as large an area as possible.

51. If $ax + (b/x) \geq c$ for all positive values of x, where a, b, and c are positive constants, show that $ab \geq c^2/4$.

52. Prove that if $ax^2 + (b/x) \geq c$ for all positive values of x, where a, b, and c are positive constants, then $27ab^2 \geq 4c^3$.

53. Given $f(x) = ax^2 + 2bx + c$ with $a > 0$. By considering the minimum, prove that $f(x) \geq 0$ for all real x if, and only if, $b^2 - ac \leq 0$.

54. In Problem 53, take

$$f(x) = (a_1x + b_1)^2 + (a_2x + b_2)^2 + \cdots + (a_nx + b_n)^2,$$

and deduce Schwarz's inequality:

$$(a_1b_1 + a_2b_2 + \cdots + a_nb_n)^2 \leq (a_1^2 + a_2^2 + \cdots + a_n^2)(b_1^2 + b_2^2 + \cdots + b_n^2).$$

55. In Problem 54, prove that equality can hold only in case there is a real number x such that $b_i = -a_ix$ for every $i = 1, 2, \ldots, n$.

56. If x is positive and m is greater than one, prove that $x^m - 1 - m(x - 1)$ is not negative.

57. What are the dimensions of the rectangular plot of greatest area which can be laid out within a triangle of base 36 ft and altitude 12 ft? Assume that one side of the rectangle lies on the base of the triangle.

58. Find the width across the top of an isosceles trapezoid of base 12 in. and slant sides 6 in. if its area is a maximum.

59. A fence h m high runs parallel to and w m from a vertical wall. Find the length of the shortest ladder that will reach from the ground across the top of the fence to the wall.

60. Assuming that the cost per hour of running the *Queen Elizabeth II* is $a + bv^n$, where a, b, and n are positive constants, $n > 1$, and v is the velocity through the water, find the speed for making the run from Liverpool to New York at minimum cost.

61. A flower bed is to be in the shape of a circular sector of radius r and central angle θ (i.e., like a piece of pie). Find r and θ if the area is fixed and the perimeter is a minimum.

62. A reservoir is to be built in the form of a right circular cone and the lateral area waterproofed. If the capacity of the reservoir is to be 72π ft^3 and one gallon of waterproofing material will cover 80 ft^2, how many gallons are required?

63. Given two concentric circles, C_1 of radius r_1 and C_2 of radius r_2, $r_2 > r_1 > 0$. Let A be the area between them.

a) How fast is A increasing (or decreasing) when $r_1 = 4$ cm and is increasing at the rate of 0.02 cm/sec while $r_2 = 6$ cm and is increasing at the rate of 0.01 cm/sec?

b) Suppose that at time $t = 0$, r_1 is 3 cm and r_2 is 5 cm, and that for $t > 0$, r_1 increases at the constant rate of a cm/sec and r_2 increases at the constant rate of b cm/sec. If $(\frac{3}{5})a < b < a$, find when the area A will be a maximum.

64. Given two concentric spheres, S_1 of radius r_1 and S_2 of radius r_2, $r_2 > r_1 > 0$. Let V be the volume between them. Suppose that at time $t = 0$, $r_1 = r$ in. and $r_2 = R$ in., and that for $t > 0$, r_1 increases at the constant rate of a in/sec and r_2 increases at the constant rate of b in/sec. If $a > b > ar^2/R^2$, find when V will be a maximum.

65. The motion of a particle in a straight line is given by $s = \lambda t - (1 + \lambda^4)t^2$. Show that the particle moves forward initially when λ is positive but ultimately retreats. Show also that for different values of λ the maximum possible distance that the particle can move forward is $\frac{1}{8}$.

66. Let $h(x) = f(x)g(x)$ be the product of two functions that have first and second derivatives and are positive; that is, $f(x) > 0$, $g(x) > 0$.

a) Is it true, if f and g both have a relative maximum at $x = a$, that h has a relative maximum at $x = a$?

b) Is it true, if f and g both have a point of inflection at $x = a$, that h has a point of inflection at $x = a$?

For both (a) and (b) either give a proof or construct a numerical example showing that the statement is false.

67. The numbers $c_1, c_2, \ldots, c_n$ are recorded in an experiment. It is desired to determine a number x with the property that

$$(c_1 - x)^2 + (c_2 - x)^2 + (c_3 - x)^2 + \cdots + (c_n - x)^2$$

shall be a minimum. Find x.

68. The four points

$$(-2, -\tfrac{1}{2}), \quad (0, 1), \quad (1, 2), \quad \text{and} \quad (3, 3)$$

are observed to lie more or less close to a straight line of equation $y = mx + 1$. Find m if the sum

$$(y_1 - mx_1 - 1)^2 + (y_2 - mx_2 - 1)^2 + (y_3 - mx_3 - 1)^2 + (y_4 - mx_4 - 1)^2$$

is to be a minimum, where $(x_1, y_1), \ldots, (x_4, y_4)$ are the coordinates of the given points.

69. The *geometric mean* of the n positive numbers $a_1, a_2, \ldots, a_n$ is the nth root of $a_1 a_2 \cdots a_n$ and the arithmetic mean is $(a_1 + a_2 + \cdots + a_n)/n$. Show that if $a_1, a_2, \ldots, a_{n-1}$ are fixed and $a_n = x$ is permitted to vary over the set of positive real numbers, the ratio of the arithmetic mean to the geometric mean is a minimum when x is the arithmetic mean of $a_1, a_2, \ldots, a_{n-1}$.

70. The curve $(y + 1)^3 = x^2$ passes through the points $(1, 0)$ and $(-1, 0)$. Does Rolle's Theorem justify the conclusion that dy/dx vanishes for some value of x in the interval $-1 \le x \le 1$? Give reasons for your answer.

71. If $a < 0 < b$ and $f(x) = x^{-1/3}$, show that there is no c that satisfies Eq. (4), Article 3–8. Illustrate with a sketch of the graph.

72. If $a < 0 < b$ and $f(x) = x^{1/3}$, show that there is a value of c that satisfies Eq. (4), Article 3–8, even though the function fails to have a derivative at $x = 0$. Illustrate with a sketch of the graph.

73. Show that the equation $f(x) = 2x^3 - 3x^2 + 6x + 6 = 0$ has exactly one real root and find its value accurate to two significant figures. [*Hint.* $f(-1) = -5$, $f(0) = +6$, and $f'(x) > 0$ for all real x.]

74. *Extended Mean Value Theorem.* Suppose $f(x)$ and its derivatives $f'(x), f''(x), \ldots, f^{(n-1)}(x)$ of order one through $(n - 1)$ are continuous on $a \le x \le b$, and $f^{(n)}(x)$ exists for $a < x < b$. If

$$F(x) = f(x) - f(a) - (x - a)f'(a) - (x - a)^2 f''(a)/2! - \cdots - \frac{(x - a)^{n-1} f^{(n-1)}(a)}{(n - 1)!} - K(x - a)^n,$$

where K is chosen so that $F(b) = 0$, show that:

a) $F(a) = F(b) = 0$,

b) $F'(a) = F''(a) = \cdots = F^{(n-1)}(a) = 0$,

c) there exist numbers $c_1, c_2, c_3, \ldots, c_n$ such that

$$a < c_n < c_{n-1} < \cdots < c_2 < c_1 < b$$

and such that

$$F'(c_1) = 0 = F''(c_2) = F'''(c_3) = \cdots = F^{(n-1)}(c_{n-1}) = F^{(n)}(c_n).$$

d) Hence, deduce that $K = [f^{(n)}(c_n)]/n!$ for c_n as above in (c); or, in other words, since $F(b) = 0$,

$$f(b) = f(a) + f'(a)(b - a) + \frac{f''(a)}{2!}(b - a)^2 + \cdots + \frac{f^{(n-1)}(a)}{(n - 1)!}(b - a)^{n-1} + \frac{f^{(n)}(c_n)}{n!}(b - a)^n$$

for some c_n, $a < c_n < b$. [*Amer. Math. Monthly*, **60** (1953), p. 415, James Wolfe.]

75. Suppose that it costs a company $y = a + bx$ dollars to produce x units per week. It can sell x units per week at a price of $P = c - ex$ dollars per unit. (a) What production level maximizes the profit? (b) What is the corresponding price? (c) What is the weekly profit at this level of production? (d) At what price should each item be sold to maximize profits if the government imposes a tax of t dollars per item sold? Comment on the difference between this price and the price before tax.

76. Evaluate the following limits.

a) $\lim\limits_{x \to 0} \dfrac{2 \sin 5x}{3x}$

b) $\lim\limits_{x \to 0} \sin 5x \cot 3x$

c) $\lim\limits_{x \to 0} x \csc^2 \sqrt{2x}$

d) $\lim\limits_{x \to \pi/2} (\sec x - \tan x)$

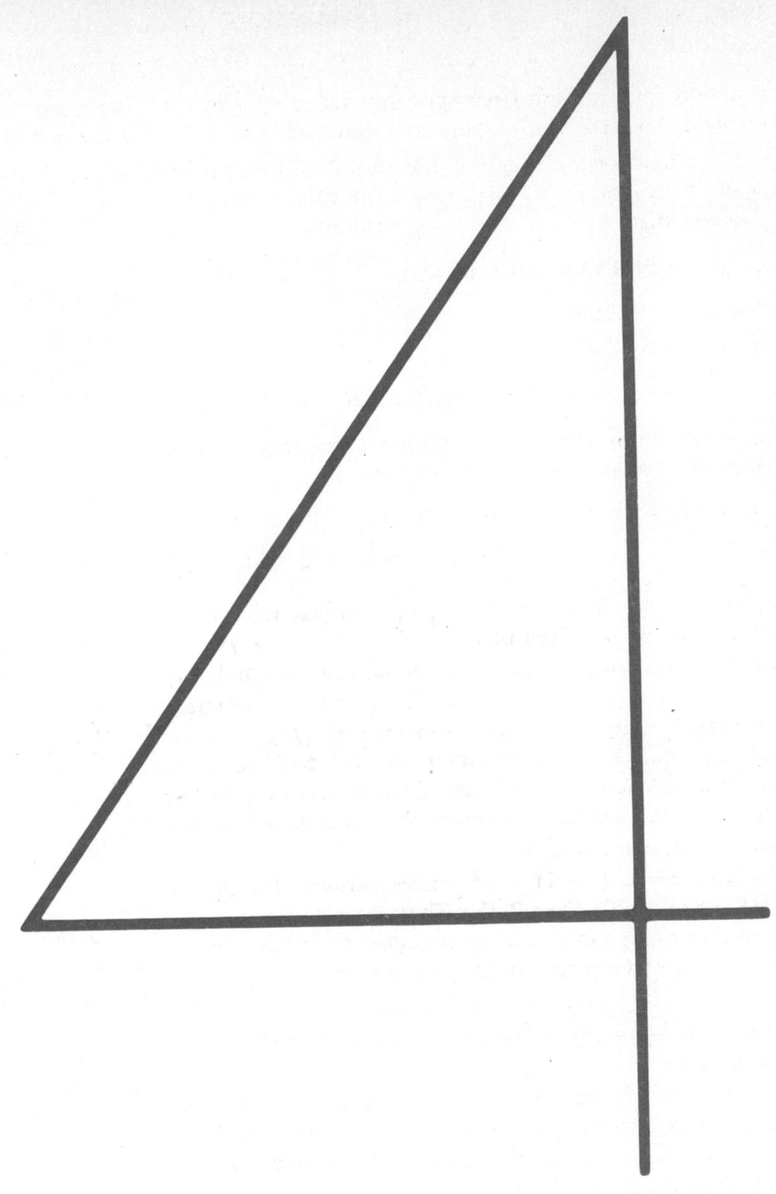

INTEGRATION

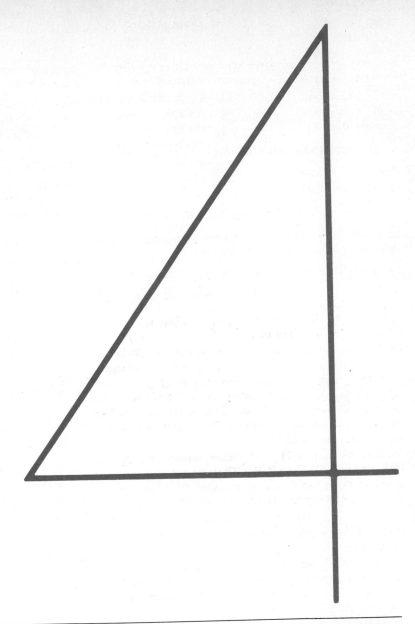

4-1 INTRODUCTION

In the preceding chapters we have pursued one of the two main branches of the calculus, namely, *differential calculus*. We shall now turn our attention to the other main branch of the subject, *integral calculus*. Today, "to integrate" has two meanings in calculus. The deeper and more fundamental meaning is nearly the same as the nontechnical definition: "to indicate the whole of; to give the sum or total of" (Webster). The mathematical meaning of the word in this sense will be amply illustrated in finding areas bounded by curves, volumes of various solids, lengths of curves, centers of gravity, and other applications.

The second mathematical meaning of the verb "to integrate" is "to find a function whose derivative is given." This is the aspect of integration that we shall discuss in the next two articles.

The two kinds of integration are called respectively *definite* and *indefinite*, and the connection between the two is given by a theorem called the *fundamental theorem* of integral calculus.

4-2 THE INDEFINITE INTEGRAL

Suppose that we are given a derivative dy/dx as a function

$$\frac{dy}{dx} = f(x), \qquad a < x < b, \tag{1}$$

and are asked to find $y = F(x)$.

For example, we might be asked to find y as a function of x if

$$\frac{dy}{dx} = 2x.$$

From our experience with derivatives, we can find one answer, namely,

$$y = x^2.$$

On the other hand, we realize that this is not the only answer, since

$$y = x^2 + 1, \qquad y = x^2 - \sqrt{2}, \qquad y = x^2 + 5\pi$$

are also valid answers. Indeed,

$$y = x^2 + C$$

is an answer if C is any constant.

Definition 1. *An equation such as* (1), *which specifies the derivative as a function of* x *(or as a function of* x *and* y*), is called a **differential equation.***

For example,

$$\frac{dy}{dx} = 2xy^2$$

is a differential equation. Second, third, and higher order derivatives may also occur in differential equations, such as

$$\frac{d^2y}{dx^2} + 6xy\frac{dy}{dx} + 3x^2y^3 = 0,$$

and so on. For the time being we shall restrict attention to the special type of differential equation considered in Eq. (1). Differential equations of more general types will be considered in Chapter 18.

***Definition* 2.** *A function $y = F(x)$ is called a* **solution** *of the differential equation* (1) *if, over the domain $a < x < b$, $F(x)$ is differentiable and*

$$\frac{dF(x)}{dx} = f(x). \tag{2}$$

We also say, in these circumstances, that $F(x)$ is **an integral** *of $f(x)$ with respect to x.*

It is clear from this definition that if $F(x)$ is an integral of $f(x)$ with respect to x, then $F(x) + C$ is also such an integral when C is any constant whatever. For if $F(x)$ satisfies Eq. (2), then

$$\frac{d}{dx}[F(x) + C] = \frac{dF(x)}{dx} + \frac{dC}{dx}$$
$$= f(x) + 0 = f(x).$$

What is not clear, however, is whether there are other integrals of $f(x)$ besides those given by the formula $F(x) + C$.

We know that $y = x^2 + C$ is a solution of the differential equation $dy/dx = 2x$ for any constant C. But are there any other solutions? This question is answered by the second corollary of the Mean Value Theorem, Article 3–8. For if both $F_1(x)$ and $F_2(x)$ are integrals of $f(x)$, then

$$\frac{dF_1(x)}{dx} = \frac{dF_2(x)}{dx} = f(x),$$

so that

$$\frac{d[F_1(x) - F_2(x)]}{dx} = 0,$$

and hence

$$F_1(x) - F_2(x) = C,$$

where C is a constant. Hence, if we take $F_2(x) = F(x)$, we have $F_1(x) = F(x) + C$.

Therefore, if

$$y = F(x)$$

is any solution whatever of Eq. (1), then *all* solutions are contained in the formula

$$y = F(x) + C,$$

where C is an arbitrary constant. This is indicated by writing

$$\int f(x)\,dx = F(x) + C, \tag{3}$$

where the symbol $\int$ is called an "integral sign" and Eq. (3) is read "The integral of $f(x)\,dx$ is $F(x)$ plus C." This is a standard notation. We may interpret it in either of two ways:

1. We may think of the symbol

$$\int \ldots dx \tag{4}$$

as meaning "integral, with respect to x, of ...." The symbol (4) is then interpreted as the inverse of the symbol

$$\frac{d}{dx}\ldots,$$

which means "derivative, with respect to x, of ...." In this interpretation the integral sign and the dx go together; the integral sign specifies the operation of integration, and the dx tells us that the *variable of integration* is x.

2. Or we may think of Eq. (2) as written in *differential* form:

$$dF(x) = f(x)\,dx, \tag{5}$$

before the operation indicated by the integral sign is performed. Then, when we introduce the integral sign in Eq. (5) (that is, when we "integrate" both sides of the equation), we get

$$\int dF(x) = \int f(x)\,dx.$$

If we compare this with Eq. (3), we have

$$\int dF(x) = F(x) + C. \tag{6}$$

In other words, when we integrate the *differential* of a function we get that function plus an arbitrary constant. In this interpretation, the symbol $\int$ for integration without the dx stands for the operation that is the inverse of the operation denoted by the symbol d for differentiation. This is the interpretation which we shall adopt in this book. We will refer to the differential $f(x)\,dx$ in Eq. (3) as the *integrand* of the integral.

EXAMPLE 1. Solve the differential equation

$$\frac{dy}{dx} = 3x^2.$$

Solution. We write the given equation in the differential form

$$dy = 3x^2\,dx.$$

Now we know, from past experience, that

$$d(x^3) = 3x^2\,dx.$$

Hence we have

$$y = \int 3x^2\,dx = \int d(x^3) = x^3 + C.$$

If both x and y occur in the differential equation, but in such a way that we can separate the variables to combine all y terms with dy and all x terms with dx, we then integrate as in the following example.

EXAMPLE 2. Solve the differential equation

$$\frac{dy}{dx} = x^2\sqrt{y}, \qquad y > 0. \tag{7}$$

Solution. We change to differentials:

$$dy = x^2\sqrt{y}\,dx.$$

We divide both sides of the equation by $\sqrt{y}$ to separate the variables and obtain

$$y^{-(1/2)}\,dy = x^2\,dx.$$

The left side of this equation is

$$d(2y^{1/2}) = y^{-(1/2)}\,dy,$$

while the right side is

$$d\left(\frac{x^3}{3}\right) = x^2\,dx.$$

Therefore

$$d(2y^{1/2}) = d\left(\frac{x^3}{3}\right).$$

When we integrate this equation, we may write

$$2y^{1/2} + C_1 = \frac{x^3}{3} + C_2$$

or

$$2y^{1/2} = \frac{x^3}{3} + C,$$

where we have combined the two constants C_1 and C_2 into a single constant

$$C = C_2 - C_1.$$

Arbitrary Constants

The equation

$$2y^{1/2} + C_1 = \frac{x^3}{3} + C_2$$

or

$$2y^{1/2} = \frac{x^3}{3} + (C_2 - C_1)$$

in Example 2 describes the family of solutions of Eq. (7). There is one solution for each value of $(C_2 - C_1)$. The equation

$$2y^{1/2} = \frac{x^3}{3} + C$$

describes the very same family of functions, one for each value of C. Clearly there is no need to describe the family with two constants when one will do, nor is any greater generality achieved by doing so.

When we integrate the two sides of a differential equation, it always suffices to add the arbitrary constant C to just one side of the equation since, in any case, if we add constants to both sides of the equation they may always be combined into a single constant.

Integration, as described above, requires the ability to guess the answer. But the following formulas help to reduce the amount of guesswork in many cases. In these formulas, u and v denote differentiable functions of some independent variable (say of x), and a, n, and C are constants.

a) $$\int du = u + C,$$

b) $$\int a\,du = a \int du,$$

c) $$\int (du + dv) = \int du + \int dv,$$

d) $$\int u^n\,du = \frac{u^{n+1}}{n+1} + C, \quad (n \neq -1).$$

In words, these formulas say that:

a) The integral of the differential of a function u is u plus an arbitrary constant C.

b) A constant may be moved across the integral sign. [*Caution.* Variables must *not* be moved across the integral sign.]

c) The integral of the sum of two differentials is the sum of their integrals. This may be extended to the sum of any *finite* number of differentials:

$$\int (du_1 + du_2 + \cdots + du_n) = \int du_1 + \int du_2 + \cdots + \int du_n.$$

d) If n is not minus one, the integral of $u^n\,du$ is obtained by adding one to the exponent, dividing by the new exponent, and adding an arbitrary constant.

EXAMPLE 3

$$\int (5x - x^2 + 2)\,dx = \frac{5}{2}x^2 - \frac{x^3}{3} + 2x + C.$$

$$\int x^{1/2}\,dx = \frac{x^{3/2}}{3/2} + C = \frac{2}{3}x^{3/2} + C.$$

CAUTION. One *must* have precisely du and u^n in order to apply formula (d).

EXAMPLE 4

$$\int \sqrt{2x+1}\,dx$$

The integral does not fit the formula

$$\int u^n\,du$$

with

$$u = 2x+1, \qquad n = \tfrac{1}{2},$$

because then

$$du = \frac{du}{dx}\cdot dx = 2\,dx$$

is *not* precisely dx. The constant factor 2 is missing from the integral. However, this factor can be introduced after the integral sign provided we compensate for it by a factor of $\frac{1}{2}$ in front of the integral sign, by (b). Thus we write

$$\begin{aligned}\int \sqrt{2x+1}\,dx &= \tfrac{1}{2}\int \sqrt{2x+1}\cdot 2\,dx \\ &= \tfrac{1}{2}\int u^{1/2}\,du \qquad [u = 2x+1, \quad du = 2\,dx] \\ &= \frac{1}{2}\frac{u^{3/2}}{3/2} + C \\ &= \tfrac{1}{3}(2x+1)^{3/2} + C.\end{aligned}$$

PROBLEMS

Solve the following differential equations. Remember to separate the variables when necessary.

1. $\dfrac{dy}{dx} = x^2 + 1$
2. $\dfrac{dy}{dx} = \dfrac{1}{x^2} + x, \quad x > 0$
3. $\dfrac{dy}{dx} = \dfrac{x}{y}, \quad y > 0$
4. $\dfrac{dy}{dx} = \sqrt{xy}, \quad x > 0, \quad y > 0$
5. $\dfrac{dy}{dx} = \sqrt[3]{y/x}, \quad x > 0, \quad y > 0$
6. $\dfrac{dy}{dx} = 2xy^2, \quad y > 0$
7. $\dfrac{dy}{dx} = 3x^2 - 2x + 5$
8. $\dfrac{ds}{dt} = 3t^2 + 4t - 6$
9. $\dfrac{dr}{dz} = (2z+1)^3$
10. $\dfrac{du}{dv} = 2u^2(4v^3 + 4v^{-3}), \quad v > 0, \quad u > 0$
11. $\dfrac{dx}{dt} = 8\sqrt{x}, \quad x > 0$
12. $\dfrac{dy}{dt} = (2t + t^{-1})^2, \quad t > 0$
13. $\dfrac{dy}{dz} = \sqrt{(z^2 - z^{-2})^2 + 4}, \quad z > 0$

Evaluate the following integrals:

14. $\int (2x+3)\,dx$
15. $\int (x^2 - \sqrt{x})\,dx$
16. $\int (3x-1)^{234}\,dx$
17. $\int (2-7t)^{2/3}\,dt$
18. $\int \sqrt{2+5y}\,dy$
19. $\displaystyle\int \frac{dx}{(3x+2)^2}$
20. $\displaystyle\int \frac{3r\,dr}{\sqrt{1-r^2}}$
21. $\int \sqrt{2x^2+1}\,x\,dx$
22. $\int t^2(1+2t^3)^{-(2/3)}\,dt$
23. $\displaystyle\int \frac{y\,dy}{\sqrt{2y^2+1}}$
24. $\displaystyle\int \left(\sqrt{x} + \frac{1}{\sqrt{x}}\right)dx$
25. $\displaystyle\int \frac{(z+1)\,dz}{\sqrt[3]{z^2+2z+2}}$

4-3 APPLICATIONS OF INDEFINITE INTEGRATION

Differential equations, such as Eq. (1) or (7) of Article 4–2, arise in chemistry, physics, mathematics, and all branches of engineering. Some of these applications will be illustrated in the examples that follow. Before proceeding with these, however, let us consider the meaning of the arbitrary constant C, which always enters when we integrate a differential equation. If we draw the integral curve $y = F(x)$ (corresponding to taking $C = 0$), then any other integral curve $y = F(x) + C$ is obtained by shifting this curve through a vertical displacement C. Thus we obtain, as in Fig. 4–1, a family of "parallel" curves. They are parallel in the sense that the slope of the tangent to any one of them, at the point of abscissa x, is $f(x)$, the same for all curves $y = F(x) + C$. Now clearly this family of parallel curves has the property that, given any point (x_0, y_0) with x_0 in the allowed domain of the independent variable x, there is one and only one curve of the family that passes through this particular point. For in order that the curve shall pass through the point, the equation must be satisfied by these particular coordinates. This uniquely specifies the value of C to be

$$C = y_0 - F(x_0).$$

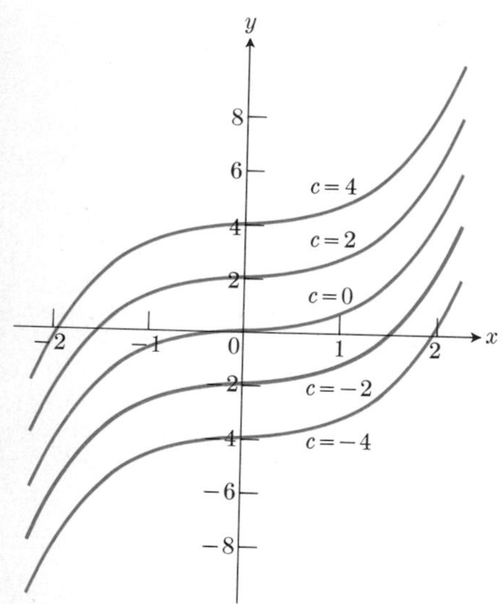

4–1 Selected curves of the family $y = x^3 + C$.

With C thus determined, we get a definite function expressing y in terms of x.

The condition imposed that $y = y_0$ when $x = x_0$ is often referred to as an *initial condition*. This is particularly appropriate in problems where time is the independent variable and initial velocities or initial positions of moving bodies are specified.

EXAMPLE 1. The velocity, at time t, of a moving body is given by

$$v = at,$$

where a is a constant. If the body's coordinate is s_0 at time $t = 0$, find the distance s as a function of t.

Solution. The velocity v is the same as the derivative ds/dt. Hence we want to solve the problem that consists of

$$\text{The differential equation:} \quad \frac{ds}{dt} = at \tag{1}$$

and

$$\text{The initial condition:} \quad s = s_0 \quad \text{when} \quad t = 0. \tag{2}$$

We write Eq. (1) in differential form,

$$ds = at\, dt,$$

and integrate:

$$s = \int at\, dt = a\frac{t^2}{2} + C.$$

The constant of integration may now be determined from the initial condition, which requires that

$$s_0 = C.$$

Hence, the solution of the problem is

$$s = a\frac{t^2}{2} + s_0.$$

EXAMPLE 2. (See Fig. 4–1.) Find the curve whose slope at the point (x, y) is $3x^2$ if the curve is also required to pass through the point $(1, -1)$.

Solution. In mathematical language, we have the following problem:

$$\text{Differential equation:}\quad \frac{dy}{dx} = 3x^2;$$

$$\text{Initial condition:}\quad y = -1 \quad \text{when} \quad x = 1.$$

First, we integrate the differential equation:

$$dy = 3x^2\, dx,$$

$$y = \int 3x^2\, dx = x^3 + C.$$

Then we impose the initial condition to evaluate the constant C:

$$-1 = 1^3 + C; \qquad C = -2.$$

We substitute the value of C into the solution of the differential equation, and obtain the particular integral curve that passes through the given point, namely,

$$y = x^3 - 2.$$

The total revenue $R(x)$ from selling x units of a product can be determined by integrating the marginal revenue dR/dx and using an initial condition to evaluate the constant of integration.

EXAMPLE 3. For quantities x up to a certain production level $x = L$, a company found that its marginal revenue was

$$\frac{dR}{dx} = 5 + \frac{4}{(2x + 1)^2}.$$

Find $R(x)$ for $0 \le x \le L$, if $R(0) = 0$.

Solution

$$\int dR = \int \left[5 + \frac{4}{(2x + 1)^2}\right] dx,$$

$$R(x) = 5x - \frac{2}{2x + 1} + C.$$

Since $R(0) = 0$,

$$0 = 0 - 2 + C, \qquad C = 2.$$

The revenue function for $0 \leq x \leq L$ is

$$R(x) = 5x - \frac{2}{2x+1} + 2.$$

PROBLEMS

In each of the following problems (1 through 6), find the position s as a function of t from the given velocity $v = ds/dt$. Evaluate the constant of integration so as to have $s = s_0$ when $t = 0$.

1. $v = 3t^2$ **2.** $v = 2t + 1$

3. $v = (t + 1)^2$ **4.** $v = (t^2 + 1)^2$

5. $v = (t + 1)^{-2}$ **6.** $v = \sqrt{2gs}$ (g = constant)

In each of the following problems (7 through 11), find the velocity v and position s as functions of t from the given acceleration $a = dv/dt$. Evaluate the constants of integration so as to have $v = v_0$ and $s = s_0$ when $t = 0$.

7. $a = g$ (constant) **8.** $a = t$

9. $a = \sqrt[3]{2t + 1}$ **10.** $a = (2t + 1)^{-3}$

11. $a = (t^2 + 1)^2$

12. The gravitational attraction exerted by the earth on a particle of mass m at distance s from the center is given by $F = -mgR^2s^{-2}$, where R is the radius of the earth and F is negative because the force acts in opposition to increasing s (Fig. 4–2). If a particle is projected vertically upward from the surface of the earth with initial velocity $v_0 = \sqrt{2gR}$, apply Newton's second law $F = ma$ with $a = v(dv/ds)$ to show that $v = v_0\sqrt{R/s}$ and that $s^{3/2} = R^{3/2}[1 + (3v_0 t/2R)]$.

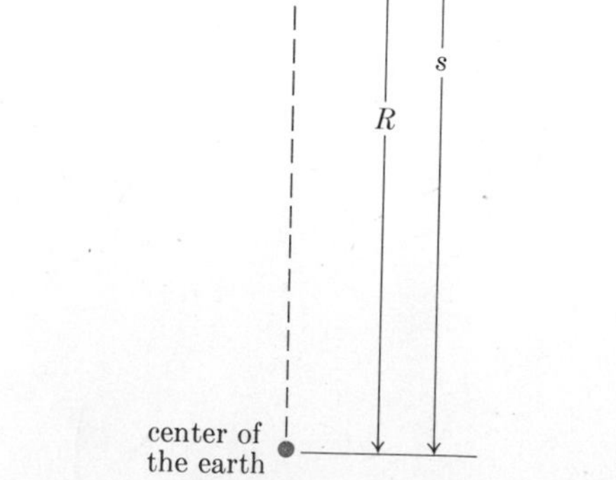

4–2 A mass m that is s km from the earth's center.

REMARK. The initial velocity $v_0 = \sqrt{2gR}$ (approximately 11.2 kilometers per second) is known as the "velocity of escape," since the displacement s tends to infinity with increasing t provided the initial velocity is this large. Actually, a somewhat larger initial velocity is required for escape from the earth's gravitational attraction, due to the retardation effect of air resistance, which we have neglected here for the sake of simplicity.

Solve the following differential equations subject to the prescribed initial conditions.

13. $\dfrac{dy}{dx} = 9x^2 - 4x + 5, \quad x = -1, \; y = 0$

14. $\dfrac{dy}{dx} = 4(x - 7)^3, \quad x = 8, \; y = 10$

15. $\dfrac{dy}{dx} = x^{1/2} + x^{1/4}, \quad x = 0, \; y = -2$

16. $\dfrac{dy}{dx} = \dfrac{x^2 + 1}{x^2}, \quad x = 1, \; y = 1$

17. $\dfrac{dy}{dx} = x\sqrt{y}, \quad x = 0, \; y = 1$

18. $\dfrac{dy}{dx} = 2xy^2, \quad x = 1, \; y = 1$

19. $\dfrac{dy}{dx} = x\sqrt{1 + x^2}, \quad x = 0, \; y = -3$

20. $\dfrac{dy}{dx} = \dfrac{4\sqrt{(1 + y^2)^3}}{y}, \quad x = 0, \; y = 1$

21. (a) Find the total revenue $R(x)$ from selling x units if the marginal revenue in dollars per unit for $0 < x \leq 400$ is

$$\frac{dR}{dx} = \frac{125}{\sqrt{x}} - \frac{100}{x^2}$$

and the revenue from selling the first 100 units is \$2400. (b) What additional income comes from selling the next 100 units?

4–4 INTEGRATION OF SINES AND COSINES

Corresponding to the derivative formulas VII and VIII (see Article 2–13), we also have the differential formulas

$$d(\sin u) = \cos u \, du, \qquad \text{VII}'$$

$$d(\cos u) = -\sin u \, du, \qquad \text{VIII}'$$

and the integration formulas

$$\int \cos u \, du = \sin u + C,$$
$$\int \sin u \, du = -\cos u + C. \qquad (1)$$

EXAMPLE 1

$$\begin{aligned}\int \cos 2t \, dt &= \tfrac{1}{2} \int \cos 2t \cdot 2 \, dt \\ &= \tfrac{1}{2} \int \cos u \, du \qquad (u = 2t) \\ &= \tfrac{1}{2} \sin u + C \\ &= \tfrac{1}{2} \sin 2t + C.\end{aligned}$$

EXAMPLE 2. Evaluate the integral

$$\int \frac{\cos 2x}{\sin^3 2x} \, dx.$$

Solution. Since

$$d(\sin 2x) = 2 \cos 2x \, dx,$$

we recognize the numerator as being

$$\tfrac{1}{2} d(\sin 2x).$$

Hence we have

$$\begin{aligned}\int \frac{\cos 2x \, dx}{\sin^3 2x} &= \int (\sin 2x)^{-3} \cdot \tfrac{1}{2} d(\sin 2x) \\ &= \tfrac{1}{2} \int u^{-3} \, du \qquad (u = \sin 2x) \\ &= \frac{1}{2} \frac{u^{-2}}{-2} + C \\ &= \frac{-1}{4 \sin^2 2x} + C.\end{aligned}$$

In Examples 1 and 2 we used a combination of substitution and algebraic manipulation to reduce the integrands to standard forms that we knew how to integrate. The standard forms available to us at the moment are

$$\int du = u + C \qquad \int u^n\, du = \frac{u^{n+1}}{n+1} + C, \quad n \neq -1 \qquad \textbf{(2)}$$

$$\int \sin u\, du = -\cos u + C \qquad \int \cos u\, du = \sin u + C,$$

and the rules we can use for algebraic manipulation of integrals are

$$\int a\, du = a \int du, \qquad \int du + dv = \int du + \int dv. \qquad \textbf{(3)}$$

However, it may not always be clear, when you first see an integral, how to find a combination of substitutions and manipulations that will reduce it to one of the standard forms. (Occasionally no such combination exists, but that will not be an issue here.)

There is a procedure you can try if you don't see how to integrate a given function right away. The procedure assumes that you have enough experience to make a reasonable guess at the answer, but it does not require you to guess absolutely right the first time. The steps are: (1) write down your guess; (2) compare its differential with the one in the integral; (3) modify your guess accordingly; and (4) check the result and make any further improvements necessary. Make sure to add a C.

We use this procedure in the next example.

EXAMPLE 3. Evaluate the integral

$$\int \sin(7x + 5)\, dx.$$

Solution. We try

$$\cos(7x + 5) + C.$$

Its differential is

$$-\sin(7x + 5) \cdot 7\, dx.$$

This differs from the original differential $\sin(7x + 5)\, dx$ by a factor of -7. We divide the trial function by -7, obtaining

$$-\frac{1}{7}\cos(7x + 5) + C.$$

The differential of this new function is

$$-\frac{1}{7} \cdot -\sin(7x + 5) \cdot 7\, dx = \sin(7x + 5)\, dx,$$

which is what we want. We conclude that

$$\int \sin(7x + 5)\, dx = -\frac{1}{7}\cos(7x + 5) + C.$$

EXAMPLE 4. Find

$$\int x \sin x\, dx.$$

Solution. We try

$$x \cos x + C.$$

Its differential is

$$\cos x\, dx - x \sin x\, dx.$$

There are two things wrong here. First, we have $-x \sin x\, dx$ when we want $+x \sin x\, dx$, and second, we have $\cos x\, dx$ which we do not want at all. Correcting the sign is easy: we just take

$$-x \cos x + C$$

as our new trial function. Now the differential is

$$-\cos x\, dx + x \sin x\, dx,$$

which is partly what we want but still has a term, $-\cos x\, dx$, that we don't want. To eliminate it we add to the trial function a term whose differential is $+\cos x\, dx$, namely, $\sin x$. This changes the trial function to

$$\sin x - x \cos x + C,$$

whose differential is

$$\cos x\, dx - \cos x\, dx + x \sin x\, dx = x \sin x\, dx.$$

This is just what we want:

$$\int x \sin x\, dx = \sin x - x \cos x + C.$$

PROBLEMS

Evaluate the following integrals.

1. $\int \sin 3x\, dx$
2. $\int \cos (2x + 4)\, dx$
3. $\int x \sin (2x^2)\, dx$
4. $\int (\cos \sqrt{x}) \frac{dx}{\sqrt{x}}$
5. $\int \sin 2t\, dt$
6. $\int \cos (3\theta - 1)\, d\theta$
7. $\int 4 \cos 3y\, dy$
8. $\int 2 \sin z \cos z\, dz$
9. $\int \sin^2 x \cos x\, dx$
10. $\int \cos^2 2y \sin 2y\, dy$
11. $\int (1 - \sin^2 3t) \cos 3t\, dt$
12. $\int \frac{\sin x\, dx}{\cos^2 x}$
13. $\int \frac{\cos x\, dx}{\sin^2 x}$
14. $\int \sqrt{2 + \sin 3t} \cos 3t\, dt$
15. $\int \frac{\sin 2t\, dt}{\sqrt{2 - \cos 2t}}$
16. $\int \sin^3 \frac{y}{2} \cos \frac{y}{2}\, dy$
17. $\int \frac{\sin [(z - 1)/3]\, dz}{\cos^2 [(z - 1)/3]}$
18. $\int \cos^2 \frac{2x}{3} \sin \frac{2x}{3}\, dx$
19. $\int (1 + \sin 2t)^{3/2} \cos 2t\, dt$
20. $\int (3 \sin 2x + 4 \cos 3x)\, dx$
21. $\int \sin t \cos t(\sin t + \cos t)\, dt$
22. $\int (\sin x + x \cos x)\, dx$

Solve the following differential equations subject to the given initial conditions.

23. $2y \frac{dy}{dx} = 5x - 3 \sin x, \qquad x = 0, \quad y = 0$
24. $\frac{dy}{dx} = \frac{\pi \cos \pi x}{\sqrt{y}}, \qquad x = \frac{1}{2}, \quad y = 1$
25. We can treat the integral of $2 \sin x \cos x\, dx$ in three different ways:

i) $\int 2 \sin x \cos x\, dx = \int 2 \sin x\, d(\sin x)$

$$= \sin^2 x + C_1$$

ii) $\int 2 \sin x \cos x \, dx = \int -2 \cos x \, d(\cos x)$

$= -\cos^2 x + C_2$

iii) $\int 2 \sin x \cos x \, dx = \int \sin 2x \, dx$

$= -\frac{1}{2} \cos 2x + C_3.$

Can all three integrations be correct? Explain.

4–5 AREA UNDER A CURVE

In geometry we learned how to find areas of certain polygons: rectangles, triangles, parallelograms, trapezoids. Indeed, the area of any polygon can be found by cutting it into triangles.

The area of a circle is easily computed from the familiar formula $A = \pi r^2$. But the idea behind this simple formula isn't so simple. In fact, it is the subtle concept of a *limit*, the area of the circle being *defined* as the limit of areas of inscribed (or circumscribed) regular polygons as the number of sides *increases without bound.* A similar idea is involved in the definition we now introduce for other plane areas.

Let $y = f(x)$ define a continuous function of x on the closed interval $a \le x \le b$. For simplicity, we shall also suppose that $f(x)$ is positive for $a \le x \le b$. We consider the problem of calculating the area bounded above by the graph of the function, on the sides by vertical lines through $x = a$ and $x = b$, and below by the x-axis (Fig. 4–3).

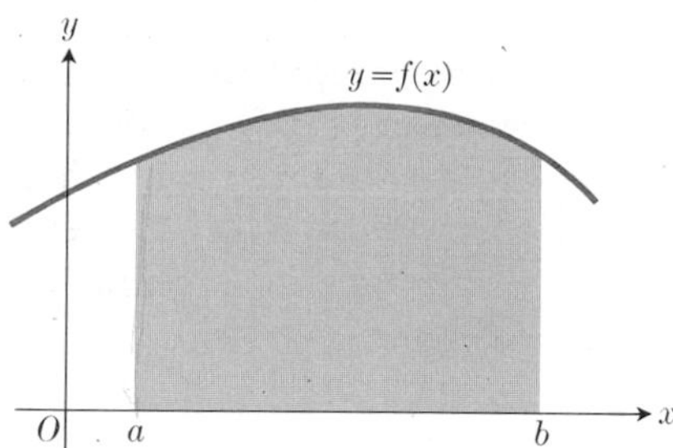

4–3 Area under a curve.

We divide the area into n thin strips of uniform width $\Delta x = (b - a)/n$ by lines perpendicular to the x-axis through the endpoints $x = a$ and $x = b$ and many intermediate points, which we number as $x_1, x_2, \ldots, x_{n-1}$ (Fig. 4–4). We use an inscribed rectangle to approximate the area in each strip. For instance, in the figure, we approximate the area of the strip $aP_0 P_1 x_1$ by the shaded rectangle of altitude aP_0 and base $a \cdots x_1$. The area of this rectangle is

$$f(a) \cdot (x_1 - a) = f(a) \cdot \Delta x,$$

since the length of the altitude aP_0 is the value of f at $x = a$, and the length of the base is $x_1 - a = \Delta x$. Similarly, the inscribed rectangle in the second strip has area

$$f(x_1) \cdot \Delta x.$$

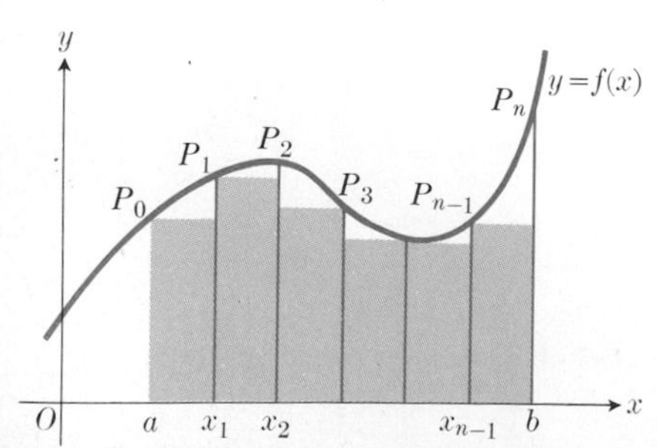

4–4 Area under a curve $y = f(x)$ divided into strips. Each strip is approximated by a rectangle.

Continuing in this fashion, we inscribe a rectangle in each strip.

If the function increases with x as in Fig. 4–5, then the altitude of each rectangle is the length of its left edge, and we have

$$\begin{aligned}
&\text{Area of first rectangle} &&= f(a)\cdot\Delta x,\\
&\text{Area of second rectangle} &&= f(x_1)\cdot\Delta x,\\
&\text{Area of third rectangle} &&= f(x_2)\cdot\Delta x,\\
&\quad\vdots\\
&\text{Area of } n\text{th and last rectangle} &&= f(x_{n-1})\cdot\Delta x.
\end{aligned}$$

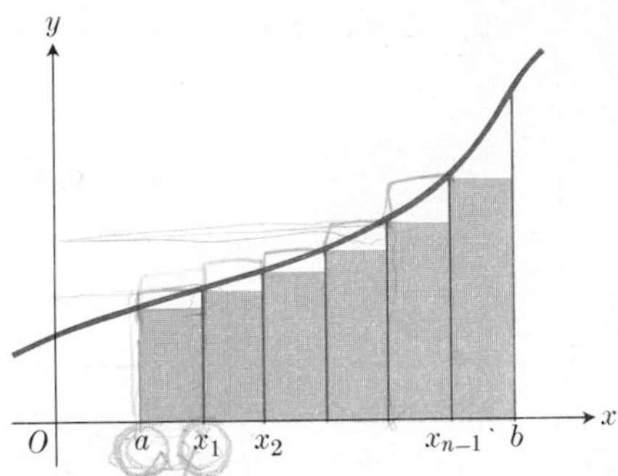

4–5 Rectangles under the graph of an increasing function.

EXAMPLE 1. Suppose $f(x) = 1 + x^2$; $a = 0$, $b = 1$, and $n = 4$. There are $n - 1 = 3$ intermediate points $x_1 = \frac{1}{4}$, $x_2 = \frac{1}{2}$, and $x_3 = \frac{3}{4}$, which divide the interval $0 \le x \le 1$ into $n = 4$ subintervals, each of length $\Delta x = \frac{1}{4}$. The inscribed rectangles (Fig. 4–6) have areas

$$\begin{aligned}
f(0)\cdot\Delta x &= 1\cdot\tfrac{1}{4} = \tfrac{16}{64}\\
f(\tfrac{1}{4})\cdot\Delta x &= \tfrac{17}{16}\cdot\tfrac{1}{4} = \tfrac{17}{64}\\
f(\tfrac{1}{2})\cdot\Delta x &= \tfrac{5}{4}\cdot\tfrac{1}{4} = \tfrac{20}{64}\\
f(\tfrac{3}{4})\cdot\Delta x &= \tfrac{25}{16}\cdot\tfrac{1}{4} = \tfrac{25}{64}\\
\text{Sum} &= \tfrac{78}{64} = 1.21875.
\end{aligned}$$

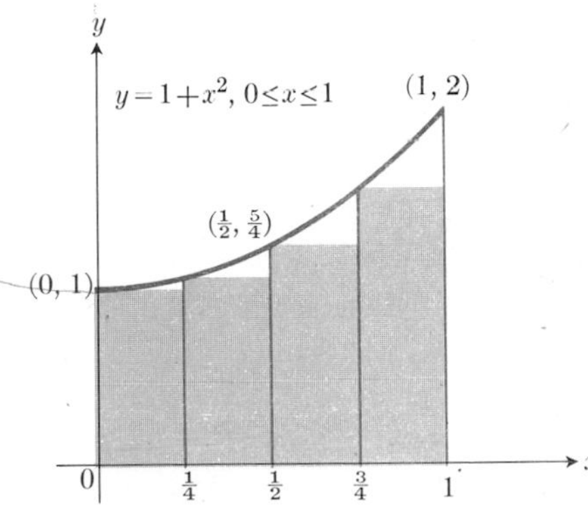

4–6 Rectangles under the graph of $y = 1 + x^2$, $0 \le x \le 1$.

Since the area under the curve is larger than the sum of the areas of these inscribed rectangles, we may expect it to be somewhat larger than 1.22. In fact, by using methods we shall soon develop, we shall find that the area is exactly $\frac{4}{3}$. Thus our estimate of 1.22 is about 8 percent too small. There are easy ways of improving the accuracy, for example by using trapezoids in place of rectangles to approximate each strip, but we defer that to a later time.

If the curve slopes downward as in Fig. 4–7, then the altitude of each inscribed rectangle is the length of its right edge, and we have areas as follows:

$$\begin{aligned}
&\text{First rectangle} && f(x_1)\cdot\Delta x,\\
&\text{Second rectangle} && f(x_2)\cdot\Delta x,\\
&\text{Third rectangle} && f(x_3)\cdot\Delta x,\\
&\quad\vdots\\
&n\text{th and last} && f(b)\cdot\Delta x.
\end{aligned}$$

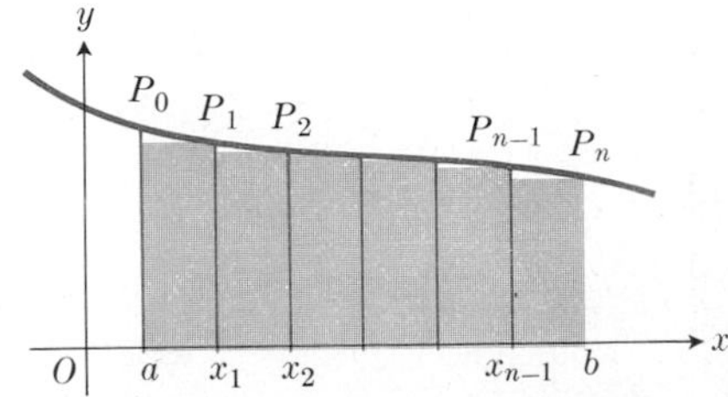

4–7 Rectangles under the graph of a decreasing function.

More generally, the curve may rise and fall between $x = a$ and $x = b$, as in Fig. 4–8. But there is a number c_1, between a and x_1 inclusive, such that the first inscribed rectangle has area $f(c_1)\cdot\Delta x$; and a number c_2 in the second closed subinterval such that the area of the second inscribed rec-

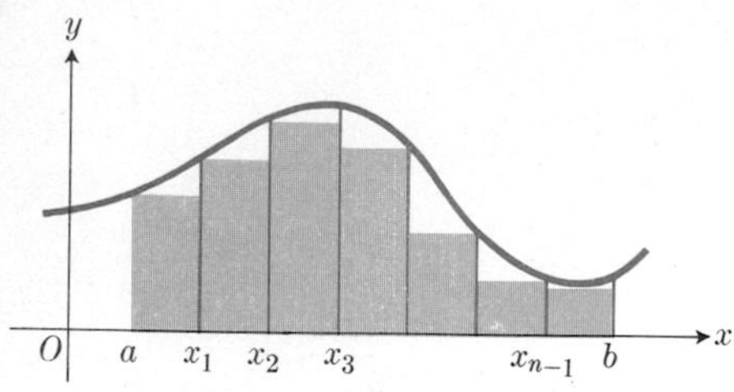

4-8 Rectangles under a curve which rises and falls between a and b.

tangle is $f(c_2) \cdot \Delta x$; and so on. The number c_1 is the place between a and x_1, inclusive, where f is minimized for the first subinterval. Similarly, the minimum value of f for x in the second subinterval is attained at c_2, and so on.

The sum of the areas of these inscribed rectangles is

$$S_n = f(c_1) \cdot \Delta x + f(c_2) \cdot \Delta x + \cdots + f(c_n) \cdot \Delta x. \tag{1}$$

We may also write this in more abbreviated form by using the sigma notation,

$$S_n = \sum_{k=1}^{n} f(c_k) \cdot \Delta x. \tag{2}$$

The Greek letter Σ (capital sigma) is used this way in mathematics to denote a sum. Note that each term of the sum in (1) is of the form $f(c_k) \cdot \Delta x$, with only the subscript on c changing from one term to another. We have indicated the subscript by k, but we could equally well have used i or j or any other symbol except a letter that is currently in use for something else. In the first term in the sum on the right side of Eq. (1) the subscript is $k = 1$; in the second, $k = 2$; and so on to the last, or nth, in which $k = n$. We indicate this by writing $k = 1$ below the Σ in (2), to say that the sum is to *start* with the term we get by replacing k in the expression that follows by 1. The n above the sigma tells us where to *stop*. For instance, if $n = 4$, we have

$$\sum_{k=1}^{4} f(c_k) \cdot \Delta x = f(c_1) \cdot \Delta x + f(c_2) \cdot \Delta x + f(c_3) \cdot \Delta x + f(c_4) \cdot \Delta x.$$

The only thing that changes from one summand to the next is the numeral in the place indicated by k. First we replace k by 1, then by 2, then 3, then 4. Then we add.

Here are a few other examples of Σ notation:

EXAMPLE 2

a) $\displaystyle\sum_{k=1}^{5} k^2 = 1^2 + 2^2 + 3^2 + 4^2 + 5^2,$

b) $\displaystyle\sum_{k=1}^{3} \frac{k}{k+1} = \frac{1}{1+1} + \frac{2}{2+1} + \frac{3}{3+1},$

c) $\displaystyle\sum_{j=0}^{2} \frac{j+1}{j+2} = \frac{0+1}{0+2} + \frac{1+1}{1+2} + \frac{2+1}{2+2},$

d) $\displaystyle\sum_{i=1}^{4} x_i = x_1 + x_2 + x_3 + x_4,$

e) $\displaystyle\sum_{k=1}^{4} x^k = x + x^2 + x^3 + x^4.$

We turn our attention once more to the area under the graph of a positive continuous function $y = f(x)$, $a \leq x \leq b$. We *define* the area to be *the limit of the sums of the areas of inscribed rectangles as their common base length Δx approaches zero and their number increases without bound.*

In symbols,

$$A = \lim_{n\to\infty} [f(c_1)\,\Delta x + f(c_2)\,\Delta x + \cdots + f(c_n)\,\Delta x]$$

$$= \lim_{n\to\infty} \sum_{k=1}^{n} f(c_k)\,\Delta x. \tag{3}$$

REMARK 1. The existence of the limit in (3) is a consequence of the continuity of f, but proving this fact is beyond the scope of our discussion and will be left to more advanced courses in mathematical analysis. However, it is a fact that, by taking larger and larger values of n and computing the sum of the areas of inscribed rectangles for each n, we get answers that differ from one another (and from what we would intuitively call the area under the curve) by amounts that become arbitrarily small as n increases.

REMARK 2. We could have used circumscribed instead of inscribed rectangles. We would then replace the c_k in Eq. (3) by other numbers, say e_k. These would be the places in the subintervals where the function takes on its *maximum* instead of minimum values. The corresponding sums would tend to overestimate the exact area, but in the limit we would get the same answer whether we used inscribed or circumscribed rectangles. The fact that the two kinds of sums of areas of rectangles give the same limit is a consequence of the *uniform continuity* of the function f over the domain $a \leq x \leq b$. Again, this is a theorem which is usually proved in more advanced courses in mathematical analysis. (It is also implied by the inequalities and equations (10) through (14) of Article 4–8.)

REMARK 3. Just as we use the simple formula $A = \pi r^2$ to find the area of a circle, rather than resorting to a calculation of the limit of areas of inscribed polygons, so with the area under a curve. We shall not compute many areas directly from the definition in Eq. (3). Rather we shall develop from it a method for getting answers very quickly and simply. But we need the definition of area, as given above, as a starting place.

PROBLEMS

In each of the following problems (1 through 5), sketch the graph of the given equation over the interval $a \leq x \leq b$. Divide the interval into $n = 4$ subintervals each of length $\Delta x = (b - a)/4$. (a) Sketch the inscribed rectangles and compute the sum of their areas. (b) Do the same using the circumscribed in place of the inscribed rectangle in each subinterval (Fig. 4–9).

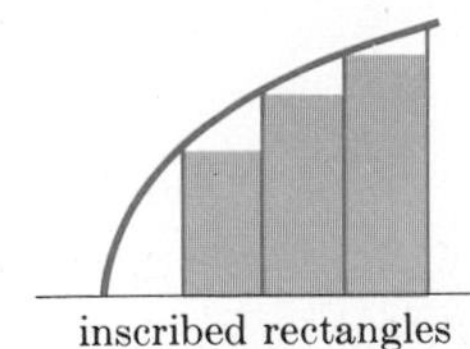

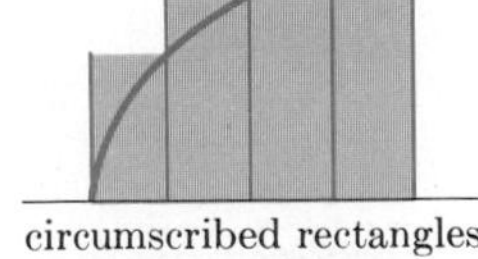

Figure 4–9

1. $y = 2x + 1, \quad a = 0, \quad b = 1.$

2. $y = x^2, \quad a = -1, \quad b = 1.$

3. $y = \sin x, \quad a = 0, \quad b = \pi.$

4. $y = 1/x, \quad a = 1, \quad b = 2.$

5. $y = \sqrt{x}, \quad a = 0, \quad b = 4.$

Write out the following sums, as in Example 2.

6. $\displaystyle\sum_{k=1}^{5} \frac{1}{k}$ **7.** $\displaystyle\sum_{i=-1}^{3} 2^i$ **8.** $\displaystyle\sum_{n=1}^{4} \cos n\pi x$

Find the value of each sum.

9. $\displaystyle\sum_{n=0}^{4} \frac{n}{4}$ **10.** $\displaystyle\sum_{k=1}^{3} \frac{k-1}{k}$ **11.** $\displaystyle\sum_{m=0}^{5} \sin \frac{m\pi}{2}$

4–6

COMPUTATION OF AREAS AS LIMITS

In Article 4–5 we defined the area under the graph of $y = f(x)$ over the interval $a \leq x \leq b$ as the *limit* of sums of areas of inscribed rectangles. We computed a few sums, but no limits. To compute the limits we need some algebraic formulas. We now develop these. Then we compute some areas as limits to show how it can be done. In Article 4–7 we show how much easier it is using integral calculus.

We need the following formulas:

$$\sum_{k=1}^{n} k = 1 + 2 + 3 + \cdots + n = \frac{n(n+1)}{2},$$

$$\sum_{k=1}^{n} k^2 = 1^2 + 2^2 + 3^2 + \cdots + n^2 = \frac{n(n+1)(2n+1)}{6},$$

which we shall prove by the method of mathematical induction. This consists of showing that each formula is true when $n = 1$, and that if the formula is true for any integer n, then it is also true for the next integer, $n + 1$. We shall also show how such formulas might be discovered.

First, consider the sum of first powers:

$$F(n) = 1 + 2 + 3 + \cdots + n.$$

Table 4–1 shows briefly how $F(n)$ increases with n. The last column exhibits $F(n)/n$, the ratio of $F(n)$ to n.

Table 4–1

n	$F(n) = 1 + 2 + 3 + \cdots + n$	$F(n)/n$
1	1	$1 = \frac{2}{2}$
2	$1 + 2 = 3$	$\frac{3}{2} = \frac{3}{2}$
3	$1 + 2 + 3 = 6$	$\frac{6}{3} = \frac{4}{2}$
4	$1 + 2 + 3 + 4 = 10$	$\frac{10}{4} = \frac{5}{2}$
5	$1 + 2 + 3 + 4 + 5 = 15$	$\frac{15}{5} = \frac{6}{2}$
6	$1 + 2 + 3 + 4 + 5 + 6 = 21$	$\frac{21}{6} = \frac{7}{2}$

The last column suggests that the ratio $F(n)/n$ is equal to $(n + 1)/2$. At least this is the case for all the entries in the table ($n = 1, 2, 3, 4, 5, 6$). In other words, the formula

$$\frac{F(n)}{n} = \frac{n+1}{2}$$

or

$$1 + 2 + 3 + \cdots + n = \frac{n(n+1)}{2} \tag{1}$$

is true for $n = 1, 2, 3, 4, 5, 6$. Suppose now that n is any integer for which (1) is known to be true (at the moment, n could be any integer from 1 through

6). Then if $(n+1)$ were added to both sides of the equation, the new equation

$$1+2+3+\cdots+n+(n+1)=\frac{n(n+1)}{2}+(n+1) \tag{2}$$

would also be true for that same n. But the right side of (2) is

$$\frac{n(n+1)}{2}+(n+1)=\frac{(n+1)}{2}(n+2)=\frac{(n+1)(n+2)}{2},$$

so that (2) becomes

$$1+2+3+\cdots+n+(n+1)=\frac{(n+1)((n+1)+1)}{2},$$

which is just like Eq. (1) except that n is replaced by $n+1$. Thus if Eq. (1) is true for an integer n, it is also true for the next integer $n+1$. Hence we now know that it is true for $n+1=7$, since it was true for $n=6$. Then we can say it is true for $n+1=8$, since it is true for $n=7$. By the principle of mathematical induction, then, it is true for every positive integer n.

Now let's consider the squares. Let

$$Q(n)=1^2+2^2+3^2+\cdots+n^2$$

be the sum of the squares of the first n positive integers. Obviously this grows faster than $F(n)$, the sum of first powers, but let us look at the ratio of $Q(n)$ to $F(n)$ to compare them. (See Table 4-2.)

Table 4-2

n	$F(n)$	$Q(n)=1^2+2^2+3^2+\cdots+n^2$	$Q(n)/F(n)$
1	1	$1^2=1$	$\frac{1}{1}=\frac{3}{3}$
2	3	$1^2+2^2=5$	$\frac{5}{3}=\frac{5}{3}$
3	6	$1^2+2^2+3^2=14$	$\frac{14}{6}=\frac{7}{3}$
4	10	$1^2+2^2+3^2+4^2=30$	$\frac{30}{10}=\frac{9}{3}$
5	15	$1^2+2^2+3^2+4^2+5^2=55$	$\frac{55}{15}=\frac{11}{3}$
6	21	$1^2+2^2+3^2+4^2+5^2+6^2=91$	$\frac{91}{21}=\frac{13}{3}$

We note how regular the last column is: $\frac{3}{3}, \frac{5}{3}, \frac{7}{3}$, and so on. In fact it is just $(2n+1)/3$ for $n=1, 2, 3, 4, 5, 6$; that is,

$$Q(n)=F(n)\cdot\frac{2n+1}{3}.$$

But from Eq. (1), $F(n)=n(n+1)/2$, and hence

$$Q(n)=1^2+2^2+3^2+\cdots+n^2=\frac{n(n+1)(2n+1)}{6} \tag{3}$$

is true for the integers n from 1 through 6. To establish it for all other positive integers, we proceed as before. Start with any n for which (3) is true and add $(n + 1)^2$. Then

$$1^2 + 2^2 + 3^2 + \cdots + n^2 + (n + 1)^2 = \frac{n(n + 1)(2n + 1)}{6} + (n + 1)^2$$

$$= \frac{(n + 1)}{6}[n(2n + 1) + 6(n + 1)]$$

$$= \frac{(n + 1)}{6}(2n^2 + 7n + 6) = \frac{(n + 1)(n + 2)(2n + 3)}{6}. \tag{4}$$

We note that the last expression in (4) is the same as the last expression in (3) with n replaced by $n + 1$. In other words, if the formula in (3) is true for any integer n, we have just shown that it is true for $n + 1$. Since we know it is true for $n = 6$, it is also true for $n + 1 = 7$. And now that we know it is true for $n = 7$, it follows that it is true for $n + 1 = 8$, and so on. It is true for every positive integer n by the principle of mathematical induction.

We now apply these formulas to find areas under two graphs.

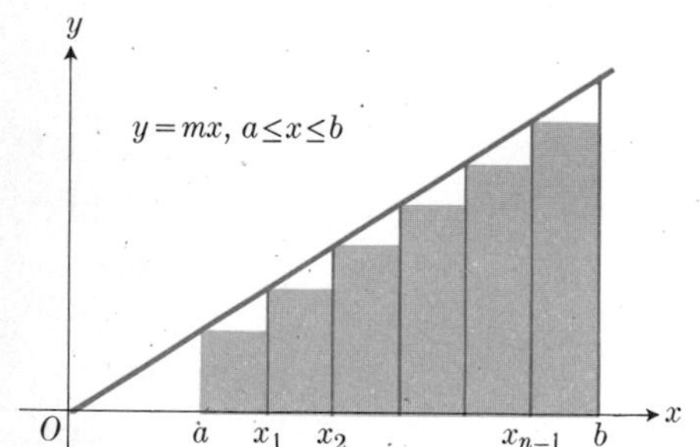

4–10 The area under $y = mx$, $a \le x \le b$.

EXAMPLE 1. Let a and b be positive numbers, with $a < b$. Find the area under the graph $y = mx$, $a \le x \le b$ (Fig. 4–10).

Solution. Let n be a positive integer and divide the interval (a, b) into n subintervals each of length $\Delta x = (b - a)/n$, by inserting the points

$$\begin{aligned} x_1 &= a + \Delta x, \\ x_2 &= a + 2\,\Delta x, \\ x_3 &= a + 3\,\Delta x, \\ &\vdots \\ x_{n-1} &= a + (n - 1)\,\Delta x. \end{aligned}$$

The inscribed rectangles have areas

$$\begin{aligned} f(a)\,\Delta x &= ma \cdot \Delta x, \\ f(x_1)\,\Delta x &= m(a + \Delta x) \cdot \Delta x, \\ f(x_2)\,\Delta x &= m(a + 2\,\Delta x) \cdot \Delta x, \\ &\vdots \\ f(x_{n-1})\,\Delta x &= m[a + (n - 1)\,\Delta x] \cdot \Delta x, \end{aligned}$$

whose sum is

$$\begin{aligned} S_n &= m[a + (a + \Delta x) + (a + 2\,\Delta x) + \cdots + (a + (n - 1)\,\Delta x)] \cdot \Delta x \\ &= m[na + (1 + 2 + \cdots + (n - 1))\,\Delta x]\,\Delta x = m\left[na + \frac{(n - 1)n}{2}\Delta x\right]\Delta x \\ &= m\left[a + \frac{n - 1}{2}\Delta x\right] n\,\Delta x \qquad \left(\Delta x = \frac{b - a}{n}\right) \\ &= m\left[a + \frac{b - a}{2} \cdot \frac{n - 1}{n}\right] \cdot (b - a). \end{aligned}$$

The area under the graph is defined to be the limit of S_n as $n \to \infty$. In the final form, the only place n appears is in the fraction

$$\frac{n-1}{n} = 1 - \frac{1}{n},$$

and $1/n \to 0$ as $n \to \infty$, so

$$\lim \frac{n-1}{n} = 1 - 0 = 1.$$

Therefore,

$$\lim S_n = m\left(a + \frac{b-a}{2}\right) \cdot (b-a)$$

$$= \frac{ma + mb}{2} \cdot (b-a).$$

This is easily interpreted as the area of a trapezoid, with "bases" (in this case vertical) ma and mb and with altitude $(b - a)$.

EXAMPLE 2. Find the area under the graph of $y = x^2$, $0 \le x \le b$ (Fig. 4–11).

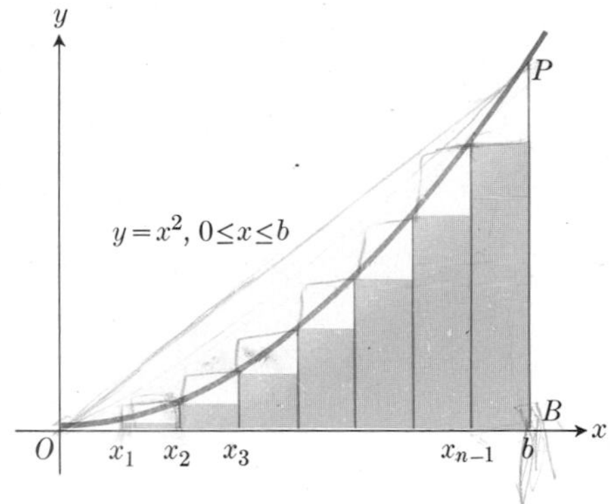

4–11 The area under $y = x^2$, $0 \le x \le b$.

Solution. Divide the interval $0 \le x \le b$ into n (> 0) subintervals each of length $\Delta x = b/n$, by inserting the points

$$x_1 = \Delta x, \quad x_2 = 2\,\Delta x, \quad x_3 = 3\,\Delta x, \quad \ldots, \quad x_{n-1} = (n-1)\,\Delta x.$$

The inscribed rectangles have areas

$$\begin{aligned}
f(0)\,\Delta x &= 0,\\
f(x_1)\,\Delta x &= (\Delta x)^2\,\Delta x,\\
f(x_2)\,\Delta x &= (2\,\Delta x)^2\,\Delta x,\\
f(x_3)\,\Delta x &= (3\,\Delta x)^2\,\Delta x,\\
&\vdots\\
f(x_{n-1})\,\Delta x &= ((n-1)\,\Delta x)^2\,\Delta x.
\end{aligned}$$

The sum of these areas is

$$\begin{aligned}
S_n &= (1^2 + 2^2 + 3^2 + \cdots + (n-1)^2)(\Delta x)^3\\
&= \frac{(n-1)n(2n-1)}{6} \cdot \left(\frac{b}{n}\right)^3\\
&= \frac{b^3}{6} \cdot \frac{n-1}{n} \cdot \frac{n}{n} \cdot \frac{2n-1}{n}\\
&= \frac{b^3}{6} \cdot \left(1 - \frac{1}{n}\right) \cdot \left(2 - \frac{1}{n}\right).
\end{aligned}$$

To find the area under the graph, we let n increase without bound and get

$$A = \lim S_n = \frac{b^3}{6} \cdot 1 \cdot 2 = \frac{b^3}{3}.$$

Therefore the area under the curve is $\frac{1}{3}$ the base b times the "altitude" b^2. The triangle OBP in Fig. 4–11 has area $\frac{1}{2}b \cdot b^2 = b^3/2$, and the area under the curve turns out to be somewhat smaller, as we should expect.

PROBLEMS

1. Verify the formula

$$\sum_{k=1}^{n} k^3 = 1^3 + 2^3 + \cdots + n^3 = \left(\frac{n(n+1)}{2}\right)^2$$

for $n = 1, 2, 3$. Then add $(n+1)^3$ and thereby prove by mathematical induction (as in the text) that the formula is true for all positive integers n.

2. Using the result of Problem 1 and the method of Example 2 in the text, show that the area under the graph of $y = x^3$ over the interval $0 \le x \le b$ is $b^4/4$.

3. Find the area under the graph of $y = mx$ over the interval $a \le x \le b$ by using *circumscribed* rectangles in place of the inscribed rectangles of Example 1 in the text.

4. Find the area under the curve $y = x^2$ over the interval $0 \le x \le b$ by using circumscribed rectangles in place of the inscribed rectangles of Example 2 in the text.

5. Do Problem 2 above by using circumscribed rectangles instead of inscribed rectangles.

6. Establish the formulas given below, for every positive integer n, by showing (a) that the formula is correct for $n = 1$, and (b) if true for n, the formula is also true for $n + 1$.

$$\sum_{k=1}^{n} (2k-1) = 1 + 3 + 5 + \cdots + (2n-1) = n^2,$$

$$\sum_{k=1}^{n} \frac{1}{k(k+1)} = \frac{1}{1 \cdot 2} + \frac{1}{2 \cdot 3} + \cdots + \frac{1}{n \cdot (n+1)} = \frac{n}{n+1}.$$

4–7 AREAS BY CALCULUS

In Article 4–5 we defined the area under a curve and showed how we could estimate it by computing sums of areas of rectangles. Nothing more than arithmetic is involved in these calculations, but we pay the price of getting only an estimate of the true area. On the other hand, in Article 4–6 we used algebraic techniques and actually computed *limits*, thus getting exact areas at the cost of fairly extensive algebraic preliminaries. In this article we shall follow the path blazed by Leibniz and Newton to show how exact areas can be computed easily by using integral calculus.

To begin we need some preliminary results. We consider a function f which is positive-valued and continuous over the domain $a \le x \le b$. Let A_a^c, A_c^b, A_a^b denote the areas under the graph and above the x-axis from a to c, from c to b, and from a to b, respectively (Fig. 4–12). If c is between a and b, we have

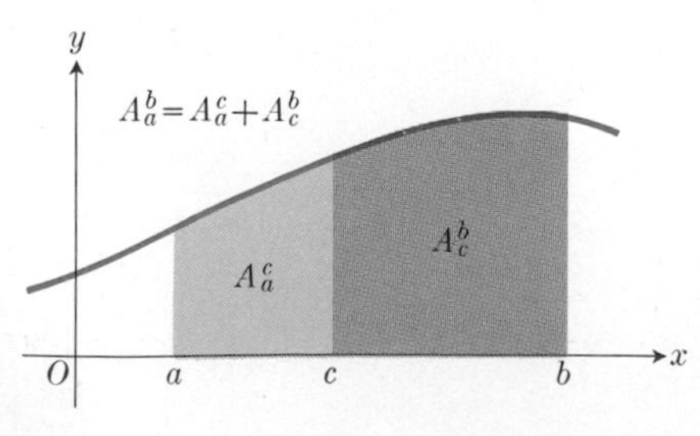

4–12 $A_a^c + A_c^b = A_a^b$.

$$A_a^c + A_c^b = A_a^b. \tag{1}$$

And this is also true when $c = a$ if we define the area from a to a to be zero,

$$A_a^a = 0. \tag{2}$$

Equation (1) is also true if c is beyond b, provided we adopt some conventions about signed areas. Let us say that area above the x-axis is positive if we go from left to right, and negative if we go from right to left. Thus, in Fig.

4–12, A_a^c, A_c^b, and A_a^b are all positive, while

$$A_c^a = -A_a^c, \qquad A_b^c = -A_c^b, \qquad A_b^a = -A_a^b \tag{3}$$

are negative. So formula (1) is also true in the form

$$A_a^b + A_b^c = A_a^c, \tag{4}$$

because adding A_b^c to A_a^b just subtracts A_c^b from the latter, leaving A_a^c.

The following theorem will also be used.

The Intermediate Value Theorem. *Let f be a positive-valued continuous function over the domain $a \le x \le b$. Let A_a^b denote the area under the graph of f over the domain. Then there is at least one number c between a and b such that*

$$A_a^b = f(c) \cdot (b - a). \tag{5}$$

Proof. Suppose m and M are respectively the minimum and maximum values of f over the domain $a \le x \le b$. Then

$$m(b - a) \le A_a^b \le M(b - a),$$

and therefore

$$m \le \frac{A_a^b}{b - a} \le M.$$

Since $A_a^b/(b - a)$ lies between the minimum and maximum values of $f(x)$ for $a \le x \le b$, there is at least one place c between a and b where

$$f(c) = \frac{A_a^b}{b - a}$$

(Article 2–11, Theorem 4). Equation (5) follows.

REMARK. The geometric interpretation of the Intermediate Value Theorem is this. A line drawn parallel to the x-axis at the right place between m and M units above the x-axis will serve as upper boundary of a rectangle having the same area as that under the curve, and it will surely cut the curve at least once between $x = a$ and $x = b$. The abscissa of that cut is a suitable value of c in Eq. (5) (See Fig. 4–13).

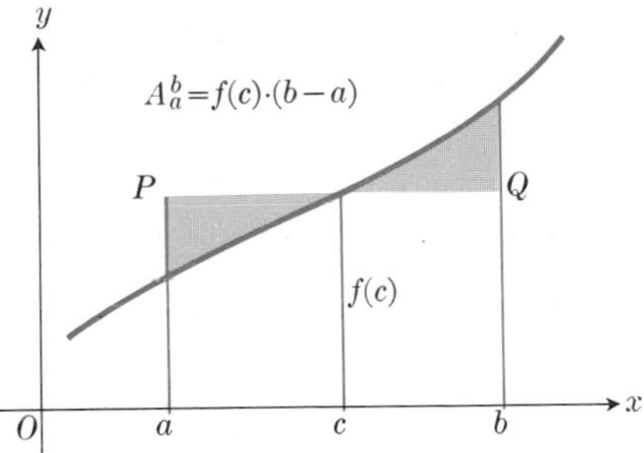

4–13 The area under the curve is equal to the area of the rectangle $aPQb$: The shaded regions above and below the curve have equal areas.

To compute the area A_a^b, we now consider any abscissa x between a and b, the area A_a^x, and the area $A_a^{x+\Delta x}$, where $\Delta x \ne 0$ (Fig. 4–14). We shall derive a differential equation for the area function A_a^x. The solution of this differential equation, with the initial condition

$$A_a^a = 0,$$

will enable us to compute the area from a to any x and, in particular, from a to b.

From Eq. (1) we have

$$A_a^x + A_x^{x+\Delta x} = A_a^{x+\Delta x},$$

so that

$$\Delta(A_a^x) = A_a^{x+\Delta x} - A_a^x = A_x^{x+\Delta x}. \tag{6a}$$

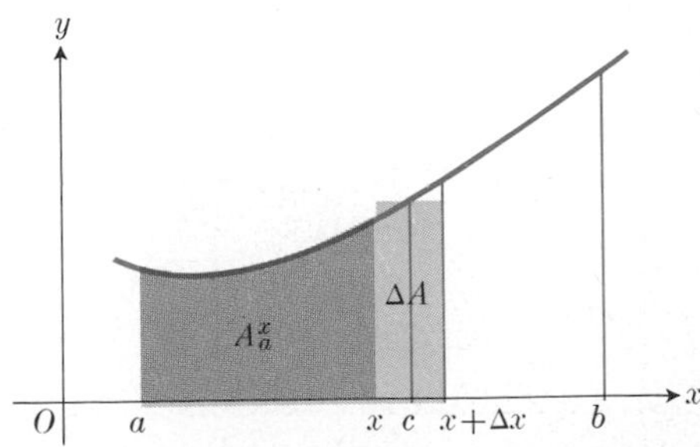

4–14 An increment of the area function.

Then, by Eq. (5),

$$A_x^{x+\Delta x} = f(c) \cdot \Delta x, \tag{6b}$$

where c is a number between x and $x + \Delta x$, which must therefore approach x as Δx approaches zero. Combining (6a) and (6b) and dividing by Δx, we get

$$\frac{\Delta A_a^x}{\Delta x} = f(c), \tag{7}$$

and therefore

$$\begin{aligned} \frac{dA_a^x}{dx} &= \lim_{\Delta x \to 0} \frac{\Delta A_a^x}{\Delta x} \\ &= \lim_{c \to x} f(c) \\ &= f(x), \end{aligned}$$

where the last line follows from the fact that f is continuous.

Therefore the area function A_a^x satisfies the differential equation

$$\frac{dA_a^x}{dx} = f(x) \tag{8a}$$

and the initial condition

$$A_a^a = 0. \tag{8b}$$

Thus if $F(x)$ is any integral of $f(x)\,dx$, we have

$$A_a^x = \int f(x)\,dx = F(x) + C. \tag{9a}$$

We also have

$$A_a^a = 0 = F(a) + C.$$

Hence

$$C = -F(a)$$

and

$$A_a^x = F(x) - F(a).$$

Finally, by taking $x = b$ we get

$$A_a^b = F(b) - F(a). \tag{9b}$$

Equations (9a) and (9b) summarize the method for finding the area under the graph of a positive-valued continuous function by integration. If the equation of the curve is $y = f(x)$, we integrate f to find

$$F(x) + C = \int f(x)\,dx. \tag{10a}$$

If the interval is $a \le x \le b$, we then compute

$$A_a^b = F(x)]_a^b = F(b) - F(a). \tag{10b}$$

The notation $F(x)]_a^b$ in Eq. (10b) simply means: first replace x by the upper value b to calculate $F(b)$, then subtract the value $F(a)$ obtained by setting $x = a$. For example,

$$2x + 3]_1^5 = 13 - 5 = 8.$$

The constant of integration may be omitted in evaluating Eq. (10b). For if we use $F(x) + C$ in place of $F(x)$ in (10b), we find

$$\begin{aligned} F(x) + C]_a^b &= [F(b) + C] - [F(a) + C] \\ &= F(b) - F(a) \\ &= F(x)]_a^b. \end{aligned}$$

EXAMPLE 1. The area under the graph of $y = mx$, $a \le x \le b$ (Fig. 4–10) is

$$\begin{aligned} \int mx\,dx\Big]_a^b = \frac{mx^2}{2}\Big]_a^b &= \frac{mb^2}{2} - \frac{ma^2}{2} \\ &= \frac{mb + ma}{2}\cdot(b - a). \end{aligned}$$

Compare the result and the method with Example 1 of Article 4–6.

EXAMPLE 2. The area under the graph of $y = x^2$, $0 \le x \le b$ (Fig. 4–11) is

$$\int x^2\,dx\Big]_0^b = \frac{x^3}{3}\Big]_0^b = \frac{b^3}{3}.$$

Compare the result and the method with Example 2 of Article 4–6.

EXAMPLE 3. Calculate the area bounded by the parabola $y = 6 - x - x^2$ and the x-axis.

Solution. We find where the curve crosses the x-axis by setting

$$y = 0 = 6 - x - x^2 = (3 + x)(2 - x),$$

which gives

$$x = -3 \qquad \text{or} \qquad x = 2.$$

The curve is sketched in Fig. 4–15.

According to Eqs. (10a, b), the area is

$$\begin{aligned} A_{-3}^2 = \int (6 - x - x^2)\,dx\Big]_{-3}^2 &= 6x - \frac{x^2}{2} - \frac{x^3}{3}\Big]_{-3}^2 \\ &= (12 - 2 - \tfrac{8}{3}) - (-18 - \tfrac{9}{2} + \tfrac{27}{3}) = 20\tfrac{5}{6}. \end{aligned}$$

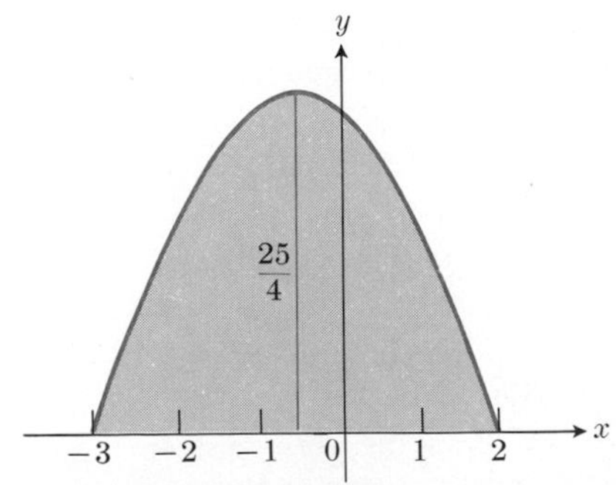

4–15 The parabolic arch $y = 6 - x - x^2$, $-3 \le x \le 2$.

The curve in Fig. 4–15 is an arch of a parabola, and it is interesting to note that the area is exactly equal to two-thirds the base times the altitude:

$$\tfrac{2}{3}(5)(\tfrac{25}{4}) = \tfrac{125}{6} = 20\tfrac{5}{6}.$$

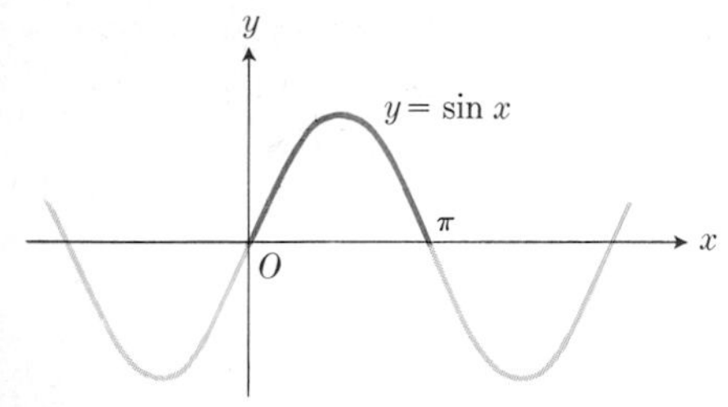

4–16 One arch of the curve $y = \sin x$.

EXAMPLE 4. Show that the area under one arch of the curve $y = \sin x$ is 2.

Solution. One arch of the sine curve extends from $x = 0$ to $x = \pi$ (Fig. 4–16). Therefore the area is

$$A_0^\pi = \int \sin x \, dx \Big]_0^\pi = -\cos x \Big]_0^\pi$$

$$= -\cos \pi - (-\cos 0) = -(-1) + 1 = 2.$$

PROBLEMS

In Problems 1 through 10, find the area bounded by the x-axis, the given curve $y = f(x)$, and the given vertical lines:

1. $y = x^2 + 1;\quad x = 0,\quad x = 3.$

2. $y = 2x + 3;\quad x = 0,\quad x = 1.$

3. $y = \sqrt{2x + 1};\quad x = 0,\quad x = 4.$

4. $y = \dfrac{1}{\sqrt{2x + 1}};\quad x = 0,\quad x = 4.$

5. $y = \dfrac{1}{(2x + 1)^2};\quad x = 1,\quad x = 2.$

6. $y = (2x + 1)^2;\quad x = -1,\quad x = 3.$

7. $y = x^3 + 2x + 1;\quad x = 0,\quad x = 2.$

8. $y = x\sqrt{2x^2 + 1};\quad x = 0,\quad x = 2.$

9. $y = \dfrac{x}{\sqrt{2x^2 + 1}};\quad x = 0,\quad x = 2.$

10. $y = \dfrac{x}{(2x^2 + 1)^2};\quad x = 0,\quad x = 2.$

11. Find the area bounded by the coordinate axes and the line $x + y = 1$.

12. Find the area between the curve $y = 4 - x^2$ and the x-axis.

13. Find the area between the curve $y = 1/\sqrt{x}$, the x-axis, and the lines $x = 1$, $x = 4$.

14. Find the area between the curve $y = \sqrt{1 - x}$ and the coordinate axes.

15. Find the area between the curve $x = 1 - y^2$ and the y-axis.

16. Find the area contained between the x-axis and one arch of the curve $y = \cos 3x$.

***17.** Take $B = A$ in Eq. (11a), Article 2–9, and show that

$$\cos 2A = \cos^2 A - \sin^2 A.$$

Combine this with the identity

$$1 = \cos^2 A + \sin^2 A$$

to show that

$$\cos^2 A = \tfrac{1}{2}(1 + \cos 2A), \qquad \sin^2 A = \tfrac{1}{2}(1 - \cos 2A).$$

Use the last of these identities to find the area contained between the x-axis and one arch of the curve $y = \sin^2 3x$.

18. The graph of $y = \sqrt{a^2 - x^2}$ over $-a \le x \le a$ is a semicircle of radius a.

a) Using this fact, explain why it is true that

$$\int \sqrt{a^2 - x^2}\, dx \Big]_{-a}^{a} = \tfrac{1}{2}\pi a^2.$$

b) Evaluate

$$\int \sqrt{a^2 - x^2}\, dx \Big]_{0}^{a}.$$

19. The integral in Problem 18 above can be evaluated by using the substitution

$$x = a \cos \theta, \qquad \pi \ge \theta \ge 0$$

to replace $\sqrt{a^2 - x^2}\, dx$ by $-a^2 \sin^2 \theta \, d\theta$. Combine this with Problem 17 above to show that

$$\int \sqrt{a^2 - x^2}\, dx \Big]_{-a}^{a} = \int -a^2 \sin^2 \theta \, d\theta \Big]_{\pi}^{0}$$

$$= -\frac{a^2}{2} \int (1 - \cos 2\theta)\, d\theta \Big]_{\pi}^{0},$$

and thus verify the result given in Problem 18(a), by evaluating this final integral.

* The method used in this problem should be used in several later problems involving integration of squares of sines and cosines.

4–8

THE DEFINITE INTEGRAL AND THE FUNDAMENTAL THEOREM OF INTEGRAL CALCULUS

In Articles 4–5, 4–6, and 4–7, we made a systematic study of the area problem. We have arrived at the following result.

If the function f is positive and continuous over the domain $a \leq x \leq b$, then the area under its graph is

$$A_a^b = \lim \sum f(c_k)\,\Delta x = \int f(x)\,dx\Big]_a^b = F(x)\Big]_a^b = F(b) - F(a). \quad (1)$$

The first part of this equation is just the definition of the area as the limit of the sum of areas of inscribed rectangles. The last part of the equation gives a short way to evaluate this limit by calculus. Therein lies one of the most powerful ideas of post-Renaissance mathematics, for the key idea is this: The limit can be evaluated by integration. This, essentially, is what is known as the *Fundamental Theorem* of integral calculus. It ties together the summation process (which Archimedes used over two thousand years ago for finding areas, volumes, and centers of gravity) and the differentiation process, from which one may find the tangent to a curve. It is a remarkable fact that the inverse of the "tangent problem" (that is, the inverse of differentiation) provides a ready tool for solving the summation problem. And its applications, as we shall see, extend far beyond the finding of areas; e.g., finding volumes of solids, lengths of curves, areas of surfaces of revolution, centers of gravity, work done by a variable force, gravitational and electrical potential, population growth, and cardiac output, to mention only a few.

While Eq. (1) above is expressed in terms of area, and up until now has been restricted to positive-valued functions, the Fundamental Theorem is less restrictive.

Fundamental Theorem of Integral Calculus. *Let f be a function that is continuous over the domain $a \leq x \leq b$. Let*

$$a,\ x_1,\ x_2,\ \ldots,\ x_{n-1},\ b \quad (2)$$

be a set of numbers $a < x_1 < x_2 < \cdots < x_{n-1} < b$, which partition the interval (a, b) into n equal subintervals each of length

$$\Delta x = \frac{(b-a)}{n}. \quad (3)$$

Let $c_1, c_2, \ldots, c_n$ be a set of n numbers, one in each subinterval,

$$a \leq c_1 \leq x_1, \quad x_1 \leq c_2 \leq x_2, \quad \ldots, \quad x_{n-1} \leq c_n \leq b. \quad (4)$$

Let

$$S_n = f(c_1)\,\Delta x + f(c_2)\,\Delta x + \cdots + f(c_n)\,\Delta x$$
$$= \sum_{k=1}^{n} f(c_k)\,\Delta x. \quad (5)$$

Finally, let $F(x)$ be any integral of $f(x)\,dx$,

$$F(x) = \int f(x)\,dx. \quad (6)$$

Then, as $n \to \infty$,

$$\lim S_n = \lim \sum f(c_k)\,\Delta x = F(b) - F(a). \tag{7}$$

Proof. We shall first prove (7) for the special set of numbers $c_1, c_2, \ldots, c_n$ that we get by applying the Mean Value Theorem of Article 3–8 to the function F in each subinterval. We can do this because F is differentiable and continuous. Thus, remembering that $F'(x) = f(x)$, we have

$$\begin{aligned}
F(x_1) - F(a) &= F'(c_1) \cdot (x_1 - a) = f(c_1)\,\Delta x,\\
F(x_2) - F(x_1) &= F'(c_2) \cdot (x_2 - x_1) = f(c_2)\,\Delta x,\\
F(x_3) - F(x_2) &= F'(c_3) \cdot (x_3 - x_2) = f(c_3)\,\Delta x,\\
&\vdots\\
F(x_{n-1}) - F(x_{n-2}) &= F'(c_{n-1}) \cdot (x_{n-1} - x_{n-2}) = f(c_{n-1})\,\Delta x,\\
F(b) - F(x_{n-1}) &= F'(c_n) \cdot (b - x_{n-1}) = f(c_n)\,\Delta x.
\end{aligned} \tag{8}$$

We add Eqs. (8), and note that $F(x_1), F(x_2), \ldots, F(x_{n-1})$ all appear twice on the left side, once positive and once negative. Hence these terms cancel out, leaving only $F(b) - F(a)$ in the sum. Thus we get

$$F(b) - F(a) = f(c_1)\,\Delta x + f(c_2)\,\Delta x + \cdots + f(c_n)\,\Delta x. \tag{9}$$

Since the left side of this equation does not in any way involve n, it remains fixed as we let $n \to \infty$, thus establishing Eq. (7), for this particular way of choosing the numbers $c_1, c_2, \ldots, c_n$.

But the theorem states that the same answer is obtained no matter how the c's are chosen in the subintervals, so long as there is one c in each subinterval. To establish this final result, we recall that the function f is continuous on the closed interval $a \le x \le b$, and therefore is *uniformly* continuous there [Article 2–11, Theorem 5]. Hence, if ϵ is any positive number, there exists a positive number δ, depending only upon ϵ, such that

$$|f(c_k) - f(c_k')| < \epsilon \tag{10}$$

whenever

$$|c_k - c_k'| < \delta. \tag{11}$$

And we can make $\Delta x = (b - a)/n < \delta$ by making

$$n > \frac{(b - a)}{\delta}. \tag{12}$$

For all sufficiently large n, (12) is satisfied. Now let c_1, c_1' be two numbers in the first subinterval, c_2, c_2' in the second, and so on. Form the sums

$$S_n = \sum_{k=1}^{n} f(c_k)\,\Delta x,$$

$$S_n' = \sum_{k=1}^{n} f(c_k')\,\Delta x.$$

Their difference is less than or equal to

$$|f(c_1)-f(c_1')|\,\Delta x+|f(c_2)-f(c_2')|\,\Delta x+\cdots+|f(c_n)-f(c_n')|\,\Delta x. \tag{13}$$

Every term in (13) is less than $\epsilon \cdot \Delta x$, by (10), and there are n terms. Therefore

$$|S_n - S_n'| < n \cdot (\epsilon \cdot \Delta x) = \epsilon \cdot (n\,\Delta x) = \epsilon \cdot (b-a), \tag{14}$$

provided condition (12) is satisfied. This inequality, (14), says that the sums S_n and S_n' that we get from two different choices of the c's in the subintervals can be made to differ by as little as we please [no more than $\epsilon \cdot (b-a)$] by making n sufficiently large. But for the particular choice of the c's in Eqs. (8), we have

$$S_n = F(b) - F(a).$$

Therefore S_n' differs arbitrarily little from $F(b) - F(a)$ when n is sufficiently large. This means that

$$\lim S_n' = F(b) - F(a). \tag{15}$$

Equation (15) completes the proof.

REMARK. The integral sign, $\int$, is a modified capital S (for sum), intended to remind us of the close connection between integration and summation.

The limit

$$\lim \sum f(c_k)\,\Delta x$$

in Eq. (7) is called the *definite integral* of *f from a to b*. It is denoted by the symbol

$$\int_a^b f(x)\,dx.$$

The numbers a and b are called the *limits of integration* of the integral, a being the *lower limit* and b the *upper limit*.

The Fundamental Theorem tells us that we can evaluate a definite integral if we know any indefinite integral $F(x)$ of the integrand $f(x)\,dx$. We just subtract $F(a)$ from $F(b)$.

EXAMPLE 1

$$\begin{aligned}\int_0^{\pi/2} \cos x\,dx &= \sin x\Big]_0^{\pi/2}\\ &= \sin\frac{\pi}{2} - \sin 0\\ &= 1.\end{aligned}$$

Three Properties of Definite Integrals

Definite integrals of continuous functions have simple algebraic properties that are often used in computations.

First, the integral of a constant multiple of a function is that same constant times the integral of the function:

(A) $$\int_a^b kf(x)\,dx = k\int_a^b f(x)\,dx, \quad k \text{ any constant.}$$

EXAMPLE 2

$$\begin{aligned}\int_0^\pi 5\sin x\,dx &= 5\int_0^\pi \sin x\,dx \\ &= 5\Big[-\cos x\Big]_0^\pi \\ &= 5[-\cos\pi + \cos 0] = 10.\end{aligned}$$

EXAMPLE 3

$$\int_0^4 -x^2\,dx = -\int_0^4 x^2\,dx = -\left[\frac{x^3}{3}\right]_0^4 = -\frac{64}{3}.$$

Second, the integral of the sum of two functions is the sum of their integrals:

(B) $$\int_a^b [f(x)+g(x)]\,dx = \int_a^b f(x)\,dx + \int_a^b g(x)\,dx.$$

A similar rule holds for the difference of two functions.

EXAMPLE 4

$$\begin{aligned}\int_1^2 \left[3-\frac{6}{x^2}\right]dx &= \int_1^2 3\,dx - \int_1^2 \frac{6}{x^2}\,dx \\ &= \Big[3x\Big]_1^2 - \left[-\frac{6}{x}\right]_1^2 \\ &= 6-3+3-6 = 0.\end{aligned}$$

Third, the sign of an integral changes when its limits of integration are interchanged.

(C) $$\int_b^a f(x)\,dx = -\int_a^b f(x)\,dx.$$

EXAMPLE 5

$$\begin{aligned}\int_1^0 [4-5x^2]\,dx &= \int_0^1 [5x^2-4]\,dx \\ &= \left[5\left(\frac{x^3}{3}\right)-4x\right]_0^1 = -\frac{7}{3}.\end{aligned}$$

As you might suspect, the first two of the three properties of definite integrals, Properties (A) and (B), are related to the analogous properties of indefinite integrals. We will make the relationship explicit when we return to the three properties later in this article. For the moment, however, we will turn our attention to the relation between definite integrals and area.

If a continuous function $f(x)$ has no negative values over $a \le x \le b$, then the definite integral

$$\int_a^b f(x)\,dx = F(x)\Big]_a^b = F(b) - F(a) \tag{16}$$

represents the area under its graph, above the x-axis, between the ordinates at $x = a$ and $x = b$. If, on the other hand, the function f were everywhere negative between a and b, the summands $f(c_k)\,\Delta x$ would all be negative (assuming $b > a$ and $\Delta x = (b - a)/n$ is positive) and the integral, (16), would be negative.

EXAMPLE 6. For $|x| < 2, f(x) = x^2 - 4$ is negative (Fig. 4–17(a)).

$$\int_{-2}^{2} f(x)\,dx = \frac{x^3}{3} - 4x\Big]_{-2}^{2} = (\tfrac{8}{3} - 8) - (-\tfrac{8}{3} + 8) = -\tfrac{32}{3}.$$

The area between the curve and the x-axis, from $x = -2$ to $x = +2$, contains $\frac{32}{3}$ units of area. The sign is negative because the curve lies below the x-axis. Clearly, the graph (Fig. 4–17(b)) of

$$y = g(x) = -f(x) = 4 - x^2, \qquad -2 \le x \le 2$$

is just the mirror image, with respect to the x-axis as mirror, of the curve in Fig. 4–17(a). The area between the graph of $y = g(x)$ and the x-axis is

$$\int_{-2}^{2} g(x)\,dx = 4x - \frac{x^3}{3}\Big]_{-2}^{2} = \tfrac{32}{3}.$$

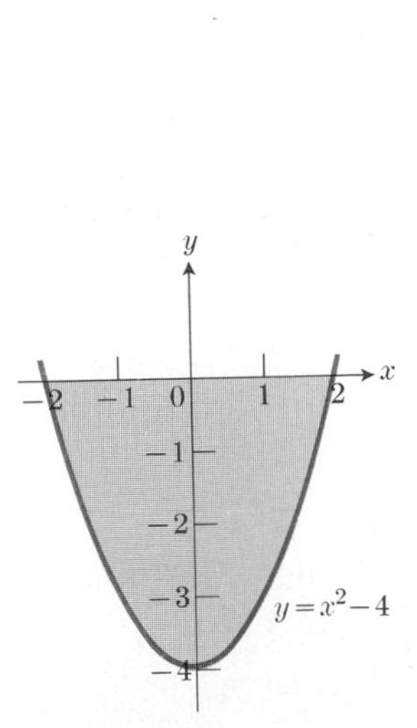

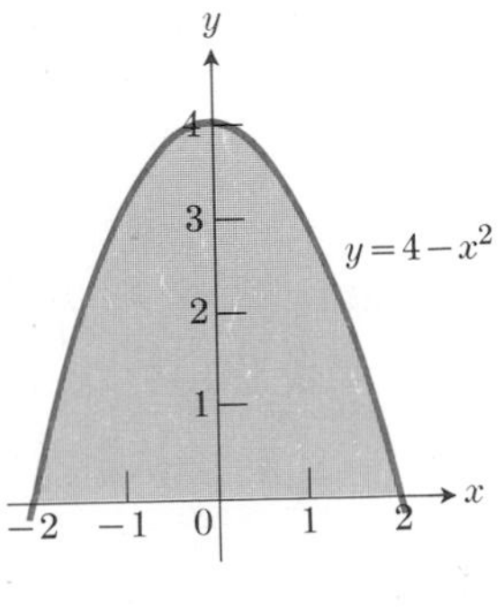

4–17 These graphs enclose the same amount of area with the x-axis, but the definite integrals of the two functions from -2 to 2 differ in sign.

The absolute value is the same as for the integral of $f(x)\,dx$ between the same limits. For $g(x)\,dx$ the sign is positive, since the area between the g-curve and the x-axis is above the axis.

If the graph of $y = f(x)$, $a \le x \le b$, is partly below and partly above the x-axis, as in Fig. 4–18, then

$$\lim \sum f(c_k)\,\Delta x = \int_a^b f(x)\,dx = F(x)\Big]_a^b = F(b) - F(a)$$

is the algebraic sum of *signed* areas, positive areas above the x-axis, negative areas below. For example, if the absolute values of the areas between the curve and the x-axis in Fig. 4–18 are A_1, A_2, A_3, A_4, then the definite integral of f from a to b is equal to

$$\int_a^b f(x)\,dx = -A_1 + A_2 - A_3 + A_4.$$

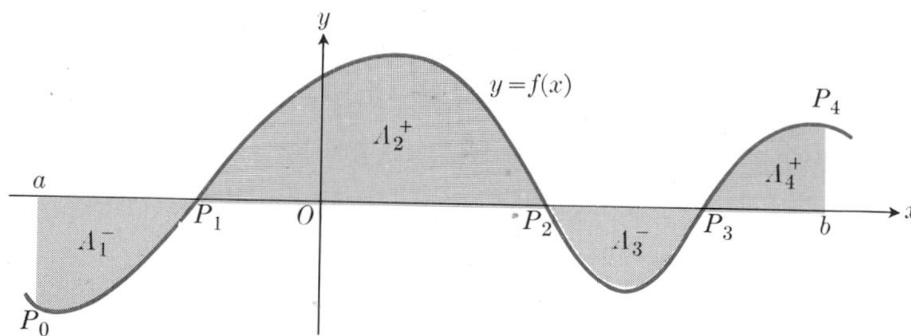

4–18 The integral $\int_a^b f(x)\,dx$ is the algebraic sum of signed areas.

Thus if we wanted the sum of the absolute values of these signed areas, that is,

$$A = |-A_1| + A_2 + |-A_3| + A_4,$$

we should need to find the abscissas s_1, s_2, s_3 of the points P_1, P_2, P_3 where the curve crosses the x-axis. We would then compute, separately,

$$-A_1 = \int_a^{s_1} f(x)\,dx, \qquad A_2 = \int_{s_1}^{s_2} f(x)\,dx,$$

$$-A_3 = \int_{s_2}^{s_3} f(x)\,dx, \qquad A_4 = \int_{s_3}^{b} f(x)\,dx,$$

and add their absolute values.

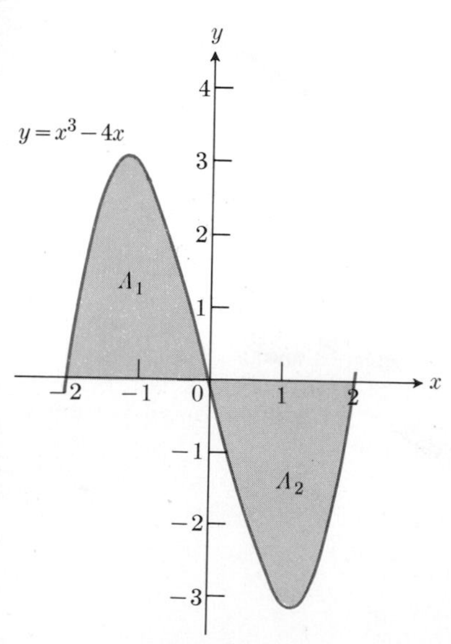

4–19 Graph of $y = x^3 - 4x$, $-2 \le x \le 2$.

EXAMPLE 7. Find the total area bounded by the curve $y = x^3 - 4x$ and the x-axis.

Solution. The graph in Fig. 4–19 lies above the x-axis from -2 to 0, below from 0 to $+2$. (The polynomial $x^3 - 4x$ factors as

$$x^3 - 4x = x(x-2)(x+2),$$

and we determine the sign of the product from the signs of the three factors.)

$$A_1 = \int_{-2}^{0} (x^3 - 4x)\, dx = \frac{x^4}{4} - 2x^2 \Big]_{-2}^{0} = 0 - (4 - 8) = +4,$$

$$-A_2 = \int_{0}^{2} (x^3 - 4x)\, dx = \frac{x^4}{4} - 2x^2 \Big]_{0}^{2} = (4 - 8) - 0 = -4,$$

$$A_1 + |-A_2| = 4 + |-4| = 8.$$

The definite integral, as a limit of sums, provides a new way of defining functions. The integral of any continuous function $f(t)$ from $t = a$ to $t = x$ defines a number

$$F(x) = \int_a^x f(t)\, dt, \tag{17a}$$

which can be computed as a limit (at least in theory). The function F defined by this formula has the property that its derivative at any x is the value of the integrand f at x:

$$F'(x) = f(x). \tag{17b}$$

To show this, we use the definition of the derivative

$$F'(x) = \lim_{\Delta x \to 0} \frac{F(x + \Delta x) - F(x)}{\Delta x}$$

$$= \lim_{\Delta x \to 0} \frac{1}{\Delta x} \int_x^{x+\Delta x} f(t)\, dt.$$

By the Intermediate Value Theorem, Article 4–7, Eq. (5), we have

$$\int_x^{x+\Delta x} f(t)\, dt = f(c)\, \Delta x$$

for some c between x and $x + \Delta x$. When we divide both sides of this equation by Δx, and then let Δx approach zero, c approaches x and $f(c)$ approaches $f(x)$. (Why?) Hence

$$F'(x) = \lim_{\Delta x \to 0} \left[\frac{1}{\Delta x} f(c) \cdot \Delta x\right] = \lim_{c \to x} f(c) = f(x).$$

In other words,

$$\frac{d}{dx}\left(\int_a^x f(t)\, dt\right) = f(x). \tag{18}$$

EXAMPLE 8. Suppose

$$F(x) = \int_0^x \sqrt{1 - t^2}\, dt, \qquad 0 < x < 1.$$

Then

$$F'(x) = \sqrt{1 - x^2}.$$

Equation (18) tells us that, if f is a continuous function, then there is a function of which it is the derivative. That is, *every continuous function has an indefinite integral.* We can use this fact to establish Properties (A), (B), and (C) for definite integrals of continuous functions.

Verification of Properties (A), (B), and (C)

Let $f(x)$ and $g(x)$ be continuous for $a \le x \le b$, and let

$$F(x) = \int f(x)\,dx, \qquad G(x) = \int g(x)\,dx.$$

These indefinite integrals have the properties that

$$\int kf(x)\,dx = kF(x) \tag{19}$$

and

$$\int [f(x) + g(x)]\,dx = F(x) + G(x). \tag{20}$$

Equations (19) and (20) lead immediately to properties (A) and (B) for definite integrals, as follows:

(A)
$$\begin{aligned}\int_a^b kf(x)\,dx = kF(x)\Big]_a^b &= kF(b) - kF(a)\\ &= k[F(b) - F(a)]\\ &= k\int_a^b f(x)\,dx.\end{aligned}$$

(B)
$$\begin{aligned}\int_a^b [f(x) + g(x)]\,dx &= \Big[F(x) + G(x)\Big]_a^b\\ &= [F(b) + G(b)] - [F(a) + G(a)]\\ &= [F(b) - F(a)] + [G(b) - G(a)]\\ &= \int_a^b f(x)\,dx + \int_a^b g(x)\,dx.\end{aligned}$$

As for Property (C), we have

(C)
$$\begin{aligned}\int_b^a f(x)\,dx &= F(a) - F(b)\\ &= -[F(b) - F(a)]\\ &= -\int_a^b f(x)\,dx.\end{aligned}$$

Two Further Properties of Definite Integrals

There are two other properties of definite integrals of continuous functions that are worth mentioning now for later use.

The first is that the integral of a nonnegative function is never negative:

(D) If $f(x) \geq 0$ for $a \leq x \leq b$, then $\int_a^b f(x)\,dx \geq 0$.

The reason is that none of the approximating sums $\sum f(c_k)$ is ever negative, so the smallest limiting value they could possibly have is zero.

The second is that integrals preserve order:

(E) If $f(x) \leq g(x)$ for $a \leq x \leq b$, then $\int_a^b f(x)\,dx \leq \int_a^b g(x)\,dx$.

The reason for (E) is that $[g(x) - f(x)] \geq 0$ for $a \leq x \leq b$, so that, by Properties (B) and (D),

$$\int_a^b g(x)\,dx - \int_a^b f(x)\,dx = \int_a^b [g(x) - f(x)]\,dx \geq 0.$$

The Fundamental Theorem is sometimes used as a tool for approximating sums. This is the reverse of what we did in Article 4–6. There we found formulas for sums of first powers, and of squares, of the positive integers 1 through n. Then we used these formulas to compute limits of sums of areas of inscribed rectangles for the graphs of $y = mx$, $a \leq x \leq b$, and of $y = x^2$, $0 \leq x \leq b$. In the following example, we work back from the definite integral (or, what amounts to the same thing, the area under the graph) to an approximation for the sum of the square roots of the integers 1 through n. The process is not completely reversible. We can go from exact formulas for sums to definite integrals by way of limits, but we cannot go back from the definite integral to an exact formula for the sum, because we don't know which terms went to zero in the limit process, and hence we cannot recover them.

EXAMPLE 9. Consider the function defined by $f(x) = \sqrt{x}$, $0 \leq x \leq 1$. Let n be a positive integer, and $\Delta x = 1/n$. In Eq. (5) take $c_1 = x_1 = \Delta x$, $c_2 = x_2 = 2\,\Delta x, \ldots, c_n = b = 1 = n\,\Delta x$. Then

$$\begin{aligned} S_n &= \sqrt{c_1}\,\Delta x + \sqrt{c_2}\,\Delta x + \cdots + \sqrt{c_n}\,\Delta x \\ &= \frac{\sqrt{1} + \sqrt{2} + \cdots + \sqrt{n}}{n^{3/2}} \\ &\to \int \sqrt{x}\,dx\Big]_0^1 = \frac{x^{3/2}}{3/2}\Big]_0^1 = \frac{2}{3}, \quad \text{as } n \to \infty. \end{aligned}$$

When n is large, S_n will be close to its limit $\frac{2}{3}$. This means that the numerator

$$\sqrt{1} + \sqrt{2} + \cdots + \sqrt{n} \text{ is approximately equal to } \tfrac{2}{3}n^{3/2}.$$

For $n = 10$, the sum of the square roots is 22.5^-, while $\frac{2}{3}n^{3/2}$ is 21.1^-, so that the approximation is in error by about 6 percent.

PROBLEMS

1. For each of the following cases, integrate the given function f to find a new function F, defined by $F(x) = \int f(x)\,dx$. Apply the Mean Value Theorem to this new function F to find an expression for c_k in terms of x_k and x_{k-1}

such that

$$F(x_k) - F(x_{k-1}) = F'(c_k)(x_k - x_{k-1}).$$

a) $f(x) = x$ **b)** $f(x) = x^2$

c) $f(x) = x^3$ **d)** $f(x) = 1/\sqrt{x}$.

2. Consider the function defined by $f(x) = x$ and take $a = 0$, $b > 0$. Show that by taking

$$c_k = \tfrac{1}{2}(x_k + x_{k-1})$$

in Eq. (5), the resulting sum has the constant value

$$S_n = \tfrac{1}{2}b^2,$$

independent of the value of n. (Let $a = x_0$ and $b = x_n$.)

3. Take $f(x) = x^2$, $a = 0$, $b > 0$, and form S_n (Eq. (5)), using

$$c_k = \sqrt{\frac{x_k^2 + x_k x_{k-1} + x_{k-1}^2}{3}}.$$

Show that no matter what value n has, the resulting sum S_n has the constant value

$$S_n = \tfrac{1}{3}b^3.$$

(Let $a = x_0$ and $b = x_n$.) What is the limit of S_n as $n \to \infty$? Note that one should substitute $x_k - x_{k-1}$ for Δx and recognize that

$$\left(\frac{x_k^2 + x_k x_{k-1} + x_{k-1}^2}{3}\right)\Delta x = \frac{x_k^3 - x_{k-1}^3}{3}.$$

4. Take $f(x) = x^3$, $a = 0$, $b > 0$, and calculate S_n (Eq. (5)), taking

$$c_k = \sqrt[3]{\frac{x_k^3 + x_k^2 x_{k-1} + x_k x_{k-1}^2 + x_{k-1}^3}{4}}.$$

Express the result in a form that is independent of the number of subdivisions n. (Let $a = x_0$ and $b = x_n$.)

5. Take $f(x) = 1/\sqrt{x}$, $a = 1$, $b > 1$. Use the intermediate values

$$c_k = \left(\frac{\sqrt{x_{k-1}} + \sqrt{x_k}}{2}\right)^2$$

and calculate S_n (Eq. (5)). Express the result in a form that is independent of the number of subdivisions. (Let $a = x_0$, and $b = x_n$.)

Evaluate each of the following definite integrals (6 through 16).

6. $\displaystyle\int_1^2 (2x + 5)\,dx$ **7.** $\displaystyle\int_0^1 (x^2 - 2x + 3)\,dx$

8. $\displaystyle\int_{-1}^1 (x + 1)^2\,dx$ **9.** $\displaystyle\int_0^2 \sqrt{4x + 1}\,dx$

10. $\displaystyle\int_0^\pi \sin x\,dx$ **11.** $\displaystyle\int_0^\pi \cos x\,dx$

12. $\displaystyle\int_{\pi/4}^{\pi/2} \frac{\cos x\,dx}{\sin^2 x}$ (Let $u = \sin x$.)

13. $\displaystyle\int_0^{\pi/6} \frac{\sin 2x}{\cos^2 2x}\,dx$ ***14.** $\displaystyle\int_0^\pi \sin^2 x\,dx$

***15.** $\displaystyle\int_0^{2\pi/\omega} \cos^2(\omega t)\,dt$ (ω constant)

16. $\displaystyle\int_0^1 \frac{dx}{(2x + 1)^3}$

17. (a) Express the area between the curves $y = x^2$, $y = 18 - x^2$ as a *limit of a sum* of areas of rectangles. (b) Evaluate the area of part (a) by Eq. (7).

In each of the following problems (18 through 21), use Eq. (18) to find $F'(x)$ for the given functions F:

18. $F(x) = \displaystyle\int_0^x \sqrt{1 + t^2}\,dt$ **19.** $F(x) = \displaystyle\int_1^x \frac{dt}{t}$

20. $F(x) = \displaystyle\int_x^1 \sqrt{1 - t^2}\,dt$ **21.** $F(x) = \displaystyle\int_0^x \frac{dt}{1 + t^2}$

22. $F(x) = \displaystyle\int_1^{2x} \cos(t^2)\,dt$

[*Hint.* Use the chain rule with $u = 2x$.]

23. $F(x) = \displaystyle\int_1^{x^2} \frac{dt}{1 + \sqrt{1 - t}}$ **24.** $F(x) = \displaystyle\int_{\sin x}^0 \frac{dt}{2 + t}$

* See Problem 17, Article 4–7.

4–9 RULES FOR APPROXIMATING INTEGRALS

Any definite integral may be thought of as an area, or an algebraic sum of signed areas, as discussed in Article 4–8. We know how to evaluate a definite integral when an indefinite integral of the integrand is known. But there are simple functions, for example $(\sin x)/x$, for which no simple indefinite integral is known. In such instances, as long as the integrand is continuous, the definite integral still exists and we may wish to evaluate it numerically. We can often obtain good accuracy by using numerical methods for approximating a definite integral. These methods are also important for computations done by machines. One of the simplest of these numerical methods is the *trapezoidal rule*, which we shall now derive. (See Fig. 4–20.)

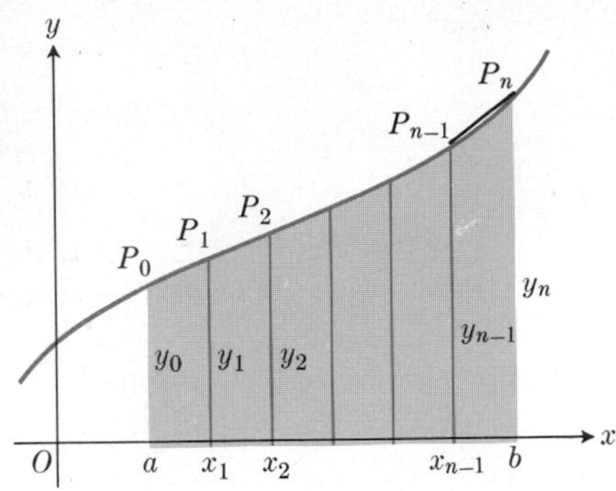

4–20 The sum of areas of trapezoids can give a good approximation of area under a curve.

Suppose that the definite integral $\int_a^b f(x)\,dx$ is to be evaluated. We divide the interval $a \le x \le b$ into n subintervals, each of length $h = (b - a)/n$, in the usual way by inserting the points

$$x_1 = a + h, \quad x_2 = a + 2h, \quad \ldots, \quad x_{n-1} = a + (n-1)h$$

between

$$x_0 = a \quad \text{and} \quad x_n = b.$$

The integral from a to b is just the sum of the integrals from a to x_1, from x_1 to x_2, etc.:

$$\int_a^b f(x)\,dx = \int_a^{x_1} f(x)\,dx + \int_{x_1}^{x_2} f(x)\,dx + \cdots + \int_{x_{n-1}}^{b} f(x)\,dx$$

$$= \sum_{k=1}^{n} \int_{x_{k-1}}^{x_k} f(x)\,dx.$$

The integral over the first subinterval is now *approximated* by the area of the trapezoid $aP_0P_1x_1$, which equals $\frac{1}{2}(y_0 + y_1)h$; over the second subinterval by the area of the trapezoid $x_1P_1P_2x_2$, which is $\frac{1}{2}(y_1 + y_2)h$; and so on. The *trapezoidal rule* is: To estimate the definite integral $\int_a^b f(x)\,dx$, use the *trapezoidal approximation* T given by

$$T = \tfrac{1}{2}(y_0 + y_1)h + \tfrac{1}{2}(y_1 + y_2)h + \cdots$$
$$+ \tfrac{1}{2}(y_{n-2} + y_{n-1})h + \tfrac{1}{2}(y_{n-1} + y_n)h$$
$$= \frac{h}{2}(y_0 + 2y_1 + 2y_2 + \cdots + 2y_{n-1} + y_n), \qquad \textbf{(1a)}$$

where

$$y_0 = f(x_0), \quad y_1 = f(x_1), \quad \ldots, \quad y_{n-1} = f(x_{n-1}), \quad y_n = f(x_n).$$

Since $h = (b - a)/n$, we may write the approximation in the following alternative form.

TRAPEZOIDAL RULE

$$\int_a^b f(x)\,dx \approx T = \frac{b-a}{2n}(y_0 + 2y_1 + 2y_2 + \cdots + 2y_{n-1} + y_n) \qquad \textbf{(1b)}$$

EXAMPLE 1. Use the trapezoidal rule with $n = 4$ to estimate $\int_1^2 x^2\,dx$ and compare this approximation with the exact value of the integral.

Solution. The exact value of this integral is

$$\int_1^2 x^2\,dx = \frac{x^3}{3}\Big]_1^2 = \frac{7}{3} \approx 2.33333.$$

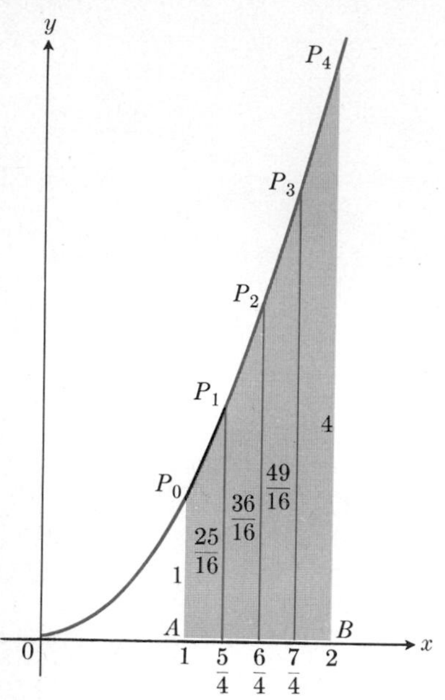

4–21 The trapezoidal approximation to the area under the graph of $y = x^2$, $1 \le x \le 2$, is a slight overestimate.

For the trapezoidal approximation we have

$$a = 1, \qquad b = 2, \qquad n = 4, \qquad h = \tfrac{1}{4},$$

so that

$$\begin{aligned}
x_0 &= a &&= 1, \qquad & y_0 &= f(x_0) = 1^2 = \tfrac{16}{16}\\
x_1 &= a + h &&= \tfrac{5}{4}, & y_1 &= f(x_1) = (\tfrac{5}{4})^2 = \tfrac{25}{16}\\
x_2 &= a + 2h &&= \tfrac{6}{4}, & y_2 &= f(x_2) = (\tfrac{6}{4})^2 = \tfrac{36}{16}\\
x_3 &= a + 3h &&= \tfrac{7}{4}, & y_3 &= f(x_3) = (\tfrac{7}{4})^2 = \tfrac{49}{16}\\
x_4 &= b &&= 2, & y_4 &= f(x_4) = (\tfrac{8}{4})^2 = \tfrac{64}{16}
\end{aligned}$$

and

$$\begin{aligned}
T &= \frac{b-a}{2n}(y_0 + 2y_1 + 2y_2 + 2y_3 + y_4)\\
&= \tfrac{1}{8}(\tfrac{75}{4}) = \tfrac{75}{32} = 2.34375.
\end{aligned}$$

Thus the approximation is too large by about half a percent. As the graph in Fig. 4–21 shows, each approximating trapezoid contains slightly more area than the corresponding strip of area under the curve.

Accuracy of the Trapezoidal Approximation

As n increases and $h = \Delta x$ approaches zero, the trapezoidal approximation approaches the exact value of the definite integral as limit. For we have

$$\begin{aligned}
T &= (y_1 + y_2 + \cdots + y_n)\,\Delta x + \tfrac{1}{2}(y_0 - y_n)\,\Delta x\\
&= \sum_{k=1}^{n} f(x_k)\,\Delta x + \tfrac{1}{2}[f(a) - f(b)]\,\Delta x. \qquad (2)
\end{aligned}$$

When n increases without bound and Δx approaches zero, the sum indicated by the sigma approaches $\int_a^b f(x)\,dx$ as limit, and the last term in (2) approaches zero. Therefore,

$$\lim T = \int_a^b f(x)\,dx.$$

This means, of course, that by taking n sufficiently large, we can make the difference between T and the integral as small as desired.

By methods studied in more advanced calculus (an extension of the Mean Value Theorem), it is possible to prove* that, if f is continuous on $a \le x \le b$, and twice differentiable on $a < x < b$, then there is a number c between a and b such that

$$\int_a^b f(x)\,dx = T - \frac{b-a}{12} f''(c) \cdot h^2. \qquad (3)$$

---

* See, for example, J. M. H. Olmsted, *Intermediate Analysis* (Appleton-Century-Crofts, 1956), p. 145.

Thus as h approaches zero, the "error," that is, the difference between the integral and the trapezoidal approximation, approaches zero as the *square* of h. By estimating the size of the second derivative of f between a and b, we can get a good estimate of how accurately T approximates the integral.

EXAMPLE 2. In Example 1, $f(x) = x^2, f''(x) = 2$, and the error predicted by (3) is

$$-\frac{b-a}{12} f''(c) \cdot h^2 = -\frac{2-1}{12} \cdot 2 \cdot \frac{1}{16} = -\frac{1}{96}.$$

This is precisely what we find when we subtract $T = \frac{75}{32}$ from $\int_1^2 x^2\,dx = \frac{7}{3}$, since $\frac{7}{3} - \frac{75}{32} = -\frac{1}{96}$. Here we are able to give the error *exactly*, since the second derivative of $f(x) = x^2$ is a constant and we have no uncertainty caused by not knowing c in the term $f''(c)$. Of course we are not always this lucky, and in most cases the best we can do is to *estimate* the difference between the integral and T.

EXAMPLE 3. Find how many subdivisions are required to approximate

$$\int_1^2 \frac{1}{x}\,dx$$

with the trapezoidal rule with an error of less than 10^{-4}.

Solution. The question is how small an h we need to make

$$E = \left| \frac{b-a}{12} f''(c) \cdot h^2 \right| < 10^{-4}.$$

Once we know this, we can decide how many subdivisions to make (the value of n). Since

$$f''(x) = 2x^{-3} = \frac{2}{x^3},$$

$f''(x)$ decreases steadily from

$$f''(1) = 2 \qquad \text{to} \qquad f''(2) = \tfrac{1}{4}.$$

Therefore, $|f''(c)| \leq 2$, and

$$E = \left| \frac{2-1}{12} f''(c) \cdot h^2 \right| \leq \frac{1}{12} \cdot 2 \cdot h^2 = \frac{h^2}{6}.$$

If we make $h^2/6 < 10^{-4}$, then E will be less than 10^{-4}. This can be achieved by taking

$$h^2 < 6 \times 10^{-4},$$

which will hold if

$$0 < h < 2.44 \times 10^{-2}.$$

Since $h = (b-a)/n = 1/n$, we can rewrite the inequality above in terms of n

and conclude that

$$n = \frac{1}{h} > 40.98.$$

The first integer beyond 40.98 is $n = 41$. With $n = 41$ subdivisions, we can guarantee $E < 10^{-4}$. Of course, any larger n will work, too.

Simpson's Rule

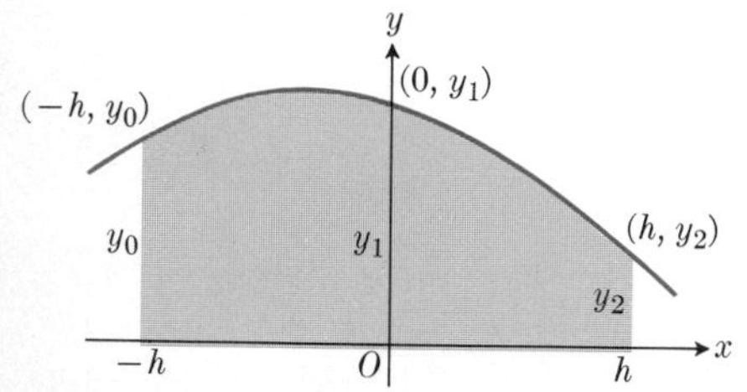

4–22 The shaded area under the parabola is $(h/3)(y_0 + 4y_1 + y_2)$.

Another method for approximating integrals, called *Simpson's method*, is based on the formula

$$A_p = \frac{h}{3}[y_0 + 4y_1 + y_2]$$

for the area under the arc of the parabola

$$y = Ax^2 + Bx + C$$

between $x = -h$ and $x = +h$, as in Fig. 4–22.*

This result is readily established as follows: In the first place,

$$\begin{aligned} A_p &= \int_{-h}^{h} (Ax^2 + Bx + C)\,dx \\ &= \frac{2Ah^3}{3} + 2Ch. \end{aligned}$$

Since the curve passes through the three points $(-h, y_0)$, $(0, y_1)$, and (h, y_2), we also have

$$y_0 = Ah^2 - Bh + C, \qquad y_1 = C, \qquad y_2 = Ah^2 + Bh + C,$$

from which there follows

$$\begin{aligned} C &= y_1, \\ Ah^2 - Bh &= y_0 - y_1, \\ Ah^2 + Bh &= y_2 - y_1, \\ 2Ah^2 &= y_0 + y_2 - 2y_1. \end{aligned}$$

Hence, expressing the area A_p in terms of the ordinates y_0, y_1, and y_2, we have

$$A_p = \frac{h}{3}[2Ah^2 + 6C] = \frac{h}{3}[(y_0 + y_2 - 2y_1) + 6y_1]$$

or

$$A_p = \frac{h}{3}[y_0 + 4y_1 + y_2]. \tag{4}$$

* We choose the interval $-h \le x \le h$ to simplify the algebra. There is no loss in generality in so doing, because the area does not depend on the location of the y-axis.

Simpson's rule follows from applying the formula for A_p to successive pieces of the curve $y = f(x)$ between $x = a$ and $x = b$. Each separate piece of the curve, covering an x-subinterval of width $2h$, is approximated by an arc of a parabola through its ends and its midpoint. The areas under the parabolic arcs are then added to give Simpson's rule.

SIMPSON'S RULE

$$\int_a^b f(x)\,dx \simeq S$$

$$= \frac{h}{3}[y_0 + 4y_1 + 2y_2 + 4y_3 + 2y_4 + \cdots + 2y_{n-2} + 4y_{n-1} + y_n] \quad \textbf{(5)}$$

The y's in Eq. (5) are the values of $y = f(x)$ at the points

$$x_0 = a, \quad x_1 = a + h, \quad x_2 = a + 2h, \quad \ldots, \quad x_n = a + nh = b,$$

corresponding to a subdivision of the interval $a \le x \le b$ into n equal subintervals of width $h = (b - a)/n$. (See Fig. 4 23.) The number n must be even in order to apply the method.

To estimate the error in the Simpson approximation, we have the formula*

$$\int_a^b f(x)\,dx = S - \frac{b-a}{180} f^{(4)}(c) \cdot h^4, \quad \textbf{(6)}$$

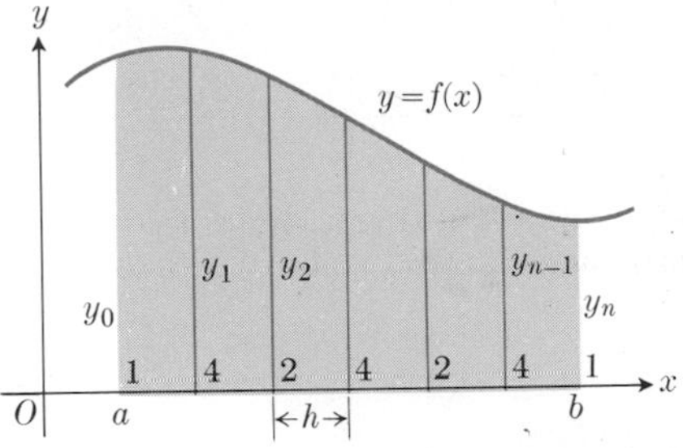

4–23 The number of subdivisions must be even if Simpson's rule is to work.

which applies when f is continuous on $a \le x \le b$ and four times differentiable on $a < x < b$. The fact that Eq. (6) has an $h^4/180$ while the estimate for the trapezoidal rule in Eq. (3) has an $h^2/12$ suggests that Simpson's rule will generally give more accurate results than the trapezoidal rule for a given h when h is small.

If $f(x)$ is a polynomial of degree less than four, then $f^{(4)}(c) = 0$ in Eq. (6) and the approximation S gives the exact value of the integral. We illustrate this in the next example, in which, for comparison, we approximate the value of an integral whose value we already know.

EXAMPLE 4. Approximate $\int_0^1 4x^3\,dx$ by the trapezoidal rule and by Simpson's rule with $n = 2$.

Solution. The exact value of the integral is

$$\int_0^1 4x^3\,dx = x^4\Big]_0^1 = 1.$$

The trapezoidal rule gives

$$T = \frac{1}{2 \cdot 2}[0 + 2 \cdot 4(\tfrac{1}{2})^3 + 4(1)^3] = \tfrac{1}{4}[1 + 4] = \tfrac{5}{4}.$$

* See, for example, J. M. H. Olmsted, *Intermediate Analysis* (Appleton-Century-Crofts), p. 146.

Simpson's rule gives

$$S = \frac{1}{2 \cdot 3}[0 + 4 \cdot 4(\tfrac{1}{2})^3 + 4(1)^3] = \tfrac{1}{6}[6] = 1.$$

Simpson's rule gives the exact value in this case because $f(x) = 4x^3$ is a polynomial of degree less than four. The fourth derivative of f is zero, and the error term in Eq. (6) vanishes.

Both of the approximation rules of this article can give good estimates of the integral of a continuous function from a table of values of the function when the increment h is small enough. Thus we can sometimes expect to obtain useful estimates of the integral of a function even when we do not know a formula for the function. This is the case in many practical applications in which the source of our information about a function is a set of specific values of the function measured in the laboratory or in the field.

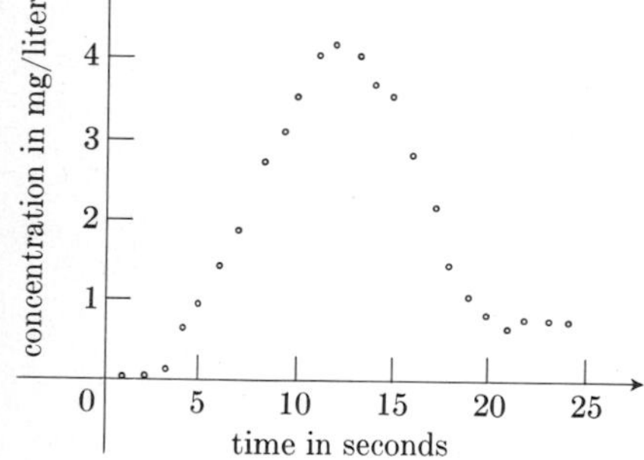

4–24 Dye concentrations measured in the aorta near the heart at one-second intervals.

EXAMPLE 5 *Measuring cardiac output.** The rate R at which a person's heart pumps blood is usually measured in liters per minute and is called the person's *cardiac output*. For a person at rest, this rate is usually about 5 liters per minute. But during strenuous exercise it can rise to more than 30 liters per minute. It can also change significantly as a result of disease.

One way to measure cardiac output is to inject a known amount D of dye into a main vein near the heart. The dyed blood circulates through the right side of the heart, the lungs, and the left side of the heart, and begins to enter the arteries. The concentration of the dye can be monitored in the aorta, say, where the first of the dye can be expected to appear a few seconds after injection. After entering the aorta, the dyed blood takes about 20 seconds to complete its trip through the body, heart, lungs and heart again, and to start past the monitoring point once more. A typical set of dye concentration readings resulting from an injection of $D = 5.0$ milligrams of dye are shown in Table 4–3 and plotted in Fig. 4–24.

Table 4–3. Data (in mg/l) for the dye-dilution method of measuring cardiac output

Seconds after injection	Concentration	Seconds after injection	Concentration	Seconds after injection	Concentration
0	0	9	3.0	18	1.5
1	0	10	3.7	19	1.1
2	0	11	4.0	20	0.9
3	0.1	12	4.1	21	0.8
4	0.6	13	4.0	22	0.9
5	0.9	14	3.8	23	0.9
6	1.4	15	3.7	24	0.9
7	1.9	16	2.9		
8	2.7	17	2.2		

* From *Measuring Cardiac Output*, by B. Horelick and S. Koont, Project UMAP, Education Development Center, Inc., 1978.

Table 4–3 shows measurements taken at the aorta every second for 24 seconds. The concentrations are recorded in milligrams of dye per liter of blood. The data show that most of the dye passed through the aorta in the first 15 or 20 seconds, but that the concentration did not taper to zero during the last three seconds. In fact, after $t = 21$ seconds, the dye concentration rose slightly. The dye that had been pumped through during the first seconds had circulated through the body and was beginning to reappear.

To measure the cardiac output, therefore, we *assume* that the concentration of first-time-through dye did taper off even though the concentration readings did not. The concentration seemed to be falling steadily just before $t = 21$, and we simply continue the trend by replacing the last three data points in the table with the three fictitious data points $A(22, 0.5)$, $B(23, 0.3)$, and $C(24, 0)$, as shown in Fig. 4–25. In Fig. 4–25 we have fitted a smooth curve to the data points to represent the dye concentration $C(t)$ as a continuous function of time. This is a reasonable thing to do because there is no reason for the dye concentration to change abruptly.

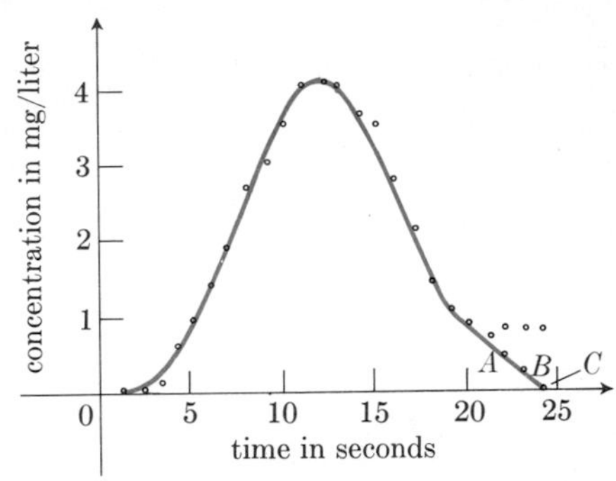

4–25 Dye concentration $C(t)$ pictured with a smooth curve that fits the real and adjusted data points.

The amount of blood that flows past the monitoring point in the aorta in a time interval Δt is $R\ \Delta t$ (rate times time). The amount of *dye* that flows past in Δt seconds is approximately $C(t_i)R\ \Delta t$, where $C(t_i)$ is the concentration observed at the beginning of the time interval. The total amount D of dye flowing by in the interval $0 \leq t \leq 24$ is approximately

$$D = \sum C(t_i)R\ \Delta t = R \sum C(t_i)\ \Delta t. \tag{7}$$

The sum on the right of Eq. (7) is an approximating sum for the definite integral

$$\int_0^{24} C(t)\, dt.$$

If we knew $C(t)$ as a continuous function of t, we could then write

$$D = R \int_0^{24} C(t)\, dt, \tag{8}$$

and compute the cardiac output R from the equation

$$R = \frac{D}{\int_0^{24} C(t)\, dt}. \tag{9}$$

However, we know $C(t)$ only at a set of isolated values of t. Fortunately, these values permit us to approximate the integral. The trapezoidal rule gives

$$\int_0^{24} C(t)\, dt \approx \frac{24 - 0}{2(24)}(0 + 0 + 0 + 0.2 + 1.2 + \cdots + 1.6 + 1.0 + 0.6 + 0)$$
$$= \tfrac{1}{2}(88.2) = 44.1. \tag{10}$$

We conclude that

$$R \approx \frac{D}{44.1} = \frac{5.0}{44.1} \approx 0.113 \text{ liters/second}$$
$$\approx 6.8 \text{ liters/minute.}$$

Simpson's rule gives

$$\int_0^{24} C(t)\,dt \approx \frac{24-0}{3(24)}[0 + 4(0) + 2(0) + 4(0.1) + 2(0.6) + 4(0.9) + \cdots + 2(0.9) + 4(0.8) + 2(0.5) + 4(0.3) + 0]$$
$$= \tfrac{1}{3}(132.2) \approx 44.1 \text{ (to the nearest tenth).} \tag{11}$$

Again, $R \approx 6.8$ liters/minute.

The fact that there is no significant difference in the results of the two rules in this case can be traced to two factors. First, the increment $h = 1$ is fairly large. The h^4 in the Simpson error formula is no smaller than the h^2 in the trapezoidal error formula. Second, the data given are nearest-tenth estimates, and are not accurate enough to justify rounding the $\frac{1}{3}(132.2)$ in the Simpson calculation to anything more refined than 44.1.

PROBLEMS

1. Interpret the meaning of the sign of the error term in Eq. (3) in case the graph of $y = f(x)$ is: (a) concave upward over $a < x < b$; (b) concave downward. Illustrate both cases with sketches.

Approximate each of the following integrals (2–7) with $n = 4$ by (a) the trapezoidal rule and (b) Simpson's rule. Compare your answers with (c) the exact value in each case. Use the error terms in (d) Eq. (3) and (e) Eq. (6) to estimate the minimum number of subdivisions needed to approximate the integral with an error of less than 10^{-5} by each of the two rules.

2. $\int_0^2 x\,dx$ **3.** $\int_0^2 x^2\,dx$ **4.** $\int_0^2 x^3\,dx$

5. $\int_1^2 \frac{1}{x^2}\,dx$ **6.** $\int_1^4 \sqrt{x}\,dx$ **7.** $\int_0^{\pi} \sin x\,dx$

8. Estimate the error in using (a) the trapezoidal rule and (b) Simpson's rule to approximate $\int_1^2 (1/x)\,dx$ with $n = 10$.

9. Repeat Example 3 with Simpson's rule in place of the trapezoidal rule.

10. In what units should one express the integral

$$\int_0^{24} C(t)\,dt$$

in Example 5?

11. (*Calculator*) Carry out the calculation in Eq. (10).

12. (*Calculator*) The rate at which flashbulbs give off light varies during the flash. For some bulbs, the light, measured in *lumens*, reaches a peak and fades quickly, as shown in Fig. 4–26(a). For other bulbs, the light, instead of reaching a peak, stays at a moderate level for a relatively longer period of time, as shown in Fig. 4–26(b). To calculate how much light reaches the film in a camera, we must know when the

a)

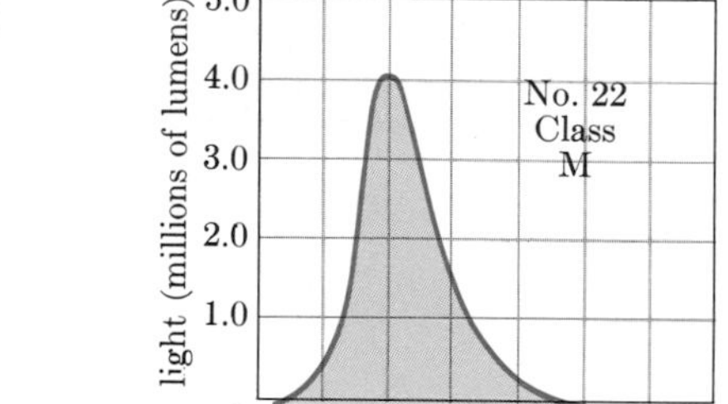

b)

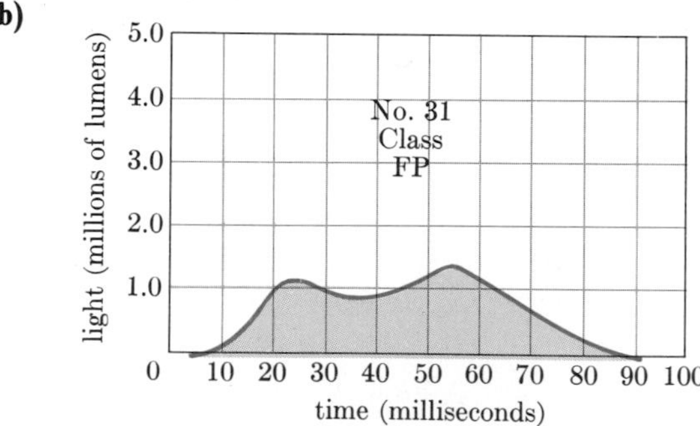

4–26 Flashbulb output data from Tables 4–4 and 4–5 plotted and connected by smooth curves.

shutter opens and closes. A typical focal-plane shutter opens 20 milliseconds and closes 70 milliseconds after the button is pressed. The amount A of light emitted by the flashbulb in this interval is

$$A = \int_{20}^{70} L(t)\, dt \quad \text{lumen-milliseconds,}$$

where $L(t)$ is the lumen output of the bulb as a function of time. Use the trapezoidal rule and the numerical data from Tables 4–4 and 4–5 to estimate A for each of the given bulbs, and find out which bulb gets more light to the film.*

* From *Integration*, by W. U. Walton, *et al.*, Project CALC, Education Development Center, Inc., Newton, MA (1975), p. 83.

Table 4–4.† Light output (in millions of lumens) vs. time (in milliseconds) for No. 22 flashbulb

Time after ignition	Light output	Time after ignition	Light output
0	0	30	1.7
5	0.2	35	0.7
10	0.5	40	0.35
15	2.6	45	0.2
20	4.2	50	0
25	3.0		

† Data from *Photographic Lamp and Equipment Guide*, P4–15P, Gen. Elec. Company, Cleveland, Ohio.

Table 4–5.‡ Light output (in millions of lumens) vs. time (in milliseconds) for No. 31 flashbulb

Time after ignition	Light output	Time after ignition	Light output	Time after ignition	Light output
0	0	35	0.9	65	1.0
5	0.1	40	1.0	70	0.8
10	0.3	45	1.1	75	0.6
15	0.7	50	1.3	80	0.3
20	1.0	55	1.4	85	0.2
25	1.2	60	1.3	90	0
30	1.0				

‡ Data from *Photographic Lamp and Equipment Guide*, P4–15P, Gen. Electric Company, Cleveland, Ohio.

4–10 SOME COMMENTS ON NOTATION

In each application of the definite integral it is reasonably easy to set up sums that approximate the answer to some physical problem. In general, it will even be possible (though not necessary) to find *particular* choices of the points c_k such that the *particular* sums

$$S_n = \sum_{k=1}^{n} f(c_k)\, \Delta x$$

give the *exact* value. Then

$$\lim_{n\to\infty} S_n = \int_a^b f(x)\, dx = F(x)\Big]_a^b = F(b) - F(a)$$

also gives the *exact* value. But since all sums S_n give the *same* answer in the limit (provided the function $f(x)$ is continuous for $a \le x \le b$, and this condition will usually be satisfied by the functions we shall encounter), we could get the same limit from

$$S_n = \sum_{k=1}^{n} f(x_k)\,\Delta x. \tag{1a}$$

Finally, we modify this notation slightly by dropping the subscript k entirely and writing simply

$$S_a^b = \sum_a^b f(x)\,\Delta x, \tag{1b}$$

where we write a and b to indicate that we have a sum of expressions, each of the form $f(x)\,\Delta x$, extending over a set of subintervals from $x = a$ to $x = b$. Of course it is not the *sum* (1b) that we are interested in, but rather the *limit* of the sum as given by the definite integral, and the notation (1b) is most suggestive of the final form, namely,

$$\lim_{\Delta x \to 0} S_a^b = \lim_{\Delta x \to 0} \sum_a^b f(x)\,\Delta x = \int_a^b f(x)\,dx = F(x)\Big]_a^b. \tag{2}$$

As remarked in Article 4–8, it was the close relationship between sums and integrals that led to the adoption of the symbol $\int$ (a modified S) to denote integration.

It should also be noted that *since it is the integral* that gives the *exact* answer in (2), and since the expression $f(x)\,dx$ after the integral sign is the same as the differential of $F(x)$,

$$\frac{dF(x)}{dx} = f(x), \tag{3a}$$

$$dF(x) = f(x)\,dx, \tag{3b}$$

we would arrive at the *correct final result* for the area under the curve $y = f(x) \geq 0$ between $x = a$ and $x = b$, say, if we were to write

$$dA = f(x)\,dx, \qquad A = \int_a^b f(x)\,dx. \tag{4}$$

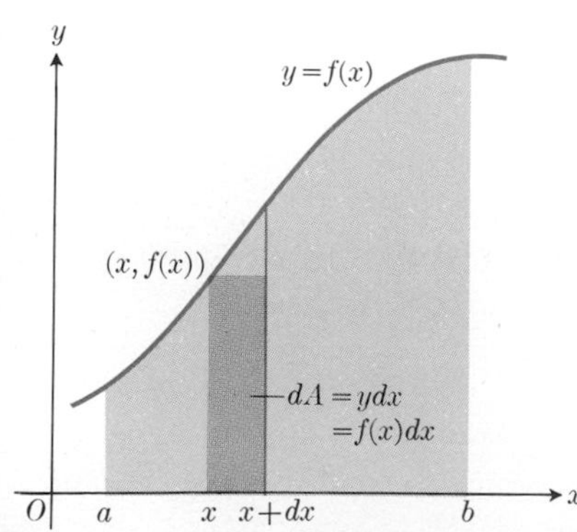

4–27 If dx is a small increment in x, then the area of the shaded rectangle is $f(x)\,dx$.

It is easy to attach a geometric interpretation to (4), but it is also easy to be misled by this interpretation into feeling that the integral in (4) gives only an approximation to the area, rather than giving its exact value. Enough has already been said on this latter point, however, so that the careful reader need not be a victim of this delusion. If we accept the interpretation simply as a shortcut for setting up the *integral whose value gives the exact result*, we may thereby gain from its simplicity. Namely, if we again think of the area from the left boundary a to a right boundary x, this area is a function of x, with derivative $dA/dx = y = f(x)$, as we found in Article 4–7. When we multiply both sides of this equation by dx, we get the result $dA = f(x)\,dx$, as in (4). But if we think of dx as a small increment in x, we may also interpret dA as the area of a small rectangle with base extending along the x-axis from x to $x + dx$, and with altitude $f(x) = y$ equal to the ordinate of the curve (see Fig. 4–27. Then this rectangle gives an *approximation* to that portion of the area under the curve lying between x and $x + dx$, and we think of the integral

$$A = \int_a^b f(x)\,dx$$

as adding together all of these small rectangles from $x = a$ to $x = b$ and then taking the *limit* of the sum so as to give the *exact value.*

It should be borne in mind that what has just been discussed should in no way obscure the fact that a *precise* formulation of the problem would involve a process of

a) subdividing the interval $a \le x \le b$,

b) forming a sum $\sum_a^b f(x)\,\Delta x$,

c) taking the limit, $\lim_{\Delta x \to 0} \sum_a^b f(x)\,\Delta x$, and

d) applying the fundamental theorem to evaluate this limit,

$$\lim_{\Delta x \to 0} \sum_a^b f(x)\,\Delta x = \int_a^b f(x)\,dx = F(x)\Big]_a^b.$$

Insofar as the shortcut described above leads to the same final answer, without leading to confusion or feelings of misgiving, it may be helpful and time-saving. But whenever we suspect that the final answer may be only an approximation instead of a mathematically exact answer, a reconsideration, along the lines that led up to the fundamental theorem, should be made. It is probably desirable, at least in the beginning, to go through the precise formulation first, and then it is but a matter of seconds to repeat the setup of the problem by the shortcut method.

SUMMARY

Much that we have done in this chapter is related to area. This is useful and gives us a way of interpreting sums like those in Eq. (5), Article 4–8, and Eq. (1a) in Article 4–10. But it is also good to express the main results in ways that don't depend upon area. In this article we shall summarize six results of major importance. Although we have appealed to the notion of area in presenting them in earlier sections, they can all be proved by purely analytical methods, with no reference to area. (See, for example, Apostol, *Modern Mathematical Analysis*, or Buck, *Advanced Calculus*, or Rudin, *Principles of Analysis.*)

Once again we start with a function f defined on an interval $a \le x \le b$. We partition the interval into n subintervals by inserting points $x_1, x_2, \ldots, x_{n-1}$ between $a = x_0$ and $b = x_n$. We do not require that the points be uniformly spaced. The kth subinterval has length $\Delta x_k = x_k - x_{k-1}$, which may vary with k. In the kth subinterval a number c_k is chosen arbitrarily, for each k from 1 through n. Then we form the sum

$$\sum_{k=1}^{n} f(c_k) \cdot (x_k - x_{k-1}). \tag{1}$$

This sum depends upon the function f, the points $x_0, x_1, x_2, \ldots, x_n$ and upon the c's. However, for a given function f and interval $[a, b]$ it may happen that all sums like (1) are nearly equal to some constant, provided the subintervals are all sufficiently short. If this is true, then that constant is called the *Riemann integral* of f from a to b, and is variously denoted by

$$R_a^b(f), \quad \text{or} \int_a^b f, \quad \text{or} \int_a^b f(x)\,dx, \quad \text{or} \int_a^b f(t)\,dt, \quad \text{or} \int_a^b f(u)\,du, \quad \text{and so on.}$$

Definition of Riemann Integral. *Let f be a function whose domain includes the interval $[a, b]$, $a < b$. Let f have the property that there exists a number $R_a^b(f)$ so related to f that to each positive number ϵ there corresponds a positive number δ such that every sum (1) differs from $R_a^b(f)$ by less than ϵ whenever all subintervals have lengths Δx_k less than δ. Then:*

a) *f is said to be **Riemann integrable** (or, more briefly, integrable) over $[a, b]$, and*

b) *$R_a^b(f)$ is called the **Riemann integral** (or, more briefly, the integral) of f from a to b.*

Theorem 1. *If f is Riemann integrable over an interval $[a, b]$, then it is also integrable over any subinterval contained in $[a, b]$.*

Theorem 2. *Every function that is continuous on a closed bounded interval $[a, b]$ is Riemann integrable there.*

REMARK. Although we are mainly interested in continuous functions, they are not the only ones that are integrable. All bounded functions that are *piecewise* continuous are also integrable. "Piecewise continuous" means that the interval can be divided into a finite number of nonoverlapping open subintervals over each of which the function is continuous. "Bounded" means that, for some finite constant M, $|f(x)| \leq M$ for all values of x in the interval. Figure 4–28 shows the graph of a bounded piecewise-continuous function over $[a, b]$. For this example, the integral $R_a^b(f)$ would be computed

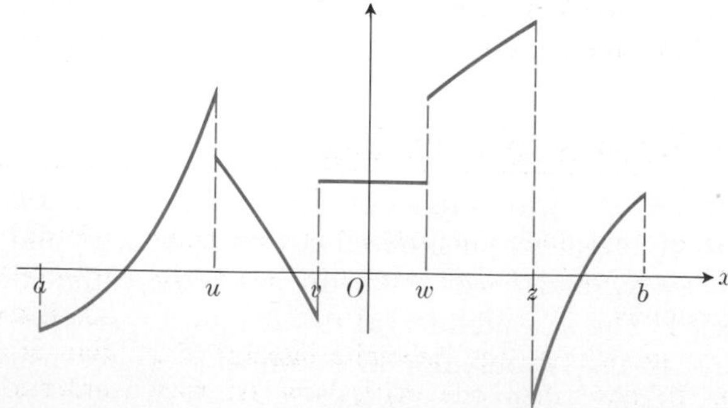

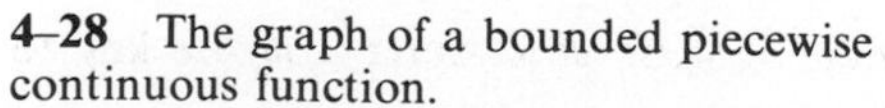
4–28 The graph of a bounded piecewise continuous function.

as the sum

$$R_a^b(f) = R_a^u(f) + R_u^v(f) + R_v^w(f) + R_w^z(f) + R_z^b(f).$$

If $b < a$ and $R_b^a(f)$ exists, then we define $R_a^b(f)$ to be its negative:

$$R_a^b(f) = -R_b^a(f). \tag{2}$$

If $a = b$, we define $R_a^a(f)$ to be zero.

Theorem 3. *Let a, b, c be three numbers belonging to an interval over which the Riemann integral of f exists. Then*

$$R_a^c(f) = R_a^b(f) + R_b^c(f). \tag{3}$$

Theorem 4. *Let f be Riemann integrable over [a, b]. Let x be any number between a and b at which f is continuous. Then $R_a^x(f)$ is differentiable at x and its derivative there is f(x):*

$$\frac{d}{dx} R_a^x(f) = f(x). \tag{4}$$

Theorem 5. The Mean Value Theorem for Integrals. *Let f be continuous on [a, b]. Then there exists at least one number c between a and b such that*

$$R_a^b(f) = f(c) \cdot (b - a). \tag{5}$$

Theorem 6. Fundamental Theorem of Integral Calculus. *Let f be Riemann integrable over [a, b]. Let F be any continuous indefinite integral of f, that is,*

$$F'(x) = f(x) \quad \text{for} \quad a < x < b.$$

Then

$$R_a^b(f) = F(b) - F(a). \tag{6}$$

PROBLEMS

1. Rewrite Eqs. (2) through (6), Article 4–11, using the notation $\int_a^b f(t)\,dt$ in place of $R_a^b(f)$ for the Riemann integral of f from a to b.

2. Sketch graphs of each of the following piecewise-continuous functions on (0, 2) and compute $\int_0^2 f(x)\,dx$:

a) $f(x) = \begin{cases} x, & \text{for } 0 \le x < 1, \\ \sin(\pi x), & \text{for } 1 \le x \le 2. \end{cases}$

b) $f(x) = \begin{cases} \sqrt{1 - x}, & \text{for } 0 \le x \le 1, \\ (7x - 6)^{-1/3}, & \text{for } 1 < x \le 2. \end{cases}$

3. Find $F'(x)$ for $x = \frac{1}{2}$ and for $x = \frac{3}{2}$ if $F(x) = \int_0^x f(t)\,dt$ and (a) f is defined as in Problem 2(a) above; (b) f is defined as in Problem 2(b) above; (c) $f(t) = (\sin(\pi t))/(1 + t)$.

REVIEW QUESTIONS AND EXERCISES

1. The process of "indefinite integration" is sometimes called "antidifferentiation." Explain why the two terms should be synonymous.

2. Can there be more than one indefinite integral of a given function? If more than one exist, how are they related? What theorem of Chapter 3 is the key to this relationship?

3. If the acceleration of a moving body is given as a function of time (t), what further information do you need in order to find the law of motion, $s = f(t)$? How is s found?

4. Write a formula for the area bounded above by the semicircle

$$y = \sqrt{r^2 - t^2},$$

below by the t-axis, on the left by the y-axis, and on the right by the line $t = x$. Without making any calculations, what do you know must be the derivative, with respect to x, of this expression? Explain.

5. What numerical methods do you know for approximating a definite integral? How can an approximation usually be improved upon to give greater accuracy?

6. What property of continuous functions is used in the proof of the Intermediate Value Theorem?

7. Is every Riemann-integrable function also differentiable? Give a reason for your answer.

8. Is the function f defined on the domain $0 \le x \le 1$ by

$$f(x) = \begin{cases} 0 & \text{when } x \text{ is rational,} \\ 1 & \text{when } x \text{ is irrational,} \end{cases}$$

Riemann-integrable over (0, 1)? Give a reason for your answer.

MISCELLANEOUS PROBLEMS

Solve the differential equations in Problems 1–5.

1. $\dfrac{dy}{dx} = xy^2$ **2.** $\dfrac{dy}{dx} = \sqrt{1 + x + y + xy}$

3. $\dfrac{dy}{dx} = \dfrac{x^2 - 1}{y^2 + 1}$ **4.** $\dfrac{dx}{dy} = \dfrac{y - \sqrt{y}}{x + \sqrt{x}}$

5. $\dfrac{dx}{dy} = \left(\dfrac{2 + x}{3 - y}\right)^2$

6. Solve each of the following differential equations subject to the prescribed initial conditions:

a) $\dfrac{dy}{dx} = x\sqrt{x^2 - 4}; \quad x = 2, \quad y = 3.$

b) $\dfrac{dy}{dx} = xy^3; \quad x = 0, \quad y = 1.$

7. Can there be a curve satisfying the following conditions? d^2y/dx^2 is everywhere equal to zero and, when $x = 0$, $y = 0$ and $dy/dx = 1$. Give a reason for your answer.

8. Find an equation of the curve whose slope at the point (x, y) is $3x^2 + 2$, if the curve is required to pass through the point $(1, -1)$.

9. A particle moves along the x-axis. Its acceleration is $a = -t^2$. At $t = 0$, the particle is at the origin. In the course of its motion, it reaches the point $x = b$, where $b > 0$, but no point beyond b. Determine its velocity at $t = 0$.

10. A particle moves with acceleration $a = \sqrt{t} - (1/\sqrt{t})$. Assuming that the velocity $v = 4/3$ and the distance $s = -4/15$ when $t = 0$, find (a) the velocity v in terms of t, (b) the distance s in terms of t.

11. A particle is accelerated with acceleration $3 + 2t$, where t is the time. At $t = 0$, the velocity is 4. Find the velocity as a function of time and the distance between the position of the particle at time zero and at time 4.

12. The acceleration of a particle moving along the x-axis is given by $d^2x/dt^2 = -4x$. If the particle starts from rest at $x = 5$, find the velocity when it first reaches $x = 3$.

13. Let $f(x)$, $g(x)$ be two continuously differentiable functions satisfying the relationships $f'(x) = g(x)$ and $f''(x) = -f(x)$. Let $h(x) = f^2(x) + g^2(x)$. If $h(0) = 5$, find $h(10)$.

14. The family of straight lines $y = ax + b$ (a, b arbitrary constants) can be characterized by the relation $y'' = 0$. Find a similar relation satisfied by the family of all circles

$$(x - h)^2 + (y - h)^2 = r^2,$$

where h and r are arbitrary constants. [*Hint.* Eliminate h and r from the set of three equations including the given one and two obtained by successive differentiation.]

15. Assume that the brakes of an automobile produce a constant deceleration of k ft/sec^2. (a) Determine what k must be to bring an automobile traveling 60 mi/hr (88 ft/sec) to rest in a distance of 100 ft from the point where the brakes are applied. (b) With the same k, how far would a car traveling 30 mi/hr travel before being brought to a stop?

16. Solve the differential equation $dy/dx = x\sqrt{1 + x^2}$ subject to the condition that $y = -2$ when $x = 0$.

17. The acceleration due to gravity is -32 ft/sec^2. A stone is thrown upward from the ground with a speed of 96 ft/sec. Find the height to which the stone rises in t sec. What is the maximum height reached by the stone?

18. (*Amer. Math. Monthly* (1955), M. S. Klamkin.) Show that the following procedure will produce a continuous polygonal "curve" whose slope at the point (x_k, y_k) will be $f(x_k)$. First, sketch the auxiliary curve C: $y = xf(x)$. Then through the point $P_0(x_0, y_0)$, construct the line $x = x_0$ intersecting C in $Q_0(x_0, x_0 f(x_0))$. Through P_0 draw a line segment P_0P_1 parallel to OQ_0. Then the slope of P_0P_1 is $f(x_0)$. Now take $P_1(x_1, y_1)$ on this segment to lie close to P_0. For example, take $x_1 = x_0 + h$, where h is small. Then find $Q_1(x_1, x_1 f(x_1))$ on C and through P_1 draw a line segment P_1P_2 parallel to OQ_1. Continue the process by taking $P_2(x_2, y_2)$ close to P_1, with $x_2 = x_1 + h$; then find $Q_2(x_2, x_2 f(x_2))$ on C and through P_2 draw a line segment P_2P_3 parallel to OQ_2; and so on.

19. (a) Apply the procedure of Problem 18 to the case $f(x) = 1/x$ with $x_0 = 1$, $y_0 = 1$, and $h = \frac{1}{4}$. Continue the process until you reach the point $P_4(x_4, y_4)$. What is your value of y_4? (b) Repeat the construction of part (a), but with $h = \frac{1}{8}$, and continue until you reach $x_8 = 2$. What is your value of y_8?

20. A body is moving with velocity 16 ft/sec when it is suddenly subjected to a deceleration. If the deceleration is proportional to the square root of the velocity, and the body comes to rest in 4 sec, (a) how fast is the body moving 2 sec after it begins decelerating, and (b) how far does the body travel before coming to rest?

Evaluate the integrals in Problems 21 through 33:

21. $\int \frac{x^3+1}{x^2}\,dx$

22. $\int y\sqrt{1+y^2}\,dy$

23. $\int t^{1/3}(1+t^{4/3})^{-7}\,dt$

24. $\int \frac{(1+\sqrt{u})^{1/2}\,du}{\sqrt{u}}$

25. $\int \frac{dr}{\sqrt[3]{(7-5r)^2}}$

26. $\int \cos 4x\,dx$

27. $\int \sin^2 3x \cos 3x\,dx$

28. $\int \frac{\cos x\,dx}{\sqrt{\sin x}}$

29. $\int \cos(2x-1)\,dx$

30. $\int \frac{y\,dy}{\sqrt{25-4y^2}}$

31. $\int \frac{dt}{t\sqrt{2t}}$

32. $\int (x^2-\sqrt{x})\,dx$

33. $\int \frac{dx}{(2-3x)^2}$

34. If one side and the opposite angle of a triangle are fixed, prove that the area is a maximum when the triangle is isosceles.

35. A light hangs above the center of a table of radius r ft. The illumination at any point on the table is directly proportional to the cosine of the angle of incidence (i.e., the angle a ray of light makes with the normal) and is inversely proportional to the square of the distance from the light. How far should the light be above the table in order to give the strongest illumination at the edge of the table?

36. If A, B, C are constants, $AB \neq 0$, prove that the graph of the curve $y = A\sin(Bx + C)$ is always concave toward the x-axis except at its points of inflection, which are its points of intersection with the x-axis.

37. Two particles move on the same straight line so that their distances from a fixed point O, at any time t, are

$$x_1 = a\sin bt \quad \text{and} \quad x_2 = a\sin[bt + (\pi/3)],$$

where a and b are constants, $ab \neq 0$. Find the greatest distance between them.

38. If the identity $\sin(x+a) = \sin x\cos a + \cos x\sin a$ is differentiated with respect to x, is the resulting equation also an identity? Does this principle apply to the equation $x^2 - 2x - 8 = 0$? Explain.

39. A revolving beacon light in a lighthouse $\frac{1}{2}$ mile offshore makes two revolutions per minute. If the shoreline is a straight line, how fast is the ray of light moving along the shore when it passes a point one mile from the lighthouse?

40. The coordinates of a moving particle are $x = a\cos^3\theta$ and $y = a\sin^3\theta$. If a is a positive constant and θ increases at the constant rate of ω rad/sec, find the magnitude of the velocity vector.

41. The area bounded by the x-axis, the curve $y = f(x)$, and the lines $x = 1$, $x = b$, is equal to $\sqrt{b^2+1} - \sqrt{2}$ for all $b > 1$. Find $f(x)$.

42. Let $f(x)$ be a continuous function. Express

$$\lim_{n\to\infty} \frac{1}{n}\left[f\left(\frac{1}{n}\right) + f\left(\frac{2}{n}\right) + \cdots + f\left(\frac{n}{n}\right)\right]$$

as a definite integral.

43. Use the result of Problem 42 to evaluate:

a) $\lim_{n\to\infty} \frac{1}{n^{16}}[1^{15} + 2^{15} + 3^{15} + \cdots + n^{15}]$,

b) $\lim_{n\to\infty} \frac{\sqrt{1}+\sqrt{2}+\sqrt{3}+\cdots+\sqrt{n}}{n^{3/2}}$,

c) $\lim_{n\to\infty} \frac{1}{n}\left[\sin\frac{\pi}{n} + \sin\frac{2\pi}{n} + \sin\frac{3\pi}{n} + \cdots + \sin\frac{n\pi}{n}\right]$

Find:

d) $\lim_{h\to 0} \frac{1}{h}\int_x^{x+h} \frac{du}{u+\sqrt{u^2+1}}$,

e) $\lim_{x\to x_1} \left[\frac{x}{x-x_1}\int_{x_1}^{x} f(t)\,dt\right]$.

44. Variables x and y are related by the equation

$$x = \int_0^y \frac{1}{\sqrt{1+4t^2}}\,dt.$$

Show that d^2y/dx^2 is proportional to y and find the constant of proportionality.

APPLICATIONS OF THE DEFINITE INTEGRAL

5–1 INTRODUCTION

In Chapter 4 we discovered a close connection between sums of the form

$$S_a^b = \sum_a^b f(x)\,\Delta x \tag{1}$$

and integration, the inverse of differentiation. When f is continuous on $a \le x \le b$, we found that the *limit* of S_a^b as Δx approaches zero is just $F(b) - F(a)$, where F is any integral of f:

$$F(x) = \int f(x)\,dx. \tag{2}$$

We applied this to the problem of computing the area between the x-axis and the graph of $y = f(x)$, $a \le x \le b$. In this chapter we shall extend the applications to the following topics: area between two curves, distance, volumes, lengths of curves, areas of surfaces of revolution, average value of a function, center of mass, centroid, work, and hydrostatic force.

5–2 AREA BETWEEN TWO CURVES

Suppose that

$$y_1 = f_1(x) \qquad \text{and} \qquad y_2 = f_2(x)$$

define two functions of x that are continuous for $a \le x \le b$, and furthermore, suppose that

$$f_1(x) \ge f_2(x) \qquad \text{for} \quad a \le x \le b.$$

Then the y_1 curve is above the y_2 curve from a to b (Fig. 5–1) and we consider the problem of finding the area bounded above by the y_1 curve, below by the y_2 curve, and on the sides by the vertical lines $x = a$, $x = b$.

If the x-interval from a to b is divided into n equal subintervals, each of width $\Delta x = (b - a)/n$, and a rectangle of width Δx and altitude extending from the y_2 curve to the y_1 curve is used to approximate that portion of the

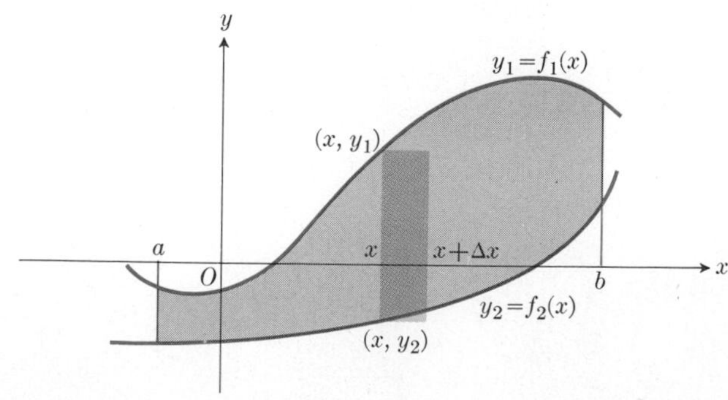

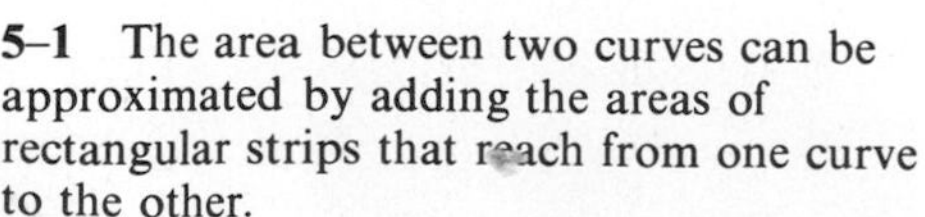
5–1 The area between two curves can be approximated by adding the areas of rectangular strips that reach from one curve to the other.

area between the curves that lies between x and $x + \Delta x$, then the area of the rectangle is

$$(y_1 - y_2)\,\Delta x = [f_1(x) - f_2(x)]\,\Delta x.$$

The total area in question is *approximated* by adding together the areas of all such rectangles

$$A \approx \sum_a^b [f_1(x) - f_2(x)]\,\Delta x.$$

Finally, if we let $\Delta x \to 0$, we obtain a number we call the exact area:

$$A = \lim_{\Delta x \to 0} \sum_a^b [f_1(x) - f_2(x)]\,\Delta x = \int_a^b [f_1(x) - f_2(x)]\,dx. \quad \textbf{(1)}$$

EXAMPLE. Find the area (Fig. 5–2) bounded by the parabola

$$y = 2 - x^2$$

and the straight line

$$y = -x.$$

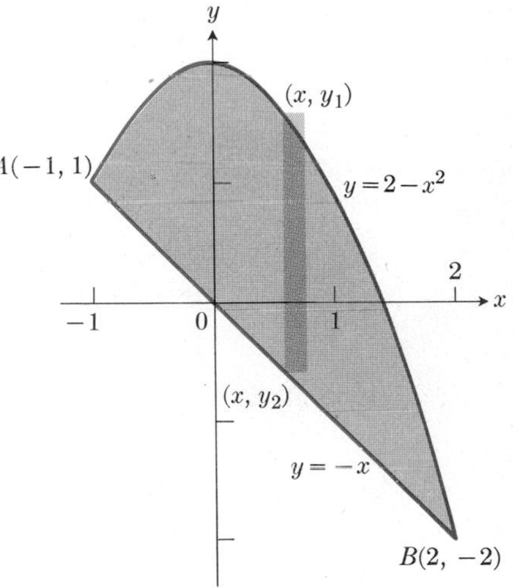

5–2 Calculating the area between $y = 2 - x^2$ and $y = -x$.

Solution. We first find where the curves intersect by finding points that satisfy both equations simultaneously. That is, we solve

$$2 - x^2 = -x$$

or

$$x^2 - x - 2 = 0, \qquad (x - 2)(x + 1) = 0, \qquad x = -1, 2.$$

The points of intersection are thus $A(-1, 1)$ and $B(2, -2)$. For all values of x between -1 and $+2$, the curve

$$y_1 = 2 - x^2$$

is above the line

$$y_2 = -x$$

by an amount

$$y_1 - y_2 = (2 - x^2) - (-x) = 2 - x^2 + x.$$

This is the altitude of a typical rectangle used to approximate that portion of the area lying between x and $x + \Delta x$. The total area is approximated by

$$A_{-1}^{2} \approx \sum_{-1}^{2} (y_1 - y_2)\,\Delta x = \sum_{-1}^{2} (2 - x^2 + x)\,\Delta x$$

and is given exactly by

$$A_{-1}^{2} = \lim_{\Delta x \to 0} \sum_{-1}^{2} (2 - x^2 + x)\,\Delta x = \int_{-1}^{2} (2 - x^2 + x)\,dx = 4\tfrac{1}{2}.$$

PROBLEMS

1. Make a sketch to represent a region that is bounded on the right by a continuous curve $x = f(y)$, on the left by a continuous curve $x = g(y)$, below by the line $y = a$, and above by the line $y = b$. Divide the region into n horizontal strips each of altitude $\Delta y = (b - a)/n$ and express the area of the region (a) as a limit of a sum of areas of rectangles, and (b) as an appropriate definite integral.

2. Find the area bounded by the x-axis and the curve $y = 2x - x^2$.

3. Find the area bounded by the y-axis and the curve $x = y^2 - y^3$.

4. Find the area bounded by the curve $y^2 = x$ and the line $x = 4$.

5. Find the area bounded by the curve $y = 2x - x^2$ and the line $y = -3$.

6. Find the area bounded by the curve $y = x^2$ and the line $y = x$.

7. Find the area bounded by the curve $x = 3y - y^2$ and the line $x + y = 3$.

8. Find the area bounded by the curves $y = x^4 - 2x^2$ and $y = 2x^2$.

9. Find the area of the "triangular" region in the first quadrant bounded by the y-axis and the curves $y = \sin x$, $y = \cos x$.

10. The area bounded by the curve $y = x^2$ and the line $y = 4$ is divided into two equal portions by the line $y = c$. Find c.

11. Find the area bounded by the curve $\sqrt{x} + \sqrt{y} = 1$ and the coordinate axes.

12. Use Simpson's rule with $n = 10$ to approximate the area between the curves $y = 1/(1 + x^2)$ and $y = -1/(1 + x^2)$, $-1 \leq x \leq 1$.

DISTANCE

As a second application of the basic principles involved in the use of the Fundamental Theorem of the calculus, we shall calculate the distance traveled by a body moving with velocity

$$v = f(t). \tag{1}$$

To simplify the discussion we shall assume that $f(t)$ is nonnegative, as well as continuous, for $a \leq t \leq b$. This means that the body moves in only one direction and does not back up.

Now there are two ways in which we can calculate the distance traveled by the body between $t = a$ and $t = b$.

FIRST METHOD. If we can integrate the differential equation

$$ds = f(t)\,dt, \tag{2}$$

which we get by substituting ds/dt for v in Eq. (1), then we can determine the position s of the body as a function of t, say

$$s = F(t) + C. \tag{3}$$

The distance traveled by the body between $t = a$ and $t = b$ is then given by

$$s\Big]_{t=a}^{t=b} = F(t) + C\Big]_a^b = F(b) - F(a).$$

We recognize this, of course, as saying that the distance is given by the definite integral

$$s\Big]_{t=a}^{t=b} = \int_a^b f(t)\,dt = F(t)\Big]_a^b = F(b) - F(a). \tag{4}$$

SECOND METHOD. In this method, we imagine the total time interval $a \leq t \leq b$ as divided into n subintervals, each of duration $\Delta t = (b - a)/n$.

The velocity at the beginning of the first subinterval is

$$v_1 = f(t_1) = f(a).$$

If Δt is small, the velocity remains nearly constant throughout the time from a to $a + \Delta t$. Hence during the first subinterval of time, the body travels a distance Δs_1 which is approximately equal to $v_1 \, \Delta t$:

$$\Delta s_1 \approx v_1 \, \Delta t = f(t_1) \, \Delta t. \tag{5}$$

If, instead of using the velocity v_1 at time t_1, we were to use the *average velocity*

$$\overline{v_1} = \frac{\Delta s_1}{\Delta t}, \tag{6a}$$

we could write

$$\Delta s_1 = \overline{v_1} \, \Delta t \tag{6b}$$

exactly. Now by the Mean Value Theorem, we know that there is some instant, say T_1, between t_1 and $t_1 + \Delta t$, where the instantaneous velocity is equal to the average velocity $\overline{v_1}$. In other words,

$$f(T_1) = \overline{v_1} \quad \text{for some } T_1, \qquad t_1 < T_1 < t_1 + \Delta t, \tag{6c}$$

and therefore

$$\Delta s_1 = f(T_1) \, \Delta t$$

exactly. By reasoning in the same manner for the second, third, ..., nth subintervals, we conclude that there are instants of time $T_2, T_3, \ldots, T_n$ in these intervals for which

$$\begin{aligned} \Delta s_2 &= f(T_2) \, \Delta t, \\ \Delta s_3 &= f(T_3) \, \Delta t, \\ &\vdots \\ \Delta s_n &= f(T_n) \, \Delta t, \end{aligned}$$

where $\Delta s_2, \Delta s_3, \ldots, \Delta s_n$ represent the distances traveled during these respective time subintervals. Therefore the total distance traveled between $t = a$ and $t = b$ is

$$\begin{aligned} s\Big]_{t=a}^{t=b} &= \Delta s_1 + \Delta s_2 + \Delta s_3 + \cdots + \Delta s_n \\ &= f(T_1) \, \Delta t + f(T_2) \, \Delta t + \cdots + f(T_n) \, \Delta t \\ &= \sum_{k=1}^{n} f(T_k) \, \Delta t. \end{aligned} \tag{7}$$

Let us now take finer and finer subdivisions Δt and let n increase without limit. For each n we select the appropriate instants of time $T_1, T_2, \ldots, T_n$ according to the method described above. Then the particular sums used in Eq. (7) tend to the definite integral

$$\lim_{n \to \infty} \sum_{k=1}^{n} f(T_k) \, \Delta t = \int_a^b f(t) \, dt \tag{8}$$

as limit, by virtue of the Fundamental Theorem. On the other hand, these sums all give the distance traveled by the body. Therefore the distance traveled is equal to the integral in Eq. (8) [or Eq. (4)].

REMARK 1. If, instead of using the velocities at the instants of time T_1, $T_2, \ldots, T_n$ described above, we had used the velocities

$$v_1 = f(t_1), \qquad v_2 = f(t_2), \qquad \ldots, \qquad v_n = f(t_n)$$

at the beginnings of the various subintervals, then we would have had n *approximations* like (5) with subscripts 1, 2, ..., n. Then we would have obtained an *approximation*

$$\Delta s_1 + \Delta s_2 + \cdots + \Delta s_n \approx f(t_1)\,\Delta t + f(t_2)\,\Delta t + \cdots + f(t_n)\,\Delta t,$$

or

$$s\Big]_{t=a}^{t=b} \approx \sum_{k=1}^{n} f(t_k)\,\Delta t. \tag{9}$$

Now since $f(t)$ is continuous, the sums (7) and (9) have the same *limit* as $n \to \infty$. In other words, the approximation (9) gets better as n increases, and the *limit* again gives the exact value, namely, the integral in Eq. (8).

REMARK 2. Of course, the two methods give the same result, Eqs. (4) and (8). The second method is useful primarily (a) because it shows how the simple formula

$$\text{Distance} = \text{Velocity} \times \text{Time},$$

which applies only to the case of *constant* velocity, can be extended to the case of variable velocity, provided we apply it to short subintervals Δt; and (b) because it can be used [in the form of the approximation (9)] to estimate the distance in cases where the velocity is given empirically by a table of values or a graph instead of by a formula $f(t)$ with known indefinite integral $F(t)$. (See Problem 15.)

REMARK 3. If the velocity changes sign during the interval (a, b), then the integral in Eq. (4) gives only the *net* change in s. This permits cancellation of distances traveled forward and backward. For example, it would give an answer of 2 miles if the body traveled forward 7 miles and backed up 5 miles. If we want to determine the total distance traveled, we calculate the integral of the *absolute value* of the velocity,

$$\int_a^b |f(t)|\,dt. \tag{10}$$

This can be done in practice by integrating separately over the intervals where v is positive and where v is negative and adding the absolute values of the results.

REMARK 4. The preceding discussion shows that the distance traveled is given by precisely the same expression as that for the area bounded by the curve

$$v = f(t)$$

and the t-axis from a to b. All of the discussion above can be interpreted geometrically. For example, T is chosen between t and $t + \Delta t$ in such a way that the area of the rectangle of base Δt and altitude $f(T)$ (Fig. 5–3(a)) is precisely equal to the area under the velocity curve between t and $t + \Delta t$. This is also the place where the slope of the curve $s = F(t)$ (Fig. 5–3(b)) is equal to the slope of the chord.

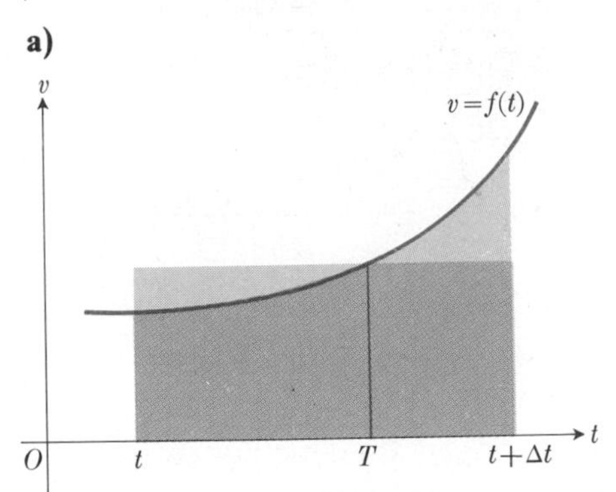

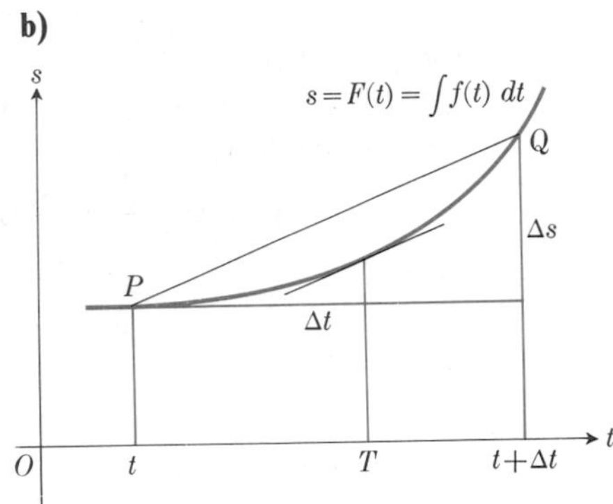

5–3 Two geometric interpretations of the equation

$$f(T)\,\Delta t = \int_t^{t+\Delta t} f(t)\,dt = F(t+\Delta t) - F(t):$$

(a) The area of the shaded rectangle equals the area under the curve between t and $(t + \Delta t)$; (b) At $t = T$ the slope $f(T)$ of the curve $s = F(t)$ equals the slope $[F(t+\Delta t) - F(t)]/\Delta t$ of the chord PQ.

PROBLEMS

In each of the following problems (1 through 8), the function $v = f(t)$ represents the velocity v (ft/sec) of a moving body as a function of the time t (sec). Sketch the graph of v versus t and find that portion of the given time interval $a \le t \le b$ in which the velocity is (a) positive, and (b) negative. Then find the total distance traveled by the body between $t = a$ and $t = b$.

1. $v = 2t + 1;\quad 0 \le t \le 2$

2. $v = t^2 - t - 2;\quad 0 \le t \le 3$

3. $v = t - \dfrac{8}{t^2};\quad 1 \le t \le 3$

4. $v = |t - 1|;\quad 0 \le t \le 2$

5. $v = 6 \sin 3t;\quad 0 \le t \le \dfrac{\pi}{2}$

6. $v = 4 \cos 2t;\quad 0 \le t \le \pi$

7. $v = \sin t + \cos t;\quad 0 \le t \le \pi$

8. $v = \sin t\sqrt{2 + 2\cos t};\quad 0 \le t \le \pi$

In each of the following problems (9 through 13), the function $a = f(t)$ represents the acceleration (ft/sec^2) of a moving body and v_0 is its velocity at time $t = 0$. Find the *distance* traveled by the body between time $t = 0$ and $t = 2$.

9. $a = \sin t;\quad v_0 = 2$

10. $a = 1 - \cos t;\quad v_0 = 0$

11. $a = g$ (const.); $\quad v_0 = 0$

12. $a = \sqrt{4t + 1};\quad v_0 = -4\frac{1}{3}$

13. $a = \dfrac{1}{\sqrt{4t + 1}};\quad v_0 = 1$

14. Suppose water flows into a tank at the rate of $f(t)$ gal/min, where f is a given, positive, continuous function of t. Let the amount of water in the tank at time $t = 0$ be Q_0 gal. Apply the Fundamental Theorem to show that the amount of water in the tank at any later time $t = b$ is

$$Q = Q_0 + \int_0^b f(t)\,dt.$$

15. (*Calculator*) Table 5–1 shows the speed of an automobile every 10 seconds from start to stop on a two-minute trip. Use Simpson's rule to estimate how far the car went.

Table 5–1. Selected speeds of a car on a two-minute trip

Time (sec)	Velocity (mph)	Time (sec)	Velocity (mph)
0	0	70	66
10	32	80	66
20	51	90	58
30	57	100	40
40	54	110	6
50	64	120	0
60	66		

5–4 VOLUMES (SLICES)

The volumes of many solids can be found by the "method of slicing." Suppose, for example, that the solid is bounded by two parallel planes perpendicular to the x-axis at $x = a$ and $x = b$. Imagine the solid cut into thin slices of thickness Δx by planes perpendicular to the x-axis. Then the total volume V of the solid is the sum of the volumes of these slices (see Fig. 5–4).

Let ΔV be the volume of a representative slice between x and $x + \Delta x$. Then if A' and A'' are, respectively, the smallest and largest cross-sectional areas of the solid between x and $x + \Delta x$, it will be seen at once that

$$A' \,\Delta x \le \Delta V \le A'' \,\Delta x$$

or

$$\Delta V = A(\bar{x})\,\Delta x,$$

where $A(\bar{x})$ denotes an appropriate intermediate cross-sectional area of the solid at some $\bar{x}$ between x and $x + \Delta x$. Then

$$V = \sum_a^b A(\bar{x})\,\Delta x$$

will give the total volume of the solid exactly. If, instead of choosing the exactly appropriate intermediate point $\bar{x}$ in the typical subinterval, we use the area $A(x)$ of the cross section at x, we have only an approximation,

$$V \approx \sum_a^b A(x)\,\Delta x.$$

But now let $\Delta x \to 0$. Then, if the cross-sectional area is a continuous function of x, all these sums will approach the same limit. Since one sequence of sums always gives the value V, it will have this value as its limit. Hence the other sums will also give the value V in the limit, that is,

$$V = \lim_{\Delta x \to 0} \sum_a^b A(x)\,\Delta x = \int_a^b A(x)\,dx. \tag{1}$$

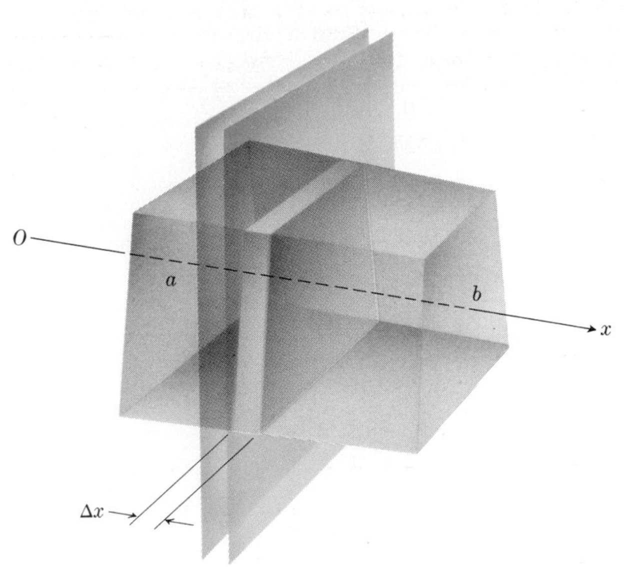

5–4 The volume of the solid is the sum of the volumes of slices of thickness Δx.

Volume of a Solid of Revolution

The solid generated by rotating a plane area about an axis in its plane is called a solid of revolution. To find the volume of a solid like the one in Fig. 5–5, we need only observe that the cross-sectional area $A(x)$ in Eq. (1) is the area of a circle of radius $r = y = f(x)$, so that

$$A(x) = \pi r^2 = \pi[f(x)]^2. \tag{2}$$

EXAMPLE 1. Suppose the curve in Fig. 5–5 represents the graph of

$$y = \sqrt{x}$$

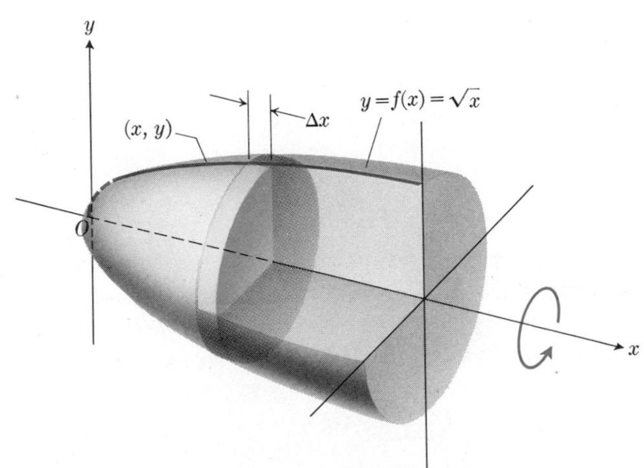

5–5 A slice perpendicular to the axis of a solid of revolution.

from (0, 0) to (4, 2). Then the volume of the representative slice is

$$\Delta V \approx \pi y^2 \, \Delta x = \pi(\sqrt{x})^2 \, \Delta x,$$

and the total volume is approximately

$$V \approx \sum_0^4 \pi x \, \Delta x.$$

Exactly, we have

$$V = \lim_{\Delta x \to 0} \sum_0^4 \pi x \, \Delta x = \int_0^4 \pi x \, dx = \pi \frac{x^2}{2}\bigg]_0^4 = 8\pi.$$

EXAMPLE 2. The circle

$$x^2 + y^2 = a^2$$

is rotated about the x-axis to generate a sphere. Find its volume.

Solution. We imagine the sphere cut into thin slices by planes perpendicular to the x-axis (Fig. 5–6). The volume of a typical slice between two planes at x and $x + \Delta x$ is approximately

$$\pi y^2 \, \Delta x = \pi(a^2 - x^2) \, \Delta x,$$

and the sum of all slices is approximately

$$V_{-a}^{a} \approx \sum_{-a}^{a} \pi(a^2 - x^2) \, \Delta x.$$

The exact volume is given by

$$V_{-a}^{a} = \lim_{\Delta x \to 0} \sum_{-a}^{a} \pi(a^2 - x^2) \, \Delta x = \int_{-a}^{a} \pi(a^2 - x^2) \, dx$$

$$= \pi \left[a^2 x - \frac{x^3}{3}\right]_{-a}^{a} = \frac{4}{3}\pi a^3.$$

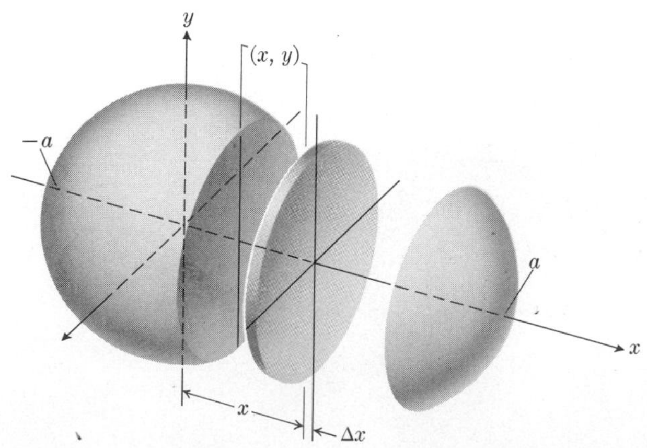

5–6 The sphere generated by rotating the circle $x^2 + y^2 = a^2$ about the x-axis.

Various methods for finding volumes are illustrated in the following examples.

EXAMPLE 3. A wedge is cut from a right circular cylinder of radius r by two planes, one perpendicular to the axis of the cylinder while the second makes an angle α with the first and intersects it at the center of the cylinder. Find the volume of the wedge.

Solution. The volume ΔV of the slice between y and $y + \Delta y$ in Fig. 5–7 is approximately

$$\Delta V \approx A(y)\, \Delta y,$$

where

$$A(y) = \tfrac{1}{2}xh$$

is the area of the triangle that forms one face of the slice and is to be expressed as a function of y. By trigonometry,

$$h = x \tan \alpha,$$

and by the theorem of Pythagoras,

$$x^2 + y^2 = r^2$$

or

$$x^2 = r^2 - y^2.$$

Hence

$$A(y) = \tfrac{1}{2}x^2 \tan \alpha = \tfrac{1}{2} \tan \alpha (r^2 - y^2).$$

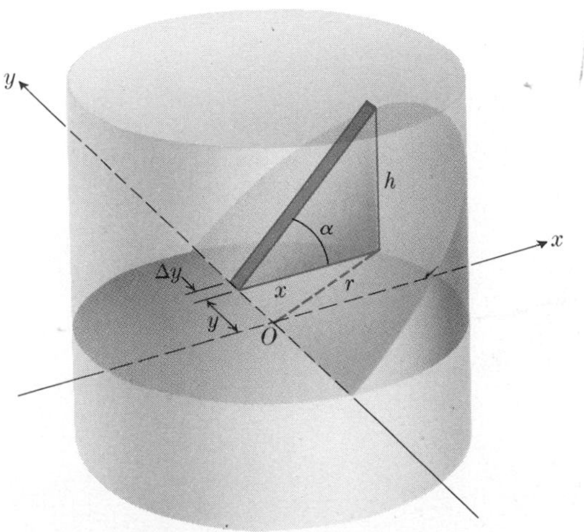

5–7 The curved wedge can be cut into triangular slices.

The total volume is given by

$$V = \lim_{\Delta y \to 0} \sum_{-r}^{r} A(y)\,\Delta y$$

$$= \int_{-r}^{r} \tfrac{1}{2}\tan\alpha(r^2 - y^2)\,dy.$$

Remembering that the factor $\frac{1}{2}\tan\alpha$ is a constant, we find

$$V = \tfrac{2}{3}r^3 \tan\alpha.$$

EXAMPLE 4. The base of the solid in Fig. 5–8 is an equilateral triangle of side s, with one vertex at the origin; one altitude of the triangle lies along the x-axis. Each plane section perpendicular to the x-axis is a square, one side of which lies in the base of the solid. Find the volume of the solid.

a)

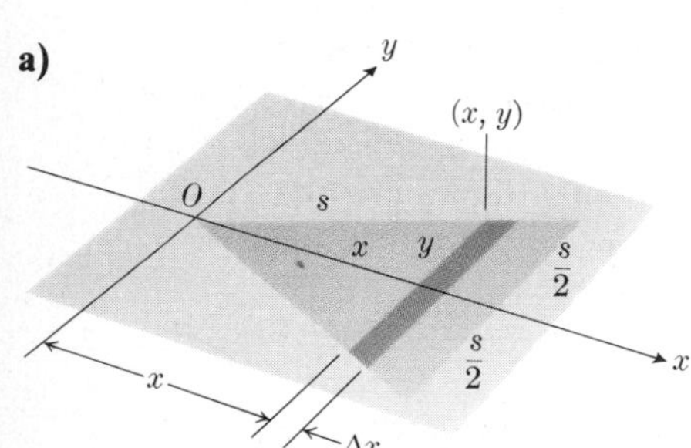

b)

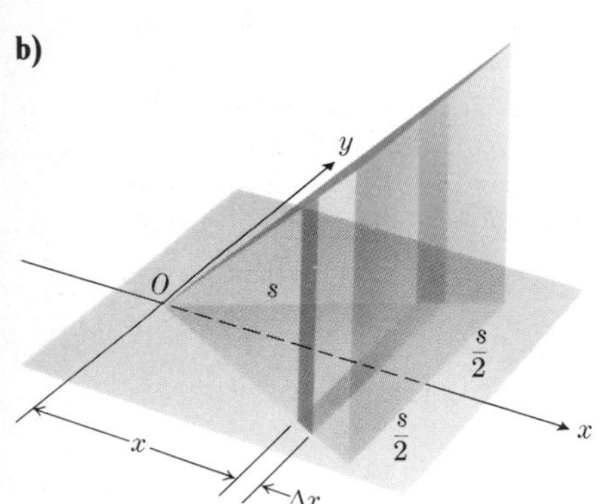

5–8 A solid with a triangular base (a), and square sections (b).

Solution. Figure 5–8(a) shows the base of the solid with a strip of width Δx, which corresponds to a slice of the solid of volume

$$\Delta V \approx A(x)\,\Delta x,$$

where

$$A(x) = (2y)^2 = 4y^2$$

is the area of a face of the slice. The slice extends upward from the xy-plane of Fig. 5–8(a). It is possible to find the required volume from the statement of the problem by reference to this figure and without visualizing the actual solid. A perspective view of the solid is, however, given in Fig. 5–8(b). It is required to find y in terms of x so that the area $A(x)$ will be given as a function of x. Since the base triangle is equilateral, its altitude h is given by

$$h^2 = s^2 - (s/2)^2 = \tfrac{3}{4}s^2$$

or

$$h = \frac{s}{2}\sqrt{3}.$$

Then, by similar triangles, we find

$$\frac{2y}{x} = \frac{s}{h} = \frac{2}{\sqrt{3}}$$

or

$$y = \frac{x}{\sqrt{3}}.$$

Then

$$V = \int_0^h A(x)\,dx$$

$$= \int_0^{s\sqrt{3}/2} \frac{4}{3}x^2\,dx = \frac{s^3}{2\sqrt{3}} = \frac{1}{3}hs^2.$$

PROBLEMS

In Problems 1 through 8, find the volumes generated when the areas bounded by the given curves and lines are rotated about the x-axis. [*Note.* $x = 0$ is the y-axis and $y = 0$ is the x-axis.]

1. $x + y = 2;\quad x = 0,\quad y = 0$

2. $y = \sin x,\quad y = 0\quad (0 \le x \le \pi)$
[See Problem 17, Article 4–7.]

3. $y = x - x^2;\quad y = 0$

4. $y = -3x - x^2;\quad y = 0$

5. $y = x^2 - 2x;\quad y = 0$

6. $y = x^3;\quad x = 2,\quad y = 0$

7. $y = x^4;\ x = 1,\ y = 0$

8. $y = \sqrt{\cos x},\ 0 \le x \le \pi/2;\quad x = 0;\quad y = 0$

9. Find the volume generated when the area bounded by $y = \sqrt{x}$, $y = 2$, and $x = 0$ is rotated (a) about the y-axis, (b) about the line $y = 2$.

10. By integration find the volume generated by rotating the triangle with vertices at $(0, 0)$, $(h, 0)$, (h, r),

a) about the x-axis, **b)** about the y-axis.

11. (a) A hemispherical bowl of radius a contains water to a depth h. Find the volume of water in the bowl. (b) (Review problem on related rates.) Water runs into a hemispherical bowl of radius 5 ft at the rate of 0.2 ft^3/sec. How fast is the water level in the bowl rising when the water is 4 ft deep?

12. A football has a volume that is approximately the same as the volume generated by rotating the area inside the ellipse $b^2x^2 + a^2y^2 = a^2b^2$ (where a and b are constants) about the x-axis. Find the volume so generated.

13. The cross sections of a certain solid by planes perpendicular to the x-axis are circles with diameters extending from the curve $y = x^2$ to the curve $y = 8 - x^2$. The solid lies between the points of intersection of these two curves. Find its volume.

14. The base of a certain solid is the circle $x^2 + y^2 = a^2$. Each plane section of the solid cut out by a plane perpendicular to the x-axis is a square with one edge of the square in the base of the solid. Find the volume of the solid.

15. Two great circles, lying in planes that are perpendicular to each other, are marked on a sphere of radius a. A portion of the sphere is then shaved off in such a manner that any plane section of the remaining solid, perpendicular to the common diameter of the two great circles, is a square with vertices on these circles. Find the volume of the solid that remains.

16. The base of a certain solid is the circle $x^2 + y^2 = a^2$. Each plane section of the solid cut out by a plane perpendicular to the y-axis is an isosceles right triangle with one leg in the base of the solid. Find the volume.

17. The base of a certain solid is the region between the x-axis and the curve $y = \sin x$ between $x = 0$ and $x = \pi/2$. Each plane section of the solid perpendicular to the x-axis is an equilateral triangle with one side in the base of the solid. Find the volume.

18. A rectangular swimming pool is 30 ft wide and 50 ft long. The depth of water h ft at distance x ft from one end of the pool is measured at 5-ft intervals and found to be as follows:

x (ft)	0	5	10	15	20	25
h (ft)	6.0	8.2	9.1	9.9	10.5	11.0
x (ft)	30	35	40	45	50	
h (ft)	11.5	11.9	12.3	12.7	13.0	

Use the trapezoidal rule to estimate the volume of water in the pool.

5–5 VOLUMES (SHELLS AND WASHERS)

Sometimes when we rotate an area about a line in the plane of the area, the volume swept out by a rectangular strip in the area is a washer or a cylinder instead of a disk. The calculation of the volume in these cases is straightforward, but involves modeling that differs enough from the examples of Article 5–4 to warrant separate attention.

Suppose the area $PQRS$ in Fig. 5–9 is revolved around the y-axis. We can compute the volume generated in the following way. Consider a strip of area between the ordinate at x and the ordinate at $x + \Delta x$. When this strip is revolved around the y-axis, it generates a hollow, thin-walled shell of inner radius x, outer radius $x + \Delta x$, and volume ΔV. The base of this shell is a ring bounded by two concentric circles. The inner radius is

$$r_1 = x$$

and the outer radius is

$$r_2 = x + \Delta x.$$

The area of the ring is

$$\Delta A = \pi(r_2^2 - r_1^2) = 2\pi\left(\frac{r_2 + r_1}{2}\right)(r_2 - r_1) = 2\pi r\, \Delta x.$$

Here

$$r = \frac{r_2 + r_1}{2} = x + \frac{\Delta x}{2}$$

is the radius of the circle midway between the inner and outer boundaries of the ring, and $2\pi r$ is its circumference.

Now if we had a cylindrical shell of constant altitude y standing on this base, its volume would be

$$\text{Altitude} \times \text{base} = y\, \Delta A.$$

In the present case, the altitude of the shell varies between y and $y + \Delta y$. Its

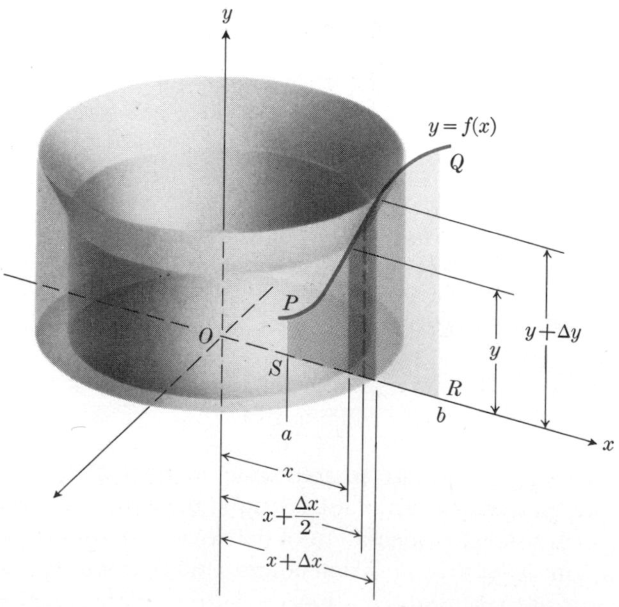

5–9 The volume swept out when $PQRS$ is revolved about the y-axis is a union of cylindrical shells like the one shown here.

volume therefore lies between $y\,\Delta A$ and $(y+\Delta y)\,\Delta A$. That is,

$$y\,\Delta A \le \Delta V \le (y+\Delta y)\,\Delta A$$

or

$$y \cdot 2\pi r\,\Delta x \le \Delta V \le (y+\Delta y)\cdot 2\pi r\,\Delta x.$$

The total volume V is contained between the "lower" sum

$$s = \sum_a^b y \cdot 2\pi\left(x + \frac{\Delta x}{2}\right)\Delta x$$

and the "upper" sum

$$S = \sum_a^b (y+\Delta y)\cdot 2\pi\left(x + \frac{\Delta x}{2}\right)\Delta x.$$

As Δx approaches zero, both of these sums approach the integral

$$\int_a^b y \cdot 2\pi x\,dx$$

as limit (see Article 5–6). Hence this limit must also be equal to the volume V, namely,

$$V = \lim_{\Delta x\to 0} s = \lim_{\Delta x\to 0} S = \int_a^b y\cdot 2\pi x\,dx = \int_a^b 2\pi x f(x)\,dx.$$

REMARK. An easy way to visualize this result is to imagine that the volume element ΔV has been cut along a generator of the cylinder and that the shell has been rolled out flat like a thin sheet of tin. The sheet then has dimensions very nearly equal to $2\pi x$ by $y = f(x)$ by Δx. Hence

$$\Delta V \approx 2\pi x \cdot f(x)\cdot \Delta x,$$

and the total volume is given approximately by

$$V \approx \sum_a^b 2\pi x \cdot f(x)\cdot \Delta x.$$

As Δx approaches zero, we obtain a limit that is equal to the exact volume:

$$V = \lim_{\Delta x\to 0} \sum_a^b 2\pi x\cdot f(x)\cdot \Delta x = \int_a^b 2\pi x f(x)\,dx.$$

EXAMPLE 1. The area bounded by $y = \sqrt{x}$, $y = 0$, and $x = 4$ is revolved about the x-axis. Find the volume swept out.

Solution. Instead of beginning with a vertical strip to generate a disk, as in Example 1 of Article 5–4, we begin with a horizontal strip of area between the lines at distances y and $y + \Delta y$ above the x-axis. (See Fig. 5–10.) The volume generated by revolving this strip around the x-axis is a hollow cylindrical shell of inner circumference $2\pi y$, inner length $4 - x$, and wall

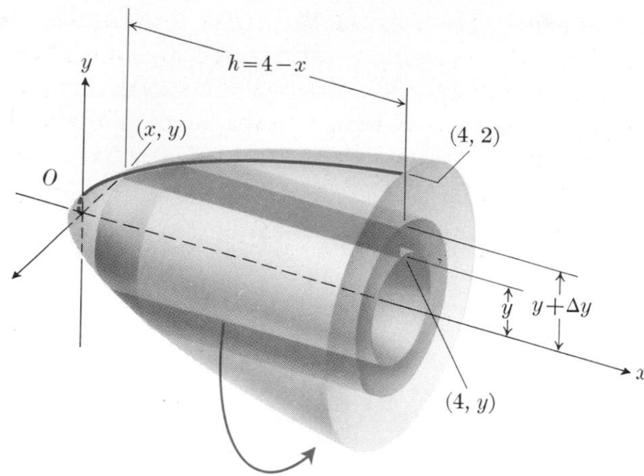

5–10 The volume of the cylindrical shell generated by the horizontal strip is about

Circumference · Length · Thickness
$\approx 2\pi y \cdot (4 - x) \cdot \Delta y$

thickness Δy. Hence, the total volume V is approximately

$$V \approx \sum_{y=0}^{2} 2\pi y(4 - x)\,\Delta y$$

and is exactly equal to the limit of this sum as Δy approaches zero:

$$V = \lim_{\Delta y \to 0} \sum_{y=0}^{2} 2\pi y(4 - x)\,\Delta y = \int_0^2 2\pi y(4 - y^2)\,dy$$

$$= 2\pi \left[2y^2 - \frac{y^4}{4}\right]_0^2 = 8\pi.$$

EXAMPLE 2. A hole of diameter a is bored through the center of the sphere in Example 2 of Article 5–4. Find the remaining volume.

Solution. The volume could be generated by rotating about the y-axis the area inside the circle $x^2 + y^2 = a^2$ lying to the right of the line $x = a/2$ (Fig. 5–11(a)). The line and the circle intersect at the points $(a/2, \pm a\sqrt{3}/2)$. There are at least three methods for finding the required volume.

METHOD 1. Figure 5–11(b) shows an exploded view of the solid sphere with the core pulled out. Note that the core is a cylinder with a spherical cap at each end. Essentially, what we shall do is subtract the volume of this core from the volume of the sphere, but we shall simplify matters slightly by imagining that the two caps have been sliced off first, by planes perpendicular to the y-axis at $y = \pm a\sqrt{3}/2$. When these two caps have been removed, the truncated sphere has a volume V_1. From this truncated sphere we remove a right circular cylinder of radius $a/2$ and altitude $2(a\sqrt{3}/2) = a\sqrt{3}$. Then the volume of this flat-ended cylinder is

$$V_2 = \pi \left(\frac{a}{2}\right)^2 (a\sqrt{3}) = \frac{\sqrt{3}}{4}\pi a^3.$$

The desired volume is $V = V_1 - V_2$. We find V_1 by the same method we used for the spherical ball in Example 2 of Article 5-4, but we keep in mind that the two caps have been removed at top and bottom. Imagine the solid as cut into slices by planes perpendicular to the y-axis. The slice between y and $y + \Delta y$ is approximated by a cylinder of altitude Δy and cross-sectional area

$$\pi x^2 = \pi(a^2 - y^2),$$

so that we have the approximation

$$V_1 \approx \sum_{-a\sqrt{3}/2}^{a\sqrt{3}/2} \pi(a^2 - y^2)\,\Delta y$$

and the exact value

$$V_1 = \int_{-a\sqrt{3}/2}^{a\sqrt{3}/2} \pi(a^2 - y^2)\,dy = \frac{3\sqrt{3}}{4}\pi a^3.$$

Thus

$$V = V_1 - V_2 = \frac{3\sqrt{3}}{4}\pi a^3 - \frac{\sqrt{3}}{4}\pi a^3 = \frac{\sqrt{3}}{2}\pi a^3.$$

METHOD 2. Instead of subtracting volumes, we may work directly with the volume required. Again we imagine the solid to be cut into thin slices by planes perpendicular to the y-axis. Each slice (Fig. 5-11(c)) is now like a washer of thickness Δy, inner radius

$$r_1 = \frac{a}{2},$$

and outer radius

$$r_2 = x = \sqrt{a^2 - y^2}.$$

The area of a face of such a washer is

$$\pi r_2^2 - \pi r_1^2 = \pi(\tfrac{3}{4}a^2 - y^2),$$

and the volume of the solid is approximately

$$V \approx \sum_{-a\sqrt{3}/2}^{a\sqrt{3}/2} \pi(\tfrac{3}{4}a^2 - y^2)\,\Delta y,$$

while its exact value is

$$\begin{aligned} V &= \lim_{\Delta y \to 0} \sum_{-a\sqrt{3}/2}^{a\sqrt{3}/2} \pi(\tfrac{3}{4}a^2 - y^2)\,\Delta y \\ &= \int_{-a\sqrt{3}/2}^{a\sqrt{3}/2} \pi(\tfrac{3}{4}a^2 - y^2)\,dy \\ &= \frac{\sqrt{3}}{2}\pi a^3. \end{aligned}$$

METHOD 3. This time we shall use the cylindrical-shell approach (see Fig. 5-11(a)). We imagine the solid to be cut into a number of hollow cylindrical

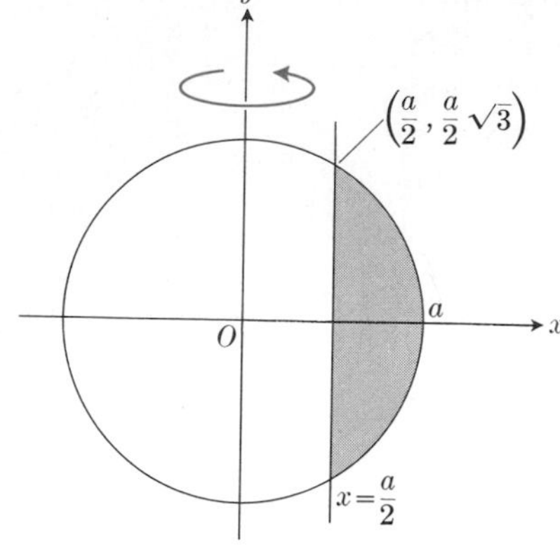

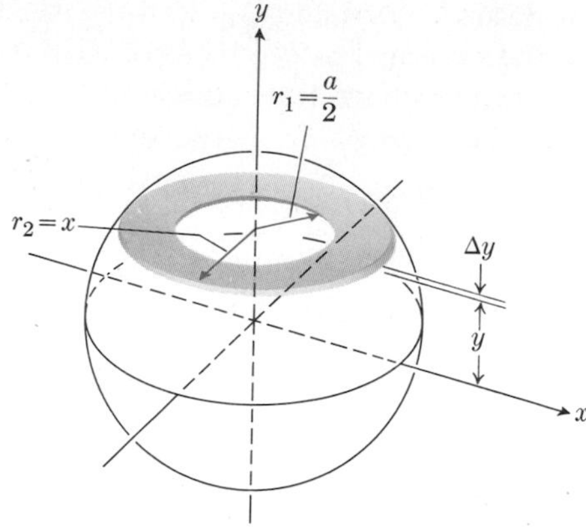

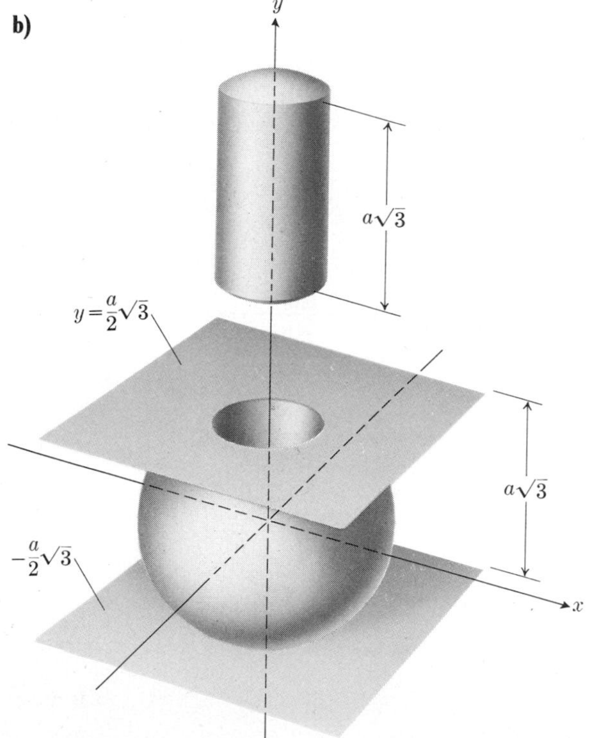

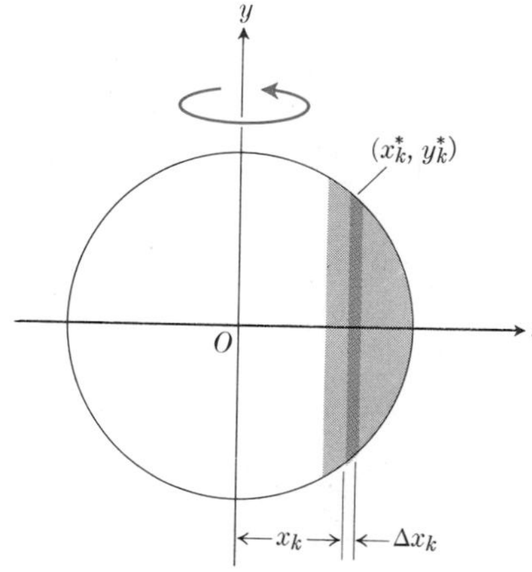

5–11 (a) The tinted region generates the volume of revolution. (b) An exploded view showing the sphere with the core removed. (c) A phantom view showing a cross-sectional slice of the sphere with core removed. (d) The strip of area indicated by darker tint generates a cylindrical shell.

shells by cylinders having the y-axis as their common axis and having radii

$$x_1 = \frac{a}{2}, \quad x_2, \quad x_3, \quad \ldots, \quad x_n, \quad x_{n+1} = a.$$

The first shell has inner radius x_1 and outer radius x_2, the second shell has inner radius x_2 and outer radius x_3, and so on, the kth shell having inner radius x_k and outer radius x_{k+1}. This kth shell fills the region swept out when the dark strip in Fig. 5–11(d) is revolved about the y-axis. If we imagine this region to have been cut along a line parallel to the y-axis and flattened out, we see that the volume V_k of the kth cylindrical shell is approximately

$$2\pi x_k^* \cdot 2y_k^* \cdot \Delta x_k = 4\pi x_k^* \sqrt{a^2 - (x_k^*)^2}\, \Delta x_k,$$

where (x_k^*, y_k^*) (Fig. 5–11(d)) is the point of abscissa

$$x_k^* = \tfrac{1}{2}(x_k - x_{k+1})$$

on the circle in the first quadrant. Then the entire volume will be approximated by

$$V \approx \sum_{k=1}^{n} 4\pi x_k^* \sqrt{a^2 - (x_k^*)^2}\, \Delta x_k$$

$$\approx \sum_{a/2}^{a} 4\pi x \sqrt{a^2 - x^2}\, \Delta x.$$

The exact value will be the *limit* of this sum, namely,

$$V = \lim_{x \to 0} \sum_{a/2}^{a} 4\pi x \sqrt{a^2 - x^2}\, \Delta x$$

$$= \int_{a/2}^{a} 4\pi x \sqrt{a^2 - x^2}\, dx.$$

To evaluate this integral, we let

$$u = a^2 - x^2;$$

then

$$V = 4\pi \int_{a/2}^{a} \sqrt{a^2 - x^2}\, (x\, dx)$$

$$= 4\pi \int u^{1/2}(-\tfrac{1}{2}\, du) = -\frac{4\pi}{3}\left[(a^2 - x^2)^{3/2}\right]_{a/2}^{a}$$

$$= \frac{\sqrt{3}}{2}\pi a^3.$$

PROBLEMS

In Problems 1–8 find the volume generated when the area bounded by the given curves and lines is rotated about the x-axis. [*Note.* $x = 0$ is the y-axis and $y = 0$ is the x-axis.]

1. $x + y = 2;\quad x = 0,\quad y = 0$
2. $x = 2y - y^2;\quad x = 0$
3. $y = 3x - x^2;\quad y = x$
4. $y = x;\quad y = 1,\quad x = 0$
5. $y = x^2;\quad y = 4$
6. $y = 3 + x^2;\quad y = 4$
7. $y = x^2 + 1;\quad y = x + 3$
8. $y = 4 - x^2;\quad y = 2 - x$

In Problems 9–16, find the volume generated by revolving the given area about the given axis.

9. The area bounded by $y = x^4$, $x = 1$, and $y = 0$ about the y-axis.
10. The area bounded by $y = x^3$, $x = 2$, and $y = 0$, about the y-axis.
11. The triangle with vertices (1, 1), (1, 2), (2, 2), (a) about the x-axis; (b) about the y-axis.
12. The area bounded by the curve $x = y - y^3$ and the lines $x = 0$, $y = 0$, $y = 1$, about the x-axis.
13. The area bounded by $y = \sqrt{x}$, $y = 2$, $x = 0$, (a) about the x-axis; (b) about the line $x = 4$.

14. The area bounded by the y-axis, and by the curves $y = \cos x$ and $y = \sin x$ for $0 \le x \le \pi/4$, about the x-axis.

15. The area bounded by $y = 0$ and the curve $y = 8x^2 - 8x^3$, $0 \le x \le 1$, about the y-axis.

16. The area between the curves $y = 2x^2$ and $y = x^4 - 2x^2$ about the y-axis.

17. Use cylindrical shells and the result of Example 4, Article 4–4, to find the volume generated by revolving about the y-axis the area bounded by $y = 0$ and the curve $y = \sin x$, $0 \le x \le \pi$.

18. The area bounded by the curve $y = x^2$ and the line $y = 4$ generates various solids of revolution when rotated as follows:

a) about the y-axis, **b)** about the line $y = 4$,
c) about the x-axis, **d)** about the line $y = -1$,
c) about the line $x = 2$.

Find the volume generated in each case.

19. The circle $x^2 + y^2 = a^2$ is rotated about the line $x = b$ $(b > a)$ to generate a torus. Find the volume generated. [*Hint.* $\int_{-a}^{a} \sqrt{a^2 - x^2}\, dx = \pi a^2/2$, since it is the area of a semicircle of radius a.]

APPROXIMATIONS

By now it is apparent that each application of the Fundamental Theorem that we have made so far has involved the following steps:

1. Select an independent variable, say x, such that the quantity U to be computed can be represented as a sum of pieces ΔU, where ΔU is that part of U that is associated with the subinterval $(x, x + \Delta x)$ of the domain $a \le x \le b$ of the variable x.

2. Subdivide the domain (a, b) into n subintervals. For simplicity we usually take the lengths all to be the same, namely, equal to $\Delta x = (b - a)/n$.

3. Approximate that portion ΔU of U that is associated with the subinterval $(x, x + \Delta x)$ by an expression of the form

$$\Delta U \approx f(X)\, \Delta x. \tag{1}$$

In this expression, X is to be some point in the subinterval $(x, x + \Delta x)$ and the function f is to be continuous over the entire domain $a \le x \le b$.

4. Then the total quantity U is *approximately*

$$U \approx \sum_a^b f(X)\, \Delta x. \tag{2}$$

5. Take the limit, as Δx approaches zero, of the sum in Eq. (2). This limit is the definite integral

$$\lim_{\Delta x \to 0} \sum_a^b f(X)\, \Delta x = \int_a^b f(x)\, dx. \tag{3}$$

Is this limit also an approximation to U or does it give U exactly?

In the case of area, distance, and volume we have seen that the *limit* in (3) does give U exactly. To be able to apply these methods to new situations as they arise, we need an answer to the following question.

QUESTION. How accurate must the approximations in (1) and (2) be to say that all of the error is squeezed out in going to the limit, (3), with the result that the exact value of U is given by the limit

$$U = \lim_{\Delta x \to 0} \sum_a^b f(X)\, \Delta x = \int_a^b f(x)\, dx? \tag{4}$$

ANSWER. Denote by $\alpha\,\Delta x$ the correction that must be added to the right side of Eq. (1) to give ΔU exactly. That is, suppose that

$$\Delta U = f(X)\,\Delta x + \alpha\,\Delta x, \tag{5}$$

exactly.

FIRST CASE. Suppose these correction terms are no larger than a constant K times $(\Delta x)^2$,

$$|\alpha\,\Delta x| \le K(\Delta x)^2,$$

where K is a constant the same for all subintervals and all methods of subdivision. Then we have

$$\Delta U = f(X)\,\Delta x + \alpha\,\Delta x,$$

$$U = \sum_a^b f(X)\,\Delta x + \sum_a^b \alpha\,\Delta x$$

and

$$\left| U - \sum_a^b f(X)\,\Delta x \right| = \left| \sum_a^b \alpha\,\Delta x \right| < \sum_a^b K(\Delta x)^2. \tag{6}$$

This last sum consists of n terms each of which is equal to $K(\Delta x)^2$, where $\Delta x = (b - a)/n$. Therefore

$$\sum_a^b K(\Delta x)^2 = nK(b - a)^2/n^2 = K(b - a)^2/n = K(b - a)\,\Delta x,$$

and (6) becomes

$$\left| U - \sum_a^b f(X)\,\Delta x \right| \le K(b - a)\,\Delta x. \tag{7}$$

In other words, if the error in the approximation (1) to each individual ΔU is no more than a constant times the *square* of Δx, then the error in the approximation (2) to the *total* U is no more than a constant times the *first power* of Δx. Now let Δx approach zero in (7). The sum on the left becomes the definite integral (3), and the term on the right becomes zero. In other words, U is exactly equal to the definite integral in this case.

SECOND CASE. Suppose the correction terms are numerically no larger than a constant K' times Δx times δy:

$$|\alpha\,\Delta x| \le K'\,\Delta x\,\delta y,$$

where K' is the same for all subintervals and all methods of subdivision, and where δy is the oscillation in the interval $(x, x + \Delta x)$ of a function $y = \phi(x)$ that is continuous over the closed interval (a, b). Then one finds in this case that the total error in the approximation (2) is no larger than

$$K'(b - a) \text{ times } (\max \delta y).$$

But the maximum δy also approaches zero when Δx does, so again we find that U is given exactly by the definite integral.

We have given criteria such as

$$|\alpha \, \Delta x| \le K(\Delta x)^2 \qquad \text{or} \qquad |\alpha \, \Delta x| \le K' \, \Delta x \, \delta y,$$

where K and K' are constants. Usually, in an application, we have a function of x in place of K or K' in these inequalities. But a function of x that is continuous over the closed interval $a \le x \le b$ has a maximum absolute value M on that interval, and we could take K (or K') equal to M in such a case. Also, the correction terms $\alpha \, \Delta x$ could involve finite combinations of the two cases discussed above, provided the inequality

$$|\alpha \, \Delta x| \le K(\Delta x)^2 + K' \, \Delta x \, \delta y$$

is satisfied for some choice of the constants K and K'.

Roughly speaking, we may say that in the approximation

$$\Delta U \approx f(X) \, \Delta x$$

we must include all first power Δx terms but we may omit higher-power terms like $(\Delta x)^2$, $(\Delta x)^3$, and so on, or we may omit such mixed terms as

$$(\Delta x)(\Delta y), \qquad (\Delta x)^2(\Delta y), \qquad (\Delta x)(\Delta y)^2,$$

and so on. If each separate piece ΔU is estimated to this degree of accuracy, then the total quantity U which is given approximately by the sum (2) will be given exactly by the limit of the sum, namely, by the integral (4).

In discussing the cylindrical shell method of finding a volume of revolution, Article 5–5, we found that we could estimate the volume ΔV in a hollow shell as follows:

$$2\pi\left(x + \frac{\Delta x}{2}\right) \cdot y \cdot \Delta x \le \Delta V \le 2\pi\left(x + \frac{\Delta x}{2}\right)(y + \Delta y) \, \Delta x. \tag{8}$$

Multiplied out, this becomes

$$2\pi xy \, \Delta x + \pi y(\Delta x)^2 \le \Delta V$$
$$\le 2\pi xy \, \Delta x + \pi y(\Delta x)^2 + 2\pi x \, \Delta x \, \Delta y + \pi \, \Delta y(\Delta x)^2.$$

If we ignore all except the first power terms in Δx, we have the approximation

$$\Delta V \approx 2\pi xy \, \Delta x,$$

with an error that involves combinations like

$$\pi y(\Delta x)^2, \qquad 2\pi x \, \Delta y \, \Delta x, \qquad \pi \, \Delta y(\Delta x)^2.$$

All such terms may be safely ignored when we go to the *limit* of the sum:

$$V = \lim_{\Delta x \to 0} \sum_a^b 2\pi xy \, \Delta x = \int_a^b 2\pi xy \, dx = \int_a^b 2\pi x f(x) \, dx.$$

Infinitesimals. A variable, such as Δx above, that approaches zero as a limit is called an infinitesimal. Terms that approach zero as the first power of Δx are said to be of the *same order* as Δx, but terms which approach zero as $(\Delta x)^2$ or as $\Delta y \, \Delta x$ are called infinitesimals of *higher order* than Δx. In setting up a definite integral, we must retain those infinitesimals that are of the same order as Δx, but we may omit those infinitesimals that are of higher order than Δx. Thus we may omit the term $\alpha\,\Delta x$, Eq. (5), if α is an infinitesimal of the same order as Δx (or higher order) or of the same order as δy (or higher order), and the *limit* in (4) will give the exact value of U.

PROBLEMS

1. In Fig. 5–9, Article 5–5, let V_a^x denote the volume generated by rotating about the y-axis the area under the curve $y = f(x)$ between the ordinate at a and the ordinate at x, $(x > a)$. Use inequality (8) to show that

$$\frac{dV_a^x}{dx} = \lim_{\Delta x\to 0} \frac{\Delta V_a^x}{\Delta x} = 2\pi x f(x).$$

From this, deduce that

$$V_a^b = \int_a^b 2\pi x f(x)\,dx.$$

2. Let U_a^x denote the amount of the quantity U associated with the interval (a, x), and let ΔU in Eq. (5) represent $U_a^{x+\Delta x} - U_a^x = U_x^{x+\Delta x}$. If the function $f(x)$ in Eq. (5) is continuous over the closed interval $a \le x \le b$ and $|\alpha\,\Delta x| \le K(\Delta x)^2$, where K is a constant, show that

$$\frac{dU_a^x}{dx} = \lim_{\Delta x\to 0} \frac{\Delta U}{\Delta x} = f(x).$$

From this, deduce that $U_a^b = \int_a^b f(x)\,dx$.

3. In Problem 2, replace the condition $|\alpha\,\Delta x| \le K(\Delta x)^2$ by the condition

$$|\alpha\,\Delta x| \le |K'\,\Delta x\,\delta y|,$$

where K' is a constant and δy is the oscillation over the interval $(x, x + \Delta x)$ of a function $y = g(x)$ that is continuous over the closed interval $a \le x \le b$. Then derive the same conclusion as in Problem 2.

5–7 LENGTH OF A PLANE CURVE

Divide the arc AB (Fig. 5–12) into n pieces and join the successive points of division by straight lines. A representative line, such as PQ, will have length

$$PQ = \sqrt{(\Delta x_k)^2 + (\Delta y_k)^2}.$$

The length of the curve AB is approximately

$$L_A^B \approx \sum_{k=1}^{n} \sqrt{(\Delta x_k)^2 + (\Delta y_k)^2}.$$

When the number of division points is increased indefinitely while the lengths of the individual segments tend to zero, we obtain

$$L_A^B = \lim_{n\to\infty} \sum_{k=1}^{n} \sqrt{(\Delta x_k)^2 + (\Delta y_k)^2}, \tag{1}$$

provided the limit exists.* The sum on the right side of (1) is not in the standard form to which we can apply the Fundamental Theorem of the integral calculus, but it can be put into such a form, as follows:

Suppose that the function $y = f(x)$ is continuous and possesses a continuous derivative at each point of the curve from $A[a, f(a)]$ to $B[b, f(b)]$. Then, by the Mean Value Theorem, there is some point $P^*(x_k^*, y_k^*)$ between P and

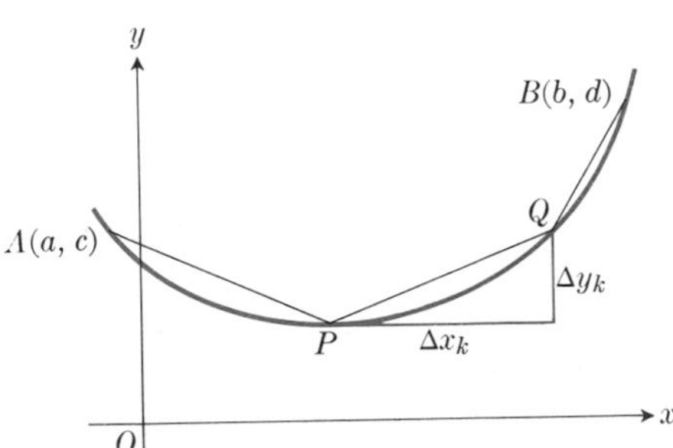

5–12 The arc AB is approximated by the polygonal path $APQB$. The length of the arc is defined to be the limit (when it exists) of the lengths of successively finer polygonal approximations.

* For most smooth curves encountered in practice, the limit does exist. Such curves are called rectifiable. An example of a continuous curve that is not rectifiable is given by the curve

$$y = \begin{cases} x \sin 1/x & \text{when } x \ne 0, \\ 0 & \text{when } x = 0, \end{cases} \qquad \frac{-\pi}{2} \le x \le \frac{\pi}{2}.$$

Q on the curve where the tangent to the curve is parallel to the chord PQ. That is,

$$f'(x_k^*) = \frac{\Delta y_k}{\Delta x_k}$$

or

$$\Delta y_k = f'(x_k^*)\,\Delta x_k.$$

Hence (1) may also be written in the form

$$L_A^B = \lim_{n\to\infty} \sum_{k=1}^{n} \sqrt{(\Delta x_k)^2 + (f'(x_k^*)\,\Delta x_k)^2}$$

$$= \lim_{\Delta x\to 0} \left(\sum_a^b \sqrt{1 + (f'(x^*))^2}\,\Delta x \right)$$

or

$$L_A^B = \int_a^b \sqrt{1 + \left(\frac{dy}{dx}\right)^2}\, dx, \tag{2a}$$

where we have written dy/dx for $f'(x)$.

It is sometimes convenient, if x can be expressed as a function of y, to interchange the roles of x and y. The analogue of Eq. (2a) in this case is

$$L_A^B = \int_c^d \sqrt{1 + \left(\frac{dx}{dy}\right)^2}\, dy. \tag{2b}$$

There is a particularly useful formula for calculating the length of a curve that is given parametrically. Let the equations of motion be

$$x = g(t), \qquad y = h(t), \tag{3}$$

and let t_k, t_{k+1} be the values of t at P and Q respectively. Suppose the arc AB is described just once by $P(x, y)$ as t goes from t_a at A to t_b at B. If the functions $g(t)$ and $h(t)$ are continuously differentiable for t between t_a and t_b inclusive, the Mean Value Theorem may be applied to Eq. (3) to give

$$\Delta x_k = x_{k+1} - x_k = g(t_{k+1}) - g(t_k) = g'(t_k')\,\Delta t_k,$$

$$\Delta y_k = y_{k+1} - y_k = h(t_{k+1}) - h(t_k) = h'(t_k'')\,\Delta t_k,$$

where t_k' and t_k'' are two suitably chosen values of t between t_k and t_{k+1}. Then (1) becomes

$$L_A^B = \lim_{n\to\infty} \sum_{k=1}^{n} \sqrt{(g'(t_k'))^2 + (h'(t_k''))^2}\,\Delta t_k$$

$$= \int_{t_a}^{t_b} \sqrt{\left(\frac{dx}{dt}\right)^2 + \left(\frac{dy}{dt}\right)^2}\, dt. \tag{4}$$

Clearly, there is nothing inherently dependent upon the fact that t stands for time in Eqs. (3) and (4). Any other variable could serve as well, and if θ is used instead of t in (3) in representing the curve, then we need only replace t by θ in (4) as well.

EXAMPLE 1. The coordinates (x, y) of a point on a circle of radius r can be expressed in terms of the central angle θ (Fig. 5–13) as

$$x = r \cos \theta, \qquad y = r \sin \theta.$$

The point $P(x, y)$ moves once around the circle as θ varies from 0 to 2π, so that the circumference of the circle is given by

$$C = \int_0^{2\pi} \sqrt{\left(\frac{dx}{d\theta}\right)^2 + \left(\frac{dy}{d\theta}\right)^2}\, d\theta.$$

We find

$$\frac{dx}{d\theta} = -r \sin \theta, \qquad \frac{dy}{d\theta} = r \cos \theta,$$

so that

$$\left(\frac{dx}{d\theta}\right)^2 + \left(\frac{dy}{d\theta}\right)^2 = r^2(\sin^2 \theta + \cos^2 \theta) = r^2,$$

and hence

$$C = \int_0^{2\pi} r\, d\theta = r[\theta]_0^{2\pi} = 2\pi r.$$

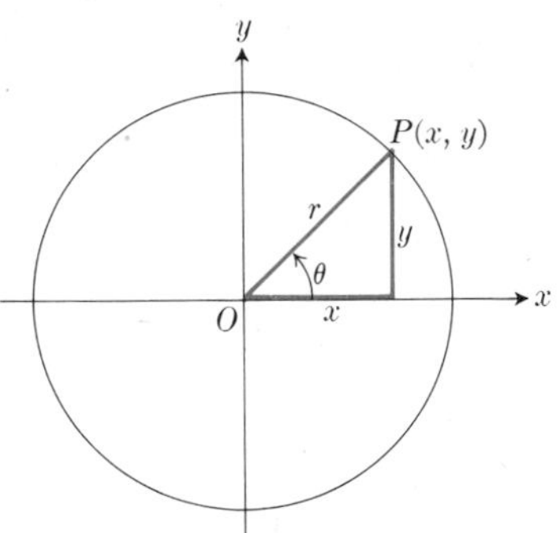

5–13 As θ grows from $\theta = 0$ to $\theta = 2\pi$, the point $P(x, y)$ travels around the circle exactly once.

Equation (4) is frequently written in terms of differentials in place of derivatives. This is done formally by writing $(dt)^2$ under the radical in place of the dt outside the radical, and then writing

$$\left(\frac{dx}{dt}\right)^2 (dt)^2 = \left(\frac{dx}{dt}\,dt\right)^2 = (dx)^2$$

and

$$\left(\frac{dy}{dt}\right)^2 (dt)^2 = \left(\frac{dy}{dt}\,dt\right)^2 = (dy)^2.$$

It is also customary to eliminate the parentheses in $(dx)^2$ and write dx^2 instead, so that Eq. (4) is written

$$L = \int \sqrt{dx^2 + dy^2}. \tag{5}$$

Of course, dx and dy must both be expressed in terms of one and the same variable, and appropriate limits must be supplied in (5) before the integration can be performed.

A useful mnemonic device for Eq. (5) is to write

$$ds = \sqrt{dx^2 + dy^2} \tag{6}$$

and treat ds as the differential of arc length, which can be integrated (between appropriate limits) to give the total length of a curve. Figure 5–14(a) gives the exact interpretation of ds corresponding to Eq. (6). Figure 5–14(b) is not strictly accurate, but is to be thought of as a simplified version of Fig.

a)

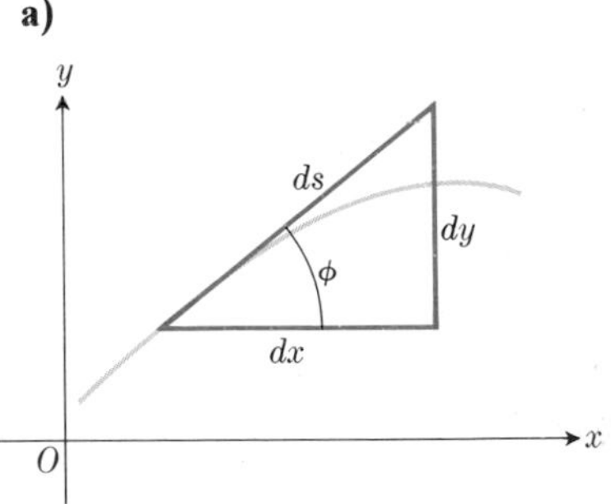

b)

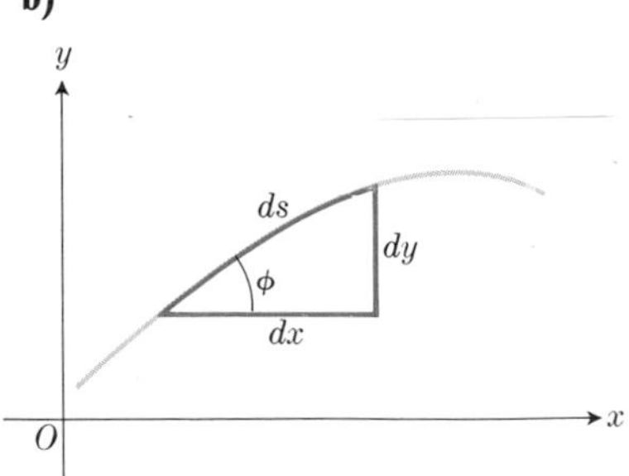

5–14 Diagrams for the equation $ds = \sqrt{dx^2 + dy^2}$.

5–14(a). The inaccuracies in this simplified version will be compensated for if the arc of the curve is treated as the hypotenuse ds of a right triangle of sides dx and dy.

EXAMPLE 2. Find the length of the curve $y = x^{2/3}$ between $x = -1$ and $x = 8$.

Solution. From the equation of the curve, we find

$$\frac{dy}{dx} = \frac{2}{3}x^{-1/3}.$$

Since this becomes infinite at the origin (see Fig. 5–15), we use Eq. (2b) instead of (2a) to find the length of the curve. Then we need to find dx/dy. Since the equation of the curve,

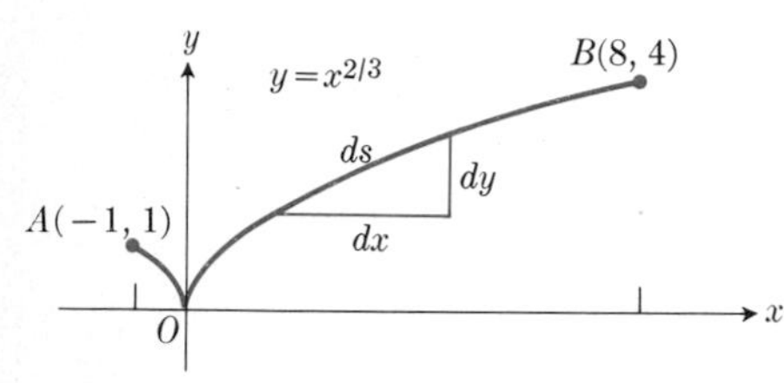

5–15 To compute the length of $y = x^{2/3}$ between A and B one writes $x = -y^{3/2}$ for the part from A to O, and $x = y^{3/2}$ for the part from O to B, and uses Eq. (2b) twice. The discussion at the end of Example 2 explains why.

$$y = x^{2/3},$$

can also be written as

$$x = \pm y^{3/2},$$

we find

$$\frac{dx}{dy} = \pm\frac{3}{2}y^{1/2},$$

or

$$dx = \pm\tfrac{3}{2}y^{1/2}\,dy.$$

Then

$$ds^2 = dx^2 + dy^2 = (\tfrac{9}{4}y + 1)\,dy^2,$$

so that

$$ds = \sqrt{\tfrac{9}{4}y + 1}\,dy.$$

The portion of the curve between $A(-1, 1)$ and the origin has length

$$L_1 = \int_0^1 \sqrt{\tfrac{9}{4}y + 1}\,dy,$$

while the rest of the curve from the origin to $B(8, 4)$ has length

$$L_2 = \int_0^4 \sqrt{\tfrac{9}{4}y + 1}\,dy,$$

and the total length is

$$L = L_1 + L_2.$$

It is necessary to calculate the length of the curve with two separate integrals since $x = \pm y^{3/2}$ needs to be separated into two distinct functions of y. For the portion AO of the curve, we have $x = -y^{3/2}$, $0 \le y \le 1$; while on the arc OB, we have $x = +y^{3/2}$, $0 \le y \le 4$.

To evaluate the given integrals, we let

$$u = \tfrac{9}{4}y + 1,$$

then

$$du = \tfrac{9}{4}\,dy, \qquad dy = \tfrac{4}{9}\,du,$$

and

$$\int (\tfrac{9}{4}y + 1)^{1/2}\,dy = \tfrac{4}{9}\int u^{1/2}\,du = \tfrac{8}{27}u^{3/2}.$$

Therefore,

$$L = \frac{8}{27}\left\{\left(\frac{9}{4}y + 1\right)^{3/2}\bigg]_0^1 + \left(\frac{9}{4}y + 1\right)^{3/2}\bigg]_0^4\right\}$$

$$= \tfrac{1}{27}(13\sqrt{13} + 80\sqrt{10} - 16) = 10.5.$$

To check against gross errors, we calculate the sum of the lengths of the two inscribed chords:

$$AO + OB = \sqrt{2} + \sqrt{80} = 10.4,$$

which appears to be satisfactory.

The curve in Fig. 5–15 has a cusp at (0, 0) where the slope becomes infinite. If we were to reconstruct the derivation of Eq. (2) for this particular curve, we would see that the crucial step that required an application of the Mean Value Theorem could not have been taken for the case of a chord PQ from a point P to the left of the cusp to a point Q to its right. For this reason, if for no other, when one or more cusps occur between the ends of a portion of a curve whose length is to be calculated, it is best to calculate the lengths of portions of the curve between cusps and add the results. We recall that the Mean Value Theorem is still valid even when the derivative becomes infinite at an extremity of the interval where it is to be applied, so that the derivation of Eq. (2) would be valid for the separate portions of a curve lying *between* cusps (or other discontinuities of dy/dx, such as occur at corners). Thus in the example just worked, we find the lengths L_1 from $A(-1, 1)$ to O (up to the cusp) and L_2 from O to $B(8, 4)$, then add the results to obtain $L = L_1 + L_2$. This was done by the sum of the two integrals. Had there been no point of discontinuity of dy/dx, it would not have been necessary to take two separate integrals, and Eq. (2a) could have been used.

EXAMPLE 3. The coordinates of the point $P(x, y)$ on the four-cusped hypocycloid are given by

$$x = a\cos^3\theta, \qquad y = a\sin^3\theta.$$

Find the total length of the curve (Fig. 5–16).

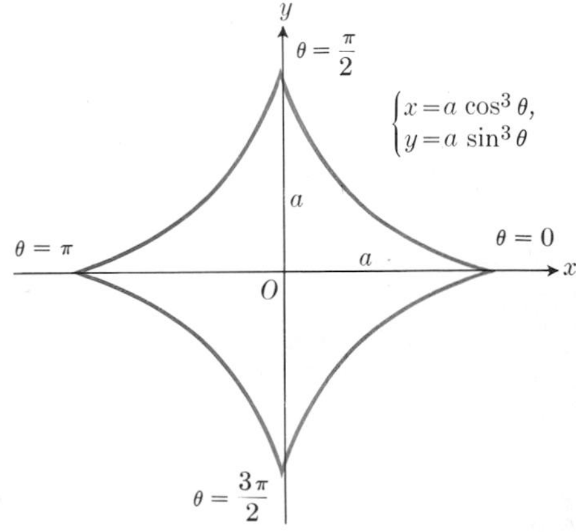

5–16 The hypocycloid $x = a\cos^3\theta$, $y = a\sin^3\theta$, $0 \le \theta \le 2$.

Solution. When θ varies from 0 to $\pi/2$, P traces out the portion of the curve in the first quadrant. Also, from the fact that

$$x^{2/3} + y^{2/3} = a^{2/3}(\cos^2\theta + \sin^2\theta) = a^{2/3},$$

it will be seen that, for every point (x, y) on the curve in the first quadrant, the corresponding points

$$(-x, y), \qquad (-x, -y), \qquad \text{and} \qquad (x, -y)$$

in the other three quadrants are also on the curve, which is therefore symmetrical about both axes. The portion of the curve in the first quadrant lies *between* two cusps and is one-quarter of the total length of the curve. Therefore

$$L = 4 \int_{\theta=0}^{\theta=\pi/2} \sqrt{dx^2 + dy^2}.$$

From the equation of the curve, we find

$$\frac{dx}{d\theta} = -3a \cos^2 \theta \sin \theta, \qquad dx = 3a \cos \theta \sin \theta(-\cos \theta)\, d\theta,$$

$$\frac{dy}{d\theta} = 3a \sin^2 \theta \cos \theta, \qquad dy = 3a \cos \theta \sin \theta(\sin \theta)\, d\theta,$$

and hence

$$ds^2 = dx^2 + dy^2 = (3a \cos \theta \sin \theta)^2(\cos^2 \theta + \sin^2 \theta)(d\theta)^2$$

or

$$ds^2 = (3a \cos \theta \sin \theta\, d\theta)^2.$$

Hence, for θ between 0 and $\pi/2$,

$$ds = 3a \cos \theta \sin \theta\, d\theta$$

and

$$L = 4 \int_0^{\pi/2} 3a \cos \theta \sin \theta\, d\theta.$$

To evaluate this integral, we let

$$u = \sin \theta, \qquad du = \cos \theta\, d\theta,$$

and

$$\int \cos \theta \sin \theta\, d\theta = \int u\, du = \tfrac{1}{2}u^2 = \tfrac{1}{2} \sin^2 \theta,$$

so that

$$L = (12a)(\tfrac{1}{2} \sin^2 \theta)\Big]_0^{\pi/2} = 6a.$$

PROBLEMS

Find the lengths of the curves in Problems 1 through 6.

1. $y = \frac{1}{3}(x^2 + 2)^{3/2}$ from $x = 0$ to $x = 3$.
2. $y = x^{3/2}$ from $(0, 0)$ to $(4, 8)$.
3. $9x^2 = 4y^3$ from $(0, 0)$ to $(2\sqrt{3}, 3)$.
4. $y = (x^3/3) + (1/4x)$ from $x = 1$ to $x = 3$.
5. $x = (y^4/4) + (1/8y^2)$ from $y = 1$ to $y = 2$.
6. $(y + 1)^2 = 4x^3$ from $x = 0$ to $x = 1$.
7. Find the distance traveled between $t = 0$ and $t = \pi/2$ by a particle $P(x, y)$ whose position at time t is given by

$$x = a \cos t + at \sin t, \qquad y = a \sin t - at \cos t,$$

where a is a positive constant.

8. Find the length of the curve

$$x = t - \sin t, \qquad y = 1 - \cos t, \qquad 0 \leq t \leq 2\pi.$$

[*Hint*. $\sqrt{2 - 2\cos t} = 2\sqrt{(1 - \cos t)/2}$.]

9. Find the distance traveled by the particle $P(x, y)$ between $t = 0$ and $t = 4$ if the position at time t is given by

$$x = \frac{t^2}{2}, \qquad y = \frac{1}{3}(2t + 1)^{3/2}.$$

10. The position of a particle $P(x, y)$ at time t is given by

$$x = \frac{1}{3}(2t + 3)^{3/2}, \qquad y = \frac{t^2}{2} + t.$$

Find the distance it travels between $t = 0$ and $t = 3$.

11. (*Calculator*) The length of one arch of the curve $y = \sin x$ is given by

$$L = \int_0^{\pi} \sqrt{1 + \cos^2 x}\, dx.$$

Estimate L by Simpson's rule with $n = 8$.

5–8 AREA OF A SURFACE OF REVOLUTION

Suppose that the curve in Fig. 5–17 is rotated about the x-axis. It will generate a surface in space. The inscribed polygonal line segments will generate inscribed frustums of cones. The sum of the lateral areas of these frustums will be an approximation to the area of the surface. To obtain an analytic expression for this approximation, we require the formula

$$A = \pi(r_1 + r_2)l \tag{1}$$

for the lateral area A of a frustum of slant height l, where r_1 and r_2 are the radii of its bases.

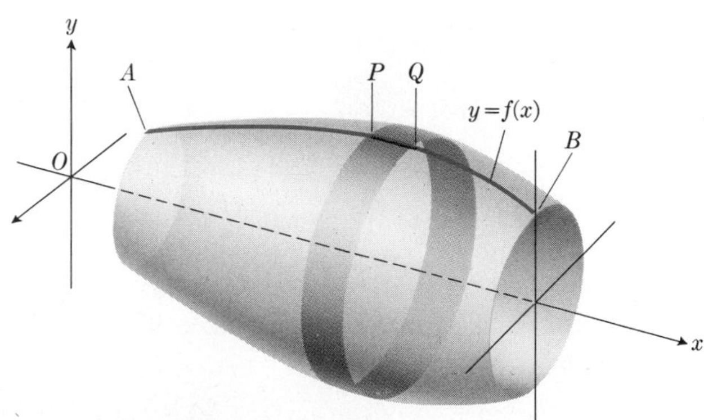

5–17 The surface swept out by a plane curve rotated about an axis in the plane of this curve is a union of bands.

To establish Eq. (1), imagine the frustum of a cone to be the limit of inscribed frustums of pyramids (see Fig. 5–18). If each base of an inscribed frustum of a pyramid is a regular polygon of n sides, and b_1 is the length of one side in the upper face, while b_2 is the length of a side in the lower face, then the lateral area will consist of n trapezoids each having an area

$$\tfrac{1}{2}(b_1 + b_2)h.$$

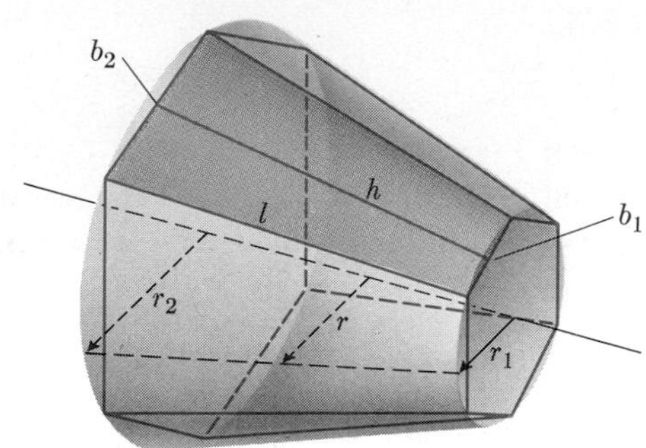

5–18 The frustum of a cone approximated by the frustum of a pyramid.

The n trapezoids have area

$$\tfrac{1}{2}(nb_1 + nb_2)h.$$

As n increases indefinitely, we have

$$\lim_{n\to\infty} nb_1 = 2\pi r_1, \qquad \lim_{n\to\infty} nb_2 = 2\pi r_2,$$

and

$$\lim_{n\to\infty} h = l,$$

so that

$$A = \lim_{n\to\infty} \tfrac{1}{2}(nb_1 + nb_2)h = \tfrac{1}{2}(2\pi r_1 + 2\pi r_2)l = \pi(r_1 + r_2)l,$$

which establishes Eq. (1). Note that if $r_1 = r_2$, Eq. (1) reduces to the correct formula for the lateral area of a cylinder, and if $r_1 = 0$, it gives the correct result for the lateral area of a cone. It can also be put into the form

$$A = 2\pi rl$$

where

$$r = \tfrac{1}{2}(r_1 + r_2)$$

is the radius of the mid-section of the frustum. In this form, (1) says that the lateral area of a frustum of a cone = (circumference of mid-section) × (slant height).

We now consider the portion of the surface ΔS generated by the arc PQ, and its inscribed frustum of a cone generated by the chord PQ. Let's call (x, y) the coordinates of P, and $(x + \Delta x, y + \Delta y)$ the coordinates of Q, and then take

$$r_1 = y, \qquad r_2 = y + \Delta y, \qquad l = \sqrt{(\Delta x)^2 + (\Delta y)^2}$$

in Eq. (1). Then we have the approximation

$$S \approx \sum_{x=a}^{b} \pi(2y + \Delta y)\sqrt{(\Delta x)^2 + (\Delta y)^2}$$

or

$$S \approx \sum_a^b 2\pi \left(y + \frac{1}{2}\Delta y\right)\sqrt{1 + \left(\frac{\Delta y}{\Delta x}\right)^2}\, \Delta x.$$

If y and dy/dx are continuous functions of x and we omit products like $(\Delta y)(\Delta x)$ and higher powers of Δx in this approximation, we have

$$S \approx \sum_a^b 2\pi y \sqrt{1 + \left(\frac{dy}{dx}\right)^2}\, \Delta x.$$

Then taking the limit as Δx tends to zero, we get

$$S = \lim_{\Delta x \to 0} \sum_a^b 2\pi y \sqrt{1 + \left(\frac{dy}{dx}\right)^2}\, \Delta x$$

or

$$S = \int_a^b 2\pi y \sqrt{1 + \left(\frac{dy}{dx}\right)^2}\, dx. \qquad (2)$$

Our end result, Eq. (2), is easily remembered if we write

$$\sqrt{1 + \left(\frac{dy}{dx}\right)^2}\, dx = ds$$

and take

$$S = \int 2\pi y\, ds. \qquad (3)$$

If we let

$$dS = 2\pi y\, ds,$$

so that

$$S = \int dS,$$

we may interpret dS as the product of a

$$\text{Circumference} = 2\pi y$$

and a

$$\text{Slant height} = ds.$$

Thus dS gives the lateral area of a frustum of a cone of slant height ds if the point (x, y) is the midpoint of the element of arc length ds (Fig. 5–19).

Why not approximate the surface area S by inscribed *cylinders* and arrive at a result

$$S = \int 2\pi y\, dx,$$

having dx instead of ds, to replace Eq. (3)? Since we know from our discussion on volume that inscribed cylinders work perfectly well for *volumes* of revolution, why not use them for *surfaces* of revolution also? The answer

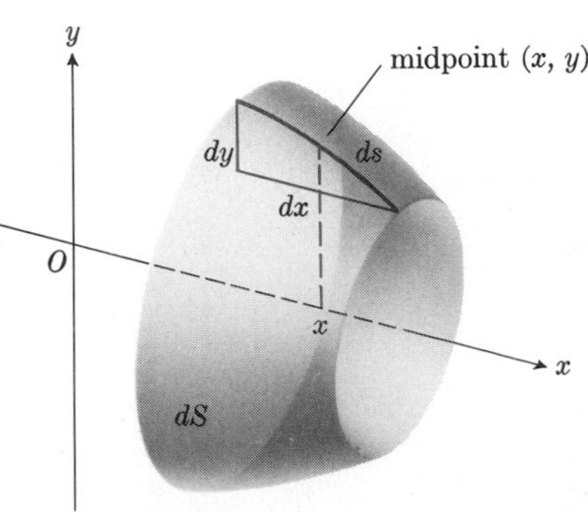

5–19 $dS = 2\pi y\, ds$.

hinges on the fact that the approximation

$$\Delta V \approx \pi y^2 \, \Delta x$$

for the volume of a slice involves, at worst, terms that are products like $(\Delta x)(\Delta y)$ and higher powers of Δx and these contribute zero to the *limit* of the sum of volumes of the inscribed cylinders. (See Article 5–6.) But the approximations

(a) $\Delta S \approx 2\pi y \, \Delta x$ (Inscribed cylinder)

and

(b) $\Delta S \approx 2\pi y \sqrt{(\Delta x)^2 + (\Delta y)^2}$ (Inscribed conical band)

for the surface area of a slice cannot *both* be this accurate. For their ratio is

$$\frac{2\pi y \sqrt{(\Delta x)^2 + (\Delta y)^2}}{2\pi y \, \Delta x} = \sqrt{1 + \left(\frac{\Delta y}{\Delta x}\right)^2},$$

which has the limiting value

$$\lim_{\Delta x \to 0} \sqrt{1 + \left(\frac{\Delta y}{\Delta x}\right)^2} = \sqrt{1 + \left(\frac{dy}{dx}\right)^2},$$

and this will be different from one (unless $dy/dx = 0$, which would not be generally true), whereas two approximations that differ only by terms involving products like $(\Delta y)(\Delta x)$ and higher powers of Δx have a ratio whose limiting value is unity. Since the approximations (a) and (b) above will usually lead to different answers when we pass to the corresponding definite integrals, they cannot both be correct, and we must abandon one or both of them. But the approximation (b) is clearly the one that corresponds to a natural way of defining the surface area of a surface of revolution and it leads to (3).

If the axis of revolution is the y-axis, the corresponding formula that replaces (3) is

$$S = \int_c^d 2\pi x \sqrt{1 + \left(\frac{dx}{dy}\right)^2} \, dy. \tag{4}$$

If the curve that sweeps out the surface is given in parametric form with x and y as functions of a third variable t that varies from t_a to t_b, then we may compute S from the formula

$$S = \int_{t_a}^{t_b} 2\pi\rho \sqrt{\left(\frac{dx}{dt}\right)^2 + \left(\frac{dy}{dt}\right)^2} \, dt, \tag{5}$$

where ρ is the distance from the axis of revolution to the element of arc length, and is expressed as a function of t.

More generally we may write

$$S = \int 2\pi\rho \, ds, \tag{6}$$

where, again, ρ is the distance from the axis of revolution to the element of arc length ds. Both ρ and ds need to be expressed in terms of some one variable and proper limits must be supplied to (6) in any particular problem.

EXAMPLE 1. The circle

$$x^2 + y^2 = r^2$$

is revolved about the x-axis (Fig. 5–20). Find the area of the sphere generated.

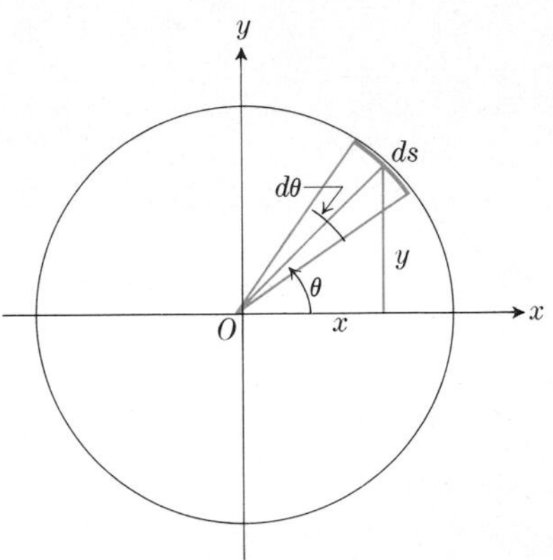

5–20 To compute the surface area of the sphere obtained by revolving the circle $x^2 + y^2 = r^2$ about the x-axis, let θ vary from $\theta = 0$ to $\theta = \pi$. The top half of the circle generates the entire sphere.

Solution. We write

$$dS = 2\pi y \; ds,$$
$$ds = \sqrt{dx^2 + dy^2},$$

and use

$$x = r \cos \theta, \qquad y = r \sin \theta$$

to represent the circle. Then

$$dx = -r \sin \theta \; d\theta, \qquad dy = r \cos \theta \; d\theta,$$

so that

$$ds = r \; d\theta$$

and

$$dS = 2\pi y \; ds = 2\pi(r \sin \theta) r \; d\theta$$
$$= 2\pi r^2 \sin \theta \; d\theta.$$

The top half of the circle generates the entire sphere, and the representative point (x, y) traces out this upper semicircle as θ varies from 0 to π. Hence

$$S = \int_0^{\pi} 2\pi r^2 \sin \theta \; d\theta$$
$$= 2\pi r^2 [-\cos \theta]_0^{\pi} = 4\pi r^2.$$

EXAMPLE 2. The circle in Example 1 is revolved about the line $y = -r$, which is tangent to the circle at the point $(0, -r)$ (Fig. 5–21). Find the area of the surface generated.

Solution. Here it takes the whole circle to generate the surface, and in terms of the previous example, this means that we must let θ vary from 0 to 2π. The radius of rotation now becomes

$$\rho = y + r,$$

and we have

$$dS = 2\pi\rho \; ds = 2\pi(y + r) r \; d\theta = 2\pi(r \sin \theta + r) r \; d\theta.$$

Hence

$$S = \int_0^{2\pi} 2\pi(\sin \theta + 1) r^2 \; d\theta = 2\pi r^2 [-\cos \theta + \theta]_0^{2\pi} = 4\pi^2 r^2.$$

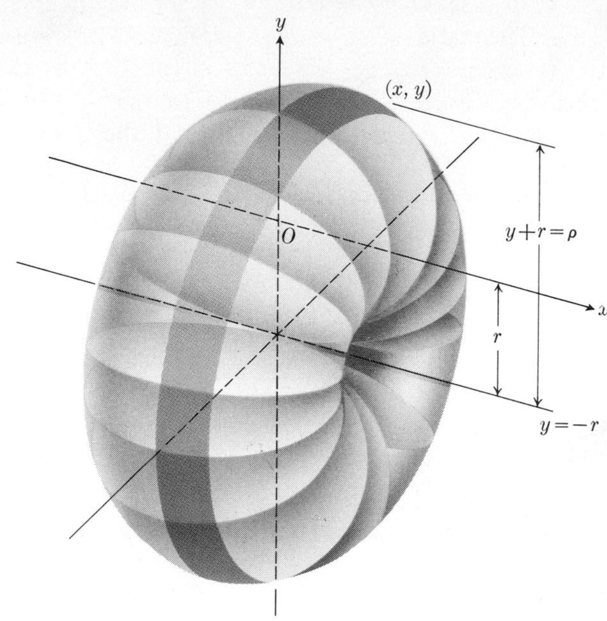

5–21 The circle of Fig. 5–20 revolved about the line $y = -r$.

PROBLEMS

1. Find the area of the surface generated by rotating the portion of the curve $y = \frac{1}{3}(x^2 + 2)^{3/2}$ between $x = 0$ and $x = 3$ about the y-axis.

2. Find the area of the surface generated by rotating about the x-axis the arc of the curve $y = x^3$ between $x = 0$ and $x = 1$.

3. Find the area of the surface generated by rotating about the y-axis the arc of the curve $y = x^2$ between $(0, 0)$ and $(2, 4)$.

4. The arc of the curve $y = (x^3/3) + (1/4x)$ from $x = 1$ to $x = 3$ is rotated about the line $y = -1$. Find the surface area generated.

5. The arc of the curve $x = (y^4/4) + (1/8y^2)$ from $y = 1$ to $y = 2$ is rotated about the x-axis. Find the surface area generated.

6. Find the area of the surface generated by rotating about the y-axis the curve $y = (x^2/2) + \frac{1}{2}$, $0 \leq x \leq 1$.

7. Find the area of the surface generated by rotating the curve $x = t^2$, $y = t$, $0 \leq t \leq 1$, about the x-axis.

8. Find the area of the surface generated by rotating the hypocycloid $x = a \cos^3 \theta$, $y = a \sin^3 \theta$, about the x-axis.

9. The curve described by the particle $P(x, y)$,

$$x = t + 1, \qquad y = \frac{t^2}{2} + t,$$

from $t = 0$ to $t = 4$, is rotated about the y-axis. Find the surface area that is generated.

10. The loop of the curve $9x^2 = y(3 - y)^2$ is rotated about the x-axis. Find the surface area generated.

5–9 AVERAGE VALUE OF A FUNCTION

The process of finding the average value of a finite number of data is familiar to all students. For example, if $y_1, y_2, \ldots, y_n$ are the grades of a class of n students on a certain calculus quiz, then the class average on that quiz is

$$y_{av} = \frac{y_1 + y_2 + \cdots + y_n}{n}. \tag{1}$$

When the number of data is infinite, it is not feasible to use Eq. (1) (since it is likely to take on the meaningless form ∞/∞). This situation arises, in particular, when the data y are given by a continuous function

$$y = f(x), \qquad a \leq x \leq b.$$

In this case, the average value of y, with respect to x, is defined to be

$$(y_{av})_x = \frac{1}{b-a}\int_a^b f(x)\,dx. \tag{2}$$

The curve in Fig. 5–22, for example, might represent temperature as a function of time over a twenty-four hour period. Equation (2) would then give the "average temperature" for the day.

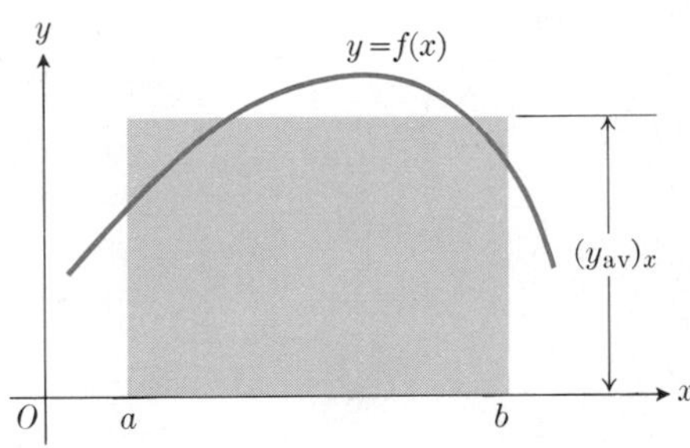

5–22 One interpretation of $(y_{av})_x = [1/(b-a)]\int_a^b f(x)\,dx$ comes from interpreting the integral as an area.

REMARK 1. It may be possible to express y as a function of x, or, alternatively, as a function of u. Then $(y_{av})_x$ and $(y_{av})_u$ need not be equal. For example, for a freely falling body starting from rest,

$$s = \tfrac{1}{2}gt^2, \qquad v = gt, \qquad v = \sqrt{2gs}.$$

Suppose we calculate the average velocity, first with respect to t and second with respect to s, from $t_1 = 0$, $s_1 = 0$, to $t_2 > 0$, $s_2 = \frac{1}{2}g(t_2)^2$. Then, by definition,

$$(v_{av})_t = \frac{1}{t_2 - 0}\int_0^{t_2} gt\,dt = \frac{1}{2}gt_2 = \frac{1}{2}v_2,$$

$$(v_{av})_s = \frac{1}{s_2 - 0}\int_0^{s_2} \sqrt{2gs}\,ds = \frac{2}{3}\sqrt{2gs_2} = \frac{2}{3}v_2.$$

REMARK 2. If both sides of Eq. (2) are multiplied by $b - a$, we have

$$(y_{av})_x \cdot (b-a) = \int_a^b f(x)\,dx. \tag{3}$$

The right side of Eq. (3) represents the area bounded above by the curve $y = f(x)$, below by the x-axis, and on the sides by the ordinates $x = a$, $x = b$. The left side of the equation can be interpreted as the area of a rectangle of altitude $(y_{av})_x$ and of base $b - a$. Hence, Eq. (3) provides a geometric interpretation of $(y_{av})_x$ as that ordinate of the curve $y = f(x)$ that should be used as altitude if one wishes to construct a rectangle whose base is the interval $a \leq x \leq b$ and whose area is equal to the area under the curve (Fig. 5–22). In the narrower sense of area, this statement is valid only when the curve lies above the x-axis. If the curve lies partly or entirely below the x-axis, we would count areas below the x-axis as negative. In such a case there might well be a certain amount of canceling of positive and negative areas.

REMARK 3. Equation (2) is a *definition*, and hence is not subject to proof. Nevertheless, some discussion may help to explain why this particular formula is used to define the average. One might arrive at it as follows. From the total "population" of x-values, $a \leq x \leq b$, we select a representative "sample," $x_1, x_2, \ldots, x_n$, uniformly distributed between a and b. Then, using Eq. (1), we calculate the average of the functional values

$$y_1 = f(x_1), \qquad y_2 = f(x_2), \qquad \ldots, \qquad y_n = f(x_n)$$

associated with these representative x's. This gives us

$$\frac{y_1 + y_2 + \cdots + y_n}{n} = \frac{f(x_1) + f(x_2) + \cdots + f(x_n)}{n}. \tag{4}$$

Since we require that the x's be uniformly distributed between a and b, let us take the spacing to be Δx, with

$$x_2 - x_1 = x_3 - x_2 = \cdots = x_n - x_{n-1} = \Delta x$$

and

$$\Delta x = \frac{b - a}{n}.$$

Then, in (4), let us replace the n in the denominator by $(b - a)/\Delta x$, thus obtaining

$$\frac{f(x_1) + f(x_2) + \cdots + f(x_n)}{(b - a)/\Delta x} = \frac{f(x_1)\,\Delta x + f(x_2)\,\Delta x + \cdots + f(x_n)\,\Delta x}{b - a}$$

If, now, n is very large and Δx small, the expression

$$f(x_1)\,\Delta x + f(x_2)\,\Delta x + \cdots + f(x_n)\,\Delta x = \sum_{k=1}^{n} f(x_k)\,\Delta x$$

is very nearly equal to $\int_a^b f(x)\,dx$. In fact, if we take limits, letting $n \to \infty$, we obtain precisely

$$\lim_{n\to\infty} \frac{f(x_1)\,\Delta x + f(x_2)\,\Delta x + \cdots + f(x_n)\,\Delta x}{b - a} = \frac{1}{b - a}\int_a^b f(x)\,dx.$$

This is the expression that defines the average value of y in Eq. (2).

EXAMPLE 1. The costs of warehouse space, utilities, insurance, and security can be a large part of the cost of doing business, and a firm's average daily inventory can play a significant role in determining these costs.

For example, suppose that a wholesale grocer receives a shipment of 1200 cases of chocolate bars every 30 days. The chocolate is sold to retailers at a steady rate; and x days after the shipment arrives, the inventory $I(x)$ of cases still on hand is

$$I(x) = 1200 - 40x.$$

From Eq. (2) we compute the average daily inventory to be

$$I_{\text{av}} = \tfrac{1}{30}\int_0^{30} (1200 - 40x)\,dx = \tfrac{1}{30}[1200x - 20x^2]_0^{30} = 600.$$

From I_{av} we can compute the firm's daily holding cost for the chocolate bars. If the cost of holding one case is 3¢ per day, then the total daily holding cost for the chocolate is

$$(600)(0.03) = \$18 \text{ per day}.$$

EXAMPLE 2 *Delesse's rule.** To find out what proportion of a tissue is composed of particles of a certain kind, life scientists sometimes study thin slices of the tissue a few thousandths of a millimeter thick. Under reasonable circumstances, for example, if the particles do not cluster and are fairly evenly distributed throughout the tissue, the proportion of the slice occupied by the traces of the particles will be the same as the proportion of the tissue occupied by the uncut particles. The equality of these proportions was discovered by a French geologist, Achille Ernest Delesse, in the 1840's. The mathematical justification for it lies in the notion of average value.

Suppose that the tissue under investigation is a cube whose sides have length L, as shown in Fig. 5–23. The particles make up a volume u less than L^3, say

$$u = kL^3, \qquad 0 < k < 1. \tag{5}$$

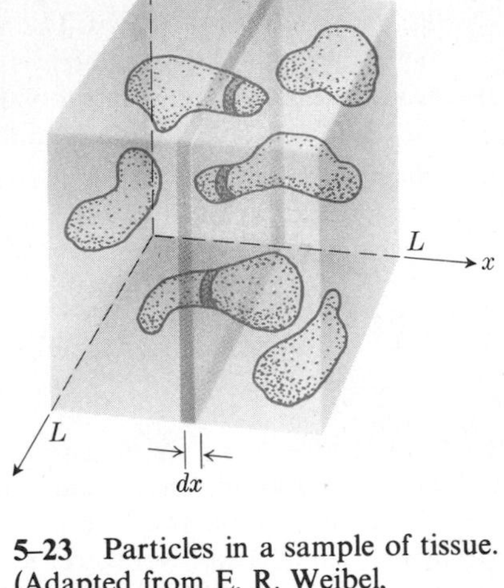

5–23 Particles in a sample of tissue. (Adapted from E. R. Weibel, *Morphometry of the Human Lung.* New York: Academic Press, 1963, p. 13.)

We wish to estimate the proportionality constant k by examining a slice of the cube of width dx perpendicular to the x-axis. The volume of the slice is

$$dV = L^2\,dx.$$

The space occupied by the traces of the particles in the slice can be written as

$$du = r(x)\,dV = r(x)L^2\,dx, \tag{6}$$

where the proportionality factor $r(x)$ depends on the location x where the slice is cut. From Eq. (2), the average value of r is

$$\bar{r} = \frac{1}{L}\int_0^L r(x)\,dx. \tag{7}$$

From Eq. (6) we have

$$u = \int_0^L r(x)L^2\,dx = L^2\int_0^L r(x)\,dx, \tag{8}$$

or, using Eq. (7),

$$u = \bar{r}L^3. \tag{9}$$

A comparison of this equation with Eq. (5) shows that

$$k = \bar{r}.$$

This is Delesse's rule.

* A. E. Delesse, "A mechanical procedure for determining the composition of rocks," *Annales des Mines*, **13**, 1848, pp. 379–388.

10, 12

PROBLEMS

In each of the following problems (1 through 5), find the average value with respect to x, over the given domain, of the given function $f(x)$. In each case, draw a graph of the curve $y = f(x)$, and sketch a rectangle whose altitude is the average ordinate.

1. a) $\sin x, \quad 0 \le x \le \pi/2$ **b)** $\sin x, \quad 0 \le x \le 2\pi$

2. a) $\sin^2 x, \quad 0 \le x \le \pi/2$ **b)** $\sin^2 x, \quad \pi \le x \le 2\pi$

3. $\sqrt{2x+1}, \quad 4 \le x \le 12$

4. $\frac{1}{2} + \frac{1}{2}\cos 2x, \quad 0 \le x \le \pi$

5. $\alpha x + \beta; \quad a \le x \le b \quad [\alpha, \beta, a, b, \text{constants}]$

6. Solon Container receives 450 drums of plastic pellets every 30 days. The inventory function (drums on hand as a function of days) is $I(x) = 450 - x^2/2$. Find the average daily inventory. If the holding cost for one drum is 2¢ per day, find the total daily holding cost.

7. Mitchell Mailorder receives a shipment of 600 cases of athletic socks every 60 days. The number of cases on hand t days after the shipment arrives is $I(t) = 600 - 20\sqrt{15t}$. Find the average daily inventory. If the holding cost for one case is $\frac{1}{2}$¢ per day, find the total daily holding cost.

8. (*Calculator*) Compute the average value of the temperature function

$$f(x) = 37 \sin\left[\frac{2\pi}{365}(x - 101)\right] + 25$$

for a 365-day year (see the Example in Article 2–9). This is one way to estimate the annual mean air temperature in Fairbanks, Alaska. The National Weather Service's official figure, a numerical average of the daily normal mean air temperatures for the year, is 25.7°F, which is slightly higher than the average value of $f(x)$. Figure 2–19 shows why.

9. (*Calculator*) (a) Use the trapezoidal rule to estimate the average lumen output of the No. 22 flashbulb of Problem 12, Article 4–9, for the time interval from $t = 0$ to $t = 60$ milliseconds. Take the data from Table 4–4. (b) How long would a 60-watt incandescent light bulb rated at 765 lumens have to burn to put out as much light as the No. 22 flashbulb did in (a)?

10. Given a circle C of radius a, and a diameter AB of C. Chords are drawn perpendicular to AB, intercepting equal segments along AB. Find the limit of the average of the lengths of these chords, as the number of chords tends to infinity. [*Hint.* $\int_{-a}^{a} \sqrt{a^2 - x^2}\, dx$ is $\frac{1}{2}\pi a^2$, since it is the area of a semicircle of radius a.]

11. Solve Problem 10 under the modified assumption that the chords intercept equal arcs along the circumference of C.

12. Solve Problem 10 using the *squares* of the lengths, in place of the lengths of the chords.

13. Solve Problem 11 using the *squares* of the lengths, in place of the lengths of the chords.

5–10 MOMENTS AND CENTER OF MASS

If masses $m_1, m_2, \ldots, m_n$ are placed along the x-axis at distances $x_1, x_2, \ldots, x_n$ from the origin (Fig. 5–24), then their moment about the origin is defined to be

$$x_1 m_1 + x_2 m_2 + \cdots + x_n m_n = \sum_{k=1}^{n} x_k m_k. \tag{1}$$

If all the mass

$$m_1 + m_2 + \cdots + m_n = \sum_{k=1}^{n} m_k \tag{2}$$

is concentrated at one point of abscissa x, the total moment is

$$x\left(\sum_{k=1}^{n} m_k\right).$$

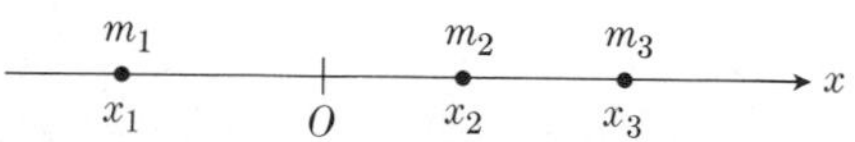

5–24 Masses on the x-axis.

The position of $\bar{x}$ for which this is the same as the total moment in (1) is called the *center of mass*. The condition

$$\bar{x} \sum_{k=1}^{n} m_k = \sum_{k=1}^{n} x_k m_k$$

thus determines

$$\bar{x} = \frac{\sum_{k=1}^{n} x_k m_k}{\sum_{k=1}^{n} m_k}. \tag{3}$$

EXAMPLE 1. The principle of a moment underlies the simple seesaw. For instance (Fig. 5-25), suppose one child weighs 80 lb and sits 5 ft from the point O, while the other child weighs 100 lb and is 4 ft from O. Then the child at the left end of the seesaw produces a moment of $5 \times 80 = 400$ ft-lb, which tends to rotate the plank counterclockwise about O. The child at the right end of the plank produces a moment of $4 \times 100 = 400$ ft-lb, which tends to rotate the plank clockwise around O. If we introduce coordinates $x_1 = -5$ and $x_2 = +4$, we find

$$\begin{aligned} x_1 m_1 + x_2 m_2 &= (-5)(80) + (4)(100) \\ &= -400 + 400 = 0 \end{aligned}$$

as the resultant moment about O. The same moment, zero, would be obtained if both children were at O, which is the center of their mass.

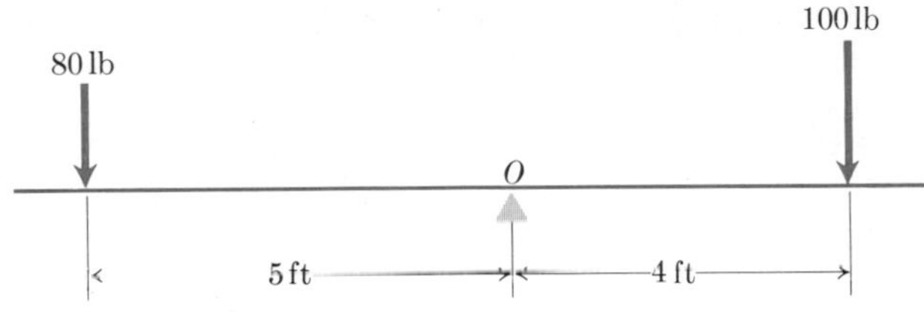

5-25 A 100-lb weight four feet to the right of O balances an 80-lb weight five feet to the left of O.

If, instead of being placed on the x-axis, the masses are located in the xy-plane at points

$$(x_1, y_1), \quad (x_2, y_2), \quad \ldots, \quad (x_n, y_n),$$

in that order, then we define their moments with respect to the y-axis and with respect to the x-axis as

$$M_y = x_1 m_1 + x_2 m_2 + \cdots + x_n m_n = \sum_{k=1}^{n} x_k m_k,$$

$$M_x = y_1 m_1 + y_2 m_2 + \cdots + y_n m_n = \sum_{k=1}^{n} y_k m_k.$$

The center of mass is the point $(\bar{x}, \bar{y})$,

$$\bar{x} = \frac{\sum x_k m_k}{\sum m_k}, \qquad \bar{y} = \frac{\sum y_k m_k}{\sum m_k}, \tag{4}$$

where the total mass could be concentrated and still give the same total moments M_y and M_x.

In space, three coordinates are needed to specify the position of a point. If the masses are located at the points

$$(x_1, y_1, z_1), \quad (x_2, y_2, z_2), \quad \ldots, \quad (x_n, y_n, z_n),$$

we define their moments with respect to the various coordinate planes as

$$M_{yz} = x_1 m_1 + x_2 m_2 + \cdots + x_n m_n = \sum_{k=1}^{n} x_k m_k,$$

$$M_{zx} = y_1 m_1 + y_2 m_2 + \cdots + y_n m_n = \sum_{k=1}^{n} y_k m_k,$$

$$M_{xy} = z_1 m_1 + z_2 m_2 + \cdots + z_n m_n = \sum_{k=1}^{n} z_k m_k.$$

(M_{yz} = Moment with respect to the yz-plane, etc.)

The center of mass $(\bar{x}, \bar{y}, \bar{z})$ is the point where the total mass could be concentrated without altering these moments. Its coordinates therefore are given by

$$\bar{x} = \frac{\sum x_k m_k}{\sum m_k}, \qquad \bar{y} = \frac{\sum y_k m_k}{\sum m_k}, \qquad \bar{z} = \frac{\sum z_k m_k}{\sum m_k}. \tag{5}$$

Now most physical objects with which we deal are composed of enormously large numbers of molecules. It would be extremely difficult, and in most cases unnecessary, for us to concern ourselves with the molecular structure of a physical object, such as a pendulum, whose motion as a whole is to be studied. Instead, we make certain simplifying assumptions which we recognize as being only approximately correct. One such assumption is that the matter in a given solid is continuously distributed throughout the solid. Furthermore, if P is a point in the solid and ΔV is an element of volume that contains P, and if Δm is the mass of ΔV, then we assume that the ratio $\Delta m/\Delta V$ tends to a definite limit

$$\delta = \lim_{\Delta V \to 0} \frac{\Delta m}{\Delta V}, \tag{6}$$

as the largest dimension of ΔV approaches zero. The limit δ is called the *density* of the solid at the point P. It is customary to write Eq. (6) in the alternative forms

$$\delta = dm/dV, \qquad dm = \delta\, dV. \tag{7}$$

If now a solid is divided into small pieces ΔV of mass Δm and if $P(\tilde{x}, \tilde{y}, \tilde{z})$ is a point in ΔV and δ is the density at P, then

$$\Delta m \approx \delta\, \Delta V.$$

The moments of Δm with respect to the coordinate planes are not defined by what we have done thus far. But now we may think of replacing the Δm that fills the volume ΔV by an equal mass all concentrated at the point P. The moments of this concentrated mass with respect to the coordinate planes are

$$\tilde{x}\, \Delta m, \qquad \tilde{y}\, \Delta m, \qquad \tilde{z}\, \Delta m.$$

Now we add the moments of all the concentrated masses in all the volume elements ΔV and take the limit as the ΔV's approach zero. This leads us to the following *definitions* of the moments M_{yz}, etc., for the mass as a whole:

$$M_{yz} = \lim_{\Delta m \to 0} \sum \tilde{x}\, \Delta m = \int \tilde{x}\, dm,$$

$$M_{zx} = \lim_{\Delta m \to 0} \sum \tilde{y}\, \Delta m = \int \tilde{y}\, dm,$$

$$M_{xy} = \lim_{\Delta m \to 0} \sum \tilde{z}\, \Delta m = \int \tilde{z}\, dm.$$

From these, we then deduce the equations

$$\bar{x} = \frac{\int \tilde{x}\, dm}{\int dm}, \qquad \bar{y} = \frac{\int \tilde{y}\, dm}{\int dm}, \qquad \bar{z} = \frac{\int \tilde{z}\, dm}{\int dm} \tag{8}$$

for the center of mass of the solid as a whole.

In theory, the element dm is approximately the mass in a volume element dV which has three small dimensions as in Fig. 5–26. In a later chapter we shall see how to evaluate the integrals (8) which arise when this is done. In practice, however, we can usually take

$$dm = \delta\, dV$$

with a volume element dV which has only one small dimension. Then we must interpret $\tilde{x}$, $\tilde{y}$, $\tilde{z}$ in the integrands in (8) as the coordinates of the *center of mass* of the *element dm*.

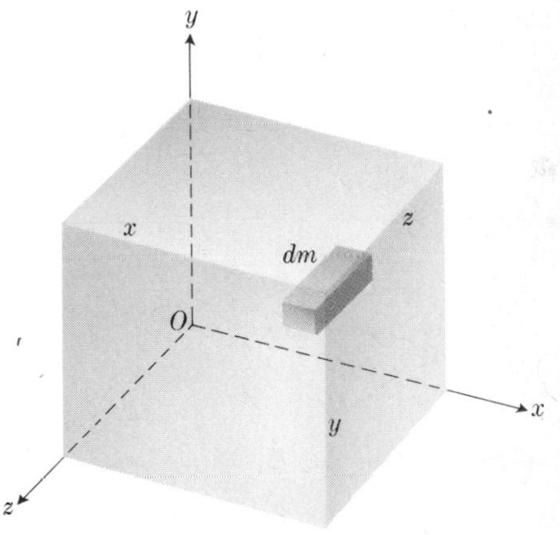

5–26 Mass dm = density × dV.

In many problems of practical importance the density δ is constant and the solid possesses a plane of symmetry. Then it is easy to see that the center of mass lies in this plane of symmetry. For we may, with no loss of generality, choose our coordinate reference frame in such a way that the yz-plane is the plane of symmetry. Then for every element of mass Δm with a positive $\tilde{x}$ there is a symmetrically located element of mass with a corresponding negative $\tilde{x}$. These two elements have moments that are equal in magnitude and of opposite signs. The whole mass is made up of such symmetric pairs of elements and the sum of their moments about the yz-plane is zero. Therefore $\bar{x} = 0$; that is, the center of mass lies in the plane of symmetry. If there are two planes of symmetry, their intersection is an axis of symmetry and the center of mass must lie on this axis, since it lies in both planes of symmetry.

The most frequently encountered distributions of mass are

a) along a thin wire or filament: $dm = \delta_1\, ds$,
b) in a thin plate or shell: $dm = \delta_2\, dA$ or $\delta_2\, dS$,
c) in a solid: $dm = \delta_3\, dV$,

where

ds = element of arc length,

δ_1 = mass per unit length of the wire,

dA or dS = element of area,

δ_2 = mass per unit area of the plate or shell,

dV = element of volume,

δ_3 = mass per unit volume of the solid.

EXAMPLE 1. Find the center of mass of a thin homogeneous triangular plate of base b and altitude h.

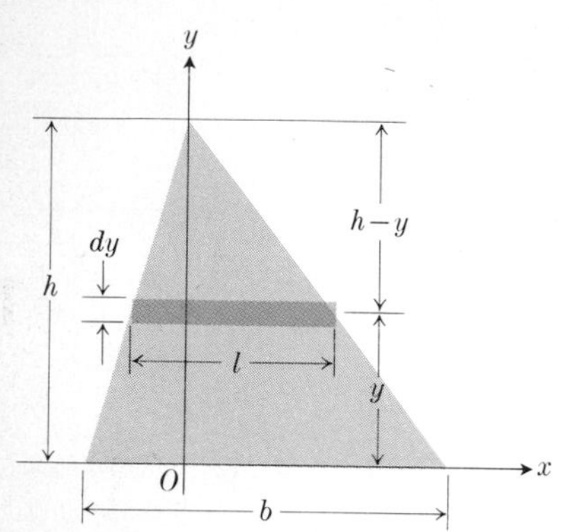

5–27 Calculating the mass of a thin triangular plate.

Solution. Divide the triangle into strips of width dy parallel to the x-axis. A representative strip is shown in Fig. 5–27. The mass of the strip is approximately

$$dm = \delta_2\, dA,$$

where

$$dA = l\, dy$$

and l is the width of the triangle at distance y above its base. By similar triangles,

$$\frac{l}{b} = \frac{h-y}{h}$$

or

$$l = \frac{b}{h}(h-y),$$

so that

$$dm = \delta_2 \frac{b}{h}(h-y)\, dy.$$

For the y-coordinate of the center of mass of the element dm, we have $\tilde{y} = y$. For the entire plate,

$$\bar{y} = \frac{\int y\, dm}{\int dm} = \frac{\int_0^h \delta_2 \frac{b}{h} y(h-y)\, dy}{\int_0^h \delta_2 \frac{b}{h}(h-y)\, dy} = \frac{1}{3}h.$$

Thus the center of mass lies above the base of the triangle at a distance one-third of the way toward the opposite vertex. By considering each side in turn as being a base of the triangle, this result shows that the center of gravity lies at the intersection of the medians.

EXAMPLE 2. A thin homogeneous wire is bent to form a semicircle of radius r (Fig. 5–28). Find its center of mass.

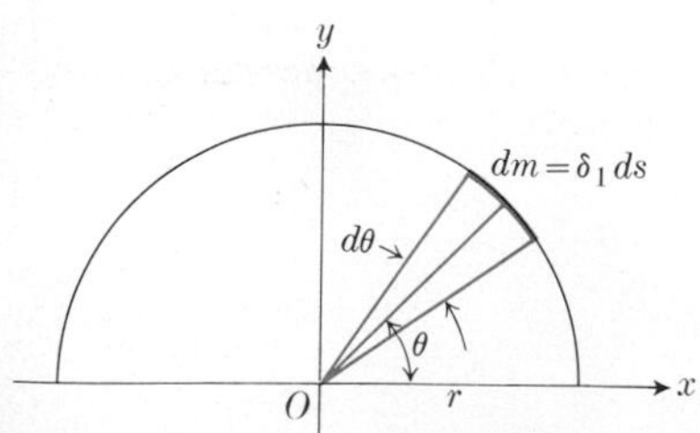

5–28 Calculating the mass of a semicircular wire.

Solution. Here we take

$$dm = \delta_1\, ds,$$

where ds is an element of arc length of the wire and

$$\delta_1 = \frac{M}{L} = \frac{M}{\pi r}$$

is the mass per unit length of the wire. In terms of the central angle θ

measured in radians (as usual), we have

$$ds = r\,d\theta$$

and

$$\tilde{x} = r\cos\theta, \qquad \tilde{y} = r\sin\theta.$$

Hence

$$\bar{x} = \frac{\int_0^\pi r\cos\theta\,\delta_1 r\,d\theta}{\int_0^\pi \delta_1 r\,d\theta} = \frac{\delta_1 r^2[\sin\theta]_0^\pi}{\delta_1 r[\theta]_0^\pi} = 0,$$

$$\bar{y} = \frac{\int_0^\pi r\sin\theta\,\delta_1 r\,d\theta}{\int_0^\pi \delta_1 r\,d\theta} = \frac{\delta_1 r^2[-\cos\theta]_0^\pi}{\delta_1 r[\theta]_0^\pi} = \frac{2}{\pi}r.$$

The center of mass is therefore on the y-axis at a distance $2/\pi$ (roughly $\frac{2}{3}$) of the way up from the origin toward the intercept $(0, r)$.

EXAMPLE 3. Find the center of mass of a solid hemisphere of radius r if its density at any point P is proportional to the distance between P and the base of the hemisphere.

Solution. Imagine the solid cut into slices of thickness dy by planes perpendicular to the y-axis (Fig. 5–29), and take

$$dm = \delta_3\,dV,$$

where

$$dV = A(y)\,dy$$

is the volume of the representative slice at distance y above the base of the hemisphere, which is in the xz-plane, and where

$$\delta_3 = ky \qquad (k = \text{constant})$$

is the density of the solid in this slice. The area of a face of the slice dV is

$$A(y) = \pi x^2,$$

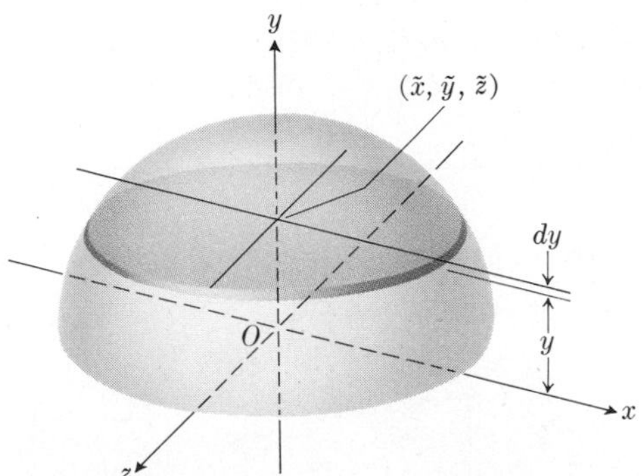

5–29 Finding the mass of a hemispherical solid by slicing parallel to its base.

where $x^2 + y^2 = r^2$; that is,

$$dV = A(y)\,dy = \pi(r^2 - y^2)\,dy;$$

so that

$$dm = k\pi(r^2 - y^2)y\,dy.$$

The center of mass of the slice may be taken at its geometric center,

$$(\tilde{x}, \tilde{y}, \tilde{z}) = (0, y, 0),$$

so that

$$\bar{x} = \bar{z} = 0$$

and

$$\bar{y} = \frac{\int y\,dm}{\int dm} = \frac{\int_0^r k\pi(r^2 - y^2)y^2\,dy}{\int_0^r k\pi(r^2 - y^2)y\,dy} = \frac{k\pi\left[\dfrac{r^2y^3}{3} - \dfrac{y^5}{5}\right]_0^r}{k\pi\left[\dfrac{r^2y^2}{2} - \dfrac{y^4}{4}\right]_0^r} = \frac{8}{15}r.$$

PROBLEMS

In each of the following problems (1 through 5), find the center of mass of a thin homogeneous plate covering the given portion of the xy-plane.

1. The first quadrant of the circle $x^2 + y^2 = a^2$.

2. The area bounded by the parabola $y = h^2 - x^2$ and the x-axis.

3. The "triangular" area in the first quadrant between the circle $x^2 + y^2 = a^2$ and the lines $x = a$, $y = a$.

4. The area between the x-axis and the curve $y = \sin x$ between $x = 0$ and $x = \pi$. [*Hint.* Take $dA = y\,dx$ and $\tilde{y} = \frac{1}{2}y$.]

5. The area between the y-axis and the curve $x = 2y - y^2$.

6. Find the distance, from the base, of the center of mass of a thin triangular plate of base b and altitude h if its density varies as the square root of the distance from the base.

7. In Problem 6, suppose that the density varies as the square of the distance.

8. Find the center of mass of a homogeneous solid right circular cone.

9. Find the center of mass of a solid right circular cone if the density varies as the distance from the base.

10. In Problem 9 suppose that the density varies as the square of the distance.

11. In Example 2 (see Fig. 5–28) suppose that the density is $\delta_1 = k \sin\theta$, k being constant. Find the center of mass.

5–11 CENTROID AND CENTER OF GRAVITY

For a mass of uniform density, Eqs. (8), Article 5–10, reduce to

$$\bar{x} = \frac{\int \tilde{x}\,\delta_3\,dV}{\int \delta_3\,dV} = \frac{\delta_3 \int \tilde{x}\,dV}{\delta_3 \int dV} = \frac{\int \tilde{x}\,dV}{\int dV},$$

$$\bar{y} = \frac{\int \tilde{y}\,dV}{\int dV}, \qquad \bar{z} = \frac{\int \tilde{z}\,dV}{\int dV} \tag{1}$$

for a solid, with similar equations having dA or ds in place of dV in the case of a plate or a wire. Since these expressions involve only the geometric objects, namely, volumes, areas, and curves, we speak of the point $(\bar{x}, \bar{y}, \bar{z})$ in such cases as the *centroid* of the object. The term *center of gravity* is also used, since the line of action of the forces due to gravity acting on the elements of the object passes through this point. (See Sears, Zemansky, Young, *University Physics*, Fifth edition (1976), Chapters 2 and 3, for a discussion of physical concepts involved.)

EXAMPLE 1. Find the center of gravity of a solid hemisphere of radius r.

Solution. As in Example 3, Article 5–10, imagine the solid (Fig. 5–29) cut into slices of thickness dy by planes perpendicular to the y-axis. The centroid of a slice is its geometric center, on the y-axis, at $(0, y, 0)$. Its moment with respect to the xz-plane is

$$\begin{aligned} dM_{xz} &= y\,dV \\ &= y\pi(r^2 - y^2)\,dy. \end{aligned}$$

Hence

$$M_{xz} = \pi \int_0^r (r^2 y - y^3)\,dy = \frac{\pi r^4}{4}.$$

Since the volume of the hemisphere is

$$V = \tfrac{2}{3}\pi r^3,$$

we have

$$\bar{y} = \frac{M_{xz}}{V} = \frac{3}{8}r.$$

EXAMPLE 2. Find the center of gravity of a thin hemispherical shell of inner radius r and thickness t.

Solution. We shall solve this problem, (a) exactly, by using the results of the preceding example; then (b) we shall see how the position of the center of gravity changes as we hold r fixed and let $t \to 0$. Finally, (c) we shall solve the problem approximately without using the results of Example 1, by considering the center of mass of an imaginary distribution of mass over the surface of the hemisphere of radius r, assuming that the thickness t is negligible in comparison with r (as, for example, the gold leaf covering the dome of the State House in Boston).

a) Let M_1, M_2, and M; V_1, V_2, and V denote, respectively, the moments with respect to the xz-plane and the volumes of the solid hemisphere of radius r, the solid hemisphere of radius $(r + t)$, and the hemispherical shell of thickness t and inner radius r. Since the moment of the sum of two masses is the sum of their moments and

$$V_1 + V = V_2,$$

we also have

$$M_1 + M = M_2;$$

that is

$$M = M_2 - M_1.$$

But, by Example 1,

$$M_2 = \frac{\pi}{4}(r+t)^4, \qquad M_1 = \frac{\pi}{4}r^4,$$

so that

$$M = \frac{\pi}{4}[(r+t)^4 - r^4]$$

$$= \frac{\pi}{4}[4r^3t + 6r^2t^2 + 4rt^3 + t^4],$$

while

$$V = V_2 - V_1 = \tfrac{2}{3}\pi[(r+t)^3 - r^3]$$
$$= \tfrac{2}{3}\pi(3r^2t + 3rt^2 + t^3);$$

hence

$$\bar{y} = \frac{M}{V} = \frac{1}{2}\frac{[r^3 + \frac{3}{2}r^2t + rt^2 + \frac{1}{4}t^3]}{[r^2 + rt + \frac{1}{3}t^2]}.$$

b) In the case of a shell where the thickness t is negligible in comparison with r, this reduces to $\bar{y} = \frac{1}{2}r$, by writing

$$\bar{y} = \frac{1}{2}\frac{r^3\left[1 + \frac{3}{2}\left(\frac{t}{r}\right) + \left(\frac{t}{r}\right)^2 + \frac{1}{4}\left(\frac{t}{r}\right)^3\right]}{r^2\left[1 + \left(\frac{t}{r}\right) + \frac{1}{3}\left(\frac{t}{r}\right)^2\right]},$$

and then letting $(t/r) \to 0$.

c) To solve the problem directly, without reference to Example 1, consider the mass of the shell to be uniformly distributed over its surface so that the mass of any portion cut from the shell will be proportional to its (inner) surface area. The proportionality factor,

$$\sigma = \delta t,$$

where δ is the volume density and t the thickness of the shell, is frequently referred to as a surface density factor. (Thus in working with sheet metal stock, say, aluminum of uniform thickness and density, we might speak of it as weighing so many pounds *per square foot*. This would be our σ, and A square feet of this particular stock would weigh σA pounds.) Then the slice of shell between planes perpendicular to the y-axis at distances y and $y + \Delta y$, respectively, above the xz-plane has mass

$$\Delta m = \sigma\,\Delta S,$$

where ΔS is the surface area of the slice (see Fig. 5–30). The moment of this slice with respect to the xz-plane then lies between

$$y\,\Delta m \qquad \text{and} \qquad (y + \Delta y)\,\Delta m,$$

and hence differs from $y\,\Delta m$ by at most $\Delta y\,\Delta m$. The sum of the moments of the slices has a limit, as Δy approaches zero, equal to $\int y\,dm$. We are thus led to

$$\bar{y} = \frac{\int y\,dm}{\int dm} = \frac{\int \sigma y\,dS}{\int \sigma\,dS} = \frac{\sigma \int y\,dS}{\sigma \int dS},$$

since σ is constant by our hypothesis. Here

$$dS = 2\pi x\,ds = 2\pi(r\cos\theta)r\,d\theta$$

if we use

$$x = r\cos\theta, \qquad y = r\sin\theta$$

to represent the circle $x^2 + y^2 = r^2$. Hence

$$\bar{y} = \frac{\int_0^{\pi/2} r\sin\theta \cdot 2\pi(r\cos\theta)\cdot r\,d\theta}{\int_0^{\pi/2} 2\pi(r\cos\theta)r\,d\theta}$$

$$= \frac{2\pi r^3 \int_0^{\pi/2} \sin\theta\cos\theta\,d\theta}{2\pi r^2 \int_0^{\pi/2}\cos\theta\,d\theta} = r\frac{[\frac{1}{2}\sin^2\theta]_0^{\pi/2}}{[\sin\theta]_0^{\pi/2}} = \frac{1}{2}r.$$

Observe that the element of arc ds which, when rotated about the y-axis, generates dS, need only move along the arc of the circle in the first quadrant, namely, $0 \le \theta \le \pi/2$, in order to give us the entire hemisphere.

By the symmetry of the shell, the center of gravity lies on the y-axis, that is,

$$(\bar{x}, \bar{y}, \bar{z}) = (0, \tfrac{1}{2}r, 0).$$

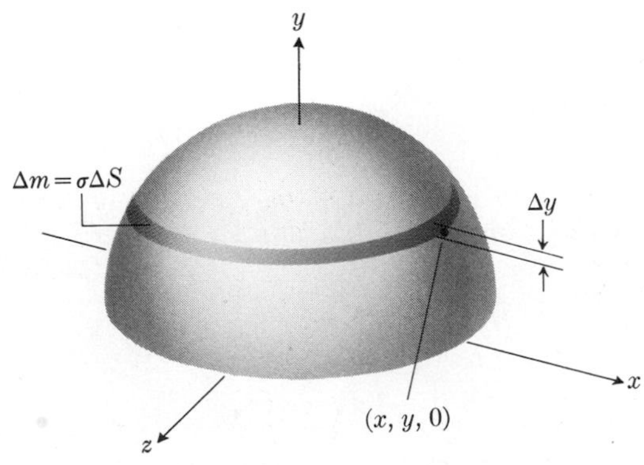

5–30 $\Delta m = \sigma\,\Delta S$, where σ is a density factor measured in mass per unit area.

PROBLEMS

In Problems 1 through 5, find the center of gravity of the areas bounded by the given curves and lines.

1. The x-axis and the curve $y = c^2 - x^2$.
2. The y-axis and the curve $x = y - y^3$, $0 \le y \le 1$.
3. The curve $y = x^2$ and the line $y = 4$.
4. The curve $y = x - x^2$ and the line $x + y = 0$.
5. The curve $x = y^2 - y$ and the line $y = x$.

6. Find the center of gravity of a solid right circular cone of altitude h and base-radius r.

7. Find the center of gravity of the solid generated by rotating, about the y-axis, the area bounded by the curve $y = x^2$ and the line $y = 4$.

8. The area bounded by the curve $x = y^2 - y$ and the line $y = x$ is rotated about the x-axis. Find the center of gravity of the solid thus generated.

9. Find the center of gravity of a very thin right circular conical shell of base-radius r and altitude h.

• **10.** Find the center of gravity of the surface area generated by rotating about the line $x = -r$, the arc of the circle $x^2 + y^2 = r^2$ that lies in the first quadrant. (Use $x = r\cos\theta$, $y = r\sin\theta$, to represent the circle.)

11. Find the moment, about the x-axis, of the arc of the parabola $y = \sqrt{x}$ lying between (0, 0) and (4, 2).

12. Find the center of gravity of the arc length of one quadrant of a circle.

5–12 THE THEOREMS OF PAPPUS

When a plane area, such as A in Fig. 5–31, is rotated about an axis in its plane that does not intersect the area, there is a useful formula that relates the volume swept out by the area to the path described by its centroid.

Theorem 1. *If a plane area is revolved about a line that lies in its plane but does not intersect the area, then the volume generated is equal to the product of the area and the distance traveled by its center of gravity.*

To prove this result, which is one of the Theorems of Pappus, let the x-axis coincide with the axis of revolution and divide the area into strips of width Δy by lines parallel to the x-axis. The entire volume is the sum of the volumes generated by these strips of area. Let $l = f(y)$ be the width of the area at distance y above the x-axis, $c \le y \le d$. By the same argument we used in Article 5–5 to justify the cylindrical shell method of computing volumes, we have

$$V = \lim_{\Delta y \to 0} \sum 2\pi y l \,\Delta y$$

$$= \int_c^d 2\pi y l \, dy. \tag{1}$$

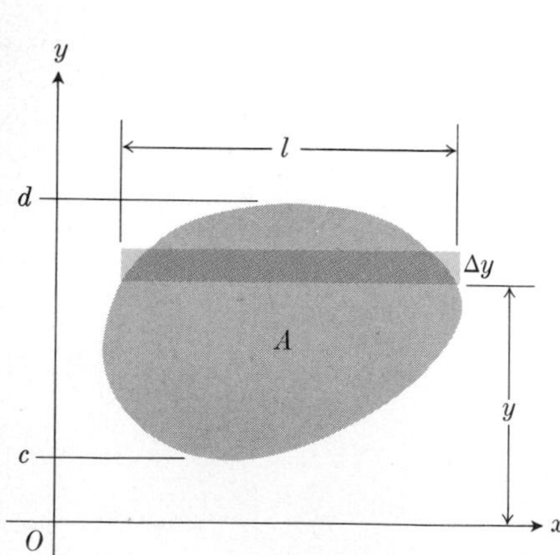

5–31 The shape above is to be revolved about the x-axis to generate a volume. A 1700-year-old theorem says that the volume can be calculated by multiplying the shape's area by the distance traveled by the shape's center of gravity.

But the ordinate $\bar{y}_A$ of the center of gravity of the area A is given by

$$\bar{y}_A = \frac{\int y\, dA}{\int dA} = \frac{\int_c^d yl\, dy}{A},$$

so that

$$\int_c^d yl\, dy = A\bar{y}_A,$$

and hence Eq. (1) becomes

$$V = 2\pi \bar{y}_A A. \tag{2}$$

Since $2\pi\bar{y}_A$ is the distance traveled by the center of gravity of the area, the theorem is established.

EXAMPLE 1. (See Fig. 5–32.) Find the volume of the torus (doughnut) generated by rotating a circle of radius r about an axis in its plane at a distance b from its center, $b > r$.

Solution. The center of the circle is its center of gravity, and this travels a distance $2\pi b$. The area of the circle is πr^2, so by Eq. (2) the volume of the torus is

$$V = (2\pi b)(\pi r^2) = 2\pi^2 b r^2.$$

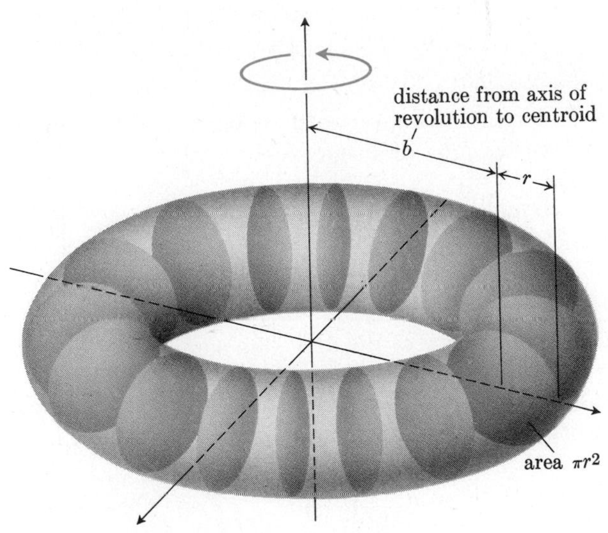

5–32 The volume swept out by the revolving disk is $(2\pi b)(\pi r^2)$.

Theorem 2. *If an arc of a plane curve is revolved about a line that lies in its plane but does not intersect the arc, then the surface area generated by the arc is equal to the product of the length of the arc and the distance traveled by its center of gravity.*

In this, another Theorem of Pappus, the center of gravity is that of the curve (or of a fine homogeneous wire whose centerline coincides with the curve), and is generally different from the center of gravity of the enclosed plane area (if the curve is a closed curve). To prove the theorem, refer the curve to x- and y-axes in its plane and let the x-axis coincide with the axis of revolution (see Fig. 5–33). Then the surface area generated is

$$S = \int_{x=a}^{x=b} 2\pi y \, ds, \tag{3}$$

as we found in Article 5–8. But the center of gravity of the curve has ordinate

$$\bar{y}_c = \frac{\int y \, ds}{\int ds} = \frac{\int y \, ds}{L},$$

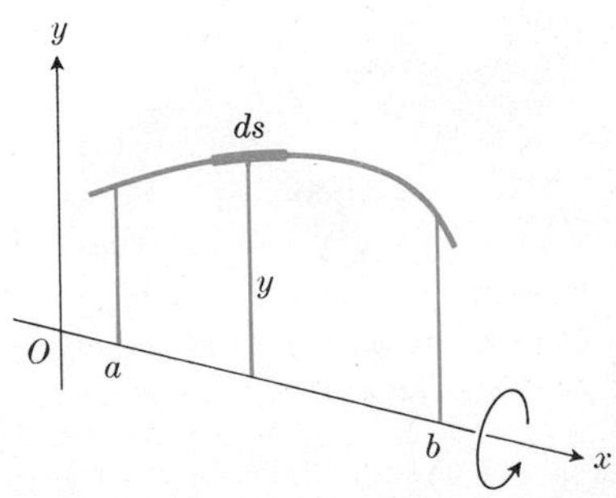

5–33 Arc of a plane curve.

where

$$L = \int ds$$

is the length of the arc. Hence

$$S = 2\pi \int_{x=a}^{x=b} y\, ds = 2\pi \bar{y}_c L. \tag{4}$$

Q.E.D.

EXAMPLE 2. The surface area of the torus in the previous example is given by

$$S = (2\pi b)(2\pi r) = 4\pi^2 br.$$

The two Theorems of Pappus can be used to determine the center of gravity of a known volume or surface.

EXAMPLE 3. Use the first Theorem of Pappus and the fact that the volume of a sphere of radius r is

$$V = \tfrac{4}{3}\pi r^3$$

to find the center of gravity of the area of a semicircle.

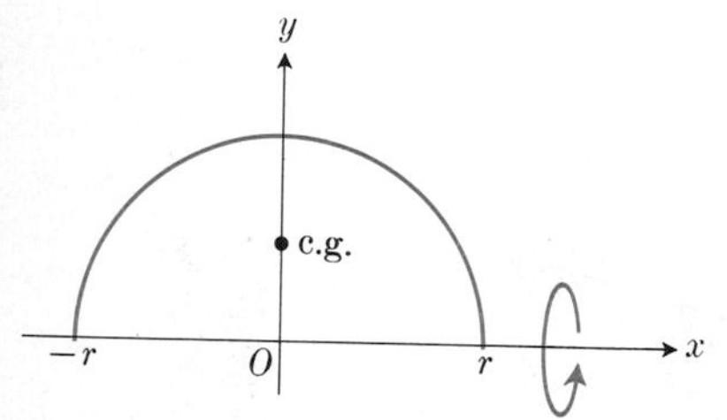

5–34 The y-coordinate of the center of gravity of a semicircular area can be calculated from Pappus' theorem without integration.

Solution. Note that we generate a sphere by rotating a semicircle about its diameter (Fig. 5–34). Then the axis of revolution does not intersect the area, and since

$$A = \tfrac{1}{2}\pi r^2,$$

while

$$V = 2\pi \bar{y} A,$$

we find

$$\bar{y} = \frac{V}{2\pi A} = \frac{\frac{4}{3}\pi r^3}{2\pi \cdot \frac{1}{2}\pi r^2} = \frac{4}{3\pi} r.$$

PROBLEMS

1. Use the Theorems of Pappus to find the lateral surface area and the volume of a right circular cone.

2. Use the second Theorem of Pappus and the fact that the surface area of a sphere of radius r is $4\pi r^2$ to find the center of gravity of the semicircular arc

$$y = \sqrt{r^2 - x^2}, \qquad -r \le x \le r.$$

3. The semicircular arc $y = \sqrt{r^2 - x^2}$, $-r \le x \le r$, is rotated about the line $y = r$. Use the second Theorem of Pappus together with the answer to the preceding problem to find the surface area generated.

4. The center of gravity of the area bounded by the x-axis and the semicircle $y = \sqrt{r^2 - x^2}$ is at $[0, (4/3\pi)r]$ (see Example 3, above). Find the volume generated when this area is rotated about the line $y = -r$.

5. The area in the preceding example is rotated about the line $y = x - r$. Find the volume generated.

6. Use the answer to Problem 2 above to find the surface area generated by rotating the semicircular arc $y = \sqrt{r^2 - x^2}$, $-r \le x \le r$, about the line $y = x - r$.

7. Find the moment about the x-axis of the area in the semicircle of Fig. 5–34, Example 3, above. (If you use results already known, you won't need to integrate.)

8. Find the moment about the line $y = -r$ of the area in the semicircle of Fig. 5–34.

9. Find the moment about the line $y = x - r$ of the area in the semicircle of Fig. 5–34.

5–13 HYDROSTATIC PRESSURE

If a flat-bottomed container is filled with water to a depth h, the force against the bottom of the container due to the pressure of the liquid is

$$F = whA, \tag{1}$$

where w is the weight-density, which is nearly 62.5 lb/ft^3, and A is the area of the bottom of the container. Obviously, the units in Eq. (1) must be compatible, say h in feet, A in square feet, w in pounds per cubic foot, giving F in pounds. It is a remarkable fact that this force does not depend upon the shape of the sides of the vessel, the force on the bottom being the same in both (a) and (b) in Fig. 5–35, for example, if both containers have the same area at their bases and both have the same "head" h. (See Sears, Zemansky, Young, *University Physics*, Fifth edition (1976), Chapter 12.) The *pressure*, or *force per unit area*, at the bottom of the container is therefore

$$p = wh. \tag{2}$$

Next, consider any body of water, such as the water in a reservoir or behind a dam. According to Pascal's principle, the pressure $p = wh$ at depth h in such a body of water is the same *in all directions*. For a flat plate submerged *horizontally*, the downward *force* acting on its upper face due to this liquid pressure is the same as that given by Eq. (1). If the plate is submerged *vertically*, however, then the pressure against it will be different at different depths and Eq. (1) no longer is usable in that form because we would have different h factors for points at different depths. We circumvent this difficulty in a manner that should by now be fairly familiar, namely, by dividing the plate into many narrow strips, the representative strip having its upper edge at depth h and its lower edge at depth $h + \Delta h$ below the surface of the water. If the area of this strip is called ΔA, and the force on one side of it ΔF, then Eq. (1) suggests that

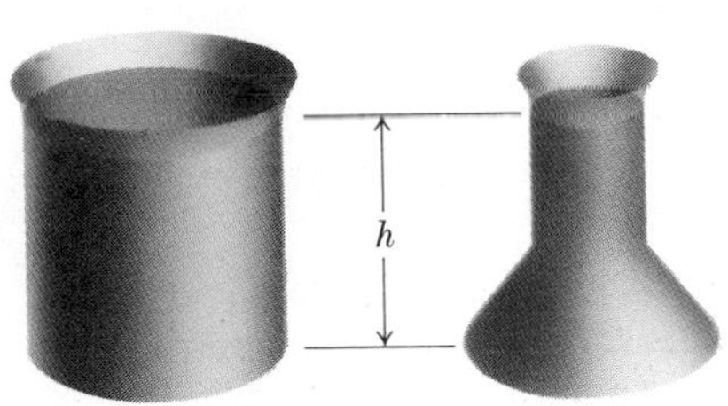

5–35 The hydrostatic pressure on the bottoms of these containers is the same.

$$wh\,\Delta A \le \Delta F \le w(h + \Delta h)\,\Delta A,$$

since the pressure will vary from wh to $w(h + \Delta h)$ in this strip. When we add the forces for all strips, then take the limit of such sums as $\Delta h \to 0$, we may disregard the infinitesimals of higher order, such as $\Delta h\,\Delta A$, and we are led to

$$F = \lim_{\Delta h \to 0} \sum_a^b wh\,\Delta A$$

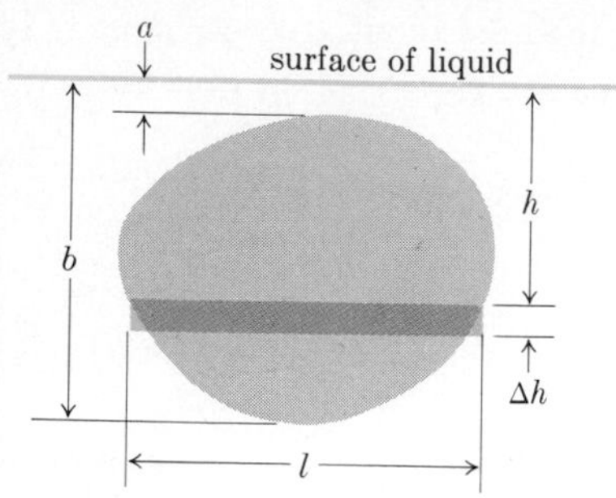

5–36 A plate submerged vertically beneath the surface of a liquid. The force exerted by the liquid on one side of the rectangular strip is approximately $whl\,\Delta h$, where w is the weight-density of the liquid.

or

$$F = \int_{h=a}^{h=b} wh\,dA = \int_a^b whl\,dh, \tag{3}$$

where $dA = l\,dh$ (see Fig. 5–36).

As a corollary of Eq. (3), if we denote the depth of the center of gravity of the area A by $\bar{h}$, then

$$\bar{h} = \frac{\int h\,dA}{\int dA} \quad \text{or} \quad \int h\,dA = \bar{h}A.$$

Since w is a constant that may be moved across the integral sign in (3), we have

$$F = w\bar{h}A. \tag{4}$$

This states that the total force of the liquid pressing against one face of the plate (an equal and opposite force presses against the other face unless the plate forms part of a wall of the container) is the same as it would be according to (1) if all of the area A were at the depth $\bar{h}$ below the surface.

Equation (4) is the working tool used most frequently by engineers in finding such hydrostatic forces as we have discussed. They can refer to a handbook to obtain the center of gravity of simple plane areas, and from this they quickly find $\bar{h}$. Of course, the location of the center of gravity given in the handbook was calculated by someone who performed an integration equivalent to evaluating the integral in Eq. (3). We recommend that, for now, you solve problems of this type by thinking through the steps which lead up to Eq. (3) by integration, and then checking your results, when you can conveniently do so, by Eq. (4).

EXAMPLE 1. A trapezoid is submerged vertically in water with its upper edge 4 ft below the surface and its lower edge 10 ft below the surface. If the upper and lower edges are respectively 6 ft and 8 ft long, find the total force on one face of the trapezoid.

Solution. In Fig. 5–37(a) we have, by similar triangles,

$$\frac{l-6}{2} = \frac{h-4}{6},$$

so that

$$l = \frac{h+14}{3}.$$

Then the force is

$$F = \int_4^{10} wh\left(\frac{h+14}{3}\right)dh = 300w.$$

Since

$$w = 62.5 \text{ lb/ft}^3 = \tfrac{1}{32} \text{ ton/ft}^3,$$

we have

$$F = 9\tfrac{3}{8} \text{ tons.}$$

Now we check by using Eq. (4). The trapezoid can be resolved into a parallelogram plus a triangle (Fig. 5–37(b)). For the parallelogram,

$$\bar{h}_1 = 7, \qquad A_1 = 36; \qquad F_1 = 252w.$$

For the triangle,

$$\bar{h}_2 = 8, \qquad A_2 = 6; \qquad F_2 = 48w.$$

For the trapezoid,

$$F = F_1 + F_2 = 300w.$$

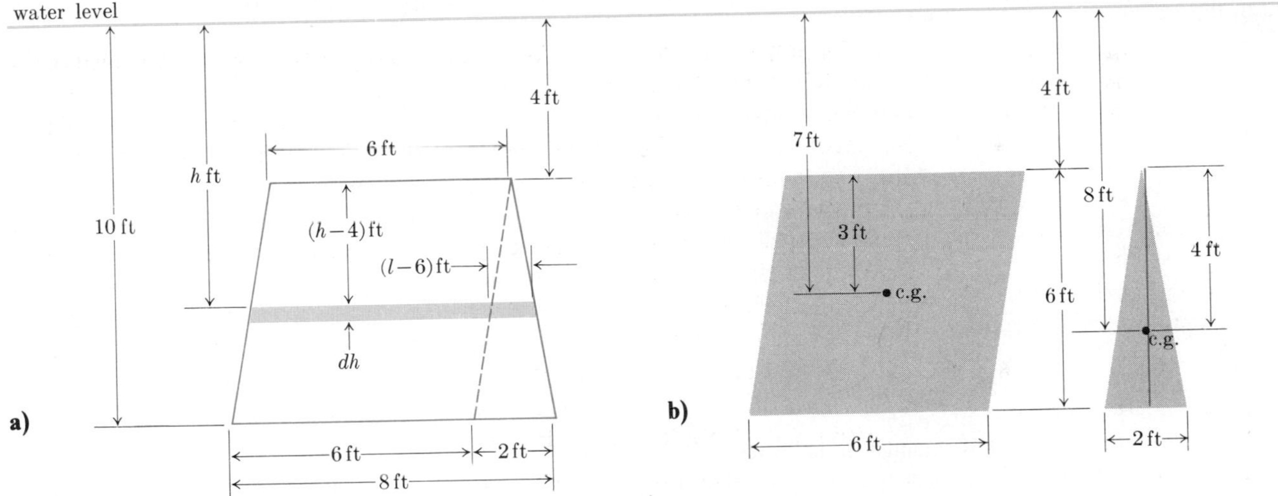

5–37 (a) The trapezoid of Example 1 submerged vertically beneath the surface of the water. (b) To calculate the force on one side, the trapezoid is divided into a parallelogram and an isosceles triangle. The resulting centroids are marked "c.g." (center of gravity).

EXAMPLE 2. Find the moment produced about the lower edge of the trapezoid by the forces in the preceding example.

Solution. The force on the representative strip may be denoted by

$$dF = wh\,dA = wh\left(\frac{h + 14}{3}\right)dh.$$

For the moment of this force about the lower edge of the trapezoid, we must multiply this force by the moment arm,

$$r = 10 - h,$$

to give the moment

$$dM = r\,dF = wh(10 - h)\frac{h + 14}{3}\,dh.$$

The total moment due to forces on all the strips is

$$M = \frac{w}{3}\int_4^{10} (140h - 4h^2 - h^3)\,dh = 732w$$

or

$$M = 22\tfrac{7}{8} \text{ foot-tons.}$$

PROBLEMS

1. The vertical ends of a water trough are isosceles triangles of base 4 ft and altitude 3 ft. Find the force on one end if the trough is full of water weighing 62.5 lb/ft³.

2. Find the force in the previous problem if the water level in the trough is lowered one foot.

3. A triangular plate ABC is submerged in water with its plane vertical. The side AB, 4 ft long, is 1 ft below the surface, while C is 5 ft below AB. Find the total force on one face of the plate.

4. Find the force on one face of the triangle ABC of Problem 3 if AB is one foot below the surface as before, but the triangle is rotated 180° about AB so as to bring the vertex C 4 ft *above* the surface.

5. A semicircular plate is submerged in water with its plane vertical and its diameter in the surface. Find the force on one face of the plate if its diameter is 2 ft.

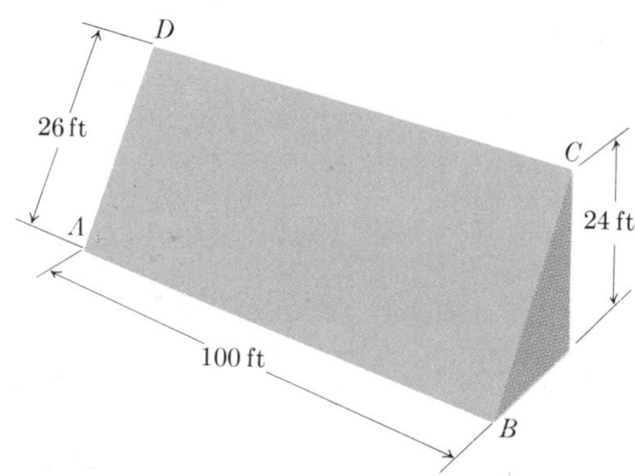

5–38 The dam of Problem 6.

6. The face of a dam is a rectangle, $ABCD$, of dimensions $AB = CD = 100$ ft, $AD = BC = 26$ ft. Instead of being vertical, the plane $ABCD$ is inclined as indicated in Fig. 5–38, so that the top of the dam is 24 ft higher than the bottom. Find the force due to water pressure on the dam when the surface of the water is level with the top of the dam.

7. Find the moment, about AB, of the force in Problem 6.

5–14 WORK

When a constant force F (pounds) acts throughout a distance s (feet), the *work* done (in foot-pounds) is the product of force and distance,

$$W = Fs. \tag{1}$$

When the force is not constant, as for instance in stretching or compressing a spring, then Eq. (1) cannot be used directly to give the work done. The law in (1) can be used, however, to estimate the work done over a *short* interval Δs if the force is a continuous function of s. The integral process then enables us to extend the law in (1) to find the total work done.

For most springs there is a range over which the amount of force F required to stretch or compress the spring from its natural length can be approximated by the equation

$$F = cx, \tag{2}$$

where x is the amount the spring has been displaced from its natural or unstressed length, and c is a constant characteristic of the spring, called the *spring constant* (Fig. 5–39(a)). Beyond this range, the metal of the spring becomes distorted and Eq. (2) is no longer a reliable description. We assume that the springs in this article are never stretched or compressed to such an extent. Equation (2) is known as *Hooke's law.*

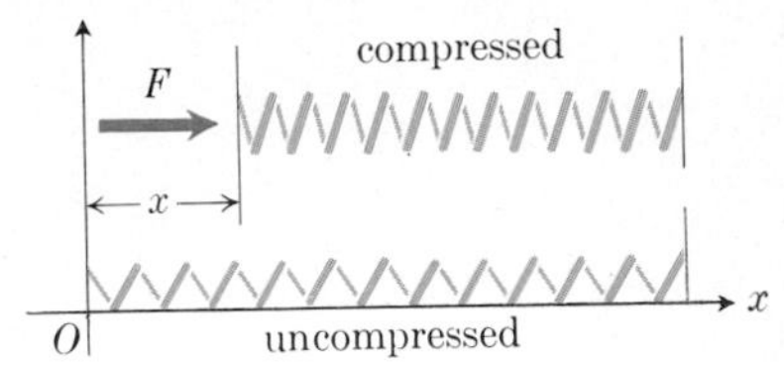

(a)

(b)

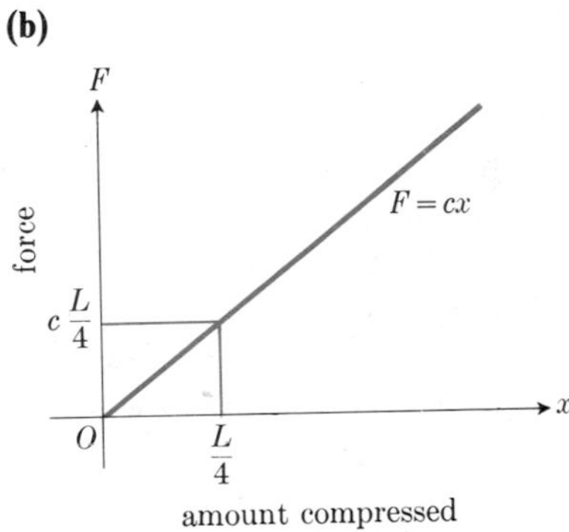

5–39 The force F required to hold a spring under compression increases linearly as the spring is compressed.

EXAMPLE 1. Find the work done in compressing a spring from its natural length L to a length of $\frac{3}{4}L$.

Solution. To compress the spring by an amount $L/4$, the force must be increased from

$$F_0 = c \times 0 = 0$$

to

$$F_1 = c\left(\frac{L}{4}\right).$$

The point of application of the force will move from $x = 0$ to $x = L/4$ as the force increases (Fig. 5–39(b)). To find the work done during the process, we imagine the x-interval from 0 to $L/4$ to be divided into a large number of subintervals, each of length Δx. As the spring is compressed from x to $x + \Delta x$, the *force* varies from cx to $c(x + \Delta x)$. Since the force acts through a *distance* Δx, the work done to achieve this small compression will lie between

$$cx\,\Delta x \qquad \text{and} \qquad c(x + \Delta x)\,\Delta x.$$

Therefore, the total work of compression is approximately

$$W \approx \sum_{x=0}^{L/4} cx\,\Delta x,$$

or

$$W = \sum_{x=0}^{L/4} c\tilde{x}\,\Delta x$$

for appropriate choices of the $\tilde{x}$ between x and $x + \Delta x$. In the limit as Δx tends to zero, we have

$$W = \lim_{\Delta x \to 0} \sum_{x=0}^{L/4} cx\,\Delta x = \int_0^{L/4} cx\,dx = \frac{cL^2}{32}$$

or

$$W = \frac{1}{2}\left(\frac{cL}{4}\right)\left(\frac{L}{4}\right).$$

In this last form, the factor $\frac{1}{2}c(L/4)$ is one-half the final value reached by F when the spring has been compressed to $\frac{3}{4}$ of its original length, and the factor $L/4$ is the total distance through which the variable force has acted. This suggests

$$W = \bar{F}s \tag{3}$$

as a suitable modification of Eq. (1) when the force is variable, where $\bar{F}$ represents the *average* value of the variable force throughout the total displacement. However, the determination of $\bar{F}$ itself involves an integration in the general case, so that it is usually as easy to apply the principles illustrated in the example just considered as it is to apply Eq. (3). In fact, Eq. (3) may be interpreted as *defining* $\bar{F}$.

In a manner entirely analogous to that in the example above, it is easily seen that

$$W = \int_a^b F\,ds \tag{4}$$

gives the work done by a variable force (which, however, always acts along a given direction) as the point of application undergoes a displacement from $s = a$ to $s = b$.

EXAMPLE 2. A spring has a natural length of $L = 3$ ft. A force of 10 lbs stretches the spring to a length of 3.5 ft. Find the spring constant. Then calculate the amount of work done in stretching the spring from its natural length to a length of 5 ft. How much work is done in stretching the spring from 4 ft to 5 ft? How far beyond its natural length will a 15-lb force stretch the spring?

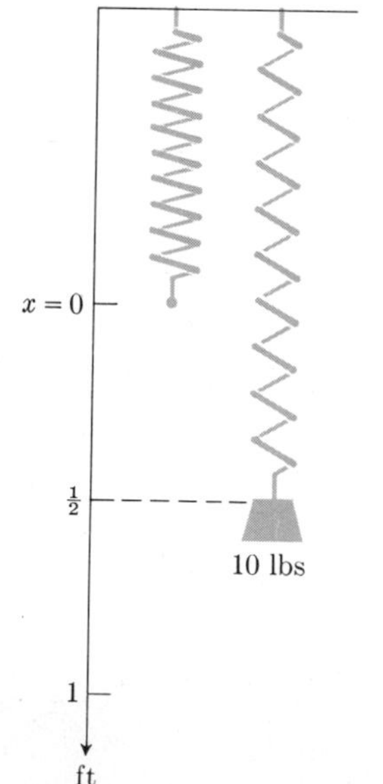

5–40 A 10-lb weight stretches the spring half a foot beyond its unstressed length.

Solution. We find the spring constant from Eq. (2). A force of 10 lbs stretches the spring 0.5 ft, so that

$$10 = c(0.5), \qquad c = 20 \text{ lb/ft}.$$

To calculate the work done in stretching the spring 2 ft beyond its natural length, imagine the spring hanging parallel to the x-axis, as shown in Fig. 5–40. Then, by Eq. (4),

$$W = \int_0^2 20x\,dx = 10x^2 \Big]_0^2 = 40 \text{ foot-pounds}.$$

To find the work done in stretching the spring from a length of 4 ft to a length of 5 ft, we calculate

$$W = \int_1^2 20x\,dx = 10x^2 \Big]_1^2 = 30 \text{ foot-pounds}.$$

To learn how far a 15 lb force will stretch the spring, we solve Eq. (1) with $F = 15$ and $c = 20$:

$$15 = 20x, \qquad x = \tfrac{15}{20} \text{ ft} = 9 \text{ in}.$$

No calculus is involved in this last computation.

Equation (4) leads to an interesting theorem of mechanics.

Theorem. *Let F denote the resultant of all forces acting on a particle of mass m. Let the direction of F remain constant. Then, whether the magnitude of F is* *constant or variable, the work done on the particle by the force F is equal to the change in the kinetic energy of the particle.*

The ingredients required for a proof of this theorem are:

a) Eq. (4), which gives the work,
b) the definition of kinetic energy, K.E. $= \frac{1}{2}mv^2$, and
c) Newton's second law: $F = m(dv/dt)$.

The fact that

$$v = \frac{ds}{dt}$$

and

$$\frac{dv}{dt} = \frac{dv}{ds}\frac{ds}{dt} = \frac{dv}{ds}v$$

and Newton's second law enable us to write Eq. (4) in the form

$$W = \int_{s=a}^{s=b} mv\frac{dv}{ds}\,ds = \int_{v=v_a}^{v=v_b} mv\,dv,$$

which leads to

$$W = \tfrac{1}{2}mv^2\Big]_{v_a}^{v_b} = \tfrac{1}{2}mv_b^2 - \tfrac{1}{2}mv_a^2.$$

That is, the work done by the force F is the kinetic energy at b minus the kinetic energy at a or, more simply, the change in kinetic energy:

$$W = \Delta(\text{K.E.}).$$

We now consider another situation where the simple Eq. (1) cannot be applied to the *total* but can be applied to a *small piece*.

EXAMPLE 3. Calculate the amount of work required to pump all the water from a full hemispherical bowl of radius r ft to a distance h ft above the top of the bowl (Fig. 5–41).

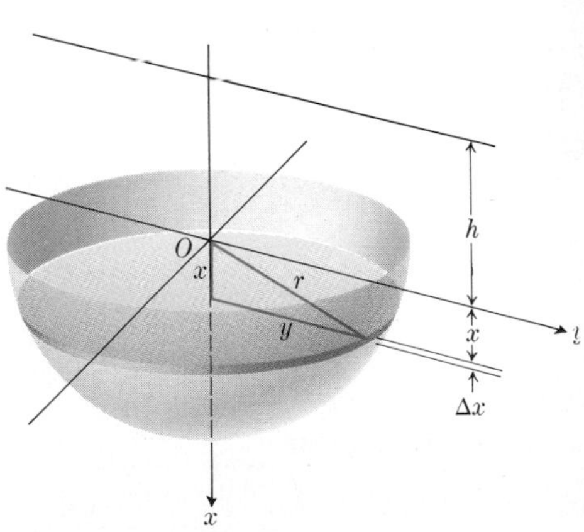

5–41 To calculate the work required to pump the water from a bowl, think of lifting the water out one slab at a time.

Solution. We introduce coordinate axes as shown in Fig. 5–41 and imagine the bowl to be divided into thin slices by planes perpendicular to the x-axis between $x = 0$ and $x = r$. The representative slice between the planes at x and $x + \Delta x$ has volume ΔV which, if we neglect only infinitesimals of higher order than Δx, is given approximately by

$$\Delta V \approx \pi y^2\,\Delta x = \pi(r^2 - x^2)\,\Delta x.$$

To the same order of approximation, the force F required to lift *this slice* is equal to its weight:

$$w\,\Delta V \approx \pi w(r^2 - x^2)\,\Delta x,$$

where w is the weight of a cubic foot of water. Finally, the *distance* through which this force must act lies between

$$h + x \qquad \text{and} \qquad h + x + \Delta x,$$

so that the work ΔW done in *lifting this one slice* is approximately

$$\Delta W \approx \pi w(r^2 - x^2)(h + x)\,\Delta x,$$

where we again have suppressed all higher powers of Δx. This is justified in the *limit* of the sum, and the total work is

$$\begin{aligned} W &= \lim_{\Delta x \to 0} \sum_0^r \pi w(r^2 - x^2)(h + x)\,\Delta x \\ &= \int_0^r \pi w(h + x)(r^2 - x^2)\,dx \\ &= hw \int_0^r \pi(r^2 - x^2)\,dx + w \int_0^r \pi x(r^2 - x^2)\,dx \\ &= hwV + \bar{x}wV. \end{aligned}$$

Here wV is the weight of the whole bowlful of water of volume V, and the second integral may be interpreted physically as giving the work required in pumping *all* the water from the depth of the center of gravity of the bowl to the level $x = 0$, while the first integral gives the work done in pumping the whole bowlful of water from the level $x = 0$ up a distance of h feet. The actual evaluation of the integrals leads to

$$W = \tfrac{2}{3}\pi r^3 w(h + \tfrac{3}{8}r).$$

Can you prove for yourself that, no matter what the shape of the container in Fig. 5–41, the total work is the sum of two terms, one of which is

$$W_1 = hw \int dV$$

and represents the total work done in lifting a bowlful of water a distance h, while the other is

$$W_2 = w \int x\,dV$$

and represents the work done in lifting a bowlful of water a distance equal to the depth of the center of gravity of the bowl?

PROBLEMS

1. If the spring in Fig. 5–39 has natural length $L = 18$ in., and a force of 10 lb is sufficient to compress it to a length of 16 in., what is the value of the "spring constant" c for the particular spring in question? How much work is done in compressing it from a length of 16 in. to a length of 12 in.?

2. A spring has a natural length of 10 in. An 800 lb force stretches the spring to 14 in. (a) Find the spring constant. (b) How much work is done in stretching the spring from 10 in. to 12 in.? (c) How far beyond its natural length will a 1600 lb force stretch the spring?

3. A 10,000 lb force compresses a spring from its natural length of 12 in. to a length of 11 in. How much work is done in compressing the spring (a) from 12 to 11.5 in.? (b) from 11.5 in. to 11 in.?

4. A spring has a natural length of 2 ft. A 1 lb force stretched the spring 5 ft (from 2 ft to 7 ft). How much work did the 1 lb force do? If the spring is stretched by a 2 lb force, what will its total length be?

5. A bathroom scale is depressed $\frac{1}{16}$ in. when a 150 lb person stands on it. Assuming that the scale behaves like a spring, find how much work is required to depress the scale $\frac{1}{8}$ in. from its natural height. How much weight is required to compress the scale this much?

6. Answer the questions of Problem 1 if the law of force is $F = c \sin(\pi x/2L)$ in place of Eq. (2).

7. Two electrons repel each other with a force inversely proportional to the square of the distance between them. Suppose one electron is held fixed at the point (1, 0) on the x-axis. Find the work required to move a second electron along the x-axis from the point $(-1, 0)$ to the origin.

8. If two electrons are held stationary at the points $(-1, 0)$ and $(1, 0)$ on the x-axis, find the work done in moving a third electron from (5, 0) to (3, 0) along the x-axis.

9. If a straight hole could be bored through the center of the earth, a particle of mass m falling in this hole would be attracted toward the center of the earth with a force $mg(r/R)$ when it is at distance r from the center. (R is the radius of earth; g is the acceleration due to gravity at the surface of the earth.) How much work is done on the particle as it falls from the surface to the center of the earth?

10. A bag of sand originally weighing 144 lb is lifted at a constant rate of 3 ft/min. The sand leaks out uniformly at such a rate that half of the sand is lost when the bag has been lifted 18 ft. Find the work done in lifting the bag this distance.

11. Gas in a cylinder of constant cross-sectional area A expands or is compressed by the motion of a piston. If p is the pressure of the gas in pounds per square inch and v is its volume in cubic inches, show that the work done by the gas as it goes from an initial state (p_1, v_1) to a second state (p_2, v_2) is

$$W = \int_{(p_1,v_1)}^{(p_2,v_2)} p\, dv \quad \text{inch-pounds.}$$

[*Hint.* Take the x-axis perpendicular to the face of the piston. Then $dv = A\, dx$ and $F = pA$.]

12. Use the result of Problem 11 to find the work done on the gas in compressing it from $v_1 = 243$ in^3 to $v_2 = 32$ in^3 if the initial pressure $p_1 = 50$ lb/in^2 and the pressure and volume satisfy the law for adiabatic change of state, $pv^{1.4} =$ constant.

13. Find the work done in pumping all the water out of a conical reservoir of radius 10 ft at the top, altitude 8 ft, to a height of 6 ft above the top of the reservoir.

14. Find the work done in Problem 13 if, at the beginning, the reservoir is filled to a depth of 5 ft and the water is pumped just to the top of the reservoir.

REVIEW QUESTIONS AND EXERCISES

1. List nine applications of the definite integral presented in this chapter.

2. How do you define the area bounded above by a curve $y = f_1(x)$, below by a curve $y = f_2(x)$, and on the sides by $x = a$ and $x = b$, $a < b$?

3. How do you define the volume generated by rotating a plane area about an axis in its plane and not intersecting the area?

4. How do you define the length of a plane curve? Can you extend this to a curve in three-dimensional space?

5. How do you define the surface area of a sphere? Of other surfaces of revolution?

6. How do you define the average value of a function over an interval?

7. How do you define center of mass?

8. How do you define work done by a variable force?

9. How do you define the hydrostatic force on the face of a dam?

MISCELLANEOUS PROBLEMS

1. Sketch the graphs of the equations $y = 2 - x^2$ and $x + y = 0$ in one diagram, and find the area bounded by them.

2. Find the maximum and minimum points of the curve $y = x^3 - 3x^2$ and find the total area bounded by this curve and the x-axis. Sketch.

In the following problems (3–15), find the area bounded by the given curves and lines. A sketch is usually helpful.

3. $y = x, \quad y = \dfrac{1}{x^2}, \quad x = 2$

4. $y = x, \quad y = \dfrac{1}{\sqrt{x}}, \quad x = 2$

5. $y = x + 1, \quad y = 3 - x^2$

6. $y = 2x^2, \quad y = x^2 + 2x + 3$

7. $x = 2y^2, \quad x = 0, \quad y = 3$

8. $4x = y^2 - 4, \quad 4x = y + 16$

9. $x^{1/2} + y^{1/2} = a^{1/2}, \quad x = 0, \quad y = 0$

10. $y = \sin x, \quad y = \sqrt{2}x/2$

11. $y^2 = 9x, \quad y = \dfrac{3x^2}{8}$

12. $y = \sin x, \quad y = x, \quad 0 \leq x \leq \frac{\pi}{4}$

13. $y = x\sqrt{2x^2 + 1}, \quad x = 0, \quad x = 2$

14. $y^2 = 4x$ and $y = 4x - 2$

15. $y = 2 - x^2$ and $y = x^2 - 6$

16. The function $v = 3t^2 - 15t + 18$ represents the velocity v (ft/sec) of a moving body as a function of the time t (sec). (a) Find that portion of the time interval $0 \leq t \leq 3$ in which the velocity is positive. (b) Find that portion where v is negative. (c) Find the total distance traveled by the body from $t = 0$ to $t = 3$.

17. The area from 0 to x under a certain graph is given to be

$$A = (1 + 3x)^{1/2} - 1, \quad x \geq 0.$$

a) Find the *average* rate of change of A with respect to x as x increases from 1 to 8.

b) Find the *instantaneous* rate of change of A with respect to x at $x = 5$.

c) Find the ordinate (height) y of the graph as a function of x.

d) Find the average value of the ordinate (height) y, with respect to x, as x increases from 1 to 8.

18. A solid is generated by rotating, about the x-axis, the area bounded by the curve $y = f(x)$, the x-axis, and the lines $x = a$, $x = b$. Its volume, for all $b > a$, is $b^2 - ab$. Find $f(x)$.

19. Find the volume generated by rotating the area bounded by the given curves and lines about the line indicated:

a) $y = x^2, \quad y = 0, \quad x = 3;$ about the x-axis.

b) $y = x^2, \quad y = 0, \quad x = 3;$ about the line $x = -3$.

c) $y = x^2, \quad y = 0, \quad x = 3;$ about the y-axis, first integrating with respect to x and then integrating with respect to y.

d) $x = 4y - y^2, \quad x = 0;$ about the y-axis.

e) $x = 4y - y^2, \quad x = 0;$ about the x-axis.

20. A solid is generated by rotating the curve $y = f(x)$, $0 \leq x \leq a$, about the x-axis. Its volume for all a is $a^2 + a$; find $f(x)$.

21. The area bounded by the curve $y^2 = 4x$ and the straight line $y = x$ is rotated about the x-axis. Find the volume generated.

22. Sketch the area bounded by the curve $y^2 = 4ax$, the line $x = a$, and the x-axis. Find the respective volumes generated by rotating this area in the following ways: (a) about the x-axis, (b) about the line $x = a$, (c) about the y-axis.

23. The area bounded by the curve $y = x/\sqrt{x^3 + 8}$, the x-axis, and the line $x = 2$ is rotated about the y-axis, generating a certain volume. Set up the integral that should be used to evaluate the volume and then evaluate the integral.

24. Find the volume of the solid generated by rotating the larger area bounded by $y^2 = x - 1$, $x = 3$, and $y = 1$ about the y-axis.

25. The area bounded by the curve $y^2 = 4ax$ and the line $x = a$ is rotated about the line $x = 2a$. Find the volume generated.

26. A twisted solid is generated as follows: We are given a fixed line L in space, and a square of side s in a plane perpendicular to L. One vertex of the square is on L. As this vertex moves a distance h along L, the square turns through a full revolution, with L as the axis. Find the volume generated by this motion. What would the volume be if the square had turned through two full revolutions in moving the same distance along L?

27. Two circles have a common diameter and lie in perpendicular planes. A square moves in such a way that its plane is perpendicular to this diameter and its diagonals are chords of the circles. Find the volume generated.

28. Find the volume generated by rotating about the x-axis the area bounded by the x-axis and one arch of the curve $y = \sin 2x$.

29. A round hole of radius $\sqrt{3}$ ft is bored through the center of a solid sphere of radius 2 ft. Find the volume cut out.

30. The cross section of a certain solid in any plane perpendicular to the x-axis is a circle having diameter AB with A on the curve $y^2 = 4x$ and B on the curve $x^2 = 4y$. Find the volume of the solid lying between the points of intersection of the curves.

31. The base of a solid is the area bounded by $y^2 = 4ax$ and $x = a$. Each cross section perpendicular to the x-axis is an equilateral triangle. Find the volume of the solid.

32. Find the length of the curve $y = (\frac{2}{3})x^{3/2} - (\frac{1}{2})x^{1/2}$ from $x = 0$ to $x = 4$.

33. Find the surface area generated when the curve of Problem 32 is rotated about the y-axis.

34. Find the length of the curve $x = (\frac{3}{5})y^{5/3} - (\frac{3}{4})y^{1/3}$ from $y = 0$ to $y = 1$.

35. Find the surface area generated when the curve of Problem 34 is rotated about the line $y = -1$.

36. Find the average value of y with respect to x for that part of the curve $y = \sqrt{ax}$ between $x = a$ and $x = 3a$.

37. Find the average value of y^2 with respect to x for the curve $ay = b\sqrt{a^2 - x^2}$ between $x = 0$ and $x = a$. Also find the average value of y with respect to x^2 for $0 \leq x \leq a$.

38. Consider the curve $y = f(x)$, $x \geq 0$ such that $f(0) = a$. Let $s(x)$ denote the arc length along the curve from $(0, a)$ to $(x, f(x))$. Find $f(x)$ if (a) $s(x) = Ax$. (What are the permissible values of A?) (b) Is it possible for $s(x)$ to equal x^n, $n > 1$? Give a reason for your answer.

39. A point moves in a straight line during the time from $t = 0$ to $t = 3$ according to the law $s = 120t - 16t^2$. (a) Find the average value of the velocity, with respect to time, for these three seconds. [Compare with the "average velocity," Article 1–9, Eq. (6).] (b) Find the average value of the velocity with respect to the distance s during the three seconds.

40. Sketch a smooth curve through the points

$$A(1, 3),\quad B(3, 5),\quad C(5, 6),\quad D(7, 6),\quad E(9, 7),\quad F(11, 10).$$

The area bounded by this curve, the x-axis, and the lines $x = 1$, $x = 11$, is rotated about the x-axis to generate a solid. Use the trapezoidal rule to approximate the volume generated. Also determine approximately the average value of the circular cross-sectional area (with respect to x.)

41. Determine the center of mass of a thin homogeneous plate covering the area enclosed by the curves $y^2 = 8x$ and $y = x^2$.

42. Find the center of mass of a homogeneous plate covering the area in the first quadrant bounded by the curve $4y = x^2$, the y-axis, and the line $y = 4$.

43. Find the center of gravity of the area bounded by the curve $y = 4x - x^2$ and the line $2x - y = 0$.

44. Find the center of mass of a thin homogeneous plate covering the portion of the xy-plane, in the first quadrant, bounded by the curve $y = x^2$, the x-axis, and the line $x = 1$.

45. Consider a thin metal plate of area A and constant density and thickness. Show that, if its first moment about the y-axis is M, its moment about the line $x = b$ is $M - bA$. Indicate why this result actually shows that the center of gravity is a physical property of the body, independent of the coordinate system used for finding its location.

46. Find the center of mass of a thin plate covering the region bounded by the curve $y^2 = 4ax$ and the line $x = a$, a = positive constant, if the density at (x, y) is directly proportional to (a) x, (b) $|y|$.

47. Find the centroid of the area, in the first quadrant, bounded by two concentric circles and the coordinate axes, if the circles have radii a and b, $b > a > 0$, and their centers are at the origin. Also find the limits of the coordinates of the centroid as a approaches b, and discuss the meaning of the result.

48. (a) Find the centroid of the arc of the curve $x = a \cos^3 \phi$, $y = a \sin^3 \phi$ that is in the first quadrant. (b) Find the centroid of the surface generated by rotating the arc of part (a) about the y-axis.

49. A triangular corner is cut from a square 1 ft on a side. The area of the cutoff triangle is 36 in^2. If the centroid of the remaining area is 7 in. from one side of the original square, how far is it from the remaining sides?

50. A triangular plate ABC is submerged in water with its plane vertical. The side AB, 4 ft long, is 6 ft below the surface of the water, while the vertex C is 2 ft below the surface. Find the force of liquid pressure on one face of the plate.

51. A dam is in the form of a trapezoid, with its two horizontal sides 200 and 100 ft, respectively, the longer side being at the top; the height is 20 ft. What is the force of pressure on the dam when the water is level with the top of the dam?

52. The center of pressure on a submerged plane area is defined to be the point at which the total force could be applied without changing its total moment about any axis in the plane. Find the depth to the center of pressure (a) on a vertical rectangle of height h and width b if its upper edge is in the surface of the water, (b) on a vertical triangle of height h and base b if the vertex opposite b is a ft, and the base b is $(a + h)$ ft below the surface of the water.

53. A container is filled with two nonmixing liquids with respective densities d_1 and d_2, $d_1 < d_2$. Find the force on one face of a square $ABCD$, $6\sqrt{2}$ feet on a side, immersed in the liquids with the diagonal AC normal to the free surface, if the highest point A of the square is 2 ft below the free surface and BD lies on the surface separating the two liquids.

54. A particle of mass M starts from rest at time $t = 0$ and is moved with constant acceleration a from $x = 0$ to $x = h$ against a variable force $F(t) = t^2$. Find the work done.

55. When a particle of mass M is at $(x, 0)$, it is attracted toward the origin with a force whose magnitude is k/x^2. If the particle starts from rest at $x = b$ and is acted upon by no other forces, find the work done on it by the time it reaches $x = a$, $0 < a < b$.

56. Below the surface of the earth the force of its gravitational attraction is directly proportional to the distance from its center. Find the work done in lifting an object, whose weight at the surface is w lb, from a distance r ft below the earth's surface to the surface.

57. A storage tank is a right circular cylinder 20 ft long and 8 ft in diameter with its axis horizontal. If the tank is half full of oil weighing w lb/ft^3, find the work done in emptying it through a pipe that runs from the bottom of the tank to an outlet that is 6 ft above the top of the tank.

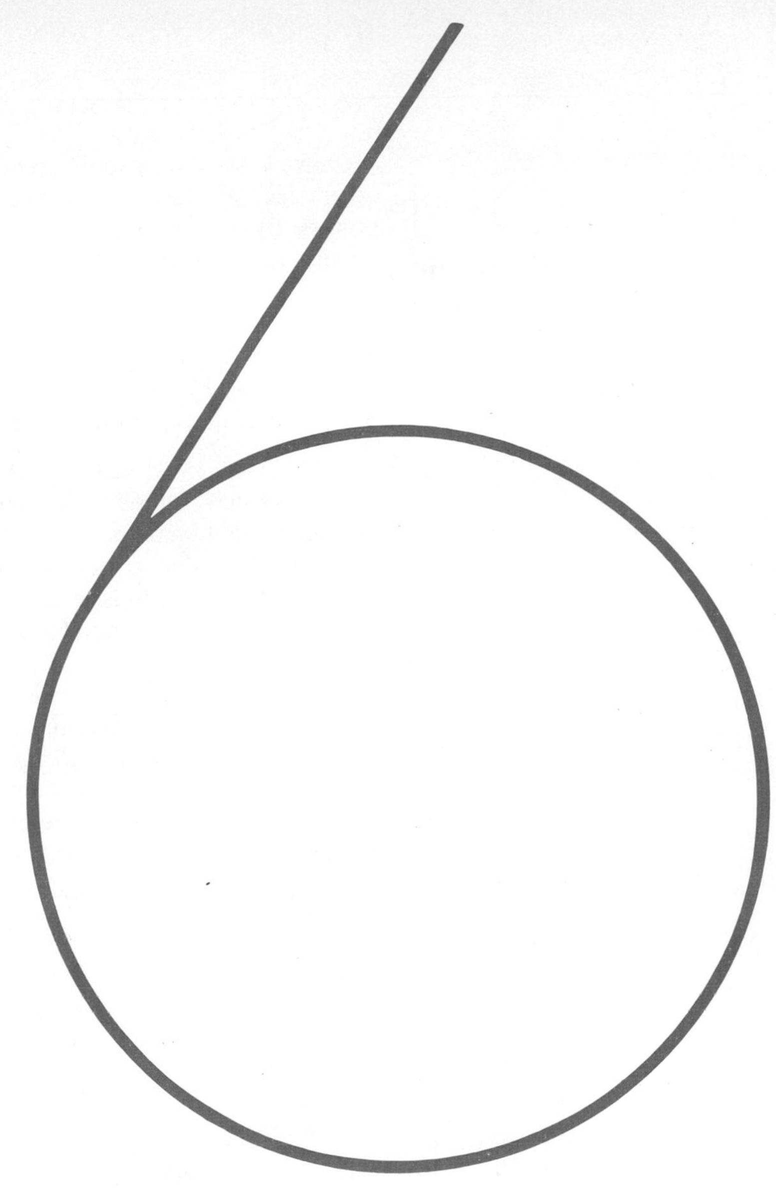

6 TRANSCENDENTAL FUNCTIONS

THE TRIGONOMETRIC FUNCTIONS

We have learned how to differentiate and integrate polynomials and certain other algebraic functions including some rational functions and fractional powers. By definition, y is an *algebraic* function of x if it is a function that satisfies an irreducible algebraic equation of the form

$$P_0(x)y^n + P_1(x)y^{n-1} + \cdots + P_{n-1}(x)y + P_n(x) = 0,$$

with n a positive integer and with coefficients $P_0(x)$, $P_1(x)$, ... that are polynomials in x. For instance, $y = \sqrt{x}$, $x > 0$, defines an algebraic function whose elements (x, y) satisfy the irreducible equation

$$y^2 - x = 0.$$

Sums, products, quotients, powers, and roots of algebraic functions are in turn algebraic functions.

A function that is not algebraic is called *transcendental.* The class of transcendental functions includes the trigonometric, logarithmic, exponential, and inverse trigonometric functions, and many more that are less familiar.

We have learned how to differentiate and integrate two transcendental functions—the sine and cosine. In this chapter we shall add to this list the derivatives of the remaining trigonometric functions, their inverse functions, and the logarithmic and exponential functions.

At this stage it is well to recall the following formulas for derivatives and differentials:

	Derivatives		**Differentials**
I.	$\dfrac{dc}{dx} = 0.$	I′.	$dc = 0.$
II.	$\dfrac{d(cu)}{dx} = c\dfrac{du}{dx}.$	II′.	$d(cu) = c\,du.$
III.	$\dfrac{d(u+v)}{dx} = \dfrac{du}{dx} + \dfrac{dv}{dx}.$	III′.	$d(u+v) = du + dv.$
IV.	$\dfrac{d(uv)}{dx} = u\dfrac{dv}{dx} + v\dfrac{du}{dx}.$	IV′.	$d(uv) = u\,dv + v\,du.$
V.	$\dfrac{d\left(\dfrac{u}{v}\right)}{dx} = \dfrac{v\dfrac{du}{dx} - u\dfrac{dv}{dx}}{v^2}.$	V′.	$d\left(\dfrac{u}{v}\right) = \dfrac{v\,du - u\,dv}{v^2}.$
VI.	$\dfrac{d(u^n)}{dx} = nu^{n-1}\dfrac{du}{dx}.$	VI′.	$d(u^n) = nu^{n-1}\,du.$
VII.	$\dfrac{d(\sin u)}{dx} = \cos u\dfrac{du}{dx}.$	VII′.	$d(\sin u) = \cos u\,du.$
VIII.	$\dfrac{d(\cos u)}{dx} = -\sin u\dfrac{du}{dx}.$	VIII′.	$d(\cos u) = -\sin u\,du.$

The first six of these formulas by themselves enable us to differentiate the *algebraic* functions, which include polynomials, ratios of polynomials, and roots or powers of either of these types. VII, VII′, VIII, and VIII′ are discussed in Article 2–10.

When we combine formulas V, VII, and VIII and apply them to the trigonometric identities

$$\tan u = \frac{\sin u}{\cos u}, \qquad \cot u = \frac{\cos u}{\sin u},$$
$$\sec u = \frac{1}{\cos u}, \qquad \csc u = \frac{1}{\sin u}, \tag{1}$$

it is a simple matter to complete the list of formulas for differentiating the trigonometric functions and, doing so, we obtain:

IX. $\dfrac{d(\tan u)}{dx} = \sec^2 u \dfrac{du}{dx}.$ IX′. $d(\tan u) = \sec^2 u\, du.$

X. $\dfrac{d(\cot u)}{dx} = -\csc^2 u \dfrac{du}{dx}.$ X′. $d(\cot u) = -\csc^2 u\, du.$

XI. $\dfrac{d(\sec u)}{dx} = \sec u \tan u \dfrac{du}{dx}.$ XI′. $d(\sec u) = \sec u \tan u\, du.$

XII. $\dfrac{d(\csc u)}{dx} = -\csc u \cot u \dfrac{du}{dx}.$ XII′. $d(\csc u) = -\csc u \cot u\, du.$

The proofs of these formulas should be carried through by the reader.

These are the forms that are customarily used, though there are alternative forms such as

$$\frac{d(\sec u)}{dx} = \frac{\sin u}{\cos^2 u} \frac{du}{dx},$$

which are obtained from the expressions given by using some trigonometric identities. One reason for preferring the numbered forms above is that they are quite easy to remember if we note that *the derivative of every cofunction* (i.e., cos, cot, csc) *can be obtained from the derivative of the corresponding function* (i.e., sin, tan, sec) by

a) *introducing a minus sign*, and
b) *replacing each function by its cofunction.*

Apply this, for example, to the formula

$$\frac{d(\sec u)}{dx} = \sec u \tan u \frac{du}{dx}.$$

Replace sec u and tan u by their cofunctions on *both sides* of the equation and put in a *minus* sign; the result is

$$\frac{d(\csc u)}{dx} = -\csc u \cot u \frac{du}{dx}.$$

Thus it is really only necessary to "memorize" the two new formulas

$$\frac{d(\tan u)}{dx} = \sec^2 u \frac{du}{dx},$$

$$\frac{d(\sec u)}{dx} = \sec u \tan u \frac{du}{dx},$$

and the rule above produces the other two.

The formulas IX′–XII′ for differentials immediately produce the four new integration formulas:

$$\int \sec^2 u\, du = \tan u + C, \qquad \int \sec u \tan u\, du = \sec u + C,$$
$$\int \csc^2 u\, du = -\cot u + C, \qquad \int \csc u \cot u\, du = -\csc u + C. \tag{2}$$

EXAMPLE 1. Find dy/dx if $y = \tan^2 3x$.

Solution. First we apply the power formula VI,

$$\frac{dy}{dx} = 2 \tan 3x \frac{d(\tan 3x)}{dx}$$

and then IX,

$$\frac{d(\tan 3x)}{dx} = \sec^2 3x \frac{d(3x)}{dx},$$

and then II,

$$\frac{d(3x)}{dx} = 3\frac{dx}{dx} = 3.$$

When these are combined, we get

$$\frac{dy}{dx} = 6 \tan 3x \sec^2 3x.$$

EXAMPLE 2. Integrate $\int \tan^2 3x\, dx$.

Solution. At first sight, this seems to be impossible with the formulas we have for integration. But the trigonometric identity

$$\sin^2 3x + \cos^2 3x = 1$$

becomes

$$\tan^2 3x + 1 = \sec^2 3x$$

when we divide both sides by $\cos^2 3x$. Hence,

$$\tan^2 3x = \sec^2 3x - 1$$

and

$$\int \tan^2 3x\, dx = \int (\sec^2 3x - 1)\, dx = \int \sec^2 3x\, dx - \int 1\, dx$$

$$= \tfrac{1}{3} \int \sec^2 3x\, d(3x) - \int 1\, dx = \tfrac{1}{3} \tan 3x - x + C.$$

EXAMPLE 3 (*Optimal branching angle for blood vessels*). When a smaller artery branches off from a larger one, it is reasonable to suppose that the angle formed by the central axes of the arteries is such as to be "best" from some energy-conserving viewpoint. We assume, for instance, that energy loss due to friction is minimized along the section AOB shown in Fig. 6–1. In this diagram, B is a given point to be reached by the smaller artery, A is a point in the larger artery upstream from B, and O is the point where branching occurs. A law due to Poiseuille states that the loss of energy due to friction in nonturbulent flow is proportional to the length of the path and inversely proportional to the fourth power of the radius. Thus, the loss along AO is $(kd_1)/R^4$ and along OB is $(kd_2)/r^4$, where k is a constant, d_1 is the length of AO, d_2 is the length of OB, R is the radius of the larger artery, and r is the radius of the smaller branch. The angle θ is to be such as to minimize the sum of these two losses:

$$L = k\frac{d_1}{R^4} + k\frac{d_2}{r^4}.$$

In our model, we assume that $AC = a$ and $BC = b$ are fixed. Thus we have the relations

$$d_1 + d_2 \cos\theta = a, \qquad d_2 \sin\theta = b,$$

so that

$$d_2 = b \csc\theta \qquad \text{and} \qquad d_1 = a - d_2 \cos\theta = a - b \cot\theta.$$

We can express the total loss L as a function of θ:

$$L = k\left(\frac{a - b\cot\theta}{R^4} + \frac{b\csc\theta}{r^4}\right). \tag{3}$$

When we differentiate Eq. (3) with respect to θ we get

$$\frac{dL}{d\theta} = k\left(\frac{b\csc^2\theta}{R^4} - \frac{b\csc\theta\cot\theta}{r^4}\right) = \frac{kb\csc^2\theta}{r^4}\left(\frac{r^4}{R^4} - \cos\theta\right).$$

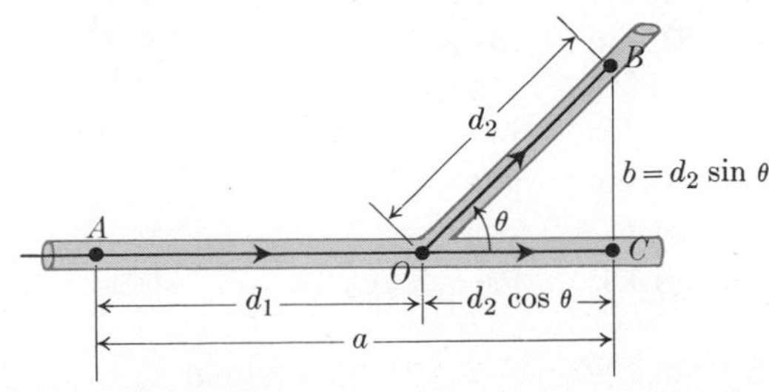

6–1 The smaller artery OB branches away from the larger artery AOC at an angle θ that minimizes the friction loss along AO and OB. The optimum angle is found to be $\theta_c = \cos^{-1}(r^4/R^4)$, where r is the radius of the smaller artery and R is the radius of the larger.

The critical value of θ, for which $dL/d\theta$ is zero, is

$$\theta_c = \cos^{-1}\left(\frac{r^4}{R^4}\right). \tag{4}$$

A slightly smaller value of θ makes $\cos\theta$ larger and $dL/d\theta$ negative, while a slightly larger θ makes $\cos\theta$ smaller and $dL/d\theta$ positive. Therefore, L has a minimum value at $\theta = \theta_c$.

PROBLEMS

Sketch the graphs of the equations in Problems 1–10.

1. $y = \sin x$ **2.** $y = \cos x$

3. $y = \tan x$ **4.** $y = \cot x$

5. $y = \sec x$ **6.** $y = \csc x$

7. $y = 3 \sin 2x$ **8.** $y = 4 \cos (x/3)$

9. $y = \sin^2 x$ **10.** $y = \frac{1}{2} + \frac{1}{2}\cos 2x$

11. a) Derive formula IX. **b)** Derive formula XI.

12. a) Derive formula X. **b)** Derive formula XII.

Find dy/dx in each of the following problems (13 through 33):

13. $y = \tan (3x^2)$ **14.** $y = \tan^2 (\cos x)$

15. $y = \cot (3x + 5)$ **16.** $y = \sqrt{\cot x}$

17. $y = \sec^2 x - \tan^2 x$ **18.** $y = \frac{1}{3}\sec^3 x$

19. $y = 3x + \tan 3x$ **20.** $y = 3 \tan 2x$

21. $y = x - \tan x$ **22.** $y = \sec^4 x - \tan^4 x$

23. $y = (\csc x + \cot x)^2$ **24.** $y = 2 \sin^2 3x$

25. $y = \frac{1}{2}x - \frac{1}{4}\sin 2x$ **26.** $y = \frac{1}{2}x + \frac{1}{4}\sin 2x$

27. $y = \sin^3 \frac{x}{3} - 3 \sin \frac{x}{3}$ **28.** $y = 3\cos^2 \frac{x}{2}$

29. $y = 2 \sin \frac{1}{2}x - x \cos \frac{1}{2}x$ **30.** $x^2 = \sin y + \sin 2y$

31. $y = \sin^3 x - \sin 3x$ **32.** $y = \frac{1}{3}\sin^3 5x - \sin 5x$

33. $x + \tan (xy) = 0$

34. Find the maximum height of the curve $y = 6 \cos x - 8 \sin x$ above the x-axis.

35. Find the maximum and minimum values of the function $y = 2 \sin x + \cos 2x$ for $0 \le x \le \pi/2$.

36. (*Calculator or tables*) If the ratio of the radii of the arteries in Example 3 is $r/R = 5/6$, estimate to the nearest degree the optimal branching angle given by Eq. (4).

37. Show that the curve $y = x \sin x$ is tangent to the line $y = x$ whenever $\sin x = 1$, and is tangent to the line $y = -x$ whenever $\sin x = -1$.

38. A revolving light 3 miles from a straight shoreline makes 8 revolutions per minute. Find the velocity of the beam of light along the shore at the instant when it makes an angle of 45° with the shoreline.

39. A rope with a ring in one end is looped over two pegs in a horizontal line. The free end, after being passed through the ring, has a weight suspended from it, so that the rope hangs taut. If the rope slips freely over the pegs and through the ring, the weight will descend as far as possible. Assume that the length of the rope is at least four times as great as the distance between the pegs, and that the configuration of the rope is symmetric with respect to the line of the vertical part of the rope. (The symmetry assumption can be justified on the grounds that the rope and weight will take a rest position that minimizes the potential energy of the system. See Problem 25, Article 8–6.) Find the angle formed at the bottom of the loop.

Evaluate the following integrals:

40. $\int \sin 3t \, dt$ **41.** $\int \sec^2 2\theta \, d\theta$

42. $\int \tan^3 x \sec^2 x \, dx$ **43.** $\int \sec^3 x \tan x \, dx$

44. $\int \sec \frac{x}{2} \tan \frac{x}{2} \, dx$ **45.** $\int \cos^2 y \, dy$

46. $\int \frac{d\theta}{\cos^2 \theta}$ **47.** $\int \frac{d\theta}{\sin^2 (\theta/3)}$

48. Find the area bounded by the curve $y = \tan x \sec^2 x$, the x-axis, and the line $x = \pi/3$.

49. The area bounded above by the curve $y = \tan x$, below by the x-axis, and on the right by the line $x = \pi/4$ is revolved about the x-axis. Find the volume generated.

Evaluate the following limits, by showing that l'Hôpital's rule may be applied, and then applying it:

50. $\lim_{h \to 0} \frac{\tan h}{3h}$ **51.** $\lim_{x \to 0} \frac{\sec x - 1}{x^2}$

52. $\lim_{y \to 0} 2y \cot y$ **53.** $\lim_{t \to \pi} \frac{t - \pi}{2 \tan 3t}$

54. Let $f(x) = (\tan x)/x$ for $0 < |x| < \pi/2$. Show that:

a) $\lim_{x \to 0} f(x) = 1$

b) $f(-x) = f(x)$

c) $f'(x) = [(\sec^2 x)/x][1 - (\sin 2x)/2x]$ and therefore $f'(x)$ is positive for $0 < x < \pi/2$.

d) $f(x)$ increases without bound as $x \to \pi/2^-$.

Use the information above to sketch the graph of $y = f(x)$.

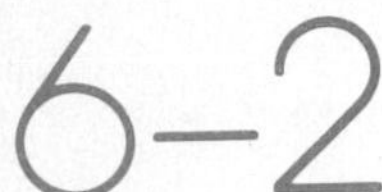

THE INVERSE TRIGONOMETRIC FUNCTIONS

There are two reasons for studying the inverses of the trigonometric functions: first, because the inverse of any function is worth some study in its own right, and second, because the derivatives of the inverse trigonometric functions lead to useful integration formulas. We recall that the inverse of the function $y=f(x)$ comes from the equation $x=f(y)$ that we get by interchanging the letters x and y in the original function. So we begin our study of the inverse of the sine function by investigating the equation

$$x = \sin y. \tag{1}$$

In this equation, infinitely many values of y correspond to each x in the range $-1 \le x \le 1$.

For example, if $x = \frac{1}{2}$ then we ask for all angles y such that $\sin y = \frac{1}{2}$. The two angles 30° and 150° in the first and second quadrants occur to us immediately. But any whole multiple of 360° may be either added to or subtracted from these and the sine of the resulting angle will still be $\frac{1}{2}$. Expressing these facts in mathematical language and using radian measure for the angles, we have $\sin y = \frac{1}{2}$ if

$$y = \begin{cases} \dfrac{\pi}{6} + 2n\pi \\ \dfrac{5\pi}{6} + 2n\pi \end{cases} \qquad n = 0, \pm 1, \pm 2, \ldots$$

Similarly, we find that $\sin y = -\frac{1}{2}$ if

$$y = \begin{cases} -\dfrac{\pi}{6} + 2n\pi \\ -\dfrac{5\pi}{6} + 2n\pi \end{cases} \qquad n = 0, \pm 1, \pm 2, \ldots$$

Now it is desirable, for some of our later applications, to adopt a rule for picking a *principal value* of y. We shall require that the rule (a) produce one and only one value of y for each x, $-1 \le x \le 1$, such that $\sin y = x$; and (b) give two "nearly equal" values of y for two "nearly equal" values of x.

To state requirement (b) more specifically, we require that if x_1 and x_2 are two values of x both between -1 and $+1$, and y_1 and y_2 are the corresponding values of y such that $\sin y = x$, then $y_2 - y_1$ should tend to zero if $x_2 - x_1$ does. The portion of the curve AOB shown heavily marked in Fig. 6–2 fulfills these requirements. For any x between -1 and $+1$ there is one and only one corresponding point (x, y) on this portion of the curve, and the y-value satisfies $\sin y = x$. Furthermore, this is a continuous curve, so that if (x_1, y_1) and (x_2, y_2) are two points on it and $(x_2 - x_1) \to 0$, then also $(y_2 - y_1) \to 0$.

To be sure that the point (x, y) stays on the portion AOB of Fig. 6–2, we need only restrict y:

$$\sin y = x, \qquad -\frac{\pi}{2} \le y \le \frac{\pi}{2}. \tag{2}$$

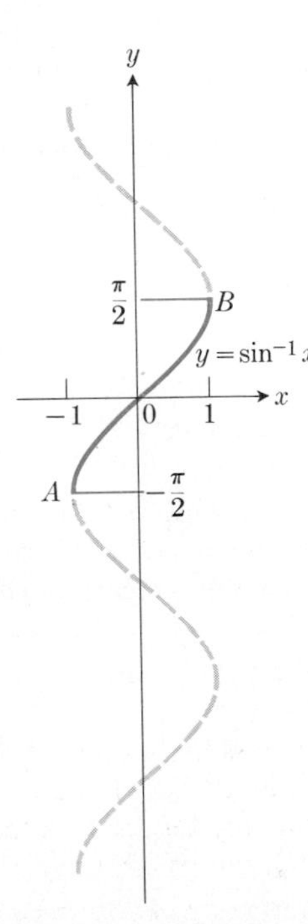

6–2 $y = \sin^{-1} x$.

The restrictions placed on y give a continuous function

$$y = \sin^{-1} x, \qquad -\frac{\pi}{2} \leq y \leq \frac{\pi}{2}, \tag{3}$$

called the "inverse sine of x," which is defined on the domain $-1 \leq x \leq 1$ and has values on the range $-\pi/2 \leq y \leq +\pi/2$. Note that the minus one in Eq. (3), although written as an exponent, does *not* mean

$$(\sin x)^{-1} = \frac{1}{\sin x} = \csc x.$$

Actually, Eq. (3) merely gives a name to the new function that is defined implicitly by Eq. (2). The symbol $f^{-1}(x)$ is often used to denote the function y defined implicitly by $f(y) = x$, that is,

$$y = f^{-1}(x).$$

The notation arcsin x is also used to represent the function that we have denoted by $\sin^{-1} x$, but the latter notation is now more commonly used. Thus,

$$\sin^{-1}\left(\frac{1}{2}\right) = \frac{\pi}{6}, \qquad \sin^{-1}\left(-\frac{1}{2}\right) = -\frac{\pi}{6}.$$

In terms of angles referred to standard position in the various quadrants, Eq. (2) and the restriction $-\pi/2 \leq y \leq \pi/2$ mean that the answer to the question: "What is the angle y whose sine is x?" is always an angle in the *first* or *fourth* quadrant, but if it is in the *fourth* quadrant, it is to be expressed as the *negative* of an angle between 0 and $\pi/2$ and not as a positive angle $\geq 3\pi/2$, since the latter would violate the restriction in (2).

At the risk of appearing to labor a point which is already clear, we also note that the inverse sine is an *odd* function of x. This means that

$$\sin^{-1}(-x) = -\sin^{-1}(x). \tag{4}$$

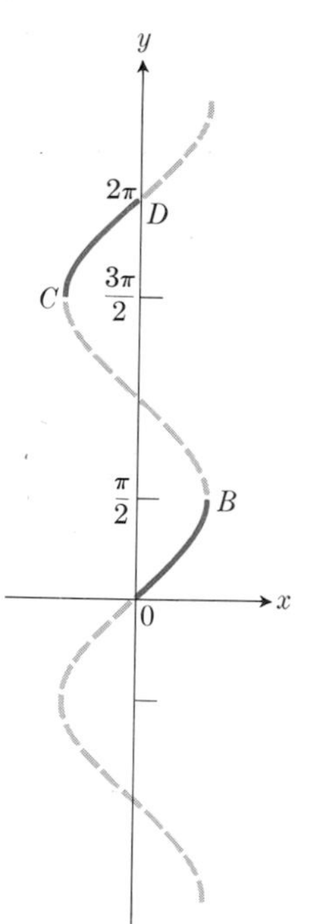

6–3 If $y = \sin^{-1} x$ were the function graphed here, it would not be continuous at $x = 0$.

Keeping this fact firmly in mind will prevent us from using values of y corresponding to points on the discontinuous curve composed of the portions OB and CD on the curve in Fig. 6–3. The objection to using these is that for a small positive value of x, say $x_1 = +0.01$, the point is near O and $y_1 \approx 0.01$; while for a small negative value of x, say $x_2 = -0.01$, the point is near D and $y_2 \approx 2\pi - 0.01$. The difference $y_2 - y_1$ is nearly $2\pi = 6.28+$, whereas the difference $x_1 - x_2$ is, in this case, only 0.02. This difficulty is not encountered if we restrict the value of y as in (3), which confines us to the *continuous* curve AOB of Fig. 6–2.

To each of the other trigonometric functions there also corresponds an *inverse* trigonometric function. In each case, we restrict the angle in such a way that the function is *single-valued.*

The reasoning that led us to adopt the particular range

$$-\frac{\pi}{2} \leq y \leq \frac{\pi}{2}$$

for the principal value of $y = \sin^{-1} x$ prompts us to adopt a similar range for the principal value of y satisfying the equation $x = \tan y$ (see Fig. 6–4). Thus we write

$$y = \tan^{-1} x, \qquad -\frac{\pi}{2} < y < \frac{\pi}{2} \tag{5a}$$

to mean the same as

$$\tan y = x, \qquad -\frac{\pi}{2} < y < \frac{\pi}{2}. \tag{5b}$$

The inverse tangent function, (5a), is defined on the *domain* $-\infty < x < +\infty$, that is, for all real x. Its *range* is $-\pi/2 < y < +\pi/2$. The values $y = \pm\pi/2$ are to be excluded, since the tangent becomes infinite as the angle approaches $\pm\pi/2$.

When we come to the inverse cosine function, we simply *define* it by the equation

$$\cos^{-1} x = \frac{\pi}{2} - \sin^{-1} x. \tag{6}$$

Sincc

$$-\frac{\pi}{2} \le \sin^{-1} x \le \frac{\pi}{2},$$

the range of principal values for (6) is

$$0 \le \cos^{-1} x \le \pi. \tag{7}$$

The *domain* of the inverse cosine function is $-1 \le x \le 1$. Its *range* is $0 \le y \le \pi$. The principal value is thus represented by the heavily marked portion of the curve

$$x = \cos y$$

shown in Fig. 6–5.

The reason for defining $\cos^{-1} x$ by Eq. (6) is as follows. In the right triangle in Fig. 6–6, the acute angles α and β are complementary, that is

$$\alpha + \beta = \frac{\pi}{2}.$$

But we also have

$$\sin \alpha = x = \cos \beta,$$

so that

$$\alpha = \sin^{-1} x, \qquad \beta = \cos^{-1} x,$$

and the relation $\alpha + \beta = \pi/2$ is the same as $\beta = \pi/2 - \alpha$; that is,

$$\cos^{-1} x = \frac{\pi}{2} - \sin^{-1} x.$$

Thus Eq. (6) expresses the fact that the angle whose cosine is x is the complement of the angle whose sine is x.

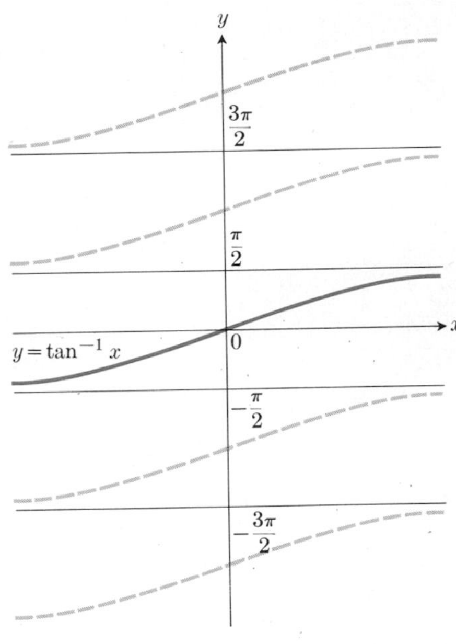

6–4 The branch chosen for $y = \tan^{-1} x$ is the one through the origin.

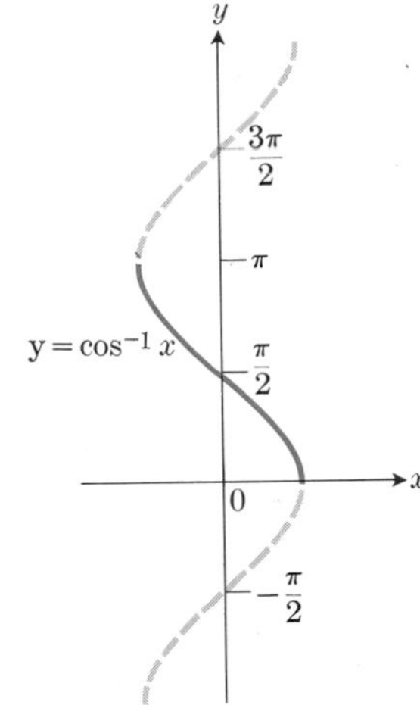

6–5 $y = \cos^{-1} x$.

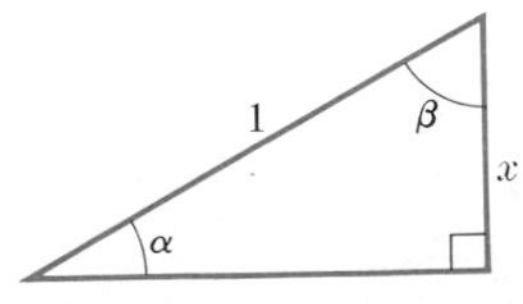

6–6 $\alpha + \beta = \pi/2$.

For exactly analogous reasons, we also define the inverse cotangent to be

$$\cot^{-1} x = \frac{\pi}{2} - \tan^{-1} x, \tag{8}$$

and we thus restrict the principal value to

$$0 < \cot^{-1} x < \pi. \tag{9}$$

The inverse secant and inverse cosecant functions will be single-valued functions of x on the domain $|x| \geq 1$ if we adopt the definitions

$$\sec^{-1} x = \cos^{-1}\left(\frac{1}{x}\right), \tag{10a}$$

$$\csc^{-1} x = \sin^{-1}\left(\frac{1}{x}\right), \tag{10b}$$

with their principal values confined to the ranges

$$0 \leq \sec^{-1} x \leq \pi, \tag{11a}$$

$$-\frac{\pi}{2} \leq \csc^{-1} x \leq \frac{\pi}{2}. \tag{11b}$$

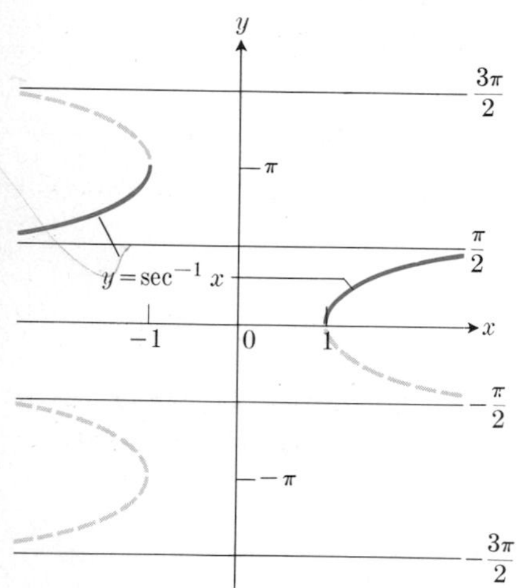

6–7 $y = \sec^{-1} x$ is defined for $|x| \geq 1$.

The reason for adopting the definitions above is the following. If $\sec y = x$, then $\cos y = 1/x$, and we simply ask that the principal values of y be the same in these two cases, that is

$$y = \sec^{-1} x = \cos^{-1}\left(\frac{1}{x}\right).$$

It should be noted, however, that some writers choose the principal value of the inverse secant of x to lie between 0 and $\pi/2$ when x is positive, and between $-\pi$ and $-\pi/2$ (hence, as a negative angle in the third quadrant) when x is negative. This latter method has the advantage of simplifying the formula for the derivative of $\sec^{-1} x$, but has the disadvantage of failing to satisfy the relationship expressed in Eq. (10a) when x is negative. Either method leads to a function that is discontinuous, as is inherent in the nature of the secant function itself, since to pass from a point where the secant is negative to a point where the secant is positive requires crossing one of the discontinuities of the curve (Fig. 6–7).

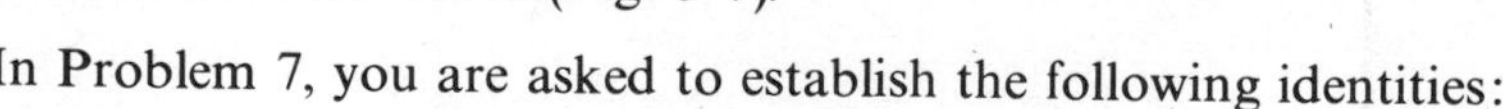

In Problem 7, you are asked to establish the following identities:

$$\tan^{-1}(-x) = -\tan^{-1} x, \tag{12a}$$

$$\cos^{-1}(-x) = \pi - \cos^{-1} x, \tag{12b}$$

$$\sec^{-1}(-x) = \pi - \sec^{-1} x. \tag{12c}$$

These are easy to interpret graphically. We list them here for future reference.

PROBLEMS

1. Given that $\alpha = \sin^{-1} \frac{1}{2}$, find $\cos \alpha$, $\tan \alpha$, $\sec \alpha$, $\csc \alpha$.

2. Given that $\alpha = \cos^{-1}(-\frac{1}{2})$, find $\sin \alpha$, $\tan \alpha$, $\sec \alpha$, $\csc \alpha$.

3. Evaluate $\sin^{-1}(1) - \sin^{-1}(-1)$.

4. Evaluate $\tan^{-1}(1) - \tan^{-1}(-1)$.

5. Evaluate $\sec^{-1}(2) - \sec^{-1}(-2)$.

6. A picture a feet high is placed on a wall with its base b feet above the level of an observer's eye. If the observer stands x feet from the wall, show that the angle of vision α subtended by the picture is given by

$$\alpha = \cot^{-1} \frac{x}{a+b} - \cot^{-1} \frac{x}{b}.$$

7. Prove:

a) $\tan^{-1}(-x) = -\tan^{-1} x$
b) $\cos^{-1}(-x) = \pi - \cos^{-1} x$
c) $\sec^{-1}(-x) = \pi - \sec^{-1} x$

8. Simplify each of the following expressions:

a) $\sin(\sin^{-1} 0.735)$ **b)** $\cos(\sin^{-1} 0.8)$
c) $\sin(2 \sin^{-1} 0.8)$ **d)** $\tan^{-1}(\tan \pi/3)$
e) $\cos^{-1}(-\sin \pi/6)$ **f)** $\sec^{-1}(\sec(-30°))$

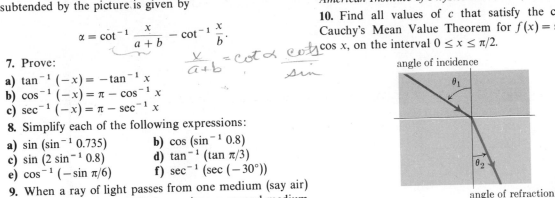

9. When a ray of light passes from one medium (say air) where it travels with a velocity c_1, into a second medium (for example, water) where it travels with velocity c_2, the angle of incidence θ_1 and angle of refraction θ_2 are related by Snell's law:

$$\frac{\sin \theta_1}{c_1} = \frac{\sin \theta_2}{c_2}$$

(Fig. 6–8). The quotient $c_1/c_2 = n_{12}$ is called the index of refraction of medium 2 with respect to medium 1. (a) Express θ_2 as a function of θ_1. (b) Find the largest value of θ_1 for which the expression for θ_2 in part (a) is defined. (For values of θ_1 larger than this, the incoming light will be reflected.) [*Remark.* Snell's law also applies in acoustics. See, for example, R. G. Lindsay and K. D. Kryter, "Acoustics," *American Institute of Physics Handbook*, 3rd Edition, 1972.]

10. Find all values of c that satisfy the conclusion of Cauchy's Mean Value Theorem for $f(x) = \sin x$, $g(x) = \cos x$, on the interval $0 \le x \le \pi/2$.

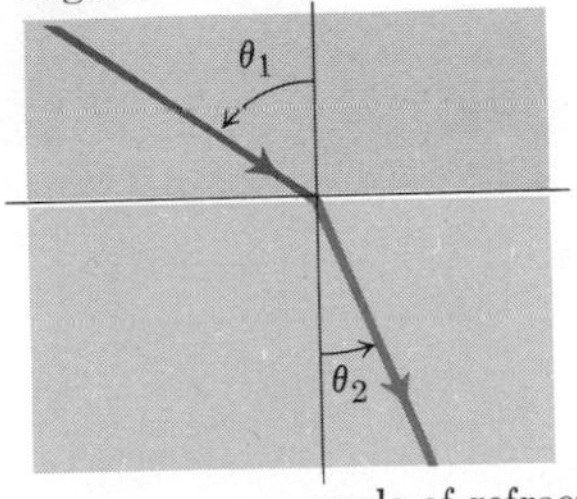

6–8 A ray refracted as it passes from one medium to another.

6–3 DERIVATIVES OF THE INVERSE TRIGONOMETRIC FUNCTIONS

The following formulas may now be derived.

XIII. $\dfrac{d(\sin^{-1} u)}{dx} = \dfrac{du/dx}{\sqrt{1-u^2}}$. XIII′. $d(\sin^{-1} u) = \dfrac{du}{\sqrt{1-u^2}}$.

XIV. $\dfrac{d(\cos^{-1} u)}{dx} = -\dfrac{du/dx}{\sqrt{1-u^2}}$. XIV′. $d(\cos^{-1} u) = -\dfrac{du}{\sqrt{1-u^2}}$.

XV. $\dfrac{d(\tan^{-1} u)}{dx} = \dfrac{du/dx}{1+u^2}$. XV′. $d(\tan^{-1} u) = \dfrac{du}{1+u^2}$.

XVI. $\dfrac{d(\cot^{-1} u)}{dx} = -\dfrac{du/dx}{1+u^2}$. XVI′. $d(\cot^{-1} u) = -\dfrac{du}{1+u^2}$.

XVII. $\dfrac{d(\sec^{-1} u)}{dx} = \dfrac{du/dx}{|u|\sqrt{u^2-1}}$. XVII′. $d(\sec^{-1} u) = \dfrac{du}{|u|\sqrt{u^2-1}}$.

XVIII. $\dfrac{d(\csc^{-1} u)}{dx} = \dfrac{-du/dx}{|u|\sqrt{u^2-1}}$. XVIII′. $d(\csc^{-1} u) = \dfrac{-du}{|u|\sqrt{u^2-1}}$.

To illustrate how these are derived, we shall prove formulas XIII and XVII. Let

$$y = \sin^{-1} u, \qquad -\frac{\pi}{2} \le y \le \frac{\pi}{2}.$$

Then

$$\sin y = u,$$

$$\cos y \frac{dy}{dx} = \frac{du}{dx}, \qquad \frac{dy}{dx} = \frac{1}{\cos y} \frac{du}{dx}.$$

To express the right side in terms of u, we use the fact that

$$\cos y = \pm\sqrt{1 - \sin^2 y} = \pm\sqrt{1 - u^2}.$$

Since $-\pi/2 \le y \le \pi/2$, $\cos y$ is not negative; hence

$$\cos y = +\sqrt{1 - u^2}$$

and

$$\frac{dy}{dx} = \frac{1}{\sqrt{1 - u^2}} \frac{du}{dx},$$

which establishes XIII.

Next, let

$$y = \sec^{-1} u, \qquad 0 \le y \le \pi.$$

Then

$$\sec y = u, \qquad \sec y \tan y \frac{dy}{dx} = \frac{du}{dx},$$

$$\frac{dy}{dx} = \frac{1}{\sec y \tan y} \frac{du}{dx}.$$

Substituting

$$\sec y = u, \qquad \tan y = \pm\sqrt{\sec^2 y - 1} = \pm\sqrt{u^2 - 1},$$

we have

$$\frac{dy}{dx} = \frac{1}{u(\pm\sqrt{u^2 - 1})} \frac{du}{dx}.$$

The ambiguous sign is determined by the sign of $\tan y$, and hence is

$$+ \quad \text{if } 0 < y < \frac{\pi}{2}, \qquad \text{that is, if } u \text{ is } +;$$

$$- \quad \text{if } \frac{\pi}{2} < y < \pi, \qquad \text{that is, if } u \text{ is } -.$$

That is,

$$\frac{dy}{dx} = \begin{cases} \dfrac{1}{u\sqrt{u^2-1}}\dfrac{du}{dx} & \text{if } u > 1, \\ \dfrac{1}{-u\sqrt{u^2-1}}\dfrac{du}{dx} & \text{if } u < -1, \end{cases}$$

and both of these are summarized in the single formula

$$\frac{dy}{dx} = \frac{1}{|u|\sqrt{u^2-1}}\frac{du}{dx}.$$

The formulas XIII to XVIII are used directly as given, but even more important are the integration formulas obtained immediately from the differential formulas XIII′ to XVIII′, namely,

$$\int \frac{du}{\sqrt{1-u^2}} = \sin^{-1} u + C, \qquad \int \frac{du}{1+u^2} = \tan^{-1} u + C,$$
$$\int \frac{du}{u\sqrt{u^2-1}} = \int \frac{d(-u)}{(-u)\sqrt{u^2-1}} = \sec^{-1} |u| + C. \tag{1}$$

Note that $\sec^{-1} u$ and $\sec^{-1} |u|$ are meaningless unless $|u| \geq 1$ (see Fig. 6–7).

REMARK. Something more should be said about the last formula in Eqs. (1). In the first place, if we are evaluating a *definite* integral of the form

$$\int_a^b \frac{dx}{x\sqrt{x^2-1}},$$

both a and b should be greater than 1 or both should be less than -1, for otherwise we would be attempting to integrate an expression that becomes infinite, or imaginary, or both, within the interval of integration. (Why?) On the other hand, if we are looking for all curves of the form $y = f(x)$ such that $f'(x) = 1/(x\sqrt{x^2-1})$, then our answer is

$$y = \begin{cases} \sec^{-1} x + C_1 & \text{if } x > 1, \\ \sec^{-1} (-x) + C_2 & \text{if } x < -1; \end{cases}$$

and the two constants C_1 and C_2 need not be the same.

We can also replace $\sec^{-1} (-x)$ by $\pi - \sec^{-1} x$ by Eq. (12c) of Article 6–2 and then let $C_2 + \pi = C'$, and write

$$y = \begin{cases} \sec^{-1} x + C & \text{if } x > 1, \\ -\sec^{-1} x + C' & \text{if } x < -1. \end{cases}$$

EXAMPLE 1. Evaluate:

a) $\displaystyle\int_0^1 \frac{dx}{1+x^2}$ and **b)** $\displaystyle\int_{2/\sqrt{3}}^{2/\sqrt{2}} \frac{dx}{x\sqrt{x^2-1}}.$

Solutions

a) $\tan^{-1} x\Big]_0^1 = \tan^{-1} 1 - \tan^{-1} 0 = \frac{\pi}{4} - 0 = \frac{\pi}{4}$.

b) $\sec^{-1} x\Big]_{2/\sqrt{3}}^{2/\sqrt{2}} = \cos^{-1}(\sqrt{2}/2) - \cos^{-1}(\sqrt{3}/2) = \frac{\pi}{4} - \frac{\pi}{6} = \frac{\pi}{12}$.

EXAMPLE 2. Find a curve whose slope at the point (x, y) is $1/(x\sqrt{x^2-1})$ and that passes through the points $(-2, -2)$ and $(\sqrt{2}, 0)$.

Solution. From the discussion above, we can write

$$y = \begin{cases} \sec^{-1} x + C & \text{if } x > 1, \quad \text{(2a)} \\ -\sec^{-1} x + C' & \text{if } x < -1. \quad \text{(2b)} \end{cases}$$

Using Eq. (2a) with $x = \sqrt{2}$ and $y = 0$, we have

$$0 = \sec^{-1}\sqrt{2} + C, \qquad C = -\sec^{-1}\sqrt{2} = -\frac{\pi}{4}.$$

To find the value of C' we use Eq. (2b) and the point $(-2, -2)$ to get

$$-2 = -\sec^{-1}(-2) + C',$$

$$C' = \sec^{-1}(-2) - 2 = \frac{2\pi}{3} - 2.$$

Therefore the curve is described by the equations

$$y = \begin{cases} \sec^{-1} x - \frac{\pi}{4} & \text{if } x > 1, \\ -\sec^{-1} x + \frac{2\pi}{3} - 2 & \text{if } x < -1. \end{cases}$$

The graph is shown in Fig. 6–9.

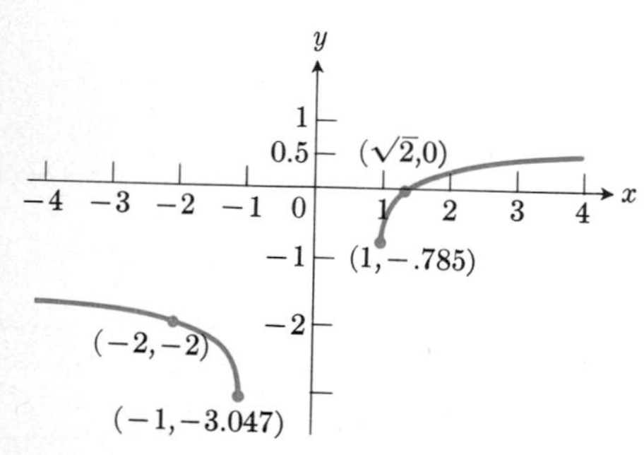

6–9 Graph of curve satisfying $dy/dx = 1/(x\sqrt{x^2-1})$ and passing through the points $(-2, -2)$ and $(\sqrt{2}, 0)$. The two branches have the same shape. Either branch can be moved up or down any number of units without changing the slope.

PROBLEMS

1. Derive formula XIV.
2. Derive formula XV.
3. Derive formula XVI.
4. Derive formula XVIII.

Find dy/dx in each of the following:

5. $y = \sin^{-1}\frac{x}{2}$
6. $y = \frac{1}{3}\tan^{-1}\frac{x}{3}$
7. $y = \sec^{-1} 5x$
8. $y = \cos^{-1} 2x$
9. $y = \cot^{-1}\frac{2}{x} + \tan^{-1}\frac{x}{2}$
10. $y = \sin^{-1}\frac{x-1}{x+1}$
11. $y = \tan^{-1}\frac{x-1}{x+1}$
12. $y = x\sin^{-1} x + \sqrt{1-x^2}$
13. $y = x(\sin^{-1} x)^2 - 2x + 2\sqrt{1-x^2}\sin^{-1} x$
14. $y = x\cos^{-1} 2x - \frac{1}{2}\sqrt{1-4x^2}$
15. How far from the wall should the observer stand in order to maximize the angle of vision α in Problem 6, Article 6–2?

Evaluate the following integrals:

16. $\int_0^{1/2} \frac{dx}{\sqrt{1-x^2}}$
17. $\int_{-1}^{1} \frac{dx}{1+x^2}$
18. $\int_{\sqrt{2}}^{2} \frac{dx}{x\sqrt{x^2-1}}$
19. $\int_{-2}^{-\sqrt{2}} \frac{dx}{x\sqrt{x^2-1}}$

20. $\displaystyle\int \frac{dx}{\sqrt{1-4x^2}}$

21. $\displaystyle\int_{1/\sqrt{3}}^{1} \frac{dx}{x\sqrt{4x^2-1}}$

22. Find a curve whose slope at $P(x, y)$ is $1/(x\sqrt{4x^2-1})$ if it contains the points $A(-1, -1)$ and $B(1, 2)$.

23. Evaluate the limits:

a) $\displaystyle\lim_{x\to 0} \frac{\sin^{-1} 2x}{x}$ **b)** $\displaystyle\lim_{x\to 0} \frac{2\tan^{-1} 3x}{5x}$

c) $\displaystyle\lim_{x\to 0} x^{-3}(\sin^{-1} x - x)$ **d)** $\displaystyle\lim_{x\to 0} x^{-3}(\tan^{-1} x - x)$

24. Use Simpson's method with $n = 2$ to approximate the area under the curve $y = \sin^{-1} x$ over the interval $[0, 1]$. Compare your answer with the trapezoidal approximation using two trapezoids, those for $0 \le x \le \frac{1}{2}$ and $\frac{1}{2} \le x \le 1$.

25. Verify that the derivative of $f(x) = x \sin^{-1} x + \sqrt{1-x^2}$ is $\sin^{-1} x$. Use this result to find the exact value of $\int_0^1 \sin^{-1} x\, dx$.

THE NATURAL LOGARITHM

We have so far studied functions that are fairly familiar. Polynomials, rational functions, and other algebraic functions result from the familiar operations of arithmetic and algebra. The trigonometric functions can be identified with coordinates of points on a unit circle and with their ratios and reciprocals. The inverse trigonometric functions are probably less familiar, but nevertheless they can be understood without any knowledge of the calculus. But we are now going to study a function, the natural logarithm,* which depends upon the calculus for its very definition.

The natural logarithm of x, which is indicated by the notation $\ln x$, is defined, for positive x, as the integral

$$\ln x = \int_1^x \frac{1}{t}\, dt. \tag{1}$$

For any x greater than 1, this integral represents the area bounded above by the curve $y = 1/t$, below by the t-axis, on the left by the line $t = 1$, and on the right by the line $t = x$. (See Fig. 6–10.)

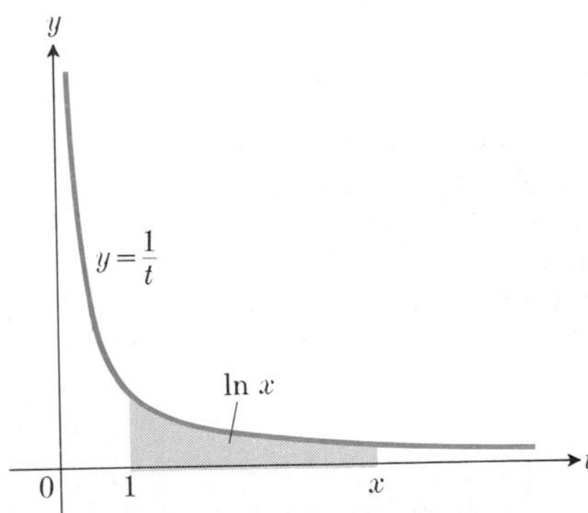

6–10 The shaded area is ln x.

If $x = 1$, the left and right boundaries of the area are identical and the area is zero,

$$\ln 1 = \int_1^1 \frac{1}{t}\, dt = 0. \tag{2}$$

If x is less than 1, then the left boundary is the line $t = x$ and the right boundary is $t = 1$. In this case,

$$\ln x = \int_1^x \frac{1}{t}\, dt = -\int_x^1 \frac{1}{t}\, dt \tag{3}$$

is the negative of the area under the curve between x and 1.

In all cases, if x is any positive number, the value of the definite integral in Eq. (1) can be calculated to as many decimal places as may be desired by using inscribed rectangles, circumscribed rectangles, or trapezoids to approximate the appropriate area. (See Chapter 4. Another method for computing natural logarithms, by means of series, will also be discussed in

---

* The first discovery of logarithms is credited to a Scottish nobleman, John Napier (1550–1617). For a biographical sketch of Napier, see the *World of Mathematics*, Vol. 1, "The Great Mathematicians," by H. W. Turnbull. New York: Simon and Schuster, 1962; pp. 121–125.

Chapter 16. Also see Problem 8 below.) In any event, Eq. (1) defines a computable function of x over the domain $0 < x < +\infty$. We study its range in Article 6–7.

REMARK. No doubt you have learned about logarithms in your earlier studies in mathematics. Common logarithms, or logarithms to the base 10, are related to the natural logarithms by a rule that we shall come to in Article 6–10. Any function $f(x)$ that is defined on the domain of positive numbers x and that satisfies the condition

$$f(ax) = f(a) + f(x)$$

may be called a logarithmic function. The function that we have introduced as $\ln x$ has these properties: that is,

$$\ln x = \int_1^x \frac{1}{t}\,dt$$

is defined for all positive values of x, and, as we shall see in Article 6–6,

$$\ln ax = \ln a + \ln x. \tag{4}$$

(One method of establishing Eq. (4) is outlined in Problem 9. We shall prove it by a different method in Article 6–6.) Fundamentally, it is the property of areas under the curve $y = 1/t$ expressed by Eq. (4) that motivates the definition of $\ln x$ that we have given.

PROBLEMS

Use trapezoids of altitude $\Delta t = 0.1$ to approximate the appropriate areas to obtain approximations to the following natural logarithms, Problems 1–4.

1. $\ln 1.2$ **2.** $\ln 1.4$

3. $\ln 2$ **4.** $\ln 0.5$

5. (a) Suppose h is small and positive. Does the approximation $\ln(1 + h) \approx h$ correspond to using an inscribed rectangle or a circumscribed rectangle to approximate the area from 1 to $1 + h$ under the curve $y = 1/t$? (b) Answer the same question in case h is negative.

6. Approximate $\ln(1 + h)$ by using the line L that is tangent to the curve $y = 1/t$ at $A(1, 1)$, as upper boundary of a trapezoid of altitude $|h|$. Sketch. Show that this leads to the approximation

$$\ln(1 + h) \approx h - \frac{h^2}{2}.$$

Use this result to approximate (a) $\ln 1.04$; (b) $\ln 0.96$.

7. Find the volume generated by rotating about the x-axis the area in the first quadrant bounded by $y = 1/\sqrt{x}$, the x-axis, the line $x = 1$, and the line $x = 2$.

Show, by long division or otherwise, that

$$\frac{1}{1+u} = 1 - u + u^2 - \frac{u^3}{1+u}.$$

(The division could be continued. We stop here only for the sake of illustration.)

b) In Eq. (1), make the substitution

$$t = 1 + u, \qquad dt = du$$

and make the corresponding change in the limits of integration, thus obtaining

$$\ln x = \int_0^{x-1} \frac{du}{1+u}.$$

c) Combine the results of (a) and (b) to obtain

$$\ln x = \int_0^{x-1} \left(1 - u + u^2 - \frac{u^3}{1+u}\right) du,$$

or

$$\ln x = (x-1) - \tfrac{1}{2}(x-1)^2 + \tfrac{1}{3}(x-1)^3 - R,$$

where

$$R = \int_0^{x-1} \frac{u^3}{1+u}\,du.$$

d) Show that, if $x > 1$ and $0 \le u \le x - 1$, then

$$\frac{u^3}{1+u} \le u^3.$$

Hence, deduce that

$$R \leq \int_0^{x-1} u^3\, du = \frac{(x-1)^4}{4}.$$

e) Combining the results of (c) and (d), show that the approximation

$$\ln x \approx (x-1) - \tfrac{1}{2}(x-1)^2 + \tfrac{1}{3}(x-1)^3$$

tends to overestimate the value of ln x, but with an error not greater than $(x-1)^4/4$.

f) Use the result of (e) to estimate ln 1.2.

9. (*A proof of Eq.* (4)) **a)** Prove that the area under the curve $y = 1/t$ over $[1, x]$ is equal to the area under the same curve over $[a, ax]$ where a is any positive constant. *Suggestion.* Take any partition of $[1, x]$ and multiply each coordinate by a to get the corresponding partition of $[a, ax]$. Sketch. If $f(t_i)\,\Delta t_i$ is the area of a rectangle over one of the subdivisions in $[1, x]$, what is the rectangle whose area is represented by $f(at_i)(a\,\Delta t_i)$? Are these two rectangles equal in area?

b) In part (a) you have shown that the area under the curve $y = 1/t$ over $[a, ax]$ is equal to ln x. By Eq. (1), the area over $[1, a]$ is ln a. Now combine these results to show that ln ax = ln a + ln x. (*Remark.* It is easier to see what goes on if you assume that both a and x are greater than 1 in the foregoing. The language has to be different if either a or x is less than 1, but the final conclusion ln ax = ln a + ln x is still true. Our proof in Article 6–6 is more straightforward and does not require special cases.)

6–5 THE DERIVATIVE OF ln x

Since the function $F(x) = \ln x$ is defined by the integral

$$F(x) = \int_1^x \frac{1}{t}\, dt \qquad (x > 0) \tag{1}$$

(see Fig. 6–11), it follows at once, from Theorem 4 of Article 4–10, that

$$F'(x) = \frac{1}{x}.$$

That is,

$$\frac{d(\ln x)}{dx} = \frac{1}{x}. \tag{2}$$

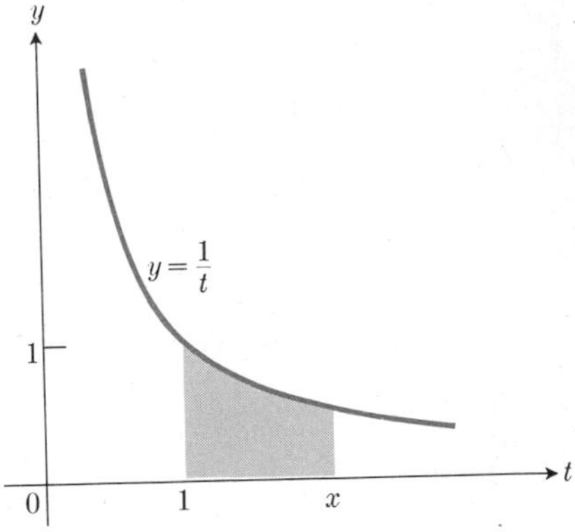

We obtain a more general formula by considering ln u, where u is a positive, differentiable function of x. By the chain rule for derivatives,

$$\frac{d \ln u}{dx} = \frac{d \ln u}{du}\frac{du}{dx} = \frac{1}{u}\frac{du}{dx}, \tag{XIX}$$

or, in terms of differentials,

$$d \ln u = \frac{du}{u}. \tag{XIX$'$}$$

6–11 $\ln x = \int_1^x \frac{1}{t}\, dt,\quad \frac{d(\ln x)}{dx} = \frac{1}{x}.$

EXAMPLE 1. Find dy/dx if $y = \ln(3x^2 + 4)$.

Solution

$$\frac{dy}{dx} = \frac{1}{3x^2+4}\frac{d(3x^2+4)}{dx} = \frac{6x}{3x^2+4}.$$

Equation (XIX′) leads at once to the integration formula

$$\int \frac{du}{u} = \ln u + C, \tag{3a}$$

provided u is positive. On the other hand, if u is negative then $-u$ is positive and

$$\int \frac{du}{u} = \int \frac{d(-u)}{-u} = \ln(-u) + C'. \tag{3b}$$

The two results (3a, b) can be combined into a single result, namely,

$$\int \frac{du}{u} = \begin{cases} \ln u + C & \text{if } u > 0, \\ \ln(-u) + C' & \text{if } u < 0, \end{cases} \tag{4a}$$

or, if u does not change sign on the given domain,

$$\int \frac{du}{u} = \ln |u| + C. \tag{4b}$$

EXAMPLE 2. Find a function $y = f(x)$ such that $dy/dx = 1/x$, and $f(1) = 1$ and $f(-1) = 2$. Sketch the solution.

Solution. There are constants C and C' such that

$$y = \begin{cases} \ln x + C & \text{if } x \text{ is positive,} \\ \ln(-x) + C' & \text{if } x \text{ is negative.} \end{cases}$$

Substituting $y = 1$ when $x = 1$, we get

$$1 = \ln 1 + C = 0 + C, \quad \text{so} \quad C = 1.$$

Likewise, putting $y = 2$ when $x = -1$, we get

$$2 = \ln(-(-1)) + C' = \ln 1 + C' = 0 + C', \quad \text{so} \quad C' = 2.$$

The complete solution is, therefore,

$$y = f(x) = \begin{cases} \ln x + 1 & \text{if } x \text{ is positive,} \\ \ln(-x) + 2 & \text{if } x \text{ is negative.} \end{cases}$$

A graph of the solution is shown in Fig. 6–12. (For a general analysis of the graph of $y = \ln x$, see Article 6–7.)

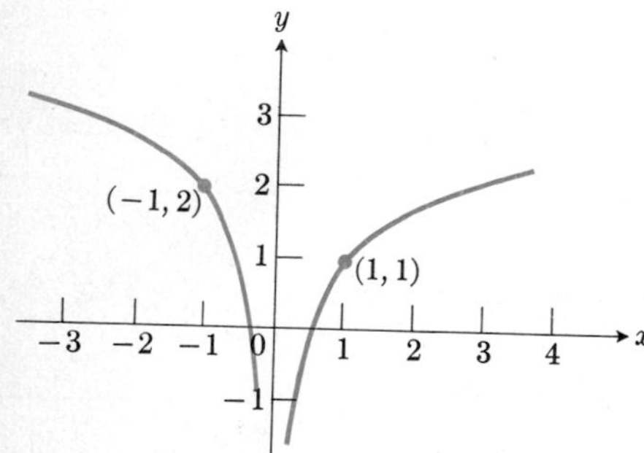

6–12 Graph of function $f(x)$ whose derivative is $1/x$ with $f(-1) = 2$ and $f(1) = 1$:

$$f(x) = \begin{cases} 2 + \ln(-x) & \text{when } x \text{ is negative,} \\ 1 + \ln x & \text{when } x \text{ is positive,} \end{cases}$$

The two constants of integration C and C' are not equal.

We recall that the formula

$$\int u^n \, du = \frac{u^{n+1}}{n+1} + C, \qquad n \neq -1$$

failed to cover one case, namely, $n = -1$. Equation (4b) now covers this for us, since it tells us that

$$\int u^{-1} \, du = \int \frac{du}{u} = \ln |u| + C.$$

It is important, of course, to remember that

$$\int \frac{dx}{x^2} = \int x^{-2}\, dx = \frac{x^{-1}}{-1} + C$$

is *not* a logarithm.

EXAMPLE 2. Integrate

$$\int \frac{\cos\theta\, d\theta}{1 + \sin\theta}.$$

Solution. In Eq. (4b), let

$$u = 1 + \sin\theta.$$

Then

$$du = \frac{du}{d\theta}\, d\theta = \cos\theta\, d\theta$$

so that

$$\int \frac{\cos\theta\, d\theta}{1 + \sin\theta} = \int \frac{du}{u} = \ln|u| + C$$
$$= \ln|1 + \sin\theta| + C.$$

PROBLEMS

Find dy/dx in each of the following problems (1 through 18).

1. $y = \ln(x^2 + 2x)$
2. $y = (\ln x)^3$
3. $y = \ln(\cos x)$
4. $y = \ln(\tan x + \sec x)$
5. $y = \ln(x\sqrt{x^2 + 1})$
6. $y = \ln(3x\sqrt{x + 2})$
7. $y = x \ln x - x$
8. $y = x^3 \ln(2x)$
9. $y = \frac{1}{2} \ln \frac{1 + x}{1 - x}$
10. $y = \frac{1}{3} \ln \frac{x^3}{1 + x^3}$
11. $y = \ln \frac{x}{2 + 3x}$
12. $y = \ln(x^2 + 4) - x \tan^{-1} \frac{x}{2}$
13. $y = \ln x - \frac{1}{2} \ln(1 + x^2) - \frac{\tan^{-1} x}{x}$
14. $y = x(\ln x)^3$
15. $y = x[\sin(\ln x) + \cos(\ln x)]$
16. $y = x \sec^{-1} x - \ln(x + \sqrt{x^2 - 1}), \quad (x > 1)$
17. $y = x \ln(a^2 + x^2) - 2x + 2a \tan^{-1} \frac{x}{a}$
18. $y = \ln(\ln x)$

Evaluate the following integrals:

19. $\int \frac{dx}{2x + 3}$
20. $\int \frac{dx}{2 - 3x}$
21. $\int \frac{x\, dx}{4x^2 + 1}$
22. $\int \frac{\sin x\, dx}{2 - \cos x}$
23. $\int \frac{\cos x\, dx}{\sin x}$
24. $\int \frac{2x - 5}{x}\, dx$
25. $\int \frac{x\, dx}{x + 1}$
26. $\int \frac{x^2\, dx}{4 - x^3}$
27. $\int \frac{x\, dx}{1 - x^2}$
28. $\int \frac{dx}{\sqrt{x}(1 + \sqrt{x})}$
29. $\int (\ln x)^2 \frac{dx}{x}$
30. $\int \frac{dx}{(2x + 3)^2}$
31. $\int \tan x\, dx$
32. $\int \frac{dx}{x \ln x}$
33. $\int \frac{\ln x}{x}\, dx$
34. Evaluate the following limits (using l'Hôpital's rule):

    a) $\lim\limits_{t \to 0} \frac{\ln(1 + 2t) - 2t}{t^2}$ b) $\lim\limits_{x \to \infty} \frac{\ln x}{x}$

    c) $\lim\limits_{h \to 0^+} h \ln h$ d) $\lim\limits_{\theta \to 0^+} \frac{\ln(\sin\theta)}{\cot\theta}$
35. Find the length of the curve $y = \ln \sec x$ from $x = 0$ to $x = \pi/4$, using at some stage the result of Problem 4.

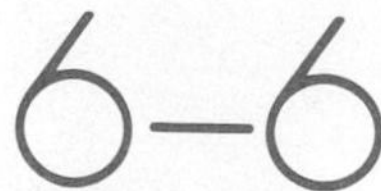

PROPERTIES OF NATURAL LOGARITHMS

In this article we shall establish the following properties of the natural logarithm:

$$\ln ax = \ln a + \ln x, \tag{1}$$

$$\ln \frac{x}{a} = \ln x - \ln a, \tag{2}$$

$$\ln x^n = n \ln x, \tag{3}$$

provided x and a are positive and n is a rational number.

The proofs of these results are all based on the fact that

$$y = \ln x$$

satisfies the differential equation

$$\frac{dy}{dx} = \frac{1}{x} \quad \text{for all} \quad x > 0,$$

plus the fact that if two functions have the same derivative for all $x > 0$, then the two functions can differ only by a constant. That is, if

$$\frac{dy_1}{dx} = \frac{dy_2}{dx} \quad \text{for all} \quad x > 0,$$

then

$$y_1 = y_2 + \text{constant} \quad \text{for all} \quad x > 0.$$

Now, to prove Eq. (1), let

$$y_1 = \ln ax, \qquad y_2 = \ln x.$$

Then

$$\frac{dy_1}{dx} = \frac{1}{ax}\frac{d(ax)}{dx} = \frac{a}{ax} = \frac{1}{x} = \frac{dy_2}{dx}. \tag{4}$$

Therefore we have

$$\ln ax = \ln x + C. \tag{5}$$

To evaluate C it suffices to substitute $x = 1$:

$$\ln a = \ln 1 + C = 0 + C,$$

which gives

$$C = \ln a.$$

Hence, by (5),

$$\ln ax = \ln x + \ln a. \qquad \text{Q.E.D.}$$

To prove Eq. (2), we first put $x = 1/a$ in Eq. (1) and recall that $\ln 1 = 0$:

$$0 = \ln 1 = \ln a + \ln \left(\frac{1}{a}\right)$$

so that

$$\ln \frac{1}{a} = -\ln a. \tag{6}$$

Now apply Eq. (1) with a replaced by $1/a$ and $\ln a$ replaced by $\ln (1/a) = -\ln a$. The result is Eq. (2).

To prove Eq. (3), let

$$y_1 = \ln x^n.$$

Then

$$\frac{dy_1}{dx} = \frac{1}{x^n} \cdot nx^{n-1} = \frac{n}{x} = \frac{d}{dx}(n \ln x).$$

Hence $y_1 = \ln x^n$ and $y_2 = n \ln x$ have equal derivatives, so they differ at most by a constant:

$$\ln x^n = n \ln x + C. \tag{7}$$

But by taking $x = 1$, and remembering that $\ln 1 = 0$, we find $C = 0$, which gives Eq. (3). In particular, if $n = 1/m$, where m is a positive integer, we have

$$\ln \sqrt[m]{x} - \ln x^{1/m} = \frac{1}{m} \ln x. \tag{8}$$

PROBLEMS

Express the following logarithms in terms of the two given logarithms $a = \ln 2$, $b = \ln 3$. [For example: $\ln 1.5 = \ln \frac{3}{2} = \ln 3 - \ln 2 = b - a$.]

1. $\ln 16$ **2.** $\ln \sqrt[3]{9}$ **3.** $\ln 2\sqrt{2}$ **4.** $\ln 0.25$ **5.** $\ln \frac{4}{9}$ **6.** $\ln 12$ **7.** $\ln \frac{9}{8}$ **8.** $\ln 36$ **9.** $\ln 4.5$ **10.** $\ln \sqrt{13.5}$

6–7 GRAPH OF $y = \ln x$

The slope of the curve

$$y = \ln x \tag{1}$$

is given by

$$\frac{dy}{dx} = \frac{1}{x}, \tag{2}$$

which is positive for all $x > 0$. Hence the graph of $y = \ln x$ steadily rises from left to right. Since the derivative is continuous, the function $\ln x$ is itself continuous, and the curve has a continuously turning tangent.

The second derivative,

$$\frac{d^2y}{dx^2} = -\frac{1}{x^2}, \tag{3}$$

is always negative, so the curve (1) is everywhere concave downward.

The curve passes through the point (1, 0), since $\ln 1 = 0$. At this point its slope is $+1$, so the tangent line at this point makes an angle of 45° with the x-axis (if we use equal units on the x- and y-axes).

If we refer to the definition of ln 2 as an integral,

$$\ln 2 = \int_1^2 \frac{1}{t}\,dt,$$

we see that it may be interpreted as the area in Fig. 6–11 with $x = 2$. By considering the areas of rectangles of base 1 and altitudes 1 or $\frac{1}{2}$, respectively circumscribed over and inscribed under the given area, we see that

$$0.5 < \ln 2 < 1.0.$$

In fact, by more extensive calculations, the value of ln 2 to 5 decimal places can be found to be

$$\ln 2 \approx 0.69315.$$

By Eq. (3) of Article 6–6 we have

$$\ln 4 = \ln 2^2 = 2 \ln 2 \approx 1.38630,$$
$$\ln 8 = \ln 2^3 = 3 \ln 2 \approx 2.07944,$$
$$\ln \tfrac{1}{2} = \ln 2^{-1} = -\ln 2 \approx -0.69315,$$
$$\ln \tfrac{1}{4} = \ln 2^{-2} = -2 \ln 2 \approx -1.38630,$$

and so on.

We now plot the points that correspond to $x = \frac{1}{4}, \frac{1}{2}, 1, 2, 4, 8$ on the curve $y = \ln x$ and connect them with a smooth curve. The curve we draw should have slope $1/x$ at the point of abscissa x and should everywhere be concave downward. The curve is shown in Fig. 6–13.

Since ln 2 is greater than 0.5 and $\ln 2^n = n \ln 2$, it is clear that

$$\ln 2^n > 0.5n,$$

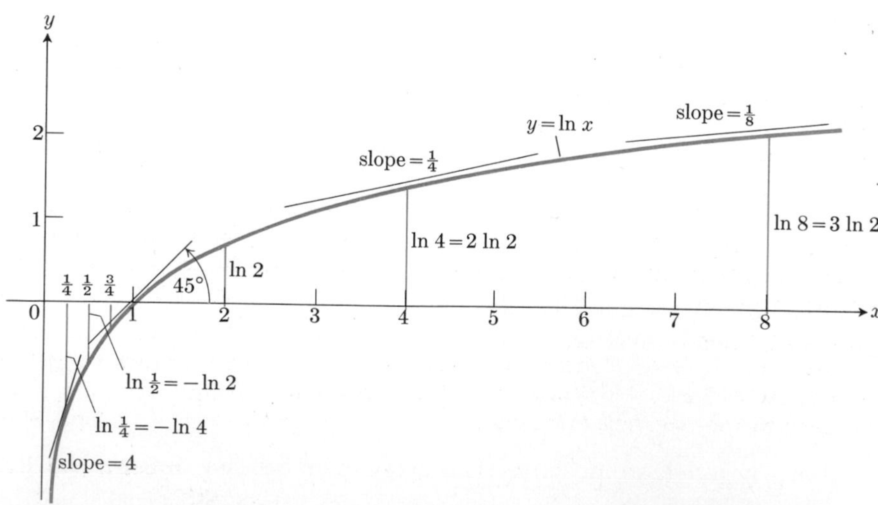

6–13 Graph of $y = \ln x$.

and hence $\ln x$ increases without limit as x does. That is,

$$\ln x \to +\infty \qquad \text{as} \qquad x \to +\infty. \tag{4}$$

On the other hand, as x approaches zero through positive values, $1/x$ tends to plus infinity. Hence, taking Eq. (6) of Article 6–6 into account, we have

$$\ln x = -\ln \frac{1}{x} \to -\infty \qquad \text{as} \qquad x \to 0^+. \tag{5}$$

Summary

The natural logarithm, $y = \ln x$, is a function with the following properties:

1. Its *domain* is the set of positive real numbers, $x > 0$.

2. Its *range* is the set of all real numbers, $-\infty < y < +\infty$.

3. It is a *continuous, increasing* function of x everywhere on its domain. If $x_1 > x_2 > 0$, then $\ln x_1 > \ln x_2$. It provides a one-to-one mapping from its domain to its range.

4. *Multiplication* of numbers in the domain corresponds to *addition* of numbers in the range. That is, if

$$x_1 > 0, \qquad y_1 = \ln x_1,$$

$$x_2 > 0, \qquad y_2 = \ln x_2,$$

then

$$x_1 x_2 > 0 \qquad \text{and} \qquad y_1 + y_2 = \ln (x_1 x_2).$$

5. The *derivative* of $y = \ln x$ is $dy/dx = 1/x$.

PROBLEMS

1. Take $\ln 3 = 1.09861$ as known. Plot the points corresponding to $x = \frac{1}{9}, \frac{1}{3}, 1, 3$, and 9 on the curve $y = \ln x$. Also construct, through each of these points, a line segment tangent to the curve. Then sketch the curve itself. From the curve, read off $\ln 2$.

2. Let x_0 be the abscissa of the point $(x_0, 1)$ in which the line $y = 1$ intersects the curve $y = \ln x$. Show that the curve $y = x \ln x$ has a minimum at $[1/x_0, -(1/x_0)]$ and sketch the curve for $x > 0$. Does this curve possess a point of inflection? If so, find it (or them), and if not, state why not. (See Problem 5.)

3. Sketch the curve $x = \ln y$ for $y > 0$. What is its slope at the point (x, y)? Is it always concave upward, or downward, or does it have inflection points? Give reasons for your answers.

4. The curve $y = \ln x$ in Fig. 6–13 has the property that y becomes infinite when x does. But the ratio $(\ln x)/x$ approaches zero as x becomes infinite. Prove this latter statement by showing, first, that for $x > 1$

$$\ln x = \int_1^x \frac{1}{t}\,dt \le \int_1^x \frac{1}{\sqrt{t}}\,dt = 2(\sqrt{x} - 1).$$

[*Hint.* Compare the areas under the curves $y_1 = 1/t$ and $y_2 = 1/\sqrt{t}$ for $1 \le t \le x$.]

5. From the result of Problem 4 that

$$\lim_{x \to +\infty} \frac{\ln x}{x} = 0,$$

deduce that $\lim_{x \to 0^+} x \ln x = 0$. [*Hint.* Let $x = 1/u$, $u \to +\infty$.]

6. Show that the curve

$$y = \ln x - (x - 1) + \tfrac{1}{2}(x - 1)^2$$

has a point of inflection and a horizontal tangent at $(1, 0)$. Sketch the curve for $0 < x < 2$. (Compare Problem 8, Article 6–4.)

7. Suppose you had a table of natural logarithms giving $\ln x$ for each $x > 0$. How could you use this to find $\log_{10} N$, where

$$\log_{10} N = b \quad \text{means} \quad N = 10^b?$$

In particular, find $\log_{10} 2$, given $\ln 2 = 0.69315$, $\ln 10 = 2.30259$.

6–8 THE EXPONENTIAL FUNCTION

In Article 6–7 we discussed and sketched the graph of the curve $y = \ln x$ (Fig. 6–13). We now make the observation that the curve $y = \ln x$ must cross the horizontal line $y = 1$ for some value of x between 2 and 4, since $\ln x$ is continuous and $\ln 2$ is less than 1 while $\ln 4$ is greater than 1. The value of x for which $\ln x = 1$ is denoted by the letter e. It is one of the most important numbers in mathematics. It satisfies the basic equation

$$\ln e = 1. \tag{1}$$

From our discussion above, it follows that e lies between 2 and 4. (In Chapter 16 we shall see how its value may be computed to any desired number of decimal places by using series.) Its value to 15 decimal places is

$$e = 2.7\ 1828\ 1828\ 45\ 90\ 45\ldots \tag{2}$$

By Eq. (3), Article 6–6, and Eq. (1) above, we have

$$\ln e^n = n \ln e = n \tag{3}$$

for any rational number n. Thus, for example, we have

$$\ln e^2 = 2, \qquad \ln e^3 = 3, \qquad \ln e^{-1} = -1, \qquad \ln \sqrt{e} = \tfrac{1}{2},$$

and so on. Since only one number can have its natural logarithm equal to n, for any given n, we may restate Eq. (3) by saying that the number whose natural logarithm is n is e^n; that is, the anti-natural-logarithm of n is e^n.

We now propose to study the antilogarithm, i.e., the *inverse of the logarithm*, as a function. To obtain this inverse function, we let

$$y = \text{Inverse natural logarithm of } x$$

or

$$x = \ln y. \tag{4}$$

The equation $x = \ln y$ defines a unique x for each positive real number y. Values of y greater than 1 correspond to x greater than zero; $y = 1$ to $x = 0$; $y < 1$ to $x < 0$. To each positive real number y there corresponds just one real number x such that $x = \ln y$. And conversely, to each real number x there corresponds just one positive real number y such that $x = \ln y$. The correspondence is one-to-one between the sets $y > 0$ and $-\infty < x < +\infty$, and hence it may be used to *define* y as a *function of* x, on the domain of all real numbers $-\infty < x < +\infty$. The *range* of this function is the set of all positive real numbers $y > 0$.

We have just seen (Eq. (3)) that $x = \ln y = n$ if and only if $y = e^n$, provided n is a rational number. That is, Eq. (4) is equivalent to the equation

$$y = e^x \tag{5}$$

for all rational values of x. We are therefore led to define e^x for all real values of x, irrational as well as rational, to be that number y whose natural logarithm is x:

$$y = e^x \quad \text{if and only if} \quad x = \ln y. \tag{6}$$

The resulting function is a continuous, single-valued function of x, defined for all real x, $-\infty < x < +\infty$. It is called the *exponential function*, with e as base and exponent x. *The exponential function is the inverse of the natural logarithm.* Its graph, Fig. 6–14 may be obtained by reflecting the curve in Fig. 6–13 across the 45° line $y = x$. Note, in particular, that $e^0 = 1$ since $\ln 1 = 0$.

To find the derivative of

$$y = e^x, \tag{7}$$

we differentiate both sides of the equivalent equation

$$x = \ln y$$

implicitly with respect to x. Then

$$1 = \frac{1}{y}\frac{dy}{dx} \quad \text{or} \quad \frac{dy}{dx} = y. \tag{8}$$

Taking account of Eq. (7), we therefore have

$$\frac{de^x}{dx} = e^x.$$

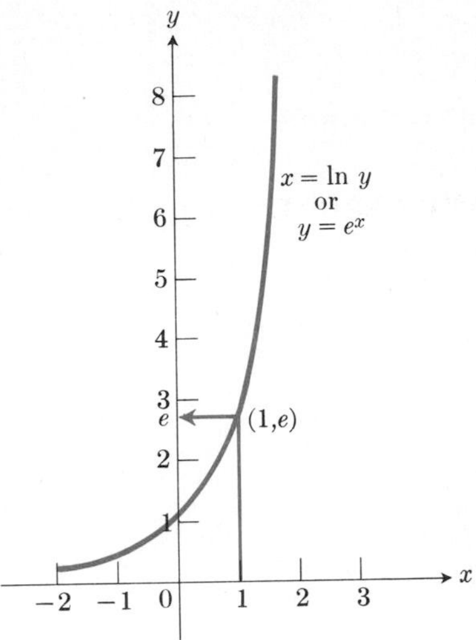

6–14 $y = e^x$ or $x = \ln y$.

Here is a function that is not changed by differentiation! It is indestructible. It can be differentiated again and again without changing. In this, the exponential function is like the story of a student who asked a guru what was holding up the earth. The answer was that the earth was upheld by an elephant, and the student naturally wanted to know what held up that elephant. The guru paused a moment, then replied "It's elephants all the way down."

In Fig. 6–15, the line QP through the points $Q(x - 1, 0)$ and $P(x, e^x)$ is tangent to the curve $y = e^x$ at P, for the slope of QP is $y/1$ and the slope of the curve, at P, is also equal to y, by Eq. (8).

We obtain a slightly more general formula for the derivative of e^u, where u is a differentiable function of x, by applying the chain rule

$$\frac{de^u}{dx} = \frac{de^u}{du}\frac{du}{dx} = e^u \frac{du}{dx}. \tag{XX}$$

In terms of differentials, we have, from XX,

$$de^u = e^u \, du. \tag{XX'}$$

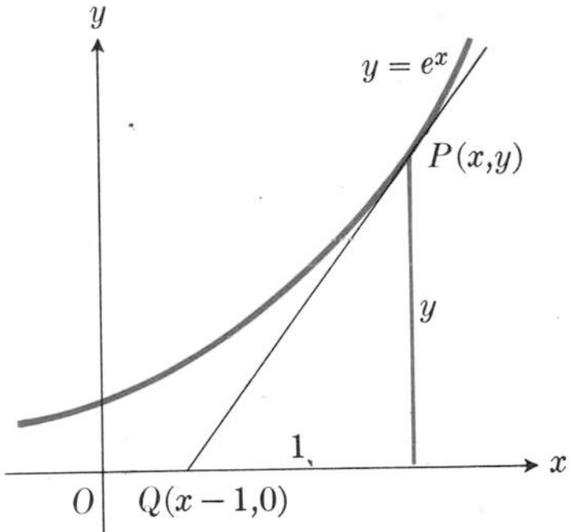

6–15 Line QP is tangent to the curve at P.

This in turn leads to the integration formula

$$\int e^u \, du = e^u + C. \tag{9}$$

EXAMPLE 1. Find dy/dx if $y = e^{\tan^{-1} x}$.

Solution

$$\frac{dy}{dx} = e^{\tan^{-1} x} \frac{d \tan^{-1} x}{dx}$$

$$= e^{\tan^{-1} x} \cdot \frac{1}{1 + x^2} \cdot \frac{dx}{dx}$$

$$= \frac{e^{\tan^{-1} x}}{1 + x^2}.$$

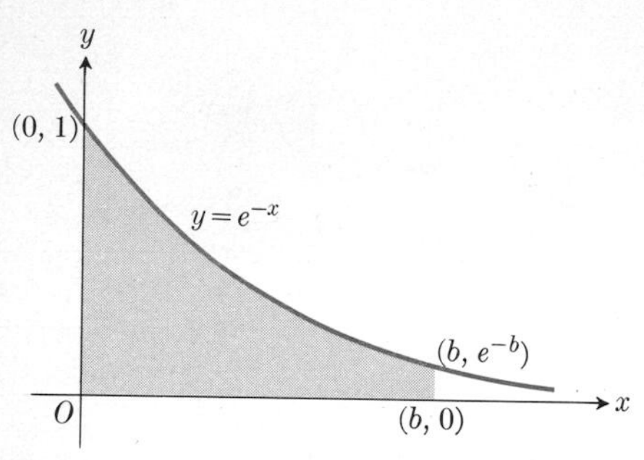

6–16 The shaded area is $1 - e^{-b}$.

EXAMPLE 2. Find the area under the curve $y = e^{-x}$ from $x = 0$ to $x = b(> 0)$ and show that this area *remains finite* as $b \to +\infty$. (See Fig. 6–16.)

Solution. The area from $x = 0$ to $x = b$ is given by

$$A_0^b = \int_0^b y\, dx = \int_0^b e^{-x}\, dx.$$

To evaluate this integral, we compare it with our standard forms and see that it is almost, but not exactly, like

$$\int e^u\, du = e^u + C.$$

To bring it into precisely this form, we let

$$u = -x, \qquad du = -dx,$$

or

$$dx = -du,$$

so that

$$\int e^{-x}\, dx = \int e^u(-du) = -\int e^u\, du = -e^u + C = -e^{-x} + C.$$

Therefore

$$A_0^b = -e^{-x}\Big]_0^b = -e^{-b} + e^0 = 1 - e^{-b}.$$

From this we see that the number of square units of area in the shaded region of Fig. 6–16 is somewhat less than unity, for b large and positive, and moreover

$$\lim_{b \to +\infty} A_0^b = \lim_{b \to +\infty} (1 - e^{-b}) = 1,$$

since [see Eq. (11) below]

$$\lim_{b \to +\infty} e^{-b} = \lim_{b \to +\infty} \frac{1}{e^b} = 0.$$

Some properties of the function

$$y = e^x$$

are worthy of additional comment.

In the first place, the exponential function satisfies the law

$$e^{x_1} \cdot e^{x_2} = e^{x_1 + x_2}. \tag{10}$$

For, if

$$y_1 = e^{x_1} \quad \text{and} \quad y_2 = e^{x_2},$$

then, by definition,

$$x_1 = \ln y_1 \quad \text{and} \quad x_2 = \ln y_2,$$

so that

$$x_1 + x_2 = \ln y_1 + \ln y_2 = \ln y_1 y_2$$

by Eq. (1), Article 6–6. Therefore, by definition,

$$y_1 y_2 = e^{x_1 + x_2},$$

which establishes Eq. (10).

Again, we have

$$e^{-x} = \frac{1}{e^x} \tag{11}$$

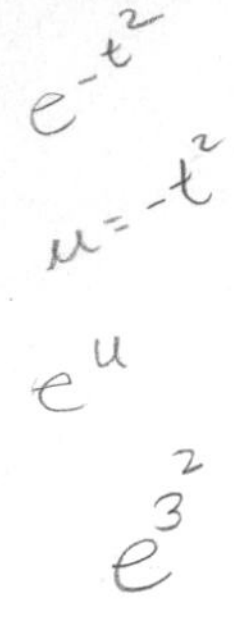

for any real number x. For, if

$$y = e^{-x}$$

then, by definition,

$$-x = \ln y$$

or, from Eq. (6), Article 6–6,

$$x = -\ln y = \ln\left(\frac{1}{y}\right).$$

Therefore

$$\frac{1}{y} = e^x \quad \text{or} \quad y = \frac{1}{e^x},$$

which establishes Eq. (11).

A table of e^x and e^{-x} is included at the end of the book for convenience and to give an appreciation of the rapid rate of increase of the exponential function for positive values of x. Many small calculators give $\ln x$ and e^x, as well as other elementary functions.

PROBLEMS

1. Simplify each of the following expressions:

a) $e^{\ln x}$ b) $\ln (e^x)$ c) $e^{-\ln (x^2)}$
d) $\ln (e^{-x^2})$ e) $\ln (e^{1/x})$ f) $\ln (1/e^x)$
g) $e^{\ln (1/x)}$ h) $e^{-\ln (1/x)}$ i) $e^{\ln 2 + \ln x}$
j) $e^{2 \ln x}$ k) $\ln (e^{x - x^2})$ l) $\ln (x^2 e^{-2x})$
m) $e^{x + \ln x}$ n) $e^{\ln x - 2 \ln y}$

Find dy/dx in each of the following problems (2 through 19).

2. $y = x^2 e^x$
3. $y = e^{2x}(2 \cos 3x + 3 \sin 3x)$
4. $y = \ln \dfrac{e^x}{1 + e^x}$
5. $y = \frac{1}{2}(e^x - e^{-x})$
6. $y = \frac{1}{2}(e^x + e^{-x})$
7. $y = \dfrac{e^x - e^{-x}}{e^x + e^{-x}}$
8. $y = e^{\sin^{-1} x}$
9. $y = (1 + 2x)e^{-2x}$
10. $y = (9x^2 - 6x + 2)e^{3x}$
11. $y = \dfrac{ax - 1}{a^2} e^{ax}$
12. $y = e^{-x^2}$
13. $y = x^2 e^{-x^2}$
14. $y = e^x \ln x$
15. $y = \tan^{-1} (e^x)$
16. $y = \sec^{-1} (e^{2x})$
17. $e^{2x} = \sin (x + 3y)$
18. $y = e^{1/x}$
19. $\tan y = e^x + \ln x$
20. (a) Show that $y = Ce^{ax}$ is a solution of the differential equation $dy/dx = ay$ for any choice of the constant C. (b) Using the result of (a), find a solution of the differential equation $dy/dt = -2y$ satisfying the initial condition $y = 3$ when $t = 0$.
21. Use l'Hôpital's rule to evaluate the following limits:

a) $\lim\limits_{h \to 0} \dfrac{e^h - (1 + h)}{h^2}$ b) $\lim\limits_{x \to \infty} \dfrac{e^x}{x^5}$

Evaluate the following integrals:

22. $\int e^{2x}\,dx$
23. $\int xe^{x^2}\,dx$
24. $\int e^{\sin x} \cos x\,dx$
25. $\int e^{x/3}\,dx$
26. $\int \dfrac{4\,dx}{e^{3x}}$
27. $\int \dfrac{e^x\,dx}{1 + 2e^x}$

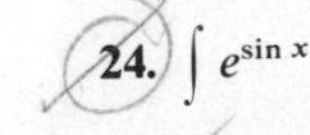

28. $\displaystyle\int_e^{e^2} \frac{dx}{x \ln x}$ **29.** $\displaystyle\int \frac{(e^x - e^{-x})\,dx}{(e^x + e^{-x})}$

30. $\displaystyle\int xe^x\,dx$ (See Example 4, Article 4–4.)

Sketch the graphs of the functions in Problems 31 through 34, taking extreme values and inflection points into account.

31. $y = x$, $y = e^x$, and $y = \ln x$ (in a common graph)

32. $y = (\ln x)/x$, $x > 0$ **33.** $y = (1 + t)e^{-t}$

34. $y = e^{-t} \cos t$, $0 \le t \le 2\pi$

35. The area between the curve $y = e^{-x}$ and the x-axis from $x = 1$ to $x = \ln 10$ is revolved about the x-axis. Find the volume thus swept out.

36. Find the length of the curve $x = e^t \sin t$, $y = e^t \cos t$, $0 \le t \le \pi$.

37. If a particle moves along the x-axis so that its position at time t is given by $x = ae^{\omega t} + be^{-\omega t}$, where a, b, ω, are constants, show that it is repelled from the origin with a force proportional to the displacement. [Assume that force = mass × acceleration.]

Problems 38–41 deal with hyperbolic functions. These are treated in greater detail in Chapter 9.

Certain combinations of e^x and e^{-x} behave in some respects like the trigonometric functions (and quite unlike the trigonometric functions in other ways). The hyperbolic cosine of x, written $\cosh x$, and hyperbolic sine of x, written $\sinh x$, are defined by the relations:

$$\cosh x = \tfrac{1}{2}(e^x + e^{-x}), \qquad \sinh x = \tfrac{1}{2}(e^x - e^{-x}).$$

Using these definitions, prove the following:

38. $\dfrac{d}{dx}(\cosh x) = \sinh x$, $\dfrac{d}{dx}(\sinh x) = \cosh x$

39. $\cosh^2 x - \sinh^2 x = 1$, $\cosh^2 x + \sinh^2 x = \cosh(2x)$

40. $\cosh(-x) = \cosh x$, $\sinh(-x) = -\sinh x$

41. Using the tables of e^x and e^{-x} in the back of the book, sketch graphs of $y = \cosh x$ and $y = \sinh x$.

6–9 THE FUNCTION a^u

If a is any positive real number and

$$b = \ln a, \tag{1a}$$

then

$$a = e^b. \tag{1b}$$

The two equations (1a, b) may be combined to give the result

$$a = e^{\ln a}. \tag{2}$$

In words, $\ln a$ *is the power to which the base e may be raised to give a.*

Suppose we now raise both sides of Eq. (2) to the power u, where u is any real number. We would like to have the law of exponents

$$(e^{\ln a})^u = e^{u \ln a}$$

be true. Hence we now make the following *definition*:

$$a^u = e^{u \ln a}. \tag{3}$$

This definition is equivalent to saying that

$$\ln a^u = u \ln a, \tag{3'}$$

since both Eqs. (3) and (3′) say that $u \ln a$ is the power to which e may be raised to produce a^u. But (3′) is the same as Eq. (3), Article 6–6, in case $u = n$ is a rational number. What we are now considering is the case where u may be any real number, rational or irrational, $-\infty < u < +\infty$. Our new definition of a^u includes the old case but goes beyond and extends it.

Equation (3) is the basis for the algorithm used by some small calculators to compute y^x. Humans have no trouble computing $(-2)^3$, because we know that it is just $-(2^3)$, or -8. But suppose that we thought we should calculate the result using Eq. (3):

$$(-2)^3 = e^{3 \ln(-2)},$$

and we have learned that -2 is not in the domain of the function $\ln x$. We would do something similar to what the calculator does: flash a signal that signifies "error." The number a in Eq. (3) should be positive.

Derivative of a^u

We are ready to calculate the derivative of $y = a^u$ in case u is a differentiable function of x. We apply formula XX, Article 6–8, and, remembering that $\ln a$ is constant when a is, we obtain

$$\frac{da^u}{dx} = \frac{de^{u \ln a}}{dx}$$

$$= e^{u \ln a} \cdot \frac{du}{dx} \cdot \ln a,$$

$$\frac{da^u}{dx} = a^u \cdot \frac{du}{dx} \cdot \ln a. \tag{4}$$

This gives us a formula for the derivative of any positive constant a raised to a variable power. There is very little reason to memorize the result, since it may always be derived very quickly by the method of logarithmic differentiation, which will presently be discussed. It illustrates the fact that the base e is the most desirable one to encounter, since $\ln e = 1$ and Eq. (4) is the same as formula XX in case $a = e$. It also enables us to write down a formula for the integral of $a^u\,du$. For, if we multiply both sides of Eq. (4) by dx to change it to differential form,

$$da^u = \ln a \cdot a^u\,du,$$

and then divide by $\ln a$, provided $a \neq 1$, we see that

$$\int a^u\,du = \int \frac{1}{\ln a}\,da^u = \frac{a^u}{\ln a} + C, \qquad a > 0, \quad a \neq 1. \tag{5}$$

Logarithmic differentiation

The properties

$$\begin{aligned} &\textbf{a)}\ \ln uv = \ln u + \ln v \\ &\textbf{b)}\ \ln \frac{u}{v} = \ln u - \ln v \\ &\textbf{c)}\ \ln u^n = n \ln u \\ &\textbf{d)}\ \ln a^u = u \ln a \end{aligned} \tag{6}$$

can be used to advantage in calculating derivatives of products, quotients, roots, and powers, as illustrated in the examples that follow. The method, known as logarithmic differentiation, is to take the natural logarithm of both sides of an equation

$$y = f(x),$$
$$\ln y = \ln f(x),$$

simplify $\ln f(x)$ as much as possible by making use of the properties in Eq. (6), and then differentiate implicitly with respect to x:

$$\frac{d}{dx} \ln y = \frac{1}{y} \frac{dy}{dx}.$$

EXAMPLE 1. Find where the curves $y = x^2$ and $y = 2^x$ intersect.

Solution. (See Fig. 6–17.) It is easy to plot points on the two curves for

$$x = -3, \quad -2, \quad -1, \quad 0, \quad 1, \quad 2, \quad 3, \quad 4, \quad 5,$$

and then sketch a smooth curve for each of the two equations. The curves obviously intersect at $x = 2$ and 4. There is a third intersection between -1 and 0. To find it, we put $f(x) = 2^x - x^2$ and use Newton's method to locate a root of $f(x) = 0$. Recall that the general procedure is to make an initial guess (we shall put $x_1 = -1$), and then use the formula

$$x_{n+1} = x_n - \frac{f(x_n)}{f'(x_n)}$$

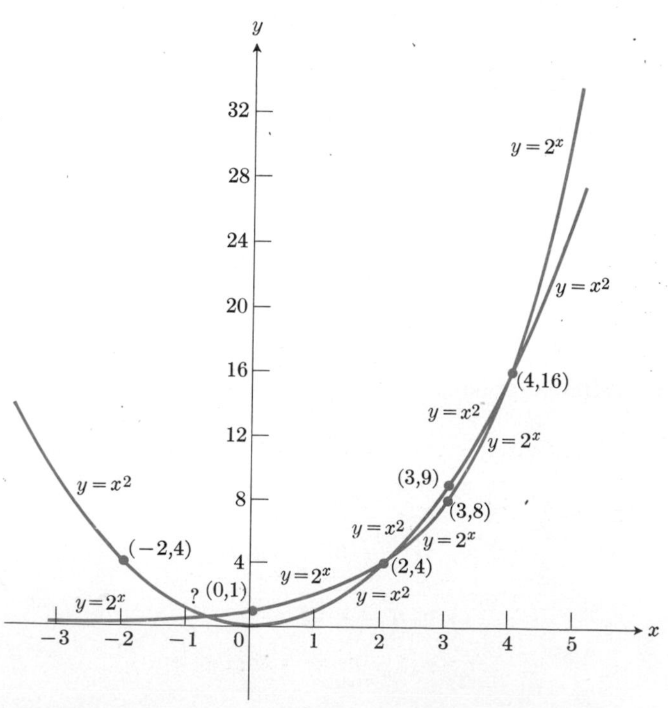

6–17 Where do the curves $y = x^2$ and $y = 2^x$ intersect? (At $x = 2$, $x = 4$, and $x = ?$.)

to get other approximations. For $f(x) = 2^x - x^2$ we get

$$x' = x - \frac{2^x - x^2}{2^x \ln 2 - 2x}$$

where, for simplicity of notation, we have written x' in place of x_{n+1} on the left and x in place of x_n on the right. The successive approximations are:

$$x_1 = -1$$
$$x_2 = -0.7869$$
$$x_3 = -0.7668$$
$$x_4 = -0.7667$$
$$x_5 = -0.766665$$
$$x_6 = -0.76666470$$
$$x_7 = -0.766664696 \qquad x_7 = x_8 \quad (x_7)^2 = 0.587774756$$
$$x_8 = -0.766664696 \qquad 2^{x_7} = 0.587774756$$

We continued the iterations until we got nine-decimal agreement. For accuracy to three decimals, $x = -0.767$, and we have the answer in three iterations.

EXAMPLE 2. If n is a real constant and u is a positive differentiable function of x, show that

$$\frac{du^n}{dx} = nu^{n-1}\frac{du}{dx}.$$

Solution. Let $y = u^n$. Then

$$\ln y = \ln u^n = n \ln u,$$

$$\frac{1}{y}\frac{dy}{dx} = n\frac{1}{u}\frac{du}{dx},$$

$$\frac{dy}{dx} = n\frac{y}{u}\frac{du}{dx} = n\frac{u^n}{u}\frac{du}{dx}$$

$$= nu^{n-1}\frac{du}{dx}. \qquad \text{Q.E.D.}$$

EXAMPLE 3. Find dy/dx if $y = x^x$, $x > 0$.

Solution. $\ln y = \ln x^x = x \ln x,$

$$\frac{1}{y}\frac{dy}{dx} = x \cdot \frac{1}{x} + \ln x = 1 + \ln x,$$

$$\frac{dy}{dx} = y(1 + \ln x) = x^x(1 + \ln x).$$

EXAMPLE 4. Find dy/dx if

$$y^{2/3} = \frac{(x^2+1)(3x+4)^{1/2}}{\sqrt[5]{(2x-3)(x^2-4)}}, \qquad (x > 2).$$

Solution

$$\ln y^{2/3} = \tfrac{2}{3} \ln y$$
$$= \ln (x^2+1) + \tfrac{1}{2} \ln (3x+4) - \tfrac{1}{5} \ln (2x-3) - \tfrac{1}{5} \ln (x^2-4) \quad \textbf{(a)}$$

and

$$\frac{2}{3} \cdot \frac{1}{y} \frac{dy}{dx} = \frac{2x}{x^2+1} + \frac{1}{2} \cdot \frac{3}{3x+4} - \frac{1}{5} \cdot \frac{2}{2x-3} - \frac{1}{5} \cdot \frac{2x}{x^2-4},$$

so that

$$\frac{dy}{dx} = \frac{3y}{2}\left[\frac{2x}{x^2+1} + \frac{\frac{3}{2}}{3x+4} - \frac{\frac{2}{5}}{2x-3} - \frac{2x/5}{x^2-4}\right].$$

REMARK. The restriction $x > 2$ ensures that all the quantities whose logarithms are indicated in (a) above are positive. If we want dy/dx at a point where y is negative, we may multiply our equation by -1 before taking logarithms; for if y is negative, then $-y$ is positive and $\ln(-y)$ is defined.

EXAMPLE 5 *Point elasticity of total cost.* Economists define the ratio of marginal cost to average cost as the point elasticity of total cost. That is, if the total cost of producing x units of a given product is $y = f(x)$ dollars, then the "average cost" is y/x dollars per unit. The "marginal cost," which is, roughly speaking, the additional cost of producing one more unit, is dy/dx. Then, by definition,

$$\text{Point elasticity of total cost} = \frac{dy/dx}{y/x} = \frac{dy/y}{dx/x} = \frac{d(\ln y)}{d(\ln x)}.$$

When the point elasticity of total cost equals one, then marginal cost equals average cost (that is, $dy/dx = y/x$) and average cost has a stationary value (that is, $d(y/x)/dx = 0$). [For further discussion, see Alpha C. Chiang, *Fundamental Methods of Mathematical Economics*, Second edition, McGraw-Hill Book Company, 1974, pp. 202ff.]

PROBLEMS

Use the method of logarithmic differentiation to find dy/dx in each of the following problems (1 through 8).

1. $y^2 = x(x+1) \quad (x > 0)$

2. $y = \sqrt[3]{\dfrac{x+1}{x-1}} \quad (x > 1)$

3. $y = \dfrac{x\sqrt{x^2+1}}{(x+1)^{2/3}} \quad (x > 0)$

4. $y = \sqrt[3]{\dfrac{x(x+1)(x-2)}{(x^2+1)(2x+3)}} \quad (x > 2)$

5. $y = x^{\sin x} \quad (x > 0)$

6. $y = (\sin x)^{\tan x} \quad (\sin x > 0)$

7. $y = 2^{\sec x}$

8. $y = x^{\ln x} \quad (x > 0)$

9. Show that $(ab)^u = a^u b^u$ if a and b are any positive numbers and u is any real number.

10. Show that the derivative of average cost is zero when marginal cost and average cost are equal.

Evaluate the following integrals (11–15):

11. $\displaystyle\int_0^{\ln 2} e^{-2x}\, dx$

12. $\displaystyle\int_0^{1.2} 3^x\, dx$

13. $\int_1^{\sqrt{2}} x2^{-x^2}\,dx$

14. $\int_0^1 5^{2t-2}\,dt$

15. $\int_0^{\pi/6} (\cos\theta)4^{-\sin\theta}\,d\theta$

16. Let a be a number greater than one. Prove that the graph of $y = a^x$ has the following characteristics:

a) If $x_1 > x_2$, then $a^{x_1} > a^{x_2}$.

b) The graph is everywhere concave upward.

c) The graph lies entirely above the x-axis.

d) The slope at any point is proportional to the ordinate there, and the proportionality factor is the slope at the y-intercept of the graph.

e) The curve approaches the negative x-axis as $x \to -\infty$.

17. Suppose that a and b are positive numbers such that $a^b = b^a$. (For example, $2^4 = 4^2$.)

a) Show that $(\ln a)/a = (\ln b)/b$.

b) Show that the graph of the function $f(x) = (\ln x)/x$ has a maximum at $x = e$, a point of inflection at $x = e^{3/2}$, approaches minus infinity as x approaches zero through positive values, and approaches zero as x approaches plus infinity. Sketch its graph.

c) Use the results of parts (a) and (b) to show that:

i) If $0 < a \le 1$ and $a^b = b^a$ then $b = a$, and

ii) If $1 < a < e$, or if $a > e$, then there is exactly one number $b \ne a$ such that $a^b = b^a$.

18. In Example 1, we found three zeros for the function $f(x) = 2^x - x^2$. Might there be others? One way to find out is to study the derived function $f'(x)$ to see how many zeros it has.

a) Show that each zero of $f'(x)$ corresponds to an intersection of the graphs of $y = 2^x \ln 2$ and $y = 2x$. Further, show that the first of these is everywhere concave upward while the second is a straight line. Sketch their graphs.

b) From the analysis of part (a), what can you conclude about the number of zeros of $f'(x)$? Of $f(x)$?

c) (*Calculator*) If you have a calculator that can easily evaluate $2^x \ln 2$ and $2^x(\ln 2)^2$, find the zeros of $f'(x)$ to three-decimal accuracy. Compare your answers with what you might expect from Fig. 6–17.

19. For what positive values of x does $x^{(x^x)} = (x^x)^x$?

6–10 THE FUNCTION $\log_a u$

We know that $\ln u$ is the power to which e may be raised to give u. For that reason, we say that e is the base of the system of natural logarithms in keeping with the following definition.

Definition. *If u is positive and a is a positive number different from* 1, *we say that y is the logarithm of u to the base a, and write*

$$y = \log_a u, \tag{1a}$$

provided y is the power to which a may be raised to give u:

$$a^y = u. \tag{1b}$$

For example,

$$\log_5 25 = 2 \quad \text{since} \quad 5^2 = 25,$$

$$\log_2 \tfrac{1}{4} = -2 \quad \text{since} \quad 2^{-2} = \tfrac{1}{4}.$$

To find $x = \log_4 8$, we rewrite the equation as

$$4^x = 2^{2x} = 8 = 2^3,$$

from which we read $2x = 3$, $x = \frac{3}{2}$. In other words,

$$\log_4 8 = \tfrac{3}{2} \quad \text{since} \quad 4^{3/2} = (\sqrt{4})^3 = 8.$$

We may solve Eq. (1b) for y, and thereby obtain an expression for $\log_a u$, by taking natural logarithms and applying Eq. (3′) of Article 6–9:

$$\ln u = \ln a^y = y \ln a.$$

If $\ln a \ne 0$ (which is the case when a is different from 1), we may solve for y.

The result is that

$$y = \frac{\ln u}{\ln a}$$

is the power to which a may be raised to produce u. In other words,

$$\log_a u = \frac{\ln u}{\ln a}. \tag{2}$$

Properties of $\log_a u$

The following properties follow readily from Eq. (2) above and the analogous properties of $\ln u$.

$$\textbf{a)}\ \log_a uv = \log_a u + \log_a v$$

$$\textbf{b)}\ \log_a \frac{u}{v} = \log_a u - \log_a v \tag{3}$$

$$\textbf{c)}\ \log_a u^v = v \log_a u$$

Equation (3c), for example, is derived as follows:

$$\log_a u^v = \frac{\ln u^v}{\ln a} = \frac{v \ln u}{\ln a} = v \log_a u,$$

where we make use of Eq. (2), then Eq. (3′) of Article 6–9, and then Eq. (2) again.

If u is a differentiable positive function of x, we may differentiate both sides of Eq. (2) and thus obtain

$$\frac{d \log_a u}{dx} = \frac{1}{u \ln a} \frac{du}{dx}. \tag{4}$$

It is clear that this formula is simpler for logarithms to the base e than for any other base. The only bases of practical importance are $a = e$ (natural logarithms) and $a = 10$ (common logarithms). Since $\ln 10 = 2.30259\ldots$, Eq. (4) is certainly less attractive for the case $a = 10$ than it is for the case $a = e$. This is the primary reason why natural logarithms are to be preferred over common logarithms in applications of the calculus.

Common logarithms are often used in scientific formulas. For example, earthquake intensity is reported on the Richter scale. Here the formula is

$$m = \log\left(\frac{a}{T}\right) + B, \tag{5}$$

where a is the amplitude of the ground motion in microns at the receiving station, T is the period of the seismic wave in seconds, and B is an empirical factor that allows for weakening of the seismic wave with increasing distance from the epicenter of the earthquake. Other familiar examples include the measurement of noise in decibels and acidity in pH values.

If y is any function of x of the general form

$$y = A \cdot C^x, \tag{6}$$

the range of values of y may be very large, especially if C is large compared to one. To compensate for such a large spread of the values of y, we can take logarithms to any base. If the base is 10, we get

$$\log y = \log A + x \log C, \tag{7}$$

so that the graph of $\log y$ as a function of x is a straight line with slope $\log C$ and with intercept $(0, \log A)$. A change of one unit in $\log y$ corresponds to multiplying or dividing y by a factor of 10.

PROBLEMS

Determine the following logarithms:

1. a) $\log_4 16$ b) $\log_8 32$
   c) $\log_5 0.04$ d) $\log_{0.5} 4$
2. a) $\log_2 4$ b) $\log_4 2$
   c) $\log_8 16$ d) $\log_{32} 4$
3. Find x if $3^x = 2^{x+1}$.
4. Find x if $3^{\log_3 7} + 2^{\log_2 5} = 5^{\log_5 x}$.
5. Show that $\log_b u = \log_a u \cdot \log_b a$ if a, b, and u are positive numbers, $a \neq 1$, $b \neq 1$.
6. Given $\ln 2 = 0.69315$, $\ln 10 = 2.30259$, and $\log_{10} 2 = 0.30103$. Find:
   a) $\log_{10} 20$, $\log_{10} 200$, $\log_{10} 0.2$, $\log_{10} 0.02$;
   b) $\ln 20$, $\ln 200$, $\ln 0.2$, $\ln 0.02$.
7. Which function is changing faster at $x = 10$,
   $$f_1(x) = \ln x \quad \text{or} \quad f_2(x) = \log_2 x?$$
8. Stirling's formula says that, if n is large, then
   $$n! \sim \sqrt{2\pi}\, n^{n+(1/2)}e^{-n}.$$
   For what value of the constant m can we replace e^{-n} by 10^{-mn} in the formula?
9. Find the derivatives of the following:
   a) $y = 3^{\tan x}$ b) $y = (x^2 + 1)^{\ln x}$
   c) $s = 2^{-t^2}$ d) $r = \theta e^{-2\theta}$

6–11

COMPOUND INTEREST AND EXPONENTIAL GROWTH

We are all familiar with arithmetic progressions and geometric progressions. In an arithmetic progression

$$a, \quad a + b, \quad a + 2b, \quad a + 3b, \quad \ldots$$

each term is a fixed amount more (or less) than the term before it. In a geometric progression

$$a, \quad ar, \quad ar^2, \quad ar^3, \quad \ldots$$

each term is a fixed *multiple* of the term before it. The way money on deposit in a savings account grows is like a geometric progression. For example, if a bank pays 6 percent annual interest and compounds interest quarterly, an amount A at the start of an interest period receives an additional

$$\frac{0.06}{4}A = \frac{r}{4}A \qquad (r = 0.06)$$

at the end of the interest period. Because the interest is added to the original amount A, the amount at the end of the period is

$$A + \frac{r}{4}A = \left(1 + \frac{r}{4}\right)A,$$

and the amounts at the ends of successive interest periods form a geometric progression

$$A, \quad \left(1 + \frac{r}{4}\right) A, \quad \left(1 + \frac{r}{4}\right)^2 A, \quad \ldots, \quad \left(1 + \frac{r}{4}\right)^n A.$$

In particular, at the end of t years the number of interest periods is $n = 4t$ and the amount is

$$A_t = \left(1 + \frac{r}{4}\right)^{4t} A_0 \qquad (t = \text{an integer}), \tag{1}$$

where A_0 is the original amount.

EXAMPLE 1. A bank agrees to pay 6 percent interest compounded quarterly for the next eight years. How much should you deposit now in order to have \$1000 in the account eight years from now?

Solution. We put $A_8 = 1000$ in Eq. (1), with $r = 0.06$ and $t = 8$:

$$1000 = A_0(1.015)^{32}$$

and solve for A_0:

$$A_0 = 1000(1.015)^{-32} = 620.9929 \quad \text{(to four decimals)}.$$

Thus a deposit of \$621 would yield \$1000 in eight years if the interest is 6 percent compounded quarterly.

More generally, suppose the rate r per year is fixed, but the number of compounding periods per year is k. Then Eq. (1) becomes

$$A_t = A_0 \left(1 + \frac{r}{k}\right)^{kt} = A_0 \left[\left(1 + \frac{r}{k}\right)^k\right]^t. \tag{2}$$

The expression

$$f(k) = \left(1 + \frac{r}{k}\right)^k \tag{3}$$

has a limit as k increases without bound. To find what that limit is, we take the natural logarithm

$$\ln f(k) = k \ln \left(1 + \frac{r}{k}\right) \tag{4}$$

and then put

$$\frac{r}{k} = h, \qquad \text{so} \quad k = \frac{r}{h}$$

and

$$\ln f(k) = \frac{r}{h} \ln (1 + h) = r \frac{\ln (1 + h)}{h}. \tag{4'}$$

As k increases without bound, h approaches zero through positive values and, by l'Hôpital's rule,

$$\lim_{h \to 0+} \frac{\ln(1+h)}{h} = \lim_{h \to 0+} \frac{1}{1+h} = 1.$$

Hence, $\ln f(k)$ in Eq. (4′) has the limit r as k approaches infinity and $f(k)$ has the limit e^r. Thus, from Eq. (2), as k increases without bound, we get

$$\lim A_t = A_0 e^{rt}. \tag{5}$$

REMARK 1. When we took the limit as k increases without bound in Eq. (2) above, we went to the extreme of compounding the interest continuously. The result is the function

$$A(t) = A_0 e^{rt}. \tag{6}$$

In this relation, we need not restrict t to be an integer—it can be any real number greater than or equal to zero. The derivative of this function is

$$\frac{dA}{dt} = rA_0 e^{rt} = rA. \tag{7}$$

If we rewrite Eq. (7) in differential form, we get

$$dA = rA\,dt = A(r\,dt). \tag{7′}$$

This equation can be interpreted as the increase that would be added to A during a very short interval of time from t to $t + dt$. The increase is jointly proportional to the amount A at time t and to the annual interest rate r multiplied by dt, which we can interpret as a very small fraction of a year.

REMARK 2. There are many physical, biological, ecological, and economic phenomena in which some quantity x grows, or declines, at a rate that is proportional to the amount that is present at time t. This is expressed by the differential equation

$$\frac{dx}{dt} = kx. \tag{8}$$

If we know the value of x at some instant of time, we take that as $t = 0$ and use the initial condition

$$x = x_0 \quad \text{when} \quad t = 0 \tag{9}$$

to determine x as a function of t.

The general solution of the differential equation

$$\frac{dx}{dt} = kx \qquad \text{with } x = x_0 \text{ when } t = 0$$

is

$$x = x_0 e^{kt}. \tag{10}$$

Positive values of k correspond to exponential growth; negative values correspond to decrease. For example, if a body of water has become polluted with some substance but the polluting source has been stopped and fresh water is being continuously introduced with thorough mixing, then we can expect the rate of decrease of the amount of the pollutant in the water to be proportional to the amount still remaining. Equation (10), with an appropriate negative value of k, would then describe the amount of pollutant at time t after the cleanup had begun.

EXAMPLE 2. Suppose \$621 is deposited in an account with interest at the rate of 6 percent and the interest is compounded continuously for eight years. Find the amount at the time $t = 8$.

Solution. The phrase "compounded continuously" corresponds mathematically to the limit we got in Eq. (5) as $k \to \infty$. Thus, we put $r = 0.06$, $t = 8$, and $A_0 = 621$, to obtain the answer

$$A_8 = 621e^{0.48} = 1003.5822 \quad \text{(to four decimals)}.$$

The effect of continuous compounding, as compared with quarterly, has been an addition of \$3.58. A bank might decide it would be worth this additional amount to be able to advertise "we compound your money every second, night and day—better than that, we compound the interest continuously."

EXAMPLE 3. Suppose that the amount of substance x follows the exponential law of Eq. (10). If x decreases by 10 percent in 18 months, how long will it be until x is less than $0.005x_0$?

Solution. Let t be measured in months and put $x = 0.9x_0$ and $t = 18$ in Eq. (10). Thus,

$$0.9x_0 = x_0 e^{18k}, \qquad 18k = \ln 0.9 = -0.1054, \qquad k = -0.0059.$$

With k known, we now substitute $x = 0.005x_0$ and solve for t:

$$0.005x_0 = x_0 e^{kt}, \qquad kt = \ln 0.005, \qquad t = \frac{\ln 0.005}{k} = \frac{-5.2983}{-0.0059},$$

or $t = 906$ months, or about 75.5 years. The 75 years is 50 times 18 months: Each 18 months corresponds to multiplying by 0.90, and $(0.90)^{50}$ is approximately 0.005.

Benjamin Franklin's Will. The Franklin Technical Institute of Boston owes its existence to a codicil to the will of Benjamin Franklin. In part, that codicil reads:

> I was born in Boston, New England and owe my first instruction in Literature to the free Grammar Schools established there: I have therefore already considered those schools in my Will.... I have considered that among Artisans good Apprentices are most likely to make good citizens ... I wish to be useful even after my Death, if possible, in forming and advancing other young men that may be serviceable to their Country in both Boston and Philadelphia. To this end I devote Two

> thousand Pounds Sterling, which I give, one thousand thereof to the Inhabitants of the Town of Boston in Massachusetts, and the other thousand to the inhabitants of the City of Philadelphia, in Trust and for the Uses, Interests and Purposes hereinafter mentioned and declared.

Franklin's plan was to lend money to young apprentices at 5 percent interest with the provision that each borrower should pay each year "with the yearly Interest, one tenth part of the Principal, which sums of Principal and Interest shall be again let to fresh Borrowers.

"If this plan is executed and succeeds as projected without interruption for one hundred Years, the Sum will then be one hundred and thirty-one thousand Pounds of which I would have the Managers of the Donation to the Inhabitants of the Town of Boston, then lay out at their discretion one hundred thousand Pounds in Public Works.... The remaining thirty-one thousand Pounds, I would have continued to be let out on Interest in the manner above directed for another hundred Years.... At the end of this second term if no unfortunate accident has prevented the operation the sum will be Four Millions and Sixty-one Thousand Pounds."

It was not always possible to find as many borrowers as Franklin had planned, but the managers of the trust did the best they could; they lent money to medical students as well as others. At the end of one hundred years from the reception of the Franklin gift, January, 1894, the fund had grown from one thousand pounds to almost exactly ninety thousand pounds. In one hundred years the original capital had multiplied about ninety times instead of the one hundred and thirty-one times Franklin had anticipated.

QUESTION. What rate of interest, compounded continuously for one hundred years, would multiply the original capital by 90?

The mathematical model we assume is that which is expressed by the equation

$$A = A_0 e^{rt},$$

where A_0 is the original capital, r is the interest rate per year (but compounded continuously), and t is the time in years. If we put $t = 100$ and $A = 90A_0$, we get

$$90A_0 = A_0 e^{100r},$$

which leads to

$$100r = \ln 90 = 4.50$$

or

$$r = 0.045 \quad \text{or} \quad 4.5 \text{ percent.}$$

PROBLEMS

1. Suppose that the GNP in a country is increasing at an annual rate of 4 percent. How many years, at that rate of growth, are required in order to double the present GNP?

2. In Benjamin Franklin's estimate that the original one thousand pounds would grow to 131 thousand in 100 years, he was using an annual rate of 5 percent and compounding once each year. What rate of interest per year when compounded continuously for 100 years would produce such a result as to multiply the original amount by 131?

3. If you use the approximation $\ln 2 \approx 0.70$ (in place of

0.69315...), you can derive a rule of thumb that says "If a quantity grows at the rate of 5 percent per year compounded continuously over the next 70 years, then it will double in about $\frac{70}{5} = 14$ years, so it will be multiplied by $2^5 = 32$ during the 70-year span. If the annual rate is r percent, it will be multiplied by about 2^r during a life span of 70 years." Show how this is derived.

4. Suppose a body of mass m moving in a straight line with velocity v encounters a resistance proportional to the velocity and this is the only force acting on the body. If the body starts with velocity v_0, how far does it travel in time t? Assume $F = d(mv)/dt$.

5. A radioactive substance disintegrates at a rate proportional to the amount present. How much of the substance remains at time t if the initial amount is Q_0?

6. If the bacteria in a culture increase continuously at a rate proportional to the number present, and the initial number is N_0, find the number at time t.

In Problems 7–10, substitute $y = e^{rx}$ and find values of the constant r for which $y = e^{rx}$ is a solution of the given differential equation.

7. $\dfrac{d^2y}{dx^2} - 4\dfrac{dy}{dx} + 3y = 0$ **8.** $\dfrac{d^2y}{dx^2} - \dfrac{dy}{dx} - 2y = 0$

9. $\dfrac{d^3y}{dx^3} + 6\dfrac{d^2y}{dx^2} + 5\dfrac{dy}{dx} = 0$ **10.** $\dfrac{d^4y}{dx^4} - 13\dfrac{d^2y}{dx^2} + 36y = 0$

REVIEW QUESTIONS AND EXERCISES

1. Review the formulas for derivatives of sums, products, quotients, powers, sines, and cosines. Using these, develop formulas for derivatives of the other trigonometric functions.

2. Define the inverse sine, inverse cosine, inverse tangent, and inverse secant functions. What is the *domain* of each? What is its *range*? What is the derivative of each? Sketch the graph of each.

3. Define the natural logarithm function. What is its domain? What is its range? What is its derivative? Sketch its graph.

4. What is the inverse function of the natural logarithm called? What is the domain of this function? What is its range? What is its derivative? Sketch its graph.

5. Define the term "algebraic function." Define "transcendental function." To which class (algebraic or transcendental) do you think the greatest integer function (Fig. 1–45) belongs?

[It is often difficult to prove that a particular function belongs to one class or the other. Numbers are also classified as algebraic and transcendental. *References:* (1) W. J. Le Veque, *Topics in Number Theory*, Addison-Wesley, Vol. II, Chap. 5, pp. 161–200; (2) I. M. Niven, *Irrational Numbers*, Carus monograph number 11 of the Mathematical Association of America, (1956). Both π and e are transcendental numbers, and proofs may be found in the references cited. That π is transcendental was first proved by Ferdinand Lindemann in 1882. One result that follows from the transcendence of π is that it is impossible to construct, with unmarked straightedge and compass alone, a square whose area is equal to the area of a given circle. The first proof that e is transcendental was published by Charles Hermite in 1873. You may also enjoy reading about an interesting related feature of the graph of $y = \ln x$ in the article on logarithms on p. 301 of Vol. 14 of the *Encyclopedia Britannica* (1956 edition).]

6. Let n be an integer greater than 1. Divide the interval $1 \le x \le n$ into n equal subintervals and write an expression for the trapezoidal approximation to the area under the graph of $y = 1/x$, $1 \le x \le n$, based on this subdivision. Is this approximation less than, equal to, or greater than $\ln n$? Give a reason for your answer.

7. Prove that $\lim_{x\to\infty} (\ln x)/x = 0$, starting with the definition of $\ln x$ as an integral.

8. The *Encyclopedia Britannica* article on logarithms begins with the statement: "By shortening processes of computation, logarithms have doubled the working speed of astronomers and engineers." What property or properties of logarithms do you think the author of the article had in mind when he made that statement?

9. What is the meaning of the differential equation $dy/dt = ky$? What is the solution of this equation that satisfies the initial condition $y = y_0$ when $t = 0$?

MISCELLANEOUS PROBLEMS

In each of the following problems (1 through 25), (a) find dy/dx, and (b) sketch the curve.

1. $y = \sin 2x$ **2.** $y = 4\cos(2x + \pi/4)$

3. $y = 2\sin x + \sin 2x$ **4.** $y = \dfrac{\sin x}{1 + \cos x}$

5. $x = \cos y$ **6.** $x = \tan y$

7. $y = 4\sin\left(\dfrac{x}{2} + \pi\right)$ **8.** $y = 1 - \sin x$

9. $y = x - \sin x$

10. $y = \dfrac{\sin x}{x}$ (What happens as $x \to 0$? As $x \to \infty$?)

11. $y = \dfrac{\sin x}{x^2}$ (What happens as $x \to 0$? As $x \to \infty$?)

12. $y = x \sin \dfrac{1}{x}$ (What happens as $x \to \infty$? As $x \to 0$?)

13. $y = x^2 \sin \dfrac{1}{x}$ (What happens as $x \to \infty$? As $x \to 0$?)

14. $x = \tan \dfrac{\pi y}{2}$ 15. $y = \dfrac{e^x - e^{-x}}{e^x + e^{-x}}$

16. $y = xe^{-x}$

17. a) $y = x \ln x$, b) $y = \sqrt{x} \ln x$

18. a) $y = \dfrac{\ln x}{x}$, b) $y = \dfrac{\ln x}{\sqrt{x}}$, c) $y = \dfrac{\ln x}{x^2}$

19. $y = e^{-x} \sin 2x$

20. a) $y = 2x - \frac{1}{2}e^{2x}$, b) $y = e^{[2x \; (1/2)e^{2x}]}$

21. a) $y = x - e^x$, b) $y = e^{(x - e^x)}$

22. $y = \ln (x + \sqrt{x^2 + 1})$ 23. $y = \frac{1}{2} \ln \dfrac{1 + x}{1 - x}$

24. $y = \ln (x^2 + 4)$ 25. $y = x \tan^{-1} \dfrac{x}{2}$

Find dy/dx in Problems 26–42.

26. $y = \dfrac{e^{2x} - e^{-2x}}{e^{2x} + e^{-2x}}$ 27. $y = \ln \dfrac{\sec x + \tan x}{\sec x - \tan x}$

28. $y = x^2 e^{2x} \sin 3x$ 29. $y = \sin^{-1} (x^2) - xe^{x^2}$

30. $y = \ln \left(\dfrac{x^4}{1 + x^3}\right) + 7^{x^{2/3}}$ 31. $y = (x^2 + 2)^{2-x}$

32. $y = \dfrac{\ln x}{e^x}$ 33. $y = \ln \dfrac{x}{\sqrt{x^2 + 1}}$

34. $y = \ln (4 - 3x)$ 35. $y = \ln (3x^2 + 4x)$

36. $y = x(\ln x)^3$ 37. $y = x \ln (x^3)$

38. $y = x^3 \ln x$ 39. $y = \ln e^x$

40. $y = x^2 e^x$ 41. $x = \ln y$

42. $y = \ln (\ln x)$

43. Find dy/dx by logarithmic differentiation for

a) $y = \dfrac{x}{x^2 + 1}$, $x > 0$; b) $y = \sqrt[3]{\dfrac{x(x - 2)}{x^2 + 1}}$, $x > 2$.

44. If $f(x) = x + e^{4x}$, find $f(0)$ and $f'(0)$, and find an approximation for $f(0.01)$.

45. Find dy/dx for each of the following:

a) $y = a^{x^2 - x}$, b) $y = \ln \dfrac{e^x}{1 + e^x}$,

c) $y = x \ln x - x$ d) $y = x^{1/x}$.

46. Sketch the graphs of $y = \ln (1 - x)$ and $y = \ln (1/x)$.

47. Sketch (in a common figure) the graphs of $y = e^{-x}$ and $y = -e^{-x}$.

48. Solve for x: $\tan^{-1} x - \cot^{-1} x = \pi/4$.

49. If $\dfrac{dy}{dx} = \dfrac{e^x - e^{-x}}{e^x + e^{-x}}$, find $\dfrac{d^2y}{dx^2}$ and y.

50. If $dy/dx = 2/e^y$ and $y = 0$ when $x = 5$, find y as a function of x.

51. $P(x_1, y_1)$ and $Q(x_2, y_2)$ are any two points (in the first quadrant) lying on the hyperbola $xy = R$ (R positive). Show that the area bounded by the arc PQ, the lines $x = x_1$, $x = x_2$, and the x-axis is equal to the area bounded by the arc PQ, the lines $y = y_1$, $y = y_2$, and the y-axis.

52. By the trapezoidal rule, find $\int_0^2 e^{-x^2} dx$, using $n = 4$.

53. In a capacitor discharging electricity, the rate of change of the voltage in volts per second is proportional to the voltage, being numerically equal to minus one-fortieth of the voltage. Express the voltage as a function of the time. In how many seconds will the voltage decrease to 10 percent of its original value?

54. A curve $y = f(x)$ goes through the points $(0, 0)$ and (x_1, y_1). It divides the rectangle $0 \le x \le x_1, 0 \le y \le y_1$ into two regions: A above the curve and B below. Find the curve if the area of A is twice the area of B for all choices of $x_1 > 0$ and $y_1 > 0$.

55. Find a curve passing through the origin and such that the length s of the curve between the origin and any point (x, y) of the curve is given by

$$s = e^x + y - 1.$$

56. A particle starts at the origin and moves along the x-axis in such a way that its velocity at the point $(x, 0)$ is given by the formula $dx/dt = \cos^2 \pi x$. How long will it take to cover the distance from the origin to the point $x = \frac{1}{4}$? Will it ever reach the point $x = \frac{1}{2}$? Why?

57. A particle moves in a straight line with acceleration $a = 4/(4 - t)^2$. If when $t = 0$ the velocity is equal to 2, find how far the particle moves between $t = 1$ and $t = 2$.

58. The velocity of a certain particle moving along the x-axis is proportional to x. At time $t = 0$ the particle is located at $x = 2$ and at time $t = 10$ it is at $x = 4$. Find its position at $t = 5$.

59. Solve the differential equation $dy/dx = y^2 e^{-x}$ if $y = 2$ when $x = 0$.

60. It is estimated that the population of a certain country is now increasing at a rate of 2 percent per year. Assuming that this (instantaneous) rate will continue indefinitely, estimate what the population N will be t years from now, if the population now is N_0. How many years will it take for the population to double?

61. If $y = (e^{2x} - 1)/(e^{2x} + 1)$, show that $dy/dx = 1 - y^2$.

62. Determine the inflection points of the curve $y = e^{-(x/a)^2}$, where a is a positive constant. Sketch the curve. (This is closely related to the normal curve used in statistics.)

63. Find the volume generated when the area bounded by $x = \sec y$, $x = 0$, $y = 0$, $y = \pi/3$, is rotated about the y-axis.

64. Find the length of the curve

$$\frac{x}{a} = \left(\frac{y}{b}\right)^2 - \frac{1}{8}\left(\frac{b^2}{a^2}\right)\ln\left(\frac{y}{b}\right)$$

from $y = b$ to $y = 3b$, assuming a and b to be positive constants.

65. Find the volume generated by rotating about the x-axis the area bounded by $y = e^x$, $y = 0$, $x = 0$, $x = 2$.

66. Find the area bounded by the curve

$$y = \left(\frac{a}{2}\right)(e^{x/a} + e^{-x/a}),$$

the x-axis, and the lines $x = -a$ and $x = +a$.

67. The portion of a tangent to a curve included between the x-axis and the point of tangency is bisected by the y-axis. If the curve passes through (1, 2), find its equation.

Evaluate the integrals in Problems 68–78.

68. $\displaystyle\int \frac{dx}{4 - 3x}$

69. $\displaystyle\int \frac{5\,dx}{x - 3}$

70. $\displaystyle\int_0^2 \frac{x\,dx}{x^2 + 2}$

71. $\displaystyle\int_0^2 \frac{x\,dx}{(x^2 + 2)^2}$

72. $\displaystyle\int \frac{x + 1}{x}\,dx$

73. $\displaystyle\int \frac{x}{2x + 1}\,dx$

74. $\displaystyle\int_0^1 \frac{x^2\,dx}{2 - x^3}$

75. $\displaystyle\int_0^3 x(e^{x^2 - 1})\,dx$

76. $\displaystyle\int_1^3 \frac{dx}{x}$

77. $\displaystyle\int_0^5 \frac{x\,dx}{x^2 + 1}$

78. $\displaystyle\int_0^1 (e^x + 1)\,dx$

79. In the inversion of raw sugar, the time rate of change of the amount of raw sugar present varies as the amount of raw sugar remaining. If 1000 lb of raw sugar has been reduced to 800 lb after 10 hr, how much raw sugar will remain after 24 hr?

80. A cylindrical tank of radius 10 ft and height 20 ft, with its axis vertical, is full of water but has a leak at the bottom. Assuming that water escapes at a rate proportional to the depth of water in the tank and that 10 percent escapes during the first hour, find a formula for the volume of water left in the tank after t hr.

81. Let p be a positive integer ≥ 2. Show that

$$\lim_{n\to\infty}\left(\frac{1}{n+1} + \frac{1}{n+2} + \cdots + \frac{1}{p \cdot n}\right) = \ln p.$$

82. (a) If $(\ln x)/x = (\ln 2)/2$, does it necessarily follow that $x = 2$? (b) If $(\ln x)/x = -2 \ln 2$, does it necessarily follow that $x = \frac{1}{2}$? Give reasons for your answers.

83. Given that $\lim_{x\to\infty} (\ln x)/x = 0$ (see Article 6–7, Problem 4). Prove that (a) $\lim_{x\to\infty} (\ln x)/x^h = 0$ if h is any positive constant, (b) $\lim_{x\to+\infty} x^n/e^x = 0$ if n is any constant.

84. Show that $\lim_{h\to 0} (e^h - 1)/h = 1$, by considering the definition of the derivative of e^x at $x = 0$.

85. Prove that if x is any positive number, $\lim_{n\to\infty} n(\sqrt[n]{x} - 1) = \ln x$. [*Hint.* Take $x = e^{nh}$ and apply Problem 84.] *Remark.* This result provides a method for finding $\ln x$ (to any desired finite number of decimal places) using nothing fancier than repeated use of the operation of extracting square roots. For we may take $n = 2^k$, and then $\sqrt[n]{x}$ is obtained from x by taking k successive square roots.

86. Show that $(x^2/4) < x - \ln(1 + x) < (x^2/2)$ if

$$0 < x < 1.$$

[*Hint.* Let $f(x) = x - \ln(1 + x)$ and show that $(x/2) < f'(x) < x$.]

87. Prove that the area under the graph of $y = 1/x$ over the interval $a \leq x \leq b$ $(a > 0)$ is the same as the area over the interval $ka \leq x \leq kb$, for any $k > 0$.

88. Find the limit, as $n \to \infty$, of

$$\frac{e^{1/n} + e^{2/n} + \cdots + e^{(n-1)/n} + e^{n/n}}{n}.$$

7

METHODS OF INTEGRATION

7–1 BASIC FORMULAS

Since indefinite integration is defined as the inverse of differentiation, evaluating an integral

$$\int f(x)\,dx \tag{1}$$

is equivalent to finding a function F such that

$$dF(x) = f(x)\,dx. \tag{2}$$

At first sight, this may seem like a hopeless task when we think of adopting a "trial-and-error" approach, and realize that it is simply impossible to try *all functions* as F in Eq. (2) hoping to find one that does the job.* In fact, it is even possible to write down fairly simple integrals, such as

$$\int \sin x^2\,dx, \qquad \int e^{-x^2}\,dx, \qquad \int \sqrt{1+x^4}\,dx, \tag{3}$$

which cannot be expressed in terms of finite combinations of the so-called "elementary functions" that we have studied thus far. We shall leave a discussion of such integrals as (3) to Chapter 16, and say simply that the words "finite combinations" must give way and an integral like (3) may then be expressed in terms of an infinite series.

In order to reduce the amount of trial and error involved in integration, it is useful to build up a table of standard types of integral formulas by inverting formulas for differentials, as we have done in the previous chapters. Then we try to match any integral that confronts us against one of the standard types. This usually involves a certain amount of algebraic manipulation.

A table of integrals, more extensive than the list of basic formulas given here, may be found inside the covers of this book. To use such a table intelligently, it is necessary to become familiar with certain basic techniques that one can apply to reduce a given integral to a form that matches an entry in the table. The examples and problems in this book should serve to develop skill with these techniques. To concentrate on the techniques without becoming entangled in a mass of algebra, these problems and examples have been kept fairly simple. In fact, *these particular problems* can frequently be solved immediately by consulting an integral table. But solving them this way right now would defeat the purpose of developing the skill likely to be needed for later work. And it is this skill that is important, rather than the specific answer to any given problem.

Perhaps a good way to develop the skill we are aiming for is to build your own table of integrals. You may, for example, make a notebook in which the various sections are headed by standard forms like

$$\int u^n\,du, \qquad \int \frac{du}{u}, \qquad \int e^u\,du, \qquad \text{etc.,}$$

* If f is continuous, then an integral function F satisfying Eq. (2) always exists. For example, for $F(x)$ we could take the area A_a^x discussed in Article 4–7. Theoretically, this, together with the fact that such an area can be calculated as a limit of sums of areas of rectangles, gives us a rule for computing $F(x)$. However, we are interested in avoiding these arithmetical calculations, if possible. Hence we prefer to find simple closed-form expressions for the integral whenever possible.

and then under each heading include several examples to illustrate the range of application of the particular formula.

Making such a notebook probably has educational value. But once it is made, it should rarely be necessary to refer to it!

Success in integration hinges on the ability to spot what part of the integrand should be called u in order that one will also have du, so that a known formula can be applied. This means that the *first requirement* for skill in integration is a thorough mastery of the formulas for differentiation. We therefore list certain formulas for differentials that have been derived in previous chapters, together with their integral counterparts. (See page 334.)

At present, let us just consider this list a handy reference and *not* a challenge to our memories! A bit of examination will probably convince us that we are already rather familiar with the first twelve formulas for *differentials* and, so far as *integration* is concerned, our training in technique will show us how to get the *integrals* in the last six cases without memorizing the formulas for the differentials of the inverse trigonometric functions.

Just what types of functions can we integrate directly with this short table of integrals?

Powers

$$\int u^n\,du, \qquad \int \frac{du}{u}.$$

Exponentials

$$\int e^u\,du, \qquad \int a^u\,du.$$

Trigonometric functions

$$\int \sin u\,du, \qquad \int \cos u\,du.$$

Algebraic functions

$$\int \frac{du}{\sqrt{1-u^2}}, \qquad \int \frac{du}{1+u^2}, \qquad \int \frac{du}{u\sqrt{u^2-1}}.$$

Of course, there are additional combinations of trigonometric functions such as $\int \sec^2 u\,du$, etc., which are integrable accidentally, so to speak.

What common types of functions are *not* included in the table?

Logarithms

$$\int \ln u\,du, \qquad \int \log_a u\,du.$$

Trigonometric functions

$$\int \tan u\,du, \qquad \int \cot u\,du, \qquad \int \sec u\,du, \qquad \int \csc u\,du.$$

Algebraic functions

$$\int \frac{du}{a^2+u^2}, \qquad \text{etc., with } a^2 \neq 1.$$

$$\int \sqrt{a^2 \pm u^2}\,du, \qquad \int \sqrt{u^2-a^2}\,du, \qquad \text{etc.}$$

Summary of Differential Formulas and Corresponding Integrals

Differential formula	Corresponding integral
1. $du = \dfrac{du}{dx}\,dx$	1. $\int du = u + C$
2. $d(au) = a\,du$	2. $\int a\,du = a \int du$
3. $d(u + v) = du + dv$	3. $\int (du + dv) = \int du + \int dv$
4. $d(u^n) = nu^{n-1}\,du$	4. $\int u^n\,du = \dfrac{u^{n+1}}{n+1} + C, \quad n \neq -1$
5. $d(\ln u) = \dfrac{du}{u}$	5. $\int \dfrac{du}{u} = \ln \lvert u \rvert + C$
6. a) $d(e^u) = e^u\,du$	6. a) $\int e^u\,du = e^u + C$
b) $d(a^u) = a^u \ln a\,du$	b) $\int a^u\,du = \dfrac{a^u}{\ln a} + C$
7. $d(\sin u) = \cos u\,du$	7. $\int \cos u\,du = \sin u + C$
8. $d(\cos u) = -\sin u\,du$	8. $\int \sin u\,du = -\cos u + C$
9. $d(\tan u) = \sec^2 u\,du$	9. $\int \sec^2 u\,du = \tan u + C$
10. $d(\cot u) = -\csc^2 u\,du$	10. $\int \csc^2 u\,du = -\cot u + C$
11. $d(\sec u) = \sec u \tan u\,du$	11. $\int \sec u \tan u\,du = \sec u + C$
12. $d(\csc u) = -\csc u \cot u\,du$	12. $\int \csc u \cot u\,du = -\csc u + C$
13. $d(\sin^{-1} u) = \dfrac{du}{\sqrt{1-u^2}}$ 14. $d(\cos^{-1} u) = \dfrac{-du}{\sqrt{1-u^2}}$	13. and 14. $\int \dfrac{du}{\sqrt{1-u^2}} = \begin{cases} \sin^{-1} u + C \\ -\cos^{-1} u + C' \end{cases}$
15. $d(\tan^{-1} u) = \dfrac{du}{1+u^2}$ 16. $d(\cot^{-1} u) = \dfrac{-du}{1+u^2}$	15. and 16. $\int \dfrac{du}{1+u^2} = \begin{cases} \tan^{-1} u + C \\ -\cot^{-1} u + C' \end{cases}$
17. $d(\sec^{-1} u) = \dfrac{du}{\lvert u \rvert \sqrt{u^2-1}}$ 18. $d(\csc^{-1} u) = \dfrac{-du}{\lvert u \rvert \sqrt{u^2-1}}$	17. and 18. $\int \dfrac{du}{u\sqrt{u^2-1}} = \begin{cases} \sec^{-1} \lvert u \rvert + C \\ -\csc^{-1} \lvert u \rvert + C' \end{cases}$

Inverse functions

$$\int \sin^{-1} u\,du, \qquad \int \tan^{-1} u\,du, \qquad \text{etc.}$$

We shall eventually see how to evaluate all of these and some others, but there are no methods that will solve *all* integration problems in terms of elementary functions.

PROBLEMS

Evaluate each of the integrals 1 through 44 by reducing the integrand to one of the standard forms. In each case, indicate what you have called u and refer by number to the standard formula used.

1. $\int \sqrt{2x+3}\,dx$
2. $\int \frac{dx}{3x+5}$
3. $\int \frac{dx}{(2x-7)^2}$
4. $\int \frac{(x+1)\,dx}{x^2+2x+3}$
5. $\int \frac{\sin x\,dx}{2+\cos x}$
6. $\int \tan^3 2x \sec^2 2x\,dx$
7. $\int \frac{x\,dx}{\sqrt{1-4x^2}}$
8. $\int x^{1/3}\sqrt{x^{4/3}-1}\,dx$
9. $\int \frac{2\,dx}{\sqrt{1-4x^2}}$
10. $\int \frac{2v\,dv}{\sqrt{1-v^4}}$
11. $\int \frac{x\,dx}{(3x^2+4)^3}$
12. $\int x^2\sqrt{x^3+5}\,dx$
13. $\int \frac{x^2\,dx}{\sqrt{x^3+5}}$
14. $\int \frac{x\,dx}{4x^2+1}$
15. $\int e^{2x}\,dx$
16. $\int e^{\cos x}\sin x\,dx$
17. $\int \frac{dx}{e^{3x}}$
18. $\int \frac{e^{\sqrt{x+1}}}{\sqrt{x+1}}\,dx$
19. $\int \frac{e^x\,dx}{1+e^{2x}}$
20. $\int \frac{dt}{1+9t^2}$
21. $\int \cos^2 x \sin x\,dx$
22. $\int \frac{\cos x\,dx}{\sin^3 x}$
23. $\int \cot^3 x \csc^2 x\,dx$
24. $\int \tan 3x \sec^2 3x\,dx$
25. $\int \frac{e^{2x}+e^{-2x}}{e^{2x}-e^{-2x}}\,dx$
26. $\int \sin 2x \cos^2 2x\,dx$
27. $\int (1+\cos\theta)^3 \sin\theta\,d\theta$
28. $\int te^{-t^2}\,dt$
29. $\int \frac{dt}{t\sqrt{4t^2-1}}$
30. $\int \frac{dx}{\sqrt{e^{2x}-1}}$ [*Hint.* Multiply numerator and denominator by e^x.]
31. $\int \frac{\cos x\,dx}{\sin x}$
32. $\int \frac{\cos x\,dx}{1+\sin x}$
33. $\int \sec^3 x \tan x\,dx$
34. $\int \frac{\sin\theta\,d\theta}{\sqrt{1+\cos\theta}}$
35. $\int e^{\tan 3x}\sec^2 3x\,dx$
36. $\int \cos 2t\sqrt{4-\sin 2t}\,dt$
37. $\int \frac{1+\cos 2x}{\sin^2 2x}\,dx$
38. $\int \frac{\sin^2 2x}{1+\cos 2x}\,dx$
39. $\int \frac{\csc^2 2t}{\sqrt{1+\cot 2t}}\,dt$
40. $\int e^{3x}\,dx$
41. $\int \frac{e^{\tan^{-1} 2t}}{1+4t^2}\,dt$
42. $\int xe^{-x^2}\,dx$
43. $\int 3^x\,dx$
44. $\int 10^{2x}\,dx$

45. Can both of the following integrations be correct? Explain.

a) $\int \frac{dx}{\sqrt{1-x^2}} = \sin^{-1} x + C$

b) $\int \frac{dx}{\sqrt{1-x^2}} = -\int \frac{-dx}{\sqrt{1-x^2}} = \cos^{-1}(-x) + C$

46. Solve for C in each of the following equations.

a) $\tan^{-1} u + \cot^{-1} u = C$
b) $\sec^{-1} |u| + \csc^{-1} |u| = C$

47. Each of the integrals in (a) through (c) may be evaluated easily for a particular numerical value of n. Choose this value and integrate. For example,

$$\int x^n \cos(x^2)\,dx$$

is evaluated easily for $n = 1$:

$$\int x\cos(x^2)\,dx = \tfrac{1}{2}\sin(x^2) + C.$$

a) $\int x^n \ln x\,dx$, b) $\int x^n e^{x^3}\,dx$, c) $\int x^n \sin\sqrt{x}\,dx$.

48. The integral $\int_a^\infty e^{-x^2}\,dx$ arises in statistics and elsewhere. It is defined to mean the same thing as

$$\lim_{b\to+\infty}\int_a^b e^{-x^2}\,dx.$$

Show that if $x > a \geq 1$, then $e^{-x^2} < e^{-ax}$. Hence, by comparing the integral from a to ∞ of e^{-x^2} with the integral of e^{-ax} and evaluating the latter integral, show that

$$\int_a^\infty e^{-x^2}\,dx < \frac{1}{a}e^{-a^2}, \qquad \text{if} \quad a \geq 1.$$

7–2 POWERS OF TRIGONOMETRIC FUNCTIONS

The formula

$$\int u^n\,du = \begin{cases} \dfrac{u^{n+1}}{n+1} + C, & n \neq -1, \\ \ln|u| + C, & n = -1, \end{cases}$$

may be used to evaluate certain integrals involving powers of the trigonometric functions, as illustrated by the examples that follow. The same methods work for powers of other functions. Pay attention to the *methods* rather than trying to remember specific results.

EXAMPLE 1

$$\int \sin^n ax \cos ax\,dx.$$

Solution. If we let $u = \sin ax$, then

$$du = \cos ax\,d(ax) = a\cos ax\,dx,$$

so that we need only multiply the integral by unity in the form of a times $1/a$. Since a and $1/a$ are constants, we may write a inside the integral sign and $1/a$ in front of the integral sign to have

$$\begin{aligned} \int \sin^n ax \cos ax\,dx &= \frac{1}{a}\int (\sin ax)^n (a\cos ax\,dx) \\ &= \frac{1}{a}\int u^n\,du \\ &= \begin{cases} \dfrac{1}{a}\dfrac{u^{n+1}}{n+1} + C, & n \neq -1, \\ \dfrac{1}{a}\ln|u| + C, & n = -1; \end{cases} \end{aligned}$$

that is,

$$\int \sin^n ax \cos ax\,dx = \frac{\sin^{n+1} ax}{(n+1)a} + C, \qquad n \neq -1, \tag{1a}$$

and if $n = -1$, we get

$$\int \cot ax\,dx = \int \frac{\cos ax\,dx}{\sin ax} = \frac{1}{a}\ln|\sin ax| + C. \tag{1b}$$

Note that the success of the method depended upon having $\cos ax$ to go with the dx as part of du.

By a similar method we can obtain

$$\int \cos^n ax \sin ax\, dx = \frac{-\cos^{n+1} ax}{(n+1)a} + C, \qquad n \neq -1, \tag{2a}$$

and, when $n = -1$,

$$\int \tan ax\, dx = \int \frac{\sin ax}{\cos ax} dx = -\frac{1}{a} \ln |\cos ax| + C. \tag{2b}$$

EXAMPLE 2

$$\int \sin^3 x\, dx.$$

Solution. The method of the previous example does not work because there is no $\cos x$ to go with dx to give du if we try letting $u = \sin x$. But if we write

$$\sin^3 x = \sin^2 x \cdot \sin x = (1 - \cos^2 x) \cdot \sin x$$

and let

$$u = \cos x, \qquad du = -\sin x\, dx,$$

we have

$$\int \sin^3 x\, dx = \int (1 - \cos^2 x) \cdot \sin x\, dx = \int (1 - u^2) \cdot (-du)$$

$$= \int (u^2 - 1)\, du = \tfrac{1}{3}u^3 - u + C = \tfrac{1}{3} \cos^3 x - \cos x + C.$$

This method may be applied whenever an *odd* power of $\sin x$ or $\cos x$ is to be integrated. For example, any positive odd power of $\cos x$ has the form

$$\cos^{2n+1} x = \cos^{2n} x \cdot \cos x = (\cos^2 x)^n \cdot \cos x = (1 - \sin^2 x)^n \cdot \cos x,$$

with n an integer ≥ 0. Then if we let $u = \sin x$, $du = \cos x\, dx$, we have

$$\int \cos^{2n+1} x\, dx = \int (1 - \sin^2 x)^n \cdot \cos x\, dx = \int (1 - u^2)^n \cdot du.$$

The expression $(1 - u^2)^n$ may now be expanded by the binomial theorem and the result evaluated as a sum of individual integrals of the type $\int u^m\, du$.

EXAMPLE 3

$$\int \sec x \tan x\, dx.$$

Solution. Of course this is a standard form already, so there is no real problem in finding an answer. But in trigonometry we often express all trigonometric functions in terms of sines and cosines, and we now investigate what this does to the integral in question:

$$\int \sec x \tan x \, dx = \int \frac{1}{\cos x} \frac{\sin x}{\cos x} dx = \int \frac{\sin x \, dx}{\cos^2 x}.$$

Taking a cue from the previous examples (keeping in mind du as well as u), we let

$$u = \cos x, \qquad du = -\sin x \, dx,$$

and then

$$\int \frac{\sin x \, dx}{\cos^2 x} = \int \frac{-du}{u^2} = -\int u^{-2} \, du = \frac{-u^{-1}}{-1} + C = \frac{1}{u} + C$$

$$= \frac{1}{\cos x} + C = \sec x + C.$$

EXAMPLE 4

$$\int \tan^4 x \, dx.$$

Solution. This does not lend itself readily to the use of sines and cosines, since both of them occur to even powers. We say: $u = \tan x$ would require $du = \sec^2 x \, dx$. Is there some way to include $\sec^2 x$? Yes; there is an identity involving tangents and secants. How does it go? Since

$$\sin^2 x + \cos^2 x = 1,$$

if we divide through by $\cos^2 x$ we get

$$\tan^2 x + 1 = \sec^2 x \qquad \text{or} \qquad \tan^2 x = \sec^2 x - 1.$$

Then

$$\int \tan^4 x \, dx = \int \tan^2 x \cdot \tan^2 x \, dx = \int \tan^2 x \cdot (\sec^2 x - 1) \, dx$$

$$= \int \tan^2 x \sec^2 x \, dx - \int \tan^2 x \, dx.$$

The first of these is all set. But how about the $\tan^2 x$? Oh, yes,

$$\tan^2 x = \sec^2 x - 1,$$

so

$$\int \tan^4 x \, dx = \int \tan^2 x \sec^2 x \, dx - \int \tan^2 x \, dx$$

$$= \int \tan^2 x \sec^2 x \, dx - \int (\sec^2 x - 1) \, dx$$

$$= \int \tan^2 x \sec^2 x \, dx - \int \sec^2 x \, dx + \int dx.$$

In the first two of these, let

$$u = \tan x, \qquad du = \sec^2 x \, dx$$

and have

$$\int u^2\,du - \int du = \tfrac{1}{3}u^3 - u + C'.$$

The other is a standard form, so

$$\int \tan^4 x\,dx = \tfrac{1}{3}\tan^3 x - \tan x + x + C.$$

This method works for any *even* power of tan x, but what is still better is a *reduction formula* derived as follows:

$$\int \tan^n x\,dx = \int \tan^{n-2} x(\sec^2 x - 1)\,dx$$

$$= \int \tan^{n-2} x \sec^2 x\,dx - \int \tan^{n-2} x\,dx$$

$$= \frac{\tan^{n-1} x}{n-1} - \int \tan^{n-2} x\,dx.$$

This reduces the problem of integrating $\tan^n x\,dx$ to the problem of integrating $\tan^{n-2} x\,dx$. Since this decreases the exponent on tan x by 2, a repetition with the same formula will reduce the exponent by 2 again, and so on. Applying this to the problem above, we have

$$n = 4: \quad \int \tan^4 x\,dx = \frac{\tan^3 x}{3} - \int \tan^2 x\,dx,$$

$$n = 2: \quad \int \tan^2 x\,dx = \frac{\tan x}{1} - \int \tan^0 x\,dx,$$

$$\int \tan^0 x\,dx = \int 1\,dx = x + C.$$

Therefore,

$$\int \tan^4 x\,dx = \tfrac{1}{3}\tan^3 x - [\tan x - x + C]$$

$$= \tfrac{1}{3}\tan^3 x - \tan x + x + C'.$$

This reduction formula works whether the original exponent n is even or odd, but if the exponent is odd, say $2m + 1$, then after m steps it will be reduced by $2m$, leaving

$$\int \tan x = -\ln|\cos x| + C$$

as the final integral to be evaluated.

These examples illustrate how it is possible to use the trigonometric identities

$$\sin^2 x + \cos^2 x = 1, \qquad \tan^2 x + 1 = \sec^2 x,$$

and others readily derived from these, to evaluate the integrals of

a) *odd* powers of $\sin x$ or $\cos x$,

b) *any* integral powers of $\tan x$ (or $\cot x$), and

c) *even* powers of $\sec x$ (or $\csc x$).

The even powers of $\sec x$, say $\sec^{2n} x$, can all be reduced to powers of $\tan x$ by employing the substitution $\sec^2 x = 1 + \tan^2 x$, and then using the reduction formula for integrating powers of $\tan x$ after expanding $\sec^{2n} x = (1 + \tan^2 x)^n$ by the binomial theorem. But it is even simpler to use the method below:

$$\int \sec^{2n} x\, dx = \int \sec^{2n-2} x \sec^2 x\, dx = \int (\sec^2 x)^{n-1} \sec^2 x\, dx$$

$$= \int (1 + \tan^2 x)^{n-1} \sec^2 x\, dx$$

$$= \int (1 + u^2)^{n-1}\, du \qquad (u = \tan x).$$

When $(1 + u^2)^{n-1}$ is expanded by the binomial theorem, the resulting polynomial in u may be integrated term by term.

For example,

$$\int \sec^6 x\, dx = \int \sec^4 x \cdot \sec^2 x\, dx = \int (1 + \tan^2 x)^2 \cdot \sec^2 x\, dx$$

$$= \int (1 + 2u^2 + u^4)\, du \qquad (u = \tan x)$$

$$= u + \frac{2u^3}{3} + \frac{u^5}{5} + C$$

$$= \tan x + 2\frac{\tan^3 x}{3} + \frac{\tan^5 x}{5} + C.$$

EXAMPLE 5

$$\int \sec x\, dx.$$

Solution. This is hard to evaluate unless one has seen the following trick!

$$\sec x = \frac{\sec x(\tan x + \sec x)}{\sec x + \tan x} = \frac{\sec x \tan x + \sec^2 x}{\sec x + \tan x}.$$

In this form the numerator is the derivative of the denominator. Therefore

$$\int \sec x\, dx = \int \frac{\sec x \tan x + \sec^2 x}{\sec x + \tan x}\, dx$$

$$= \int \frac{du}{u} \qquad (u = \sec x + \tan x)$$

$$= \ln |u| + C.$$

That is,

$$\int \sec x\, dx = \ln |\sec x + \tan x| + C. \tag{3}$$

EXAMPLE 6 *Mercator's world map.* The integral of the secant plays an important role in making maps for compass navigation. The easiest course for a sailor to steer is a course whose compass heading is constant. This might be a course of 45° (northeast), for example, or a course of 225° (southwest), or whatever. Such a course will lie along a spiral that winds around the globe toward one of the poles (Fig. 7–1), unless the course runs due north or south, or lies parallel to the equator.

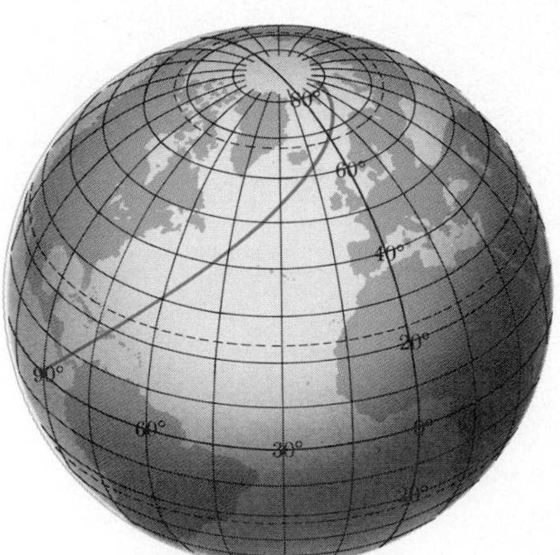

7–1 A flight with a constant bearing of 45° E of N from the Galapagos Islands in the Pacific to Franz Josef Land in the Arctic Ocean.

In 1569, Gerhard Krämer, a Flemish surveyor and geographer known to us by his Latinized last name, Mercator, made a world map on which all spirals of constant compass heading appeared as straight lines (Fig. 7–2).

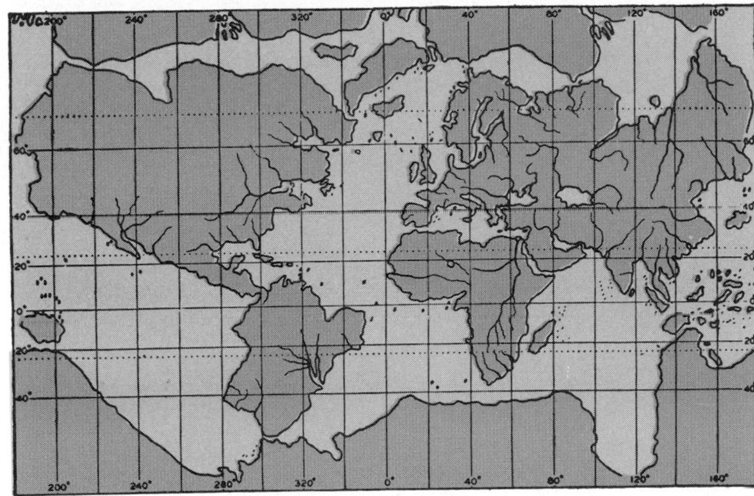

7–2 Sketch of Mercator's map of 1569.

This fantastic achievement met what must have been one of the most pressing navigational needs of all time. For a sailor could then read the compass heading for a voyage between any two points from the direction of a straight line connecting them on Mercator's map (Fig. 7–3).

If you look closely at Fig. 7–3, you will see that the vertical lines of longitude that meet at the poles on a globe have been spread apart to lie parallel on the map. The horizontal lines of latitude that are shown every 10° are parallel also, as they are on the globe, but they are not evenly spaced. The spacing between them increases toward the poles.

The secant function plays a role in determining the correct spacing of all these lines. The scaling factor by which horizontal distances are increased at a fixed latitude $\theta°$ to spread the lines of longitude apart is precisely $\sec\theta$. There is no spread at the equator, where $\sec 0° = 1$. At latitude 30° north or south, the spreading is accomplished by multiplying all horizontal distances by the factor $\sec 30° = 2/\sqrt{3} \approx 1.15$. At 60°, the factor is $\sec 60° = 2$. The closer you move toward the poles, the more the longitudes have to be spread to be parallel. The lines of latitude are spread apart toward the poles to match the spreading of the longitudes, but the formula for the spreading is complicated by the fact that the scaling factor $\sec\theta$ increases with the latitude θ. Thus, the factor to be used for stretching an interval of latitude is not a constant on the interval. This difficulty is overcome by integration. If R is the radius of the globe being modeled (Fig. 7–4), then the distance D between

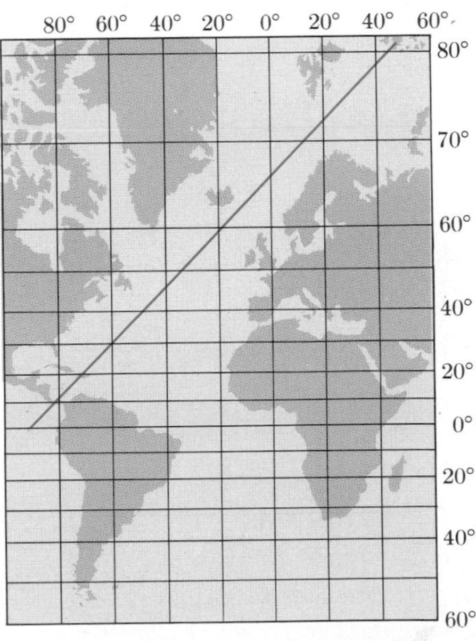

7–3 The flight of Fig. 1 traced on a Mercator map.

the lines that are drawn on the map to show the equator and the latitude $\alpha°$ is R times the integral of the secant from zero to α:

$$D = R \int_0^{\alpha} \sec x \, dx. \tag{4}$$

Therefore, the map distance between two lines of north latitude, say, at $\alpha°$ and $\beta°$ $(\alpha < \beta)$ is

$$R \int_0^{\beta} \sec x \, dx - R \int_0^{\alpha} \sec x \, dx = R \int_{\alpha}^{\beta} \sec x \, dx$$

$$= R \ln |\sec x + \tan x| \Big]_{\alpha}^{\beta}. \tag{5}$$

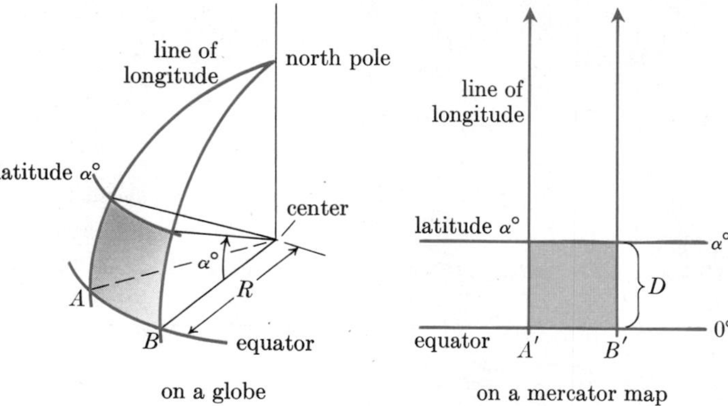

7–4 Lines of latitude and longitude.

EXAMPLE 7. Suppose that the equatorial length of a Mercator map just matches the equator of a globe of radius 25 cm. Then Eq. (4) gives the spacing on the map between the equator and the latitude 20° north as

$$25 \int_0^{20°} \sec x \, dx = 25 \ln |\sec x + \tan x| \Big]_0^{20°} \approx 9 \text{ cm.}$$

The spacing between 60° and 80° north is given by Eq. (5) as

$$25 \int_{60°}^{80°} \sec x \, dx = 25 \ln |\sec x + \tan x| \Big]_{60°}^{80°} \approx 28 \text{ cm.}$$

The navigational properties of a Mercator map are achieved at the expense of a considerable distortion of distance. (For a very readable derivation and discussion of the formula in Eq. (4), see Philip Tuchinsky's *Mercator's World Map and the Calculus*, Project UMAP, Education Development Center, Newton, MA, 1978.)

PROBLEMS

Evaluate the integrals 1 through 33.

1. $\int \sin^{3/2} x \cos x \, dx$

2. $\int \sqrt{\cos x} \sin x \, dx$

3. $\int \sin t \sqrt{1 + \cos t} \, dt$

4. $\int \frac{\sin \theta \, d\theta}{2 - \cos \theta}$

5. $\int \frac{\sec^2 2x \, dx}{1 + \tan 2x}$

6. $\int \tan 3x \, dx$

7. $\int \cos^3 x\,dx$

8. $\int \tan^2 4\theta\,d\theta$

9. a) $\int \sin^3 x \cos^2 x\,dx$

b) $\int \frac{\sin^3 x\,dx}{\cos^2 x}$

10. $\int \sec^n x \tan x\,dx$

11. $\int \tan^n x \sec^2 x\,dx$

12. $\int \sin^n x \cos x\,dx$

13. $\int \cos^n x \sin x\,dx$

14. $\int \sin^2 3x \cos 3x\,dx$

15. $\int \cos^3 2x \sin 2x\,dx$

16. $\int \sec^4 3x \tan 3x\,dx$

17. $\int \sec^4 3x\,dx$

18. $\int \cos^3 2x\,dx$

19. $\int \tan^3 2x\,dx$

20. $\int \tan^3 x \sec x\,dx$

21. $\int \sin^3 x\,dx$

22. $\int \frac{\cos x\,dx}{(1 + \sin x)^2}$

23. $\int \frac{\sec^2 x\,dx}{2 + \tan x}$

24. $\int \frac{\cos^3 t\,dt}{\sin^2 t}$

25. $\int \frac{e^x\,dx}{1 + e^x}$

26. $\int (\ln ax)^n \frac{dx}{x}$

27. $\int \frac{dx}{x \ln 3x}$

28. $\int \cot^3 x\,dx$

29. $\int \csc^3 2t \cot 2t\,dt$

30. $\int \csc^4 x\,dx$

31. $\int \frac{dx}{\cos x}$

32. $\int_0^{\pi/4} \frac{dx}{\sqrt{1 - \sin^2 x}}$

33. $\int \csc \theta\,d\theta$ [*Hint.* Repeat Example 5 with cofunctions.]

34. (*Calculator, or tables*) How far apart should the following lines of latitude be on the Mercator map of Example 7?
a) 30° and 45° north (about the latitudes of New Orleans, La., and Minneapolis, Minn.);
b) 45° and 60° north (about the latitudes of Salem, Ore., and Seward, Al.).

35. Find the area of the surface generated by revolving the arc

$$x = t^{2/3}, \quad y = t^2/2, \quad 0 \le t \le 2,$$

about the x-axis.

36. Derive a reduction formula for $\int \cot^n ax\,dx$ and use the result to evaluate $\int \cot^4 3x\,dx$.

37. Find the length of the curve

$$y = \ln(\cos x), \quad 0 \le x \le \pi/3.$$

7–3 EVEN POWERS OF SINES AND COSINES

In Article 7–2 we saw how to evaluate integrals of odd powers of sines and cosines. Indeed, any integral of the form

$$\int \sin^m x \cos^n x\,dx, \tag{1}$$

in which at least one of the exponents m and n is a positive odd integer, may be evaluated by these methods.

To set the stage for our discussion of even powers, we begin by looking at the technique we would normally use for odd powers, and then examine what goes wrong when we try to use the same technique for even powers.

EXAMPLE 1

$$\int \cos^{2/3} x \sin^5 x\,dx.$$

Solution. Here we have $\sin x$ to an *odd* power. So we put one factor of $\sin x$ with dx and the remaining sine factors, namely $\sin^4 x$, can be expressed in terms of $\cos x$ without introducing any square roots, as follows:

$$\sin^4 x = (\sin^2 x)^2 = (1 - \cos^2 x)^2.$$

The sin x goes well with dx when we take

$$u = \cos x, \qquad du = -\sin x \, dx$$

and evaluate the integral as follows:

$$\int \cos^{2/3} x \sin^5 x \, dx = \int \cos^{2/3} x(1 - \cos^2 x)^2 \sin x \, dx$$

$$= \int u^{2/3}(1 - u^2)^2(-du)$$

$$= -\int (u^{2/3} - 2u^{8/3} + u^{14/3}) \, du$$

$$= -[\tfrac{3}{5}u^{5/3} - \tfrac{6}{11}u^{11/3} + \tfrac{3}{17}u^{17/3}] + C$$

$$= -\cos^{5/3} x \, [\tfrac{3}{5} - \tfrac{6}{11} \cos^2 x + \tfrac{3}{17} \cos^4 x] + C.$$

DISCUSSION. If sin x had appeared to an *even* power in the integral, as it does, say, in the integral

$$\int \cos^{2/3} x \sin^4 x \, dx,$$

then the method above would not work. The substitution $\sin^4 x = (1 - \cos^2 x)^2$ would reduce the integral to

$$\int \cos^{2/3} x \sin^4 x \, dx = \int \cos^{2/3} x(1 - \cos^2 x)^2 \, dx,$$

and there would be no $-\sin x \, dx = du$ to go with the $\cos x = u$.

When both the exponents m and n in the integral (1) are even integers, we turn to one or both of the following trigonometric identities:

$$\sin^2 A = \tfrac{1}{2}(1 - \cos 2A), \tag{2a}$$

$$\cos^2 A = \tfrac{1}{2}(1 + \cos 2A). \tag{2b}$$

These identities may be derived by adding or subtracting the equations

$$\cos^2 A + \sin^2 A = 1, \qquad \cos^2 A - \sin^2 A = \cos 2A,$$

and dividing by two.

EXAMPLE 2

$$\int \cos^4 x \, dx = \int (\cos^2 x)^2 \, dx = \int \tfrac{1}{4}(1 + \cos 2x)^2 \, dx \tag{a}$$

$$= \tfrac{1}{4} \int (1 + 2 \cos 2x + \cos^2 2x) \, dx \tag{b}$$

$$= \tfrac{1}{4} \int [1 + 2 \cos 2x + \tfrac{1}{2}(1 + \cos 4x)] \, dx$$

$$= \tfrac{3}{8}x + \tfrac{1}{4} \sin 2x + \tfrac{1}{32} \sin 4x + C.$$

In (a), we used Eq. (2b) with $A = x$, and in (b), we used Eq. (2b) with $A = 2x$. The final integrations involve

$$\int \cos ax\, dx = \frac{1}{a}\int \cos ax\, d(ax) = \frac{1}{a}\sin ax + C'.$$

An integral like

$$\int \sin^2 x \cos^4 x\, dx,$$

which involves even powers of both sin x and cos x, can be changed to a sum of integrals that involve only powers of one of them. Then these may be handled by the method of Example 2.

EXAMPLE 3

$$\int \sin^2 x \cos^4 x\, dx = \int (1 - \cos^2 x) \cos^4 x\, dx = \int \cos^4 x\, dx - \int \cos^6 x\, dx.$$

We evaluated $\int \cos^4 x\, dx$ above, and

$$\int \cos^6 x\, dx = \int (\cos^2 x)^3\, dx = \tfrac{1}{8}\int (1 + \cos 2x)^3\, dx$$

$$= \tfrac{1}{8}\int (1 + 3\cos 2x + 3\cos^2 2x + \cos^3 2x)\, dx.$$

We now know how to handle each term of the integrand. The result is

$$\int \cos^6 x\, dx = \tfrac{5}{16}x + \tfrac{1}{4}\sin 2x + \tfrac{3}{64}\sin 4x - \tfrac{1}{48}\sin^3 2x + C.$$

Combining this with the result of Example 2 gives:

$$\int \sin^2 x \cos^4 x\, dx = \int \cos^4 x\, dx - \int \cos^6 x\, dx$$

$$= \tfrac{1}{16}x - \tfrac{1}{64}\sin 4x + \tfrac{1}{48}\sin^3 2x + C.$$

PROBLEMS

Evaluate the following integrals:

1. $\int \sin^2 x \cos^2 x\, dx$
2. $\int \sin^4 y \cos^2 y\, dy$
3. $\int \sin^2 2t\, dt$
4. $\int \cos^2 3\theta\, d\theta$
5. $\int \sin^4 ax\, dx$
6. $\int \dfrac{\sin^4 x\, dx}{\cos^2 x}$
7. $\int \dfrac{dx}{\cos^2 x}$
8. $\int \dfrac{dx}{\sin^4 x}$
9. $\int \dfrac{\cos 2t\, dt}{\sin^4 2t}$
10. $\int \sin^6 x\, dx$
11. $\int_0^{2\pi} \sqrt{\dfrac{1 - \cos t}{2}}\, dt$
12. $\int_0^{\pi} \sqrt{1 - \cos 2x}\, dx$
13. $\int_0^{\pi/10} \sqrt{1 + \cos 5\theta}\, d\theta$
14. $\int_0^{2\pi} \sqrt{1 + \cos (y/4)}\, dy$
15. The graph of $x = t - \sin t$, $y = 1 - \cos t$, $0 \le t \le 2\pi$, is an arch standing on the x-axis. Find the surface area generated by rotating the arch about the axis.
16. Find the volume generated by revolving one arch of the curve $y = \sin x$ about the x-axis.

7–4

INTEGRALS INVOLVING $\sqrt{a^2 - u^2}$, $\sqrt{a^2 + u^2}$, $\sqrt{u^2 - a^2}$, $a^2 + u^2$, and $a^2 - u^2$

Some of these follow directly from the integral formulas in Article 7–1. For example, we have

$$\int \frac{du}{1 + u^2} = \tan^{-1} u + C, \tag{1}$$

and, to evaluate

$$\int \frac{du}{a^2 + u^2}, \tag{2}$$

we factor a^2 out of the denominator and proceed as follows:

$$\int \frac{du}{a^2 + u^2} = \int \frac{du}{a^2\left[1 + \left(\frac{u}{a}\right)^2\right]} = \frac{1}{a^2} \int \frac{ad\left(\frac{u}{a}\right)}{1 + \left(\frac{u}{a}\right)^2} = \frac{1}{a} \int \frac{dz}{1 + z^2}$$

$$= \frac{1}{a} \tan^{-1} z + C = \frac{1}{a} \tan^{-1} \frac{u}{a} + C \qquad \left[z = \frac{u}{a}\right].$$

That is,

$$\int \frac{du}{a^2 + u^2} = \frac{1}{a} \tan^{-1} \frac{u}{a} + C. \tag{3}$$

The essential feature here was the introduction of a new variable by the substitution

$$z = \frac{u}{a} \qquad \text{or} \qquad u = az.$$

Such a substitution allows the a terms to be brought outside the integral sign, and the resulting integral may then match one of the inverse trigonometric formulas.

An alternative approach will show, however, that one may bypass the job of learning these formulas. In addition, this method, which we shall soon illustrate, permits the evaluation of many additional integrals.

The method uses the following identities.

$$\begin{aligned} 1 - \sin^2 \theta &= \cos^2 \theta, \\ 1 + \tan^2 \theta &= \sec^2 \theta, \\ \sec^2 \theta - 1 &= \tan^2 \theta. \end{aligned} \tag{4}$$

These identities may be multiplied by a^2, with the result that the substitutions listed below have the following effects:

a) $u = a \sin \theta$ replaces $a^2 - u^2$ by $a^2 \cos^2 \theta$.

b) $u = a \tan \theta$ replaces $a^2 + u^2$ by $a^2 \sec^2 \theta$. **(5)**

c) $u = a \sec \theta$ replaces $u^2 - a^2$ by $a^2 \tan^2 \theta$.

It is thus seen that corresponding to each of the *binomial* expressions

$$a^2 - u^2, \qquad a^2 + u^2, \qquad \text{and} \qquad u^2 - a^2,$$

we have a substitution that replaces the binomial by a single squared term. The particular substitution to use will depend upon the form of the integrand. In the examples that follow, a is a positive constant.

EXAMPLE 1

$$\int \frac{du}{\sqrt{a^2-u^2}}, \qquad |a|>|u|.$$

Solution. We try the substitution (5a):

$$u = a \sin\theta, \qquad du = a\cos\theta\, d\theta,$$
$$a^2-u^2 = a^2(1-\sin^2\theta) = a^2\cos^2\theta.$$

Then

$$\int \frac{du}{\sqrt{a^2-u^2}} = \int \frac{a\cos\theta\, d\theta}{\sqrt{a^2\cos^2\theta}} = \int \frac{a\cos\theta\, d\theta}{\pm a\cos\theta} \quad (\pm \text{ depends on sign of } \cos\theta)$$
$$= \pm\int d\theta = \pm(\theta + C).$$

Since $\sin\theta = u/a$,

$$\theta = \sin^{-1}\frac{u}{a}$$

and

$$\int \frac{du}{\sqrt{a^2-u^2}} = \pm\left(\sin^{-1}\frac{u}{a} + C\right).$$

Using only the *principal value* of $\sin^{-1} u/a$ means that θ will lie between $-\pi/2$ and $\pi/2$; hence $\cos\theta \geq 0$ and the ambiguous sign is $+$; that is,

$$\int \frac{du}{\sqrt{a^2-u^2}} = \sin^{-1}\frac{u}{a} + C. \qquad \textbf{(6)}$$

EXAMPLE 2

$$\int \frac{du}{\sqrt{a^2+u^2}}, \qquad a>0.$$

Solution. This time we try

$$u = a\tan\theta,$$
$$du = a\sec^2\theta\, d\theta,$$
$$a^2+u^2 = a^2(1+\tan^2\theta) = a^2\sec^2\theta.$$

Then

$$\int \frac{du}{\sqrt{a^2+u^2}} = \int \frac{a\sec^2\theta\, d\theta}{\sqrt{a^2\sec^2\theta}}$$
$$= \pm\int \sec\theta\, d\theta \quad (\pm \text{ depends on sign of } \sec\theta).$$

By Eq. (3), Article 7–2, we know that

$$\int \sec\theta\, d\theta = \ln\,|\sec\theta + \tan\theta| + C.$$

If we take

$$\theta = \tan^{-1}\frac{u}{a}, \qquad -\frac{\pi}{2} < \theta < \frac{\pi}{2},$$

then $\sec\theta$ is positive, and

$$\begin{aligned}\int \frac{du}{\sqrt{a^2+u^2}} &= \int \sec\theta\, d\theta \\ &= \ln\,|\sec\theta + \tan\theta| + C = \ln\left|\frac{\sqrt{a^2+u^2}}{a} + \frac{u}{a}\right| + C \\ &= \ln\,|\sqrt{a^2+u^2} + u| + C',\end{aligned}$$

where

$$C' = C - \ln a.$$

That is,

$$\int \frac{du}{\sqrt{a^2+u^2}} = \ln|\sqrt{a^2+u^2} + u| + C'. \tag{7}$$

EXAMPLE 3

$$\int \frac{du}{\sqrt{u^2-a^2}}, \qquad |u| > a > 0.$$

Solution. We try the substitution

$$\begin{aligned} u &= a\sec\theta, \\ du &= a\sec\theta\tan\theta\, d\theta, \\ u^2 - a^2 &= a^2(\sec^2\theta - 1) = a^2\tan^2\theta. \end{aligned}$$

Then

$$\begin{aligned}\int \frac{du}{\sqrt{u^2-a^2}} &= \int \frac{a\sec\theta\tan\theta\, d\theta}{\sqrt{a^2\tan^2\theta}} \\ &= \pm\int \sec\theta\, d\theta \quad (\pm \text{ depends on sign of } \tan\theta).\end{aligned}$$

If we take

$$\theta = \sec^{-1}\frac{u}{a}, \qquad 0 \le \theta \le \pi,$$

then

$$\begin{aligned} &\tan\theta \text{ is positive} \quad \text{if } 0 < \theta < \pi/2, \\ &\tan\theta \text{ is negative} \quad \text{if } \pi/2 < \theta < \pi, \end{aligned}$$

and, from Eq. (3) of Article 7–2,

$$\pm\int \sec\theta\, d\theta = \pm\ln\,|\sec\theta + \tan\theta| + C.$$

When $\tan\theta$ is positive, we must use the plus sign; when $\tan\theta$ is negative, the minus sign. Moreover,

$$\sec\theta = \frac{u}{a}, \qquad \tan\theta = \pm\frac{\sqrt{u^2 - a^2}}{a}.$$

So we have

$$\int \frac{du}{\sqrt{u^2 - a^2}} = \pm\ln\left|\frac{u}{a} \pm \frac{\sqrt{u^2 - a^2}}{a}\right| + C$$

$$= \begin{cases} \ln\left|\dfrac{u}{a} + \dfrac{\sqrt{u^2 - a^2}}{a}\right| + C \\ \text{or} \\ -\ln\left|\dfrac{u}{a} - \dfrac{\sqrt{u^2 - a^2}}{a}\right| + C. \end{cases}$$

But the two forms are actually equal, because

$$-\ln\left|\frac{u}{a} - \frac{\sqrt{u^2 - a^2}}{a}\right| = \ln\left|\frac{a}{u - \sqrt{u^2 - a^2}}\right|$$

$$= \ln\left|\frac{a(u + \sqrt{u^2 - a^2})}{(u - \sqrt{u^2 - a^2})(u + \sqrt{u^2 - a^2})}\right|$$

$$= \ln\left|\frac{a(u + \sqrt{u^2 - a^2})}{a^2}\right|$$

$$= \ln\left|\frac{u + \sqrt{u^2 - a^2}}{a}\right|.$$

Therefore

$$\int \frac{du}{\sqrt{u^2 - a^2}} = \ln|u + \sqrt{u^2 - a^2}| + C', \tag{8}$$

where we have replaced $C - \ln a$ by C'.

EXAMPLE 4

$$\int \frac{du}{a^2 + u^2}, \qquad a > 0.$$

Solution. We try

$$u = a\tan\theta, \qquad du = a\sec^2\theta\, d\theta,$$

$$a^2 + u^2 = a^2(1 + \tan^2\theta) = a^2\sec^2\theta.$$

Then

$$\int \frac{du}{a^2 + u^2} = \int \frac{a\sec^2\theta\, d\theta}{a^2\sec^2\theta}$$

$$= \frac{1}{a}\int d\theta = \frac{1}{a}\theta + C.$$

Since $u = a \tan \theta$,

$$\tan \theta = \frac{u}{a}, \qquad \theta = \tan^{-1} \frac{u}{a},$$

and

$$\int \frac{du}{a^2 + u^2} = \frac{1}{a} \tan^{-1} \frac{u}{a} + C. \tag{9}$$

EXAMPLE 5

$$\int \frac{x^2\, dx}{\sqrt{9 - x^2}}.$$

Solution. If we substitute

$$x = 3 \sin \theta, \qquad \frac{-\pi}{2} < \theta < \frac{\pi}{2},$$

$$dx = 3 \cos \theta\, d\theta,$$

$$9 - x^2 = 9(1 - \sin^2 \theta) = 9 \cos^2 \theta,$$

then we find

$$\int \frac{x^2\, dx}{\sqrt{9 - x^2}} = \int \frac{9 \sin^2 \theta \cdot 3 \cos \theta\, d\theta}{3 \cos \theta} = 9 \int \sin^2 \theta\, d\theta.$$

This is considerably simpler than the integral we started with. To evaluate it, we use the identity

$$\sin^2 \theta = \tfrac{1}{2}(1 - \cos 2\theta).$$

Then

$$\int \sin^2 \theta\, d\theta = \tfrac{1}{2} \int (1 - \cos 2\theta)\, d\theta = \tfrac{1}{2}[\theta - \tfrac{1}{2} \sin 2\theta] + C$$

$$= \tfrac{1}{2}[\theta - \sin \theta \cos \theta] + C.$$

Substituting this above, we get

$$\int \frac{x^2\, dx}{\sqrt{9 - x^2}} = \frac{9}{2}[\theta - \sin \theta \cos \theta] + C$$

$$= \frac{9}{2}\left[\sin^{-1} \frac{x}{3} - \frac{x\sqrt{9 - x^2}}{9}\right] + C.$$

The trigonometric substitutions (a), (b), and (c) of Eq. (5) can be remembered by thinking of the theorem of Pythagoras and taking a and u as two of the sides and θ as an angle in a right triangle. Thus $\sqrt{a^2 - u^2}$ suggests a as hypotenuse and u as a leg, $\sqrt{a^2 + u^2}$ suggests a and u as the legs, and $\sqrt{u^2 - a^2}$ suggests u as hypotenuse and a as a leg. These situations are shown in Fig. 7–5.

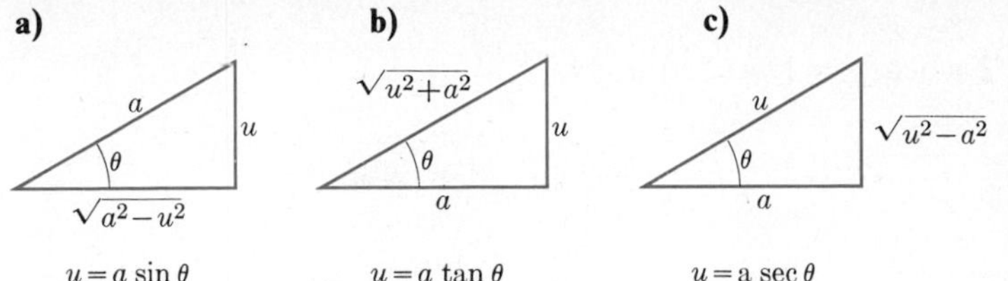

7–5 If $u = a \sin \theta$, then the values of the trigonometric functions of θ can be read from Triangle (a). Triangles (b) and (c) give the values of the trigonometric functions of θ for the substitutions $u = a \tan \theta$ and $u = a \sec \theta$.

The trigonometric identities, Eqs. (4), are simply equivalent expressions of the theorem of Pythagoras applied to the right triangles in Fig. 7–6.

Note that whenever we evaluate an indefinite integral by changing variables, i.e., by substitution, we express the final result in terms of the original variable of integration. When we integrate

$$\int \frac{du}{a^2 + u^2}$$

by substituting $u = a \tan \theta$, we state the final result as

$$\int \frac{du}{a^2 + u^2} = \frac{1}{a} \tan^{-1} \frac{u}{a} + C,$$

and not as

$$\int \frac{du}{a^2 + u^2} = \frac{1}{a} \theta + C.$$

However, when we have a definite integral to evaluate, there is another course of action open to us. We can transform the limits of integration by the same formula we use to change the variable of integration, and then evaluate the transformed integral with the transformed limits. We do this in the next example.

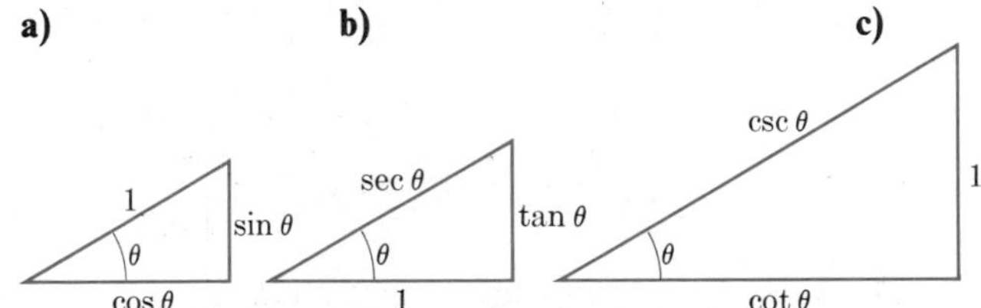

7–6 The triangles in (b) and (c) are obtained from the basic triangle in (a) by dividing its sides all by $\cos \theta$ or $\sin \theta$, respectively, to obtain similar triangles.

EXAMPLE 6. Find the area of the quarter circle bounded by the curve $y = \sqrt{1 - x^2}$ in the first quadrant.

Solution. The area of the quarter circle is

$$\int_0^1 \sqrt{1 - x^2}\, dx.$$

If we substitute $x = \sin \theta$, $dx = \cos \theta \, d\theta$, then $\theta = 0$ when $x = 0$, and

$\theta = \pi/2$ when $x = 1$. Accordingly,

$$\int_0^1 \sqrt{1-x^2}\,dx = \int_0^{\pi/2} \sqrt{1-\sin^2\theta}\cos\theta\,d\theta$$

$$= \int_0^{\pi/2} \cos^2\theta\,d\theta$$

$$= \int_0^{\pi/2} \frac{1+\cos 2\theta}{2}\,d\theta = \frac{\theta}{2} + \frac{\sin 2\theta}{4}\Bigg]_0^{\pi/2} = \frac{\pi}{4} + 0 = \frac{\pi}{4}.$$

REMARK. We could have calculated the area of the quarter circle in Example 6 by expressing

$$\frac{\theta}{2} + \frac{\sin 2\theta}{4}$$

in terms of x and evaluating the result in terms of the original limits, but it would have been more work to do so. In some integrations, however, finding the new limits of integration after a change of variable seems to take as much work as changing the result of the integration back into an expression involving the original variable. You will have to use your own judgment about which course to take in any given instance.

PROBLEMS

Evaluate the integrals 1 through 20.

1. $\displaystyle\int_0^{0.6a} \frac{x\,dx}{\sqrt{a^2-x^2}}$

2. $\displaystyle\int \frac{dx}{\sqrt{1-4x^2}}$

3. $\displaystyle\int_0^a \sqrt{a^2-x^2}\,dx$

4. $\displaystyle\int \frac{dx}{\sqrt{4-(x-1)^2}}$

5. $\displaystyle\int \sec 2t\,dt$

6. $\displaystyle\int_0^2 \frac{dx}{\sqrt{4+x^2}}$

7. $\displaystyle\int_0^1 \frac{dx}{\sqrt{4-x^2}}$

8. $\displaystyle\int \frac{x\,dx}{\sqrt{4+x^2}}$

9. $\displaystyle\int_0^2 \frac{x\,dx}{4+x^2}$

10. $\displaystyle\int_0^2 \frac{dx}{4+x^2}$

11. $\displaystyle\int_0^1 \frac{dx}{4-x^2}$

12. $\displaystyle\int_0^1 \frac{x^3\,dx}{\sqrt{x^2+1}}$

13. $\displaystyle\int \frac{dx}{x\sqrt{a^2+x^2}}$

14. $\displaystyle\int \frac{x+1}{\sqrt{4-x^2}}\,dx$

15. $\displaystyle\int \frac{dx}{\sqrt{2-5x^2}}$

16. $\displaystyle\int \frac{\sin\theta\,d\theta}{\sqrt{2-\cos^2\theta}}$

17. $\displaystyle\int \frac{dx}{x\sqrt{x^2-a^2}}$

18. $\displaystyle\int \frac{dx}{x\sqrt{a^2-x^2}}$

19. $\displaystyle\int \frac{dx}{(a^2-x^2)^{3/2}}$

20. $\displaystyle\int \frac{dx}{(a^2+x^2)^2}$

21. Find the area bounded by the curve $y = \sqrt{1-(x^2/9)}$ in the first quadrant.

22. Find the area between the x-axis and the curve $y = \sqrt{1+\cos 4x}$, $0 \le x \le \pi$.

23. Suppose $\theta = \sin^{-1}(u/2)$. Express $\cos\theta$ and $\tan\theta$ in terms of u. (See Fig. 7–5.)

24. Express in terms of u and a:

a) $\sin\left(\tan^{-1}\dfrac{u}{a}\right)$

b) $\cos\left(\sec^{-1}\dfrac{u}{a}\right)$

7–5

INTEGRALS INVOLVING $ax^2 + bx + c$

The general quadratic

$$f(x) = ax^2 + bx + c, \qquad a \neq 0 \tag{1}$$

can be reduced to the form $a(u^2 + B)$ by completing the square, as follows:

$$\begin{aligned} ax^2 + bx + c = a\left(x^2 + \frac{b}{a}x\right) + c &= a\left(x^2 + \frac{b}{a}x + \frac{b^2}{4a^2}\right) + c - \frac{b^2}{4a} \\ &= a\left(x + \frac{b}{2a}\right)^2 + \frac{4ac - b^2}{4a}, \end{aligned}$$

and then substituting

$$u = x + \frac{b}{2a}, \qquad B = \frac{4ac - b^2}{4a^2}, \tag{2}$$

which gives us

$$f(x) = ax^2 + bx + c = a(u^2 + B).$$

When the integrand involves the square root of $f(x) = ax^2 + bx + c$, we restrict attention to the case where $f(x)$ is not negative. If a is negative and B is positive, the square root is imaginary. We disregard this case, and consider

$$\sqrt{a(u^2 + B)}$$

1. when a is positive, and
2. when a and B are both negative.

In the first case, the relation

$$\sqrt{a(u^2 + B)} = \sqrt{a}\sqrt{u^2 + B}$$

allows us to reduce the problem to a consideration of $\sqrt{u^2 + B}$, which we handle by the methods of Article 7–4. In the second case, when a and B are both negative, then $-a$ and $-B$ are positive and

$$\begin{aligned} \sqrt{a(u^2 + B)} &= \sqrt{-a(-B - u^2)} \\ &= \sqrt{-a}\sqrt{-B - u^2} \qquad (-a > 0,\ -B > 0), \end{aligned}$$

and, taking $-B = A^2$, say, we consider $\sqrt{A^2 - u^2}$ as in Article 7–4.

When the integrand does not involve an even root of $f(x)$, there need be no restriction on the signs of a and B. In these cases also, we try to use the trigonometric substitutions of the previous section, or to apply the integration formulas derived there.

EXAMPLE 1

$$\int \frac{dx}{\sqrt{2x - x^2}}.$$

Solution. The algebraic transformations proceed as follows:

$$\begin{aligned} \sqrt{2x - x^2} = \sqrt{-(x^2 - 2x)} &= \sqrt{-(x^2 - 2x + 1) + 1} \\ &= \sqrt{1 - u^2} \qquad (u = x - 1). \end{aligned}$$

Then, with $u = x - 1$,

$$du = dx$$

and

$$\int \frac{dx}{\sqrt{2x - x^2}} = \int \frac{du}{\sqrt{1 - u^2}} = \sin^{-1} u + C;$$

that is,

$$\int \frac{dx}{\sqrt{2x - x^2}} = \sin^{-1}(x - 1) + C.$$

EXAMPLE 2

$$\int \frac{dx}{4x^2 + 4x + 2}.$$

Solution. Again we start with the algebraic transformations:

$$\begin{aligned} 4x^2 + 4x + 2 &= 4(x^2 + x) + 2 \\ &= 4(x^2 + x + \tfrac{1}{4}) + (2 - \tfrac{4}{4}) \\ &= 4(x + \tfrac{1}{2})^2 + 1. \end{aligned}$$

Then we let

$$u = x + \tfrac{1}{2}, \qquad du = dx,$$

and

$$\begin{aligned} \int \frac{dx}{4x^2 + 4x + 2} &= \int \frac{du}{4u^2 + 1} \\ &= \frac{1}{4}\int \frac{du}{u^2 + \frac{1}{4}} \\ &= \frac{1}{4}\int \frac{du}{u^2 + a^2} \qquad (a = \tfrac{1}{2}) \\ &= \frac{1}{4}\frac{1}{a}\tan^{-1}\frac{u}{a} + C \\ &= \frac{1}{2}\tan^{-1}(2x + 1) + C. \end{aligned}$$

EXAMPLE 3

$$\int \frac{(x + 1)\,dx}{\sqrt{2x^2 - 6x + 4}}.$$

Solution. The quadratic part may be reduced as follows:

$$\begin{aligned} 2x^2 - 6x + 4 &= 2(x^2 - 3x) + 4 \\ &= 2(x^2 - 3x + \tfrac{9}{4}) + 4 - \tfrac{9}{2} = 2(u^2 - a^2) \end{aligned}$$

with

$$u = x - \tfrac{3}{2}, \qquad a = \tfrac{1}{2}.$$

Then

$$x = u + \tfrac{3}{2}, \qquad dx = du, \qquad x + 1 = u + \tfrac{5}{2},$$

and

$$\int \frac{(x+1)\,dx}{\sqrt{2x^2 - 6x + 4}} = \int \frac{(u + \frac{5}{2})\,du}{\sqrt{2(u^2 - a^2)}}$$
$$= \frac{1}{\sqrt{2}} \int \frac{u\,du}{\sqrt{u^2 - a^2}} + \frac{5}{2\sqrt{2}} \int \frac{du}{\sqrt{u^2 - a^2}}.$$

In the former of these, we let

$$z = u^2 - a^2, \qquad dz = 2u\,du, \qquad u\,du = \tfrac{1}{2}\,dz,$$

and to the latter we apply Eq. (8), Article 7–4. That is,

$$\frac{1}{\sqrt{2}} \int \frac{u\,du}{\sqrt{u^2 - a^2}} = \frac{1}{2\sqrt{2}} \int \frac{dz}{\sqrt{z}} = \frac{1}{2\sqrt{2}} \int z^{-(1/2)}\,dz = \frac{1}{2\sqrt{2}} \frac{z^{1/2}}{\frac{1}{2}} + C_1$$
$$= \sqrt{\frac{u^2 - a^2}{2}} + C_1$$

and

$$\frac{5}{2\sqrt{2}} \int \frac{du}{\sqrt{u^2 - a^2}} = \frac{5}{2\sqrt{2}} \ln\,|u + \sqrt{u^2 - a^2}| + C_2,$$

so that

$$\int \frac{(x+1)\,dx}{\sqrt{2x^2 - 6x + 4}}$$
$$= \sqrt{\frac{u^2 - a^2}{2}} + \frac{5}{2\sqrt{2}} \ln\,|u + \sqrt{u^2 - a^2}| + C$$
$$= \sqrt{\frac{x^2 - 3x + 2}{2}} + \frac{5}{2\sqrt{2}} \ln\left|x - \frac{3}{2} + \sqrt{x^2 - 3x + 2}\right| + C.$$

PROBLEMS

1. $\displaystyle\int_1^3 \frac{dx}{x^2 - 2x + 5}$

2. $\displaystyle\int \frac{x\,dx}{\sqrt{x^2 - 2x + 5}}$

3. $\displaystyle\int \frac{(x+1)\,dx}{\sqrt{2x - x^2}}$

4. $\displaystyle\int \frac{(x-1)\,dx}{\sqrt{x^2 - 4x + 3}}$

5. $\displaystyle\int \frac{x\,dx}{\sqrt{5 + 4x - x^2}}$

6. $\displaystyle\int \frac{dx}{\sqrt{x^2 - 2x - 8}}$

7. $\displaystyle\int \frac{(1-x)\,dx}{\sqrt{8 + 2x - x^2}}$

8. $\displaystyle\int \frac{x\,dx}{\sqrt{x^2 + 4x + 5}}$

9. $\displaystyle\int \frac{x\,dx}{x^2 + 4x + 5}$

10. $\displaystyle\int \frac{(2x+3)\,dx}{4x^2 + 4x + 5}$

7–6 INTEGRATION BY THE METHOD OF PARTIAL FRACTIONS

In algebra we learned how to combine fractions over a common denominator. In integration, it is desirable to reverse the process and split a fraction into a sum of fractions with simpler denominators. The technique of doing this is called the *method of partial fractions.*

EXAMPLE 1

$$\frac{2}{x+1}+\frac{3}{x-3}=\frac{2(x-3)+3(x+1)}{(x+1)(x-3)}=\frac{5x-3}{(x+1)(x-3)}.$$

The reverse process consists in finding constants A and B such that

$$\frac{5x-3}{(x+1)(x-3)}=\frac{A}{x+1}+\frac{B}{x-3}.$$

(Pretend, for a moment, that we don't know that $A = 2$, $B = 3$ will work. We call A and B *undetermined coefficients.*) Clearing of fractions, we have

$$\begin{aligned}5x-3&=A(x-3)+B(x+1)\\&=(A+B)x-3A+B.\end{aligned}$$

This will be an identity in x if and only if coefficients of like powers of x on the two sides of the equation are equal:

$$A+B=5, \qquad -3A+B=-3.$$

These two equations in two unknowns determine

$$A=2, \qquad B=3.$$

More generally, suppose we wish to separate a rational function

$$\frac{f(x)}{g(x)} \tag{1}$$

into a sum of partial fractions. Success in doing so hinges upon two things:

1. *The degree of $f(x)$ should be less than the degree of $g(x)$.* (If this is not the case, we first perform a long division, then work with the remainder term. This remainder can always be put into the required form.)

2. *The factors of $g(x)$ should be known.* (Theoretically, any polynomial $g(x)$ with real coefficients can be expressed as a product of real linear and quadratic factors. In practice, it may be difficult to perform the factorization.)

If these two conditions prevail we can carry out the following steps.

FIRST. Let $x - r$ be a linear factor of $g(x)$. Suppose $(x - r)^m$ is the highest power of $x - r$ that divides $g(x)$. Then assign the sum of m partial fractions to this factor, as follows:

$$\frac{A_1}{x-r}+\frac{A_2}{(x-r)^2}+\cdots+\frac{A_m}{(x-r)^m}.$$

Do this for each distinct linear factor of $g(x)$.

SECOND. Let $x^2 + px + q$ be a quadratic factor of $g(x)$. Suppose

$$(x^2 + px + q)^n$$

is the highest power of this factor that divides $g(x)$. Then, to this factor, assign the sum of the n partial fractions:

$$\frac{B_1x + C_1}{x^2 + px + q} + \frac{B_2x + C_2}{(x^2 + px + q)^2} + \cdots + \frac{B_nx + C_n}{(x^2 + px + q)^n}.$$

Do this for each distinct quadratic factor of $g(x)$.

THIRD. Set the original fraction $f(x)/g(x)$ equal to the sum of all these partial fractions. Clear the resulting equation of fractions and arrange the terms in decreasing powers of x.

FOURTH. Equate the coefficients of corresponding powers of x, and solve the resulting equations for the undetermined coefficients.

EXAMPLE 2. Express

$$\frac{f(x)}{g(x)} = \frac{-2x + 4}{(x^2 + 1)(x - 1)^2}$$

as a sum of partial fractions.

Solution. The degree of $f(x)$ is less than the degree of $g(x)$, and $g(x)$ is already written as a product of linear and quadratic factors. To carry out the steps listed above, we write

$$\frac{-2x + 4}{(x^2 + 1)(x - 1)^2} = \frac{Ax + B}{x^2 + 1} + \frac{C}{x - 1} + \frac{D}{(x - 1)^2}.$$

Then

$$\begin{aligned} -2x + 4 &= (Ax + B)(x - 1)^2 + C(x - 1)(x^2 + 1) + D(x^2 + 1) \\ &= (A + C)x^3 + (-2A + B - C + D)x^2 \\ &\quad + (A - 2B + C)x + (B - C + D). \end{aligned}$$

In order for this to be an identity in x, it is both necessary and sufficient that the coefficient of each power of x be the same on the left side of the equation as it is on the right side. Equating these coefficients leads to the following equations:

Coefficient of x^3: $\quad 0 = A + C,$

Coefficient of x^2: $\quad 0 = -2A + B - C + D$

Coefficient of x^1: $\quad -2 = A - 2B + C,$

Coefficient of x^0: $\quad 4 = B - C + D.$

If we subtract the fourth equation from the second, we obtain

$$-4 = -2A, \qquad A = 2.$$

Then from the first equation, we have

$$C = -A = -2.$$

Knowing A and C, we find B from the third equation,

$$B = 1.$$

Finally, from the fourth equation, we have

$$D = 4 - B + C = 1.$$

Hence

$$\frac{-2x + 4}{(x^2 + 1)(x - 1)^2} = \frac{2x + 1}{x^2 + 1} - \frac{2}{x - 1} + \frac{1}{(x - 1)^2}.$$

EXAMPLE 3. Evaluate

$$\int \frac{x^5 - x^4 - 3x + 5}{x^4 - 2x^3 + 2x^2 - 2x + 1} dx.$$

Solution. The integrand is a fraction, but not a proper fraction. Hence we divide first, obtaining

$$\frac{x^5 - x^4 - 3x + 5}{x^4 - 2x^3 + 2x^2 - 2x + 1} = x + 1 + \frac{-2x + 4}{x^4 - 2x^3 + 2x^2 - 2x + 1}. \tag{2}$$

The denominator factors as follows:

$$x^4 - 2x^3 + 2x^2 - 2x + 1 = (x^2 + 1)(x - 1)^2.$$

By the result of Example 2, we have, for the remainder term,

$$\frac{-2x + 4}{(x^2 + 1)(x - 1)^2} = \frac{2x + 1}{x^2 + 1} - \frac{2}{x - 1} + \frac{1}{(x - 1)^2}. \tag{3}$$

Hence, substituting from (3) into (2), multiplying by dx, and integrating, we have

$$\begin{aligned}
&\int \frac{x^5 - x^4 - 3x + 5}{x^4 - 2x^3 + 2x^2 - 2x + 1} dx \\
&\quad = \int \left[x + 1 + \frac{2x + 1}{x^2 + 1} - \frac{2}{x - 1} + \frac{1}{(x - 1)^2} \right] dx \\
&\quad = \int \left[x + 1 + \frac{2x}{x^2 + 1} + \frac{1}{x^2 + 1} - \frac{2}{x - 1} + \frac{1}{(x - 1)^2} \right] dx \\
&\quad = \frac{x^2}{2} + x + \ln (x^2 + 1) + \tan^{-1} x - 2 \ln |x - 1| - \frac{1}{x - 1} + C.
\end{aligned}$$

In theory, any rational function of x can be integrated by the method of partial fractions. Once the necessary algebra has been done, the problem reduces to that of evaluating integrals of the following two types:

$$\int \frac{dx}{(x-r)^h}, \tag{4a}$$

$$\int \frac{(ax+b)\,dx}{(x^2+px+q)^k}. \tag{4b}$$

The first of these becomes simply $\int u^{-h}\,du$ when we let $u = x - r$. In the second type it is preferable to complete the square in the denominator:

$$x^2 + px + q = \left(x + \frac{p}{2}\right)^2 + q - \frac{p^2}{4}.$$

The quadratic $x^2 + px + q$ has no real roots. (If it had real roots, it would have been replaced by its linear factors in the original partial-fractions expansion.) Its discriminant, $p^2 - 4q$, is therefore negative. In other words,

$$4q - p^2 > 0, \qquad \text{or} \qquad q - \frac{p^2}{4} > 0.$$

Let

$$u = x + \frac{p}{2}, \qquad c^2 = q - \frac{p^2}{4}.$$

Then

$$ax + b = a\left(u - \frac{p}{2}\right) + b = au + b', \qquad b' = b - a\frac{p}{2},$$

and we consider

$$\int \frac{au+b'}{(u^2+c^2)^k}\,du = \frac{a}{2}\int (u^2+c^2)^{-k}(2u\,du) + b'\int \frac{du}{(u^2+c^2)^k}. \tag{5}$$

The first integral on the right in (5) readily yields to the substitution $z = u^2 + c^2$. In the second integral, we let

$$u = c\tan\theta, \qquad du = c\sec^2\theta\,d\theta, \qquad u^2 + c^2 = c^2\sec^2\theta,$$

and obtain

$$\int \frac{du}{(u^2+c^2)^k} = c^{1-2k}\int \cos^{2k-2}\theta\,d\theta \qquad \left(\theta = \tan^{-1}\frac{u}{c}\right). \tag{6}$$

In the next article we shall obtain a reduction formula for $\int \cos^n\theta\,d\theta$, which may be used to evaluate the integral in (6). The trigonometric identity

$$\cos^2\theta = \frac{1+\cos 2\theta}{2} \tag{7}$$

may also be used to advantage.

The Heaviside Method

When the degree of the polynomial $f(x)$ is less than the degree of $g(x)$, and

$$g(x) = (x-r_1)(x-r_2)\cdots(x-r_n) \tag{8}$$

is a product of n different linear factors, each to the first power, there is a quick way to expand $f(x)/g(x)$ by partial fractions.

EXAMPLE 4. Find A, B and C in the partial-fractions expansion

$$\frac{x^2+1}{(x-1)(x-2)(x-3)} = \frac{A}{x-1} + \frac{B}{x-2} + \frac{C}{x-3}. \tag{9}$$

Solution. If we multiply both sides of Eq. (9) by $(x-1)$ to get

$$\frac{x^2+1}{(x-2)(x-3)} = A + \frac{B(x-1)}{x-2} + \frac{C(x-1)}{x-3}, \tag{10}$$

and set $x = 1$, the resulting equation gives the value of A:

$$\frac{(1)^2+1}{(1-2)(1-3)} = A + 0 + 0,$$

$$A = 1.$$

Thus, the value of A is the number we would have obtained if we had covered the factor $x - 1$ in the denominator of the original fraction

$$\frac{x^2+1}{(x-1)(x-2)(x-3)} \tag{11}$$

and evaluated what was left at $x = 1$. Similarly, we can find the value of B in Eq. (9) by covering up the factor $x - 2$ in (11) and evaluating the result,

$$\frac{x^2+1}{(x-1)(x-3)}, \tag{12}$$

at $x = 2$. That is,

$$B = \frac{(2)^2+1}{(2-1)(2-3)} = -5.$$

Finally, the value of C can be found by covering the factor $x - 3$ in (11) to get

$$\frac{x^2+1}{(x-1)(x-2)}, \tag{13}$$

and evaluating this fraction at $x = 3$:

$$C = \frac{(3)^2+1}{(3-1)(3-2)} = 5.$$

In general, to expand a quotient of polynomials $f(x)/g(x)$ by partial fractions when the degree of $f(x)$ is less than the degree of $g(x)$, and $g(x)$ is the product of n linear factors, each to the first power, one may proceed in the following way. First, write the quotient with $g(x)$ factored:

$$\frac{f(x)}{g(x)} = \frac{f(x)}{(x-r_1)(x-r_2)\cdots(x-r_n)}. \tag{14}$$

Then, cover the factors $(x - r_i)$ of $g(x)$ in (14) one at a time, each time replacing all the uncovered x's by the number r_i. This gives a number A_i for each root r_i:

$$A_1 = \frac{f(r_1)}{(r_1 - r_2)\cdots(r_1 - r_n)},$$

$$A_2 = \frac{f(r_2)}{(r_2 - r_1)(r_2 - r_3)\cdots(r_2 - r_n)}, \tag{15}$$

$$\vdots$$

$$A_n = \frac{f(r_n)}{(r_n - r_1)(r_n - r_2)\cdots(r_n - r_{n-1})}.$$

The partial-fraction expansion of $f(x)/g(x)$ is then

$$\frac{f(x)}{g(x)} = \frac{A_1}{(x - r_1)} + \frac{A_2}{(x - r_2)} + \cdots + \frac{A_n}{(x - r_n)}. \tag{16}$$

EXAMPLE 5. Evaluate

$$\int \frac{x + 4}{x^3 + 3x^2 - 10x}\,dx.$$

Solution. The degree of $f(x) = x + 4$ is less than the degree of $g(x) = x^3 + 3x^2 - 10x$, and, with $g(x)$ factored,

$$\frac{x + 4}{x^3 + 3x^2 - 10x} = \frac{x + 4}{x(x - 2)(x + 5)}.$$

The roots of $g(x)$ are $r_1 = 0$, $r_2 = 2$, and $r_3 = -5$. We find

$$A_1 = \frac{0 + 4}{(0 - 2)(0 + 5)} = -\frac{2}{5},$$

$$A_2 = \frac{2 + 4}{2(2 + 5)} = \frac{3}{7},$$

$$A_3 = \frac{-5 + 4}{(-5)(-5 - 2)} = -\frac{1}{35}.$$

Therefore,

$$\frac{x + 4}{x(x - 2)(x + 5)} = -\frac{2}{5x} + \frac{3}{7(x - 2)} - \frac{1}{35(x + 5)},$$

and

$$\int \frac{x + 4}{x(x - 2)(x + 5)}\,dx = -\frac{2}{5}\ln|x| + \frac{3}{7}\ln|x - 2| - \frac{1}{35}\ln|x + 5| + C.$$

EXAMPLE 6. The equation that describes the autocatalytic reaction of Example 2, Article 3–6, can be written as

$$\frac{dx}{dt} = kx(a - x).$$

Find x as a function of t if the initial amount of product is x_0; that is, $x = x_0$ when $t = 0$.

Solution. We separate variables to obtain

$$\frac{dx}{x(a-x)} = k\,dt, \tag{17}$$

and integrate both sides of the equation:

$$\int \frac{dx}{x(a-x)} = kt + C. \tag{18}$$

Since

$$\frac{1}{x(a-x)} = \frac{1}{ax} + \frac{1}{a(a-x)},$$

the integral on the left of Eq. (18) is

$$\int \frac{dx}{x(a-x)} = \frac{1}{a}\ln x - \frac{1}{a}\ln(a-x) + C = \frac{1}{a}\ln\frac{x}{a-x} + C. \tag{19}$$

We can omit the usual absolute-value signs because neither x nor $a - x$ is negative in the context of this application. Equations (18) and (19) together give

$$\frac{1}{a}\ln\frac{x}{a-x} = kt + C. \tag{20}$$

Substituting $x = x_0$, $t = 0$, in this equation, we find that

$$\frac{1}{a}\ln\frac{x_0}{a-x_0} = C.$$

When we substitute this expression for C in Eq. (20) and simplify the equation, the result is

$$\ln\frac{x(a-x_0)}{x_0(a-x)} = akt. \tag{21}$$

PROBLEMS

Evaluate the integrals 1 through 18.

1. $\int \frac{dx}{1-x^2}$
2. $\int \frac{d\theta}{\theta^3+\theta^2-2\theta}$
3. $\int \frac{x\,dx}{x^2+4x-5}$
4. $\int \frac{x\,dx}{x^2-2x-3}$
5. $\int \frac{(x+1)\,dx}{x^2+4x-5}$
6. $\int \frac{x^2\,dx}{x^2+2x+1}$
7. $\int \frac{dx}{x(x+1)^2}$
8. $\int \frac{dx}{(x+1)(x^2+1)}$
9. $\int \frac{(x+3)\,dx}{2x^3-8x}$
10. $\int \frac{\cos x\,dx}{\sin^2 x+\sin x-6}$
11. $\int \frac{5x^2\,dx}{x^2+1}$
12. $\int \frac{x^3\,dx}{x^2-2x+1}$
13. $\int \frac{dx}{x(x^2+x+1)}$
14. $\int \frac{\sin\theta\,d\theta}{\cos^2\theta+\cos\theta-2}$
15. $\int \frac{e^t\,dt}{e^{2t}+3e^t+2}$
16. $\int \frac{dx}{(x^2+1)^2}$

17. $\int \frac{x^4\,dx}{(x^2+1)^2}$

18. $\int \frac{(4x^3 - 20x)\,dx}{x^4 - 10x^2 + 9}$

19. To integrate $\int x^2\,dx/(x^2-1)$ by partial fractions, we would first divide x^2 by $x^2 - 1$ to get

$$\frac{x^2}{x^2-1} = 1 + \frac{1}{x^2-1}.$$

Suppose that we ignore the fact that x^2 and $x^2 - 1$ have the same degree, and try to write

$$\frac{x^2}{x^2-1} = \frac{x^2}{(x-1)(x+1)} = \frac{A}{x-1} + \frac{B}{x+1}$$

What goes wrong? Find out by trying to solve for A and B.

20. Many chemical reactions are the result of an interaction of two molecules that undergo a change to produce a new product. The rate of the reaction typically depends on the concentration of the two kinds of molecules. If a is the amount of substance A and b is the amount of substance B at time $t = 0$ and if x is the amount of product at time t, then the rate of formation of x may be given by the differential equation

$$\frac{dx}{dt} = k(a-x)(b-x),$$

where k is a positive constant. Find a relation between x and t, (a) if $a = b$, and (b) if $a \neq b$. [See Example 6.]

7–7 INTEGRATION BY PARTS

There are really just two general methods of integration. One of these is the method of substitution, which we have illustrated in Articles 7–2 through 7–5. The method of partial fractions is really not a method of integration so much as it is a method of algebraic transformation of a rational function into an integrable form. The second general method of integration, called *integration by parts*, depends upon the formula for the differential of a product:

$$d(uv) = u\,dv + v\,du$$

or

$$u\,dv = d(uv) - v\,du.$$

When this is integrated, we have

$$\int u\,dv = uv - \int v\,du + C. \tag{1}$$

Formula (1) expresses one integral, $\int u\,dv$, in terms of a second integral, $\int v\,du$. If, by proper choice of u and dv, the second integral is simpler than the first, we may be able to evaluate it quite simply and thus arrive at an answer.

REMARK. In a definite integral, appropriate limits must be supplied. We may then interpret the formula for integration by parts,

$$\int_{v_1}^{v_2} u\,dv = (u_2 v_2 - u_1 v_1) - \int_{u_1}^{u_2} v\,du,$$

geometrically in terms of areas (see Fig. 7–7).

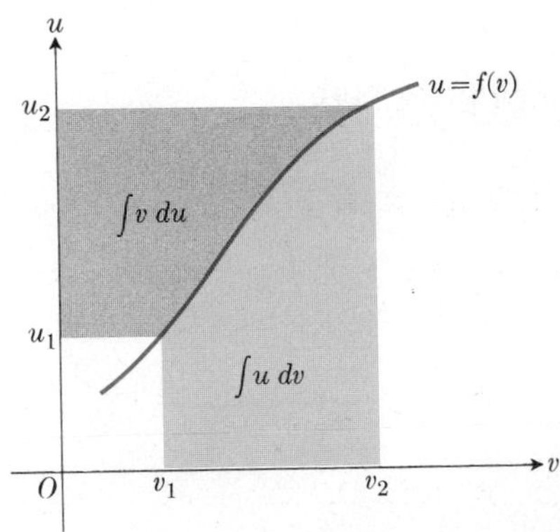

7–7 $\int_{v_1}^{v_2} u\,dv = (u_2 v_2 - u_1 v_1) - \int_{u_1}^{u_2} v\,du.$

EXAMPLE 1

$$\int \ln x\,dx.$$

Solution. If we try to match $\ln x\, dx$ with $u\, dv$, we may take $u = \ln x$ and $dv = dx$. Then, to use (1), we see that we also require

$$du = d(\ln x) = \frac{dx}{x}$$

and

$$v = \int dv = \int dx = x + C_1,$$

so that

$$\int \ln x\, dx = (\ln x)(x + C_1) - \int (x + C_1)\frac{dx}{x} + C_2$$

$$= x \ln x + C_1 \ln x - \int dx - \int C_1 \frac{dx}{x} + C_2$$

$$= x \ln x + C_1 \ln x - x - C_1 \ln x + C_2 = x \ln x - x + C_2.$$

Note that the first constant of integration C_1 does not appear in the final answer. This is generally true, for if we write $v + C_1$ in place of v in the right side of (1), we obtain

$$u(v + C_1) - \int (v + C_1)\, du = uv + C_1 u - \int v\, du - \int C_1\, du = uv - \int v\, du,$$

where it is understood that a constant of integration must still be added in the final result. It is therefore customary to drop the first constant of integration when determining v as $\int dv$.

EXAMPLE 2

$$\int \tan^{-1} x\, dx.$$

Solution. This is typical of the inverse trigonometric functions. Let

$$u = \tan^{-1} x \qquad \text{and} \qquad dv = dx;$$

then

$$du = \frac{dx}{1 + x^2} \qquad \text{and} \qquad v = x,$$

so that

$$\int \tan^{-1} x\, dx = x \tan^{-1} x - \int \frac{x\, dx}{1 + x^2} = x \tan^{-1} x - \frac{1}{2} \ln (1 + x^2) + C.$$

Sometimes an integration by parts must be repeated to obtain an answer, as in the following example.

EXAMPLE 3

$$\int x^2 e^x\, dx.$$

Solution. Let

$$u = x^2 \quad \text{and} \quad dv = e^x\,dx.$$

Then

$$du = 2x\,dx \quad \text{and} \quad v = e^x,$$

so that

$$\int x^2 e^x\,dx = x^2 e^x - 2\int x e^x\,dx.$$

The integral on the right is similar to the original integral, except that we have reduced the power of x from 2 to 1. If we could now reduce it from 1 to 0, we could see success ahead. In $\int x e^x\,dx$, we therefore let

$$U = x \quad \text{and} \quad dV = e^x\,dx,$$

so that

$$dU = dx \quad \text{and} \quad V = e^x.$$

Then

$$\int x e^x\,dx = x e^x - \int e^x\,dx = x e^x - e^x + C,$$

and

$$\int x^2 e^x\,dx = x^2 e^x - 2x e^x + 2e^x + C.$$

EXAMPLE 4. Obtain a reduction formula for the integral

$$J_n = \int \cos^n x\,dx.$$

Solution. We may think of $\cos^n x$ as $\cos^{n-1} x \cdot \cos x$. Then we let

$$u = \cos^{n-1} x \quad \text{and} \quad dv = \cos x\,dx,$$

so that

$$du = (n-1)\cos^{n-2} x(-\sin x\,dx) \quad \text{and} \quad v = \sin x.$$

Hence

$$J_n = \cos^{n-1} x \sin x + (n-1)\int \sin^2 x \cos^{n-2} x\,dx$$

$$= \cos^{n-1} x \sin x + (n-1)\int (1 - \cos^2 x)\cos^{n-2} x\,dx,$$

or

$$\int \cos^n x\,dx$$

$$= \cos^{n-1} x \sin x + (n-1)\int \cos^{n-2} x\,dx - (n-1)\int \cos^n x\,dx.$$

The last integral on the right may now be transposed to the left to give

$$[1 + (n-1)]J_n = nJ_n.$$

We then divide by n, and the final result is

$$\int \cos^n x\, dx = \frac{\cos^{n-1} x \sin x}{n} + \frac{n-1}{n} \int \cos^{n-2} x\, dx. \tag{2}$$

This allows us to reduce the exponent on $\cos x$ by 2 and is a very useful formula. When n is a positive integer, we may apply the formula repeatedly until the remaining integral is either

$$\int \cos x\, dx = \sin x + C \qquad \text{or} \qquad \int \cos^0 x\, dx = \int dx = x + C.$$

For example, with $n = 4$, we get

$$\int \cos^4 x\, dx = \frac{\cos^3 x \sin x}{4} + \frac{3}{4} \int \cos^2 x\, dx,$$

and with $n = 2$,

$$\int \cos^2 x\, dx = \frac{\cos x \sin x}{2} + \frac{1}{2} \int dx.$$

Therefore,

$$\int \cos^4 x\, dx = \frac{\cos^3 x \sin x}{4} + \frac{3}{4}\left(\frac{\cos x \sin x}{2} + \tfrac{1}{2}x\right) + C.$$

You may find it instructive to derive the companion formula:

$$\int \sin^n x\, dx = -\frac{\sin^{n-1} x \cos x}{n} + \frac{n-1}{n} \int \sin^{n-2} x\, dx. \tag{3}$$

The integral in the following example occurs in electrical engineering problems. Its evaluation requires two integrations by parts, followed by solving for the unknown integral in a method analogous to that used above in finding reduction formulas.

EXAMPLE 5

$$\int e^{ax} \cos bx\, dx.$$

Solution. Let

$$u = e^{ax} \qquad \text{and} \qquad dv = \cos bx\, dx.$$

Then

$$du = ae^{ax}\, dx \qquad \text{and} \qquad v = \frac{1}{b} \sin bx,$$

so that

$$\int e^{ax} \cos bx\, dx = \frac{e^{ax} \sin bx}{b} - \frac{a}{b} \int e^{ax} \sin bx\, dx.$$

The second integral is like the first except that it has sin bx in place of cos bx. If we apply integration by parts to it, letting

$$U = e^{\ x} \quad \text{and} \quad dV = \sin bx\, dx,$$

then

$$dU = ae^{ax}\, dx \quad \text{and} \quad V = -\frac{1}{b}\cos bx,$$

so that

$$\int e^{ax} \cos bx\, dx = \frac{e^{ax} \sin bx}{b} - \frac{a}{b}\left[-\frac{e^{ax}\cos bx}{b} + \frac{a}{b}\int e^{ax}\cos bx\, dx\right].$$

Now the unknown integral appears on the left with a coefficient of unity and on the right with a coefficient of $-a^2/b^2$. Transposing this term to the left and dividing by the new coefficient

$$1 + \frac{a^2}{b^2} = \frac{a^2 + b^2}{b^2},$$

we have

$$\int e^{ax} \cos bx\, dx = e^{ax}\left(\frac{b \sin bx + a \cos bx}{a^2 + b^2}\right) + C. \qquad (4)$$

PROBLEMS

Evaluate the integrals 1 through 16.

1. $\int x \ln x\, dx$
2. $\int x^n \ln ax\, dx \quad (n \neq -1)$
3. $\int x \tan^{-1} x\, dx$
4. $\int \sin^{-1} ax\, dx$
5. $\int x \sin ax\, dx$
6. $\int x^2 \cos ax\, dx$
7. $\int x \sec^2 ax\, dx$
8. $\int e^{ax} \sin bx\, dx$
9. $\int \sin (\ln x)\, dx$
10. $\int \cos (\ln x)\, dx$
11. $\int \ln (a^2 + x^2)\, dx$
12. $\int x \cos (2x + 1)\, dx$
13. $\int x \sin^{-1} x\, dx$
14. $\int_1^2 x \sec^{-1} x\, dx$
15. $\int_1^4 \sec^{-1} \sqrt{x}\, dx$
16. $\int x^2 \tan^{-1} x\, dx$

Derive the reduction formulas given in part (a) of each of the following problems, and apply each one to the specific problems given there.

17. a) $\displaystyle\int x^m (\ln x)^n\, dx = \frac{x^{m+1}(\ln x)^n}{m+1} - \frac{n}{m+1}\int x^m (\ln x)^{n-1}\, dx$

 b) $\int x^3 (\ln x)^2\, dx$

18. a) $\displaystyle\int \sin^n x\, dx = -\frac{\sin^{n-1} x \cos x}{n} + \frac{n-1}{n}\int \sin^{n-2} x\, dx$

 b) $\displaystyle\int_0^{\pi/6} \sin^4 3x\, dx$

19. a) $\int x^n e^x\, dx = x^n e^x - n \int x^{n-1} e^x\, dx$; b) $\int x^3 e^x\, dx$

20. **a)** $\int \sec^n x\,dx = \dfrac{\sec^{n-2} x \tan x}{(n-1)} + \dfrac{n-2}{n-1}\int \sec^{n-2} x\,dx$

b) $\int \sec^3 x\,dx$ [See Eq. (3), Article 7–2.]

c) $\int \sqrt{a^2 + x^2}\,dx$ [*Hint.* Let $x = a \tan \theta$.]

21. Find the second degree polynomial $P(x)$ that has the following properties: (a) $P(0) = 1$, (b) $P'(0) = 0$, and (c) the indefinite integral

$$\int \frac{P(x)\,dx}{x^3(x-1)^2}$$

is a rational function. (That is, no logarithmic terms occur in the answer.)

22. Use cylindrical shells to find the volume of the solid obtained by revolving the area bounded by $x = 0$, $y = 0$, and $y = \cos x$, $0 \le x \le \pi/2$, about the y-axis.

23. Find the centroid of the area bounded by $y = x^2 e^x$, $y = 0$, $x = 1$.

24. Find the centroid of the area bounded by $y = \ln x$, $x = 1$, $y = 1$.

25. Evaluate $\int_0^1 e^{\sqrt{x}}\,dx$.

7–8 INTEGRATION OF RATIONAL FUNCTIONS OF sin *x* AND cos *x*, AND OTHER TRIGONOMETRIC INTEGRALS

It has been discovered that the substitution

$$z = \tan \frac{x}{2} \tag{1}$$

enables us to reduce the problem of integrating any rational function of $\sin x$ and $\cos x$ to a problem involving a rational function of z. This in turn can be integrated by the method of partial fractions discussed in Article 7–6. Thus the substitution (1) is a very powerful tool. This method is cumbersome, however, and is used only when the simpler methods outlined previously have failed.

To see the effect of the substitution, we calculate

$$\cos x = 2\cos^2 \frac{x}{2} - 1 = \frac{2}{\sec^2 (x/2)} - 1$$
$$= \frac{2}{1 + \tan^2 (x/2)} - 1 = \frac{2}{1 + z^2} - 1$$

or

$$\cos x = \frac{1 - z^2}{1 + z^2}, \tag{2a}$$

and

$$\sin x = 2 \sin \frac{x}{2} \cos \frac{x}{2} = 2\,\frac{\sin (x/2)}{\cos (x/2)} \cdot \cos^2 \frac{x}{2}$$
$$= 2 \tan \frac{x}{2} \cdot \frac{1}{\sec^2 (x/2)} = \frac{2 \tan (x/2)}{1 + \tan^2 (x/2)}$$

or

$$\sin x = \frac{2z}{1 + z^2}. \tag{2b}$$

Finally,

$$x = 2 \tan^{-1} z,$$

so that

$$dx = \frac{2\,dz}{1+z^2}. \tag{2c}$$

EXAMPLE 1

$$\int \sec x\,dx = \int \frac{dx}{\cos x} \qquad \text{becomes} \qquad \int \frac{2\,dz}{1+z^2}\cdot\frac{1+z^2}{1-z^2} = \int \frac{2\,dz}{1-z^2}.$$

To this we apply the method of partial fractions:

$$\frac{2}{1-z^2} = \frac{A}{1-z} + \frac{B}{1+z},$$

$$2 = A(1+z) + B(1-z)$$

$$= (A+B) + (A-B)z,$$

which requires

$$A + B = 2, \qquad A - B = 0.$$

Hence

$$A = B = 1$$

and

$$\int \frac{2\,dz}{1-z^2} = \int \frac{dz}{1-z} + \int \frac{dz}{1+z} = -\ln|1-z| + \ln|1+z| + C$$

$$= \ln\left|\frac{1+z}{1-z}\right| + C$$

$$= \ln\left|\frac{1+\tan(x/2)}{1-\tan(x/2)}\right| + C$$

$$= \ln\left|\frac{\tan(\pi/4)+\tan(x/2)}{1-\tan(\pi/4)\tan(x/2)}\right| + C$$

$$= \ln\left|\tan\left(\frac{\pi}{4}+\frac{x}{2}\right)\right| + C.$$

That is,

$$\int \sec x\,dx = \ln\left|\tan\left(\frac{\pi}{4}+\frac{x}{2}\right)\right| + C \tag{3}$$

is an alternative form, which may be used in place of Eq. (3), Article 7–2.

EXAMPLE 2

$$\int \frac{dx}{1+\cos x} = \int \frac{2\,dz}{1+z^2}\,\frac{1+z^2}{2} = \int dz = z + C = \tan\frac{x}{2} + C.$$

EXAMPLE 3

$$\int \frac{dx}{2+\sin x} = \int \frac{2\,dz}{1+z^2}\left[\frac{1+z^2}{2+2z+2z^2}\right] = \int \frac{dz}{z^2+z+1} = \int \frac{dz}{(z+\frac{1}{2})^2+\frac{3}{4}}$$

$$= \int \frac{du}{u^2+a^2} \qquad \left[u = z+\frac{1}{2},\quad a = \frac{\sqrt{3}}{2}\right]$$

$$= \frac{1}{a}\tan^{-1}\frac{u}{a} + C = \frac{2}{\sqrt{3}}\tan^{-1}\frac{2z+1}{\sqrt{3}} + C$$

$$= \frac{2}{\sqrt{3}}\tan^{-1}\frac{1+2\tan(x/2)}{\sqrt{3}} + C.$$

We have already made repeated use of trigonometric identities to aid us in evaluating integrals. The following types of integrals:

$$\int \sin mx \sin nx\,dx, \qquad \int \sin mx \cos nx\,dx, \qquad \int \cos mx \cos nx\,dx, \tag{4}$$

arise in connection with alternating-current theory, heat transfer problems, bending of beams, cable stress analysis in suspension bridges, and many other places where trigonometric series (or Fourier series) are applied to problems in mathematics, science, and engineering. The integrals in (4) can be evaluated by the method of integration by parts, but two such integrations are required in each case. A simpler way to evaluate them is to exploit the trigonometric identities

a) $\sin mx \sin nx = \frac{1}{2}[\cos(m-n)x - \cos(m+n)x]$,

b) $\sin mx \cos nx = \frac{1}{2}[\sin(m-n)x + \sin(m+n)x]$, **(5)**

c) $\cos mx \cos nx = \frac{1}{2}[\cos(m-n)x + \cos(m+n)x]$.

These identities follow at once from

$$\begin{aligned}\cos(A+B) &= \cos A\cos B - \sin A\sin B,\\ \cos(A-B) &= \cos A\cos B + \sin A\sin B,\end{aligned} \tag{6a}$$

and

$$\begin{aligned}\sin(A+B) &= \sin A\cos B + \cos A\sin B,\\ \sin(A-B) &= \sin A\cos B - \cos A\sin B.\end{aligned} \tag{6b}$$

For example, if we add the two equations in (6a) and then divide by 2, we obtain (5c) by taking $A = mx$ and $B = nx$. The identity in (5a) is obtained in a similar fashion by subtracting the first equation in (6a) from the second equation. Finally, if we add the two equations in (6b) we are led to the identity in (5b).

EXAMPLE 4

$$\int \sin 3x \cos 5x\, dx = \tfrac{1}{2}\int [\sin(-2x) + \sin 8x]\, dx$$

$$= \tfrac{1}{2}\int (\sin 8x - \sin 2x)\, dx$$

$$= -\frac{\cos 8x}{16} + \frac{\cos 2x}{4} + C.$$

PROBLEMS

Evaluate integrals 1 through 8.

1. $\displaystyle\int_0^{\pi} \frac{dx}{1+\sin x}$
2. $\displaystyle\int_{\pi/2}^{\pi} \frac{dx}{1-\cos x}$
3. $\displaystyle\int \frac{dx}{1-\sin x}$
4. $\displaystyle\int_0^{\pi/2} \frac{dx}{2+\cos x}$
5. $\displaystyle\int \frac{\cos x\, dx}{2-\cos x}$
6. $\displaystyle\int_0^{\pi/2} \cos 3x \sin 2x\, dx$
7. $\displaystyle\int_{-\pi}^{\pi} \sin 3x \sin 2x\, dx$
8. $\displaystyle\int_{-\pi}^{\pi} \sin^2 3x\, dx$

9. Two functions f and g are said to be *orthogonal* on an interval $a \le x \le b$ if $\int_a^b f(x)g(x)\, dx = 0$. (a) Prove that $\sin mx$ and $\sin nx$ are orthogonal on any interval of length 2π provided m and n are integers such that $m^2 \ne n^2$. (b) Prove the same for $\cos mx$ and $\cos nx$. (c) Prove the same for $\sin mx$ and $\cos nx$ even if $m = n$.

7–9 FURTHER SUBSTITUTIONS

Some integrals involving fractional powers of the variable x may be simplified by substituting $x = z^n$, where n is the least common multiple of the denominators of the exponents.

For example

$$\int \frac{\sqrt{x}\, dx}{1+\sqrt[4]{x}}$$

may be simplified by taking

$$x = z^4, \qquad dx = 4z^3\, dz.$$

This leads to

$$\int \frac{\sqrt{x}\, dx}{1+\sqrt[4]{x}} = \int \frac{z^2 \cdot 4z^3\, dz}{1+z}$$

$$= 4\int \left(z^4 - z^3 + z^2 - z + 1 - \frac{1}{z+1}\right) dz$$

$$= 4\left[\frac{z^5}{5} - \frac{z^4}{4} + \frac{z^3}{3} - \frac{z^2}{2} + z - \ln|z+1|\right] + C$$

$$= \tfrac{4}{5}x^{5/4} - x + \tfrac{4}{3}x^{3/4} - 2x^{1/2} + 4x^{1/4} - 4\ln|1 + x^{-1/4}| + C.$$

In $\int x^3\sqrt{x^2+a^2}\, dx$, on the other hand, the substitution

$$z^2 = x^2 + a^2$$

or

$$x^2 = z^2 - a^2$$

and

$$2x\,dx = 2z\,dz$$

leads to

$$\int x^3\sqrt{x^2 + a^2}\,dx = \int x^2\sqrt{x^2 + a^2} \cdot x\,dx = \int (z^2 - a^2) \cdot z^2 \cdot dz$$

$$= \int (z^4 - a^2z^2)\,dz$$

$$= \tfrac{1}{5}(x^2 + a^2)^{5/2} - \tfrac{1}{3}a^2(x^2 + a^2)^{3/2} + C$$

$$= \frac{3x^2 - 2a^2}{15}(x^2 + a^2)^{3/2} + C.$$

Even when it is not clear at the start that a substitution will work, it is advisable to try one that seems reasonable and pursue it until it either gives results or appears to make matters worse. In the latter case, try something else! Sometimes a chain of substitutions

$$u = f(x), \qquad v = g(u), \qquad z = h(v), \qquad \text{etc.},$$

will produce results when it is by no means obvious that this will work. The criterion of success is whether the new integrals so obtained appear to be simpler than the original integral. In this regard, it is handy to remember that any rational function of x can be integrated by the method of partial fractions and that any rational function of $\sin x$ and $\cos x$ can be integrated by using the substitution $z = \tan x/2$. If we can reduce a given integral to one of these types, we then know how to finish the job.

Even in these cases, however, it is frequently simpler to use special methods suggested by the particular integrand rather than to use the general methods. For instance, one would hardly let $z = \tan x/2$ in order to evaluate $\int \sin x\,dx = -\cos x + C$. And reference to Eqs. (5) and (6), Article 7–6, and the accompanying discussion shows that a trigonometric substitution is used to evaluate certain of the integrals that arise in the method of partial fractions. It may be more convenient to use the same substitution *before* going through the algebraic reductions instead of *after* doing so.

For example, consider the integral

$$\int_{-1}^{0} \sqrt{\frac{1 + x}{1 - x}}\,dx. \tag{1}$$

If we let

$$\frac{1 + x}{1 - x} = z^2, \tag{2}$$

we shall, of course, get rid of the radical. Whether this is really a good substitution or not depends upon how complicated the expression is for dx

in terms of z and dz. To settle this question, we solve for x as follows:

$$1 + x = z^2 - xz^2,$$

$$x(z^2 + 1) = z^2 - 1,$$

$$x = \frac{z^2 - 1}{z^2 + 1}. \tag{3}$$

Hence

$$dx = \frac{4z\,dz}{(z^2 + 1)^2}$$

and the integral becomes

$$\int \sqrt{\frac{1 + x}{1 - x}}\,dx = \int \frac{4z^2\,dz}{(z^2 + 1)^2}.$$

Now the integrand on the right is a rational function of z and we could proceed by the method of partial fractions. But the $z^2 + 1$ in the denominator also lends itself to the substitution

$$z = \tan\theta. \tag{4}$$

We try this, and have

$$dz = \sec^2\theta\,d\theta, \qquad z^2 + 1 = \tan^2\theta + 1 = \sec^2\theta,$$

so that

$$\int \frac{4z^2\,dz}{(z^2 + 1)^2} = \int \frac{4\tan^2\theta \cdot \sec^2\theta\,d\theta}{\sec^4\theta}$$

$$= 4\int \frac{\sin^2\theta}{\cos^2\theta} \cdot \frac{1}{\sec^2\theta}\,d\theta = 4\int \sin^2\theta\,d\theta,$$

and the last integral can now be evaluated at once to give

$$4\int \sin^2\theta\,d\theta = 2\left[\theta - \frac{\sin 2\theta}{2}\right] + C. \tag{5}$$

We now have two alternative courses of action for evaluating the *definite integral*, (1): namely,

a) we may reverse the substitutions (3) and (4) and replace (5) by its equivalent in terms of x. Then the definite integral (1) could be evaluated by substituting the original limits of integration; or,

b) we may determine new limits of integration corresponding to the new variable of integration.

We illustrate the second line of attack. In the original integral, (1), x varies from -1 to 0. As this happens, the left side of (2) varies from 0 to 1, and since we have tacitly taken

$$z = \sqrt{\frac{1 + x}{1 - x}}$$

as the *positive* square root, we see that then z varies from 0 to 1. Finally, from (4) we have $\theta = \tan^{-1} z$, so that θ varies from 0 to $\pi/4$ as z varies from 0 to 1. Combining these results, we have

$$\int_{-1}^{0} \sqrt{\frac{1+x}{1-x}}\,dx = \int_{0}^{1} \frac{4z^2\,dz}{(z^2+1)^2} \qquad \left[z = \sqrt{\frac{1+x}{1-x}}\right]$$

$$= 4\int_{0}^{\pi/4} \sin^2\theta\,d\theta \qquad [\theta = \tan^{-1} z]$$

$$= 2\left[\theta - \frac{\sin 2\theta}{2}\right]_{0}^{\pi/4} = \frac{\pi}{2}.$$

It is also instructive to evaluate the integral in (1) by making the alternative substitution

$$x = \cos 2t, \qquad dx = -2\sin 2t\,dt = -4\sin t\cos t\,dt,$$

which is particularly well adapted to the integrand in question, since

$$1 + \cos 2t = 2\cos^2 t$$

and

$$1 - \cos 2t = 2\sin^2 t.$$

But the shortest way of all is to notice that for the interval of integration $-1 \le x \le 0$ we have

$$\sqrt{\frac{1+x}{1-x}} = \frac{1+x}{\sqrt{1-x^2}},$$

and hence

$$\int \sqrt{\frac{1+x}{1-x}}\,dx = \int \frac{1+x}{\sqrt{1-x^2}}\,dx$$

$$= \sin^{-1} x - \sqrt{1-x^2} + C. \qquad (6)$$

PROBLEMS

1. $\int \frac{1-\sqrt{x}}{1+\sqrt{x}}\,dx$

2. $\int \frac{dx}{a+b\sqrt{x}}$ (a and b constants)

3. $\int x^2\sqrt{x+a}\,dx$

4. $\int \frac{\sqrt{x+a}\,dx}{x+b}$ $(b > a)$

5. $\int \sqrt{\frac{a+x}{b+x}}\,dx$ $(b \ne a)$

6. $\int \frac{dx}{x+\sqrt{x^2+a^2}}$ $(a > 0)$

7. $\int_0^1 \frac{x^3\,dx}{(x^2+1)^{3/2}}$

8. $\int \frac{dx}{x(ax^n+c)}$ $(anc \ne 0)$

9. $\int_3^8 \frac{(t+2)\,dt}{t\sqrt{t+1}}$

10. $\int \frac{dx}{x-x^{2/3}}$

11. $\int_0^3 \frac{\sqrt{x+1}-1}{\sqrt{x+1}+1}\,dx$

12. $\int \frac{dx}{x(1-\sqrt[4]{x})}$

13. $\int \frac{y^{2/3}\,dy}{y+1}$

14. $\int \frac{z^5\,dz}{\sqrt{1+z^3}}$

15. $\int \frac{\sqrt{t^3-1}}{t}\,dt$

16. $\int_0^{\ln 2} \frac{dw}{(1+e^w)}$

17. $\int_0^{\pi/2} \frac{\sin 2\theta\,d\theta}{2+\cos\theta}$

18. $\int \frac{\sin x\,dx}{\tan x+\cos x}$

19. $\int \frac{dx}{x^3+1}$

20. $\int \frac{dy}{y^{1/3}-y^{1/2}}$

7–10 IMPROPER INTEGRALS

When the integral discussed in the previous article is changed to

$$\int_{-1}^{+1} \sqrt{\frac{1+x}{1-x}}\, dx,$$

which arises in the so-called "lifting line theory" in aerodynamics, the result is called an *improper* integral because the integrand

$$f(x) = \sqrt{\frac{1+x}{1-x}}$$

becomes infinite at one of the limits of integration, in this case at $x = +1$. More generally, integrals of the following two types are called improper integrals:

a) $\int_a^b f(x)\, dx$, where $f(x)$ becomes infinite at a value of x between a and b inclusive,

b) $\int_a^\infty f(x)\, dx$ or $\int_{-\infty}^b f(x)\, dx$, where one or both of the limits of integration are infinite.

EXAMPLE 1

$$\int_{-1}^{1} \sqrt{\frac{1+x}{1-x}}\, dx = \int_0^\infty \frac{4z^2\, dz}{(z^2+1)^2} \qquad \left[z = \sqrt{\frac{1+x}{1-x}}\right],$$

where the integral on the left is an improper integral of the first type and the integral on the right is an improper integral of the second type.

An integral can be improper for more than one reason.

EXAMPLE 2. In

$$\int_0^\infty \frac{1}{x^3}\, dx,$$

the function $1/x^3$ becomes infinite as x approaches 0, and also one of the limits of integration is infinite.

Figure 7–8 illustrates another case where the function becomes infinite at one of the limits of integration. If we interpret the integral in Example 1 in terms of area under the curve $y = f(x)$, say from -1 to $+1$, we see that the curve extends to infinity as x approaches 1 and the area from -1 to $+1$ is not well defined. Nevertheless, we can certainly define the area from $x = -1$ to $x = b$, where b is any positive number *less* than one; for example, we can take $b = 0.999$. This defines a function of b:

$$g(b) = \int_{-1}^{b} f(x)\, dx.$$

If this function has a finite limit as b approaches $+1$ from the left, we *define*

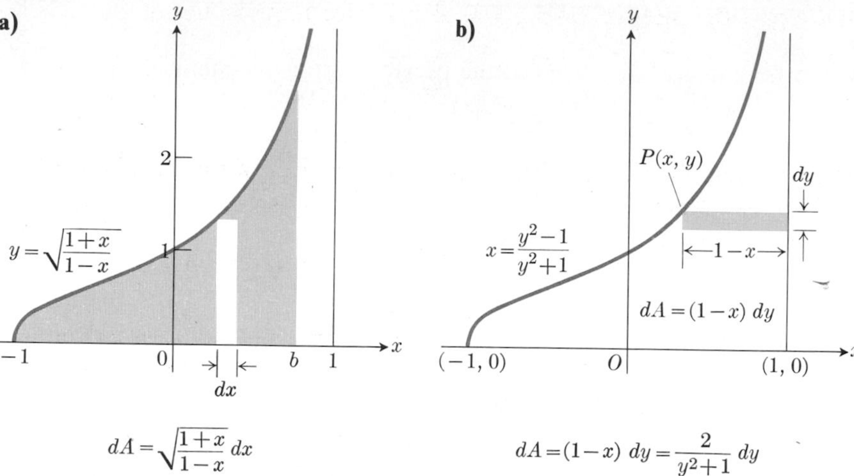

7–8 Two schemes for calculating $\int_{-1}^{1}\sqrt{(1+x)/(1-x)}\,dx$ as an area.

the value of the improper integral to be this limit:

$$\int_{-1}^{+1} f(x)\,dx = \lim_{b\to 1^-}\int_{-1}^{b} f(x)\,dx.$$

In this case we also say that the improper integral *converges*. On the other hand, we say that the integral *diverges* if the function g has no definite finite limit as $b \to 1^-$.

EXAMPLE 3. We find from Eq. (6) of Article 7–9 that

$$\int_{-1}^{b}\sqrt{\frac{1+x}{1-x}}\,dx = \sin^{-1}x - \sqrt{1-x^2}\Big]_{-1}^{b}$$

$$= \sin^{-1}b - \sqrt{1-b^2} + \frac{\pi}{2}.$$

This is the number denoted above by $g(b)$. When b is slightly less than $+1$, $\sin^{-1}b$ is slightly less than $\pi/2$ and $\sqrt{1-b^2}$ is nearly zero. Hence,

$$\lim_{b\to 1^-}\int_{-1}^{b}\sqrt{\frac{1+x}{1-x}}\,dx = \lim_{b\to 1^-}\left[\sin^{-1}b - \sqrt{1-b^2} + \frac{\pi}{2}\right]$$

$$= \frac{\pi}{2} - 0 + \frac{\pi}{2} = \pi.$$

The given integral therefore converges and its value is π.

The same result is obtained if, instead of finding the area by summing vertical elements (Fig. 7–8(a)), we sum horizontal elements (Fig. 7–8(b)). Then we find

$$A = \int_{y=0}^{\infty}(1-x)\,dy = \int_{0}^{\infty}\frac{2}{y^2+1}\,dy.$$

This time, the integral to be evaluated is an improper integral of the second type because the range of integration extends to infinity. In this case we investigate the integral from $y = 0$ to $y = c$ for large values of c:

$$\int_0^c \frac{2\,dy}{y^2+1} = 2\tan^{-1} c,$$

and we *define* the integral from 0 to ∞ as the limit of this as $c \to \infty$ (if the limit exists). That is,

$$\int_0^\infty \frac{2\,dy}{y^2+1} = \lim_{c\to\infty} \int_0^c \frac{2\,dy}{y^2+1} = \lim_{c\to\infty} (2\tan^{-1} c) = \pi.$$

The limit does exist, since $\tan^{-1} c$ approaches $\pi/2$ as c increases indefinitely.

EXAMPLE 4. In the integral

$$\int_0^1 \frac{dx}{x},$$

the function f is defined by

$$f(x) = \frac{1}{x},$$

which becomes infinite at $x = 0$. We cut off the point $x = 0$ and start our integration at some positive number $b < 1$. (See Fig. 7–9.) That is, we consider the integral

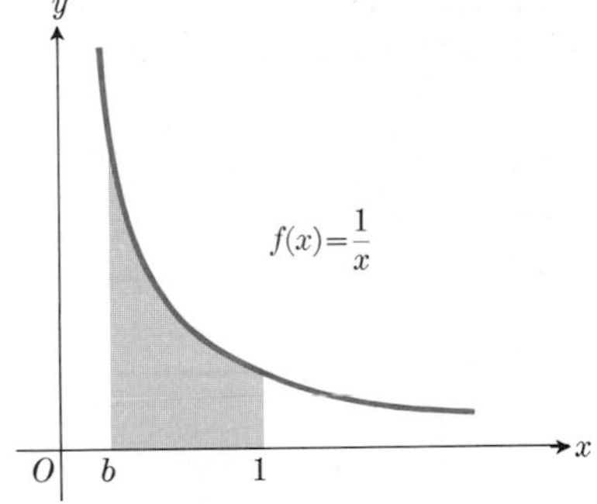

7–9 $\int_0^1 \frac{dx}{x} = \lim_{b\to 0^+} \int_b^1 \frac{dx}{x}.$

$$\int_b^1 \frac{dx}{x} = \ln x\Big]_b^1 = \ln 1 - \ln b = \ln \frac{1}{b},$$

and investigate its behavior as b approaches zero from the right. Since

$$\lim_{b\to 0^+} \int_b^1 \frac{dx}{x} = \lim_{b\to 0^+} \left(\ln \frac{1}{b}\right) = +\infty,$$

we say that the integral from $x = 0$ to $x = 1$ *diverges*.

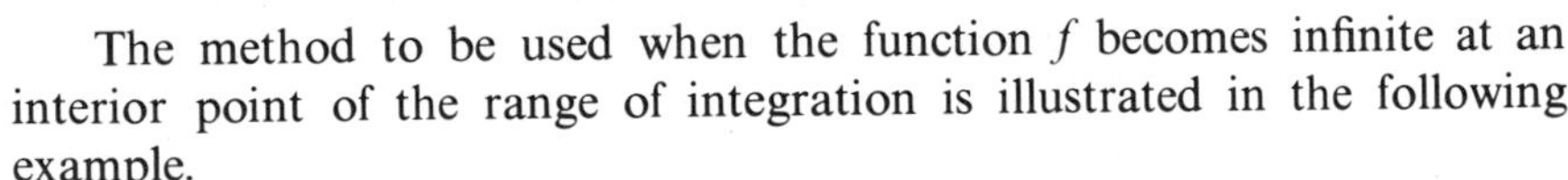

The method to be used when the function f becomes infinite at an interior point of the range of integration is illustrated in the following example.

EXAMPLE 5. In the integral

$$\int_0^3 \frac{dx}{(x-1)^{2/3}},$$

the function

$$f(x) = \frac{1}{(x-1)^{2/3}}$$

becomes infinite at $x = 1$, which lies between the limits of integration 0 and 3. In such a case, we again cut out the point where $f(x)$ becomes infinite. This time we integrate from 0 to b, where b is slightly less than 1, and start again on the other side of 1 at c and integrate from c to 3 (Fig. 7–10). Then we get the two integrals

$$\int_0^b \frac{dx}{(x-1)^{2/3}} \quad \text{and} \quad \int_c^3 \frac{dx}{(x-1)^{2/3}}$$

to investigate. If the first of these has a definite limit as $b \to 1^-$ and if the second also has a definite limit as $c \to 1^+$, then we say that the improper integral converges and that its value is given by

$$\int_0^3 \frac{dx}{(x-1)^{2/3}} = \lim_{b \to 1^-} \int_0^b \frac{dx}{(x-1)^{2/3}} + \lim_{c \to 1^+} \int_c^3 \frac{dx}{(x-1)^{2/3}}.$$

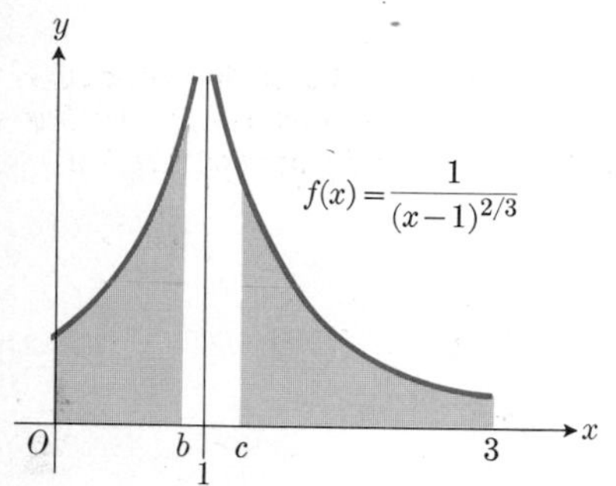

7–10 $\int_0^3 f(x)\,dx = \lim_{b \to 1^-} \int_0^b f(x)\,dx + \lim_{c \to 1^+} \int_c^3 f(x)\,dx.$

If either limit fails to exist, we say that the given improper integral *diverges*. For this example,

$$\lim_{b \to 1^-} \int_0^b (x-1)^{-2/3}\,dx = \lim_{b \to 1^-} [3(b-1)^{1/3} - 3(0-1)^{1/3}] = +3$$

and

$$\lim_{c \to 1^+} \int_c^3 (x-1)^{-2/3}\,dx = \lim_{c \to 1^+} [3(3-1)^{1/3} - 3(c-1)^{1/3}] = 3\sqrt[3]{2}.$$

Since both limits exist and are finite, the original integral is said to converge and its value is $3 + 3\sqrt[3]{2}$.

The convergence of the integral

$$\int_1^\infty \frac{dx}{x^p}$$

depends on the size of the exponent p. The next example illustrates this with $p = 1$ and $p = 2$.

EXAMPLE 6. Determine whether the following improper integrals converge or diverge:

$$\int_1^\infty \frac{dx}{x} \quad \text{and} \quad \int_1^\infty \frac{dx}{x^2}.$$

Solution. The two curves

$$y_1 = \frac{1}{x} \quad \text{and} \quad y_2 = \frac{1}{x^2}$$

both approach the x-axis as $x \to \infty$ (Fig. 7–11). In the first case,

$$\int_1^b \frac{dx}{x} = \ln x \Big]_1^b = \ln b.$$

If we now let b take on larger and larger positive values, the logarithm of b increases indefinitely and

$$\lim_{b \to \infty} \int_1^b \frac{dx}{x} = \infty.$$

a)

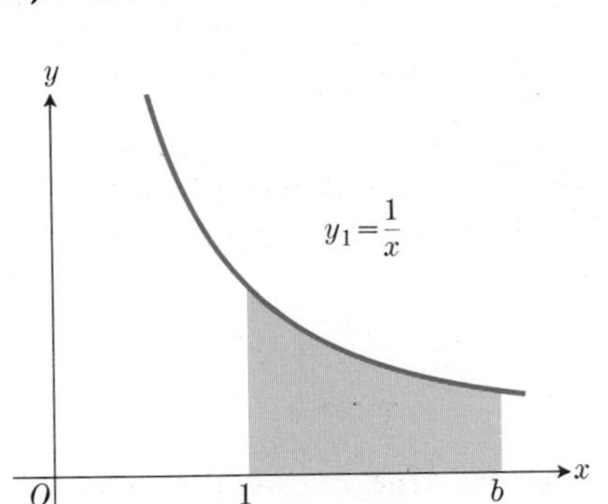

b)

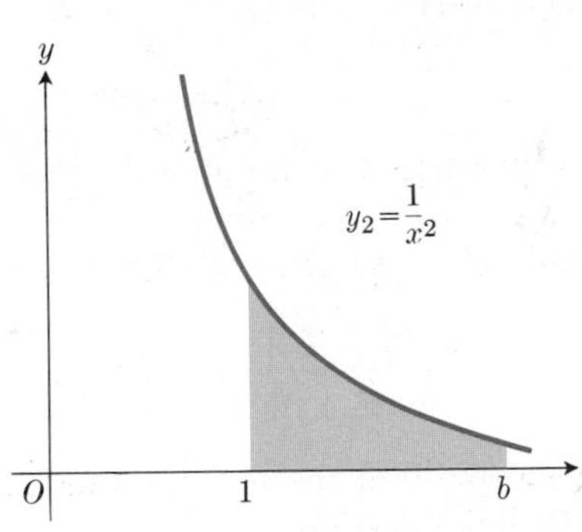

7–11 (a) The shaded area, ln b, does not approach a finite limit as $b \to \infty$. (b) The shaded area, $1 - (1/b)$, approaches 1 as $b \to \infty$.

We therefore say that

$$\int_1^\infty \frac{dx}{x} = \infty$$

and that the integral *diverges.*

In the second case,

$$\int_1^b \frac{dx}{x^2} = -\frac{1}{x}\Big]_1^b = 1 - \frac{1}{b}.$$

This does have a definite limit, namely 1, as b increases indefinitely, and we say that the integral from 1 to ∞ converges and that its value is 1. That is,

$$\int_1^\infty \frac{dx}{x^2} = \lim_{b\to\infty} \int_1^b \frac{dx}{x^2} = \lim_{b\to\infty}\left(1 - \frac{1}{b}\right) = 1.$$

More generally, the integral

$$\int_1^\infty \frac{dx}{x^p}$$

converges when $p > 1$ but diverges when $p \leq 1$ (Problem 22).

Sometimes we can determine whether a given integral converges or diverges by comparing it with a simpler integral. This is the case with the integral in the next example, an integral that is central to the study of continuous probability.

EXAMPLE 7. Determine whether the integral

$$\int_1^\infty e^{-x^2}\,dx$$

converges or diverges.

Solution. Even though we cannot find any simpler expression for

$$I(b) \equiv \int_1^b e^{-x^2}\,dx,$$

we can show that

$$\lim_{b\to\infty} I(b)$$

exists and is finite, for the function $I(b)$ represents the area between the x-axis and the curve

$$y = e^{-x^2}$$

between $x = 1$ and $x = b$. Clearly, this is an increasing function of b, so that there are two alternatives: either

a) $I(b)$ becomes infinite as $b \to \infty$,

or

b) $I(b)$ has a finite limit as $b \to \infty$.

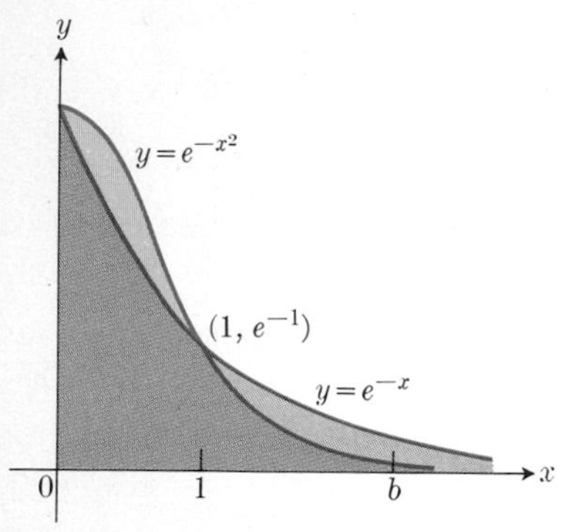

7–12 The graphs of $y = e^{-x^2}$ and $y = e^{-x}$.

We show that the first alternative cannot be the true one. We do this by comparing the area under the given curve $y = e^{-x^2}$ with the area under the curve $y = e^{-x}$ (Fig. 7–12). The latter area, from $x = 1$ to $x = b$, is given by the integral

$$\int_1^b e^{-x}\,dx = -e^{-x}\Big]_1^b = e^{-1} - e^{-b},$$

which approaches the finite limit e^{-1} as $b \to \infty$. Since e^{-x^2} is less than e^{-x} for all x greater than one, the area under the given curve is certainly no greater than e^{-1} no matter how large b is.

The discussion above is summarized in the following inequalities:

$$I(b) = \int_1^b e^{-x^2}\,dx \le \int_1^b e^{-x}\,dx = e^{-1} - e^{-b} \le e^{-1};$$

that is,

$$I(b) \le e^{-1} < 0.37.$$

Therefore $I(b)$ does not become infinite as $b \to \infty$, so alternative (a) is ruled out and alternative (b) must hold; that is,

$$\int_1^\infty e^{-x^2}\,dx = \lim_{b\to\infty} \int_1^b e^{-x^2}\,dx$$

converges to a definite finite value. We have not calculated what this limit is, but we know that it exists and is less than 0.37.

An improper integral may diverge without becoming infinite.

EXAMPLE 8. The integral

$$\int_0^b \cos x\,dx = \sin b$$

takes all values between -1 and $+1$ as b varies between $2n\pi - \pi/2$ and $2n\pi + \pi/2$, where n is any integer. Hence,

$$\lim_{b\to\infty} \int_0^b \cos x\,dx$$

does not exist. We might say that this integral "diverges by oscillation."

Improper integrals appear in the study of economics in several ways. We illustrate one of them in the next example.

EXAMPLE 9 (*Discounting and present value*). If P dollars are invested at an interest rate r compounded continuously for t years, then the value of the asset at the end of the compounding process is

$$A = Pe^{rt}. \tag{1}$$

For instance, \$60.65 invested at 5 percent compounded continuously will be worth

$$A = 60.65e^{0.05 \times 10} = 60.65e^{0.5} \approx 100 \text{ dollars}$$

in ten years.

Closely related to compounding interest is the concept of *discounting.* The problem of discounting is that of finding the *present value* P of an amount of money A that will become available in t years. What is a 5 percent savings bond that will pay \$100 ten years from now worth today? It is worth what we would have to bank today at 5 percent to accumulate \$100 in ten years. That is, the bond is worth $P = \$60.65$. More generally, the present value of an investment that will pay A dollars after t years of continuous compounding at rate r is

$$P = Ae^{-rt}, \tag{2}$$

an equation obtained by solving Eq. (1) for P. The amount P is the present value of *A discounted at the rate of r per year.* Thus, $P = \$60.65$ is the present value of $A = \$100$ payable ten years from now discounted at 5 percent per year.

Many investments operate differently from savings accounts. Rather than compounding interest on the investment continuously, they make periodic payments to the investor. How is the present value of all the future revenue from such an investment to be calculated? If the revenue from the investment is given as a function of time $R(t)$, then the amount paid in a future time interval of length Δt will be $R(t)\,\Delta t$ for some t in that interval. The present value of this part of the total revenue, when discounted at the rate of r per year, is about $R(t)e^{-rt}\,\Delta t$. The present value of the revenue from the whole investment period is then approximately

$$\sum R(t)e^{-rt}\,\Delta t. \tag{3}$$

In the limit, we can calculate this value as

$$P(T) = \int_0^T R(t)e^{-rt}\,dt, \tag{4}$$

where T is the duration of the investment. If the investment is a perpetual bond or an indestructible capital asset like land, then the present value of the total revenue from the investment may be taken to be

$$P = \int_0^\infty R(t)e^{-rt}\,dt. \tag{5}$$

For instance, if $R(t)$ is a constant C dollars a year, then

$$P = \int_0^\infty Ce^{-rt}\,dt = \lim_{b\to\infty} -\frac{C}{r}e^{-rt}\Big]_0^b$$
$$= \lim_{b\to\infty} \frac{C}{r}(1 - e^{-rb})$$
$$= \frac{C}{r}.$$

PROBLEMS

Show that the following improper integrals converge and evaluate them.

1. $\int_0^\infty \frac{dx}{x^2+1}$ **2.** $\int_0^1 \frac{dx}{\sqrt{x}}$

3. $\int_{-1}^1 \frac{dx}{x^{2/3}}$ **4.** $\int_1^\infty \frac{dx}{x^{1.001}}$

5. $\int_0^4 \frac{dx}{\sqrt{4-x}}$ **6.** $\int_0^1 \frac{dx}{\sqrt{1-x^2}}$

7. $\int_0^\infty e^{-x}\cos x\,dx$ **8.** $\int_0^1 \frac{dx}{x^{0.999}}$

Determine whether each of the following improper integrals converges or diverges.

9. $\int_1^\infty \frac{dx}{\sqrt{x}}$ **10.** $\int_1^\infty \frac{dx}{x^3}$

11. $\int_1^\infty \frac{dx}{x^3+1}$ **12.** $\int_0^\infty \frac{dx}{x^3}$

13. $\int_0^\infty \frac{dx}{x^3+1}$ **14.** $\int_0^\infty \frac{dx}{1+e^x}$

15. $\int_0^{\pi/2} \tan x\,dx$ **16.** $\int_{-1}^1 \frac{dx}{x^2}$

17. $\int_{-1}^1 \frac{dx}{x^{2/5}}$ **18.** $\int_0^\infty \frac{dx}{\sqrt{x}}$

19. $\int_0^\infty \frac{dx}{\sqrt{x+x^4}}$ [*Hint.* Compare the integral with $\int dx/\sqrt{x}$ for x near zero and with $\int dx/x^2$ for large x.]

20. Show that

$$\int_3^\infty e^{-3x}\,dx = \tfrac{1}{3}e^{-9} = 0.000041,$$

and hence that $\int_3^\infty e^{-x^2}\,dx < 0.000041$. Therefore, $\int_0^\infty e^{-x^2}\,dx$ can be replaced by $\int_0^3 e^{-x^2}\,dx$ without introducing any errors in the first three decimal places of the answer. Evaluate this last integral by Simpson's rule with $n = 6$. (This illustrates one method by which a convergent improper integral may be approximated numerically.)

21. As Example 6 shows, the integral $\int_1^\infty (dx/x)$ diverges. This means that the integral

$$\int_1^\infty 2\pi\frac{1}{x}\sqrt{1+\frac{1}{x^4}}\,dx,$$

which measures the surface area of the solid of revolution traced out by revolving the curve $y = 1/x$, $1 \le x$, about the x-axis, diverges also. For, by comparing the two integrals, we see that, for every finite value b,

$$\int_1^b 2\pi\frac{1}{x}\sqrt{1+\frac{1}{x^4}}\,dx > \int_1^b \frac{dx}{x}.$$

However, the integral

$$\int_1^\infty \pi\left(\frac{1}{x}\right)^2 dx$$

for the volume of the solid converges. Calculate it. This solid of revolution is sometimes described as a can that does not hold enough paint to cover its own outside surface.

22. Show that

$$\int_1^\infty \frac{dx}{x^p} = \frac{1}{p-1} \quad \text{when } p > 1,$$

but that the integral is infinite when $p < 1$. Example 6 shows what happens when $p = 1$.

23. Find the present value of the revenue from a perpetual bond that pays \$300 a year discounted at 6 percent per year.

24. A U.S. savings bond that will yield \$25 in 5 years can be purchased for \$18.75. Assuming that the interest is compounded continuously, find the rate at which the bond has been discounted.

25. A perpetual investment pays \$100 a year, but, to compensate for inflation, the revenue function $R(t)$ of Example 9 is chosen to be $R(t) = 100(0.95)^t$.

a) Estimate the present value of the revenue from this investment discounted at 5 percent a year.

b) What would the present value of the revenue be if there were no inflation?

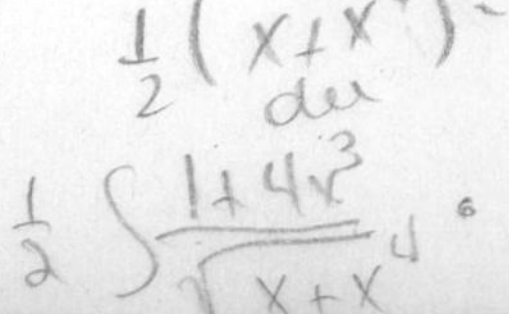

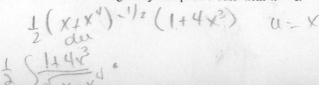

REVIEW QUESTIONS AND EXERCISES

1. What are some of the general methods presented in this chapter for finding an indefinite integral?

2. What substitution(s) would you consider trying if the integrand contained the following?

a) $\sqrt{x^2+9}$ **b)** $\sqrt{x^2-9}$

c) $\sqrt{9-x^2}$ **d)** $\sin^3 x \cos^2 x$

e) $\sin^2 x \cos^2 x$ **f)** $\dfrac{1+\sin\theta}{2+\cos\theta}$

3. What method(s) would you try if the integrand contained the following?

a) $\sin^{-1} x$ **b)** $\ln x$

c) $\sqrt{1+2x-x^2}$ **d)** $x \sin x$

e) $\dfrac{2x+3}{x^2-5x+6}$ **f)** $\sin 5x \cos 3x$

g) $\dfrac{1-\sqrt{x}}{1+\sqrt[4]{x}}$ **h)** $x\sqrt{2x+3}$

4. Discuss two types of improper integral. Define convergence and divergence of each type. Give examples of convergent and divergent integrals of each type.

MISCELLANEOUS PROBLEMS

Evaluate the following integrals:

1. $\displaystyle\int \frac{\cos x\,dx}{\sqrt{1+\sin x}}$ **2.** $\displaystyle\int \frac{\sin^{-1} x\,dx}{\sqrt{1-x^2}}$

3. $\displaystyle\int \frac{\tan x\,dx}{\cos^2 x}$ **4.** $\displaystyle\int \frac{dx}{1-\sin x}$

5. $\displaystyle\int e^{\ln\sqrt{x}}\,dx$ **6.** $\displaystyle\int \frac{\cos\sqrt{x}}{\sqrt{x}}\,dx$

7. $\displaystyle\int \frac{dx}{\sqrt{x^2+2x+2}}$ **8.** $\displaystyle\int \frac{(3x-7)\,dx}{(x-1)(x-2)(x-3)}$

9. $\displaystyle\int x^2 e^x\,dx$ **10.** $\displaystyle\int \sqrt{x^2+1}\,dx$

11. $\displaystyle\int \frac{e^t\,dt}{1+e^{2t}}$ **12.** $\displaystyle\int \frac{dx}{e^x+e^{-x}}$

13. $\displaystyle\int \frac{dx}{1+\sqrt{x}}$ **14.** $\displaystyle\int \frac{dx}{\sqrt{1+\sqrt{x}}}$

15. $\displaystyle\int t^{2/3}(t^{5/3}+1)^{2/3}\,dt$ **16.** $\displaystyle\int \frac{\cot x\,dx}{\ln(\sin x)}$

17. $\displaystyle\int \frac{dt}{\sqrt{e^t+1}}$ **18.** $\displaystyle\int \frac{dt}{\sqrt{1-e^{-t}}}$

19. $\displaystyle\int \frac{\sin x e^{\sec x}}{\cos^2 x}\,dx$ **20.** $\displaystyle\int \frac{\cos x\,dx}{1+\sin^2 x}$

21. $\displaystyle\int \frac{dx}{\sqrt{2x-x^2}}$ **22.** $\displaystyle\int \frac{\sin x\,dx}{1+\cos^2 x}$

23. $\displaystyle\int \frac{\cos 2t}{1+\sin 2t}\,dt$ **24.** $\displaystyle\int \frac{dx}{\sin x \cos x}$

25. $\displaystyle\int \sqrt{1+\sin x}\,dx$ **26.** $\displaystyle\int \sqrt{1-\sin x}\,dx$

27. $\displaystyle\int \frac{dx}{\sqrt{(a^2-x^2)^3}}$ **28.** $\displaystyle\int \frac{dx}{\sqrt{(a^2+x^2)^3}}$

29. $\displaystyle\int \frac{\sin x\,dx}{\cos^2 x - 5\cos x + 4}$ **30.** $\displaystyle\int \frac{e^{2x}\,dx}{\sqrt[3]{1+e^x}}$

31. $\displaystyle\int \frac{dx}{x(x+1)(x+2)\cdots(x+m)}$

32. $\displaystyle\int \frac{dx}{x^6-1}$

33. $\displaystyle\int \frac{dy}{y(2y^3+1)^2}$ **34.** $\displaystyle\int \frac{x\,dx}{1+\sqrt{x}}$

35. $\displaystyle\int \frac{dx}{x(x^2+1)^2}$ **36.** $\displaystyle\int \ln\sqrt{x-1}\,dx$

37. $\displaystyle\int \frac{dx}{e^x-1}$ **38.** $\displaystyle\int \frac{d\theta}{1-\tan^2\theta}$

39. $\displaystyle\int \frac{(x+1)\,dx}{x^2(x-1)}$ **40.** $\displaystyle\int \frac{x\,dx}{x^2+4x+3}$

41. $\displaystyle\int \frac{du}{(e^u-e^{-u})^2}$ **42.** $\displaystyle\int \frac{4\,dx}{x^3+4x}$

43. $\displaystyle\int \frac{dx}{5x^2+8x+5}$ **44.** $\displaystyle\int \frac{\sqrt{x^2-a^2}}{x}\,dx$

45. $\displaystyle\int e^x \cos 2x\,dx$ **46.** $\displaystyle\int \frac{dx}{x(3\sqrt{x}+1)}$

47. $\displaystyle\int \frac{dx}{x(1+\sqrt[3]{x})}$ **48.** $\displaystyle\int \frac{\cot\theta\,d\theta}{1+\sin^2\theta}$

49. $\displaystyle\int \frac{z^5\,dz}{\sqrt{1+z^2}}$ **50.** $\displaystyle\int \frac{e^{4t}\,dt}{(1+e^{2t})^{2/3}}$

51. $\int \frac{dx}{x^{1/5}\sqrt{1+x^{4/5}}}$

52. $\int x \sec^2 x\,dx$

53. $\int x \sin^{-1} x\,dx$

54. $\int \frac{(x^3+x^2)\,dx}{x^2+x-2}$

55. $\int \frac{x^3+1}{x^3-x}\,dx$

56. $\int \frac{x\,dx}{(x-1)^2}$

57. $\int \frac{(2e^{2x}-e^x)\,dx}{\sqrt{3e^{2x}-6e^x-1}}$

58. $\int \frac{(x+1)\,dx}{(x^2+2x-3)^{2/3}}$

59. $\int \frac{dy}{(2y+1)\sqrt{y^2+y}}$

60. $\int \frac{dx}{x^2\sqrt{a^2-x^2}}$

61. $\int (1-x^2)^{3/2}\,dx$

62. $\int \ln (x+\sqrt{1+x^2})\,dx$

63. $\int x \tan^2 x\,dx$

64. $\int \frac{\tan^{-1} x}{x^2}\,dx$

65. $\int x \cos^2 x\,dx$

66. $\int x^2 \sin x\,dx$

67. $\int x \sin^2 x\,dx$

68. $\int \frac{dt}{t^4+4t^2+3}$

69. $\int \frac{du}{e^{4u}+4e^{2u}+3}$

70. $\int x \ln \sqrt{x+2}\,dx$

71. $\int (x+1)^2 e^x\,dx$

72. $\int \sec^{-1} x\,dx$

73. $\int \frac{8\,dx}{x^4+2x^3}$

74. $\int \frac{x\,dx}{x^4-16}$

75. $\int_0^{\pi/2} \frac{\cos x\,dx}{\sqrt{1+\cos x}}$

76. $\int \frac{\cos x\,dx}{\sin^3 x - \sin x}$

77. $\int \frac{du}{(e^u+e^{-u})^2}$

78. $\int \frac{x\,dx}{1+\sqrt{x}+x}$

79. $\int \frac{\sec^2 t\,dt}{\sec^2 t - 3\tan t + 1}$

80. $\int \frac{dt}{\sec^2 t + \tan^2 t}$

81. $\int \frac{dx}{1+\cos^2 x}$

82. $\int e^{2t} \cos (e^t)\,dt$

83. $\int \ln \sqrt{x^2+1}\,dx$

84. $\int x \ln (x^3+x)\,dx$

85. $\int x^3 e^{x^2}\,dx$

86. $\int \frac{\cos x\,dx}{\sqrt{4-\cos^2 x}}$

87. $\int \frac{\sec^2 x\,dx}{\sqrt{4-\sec^2 x}}$

88. $\int x^2 \sin (1-x)\,dx$

89. $\int \frac{dx}{1+\sin x}$

90. $\int \frac{dx}{1+2\sin x}$

91. $\int \frac{dx}{\sin^3 x}$

92. $\int \frac{dx}{\cot^3 x}$

93. $\int (\sin^{-1} x)^2\,dx$

94. $\int x \ln \sqrt[3]{3x+1}\,dx$

95. $\int \frac{x^3\,dx}{(x^2+1)^2}$

96. $\int \frac{x\,dx}{\sqrt{1-x}}$

97. $\int x\sqrt{2x+1}\,dx$

98. $\int \ln (x+\sqrt{x^2-1})\,dx$

99. $\int \ln (x-\sqrt{x^2-1})\,dx$

100. $\int \frac{dt}{t-\sqrt{1-t^2}}$

101. $\int e^{-x} \tan^{-1} (e^x)\,dx$

102. $\int \sin^{-1} \sqrt{x}\,dx$

103. $\int \ln (x+\sqrt{x})\,dx$

104. $\int \tan^{-1} \sqrt{x}\,dx$

105. $\int \ln (x^2+x)\,dx$

106. $\int \ln (\sqrt{x}+\sqrt{1+x})\,dx$

107. $\int \cos \sqrt{x}\,dx$

108. $\int \sin \sqrt{x}\,dx$

109. $\int \tan^{-1} \sqrt{x+1}\,dx$

110. $\int \sqrt{1-x^2} \sin^{-1} x\,dx$

111. $\int x \sin^2 (2x)\,dx$

112. $\int \frac{\tan x\,dx}{\tan x + \sec x}$

113. $\int \frac{dt}{\sqrt{e^{2t}+1}}$

114. $\int \frac{dx}{(\cos^2 x + 4\sin x - 5)\cos x}$

115. $\int \frac{dt}{a+be^{ct}}$, $\quad a, b, c \neq 0$

116. $\int \sqrt{\frac{1-\cos x}{\cos \alpha - \cos x}}\,dx$, $\quad \alpha$ constant, $0 < \alpha < x < \pi$

117. $\int \frac{dx}{\sin x - \cos x}$

118. $\int \ln \sqrt{1+x^2}\,dx$

119. $\int \ln (2x^2+4)\,dx$

120. $\int \frac{x^3}{\sqrt{1-x^2}}\,dx$

121. $\int \frac{dx}{x(2+\ln x)}$

122. $\int \frac{\cos 2x - 1}{\cos 2x + 1}\,dx$

123. $\int \frac{dx}{x^3+1}$

124. $\int \frac{e^{2x}\,dx}{\sqrt[4]{e^x+1}}$

125. $\int \frac{e^x\,dx}{1+e^{2x}}$

126. $\int e^{\sqrt{t}}\,dt$

127. $\int \sin \sqrt{x+1}\,dx$

128. $\int \cos \sqrt{1-x}\,dx$

Evaluate each of the following limits, Problems 129–135, by identifying it with an appropriate definite integral and evaluating the latter.

129. $\lim_{n\to\infty}\left(\frac{1}{n+1}+\frac{1}{n+2}+\cdots+\frac{1}{2n}\right)$

130. $\lim_{n\to\infty}\left(\frac{1}{\sqrt{n^2}}+\frac{1}{\sqrt{n^2+n}}+\frac{1}{\sqrt{n^2+2n}}+\cdots+\frac{1}{\sqrt{n^2+(n-1)n}}\right)$

131. $\lim_{n\to\infty}\left(\sin 0+\sin(\pi/n)+\sin(2\pi/n)+\cdots+\sin[(n-1)\pi/n]\right)/n$

132. $\lim_{n\to\infty}\left(\frac{1+\sqrt[n]{e}+\sqrt[n]{e^2}+\sqrt[n]{e^3}+\cdots+\sqrt[n]{e^{n-1}}}{n}\right)$

133. $\lim_{n\to\infty}\left(\frac{n}{n^2+0^2}+\frac{n}{n^2+1^2}+\frac{n}{n^2+2^2}+\cdots+\frac{n}{n^2+(n-1)^2}\right)$

134. $\lim_{n\to\infty}\sum_{k=1}^{n}\ln\sqrt[n]{1+\frac{k}{n}}$

135. $\lim_{n\to\infty}\sum_{k=0}^{n-1}\frac{1}{\sqrt{n^2-k^2}}$

136. Show that $\int_0^\infty x^3e^{-x^2}\,dx$ is a convergent integral, and evaluate it.

137. Show that $\int_0^1 \ln x\,dx$ is a convergent integral and find its value. Sketch the integrand $y=\ln x$ for $0<x\leq 1$.

138. Assuming that $|\alpha|\neq|\beta|$, prove that

$$\lim_{T\to\infty}\frac{1}{T}\int_0^T \sin\alpha x\sin\beta x\,dx=0.$$

139. Evaluate

$$\lim_{h\to 0}\frac{1}{h}\int_2^{2+h} e^{-x^2}\,dx.$$

140. At points of the curve $y^2=4px$, lines of length $h=y$ are drawn perpendicular to its plane. Find the area of the surface formed by these lines at points of the curve between $(0,0)$ and $(p,2p)$.

141. A plane figure is bounded by a 90° arc of a circle of radius r and a straight line. Find its area and its centroid.

142. Find the coordinates of the center of gravity of the area bounded by the curves $y=e^x$, $x=1$, and $y=1$.

143. At points on a circle of radius r, perpendiculars to its plane are erected, the perpendicular at each point P being of length ks, where s is the arc of the circle from a fixed point A to P. Find the area of the surface formed by the perpendiculars along the arc beginning at A and extending once around the circle.

144. A plate in the first quadrant, bounded by the curves $y=e^x$, $y=1$, and $x=4$, is submerged vertically in water with its upper corner on the surface. The surface of the water is given by the line $y=e^4$. Find the total force on one side of the plate if the weight of water is 62.5 lb/ft^3, and if the units of x and y are also measured in feet.

145. The area under the curve $y=e^{-x}$, for $x\geq 0$, is rotated about the x-axis. If A is the area under the curve, V is the volume generated, and S is the surface area of this volume: (a) is A finite? (b) is V finite? (c) is S finite? Give reasons for your answers.

146. Find the length of arc of $y=\ln x$ from $x=1$ to $x=e$.

147. The arc of Problem 146 is rotated about the y-axis. Find the surface area generated. Check your answer by comparing it with the area of a frustum of a suitably related cone.

148. Find the length of arc of the curve $y=e^x$ from $x=0$ to $x=2$.

149. The arc of Problem 148 is rotated about the x-axis. Find the surface area generated. Compare this area with the area of a suitably related frustum of a cone to check your answer.

150. One arch of the curve $y=\cos x$ is rotated about the x-axis. Find the surface area generated.

151. Use Simpson's rule with $n=8$ to approximate the length of arc of $y=\cos x$ from $x=0$ to $x=\pi/2$. Check your answer by consulting a table of elliptic integrals if one is available.

152. A thin wire is bent into the shape of one arch of the curve $y=\cos x$. Find its center of mass (see Problems 150, 151).

153. The area between the graph of $y=\ln(1/x)$, the x-axis, and the y-axis is revolved around the x-axis. Find the volume of the solid it generates.

154. Find the total perimeter of the curve $x^{2/3}+y^{2/3}=a^{2/3}$.

155. Find the area of the surface generated by rotating the curve $x^{2/3}+y^{2/3}=a^{2/3}$ about the x-axis.

156. A thin homogeneous wire is bent into the shape of one arch of the curve $x^{2/3}+y^{2/3}=a^{2/3}$. Find its center of mass (see Problems 154, 155).

157. Determine whether the integral $\int_1^\infty \ln x(dx/x^2)$ converges or diverges.

158. Sketch the curves:

a) $y=x-e^x$; show behavior for large $|x|$;

b) $y=e^{(x-e^x)}$; show behavior for large $|x|$.

Show that the following integrals converge and compute their values:

c) $\int_{-\infty}^{b} e^{(x-e^x)}\,dx$ d) $\int_{-\infty}^{\infty} e^{(x-e^x)}\,dx$

159. The gamma function $\Gamma(x)$ is defined, for $x > 0$, by the definite integral

$$\Gamma(x) = \int_0^{\infty} t^{x-1}e^{-t}\,dt.$$

a) Sketch graphs of the integrand $y = t^{x-1}e^{-t}$ vs. t, $t > 0$, for the three typical cases $x = \frac{1}{2}, 1, 3$. Find maxima, minima, and points of inflection (if they exist).

b) Show that the integral converges if $x > 0$.

c) Show that the integral diverges if $x \le 0$.

d) Using integration by parts, show that $\Gamma(x+1) = x\Gamma(x)$, for $x > 0$.

e) Using the result of part (d), show that, if n is a positive integer, $\Gamma(n) = (n-1)!$, where $0! = 1$ (by definition) and if m is a positive integer, $m!$ is the product of the positive integers from 1 through m inclusive.

f) Discuss how one might compute a table of values of $\Gamma(x)$ for the domain $1 \le x \le 2$, say. Consult such a table, if available, and sketch the graph of $y = \Gamma(x)$ for $0 < x \le 3$.

160. Determine whether the integral $\int_0^{\infty} t^{x-1}(\ln t)e^{-t}\,dt$ converges or diverges for fixed $x > 0$. Sketch the integrand $y = t^{x-1}\ln te^{-t}$ vs. t, $t > 0$, for the two cases $x = \frac{1}{2}$ and $x = 3$.

161. Solve the differential equation $d^2x/dt^2 = -k^2x$, subject to the initial conditions $x = a$, $dx/dt = 0$ when $t = 0$. [*Hint.* Let $dx/dt = v$, $d^2x/dt^2 = dv/dt = v\,dv/dx$.]

162. Find $\lim_{n\to\infty} \int_0^1 \frac{ny^{n-1}}{1+y}\,dy.$

163. Prove that if n is a positive integer, or zero, then

$$\int_{-1}^{1} (1-x^2)^n\,dx = \frac{2^{2n+1}(n!)^2}{(2n+1)!},$$

with $0! = 1$; $n! = 1 \cdot 2 \cdots n$ for $n \ge 1$.

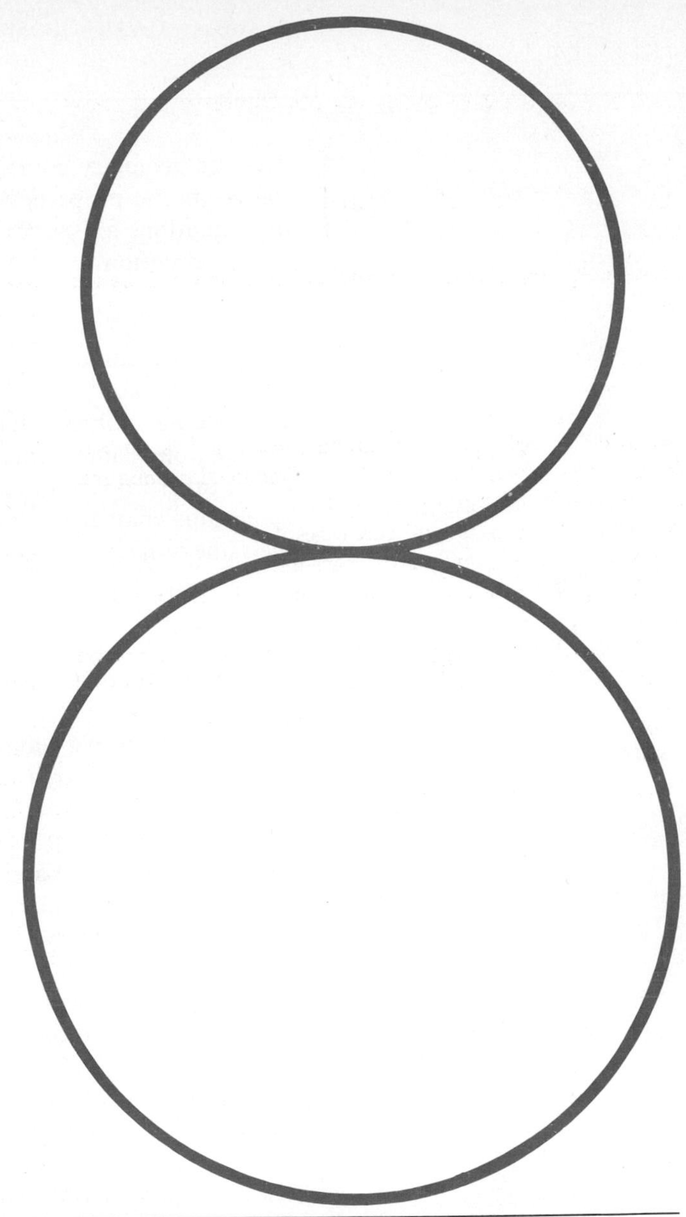

PLANE ANALYTIC GEOMETRY

8–1 CURVES AND EQUATIONS

a)

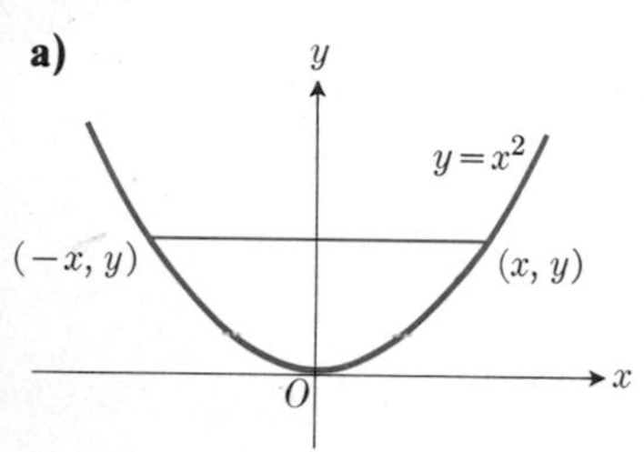

symmetry about the y-axis

b)

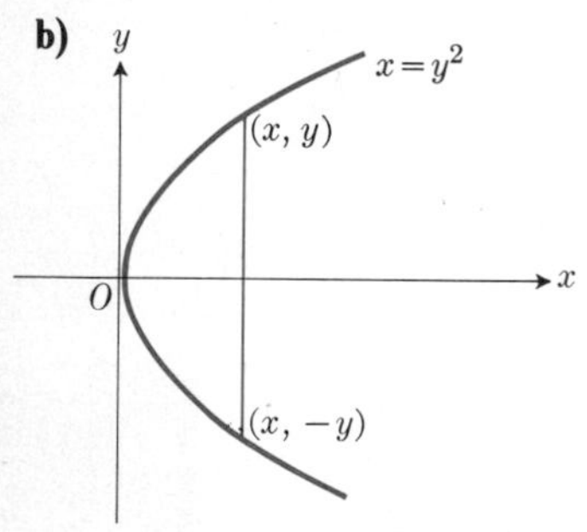

symmetry about the x-axis

c)

y

$y=x^3$

(x, y)

O

x

$(-x, -y)$

symmetry about the origin

d)

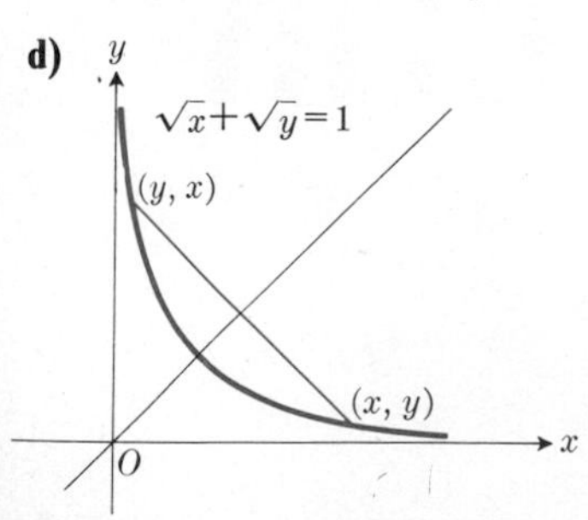

symmetry about the line $y = x$

8–1 Coordinate tests for symmetry.

Analytic geometry combines algebra and calculus with geometry to study the geometric properties of curves when their equations are given, and to find equations for curves when their geometric properties are known.

An equation

$$F(x, y) = 0 \tag{1}$$

determines a curve that is the set of all and only those points $P(x, y)$ whose coordinates satisfy the equation. This curve is called the graph of the equation. We have already had some experience in analyzing equations to find turning points and points of inflection. We shall now see how equations may reveal other important characteristics of curves as well.

In this chapter we shall assume that the scales on the x- and y-axes are the same, unless we specifically note otherwise.

Symmetry

Symmetries that are easily detected are:

Symmetry about the y-axis. If the equation of the curve is unaltered when x is replaced by $-x$, that is, if

$$F(x, y) = F(-x, y),$$

then the points (x, y) and $(-x, y)$ both lie on the curve when either one of them does. In particular, an equation that contains only even powers of x represents such a curve (Fig. 8–1(a)).

Symmetry about the x-axis if the equation is unaltered when y is replaced by $-y$; in particular if only even powers of y occur (Fig. 8–1(b)).

Symmetry about the origin if the equation is unaltered when x and y are replaced by $-x$ and $-y$, respectively (Fig. 8–1(c)).

Symmetry about the 45° line $y = x$ if the equation is unaltered when x and y are interchanged (Fig. 8–1(d)).

EXAMPLE 1

$$x^2 + y^2 = 1.$$

Symmetric about both axes, about the origin, and about the line $y = x$.

EXAMPLE 2

$$x^2 - y^2 = 1.$$

Symmetric about both axes and the origin. Not symmetric about the line $y = x$.

EXAMPLE 3

$$xy = 1.$$

Not symmetric about either axis. Symmetric about the origin and about the line $y = x$.

Extent

Only real values of x and y are considered in determining the points (x, y) whose coordinates satisfy a given equation. When even powers of a variable appear in the equation, the solution for that variable may involve square roots (or other even roots). The *extent* of the curve may then be limited by the condition that negative numbers do not have real square roots.

EXAMPLE 4

$$x^2 + y^2 = 1.$$

When this equation is solved for y, we get

$$y = \pm\sqrt{1 - x^2}.$$

The quantity under the radical is negative if $|x| > 1$. The extent of the curve in the x-direction is therefore limited to the interval $-1 \leq x \leq 1$. By symmetry about the line $y = x$, the curve is also limited in the y-direction to $-1 \leq y \leq 1$.

EXAMPLE 5

$$x^2 - y^2 = 1.$$

Solving for y, we get

$$y = \pm\sqrt{x^2 - 1}.$$

In this case, y is imaginary unless $|x| \geq 1$. No portion of the curve lies between the two lines $x = -1$ and $x = +1$. Solving for x, we get

$$x = \pm\sqrt{1 + y^2}.$$

The quantity under the radical is positive (actually it is greater than or equal to one) for all real values of y, $-\infty < y < +\infty$. The extent of this curve is not limited in the y-direction.

Intercepts

The point or points where a given curve crosses the x-axis can be found by setting $y = 0$ in the equation and solving for x. These points are called the *x-intercepts*. The y-intercepts are found in an analogous way by setting $x = 0$. If the labor involved in finding the intercepts is not excessive, they are worth determining to give specific points on the curve.

EXAMPLE 6

$$x^2 + y^2 = 1.$$

Setting $y = 0$, we have $x^2 = 1$. Therefore $(1, 0)$ and $(-1, 0)$ are the x-intercepts. By symmetry, $(0, 1)$ and $(0, -1)$ are the y-intercepts.

EXAMPLE 7

$$x^2 - y^2 = 1.$$

Setting $y = 0$, we find the x-intercepts are $(1, 0)$ and $(-1, 0)$. Setting $x = 0$, we obtain $y^2 = -1$, which has no real solutions. The curve does not have intercepts on the y-axis (see Example 5).

EXAMPLE 8

$$xy = 1.$$

Setting either $x = 0$ or $y = 0$ leads to the equation $0 = 1$, which has no solutions. There are no x- or y-intercepts.

Asymptotes

As the point $P(x, y)$ on a given curve moves farther and farther away from the vicinity of the origin, it may happen that the distance between P and some fixed line tends to zero. In such a case the line is called an *asymptote* of the curve. More generally, if the equation of the curve has the form

$$y = \frac{N(x)}{D(x)}, \tag{2}$$

where $N(x)$ and $D(x)$ are polynomials without any factors in common, and if $x = c$ is a root of the equation

$$D(x) = 0, \tag{3}$$

then as the x-coordinate of the tracing point $P(x, y)$ approaches c, two things will occur:

1. $y \to \infty$; hence the distance $OP \to \infty$; and
2. the horizontal distance $P'P$ between the curve and the vertical line $x = c$ tends to zero (Fig. 8–2).

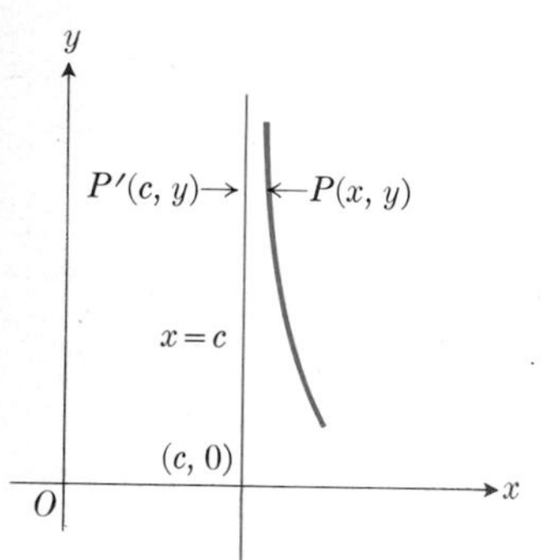

8–2 As $x \to c$, the point $P(x, y)$ rises along the curve toward the line $x = c$.

In other words, *the line $x = c$ is an asymptote of the graph of Eq. (2) if $x = c$ makes the denominator $D(x)$ vanish.* Such asymptotes are found by solving the equation explicitly for y in terms of x. If the result is a fraction, we set the denominator of the fraction equal to zero and solve for the numerical values of x. A similar procedure with the roles of x and y reversed shows that values of y that cause the denominator to vanish in the expression

$$x = \frac{f(y)}{g(y)} \tag{4}$$

may give horizontal asymptotes of the curve. An alternate method for finding such asymptotes is to let $x \to \pm\infty$ in Eq. (2)—provided the extent of the curve does not prohibit this—and find the limiting values of y.

EXAMPLE 9. (See Fig. 8–3.)

$$y^2(x^2 - x) = x^2 + 1. \tag{5}$$

We solve for y to obtain

$$y = \pm\sqrt{\frac{x^2 + 1}{x(x - 1)}}. \tag{6}$$

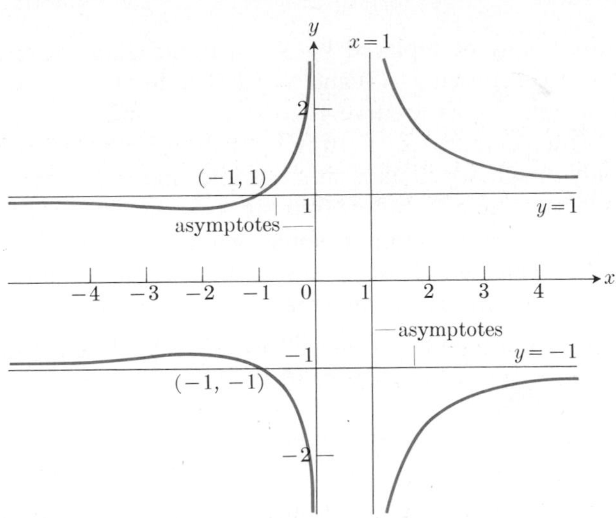

8–3 The graph of $y^2(x^2 - x) = x^2 + 1$ has four asymptotes.

The expression under the radical must not be negative, so no portion of the curve lies between the lines $x = 0$ and $x = 1$. But all values of $x > 1$ and all negative values of x, that is, $x < 0$, are permissible. As x approaches zero *from the left*, $y \to \pm\infty$ and as x approaches one *from the right*, $y \to \pm\infty$. The lines $x = 0$ and $x = 1$ are asymptotes of the curve. Since arbitrarily large values of $|x|$ are permitted, we also investigate the behavior of the curve as $x \to -\infty$ and again as $x \to +\infty$. The expression

$$\frac{\infty^2 + 1}{\infty(\infty - 1)},$$

which appears if we substitute $x = \infty$ directly into (6), is meaningless, but if we write the equation of the curve in the equivalent form

$$y^2 = \frac{x^2 + 1}{x^2 - x} = \frac{1 + (1/x^2)}{1 - (1/x)}, \tag{7}$$

we readily see that $y^2 \to 1$ as $x \to \infty$ or as $x \to -\infty$. Thus the lines $y = 1$ and $y = -1$ are also asymptotes of the curve. We reexamine Eq. (7) to see if y^2 is necessarily always greater than one, or always less than one, or may be equal to one. Certainly when x tends to $+\infty$, the numerator in (7) is greater than one, while the denominator is less than one; hence the fraction is larger than one, that is,

$$y^2 > 1, \qquad y^2 \to 1 \quad \text{as} \quad x \to +\infty. \tag{8}$$

On the other hand, when x tends to $-\infty$, both $1/x^2$ and $-1/x$ are positive, so that both the numerator and denominator in (7) are greater than one. However, $1/x^2$ will be less than $-1/x$, so that the numerator is less than the denominator; that is,

$$y^2 < 1, \qquad y^2 \to 1 \quad \text{as} \quad x \to -\infty. \tag{9}$$

To determine whether y^2 may ever equal 1, we try it, say in (5), and find

$$y^2 = 1 \qquad \text{when} \quad x = -1. \tag{10}$$

We now have quite a bit of information about the curve represented by Eq. (5). It is immediately evident that the curve is symmetric about the

x-axis, because y may be replaced by $-y$ without changing the equation. There is no curve between $x = 0$ and $x = 1$. The lines $x = 0$, $x = 1$, $y = 1$, $y = -1$ are asymptotes of the curve. It crosses $y = 1$ and $y = -1$ at $x = -1$. There is no x-intercept, because putting $y = 0$ in Eq. (5) requires $0 = x^2 + 1$, which has only imaginary roots. Using this information, we may sketch the curve with a fair degree of accuracy (see Fig. 8–3). In fact, it becomes apparent that the curve has a minimum somewhat to the left of $x = -1$, and a symmetrically located maximum, and that there is also a point of inflection to the left of this turning point. To find these points accurately requires that we determine dy/dx and d^2y/dx^2. The turning points will be found to occur at $(-1 - \sqrt{2}, \pm\sqrt{2\sqrt{2} - 2})$. The algebra involved in finding the points of inflection is excessive.

Direction at a Point

The three curves

$$\begin{array}{lll} \textbf{a)} & y = x, & dy/dx = 1, \\ \textbf{b)} & y = x^2, & dy/dx = 2x, \\ \textbf{c)} & y = \sqrt{x}, & dy/dx = 1/(2\sqrt{x}) \end{array}$$

all pass through the origin and the point (1, 1). But their behavior for small values of x is radically different. The individual nature of any one of them in the vicinity of (0, 0) is better indicated if the *direction* of the curve at that point is also given. This, of course, means that it is desirable to find the slope of each of them at (0, 0). We find that the inclination angles are respectively 45°, 0°, and 90° (see Fig. 8–4).

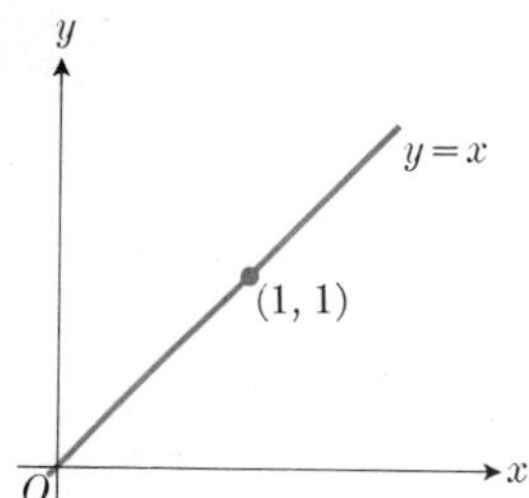

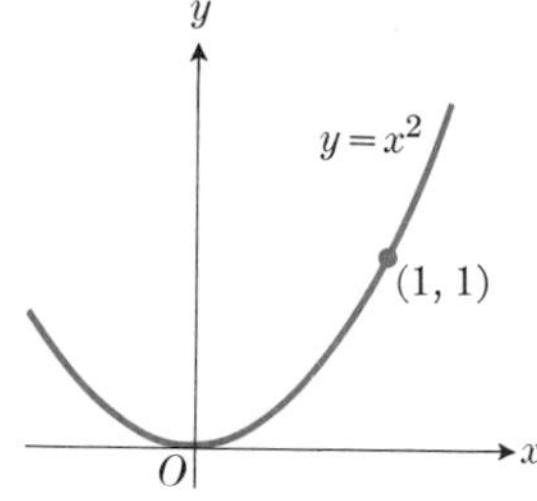

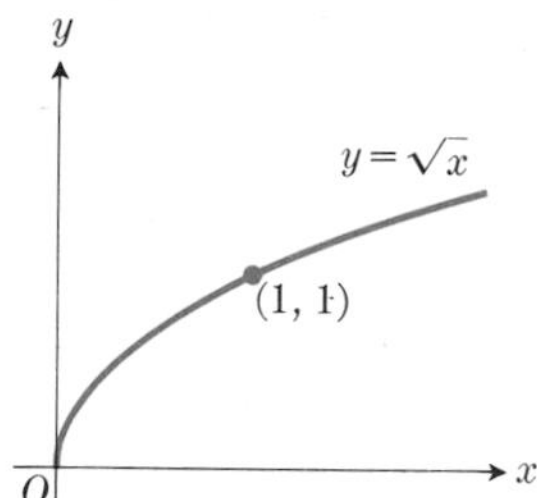

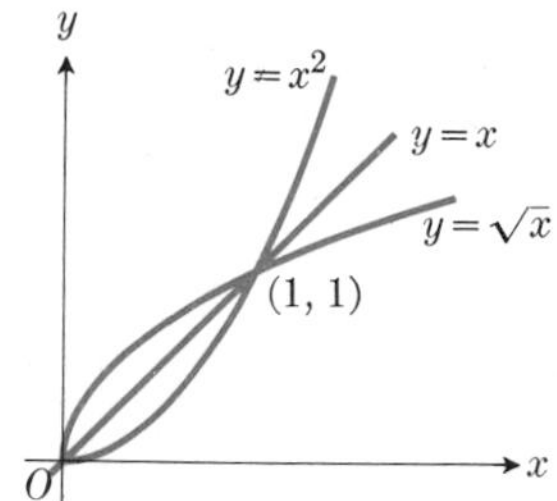

8–4 The curves $y = x$, $y = x^2$, and $y = \sqrt{x}$ have different directions at the origin.

EXAMPLE 10. (See Fig. 8–5.)

$$y^2 = x^2(1 - x^2).$$

This curve has symmetry with respect to both axes and the origin. Its extent in the x-direction is limited to $|x| \le 1$. Differentiating implicitly, we find

$$y' = \frac{x - 2x^3}{y}.$$

At one x-intercept, $(1, 0)$, the slope is infinite. At the origin, which is another intercept, the expression we have for y' becomes $0/0$, which is meaningless. However, if we replace y in the denominator by its equivalent expression in terms of x, we obtain

$$y' = \frac{x(1-2x^2)}{\pm x\sqrt{1-x^2}} = \pm\frac{1-2x^2}{\sqrt{1-x^2}}.$$

At $x = 0$, this gives $y' = \pm 1$. The same result can be obtained by considering the limit, as P approaches the origin O, of the slope of the secant line through O and a second point $P(x, y)$ on the curve. Denoting this slope by m_{sec}, we have

$$m_{\text{sec}} = \frac{\text{rise}}{\text{run}} = \frac{y-0}{x-0} = \pm\sqrt{1-x^2}.$$

When $P \to O$, $x \to 0$, and $m_{\text{sec}} \to \pm 1$. The double sign means, of course, that if P approaches O along the branch of the curve given by

$$y = x\sqrt{1-x^2},$$

the limit of the slope of the secant is $+1$, while the branch given by

$$y = -x\sqrt{1-x^2}$$

has slope -1 at the origin (Fig. 8–5). We also find turning points at $x = \pm\sqrt{\frac{1}{2}}$, $y = \pm\frac{1}{2}$. We may determine the extent of the curve in the y-direction by comparing the equation of the curve in the form

$$x^4 - x^2 + y^2 = 0$$

with the quadratic equation

$$az^2 + bz + c = 0,$$

whose solutions are

$$z = \frac{-b \pm \sqrt{b^2 - 4ac}}{2a}.$$

Taking $z = x^2$, $a = 1$, $b = -1$, and $c = y^2$, this leads to

$$x^2 = \frac{1 \pm \sqrt{1-4y^2}}{2}.$$

This requires $1 - 4y^2 \geq 0$, so there is no portion of the curve above the line $y = \frac{1}{2}$ or below the line $y = -\frac{1}{2}$.

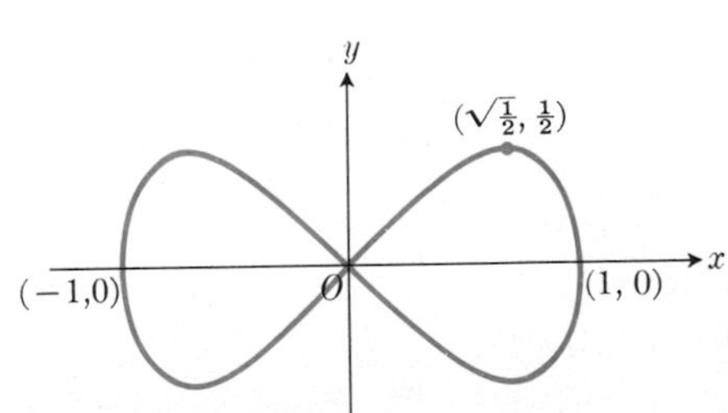

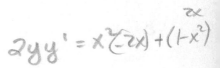

8–5 The graph of $y^2 = x^2(1 - x^2)$.

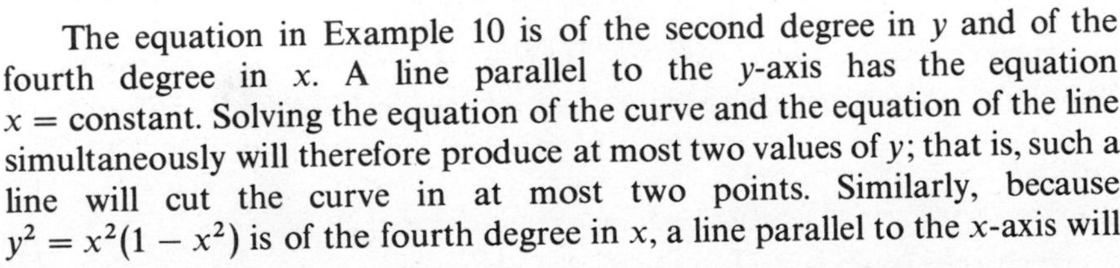

The equation in Example 10 is of the second degree in y and of the fourth degree in x. A line parallel to the y-axis has the equation $x =$ constant. Solving the equation of the curve and the equation of the line simultaneously will therefore produce at most two values of y; that is, such a line will cut the curve in at most two points. Similarly, because $y^2 = x^2(1 - x^2)$ is of the fourth degree in x, a line parallel to the x-axis will cut the curve in at most four points. The line $y = c$ and the curve will, in fact, have

a) no intersections if $|c| > \frac{1}{2}$,
b) two intersections if $|c| = \frac{1}{2}$,
c) four intersections if $0 < |c| < \frac{1}{2}$,
d) three intersections if $c = 0$.

The results in cases (b) and (d) may be interpreted as limiting cases of (c) with some of the intersections coinciding.

PROBLEMS

Analyze each of the equations below to investigate the following properties of the curve: (a) symmetry, (b) extent, (c) intercepts, (d) asymptotes, (e) slope at the intercepts. Locate a few points, and sketch the curve, taking into account the information discovered above.

1. $y^2 = x(x-2)$

2. $y^2 = \dfrac{x}{x-2}$

3. $x^4 + y^4 = 1$

4. $x^2 = \dfrac{1+y^2}{1-y^2}$

5. $x^2 = \dfrac{y^2+1}{y^2-1}$

6. $y = x + \dfrac{1}{x}$

7. $y = x^2 + 1$

8. $y = \dfrac{1}{x^2+1}$

9. $y = x^2 - 1$

10. $y = \dfrac{1}{x^2-1}$

8–2 TANGENTS AND NORMALS

In Chapter 1 we learned that

$$y - y_1 = m(x - x_1) \tag{1}$$

is an equation for the line of slope m which passes through the point (x_1, y_1). The equation of a line *tangent* to a given curve $y = f(x)$ at a given point (x_1, y_1) on the curve can be found by taking

$$m = \left(\frac{dy}{dx}\right)_{(x_1, y_1)} = f'(x_1)$$

in Eq. (1). Equation (1) then becomes:

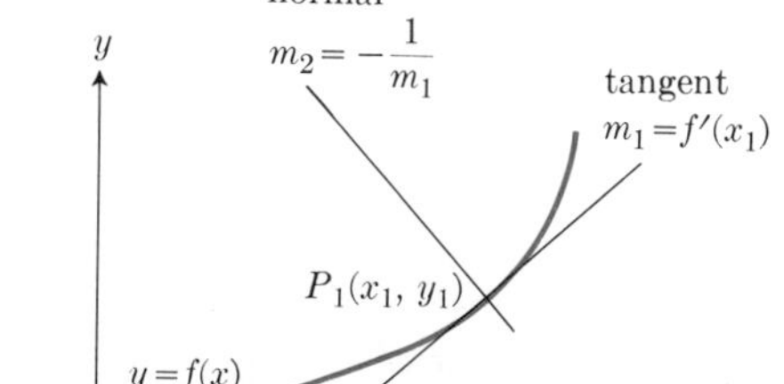

8–6 The normal and tangent to a smooth curve.

Tangent

$$y - y_1 = f'(x_1)(x - x_1). \tag{2}$$

The numbers x_1, y_1, and $f'(x_1)$ are all *constants* in this equation.

The line through $P_1(x_1, y_1)$ perpendicular to the tangent line is called the *normal* to the curve at P_1 (Fig. 8–6). Its slope m_2 is the negative reciprocal of the slope m_1 of the tangent; that is,

$$m_2 = -\frac{1}{m_1} = \frac{-1}{f'(x_1)}.$$

The point slope equation of the *normal* is therefore:

Normal

$$y - y_1 = \frac{-1}{f'(x_1)}(x - x_1). \tag{3}$$

EXAMPLE 1. Find the lines tangent and normal to the curve

$$y^2 - 6x^2 + 4y + 19 = 0 \tag{4}$$

at the point (2, 1).

Solution. We differentiate both sides of the equation with respect to x and solve for (dy/dx):

$$2y\frac{dy}{dx} - 12x + 4\frac{dy}{dx} = 0, \tag{5}$$

$$\frac{dy}{dx}(2y + 4) = 12x,$$

$$\frac{dy}{dx} = \frac{6x}{y + 2}.$$

We then evaluate the derivative at $x = 2$, $y = 1$, to obtain

$$\left.\frac{dy}{dx}\right|_{(2,1)} = \left.\frac{6x}{y + 2}\right|_{(2,1)} = \frac{12}{3} = 4. \tag{6}$$

Therefore, the tangent to the curve at the point (2, 1) is

$$y - 1 = 4(x - 2),$$

and the normal is

$$y - 1 = -\tfrac{1}{4}(x - 2).$$

EXAMPLE 2. Find the tangents to the curve $y = x^3 - 7x$ that are parallel to the line $y = 5x - 1$.

Solution. The slope of the curve at a point (x, y) on the curve is

$$y' = 3x^2 - 7.$$

The slope of the given line is $m = 5$. We equate the two slopes to get

$$3x^2 - 7 = 5,$$

$$x^2 = \tfrac{12}{3} = 4,$$

$$x = \pm 2.$$

Thus, the tangents to the curve have slope 5 when $x = +2$ and $x = -2$. The y-coordinate of the point on the curve at $x = +2$ is

$$y = (2)^3 - 7(2) = -6.$$

The point–slope equation of the tangent at the point $(2, -6)$ is therefore

$$y + 6 = 5(x - 2).$$

The slope–intercept equation of this line is

$$y = 5x - 16.$$

When $x = -2$ on the curve,

$$y = (-2)^3 - 7(-2) = 6.$$

The tangent to the curve at the point $(-2, 6)$ is

$$y - 6 = 5(x + 2),$$

or

$$y = 5x + 16.$$

EXAMPLE 3. Show that the normal to the curve

$$x^2 + y^2 = a^2 \tag{7}$$

at any point (x_1, y_1) on it passes through the origin.

Solution. Differentiating (7) implicitly and solving for dy/dx, wc find

$$\frac{dy}{dx} = -\frac{x}{y}$$

as the slope of the *tangent* at (x, y). The slope of the *normal* at (x_1, y_1) is therefore

$$m = \frac{y_1}{x_1},$$

and the equation of the normal is

$$y - y_1 = \frac{y_1}{x_1}(x - x_1). \tag{8}$$

When we clear of fractions, (8) reduces to

$$x_1 y = y_1 x.$$

Clearly, the origin lies on this line, since the coordinates $x = 0$, $y = 0$ satisfy the equation.

EXAMPLE 4. Show that the number of tangent lines that can be drawn from the point $Q(h, k)$ to the curve

$$y = x^2 \tag{9}$$

is two, one, or zero according as k is less than h^2, equal to h^2, or greater than h^2, respectively.

Solution. Figure 8–7 represents the curve and the three cases $k < h^2$, $k = h^2$, $k > h^2$. From the fact that $d^2y/dx^2 = 2$ is always positive, so that the curve is concave upward, we see that the results stated are equivalent to saying that two tangents can be drawn from a point on the convex side of the curve, no tangents from a point on the concave side of the curve, and only one tangent from a point on the curve. This is geometrically evident, but we shall adopt an analytical approach as follows.

Suppose that a tangent *can* be drawn to the curve from Q, touching the curve at some point $P_1(x_1, y_1)$ which is at present not known. Then, using Eq. (2), we find the equation of this tangent line to be

$$y - y_1 = 2x_1(x - x_1).$$

a)

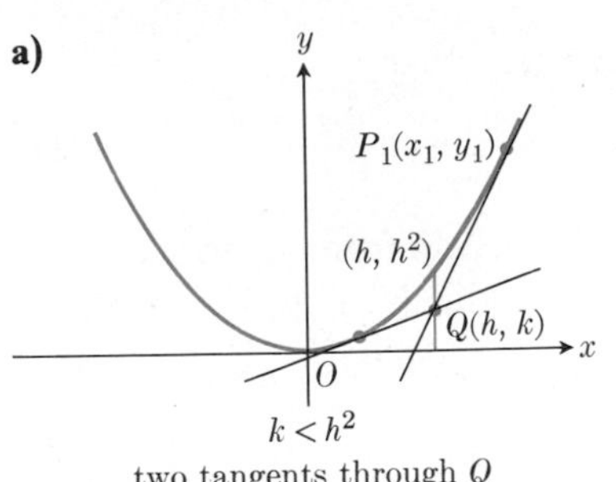

$k < h^2$
two tangents through Q

b)

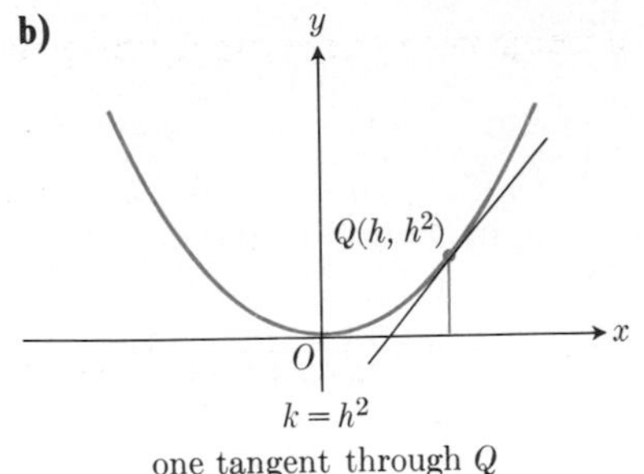

$k = h^2$
one tangent through Q

c)

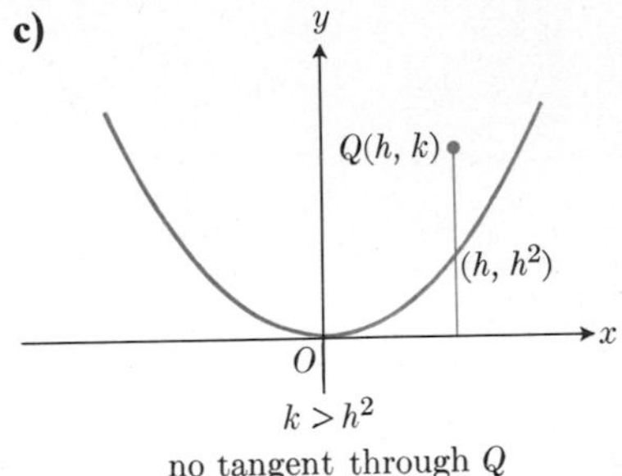

$k > h^2$
no tangent through Q

Figure 8–7

Since $Q(h, k)$ is *on this line*, its coordinates must satisfy the equation

$$k - y_1 = 2x_1(h - x_1). \qquad \textbf{(10a)}$$

Also, since (x_1, y_1) is *on the curve*, its coordinates must satisfy the equation

$$y_1 = x_1^2. \qquad \textbf{(10b)}$$

Now in reality, h and k are known to us but x_1 and y_1 are not. We therefore have two equations, (10a) and (10b), for two unknowns, x_1 and y_1. We eliminate y_1 between them and obtain

$$k - x_1^2 = 2hx_1 - 2x_1^2$$

or

$$x_1^2 - 2hx_1 + k = 0.$$

If we solve this for x_1 by means of the quadratic formula, we obtain

$$x_1 = h \pm \sqrt{h^2 - k}. \qquad \textbf{(10c)}$$

Only real values of x_1 correspond to points P_1 on the curve; hence no tangent may be drawn if $h^2 - k$ is negative, which is the same condition as saying k is greater than h^2. If $h^2 = k$, then the two roots in (10c) coincide and give only one point, namely $x_1 = h$, $y_1 = k = h^2$, to which the tangent can be drawn. But if $k < h^2$, the two roots in (10c) are distinct and each root gives a value of x_1 which with $y_1 = x_1^2$ determines a point P_1 such that the line QP_1 is tangent to the curve, so that two tangents may be drawn.

Angle between Two Curves

Let C_1 and C_2 be two curves that intersect at a point P. Then the angle between C_1 and C_2 at P is, by definition, the angle β between their tangents at P (Fig. 8–8). If these tangents are, respectively, L_1 and L_2, they have slopes

$$m_1 = \tan \phi_1, \qquad m_2 = \tan \phi_2.$$

Then $\tan \beta$ can be found from m_1 and m_2 as follows. Since

$$\beta = \phi_2 - \phi_1,$$

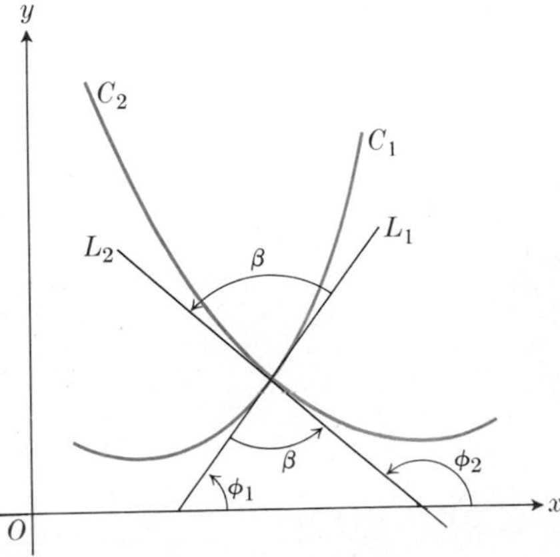

8–8 The angle between two smooth curves C_1 and C_2 at a point of intersection is the angle β between their tangents there. It is measured counterclockwise from C_1 to C_2.

we have

$$\tan \beta = \tan (\phi_2 - \phi_1) = \frac{\tan \phi_2 - \tan \phi_1}{1 + \tan \phi_2 \tan \phi_1} = \frac{m_2 - m_1}{1 + m_2 m_1}. \tag{11}$$

Here β is measured in the counterclockwise direction from L_1 to L_2.

We recall that the lines L_1 and L_2 are perpendicular if $m_2 = -1/m_1$. In this case we say that the curves C_1 and C_2 are *orthogonal.*

EXAMPLE 5. Show that every curve of the family

$$xy = a, \qquad a \neq 0, \tag{12a}$$

is orthogonal to every curve of the family

$$x^2 - y^2 = b, \qquad b \neq 0. \tag{12b}$$

Solution. The two families of curves are sketched in Fig. 8–9. At a point $P(x, y)$ on any curve of (12a), the slope is

$$\frac{dy}{dx} = -\frac{y}{x}, \tag{13a}$$

and on any curve of (12b) the slope is

$$\frac{dy}{dx} = \frac{x}{y}. \tag{13b}$$

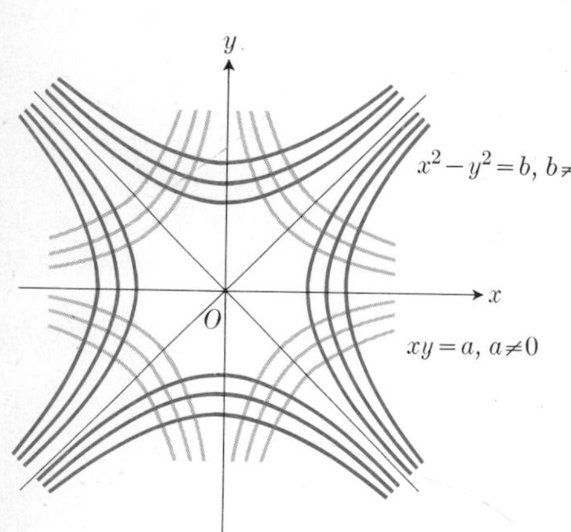

8–9 Each curve is orthogonal to every curve it meets in the other family.

At a point of intersection, the values of x and y in (13b) are the same as in (13a), and the two curves are orthogonal because these slopes are negative reciprocals of each other. The cases $x = 0$ or $y = 0$ cannot occur in Eqs. (13) if (x, y) is a point of intersection of any curve (12a) and a curve (12b), since a and b are restricted to be constants different from zero. That every curve in (12a) does in fact intersect every curve in (12b) follows from the fact that the equation

$$x^2 - \frac{a^2}{x^2} = b,$$

which results from eliminating y between (12a) and (12b), has real roots for every pair of nonzero real constants a and b.

The curves in (12b) are called *orthogonal trajectories* of the curves in (12a). Such mutually orthogonal systems of curves are of particular importance in physical problems related to electrical potential, where the curves in one family correspond to lines of flow and those in the other family correspond to lines of constant potential. They also occur in hydrodynamics and in heat-flow problems.

PROBLEMS

1. Find the tangent to the curve $y^2 - 2x - 4y - 1 = 0$ at the point $(-2, 1)$.

2. Find the normal to the curve $xy + 2x - 5y - 2 = 0$ at the point $(3, 2)$.

3. Find the tangents to the curve $y = x^3 - 6x + 2$ that are parallel to the line $y = 6x - 2$.

4. Find the normals to the curve $xy + 2x - y = 0$ that are parallel to the line $2x + y = 0$.

5. Show that the two lines that are drawn from $(\frac{3}{2}, 0)$ tangent to the curve $x^2 - 4y + 4 = 0$ are perpendicular.

6. There are three normals through the point $(\frac{3}{4}, 0)$ to the curve $y^2 = x$. One of them is the x-axis. Show that the other two are perpendicular.

7. Does the line that is tangent to the curve $y = x^3$ at the point $(1, 1)$ intersect the curve at any other point? If so, find the point.

8. A line is drawn from the point $P_0(1, 5)$ tangent to the curve $y = x^3$ at a point $P_1(x_1, y_1)$ on it. Find the coordinates of P_1. Is there more than one possibility for the point P_1? Why?

9. Find all lines that can be drawn normal to the curve $x^2 - y^2 = 5$ and parallel to the line $2x + 3y = 10$. Sketch the curve and the lines.

10. Find all lines that can be drawn tangent to the curve $4xy = 1$ from the point $P(-1, 2)$. Sketch the curve and the lines.

11. The line that is normal to the curve $y = x^2 + 2x - 3$ at $(1, 0)$ intersects the curve at what other point?

12. If l represents the distance between a fixed point $P_1(x_1, y_1)$ and a variable point $P(x, y)$ on a curve $y = f(x)$ (Fig. 8–10), then

$$l^2 = (x - x_1)^2 + [f(x) - y_1]^2.$$

Show that the derivative $d(l^2)/dx$ is equal to zero when $x = x_2$ if and only if the line P_1P_2 is normal to the curve at $P_2[x_2, f(x_2)]$.

13. Show that the curve $2x^2 + 3y^2 = 5$ and the curve $y^2 = x^3$ intersect at right angles.

14. Let $P_1(x_1, y_1)$ and $P_2(x_2, y_2)$ be any two points on the curve

$$y = ax^2 + bx + c, \qquad a \neq 0.$$

If a line is drawn tangent to the curve at (x_0, y_0) and is parallel to the chord P_1P_2, show that $x_0 = (x_1 + x_2)/2$.

15. For what values of b is the line $y = 12x + b$ tangent to the curve $y = x^3$?

16. For what values of m is the line $y = mx$ tangent to the curve

$$y^2 + x^2 - 4x + 3 = 0?$$

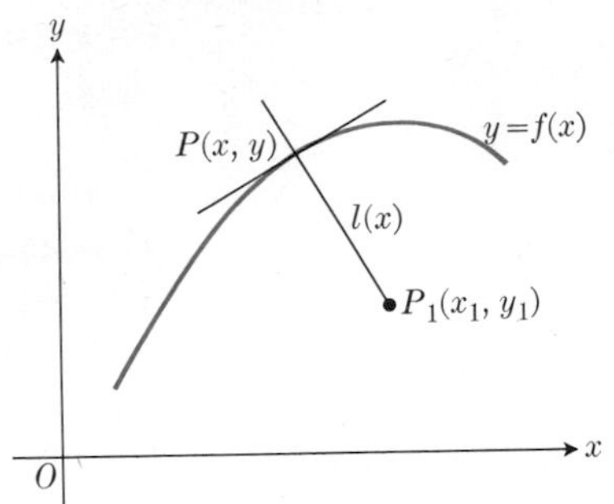

8–10 The values of x where the line P_1P is normal to the curve are critical values of the function $l(x)$.

17. Find the interior angles of the triangle whose vertices are $A(1, 1)$, $B(3, -1)$, and $C(5, 2)$.

18. Find the slope of the line that bisects the angle ACB in the previous problem.

19. Let A, B, C be the interior angles of a triangle in which no angle is a right angle. By calculating $\tan(A + B + C)$ and observing that

$$A + B + C = 180°,$$

show that the equation

$$\tan A + \tan B + \tan C = \tan A \tan B \tan C$$

must be satisfied.

20. Calculate the interior angles of the triangle whose vertices are $A(1, 2)$, $B(2, -1)$, and $C(-1, 1)$, and check your results by showing that they satisfy the equation

$$\tan A + \tan B + \tan C = \tan A \tan B \tan C.$$

(See Problem 19, above.)

21. Find the angles between the following pairs of curves:

a) $3x + y = 5, \quad 2x - y = 4,$

b) $y = x^2, \quad xy = 1,$

c) $x^2 + y^2 = 16, \quad y^2 = 6x,$

d) $x^2 + xy + y^2 = 7, \quad y = 2x.$

8–3 DISTANCE BETWEEN TWO POINTS. EQUATIONS

It is at once apparent from Fig. 8–11 and the theorem of Pythagoras that the distance d between the two points $P_1(x_1, y_1)$ and $P_2(x_2, y_2)$ is given by

$$d = \sqrt{(x_2 - x_1)^2 + (y_2 - y_1)^2}. \qquad (1)$$

This formula is particularly useful in finding the equation of a curve whose geometric character depends upon one or more distances, as in the example below.

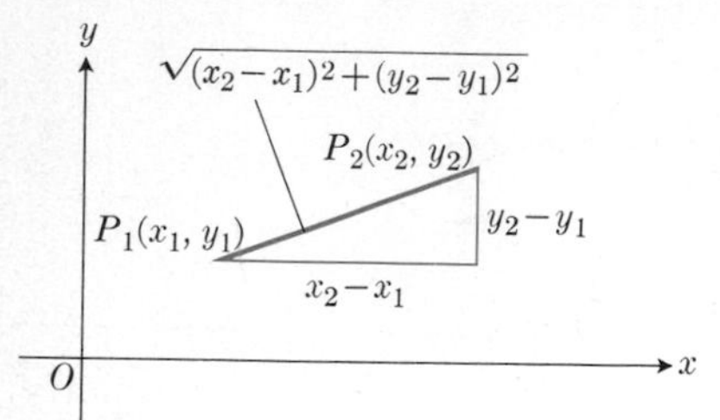

8–11 The distance between two points P_1 and P_2 is computed from their coordinates.

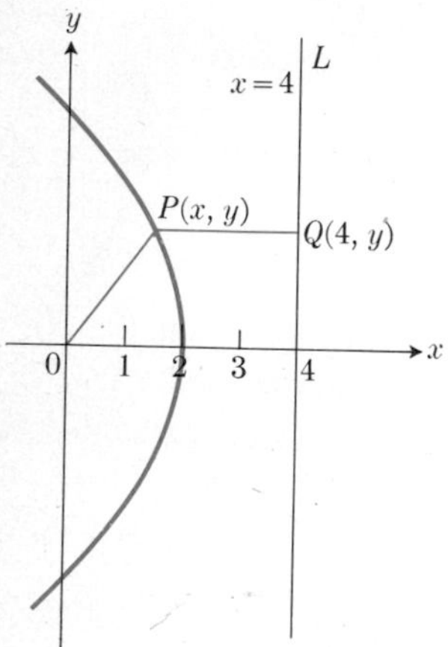

8–12 The curve traced by a point P that stays equidistant from point O and from line L.

EXAMPLE 1. Find an equation for the set of points $P(x, y)$ that are equidistant from the origin O and the line L: $x = 4$.

Solution. The distance between P and L is the perpendicular distance PQ between $P(x, y)$ and the point $Q(4, y)$ on L that has the same ordinate as P. (See Fig. 18–12.) Thus,

$$PQ = \sqrt{(4-x)^2 + (y-y)^2} = |4-x|.$$

The distance OP is

$$OP = \sqrt{x^2 + y^2}.$$

The condition to be satisfied by P is $OP = PQ$, or

$$\sqrt{x^2 + y^2} = |4-x|. \tag{2}$$

If (2) holds, so does the equation we get by squaring:

$$x^2 + y^2 = 16 - 8x + x^2$$

or

$$y^2 = 16 - 8x. \tag{3}$$

That is, if a point is equidistant from O and L, then its coordinates must satisfy Eq. (3). The converse is also true, for if Eq. (3) holds, then

$$\begin{aligned}\sqrt{x^2 + y^2} &= \sqrt{x^2 + (16 - 8x)}\\ &= \sqrt{(x-4)^2}\\ &= |x-4|\\ &= |4-x|,\end{aligned}$$

and hence

$$OP = PQ.$$

Therefore Eq. (3) expresses both the necessary and sufficient condition on the coordinates of $P(x, y)$ for P to be equidistant from O and L.

PROBLEMS

In Problems 1–8, use the distance formula to derive equations for the sets of points $P(x, y)$ that satisfy the specified conditions. Analyze each equation and sketch its graph.

1. P is equidistant from the two points $A(-2, 1)$ and $B(2, -3)$.

2. The distance from P to $F_1(-1, 0)$ is twice its distance to $F_2(2, 0)$.

3. The product of its distances from $F_1(-2, 0)$ and $F_2(2, 0)$ is 4.

4. The sum of the distances from P to $F_1(1, 0)$ and $F_2(0, 1)$ is constant and the curve passes through the origin.

5. The distance of P from the line $x = -2$ is 2 times its distance from the point (2, 0).

6. The distance of P from the point $(-3, 0)$ is 4 more than its distance from the point (3, 0).

7. The distance of P from the line $y = 1$ is 3 less than its distance from the origin.

8. P is 3 units from the point (2, 3).

9. Find a point that is equidistant from the three points $A(0, 1)$, $B(1, 0)$, $C(4, 3)$. What is the radius of the circle through A, B, and C?

10. Find the distance between the point $P_1(x_1, y_1)$ and the straight line $Ax + By + C = 0$.

8–4 THE CIRCLE

Definition. *A circle is the set of points in a plane whose distance from a given fixed point in the plane is a constant.*

Equation of a Circle

Let $C(h, k)$ be the given fixed point, the *center* of the circle. Let r be the constant distance, the *radius* of the circle. Let $P(x, y)$ be a point on the circle (Fig. 8–13). Then

$$\overline{CP} = r, \tag{1}$$

or

$$\sqrt{(x-h)^2 + (y-k)^2} = r,$$

or

$$(x-h)^2 + (y-k)^2 = r^2. \tag{2}$$

If (1) is satisfied, so is (2), and conversely. Therefore (2) is an equation for the circle.

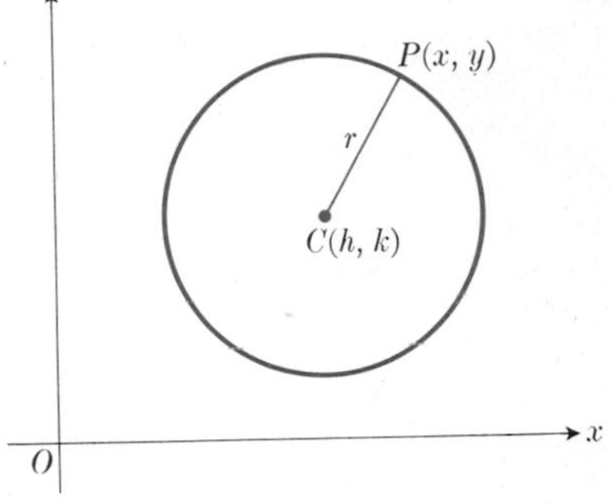

8–13 $(x-h)^2 + (y-k)^2 = r^2$.

EXAMPLE 1. Find an equation for the circle with center at the origin and with radius r.

Solution. If $h = k = 0$, Eq. (2) becomes

$$x^2 + y^2 = r^2. \tag{3}$$

EXAMPLE 2. Find the circle through the origin with center at $C(2, -1)$.

Solution. Its equation, (2), is of the form

$$(x-2)^2 + (y+1)^2 = r^2.$$

Since the circle goes through the origin, $x = y = 0$ must satisfy the equation. Hence

$$(0-2)^2 + (0+1)^2 = r^2$$

or

$$r^2 = 5.$$

The equation is

$$(x-2)^2 + (y+1)^2 = 5.$$

EXAMPLE 3. What points $P(x, y)$ satisfy the inequality

$$(x-h)^2 + (y-k)^2 < r^2? \tag{4}$$

Solution. The left side of (4) is the square of the distance CP from $C(h, k)$ to $P(x, y)$. The inequality is satisfied if and only if

$$\overline{CP} < r;$$

that is, if P lies inside the circle of radius r with center at $C(h, k)$, Fig. 8–14.

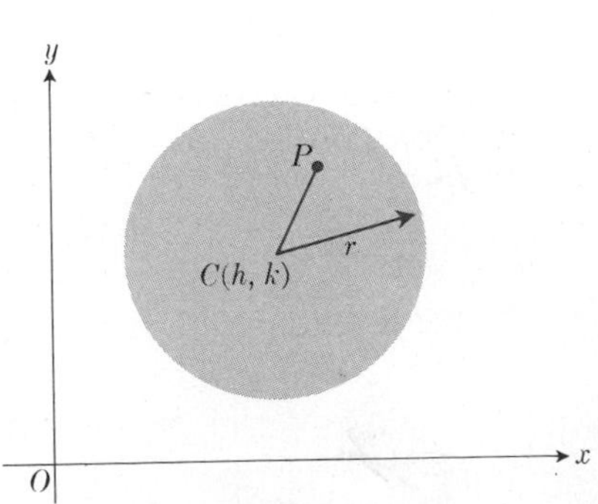

8–14 The region $(x-h)^2 + (y-k)^2 < r^2$ is the interior of the circle with center $C(h, k)$ and radius r.

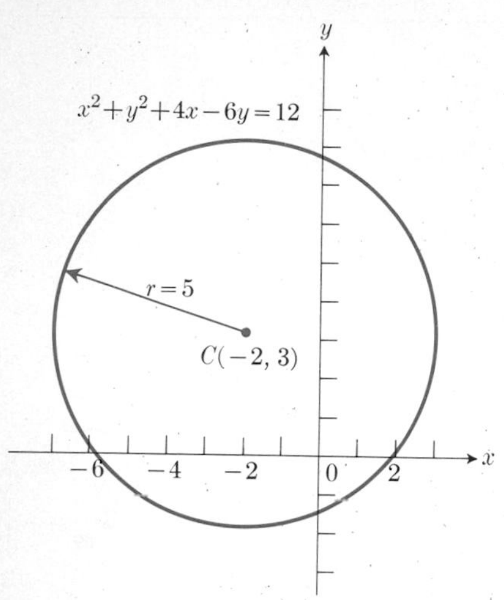

8–15 The graph of $x^2 + y^2 + 4x - 6y = 12$.

EXAMPLE 4. Analyze the equation

$$x^2 + y^2 + 4x - 6y = 12.$$

Solution. We complete the squares in the x terms and y terms and get

$$(x^2 + 4x + 4) + (y^2 - 6y + 9) = 12 + 4 + 9$$

or

$$(x + 2)^2 + (y - 3)^2 = 25.$$

This is of the same form as Eq. (2); therefore it represents a circle with center $C(-2, 3)$ and radius $r = 5$. Its graph is shown in Fig. 8–15.

REMARK 1. An equation of the form

$$Ax^2 + Ay^2 + Dx + Ey + F = 0, \qquad A \neq 0, \tag{5}$$

can often be reduced to the form of Eq. (2) by completing the squares as we did in Example 4. More specifically, we may divide (5) by A and write

$$\left(x^2 + \frac{D}{A}x\right) + \left(y^2 + \frac{E}{A}y\right) = -\frac{F}{A}. \tag{6}$$

To complete the squares for x, add $(D/2A)^2 = D^2/(4A^2)$; and for y add $(E/2A)^2 = E^2/(4A^2)$. Of course we must add to both sides of Eq. (6), thus obtaining

$$\left(x + \frac{D}{2A}\right)^2 + \left(y + \frac{E}{2A}\right)^2 = -\frac{F}{A} + \frac{D^2 + E^2}{4A^2}$$

$$= \frac{D^2 + E^2 - 4AF}{4A^2}. \tag{7}$$

Equation (7) is like Eq. (2), with

$$r^2 = \frac{D^2 + E^2 - 4AF}{4A^2}, \tag{8}$$

provided this expression is positive. Then (5) represents a circle with center at $(-D/2A, -E/2A)$ and radius $r = \sqrt{(D^2 + E^2 - 4AF)/(4A^2)}$.

If (8) is equal to zero, the curve reduces to a single point, and if it is negative, there are no points (with real coordinates) that satisfy Eq. (7) or Eq. (5).

We recommend that you apply the method of Example 4, and not use formulas, to handle problems of this type. The thing to remember is that an equation like (5), which is *quadratic in x and in y, with equal coefficients of x^2 and y^2, and with no xy term, represents a circle* (or a single point, or no real locus).

REMARK 2. Equation (5) can be divided by A and be replaced by an equation of the form

$$x^2 + y^2 + C_1x + C_2y + C_3 = 0, \tag{9}$$

where C_1, C_2, C_3 are three constants. The three coefficients in (9) can often be determined so as to satisfy three prescribed conditions. Typical conditions might be that the circle go through three given (noncollinear) points; or be tangent to three given nonconcurrent lines; or be tangent to two lines and pass through a given point not on either line.

EXAMPLE 5. Find the circle through the three points $A(1, 0)$, $B(0, 1)$, and $C(2, 2)$.

Solution. Let Eq. (9) be the equation of the circle. Then substitute for x and y the coordinates of A, B, and C, since these points are to be on the circle.

Point	$x^2 + y^2 + C_1x + C_2y + C_3 = 0$	
$A(1, 0)$	$1 + C_1 + C_3 = 0$	
$B(0, 1)$	$1 + C_2 + C_3 = 0$	**(10)**
$C(2, 2)$	$4 + 4 + 2C_1 + 2C_2 + C_3 = 0$	

Equations (10) are three equations for the three unknowns. We solve them for C_1, C_2, and C_3. Subtract the second equation from the first to get

$$C_2 = C_1.$$

Substitute C_1 for C_2 in the third equation:

$$8 + 4C_1 + C_3 = 0.$$

Subtract the first equation from this:

$$7 + 3C_1 = 0.$$

Hence

$$C_2 = C_1 = -\tfrac{7}{3}$$

and

$$C_3 = -1 - C_1 = \tfrac{4}{3}.$$

Therefore, the equation of the circle through C_1, C_2, and C_3 is

$$x^2 + y^2 - \tfrac{7}{3}x - \tfrac{7}{3}y + \tfrac{4}{3} = 0$$

or

$$3x^2 + 3y^2 - 7x - 7y + 4 = 0.$$

Of course this example could equally well have been solved starting with Eq. (2), which contains the three unknowns h, k, and r. Or we could have found the center Q of the circle by locating the point of intersection of the perpendicular bisectors of the segments AB and BC. The radius is the distance from the center Q to any one of the three points A, B, or C.

PROBLEMS

In each of the following problems (1 through 4), find the equation of the circle having the given center $C(h, k)$ and radius r.

1. $C(0, 2)$, $r = 2$ **2.** $C(-2, 0)$, $r = 3$

3. $C(3, -4)$, $r = 5$ **4.** $C(1, 1)$, $r = \sqrt{2}$

5. Write an inequality that describes the points that lie inside the circle with center $C(-2, -1)$ and radius $r = \sqrt{6}$.

6. Write an inequality that describes the points that lie outside the circle with center $C(-4, 2)$ and radius $r = 4$.

In each of the following problems (7 through 10), find the center and radius of the given circle.

7. $x^2 + y^2 - 2y = 3$ **8.** $x^2 + y^2 + 2x = 8$

9. $3x^2 + 3y^2 + 6x = 1$ **10.** $2x^2 + 2y^2 + x + y = 0$

What points satisfy the inequalities in Problems 11 and 12?

11. $x^2 + y^2 + 2x - 4y + 5 \le 0$

12. $x^2 + y^2 + 4x + 4y + 9 \ge 0$

13. The center of a circle is $C(2, 2)$. The circle goes through the point $A(4, 5)$. Find its equation.

14. The center of a circle is $C(-1, 1)$. The circle is tangent to the line $x + 2y = 4$. Find its equation.

15. A circle passes through the points $A(2, -2)$ and $B(3, 4)$. Its center is on the line $x + y = 2$. Find its equation.

16. Show geometrically that the lines that are drawn from the exterior point $P_1(x_1, y_1)$ tangent to the circle $(x - h)^2 + (y - k)^2 = r^2$ have length l given by

$$l^2 = (x_1 - h)^2 + (y_1 - k)^2 - r^2.$$

17. Find the equation of the circle that passes through the three points, $A(2, 3)$, $B(3, 2)$, and $C(-4, 3)$.

18. Find an equation for the coordinates of the point $P(x, y)$ if the sum of the squares of its distances from the two points $(-5, 2)$ and $(1, 4)$ is always 52. Identify and sketch the curve.

19. Is the point $(0.1, 3.1)$ inside, outside, or on the circle

$$x^2 + y^2 - 2x - 4y + 3 = 0?$$

Why?

20. If the distance from $P(x, y)$ to the point $(6, 0)$ is twice its distance from the point $(0, 3)$, show that P lies on a circle and find the center and radius.

21. Find the circle inscribed in the triangle whose sides are the lines $4x + 3y = 24$, $3x - 4y = 18$, $4x - 3y + 32 = 0$. [*Hint.* The distance between the point (h, k) and the line $ax + by = c$ is

$$\frac{|ah + bk - c|}{\sqrt{a^2 + b^2}}$$

by the answer to Problem 10, Article 8–3.]

22. Let P be a point outside a given circle C. Let PT be tangent to C at T. Let the line PN from P through the center of C intersect C at M and N. Prove that $PM \cdot PN = (PT)^2$.

23. It is known that any angle inscribed in a semicircle is a right angle. Prove the converse: i.e., if for every choice of the point $P(x, y)$ on a curve C joining O and A, the angle OPA is a right angle, then the curve is a circle or a semicircle having OA as diameter.

24. Suppose that Eqs. (2) and (9) represent the same circle. (a) Express C_1, C_2, and C_3 in terms of h, k, and r. (b) Express h, k, and r in terms of C_1, C_2, and C_3.

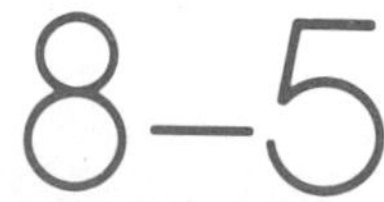

THE PARABOLA

Definition. *A parabola is the set of points in a plane that are equidistant from a given fixed point and fixed line in the plane.*

The Equation of a Parabola

The fixed point is called the *focus* of the parabola and the fixed line the *directrix*. If the focus F lies on the directrix L, then the parabola is nothing more than the line through F perpendicular to L. (We consider this to be a degenerate case.) If F does not lie on L, then we may choose a coordinate system that results in a simple equation for the parabola by taking the y-axis through F perpendicular to L, and taking the origin halfway between F and L. If the distance between F and L is $2p$, we may assign F coordinates $(0, p)$ and the equation of L is $y = -p$, as in Fig. 8–16. Then a point $P(x, y)$ lies on the parabola if and only if the distances PF and PQ are equal:

$$PF = PQ, \tag{1}$$

where $Q(x, -p)$ is the foot of the perpendicular from P to L. From the distance formula,

$$PF = \sqrt{x^2 + (y - p)^2} \quad \text{and} \quad PQ = \sqrt{(y + p)^2}.$$

When we equate these two expressions, square, and simplify, we get

$$x^2 = 4py. \tag{2}$$

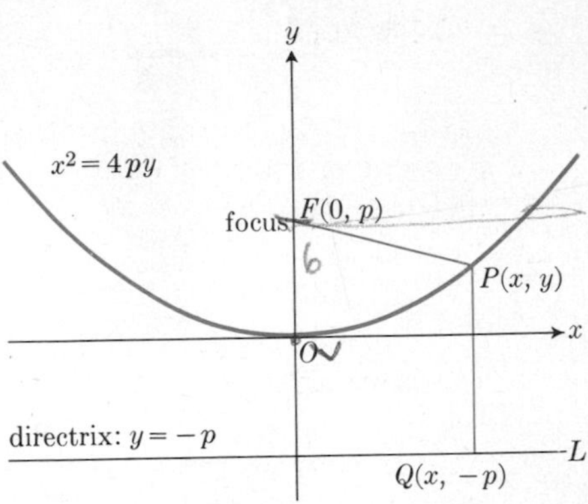

8–16 The parabola $x^2 = 4py$.

This equation must be satisfied by any point on the parabola. Conversely, if (2) is satisfied, then

$$\begin{aligned} PF &= \sqrt{x^2 + (y - p)^2} \\ &= \sqrt{4py + (y^2 - 2py + p^2)} \\ &= \sqrt{(y + p)^2} \\ &= PQ, \end{aligned}$$

and $P(x, y)$ is on the parabola.

DISCUSSION. In Eq. (2) assume p is positive. Then y cannot be negative, for real x, and the curve lies above the x-axis. It is symmetric about the y-axis, since x appears only to an even power.

The axis of symmetry of the parabola is also called the "axis of the parabola." The point on this axis midway between the focus and the directrix is on the parabola, since it is equidistant from the focus and the directrix. It is called the *vertex* of the parabola. The origin is the vertex of the parabola in Fig. 8–16. The tangent to a parabola at its vertex is parallel to the directrix. From Eq. (2) we find the slope of the tangent at any point is $dy/dx = x/2p$, and this is zero at the origin. The second derivative is $d^2y/dx^2 = 1/2p$, which is positive, so the curve is concave upward.

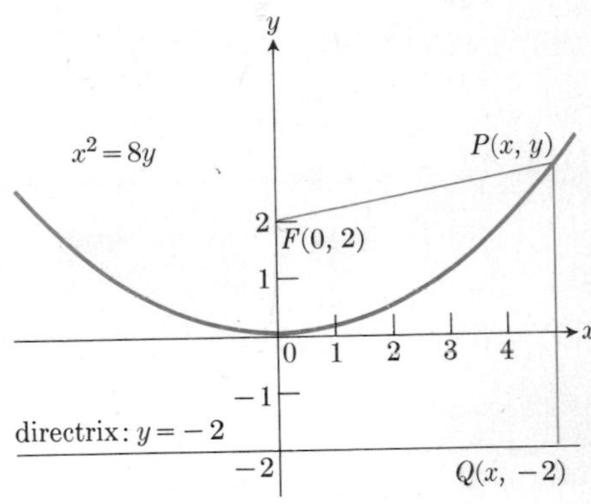

8–17 The parabola $x^2 = 8y$.

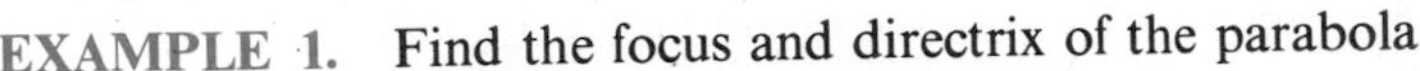

EXAMPLE 1. Find the focus and directrix of the parabola

$$x^2 = 8y. \tag{3}$$

Solution. Equation (3) matches (2) if we take $4p = 8$, $p = 2$. The focus is on the axis of symmetry (the y-axis), p units from the vertex, that is, at $F(0, 2)$. The directrix is the line $y = -2$. Every point on the graph of (3) is equidistant from $F(0, 2)$ and the line $y = -2$ (Fig. 8–17).

REMARK 1. Suppose the parabola opens downward, as in Fig. 8–18, with its focus $F(0, -p)$ and directrix the line $y = p$. The effect is to change the sign of p in Eq. (2), which now becomes

$$x^2 = -4py. \tag{4}$$

We may also interchange the roles of x and y in Eqs. (2) and (4). The resulting equations

$$y^2 = 4px \tag{5a}$$

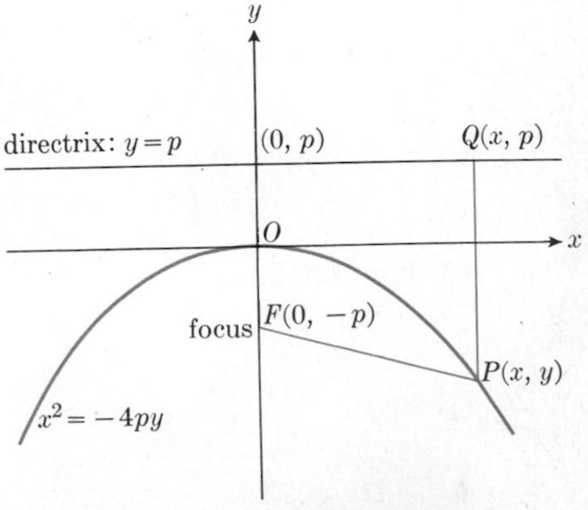

8–18 The parabola $x^2 = -4py$.

and

$$y^2 = -4px \tag{5b}$$

also represent parabolas, but now they are symmetric about the x-axis because y appears only to an even power. The *vertex* is still at the origin. The directrix is perpendicular to the axis of symmetry, and p units from the vertex. The focus is on the axis of symmetry, also p units from the vertex, and "inside" the curve. If we assume that p is positive in Eqs. (5), then (5a) opens toward the right, because x must be greater than or equal to zero, while (5b) opens toward the left. Figure 8–19 shows graphs of parabolas of these two types.

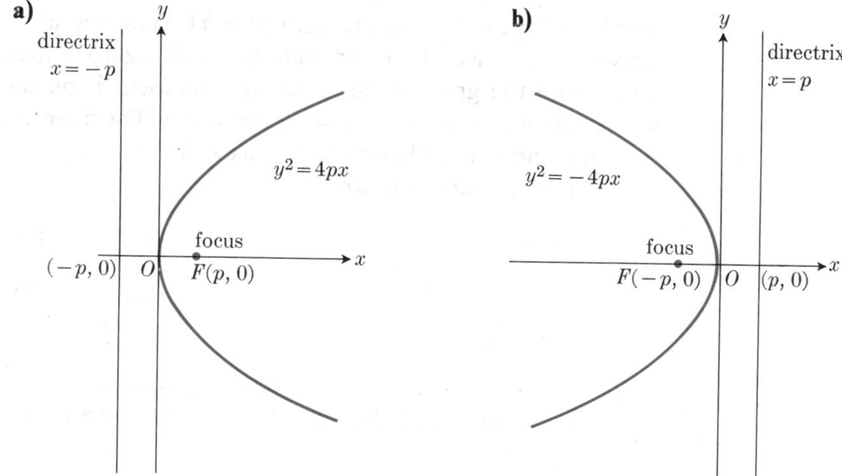

8–19 (a) The parabola $y^2 = 4px$. (b) The parabola $y^2 = -4px$.

Translation of Axes

If the vertex of the parabola is at the point $V(h, k)$, Eqs. (2), (4), and (5) no longer apply in those forms. However, it is easy to determine what the appropriate equation is, by introducing a new coordinate system, with its origin O' at V, and axes parallel to the original axes. Every point P in the plane then has two sets of coordinates, say x and y in the original system, and x', y' in the new. To go from O to P, we have a horizontal displacement x and a vertical displacement y. The abscissa may be resolved into two horizontal displacements: h from O to O' and x' from O' to P (Fig. 8–20). Similarly, the ordinate is the resultant of two vertical displacements: k from O to O' and y' from O' to P. Thus the two sets of coordinates are related as follows:

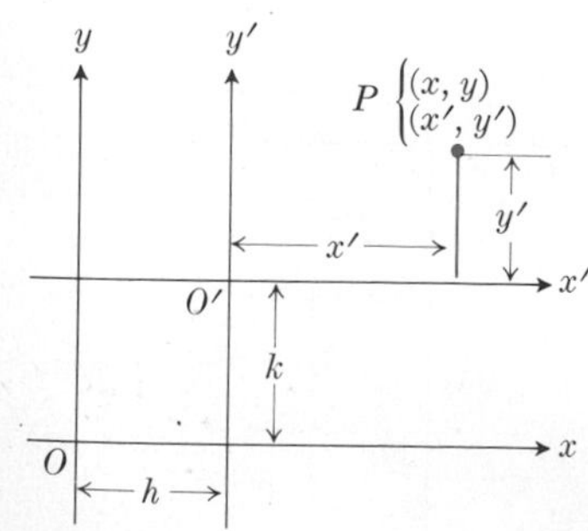

8–20 Translation of axes.

$$\begin{Bmatrix} x = x' + h \\ y = y' + k \end{Bmatrix} \tag{6a}$$

or

$$\begin{Bmatrix} x' = x - h \\ y' = y - k \end{Bmatrix}. \tag{6b}$$

Equations (6) are called the equations for *translation of axes*, because the new coordinate axes may be obtained by moving the old axes to the position of the new ones in a motion known as a pure translation without rotation.

Suppose, now, we consider a parabola, with vertex $V(h, k)$ and opening upward as in Fig. 8–21. In terms of $x'y'$-coordinates, Eq. (2) provides us with the equation of the parabola in the form

$$(x')^2 = 4py'. \tag{7}$$

By using Eqs. (6), we may express this in xy-coordinates by the equation

$$(x - h)^2 = 4p(y - k). \tag{8a}$$

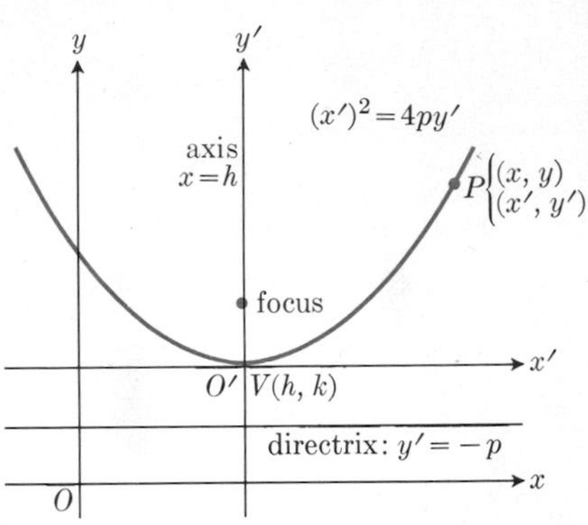

8–21 Parabola with vertex at $V(h, k)$.

The axis of symmetry of the parabola in (8a) is the line $x = h$. The equation of this line is obtained by setting the quadratic term $(x - h)^2$ in (8a) equal to zero. When p is positive, $y - k$ must be greater than or equal to zero in (8a), for real $x - h$, and therefore the graph opens upward. The focus is on the axis of symmetry, p units above the vertex at $x = h$, $y = k + p$. The directrix is p units below the vertex and perpendicular to the axis of symmetry.

Other forms of equations of parabolas are:

$$(x - h)^2 = -4p(y - k), \tag{8b}$$

$$(y - k)^2 = 4p(x - h), \tag{8c}$$

$$(y - k)^2 = -4p(x - h). \tag{8d}$$

Equation (8b) has a graph symmetric about $x = h$, opening downward; (8c) symmetric about $y = k$ and opening to the right $(x \geq h)$; (8d) symmetric about $y = k$ and opening to the left $(x \leq h)$.

EXAMPLE 2. Discuss the parabola

$$y = x^2 + 4x. \tag{9}$$

Solution. We complete the square in the x terms by adding 4 to both sides of Eq. (9):

$$y + 4 = x^2 + 4x + 4 = (x + 2)^2.$$

This has the form

$$(x - h)^2 = 4p(y - k)$$

with

$$h = -2, \qquad k = -4,$$

$$4p = 1, \qquad p = \tfrac{1}{4}.$$

The vertex of the parabola is $V(-2, -4)$; its axis of symmetry $(x + 2)^2 = 0$; and it opens upward because $y \geq -4$ for real x. The graph is shown in Fig. 8–22. The focus is on the axis of symmetry, $\frac{1}{4}$ unit above the vertex, at $F(-2, -3\frac{3}{4})$. The directrix is parallel to the x-axis, $\frac{1}{4}$ unit below the vertex. Its equation is $y = -4\frac{1}{4}$.

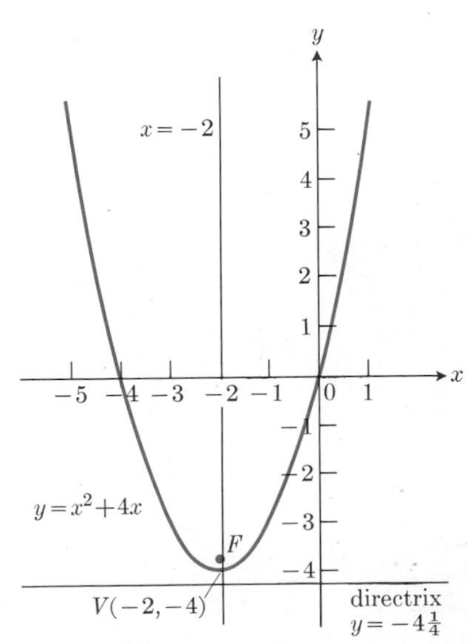

8–22 The parabola $y = x^2 + 4x$.

The key feature of an equation of a parabola is that it is quadratic in one of the coordinates and linear in the other. Whenever we have such an equation we may reduce it to one of the standard forms (8a, b, c, d) by completing the square in the coordinate that appears quadratically. We then put the linear terms in the form $\pm 4p(x-h)$ or $\pm 4p(y-k)$. Then the information about vertex, distance from vertex to focus, axis of symmetry, and direction the curve opens can all be read from the equation in this standard form.

EXAMPLE 3. Discuss the equation

$$2x^2 + 5y - 3x + 4 = 0.$$

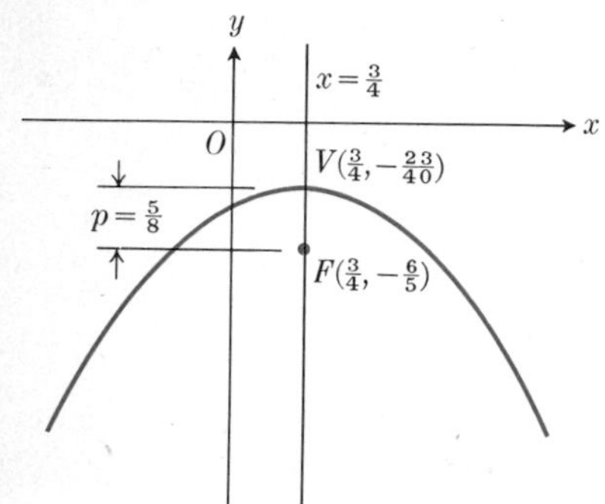

8–23 The parabola $2x^2 + 5y - 3x + 4 = 0$.

Solution. This equation is quadratic in x, linear in y. We divide by 2, the coefficient of x^2, and collect all the x terms on one side of the equation:

$$x^2 - \tfrac{3}{2}x = -\tfrac{5}{2}y - 2.$$

Now we complete the square by adding $(-\frac{3}{4})^2 = \frac{9}{16}$ to both sides:

$$\begin{aligned}(x - \tfrac{3}{4})^2 &= -\tfrac{5}{2}y - 2 + \tfrac{9}{16}\\ &= -\tfrac{5}{2}y - \tfrac{23}{16}.\end{aligned}$$

To get the y terms in the form $-4p(y-k)$, we factor out $-\frac{5}{2}$, and write

$$(x - \tfrac{3}{4})^2 = -\tfrac{5}{2}(y + \tfrac{23}{40}).$$

This has the form

$$(x-h)^2 = -4p(y-k)$$

with

$$h = \tfrac{3}{4}, \qquad k = -\tfrac{23}{40}, \qquad 4p = \tfrac{5}{2}.$$

Hence the vertex is $V(\frac{3}{4}, -\frac{23}{40})$. The axis of symmetry is $(x - \frac{3}{4})^2 = 0$, or $x = \frac{3}{4}$; and the distance from the vertex to the focus is

$$p = \tfrac{5}{8}.$$

Since $y - k$ must here be ≤ 0 for real x, the curve opens downward, and the focus is p units below the vertex at $F(\frac{3}{4}, -\frac{6}{5})$. The graph is shown in Fig. 8–23.

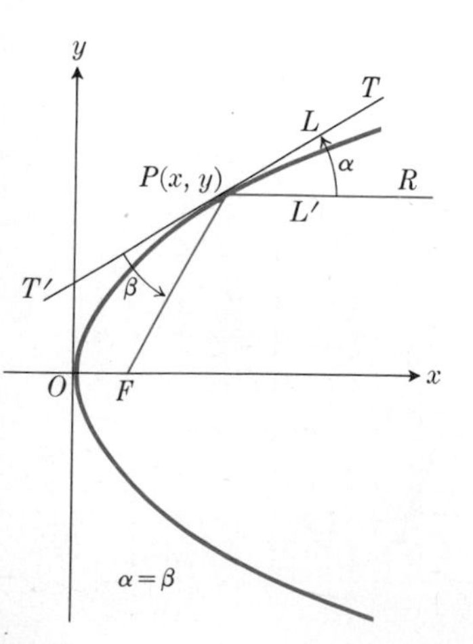

8–24 In a parabolic reflector, the angles α and β are equal.

REMARK 3. In Fig. 8–24, $T'PT$ is tangent to the parabola, F is the focus, and PL' is parallel to the axis of the parabola. The angles $\alpha = \angle L'PT$ and $\beta = \angle T'PF$ are equal (see Problem 31). This accounts for the property of a parabolic reflector that rays originating from the focus are reflected parallel to the axis, or rays coming into the reflector parallel to the axis are reflected to the focus. This property is used in parabolic mirrors of telescopes and in parabolic radar antennas.

EXAMPLE 4. The equation $x + 6p = 20$ gives the relation between the wholesale price p of coffee (dollars per pound) and the number of pounds x consumed per person in the United States from 1960 through 1974. The number x is called the *demand* for the coffee, and the equation $x + 6p = 20$ is called the *demand law*. (See Problem 19, Article 1–5.) The revenue from coffee sales under this demand law is

$$R = xp = (20 - 6p)p = 20p - 6p^2 \quad \text{dollars per person.}$$

The graph of the revenue function is a parabola (Fig. 8–25), but only the portion in the first quadrant is meaningful in the present economic context. When we complete the square in p, we find

$$p^2 - \frac{10}{3}p = -\frac{R}{6},$$

$$p^2 - \frac{10}{3}p + \frac{25}{9} = -\frac{R}{6} + \frac{25}{9},$$

$$(p - \tfrac{5}{3})^2 = -\tfrac{1}{6}(R - \tfrac{50}{3}).$$

The vertex is $V(\frac{5}{3}, \frac{50}{3})$ and the axis of symmetry is the line $p = \frac{5}{3}$.

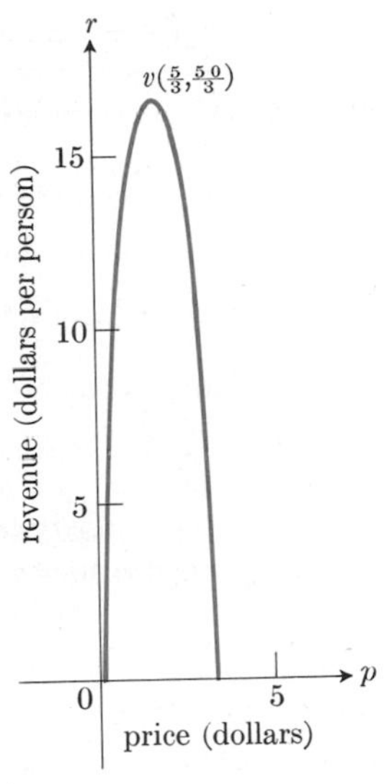

8–25 Revenue vs. price for the coffee demand law of Example 4.

Construction

A parabola can be constructed with straightedge and compass in the following way (Fig. 8–26):

a) Construct a family of lines parallel to the directrix L.

b) Set a compass to measure the distance d from the directrix to one of these lines L'. With the focus as center, construct an arc of radius d intersecting L' in points A' and B'.

c) Repeat the process with other lines L'', L''', and so on, constructing points A'', B'', A''', B''', and so on. The points constructed this way are all equidistant from L and F.

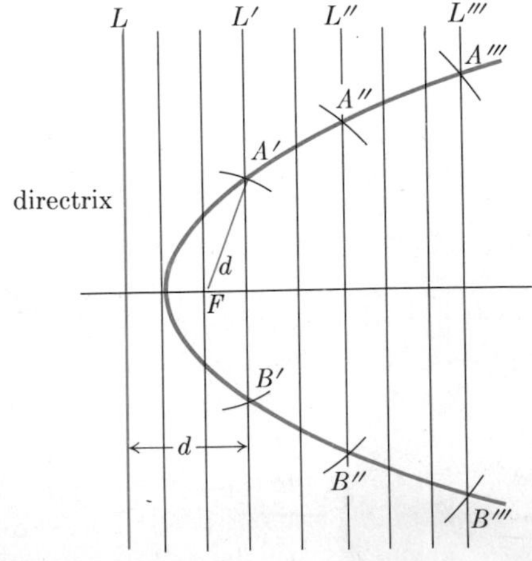

8–26 Construction of points on a parabola with focus F and directrix L.

PROBLEMS

In each of the following problems (1 through 6), the vertex V and focus F of a parabola are given. Find the equation of the parabola and of its directrix. Sketch the graph showing the focus, vertex, and directrix.

1. $V(0, 0)$, $F(0, 2)$
2. $V(0, 0)$, $F(-2, 0)$
3. $V(-2, 3)$, $F(-2, 4)$
4. $V(0, 3)$, $F(-1, 3)$
5. $V(-3, 1)$, $F(0, 1)$
6. $V(1, -3)$, $F(1, 0)$

In each of the following problems (7 through 12), the vertex V and directrix L of a parabola are given. Find the equation of the parabola and its focus. Sketch the graph showing the focus, vertex, and directrix.

7. $V(2, 0)$; L is the y-axis.
8. $V(1, -2)$; L is the x-axis.
9. $V(-3, 1)$; L is the line $x = 1$.
10. $V(-2, -2)$; L is the line $y = -3$.
11. $V(0, 1)$; L is the line $x = -1$.
12. $V(0, 1)$; L is the line $y = 2$.

In each of the following problems (13 through 22), find the vertex, axis of symmetry, focus, and directrix of the given parabola. Sketch the curve, showing these features.

13. $x^2 + 8y - 2x = 7$
14. $x^2 - 2y + 8x + 10 = 0$
15. $y^2 + 4x = 8$
16. $x^2 - 8y = 4$
17. $x^2 + 2x - 4y - 3 = 0$
18. $y^2 + x + y = 0$
19. $4y^2 - 8y + 3x - 2 = 0$
20. $y^2 + 6y + 2x + 5 = 0$
21. $3x^2 - 8y - 12x = 4$
22. $3x - 2y^2 - 4y + 7 = 0$
23. What points satisfy the inequality $x^2 < 8y$? Sketch.
24. (a) Do Problem 19 of Article 1–5 if you have not done so already. (b) At what price is the revenue from coffee sales under the demand law of Example 4 the greatest? What per capita consumption does the demand law give for this price?
25. A clothing-store chain has found that the daily revenue R from sales of a particular style of shirt is related to the dollar price p per shirt by the equation $R = -(\frac{1}{5})p^3 + 125p$. (a) Express the daily demand x as a function of p (see Example 4). Graph x as a function of p in the first quadrant. (b) At what price is the revenue R the greatest?
26. Find the length of the chord perpendicular to the axis of the parabola $y^2 = 4px$ and passing through the focus. (This chord is called the "latus rectum" of the parabola.)
27. Find the equation of the parabolic arch of base b and altitude h in Fig. 8–27.
28. Given the three points $(-1, 2)$, $(1, -1)$, and $(2, 1)$. (a) Find a parabola passing through the given points and having its axis parallel to the x-axis. (b) Find a parabola passing through the given points and having its axis parallel to the y-axis.

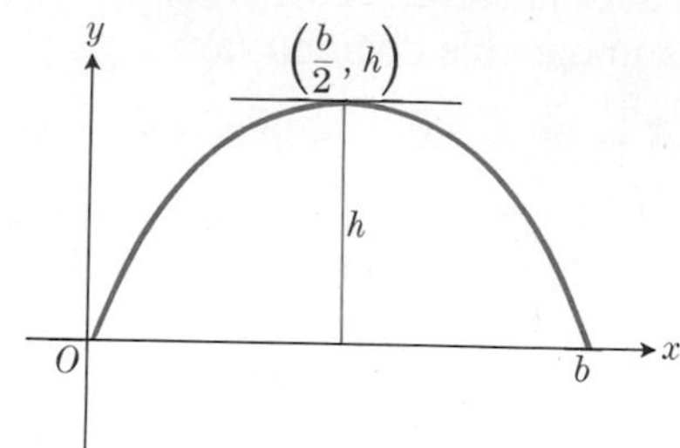

8–27 The parabolic arch of Problem 27.

29. Suppose a and b are positive numbers. Sketch the parabolas

$$y^2 = 4a^2 - 4ax \quad \text{and} \quad y^2 = 4b^2 + 4bx$$

in the same diagram. Show that they have a common focus, the same for any a and b. Show that they intersect at $(a - b, \pm 2\sqrt{ab})$, and that each "a-parabola" is orthogonal to every "b-parabola." (Using different values of a and b, we obtain families of confocal parabolas. Each family is a set of orthogonal trajectories of the other family. See Article 8–2.)

30. What points satisfy the equation

$$(2x + y - 3)(x^2 + y^2 - 4)(x^2 - 8y) = 0?$$

Give a reason for your answer.

31. Prove that the angles α and β in Fig. 8–24 are equal.
32. Prove that the tangent to the parabola $y^2 = 4px$ at $P_1(x_1, y_1)$ intersects the axis of symmetry x_1 units to the left of the vertex. (This provides a simple method for constructing the tangent to a parabola at any point on it.)
33. Show that the area of a parabolic segment of altitude h and base b is $\frac{2}{3}bh$ (see Problem 27).
34. Show that the volume generated by rotating the area bounded by the parabola $y = (4h/b^2)x^2$ and the line $y = h$ about the y-axis is equal to one and one-half times the volume of the corresponding inscribed cone.
35. The condition for equilibrium of the section OP of a cable that supports a weight of w pounds per foot measured along the horizontal (Fig. 8–28) is

$$\frac{dy}{dx} = \frac{wx}{H} \left(= \frac{T \sin \phi}{T \cos \phi} \right),$$

where the origin O is taken at the low point of the cable and H is the horizontal tension at O. Show that the curve in which the cable hangs is a parabola.

36. (*Reflective property of parabolas*) Assume, from optics, that when a ray of light is reflected by a mirror the angle of

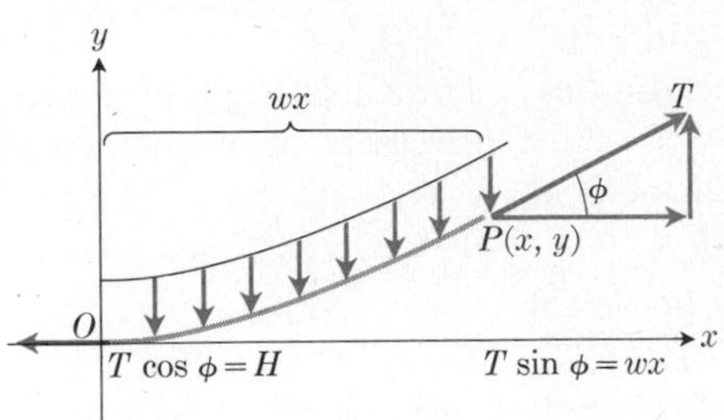

8–28 Diagram of a cable supporting a load of w pounds per horizontal foot.

incidence is equal to the angle of reflection. If a mirror is formed by rotating a parabola about its axis and silvering the resulting surface, show that a ray of light emanating from the focus of the parabola is reflected parallel to the axis.

37. Construct the graph of the parabola with focus $F(2, 2)$ and directrix the line $x + y = 0$.

38. Find the equation of the parabola of Problem 37. [Assume that the distance between a point (x, y) and the line $Ax + By + C = 0$ is $|Ax + By + C|/\sqrt{A^2 + B^2}$.]

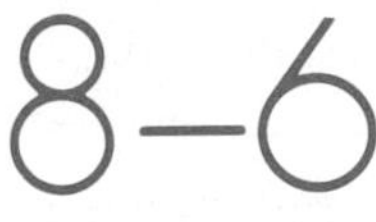

THE ELLIPSE

Definition. *An ellipse is the set of points in a plane whose distances from two fixed points in the plane have a constant sum.*

The Equation of an Ellipse

If the two fixed points, called *foci*, are taken at $F_1(-c, 0)$ and $F_2(c, 0)$ (Fig. 8–29), and the sum of the distances $PF_1 + PF_2$ is denoted by $2a$, then the coordinates of a point $P(x, y)$ on the ellipse must satisfy the equation

$$\sqrt{(x + c)^2 + y^2} + \sqrt{(x - c)^2 + y^2} = 2a.$$

To simplify this expression, we transpose the second radical to the right side of the equation, square, and simplify, to obtain

$$a - \frac{c}{a}x = \sqrt{(x - c)^2 + y^2}.$$

Again we square and simplify, and obtain

$$\frac{x^2}{a^2} + \frac{y^2}{a^2 - c^2} = 1. \tag{1}$$

Since the sum $PF_1 + PF_2 = 2a$ of two sides of the triangle F_1F_2P is greater than the third side $F_1F_2 = 2c$, the term $(a^2 - c^2)$ in (1) is positive and has a real positive square root, which we denote by b:

$$b = \sqrt{a^2 - c^2}. \tag{2}$$

Then (1) takes the more compact form

$$\frac{x^2}{a^2} + \frac{y^2}{b^2} = 1, \tag{3}$$

from which it is readily seen that the curve is symmetric about both axes and lies inside the rectangle bounded by the lines $x = a$, $x = -a$, $y = b$, $y = -b$. The intercepts of the curve are at $(\pm a, 0)$ and $(0, \pm b)$. The curve intersects each axis at an angle of 90°, since

$$\frac{dy}{dx} = \frac{-b^2x}{a^2y}$$

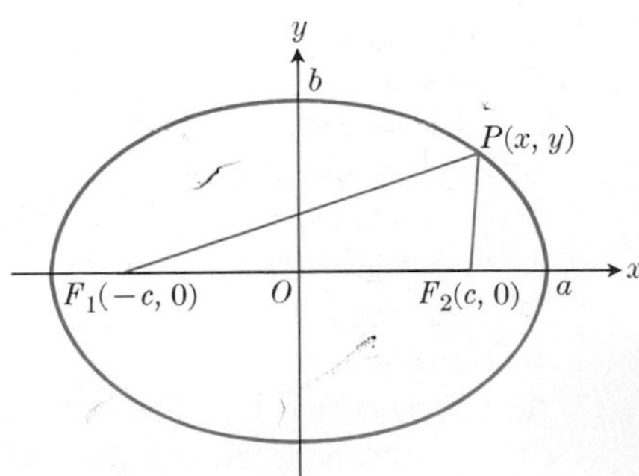

8–29 The ellipse $(x^2/a^2) + (y^2/b^2) = 1$, $a > b$.

is zero at $x = 0$, $y = \pm b$ and is infinite at $y = 0$, $x = \pm a$.

We have shown that the coordinates of P must satisfy (1) if P satisfies the geometric condition $PF_1 + PF_2 = 2a$. Conversely, if x and y satisfy the algebraic equation (1) with $0 < c < a$, then

$$y^2 = (a^2 - c^2)\frac{a^2 - x^2}{a^2},$$

and substituting this in the radicals below, we find that

$$PF_1 = \sqrt{(x + c)^2 + y^2} = \left| a + \frac{c}{a}x \right| \tag{4a}$$

and

$$PF_2 = \sqrt{(x - c)^2 + y^2} = \left| a - \frac{c}{a}x \right|. \tag{4b}$$

Since x is restricted to the range $-a \le x \le a$, the value of $(c/a)x$ lies between $-c$ and c, so that both $a + (c/a)x$ and $a - (c/a)x$ are positive, both being between $a + c$ and $a - c$. Hence the absolute values in (4a) and (4b) yield

$$PF_1 = a + \frac{c}{a}x, \qquad PF_2 = a - \frac{c}{a}x, \tag{5}$$

and, adding these, we see that $PF_1 + PF_2$ has a value $2a$ independent of the position of P on the curve. Thus the *geometric property* and *algebraic equation* are equivalent.

In Eq. (3), $b^2 = a^2 - c^2$ is less than a^2. The *major axis* of the ellipse is the segment of length $2a$ between the x-intercepts $(\pm a, 0)$. The *minor axis* is the segment of length $2b$ between the y-intercepts $(0, \pm b)$. The numbers a and b are also referred to respectively as *semimajor axis* and *semiminor axis*. If these semiaxes are $a = 4$, $b = 3$, then Eq. (3) is

$$\frac{x^2}{16} + \frac{y^2}{9} = 1. \tag{6a}$$

On the other hand, if we interchange the roles of x and y in (6a), we get the equation

$$\frac{x^2}{9} + \frac{y^2}{16} = 1, \tag{6b}$$

which must also represent an ellipse, but one with its major axis vertical rather than horizontal. Graphs of Eqs. (6a) and (6b) are given in Fig. 8–30 (a) and (b).

There is never any need for confusion in analyzing equations like (6a) and (6b). We simply find the intercepts on the axes of symmetry; then we know which way the major axis runs. The foci are always on the major axis. And if we use the letters a, b, and c to represent the lengths of semimajor axis, semiminor axis, and half-distance between foci, then Eq. (2) tells us that

$$b^2 = a^2 - c^2$$

or

$$a^2 = b^2 + c^2. \tag{7}$$

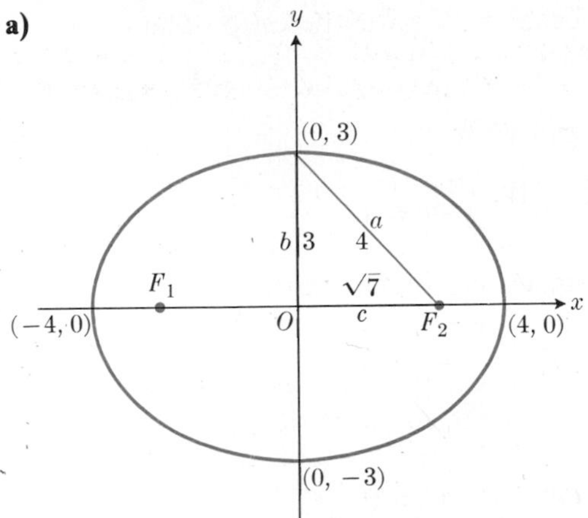

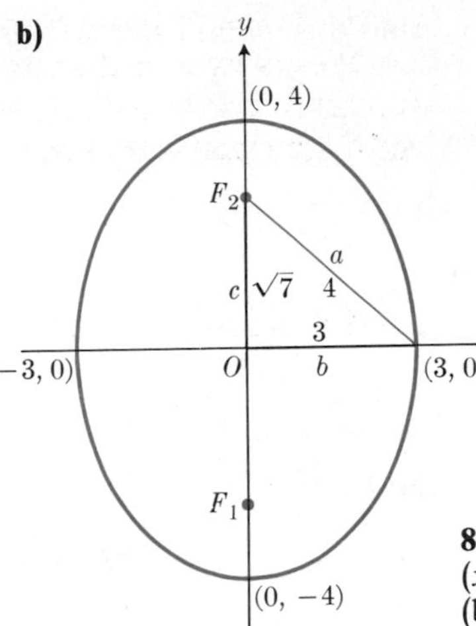

8–30 (a) The major axis of $(x^2/16) + (y^2/9) = 1$ is horizontal. (b) The major axis of $(x^2/9) + (y^2/16) = 1$ is vertical.

Hence a is the hypotenuse of a right triangle of sides b and c, as in Fig. 8–30. When we start with an equation like (6a) or (6b), we can read off a^2 and b^2 from it at once. Then Eq. (7) determines c^2 as their difference. So in either of Eqs. (6a) and (6b) we have

$$c^2 = 16 - 9 = 7.$$

Therefore the foci are $\sqrt{7}$ units from the center of the ellipse as shown.

Center not at the Origin

The *center* of an ellipse is defined as the point of intersection of its axes of symmetry. If the center is at $C(h, k)$, and the axes of the ellipse are parallel to the x- and y-axes, then we may introduce new coordinates

$$x' = x - h, \qquad y' = y - k, \tag{8}$$

using C as origin O' of $x'y'$-coordinates. The equation of the ellipse in the new coordinates is either

$$\frac{x'^2}{a^2} + \frac{y'^2}{b^2} = 1 \tag{9a}$$

or

$$\frac{x'^2}{b^2} + \frac{y'^2}{a^2} = 1, \tag{9b}$$

depending upon which way the major axis runs.

EXAMPLE 1. Analyze the equation $9x^2 + 4y^2 + 36x - 8y + 4 = 0$.

Solution. In order to complete the squares, we collect the x terms and the y terms separately, thus

$$9(x^2 + 4x) + 4(y^2 - 2y) = -4,$$

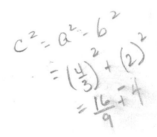

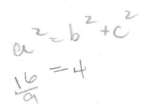

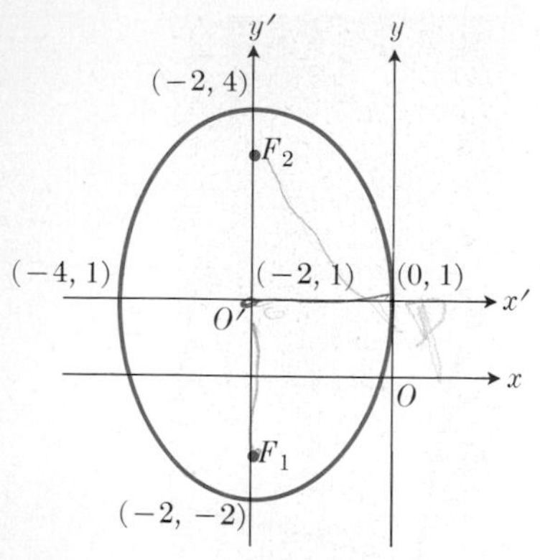

8–31 The ellipse $9x^2 + 4y^2 + 36x - 8y + 4 = 0$.

and then complete the square in each set of parentheses to obtain

$$9(x^2 + 4x + 4) + 4(y^2 - 2y + 1) = -4 + 36 + 4.$$

We now divide both sides by 36 and write

$$\frac{(x+2)^2}{4} + \frac{(y-1)^2}{9} = 1.$$

Setting

$$x' = x + 2, \qquad y' = y - 1,$$

we see that the new origin $x' = 0$, $y' = 0$, is the same as the point $x = -2$, $y = 1$. In terms of the new coordinates, the equation is

$$\frac{x'^2}{4} + \frac{y'^2}{9} = 1,$$

which represents an ellipse with intercepts at $(0, \pm 3)$ on the y'-axis and $(\pm 2, 0)$ on the x'-axis (Fig. 8–31). To locate the foci, we use the relation

$$b = \sqrt{a^2 - c^2}$$

to find

$$c = \sqrt{a^2 - b^2}.$$

Here

$$a^2 = 9, \qquad b^2 = 4,$$

so

$$c = \sqrt{5}.$$

The foci are at the points $(0, \pm\sqrt{5})$ on the y'-axis or at $(-2, 1 \pm \sqrt{5})$ in terms of the original coordinates.

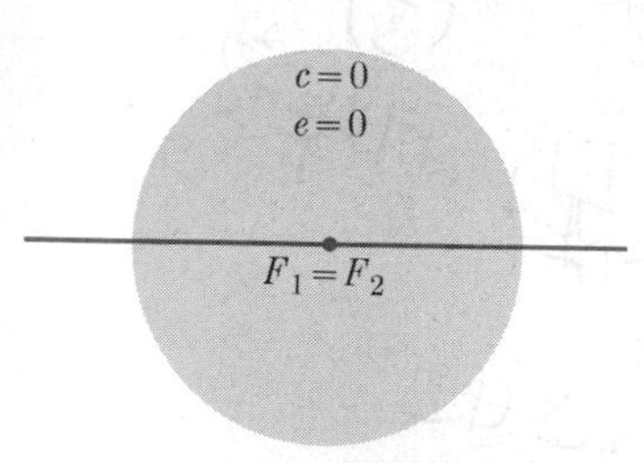

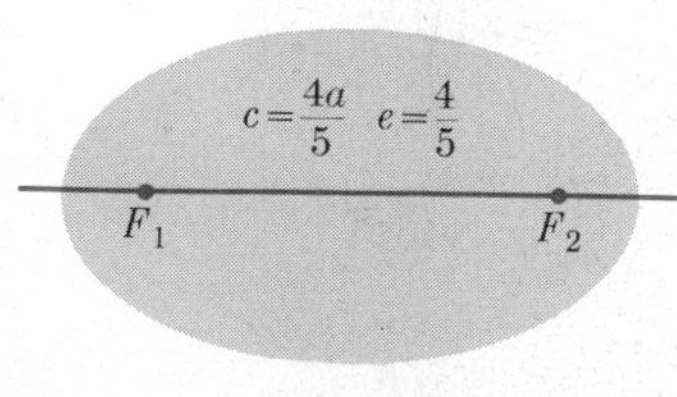

F1 c=a F2
e=1

8–32 The eccentricity of an ellipse describes its shape.

We recall (Fig. 8–29) that the essential *geometric* property of an ellipse is that the sum of the distances from any point on it to the two foci is a constant, namely,

$$PF_1 + PF_2 = 2a.$$

The essential *algebraic* property of its equation, when written in the form of a quadratic without a cross-product term, is that the x^2 and y^2 terms have the same sign.

In order to discuss the properties of the ellipse in more detail, we shall assume that its equation has been reduced to the form

$$\frac{x^2}{a^2} + \frac{y^2}{b^2} = 1, \qquad a > b > 0. \tag{10}$$

Although the distance c from the center of the ellipse to a focus does not appear in its equation, we may still determine c as in the examples above from the equation

$$c^2 = a^2 - b^2, \tag{11}$$

which simply comes from rewriting Eq. (7).

Eccentricity

If we keep a fixed and vary c over the range $0 \leq c \leq a$, the resulting ellipses will vary in shape. They are circular when $c = 0$ (so that $a = b$), and become flatter as c increases, until in the extreme case $c = a$, the "ellipse" reduces to the line segment F_1F_2 joining the two foci (Fig. 8–32). The ratio

$$e = \frac{c}{a}, \tag{12}$$

called the *eccentricity* of the ellipse, varies from 0 to 1 and indicates the degree of departure from circularity.

The planets in the solar system revolve around the sun in elliptical orbits with the sun at one focus. Most of the planets, including the earth, have orbits that are nearly circular, as can be seen from the eccentricities in Table 8–1. Pluto, however, has a fairly eccentric orbit, with $e = 0.25$, as does Mercury, with $e = 0.21$. Other members of the solar system have orbits that are even more eccentric. Icarus, an asteroid about one mile wide that revolves around the sun every 409 earth days, has an orbital eccentricity of 0.83 (Fig. 8–33).

Table 8–1. Eccentricities of planetary orbits

Mercury	0.21	Saturn	0.06
Venus	0.01	Uranus	0.05
Earth	0.02	Neptune	0.01
Mars	0.09	Pluto	0.25
Jupiter	0.05		

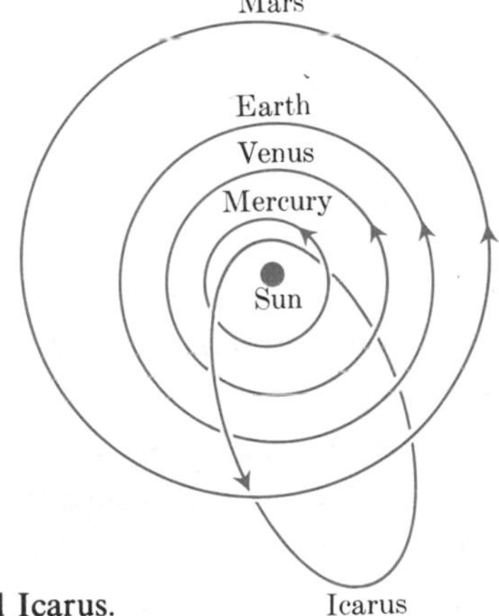

8–33 The orbit of the asteroid Icarus.

EXAMPLE 2. The dimensions of the orbit of the comet Kohoutek (Fig. 8–34) are approximately 44 astronomical units wide by 3,600 astronomical units long. (One astronomical unit (AU) is the earth's mean distance from the sun, about 92,600,000 miles.) Find the eccentricity of the orbit.

Solution

$$e = \frac{\sqrt{a^2 - b^2}}{a} = \frac{\sqrt{(1800)^2 - (22)^2}}{1800} \approx 0.99993.$$

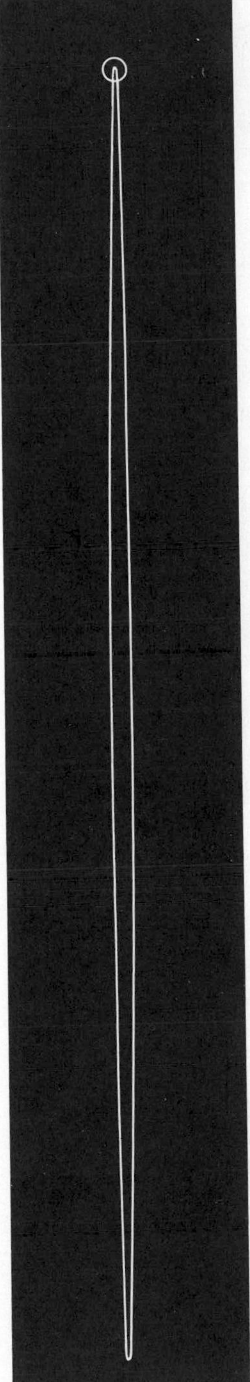

8–34 The orbit of Comet Kohoutek, shown approximately to scale. The small circle shows the outer limit of the orbit of Pluto.

We recall that a parabola has one focus and one directrix. Each ellipse has two foci and two directrices. The directrices are lines perpendicular to the major axis of the ellipse at distances $\pm a/e$ from its center. The *parabola* has the property that

$$PF = 1 \cdot PD \tag{13}$$

for any point P on it, where F is the focus and D is the point nearest P on the directrix. For an *ellipse*, it is not difficult to show that the equations which take the place of (13) are

$$PF_1 = e \cdot PD_1, \qquad PF_2 = e \cdot PD_2. \tag{14}$$

Here e is the eccentricity, P is any point on the ellipse, F_1 and F_2 are the foci, and D_1 and D_2 are the points nearest P on the two directrices. In Eq. (14), the corresponding directrix and focus must be used; that is, if one uses the distance from P to the focus F_1, one must also use the distance from P to the directrix at the same end of the ellipse (see Fig. 8–35). We thus associate the directrix $x = -a/e$ with the focus $F_1(-c, 0)$, and the directrix $x = a/e$ with the focus $F_2(c, 0)$. In terms of the semimajor axis a and eccentricity $e < 1$, as one goes away from the center along the major axis, one finds successively

a *focus* at distance ae from the center,

a *vertex* at distance a from the center,

a *directrix* at distance a/e from the center.

The "focus-and-directrix" property furnishes a common bond uniting the parabola, ellipse, and hyperbola. Namely, if a point $P(x, y)$ is such that its distance PF from a fixed point (the focus) is proportional to its distance PD from a fixed line (the directrix), that is, so that

$$PF = e \cdot PD, \tag{15}$$

where e is a constant of proportionality, then the locus of P is

a) a *parabola* if $e = 1$,
b) an *ellipse* of eccentricity e if $e < 1$, and
c) a *hyperbola* of eccentricity e if $e > 1$.

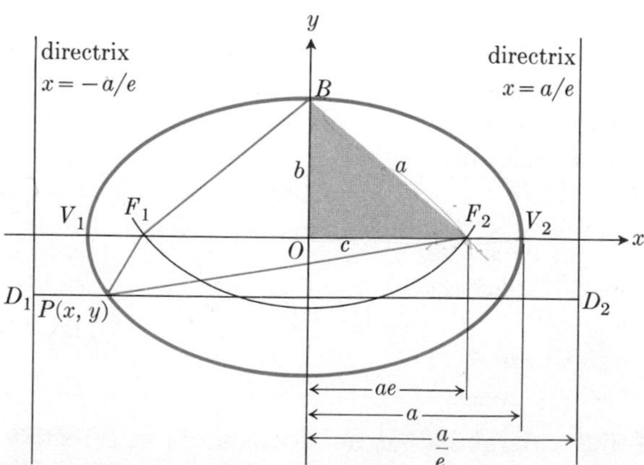

8–35 The ellipse $(x^2/a^2) + (y^2/b^2) = c^2$.

Constructions

There are several ways to construct an ellipse. One of these uses the definition directly. The two ends of a string of length $2a$ are held fixed at the foci F_1 and F_2 and a pencil traces the curve as it is held taut against the string (see Fig. 8–36).

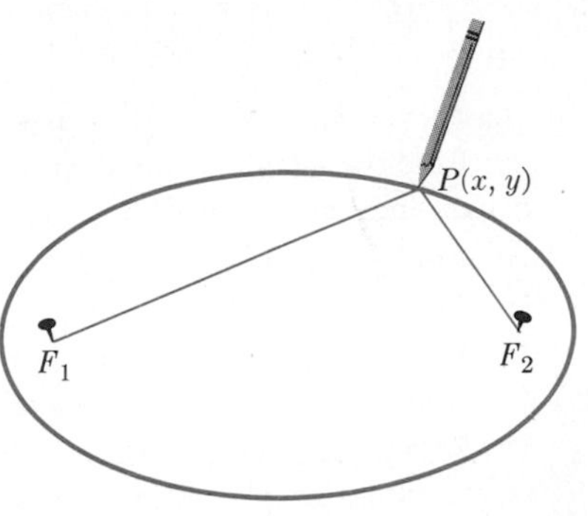

8–36 $PF_1 + PF_2 = 2a$.

A second method uses a straightedge AB of length $a + b$. Place point A on the y-axis and B on the x-axis, and on the graph paper, make a dot at $P(x, y)$ at distance a from A (see Fig. 8–37). In terms of the angle θ that line AB makes with the (negative) x-axis, we have

$$x = a \cos \theta, \qquad y = b \sin \theta, \tag{16}$$

and hence

$$\frac{x^2}{a^2} + \frac{y^2}{b^2} = \cos^2 \theta + \sin^2 \theta = 1.$$

Therefore $P(x, y)$ is on the ellipse, Eq. (10).

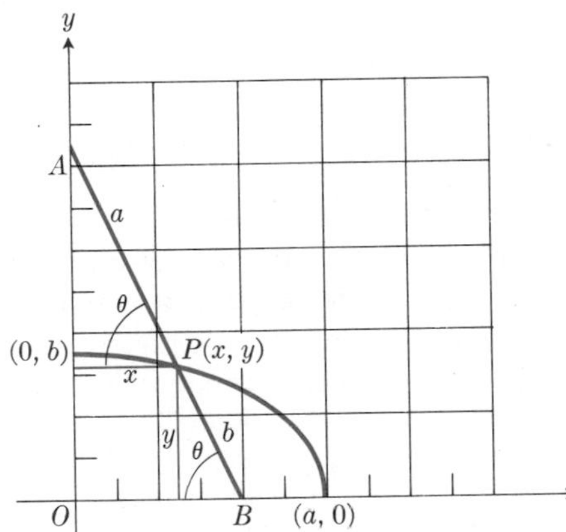

8–37 As B moves out from the origin, and A slides downward, the point P traces out part of an ellipse.

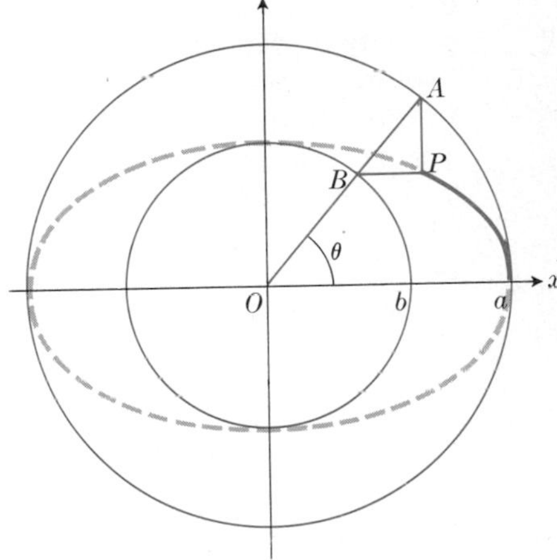

8–38 As θ increases from 0 to 2π, the point P at the intersection of the vertical line through A and the horizontal line through B traces out an ellipse.

A third method is to construct two concentric circles of radii a and b (Fig. 8–38). A line making an angle θ with the horizontal is drawn from the center cutting the two circles in points A and B respectively. The vertical line through A and the horizontal line through B intersect in a point P whose coordinates also satisfy (16). By varying the angle θ from 0 to 2π, we may obtain as many points on the ellipse as we desire.

PROBLEMS

In each of the following problems (1 through 5), find the equation of an ellipse having the given center C, focus F, and semimajor axis a. Sketch the graph and give the eccentricity of each ellipse.

1. $C(0, 0)$, $F(0, 2)$, $a = 4$

2. $C(0, 0)$, $F(-3, 0)$, $a = 5$

3. $C(0, 2)$, $F(0, 0)$, $a = 3$

4. $C(-3, 0)$, $F(-3, -2)$, $a = 4$

5. $C(2, 2)$, $F(-1, 2)$, $a = \sqrt{10}$

6. The endpoints of the major and minor axes of an ellipse are $(1, 1)$, $(3, 4)$, $(1, 7)$, and $(-1, 4)$. Sketch the ellipse, give its equation, and find its foci.

7. Find the center, vertices, and foci of the ellipse

$$25x^2 + 9y^2 - 100x + 54y - 44 = 0.$$

Sketch the curve.

8. Sketch each of the following ellipses:

a) $9x^2 + 4y^2 = 36$ **b)** $4x^2 + 9y^2 = 144$

c) $\dfrac{(x-1)^2}{16} + \dfrac{(y+2)^2}{4} = 1$

d) $4x^2 + y^2 = 1$

e) $16(x-2)^2 + 9(y+3)^2 = 144$

9. Find the equation of the ellipse that passes through the origin and has foci at $(-1, 1)$ and $(1, 1)$.

10. Find the eccentricity and the directrices of the ellipse $(x^2/7) + (y^2/16) = 1$.

11. Find the volume generated by rotating an ellipse of semi-axes a and b $(a > b)$ about its major axis.

12. Set up the integrals that give (a) the area of a quadrant of the circle $x^2 + y^2 = a^2$, (b) the area of a quadrant of the ellipse $b^2x^2 + a^2y^2 = a^2b^2$. Show that the integral in (b) is b/a times the integral in (a), and deduce the area of the ellipse from the known area of the circle.

13. (*Reflective property of ellipses*) An ellipsoid is generated by rotating an ellipse about its major axis. The inside surface of the ellipsoid is silvered to produce a mirror. Show that a ray of light emanating from one focus will be reflected to the other focus. (Sound waves also follow such paths, and this property of ellipsoids accounts for phenomena in certain "whispering galleries.")

14. Find the length of the chord perpendicular to the major axis of the ellipse $b^2x^2 + a^2y^2 = a^2b^2$ and passing through a focus. (This chord is called the "latus rectum" of the ellipse.)

15. Find the equation of an ellipse of eccentricity $\frac{2}{3}$ if the line $x = 9$ is one directrix and the corresponding focus is at $(4, 0)$.

16. Find the values of the constants A, B, and C if the ellipse

$$4x^2 + y^2 + Ax + By + C = 0$$

is to be tangent to the x-axis at the origin and to pass through the point $(-1, 2)$.

17. Show that the line tangent to the ellipse $(x^2/a^2) + (y^2/b^2) = 1$ at the point $P_1(x_1, y_1)$ on it is

$$\frac{xx_1}{a^2} + \frac{yy_1}{b^2} = 1.$$

In Problems 18–20, graph the sets of points whose coordinates satisfy the given inequality or equation.

18. $9x^2 + 16y^2 < 144$.

19. $(x^2+4y)(2x-y-3)(x^2+y^2-25)(x^2+4y^2-4)=0$.

20. $(x^2 + y^2 - 1)(9x^2 + 4y^2 - 36) < 0$.

21. Draw an ellipse of eccentricity $\frac{4}{5}$.

22. Draw the orbit of Pluto to scale.

23. (*Calculator*) The orbit of Halley's Comet (expected to return in 1986) is about 9.12 AU wide and 36.18 AU long. Find its eccentricity. (See Example 2.)

24. (*Calculator*) The equations $x = a \cos \theta$, $y = b \sin \theta$, $0 \le \theta \le 2\pi$, are parametric equations for an ellipse.

a) Show that $(x^2/a^2) + (y^2/b^2) = 1$.

b) Show that the total length (perimeter) of the ellipse is

$$4a \int_0^{\pi/2} \sqrt{1 - e^2 \cos^2 \theta}\, d\theta,$$

where e is the eccentricity of the ellipse.

c) The integral in (b) is called an *elliptic integral*. It has no elementary antiderivative. Estimate the length of the ellipse when $a = 1$ and $e = \frac{1}{2}$ by the trapezoidal rule with $n = 10$.

d) The absolute value of the second derivative of $f(\theta) = \sqrt{1 - e^2 \cos^2 \theta}$ is less than one. Based on this, what estimate does Eq. (3), Article 4–9, give of the error in the approximation in (c)?

25. Problem 39, Article 6–1, considered a rope with a ring at one end looped over two pegs in a horizontal line. The free end of the rope passed through the ring to a weight that pulled the rope taut. It was assumed that the rope, which slipped freely over the pegs and through the ring, would come to rest in a configuration symmetric with respect to the line of the vertical part of the rope.

a) Show that for each fixed position of the ring on the rope the possible locations of the ring in space lie on an ellipse with foci at the pegs.

b) Justify the original symmetry assumption by combining the result in (a) with the assumption that the rope and weight will take a rest position of minimal potential energy.

8–7 THE HYPERBOLA

Definition. *A hyperbola is the set of points in a plane whose distances from two fixed points in the plane have a constant difference.*

The Equation of a Hyperbola

If we take the two fixed points, called *foci*, at $F_1(-c, 0)$ and $F_2(c, 0)$ and the constant equal to $2a$ (see Fig. 8–39), then a point $P(x, y)$ lies on the hyperbola if and only if

$$\sqrt{(x+c)^2+y^2}-\sqrt{(x-c)^2+y^2}=2a$$

or

$$\sqrt{(x-c)^2+y^2}-\sqrt{(x+c)^2+y^2}=2a.$$

The second equation is like the first, with $2a$ replaced by $-2a$. Hence we write the first one with $\pm 2a$, transpose one radical to the right side of the equation, square, and simplify. One radical still remains. We isolate it and square again. We then obtain the equation

$$\frac{x^2}{a^2}+\frac{y^2}{a^2-c^2}=1. \tag{1}$$

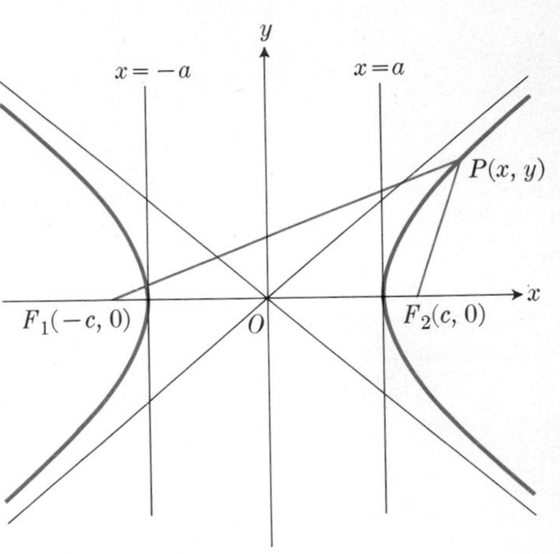

8–39 $PF_1 - PF_2 = 2a$.

So far, this is just like the equation for an ellipse. But now $a^2 - c^2$ is negative, because the *difference* in two sides of the triangle F_1F_2P is less than the third side:

$$2a < 2c.$$

So in this case $c^2 - a^2$ is positive and has a real positive square root, which we call b:

$$b=\sqrt{c^2-a^2}, \tag{2a}$$

or

$$a^2-c^2=-b^2. \tag{2b}$$

The equation of the hyperbola now becomes

$$\frac{x^2}{a^2}-\frac{y^2}{b^2}=1, \tag{3}$$

which is analogous to the equation of an ellipse. The only differences are the minus sign in the equation of the hyperbola, and the new relation among a, b, and c given by Eq. (2b). The hyperbola, like the ellipse, is symmetric with respect to both axes and the origin, but it has no real y-intercepts and in fact no portion of the curve lies between the lines $x = a$ and $x = -a$.

If we start with a point $P(x, y)$ whose coordinates satisfy Eq. (3), the distances PF_1 and PF_2 will be given by

$$PF_1=\sqrt{(x+c)^2+y^2}=\left|a+\frac{c}{a}x\right|, \tag{4a}$$

$$PF_2=\sqrt{(x-c)^2+y^2}=\left|a-\frac{c}{a}x\right|, \tag{4b}$$

as for the ellipse. But now c is greater than a, and P is either to the right of the line $x = a$, that is

$$x > a,$$

or else P is to the left of the line $x = -a$, and then

$$x < -a.$$

The absolute values in Eqs. (4) work out to be

$$\left.\begin{aligned} PF_1 &= a + \frac{c}{a}x \\ PF_2 &= \frac{c}{a}x - a \end{aligned}\right\} \text{ if } x > a \tag{5a}$$

and

$$\left.\begin{aligned} PF_1 &= -\left(a + \frac{c}{a}x\right) \\ PF_2 &= a - \frac{c}{a}x \end{aligned}\right\} \text{ if } x < -a. \tag{5b}$$

Thus, when P is to the right of the line $x = a$, the condition $PF_1 - PF_2 = 2a$ is satisfied, while if P is to the left of $x = -a$, the condition $PF_2 - PF_1 = 2a$ is fulfilled (Fig. 8–39). In either case, *any point P that satisfies the geometric conditions must satisfy Eq.* (3). *Conversely, any point that satisfies Eq.* (3) *also satisfies the geometric conditions.*

Asymptotes

The left side of (3) can be factored and the equation written in the form

$$\left(\frac{x}{a} - \frac{y}{b}\right)\left(\frac{x}{a} + \frac{y}{b}\right) = 1$$

or

$$\frac{x}{a} - \frac{y}{b} = \frac{ab}{bx + ay}. \tag{6a}$$

Analysis of (3) shows that one branch of the curve lies in the first quadrant and has infinite extent. If the point P moves along this branch so that x and y both become infinite, then the right side of (6a) tends to zero; hence the left side must do likewise. That is

$$\lim_{\substack{x \to \infty \\ y \to \infty}} \left(\frac{x}{a} - \frac{y}{b}\right) = 0, \tag{6b}$$

which leads us to speculate that the straight line

$$\frac{x}{a} - \frac{y}{b} = 0 \tag{7a}$$

may be an asymptote of the curve. To see that this is definitely so, we investigate the vertical distance $(y_2 - y_1)$ between the curve and the line where we take

$$y_2 = \frac{b}{a}x$$

on the line, and

$$y_1 = \frac{b}{a}\sqrt{x^2 - a^2}$$

on the curve (Fig. 8–40). We then multiply both sides of Eq. (6b) by b, and see that

$$\lim_{x\to\infty} (y_2 - y_1) = 0.$$

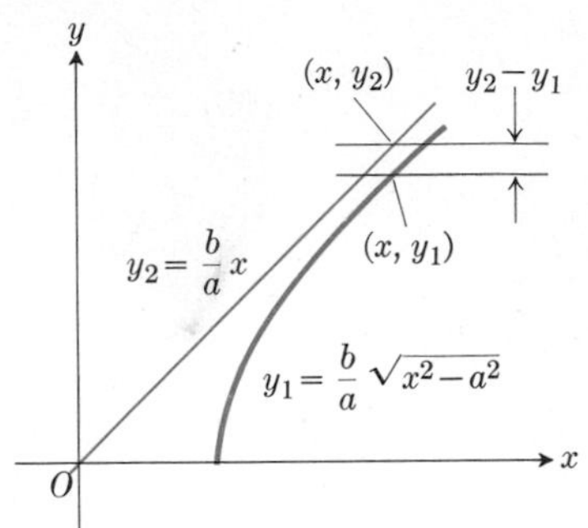

8–40 As $x \to \infty$, the point (x, y_1) rises on the hyperbola toward the asymptote $y_2 = (b/a)x$.

Since this vertical distance tends to zero, certainly the perpendicular distance from the line to the curve also approaches zero, and the line in Eq. (7a) is an asymptote of the hyperbola.

By symmetry, the line

$$\frac{x}{a} + \frac{y}{b} = 0 \tag{7b}$$

is also an asymptote of the hyperbola. Both asymptotes may be obtained by replacing the "one" on the right side of (3) by a zero and then factoring. In sketching a hyperbola (Fig. 8–41), it is convenient to mark off distances a to the right and to the left of the origin along the x-axis and distances b above and below the origin along the y-axis, and to construct a rectangle whose sides pass through these points, parallel to the coordinate axes. The diagonals of this rectangle, extended, are the asymptotes of the hyperbola. The semidiagonal

$$c = \sqrt{a^2 + b^2}$$

can also be used as the radius of a circle that will cut the x-axis in two points, $F_1(-c, 0)$ and $F_2(c, 0)$, which are the foci of the hyperbola.

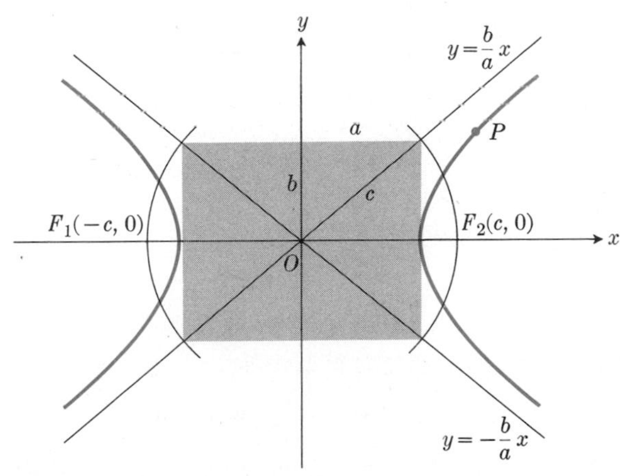

8–41 The hyperbola $(x^2/a^2) - (y^2/b^2) = 1$.

If we interchange x and y in Eq. (3), the new equation

$$\frac{y^2}{a^2} - \frac{x^2}{b^2} = 1 \tag{8}$$

represents a hyperbola with foci on the y-axis. Its graph is shown in Fig. 8–42.

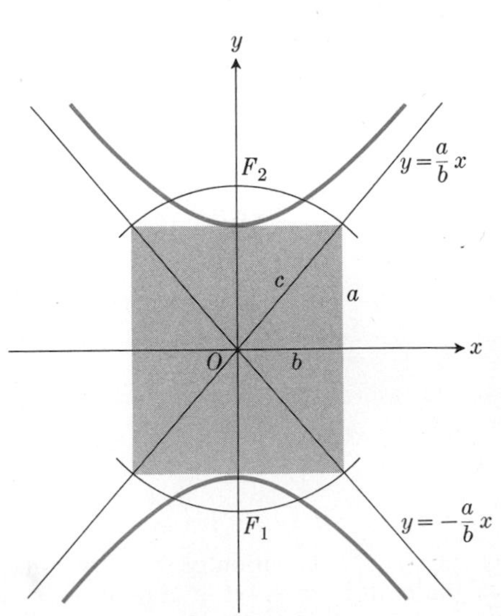

8–42 The hyperbola $(y^2/a^2) - (x^2/b^2) = 1$.

Center not at the Origin

The *center* of a hyperbola is the point of intersection of its axes of symmetry. If the center is $C(h, k)$, we may introduce a translation to new coordinates

$$x' = x - h, \qquad y' = y - k \tag{9}$$

with origin O' at the center. In terms of the new coordinates, the equation of the hyperbola is either

$$\frac{x'^2}{a^2} - \frac{y'^2}{b^2} = 1 \tag{10a}$$

or

$$\frac{y'^2}{a^2} - \frac{x'^2}{b^2} = 1. \tag{10b}$$

EXAMPLE 1. Analyze the equation $x^2 - 4y^2 + 2x + 8y - 7 = 0$.

Solution. We complete the squares in the x and y terms separately and reduce to standard form:

$$(x^2 + 2x) - 4(y^2 - 2y) = 7,$$
$$(x^2 + 2x + 1) - 4(y^2 - 2y + 1) = 7 + 1 - 4,$$
$$\frac{(x + 1)^2}{4} - (y - 1)^2 = 1.$$

The translation of axes

$$x' = x + 1, \qquad y' = y - 1$$

reduces the equation to

$$\frac{x'^2}{4} - \frac{y'^2}{1} = 1,$$

which represents a hyperbola with center at $x' = 0$, $y' = 0$, or $x = -1$, $y = 1$, having

$$a^2 = 4, \qquad b^2 = 1, \qquad c^2 = a^2 + b^2 = 5$$

and asymptotes

$$\frac{x'}{2} - y' = 0, \qquad \frac{x'}{2} + y' = 0.$$

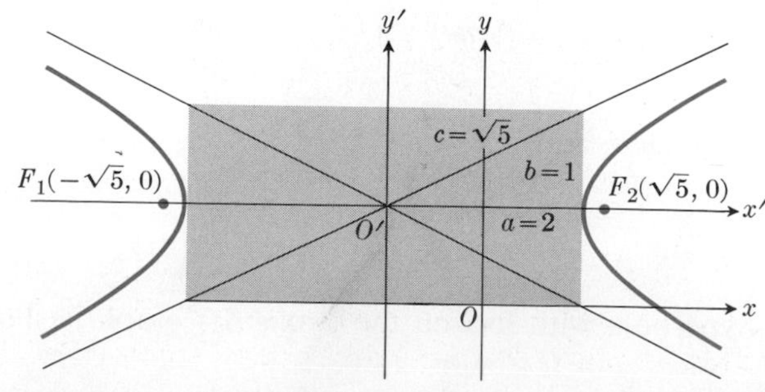

8–43 The xy-equation of the hyperbola shown to the right is $x^2 - 4y^2 + 2x + 8y - 7 = 0$. The $x'y'$-equation is $(x'^2/4) - (y'^2/1) = 1$.

The foci have coordinates $(\pm\sqrt{5}, 0)$ relative to the new axes or, since

$$x = x' - 1, \qquad y = y' + 1,$$

the coordinates relative to the original axes are $(-1 \pm \sqrt{5}, 1)$. The curve is sketched in Fig. 8–43.

EXAMPLE 2

$$x^2 - 4y^2 - 2x + 8y - 2 = 0.$$

Proceeding as before, we obtain

$$(x-1)^2 - 4(y-1)^2 = 2 + 1 - 4 = -1.$$

The standard form requires a plus one on the right side of the equation, so we change signs and have

$$4(y-1)^2 - (x-1)^2 = 1.$$

Comparison with (10) indicates that we should write the first term of this equation as $(y-1)^2$ divided by 0.25:

$$\frac{(y-1)^2}{0.25} - \frac{(x-1)^2}{1} = 1.$$

The translation $x' = x - 1$, $y' = y - 1$ replaces this by

$$\frac{y'^2}{0.25} - \frac{x'^2}{1} = 1,$$

which represents a hyperbola with center at $x' = y' = 0$, or $x = y = 1$. The curve has intercepts at $(0, \pm 0.5)$ on the y'-axis but does not cross the x'-axis. Here (10b) applies, with

$$a^2 = 0.25, \qquad b^2 = 1, \qquad c^2 = a^2 + b^2 = 1.25.$$

The lines (Fig. 8–44)

$$\frac{y'}{0.5} - x' = 0, \qquad \frac{y'}{0.5} + x' = 0$$

are the asymptotes, while the foci are at $(0, \pm\sqrt{1.25})$ on the y'-axis.

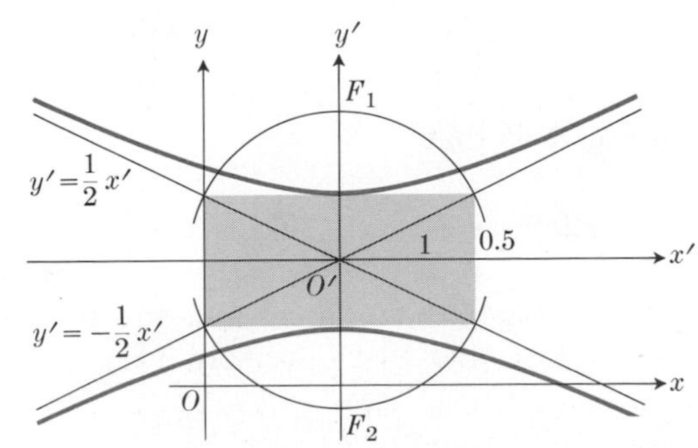

8–44 The hyperbola $(y'^2/0.25) - (x'^2/1) = 1$.

There is no restriction $a > b$ for the hyperbola as there is for the ellipse, and the direction in which the hyperbola opens is controlled by the *signs* rather than by the relative *sizes* of the coefficients of the quadratic terms.

In our further discussion of the hyperbola, we shall assume that it has been referred to axes through its center and that its equation has the form

$$\frac{x^2}{a^2} - \frac{y^2}{b^2} = 1. \tag{11}$$

Then

$$b = \sqrt{c^2 - a^2}$$

and

$$c^2 = a^2 + b^2. \tag{12}$$

As for the ellipse, we define the *eccentricity* e to be

$$e = \frac{c}{a}.$$

Since $c \geq a$, the eccentricity of a hyperbola is never less than one. The lines

$$x = \frac{a}{e}, \qquad x = -\frac{a}{e}$$

are the *directrices.*

We shall now verify that a point $P(x, y)$ whose coordinates satisfy Eq. (11) also has the property that

$$PF_1 = e \cdot PD_1 \tag{13a}$$

and

$$PF_2 = e \cdot PD_2, \tag{13b}$$

where $F_1(-c, 0)$ and $F_2(c, 0)$ are the foci while $D_1(-a/e, y)$ and $D_2(a/e, y)$ are the points nearest P on the directrices.

We shall content ourselves with establishing the results (13a, b) for any point P on the right branch of the hyperbola; the method is the same when P is on the left branch. Reference to Eqs. (5a) then shows that

$$\begin{aligned} PF_1 &= \frac{c}{a}x + a = e\left(x + \frac{a}{e}\right), \\ PF_2 &= \frac{c}{a}x - a = e\left(x - \frac{a}{e}\right), \end{aligned} \tag{14a}$$

while we see from Fig. 8–45 that

$$PD_1 = x + \frac{a}{e}, \qquad PD_2 = x - \frac{a}{e}. \tag{14b}$$

These results combine to establish the "focus-and-directrix" properties of the hyperbola expressed in Eqs. (13a, b). Conversely, if Eqs. (14a) are satisfied, it is also true that

$$PF_1 - PF_2 = 2a;$$

that is, P satisfies the requirement that the difference of its distances from the two foci is constant.

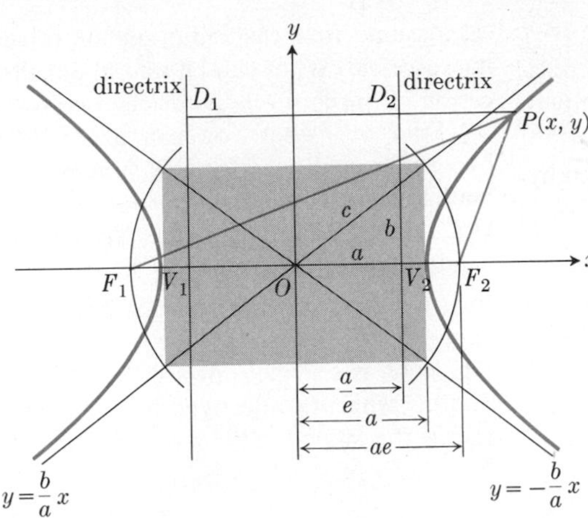

8–45 $PF_1 = e \cdot PD_1$ and $PF_2 = e \cdot PD_2$.

Construction

There are various schemes for sketching hyperbolas. One of them (see Fig. 8–46) exploits the equation

$$PF_1 = 2a + PF_2$$

as follows: Construct a circle of radius r centered at F_2 and a circle of radius $(2a + r)$ centered at F_1. The points P, P', where the two circles cross, are points on the hyperbola. By varying r, we may obtain as many points on the hyperbola as desired. Interchanging the roles of the two foci F_1 and F_2 will give points on the other branch.

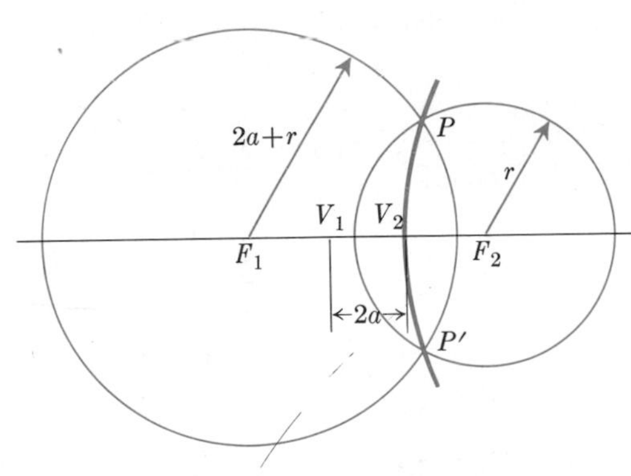

8–46 The points P and P' are on the hyperbola $PF_1 = 2a + PF_2$.

PROBLEMS

1. Sketch each of the following hyperbolas:

a) $\frac{x^2}{9} - \frac{y^2}{16} = 1,$ b) $\frac{x^2}{16} - \frac{y^2}{9} = 1,$

c) $\frac{y^2}{9} - \frac{x^2}{16} = 1,$ d) $\frac{x^2}{9} - \frac{y^2}{16} = -1.$

In each of the following problems (2 through 8), find the center, vertices, foci, and asymptotes of the given hyperbola. Sketch the curve.

2. $9(x - 2)^2 - 4(y + 3)^2 = 36$
3. $4(x - 2)^2 - 9(y + 3)^2 = 36$
4. $4(y + 3)^2 - 9(x - 2)^2 = 1$
5. $5x^2 - 4y^2 + 20x + 8y = 4$
6. $4x^2 = y^2 - 4y + 8$
7. $4y^2 = x^2 - 4x$

8. $4x^2 - 5y^2 - 16x + 10y + 31 = 0$

9. Show that the line tangent to the hyperbola $b^2x^2 - a^2y^2 = a^2b^2$ at a point $P(x_1, y_1)$ on it has an equation that may be written in the form $b^2xx_1 - a^2yy_1 = a^2b^2$.

10. Find the volume generated when the area bounded by the hyperbola $b^2x^2 - a^2y^2 = a^2b^2$ and the line $x = c$, through its focus $(c, 0)$, is rotated about the y-axis.

11. Show that the equation

$$\frac{x^2}{9 - C} + \frac{y^2}{5 - C} = 1$$

represents (a) an ellipse if C is any constant less than 5, (b) a hyperbola if C is any constant between 5 and 9, (c) no real locus if C is greater than 9. Show that each ellipse in (a) and each hyperbola in (b) has foci at the two points $(\pm 2, 0)$, independent of the value of C.

12. Find the equation of the hyperbola with foci at (0, 0) and (0, 4) if it is required to pass through the point (12, 9).

13. One focus of a hyperbola is located at the point $(1, -3)$ and the corresponding directrix is the line $y = 2$. Find the equation of the hyperbola if its eccentricity is $\frac{3}{2}$.

14. Find out what you can about the DECCA system of air navigation. [See *Time*, Feb. 23, 1959, p. 87, or the reference in Problem 15.]

15. A radio signal was sent simultaneously from towers A and B located several hundred miles apart on the California coast. A ship offshore received the signal from A 1400 microseconds before it received the signal from B.

a) Assume that the radio signals traveled at 980 ft per microsecond. What can be said about the approximate location of the ship relative to the two towers?

b) Find out what you can about LORAN and other hyperbolic radio-navigation systems. [See, for example, Nathaniel Bowditch's *American Practical Navigator*, Vol. I, U.S. Defense Mapping Agency Hydrographic Center, Publication No. 9, 1977, Chapter XLIII.]

16. (*Reflective property of hyperbolas*) Show that a ray of light directed toward one focus of a hyperbolic mirror, as in Fig. 8–47, is reflected toward the other focus. [*Hint.* Show that the tangent to the hyperbola at the point P in Fig. 8–47 bisects the angle made by the segments PF_1 and PF_2.]

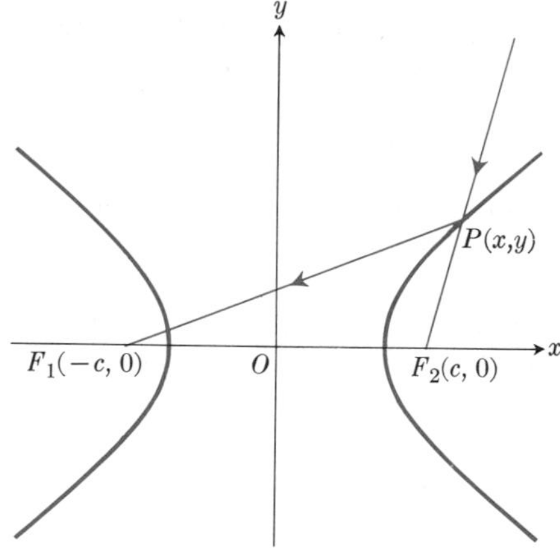

8–47 Reflective property of hyperbolas.

SECOND DEGREE CURVES

The equations of the circle, parabola, ellipse, and hyperbola are special cases of the general second degree equation

$$Ax^2 + Bxy + Cy^2 + Dx + Ey + F = 0, \tag{1}$$

in which the coefficients A, B, and C are not all zero. For example, the circle

$$(x - h)^2 + (y - k)^2 = r^2$$

may be obtained from Eq. (1) by taking

$$A = C = 1, \quad B = 0, \quad D = -2h,$$
$$E = -2k, \quad F = h^2 + k^2 - r^2,$$

and the parabola

$$x^2 = 4py$$

is obtained by taking

$$A = 1, \quad E = -4p, \quad B = C = D = F = 0.$$

In fact, even the straight line is a special case of (1) with $A = B = C = 0$, but this reduces (1) to a *linear* equation instead of maintaining its status as a second degree equation. The terms Ax^2, Bxy, and Cy^2 are the second degree, or quadratic terms, and we shall presently investigate the nature of the curve represented by Eq. (1) when at least one of these quadratic terms is present.

The so-called "cross-product" term, Bxy, has not appeared in the equations we found in Articles 8–4 to 8–7. This is a consequence of the way in which we chose coordinate axes, namely, such that at least one of them is parallel to an axis of symmetry of the curve in question. However, suppose we seek to find the equation of a hyperbola with foci at $F_1(-a, -a)$ and $F_2(a, a)$, for example, and with $|PF_1 - PF_2| = 2a$ (Fig. 8–48). Then

$$\sqrt{(x + a)^2 + (y + a)^2} - \sqrt{(x - a)^2 + (y - a)^2} = \pm 2a,$$

and when we transpose one radical, square, solve for the radical that still appears, and square again, this reduces to

$$2xy = a^2, \tag{2}$$

which is a special case of Eq. (1) in which the cross-product term is present. The asymptotes of the hyperbola in Eq. (2) are the x- and y-axes, and the transverse axis of the hyperbola (the axis of symmetry on which the foci lie) makes an angle of 45° with the coordinate axes. In fact, the cross-product term is present only in some similar circumstance, where the axes of the conic are tilted.

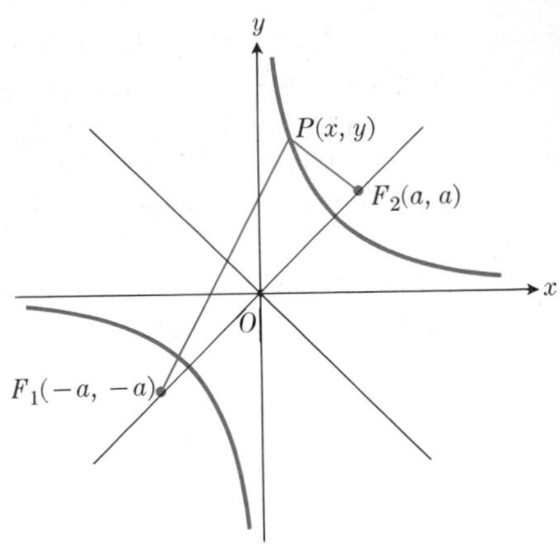

8–48 The hyperbola $2xy = a^2$.

Rotation of Axes

The equation of a curve can be modified by referring it to $x'y'$-axes by a rotation through an angle α in the counterclockwise direction. In the notation of Fig. 8–49, we have

$$x = OM = OP \cos(\theta + \alpha),$$
$$y = MP = OP \sin(\theta + \alpha), \tag{3a}$$

while

$$x' = OM' = OP \cos\theta,$$
$$y' = M'P = OP \sin\theta. \tag{3b}$$

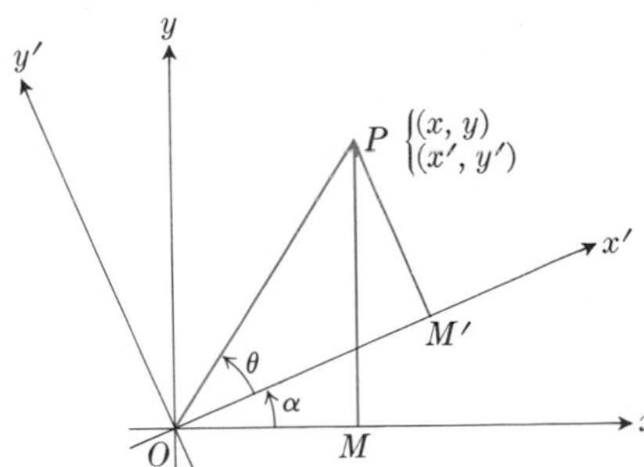

8–49 A counterclockwise rotation through angle α.

Using the relationships

$$\cos(\theta + \alpha) = \cos\theta\cos\alpha - \sin\theta\sin\alpha,$$
$$\sin(\theta + \alpha) = \sin\theta\cos\alpha + \cos\theta\sin\alpha,$$

in (3a) and taking account of (3b), we find

Equations for Rotation of Axes

$$x = x'\cos\alpha - y'\sin\alpha,$$
$$y = x'\sin\alpha + y'\cos\alpha. \tag{4}$$

EXAMPLE 1. The x- and y-axes are rotated $\alpha = 45°$ about the origin. Find the equation of the hyperbola of Eq. (2) in terms of the new coordinates.

Solution. Since $\cos 45° = \sin 45° = \sqrt{\frac{1}{2}}$, we substitute

$$x = \frac{x' - y'}{\sqrt{2}}, \qquad y = \frac{x' + y'}{\sqrt{2}}$$

into Eq. (2) and obtain

$$(x')^2 - (y')^2 = a^2,$$

which is equivalent to Eq. (3), Article 8–7, with $b = a$.

If we apply the equations for rotation of axes (4) to the general quadratic equation (1), we obtain a new quadratic equation of the form

$$A'x'^2 + B'x'y' + Cy'^2 + D'x' + E'y' + F' = 0. \tag{5}$$

The new coefficients are related to the old as follows:

$$\left.\begin{aligned} A' &= A\cos^2\alpha + B\cos\alpha\sin\alpha + C\sin^2\alpha, \\ B' &= B(\cos^2\alpha - \sin^2\alpha) + 2(C - A)\sin\alpha\cos\alpha, \\ C' &= A\sin^2\alpha - B\sin\alpha\cos\alpha + C\cos^2\alpha, \\ D' &= D\cos\alpha + E\sin\alpha, \\ E' &= -D\sin\alpha + E\cos\alpha, \\ F' &= F. \end{aligned}\right\} \tag{6}$$

If we start with an equation for a curve in which the cross-product term is present ($B \neq 0$), we can always find an angle of rotation α such that the cross-product term does not appear in the new equation ($B' \neq 0$). To find the angle α that eliminates the cross-product term, we put $B' = 0$ in the second equation in (6) and solve for α. It is easier to do this if we note that

$$\cos^2\alpha - \sin^2\alpha = \cos 2\alpha,$$

$$2\sin\alpha\cos\alpha = \sin 2\alpha,$$

so that

$$B' = B\cos 2\alpha + (C - A)\sin 2\alpha.$$

Hence B' will vanish if we choose α so that

$$\cot 2\alpha = \frac{A - C}{B}. \tag{7}$$

EXAMPLE 2. The coordinate axes are to be rotated through an angle α so that the new equation for the curve

$$x^2 + xy + y^2 = 3 \tag{8}$$

has no cross-product term. Find α and the new equation.

Solution. The equation (8) has $A = B = C = 1$. Choose α according to Eq. (7):

$$\cot 2\alpha = 0, \qquad 2\alpha = 90°, \qquad \alpha = 45°.$$

Substitute this value for α into Eq. (4) to obtain

$$x = \frac{x' - y'}{\sqrt{2}}, \qquad y = \frac{x' + y'}{\sqrt{2}}.$$

When these values are substituted in the original equation (8), we find that

$$3(x')^2 + (y')^2 = 6.$$

This is the equation of an ellipse with foci on the new y'-axis.

Since axes may always be rotated to eliminate the cross-product term, there is no loss in generality in assuming that this has been done. Then the quadratic equation (5), with $B' = 0$, will look like Eq. (1), with $B = 0$:

$$Ax^2 + Cy^2 + Dx + Ey + F = 0. \tag{9}$$

Equation (9) represents:

a) A straight line if $A = C = 0$, and not both D and E vanish.

b) A circle if $A = C \neq 0$. In special cases the locus may reduce to a single point, or no real locus.

c) A parabola if (9) is quadratic in one variable, linear in the other.

d) An ellipse if A and C are both positive or both negative. In special cases the locus may reduce to a single point, or no real locus.

e) A hyperbola if A and C are of opposite signs, both different from zero. In special cases the locus may reduce to a pair of intersecting straight lines. (For example: $x^2 - y^2 = 0$.)

We have already seen how to reduce (9) to the standard form for the equation of a circle, parabola, ellipse, or hyperbola by completing the squares (as needed) and translating to new axes.

Summary

Any second degree equation in x and y represents a circle, parabola, ellipse, or hyperbola (except for certain special cases in which the locus may reduce to a point, a line, a pair of lines, or fail to exist, as noted above). Conversely, any of these curves has an equation of the second degree. To find the curve, given its equation, we

FIRST. Rotate axes (if necessary) to eliminate the cross-product term,

SECOND. Translate axes (if desired) to reduce the equation to a standard form that we recognize.

PROBLEMS

Transform each of the following equations by a rotation of axes into an equation that has no cross-product term.

1. $xy = 2$
2. $x^2 + xy + y^2 = 1$
3. $2y^2 + \sqrt{3}\,xy - x^2 = 2$
4. $3x^2 + 2xy + 3y^2 - 19$
5. $x^2 - 3xy + y^2 = 5$
6. $3x^2 + 4\sqrt{3}\,xy - y^2 = 7$
7. Use the definition of an ellipse to write an equation for the ellipse with foci at $F_1(-1, 0)$ and $F_2(0, \sqrt{3})$ if it passes through the point $(1, 0)$. Through what angle α should the

axes be rotated to eliminate the cross-product term from the equation found? (Do not carry out the rotation.)

8. Show that the equation $x^2 + y^2 = r^2$ becomes $x'^2 + y'^2 = r^2$ for every choice of the angle α in the equations for rotation of axes.

9. Show that $A' + C' = A + C$ for every choice of the angle α in Eqs. (6).

10. Show that $B'^2 - 4A'C' = B^2 - 4AC$ for every choice of the angle α in Eqs. (6).

11. Show that a rotation of the axes through 45° will eliminate the cross-product term from Eq. (1) whenever $A = C$.

12. Find the equation of the curve $x^2 + 2xy + y^2 = 1$ after a rotation of axes which makes $A' = 0$ in Eq. (6).

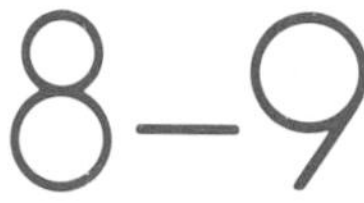

8–9 INVARIANTS AND THE DISCRIMINANT

The equation

$$Ax^2 + Bxy + Cy^2 + Dx + Ey + F = 0 \tag{1}$$

is a quadratic equation when at least one of the coefficients A, B, and C is different from zero. There is a criterion we may apply to tell whether the curve represented by such a quadratic equation is a parabola, an ellipse, or a hyperbola, without first performing a rotation of axes to eliminate the cross-product term. Our discussion has shown that if $B \neq 0$ then a rotation of axes through an angle α determined by

$$\cot 2\alpha = \frac{A - C}{B} \tag{2}$$

will transform the equation to the equivalent form

$$A'x'^2 + B'x'y' + C'y'^2 + D'x' + E'y' + F' = 0 \tag{3}$$

with new coefficients $A', \ldots, F'$ related to the old as in Eq. (6), Article 8–8, and with $B' = 0$ for the particular choice of α satisfying Eq. (2) above.

Now the nature of the curve whose equation is (3) with cross-product term removed is determined as follows:

a) a *parabola* if A' or $C' = 0$, that is, if $A'C' = 0$;
b) an *ellipse* if A' and C' have the same sign, that is, if $A'C' > 0$; and
c) a *hyperbola* if A' and C' have opposite signs, that is, if $A'C' < 0$.

But it has been discovered and can easily be verified by use of Eq. (6), Article 8–8, that the coefficients A, B, C, and A', B', C' satisfy the following condition:

$$B^2 - 4AC = B'^2 - 4A'C' \tag{4}$$

for *any* rotation of axes. That is, the quantity $B^2 - 4AC$ is *invariant* under a rotation of axes. But when the particular rotation is performed that makes $B' = 0$, the right side of (4) becomes simply $-4A'C'$. The criteria above, expressed in terms of A' and C', can now be expressed in terms of the *discriminant*:

$$\text{Discriminant} = B^2 - 4AC. \tag{5}$$

Namely, the curve is

a) a *parabola* if $B^2 - 4AC = 0$,

b) an *ellipse* if $B^2 - 4AC < 0$,

c) a *hyperbola* if $B^2 - 4AC > 0$,

with the understanding that certain degenerate cases may arise.

Another invariant associated with Eqs. (1) and (3) is the sum of the coefficients of the squared terms. For it is evident from Eq. (6), Article 8–8, that

$$A' + C' = A(\cos^2 \alpha + \sin^2 \alpha) + C(\sin^2 \alpha + \cos^2 \alpha)$$

or

$$A' + C' = A + C, \tag{6}$$

since

$$\sin^2 \alpha + \cos^2 \alpha = 1 \qquad \text{for any angle } \alpha.$$

The two invariants (4) and (6) may be used as a check against numerical errors in performing a rotation of axes of a quadratic equation. They may also be used to find the new coefficients of the quadratic terms

$$A'x'^2 + B'x'y' + C'y'^2,$$

with

$$B' = 0,$$

as in the following example.

EXAMPLE. Determine the equation to which

$$x^2 + xy + y^2 = 1$$

reduces when the axes are rotated to eliminate the cross-product term.

Solution. From the original equation we find

$$B^2 - 4AC = -3, \qquad A + C = 2.$$

Then, taking $B' = 0$, we have from (4) and (6),

$$-4A'C' = -3, \qquad A' + C' = 2.$$

Substituting $C' = 2 - A'$ from the second of these into the first, we obtain the quadratic equation

$$4A'^2 - 8A' + 3 = 0,$$

which factors into

$$(2A' - 3)(2A' - 1) = 0$$

and gives

$$A' = \tfrac{3}{2} \qquad \text{or} \qquad A' = \tfrac{1}{2}.$$

The corresponding values of C' are

$$C' = \tfrac{1}{2} \quad \text{or} \quad C' = \tfrac{3}{2}.$$

The equation therefore is

$$\tfrac{3}{2}x'^2 + \tfrac{1}{2}y'^2 = 1$$

or

$$\tfrac{1}{2}x'^2 + \tfrac{3}{2}y'^2 = 1$$

in the new coordinates. Hence the curve is an ellipse.

It should be noted that when no first-power terms are present in the original equation, they will also be absent in the new equation. This is due to the fact that a rotation of axes preserves the algebraic degree of each term of the equation; or we may refer to Eq. (6), Article 8–8, which shows that D' and E' are both zero if D and E are zero.

PROBLEMS

Use the discriminant and classify each of the following second degree equations as representing a circle, an ellipse, a parabola, or a hyperbola.

1. $x^2 + y^2 + xy + x - y = 3$
2. $2x^2 - y^2 + 4xy - 2x + 3y = 6$
3. $x^2 + 4xy + 4y^2 - 3x = 6$
4. $x^2 + y^2 + 3x - 2y = 10$
5. $xy + y^2 - 3x = 5$
6. $3x^2 + 6xy + 3y^2 - 4x + 5y = 12$
7. $x^2 - y^2 = 1$
8. $2x^2 + 3y^2 - 4x = 7$
9. $x^2 - 3xy + 3y^2 + 6y = 7$

10. When $B^2 - 4AC$ is negative, the equation
$$Ax^2 + Bxy + Cy^2 = 1$$
represents an ellipse. If the semiaxes have lengths a and b, the area of the ellipse is πab. Show that the area of the ellipse given above is $2\pi/\sqrt{4AC - B^2}$

11. Show, by reference to Eq. (6), Article 8–8, that
$$D'^2 + E'^2 = D^2 + E^2$$
for every angle of rotation α.

12. If $C = -A$ in Eq. (1), show that there is a rotation of axes for which $A' = C' = 0$ in the resulting Eq. (3). Find the angle α that makes $A' = C' = 0$ in this case. [*Hint.* Since $A' + C' = 0$, one need only make the further requirement that $A' = 0$ in Eq. (3).]

8–10 SECTIONS OF A CONE

The circle, parabola, ellipse, and hyperbola are known as *conic* sections because each may be obtained by cutting a cone by a plane. If the cutting plane is perpendicular to the axis of the cone, the section is a circle.

In general, suppose the cutting plane makes an angle α with the axis of the cone and let the generating angle of the cone be β (see Fig. 8–50). Then the section is

i) a circle, if $\alpha = 90°$;
ii) an ellipse, if $\beta < \alpha < 90°$;
iii) a parabola, if $\alpha = \beta$;
iv) a hyperbola, if $0 \leq \alpha < \beta$.

The connection between these curves as we have defined them and the sections from a cone is readily made by reference to Fig. 8–51. The figure is

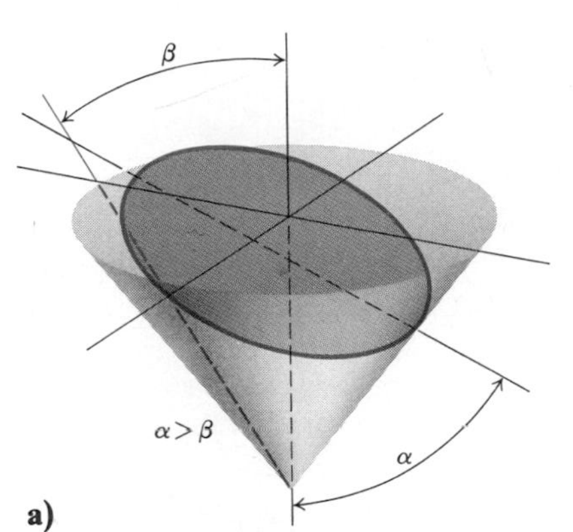

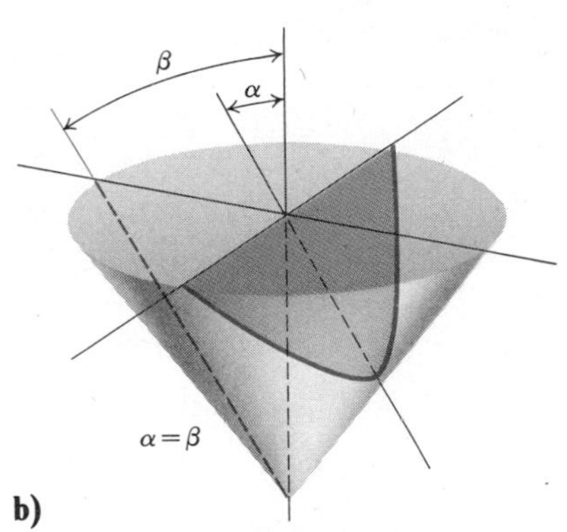

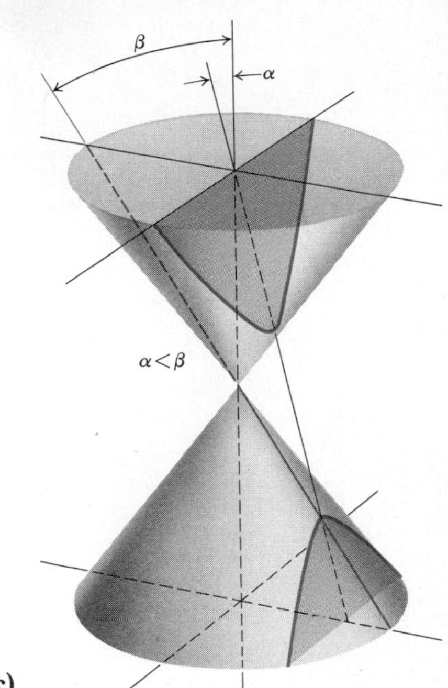

8–50 Plane intersecting a cone in (a) an ellipse, (b) a parabola, (c) a hyperbola.

drawn to illustrate the case of an ellipse, but the argument holds for the other cases as well.

A sphere is inscribed tangent to the cone along a circle C, and tangent to the cutting plane at a point F. Point P is any point on the conic section. We shall see that F is a focus, and that the line L, in which the cutting plane and the plane of the circle C intersect, is a directrix of the curve. To this end let Q be the point where the line through P parallel to the axis of the cone intersects the plane of C, let A be the point where the line joining P to the vertex of the cone touches C, and let PD be perpendicular to line L at D. Then PA and PF are two lines tangent to the same sphere from a common point P and hence have the same length:

$$PA = PF.$$

Also, from the right triangle PQA, we have

$$PQ = PA \cos \beta;$$

and from the right triangle PQD, we find that

$$PQ = PD \cos \alpha.$$

Hence

$$PA \cos \beta = PD \cos \alpha,$$

or

$$\frac{PA}{PD} = \frac{\cos \alpha}{\cos \beta}.$$

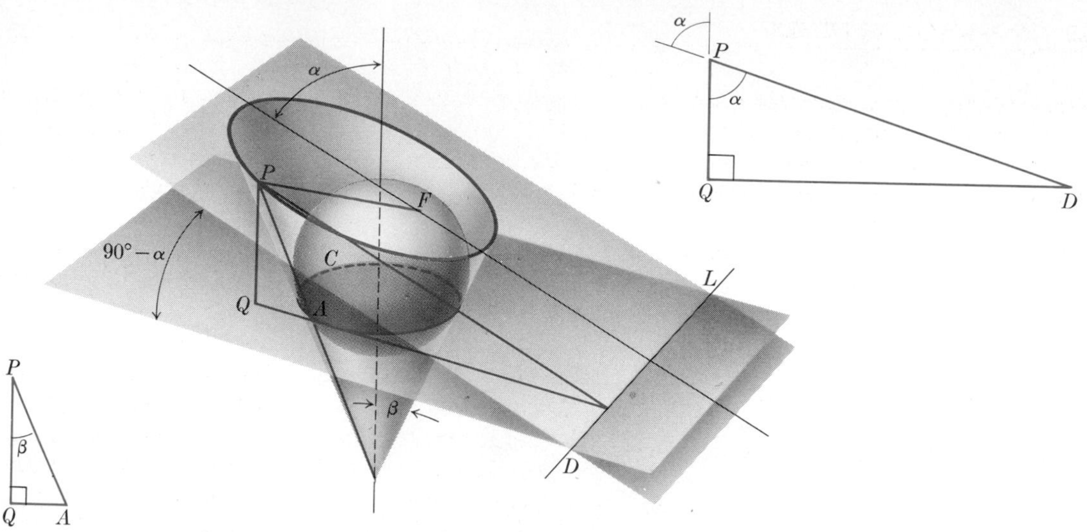

8–51 The line L is the directrix that corresponds to the focus F of the ellipse.

But since $PA = PF$, this means that

$$\frac{PF}{PD} = \frac{\cos \alpha}{\cos \beta}. \tag{1}$$

Since α and β are constant for a given cone and a given cutting plane, Eq. (1) has the form

$$PF = e \cdot PD.$$

This characterizes P as belonging to a parabola, an ellipse, or a hyperbola, with focus at F and directrix L, accordingly as $e = 1$, $e < 1$, or $e > 1$, respectively, where

$$e = \frac{\cos \alpha}{\cos \beta}$$

is thus identified with the eccentricity.

PROBLEMS

1. Sketch a figure similar to Fig. 8–51 when the conic section is a parabola, and carry through the argument of this article on the basis of such a figure.

2. Sketch a figure similar to Fig. 8–51 when the conic section is a hyperbola and carry through the argument of this article on the basis of such a figure.

3. Which parts of the construction described in this article become impossible when the conic section is a circle?

4. Let one directrix be the line $x = -p$ and take the corresponding focus at the origin. Using Eq. (15) of Article 8–6, derive the equation of the general conic section of eccentricity e. If e is neither 0 nor 1, show that the center of the conic section has coordinates

$$\left(\frac{pe^2}{1 - e^2}, 0\right).$$

REVIEW QUESTIONS AND EXERCISES

1. Discuss criteria for symmetry of a curve with respect to: (a) the x-axis, (b) the y-axis, (c) the origin, (d) the line $y = x$.

2. Define *asymptote*. How do you find vertical and horizontal asymptotes of a curve if its equation is given in the form $y = f(x)/g(x)$?

3. How do you find the extent of a curve (or, alternatively, strips of the plane from which the curve is excluded)?

4. Name the conic sections.

5. What kind of equation characterizes the conic sections?

6. If the equation of a conic section is given, and it contains no xy-term, how can you tell by inspection whether it is a parabola, circle, ellipse, or hyperbola? How can you tell what the curve is if there is an xy-term in the equation?

7. What are the equations of transformation of coordinates:

a) for a translation of axes? **b)** for a rotation of axes? Illustrate with diagrams.

8. What two quantities that are associated with the equation of a conic section remain invariant under a rotation of axes?

9. Sketch a parabola and label its vertex, focus, axis, and directrix. What is the definition of a parabola? What is the equation of your parabola?

10. Sketch an ellipse and label its vertices, foci, axes, and directrices. What is the definition of an ellipse? What is the equation of your ellipse?

11. Sketch a hyperbola and label its vertices, foci, axes, asymptotes, and directrices. What is the definition of a hyperbola? What is the equation of your hyperbola?

12. A ripple tank is made by bending a strip of tin around the perimeter of an ellipse for the wall of the tank and soldering a flat bottom onto this. An inch or two of water is put in the tank and the experimenter pokes a finger into it, right at one focus of the ellipse. Ripples radiate outward through the water, reflect from the strip around the edge of the tank, and (in a short time) a drop of water spurts up at the second focus. Why?

MISCELLANEOUS PROBLEMS

In Problems 1 through 9, determine the following properties of the curves whose equations are given: (A) symmetry, (B) extent, (C) intercepts, (D) asymptotes, (E) slope at intercepts. Use this information in sketching the curves.

1. a) $y^2 = x(4 - x)$ **b)** $y^2 = x(x - 4)$

c) $y^2 = \dfrac{x}{4 - x}$

2. a) $y = x + \dfrac{1}{x^2}$ **b)** $y^2 = x + \dfrac{1}{x^2}$

c) $y = x^2 + \dfrac{1}{x}$

3. a) $y = x(x + 1)(x - 2)$ **b)** $y^2 = x(x + 1)(x - 2)$

4. a) $y = \dfrac{8}{4 + x^2}$ **b)** $y = \dfrac{8}{4 - x^2}$ **c)** $y = \dfrac{8x}{4 + x^2}$

5. a) $xy = x^2 + 1$ **b)** $y = \dfrac{x^2}{x - 1}$

6. a) $y^2 = x^4 - x^2$ **b)** $y^2 = \dfrac{x - 1}{x - 2}$

7. $x^2y - y = 4(x - 2)$ **8.** $y = \dfrac{x^2 + 1}{x^2 - 1}$

9. $x^2 + xy + y^2 = 3$

10. Let C be the curve in Problem 9. Let $P(x, y)$ be a point on C. Let $P'(kx, ky)$ be a point on the line OP from the origin to P. If k is held constant, what is the equation of the curve described by P' as P traces out the curve C?

11. Sketch the graph whose equation is

$$(y - x + 2)(2y + x - 4) = 0.$$

12. A certain graph has an equation of the form

$$ay^2 + by = \frac{cx + d}{ex^2 + fx + g},$$

where a, b, c, d, e, f, and g are constants whose value in each case is either 0 or 1. From the following information about the graph, determine the constants and give a reason for your choice in each case:

Extent. The curve does not exist for $x < -1$. All values of y are permissible.

Symmetry. The curve is symmetric about the x-axis.

Intercepts. No y-intercept; x-intercept at $(-1, 0)$.

Asymptotes. Both axes; no others.

Sketch the graph.

13. Each of the following inequalities describes one or more regions of the xy-plane. Sketch first the curve obtained by replacing the inequality sign by an equal sign; then indicate the region that contains the points whose coordinates satisfy the given inequality.

a) $x < 3$ **b)** $x < y$ **c)** $x^2 < y$

d) $x^2 + y^2 > 4$ **e)** $x^2 + xy + y^2 < 3$

f) $x^2 + xy + y^2 > 3$ **g)** $y^2 < \dfrac{x}{4 - x}$

14. Write an equation of the tangent, at (2, 2), to the curve

$$x^2 - 2xy + y^2 + 2x + y - 6 = 0.$$

15. Sketch the curves $xy = 2$ and $x^2 - y^2 = 3$ in one diagram, and show that they intersect orthogonally.

16. Find equations of the lines that are tangent to the curve

$$y = x^3 - 6x + 2$$

and are parallel to the line $y = 6x - 2$.

17. Prove that if a line is drawn tangent to the curve $y^2 = kx$ at a point $P(x, y)$ not at the origin, then the portion of the tangent that lies between the x-axis and P is bisected by the y-axis.

18. Through the point $P(x, y)$ on the curve $y^2 = kx$, lines are drawn parallel to the axes. The rectangular area bounded by these two lines and the axes is divided into two portions by the given curve. (a) If these two areas are rotated about the y-axis, show that they generate two solids whose volumes are in the ratio of four to one. (b) What is the ratio of the volumes of the solids generated when these areas are rotated about the x-axis?

19. Show that the curves $2x^2 + 3y^2 = a^2$ and $ky^2 = x^3$ are orthogonal for all values of the constants a and k ($a \neq 0$, $k \neq 0$). Sketch the four curves corresponding to $a = 2$, $a = 4$, $k = \frac{1}{2}$, $k = -2$ in one diagram.

20. Show, analytically, that an angle inscribed in a semicircle is a right angle.

21. Two points P, Q are called symmetric with respect to a circle if P and Q lie on the same ray through the center and if the product of their distances from the center is equal to the square of the radius. Given that Q describes the straight line $x + 2y - 5 = 0$, find the locus of the point P that is symmetric to Q with respect to the circle $x^2 + y^2 = 4$.

22. A point $P(x, y)$ moves so that the ratio of its distances from two fixed points is a constant k. Show that the point traces a circle if $k \neq 1$, and a straight line if $k = 1$.

23. Show that the centers of all chords of the parabola $x^2 = 4py$ with slope m lie on a straight line, and find its equation.

24. The line through the focus F and the point $P(x_1, y_1)$ on the parabola $y^2 = 4px$ intersects the parabola in a second point $Q(x_2, y_2)$. Find the coordinates of Q in terms of y_1 and p. If O is the vertex and PO cuts the directrix at R, prove that QR is parallel to the axis of the parabola.

25. Find the point (or points) on the curve $x^2 = y^3$ nearest the point $P(0, 4)$. Sketch the curve and the shortest line from P to the curve.

26. Prove that every line through the center of the circle

$$(x - h)^2 + (y - k)^2 = r^2$$

is orthogonal to the circle.

27. Find all points on the curve $x^2 + 2xy + 3y^2 = 3$, where the tangent line is perpendicular to the line $x + y = 1$.

28. A line PT is drawn tangent to the curve $xy = x + y$ at the point $P(-2, \frac{2}{3})$. Find equations of two lines that are normal to the curve and perpendicular to PT.

29. Graph each of the following equations:

a) $(x + y)(x^2 + y^2 - 1) = 0$;

b) $(x + y)(x^2 + y^2 - 1) = 1$.

[*Hint.* In part (b), consider intersections of the curve with the line $x + y = k$ for different values of the constant k.]

30. Find the center and radius of the circle through the two points $A(2, 0)$ and $B(6, 0)$ and tangent to the curve $y = x^2$.

31. Find the center of the circle that passes through the point (0, 1) and is tangent to the curve $y = x^2$ at (2, 4).

32. Let L_1, L_2, L_3 be three straight lines, no two of which are parallel. Let $E_i = a_i x + b_i y + c_i = 0$, $i = 1, 2, 3$, be the equation of the line L_i.

a) Describe the graph of the equation $E_1 E_2 + hE_2 E_3 + kE_1 E_3 = 0$, assuming h and k are constants.

b) Use the method of part (a) and determine h and k so that the equation represents a circle through the points of intersection of the lines

$$x + y - 2 = 0, \qquad x - y + 2 = 0, \qquad y - 2x = 0.$$

c) Find a parabola, axis vertical, through the points of intersection of the lines in (b).

33. A comet moves in a parabolic orbit with the sun at the focus. When the comet is 4×10^7 miles from the sun, the line from the sun to it makes an angle of 60° with the axis of the orbit (drawn in the direction in which the orbit opens). How near does the comet come to the sun?

34. Sketch in one diagram the curves $y^2 = 4x + 4$, $y^2 = 64 - 16x$, and find the angles at which they intersect.

35. Find an equation of the curve such that the distance from any point $P(x, y)$ on the curve to the line $x = 3$ is the same as its distance to the point (4, 0). Sketch the curve.

36. Two radar stations lying along an east–west line are separated by 20 mi. Choose a coordinate system such that their positions are (−10, 0) and (10, 0). A low-flying plane traveling from west to east is known to have a speed of v_0 mi/sec. At $t = 0$ a signal is sent from the station at (−10, 0), bounces off the plane, and is received at (10, 0) $30/c$ sec later (c is the velocity of the signal). When $t = 10/v_0$, another signal is sent out from the station at (−10, 0), reflects off the plane, and is once again received $30/c$ sec later by the other station. What is the position of the plane when it reflects the second signal, providing that one assumes $v_0 \ll c$ (that is, v_0 is much less than c)?

37. A line is drawn tangent to the parabola $y^2 = 4px$ at a point $P(x, y)$ on the curve. Let A be the point where this tangent line crosses the axis of the parabola, let F be the

focus, and let PD be the line parallel to the axis of the parabola and intersecting the directrix at D. Prove that $AFPD$ is a rhombus.

38. Find the equation of the locus of a point $P(x, y)$ if the distance from P to the vertex is twice the distance from P to the focus of the parabola $x^2 = 8y$. Name the locus.

39. Prove that the tangent to a parabola at a point P cuts the axis of the parabola at a point whose distance from the vertex equals the distance from P to the tangent at the vertex.

40. Discuss and sketch the graph of the equation $x^4 - (y^2 - 9)^2 = 0$.

41. Show that the curve C: $x^4 - (y^2 - 9)^2 = 1$ approaches part of the curve $x^4 - (y^2 - 9)^2 = 0$ as the point $P(x, y)$ moves farther and farther away from the origin. Sketch. Do any points of C lie inside the circle $x^2 + y^2 = 9$? Give a reason for your answer.

42. The ellipse $(x^2/a^2) + (y^2/b^2) = 1$ divides the plane into two regions; one inside the ellipse, the other outside. Show that points in one of these regions have coordinates that satisfy the inequality $(x^2/a^2) + (y^2/b^2) < 1$, while in the other, $(x^2/a^2) + (y^2/b^2) > 1$. (Consider the effect of replacing x, y in the given equation by $x' = kx$, $y' = ky$, with $k < 1$ in one case and $k > 1$ in the other.)

43. Find an equation of an ellipse with foci at (1, 0) and (5, 0), and one vertex at the origin.

44. Let $F_1 = (3, 0)$, $F_2 = (0, 5)$, $P = (-1, 3)$. (a) Find the distances F_1P and F_2P. (b) Does the origin O lie inside or outside the ellipse that has F_1 and F_2 as its foci and that passes through the point P? Why?

45. Find the greatest area of a rectangle inscribed in the ellipse $(x^2/a^2) + (y^2/b^2) = 1$, with sides parallel to the coordinate axes.

46. Show that the line $y = mx + c$ is tangent to the conic section $Ax^2 + y^2 = 1$ if and only if the constants A, m, and c satisfy the condition $A(c^2 - 1) = m^2$.

47. Starting from the general equation for the conic, find the equation of the conic with the following properties: (a) it is symmetric with respect to the origin; (b) it passes through the point (1, 0); (c) the tangent to it at the point (−2, 1) on it is the line $y = 1$.

48. Find an ellipse with one vertex at the point (3, 1), the nearer focus at the point (1, 1), and eccentricity $\frac{2}{3}$.

49. By a suitable rotation of axes, show that the equation $xy - x - y = 1$ represents a hyperbola. Sketch.

50. Find an equation of a hyperbola with eccentricity equal to $\sqrt{2}$ and with vertices at the points (2, 0) and (−2, 0).

51. Sketch the conic $\sqrt{2}\,y - 2xy = 3$. Locate its center and find its eccentricity.

52. If c is a fixed positive constant, then

$$\frac{x^2}{t^2} + \frac{y^2}{t^2 - c^2} = 1 \qquad (c^2 < t^2)$$

defines a family of ellipses, any member of which is characterized by a particular value of t. Show that every member of the family

$$\frac{x^2}{t^2} - \frac{y^2}{c^2 - t^2} = 1 \qquad (t^2 < c^2)$$

intersects any member of the first family at right angles.

53. Graph the equation $|x| + |y| = 1$ and find the area it encloses.

54. Show that if the tangent to a curve at a point $P(x, y)$ passes through the origin, then $dy/dx = y/x$ at the point. Hence show that no tangent can be drawn from the origin to the hyperbola $x^2 - y^2 = 1$.

55. (a) Find the coordinates of the center and the foci, the lengths of the axes, and the eccentricity of the ellipse $x^2 + 4y^2 - 4x + 8y - 1 = 0$. (b) Do likewise with the hyperbola $3x^2 - y^2 + 12x - 3y = 0$, and in addition find equations of its asymptotes.

56. If the ends of a line segment of constant length move along perpendicular lines, show that a point P on the segment, at distances a and b from the ends, describes an ellipse.

57. Sketch the curves:

a) $(9x^2 + 4y^2 - 36)(4x^2 + 9y^2 - 36) = 0$,
b) $(9x^2 + 4y^2 - 36)(4x^2 + 9y^2 - 36) = 1$.

Is the curve in (b) bounded or does it extend to points arbitrarily far from the origin? Give a reason for your answer.

58. Let p, q be positive numbers such that $q < p$. If r is a third number, prove that the equation $[x^2/(p - r)] + [y^2/(q - r)] = 1$ represents (a) an ellipse if $r < q$, (b) a hyperbola if $q < r < p$, (c) nothing if $p < r$. Prove that all these ellipses and hyperbolas have the same foci, and find these foci.

59. Find the eccentricity of the hyperbola $xy = 1$.

60. On a level plane the sound of a rifle and that of the bullet striking the target are heard at the same instant. What is the location of the hearer?

61. Show that any tangent to the hyperbola $xy = a^2$ determines with its asymptotes a triangle of area $2a^2$.

62. Given the hyperbola $9x^2 - 4y^2 - 18x - 16y + 29 = 0$. Find the coordinates of the center and foci, and the equations of the asymptotes. Sketch.

63. By an appropriate rotation, eliminate the xy-term from the equation,

$$7x^2 - 8xy + y^2 = 9.$$

64. Show that the tangent to the conic section

$$Ax^2 + Bxy + Cy^2 + Dx + Ey + F = 0$$

at a point (x_1, y_1) on it has an equation that may be written in the form

$$Axx_1 + B\left(\frac{x_1 y + x y_1}{2}\right) + Cyy_1 + D\left(\frac{x + x_1}{2}\right) + E\left(\frac{y + y_1}{2}\right) + F = 0.$$

65. a) Find the eccentricity and center of the conic

$$x^2 + 12y^2 - 6x - 48y + 9 = 0.$$

b) Find the vertex of the conic

$$x^2 - 6x - 12y + 9 = 0.$$

c) Sketch the conics in one diagram.

different eccentricity. Why

66. Find an equation of the circle passing through the three points common to the conics of Problem 65.

67. Two vertices A, B of a triangle are fixed and the vertex $C(x, y)$ moves in such a way that $\angle A = 2(\angle B)$. Find the path traced by C.

68. Find the equation into which $x^{1/2} + y^{1/2} = a^{1/2}$ is transformed by a rotation of axes through 45° and elimination of radicals.

69. Show that $dx^2 + dy^2$ is invariant under any rotation of axes about the origin.

70. Show that $x\,dy - y\,dx$ is invariant under any rotation of axes about the origin.

71. Graph the equation $x^{2n} + y^{2n} = a^{2n}$ for the following values of n: (a) 1, (b) 2, (c) 100. In each instance find where the curve cuts the line $y = x$.

a. $x^2 - 6x + 9 + 12(y^2 - 4y + 4) = -9 + 9 + 48$

$$\frac{(x-3)^2}{48} + \frac{12(y-2)^2}{48} = \frac{48}{48}$$

$$\frac{(x-3)^2}{48} + \frac{(y-2)^2}{4} = 1$$

$e = \frac{c}{a}$ $\quad c^2 = a^2 + b^2 = 48 + 4 = 52 \quad c = \sqrt{52} = \sqrt{4 \cdot 13} = 2\sqrt{13}$

$a = \sqrt{48} = \sqrt{4 \cdot 12} = 2\sqrt{12} = 2\sqrt{4 \cdot 3} = 4\sqrt{3}$

$e = \frac{2\sqrt{13}}{4\sqrt{3}} = \frac{\sqrt{13}}{2\sqrt{3}} = 1.04$

b. $x^2 - 6x + 9 - 12y =$

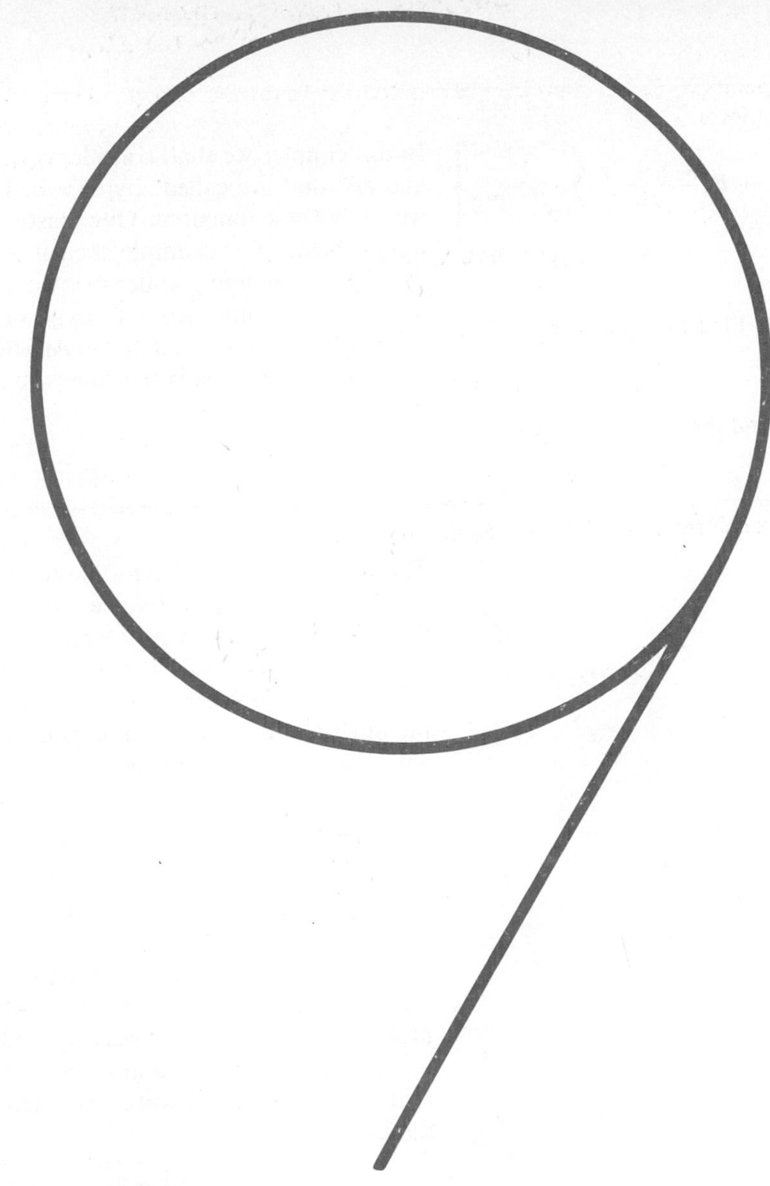

HYPERBOLIC FUNCTIONS

9–1 INTRODUCTION

In this chapter we shall consider certain combinations of the exponentials e^x and e^{-x} that are called "hyperbolic functions." There are two reasons why we study these functions. One reason is that they are used to solve engineering problems. For example, the tension at any point in a cable, suspended by its ends and hanging under its own weight (such as an electric transmission line) may be computed with hyperbolic functions. We shall investigate the hanging cable in some detail in Article 9–6. A second reason for studying the hyperbolic functions is that they are useful in solving differential equations.

9–2 DEFINITIONS AND IDENTITIES

The combinations $\frac{1}{2}(e^u + e^{-u})$ and $\frac{1}{2}(e^u - e^{-u})$ occur so frequently that it has been found convenient to give special names to them. It may not be clear at this particular time why the names about to be introduced are especially appropriate. But it will become apparent as we proceed that these functions are related to each other by rules that are very much like the rules that relate the functions cos u and sin u. And just as cos u and sin u may be identified with the point (x, y) on the unit circle $x^2 + y^2 = 1$, the functions

$$\cosh u = \tfrac{1}{2}(e^u + e^{-u}),\qquad \sinh u = \tfrac{1}{2}(e^u - e^{-u}), \tag{1}$$

may be identified with the coordinates of the point (x, y) on the *unit hyperbola* $x^2 - y^2 = 1$.

Equations (1) are the *definitions* of the *hyperbolic cosine* and *hyperbolic sine* of u (cosh u is often pronounced to rhyme with "gosh you," and sinh u pronounced as though it were spelled "cinch u").

To check that the point (x, y) with $x = \cosh u$ and $y = \sinh u$ lies on the unit hyperbola, we substitute the defining relations (1) into the equation of the hyperbola:

$$x^2 - y^2 = 1,$$
$$\cosh^2 u - \sinh^2 u \overset{?}{=} 1,$$
$$\tfrac{1}{4}(e^{2u} + 2 + e^{-2u}) - \tfrac{1}{4}(e^{2u} - 2 + e^{-2u}) \overset{?}{=} 1,$$
$$\tfrac{1}{4}(e^{2u} + 2 + e^{-2u} - e^{2u} + 2 - e^{-2u}) \overset{?}{=} 1,$$
$$\tfrac{1}{4}(4) \overset{?}{=} 1. \qquad \text{(Yes!)}$$

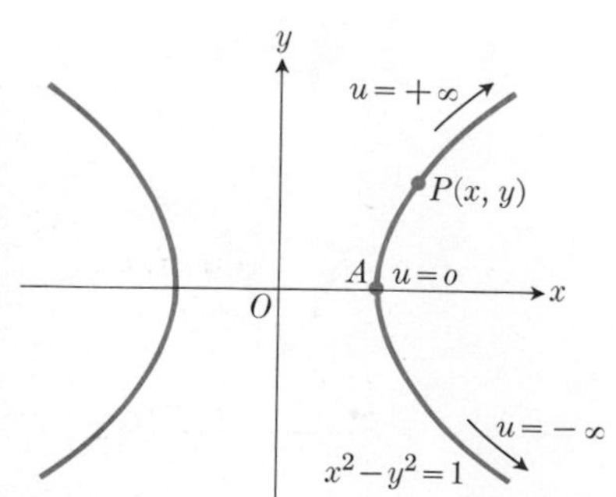

9–1 The equations $x = \cosh u$, $y = \sinh u$, $-\infty < u < \infty$, are parametric equations for the righthand branch of the unit hyperbola $x^2 - y^2 = 1$.

Actually, if we let

$$x = \cosh u = \tfrac{1}{2}(e^u + e^{-u}),\qquad y = \sinh u = \tfrac{1}{2}(e^u - e^{-u}), \tag{2}$$

then when u varies from $-\infty$ to $+\infty$, the point $P(x, y)$ describes the right-hand branch of the hyperbola $x^2 - y^2 = 1$. The sense in which the curve is described is shown by the arrows in Fig. 9–1. Since e^u is always positive and $e^{-u} = 1/e^u$ is also positive, it follows that $x = \cosh u = \frac{1}{2}(e^u + e^{-u})$ is positive for all real values of u, $-\infty < u < +\infty$. Hence the point (x, y) remains always to the right of the y-axis.

The first bit of hyperbolic trigonometry that we have just established is the basic identity

$$\cosh^2 u - \sinh^2 u = 1. \tag{3}$$

This is analogous to, but not the same as the ordinary trigonometric identity, $\cos^2 u + \sin^2 u = 1$.

The remaining hyperbolic functions are *defined* in terms of $\sinh u$ and $\cosh u$ as follows:

$$\begin{aligned}
\tanh u &= \frac{\sinh u}{\cosh u} = \frac{e^u - e^{-u}}{e^u + e^{-u}},\\
\coth u &= \frac{\cosh u}{\sinh u} = \frac{e^u + e^{-u}}{e^u - e^{-u}},\\
\operatorname{sech} u &= \frac{1}{\cosh u} = \frac{2}{e^u + e^{-u}},\\
\operatorname{csch} u &= \frac{1}{\sinh u} = \frac{2}{e^u - e^{-u}}.
\end{aligned} \tag{4}$$

If we divide the identity (3) by $\cosh^2 u$, we get

$$1 - \tanh^2 u = \operatorname{sech}^2 u, \tag{5a}$$

and if we divide it by $\sinh^2 u$, we get

$$\coth^2 u - 1 = \operatorname{csch}^2 u. \tag{5b}$$

Since from (1) we find

$$\cosh u + \sinh u = e^u, \tag{6a}$$

$$\cosh u - \sinh u = e^{-u}, \tag{6b}$$

it is apparent that *any* combination of the exponentials e^u and e^{-u} can be replaced by a combination of $\sinh u$ and $\cosh u$, and conversely. Also, since e^{-u} is positive, (6b) shows that $\cosh u$ is always greater than $\sinh u$. But for large values of u, e^{-u} is small, and $\cosh u \approx \sinh u$.

The graphs of the hyperbolic functions are shown in Fig. 9–2(a) through (d).

At $x = 0$, $\cosh x = 1$ and $\sinh x = 0$, so the hyperbolic functions all have the same values at 0 that the corresponding trigonometric functions have. The hyperbolic cosine is an *even function*, that is,

$$\cosh(-x) = \cosh x, \tag{7}$$

and the hyperbolic sine is an *odd function*, that is,

$$\sinh(-x) = -\sinh x; \tag{8}$$

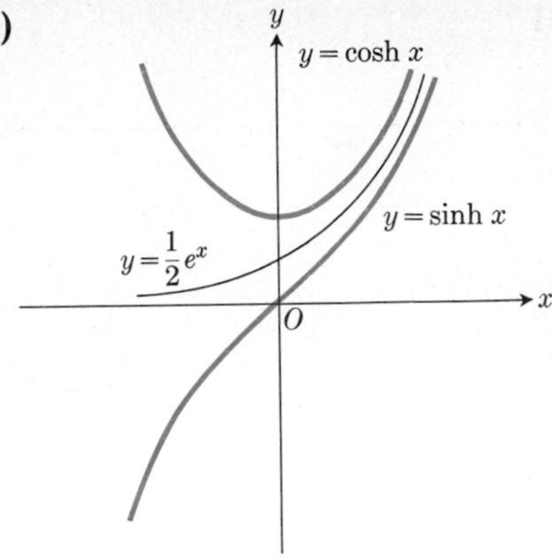

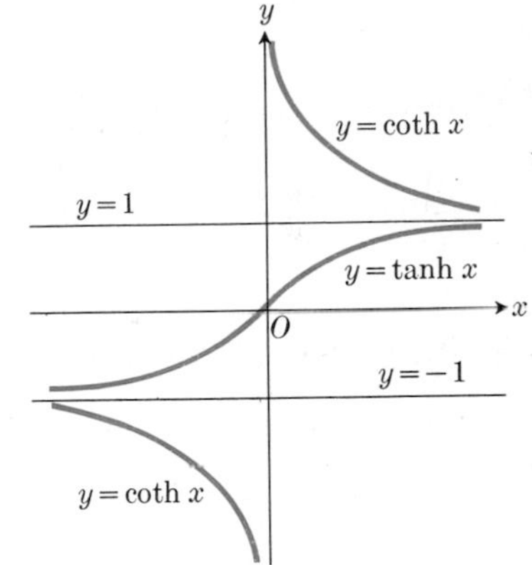

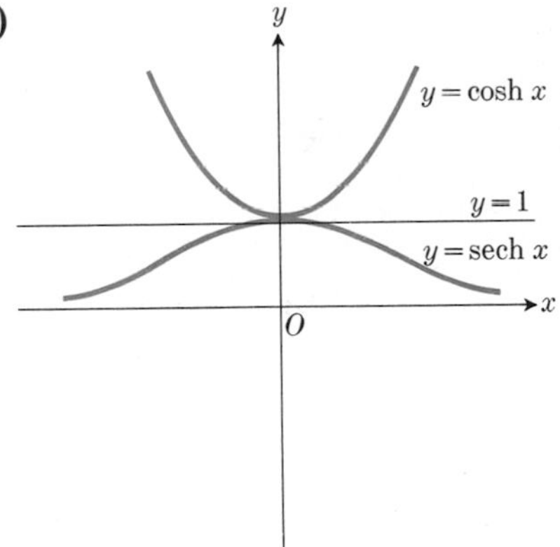

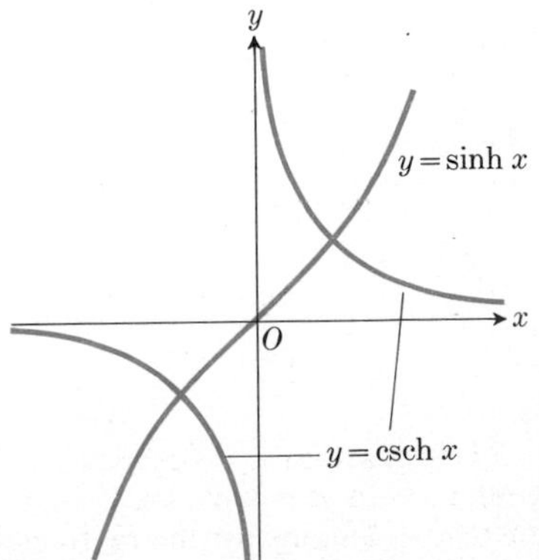

9–2 Graphs of the six hyperbolic functions.

so one curve is symmetric about the y-axis and the other is symmetric with respect to the origin. Here again the hyperbolic functions behave like the ordinary trigonometric (or circular) functions.

Certain major differences between the hyperbolic and the circular functions should be noted. For example, the circular functions are periodic: $\sin(x + 2\pi) = \sin x$, $\tan(x + \pi) = \tan x$, etc. But *the hyperbolic functions are not periodic.* Again, they differ greatly in the range of values they assume:

$\sin x$ varies between -1 and $+1$, oscillates;
$\sinh x$ varies from $-\infty$ to $+\infty$, steadily increases;

$\cos x$ varies between -1 and $+1$, oscillates;
$\cosh x$ varies from $+\infty$ to $+1$ to $+\infty$;

$|\sec x|$ is never less than unity;
$\operatorname{sech} x$ is never greater than unity, is always positive;

$\tan x$ varies from $-\infty$ to $+\infty$;
$\tanh x$ varies from -1 to $+1$.

Another difference lies in the behavior of the functions as $x \to \pm\infty$. We can say nothing very specific about the behavior of the circular functions $\sin x$, $\cos x$, $\tan x$, etc., for large values of x. But the hyperbolic functions behave very much like $e^x/2$, $e^{-x}/2$, unity, or zero, as follows:

For x large and positive:	**For x negative, $\|x\|$ large:**	
$\cosh x \approx \sinh x \approx \frac{1}{2}e^x$	$\cosh x \approx -\sinh x \approx \frac{1}{2}e^{-x}$	
$\tanh x \approx \coth x \approx 1$	$\tanh x \approx \coth x \approx -1$	
$\operatorname{sech} x \approx \operatorname{csch} x \approx 2e^{-x} \approx 0$	$\operatorname{sech} x \approx -\operatorname{csch} x \approx 2e^x \approx 0$	**(9)**

Additional analogies will be apparent when we study the calculus of hyperbolic functions in the next article. We conclude this article with a number of formulas that are easily checked.

It requires only the definitions in (1) and a bit of routine algebra to produce the identities

$$\sinh(x + y) = \sinh x \cosh y + \cosh x \sinh y$$

$$\cosh(x + y) = \cosh x \cosh y + \sinh x \sinh y \tag{10}$$

These in turn give

$$\sinh 2x = 2 \sinh x \cosh x, \tag{11a}$$

$$\cosh 2x = \cosh^2 x + \sinh^2 x, \tag{11b}$$

when we take $y = x$. The second of these leads to useful "half-angle" formulas when we combine it with the basic identity

$$1 = \cosh^2 x - \sinh^2 x. \tag{3}$$

For if we add (11b) and (3), we have

$$\cosh 2x + 1 = 2 \cosh^2 x, \tag{12a}$$

while if we subtract (3) from (11b), we get

$$\cosh 2x - 1 = 2 \sinh^2 x. \tag{12b}$$

PROBLEMS

1. Show that $x = -\cosh u$, $y = \sinh u$ represents a point on the left branch of the hyperbola $x^2 - y^2 = 1$.

2. Using the definitions of $\cosh u$ and $\sinh u$ given by Eq. (1), show that $\cosh(-u) = \cosh u$ and $\sinh(-u) = -\sinh u$.

3. Verify Eqs. (10) for $\sinh(x + y)$ and $\cosh(x + y)$.

4. Show that $(\cosh x + \sinh x)^n = \cosh nx + \sinh nx$.

5. Let L be the line tangent to the hyperbola $x^2 - y^2 = 1$ at the point $P_1(x_1, y_1)$, where $x_1 = \cosh u$, $y_1 = \sinh u$. Show that L cuts the x-axis at the point $(\operatorname{sech} u, 0)$ and the y-axis at $(0, -\operatorname{csch} u)$.

6. In each of the following problems, one of the six hyperbolic functions of u is given; determine the remaining five.

a) $\sinh u = -\frac{3}{4}$, **b)** $\cosh u = \frac{17}{15}$,
c) $\tanh u = -\frac{7}{25}$, **d)** $\coth u = \frac{13}{12}$,
e) $\operatorname{sech} u = \frac{3}{5}$, **f)** $\operatorname{csch} u = \frac{5}{12}$.

7. Show that the distance r from the origin O to the point $P(\cosh u, \sinh u)$ on the hyperbola $x^2 - y^2 = 1$ is $r = \sqrt{\cosh 2u}$.

8. Show that the line tangent to the hyperbola at its vertex A in Fig. 9–1 intersects the line OP in the point $(1, \tanh u)$. This gives a geometric representation of $\tanh u$.

9. If θ lies in the interval $-\pi/2 < \theta < \pi/2$ and $\sinh x = \tan \theta$, show that $\cosh x = \sec \theta$, $\tanh x = \sin \theta$, $\coth x = \csc \theta$, $\operatorname{csch} x = \cot \theta$, and $\operatorname{sech} x = \cos \theta$.

9–3 DERIVATIVES AND INTEGRALS

Let u be a differentiable function of x and differentiate

$$\sinh u = \tfrac{1}{2}(e^u - e^{-u}), \qquad \cosh u = \tfrac{1}{2}(e^u + e^{-u}), \tag{1}$$

with respect to x. Applying the formulas

$$\frac{de^u}{dx} = e^u \frac{du}{dx}, \qquad \frac{de^{-u}}{dx} = e^{-u}\frac{d(-u)}{dx} = -e^{-u}\frac{du}{dx},$$

we get

$$\frac{d(\sinh u)}{dx} = \cosh u \frac{du}{dx}, \tag{XXI}$$

$$\frac{d(\cosh u)}{dx} = \sinh u \frac{du}{dx}. \tag{XXII}$$

Then, if we let

$$y = \tanh u = \frac{\sinh u}{\cosh u}$$

and differentiate as a fraction, we get

$$\begin{aligned}\frac{d(\tanh u)}{dx} &= \frac{\cosh u[d(\sinh u)/dx] - \sinh u[d(\cosh u)/dx]}{\cosh^2 u} \\ &= \frac{\cosh^2 u(du/dx) - \sinh^2 u(du/dx)}{\cosh^2 u} \\ &= \frac{(\cosh^2 u - \sinh^2 u)(du/dx)}{\cosh^2 u} = \frac{1}{\cosh^2 u}\frac{du}{dx} \\ &= \operatorname{sech}^2 u \frac{du}{dx}.\end{aligned}$$

In a similar manner, we may establish the rest of the formulas in the following list:

$$\frac{d(\tanh u)}{dx} = \operatorname{sech}^2 u \frac{du}{dx}, \qquad \text{XXIII}$$

$$\frac{d(\coth u)}{dx} = -\operatorname{csch}^2 u \frac{du}{dx}, \qquad \text{XXIV}$$

$$\frac{d(\operatorname{sech} u)}{dx} = -\operatorname{sech} u \tanh u \frac{du}{dx}, \qquad \text{XXV}$$

$$\frac{d(\operatorname{csch} u)}{dx} = -\operatorname{csch} u \coth u \frac{du}{dx}. \qquad \text{XXVI}$$

Aside from the pattern of algebraic signs, these formulas are the exact analogs of the formulas for the corresponding circular functions. Exactly half of them have minus signs, but we no longer attach the minus signs to the derivatives of the cofunctions. The first three, sinh u, cosh u, tanh u, have positive derivatives and the last three have negative derivatives.

Each of these derivative formulas has a matching differential formula. These in turn may be integrated at once to produce the following integration formulas:

1. $$\int \sinh u \, du = \cosh u + C.$$

2. $$\int \cosh u \, du = \sinh u + C.$$

3. $$\int \operatorname{sech}^2 u \, du = \tanh u + C.$$

4. $$\int \operatorname{csch}^2 u \, du = -\coth u + C.$$ **(2)**

5. $$\int \operatorname{sech} u \tanh u \, du = -\operatorname{sech} u + C.$$

6. $$\int \operatorname{csch} u \coth u \, du = -\operatorname{csch} u + C.$$

EXAMPLE 1. Show that $y = a \cosh (x/a)$ satisfies the differential equation

$$\frac{d^2y}{dx^2} = \frac{w}{H}\sqrt{1 + \left(\frac{dy}{dx}\right)^2}, \qquad (3)$$

provided $a = H/w$, where H and w are constants.

Solution. By differentiating $y = a \cosh (x/a)$, we find

$$\frac{dy}{dx} = a\left(\sinh \frac{x}{a}\right)\frac{1}{a} = \sinh \frac{x}{a}, \qquad \frac{d^2y}{dx^2} = \left(\cosh \frac{x}{a}\right)\frac{1}{a}.$$

We substitute these into (3) and obtain

$$\frac{1}{a}\cosh\frac{x}{a} \stackrel{?}{=} \frac{w}{H}\sqrt{1+\sinh^2\frac{x}{a}} \qquad \textbf{(a)}$$

$$= \frac{w}{H}\sqrt{\cosh^2\frac{x}{a}} \qquad \textbf{(b)}$$

$$= \frac{w}{H}\cosh\frac{x}{a}, \qquad \textbf{(c)}$$

which is a true equation provided $a = H/w$.

REMARK 1. In going from (a) to (b) above, we used the fundamental identity

$$\cosh^2 u - \sinh^2 u = 1$$

in the form

$$1 + \sinh^2 u = \cosh^2 u.$$

In going from (b) to (c), we used the fact that $\cosh u$ is always positive, and hence

$$\sqrt{\cosh^2 u} = |\cosh u| = \cosh u.$$

REMARK 2. The differential equation (3) expresses the condition for equilibrium of forces acting on a section AP of a hanging cable (Fig. 9–3). We imagine the rest of the cable as having been removed and the section AP from the lowest point A to the representative point $P(x, y)$ as being in equilibrium under the forces

1. H = horizontal tension pulling on the cable at A,
2. T = tangential tension pulling on the cable at P,
3. $W = ws$ = weight of s feet of the cable at w pounds per foot of length from A to P.

Then equilibrium of the cable requires that the horizontal and vertical components of T just balance H and W:

$$T\cos\phi = H, \qquad T\sin\phi = W = ws. \qquad \textbf{(4)}$$

By division, we get

$$\frac{T\sin\phi}{T\cos\phi} = \tan\phi = \frac{W}{H}$$

or

$$\frac{dy}{dx} = \frac{ws}{H}, \qquad \textbf{(5)}$$

since $\tan\phi = dy/dx$. The arc length s in Eq. (5) would be found by integrating

$$ds = \sqrt{1 + \left(\frac{dy}{dx}\right)^2}\,dx$$

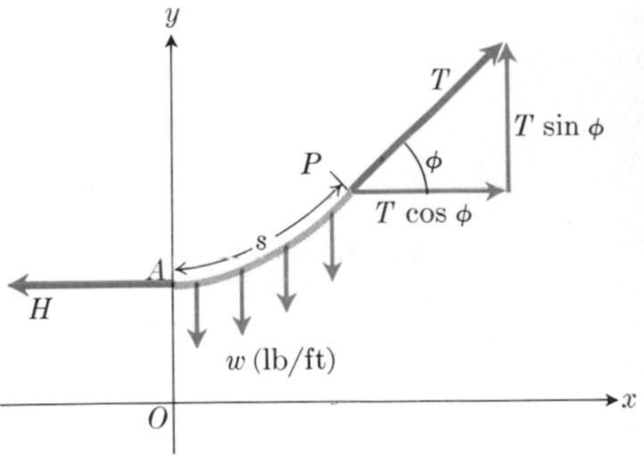

9–3 Forces acting on a section AP of a flexible hanging cable weighing w lb/ft. The load on the cable is uniform along the cable but is not uniform per horizontal foot.

from A to P. But instead of doing so, we may differentiate Eq. (5) with respect to x:

$$\frac{d^2y}{dx^2} = \frac{w}{H}\frac{ds}{dx},$$

and then substitute $\sqrt{1 + (dy/dx)^2}$ in place of ds/dx to obtain Eq. (3) above.

REMARK 3. In Example 1, above, we pulled the equation $y = a \cosh (x/a)$ out of the hat, so to speak, and showed by substitution that it satisfies the differential equation (3). In Article 9–6, we shall adopt the more straightforward approach of simply solving Eq. (3) subject to the initial conditions

$$\frac{dy}{dx} = 0 \quad \text{and} \quad y = y_0 \quad \text{when} \quad x = 0.$$

By choosing the origin so that $y_0 = a = H/w$, we shall find that the solution is indeed the one given above, namely,

$$y = a \cosh \frac{x}{a} \quad \text{with} \quad a = \frac{H}{w}. \tag{6}$$

EXAMPLE 2. Suppose that the height $y(0)$ of the curve $y = a \cosh (x/a)$ above the x-axis is chosen to be $y(0) = H/w$. (This can be done by letting $a = H/w$.) Show that the tension in the cable at $P(x, y)$ in Fig. 9–3 is

$$T = wy.$$

Solution. We make use of the fact that

$$\frac{dy}{dx} = \tan \phi,$$

since T acts along the tangent, and

$$T = \frac{H}{\cos \phi} = H \sec \phi,$$

by Eq. (4a). Then, differentiating (6), we have

$$\tan \phi = \frac{dy}{dx} = \sinh \frac{x}{a}$$

and

$$\sec \phi = \sqrt{\sec^2 \phi} = \sqrt{1 + \tan^2 \phi} = \sqrt{1 + \left(\frac{dy}{dx}\right)^2}$$

$$= \sqrt{1 + \sinh^2 \frac{x}{a}} = \sqrt{\cosh^2 \frac{x}{a}} = \cosh \frac{x}{a}.$$

Therefore

$$T = H \sec \phi = H \cosh \frac{x}{a}, \tag{7a}$$

where

$$a = \frac{H}{w} \quad \text{or} \quad H = wa. \tag{7b}$$

Combining (7a) and (7b), we have

$$T = wa \cosh \frac{x}{a}$$

or, when we take account of Eq. (6),

$$T = wy.$$

This means that the tension at P is equal to the weight of y feet of the cable. Thus if the end of the cable to the right of P is allowed to hang down over a smooth peg while the cable is held at P so that it does not slip, and if the cable is then cut off at the point Q where it crosses the x-axis (Fig. 9–4), it may then be released at P and the weight wy of the section of cable PQ will be just sufficient to prevent the cable from slipping. If this is carried out at two different points P and P', the cable may be draped over two smooth pegs without slipping, provided the free ends reach just to the x-axis. The curve $y = a \cosh (x/a)$ is called a *catenary* from the Latin word *catena*, meaning chain. The x-axis is called the directrix of the catenary.

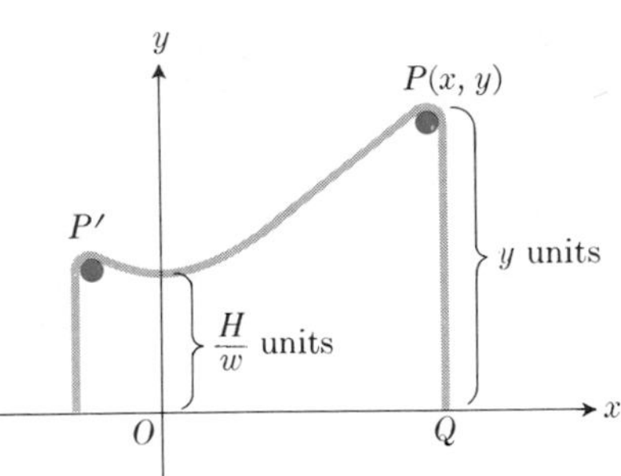

9–4 If the axes are positioned so that the lowest point of the uniform cable is H/w units above the x-axis, then the tension at each point $P(x, y)$ on the cable is exactly equal to the weight of a piece of cable y units long.

PROBLEMS

1. Establish the validity of the formulas XXIV–XXVI.

Find dy/dx in each of the following:

2. $y = \sinh 3x$

3. $y = \cosh^2 5x$

4. $y = \cosh^2 5x - \sinh^2 5x$

5. $y = \tanh 2x$

6. $y = \coth (\tan x)$

7. $y = \operatorname{sech}^3 x$

8. $y = 4 \operatorname{csch} (x/4)$

9. $\sinh y = \tan x$

Integrate each of the following:

10. $\int \cosh (2x + 1)\, dx$

11. $\int \tanh x\, dx$

12. $\int \frac{\sinh x}{\cosh^4 x}\, dx$

13. $\int \frac{4\, dx}{(e^x + e^{-x})^2}$

14. $\int \frac{e^x - e^{-x}}{e^x + e^{-x}}\, dx$

15. $\int \tanh^2 x\, dx$

16. $\int \frac{\sinh \sqrt{x}}{\sqrt{x}}\, dx$

17. $\int \cosh^2 3x\, dx$

18. $\int \sqrt{\cosh x - 1}\, dx$

19. Find the area of the hyperbolic sector AOP bounded by the arc AP and the lines OA, OP through the origin, in Fig. 9–1.

20. Find the length of $y = \cosh x$, $0 \le x \le 1$.

21. (*Calculator*) The line $y = (x/2) + 1$ crosses the catenary $y = \cosh x$ at the point (0, 1). Experiment with a calculator to collect evidence for the fact that the line also crosses the catenary approximately at the point (0.9308, 1.4654).

22. (*Calculator*) Two successive poles supporting an electric power line are 100 feet apart, the supporting members being at the same level. If the wire dips 25 feet at the center, (a) find the length of the wire between supports, and (b) find the tension in the wire at its lowest point if its weight is $w = 0.3$ lb/ft. [*Hint.* First approximate a from the equation $(25/a) + 1 = \cosh (50/a)$, which can be related to Problem 21 with $x = 50/a$.]

23. The equation $\sinh x = \tan \theta$, $-\pi/2 < \theta < \pi/2$, defines θ as a function of x:

$$\theta = \tan^{-1} (\sinh x),$$

to which the name "gudermannian of x" has been attached, written

$$\theta = \operatorname{gd} x.$$

Show that

$$\frac{d\theta}{dx} = \frac{1}{\cosh x} = \frac{1}{\sec \theta},$$

so that $\sec \theta\, d\theta = dx$ and

$$\int \sec \theta\, d\theta = \operatorname{gd}^{-1} \theta + C = \sinh^{-1} (\tan \theta) + C.$$

24. Sketch the curve $\theta = \operatorname{gd} x$ (see Problem 23) by the following procedure: First sketch the curves $y = \sinh x$ and $y = \tan \theta$ $(-\pi/2 < \theta < \pi/2)$ on separate xy- and θy-planes. Starting in the xy-plane with any value of x, $-\infty < x < +\infty$, determine the corresponding value of y from the curve $y = \sinh x$. Transfer this y reading to the y-axis in the θy-plane and determine the corresponding value of θ from the curve $y = \tan \theta$. Use this value of θ as ordinate and the original value of x as abscissa to plot a point on the curve $\theta = \operatorname{gd} x$.

25. Show that the curve $\theta = \operatorname{gd} x$ (see Problems 23 and 24) has the lines $\theta = \pm\pi/2$ as horizontal asymptotes, is always rising (from left to right), has a point of inflection at the origin, and is symmetric with respect to the origin.

*9–4 GEOMETRIC SIGNIFICANCE OF THE HYPERBOLIC RADIAN

We are now in a position to illustrate the meaning of the variable u in the equations

$$x = \cosh u, \qquad y = \sinh u \tag{1}$$

as they relate to the point $P(x, y)$ on the unit hyperbola

$$x^2 - y^2 = 1. \tag{2}$$

Before we do so, however, we shall find the analogous meaning of the variable θ in the equations

$$x = \cos \theta, \qquad y = \sin \theta \tag{3}$$

as they relate to the point $P(x, y)$ on the unit circle

$$x^2 + y^2 = 1. \tag{4}$$

The most familiar interpretation of θ is, of course, that it is the radian measure of the angle AOP in Fig. 9–5, that is

$$\theta = \frac{\text{arc } AP}{\text{radius } OA}.$$

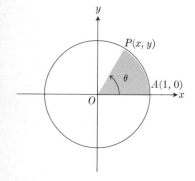

9–5 A sector of the unit circle $x^2 + y^2 = 1$. The number θ is twice the number of units of shaded area.

But we also recall that the area of a circular sector of radius r and central angle θ (radians) is given by $(\frac{1}{2})r^2\theta$. Since we are here dealing with a unit circle, this says that

$$\text{Area of sector } AOP = \tfrac{1}{2}\theta$$

or, if we solve this for θ,

$$\theta = \text{twice the area of the sector } AOP. \tag{5}$$

Of course we must realize that θ is a pure (dimensionless) number and Eq. (5) really says that the value of θ which Eqs. (3) associate with the point $P(x, y)$ on the unit circle is twice the *number* of square units of area that the radius vector OP sweeps out as P moves along the circle from A to its final position P. Thus when the area of the sector AOP is one-half the area of a square having OA as a side, then $\theta = 1$ and the coordinates of P represent cos 1 and sin 1. Negative values of θ would be interpreted as corresponding to areas swept over in a *clockwise* rotation of OP.

Now for the unit hyperbola,

$$x^2 - y^2 = 1,$$

we shall find an analogous interpretation for the variable u in the equations

$$x = \cosh u, \qquad y = \sinh u.$$

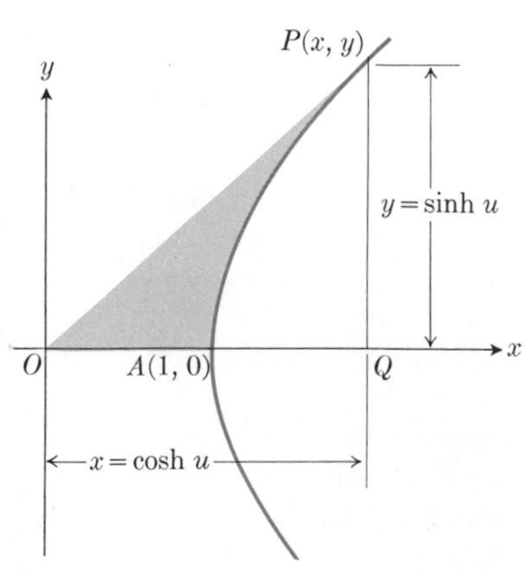

9–6 A "sector" of the unit hyperbola $x^2 - y^2 = 1$. The number u is twice the number of units of shaded area. (The text explains why.)

To see that this is indeed the case, we shall calculate the area of the sector AOP in Fig. 9–6. This area is clearly equal to the area of the triangle OQP minus the area AQP bounded above by the curve, below by the x-axis, and

---

* Starred sections may be omitted without loss of continuity.

on the right by the vertical line QP. But this area is simply

$$\text{area } AQP = \int_A^P y\,dx = \int_A^P \sinh u\, d(\cosh u)$$
$$= \int_A^P \sinh^2 u\, du = \tfrac{1}{2}\int_A^P (\cosh 2u - 1)\,du \qquad \text{[Eq. (12b), Article 9–2]}$$
$$= \tfrac{1}{2}\left[\tfrac{1}{2}\sinh 2u - u\right]_{A(u=0)}^{P(u=u)}$$
$$= \tfrac{1}{4}\sinh 2u - \tfrac{1}{2}u = \tfrac{1}{2}\sinh u \cosh u - \tfrac{1}{2}u.$$

Hence,

$$\text{Area of sector } AOP = \text{Area of } OQP - \text{Area of } AQP$$
$$= \tfrac{1}{2}\sinh u \cosh u - \left(\tfrac{1}{2}\sinh u \cosh u - \tfrac{1}{2}u\right)$$
$$= \tfrac{1}{2}u,$$

or, solving for u,

$$u = \text{twice the area of the sector } AOP. \tag{6}$$

As for the circle, a positive value of u is associated with an area above the x-axis and a negative value with an area below the x-axis, and areas are to be measured in terms of the unit square having OA as side. The term *hyperbolic radian* is sometimes used in connection with the variable u in Eq. (6), but here again, u is just a dimensionless real number. For example, cosh 2 and sinh 2 may be interpreted as the coordinates of P when the area of the sector AOP is just equal to the area of a square having OA as side.

9–5 THE INVERSE HYPERBOLIC FUNCTIONS

If we start with

$$x = \sinh y, \tag{1}$$

then as y varies continuously from $-\infty$ to $+\infty$, x does likewise. Graphically, this means that we may start with any real value on the y-axis in Fig. 9–7(a) and draw a horizontal line to the curve. Then a vertical line to the x-axis locates exactly one value of x such that the point (x, y) is on the curve. On the other hand, we could equally well reverse these steps and start with any real value x on the x-axis, go along a vertical line to the curve, then on a horizontal line to the y-axis. This latter procedure gives us y as a function of x, and the notation we use is

$$y = \sinh^{-1} x. \tag{2}$$

Here we have no problem about principal values, as we did in the case of the inverses of the circular functions, since the correspondence between the real numbers x and the real numbers y in Eq. (1) is one-to-one. Equation (1) says exactly the same thing as Eq. (2).

$$y = \sinh^{-1} x \quad \text{means} \quad x = \sinh y. \tag{3}$$

a)

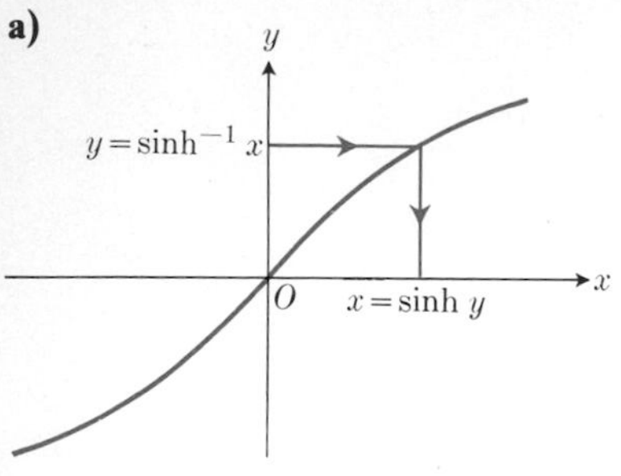

b)

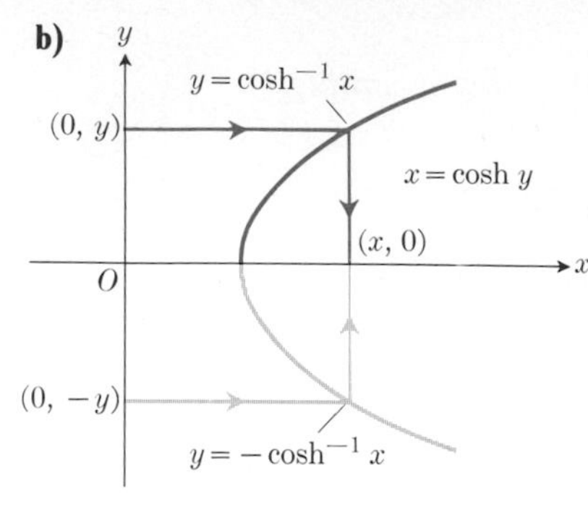

c)

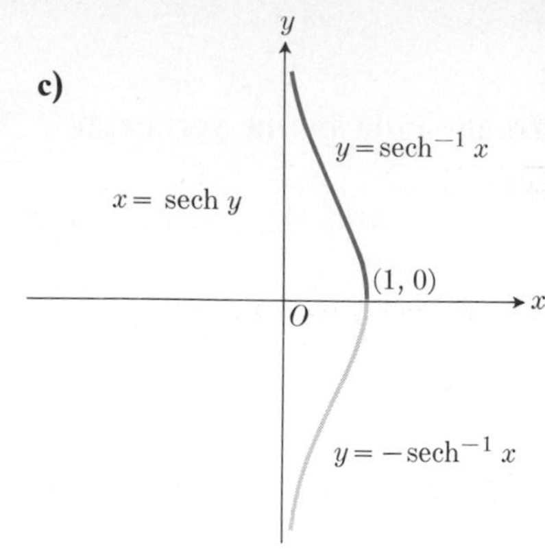

d)

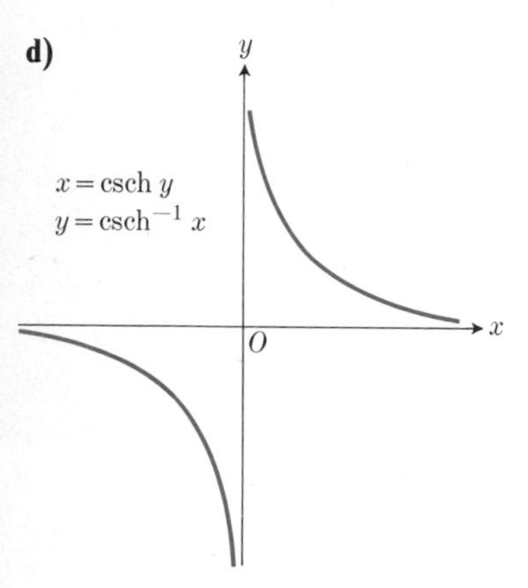

e)

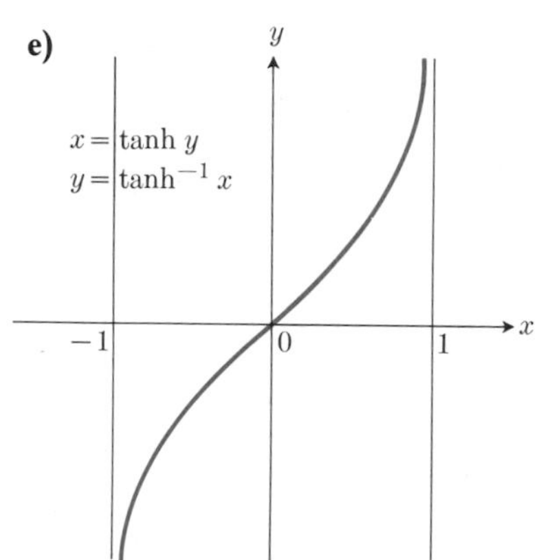

f)

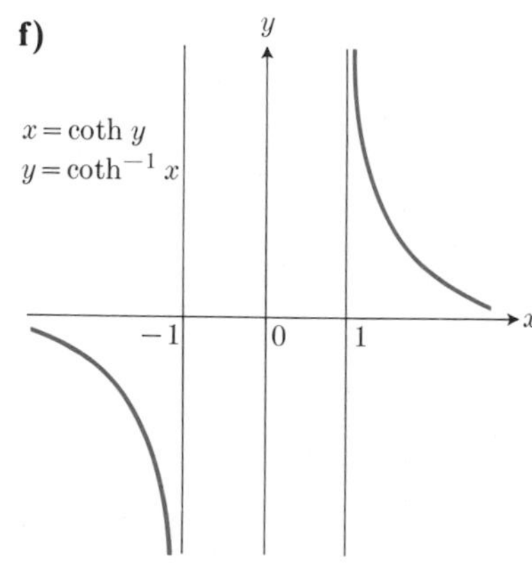

9–7 Graphs of the inverse hyperbolic functions.

The inverse hyperbolic cosine, however, is double-valued and it is desirable to prescribe a principal branch. For if we start with the equation

$$x = \cosh y,$$

then y and $-y$ both give the same value of x; that is, the correspondence between y-values and x-values is two-to-one, so that if x is considered the independent variable, there are *two* corresponding values of y. This is analogous to the situation surrounding the equation $x = y^2$, which defines x as a single-valued function of y; but when x is given and we ask for y, the result is $y = \pm\sqrt{x}$. In the case of the inverse hyperbolic cosine, we take the positive values of y as the principal branch:

$$y = \cosh^{-1} x \qquad \text{means} \quad x = \cosh y, \quad y \geq 0, \quad x \geq 1. \tag{4}$$

Thus in Fig. 9–7(b) the equation $x = \cosh y$ represents the entire curve, but $y = \cosh^{-1} x$ represents only that portion above the x-axis, while the portion below the x-axis is given by $y = -\cosh^{-1} x$.

Reference to Fig. 9–2 shows that the only other double-valued inverse is the inverse hyperbolic secant, and again we select the positive branch. That is,

$$y = \operatorname{sech}^{-1} x, \qquad y > 0, \qquad 0 < x \leq 1 \tag{5}$$

defines the principal branch and the numbers x and y satisfy

$$x = \operatorname{sech} y. \tag{6}$$

Since

$$\operatorname{sech} y = \frac{1}{\cosh y},$$

Eq. (6) is equivalent to

$$\cosh y = \frac{1}{x}$$

and the restriction $y > 0$ defines the same branch as in (5), so that

$$y = \cosh^{-1} \frac{1}{x}.$$

That is,

$$\operatorname{sech}^{-1} x = \cosh^{-1} \frac{1}{x}.$$

Similarly, we see that

$$y = \operatorname{csch}^{-1} x = \sinh^{-1} \frac{1}{x} \quad \text{means} \quad \operatorname{csch} y = x. \tag{7}$$

Also,

$$y = \tanh^{-1} x \quad \text{means} \quad x = \tanh y, \tag{8a}$$

and

$$y = \coth^{-1} x \quad \text{means} \quad x = \coth y. \tag{8b}$$

The graphs of the inverse hyperbolic functions are given in Fig. 9–7. Numerical values of $\sinh^{-1} x$, $\cosh^{-1} x$, and $\tanh^{-1} x$ are given in tables such as *Handbook of Mathematical Functions* (formerly published by the National Bureau of Standards, now printed by Dover Publications), which gives their values to ten decimal places. They are also given by many scientific calculators to eight or ten places.

When hyperbolic function keys are not available on a calculator, it is still possible to evaluate the inverse hyperbolic functions by expressing them in terms of logarithms, as illustrated below for $\tanh^{-1} x$. Let $y = \tanh^{-1} x$; then $\tanh y = x$ or

$$x = \frac{\sinh y}{\cosh y} = \frac{\frac{1}{2}(e^y - e^{-y})}{\frac{1}{2}(e^y + e^{-y})} = \frac{e^y - (1/e^y)}{e^y + (1/e^y)} = \frac{e^{2y} - 1}{e^{2y} + 1}.$$

We now solve this equation for e^{2y}:

$$xe^{2y} + x = e^{2y} - 1$$

or

$$1 + x = e^{2y}(1 - x),$$

and

$$e^{2y} = \frac{1 + x}{1 - x}.$$

Hence

$$y = \tanh^{-1} x = \frac{1}{2} \ln \frac{1+x}{1-x}, \qquad |x| < 1. \tag{9}$$

The variable x in Eq. (9) is restricted to the domain $|x| < 1$, since $x = \tanh y$ lies in this interval for all real values of y, $-\infty < y < +\infty$.

EXAMPLE 1

$$\tanh^{-1} 0.25 = \frac{1}{2} \ln \frac{1.25}{0.75} = \frac{1}{2} \ln \frac{5}{3}$$
$$= \tfrac{1}{2}(\ln 5 - \ln 3) \approx 0.25541.$$

The expressions for the other inverse hyperbolic functions in terms of logarithms are found in a similar manner. They are:

$$\begin{aligned}
\sinh^{-1} x &= \ln (x + \sqrt{x^2 + 1}), \quad -\infty < x < \infty, \\
\cosh^{-1} x &= \ln (x + \sqrt{x^2 - 1}), \quad x \geq 1, \\
\operatorname{sech}^{-1} x &= \ln \left(\frac{1 + \sqrt{1 - x^2}}{x} \right) = \cosh^{-1} \left(\frac{1}{x} \right), \quad 0 < x \leq 1, \\
\operatorname{csch}^{-1} x &= \ln \left(\frac{1}{x} + \frac{\sqrt{1 + x^2}}{|x|} \right) = \sinh^{-1} \left(\frac{1}{x} \right), \quad x \neq 0, \\
\coth^{-1} x &= \frac{1}{2} \ln \frac{x+1}{x-1} = \tanh^{-1} \left(\frac{1}{x} \right), \quad |x| > 1.
\end{aligned} \tag{10}$$

These logarithmic expressions are, on the whole, rather cumbersome, and the inverse hyperbolic functions provide a useful shorthand wherever these expressions arise.

The chief merit of the inverse hyperbolic functions lies in their usefulness in integration. This will easily be understood after we have derived the following formulas for their derivatives:

$$\frac{d(\sinh^{-1} u)}{dx} = \frac{1}{\sqrt{1 + u^2}} \frac{du}{dx}, \tag{XXVII}$$

$$\frac{d(\cosh^{-1} u)}{dx} = \frac{1}{\sqrt{u^2 - 1}} \frac{du}{dx}, \tag{XXVIII}$$

$$\frac{d(\tanh^{-1} u)}{dx} = \frac{1}{1 - u^2} \frac{du}{dx}, \quad |u| < 1, \tag{XXIX}$$

$$\frac{d(\coth^{-1} u)}{dx} = \frac{1}{1 - u^2} \frac{du}{dx}, \quad |u| > 1, \tag{XXX}$$

$$\frac{d(\operatorname{sech}^{-1} u)}{dx} = \frac{-du/dx}{u\sqrt{1 - u^2}}, \tag{XXXI}$$

$$\frac{d(\operatorname{csch}^{-1} u)}{dx} = \frac{-du/dx}{|u|\sqrt{1 + u^2}}. \tag{XXXII}$$

The proofs of these all follow the same method. We illustrate the case of $\cosh^{-1} u$. To this end, let

$$y = \cosh^{-1} u;$$

then

$$\cosh y = u,$$

$$\sinh y \frac{dy}{dx} = \frac{du}{dx},$$

and

$$\frac{dy}{dx} = \frac{1}{\sinh y} \frac{du}{dx}.$$

But

$$\cosh^2 y - \sinh^2 y = 1,$$
$$\cosh y = u,$$

so that

$$\sinh y = \pm\sqrt{\cosh^2 y - 1}$$
$$= \pm\sqrt{u^2 - 1}$$

and

$$\frac{dy}{dx} = \frac{1}{\pm\sqrt{u^2 - 1}} \frac{du}{dx}.$$

The ambiguous sign will be + if we restrict attention to the principal value, $y = \cosh^{-1} u$, $y \geq 0$, for then $\sinh y \geq 0$ and the ambiguous sign is the same as the sign of $\sinh y$. Thus XXVIII is established. The identities (5a) and (5b) of Article 9–2, with y in place of u, will be found to be useful in proving formulas XXIX to XXXII. The derivation is straightforward.

The restrictions $|u| < 1$ and $|u| > 1$ in XXIX and XXX, respectively, are due to the fact that if

$$y = \tanh^{-1} u,$$

then

$$u = \tanh y,$$

and since

$$-1 < \tanh y < 1,$$

this means $|u| < 1$. Similarly,

$$y = \coth^{-1} u, \qquad u = \coth y$$

requires $|u| > 1$. The distinction becomes important when we invert the formulas to get integration formulas, since otherwise we would be unable to tell whether we should write $\tanh^{-1} u$ or $\coth^{-1} u$ for

$$\int \frac{du}{1-u^2}.$$

The following integration formulas follow at once from the differential formulas XXVII′ to XXXII′, that are obtained by multiplying both sides of XXVII to XXXII by dx:

$$\begin{aligned}
&\textbf{1.} \quad \int \frac{du}{\sqrt{1+u^2}} = \sinh^{-1} u + C,\\
&\textbf{2.} \quad \int \frac{du}{\sqrt{u^2-1}} = \cosh^{-1} u + C,\\
&\textbf{3.} \quad \int \frac{du}{1-u^2} = \begin{cases} \tanh^{-1} u + C & \text{if } |u| < 1 \\ \coth^{-1} u + C & \text{if } |u| > 1 \end{cases} = \frac{1}{2} \ln \left| \frac{1+u}{1-u} \right| + C, \qquad \textbf{(11)}\\
&\textbf{4.} \quad \int \frac{du}{u\sqrt{1-u^2}} = -\operatorname{sech}^{-1} |u| + C = -\cosh^{-1}\left(\frac{1}{|u|}\right) + C,\\
&\textbf{5.} \quad \int \frac{du}{u\sqrt{1+u^2}} = -\operatorname{csch}^{-1} |u| + C = -\sinh^{-1}\left(\frac{1}{|u|}\right) + C.
\end{aligned}$$

PROBLEMS

1. Solve the equation $x = \sinh y = \frac{1}{2}(e^y - e^{-y})$ for e^y in terms of x, and thus show that $y = \ln(x + \sqrt{1+x^2})$. (This equation expresses $\sinh^{-1} x$ as a logarithm.)

2. Express $\cosh^{-1} x$ in terms of logarithms by using the method of Problem 1.

3. Establish formula XXVII.

4. Establish formula XXIX.

5. Establish formula XXXI.

Find dy/dx in each of the following:

6. $y = \sinh^{-1}(2x)$ **7.** $y = \tanh^{-1}(\cos x)$

8. $y = \cosh^{-1}(\sec x)$ **9.** $y = \coth^{-1}(\sec x)$

10. $y = \operatorname{sech}^{-1}(\sin 2x)$

Evaluate each of the following integrals:

11. $\int \frac{dx}{\sqrt{1+4x^2}}$ **12.** $\int \frac{dx}{\sqrt{4+x^2}}$ **13.** $\int_0^{0.5} \frac{dx}{1-x^2}$

14. $\int_{5/4}^{2} \frac{dx}{1-x^2}$ **15.** $\int \frac{dx}{x\sqrt{4+x^2}}$

16. (*Retarded free fall*) If a body of mass m falling from rest under the action of gravity encounters an air resistance proportional to the square of the velocity, then the velocity v at time t satisfies the differential equation

$$m\left(\frac{dv}{dt}\right) = mg - kv^2,$$

where k is a constant of proportionality and $v = 0$ when $t = 0$. Show that

$$v = \sqrt{\frac{mg}{k}} \tanh\left(\sqrt{\frac{gk}{m}}\, t\right),$$

and hence deduce that the body approaches a "limiting velocity" equal to $\sqrt{mg/k}$ as $t \to \infty$.

*9-6 THE HANGING CABLE

We conclude this chapter by deriving the solution of the differential equation

$$\frac{d^2y}{dx^2} = \frac{w}{H}\sqrt{1 + \left(\frac{dy}{dx}\right)^2}, \qquad \textbf{(1)}$$

which is the equation of equilibrium of forces on a hanging cable discussed in Article 9–3, Example 1. Since Eq. (1) involves the second derivative, we shall require two conditions to determine the constants of integration. By choosing the y-axis to be the vertical line through the lowest point of the cable (Fig. 9–8), one condition becomes

$$\frac{dy}{dx} = 0 \quad \text{when} \quad x = 0. \tag{2a}$$

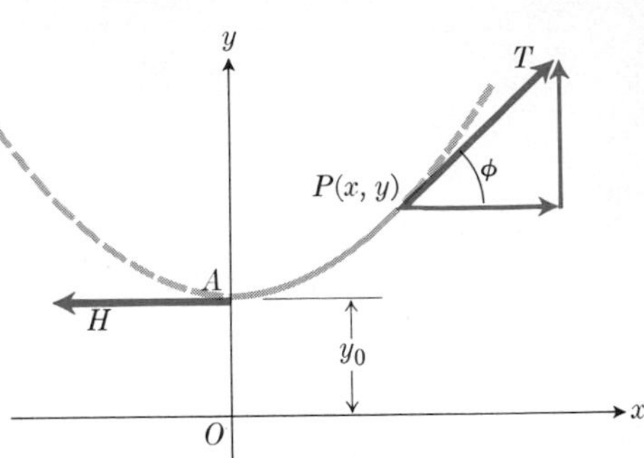

9–8 A section of hanging cable.

Then we may still move the x-axis up or down to suit our convenience. That is, we let

$$y = y_0 \quad \text{when} \quad x = 0, \tag{2b}$$

and we may choose y_0 so as to give us the simplest form in our final answer.

It is customary, when solving an equation such as (1), to introduce a single letter to represent dy/dx. The letter p is most often used. Thus we let

$$\frac{dy}{dx} = p, \tag{3a}$$

and then we may write

$$\frac{d^2y}{dx^2} = \frac{dp}{dx}, \tag{3b}$$

so that Eq. (1) takes the form

$$\frac{dp}{dx} = \frac{w}{H}\sqrt{1+p^2}.$$

We may now separate the variables to get

$$\frac{dp}{\sqrt{1+p^2}} = \frac{w}{H}\,dx$$

or

$$\int \frac{dp}{\sqrt{1+p^2}} = \frac{w}{H}x + C_1. \tag{4a}$$

The integral on the left is of the same form, with p in place of u, as the first formula in (11), Article 9–5. Hence (4a) becomes

$$\sinh^{-1} p = \frac{w}{H}x + C_1. \tag{4b}$$

Since $p = dy/dx = 0$ when $x = 0$, we determine the constant of integration

$$\sinh^{-1} 0 = C_1,$$

from which (see Fig. 9–7)

$$C_1 = 0.$$

Hence

$$\sinh^{-1} p = \frac{w}{H}x$$

or

$$p = \sinh\left(\frac{w}{H}x\right). \tag{5a}$$

We substitute $p = dy/dx$, multiply by dx, and have

$$dy = \sinh\left(\frac{w}{H}x\right)dx$$

or

$$\begin{aligned} y &= \int \sinh\left(\frac{w}{H}x\right)dx \\ &= \frac{H}{w}\int \sinh\left(\frac{w}{H}x\right)d\left(\frac{w}{H}x\right) \\ &= \frac{H}{w}\cosh\left(\frac{w}{H}x\right) + C_2. \end{aligned} \tag{5b}$$

The condition $y = y_0$ when $x = 0$ determines C_2:

$$y_0 = \frac{H}{w}\cosh 0 + C_2,$$

$$C_2 = y_0 - \frac{H}{w}, \tag{5c}$$

and hence

$$y = \frac{H}{w}\cosh\left(\frac{w}{H}x\right) + y_0 - \frac{H}{w}. \tag{5d}$$

Clearly, this equation will have a simpler form if we choose y_0 so that

$$y_0 = \frac{H}{w}.$$

We do so. The answer then takes the form

$$y = \frac{H}{w}\cosh\left(\frac{w}{H}x\right)$$

or

$$y = a\cosh\frac{x}{a} \quad \text{with} \quad a = \frac{H}{w}. \tag{6}$$

PROBLEMS

1. Find the length of arc of the catenary $y = a\cosh x/a$ from $A(0, a)$ to $P_1(x_1, y_1)$, $x_1 > 0$.

2. Show that the area bounded by the x-axis, the catenary $y = a\cosh x/a$, the y-axis, and the vertical line through $P_1(x_1, y_1)$, $x_1 > 0$, is the same as the area of a rectangle of altitude a and base s, where s is the length of the arc from $A(0, a)$ to P_1. (See Problem 1.)

3. The catenary $y = a\cosh x/a$ is revolved about the x-axis. Find the surface area generated by the portion of the curve between the points $A(0, a)$ and $P_1(x_1, y_1)$, $x_1 > 0$. (Incidentally, of all continuously differentiable curves $y = f(x)$, $f(x) > 0$, from $A(0, a)$ to $P(x_1, y_1)$, the catenary generates the surface of revolution of least area.)

4. Find the center of gravity of the arc of the catenary

$y = a \cosh x/a$ between two symmetrically located points $P_0(-x_1, y_1)$ and $P_1(x_1, y_1)$.

5. Find the volume generated when the area of Problem 2 is revolved about the x-axis.

6. The length of the arc AP (Fig. 9–8) is $s = a \sinh x/a$. (See Problem 1.)

a) Show that the coordinates of $P(x, y)$ may be expressed as functions of the arc length s, as follows:

$$x = a \sinh^{-1} \frac{s}{a}, \qquad y = \sqrt{s^2 + a^2}.$$

b) Calculate dx/ds and dy/ds from part (a) above and verify that $(dx/ds)^2 + (dy/ds)^2 = 1$.

7. (*Calculator or tables*) A cable 32 feet long and weighing 2 pounds per foot has its ends fastened at the same level to two posts 30 feet apart.

a) Show that the constant a in Eq. (6) must satisfy the equation

$$\sinh u = \frac{16}{15} u, \qquad u = \frac{15}{a}. \qquad \text{(See Problem 6a.)}$$

b) Sketch graphs of the curves $y_1 = \sinh u$, $y_2 = (16/15)u$ and show (with the aid of a calculator or tables) that they intersect at $u = 0$ and $u = \pm 0.6$ (approximately).

c) Using the results of part (b), find the dip in the cable at its center.

d) Using the results of part (b), find the tension in the cable at its lowest point.

REVIEW QUESTIONS AND EXERCISES

1. Define each of the hyperbolic functions.

2. State three trigonometric identities [such as formulas for $\sin(A + B)$, $\cos(A - B)$, $\cos^2 A + \sin^2 A = 1$, etc.]. What are the corresponding hyperbolic identities? Verify them.

3. Develop formulas for derivatives of the six hyperbolic functions.

4. What is the domain of the hyperbolic sine? What is its range?

5. What are the domain and range of the hyperbolic cosine? Of the hyperbolic tangent?

6. State some differences between the graphs of the trigonometric functions and their hyperbolic counterparts (for example, sine and sinh, cosine and cosh, tangent and tanh).

7. If $y = A \sin(at) + B \cos(at)$, then $y'' = -a^2 y$. What is the corresponding differential equation satisfied by $y = A \sinh(at) + B \cosh(at)$?

8. Define $\sinh^{-1}$ and $\cosh^{-1}$ functions. What are their domains? What are their ranges? What are their derivatives?

MISCELLANEOUS PROBLEMS

1. Prove the hyperbolic identity $\cosh 2x = \cosh^2 x + \sinh^2 x$.

2. Verify that $\tanh x = \sinh 2x/(1 + \cosh 2x)$.

3. Sketch the curves $y = \cosh x$ and $y = \sinh x$ in one diagram. To each positive value of x corresponds a point P on $y = \sinh x$ and a point Q on $y = \cosh x$. Calculate the limit of the distance PQ as x becomes infinitely large.

4. If $\cosh x = \frac{5}{4}$, find $\sinh x$ and $\tanh x$.

5. If $\operatorname{csch} x = -\frac{9}{40}$, find $\cosh x$ and $\tanh x$.

6. If $\tanh x > \frac{5}{13}$, show that $\sinh x > 0.4$ and $\operatorname{sech} x < 0.95$.

7. Let $P(x, y)$ be a point on the curve $y = \tanh x$ (Fig. 9–2(b)). Let AB be the vertical line segment through P with A and B on the asymptotes of the curve. Let C be a semicircle with AB as diameter. Let L be a line through P perpendicular to AB and cutting C in a point Q. Show that $PQ = \operatorname{sech} x$.

8. Prove that $\sinh 3u = 3 \sinh u + 4 \sinh^3 u$.

9. Find equations of the asymptotes of the hyperbola represented by the equation $y = \tanh(\frac{1}{2} \ln x)$.

10. A particle moves along the x-axis according to one of the following laws: (a) $x = a \cos kt + b \sin kt$, (b) $x = a \cosh kt + b \sinh kt$. In both cases, show that the acceleration is proportional to x, but that in the first case it is always directed toward the origin while in the second case it is directed away from the origin.

11. Show that $y = \cosh x$, $\sinh x$, $\cos x$, and $\sin x$ all satisfy the relationship $d^4y/dx^4 = y$.

Find dy/dx in each of Problems 12–21.

12. $y = \sinh^2 3x$

13. $\tan x = \tanh^2 y$

14. $\sin^{-1} x = \operatorname{sech} y$

15. $\sinh y = \sec x$

16. $\tan^{-1} y = \tanh^{-1} x$

17. $y = \tanh(\ln x)$

18. $x = \cosh(\ln y)$

19. $y = \sinh(\tan^{-1} e^{3x})$

20. $y = \sinh^{-1}(\tan x)$

21. $y^2 + x \cosh y + \sinh^2 x = 50$

Evaluate each of the following integrals, Problems 22–31:

22. $\int \frac{d\theta}{\sinh \theta + \cosh \theta}$

23. $\int \frac{\cosh \theta \, d\theta}{\sinh \theta + \cosh \theta}$

24. $\int \sinh^3 x \, dx$

25. $\int e^x \sinh 2x \, dx$

26. $\int \frac{e^{2x} - 1}{e^{2x} + 1} dx$

27. $\int_0^1 \frac{dx}{4 - x^2}$

28. $\int_3^5 \frac{dx}{4 - x^2}$

29. $\int \frac{e^t \, dt}{\sqrt{1 + e^{2t}}}$

30. $\int \frac{\sin x \, dx}{1 - \cos^2 x}$

31. $\int \frac{\sec^2 \theta \, d\theta}{\sqrt{\tan^2 \theta - 1}}$

Sketch the following curves, Problems 32–34:

32. $y = \frac{1}{2} \ln \frac{1 + \tanh x}{1 - \tanh x}$

33. $y = \tan \left(\frac{\pi}{2} \tanh x \right)$

34. $\cosh y = 1 + \frac{x^2}{2}$

35. If the arc s of the catenary $y = a \cosh (x/a)$ is measured from the lowest point, show that $dy/dx = s/a$.

36. A body starting from rest falls under the attraction of gravity but encounters resistance proportional to the square of its velocity. Show that if the body could continue to fall indefinitely under these same conditions, its velocity would approach a limiting value, and find the distance it would fall in time t.

37. Evaluate the limit, as $x \to \infty$, of $\cosh^{-1} x - \ln x$.

38. Evaluate

$$\lim_{x \to \infty} \int_1^x \left(\frac{1}{\sqrt{1 + t^2}} - \frac{1}{t} \right) dt.$$

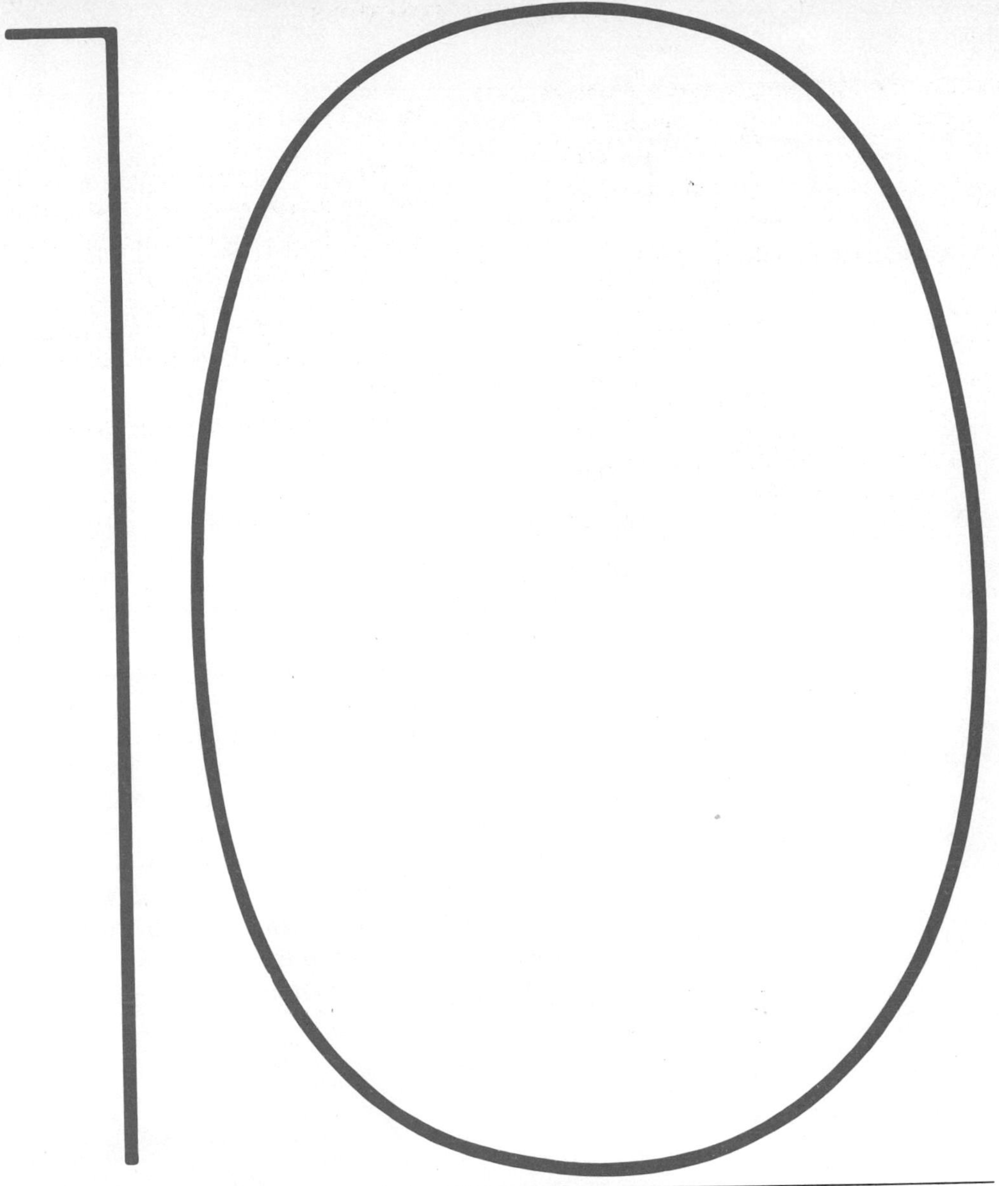

POLAR COORDINATES

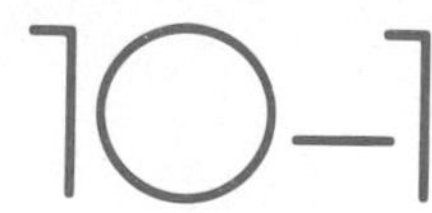

10-1 THE POLAR COORDINATE SYSTEM

We know that a point can be located in a plane by giving its abscissa and ordinate relative to a given coordinate system. Such x- and y-coordinates are called *cartesian* coordinates, in honor of the French mathematician-philosopher René Descartes* (1596–1650), who is credited with discovering this method of describing the position of a point in a plane.

Another useful way to locate a point in a plane is by *polar coordinates*, Fig. 10–1. First, we fix an *origin O* and an *initial ray*† from O. The point P has polar coordinates r, θ, with

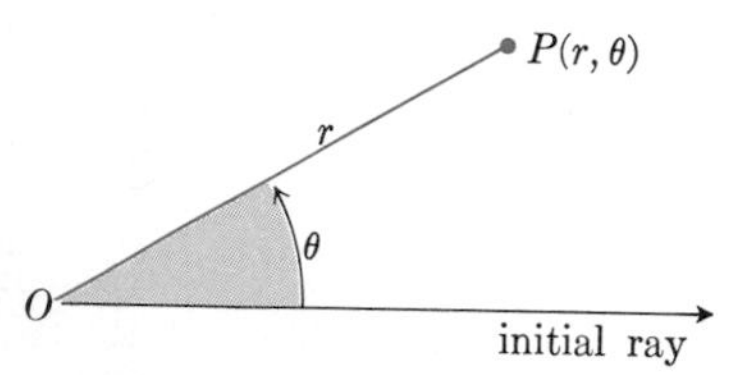

10–1 Polar coordinates.

$$r = \text{Directed distance from } O \text{ to } P, \tag{1a}$$

and

$$\theta = \text{Directed angle from initial ray to } OP. \tag{1b}$$

As in trigonometry, the angle θ is *positive* when measured counterclockwise and negative when measured clockwise (Fig. 10–1). But the angle associated with a given point is not unique (Fig. 10–2). For instance, the point 2 units from the origin, along the ray $\theta = 30°$, has polar coordinates $r = 2$, $\theta = 30°$. It also has coordinates $r = 2$, $\theta = -330°$, or $r = 2$, $\theta = 390°$.

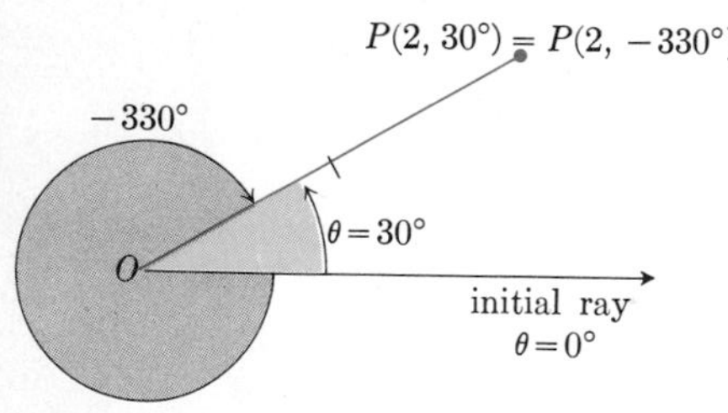

10–2 The ray $\theta = 30°$ is the same as the ray $\theta = -330°$.

There are occasions when we wish to allow r to be negative. That is why we say "directed distance" in Eq. (1a). The ray $\theta = 30°$ and the ray $\theta = 210°$ together make up a complete line through O (Fig. 10–3). The point $P(2, 210°)$ two units from O on the ray $\theta = 210°$ has polar coordinates $r = 2$, $\theta = 210°$. It can be reached by standing at O and facing out along the initial ray, if you first turn 210° counterclockwise, and then go forward two units. You would reach the same point by turning only 30° counterclockwise from the initial ray and then going *backward* two units. So we say that the point also has polar coordinates $r = -2$, $\theta = 30°$.

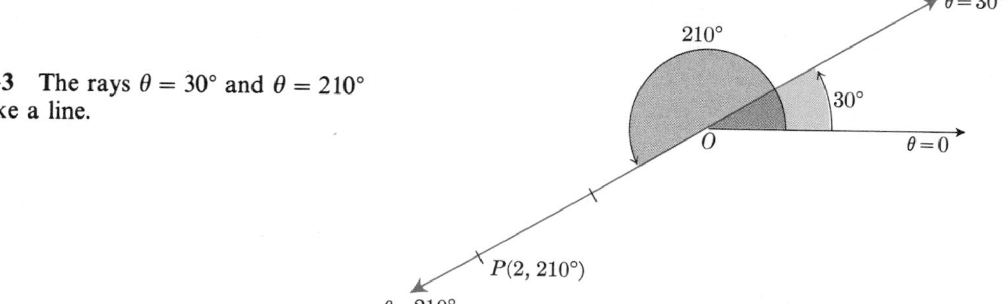

10–3 The rays $\theta = 30°$ and $\theta = 210°$ make a line.

Whenever the angle between two rays is 180°, the rays actually make a straight line. We then say that each ray is the negative of the other. Points on the ray $\theta = \alpha$ have polar coordinates (r, α) with $r \geq 0$. Points on the

* For an interesting biographical account, together with an excerpt from Descartes' own writings, see *World of Mathematics*, Vol. 1, pp. 235–253.

† A *ray* is a half-line consisting of a vertex and points of a line on one side of the vertex. For example, the origin and positive x-axis make up a ray. The set of points on the line $y = 2x + 3$ with $x \geq 1$ is another ray; its vertex is (1, 5).

negative ray, $\theta = \alpha + 180°$, have coordinates (r, α) with $r \leq 0$. The origin is $r = 0$. (See Fig. 10–4 for the ray $\theta = 30°$ and its negative. *Caution.* The "negative" of the ray $\theta = 30°$ is the ray $\theta = 30° + 180° = 210°$ and *not* the ray $\theta = -30°$. "Negative" refers to the directed distance r.)

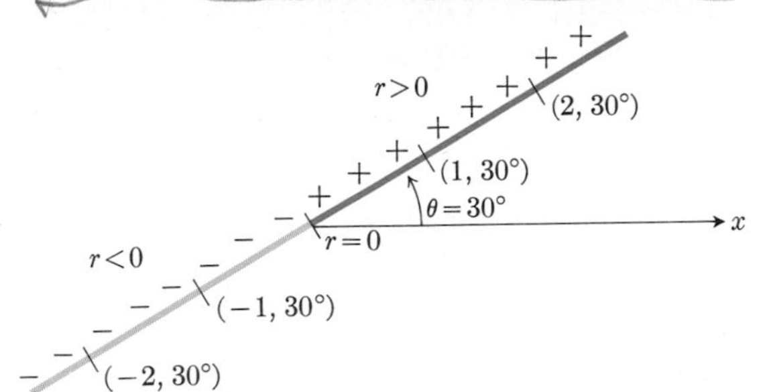

10–4 The terminal ray $\theta = \pi/6$ and its negative.

There is a great advantage in being able to use both polar and cartesian coordinates. To do this, we use a common origin and take the initial ray as the positive x-axis, the ray $\theta = 90°$ as the positive y-axis. The coordinates (Fig. 10–5) are then related by the equations

$$x = r \cos \theta, \qquad y = r \sin \theta. \tag{2}$$

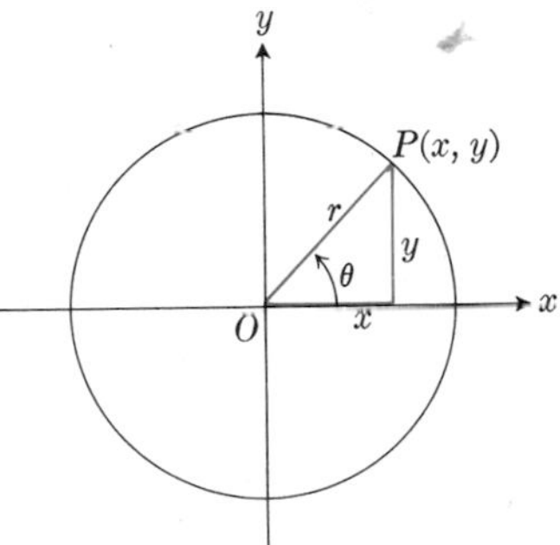

10–5 Polar and cartesian coordinates.

These are the equations that define $\sin \theta$ and $\cos \theta$ when r is positive. They are also valid if r is negative, because $\cos(\theta + 180°) = -\cos \theta$, $\sin(\theta + 180°) = -\sin \theta$, so positive r's on the ray $\theta + 180°$ correspond to negative r's associated with the ray θ. When $r = 0$, then $x = y = 0$, and P is the origin.

If we impose the condition

$$r = a \qquad (a \text{ constant}), \tag{3}$$

then the locus of P is a circle with center O, radius a, and P describes the circle once as θ varies from 0 to 360° (Fig. 10–6). On the other hand, if we let r vary and hold θ fixed, say

$$\theta = 30°, \tag{4}$$

the locus of P is the straight line shown in Fig. 10–4.

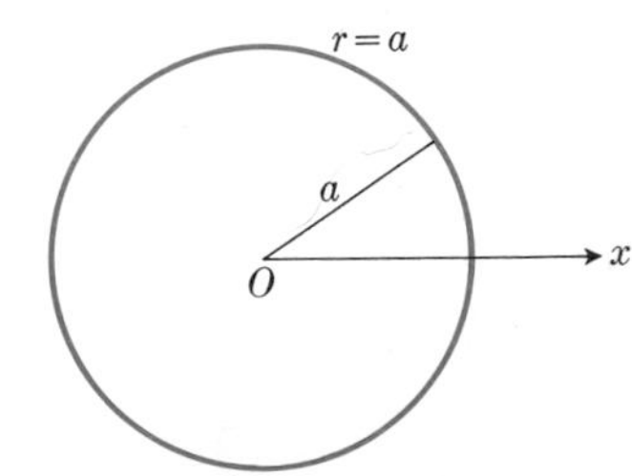

10–6 The polar equation for the circle shown above is $r = a$.

We adopt the convention that r may be any real number, $-\infty < r < \infty$. Then $r = 0$ corresponds to $x = 0$, $y = 0$ in Eqs. (2), regardless of θ. That is,

$$r = 0, \qquad \theta \text{ any value} \tag{5}$$

is the origin. Positive values of r with θ fixed give points on the terminal side of the angle θ; *negative* values of r give points on the negative ray.

The same point may be represented in several different ways in polar coordinates. For example, the point (2, 30°), or $(2, \pi/6)$, has the following representations:

$$(2, 30°), \qquad (2, -330°), \qquad (-2, 210°), \qquad (-2, -150°).$$

These and all others are summarized in the two formulas

$$(2, 30° + n360°), \qquad (-2, 210° + n360°) \qquad [n = 0, \pm 1, \pm 2, \ldots]$$

or, if we measure the angles in radians,

$$\left(2, \frac{\pi}{6} + 2n\pi\right), \qquad \left(-2, \frac{7\pi}{6} + 2n\pi\right) \qquad [n = 0, \pm 1, \pm 2, \ldots].$$

The fact that the same point may be represented in several different ways in polar coordinates makes added care necessary in certain situations. For example, the point $(2a, \pi)$ is on the curve

$$r^2 = 4a^2 \cos \theta \tag{6}$$

even though its coordinates as given do not satisfy the equation, because the same point is represented by $(-2a, 0)$ and these coordinates do satisfy the equation. The same point $(2a, \pi)$ is on the curve

$$r = a(1 - \cos \theta), \tag{7}$$

and hence this point should be included among the points of intersection of the two curves represented by Eqs. (6) and (7). But if we solve the equations simultaneously by substituting $\cos \theta = r^2/4a^2$ from (6) into (7) and then solving the resulting quadratic equation

$$\left(\frac{r}{a}\right)^2 + 4\left(\frac{r}{a}\right) - 4 = 0$$

for

$$\frac{r}{a} = -2 \pm 2\sqrt{2}, \tag{8}$$

we do *not* obtain the point $(2a, \pi)$ as a point of intersection. The reason is simple enough; namely, the point is not on the curves "simultaneously" in the sense of being reached at the same value of θ, since it is reached in the one case when $\theta = 0$ and in the other case when $\theta = \pi$. It is as though two ships describe paths that intersect at a point, but the ships do not collide because they reach the point of intersection at different times! The curves represented by Eqs. (6) and (7) are shown in Fig. 10–10(c), and they are seen to intersect at the four points

$$(0, 0), \qquad (2a, \pi), \qquad (r_1, \theta_1), \qquad (r_1, -\theta_1), \tag{9a}$$

where

$$r_1 = (-2 + 2\sqrt{2})a,$$
$$\cos \theta_1 = 1 - \frac{r_1}{a} = 3 - 2\sqrt{2}. \tag{9b}$$

Only the last two of these points are found from the simultaneous solution; the first two are disclosed only by graphing the curves.

REMARK. Karl von Frisch has advanced the following theory about how bees communicate information about newly discovered sources of food. A scout returning to the hive from a flower bed gives away samples of the food and then, if the bed is more than about a hundred yards away, performs a dance to show where the flowers are. The bee runs straight ahead for a centimeter or so, waggling from side to side, and circles back to the starting place. The bee then repeats the straight run, circling back in the opposite direction (Fig. 10–7). The dance continues this way in regular alternation. Exceptionally excited bees have been observed to dance for more than three and a half hours.

If the dance is performed outside the hive, the straight run points to the flowers. If the dance is performed inside, it is performed on the vertical wall of a honeycomb, with gravity substituting for the sun's position. A vertical straight run means that the food is in the direction of the sun. A run 30° to the right of vertical means that the food is 30° to the right of the sun, and so on. Distance (more accurately, the amount of energy required to reach the food) is communicated by the duration of the straight-run portions of the dance. Straight runs lasting three seconds each are typical for distances of about a half-mile from the hive. Straight runs that last five seconds each mean about two miles. (See E. O. Wilson's *The Insect Societies*, Belknap Press of Harvard University Press, Cambridge, MA, 1971, for details.)

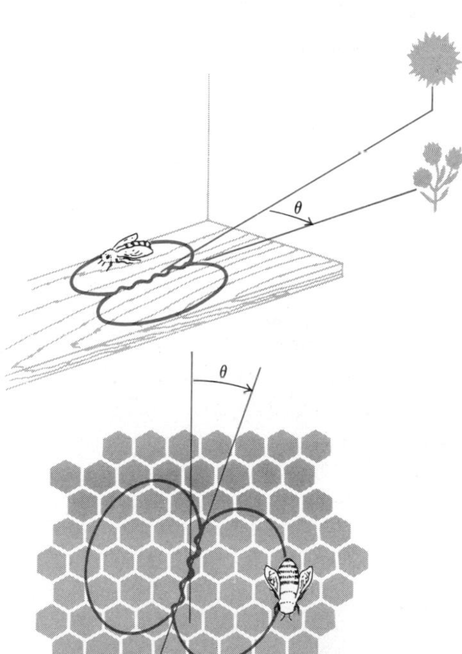

10–7 The waggle dance of a scout bee.

PROBLEMS

1. Plot the following points, given in polar form, and find *all* polar coordinates of each point:

a) $(3, \pi/4)$ **b)** $(-3, \pi/4)$ **c)** $(3, -\pi/4)$ **d)** $(-3, -\pi/4)$

In Problems 2–9, graph the set of points $P(r, \theta)$ whose polar coordinates satisfy the given equation, inequality or inequalities.

2. $r = 2$

3. $0 \leq r \leq 2$

4. $r > 1$

5. $1 < r < 2$

6. $0° \leq \theta \leq 30°, \quad r \geq 0$

7. $\theta = 120°, \quad r \leq -2$

8. $\theta = 60°, \quad -1 \leq r \leq 3$

9. $\theta = 495°, \quad r \geq -1$

10. Find cartesian coordinates for the points in Problem 1.

In Problems 11–14, use Eq. (2) to write cartesian equations equivalent to the given polar equations. Then graph the equations.

11. $r \cos \theta = 2$

12. $r \sin \theta = -1$

13. $r \cos \theta + r \sin \theta = 1$

14. $r \sin \theta = r \cos \theta$

In Problems 15–18, use the trigonometric formulas in Eqs. (11a–e) of Article 2–9 to expand the left side of each equation. Then replace the resulting polar equation by an equivalent cartesian equation, and sketch the graph.

15. $r \cos (\theta - 60°) = 3$

16. $r \sin (\theta + 45°) = 4$

17. $r \sin (45° - \theta) = \sqrt{2}$

18. $r \cos (30° - \theta) = 0$

19. Show that $(2, \frac{3}{4}\pi)$ is on the curve $r = 2 \sin 2\theta$.

20. Show that $(\frac{1}{2}, \frac{3}{2}\pi)$ is on the curve $r = -\sin (\theta/3)$.

21. Show that the equations $r = \cos \theta + 1$, $r = \cos \theta - 1$, represent the same curve.

Find some intersections of the following pairs of curves (a = constant):

22. $r^2 = 2a^2 \sin 2\theta, \quad r = a$

23. $r = a \sin \theta, \quad r = a \cos \theta$

24. $r = a(1 + \cos \theta), \quad r = a(1 - \sin \theta)$

25. $r = a(1 + \sin \theta), \quad r = 2a \cos \theta$

26. $r = a \cos 2\theta, \quad r = a(1 + \cos \theta)$

10-2 GRAPHS OF POLAR EQUATIONS

The graph of an equation

$$F(r, \theta) = 0$$

consists of all those points whose coordinates (in some form) satisfy the equation. Frequently the equation gives r explicitly in terms of θ, as

$$r = f(\theta).$$

As many points as desired may then be obtained by substituting values of θ and calculating the corresponding values of r. In particular, it is desirable to plot the points where r is a maximum or a minimum and to find the values of θ when the curve passes through the origin, if that occurs.

Certain types of *symmetry* are readily detected. For example, the curve is:

a) symmetric about the origin if the equation is unchanged when r is replaced by $-r$;

b) symmetric about the x-axis if the equation is unchanged when θ is replaced by $-\theta$;

c) symmetric about the y-axis if the equation is unchanged when θ is replaced by $\pi - \theta$.

These and certain other tests for symmetry are readily verified by considering the symmetrically located points in Fig. 10–8.

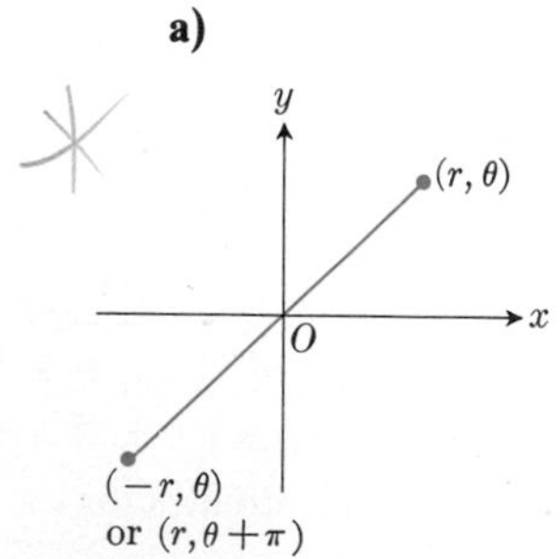

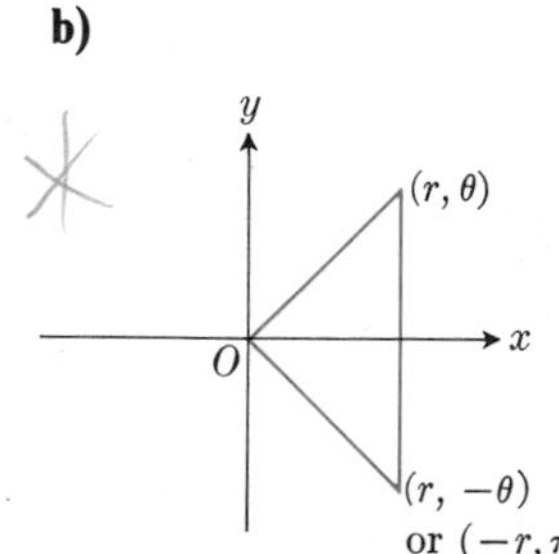

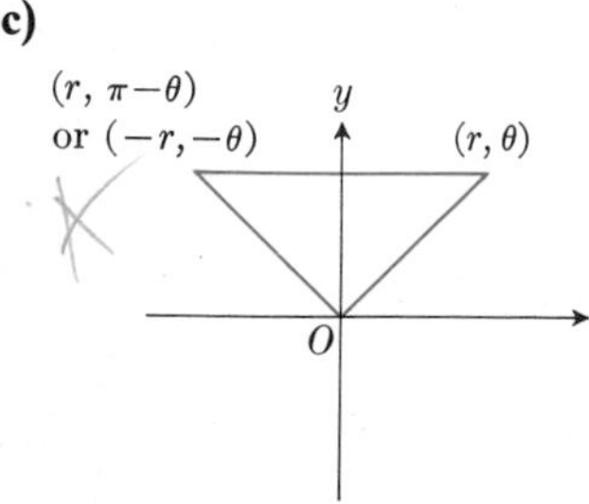

10–8 Some of the polar coordinate tests for symmetry.

EXAMPLE 1. Discuss and sketch the curve $r = a(1 - \cos\theta)$, where a is a positive constant.

Discussion. Since $\cos(-\theta) = \cos\theta$, the equation is unaltered when θ is replaced by $-\theta$; hence the curve is symmetric about the x-axis (Fig. 10–8b). Also, since

$$-1 \le \cos\theta \le 1,$$

the values of r vary between 0 and $2a$. The minimum value, $r = 0$, occurs at $\theta = 0$, and the maximum value, $r = 2a$, occurs at $\theta = \pi$. Moreover, as θ varies from 0 to π, $\cos\theta$ decreases from 1 to -1; hence $1 - \cos\theta$ increases from 0 to 2. That is, r increases from 0 to $2a$ as the radius vector OP swings from $\theta = 0$ to $\theta = \pi$. We make a table of values (Table 10–1) and plot the corresponding points.

Table 10–1. Values of $r = a(1 - \cos\theta)$ for selected values of θ

θ:	0	60°	90°	120°	180°
r:	0	$a/2$	a	$3a/2$	$2a$

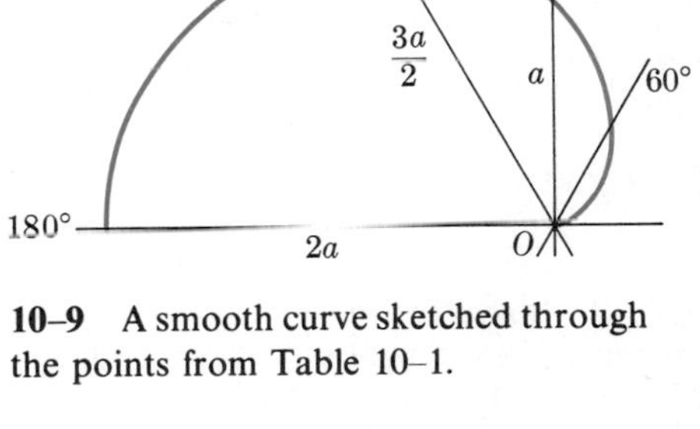

10–9 A smooth curve sketched through the points from Table 10–1.

Now we sketch a smooth curve through them (Fig. 10–9) in such a way that r increases as θ increases, since

$$\frac{dr}{d\theta} = a\sin\theta$$

is positive for $0 < \theta < \pi$. Then we exploit the symmetry of the curve and reflect this portion across the x-axis. The result is the curve shown in Fig. 10–10(a), which is called a *cardioid* because of its heart-shaped appearance. Its behavior at the origin and the angles between its tangents and the coordinate axes at the other intercepts are more easily discussed at a later time. However, we may investigate the slope of the cardioid at the origin as follows: Let P be a point on the curve in the first quadrant, where P is

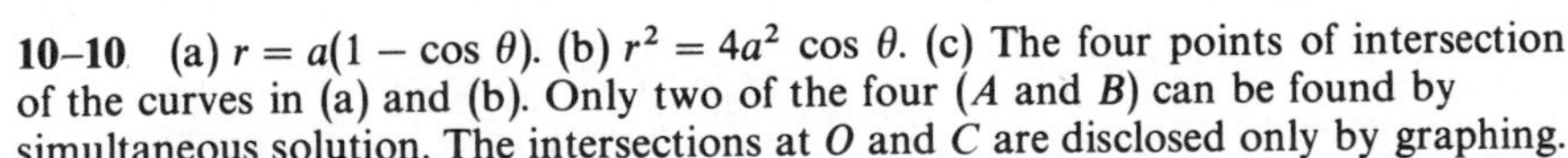

10–10 (a) $r = a(1 - \cos\theta)$. (b) $r^2 = 4a^2\cos\theta$. (c) The four points of intersection of the curves in (a) and (b). Only two of the four (A and B) can be found by simultaneous solution. The intersections at O and C are disclosed only by graphing.

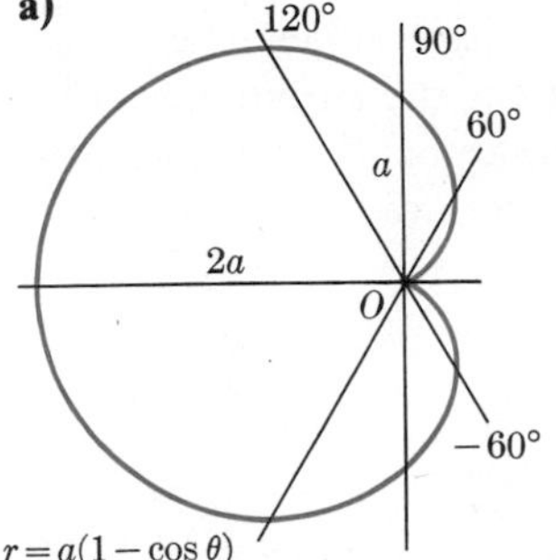

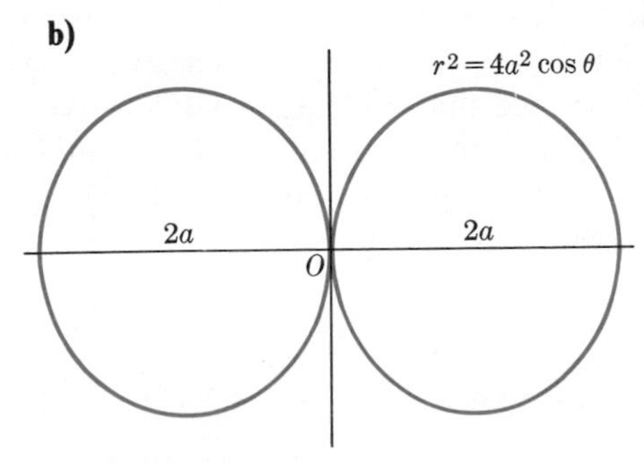

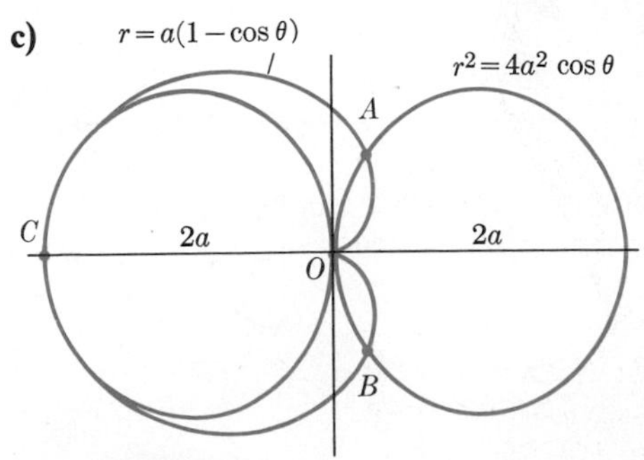

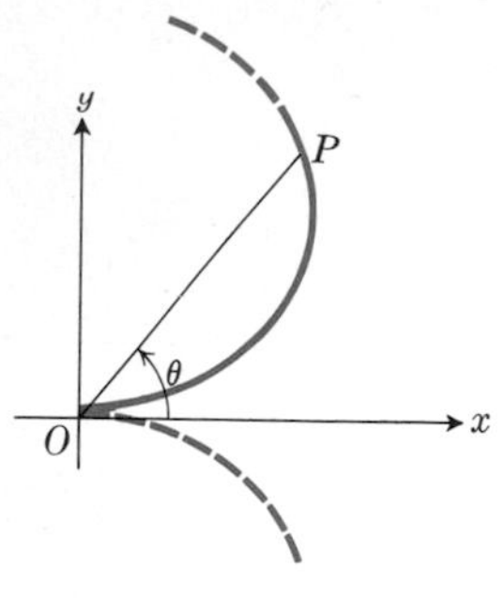

10–11 As $P \to O$ along the cardioid, $\theta \to 0$. At the origin, the cardioid has a horizontal tangent.

destined to approach O along the curve (see Fig. 10–11). Then, as $P \to O$, the slope of OP ($= \tan\theta$) approaches the slope of the tangent at O. Since $P \to O$ as $\theta \to 0$,

$$\lim_{\theta\to 0} (\text{slope of } OP) = \lim_{\theta\to 0} \tan\theta = 0.$$

That is, the slope of the tangent to the curve at the origin is zero.

The process by which we found the tangent to the cardioid at the origin at the end of Example 1 works for any smooth curve through the origin. If the curve passes through the origin when $\theta = \theta_0$, then the discussion in Example 1 would be modified only to the extent of saying that $P \to O$ along the curve as $\theta \to \theta_0$, and hence

$$\left(\frac{dy}{dx}\right)_{\theta=\theta_0} = \lim_{\theta\to\theta_0} (\tan\theta) = \tan\theta_0.$$

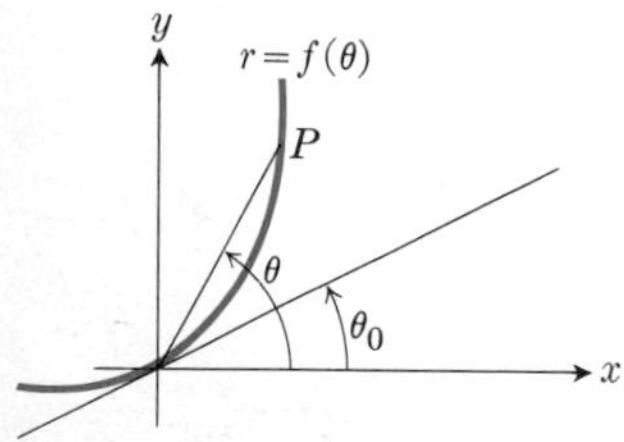

10–12 If the curve $r = f(\theta)$ passes through the origin at $\theta = \theta_0$, and if f has a derivative at $\theta = \theta_0$, then the line $\theta = \theta_0$ is tangent to the curve at the origin.

But $(dy/dx)_{\theta=\theta_0}$ is also the tangent of the angle between the x-axis and the curve at this point. Hence the line $\theta = \theta_0$ is tangent to the curve at the origin. In other words, whenever a curve passes through the origin for a value θ_0 of θ and the derivative $dr/d\theta$ exists at that point, it does so *tangent* to the line $\theta = \theta_0$. See Fig. 10–12.

EXAMPLE 2. $r^2 = 4a^2 \cos\theta$. This curve is symmetric about the origin. Two values,

$$r = \pm 2a\sqrt{\cos\theta},$$

correspond to each value of θ for which $\cos\theta > 0$, namely,

$$-\frac{\pi}{2} < \theta < \frac{\pi}{2}.$$

Furthermore, the curve is symmetric about the x-axis, since θ may be replaced by $-\theta$ without altering the value of $\cos\theta$. The curve passes through the origin at $\theta = \pi/2$ and is tangent to the y-axis at this point. Since $\cos\theta$ never exceeds unity, the maximum value of r is $2a$, which occurs at $\theta = 0$. As θ increases from 0 to $\pi/2$, $|r|$ decreases from $2a$ to 0. The curve is sketched in Fig. 10–10(b).

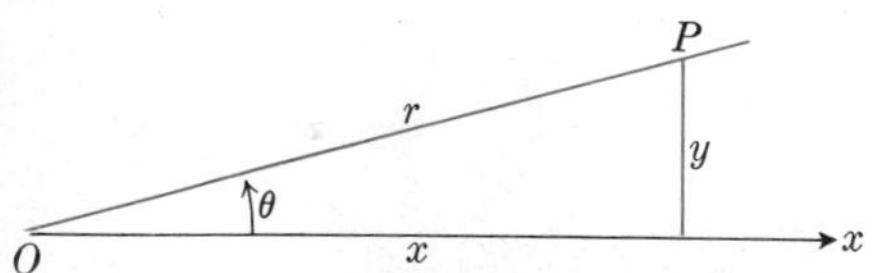

10–13 As $\theta \to 0$, P can be kept away from the axis by increasing r.

EXAMPLE 3. $r\theta = a$, where a is a positive constant. When $\theta = 0$ the equation becomes $0 = a$, which is not true. That is, there is no point on the curve for $\theta = 0$. However, suppose θ is a *small* positive angle. Then from $r = a/\theta$, we see that r is large and positive. Consider the situation in Fig. 10–13. No matter how small the positive angle θ may be, if r is sufficiently large the point P may be far above the x-axis. In fact, we need to see what happens to

$$y = r\sin\theta = \frac{a}{\theta}\sin\theta$$

for small positive values of θ. We know, of course, that

$$\lim_{\theta\to 0} \frac{\sin\theta}{\theta} = 1;$$

hence

$$\lim_{\theta \to 0} y = \lim_{\theta \to 0} a \frac{\sin \theta}{\theta} = a.$$

This shows that the line $y = a$ is an asymptote of this curve. So we think of the curve being traced by a point P that starts far out near the line $y = a$ for $\theta = 0^+$ and moves in the direction indicated by the arrows in Fig. 10–14(a) as θ increases and r decreases. As the radius vector OP continues to rotate about the origin, it shrinks in length, and P describes a spiral, which coils around the origin with r tending to zero as θ increases indefinitely.

When r and θ are replaced by $-r$ and $-\theta$, respectively, the equation is unaltered. Hence for every point (r_1, θ_1) on the curve in Fig. 10–14(a), there is a point $(-r_1, -\theta_1)$ symmetrically located with respect to the y-axis, also on the curve $r\theta = a$. We therefore reflect the curve in Fig. 10–14(a) in the y-axis, obtaining another spiral which coils around the origin in the clockwise sense as θ approaches minus infinity. The complete curve is indicated in Fig. 10–14(b). It is called a *hyperbolic spiral*, the adjective "hyperbolic" being used because the equation $r\theta = a$ is analogous to the equation $xy = a$, which represents a hyperbola in cartesian coordinates.

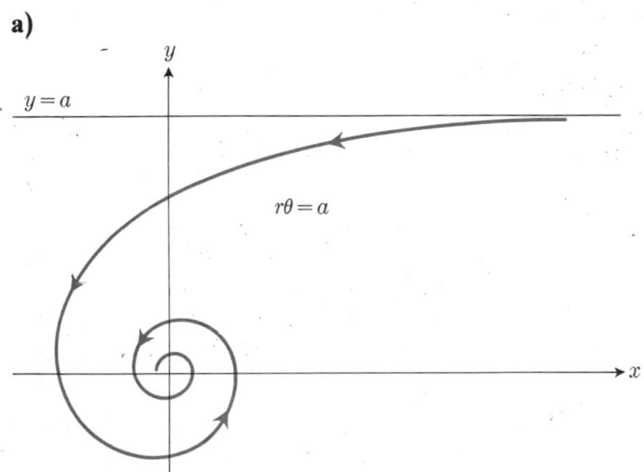

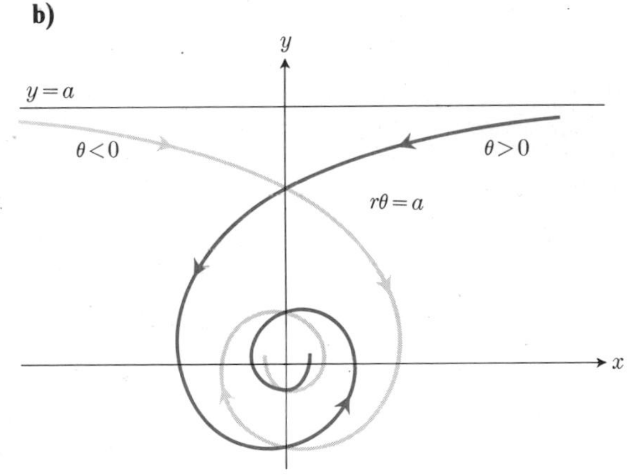

10–14 The hyperbolic spiral $r\theta = a$.

PROBLEMS

1. Find the polar form of the equation of the line $3x + 4y = 5$.

2. If the polar coordinates (r, θ) of a point P satisfy the equation $r = 2a \cos \theta$, what equation is satisfied by the cartesian coordinates (x, y) of P?

Discuss and sketch each of the following curves;

3. $r = a(1 + \cos \theta)$ **4.** $r = a(1 - \sin \theta)$

5. $r = a \sin 2\theta$ **6.** $r^2 = 2a^2 \cos 2\theta$

7. $r = a(2 + \sin \theta)$ **8.** $r = a(1 + 2 \sin \theta)$

9. $r = \theta$ **10.** $r = a \sin \theta/2$

11. Find the points on the curve $r = a(1 + \cos \theta)$, where the tangent is (a) parallel to the x-axis, (b) parallel to the y-axis. [*Hint*. Express x and y in terms of θ. Then calculate dy/dx.]

12. Sketch the curves $r = a(1 + \cos \theta)$ and $r = 3a \cos \theta$ in one diagram and find the angle between their tangents at the point of intersection that lies in the first quadrant.

13. What kind of symmetry occurs in the graph of $r = f(\theta)$ if the equation is unaltered when r and θ are replaced by $-r$ and $-\theta$, respectively?

POLAR EQUATIONS OF THE CONIC SECTIONS AND OTHER CURVES

The relationships given in Article 10–1 between cartesian and polar coordinates enable us to change any cartesian equation into a polar equation for the same curve.

For example, the circle

$$x^2 + y^2 - 2ax = 0, \tag{1}$$

with center at $(a, 0)$ and radius a (Fig. 10–15a) becomes

$$(r \cos \theta)^2 + (r \sin \theta)^2 - 2a(r \cos \theta) = 0,$$

which reduces to

$$r(r - 2a \cos \theta) = 0.$$

The graph obtained by putting the first factor equal to zero, $r = 0$, is just one point, the origin. The other factor vanishes when

$$r = 2a \cos \theta. \tag{2}$$

This includes the origin among its points and hence represents the entire graph of Eq. (1).

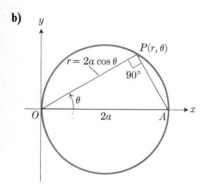

10–15 The circle $r = 2a \cos \theta$.

The example illustrates one method of finding the polar equation for a curve, namely by transforming its cartesian equation into polar form. An alternative method is to derive the polar equation directly from some geometric property. For example, take the circle in Fig. 10–15(b) and let $P(r, \theta)$ be a representative point on the circle. Then angle OPA is a right angle (why?) and from the right triangle OPA, we read

$$\frac{r}{2a} = \cos \theta \qquad \text{or} \qquad r = 2a \cos \theta,$$

which is the same equation obtained above.

We shall apply this second method to obtain equations of various curves in the following examples.

EXAMPLE 1. Find the polar equation of the circle of radius a with center at (b, β).

Solution. We let $P(r, \theta)$ be a representative point on the circle and apply the law of cosines to the triangle OCP (Fig. 10–16) to obtain

$$a^2 = b^2 + r^2 - 2br \cos (\theta - \beta). \tag{3}$$

If the circle passes through the origin, then $b = a$ and the equation takes the simpler form

$$r[r - 2a \cos (\theta - \beta)] = 0$$

or

$$r = 2a \cos (\theta - \beta). \tag{4}$$

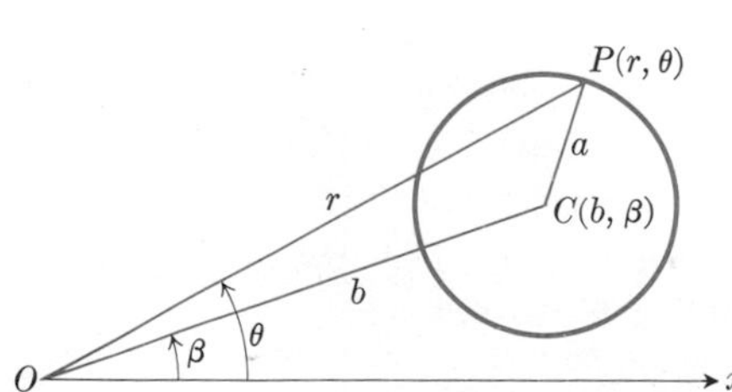

10–16 To find an equation for the circle shown above, apply the law of cosines to triangle OCP.

In particular, if $\beta = 0$, Eq. (4) reduces to the result we have obtained before, while if $\beta = 90°$, so that the center of the circle lies on the y-axis (Fig. 10–17), Eq. (4) reduces to

$$r = 2a \sin \theta. \tag{5}$$

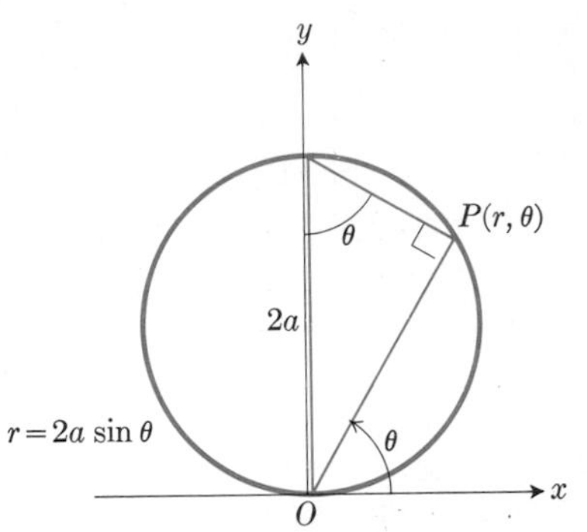

10–17 $r = 2a \sin \theta$ **is the equation of a circle through the origin with its center on the positive** y**-axis.**

EXAMPLE 2. The normal from the origin to the line L intersects L at the point $N(p, \beta)$. Find the polar equation of L.

Solution. We let $P(r, \theta)$ be a representative point on the line L in Fig. 10–18 and, from the right triangle ONP, read the result

$$r \cos (\theta - \beta) = p. \tag{6}$$

This equation is simply a more general form of the equation

$$r \cos \theta = p, \tag{7}$$

which is the polar form of the line

$$x = p.$$

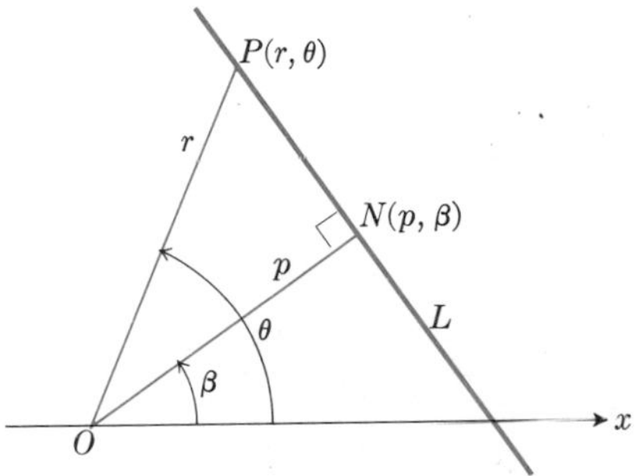

10–18 The relation $p/r = \cos (\theta - \beta)$ can be read from the triangle ONP.

In fact, if we perform a rotation of axes as in Fig. 10–19, the new polar coordinates (r', θ') are related to the old polar coordinates as follows:

$$r' = r, \qquad \theta' = \theta - \beta. \tag{8}$$

If we apply this rotation to Eq. (6), we get

$$r' \cos \theta' = p.$$

But

$$r' \cos \theta' = x',$$

so the equation is the same as

$$x' = p,$$

which represents a straight line p units from and parallel to the y'-axis.

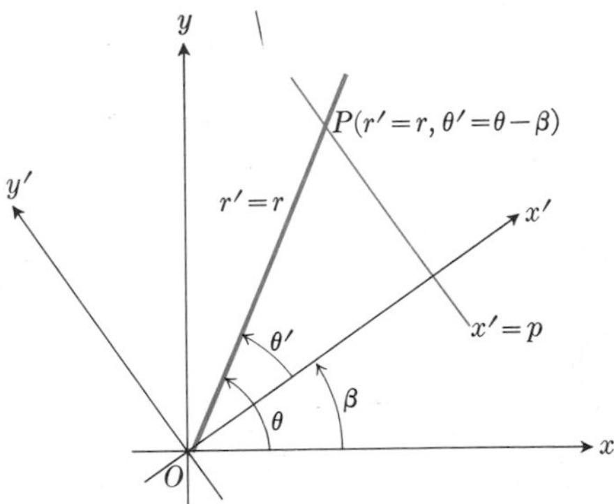

10–19 Another equation of the line L of Fig. 10–18 is $x' = p$.

EXAMPLE 3. Find a polar equation for the path of a point P that moves in such a way that the product of its distances from the two points $F_1(a, \pi)$ and $F_2(a, 0)$ is a constant, say b^2.

Solution. We let $P(r, \theta)$ be a representative point on the locus and determine the equation satisfied by the coordinates r and θ in order to fulfill the requirement

$$d_1 d_2 = b^2, \tag{9}$$

where $d_1 = PF_1$ and $d_2 = PF_2$ (Fig. 10–20). We apply the law of cosines twice: once to the triangle OPF_2,

$$d_2^2 = r^2 + a^2 - 2ar \cos \theta,$$

and again to the triangle OPF_1,

$$d_1^2 = r^2 + a^2 - 2ar \cos (\pi - \theta).$$

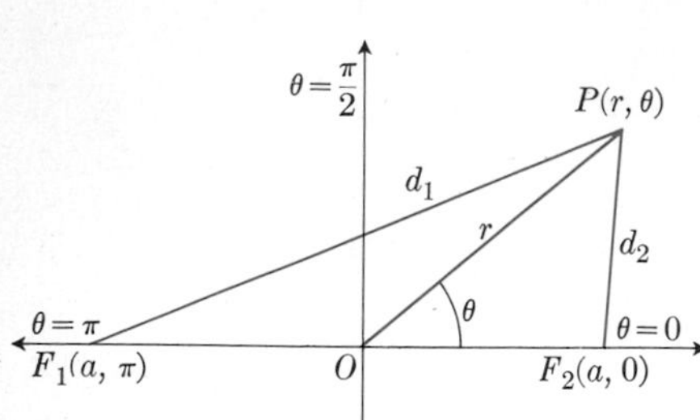

10–20 Example 3 shows that if P is constrained to move so that $PF_1 \cdot PF_2 = b^2$ (a positive constant), then P traces out the curve $b^4 = a^4 + r^4 - 2a^2r^2 \cos 2\theta$.

But

$$\cos(\pi - \theta) = -\cos \theta,$$

so that

$$d_1^2 = r^2 + a^2 + 2ar \cos \theta.$$

Hence

$$d_1^2 d_2^2 = (r^2 + a^2)^2 - (2ar \cos \theta)^2$$

or

$$b^4 = a^4 + r^4 + 2a^2r^2(1 - 2\cos^2 \theta).$$

The trigonometric identity $\cos 2\theta = 2\cos^2 \theta - 1$ enables us to put our equation in the form

$$b^4 = a^4 + r^4 - 2a^2r^2 \cos 2\theta. \tag{10}$$

One special case allows the locus to pass through the origin, namely, if $b = a$. Then the equation simplifies still further to the form

$$r^2 = 2a^2 \cos 2\theta. \tag{11}$$

The graphs of the curves represented by (10) for different values of $PF_1 \cdot PF_2$ are shown in Fig. 10–21(a)–(c). The curves in both (a) and (b) are called lemniscates, and the curve in (c) consists of two separate closed portions known as "ovals of Cassini."

Figure 10–21

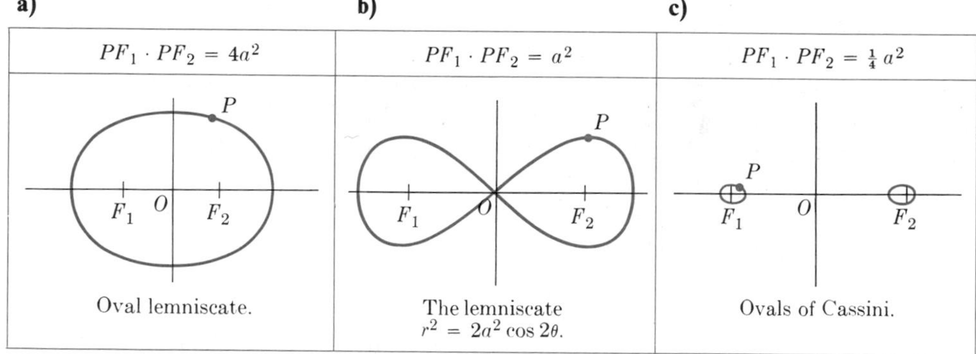

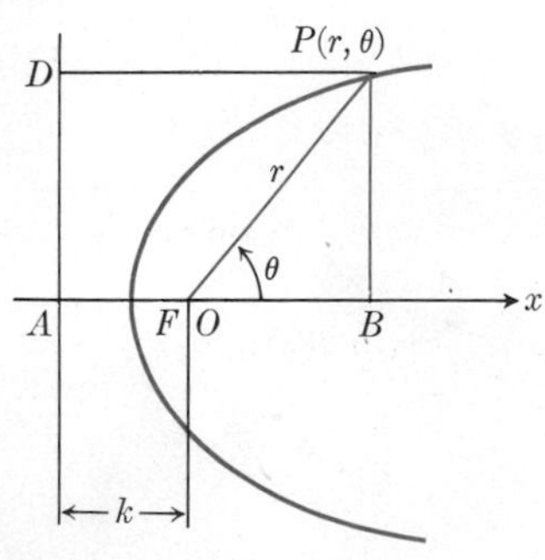

10–22 If $PF = e \cdot PD$, then $r = e(k + r\cos\theta)$.

EXAMPLE 4. Find the polar equation of the conic section of eccentricity e if the focus is at the origin and the associated directrix is the line $x = -k$.

Solution. We adopt the notation of Fig. 10–22 and use the focus-and-directrix property

$$PF = e \cdot PD, \tag{12}$$

which allows us to handle the parabola, ellipse, and hyperbola all at the same time.

By taking the origin at the focus F, we have

$$PF = r,$$

while

$$PD = AB$$

and

$$AB = AF + FB = k + r \cos \theta.$$

Then Eq. (12) is the same as

$$r = e(k + r \cos \theta).$$

If we solve this equation for r, we get

$$r = \frac{ke}{1 - e \cos \theta}. \tag{13}$$

Typical special cases of (13) are obtained by taking

$$e = 1, \qquad r = \frac{k}{1 - \cos \theta} = \frac{k}{2} \csc^2 \frac{\theta}{2}, \tag{14a}$$

which represents a *parabola*;

$$e = \frac{1}{2}, \qquad r = \frac{k}{2 - \cos \theta}, \tag{14b}$$

which represents an *ellipse*; and

$$e = 2, \qquad r = \frac{2k}{1 - 2 \cos \theta}, \tag{14c}$$

which represents a *hyperbola*.

It is worth noting that the denominator in Eq. (14b) for the ellipse can never vanish, so that r remains finite for all values of θ. But r becomes infinite as θ approaches 0 in (14a) and as θ approaches $\pi/3$ in (14c).

By replacing the constant ke in Eq. (13) by its equivalent value

$$ke = a(1 - e^2)$$

when $e < 1$, we may let $e \to 0$ and get

$$r = a$$

in the limit. That is, the circle of radius a and center at O is a limiting case of the curves represented by Eq. (13).

PROBLEMS

1. A line segment of length $2a$ slides with its ends on the x- and y-axes. Find the polar equation of the locus described by the point $P(r, \theta)$ in which the perpendicular from the origin intersects the moving line. Sketch the curve.

2. OA is a diameter of a circle of radius a, AC is tangent to the circle, and OC intersects the circle at B. On OC the point $P(r, \theta)$ is found such that $OP = BC$. With O as origin, OA as x-axis, and angle AOP as θ, find the polar equation of the locus of P and sketch the curve. Show that the line $x = 2a$ is an asymptote. The curve is called a "cissoid," meaning "ivy-like."

In Problems 3–7 determine the polar equation and sketch the given curve.

3. $x^2 + y^2 - 2ay = 0$

4. $(x^2 + y^2)^2 + 2ax(x^2 + y^2) - a^2y^2 = 0$

5. $x \cos \alpha + y \sin \alpha = p \qquad (\alpha, p \text{ constants})$

6. $y^2 = 4ax + 4a^2$

7. $(x^2 + y^2)^2 = x^2 - y^2$

In Problems 8–13 determine the cartesian equation and sketch the given curve.

8. $r = 4 \cos \theta$ **9.** $r = 6 \sin \theta$
10. $r = \sin 2\theta$ **11.** $r^2 = 2a^2 \cos 2\theta$
12. $r = 8/(1 - 2 \cos \theta)$ **13.** $r = a(1 + \sin \theta)$

14. Sketch the following curves:
a) $r = 2 \cos (\theta + 45°)$, **b)** $r = 4 \csc (\theta - 30°)$,
c) $r = 5 \sec (60° - \theta)$, **d)** $r = 3 \sin (\theta + 30°)$,
e) $r = a + a \cos (\theta - 30°)$, **f)** $0 \leq r \leq 2 - 2 \cos \theta$.

Each of the graphs in Problems 15–22 is the graph of exactly one of the equations (a)–(l) in the list below. Find the equation for each graph.

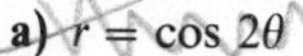

a) $r = \cos 2\theta$ **g)** $r = 1 + \cos \theta$
b) $r \cos \theta = 1$ **h)** $r = 1 - \sin \theta$
c) $r = \dfrac{6}{1 - 2 \cos \theta}$ **i)** $r = \dfrac{2}{1 - \cos \theta}$
d) $r = \sin 2\theta$ **j)** $r^2 = \sin 2\theta$
e) $r = \theta$ **k)** $r = -\sin \theta$
f) $r^2 = \cos 2\theta$ **l)** $r = 2 \cos \theta + 1$

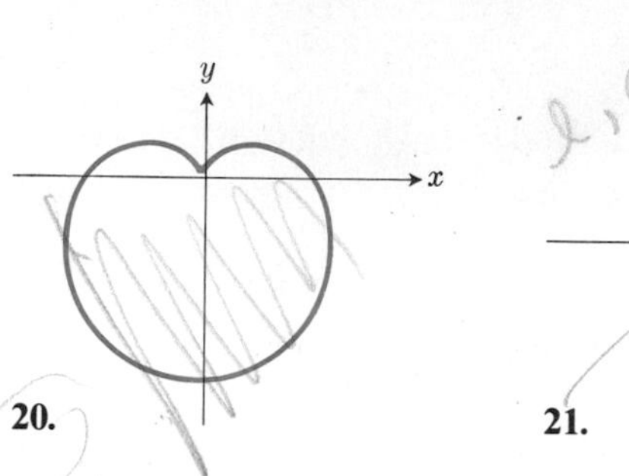

20.

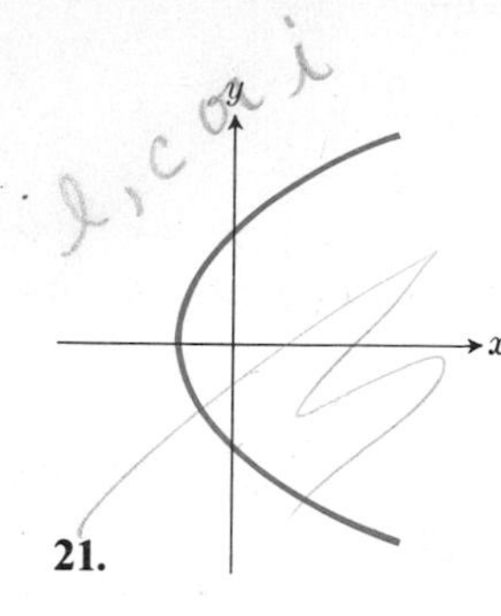

21.

22.

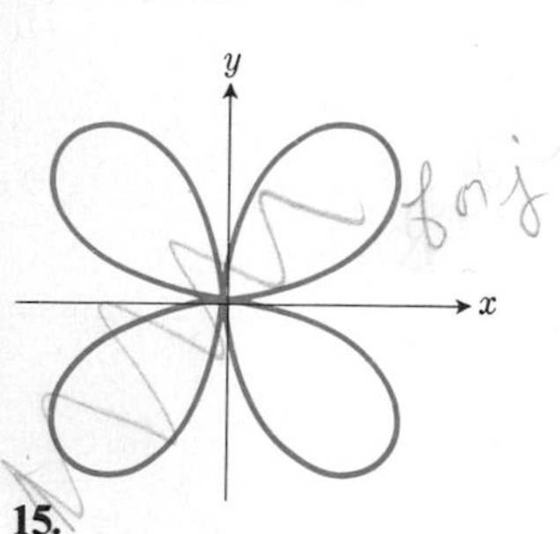

15.

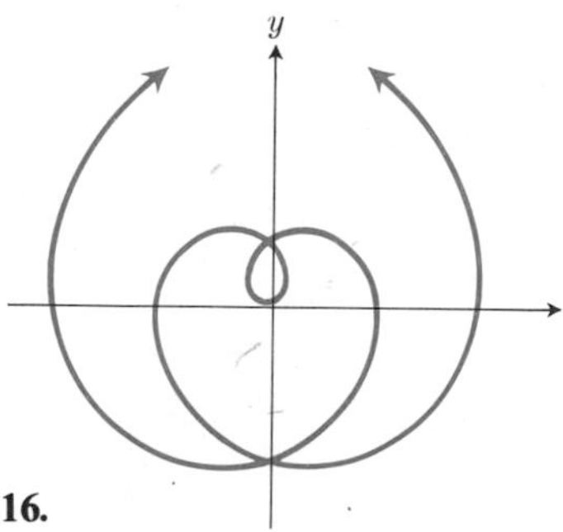

16.

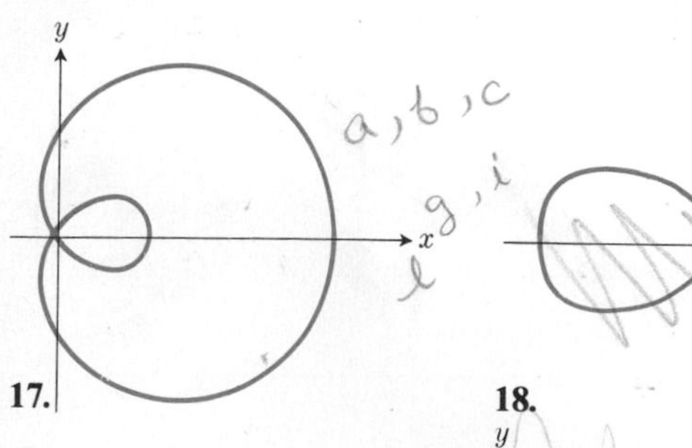

17. **18.**

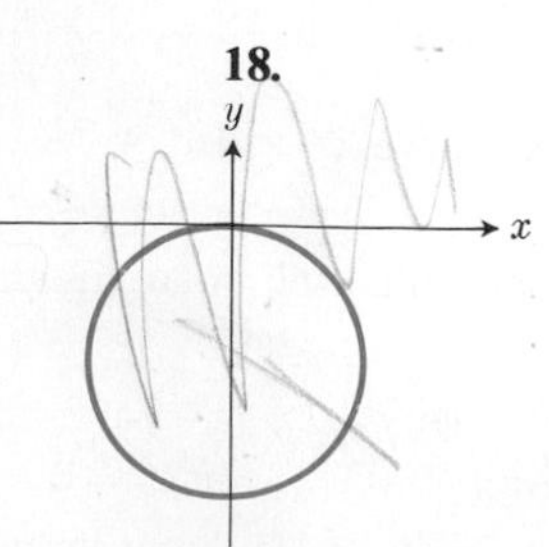

19.

Figure 10–23

23. (a) How can the angle β and the distance p [see Fig. 10–18 and Eq. (6)] be determined from the cartesian equation $ax + by = c$ for a straight line? (b) Specifically, find p, β, and the polar equation for the straight line $\sqrt{3}\,x + y = 6$.

24. The focus of a parabola is at the origin and its directrix is the line $r \cos \theta = -4$. Find the polar equation of the parabola.

25. One focus of a hyperbola of eccentricity $\frac{5}{4}$ is at the origin and the corresponding directrix is the line $r \cos \theta = 9$. Find the polar coordinates of the second focus. Also determine the polar equation of the hyperbola and sketch.

26. One focus of an ellipse of eccentricity $\frac{1}{4}$ is at the origin. The corresponding directrix is the line $r \cos \theta = 8$. Find the coordinates of the other focus. Write a polar equation for the ellipse, and sketch.

27. Find the maximum and minimum values of r that satisfy Eq. (10), first in terms of a and b, and then specifically for the cases $b = 2a$, $b = a$, and $b = a/2$.

28. Determine the slopes of the lines that are tangent to the lemniscate $r^2 = 2a^2 \cos 2\theta$ at the origin.

29. Equation (14b), $r = k/(2 - \cos \theta)$, represents an ellipse with one focus at the origin. Sketch the curve and its directrices for the case $k = 2$ and locate the center of the ellipse.

30. In the case $e > 1$, Eq. (13) represents a hyperbola. From the polar form of the equation, determine the slopes of the asymptotes of the hyperbola of eccentricity e.

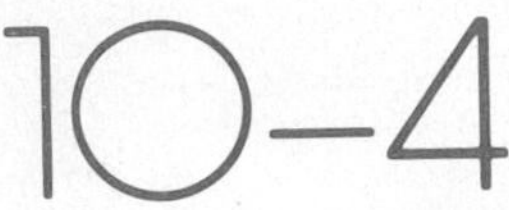

10–4 THE ANGLE ψ BETWEEN THE RADIUS VECTOR AND THE TANGENT LINE

In cartesian coordinates, when we want to discuss the direction of a curve at a point, we use the angle ϕ from the positive x-axis to the tangent line. In polar coordinates, it is more convenient to make use of the angle ψ (psi) from the *radius vector* to the tangent line. Then the relationship

$$\phi = \theta + \psi, \tag{1}$$

which can be read from Fig. 10–24, makes it a simple matter to find ϕ if that angle is desired instead of ψ.

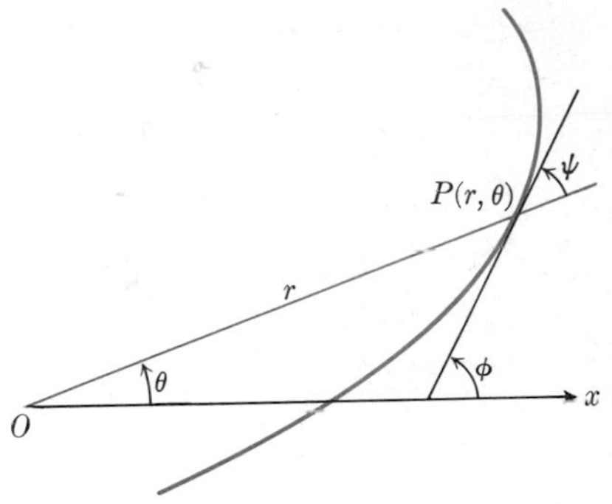

10–24 The angle ψ between the tangent vector and the radius vector.

Suppose the equation of the curve is given in the form $r = f(\theta)$, where $f(\theta)$ is a differentiable function of θ. Then from

$$x = r\cos\theta, \qquad y = r\sin\theta, \tag{2}$$

we see that x and y are differentiable functions of θ with

$$\begin{aligned} \frac{dx}{d\theta} &= -r\sin\theta + \cos\theta\,\frac{dr}{d\theta}, \\ \frac{dy}{d\theta} &= r\cos\theta + \sin\theta\,\frac{dr}{d\theta}. \end{aligned} \tag{3}$$

Since $\psi = \phi - \theta$ from (1),

$$\tan\psi = \tan(\phi - \theta) = \frac{\tan\phi - \tan\theta}{1 + \tan\phi\tan\theta},$$

while

$$\tan\phi = \frac{dy/d\theta}{dx/d\theta}, \qquad \tan\theta = \frac{y}{x}.$$

Hence

$$\tan\psi = \frac{\dfrac{dy/d\theta}{dx/d\theta} - \dfrac{y}{x}}{1 + \dfrac{y}{x}\dfrac{dy/d\theta}{dx/d\theta}} = \frac{x\dfrac{dy}{d\theta} - y\dfrac{dx}{d\theta}}{x\dfrac{dx}{d\theta} + y\dfrac{dy}{d\theta}}. \tag{4}$$

The numerator in the last expression in Eq. (4) is found by substitution from Eqs. (2) and (3) to be

$$x\frac{dy}{d\theta} - y\frac{dx}{d\theta} = r^2.$$

Similarly, the denominator is

$$x\frac{dx}{d\theta} + y\frac{dy}{d\theta} = r\frac{dr}{d\theta}.$$

When we substitute these into Eq. (4), we obtain the very simple final result

$$\tan\psi = \frac{r}{dr/d\theta}. \tag{5}$$

REMARK. This formula for $\tan \psi$ is much simpler than the formula

$$\tan \phi = \frac{r \cos \theta + (\sin \theta)\, dr/d\theta}{-r \sin \theta + (\cos \theta)\, dr/d\theta}, \tag{6}$$

that one obtains by calculating

$$\frac{dy}{dx} = \frac{dy/d\theta}{dx/d\theta}$$

from (3). This is why it is usually preferable to work with the angle ψ rather than with ϕ in the case of polar coordinates.

One may obtain a simple expression for the differential element of arc length ds by squaring and adding the differentials

$$dx = -r \sin \theta \, d\theta + \cos \theta \, dr,$$

$$dy = r \cos \theta \, d\theta + \sin \theta \, dr.$$

We find that

$$ds^2 = dx^2 + dy^2 = r^2 \, d\theta^2 + dr^2.$$

This result and the result for $\tan \psi$ are both easily remembered in the form

$$\tan \psi = \frac{r \, d\theta}{dr}, \tag{7a}$$

$$ds^2 = r^2 \, d\theta^2 + dr^2 \tag{7b}$$

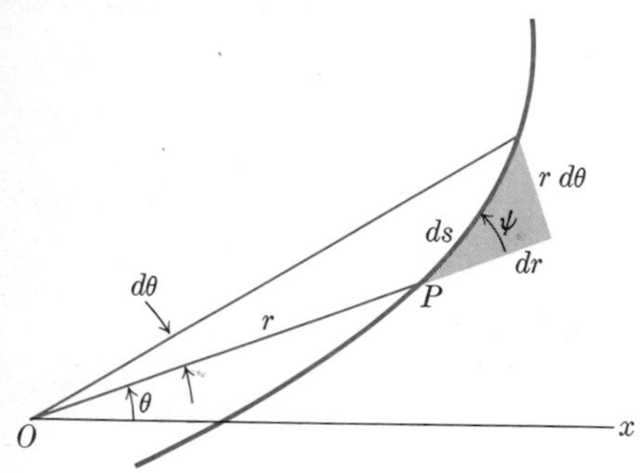

10–25 Arc length: $ds^2 = r^2 \, d\theta^2 + dr^2$.

if we refer to the "differential triangle" shown in Fig. 10–25. We simply treat dr and $r \, d\theta$ as the two legs and ds as the hypotenuse of an ordinary right triangle with the angle ψ opposite the side $r \, d\theta$. If we realize that certain terms of higher order are being neglected, we may think of dr as the component of displacement along the radius vector and $r \, d\theta$ as the component at right angles to this produced by the displacement ds along the curve. The relationships (7) may be read at once from this triangle. We should realize, of course, that the *proof* of these equations did not depend upon any such "differential triangle" and that the latter is only a mnemonic device.

To find the angle ψ, we use the first equation in (7). To find the length of a polar curve, we find ds from the second equation in (7) and integrate between appropriate limits as in the following examples.

EXAMPLE 1. Find the angle ψ for the cardioid (Fig. 10–26),

$$r = a(1 - \cos \theta). \tag{8a}$$

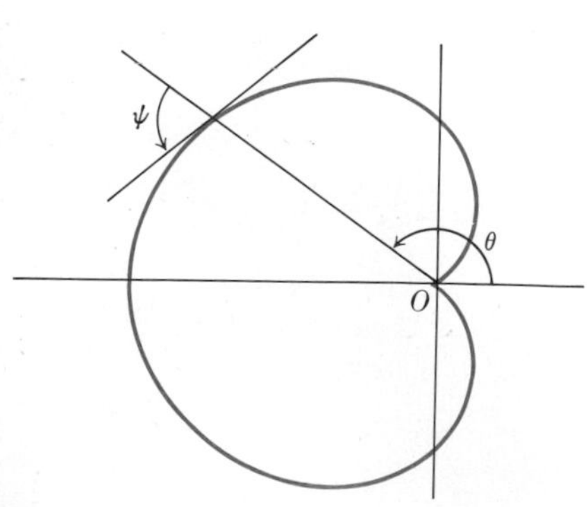

10–26 Cardioid: $r = a(1 - \cos \theta)$.

Solution. From the equation of the curve, we get

$$dr = a \sin \theta \, d\theta, \tag{8b}$$

so that

$$\tan \psi = \frac{r \, d\theta}{dr} = \frac{a(1 - \cos \theta)\, d\theta}{a \sin \theta \, d\theta} = \tan \frac{\theta}{2}.$$

As θ varies from 0 to 2π, the angle ψ varies from 0 to π according to the equation $\psi = \theta/2$. Thus at the y-intercepts the tangent line makes an angle of

45° with the vertical, at the origin the curve is tangent to the x-axis, and at $(2a, \pi)$ the tangent line makes an angle of 90° with the negative x-axis.

Suppose we ask for the points on the cardioid where the tangent line is vertical. Denoting the inclination angle of the tangent line by ϕ and recalling that

$$\phi = \psi + \theta \qquad \text{and} \qquad \psi = \tfrac{1}{2}\theta,$$

we get

$$\phi = \tfrac{3}{2}\theta.$$

Since the tangent is vertical when

$$\phi = \frac{\pi}{2} + n\pi,$$

the values of θ satisfy

$$\theta = \frac{2}{3}\phi = \frac{\pi}{3} + \frac{2}{3}n\pi.$$

Taking $n = 0, -1, 1, -2, 2, \ldots$, we obtain

$$\theta = \frac{\pi}{3}, \quad \frac{-\pi}{3}, \quad \pi, \quad -\pi, \quad \tfrac{5}{3}\pi, \quad \ldots$$

These lead to three distinct points, namely,

$$\left(\frac{a}{2}, \pm\frac{\pi}{3}\right) \quad \text{and} \quad (2a, \pi),$$

whose radius vectors are spaced 120° apart. (See Fig. 10–27.)

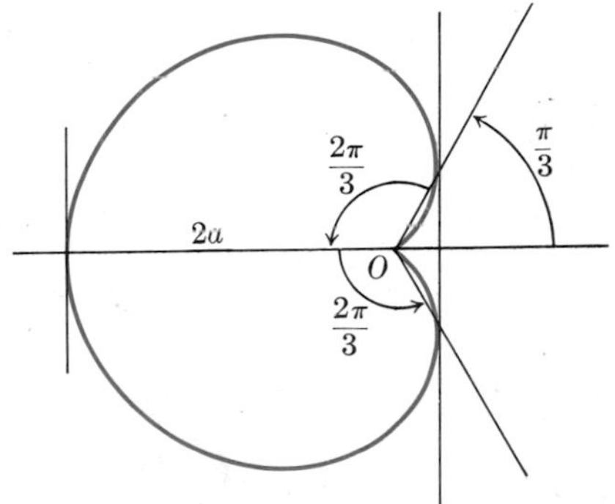

10–27 Vertical tangents to the cardioid $r = a(1 - \cos\theta)$.

EXAMPLE 2. Find the length of the cardioid $r = a(1 - \cos\theta)$.

Solution. Substituting dr and r from (8b, a) into the second equation in (7), we have

$$\begin{aligned} ds^2 &= a^2\,d\theta^2[\sin^2\theta + (1 - \cos\theta)^2] \\ &= 2a^2\,d\theta^2(1 - \cos\theta) \end{aligned}$$

and

$$ds = a\sqrt{2}\,\sqrt{1 - \cos\theta}\,d\theta.$$

To integrate the expression on the right, we substitute

$$1 - \cos\theta = 2\sin^2\frac{\theta}{2}$$

so that

$$ds = 2a\left|\sin\frac{\theta}{2}\right|d\theta.$$

Since $\sin \theta/2$ is not negative when θ varies from 0 to 2π, we obtain

$$s = \int_0^{2\pi} 2a \sin \frac{\theta}{2}\, d\theta$$

$$= -4a \cos \frac{\theta}{2}\Big]_0^{2\pi} = 8a.$$

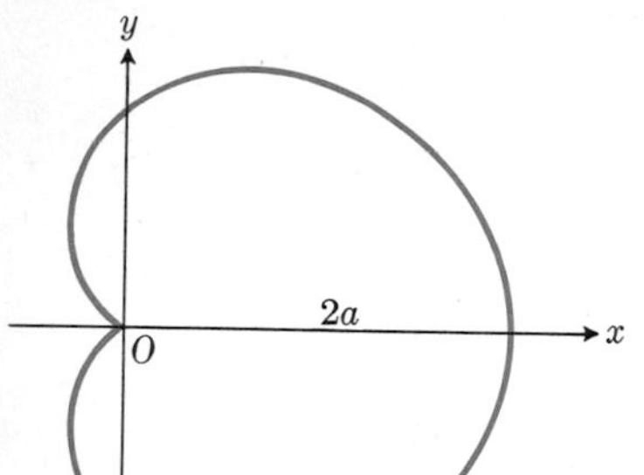

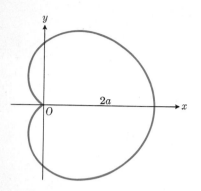

10–28 Cardioid: $r = a(1 + \cos \theta)$.

In letting θ range from 0 to 2π, we start at the cusp at the origin, go once around the smooth portion of the cardioid and return to the cusp. In doing this we do not pass *across* the cusp (Fig. 10–26). If, on the other hand, we take the cardioid $r = a(1 + \cos \theta)$, the appropriate procedure for avoiding the cusp (Fig. 10–28) is to let θ increase from $-\pi$ to π, or we may use the symmetry of the curve and calculate half of the total length by letting θ vary from 0 to π.

EXAMPLE 3. The lemniscate

$$r^2 = 2a^2 \cos 2\theta$$

is revolved about the y-axis. Find the area of the surface generated.

Solution. An element of arc length ds (Fig. 10–29) generates a portion of surface area

$$dS = 2\pi x\, ds,$$

where

$$x = r \cos \theta, \qquad ds = \sqrt{dr^2 + r^2\, d\theta^2}.$$

That is,

$$dS = 2\pi r \cos \theta \sqrt{dr^2 + r^2\, d\theta^2} = 2\pi \cos \theta \sqrt{r^2\, dr^2 + r^4\, d\theta^2}.$$

From the equation of the curve, we get

$$r\, dr = -2a^2 \sin 2\theta\, d\theta.$$

Then

$$(r^2\, dr^2 + r^4\, d\theta^2) = (2a^2\, d\theta)^2(\sin^2 2\theta + \cos^2 2\theta)$$

and

$$dS = 4\pi a^2 \cos \theta\, d\theta.$$

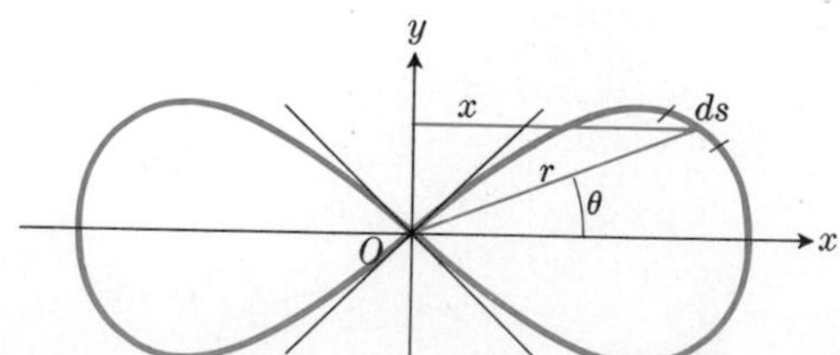

10–29 Lemniscate: $r^2 = 2a^2 \cos 2\theta$.

The total surface area is generated by the loop of the lemniscate to the right of the y-axis between $\theta = -\pi/4$ and $\theta = +\pi/4$, so that

$$S = \int_{-\pi/4}^{\pi/4} 4\pi a^2 \cos\theta\, d\theta = 4\pi a^2\sqrt{2}.$$

PROBLEMS

1. For the hyperbolic spiral $r\theta = a$ show that $\psi = 135°$ when $\theta = 1$ radian, and that $\psi \to 90°$ as the spiral winds around the origin. Sketch the curve and indicate ψ for $\theta = 1$ radian.

2. Show, by reference to a figure, that the angle β between the tangents to two curves at a point of intersection may be found from the formula

$$\tan\beta = \frac{\tan\psi_2 - \tan\psi_1}{1 + \tan\psi_2 \tan\psi_1}.$$

When will the two curves intersect orthogonally?

3. Find a point of intersection of the parabolas

$$r = \frac{1}{1-\cos\theta} \quad \text{and} \quad r = \frac{3}{1+\cos\theta}$$

and find the angle between the tangents to these curves at this point.

4. Find points on the cardioid $r = a(1 + \cos\theta)$ where the tangent line is horizontal.

5. Find the length of the cardioid $r = a(1 + \cos\theta)$. [*Hint.* $\int \sqrt{1+\cos\theta}\, d\theta = \int \sqrt{2}\,|\cos\theta/2|\, d\theta$.]

6. A thin, uniform wire is bent into the shape of the cardioid $r = a(1 + \cos\theta)$. Find its center of gravity $(\bar{x}, \bar{y})$. [*Hint.* $\int \cos\theta \cos\theta/2\, d\theta$ can be evaluated by substituting $\cos\theta = 1 - 2\sin^2\theta/2$ and then letting $u = \sin\theta/2$.]

7. The lemniscate $r^2 = 2a^2\cos 2\theta$ is rotated about the x-axis. Find the area of the surface generated.

8. Find the length of the curve $r = a\sin^2\theta/2$ from $\theta = 0$ to $\theta = \pi$. Sketch the curve.

9. Find the length of the parabolic spiral $r = a\theta^2$ between $\theta = 0$ and $\theta = \pi$. Sketch the curve.

10. Find the length of the curve $r = a\sin^3\theta/3$ between $\theta = 0$ and $\theta = \pi$. Sketch the curve.

11. Find the surface area generated by rotating the curve $r = 2a\cos\theta$ about the line $\theta = \pi/2$. Sketch.

10–5 PLANE AREAS IN POLAR COORDINATES

The area AOB in Fig. 10–30 is bounded by the rays $\theta = \alpha$, $\theta = \beta$, and the curve $r = f(\theta)$. We imagine the angle AOB as being divided into n parts

$$\Delta\theta = \frac{\beta - \alpha}{n},$$

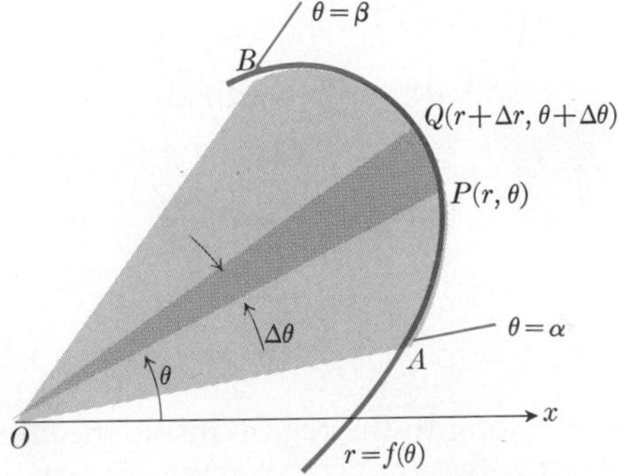

10–30 To derive a formula for the area swept out by the radius vector OP as P moves from A to B along the curve, the area is divided into sectors.

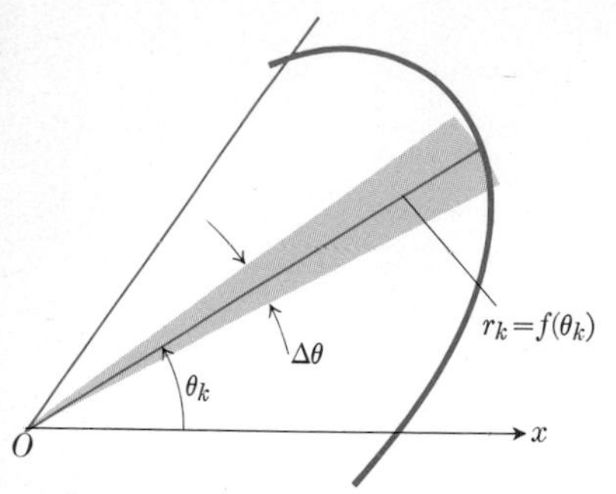

10–31 For some θ_k between θ and $\theta + \Delta\theta$, the area of the shaded circular sector just equals the area of the sector POQ bounded by the curve shown in Fig. 10–30.

and we approximate the area in a typical sector POQ by the area of a *circular* sector of radius r and central angle $\Delta\theta$ (Fig. 10–31). That is,

$$\text{Area of } POQ \approx \tfrac{1}{2}r^2\,\Delta\theta,$$

and hence the entire area AOB is approximately

$$\sum_{\theta=\alpha}^{\beta} \tfrac{1}{2}r^2\,\Delta\theta.$$

In fact, if the function $r = f(\theta)$ which represents the polar curve is a continuous function of θ for $\alpha \le \theta \le \beta$, then there is a θ_k between θ and $\theta + \Delta\theta$ such that the circular sector of radius

$$r_k = f(\theta_k)$$

and central angle $\Delta\theta$ gives the *exact* area of POQ (Fig. 10–31). Then the entire area is given exactly by

$$A = \sum \tfrac{1}{2}r_k^2\,\Delta\theta = \sum \tfrac{1}{2}[f(\theta_k)]^2\,\Delta\theta.$$

If we let $\Delta\theta \to 0$, we may apply the Fundamental Theorem of the integral calculus and obtain

$$A = \lim_{\Delta\theta\to 0} \sum \tfrac{1}{2}[f(\theta_k)]^2\,\Delta\theta = \tfrac{1}{2}\int_{\alpha}^{\beta} [f(\theta)]^2\,d\theta,$$

or

$$A = \int_{\alpha}^{\beta} \tfrac{1}{2}r^2\,d\theta. \tag{1}$$

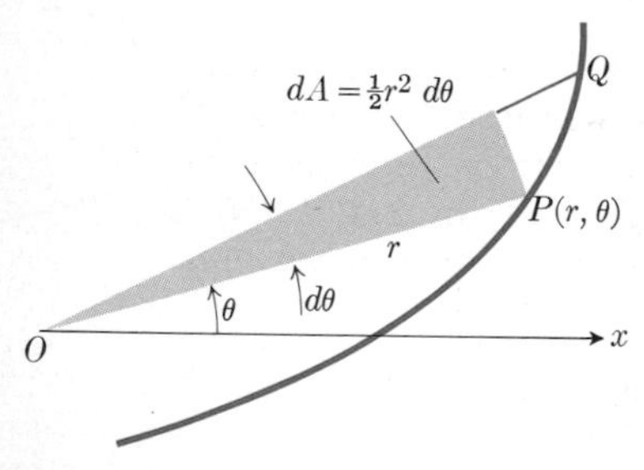

10–32 The area of the sector POQ is approximated by the area of the shaded circular sector.

This result may also be remembered as the integral of the differential element of area (Fig. 10–32):

$$dA = \tfrac{1}{2}r^2\,d\theta,$$

taken between the appropriate limits on θ.

EXAMPLE. Find the area that is inside the circle $r = a$ and outside the cardioid $r = a(1 - \cos\theta)$. (See Fig. 10–33.)

Solution. We take a representative element of area

$$dA = dA_1 - dA_2,$$

where

$$dA_1 = \tfrac{1}{2}r_1^2\,d\theta, \qquad dA_2 = \tfrac{1}{2}r_2^2\,d\theta$$

with

$$r_1 = a, \qquad r_2 = a(1 - \cos\theta).$$

Such elements of area belong to the region inside the circle and outside the cardioid provided θ lies between

$$-\frac{\pi}{2} \quad\text{and}\quad +\frac{\pi}{2},$$

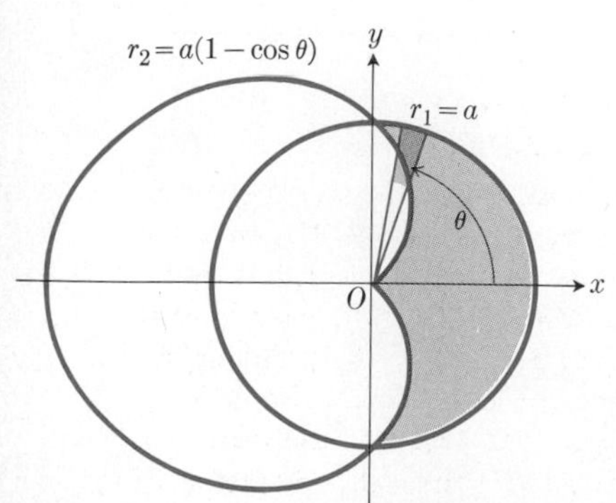

10–33 The shaded area is obtained from the integral $\int_{-\pi/2}^{\pi/2} \frac{1}{2}(r_1^2 - r_2^2)\,d\theta$.

where the curves intersect. Hence

$$A = \int_{-\pi/2}^{\pi/2} \tfrac{1}{2}(r_1^2 - r_2^2)\, d\theta$$

$$= \int_{-\pi/2}^{\pi/2} \frac{a^2}{2}(2\cos\theta - \cos^2\theta)\, d\theta$$

$$= a^2 \int_{-\pi/2}^{\pi/2} \cos\theta\, d\theta - \frac{a^2}{2}\int_{-\pi/2}^{\pi/2} \frac{1+\cos 2\theta}{2}\, d\theta$$

$$= a^2\left(2 - \frac{\pi}{4}\right).$$

As a check against gross errors, we observe that this is roughly 80 percent of the area of a semicircle of radius a, and this seems reasonable when we look at the area in Fig. 10–33.

PROBLEMS

[*Note.* The trigonometric identities

$$\sin^2\theta = \tfrac{1}{2}(1 - \cos 2\theta), \qquad \cos^2\theta = \tfrac{1}{2}(1 + \cos 2\theta)$$

should be used to evaluate $\int \sin^2\theta\, d\theta$ and $\int \cos^2\theta\, d\theta$ in certain of the problems that follow.]

1. Find the total area inside the cardioid $r = a(1 + \cos\theta)$.

2. Find the total area inside the circle $r = 2a\sin\theta$.

3. Find the total area inside the lemniscate $r^2 = 2a^2\cos 2\theta$.

4. Find that portion of the area inside the lemniscate $r^2 = 2a^2\cos 2\theta$ that is not included in the circle $r = a$. Sketch.

5. Find the area inside the curve $r = a(2 + \cos\theta)$.

6. Find the area common to the circles $r = 2a\cos\theta$ and $r = 2a\sin\theta$. Sketch.

7. Find the area inside the circle $r = 3a\cos\theta$ and outside the cardioid $r = a(1 + \cos\theta)$.

8. Since the center of gravity of a triangle is located on a median at a distance $\frac{2}{3}$ of the way from a vertex to the opposite base, the lever arm for the moment about the x-axis of the area of triangle POQ in Fig. 10–30 is $\frac{2}{3}r\sin\theta + \epsilon$, where $\epsilon \to 0$ as $\Delta\theta \to 0$. Deduce that the center of gravity of the area AOB in the figure is given by

$$\bar{y} = \frac{\int \frac{2}{3}r\sin\theta \cdot \frac{1}{2}r^2\, d\theta}{\int \frac{1}{2}r^2\, d\theta}$$

and similarly,

$$\bar{x} = \frac{\int \frac{2}{3}r\cos\theta \cdot \frac{1}{2}r^2\, d\theta}{\int \frac{1}{2}r^2\, d\theta},$$

with limits $\theta = \alpha$ to $\theta = \beta$ on all integrals.

9. Use the results of Problem 8 to find the center of gravity of the area bounded by the cardioid $r = a(1 + \cos\theta)$.

10. Use the results of Problem 8 to find the center of gravity of the area of a semicircle of radius a.

REVIEW QUESTIONS AND EXERCISES

1. Make a diagram to show the standard relations between cartesian coordinates (x, y) and polar coordinates (r, θ). Express each set of coordinates in terms of the other kind.

2. If a point has polar coordinates (r_1, θ_1), what other polar coordinates represent the same point?

3. What is the expression for area between curves in polar coordinates?

4. What is the expression for length of arc of a curve in polar coordinates? For area of a surface of revolution?

5. What are some criteria for symmetry of a curve if its polar coordinates satisfy the equation $r = f(\theta)$? Illustrate your discussion with specific examples.

6. An artificial satellite is in an orbit that passes over the North and South Poles of the earth. When it is over the North Pole it is at the highest point of its orbit, 1000 miles above the earth's surface. Above the South Pole it is at the lowest point of its orbit, 300 miles above the earth's surface. (a) Assuming that the orbit (with reference to the earth) is an ellipse with one focus at the center of the earth, find its eccentricity. (Take the diameter of the earth to be 8000 miles.) (b) Using the north–south axis of the earth as polar axis, and the center of the earth as origin, find a polar equation of the orbit.

MISCELLANEOUS PROBLEMS

Discuss and sketch each of the curves in Problems 1–13 (where a is a positive constant).

1. $r = a\theta$ **2.** $r = a(1 + \cos 2\theta)$

3. a) $r = a \sec \theta$ **b)** $r = a \csc \theta$

c) $r = a \sec \theta + a \csc \theta$

4. $r = a \sin\left(\theta + \frac{\pi}{3}\right)$

5. $r^2 + 2r(\cos \theta + \sin \theta) = 7$

6. $r = a \cos \theta - a \sin \theta$ **7.** $r \cos \frac{\theta}{2} = a$

8. $r^2 = a^2 \sin \theta$ **9.** $r^2 = 2a^2 \sin 2\theta$

10. $r = a(1 - 2 \sin 3\theta)$ **11. a)** $r = \cos 2\theta$

b) $r^2 = \cos 2\theta$

12. a) $r = 1 + \cos \theta$ **b)** $r = \frac{1}{1 + \cos \theta}$

13. a) $r = \frac{2}{1 - \cos \theta}$ **b)** $r = \frac{2}{1 + \sin \theta}$

14. Sketch and discuss the graph whose equation in polar coordinates is

$$r = 1 - \tan^2 \theta.$$

Show that it has no vertical asymptotes.

Sketch each of the pairs of curves in Problems 15–20, and find all points of intersection and the angle between their tangents at each point of intersection.

15. $r = a, \quad r = 2a \sin \theta$

16. $r = a, \quad r = a(1 - \sin \theta)$

17. $r = a \sec \theta, \quad r = 2a \sin \theta$

18. $r = a \cos \theta, \quad r = a(1 + \cos \theta)$

19. $r = a(1 + \cos 2\theta), \quad r = a \cos 2\theta$

20. $r^2 = 4 \cos 2\theta, \quad r^2 = \sec 2\theta$

21. Find the equation, in polar coordinates, of a parabola whose focus is at $r = 0$ and whose vertex is at $r = 1, \theta = 0$.

22. Find the polar equation of the straight line with intercepts a and b on the lines $\theta = 0, \theta = \pi/2$.

23. Find the equation of a circle with center on the line $\theta = \pi$, of radius a, and passing through the origin.

24. Find the polar equation of a parabola with focus at the origin and vertex at $(a, \pi/4)$.

25. Find the polar equation of an ellipse with one focus at the origin, the other at $(2, 0)$, and a vertex at $(4, 0)$.

26. Find the polar equation of a hyperbola with one focus at the origin, center at $(2, \pi/2)$, and vertex at $(1, \pi/2)$.

27. Three LORAN stations are located (in polar coordinates) at $(a, 0)$, $(0, 0)$, and $(a, \pi/4)$. Radio signals are sent out from the three stations simultaneously. A ship receiving the signals notes that the signals from the second and third stations arrive $a/2v$ sec later than that from the first. If v is the velocity of a radio signal, what is the location of the ship in polar coordinates?

28. Show that the parabolas $r = a/(1 + \cos \theta)$, $r = b/(1 - \cos \theta)$ are orthogonal at each point of intersection ($ab \neq 0$).

29. Find the angle between the line $\theta = \pi/2$ and the cardioid $r = a(1 - \cos \theta)$ at their intersection.

30. Find the angle between the line $r = 3 \sec \theta$ and the curve $r = 4(1 + \cos \theta)$ at one of their intersections.

31. Find the slope of the tangent line to the curve $r = a \tan(\theta/2)$ at $\theta = \pi/2$.

32. Check that the two curves $r = 1/(1 - \cos \theta)$ and $r = 3/(1 + \cos \theta)$ intersect at the point $(2, \pi/3)$. Find the angle between the tangents to these curves at this point.

33. The equation $r^2 = 2 \csc 2\theta$ represents a curve in polar coordinates. (a) Sketch the curve. (b) Find the equation of the curve in rectangular coordinates. (c) Find the angle at which the curve intersects the line $\theta = \pi/4$.

34. A given curve cuts all rays θ = constant at the constant angle α.

a) Show that the area bounded by the curve and two rays $\theta = \theta_1, \theta = \theta_2$, is proportional to $r_2^2 - r_1^2$, where (r_1, θ_1) and (r_2, θ_2) are polar coordinates of the ends of the arc of the curve between these rays. Find the factor of proportionality.

b) Show that the length of the arc of the curve in part (a) is proportional to $r_2 - r_1$ and find the proportionality constant.

35. The cardioid $r = a(1 - \cos \theta)$ is rotated about the initial line.

a) Find the area of the surface generated. [*Hint.* You may use the fact that $\sin \theta = 2 \sin(\theta/2) \cos(\theta/2)$, and $1 - \cos \theta = 2 \sin^2(\theta/2)$ to evaluate your integral.]

b) Set up the definite integral (or integrals) that would be used to find the centroid of the area in part (a).

c) Find the centroid of the area in part (a).

36. Let P be a point on the hyperbola $r^2 \sin 2\theta = 2a^2$. Show that the triangle formed by OP, the tangent at P, and the initial line is isosceles.

37. Verify that the formula for finding the length of a curve in polar form gives the correct result for the circumference of the circles (a) $r = a$, (b) $r = a \cos \theta$, (c) $r = a \sin \theta$.

38. If $r = a \cos^3(\theta/3)$, show that $ds = a \cos^2(\theta/3)\, d\theta$ and determine the perimeter of the curve.

39. Find the area that lies inside the curve $r = 2a \cos 2\theta$ and outside the curve $r = a\sqrt{2}$.

40. Sketch the curves

$$r = 2a \cos^2 (\theta/2) \quad \text{and} \quad r = 2a \sin^2 (\theta/2),$$

and find the area they have in common.

Find the total area enclosed by each of the curves in Problems 41–47.

41. $r^2 = a^2 \cos 2\theta$

42. $r = a(2 - \cos \theta)$

43. $r = a(1 + \cos 2\theta)$

44. $r = 2a \cos \theta$

45. $r = 2a \sin 3\theta$

46. $r^2 = 2a^2 \sin 3\theta$

47. $r^2 = 2a^2 \cos^2 (\theta/2)$

48. Find the area that is inside the cardioid $r = a(1 + \sin \theta)$ and outside the circle $r = a \sin \theta$.

11

VECTORS AND PARAMETRIC EQUATIONS

11–1 VECTOR COMPONENTS AND THE UNIT VECTORS i AND j

Some physical quantities, like length and mass, are completely determined when their magnitudes are given in terms of specific units. Such quantities are called *scalars*. Other quantities, like forces and velocities, in which the direction as well as the magnitude is important, are called *vectors*. It is customary to represent a vector by a directed line segment whose direction represents the direction of the vector and whose length, in terms of some chosen unit, represents its magnitude.

The most satisfactory algebra of vectors is based on a representation of each vector in terms of its components parallel to the axes of a cartesian coordinate system. This is accomplished by using the same unit of length on the two axes, with vectors of unit length along the axes used as basic vectors in terms of which the other vectors in the plane may be expressed. Along the x-axis we choose the vector $\mathbf{i}$ from (0, 0) to (1, 0).* Along the y-axis we choose the vector $\mathbf{j}$ from (0, 0) to (0, 1). (See Fig. 11–1.) Then $a\mathbf{i}$, a being a scalar, represents a vector parallel to the x-axis, having magnitude $|a|$ and pointing to the right if a is positive, to the left if a is negative. Similarly, $b\mathbf{j}$ is a vector parallel to the y-axis and having the same direction as $\mathbf{j}$ if b is positive, or the opposite direction if b is negative.

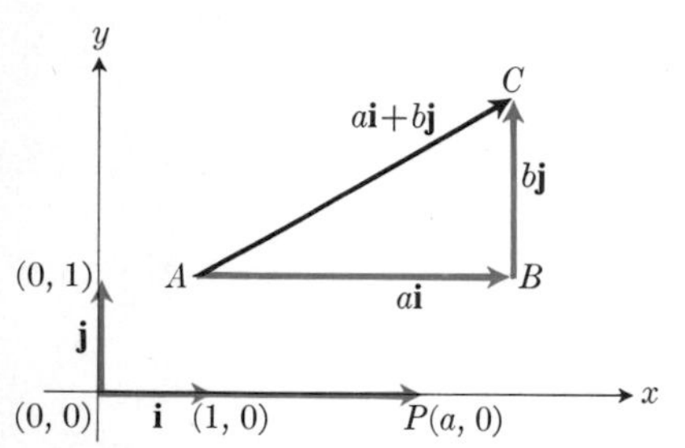

11–1 The vector $\overrightarrow{AC}$ expressed as a multiple of **i** plus a multiple of **j**.

We shall ordinarily deal with "free vectors," meaning that a vector is free to move about under parallel displacements. We say that two vectors are *equal* if they have the same direction and the same magnitude. This condition may be expressed algebraically by saying that

$$a\mathbf{i} + b\mathbf{j} = a'\mathbf{i} + b'\mathbf{j} \quad \text{if and only if} \quad a = a' \quad \text{and} \quad b = b'.$$

That is, two vectors are equal if and only if their corresponding *components* are equal. Thus, in Fig. 11–1, the vector $\overrightarrow{AB}$ and the vector $\overrightarrow{OP}$ from (0, 0) to $(a, 0)$ are both equal to $a\mathbf{i}$.

Addition

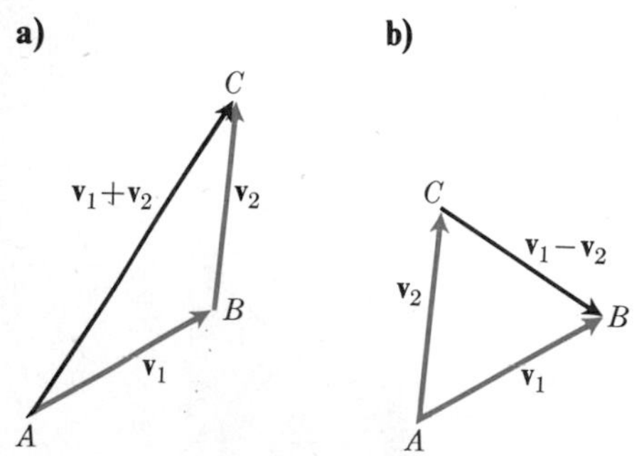

11–2 The sum (a) and difference (b) of two vectors.

Two vectors, $\mathbf{v}_1$ and $\mathbf{v}_2$ are *added* by drawing a vector $\mathbf{v}_1$, say from A to B in Fig. 11–2(a), and then a vector equal to $\mathbf{v}_2$ starting from the terminal point of $\mathbf{v}_1$; thus $\mathbf{v}_2 = \overrightarrow{BC}$ in Fig. 11–2(a). The sum $\mathbf{v}_1 + \mathbf{v}_2$ is then the vector from the starting point A of $\mathbf{v}_1$ to the terminal point C of $\mathbf{v}_2$:

$$\mathbf{v}_1 = \overrightarrow{AB}, \qquad \mathbf{v}_2 = \overrightarrow{BC},$$

$$\mathbf{v}_1 + \mathbf{v}_2 = \overrightarrow{AB} + \overrightarrow{BC} = \overrightarrow{AC}.$$

If we apply this principle to the vectors $a\mathbf{i}$ and $b\mathbf{j}$ in Fig. 11–1, we see that $a\mathbf{i} + b\mathbf{j}$ is the vector hypotenuse of a right triangle whose vector sides are $a\mathbf{i}$ and $b\mathbf{j}$. If the vectors $\mathbf{v}_1$ and $\mathbf{v}_2$ are given in terms of components

$$\mathbf{v}_1 = a_1\mathbf{i} + b_1\mathbf{j},$$

$$\mathbf{v}_2 = a_2\mathbf{i} + b_2\mathbf{j},$$

* Vectors are indicated by bold-faced Roman letters. In handwritten work it is customary to draw small arrows over letters that represent vectors.

then

$$\mathbf{v}_1 + \mathbf{v}_2 = (a_1 + a_2)\mathbf{i} + (b_1 + b_2)\mathbf{j} \quad (1)$$

has x- and y-components obtained by adding the x- and y-components of $\mathbf{v}_1$ and $\mathbf{v}_2$.

Subtraction

To *subtract* one vector $\mathbf{v}_2$ from another vector $\mathbf{v}_1$ geometrically, we draw them both from a common initial point and then draw the vector from the tip of $\mathbf{v}_2$ to the tip of $\mathbf{v}_1$. Thus in Fig. 11–2(b), we have

$$\mathbf{v}_1 = \overrightarrow{AB}, \qquad \mathbf{v}_2 = \overrightarrow{AC},$$

and

$$\mathbf{v}_1 - \mathbf{v}_2 = -\mathbf{v}_2 + \mathbf{v}_1 = \overrightarrow{CA} + \overrightarrow{AB} = \overrightarrow{CB}.$$

In terms of components, vector subtraction follows the simple algebraic law

$$\mathbf{v}_1 - \mathbf{v}_2 = (a_1 - a_2)\mathbf{i} + (b_1 - b_2)\mathbf{j}, \quad (2)$$

which says that corresponding components are subtracted.

Length of a Vector

The length of the vector $\mathbf{v} = a\mathbf{i} + b\mathbf{j}$ is usually denoted by $|\mathbf{v}|$, which may be read "the magnitude of v." Figure 11–1 shows that $\mathbf{v}$ is the hypotenuse of a right triangle whose legs have lengths $|a|$ and $|b|$. Hence we may apply the theorem of Pythagoras to obtain

$$|\mathbf{v}| = |a\mathbf{i} + b\mathbf{j}| = \sqrt{a^2 + b^2}.$$

Multiplication by Scalars

The algebraic operation of multiplying a vector $\mathbf{v} = a\mathbf{i} + b\mathbf{j}$ by a scalar c is also simple, namely

$$c(a\mathbf{i} + b\mathbf{j}) = (ca)\mathbf{i} + (cb)\mathbf{j}.$$

Note how the unit vectors $\mathbf{i}$ and $\mathbf{j}$ allow us to keep the components separated from one another when we operate on vectors algebraically. Geometrically, $c\mathbf{v}$ is a vector whose length is $|c|$ times the length of $\mathbf{v}$:

$$|c\mathbf{v}| = |(ca)\mathbf{i} + (cb)\mathbf{j}| = \sqrt{(ca)^2 + (cb)^2} = |c|\sqrt{a^2 + b^2} = |c|\,|\mathbf{v}|. \quad (3)$$

The direction of $c\mathbf{v}$ agrees with that of $\mathbf{v}$ if c is positive, and is opposite to that of $\mathbf{v}$ if c is negative (Fig. 11–3). If $c = 0$, the vector $c\mathbf{v}$ has no direction.

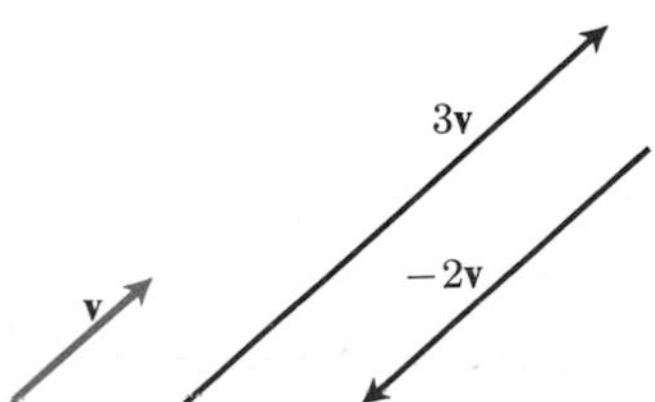

11–3 Scalar multiples of v.

Zero Vector

Any vector whose length is zero is called the *zero vector*, $\mathbf{0}$. The vector

$$a\mathbf{i} + b\mathbf{j} = \mathbf{0}, \qquad \text{if and only if} \quad a = b = 0.$$

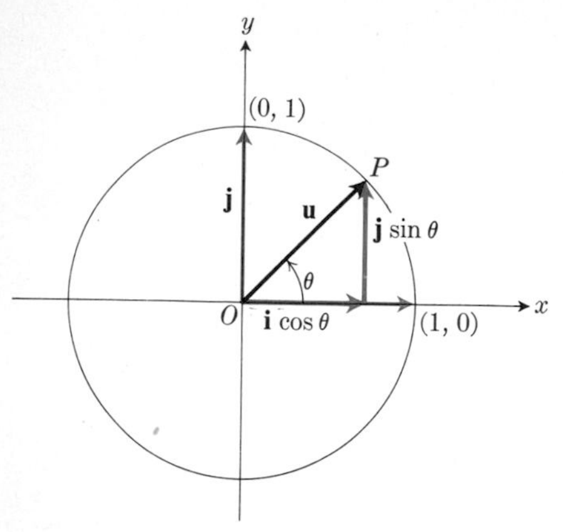

11–4 $\mathbf{u} = \mathbf{i}\cos\theta + \mathbf{j}\sin\theta$.

Unit Vector

Any vector **u** whose length is equal to the unit of length used along the coordinate axes is called a *unit vector*. If **u** is the unit vector obtained by rotating **i** through an angle θ in the positive direction, then (Fig. 11–4) **u** has a horizontal component

$$u_x = \cos\theta$$

and a vertical component

$$u_y = \sin\theta,$$

so that

$$\mathbf{u} = \mathbf{i}\cos\theta + \mathbf{j}\sin\theta. \tag{4}$$

If we allow the angle θ in Eq. (4) to vary from 0 to 2π, then the point P in Fig. 11–6 traces the unit circle $x^2 + y^2 = 1$ once in the counterclockwise direction. Every unit vector in the plane is described by Eq. (4) for some value of θ.

To find a unit vector in the direction of a given nonzero vector **v**, we divide **v** by its own length, $|\mathbf{v}|$. This amounts to multiplying **v** by the scalar $1/|\mathbf{v}|$. The result has length 1 because

$$\left|\frac{\mathbf{v}}{|\mathbf{v}|}\right| = \frac{1}{|\mathbf{v}|}\,|\mathbf{v}| = 1. \tag{5}$$

Two vectors are said to be *parallel* if the line segments representing them are parallel. Similarly, a vector is parallel to a line if the segments that represent the vector are parallel to the line. When we talk of a vector's being *tangent* or *normal* to a curve at a point, we mean that the vector is parallel to the line that is tangent or normal to the curve at the point. The next example shows how such a vector may be found.

EXAMPLE 1. Find unit vectors tangent and normal to the curve $y = (x^3/2) + \frac{1}{2}$ at the point (1, 1).

Solution. The slope of the line tangent to the curve at the point (1, 1) is

$$y' = \left.\frac{3x^2}{2}\right|_{x=1} = \frac{3}{2}.$$

We find a unit vector with this slope. The vector $\mathbf{v} = 2\mathbf{i} + 3\mathbf{j}$ has slope $\frac{3}{2}$ (Fig. 11–5), as does every nonzero multiple of **v**. To find a multiple of **v** that is a unit vector, we divide **v** by its length,

$$|\mathbf{v}| = \sqrt{2^2 + 3^2} = \sqrt{13}.$$

This produces the unit vector

$$\mathbf{u} = \frac{\mathbf{v}}{|\mathbf{v}|} = \frac{2}{\sqrt{13}}\mathbf{i} + \frac{3}{\sqrt{13}}\mathbf{j}.$$

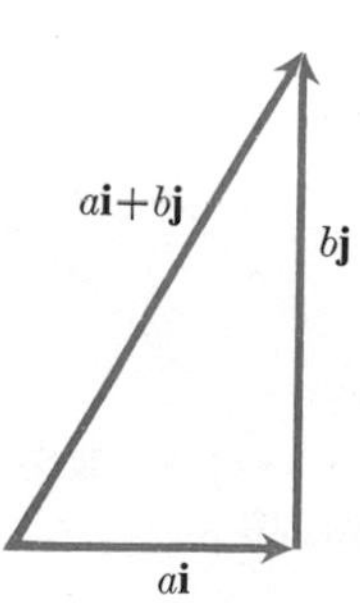

11–5 If $a \neq 0$, the vector $a\mathbf{i} + b\mathbf{j}$ has slope b/a.

The vector **u** is tangent to the curve at (1, 1) because it has the same direction as **v**. Of course, the vector

$$-\mathbf{u} = -\frac{2}{\sqrt{13}}\mathbf{i} - \frac{3}{\sqrt{13}}\mathbf{j},$$

which points in the direction opposite to **u**, is also tangent to the curve at (1, 1). Without some additional requirement, there is no reason to prefer one of these vectors to the other.

To find unit vectors normal to the curve at (1, 1), we look for unit vectors whose slopes are the negative reciprocal of the slope of **u**. This is quickly done by interchanging the components of **u** and changing the sign of one of them. We obtain

$$\mathbf{n} = \frac{3}{\sqrt{13}}\mathbf{i} - \frac{2}{\sqrt{13}}\mathbf{j}, \quad \text{and} \quad -\mathbf{n} = -\frac{3}{\sqrt{13}}\mathbf{i} + \frac{2}{\sqrt{13}}\mathbf{j}.$$

Again, either one will do.

PROBLEMS

In Problems 1–10 express each of the vectors in the form $a\mathbf{i} + b\mathbf{j}$. Indicate all quantities graphically.

1. $\overrightarrow{P_1P_2}$ if P_1 is the point (1, 3) and P_2 is the point (2, −1).

2. $\overrightarrow{OP_3}$ if O is the origin and P_3 is the midpoint of the vector $\overrightarrow{P_1P_2}$ joining $P_1(2, -1)$ and $P_2(-4, 3)$.

3. The vector from the point $A(2, 3)$ to the origin.

4. The sum of the vectors $\overrightarrow{AB}$ and $\overrightarrow{CD}$, given the four points $A(1, -1)$, $B(2, 0)$, $C(-1, 3)$, and $D(-2, 2)$.

5. A unit vector making an angle of 30° with the positive x-axis.

6. The unit vector obtained by rotating **j** through 120° in the clockwise direction.

7. A unit vector having the same direction as the vector $3\mathbf{i} - 4\mathbf{j}$.

8. A unit vector tangent to the curve $y = x^2$ at the point (2, 4).

9. A unit vector normal to the curve $y = x^2$ at the point $P(2, 4)$ and pointing from P toward the concave side of the curve (that is, an "inner" normal).

10. A unit vector tangent to the unit circle. [*Hint.* See Eq. (4).]

Find the lengths of each of the following vectors and the angle that each makes with the positive x-axis.

11. $\mathbf{i} + \mathbf{j}$ **12.** $2\mathbf{i} - 3\mathbf{j}$ **13.** $\sqrt{3}\,\mathbf{i} + \mathbf{j}$

14. $-2\mathbf{i} + 3\mathbf{j}$ **15.** $5\mathbf{i} + 12\mathbf{j}$ **16.** $-5\mathbf{i} - 12\mathbf{j}$

17. Let A, B, C, D be the vertices, in order, of a quadrilateral. Let A', B', C', D' be the midpoints of the sides AB, BC, CD, and DA, in order. Prove that $A'B'C'D'$ is a parallelogram. [*Hint.* First show that $\overrightarrow{A'B'} = \overrightarrow{D'C'} = \frac{1}{2}\overrightarrow{AC}$.]

18. Using vectors, show that the diagonals of a parallelogram bisect each other. [*Method.* Let A be one vertex and let M and N be the midpoints of the diagonals. Then show that $\overrightarrow{AM} = \overrightarrow{AN}$.]

11–2 PARAMETRIC EQUATIONS IN KINEMATICS

In newtonian mechanics, the motion of a particle in a plane is usually described by a pair of differential equations

$$F_x = \frac{d(mv_x)}{dt}, \qquad F_y = \frac{d(mv_y)}{dt} \tag{1}$$

that express Newton's second law of motion

$$\mathbf{F} = \frac{d(m\mathbf{v})}{dt} \tag{2}$$

in parametric form. Here, **F** is a vector that represents a force acting on a particle of mass m at time t. The vector **v** is the velocity vector of the particle

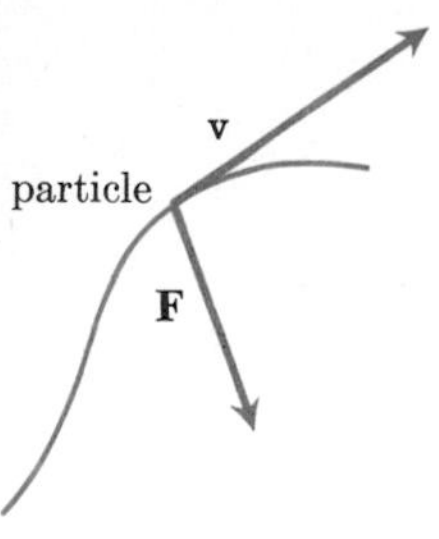

The force and velocity vectors of the motion of a particle in a plane might look like this at a particular time t.

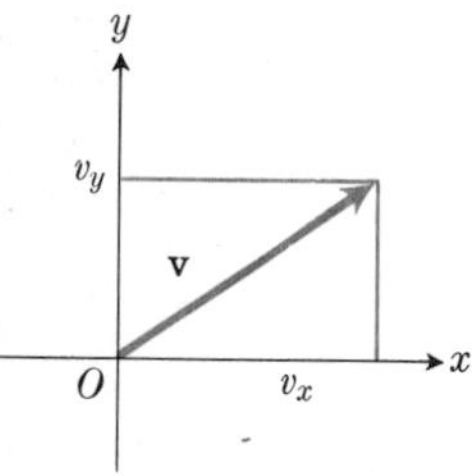

The components v_x and v_y of **v**

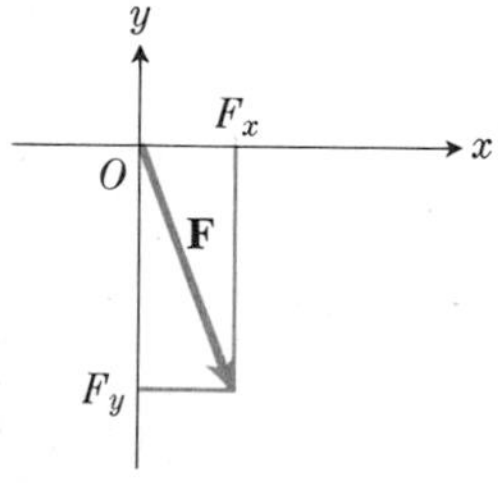

The components F_x and F_y of **F**

11–6 Motion of a particle in a plane.

at time t (Fig. 11–6). The quantities F_x and F_y are the x- and y-components of **F**, while v_x and v_y are the components of **v**.

If we know the position and velocity of the particle at some given instant, then the position of the particle at all later instants can usually be found by integrating Eqs. (1) with respect to time. The constants of integration are determined from given initial conditions. The result is another pair of parametric equations

$$x = f(t), \qquad y = g(t) \tag{3}$$

that give the coordinates x and y of the particle as functions of t.

The equations in (3) contain more information about the motion of the particle than the cartesian equation

$$y = F(x) \tag{4}$$

that we get from (3) by eliminating t. The parametric equations tell where the particle goes and *when* it gets to any given place, whereas the cartesian equation only tells the curve along which the particle travels. (Sometimes, too, a parametric representation of a curve is all that is possible; that is, a parameter cannot always be eliminated in practice.)

EXAMPLE 1. A projectile is fired with an initial velocity v_0 ft/sec at an angle of elevation α. Assuming that gravity is the only force acting on the projectile, find its motion.

Solution. We introduce coordinate axes with the origin at the point where the projectile begins its motion (Fig. 11–7). The distance traveled by the projectile over the ground is measured along the x-axis, and the height of the projectile above the ground is measured along the y-axis. At any time t, the projectile's position is given by a coordinate pair $x(t)$, $y(t)$, that we assume to be differentiable functions of t. If we measure distance in feet and time in seconds, with $t = 0$ at the instant the projectile is fired, then the initial conditions for the projectile's motion are

$$t = 0 \text{ sec}, \qquad x = 0 \text{ ft}, \qquad y = 0 \text{ ft},$$
$$v_x(0) = \frac{dx}{dt}(0) = v_0 \cos\alpha \quad \text{ft/sec}, \qquad v_y(0) = \frac{dy}{dt}(0) = v_0 \sin\alpha \quad \text{ft/sec}. \tag{5}$$

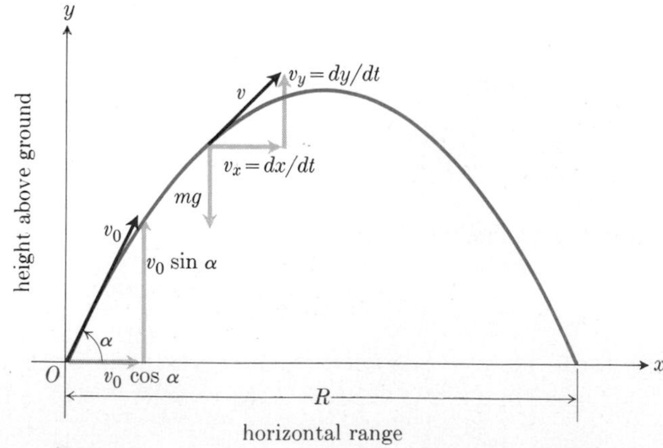

11–7 Ideal projectiles move along parabolas.

If the projectile is to travel only a few miles, and not go very high, it will cause no serious error to model the force of gravity with a constant vector **F** that points straight down. Its x- and y-components are

$$F_x = 0 \text{ lb}, \qquad F_y = -mg \text{ lb},$$

where m is the mass of the projectile and g is the acceleration of gravity. With these values for F_x and F_y, the equations in (1) become

$$0 = m\frac{d^2x}{dt^2}, \qquad -mg = m\frac{d^2y}{dt^2}. \tag{6}$$

To solve these equations for x and y, we integrate each one twice. This introduces four constants of integration, which may be evaluated by using the initial conditions (5). From the first equation in (6), we get

$$\frac{d^2x}{dt^2} = 0 \text{ ft/sec}^2, \qquad \frac{dx}{dt} = c_1 \text{ ft/sec}, \qquad x = c_1t + c_2 \text{ ft}, \tag{7a}$$

and from the second equation in (6),

$$\frac{d^2y}{dt^2} = -g \text{ ft/sec}^2, \qquad \frac{dy}{dt} = -gt + c_3 \text{ ft/sec}, \qquad y = -\tfrac{1}{2}gt^2 + c_3t + c_4 \text{ ft}. \tag{7b}$$

From the initial conditions, we find

$$c_1 = v_0 \cos\alpha \text{ ft/sec}, \qquad c_2 = 0 \text{ ft}, \qquad c_3 = v_0 \sin\alpha \text{ ft/sec}, \qquad c_4 = 0 \text{ ft}. \tag{7c}$$

The position of the projectile t seconds after firing is

$$x = (v_0 \cos\alpha)\,t \text{ ft}, \qquad y = -\tfrac{1}{2}gt^2 + (v_0 \sin\alpha)t \text{ ft}. \tag{8}$$

For a given angle of elevation α and a given muzzle velocity v_0, the position of the projectile at any time may be determined from the parametric equations in (8). These equations may be used to answer such questions as:

1. How high does the projectile rise?

2. How far away does the projectile land, and how does the horizontal range R vary with the angle of elevation?

3. What angle of elevation gives the maximum range?

First, the projectile will reach its highest point when its y-(vertical) velocity component is zero, that is, when

$$\frac{dy}{dt} = -gt + v_0 \sin\alpha = 0 \text{ ft/sec}$$

or

$$t - t_m = \frac{v_0 \sin\alpha}{g} \text{ sec.}$$

For this value of t, the value of y is

$$y_{\max} = -\frac{1}{2}g(t_m)^2 + (v_0 \sin\alpha)t_m = \frac{(v_0 \sin\alpha)^2}{2g} \text{ ft.}$$

Second, to find R we first find the time when the projectile strikes the ground. That is, we find the value of t for which $y = 0$. We then find the value of x for this value of t:

$$y = t(-\tfrac{1}{2}gt + v_0 \sin \alpha) = 0 \text{ ft}$$

when

$$t = 0 \qquad \text{or} \qquad t = \frac{2v_0 \sin \alpha}{g} = 2t_m \text{ sec.}$$

Since $t = 0$ is the instant when the projectile is fired, $t = 2t_m$ is the time when the projectile hits the ground. The corresponding value of x is

$$R = (v_0 \cos \alpha)(2t_m) = v_0 \cos \alpha \frac{2v_0 \sin \alpha}{g} = \frac{v_0^2}{g} \sin 2\alpha \text{ ft.}$$

Finally, the formula just given for R shows that the maximum range for a given muzzle velocity is obtained when $\sin 2\alpha = 1$, or $\alpha = 45°$.

The cartesian equation of the path of the projectile is readily obtained from (8). We need only substitute

$$t = \frac{x}{v_0 \cos \alpha}$$

from the first into the second equation of (8) to eliminate t and obtain

$$y = -\left(\frac{g}{2v_0^2 \cos^2 \alpha}\right)x^2 + (\tan \alpha)x. \tag{9}$$

Since this equation is linear in y and quadratic in x, it represents a *parabola*. Thus the path of a projectile (neglecting air resistance) is a parabola.

Differential equations that take air resistance into account are usually too complicated for straightforward integration. The M.I.T. differential analyzers were used to solve such equations during War II to build up "range tables." In following moving targets, keeping track of *time* is of great importance, so that equations or tables that give x and y in terms of t are preferred over other forms.

PROBLEMS

In Problems 1–4, the projectile is assumed to obey the laws of motion discussed above, in which air resistance is neglected.

1. Find two values of the angle of elevation that will enable a projectile to reach a target on the same level as the gun and 25,000 feet distant from it if the initial velocity is 1000 ft/sec. Determine the times of flight corresponding to these two angles.

2. Show that doubling the initial velocity of a projectile multiplies both the maximum height and the range by a factor of four.

3. Show that a projectile attains three-quarters of its maximum height in one-half the time required to reach that maximum.

4. Suppose a target moving at the constant rate of a ft/sec is level with and b ft away from a gun at the instant the gun is fired. If the target moves in a horizontal line directly away from the gun, show that the muzzle velocity v_0 and angle of elevation α must satisfy the equation.

$$v_0^2 \sin 2\alpha - 2av_0 \sin \alpha - bg = 0$$

if the projectile is to strike the target.

In Problems 5–7, find parametric equations and sketch the curve described by the point $P(x, y)$ for $t \geq 0$ if its coordinates satisfy the given differential equations and initial conditions.

5. $\dfrac{dx}{dt} = x, \quad \dfrac{dy}{dt} = -x^2; \quad t = 0, \quad x = 1, \quad y = -4.$

   [*Hint.* Solve for x first.]

6. $\dfrac{dx}{dt} = y, \quad \dfrac{dy}{dt} = y^2; \quad t = 0, \quad x = 0, \quad y = 1.$

7. $\dfrac{dx}{dt} = \sqrt{1 - x^2}, \quad \dfrac{dy}{dt} = x^2; \quad t = 0, \quad x = 0, \quad y = 1.$

11–3 PARAMETRIC EQUATIONS IN ANALYTIC GEOMETRY

The solutions of differential equations of motion are not the only ways in which parametric equations arise. For example, we have already used the equations

$$x = a \cos \theta, \qquad y = a \sin \theta, \qquad 0 \leq \theta \leq 2\pi, \tag{1}$$

to represent the circle of radius a whose center is at the origin (Fig. 11–8). Similarly, the equations

$$x = a \cos \phi, \qquad y = b \sin \phi, \qquad 0 \leq \phi \leq 2\pi, \tag{2}$$

are parametric equations for the ellipse whose cartesian equation is

$$\frac{x^2}{a^2} + \frac{y^2}{b^2} = 1.$$

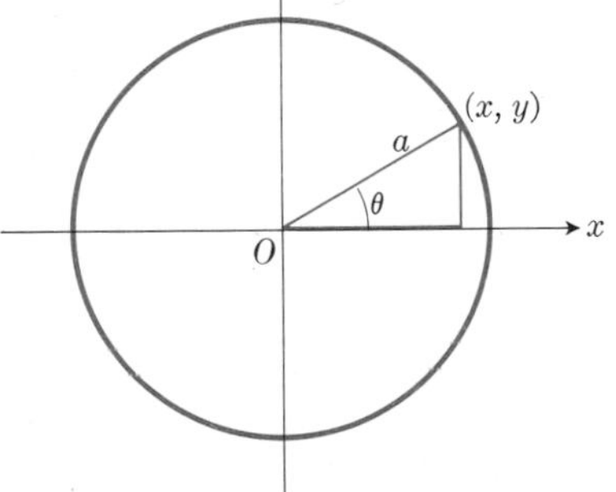

11–8 $x = a \cos \theta$, $y = a \sin \theta$.

EXAMPLE 1. Find parametric equations for the parabola

$$y^2 = 4px. \tag{3}$$

Solution. The parabola can be parametrized in several ways. One way is to use the slope

$$t = \frac{dy}{dx}$$

of the tangent to the curve at (x, y) as a parameter (Fig. 11–9(a)). Since

$$2y \frac{dy}{dx} = 4p \qquad \text{or} \qquad \frac{dy}{dx} = \frac{2p}{y},$$

a)

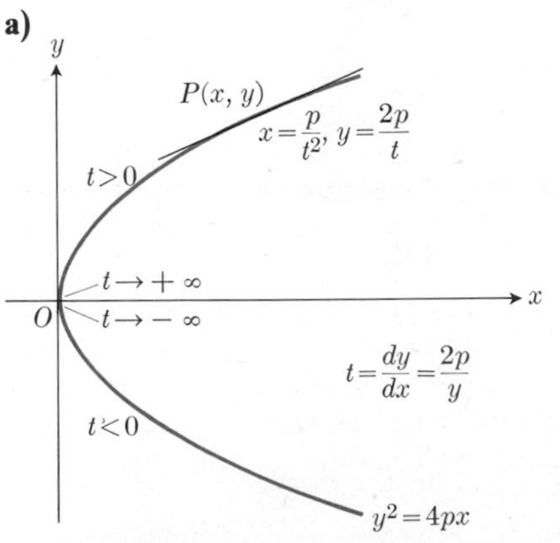

parameter t: slope of the tangent at P

b)

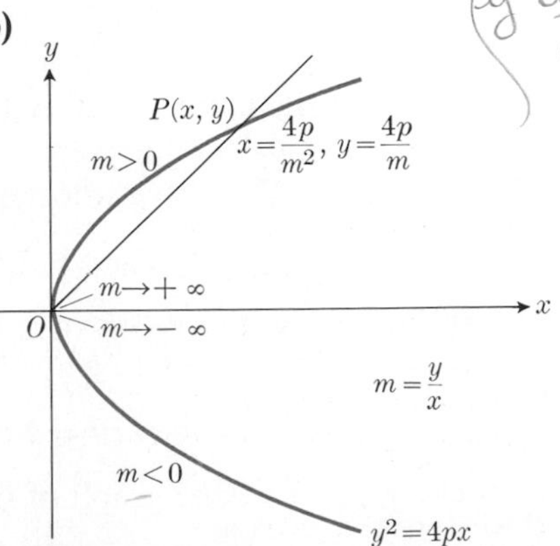

parameter m: slope of OP

11–9 Parametrizations of the parabola $y^2 = 4px$.

the parametric equations in this case are

$$y = \frac{2p}{t}, \qquad x = \frac{p}{t^2}. \tag{4}$$

If we use the parameter

$$m = \frac{y}{x},$$

(Fig. 11–9(b)), which is the slope of the line joining the origin to the point $P(x, y)$ on the parabola, we have

$$y^2 = m^2x^2 \qquad \text{and} \qquad y^2 = 4px,$$

which lead to

$$x = \frac{4p}{m^2}, \qquad y = \frac{4p}{m} \tag{5}$$

as the parametric equations.

Sometimes the parametric equations of a curve and the cartesian equation are not coextensive.

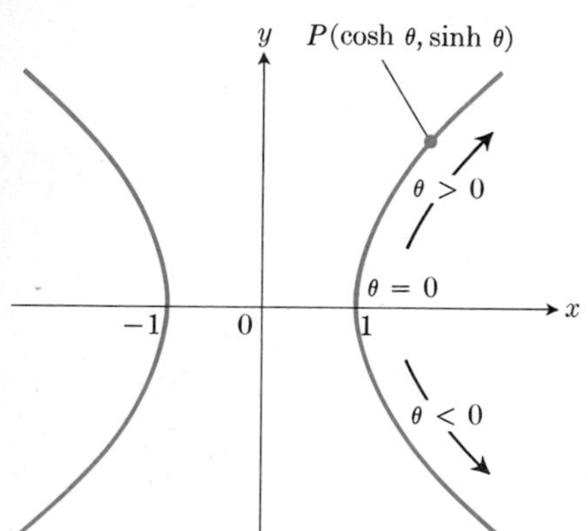

11–10 The parametric equations $x = \cosh\theta$, $y = \sinh\theta$, $-\infty < \theta < \infty$, give only the right branch of the hyperbola $x^2 - y^2 = 1$, because $\cosh\theta \geq 1$.

EXAMPLE 2. Suppose the parametric equations of a curve are

$$x = \cosh\theta, \qquad y = \sinh\theta. \tag{6}$$

Then the hyperbolic identity

$$\cosh^2\theta - \sinh^2\theta = 1$$

enables us to eliminate θ and write

$$x^2 - y^2 = 1 \tag{7}$$

as a cartesian equation of the curve. Closer scrutiny, however, shows that Eq. (7) *includes too much*, for $x = \cosh\theta$ is always positive, so the parametric equations represent a curve lying wholly to the right of the y-axis, whereas the cartesian equation (7) represents both the right- and lefthand branches of the hyperbola (Fig. 11–10). The lefthand branch could be excluded by taking only positive values of x. That is,

$$x = \sqrt{1 + y^2} \tag{8}$$

does represent the curve given by (6).

EXAMPLE 3. The curve whose parametric equations are

$$x = \cos 2\theta, \qquad y = \cos\theta, \tag{9}$$

lies within the square $-1 \leq x \leq 1$, $-1 \leq y \leq 1$. We may eliminate θ as follows:

$$x = \cos 2\theta = 2\cos^2\theta - 1 = 2y^2 - 1.$$

Thus every point on the graph of (9) also lies on the curve

$$x = 2y^2 - 1. \tag{10}$$

If we omit the restrictions

$$|x| \leq 1, \qquad |y| \leq 1,$$

then Eq. (10) represents the complete parabola

$$y^2 = \tfrac{1}{2}(x + 1)$$

shown in Fig. 11–11. The parametric equations, however, represent only the arc ABC. From (9), we see that the point starts at $A(1, 1)$ when $\theta = 0$, moves along AB to $B(-1, 0)$ as θ varies from 0 to $\pi/2$, and continues to $C(1, -1)$ as θ increases to π. As θ varies from π to 2π, the point traverses the arc CBA back to A. Since both x and y are periodic, x of period π and y of period 2π, further variations in θ result in retracing the same portion of the parabola.

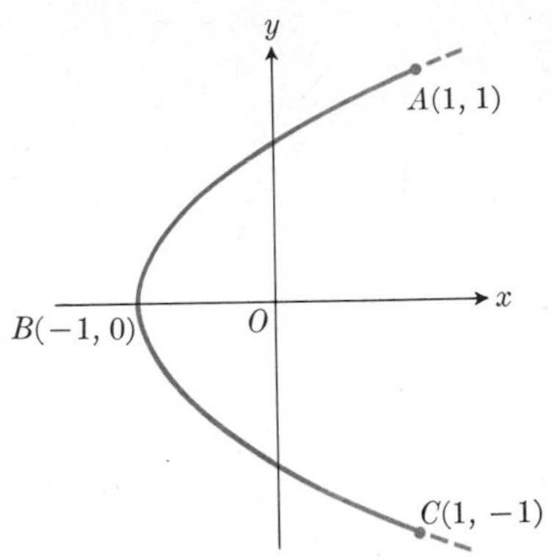

11–11 $x = \cos 2\theta$, $y = \cos \theta$.

EXAMPLE 4. A wheel of radius a rolls along a horizontal straight line without slipping. Find the curve traced by a point P on a spoke of the wheel b units from its center. Such a curve is called a *trochoid* (one Greek word for wheel is *trochos*). When $b = a$, P is on the circumference and the curve is called a *cycloid*. This is like the path traveled by the head of a nail in a tire.

Solution. In Fig. 11–12 we take the x-axis to be the line the wheel rolls along, with the y-axis through a low point of the trochoid. It is customary to use the angle ϕ through which CP has rotated as the parameter. Since the circle rolls without slipping, the distance OM that the wheel has moved horizontally is just equal to the circular arc $MN = a\phi$. (Roll the wheel back. Then N will fall at the origin O.) The xy-coordinates of C are therefore

$$h = a\phi, \qquad k = a. \tag{11}$$

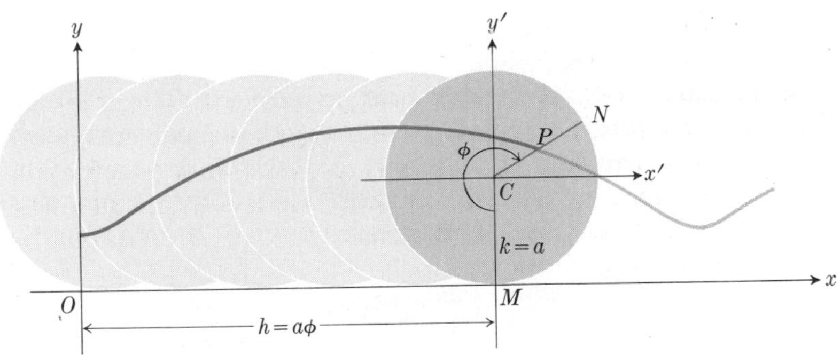

11–12 Trochoid: $x = a\phi - b \sin \phi$, $y = a - b \cos \phi$.

We now introduce $x'y'$-axes parallel to the xy-axes and having their origin at C (Fig. 11–13). The xy- and $x'y'$-coordinates of P are related by the equations

$$x = h + x', \qquad y = k + y'. \tag{12}$$

From Fig. 11–13 we may immediately read

$$x' = b \cos \theta, \qquad y' = b \sin \theta,$$

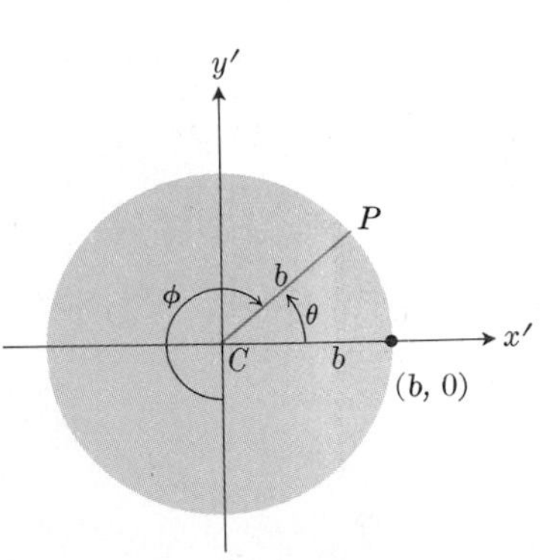

11–13 The $x'y'$-coordinates of P are $x' = b \cos \theta$, $y = b \sin \theta$.

or, since

$$\theta = \frac{3\pi}{2} - \phi,$$

$$x' = -b \sin \phi, \qquad y' = -b \cos \phi. \tag{13}$$

We substitute these results and Eqs. (12) into (11) and obtain

$$x = a\phi - b \sin \phi,$$
$$y = a - b \cos \phi \tag{14}$$

as parametric equations of the trochoid.

a)

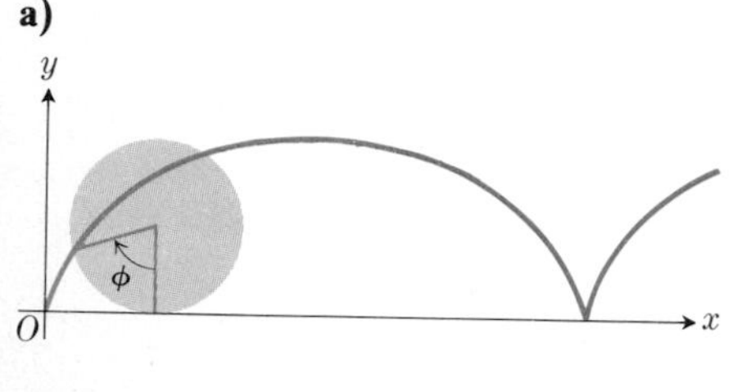

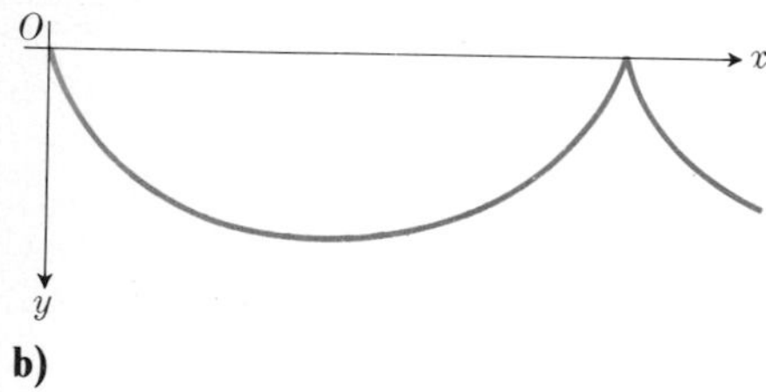

b)

11–14 Cycloid: $x = a(\phi - \sin \phi)$, $y = a(1 - \cos \phi)$.

The cycloid (Fig. 11–14(a)),

$$x = a(\phi - \sin \phi), \qquad y = a(1 - \cos \phi), \tag{15}$$

obtained from (14) by taking $b = a$, is the most important special case.

Brachistochrones and Tautochrones

If we reflect both the cycloid and the y-axis across the x-axis, Eqs. (15) still apply, and the resulting curve (Fig. 11–14(b)) has several interesting properties, one of which we shall now discuss without proof. The proofs belong to a branch of mathematics known as the calculus of variations. Much of the fundamental theory of this subject is attributed to the Bernoulli brothers, John and James, who were friendly rivals and stimulated each other with mathematical problems in the form of challenges. One of these, the brachistochrone problem, was: Among all smooth curves joining two given points, to find that one along which a bead, subject only to the force of gravity, might slide *in the shortest time.*

The two points, labeled P_0 and P_1 in Fig. 11–15, may be taken to lie in a vertical plane at the origin and at (x_1, y_1), respectively. We can formulate the problem in mathematical terms as follows. The kinetic energy of the bead at the start is zero, since its velocity is zero. The work done by gravity in moving the particle from (0, 0) to any point (x, y) is mgy and this must be equal to the change in kinetic energy; that is,

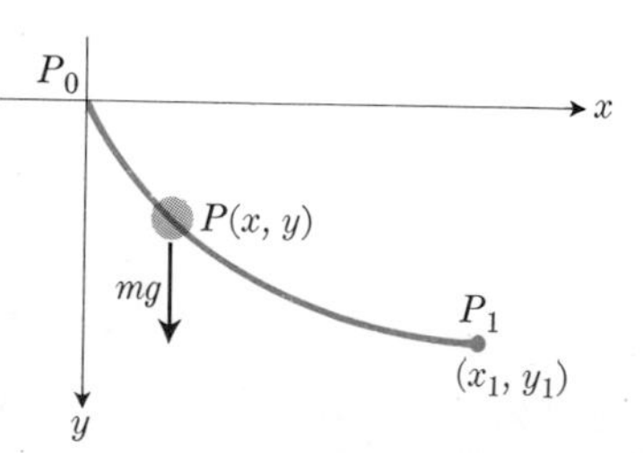

11–15 A bead sliding down a cycloid.

$$mgy = \tfrac{1}{2}mv^2 - \tfrac{1}{2}m(0)^2.$$

Thus the velocity

$$v = ds/dt$$

that the particle has when it reaches $P(x, y)$ is

$$v = \sqrt{2gy}.$$

That is,

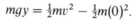

$$\frac{ds}{dt} = \sqrt{2gy} \qquad \text{or} \qquad dt = \frac{ds}{\sqrt{2gy}} = \frac{\sqrt{1 + \left(\dfrac{dy}{dx}\right)^2}\, dx}{\sqrt{2gy}}.$$

The time t_1 required for the bead to slide from P_0 to P_1 depends upon the particular curve $y = f(x)$ along which it moves and is given by

$$t_1 = \int_0^{x_1} \sqrt{\frac{1 + (f'(x))^2}{2gf(x)}}\, dx. \tag{16}$$

The problem is *to find the curve* $y = f(x)$ that passes through the points $P_0(0, 0)$ and $P_1(x_1, y_1)$ and minimizes the value of the integral in Eq. (16). (*Brachistochrone* is derived from two Greek words that together mean "shortest time.")

At first sight, one might guess that the straight line joining P_0 and P_1 would also yield the shortest time, but a moment's reflection will cast some doubt on this conjecture, for there may be some gain in time by having the particle start to fall vertically at first, thereby building up its velocity more quickly than if it were to slide along an inclined path. With this increased velocity, one may be able to afford to travel over a longer path and still reach P_1 in a shorter time. The solution of the problem is beyond the present book, but the brachistochrone curve is actually an arc of a cycloid through P_0 and P_1, having a cusp at the origin.

If we write Eq. (16) in the equivalent form

$$t_1 = \int \sqrt{\frac{dx^2 + dy^2}{2gy}}$$

and then substitute Eqs. (15) into this, we obtain

$$t_1 = \int_{\phi=0}^{\phi_1} \sqrt{\frac{a^2(2 - 2\cos\phi)}{2ga(1 - \cos\phi)}}\, d\phi = \phi_1 \sqrt{\frac{a}{g}}$$

as the time required for the particle to slide from P_0 to P_1. The time required to reach the bottom of the arc is obtained by taking $\phi_1 = \pi$. Now it is a remarkable fact, which we shall soon demonstrate, that the time required to slide along the cycloid from (0, 0) to the lowest point $(a\pi, 2a)$ is the same as the time required for the particle, starting from rest, to slide from *any intermediate point* of the arc, say (x_0, y_0), to $(a\pi, 2a)$. For the latter case, one has

$$v = \sqrt{2g(y - y_0)}$$

as the velocity at $P(x, y)$, and the time required is

$$T = \int_{\phi_0}^{\pi} \sqrt{\frac{a^2(2 - 2\cos\phi)}{2ag(\cos\phi_0 - \cos\phi)}}\, d\phi = \sqrt{\frac{a}{g}} \int_{\phi_0}^{\pi} \sqrt{\frac{1 - \cos\phi}{\cos\phi_0 - \cos\phi}}\, d\phi$$

$$= \sqrt{\frac{a}{g}} \int_{\phi_0}^{\pi} \sqrt{\frac{2\sin^2(\phi/2)}{[2\cos^2(\phi_0/2) - 1] - [2\cos^2(\phi/2) - 1]}}\, d\phi$$

$$= 2\sqrt{\frac{a}{g}} \left[-\sin^{-1} \frac{\cos(\phi/2)}{\cos(\phi_0/2)} \right]_{\phi_0}^{\pi} = 2\sqrt{\frac{a}{g}} (-\sin^{-1} 0 + \sin^{-1} 1) = \pi \sqrt{\frac{a}{g}}.$$

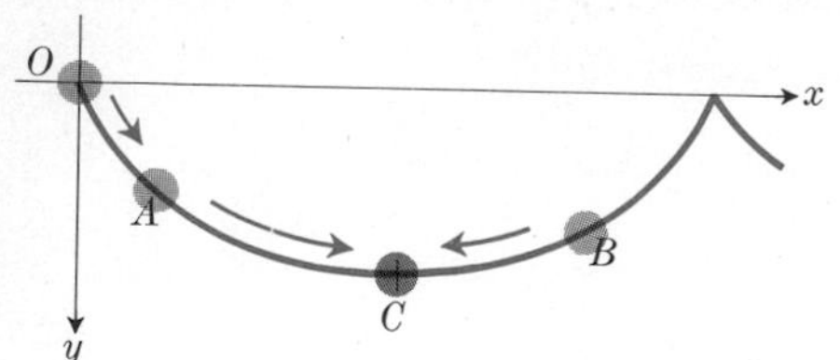

11–16 Beads released on the cycloid at O, A, and B will take the same amount of time to reach C.

Since this answer is independent of the value of ϕ_0, it follows that the same length of time is required to reach the lowest point on the cycloid no matter where on the arc the particle is released from rest. Thus, in Fig. 11–16, three particles which start at the same time from O, A, and B will reach C simultaneously. In this sense, the cycloid is also a *tautochrone* (meaning "the same time") as well as being a brachistochrone.

Pendulum Clocks

One trouble with pendulum clocks is that the rate at which the pendulum swings changes with the size of the swing. The wider the swing, the longer it takes the pendulum to return. This would create no problem if clocks never ran down, but they do. As the spring unwinds, the force exerted on the pendulum decreases, the pendulum swings through increasingly shorter arcs, and the clock speeds up. The ticks come faster as the clock winds down. Christiaan Huygens, a seventeenth-century Dutch mathematician, physicist and astronomer, needed an accurate clock to make careful astronomical measurements. In 1673 he published the first description of an ideal pendulum clock whose bob swings in a cycloid. The period of the swing of Huygens' clock did not depend on the amplitude, and would not change as the clock wound down.

How does one make a pendulum bob swing in a cycloid? Hang it from a fine wire constrained by "cheeks" (Fig. 11–17), which cause the bob to draw up as it swings to the side. And what is the shape of the cheeks? They are cycloids.

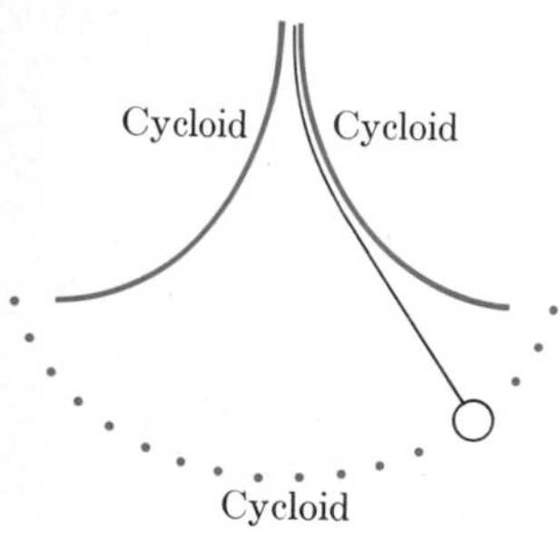

11–17 A flexible pendulum constrained by cycloids swings in a cycloid.

PROBLEMS

In each of Problems 1–10, sketch the graph of the curve described by the point $P(x, y)$ as the parameter t varies over the domain given. Also find a cartesian equation of the curve in each case.

1. $x = \cos t,\quad y = \sin t,\quad 0 \le t \le 2\pi$
2. $x = \cos 2t,\quad y = \sin t,\quad 0 \le t \le 2\pi$
3. $x = \sec t,\quad y = \tan t,\quad -\pi/2 < t < \pi/2$
4. $x = 2 + 4 \sin t,\quad y = 3 - 2 \cos t,\quad 0 \le t \le 2\pi$
5. $x = 2t + 3,\quad y = 4t^2 - 9,\quad -\infty < t < \infty$
6. $x = \cosh t,\quad y = 2 \sinh t,\quad 0 \le t < \infty$
7. $x = 2 + 1/t,\quad y = 2 - t,\quad 0 < t < \infty$
8. $x = t + 1,\quad y = t^2 + 4,\quad 0 \le t < \infty$
9. $x = t^2 + t,\quad y = t^2 - t,\quad -\infty < t < \infty$
10. $x = 3 + 2 \operatorname{sech} t,\quad y = 4 - 3 \tanh t,\quad -\infty < t < \infty$
11. Find parametric equations of the semicircle
$$x^2 + y^2 = a^2, \qquad y > 0,$$
using as parameter the slope $t = dy/dx$ of the tangent to the curve at (x, y).
12. Find parametric equations of the semicircle
$$x^2 + y^2 = a^2, \qquad y > 0,$$
using as parameter the variable θ defined by the equation $x = a \tanh \theta$.
13. Find parametric equations of the circle
$$x^2 + y^2 = a^2,$$
using as parameter the arc length s measured counterclockwise from the point $(a, 0)$ to the point (x, y).
14. Find parametric equations of the catenary $y = a \cosh x/a$, using as parameter the length of arc s from the point $(0, a)$ to the point (x, y), with the sign of s taken to be the same as the sign of x.
15. If a string wound around a fixed circle is unwound while held taut in the plane of the circle, its end traces an *involute* of the circle (Fig. 11–18). Let the fixed circle be located with its center at the origin O and have radius a. Let the initial position of the tracing point P be $A(a, 0)$ and let the unwound portion of the string PT be tangent to the

circle at T. Derive parametric equations of the involute, using the angle AOT as the parameter t.

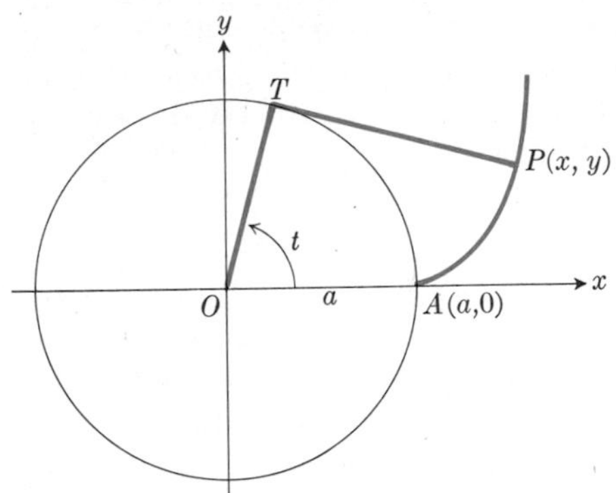

11–18 Involute of a circle.

16. When a circle rolls externally on the circumference of a second, fixed circle, any point P on the circumference of the rolling circle describes an *epicycloid* (Fig. 11–19). Let the fixed circle have its center at the origin O and have radius a. Let the radius of the rolling circle be b and let the initial position of the tracing point P be $A(a, 0)$. Determine parametric equations of the epicycloid, using as parameter the angle θ from the positive x-axis to the line of centers.

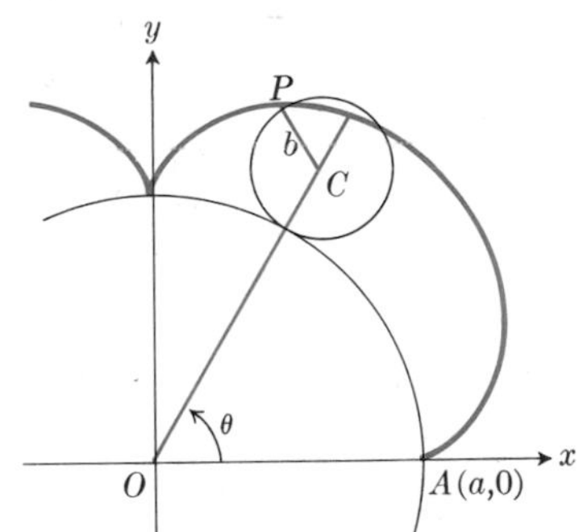

11–19 Epicycloid, with $b = a/4$.

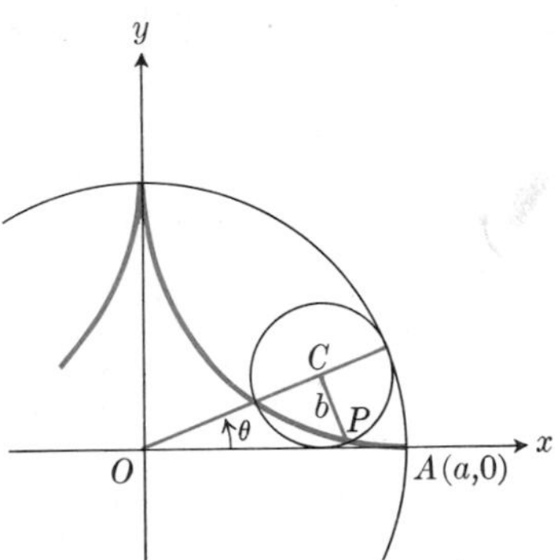

11–20 Hypocycloid, with $b = a/4$.

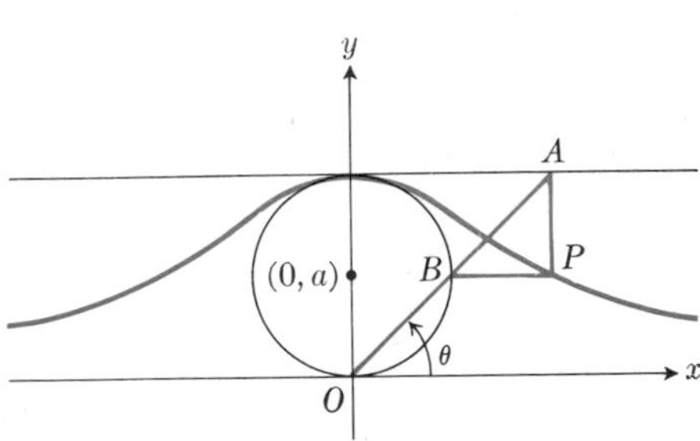

11–21 The witch of Maria Agnesi.

17. When a circle rolls on the inside of a fixed circle any point P on the circumference of the rolling circle describes a *hypocycloid*. Let the fixed circle be $x^2 + y^2 = a^2$, let the radius of the rolling circle be b, and let the initial position of the tracing point P be $A(a, 0)$. Use the angle θ from the positive x-axis to the line of centers as parameter and determine parametric equations of the hypocycloid. In particular, if $b = a/4$, as in Fig. 11–20, show that

$$x = a \cos^3 \theta, \qquad y = a \sin^3 \theta.$$

18. Find the length of one arch of the cycloid

$$x = a(\phi - \sin \phi),$$
$$y = a(1 - \cos \phi).$$

19. Show that the slope of the cycloid

$$x = a(\phi - \sin \phi),$$
$$y = a(1 - \cos \phi)$$

is $dy/dx = \cot \phi/2$. In particular, the tangent to the cycloid is vertical when ϕ is 0 or 2π.

20. Show that the slope of the trochoid

$$x = a\phi - b \sin \phi, \qquad y = a - b \cos \phi$$

is always finite if $b < a$.

21. The *witch of Maria Agnesi* is a bell-shaped curve that may be constructed as follows: Let C be a circle of radius a having its center at $(0, a)$ on the y-axis (Fig. 11–21). The variable line OA through the origin O intersects the line $y = 2a$ in the point A and intersects the circle in the point B. A point P on the witch is now located by taking the intersection of lines through A and B parallel to the y- and x-axes, respectively. (a) Find parametric equations of the witch, using as parameter the angle θ from the x-axis to the line OA.
(b) Also find the cartesian equation for the witch.

22. (*Calculator*) An automobile tire of radius 1 ft has a pebble stuck in the tread. Estimate to the nearest foot how far the pebble travels when the car goes one mile. Start by finding the ratio of the length of one arch of a cycloid to its base length.

11–4 SPACE COORDINATES

A. Cartesian Coordinates

Figure 11–22 shows a system of mutually orthogonal coordinate axes, Ox, Oy, and Oz. The system is called *righthanded* because a right-threaded screw pointing along Oz will advance when turned from Ox to Oy through an angle, say, of 90°. The cartesian coordinates of a point $P(x, y, z)$ in space may be read from the coordinate axes by passing planes through P perpendicular to each axis. The points on the x-axis have their y- and z-coordinates both zero. That is, they have coordinates of the form $(x, 0, 0)$. Points in a plane perpendicular to the z-axis, say, all have the same z-coordinate. Thus the points in the plane perpendicular to the z-axis and 5 units above the xy-plane all have coordinates of the form $(x, y, 5)$. We can write $z = 5$ as an equation for this plane. The three planes

$$x = 2, \qquad y = 3, \qquad z = 5$$

intersect in the point $P(2, 3, 5)$. The points of the yz-plane are obtained by setting $x = 0$. The three coordinate planes $x = 0$, $y = 0$, $z = 0$ divide the space into eight cells, called octants. The octant in which all three coordinates are positive is called the *first octant*, but there is no conventional numbering of the remaining seven octants.

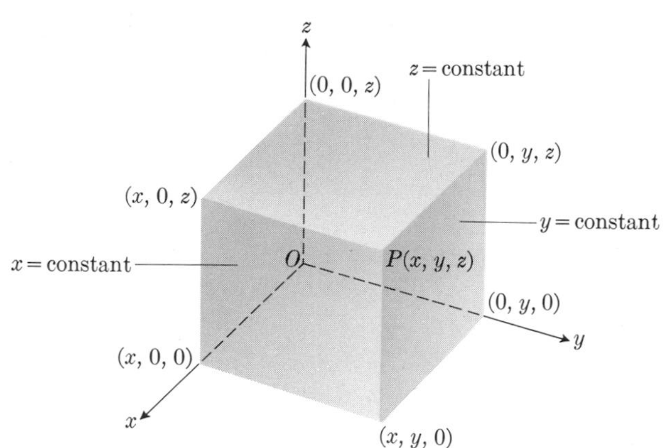

11–22 Righthanded coordinate system.

B. Cylindrical Coordinates

It is frequently convenient to use cylindrical coordinates (r, θ, z) to locate a point in space. These are just the polar coordinates (r, θ) used instead of (x, y) in the plane $z = 0$, coupled with the z-coordinate. Cylindrical and cartesian coordinates are related by the familiar equations (Fig. 11–23)

$$\begin{aligned} x &= r\cos\theta, & r^2 &= x^2 + y^2, \\ y &= r\sin\theta, & \tan\theta &= y/x, \\ & & z &= z. \end{aligned} \tag{1}$$

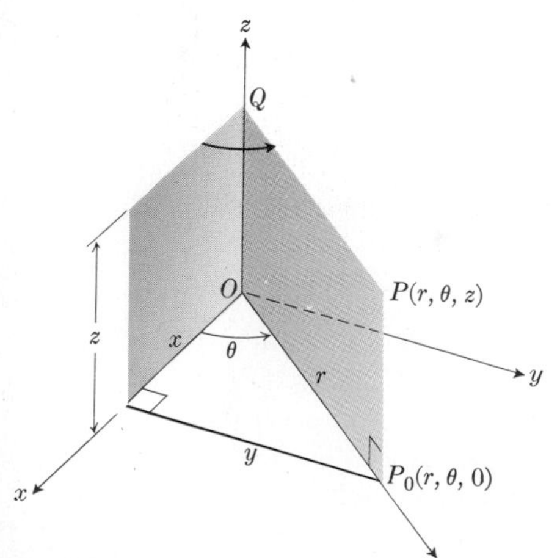

11–23 Cylindrical coordinates.

The equation $r =$ constant describes a right circular cylinder of radius r whose axis is the z-axis, $r = 0$ being an equation for the z-axis itself. The equation $\theta =$ constant describes a plane containing the z-axis and making an angle θ with the xz-plane (Fig. 11–24). (Some authors require the values of r in cylindrical coordinates to be nonnegative. In this case, the equation $\theta =$ constant describes a half-plane fanning out from the z-axis.)

Cylindrical coordinates are convenient when there is an axis of symmetry in a physical problem.

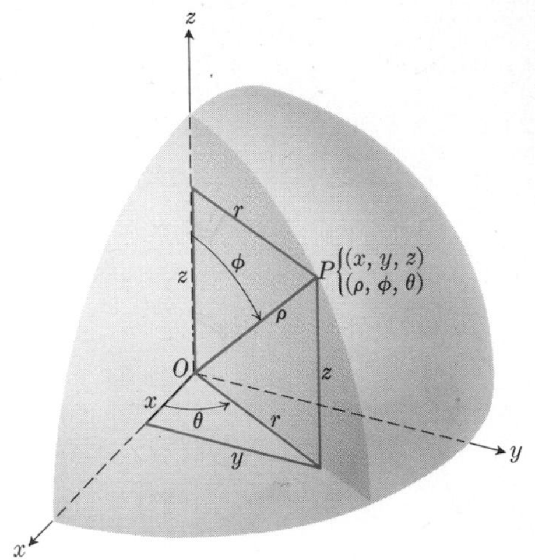

11–25 Spherical coordinates.

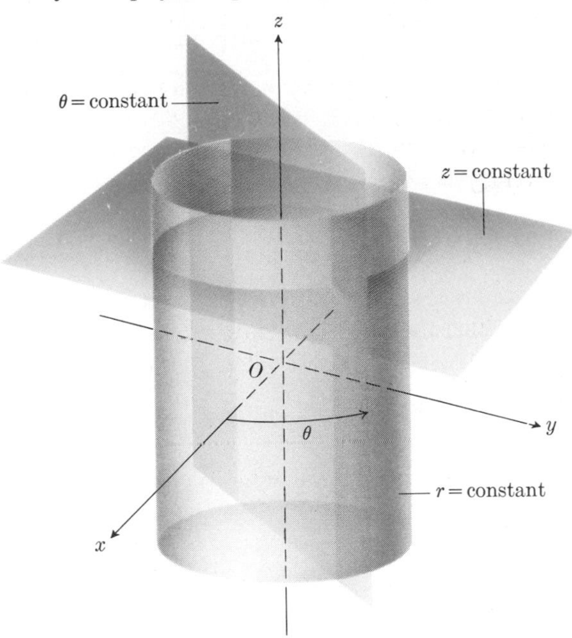

11–24 Some planes and cylinders have simple equations in cylindrical coordinates.

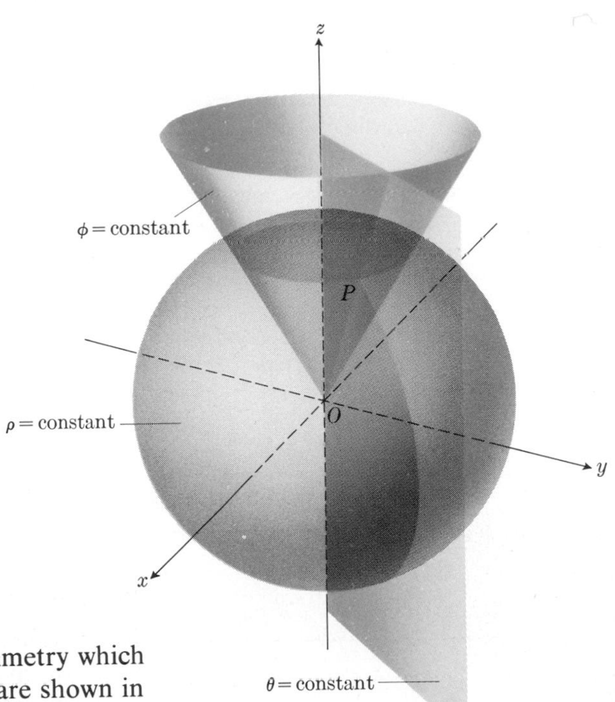

11–26 Spheres and cones whose centers are at the origin have simple equations in spherical coordinates.

C. Spherical Coordinates

Spherical coordinates are useful when there is a center of symmetry which we can take as the origin. The *spherical coordinates* (ρ, ϕ, θ) are shown in Fig. 11–25. The first coordinate $\rho = |OP|$ is the distance from the origin to the point P. It is never negative. The equation $\rho =$ constant describes the surface of a sphere of radius ρ with center at O (Fig. 11–26). The second spherical coordinate, ϕ, is the angle measured down from the z-axis to the line OP. The equation $\phi =$ constant describes a cone with vertex at O, axis Oz, and generating angle ϕ, provided we broaden our interpretation of the word "cone" to include the xy-plane for which $\phi = \pi/2$ and cones with generating angles greater than $\pi/2$. The third spherical coordinate θ is the same as the angle θ in cylindrical coordinates, namely, the angle from the xz-plane to the plane through P and the z-axis. But, in contrast with cylindrical coordinates, the equation $\theta =$ constant in spherical coordinates defines a half-plane (Fig. 11–26).

From Fig. 11–25 we may read the following relationships between the cartesian, cylindrical, and spherical coordinate systems:

$$\begin{aligned} r &= \rho \sin \phi, & x &= r \cos \theta, & x &= \rho \sin \phi \cos \theta, \\ z &= \rho \cos \phi, & y &= r \sin \theta, & y &= \rho \sin \phi \sin \theta, \\ \theta &= \theta, & z &= z, & z &= \rho \cos \phi. \end{aligned} \tag{2}$$

Every point in space can be given spherical coordinates restricted to the ranges

$$\rho \geq 0, \qquad 0 \leq \phi \leq \pi, \qquad 0 \leq \theta < 2\pi. \tag{3}$$

Because of the analogy between the surface of a sphere and the earth's surface, the z-axis is sometimes called the *polar axis*, while ϕ is referred to as *co-latitude* and θ as *longitude*. One also speaks of *meridians*, *parallels*, and the *northern* and *southern hemispheres*.

PROBLEMS

In Problems 1–4, describe the set of points $P(x, y, z)$ whose cartesian coordinates satisfy the given pairs of simultaneous equations. Sketch.

1. $x =$ constant, $y =$ constant
2. $y = x$, $z = 5$
3. $x^2 + y^2 = 4$, $z = -2$
4. $x = 0$, $\dfrac{y^2}{a^2} + \dfrac{z^2}{b^2} = 1$

In Problems 5–8, describe the set of points $P(r, \theta, z)$ whose cylindrical coordinates satisfy the given pairs of simultaneous equations. Sketch.

5. $r = 2$, $z = 3$
6. $\theta = \pi/6$, $z = r$
7. $r = 3$, $z = 2\theta$
8. $r = 2\theta$, $z = 3\theta$

In Problems 9–12, describe the set of points $P(\rho, \phi, \theta)$ whose spherical coordinates satisfy the given pairs of simultaneous equations. Sketch.

9. $\rho = 5$, $\theta = \pi/4$
10. $\rho = 5$, $\phi = \pi/4$
11. $\theta = \pi/4$, $\phi = \pi/4$
12. $\theta = \pi/2$, $\rho = 4 \cos \phi$

Translate the following equations from the given coordinate system (cartesian, cylindrical, or spherical) into forms that are appropriate to the other two systems.

13. $x^2 + y^2 + z^2 = 4$
14. $x^2 + y^2 + z^2 = 4z$
15. $z^2 = r^2$
16. $\rho = 6 \cos \phi$

Describe the following sets.

17. $x \geq 0$
18. $3 \leq \rho \leq 5$
19. $r \geq 2$, $\rho \leq 5$
20. $0 \leq \theta \leq \pi/4$, $0 \leq \phi \leq \pi/4$, $\rho \geq 0$
21. $4x^2 + 9y^2 \leq 36$

11–5 VECTORS IN SPACE

Vectors in space are the three-dimensional analog of vectors in the plane, and are subject to the same rules of addition, subtraction, and scalar multiplication that govern vectors in the plane. The vectors from the origin to the points whose cartesian coordinates are (1, 0, 0), (0, 1, 0), and (0, 0, 1) are the basic unit vectors. We denote them by **i**, **j**, and **k**, and write the vector from the origin O to the point $P(x, y, z)$ as

$$\mathbf{R} = \overrightarrow{OP} = \mathbf{i}x + \mathbf{j}y + \mathbf{k}z. \tag{1}$$

If $P_1(x_1, y_1, z_1)$ and $P_2(x_2, y_2, z_2)$ are two points in space (Fig. 11–27), then the vector from P_1 to P_2 is the vector sum

$$\overrightarrow{P_1P_2} = \overrightarrow{P_1O} + \overrightarrow{OP_2}.$$

Since

$$\overrightarrow{P_1O} = -\overrightarrow{OP_1},$$

this is the same as

$$\overrightarrow{P_1P_2} = \overrightarrow{OP_2} - \overrightarrow{OP_1}$$

or

$$\overrightarrow{P_1P_2} = \mathbf{i}(x_2 - x_1) + \mathbf{j}(y_2 - y_1) + \mathbf{k}(z_2 - z_1). \tag{2}$$

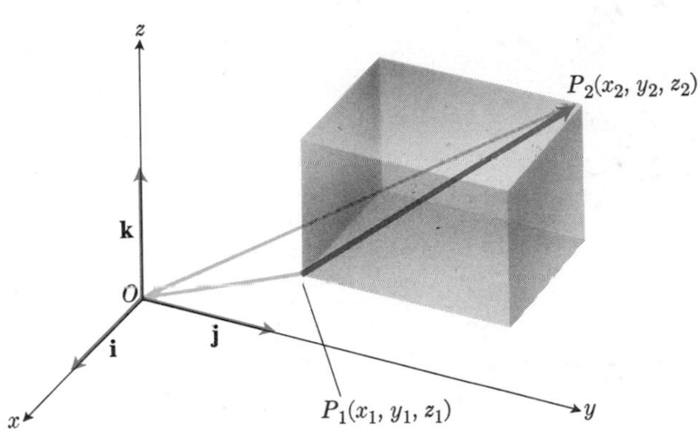

11–27 $\overrightarrow{P_1P_2} = \overrightarrow{P_1O} + \overrightarrow{OP_2}$.

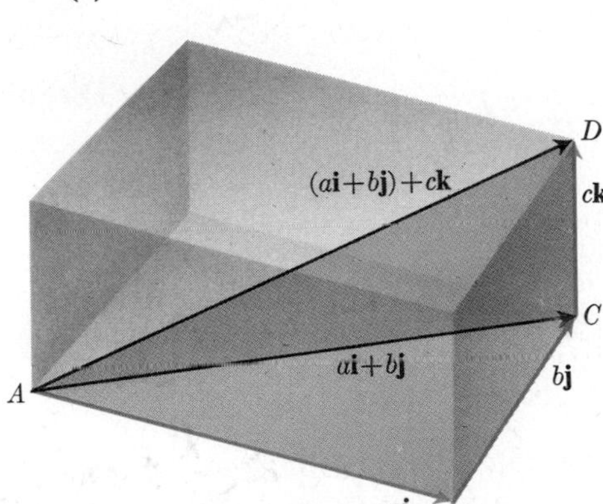

11–28 $|\overrightarrow{AD}|$ can be determined from the right triangles ABC and ACD.

The length of any vector

$$\mathbf{A} = a\mathbf{i} + b\mathbf{j} + c\mathbf{k}$$

is readily determined by applying the theorem of Pythagoras twice. In the right triangle ABC (Fig. 11–28),

$$|\overrightarrow{AC}| = |a\mathbf{i} + b\mathbf{j}| = \sqrt{a^2 + b^2},$$

and in the right triangle ACD,

$$|\overrightarrow{AD}| = \sqrt{|\overrightarrow{AC}|^2 + |\overrightarrow{CD}|^2} = \sqrt{(a^2 + b^2) + c^2}.$$

That is,

$$|a\mathbf{i} + b\mathbf{j} + c\mathbf{k}| = \sqrt{a^2 + b^2 + c^2}. \tag{3}$$

If we apply this result to the vector $\overrightarrow{P_1P_2}$ of Eq. (2), we obtain a formula for the distance between two points:

$$|\overrightarrow{P_1P_2}| = \sqrt{(x_2 - x_1)^2 + (y_2 - y_1)^2 + (z_2 - z_1)^2}. \tag{4}$$

Equation (4) may be used to determine an equation for the sphere of radius a with center at $P_0(x_0, y_0, z_0)$ (Fig. 11–29). The point P is on the sphere if and only if

$$|\overrightarrow{P_0P}| = a,$$

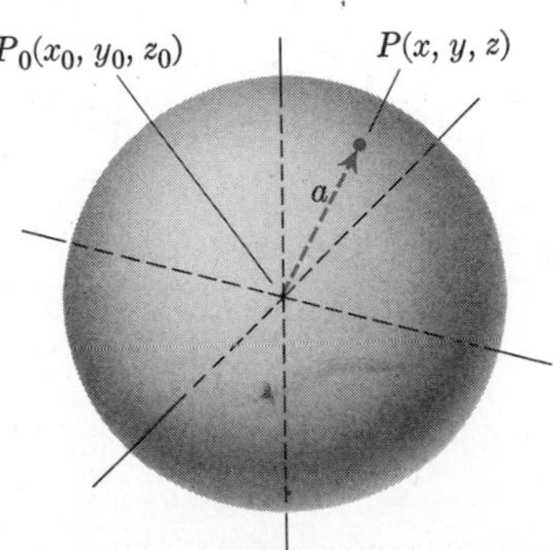

11–29 The sphere $(x - x_0)^2 + (y - y_0)^2 + (z - z_0)^2 = a^2$.

or

$$(x - x_0)^2 + (y - y_0)^2 + (z - z_0)^2 = a^2. \tag{5}$$

EXAMPLE 1. Find the center and radius of the sphere

$$x^2 + y^2 + z^2 + 2x - 4y = 0.$$

Solution. Complete the squares in the given equation to obtain

$$x^2 + 2x + 1 + y^2 - 4y + 4 + z^2 = 0 + 1 + 4$$

$$(x + 1)^2 + (y - 2)^2 + z^2 = 5.$$

Comparison with Eq. (5) shows that $x_0 = -1$, $y_0 = 2$, $z_0 = 0$, and $a = \sqrt{5}$. The center is $(-1, 2, 0)$ and the radius is $\sqrt{5}$.

Direction

For any nonzero vector **A**, we obtain a unit vector called *the direction of* **A** by dividing **A** by its own length:*

$$\text{Direction of } \mathbf{A} = \frac{\mathbf{A}}{|\mathbf{A}|}. \tag{6}$$

EXAMPLE 2. If

$$\mathbf{A} = 2\mathbf{i} - 3\mathbf{j} + 7\mathbf{k},$$

then its length is $\sqrt{4 + 9 + 49} = \sqrt{62}$, and

$$\text{Direction of } (2\mathbf{i} - 3\mathbf{j} + 7\mathbf{k}) = \frac{2\mathbf{i} - 3\mathbf{j} + 7\mathbf{k}}{\sqrt{62}}.$$

* The authors credit Professor Arthur P. Mattuck with this definition.

PROBLEMS

Find the centers and radii of the spheres in Problems 1–4.

1. $x^2 + y^2 + z^2 + 4x - 4z = 0$
2. $2x^2 + 2y^2 + 2z^2 + x + y + z = 9$
3. $x^2 + y^2 + z^2 - 2az = 0$
4. $3x^2 + 3y^2 + 3z^2 + 2y - 2z = 9$
5. Find the distance between the point $P(x, y, z)$ and (a) the x-axis, (b) the y-axis, (c) the z-axis, (d) the xy-plane.
6. The distance from $P(x, y, z)$ to the origin is d_1 and the distance from P to $A(0, 0, 3)$ is d_2. Write an equation for the coordinates of P if

   a) $d_1 = 2d_2$, b) $d_1 + d_2 = 6$, c) $|d_1 - d_2| = 2$.

Find the lengths of the following vectors.

7. $2\mathbf{i} + \mathbf{j} - 2\mathbf{k}$
8. $3\mathbf{i} - 6\mathbf{j} + 2\mathbf{k}$
9. $\mathbf{i} + 4\mathbf{j} - 8\mathbf{k}$
10. $9\mathbf{i} - 2\mathbf{j} + 6\mathbf{k}$
11. Find the direction of $4\mathbf{i} + 3\mathbf{j} + 12\mathbf{k}$.
12. Find the vector from the origin O to the point of intersection of the medians of the triangle whose vertices are the three points

    $A(1, -1, 2)$, $B(2, 1, 3)$, $C(-1, 2, -1)$.
13. A bug is crawling straight up the side of a rotating right circular cylinder of radius 2 ft. At time $t = 0$, it is at the point $(2, 0, 0)$ relative to a fixed set of xyz-axes. The axis of the cylinder lies along the z-axis. Assume that the bug travels on the cylinder along a line parallel to the z-axis at the rate of c ft/sec, and that the cylinder rotates (counterclockwise as viewed from above) at the rate of b radians/sec. If $P(x, y, z)$ is the bug's position at the end of t seconds, show that

    $$\overrightarrow{OP} = \mathbf{i}(2 \cos bt) + \mathbf{j}(2 \sin bt) + \mathbf{k}(ct).$$

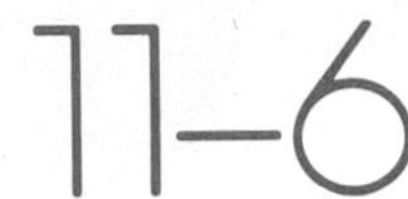

THE SCALAR PRODUCT OF TWO VECTORS

The *scalar product* of two vectors **A** and **B** is a scalar defined by the equation

$$\mathbf{A} \cdot \mathbf{B} = |\mathbf{A}|\,|\mathbf{B}| \cos \theta, \tag{1}$$

where θ measures the smallest angle determined by **A** and **B** when their initial points coincide, as in Fig. 11–30. This product is also called the *dot product*, because of the dot used to denote it. The definition of the dot product given here is "coordinate-free," in the sense that it is independent of whatever reference frame we might use to describe the vectors in terms of coordinates.

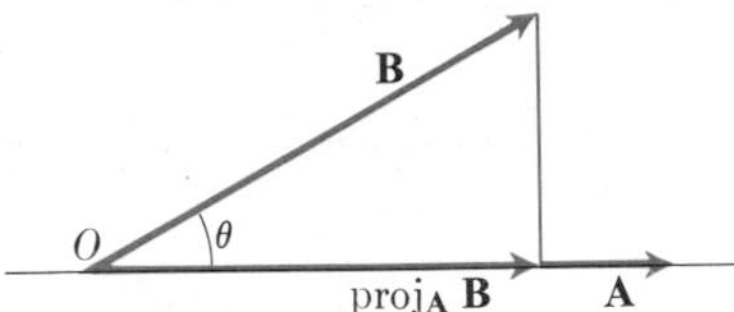

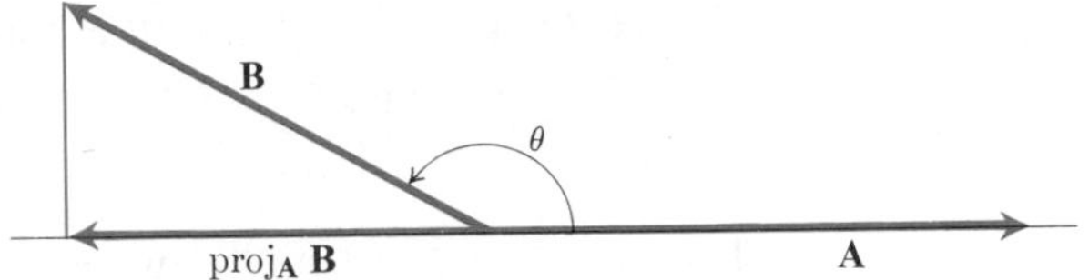

11–30 Vector projections of **B** onto **A**. In (a), the component of **B** in the direction of **A** is the length of the vector projection. In (b), it is *minus* the length of the vector projection.

It is clear from Eq. (1) that interchanging the two factors **A** and **B** does not change the dot product. That is,

$$\mathbf{A} \cdot \mathbf{B} = \mathbf{B} \cdot \mathbf{A}. \tag{2}$$

The operation of scalar multiplication is commutative.

The vector that we get by projecting **B** onto the line through **A** is called the *vector projection of* **B** *onto* **A**. We denote it by $\text{proj}_{\mathbf{A}}\, \mathbf{B}$ (Fig. 11–30).

The *component of* **B** *in the direction of* **A** is a number that is plus or minus the length of the vector projection of **B** onto **A**. The sign is plus if $\text{proj}_{\mathbf{A}}\, \mathbf{B}$ has the same direction as $+\mathbf{A}$, and is minus if it has the same direction as $-\mathbf{A}$. In either case, the component of **B** in the direction of **A** is equal to $|\mathbf{B}| \cos \theta$ (see Fig. 11–30 again).

The dot product gives a convenient way to calculate the component of **B** in the direction of **A**. We solve Eq. (1) for $|\mathbf{B}| \cos \theta$ to get

$$\mathbf{B}\text{-component in }\mathbf{A}\text{-direction} = |\mathbf{B}| \cos \theta = \frac{\mathbf{A} \cdot \mathbf{B}}{|\mathbf{A}|}. \tag{3}$$

Multiplying both sides of Eq. (3) by $|\mathbf{A}|$ leads to a geometric interpretation of $\mathbf{A} \cdot \mathbf{B}$:

$$\begin{aligned}\mathbf{A} \cdot \mathbf{B} &= |\mathbf{A}|(|\mathbf{B}| \cos \theta)\\ &= (\text{length of } \mathbf{A}) \text{ times } (\mathbf{B}\text{-component in } \mathbf{A}\text{-direction}).\end{aligned}$$

Of course we may interchange the roles of $|\mathbf{A}|$ and $|\mathbf{B}|$ and write the dot product in the alternative form of

$$\begin{aligned}\mathbf{A} \cdot \mathbf{B} &= |\mathbf{B}|(|\mathbf{A}| \cos \theta)\\ &= (\text{length of } \mathbf{B}) \text{ times } (\mathbf{A}\text{-component in } \mathbf{B}\text{-direction}).\end{aligned}$$

To calculate $\mathbf{A} \cdot \mathbf{B}$ from the components of **A** and **B**, we let

$$\mathbf{A} = a_1\mathbf{i} + a_2\mathbf{j} + a_3\mathbf{k},$$
$$\mathbf{B} = b_1\mathbf{i} + b_2\mathbf{j} + b_3\mathbf{k}, \tag{4}$$

and

$$\mathbf{C} = \mathbf{B} - \mathbf{A}$$
$$= (b_1 - a_1)\mathbf{i} + (b_2 - a_2)\mathbf{j} + (b_3 - a_3)\mathbf{k}.$$

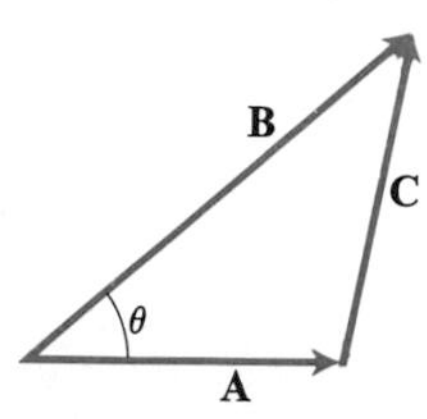

11–31 Equation (6) is obtained by applying the law of cosines to a triangle whose sides represent **A**, **B**, and **C** = **B** − **A**.

Then we apply the law of cosines to a triangle whose sides represent the vectors **A**, **B**, and **C** (Fig. 11–31) and obtain

$$|\mathbf{C}|^2 = |\mathbf{A}|^2 + |\mathbf{B}|^2 - 2|\mathbf{A}|\,|\mathbf{B}| \cos \theta,$$
$$|\mathbf{A}|\,|\mathbf{B}| \cos \theta = \frac{|\mathbf{A}|^2 + |\mathbf{B}|^2 - |\mathbf{C}|^2}{2}. \tag{5}$$

The left side of this equation is $\mathbf{A} \cdot \mathbf{B}$, and we may calculate all terms on the right side of (5) by applying Eq. (3) of Article 11–5 to find the lengths of **A**, **B**, and **C**. The result of this algebra is the formula

$$\mathbf{A} \cdot \mathbf{B} = a_1 b_1 + a_2 b_2 + a_3 b_3. \tag{6}$$

Thus, to find the scalar product of two given vectors we multiply their *corresponding* components together and add the results.

EXAMPLE 1. Find the angle θ between $\mathbf{A} = \mathbf{i} - 2\mathbf{j} - 2\mathbf{k}$ and $\mathbf{B} = 6\mathbf{i} + 3\mathbf{j} + 2\mathbf{k}$. Also, find the component of **B** in the direction of **A**.

Solution

$$\mathbf{A} \cdot \mathbf{B} = 6 - 6 - 4 = -4$$

from Eq. (6), while

$$\mathbf{A} \cdot \mathbf{B} = |\mathbf{A}|\,|\mathbf{B}| \cos \theta$$

from Eq. (1). Since $|\mathbf{A}| = \sqrt{1 + 4 + 4} = 3$ and $|\mathbf{B}| = \sqrt{36 + 9 + 4} = 7$, we have

$$\cos \theta = \frac{\mathbf{A} \cdot \mathbf{B}}{|\mathbf{A}|\,|\mathbf{B}|} = \frac{-4}{21},$$

$$\theta = \cos^{-1} \frac{-4}{21} \approx 101°.$$

The component of **B** in the direction of **A** is

$$\frac{\mathbf{A} \cdot \mathbf{B}}{|\mathbf{A}|} = -\frac{4}{3}.$$

This is the negative of the length of the vector projection of **B** onto **A**.

From Eq. (6), it is readily seen that if

$$\mathbf{C} = c_1\mathbf{i} + c_2\mathbf{j} + c_3\mathbf{k}$$

is any third vector, then

$$\begin{aligned}\mathbf{A}\cdot(\mathbf{B}+\mathbf{C}) &= a_1(b_1+c_1)+a_2(b_2+c_2)+a_3(b_3+c_3)\\ &= (a_1b_1+a_2b_2+a_3b_3)+(a_1c_1+a_2c_2+a_3c_3)\\ &= \mathbf{A}\cdot\mathbf{B}+\mathbf{A}\cdot\mathbf{C}.\end{aligned}$$

Hence scalar multiplication obeys the *distributive* law:

$$\mathbf{A}\cdot(\mathbf{B}+\mathbf{C}) = \mathbf{A}\cdot\mathbf{B}+\mathbf{A}\cdot\mathbf{C}. \tag{7}$$

If we combine this with the commutative law, Eq. (2), it is also evident that

$$(\mathbf{A}+\mathbf{B})\cdot\mathbf{C} = \mathbf{A}\cdot\mathbf{C}+\mathbf{B}\cdot\mathbf{C}. \tag{8}$$

Equations (7) and (8) together permit us to multiply sums of vectors by the familiar laws of algebra. For example,

$$(\mathbf{A}+\mathbf{B})\cdot(\mathbf{C}+\mathbf{D}) = \mathbf{A}\cdot\mathbf{C}+\mathbf{A}\cdot\mathbf{D}+\mathbf{B}\cdot\mathbf{C}+\mathbf{B}\cdot\mathbf{D}. \tag{9}$$

Orthogonal Vectors

It is clear from Eq. (1) that the dot product of two vectors is zero when the vectors are perpendicular, since $\cos 90° = 0$. Conversely, if $\mathbf{A}\cdot\mathbf{B} = 0$ then one of the vectors is zero or else the vectors are perpendicular. The zero vector has no specified direction, and we can adopt the convention that it is perpendicular to any vector. Then we can say that $\mathbf{A}\cdot\mathbf{B} = 0$ if and only if the vectors **A** and **B** are perpendicular. Perpendicular vectors are also said to be *orthogonal.*

If the scalar product is negative, then $\cos\theta$ is negative and the angle between the vectors is greater than 90°.

If $\mathbf{B} = \mathbf{A}$, then $\theta = 0$ and $\cos\theta = 1$, so that $\mathbf{A}\cdot\mathbf{A} = |\mathbf{A}|^2$.

EXAMPLE 2. Write the vector **B** as the sum of a vector $\mathbf{B}_1$ parallel to **A** and a vector $\mathbf{B}_2$ perpendicular to **A** (Fig. 11-32).

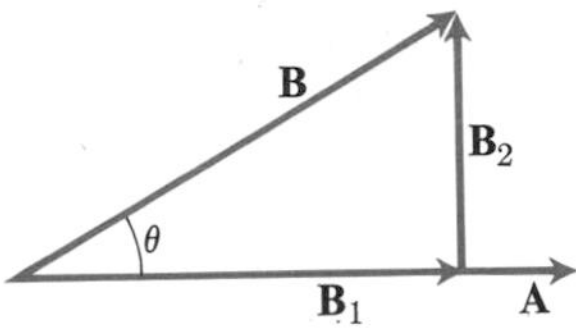

11-32 The vector **B** as the sum of vectors parallel and perpendicular to **A**.

Solution. Let

$$\mathbf{B} = \mathbf{B}_1 + \mathbf{B}_2,$$

with $\mathbf{B}_1 = c\mathbf{A}$ and $\mathbf{B}_2\cdot\mathbf{A} = 0$. Then, substituting $c\mathbf{A}$ for $\mathbf{B}_1$, we have

$$\mathbf{B} = c\mathbf{A} + \mathbf{B}_2$$

and

$$0 = \mathbf{B}_2\cdot\mathbf{A} = (\mathbf{B}-c\mathbf{A})\cdot\mathbf{A} = \mathbf{B}\cdot\mathbf{A} - c(\mathbf{A}\cdot\mathbf{A})$$

or

$$c = \frac{\mathbf{B}\cdot\mathbf{A}}{\mathbf{A}\cdot\mathbf{A}}.$$

Then

$$\mathbf{B}_2 = \mathbf{B}-\mathbf{B}_1 = \mathbf{B}-c\mathbf{A} = \mathbf{B}-\frac{\mathbf{B}\cdot\mathbf{A}}{\mathbf{A}\cdot\mathbf{A}}\mathbf{A}$$

is perpendicular to **A** because c was chosen to make $\mathbf{B}_2\cdot\mathbf{A} = 0$.

For example, if

$$\mathbf{B} = 2\mathbf{i} + \mathbf{j} - 3\mathbf{k} \quad \text{and} \quad \mathbf{A} = 3\mathbf{i} - \mathbf{j},$$

then

$$c = \frac{\mathbf{B} \cdot \mathbf{A}}{\mathbf{A} \cdot \mathbf{A}} = \frac{6 - 1}{9 + 1} = \frac{1}{2},$$

and

$$\mathbf{B}_1 = \tfrac{1}{2}\mathbf{A} = \tfrac{3}{2}\mathbf{i} - \tfrac{1}{2}\mathbf{j}$$

is parallel to **A**, while

$$\mathbf{B}_2 = \mathbf{B} - \mathbf{B}_1 = \tfrac{1}{2}\mathbf{i} + \tfrac{3}{2}\mathbf{j} - 3\mathbf{k}$$

is perpendicular to **A**.

EXAMPLE 3. Show that the vector $\mathbf{N} = a\mathbf{i} + b\mathbf{j}$ is perpendicular to the line $ax + by = c$ in the xy-plane (Fig. 11–33).

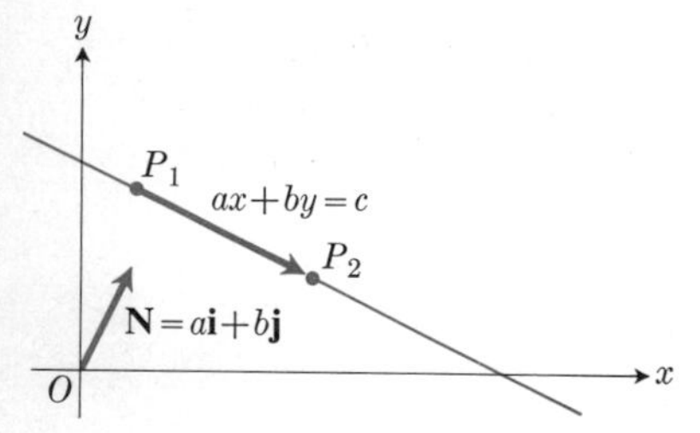

11–33 The vector $\mathbf{N} = a\mathbf{i} + b\mathbf{j}$ is normal to the line $ax + by = c$. Example 3 explains why.

Solution. Let $P_1(x_1, y_1)$ and $P_2(x_2, y_2)$ be any two points on the line; that is,

$$ax_1 + by_1 = c, \qquad ax_2 + by_2 = c.$$

By subtraction, we eliminate c and obtain

$$a(x_2 - x_1) + b(y_2 - y_1) = 0,$$

or

$$(a\mathbf{i} + b\mathbf{j}) \cdot [(x_2 - x_1)\mathbf{i} + (y_2 - y_1)\mathbf{j}] = 0. \tag{10}$$

Now $(x_2 - x_1)\mathbf{i} + (y_2 - y_1)\mathbf{j} = \overrightarrow{P_1P_2}$ is a vector joining two points on the line, while $\mathbf{N} = a\mathbf{i} + b\mathbf{j}$ is the given vector. Equation (10) says that either $\mathbf{N} = \mathbf{0}$, or $\overrightarrow{P_1P_2} = \mathbf{0}$, or else $\mathbf{N} \perp \overrightarrow{P_1P_2}$. But $ax + by = c$ is assumed to be an honest equation of a straight line, so that a and b are not both zero and $\mathbf{N} \neq \mathbf{0}$. Furthermore, we may surely choose P_2 different from P_1 on the line to make $\overrightarrow{P_1P_2} \neq \mathbf{0}$. Hence $\mathbf{N} \perp \overrightarrow{P_1P_2}$.

For example, $\mathbf{N} = 2\mathbf{i} - 3\mathbf{j}$ is normal to the line $2x - 3y = 5$.

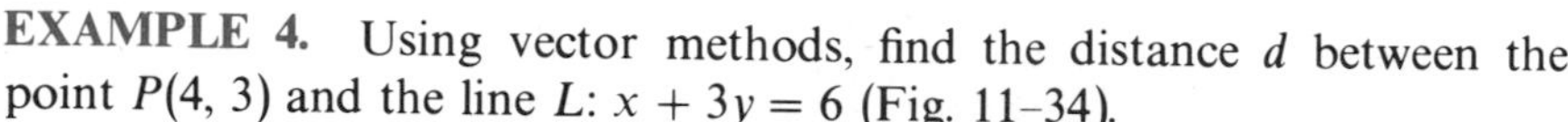

EXAMPLE 4. Using vector methods, find the distance d between the point $P(4, 3)$ and the line L: $x + 3y = 6$ (Fig. 11–34).

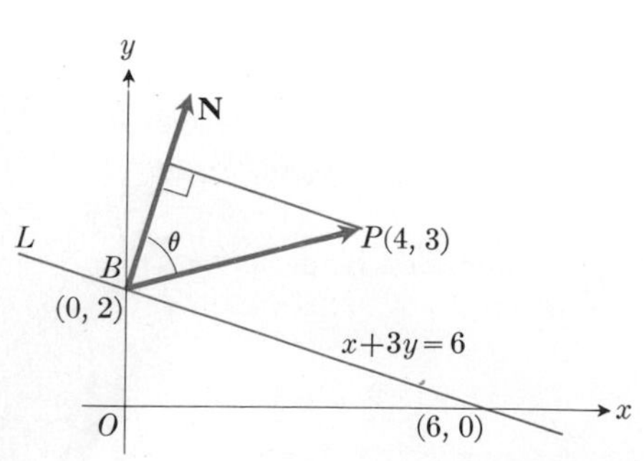

11–34 The distance from P to line L is the length of the vector projection of $\overrightarrow{BP}$ onto **N**.

Solution. The line cuts the y-axis at $B(0, 2)$. At B, draw the vector

$$\mathbf{N} = \mathbf{i} + 3\mathbf{j}$$

normal to L (see Example 3). Then the distance between P and L is the component of $\overrightarrow{BP}$ in the direction of **N**. Since

$$\overrightarrow{BP} = (4 - 0)\mathbf{i} + (3 - 2)\mathbf{j} = 4\mathbf{i} + \mathbf{j},$$

we have

$$d = \text{proj}_{\mathbf{N}} \overrightarrow{BP} = \frac{\mathbf{N} \cdot \overrightarrow{BP}}{|\mathbf{N}|} = \frac{4 + 3}{\sqrt{10}} = \frac{7\sqrt{10}}{10}.$$

The dot product is useful in mechanics, where it is used in calculating the work done by a force **F** when the point of application of **F** undergoes a displacement $\overrightarrow{AB}$. If the force remains constant in direction and magnitude, this work is given by (Fig. 11–35)

$$\text{Work} = (|\mathbf{F}| \cos \theta)|\overrightarrow{AB}|$$
$$= \mathbf{F} \cdot \overrightarrow{AB}.$$

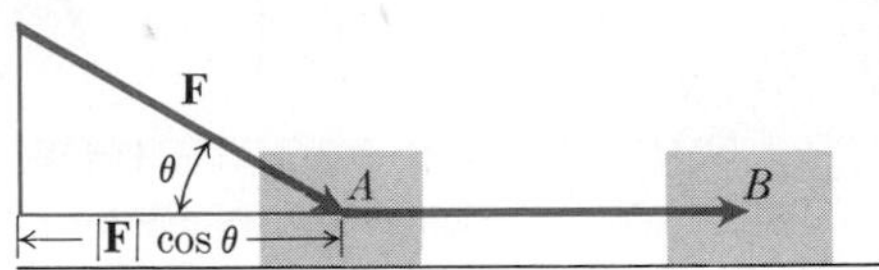

11–35 The work done by **F** during a displacement $\overrightarrow{AB}$ is $\mathbf{F} \cdot \mathbf{AB} = (|F| \cos \theta)|\overrightarrow{AB}|$.

The concept of work also enters into the study of electricity and magnetism and the scalar product again plays a basic role. (See Sears, Zemansky, Young, *University Physics* (1976), Chapter 26.)

PROBLEMS

1. Suppose it is known that $\mathbf{A} \cdot \mathbf{B}_1 = \mathbf{A} \cdot \mathbf{B}_2$, and **A** is not zero, but nothing more is known about the vectors $\mathbf{B}_1$ and $\mathbf{B}_2$. Is it permissible to cancel **A** from both sides of the equation? Give a reason for your answer.

2. (a) Express the vector projection of **B** onto **A** in a vector form that is convenient for calculation. (b) Find the vector projection of $\mathbf{B} = \mathbf{i} + 3\mathbf{j} + 4\mathbf{k}$ onto the vector $\mathbf{A} = 10\mathbf{i} + 11\mathbf{j} - 2\mathbf{k}$.

3. Find the interior angles of the triangle ABC whose vertices are the points $A(-1, 0, 2)$, $B(2, 1, -1)$, and $C(1, -2, 2)$.

4. Find the point $A(a, a, 0)$ on the line $y = x$ in the xy-plane such that the vector $\overrightarrow{AB}$ is perpendicular to the line OA. Here O is the origin and B is the point $(2, 4, -3)$.

5. Find the component of $\mathbf{A} = 2\mathbf{i} + 2\mathbf{j} + \mathbf{k}$ in the direction of $\mathbf{B} = 2\mathbf{i} + 10\mathbf{j} - 11\mathbf{k}$.

6. Find the angle between the diagonal of a cube and one of its edges.

7. Find the angle between the diagonal of a cube and a diagonal of one of its faces.

8. Find the angle between vectors **A** and **B** of Problem 5.

9. How many lines through the origin make angles of 60° with both the y- and z-axes? What angles do they make with the positive x-axis?

10. If $a = |\mathbf{A}|$ and $b = |\mathbf{B}|$, show that the vector

$$\mathbf{C} = \frac{a\mathbf{B} + b\mathbf{A}}{a + b}$$

bisects the angle between **A** and **B**.

11. With the same notation as in Problem 10, show that the vectors $a\mathbf{B} + b\mathbf{A}$ and $\mathbf{A}b - \mathbf{B}a$ are perpendicular.

12. If **R** is the vector from the origin O to $P(x, y, z)$ and **k** is the unit vector along the z-axis, show geometrically that the equation

$$\frac{\mathbf{R} \cdot \mathbf{k}}{|\mathbf{R}|} = \cos 45°$$

represents a cone with vertex at the origin and generating angle of 45°. Express the equation in cartesian form.

13. Find the work done by a force $\mathbf{F} = -w\mathbf{k}$ as its point of application moves from the point $P_1(x_1, y_1, z_1)$ to a second point $P_2(x_2, y_2, z_2)$ along the straight line P_1P_2.

14. Using vector methods, show that the distance d between the point (x_1, y_1) and the line $ax + by + c = 0$ is

$$d = \frac{|ax_1 + by_1 + c|}{\sqrt{a^2 + b^2}}.$$

15. *Direction cosines.* If the vector $\mathbf{A} = a\mathbf{i} + b\mathbf{j} + c\mathbf{k}$ makes angles α, β, and γ, respectively, with the positive x-, y-, and z-axes, then $\cos \alpha$, $\cos \beta$, $\cos \gamma$ are called its *direction cosines.* Show that

a) $$\cos \alpha = \frac{a}{\sqrt{a^2 + b^2 + c^2}},$$

$$\cos \beta = \frac{b}{\sqrt{a^2 + b^2 + c^2}},$$

$$\cos \gamma = \frac{c}{\sqrt{a^2 + b^2 + c^2}};$$

b) $\cos^2 \alpha + \cos^2 \beta + \cos^2 \gamma = 1$;

c) $\mathbf{u} = \mathbf{i} \cos \alpha + \mathbf{j} \cos \beta + \mathbf{k} \cos \gamma$ is a unit vector having the same direction as **A**.

16. Show that scalar multiplication is *positive definite*; that is, $\mathbf{A} \cdot \mathbf{A} \geq 0$ for every vector **A**, and $\mathbf{A} \cdot \mathbf{A} = 0$ if and only if **A** is the zero vector.

17. Show that if r is a scalar, then $(r\mathbf{A}) \cdot \mathbf{B} = r(\mathbf{A} \cdot \mathbf{B})$.

18. In Fig. 11–2 it looks as if $\mathbf{v}_1 + \mathbf{v}_2$ and $\mathbf{v}_1 - \mathbf{v}_2$ are orthogonal. Is this mere coincidence, or are there circumstances under which we may expect the sum of two vectors to be perpendicular to the difference of the same two vectors? Find out by expanding the left side of the equation

$$(\mathbf{v}_1 + \mathbf{v}_2) \cdot (\mathbf{v}_1 - \mathbf{v}_2) = 0.$$

11–7 THE VECTOR PRODUCT OF TWO VECTORS IN SPACE

Two nonzero vectors **A** and **B** in space may be subjected to parallel displacements, if necessary, to bring their initial points into coincidence. Suppose that this has been done and let θ be the angle from **A** to **B**, with $0 \leq \theta \leq \pi$. Then, unless **A** and **B** are parallel, they now determine a plane. Let **n** be a unit vector perpendicular to this plane and pointing in the direction a right-threaded screw advances when its head is rotated from **A** to **B** through the angle θ. The *vector product*, or *cross product*, of **A** and **B**, in that order, is then defined by the equation (Fig. 11–36(a))

$$\mathbf{A} \times \mathbf{B} = \mathbf{n}|\mathbf{A}|\,|\mathbf{B}| \sin \theta. \tag{1}$$

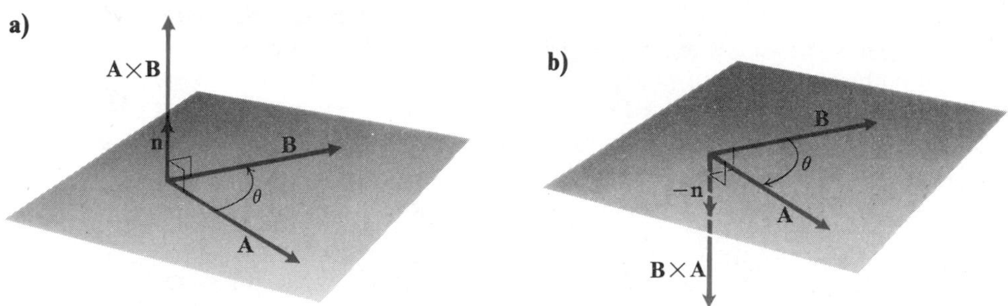

11–36 **A** × **B** and **B** × **A** have the same magnitude but point in opposite directions from the plane of **A** and **B**.

Like the definition of the scalar product of two vectors, given in Article 11–6, the definition of the vector product given here is coordinate-free. We emphasize, however, that the vector product **A** × **B** is a *vector*, while the scalar product **A** · **B** is a *scalar*. (Applications of the cross product to electricity and magnetism are discussed in Sears, Zemansky, Young, *University Physics* (1976), Chapters 26 and 30.)

If **A** and **B** are parallel, then $\theta = 0$ or 180° and $\sin \theta = 0$, so that $\mathbf{A} \times \mathbf{B} = \mathbf{0}$. In this case, the direction of **n** is not determined, but this is immaterial, since the zero vector has no specific direction. In all other cases, however, **n** is determined and the cross product is a vector having the same direction as **n** and having magnitude equal to the area, $|\mathbf{A}|\,|\mathbf{B}| \sin \theta$, of the parallelogram determined by the vectors **A** and **B** (Fig. 11–37).

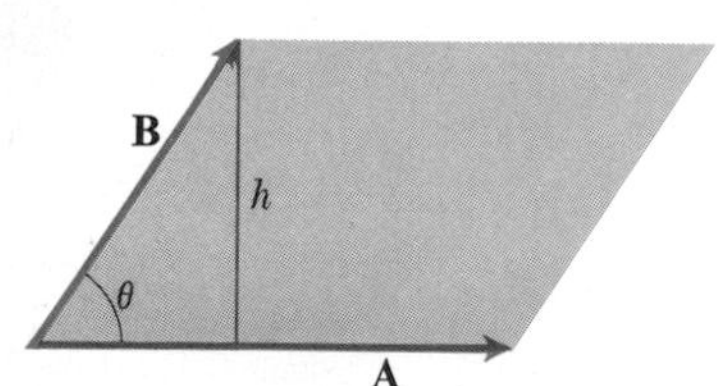

11–37 The area of the parallelogram is $|\mathbf{A} \times \mathbf{B}|$.

If the order of the factors **A** and **B** is reversed in the construction of the cross product, the direction of the unit vector perpendicular to their plane is reversed (Fig. 11–36(b)). This is because the righthanded screw that turns through θ from **B** to **A** points the other way. The original unit vector **n** is now replaced by $-\mathbf{n}$, with the result that

$$\mathbf{B} \times \mathbf{A} = -\mathbf{A} \times \mathbf{B}. \tag{2}$$

Thus, cross product multiplication is not commutative. Reversing the order of the factors changes the product.

When the definition is applied to the unit vectors **i**, **j**, and **k**, one readily finds that

$$\begin{aligned} \mathbf{i} \times \mathbf{j} &= -\mathbf{j} \times \mathbf{i} = \mathbf{k}, \\ \mathbf{j} \times \mathbf{k} &= -\mathbf{k} \times \mathbf{j} = \mathbf{i}, \\ \mathbf{k} \times \mathbf{i} &= -\mathbf{i} \times \mathbf{k} = \mathbf{j}, \end{aligned} \tag{3}$$

while

$$\mathbf{i} \times \mathbf{i} = \mathbf{j} \times \mathbf{j} = \mathbf{k} \times \mathbf{k} = \mathbf{0}.$$

Our next objective is to express $\mathbf{A} \times \mathbf{B}$ in terms of the components of $\mathbf{A}$ and $\mathbf{B}$. First we note that the associative law

$$(r\mathbf{A}) \times (s\mathbf{B}) = (rs)\mathbf{A} \times \mathbf{B}, \tag{4}$$

follows from the geometric meaning of the cross product. Secondly, we adopt a geometric argument to establish the distributive law

$$\mathbf{A} \times (\mathbf{B} + \mathbf{C}) = \mathbf{A} \times \mathbf{B} + \mathbf{A} \times \mathbf{C}. \tag{5}$$

Proof. To see that Eq. (5) is valid, we interpret the cross product $\mathbf{A} \times \mathbf{B}$ in a slightly different way. The vectors $\mathbf{A}$ and $\mathbf{B}$ are drawn from the common point O and a plane M is constructed perpendicular to $\mathbf{A}$ at O (Fig. 11–38). Vector $\mathbf{B}$ is now projected orthogonally onto M, yielding a vector $\mathbf{B}'$ whose length is $|\mathbf{B}| \sin \theta$. The vector $\mathbf{B}'$ is then rotated 90° about $\mathbf{A}$ in the positive sense to produce a vector $\mathbf{B}''$. Finally, $\mathbf{B}''$ is multiplied by the length of $\mathbf{A}$. The resulting vector $|\mathbf{A}|\mathbf{B}''$ is equal to $\mathbf{A} \times \mathbf{B}$ since $\mathbf{B}''$ has the same direction as $\mathbf{n}$ by its construction (Fig. 11–38) and

$$|\mathbf{A}|\,|\mathbf{B}''| = |\mathbf{A}|\,|\mathbf{B}'| = |\mathbf{A}|\,|\mathbf{B}| \sin \theta = |\mathbf{A} \times \mathbf{B}|.$$

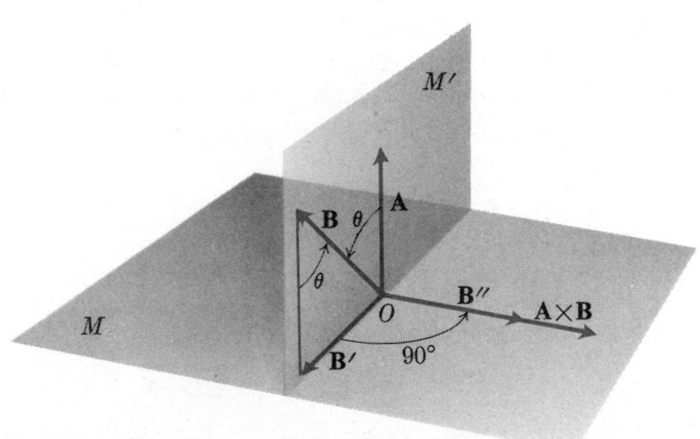

11–38 For reasons explained above, $\mathbf{A} \times \mathbf{B} = |\mathbf{A}|\mathbf{B}''$.

Now each of these three operations, namely,

1. projection onto M,
2. rotation about $\mathbf{A}$ through 90°,
3. multiplication by the scalar $|\mathbf{A}|$,

when applied to a triangle, will produce another triangle. If we start with the triangle whose sides are **B**, **C**, and **B** + **C** (Fig. 11–39) and apply these three steps, we successively obtain:

1. a triangle whose sides are $\mathbf{B}'$, $\mathbf{C}'$, and $(\mathbf{B}+\mathbf{C})'$ satisfying the vector equation

$$\mathbf{B}' + \mathbf{C}' = (\mathbf{B} + \mathbf{C})';$$

2. a triangle whose sides are $\mathbf{B}''$, $\mathbf{C}''$, and $(\mathbf{B}+\mathbf{C})''$ satisfying the vector equation

$$\mathbf{B}'' + \mathbf{C}'' = (\mathbf{B} + \mathbf{C})'';$$

(the double-prime on each vector has the same meaning as in Fig. 11–38); and finally,

3. a triangle whose sides are $|\mathbf{A}|\mathbf{B}''$, $|\mathbf{A}|\mathbf{C}''$, and $|\mathbf{A}|(\mathbf{B}+\mathbf{C})''$ satisfying the vector equation

$$|\mathbf{A}|\mathbf{B}'' + |\mathbf{A}|\mathbf{C}'' = |\mathbf{A}|(\mathbf{B} + \mathbf{C})''. \tag{6}$$

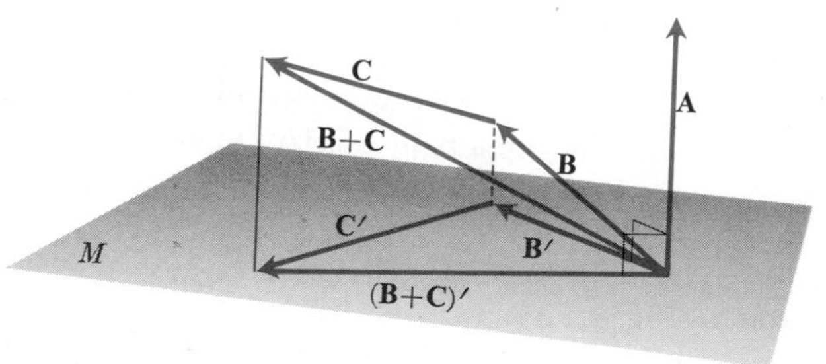

11–39 The vectors of Eq. (7) projected onto a plane perpendicular to **A**.

When we use the equations $|\mathbf{A}|\mathbf{B}'' = \mathbf{A} \times \mathbf{B}$, $|\mathbf{A}|\mathbf{C}'' = \mathbf{A} \times \mathbf{C}$ and $|\mathbf{A}|(\mathbf{B}+\mathbf{C})'' = \mathbf{A} \times (\mathbf{B} + \mathbf{C})$, which result from our discussion above, Eq. (6) becomes

$$\mathbf{A} \times \mathbf{B} + \mathbf{A} \times \mathbf{C} = \mathbf{A} \times (\mathbf{B} + \mathbf{C}),$$

which is the distributive law, (5), that we wanted to establish.

The companion law

$$(\mathbf{B} + \mathbf{C}) \times \mathbf{A} = \mathbf{B} \times \mathbf{A} + \mathbf{C} \times \mathbf{A} \tag{7}$$

now follows at once from Eq. (5) if we multiply both sides of Eq. (5) by minus one and take account of the fact that interchanging the two factors in a cross product changes the sign of the result.

From Eqs. (4), (5), and (7), we may conclude that cross-product multiplication of vectors follows the ordinary laws of algebra, *except that the order of the factors is not reversible.* If we apply these results to calculate $\mathbf{A} \times \mathbf{B}$ with

$$\mathbf{A} = a_1\mathbf{i} + a_2\mathbf{j} + a_3\mathbf{k},$$

$$\mathbf{B} = b_1\mathbf{i} + b_2\mathbf{j} + b_3\mathbf{k},$$

we obtain

$$\begin{aligned}\mathbf{A}\times\mathbf{B} &= (a_1\mathbf{i}+a_2\mathbf{j}+a_3\mathbf{k})\times(b_1\mathbf{i}+b_2\mathbf{j}+b_3\mathbf{k})\\ &= a_1b_1\mathbf{i}\times\mathbf{i}+a_1b_2\mathbf{i}\times\mathbf{j}+a_1b_3\mathbf{i}\times\mathbf{k}+a_2b_1\mathbf{j}\times\mathbf{i}\\ &\quad + a_2b_2\mathbf{j}\times\mathbf{j}+a_2b_3\mathbf{j}\times\mathbf{k}+a_3b_1\mathbf{k}\times\mathbf{i}\\ &\quad + a_3b_2\mathbf{k}\times\mathbf{j}+a_3b_3\mathbf{k}\times\mathbf{k}\\ &= \mathbf{i}(a_2b_3-a_3b_2)+\mathbf{j}(a_3b_1-a_1b_3)+\mathbf{k}(a_1b_2-a_2b_1), \qquad \textbf{(8)}\end{aligned}$$

where Eqs. (3) have been used to evaluate the products $\mathbf{i}\times\mathbf{i}=\mathbf{0}$, $\mathbf{i}\times\mathbf{j}=\mathbf{k}$, etc. The terms on the right side of Eq. (8) are the same as the terms in the expansion of the third-order determinant below, so that the cross product may conveniently be calculated from the equation

$$\mathbf{A}\times\mathbf{B}=\begin{vmatrix}\mathbf{i} & \mathbf{j} & \mathbf{k}\\ a_1 & a_2 & a_3\\ b_1 & b_2 & b_3\end{vmatrix}. \qquad \textbf{(9)}$$

EXAMPLE 1. Find the area of the triangle whose vertices are $A(1, -1, 0)$, $B(2, 1, -1)$, and $C(-1, 1, 2)$ (Fig. 11–40).

Solution. Two sides of the given triangle are represented by the vectors

$$\mathbf{a}=\overrightarrow{AB}=(2-1)\mathbf{i}+(1+1)\mathbf{j}+(-1-0)\mathbf{k}=\mathbf{i}+2\mathbf{j}-\mathbf{k},$$

$$\mathbf{b}=\overrightarrow{AC}=(-1-1)\mathbf{i}+(1+1)\mathbf{j}+(2-0)\mathbf{k}=-2\mathbf{i}+2\mathbf{j}+2\mathbf{k}.$$

The area of the triangle is one-half the area of the parallelogram represented by these vectors. The area of the parallelogram is the magnitude of the vector

$$\mathbf{c}=\mathbf{a}\times\mathbf{b}=\begin{vmatrix}\mathbf{i} & \mathbf{j} & \mathbf{k}\\ 1 & 2 & -1\\ -2 & 2 & 2\end{vmatrix}$$

$$=\mathbf{i}\begin{vmatrix}2 & -1\\ 2 & 2\end{vmatrix}-\mathbf{j}\begin{vmatrix}1 & -1\\ -2 & 2\end{vmatrix}+\mathbf{k}\begin{vmatrix}1 & 2\\ -2 & 2\end{vmatrix}=6\mathbf{i}+6\mathbf{k},$$

which is $|\mathbf{c}|=\sqrt{6^2+6^2}=6\sqrt{2}$. Therefore, the area of the triangle is $\frac{1}{2}|\mathbf{a}\times\mathbf{b}|=3\sqrt{2}$.

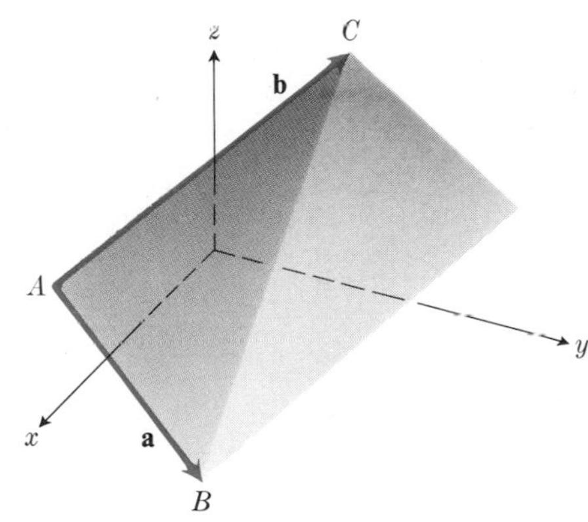

11–40 The area of $\triangle ABC$ is half of $|\mathbf{a}\times\mathbf{b}|$.

EXAMPLE 2. Find a unit vector perpendicular to both $\mathbf{A}=2\mathbf{i}+\mathbf{j}-\mathbf{k}$ and $\mathbf{B}=\mathbf{i}-\mathbf{j}+2\mathbf{k}$.

Solution. The vector $\mathbf{N}=\mathbf{A}\times\mathbf{B}$ is perpendicular to both $\mathbf{A}$ and $\mathbf{B}$. We divide $\mathbf{N}$ by $|\mathbf{N}|$ to obtain a unit vector $\mathbf{u}$ that has the same direction as $\mathbf{N}$:

$$\mathbf{u}=\frac{\mathbf{N}}{|\mathbf{N}|}=\frac{\mathbf{A}\times\mathbf{B}}{|\mathbf{A}\times\mathbf{B}|}=\frac{\mathbf{i}-5\mathbf{j}-3\mathbf{k}}{\sqrt{1^2+(-5)^2+(-3)^2}}=\frac{\mathbf{i}-5\mathbf{j}-3\mathbf{k}}{\sqrt{35}}.$$

Either $\mathbf{u}$ or its negative will do.

PROBLEMS

1. Find $\mathbf{A} \times \mathbf{B}$ if $\mathbf{A} = 2\mathbf{i} - 2\mathbf{j} - \mathbf{k}$, $\mathbf{B} = \mathbf{i} + \mathbf{j} + \mathbf{k}$.

2. Find a vector $\mathbf{N}$ perpendicular to the plane determined by the points $A(1, -1, 2)$, $B(2, 0, -1)$, and $C(0, 2, 1)$.

3. Find the area of the triangle ABC of Problem 2.

4. Find the distance between the origin and the plane ABC of Problem 2 by projecting $\overrightarrow{OA}$ onto the normal vector $\mathbf{N}$.

5. Find a vector that is perpendicular to both of the vectors $\mathbf{A} = \mathbf{i} + \mathbf{j} + \mathbf{k}$ and $\mathbf{B} = \mathbf{i} + \mathbf{j}$.

6. Vectors from the origin to the points A, B, C are given by $\mathbf{A} = \mathbf{i} - \mathbf{j} + \mathbf{k}$, $\mathbf{B} = 2\mathbf{i} + 3\mathbf{j} - \mathbf{k}$, $\mathbf{C} = -\mathbf{i} + 2\mathbf{j} + 2\mathbf{k}$. Find all points $P(x, y, z)$ that satisfy the following requirements: $\overrightarrow{OP}$ is a unit vector perpendicular to $\mathbf{C}$ and P lies in the plane determined by $\mathbf{A}$ and $\mathbf{B}$.

7. Using vector methods, find the distance between the line L_1 determined by the two points $A(1, 0, -1)$, $B(-1, 1, 0)$ and the line L_2 determined by the points $C(3, 1, -1)$, $D(4, 5, -2)$. The distance is to be measured along a line perpendicular to both L_1 and L_2.

8. $\mathbf{A} = 3\mathbf{i} + \mathbf{j} - \mathbf{k}$ is normal to a plane M_1 and $\mathbf{B} = 2\mathbf{i} - \mathbf{j} + \mathbf{k}$ is normal to a second plane M_2. (a) Find the angle between the two normals. (b) Do the two planes intersect? Give a reason for your answer. (c) If the two planes do intersect, find a vector parallel to their line of intersection.

9. Let $\mathbf{A}$ be a nonzero vector. Show that (a) $\mathbf{A} \times \mathbf{B} = \mathbf{A} \times \mathbf{C}$ does not guarantee $\mathbf{B} = \mathbf{C}$ (see Problem 1, Article 11–6); (b) $\mathbf{A} \cdot \mathbf{B} = \mathbf{A} \cdot \mathbf{C}$ and $\mathbf{A} \times \mathbf{B} = \mathbf{A} \times \mathbf{C}$ together imply $\mathbf{B} = \mathbf{C}$.

11–8 EQUATIONS OF LINES AND PLANES

Lines

Suppose L is a line in space that passes through a given point $P_1(x_1, y_1, z_1)$ and is parallel to a given nonzero vector

$$\mathbf{v} = A\mathbf{i} + B\mathbf{j} + C\mathbf{k}.$$

Then L is the set of all points $P(x, y, z)$ for which the vector $\overrightarrow{P_1P}$ is parallel to the given vector $\mathbf{v}$ (Fig. 11–41).

That is, P is on the line L if and only if there is a scalar t such that

$$\overrightarrow{P_1P} = t\mathbf{v}. \tag{1}$$

When we separate the components in Eq. (1), we have

$$x - x_1 = tA, \qquad y - y_1 = tB, \qquad z - z_1 = tC. \tag{2}$$

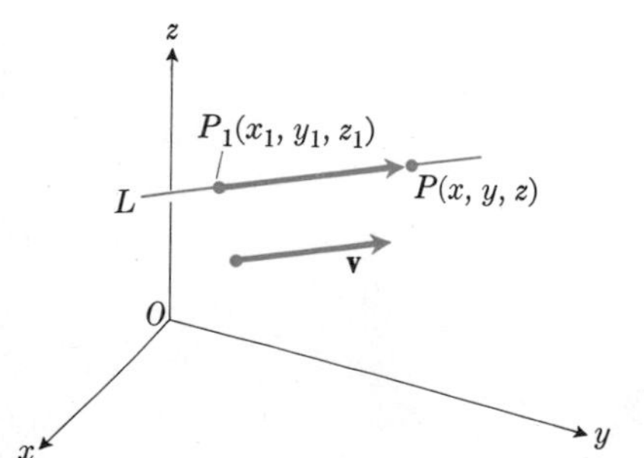

11–41 P is on the line through P_1 parallel to $\mathbf{v}$ if and only if $\overrightarrow{P_1P}$ is a scalar multiple of $\mathbf{v}$.

These equations are parametric equations for the line. If we allow t to vary from $-\infty$ to $+\infty$, the point $P(x, y, z)$ given by Eqs. (2) will traverse the line L through P_1.

We may eliminate t from the equations in (2) to obtain the following cartesian equations for the line:

$$\frac{x - x_1}{A} = \frac{y - y_1}{B} = \frac{z - z_1}{C}. \tag{3}$$

If any one of the constants A, B, or C is zero in Eqs. (3), the corresponding numerator is also zero. This follows at once from the parametric form, Eqs. (2), which shows, for example, that

$$x - x_1 = tA \qquad \text{and} \qquad A = 0$$

together imply that

$$x - x_1 = 0.$$

Thus, when one of the denominators in Eqs. (3) is zero, we interpret the equations to say that the corresponding numerator is zero. With this interpretation, Eqs. (3) may always be used.

Planes

To obtain an equation for a *plane*, we suppose that a point $P_1(x_1, y_1, z_1)$ on the plane and a nonzero vector

$$\mathbf{N} = A\mathbf{i} + B\mathbf{j} + C\mathbf{k} \tag{4}$$

perpendicular to the plane are given (Fig. 11–42). Then the point $P(x, y, z)$ will lie in the plane if and only if the vector $\overrightarrow{P_1P}$ is perpendicular to $\mathbf{N}$; that is, if and only if

$$\mathbf{N} \cdot \overrightarrow{P_1P} = 0$$

or

$$A(x - x_1) + B(y - y_1) + C(z - z_1) = 0. \tag{5}$$

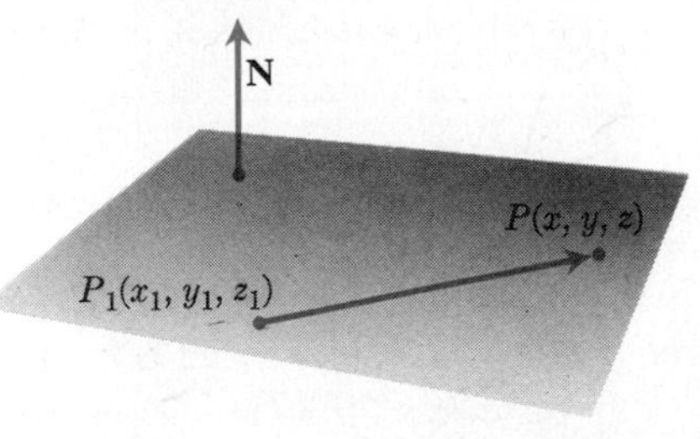

11–42 P lies in the plane through P_1 perpendicular to $\mathbf{N}$ if and only if $\overrightarrow{P_1P} \cdot \mathbf{N} = 0$.

This equation may also be put in the form

$$Ax + By + Cz = D, \tag{6}$$

where D is the constant $Ax_1 + By_1 + Cz_1$. Conversely, if we start from any linear equation such as (6), we may find a point $P_1(x_1, y_1, z_1)$ whose coordinates do satisfy it; that is, such that

$$Ax_1 + By_1 + Cz_1 = D.$$

Then, by subtraction, we may put the given equation (6) into the form of Eq. (5) and factor it into the dot product

$$\mathbf{N} \cdot \overrightarrow{P_1P} = 0,$$

with $\mathbf{N}$ as in Eq. (4). This says that the constant vector $\mathbf{N}$ is perpendicular to the vector $\overrightarrow{P_1P}$ for every pair of points P_1 and P whose coordinates satisfy the equation. Hence the set of points $P(x, y, z)$ whose coordinates satisfy such a linear equation is a plane and the vector $A\mathbf{i} + B\mathbf{j} + C\mathbf{k}$, with the same coefficients that x, y, and z have in the given equation, is normal to the plane.

EXAMPLE 1. Find the distance d between the point $P(2, -3, 4)$ and the plane $x + 2y + 2z = 13$.

Solution 1. Carry out the following steps:

First. Find a line L through P normal to the plane.

Second. Find the coordinates of the point Q in which the line meets the plane.

Third. Compute the distance between P and Q.

The vector $\mathbf{N} = \mathbf{i} + 2\mathbf{j} + 2\mathbf{k}$ is normal to the given plane, and the line

$$L: \quad \frac{x - 2}{1} = \frac{y + 3}{2} = \frac{z - 4}{2}$$

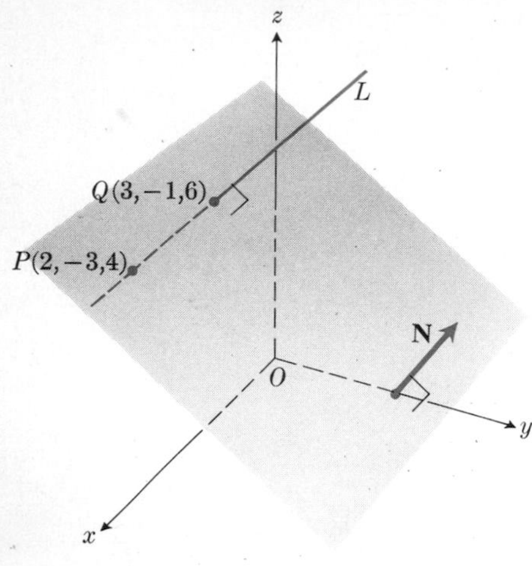

11–43 The distance between P and the plane is the distance between P and Q.

goes through P and is parallel to $\mathbf{N}$. Hence L is normal to the plane.

If we denote the common ratio in the equations for L by t,

$$\frac{x-2}{1}=\frac{y+3}{2}=\frac{z-4}{2}=t,$$

we have

$$x=t+2, \qquad y=2t-3, \qquad z=2t+4$$

as parametric equations of the line in terms of the parameter t. Substituting these into the equation of the plane, we obtain

$$(t+2)+2(2t-3)+2(2t+4)=13,$$

or $t=1$ at the point of intersection of the plane and the line L. That is, $Q(3,-1,6)$ is the point of intersection.

The distance between the point and the plane is the distance between $P(2,-3,4)$ and $Q(3,-1,6)$ (Fig. 11–43). Hence

$$d=\sqrt{(3-2)^2+(-1+3)^2+(6-4)^2}=3.$$

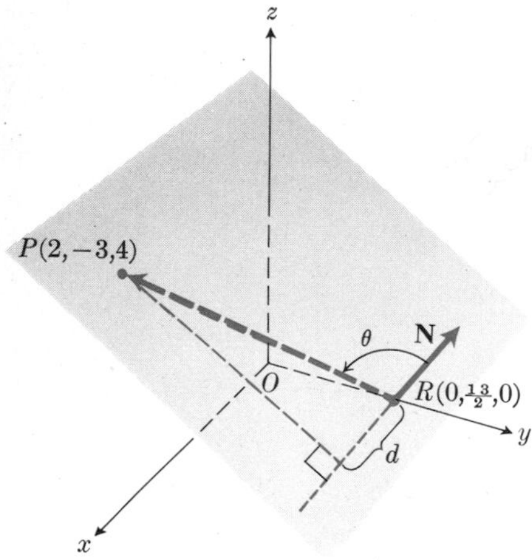

11–44 d is the length of $\text{proj}_{\mathbf{N}}\,\overrightarrow{RP}$.

Solution 2. Let R be any point in the plane, and find the component of $\overrightarrow{RP}$ in the direction of $\mathbf{N}$. This will be plus d or minus d, the sign depending on the direction of the vector projection of $\overrightarrow{RP}$ onto $\mathbf{N}$. Figure 11–44 shows that the component is negative in this case, but we do not need to know this to find d.

Since R can be any point in the given plane, we might as well choose R to be a point whose coordinates are simple, say the point $R(0,\frac{13}{2},0)$ where the plane meets the y-axis. Then,

$$\begin{aligned}\overrightarrow{RP}&=(2-0)\mathbf{i}+(-3-\tfrac{13}{2})\mathbf{j}+(4-0)\mathbf{k}\\&=2\mathbf{i}-\tfrac{19}{2}\mathbf{j}+4\mathbf{k}.\end{aligned}$$

The component of $\overrightarrow{RP}$ in the direction of $\mathbf{N}=\mathbf{i}+2\mathbf{j}+2\mathbf{k}$ is

$$\frac{\mathbf{N}\cdot\overrightarrow{RP}}{|\mathbf{N}|}=\frac{2-19+8}{\sqrt{(1)^2+(2)^2+(2)^2}}=\frac{-9}{\sqrt{9}}=-3.$$

Therefore, $d=3$.

EXAMPLE 2. Find the angle between the two planes $3x-6y-2z=7$ and $2x+y-2z=5$.

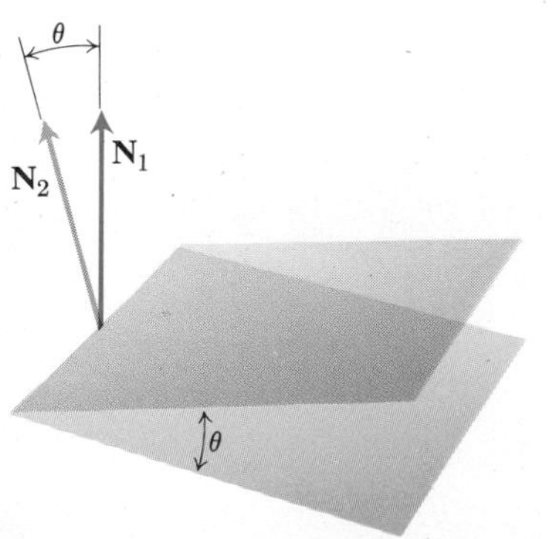

11–45 The angle between two planes can be obtained from their normals.

Solution. Clearly the angle between two planes (Fig. 11–45) is the same as the angle between their normals. (Actually there are two angles in each case, namely θ and $180°-\theta$.) From the equations of the planes we may read off their normal vectors:

$$\mathbf{N}_1=3\mathbf{i}-6\mathbf{j}-2\mathbf{k}, \qquad \mathbf{N}_2=2\mathbf{i}+\mathbf{j}-2\mathbf{k}.$$

Then

$$\cos\theta=\frac{\mathbf{N}_1\cdot\mathbf{N}_2}{|\mathbf{N}_1|\,|\mathbf{N}_2|}=\frac{4}{21}, \qquad \theta=\cos^{-1}\left(\frac{4}{21}\right)\approx 79°.$$

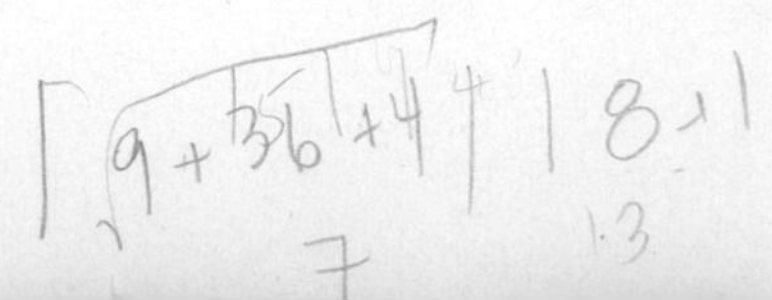

EXAMPLE 3. Find a vector parallel to the line of intersection of the two planes in Example 2.

Solution. The requirements are met by the vector

$$\mathbf{v} = \mathbf{N}_1 \times \mathbf{N}_2 = \begin{vmatrix} \mathbf{i} & \mathbf{j} & \mathbf{k} \\ 3 & -6 & -2 \\ 2 & 1 & -2 \end{vmatrix} = 14\mathbf{i} + 2\mathbf{j} + 15\mathbf{k}.$$

The vector $\mathbf{v}$ is perpendicular to both of the normals $\mathbf{N}_1$ and $\mathbf{N}_2$, and is therefore parallel to both planes.

The equations of two intersecting planes in space are satisfied simultaneously by the coordinates of all and only those points that lie on the line of intersection of the two planes. Hence, a pair of simultaneous linear equations may be interpreted as equations for a line. For example, recall the Eqs. (3),

$$\frac{x - x_1}{A} = \frac{y - y_1}{B} = \frac{z - z_1}{C},$$

which we found for the line L through the point $P_1(x_1, y_1, z_1)$ and parallel to the vector $\mathbf{v} = A\mathbf{i} + B\mathbf{j} + C\mathbf{k}$. This is equivalent to the three simultaneous equations

$$\begin{aligned} B(x - x_1) &= A(y - y_1), \\ C(x - x_1) &= A(z - z_1), \\ C(y - y_1) &= B(z - z_1). \end{aligned} \tag{7}$$

Each of these equations represents a plane. Any pair of them represents the line of intersection of the corresponding pair of planes. There are three such pairs of planes, namely 1st and 2nd, 1st and 3rd, 2nd and 3rd. But the three lines of intersection so determined are all identical; that is, there is just *one* line of intersection.

To see that this is so, we consider three separate cases.

CASE 1. If any two of the three coefficients A, B, C are zero and the third one is different from zero, then one of the three equations in (7) reduces to $0 = 0$, which imposes no restriction on (x, y, z), while the other two equations represent two planes that intersect in a common line.

CASE 2. If only one of the coefficients is zero, say $A = 0$ and $BC \neq 0$, then the first two of Eqs. (7) say simply that $x = x_1$. These two equations thus represent just one plane and the intersection of this plane with the plane

$$C(y - y_1) = B(z - z_1)$$

is the line L.

CASE 3. If $A \neq 0$, we may multiply the first equation in (7) by C/A and the second by B/A and subtract one from the other to obtain the third equation in (7). Thus we might just as well ignore the third equation, since it contains no new information.

In all cases, we see that the three Eqs. (7) reduce to just two independent equations, and the three planes intersect in one straight line.

The Eqs. (3) for a line are said to be in *standard form.*

EXAMPLE 4. Write a standard form equation for the line determined by the planes of Example 2.

Solution. First find the coordinates of a point common to both planes, say (9, 1, 7). Then obtain the A, B, and C of Eqs. (3) from the coefficients of $\mathbf{v} = \mathbf{N}_1 \times \mathbf{N}_2 = 14\mathbf{i} + 2\mathbf{j} + 15\mathbf{k}$. Finally, substitute all these values in Eqs. (3) to obtain

$$\frac{x-9}{14} = \frac{y-1}{2} = \frac{z-7}{15}.$$

EXAMPLE 5. Find an equation of the plane that passes through the two points $P_1(1, 0, -1)$ and $P_2(-1, 2, 1)$ and is parallel to the line of intersection of the planes $3x + y - 2z = 6$ and $4x - y + 3z = 0$.

Solution. The coordinates of either one of the points P_1 or P_2 will do for the x_1, x_2, and x_3 in Eq. (5). What remains, then, is to find a vector $\mathbf{N}$ normal to the plane in question to furnish the coefficients A, B, and C of Eq. (5) (Fig. 11–46).

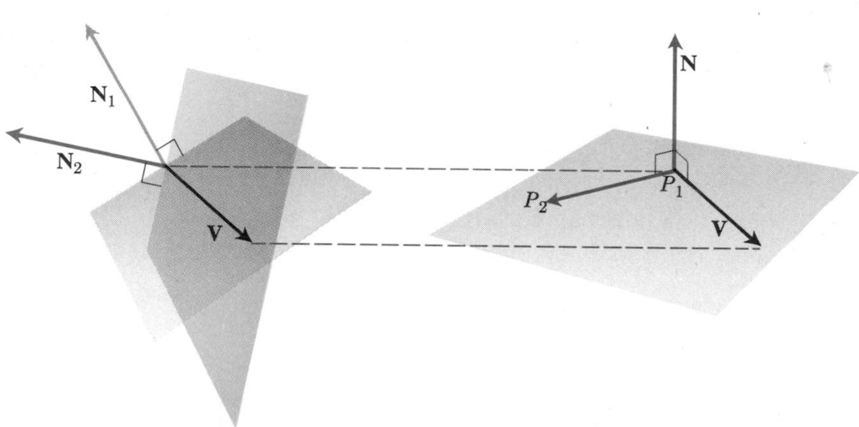

11–46 Constructing a plane through P_1 and P_2 that is parallel to the line of intersection of two other planes.

The line of intersection of the two given planes is parallel to the vector

$$\mathbf{v} = \mathbf{N}_1 \times \mathbf{N}_2 = \begin{vmatrix} \mathbf{i} & \mathbf{j} & \mathbf{k} \\ 3 & 1 & -2 \\ 4 & -1 & 3 \end{vmatrix} = \mathbf{i} - 17\mathbf{j} - 7\mathbf{k},$$

where $\mathbf{N}_1$ and $\mathbf{N}_2$ are normals to the two given planes. The vector

$$\overrightarrow{P_1P_2} = -2\mathbf{i} + 2\mathbf{j} + 2\mathbf{k}$$

is to lie in the required plane. Now we may slide $\mathbf{v}$ parallel to itself until it also lies in the required plane (since the plane is to be parallel to $\mathbf{v}$). Hence we may take

$$\mathbf{N} = \overrightarrow{P_1P_2} \times \mathbf{v} = 20\mathbf{i} - 12\mathbf{j} + 32\mathbf{k}$$

as a vector normal to the plane. Actually, $\frac{1}{4}\mathbf{N} = 5\mathbf{i} - 3\mathbf{j} + 8\mathbf{k}$ serves just as well. From this normal vector, we may substitute

$$A = 5, \qquad B = -3, \qquad C = 8$$

in Eq. (5), together with $x_1 = 1$, $y_1 = 0$, $z_1 = -1$, since $P_1(1, 0, -1)$ is to lie in the plane. The required plane is therefore

$$5(x - 1) - 3(y - 0) + 8(z + 1) = 0$$

or

$$5x - 3y + 8z + 3 = 0.$$

PROBLEMS

1. Find the coordinates of the point P in which the line

$$\frac{x-1}{2} = \frac{y+1}{-1} = \frac{z}{3}$$

intersects the plane $3x + 2y - z = 5$.

2. Find parametric and cartesian equations of the line joining the points $A(1, 2, -1)$ and $B(-1, 0, 1)$.

3. Show, by vector methods, that the distance from the point $P_1(x_1, y_1, z_1)$ to the plane $Ax + By + Cz - D = 0$ is

$$\frac{|Ax_1 + By_1 + Cz_1 - D|}{\sqrt{A^2 + B^2 + C^2}}.$$

4. (a) What is meant by the angle between a line and a plane? (b) Find the acute angle between the line

$$\frac{x+1}{2} = \frac{y}{3} = \frac{z-3}{6}$$

and the plane $10x + 2y - 11z = 3$.

5. Find a plane that passes through the point $(1, -1, 3)$ and is parallel to the plane $3x + y + z = 7$.

6. Show that the planes obtained by substituting different values for the constant D in the equation

$$2x + 3y - 6z = D$$

are parallel. Find the distance between two of these planes, one corresponding, say, to $D = D_1$ and the other to $D = D_2$.

7. Prove that the line

$$\frac{x-1}{2} = \frac{y+1}{3} = \frac{z-2}{4}$$

is parallel to the plane $x - 2y + z = 6$.

8. Find a plane through the points $A(1, 1, -1)$, $B(2, 0, 2)$, and $C(0, -2, 1)$.

9. Let $P_i(x_i, y_i, z_i)$, $i = 1, 2, 3$, be three points. What set is described by the equation

$$\begin{vmatrix} x & y & z & 1 \\ x_1 & y_1 & z_1 & 1 \\ x_2 & y_2 & z_2 & 1 \\ x_3 & y_3 & z_3 & 1 \end{vmatrix} = 0?$$

10. Find a plane through $A(1, -2, 1)$ perpendicular to the vector from the origin to A.

11. Find a plane through $P_0(2, 1, -1)$ perpendicular to the line of intersection of the planes $2x + y - z = 3$, $x + 2y + z = 2$.

12. Find a plane through the points $P_1(1, 2, 3)$ and $P_2(3, 2, 1)$ perpendicular to the plane $4x - y + 2z = 7$.

13. Find the distance between the origin and the line

$$\frac{x-2}{3} = \frac{y-1}{4} = \frac{2-z}{5}.$$

14. (a) Prove that three points A, B, C are collinear if and only if $\overrightarrow{AC} \times \overrightarrow{AB} = 0$. (b) Are the points $A(1, 2, -3)$, $B(3, 1, 0)$, $C(-3, 4, -9)$ collinear?

15. Prove that four points A, B, C, D are coplanar if and only if $\overrightarrow{AD} \cdot (\overrightarrow{AB} \times \overrightarrow{BC}) = 0$.

16. Show that the line of intersection of the planes

$$x + 2y - 2z = 5 \quad \text{and} \quad 5x - 2y - z = 0$$

is parallel to the line

$$\frac{x+3}{2} = \frac{y}{3} = \frac{z-1}{4}.$$

Find the plane determined by these two lines.

17. Show that the lines

$$\frac{x-2}{1}=\frac{y-2}{3}=\frac{z-3}{1} \quad \text{and} \quad \frac{x-2}{1}=\frac{y-3}{4}=\frac{z-4}{2}$$

intersect. Find the plane determined by these two lines.

18. Find the direction cosines (Article 11–6, Problem 15) of the line $2x + y - z = 5$, $x - 3y + 2z = 2$.

19. The equation $\mathbf{N} \cdot \overrightarrow{P_1P} = 0$ represents a plane through P_1 perpendicular to $\mathbf{N}$. What set does the inequality $\mathbf{N} \cdot \overrightarrow{P_1P} > 0$ represent? Give a reason for your answer.

20. The unit vector $\mathbf{u}$ makes angles α, β, γ, respectively, with the positive x-, y-, z-axes. Find the plane normal to $\mathbf{u}$ through $P_0(x_0, y_0, z_0)$.

11–9 PRODUCTS OF THREE VECTORS OR MORE

Products that involve three vectors or more often arise in physical and engineering problems. For example (see Sears, Zemansky, Young, *University Physics* (1976), Chapter 33), the electromotive force $\overrightarrow{dE}$ induced in an element of a conducting wire $\overrightarrow{dl}$ moving with velocity $\mathbf{v}$ through a magnetic field at a point where the flux density is $\mathbf{B}$ is given by $\overrightarrow{dE} = (\mathbf{B} \times \overrightarrow{dl}) \cdot \mathbf{v}$. Here the factor in parentheses is a vector, and the result of forming the scalar product of this vector and $\mathbf{v}$ is a scalar. It is a real economy in thinking to represent the result in the compact vector form which removes the necessity of carrying factors such as the sine of the angle between $\mathbf{B}$ and $\overrightarrow{dl}$ and the cosine of the angle between the normal to their plane and the velocity vector $\mathbf{v}$. All of these are automatically taken account of by the given product of three vectors.

Triple Scalar Product

The product $(\mathbf{A} \times \mathbf{B}) \cdot \mathbf{C}$, called the *triple scalar product*, has the following geometrical significance. The vector $\mathbf{N} = \mathbf{A} \times \mathbf{B}$ is normal to the base of the parallelepiped determined by the vectors $\mathbf{A}$, $\mathbf{B}$, and $\mathbf{C}$ in Fig. 11–47. The magnitude of $\mathbf{N}$ equals the area of the base determined by $\mathbf{A}$ and $\mathbf{B}$. Thus

$$(\mathbf{A} \times \mathbf{B}) \cdot \mathbf{C} = \mathbf{N} \cdot \mathbf{C} = |\mathbf{N}|\,|\mathbf{C}| \cos\theta$$

is, except perhaps for sign, the *volume of a box* of edges $\mathbf{A}$, $\mathbf{B}$, and $\mathbf{C}$, since

$$|\mathbf{N}| = |\mathbf{A} \times \mathbf{B}| = \text{area of base}$$

and

$$|\mathbf{C}| \cos\theta = \pm h = \pm\text{altitude of box.}$$

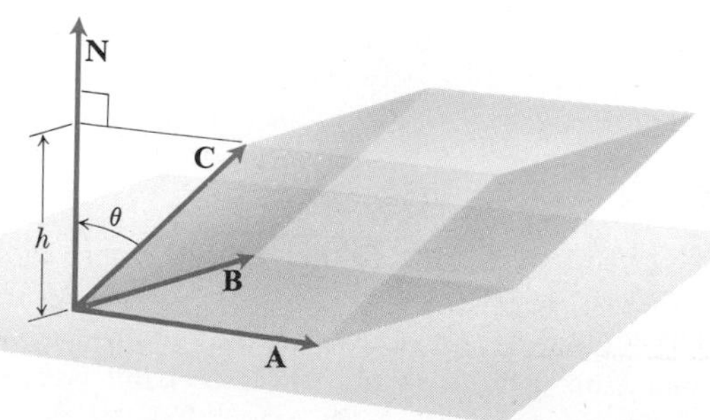

11–47 Except perhaps for sign, the number $(\mathbf{A} \times \mathbf{B}) \cdot \mathbf{C}$ is the volume of the parallelopiped shown here.

If **C** and **A** × **B** lie on the same side of the plane determined by **A** and **B**, the triple scalar product will be positive. But if the vectors **A**, **B**, and **C** form a lefthanded system, then (**A** × **B**) · **C** is negative. By successively considering the plane of **B** and **C**, then the plane of **C** and **A**, as the base of the parallelepiped, we can readily see that

$$(\mathbf{A} \times \mathbf{B}) \cdot \mathbf{C} = (\mathbf{B} \times \mathbf{C}) \cdot \mathbf{A} = (\mathbf{C} \times \mathbf{A}) \cdot \mathbf{B}. \tag{1}$$

Since the dot product is commutative, we also have

$$(\mathbf{B} \times \mathbf{C}) \cdot \mathbf{A} = \mathbf{A} \cdot (\mathbf{B} \times \mathbf{C}),$$

so that Eq. (1) gives the result

$$(\mathbf{A} \times \mathbf{B}) \cdot \mathbf{C} = \mathbf{A} \cdot (\mathbf{B} \times \mathbf{C}). \tag{2}$$

Equation (2) says that the dot and the cross may be interchanged in the triple scalar product, provided only that the multiplications are performed in a way that "makes sense." Thus (**A** · **B**) × **C** is excluded on the ground that (**A** · **B**) is a scalar and we never "cross" a scalar and a vector.

The triple scalar product in Eq. (2) is conveniently expressed in determinant form as follows:

$$\begin{aligned}
\mathbf{A} \cdot (\mathbf{B} \times \mathbf{C}) &= A \cdot \left[\begin{vmatrix} b_2 & b_3 \\ c_2 & c_3 \end{vmatrix} \mathbf{i} - \begin{vmatrix} b_1 & b_3 \\ c_1 & c_3 \end{vmatrix} \mathbf{j} + \begin{vmatrix} b_1 & b_2 \\ c_1 & c_2 \end{vmatrix} \mathbf{k} \right] \\
&= a_1 \begin{vmatrix} b_2 & b_3 \\ c_2 & c_3 \end{vmatrix} - a_2 \begin{vmatrix} b_1 & b_3 \\ c_1 & c_3 \end{vmatrix} + a_3 \begin{vmatrix} b_1 & b_2 \\ c_1 & c_2 \end{vmatrix} \\
&= \begin{vmatrix} a_1 & a_2 & a_3 \\ b_1 & b_2 & b_3 \\ c_1 & c_2 & c_3 \end{vmatrix}.
\end{aligned} \tag{3}$$

A product that involves three vectors but is much simpler than the triple scalar product is (**A** · **B**)**C**. Here the scalar s = **A** · **B** multiplies the vector **C**.

Triple Vector Product

The triple vector products (**A** × **B**) × **C** and **A** × (**B** × **C**) are usually not equal, but each of them can be evaluated rather simply by formulas which we shall now derive.

We start by showing that the vector product (**A** × **B**) × **C** is given by

$$(\mathbf{A} \times \mathbf{B}) \times \mathbf{C} = (\mathbf{A} \cdot \mathbf{C})\mathbf{B} - (\mathbf{B} \cdot \mathbf{C})\mathbf{A}. \tag{4}$$

CASE 1. If one of the vectors is the zero vector, Eq. (4) is true because both sides of it are zero.

CASE 2. If none of the vectors is zero, but if **B** = s**A** for some scalar s, then both sides of Eq. (4) are zero again.

CASE 3. Suppose that none of the vectors is zero and that **A** and **B** are not parallel. The vector on the left of Eq. (4) is parallel to the plane determined by **A** and **B**, so that it is possible to find scalars m and n such that

$$(\mathbf{A} \times \mathbf{B}) \times \mathbf{C} = m\mathbf{A} + n\mathbf{B}. \tag{5}$$

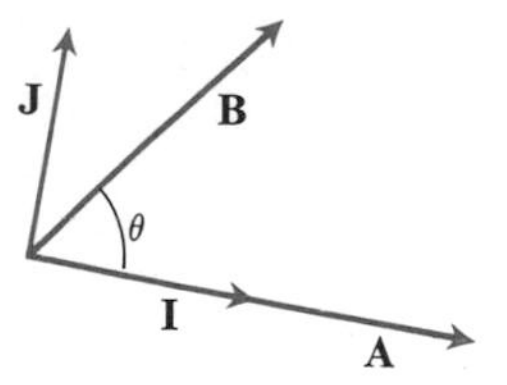

11–48 Orthogonal vectors **I** and **J** in the plane of **A** and **B**.

To calculate m and n, we introduce orthogonal unit vectors **I** and **J** in the plane of **A** and **B** with $\mathbf{I} = \mathbf{A}/|\mathbf{A}|$ (Fig. 11–48). We also introduce a third unit vector $\mathbf{K} = \mathbf{I} \times \mathbf{J}$, and write all our vectors in terms of these unit vectors **I**, **J**, and **K**:

$$\begin{aligned}\mathbf{A} &= a_1\mathbf{I},\\ \mathbf{B} &= b_1\mathbf{I} + b_2\mathbf{J},\\ \mathbf{C} &= c_1\mathbf{I} + c_2\mathbf{J} + c_3\mathbf{K}.\end{aligned} \tag{6}$$

Then

$$\mathbf{A} \times \mathbf{B} = a_1 b_2 \mathbf{K}$$

and

$$(\mathbf{A} \times \mathbf{B}) \times \mathbf{C} = a_1 b_2 c_1 \mathbf{J} - a_1 b_2 c_2 \mathbf{I}. \tag{7}$$

Comparing this with the right side of Eq. (5), we have

$$m(a_1\mathbf{I}) + n(b_1\mathbf{I} + b_2\mathbf{J}) = a_1 b_2 c_1 \mathbf{J} - a_1 b_2 c_2 \mathbf{I}.$$

This is equivalent to the pair of scalar equations

$$\begin{aligned} ma_1 + nb_1 &= -a_1 b_2 c_2,\\ nb_2 &= a_1 b_2 c_1.\end{aligned}$$

If b_2 were equal to zero, **A** and **B** would be parallel, contrary to hypothesis. Hence b_2 is not zero and we may solve the last equation for n. We find

$$n = a_1 c_1 = \mathbf{A} \cdot \mathbf{C}.$$

Then, by substitution,

$$\begin{aligned} ma_1 &= -nb_1 - a_1 b_2 c_2\\ &= -a_1 c_1 b_1 - a_1 b_2 c_2,\end{aligned}$$

and since $|\mathbf{A}| = a_1 \neq 0$, we may divide by a_1 and have

$$m = -(b_1 c_1 + b_2 c_2) = -(\mathbf{B} \cdot \mathbf{C}).$$

When these values are substituted for m and n in Eq. (5), we obtain the result given in Eq. (4).

The identity

$$(\mathbf{B} \times \mathbf{C}) \times \mathbf{A} = (\mathbf{B} \cdot \mathbf{A})\mathbf{C} - (\mathbf{C} \cdot \mathbf{A})\mathbf{B} \tag{8a}$$

follows from Eq. (4) by a simple interchange of the letters **A**, **B**, and **C**. If we now interchange the factors $\mathbf{B} \times \mathbf{C}$ and **A** we must change the sign on the right side of the equation. This gives the following identity, which is a companion of Eq. (4):

$$\mathbf{A} \times (\mathbf{B} \times \mathbf{C}) = (\mathbf{A} \cdot \mathbf{C})\mathbf{B} - (\mathbf{A} \cdot \mathbf{B})\mathbf{C}. \tag{8b}$$

EXAMPLE 1. Verify Eq. (4) for the vectors

$$\begin{aligned}\mathbf{A} &= \mathbf{i} - \mathbf{j} + 2\mathbf{k},\\ \mathbf{B} &= 2\mathbf{i} + \mathbf{j} + \mathbf{k},\\ \mathbf{C} &= \mathbf{i} + 2\mathbf{j} - \mathbf{k}.\end{aligned}$$

Solution. Since

$$\mathbf{A} \cdot \mathbf{C} = -3, \qquad \mathbf{B} \cdot \mathbf{C} = 3,$$

the right side of Eq. (4) is

$$(\mathbf{A} \cdot \mathbf{C})\mathbf{B} - (\mathbf{B} \cdot \mathbf{C})\mathbf{A} = -3\mathbf{B} - 3\mathbf{A} = -3(3\mathbf{i} + 3\mathbf{k}) = -9\mathbf{i} - 9\mathbf{k}.$$

To calculate the left side of Eq. (4) we have

$$\mathbf{A} \times \mathbf{B} = \begin{vmatrix} \mathbf{i} & \mathbf{j} & \mathbf{k} \\ 1 & -1 & 2 \\ 2 & 1 & 1 \end{vmatrix} = -3\mathbf{i} + 3\mathbf{j} + 3\mathbf{k},$$

so that

$$(\mathbf{A} \times \mathbf{B}) \times \mathbf{C} = \begin{vmatrix} \mathbf{i} & \mathbf{j} & \mathbf{k} \\ -3 & 3 & 3 \\ 1 & 2 & -1 \end{vmatrix} = -9\mathbf{i} - 9\mathbf{k}.$$

EXAMPLE 2. Use Eqs. (4) and (8b) to express

$$(\mathbf{A} \times \mathbf{B}) \times (\mathbf{C} \times \mathbf{D})$$

in terms of scalar multiplication and cross products involving no more than two factors.

Solution. Write, for convenience,

$$\mathbf{C} \times \mathbf{D} = \mathbf{V}.$$

Then use Eq. (4) to evaluate

$$(\mathbf{A} \times \mathbf{B}) \times \mathbf{V} = (\mathbf{A} \cdot \mathbf{V})\mathbf{B} - (\mathbf{B} \cdot \mathbf{V})\mathbf{A}$$

or

$$(\mathbf{A} \times \mathbf{B}) \times (\mathbf{C} \times \mathbf{D}) = (\mathbf{A} \cdot \mathbf{C} \times \mathbf{D})\mathbf{B} - (\mathbf{B} \cdot \mathbf{C} \times \mathbf{D})\mathbf{A}.$$

The result, as written, expresses the answer as a scalar times **B** minus a scalar times **A**. One could also represent the answer as a scalar times **C** minus a scalar times **D**. Geometrically, the vector is parallel to the line of intersection of the **A**, **B**-plane and the **C**, **D**-plane.

EXAMPLE 3. (See Fig. 11–49.) Let

$$\mathbf{A} = \overrightarrow{PQ}, \qquad \mathbf{B} = \overrightarrow{PS}$$
$$\mathbf{A}' = \overrightarrow{P'Q'}, \qquad \mathbf{B}' = \overrightarrow{P'S'}$$

be sides of parallelograms $PQRS$ and $P'Q'R'S'$ that are related in such a way that PP', QQ', and SS' are parallel to one another and to the unit vector **n**. Show that

$$(\mathbf{A} \times \mathbf{B}) \cdot \mathbf{n} = (\mathbf{A}' \times \mathbf{B}') \cdot \mathbf{n} \tag{9}$$

and discuss the geometrical meaning of this identity.

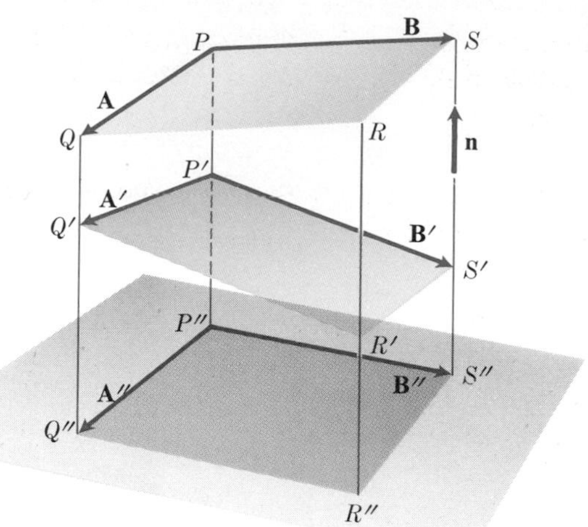

11–49 If $|\mathbf{n}| = 1$, then $(\mathbf{A} \times \mathbf{B}) \cdot \mathbf{n}$ is the area of the projection of the parallelogram determined by $\mathbf{A}$ and $\mathbf{B}$ on a plane perpendicular to $\mathbf{n}$.

Verification of Eq. (9)

From the way the parallelograms are related, it follows that

$$\begin{aligned}\mathbf{A} &= \overrightarrow{PQ} = \overrightarrow{PP'} + \overrightarrow{P'Q'} + \overrightarrow{Q'Q} \\ &= \overrightarrow{P'Q'} + (\overrightarrow{PP'} - \overrightarrow{QQ'}) = \mathbf{A}' + s\mathbf{n}\end{aligned}$$

for some scalar s, since both $\overrightarrow{PP'}$ and $\overrightarrow{QQ'}$ are parallel to $\mathbf{n}$. Similarly,

$$\mathbf{B} = \mathbf{B}' + t\mathbf{n}$$

for some scalar t. Hence

$$\begin{aligned}\mathbf{A} \times \mathbf{B} &= (\mathbf{A}' + s\mathbf{n}) \times (\mathbf{B}' + t\mathbf{n}) \\ &= \mathbf{A}' \times \mathbf{B}' + t(\mathbf{A}' \times \mathbf{n}) + s(\mathbf{n} \times \mathbf{B}') + st(\mathbf{n} \times \mathbf{n}). \qquad (10)\end{aligned}$$

But $\mathbf{n} \times \mathbf{n} = 0$, while $\mathbf{A}' \times \mathbf{n}$ and $\mathbf{n} \times \mathbf{B}'$ are both perpendicular to $\mathbf{n}$. Therefore when we dot both sides of (10) with $\mathbf{n}$ we get Eq. (9).

Geometrical Meaning of Eq. (9)

The result (9) says that when the parallelograms $PQRS$ and $P'Q'R'S'$ are any two plane sections of a prism with sides parallel to $\mathbf{n}$, then the box determined by $\mathbf{A}$, $\mathbf{B}$, and $\mathbf{n}$ has the same volume as the box determined by $\mathbf{A}'$, $\mathbf{B}'$, and $\mathbf{n}$. Thus, in particular, we may replace the right side of (9) by $(\mathbf{A}'' \times \mathbf{B}'') \cdot \mathbf{n}$, where $\mathbf{A}''$ and $\mathbf{B}''$ are sides of a *right* section $P''Q''R''S''$ as in Fig. 11–49. Then $\mathbf{A}'' \times \mathbf{B}''$ is parallel to $\mathbf{n}$, and

$$\mathbf{A}'' \times \mathbf{B}'' = (\text{Area right section})\, \mathbf{n}$$

and

$$(\mathbf{A}'' \times \mathbf{B}'') \cdot \mathbf{n} = \text{Area right section}.$$

Therefore, by Eq. (9), we have the following interpretation:

$(\mathbf{A} \times \mathbf{B}) \cdot \mathbf{n}$ is the area of the orthogonal projection of the parallelogram determined by $\mathbf{A}$ and $\mathbf{B}$ onto a plane whose unit normal is $\mathbf{n}$. **(11)**

This assumes that $\mathbf{A} \times \mathbf{B}$ and $\mathbf{n}$ lie on the same side of the plane $PQRS$. If they are on opposite sides, take the absolute value to get the area. Except possibly for sign, then,

$$(\mathbf{A} \times \mathbf{B}) \cdot \mathbf{k} = \text{Area of projection in the } xy\text{-plane}, \tag{12a}$$

$$(\mathbf{A} \times \mathbf{B}) \cdot \mathbf{j} = \text{Area of projection in the } xz\text{-plane}, \tag{12b}$$

$$(\mathbf{A} \times \mathbf{B}) \cdot \mathbf{i} = \text{Area of projection in the } yz\text{-plane}. \tag{12c}$$

PROBLEMS

In Problems 1–3, take

$$\mathbf{A} = 4\mathbf{i} - 8\mathbf{j} + \mathbf{k},$$

$$\mathbf{B} = 2\mathbf{i} + \mathbf{j} - 2\mathbf{k},$$

$$\mathbf{C} = 3\mathbf{i} - 4\mathbf{j} + 12\mathbf{k}.$$

1. Find $(\mathbf{A} \cdot \mathbf{B})\mathbf{C}$ and $\mathbf{A}(\mathbf{B} \cdot \mathbf{C})$.

2. Find the volume of the box having $\mathbf{A}$, $\mathbf{B}$, $\mathbf{C}$ as three co-terminous edges.

3. (a) Find $\mathbf{A} \times \mathbf{B}$ and use the result to find $(\mathbf{A} \times \mathbf{B}) \times \mathbf{C}$. (b) Find $(\mathbf{A} \times \mathbf{B}) \times \mathbf{C}$ by another method.

4. Prove that any vector $\mathbf{A}$ satisfies the identity

$$\mathbf{A} = \tfrac{1}{2}[\mathbf{i} \times (\mathbf{A} \times \mathbf{i}) + \mathbf{j} \times (\mathbf{A} \times \mathbf{j}) + \mathbf{k} \times (\mathbf{A} \times \mathbf{k})].$$

5. Express the product $\mathbf{R} = (\mathbf{A} \times \mathbf{B}) \times (\mathbf{C} \times \mathbf{D})$ in the form $a\mathbf{C} + b\mathbf{D}$ with scalars a and b.

6. Find the volume of the tetrahedron with vertices at $(0, 0, 0)$, $(1, -1, 1)$, $(2, 1, -2)$, and $(-1, 2, -1)$.

7. Use Eq. (3) to show that

a) $\mathbf{A} \cdot (\mathbf{C} \times \mathbf{B}) = -\mathbf{A} \cdot (\mathbf{B} \times \mathbf{C})$, **b)** $\mathbf{A} \cdot (\mathbf{A} \times \mathbf{B}) = 0$,
c) $(\mathbf{A} + \mathbf{D}) \cdot (\mathbf{B} \times \mathbf{C}) = \mathbf{A} \cdot (\mathbf{B} \times \mathbf{C}) + \mathbf{D} \cdot (\mathbf{B} \times \mathbf{C})$.

Interpret the results geometrically.

8. Explain the statement in the text that $(\mathbf{A} \times \mathbf{B}) \times \mathbf{C}$ is parallel to the plane determined by $\mathbf{A}$ and $\mathbf{B}$. Illustrate with a sketch.

9. Explain the statement, at the end of Example 2, that $(\mathbf{A} \times \mathbf{B}) \times (\mathbf{C} \times \mathbf{D})$ is parallel to the line of intersection of the $\mathbf{A}$, $\mathbf{B}$-plane and the $\mathbf{C}$, $\mathbf{D}$-plane. Illustrate with a sketch.

10. Find a line in the plane of $P_0(0, 0, 0)$, $P_1(2, 2, 0)$, $P_2(0, 1, -2)$, and perpendicular to the line

$$\frac{x+1}{3} = \frac{y-1}{2} = 2z.$$

11. Let $P(1, 2, -1)$, $Q(3, -1, 4)$, and $R(2, 6, 2)$ be three vertices of a parallelogram $PQRS$.

a) Find the coordinates of S.
b) Find the area of $PQRS$.
c) Find the area of the projection of $PQRS$ in the xy-plane; in the yz-plane; in the xz-plane.

12. Show that the area of a parallelogram in space is the square root of the sum of the squares of the areas of its projections on any three mutually orthogonal planes.

11–10 CYLINDERS

In this article and the next, we shall consider some extensions of analytic geometry to space. We begin with the notion of a surface.

The set of points $P(x, y, z)$ that satisfy an equation

$$F(x, y, z) = 0 \tag{1}$$

may be interpreted in a broad sense as being a surface. The simplest examples of surfaces are planes, which have equations of the form $Ax + By + Cz - D = 0$. Almost as simple as planes are the surfaces called *cylinders.*

In general, a cylinder is a surface that is generated by moving a straight line along a given curve while holding the line parallel to a given fixed line.

EXAMPLE 1. The *parabolic cylinder* of Fig. 11–50 is generated by a line parallel to the z-axis that moves along the curve $y = x^2$ in the xy-plane. If a point $P_0(x, y, 0)$ lies on the parabola, then every point $P(x, y, z)$ with the same x- and y-coordinates lies on the line through P_0 parallel to the z-axis, and hence belongs to the surface. Conversely, if $P(x, y, z)$ lies on the surface, its projection $P_0(x, y, 0)$ on the xy-plane lies on the parabola $y = x^2$, so that its coordinates satisfy the equation $y = x^2$. Regardless of the value of z, the points of the surface are the points whose coordinates satisfy this equation. Thus, the equation $y = x^2$ is an equation for the cylinder as well as for the generating parabola. The cross sections of the cylinder perpendicular to the z-axis are parabolas, too, all of them congruent to the parabola in the xy-plane.

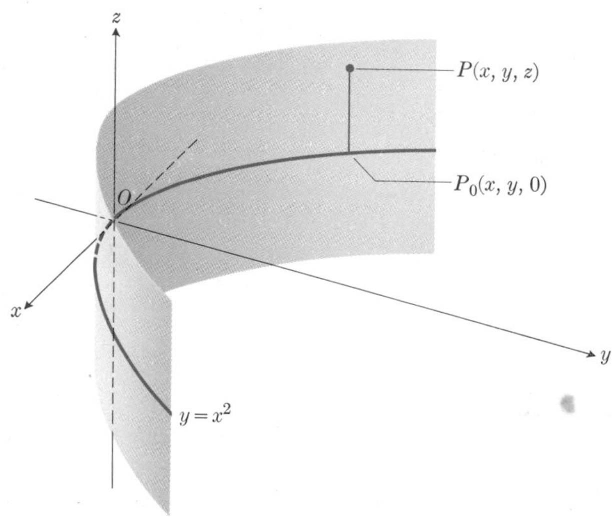

11–50 Parabolic cylinder.

In general, any curve

$$f(x, y) = 0 \tag{2}$$

in the xy-plane defines a cylinder in space whose equation is also $f(x, y) = 0$, and which is made up of the points of the lines through the curve that are parallel to the z-axis. The lines are sometimes called *elements* of the cylinder.

The discussion above can be carried through for cylinders with elements parallel to the other coordinate axes, and the result is summarized by saying that *an equation in cartesian coordinates, from which one letter is missing, represents a cylinder with elements parallel to the axis associated with the missing letter.*

EXAMPLE 2. The surface

$$y^2 + 4z^2 = 4$$

is an *elliptic cylinder* with elements parallel to the x-axis. It extends indefinitely in both the negative and positive directions along the x-axis, which is the axis of the cylinder, since it passes through the centers of the elliptical cross sections of the cylinder (Fig. 11–51).

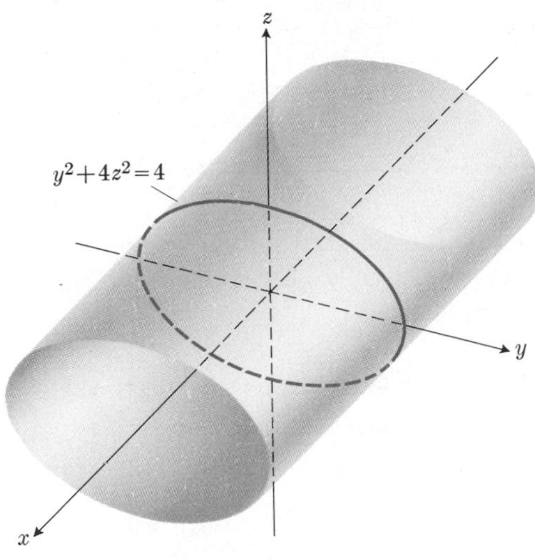

11–51 Elliptic cylinder.

EXAMPLE 3. The surface

$$r^2 = 2a \cos 2\theta$$

in cylindrical coordinates is a cylinder with elements parallel to the z-axis. Each section perpendicular to the z-axis is a lemniscate. The cylinder extends indefinitely in both the positive and negative directions along the z-axis (Fig. 11–52).

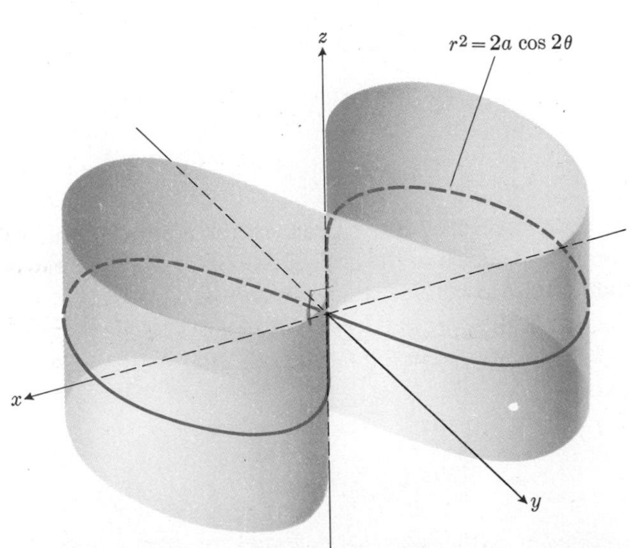

11–52 A cylinder whose cross sections are lemniscates.

PROBLEMS

Describe and sketch each of the following surfaces [(r, θ, z) are cylindrical coordinates].

1. $x^2 + z^2 = 1$
2. $z = x^2$
3. $x = -y^2$
4. $4x^2 + y^2 = 4$
5. $z = -y$
6. $y^2 - x^2 = 1$
7. $x^2 - z^2 = 1$
8. $z^2 - y^2 = 1$
9. $r = 4$
10. $r = \sin\theta$
11. $r = \cos\theta$
12. $r = 1 + \cos\theta$
13. $x^2 + y^2 = a^2$
14. $y^2 + z^2 - 4z = 0$
15. $x^2 + 4z^2 - 4z = 0$

11-11 QUADRIC SURFACES

A surface whose equation is a quadratic in the variables x, y, and z is called a *quadric* surface. We indicate briefly how some of the simpler ones may be recognized from their equations.

The *sphere*

$$(x - h)^2 + (y - k)^2 + (z - m)^2 = a^2 \tag{1}$$

with center at (h, k, m) and radius a has already been mentioned in Article 11-5. Likewise, the various *cylinders*

$$Ax^2 + Bxy + Cy^2 + Dx + Ey + F = 0 \tag{2}$$

with elements parallel to the z-axis, and others with elements parallel to the other coordinate axes, are familiar and will not be further discussed. In the examples that follow, we shall refer the surfaces discussed to coordinate axes that yield simple forms of the equations. For example, we take the origin to be at the center of the ellipsoid in Example 1 below. If the center were at (h, k, m) instead, the equation would simply have $x - h$, $y - k$, and $z - m$, in place of x, y, z, respectively. We take a, b, and c to be positive constants in every case.

EXAMPLE 1. *The ellipsoid*

$$\frac{x^2}{a^2} + \frac{y^2}{b^2} + \frac{z^2}{c^2} = 1 \tag{3}$$

cuts the coordinate axes at $(\pm a, 0, 0)$, $(0, \pm b, 0)$, and $(0, 0, \pm c)$. It lies inside the rectangular box

$$|x| \le a, \qquad |y| \le b, \qquad |z| \le c.$$

Since only even powers of x, y, and z occur in the equation, this surface is symmetric with respect to each of the coordinate planes. The sections cut out by the coordinate planes are ellipses. For example,

$$\frac{x^2}{a^2} + \frac{y^2}{b^2} = 1 \quad \text{when} \quad z = 0.$$

Each section cut out by a plane

$$z = z_1, \qquad |z_1| < c$$

is an ellipse

$$\frac{x^2}{a^2[1 - (z_1^2/c^2)]} + \frac{y^2}{b^2[1 - (z_1^2/c^2)]} = 1$$

with center on the z-axis and having semiaxes

$$\frac{a}{c}\sqrt{c^2 - z_1^2} \quad \text{and} \quad \frac{b}{c}\sqrt{c^2 - z_1^2}.$$

The surface is sketched in Fig. 11–53. When two of the three semiaxes a, b, and c are equal, the surface is an ellipsoid of revolution, and when all three are equal, it is a sphere.

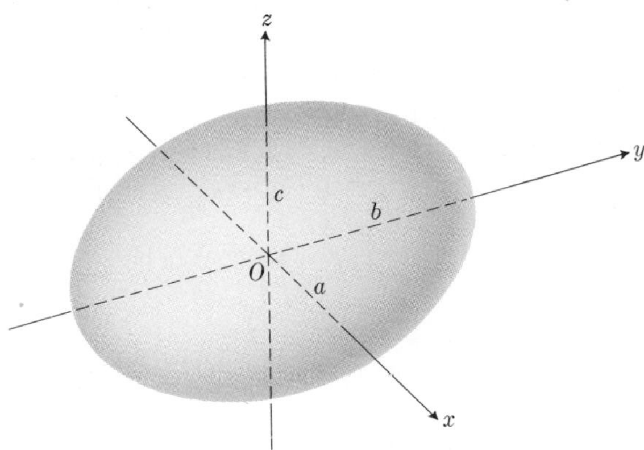

11–53 Ellipsoid.

EXAMPLE 2. *The elliptic paraboloid* (Fig. 11–54)

$$\frac{x^2}{a^2} + \frac{y^2}{b^2} = \frac{z}{c} \tag{4}$$

is symmetric with respect to the planes $x = 0$ and $y = 0$. The only intercept on the axes is at the origin. Since the left side of the equation is nonnegative, the surface is limited to the region $z \geq 0$. That is, away from the origin it lies above the xy-plane. The section cut out from the surface by the yz-plane is

$$x = 0, \qquad y^2 = \frac{b^2}{c} z,$$

which is a parabola with vertex at the origin and opening upward. Similarly, one finds that when $y = 0$,

$$x^2 = \frac{a^2}{c} z,$$

which is also such a parabola. When $z = 0$, the cut reduces to the single point (0, 0, 0). Each plane $z = z_1 > 0$ perpendicular to the z-axis cuts the surface in an ellipse of semiaxes

$$a\sqrt{z_1/c} \quad \text{and} \quad b\sqrt{z_1/c}.$$

These semiaxes increase in magnitude as z_1 increases. The paraboloid extends indefinitely upward.

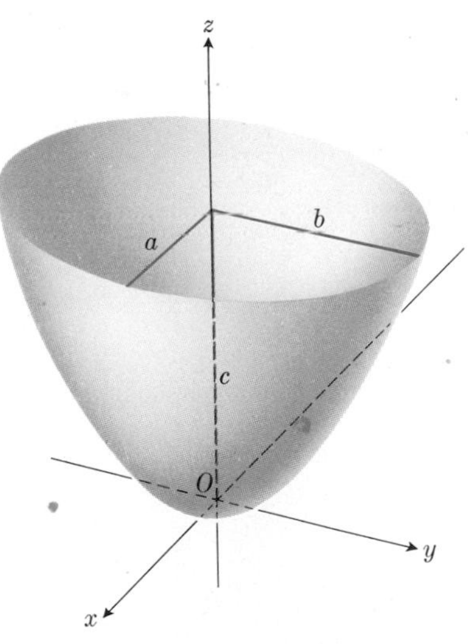

11–54 Elliptic paraboloid.

EXAMPLE 3. *Circular paraboloid, or paraboloid of revolution:*

$$\frac{x^2}{a^2} + \frac{y^2}{a^2} = \frac{z}{c}. \tag{5a}$$

The equation is obtained by taking $b = a$ in Eq. (4) for the elliptic paraboloid. The cross sections of the surface by planes perpendicular to the z-axis are circles centered on the z-axis. The cross sections by planes containing the z-axis are congruent parabolas with a common focus at the point $(0, 0, a^2/4c)$. In cylindrical coordinates, (5a) becomes

$$\frac{r^2}{a^2} = \frac{z}{c}. \tag{5b}$$

Shapes cut from circular paraboloids are used for antennae in radio telescopes, satellite trackers, and microwave radio links (Fig. 11–55).

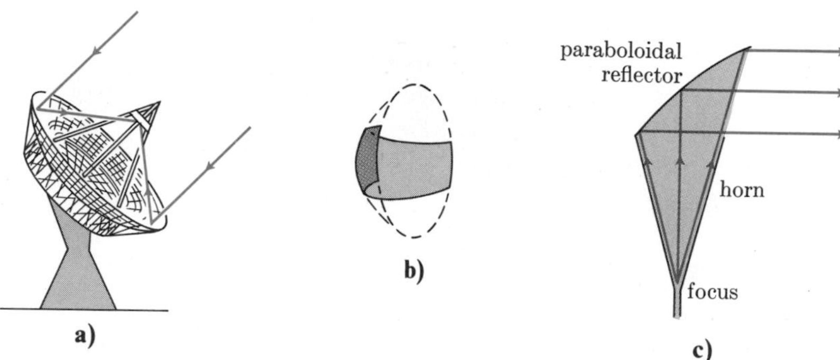

11–55 Antennas shaped like pieces of paraboloids of revolution. (a) Radio telescopes use the same principles as optical telescopes. (b) A "rectangular-cut" radar reflector. (c) Horn antenna in a microwave radio link.

EXAMPLE 4. *The elliptic cone* (Fig. 11–56)

$$\frac{x^2}{a^2} + \frac{y^2}{b^2} = \frac{z^2}{c^2} \tag{6}$$

is symmetric with respect to all three coordinate planes. The plane $z = 0$ cuts the surface in the single point (0, 0, 0). The plane $x = 0$ cuts it in the two intersecting straight lines

$$x = 0, \qquad \frac{y}{b} = \pm\frac{z}{c} \tag{7}$$

and when

$$y = 0, \qquad \frac{x}{a} = \pm\frac{z}{c}. \tag{8}$$

The section cut out by a plane $z = z_1 > 0$ is an ellipse with center on the z-axis and vertices lying on the straight lines (7) and (8). In fact, the whole surface is generated by a straight line L which passes through the origin and a point Q on the ellipse

$$z = c, \qquad \frac{x^2}{a^2} + \frac{y^2}{b^2} = 1.$$

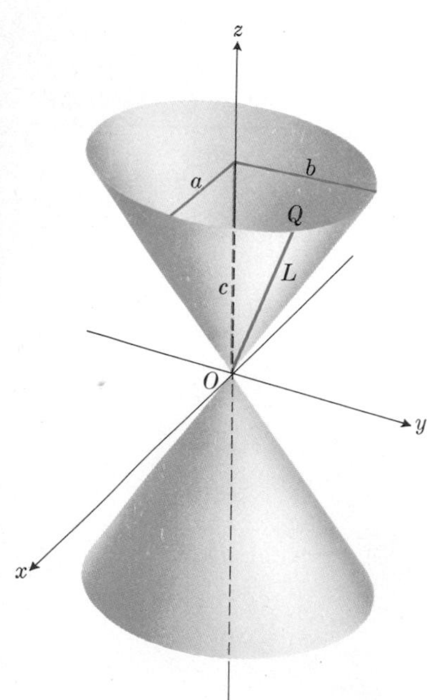

11–56 Elliptic cone.

As the point Q traces out the ellipse, the infinite line L generates the surface, which is a cone with elliptic cross sections. To see why, suppose that $Q(x_1, y_1, z_1)$ is a point on the surface and t is any scalar. Then the vector from O to the point $P(tx_1, ty_1, tz_1)$ is simply t times $\overrightarrow{OQ}$, so that as t varies from $-\infty$ to $+\infty$ the point P traces out the infinite line L. But since Q is assumed to be on the surface, the equation

$$\frac{x_1^2}{a^2} + \frac{y_1^2}{b^2} = \frac{z_1^2}{c^2}$$

is satisfied. Multiplying both sides of this equation by t^2 shows that the point $P(tx_1, ty_1, tz_1)$ is also on the surface. This establishes the validity of the remark that the surface is a cone generated by the line L through O and the point Q on the ellipse.

In case $a = b$, the cone is a right circular cone and its equation in cylindrical coordinates is simply

$$\frac{r}{a} = \frac{z}{c}. \quad (9)$$

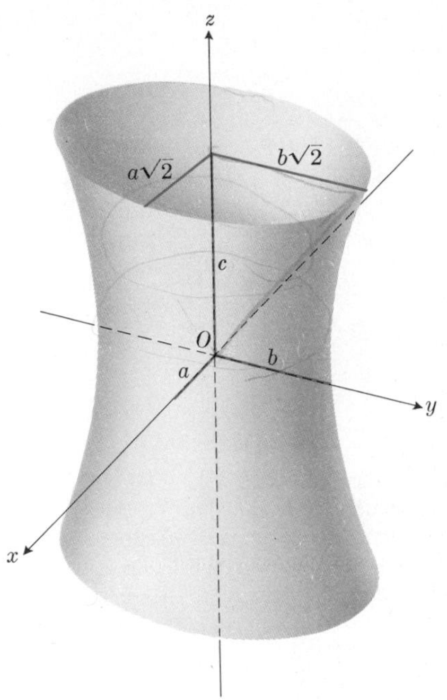

11–57 Hyperboloid of one sheet.

EXAMPLE 5. *The hyperboloid of one sheet* (Fig. 11–57)

$$\frac{x^2}{a^2} + \frac{y^2}{b^2} - \frac{z^2}{c^2} = 1 \quad (10)$$

is symmetric with respect to each of the three coordinate planes. The sections cut out by the coordinate planes are:

$$x = 0: \text{ the hyperbola } \frac{y^2}{b^2} - \frac{z^2}{c^2} = 1,$$

$$y = 0: \text{ the hyperbola } \frac{x^2}{a^2} - \frac{z^2}{c^2} = 1, \quad (11)$$

$$z = 0: \text{ the ellipse } \frac{x^2}{a^2} + \frac{y^2}{b^2} = 1.$$

The plane $z = z_1$ cuts the surface in an ellipse with center on the z-axis and vertices on the hyperbolas in (11). The surface is connected, meaning that it is possible to travel from any point on it to any other point on it without leaving the surface. For this reason, it is said to have *one* sheet, in contrast to the next example, which consists of *two* sheets. In the special case where $a = b$, the surface is a hyperboloid of revolution with equation given in cylindrical coordinates by

$$\frac{r^2}{a^2} - \frac{z^2}{c^2} = 1. \quad (12)$$

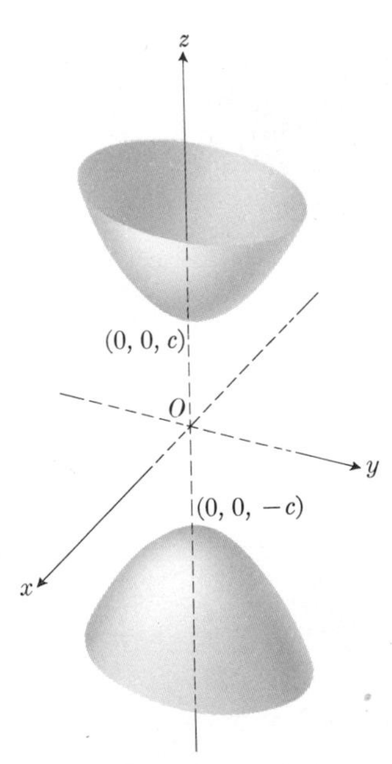

11–58 Hyperboloid of two sheets.

EXAMPLE 6. *The hyperboloid of two sheets* (Fig. 11–58)

$$\frac{z^2}{c^2} - \frac{x^2}{a^2} - \frac{y^2}{b^2} = 1 \quad (13)$$

is symmetric with respect to the three coordinate planes. The plane $z = 0$ does not intersect the surface; in fact, one must have

$$|z| \geq c$$

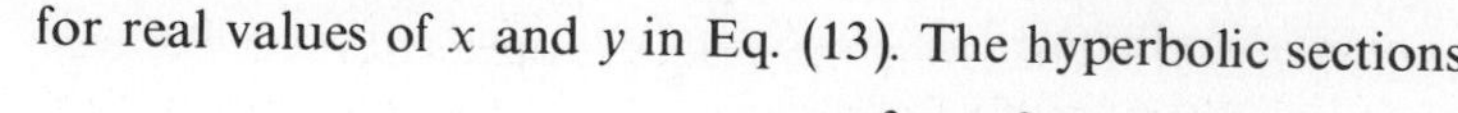

for real values of x and y in Eq. (13). The hyperbolic sections

$$x = 0: \quad \frac{z^2}{c^2} - \frac{y^2}{b^2} = 1,$$

$$y = 0: \quad \frac{z^2}{c^2} - \frac{x^2}{a^2} = 1$$

have their vertices and foci on the z-axis. The surface is separated into two portions, one above the plane $z = c$ and the other below the plane $z = -c$. This accounts for its name.

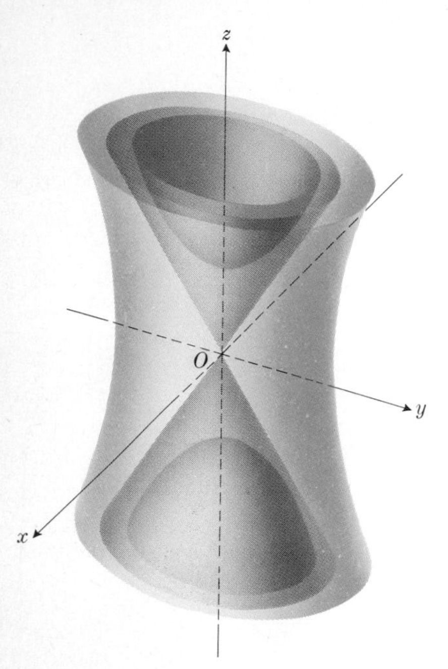

11–59 Cone asymptotic to hyperboloid of one sheet and hyperboloid of two sheets.

Equations (10) and (13) differ in the number of negative terms that each contains on the left side when the right side is $+1$. The number of negative signs is the same as the number of sheets of the hyperboloid. If we compare with Eq. (6), we see that replacing the unity on the right side of either Eq. (10) or (13) by zero gives the equation of a cone. This cone (Fig. 11–59) is, in fact, asymptotic to both of the hyperboloids (10) and (13) in the same way that the lines

$$\frac{x^2}{a^2} - \frac{y^2}{b^2} = 0$$

are asymptotic to the two hyperbolas

$$\frac{x^2}{a^2} - \frac{y^2}{b^2} = \pm 1$$

in the xy-plane.

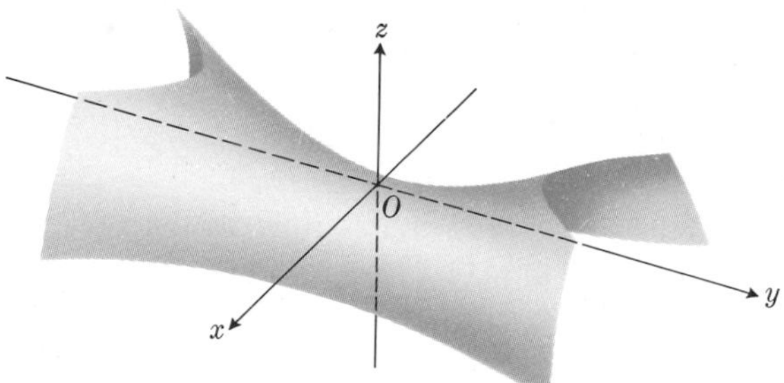

11–60 Hyperbolic paraboloid.

EXAMPLE 7. *The hyperbolic paraboloid* (Fig. 11–60)

$$\frac{y^2}{b^2} - \frac{x^2}{a^2} = \frac{z}{c} \tag{14}$$

has symmetry with respect to the planes $x = 0$ and $y = 0$. The sections in these planes are

$$x = 0: \quad y^2 = b^2 \frac{z}{c}, \tag{15a}$$

$$y = 0: \quad x^2 = -a^2 \frac{z}{c}, \tag{15b}$$

which are parabolas. In the plane $x = 0$, the parabola opens upward and has vertex at the origin. The parabola in the plane $y = 0$ has the same vertex, but it opens downward. If we cut the surface by a plane $z = z_1 > 0$, the section is a hyperbola,

$$\frac{y^2}{b^2} - \frac{x^2}{a^2} = \frac{z_1}{c}, \tag{16}$$

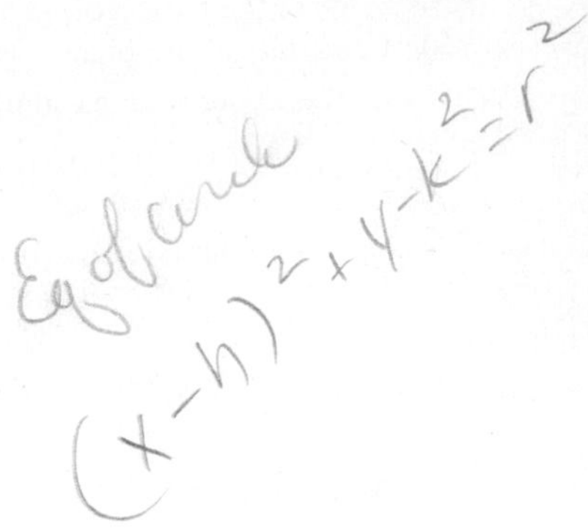

whose focal axis is parallel to the y-axis and which has its vertices on the parabola in (15a). If, on the other hand, z_1 is negative in Eq. (16), then the focal axis of the hyperbola is parallel to the x-axis, and its vertices lie on the parabola in (15b). Near the origin the surface is shaped like a saddle. To a person traveling along the surface in the yz-plane, the origin looks like a minimum. To a person traveling in the xz-plane, on the other hand, the origin looks like a maximum. Such a point is called a *minimax* or *saddle point* of a surface (Fig. 11–60). We shall discuss maximum and minimum points on surfaces in the next chapter.

If $a = b$ in Eq. (14), the surface is not a surface of revolution, but it is possible to express the equation in the alternative form

$$\frac{2x'y'}{a^2} = \frac{z}{c} \tag{17}$$

if we refer it to $x'y'$-axes obtained by rotating the xy-axes through 45°.

PROBLEMS

Describe and sketch each of the following surfaces [(r, θ, z) are cylindrical coordinates]. Complete the square, when necessary, to put the equation into one of the standard forms shown in the examples.

1. $x^2 + y^2 = z - 1$

2. $x^2 + y^2 + z^2 + 4x - 6y = 3$

3. $x^2 + 4y^2 + z^2 = 4$

4. $x^2 + 4y^2 + z^2 - 8y = 0$

5. $4x^2 + 4y^2 + 4z^2 - 8y = 0$

6. $x^2 - y^2 + z^2 + 4x - 6y = 9$

7. $x^2 - y^2 - z^2 + 4x - 6y = 9$

8. $z^2 = 4x$

9. $z^2 = 4xy$ **10.** $z = 4xy$

11. $z = r^2$ **12.** $z = r$

13. $z^2 = r$ **14.** $z^2 = x^2 + 4y^2$

15. $z^2 = x^2 - 4y^2$ **16.** $z^2 = 4y^2 - x^2$

17. $z^2 = x^2 + 4y^2 - 2x + 8y + 4z$

18. $z^2 = x^2 + 4y^2 - 2x + 8y + 4z + 1$

19. $x^2 + 4z^2 = 4$ **20.** $x = y^2 + 4z^2 + 1$

21. $z = r \cos \theta$ **22.** $z = r \sin \theta$

23. $z = \sin \theta \ (0 \le \theta \le \pi/2)$ **24.** $z = \cosh \theta \ (0 \le \theta \le \pi/2)$

25. (a) Express the area, $A(z_1)$, of the cross section cut from the ellipsoid

$$\frac{x^2}{a^2} + \frac{y^2}{b^2} + \frac{z^2}{c^2} = 1$$

by the plane $z = z_1$, as a function of z_1. (The area of an ellipse of semiaxes A and B is πAB.) (b) By integration, find the volume of the ellipsoid of part (a). Consider slices made by planes perpendicular to the z-axis. Does your answer give the correct volume of a sphere in case $a = b = c$?

26. By integration, prove that the volume of the segment of the elliptic paraboloid

$$\frac{x^2}{a^2} + \frac{y^2}{b^2} = \frac{z}{c}$$

cut off by the plane $z = h$ is equal to one-half the area of its base times its altitude.

27. Given the hyperboloid of one sheet of Eq. (10),

a) By integration, find the volume between the plane $z = 0$ and the plane $z = h$, enclosed by the hyperboloid.

b) Express your answer to (a) in terms of the altitude h and the areas A_0 and A_h of the plane ends of the segment of the hyperboloid.

c) Verify that the volume of (a) is also given exactly by the prismoid formula

$$V = h(A_0 + 4A_m + A_h)/6,$$

where A_0 and A_h are the areas of the plane ends of the segment of the hyperboloid and A_m is the area of its midsection cut out by the plane $z = h/2$.

28. If the hyperbolic paraboloid

$$\frac{y^2}{b^2} - \frac{x^2}{a^2} = \frac{z}{c}$$

is cut by the plane $y = y_1$, the resulting curve is a parabola. Find its vertex and focus.

29. What is the nature, in general, of a surface whose equation in spherical coordinates has the form $\rho = F(\phi)$? Give reasons for your answer.

Describe and sketch the following surfaces, which are special cases of Exercise 29.

30. $\rho = a \cos \phi$ **31.** $\rho = a(1 + \cos \phi)$

REVIEW QUESTIONS AND EXERCISES

1. When are two vectors equal?

2. How are two vectors added? Subtracted?

3. If a vector is multiplied by a scalar, how is the result related to the original vector? In your discussion include all possible values of the scalar: positive, negative, and zero.

4. In a single diagram, show the cartesian, cylindrical, and spherical coordinates of an arbitrary point P, and write the expressions for each set of coordinates in terms of the other two kinds.

5. What set in space is described by:

a) $x =$ constant, **b)** $r =$ constant,
c) $\theta =$ constant, **d)** $\rho =$ constant,
e) $\phi =$ constant, **f)** $ax + by + cz = d$,
g) $ax^2 + by^2 + cz^2 = d$?

6. What is the length of the vector $a\mathbf{i} + b\mathbf{j} + c\mathbf{k}$? On what theorem of plane geometry does this result depend?

7. Define *scalar product* of two vectors. Which algebraic laws (commutative, associative, distributive) are satisfied by the operations of addition and scalar multiplication of vectors? Which of these laws is (are) not satisfied? Explain. When is the scalar product equal to zero?

8. Suppose that $\mathbf{i}, \mathbf{j}, \mathbf{k}$ is one set of mutually orthogonal unit vectors and that $\mathbf{i}', \mathbf{j}', \mathbf{k}'$ is another set of such vectors. Suppose that all the scalar products of a unit vector from one set with a unit vector from the other set are known. Let

$$\mathbf{A} = a\mathbf{i} + b\mathbf{j} + c\mathbf{k} = a'\mathbf{i}' + b'\mathbf{j}' + c'\mathbf{k}'$$

and express a, b, c in terms of a', b', c'; and conversely. (Expressions involve $\mathbf{i} \cdot \mathbf{i}', \mathbf{i} \cdot \mathbf{j}', \mathbf{i} \cdot \mathbf{k}'$, and so forth.)

9. List four applications of the scalar product.

10. Define *vector product* of two vectors. Which algebraic laws (commutative, associative, distributive) are satisfied by the vector product operation (combined with addition), and which are not? Explain. When is the vector product equal to zero?

11. Derive the formula for expressing the vector product of two vectors as a determinant. What is the effect of interchanging the order of the two vectors and the corresponding rows of the determinant?

12. How may vector and scalar products be used to find the equation of a plane through three given points?

13. With the book closed, develop equations for a line

a) through two given points,
b) through one point and parallel to a given line.

14. With the book closed, develop the equation of a plane

a) through a given point and normal to a given vector,
b) through one point and parallel to a given plane,
c) through a point and perpendicular to each of two given planes.

15. What is the geometrical interpretation of

$$\mathbf{A} \cdot (\mathbf{B} \times \mathbf{C})?$$

When is this triple scalar product equal to zero?

16. What is the meaning of

a) $\mathbf{A} \times (\mathbf{B} \times \mathbf{C})$, **b)** $\mathbf{A} \times (\mathbf{B} \cdot \mathbf{C})$, **c)** $\mathbf{A} \cdot (\mathbf{B} \cdot \mathbf{C})$?

17. Given a parallelogram $PQRS$ in space, how could you find a vector normal to its plane and with length equal to its area?

18. What set in space is described by an equation of the form

a) $f(x, y) = 0$, **b)** $f(z, r) = 0$,
c) $z = f(\theta)$, $0 \le \theta \le 2\pi$?

19. Define *quadric surface*. Name and sketch six different quadric surfaces and indicate their equations.

MISCELLANEOUS PROBLEMS

In Exercises 1 through 10, find parametric equations of the path traced by the point $P(x, y)$ for the data given.

1. $\dfrac{dx}{dt} = x^2$, $\dfrac{dy}{dt} = x$; $t = 0, x = 1, y = 1$

2. $\frac{dx}{dt} = \cos^2 x, \quad \frac{dy}{dt} = x; \quad t = 0, x = \frac{\pi}{4}, y = 0$

3. $\frac{dx}{dt} = e^t, \quad \frac{dy}{dt} = xe^x; \quad t = 0, x = 1, y = 0$

4. $\frac{dx}{dt} = 6 \sin 2t, \quad \frac{dy}{dt} = 4 \cos 2t; \quad t = 0, x = 0, y = 4$

5. $\frac{dx}{dt} = 1 - \cos t, \quad \frac{dy}{dt} = \sin t; \quad t = 0, x = 0, y = 0$

6. $\frac{dx}{dt} = \sqrt{1 + y}, \quad \frac{dy}{dt} = y; \quad t = 0, x = 0, y = 1$

7. $\frac{dx}{dt} = \text{sech } x, \quad \frac{dy}{dt} = x; \quad t = 0, x = 0, y = 0$

8. $\frac{dx}{dt} = \cosh \frac{t}{2}, \quad \frac{dy}{dt} = x; \quad t = 0, x = 2, y = 0$

9. $\frac{dx}{dt} = y, \quad \frac{dy}{dt} = -x; \quad t = 0, x = 0, y = 4$

10. $\frac{d^2x}{dt^2} = -\frac{dx}{dt}, \quad \frac{dy}{dt} = x; \quad t = 0, x = 1, y = 1, \frac{dx}{dt} = 1$

11. A particle is projected with velocity v at an angle α to the horizontal from a point that is at the foot of a hill inclined at an angle ϕ to the horizontal, where

$$0 < \phi < \alpha < (\pi/2).$$

Show that it reaches the ground at a distance

$$\frac{2v^2 \cos \alpha}{g \cos^2 \phi} \sin (\alpha - \phi)$$

measured up the face of the hill. Hence show that the greatest range achieved for a given v is when $\alpha = (\phi/2) + (\pi/4)$.

12. A wheel of radius 4 in. rolls along the x-axis with angular velocity 2 rad/sec. Find the curve described by a point on a spoke and 2 in. from the center of the wheel if it starts from the point (0, 2) at time $t = 0$.

13. OA is the diameter of a circle of radius a. AN is tangent to the circle at A. A line through O making angle θ with diameter OA intersects the circle at M and tangent line at N. On ON a point P is located so that $OP = MN$. Taking O as origin, OA along the y-axis, and angle θ as parameter, find parametric equations of the locus described by P.

14. Let a line AB be the x-axis of a system of rectangular coordinates. Let the point C be the point (0, 1). Let the line DE through C intersect AB at F. Let P and P' be the points on DE such that $PF = P'F = a$. Express the coordinates of P and P' in terms of the angle $\theta = \angle CFB$.

15. For the curve

$$x = a(t - \sin t), \qquad y = a(1 - \cos t),$$

find the following quantities.

a) The area bounded by the x-axis and one loop of the curve

b) The length of one loop

c) The area of the surface of revolution obtained by rotating one loop about the x-axis

d) The coordinates of the centroid of the area in (a).

16. In Fig. 11–61, D is the midpoint of side AB and E is one-third of the way between C and B. *Using vectors*, prove that F is midpoint of the line CD.

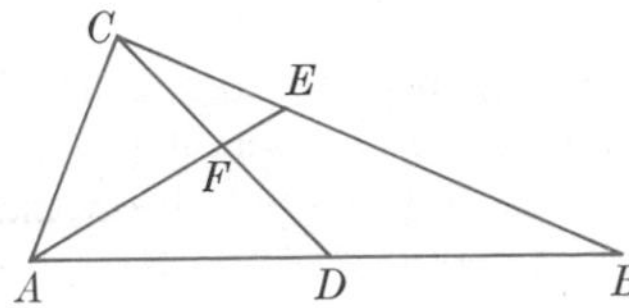

Figure 11–61

17. The vectors $2\mathbf{i} + 3\mathbf{j}$, $4\mathbf{i} + \mathbf{j}$, and $5\mathbf{i} + y\mathbf{j}$ have their initial points at the origin. Find the value of y so that the vectors terminate on one straight line.

18. $\mathbf{A}$ and $\mathbf{B}$ are vectors from the origin to the two points A and B. The point P is determined by the vector $\overrightarrow{OP} = x\mathbf{A} + y\mathbf{B}$, where x and y are positive quantities, neither of which is zero, and whose sum is equal to one. Prove that P lies on the line segment AB.

19. Using vector methods, prove that the segment joining the midpoints of two sides of a triangle is parallel to, and half the length of, the third side.

20. Let ABC be a triangle and let M be the midpoint of AB. Let P be the point on CM that is two-thirds of the way from C to M. Let O be any point in space.

a) Show that

$$\overrightarrow{OP} = \left(\frac{\overrightarrow{OA} + \overrightarrow{OB} + \overrightarrow{OC}}{3}\right).$$

b) Show how the result in (a) leads to the conclusion that the medians of a triangle meet in a point.

21. A, B, C are the vertices of a triangle and a, b, c are the midpoints of the opposite sides. Show that

$$\overrightarrow{Aa} + \overrightarrow{Bb} + \overrightarrow{Cc} = \mathbf{0}.$$

Interpret the result geometrically.

22. Vectors are drawn from the center of a regular polygon to its vertices. Show that their sum is zero.

23. Let $\mathbf{A}$, $\mathbf{B}$, $\mathbf{C}$ be vectors from a common point O to points A, B, C.

a) If A, B, C are collinear, show that three constants x, y, z (not all zero) exist such that

$$x + y + z = 0 \qquad \text{and} \qquad x\mathbf{A} + y\mathbf{B} + z\mathbf{C} = \mathbf{0}.$$

b) Conversely, if three constants x, y, z (not all zero) exist such that

$$x + y + z = 0 \quad \text{and} \quad x\mathbf{A} + y\mathbf{B} + z\mathbf{C} = \mathbf{0},$$

show that A, B, C are collinear.

24. Find the vector projection of **B** onto **A** if

$$\mathbf{A} = 3\mathbf{i} - \mathbf{j} + \mathbf{k}, \quad \mathbf{B} = 2\mathbf{i} + \mathbf{j} - 2\mathbf{k}.$$

25. Find the cosine of the angle between the line

$$\frac{1 - x}{4} = \frac{y}{3} = -\frac{z}{5}$$

and the vector $\mathbf{i} + \mathbf{j}$.

26. Given two noncollinear vectors **A** and **B**. Given also that **A** can be expressed in the form $\mathbf{A} = \mathbf{C} + \mathbf{D}$, where **C** is a vector parallel to **B**, and **D** is a vector perpendicular to **B**. Express **C** and **D** in terms of **A** and **B**.

27. The curve whose vector equation is

$$\mathbf{r} = (t^4 + 2t^2 + 1)\mathbf{i} + (1 + 4t - t^4)\mathbf{j}$$

intersects the line $x + y = 0$, $z = 0$. Find the cosine of the angle which the acceleration vector makes with the radius vector at the point of intersection.

28. *Using vectors*, prove that for any four numbers a, b, c, d we have the inequality

$$(a^2 + b^2)(c^2 + d^2) \geq (ac + bd)^2.$$

(*Hint*. Consider $\mathbf{A} = a\mathbf{i} + b\mathbf{j}$ and $\mathbf{B} = c\mathbf{i} + d\mathbf{j}$.)

29. Find a vector parallel to the plane $2x - y - z = 4$ and perpendicular to the vector $\mathbf{i} + \mathbf{j} + \mathbf{k}$.

30. Find a vector which is normal to the plane determined by the points

$$A(1, 0, -1), \quad B(2, -1, 1), \quad C(-1, 1, 2).$$

31. Given vectors

$$\mathbf{A} = 2\mathbf{i} - \mathbf{j} + \mathbf{k},$$
$$\mathbf{B} = \mathbf{i} + 2\mathbf{j} - \mathbf{k},$$
$$\mathbf{C} = \mathbf{i} + \mathbf{j} - 2\mathbf{k},$$

find a *unit* vector in the plane of **B** and **C** that is $\perp$**A**.

32. By forming the cross product of two appropriate vectors, derive the trigonometric identity

$$\sin(\alpha - \beta) = \sin\alpha\cos\beta - \cos\alpha\sin\beta.$$

33. Find a vector of *length two* parallel to the line

$$x + 2y + z - 1 = 0, \quad x - y + 2z + 7 = 0.$$

34. Given a tetrahedron with vertices O, A, B, C. A vector is constructed normal to each face, pointing outwards, and having a length equal to the area of the face. Using cross products, prove that the sum of these four outward normals is the zero vector.

35. What angle does the line of intersection of the two planes

$$2x + y - z = 0, \quad x + y + 2z = 0$$

make with the x-axis?

36. Let **A** and **C** be given vectors in space, with $\mathbf{A} \neq \mathbf{0}$ and $\mathbf{A} \cdot \mathbf{C} = 0$, and let d be a given scalar. Find a vector **B** that satisfies both equations $\mathbf{A} \times \mathbf{B} = \mathbf{C}$ and $\mathbf{A} \cdot \mathbf{B} = d$ simultaneously. The answer should be given as a formula involving **A**, **C**, and d.

37. Given any two vectors

$$\mathbf{A} = a_1\mathbf{i} + a_2\mathbf{j}, \quad \mathbf{B} = b_1\mathbf{i} + b_2\mathbf{j}$$

in the plane, define a new vector, $\mathbf{A} \otimes \mathbf{B}$, called their "circle product," as follows:

$$\mathbf{A} \otimes \mathbf{B} = (a_1 b_1 - a_2 b_2)\mathbf{i} + (a_1 b_2 + a_2 b_1)\mathbf{j}.$$

This product satisfies the following algebraic laws.

a) $\mathbf{A} \otimes \mathbf{B} = \mathbf{B} \otimes \mathbf{A}$
b) $\mathbf{A} \otimes (\mathbf{B} \otimes \mathbf{C}) = (\mathbf{A} \otimes \mathbf{B}) \otimes \mathbf{C}$
c) $\mathbf{A} \otimes (\mathbf{B} + \mathbf{C}) = (\mathbf{A} \otimes \mathbf{B}) + (\mathbf{A} \oplus \mathbf{C})$
d) $|\mathbf{A} \otimes \mathbf{B}| = |\mathbf{A}|\,|\mathbf{B}|$

Prove (a) and (d).

38. Find the equations of the straight line that passes through the point (1, 2, 3) and makes an angle of 30° with the x-axis and an angle of 60° with the y-axis.

39. The line L, whose equations are

$$x - 2z - 3 = 0, \quad y - 2z = 0,$$

intersects the plane

$$x + 3y - z + 4 = 0.$$

Find the point of intersection P and find the equation of that line in this plane that passes through P and is perpendicular to L.

40. Find the distance between the point (2, 2, 3) and the plane $2x + 3y + 5z = 0$.

41. Given the two parallel planes

$$Ax + By + Cz + D_1 = 0, \quad Ax + By + Cz + D_2 = 0,$$

show that the distance between them is given by the formula

$$\frac{|D_1 - D_2|}{|A\mathbf{i} + B\mathbf{j} + C\mathbf{k}|}.$$

42. Consider the straight line through the point (3, 2, 1) and perpendicular to the plane

$$2x - y + 2z + 2 = 0.$$

Compute the coordinates of the point of intersection of that line and that plane.

43. Find the distance between the point (2, 2, 0) and the line

$$x + y = 0, \qquad y - z = 1.$$

44. Find an equation of the plane parallel to the plane $2x - y + 2z + 4 = 0$ if the point $(3, 2, -1)$ is equidistant from both planes.

45. Given the four points

$$A = (-2, 0, -3),$$
$$B = (1, -2, 1),$$
$$C = (-2, -\tfrac{13}{5}, \tfrac{26}{5}),$$
$$D = (\tfrac{16}{5}, -\tfrac{13}{5}, 0).$$

a) Find the equation of the plane through AB that is parallel to CD.
b) Compute the shortest distance between the lines AB and CD.

46. The three vectors

$$\mathbf{A} = 3\mathbf{i} - \mathbf{j} + \mathbf{k},$$
$$\mathbf{B} = \mathbf{i} + 2\mathbf{j} - \mathbf{k},$$
$$\mathbf{C} = \mathbf{i} + \mathbf{j} + \mathbf{k},$$

are all drawn from the origin. Find an equation for the plane through their endpoints.

47. Show that the plane through the three points

$$(x_1, y_1, z_1), \qquad (x_2, y_2, z_2), \qquad (x_3, y_3, z_3)$$

is given by

$$\begin{vmatrix} x_1 - x & y_1 - y & z_1 - z \\ x_2 - x & y_2 - y & z_2 - z \\ x_3 - x & y_3 - y & z_3 - z \end{vmatrix} = 0.$$

48. Given the two straight lines

$$x = a_1 t + b_1, \qquad y = a_2 t + b_2, \qquad z = a_3 t + b_3,$$
$$x = c_1 \tau + d_1, \qquad y = c_2 \tau + d_2, \qquad z = c_3 \tau + d_3,$$

where t and τ are parameters. Show that the necessary and sufficient condition that the two lines either intersect or are parallel is

$$\begin{vmatrix} a_1 & c_1 & b_1 - d_1 \\ a_2 & c_2 & b_2 - d_2 \\ a_3 & c_3 & b_3 - d_3 \end{vmatrix} = 0.$$

49. Given the vectors

$$\mathbf{A} = \mathbf{i} + \mathbf{j} - \mathbf{k},$$
$$\mathbf{B} = 2\mathbf{i} + \mathbf{j} + \mathbf{k},$$
$$\mathbf{C} = -\mathbf{i} - 2\mathbf{j} + 3\mathbf{k},$$

evaluate

a) $\mathbf{A} \cdot (\mathbf{B} \times \mathbf{C})$, **b)** $\mathbf{A} \times (\mathbf{B} \times \mathbf{C})$.

50. Given four points

$$A = (1, 1, 1),$$
$$B = (0, 0, 2),$$
$$C = (0, 3, 0),$$
$$D = (4, 0, 0),$$

find the volume of the tetrahedron with vertices at A, B, C, D, and find the angle between the edges AB and AC.

51. Prove or disprove the formula

$$\mathbf{A} \times [\mathbf{A} \times (\mathbf{A} \times \mathbf{B})] \cdot \mathbf{C} = -|\mathbf{A}|^2 \mathbf{A} \cdot \mathbf{B} \times \mathbf{C}.$$

52. If the four vectors **A**, **B**, **C**, **D** are coplanar, show that

$$(\mathbf{A} \times \mathbf{B}) \times (\mathbf{C} \times \mathbf{D}) = \mathbf{0}.$$

53. Prove the following identities, in which **i**, **j**, **k** are three mutually perpendicular unit vectors, and **A**, **B**, **C** are any vectors.

a) $\mathbf{A} \times (\mathbf{B} \times \mathbf{C}) + \mathbf{B} \times (\mathbf{C} \times \mathbf{A}) + \mathbf{C} \times (\mathbf{A} \times \mathbf{B}) = \mathbf{0}$.
b) $\mathbf{A} \times \mathbf{B} = [\mathbf{A} \cdot (\mathbf{B} \times \mathbf{i})]\mathbf{i} + [\mathbf{A} \cdot (\mathbf{B} \times \mathbf{j})]\mathbf{j} + [\mathbf{A} \cdot (\mathbf{B} \times \mathbf{k})]\mathbf{k}$.

54. Show that

$$(\mathbf{a} \times \mathbf{b}) \cdot (\mathbf{c} \times \mathbf{d}) = \begin{vmatrix} \mathbf{a} \cdot \mathbf{c} & \mathbf{b} \cdot \mathbf{c} \\ \mathbf{a} \cdot \mathbf{d} & \mathbf{b} \cdot \mathbf{d} \end{vmatrix}.$$

55. Sketch the surfaces

a) $(x - 1)^2 + 4(y^2 + z^2) = 16$,
b) $z = r^2$ (cylindrical coordinates),
c) $\rho = a \sin \phi$ (spherical coordinates).

56. Find an equation for the set of points in space whose distance from the point $(2, -1, 3)$ is twice their distance from the xy-plane. Name the surface and find its center of symmetry.

57. Find an equation of the sphere that has the two planes

$$x + y + z - 3 = 0, \qquad x + y + z - 9 = 0$$

as tangent planes, if the two planes

$$2x - y = 0, \qquad 3x - z = 0$$

pass through the center of the sphere.

58. The two cylinders $z^3 - x = 0$ and $x^2 - y = 0$ intersect in a curve C. Find an equation of a cylinder parallel to the x-axis which passes through C. This cylinder traces out a curve C' in the yz-plane. Rotate C' about the y-axis and obtain the equation of the surface so generated.

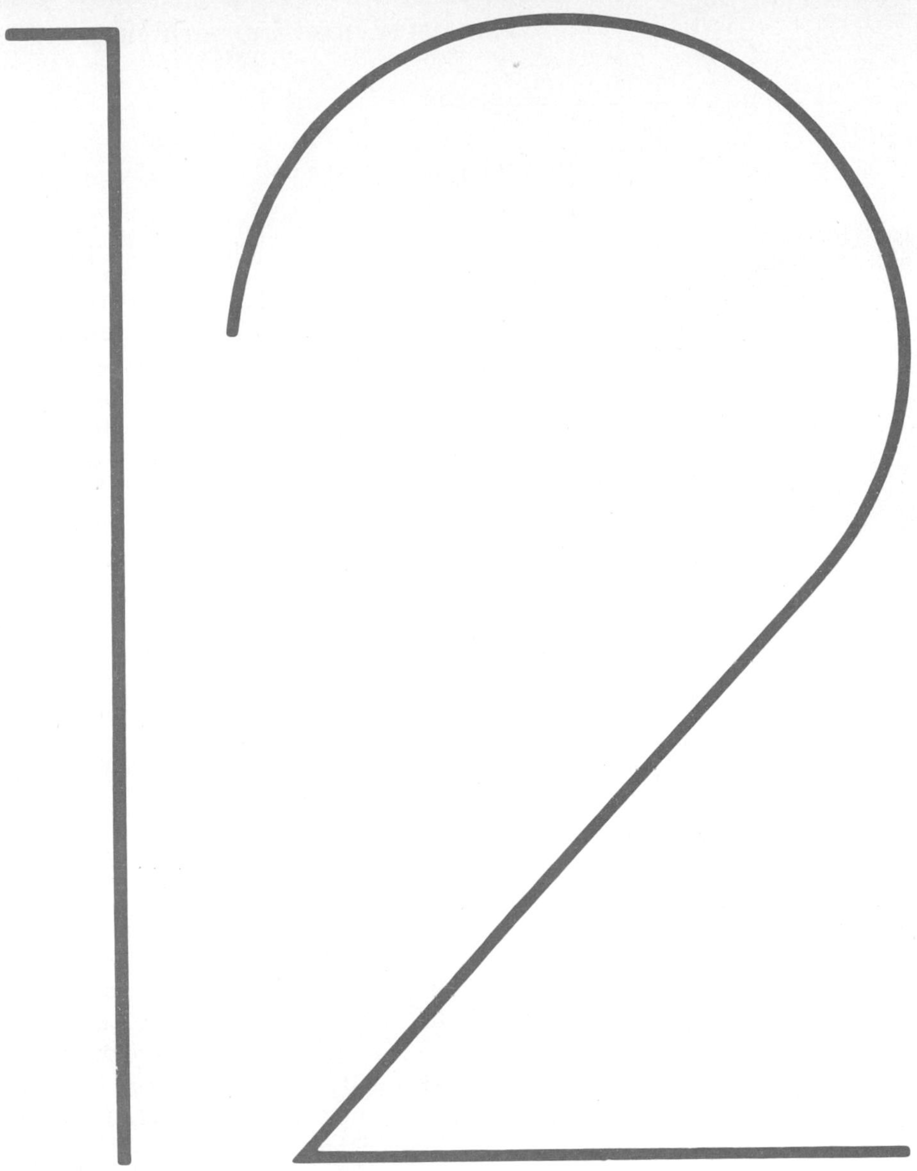

12 VECTOR FUNCTIONS AND THEIR DERIVATIVES

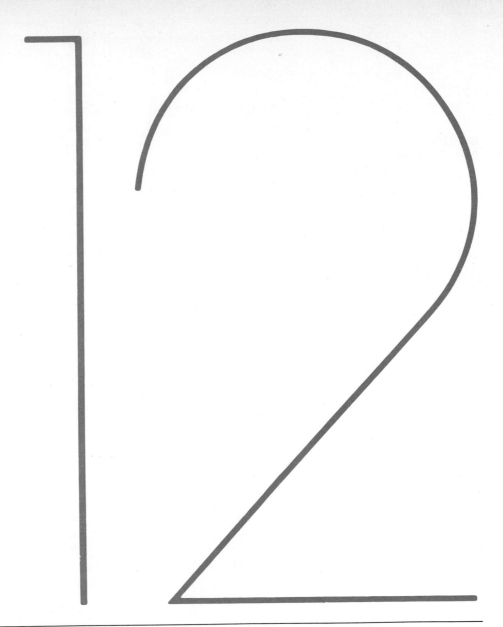

12–1 INTRODUCTION

Let **i**, **j**, and **k** be the unit vectors along the x-, y-, and z-axes in space. Then a function

$$\mathbf{F}(t) = \mathbf{i}x(t) + \mathbf{j}y(t) + \mathbf{k}z(t), \tag{1}$$

where $x(t)$, $y(t)$, and $z(t)$ are real-valued functions of the real variable t, is a vector function of t. We shall be interested primarily in using such functions to describe the motion of a particle in space or the plane. When the motion is in the plane, we shall ordinarily assume that coordinates are chosen to make the plane of motion the xy-plane. This allows us to consider motion in the xy-plane as a special case of motion in space, the special condition being that the z-coordinate of the particle is zero.

EXAMPLE 1. The position of a particle in the xy-plane at time t is given by

$$x = e^t, \qquad y = te^t.$$

Let

$$\mathbf{R}(t) = \mathbf{i}x + \mathbf{j}y = \mathbf{i}e^t + \mathbf{j}te^t.$$

Where is the particle at time $t = 0$, and how fast is it moving and in what direction?

Solution. At $t = 0$, we have $x = 1$ and $y = 0$, so

$$\mathbf{R}(0) = \mathbf{i}.$$

This is the vector from the origin to the position of the particle at time $t = 0$. Next, how can we find the speed and direction of motion? If you have studied particle mechanics from a vector viewpoint, then you probably know the answer. If not, think where the particle might be a short time after $t = 0$: Both x and y will have increased somewhat, and there will be a vector to the new position. The vector between the two positions is

$$\Delta\mathbf{R} = \mathbf{i}\,\Delta x + \mathbf{j}\,\Delta y.$$

For a small Δt, this vector gives, approximately, the direction of motion. Also, $|\Delta\mathbf{R}/\Delta t|$ gives the speed, approximately. Now for small values of Δt, we know that

$$\Delta x \approx \frac{dx}{dt}\Delta t \qquad \text{and} \qquad \Delta y \approx \frac{dy}{dt}\Delta t.$$

Therefore

$$\Delta\mathbf{R} \approx \mathbf{i}\frac{dx}{dt}\Delta t + \mathbf{j}\frac{dy}{dt}\Delta t = \left(\mathbf{i}\frac{dx}{dt} + \mathbf{j}\frac{dy}{dt}\right)\Delta t,$$

which leads to the conclusion that

$$\frac{\Delta\mathbf{R}}{\Delta t} \approx \mathbf{i}\frac{dx}{dt} + \mathbf{j}\frac{dy}{dt}.$$

From this line of reasoning (which we shall make more precise in the next article), it seems reasonable to use

$$\mathbf{i}\frac{dx}{dt} + \mathbf{j}\frac{dy}{dt} = \mathbf{i}(e^t) + \mathbf{j}(te^t + e^t),$$

evaluated at $t = 0$, as the vector whose magnitude gives the speed, and whose direction gives the direction of motion at the instant $t = 0$. The vector is $\mathbf{i} + \mathbf{j}$, so

$$\text{Speed} = |\mathbf{i} + \mathbf{j}| = \sqrt{2},$$

$$\text{Direction} = \frac{\mathbf{i} + \mathbf{j}}{\sqrt{2}}.$$

Naturally, the vector $\mathbf{i} + \mathbf{j}$ is called the *velocity vector* at $t = 0$. Its components are just the derivatives of the components of the *position vector* $\mathbf{R} = \overrightarrow{OP}$ at $t = 0$. (See Fig. 12–1.)

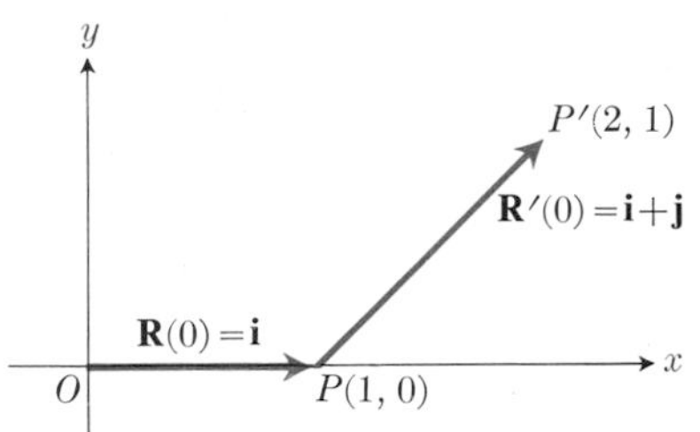

12–1 At $t = 0$, the position vector of the motion described in Example 1 is $\mathbf{R} = \mathbf{i}$, and the velocity vector is $\mathbf{R}' = \mathbf{i} + \mathbf{j}$.

REMARK. It is clear that we shall want to define the derivative of a vector function $\mathbf{R}(t)$. This in turn means that we need to define a limit such as

$$\lim_{h \to a} \mathbf{F}(h),$$

where $\mathbf{F}(h)$ is a *vector function* of h. For this definition, we assume that

$$\mathbf{F}(t) = \mathbf{i}f_1(t) + \mathbf{j}f_2(t) + \mathbf{k}f_3(t),$$

where each of the components $f_1(t)$, $f_2(t)$, and $f_3(t)$ is a function whose domain includes all points of some open interval about a, except perhaps the point a itself. We then restrict h to lie in the intersection of these open intervals, and say that $\mathbf{F}$ has a limit, as $h \to a$, if and only if each component of $\mathbf{F}$ has a limit. If, as $h \to a$,

$$\lim f_1(t) = L_1, \qquad \lim f_2(t) = L_2, \qquad \lim f_3(t) = L_3, \tag{2a}$$

then we *define the limit* of $\mathbf{F}(h)$ to be

$$\lim_{h \to a} \mathbf{F}(h) = \mathbf{i}L_1 + \mathbf{j}L_2 + \mathbf{k}L_3. \tag{2b}$$

EXAMPLE 2. Let

$$\mathbf{F}(h) = \mathbf{i}e^h + \mathbf{j}\left(\frac{\sin h}{h}\right).$$

Then, as $h \to 0$,

$$\lim e^h = e^0 = 1, \qquad \lim \frac{\sin h}{h} = 1,$$

and

$$\lim_{h \to 0} \mathbf{F}(h) = \mathbf{i} + \mathbf{j}.$$

Continuity

The vector function **F** is *continuous* at a if and only if each of its components is continuous there. This is equivalent to the ϵ, δ-requirement stated in the following definition.

Definition. *The vector function* $\mathbf{F}(t) = \mathbf{i}f_1(t) + \mathbf{j}f_2(t) + \mathbf{k}f_3(t)$ *is said to be continuous at* $h = a$ *if and only if, to each* $\epsilon > 0$, *there corresponds a* $\delta > 0$ *such that*

$$|\mathbf{F}(h) - \mathbf{F}(a)| < \epsilon \quad \text{when} \quad |h - a| < \delta. \tag{3}$$

The following inequalities enable us to show that this is equivalent to the continuity, at $h = a$, of every component of **F**:

$$\begin{aligned} |f_i(h) - f_i(a)| &= \sqrt{[f_i(h) - f_i(a)]^2} \\ &\leq \sqrt{[f_1(h) - f_1(a)]^2 + [f_2(h) - f_2(a)]^2 + [f_3(h) - f_3(a)]^2} \qquad (4) \\ &= |\mathbf{F}(h) - \mathbf{F}(a)|; \end{aligned}$$

$$\begin{aligned} |\mathbf{F}(h) - \mathbf{F}(a)| &= \sqrt{[f_1(h) - f_1(a)]^2 + [f_2(h) - f_2(a)]^2 + [f_3(h) - f_3(a)]^2} \\ &\leq |f_1(h) - f_1(a)| + |f_2(h) - f_2(a)| + |f_3(h) - f_3(a)|. \end{aligned} \tag{5}$$

The first inequality holds in turn for each component $f_i = f_1, f_2$, and f_3, because the summands under the radical are all nonnegative, so their sum is greater than or equal to any one of them. The second inequality is of the form

$$\sqrt{a^2 + b^2 + c^2} \leq |a| + |b| + |c|. \tag{6}$$

The latter inequality can be proved by squaring both sides and then taking square roots.

Now let us suppose that each component of **F** is a continuous function at $h = a$. Then, given $\epsilon > 0$, there corresponds to each integer $j = 1, 2, 3$, a positive number δ_j such that

$$|f_j(h) - f_j(a)| < \epsilon/3 \quad \text{when} \quad |h - a| < \delta_j.$$

If $\delta = \min\{\delta_1, \delta_2, \delta_3\}$, then each term in the summation in (5) is less than $\epsilon/3$ when $|h - a| < \delta$, so their sum is less than ϵ, and condition (3) is satisfied. Conversely, suppose that we had started with condition (3). Then the inequality in (4) would give

$$|f_i(h) - f_i(a)| < \epsilon \quad \text{when} \quad |h - a| < \delta;$$

hence f_i is continuous at $h = a$ for any i from 1 through 3.

Working rule. A vector function is continuous at a point of its domain at which *all* of its components are continuous.

Derivative of a Vector Function

We shall define the derivative of **F** by the same type of limit equation we use for scalar functions:

$$\mathbf{F}'(c) = \lim_{h \to 0} \frac{\mathbf{F}(c+h) - \mathbf{F}(c)}{h}, \tag{7}$$

provided that this limit exists. The following theorem provides a statement of the necessary and sufficient condition.

Theorem. *Let*

$$\mathbf{F}(t) = \mathbf{i} f_1(t) + \mathbf{j} f_2(t) + \mathbf{k} f_3(t)$$

be a vector function whose component functions are defined in some neighborhood of c. Then **F** *is differentiable at c if and only if each of its components is differentiable there. If this condition is met, then*

$$\mathbf{F}'(c) = \mathbf{i} f'_1(c) + \mathbf{j} f'_2(c) + \mathbf{k} f'_3(c). \tag{8}$$

Proof. The difference quotient we need to consider is

$$\frac{\mathbf{F}(c+h) - \mathbf{F}(c)}{h} = \mathbf{i}\left(\frac{f_1(c+h) - f_1(c)}{h}\right) + \mathbf{j}\left(\frac{f_2(c+h) - f_2(c)}{h}\right) + \mathbf{k}\left(\frac{f_3(c+h) - f_3(c)}{h}\right). \tag{9}$$

The left side of this equation has a limit if and only if each component on the right side has a limit, as $h \to 0$. The ith component on the right has a limit if and only if f_i is differentiable at c. If each component is differentiable at c, then, as $h \to 0$ and we pass to the limit in Eq. (9), we get Eq. (8). This concludes the proof.

EXAMPLE 3. At what values of t is the vector function

$$\mathbf{F}(t) = \mathbf{i} \sin t + \mathbf{j} \ln t + \mathbf{k} \tan^{-1} 3t$$

differentiable, and what is its derivative at these values?

Solution. The first component, $\sin t$, is everywhere differentiable, and its derivative is $\cos t$. The second component, $\ln t$, is differentiable for $t > 0$, and its derivative is $1/t$. The third component, $\tan^{-1} 3t$, is everywhere differentiable, and its derivative is

$$\frac{3}{(1 + 9t^2)}.$$

Hence the vector function is differentiable for $t > 0$, and its derivative is

$$\mathbf{F}'(t) = \mathbf{i} \cos t + \mathbf{j}\frac{1}{t} + \mathbf{k}\left(\frac{3}{1 + 9t^2}\right), \qquad t > 0.$$

PROBLEMS

In Problems 1 through 5, find the derivative of the given vector function and state the domain of the derived function.

1. $\mathbf{i}e^{2t} + \mathbf{j}te^{-t}$

2. $\mathbf{i} \ln \sqrt{1+t} + \mathbf{j}\sqrt{1-t^2}$

3. $\mathbf{i} \sin^{-1} 2t + \mathbf{j} \tan 3t + \mathbf{k}\left(\frac{1}{t}\right)$

4. $\mathbf{i} \sec^{-1} 3x + \mathbf{j} \cosh 2x + \mathbf{k} \tanh 4x$

5. $\mathbf{i}\left(\frac{2t-1}{2t+1}\right) + \mathbf{j} \ln (1 - 4t^2)$

6. Show that the inequality $\sqrt{a^2 + b^2 + c^2} \leq |a| + |b| + |c|$ holds for any real numbers a, b, and c.

12–2 VELOCITY AND ACCELERATION

We shall be interested in applications of vectors to problems in physics. For applications to *statics*, we need only a knowledge of the *algebra* of vectors. But for applications to *dynamics*, we also require a knowledge of the *calculus* of vectors. In this article we shall study motion of a particle in a plane, for simplicity, but most of the ideas can easily be extended to motion in space.

Position Vector

Suppose the point P moves along a curve in the xy-plane, and suppose we know its position at any time t. This means that the motion of P is described by a pair of functions f and g:

$$x = f(t), \qquad y = g(t). \tag{1}$$

The vector from the origin to P is customarily called the *position vector* of P, although it might be appropriate to call it the "radar" vector. This vector is a function of t given by

$$\mathbf{R} = \mathbf{i}x + \mathbf{j}y, \tag{2a}$$

or

$$\mathbf{R} = \mathbf{i}f(t) + \mathbf{j}g(t). \tag{2b}$$

Velocity Vector

We now ask what physical meaning we might attach to the *derivative* of $\mathbf{R}$ with respect to t. Mathematically, we have already *defined* the derivative to be

$$\frac{d\mathbf{R}}{dt} = \lim_{\Delta t \to 0} \frac{\Delta \mathbf{R}}{\Delta t}, \tag{3}$$

where $\mathbf{R}$ is given by (2a) and

$$\mathbf{R} + \Delta\mathbf{R} = \mathbf{i}(x + \Delta x) + \mathbf{j}(y + \Delta y). \tag{4}$$

Here $P(x, y)$ represents the position of the particle at time t, while $Q(x + \Delta x, y + \Delta y)$ gives its position at time $t + \Delta t$. By subtracting (2a) from (4), we obtain

$$\Delta\mathbf{R} = \mathbf{i}\,\Delta x + \mathbf{j}\,\Delta y, \tag{5}$$

which is the vector $\overrightarrow{PQ}$ in Fig. 12–2. The remaining calculations needed to give $d\mathbf{R}/dt$ proceed as follows:

$$\frac{\Delta \mathbf{R}}{\Delta t} = \mathbf{i}\frac{\Delta x}{\Delta t} + \mathbf{j}\frac{\Delta y}{\Delta t},$$

$$\lim_{\Delta t \to 0} \frac{\Delta \mathbf{R}}{\Delta t} = \lim_{\Delta t \to 0} \left(\mathbf{i}\frac{\Delta x}{\Delta t} + \mathbf{j}\frac{\Delta y}{\Delta t}\right)$$

$$= \mathbf{i} \lim_{\Delta t \to 0} \frac{\Delta x}{\Delta t} + \mathbf{j} \lim_{\Delta t \to 0} \frac{\Delta y}{\Delta t},$$

$$\frac{d\mathbf{R}}{dt} = \mathbf{i}\frac{dx}{dt} + \mathbf{j}\frac{dy}{dt}. \tag{6}$$

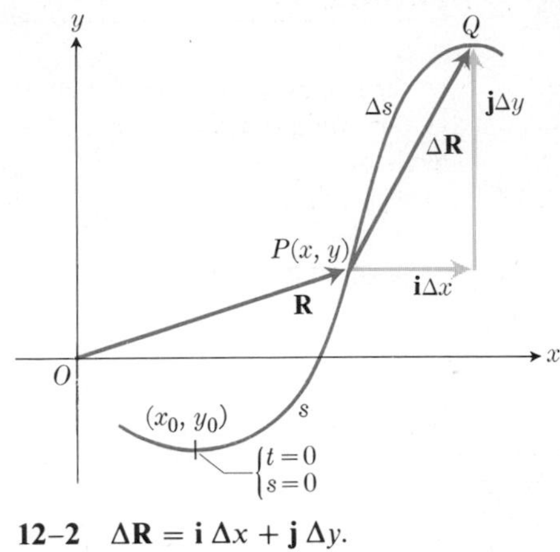

12–2 $\Delta \mathbf{R} = \mathbf{i}\,\Delta x + \mathbf{j}\,\Delta y$.

The result (6) is equivalent to what would be obtained by differentiating both sides of (2a) with respect to t, holding **i** and **j** constant. The geometric significance of (6) may be learned by calculating the slope and the magnitude of $d\mathbf{R}/dt$:

$$\text{Slope of } \frac{d\mathbf{R}}{dt} = \frac{\text{rise}}{\text{run}} = \frac{dy/dt}{dx/dt} = \frac{dy}{dx},$$

$$\text{Magnitude of } \frac{d\mathbf{R}}{dt} = \left|\frac{d\mathbf{R}}{dt}\right| = \left|\mathbf{i}\frac{dx}{dt} + \mathbf{j}\frac{dy}{dt}\right| \tag{7}$$

$$= \sqrt{\left(\frac{dx}{dt}\right)^2 + \left(\frac{dy}{dt}\right)^2} = \left|\frac{ds}{dt}\right|.$$

Here s represents arc length along the curve measured from some starting point (x_0, y_0).

If we draw a vector equal to $d\mathbf{R}/dt$, placing its initial point at P, the resulting vector will

a) be tangent to the curve at P, since its slope equals dy/dx, which is the same as the slope of the curve at P, and

b) have magnitude $= |ds/dt|$, which gives the instantaneous speed of the particle at P.

Thus, the vector $d\mathbf{R}/dt$, when drawn from P, is a suitable representation of the *velocity vector*, which has the same two properties (a) and (b).

In short, if we differentiate the position vector

$$\mathbf{R} = \mathbf{i}x + \mathbf{j}y$$

with respect to time, we get the *velocity vector*

$$\mathbf{v} = \frac{d\mathbf{R}}{dt} = \mathbf{i}\frac{dx}{dt} + \mathbf{j}\frac{dy}{dt}.$$

It is customary to draw the velocity vector at the point P (Fig. 12–3).

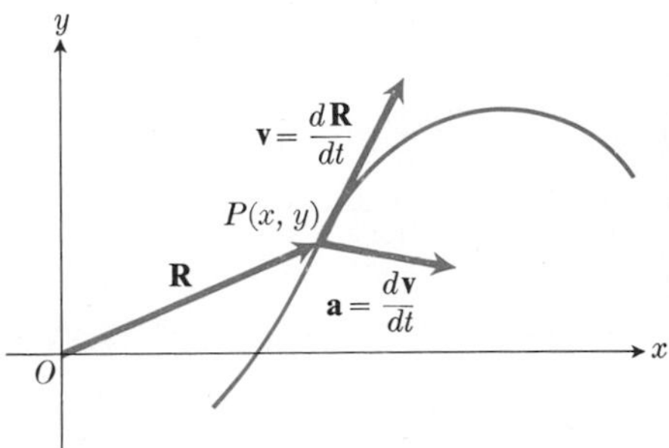

12–3 Typical position (**R**), velocity (**v**), and acceleration (**a**) vectors of a particle moving from left to right on a plane curve.

Acceleration

The acceleration vector **a** is obtained from **v** by a further differentiation:

$$\mathbf{a} = \frac{d\mathbf{v}}{dt} = \mathbf{i}\frac{d^2x}{dt^2} + \mathbf{j}\frac{d^2y}{dt^2}. \tag{8}$$

For a particle of constant mass m moving under the action of an applied force **F**, Newton's second law of motion states that

$$\mathbf{F} = m\mathbf{a}. \tag{9}$$

Since one ordinarily visualizes the force vector as being *applied at P*, it is customary to adopt the same viewpoint about the acceleration vector **a** (Fig. 12–3).

EXAMPLE 1. A particle $P(x, y)$ moves on the hyperbola

$$x = r \cosh \omega t, \qquad y = r \sinh \omega t, \tag{10}$$

where r and ω are positive constants. Then

$$\mathbf{R} = \mathbf{i}(r \cosh \omega t) + \mathbf{j}(r \sinh \omega t),$$

$$\mathbf{v} = \frac{d\mathbf{R}}{dt} = \mathbf{i}(\omega r \sinh \omega t) + \mathbf{j}(\omega r \cosh \omega t)$$

and

$$\mathbf{a} = \mathbf{i}(\omega^2 r \cosh \omega t) + \mathbf{j}(\omega^2 r \sinh \omega t)$$
$$= \omega^2 \mathbf{R}.$$

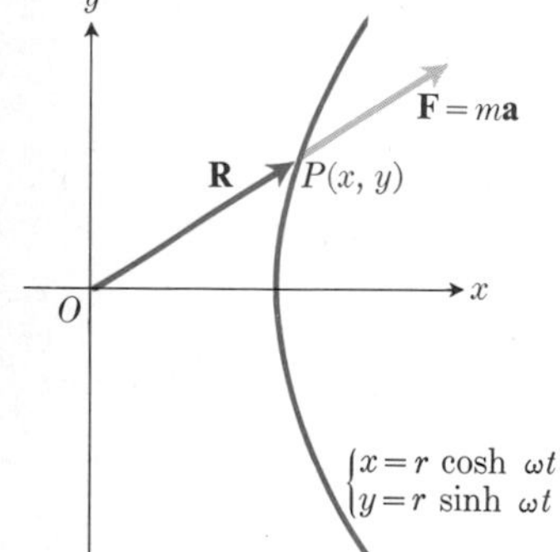

12–4 The force acting on the particle of Example 1 points directly away from O at all times.

This means that the force $\mathbf{F} = m\mathbf{a} = m\omega^2\mathbf{R}$ has a magnitude $m\omega^2|\mathbf{R}| = m\omega^2|\overrightarrow{OP}|$ which is directly proportional to the distance OP, and that its direction is the same as the direction of **R**. Thus the force is directed away from O (Fig. 12–4).

The next example illustrates how we obtain the path of motion by integrating Eq. (9) when the force **F** is a given function of time, and the initial position and initial velocity of the particle are given. In general, the force **F** may depend upon the position of P as well as upon the time, and the problem of integrating the differential equations so obtained is usually discussed in textbooks on that subject. [For example, see Martin and Reissner, *Elementary Differential Equations*, Addison-Wesley, 1961.]

EXAMPLE 2. (Fig. 12–5.) The force acting on a particle P of mass m is given as a function of t by

$$\mathbf{F} = \mathbf{i} \cos t + \mathbf{j} \sin t.$$

If the particle starts at the point $(c, 0)$ with initial velocity $v_0\mathbf{j}$, find its path.

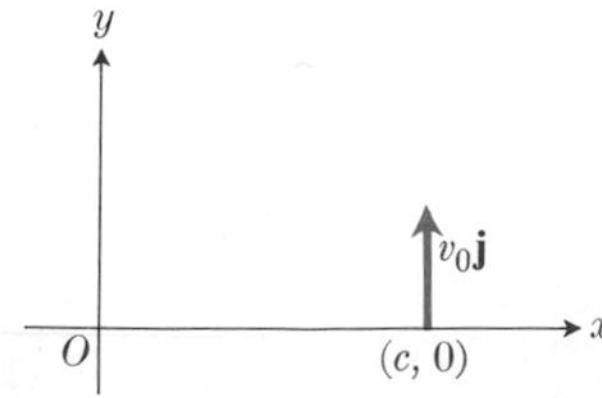

12–5 The particle of Example 2 leaves the x-axis with an initial velocity $v_0\mathbf{j}$.

Solution. If we denote the position vector by

$$\mathbf{R} = \mathbf{i}x + \mathbf{j}y,$$

we may restate the problem as follows. Find **R** if

$$\mathbf{F} = m\frac{d^2\mathbf{R}}{dt^2} = \mathbf{i}\cos t + \mathbf{j}\sin t \tag{11}$$

and, at $t = 0$,

$$\mathbf{R} = \mathbf{i}c, \qquad \frac{d\mathbf{R}}{dt} = \mathbf{j}v_0. \tag{12}$$

In (11) we let $\mathbf{v} = d\mathbf{R}/dt$, and separate the variables to obtain

$$m\,d\mathbf{v} = (\mathbf{i}\cos t + \mathbf{j}\sin t)\,dt.$$

Integrating this, we have

$$m\mathbf{v} = m\frac{d\mathbf{R}}{dt} = \mathbf{i}\sin t - \mathbf{j}\cos t + \mathbf{C}_1, \tag{13}$$

where the constant of integration is a *vector* denoted by $\mathbf{C}_1$. The value of $\mathbf{C}_1$ may be found by using the initial velocity, the righthand equation in (12), in Eq. (13), with $t = 0$:

$$m\mathbf{j}v_0 = -\mathbf{j} + \mathbf{C}_1,$$

$$\mathbf{C}_1 = (mv_0 + 1)\mathbf{j}.$$

Substituting this into (13), we have

$$m\frac{d\mathbf{R}}{dt} = \mathbf{i}\sin t + (mv_0 + 1 - \cos t)\mathbf{j}.$$

Another integration gives

$$m\mathbf{R} = -\mathbf{i}\cos t + \mathbf{j}(mv_0 t + t - \sin t) + \mathbf{C}_2.$$

The initial condition $\mathbf{R} = \mathbf{i}c$ (Eq. 12) enables us to evaluate $\mathbf{C}_2$:

$$mc\mathbf{i} = -\mathbf{i} + \mathbf{C}_2, \qquad \mathbf{C}_2 = \mathbf{i}(mc + 1),$$

so that the position vector **R** is given by

$$\mathbf{R} = \frac{1}{m}[\mathbf{i}(mc + 1 - \cos t) + \mathbf{j}(mv_0 t + t - \sin t)].$$

The parametric equations of the curve are found by equating components of this expression for **R** with

$$\mathbf{R} = \mathbf{i}x + \mathbf{j}y,$$

which gives

$$x = c + \frac{1 - \cos t}{m}, \qquad y = v_0 t + \frac{t - \sin t}{m}.$$

The foregoing equations for velocity and acceleration in two dimensions would be appropriate for describing the motion of a particle moving on a flat surface, such as a water bug skimming over the surface of a pond, or a hockey puck sliding on ice. But to describe the flight of a bumblebee or a rocket, we need three coordinates. Thus, if

$$\mathbf{R}(t) = \mathbf{i}x + \mathbf{j}y + \mathbf{k}z, \tag{14a}$$

where x, y, z are functions of t that are twice-differentiable, then the velocity of $P(x, y, z)$ is

$$\mathbf{v} = \frac{d\mathbf{R}}{dt} = \mathbf{i}\frac{dx}{dt} + \mathbf{j}\frac{dy}{dt} + \mathbf{k}\frac{dz}{dt}, \tag{14b}$$

and the acceleration is

$$\mathbf{a} = \mathbf{i}\frac{d^2x}{dt^2} + \mathbf{j}\frac{d^2y}{dt^2} + \mathbf{k}\frac{d^2z}{dt^2}. \tag{14c}$$

PROBLEMS

In Problems 1–8, $\mathbf{R} = \mathbf{i}x + \mathbf{j}y$ is the vector from the origin to the moving point $P(x, y)$ at time t. Find the velocity and acceleration vectors for any t. Also find these vectors and the speed at the particular instant given.

1. $\mathbf{R} = (a \cos \omega t)\mathbf{i} + (a \sin \omega t)\mathbf{j}$, a and ω being positive constants; $t = \pi/(3\omega)$.

2. $\mathbf{R} = (2 \cos t)\mathbf{i} + (3 \sin t)\mathbf{j}$, $t = \pi/4$

3. $\mathbf{R} = (t + 1)\mathbf{i} + (t^2 - 1)\mathbf{j}$, $t = 2$

4. $\mathbf{R} = (\cos 2t)\mathbf{i} + (2 \sin t)\mathbf{j}$, $t = 0$

5. $\mathbf{R} = e^t\mathbf{i} + e^{-2t}\mathbf{j}$, $t = \ln 3$

6. $\mathbf{R} = (\sec t)\mathbf{i} + (\tan t)\mathbf{j}$, $t = \pi/6$

7. $\mathbf{R} = (\cosh 3t)\mathbf{i} + (2 \sinh t)\mathbf{j}$, $t = 0$

8. $\mathbf{R} = [\ln (t + 1)]\mathbf{i} + t^2\mathbf{j}$, $t = 1$

9. If the force that acts on a particle P of mass m is

$$\mathbf{F} = -mg\mathbf{j},$$

where m and g are constants, and the particle starts from the origin with velocity

$$\mathbf{v}_0 = (v_0 \cos \alpha)\mathbf{i} + (v_0 \sin \alpha)\mathbf{j}$$

at time $t = 0$, find the vector $\mathbf{R} = \mathbf{i}x + \mathbf{j}y$ from the origin to P at time t.

10. Problem 9 describes the motion of a projectile *in vacuo*. If the projectile encounters a resistance proportional to the velocity, the force is

$$\mathbf{F} = -mg\mathbf{j} - k\frac{d\mathbf{R}}{dt}.$$

Show that one integration of $\mathbf{F} = md^2\mathbf{R}/dt^2$ leads to the differential equation

$$\frac{d\mathbf{R}}{dt} + \frac{k}{m}\mathbf{R} = \mathbf{v}_0 - gt\mathbf{j}.$$

(To solve this equation, one can multiply both sides of the equation by $e^{(k/m)t}$. Then the left side is the derivative of the product $\mathbf{R}e^{(k/m)t}$ and both sides can be integrated.)

Find the velocity $\mathbf{v}$ and the acceleration $\mathbf{a}$ for the motion in Problems 11 through 13. Also, find the angle θ between $\mathbf{v}$ and $\mathbf{a}$ at time $t = 0$.

11. $x = e^t$, $y = e^t \sin t$, $z = e^t \cos t$

12. $x = \tan t$, $y = \sinh 2t$, $z = \operatorname{sech} 3t$

13. $x = \ln (t^2 + 1)$, $y = \tan^{-1} t$, $z = \sqrt{t^2 + 1}$

14. The plane $z = 2x + 3y$ intersects the cylinder $x^2 + y^2 = 9$ in an ellipse.

a) Express the position of a point $P(x, y, z)$ on this ellipse as a vector function $\mathbf{R} = \overrightarrow{OP} = \mathbf{R}(\theta)$, where θ is a measure of the dihedral angle between the xz-plane and the plane containing the z-axis and P.

b) Using the equations of (a), find the velocity and acceleration of P, assuming that $d\theta/dt = \omega$ is constant.

12–3 TANGENTIAL VECTORS

As the point P moves along a given curve in the xy-plane, we may imagine its position as being specified by the length of arc s from some arbitrarily chosen reference point P_0 on the curve. The vector

$$\mathbf{R} = \mathbf{i}x + \mathbf{j}y$$

from O to $P(x, y)$ is therefore a function of s and we shall now investigate the properties of $d\mathbf{R}/ds$. To this end, let P have coordinates (x, y) corresponding to the value s, while $Q(x + \Delta x,\ y + \Delta y)$ corresponds to $s + \Delta s$. Then

$$\frac{\Delta \mathbf{R}}{\Delta s} = \mathbf{i}\frac{\Delta x}{\Delta s} + \mathbf{j}\frac{\Delta y}{\Delta s} = \frac{\overrightarrow{PQ}}{\Delta s} \tag{1}$$

is a *vector* whose magnitude is chord PQ divided by arc PQ, and this approaches unity as $\Delta s \to 0$. Hence

$$\frac{d\mathbf{R}}{ds} = \lim_{\Delta s \to 0} \frac{\Delta \mathbf{R}}{\Delta s} \tag{2}$$

is a *unit* vector. The *direction* of this unit vector is the limiting direction approached by the direction of $\Delta\mathbf{R}/\Delta s$ as $\Delta s \to 0$. Now

$$\frac{\Delta \mathbf{R}}{\Delta s} = \frac{\overrightarrow{PQ}}{\Delta s}$$

has the same direction as $\overrightarrow{PQ}$ in case (a) when Δs is positive, or else it has the same direction as $\overrightarrow{QP}$ in case (b) when Δs is negative. Figures 12–6(a) and (b) illustrate these two cases and show that in *either* case, $\Delta\mathbf{R}/\Delta s$ is directed along the chord through P and Q and points in the direction of increasing s (that is, upward to the right, although $\Delta\mathbf{R}$ points downward and to the left in Fig. 12–6(b)).

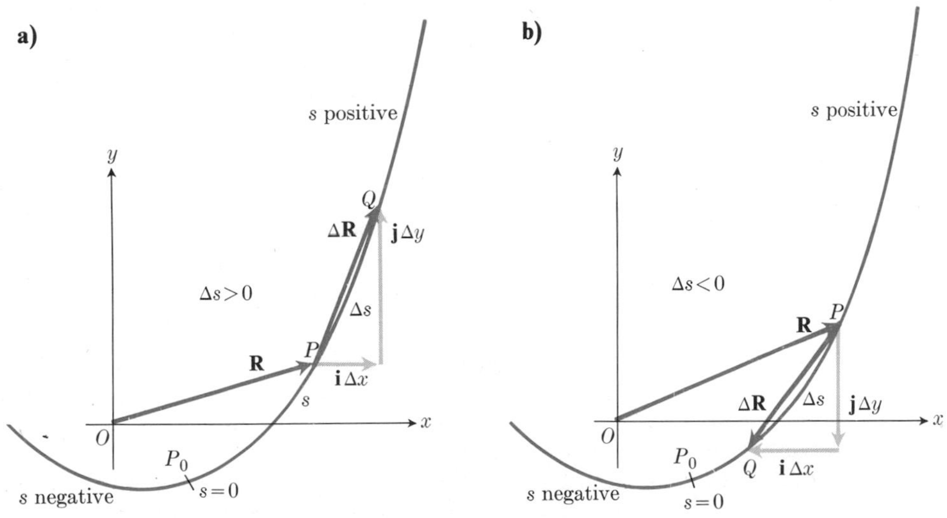

12–6 $\Delta\mathbf{R}/\Delta s$ will point in the direction of increasing s in both (a) and (b). Thus, the direction of $\Delta\mathbf{R}/\Delta s$, and of $\mathbf{T} = d\mathbf{R}/ds$ (part c), is determined by how we decide to measure s, as well as by the geometry of the curve.

As $\Delta s \to 0$ and $Q \to P$, the direction of the chord through P and Q approaches the direction of the *tangent* to the curve at P. Thus the limiting direction of $\Delta\mathbf{R}/\Delta s$, in other words the *direction of* $d\mathbf{R}/ds$, is along the *tangent to the curve at* P, and its sense is that which points in the direction of increasing arc length s. It points away from P_0 when s is positive, and toward P_0 when s is negative.

Whichever way it points, the vector

$$\frac{d\mathbf{R}}{ds} = \mathbf{T} \tag{3}$$

is a *unit vector, tangent to the curve at* P (Fig. 12–6(c)).

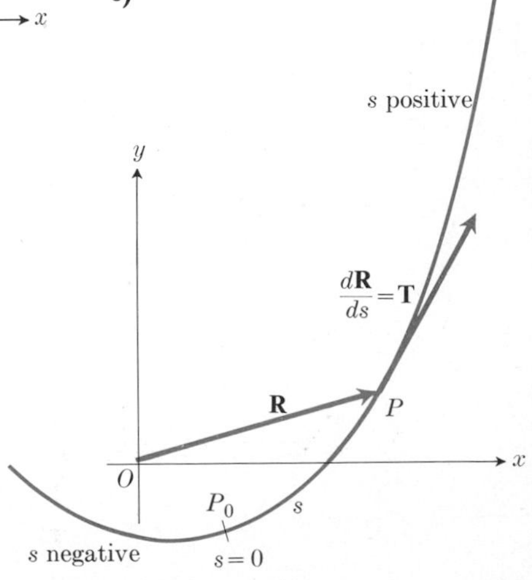

If we let $\Delta s \to 0$ in Eq. (1), we find that

$$\frac{d\mathbf{R}}{ds} = \mathbf{i}\frac{dx}{ds} + \mathbf{j}\frac{dy}{ds}, \tag{4}$$

and this may be used to find $\mathbf{T}$ at any point of a curve whose equation is given. However, the natural parametrization of a motion in many cases is likely to be time and not arc length. If $\mathbf{R} = x(t)\mathbf{i} + y(t)\mathbf{j}$ and t is not arc length, then the best way to find $\mathbf{T}$ is to normalize $\mathbf{v} = d\mathbf{R}/dt$. That is, first find $\mathbf{v}$ and then divide $\mathbf{v}$ by $|\mathbf{v}|$ to obtain

$$\mathbf{T} = \frac{\mathbf{v}}{|\mathbf{v}|}.$$

This works in all cases, except when $\mathbf{v} = \mathbf{0}$ at a point.

EXAMPLE 1. Find $\mathbf{T}$ for the motion

$$\mathbf{R} = (\cos t + t \sin t)\mathbf{i} + (\sin t - t \cos t)\mathbf{j}, \qquad t \geq 0.$$

Solution

$$\begin{aligned} \mathbf{v} = \frac{d\mathbf{R}}{dt} &= (-\sin t + t \cos t + \sin t)\mathbf{i} + (\cos t + t \sin t - \cos t)\mathbf{j} \\ &= (t \cos t)\mathbf{i} + (t \sin t)\mathbf{j}; \\ |\mathbf{v}| &= \sqrt{t^2 \cos^2 t + t^2 \sin^2 t} = t; \\ \mathbf{T} &= \frac{\mathbf{v}}{|\mathbf{v}|} = (\cos t)\mathbf{i} + (\sin t)\mathbf{j}. \end{aligned}$$

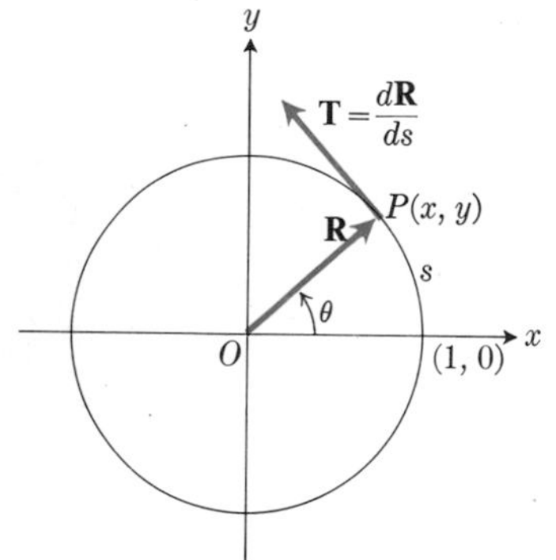

12–7 $\mathbf{R} = \mathbf{i} \cos \theta + \mathbf{j} \sin \theta$.

EXAMPLE 2. For the counterclockwise motion

$$\mathbf{R} = \mathbf{i} \cos \theta + \mathbf{j} \sin \theta$$

around the unit circle, we find that

$$\mathbf{v} = (-\sin \theta)\mathbf{i} + (\cos \theta)\mathbf{j}$$

is already a unit vector, so that $\mathbf{v} = \mathbf{T}$. In fact, $\mathbf{T}$ is $\mathbf{R}$ rotated 90° counterclockwise (Fig. 12–7).

Space Curves and Arc Length

All that has been done above for two-dimensional motion in a plane can be extended to three-dimensional motion in space. To this end, let $P(x, y, z)$ be a point whose position in space is given by the equations

$$x = f(t), \qquad y = g(t), \qquad z = h(t), \tag{5}$$

where f, g, and h are differentiable functions of t. As t varies continuously, P traces a curve in space.

EXAMPLE 3. The equations

$$x = a \cos \omega t, \qquad y = a \sin \omega t, \qquad z = bt, \tag{6}$$

where a, b, and ω are positive constants, represent a circular helix (Fig. 12–8). The projection of the point $P(x, y, z)$ onto the xy-plane moves around the circle $x^2 + y^2 = a^2$, $z = 0$, as t varies, while the distance between P and the xy-plane changes steadily with t.

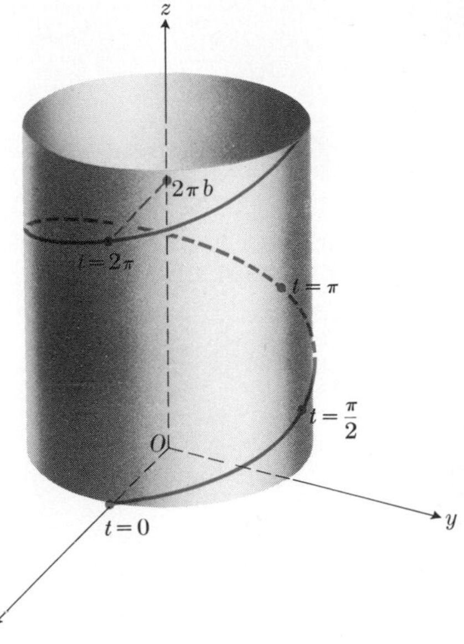

12–8 The helix $x = a \cos \omega t$, $y = a \sin \omega t$, $z = bt$, spirals up from the xy-plane as t increases from zero.

Let P_0 be any fixed point on the space curve, and adopt a positive direction for measuring the distance along the curve from P_0. To do this we can let P_0 be the position of P when $t = 0$, say, and measure arc length in the direction in which P first moves away from P_0 as t takes on positive values. Then the position of P on the curve becomes a function of the arc length s from P_0 to P.

The vector

$$\mathbf{R} = \mathbf{i}x + \mathbf{j}y + \mathbf{k}z \tag{7}$$

from the origin to P is also a function of s and we propose to discuss the geometrical significance of the derivative,

$$\frac{d\mathbf{R}}{ds} = \mathbf{i}\frac{dx}{ds} + \mathbf{j}\frac{dy}{ds} + \mathbf{k}\frac{dz}{ds}. \tag{8}$$

If we calculate the derivative from the definition

$$\frac{d\mathbf{R}}{ds} = \lim_{\Delta s \to 0} \frac{\Delta \mathbf{R}}{\Delta s},$$

we have (Fig. 12–9)

$$\frac{\Delta \mathbf{R}}{\Delta s} = \text{a vector of magnitude } \frac{\text{chord } PQ}{\text{arc } PQ} \text{ directed along the secant line } PQ.$$

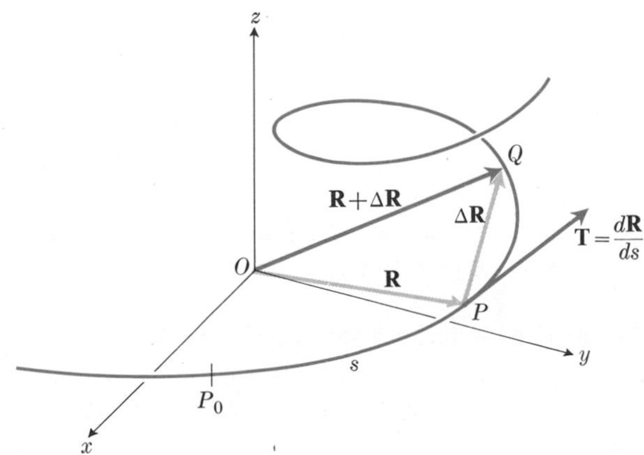

12–9 If $\mathbf{R}$ is differentiable, then $\lim_{\Delta s \to 0} \Delta\mathbf{R}/\Delta s$ is a unit vector tangent to the curve traced out by P.

As $Q \to P$ and $\Delta s \to 0$, the direction of the secant line approaches the direction of the tangent to the curve at P, while the ratio of chord to arc approaches unity (for a "smooth" curve). Therefore the limit of $\Delta\mathbf{R}/\Delta s$ is a unit vector tangent to the curve at P and pointing in the direction in which arc length increases along the curve. In other words, the vector $\mathbf{T}$, which is defined by the equation

$$\frac{d\mathbf{R}}{ds} = \mathbf{T}, \tag{9}$$

is a *unit* vector *tangent* to the space curve described by the endpoint P of the vector $\mathbf{R} = \overrightarrow{OP}$.

To find $\mathbf{T}$ we do not need to express the components of $\mathbf{R}$ in terms of s. As with motion in the plane, the fact that $\mathbf{T}$ is a unit vector lets us compute $\mathbf{T}$ from the velocity vector $\mathbf{v} = d\mathbf{R}/dt$ by the formula

$$\mathbf{T} = \frac{\mathbf{v}}{|\mathbf{v}|}. \tag{10}$$

EXAMPLE 4. Find $\mathbf{T}$ for the helix of Example 3.

Solution. The velocity vector is

$$\mathbf{v} = \mathbf{i}(-a\omega \sin \omega t) + \mathbf{j}(a\omega \cos \omega t) + \mathbf{k}(b),$$

whose length is

$$|\mathbf{v}| = \sqrt{a^2\omega^2 \sin^2 \omega t + a^2\omega^2 \cos^2 \omega t + b^2} = \sqrt{a^2\omega^2 + b^2}.$$

Therefore,

$$\mathbf{T} = \frac{\mathbf{v}}{|\mathbf{v}|} = \frac{a\omega(-\mathbf{i} \sin \omega t + \mathbf{j} \cos \omega t) + b\mathbf{k}}{\sqrt{a^2\omega^2 + b^2}}.$$

If we combine the results of Eqs. (8) and (9), we have

$$\mathbf{T} = \mathbf{i}\frac{dx}{ds} + \mathbf{j}\frac{dy}{ds} + \mathbf{k}\frac{dz}{ds}, \tag{11}$$

and since

$$\mathbf{T} \cdot \mathbf{T} = 1,$$

this means that

$$ds = \pm\sqrt{dx^2 + dy^2 + dz^2}. \tag{12}$$

The length of an arc of a curve may be calculated by computing ds from (12) and integrating between appropriate limits.

EXAMPLE 5. For the helix in Examples 3 and 4,

$$ds = \sqrt{a^2\omega^2 + b^2}\, dt$$

and

$$s = \sqrt{a^2\omega^2 + b^2} \int dt,$$

where appropriate limits of integration are to be supplied. Thus the length of one full turn of the helix

$$x = \cos t, \qquad y = \sin t, \qquad z = t,$$

for which $a = b = \omega = 1$, is

$$\sqrt{2}\int_0^{2\pi} dt = 2\pi\sqrt{2}.$$

This is $\sqrt{2}$ times the length of the unit circle in the xy-plane over which the helix stands.

PROBLEMS

In each of the following problems (1 through 8), $\mathbf{R} = \mathbf{i}x + \mathbf{j}y$ is the vector from the origin O to $P(x, y)$. For each of these motions, find the unit tangent vector $\mathbf{T} = d\mathbf{R}/ds$.

1. $\mathbf{R} = 2\mathbf{i}\cos t + 2\mathbf{j}\sin t$

2. $\mathbf{R} = e^t\mathbf{i} + t^2\mathbf{j}$

3. $\mathbf{R} = (\cos^3 t)\mathbf{i} + (\sin^3 t)\mathbf{j}$

4. $\mathbf{R} = \mathbf{i}x + \mathbf{j}x^2$

5. $\mathbf{R} = (\cos 2t)\mathbf{i} + (2\cos t)\mathbf{j}$

6. $\mathbf{R} = \dfrac{t^3}{3}\mathbf{i} + \dfrac{t^2}{2}\mathbf{j}$

7. $\mathbf{R} = (e^t\cos t)\mathbf{i} + (e^t\sin t)\mathbf{j}$

8. $\mathbf{R} = \cosh t\mathbf{i} + t\mathbf{j}$

In Problems 9 through 12, $\mathbf{R} = \mathbf{i}x + \mathbf{j}y + \mathbf{k}z$. Find the unit tangent vector $\mathbf{T}$ for each space curve.

9. $x = 6\sin 2t,\quad y = 6\cos 2t,\quad z = 5t$

10. $x = e^t\cos t,\quad y = e^t\sin t,\quad z = e^t$

11. $x = 3\cosh 2t,\quad y = 3\sinh 2t,\quad z = 6t$

12. $x = 3t\cos t,\quad y = 3t\sin t,\quad z = 4t$

For the curves in Problems 13–16, find the length of the curve between $t = 0$ and $t = \pi$.

13. The curve of Problem 9

14. The curve of Problem 10

15. The curve of Problem 11

16. The curve of Problem 12

12–4 CURVATURE AND NORMAL VECTORS

Our next step is to consider the rate of change of the unit tangent vector $\mathbf{T}$ as P moves along the curve. Of course, the length of $\mathbf{T}$ is constant, always being equal to one. But the direction of $\mathbf{T}$ changes, since it is tangent to the curve and the tangent changes direction from point to point except where the curve is straight.

Motion in a Plane

If P moves along a curve in the xy-plane, we measure the direction of $\mathbf{T}$ by the angle ϕ from the positively directed x-axis to $\mathbf{T}$ (Fig. 12–10). We may then measure the rate at which $\mathbf{T}$ turns to one side or the other as we move along the curve by keeping track of the change in ϕ. The absolute value of the derivative $d\phi/ds$ of ϕ with respect to arc length (measured in radians per unit of length) is called the *curvature function* of the curve, and its value at any given point is called the curvature at that point. The usual notation for curvature is the Greek letter κ (kappa):

$$\kappa = \left|\frac{d\phi}{ds}\right|, \tag{1}$$

where

$$\tan\phi = \frac{dy}{dx}$$

and

$$ds = \pm\sqrt{dx^2 + dy^2}.$$

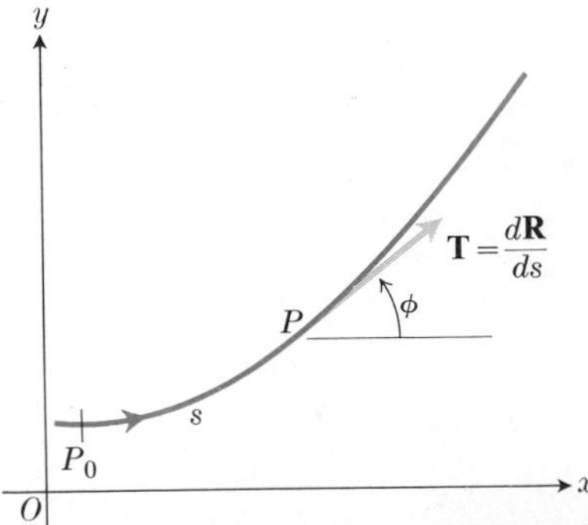

12–10 The value of $|d\phi/ds|$ at P is called the curvature of the curve at P.

One may derive a formula for κ from the equations above in a straightforward manner. Namely,

$$\phi = \tan^{-1} \frac{dy}{dx},$$

$$\frac{d\phi}{dx} = \frac{d^2y/dx^2}{1 + (dy/dx)^2},$$

and

$$\frac{ds}{dx} = \pm\sqrt{1 + (dy/dx)^2},$$

so that

$$\kappa = \left|\frac{d\phi}{ds}\right| = \left|\frac{d\phi/dx}{ds/dx}\right| = \frac{|d^2y/dx^2|}{[1 + (dy/dx)^2]^{3/2}}. \tag{2a}$$

We may arrive at a formula for κ in terms of dx/dy and d^2x/dy^2 if we use

$$\phi = \cot^{-1} \frac{dx}{dy}$$

and

$$\kappa = \left|\frac{d\phi}{ds}\right| = \left|\frac{d\phi/dy}{ds/dy}\right|$$

The result, which corresponds to (2a), is

$$\kappa = \frac{|d^2x/dy^2|}{[1 + (dx/dy)^2]^{3/2}}. \tag{2b}$$

If the equation of the curve is given in parametric form,

$$x = f(t), \qquad y = g(t),$$

then

$$\phi = \tan^{-1}\left(\frac{dy/dt}{dx/dt}\right),$$

and if we use

$$\kappa = \left|\frac{d\phi/dt}{ds/dt}\right|,$$

the calculations are as follows:

$$\frac{d\phi}{dt} = \frac{1}{1 + \left(\dfrac{dy/dt}{dx/dt}\right)^2} \frac{\dfrac{dx}{dt}\dfrac{d^2y}{dt^2} - \dfrac{dy}{dt}\dfrac{d^2x}{dt^2}}{\left(\dfrac{dx}{dt}\right)^2} = \frac{\dot{x}\ddot{y} - \dot{y}\ddot{x}}{\dot{x}^2 + \dot{y}^2} \qquad \left[\dot{x} = \frac{dx}{dt},\ \ddot{x} = \frac{d^2x}{dt^2}\right]$$

and

$$\frac{ds}{dt} = \pm\sqrt{\dot{x}^2 + \dot{y}^2},$$

so that

$$\kappa = \frac{|\dot{x}\ddot{y} - \dot{y}\ddot{x}|}{[\dot{x}^2 + \dot{y}^2]^{3/2}}. \tag{2c}$$

EXAMPLE 1. *The curvature of a straight line is* 0.
On a straight line, ϕ is constant. Therefore $d\phi/ds$ in Eq. (2a) is zero.

EXAMPLE 2. *The curvature of a circle of radius a is* $1/a$.
We place the center of the circle at the origin to make its equation simple (Fig. 12–11).

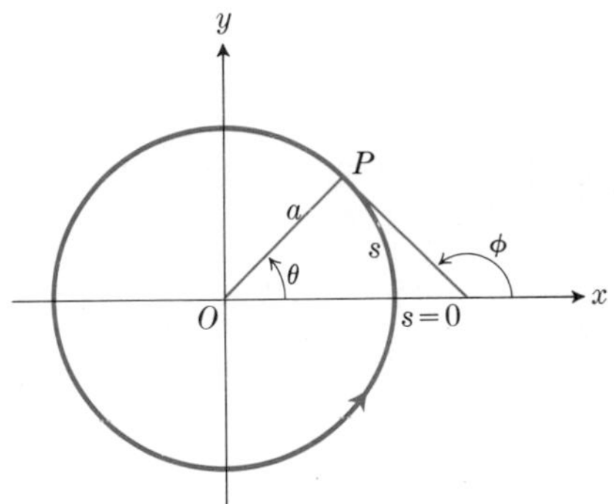

12–11 P: $x = a \cos \theta$, $y = a \sin \theta$.

METHOD 1. Parametrize the circle with the equations

$$x = a \cos \theta, \qquad y = a \sin \theta.$$

Then,

$$\dot{x} = -a \sin \theta, \qquad \dot{y} = a \cos \theta,$$

$$\ddot{x} = -a \cos \theta, \qquad \ddot{y} = -a \sin \theta.$$

From Eq. (2c) we have

$$\kappa = \frac{|(-a \sin \theta)(-a \sin \theta) - (a \cos \theta)(-a \cos \theta)|}{[a^2 \sin^2 \theta + a^2 \cos^2 \theta]^{3/2}}$$

$$= \frac{a^2}{a^3} = \frac{1}{a}.$$

METHOD 2. (Special to the circle) The geometry of Fig. 12–11 allows s and ϕ to be expressed in terms of θ as follows:

$$s = a\theta, \qquad \phi = \theta + \frac{\pi}{2}. \tag{3}$$

Equation (1) then gives

$$\kappa = \left|\frac{d\phi}{ds}\right| = \left|\frac{d\theta}{a\, d\theta}\right| = \frac{1}{a}.$$

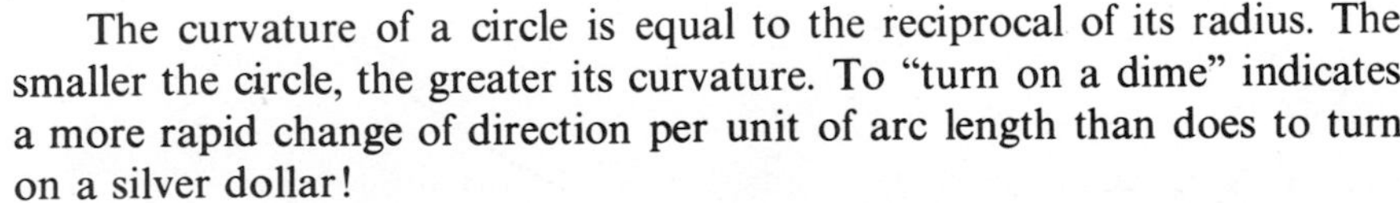
The curvature of a circle is equal to the reciprocal of its radius. The smaller the circle, the greater its curvature. To "turn on a dime" indicates a more rapid change of direction per unit of arc length than does to turn on a silver dollar!

Circle and Radius of Curvature

The circle that is tangent to a plane curve at P, whose center lies on the concave side of the curve and that has the same curvature as the curve has at P, is called the *circle of curvature*. Its radius is $1/\kappa$, from Example 2. We define the *radius of curvature* ρ at P to be

$$\rho = \frac{1}{\kappa} = \frac{[1 + (dy/dx)^2]^{3/2}}{|d^2y/dx^2|}. \tag{4}$$

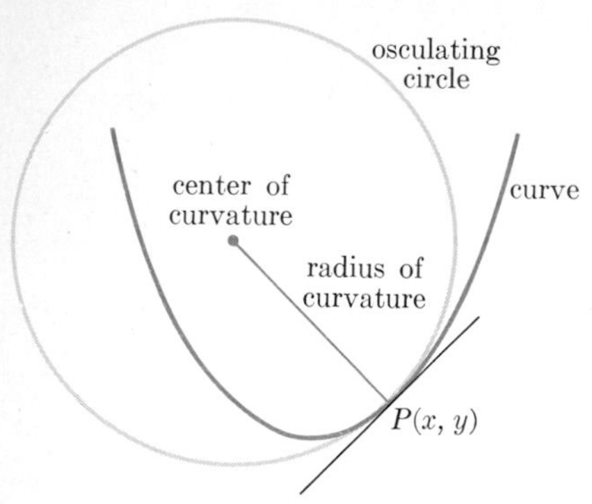

12–12 The osculating circle or circle of curvature at $P(x, y)$.

The center of the circle of curvature is called the center of curvature. The circle of curvature has its first and second derivatives equal, respectively, to the first and second derivatives of the curve itself at this point. For this reason it has a higher degree of contact with the curve at P than has any other circle, so it is also called the *osculating* circle! (See Fig. 12–12.) Since velocity and acceleration involve only the first and second time derivatives of the coordinates of P, it is natural to anticipate that the instantaneous velocity and acceleration of a particle moving on any curve may be expressed in terms of instantaneous velocity and acceleration of an associated particle moving on the osculating circle. This will be investigated in the next article.

Unit Normal Vector

We return once more to the question of the rate of change of the unit vector $\mathbf{T}$ as P moves along the curve. In terms of the slope angle ϕ (Fig. 12–13), we may write

$$\mathbf{T} = \mathbf{i} \cos \phi + \mathbf{j} \sin \phi, \tag{5}$$

and then the derivative

$$\frac{d\mathbf{T}}{d\phi} = -\mathbf{i} \sin \phi + \mathbf{j} \cos \phi \tag{6}$$

has magnitude

$$\left|\frac{d\mathbf{T}}{d\phi}\right| = \sqrt{\sin^2 \phi + \cos^2 \phi} = 1.$$

From Eqs. (5) and (6) we see that

$$\mathbf{T} \cdot \frac{d\mathbf{T}}{d\phi} = 0.$$

Therefore $d\mathbf{T}/d\phi$ is perpendicular to $\mathbf{T}$. In fact, we see from Eq. (6) that

$$\frac{d\mathbf{T}}{d\phi} = \mathbf{N}, \tag{7}$$

where

$$\mathbf{N} = \mathbf{i} \cos (\phi + 90°) + \mathbf{j} \sin (\phi + 90°) = -\mathbf{i} \sin \phi + \mathbf{j} \cos \phi$$

is the *unit normal* vector obtained by rotating the unit tangent vector $\mathbf{T}$ counterclockwise through 90° (Fig. 12–13).

A comparison of Eqs. (5) and (6) shows that $\mathbf{N}$ can be found from $\mathbf{T}$ by interchanging components and changing the sign of the new first component.

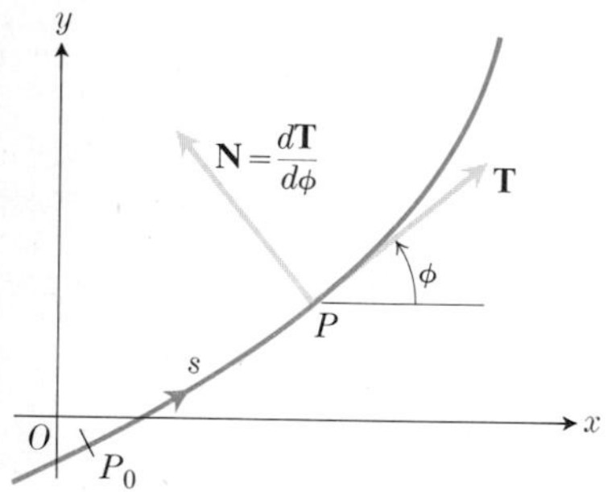

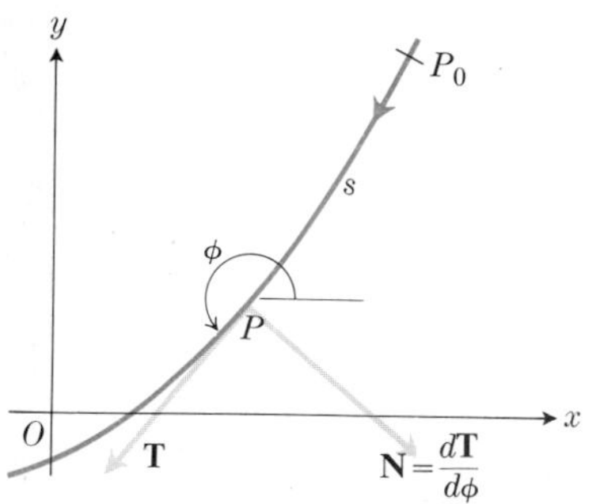

12–13 Turn $\mathbf{T}$ counterclockwise 90° to get $\mathbf{N}$.

EXAMPLE 3. Find $\mathbf{N}$ for the curve traced by

$$\mathbf{R} = (2t + 3)\mathbf{i} + (t^2 - 1)\mathbf{j}.$$

Solution. We first find **T**:

$$\mathbf{v} = 2\mathbf{i} + 2t\mathbf{j},$$

$$|\mathbf{v}| = \sqrt{4 + 4t^2} = 2\sqrt{1 + t^2},$$

$$\mathbf{T} = \frac{\mathbf{v}}{|\mathbf{v}|} = \frac{1}{\sqrt{1 + t^2}}\mathbf{i} + \frac{t}{\sqrt{1 + t^2}}\mathbf{j}.$$

We then interchange the components of **T** and change the sign of the new first component, to get

$$\mathbf{N} = -\frac{t}{\sqrt{1 + t^2}}\mathbf{i} + \frac{1}{\sqrt{1 + t^2}}\mathbf{j}.$$

For a curve in 3-space, the direction of the unit tangent vector **T** is not determined by a single angle such as ϕ. Instead, we shall use arc length, s, as the parameter for the theoretical study of **T**. In Article 12–5, we shall see that **T** and $d\mathbf{T}/ds$ are orthogonal vectors. If $d\mathbf{T}/ds$ is not the zero vector, we then use its direction to specify the *principal normal* to the curve. In the two-dimensional case, we have (from the chain rule)

$$\frac{d\mathbf{T}}{ds} = \frac{d\mathbf{T}}{d\phi}\frac{d\phi}{ds} = \mathbf{N}(\pm\kappa).$$

If we direct the curve so that ϕ is an *increasing function* of s, then

$$\frac{d\phi}{ds} = \kappa,$$

and

$$\frac{d\mathbf{T}}{ds} = \frac{d\mathbf{T}}{d\phi}\frac{d\phi}{ds} = \mathbf{N}\kappa. \tag{8}$$

To combine both the two-dimensional and three-dimensional curves in one equation, we drop the middle part of Eq. (8) and obtain the simple equation

$$\frac{d\mathbf{T}}{ds} = \mathbf{N}\kappa. \tag{9}$$

In Eq. (9), κ is the magnitude of $d\mathbf{T}/ds$:

$$\kappa = \left|\frac{d\mathbf{T}}{ds}\right|. \tag{10}$$

This number is called the *curvature* of the space curve. Such a definition is consistent with Eq. (1) for a plane curve, and extends the concept of curvature to curves in space. Equations (9) and (10) together define the unit principal normal vector **N**, whenever $d\mathbf{T}/ds \neq \mathbf{0}$:

$$\mathbf{N} = \frac{d\mathbf{T}/ds}{|d\mathbf{T}/ds|}. \tag{11}$$

EXAMPLE 4. Find the curvature and principal normal of the helix of Examples 3 and 4 of Article 12–3.

Solution. In Example 4, Article 12–3, we found

$$\mathbf{T} = \frac{a\omega(-\mathbf{i}\sin\omega t + \mathbf{j}\cos\omega t) + b\mathbf{k}}{\sqrt{a^2\omega^2 + b^2}} \tag{12}$$

and

$$\frac{ds}{dt} = \sqrt{a^2\omega^2 + b^2}.$$

Hence

$$\frac{d\mathbf{T}}{ds} = \frac{d\mathbf{T}/dt}{ds/dt}$$

$$= \frac{-a\omega^2}{a^2\omega^2 + b^2}(\mathbf{i}\cos\omega t + \mathbf{j}\sin\omega t),$$

and

$$\kappa = \left|\frac{d\mathbf{T}}{ds}\right| = \frac{a\omega^2}{a^2\omega^2 + b^2}. \tag{13}$$

Two limiting cases of Eq. (13) are worth checking. First, if $b = 0$, then $z = 0$, and the helix reduces to a circle of radius a in the xy-plane, while Eq. (13) reduces to $\kappa = 1/a$ as it should. Second, if $a = 0$, then $x = y = 0$ and $z = bt$. This tells us that the point moves along the z-axis. Again Eq. (13) gives the correct curvature, namely $\kappa = 0$. In the general case, the curvature of a circular helix is constant and less than the curvature of the circle that is the cross section of the cylinder around which the helix winds (Fig. 12–8).

The principal normal of the helix is the vector

$$\mathbf{N} = \frac{d\mathbf{T}/ds}{|d\mathbf{T}/ds|} = -(\mathbf{i}\cos\omega t + \mathbf{j}\sin\omega t)$$

$$= -\frac{\mathbf{i}x + \mathbf{j}y}{a}, \tag{14}$$

which is parallel to the vector from the point $(0, 0, z)$ on the z-axis to the point $P(x, y, z)$ on the helix.

Once the unit vectors $\mathbf{T}$ and $\mathbf{N}$ have been determined, it is a simple matter to define a third unit vector, perpendicular to both $\mathbf{T}$ and $\mathbf{N}$, by the equation

$$\mathbf{B} = \mathbf{T} \times \mathbf{N}. \tag{15}$$

The vector $\mathbf{B}$ so defined may be thought of as lying in the plane normal to $\mathbf{T}$ at P (Fig. 12–14) and is called the *binormal* at P. The three unit vectors, $\mathbf{T}$, $\mathbf{N}$, and $\mathbf{B}$, form a righthanded system of mutually orthogonal unit vectors which are useful in more thorough investigations of space curves. (Struik, *Differential Geometry*, Chapter 1; Addison-Wesley.)

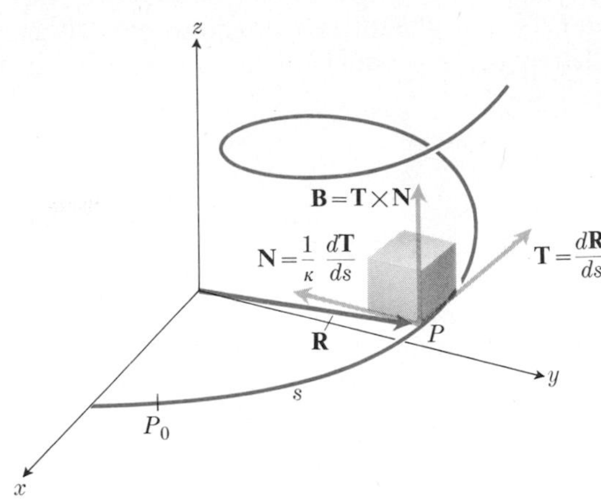

12–14 **T**, **N**, and **B** form a righthanded coordinate frame.

PROBLEMS

Find the curvature of each of the curves in Problems 1–12.

1. $y = a \cosh (x/a)$

2. $y = \ln (\cos x)$

3. $y = e^{2x}$

4. $x = a \cos^3 t, \quad y = a \sin^3 t$

5. $x = a(\cos \theta + \theta \sin \theta)$, $y = a(\sin \theta - \theta \cos \theta)$

6. $x = a(\theta - \sin \theta)$, $y = a(1 - \cos \theta)$

7. $x = \ln \sec y$

8. $x = \frac{1}{3}(y^2 + 2)^{3/2}$

9. $x = \dfrac{y^4}{4} + \dfrac{1}{8y^2}$

10. $x = 2t + 3, \quad y = 5 - t^2$

11. $x = \dfrac{t^3}{3}, \quad y = \dfrac{t^2}{2}$

12. $x = e^t \cos t, \quad y = e^t \sin t$

13. Find the equation of the osculating circle associated with the curve $y = e^x$ at the point (0, 1). By calculating dy/dx and d^2y/dx^2 at the point (0, 1) from the equation of this circle, verify that these derivatives have the same values there as do the corresponding derivatives for the curve $y = e^x$. Sketch the curve and the osculating circle.

14. Show that when x and y are considered as functions of arc length s, the unit vectors **T** and **N** may be expressed as follows:

$$\mathbf{T} = \mathbf{i}\frac{dx}{ds} + \mathbf{j}\frac{dy}{ds}, \qquad \mathbf{N} = -\mathbf{i}\frac{dy}{ds} + \mathbf{j}\frac{dx}{ds},$$

where $dx/ds = \cos \phi$, $dy/ds = \sin \phi$, and ϕ is the angle from the positive x-axis to the tangent line.

In Problems 15–17, find the principal normal vector **N**, the curvature κ, and the unit binormal vector **B**.

15. The curve of Problem 9, Article 12–3

16. The curve of Problem 10, Article 12–3

17. The curve of Problem 11, Article 12–3

18. Let $\mathbf{R} = \overrightarrow{OP}$ be the vector from the origin to a moving point P. Let **T** and **N** be the unit tangent and principal normal vectors, respectively, for the curve described by P. Express the velocity and acceleration vectors $d\mathbf{R}/dt$ and $d^2\mathbf{R}/dt^2$ in terms of their **T**- and **N**-components.

12–5 DIFFERENTIATION OF PRODUCTS OF VECTORS

If the components of a vector are differentiable functions of a scalar variable t, then we know that the vector is a differentiable function of t, and its derivative is obtained by differentiating the components (Article 12–1, Eq. 8).

It is also convenient to develop formulas for the derivative of the dot and cross products of two vectors that are differentiable functions of t. Suppose, for example, that

$$\mathbf{U} = \mathbf{i}f_1(t) + \mathbf{j}f_2(t) + \mathbf{k}f_3(t),$$
$$\mathbf{V} = \mathbf{i}g_1(t) + \mathbf{j}g_2(t) + \mathbf{k}g_3(t), \tag{1}$$

where the f's and g's are differentiable functions of t. Then, by the ordinary formulas for differentiating products of scalar functions, it is easy to verify that

$$\frac{d}{dt}(\mathbf{U}\cdot\mathbf{V}) = \frac{d\mathbf{U}}{dt}\cdot\mathbf{V} + \mathbf{U}\cdot\frac{d\mathbf{V}}{dt}, \tag{2}$$

$$\frac{d}{dt}(\mathbf{U}\times\mathbf{V}) = \frac{d\mathbf{U}}{dt}\times\mathbf{V} + \mathbf{U}\times\frac{d\mathbf{V}}{dt}. \tag{3}$$

However, instead of appealing to the component-wise verification of the identities in Eqs. (2) and (3), it is instructive to establish these equations by the Δ-process. For example, let

$$\mathbf{W} = \mathbf{U}\times\mathbf{V},$$

where t has some specific value. Then give t an increment Δt and denote the new values of the vectors by $\mathbf{U} + \Delta\mathbf{U}$, etc., so that

$$\begin{aligned}\mathbf{W} + \Delta\mathbf{W} &= (\mathbf{U} + \Delta\mathbf{U})\times(\mathbf{V} + \Delta\mathbf{V})\\ &= \mathbf{U}\times\mathbf{V} + \mathbf{U}\times\Delta\mathbf{V} + \Delta\mathbf{U}\times\mathbf{V} + \Delta\mathbf{U}\times\Delta\mathbf{V},\end{aligned}$$

and

$$\frac{\Delta\mathbf{W}}{\Delta t} = \mathbf{U}\times\frac{\Delta\mathbf{V}}{\Delta t} + \frac{\Delta\mathbf{U}}{\Delta t}\times\mathbf{V} + \frac{\Delta\mathbf{U}}{\Delta t}\times\Delta\mathbf{V}.$$

Now take limits as $\Delta t \to 0$, noting that

$$\lim\frac{\Delta\mathbf{W}}{\Delta t} = \frac{d\mathbf{W}}{dt}, \qquad \lim\frac{\Delta\mathbf{U}}{\Delta t} = \frac{d\mathbf{U}}{dt}, \qquad \lim\Delta\mathbf{V} = \lim\frac{\Delta\mathbf{V}}{\Delta t}\cdot\lim\Delta t = 0,$$

so that

$$\frac{d\mathbf{W}}{dt} = \mathbf{U}\times\frac{d\mathbf{V}}{dt} + \frac{d\mathbf{U}}{dt}\times\mathbf{V},$$

which is equivalent to Eq. (3).

Equations (2) and (3) are both like the equation for the derivative of the product of two scalar functions u and v. Indeed, the proofs by the Δ-process are the same for vectors as for scalars. The only place we need to be careful is in a derivative involving a cross product. The relative order of the factors must be preserved, because reversing the order changes the sign of the product.

EXAMPLE 1. The formula for the derivative of the triple scalar product leads to an interesting identity for the derivative of a determinant of order three. Let

$$\begin{aligned}\mathbf{U} &= u_1\mathbf{i} + u_2\mathbf{j} + u_3\mathbf{k},\\ \mathbf{V} &= v_1\mathbf{i} + v_2\mathbf{j} + v_3\mathbf{k},\\ \mathbf{W} &= w_1\mathbf{i} + w_2\mathbf{j} + w_3\mathbf{k},\end{aligned} \tag{4}$$

where the components are differentiable functions of a scalar t. Then the identity

$$\frac{d}{dt}(\mathbf{U} \cdot \mathbf{V} \times \mathbf{W}) = \frac{d\mathbf{U}}{dt} \cdot \mathbf{V} \times \mathbf{W} + \mathbf{U} \cdot \frac{d\mathbf{V}}{dt} \times \mathbf{W} + \mathbf{U} \cdot \mathbf{V} \times \frac{d\mathbf{W}}{dt} \tag{5}$$

is equivalent to

$$\frac{d}{dt}\begin{vmatrix} u_1 & u_2 & u_3 \\ v_1 & v_2 & v_3 \\ w_1 & w_2 & w_3 \end{vmatrix} = \begin{vmatrix} \frac{du_1}{dt} & \frac{du_2}{dt} & \frac{du_3}{dt} \\ v_1 & v_2 & v_3 \\ w_1 & w_2 & w_3 \end{vmatrix} + \begin{vmatrix} u_1 & u_2 & u_3 \\ \frac{dv_1}{dt} & \frac{dv_2}{dt} & \frac{dv_3}{dt} \\ w_1 & w_2 & w_3 \end{vmatrix} + \begin{vmatrix} u_1 & u_2 & u_3 \\ v_1 & v_2 & v_3 \\ \frac{dw_1}{dt} & \frac{dw_2}{dt} & \frac{dw_3}{dt} \end{vmatrix} \tag{6}$$

This says that the derivative of a determinant of order three is the sum of three determinants obtained from the original determinant by differentiating one row at a time. The result may be extended to determinants of any order n.

Derivatives of Vectors of Constant Length

An interesting geometrical result is obtained by differentiating the identity

$$\mathbf{V} \cdot \mathbf{V} = |\mathbf{V}|^2 \tag{7a}$$

when $\mathbf{V}$ is a vector of constant magnitude, for then $|\mathbf{V}|^2$ is a constant, so its derivative is zero, and one has

$$\mathbf{V} \cdot \frac{d\mathbf{V}}{dt} + \frac{d\mathbf{V}}{dt} \cdot \mathbf{V} = 0$$

or, since the scalar product is commutative,

$$2\mathbf{V} \cdot \frac{d\mathbf{V}}{dt} = 0. \tag{7b}$$

This means that either $\mathbf{V}$ is zero, $d\mathbf{V}/dt$ is zero (and hence $\mathbf{V}$ is constant in direction as well as magnitude), or else that $d\mathbf{V}/dt$ is perpendicular to $\mathbf{V}$.

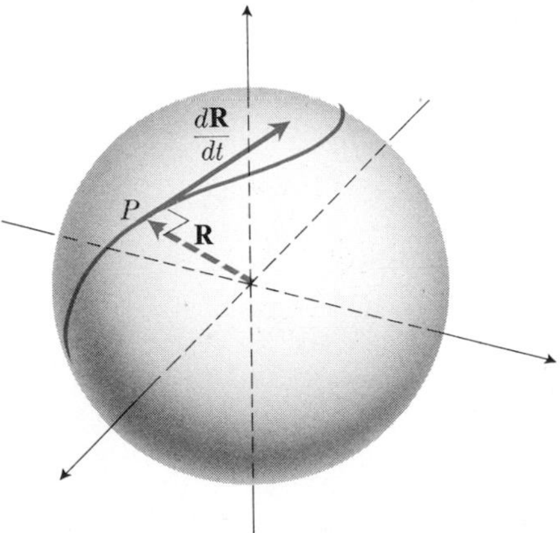

12–15 The velocity vector of a particle P that moves on the surface of a sphere is tangent to the sphere.

EXAMPLE 2. Suppose that a point P moves about on the surface of a sphere. Then the magnitude of the vector $\mathbf{R}$ from the center to P is a constant equal to the radius of the sphere. Therefore, the velocity vector $d\mathbf{R}/dt$ is always perpendicular to $\mathbf{R}$ (Fig. 12–15).

We can also use the foregoing results to show that the derivative of the unit tangent vector $\mathbf{T}$ is orthogonal to $\mathbf{T}$. Because $|\mathbf{T}| = 1$, we have

$$\mathbf{T} \cdot \mathbf{T} = 1,$$

so that, by the same kind of reasoning we used in going from Eq. (7a) to (7b), we can deduce that

$$\mathbf{T} \cdot \frac{d\mathbf{T}}{ds} = 0.$$

This validates our earlier statement that $d\mathbf{T}/ds$ is perpendicular to $\mathbf{T}$, so that the definition

$$\frac{d\mathbf{T}}{ds} = \mathbf{N}\kappa, \tag{8}$$

as given in Eq. (9), Article 12–4, with $\kappa = |d\mathbf{T}/ds|$, produces a vector $\mathbf{N}$ orthogonal to $\mathbf{T}$.

Tangential and Normal Components of the Velocity and Acceleration Vectors

In mechanics it is useful to be able to discuss the motion of a particle P in terms of its instantaneous speed ds/dt, acceleration along its path d^2s/dt^2, and the curvature of the path. This is easy if we refer the velocity and acceleration vectors to the unit vectors $\mathbf{T}$ and $\mathbf{N}$.

In Article 12–2 we found the velocity vector to be given by

$$\mathbf{v} = \frac{d\mathbf{R}}{dt}, \tag{9}$$

where $\mathbf{R} = \mathbf{i}x + \mathbf{j}y + \mathbf{k}z$ is the position vector $\overrightarrow{OP}$. We may also write this in the form

$$\mathbf{v} = \frac{d\mathbf{R}}{dt} = \frac{d\mathbf{R}}{ds}\frac{ds}{dt}$$

or

$$\mathbf{v} = \mathbf{T}\frac{ds}{dt} \tag{10}$$

if we use the result of Eq. (9), Article 12–3. This is in keeping with our earlier remark that the velocity vector is tangent to the curve and has magnitude $|\mathbf{v}| = |ds/dt|$. (See Fig. 12–16.)

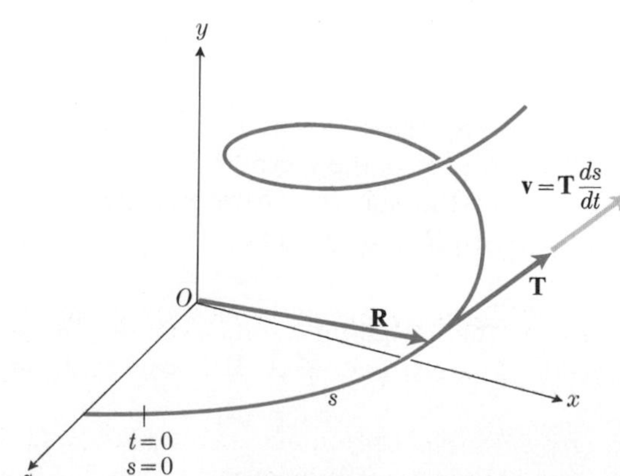

12–16 Divide $\mathbf{v}$ by ds/dt to get $\mathbf{T}$.

To obtain the acceleration vector, we differentiate Eq. (10) with respect to t:

$$\mathbf{a} = \frac{d\mathbf{v}}{dt} = \mathbf{T}\frac{d^2s}{dt^2} + \frac{d\mathbf{T}}{dt}\frac{ds}{dt}.$$

By Eq. (8),

$$\frac{d\mathbf{T}}{dt} = \frac{d\mathbf{T}}{ds}\frac{ds}{dt} = \mathbf{N}\kappa\frac{ds}{dt},$$

so that

$$\mathbf{a} = \mathbf{T}\frac{d^2s}{dt^2} + \mathbf{N}\kappa\left(\frac{ds}{dt}\right)^2. \tag{11}$$

Equation (11) expresses the acceleration vector in terms of its tangential and normal components. The *tangential component*, $a_T = d^2s/dt^2$, is simply the derivative of the speed ds/dt of the particle in its path. The *normal component* $a_N = \kappa(ds/dt)^2$ is directed toward the concave side of the curve and has magnitude

$$a_N = \kappa\left(\frac{ds}{dt}\right)^2 = \frac{(ds/dt)^2}{\rho} = \frac{v^2}{\rho},$$

where v is the instantaneous speed of the particle and ρ is the radius of curvature of the path at the point in question. This explains why a large normal force, which must be supplied by friction between the tires and the roadway, is required to hold an automobile on a level road if it makes a sharp turn (small ρ) or a moderate turn at high speed (large v^2). (See Sears, Zemansky, Young, *University Physics* (1976), Chapter 6, for a discussion of the banking of curves.)

If the particle is moving in a circle with *constant* speed $v = ds/dt$, then d^2s/dt^2 is zero, and the only acceleration is the normal acceleration v^2/ρ toward the center of the circle. If the speed is not constant, the acceleration vector **a** is the resultant of the tangential and normal components, as in Fig. 12–17.

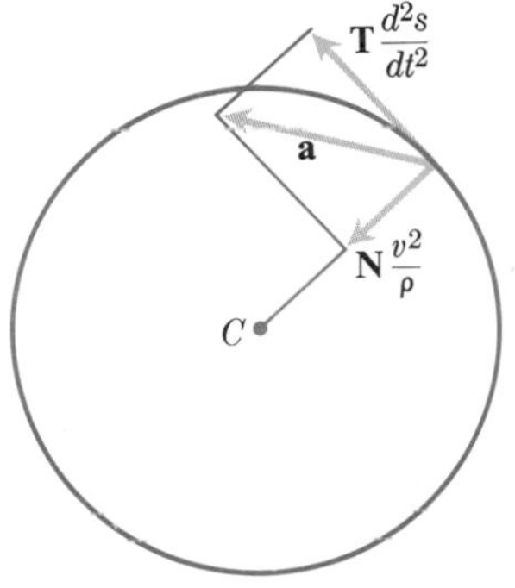

12–17 Tangential and normal components of an acceleration vector.

The following example illustrates how the tangential and normal components of velocity and acceleration may be computed when the equations of motion are known. In particular, it should be noted that the equation

$$|\mathbf{a}|^2 = a_x^2 + a_y^2 = a_T^2 + a_N^2 \tag{12}$$

is used to determine the normal component of acceleration

$$a_N = \sqrt{|\mathbf{a}|^2 - a_T^2}. \tag{13}$$

Note that Eq. (13) gives a way to find a_N without having to find κ first.

EXAMPLE 3. The coordinates of a moving particle at time t are given by

$$x = \cos t + t\sin t, \qquad y = \sin t - t\cos t.$$

Find the velocity and acceleration vectors, the speed ds/dt, and the normal and tangential components of acceleration.

Solution

$$\mathbf{v} = \mathbf{i}\frac{dx}{dt} + \mathbf{j}\frac{dy}{dt} = \mathbf{i}[-\sin t + t\cos t + \sin t] + \mathbf{j}[\cos t + t\sin t - \cos t]$$

$$= \mathbf{i}t\cos t + \mathbf{j}t\sin t$$

and

$$\mathbf{a} = \frac{d\mathbf{v}}{dt} = \mathbf{i}[-t\sin t + \cos t] + \mathbf{j}[t\cos t + \sin t].$$

Now the tangential component of velocity is

$$\frac{ds}{dt} = |\mathbf{v}| = \sqrt{(t\cos t)^2 + (t\sin t)^2} = t$$

and the tangential component of acceleration is

$$a_{\mathrm{T}} = \frac{d^2s}{dt^2} = \frac{d}{dt}\left(\frac{ds}{dt}\right) = \frac{d}{dt}(t) = 1.$$

We use Eq. (13) to determine the normal component of acceleration:

$$a_{\mathrm{N}} = \sqrt{|\mathbf{a}|^2 - a_{\mathrm{T}}^2} = \sqrt{(-t\sin t + \cos t)^2 + (t\cos t + \sin t)^2 - 1} = t.$$

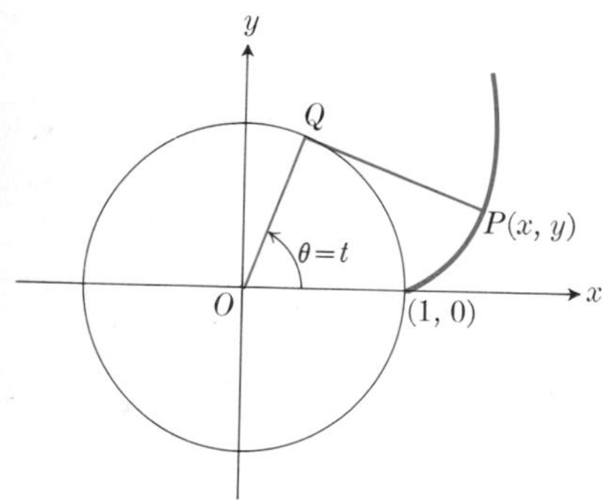

12–18 Involute of a circle.

Here the tangential acceleration has constant magnitude and the normal acceleration starts with zero magnitude at $t = 0$ and increases with time. The equations of motion are the same as the parametric equations for the *involute* of a circle of unit radius. This is the path of the endpoint P of a string that is held taut as it is unwound from the circle. To get the parametrization, the origin is taken as the center of the circle (Fig. 12–18), with (1, 0) being the position where P starts. The angle t is measured from the positively directed x-axis counterclockwise to the ray from O to the point of tangency Q.

We can find the radius of curvature from the equation $a_{\mathrm{N}} = v^2/\rho$, since $v^2 = |\mathbf{v}|^2 = t^2$ and $a_{\mathrm{N}} = t$ and hence

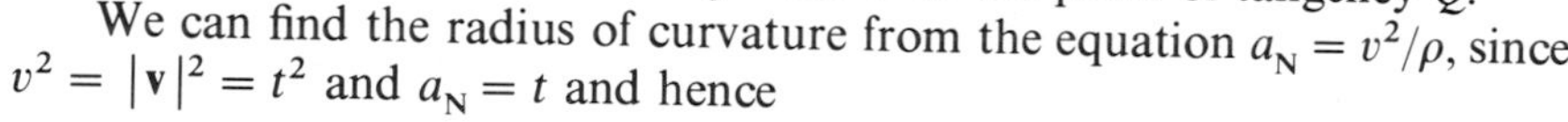

$$\rho = \frac{v^2}{a_{\mathrm{N}}} = \frac{t^2}{t} = t.$$

Equations (10) and (11) can be used to find a formula for the curvature κ in terms of the velocity and acceleration. First, we compute the cross product of the velocity and acceleration vectors. We obtain

$$\mathbf{v}\times\mathbf{a} = \mathbf{T}\frac{ds}{dt}\times\left[\mathbf{T}\frac{d^2s}{dt^2} + \mathbf{N}\kappa\left(\frac{ds}{dt}\right)^2\right]$$

$$= \mathbf{T}\times\mathbf{N}\kappa\left(\frac{ds}{dt}\right)^3 \tag{14}$$

because we can apply the distributive law for the cross product, and $\mathbf{T}\times\mathbf{T} = \mathbf{0}$. Moreover, $\mathbf{T}\times\mathbf{N}$ is the unit binormal vector $\mathbf{B}$, as given by Eq. (15), Article 12–4. Therefore

$$\mathbf{v}\times\mathbf{a} = \mathbf{B}\kappa\left(\frac{ds}{dt}\right)^3. \tag{15}$$

Since $\mathbf{B}$ is a *unit* vector, the magnitude of $\mathbf{v} \times \mathbf{a}$ is

$$|\mathbf{v} \times \mathbf{a}| = \kappa \left| \frac{ds}{dt} \right|^3 = \kappa |\mathbf{v}|^3.$$

Finally, if $|\mathbf{v}| \neq 0$, we get (by division)

$$\kappa = \frac{|\mathbf{v} \times \mathbf{a}|}{|\mathbf{v}|^3}. \tag{16}$$

How do we use this equation? Given the motion in the form $\mathbf{R} = \mathbf{i}x + \mathbf{j}y + \mathbf{k}z$, we differentiate with respect to time to get $\mathbf{v}$, then differentiate again to get $\mathbf{a}$, and compute $\mathbf{v} \times \mathbf{a}$ using a determinant of order 3 in the usual way for cross products. We then divide the length of this vector by the cube of the length of $\mathbf{v}$.

EXAMPLE 4. Use Eq. (16) to find the curvature of the curve of the preceding example.

Solution. In that example, we found the velocity

$$\mathbf{v} = \mathbf{i}t \cos t + \mathbf{j}t \sin t,$$

and acceleration

$$\mathbf{a} = \mathbf{i}(-t \sin t + \cos t) + \mathbf{j}(t \cos t + \sin t).$$

Therefore

$$\mathbf{v} \times \mathbf{a} = \begin{vmatrix} \mathbf{i} & \mathbf{j} & \mathbf{k} \\ t \cos t & t \sin t & 0 \\ (-t \sin t + \cos t) & (t \cos t + \sin t) & 0 \end{vmatrix};$$

this leads to

$$\begin{aligned} \mathbf{v} \times \mathbf{a} &= \mathbf{k}(t^2 \cos^2 t + t \cos t \sin t + t^2 \sin^2 t - t \sin t \cos t) \\ &= \mathbf{k}t^2, \end{aligned}$$

and

$$\kappa = \frac{|\mathbf{v} \times \mathbf{a}|}{|\mathbf{v}|^3} = \frac{t^2}{t^3} = \frac{1}{t}.$$

This result is valid for $t > 0$. If the curve and the motion also exist for $t < 0$, we should replace t by $|t|$ for $t < 0$.

PROBLEMS

1. Derive Eq. (2) by the Δ-process.

2. Apply Eqs. (2) and (3) to $\mathbf{U} \cdot \mathbf{V}_1$ with $\mathbf{V}_1 = \mathbf{V} \times \mathbf{W}$ and thereby derive Eq. (5) for

$$\frac{d}{dt}[\mathbf{U} \cdot (\mathbf{V} \times \mathbf{W})].$$

3. If $\mathbf{F}(t) = \mathbf{i}f(t) + \mathbf{j}g(t) + \mathbf{k}h(t)$, where f, g, and h are functions of t that have derivatives of orders one, two, and three, show that

$$\frac{d}{dt}\left[\mathbf{F} \cdot \left(\frac{d\mathbf{F}}{dt} \times \frac{d^2\mathbf{F}}{dt^2}\right)\right] = \mathbf{F} \cdot \left(\frac{d\mathbf{F}}{dt} \times \frac{d^3\mathbf{F}}{dt^3}\right).$$

Explain why the answer contains just this one term rather than the three terms that one might expect.

4. With the book closed, derive vector expressions for the velocity and acceleration in terms of tangential and normal components. Check your derivations with those given in the text.

In Problems 5 through 9, find the velocity and acceleration vectors, and then find the speed ds/dt and the tangential and normal components of acceleration.

5. $\mathbf{R} = \mathbf{i} \cosh 2t + \mathbf{j} \sinh 2t$

6. $\mathbf{R} = (2t + 3)\mathbf{i} + (t^2 - 1)\mathbf{j}$

7. $\mathbf{R} = (a \cos \omega t)\mathbf{i} + (a \sin \omega t)\mathbf{j}$, a and ω positive constants

8. $\mathbf{R} = \mathbf{i} \ln (t^2 + 1) + \mathbf{j}(t - 2 \tan^{-1} t)$

9. $\mathbf{R} = \mathbf{i}e^t \cos t + \mathbf{j}e^t \sin t$

10. Deduce from Eq. (11) that a particle will move in a straight line if the normal component of acceleration is identically zero.

11. Show that the radius of curvature of a plane curve is given by

$$\rho = \frac{(\dot{x}^2 + \dot{y}^2)}{\sqrt{\ddot{x}^2 + \ddot{y}^2 - \ddot{s}^2}},$$

where

$$\dot{x} = \frac{dx}{dt}, \qquad \ddot{x} = \frac{d^2x}{dt^2}, \qquad \ldots$$

and

$$\ddot{s} = \frac{d}{dt}(\sqrt{\dot{x}^2 + \dot{y}^2}).$$

12. If a particle moves in a curve with constant speed, show that the force is always directed along the normal.

13. If the force acting on a particle is at all times perpendicular to the direction of motion, show that the speed remains constant.

14. Use Eq. (16) to find the curvature of the helix $x = \cos t$, $y = \sin t$, $z = t$.

12–6 POLAR COORDINATES

When a particle P moves on a curve whose equation is given in polar coordinates, it is convenient to express the velocity and acceleration vectors in terms of the unit vectors

$$\mathbf{u}_r = \mathbf{i} \cos \theta + \mathbf{j} \sin \theta, \qquad \mathbf{u}_\theta = -\mathbf{i} \sin \theta + \mathbf{j} \cos \theta. \tag{1}$$

The vector $\mathbf{u}_r$ points along the radius vector $\overrightarrow{OP}$, and $\mathbf{u}_\theta$ points at right angles to $\overrightarrow{OP}$ and in the direction of increasing θ, as shown in Fig. 12–19. From (1), we find that

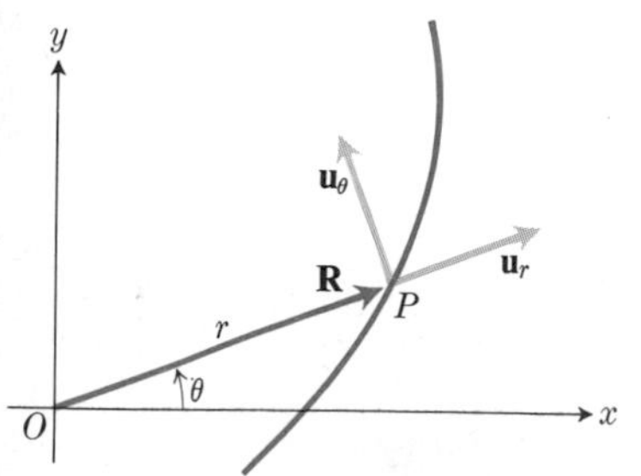

12–19 The unit vectors $\mathbf{u}_r$ and $\mathbf{u}_\theta$.

$$\begin{aligned} \frac{d\mathbf{u}_r}{d\theta} &= -\mathbf{i} \sin \theta + \mathbf{j} \cos \theta = \mathbf{u}_\theta, \\ \frac{d\mathbf{u}_\theta}{d\theta} &= -\mathbf{i} \cos \theta - \mathbf{j} \sin \theta = -\mathbf{u}_r. \end{aligned} \tag{2}$$

This says that differentiating either $\mathbf{u}_r$ or $\mathbf{u}_\theta$ with respect to θ is equivalent to rotating that vector 90° counterclockwise.

Since the vectors $\mathbf{R} = \overrightarrow{OP}$ and $r\mathbf{u}_r$ have the same direction, and the length of $\mathbf{R}$ is the absolute value of the polar coordinate r of $P(r, \theta)$, we have

$$\mathbf{R} = r\mathbf{u}_r. \tag{3}$$

We differentiate this equation with respect to t to obtain the velocity, remembering that both r and $\mathbf{u}_r$ may be variables. From (2) and the chain rule we get

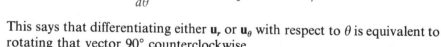

$$\frac{d\mathbf{u}_r}{dt} = \frac{d\mathbf{u}_r}{d\theta}\frac{d\theta}{dt} = \mathbf{u}_\theta \frac{d\theta}{dt}, \qquad \frac{d\mathbf{u}_\theta}{dt} = \frac{d\mathbf{u}_\theta}{d\theta}\frac{d\theta}{dt} = -\mathbf{u}_r \frac{d\theta}{dt}. \tag{4}$$

Hence,

$$\mathbf{v} = \frac{d\mathbf{R}}{dt} = \mathbf{u}_r \frac{dr}{dt} + r \frac{d\mathbf{u}_r}{dt}$$

becomes

$$\mathbf{v} = \mathbf{u}_r \frac{dr}{dt} + \mathbf{u}_\theta r \frac{d\theta}{dt}. \tag{5}$$

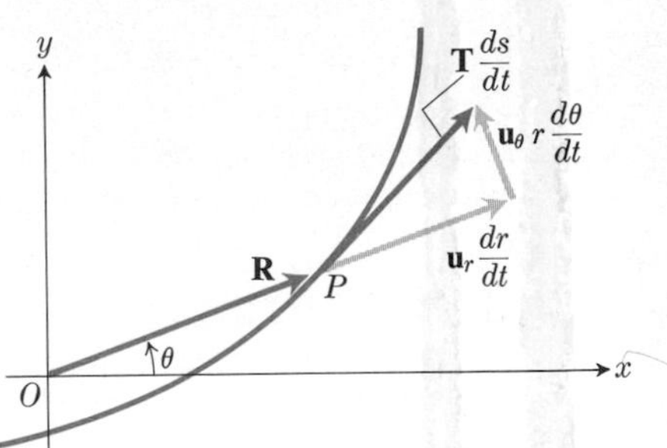

12–20 $\mathbf{u}_r \frac{dr}{dt} + \mathbf{u}_\theta r \frac{d\theta}{dt}$ is the velocity vector.

Of course this velocity vector is tangent to the curve at P and has magnitude

$$|\mathbf{v}| = \sqrt{(dr/dt)^2 + r^2(d\theta/dt)^2} = |ds/dt|.$$

In fact, if the three sides of the "differential triangle" of sides dr, $r\,d\theta$, and ds are all divided by dt (Fig. 12–20), the result will be a similar triangle having sides dr/dt, $r\,d\theta/dt$, and ds/dt, which illustrates the vector equation

$$\mathbf{v} = \mathbf{T}\frac{ds}{dt} = \mathbf{u}_r \frac{dr}{dt} + \mathbf{u}_\theta r \frac{d\theta}{dt}.$$

The acceleration vector is found by differentiating the velocity vector in (5) as follows:

$$\mathbf{a} = \frac{d\mathbf{v}}{dt} = \left(\mathbf{u}_r \frac{d^2r}{dt^2} + \frac{d\mathbf{u}_r}{dt}\frac{dr}{dt}\right) + \left(\mathbf{u}_\theta r \frac{d^2\theta}{dt^2} + \mathbf{u}_\theta \frac{dr}{dt}\frac{d\theta}{dt} + \frac{d\mathbf{u}_\theta}{dt} r \frac{d\theta}{dt}\right).$$

When Eqs. (4) are used to evaluate the derivatives of $\mathbf{u}_r$ and $\mathbf{u}_\theta$ and the components are separated, the result becomes

$$\mathbf{a} = \mathbf{u}_r \left[\frac{d^2r}{dt^2} - r\left(\frac{d\theta}{dt}\right)^2\right] + \mathbf{u}_\theta \left[r\frac{d^2\theta}{dt^2} + 2\frac{dr}{dt}\frac{d\theta}{dt}\right]. \tag{6}$$

The polar form is particularly convenient in discussing the motion of a particle in what is called a "central force field." By this we mean that the force acting on the particle is always directed toward a single point, the center of force, which we choose as origin (Fig. 12–21). Then from $\mathbf{F} = m\mathbf{a}$, we see that the $\mathbf{u}_\theta$ component of acceleration must vanish. That is, in any central force field,

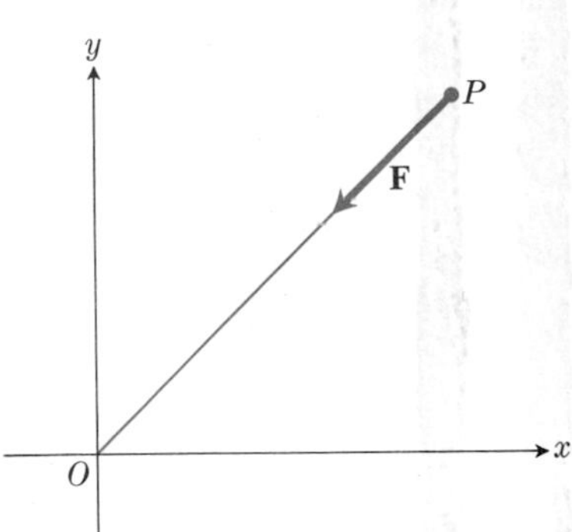

12–21 $\mathbf{F}$ is a central force if it points toward a fixed point (here the origin) no matter how P moves.

$$r\frac{d^2\theta}{dt^2} + 2\frac{dr}{dt}\frac{d\theta}{dt} = 0, \tag{7}$$

where the origin is at the center of force. (For instance, the sun would be chosen as the origin in discussing the gravitational attraction between the sun and a planet.) To integrate (7), let

$$u = \frac{d\theta}{dt}.$$

Then

$$r\frac{du}{dt} + 2u\frac{dr}{dt} = 0,$$

or

$$r\,du = -2u\,dr, \qquad \frac{du}{u} = -2\frac{dr}{r},$$

$$\ln|u| = -2\ln|r| + c_1,$$

$$\ln|ur^2| = c_1, \qquad |ur^2| = e^{c_1} = C,$$

or

$$r^2\frac{d\theta}{dt} = \pm C. \tag{8}$$

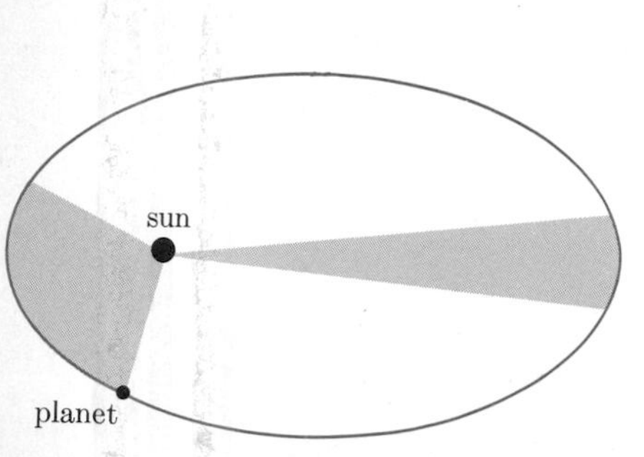

12–22 The line joining a planet and its sun sweeps over equal areas in equal times.

The left side of this equation is $2\,dA/dt$, where $dA = \frac{1}{2}r^2\,d\theta$ is the area swept over as the radius vector $\overrightarrow{OP}$ rotates through a small angle $d\theta$. Hence, Eq. (8) says that the radius vector *sweeps over area at a constant rate* in a central force field. Kepler's second law of planetary motion is thus a consequence of the fact that the field of gravitational attraction of the sun for the planets is a central force field (Fig. 12–22).

PROBLEMS

1. With the book closed, derive vector expressions for the velocity and acceleration in terms of components along and at right angles to the radius vector. Check your derivations with those given in the text.

In Problems 2–6, find the velocity and acceleration vectors in terms of $\mathbf{u}_r$ and $\mathbf{u}_\theta$.

2. $r = a(1 - \cos\theta)$ and $\dfrac{d\theta}{dt} = 3$

3. $r = a\sin 2\theta$ and $\dfrac{d\theta}{dt} = 2t$

4. $r = e^{a\theta}$ and $\dfrac{d\theta}{dt} = 2$

5. $r = a(1 + \sin t)$ and $\theta = 1 - e^{-t}$

6. $r = 2\cos 4t$ and $\theta = 2t$

7. If a particle moves in an ellipse whose polar equation is $r = c/(1 - e\cos\theta)$ and the force is directed toward the origin, show that the magnitude of the force is proportional to $1/r^2$.

REVIEW QUESTIONS AND EXERCISES

1. Define the derivative of a vector function.

2. Develop formulas for the derivatives, with respect to θ, of the unit vectors $\mathbf{u}_r$ and $\mathbf{u}_\theta$.

3. Develop vector formulas for velocity and acceleration of a particle moving in a plane curve:

a) in terms of cartesian coordinates,

b) in terms of polar coordinates,

c) in terms of distance traveled along the curve and unit vectors tangent and normal to the curve.

4. a) Define curvature of a plane curve.

b) Define radius of curvature.

c) Define center of curvature.

d) Define osculating circle.

5. Develop a formula for the curvature of a curve whose parametric equations are $x = f(t)$, $y = g(t)$.

6. In what way does the curvature of a curve affect the acceleration of a particle moving along the curve? In particular, discuss the case of constant-speed motion along a curve.

7. State and derive Kepler's second law concerning motion in a central force field.

8. If a vector $\mathbf{V}$ is a differentiable function of t and $|\mathbf{V}| =$ constant, what do you know about $d\mathbf{V}/dt$?

9. Define arc length and curvature of a space curve.

10. For a space curve, explain how to find the unit tangent vector, unit principal normal, and unit binormal.

MISCELLANEOUS PROBLEMS

1. A particle moves in the xy-plane according to the time law

$$x = 1/\sqrt{1 + t^2}, \qquad y = t/\sqrt{1 + t^2}.$$

a) Compute the velocity vector and acceleration vector when $t = 1$.
b) At what time is the speed of the particle a maximum?

2. A circular wheel with unit radius rolls along the x-axis uniformly, rotating one half-turn per second. The position of a point P on the circumference is given by the formula

$$\overrightarrow{OP} = \mathbf{R} = \mathbf{i}(\pi t - \sin \pi t) + \mathbf{j}(1 - \cos \pi t).$$

a) Determine the velocity (*vector*) $\mathbf{v}$ and the acceleration (*vector*) $\mathbf{a}$ at time t.
b) Determine the slopes (as functions of t) of the two straight lines PC and PQ joining P to the center C of the wheel and to the point Q that is topmost at the instant.
c) Show that the directions of the vectors $\mathbf{v}$ and $\mathbf{a}$ can be expressed in terms of the straight lines described in (b).

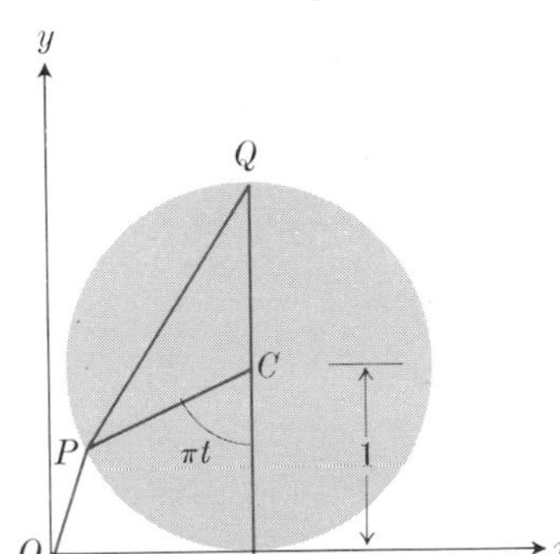

Figure 12–23

3. The motion of a particle in the xy-plane is given by

$$\mathbf{R} = \mathbf{i}at \cos t + \mathbf{j}at \sin t.$$

Find the speed, and the tangential and normal components of the acceleration.

4. A particle moves in the xy-plane in such a manner that the derivative of the position vector is always perpendicular to the position vector. Show that the particle moves on a circle with center at the origin.

5. The position of a point at time t is given by the formulas $x = e^t \cos t$, $y = e^t \sin t$.
a) Show that $\mathbf{a} = 2\mathbf{v} - 2\mathbf{r}$.
b) Show that the angle between the radius vector $\mathbf{r}$ and the acceleration vector $\mathbf{a}$ is constant, and find this angle.

6. Given the instantaneous velocity $\mathbf{v} = a\mathbf{i} + b\mathbf{j}$ and acceleration $\mathbf{a} = c\mathbf{i} + d\mathbf{j}$ of a particle at a point P on its path of motion, determine the curvature of the path at P.

7. Find the parametric equations, in terms of the parameter θ, of the position of the center of curvature of the cycloid

$$x = a(\theta - \sin \theta), \qquad y = a(1 - \cos \theta).$$

8. Find the point on the curve $y = e^x$ for which the radius of curvature is a minimum.

9. Given a closed curve having the property that every line parallel to the x-axis or the y-axis has at most two points in common with the curve. Let

$$x = x(t), \qquad y = y(t), \qquad \alpha \le t \le \beta,$$

be equations of the curve.
a) Prove that if dx/dt and dy/dt are continuous, then the area bounded by the curve is

$$\frac{1}{2}\left|\int_\alpha^\beta \left[x(t)\frac{dy}{dt} - y(t)\frac{dx}{dt}\right] dt\right|.$$

b) Use the result of (a) to find the area inside the ellipse

$$x = a \cos \phi, \qquad y = b \sin \phi, \qquad 0 \le \phi \le 2\pi.$$

What does the answer become when $a = b$?

10. For the curve defined by the equations

$$x = \int_0^\theta \cos\left(\tfrac{1}{2}\pi t^2\right) dt, \qquad y = \int_0^\theta \sin\left(\tfrac{1}{2}\pi t^2\right) dt,$$

calculate the curvature κ as a function of the length of arc s, where s is measured from $(0, 0)$.

11. The curve for which the length of the tangent intercepted between the point of contact and the y-axis is always equal to 1 is called the *tractrix*. Find its equation. Show that the radius of curvature at each point of the curve is inversely proportional to the length of the normal intercepted between the point on the curve and the y-axis. Calculate the length of arc of the tractrix, and find the parametric equations in terms of the length of arc.

12. Let $x = x(t)$, $y = y(t)$ be a closed curve. A constant length p is measured off along the normal to the curve. The extremity of this segment describes a curve which is called a *parallel curve* to the original curve. Find the length of arc, the radius of curvature, and the area enclosed by the parallel curve. Assume that the appropriate derivatives exist and are continuous.

13. Given the curve represented by the parametric equations

$$x = 32t, \qquad y = 16t^2 - 4.$$

a) Calculate the radius of curvature of the curve at the point where $t = 3$.
b) Find the length of the curve between the points where $t = 0$ and $t = 1$.

14. Find the velocity, acceleration, and speed of a particle whose position at time t is

$$x = 3 \sin t, \qquad y = 2 \cos t.$$

Also find the tangential and normal components of the acceleration.

15. The position of a particle at time t is given by the equations

$$x = 1 + \cos 2t, \qquad y = \sin 2t.$$

Find:

a) the normal and tangential components of acceleration at time t;

b) the radius of curvature of the path;

c) the equation of the path in polar coordinates, using the x-axis as the line $\theta = 0$ and the y-axis as the line $\theta = \pi/2$.

16. A particle moves so that its position at time t has the polar coordinates $r = t$, $\theta = t$. Find the velocity $\mathbf{v}$, the acceleration $\mathbf{a}$, and the curvature κ at any time t.

17. Find an expression for the curvature of the curve whose equation in polar coordinates is $r = f(\theta)$.

18. a) Find the equation in *polar coordinates* of the curve

$$x = e^{2t} \cos t, \qquad y = e^{2t} \sin t.$$

b) Find the length of this curve from $t = 0$ to $t = 2\pi$.

19. Express the velocity vector in terms of $\mathbf{u}_r$ and $\mathbf{u}_\theta$ for a point moving in the xy-plane according to the law

$$\mathbf{r} = (t + 1)\mathbf{i} + (t - 1)\mathbf{j}.$$

20. The polar coordinates of a particle at time t are

$$r = e^{\omega t} + e^{-\omega t}, \qquad \theta = t,$$

where ω is a constant. Find the acceleration vector when $t = 0$.

21. A slender rod, passing through the fixed point O, is rotating about O in a plane at the constant rate of 3 rad/min. An insect is crawling along the rod toward O at the constant rate of 1 in/min. Use polar coordinates in the plane, with point O as the origin, and assume that the insect starts at the point $r = 2$, $\theta = 0$.

a) Find, in polar form, the vector velocity and vector acceleration of the insect when it is halfway to the origin.

b) What will be the length of the path, in the plane, that the insect has traveled when it reaches the origin?

22. A smooth ball rolls inside a long hollow tube while the tube rotates with constant angular velocity ω about an axis perpendicular to the axis of the tube. Assuming no friction between the ball and the sides of the tube, show that the distance r from the axis of rotation to the ball satisfies the differential equation

$$d^2r/dt^2 - \omega^2 r = 0.$$

If at time $t = 0$ the ball is at rest (relative to the tube) at $r = a > 0$, find r as a function of t.

In Problems 23–26, r, θ, and z are cylindrical coordinates of a moving point P. The vectors $\mathbf{u}_r = \mathbf{i} \cos \theta + \mathbf{j} \sin \theta$ and $\mathbf{u}_\theta = -\mathbf{i} \sin \theta + \mathbf{j} \cos \theta$ are the usual unit vectors used with polar coordinates, as in Article 12–6.

23. Express the vector $\mathbf{R} = \overrightarrow{OP}$ in terms of cylindrical coordinates and the unit vectors $\mathbf{u}_r$, $\mathbf{u}_\theta$, and $\mathbf{k}$.

24. Derive formulas for the velocity $\mathbf{v} = d\mathbf{R}/dt$ and acceleration $\mathbf{a} = d\mathbf{v}/dt$ in terms of cylindrical coordinates and the unit vectors $\mathbf{u}_r$, $\mathbf{u}_\theta$, and $\mathbf{k}$.

25. A particle P slides without friction along a coil spring having the form of a right circular helix. If the positive z-axis is taken downward, the cylindrical coordinates of P at time t are $r = a$, $z = b\theta$, where a and b are positive constants. If the particle starts at $r = a$, $\theta = 0$ with zero velocity and falls under gravity, the law of conservation of energy then tells us that its speed after it has fallen a vertical distance z is $\sqrt{2gz}$.

a) Find the angular velocity $d\theta/dt$ when $\theta = 2\pi$.

b) Express θ and z as functions of the time t.

c) Determine the tangential and normal components of the velocity $d\mathbf{R}/dt$ and acceleration $d^2\mathbf{R}/dt^2$ as functions of t. Is there any component of acceleration in the direction of the binormal $\mathbf{B}$?

26. Suppose the curve in Problem 25 is replaced by the conical helix

$$r = a\theta, \qquad z = b\theta.$$

a) Express the angular velocity $d\theta/dt$ as a function of θ.

b) Express the distance that the particle travels along this helix as a function of θ.

27. Hold two of the three spherical coordinates ρ, ϕ, θ of point P in Fig. 11–25 constant while letting the other coordinate increase. Let $\mathbf{u}$, with subscript corresponding to the coordinate that is permitted to vary, denote the unit vector that points in the direction in which P starts to move under these conditions.

a) Express the three unit vectors $\mathbf{u}_\rho$, $\mathbf{u}_\phi$, $\mathbf{u}_\theta$ which are obtained in this manner, in terms of ρ, ϕ, θ, and the unit vectors $\mathbf{i}$, $\mathbf{j}$, $\mathbf{k}$.

b) Show that $\mathbf{u}_\rho \cdot \mathbf{u}_\phi = 0$.

c) Show that $\mathbf{u}_\theta = \mathbf{u}_\rho \times \mathbf{u}_\phi$.

d) Do the vectors $\mathbf{u}_\rho$, $\mathbf{u}_\phi$, $\mathbf{u}_\theta$ form a system of mutually orthogonal vectors? Is the system, in the order given, a righthanded or a lefthanded system?

28. If the spherical coordinates ρ, ϕ, θ of a moving point P are differentiable functions of the time t, and $\mathbf{R} = \overrightarrow{OP}$ is the vector from the origin to P, express $\mathbf{R}$ and $d\mathbf{R}/dt$ in terms of ρ, ϕ, θ and their derivatives and the unit vectors $\mathbf{u}_\rho$, $\mathbf{u}_\phi$, $\mathbf{u}_\theta$ of Problem 27.

29. Express $ds^2 = dx^2 + dy^2 + dz^2$ in terms of

a) cylindrical coordinates r, θ, z,
b) spherical coordinates ρ, ϕ, θ (see Problem 28).

Interpret your results geometrically in terms of the sides and a diagonal of a rectangular box. Sketch.

30. Using the results of Problem 29, find the lengths of the following curves between $\theta = 0$ and $\theta = \ln 8$.

a) $z = r = ae^{\theta}$
b) $\phi = \pi/6, \quad \rho = 2e^{\theta}$

31. Determine parametric equations giving x, y, z in terms of the parameter θ for the curve of intersection of the sphere $\rho = a$ and the plane $y + z = 0$, and find its length.

32. In Article 12–6, we found the velocity vector of a particle moving in a plane to be

$$\mathbf{v} = \frac{d\mathbf{R}}{dt} = \mathbf{i}\frac{dx}{dt} + \mathbf{j}\frac{dy}{dt}$$

$$= \mathbf{u}_r\frac{dr}{dt} + \mathbf{u}_\theta\frac{r\,d\theta}{dt}.$$

a) Express dx/dt and dy/dt in terms of dr/dt and $r\,d\theta/dt$ by computing $\mathbf{v} \cdot \mathbf{i}$ and $\mathbf{v} \cdot \mathbf{j}$.
b) Express dr/dt and $r\,d\theta/dt$ in terms of dx/dt and dy/dt by computing $\mathbf{v} \cdot \mathbf{u}_r$ and $\mathbf{v} \cdot \mathbf{u}_\theta$.

33. The line through OA, A being the point $(1, 1, 1)$, is the axis of rotation of a rigid body that is rotating with a constant angular speed of 6 rad/sec. The rotation appears clockwise when we look towards the origin from A. Find the velocity vector of the point of the body that is at the position $(1, 3, 2)$ (see Example 5, Article 2–10).

34. Consider the space curve whose parametric equations are

$$x = t, \qquad y = t, \qquad z = \tfrac{2}{3}t^{3/2}.$$

Compute the equation of the plane that passes through the point $(1, 1, \frac{2}{3})$ of this curve, and is perpendicular to the tangent of this curve at the same point.

35. A curve is given by the parametric equations

$$x = e^t \sin 2t, \qquad y = e^t \cos 2t, \qquad z = 2e^t.$$

Let P_0 be the point where $t = 0$. Determine

a) the direction cosines of the tangent, principal normal, and binormal at P_0;
b) the curvature at P_0.

36. The *normal plane* to a space curve at any point P of the curve is defined as the plane through P that is perpendicular to the tangent vector. The *osculating plane* at P is the plane containing the tangent and the principal normal. Given the space curve whose vector equation is

$$\mathbf{r}(t) = t\mathbf{i} + t^2\mathbf{j} + t^3\mathbf{k},$$

find:

a) the equation of the normal plane at $(1, 1, 1)$;
b) the equation of the osculating plane at $(1, 1, 1)$.

37. Given the curve whose vector is

$$\mathbf{r}(t) = (3t - t^3)\,\mathbf{i} + 3t^2\mathbf{j} + (3t + t^3)\mathbf{k},$$

compute the curvature.

38. Show that the length of the arc described by the endpoint of

$$\mathbf{R} = (3 \cos t)\,\mathbf{i} + (3 \sin t)\,\mathbf{j} + t^2\mathbf{k},$$

as t varies from 0 to 2, is $5 + \frac{9}{4} \ln 3$.

39. The curve whose vector equation is

$$\mathbf{r}(t) = (2\sqrt{t} \cos t)\,\mathbf{i} + (3\sqrt{t} \sin t)\mathbf{j} + \sqrt{1 - t}\,\mathbf{k}, \qquad 0 \le t \le 1,$$

lies on a quadric surface. Find the equation of this surface and describe it.

40. Find the orbit of a planet relative to the sun, assuming the sun to be fixed at the origin and the force acting on the planet to be directed toward the sun with magnitude $\gamma mM/r^2$, where γ is the universal gravitational constant, M is the mass of the sun, m is the mass of the planet, and r is its distance from the sun. Choose the initial line to pass through the perihelion point of the orbit, and assume the velocity at perihelion is v_0. Show that the path is a circle, ellipse, parabola, or hyperbola according as $v_0^2 r_0/\gamma M$ equals one, lies between one and two, equals two, or is greater than two.

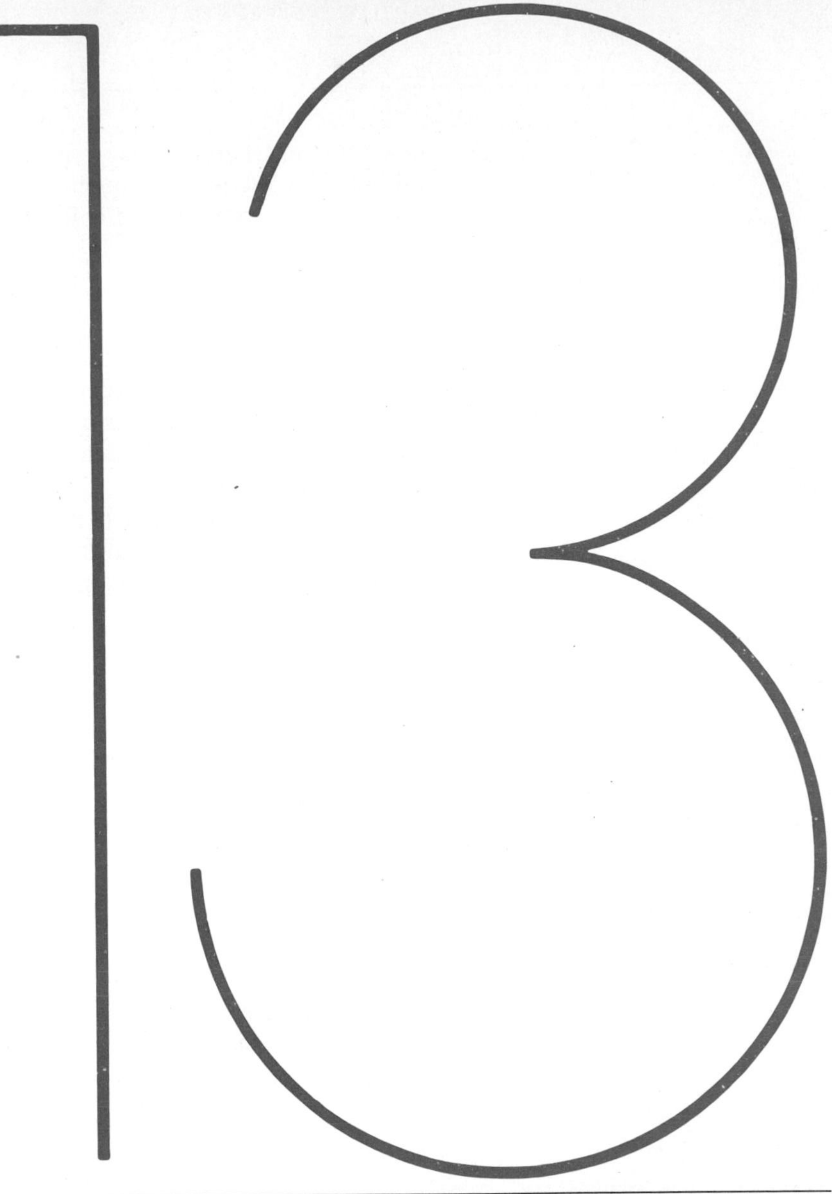

PARTIAL DIFFERENTIATION

13-1 FUNCTIONS OF TWO OR MORE VARIABLES

As we saw in Chapter 1, there are many instances in science, engineering, and everyday life where a quantity w is determined by a number of other quantities. For example, the volume of a right circular cone of radius r and altitude h is

$$V = \tfrac{1}{3}\pi r^2 h. \tag{1}$$

The values of r and h in this formula can be assigned independently of each other and, once they have been assigned, the corresponding value of V is determined. We say that *V is a function of r* and h, and we call r and h the *independent* variables of the function. The variable V is the *dependent* variable of the function.

In general, if w is uniquely determined when the values of two independent variables x and y are given, we say that w is a function of x and y, and indicate this fact by writing some such notation as

$$w = f(x, y). \tag{2}$$

The set of pairs (x, y) for which w is defined is called the domain of w, and the set of values that w assumes for the pairs in its domain is called the range of w.

The notation

$$w = f(x, y, z) \tag{3}$$

means, similarly, that the value of w is determined by assigning values to three independent variables x, y, and z. For example, if

$$\rho = \sqrt{x^2 + y^2 + z^2}, \tag{4}$$

as in the relationship between $\rho = |\overrightarrow{OP}|$ and the cartesian coordinates of $P(x, y, z)$, then the assignment of values to the coordinates x, y, and z determines a unique value of ρ.

Continuity

A function $w = f(x, y)$ is *continuous* at a point (x_0, y_0) in its domain if and only if

$$w \to w_0 = f(x_0, y_0)$$

as

$$(x, y) \to (x_0, y_0),$$

or

$$\lim_{\substack{x \to x_0 \\ y \to y_0}} f(x, y) = f(x_0, y_0).$$

In other words, w is continuous at (x_0, y_0) provided $|w - w_0|$ can be made arbitrarily small by making both $|x - x_0|$ and $|y - y_0|$ small. This is like the definition of continuity for functions of one variable, except that there are two independent variables involved instead of one.

EXAMPLE 1. The function $w = xy$ is continuous at any (x_0, y_0) since

$$\begin{aligned}|w - w_0| &= |xy - x_0 y_0| \\ &= |xy - xy_0 + xy_0 - x_0 y_0| \\ &= |x(y - y_0) + y_0(x - x_0)|\end{aligned}$$

can be made arbitrarily small by making both $|x - x_0|$ and $|y - y_0|$ small.

EXAMPLE 2. The function w defined by

$$w(x, y) = \begin{cases} \dfrac{xy}{x^2 + y^2} & \text{when } (x, y) \neq (0, 0), \\ 0 & \text{when } (x, y) = (0, 0) \end{cases}$$

is not continuous at (0, 0). For, if we take

$$x = r \cos \theta, \qquad y = r \sin \theta, \qquad (r \neq 0),$$

we have

$$w = \sin \theta \cos \theta = \tfrac{1}{2} \sin 2\theta,$$

so that w takes all values between $-\frac{1}{2}$ and $+\frac{1}{2}$ as the point (x, y), or (r, θ), moves around the origin, no matter how small r may be. We cannot make w stay close to zero simply by keeping (x, y) close to (0, 0).

In most cases, the so-called elementary functions, which include functions given by algebraic combinations of polynomials, trigonometric functions, logarithms, or exponentials, are continuous, except possibly where a denominator is zero or the function is otherwise undefined.

PROBLEMS

1. How close to the point (0, 0) should one take the point (x, y) in order to make $|f(x, y) - f(0, 0)| < \varepsilon$ if:

a) $f(x, y) = x^2 + y^2$ and $\varepsilon = 0.01$?

b) $f(x, y) = \dfrac{y}{x^2 + 1}$ and $\varepsilon = 0.001$?

2. (a) How close to the point (0, 0, 0) should one take the point (x, y, z) in order to make $|f(x, y, z) - f(0, 0, 0)| < \varepsilon$ if $f(x, y, z) = x^2 + y^2 + z^2$ and $\varepsilon = 0.01$? If $f(x, y, z) = xyz$ and $\varepsilon = 0.008$? (b) Is the function $f(x, y, z) = x^2 + y^2 + z^2$ continuous at (0, 0, 0)? Give reasons for your answer.

3. Let $f(x, y) = (x + y)/(x^2 + y)$ when $x^2 + y \neq 0$.

a) Is it possible to define $f(1, -1)$ in such a way that $f(x, y) \to f(1, -1)$ as $(x, y) \to (1, -1)$ along the line $x = 1$? Along the line $y = -1$?

b) Is it possible to define $f(1, -1)$ in such a way that f is continuous at $(1, -1)$?

Give the reasons for your answers.

The functions in Problems 4–7 are modifications of the function in Example 2. Express each one in polar coordinates and see whether it has a limit as (x, y) approaches (0, 0). If the limit exists, say what it is; if it does not exist, say why not.

4. $g(x, y) = \dfrac{x^2 y}{x^2 + y^2}$

5. $h(x, y) = \dfrac{x^2}{x^2 + y^2}$

6. $w(x, y) = \dfrac{x^2 - y^2}{x^2 + y^2}$

7. $z(x, y) = \dfrac{xy}{\sqrt{x^2 + y^2}}$

Find the limits in Problems 8 and 9.

8. $\displaystyle\lim_{\substack{x \to 0 \\ y \to 0}} \frac{3x^2 - y^2 + 5}{x^2 + y^2 + 1}$

9. $\displaystyle\lim_{\substack{x \to 0 \\ y \to 0}} \frac{e^y \sin x}{x}$

Find the largest possible domain in the xy-plane for each of the following functions, if w is to be a real variable.

10. $w = e^{x-y}$

11. $w = \ln (x^2 + y^2)$

12. $w = \dfrac{\sin xy}{xy}$

13. $w = \dfrac{x}{\sqrt{y}}$

13–2 THE DIRECTIONAL DERIVATIVE: SPECIAL CASES

Let f be a function of two independent variables x and y and denote the dependent variable by w. The equation

$$w = f(x, y) \tag{1}$$

may be interpreted as defining a surface in xyw-space. In particular, we might imagine that the equation represents the elevation of points on a hill above the plane $w = 0$, as in Fig. 13–1.

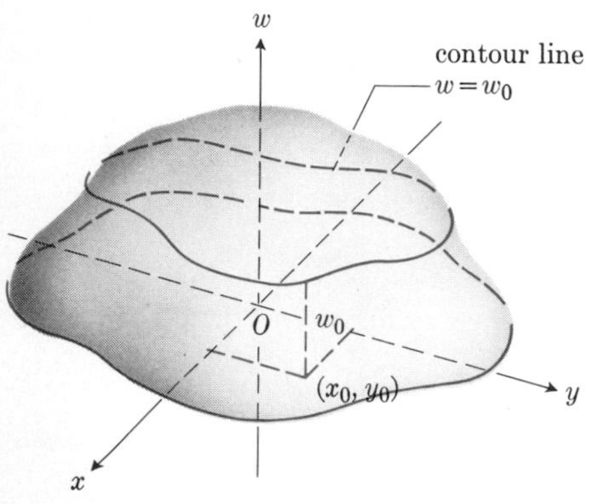

13–1 Contour line.

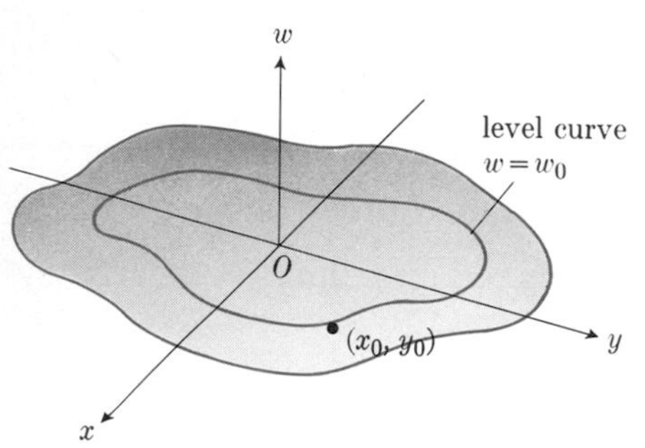

13–2 Level curve.

If we cut the surface with a plane $w = w_0$, a constant, we get a *contour line* on the surface. And if we project this contour line straight down onto the xy-plane, we obtain a *level curve* in the domain of w (Fig. 13–2).* The level curve consists of the points in the domain where f has the value w_0. An equation for the level curve is obtained by setting $f(x, y) = w_0$.

EXAMPLE 1. The function

$$w = 100 - x^2 - y^2, \qquad w \geq 0. \tag{2}$$

Figure 13–3 shows the plane $w = 75$ cutting the surface (a paraboloid of revolution) defined by the function, in a contour line. The corresponding level curve is

$$100 - x^2 - y^2 = 75,$$

or

$$x^2 + y^2 = 25,$$

a circle in the xy-plane. This is the circle that carries the marker $w = 75$ in Fig. 13–4.

Level curves are particularly useful in engineering applications. For instance, if Eq. (2) gave the celsius temperature at each point in a flat circular plate, then the level curves would be the isotherms of the temperature distribution.

Along with the launching and positioning of satellites has come an increased interest in mapping the variations in the earth's gravitational field. The strength of the field may vary significantly from place to place on the surface of the earth. In fact, changes in the performance of pendulum clocks taken by voyagers from Europe to other continents are said to have provided early supporting evidence for Newton's law of gravitation. If one takes the strength of the field at mean sea level as a standard, then the points in the earth's gravitational field that have the same gravitational potential as the standard value constitute a potato-shaped surface that geophysicists call the *geoid*. The geoid differs from the surface of the earth itself in most places, and it also differs from the ellipsoid that is normally used to approximate the surface of the earth (Fig. 13–5). The height of the geoid above or below the

* There seems to be no firm agreement about the language to use here, for level curves may also be called *contours*.

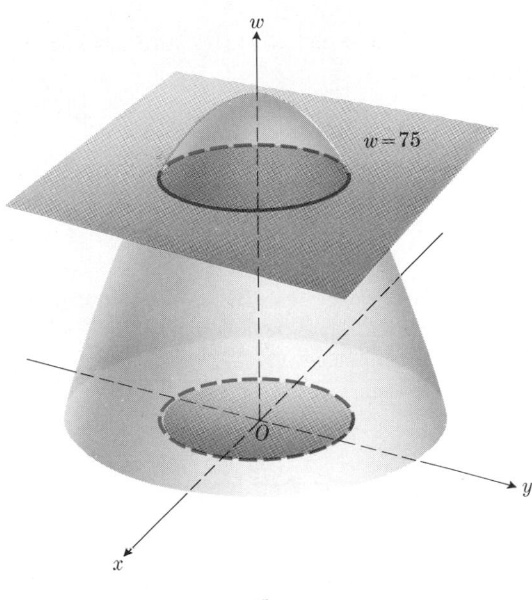

13–3 Contour line $w = 75$ on the surface $w = 100 - x^2 - y^2$, $w \geq 0$.

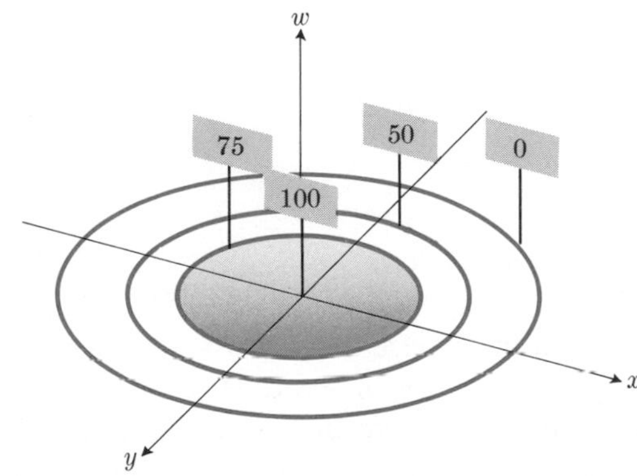

13–4 Level curves in the domain of $w = 100 - x^2 - y^2$, $w \geq 0$.

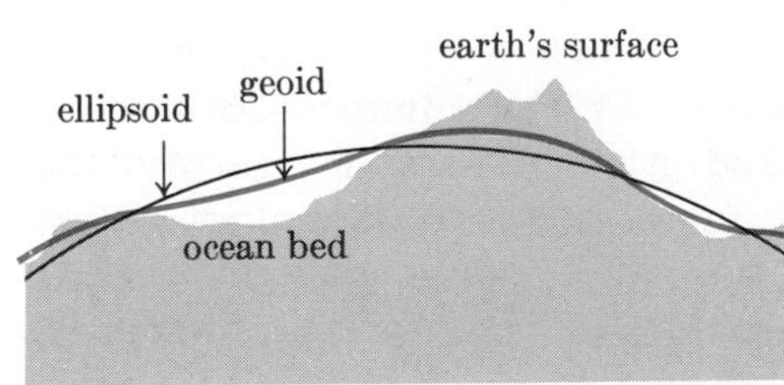

13–5 Surfaces of the earth, geoid, and ellipsoid.

ellipsoid is called the *geoidal height*. Geoidal heights are counted as positive when the geoid rises above the ellipsoid, and negative when it dips below the ellipsoid. Figure 13–6 shows contours of geoidal height on a Mercator map of the earth. These contours are the level curves of the geoidal height function.

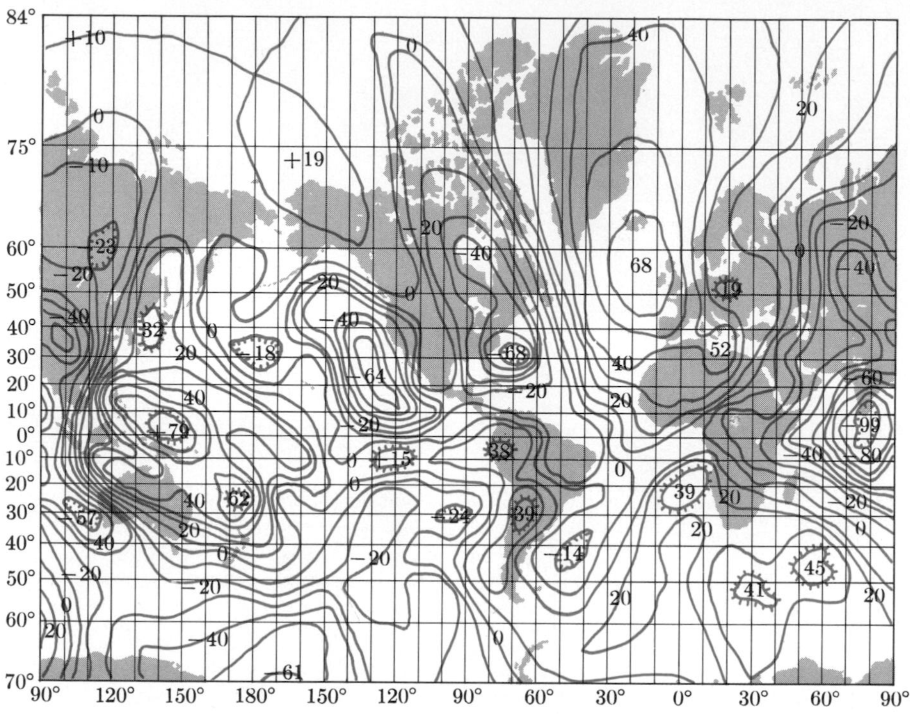

13–6 Contour map of geoidal height (meters).

EXAMPLE 2. *Potential wells.* Newton's law of gravitation says that the magnitude of the force with which an object, say a space vehicle, is attracted to the sun is inversely proportional to the square of the distance r between the object and the sun's center. If we denote the magnitude of the force by k/r^2, then the amount of work required to move the vehicle from a unit distance $r = 1$ from the sun out to a distance $r = b$ from the sun is

$$w = \int_{r=1}^{r=b} \frac{k}{r^2}\,dr = -\frac{k}{r}\bigg]_1^b = k\left(1 - \frac{1}{b}\right). \tag{3}$$

Figure 13–7 shows a graph of w as a function of r in the wr-plane. However, we may also think of $w = k(1 - (1/r))$ as a function of the two polar coordinate variables r and θ, and graph w as a surface over the $r\theta$-plane. When we do so, we obtain the funnel-shaped surface of revolution shown in Fig. 13–8. The amount of work W_a^b required to move a mass against gravity from a position $r = a$ units from the sun to a position $r = b$ units from the sun can then be pictured as a change in elevation on this surface. Specifically, W_a^b is the difference in height between the contour lines that lie above the level curves $r = a$ and $r = b$. To see that this is so, we calculate

$$W_a^b = \int_a^b \frac{k}{r^2}\,dr = \int_1^b \frac{k}{r^2}\,dr - \int_1^a \frac{k}{r^2}\,dr = k\left(1 - \frac{1}{b}\right) - k\left(1 - \frac{1}{a}\right). \tag{4}$$

Therefore, if we think of the surface as a well, then W_a^b is the amount of work

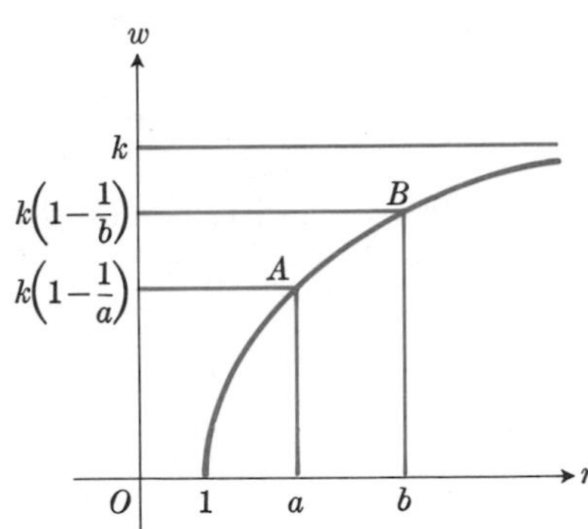

13–7 Graph of $w = k(1 - (1/r))$, $r \geq 1$.

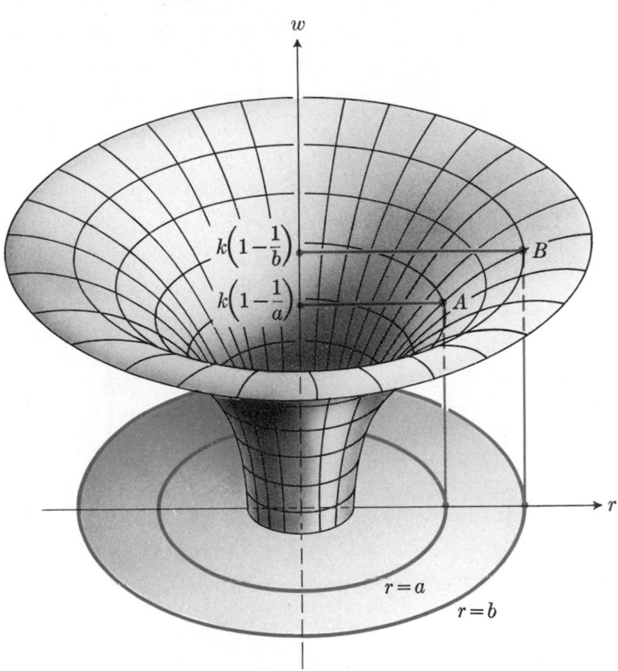

13–8 The potential well $w = k(1 - (1/r))$, $r \geq 1$, is obtained by revolving the curve of Fig. 13–7 about the w-axis.

it would take to move a unit mass up the side of the well from contour A to contour B against a constant downward unit force. Since W_a^b is the difference in the potential energies possessed by a unit mass at distances $r = a$ and $r = b$ from the sun, the surface in Fig. 13–8 is often called a *potential well*, and the contour rings around it *equipotential* curves. The level curves of the potential function $w = k(1 - (1/r))$ are concentric circles around the origin that represents the sun in the polar coordinate plane.

Suppose now that w is a function of x and y, defined for points (x, y) in some domain D in the xy-plane. Let $P_0(x_0, y_0)$ and $P_1(x_1, y_1)$ be any two points of D. Then the increment in w in going from w_0 at P_0 to w_1 at P_1 is

$$\Delta w = w_1 - w_0 = f(x_1, y_1) - f(x_0, y_0) \tag{5}$$

corresponding to

$$\Delta x = x_1 - x_0, \qquad \Delta y = y_1 - y_0.$$

Keeping P_0 fixed, suppose we require P_1 to approach it along some specific smooth curve in the xy-plane. This curve would in general not be one of the level curves referred to above, but would instead cut across these level curves. To be definite, suppose P_1 approaches P_0 along a straight line L, making an angle ϕ with the x-axis (Fig. 13–9). Then, if the limit

$$\frac{dw}{ds} = \lim_{\Delta s \to 0} \frac{\Delta w}{\Delta s} = \lim_{P_1 \to P_0} \frac{f(x_1, y_1) - f(x_0, y_0)}{\sqrt{\Delta x^2 + \Delta y^2}} \tag{6}$$

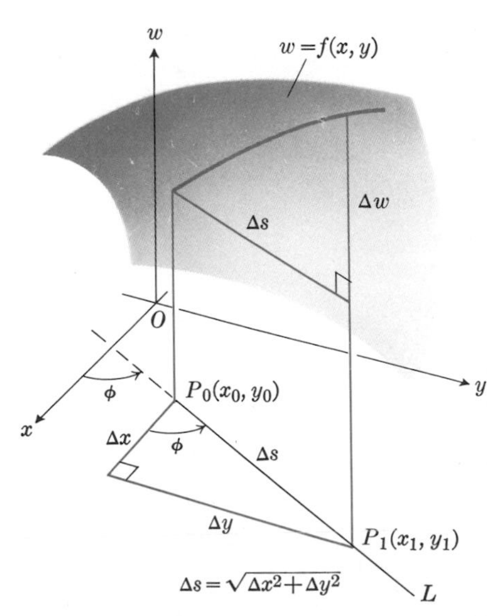

13–9 The derivative of $w = f(x, y)$ at P_0 in the direction of $\overrightarrow{P_0P_1}$ is the limit of $\Delta w/\Delta s$ as P_1 approaches P_0 along L.

exists, its value is called the *directional derivative* of $w = f(x, y)$ at (x_0, y_0) in the direction of $\overrightarrow{P_0 P_1}$. The adjective *directional* is used because the value of the limit in (6) may depend not only on the function and the point P_0 but also on the direction from which P_1 approaches P_0.

Before investigating the directional derivative, we look at two closely related limits. The first is the limit as P_1 is allowed to approach P_0 from either side on the line $y = y_0$ parallel to the x-axis. The second is the limit as P_1 is allowed to approach P_0 from either side on the line $x = x_0$ parallel to the y-axis. These cases are not as restrictive as they might seem at first, for it turns out that we can calculate all directional derivatives in terms of these two special limits whenever the surface $w = f(x, y)$ is smooth enough to have a unique tangent plane at P_0. (The theorems in Articles 13–4 and 13–5 give the details.)

In the case where P_1 is allowed to approach P_0 from either side on the line $y = y_0$, we write

$$f_x(x_0, y_0) = \lim_{\Delta x \to 0} \frac{f(x_0 + \Delta x, y_0) - f(x_0, y_0)}{\Delta x}, \tag{7}$$

and call the limit, when it exists, the *partial derivative of* $w = f(x, y)$ *with respect to* x *at* $P_0(x_0, y_0)$. This is just the usual derivative with respect to x of the function $f(x, y_0)$ obtained from $f(x, y)$ by holding the value of y constant. It measures the instantaneous rate of change in f per unit change in x at P_0. We sometimes write $\partial w/\partial x$ for f_x.

If we delete the subscript 0 in (7), the result is the definition of the partial derivative of f with respect to x at an arbitrary point (x, y):

$$\frac{\partial w}{\partial x} = f_x(x, y) = \lim_{\Delta x \to 0} \frac{f(x + \Delta x, y) - f(x, y)}{\Delta x}. \tag{8}$$

Note. In passing to the limit in Eq. (7) or (8) it is understood that Δx may be either positive or negative. In certain "pathological" cases, a function may have a directional derivative from the right ($\Delta x > 0$) but not from the left ($\Delta x < 0$); or it may have both directional derivatives but the two may fail to have the same magnitude. In either of these cases, the partial derivative f_x would not exist. If, however, f_x does exist, then it gives the directional derivative from the right, while $-f_x$ gives the directional derivative from the left. The change in sign is due to the fact that when Δx is negative, $\Delta x = -\sqrt{\Delta x^2}$, and Eq. (8) gives the negative of what Eq. (6) gives. Thus, if f_x exists at a point, then both the right and left directional derivatives exist at that point, and they have the same magnitude but opposite signs.

To calculate f_x we hold y constant and apply the rules for ordinary differentiation with respect to x.

EXAMPLE 3. If

$$w = 100 - x^2 - y^2,$$

then

$$\frac{\partial w}{\partial x} = 0 - 2x - 0 = -2x.$$

If w is the celsius temperature of a steel plate at (x, y), where x and y are in centimeters, then the temperature at (3, 4) is 75°C and

$$\frac{\partial w}{\partial x} = -6 \text{ °C/cm}.$$

That is, a small positive change in x would decrease the temperature at the rate of 6°C per cm change in x, while a negative change in x would increase w at the same rate.

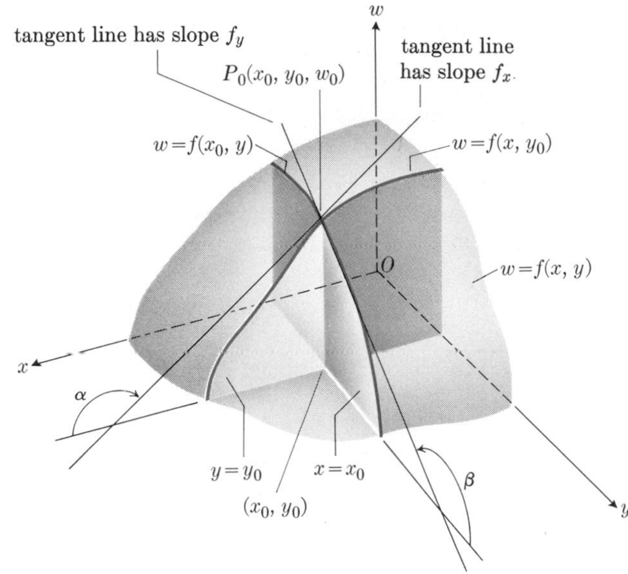

13–10 The plane $y = y_0$ cuts the surface $w = f(x, y)$ in the curve $w = f(x, y_0)$. At each x, the slope of this curve is $f_x(x, y_0)$. Similarly, the plane $x = x_0$ cuts the surface in a curve whose slope is $f_y(x_0, y)$.

The geometric interpretation of Eq. (5), (Fig. 13–10), is that

$$f_x(x_0, y_0) = \left(\frac{\partial w}{\partial x}\right)_{(x_0, y_0)}$$

gives the slope at (x_0, y_0, w_0) of the curve $w = f(x, y_0)$ in which the plane $y = y_0$ cuts the surface $w = f(x, y)$.

Thus, in Fig. 13–10, if x, y, and w are measured in the same units,

$$\tan \alpha = \left(\frac{\partial w}{\partial x}\right)_{(x_0, y_0)} = f_x(x_0, y_0).$$

Similarly,

$$\tan \beta = \left(\frac{\partial w}{\partial y}\right)_{(x_0, y_0)} = f_y(x_0, y_0).$$

Here the partial derivative of $w = f(x, y)$ with respect to y is denoted either by $\partial w/\partial y$ or by $f_y(x, y)$ and we have the definitions

$$f_y(x_0, y_0) = \lim_{\Delta y \to 0} \frac{f(x_0, y_0 + \Delta y) - f(x_0, y_0)}{\Delta y},$$

$$\frac{\partial w}{\partial y} = f_y(x, y) = \lim_{\Delta y \to 0} \frac{f(x, y + \Delta y) - f(x, y)}{\Delta y}. \qquad \textbf{(9)}$$

There are similar definitions for $\partial w/\partial x$, $\partial w/\partial y$, $\partial w/\partial z$, $\partial w/\partial u$, and $\partial w/\partial v$ in case $w = f(x, y, z, u, v)$. To compute them, we hold all but one of the variables constant while differentiating with respect to that one. The alternative subscript notation has the advantage of permitting us to exhibit the values of the variables where the derivative is to be evaluated. For example, $f_u(x_0, y_0, z_0, u_0, v_0)$ is the partial derivative of $w = f(x, y, z, u, v)$ with respect to u at $(x_0, y_0, z_0, u_0, v_0)$. This can also be denoted by $(\partial w/\partial u)_{(x_0, y_0, z_0, u_0, v_0)}$, or simply by $(\partial w/\partial u)_0$ when no confusion will result.

EXAMPLE 4. Three resistors of resistances R_1, R_2, and R_3 connected in parallel produce a resistance R given by

$$\frac{1}{R} = \frac{1}{R_1} + \frac{1}{R_2} + \frac{1}{R_3}.$$

Find $\partial R/\partial R_2$.

Solution. Treat R_1 and R_3 as constants and differentiate both sides of the equation with respect to R_2. Then

$$-\frac{1}{R^2}\frac{\partial R}{\partial R_2} = -\frac{1}{R_2^2}$$

or

$$\frac{\partial R}{\partial R_2} = \left(\frac{R}{R_2}\right)^2.$$

EXAMPLE 5. If $w = (xy)^z$, find $\partial w/\partial z$.

Solution. Here, we treat x and y, and hence xy, as constant and apply the law

$$\frac{d(a^u)}{dz} = a^u \ln a \frac{du}{dz}.$$

Hence

$$\frac{\partial w}{\partial z} = (xy)^z \ln (xy).$$

PROBLEMS

In Problems 1–5, show two ways to represent the function $w = f(x, y)$, (a) by sketching a surface in xyw-space, and (b) by drawing a family of level curves, $f(x, y) = \text{constant}$.

1. $f(x, y) = x$

2. $f(x, y) = y$

3. $f(x, y) = x^2 + y^2$

4. $f(x, y) = x^2 - y^2$

5. $f(x, y) = ye^x$

In each of the following problems (6–10), find $\partial w/\partial x$ and $\partial w/\partial y$:

6. $w = e^x \cos y$

7. $w = e^x \sin y$

8. $w = \tan^{-1} \dfrac{y}{x}$

9. $w = \ln \sqrt{x^2 + y^2}$

10. $w = \cosh (y/x)$

In Problems 11–16, find the partial derivatives of the given function with respect to each variable.

11. $f(x, y, z, w) = x^2 e^{2y+3z} \cos (4w)$

12. $f(x, y, z) = z \sin^{-1} (y/x)$

13. $f(u, v, w) = \dfrac{u^2 - v^2}{v^2 + w^2}$

14. $f(r, \theta, z) = \dfrac{r(2 - \cos 2\theta)}{r^2 + z^2}$

15. $f(x, y, u, v) = \dfrac{x^2 + y^2}{u^2 + v^2}$

16. $f(x, y, r, s) = \sin 2x \cosh 3r + \sinh 3y \cos 4s$

In Problems 17 and 18, A, B, C are the angles of a triangle and a, b, c are the respective opposite sides.

17. Express A (explicitly or implicitly) as a function of a, b, c and calculate $\partial A/\partial a$ and $\partial A/\partial b$.

18. Express a (explicitly or implicitly) as a function of A, b, B and calculate $\partial a/\partial A$ and $\partial a/\partial B$.

In Problems 19–24, express the spherical coordinates ρ, ϕ, θ as functions of the cartesian coordinates x, y, z and calculate:

19. $\partial\rho/\partial x$ **20.** $\partial\phi/\partial z$ **21.** $\partial\theta/\partial y$

22. $\partial\theta/\partial z$ **23.** $\partial\phi/\partial x$ **24.** $\partial\theta/\partial x$

In Problems 25–27, let $\mathbf{R} = \mathbf{i}x + \mathbf{j}y + \mathbf{k}z$ be the vector from the origin to (x, y, z). Express x, y, z as functions of the spherical coordinates ρ, ϕ, θ, and calculate:

25. $\partial\mathbf{R}/\partial\rho$ **26.** $\partial\mathbf{R}/\partial\phi$ **27.** $\partial\mathbf{R}/\partial\theta$

28. Express the answers to Problems 25–27 in terms of the unit vectors $\mathbf{u}_\rho$, $\mathbf{u}_\phi$, $\mathbf{u}_\theta$ discussed in Miscellaneous Problem 27, Chapter 12.

29. In Fig. 13–10, let

$$\mathbf{R} = \mathbf{i}x + \mathbf{j}y + \mathbf{k}f(x, y)$$

be the vector from the origin to (x, y, w). What can you say about the direction of the vector (a) $\partial\mathbf{R}/\partial x$, (b) $\partial\mathbf{R}/\partial y$? (c) Calculate the vector product

$$\mathbf{v} = \left(\frac{\partial\mathbf{R}}{\partial x}\right) \times \left(\frac{\partial\mathbf{R}}{\partial y}\right).$$

What can you say about the direction of this vector $\mathbf{v}$ with respect to the surface $w = f(x, y)$?

13–3 TANGENT PLANE AND NORMAL LINE

In Article 13–2 we saw that the partial derivatives

$$f_x(x_0, y_0) = \left(\frac{\partial w}{\partial x}\right)_{(x_0, y_0)} \quad \text{(1a)}$$

and

$$f_y(x_0, y_0) = \left(\frac{\partial w}{\partial y}\right)_{(x_0, y_0)} \quad \text{(1b)}$$

give the slopes of the lines L_1 and L_2 which are tangent to the curves C_1 and C_2 that are cut from the surface $w = f(x, y)$ by the planes $y = y_0$ and $x = x_0$. The lines L_1 and L_2 determine a plane. If the surface is sufficiently smooth near $P_0(x_0, y_0, w_0)$, this plane will be tangent to the surface at P_0.

Definition. Tangent plane. *Let $w = f(x, y)$ be the equation of a surface S. Let $P_0(x_0, y_0, w_0)$ be a point on the surface. Let T be a plane through P_0. Let $P(x, y, w)$ be any other point on S. If the angle between T and the line P_0P approaches zero as P approaches P_0 along the surface, we say that T is tangent to S at P_0 (Fig. 13–11).*

The line through P_0 normal to the tangent plane is called the *normal line* to the surface at P_0.

REMARK 1. If a surface has a tangent plane at $P_0(x_0, y_0, w_0)$, the lines L_1 and L_2 that are tangent to the curves C_1 and C_2 must lie in it. Since two intersecting lines determine a plane, the plane determined by L_1 and L_2 is the tangent plane, if there is one.

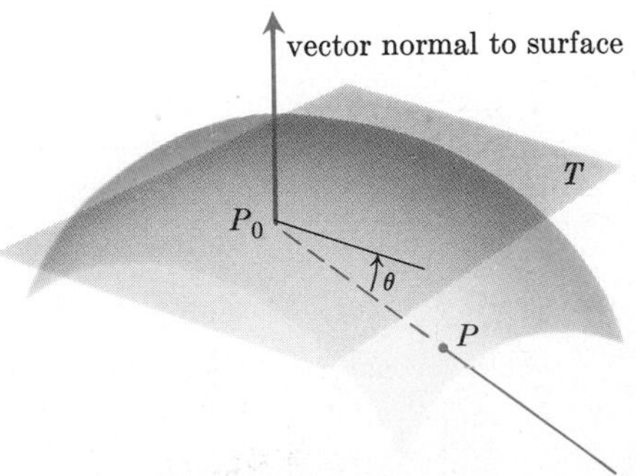

13–11 If θ approaches zero as P approaches P_0 along the surface, then the plane T is tangent to the surface at P_0.

REMARK 2. The curves C_1 and C_2, cut from the surface by the planes $x = x_0$ and $y = y_0$, may be smooth enough to have tangent lines L_1 and L_2 and the surface still not have a tangent plane at P_0. In other words, the plane determined by L_1 and L_2 may fail to be tangent to the surface. This would happen, for example, if the curves cut from the surface by other planes, such as the planes $y - y_0 = \pm(x - x_0)$, either failed to have tangent lines, or had tangent lines L', L'' which did not lie in the plane determined by L_1 and L_2. In the next article, we shall show that this does not happen if the partial derivatives $f_x(x, y)$, $f_y(x, y)$ exist in some rectangle centered at (x_0, y_0) and are continuous at (x_0, y_0).

We shall assume for now that the surface does have a tangent plane and a normal line and see how to find their equations. They may easily be written down once we have found a vector $\mathbf{N}$ perpendicular to the plane of L_1 and L_2. For such a vector $\mathbf{N}$, we may use the cross product of vectors $\mathbf{v}_1$ and $\mathbf{v}_2$ along the lines L_1 and L_2. So we now consider how to find $\mathbf{v}_1$ and $\mathbf{v}_2$.

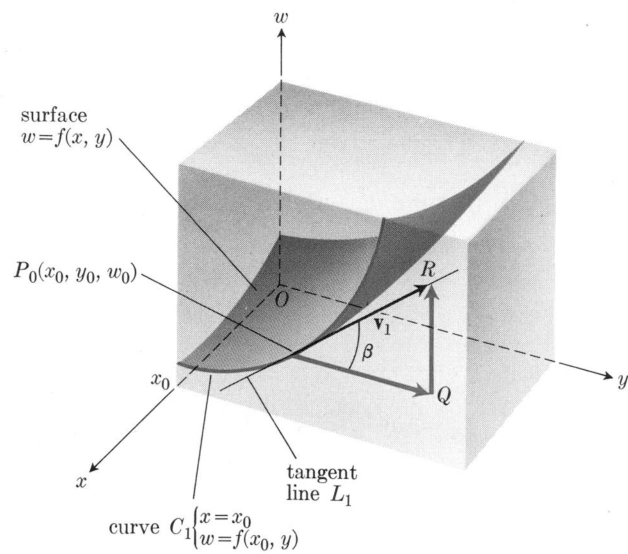

13–12 $\mathbf{v}_1 = \mathbf{j} + f_y(x_0, y_0)\mathbf{k}$ is tangent to C_1 at (x_0, y_0) because its slope is $f_y(x_0, y_0)$.

Figure 13–12 shows part of the curve C_1 cut from the surface by the plane $x = x_0$. Triangle P_0QR is a right triangle with hypotenuse P_0R lying along the tangent line L_1. The slope of L_1 is

$$\tan \beta = \frac{QR}{P_0Q} = f_y(x_0, y_0).$$

Therefore, if we take $P_0Q = 1$ y-unit, QR will be equal to $f_y(x_0, y_0)$ w-units. In terms of vectors, we may take

$$\overrightarrow{P_0Q} = 1\mathbf{j}, \qquad \overrightarrow{QR} = f_y(x_0, y_0)\mathbf{k}$$

and

$$\mathbf{v}_1 = \overrightarrow{P_0Q} + \overrightarrow{QR} = \mathbf{j} + f_y(x_0, y_0)\mathbf{k}, \tag{2a}$$

where **i**, **j**, and **k** will be used to denote unit vectors along the x-, y-, and w-axes, respectively.

Similarly, by considering the curve C_2 cut from the surface by the plane $y = y_0$, we see that the vector

$$\mathbf{v}_2 = \mathbf{i} + f_x(x_0, y_0)\mathbf{k} \tag{2b}$$

is parallel to the line L_2.

For the normal vector **N** we may therefore take

$$\mathbf{N} = \mathbf{v}_1 \times \mathbf{v}_2 = \begin{vmatrix} \mathbf{i} & \mathbf{j} & \mathbf{k} \\ 0 & 1 & f_y(x_0, y_0) \\ 1 & 0 & f_x(x_0, y_0) \end{vmatrix} = \mathbf{i} f_x(x_0, y_0) + \mathbf{j} f_y(x_0, y_0) - \mathbf{k}. \tag{3}$$

The equations of the tangent plane and normal line at $P_0(x_0, y_0, w_0)$ may now be written down with coefficients taken from the normal vector **N**:

Tangent plane: $$A(x - x_0) + B(y - y_0) + C(w - w_0) = 0, \tag{4a}$$

Normal line: $$\frac{x - x_0}{A} = \frac{y - y_0}{B} = \frac{w - w_0}{C}, \tag{4b}$$

Coefficients: $$A = f_x(x_0, y_0), \quad B = f_y(x_0, y_0), \quad C = -1. \tag{4c}$$

PROBLEMS

In Problems 1–5, find the plane that is tangent to the given surface $z = f(x, y)$ at the given point P_0. Also find the line normal to the surface at P_0.

1. $z = x^2 + y^2$; $(3, 4, 25)$
2. $z = \sqrt{9 - x^2 - y^2}$; $(1, -2, 2)$
3. $z = x^2 - xy - y^2$; $(1, 1, -1)$
4. $z = \tan^{-1} \dfrac{y}{x}$; $(1, 1, \pi/4)$
5. $z = x/\sqrt{x^2 + y^2}$; $(3, -4, \frac{3}{5})$
6. (a) If the equation of a surface is given in the form $x = f(y, z)$, what takes the place of Eq. (3) for a vector **N** normal to the surface at a point $P_0(x_0, y_0, z_0)$? (b) Find the tangent plane and normal line to the surface $x = e^{2y-z}$ at the point $(1, 1, 2)$.
7. Show that there is a line on the cone $z^2 = 2x^2 + 4y^2$ where the tangent plane is parallel to the plane $12x + 14y + 11z = 25$. Find the line and the tangent plane.
8. At each point of the curve of intersection of the paraboloid $z = x^2 + y^2$ and the plane $z = z_0$ (> 0), a linc is drawn normal to the paraboloid. Show that these lines generate a cone and find its vertex. Sketch the paraboloid and the associated cone.
9. The intersection of the surface $z = f(x, y)$ and the surface $z = g(x, y)$ is a curve C. Find a vector tangent to C at a point $P_0(x_0, y_0, z_0)$ on it. Express the result in terms of partial derivatives of f and g at P_0.
10. Apply the result of Problem 9 to find a vector of length $\sqrt{3}$ tangent to the curve of intersection of the cone $z^2 = 4x^2 + 9y^2$ and the plane $6x + 3y + 2z = 5$ at the point $P_0(2, 1, -5)$.

13–4 APPROXIMATE VALUE OF Δw

We saw in the previous article, Eqs. (4a, c), that if the surface $w = f(x, y)$ has a tangent plane at $P_0(x_0, y_0, w_0)$, then the equation of the tangent plane is

$$w - w_0 = f_x(x_0, y_0)(x - x_0) + f_y(x_0, y_0)(y - y_0). \tag{1}$$

In this equation, (x_0, y_0, w_0) are coordinates of a point on the surface, while

(x, y, w) are coordinates of a point on the *tangent plane.* If we take

$$x = x_0 + \Delta x,$$
$$y = y_0 + \Delta y$$

in Eq. (1), and denote the change, $w - w_0$, by $\Delta w_{\tan}$, we have

$$\Delta w_{\tan} = f_x(x_0, y_0)\,\Delta x + f_y(x_0, y_0)\,\Delta y. \tag{2}$$

This equation tells how much change is produced in w, corresponding to the changes Δx and Δy, when we move along the *tangent plane.* In this article we shall see that, under suitable restrictions on the function f, (a) the surface does have a tangent plane, and (b) the change in w *on the surface* $w = f(x, y)$ differs from $\Delta w_{\tan}$ by an amount $\epsilon_1\,\Delta x + \epsilon_2\,\Delta y$, where both ϵ_1 and ϵ_2 are small when Δx and Δy are small. We shall discuss the suitable restrictions on f and then prove the theorem below.

Theorem 1. *Let the function $w = f(x, y)$ be continuous and have partial derivatives f_x, f_y throughout a region*

$$R\colon\ |x - x_0| < h, \qquad |y - y_0| < k$$

of the xy-plane. Let f_x and f_y be continuous at (x_0, y_0). Let

$$\Delta w = f(x_0 + \Delta x, y_0 + \Delta y) - f(x_0, y_0). \tag{3}$$

Then

$$\Delta w = f_x(x_0, y_0)\,\Delta x + f_y(x_0, y_0)\,\Delta y + \epsilon_1\,\Delta x + \epsilon_2\,\Delta y, \tag{4}$$

where

$$\epsilon_1 \text{ and } \epsilon_2 \to 0 \qquad \text{when} \quad \Delta x \text{ and } \Delta y \to 0. \tag{5}$$

The region R is a rectangle with center (x_0, y_0) and sides $2h$ by $2k$. We shall restrict Δx and Δy to be so small that the points

$$(x_0, y_0),\quad (x_0 + \Delta x, y_0 + \Delta y),\quad (x_0 + \Delta x, y_0),\quad (x_0, y_0 + \Delta y)$$

all lie inside this rectangle R. The function f is assumed to be continuous and to have partial derivatives f_x and f_y throughout R. In particular, these functions are well behaved at each of the points listed above and along the segments joining them. This is sufficient to make valid the applications of the Mean Value Theorem in the proof below.

Proof. The key to the proof is a double application of the Mean Value Theorem. The increment Δw is the change in f from $A(x_0, y_0)$ to $B(x_0 + \Delta x, y_0 + \Delta y)$ in R. We resolve this into two parts

$$\Delta w_1 = f(x_0 + \Delta x, y_0) - f(x_0, y_0) \tag{6}$$

and

$$\Delta w_2 = f(x_0 + \Delta x, y_0 + \Delta y) - f(x_0 + \Delta x, y_0). \tag{7}$$

The first is the change in w from A to C; the second, from C to B (Fig.

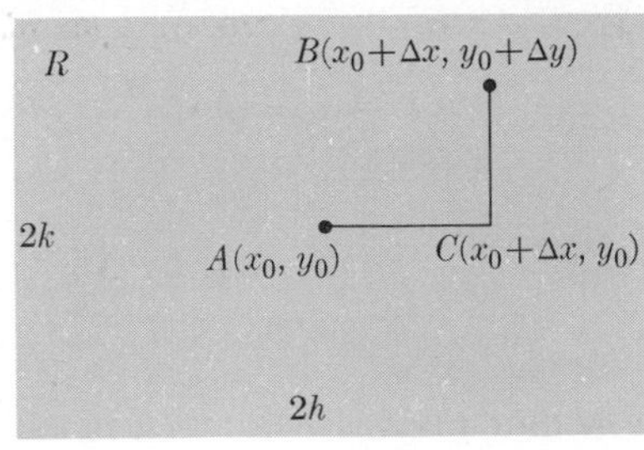

13–13 The region R of Theorem 1.

13–13). Their sum is

$$\begin{aligned}\Delta w_2 + \Delta w_1 &= f(x_0 + \Delta x, y_0 + \Delta y) - f(x_0 + \Delta x, y_0) \\ &\quad + f(x_0 + \Delta x, y_0) - f(x_0, y_0) \qquad \textbf{(8)} \\ &= f(x_0 + \Delta x, y_0 + \Delta y) - f(x_0, y_0) = \Delta w.\end{aligned}$$

In Δw_1, we hold $y = y_0$ fixed and have an increment of a function of x that is continuous and differentiable. The Mean Value Theorem is therefore applicable, and yields

$$\Delta w_1 = f(x_0 + \Delta x, y_0) - f(x_0, y_0) = f_x(x_1, y_0)\, \Delta x \qquad \textbf{(9)}$$

for some x_1 between x_0 and $x_0 + \Delta x$.

Similarly, in Δw_2 we hold $x = x_0 + \Delta x$ fixed and have an increment of a function of y that is continuous and differentiable. By the Mean Value Theorem,

$$\Delta w_2 = f(x_0 + \Delta x, y_0 + \Delta y) - f(x_0 + \Delta x, y_0) = f_y(x_0 + \Delta x, y_1)\, \Delta y \qquad \textbf{(10)}$$

for some y_1 between y_0 and $y_0 + \Delta y$. Hence

$$\Delta w = f_x(x_1, y_0)\, \Delta x + f_y(x_0 + \Delta x, y_1)\, \Delta y \qquad \textbf{(11)}$$

for some x_1 between x_0 and $x_0 + \Delta x$, and y_1 between y_0 and $y_0 + \Delta y$.

We now use the hypothesis that f_x and f_y are continuous at $P_0(x_0, y_0)$. This means that

$$f_x(x_1, y_0) \to f_x(x_0, y_0) \qquad \textbf{(12a)}$$

and

$$f_y(x_0 + \Delta x, y_1) \to f_y(x_0, y_0) \qquad \textbf{(12b)}$$

as Δx and Δy approach zero. Therefore

$$f_x(x_1, y_0) = f_x(x_0, y_0) + \epsilon_1, \qquad \textbf{(13a)}$$

$$f_y(x_0 + \Delta x, y_1) = f_y(x_0, y_0) + \epsilon_2, \qquad \textbf{(13b)}$$

where ϵ_1 and ϵ_2 both approach zero as Δx and Δy approach zero. Substituting (13a, b) into (11) gives the desired result,

$$\Delta w = [f_x(x_0, y_0) + \epsilon_1]\, \Delta x + [f_y(x_0, y_0) + \epsilon_2]\, \Delta y,$$

while (12a) and (12b) guarantee that ϵ_1 and $\epsilon_2 \to 0$ when Δx and $\Delta y \to 0$.

Q.E.D.

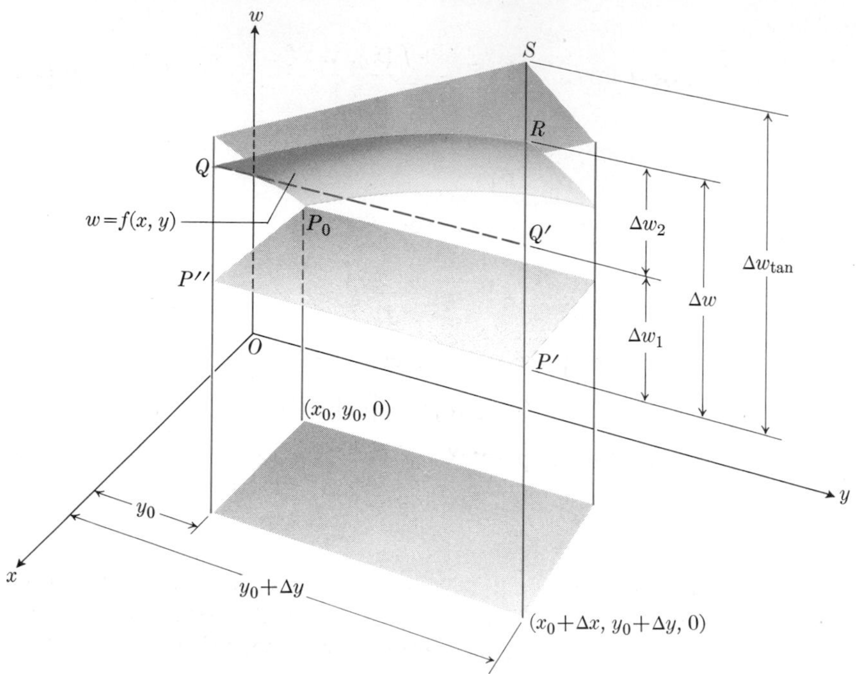

13–14 Part of the surface $w = f(x, y)$ near $P_0(x_0, y_0, w_0)$, and part of the plane tangent to the surface at P_0. The points P_0, P', and P'' have the same height $w_0 = f(x_0, y_0)$ above the xy-plane. The change in w on the surface is $\Delta w = P'R$, and the change in w on the tangent plane is $\Delta w_{\tan} = P'S$. The change

$\Delta w_1 = f(x_0 + \Delta x, y_0) - f(x_0, y_0)$,

shown as $P''Q = P'Q'$, is caused by changing x from x_0 to $x_0 + \Delta x$ while holding y equal to y_0. Then, with x held equal to $x_0 + \Delta x$,

$\Delta w_2 = f(x_0 + \Delta x, y_0 + \Delta y) - f(x_0 + \Delta x, y_0)$

is the change in w caused by changing y from y_0 to $y_0 + \Delta y$. This is represented by $Q'R$. The total change in w is the sum of Δw_1 and Δw_2.

For a pictorial representation of Δw, $\Delta w_{\tan}$, Δw_1, and Δw_2, see Fig. 13–14.

Theorem 2. *Let $w = f(x, y)$ be continuous in a region R: $|x - x_0| < h$, $|y - y_0| < k$. Let f_x and f_y exist in R and be continuous at (x_0, y_0). Let $P_0(x_0, y_0, w_0)$ be a point on the surface $w = f(x, y)$. Then the plane T through P_0 normal to the vector*

$$\mathbf{N} = \mathbf{i} f_x(x_0, y_0) + \mathbf{j} f_y(x_0, y_0) - \mathbf{k} \tag{14}$$

is tangent to the surface.

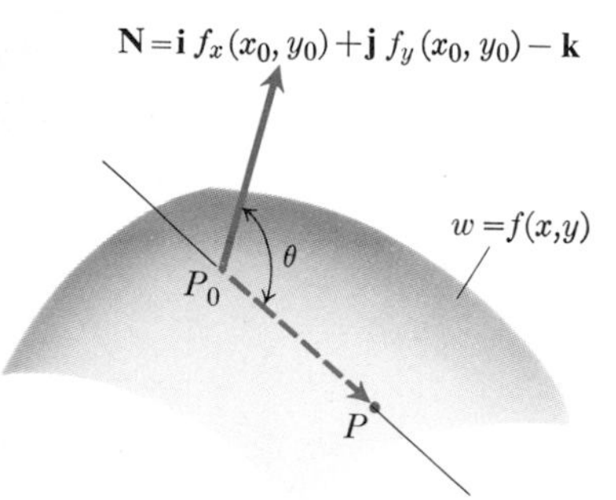

13–15 If f, f_x, and f_y are continuous in a region about (x_0, y_0), then $\theta \to 90°$ as $P \to P_0$.

Proof. We show that the plane T satisfies the requirement set forth in the tangent-plane definition in Article 13–3. Namely, we show that if P is any point on the surface other than P_0, then the angle between $\overrightarrow{P_0P}$ and T approaches 0 as $P \to P_0$. This is done by showing that the angle between $\overrightarrow{P_0P}$ and $\mathbf{N}$ approaches 90° as $P \to P_0$ (Fig. 13–15).

The cosine of the angle θ between $\overrightarrow{P_0P}$ and $\mathbf{N}$ is

$$\cos\theta = \frac{\overrightarrow{P_0P} \cdot \mathbf{N}}{|\overrightarrow{P_0P}|\,|\mathbf{N}|}. \tag{15}$$

Now

$$\begin{aligned}\overrightarrow{P_0P} &= \mathbf{i}(x - x_0) + \mathbf{j}(y - y_0) + \mathbf{k}(w - w_0)\\ &= \mathbf{i}\,\Delta x + \mathbf{j}\,\Delta y + \mathbf{k}\,\Delta w.\end{aligned} \tag{16}$$

Therefore

$$\cos\theta = \frac{f_x(x_0, y_0)\,\Delta x + f_y(x_0, y_0)\,\Delta y - \Delta w}{|\overrightarrow{P_0P}|\,|\mathbf{N}|} \tag{17}$$

$$= \frac{-\epsilon_1\,\Delta x - \epsilon_2\,\Delta y}{|\overrightarrow{P_0P}|\,|\mathbf{N}|}.$$

From (14) we see that $|\mathbf{N}| \geq 1$, and from (16)

$$\frac{|\Delta x|}{|\overrightarrow{P_0P}|} \leq 1, \qquad \frac{|\Delta y|}{|\overrightarrow{P_0P}|} \leq 1.$$

Hence, from (17) and the previous theorem,

$$|\cos\theta| \leq |\epsilon_1| + |\epsilon_2| \to 0$$

as $P \to P_0$. Therefore, for any point $P \neq P_0$ on the surface, the angle between the vector $\overrightarrow{P_0P}$ and the vector $\mathbf{N}$, Eq. (14), approaches 90°. This concludes the proof.

REMARK 1. The hypotheses of Theorems 1 and 2 are more refined than we usually need. It is usually enough to remember that the conclusions of these two theorems hold when f, f_x, and f_y are all continuous throughout R.

The power of Theorem 1 lies in Eqs. (4) and (5), which say that

$$\Delta w = \Delta w_{\tan} + \epsilon_1\,\Delta x + \epsilon_2\,\Delta y$$

consists of a part $\Delta w_{\tan}$, which is *linear* in Δx and Δy, plus error terms $\epsilon_1\,\Delta x$ and $\epsilon_2\,\Delta y$ that are *products* of small terms when Δx and Δy are small.

EXAMPLE 1. If

$$w = x^2 + y^2 = f(x, y),$$

then

$$\Delta w = (x + \Delta x)^2 + (y + \Delta y)^2 - (x^2 + y^2)$$

$$= \underbrace{2x\,\Delta x + 2y\,\Delta y}_{\Delta w_{\tan}} + \underbrace{(\Delta x)^2 + (\Delta y)^2}_{\epsilon_1\,\Delta x + \epsilon_2\,\Delta y}.$$

Since $f_x = 2x$, $f_y = 2y$, the part $2x\,\Delta x + 2y\,\Delta y$ is the same as $\Delta w_{\tan}$. Then $\Delta w - \Delta w_{\tan}$ is $(\Delta x)^2 + (\Delta y)^2$. This agrees with Eq. (4) with $\epsilon_1 = \Delta x$ and $\epsilon_2 = \Delta y$, which approach zero when Δx and Δy do.

Theorem 1 sometimes lets us approximate a complicated function $w = f(x, y)$ by a linear function that we can construct from it. The approximation comes from Eq. (4). If we replace Δw in Eq. (4) by $f(x, y) - f(x_0, y_0)$, and add $f(x_0, y_0)$ to both sides, we see that

$$f(x, y) = f(x_0, y_0) + f_x(x_0, y_0)\,\Delta x + f_y(x_0, y_0)\,\Delta y + \epsilon_1\,\Delta x + \epsilon_2\,\Delta y. \tag{18}$$

Theorem 1 then says that

$$f(x, y) \approx f(x_0, y_0) + f_x(x_0, y_0)\,\Delta x + f_y(x_0, y_0)\,\Delta y \tag{19}$$

when Δx and Δy are small. Finally, when we replace Δx and Δy by $x - x_0$ and $y - y_0$, we obtain the following linear approximation to $f(x, y)$ near the point (x_0, y_0):

$$f(x, y) \approx f(x_0, y_0) + f_x(x_0, y_0)(x - x_0) + f_y(x_0, y_0)(y - y_0). \tag{20}$$

EXAMPLE 2. Show that

$$\frac{1}{1 + x - y} \approx 1 - x + y \tag{21}$$

when x and y are very small.

Solution. The function $f(x, y) = 1/(1 + x - y)$ is certainly continuous for $|x - y| < 1$, as are the derivatives

$$f_x(x, y) = \frac{-1}{(1 + x - y)^2}, \qquad f_y(x, y) = \frac{1}{(1 + x - y)^2}. \tag{22}$$

Thus the conclusion of Theorem 1 holds for f when $|x - y| < 1$.

If we take $(x_0, y_0) = (0, 0)$ in (20), the equation becomes

$$f(x, y) \approx f(0, 0) + xf_x(0, 0) + yf_y(0, 0).$$

Evaluating this equation gives

$$\frac{1}{1 + x - y} \approx 1 + x(-1) + y(1) = 1 - x + y,$$

which is the desired result.

To estimate the error in the approximation, we could estimate ϵ_1 and ϵ_2 from Eqs. (13a) and (13b), and calculate

$$\epsilon_1\, \Delta x + \epsilon_2\, \Delta y = \epsilon_1 x + \epsilon_2 y.$$

The calculation is a long one, however, and we need not go into it in this case because it is easier to find the remainder that results from dividing $1 + x - y$ into 1 directly by long division. When the result of the division is simplified, we find that

$$\frac{1}{1 + x - y} = 1 - x + y + \frac{(x - y)^2}{1 + x - y}.$$

Thus, the error in the approximation (21) is exactly $(x - y)^2/(1 + x - y)$. To estimate this error when $|x - y| < \frac{1}{2}$, for instance, we have

$$0 \le \frac{(x - y)^2}{1 + x - y} \le \frac{(x - y)^2}{1 - \frac{1}{2}} = 2(x - y)^2. \tag{23}$$

Note that the accuracy of (21) does not depend on x and y being small, but on $|x - y|$ being small (see Problem 3).

Example 2 gives a linear approximation to $f(x, y) = 1/(1 + x - y)$ when the point (x, y) is near the point $(0, 0)$. The next example gives a linear approximation to f that works when the point (x, y) is close to the point $(2, 1)$.

EXAMPLE 3. Find a linear function that approximates $1/(1 + x - y)$ near the point $(2, 1)$.

Solution. We begin by taking $(x_0, y_0) = (2, 1)$ in Eq. (20), which then becomes

$$f(x, y) \approx f(2, 1) + f_x(2, 1)(x - 2) + f_y(2, 1)(y - 1). \qquad (24)$$

We then use the formulas for f and its partial derivatives, Eq. (22), to evaluate both sides of (24), obtaining

$$\frac{1}{1 + x - y} \approx \frac{1}{2} + \left(-\frac{1}{4}\right)(x - 2) + \left(\frac{1}{4}\right)(y - 1) = \frac{3}{4} - \frac{x}{4} + \frac{y}{4}. \qquad (25)$$

REMARK 2. The surface

$$w = f(x_0, y_0) + f_x(x_0, y_0)(x - x_0) + f_y(x_0, y_0)(y - y_0) \qquad (26)$$

generated by the right side of (20) is the plane that is tangent to the surface $w = f(x, y)$ at the point (x_0, y_0). Thus the plane $w = 1 - x + y$ in Example 2 is tangent to the surface $w = 1/(1 + x - y)$ at the point $(0, 0)$. The plane

$$w = \frac{3}{4} - \frac{x}{4} + \frac{y}{4}$$

in Example 3 is tangent to the surface at the point $(2, 1)$. What we did in making the approximations in Examples 2 and 3 was to substitute heights on the tangent plane for heights on the surface near the point of tangency.

The approximation

$$\Delta w \approx \Delta w_{\tan} = f_x(x_0, y_0)\,\Delta x + f_y(x_0, y_0)\,\Delta y, \qquad (27)$$

which we get from Eq. (4), gives a way to see how *sensitive* $w = f(x, y)$ is to changes in its variables near the point (x_0, y_0). This is illustrated in the next example.

EXAMPLE 4. For the volume

$$V = \pi r^2 h$$

of a right circular cylinder, Eq. (27) gives

$$\Delta V \approx V_r(r_0, h_0)\,\Delta r + V_h(r_0, h_0)\,\Delta h. \qquad (28)$$

Therefore, near the point $r_0 = 1$, $h_0 = 5$, ΔV is related to Δr and Δh by the approximation

$$\Delta V \approx V_r(1, 5)\,\Delta r + V_h(1, 5)\,\Delta h. \qquad (29)$$

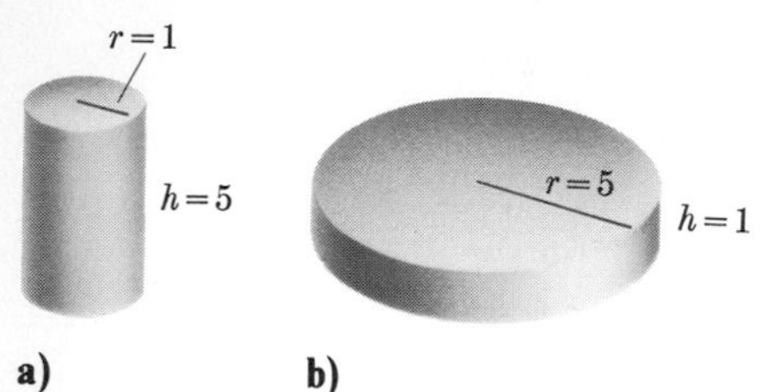

13–16 The volume of cylinder (a) is more sensitive to a small change in r than it is to an equally small change in h. The volume of cylinder (b) is more sensitive to small changes in h than it is to small changes in r.

Since

$$V_r(1, 5) = 2\pi rh\,|_{(1,5)} = 10\pi,$$
$$V_h(1, 5) = \pi r^2\,|_{(1,5)} = \pi$$

at the point (1, 5), Eq. (29) gives

$$\Delta V \approx 10\pi\ \Delta r + \pi\ \Delta h.$$

A one-unit change in r will change V by about 10π units. A one-unit change in h will change V by only about π units. The volume of a cylinder with radius 1 and height 5 is nearly ten times more sensitive to a small change in r than it is to a change of the same size in h (Fig. 13–16).

In contrast, if the given values of r and h are reversed, so that $r = 5$ and $h = 1$, then

$$V_r = 2\pi rh\,|_{(5,1)} = 10\pi, \qquad V_h = \pi r^2\,|_{(5,1)} = 25\pi,$$

and Eq. (28) becomes

$$\Delta V \approx 10\pi\ \Delta r + 25\pi\ \Delta h.$$

The volume is more sensitive now to a small change in h than it is to an equally small change in r.

There is a general rule to be learned from Example 4. Namely, a differentiable function is most sensitive to small changes in the variables with respect to which it has the largest partial derivatives.

Functions of More Variables

Analogous results hold for functions of any finite number of independent variables. For a function of three variables

$$w = f(x, y, z),$$

that is continuous and has partial derivatives f_x, f_y, f_z at and in some neighborhood of the point (x_0, y_0, z_0), and whose derivatives are continuous at the point, we have

$$\begin{aligned}\Delta w &= f(x_0 + \Delta x, y_0 + \Delta y, z_0 + \Delta z) - f(x_0, y_0, z_0)\\ &= f_x\ \Delta x + f_y\ \Delta y + f_z\ \Delta z + \epsilon_1\ \Delta x + \epsilon_2\ \Delta y + \epsilon_3\ \Delta z,\end{aligned} \tag{30}$$

where

$$\epsilon_1, \epsilon_2, \epsilon_3 \to 0 \quad \text{when} \quad \Delta x, \Delta y, \text{and } \Delta z \to 0.$$

The partial derivatives f_x, f_y, f_z in this formula are to be evaluated at the point (x_0, y_0, z_0).

Note. The result (30) may be proved by treating Δw as the sum of three increments,

$$\Delta w_1 = f(x_0 + \Delta x, y_0, z_0) - f(x_0, y_0, z_0), \tag{31a}$$

$$\Delta w_2 = f(x_0 + \Delta x, y_0 + \Delta y, z_0) - f(x_0 + \Delta x, y_0, z_0), \tag{31b}$$

$$\Delta w_3 = f(x_0 + \Delta x, y_0 + \Delta y, z_0 + \Delta z) - f(x_0 + \Delta x, y_0 + \Delta y, z_0), \tag{31c}$$

and applying the Mean Value Theorem to each of these separately. Note that two coordinates remain constant and only one varies in each of these partial increments $\Delta w_1, \Delta w_2, \Delta w_3$. For example, in (31b), only y varies, since x is held equal to $x_0 + \Delta x$ and z is held equal to z_0. Since the function $f(x_0 + \Delta x, y, z_0)$ is a continuous function of y with a derivative f_y, it is subject to the Mean Value Theorem, and we have

$$\Delta w_2 = f_y(x_0 + \Delta x, y_1, z_0)\,\Delta y$$

for some y_1 between y_0 and $y_0 + \Delta y$.

The formula

$$\Delta w_{\tan} = f_x(x_0, y_0, z_0)\,\Delta x + f_y(x_0, y_0, z_0)\,\Delta y + f_z(x_0, y_0, z_0)\,\Delta z$$

$$= \left(\frac{\partial w}{\partial x}\right)_0 \Delta x + \left(\frac{\partial w}{\partial y}\right)_0 \Delta y + \left(\frac{\partial w}{\partial z}\right)_0 \Delta z, \tag{32}$$

gives a good approximation to Δw when the increments in the independent variables are small.

EXAMPLE 5. *Deflection of loaded beams.* A rectangular beam that is supported at its two ends (Fig. 13–17) will sag in the middle when subjected to a uniform load. The amount S of sag, called the *deflection* of the beam, may be estimated from the formula

$$S = C\frac{p\ell^4}{wh^3} \quad \text{(m)}, \tag{33}$$

13–17 Beam supported at ends.

where

$p =$ the load (kg/meter of beam length),
$\ell =$ the length between supports (m),
$w =$ the width of the beam (m),
$h =$ the height of the beam (m),
$C =$ a constant that depends on the units of measurement and on the material from which the beam is made.

When

$$\Delta S \approx \Delta S_{\tan} = S_p\,\Delta p + S_\ell\,\Delta\ell + S_w\,\Delta w + S_h\,\Delta h$$

is written out for a particular set of values p_0, ℓ_0, w_0, h_0, and simplified, the resulting approximation is

$$\Delta S \approx S_0\left[\frac{\Delta p}{p_0} + \frac{4\,\Delta\ell}{\ell_0} - \frac{\Delta w}{w_0} - \frac{3\,\Delta h}{h_0}\right], \tag{34}$$

where $S_0 = S(p_0, \ell_0, h_0, w_0) = Cp_0\ell_0^4/w_0h_0^3$.

At $p_0 = 100$ kg/m, $\ell_0 = 4$ m, $w_0 = 0.1$ m, and $h_0 = 0.2$ m,

$$\Delta S \approx S_0\left[\frac{\Delta p}{100} + \Delta\ell - 10\,\Delta w - 15\,\Delta h\right]. \tag{35}$$

13–18 The dimensions of the beam in Example 5.

(See Fig. 13–18.)

Conclusions about this beam from Eq. (35). Since Δp and $\Delta \ell$ appear with positive coefficients in Eq. (35), increases in p and in ℓ will increase the sag. But Δw and Δh appear with negative coefficients, so that increases in w and h will *decrease* the sag (make the beam stiffer). The sag is not very sensitive to small changes in load, because the coefficient of Δp is 1/100. The coefficient of Δh is a negative number of greater magnitude than the coefficient of Δw. Therefore, making the beam $\Delta h = 1$ cm higher will decrease the sag more than making the beam $\Delta w = 1$ cm wider.

PROBLEMS

1. Find $\Delta w_{\tan}$ and Δw if $w = x^2 - xy + y^2$, $(x_0, y_0) = (1, -2)$, $\Delta x = 0.01$, $\Delta y = 0.02$.

2. Calculate Δw, $\Delta w_{\tan}$, ϵ_1, and ϵ_2 at the general point (x, y) for the function $w = x^2 + xy$.

3. (a) Sketch the region in the xy-plane whose coordinates satisfy the inequality $|x - y| < \frac{1}{2}$. (b) Based on inequality (23) at the end of Example 2, how small should one make $|x - y|$ to be sure that the error in the approximation $1/(1 + x - y) \approx 1 - x + y$ is less than 10^{-3}?

4. (*Calculator*) Evaluate both sides of Eq. (25) for (a) $(x, y) = (2.1, 1.1)$; (b) $(x, y) = (2.1, 0.9)$.

In Problems 5–7, use Eq. (20) to find linear approximations to the given functions near the given points. If you have a *calculator*, check your approximations for an assortment of values of x and y.

5. $f(x, y) = \sqrt{x^2 + y^2}$;
near (a) $(1, 0)$; (b) $(0, 1)$; (c) $(1, 1)$.

6. $f(x, y) = (\sin x)/y$; near (a) $(\pi/2, 1)$; (b) $(0, 1)$.

7. $f(x, y) = e^x \cos y$; near (a) $(0, 0)$; (b) $(0, \pi/2)$.

8. What relationship must hold between the r and h in Example 4 if the volume of the cylinder is to be equally sensitive to small changes in the two variables?

9. The beam of Example 5 is tipped on its side, so that $h = 0.1$ m and $w = 0.2$ m. (a) What is the approximation for ΔS now? (b) Compare the sensitivity of the beam to a small change in height with its sensitivity to a change of the same amount in width.

10. Use $\Delta w_{\tan}$ to calculate how much an error of 2 percent in each of the factors a, b, c may affect the product abc.

11. (*Calculator*) Let $Q = \sqrt{2KM/h}$ be the economic order quantity of Example 24, Article 1–6. (a) Write an approximation for ΔQ, with partial derivatives evaluated at $K_0 = \$2.00$, $M_0 = 20$ radios/week, and $h_0 = \$0.05$. (b) At the values for K_0, M_0, h_0, given in (a), to which variable is Q most sensitive? least sensitive?

12. The dimensions of a rectangular box are measured as 3, 4, and 12 in. If the measurements may be in error by ± 0.01, ± 0.01, and ± 0.03 in., respectively, calculate the length of the diagonal and estimate the possible error in this length.

13. Carry through the details of deriving Eq. (11).

14. A function $w = f(x, y)$ is said to be *differentiable* at $P(a, b)$ if there are constants M and N (possibly depending on f and P) such that

$$\Delta w = M\,\Delta x + N\,\Delta y + \alpha[|\Delta x| + |\Delta y|]$$

and $\alpha \to 0$ as $|\Delta x| + |\Delta y| \to 0$. Here $\Delta w = f(a + \Delta x, b + \Delta y) - f(a, b)$. Prove that if f is differentiable at (a, b), then $M = f_x(a, b)$ and $N = f_y(a, b)$.

15. If the function $w = f(x, y)$ is differentiable at $P(a, b)$ (see Problem 14), prove it is continuous there.

13–5

THE DIRECTIONAL DERIVATIVE: GENERAL CASE

Let us return once more to Fig. 13–9 and the problem of determining the instantaneous rate of change at $P_0(x_0, y_0)$ of a function $w = f(x, y)$, measured in units of change of w per unit of distance along a ray L with vertex at P_0 and making an angle ϕ with the positive x-axis. Hold $P_0(x_0, y_0)$ fixed, and let $P_1(x_1, y_1)$ be a point on L near P_0. Let

$$\Delta x = x_1 - x_0,$$

$$\Delta y = y_1 - y_0.$$

The ratio

$$\frac{\Delta w}{\Delta s} = \frac{w_1 - w_0}{\sqrt{\Delta x^2 + \Delta y^2}} = \frac{f(x_1, y_1) - f(x_0, y_0)}{\sqrt{(x_1 - x_0)^2 + (y_1 - y_0)^2}}$$

is the average rate of change of w along L from P_0 to P_1. If $\Delta w/\Delta s$ has a limit as $P_1 \to P_0$ along L, we denote the limit by dw/ds and call it the *directional derivative of w at P_0 in the direction of* $\overrightarrow{P_0P_1}$. The next theorem tells how to calculate this derivative from the partial derivatives of f.

Theorem. *Let $w = f(x, y)$ be continuous and possess partial derivatives f_x, f_y throughout some neighborhood of the point $P_0(x_0, y_0)$. Let f_x and f_y be continuous at P_0. Then the directional derivative at P_0 exists for any direction angle ϕ, and is given by*

$$\frac{dw}{ds} = f_x(x_0, y_0) \cos \phi + f_y(x_0, y_0) \sin \phi. \tag{1}$$

Note that the special cases $\phi = 0, \pi/2, \pi, 3\pi/2$, respectively, lead to

$$\frac{dw}{ds} = \frac{\partial f}{\partial x}, \quad \frac{\partial f}{\partial y}, \quad -\frac{\partial f}{\partial x}, \quad -\frac{\partial f}{\partial y},$$

in harmony with our earlier discussion.

Proof of the theorem. Equation (4) of the previous article is valid under the hypotheses we have made for the continuity of $f(x, y)$, $\partial f/\partial x$, and $\partial f/\partial y$. Hence,

$$\frac{\Delta w}{\Delta s} = f_x(x_0, y_0)\frac{\Delta x}{\Delta s} + f_y(x_0, y_0)\frac{\Delta y}{\Delta s} + \epsilon_1 \frac{\Delta x}{\Delta s} + \epsilon_2 \frac{\Delta y}{\Delta s},$$

where

$$\epsilon_1 \text{ and } \epsilon_2 \to 0 \quad \text{as} \quad \Delta x \text{ and } \Delta y \to 0.$$

Now, if $P_1 \to P_0$ along L, or even along a smooth curve that is tangent to L at P_0, we have

$$\lim \frac{\Delta x}{\Delta s} = \frac{dx}{ds} = \cos \phi,$$

$$\lim \frac{\Delta y}{\Delta s} = \frac{dy}{ds} = \sin \phi$$

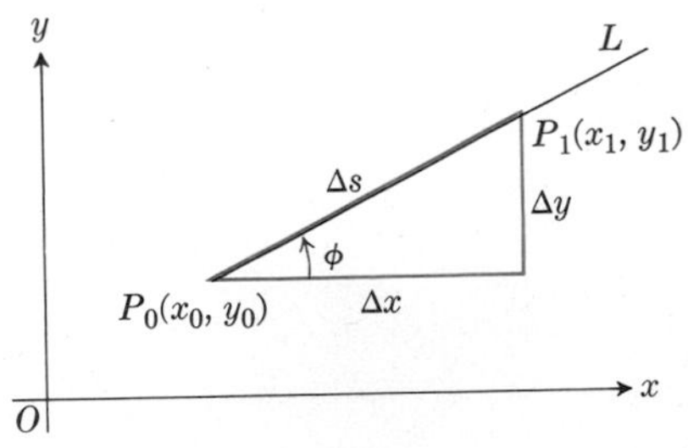

13–19 As $P_1 \to P_0$ on L, $\Delta x/\Delta s = \cos \phi$ and $\Delta y/\Delta s = \sin \phi$.

(Fig. 13–19), and hence

$$\frac{dw}{ds} = \lim \frac{\Delta w}{\Delta s} = f_x(x_0, y_0) \cos \phi + f_y(x_0, y_0) \sin \phi. \qquad \text{Q.E.D.}$$

EXAMPLE 1. Let $w = 100 - x^2 - y^2$. If one starts from the point $P_0(3, 4)$, in which direction should one go to make w increase most rapidly?

Solution. We have

$$f(x, y) = 100 - x^2 - y^2,$$

$$f_x(3, 4) = -6, \qquad f_y(3, 4) = -8,$$

and

$$\left(\frac{dw}{ds}\right)_{(3,4)} = -6 \cos \phi - 8 \sin \phi.$$

To make w increase most rapidly, we seek the angle ϕ for which the function

$$F(\phi) = -6 \cos \phi - 8 \sin \phi$$

has a maximum. Since

$$F'(\phi) = 6 \sin \phi - 8 \cos \phi$$

is zero when

$$\tan \phi = \tfrac{4}{3},$$

$$\sin \phi = \pm\tfrac{4}{5},$$

$$\cos \phi = \pm\tfrac{3}{5},$$

while

$$F''(\phi) = 6 \cos \phi + 8 \sin \phi$$

is negative in case both $\sin \phi$ and $\cos \phi$ are negative, we observe that the maximum value of $F(\phi)$ is attained when

$$\cos \phi = -\tfrac{3}{5},$$

$$\sin \phi = -\tfrac{4}{5}.$$

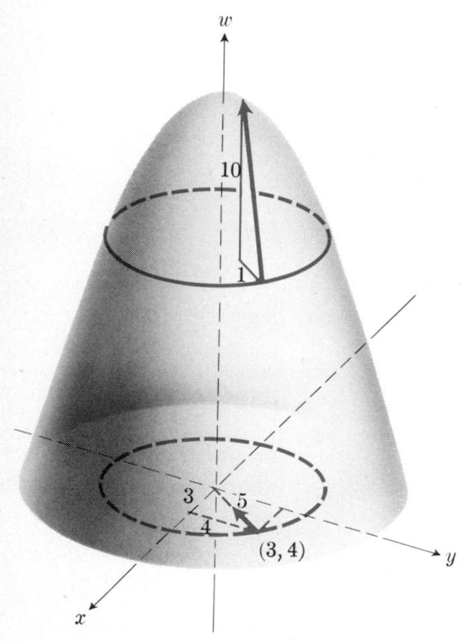

13–20 At (3, 4) the change in $w = 100 - x^2 - y^2$ is greatest in the direction toward the origin. This corresponds to the direction of steepest ascent on the surface.

The geometric meaning of this result is that w increases most rapidly in the direction from $P_0(3, 4)$ toward the origin (Fig. 13–20). The derivative of w in this direction is found to be

$$\left.\frac{dw}{ds}\right|_{(3,4)} = -6(-\tfrac{3}{5}) - 8(-\tfrac{4}{5}) = 10.$$

The notion of the directional derivative can easily be extended from the case of functions of two independent variables to the case of functions of three independent variables. To this end, consider the values of a function

$$w = f(x, y, z)$$

at $P_0(x_0, y_0, z_0)$ and at a nearby point $P_1(x_1, y_1, z_1)$ lying on a ray L emanating from P_0. It will be convenient to specify the direction of L by a unit vector $\mathbf{u}$. To find such a vector, we let

$$x_1 - x_0 = \Delta x, \qquad y_1 - y_0 = \Delta y, \qquad z_1 - z_0 = \Delta z,$$

so that

$$\overrightarrow{P_0P_1} = \mathbf{i}\,\Delta x + \mathbf{j}\,\Delta y + \mathbf{k}\,\Delta z.$$

Since the length of $\overrightarrow{P_0P_1}$ is

$$\Delta s = \sqrt{(\Delta x)^2 + (\Delta y)^2 + (\Delta z)^2},$$

the direction of $\overrightarrow{P_0P_1}$ is given by

$$\frac{\overrightarrow{P_0P_1}}{\Delta s} = \mathbf{u}.$$

That is,

$$\mathbf{u} = \mathbf{i}\frac{\Delta x}{\Delta s} + \mathbf{j}\frac{\Delta y}{\Delta s} + \mathbf{k}\frac{\Delta z}{\Delta s} = \mathbf{i}\cos\alpha + \mathbf{j}\cos\beta + \mathbf{k}\cos\gamma,$$

or

$$\frac{\Delta x}{\Delta s} = \cos\alpha, \qquad \frac{\Delta y}{\Delta s} = \cos\beta, \qquad \frac{\Delta z}{\Delta s} = \cos\gamma.$$

These direction cosines of $\overrightarrow{P_0P_1}$ remain constant as P_1 approaches P_0 along L. Hence, in the limit as $\Delta s \to 0$, we also have

$$\frac{dx}{ds} = \cos\alpha, \qquad \frac{dy}{ds} = \cos\beta, \qquad \frac{dz}{ds} = \cos\gamma.$$

With these geometrical considerations out of the way, we now define the directional derivative of w at P_0 in the direction $\mathbf{u}$ to be the limit, as P_1 approaches P_0 along L, of the average rate of change of w with respect to distance:

$$\frac{dw}{ds} = \lim_{\Delta s \to 0} \frac{\Delta w}{\Delta s} = \lim_{P_1 \to P_0} \frac{f(x_1, y_1, z_1) - f(x_0, y_0, z_0)}{\sqrt{(x_1 - x_0)^2 + (y_1 - y_0)^2 + (z_1 - z_0)^2}}.$$

If f, f_x, f_y, and f_z are all continuous functions of x, y, z in some neighborhood of the point $P_0(x_0, y_0, z_0)$, then Eq. (30) of Article 13–4 applies, and we find that the directional derivative of $w = f(x, y, z)$ at P_0 in the direction of $\mathbf{u} = \mathbf{i}\cos\alpha + \mathbf{j}\cos\beta + \mathbf{k}\cos\gamma$ is

$$\frac{dw}{ds} = f_x(x_0, y_0, z_0)\cos\alpha + f_y(x_0, y_0, z_0)\cos\beta + f_z(x_0, y_0, z_0)\cos\gamma. \tag{2}$$

This can be expressed as the dot product of the vector $\mathbf{u}$ above and the vector

$$\mathbf{v} = \mathbf{i}f_x(x_0, y_0, z_0) + \mathbf{j}f_y(x_0, y_0, z_0) + \mathbf{k}f_z(x_0, y_0, z_0). \tag{3}$$

That is,

$$\frac{dw}{ds} = \mathbf{u} \cdot \mathbf{v}. \tag{4}$$

This factorization separates the directional derivative into a part $\mathbf{u}$ which depends only upon the *direction* and a part $\mathbf{v}$ which depends only upon the *function and the point P*. The vector $\mathbf{v}$ is called the *gradient* of f at P_0. It will be considered in detail in the next article. Equation (4) applies also in two dimensions as well as in three and includes Eq. (1) as a special case, with $\gamma = 90°$, $\cos\gamma = 0$.

EXAMPLE 2. Find the directional derivative of

$$f(x, y, z) = x^3 - xy^2 - z$$

at $P_0(1, 1, 0)$ in the direction of the vector $\mathbf{A} = 2\mathbf{i} - 3\mathbf{j} + 6\mathbf{k}$.

Solution. The partial derivatives of f at P_0 are

$$f_x = 3x^2 - y^2 \big|_{(1,1,0)} = 2,$$

$$f_y = -2xy \big|_{(1,1,0)} = -2,$$

$$f_z = -1 \big|_{(1,1,0)} = -1.$$

Therefore, the gradient of f at $(1, 1, 0)$ is

$$\mathbf{v} = 2\mathbf{i} - 2\mathbf{j} - \mathbf{k}.$$

Since

$$|\mathbf{A}| = \sqrt{2^2 + 3^2 + 6^2} = \sqrt{49} = 7,$$

the direction of $\mathbf{A}$ is

$$\mathbf{u} = \frac{\mathbf{A}}{|\mathbf{A}|} = \frac{2}{7}\mathbf{i} - \frac{3}{7}\mathbf{j} + \frac{6}{7}\mathbf{k}.$$

The derivative of f in the direction of $\mathbf{A}$ can now be calculated from Eq. (4) as

$$\mathbf{u} \cdot \mathbf{v} = 2(\tfrac{2}{7}) + 2(\tfrac{3}{7}) - 1(\tfrac{6}{7}) = \tfrac{4}{7}.$$

PROBLEMS

In Problems 1–4, find the directional derivative of the given function, $f = f(x, y, z)$, at the given point, and in the direction of the given vector $\mathbf{A}$.

1. $f = e^x \cos(yz)$, $P_0(0, 0, 0)$, $\mathbf{A} = 2\mathbf{i} + \mathbf{j} - 2\mathbf{k}$.
2. $f = \ln \sqrt{x^2 + y^2 + z^2}$, $P_0(3, 4, 12)$, $\mathbf{A} = 3\mathbf{i} + 6\mathbf{j} - 2\mathbf{k}$.
3. $f = x^2 + 2y^2 + 3z^2$, $P_0(1, 1, 1)$, $\mathbf{A} = \mathbf{i} + \mathbf{j} + \mathbf{k}$.
4. $f = xy + yz + zx$, $P_0(1, -1, 2)$, $\mathbf{A} = 10\mathbf{i} + 11\mathbf{j} - 2\mathbf{k}$.

5. In which direction should one travel, starting from $P_0(1, 1, 0)$, to obtain the most rapid rate of decrease of the function

$$f = (x + y - 2)^2 + (3x - y - 6)^2?$$

6. The directional derivative of a given function $w = f(x, y)$ at $P_0(1, 2)$ in the direction toward $P_1(2, 3)$ is $+2\sqrt{2}$, and in the direction toward $P_2(1, 0)$ it is -3. What is the value of dw/ds at P_0 in the direction toward the origin?

7. Investigate the following graphical method of representing the directional derivative. Let $w = f(x, y)$ be a given function and let $P_0(x_0, y_0)$ be a given point. Through P_0 draw any ray making an angle θ with the positive x-direction, $0 \le \theta \le 2\pi$. On this directed line (or on its backward extension through P_0, if r is negative), mark the point Q such that the polar coordinates of Q relative to P_0 are (r, θ) with $r = (dw/ds)_0$. Show that Q is located on a circle of diameter

$$\sqrt{\left(\frac{\partial w}{\partial x}\right)_0^2 + \left(\frac{\partial w}{\partial y}\right)_0^2}.$$

Show that P_0 and

$$P_1\left(x_0 + \left(\frac{\partial w}{\partial x}\right)_0, y_0 + \left(\frac{\partial w}{\partial y}\right)_0\right)$$

are opposite ends of one diameter of the circle. (This gives an easy way to construct the circle: Locate P_0 and P_1, and then draw the circle with diameter P_0P_1. This circle is analogous to the Mohr circle in mechanics.)

8. Find the directional derivative of $f(x, y) = x \tan^{-1} y/x$ at $(1, 1)$ in the direction of $\mathbf{A} = 2\mathbf{i} - \mathbf{j}$.

9. In which direction is the directional derivative of

$$f(x, y) = \frac{x^2 - y^2}{x^2 + y^2}$$

at $(1, 1)$ equal to zero?

13–6 THE GRADIENT

In the previous article we found that the directional derivative of a function $w = f(x, y, z)$ could be expressed as the dot product of a unit vector $\mathbf{u}$ specifying the direction and the vector $\mathbf{v}$ of Eq. (3). This latter vector depends only upon the values of the partial derivatives of w at P_0 and is called the *gradient* of w. Two symbols are commonly used to denote the gradient, namely, grad w and ∇w, where ∇ is an inverted capital delta and is generally called *del*. The gradient is defined by the equation

$$\text{grad } w = \nabla w = \mathbf{i}\frac{\partial w}{\partial x} + \mathbf{j}\frac{\partial w}{\partial y} + \mathbf{k}\frac{\partial w}{\partial z}. \tag{1}$$

The del operator

$$\nabla = \mathbf{i}\frac{\partial}{\partial x} + \mathbf{j}\frac{\partial}{\partial y} + \mathbf{k}\frac{\partial}{\partial z} \tag{2}$$

is akin to, but somewhat more complex than, the familiar differentiation operator d/dx. When del operates on a differentiable function $w = f(x, y, z)$, it produces a vector, namely the vector grad w or grad f given by Eq. (1).

In courses in advanced calculus and vector analysis, a detailed study is made of the operator ∇, including not only the operation of forming the gradient of a scalar function w but also the additional operations of forming the dot and cross products of the vector operator del with other vectors.

In this article we develop some of the geometric properties of the gradient.

The Connection between the Gradient and the Directional Derivative

Using ∇w to represent the gradient, we may write Eq. (2) of Article 13–5 as

$$\left(\frac{dw}{ds}\right)_0 = (\nabla w)_0 \cdot \mathbf{u}, \tag{3}$$

where the subscript 0 is used to show that both ∇w and dw/ds are to be evaluated at the point $P_0(x_0, y_0, z_0)$.

From Eq. (3) and the geometric significance of the dot product of two vectors, we can say that

$$\begin{aligned}\left(\frac{dw}{ds}\right)_0 &= |(\nabla w)_0|\,|\mathbf{u}| \cos\theta \\ &= |(\nabla w)_0| \cos\theta,\end{aligned} \tag{4}$$

where θ is the angle between the vector $(\nabla w)_0$ and the unit vector $\mathbf{u}$. That is, $(dw/ds)_0$ is just the component of grad w at P_0, in the direction $\mathbf{u}$ (Fig. 13–21a). Since this component is largest when $\cos\theta = 1$ in Eq. (4), that is, when $\mathbf{u}$ and ∇w have the same direction, we can say:

The function $w = f(x, y, z)$ changes most rapidly in the direction given by the vector grad w. Moreover, the directional derivative in this direction is equal to the magnitude of the gradient.

---

a)

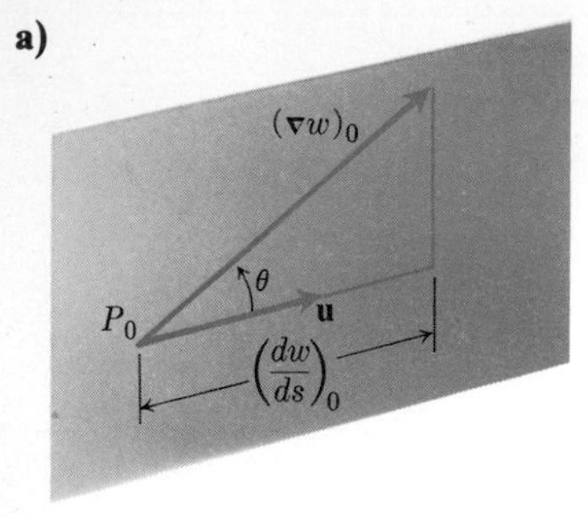

dw/ds is the component of ∇w in the direction of **u**.

b)

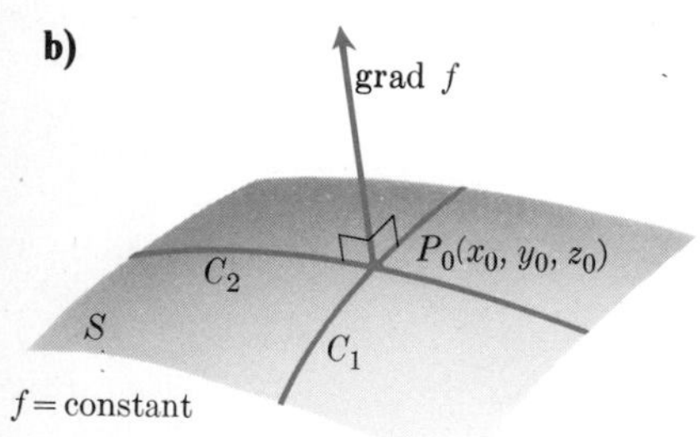

$(\text{grad } f)_0$ is perpendicular to the surface $f(x, y, z) = w_0$ at $P_0(x_0, y_0, z_0)$.

Figure 13–21

We may therefore characterize the gradient of the function $w = f(x, y, z)$ at the point $P_0(x_0, y_0, z_0)$ as a vector

a) whose *direction* is that in which $(dw/ds)_0$ has its maximum value, and
b) whose *magnitude* is equal to that maximum value of $(dw/ds)_0$.

The Connection between $(\nabla w)_0$ and the Surface $f(x, y, z) = w_0$

The points at which the function $w = f(x, y, z)$ has a constant value w_0 will generally constitute a surface in space. The equation of this surface is

$$f(x, y, z) = w_0, \tag{5a}$$

or

$$f(x, y, z) - w_0 = 0. \tag{5b}$$

If w represents temperature, the surface given by Eq. (5) is an isothermal surface. If w represents electrical or gravitational potential, then the surface is an equipotential surface. What we now wish to establish is that the gradient vector is normal to this isothermal or potential surface, as shown in Fig. 13–21(b). To see that this is so, we consider any curve C on the surface S of Eq. (5) and passing through the point $P_0(x_0, y_0, z_0)$ on S. We calculate the directional derivative $(dw/ds)_0$ in the direction of the tangent vector to C at P_0. This derivative is zero because w remains constant on C and hence $(\Delta w)_C = 0$, so that

$$\left(\frac{dw}{ds}\right)_0 = \lim \frac{\Delta w}{\Delta s} = 0.$$

If we compare this result with Eq. (4), we see that at any point P_0 where $(\nabla w)_0$ is not zero, $\cos\theta$ vanishes; that is,

$$(\nabla w)_0 \text{ is perpendicular to } \mathbf{u},$$

where **u** is a unit vector tangent to C at P_0. Now since C could be any curve on S through P_0, we have the result that

---

The gradient $(\nabla w)_0$ of the function $w = f(x, y, z)$ is normal to the surface

$$f(x, y, z) = w_0$$

at the point $P_0(x_0, y_0, z_0)$.

In the exceptional case where $(\nabla w)_0$ is the zero vector, it has no definite direction. But if we adopt the convention that the zero vector is orthogonal to every direction, then we may say without exception that the gradient of a function $f(x, y, z)$ at a point $P_0(x_0, y_0, z_0)$ is orthogonal to the surface $f(x, y, z) =$ constant passing through that point.

EXAMPLE. Find the plane which is tangent to the surface $z = x^2 + y^2$ at the point $P_0(1, -2, 5)$.

Solution. Let $w = f(x, y, z) = x^2 + y^2 - z$, so that the equation of the surface has the form

$$f(x, y, z) = \text{constant},$$

where the constant in this case is zero. Then the vector

$$(\text{grad } f)_0 = \left(\mathbf{i}\frac{\partial f}{\partial x} + \mathbf{j}\frac{\partial f}{\partial y} + \mathbf{k}\frac{\partial f}{\partial z}\right)_0$$

$$= (\mathbf{i}2x + \mathbf{j}2y - \mathbf{k})_{(1,-2,5)} = 2\mathbf{i} - 4\mathbf{j} - \mathbf{k}$$

is *normal* to the surface at P_0. But we recall that the equation of the plane through $P_0(x_0, y_0, z_0)$ normal to the vector

$$\mathbf{N} = A\mathbf{i} + B\mathbf{j} + C\mathbf{k}$$

is

$$A(x - x_0) + B(y - y_0) + C(z - z_0) = 0.$$

For the particular case at hand, we therefore have

$$2(x - 1) - 4(y + 2) - (z - 5) = 0,$$

or

$$2x - 4y - z = 5,$$

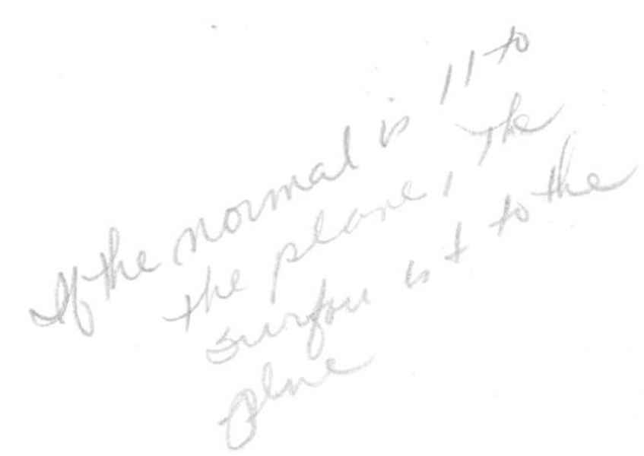

as the equation of the tangent plane.

Note that the equation of the surface should be put into the form

$$f(x, y, z) = \text{constant}$$

in order to find the normal vector, grad f.

PROBLEMS

In Problems 1–7, find the electric intensity vector $\mathbf{E} = -\text{grad } V$ from the given potential function V, at the given point:

1. $V = x^2 + y^2 - 2z^2 \quad (1, 1, 1)$

2. $V = 2z^3 - 3(x^2 + y^2)z \quad (1, 1, 1)$

3. $V = e^{-2y} \cos 2x \quad (\pi/4, 0, 0)$

4. $V = \ln \sqrt{x^2 + y^2} \quad (3, 4, 0)$

5. $V = (x^2 + y^2 + z^2)^{-(1/2)} \quad (1, 2, -2)$

6. $V = e^{3x+4y} \cos 5z \quad (0, 0, \pi/6)$

7. $V = \cos 3x \cos 4y \sinh 5z \quad (0, \pi/4, 0)$

8. Find equations of the line normal to the surface $z^2 = x^2 + y^2$ at $(3, 4, -5)$.

9. Lines are drawn through the origin and normal to the surface $xy + z = 2$. (a) Find equations of all such lines. (b) Find all points of intersection of these lines with the surface.

10. Find the points on the surface

$$(y + z)^2 + (z - x)^2 = 16,$$

where the normal is parallel to the yz-plane.

11. Find the tangent plane and normal to the hyperboloid $x^2 + y^2 - z^2 = 18$ at $(3, 5, -4)$.

12. In which direction should one travel, starting from the point $P_0(2, -1, 2)$, in order to obtain the most rapid rate of increase of the function $f = (x + y)^2 + (y + z)^2 + (z + x)^2$? What is the instantaneous rate of change of f per unit of distance in this direction?

13. Suppose cylindrical coordinates r, θ, z are introduced into a function $w = f(x, y, z)$ to yield $w = F(r, \theta, z)$. Show that the gradient may be expressed in terms of cylindrical coordinates and the unit vectors $\mathbf{u}_r, \mathbf{u}_\theta, \mathbf{k}$ as follows:

$$\nabla w = \mathbf{u}_r \frac{\partial w}{\partial r} + \frac{1}{r}\mathbf{u}_\theta \frac{\partial w}{\partial \theta} + \mathbf{k}\frac{\partial w}{\partial z}.$$

[*Hint.* The component of ∇w in the direction of $\mathbf{u}_r$ is equal to the directional derivative dw/ds in that direction. But this is precisely $\partial w/\partial r$. Reason similarly for the components of ∇w in the directions of $\mathbf{u}_\theta$ and $\mathbf{k}$.]

14. Express the gradient in terms of spherical coordinates and the appropriate unit vectors $\mathbf{u}_\rho$, $\mathbf{u}_\phi$, $\mathbf{u}_\theta$. Use a geometrical argument to determine the component of ∇w in each of these directions. (See hint for Problem 13.)

15. (a) In the case of a function $w = f(x, y)$ of two independent variables, what is the expression for grad f? (b) Find the direction in which the function $w = x^2 + xy + y^2$ increases most rapidly, at the point $(-1, 1)$. What is the magnitude of dw/ds in this direction?

In Problems 16–23, verify that the function V satisfies Laplace's equation

$$\frac{\partial^2 V}{\partial x^2} + \frac{\partial^2 V}{\partial y^2} + \frac{\partial^2 V}{\partial z^2} = 0,$$

where V is as given:

16. In Problem 1
17. In Problem 2
18. In Problem 3
19. In Problem 4
20. In Problem 5
21. In Problem 6
22. In Problem 7

23. *Method of steepest descent.* Suppose it is desired to find a solution of the equation $f(x, y, z) = 0$. Let $P_0(x_0, y_0, z_0)$ be a first guess, and suppose $f(x_0, y_0, z_0) = f_0$ is not zero. Let $(\nabla f)_0$ be the gradient vector normal to the surface $f(x, y, z) = f_0$ at P_0. If f_0 is positive, we want to decrease the value of f. The gradient points in the direction of most rapid increase, its negative in the direction of "steepest descent." We therefore take as next approximation

$$x_1 = x_0 - hf_x(x_0, y_0, z_0),$$
$$y_1 = y_0 - hf_y(x_0, y_0, z_0),$$
$$z_1 = z_0 - hf_z(x_0, y_0, z_0).$$

What value of h corresponds to making $\Delta f_{\tan} = -f_0$? What change is suggested if f_0 is negative? [The method could be applied to the problem of solving the simultaneous equations

$$x - y + z = 3,$$
$$x^2 + y^2 + z^2 = 20,$$
$$xyz = 8,$$

by writing

$$f(x, y, z) = (x - y + z - 3)^2 + (x^2 + y^2 + z^2 - 20)^2 + (xyz - 8)^2.]$$

13–7 THE CHAIN RULE FOR PARTIAL DERIVATIVES

The formula

$$\frac{dy}{dt} = \frac{dy}{dx}\frac{dx}{dt}, \tag{1}$$

developed in Chapter 2, expresses the chain rule for differentiating a function

$$y = f(x) \tag{2}$$

with respect to t, when x is a function of t,

$$x = g(t). \tag{3}$$

Substituting Eq. (3) into Eq. (2) gives y as a function of t:

$$y = f[g(t)] = F(t). \tag{4}$$

Equation (1) in turn tells us that

$$F'(t) = f'(x)g'(t) \tag{5a}$$

or, in subscript notation, that

$$F_t = f_x g_t, \tag{5b}$$

or

$$y_t = y_x x_t. \tag{5c}$$

In this article we extend the chain rule to functions of several variables. We start with a function

$$w = f(x, y, z) \tag{6}$$

that has continuous partial derivatives

$$\frac{\partial w}{\partial x} = f_x, \qquad \frac{\partial w}{\partial y} = f_y, \qquad \frac{\partial w}{\partial z} = f_z \tag{7}$$

throughout some region R of xyz-space. Suppose we want to study the behavior of the function f along a curve C lying in R and given by parametric equations

$$x = x(t), \qquad y = y(t), \qquad z = z(t). \tag{8}$$

Such a situation arises, for example, in studying the pressure or density in a moving fluid. Then the equation that takes the place of Eq. (1) or (5) is

$$\frac{dw}{dt} = \frac{\partial w}{\partial x}\frac{dx}{dt} + \frac{\partial w}{\partial y}\frac{dy}{dt} + \frac{\partial w}{\partial z}\frac{dz}{dt}, \tag{9}$$

as we shall now show. Let t_0 be a value of t that corresponds to a point P_0 in R and let Δt be an increment in t such that the point P that corresponds to $t_0 + \Delta t$ also lies in R. Let Δx, Δy, Δz, Δw denote the increments in x, y, z, w. Then, by Eq. (30) of Article 13–4, we may write

$$\frac{\Delta w}{\Delta t} = \left(\frac{\partial w}{\partial x}\right)_0 \frac{\Delta x}{\Delta t} + \left(\frac{\partial w}{\partial y}\right)_0 \frac{\Delta y}{\Delta t} + \left(\frac{\partial w}{\partial z}\right)_0 \frac{\Delta z}{\Delta t} + \epsilon_1 \frac{\Delta x}{\Delta t} + \epsilon_2 \frac{\Delta y}{\Delta t} + \epsilon_3 \frac{\Delta z}{\Delta t}, \tag{10}$$

where the subscript zero shows that the partial derivatives are to be evaluated at P_0, and where

$$\epsilon_1, \epsilon_2, \epsilon_3 \to 0 \quad \text{as} \quad \Delta x, \Delta y, \Delta z \to 0.$$

Suppose we now let $\Delta t \to 0$ in Eq. (10) and assume that the curve C given by Eqs. (8) has derivatives dx/dt, dy/dt, dz/dt at t_0. Then

$$\Delta x, \Delta y, \Delta z \to 0 \quad \text{as} \quad \Delta t \to 0$$

and the three terms in Eq. (10) that involve the epsilons go to zero, while the other terms give

$$\left(\frac{dw}{dt}\right)_0 = \left(\frac{\partial w}{\partial x}\right)_0 \left(\frac{dx}{dt}\right)_0 + \left(\frac{\partial w}{\partial y}\right)_0 \left(\frac{dy}{dt}\right)_0 + \left(\frac{\partial w}{\partial z}\right)_0 \left(\frac{dz}{dt}\right)_0.$$

This is Eq. (9) with all derivatives evaluated for $t = t_0$, $x = x_0$, $y = y_0$, and $z = z_0$.

EXAMPLE 1. Express dw/dt as a function of t if $w = xy + z$ and $x = \cos t$, $y = \sin t$, $z = t$. (This derivative shows how w varies along a particular helix in its domain.)

Solution. Starting with Eq. (9) we have

$$\begin{aligned}\frac{dw}{dt} &= \frac{\partial w}{\partial x}\frac{dx}{dt} + \frac{\partial w}{\partial y}\frac{dy}{dt} + \frac{\partial w}{\partial z}\frac{dz}{dt} \\ &= y(-\sin t) + x(\cos t) + 1(1) \\ &= -\sin^2 t + \cos^2 t + 1 \\ &= 1 + \cos 2t.\end{aligned}$$

No essential complication is introduced by considering the behavior of the function w in Eq. (6) on a *surface* S lying in R. We usually use *two* parameters to give the equations of a surface (for example, *latitude* and *longitude* on the surface of a sphere). Hence, consider the case where x, y, and z are functions of two parameters, say r and s,

$$x = x(r, s), \qquad y = y(r, s), \qquad z = z(r, s), \tag{11}$$

and calculate

$$\frac{\partial w}{\partial r} = \lim_{\Delta r \to 0} \frac{\Delta w}{\Delta r} \tag{12}$$

with s held constant. In this case Eq. (10) is to be replaced by a similar equation with Δr in place of Δt throughout. When $\Delta r \to 0$ (s held constant), we have

$$\lim_{\Delta r \to 0} \frac{\Delta x}{\Delta r} = \frac{\partial x}{\partial r}$$

and two similar expressions with y and z in place of x. Thus when $\Delta r \to 0$, the result is

$$\frac{\partial w}{\partial r} = \frac{\partial w}{\partial x}\frac{\partial x}{\partial r} + \frac{\partial w}{\partial y}\frac{\partial y}{\partial r} + \frac{\partial w}{\partial z}\frac{\partial z}{\partial r}. \tag{13}$$

We could also derive a similar expression, with s in place of r, for $\partial w/\partial s$.

EXAMPLE 2. Find $\partial w/\partial r$ and $\partial w/\partial s$ as functions of r and s if $w = x + 2y + z^2$, and $x = r/s$, $y = r^2 + e^s$, $z = 2r$.

Solution. From Eq. (13),

$$\begin{aligned} \frac{\partial w}{\partial r} &= \frac{\partial w}{\partial x}\frac{\partial x}{\partial r} + \frac{\partial w}{\partial y}\frac{\partial y}{\partial r} + \frac{\partial w}{\partial z}\frac{\partial z}{\partial r} \\ &= 1\left(\frac{1}{s}\right) + 2(2r) + 2z(2) = \frac{1}{s} + 12r. \end{aligned}$$

Similarly,

$$\begin{aligned} \frac{\partial w}{\partial s} &= \frac{\partial w}{\partial x}\frac{\partial x}{\partial s} + \frac{\partial w}{\partial y}\frac{\partial y}{\partial s} + \frac{\partial w}{\partial z}\frac{\partial z}{\partial s} \\ &= 1\left(-\frac{r}{s^2}\right) + 2(e^s) + 2z(0) = -\frac{r}{s^2} + 2e^s. \end{aligned}$$

EXAMPLE 3. We may use the chain rule to solve the partial differential equation

$$\frac{\partial w}{\partial x} - a\frac{\partial w}{\partial y} = 0$$

for $w = f(x, y)$, given that a is a constant different from zero. We introduce new independent variables r, s such that

$$y - ax = r, \qquad y + ax = s.$$

Now we think of w as a function of r, s,

$$w = F(r, s),$$

and apply the chain rule in the form

$$\frac{\partial w}{\partial x} = \frac{\partial w}{\partial r}\frac{\partial r}{\partial x} + \frac{\partial w}{\partial s}\frac{\partial s}{\partial x} = -a\frac{\partial w}{\partial r} + a\frac{\partial w}{\partial s},$$

$$\frac{\partial w}{\partial y} = \frac{\partial w}{\partial r}\frac{\partial r}{\partial y} + \frac{\partial w}{\partial s}\frac{\partial s}{\partial y} = \frac{\partial w}{\partial r} + \frac{\partial w}{\partial s}.$$

When we substitute these expressions for $\partial w/\partial x$ and $\partial w/\partial y$ into the partial differential equation

$$\frac{\partial w}{\partial x} - a\frac{\partial w}{\partial y} = 0,$$

we obtain

$$-2a\frac{\partial w}{\partial r} = 0 \qquad \text{or} \qquad \frac{\partial w}{\partial r} = 0.$$

But this equation is *easy* to solve! It simply requires $w = F(r, s)$ to be a constant when s is constant and r is allowed to vary. That is, w must be a function of s alone:

$$\begin{aligned} w &= \phi(s) \\ &= \phi(y + ax). \end{aligned}$$

Here $\phi(s)$ is *any* differentiable function of s whatever; for example,

$$\phi(s) = e^{2s} + \tan^{-1}(s^2) + \sqrt{s^2 + 4}$$

would be a suitable function. For this special case, we have

$$w = \phi(y + ax) = e^{2y+2ax} + \tan^{-1}(y + ax)^2 + \sqrt{(y + ax)^2 + 4}$$

as a function that satisfies the original partial differential equation.

Functions of Many Variables

More generally, we may consider a function

$$w = f(x, y, z, u, \ldots, v)$$

of any number of variables $x, y, z, u, \ldots, v$ and study the behavior of this function when these variables are related to any number of other variables $p, q, r, s, \ldots, t$ by equations

$$\begin{aligned} x &= x(p, q, r, s, \ldots, t), \\ y &= y(p, q, r, s, \ldots, t), \\ &\vdots \\ v &= v(p, q, r, s, \ldots, t). \end{aligned}$$

Then, suppose we are required to find $\partial w/\partial p, \partial w/\partial q, \partial w/\partial r, \ldots, \partial w/\partial t$. By the methods used above, we find

$$\frac{\partial w}{\partial p} = \frac{\partial w}{\partial x}\frac{\partial x}{\partial p} + \frac{\partial w}{\partial y}\frac{\partial y}{\partial p} + \frac{\partial w}{\partial z}\frac{\partial z}{\partial p} + \cdots + \frac{\partial w}{\partial v}\frac{\partial v}{\partial p}, \tag{14}$$

or, in terms of the subscript notation for partial derivatives,

$$w_p = w_x x_p + w_y y_p + w_z z_p + \cdots + w_v v_p.$$

There are analogous equations for $\partial w/\partial q, \ldots, \partial w/\partial t$ obtained by replacing p by $q, \ldots, t$, respectively. This "chain rule" may be summarized as follows:

Let w be a differentiable function of the variables $x, y, \ldots, v$ and let these in turn be differentiable functions of a second set of variables $p, q, \ldots, t$:

First set of variables: $x, y, z, \ldots, v,$

Second set of variables: $p, q, r, \ldots, t.$

Then the derivative of w with respect to any one of the variables in the second set, say p, may be obtained by the following procedure:

1. Differentiate w with respect to each one of the variables in the first set; that is, calculate

$$\frac{\partial w}{\partial x}, \quad \frac{\partial w}{\partial y}, \quad \ldots, \quad \frac{\partial w}{\partial v}.$$

2. Differentiate each variable of the first set with respect to the one variable of the second set, in this case p; that is, calculate

$$\frac{\partial x}{\partial p}, \quad \frac{\partial y}{\partial p}, \quad \ldots, \quad \frac{\partial v}{\partial p}.$$

3. Form the products of the corresponding derivatives in 1 and 2, such as $(\partial w/\partial x)(\partial x/\partial p)$, $(\partial w/\partial y)(\partial y/\partial p)$, etc., and add these products together. Their sum gives $\partial w/\partial p$ [Eq. (14)].

PROBLEMS

In each of the following problems (1–3), find dw/dt (a) by expressing w explicitly as a function of t and then differentiating, and (b) by using the chain rule.

1. $w = x^2 + y^2 + z^2, \quad x = e^t \cos t, \quad y = e^t \sin t, \quad z = e^t$

2. $w = \dfrac{xy}{x^2 + y^2}, \quad x = \cosh t, \quad y = \sinh t$

3. $w = e^{2x+3y} \cos 4z, \quad x = \ln t, \quad y = \ln (t^2 + 1), \quad z = t$

4. If $w = \sqrt{x^2 + y^2 + z^2}$, $x = e^r \cos s$, $y = e^r \sin s$, $z = e^s$, find $\partial w/\partial r$ and $\partial w/\partial s$ by the chain rule, and check your answer by using a different method.

5. If $w = \ln (x^2 + y^2 + 2z)$, $x = r + s$, $y = r - s$, $z = 2rs$, find $\partial w/\partial r$ and $\partial w/\partial s$ by the chain rule, and check your answer by using a different method.

6. If a and b are constants and

$$w = (ax + by)^3 + \tanh (ax + by) + \cos (ax + by),$$

show that

$$a\frac{\partial w}{\partial y} = b\frac{\partial w}{\partial x}.$$

7. If a and b are constants and $w = f(ax + by)$ is a differentiable function of $u = ax + by$, show that

$$a\frac{\partial w}{\partial y} = b\frac{\partial w}{\partial x}.$$

[*Hint.* Apply the chain rule with u as the only independent variable in the first set of variables.]

8. If $w = f[xy/(x^2 + y^2)]$ is a differentiable function of

$u = xy/(x^2 + y^2)$, show that $x(\partial w/\partial x) + y(\partial w/\partial y) = 0$. (See the hint for Problem 7.)

9. If $w = f(x + y, x - y)$ has continuous partial derivatives with respect to $u = x + y$, $v = x - y$, show that

$$\frac{\partial w}{\partial x}\frac{\partial w}{\partial y} = \left(\frac{\partial f}{\partial u}\right)^2 - \left(\frac{\partial f}{\partial v}\right)^2.$$

10. Verify the result given in Problem 13, Article 13–6, by transforming the given expression on the right side of the equation into **i**, **j**, **k** components and replacing the cylindrical coordinates r, θ by cartesian coordinates x, y, and making use of the chain rule for partial derivatives.

11. Verify the answer obtained in Problem 14, Article 13–6, by transforming the expression you obtained in spherical coordinates back into cartesian coordinates. Make use of the chain rule for partial derivatives.

12. If we substitute polar coordinates $x = r\cos\theta$ and $y = r\sin\theta$ in a function $w = f(x, y)$, show that

$$\frac{\partial w}{\partial r} = f_x \cos\theta + f_y \sin\theta,$$

$$\frac{1}{r}\frac{\partial w}{\partial \theta} = -f_x \sin\theta + f_y \cos\theta.$$

13. Using determinants, solve the equations given in Problem 12 for f_x and f_y in terms of $(\partial w/\partial r)$ and $(\partial w/\partial\theta)$.

14. In connection with Problem 12, show that

$$\left(\frac{\partial w}{\partial r}\right)^2 + \frac{1}{r^2}\left(\frac{\partial w}{\partial \theta}\right)^2 = f_x^2 + f_y^2.$$

13–8 THE TOTAL DIFFERENTIAL

The differential of a function

$$w = f(x, y, z) \tag{1}$$

is defined to be

$$dw = \frac{\partial w}{\partial x}dx + \frac{\partial w}{\partial y}dy + \frac{\partial w}{\partial z}dz. \tag{2}$$

The chain rule [Eq. (9), Article 13–7] tells us that we may formally divide both sides of Eq. (2) by dt to calculate dw/dt in case x, y, z are differentiable functions of t. Or, if x, y, z are functions of the independent variables r, s, and we want to calculate $\partial w/\partial r$, we hold s constant in calculating dx, dy, dz and divide both sides of Eq. (2) by dr, but write $\partial w/\partial r$, etc., in place of dw/dr, etc., to show that s has been held constant.

The separate terms

$$\frac{\partial w}{\partial x}dx, \qquad \frac{\partial w}{\partial y}dy, \qquad \frac{\partial w}{\partial z}dz$$

are sometimes called "partial differentials" of w with respect to x, y, z. The sum dw of these partial differentials, Eq. (2), is called the *total differential of* w.

In general, the total differential of a function

$$w = F(x, y, z, u, \ldots, v)$$

is defined to be the sum of all its partial differentials

$$dw = F_x\,dx + F_y\,dy + F_z\,dz + F_u\,du + \cdots + F_v\,dv.$$

If x, y, and z are independent variables in Eq. (1), then dx, dy, and dz are three *new independent variables* in Eq. (2). But in any problem involving increments we shall agree to take

$$dx = \Delta x, \qquad dy = \Delta y, \qquad dz = \Delta z, \tag{3}$$

in order to be able to use the differential dw as a good approximation to Δw [see Eq. (32), Article 13–4]. When x, y, and z are *not* independent variables but are themselves given by equations such as

$$x = x(t), \qquad x = x(r, s),$$
$$y = y(t), \quad \text{or} \quad y = y(r, s),$$
$$z = z(t), \qquad z = z(r, s),$$

then in the first case we have

$$dx = x'(t)\,dt, \qquad dy = y'(t)\,dt, \qquad dz = z'(t)\,dt,$$

and in the second case,

$$\begin{aligned} dx &= \frac{\partial x}{\partial r}\,dr + \frac{\partial x}{\partial s}\,ds, \\ dy &= \frac{\partial y}{\partial r}\,dr + \frac{\partial y}{\partial s}\,ds, \\ dz &= \frac{\partial z}{\partial r}\,dr + \frac{\partial z}{\partial s}\,ds, \end{aligned} \tag{4}$$

if we are to be consistent.

Suppose we consider the second case in more detail. If we consider

$$w = f[x(r, s), y(r, s), z(r, s)] = F(r, s)$$

as a function of r and s, then instead of Eq. (2) we should have

$$dw = \frac{\partial w}{\partial r}\,dr + \frac{\partial w}{\partial s}\,ds, \tag{5}$$

where

$$\frac{\partial w}{\partial r} = F_r(r, s), \qquad \frac{\partial w}{\partial s} = F_s(r, s).$$

Is the dw given by Eq. (2) the same as the dw given by Eq. (5)? The answer, which is "yes, they are the same," is a consequence of the chain rule for derivatives. For, if we start with the dw given by Eq. (2) and into it substitute dx, dy, dz given by Eq. (4), we obtain

$$\begin{aligned} dw &= \frac{\partial w}{\partial x}\left(\frac{\partial x}{\partial r}\,dr + \frac{\partial x}{\partial s}\,ds\right) + \frac{\partial w}{\partial y}\left(\frac{\partial y}{\partial r}\,dr + \frac{\partial y}{\partial s}\,ds\right) + \frac{\partial w}{\partial z}\left(\frac{\partial z}{\partial r}\,dr + \frac{\partial z}{\partial s}\,ds\right) \\ &= \left(\frac{\partial w}{\partial x}\frac{\partial x}{\partial r} + \frac{\partial w}{\partial y}\frac{\partial y}{\partial r} + \frac{\partial w}{\partial z}\frac{\partial z}{\partial r}\right)dr + \left(\frac{\partial w}{\partial x}\frac{\partial x}{\partial s} + \frac{\partial w}{\partial y}\frac{\partial y}{\partial s} + \frac{\partial w}{\partial z}\frac{\partial z}{\partial s}\right)ds. \end{aligned}$$

The expressions in parentheses which here multiply dr and ds are the same as $\partial w/\partial r$ and $\partial w/\partial s$, respectively, by virtue of the chain rule for derivatives. Thus, starting with the expression for dw given by Eq. (2), we have transformed it into the expression for dw given by Eq. (5), thereby establishing the equivalence of the two.

It should be pointed out that in the case just discussed, where r and s are the *independent* variables, we are to treat dr and ds also as independent variables, but *not* dx, dy, and dz, which indeed are given by Eqs. (4). Thus, in a problem involving increments, we could, for convenience, take

$$dr = \Delta r \qquad \text{and} \qquad ds = \Delta s,$$

but we should *not* take $dx = \Delta x$, $dy = \Delta y$, and $dz = \Delta z$, since we are bound by Eqs. (4). The differentials dx, dy, and dz will, however, usually be reasonably good *approximations* to the increments Δx, Δy, and Δz when Δr and Δs are small (Article 13–4).

EXAMPLE 1. Find the total differential of

$$w = x^2 + y^2 + z^2$$

if

$$x = r \cos s, \qquad y = r \sin s, \qquad z = r.$$

Solution. If we use Eq. (2), we have

$$dw = 2(x\,dx + y\,dy + z\,dz)$$

with

$$dx = \cos s\,dr - r \sin s\,ds,$$
$$dy = \sin s\,dr + r \cos s\,ds,$$
$$dz = dr,$$

and hence

$$\begin{aligned} dw &= 2(x \cos s + y \sin s + z)\,dr + 2(-xr \sin s + yr \cos s)\,ds \\ &= 2(r \cos^2 s + r \sin^2 s + r)\,dr + 2(-r^2 \cos s \sin s + r^2 \sin s \cos s)\,ds \\ &= 4r\,dr. \end{aligned}$$

On the other hand, if we first express w directly in terms of r and s, we obtain

$$w = r^2 \cos^2 s + r^2 \sin^2 s + r^2 = 2r^2,$$

from which we also obtain

$$dw = 4r\,dr.$$

EXAMPLE 2. Show that the slope at the point (x, y) of the plane curve whose equation is given implicitly by

$$F(x, y) = 0$$

is

$$\frac{dy}{dx} = \frac{-F_x(x, y)}{F_y(x, y)} \qquad \text{if} \quad F_y(x, y) \neq 0.$$

Solution. Let $w = F(x, y)$ and consider the directional derivative of w at the point (x, y) in the direction of the tangent to the curve. If s denotes arc length

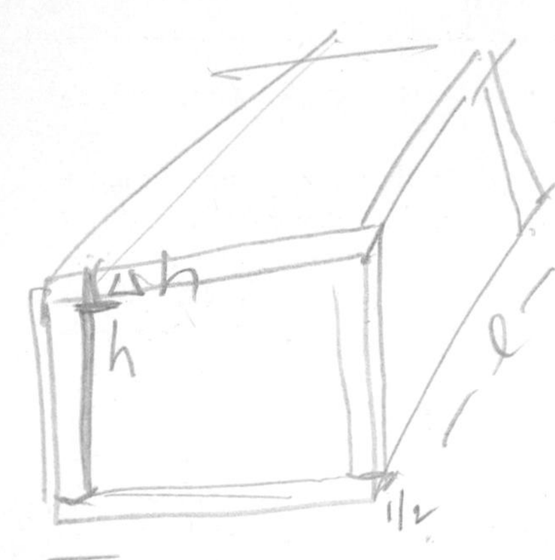

along the curve, the directional derivative is

$$\frac{dF}{ds} = F_x \frac{dx}{ds} + F_y \frac{dy}{ds}.$$

But along the given curve F is constant, so that

$$\frac{dF}{ds} = \lim_{\Delta s \to 0} \frac{\Delta F}{\Delta s} = 0.$$

Therefore

$$F_x \frac{dx}{ds} + F_y \frac{dy}{ds} = 0,$$

and hence

$$\frac{dy}{dx} = \frac{dy/ds}{dx/ds} = \frac{-F_x}{F_y}.$$

EXAMPLE 3. Let $w = F(x, y, z)$ be *constant* along a curve C passing through $P_0(x_0, y_0, z_0)$. Let dx, dy, dz be such that the vector

$$d\mathbf{R} = \mathbf{i}\,dx + \mathbf{j}\,dy + \mathbf{k}\,dz$$

is tangent to C at P_0. Show that

$$dw = \text{grad } F \cdot d\mathbf{R} = 0.$$

Solution. By definition,

$$\begin{aligned} dw &= F_x\,dx + F_y\,dy + F_z\,dz \\ &= (\mathbf{i}F_x + \mathbf{j}F_y + \mathbf{k}F_z) \cdot (\mathbf{i}\,dx + \mathbf{j}\,dy + \mathbf{k}\,dz) \\ &= \text{grad } F \cdot d\mathbf{R}. \end{aligned}$$

Also, the directional derivative of w, at P_0, in the direction of $d\mathbf{R}$ is

$$\frac{dw}{ds} = \text{grad } F \cdot \mathbf{u},$$

where

$$\mathbf{u} = \frac{d\mathbf{R}}{|d\mathbf{R}|}$$

is a unit vector in the direction of $d\mathbf{R}$. Along C, w remains constant and $dw/ds = 0$. Therefore

$$\begin{aligned} dw &= \text{grad } F \cdot d\mathbf{R} \\ &= \text{grad } F \cdot \mathbf{u}\,|d\mathbf{R}| \\ &= \frac{dw}{ds}\,|d\mathbf{R}| = 0. \end{aligned}$$

PROBLEMS

1. Show that the formulas

a) $d(u + v) = du + dv,$ **b)** $d(uv) = v\,du + u\,dv,$

c) $d\left(\dfrac{u}{v}\right) = \dfrac{v\,du - u\,dv}{v^2}$

are valid for total differentials, in case u and v are independent variables or if they are functions of any number of independent variables, such as $u = u(x, y, \ldots, p)$, $v = v(x, y, \ldots, p)$.

2. Using differentials to approximate increments, find the amount of material in a hollow rectangular box whose inside measurements are 5 ft long, 3 ft wide, 2 ft deep, if the box is made of lumber that is $\frac{1}{2}$ in. thick and the box has no top.

3. The area of a triangle is $A = \frac{1}{2}ab \sin C$, where a and b are two sides of the triangle and C is the included angle. In surveying a particular triangular plot of land, a and b are measured to be 150 ft and 200 ft, respectively, and C is read to be 60°. By how much (approximately) is the computed area in error if a and b are in error by $\frac{1}{2}$ ft each and C is in error by 2°?

4. (a) Given $x = r \cos \theta$, $y = r \sin \theta$, express dx and dy in terms of dr and $d\theta$. (b) Solve the equations of part (a) for dr and $d\theta$ in terms of dx and dy. (c) In the answer to part (b), suppose A and B are the coefficients of dx and dy in the expression for dr, that is,

$$dr = A\,dx + B\,dy.$$

Verify by direct computation that $A = \partial r/\partial x$ and $B = \partial r/\partial y$, where $r^2 = x^2 + y^2$.

5. Given $x = f(u, v)$, $y = g(u, v)$. If these equations are considered as implicitly defining u and v as functions of x and y,

a) Express dx and dy in terms of du and dv;

b) Use determinants to solve the equations of part (a) for du and dv in terms of dx and dy;

c) Show that

$$\frac{\partial u}{\partial x} = \frac{g_v}{f_u g_v - f_v g_u},$$

provided $f_u g_v - f_v g_u \neq 0.$

6. a) Given $x = \rho \sin \phi \cos \theta,$

$$y = \rho \sin \phi \sin \theta,$$

$$z = \rho \cos \phi,$$

express dx, dy, dz in terms of $d\rho, d\phi, d\theta$.

b) Solve the equations of part (a) for $d\rho$ in terms of dx, dy, dz by the use of determinants.

c) From your answers to part (b), read off $\partial\rho/\partial x$, considering ρ, ϕ, θ as functions of x, y, z that are given implicitly by the equations of part (a).

7. *Newton's method.* It is desired to find values of x and y that satisfy the pair of equations $f(x, y) = 0$ and $g(x, y) = 0$ simultaneously. Suppose that, by trial and error or otherwise, it is found that $u_0 = f(x_0, y_0)$ and $v_0 = g(x_0, y_0)$ are both small in absolute value. It is now desired to find "corrections" dx and dy such that $f(x_0 + dx, y_0 + dy) = g(x_0 + dx, y_0 + dy) = 0$. Using $u_0 + df$ and $v_0 + dg$ to approximate $f(x_0 + dx, y_0 + dy)$ and $g(x_0 + dx, y_0 + dy)$ respectively, determine approximate values of dx and dy. The procedure may be repeated with (x_0, y_0) replaced by $(x_1, y_1) = (x_0 + dx, y_0 + dy)$.

8. Generalize the method of Problem 7 to the case of three equations in three unknowns: $f(x, y, z) = 0$, $g(x, y, z) = 0$, $h(x, y, z) = 0$, assuming that

$$u_0 = f(x_0, y_0, z_0),$$

$$v_0 = g(x_0, y_0, z_0),$$

$$w_0 = h(x_0, y_0, z)$$

are small in absolute value.

9. Suppose $P_0(x_0, y_0, z_0)$ is a point on the surface S: $F(x, y, z) = 0$. Let dx and dy be arbitrary except that at least one of them should be different from zero. Show that a dz can be found, provided $F_z(x_0, y_0, z_0) \neq 0$, such that the vector $d\mathbf{R} = \mathbf{i}\,dx + \mathbf{j}\,dy + \mathbf{k}\,dz$ is tangent to the surface S at P_0. Find an expression for such a dz. Also show that, for such a vector $d\mathbf{R}$, dF is zero at P_0.

10. In Problem 9, consider the equation $F(x, y, z) = 0$ as determining z implicitly as a function of x and y, say $z = \phi(x, y)$. Show that

$$\phi_x = -\frac{F_x}{F_z}, \qquad \phi_y = -\frac{F_y}{F_z}$$

at any point where $F_z \neq 0$.

11. *Ruled surfaces.* [See "Rulings," by C. S. Ogilvy, *The American Mathematical Monthly*, **59** (1952), pp. 547–549.] The surface $z = f(x, y)$ is said to have *rulings* if through the point $P_0(x_0, y_0, z_0)$ there is a straight line segment all of whose points are on the surface. This happens if through the point $(x_0, y_0, 0)$ in the xy-plane there is a line of points $(x_0 + h, y_0 + k, 0)$ such that along this line dz and Δz are equal. This happens if and only if

$$f(x_0 + h, y_0 + k) - f(x_0, y_0) = \left(\frac{\partial f}{\partial x}\right)_0 h + \left(\frac{\partial f}{\partial y}\right)_0 k$$

when $h = \Delta x = dx$ and $k = \Delta y = dy$. Show that (a) the surface $z = \sqrt{1 + xy}$ has rulings through the point $P_0(2, 4, 3)$, given by the conditions $h = k$ or $4h = k$, (b) the surface $z = x^2 - y^2$ has rulings through any point $P_0(x_0, y_0, z_0)$, given by $h = \pm k$.

13–9 MAXIMA AND MINIMA OF FUNCTIONS OF TWO INDEPENDENT VARIABLES

In Chapter 3 we learned how to use the differential calculus to solve max-min problems for functions $y = f(x)$ of a single independent variable. In this article we shall extend the method to problems involving more than one independent variable.

We discuss the method in terms of finding high and low points on a smooth surface,

$$z = f(x, y). \tag{1}$$

The function f is assumed to be continuous and to have continuous partial derivatives with respect to x and y in some region R in the xy-plane. If there is a point (a, b) in R such that

$$f(x, y) \geq f(a, b) \tag{2}$$

for all points (x, y) sufficiently near to the point (a, b), then the function f is said to have a *local*, or *relative*, *minimum* at (a, b). If the inequality (2) holds for all points (x, y) in R, then f has an absolute minimum over R at (a, b). If the inequality in (2) is reversed, f then has a maximum (relative or absolute) at (a, b).

Suppose that the maximum (or minimum) value of f, over the region R, occurs at a point (a, b) that is not on the boundary of R; and that both $\partial f/\partial x$ and $\partial f/\partial y$ exist at (a, b). Then the first *necessary condition* that must be satisfied is that

$$\frac{\partial f}{\partial x} = 0 \quad \text{and} \quad \frac{\partial f}{\partial y} = 0 \quad \text{at } (a, b),$$

as we shall now show, for the section of the surface $z = f(x, y)$ lying in the plane $y = b$ is simply the curve

$$z = f(x, b), \qquad y = b,$$

and this curve has a high or low turning point at $x = a$ (Fig. 13–22). Hence

$$\left(\frac{\partial z}{\partial x}\right)_{x=a, y=b} = 0.$$

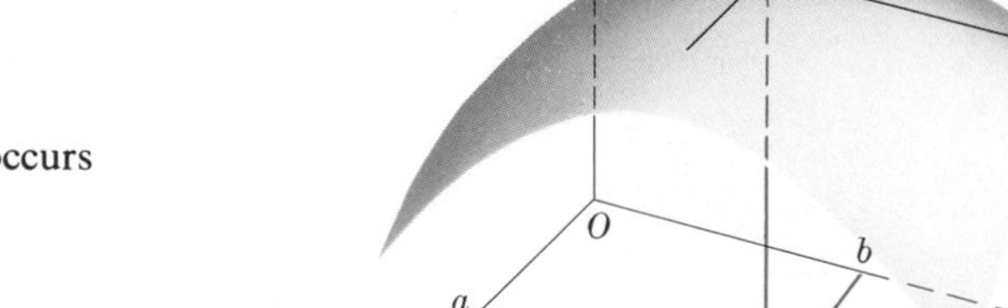

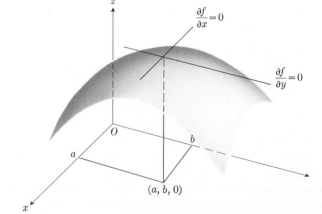

13–22 The maximum of f on R occurs at $x = a$, $y = b$.

Similarly, the curve

$$z = f(a, y), \qquad x = a,$$

in which the plane $x = a$ intersects the surface, also has a high or low turning point when $y = b$, so that

$$\left(\frac{\partial z}{\partial y}\right)_{x=a, y=b} = 0.$$

We shall not at this time enter into a detailed discussion of second derivative tests for distinguishing between maxima and minima. The fundamental principle used in deriving such a test is that the difference

$$D = f(x, y) - f(a, b)$$

should be nonnegative (that is, positive or zero) for all points (x, y) close to the point (a, b) in case of a minimum at (a, b), or nonpositive in the case of a maximum. One way to test for a maximum or a minimum is to take

$$x = a + h, \qquad y = b + k,$$

and to examine the difference D for small values of h and k, as in the example that follows.

EXAMPLE. Find the high and low points on the surface

$$z = x^2 - xy + y^2 + 2x + 2y - 4 = f(x, y).$$

Solution. We apply the first necessary condition for a maximum or minimum of z, namely,

$$\frac{\partial z}{\partial x} = 0 \quad \text{and} \quad \frac{\partial z}{\partial y} = 0.$$

This leads to the simultaneous equations

$$2x - y = -2, \qquad -x + 2y = -2,$$

with solution

$$x = y = -2.$$

Thus, $(-2, -2)$ is the point that we have been calling (a, b). The corresponding value of z is

$$f(-2, -2) = -8.$$

To examine the behavior of the difference $D = f(x, y) - f(-2, -2)$, we let

$$x = -2 + h, \qquad y = -2 + k$$

and obtain

$$\begin{aligned} D &= f(-2 + h, -2 + k) - f(-2, -2) = h^2 - hk + k^2 \\ &= \left(h - \frac{k}{2}\right)^2 + \frac{3k^2}{4} \end{aligned}$$

This is readily seen to be positive for all values of h, k, except $h = k = 0$. That is,

$$f(x, y) \geq f(-2, -2)$$

for all (x, y) different from $(-2, -2)$. Thus the surface has a *low* point at $(-2, -2, -8)$. The given function has an absolute minimum -8.

REMARK. As with functions of a single independent variable, it is often possible to see that the function $z = f(x, y)$ has exactly one maximum (or minimum), that it occurs at an interior point of the domain of f, and that f everywhere possesses partial derivatives that must be zero at the critical point. No further test is then required. This is true, for instance, in the example above.

PROBLEMS

Examine the following surfaces for high and low points:

1. $z = x^2 + xy + y^2 + 3x - 3y + 4$
2. $z = x^2 + 3xy + 3y^2 - 6x + 3y - 6$
3. $z = 5xy - 7x^2 - y^2 + 3x - 6y + 2$
4. $z = 2xy - 5x^2 - 2y^2 + 4x + 4y - 4$
5. $z = x^2 + xy + 3x + 2y + 5$
6. $z = y^2 + xy - 2x - 2y + 2$
7. Sketch the surface

$$z = \sqrt{x^2 + y^2}$$

over the region R: $|x| \leq 1$, $|y| \leq 1$. Find the high and low points of the surface over R. Discuss the existence, and the values, of $\partial z/\partial x$ and $\partial z/\partial y$ at these points.

13–10 THE METHOD OF LEAST SQUARES

An important application of minimizing a function of two variables is the *method of least squares* for fitting a straight line

$$y = mx + b \tag{1}$$

to a set of experimentally observed points $(x_1, y_1), (x_2, y_2), \ldots, (x_n, y_n)$ (Fig. 13–23). Corresponding to each observed value of x there are two values of y, namely, the observed value y_{obs} and the value predicted by the straight line $mx_{\text{obs}} + b$. We call the difference,

$$y_{\text{obs}} - (mx_{\text{obs}} + b), \tag{2}$$

a *deviation*. Each deviation measures the amount by which the predicted value of y falls short of the observed value. The set of all deviations

$$d_1 = y_1 - (mx_1 + b), \quad \ldots, \quad d_n = y_n - (mx_n + b) \tag{3}$$

gives a picture of how closely the line of Eq. (1) fits the observed data. The line is a perfect fit if and only if all of these deviations are zero. But in general no straight line will give a perfect fit. Then we are confronted with the problem of finding a line that fits *best* in some sense or other. Here is where the method of least squares comes in.

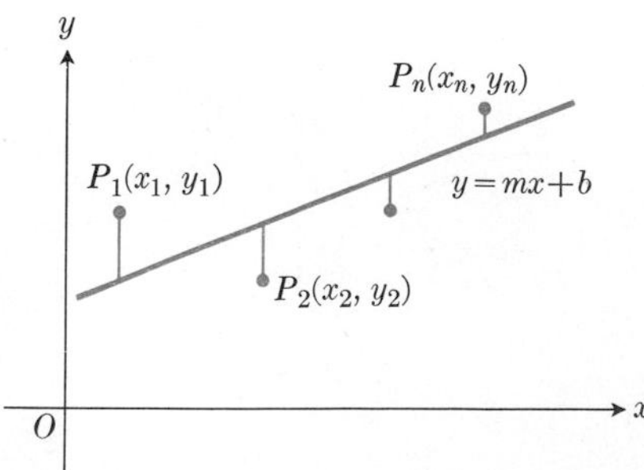

13–23 To fit a line to noncollinear points, we may choose a line that minimizes the sum of the squares of the deviations.

For a straight line that comes *close* to fitting all of the observed points, some of the deviations will probably be positive and some will be negative. But their squares will all be positive, and the expression

$$f(m, b) = (y_1 - mx_1 - b)^2 + (y_2 - mx_2 - b)^2 + \cdots + (y_n - mx_n - b)^2$$

counts a positive deviation d and a negative deviation $-d$ equally. This sum of squares of the deviations depends upon the choice of m and b. It is never negative and it can be zero only if m and b have values that produce a straight line that is a perfect fit.

Whether such a perfectly fitting line can be found or not, the method of least squares says, "*take as the line $y = mx + b$ of best fit that one for which the sum of squares of the deviations*

$$f(m, b) = d_1^2 + d_2^2 + \cdots + d_n^2$$

is a minimum." Thus we try to find the values of m and b where the surface

$$w = f(m, b)$$

in mbw-space has a low point (Fig. 13–24). To do this, we solve the equations

$$\frac{\partial f}{\partial m} = 0 \quad \text{and} \quad \frac{\partial f}{\partial b} = 0$$

simultaneously.

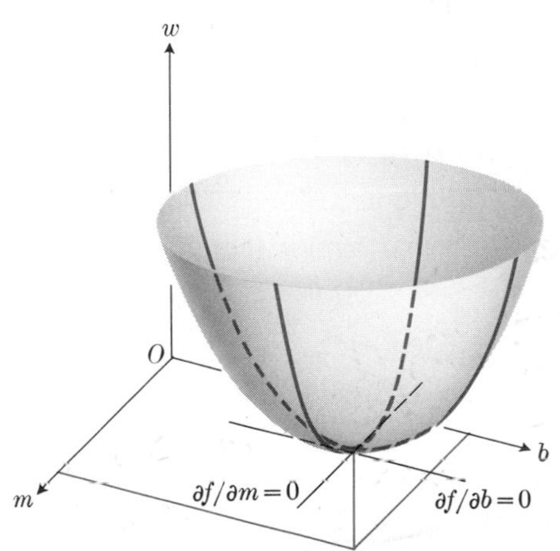

13–24 The sum $f(m, b)$ of the squares of the deviations has a minimum when $\partial f/\partial m$ and $\partial f/\partial b$ are both zero.

EXAMPLE. Find the straight line that best fits the points (0, 1), (1, 3), (2, 2), (3, 4), (4, 5) according to the method of least squares.

Solution. The sum of squares of the deviations is

$$f(m, b) = \sum (y_{\text{obs}} - mx_{\text{obs}} - b)^2,$$

where y_{obs} and x_{obs} are the observed (or given) coordinates of the points to be fitted by the line $y = mx + b$.

We list these, together with the deviations and their squares, in Table 13–1.

We differentiate the formula in the last line of Table 13–1, and find

$$\frac{\partial f}{\partial m} = -78 + 20b + 60m,$$

$$\frac{\partial f}{\partial b} = -30 + 10b + 20m.$$

Table 13–1

x_{obs}	y_{obs}	dev = $y_{obs} - mx_{obs} - b$	$(\text{dev})^2$
0	1	$1 - b$	$1 - 2b + b^2$
1	3	$3 - m - b$	$9 - 6b + b^2 - 6m + 2mb + m^2$
2	2	$2 - 2m - b$	$4 - 4b + b^2 - 8m + 4mb + 4m^2$
3	4	$4 - 3m - b$	$16 - 8b + b^2 - 24m + 6mb + 9m^2$
4	5	$5 - 4m - b$	$25 - 10b + b^2 - 40m + 8mb + 16m^2$

$$\sum (\text{dev})^2 = 55 - 30b + 5b^2 - 78m + 20mb + 30m^2 = f(m, b)$$

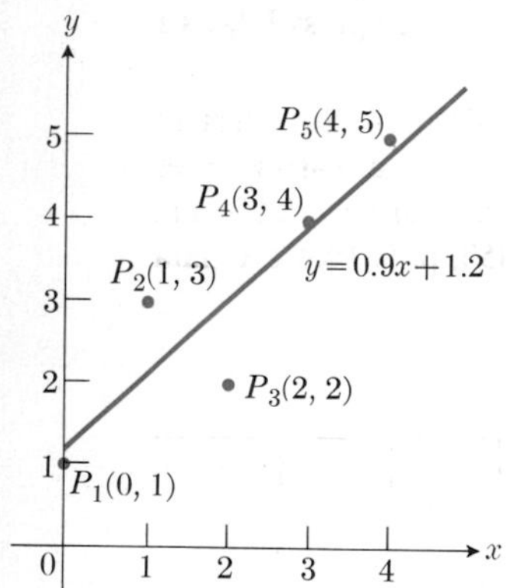

13–25 The least-squares line for the data in Table 13–1.

The values of m and b for which f has a minimum must satisfy the simultaneous equations

$$\frac{\partial f}{\partial m} = 0, \qquad 20b + 60m = 78,$$

$$\frac{\partial f}{\partial b} = 0, \qquad 10b + 20m = 30.$$

The only solution is $m = 0.9$, $b = 1.2$. The "best-fitting" line (in the sense of least sum of squares of deviations) is therefore

$$y = 0.9x + 1.2.$$

(See Fig. 13–25.)

To verify that these values of m and b do in fact correspond to a minimum, we let

$$m = 0.9 + h, \qquad b = 1.2 + k$$

and calculate

$$\Delta = f(0.9 + h, 1.2 + k) - f(0.9, 1.2).$$

Doing this algebraically, we find

$$\begin{aligned}\Delta f &= f(m + h, b + k) - f(m, b)\\ &= (-30 + 10b + 20m)k + (-78 + 20b + 60m)h + 5k^2 + 20kh + 30h^2.\end{aligned}$$

The expressions in parentheses are $\partial f/\partial b$ and $\partial f/\partial m$, respectively, and these are zero if $m = 0.9$ and $b = 1.2$. Hence

$$\begin{aligned}f(0.9 + h, 1.2 + k) - f(0.9, 1.2) &= 5k^2 + 20kh + 30h^2\\ &= 5(k + 2h)^2 + 10h^2.\end{aligned}$$

This is greater than zero for all values of h and k other than $h = k = 0$. That is,

$$f(0.9 + h, 1.2 + k) \geq f(0.9, 1.2),$$

and we have found the values of m and b for which the function $f(m, b)$ is an absolute minimum.

It is customary to omit the details of testing the answer obtained in solving a problem in least squares. Indeed, it can be shown that, for the case of fitting a straight line, the answer *always* corresponds to a minimum.

The method of least squares may also be applied to equations that are more complicated than the equation of a straight line, and the method has been widely extended. It is even the basis of departure for the modern theory of cybernetics developed originally by Professor Norbert Wiener of M.I.T.

PROBLEMS

1. The observed points (x_i, y_i), $i = 1, 2, \ldots, n$, are to be fitted by a straight line $y = mx + b$ by the method of least squares. The sum of squares of the deviations is

$$f(m, b) = \sum_{i=1}^{n} (mx_i + b - y_i)^2.$$

a) Show that the equations $\partial f/\partial b = 0$ and $\partial f/\partial m = 0$ are equivalent to

$$m(\sum x_i) + nb = \sum y_i,$$

$$m(\sum x_i^2) + b(\sum x_i) = \sum x_i y_i,$$

where all sums run from $i = 1$ to $i = n$. (b) Express the solutions b, m of the equations of part (a) in terms of determinants.

In Problems 2–4, apply the method of least squares to obtain the line $y = mx + b$ that best fits the three given points. [The computations can be systematized by making use of the results of Problem 1.]

2. $(-1, 2)$, $(0, 1)$, $(3, -1)$ **3.** $(-2, 0)$, $(0, 2)$, $(2, 3)$

4. $(0, 0)$, $(1, 2)$, $(2, 3)$

5. (*Calculator*) To determine the intermolecular potential between potassium ions and xenon gas, Budenholzer, Gislason, and Jorgensen (June 1, 1977, *Journal of Chemical Physics*, **66**, No. 11; p. 4832) accelerated a beam of potassium ions toward a cell containing xenon, and measured the current I of ions leaving the cell as a percentage of the current I_0 entering the cell. This fraction, which is a function of xenon gas pressure, was recorded at five different pressures, with the results shown in Table 13–2.

As a step in their determination, the authors used the method of least squares to find the slope m and intercept b of a line $y = mx + b$, where $y = \ln (I/I_0)$. In particular, they hoped to find that, within the limits of experimental error, b was zero. (a) Write down the value of y for each x in the table and fit a least-squares line to the (x, y) data points. Round m and b to three decimal places. (b) Express I/I_0 as a function of x.

Table 13–2. Scattering of potassium ions by xenon

x (pressure in millitorr)	0.165	0.399	0.573	0.930	1.281
I/I_0	0.940	0.862	0.810	0.712	0.622

6. (*Calculator*) Write a linear equation for the effect of irrigation on the yield of alfalfa by fitting a least-squares line to the following data from the University of California Experimental Station, *Bulletin* No. 450, p. 8. Plot the data and draw the line.

Table 13–3. Growth of alfalfa

x (total seasonal depth of water applied (in.))	12	18	24	30	36	42
y (average alfalfa yield (tons/acre))	5.27	5.68	6.25	7.21	8.20	8.71

7. (*Calculator*) *Hubble's law* for the expansion of the universe is the linear equation

$$\text{Velocity} = \text{the Hubble constant} \cdot \text{distance}$$

or

$$v = Hx.$$

It says that the velocity with which a galaxy appears to move away from us is proportional to how far away the galaxy lies. The farther away it lies, the faster it recedes. If the velocity is measured in kilometers per second and the distance in millions of light-years, then Hubble's constant is given in kilometers per second per million light-years. H is the rate at which the universe appears to be expanding. For

Table 13–4. Observed velocities and distances of five receding galaxies

Galaxy	A	B	C	D	E
Observed distance (10^6 l-yr)	500	1,400	2,100	2,900	3,000
Recession velocity (km/s)	9,000	22,000	39,000	51,000	49,000

every extra million light-years of distance, the galaxies we can observe recede faster by H kilometers per second.

The table above lists the observed distances and velocities for five galaxies. Discover Hubble's constant H by fitting a least-squares line to the data (Fig. 13–26). Round your answer to the nearest integer. You will find that the y-intercept of the line is 240 km/s when rounded to the nearest integer, and not zero. A discrepancy in the intercept is to be expected, given the uncertainties in measurement and, here, the small size of the sample. Note that the discrepancy is a small percentage of the observed recession velocities. (For more information, see Jastrow and Thompson's *Astronomy: Fundamentals and Frontiers*, Second Edition, John Wiley and Sons, Inc., 1974, Chapter 11.)

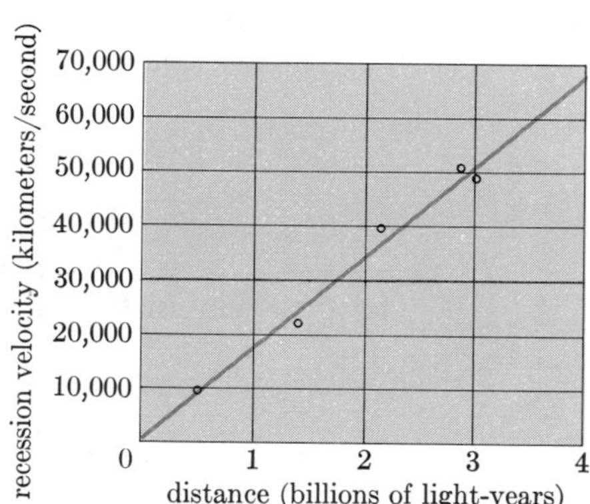

13–26 Velocity vs. distance observed for the galaxies in Table 13–4.

8. (*Calculator*) *Craters of Mars.* One theory of crater formation suggests that the frequency of large craters should fall off as the square of the diameter (Marcus, *Science*, June 21, 1968, p. 1334). Pictures from Mariner IV show the frequencies listed in Table 13–5.

Table 13–5. Crater sizes on Mars

Diameter in km, D	32–45	45–64	64–90	90–128
$1/D^2$ (for left value of class interval)	0.001	0.0005	0.00025	0.000125
Frequency, F	53	22	14	3

Fit a line of the form $F = m(1/D^2) + b$ to the data. Plot the data and draw the line.

9. If $y = mx + b$ is the best-fitting straight line, in the sense of least squares, show that the sum of deviations

$$\sum_{i=1}^{n} (y_i - mx_i - b)$$

is zero. (This means that positive and negative deviations cancel.)

10. Show that the point

$$(\bar{x}, \bar{y}) = \left[\frac{1}{n}\left(\sum_{i=1}^{n} x_i\right), \frac{1}{n}\left(\sum_{i=1}^{n} y_i\right)\right]$$

lies on the straight line $y = mx + b$ that is determined by the method of least squares. (This means that the "best-fitting" line passes through the center of gravity of the n points.)

13–11

MAXIMA AND MINIMA OF FUNCTIONS OF SEVERAL INDEPENDENT VARIABLES. LAGRANGE MULTIPLIERS

In certain applications, particularly in statistics, it becomes necessary to find maximum or minimum values of a function

$$w = f(x, y, z, u, \dots, v)$$

of several independent variables. If the given function has an extreme value at an interior point of the domain, say at

$$x = a, \qquad y = b, \qquad z = c, \qquad \dots, \qquad v = e,$$

then by setting $y = b$, $z = c$, $\dots$, $v = e$ we obtain a function of x alone,

$$F(x) = f(x, b, c, d, \dots, e),$$

which has an extreme value at $x = a$. Hence, if f has a partial derivative with respect to x at $x = a$, $y = b$, $\dots$, $v = e$, that partial derivative must be zero by virtue of the theory for max-min for functions $F(x)$ of a single independent variable. That is,

$$\frac{\partial f}{\partial x} = 0 \quad \text{at } (a, b, c, \dots, e).$$

By similar reasoning, we arrive at the first necessary condition for extreme values of a function of several independent variables, namely,

$$\frac{\partial f}{\partial x} = 0, \qquad \frac{\partial f}{\partial y} = 0, \qquad \dots, \qquad \frac{\partial f}{\partial v} = 0 \quad \text{at } (a, b, \dots, e).$$

The number of simultaneous equations $\partial f/\partial x = 0$, etc., which are thus obtained is precisely equal to the number of *independent variables* $x, y, \dots, v$. Of course the solutions of this system of equations may correspond to maximum values of f, or to minimum values, or neither, in much the same way as for solutions of the equation $dy/dx = 0$.

Occasionally, the problem arises of finding the extreme value of one function, say

$$w = f(x, y, z, u, \dots, v),$$

subject to *side conditions* or *constraints* given by equations like

$$g(x, y, z, u, \dots, v) = 0,$$
$$h(x, y, z, u, \dots, v) = 0, \dots$$

(see Fig. 13–27). The theory behind such problems is discussed in most books on advanced calculus. (See Kaplan, *Advanced Calculus*, Second edition (1973, Addison-Wesley), p. 184). Here we shall do no more than point out that the equations representing the side restrictions may be used to express some of the variables $x, y, z, \dots, v$ in terms of the remaining ones before we take partial derivatives. This is done so that the variables that remain may be *independent*. After the next two problems, which show how this method works, we shall present a second method, that of Lagrange multipliers.

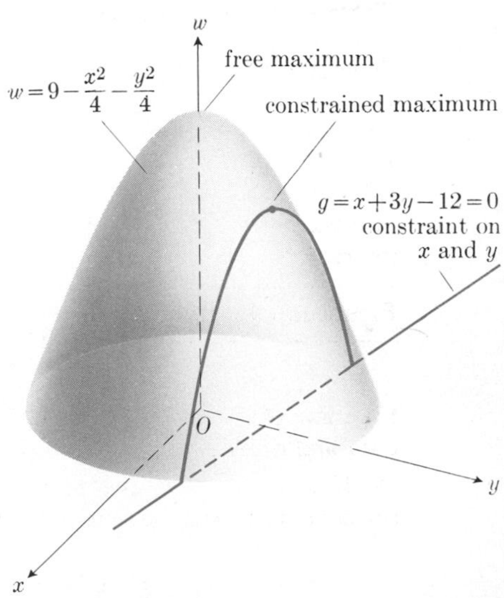

13–27 $f(x, y) = 9 - (x^2/4) - (y^2/4)$, subject to the constraint $g(x, y) = x + 3y - 12 = 0$.

EXAMPLE 1. Find the minimum distance from the origin to the plane

$$2x + y - z = 5.$$

Solution. If $P(x, y, z)$ is any point on the plane, then the distance from the origin to P is

$$|\overrightarrow{OP}| = \sqrt{x^2 + y^2 + z^2},$$

and clearly this has a minimum wherever the function

$$f(x, y, z) = |\overrightarrow{OP}|^2 = x^2 + y^2 + z^2$$

does. (The latter is simpler to work with since it does not involve radicals.) But the three variables x, y, z are not all independent, since P is to lie on the plane

$$2x + y - z = 5.$$

If we solve this equation for z, we find

$$z = 2x + y - 5,$$

and we may treat x and y as independent variables and minimize the function

$$g(x, y) = x^2 + y^2 + (2x + y - 5)^2.$$

The necessary conditions

$$\frac{\partial g}{\partial x} = 0 \quad \text{and} \quad \frac{\partial g}{\partial y} = 0$$

lead to the equations

$$10x + 4y - 20 = 0, \qquad 4x + 4y - 10 = 0,$$

with solution $x = \frac{5}{3}$, $y = \frac{5}{6}$. The z-coordinate of the corresponding point P is $z = -\frac{5}{6}$, and thus we have found the point $(\frac{5}{3}, \frac{5}{6}, -\frac{5}{6})$ as the *only* point on the plane that satisfies the *necessary* conditions. That is, if the given problem has an answer, this is it. From our knowledge of solid geometry we know that the problem does have an answer; hence we have found it. Of course, we may solve this same problem by strictly geometrical methods, but our purpose is not so much to solve this specific problem as it is to illustrate the *method* of solving such problems by partial differentiation. We may check our answer by noting that the vector from the origin to $P(\frac{5}{3}, \frac{5}{6}, -\frac{5}{6})$ is

$$\overrightarrow{OP} = \tfrac{5}{6}(2\mathbf{i} + \mathbf{j} - \mathbf{k}),$$

which is normal to the plane, as it should be.

REMARK 1. The mechanics of setting $f_x = 0, f_y = 0$, and so forth may lead to a point not in the region where the function f is defined. Sometimes it is desirable to choose a different set of independent variables when this happens. We do this in the next example.

EXAMPLE 2. Find the minimum distance from the origin to the surface $x^2 - z^2 = 1$.

Solution. We seek to minimize

$$w = x^2 + y^2 + z^2,$$

where $x^2 = 1 + z^2$, or $z^2 = x^2 - 1$. If we eliminate z^2, we have

$$w = 2x^2 + y^2 - 1,$$

whose partial derivatives,

$$\frac{\partial w}{\partial x} = 4x, \qquad \frac{\partial w}{\partial y} = 2y,$$

are zero only at $x = 0$, $y = 0$. But then we run into trouble, for $z^2 = x^2 - 1 = -1$ means that z is imaginary when $x = 0$. In fact, the point $P(x, y, z)$ is on the surface $z^2 = x^2 - 1$ only when $|x| \geq 1$.

If we eliminate x^2, however, and express w as a function of y and z, then the function

$$w = 1 + y^2 + 2z^2$$

has partial derivatives

$$\frac{\partial w}{\partial y} = 2y, \qquad \frac{\partial w}{\partial z} = 4z,$$

which are both zero when $y = z = 0$. This leads to

$$x^2 = 1 + z^2 = 1, \qquad x = \pm 1.$$

It is obvious from the expression $w = 1 + y^2 + 2z^2$ that $w \geq 1$ for all real values of y and z, since $y^2 + 2z^2 \geq 0$. Therefore the two points $(\pm 1, 0, 0)$ are nearer the origin than are any other points on the surface. The minimum distance from the surface to the origin is 1.

By expressing w in terms of y and z as independent variables, we obtained variables which can take all real values

$$-\infty < y < \infty, \qquad -\infty < z < \infty.$$

The surface is a two-sheeted hyperbolic cylinder with elements parallel to the y-axis (Fig. 13–28).

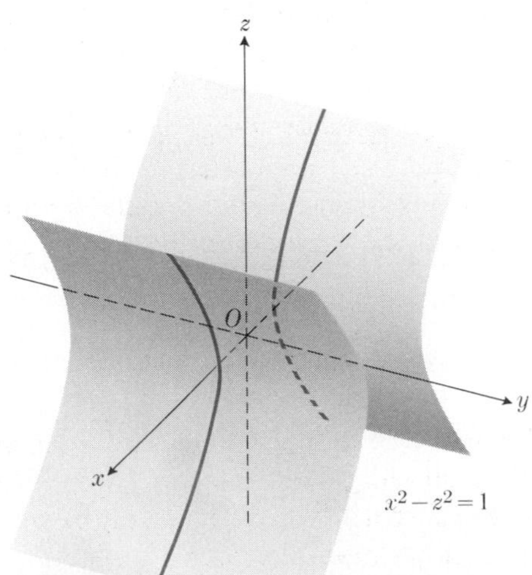

13–28 The surface $x^2 - z^2 = 1$.

Method of Lagrange Multipliers

In Example 2, we wanted to minimize the function

$$f(x, y, z) = x^2 + y^2 + z^2,$$

subject to the constraint

$$g(x, y, z) = x^2 - z^2 - 1 = 0.$$

The method of Lagrange multipliers applies to problems of this type. This is how it goes:

To minimize (or maximize) a function $f(x, y, z)$, subject to the constraint $g(x, y, z) = 0$, construct the auxiliary function

$$H(x, y, z, \lambda) = f(x, y, z) - \lambda g(x, y, z), \qquad \textbf{(1a)}$$

and find values of x, y, z, λ for which the partial derivatives of H are all zero:

$$H_x = 0, \qquad H_y = 0, \qquad H_z = 0, \qquad H_\lambda = 0. \qquad \textbf{(1b)}$$

We shall discuss the theory behind the method after the next problem, which demonstrates how to use it.

EXAMPLE 3. Find the point on the plane

$$2x - 3y + 5z = 19$$

that is nearest the origin, using the method of Lagrange multipliers.

Solution. As before, the function to be minimized can be taken to be the square of the distance from the origin to $P(x, y, z)$:

$$f(x, y, z) = x^2 + y^2 + z^2. \qquad \textbf{(2a)}$$

The constraint is

$$g(x, y, z) = 2x - 3y + 5z - 19 = 0. \qquad \textbf{(2b)}$$

We let

$$H(x, y, z, \lambda) = x^2 + y^2 + z^2 - \lambda(2x - 3y + 5z - 19). \qquad \textbf{(2c)}$$

Then

$$H_x = 2x - 2\lambda = 0, \qquad H_y = 2y + 3\lambda = 0, \qquad H_z = 2z - 5\lambda = 0, \quad \textbf{(3a)}$$

and

$$H_\lambda = -g(x, y, z) = -(2x - 3y + 5z - 19) = 0. \qquad \textbf{(3b)}$$

From Eqs. (3a), we get

$$x = \lambda, \qquad y = -\tfrac{3}{2}\lambda, \qquad z = \tfrac{5}{2}\lambda, \qquad \textbf{(3c)}$$

and when these are substituted in Eq. (3b), or (2b), we get

$$2\lambda + \tfrac{9}{2}\lambda + \tfrac{25}{2}\lambda = 19,$$

so

$$\lambda = 1. \qquad \textbf{(3d)}$$

Substituting $\lambda = 1$ in Eqs. (3c), we get the point $P_0 = (1, -\frac{3}{2}, \frac{5}{2})$. To see that the vector

$$\overrightarrow{OP_0} = \mathbf{i} - \tfrac{3}{2}\mathbf{j} + \tfrac{5}{2}\mathbf{k}$$

is normal to the plane

$$2x - 3y + 5z = 19,$$

we have only to divide both sides of the latter equation by 2. Therefore, $|\overrightarrow{OP_0}| = \frac{1}{2}\sqrt{38}$ is the minimum distance from the origin to the plane. (We could have found this answer using the normal vector

$$\mathbf{N} = 2\mathbf{i} - 3\mathbf{j} + 5\mathbf{k}$$

and no calculus.)

Discussion of the Method and Why It Works

We pass now to the general situation. Assume that the equation representing the constraint

$$g(x, y, z) = 0 \tag{4a}$$

can be solved for z as a function of (x, y):

$$z = \phi(x, y), \tag{4b}$$

throughout some neighborhood of the point $P_0(x_0, y_0)$. Assume, further, that this point minimizes the function

$$w = f(x, y, \phi(x, y)) \tag{5}$$

that we get by substituting for z (Eq. 4b) into the function $f(x, y, z)$. For convenience, we shall use subscripts 1, 2, and 3 to denote partial derivatives of f and g with respect to the first, second, and third variables, respectively:

$$\begin{aligned} f_1(x, y, z) &= f_x(x, y, z), \qquad & g_1(x, y, z) &= g_x(x, y, z), \\ f_2(x, y, z) &= f_y(x, y, z), \qquad & g_2(x, y, z) &= g_y(x, y, z), \\ f_3(x, y, z) &= f_z(x, y, z), \qquad & g_3(x, y, z) &= g_z(x, y, z). \end{aligned}$$

Also, in the calculations that follow, we assume that

$$g_3[x, y, \phi(x, y)] \neq 0 \quad \text{near } P_0 \text{ and at } P_0.$$

We next differentiate both sides of Eq. (4a) implicitly with respect to x, holding y constant, and treating z as a differentiable function, as in Eq. (4b). This gives

$$g_1 + g_3 \frac{\partial z}{\partial x} = 0, \qquad \text{or} \qquad \frac{\partial z}{\partial x} = -\frac{g_1}{g_3}. \tag{6a}$$

Likewise, if we differentiate with respect to y, holding x constant, we get

$$g_2 + g_3 \frac{\partial z}{\partial y} = 0, \qquad \text{or} \qquad \frac{\partial z}{\partial y} = -\frac{g_2}{g_3}. \tag{6b}$$

In Eqs. (6a, b), the partial derivatives g_1, g_2, and g_3 are to be evaluated at $(x, y, \phi(x, y))$ for (x, y) in some suitably restricted neighborhood of $P_0(x_0, y_0)$.

Now we turn our attention to the function in Eq. (5), whose extreme value is assumed to occur at P_0. The necessary condition [assuming that the righthand side of Eq. (5) is differentiable at P_0] for such a minimum or maximum is

$$f_1 + f_3 \frac{\partial \phi}{\partial x} = 0, \qquad f_2 + f_3 \frac{\partial \phi}{\partial y} = 0, \quad \text{at } P_0. \tag{7}$$

Substituting from Eqs. (6a, b) for

$$\frac{\partial z}{\partial x} = \frac{\partial \phi}{\partial x} = \frac{-g_1}{g_3}, \qquad \frac{\partial z}{\partial y} = \frac{\partial \phi}{\partial y} = \frac{-g_2}{g_3},$$

we get

$$f_1 - f_3 \left(\frac{g_1}{g_3}\right) = 0, \qquad f_2 - f_3 \left(\frac{g_2}{g_3}\right) = 0, \quad \text{at } P_0.$$

Thus at

$$(x_0, y_0, \phi(x_0, y_0)) = (x_0, y_0, z_0),$$

the following conditions hold:

$$f_1 = g_1 \left(\frac{f_3}{g_3}\right), \qquad f_2 = g_2 \left(\frac{f_3}{g_3}\right), \tag{8a}$$

and, of course,

$$f_3 = g_3 \left(\frac{f_3}{g_3}\right). \tag{8b}$$

Suppose, therefore, that we denote the ratio f_3/g_3 by λ. Then Eqs. (8a, b) can be combined into one vector equation:

$$\mathbf{i}f_1 + \mathbf{j}f_2 + \mathbf{k}f_3 = \lambda(\mathbf{i}g_1 + \mathbf{j}g_2 + \mathbf{k}g_3),$$

or

$$\nabla f = \lambda \nabla g \quad \text{at } (x_0, y_0, z_0), \tag{9}$$

and (x_0, y_0, z_0) is a point whose coordinates satisfy the constraint

$$g(x_0, y_0, z_0) = 0. \tag{10}$$

Equations (9, 10) are just the same as Eqs. (1a, b) in different form, because

$$\left.\begin{aligned} H_x &= f_x - \lambda g_x = 0 \\ H_y &= f_y - \lambda g_y = 0 \\ H_z &= f_z - \lambda g_z = 0 \end{aligned}\right\} \Leftrightarrow \nabla f = \lambda \nabla g,$$

and

$$H_\lambda = -g = 0 \Leftrightarrow g = 0.$$

REMARK 2. We could make Eq. (9) seem plausible by a geometric argument. Let us imagine that we are traveling around on the surface S, whose equation is $g = 0$, noting the values of f as we go. In particular, we note that the *level surfaces* of f (which we shall call *iso-f surfaces*) intersect the surface S in curves along which f remains constant. To find either a maximum or a minimum of f on S, we should take a route that crosses these iso-f *curves* in a direction in which f-values increase or decrease; specifically, if we are searching for a maximum, we should look for a direction in which f-values increase, and if we are searching for a minimum, we should look for a direction in which f-values decrease. When we have once arrived at a maximum of f on S, there will be no direction in which we can travel to get to an iso-f curve with a larger f-value. Equation (9) says that at this point ∇f and ∇g must have the same direction (or *opposite* directions, if λ is *negative*). This means that S and the surface $f =$ constant are *tangent* at that point: For a slightly smaller f-value, there would be a curve of intersection of the iso-f surface and S, and for a larger f-value, there would be no intersection. For the maximum, there is just one point at which the surface S and the iso-f surface touch, and at that point it does indeed seem plausible that the two surfaces are tangent.

REMARK 3. If there are two constraints, say

$$g(x, y, z) = 0 \qquad \text{and} \qquad h(x, y, z) = 0,$$

we introduce two Lagrange multipliers λ and μ, and work with the auxiliary function

$$H(x, y, z, \lambda, \mu) = f(x, y, z) - \lambda g(x, y, z) - \mu h(x, y, z).$$

We then treat x, y, z, λ, μ as five independent variables for H, and set the five first-order partial derivatives of H equal to zero:

$$H_x = 0, \qquad H_y = 0, \qquad H_z = 0, \qquad H_\lambda = 0, \qquad H_\mu = 0.$$

These results are equivalent to

$$\nabla f = \lambda \nabla g + \mu \nabla h \quad \text{at } (x_0, y_0, z_0), \tag{11a}$$

$$g(x_0, y_0, z_0) = 0 \qquad \text{and} \qquad h(x_0, y_0, z_0) = 0. \tag{11b}$$

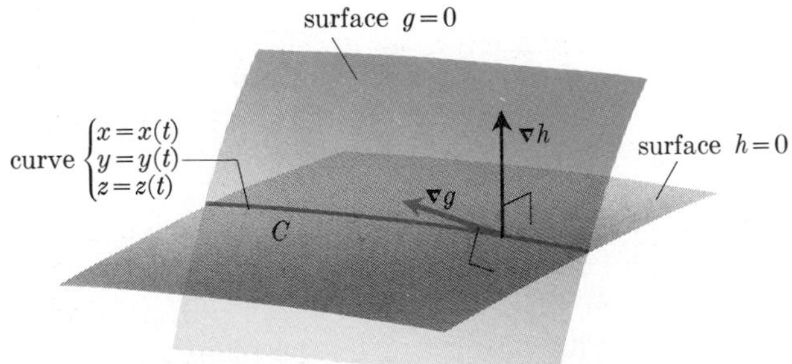

13–29 Vectors ∇g and ∇h are in a plane perpendicular to curve C because ∇g is normal to the surface $g = 0$, and ∇h is normal to the surface $h = 0$.

The vector equation (11a) says that the gradient of f lies in the plane of the gradients of g and h at $Q_0 = (x_0, y_0, z_0)$, and this has a fairly simple geometrical interpretation (Fig. 13–29). First, we know that ∇g is normal to the surface $g = 0$, and that ∇h is normal to the surface $h = 0$. The intersection of these two surfaces is usually a curve. On this curve, say C, we can think of x, y, and z as functions of one variable, for example, time (t) or arc length. Then $w = f(x, y, z)$ is a function of a single variable, say t, on C, and we want to find points where

$$\frac{dw}{dt} = 0.$$

We also know, from the chain rule, that

$$\frac{dw}{dt} = \nabla f \cdot \mathbf{v},$$

where

$$\mathbf{v} = \mathbf{i}\frac{dx}{dt} + \mathbf{j}\frac{dy}{dt} + \mathbf{k}\frac{dz}{dt}$$

is a vector *tangent* to C. To make $dw/dt = 0$, we therefore want to find a point Q_0 on C where ∇f is orthogonal to the tangent vector. This means, however, that ∇f should lie in a plane that is perpendicular to C at Q_0. This is just the plane that contains the two vectors $(\nabla g)_0$ and $(\nabla h)_0$, so $(\nabla f)_0$ should be a linear combination of them. Equation (11a) expresses this relationship. Equations (11b) represent the constraints that put Q_0 on C.

EXAMPLE 4. The cone $z^2 = x^2 + y^2$ is cut by the plane $z = 1 + x + y$ in a curve C. Find the points on C that are nearest to, and farthest from, the origin.

Solution. The function $f(x, y, z) = x^2 + y^2 + z^2$ is to be a minimum (or maximum) subject to the constraints

$$g(x, y, z) = x^2 + y^2 - z^2 = 0, \tag{12a}$$

$$h(x, y, z) = 1 + x + y - z = 0. \tag{12b}$$

We use Eq. (11a). For the critical points, we have

$$2x\mathbf{i} + 2y\mathbf{j} + 2z\mathbf{k} = \lambda(2x\mathbf{i} + 2y\mathbf{j} - 2z\mathbf{k}) + \mu(\mathbf{i} + \mathbf{j} - \mathbf{k}),$$

or, because components must agree,

$$\left.\begin{array}{l} 2x = 2x\lambda + \mu \\ 2y = 2y\lambda + \mu \\ 2z = -2z\lambda - \mu \end{array}\right\} \quad \begin{array}{l} \Rightarrow \quad x - y = (x - y)\lambda \\ \Rightarrow \quad y + z = (y - z)\lambda \end{array}$$

The equation $x - y = (x - y)\lambda$ is satisfied if $x = y$ or if $x \neq y$ and $\lambda = 1$. This latter case cannot apply: The case $\lambda = 1$ implies $y + z = y - z$, from which it follows that $z = 0$. From Eq. (12a), however, $z = 0$ gives $x^2 + y^2 = 0$, or $x = y = 0$. But the point $(0, 0, 0)$ is not on the plane $z = 1 + x + y$. Therefore $\lambda \neq 1$, and we must have $x = y$. The intersection of this plane with the plane $z = 1 + x + y$ is a line that cuts the cone in just two points. We find these points by substituting $y = x$ and $z = 1 + 2x$:

$$x^2 + x^2 = (1 + 2x)^2, \quad 2x^2 + 4x + 1 = 0,$$

$$x = -1 \pm \tfrac{1}{2}\sqrt{2}.$$

The points are

$$A = (-1 - \sqrt{\tfrac{1}{2}}, -1 - \sqrt{\tfrac{1}{2}}, -1 - \sqrt{2}), \tag{13a}$$

$$B = (-1 + \sqrt{\tfrac{1}{2}}, -1 + \sqrt{\tfrac{1}{2}}, -1 + \sqrt{2}). \tag{13b}$$

In Example 4, we know that C is either an ellipse or a hyperbola. If it is an ellipse, we would conclude that B is the point on it nearest the origin, and A the point farthest from the origin. But if it is a hyperbola, then there is no point on it that is farthest away from the origin, and the points A and B are the points on the two branches that are nearest the origin. Problem 13 asks you to think about these possibilities and decide between them. It seems obvious that the critical points should satisfy the condition $x = y$ because all three of the functions f, g, and h treat x and y alike.

As a last example, we apply the method of Lagrange multipliers to find the extreme values of a function of two variables. The problem is one that can be solved by eliminating one variable by direct substitution, but the geometry of the Lagrange solution is worth looking at.

EXAMPLE 5. Find the extreme values of the function $f(x, y) = xy$ subject to the constraint

$$g(x, y) = \frac{x^2}{8} + \frac{y^2}{2} - 1 = 0.$$

Solution. We form

$$H(x, y, \lambda) = xy - \lambda\left(\frac{x^2}{8} + \frac{y^2}{2} - 1\right)$$

and find

$$H_x = y - \frac{\lambda x}{4}, \qquad H_y = x - \lambda y, \qquad H_\lambda = -\frac{x^2}{8} - \frac{y^2}{2} + 1.$$

Setting these equal to zero gives

$$y = \frac{\lambda x}{4}, \qquad x = \lambda y, \qquad x^2 + 4y^2 = 8.$$

The two equations on the left give

$$y = \frac{\lambda}{4}(\lambda y), \qquad y = \frac{\lambda^2}{4}y, \qquad \lambda = \pm 2.$$

Therefore, $x = \pm 2y$. Substituting this in the equation $x^2 + 4y^2 = 8$, we get

$$4y^2 + 4y^2 = 8,$$
$$y = \pm 1.$$

The function $f(x, y)$ takes on its extreme values at $x = \pm 2$, $y = \pm 1$. These values are $xy = 2$ and $xy = -2$.

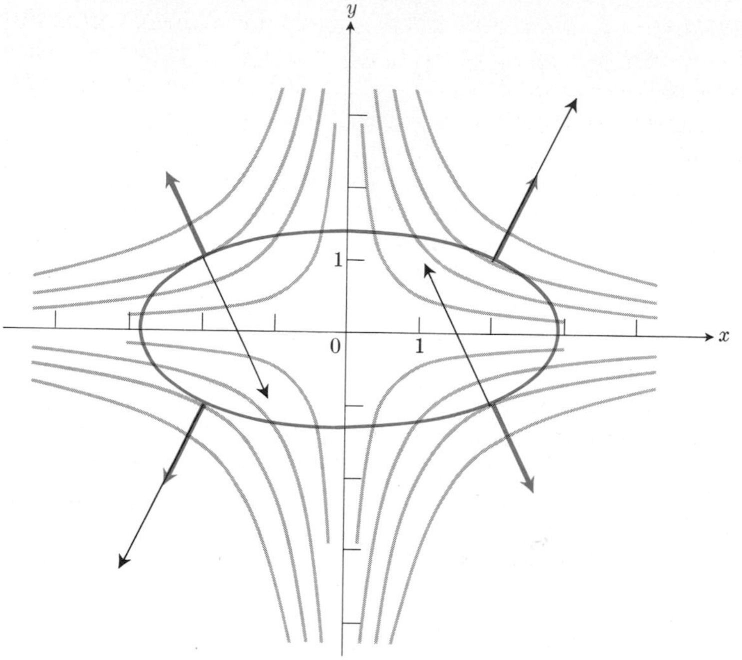

13–30 When subjected to the constraint $g(x, y) = x^2/8 + y^2/2 - 1 = 0$, the function $f(x, y) = xy$ takes on extreme values at the four points $(\pm 2, \pm 1)$.

Geometric interpretation of the solution (see Fig. 13–30). The level curves of the function $f(x, y) = xy$ are the hyperbolas $xy = c$. The farther they are from the origin, the larger the absolute value of f. We want to find the extreme values of $f(x, y)$, given that the point (x, y) also lies on the ellipse $x^2 + 4y^2 = 8$. Which hyperbolas intersecting the ellipse are farthest from the origin? The hyperbolas that just graze the ellipse, the ones that are tangent to the ellipse at the four points $(\pm 2, \pm 1)$. At these points,

a) the normal to the level curve of f is normal to the ellipse;
b) the gradient

$$\nabla f = y\mathbf{i} + x\mathbf{j}$$

is a multiple ($\lambda = \pm 2$) of the gradient

$$\nabla g = \frac{x}{4}\mathbf{i} + y\mathbf{j}.$$

For example, at the point (2, 1),

$$\nabla f = \mathbf{i} + 2\mathbf{j} \quad \text{and} \quad \nabla g = \tfrac{1}{2}\mathbf{i} + \mathbf{j},$$

so that $\nabla f = 2\nabla g$. At the point $(-2, 1)$,

$$\nabla f = \mathbf{i} - 2\mathbf{j} \quad \text{and} \quad \nabla g = -\tfrac{1}{2}\mathbf{i} + \mathbf{j},$$

so that $\nabla f = -2\nabla g$.

As mentioned earlier in this article, and in Article 13–11, the condition that the first partial derivatives of a function be zero at a point where the function has an extreme value is only a necessary condition. It is not a sufficient condition. The partial derivatives of a function may be zero at a point that is neither a maximum nor a minimum of the function. For example, the partial derivatives of the function $z = y^2 - x^2$, which defines a surface like the one shown in Fig. 11–60, are zero at the origin, but the function clearly has no maximum or minimum value there.

As with functions of a single variable, there are second derivative tests that sometimes help to distinguish maxima and minima from each other and from other points where the first partial derivatives of a function are zero. A discussion of one such test in connection with Lagrange multipliers may be found in the appendix to Chapter III of Courant and John's *Introduction to Calculus and Analysis*, Vol. II (Wiley–Interscience, 1974). See Article 16–11, also.

PROBLEMS

1. Find the extreme values of $f(x, y) = xy$ subject to the constraint $g(x, y) = x^2 + y^2 - 10 = 0$.

2. Use the method of Lagrange multipliers to find (a) the minimum value of $x + y$, subject to the constraint $xy = 16$; (b) the maximum value of xy, subject to the constraint $x + y = 16$. Comment on the geometry of each solution.

3. Find the maximum of $f(x, y) = 9 - (x^2/4) - (y^2/4)$ subject to the constraint $g(x, y) = x + 3y - 12 = 0$. (See Fig. 13–27.)

4. Find the point on the surface $z = xy + 1$ that is nearest the origin.

5. A rectangular box, open at the top, is to hold 256 in^3. Find the dimensions of the box for which the surface area is a minimum.

6. The base of a rectangular box costs three times as much per square foot as do the sides and top. Find the relative dimensions for the most economical box of given volume.

7. Find the equation of the plane through the point (2, 1, 1) that cuts off the least volume from the first octant. (Consider only those planes whose intercepts with the coordinate axes are positive.)

8. A pentagon is composed of a rectangle surmounted by an isosceles triangle. If the area is fixed, what are the dimensions for which the perimeter is a minimum?

9. A plane of the form

$$z = Ax + By + C$$

is to be "fitted" to the following points (x_i, y_i, z_i):

$$(0, 0, 0), \quad (0, 1, 1), \quad (1, 1, 1), \quad (1, 0, -1).$$

Find the plane that minimizes the sum of squares of the deviations

$$\sum_{i=1}^{4} (Ax_i + By_i + C - z_i)^2.$$

10. Consider the geometric argument in Remark 2 for the minimization problem of Example 3.

a) Describe the family of surfaces $f =$ constant.

b) Do all of the surfaces of (a) intersect the plane $2x - 3y + 5z = 19$?

c) If a particular surface $f = k$ intersects the plane, what is the locus of intersection, geometrically? If $k' > k$, does the surface $f = k'$ also intersect the plane? In what kind of curve?

d) Does the geometric plausibility argument apply to this example?

11. Use the method of Lagrange multipliers to find the points nearest to, and farthest from, the origin and lying on the curve $x^2 + 2xy + 3y^2 = 9$ in the xy-plane.

12. Use the method of Lagrange multipliers to find the points on the surface $x^2 + y^2 + z^2 = 25$, where the function $f(x, y, z) = x + 2y + 3z$ is:

a) a minimum, **b)** a maximum.

Comment on the geometric interpretation of $\nabla f = \lambda \nabla g$ at these points.

13. In the solution of Example 4, two points A and B were located as candidates for maximum or minimum distances from the origin. Use cylindrical coordinates r, θ, z to express the equations of the cone, the plane $z = 1 + x + y$, and the cylinder that contains their curve of intersection and has elements parallel to the z-axis. Is this cylinder circular, elliptical, parabolic, or hyperbolic? (Consider its intersection with the xy-plane.) Express the distance from the origin to a point on the curve of intersection of the cone and the plane as a function of θ. Does it have a minimum? A maximum? What can you now say about the points A and B of Eqs. (13a, b) as solutions in Example 4?

14. In Example 4, the extrema for $f(x, y, z)$ on the cone $z^2 = x^2 + y^2$ and the plane $z = 1 + x + y$ were found to satisfy $y = x$ as well. Thus $z = 1 + 2x$, and the function to be made a maximum or minimum is $x^2 + y^2 + z^2 = x^2 + x^2 + (1 + 2x)^2$, which can also be written as $6(x + \frac{1}{3})^2 + \frac{1}{3}$. This is obviously a minimum when $x = -\frac{1}{3}$. But the point we get with

$$y = x, \qquad z = 1 + 2x, \qquad x = -\tfrac{1}{3},$$

is $(-\frac{1}{3}, -\frac{1}{3}, \frac{1}{3})$, which is not on the cone. What's wrong? (A sketch of the situation in the plane $y = x$ may throw some light on the question.)

15. In Example 4, we can determine that, for all points on the cone $z^2 = x^2 + y^2$, the square of the distance from the origin to $P(x, y, z)$ is $w = 2(x^2 + y^2)$, which is a function of two independent variables, x and y. But if P is also to be on the plane

$$z = 1 + x + y$$

as well as the cone, then

$$(1 + x + y)^2 = x^2 + y^2.$$

Show that these points have coordinates that satisfy the equation

$$2xy + 2x + 2y + 1 = 0.$$

Interpret this equation in two ways:

a) as a curve in the xy-plane, and

b) as a set of points on a cylinder in 3-space.

Sketch the curve of (a) and find the point or points on it for which w is a minimum. Are there points on this curve for which w is a maximum? Use the information you now have to complete the discussion of Example 4.

13–12 HIGHER-ORDER DERIVATIVES

Partial derivatives of the second order are denoted by such symbols as

$$\frac{\partial^2 f}{\partial x^2}, \quad \frac{\partial^2 f}{\partial y^2}, \quad \frac{\partial^2 f}{\partial x\, \partial y}, \quad \frac{\partial^2 f}{\partial y\, \partial x}$$

or by

$$f_{xx}, \quad f_{yy}, \quad f_{yx}, \quad f_{xy},$$

where these are defined by the equations

$$\frac{\partial^2 f}{\partial x^2} = \frac{\partial}{\partial x}\left(\frac{\partial f}{\partial x}\right), \qquad \frac{\partial^2 f}{\partial x\, \partial y} = \frac{\partial}{\partial x}\left(\frac{\partial f}{\partial y}\right),$$

and so forth.

EXAMPLE. If

$$f(x, y) = x \cos y + ye^x,$$

then

$$\frac{\partial f}{\partial x} = \cos y + ye^x,$$

$$\frac{\partial}{\partial y}\left(\frac{\partial f}{\partial x}\right) = -\sin y + e^x = \frac{\partial^2 f}{\partial y\, \partial x},$$

$$\frac{\partial}{\partial x}\left(\frac{\partial f}{\partial x}\right) = ye^x = \frac{\partial^2 f}{\partial x^2},$$

$$\frac{\partial}{\partial x}\left(\frac{\partial^2 f}{\partial x^2}\right) = ye^x = \frac{\partial^3 f}{\partial x^3},$$

$$\frac{\partial}{\partial y}\left(\frac{\partial^2 f}{\partial x^2}\right) = e^x = \frac{\partial^3 f}{\partial y\, \partial x^2},$$

and so on; while

$$\frac{\partial f}{\partial y} = -x \sin y + e^x,$$

$$\frac{\partial}{\partial x}\left(\frac{\partial f}{\partial y}\right) = -\sin y + e^x = \frac{\partial^2 f}{\partial x\, \partial y},$$

$$\frac{\partial}{\partial y}\left(\frac{\partial f}{\partial y}\right) = -x \cos y = \frac{\partial^2 f}{\partial y^2},$$

$$\frac{\partial}{\partial x}\left(\frac{\partial^2 f}{\partial x\, \partial y}\right) = e^x = \frac{\partial^3 f}{\partial x^2\, \partial y},$$

and so on.

The example shows how the order of differentiation is indicated by the notation. Thus, in calculating $\partial^2 f/\partial y\, \partial x$, we differentiate first with respect to x and then with respect to y. This might also be indicated by $(f_x)_y$ or f_{xy}. Now it is a remarkable fact that the so-called "mixed" second-order partial derivatives

$$\frac{\partial^2 f}{\partial y\, \partial x} \quad \text{and} \quad \frac{\partial^2 f}{\partial x\, \partial y}$$

are generally equal, just as they are seen to be equal in the example above. That is, we arrive at the same result whether we differentiate first with respect to x and then with respect to y, or do the differentiation in the reverse order. The following theorem supports this assertion under suitable hypotheses.

Theorem. *If the function $w = f(x, y)$, together with the partial derivatives f_x, f_y, f_{xy}, and f_{yx}, is continuous, then*

$$\frac{\partial}{\partial x}\left(\frac{\partial f}{\partial y}\right) = \frac{\partial}{\partial y}\left(\frac{\partial f}{\partial x}\right).$$

Proof. Let (a, b) be a point in the interior of a rectangle R in the xy-plane on which f, f_x, f_y, f_{xy}, and f_{yx} are all continuous. Then the fact that

$$f_{xy}(a, b) = f_{yx}(a, b) \tag{1}$$

can be proved by repeated application of the Mean Value Theorem, as follows. We let h and k be numbers such that the point $(a + h, b + k)$ also lies in the rectangle R, and consider the difference

$$\Delta = F(a + h) - F(a), \tag{2}$$

where we define $F(x)$ in terms of $f(x, y)$ by the equation

$$F(x) = f(x, b + k) - f(x, b). \tag{3}$$

We apply the Mean Value Theorem to the function $F(x)$, and Eq. (2) becomes

$$\Delta = hF'(c_1), \tag{4}$$

where c_1 lies between a and $a + h$. From Eq. (3),

$$F'(x) = f_x(x, b + k) - f_x(x, b),$$

so Eq. (4) becomes

$$\Delta = h[f_x(c_1, b + k) - f_x(c_1, b)]. \quad \textbf{(5)}$$

Now we apply the Mean Value Theorem to the function $g(y) = f_x(c_1, y)$ and have

$$g(b + k) - g(b) = kg'(d_1) \quad \textbf{(6a)}$$

or

$$f_x(c_1, b + k) - f_x(c_1, b) = kf_{xy}(c_1, d_1), \quad \textbf{(6b)}$$

for some d_1 between b and $b + k$. By substituting this into Eq. (5), we get

$$\Delta = hkf_{xy}(c_1, d_1), \quad \textbf{(7)}$$

for some point (c_1, d_1) in the rectangle R' whose vertices are the four points (a, b), $(a + h, b)$, $(a + h, b + k)$, and $(a, b + k)$. (See Fig. 13–31.)

On the other hand, by substituting from Eq. (3) into Eq. (2), we may also write

$$\begin{aligned}\Delta &= f(a + h, b + k) - f(a + h, b) - f(a, b + k) + f(a, b)\\ &= [f(a + h, b + k) - f(a, b + k)] - [f(a + h, b) - f(a, b)]\\ &= \phi(b + k) - \phi(b),\end{aligned} \quad \textbf{(8)}$$

where

$$\phi(y) = f(a + h, y) - f(a, y). \quad \textbf{(9)}$$

The Mean Value Theorem applied to Eq. (8) now gives

$$\Delta = k\phi'(d_2), \quad \textbf{(10)}$$

for some d_2 between b and $b + k$. By Eq. (9),

$$\phi'(y) = f_y(a + h, y) - f_y(a, y). \quad \textbf{(11)}$$

Substituting from Eq. (11) into Eq. (10), we have

$$\Delta = k[f_y(a + h, d_2) - f_y(a, d_2)]. \quad \textbf{(12)}$$

Finally, we apply the Mean Value Theorem to the expression in brackets and get

$$\Delta = khf_{yx}(c_2, d_2), \quad \textbf{(13)}$$

for some c_2 between a and $a + h$.

A comparison of Eqs. (7) and (13) shows that

$$f_{xy}(c_1, d_1) = f_{yx}(c_2, d_2), \quad \textbf{(14)}$$

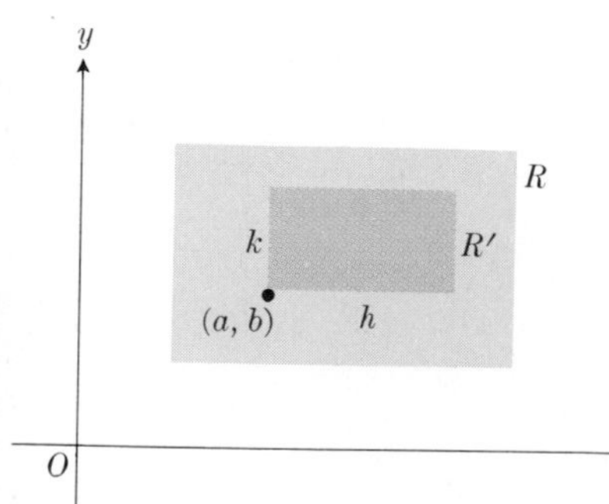

13–31 The key to proving $f_{xy}(a, b) = f_{yx}(a, b)$ is the fact that no matter how small R' is, f_{xy} and f_{yx} take on equal values somewhere inside R' (although not necessarily at the same point of R').

where (c_1, d_1) and (c_2, d_2) both lie in the rectangle R' (Fig. 13–31). Equation (14) is not quite the result we want, since it says only that the mixed derivative f_{xy} has the same value at (c_1, d_1) that the derivative f_{yx} has at (c_2, d_2). But the numbers h and k in our discussion may be made as small as we wish. The hypothesis that f_{xy} and f_{yz} are both continuous throughout R then means that

$$f_{xy}(c_1, d_1) = f_{xy}(a, b) + \epsilon_1$$

and

$$f_{yx}(c_2, d_2) = f_{yx}(a, b) + \epsilon_2,$$

where

$$\epsilon_1, \epsilon_2 \to 0$$

as

$$h, k \to 0.$$

Hence, if we let h and $k \to 0$, we have

$$f_{xy}(a, b) = f_{yx}(a, b).$$

Q.E.D.

The proof just completed hinges upon the consideration of the so-called "second difference" Δ given by Eq. (8). The reason for calling this a *second* difference is to be found from a closer examination of Eqs. (2) and (3). Note that both

$$F(a) = f(a, b + k) - f(a, b)$$

and

$$F(a + h) = f(a + h, b + k) - f(a + h, b)$$

are themselves differences ("first" differences), while

$$\Delta = F(a + h) - F(a)$$

is the difference between these first differences.

An interesting byproduct of the proof of the theorem is the fact that this second difference may, under the hypotheses of the theorem, be approximated by

$$\Delta \approx hkf_{xy}(a, b),$$

where the accuracy of the approximation depends upon the size of h and k.

If we refer once more to the example at the beginning of this article, we note not only that

$$\frac{\partial^2 f}{\partial x\, \partial y} = \frac{\partial^2 f}{\partial y\, \partial x},$$

but also that

$$\frac{\partial^3 f}{\partial x^2\, \partial y} = \frac{\partial^3 f}{\partial y\, \partial x^2}.$$

This equality may be derived from the theorem above as follows:

$$\begin{aligned}\frac{\partial^3 f}{\partial x^2\, \partial y} &= \frac{\partial}{\partial x}\left(\frac{\partial^2 f}{\partial x\, \partial y}\right) = \frac{\partial}{\partial x}\left(\frac{\partial^2 f}{\partial y\, \partial x}\right) \\ &= \frac{\partial}{\partial x}\left(\frac{\partial}{\partial y} f_x\right) = \frac{\partial}{\partial y}\left(\frac{\partial}{\partial x} f_x\right) \\ &= \frac{\partial}{\partial y}\left(\frac{\partial^2 f}{\partial x^2}\right) = \frac{\partial^3 f}{\partial y\, \partial x^2}.\end{aligned}$$

In fact, if all the partial derivatives that appear are continuous, the notation

$$\frac{\partial^{m+n} f}{\partial x^m \, \partial y^n}$$

may be used to denote the result of differentiating the function $f(x, y)$ m times with respect to x and n times with respect to y, the order in which these differentiations are performed being entirely arbitrary. For example, $\partial^5 f/(\partial x^2 \, \partial y^3)$ is the result of five successive differentiations, two with respect to x and three with respect to y, such as f_{xyyxy}, where the latter notation means differentiation first with respect to x, then twice with respect to y, then again with respect to x, and finally with respect to y. (The subscripts are read from left to right.)

PROBLEMS

1. If $w = \cos(x + y) + \sin(x - y)$, show that

$$\frac{\partial^2 w}{\partial x^2} = \frac{\partial^2 w}{\partial y^2}.$$

2. If $w = \ln(2x + 2y) + \tan(2x - 2y)$, show that

$$\frac{\partial^2 w}{\partial x^2} = \frac{\partial^2 w}{\partial y^2}.$$

3. If $w = f(x + y) + g(x - y)$, where $f(u)$ and $g(v)$ are twice-differentiable functions of $u = x + y$ and $v = x - y$, respectively, show that

$$\frac{\partial^2 w}{\partial x^2} = \frac{\partial^2 w}{\partial y^2} = f''(u) + g''(v).$$

(Problems 1 and 2 are special examples of this result.)

4. If c is a constant and $w = \sin(x + ct) + \cos(2x + 2ct)$, show that $(\partial^2 w/\partial t^2) = c^2(\partial^2 w/\partial x^2)$.

5. If c is a constant and

$$w = 5\cos(3x + 3ct) - 7\sinh(4x - 4ct),$$

show that $(\partial^2 w/\partial t^2) = c^2(\partial^2 w/\partial x^2)$.

6. If c is a constant and $w = f(x + ct) + g(x - ct)$, where $f(u)$ and $g(v)$ are twice-differentiable functions of $u = x + ct$ and $v = x - ct$, respectively, show that

$$\frac{\partial^2 w}{\partial t^2} = c^2 \frac{\partial^2 w}{\partial x^2} = c^2(f''(u) + g''(v)).$$

(Note that Problems 4 and 5 are special cases. The equation $(\partial^2 w/\partial t^2) = c^2(\partial^2 w/\partial x^2)$ describes the motion of a wave that travels with velocity c. See Sears, Zemansky, Young, *University Physics*, Fifth edition (1976, Addison-Wesley, Chapter 21.)

In each of the following problems (7–13), verify that V satisfies Laplace's equation

$$\frac{\partial^2 V}{\partial x^2} + \frac{\partial^2 V}{\partial y^2} + \frac{\partial^2 V}{\partial z^2} = 0.$$

7. $V = x^2 + y^2 - 2z^2$

8. $V = 2z^3 - 3(x^2 + y^2)z$

9. $V = e^{-2y}\cos 2x$

10. $V = \ln\sqrt{x^2 + y^2}$

11. $V = (x^2 + y^2 + z^2)^{-1/2}$

12. $V = e^{3x+4y}\cos 5z$

13. $V = \cos 3x \cos 4y \sinh 5z$

In each of the following problems (14–17), verify that $w_{xy} = w_{yx}$.

14. $w = e^x \sinh y + \cos(2x - 3y)$

15. $w = \ln(2x + 3y)$

16. $w = \tan^{-1}(y/x)$

17. $w = xy^2 + x^2y^3 + x^3y^4$

18. Let $f(x, y) = x^3y^2$. Following the notation in Eqs. (2) through (7), find:

a) $F(x)$, b) c_1, c) $g(y)$, d) d_1

and thus verify Eq. (7) for this particular case. Also show that $f_{xy}(c_1, d_1) \to f_{xy}(a, b)$ as $(h, k) \to (0, 0)$.

19. Use the function $f = x^3y^2$ and carry out the steps of Eqs. (8) to (13). In particular, find (c_2, d_2) and show that $f_{yx}(c_2, d_2) \to f_{xy}(a, b)$ as $(h, k) \to (0, 0)$.

13–13 EXACT DIFFERENTIALS

We have seen that on numerous occasions the result of translating a physical problem into mathematical terms is a differential equation to be integrated. In the simplest cases, we may be able to separate the variables and write the differential equation in a form such as

$$f(x)\,dx = g(y)\,dy,$$

which we can solve if we are able to evaluate $\int f(x)\,dx$ and $\int g(y)\,dy$. Sometimes, however, we are not able to separate the variables, as in the equations

$$(x^2 + y^2)\,dx + 2xy\,dy = 0 \tag{1a}$$

and

$$(x^2 + y^2)\,dx - 2xy\,dy = 0. \tag{1b}$$

More generally, we may be led to a differential equation of the form

$$M(x, y)\,dx + N(x, y)\,dy = 0, \tag{2}$$

where $M(x, y)$ and $N(x, y)$ are functions of x and y. (In most cases, these functions will be continuous and have continuous partial derivatives with respect to x and y.) The differential equation (2) can be solved quite easily, provided that it is possible to find a function

$$w = f(x, y) \tag{3}$$

such that the left side of Eq. (2) is the total differential of w. For if such is the case, then Eq. (2) becomes

$$dw = 0,$$

and the solution of this equation is simply

$$w = C,$$

and the solution of Eq. (2) is

$$f(x, y) = C,$$

where C is an arbitrary constant.

Now, expressions of the form given in Eq. (2) aren't always differentials of functions. In fact, of the two expressions in Eq. (1a, b), we shall see that the first is such a differential while the second is not.

The following terminology is commonly used: An expression

$$M(x, y)\,dx + N(x, y)\,dy \tag{4}$$

is called an *exact differential* if and only if there exists a function $w = f(x, y)$ with

$$df(x, y) = M(x, y)\,dx + N(x, y)\,dy. \tag{5}$$

If no such function exists, the expression is not an exact differential.

Three questions naturally present themselves:

a) How can we tell whether a given expression is or is not an exact differential?

b) If the expression is exact, how do we find the function $f(x, y)$ of which it is the differential?

c) If the expression is not exact, how can we solve the differential equation (2)?

In the proof of the theorem below, we shall give answers to the first two of these questions. (Differential equations are discussed in more detail in Chapter 18.)

The theorem introduces a mild restriction on the geometric nature of the

Connected and simply connected.

Connected but not simply connected.

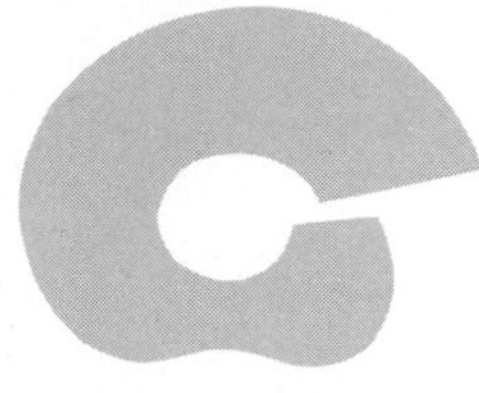

Connected and simply connected.

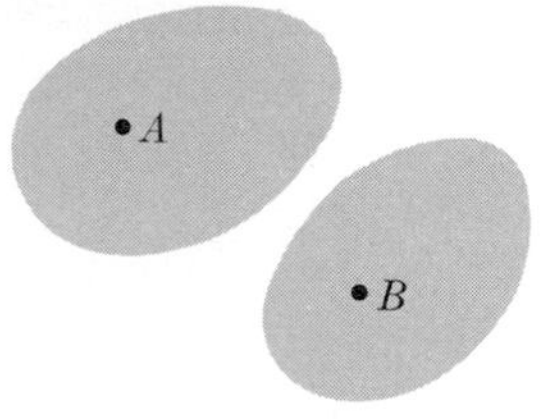

Simply connected but not connected. No path from A to B lies entirely in the region.

13–32 Regions.

set R on which the functions $M(x, y)$ and $N(x, y)$ are defined. Specifically, R is required to be a simply connected region. The word *region* has the technical meaning here of "connected open set." A subset of the plane is *open* if each of its points is the center of a circle whose interior lies entirely in the set. An *open* subset of the plane is *connected* if every two of its points can be joined by a path that lies entirely in the set. A subset R of the plane is *simply connected* if no simple closed curve in R surrounds points not in R. When you read "simply connected," think "no holes." (See Fig. 13–32.) You need not be concerned with these technicalities now. The plane domains on which most of the functions in this book are defined really are regions or unions of regions, and most of them are simply connected. It will not be necessary to test every function that comes along. But without these conditions on R (which are usually met in practice), or others like them, some of the most useful theorems of calculus would not be true.

Theorem. Test for exactness. *Suppose that the functions $M(x, y)$ and $N(x, y)$ and their partial derivatives M_x, M_y, N_x, and N_y are continuous for all real values of x and y in a simply connected region R. Then a necessary and sufficient condition for*

$$M(x, y)\,dx + N(x, y)\,dy$$

to be an exact differential in R is

$$\frac{\partial M}{\partial y} = \frac{\partial N}{\partial x}.$$

Proof. We shall first prove that the condition is necessary. Suppose the expression is an exact differential; that is, suppose a function $f(x, y)$ exists such that Eq. (5) is satisfied at all points in R. We also know that

$$df = \frac{\partial f}{\partial x}\,dx + \frac{\partial f}{\partial y}\,dy. \tag{6}$$

In Eqs. (5) and (6), dx and dy are independent variables, and we may set either dx or dy equal to zero and keep the other one different from zero. Then the only way that both equations can hold is to have

$$\frac{\partial f}{\partial x} = M(x, y), \qquad \frac{\partial f}{\partial y} = N(x, y). \tag{7}$$

Now, by the theorem of Article 13–12, we know that if M and N are continuous and have continuous partial derivatives in R, then

$$\frac{\partial}{\partial y}\left(\frac{\partial f}{\partial x}\right) = \frac{\partial}{\partial x}\left(\frac{\partial f}{\partial y}\right),$$

so that the condition

$$\frac{\partial M}{\partial y} = \frac{\partial N}{\partial x} \tag{8}$$

is a necessary condition if Eq. (7) is to be satisfied.

EXAMPLE 1. The condition given in Eq. (8) is satisfied by the expression in Eq. (1a), where

$$M = x^2 + y^2, \qquad N = 2xy.$$

Here

$$\frac{\partial M}{\partial y} = 2y = \frac{\partial N}{\partial x}.$$

We have not yet proved that this condition is sufficient, however, so we cannot at this point say that the expression is exact.

For Eq. (1b), we have

$$M = x^2 + y^2, \qquad N = -2xy$$

and

$$\frac{\partial M}{\partial y} = 2y, \qquad \frac{\partial N}{\partial x} = -2y,$$

so that

$$\frac{\partial M}{\partial y} \neq \frac{\partial N}{\partial x}.$$

Since Eq. (8) is a necessary condition, we can say that the expression in (1b) is not an exact differential.

As Example 1 suggests, it is usually a simple matter to apply the condition of Eq. (8) to test $M(x, y)\,dx + N(x, y)\,dy$ for exactness. What we have not shown yet, however, is that the condition is sufficient as well as necessary. It is here that the simple connectivity of the region R comes in, but it is also here that the argument becomes so technical that it will not be presented in full detail. We shall show how to find the function f, first in general terms, and then by example; but we will not go into the details of why one should expect the function f to exist. The full story can be found in most advanced calculus texts.

The basic fact to establish is that, if

$$\frac{\partial M}{\partial y} = \frac{\partial N}{\partial x} \quad \text{in } R,$$

then there is a function $w = f(x, y)$ whose domain includes R and which is such that

$$df = M\,dx + N\,dy.$$

We shall establish this result by showing how to find the function $f(x, y)$ and this will also answer the second question previously raised.

From Eq. (6), we see that our sought-for function must have the property expressed by Eqs. (7):

$$\frac{\partial f}{\partial x} = M(x, y), \qquad \frac{\partial f}{\partial y} = N(x, y).$$

Integrating the first of these with respect to x, we find

$$f(x, y) = \int_x M(x, y)\, dx + g(y), \tag{9}$$

where $g(y)$ represents an unknown function of y that plays the role of an arbitrary constant of integration. The integral $\int_x M(x, y)\, dx$ is an ordinary indefinite integral with respect to x with y held constant during the integration. The function $f(x, y)$ produced by Eq. (9) satisfies the condition

$$\frac{\partial f}{\partial x} = M(x, y)$$

for any choice of the function $g(y)$, because $g(y)$ acts as a constant under partial differentiation with respect to x. To see how we may satisfy the second condition, $\partial f/\partial y = N(x, y)$, we differentiate both sides of Eq. (9) with respect to y, holding x fixed, and obtain

$$\frac{\partial f}{\partial y} = \frac{\partial}{\partial y} \int_x M(x, y)\, dx + \frac{\partial g(y)}{\partial y}. \tag{10}$$

Actually, since $g(y)$ is a function of y alone, we may write dg/dy instead of $\partial g/\partial y$. We then set $\partial f/\partial y$ from Eq. (10) equal to $N(x, y)$ and have

$$N(x, y) = \frac{\partial}{\partial y} \int_x M(x, y)\, dx + \frac{dg(y)}{dy},$$

or

$$\frac{dg(y)}{dy} = N(x, y) - \frac{\partial}{\partial y} \int_x M(x, y)\, dx. \tag{11}$$

We use this differential equation to determine $g(y)$ by simply integrating its righthand member with respect to y and then substituting the result back into Eq. (9), to obtain our final answer, namely $f(x, y)$. Success of the method hinges on the fact that the expression on the righthand side of Eq. (11) *is a function of y alone, provided that the condition*

$$\frac{\partial M(x, y)}{\partial y} = \frac{\partial N(x, y)}{\partial x}$$

is satisfied. [If the righthand side of Eq. (11) depended on x as well as on y, it could not be equal to dg/dy, which involves only y.]

But how, in general, can we prove that the expression in question is independent of x? We can prove this by showing that its partial derivative with respect to x is identically zero. That is, we must calculate

$$\begin{aligned}
\frac{\partial}{\partial x}\left(N(x, y) - \frac{\partial}{\partial y} \int_x M(x, y)\, dx\right) &= \frac{\partial N}{\partial x} - \frac{\partial^2}{\partial x\, \partial y} \int_x M(x, y)\, dx \\
&= \frac{\partial N}{\partial x} - \frac{\partial}{\partial y}\left(\frac{\partial}{\partial x} \int_x M(x, y)\, dx\right) \\
&= \frac{\partial N}{\partial x} - \frac{\partial}{\partial y}(M),
\end{aligned}$$

which vanishes if it is true that

$$\frac{\partial N}{\partial x} = \frac{\partial M}{\partial y},$$

as we have assumed.

EXAMPLE 2. Find a function $f(x, y)$ whose differential is

$$df = (x^2 + y^2)\,dx + 2xy\,dy.$$

Solution. We set

$$M = x^2 + y^2, \qquad N = 2xy,$$

and note that the condition

$$\frac{\partial M}{\partial y} = \frac{\partial N}{\partial x}$$

is satisfied. We seek $f(x, y)$ such that

$$\frac{\partial f}{\partial x} = x^2 + y^2, \qquad \frac{\partial f}{\partial y} = 2xy.$$

Integrating the first of these with respect to x while holding y constant and adding $g(y)$ as our "constant of integration," we have

$$f(x, y) = \tfrac{1}{3}x^3 + y^2x + g(y).$$

Differentiating this with respect to y with x held constant and setting the result equal to $2xy$, we have

$$2xy = 2yx + \frac{dg}{dy}, \qquad \text{or} \qquad \frac{dg}{dy} = 0,$$

so that $g(y) = C$ must be a pure constant. Hence

$$f(x, y) = \tfrac{1}{3}x^3 + y^2x + C.$$

Note three things about Example 2:

1. The method was easy to apply.

2. We found infinitely many functions with the differential $(x^2 + y^2)\,dx + 2xy\,dy$, one for each value of C.

3. We were able to tell that $(x^2 + y^2)\,dx + 2xy\,dy$ was an exact differential *without knowing f in advance.* This and the ease of application are why the theorem of this article is so useful.

PROBLEMS

In Problems 1 through 7, determine whether the given expression is or is not an exact differential. If the expression is the differential of a function $f(x, y)$, find f.

1. $2x(x^3 + y^3)\,dx + 3y^2(x^2 + y^2)\,dy$

2. $e^y\,dx + x(e^y + 1)\,dy$

3. $(2x + y)\,dx + (x + 2y)\,dy$

4. $(\cosh y + y \cosh x)\,dx + (\sinh x + x \sinh y)\,dy$

5. $(\sin y + y \sin x)\,dx + (\cos x + x \cos y)\,dy$

6. $(1 + e^x)\,dy + e^x(y - x)\,dx$

7. $(e^{x+y} + e^{x-y})(dx + dy)$

13–14 DERIVATIVES OF INTEGRALS

From the Fundamental Theorem of integral calculus we know that if f is a continuous function on $a \le t \le b$, then

$$\frac{d}{dx}\int_a^x f(t)\,dt = f(x). \tag{1}$$

For example,

$$\frac{d}{dx}\int_0^x e^{-t^2}\,dt = e^{-x^2},$$

and

$$\frac{d}{dx}\int_1^x \frac{1}{t}\,dt = \frac{1}{x}, \qquad (x > 0).$$

Similarly, since

$$\int_x^b f(t)\,dt = -\int_b^x f(t)\,dt,$$

we have

$$\frac{d}{dx}\int_x^b f(t)\,dt = -f(x). \tag{2}$$

Equations (1) and (2) may be combined to give the following result.

Theorem. *Let f be continuous on $a \le t \le b$. Let u and v be differentiable functions of x such that $u(x)$ and $v(x)$ lie between a and b. Then*

$$\frac{d}{dx}\int_{u(x)}^{v(x)} f(t)\,dt = f(v(x))\frac{dv}{dx} - f(u(x))\frac{du}{dx}. \tag{3}$$

Proof. Let $F(u, v) = \int_u^v f(t)\,dt$. Then, by Eq. (1),

$$\frac{\partial F}{\partial v} = f(v), \tag{4a}$$

and, by Eq. (2),

$$\frac{\partial F}{\partial u} = -f(u), \tag{4b}$$

provided u and v lie between a and b. If u and v are differentiable functions of x, and $u(x)$, $v(x)$ are between a and b, we may apply the chain rule:

$$\frac{dF}{dx} = \frac{\partial F}{\partial u}\frac{du}{dx} + \frac{\partial F}{\partial v}\frac{dv}{dx}. \tag{5}$$

The result of substituting from Eqs. (4a, b) into Eq. (5) is

$$\frac{dF}{dx} = f(v)\frac{dv}{dx} - f(u)\frac{du}{dx}.$$

This establishes Eq. (3). Q.E.D.

EXAMPLE. Verify Eq. (3) for

$$\frac{d}{dx}\int_x^{2x} \frac{1}{t}\,dt, \qquad (x > 0).$$

Solution. Let $F(u, v) = \int_u^v (1/t)\,dt = \ln v - \ln u$. Then $\partial F/\partial u = -1/u$ and $\partial F/\partial v = 1/v$. If $u = x$ and $v = 2x$, then

$$\frac{du}{dx} = 1, \qquad \frac{dv}{dx} = 2,$$

and

$$\begin{aligned}\frac{dF}{dx} &= \frac{\partial F}{\partial u}\cdot\frac{du}{dx} + \frac{\partial F}{\partial v}\cdot\frac{dv}{dx}\\ &= -\frac{1}{u} + \frac{2}{v}\\ &= -\frac{1}{x} + \frac{2}{2x} = 0.\end{aligned}$$

Alternatively,

$$\begin{aligned}F(x, 2x) &= \int_x^{2x} \frac{1}{t}\,dt = \ln t\Big]_x^{2x} = \ln 2x - \ln x\\ &= \ln\frac{2x}{x} = \ln 2, \qquad (0 < x)\end{aligned}$$

and

$$\frac{d}{dx}F(x, 2x) = \frac{d}{dx}(\ln 2) = 0.$$

PROBLEMS

Find the derivative, with respect to x, of each of the following (assuming $x > 0$):

1. $\int_x^{x^2} \frac{1}{t}\,dt$
2. $\int_x^{2x} \frac{1}{t^2}\,dt$
3. $\int_{2x}^{x^2} \frac{1}{t^2}\,dt$
4. $\int_0^{\sin^{-1} x} \frac{\sin t}{t}\,dt$
5. $\int_x^{x^2} \ln t\,dt$
6. If u and v are differentiable functions of x and $u(x) > 0$, show (by two different methods) that

$$\frac{d}{dx}[(u(x))^{v(x)}] = u^v\left[\frac{v}{u}\cdot\frac{du}{dx} + \frac{dv}{dx}\cdot\ln u\right].$$

Find dy/dx if:

7. $y = (e^x)^x$
8. $y = (\cosh x)^{x^2}$
9. $y = (x^2 + 1)^{1/x}$
10. $y = (4x^2 + 4x + 3)^{\int_x^{x^2} \ln t\,dt}$

REVIEW QUESTIONS AND EXERCISES

1. Let $w = f(x, y)$ define a function of two independent variables, for values of (x, y) in some region G of the xy-plane (the domain of f). Describe two geometrical ways of representing the function.

2. When is a function of two variables continuous at a point of its domain? Give an example, different from those in the text, of a function that is discontinuous at some point(s) of its domain.

3. Let $w = f(x, y)$. Define $\partial w/\partial x$ and $\partial w/\partial y$ at a point (x_0, y_0) in the domain of f.

4. When is a function of three variables continuous at a point of its domain? Give an example of a function of three independent variables that is continuous at some points of its domain and discontinuous at at least one place in its domain. Give an example that is discontinuous at all points of a surface $F(x, y, z) = 0$; at all points of a line.

5. Define the directional derivative, at a point in its domain, of a function of three independent variables. Write a formula for the directional derivative in vector form. What is the analogous formula for a function of two variables?

6. Define tangent plane, and normal line, to a surface S at a point P_0 on S. Derive equations of the tangent plane and normal line in terms of the equations of the surface.

7. Write an expression for the tangent plane approximation to the increment of a function of two independent variables. What is the corresponding expression approximating the increment of a function of three variables?

8. Define *gradient* of a scalar function. Give two properties of the gradient that you consider to be important.

9. State the chain rule for partial derivatives of functions of several variables.

10. Define the *total differential* of a function of several variables.

11. Outline a method for finding local maxima or minima of a function of two or three independent variables.

12. Outline the "method of least squares" as applied to fitting a straight line to a set of observations.

13. Describe the method of Lagrange multipliers as it applies to the problem of maximizing or minimizing a function $f(x, y, z)$,

a) subject to a constraint

$$g(x, y, z) = 0,$$

b) subject to two constraints,

$$g(x, y, z) = 0 \quad \text{and} \quad h(x, y, z) = 0.$$

14. Sketch some of the contour curves for the function $f(x, y) = 2x + 3y$. Find points on the curve C: $x^2 + xy + y^2 = 3$ that

a) maximize f, **b)** minimize f.

Does it seem reasonable on geometric grounds that the level curve of f at each one of these points is tangent to C at that point? Is it true?

MISCELLANEOUS PROBLEMS

1. Let $f(x, y) = (x^2 - y^2)/(x^2 + y^2)$ for $x^2 + y^2 \neq 0$. Is it possible to define the value of f at $x = 0$, $y = 0$, in such a way that the function would be continuous at $x = 0$, $y = 0$? Why?

2. Let the function $f(x, y)$ be defined by the relations

$$f(x, y) = \frac{\sin^2(x - y)}{|x| + |y|} \quad \text{for } |x| + |y| \neq 0, \quad f(0, 0) = 0.$$

Is f continuous at $x = 0$, $y = 0$?

3. Prove that if $f(x, y)$ is defined for all x, y, by

$$f(x, y) = \begin{cases} \dfrac{2xy}{x^2 + y^2} & \text{if } (x, y) \neq (0, 0), \\ 0 & \text{if } x = y = 0, \end{cases}$$

then (a) for any fixed x, $f(x, y)$ is a continuous function of y; (b) for any fixed y, $f(x, y)$ is a continuous function of x; (c) $f(x, y)$ is not continuous at (0, 0); (d) $\partial f/\partial x$ and $\partial f/\partial y$ exist at (0, 0) but are not continuous there. (This example shows that a function may possess partial derivatives at all points of a region, yet not be continuous in the region.) Contrast the case of a function of one variable, where the existence of a derivative implies continuity.

4. Let $f(x, y)$ be defined and continuous for all x, y (differentiability not assumed). Show that it is always possible to find arbitrarily many points (x_1, y_1), (x_2, y_2), $\ldots$, (x_n, y_n) such that the function has the same value at each of them.

5. Find the first partial derivatives of the following functions:

a) $(\sin xy)^2$, **b)** $\sin[(xy)^2]$.

6. Let α, β, γ be the direction angles of a line and consider γ as a function of α and β. Find the value of $\partial\gamma/\partial\alpha$ when $\alpha = \pi/4$, $\beta = \pi/3$, $\gamma = \pi/3$.

7. Let (r, θ) and (x, y) be polar coordinates and cartesian coordinates in the plane. Show geometrically why $\partial r/\partial x$ is not equal to $(\partial x/\partial r)^{-1}$, by appealing to the definitions of these derivatives.

8. Consider the surface whose equation is $x^3z + y^2x^2 + \sin(yz) + 54 = 0$. Give an equation of the tangent plane to the surface at the point $P(3, 0, -2)$, and give equations of the straight line through P normal to the surface. Determine direction cosines of the line.

9. (a) Sketch and name the surface $x^2 - y^2 + z^2 = 4$. (b) Find a vector that is normal to this surface at $(2, -3, 3)$. (c) Find equations of the surface's tangent plane and normal line at $(2, -3, 3)$.

10. (a) Find an equation of the plane tangent to the surface

$$x^3 + xy^2 + y^3 + z^3 + 1 = 0$$

at the point $(-2, 1, 2)$. (b) Find equations of the straight line perpendicular to the plane above at the point $(-2, 1, 2)$.

11. The directional derivative of a given function $w = f(x, y)$ at the point $P_0(1, 2)$ in the direction toward $P_1(2, 3)$ is $2\sqrt{2}$, and in the direction toward $P_2(1, 0)$ it is -3. Compute $\partial f/\partial x$ and $\partial f/\partial y$ at $P_0(1, 2)$, and compute the directional derivative dw/ds at $P_0(1, 2)$ in the direction toward $P_3(4, 6)$.

12. Let $z = f(x, y)$ have continuous first partial derivatives. Let C be any curve lying on the surface and passing through (x_0, y_0, z_0). Prove that the tangent line to C at (x_0, y_0, z_0) must lie wholly in the plane determined by the tangent lines to the curves C_x and C_y, where C_x is the curve of intersection of $y = y_0$ and $z = f(x, y)$, and C_y is the curve of intersection of $x = x_0$ and the surface.

13. Let $u = xyz$. Show that if x and y are the independent variables (so u and z are functions of x and y), then

$$\partial u/\partial x = xy\,(\partial z/\partial x) + yz;$$

but that if x, y, and z are the independent variables,

$$\partial u/\partial x = yz.$$

14. Let

$$\mathbf{u} = u_1\mathbf{i} + u_2\mathbf{j} + u_3\mathbf{k}$$

and

$$\mathbf{v} = v_1\mathbf{i} + v_2\mathbf{j} + v_3\mathbf{k}$$

be given constant unit vectors and let $f(x, y, z)$ be a given scalar function. Compute (a) the directional derivative $D_u f$, and (b) the directional derivative $D_v(D_u f)$, in terms of derivatives of f and the components of **u** and **v**. (Here $D_u f$ denotes df/ds in the direction of **u**.)

15. Consider the function $w = xyz$. (a) Compute the directional derivative of w at the point $(1, 1, 1)$ in the direction of the vector $\mathbf{i} + \mathbf{j} + \mathbf{k}$. (b) Compute the largest value of the directional derivative of w at the point $(1, 1, 1)$.

16. The function $w = f(x, y)$ has, at the point $(1, 2)$, directional derivatives that are equal to $+2$ in the direction toward $(2, 2)$, and -2 in the direction toward $(1, 1)$. What is its directional derivative at $(1, 2)$ in the direction toward $(4, 6)$?

17. Given the function $f(x, y, z) = x^2 + y^2 - 3z$, what is the maximum value of the directional derivative df/ds at the point $(1, 3, 5)$?

18. Given the function

$$(x - 1)^2 + 2(y + 1)^2 + 3(z - 2)^2 - 6.$$

Find the directional derivative of the function at the point $(2, 0, 1)$ in the direction of the vector $\mathbf{i} - \mathbf{j} + 2\mathbf{k}$.

19. Find the derivative of the function

$$f(x, y, z) = x^2 - 2y^2 + z^2$$

at the point $(3, 3, 1)$ in the direction of the vector $2\mathbf{i} + \mathbf{j} - \mathbf{k}$.

20. The two equations

$$e^u \cos v - x = 0 \quad \text{and} \quad e^u \sin v - y = 0$$

define u and v as functions of x and y, say $u = u(x, y)$ and $v = v(x, y)$. Show that the angle between the two vectors

$$\left(\frac{\partial u}{\partial x}\right)\mathbf{i} + \left(\frac{\partial u}{\partial y}\right)\mathbf{j} \quad \text{and} \quad \left(\frac{\partial v}{\partial x}\right)\mathbf{i} + \left(\frac{\partial v}{\partial y}\right)\mathbf{j}$$

is constant.

21. (a) Find a vector $\mathbf{N}(x, y, z)$ normal to the surface $z = \sqrt{x^2 + y^2} + (x^2 + y^2)^{3/2}$ at the point (x, y, z) of the surface. (b) Find the cosine of the angle γ between $\mathbf{N}(x, y, z)$ and the z-axis. Find the limit of $\cos\gamma$ as $(x, y, z) \to (0, 0, 0)$.

22. Find all points (a, b, c) in space for which the spheres

$$(x - a)^2 + (y - b)^2 + (z - c)^2 = 1$$

and

$$x^2 + y^2 + z^2 = 1$$

will intersect orthogonally. (Their tangents are to be perpendicular at each point of intersection.)

23. (a) Find the gradient, at $P_0(1, -1, 3)$, of the function

$$x^2 + 2xy - y^2 + z^2.$$

(b) Find the plane that is tangent to the surface $x^2 + 2xy - y^2 + z^2 = 7$ at $P_0(1, -1, 3)$.

24. Find a unit vector normal to the surface $x^2 + y^2 = 3z$ at the point $(1, 3, \frac{10}{3})$.

25. In a flowing fluid, the density $\rho(x, y, z, t)$ depends on position and time. If

$$\mathbf{V} = \mathbf{V}(x, y, z, t)$$

is the velocity of the fluid particle at the point (x, y, z) at time t, then

$$\frac{d\rho}{dt} = \mathbf{V} \cdot \nabla\rho + \frac{\partial\rho}{\partial t} = V_1\frac{\partial\rho}{\partial x} + V_2\frac{\partial\rho}{\partial y} + V_3\frac{\partial\rho}{\partial z} + \frac{\partial\rho}{\partial t},$$

where $\mathbf{V} = V_1\mathbf{i} + V_2\mathbf{j} + V_3\mathbf{k}$. Explain the physical and geometrical meaning of this relation.

26. Find a constant a such that, at any point of intersection of the two spheres

$$(x - a)^2 + y^2 + z^2 = 3 \quad \text{and} \quad x^2 + (y - 1)^2 + z^2 = 1,$$

their tangent planes will be perpendicular to each other.

27. If the gradient of a function $f(x, y, z)$ is always parallel to the vector $x\mathbf{i} + y\mathbf{j} + z\mathbf{k}$, show that the function must assume the same value at the points $(0, 0, a)$ and $(0, 0, -a)$.

28. Let $f(P)$ denote a function defined for points P in the plane; i.e., to each point P there is attached a real number $f(P)$. Explain how one could introduce the notions of continuity and differentiability of the function and define the vector ∇f *without* introducing a coordinate system. If one introduces a polar coordinate system $r, \theta, \mathbf{U}_r, \mathbf{U}_\theta$, what form does the vector $\nabla f(r, \theta)$ take?

29. Show that the directional derivative of

$$r = \sqrt{x^2 + y^2 + z^2}$$

equals unity in any direction at the origin, but that r does not have a gradient vector at the origin.

30. Let $\mathbf{R} = x\mathbf{i} + y\mathbf{j} + z\mathbf{k}$ and $r = |\mathbf{R}|$. (a) From its geometrical interpretation, show that $\nabla r = \mathbf{R}/r$. (b) Show that $\nabla(r^n) = nr^{n-2}\mathbf{R}$. (c) Find a function with gradient equal to $\mathbf{R}$. (d) Show that $\mathbf{R} \cdot d\mathbf{R} = r\,dr$. (e) If $\mathbf{A}$ is a constant vector, show that $\nabla(\mathbf{A} \cdot \mathbf{R}) = \mathbf{A}$.

31. If θ is the polar coordinate in the xy-plane, find the direction and magnitude of $\nabla\theta$.

32. If r_1, r_2 are the distances from the point $P(x, y)$ on an ellipse to its foci, show that the equation $r_1 + r_2 =$ const., satisfied by these distances, requires $\mathbf{U} \cdot \nabla(r_1 + r_2) = 0$, where $\mathbf{U}$ is a unit tangent to the curve. By geometrical interpretation, show that the tangent makes equal angles with the lines to the foci.

33. If A, B are fixed points and θ is the angle at $P(x, y, z)$ subtended by the line segment AB, show that $\nabla\theta$ is normal to the circle through A, B, P.

34. Find the general solution of the partial differential equations:

a) $af_x + bf_y = 0$, a, b constants, **b)** $yf_x - xf_y = 0$.

[*Hint.* Consider the geometrical meaning of the equations.]

35. When y is eliminated from the two equations $z = f(x, y)$ and $g(x, y) = 0$, the result is expressible in the form $z = h(x)$. Express the derivative $h'(x)$ in terms of $\partial f/\partial x$, $\partial f/\partial y$, $\partial g/\partial x$, $\partial g/\partial y$. Check your formula by computing $h(x)$ and $h'(x)$ explicitly in the example where $f(x, y) = x^2 + y^2$ and $g(x, y) = x^3 + y^2 - x$.

36. Suppose the equation $F(x, y, z) = 0$ defines z as a function of x and y, say $z = f(x, y)$, with derivatives $\partial f/\partial x$ and $\partial f/\partial y$. Suppose also that the same equation $F(x, y, z) = 0$ defines x as a function of y and z, say $x = g(y, z)$, with derivatives $\partial g/\partial y$ and $\partial g/\partial z$. Prove that

$$\frac{\partial g}{\partial y} = -\frac{\partial f/\partial y}{\partial f/\partial x},$$

and also express $\partial g/\partial z$ in terms of $\partial f/\partial x$ and $\partial f/\partial y$.

37. Given $z = x \sin x - y^2$, $\cos y = y \sin z$, find dx/dz.

38. If

$$z = f\left(\frac{x - y}{y}\right),$$

show that $x(\partial z/\partial x) + y(\partial z/\partial y) = 0$.

39. If the substitution $u = (x - y)/2$, $v = (x + y)/2$, changes $f(u, v)$ into $F(x, y)$, express $\partial F/\partial x$ and $\partial F/\partial y$ in terms of the derivatives of $f(u, v)$ with respect to u and v.

40. Given $w = f(x, y)$ with $x = u + v$, $y = u - v$, show that

$$\frac{\partial^2 w}{\partial u\,\partial v} = \frac{\partial^2 w}{\partial x^2} - \frac{\partial^2 w}{\partial y^2}.$$

41. Suppose $f(x, y, z)$ is a function that has continuous partial derivatives and satisfies $f(tx, ty, tz) = t^n f(x, y, z)$ for every quadruple of numbers x, y, z, t (where n is a fixed integer). Show the identity

$$\frac{\partial f}{\partial x}x + \frac{\partial f}{\partial y}y + \frac{\partial f}{\partial z}z = nf.$$

[*Hint.* Differentiate with respect to t; then set $t = 1$.]

42. The substitution $u = x + y$, $v = xy^2$ changes the function $f(u, v)$ into $F(x, y)$. Express the partial derivative $\partial^2 F/\partial x\,\partial y$ in terms of x, y, and the partial derivatives of $f(u, v)$ with respect to u, v.

43. Given $z = u(x, y) \cdot e^{ax+by}$, where $u(x, y)$ is a function of x and y such that $\partial^2 u/\partial x\,\partial y = 0$, ($a$, b constants). Find values of a and b that will make the expression $\partial^2 z/\partial x\,\partial y - \partial z/\partial x - \partial z/\partial y + z$ identically zero.

44. Introducing polar coordinates, $x = r\cos\theta$, $y = r\sin\theta$, changes $f(x, y)$ into $g(r, \theta)$. Compute the value of the second derivative $\partial^2 g/\partial\theta^2$ at the point where $r = 2$ and $\theta = \pi/2$, given that $\partial f/\partial x = \partial f/\partial y = \partial^2 f/\partial x^2 = \partial^2 f/\partial y^2 = 1$ at that point.

45. Let $w = f(u, v)$ be a function of u, v with continuous partial derivatives, where u, v in turn are functions of independent variables, x, y, z, with continuous partial derivatives. Show that if w is regarded as a function of x, y, z, its gradient at any point (x_0, y_0, z_0) lies in a common plane with the gradients of $u = u(x, y, z)$ and $v = v(x, y, z)$.

46. Show that if a function u has first derivatives that satisfy a relation of the form $F(u_x, u_y) = 0$, and if $\partial F/\partial u_x$ and $\partial F/\partial u_y$ are not both zero, then u also satisfies $u_{xx}u_{yy} - u_{xy}^2 = 0$. [*Hint.* Differentiate $F = 0$ with respect to x and y.]

47. If $f(x, y) = 0$, find d^2y/dx^2.

48. If $F(x, y, z) = 0$, show that $(\partial x/\partial y)_z(\partial y/\partial z)_x \times (\partial z/\partial x)_y = -1$. [Here $(\partial x/\partial y)_z$ denotes that z is held constant while we compute the partial derivative of x with respect to y, etc.]

49. If $f(x, y, z) = 0$ and $z = x + y$, find dz/dx.

50. The function $v(x, t)$ is defined for $0 \leq x \leq 1$, $0 \leq t$ and

satisfies the partial differential equation

$$v_t = v_x(v - x) + av_{xx}$$

(a = constant > 0) and the boundary conditions $v(0, t) = 0$, $v(1, t) = 1$. Suppose that for each fixed t, $v(x, t)$ is a strictly increasing function of x; that is, $v_x(x, t) > 0$. Show that v and t may be introduced as independent variables and x as dependent variable, and find the partial differential equation satisfied by the function $x(v, t)$. Find also the region of definition of $x(v, t)$ and boundary values that it satisfies. By considering level curves, show geometrically why the assumption $v_x(x, t) > 0$ is necessary for the success of this transformation.

51. Let $f(x, y, z)$ be a function depending only on $r = \sqrt{x^2 + y^2 + z^2}$; that is, $f(x, y, z) = g(r)$. Prove that if $f_{xx} + f_{yy} + f_{zz} = 0$, it follows that

$$f = \left(\frac{a}{r}\right) + b,$$

where a and b are constants.

52. A function $f(x, y)$, defined and differentiable for all x, y, is said to be homogeneous of degree n (a nonnegative integer) if $f(tx, ty) = t^n f(x, y)$ for all t, x, and y. For such a function prove: (a) $x(\partial f/\partial x) + y(\partial f/\partial y) = nf(x, y)$ and express this in vector form; (b) $x^2(\partial^2 f/\partial x^2) + 2xy(\partial^2 f/\partial x\, \partial y) + y^2(\partial^2 f/\partial y^2) = n(n-1)f$, if f has continuous second partial derivatives; (c) a homogeneous function of degree zero is a constant.

53. Prove the Mean Value Theorem for functions of two variables

$$f(x + h, y + k) - f(x, y) = f_x(x + \theta h, y + \theta k)h + f_y(x + \theta h, y + \theta k)k, \quad 0 < \theta < 1,$$

with suitable assumptions about f. What assumptions? [*Hint.* Apply the Mean Value Theorem for functions of one variable to $F(t) = f(x + ht, y + kt)$.]

54. Prove the theorem: If $f(x, y)$ is defined in a region R, and f_x, f_y exist and are bounded in R, then $f(x, y)$ is continuous in R. (The assumption of boundedness is essential.)

55. Using differentials, find a reasonable approximation to the value of

$$w = xy\sqrt{x^2 + y^2}$$

at $x = 2.98$, $y = 4.04$.

56. A flat circular plate has the shape of the region $x^2 + y^2 \leq 1$. The plate (including the boundary, where $x^2 + y^2 = 1$) is heated so that the temperature T at any point (x, y) is

$$T = x^2 + 2y^2 - x.$$

Locate the hottest and coldest point of the plate and find the temperature at each of these points.

57. The temperature T at any point (x, y, z) in space is $T = 400xyz^2$. Find the highest temperature on the surface of the unit sphere

$$x^2 + y^2 + z^2 = 1.$$

58. For each of the following three surfaces, find all the values of x and y for which z is a maximum or minimum (if there are any). Give complete reasonings.

a) $x^2 + y^2 + z^2 = 3$, **b)** $x^2 + y^2 = 2z$, **c)** $x^2 - y^2 = 2z$.

59. Find the point(s) on the surface $xyz = 1$ whose distance from the origin is a minimum.

60. A closed rectangular box is to be made to hold a given volume, V in^3. The cost of the material used in the box is a cents/in^2 for top and bottom, b cents/in^2 for front and back, c cents/in^2 for the remaining two sides. What dimensions make the total cost of materials a minimum?

61. Find the maximum value of the function $xye^{-(2x+3y)}$ in the first quadrant.

62. A surface is defined by $z = x^3 + y^3 - 9xy + 27$. Prove that the only possible maxima and minima of z occur at $(0, 0)$ or $(3, 3)$. Prove that $(0, 0)$ is neither a maximum nor a minimum. Determine whether $(3, 3)$ is a maximum or a minimum.

63. Given n positive numbers $a_1, a_2, \ldots, a_n$. Find the maximum value of the expression $a_1x_1 + a_2x_2 + \cdots + a_nx_n$ if the variables $x_1, x_2, \ldots, x_n$ are restricted so that the sum of their squares is 1.

64. Find the minimum volume bounded by the planes $x = 0$, $y = 0$, $z = 0$, and a plane that is tangent to the ellipsoid

$$\frac{x^2}{a^2} + \frac{y^2}{b^2} + \frac{z^2}{c^2} = 1$$

at a point in the octant $x > 0$, $y > 0$, $z > 0$.

65. Among the points $P(x, y)$ on the level curve $\phi(x, y) = 0$, it is desired to find one where the function $f(x, y)$ has a (relative) maximum. Assuming that such a point, p_0, exists, show that at p_0 the vectors ∇f and $\nabla\phi$ are parallel so that there is a number λ_0 such that $(\nabla f)_0 = \lambda_0(\nabla\phi)_0$. Explain geometrically by considering the level curves of f and ϕ.

66. Let z be defined implicitly as a function of x and y by the equation $\sin(x + y) + \sin(y + z) = 1$. Compute $\partial^2 z/\partial x\, \partial y$ in terms of x, y, and z.

67. Given $z = xy^2 - y \sin x$, calculate the value of $y(\partial^2 z/\partial y\, \partial x) - \partial z/\partial x$.

68. Let $w = z \tan^{-1}(x/y)$. Compute

$$\frac{\partial^2 w}{\partial x^2} + \frac{\partial^2 w}{\partial y^2} + \frac{\partial^2 w}{\partial z^2}.$$

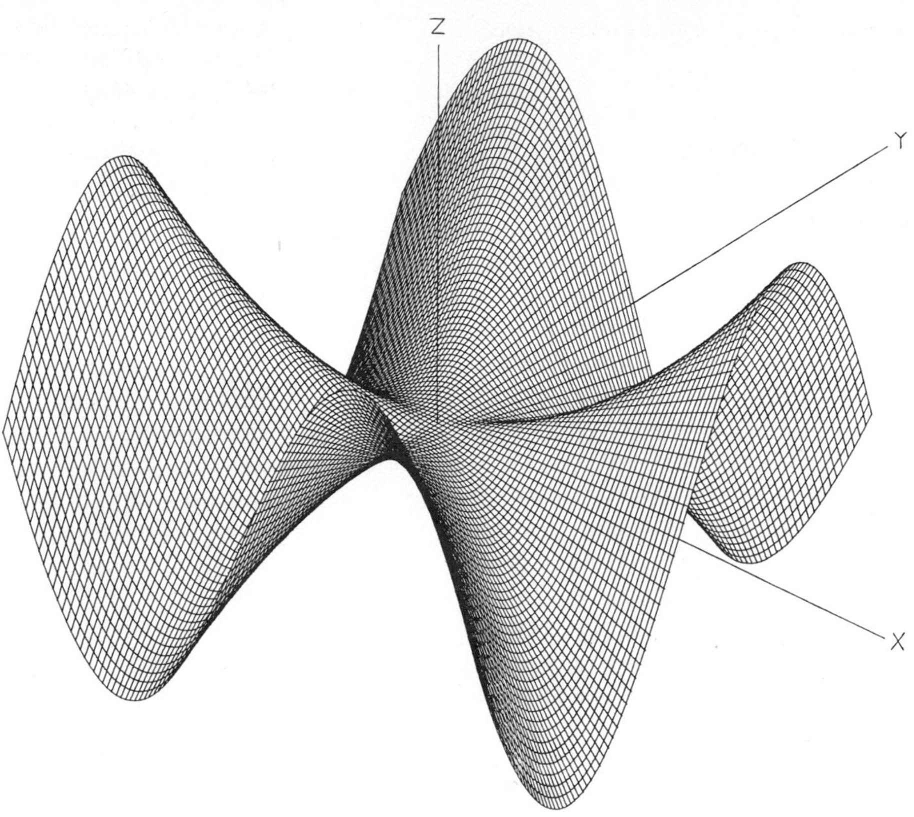

Figure 13–33. The surface of Problem 70. (Courtesy of Norton Starr, Amherst College.)

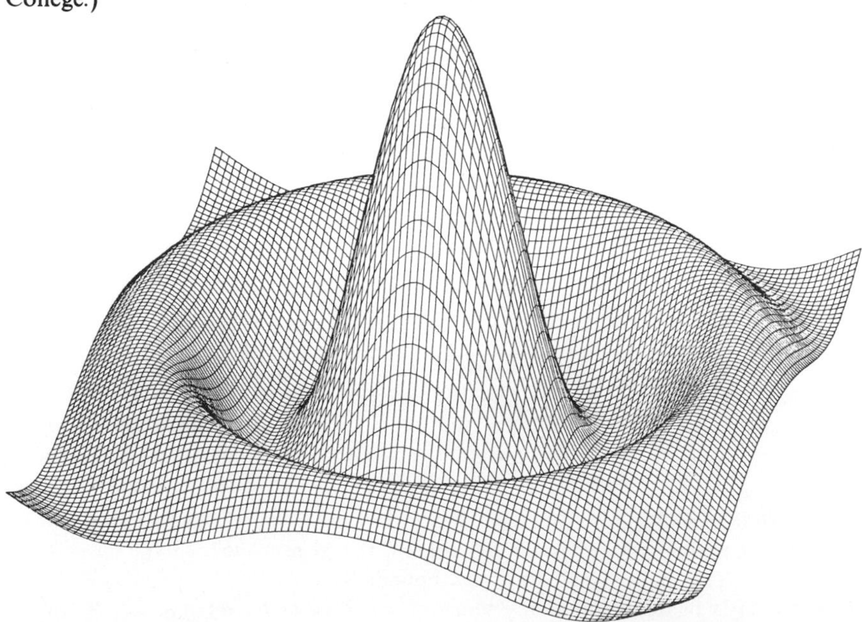

Figure 13–34. The surface of Problem 75. (Courtesy of Norton Starr, Amherst College.)

69. Show that the function satisfies the equation:

a) $\log\sqrt{x^2+y^2}$, $f_{xx}+f_{yy}=0$

b) $\sqrt{(x^2+y^2+z^2)^{-1}}$, $f_{xx}+f_{yy}+f_{zz}=0$

c) $\int_0^{x/2\sqrt{kt}} e^{-\sigma^2}\,d\sigma$, $kf_{xx}-f_t=0$ (k const.)

d) $\phi(x+at)+\psi(x-at)$, $f_{tt}=a^2 f_{xx}$

70. Consider the function defined by

$$f(x,y)=\begin{cases} xy\dfrac{x^2-y^2}{x^2+y^2}, & (x,y)\neq(0,0),\\ 0, & (x,y)=(0,0). \end{cases}$$

Then find $f_{yx}(0,0)$ and $f_{xy}(0,0)$. See Fig. 13–33.

71. Is $2x(x^3+y^3)\,dx+3y^2(x^2+y^2)\,dy$ the total differential df of a function $f(x,y)$? If so, find the function.

72. Find a function $f(x,y)$ whose differential is

$$df=\left(\frac{y}{x}+e^y\right)dx+(\ln x+2y+xe^y)\,dy,$$

or else show that no such function exists.

73. Find a function $w=f(x,y)$ such that $\partial w/\partial x=1+e^x\cos y$ and $\partial w/\partial y=2y-e^x\sin y$, or else explain why no such function exists.

74. In thermodynamics the five quantities S, T, u, p, v are such that any two of them may be considered independent variables, the others then being determined. They are connected by the differential relation $T\,dS=du+p\,dv$. Show that

$$\left(\frac{\partial S}{\partial v}\right)_T=\left(\frac{\partial p}{\partial T}\right)_v \quad\text{and}\quad \left(\frac{\partial v}{\partial S}\right)_p=\left(\frac{\partial T}{\partial p}\right)_S.$$

75. Let

$$f(r,\theta)=\begin{cases} \dfrac{\sin 6r}{6r}, & r\neq 0\\ 1, & r=0. \end{cases}$$

(See Fig. 13–34.) Find (a) $\lim_{r\to 0} f(r,\theta)$, (b) $f_r(0,0)$, (c) $f_\theta(r,\theta)$, $r\neq 0$.

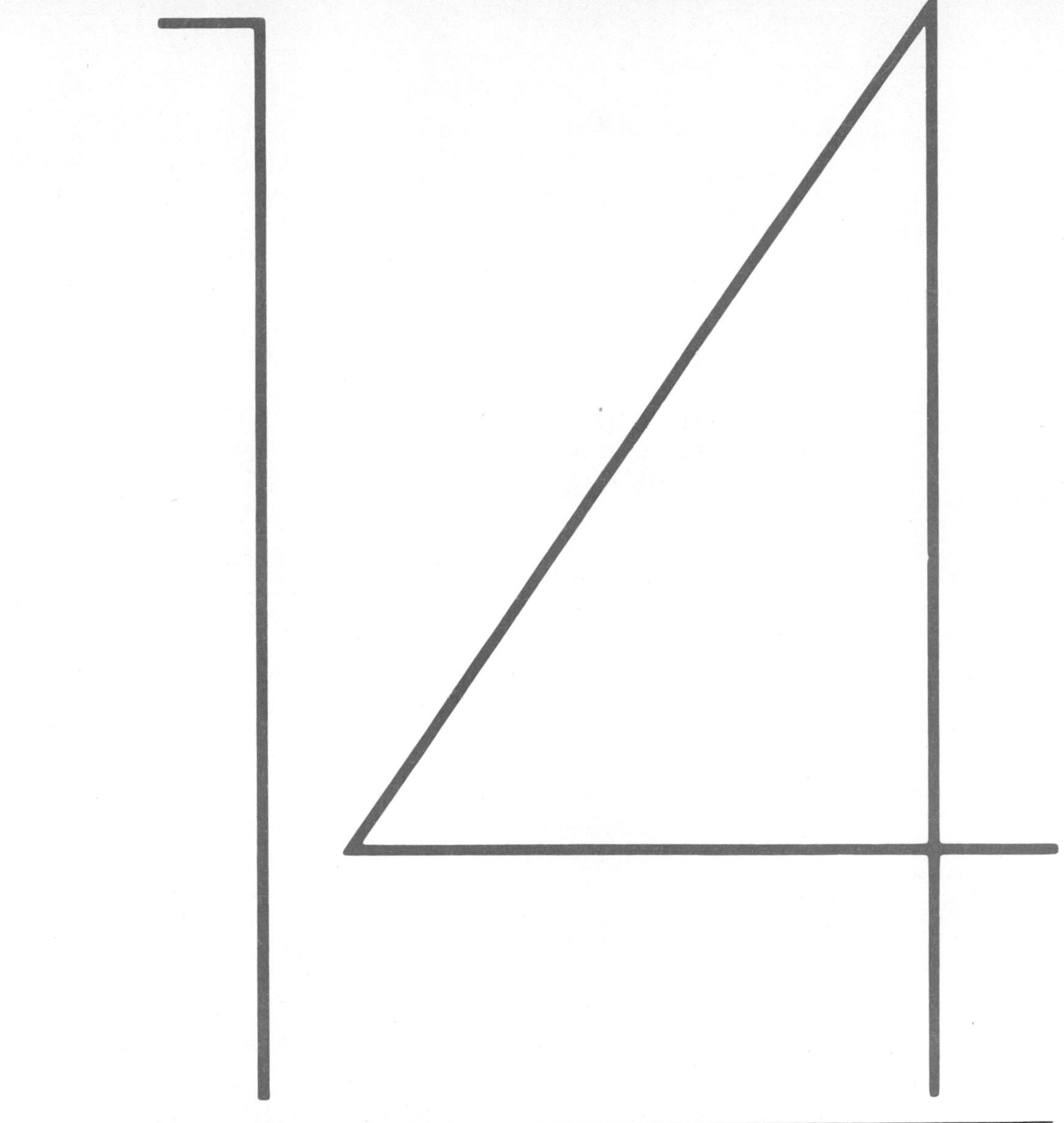

MULTIPLE INTEGRALS

14–1 DOUBLE INTEGRALS

We shall show how to use the method of double integration to calculate the area or center of gravity of the region A (Fig. 14–1) which is bounded above by the curve $y = f_2(x)$, below by $y = f_1(x)$, on the left by the line $x = a$, and on the right by $x = b$. Before taking up the specific applications referred to, we shall first define what we mean by the double integral of a function $F(x, y)$ of two variables x and y. Then the specific applications follow at once by specializing the function $F(x, y)$ to be

a) $F(x, y) = 1$, or **b)** $F(x, y) = y$

for the calculation of

a) the area, or

b) the moment of the area about the x-axis.

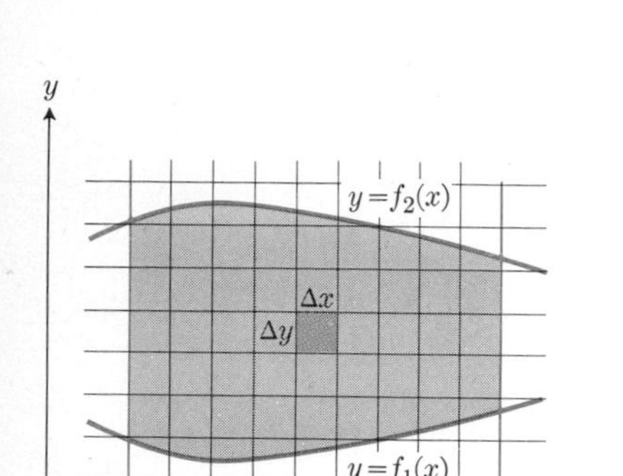

14–1 Region with rectangular grid.

The notation

$$\iint_A F(x, y)\, dA, \tag{1}$$

is used to denote the double integral, over the region A, of the function $F(x, y)$.

We imagine the region A to be covered by a grid of lines parallel to the x- and y-axes. These lines divide the plane into small pieces of area

$$\Delta A = \Delta x\, \Delta y = \Delta y\, \Delta x, \tag{2}$$

some of which lie entirely within the given region, some entirely outside of the region, and some of which are intersected by the boundary of the region. We disregard all those that lie outside the region and may or may not take into account those that lie only partly inside, but we do take into consideration all the ΔA pieces that lie completely inside. We number these in some order, as

$$\Delta A_1, \quad \Delta A_2, \quad \ldots, \quad \Delta A_n, \tag{3}$$

choose a point (x_k, y_k) in each ΔA_k, and form the sum

$$S_n = \sum_{k=1}^{n} F(x_k, y_k)\, \Delta A_k. \tag{4}$$

If the function $F(x, y)$ is continuous throughout A and if the curves that form the boundary of A are continuous and have a finite total length, then, as we refine the mesh width in such a way that Δx and Δy tend to zero (we may, for example, take $\Delta y = 2\,\Delta x$ and then make $\Delta x \to 0$), the limit

$$I = \lim_{\Delta A \to 0} \sum_{k=1}^{n} F(x_k, y_k)\, \Delta A_k \tag{5}$$

exists. It is this limit that is indicated by the notation in Eq. (1).

The double integral (1) can also be interpreted as a volume, at least in the case where $F(x, y)$ is positive. Suppose, for example, that the region A is the base of a solid (Fig. 14–2) whose altitude above the point (x, y) is given by

$$z = F(x, y).$$

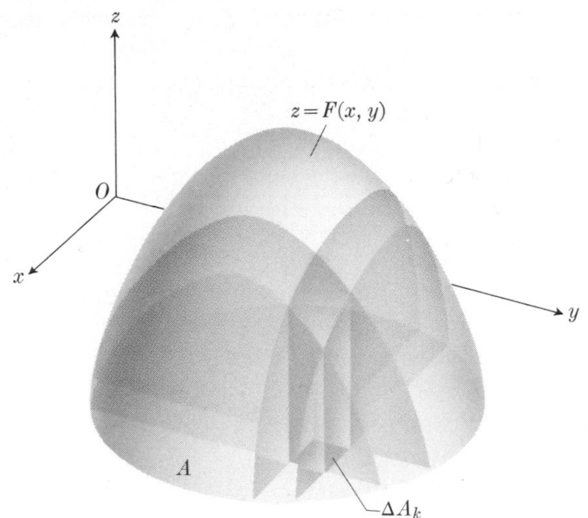

14–2 Approximating a volume by vertical prisms.

Then the term

$$F(x_k, y_k)\,\Delta A_k$$

is a reasonable approximation to the volume of that portion of the solid that rests upon the base ΔA_k. The sum S_n in Eq. (4) then gives an approximation to the total volume of the solid, and the limit in Eq. (5) gives what we call the exact volume.

Just as with integrals in one variable, the use of double integrals would be severely limited if it were necessary to calculate them directly from the definition in Eq. (5). Fortunately, it is possible to evaluate double integrals by evaluating successive single integrals. That is, in practice, the double integral in (1) is evaluated by calculating either one of the two *iterated integrals*

$$\int_A\!\int F(x, y)\,dx\,dy \qquad \text{or} \qquad \int_A\!\int F(x, y)\,dy\,dx, \tag{6}$$

as we shall explain below. A theorem of analysis, which we shall not prove here, asserts that the iterated integrals (6) are equal to each other and to the double integral (1) whenever the function $F(x, y)$ is continuous over A and the boundary of A is not too complicated. The necessary conditions are fulfilled in the examples and problems in this book. [For more details see Franklin, *A Treatise on Advanced Calculus* (Dover, 1961); Chapter XI.]

The iterated integral

$$\int_A\!\int F(x, y)\,dy\,dx$$

is the result of:

a) integrating $\int F(x, y)\,dy$ with respect to y (with x held fixed) and evaluating the resulting integral between the limits $y = f_1(x)$ and $y = f_2(x)$; then

b) integrating the result of (a) with respect to x between the limits $x = a$ and $x = b$.

That is, we start with the innermost integral and perform successive integrations as follows:

$$\int_A\int F(x, y)\, dy\, dx = \int_a^b \left(\int_{f_1(x)}^{f_2(x)} F(x, y)\, dy\right) dx, \tag{7}$$

treating x as a constant while we perform the y integration.

We can gain some insight into the geometrical significance of Eq. (7) as follows: We may again think of a solid with base covering the region A of the xy-plane and having altitude $z = F(x, y)$ at the point (x, y) of A. (Assume, for sake of simplicity, that F is positive.) Then imagine a slice cut from the solid by planes perpendicular to the x-axis at x and at $x + dx$. We may think of this as approximated by the differential of volume given by

$$dV = A(x)\, dx,$$

where $A(x)$ is the cross-sectional area cut from the solid by the plane at x. Now this cross-sectional area (Fig. 14–3) is given by the integral

$$A(x) = \int_{f_1(x)}^{f_2(x)} z\, dy = \int_{f_1(x)}^{f_2(x)} F(x, y)\, dy,$$

where x is held fixed and the limits of integration depend upon where the cutting plane is taken. That is, the y-limits are functions of x, the functions that represent the boundary curves. Then, finally, we see that the iterated integral in Eq. (7) is the same as

$$V = \int_a^b A(x)\, dx = \int_a^b \left(\int_{f_1(x)}^{f_2(x)} F(x, y)\, dy\right) dx.$$

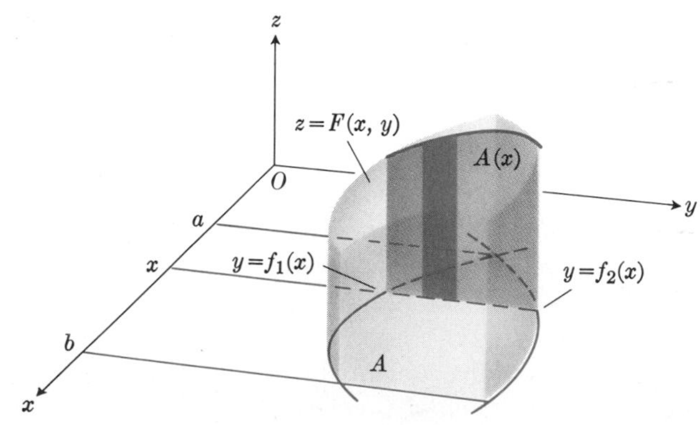

14–3 The area of the vertical slice shown above is

$$A(x) = \int_{f_1(x)}^{f_2(x)} F(x, y)\, dy.$$

This area is integrated from a to b to calculate the volume.

EXAMPLE 1. Find the volume of the solid whose base is in the xy-plane and is the triangle bounded by the x-axis, the line $y = x$, and the line $x = 1$, while the top of the solid is in the plane

$$z = F(x, y) = 3 - x - y.$$

Solution. The volume dV of a representative prism of altitude z and base $dy\,dx$ is

$$dV = (3 - x - y)\,dy\,dx.$$

For any x between 0 and 1, y may vary from $y = 0$ to $y = x$ (Fig. 14–4). Hence,

$$V = \int_0^1 \int_0^x (3 - x - y)\,dy\,dx = \int_0^1 \left[3y - xy - \frac{y^2}{2}\right]_{y=0}^{y=x} dx$$

$$= \int_0^1 \left(3x - \frac{3x^2}{2}\right) dx = \frac{3x^2}{2} - \frac{x^3}{2}\bigg]_{x=0}^{x=1} = 1.$$

When the order of integration is reversed, the integral for the volume is

$$V = \int_0^1 \int_y^1 (3 - x - y)\,dx\,dy = \int_0^1 \left[3x - \frac{x^2}{2} - xy\right]_{x=y}^{x=1} dy$$

$$= \int_0^1 \left(3 - \frac{1}{2} - y - 3y + \frac{y^2}{2} + y^2\right) dy$$

$$= \int_0^1 \left(\frac{5}{2} - 4y + \frac{3}{2}y^2\right) dy = \frac{5}{2}y - 2y^2 + \frac{y^3}{2}\bigg]_{y=0}^{y=1} = 1.$$

The two integrals are equal, as they should be.

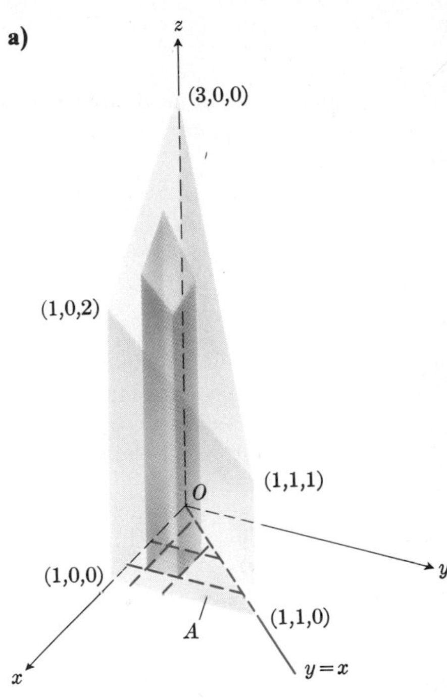

Prism with a triangular base in the xy-plane.

While the iterated integrals in Eq. (6) both give the value of the double integral, they may not be equally easy to compute. The next example shows one way this can happen.

EXAMPLE 2. Calculate

$$\iint_A \frac{\sin x}{x}\,dA,$$

where A is the triangle in the xy-plane bounded by the x-axis, the line $y = x$, and the line $x = 1$.

Solution. The region of integration is the same as the one in Example 1. If we integrate first with respect to y and then with respect to x, we find

$$\int_0^1 \left(\int_0^x \frac{\sin x}{x}\,dy\right) dx = \int_0^1 \left(y\frac{\sin x}{x}\bigg]_{y=0}^{y=x}\right) dx$$

$$= \int_0^1 \sin x\,dx = -\cos(1) + 1 \approx 0.46.$$

If we reverse the order of integration, and attempt to calculate

$$\int_0^1 \int_y^1 \frac{\sin x}{x}\,dx\,dy,$$

we are stopped by the fact that $\int (\sin x/x)\,dx$ cannot be expressed in terms of elementary functions.

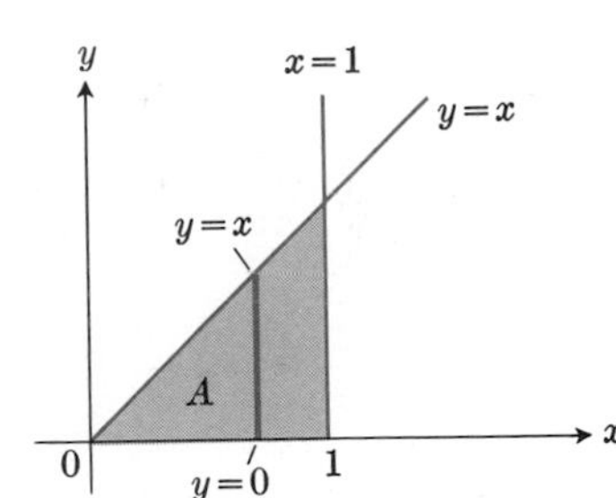

Integration limits of $\int_{x=0}^{x=1} \int_{y=0}^{y=x} F(x, y)\,dy\,dx$

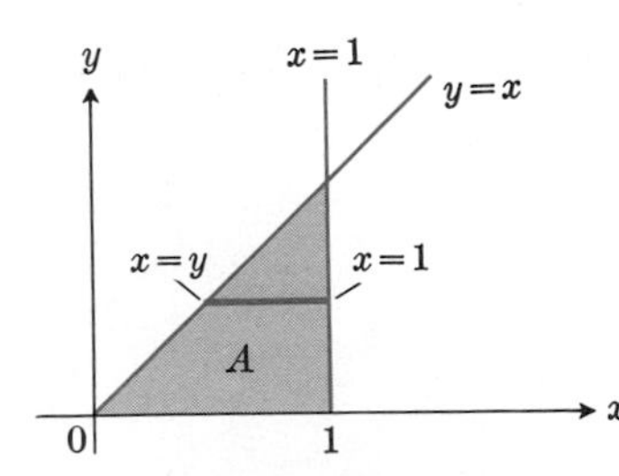

Integration limits of $\int_{y=0}^{y=1} \int_{x=y}^{x=1} F(x, y)\,dx\,dy$

Figure 14–4

PROBLEMS

Evaluate each of the double integrals in Problems 1–4. Also sketch the region A over which the integration extends.

1. $\int_0^{\pi}\int_0^{x} x \sin y \, dy\, dx$

2. $\int_1^{\ln 8}\int_0^{\ln y} e^{x+y}\, dx\, dy$

3. $\int_0^{\pi}\int_0^{\sin x} y\, dy\, dx$

4. $\int_1^{2}\int_y^{y^2} dx\, dy$

Write an equivalent double integral with the order of integration reversed for each of Problems 5–8. Check your answer by evaluating *both* double integrals. Also, sketch the region A over which the integration takes place.

5. $\int_0^{2}\int_1^{e^x} dy\, dx$

6. $\int_0^{1}\int_{\sqrt{y}}^{1} dx\, dy$

7. $\int_0^{\sqrt{2}}\int_{-\sqrt{4-2y^2}}^{\sqrt{4-2y^2}} y\, dx\, dy$

8. $\int_{-2}^{1}\int_{x^2+4x}^{3x+2} dy\, dx$

9. Find the volume of the solid whose base is the region in the xy-plane that is bounded by the parabola $y = 4 - x^2$ and the line $y = 3x$, while the top of the solid is bounded by the plane $z = x + 4$.

10. The base of a solid is the region in the xy-plane that is bounded by the circle $x^2 + y^2 = a^2$, while the top of the solid is bounded by the paraboloid $az = x^2 + y^2$. Find the volume.

14–2 AREA BY DOUBLE INTEGRATION

The simplest application of double integration is that of finding the area of a region of the xy-plane. The area is given by either of the integrals

$$A = \iint dx\, dy = \iint dy\, dx, \tag{1}$$

with proper limits of integration to be supplied. We have already illustrated how this is done for the area shown in Fig. 14–1 when the integrations are carried out in the order of first y and then x, namely,

$$A = \int_a^b \int_{f_1(x)}^{f_2(x)} dy\, dx. \tag{2}$$

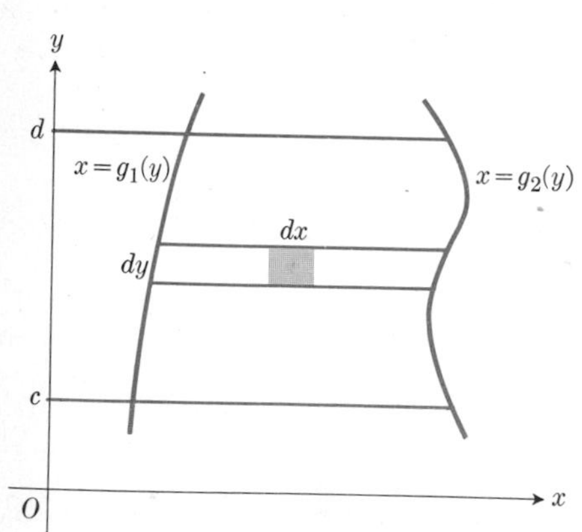

14–5 Area: $\int_c^d \int_{g_1(y)}^{g_2(y)} dx\, dy.$

If, however, the area is bounded on the left by the curve $x = g_1(y)$, on the right by $x = g_2(y)$, below by the line $y = c$, and above by the line $y = d$ (Fig. 14–5), then it is better to integrate first with respect to x [which may vary from $g_1(y)$ to $g_2(y)$] and then with respect to y. That is,

$$A = \int_c^d \int_{g_1(y)}^{g_2(y)} dx\, dy. \tag{3}$$

The first integration, with respect to x, may be visualized as adding together all the representative elements

$$dA = dx\, dy$$

that lie in a horizontal strip that extends from the curve $x = g_1(y)$ on the left to the curve $x = g_2(y)$ on the right. The evaluation of this integral gives

$$A = \int_c^d \int_{g_1(y)}^{g_2(y)} dx\, dy = \int_c^d [x]_{g_1(y)}^{g_2(y)} dy = \int_c^d [g_2(y) - g_1(y)]\, dy.$$

This latter integral could have been written down at once, since it merely expresses the area as the limit of the sum of horizontal strips of area.

EXAMPLE 1. The integral

$$\int_0^1 \int_{x^2}^{x} dy\, dx$$

represents the area of a region of the xy-plane. Sketch the region and express the same area as a double integral with the order of integration reversed.

Solution. In the inner integral, y varies from the curve $y = x^2$ to the line $y = x$. This gives the area of a vertical strip between x and $x + dx$, for values of x from $x = 0$ to $x = 1$. The region of integration is shown in Fig. 14–6. If we integrate in the other order, taking the x integration first, then x varies from the line $x = y$ to the parabola $x = \sqrt{y}$ to fill out a horizontal strip between y and $y + dy$. These strips must then be added together for values of y from 0 to 1. Hence

$$A = \int_0^1 \int_y^{\sqrt{y}} dx\, dy.$$

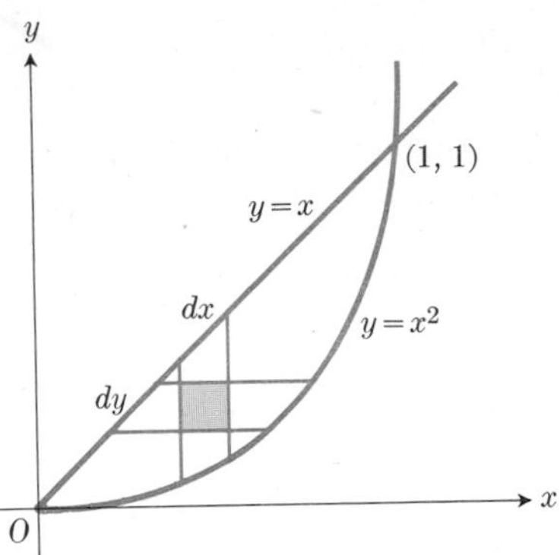

14–6 Area: $\int_0^1 \int_{x^2}^{x} dy\, dx.$

As a check, we evaluate the area by both integrals, and find

$$A = \int_0^1 \int_{x^2}^{x} dy\, dx = \int_0^1 (x - x^2)\, dx = \frac{x^2}{2} - \frac{x^3}{3}\Big]_0^1 = \frac{1}{6}$$

and

$$A = \int_0^1 \int_y^{\sqrt{y}} dx\, dy = \int_0^1 (\sqrt{y} - y)\, dy = \frac{2}{3} y^{3/2} - \frac{y^2}{2}\Big]_0^1 = \frac{1}{6}.$$

EXAMPLE 2. Find the area bounded by the parabola $y = x^2$ and the line $y = x + 2$.

Solution. The area to be found is shown in Fig. 14–7. We imagine a representative element of area

$$dA = dx\, dy = dy\, dx$$

lying in the region and ask ourselves what order of integration we should choose. We see that *horizontal* strips sometimes go from the line to the right branch of the parabola (if $1 \le y \le 4$) but sometimes go from the left branch of the parabola to its right side (if $0 \le y \le 1$). Thus integration in the order of first x and then y requires that the area be taken in two separate pieces, with the result given by

$$A = \int_0^1 \int_{-\sqrt{y}}^{\sqrt{y}} dx\, dy + \int_1^4 \int_{y-2}^{\sqrt{y}} dx\, dy.$$

On the other hand, *vertical* strips always go from the parabola as lower boundary up to the line, and the area is given by

$$A = \int_{-1}^{2} \int_{x^2}^{x+2} dy\, dx.$$

Clearly, this result is simpler and is the only one we would bother to write

a)

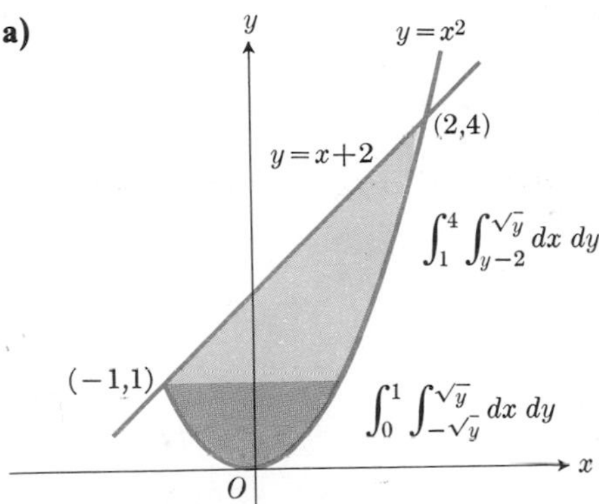

b)

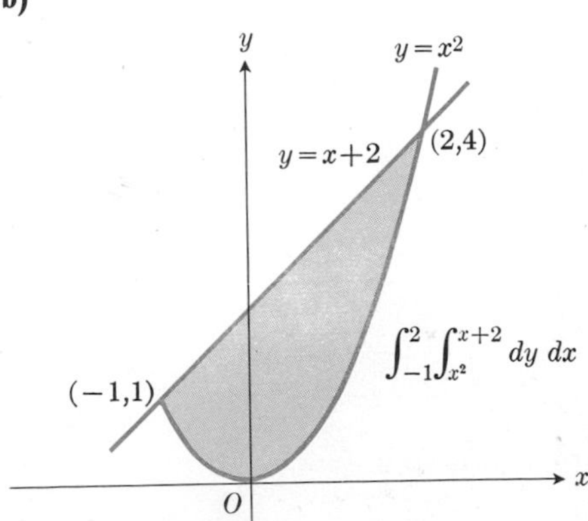

14–7 Calculating the area shown above takes (a) two integrals if the first integration is with respect to x, but (b) only one if the first integration is with respect to y.

down in practice. Evaluation of this integral leads to the result

$$A = \int_{-1}^{2} y\Big]_{x^2}^{x+2} dx$$
$$= \int_{-1}^{2} (x + 2 - x^2)\, dx = \tfrac{9}{2}.$$

PROBLEMS

In each of these problems, find the area of the region bounded by the given curves and lines by means of double integration.

1. The coordinate axes and the line $x + y = a$.
2. The x-axis, the curve $y = e^x$, and the lines $x = 0$, $x = 1$.
3. The y-axis, the line $y = 2x$, and the line $y = 4$.
4. The curve $y^2 + x = 0$, and the line $y = x + 2$.
5. The curves $x = y^2$, $x = 2y - y^2$.
6. The semicircle $y = \sqrt{a^2 - x^2}$, the lines $x = \pm a$, and the line $y = -a$.
7. The parabola $x = y - y^2$ and the line $x + y = 0$.

The integrals in Problems 8–12 give areas of regions in the xy-plane. Sketch each region. Label each bounding curve with its equation, and give the coordinates of the boundary points where the curves intersect.

8. $\int_0^1 \int_y^{\sqrt{y}} dx\, dy$
9. $\int_0^3 \int_{-x}^{x(2-x)} dy\, dx$
10. $\int_0^{\pi/4} \int_{\sin x}^{\cos x} dy\, dx$
11. $\int_{-1}^{2} \int_{y^2}^{y+2} dx\, dy$
12. $\int_{-1}^{0} \int_{-2x}^{1-x} dy\, dx + \int_0^2 \int_{-x/2}^{1-x} dy\, dx$

14-3 PHYSICAL APPLICATIONS

If the representative element of mass dm in a mass that is continuously distributed over some region A of the xy-plane is taken to be

$$dm = \delta(x, y)\, dy\, dx$$
$$= \delta(x, y)\, dA, \tag{1}$$

where $\delta = \delta(x, y)$ is the density at the point (x, y) of A (Fig. 14–8), then double integration may be used to calculate:

a) the mass,
$$M = \iint \delta(x, y)\, dA, \tag{2}$$

b) the first moment of the mass with respect to the x-axis,
$$M_x = \iint y\, \delta(x, y)\, dA, \tag{3a}$$

c) its first moment with respect to the y-axis,
$$M_y = \iint x\, \delta(x, y)\, dA. \tag{3b}$$

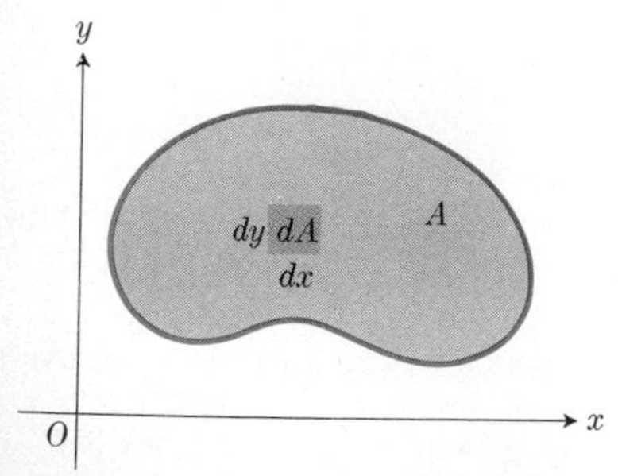

14–8 Area element $dA = dx\, dy$.

From (2) and (3) we get the coordinates of the center of mass,

$$\bar{x} = \frac{M_y}{M}, \qquad \bar{y} = \frac{M_x}{M}.$$

Other moments of importance in physical application are the *moments of inertia* of the mass. These are the *second* moments that we get by using the squares instead of the first powers of the "lever-arm" distances x and y. Thus the moment of inertia about the x-axis, denoted by I_x, is defined by

$$I_x = \iint y^2\, \delta(x, y)\, dA. \tag{4}$$

The moment of inertia about the y-axis is

$$I_y = \iint x^2\, \delta(x, y)\, dA. \tag{5}$$

Also of interest is the *polar moment of inertia* about the origin, I_0, given by

$$I_0 = \iint r^2\, \delta(x, y)\, dA. \tag{6}$$

Here $r^2 = x^2 + y^2$ is the square of the distance from the origin to the representative point (x, y) in the element of mass dm.

In all of these integrals, the same limits of integration are to be supplied as would be called for if one were calculating only the area of A.

REMARK 1. When a particle of mass m is rotating about an axis in a circle of radius r with angular velocity ω and linear velocity $v = \omega r$, its kinetic energy is

$$\tfrac{1}{2}mv^2 = \tfrac{1}{2}mr^2\omega^2.$$

If a system of particles of masses $m_1, m_2, \ldots, m_n$, all rotate about the same axis with the same angular velocity ω but their respective distances from the axis of rotation are $r_1, r_2, \ldots, r_n$, then the kinetic energy of the system of particles is

$$\text{K.E.} = \tfrac{1}{2}(m_1 v_1^2 + \cdots + m_n v_n^2) = \tfrac{1}{2}\omega^2 \sum_{k=1}^{n} m_k r_k^2 = \tfrac{1}{2}\omega^2 I, \tag{7}$$

where

$$I = \sum_{k=1}^{n} m_k r_k^2 \tag{8}$$

is the *moment of inertia* of the system about the axis in question. It depends only upon the magnitudes m_k of the masses and their distances r_k from the axis. When a mass m is moving in a straight line with velocity v, its kinetic energy is $\tfrac{1}{2}mv^2$, and an amount of work equal to this must be expended to stop the object and bring it to rest. Similarly, when a system of mass is moving in a *rotational* motion (like a turning shaft), the kinetic energy it possesses is

$$\text{K.E.} = \tfrac{1}{2}I\omega^2, \tag{9}$$

and this amount of work is required to stop the rotating system. It is seen that I here plays the role that m plays in the case of motion in a straight line. In a sense, the *moment of inertia* of a large shaft is what makes it hard to start or to stop the rotation of the shaft, in the same way that the *mass* of an automobile is what makes it hard to start or to stop its motion.

If, instead of a system of discrete mass particles as in (7) and (8), we have a continuous distribution of mass in a fine wire, or spread out in a thin film or plate over an area, or distributed throughout a solid, then we may divide the total mass into small elements of mass Δm such that if r represents the distance of some *one* point of the element Δm from an axis, then *all* points of that element will be within a distance $r \pm \epsilon$ of the axis, where $\epsilon \to 0$ as the largest dimension of the elements $\Delta m \to 0$. Then we define the moment of inertia of the total mass about the axis in question to be

$$I = \lim_{\Delta m \to 0} \sum r^2 \, \Delta m = \int r^2 \, dm. \tag{10}$$

Thus, for example, the polar moment of inertia, given by Eq. (6), is the moment of inertia with respect to a z-axis through O perpendicular to the xy-plane.

In addition to its importance in connection with the kinetic energy of rotating bodies, the moment of inertia plays an important part in the theory of the deflection of beams under transverse loading, where the "stiffness factor" is given by EI, where E is Young's modulus, and I is the moment of inertia of a cross section of the beam with respect to a horizontal axis through its center of gravity. The greater the value of I, the stiffer the beam and the less it will deflect. This fact is exploited in so-called I-beams, where the flanges at the top and bottom of the beam are at relatively large distances from the center and hence correspond to large values of r^2 in Eq. (10), thereby contributing a larger amount to the moment of inertia than would be the case if the same mass were all distributed uniformly, say in a beam with a square cross section.

REMARK 2. Moments are also of importance in statistics. The *first moment* is used in computing the mean (i.e., average) value of a given set of data. The *second moment* (which corresponds to the moment of inertia) is used in computing the variance (σ^2) or standard deviation (σ). Third and fourth moments are also used for computing statistical quantities known as skewness and kurtosis. The tth moment is defined as

$$M_t = \sum_{k=1}^{n} m_k r_k^t.$$

Here r_k ranges over the values of the statistic under consideration (e.g., r_k might represent height in quarter inches, or weight in ounces, or quiz grades in calculus in percentage points, etc.), while m_k is the number of individuals in the entire group whose "measurements" equal r_k. (For example, if 5 students get a grade of 75 on a quiz, then corresponding to $r_k = 75$ we would have $m_k = 5$.) A table of values of m_k versus r_k is called a "frequency distribution," and one refers to M_t as the tth moment of this frequency distribution. The mean value $\bar{r}$ is defined by

$$\bar{r} = \frac{\sum m_k r_k}{\sum m_k} = \frac{M_1}{m}, \tag{11}$$

where M_1 is the first moment and $m = \sum m_k$ is the total number of individuals in the "population" under consideration. The *variance* σ^2 involves the second moment about the mean. It is defined by

$$\sigma^2 = \frac{\sum (r_k - \bar{r})^2 m_k}{\sum m_k}, \tag{12a}$$

where σ is the so-called *standard deviation*. Both the variance and standard deviation are measures of the way in which the r values tend to bunch up close to $\bar{r}$ (small values of σ) or to be spread out (large values of σ). Algebraic manipulations with (12a) permit one also to write the variance in the alternative form

$$\sigma^2 = \frac{M_2}{m} - \bar{r}^2. \tag{12b}$$

There is a significant difference between the meaning attached to y in the case of the formula

$$A = \int_a^b y\, dx, \tag{13}$$

meaning the area (Fig. 14–9) under a curve $y = f(x)$ from $x = a$ to $x = b$, and the meaning attached to y in these double integrals, Eqs. (2)–(6). In Eq. (13), one must replace y by $f(x)$ from the equation of the curve *before* integrating, because y means the ordinate of the point (x, y) *on* the curve $y = f(x)$. But in the case of the double integrals (2)–(6), one must *not* replace y by a function of x before integrating because the point (x, y) is, in general, a point of the element $dA = dy\, dx$ and both x and y are *independent* variables. The equations of the boundary curves of the region A enter only as the *limits of integration*. Thus:

1. In the case of *single* integrals, such as

$$A = \int_a^b y\, dx, \tag{14}$$

we do not integrate with respect to y and hence we must substitute for it.

2. In the case of *double* integrals, such as

$$I_x = \iint y^2\, \delta\, dy\, dx, \tag{15}$$

we *do* integrate with respect to y and hence we do not substitute for it before performing the y integration. The equations $y = f_1(x)$ and $y = f_2(x)$ of the boundary curves are used as limits of integration and are only to be substituted after the y integration is performed.

a)

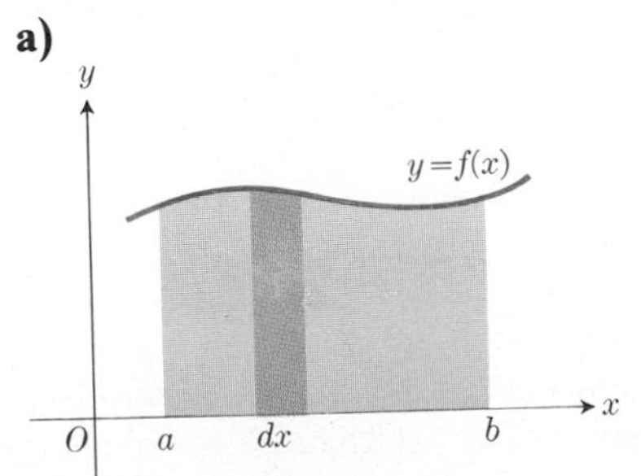

b)

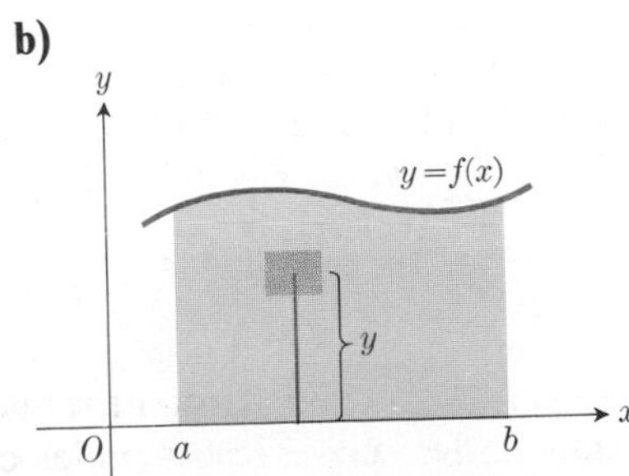

14–9 (a) To calculate $A = \int_a^b y\, dx$, substitute $f(x)$ for y before integrating. (b) To calculate $I_x = \int_a^b \int_0^{f(x)} y^2\, \delta\, dy\, dx$, integrate with respect to y before substituting $f(x)$ for y.

EXAMPLE. A thin plate of uniform thickness and density covers the region of the xy-plane shown in Fig. 14–7. Find its moment of inertia I_y about the y-axis.

Solution. Integrating in the order of first y and then x, we have

$$I_y = \int_{-1}^{2} \int_{x^2}^{x+2} x^2 \, \delta \, dy \, dx$$

$$= \delta \int_{-1}^{2} x^2 y \Big]_{y=x^2}^{y=x+2} dx$$

$$= \delta \int_{-1}^{2} (x^3 + 2x^2 - x^4) \, dx = \tfrac{63}{20} \, \delta.$$

The equation

$$I_y = MR_y^2$$

defines a number

$$R_y = \sqrt{I_y/M},$$

called the *radius of gyration* with respect to the y-axis. It tells how far from the y-axis the entire mass M might be concentrated and still give the same I_y. The mass of the plate in the example above is

$$M = \int_{-1}^{2} \int_{x^2}^{x+2} \delta \, dy \, dx = \tfrac{9}{2} \, \delta.$$

Hence

$$R_y = \sqrt{I_y/M} = \sqrt{7/10}.$$

Note that the density δ in this problem is a constant, and hence we were able to move it outside the integral signs. If the density had been given instead as some variable function of x and y, then we would have taken this into account, in both I_y and M, by simply substituting this function for δ before integrating.

PROBLEMS

1. Find the center of gravity of the area of Problem 1, Article 14–2.

2. Find the moment of inertia, about the x-axis, of the area of Problem 2, Article 14–2. [For an area, we take $\delta = 1$.]

3. Find the polar moment of inertia, about an axis through O perpendicular to the xy-plane, for the area of Problem 3, Article 14–2.

4. Find the center of gravity of the area of Problem 4, Article 14–2.

5. Find the moment of inertia about the x-axis of the area in Problem 5, Article 14–2, if the density at (x, y) is $\delta = y + 1$.

6. Find the center of gravity of the area of Problem 6, Article 14–2, if the density at (x, y) is $\delta = y + a$.

7. Find the moment of inertia, about the x-axis, of the area of Problem 7, Article 14–2, if the density at (x, y) is $\delta = x + y$.

8. For any area in the xy-plane, show that its polar moment of inertia I_0 about an axis through O perpendicular to the xy-plane is equal to $I_x + I_y$.

14–4

POLAR COORDINATES

Let A be a region of the plane bounded by rays $\theta = \alpha$, $\theta = \beta$, and curves $r = f_1(\theta)$, $r = f_2(\theta)$, as in Fig. 14–10. Suppose that A is completely contained in the wedge R

$$R: \quad 0 \le r \le a, \quad \alpha \le \theta \le \beta.$$

Let m and n be positive integers and take

$$\Delta r = \frac{a}{m}, \qquad \Delta\theta = \frac{\beta - \alpha}{n}.$$

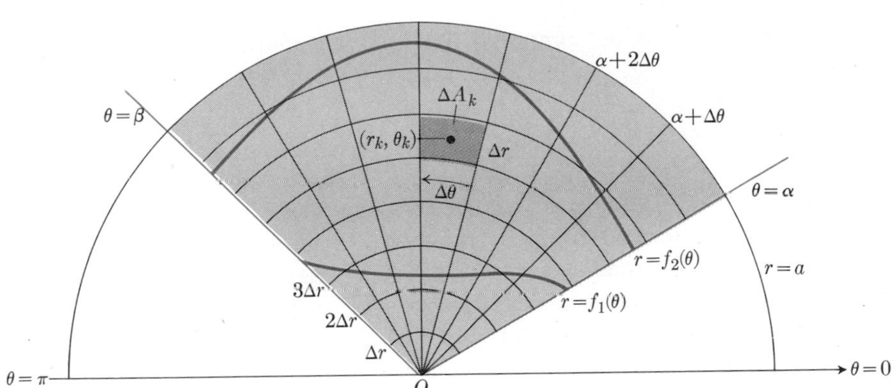

14–10 Subdivision of the region $R: 0 \le r \le a$, $\alpha \le \theta \le \beta$, in polar coordinates: $\Delta A_k = r_k \, \Delta\theta \, \Delta r$.

Now cover R by a grid of circular arcs with centers at O and radii Δr, $2\,\Delta r, \ldots, m\,\Delta r$, and rays through O along $\theta = \alpha$, $\alpha + \Delta\theta$, $\alpha + 2\,\Delta\theta, \ldots$, $\alpha + n\,\Delta\theta = \beta$. This grid partitions R into subregions of three kinds: (a) those exterior to A, (b) those interior to A, and (c) those that intersect the boundary of A. We henceforth ignore those of the first type, but we want to include all those of the second kind, and may include some, none, or all of those of the third kind. Those that are to be included may now be numbered in some order 1, 2, 3, …, N. In the kth subregion so included, let (r_k, θ_k) be the coordinates of its center.* We multiply the value of F at each of these centers by the area of the corresponding subregion and add the products. That is, we consider the sum

$$S = \sum_{k=1}^{N} F(r_k, \theta_k) \cdot \Delta A_k$$

$$= \sum_{k=1}^{N} F(r_k, \theta_k) \cdot r_k \, \Delta\theta \, \Delta r, \tag{1}$$

since

$$\Delta A_k = r_k \, \Delta\theta \, \Delta r, \tag{2}$$

as we shall now see. The radius of the inner arc bounding ΔA_k is $r_k - \frac{1}{2}\Delta r$; of

* We mean the point halfway between the circular arcs, and on the ray that bisects them.

the outer arc, $r_k + \frac{1}{2}\Delta r$. Hence

$$\Delta A_k = \tfrac{1}{2}(r_k + \tfrac{1}{2}\Delta r)^2\,\Delta\theta - \tfrac{1}{2}(r_k - \tfrac{1}{2}\Delta r)^2\,\Delta\theta,$$

and simple algebra reduces this to Eq. (2).

We now imagine this process repeated over and over again with finer and finer grids, and consider the limit of the sums (1) as the diagonals of all subregions approach zero. If the function F is continuous, and the region A is bounded by continuous, rectifiable curves, the sums approach as limit the double integral of F over A:

$$\lim_{N\to\infty} \sum_{k=1}^{N} F(r_k, \theta_k) r_k\,\Delta\theta\,\Delta r = \int_A\!\!\int F(r, \theta)\,dA. \tag{3}$$

This limit may also be computed from the iterated integral on the right below:

$$\int_A\!\!\int F(r, \theta)\,dA = \int_{\theta=\alpha}^{\beta} \int_{r=f_1(\theta)}^{f_2(\theta)} F(r, \theta) r\,dr\,d\theta. \tag{4}$$

The question naturally arises whether one might first set up the double integral in Cartesian coordinates and then change to polar coordinates.

A rigorous treatment of the problem of changing the variables in a double integral may be found in Franklin, *A Treatise on Advanced Calculus*, p. 368. We shall here be content with citing the result and showing how it leads to Eq. (4) in the case of polar coordinates. In general, equations of the form

$$x = f(u, v), \qquad y = g(u, v), \tag{5}$$

may be interpreted as mapping a region A of the xy-plane into a region G of the uv-plane. Then, under suitable restrictions on the functions f and g, the following equation gives the formula for changing from xy-coordinates to uv-coordinates in a double integral, namely,

$$\int_A\!\!\int \phi(x, y)\,dx\,dy = \int_G\!\!\int \phi[f(u, v), g(u, v)] \frac{\partial(x, y)}{\partial(u, v)}\,du\,dv, \tag{6}$$

where the symbol $\partial(x, y)/\partial(u, v)$ denotes the so-called "Jacobian" of the transformation (5) and is defined by the determinant

$$\frac{\partial(x, y)}{\partial(u, v)} = \begin{vmatrix} \dfrac{\partial x}{\partial u} & \dfrac{\partial x}{\partial v} \\[2mm] \dfrac{\partial y}{\partial u} & \dfrac{\partial y}{\partial v} \end{vmatrix}. \tag{7}$$

In the case of polar coordinates, we have r and θ in place of u and v,

$$x = r\cos\theta, \qquad y = r\sin\theta,$$

and

$$\frac{\partial(x, y)}{\partial(r, \theta)} = \begin{vmatrix} \cos\theta & -r\sin\theta \\ \sin\theta & r\cos\theta \end{vmatrix} = r(\cos^2\theta + \sin^2\theta) = r.$$

Hence, Eq. (6) becomes

$$\iint \phi(x, y)\,dx\,dy = \iint \phi(r\cos\theta, r\sin\theta)r\,dr\,d\theta, \tag{8}$$

which corresponds to Eq. (4).

EXAMPLE 1. Find the polar moment of inertia about the origin of a thin plate of density $\delta = 1$ bounded by the circle $x^2 + y^2 = 1$.

Solution

In cartesian coordinates — In polar coordinates

$$\int_{-1}^{1}\int_{-\sqrt{1-x^2}}^{\sqrt{1-x^2}} (x^2 + y^2)\,dy\,dx = \int_0^{2\pi}\int_0^1 (r^2)r\,dr\,d\theta$$

$$= \int_0^{2\pi}\left[\frac{r^4}{4}\right]_{r=0}^{r=1} d\theta$$

$$= \int_0^{2\pi} \frac{1}{4}\,d\theta = \frac{\pi}{2}.$$

To convert from the cartesian integral to the polar integral, we took $\phi(x, y) = x^2 + y^2$ in Eq. (8), and used polar-coordinate limits that described the circle. The polar integral is much easier to evaluate than the cartesian integral.

The total area of a region is given by each of the double integrals

$$A = \iint dx\,dy = \iint r\,dr\,d\theta \tag{9}$$

with appropriate limits. This means, essentially, that the given region can be divided into pieces of area

$$dA_{xy} = dx\,dy$$

by lines parallel to the x- and y-axes, or that it can be divided into pieces of area

$$dA_{r\theta} = r\,dr\,d\theta$$

by radial lines and circular arcs, and that the total area can be found by adding together all of the elements of area of either type. But it is not to be expected that the *individual pieces* dA_{xy} and $dA_{r\theta}$ will be equal. In fact, an elementary calculation shows that

$$dA_{xy} = dx\,dy = d(r\cos\theta)\,d(r\sin\theta) \neq r\,dr\,d\theta = dA_{r\theta}.$$

EXAMPLE 2. Find the moment of inertia, about the y-axis, of the area enclosed by the cardioid (see Fig. 14–11):

$$r = a(1 - \cos\theta).$$

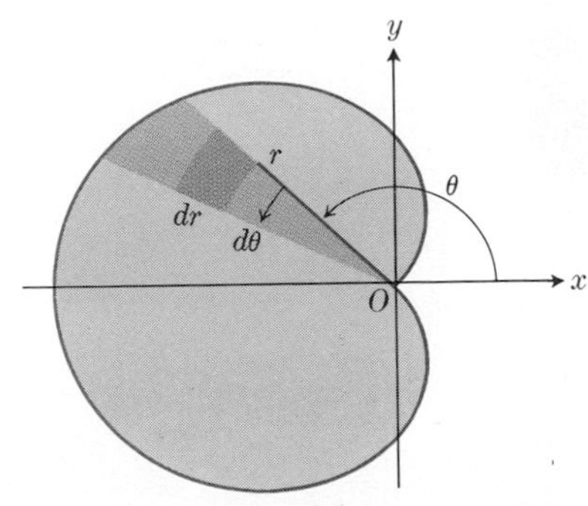

14–11 The cardioid $r = a(1 - \cos\theta)$.

Solution. It is customary to take the density as unity when working with a geometrical area. Thus we have

$$I_y = \int_A \int x^2 \, dA,$$

with

$$x = r \cos \theta, \qquad dA = r \, dr \, d\theta.$$

If we integrate first with respect to r, then, for any θ between 0 and 2π, r may vary from 0 to $a(1 - \cos \theta)$. This permits the integration to extend over those elements of area lying in the wedge between the radius lines θ and $\theta + d\theta$. Next we integrate with respect to θ from 0 to 2π to allow these wedges to cover the entire area. Hence

$$I_y = \int_0^{2\pi} \int_0^{a(1-\cos\theta)} r^3 \cos^2 \theta \, dr \, d\theta$$

$$= \int_0^{2\pi} \frac{a^4}{4} \cos^2 \theta (1 - \cos \theta)^4 \, d\theta.$$

The evaluation of the integrals

$$\int_0^{2\pi} \cos^n \theta \, d\theta \quad (n = 2, 3, 4, 5, 6)$$

is made easier by use of the reduction formula

$$\int_0^{2\pi} \cos^n \theta \, d\theta = \frac{\cos^{n-1} \theta \sin \theta}{n} \Bigg]_0^{2\pi} + \frac{n-1}{n} \int_0^{2\pi} \cos^{n-2} \theta \, d\theta$$

or, since $\sin \theta$ vanishes at both limits,

$$\int_0^{2\pi} \cos^n \theta \, d\theta = \frac{n-1}{n} \int_0^{2\pi} \cos^{n-2} \theta \, d\theta.$$

Thus

$$\int_0^{2\pi} \cos^2 \theta \, d\theta = \tfrac{1}{2} \int_0^{2\pi} d\theta = \pi,$$

$$\int_0^{2\pi} \cos^3 \theta \, d\theta = \tfrac{2}{3} \int_0^{2\pi} \cos \theta \, d\theta = \tfrac{2}{3} \sin \theta \Bigg]_0^{2\pi} = 0,$$

$$\int_0^{2\pi} \cos^4 \theta \, d\theta = \frac{3}{4} \int_0^{2\pi} \cos^2 \theta \, d\theta = \frac{3\pi}{4},$$

$$\int_0^{2\pi} \cos^5 \theta \, d\theta = \frac{4}{5} \int_0^{2\pi} \cos^3 \theta \, d\theta = 0,$$

$$\int_0^{2\pi} \cos^6 \theta \, d\theta = \frac{5}{6} \int_0^{2\pi} \cos^4 \theta \, d\theta = \frac{5\pi}{8}.$$

Therefore

$$I_y = \frac{a^4}{4}\int_0^{2\pi} (\cos^2\theta - 4\cos^3\theta + 6\cos^4\theta - 4\cos^5\theta + \cos^6\theta)\, d\theta$$

$$= \frac{a^4}{4}\left[1 + \frac{18}{4} + \frac{5}{8}\right]\pi = \frac{49\pi a^4}{32}.$$

PROBLEMS

Change each of the double integrals of Problems 1–6 to an equivalent double integral in terms of polar coordinates; then evaluate the integrals thus obtained.

1. $\int_{-a}^{a}\int_{-\sqrt{a^2-x^2}}^{\sqrt{a^2-x^2}} dy\, dx$ **2.** $\int_0^a \int_0^{\sqrt{a^2-y^2}} (x^2+y^2)\, dx\, dy$

3. $\int_0^{a/\sqrt{2}}\int_y^{\sqrt{a^2-y^2}} x\, dx\, dy$ **4.** $\int_0^{\infty}\int_0^{\infty} e^{-(x^2+y^2)}\, dx\, dy$

5. $\int_0^2\int_0^x y\, dy\, dx$ **6.** $\int_0^{2a}\int_0^{\sqrt{2ax-x^2}} x^2\, dy\, dx$

7. By double integration, find the area that lies inside the cardioid $r = a(1+\cos\theta)$ and outside the circle $r = a$.

8. Find the center of gravity of the area of Problem 7.

9. Find the polar moment of inertia I_0 with respect to an axis through O perpendicular to the xy-plane, for the area of Problem 7.

10. The base of a solid right cylinder is the area of Problem 7. The top is bounded by the plane $z = x$. Find the volume.

11. Using double integration, find the total area enclosed by the lemniscate $r^2 = 2a^2\cos 2\theta$.

12. The base of a solid is the area of Problem 11, while its top is bounded by the sphere $z = \sqrt{2a^2 - r^2}$. Find the volume.

14–5 TRIPLE INTEGRALS. VOLUME

Consider a region V, in xyz-space, completely contained within the box B bounded by the planes $x = a$, $x = b$, $y = c$, $y = d$, $z = e$, and $z = f$, with $a < b$, $c < d$, and $e < f$. Let $F(x, y, z)$ be a function whose domain includes V. Let m, n, p be positive integers, and let

$$\Delta x = \frac{b-a}{m}, \qquad \Delta y = \frac{d-c}{n}, \qquad \Delta z = \frac{f-e}{p}.$$

Divide B into mnp subregions each with dimensions Δx by Δy by Δz, by planes

$$x = a,\quad a + \Delta x,\quad a + 2\,\Delta x,\quad \ldots,\quad a + m\,\Delta x;$$

$$y = c,\quad c + \Delta y,\quad c + 2\,\Delta y,\quad \ldots,\quad c + n\,\Delta y;$$

$$z = e,\quad e + \Delta z,\quad e + 2\,\Delta z,\quad \ldots,\quad e + p\,\Delta z.$$

These subregions are of three kinds: (a) those interior to V, (b) those exterior to V, and (c) those intersecting the boundary of V. We include all those of type (a), exclude all those of type (b), and include some, none, or all those of type (c). Then we number the included subregions 1, 2, 3, ..., N. Let (x_k, y_k, z_k) be a point in the kth subregion; multiply the value of F at that point by the volume ΔV_k of the subregion, and form the sum

$$S = \sum_{k=1}^{N} F(x_k, y_k, z_k)\,\Delta V_k$$

$$= \sum_{k=1}^{N} F(x_k, y_k, z_k)\,\Delta x\,\Delta y\,\Delta z. \tag{1}$$

Finally, suppose that the function F is continuous throughout V and on its boundary. Then, if the boundary of V is sufficiently "tame," the sums (1) have a limit as $\sqrt{(\Delta x)^2 + (\Delta y)^2 + (\Delta z)^2}$ approaches zero, and this limit is called the (Riemann) triple integral of F over V:

$$\iiint_V F\,dV = \lim \sum_{k=1}^{N} F(x_k, y_k, z_k)\,\Delta x\,\Delta y\,\Delta z. \tag{2}$$

REMARK 1. There are many possible interpretations of (2). If $F(x, y, z) = 1$ for all points in V, the integral is just the volume of V. If $F(x, y, z) = x$, the integral is the first moment of the volume V with respect to the yz-plane. If $F(x, y, z)$ is the density at (x, y, z), then the integral is the mass in V. If $F(x, y, z)$ is the product of the density at (x, y, z) and the square of the distance from (x, y, z) to an axis L, then the integral is the moment of inertia of the mass with respect to L.

REMARK 2. The triple integral is seldom evaluated directly from its definition as a limit. Instead, it is usually evaluated as an iterated integral. For example, suppose V is bounded below by a surface

$$z = f_1(x, y),$$

above by the surface

$$z = f_2(x, y),$$

and laterally by a cylinder C with elements parallel to the z-axis (Fig. 14–12). Let A denote the region of the xy-plane enclosed by the cylinder C. (That is, A is the region covered by the orthogonal projection of the solid into the xy-plane.) Then the *volume* of the region V (which we shall also denote by V) can be found by evaluating the triply iterated integral

$$V = \int_A \iint_{f_1(x,y)}^{f_2(x,y)} dz\,dy\,dx. \tag{3}$$

The z-limits of integration indicate that for every (x, y) in the region A, z may extend from the lower surface $z = f_1(x, y)$ to the upper surface $z = f_2(x, y)$. The y- and x-limits of integration have not been given explicitly in Eq. (3), but are indicated as extending over the region A. The problem of supplying these limits is precisely the problem we have previously considered in connection with *double* integrals. It is usually desirable to draw the xy-projection of the solid in order to see more easily what these limits are.

In case the lateral surface of the cylinder reduces to zero (as in the example that follows), one may find the equation of the boundary of the region A by eliminating z between the two equations $z = f_1(x, y)$ and $z = f_2(x, y)$, thus obtaining an equation

$$f_1(x, y) = f_2(x, y), \tag{4}$$

which contains no z. Such an equation, interpreted as the equation of a surface in xyz-space, represents a cylinder with elements parallel to the z-axis. If we interpret it as an equation in the xy-plane, Eq. (4) represents the boundary of the region A.

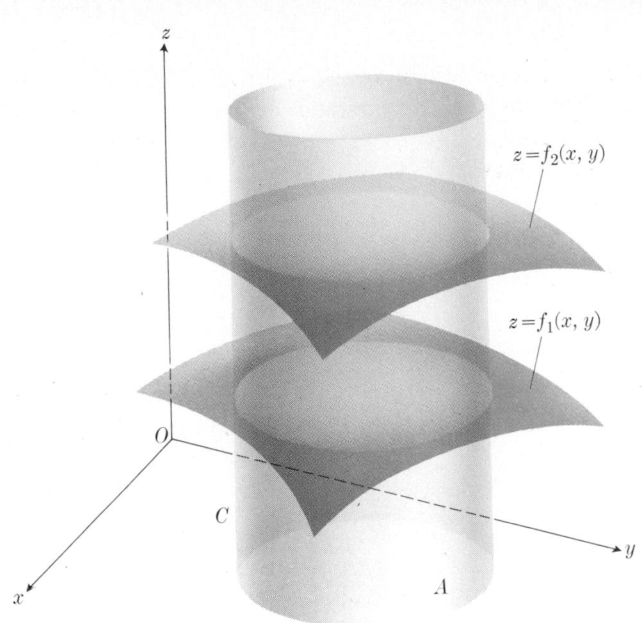

14–12 The enclosed volume can be found by evaluating $V = \int_A \int \int_{f_1(x,y)}^{f_2(x,y)} dz\, dy\, dx.$

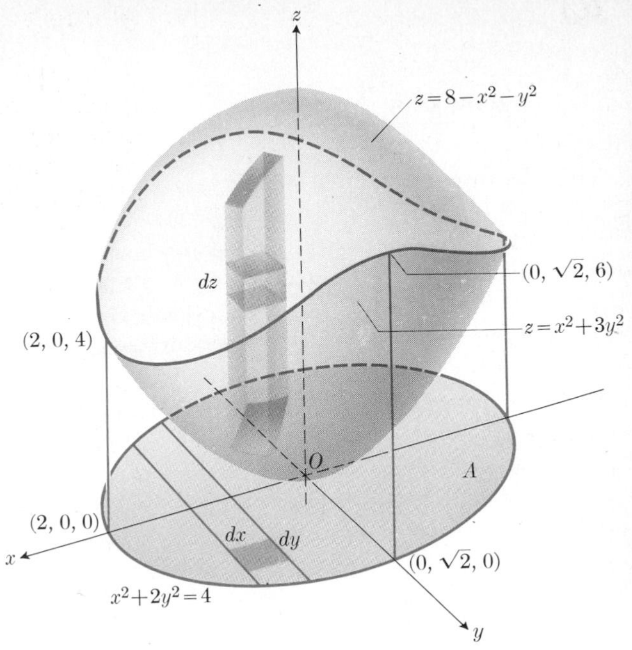

14–13 The volume between two paraboloids.

EXAMPLE. Find the volume enclosed between the two surfaces

$$z = 8 - x^2 - y^2 \quad \text{and} \quad z = x^2 + 3y^2.$$

Solution. The two surfaces (Fig. 14–13) intersect on the elliptic cylinder

$$x^2 + 2y^2 = 4.$$

The volume projects into the region A (in the xy-plane) that is enclosed by the ellipse having this same equation. In the double integral with respect to y and x over this region A, if we integrate first with respect to y, holding x and dx fixed, we see that y varies from $-\sqrt{(4 - x^2)/2}$ to $+\sqrt{(4 - x^2)/2}$. Then x varies from -2 to $+2$. Thus we have

$$V = \int_{-2}^{2} \int_{-\sqrt{(4-x^2)/2}}^{\sqrt{(4-x^2)/2}} \int_{x^2+3y^2}^{8-x^2-y^2} dz\, dy\, dx$$

$$= \int_{-2}^{2} \int_{-\sqrt{(4-x^2)/2}}^{\sqrt{(4-x^2)/2}} (8 - 2x^2 - 4y^2)\, dy\, dx$$

$$= \int_{-2}^{2} \left[2(8 - 2x^2) \sqrt{\frac{4 - x^2}{2}} - \frac{8}{3}\left(\frac{4 - x^2}{2}\right)^{3/2} \right] dx$$

$$= \frac{4\sqrt{2}}{3} \int_{-2}^{2} (4 - x^2)^{3/2}\, dx = 8\pi\sqrt{2}.$$

PROBLEMS

By triple integration, find the volume in each of the following problems.

1. The volume of the tetrahedron bounded by the plane $x/a + y/b + z/c = 1$ and the coordinate planes.

2. The volume between the cylinder $z = y^2$ and the xy-plane that is bounded by the four vertical planes $x = 0$, $x = 1$, $y = -1$, $y = 1$.

3. The volume in the first octant bounded by the planes $x + z = 1$, $y + 2z = 2$.

4. The volume in the first octant bounded by the cylinder $x = 4 - y^2$ and the planes $z = y$, $x = 0$, $z = 0$.

5. The volume enclosed by the cylinders $z = 5 - x^2$, $z = 4x^2$, and the planes $y = 0$, $x + y = 1$.

6. The volume enclosed by the cylinder $y^2 + 4z^2 = 16$ and the planes $x = 0$, $x + y = 4$.

7. The volume bounded below by the plane $z = 0$, laterally by the elliptic cylinder $x^2 + 4y^2 = 4$, and above by the plane $z = x + 2$.

8. The volume common to the two cylinders $x^2 + y^2 = a^2$ and $x^2 + z^2 = a^2$. (See Fig. 14–14.)

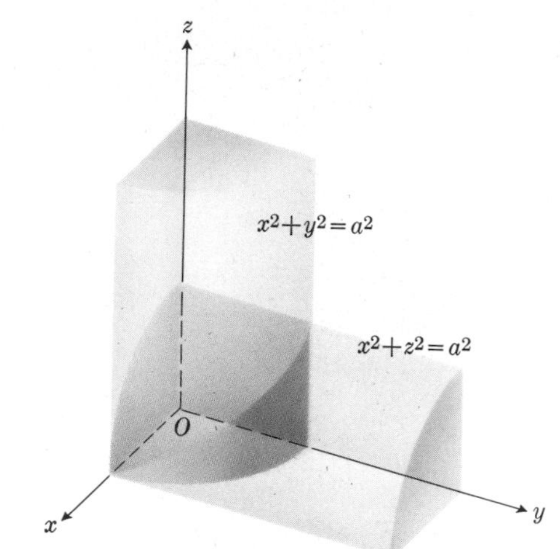

14–14 One-eighth of the volume common to the cylinders $x^2 + y^2 = a^2$, $x^2 + z^2 = a^2$.

9. The volume bounded by the elliptic paraboloids $z = x^2 + 9y^2$ and $z = 18 - x^2 - 9y^2$.

10. The volume of an ellipsoid of semiaxes a, b, c.

14–6 CYLINDRICAL COORDINATES

Instead of using an element of volume

$$dV_{xyz} = dz\,dy\,dx, \tag{1}$$

as we have done, we may use an element

$$dV_{r\theta z} = dz\,r\,dr\,d\theta. \tag{2}$$

Equation (2) may be visualized as giving the volume of an element having cross-sectional area $r\,dr\,d\theta$, such as that used with polar coordinates in Article 14–4, and altitude dz. Cylindrical coordinates, r, θ, z, are particularly useful in problems where there is an axis of symmetry of the solid. By proper choice of axes, this axis of symmetry may be taken to be the z-axis.

EXAMPLE. Find the center of gravity of a homogeneous solid hemisphere of radius a.

Solution. We may choose the origin at the center of the sphere and consider the hemisphere that lies above the xy-plane. (See Fig. 14–15.) The equation of the hemispherical surface is

$$z = \sqrt{a^2 - x^2 - y^2}$$

or, in terms of cylindrical coordinates,

$$z = \sqrt{a^2 - r^2}.$$

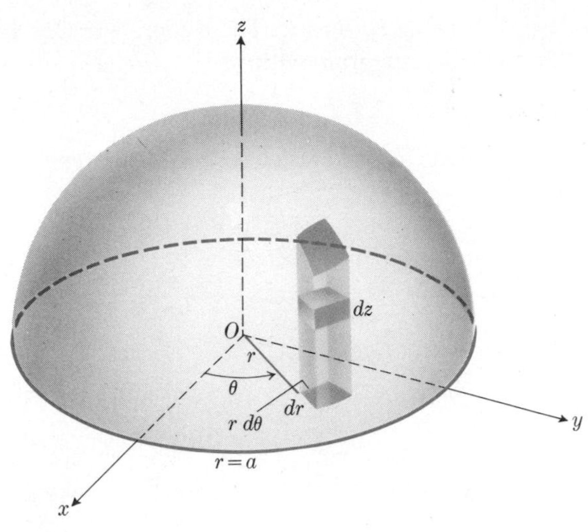

14–15 The volume element in cylindrical coordinates is $dV = dz\, r\, dr\, d\theta$.

By symmetry we have

$$\bar{x} = \bar{y} = 0.$$

We calculate $\bar{z}$:

$$\bar{z} = \frac{\iiint z\, dV}{\iiint dV} = \frac{\int_0^{2\pi} \int_0^a \int_0^{\sqrt{a^2-r^2}} z\, dz\, r\, dr\, d\theta}{\frac{2}{3}\pi a^3} = \frac{3a}{8}.$$

PROBLEMS

By triple integration, find the volume in each of the following problems.

1. The volume bounded above by the paraboloid $z = 5 - x^2 - y^2$ and below by the paraboloid $z = 4x^2 + 4y^2$.

2. The volume that is bounded above by the paraboloid $z = 9 - x^2 - y^2$, below by the xy-plane, and that lies *outside* the cylinder $x^2 + y^2 = 1$.

3. The volume cut from the sphere $x^2 + y^2 + z^2 \leq 4a^2$ by the cylinder $x^2 + y^2 \leq a^2$.

4. The volume bounded below by the paraboloid $z = x^2 + y^2$ and above by the plane $z = 2y$.

5. The volume bounded above by the sphere $x^2 + y^2 + z^2 = 2a^2$ and below by the paraboloid $az = x^2 + y^2$.

6. The volume in the first octant bounded by the cylinder $x^2 + y^2 = a^2$ and the planes $x = a$, $y = a$, $z = 0$, $z = x + y$.

14–7 PHYSICAL APPLICATIONS OF TRIPLE INTEGRATION

The mass, center of gravity, and moments of inertia of a mass M distributed over a region V of xyz-space and having density $\delta = \delta(x, y, z)$ at the point (x, y, z) of V (see Fig. 14–16) are given by integrals of the type

$$M = \iiint \delta\, dV, \tag{1}$$

$$\bar{x} = \frac{\iiint x\, \delta\, dV}{\iiint \delta\, dV}, \tag{2}$$

$$I_z = \iiint (x^2 + y^2)\, \delta\, dV, \tag{3}$$

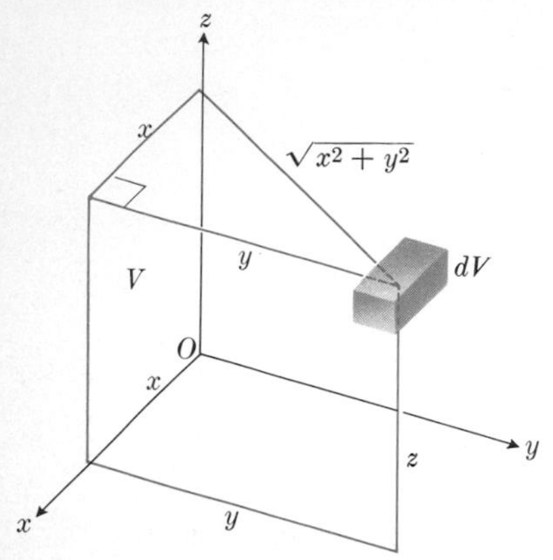

14–16 Distances of dV from the coordinate planes and the z-axis.

with similar integrals for $\bar{y}$, $\bar{z}$, I_x, and I_y. The integrals in Eqs. (1) through (3) may be evaluated as triple integrals with

$$dV = dz\ dy\ dx$$

or, if it is more convenient to use cylindrical coordinates,

$$dV = dz\ r\ dr\ d\theta.$$

Limits of integration are to be supplied so that the element of volume ranges over the volume V as discussed above.

EXAMPLE. A solid is bounded below by the xy-plane, above by the sphere $x^2 + y^2 + z^2 = 4a^2$, and laterally by the cylinder $r = 2a \cos \theta$. Find its moment of inertia I_z.

Solution. The solid lies in front of the yz-plane, as shown in Fig. 14–17. It projects orthogonally into the interior of the circle $r = 2a \cos \theta$ in the xy-plane. Taking an element of volume $dV = dz\ r\ dr\ d\theta$ enclosing a point r, θ, z, we have

$$dI_z = r^2\ dV = dz\ r^3\ dr\ d\theta.$$

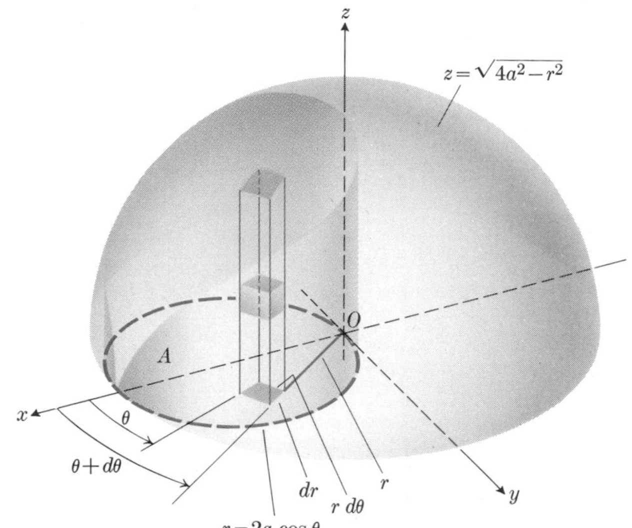

14–17 The solid bounded by the xy-plane, the sphere $x^2 + y^2 + z^2 = 4a^2$, and the cylinder $r = 2a \cos \theta$.

When we integrate with respect to z, we use as lower limit $z = 0$ (the plane) and as upper limit $z = \sqrt{4a^2 - r^2}$ (the sphere). This integral gives the moment of inertia of the elements dV in a prism extending from the xy-plane to the sphere and having its base inside the circle $r = 2a \cos \theta$. In order to add the moments of all of the prisms, we examine this region by itself to see what the appropriate r and θ limits are. If we were finding only the *area* of this region (Fig. 14–17), we would have

$$A = \int_{-\pi/2}^{\pi/2} \int_0^{2a \cos \theta} r\ dr\ d\theta.$$

In the present problem, we are finding the moment of inertia I_z of a solid standing on this area as a base, but *the same limits of integration* apply to the r and θ integrations. Therefore

$$I_z = \int_{-\pi/2}^{\pi/2} \int_0^{2a\cos\theta} \int_0^{\sqrt{4a^2 - r^2}} dz\, r^3\, dr\, d\theta = \frac{64a^5}{15}\left[\pi - \frac{26}{15}\right].$$

PROBLEMS

1. Find the moment of inertia about the x-axis for the volume of Problem 3, Article 14–6.

2. Find the moment of inertia about the z-axis for the volume of Problem 4, Article 14–6.

3. Find the x-coordinate of the center of gravity of the volume of Problem 7, Article 14–5.

4. Find the center of gravity of the volume of Problem 5, Article 14–6.

5. Use cylindrical coordinates to find the moment of inertia of a sphere of radius a and mass M about a diameter.

6. Find the volume generated by rotating the cardioid $r = a(1 - \cos\theta)$ about the x-axis. [*Hint.* Use *double* integration. Rotate an area element dA around the x-axis to generate a volume element dV.]

7. Find the moment of inertia, about the x-axis, of the volume of Problem 6.

8. Find the moment of inertia of a right circular cone of base radius a, altitude h, and mass M about an axis through the vertex and parallel to the base.

9. Find the moment of inertia of a sphere of radius a and mass M with respect to a tangent line.

10. Find the center of gravity of that portion of the volume of the sphere $r^2 + z^2 = a^2$ that lies between the planes $\theta = -(\pi/4)$ and $\theta = \pi/4$.

11. A torus of mass M is generated by rotating a circle of radius a about an axis in its plane at distance b from the center (b greater than a). Find its moment of inertia about the axis of revolution.

14–8 SPHERICAL COORDINATES

In a problem where there is symmetry with respect to a point, it may be convenient to choose that point as origin and to use spherical coordinates (Fig. 14–18). These are related to the cartesian system by the equations

$$x = \rho \sin\phi \cos\theta, \qquad y = \rho \sin\phi \sin\theta, \qquad z = \rho \cos\phi. \tag{1}$$

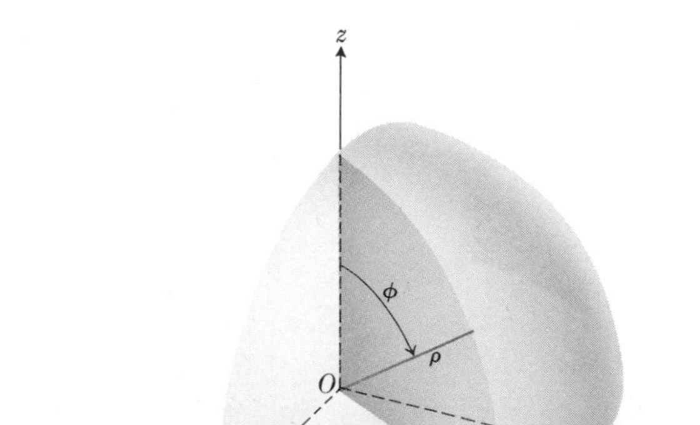

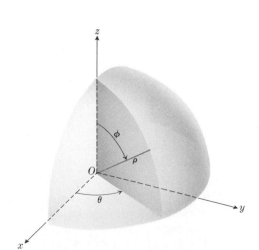

14–18 Spherical coordinates.

If we give ρ, ϕ, and θ increments $d\rho$, $d\phi$, and $d\theta$, we are led to consider the volume element (Fig. 14–19).

$$dV_{\rho\phi\theta} = d\rho \cdot \rho\, d\phi \cdot \rho \sin \phi\, d\theta = \rho^2 \sin \phi\, d\rho\, d\phi\, d\theta \tag{2}$$

and triple integrals of the form

$$\iiint F(\rho, \phi, \theta)\rho^2 \sin \phi\, d\rho\, d\phi\, d\theta. \tag{3}$$

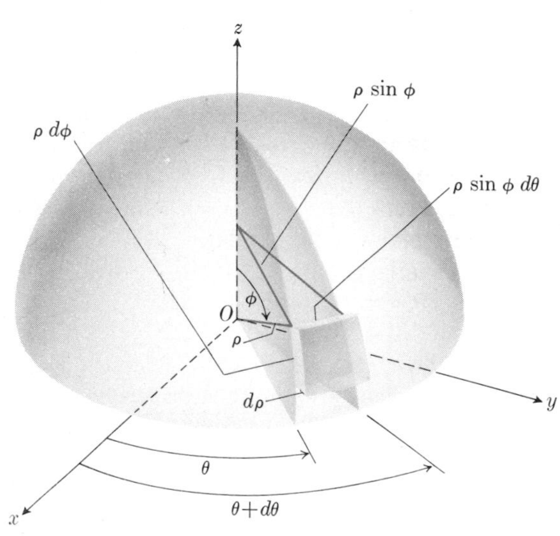

14–19 The volume element in spherical coordinates is $dV = d\rho \cdot \rho\, d\phi \cdot \rho \sin \phi\, d\theta$.

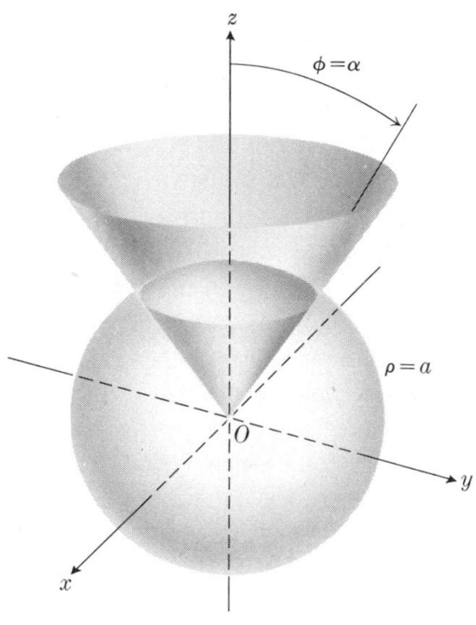

14–20 The volume cut from the sphere $\rho = a$ by the cone $\phi = \alpha$.

EXAMPLE. Find the volume cut from the sphere $\rho = a$ by the cone $\phi = \alpha$. (See Fig. 14–20.)

Solution. The volume is given by

$$V = \int_0^{2\pi} \int_0^{\alpha} \int_0^{a} \rho^2 \sin \phi\, d\rho\, d\phi\, d\theta = \frac{2\pi a^3}{3}(1 - \cos \alpha).$$

As a check, we note that the special cases $\alpha = \pi/2$ and $\alpha = \pi$ correspond to the cases of a hemisphere and a sphere, of volumes $2\pi a^3/3$ and $4\pi a^3/3$, respectively.

PROBLEMS

1. Find the smaller volume cut from the sphere $\rho = 2$ by the plane $z = \sqrt{2}$.

2. Find the center of gravity of the volume (which resembles a filled ice cream cone) that is bounded above by the sphere $\rho = a$ and below by the cone $\phi = \pi/6$.

3. Find the volume enclosed by the surface $\rho = a(1 - \cos \phi)$. Compare with Problem 6, Article 14–7.

4. Find the radius of gyration, with respect to a diameter, of a spherical shell of mass M bounded by the spheres $\rho = a$ and $\rho = 2a$ if the density is $\delta = \rho^2$.

5. Sketch the space curve $\rho = 1$, $\phi = \theta$ for $0 \le \theta \le \pi/2$. Label the point $(\rho, \phi, \theta) = (1, 0, 0)$.

14–9 SURFACE AREA

Let G be a region of the xy-plane and let the function

$$z = f(x, y), \qquad (x, y) \in G, \tag{1}$$

together with its first partial derivatives, be continuous in G. For simplicity, suppose that the surface represented by Eq. (1) has a normal $\mathbf{N}$ that is never parallel to the xy-plane. The area of the surface may then be computed in the following way:

Divide the region G into rectangles of dimensions Δx by Δy, by a grid of lines parallel to the x- and y-axes. Project a typical rectangle of area

$$\Delta A = \Delta y \, \Delta x \tag{2}$$

vertically upward onto the surface and call the corresponding area on the surface ΔS. (See Fig. 14–21.) Choose any point Q on ΔS and consider the plane tangent to the surface at Q. Project the area ΔA vertically upward onto the plane tangent to S at Q. Call the corresponding area in the tangent plane ΔP. We use ΔP to approximate ΔS. If this procedure is carried out for all of the pieces of area ΔA lying in G, and we add all the pieces of area ΔP, the result will approximate the total surface area S. That is,

$$S \approx \sum \Delta P. \tag{3}$$

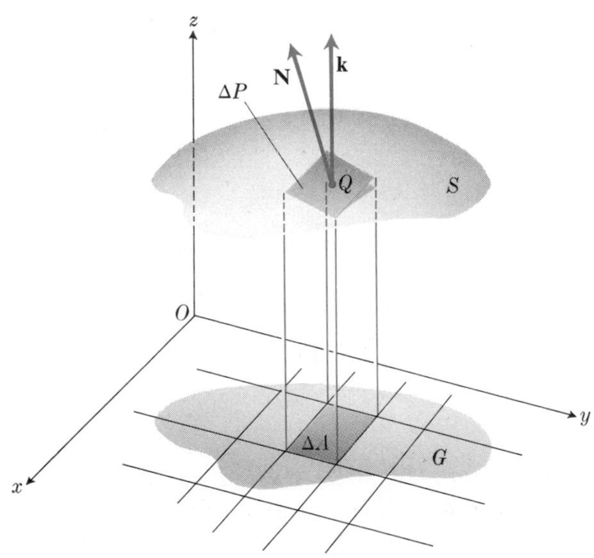

14–21 The area ΔP is the projection of ΔA in G onto the plane tangent to the surface S at the arbitrarily chosen point Q.

The approximation improves as Δx and Δy approach zero. We take the limit of the sum in (3) as the *definition of the surface area S*. That is,

$$S = \lim_{\Delta x, \Delta y \to 0} \sum_G \Delta P. \tag{4}$$

To calculate S we need an analytic expression for ΔP as a function of x, y, Δx, and Δy. Let

$$(x, y, 0), \qquad (x + \Delta x, y, 0), \qquad (x, y + \Delta y, 0),$$

and

$$(x + \Delta x, y + \Delta y, 0)$$

be the corners of the rectangle in G whose area ΔA projects onto the area ΔP in the tangent plane (Fig. 14–22). For simplicity, let Q be the point $(x, y, f(x, y))$ on the surface (1). Let **u**, **v** be vectors from Q forming two adjacent sides of the parallelogram whose area is ΔP. Then

$$\mathbf{u} = \mathbf{i}\,\Delta x + \mathbf{k} f_x(x, y)\,\Delta x,$$
$$\mathbf{v} = \mathbf{j}\,\Delta y + \mathbf{k} f_y(x, y)\,\Delta y.$$

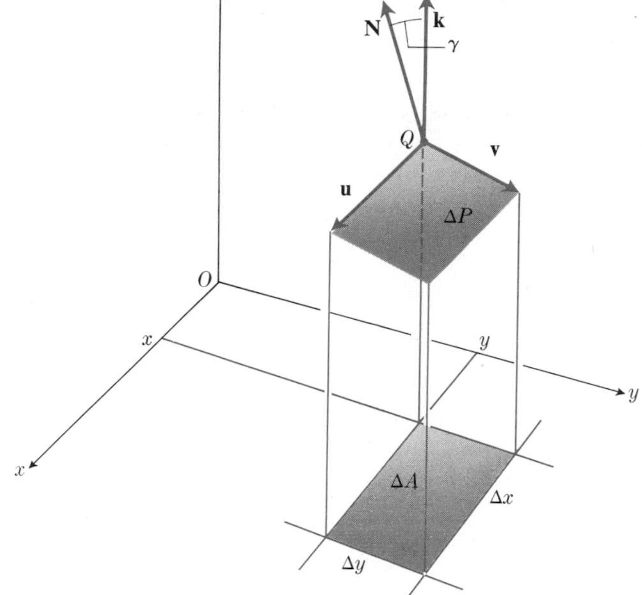

14–22 The area $\Delta P = |\mathbf{u} \times \mathbf{v}|$ is the projection of ΔA onto the tangent plane at Q: $\Delta P = \Delta A/\cos\gamma$.

A vector normal to the surface at Q, with magnitude equal to the area ΔP, is

$$\mathbf{N} = \mathbf{u} \times \mathbf{v} = \begin{vmatrix} \mathbf{i} & \mathbf{j} & \mathbf{k} \\ \Delta x & 0 & f_x(x, y)\,\Delta x \\ 0 & \Delta y & f_y(x, y)\,\Delta y \end{vmatrix}$$
$$= \Delta x\,\Delta y(-\mathbf{i} f_x(x, y) - \mathbf{j} f_y(x, y) + \mathbf{k}). \tag{5}$$

Therefore,

$$\Delta P = |\mathbf{u} \times \mathbf{v}| = \Delta x\,\Delta y\sqrt{f_x^2(x, y) + f_y^2(x, y) + 1}. \tag{6}$$

Equations (4) and (6) together say that the area of the surface S above the region G in the xy-plane is given by the integral

$$S = \iint_G \sqrt{\left(\frac{\partial f}{\partial x}\right)^2 + \left(\frac{\partial f}{\partial y}\right)^2 + 1}\; dx\,dy. \tag{7}$$

EXAMPLE 1. Find the surface area S of the paraboloid $z = x^2 + y^2$ below the plane $z = 1$.

Solution. The surface area S projects onto the interior G of the circle

$$x^2 + y^2 = 1,$$

in the xy-plane (Fig. 14–23). Here

$$z = f(x, y) = x^2 + y^2,$$

so that

$$\frac{\partial f}{\partial x} = 2x, \qquad \frac{\partial f}{\partial y} = 2y$$

and

$$S = \iint\limits_{x^2+y^2 \leq 1} \sqrt{4x^2 + 4y^2 + 1}\, dy\, dx. \tag{8}$$

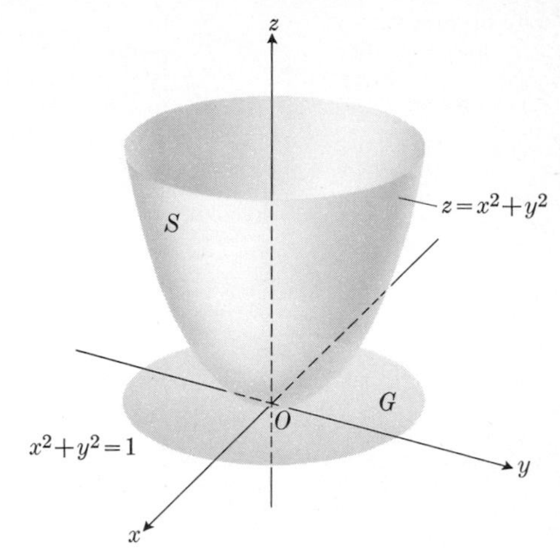

14–23 The area of the parabolic surface above is calculated in Example 1.

Now the double integral (8) is easier to evaluate in polar coordinates, since the combination $x^2 + y^2$ may be replaced by r^2. Taking the element of area to be

$$dA = r\, dr\, d\theta$$

in place of $dy\, dx$, we thus have

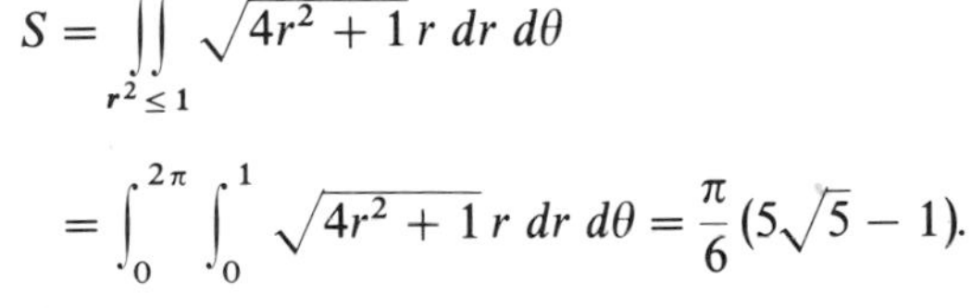

$$S = \iint\limits_{r^2 \leq 1} \sqrt{4r^2 + 1}\, r\, dr\, d\theta$$

$$= \int_0^{2\pi} \int_0^1 \sqrt{4r^2 + 1}\, r\, dr\, d\theta = \frac{\pi}{6}(5\sqrt{5} - 1).$$

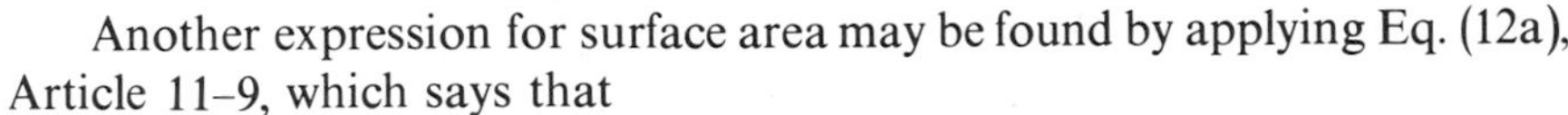

Another expression for surface area may be found by applying Eq. (12a), Article 11–9, which says that

$$(\mathbf{u} \times \mathbf{v}) \cdot \mathbf{k} = \text{area of projection of } \Delta P \text{ in } xy\text{-plane.}$$

This also agrees with Eq. (5), above, which gives

$$(\mathbf{u} \times \mathbf{v}) \cdot \mathbf{k} = \Delta x\, \Delta y = \Delta A. \tag{9a}$$

From the definition of the dot product, we also know that

$$(\mathbf{u} \times \mathbf{v}) \cdot \mathbf{k} = |\mathbf{u} \times \mathbf{v}|\, |\mathbf{k}| \cos \gamma \tag{9b}$$
$$= \Delta P \cos \gamma,$$

where γ is the angle between $\mathbf{N} = \mathbf{u} \times \mathbf{v}$ and $\mathbf{k}$. Equations (9a) and (9b) give the result

$$\Delta P = \frac{\Delta A}{\cos \gamma}, \tag{10}$$

and from Eqs. (4) and (10) we have

$$S = \int_G \int \frac{dA}{\cos \gamma}. \tag{11}$$

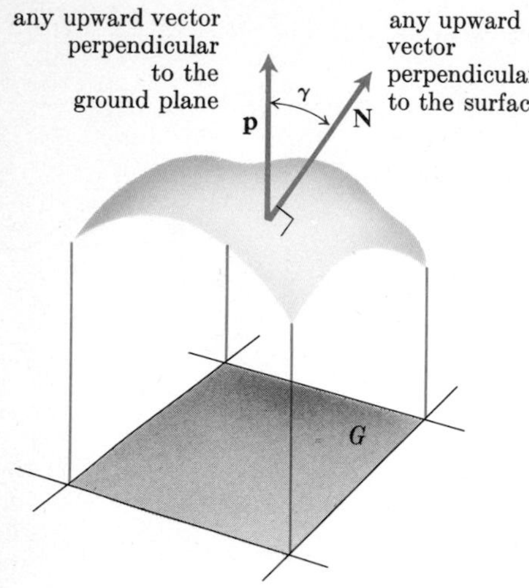

14–24 Surface area: $\iint_G (dA/\cos\gamma)$.

Equation 11 does not depend on which particular coordinates are used in the ground plane above which the surface lies. The essential ingredient is that γ be the angle between some upward normal $\mathbf{N}$ to the surface and some upward vector $\mathbf{p}$ perpendicular to the ground plane, as shown in Fig. 14–24. If the surface is given by

$$F(x, y, z) = 0,$$

then $\pm\nabla F$ will do for $\mathbf{N}$ (Article 13–6), and we may take

$$\cos\gamma = \frac{|\nabla F \cdot \mathbf{p}|}{|\nabla F|\,|\mathbf{p}|}. \tag{12}$$

If we choose $\mathbf{p}$ to be a unit vector, then Eq. (12) simplifies to

$$\cos\gamma = \frac{|\nabla F \cdot \mathbf{p}|}{|\nabla F|}. \tag{13}$$

With this expression substituted for $\cos\gamma$ in Eq. (11), we get

$$S = \iint_G \frac{dA}{\cos\gamma} = \iint_G \frac{|\nabla F|}{|\nabla F \cdot \mathbf{p}|}\,dA. \tag{14}$$

EXAMPLE 2. Evaluate Eq. (14) for the surface

$$z = f(x, y), \qquad (x, y) \in G,$$

of Eq. (1).

Solution. We take

$$F(x, y, z) = z - f(x, y) = 0.$$

Then,

$$\begin{aligned}\nabla F &= F_x\mathbf{i} + F_y\mathbf{j} + F_z\mathbf{k}\\ &= -f_x\mathbf{i} - f_y\mathbf{j} + \mathbf{k},\end{aligned}$$

and

$$|\nabla F| = \sqrt{f_x^2 + f_y^2 + 1}.$$

The upward unit normal to the ground plane is $\mathbf{p} = \mathbf{k}$, so that

$$\nabla F \cdot \mathbf{p} = \nabla F \cdot \mathbf{k} = 1.$$

Substituting these values for $|\nabla F|$ and $\nabla F \cdot \mathbf{p}$ in Eq. (14) gives

$$\begin{aligned}S &= \iint_G \frac{|\nabla F|}{|\nabla F \cdot \mathbf{p}|}\,dA\\ &= \iint_G \sqrt{f_x^2 + f_y^2 + 1}\;dx\,dy.\end{aligned}$$

Thus we have recovered Eq. (7).

PROBLEMS

1. Use the method of Example 2 to derive the following formulas.

a) The area of a smooth surface $x = f(y, z)$ above a region G in the yz-plane is

$$S = \iint_G \sqrt{f_y^2 + f_z^2 + 1}\, dy\, dz.$$

b) The area of a smooth surface $y = f(x, z)$ above a region G in the xz-plane is

$$S = \iint_G \sqrt{f_x^2 + f_z^2 + 1}\, dx\, dz.$$

2. Find, by integration, the area of the triangle cut from the plane $x/a + y/b + z/c = 1$ by the coordinate planes. Check your answer by vector methods.

3. Find, by integration, the area of that portion of the surface of the sphere $x^2 + y^2 + z^2 = a^2$ that lies in the first octant.

4. Find the area of the surface of that portion of the sphere $x^2 + y^2 + z^2 = 4a^2$ that lies inside the cylinder $x^2 + y^2 = 2ax$. (Figure 14–17 shows the top half.)

5. Find the area cut from the paraboloid $z = 9 - x^2 - y^2$ by the planes $z = 0$, $z = 8$.

6. Find the area of that portion of the sphere $x^2 + y^2 + z^2 = 2a^2$ that is cut out by the upper nappe of the cone $x^2 + y^2 = z^2$.

7. Find the area cut from the plane $z = cx$ by the cylinder $x^2 + y^2 = a^2$.

8. Find the area of that portion of the cylinder $x^2 + z^2 = a^2$ that lies between the planes $y = \pm a/2$, $x = \pm a/2$.

9. Find the area cut from the surface $az = y^2 - x^2$ by the cylinder $x^2 + y^2 = a^2$.

10. Find the area of that portion of the cylinder in Problem 4 that lies inside the sphere. [*Hint.* Project the area into the xz-plane. Or use single integration, $\int h\, ds$, where h is the altitude of the cylinder and ds is the element of arc length in the xy-plane.]

REVIEW QUESTIONS AND EXERCISES

1. Define the double integral of a function of two variables. What geometric interpretation may be given to the integral?

2. List four applications of multiple integration.

3. Define *moment of inertia* and *radius of gyration*.

4. How does a double integral in polar coordinates differ from a double integral in cartesian coordinates? In what way are they alike?

5. What are the fundamental volume elements for triple integrals (a) in cartesian coordinates, (b) in cylindrical coordinates, (c) in spherical coordinates?

6. How is surface area defined? Which formula of Article 14–9 is the most general one for computing surface area, in the sense that it includes many others as special cases?

7. How would you define $\iint_S F\, dS$, when S is a surface in space and F is a function defined at points on the surface? Illustrate when S is the hemisphere

$$z = \sqrt{1 - x^2 - y^2},$$
$$x^2 + y^2 \le 1,$$

and

$$F(x, y, z) = z.$$

What is the geometrical interpretation of $\iint z\, dS$?

MISCELLANEOUS PROBLEMS

1. Reverse the order of integration and evaluate $\int_0^4 \int_{-\sqrt{4-y}}^{(y-4)/2} dx\, dy$.

2. Sketch the region over which the integral $\int_0^1 \int_{\sqrt{y}}^{2-\sqrt{y}} xy\, dx\, dy$ is to be evaluated and find its value.

3. The integral $\int_{-1}^{1} \int_{x^2}^{1} dy\, dx$ represents the area of a region of the xy-plane. Sketch the region and express the same area as a double integral with the order of integration reversed.

4. The base of a pile of sand covers the region in the xy-plane that is bounded by the parabola $x^2 + y = 6$ and the line $y = x$. The depth of the sand above the point (x, y) is x^2. Sketch the base of the sand pile and a representative element of volume dV, and find the volume of sand in the pile by double integration.

5. In setting up a double integral for the volume V under the paraboloid $z = x^2 + y^2$ and above a certain region R of the xy-plane, the following sum of iterated integrals was obtained:

$$V = \int_0^1 \left(\int_0^y (x^2 + y^2)\, dx \right) dy + \int_1^2 \left(\int_0^{2-y} (x^2 + y^2)\, dx \right) dy.$$

Sketch the region R in the xy-plane and express V as an iterated integral in which the order of integration is reversed.

6. By change of order of integration, show that the following double integral can be reduced to a single integral

$$\int_0^x du \int_0^u e^{m(x-t)} f(t)\, dt = \int_0^x (x-t) e^{m(x-t)} f(t)\, dt.$$

Similarly, it can be shown that

$$\int_0^x dv \int_0^v du \int_0^u e^{m(x-t)} f(t)\, dt = \int_0^x \frac{(x-t)^2}{2!} e^{m(x-t)} f(t)\, dt.$$

Evaluate integrals for the case $f(t) = \cos at$. (This example illustrates that such reductions usually make calculation easier.)

7. Sometimes a multiple integral with variable limits may be changed into one with constant limits. By changing the order of integration, show that

$$\int_0^1 f(x)\, dx \int_0^x \log(x-y) f(y)\, dy$$

$$= \int_0^1 f(y)\, dy \int_y^1 \log(x-y)\, f(x)\, dx$$

$$= \tfrac{1}{2} \int_0^1 \int_0^1 \log|x-y|\, f(x)\, f(y)\, dx\, dy.$$

8. Evaluate the integral

$$\int_0^\infty \frac{e^{-ax} - e^{-bx}}{x}\, dx.$$

[*Hint.* Use the relation

$$\frac{e^{-ax} - e^{-bx}}{x} = \int_a^b e^{-xy}\, dy$$

to form a double integral, and evaluate it by change of the order of integration.]

9. By double integration, find the center of gravity of that part of the area of the circle $x^2 + y^2 = a^2$ contained in the first quadrant.

10. Determine the centroid of the plane area that is given in polar coordinates by $0 \le r \le a$, $-\alpha \le \theta \le \alpha$.

11. Find the centroid of the area bounded by the lines $\theta = 0°$ and $\theta = 45°$, and by the circles $r = 1$ and $r = 2$.

12. By double integration, find the center of gravity of the area between the parabola $x + y^2 - 2y = 0$ and the line $x + 2y = 0$.

13. For a solid body of constant density, having its center of gravity at the origin, show that the moment of inertia about an axis parallel to Oz through (x_0, y_0) is equal to the moment of inertia about Oz plus $M(x_0^2 + y_0^2)$, where M is the mass of the body.

14. Find the moment of inertia of the angle section shown in Fig. 14–25, (a) with respect to the horizontal base; (b) with respect to a horizontal line through its centroid.

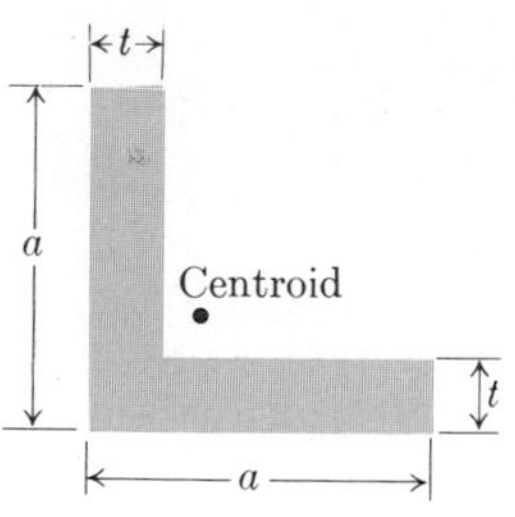

Figure 14–25

15. Show that, for a uniform elliptic lamina of semiaxes a, b, the moment of inertia about an axis in its plane through the center of the ellipse making an angle α with the axis of length $2a$ is $\frac{1}{4}M(a^2 \sin^2 \alpha + b^2 \cos^2 \alpha)$, where M is the mass of the lamina.

16. A counterweight of a flywheel has the form of the smaller segment cut from a circle of radius a by a chord at a distance b from the center $(b < a)$. Find the area of this counterweight and its polar moment of inertia about the center of the circle.

17. The radius of gyration of a body with volume V is defined by $K = \sqrt{I/V}$, where K and its moment of inertia I are referred to the same axis. Consider an ellipse $(x^2/a^2) + (y^2/b^2) = 1$ revolving about the x-axis to generate an ellipsoid. Find the radius of gyration of the ellipsoid with respect to the x-axis.

18. Find the radii of gyration about $\theta = 0$ and $\theta = \pi/2$ for the area of a loop of the curve $r^2 = a^2 \cos 2\theta$, $(a > 0)$.

19. The hydrostatic pressure at a depth y in a fluid is wy. Taking the x-axis in the surface of the fluid and the y-axis vertically downward, consider a semicircular lamina, radius a, completely immersed with its bounding diameter horizontal, uppermost, and at a depth c. Show that the depth of the center of pressure is

$$\frac{3\pi a^2 + 32ac + 12\pi c^2}{4(4a + 3\pi c)}.$$

The center of pressure is defined as the point where the entire hydrostatic force could be concentrated so as to produce the same first moment of force.

20. Show that

$$\iint \frac{\partial^2 F(x, y)}{\partial x\, \partial y}\, dx\, dy$$

over the rectangle $x_0 \le x \le x_1$, $y_0 \le y \le y_1$, is

$$F(x_1, y_1) - F(x_0, y_1) - F(x_1, y_0) + F(x_0, y_0).$$

21. Change the following double integral to an equivalent double integral in polar coordinates, and sketch the region of integration.

$$\int_{-a}^{a} \int_0^{\sqrt{a^2 - y^2}} x\, dx\, dy.$$

22. A customary method of evaluating the improper integral $I = \int_0^\infty e^{-x^2}\,dx$ is to calculate its square,

$$I^2 = \left(\int_0^\infty e^{-x^2}\,dx\right)\left(\int_0^\infty e^{-y^2}\,dy\right) = \int_0^\infty \int_0^\infty e^{-(x^2+y^2)}\,dx\,dy.$$

Introduce polar coordinates in the last expression and show that

$$I = \int_0^\infty e^{-x^2}\,dx = \frac{\sqrt{\pi}}{2}.$$

23. By transformation of variables $u = x - y$, $v = y$, show that

$$\int_0^\infty e^{-sx}\,dx \int_0^x f(x-y, y)\,dy = \int_0^\infty \int_0^\infty e^{-s(u+v)} f(u, v)\,du\,dv.$$

24. How must a, b, c be chosen in order that $\int_{-\infty}^{\infty}\int_{-\infty}^{\infty} e^{-(ax^2+2bxy+cy^2)}\,dx\,dy = 1$? [*Hint.* Introduce the transformation

$$\xi = \alpha x + \beta y, \qquad \eta = \gamma x + \delta y$$

where $(\alpha\delta - \beta\gamma)^2 = ac - b^2$; then

$$ax^2 + 2bxy + cy^2 = \xi^2 + \eta^2.]$$

25. Find the area enclosed by the lemniscate $r^2 = 2a^2 \cos 2\theta$. Also find the moment of inertia of this area about the y-axis.

26. Evaluate the integral

$$\iint \frac{dx\,dy}{(1 + x^2 + y^2)^2}$$

taken (a) over one loop of the lemniscate $(x^2 + y^2)^2 - (x^2 - y^2) = 0$, (b) over the triangle with vertices $(0, 0)$, $(2, 0)$, $(1, \sqrt{3})$. [*Hint.* Transform to polar coordinates.]

27. Show, by transforming to polar coordinates, that

$$K(a) = \int_0^{a \sin\beta} dy \int_{y \cot\beta}^{\sqrt{a^2-y^2}} \ln(x^2 + y^2)\,dx = a^2\beta(\ln a - \tfrac{1}{2}),$$

where $0 < \beta < \pi/2$. Changing the order of integration, what expression do you obtain?

28. Find the volume bounded by the cylinder $y = \cos x$ and the planes

$$z = y, \qquad x = 0, \qquad x = \pi/2, \qquad \text{and} \qquad z = 0.$$

29. Find the center of mass of the homogeneous pyramid whose base is the square enclosed by the lines $x = 1$, $x = -1$, $y = 1$, $y = -1$, in the plane $z = 0$, and whose vertex is at the point $(0, 0, 1)$.

30. Find the volume bounded above by the sphere $x^2 + y^2 + z^2 = 2a^2$ and below by the paraboloid $az = x^2 + y^2$.

31. Find the volume bounded by the surfaces

$$z = x^2 + y^2 \qquad \text{and} \qquad z = \tfrac{1}{2}(x^2 + y^2 + 1).$$

32. Determine by triple integration the volume enclosed by the two surfaces $x = y^2 + z^2$ and $x = 1 - y^2$.

33. Find the moment of inertia, with respect to the z-axis, of a solid that is bounded below by the paraboloid $3az = x^2 + y^2$ and above by the sphere $x^2 + y^2 + z^2 = 4a^2$, if its density is constant.

34. Find by integration the volume of the ellipsoid

$$\frac{x^2}{a^2} + \frac{y^2}{b^2} + \frac{z^2}{c^2} = 1.$$

35. Evaluate the integral $\iiint |xyz|\,dx\,dy\,dz$ taken throughout the ellipsoid $x^2/a^2 + y^2/b^2 + z^2/c^2 \le 1$. [*Hint.* Introduce new coordinates:

$$x = a\xi, \qquad y = b\eta, \qquad z = c\zeta.]$$

36. Two cylinders of radius a have their axes along the x- and y-axes, respectively. Find the volume that they have in common.

37. The volume of a certain solid is given by the triple integral

$$\int_0^2 \left[\int_0^{\sqrt{2x-x^2}} \left(\int_{-\sqrt{4-x^2-y^2}}^{\sqrt{4-x^2-y^2}} dz\right) dy\right] dx.$$

(a) Describe the solid by giving the equations of all the surfaces that form its boundary. (b) Express the volume as a triple integral in cylindrical coordinates. Give the limits of integration explicitly, but do not evaluate the integral.

38. A square hole of side $2b$ is cut symmetrically through a sphere of radius a $(a > b\sqrt{2})$. Find the volume removed.

39. A hole is bored through a sphere, the axis of the hole being a diameter of the sphere. The volume of the solid remaining is given by the integral

$$V = 2\int_0^{2\pi} \int_0^{\sqrt{3}} \int_1^{\sqrt{4-z^2}} r\,dr\,dz\,d\theta.$$

(a) By inspecting the given integral, determine the radius of the hole and the radius of the sphere. (b) Calculate the numerical value of the integral.

40. Set up an equivalent triple integral in rectangular coordinates. (Arrange the order so that the first integration is with respect to z, the second with respect to y, and the last with respect to x.)

$$\int_0^{\pi/2} \int_1^{\sqrt{3}} \int_1^{\sqrt{4-r^2}} r^3 \sin\theta \cos\theta\, z^2\,dz\,dr\,d\theta.$$

41. Find the volume bounded by the plane $z = 0$, the cylinder $x^2 + y^2 = a^2$, and the cylinder $az = a^2 - x^2$.

42. Find the volume of that portion of the sphere $r^2 + z^2 = a^2$ that is inside the cylinder $r = a \sin\theta$. (Here r, θ, z are cylindrical coordinates.)

43. Find the moment of inertia, about the z-axis, of the volume that is bounded above by the sphere $\rho = a$ and below by the cone $\phi = \pi/3$. (ρ, ϕ, θ are spherical coordinates.)

44. Find the volume enclosed by the surface $\rho = a \sin \phi$, in spherical coordinates.

45. Find the moment of inertia of the solid of constant density δ bounded by two concentric spheres of radii a and b ($a < b$), about a diameter.

46. Let S be a solid homogeneous sphere of radius a, constant density δ, mass $M = \frac{4}{3}\pi a^3 \delta$. Let P be a particle of mass m situated at distance b ($b > a$) from the center of S. According to Newton, the force of gravitational attraction of the sphere for P is given by the equation

$$\mathbf{F} = \gamma m \iiint \frac{\mathbf{u}\, \delta\, dV}{r^2},$$

where γ is the gravitational constant, $\mathbf{u}$ is a unit vector in the direction from P toward the volume element dV in S, r^2 is the square of the distance from P to dV, and the integration is extended throughout S. Take the origin at the center of the sphere and P at $(0, 0, b)$ on the z-axis, and show that $\mathbf{F} = -(\gamma M m/b^2)\mathbf{k}$. [*Remark*. This result shows that the force is the same as it would be if all the mass of the sphere were concentrated at its center.]

47. The density at P, a point of a solid sphere of radius a and center O, is given to be

$$\rho_0\{1 + \epsilon \cos \theta + \tfrac{1}{2}\epsilon^2(3 \cos \theta - 1)\},$$

where θ is the angle OP makes with a fixed radius OQ, and ρ_0 and ϵ are constants. Find the average density of the sphere.

48. Find the area of the surface $y^2 + z^2 = 2x$ cut off by the plane $x = 1$.

49. Find the area cut from the plane $x + y + z = 1$ by the cylinder $x^2 + y^2 = 1$.

50. Find the area above the xy-plane cut from the cone $x^2 + y^2 = z^2$ by the cylinder $x^2 + y^2 = 2ax$.

51. Find the surface area of that portion of the sphere $r^2 + z^2 = a^2$ that is inside the cylinder $r = a \sin \theta$. (r, θ, z are cylindrical coordinates.)

52. The cylinder $x^2 + y^2 = 2x$ cuts out a portion of a surface S from the upper nappe of the cone $x^2 + y^2 = z^2$. Compute the value of the surface integral

$$\iint_S (x^4 - y^4 + y^2z^2 - z^2x^2 + 1)\, dS.$$

53. The sphere $x^2 + y^2 + z^2 = 25$ is cut by the plane $z = 3$, the smaller portion cut off forming a solid V, which is bounded by a closed surface S_0 made up of two parts, the spherical part S_1 and the planar part S_2. If $(\cos \alpha)\mathbf{i} + (\cos \beta)\mathbf{j} + (\cos \gamma)\mathbf{k}$ is the unit outer normal of S_0, find the value of the surface integral

$$\iint_S (xz \cos \alpha + yz \cos \beta + \cos \gamma)\, dS$$

(a) if S is the spherical cap S_1; (b) if S is the planar base S_2; (c) if S is the complete boundary S_0.

54. Obtain the double integral expressing the surface area cut from the cylinder $z = a^2 - y^2$ by the cylinder $x^2 + y^2 = a^2$, and reduce this double integral to a definite single integral with respect to the variable y.

55. A square hole of side $2\sqrt{2}$ is cut symmetrically through a sphere of radius 2. Show that the area of the surface removed is $16\pi(\sqrt{2} - 1)$.

56. A torus surface is generated by moving a sphere of unit radius whose center travels on a closed plane circle of radius 2. Calculate the area of this surface.

57. Calculate the area of the surface $(x^2 + y^2 + z^2)^2 = x^2 - y^2$. [*Hint*. Use polar coordinates.]

58. Calculate the area of the spherical part of the boundary of the region

$$x^2 + y^2 + z^2 = r^2, \quad x^2 + y^2 - rx \geq 0, \quad x^2 + y^2 + rx \geq 0.$$

[*Hint*. Integrate first with respect to x and y.]

59. Prove that the potential of a circular disk of mass m per unit area, and of radius a, at a point distant h from the center and on the normal to the disk through the center, is $2\pi m(\sqrt{(a^2 + h^2)} - h)$. (The potential at a point P due to a mass Δm at Q is $\Delta m/r$, where r is the distance from P to Q.)

60. Find the attraction, at the vertex, of a solid right circular cone of mass M, height h, and radius of base a. (The attraction at P due to a mass Δm at Q is $(\Delta m/r^2)\mathbf{u}$, where r is the distance from P to Q, and $\mathbf{u}$ is a unit vector in the direction of $\overrightarrow{PQ}$.)

61. The solid angle sustained by a surface Σ bounded by a closed curve is defined with respect to the origin as

$$\Omega = \left| \iint_\Sigma \frac{\cos \theta}{r^2}\, dS \right|,$$

where the area element dS is located at the end of the position vector $\mathbf{R}$, θ is the angle between $\mathbf{R}$ and the normal to dS, and $r = |\mathbf{R}|$. Show that, in cartesian coordinates,

$$\Omega = \left| \iint_\Sigma \frac{x\, dy\, dz + y\, dz\, dx + z\, dx\, dy}{(x^2 + y^2 + z^2)^{3/2}} \right|.$$

62. Prove by direct integration that

$$\int_{-\infty}^{\infty} \int_{-\infty}^{\infty} \frac{dx\, dy}{(x^2 + y^2 + 1)^{3/2}} = 2\pi.$$

Interpret this integral as a solid angle sustained by a surface. What surface is this?

63. Show that the average distance of the points of the surface of a sphere of radius a from a point on the surface is $4a/3$.

VECTOR ANALYSIS

15–1 INTRODUCTION: VECTOR FIELDS

Suppose that a certain region G of 3-space is occupied by a moving fluid: air, for example, or water. We may imagine that the fluid is made up of an infinite number of particles, and that at time t, the particle that is in position P at that instant has a velocity $\mathbf{v}$. If we stay at P and observe new particles that pass through it, we shall probably see that they have different velocities. This would surely be true, for example, in turbulent motions caused by high winds or stormy seas. Again, if we could take a picture of the velocities of particles at different places at the same instant, we would expect to find that these velocities vary from place to place. Thus the velocity at position P at time t is, in general, a function of both position and time:

$$\mathbf{v} = \mathbf{F}(x, y, z, t). \tag{1}$$

Equation (1) indicates that the velocity $\mathbf{v}$ is a vector function $\mathbf{F}$ of the four independent variables x, y, z, and t. Such functions have many applications, particularly in treatments of flows of material. In hydrodynamics, for example, if $\delta = \delta(x, y, z, t)$ is the *density* of the fluid at (x, y, z) at time t, and we take $\mathbf{F} = \mathbf{i}u + \mathbf{j}v + \mathbf{k}w$ to be the velocity expressed in terms of components, then we are able to derive the Euler partial differential equation of continuity of motion:

$$\frac{\partial \delta}{\partial t} + \frac{\partial(\delta u)}{\partial x} + \frac{\partial(\delta v)}{\partial y} + \frac{\partial(\delta w)}{\partial z} = 0.$$

(We are not prepared to deal with this subject* in any detail; we mention it as one important field in which the ideas presented in this chapter are applied.) Such functions are also applied in physics and electrical engineering; for example, in the study of propagation of electromagnetic waves. Also, much current research activity in applied mathematics has to do with such functions.

Steady-State Flows

In this chapter, we shall deal only with those flows for which the velocity function, Eq. (1), does not depend on the time t. Such flows are called steady-state flows. They exemplify *vector fields.*

Definition. *If, to each point P in some region G, a vector $\mathbf{F}(P)$ is assigned, the collection of all such vectors is called a vector field.*

In addition to the vector fields that are associated with fluid flows, there are vector *force* fields that are associated with gravitational attraction, magnetic force fields, electric fields, and purely mathematical fields.

EXAMPLE 1. Imagine an idealized fluid flowing with steady-state flow in a long cylindrical pipe of radius a, so that particles at distance r from the long axis are moving parallel to the axis with speed $|\mathbf{v}| = a^2 - r^2$ (Fig. 15–1). Describe this field by a formula for $\mathbf{v}$.

---

* Some of the laws of hydrodynamics can be found in the article "Hydromechanics" in the *Encyclopaedia Britannica.*

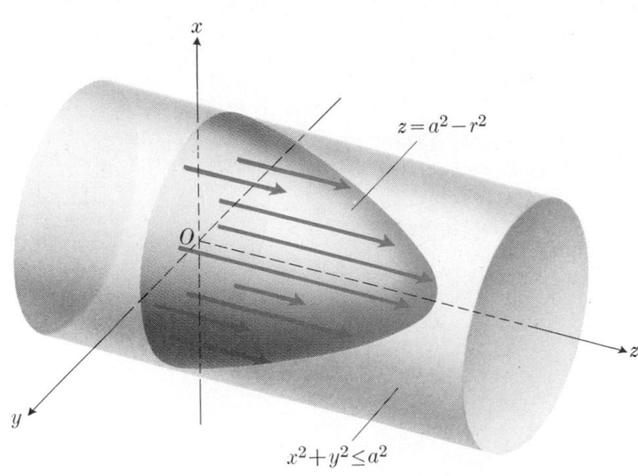

15–1 The flow of fluid in a long cylindrical pipe. The vectors $\mathbf{v} = (a^2 - r^2)\mathbf{k}$ inside the cylinder have their bases in the xy-plane and their tips on the paraboloid $z = a^2 - r^2$.

Solution. Let the z-axis lie along the axis of the pipe, with positive direction in the direction of the flow. Then, in the usual way, introduce a righthanded cartesian coordinate system with unit vectors along the axes. By hypothesis, the **k**-component of the flow is the only one different from zero, so

$$\mathbf{v} = (a^2 - r^2)\mathbf{k} = (a^2 - x^2 - y^2)\mathbf{k}$$

for points inside the pipe. This vector field is not defined outside the cylinder $x^2 + y^2 = a^2$. If we were to draw the velocity vectors at all points in the disk

$$x^2 + y^2 \leq a^2, \qquad z = 0,$$

their tips would describe the surface

$$z = a^2 - r^2$$

(cylindrical coordinates) for $z \geq 0$. Since this field does not depend on z, a similar figure would illustrate the flow field across any cross section of the pipe made by a plane perpendicular to its axis.

EXAMPLE 2. In another flow, a fluid is rotating about the z-axis with constant angular velocity ω. Hence every particle at a distance r from the z-axis and in a plane perpendicular to the z-axis traces a circle of radius r, and each such particle has constant speed $|\mathbf{v}| = \omega r$. Describe this field by writing an equation for the velocity at $P(x, y, z)$.

Solution. (See Fig. 15–2.) Each particle travels in a circle parallel to the xy-plane. Therefore it is convenient to begin by looking at the projection of such a circle onto this plane. The point $P(x, y, z)$ in space projects onto the image point $P'(x, y, 0)$, and the velocity vector $\mathbf{v}$ of a particle at P projects onto the velocity vector $\mathbf{v}'$ of a particle at P'. We assume that the motion is in the positive, or counterclockwise, direction, as indicated in the figure. The position vector of P' is $\mathbf{R}' = \mathbf{i}x + \mathbf{j}y$, and the vectors $-\mathbf{i}y + \mathbf{j}x$ and $\mathbf{i}y - \mathbf{j}x$ are both perpendicular to $\mathbf{R}'$. All three of these vectors have magnitude

$$\sqrt{x^2 + y^2} = r.$$

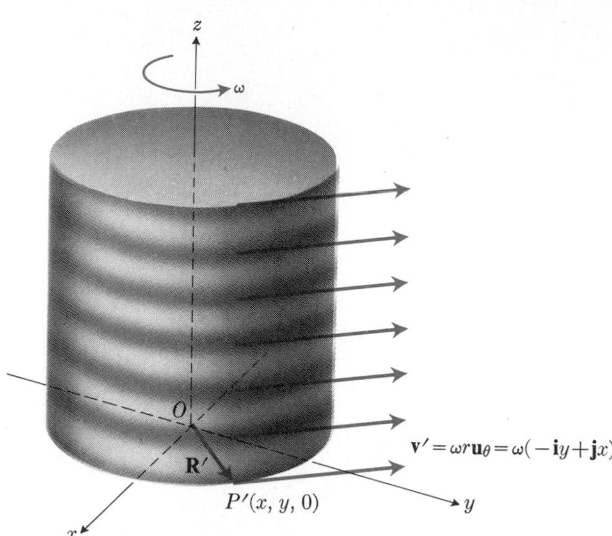

15–2 A steady flow parallel to the xy-plane, with constant angular velocity ω in the positive direction.

The velocity vector we want has magnitude ωr, is perpendicular to $\mathbf{R}'$, and points in the direction of motion. When x and y are both positive (that is, when the particle is in the first quadrant), the velocity should have a negative **i**-component and a positive **j**-component. The vector that has these properties is

$$\mathbf{v}' = \omega r \mathbf{u}_\theta = \omega(-\mathbf{i}y + \mathbf{j}x). \tag{2a}$$

This formula can be verified for P' in the other three quadrants as well; for example, in the third quadrant both x and y are negative, so Eq. (2a) gives a vector with a positive **i**-component and a negative **j**-component, which is correct. Also, because the motion of P is in a circle parallel to that described by P', and has the same velocity, we have

$$\mathbf{v} = \omega(-\mathbf{i}y + \mathbf{j}x) \tag{2b}$$

for any point in the fluid.

EXAMPLE 3. A fluid has a velocity vector, at every point in space, that is the sum of a constant velocity vector parallel to the z-axis and a rotational velocity vector given by Eq. (2b). Describe the field.

Solution. Let the constant component parallel to the z-axis be $c\mathbf{k}$. Then the resultant field is

$$\mathbf{v} = \omega(-\mathbf{i}y + \mathbf{j}x) + c\mathbf{k}. \tag{3}$$

EXAMPLE 4. The gravitational force field induced at the point $P(x, y, z)$ in space by a mass M that is taken to lie at an origin is defined to be the force with which M would attract a particle of *unit* mass at P. Describe this field mathematically, assuming the inverse-square law.

Solution. Because we are now assuming that both M and the unit mass at P are *point* masses, we don't have to integrate anything; we just write down the force:

$$\mathbf{F} = \frac{GM(1)}{|\overrightarrow{OP}|^2}\mathbf{u}, \tag{4a}$$

where G is the gravitational constant, and

$$\mathbf{u} = -\frac{\overrightarrow{OP}}{|\overrightarrow{OP}|}$$

is a unit vector directed *from P toward O*. The position vector of P is $\overrightarrow{OP} = \mathbf{i}x + \mathbf{j}y + \mathbf{k}z$, so we find that

$$\mathbf{F} = \frac{-GM(\mathbf{i}x + \mathbf{j}y + \mathbf{k}z)}{(x^2 + y^2 + z^2)^{3/2}} \tag{4b}$$

gives the gravitational force field in question. Its graph would consist of infinitely many vectors, one starting from each point P (except the origin), and pointing straight toward the origin. If P is near the origin, the associated vector is longer than for points farther away from O. For points P on a ray through the origin, the $\mathbf{F}$-vectors would lie along that same ray, and decrease in length in proportion to the square of the distance from O. Figure 15–3 is a partial representation of this field. As you look at the figure, however, you should also imagine that an $\mathbf{F}$-vector is attached to *every* point $P \neq O$, and not just to those shown. At points on the surface of the sphere $|\overrightarrow{OP}| = a$, the vectors all have the same length, and all point toward the center of the sphere.

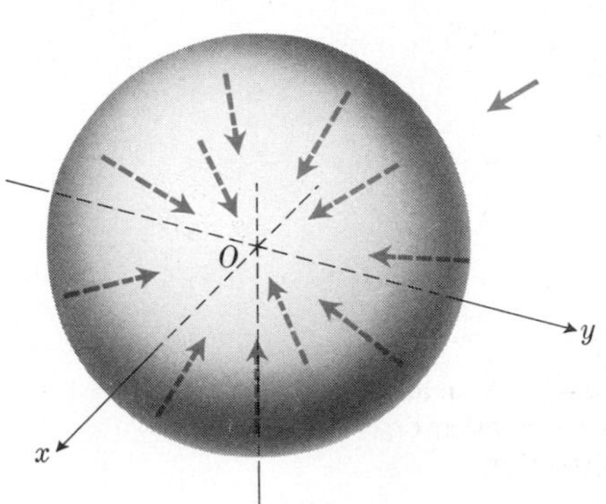

15–3 Some of the vectors of the gravitational field of Example 4.

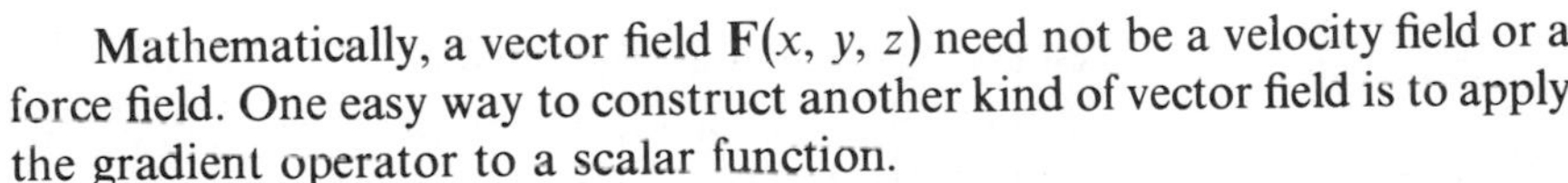

Mathematically, a vector field $\mathbf{F}(x, y, z)$ need not be a velocity field or a force field. One easy way to construct another kind of vector field is to apply the gradient operator to a scalar function.

EXAMPLE 5. Suppose that the temperature T at each point $P(x, y, z)$ in some region of space is

$$T = 100 - x^2 - y^2 - z^2, \tag{5a}$$

and that $\mathbf{F}(x, y, z)$ is defined to be the gradient of T:

$$\mathbf{F} = \nabla T. \tag{5b}$$

Find this vector field and discuss some of its properties.

Solution. From the definition of grad T we have

$$\begin{aligned} \mathbf{F} = \nabla T = \text{grad } T &= \mathbf{i}\frac{\partial T}{\partial x} + \mathbf{j}\frac{\partial T}{\partial y} + \mathbf{k}\frac{\partial T}{\partial z} \\ &= -2x\mathbf{i} - 2y\mathbf{j} - 2z\mathbf{k} \\ &= -2\mathbf{R}, \end{aligned} \tag{5c}$$

where

$$\mathbf{R} = \overrightarrow{OP} = \mathbf{i}x + \mathbf{j}y + \mathbf{k}z$$

is the position vector of $P(x, y, z)$. This field is like a central force field, all vectors $\mathbf{F}$ being directed toward the origin. At points on a sphere with $|\overrightarrow{OP}|$

equal to a constant, the magnitude of the field vectors is a constant equal to twice the radius of the sphere. So, to represent the field, we could construct any sphere with center at O and draw a vector from any point P on the surface straight through O to the other side of the sphere. The collection of all such vectors, for points in the domain of the function T of Eq. (5a), constitutes the *gradient field* of this particular scalar function.

REMARK. An *isothermal* surface for Eq. (5a) is any surface on which T is constant. For Example 5, such a surface would be any sphere with center at the origin and radius $\sqrt{100 - T}$. Our calculation of $\mathbf{F} = \nabla T = -2\mathbf{R}$ has verified that the gradient of T at P is *normal* to the isothermal surface through P, because the diameter of such a spherical surface is always normal to the surface. [See Fig. 13–21(b) for the general picture of grad f normal to the surface $f =$ constant.]

PROBLEMS

1. In Example 1, where is the speed (a) the greatest? (b) the least?

2. Suppose the density of the fluid is $\delta =$ constant at $P(x, y, z)$ in Example 1. Explain why the double integral

$$\int_0^a \int_0^{2\pi} \delta(a^2 - r^2)r \, d\theta \, dr$$

represents the *mass transport* (amount of mass per unit of time) flowing across the surface

$$x^2 + y^2 \leq a^2, \qquad z = 0.$$

Evaluate the integral.

3. In Example 2, the position vector of P is

$$\mathbf{R} = \mathbf{R}' + z\mathbf{k}.$$

Show that for the motion described, it is correct to say that

$$\frac{d\mathbf{R}}{dt} = \mathbf{v} = \frac{d\mathbf{R}'}{dt} = \mathbf{v}'.$$

4. Describe, in words, the motion of the fluid discussed in Example 3. What path in space is described by a particle of the fluid that goes through the point $A(a, 0, 0)$ at time $t = 0$? Prove your result by integrating the vector equation

$$\frac{d\mathbf{R}}{dt} = \omega(-\mathbf{i}y + \mathbf{j}x) + c\mathbf{k}.$$

You may find cylindrical coordinates helpful.

5. In Example 4, suppose that the mass M is at the point (x_0, y_0, z_0) rather than at the origin. How should Eq. (4b) be modified to describe this new gravitational force field?

In Problems 6 through 10, find the gradient fields $\mathbf{F}(x, y, z) = \nabla f$ for the given functions f.

6. $f(x, y, z) = x^2 \exp(2y + 3z)$
7. $f(x, y, z) = \ln(x^2 + y^2 + z^2)$
8. $f(x, y, z) = \tan^{-1}(xy/z)$
9. $f(x, y, z) = 2x - 3y + 5z$
10. $f(x, y, z) = (x^2 + y^2 + z^2)^{n/2}$

15–2 SURFACE INTEGRALS

We know how to calculate the area of a surface in space by projecting it onto one of the coordinate planes and integrating a suitable function over this shadow region. For a surface described by

$$z = f(x, y) \tag{1}$$

that projects into a region R in the xy-plane, the surface area is

$$\iint_R \sqrt{1 + f_x^2 + f_y^2} \, dx \, dy. \tag{2}$$

The development in Article 14–9 also showed that we could interpret the integrand

$$g(x, y) = \sqrt{1 + f_x^2 + f_y^2} \tag{3a}$$

as the amount by which we need to multiply the area of a small portion of R to obtain the area of the corresponding small portion of a tangent plane approximating the surface at $P(x, y, f(x, y))$. In such cases, it is customary to use differential notation and simply write

$$d\sigma = g(x, y)\, dA, \tag{3b}$$

where we consider $d\sigma$ to be an element of surface area in the tangent plane that approximates the corresponding portion $\Delta\sigma$ of the surface itself. This is precisely analogous to taking

$$ds = \sqrt{1 + f_x^2}\, dx$$

as an approximation of a portion Δs of arc length of a curve. Furthermore, just as $\int ds$ gives the length of a curve, so $\iint d\sigma$ gives the area of a surface. The dA in Eq. (3b) represents an element of area $dx\, dy$, or $r\, d\theta\, dr$, in the xy-plane, and Eq. (2) could be written as

$$\iint_S d\sigma = \iint_R g(x, y)\, dA. \tag{4}$$

The symbol S under the integrals on the lefthand side in Eq. (4) symbolizes the surface in space over which we integrate, just as R on the righthand side symbolizes that region of the xy-plane over which the calculations are made according to Eq. (2).

We often want to evaluate such an integral as

$$\iint_S h(x, y, z)\, d\sigma, \tag{5}$$

and understand its meaning and applications. For example, if h gives the charge density per unit area in some electrostatic field, then this integral could be interpreted as total charge on the surface S; or, if h represents the amount of fluid flowing in the direction of the normal to S at $P(x, y, z)$ per unit area, per unit time, then the integral could be interpreted as the total fluid flow across S per unit time. Many other interpretations are possible, some of which will be brought out in examples and problems. You may encounter others in your studies in physics or engineering, or in other courses in mathematics.

Definition of the Surface Integral as a Limit of Sums

Although you should have no difficulty interpreting and using the surface integral indicated by (5), we ought first to give a mathematical definition of it. As in a discussion of surface area, therefore, we consider a surface consisting of those points $P(x, y, z)$ whose coordinates satisfy

$$z = f(x, y) \qquad \text{for} \quad (x, y) \in R, \tag{6}$$

where R is a closed, bounded region of the xy-plane. We assume that f and its first partial derivatives f_x and f_y are continuous functions throughout R

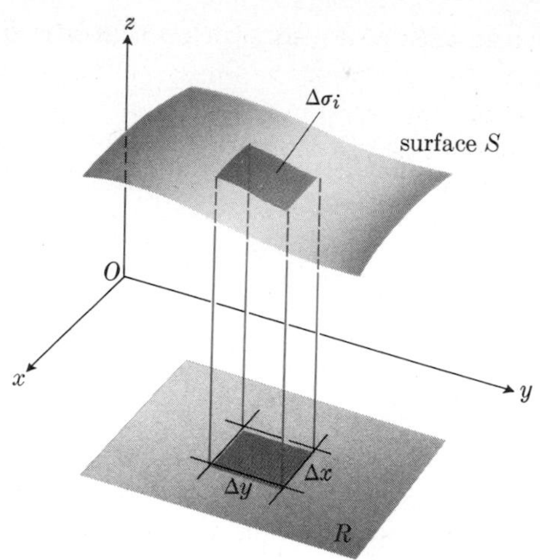

15–4 The surface S in space projects onto the region R in the xy-plane. A subregion of S with area $\Delta\sigma$ projects onto a subregion of R with area $\Delta x\,\Delta y$:

$$\iint_S h(x, y, z)\,d\sigma = \lim \sum h(x_i, y_i, z_i)\,\Delta\sigma_i.$$

and on its boundary. We subdivide the region R into a finite number N of nonoverlapping subregions. We can do this, for example, by lines parallel to the y-axis spaced Δx apart, and lines parallel to the x-axis spaced Δy apart. When these subregions of R are projected vertically upward on the surface S (see Fig. 15–4), they induce a subdivision of S into N subregions. Let the areas of these subregions be numbered

$$\Delta\sigma_1, \quad \Delta\sigma_2, \quad \ldots, \quad \Delta\sigma_N. \tag{7}$$

Next, we suppose that a point $P_i(x_i, y_i, z_i)$ is chosen on the surface in the ith subregion, and the product

$$h(x_i, y_i, z_i)\,\Delta\sigma_i$$

is formed for each i from 1 through N. Now consider the sum

$$\sum_{i=1}^{N} h(x_i, y_i, z_i)\,\Delta\sigma_i. \tag{8}$$

If such sums as (8) have a common limit L as the number N tends to infinity and the largest dimension of the subregions of R tends to zero, independently of the way in which the points P_i are selected within the subregions $\Delta\sigma_i$ on the surface, then that limit is called the *surface integral* of h over S, and it is represented by the notation (5). Although we shall not prove it here, it is true that for surfaces S of the type described, and for continuous functions h, the limit does exist as specified. We now turn to the practical matter of evaluating such surface integrals.

Evaluation of Surface Integrals

Continuing with the assumptions about S and h just mentioned, we see that the area $\Delta\sigma_i$ in the sum (8) is approximated by

$$g(x_i, y_i)\,\Delta A_i,$$

where g is the function defined by Eq. (3a) and ΔA_i is the area of the ith subregion of R. For the subregions completely inside R, away from the boundary, we could take $\Delta A_i = \Delta x \, \Delta y$; but for subregions along the boundary, we might (at least in theory) compute ΔA_i itself by a separate double integration in the xy-plane. However, as $\Delta x \to 0$ and $\Delta y \to 0$, if the boundary of R is a curve of finite arc length, these broken subregions can, in fact, simply be ignored. We do this, and let N denote the number of little rectangles that lie completely inside the boundary of R. The sum (8) is thus to be replaced by a sum of the form

$$\sum_{i=1}^{N} h(x_i, y_i, z_i) g(x_i, y_i) \, \Delta x \, \Delta y,$$

with $z_i = f(x_i, y_i)$, and g as given by Eq. (3a). Let Δx and Δy approach zero in this last sum: Then the approximations we have used for $\Delta\sigma_i$ become more and more accurate, and the limit is the same as

$$\iint_R h[x, y, f(x, y)] g(x, y) \, dx \, dy, \tag{9}$$

where

$$g(x, y) = \sqrt{1 + f_x^2 + f_y^2}.$$

As a practical procedure for evaluating the surface integral (5), replace z by its value $f(x, y)$ on the surface, and replace $d\sigma$ by

$$d\sigma = \sqrt{1 + f_x^2 + f_y^2} \, dA,$$

where dA is $dx \, dy$, $dy \, dx$, or $r \, d\theta \, dr$, and evaluate the resulting double integral over the region R in the xy-plane into which S projects.

EXAMPLE 1. Evaluate $\iint z \, d\sigma$ over the hemisphere

$$z = \sqrt{a^2 - x^2 - y^2}, \qquad x^2 + y^2 \le a^2.$$

Solution

$$\frac{\partial z}{\partial x} = \frac{-x}{z}, \qquad \frac{\partial z}{\partial y} = \frac{-y}{z}.$$

Hence

$$d\sigma = \sqrt{1 + (x^2/z^2) + (y^2/z^2)} \, dA$$

$$= \frac{a}{z} dA,$$

because $x^2 + y^2 + z^2 = a^2$ on S. Since the integrand is $z \, d\sigma = a \, dA$, we can omit substituting the radical expression for z, and simply get

$$\iint_S z \, d\sigma = \iint_R a \, dA$$

$$= a(\pi a^2) = \pi a^3.$$

We skip the detailed evaluation of the double integral of dA over the interior of the circle $r = a$ in the plane, because we know it is just the area πa^2.

EXAMPLE 2. Evaluate $\iint (x^2 + y^2)\, d\sigma$ over hemisphere S of Example 1.

Solution. From Example 1, we have

$$d\sigma = \frac{a}{z}\, dA,$$

and so our integral is

$$\iint_S (x^2 + y^2)\, d\sigma = \iint_R (x^2 + y^2)(a/z)\, dA,$$

with

$$z = \sqrt{a^2 - x^2 - y^2}.$$

This integral is an obvious candidate for polar coordinates, with

$$x^2 + y^2 = r^2, \qquad dA = r\, dr\, d\theta, \qquad z = \sqrt{a^2 - r^2}.$$

Thus we obtain

$$\iint_S (x^2 + y^2)\, d\sigma = \int_0^{2\pi} \int_0^a \frac{ar^3\, dr\, d\theta}{(a^2 - r^2)^{1/2}}.$$

The r-integration is done using the substitutions

$$u = (a^2 - r^2)^{1/2}, \qquad u^2 = a^2 - r^2,$$
$$r^2 = a^2 - u^2, \qquad r\, dr = -u\, du,$$

so that

$$\int r^3 (a^2 - r^2)^{-1/2}\, dr = -\int (a^2 - u^2) u^{-1} u\, du$$
$$= -a^2 u + \tfrac{1}{3} u^3.$$

If $r = 0$, then $u = a$, and if $r = a$, then $u = 0$; and with another two or three simple steps, we get

$$2\pi a(a^3 - \tfrac{1}{3}a^3) = \tfrac{4}{3}\pi a^4$$

as the final answer.

REMARK 1. There is a very easy way to check this result: If we were to integrate $x^2 + y^2$ over the entire sphere, we should get twice what we get for the integral over the top half. Also, because the sphere has so much symmetry, we see that

$$\iint x^2\, d\sigma = \iint y^2\, d\sigma = \iint z^2\, d\sigma$$
$$= \tfrac{1}{3} \iint (x^2 + y^2 + z^2)\, d\sigma,$$

if all integrals are extended over the entire surface of the sphere. But we can easily evaluate the last of these four integrals without integration, because

$x^2 + y^2 + z^2 = a^2$ is constant on the sphere: We have

$$\iint a^2 \, d\sigma = a^2 \iint d\sigma = a^2(4\pi a^2) = 4\pi a^4.$$

For Example 2, we have to multiply this by $\frac{1}{3}$, then by 2 (for $x^2 + y^2$), and finally by $\frac{1}{2}$, because we want the value of the integral over a hemisphere. The result of this multiplication is $\frac{4}{3}\pi a^4$, which agrees with our earlier calculation.

REMARK 2. If the equation of a surface S has the form $F(x, y, z) = 0$, we can let

$$\mathbf{N} = \mathbf{i}F_x + \mathbf{j}F_y + \mathbf{k}F_z$$

be a normal to S, and then take $d\sigma = dA/|\cos\phi|$, where ϕ is an angle between $\mathbf{N}$ and a vector normal to the plane onto which S is projected. If we project S into the xy-plane, we then take dA to be equal to $dx\,dy$, and ϕ to be the angle between $\mathbf{N}$ and $\mathbf{k}$, so that

$$d\sigma = \left(\frac{\sqrt{F_x^2 + F_y^2 + F_z^2}}{|F_z|}\right) dx\,dy. \tag{10}$$

(See Fig. 15–5.) To evaluate the surface integral

$$\iint_S h(x, y, z)\, d\sigma,$$

we use the equation of the surface to eliminate z in the integrand and in Eq. (10), thereby obtaining a function of x and y to be integrated, as usual, over the projection in the xy-plane. Two other equations can be derived from Eq. (10) by simply permuting the letters x, y, and z. These can bc used whenever it is easier to work with the projection of S onto one of the other coordinate planes.

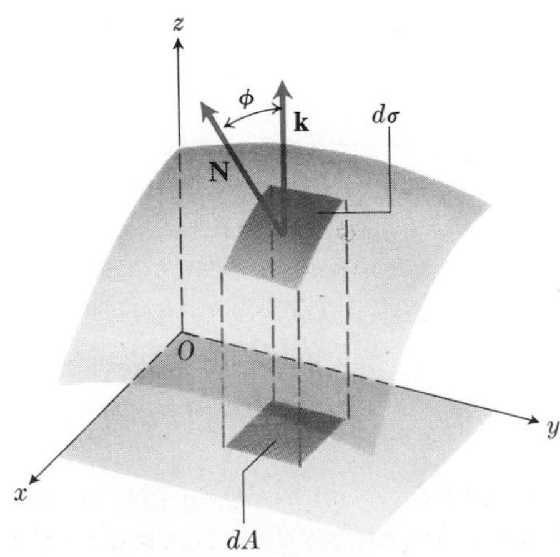

15–5 The element of area $d\sigma$ on the surface S and the element of area dA in the xy-plane satisfy the relation $d\sigma = dA/|\cos\phi|$, where ϕ is the angle between $\mathbf{N} = \mathbf{i}F_x + \mathbf{j}F_y + \mathbf{k}F_z$ and $\mathbf{k}$.

PROBLEMS

In Problems 1 through 3, explain briefly, with reference to the definition of the surface integral as a limit, why the stated result should be true if c is a constant and F and G are continuous functions.

1. $\iint_S c\, d\sigma = c \times (\text{area of } S)$

2. $\iint_S [F(x, y, z) + G(x, y, z)]\, d\sigma$
$$= \iint_S F(x, y, z)\, d\sigma + \iint_S G(x, y, z)\, d\sigma$$

3. $\iint_S cF(x, y, z)\, d\sigma = c \iint_S F(x, y, z)\, d\sigma$

4. (*Spherical coordinates.*) Suppose that the surface of the hemisphere in Example 1 is subdivided by arcs of great circles on which the spherical coordinate θ remains constant (meridians of longitude), and by circles parallel to the xy-plane on which ϕ remains constant (parallels of latitude). Let the angular spacings be $\Delta\theta$ and $\Delta\phi$, respectively. Express the integral of Example 1 in the form
$$\lim_{\substack{\Delta\theta \to 0 \\ \Delta\phi \to 0}} \sum F(\theta, \phi)\, \Delta\theta\, \Delta\phi = \iint F(\theta, \phi)\, d\theta\, d\phi,$$
with appropriate limits of integration, and evaluate. (*Hint.* You should get
$$d\sigma = (r\, d\theta) \cdot (\rho\, d\phi) = \rho^2 \sin\phi\, d\theta\, d\phi,$$
where ρ, ϕ, θ are spherical coordinates.)

In Problems 5 and 6, let $h(x, y, z) = x + y + z$ and let S be the portion of the plane $z = 2x + 3y$ for which $x \geq 0$, $y \geq 0$, $x + y \leq 2$.

5. Evaluate $\iint_S h\, d\sigma$ by projecting S into the xy-plane. Sketch the projection.

6. Evaluate $\iint_S h\, d\sigma$ by projecting S into the yz-plane. Sketch the projection and its boundaries.

In Problems 7 through 10, you are asked to evaluate integrals of the form
$$\iint_S \mathbf{F} \cdot \mathbf{n}\, d\sigma$$
for specific vector fields $\mathbf{F}$, given that S, lying in the first octant, is one-eighth of the sphere $x^2 + y^2 + z^2 = a^2$, and $\mathbf{n}$ is a unit vector normal to S and pointing away from the origin. (Thus both $\mathbf{F}$ and $\mathbf{n}$ are vector functions of position on the sphere.)

7. $\mathbf{F} = \mathbf{n}$

8. $\mathbf{F} = -\mathbf{i}y + \mathbf{j}x$

9. $\mathbf{F} = z\mathbf{k}$

10. $\mathbf{F} = \mathbf{i}x + \mathbf{j}y$

15–3 LINE INTEGRALS

Suppose that C is a directed curve in space from A to B, and that $w = w(x, y, z)$ is a scalar function of position that is continuous in a region D that contains C. Figure 15–6 illustrates such a directed curve. It is the locus of points (x, y, z) such that
$$x = f(t), \quad y = g(t), \quad z = h(t), \quad t_A \leq t \leq t_B. \tag{1}$$

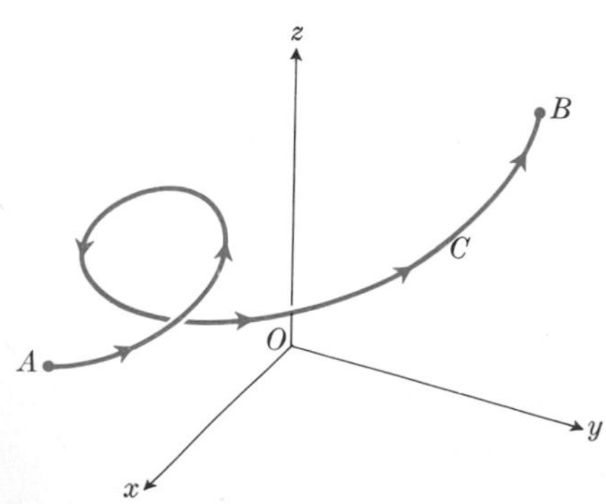

15–6 The directed curve C from A to B.

We assume that the functions f, g, h are continuous and have bounded and piecewise-continuous first derivatives on $[t_A, t_B]$. It is a theorem of higher mathematics that the object to be defined below, $\int_C w\, ds$, does not actually depend on the particular parametrization of C: All parametrizations satisfying the hypotheses stated for f, g, h give the same answer. Indeed, it is possible to define the integral without reference to parametric equations, but evaluations of line integrals are almost always carried out in terms of some parametrization or other. So we proceed as follows:

We divide the interval $[t_A, t_B]$ into N subintervals of lengths
$$\Delta t_1, \quad \Delta t_2, \quad \ldots, \quad \Delta t_N.$$
The points of subdivision also correspond to points on C which divide it into

subarcs of lengths

$$\Delta s_1, \quad \Delta s_2, \quad \ldots, \quad \Delta s_N.$$

Let $P_i(x_i, y_i, z_i)$ be an arbitrary point on the ith subarc, and form the sum

$$\sum_{i=1}^{N} w(x_i, y_i, z_i)\,\Delta s_i. \tag{2}$$

If these sums have a limit L, as $N \to \infty$ and the largest $\Delta t_i \to 0$, and if this limit is the same for *all* ways of subdividing $[t_A, t_B]$ and all choices of the points P_i, then we call this limit the *line integral* of w along C from A to B, and express it by the notation

$$\int_C w\,ds = \lim \sum_{i=1}^{N} w(x_i, y_i, z_i)\,\Delta s_i. \tag{3a}$$

It is also a theorem that, under the hypotheses stated for w and C, the line integral exists, and is the same as

$$\int_{t_A}^{t_B} w[f(t), g(t), h(t)]\sqrt{[f'(t)]^2 + [g'(t)]^2 + [h'(t)]^2}\,dt. \tag{3b}$$

Although we shall not prove this theorem, we shall show how line integrals are evaluated in practice, and illustrate some of their physical applications. Although Eq. (3b) looks quite complicated, it is just the result of substituting the parametric equations for x, y, z in w and using the standard formula for ds. In our first example, we use a curve in the xy-plane for which the formula simplifies a bit.

EXAMPLE 1. Let C be the line segment from $A(0, 0)$ to $B(1, 1)$, and let $w = x + y^2$. Evaluate $\int_C w\,ds$ for two different parametrizations of C.

Solution 1. If we let

$$x = t \quad \text{and} \quad y = t, \quad 0 \le t \le 1,$$

then we get

$$\int_C w\,ds = \int_0^1 (t + t^2)\sqrt{1 + 1}\,dt$$
$$= \sqrt{2}\left[\frac{t^2}{2} + \frac{t^3}{3}\right]_0^1 = \frac{5\sqrt{2}}{6}.$$

Solution 2. As a second parametrization of the given segment of the line $y = x$, we let

$$x = \sin t \quad \text{and} \quad y = \sin t, \quad 0 \le t \le \pi/2,$$

and get

$$\int_C w\,ds = \int_0^{\pi/2} (\sin t + \sin^2 t)\sqrt{2\cos^2 t}\,dt$$
$$= \sqrt{2}\left[\frac{\sin^2 t}{2} + \frac{\sin^3 t}{3}\right]_0^{\pi/2} = \frac{5\sqrt{2}}{6}.$$

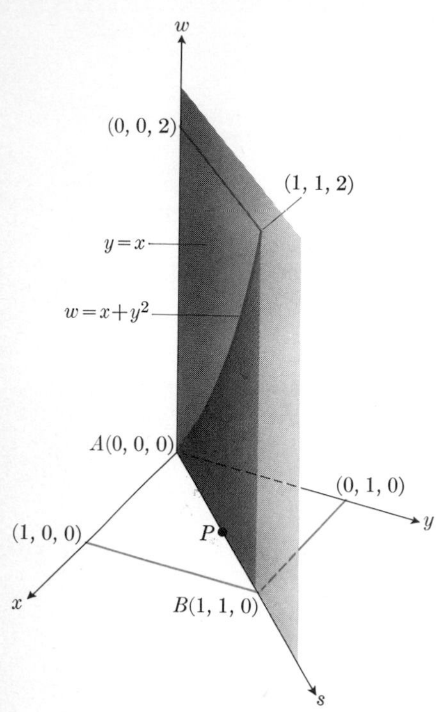

15–7 Area in the plane $y = x$ under the surface $w = x + y^2$ for $0 \le x \le 1$.

REMARK 1. The line integral of Example 1 can be interpreted as the area of the region R that lies in the plane $y = x$, above the plane $w = 0$, and under the surface $w = x + y^2$. We can, in fact, introduce an s-axis along the intersection of the planes $w = 0$ and $y = x$, as shown in Fig. 15–7. The s-coordinate of the point $P(x, x, 0)$ between $A(0, 0, 0)$ and $B(1, 1, 0)$ on C is

$$s = \sqrt{x^2 + x^2} = x\sqrt{2}.$$

Thus we can use the arc length s itself as parameter for C:

$$x = \frac{s}{\sqrt{2}}, \qquad y = \frac{s}{\sqrt{2}}, \qquad 0 \le s \le \sqrt{2}.$$

The upper boundary of R is the intersection of the surface $w = x + y^2$ and the plane $y = x$. In the sw-plane, this curve has equation

$$w = \frac{s}{\sqrt{2}} + \frac{s^2}{2},$$

and the area of R is given by

$$\int_C w\, ds = \int_0^{\sqrt{2}} \left(\frac{s}{\sqrt{2}} + \frac{s^2}{2}\right) ds$$

$$= \frac{s^2}{2\sqrt{2}} + \frac{s^3}{6}\bigg]_0^{\sqrt{2}} = \frac{1}{\sqrt{2}} + \frac{2\sqrt{2}}{6} = \frac{5\sqrt{2}}{6}.$$

Whenever C is a *plane* curve, we can interpret the line integral $\int_C w\, ds$ as the area of a portion of a cylinder (or as the difference between areas above and below C, if w has both positive and negative values along C). Even if C is curved, one can at least think of measuring the distance s along C, starting with $s = 0$ at A and increasing to $s = \ell$ at B, where ℓ is the length of arc of C from A to B. Because s increases along C, there is one and only one point on C for any value of $s \in [0, \ell]$, and we can imagine the parametric equations of C being given in terms of s; say,

$$x = x(s), \qquad y = y(s), \qquad z = z(s), \qquad 0 \le s \le \ell.$$

Then, along C, $w = w[x(s), y(s), z(s)]$ is a function of s: $w = \phi(s)$. The way in which the line integral is defined as a limit of sums ensures that $\int_C w\, ds$ is just the integral of this function ϕ with respect to s:

$$\int_C w\, ds = \int_0^{\ell} \phi(s)\, ds. \tag{4}$$

Equation (4) also suggests that we can think of the cylinder as having the plane curve C as base, and the curve $w = \phi(s)$ as upper boundary. We can then flatten the cylinder so that C becomes the segment $[0, \ell]$ of the s-axis in an sw-plane. Figure 15–8 illustrates this idea.

Line Integrals and Work

If the point of application of a force

$$\mathbf{F} = \mathbf{i}M(x, y, z) + \mathbf{j}N(x, y, z) + \mathbf{k}P(x, y, z) \tag{5}$$

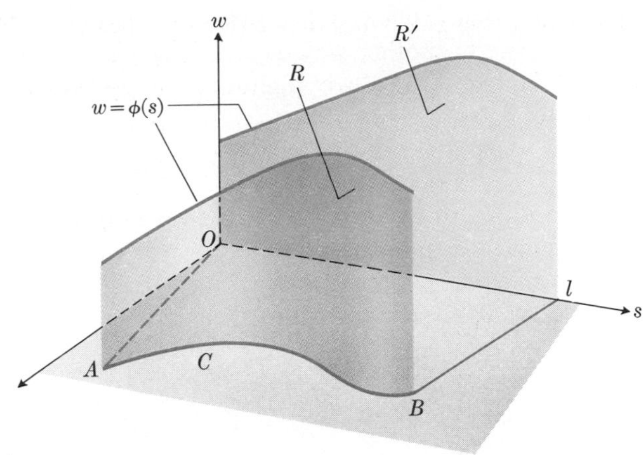

15–8 The region R above the curve C on the cylindrical surface maps onto the region R' in the sw-plane.

moves along a curve C from a point $A(a_1, a_2, a_3)$ to a point $B(b_1, b_2, b_3)$, then the work done by the force is

$$W = \int_C \mathbf{F} \cdot d\mathbf{R}, \tag{6}$$

where

$$\mathbf{R} = \mathbf{i}x + \mathbf{j}y + \mathbf{k}z \tag{7}$$

is the vector from the origin to the point (x, y, z), and

$$d\mathbf{R} = \frac{d\mathbf{R}}{ds}\,ds = \mathbf{i}\,dx + \mathbf{j}\,dy + \mathbf{k}\,dz. \tag{8}$$

If we calculate the dot product of the vectors $\mathbf{F}$ and $d\mathbf{R}$ from Eqs. (5) and (8), then we may write Eq. (6) in the alternative form

$$W = \int_C M\,dx + N\,dy + P\,dz, \tag{9}$$

where M, N, and P are functions of x, y, and z, and the subscript C on the integral refers to the curve C along which the integral is taken. Such an integral as Eq. (9) is also called a line integral (*curve integral* would perhaps be a more descriptive name). Because

$$\frac{d\mathbf{R}}{ds} = \mathbf{T} = \text{unit tangent vector},$$

Eq. (6) is just another way of saying that the work is the value of the line integral along C of the *tangential component* of the force field $\mathbf{F}$. This tangential component is a scalar function, say w, of position along C:

$$w = \mathbf{F} \cdot \mathbf{T} = w(x, y, z).$$

Therefore

$$W = \int_C \mathbf{F} \cdot d\mathbf{R} = \int_C \mathbf{F} \cdot \mathbf{T}\,ds = \int_C w(x, y, z)\,ds.$$

This is just the kind of line integral defined by Eq. (3a), but the form of the integral in Eq. (9) suggests another way of evaluating it.

To evaluate the integral in (9) we might express the equations of C in terms of a parameter t:

$$x = x(t), \qquad y = y(t), \qquad z = z(t), \tag{10}$$

such that the curve is described from A to B as t varies from a value t_1 to a value t_2. Then *all* quantities in the integral may be expressed in terms of one variable t and the result evaluated in the usual manner as a definite integral with respect to t from t_1 to t_2. In general, the value of the integral depends on the path C as well as on its endpoints.

EXAMPLE 2. A force is given by

$$\mathbf{F} = \mathbf{i}(x^2 - y) + \mathbf{j}(y^2 - z) + \mathbf{k}(z^2 - x),$$

and its point of application moves from the origin O to the point $A(1, 1, 1)$,

a) along the straight line OA, and

b) along the curve

$$x = t, \qquad y = t^2, \qquad z = t^3, \qquad 0 \le t \le 1.$$

Find the work done in the two cases.

Solution. **a)** Equations for the line OA are

$$x = y = z.$$

The integral to be evaluated is

$$W = \int_C (x^2 - y)\,dx + (y^2 - z)\,dy + (z^2 - x)\,dz,$$

which, for the path OA, becomes

$$W = \int_0^1 3(x^2 - x)\,dx = -\tfrac{1}{2}.$$

b) Along the curve, we get

$$W = \int_0^1 2(t^4 - t^3)t\,dt + 3(t^6 - t)t^2\,dt = -\tfrac{29}{60}.$$

Now, under certain conditions, the line integral between two points A and B is independent of the path C joining them. That is, the integral in Eq. (6) has the same value for any two paths C_1 and C_2 joining A and B. This happens when the force field $\mathbf{F}$ is a *gradient field*, that is, when

$$\mathbf{F}(x, y, z) = \nabla f = \mathbf{i}\frac{\partial f}{\partial x} + \mathbf{j}\frac{\partial f}{\partial y} + \mathbf{k}\frac{\partial f}{\partial z},$$

for some differentiable function f. We state this as a formal theorem and prove the sufficiency and necessity of the conditions, with some interpolated remarks.

Theorem 1. *Let* **F** *be a vector field with components M, N, P, that are continuous throughout some connected region D. Then a necessary and sufficient condition for the integral*

$$\int_A^B \mathbf{F}\cdot d\mathbf{R}$$

to be independent of the path joining the points A and B in D is that there exist a differentiable function f such that

$$\mathbf{F}=\nabla f=\mathbf{i}\frac{\partial f}{\partial x}+\mathbf{j}\frac{\partial f}{\partial y}+\mathbf{k}\frac{\partial f}{\partial z} \tag{11}$$

throughout D.

Proof. Sufficiency. First, we suppose that Eq. (11) is satisfied, and then consider A and B to be two points in D (see Fig. 15–9). Suppose that C is any piecewise smooth curve joining A and B:

$$x=x(t),\qquad y=y(t),\qquad z=z(t),\qquad t_1\le t\le t_2.$$

Along $C, f=f[x(t), y(t), z(t)]$ is a function of t to which we may apply the chain rule to differentiate with respect to t:

$$\begin{aligned}\frac{df}{dt}&=\frac{\partial f}{\partial x}\frac{dx}{dt}+\frac{\partial f}{\partial y}\frac{dy}{dt}+\frac{\partial f}{\partial z}\frac{dz}{dt}\\ &=\nabla f\cdot\left(\mathbf{i}\frac{dx}{dt}+\mathbf{j}\frac{dy}{dt}+\mathbf{k}\frac{dz}{dt}\right)\\ &=\nabla f\cdot\frac{d\mathbf{R}}{dt}.\end{aligned} \tag{12a}$$

15–9 A piecewise smooth curve C joining points A and B in the region D of Theorem 1.

Because Eq. (11) holds, we also have

$$\mathbf{F}\cdot d\mathbf{R}=\nabla f\cdot d\mathbf{R}=\nabla f\cdot\frac{d\mathbf{R}}{dt}\,dt=\frac{df}{dt}\,dt. \tag{12b}$$

We now use this result to integrate $\mathbf{F}\cdot d\mathbf{R}$ along C from A to B:

$$\begin{aligned}\int_C \mathbf{F}\cdot d\mathbf{R}&=\int_{t_1}^{t_2}\frac{df}{dt}\,dt\\ &=\int_{t_1}^{t_2}\frac{d}{dt}f[x(t), y(t), z(t)]\,dt\\ &=f[x(t), y(t), z(t)]\Big]_{t_1}^{t_2}\\ &=f[x(t_2), y(t_2), z(t_2)]-f[x(t_1), y(t_1), z(t_1)]\\ &=f(B)-f(A).\end{aligned}$$

Therefore, if $\mathbf{F}=\nabla f$, we have the result

$$\int_A^B \mathbf{F}\cdot d\mathbf{R}=\int_A^B \nabla f\cdot d\mathbf{R}=f(B)-f(A). \tag{13}$$

The value of the integral $f(B)-f(A)$ does not depend on the path C at all. Equation (13) is the space analog of the Fundamental Theorem of Integral Calculus (see Article 4–8):

$$\int_a^b f'(x)\,dx = f(b) - f(a).$$

The only difference is that we have $\nabla f \cdot d\mathbf{R}$ in place of $f'(x)\,dx$. This analogy suggests that perhaps there is also a space analog of the fact that any continuous function of a single real variable is the derivative with respect to x of its integral from a to x (again, see Article 4–8). In other words, if we define a function f by the rule

$$f(x', y', z') = \int_A^{(x',y',z')} \mathbf{F} \cdot d\mathbf{R}, \tag{14a}$$

perhaps it will be true that

$$\nabla f = \mathbf{F}. \tag{14b}$$

Equation (14b) is indeed true when the righthand side of Eq. (14a) is path-independent, and the proof of this fact will complete our theorem.

Proof. Necessity. We now assume that the line integral in (14a) is path-independent, and prove that $\mathbf{F} = \nabla f$ for the function f defined by Eq. (14a). We first write $\mathbf{F}$ in terms of its $\mathbf{i}$-, $\mathbf{j}$-, and $\mathbf{k}$-components:

$$\mathbf{F}(x, y, z) = \mathbf{i}M(x, y, z) + \mathbf{j}N(x, y, z) + \mathbf{k}P(x, y, z), \tag{15}$$

and fix the points A and $B(x', y', z')$ in D. To establish Eq. (14b), we need to show that *the equalities*

$$\frac{\partial f}{\partial x} = M, \qquad \frac{\partial f}{\partial y} = N, \qquad \frac{\partial f}{\partial z} = P \tag{16}$$

hold at each point of D. In what follows, we either assume that D is an open set, so that all of its points are interior points, or we restrict our attention to interior points.

The point $B(x', y', z')$ is the center of some small sphere whose interior lies entirely inside D. We let $h \neq 0$ be small enough so that all points on the ray from B to $B'(x'+h, y', z')$ lie in D (see Fig. 15–9), and consider the difference quotient

$$\frac{f(x'+h, y', z') - f(x', y', z')}{h} = \frac{1}{h}\int_B^{B'} \mathbf{F} \cdot d\mathbf{R}. \tag{17}$$

Since the integral does not depend on a particular path, we choose one convenient for our purpose:

$$x = x' + th, \qquad y = y', \qquad z = z', \qquad 0 \le t \le 1,$$

along which neither y nor z varies, and along which $d\mathbf{R} = \mathbf{i}\,dx = \mathbf{i}h\,dt$. When this is substituted into Eq. (17), along with $\mathbf{F}$ from Eq. (15), we get

$$\frac{f(x'+h, y', z') - f(x', y', z')}{h} = \frac{1}{h}\int_0^1 M(x'+ht, y', z')h\,dt$$

$$= \int_0^1 M(x'+ht, y', z')\,dt. \tag{18}$$

By hypothesis, **F** is continuous, so each component is a continuous function. Thus, given any $\epsilon > 0$, there is a $\delta > 0$ such that

$$|M(x' + ht, y', z') - M(x', y', z')| < \epsilon \qquad \text{when} \quad |ht| < \delta.$$

This implies that when $|h| < \delta$, the integral in Eq. (18) also differs from

$$\int_0^1 M(x', y', z')\, dt = M(x', y', z') \tag{19}$$

by less than ϵ. The equality in (19) follows from the fact that the integrand is a constant, and

$$\int_0^1 dt = 1.$$

Therefore, as $h \to 0$ in Eq. (18), the righthand side has as limit $M(x', y', z')$, so the lefthand side must have the same limit. That, however, is just the partial derivative of f with respect to x at $B(x', y', z')$. Therefore

$$\frac{\partial f}{\partial x} = M \tag{20}$$

holds at each interior point of D.

Equation (20) is the first of the three equalities, Eqs. (16), that are needed to establish Eq. (14b). Proofs of the remaining two equalities in (16) are very similar, and you are asked to prove one of them in Problem 7. One sets up a difference quotient like Eq. (17), but takes

$$B' = (x', y' + h, z') \qquad \text{or} \qquad B' = (x', y', z' + h).$$

In other words, from B, one integrates along a path parallel to the y-axis or parallel to the z-axis. On the former path, $d\mathbf{R} = \mathbf{j}h\, dt$, and on the latter, $d\mathbf{R} = \mathbf{k}h\, dt$. This concludes the proof.

EXAMPLE 3. Find a function f such that

if

$$\mathbf{F} = 2x\mathbf{i} + 2y\mathbf{j} + 2z\mathbf{k}, \tag{21a}$$

then

$$\mathbf{F} = \nabla f. \tag{21b}$$

Solution. We might be lucky and guess

$$f(x, y, z) = x^2 + y^2 + z^2, \tag{22}$$

because $2x$, $2y$, $2z$ are its partial derivatives with respect to x, y, and z. But if we weren't so inspired, then we might try something like Eq. (14a). In the first place, the functions $2x$, $2y$, $2z$ are everywhere continuous, so the region D can be all of space. Of course we don't know, until *after* we find that **F** is a gradient, that the integral in (14a) is path-independent, but we proceed on faith (or at least with hope). The choice of A is up to us, so we make life easy for ourselves by taking $A = (0, 0, 0)$. For the path of integration from A to $B(x', y', z')$, we take the line segment

$$x = x't, \qquad y = y't, \qquad z = z't, \qquad 0 \le t \le 1,$$

along which

$$d\mathbf{R} = (x'\mathbf{i} + y'\mathbf{j} + z'\mathbf{k})\, dt$$

and

$$\mathbf{F} \cdot d\mathbf{R} = (2xx' + 2yy' + 2zz')\,dt$$
$$= (2x'^2 + 2y'^2 + 2z'^2)t\,dt.$$

Therefore, when we substitute into Eq. (14a), we get

$$f(x', y', z') = \int_{(0,0,0)}^{(x',y',z')} \mathbf{F} \cdot d\mathbf{R}$$
$$= [x'^2 + y'^2 + z'^2] \int_0^1 2t\,dt$$
$$= x'^2 + y'^2 + z'^2.$$

If we delete the primes, this equation is identical with Eq. (22).

REMARK 2. The upper limit of integration in Eq. (14a) is an arbitrary point in the domain of **F**, but we use (x', y', z') to designate it, rather than (x, y, z), because the latter is used for the running point that covers the arc C from A to B during the integration. After we have completed the computation of $f(x', y', z')$, we then delete the primes to express the result as $f(x, y, z)$. The analog in one dimension would be

$$\ln x' = \int_1^{x'} \frac{1}{x}\,dx.$$

We must be careful not to confuse the variable of integration x with the limit of integration x'. We distinguished between these two things in a slightly different manner in Eq. (1), Article 6–4, where we wrote

$$\ln x = \int_1^x \frac{1}{t}\,dt.$$

Our purpose there was the same as it is here, however: to maintain a notational difference between the variable *upper limit* and the *variable of integration.*

REMARK 3. So far we have only the criterion

$$\mathbf{F} = \nabla f$$

for deciding whether

$$\int_A^B \mathbf{F} \cdot d\mathbf{R}$$

is path-independent. We shall discover another criterion in Eqs. (26) below. If we follow the method indicated by Eq. (14a) and illustrated in Example 3 for a field **F** that is *not* path-independent, then we should discover, on trying to verify that $\mathbf{F} = \nabla f$, that it isn't so. The next example illustrates exactly this situation.

EXAMPLE 4. Show that there is no function f such that

$$\mathbf{F} = \nabla f \quad \text{if} \quad \mathbf{F} = y\mathbf{i} - x\mathbf{j}.$$

Solution. Here's one way to show it: If there were such a function f, then

$$\frac{\partial f}{\partial x} = y \quad \text{and} \quad \frac{\partial f}{\partial y} = -x,$$

from which we would get

$$\frac{\partial^2 f}{\partial y\, \partial x} = \frac{\partial(y)}{\partial y} = 1 \neq \frac{\partial^2 f}{\partial x\, \partial y} = \frac{\partial(-x)}{\partial x} = -1.$$

But we should have $f_{xy} = f_{yx}$, because

$$f_x = y \quad \text{and} \quad f_y = -x$$

are everywhere continuously differentiable. This contradiction shows that no such f exists.

Another method would be to compute $\int \mathbf{F} \cdot d\mathbf{R}$ between two points, say $A(0, 0, 0)$ and $B(1, 1, 0)$, along two different paths. If the answers turn out to be the same, we haven't proved a thing. But if they turn out to be different, then we know that **F** is not a gradient field. Problem 5 asks you to do this for two specific paths.

A third method is to proceed blithely with Eq. (14a), and get a function f that satisfies Eq. (14a) for a particular path, but that fails to satisfy $\mathbf{F} = \nabla f$. Once again we would choose an origin $A = (0, 0, 0)$ and let $B = (x', y', z')$, and then integrate along the segment

$$x = x't, \qquad y = y't, \qquad z = z't, \qquad 0 \le t \le 1.$$

We would get

$$\begin{aligned} \mathbf{F} \cdot d\mathbf{R} &= (y\mathbf{i} - x\mathbf{j}) \cdot (\mathbf{i}\, dx + \mathbf{j}\, dy + \mathbf{k}\, dz) \\ &= y\, dx - x\, dy \\ &= (y't)(x'\, dt) - (x't)(y'\, dt) \\ &= t(x'y' - x'y')\, dt = 0\, dt. \end{aligned}$$

Therefore Eq. (14a) produces

$$f(x', y', z') = 0 \qquad \text{for all } (x', y', z').$$

This constant function obviously won't have a gradient equal to $y\mathbf{i} - x\mathbf{j}$. In Problem 6 you are asked to explain why this also means that no other function exists whose gradient is the given **F**.

Conservative Fields

When **F** is a force field such that the work integral from A to B is the same for all paths joining them, the field is said to be *conservative*. Theorem 1 therefore shows that a force field is *conservative* if and only if it is a *gradient* field:

$$\mathbf{F} \text{ is conservative} \quad \Leftrightarrow \quad \mathbf{F} = \nabla f. \tag{23}$$

If the field **F** is conservative, the integrand in the work integral,

$$\mathbf{F} \cdot d\mathbf{R} = M\, dx + N\, dy + P\, dz. \tag{24a}$$

is an *exact differential.* By this we mean that there is a function f whose total differential is equal to the given integrand:

$$df = M\,dx + N\,dy + P\,dz, \tag{24b}$$

which holds if and only if

$$M = \frac{\partial f}{\partial x}, \qquad N = \frac{\partial f}{\partial y}, \qquad P = \frac{\partial f}{\partial z}. \tag{25}$$

In Article 13–13, we discussed exact differentials of functions $f(x, y)$ of two variables. The criterion for an exact differential stated in the theorem of that article is easily extended to functions of three or more variables. For functions of three variables, it goes as follows.

Theorem 2. *Let $M(x, y, z)$, $N(x, y, z)$, and $P(x, y, z)$ be continuous, together with their first-order partial derivatives. Then a necessary condition for the expression*

$$M\,dx + N\,dy + P\,dz$$

to be an exact differential is that the following equations all be satisfied:

$$\frac{\partial M}{\partial y} = \frac{\partial N}{\partial x}, \qquad \frac{\partial M}{\partial z} = \frac{\partial P}{\partial x}, \qquad \frac{\partial N}{\partial z} = \frac{\partial P}{\partial y}. \tag{26}$$

This theorem is a straightforward extension of the theorem of Article 13–13 from the two-dimensional to the three-dimensional case. We shall omit the proof, since it is similar to the proof of the earlier theorem.

EXAMPLE 5. Suppose

$$\mathbf{F} = \mathbf{i}(e^x \cos y + yz) + \mathbf{j}(xz - e^x \sin y) + \mathbf{k}(xy + z).$$

Is $\mathbf{F}$ conservative? If so, find f such that $\mathbf{F} = \nabla f$.

Solution. We apply the test of Eqs. (26) to the expression

$$\mathbf{F} \cdot d\mathbf{R} = (e^x \cos y + yz)\,dx + (xz - e^x \sin y)\,dy + (xy + z)\,dz.$$

We let

$$M = e^x \cos y + yz, \qquad N = xz - e^x \sin y, \qquad P = xy + z,$$

and calculate

$$\frac{\partial M}{\partial z} = y = \frac{\partial P}{\partial x}, \qquad \frac{\partial N}{\partial z} = x = \frac{\partial P}{\partial y}, \qquad \frac{\partial M}{\partial y} = -e^x \sin y + z = \frac{\partial N}{\partial x}.$$

The theorem tells us that there may be a function $f(x, y, z)$ such that

$$\mathbf{F} \cdot d\mathbf{R} = df.$$

We would find f by integrating the system of equations

$$\frac{\partial f}{\partial x} = e^x \cos y + yz, \qquad \frac{\partial f}{\partial y} = xz - e^x \sin y, \qquad \frac{\partial f}{\partial z} = xy + z. \tag{27}$$

We integrate the first of these with respect to x, holding y and z constant, and add an arbitrary function $g(y, z)$ as the "constant of integration"; we thus obtain

$$f(x, y, z) = e^x \cos y + xyz + g(y, z). \tag{28}$$

Next we differentiate this with respect to y and set it equal to $\partial f/\partial y$ as given by the second of Eqs. (27):

$$xz - e^x \sin y = -e^x \sin y + xz + \frac{\partial g}{\partial y},$$

or

$$\frac{\partial g(y, z)}{\partial y} = 0. \tag{29}$$

Integrating Eq. (29) with respect to y, holding z constant, and adding an arbitrary function $h(z)$ as constant of integration, we obtain

$$g(y, z) = h(z). \tag{30}$$

We substitute this into Eq. (28) and then calculate $\partial f/\partial z$, which we compare with the third of Eqs. (27). We find that

$$xy + z = xy + \frac{dh(z)}{dz} \quad \text{or} \quad \frac{dh(z)}{dz} = z,$$

so that

$$h(z) = \frac{z^2}{2} + C.$$

Hence we may write Eq. (28) as

$$f(x, y, z) = e^x \cos y + xyz + (z^2/2) + C.$$

Then, for this function, it is easy to see that

$$\mathbf{F} = \nabla f.$$

A function $f(x, y, z)$ that has the property that its gradient gives the force vector $\mathbf{F}$ is called a "potential" function. (Sometimes a minus sign is introduced. For example, the electric intensity of a field is the negative of the potential gradient in the field. See Sears, Zemansky, Young, *University Physics* (Fifth edition); Addison-Wesley, 1976; pp. 446–447.)

PROBLEMS

1. In Example 1, let C be given by

$$x = t^2, \quad y = t^2, \quad 0 \le t \le 1,$$

and evaluate $\int_C w\,ds$ for $w = x + y^2$.

2. In Example 1, let C be given by $x = f(t) = y$, where $f(0) = 0$ and $f(1) = 1$. Show that if $f'(t)$ is continuous on $[0, 1]$, then $\int_C w\,ds = (5\sqrt{2})/6$, no matter what the particular function f may be.

3. Evaluate $\int \mathbf{F} \cdot d\mathbf{R}$ around the circle

$$x = \cos t, \quad y = \sin t, \quad z = 0, \quad 0 \le t \le 2\pi$$

for the force given in Example 2.

4. In Example 3, evaluate $\int \mathbf{F} \cdot d\mathbf{R}$ along a curve C lying on the sphere $x^2 + y^2 + z^2 = a^2$. Do you need to know anything more about C? Why?

5. Assume $\mathbf{F} = y\mathbf{i} - x\mathbf{j}$, as in Example 4, and take $A = (0, 0, 0)$, $B = (1, 1, 0)$. Evaluate $\int \mathbf{F} \cdot d\mathbf{R}$ for:

a) $x = y = t, \quad 0 \le t \le 1;$
b) $x = t, \quad y = t^2, \quad 0 \le t \le 1.$

Comment on the meaning of your answers.

6. In Example 4, when we considered $\mathbf{F} = y\mathbf{i} - x\mathbf{j}$, we found a function $f(x', y', z') = 0$ which expresses the value of the integral

$$\int_{(0,0,0)}^{(x',y',z')} \mathbf{F} \cdot d\mathbf{R}$$

along the line segment from $(0, 0, 0)$ to an arbitrary point (x', y', z'). Using this result, and the first half of the proof of Theorem 1, prove that if $\mathbf{F}$ were a gradient field, say $\mathbf{F} = \nabla g$, then $g - f =$ constant. From this, show that no such g exists for the given $\mathbf{F}$.

7. Using the notations of Eqs. (14a) and (15), show that $\partial f/\partial y = N$ holds at each point of D if $\mathbf{F}$ is continuous and if the integral in (14a) is path-independent in D.

8. Let $\rho = (x^2 + y^2 + z^2)^{1/2}$. Show that

$$\nabla(\rho^n) = n\rho^{n-2}\mathbf{R},$$

where $\mathbf{R} = \mathbf{i}x + \mathbf{j}y + \mathbf{k}z$. Is there a value of n for which $\mathbf{F} = \nabla(\rho^n)$ represents the "inverse-square law" field? If so, what is this value of n?

In Problems 9 through 13, find the work done by the given force $\mathbf{F}$ as the point of application moves from $(0, 0, 0)$ to $(1, 1, 1)$,

a) along the straight line $x = y = z$;
b) along the curve $x = t$, $y = t^2$, $z = t^4$; and
c) along the x-axis to $(1, 0, 0)$, then in a straight line to $(1, 1, 0)$, and from there in a straight line to $(1, 1, 1)$.

9. $\mathbf{F} = 2x\mathbf{i} + 3y\mathbf{j} + 4z\mathbf{k}$

10. $\mathbf{F} = \mathbf{i}x \sin y + \mathbf{j} \cos y + \mathbf{k}(x + y)$

11. $\mathbf{F} = \mathbf{i}(y + z) + \mathbf{j}(z + x) + \mathbf{k}(x + y)$

12. $\mathbf{F} = e^{y+2z}(\mathbf{i} + \mathbf{j}x + 2\mathbf{k}x)$

13. $\mathbf{F} = \mathbf{i}y \sin z + \mathbf{j}x \sin z + \mathbf{k}xy \cos z$

In Problems 14 through 17, find a function $f(x, y, z)$ such that $\mathbf{F} = \text{grad}\, f$ for the $\mathbf{F}$ given in the exercise named.

14. Problem 9 **15.** Problem 11

16. Problem 12 **17.** Problem 13

18. If A and B are given, prove that the line integral

$$\int_A^B (z^2\, dx + 2y\, dy + 2xz\, dz)$$

is independent of the path of integration.

19. If $\mathbf{F} = y\mathbf{i} + x\mathbf{j}$, evaluate the line integral $\int_A^B \mathbf{F} \cdot d\mathbf{R}$ along the straight line from $A(1, 1, 1)$ to $B(3, 3, 3)$.

20. If $\mathbf{F} = \mathbf{i}x^2 + \mathbf{j}yz + \mathbf{k}y^2$, compute $\int_A^B \mathbf{F} \cdot d\mathbf{R}$, where $A = (0, 0, 0)$, $B = (0, 3, 4)$, along the straight line connecting these points.

21. Let C denote the plane curve whose vector equation is

$$\mathbf{r}(t) = (e^t \cos t)\mathbf{i} + (e^t \sin t)\mathbf{j}.$$

Evaluate the line integral

$$\int \frac{x\, dx + y\, dy}{(x^2 + y^2)^{3/2}}$$

along that arc of C from the point $(1, 0)$ to the point $(e^{2\pi}, 0)$.

22. If the density $\rho(x, y, z)$ of a fluid is a function of the pressure $p(x, y, z)$, and

$$\phi(x, y, z) = \int_{p_0}^{p} (dp/\rho),$$

where p_0 is constant, show that $\nabla\phi = \nabla p/\rho$.

23. If $\mathbf{F} = y\mathbf{i}$, show that the line integral $\int_A^B \mathbf{F} \cdot d\mathbf{R}$ along an arc AB in the xy-plane is equal to an area bounded by the x-axis, the arc, and the ordinates at A and B.

Remark. Despite similarity of appearance and identity of value, the integral of this problem and the integral of earlier calculus are conceptually distinct. The latter is a line integral for which the path lies along the x-axis.

24. The "curl" of a vector field

$$\mathbf{F} = \mathbf{i}f(x, y, z) + \mathbf{j}g(x, y, z) + \mathbf{k}h(x, y, z)$$

is defined to be del cross $\mathbf{F}$; that is,

$$\text{curl } \mathbf{F} \equiv \nabla \times \mathbf{F} \equiv \begin{vmatrix} \mathbf{i} & \mathbf{j} & \mathbf{k} \\ \dfrac{\partial}{\partial x} & \dfrac{\partial}{\partial y} & \dfrac{\partial}{\partial z} \\ f & g & h \end{vmatrix},$$

or

$$\text{curl } \mathbf{F} \equiv \mathbf{i}\left(\frac{\partial h}{\partial y} - \frac{\partial g}{\partial z}\right) + \mathbf{j}\left(\frac{\partial f}{\partial z} - \frac{\partial h}{\partial x}\right) + \mathbf{k}\left(\frac{\partial g}{\partial x} - \frac{\partial f}{\partial y}\right),$$

and the "divergence" of a vector field

$$\mathbf{V} = \mathbf{i}u(x, y, z) + \mathbf{j}v(x, y, z) + \mathbf{k}w(x, y, z)$$

is defined to be del dot $\mathbf{V}$; that is,

$$\text{div } \mathbf{V} \equiv \nabla \cdot \mathbf{V} \equiv \frac{\partial u}{\partial x} + \frac{\partial v}{\partial y} + \frac{\partial w}{\partial z}.$$

If the components f, g, h of $\mathbf{F}$ are functions that possess continuous mixed partial derivatives

$$\frac{\partial^2 h}{\partial x\, \partial y}, \quad \ldots,$$

show that

$$\text{div (curl } \mathbf{F}) = 0.$$

25. Assume the notation of Problem 24.

a) Prove that if ϕ is a scalar function of x, y, z, then

$$\text{curl}\ (\text{grad}\ \phi) = \nabla \times (\nabla\phi) = \mathbf{0}.$$

b) State in terms of the vector field $\nabla \times \mathbf{F}$ how you would express the condition that $\mathbf{F} \cdot d\mathbf{r}$ be an exact differential.

Prove the following results: If

$$\mathbf{r} = x\mathbf{i} + y\mathbf{j} + z\mathbf{k},$$

c) $\text{div}\ (\phi\mathbf{F}) \equiv \nabla \cdot (\phi\mathbf{F}) = \phi\nabla \cdot \mathbf{F} + \mathbf{F} \cdot \nabla\phi$;

d) $\nabla \times (\phi\mathbf{F}) = \phi\nabla \times \mathbf{F} + (\nabla\phi) \times \mathbf{F}$;

e) $\nabla \cdot (\mathbf{F}_1 \times \mathbf{F}_2) = \mathbf{F}_2 \cdot \nabla \times \mathbf{F}_1 - \mathbf{F}_1 \cdot \nabla \times \mathbf{F}_2$;

f) $\nabla \cdot \mathbf{r} = 3$ and $\nabla \times \mathbf{r} = 0$.

15–4

TWO-DIMENSIONAL FIELDS: LINE INTEGRALS IN THE PLANE AND THEIR RELATION TO SURFACE INTEGRALS ON CYLINDERS

In this article, we turn our attention to two-dimensional vector fields of the form

$$\mathbf{F} = \mathbf{i}M(x, y) + \mathbf{j}N(x, y). \tag{1}$$

Figure 15–10 shows how such a two-dimensional vector field might look in space. In the figure, for example, $\mathbf{F}$ might represent a fluid flow in which each particle travels in a circle parallel to the xy-plane in such a way that all particles on a given line perpendicular to the xy-plane travel with the same velocity. Example 1 provides another instance, that of an electric field with field strength

$$\mathbf{E} = \frac{\mathbf{i}x + \mathbf{j}y}{x^2 + y^2}. \tag{2}$$

Note that this formulation is like the righthand side of Eq. (1), with

$$M(x, y) = \frac{x}{x^2 + y^2}, \qquad N(x, y) = \frac{y}{x^2 + y^2}.$$

The essential features of a two-dimensional field are (1) the vectors in $\mathbf{F}$ are all parallel to one plane, which we have taken to be the xy-plane, and (2) in every plane parallel to the xy-plane, the field is the same as it is in that plane. In Eq. (1), the field has a zero $\mathbf{k}$-component everywhere, which makes the vectors parallel to the xy-plane. The $\mathbf{i}$- and $\mathbf{j}$-components do not depend on z, so they are the same in all planes parallel to the xy-plane.

EXAMPLE 1. An infinitely long, thin, straight wire has a uniform electric charge density δ_0. Using Coulomb's law, find the electric field intensity around the wire due to this charge.

Solution. From a physics textbook,* we find that *Coulomb's law* is an inverse-square law. It says that the force acting on a positive test charge q_0 placed at a distance r from a positive *point charge* q is directed away from q and has magnitude $(4\pi\epsilon_0)^{-1}(qq_0)/r^2$, where ϵ_0 is a certain constant called the *permittivity*. For the charged wire, we have a distributed charge instead of a point charge, but we handle it in the familiar way: We replace this distributed charge by a large number of tiny elements, add, and take limits.

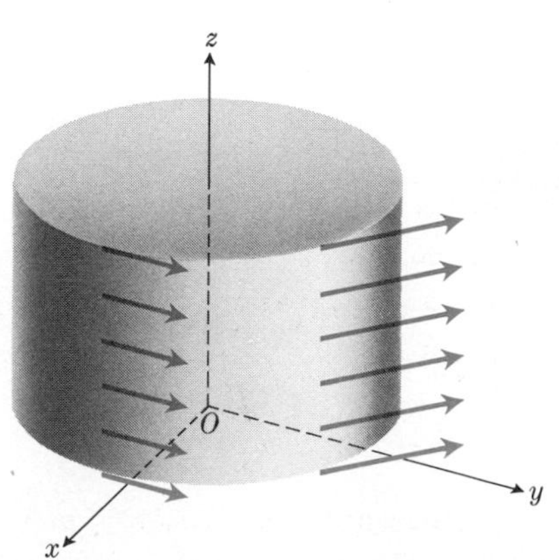

15–10 A two-dimensional vector field in space.

* For example, Sears, Zemansky, Young, *University Physics* (Fifth edition, 1976), p. 412.

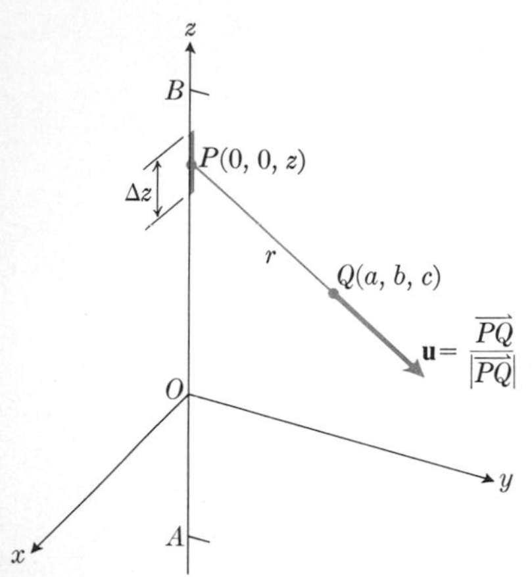

15–11 According to Coulomb's law, a charge $\delta_0\,\Delta z$ at $P(0, 0, z)$ produces a field $\Delta\mathbf{F}$ on a test charge q at $Q(a, b, c)$.

More specifically, suppose that the wire runs along the z-axis from $-\infty$ to $+\infty$. Take a long but finite piece of the wire and divide it into a lot of small segments. One of these is indicated in Fig. 15–11, with its center at $P(0, 0, z)$, and its length equal to Δz. We assume that Δz is so small that we can treat the charge $\delta_0\,\Delta z$ on this segment of the wire as a point charge at P. Now let $Q(a, b, c)$ be any point not on the z-axis, and let $\Delta\mathbf{F}$ denote the force at Q due to the point charge at P:

$$\Delta\mathbf{F} = \frac{\delta_0 q_0}{4\pi\epsilon_0}\frac{\Delta z\mathbf{u}}{a^2 + b^2 + (c - z)^2}, \tag{3a}$$

where $\mathbf{u}$ is a unit vector having the direction of $\overrightarrow{PQ}$:

$$\mathbf{u} = \frac{\mathbf{i}a + \mathbf{j}b + \mathbf{k}(c - z)}{[a^2 + b^2 + (c - z)^2]^{1/2}}. \tag{3b}$$

When we add the vector forces $\Delta\mathbf{F}$ for pieces of wire between $z = A$ and $z = B$ and take the limit as $\Delta z \to 0$, we get an integral of the form

$$\frac{\delta_0 q_0}{4\pi\epsilon_0}\int_A^B \frac{\mathbf{i}a + \mathbf{j}b + \mathbf{k}(c - z)}{[a^2 + b^2 + (c - z)^2]^{3/2}}\,dz. \tag{3c}$$

The denominator of the integrand behaves about like $|z|^3$ as $|z| \to \infty$, so the three component integrals in (3c) converge as $A \to -\infty$ and $B \to \infty$. As our final integral representation of the field, therefore, we get

$$\mathbf{F} = \frac{\delta_0 q_0}{4\pi\epsilon_0}\int_{-\infty}^{+\infty} \frac{\mathbf{i}a + \mathbf{j}b + \mathbf{k}(c - z)}{[a^2 + b^2 + (c - z)^2]^{3/2}}\,dz. \tag{4}$$

There are three separate integrals, but two are essentially the same except for the constant coefficients a and b, and the third is zero. It is easy to do the integration by making the substitutions

$$\sqrt{a^2 + b^2} = m,$$

$$z - c = m \tan\theta, \qquad \theta = \tan^{-1}\left(\frac{z - c}{m}\right),$$

$$dz = m \sec^2\theta\, d\theta,$$

and observing that the limits for θ are from $-\pi/2$ to $\pi/2$. In Problem 1 you are asked to finish these calculations and to show that the following result is correct:

$$\mathbf{F} = \frac{\delta_0 q_0}{2\pi\epsilon_0}\left(\frac{\mathbf{i}a + \mathbf{j}b}{a^2 + b^2}\right). \tag{5}$$

We observe that the result is a two-dimensional field that does not depend on $\mathbf{k}$ or on c. If we write the resultant field strength $\mathbf{E} = \mathbf{F}/q_0$ as a function of position (x, y, z) instead of (a, b, c), we have

$$\mathbf{E} = k_0\left(\frac{\mathbf{i}x + \mathbf{j}y}{x^2 + y^2}\right), \qquad \text{where } k_0 = \frac{\delta_0}{2\pi\epsilon_0}. \tag{6}$$

REMARK 1. There is also a fluid-flow interpretation for the field in Eq. (6) (or Eq. 2). To arrive at that interpretation, imagine a long, thin pipe running along the z-axis, and perforated with a very large number of little holes through which it supplies fluid at a constant rate. (It helps to be a bit vague about the actual physics of this: Don't try to be too literal-minded.) In other words, the z-axis is to be thought of as a *source* from which water flows radially outward and so produces a velocity field that is characterized by

$$\mathbf{v} = f(r)\mathbf{u}_r, \tag{7a}$$

where $\mathbf{u}_r$ is the usual unit vector associated with the cylindrical coordinates r, θ, z, and $f(r)$ is a function of r alone. Thus the velocity is all perpendicular to the z-axis, and it is independent of both θ and z. (These are our present interpretations of the phrases "at a constant rate" and "radially outward.") Now consider the amount of fluid that flows out through the cylinder $r = a$ between the planes $z = 0$ and $z = 1$ in a short interval of time, from t to $t + \Delta t$. According to the law expressed by Eq. (7a), every particle of water that is on the surface $r = a$ moves radially outward a distance Δr, which is approximately $f(a)\,\Delta t$. Thus the volume of fluid that crosses the boundary $r = a$ between $z = 0$ and $z = 1$ in this time interval is approximately the volume between the cylinders $r = a$ and $r = a + f(a)\,\Delta t$, or $2\pi a f(a)\,\Delta t$. If we multiply this by the density δ_1, we get the *mass* transported through a unit length of the cylinder $r = a$ in the interval from t to $t + \Delta t$:

$$\Delta m \approx \delta_1 2\pi a f(a)\,\Delta t. \tag{7b}$$

If we divide both sides of Eq. (7b) by Δt and take the limit as $\Delta t \to 0$, we get the *rate* at which fluid is flowing across the unit length of the cylinder $r = a$:

$$\frac{dm}{dt} = \delta_1 2\pi a f(a). \tag{7c}$$

For an incompressible fluid such as water, all fluid that flows across the cylinder $r = a$ flows across the cylinder $r = b$ as well (unless, of course, there are other sources or sinks between the two cylinders). Therefore, for the model under discussion, the rate of mass transport given by Eq. (7c) is independent of a, and its value for any radius $r = a$ is the same as for $r = 1$:

$$\delta_1 2\pi f(1) = \delta_1 2\pi a f(a). \tag{7d}$$

From Eq. (7d), we get

$$f(a) = f(1)/a \qquad \text{for any } a > 0.$$

Writing r in place of a and substituting C for $f(1)$, we can rewrite the velocity field (7a) in the form

$$\mathbf{v} = (C/r)\mathbf{u}_r. \tag{8}$$

If we recall that the position vector in cylindrical coordinates is

$$\mathbf{R} = \overrightarrow{OP} = r\mathbf{u}_r + \mathbf{k}z$$

and that this must also be equal to $\mathbf{R} = \mathbf{i}x + \mathbf{j}y + \mathbf{k}z$, then we conclude that

$$r\mathbf{u}_r = \mathbf{i}x + \mathbf{j}y, \qquad \text{or} \qquad \mathbf{u}_r = \frac{\mathbf{i}x + \mathbf{j}y}{r},$$

where

$$r = \sqrt{x^2 + y^2}. \tag{9}$$

Therefore, Eqs. (6) and (8) describe the same field if $C = k_0$.

REMARK 2. Instead of interpreting the two-dimensional vector fields as we have done in 3-space, we can interpret them simply as fields in the xy-plane itself. Then r in Eqs. (8) and (9) is just the distance from the origin to the point $P(x, y)$ in the plane, and the unit vector is

$$\mathbf{u}_r = \frac{(\mathbf{i}x + \mathbf{j}y)}{r} = \mathbf{i} \cos \theta + \mathbf{j} \sin \theta,$$

where $r > 0$ and θ measures the angle from the positive x-axis to the position vector $\overrightarrow{OP}$. Equation (8) then describes a vector field in the plane that is directed radially outward and whose strength decreases like $1/r$ as r increases. We still use the language of flow across boundaries, but in this interpretation the boundary would be a *curve* in the plane, rather than a unit length of a cylinder. Equation (7d) would be interpreted as saying that the amount of fluid flowing across the unit circle $r = 1$ per unit time is equal to the amount of fluid flowing across the circle $r = a$ in the same time. (This describes conditions after the flow has reached steady state, not during the transient phase.)

We can easily go back and forth between the two interpretations of two-dimensional fields, but henceforth we shall usually treat them as existing just in the xy-plane and ignore the fact that we can project the field onto any plane parallel to the xy-plane and thereby go to the 3-space view.

EXAMPLE 2. Given the velocity field $\mathbf{v} = (\mathbf{i}x + \mathbf{j}y)/r^2$, calculate the mass-transport rate across the line segment AB joining the points $A(1, 0)$ and $B(0, 1)$.

Solution. Let δ denote the density factor by which we multiply the area of a region to get the mass of fluid in that region. (We assume the density to be constant.) Consider a segment of the line having length Δs, with its center at $P(x, y)$ on AB. In Remark 3 below, we see that the mass of fluid Δm that flows across the segment in time Δt is given, approximately, by

$$\Delta m \approx (\mathbf{v} \cdot \mathbf{n})(\Delta t \, \Delta s) \, \delta, \tag{10}$$

where $\mathbf{n}$ is a unit vector normal to the line AB at P, and pointing away from the origin:

$$\mathbf{n} = \frac{\mathbf{i} + \mathbf{j}}{\sqrt{2}}.$$

If we divide both sides of Eq. (10) by Δt, then sum for all the pieces Δs of the segment AB, and take the limit as $\Delta s \to 0$, we get the *average rate* of mass transport across AB:

$$\frac{\Delta M}{\Delta t} \approx \int_{AB} \delta(\mathbf{v} \cdot \mathbf{n}) \, ds.$$

Finally, letting $\Delta t \to 0$ and substituting for $\mathbf{v}$, $\mathbf{n}$, and ds, with

$$x = t, \qquad y = 1 - t, \qquad 0 \le t \le 1$$

as parametrization of the segment AB, we get as the *instantaneous* mass-transport rate

$$\frac{dM}{dt} = \delta \int_0^1 \frac{x+y}{r^2\sqrt{2}}(\sqrt{2}\,dt)$$

$$= \delta \int_0^1 \frac{dt}{t^2 + (1-t)^2} \tag{11a}$$

$$= \delta(\pi/2). \tag{11b}$$

[In Exercise 2 you are asked to verify that the integral in (11a) yields the result (11b).]

REMARK 3. The terms on the righthand side of Eq. (10) are explained this way (see Fig. 15–12): The quantity $\mathbf{v}\,\Delta t$ is, very nearly, the vector displacement of all particles of fluid that were on the segment Δs at time t; hence those particles have swept over a parallelogram with dimensions Δs and $|\mathbf{v}\,\Delta t|$. The $\mathbf{n}$-component of $\mathbf{v}\,\Delta t$ is the altitude h of this parallelogram. Its area is therefore approximately

$$(\mathbf{v}\,\Delta t)\cdot\mathbf{n} \text{ times } \Delta s,$$

and the mass of fluid that fills this parallelogram is what flows across the tiny segment Δs between t and $t + \Delta t$.

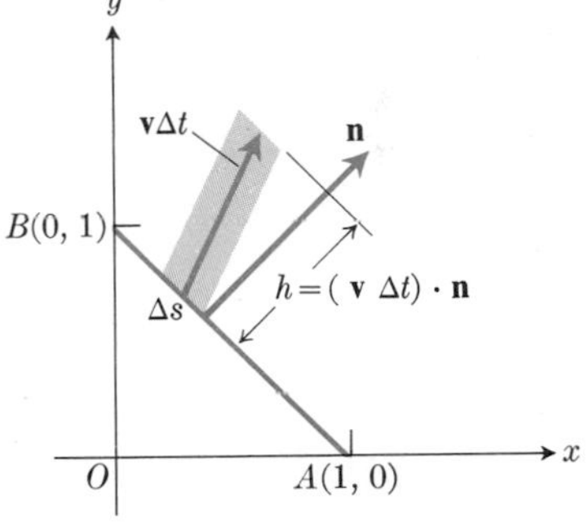

15–12 Fluid that flows across Δs in time Δt fills the parallelogram whose altitude is $h = (\mathbf{v}\,\Delta t)\cdot\mathbf{n}$.

This same line of reasoning would apply to flows in the xy-plane in general. It leads to the result

$$\frac{dM}{dt} = \int_C \delta(\mathbf{v}\cdot\mathbf{n})\,ds, \tag{12}$$

where dM/dt is the *rate* at which mass is being transported across the curve C, in the direction of the unit normal vector $\mathbf{n}$. One can interpret M as the amount of mass that has crossed C up to time t.

If the oppositely directed normal $\mathbf{n}' = -\mathbf{n}$ is substituted in place of $\mathbf{n}$ in the integral in Eq. (12), the sign of the answer changes. This just means that if flow in one direction across C is considered to be in the positive sense, then flow in the opposite direction is then considered to be negative. If C is a simple closed curve, we usually choose $\mathbf{n}$ to point outward. In Eqs. (11a, b), we chose the normal to point away from the origin; we got a positive answer because the flow in the first quadrant is generally upward and to the right for the given $\mathbf{v}$.

To simplify further discussion, we take

$$\delta\mathbf{v} = \mathbf{F}(x, y)$$

in Eq. (12), and call the resulting integral the *flux* of $\mathbf{F}$ across C:

$$\text{Flux of } \mathbf{F} \text{ across } C = \int_C \mathbf{F}\cdot\mathbf{n}\,ds. \tag{13}$$

We shall use this terminology even when the field $\mathbf{F}$ has nothing to do with a fluid flow, but you may wish to keep the fluid-flow interpretation in mind too.

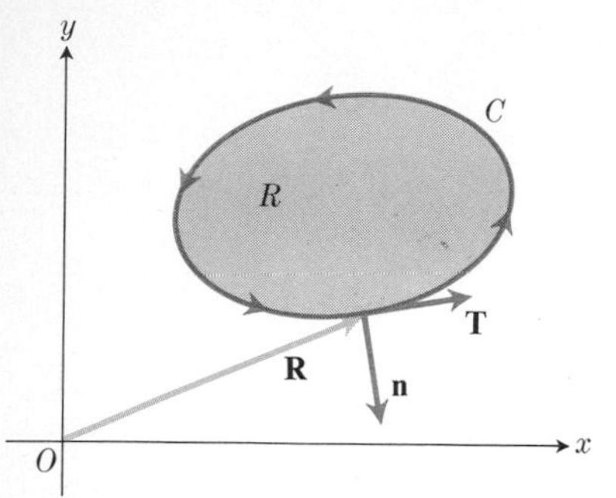

15–13 The position vector $\mathbf{R} = \mathbf{i}x + \mathbf{j}y$, the unit tangent vector $\mathbf{T} = d\mathbf{R}/ds$, and the unit normal vector $\mathbf{n} = \mathbf{T} \times \mathbf{k}$.

The curve C in Eq. (13) is to have a direction along it that is called the *positive* direction. For theoretical purposes, we find it convenient to use the arc length s, measured from some arbitrary point on C. Then s should *increase* as we proceed in the positive direction along C. (We assume that C is piecewise smooth enough to have a tangent.) Then the position vector $\mathbf{R} = \mathbf{i}x + \mathbf{j}y$ has derivative $d\mathbf{R}/ds = \mathbf{T}$, where $\mathbf{T}$ is a *unit tangent vector* pointing in the positive direction along C. (At a cusp or corner on C, the tangent will not exist, but this won't matter for most of our applications that involve integrals.) Because we often want the flux integral to represent flow outward from a region R bounded by a simple closed curve C, we choose the counterclockwise direction on C as positive, and choose the *outward*-pointing unit normal vector as $\mathbf{n}$. From Fig. 15–13, we can see that, because

$$\mathbf{T} = \frac{dx}{ds}\mathbf{i} + \frac{dy}{ds}\mathbf{j}, \tag{14a}$$

for the indicated choice of $\mathbf{n}$ we should choose $\mathbf{n} = \mathbf{T} \times \mathbf{k}$, so that

$$\mathbf{n} = \frac{dy}{ds}\mathbf{i} - \frac{dx}{ds}\mathbf{j}. \tag{14b}$$

As a check, it is easy to see that the dot product of the vectors in Eqs. (14a) and (14b) is zero, that both have unit length, and that when $\mathbf{T}$ points upward and to the right, $\mathbf{n}$ has a positive $\mathbf{i}$-component and a negative $\mathbf{j}$-component. If we proceed around the curve C in the direction in which $\mathbf{T}$ points, with the interior toward our left, then $\mathbf{n}$, as given by Eq. (14b), points to our right, as it should.

We now use Eq. (14b) to write the flux integral. We assume that

$$\mathbf{F}(x, y) = \mathbf{i}M(x, y) + \mathbf{j}N(x, y).$$

Then it follows that

$$\begin{aligned} \text{Flux across } C &= \int_C \mathbf{F} \cdot \mathbf{n}\, ds \\ &= \int_C \left(M\frac{dy}{ds} - N\frac{dx}{ds}\right) ds \\ &= \int_C (M\, dy - N\, dx). \end{aligned} \tag{15}$$

The virtue of the final integral in Eq. (15) is this: It can be evaluated using *any* reasonable parametrization of C; we aren't restricted to using the arc length s, provided we integrate in the positive direction along C.

EXAMPLE 3. Find the flux of the field

$$\mathbf{F} = 2x\mathbf{i} - 3y\mathbf{j}$$

outward across the ellipse

$$x = \cos t, \qquad y = 4 \sin t, \qquad 0 \le t \le 2\pi.$$

Solution. By Eq. (15), for the flux we have

$$\int_C (M\,dy - N\,dx) = \int_C (2x\,dy + 3y\,dx)$$

$$= \int_0^{2\pi} (8\cos^2 t - 12\sin^2 t)\,dt$$

$$= \int_0^{2\pi} [4(1+\cos 2t) - 6(1-\cos 2t)]\,dt$$

$$= -4\pi.$$

The negative answer just means that the net flux is inward.

REMARK 4. The integral that we have just evaluated was set up as a flux integral, but it can also be interpreted as a work integral of the form

$$\int_C \mathbf{G}\cdot d\mathbf{R} = \int_C (3y\mathbf{i} + 2x\mathbf{j})\cdot(\mathbf{i}\,dx + \mathbf{j}\,dy).$$

Conversely, any work integral in the plane can be reinterpreted as a flux integral of a related field. Problem 7 asks you to supply the details.

PROBLEMS

1. In Example 1, complete the calculations that lead from Eq. (4) to Eq. (5).

2. Evaluate

$$\int_0^1 \frac{dt}{2t^2 - 2t + 1}$$

by changing it to

$$\int_0^1 \frac{2\,dt}{(2t-1)^2 + 1}$$

and making a change of variables. You will thereby verify the answer given in Eq. (11b).

3. Find the rate of mass transport outward across the circle $r = a$ for the (velocity) flow field of Example 2. [The calculations are trivial if you interpret Eq. (12) correctly.]

4. In a three-dimensional velocity field, let S be a closed surface bounding a region D in its interior. Explain why

$$\iint_S \delta(\mathbf{v}\cdot\mathbf{n})\,d\sigma$$

can be interpreted as the rate of mass transport outward through S if $\mathbf{n}$ is the outward-pointing unit vector normal to S.

In Problems 5 and 6, use the result of Problem 4 to find the rate of mass transport outward through the surface given, if the flow vector $\mathbf{F} = \delta\mathbf{v}$ is:

a) $\mathbf{F} = -\mathbf{i}y + \mathbf{j}x$,

b) $\mathbf{F} = (x^2 + y^2 + z^2)^{-3/2}(\mathbf{i}x + \mathbf{j}y + \mathbf{k}z)$.

5. S is the sphere $x^2 + y^2 + z^2 = a^2$.

6. S is the closed cylinder $x^2 + y^2 = a^2$, $-h \le z \le h$, plus the end disks $z = \pm h$, $x^2 + y^2 \le a^2$.

7. Suppose that C is a directed curve with unit tangent and normal vectors $\mathbf{T}$ and $\mathbf{n}$ related as in the text, and suppose that $\mathbf{F}$ and $\mathbf{G}$ are two-dimensional fields:

$$\mathbf{F}(x, y) = \mathbf{i}M(x, y) + \mathbf{j}N(x, y),$$

$$\mathbf{G}(x, y) = -\mathbf{i}N(x, y) + \mathbf{j}M(x, y).$$

Show that

$$\int_C \mathbf{F}\cdot\mathbf{n}\,ds = \int_C \mathbf{G}\cdot\mathbf{T}\,ds.$$

Which integral represents work? Which represents flux?

15–5 GREEN'S THEOREM

This theorem asserts that under suitable conditions the line integral

$$\oint (M\,dx + N\,dy) \tag{1}$$

around a simple closed curve C in the xy-plane is equal to the double integral

$$\iint_R \left(\frac{\partial N}{\partial x} - \frac{\partial M}{\partial y}\right) dx\,dy \tag{2}$$

over the region R that lies inside C.

NOTATION. The symbol $\oint$ is used only when the curve C is *closed*.

EXAMPLE 1. Let C be the circle $x = a\cos\theta$, $y = a\sin\theta$, $0 \le \theta \le 2\pi$, and let $M = -y$, $N = x$. Then (1) is

$$\oint_C (-y\,dx + x\,dy) = \int_0^{2\pi} a^2(\sin^2\theta + \cos^2\theta)\,d\theta = 2\pi a^2,$$

and the double integral (2) is

$$\iint_{x^2+y^2\le a^2} 2\,dx\,dy = 2\int_{\theta=0}^{2\pi}\int_0^a r\,dr\,d\theta = 2\pi a^2.$$

Both integrals equal twice the area inside the circle.

Green's theorem. *Let C be a simple closed curve in the xy-plane such that a line parallel to either axis cuts C in at most two points. Let M, N, $\partial N/\partial x$, and $\partial M/\partial y$ be continuous functions of (x, y) inside and on C. Let R be the region inside C. Then*

$$\oint M\,dx + N\,dy = \iint_R \left[\frac{\partial N}{\partial x} - \frac{\partial M}{\partial y}\right] dx\,dy. \tag{3}$$

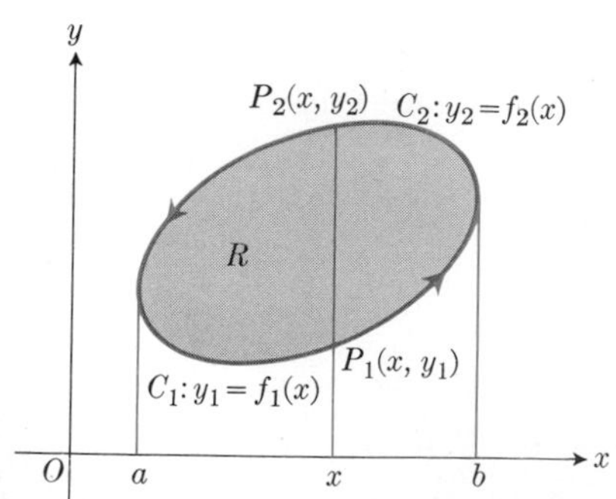

15–14 The boundary curve C, made up of C_1: $y = f_1(x)$ and C_2: $y = f_2(x)$.

DISCUSSION. We indicate that the line integral on the left side of Eq. (3) is to be taken counterclockwise, the usual positive direction in the plane. We did this automatically in Example 1 by letting θ vary from 0 to 2π in the parametric representation of the circle. Figure 15–14 shows a curve C made up of two parts,

$$C_1:\quad a \le x \le b, \qquad y_1 = f_1(x),$$
$$C_2:\quad b \ge x \ge a, \qquad y_2 = f_2(x).$$

We use this notation in the proof.

Proof. Consider the double integral of $\partial M/\partial y$ over R in Fig. 15–14. For any x between a and b, we first integrate with respect to y from $y_1 = f_1(x)$ to

$y_2 = f_2(x)$ and obtain

$$\int_{y_1}^{y_2} \frac{\partial M}{\partial y}\, dy = M(x, y)\Big]_{y=f_1(x)}^{y=f_2(x)} = M(x, f_2(x)) - M(x, f_1(x)). \tag{4}$$

Next we integrate this with respect to x from a to b:

$$\begin{aligned}\int_a^b \int_{f_1(x)}^{f_2(x)} \frac{\partial M}{\partial y}\, dy\, dx &= \int_a^b \{M(x, f_2(x)) - M(x, f_1(x))\}\, dx \\ &= -\int_b^a M(x, f_2(x))\, dx - \int_a^b M(x, f_1(x))\, dx \\ &= -\int_{C_2} M\, dx - \int_{C_1} M\, dx \\ &= -\oint_C M\, dx.\end{aligned}$$

Therefore

$$\oint_C M\, dx = \iint_R \left(-\frac{\partial M}{\partial y}\right) dx\, dy. \tag{5}$$

Equation (5) is half the result we need for Eq. (3). Problem 1 asks you to derive the other half, by integrating $\partial N/\partial x$ first with respect to x and then with respect to y, as suggested by Fig. 15–15. This shows the curve C of Fig. 15–14, decomposed into the two directed parts,

$$C_1':\quad c \le y \le d, \qquad x = g_1(y),$$

$$C_2':\quad d \ge y \ge c, \qquad x = g_2(y).$$

The result of this double integration is expressed by

$$\oint_C N\, dy = \iint_R \frac{\partial N}{\partial x}\, dx\, dy. \tag{6}$$

Combining Eqs. (5) and (6), we get Eq. (3). This concludes the proof.

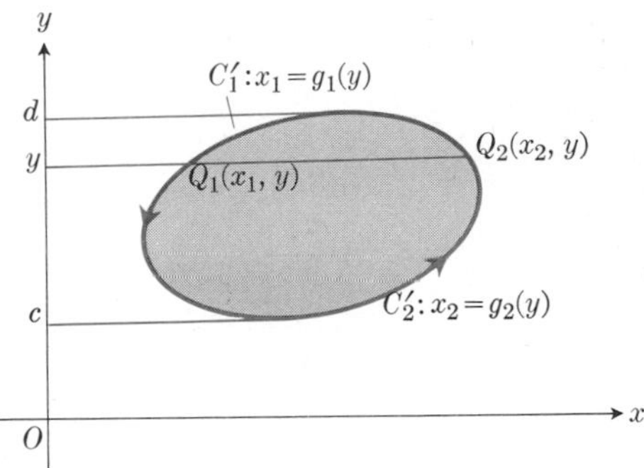

15–15 The boundary curve C', made up of C_1': $x_1 = g_1(y)$ and C_2': $x_2 = g_2(y)$.

EXAMPLE 2. Use Green's theorem to find the area enclosed by the ellipse

$$x = a \cos\theta, \qquad y = b \sin\theta, \qquad 0 \le \theta \le 2\pi.$$

Solution. If we take $M = -y$, $N = x$, as in Example 1, and apply Green's theorem, we obtain

$$\begin{aligned}\oint M\, dx + N\, dy &= \int_{\theta=0}^{2\pi} -y\, dx + x\, dy \\ &= \int_0^{2\pi} ab(\sin^2\theta + \cos^2\theta)\, d\theta \\ &= \int_0^{2\pi} ab\, d\theta = 2\pi ab,\end{aligned}$$

and

$$\iint_R \left(\frac{\partial N}{\partial x} - \frac{\partial M}{\partial y}\right) dx\, dy = \iint_R 2\, dx\, dy$$

$$= 2 \times (\text{area inside ellipse}).$$

Therefore

$$\text{Area inside ellipse} = \tfrac{1}{2} \oint (-y\, dx + x\, dy)$$

$$= \pi ab.$$

Corollary to Green's theorem. *If C is a simple closed curve such that a line parallel to either axis cuts it in at most two points, then the area enclosed by C is equal to*

$$\tfrac{1}{2} \oint_C (x\, dy - y\, dx).$$

Proof. If we take $M = -y/2$, $N = x/2$, we obtain

$$\oint_C (\tfrac{1}{2}x\, dy - \tfrac{1}{2}y\, dx) = \iint_R (\tfrac{1}{2} + \tfrac{1}{2})\, dx\, dy \tag{7}$$

$$= \text{Area of } R.$$

REMARK 1. Green's theorem may apply to curves and regions that don't meet all of the requirements stated in it. For example, C could be a rectangle, as shown in Fig. 15–16. Here C is considered as composed of four directed parts:

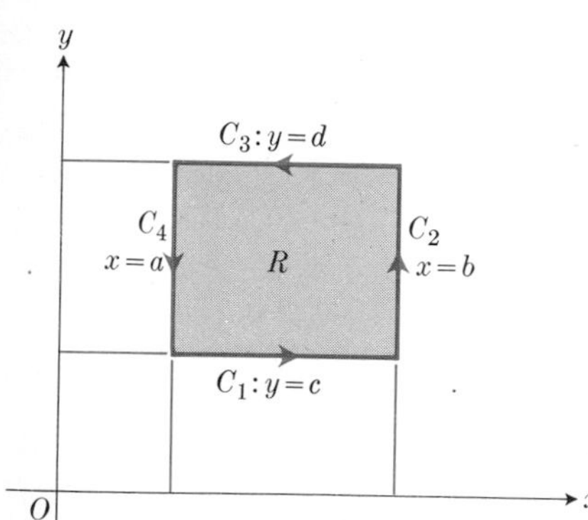

15–16 The rectangle made up of the four segments C_1, C_2, C_3, C_4.

$$\begin{aligned} C_1&: \quad y = c, \qquad a \le x \le b,\\ C_2&: \quad x = b, \qquad c \le y \le d,\\ C_3&: \quad y = d, \qquad b \ge x \ge a,\\ C_4&: \quad x = a, \qquad d \ge y \ge c. \end{aligned}$$

The lines $x = a$ and $x = b$ intersect C in more than two points, and so do the boundaries $y = c$ and $y = d$.

Proceeding as in the proof of Eq. (6), we have

$$\int_{y=c}^{d} \int_{x=a}^{b} \frac{\partial N}{\partial x}\, dx\, dy = \int_c^d [N(b, y) - N(a, y)]\, dy$$

$$= \int_c^d N(b, y)\, dy + \int_d^c N(a, y)\, dy$$

$$= \int_{C_2} N\, dy + \int_{C_4} N\, dy. \tag{8}$$

Because y is constant along C_1 and C_3,

$$\int_{C_1} N\,dy = \int_{C_3} N\,dy = 0,$$

so we can add

$$\int_{C_1} N\,dy + \int_{C_3} N\,dy$$

to the righthand side of Eq. (8) without changing the equality. Doing so, we have

$$\int_c^d \int_a^b \frac{\partial N}{\partial x}\,dx\,dy = \oint_C N\,dy. \tag{9}$$

Similarly we could show that

$$\int_a^b \int_c^d \frac{\partial M}{\partial y}\,dy\,dx = -\oint_C M\,dx. \tag{10}$$

Subtracting (10) from (9), we again arrive at

$$\oint_C M\,dx + N\,dy = \iint_R \left(\frac{\partial N}{\partial x} - \frac{\partial M}{\partial y}\right) dx\,dy.$$

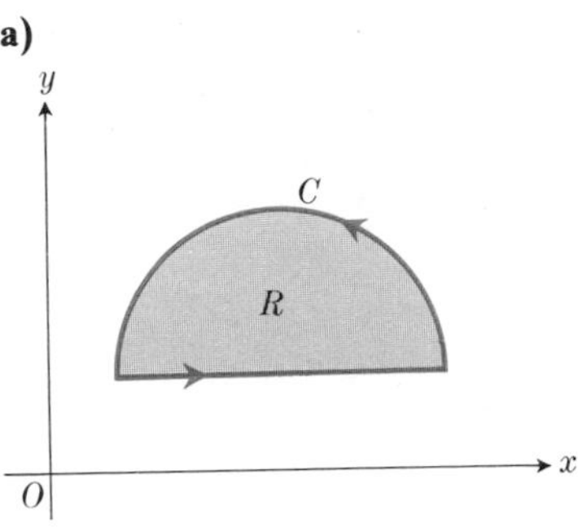

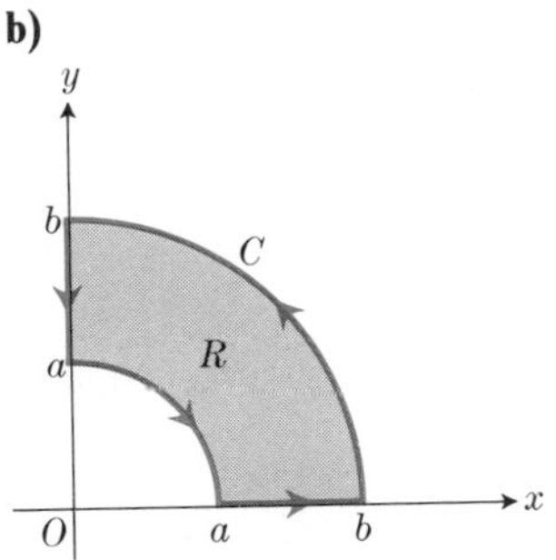

15–17 Other regions to which Green's theorem applies.

Regions such as those shown in Fig. 15–17 can be handled with no greater difficulty. Equation (3) still applies. It also applies to the horseshoe-shaped region R shown in Fig. 15–18, as we see by putting together the regions R_1 and R_2 and their boundaries. Green's theorem applies to C_1, R_1, and to C_2, R_2, yielding

$$\int_{C_1} M\,dx + N\,dy = \iint_{R_1} \left(\frac{\partial N}{\partial x} - \frac{\partial M}{\partial y}\right) dx\,dy,$$

$$\int_{C_2} M\,dx + N\,dy = \iint_{R_2} \left(\frac{\partial N}{\partial x} - \frac{\partial M}{\partial y}\right) dx\,dy.$$

When we add, the line integral along the y-axis from b to a for C_1 cancels the integral over the same segment but in the opposite direction for C_2. Hence

$$\oint_C (M\,dx + N\,dy) = \iint_R \left(\frac{\partial N}{\partial x} - \frac{\partial M}{\partial y}\right) dx\,dy,$$

where C consists of the two segments of the x-axis from $-b$ to $-a$ and from a to b, and of the two semicircles, and where R is the region inside C.

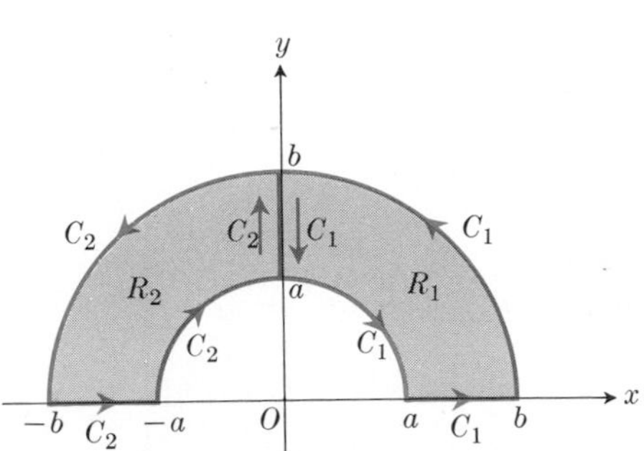

15–18 A region R that combines regions R_1 and R_2.

The device of adding line integrals over separate boundaries to build up an integral over a single boundary can be extended to any finite number of subregions. In Fig. 15–19(a), let C_1 be the boundary of the region R_1 in the first quadrant. Similarly for the other three quadrants: C_i is the boundary of the region R_i, $i = 1, 2, 3, 4$. By Green's theorem,

$$\oint_{C_i} M\,dx + N\,dy = \iint_{R_i} \left(\frac{\partial N}{\partial x} - \frac{\partial M}{\partial y}\right) dx\,dy. \tag{11}$$

We add Eqs. (11) for $i = 1, 2, 3, 4$, and get

$$\oint_{r=b} (M\,dx + N\,dy) + \oint_{r=a} (M\,dx + N\,dy) = \iint_{a \le r \le b} \left(\frac{\partial N}{\partial x} - \frac{\partial M}{\partial y}\right) dx\,dy. \tag{12}$$

Equation (12) says that the double integral of

$$\left(\frac{\partial N}{\partial x} - \frac{\partial M}{\partial y}\right) dx\,dy$$

over the annular ring R is equal to the line integral of $M\,dx + N\,dy$ over the *entire* boundary of R, in that *direction* along the boundary that keeps the region R on one's left as one progresses. Figure 15–19(b) shows R and its boundary (two concentric circles) and the positive direction on the boundary.

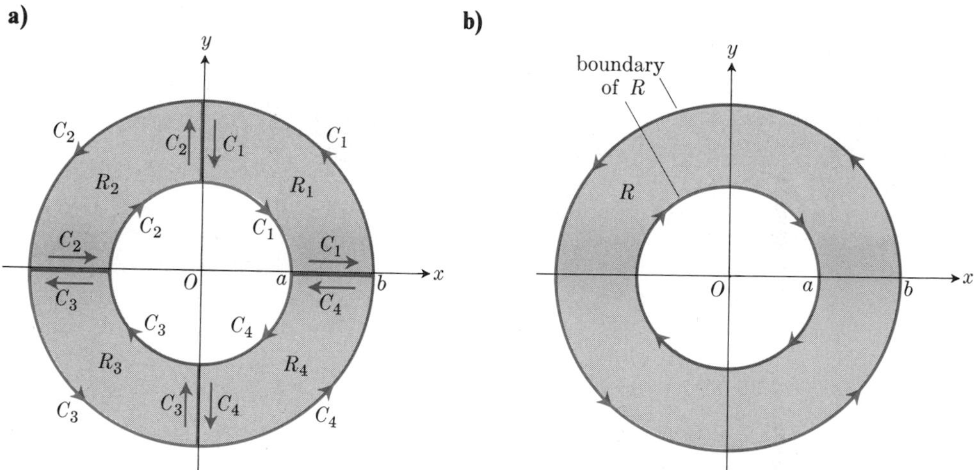

15–19 The annular region R combines four smaller regions.

EXAMPLE 3. Verify that Eq. (3) holds if

$$M = \frac{-y}{x^2 + y^2}, \qquad N = \frac{x}{x^2 + y^2},$$

$$R = \{(x, y): h^2 \le x^2 + y^2 \le 1\},$$

where $0 < h < 1$.

Solution. (See Fig. 15–20.) The boundary of R consists of the circle C_1:

$$x = \cos\theta, \qquad y = \sin\theta, \qquad 0 \le \theta \le 2\pi,$$

around which we shall integrate counterclockwise, and the circle C_h:

$$x = h \cos \phi, \qquad y = h \sin \phi, \qquad 2\pi \geq \phi \geq 0,$$

around which we shall integrate in the clockwise direction. Note that the origin is not included in R, because h is positive. For all $(x, y) \neq (0, 0)$, the functions M and N and their partial derivatives are continuous. Moreover,

$$\frac{\partial M}{\partial y} = \frac{(x^2 + y^2)(-1) + y(2y)}{(x^2 + y^2)^2} = \frac{y^2 - x^2}{(x^2 + y^2)^2} = \frac{\partial N}{\partial x},$$

so

$$\iint_R \left(\frac{\partial N}{\partial x} - \frac{\partial M}{\partial y} \right) dx\, dy = \iint_R 0\, dx\, dy = 0.$$

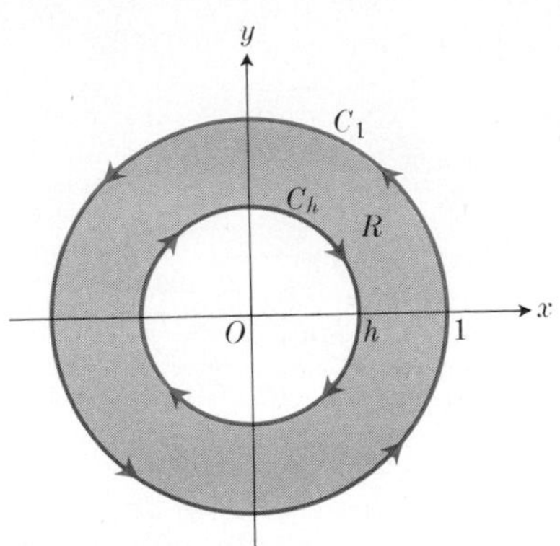

15–20 Green's theorem may be applied to the annulus R by integrating along the boundaries as shown.

The line integral is

$$\int_C M\, dx + N\, dy = \oint_{C_1} \frac{x\, dy - y\, dx}{x^2 + y^2} + \oint_{C_h} \frac{x\, dy - y\, dx}{x^2 + y^2}$$

$$= \int_0^{2\pi} (\cos^2 \theta + \sin^2 \theta)\, d\theta + \int_{2\pi}^{0} \frac{h^2(\cos^2 \phi + \sin^2 \phi)\, d\phi}{h^2}$$

$$= 2\pi - 2\pi = 0.$$

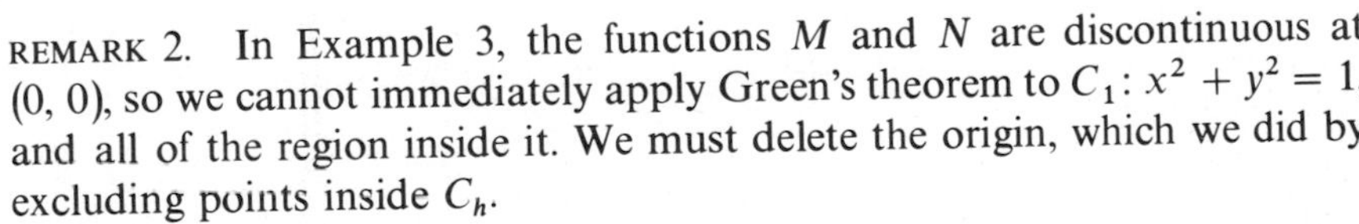

REMARK 2. In Example 3, the functions M and N are discontinuous at $(0, 0)$, so we cannot immediately apply Green's theorem to C_1: $x^2 + y^2 = 1$, and all of the region inside it. We must delete the origin, which we did by excluding points inside C_h.

REMARK 3. In Example 3, we could replace the outer circle C_1 by an ellipse or any other simple closed curve Γ that lies outside C_h (for some positive h). The result would be

$$\oint_\Gamma (M\, dx + N\, dy) + \oint_{C_h} (M\, dx + N\, dy) = 0,$$

which leads to the conclusion

$$\oint_\Gamma \frac{x\, dy - y\, dx}{x^2 + y^2} = 2\pi.$$

This result is easily accounted for if we change to polar coordinates for Γ:

$$x = r \cos \theta, \qquad y = r \sin \theta,$$

$$dx = -r \sin \theta\, d\theta + \cos \theta\, dr,$$

$$dy = r \cos \theta\, d\theta + \sin \theta\, dr.$$

For then

$$\frac{x\, dy - y\, dx}{x^2 + y^2} = \frac{r^2(\cos^2 \theta + \sin^2 \theta)\, d\theta}{r^2} = d\theta;$$

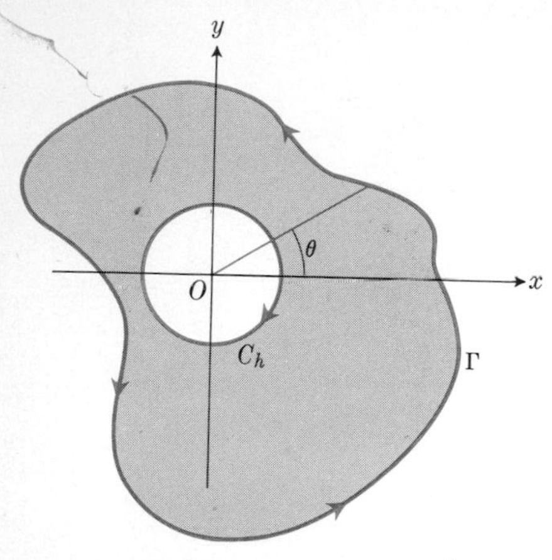

15–21 The region bounded by the circle C_h and the curve Γ.

and θ increases by 2π as we progress once around Γ counterclockwise (see Fig. 15–21).

Green's Theorem in Vector Form

Let

$$\mathbf{F} = M\mathbf{i} + N\mathbf{j} + P\mathbf{k} \qquad \text{and} \qquad \mathbf{R} = x\mathbf{i} + y\mathbf{j}.$$

Then the lefthand side of Eq. (3) is given by

$$\oint_C \mathbf{F} \cdot d\mathbf{R} = \oint_C (M\,dx + N\,dy).$$

To express the righthand side of Eq. (3) in vector form, we use the symbolic vector operator

$$\nabla = \mathbf{i}\frac{\partial}{\partial x} + \mathbf{j}\frac{\partial}{\partial y} + \mathbf{k}\frac{\partial}{\partial z}.$$

We met the del operator in Article 13–6, where we saw that if

$$w = f(x, y, z)$$

is a differentiable scalar function, then ∇w is the gradient of w:

$$\text{grad } w = \nabla w = \mathbf{i}\frac{\partial w}{\partial x} + \mathbf{j}\frac{\partial w}{\partial y} + \mathbf{k}\frac{\partial w}{\partial z}.$$

Other uses of the del operator are given in Problem 24, Article 15–3, where the curl of a vector $\mathbf{F}$ is defined to be del cross $\mathbf{F}$. Hence, if $\mathbf{F} = M\mathbf{i} + N\mathbf{j} + P\mathbf{k}$, then

$$\text{curl } \mathbf{F} = \nabla \times \mathbf{F} = \begin{vmatrix} \mathbf{i} & \mathbf{j} & \mathbf{k} \\ \dfrac{\partial}{\partial x} & \dfrac{\partial}{\partial y} & \dfrac{\partial}{\partial z} \\ M & N & P \end{vmatrix}$$

$$= \mathbf{i}\left(\frac{\partial P}{\partial y} - \frac{\partial N}{\partial z}\right) + \mathbf{j}\left(\frac{\partial M}{\partial z} - \frac{\partial P}{\partial x}\right) + \mathbf{k}\left(\frac{\partial N}{\partial x} - \frac{\partial M}{\partial y}\right).$$

The component of curl $\mathbf{F}$ that is normal to the region R in the xy-plane is

$$(\nabla \times \mathbf{F}) \cdot \mathbf{k} = \frac{\partial N}{\partial x} - \frac{\partial M}{\partial y}.$$

Hence Green's theorem can be written in vector form as

$$\oint_C \mathbf{F} \cdot d\mathbf{R} = \iint_R (\nabla \times \mathbf{F}) \cdot d\mathbf{A}, \tag{13}$$

where $d\mathbf{A} = \mathbf{k}\,dx\,dy$ is a vector normal to the region R and of magnitude $|d\mathbf{A}| = dx\,dy$. In words, Green's theorem states that the integral around C of the tangential component of $\mathbf{F}$ is equal to the integral, over the region R bounded by C, of the component of curl $\mathbf{F}$ that is normal to R; this integral, specifically, is the flux through R of curl **F**. We shall later extend this result to more general curves and surfaces in a formulation that is known as Stokes's theorem.

There is a second, *normal*, vector form for Green's theorem. It involves the gradient operator ∇ in another form, one that produces the *divergence*. Now the integrand of the line integral of Eq. (13) is the *tangential* component of the field **F** because

$$\mathbf{F} \cdot d\mathbf{R} = \left(\mathbf{F} \cdot \frac{d\mathbf{R}}{ds}\right) ds = (\mathbf{F} \cdot \mathbf{T})\, ds.$$

As in Article 15–4, if we let

$$\mathbf{F} = \mathbf{i}M(x, y) + \mathbf{j}N(x, y),$$

and let **G** be the orthogonal field given by

$$\mathbf{G} = \mathbf{i}N(x, y) - \mathbf{j}M(x, y),$$

then it follows that

$$\mathbf{F} \cdot \mathbf{T} = \mathbf{G} \cdot \mathbf{n} = M\frac{dx}{ds} + N\frac{dy}{ds}$$

because

$$\mathbf{T} = \mathbf{i}\frac{dx}{ds} + \mathbf{j}\frac{dy}{ds}, \qquad \mathbf{n} = \mathbf{i}\frac{dy}{ds} - \mathbf{j}\frac{dx}{ds}.$$

Therefore Green's theorem, which says that

$$\oint_C (M\,dx + N\,dy) = \iint_R \left[\frac{\partial N}{\partial x} - \frac{\partial M}{\partial y}\right] dx\,dy,$$

also says that

$$\oint_C \mathbf{G} \cdot \mathbf{n}\,ds = \iint_R \nabla \cdot \mathbf{G}\,dx\,dy, \tag{14}$$

where

$$\nabla \cdot \mathbf{G} = \text{div}\,\mathbf{G} = \frac{\partial N}{\partial x} + \frac{\partial(-M)}{\partial y}.$$

In words, Eq. (14) says that the line integral of the *normal* component of any vector field **G** around the boundary of a region R in which **G** is continuous and has continuous partial derivatives is equal to the double integral of the *divergence* of **G** over R. In the next article, we shall extend this result to three-dimensional vector fields and discuss the physical interpretation of the divergence. For such vector fields

$$\mathbf{F}(x, y, z) = \mathbf{i}M(x, y, z) + \mathbf{j}N(x, y, z) + \mathbf{k}P(x, y, z),$$

the *divergence* is defined to be

$$\text{div}\,\mathbf{F} = \nabla \cdot \mathbf{F} = \frac{\partial M}{\partial x} + \frac{\partial N}{\partial y} + \frac{\partial P}{\partial z}. \tag{15}$$

PROBLEMS

1. Supply the details necessary to establish Eq. (6).

2. Supply the steps necessary to establish Eq. (10).

In Problems 3 through 7, C is the circle $x^2 + y^2 = a^2$ and R is C plus its interior. Verify that

$$\oint_C M\,dx + N\,dy = \iint_R \left(\frac{\partial N}{\partial x} - \frac{\partial M}{\partial y}\right) dx\,dy,$$

given the condition stated in each problem.

3. $M = x,\ N = y$ **4.** $M = N = xy$

5. $M = -x^2y,\ N = xy^2$ **6.** $M = N = e^{x+y}$

7. $M = y,\ N = 0$

8. Suppose that

$$R = \{(x, y): 0 \le y \le \sqrt{a^2 - x^2}, \quad -a \le x \le a\},$$

and that C is the boundary of R.

a) Sketch R and C.

b) Write out the proof of Green's formula for this region.

Definition. *A region R is said to be simply connected if every simple closed curve lying in R can be continuously contracted to a point without its touching any part of the boundary of R. Examples are the interiors of circles, ellipses, cardioids, and rectangles; and, in three dimensions, the region between two concentric spheres. (The annular ring in Fig. 15–20 is not simply connected.)*

9. Show, by a geometric argument, that Green's formula, Eq. (3), holds for any simply connected region R whose boundary is a simple closed curve C, provided R can be decomposed into a finite number of nonoverlapping regions $R_1, R_2, \ldots, R_n$ with boundaries $C_1, C_2, \ldots, C_n$ of a type for which the formula (3) is true for each R_i and C_i, $i = 1, \ldots, n$.

10. Suppose R is a region in the xy-plane, C is its boundary, and the area of R is given by

$$A(R) = \oint_C \tfrac{1}{2}(x\,dy - y\,dx).$$

Suppose the equations $x = f(u, v)$, $y = g(u, v)$ map R and C in a continuous and one-to-one manner onto a region R' and curve C', respectively, in the uv-plane. Use Green's formula to show that

$$\iint_R dx\,dy = \iint_{R'} \begin{vmatrix} f_u & f_v \\ g_u & g_v \end{vmatrix} du\,dv$$

$$= \iint_R \left(\frac{\partial f}{\partial u}\frac{\partial g}{\partial v} - \frac{\partial f}{\partial v}\frac{\partial g}{\partial u}\right) du\,dv.$$

[*Hint.* Note that

$$\iint_R dx\,dy = \tfrac{1}{2}\int_C (x\,dy - y\,dx)$$

$$= \frac{1}{2}\int_{C'} \left[f(u, v)\left(\frac{\partial g}{\partial u}du + \frac{\partial g}{\partial v}dv\right)\right.$$

$$\left. - g(u, v)\left(\frac{\partial f}{\partial u}du + \frac{\partial f}{\partial v}dv\right)\right],$$

and apply Green's formula to C' and R'.]

In Problems 11 and 12, with C as given, evaluate the line integrals by applying Green's formula.

11. C is the triangle bounded by $x = 0$, $x + y = 1$, $y = 0$:

$$\int_C (y^2\,dx + x^2\,dy).$$

12. C is the boundary of $0 \le x \le \pi$, $0 \le y \le \sin x$:

$$\int_C (3y\,dx + 2x\,dy).$$

13. Rewrite Eq. (14) in nonvector notation for a vector field $\mathbf{F} = \mathbf{i}M(x, y) + \mathbf{j}N(x, y)$ in place of $\mathbf{G}$. (In other words, first write it in vector form with $\mathbf{F}$ in place of $\mathbf{G}$, and then translate the result into nonvector notation.)

THE DIVERGENCE THEOREM

This theorem states that under appropriate conditions, the triple integral

$$\iiint_D \operatorname{div} \mathbf{F}\,dV \tag{1}$$

is equal to the double integral

$$\iint_S \mathbf{F}\cdot\mathbf{n}\,d\sigma. \tag{2}$$

Here $\mathbf{F} = \mathbf{i}M + \mathbf{j}N + \mathbf{k}P$, with M, N, and P continuous functions of (x, y, z) that have continuous first-order partial derivatives:

$$\operatorname{div} \mathbf{F} = \frac{\partial M}{\partial x} + \frac{\partial N}{\partial y} + \frac{\partial P}{\partial z};$$

$\mathbf{n}\, d\sigma$ is a vector element of surface area directed along the unit outer normal vector $\mathbf{n}$; and S is the surface enclosing the region D. We shall first show that (1) and (2) are equal if D is some convex region with no holes, such as the interior of a sphere, or a cube, or an ellipsoid, and if S is a piecewise smooth surface. In addition, we assume that the projection of D into the xy-plane is a simply connected region R_{xy} and that any line perpendicular to the xy-plane at an interior point of R_{xy} intersects the surface S in at most two points, producing surfaces S_1 and S_2:

$$S_1: \quad z_1 = f_1(x, y), \quad (x, y) \text{ in } R_{xy},$$

$$S_2: \quad z_2 = f_2(x, y), \quad (x, y) \text{ in } R_{xy},$$

with $z_1 \le z_2$. Similarly for the projection of D onto the other coordinate planes.

If we write the unit normal vector $\mathbf{n}$ in terms of its direction cosines, as

$$\mathbf{n} = \mathbf{i} \cos \alpha + \mathbf{j} \cos \beta + \mathbf{k} \cos \gamma,$$

then

$$\mathbf{F} \cdot (\mathbf{n}\, d\sigma) = (\mathbf{F} \cdot \mathbf{n})\, d\sigma = (M \cos \alpha + N \cos \beta + P \cos \gamma)\, d\sigma; \qquad \textbf{(3)}$$

and the divergence theorem states that

$$\iiint_D \left(\frac{\partial M}{\partial x} + \frac{\partial N}{\partial y} + \frac{\partial P}{\partial z} \right) dx\, dy\, dz = \iint_S (M \cos \alpha + N \cos \beta + P \cos \gamma)\, d\sigma. \qquad \textbf{(4)}$$

We see that both sides of Eq. (4) are additive with respect to M, N, and P, and that our task is to prove

$$\iiint \frac{\partial M}{\partial x}\, dx\, dy\, dz = \iint M \cos \alpha\, d\sigma, \qquad \textbf{(5a)}$$

$$\iiint \frac{\partial N}{\partial y}\, dx\, dy\, dz = \iint N \cos \beta\, d\sigma, \qquad \textbf{(5b)}$$

$$\iiint \frac{\partial P}{\partial z}\, dx\, dy\, dz = \iint P \cos \gamma\, d\sigma. \qquad \textbf{(5c)}$$

We shall establish (5c) in detail.

Figure 15–22 illustrates the projection of D into the xy-plane. The surface S consists of the *upper part*

$$S_2: \quad z = f_2(x, y), \quad (x, y) \text{ in } R_{xy},$$

and the *lower part*:

$$S_1: \quad z = f_1(x, y), \quad (x, y) \text{ in } R_{xy}.$$

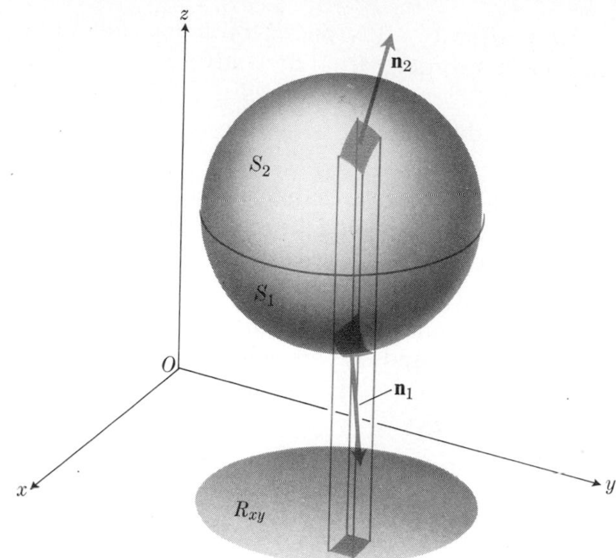

15–22 Regions S_1 and S_2 project onto R_{xy}.

On the surface S_2, the outer normal has a positive **k**-component, and

$$\cos \gamma_2 \, d\sigma_2 = dx \, dy \tag{6a}$$

is the projection of $d\sigma$ into R_{xy}. On the surface S_1, the outer normal has a negative **k**-component, and

$$\cos \gamma_1 \, d\sigma_1 = -dx \, dy. \tag{6b}$$

Therefore we can evaluate the surface integral on the righthand side of Eq. (5c):

$$\begin{aligned}\iint P \cos \gamma \, d\sigma &= \iint_{S_2} P_2 \cos \gamma_2 \, d\sigma_2 + \iint_{S_1} P_1 \cos \gamma_1 \, d\sigma_1 \\ &= \iint_{R_{xy}} P(x, y, z_2) \, dx \, dy - \iint_{R_{xy}} P(x, y, z_1) \, dx \, dy \\ &= \iint_{R_{xy}} [P(x, y, z_2) - P(x, y, z_1)] \, dx \, dy \\ &= \iint_{R_{xy}} \left[\int_{z_1}^{z_2} \frac{\partial P}{\partial z} dz\right] dx \, dy \\ &= \iiint_D \frac{\partial P}{\partial z} dz \, dx \, dy. \end{aligned} \tag{7}$$

Thus we have established Eq. (5c). Proofs for (5a) and (5b) follow the same pattern; or just permute x, y, z; M, N, P; α, β, γ, in order, and get those results from (5c) by renaming the axes. Finally, by addition of (5a, b, c), we get Eq. (4):

$$\iiint_D \text{div } \mathbf{F} \, dV = \iint_S \mathbf{F} \cdot \mathbf{n} \, d\sigma. \tag{8}$$

EXAMPLE 1. Verify Eq. (8) for the sphere

$$x^2 + y^2 + z^2 = a^2$$

if

$$\mathbf{F} = \mathbf{i}x + \mathbf{j}y + \mathbf{k}z.$$

Solution

$$\text{div } \mathbf{F} = \frac{\partial x}{\partial x} + \frac{\partial y}{\partial y} + \frac{\partial z}{\partial z} = 3,$$

so

$$\iiint_D \text{div } \mathbf{F} \, dV = \iiint_D 3 \, dV = 3(\tfrac{4}{3}\pi a^3) = 4\pi a^3.$$

To find a unit vector $\mathbf{n}$ normal to the surface S, we first write the equation of S in the form $f(x, y, z) = 0$, and then (see Article 13–6) use

$$\mathbf{n} = \pm \frac{\text{grad } f}{|\text{grad } f|}.$$

Here

$$f(x, y, z) = x^2 + y^2 + z^2 - a^2;$$

the outer unit normal is

$$\mathbf{n} = \frac{2(x\mathbf{i} + y\mathbf{j} + z\mathbf{k})}{\sqrt{4(x^2 + y^2 + z^2)}} = \frac{x\mathbf{i} + y\mathbf{j} + z\mathbf{k}}{a},$$

and

$$\mathbf{F} \cdot \mathbf{n} \, d\sigma = \frac{x^2 + y^2 + z^2}{a} d\sigma = \frac{a^2}{a} d\sigma = a \, d\sigma,$$

because $x^2 + y^2 + z^2 = a^2$ on the surface. Therefore

$$\iint_S \mathbf{F} \cdot d\boldsymbol{\sigma} = \iint_S a \, d\sigma = a(4\pi a^2) = 4\pi a^3.$$

EXAMPLE 2. Show that Eq. (8) holds for the cube with faces in the planes

$$x = x_0, \qquad x = x_0 + h,$$

$$y = y_0, \qquad y = y_0 + h,$$

$$z = z_0, \qquad z = z_0 + h,$$

where h is a positive constant.

Solution. We compute $\iint \mathbf{F} \cdot \mathbf{n}\, d\sigma$ as the sum of the integrals over the six faces separately. We begin with the two faces perpendicular to the x-axis. For the face $x = x_0$ and the face $x = x_0 + h$, respectively, we have the first and second lines of the following table.

Range of integration	Outward unit normal	$\iint (\mathbf{F} \cdot \mathbf{n})\, d\sigma$
$y_0 \le y \le y_0 + h,\ z_0 \le z \le z_0 + h$	$-\mathbf{i}$	$-\iint M(x_0, y, z)\, dy\, dz$
$y_0 \le y \le y_0 + h,\ z_0 \le z \le z_0 + h$	$\mathbf{i}$	$+\iint M(x_0 + h, y, z)\, dy\, dz$

The sum of the surface integrals over these two faces is

$$\begin{aligned}\iint (\mathbf{F} \cdot \mathbf{n})\, d\sigma &= \iint [M(x_0 + h, y, z) - M(x_0, y, z)]\, dy\, dz \\ &= \iint \left(\int_{x_0}^{x_0+h} \frac{\partial M}{\partial x}\, dx \right) dy\, dz \\ &= \iiint_D \frac{\partial M}{\partial x}\, dV.\end{aligned}$$

Similarly the sum of the surface integrals over the two faces perpendicular to the y-axis is equal to

$$\iiint (\partial N/\partial y)\, dV;$$

and the sum of the surface integrals over the other two faces is equal to $\iiint (\partial P/\partial z)\, dV$. Hence the surface integral over the six faces is equal to the sum of the three volume integrals, and Eq. (8) holds for the cube:

$$\begin{aligned}\iint_S \mathbf{F} \cdot \mathbf{n}\, d\sigma &= \iiint_D \left(\frac{\partial M}{\partial x} + \frac{\partial N}{\partial y} + \frac{\partial P}{\partial z} \right) dV \\ &= \iiint_D \operatorname{div} \mathbf{F}\, dV.\end{aligned}$$

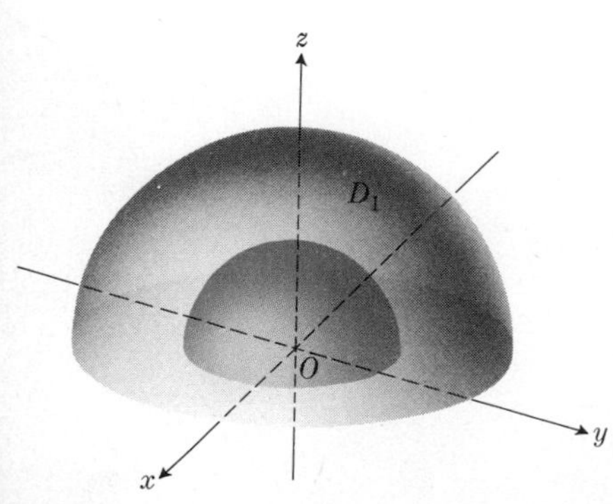

15–23 Upper half of the region between two spheres.

REMARK 1. The divergence theorem can be extended to more complex regions that can be split up into a finite number of simple regions of the type discussed, and to regions that can be defined by certain limiting processes. For example, suppose D is the region between two concentric spheres, and $\mathbf{F}$ has continuously differentiable components throughout D and on the bounding surfaces. Split D by an equatorial plane and apply the divergence theorem to each half separately. The top half, D_1, is shown in Fig. 15–23. The surface that bounds D_1 consists of an outer hemisphere, a plane washer-shaped base, and an inner hemisphere. The divergence theorem says that

$$\iiint_{D_1} \operatorname{div} \mathbf{F}\, dV_1 = \iint_{S_1} \mathbf{F} \cdot \mathbf{n}_1\, d\sigma_1. \tag{9a}$$

The unit normal $\mathbf{n}_1$ that points outward from D_1 points away from the origin along the outer surface, points down along the flat base, and points toward the origin along the inner surface. Next apply the divergence theorem to D_2, as shown in Fig. 15–24:

$$\iiint_{D_2} \text{div } \mathbf{F}\, dV_2 = \iint_{S_2} \mathbf{F} \cdot \mathbf{n}_2 \, d\sigma_2. \tag{9b}$$

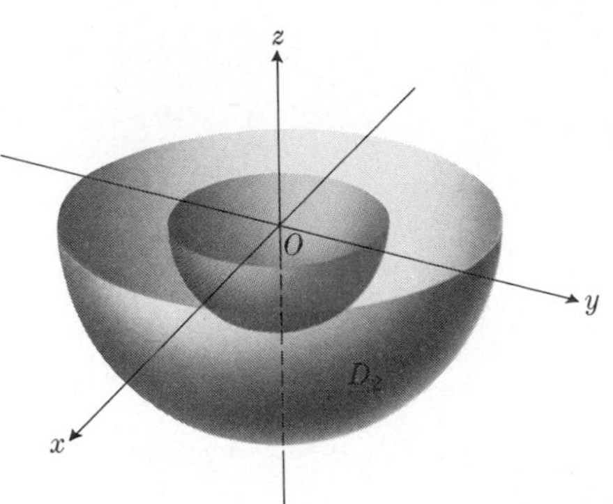

15–24 Lower half of the region between two spheres.

As we follow $\mathbf{n}_2$ over S_2, pointing outward from D_2, we see that $\mathbf{n}_2$ points upward along the flat surface in the xy-plane, points away from the origin on the outer sphere, and points toward the origin on the inner sphere. When we add (9a) and (9b), the surface integrals over the flat base cancel because of the opposite signs of $\mathbf{n}_1$ and $\mathbf{n}_2$. We thus arrive at the result

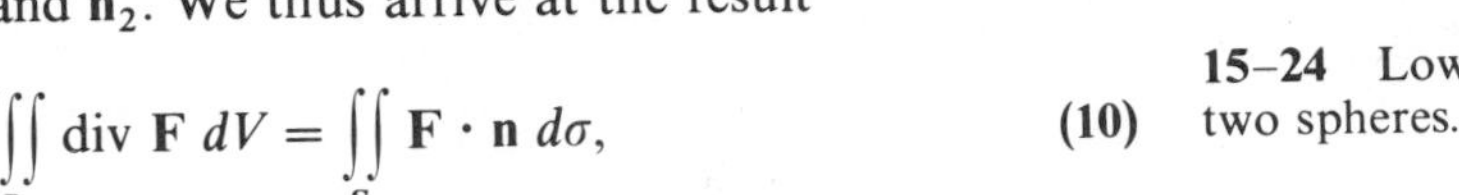

$$\iiint_{D} \text{div } \mathbf{F}\, dV = \iint_{S} \mathbf{F} \cdot \mathbf{n} \, d\sigma, \tag{10}$$

with D the region between the spheres, S the boundary of D consisting of two spheres, and $\mathbf{n}$ the unit normal to S directed outward from D.

EXAMPLE 3. Verify Eq. (10) for the region

$$1 \le x^2 + y^2 + z^2 \le 4$$

if

$$\mathbf{F} = -\frac{\mathbf{i}x + \mathbf{j}y + \mathbf{k}z}{\rho^3}, \qquad \rho = \sqrt{x^2 + y^2 + z^2}.$$

Solution. Observe that

$$\frac{\partial \rho}{\partial x} = \frac{x}{\rho}$$

and

$$\frac{\partial}{\partial x}(x\rho^{-3}) = \rho^{-3} - 3x\rho^{-4}\frac{\partial \rho}{\partial x} = \frac{1}{\rho^3} - \frac{3x^2}{\rho^5}.$$

Thus, throughout the region $1 \le \rho \le 2$, all functions considered are continuous, and

$$\text{div } \mathbf{F} = \frac{-3}{\rho^3} + \frac{3}{\rho^5}(x^2 + y^2 + z^2) = -\frac{3}{\rho^3} + \frac{3\rho^2}{\rho^5} = 0.$$

Therefore

$$\iiint_{D} \text{div } \mathbf{F}\, dV = 0. \tag{11}$$

On the outer sphere ($\rho = 2$), the positive unit normal is

$$\mathbf{n} = \frac{\mathbf{i}x + \mathbf{j}y + \mathbf{k}z}{\rho},$$

and

$$\mathbf{F} \cdot \mathbf{n}\, d\sigma = -\frac{x^2 + y^2 + z^2}{\rho^4}\, d\sigma = -\frac{1}{\rho^2}\, d\sigma.$$

Hence

$$\iint_{\rho=2} \mathbf{F} \cdot \mathbf{n}\, d\sigma = -\tfrac{1}{4} \iint_{\rho=2} d\sigma$$

$$= -\tfrac{1}{4} \cdot 4\pi\rho^2 = -\pi\rho^2 = -4\pi. \tag{12a}$$

On the inner sphere ($\rho = 1$), the positive unit normal points toward the origin; its equation is

$$\mathbf{n} = \frac{-(\mathbf{i}x + \mathbf{j}y + \mathbf{k}z)}{\rho}.$$

Hence

$$\mathbf{F} \cdot \mathbf{n}\, d\sigma = +\frac{x^2 + y^2 + z^2}{\rho^4} = \frac{1}{\rho^2}\, d\sigma.$$

Thus

$$\iint_{\rho=1} \mathbf{F} \cdot \mathbf{n}\, d\sigma = \iint_{\rho=1} \frac{1}{\rho^2}\, d\sigma$$

$$= \frac{1}{\rho^2} \cdot 4\pi\rho^2 = 4\pi. \tag{12b}$$

The sum of (12a) and (12b) is the surface integral over the complete boundary of D:

$$-4\pi + 4\pi = 0,$$

which agrees with (11), as it should.

REMARK 2. We can also conclude that if div $\mathbf{F}$ is continuous at a point Q, then

$$(\text{div } \mathbf{F})_Q = \lim_{\rho \to 0} \left(\frac{3}{4\pi\rho^3} \iint_S \mathbf{F} \cdot \mathbf{n}\, d\sigma \right). \tag{13}$$

Here S is a sphere of radius ρ centered at Q. We take D to be the interior of such a sphere and apply the divergence theorem. The argument is this: If div $\mathbf{F}$ is continuous at Q, then its average value throughout V approaches the value at Q as $\rho \to 0$:

$$\lim_{\rho \to 0} \left(\frac{1}{\frac{4}{3}\pi\rho^3} \iiint_D \text{div } \mathbf{F}\, dV \right) = (\text{div } \mathbf{F})_Q.$$

We substitute

$$\iint_S \mathbf{F} \cdot \mathbf{n}\, d\sigma \qquad \text{for} \qquad \iiint_D \text{div}\, \mathbf{F}\, dV$$

to get Eq. (13). Equation (13) can be taken as the definition of div **F**, and often is. Such a definition has the advantage of being coordinate-free. If one starts with Eq. (13) as a definition, one can then prove the divergence theorem and the coordinate representation of div **F** as

$$\frac{\partial F_x}{\partial x} + \frac{\partial F_y}{\partial y} + \frac{\partial F_z}{\partial z}.$$

However, we take Eq. (13) as a derived result, and see that it leads to the following interpretation of div **F**. Suppose **v** is the velocity field of a moving fluid, and δ is the density. If $\mathbf{F} = \delta \mathbf{v}$, then **F** specifies the mass flow per unit of time, and $\mathbf{F} \cdot \mathbf{n}$ is the component of flow normal to S; hence

$$\iint_S \mathbf{F} \cdot \mathbf{n}\, d\sigma$$

gives the net rate of flow per unit time from the region bounded by S. If we divide this by the volume of that region (that is, by $\frac{4}{3}\pi\rho^3$, assuming that S is a sphere of radius ρ), then the result is the net outflow per unit of time, per unit volume. Thus $(\text{div}\, \mathbf{F})_Q$ is the strength of the *source* at Q, if there is one. (A *sink* corresponds to a negative value of the divergence.) If we multiply $(\text{div}\, \mathbf{F})_Q$ by ΔV, the result is approximately the rate of flow out from ΔV per unit time (say, in pounds per second).

For an incompressible fluid (δ = constant), if there are no sources or sinks in a region D, then the flow into D over its entire boundary just balances the flow out, so that the net flow is zero:

$$\iint \mathbf{F} \cdot \mathbf{n}\, d\sigma = 0.$$

Equation (13) then leads to the conclusion that

$$\text{div}\, \mathbf{F} = \text{div}\, (\delta \mathbf{v}) = \delta\, \text{div}\, \mathbf{v} = 0$$

at each interior point of D. In words, the divergence of the velocity of an incompressible fluid is zero in a region where there are no sources or sinks.

PROBLEMS

In Problems 1 through 5, verify the divergence theorem for the cube with center at the origin and faces in the planes $x = \pm 1$, $y = \pm 1$, $z = \pm 1$, and **F** as given.

1. $\mathbf{F} = 2\mathbf{i} + 3\mathbf{j} + 4\mathbf{k}$
2. $\mathbf{F} = \mathbf{i}x + \mathbf{j}y + \mathbf{k}z$
3. $\mathbf{F} = \mathbf{i}yz + \mathbf{j}xz + \mathbf{k}xy$
4. $\mathbf{F} = \mathbf{i}(x - y) + \mathbf{j}(y - z) + \mathbf{k}(x - y)$
5. $\mathbf{F} = \mathbf{i}x^2 + \mathbf{j}y^2 + \mathbf{k}z^2$

In Problems 6 through 10, compute both

$$\iiint_D \text{div}\, \mathbf{F}\, dV \qquad \text{and} \qquad \iint_S \mathbf{F} \cdot \mathbf{n}\, d\sigma$$

directly. Compare the results with the divergence theorem expressed by Eq. (8), given that

$$\mathbf{F} = \mathbf{i}(x + y) + \mathbf{j}(y + z) + \mathbf{k}(z + x),$$

and given that S bounds the region D given in the problem.

6. $0 \le z \le 4 - x^2 - y^2, \quad 0 \le x^2 + y^2 \le 4$

7. $-4 + x^2 + y^2 \le z \le 4 - x^2 - y^2, \quad 0 \le x^2 + y^2 \le 4$

8. $0 \le x^2 + y^2 \le 9, \quad 0 \le z \le 5$

9. $0 \le x^2 + y^2 + z^2 \le a^2$

10. $|x| \le 1, \quad |y| \le 1, \quad |z| \le 1$

11. A function f is said to be *harmonic* in a region D if, throughout D,

$$\frac{\partial^2 f}{\partial x^2} + \frac{\partial^2 f}{\partial y^2} + \frac{d^2 f}{\partial z^2} = 0.$$

Suppose f is harmonic throughout D, S is the boundary of D, $\mathbf{n}$ is the positive unit normal on S, and $\partial f/\partial n$ is the directional derivative of f in the direction of $\mathbf{n}$. Prove that

$$\iint_S \frac{\partial f}{\partial n}\, d\sigma = 0.$$

(*Hint.* Let $\mathbf{F} = \text{grad } f$.)

12. Prove that if f is harmonic in D (see Problem 11), then

$$\iint_S f \frac{\partial f}{\partial n}\, d\sigma = \iiint_D |\text{grad } f|^2\, dV.$$

(*Hint.* Let $\mathbf{F} = f \text{ grad } f$.)

13. A function of two variables is harmonic in a region R of the xy-plane if

$$\frac{\partial^2 f}{\partial x^2} + \frac{\partial^2 f}{\partial y^2} = 0$$

throughout R. Let f be

a) the real part, or **b)** the imaginary part

of $(x + iy)^3$, where $i = \sqrt{-1}$ and x and y are real. Prove that f is harmonic in the entire xy-plane in both (a) and (b).

15–7 STOKES'S THEOREM

Stokes's theorem is an extension of Green's theorem in vector form to surfaces and curves in three dimensions. It says that the line integral

$$\oint \mathbf{F} \cdot d\mathbf{R} \tag{1}$$

is equal to the surface integral

$$\iint_S (\text{curl } \mathbf{F}) \cdot \mathbf{n}\, d\sigma, \tag{2}$$

under suitable restrictions (i) on the vector

$$\mathbf{F} = \mathbf{i}M + \mathbf{j}N + \mathbf{k}P, \tag{3}$$

(ii) on the simple closed curve C:

$$x = f(t), \qquad y = g(t), \qquad z = h(t), \qquad 0 \le t \le 1, \tag{4}$$

(iii) on the surface

$$S\colon \phi(x, y, z) = 0 \tag{5}$$

bounded by C.

EXAMPLE 1. Let S be the hemisphere

$$z = \sqrt{4 - x^2 - y^2}, \qquad 0 \le x^2 + y^2 \le 4, \tag{6}$$

lying above the xy-plane, with center at the origin. The boundary of this hemisphere is the circle C:

$$z = 0, \qquad x^2 + y^2 = 4. \tag{7}$$

Let

$$\mathbf{F} = \mathbf{i}y - \mathbf{j}x. \tag{8}$$

The integrand in the line integral (1) is

$$\begin{aligned}\mathbf{F} \cdot d\mathbf{R} &= \mathbf{F} \cdot (\mathbf{i}\, dx + \mathbf{j}\, dy + \mathbf{k}\, dz) \\ &= y\, dx - x\, dy.\end{aligned} \tag{9}$$

By Green's theorem for *plane* curves and surfaces, we have

$$\begin{aligned}\oint \mathbf{F} \cdot dr &= \oint_C (y\, dx - x\, dy) \\ &= \iint_{x^2+y^2 \le 4} -2\, dx\, dy \\ &= -8\pi.\end{aligned} \tag{10}$$

To evaluate the surface integral (2), we need to compute

$$\operatorname{curl} \mathbf{F} = \mathbf{i}\left(\frac{\partial P}{\partial y} - \frac{\partial N}{\partial z}\right) + \mathbf{j}\left(\frac{\partial M}{\partial z} - \frac{\partial P}{\partial x}\right) + \mathbf{k}\left(\frac{\partial N}{\partial x} - \frac{\partial M}{\partial y}\right), \tag{11}$$

where

$$M = y, \qquad N = -x, \qquad P = 0. \tag{12}$$

Substituting from (12) into (11), we get

$$\operatorname{curl} \mathbf{F} = -2\mathbf{k}. \tag{13}$$

The unit outer normal to the hemisphere of Eq. (6) is

$$\mathbf{n} = \frac{\mathbf{i}x + \mathbf{j}y + \mathbf{k}z}{\sqrt{x^2 + y^2 + z^2}} = \frac{\mathbf{i}x + \mathbf{j}y + \mathbf{k}z}{2}. \tag{14}$$

Therefore

$$\operatorname{curl} \mathbf{F} \cdot \mathbf{n}\, d\sigma = -z\, d\sigma. \tag{15}$$

For element of surface area $d\sigma$ (Article 14–9), we use

$$d\sigma = \sqrt{1 + \left(\frac{\partial z}{\partial x}\right)^2 + \left(\frac{\partial z}{\partial y}\right)^2}\, dx\, dy, \tag{16}$$

with

$$\frac{\partial z}{\partial x} = \frac{-x}{\sqrt{4 - x^2 - y^2}} \quad \text{and} \quad \frac{\partial z}{\partial y} = \frac{-y}{\sqrt{4 - x^2 - y^2}},$$

or

$$\frac{\partial z}{\partial x} = \frac{-x}{z} \quad \text{and} \quad \frac{\partial z}{\partial y} = \frac{-y}{z}. \tag{17}$$

From (15), (16), and (17), we get

$$\text{curl } \mathbf{F} \cdot \mathbf{n} \, d\sigma = -z \, d\sigma = -z \sqrt{1 + \frac{x^2}{z^2} + \frac{y^2}{z^2}} \, dx \, dy. \tag{18}$$

Therefore

$$\iint_S \text{curl } \mathbf{F} \cdot \mathbf{n} \, d\sigma = \iint_{x^2+y^2 \leq 4} -2 \, dx \, dy = -8\pi, \tag{19}$$

which agrees with the result found for the line integral in Eq. (10).

REMARK 1. In this example, the surface integral (19) taken over the *hemisphere* turns out to have the same value as a surface integral taken over the *plane base* of that hemisphere. The underlying reason for this equality is that both surface integrals are equal to the line integral around the circle that is their common boundary.

REMARK 2. In Stokes's theorem, we require that the surface be *orientable* and *simply connected*. By "simply connected," once again, we mean that any simple closed curve lying on the surface can be continuously contracted to a point (while staying on the surface) without its touching any part of the boundary of S. By "orientable," we mean that it is possible to consistently assign a unique direction, called *positive*, at each point of S, and that there exists a unit normal $\mathbf{n}$ pointing in this direction. As we move about over the surface S without touching its boundary, the direction cosines of the unit vector $\mathbf{n}$ should vary continuously. Also, when we return to the starting position, $\mathbf{n}$ should return to its initial direction. This rules out such a surface as a Möbius strip, which can be constructed by taking a rectangular strip of paper $abcd$, giving the end bc a single twist to interchange the positions of the vertices b and c, and then pasting the ends of the strip together so as to bring vertices a and c together, and also b and d (see Fig. 15–25). The resulting surface is nonorientable because a unit normal vector (think of the shaft of a thumbtack) can be continuously moved around the surface with-

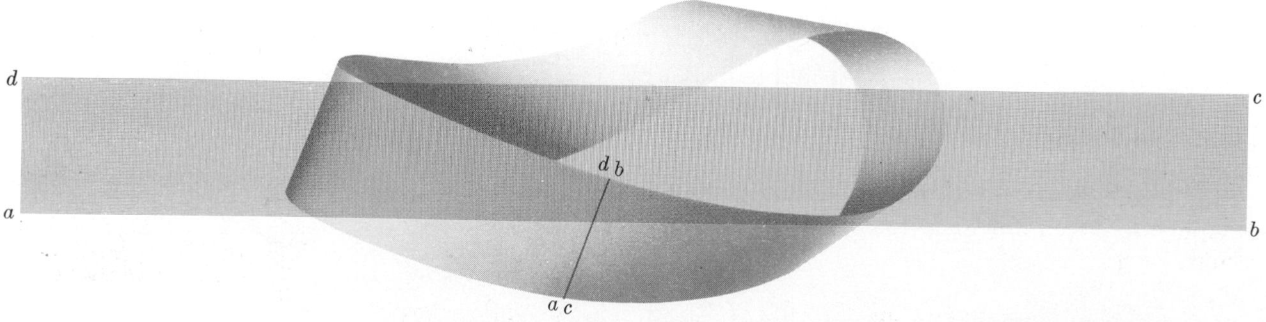

15–25 The construction of a Möbius strip.

out its touching the boundary of the surface, and in such a way that when it is returned to its initial position it will point in a direction *exactly opposite* to its initial direction.

REMARK 3. We also want C to have a positive direction that is related to the positive direction on S. We imagine a simple closed curve Γ on S, near the boundary C (see Fig. 15–26), and let $\mathbf{n}$ be normal to S at some point inside Γ. We then assign to Γ a positive direction, the counterclockwise direction as viewed by an observer who is at the end of $\mathbf{n}$ and looking down. (Note that such a direction keeps the interior of Γ on the observer's left as he progresses around Γ. We could equally well have specified $\mathbf{n}$'s direction by this condition.) Now we move Γ about on S until it touches and is tangent to C. The direction of the positive tangent to Γ at this point of common tangency we shall take to be the positive direction along C. It is a consequence of the orientability of S that a consistent assignment of positive direction along C is induced by this process. The same positive direction is assigned all the way around C, no matter where on S the process is begun. This would not be true of the (nonorientable) Möbius strip.

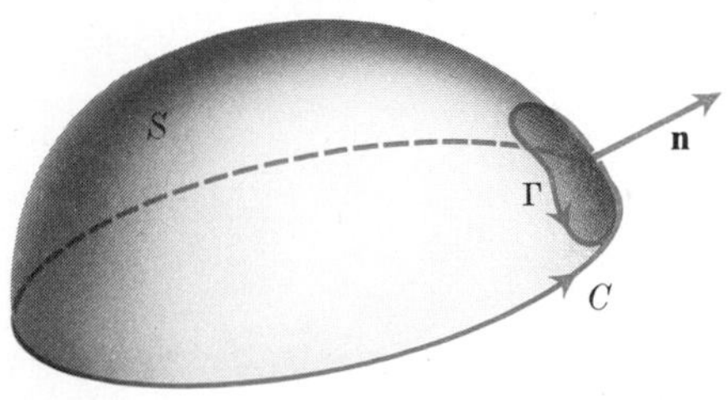

15–26 Orientation of the boundary of an oriented surface.

Stokes's Theorem. *Let S be a smooth, simply connected, orientable surface bounded by a simple closed curve C. Let*

$$\mathbf{F} = \mathbf{i}M + \mathbf{j}N + \mathbf{k}P, \tag{20}$$

where M, N, and P are continuous functions of (x, y, z), together with their first-order partial derivatives, throughout a region D containing S and C in its interior. Let $\mathbf{n}$ be a positive unit vector normal to S, and let the positive direction around C be the one induced by the positive orientation of S. Then

$$\oint_C \mathbf{F} \cdot d\mathbf{R} = \iint_S \operatorname{curl} \mathbf{F} \cdot \mathbf{n}\, d\sigma, \tag{21a}$$

where

$$d\mathbf{R} = \mathbf{i}\, dx + \mathbf{j}\, dy + \mathbf{k}\, dz = \mathbf{T}\, ds \tag{21b}$$

and

$$\mathbf{n}\, d\sigma = (\mathbf{i} \cos \alpha + \mathbf{j} \cos \beta + \mathbf{k} \cos \gamma)\, d\sigma. \tag{21c}$$

Proof for a polyhedral surface S. Let the surface S be a polyhedral surface consisting of a finite number of plane regions. (This polyhedral surface S might resemble a Buckminster Fuller geodesic dome.) We apply Green's theorem to each separate panel of S. There are two types of panels:

1. those that are surrounded on all sides by other panels, and
2. those that have one or more edges that are not adjacent to other panels.

Let Δ be part of the boundary of S that consists of those edges of the type 2 panels that are not adjacent to other panels. In Fig. 15–27, the triangles ABE, BCE, and CDE represent a part of S, with $ABCD$ part of the boundary Δ. Applying Green's theorem to the three triangles in turn and adding the results, we get

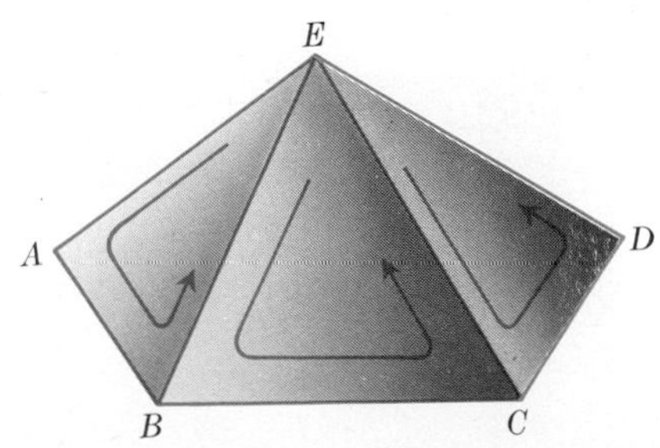

15–27 Part of a polyhedral surface.

$$\left(\oint_{ABE} + \oint_{BCE} + \oint_{CDE}\right) \mathbf{F} \cdot d\mathbf{R} = \left(\iint_{ABE} + \iint_{BCE} + \iint_{CDE}\right) \operatorname{curl} \mathbf{F} \cdot \mathbf{n}\, d\sigma. \tag{22}$$

The three line integrals on the lefthand side of Eq. (22) combine into a single line integral taken around the periphery $ABCDE$, because the integrals along interior segments cancel in pairs. For example, the integral along the segment BE in triangle ABE is opposite in sign to the integral along the same segment in triangle EBC. Similarly for the segment CE. Hence (22) reduces to

$$\oint_{ABCDE} \mathbf{F} \cdot d\mathbf{R} = \iint_{ABCDE} \text{curl } \mathbf{F} \cdot \mathbf{n} \, d\sigma.$$

In general, when we apply Green's theorem to all the panels and add the results, we get

$$\oint_{\Delta} \mathbf{F} \cdot d\mathbf{R} = \iint_{S} \text{curl } \mathbf{F} \cdot \mathbf{n} \, d\sigma. \tag{23}$$

This is Stokes's theorem for a polyhedral surface S.

REMARK 4. A rigorous proof of Stokes's theorem for more general surfaces is beyond the level of a beginning calculus course. (See, for example, Buck, *Advanced Calculus*, or Apostol, *Mathematical Analysis*.) However, the following intuitive argument shows why one would expect Eq. (21a) to be true. Imagine a sequence of polyhedral surfaces

$$S_1, \quad S_2, \quad \ldots,$$

and their corresponding boundaries $\Delta_1, \Delta_2, \ldots$. The surface S_n should be constructed in such a way that its boundary Δ_n is inscribed in or tangent to C, the boundary of S, and so that the length of Δ_n approaches the length of C as $n \to \infty$. C needs to be rectifiable if this is to hold. The faces of S_n might be polygonal regions, approximating pieces of S, and such that the area of S_n approaches the area of S as $n \to \infty$. S also needs to have finite area. Assuming that M, N, P, and their partial derivatives are continuous in a region D containing S and C, it is plausible to expect that

$$\oint_{\Delta_n} \mathbf{F} \cdot d\mathbf{R} \qquad \text{approaches} \qquad \oint_C \mathbf{F} \cdot d\mathbf{R}$$

and that

$$\iint_{S_n} \text{curl } \mathbf{F} \cdot \mathbf{n} \, d\sigma_n \qquad \text{approaches} \qquad \iint_S \text{curl } \mathbf{F} \cdot \mathbf{n} \, d\sigma$$

as $n \to \infty$. But if

$$\oint_{\Delta_n} \mathbf{F} \cdot d\mathbf{R} \to \oint_C \mathbf{F} \cdot d\mathbf{R} \tag{24a}$$

and

$$\iint_{S_n} \text{curl } \mathbf{F} \cdot \mathbf{n} \, d\sigma \to \iint_S \text{curl } \mathbf{F} \cdot \mathbf{n} \, d\sigma, \tag{24b}$$

and if the lefthand sides of (24a) and (24b) are equal by Stokes's theorem for polyhedra, we then have equality of their limits.

EXAMPLE 2. Let S be the portion of the paraboloid $z = 4 - x^2 - y^2$ that lies above the plane $z = 0$. Let C be their curve of intersection, and let

$$\mathbf{F} = \mathbf{i}(z - y) + \mathbf{j}(z + x) - \mathbf{k}(x + y).$$

Compute

$$\oint_C \mathbf{F} \cdot d\mathbf{R} \qquad \text{and} \qquad \iint_S \text{curl } \mathbf{F} \cdot \mathbf{n}\, d\sigma$$

and compare with Eq. (21a).

Solution. The curve C lies in the xy-plane; it is the circle $x^2 + y^2 = 4$. We introduce a parameter θ such that

$$x = 2 \cos \theta, \qquad y = 2 \sin \theta, \qquad 0 \le \theta \le 2\pi.$$

Along C, we have

$$\mathbf{F} \cdot d\mathbf{R} = (z - y)\, dx + (z + x)\, dy - (x + y)\, dz,$$

or, since $z = 0$, $x = 2 \cos \theta$, $y = 2 \sin \theta$,

$$\begin{aligned} \mathbf{F} \cdot d\mathbf{R} &= -y\, dx + x\, dy \\ &= -2 \sin \theta \cdot (-2 \sin \theta\, d\theta) + 2 \cos \theta \cdot (2 \cos \theta\, d\theta) \\ &= 4\, d\theta \end{aligned}$$

and

$$\oint_C \mathbf{F} \cdot d\mathbf{R} = \int_0^{2\pi} 4\, d\theta = 8\pi.$$

For the surface integral, we compute

$$\begin{aligned} \text{curl } \mathbf{F} &= \begin{vmatrix} \mathbf{i} & \mathbf{j} & \mathbf{k} \\ \dfrac{\partial}{\partial x} & \dfrac{\partial}{\partial y} & \dfrac{\partial}{\partial z} \\ z - y & z + x & -x - y \end{vmatrix} \\ &= -2\mathbf{i} + 2\mathbf{j} + 2\mathbf{k}. \end{aligned}$$

For a positive unit normal on the surface

$$S\colon\; f(x, y, z) = z - 4 + x^2 + y^2 = 0,$$

we take

$$\mathbf{n} = \frac{\text{grad } f}{|\text{grad } f|} = \frac{2x\mathbf{i} + 2y\mathbf{j} + \mathbf{k}}{\sqrt{4x^2 + 4y^2 + 1}}.$$

The projection of S onto the xy-plane is the region

$$x^2 + y^2 \le 4,$$

and for element of surface area $d\sigma$, we take

$$d\sigma = \sqrt{\left(\frac{\partial z}{\partial x}\right)^2 + \left(\frac{\partial z}{\partial y}\right)^2 + 1}\, dx\, dy$$

$$= \sqrt{4x^2 + 4y^2 + 1}\, dx\, dy.$$

Thus

$$\iint_S \text{curl } \mathbf{F} \cdot \mathbf{n}\, d\sigma = \iint_{x^2+y^2 \le 4} (-4x + 4y + 2)\, dx\, dy \qquad (\alpha)$$

$$= \iint_{x^2+y^2 \le 4} 2\, dx\, dy = 8\pi, \qquad (\beta)$$

where (β) follows from (α) because odd powers of x or y integrate to zero over the interior of the circle.

REMARK 5. Stokes's theorem can also be extended to a surface S that has one or more holes in it (like a curved slice of Swiss cheese), in a way exactly analogous to Green's theorem: The surface integral over S of the *normal component* of curl $\mathbf{F}$ is equal to the line integral around all the boundaries of S (including boundaries of the holes) of the *tangential component* of $\mathbf{F}$, where the boundary curves are to be traced in the positive direction induced by the positive orientation of S.

REMARK 6. Stokes's theorem provides the following vector interpretation for curl $\mathbf{F}$. As in the discussion of divergence, let $\mathbf{v}$ be the velocity field of a moving fluid, δ the density, and $\mathbf{F} = \delta\mathbf{v}$. Then

$$\oint_C \mathbf{F} \cdot \mathbf{T}\, ds$$

is a measure of the *circulation* of fluid around the closed curve C. By Stokes's theorem, this circulation is also equal to the flux of curl $\mathbf{F}$ through a surface S spanning C:

$$\oint_C \mathbf{F} \cdot d\mathbf{R} = \iint_S \text{curl } \mathbf{F} \cdot \mathbf{n}\, d\sigma.$$

Suppose we fix a point Q and a direction $\mathbf{u}$ at Q. Let C be a circle of radius ρ, with center at Q, whose plane is normal to $\mathbf{u}$. If curl $\mathbf{F}$ is continuous at Q, then the average value of the $\mathbf{u}$-component of curl $\mathbf{F}$ over the circular disk bounded by C approaches the $\mathbf{u}$-component of curl $\mathbf{F}$ at Q as $\rho \to 0$:

$$(\text{curl } \mathbf{F} \cdot \mathbf{u})_Q = \lim_{\rho \to 0} \frac{1}{\pi\rho^2} \iint_S \text{curl } \mathbf{F} \cdot \mathbf{u}\, d\sigma. \qquad \textbf{(25)}$$

If we replace the double integral on the righthand side of Eq. (25) by the circulation, we get

$$(\text{curl } \mathbf{F} \cdot \mathbf{u})_Q = \lim_{\rho \to 0} \frac{1}{\pi\rho^2} \oint_C \mathbf{F} \cdot d\mathbf{R}. \tag{26}$$

The lefthand side of Eq. (26) is a maximum at Q when $\mathbf{u}$ has the same direction as curl $\mathbf{F}$. When ρ is small, the righthand side of Eq. (26) is approximately equal to

$$\frac{1}{\pi\rho^2} \oint_C \mathbf{F} \cdot d\mathbf{R},$$

which is the circulation around C divided by the area of the disk. Suppose that a small paddle wheel, of radius ρ, is introduced into the fluid at Q, with its axle directed along $\mathbf{u}$. The circulation of the fluid around C will affect the rate of spin of the paddle wheel. The wheel will spin fastest when the circulation integral is maximized; therefore it will spin fastest when the axle of the paddle wheel points in the direction of curl $\mathbf{F}$. (See Fig. 15–28.)

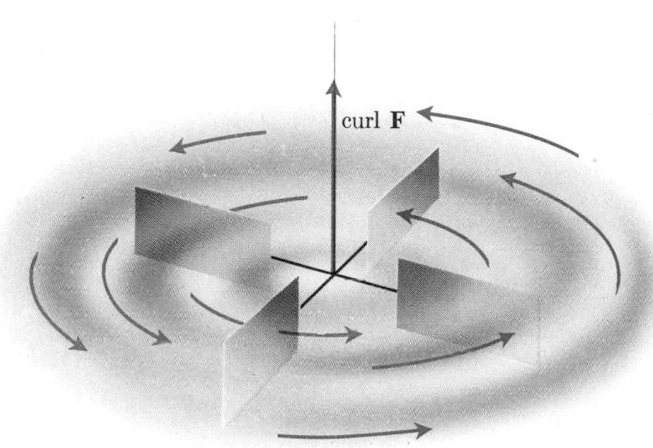

15–28 The paddle-wheel interpretation of curl $\mathbf{F}$.

EXAMPLE 3. A fluid of constant density δ rotates around the z-axis with velocity $\mathbf{v} = \omega(\mathbf{j}x - \mathbf{i}y)$, where ω is a positive constant. If $\mathbf{F} = \delta\mathbf{v}$, find curl $\mathbf{F}$, and comment.

Solution

$$\mathbf{F} = \delta\omega(\mathbf{j}x - \mathbf{i}y),$$

and

$$\text{curl } \mathbf{F} = \begin{vmatrix} \mathbf{i} & \mathbf{j} & \mathbf{k} \\ \dfrac{\partial}{\partial x} & \dfrac{\partial}{\partial y} & \dfrac{\partial}{\partial z} \\ -\delta\omega y & \delta\omega x & 0 \end{vmatrix} = 2\,\delta\omega\mathbf{k}.$$

The work done by a force equal to $\mathbf{F}$, as the point of application moves around a circle C of radius ρ, is

$$\oint_C \mathbf{F} \cdot d\mathbf{R}.$$

If C is in a plane parallel to the xy-plane, Stokes's theorem gives the result

$$\oint_C \mathbf{F} \cdot d\mathbf{R} = \iint_S \operatorname{curl} \mathbf{F} \cdot \mathbf{n}\, d\sigma = \iint 2\, \delta\omega \mathbf{k} \cdot \mathbf{k}\, dx\, dy$$

$$= (2\, \delta\omega)(\pi\rho^2).$$

We note that

$$(\operatorname{curl} \mathbf{F}) \cdot \mathbf{k} = 2\, \delta\omega = \frac{1}{\pi\rho^2} \oint_C \mathbf{F} \cdot d\mathbf{r},$$

in agreement with Eq. (26) with $\mathbf{u} = \mathbf{k}$.

PROBLEMS

In Problems 1 through 4, verify the result of Stokes's theorem for the vector

$$\mathbf{F} = \mathbf{i}(y^2 + z^2) + \mathbf{j}(x^2 + z^2) + \mathbf{k}(x^2 + y^2)$$

for the given surface S and boundary C.

1. S: $z = \sqrt{1 - x^2}$, $-1 \le x \le 1$, $-2 \le y \le 2$,
$y = 2$, $0 \le z \le \sqrt{1 - x^2}$, $-1 \le x \le 1$,
$y = -2$, $0 \le z \le \sqrt{1 - x^2}$, $-1 \le x \le 1$;
C: $z = 0$,
$x = \pm 1$, $-2 \le y \le 2$,
$y = \pm 2$, $-1 \le x \le 1$

2. The surface S is the surface of the upper half of the cube with one vertex at (1, 1, 1), center at the origin, and edges parallel to the axes; the curve C is the intersection of S with the xy-plane.

3. The surface S is as in Problem 2, with a hole cut out of the top face by the circular disk whose cylindrical coordinates satisfy

$$z = 1, \qquad 0 \le r \le \cos\theta, \qquad -\tfrac{1}{2}\pi \le \theta \le \tfrac{1}{2}\pi.$$

(The circle $z = 1$, $r = \cos\theta$ becomes part of the boundary of S.)

4. The surface S is the surface (excluding the face in the yz-plane) of a pyramid with vertices at the origin O and at $A(1, 0, 0)$, $B(0, 1, 0)$, and $D(0, 0, 1)$; the boundary curve C is the triangle OBD in the yz-plane.

5. Suppose $\mathbf{F} = \operatorname{grad} \phi$ is the gradient of a scalar function ϕ having continuous second-order partial derivatives

$$\frac{\partial^2 \phi}{\partial x^2}, \quad \frac{\partial^2 \phi}{\partial x\, \partial y}, \quad \ldots$$

throughout a simply connected region D that contains the surface S and its boundary C in the interior of D. What constant value does

$$\oint_C \mathbf{F} \cdot d\mathbf{R}$$

have in such circumstances? Explain.

6. Let $\phi = (x^2 + y^2 + z^2)^{-1/2}$. Let V be the spherical shell $1 \le x^2 + y^2 + z^2 \le 4$. Let $\mathbf{F} = \operatorname{grad} \phi$. If $1 < a < 2$ and C is the circle $z = 0$, $x^2 + y^2 = a^2$, show that

$$\oint_C \mathbf{F} \cdot d\mathbf{R} = 0$$

a) by direct evaluation of the integral, and
b) by applying Stokes's theorem with S the hemisphere

$$z = \sqrt{a^2 - x^2 - y^2}, \qquad x^2 + y^2 \le a^2.$$

7. If the components of $\mathbf{F}$ have continuous second-order partial derivatives of all types, prove that

$$\operatorname{div}(\operatorname{curl} \mathbf{F}) = 0.$$

8. Use the result of Problem 7 and the divergence theorem to show that

$$\iint_S \operatorname{curl} \mathbf{F} \cdot \mathbf{n}\, d\sigma = 0$$

if the components of $\mathbf{F}$ have continuous second-order derivatives and S is a closed surface like a sphere, an ellipsoid, or a cube.

9. By Stokes's theorem, if S_1 and S_2 are two oriented surfaces having the same positively oriented curve C as boundary, then

$$\iint_{S_1} \operatorname{curl} \mathbf{F} \cdot \mathbf{n}_1\, d\sigma_1 = \oint_C \mathbf{F} \cdot d\mathbf{r} = \iint_{S_2} \operatorname{curl} \mathbf{F} \cdot \mathbf{n}_2\, d\sigma_2.$$

Deduce that

$$\iint_S \operatorname{curl} \mathbf{F} \cdot \mathbf{n}\, d\sigma$$

has the same value for all oriented surfaces S that span C and that induce the same positive direction on C.

10. Use Stokes's theorem to deduce that if $\operatorname{curl} \mathbf{F} = \mathbf{0}$ throughout a simply connected region D, then

$$\int_{P_1}^{P_2} \mathbf{F} \cdot d\mathbf{R}$$

has the same value for all simple paths lying in D and joining P_1 and P_2. In other words, $\mathbf{F}$ is conservative.

REVIEW QUESTIONS AND EXERCISES

1. What is a vector field? Give an example of a two-dimensional vector field; of a three-dimensional field.

2. What is the velocity vector field for a fluid rotating about the x-axis if the angular velocity is a constant ω and the flow is counterclockwise as viewed by an observer at (1, 0, 0) looking toward (0, 0, 0)?

3. Give examples of gradient fields

a) in the plane, **b)** in space.

State a property that gradient fields have and other fields do not.

4. If $\mathbf{F} = \nabla f$ is a gradient field, S is a level surface for f, and C is a curve on S, why is it true (or not true) that $\int_C \mathbf{F} \cdot d\mathbf{R} = 0$?

5. Suppose that S is a portion of a level surface of a function $f(x, y, z)$. How could you select an orientation (if S is orientable) on S such that

$$\iint_S \nabla f \cdot \mathbf{n}\, d\sigma = \iint_S |\nabla f|\, d\sigma?$$

Why is the hypothesis that S is a level surface of f important?

6. If $f(x, y, z) = 2x - 3y + e^z$, and C is any smooth curve from $A(0, 0, 0)$ to $(1, 2, \ln 3)$, what is the value of $\int_C \nabla f \cdot d\mathbf{R}$? Why doesn't the answer depend on C?

7. Write a formula for a vector field $\mathbf{F}(x, y, z)$ such that $\mathbf{F} = f(\rho)\mathbf{R}$, where $\rho = |\mathbf{R}|$ and $\mathbf{R} = \mathbf{i}x + \mathbf{j}y + \mathbf{k}z$, if it is true that

a) $\mathbf{F}$ is directed radially outward from the origin and $|\mathbf{F}| = \rho^{-n}$,

b) $\mathbf{F}$ is directed toward the origin and $|\mathbf{F}| = 2$,

c) $\mathbf{F}$ is a gravitational attraction field for a mass M at the origin in which an inverse-*cube* law applies. (Don't worry about the possible nonexistence of such a field.)

8. Give one physical and one geometrical interpretation for a surface integral

$$\iint_S h\, d\sigma.$$

9. State both the normal form and the tangential form of Green's theorem in the plane.

10. State the divergence theorem and show that it applies to the region D described by $1 \le |\mathbf{R}| \le 2$, assuming that S is the total boundary of this region, $\mathbf{n}$ is directed away from D at each point, and $\mathbf{F} = \nabla(1/|\mathbf{R}|)$, $\mathbf{R} = \mathbf{i}x + \mathbf{j}y + \mathbf{k}z$.

MISCELLANEOUS PROBLEMS

In Problems 1 through 4, describe the vector fields in words and with graphs.

1. $\mathbf{F} = x\mathbf{i} + y\mathbf{j} + z\mathbf{k}$

2. $\mathbf{F} = -x\mathbf{i} - y\mathbf{j} - z\mathbf{k}$

3. $\mathbf{F} = (x - y)\mathbf{i} + (x + y)\mathbf{j}$

4. $\mathbf{F} = (x\mathbf{i} + y\mathbf{j})/(x^2 + y^2)$

In Problems 5 through 8, evaluate the surface integrals

$$\iint_S h\, d\sigma$$

for the given functions and surfaces.

5. The surface S is the hemisphere $x^2 + y^2 + z^2 = a^2$, $z \ge 0$, and $h(x, y, z) = x + y$.

6. The surface S is the portion of the plane $z = x + y$ for which $x \ge 0$, $y \ge 0$, $z \le \pi$, and

$$h(x, y, z) = \sin z.$$

7. The surface S is $z = 4 - x^2 - y^2$, $z \ge 0$; $h = z$.

8. The surface S is the sphere $\rho = a$, and $h = z^2$. (You might do the upper and lower hemispheres separately and add; or use spherical coordinates and not project the surface.)

For the functions and surfaces given in Problems 9 through 12, evaluate

$$\iint_S \frac{\partial f}{\partial n}\, d\sigma,$$

where $\partial f/\partial n$ is the directional derivative of f in the direction of the normal $\mathbf{n}$ in the sense specified.

9. The surface S is the sphere $x^2 + y^2 + z^2 = a^2$, $\mathbf{n}$ is directed outward on S, and $f = x^2 + y^2 + z^2$.

10. The surface and normal are as in Exercise 9, and $f = (x^2 + y^2 + z^2)^{-1}$.

11. The surface S is the portion of the plane

$$z = 2x + 3y$$

for which $x \ge 0$, $y \ge 0$, $z \le 5$, $\mathbf{n}$ has a positive $\mathbf{k}$-component, and $f = x + y + z$.

12. The surface S is the one-eighth of the sphere $x^2 + y^2 + z^2 = a^2$ that lies in the first octant, $\mathbf{n}$ is directed inward with respect to the sphere, and

$$f = \ln (x^2 + y^2 + z^2)^{1/2}.$$

In Problems 13 through 20, evaluate the line integrals

$$\int_C \mathbf{F} \cdot d\mathbf{R}$$

for the given fields $\mathbf{F}$ and paths C.

13. The field $\mathbf{F} = x\mathbf{i} + y\mathbf{j}$ and the circle C:

$$x = \cos t, \qquad y = \sin t, \qquad 0 \le t \le 2\pi.$$

14. The field $\mathbf{F} = -y\mathbf{i} + x\mathbf{j}$ and C as in Problem 13.

15. The field $\mathbf{F} = (x - y)\mathbf{i} + (x + y)\mathbf{j}$ and the circle C in Problem 13.

16. The field $\mathbf{F} = x\mathbf{i} + y\mathbf{j} + z\mathbf{k}$ and the ellipse C, in which the plane $z = 2x + 3y$ cuts the cylinder $x^2 + y^2 = 12$, counterclockwise as viewed from the positive end of the z-axis looking toward the origin.

17. The field $\mathbf{F} = \nabla(xy^2z^3)$ and C as in Problem 16.

18. The field $\mathbf{F} = \nabla \mathbf{x}(x\mathbf{i} + y\mathbf{j} + z\mathbf{k})$ and C as in Problem 13.

19. The field $\mathbf{F}$ as in Problem 18 and C the line segment from the origin to the point (1, 2, 3).

20. The field $\mathbf{F}$ as in Problem 17 and C the line segment from (1, 1, 1) to (2, 1, −1).

21. Heat flows from a hotter body to a cooler body. In three-dimensional heat flow, the fundamental equation for the rate at which heat flows out of D is

$$\iint_S K \frac{\partial u}{\partial n}\, d\sigma = \iiint_D c\delta \frac{\partial u}{\partial t}\, dV. \qquad \textbf{(1)}$$

The symbolism in this equation is as follows:

$u = u(x, y, z, t)$ the temperature at the point (x, y, z) at time t,

K the thermal conductivity coefficient,

δ the mass density,

c the specific heat coefficient. This is the amount of heat required to raise one unit of mass of the material of the body one degree,

S the boundary surface of the region D,

$\dfrac{\partial u}{\partial n}$ the directional derivative in the direction of the outward normal to S.

How is $\partial u/\partial n$ related to the *gradient* of the temperature? In which direction (described in words) does ∇u point? Why does the lefthand side of Eq. (1) appear to make sense as a measure of the rate of flow? Now look at the righthand side of Eq. (1): If ΔV is a small volume element in D, what does $\delta\, \Delta V$ represent? If the temperature of this element changes by an amount Δu in time Δt, what is

a) the amount, **b)** the average rate

of change of heat in the element? In words, what does the right side of Eq. (1) represent physically? Is it reasonable to interpret Eq. (1) as saying that the rate at which heat flows out through the boundary of D is equal to the rate at which heat is being supplied from D?

22. Assuming Eq. (1), Problem 21, and assuming that there is no heat source or sink in D, derive the equation

$$\nabla \cdot (K\nabla u) = c\delta \frac{\partial u}{\partial t} \qquad \textbf{(2)}$$

as the equation that must be satisfied at each point in D.

Suggestion. Apply the divergence theorem to the lefthand side of Eq. (1), and make D be a sphere of radius ϵ; then let $\epsilon \to 0$.

23. Assuming the result of Problem 22, and assuming that K, c, and δ are constants, deduce that the condition for steady-state temperature in D is Laplace's equation

$$\nabla^2 u = 0, \qquad \text{or} \qquad \text{div (grad } u) = 0.$$

In higher mathematics, the symbol Δ is used for the *Laplace operator:*

$$\Delta u = \frac{\partial^2 u}{\partial x^2} + \frac{\partial^2 u}{\partial y^2} + \frac{\partial^2 u}{\partial z^2}.$$

Thus, in this notation,

$$\Delta u = \nabla^2 u = \nabla \cdot \nabla u = \text{div (grad } u).$$

Using the divergence theorem, and assuming that the functions u and v and their first- and second-order partial derivatives are continuous in the regions considered, verify the formulas in Problems 24 through 27. Assume that S is the boundary surface of the simply connected region D.

24. $\displaystyle\iint_S u\nabla v \cdot d\sigma = \iiint_D [u\, \Delta v + (\nabla u) \cdot (\nabla v)]\, dV$

25. $\displaystyle\iint_S \left(u\frac{\partial v}{\partial n} - v\frac{\partial u}{\partial n}\right) d\sigma = \iiint_D (u\, \Delta v - v\, \Delta u)\, dV$

Suggestion. Use the result of Problem 24 as given and in the form you get by interchanging u and v.

26. $\displaystyle\iint_S u\frac{\partial u}{\partial n}\, d\sigma = \iiint_D [u\, \Delta u + |\nabla u|^2]\, dV$

Suggestion. Use the result of Problem 24 with $v = u$.

27. $\displaystyle\iint_S \frac{\partial u}{\partial n}\, d\sigma = \iiint_D \Delta u\, dV$

Suggestion. Use the result of Problem 25 with $v = -1$.

28. A function u is *harmonic* in a region D if and only if it satisfies *Laplace's equation* $\Delta u = 0$ throughout D. Use the identity in Exercise 26 to deduce that if u is harmonic in D and either $u = 0$ or $\partial u/\partial n = 0$ at all points on the surface S that is the boundary of D, then $\nabla u = \mathbf{0}$ throughout D, and therefore u is constant throughout D.

29. The result of Problem 28 can be used to establish the uniqueness of solutions of Laplace's equation in D, provided that either (i) the value of u is prescribed at each point on S, or (ii) the value of $\partial u/\partial n$ is prescribed at each point of S. This is done by supposing that u_1 and u_2 are harmonic in D and that both satisfy the same boundary conditions, and then letting $u = u_1 - u_2$. Complete this uniqueness proof.

30. Problems 21 through 23 deal with heat flow. Assume that K, c, and δ are constant and that the temperature $u = u(x, y, z)$ does not vary with time. Use the results of Problems 23 and 27 to conclude that the net rate of outflow of heat through the surface S is zero.

Note. This result might apply, for example, to the region D between two concentric spheres if the inner one were maintained at 100° and the outer one at 0°, so that heat would flow into D through the inner surface and out through the outer surface at the same rate.

31. Let $\rho = (x^2 + y^2 + z^2)^{1/2}$. Show that

$$u = C_1 + \frac{C_2}{\rho}$$

is harmonic where $\rho > 0$, if C_1 and C_2 are constants. Find values of C_1 and C_2 so that the following boundary conditions are satisfied:

a) $u = 100$ when $\rho = 1$, and $u = 0$ when $\rho = 2$;
b) $u = 100$ when $\rho = 1$, and $\partial u/\partial n = 0$ when $\rho = 2$.

Note. Part (a) refers to a steady-state heat flow problem that is like the one discussed at the end of Problem 30; part (b) refers to an insulated boundary on the sphere $\rho = 2$.

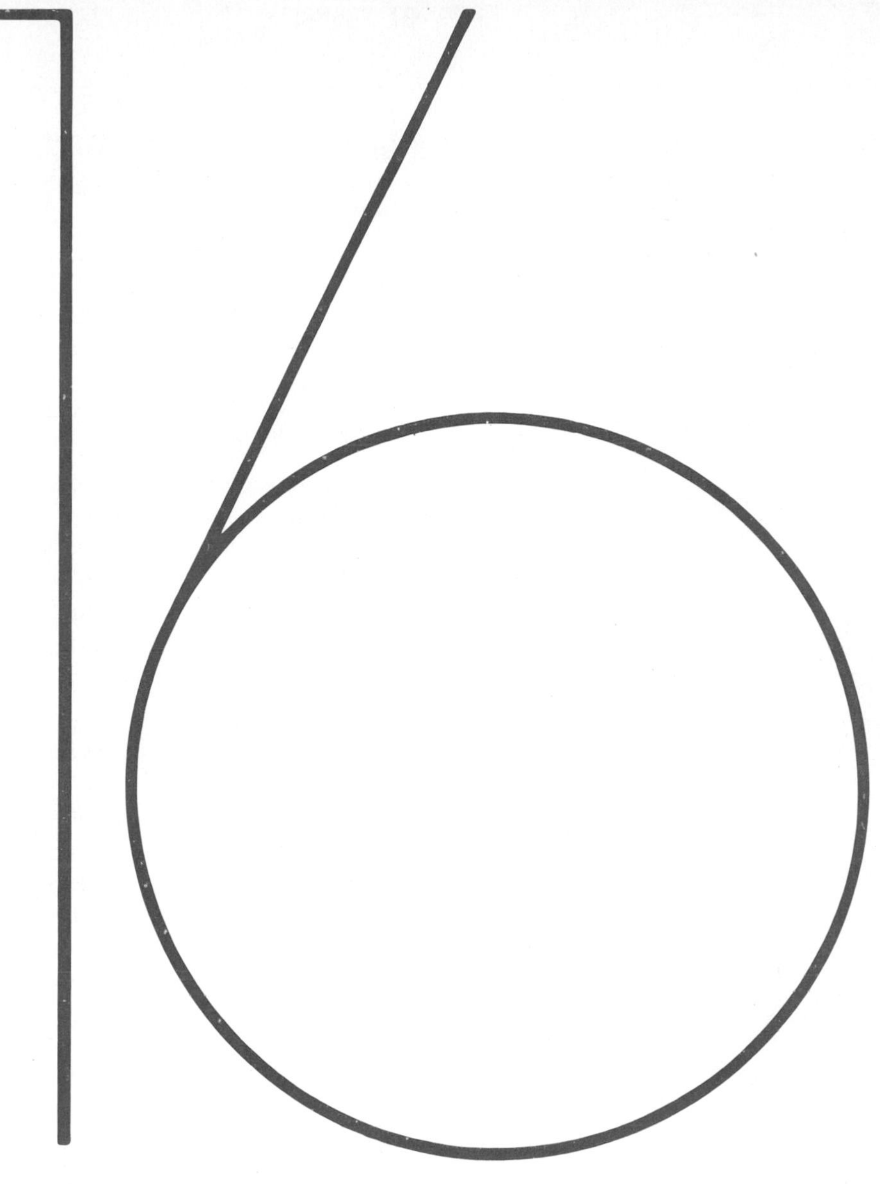

INFINITE SERIES

16-1 INTRODUCTION

The division of $1 - x^{n+1}$ by $1 - x$ results in the equation

$$\frac{1 - x^{n+1}}{1 - x} = 1 + x + x^2 + \cdots + x^n. \tag{1}$$

But when $|x|$ is small enough for x^{n+1} to be omitted from the numerator on the left without disturbing the results of some practical application, we may replace the equality (1) by the approximation

$$\frac{1}{1 - x} \approx 1 + x + x^2 + \cdots + x^n. \tag{2}$$

When $|x| < 1$, this approximation can be used in computing, as an alternative to division by $1 - x$.

Just how reliable this approximation is depends on how small x is and on how large we take n. In general, when $|x| < 1$, the more terms we add the better the approximation becomes, and it is natural to ask what would happen if we could just keep on adding. As long as we kept $|x| < 1$, so that the successive powers of x in (2) became smaller and smaller, couldn't we actually write

$$\frac{1}{1 - x} = 1 + x + x^2 + \cdots + x^n + \cdots ? \tag{3}$$

The answer is "Yes." For functions like $1/(1 - x)$ that have derivatives of all orders, we can write equalities like the one in (3) if we are careful about the domain of x and about what we mean by the sum of infinitely many terms.

The study of such sums, of what functions they represent on what domains, of how we can compute with them, and of what we can do with such sums that we could not do before we had them, is what this chapter is about. We will see why, for example, the approximation

$$\sin x \approx x - \frac{x^3}{6} \tag{4}$$

underestimates $\sin x$ by less than 0.0003 when $0 \leq x \leq 0.5$. And we will at last be able to find convenient expressions for estimating integrals like $\int_0^1 \sin x^2 \, dx$.

The way we proceed is to define an infinite sum like

$$1 + x + x^2 + x^3 + \cdots \tag{5}$$

for each x to be the limiting value of a sequence of partial sums

$$\begin{array}{cccc} \text{First} & \text{Second} & \text{Third} & \\ 1 + x, & 1 + x + x^2, & 1 + x + x^2 + x^3, & \ldots. \end{array} \tag{6}$$

The additions within the partial sums pose no problem because there are only finitely many of them at each stage, so that it only remains to make clear what we mean by the limit of a sequence of such sums. This is best done by studying sequences in their own right; in the next article, therefore, we address the questions of what we mean by a sequence and the limit of a sequence, and of how to tell when a sequence has a limit.

16–2 SEQUENCES

We begin our study of sequences with a definition.

Definition 1. *A **sequence** is a function whose domain is the set of positive integers.*

Sequences are defined by rules the way other functions are, typical rules being

$$a(n) = n - 1, \qquad a(n) = 1 - \frac{1}{n}, \qquad a(n) = \frac{\ln n}{n^2}. \tag{1}$$

To signal the fact that the domains are restricted to the set of positive integers, it is conventional to use a letter like n from the middle of the alphabet for the independent variable instead of the x, y, z, and t used so widely in other contexts. The formulas in the defining rules, however, like the ones above, are often valid for domains much larger than the set of positive integers. This can prove to be an advantage, as we shall see at the end of this article.

The numbers in the range of a sequence are called the *terms* of the sequence, the number $a(n)$ being called the *nth term*, or the term with *index n*. For example, if $a(n) = (n + 1)/n$, then the terms are:

First term	Second term	Third term		*n*th term	
$a(1) = 2,$	$a(2) = \frac{3}{2},$	$a(3) = \frac{4}{3},$	$\ldots,$	$a(n) = \frac{n+1}{n},$	$\ldots$ (2)

When we use the simpler notation a_n for $a(n)$, the sequence in (2) becomes

$$a_1 = 2, \qquad a_2 = \tfrac{3}{2}, \qquad a_3 = \tfrac{4}{3}, \qquad \ldots, \qquad a_n = \frac{n+1}{n}, \qquad \ldots \tag{3}$$

To describe sequences, we often write the first few terms as well as a formula for the nth term.

EXAMPLE 1

We write:	For the sequence whose defining rule is:
$0,\ 1,\ 2,\ \ldots,\ n-1,\ \ldots$	$a_n = n - 1$
$1,\ \frac{1}{2},\ \frac{1}{3},\ \ldots,\ \frac{1}{n},\ \ldots$	$a_n = \frac{1}{n}$
$1,\ -\frac{1}{2},\ \frac{1}{3},\ -\frac{1}{4},\ \ldots,\ (-1)^{n+1}\frac{1}{n},\ \ldots$	$a_n = (-1)^{n+1}\frac{1}{n}$
$0,\ \frac{1}{2},\ \frac{2}{3},\ \frac{3}{4},\ \ldots,\ 1-\frac{1}{n},\ \ldots$	$a_n = 1 - \frac{1}{n}$
$0,\ -\frac{1}{2},\ \frac{2}{3},\ -\frac{3}{4},\ \ldots,\ (-1)^{n+1}\left(1-\frac{1}{n}\right),\ \ldots$	$a_n = (-1)^{n+1}\left(1 - \frac{1}{n}\right)$
$3,\ 3,\ 3,\ \ldots,\ 3,\ \ldots$	$a_n = 3$

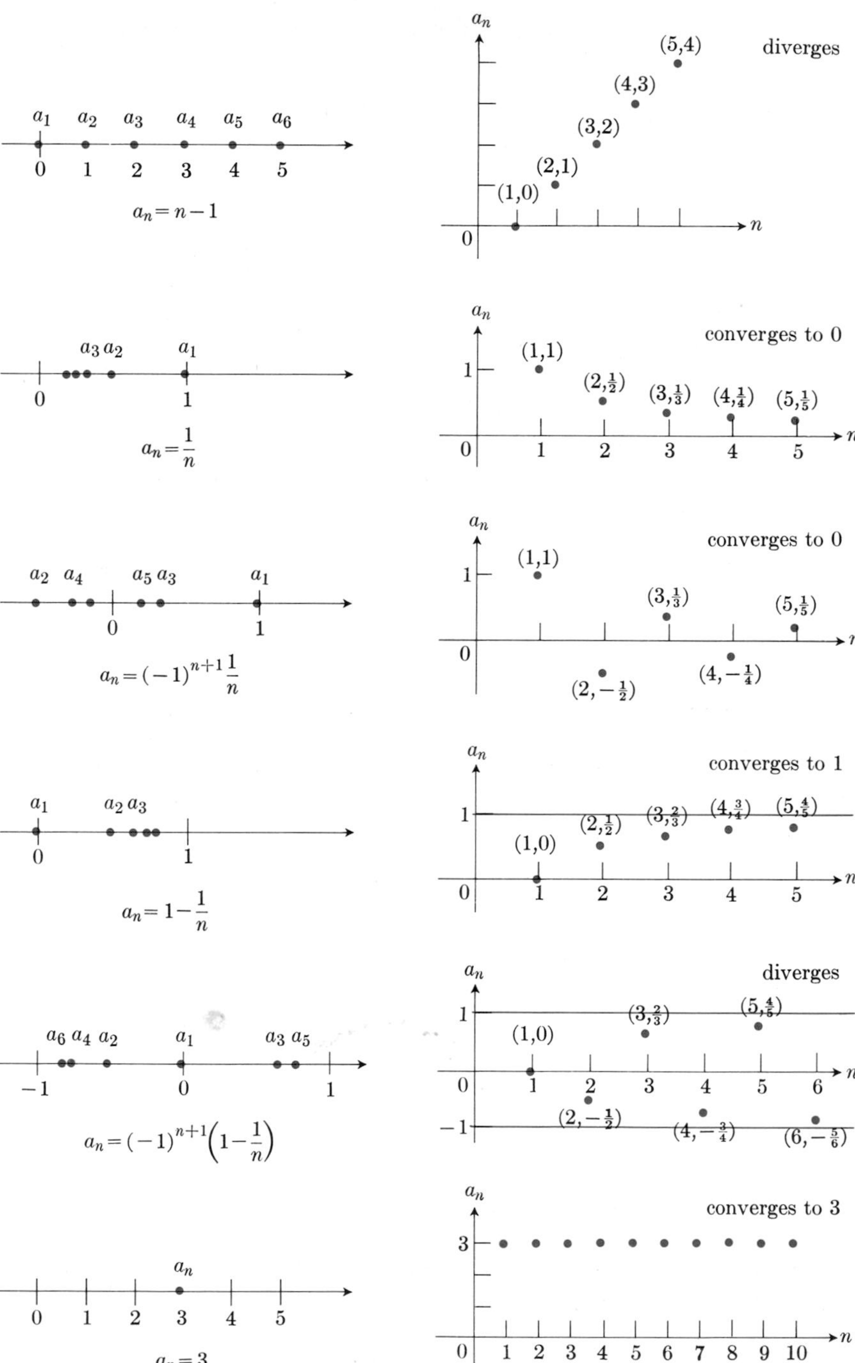

16–1 The sequences of Example 1 are graphed here in two different ways: by plotting the numbers a_n on a horizontal axis, and by plotting the points (n, a_n) in the coordinate plane.

We can, of course, use set notation to describe sequences, writing:

$\{(n, a_n)\}$ The sequence whose ordered pairs are (n, a_n)

or even

$\{a_n\}$ The sequence a_n

when such an abbreviation will not cause trouble. Both choices of notation lead to graphs, for we can either plot the ordered pairs (n, a_n) in the coordinate plane, or plot the numbers a_n on a single axis (shown as a horizontal axis in Fig. 16–1). Plotting just the number a_n has the advantage of simplicity. A potential disadvantage, however, is the fact that several a_n's may turn out to be the same for different values of n, as they are in the sequence defined by the rule $a_n = 3$, in which every term is 3. The points (n, a_n) are distinct for different values of n.

As Fig. 16–1 shows, the sequences of Example 1 exhibit different kinds of behavior. The sequences $\{1/n\}$, $\{(-1)^{n+1}(1/n)\}$, and $\{1 - 1/n\}$ seem to approach single limiting values as n increases, and the sequence $\{3\}$ is already at a limiting value from the very first. On the other hand, terms of the sequence $\{(-1)^{n+1}(1 - 1/n)\}$ seem to accumulate near two different values, -1 and 1, while the terms of $\{n - 1\}$ get larger and larger and do not accumulate anywhere.

To distinguish sequences that approach a unique limiting value L, as n increases, from those that do not, we say that they *converge*, according to the following definition.

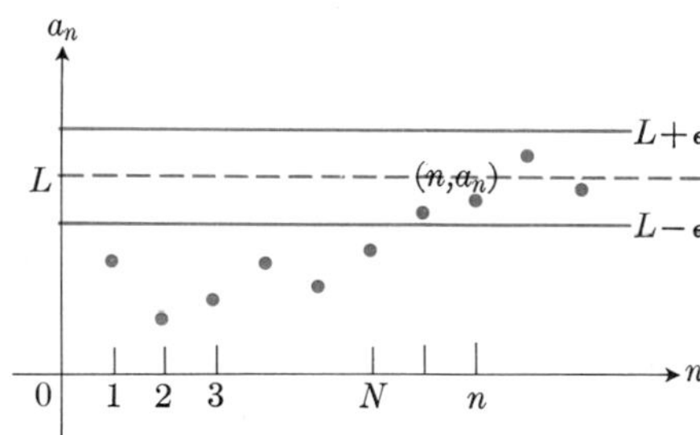

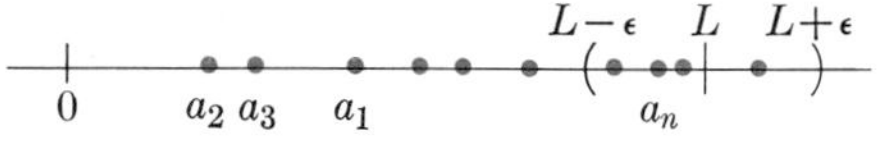

16–2 $a_n \to L$ if L is a horizontal asymptote of $\{(n, a_n)\}$. In this figure, all the a_n's after a_N are within ϵ of L.

Definition 2. *The sequence $\{(n, a_n)\}$ converges to the number L if to every positive number ϵ there corresponds an index N such that*

$$|a_n - L| < \epsilon \qquad \textit{for all} \quad n > N. \tag{4}$$

In other words, $\{(n, a_n)\}$ converges to L if, for every positive ϵ, there is an index N such that all the terms after the Nth lie within ϵ of L. (See Fig. 16–2, and look once more at the sequences in Fig. 16–1.) We indicate the fact that $\{(n, a_n)\}$ converges to L by writing

$$\lim_{n\to\infty} a_n = L \qquad \text{or} \qquad a_n \to L \quad \text{as } n \to \infty,$$

and we call L the *limit* of the sequence $\{a_n\}$. If no such limit exists, we say that $\{a_n\}$ *diverges*.

EXAMPLE 2. $\{1/n\}$ converges to 0.

To see why, we begin by writing down the inequality (4), with $a_n = 1/n$ and $L = 0$. This gives

$$|a_n - L| = \left|\frac{1}{n} - 0\right| = \frac{1}{n} < \epsilon, \tag{5}$$

and therefore we seek an integer N such that

$$\frac{1}{n} < \epsilon \qquad \text{for all} \quad n > N. \tag{6}$$

Certainly

$$\frac{1}{n} < \epsilon \qquad \text{for all} \quad n > \frac{1}{\epsilon}, \tag{7}$$

but there is no reason to expect $1/\epsilon$ to be an integer. This minor difficulty is easily overcome: We just choose any integer $N > 1/\epsilon$. Then every index n greater than N will automatically be greater than $1/\epsilon$. In short, for this choice of N we can guarantee (6). The criterion set forth in Definition 2 for convergence to 0 is satisfied.

EXAMPLE 3. If k is any number, then the constant sequence $\{k\}$, defined by $a_n = k$ for all n, converges to k.

When we take both $a_n = k$ and $L = k$ on the left of the inequality in (4), we find

$$|a_n - L| = |k - k| = 0, \tag{8}$$

which is less than every positive ϵ for every $n \geq 1$.

EXAMPLE 4. The sequence $\{(-1)^{n+1}(1 - 1/n)\}$ diverges. To see why, pick a positive ϵ smaller than 1 so that the bands shown in Fig. 16–3 about the lines $y = 1$ and $y = -1$ do not overlap. Any $\epsilon < 1$ will do. Convergence to 1 would require every point of the graph from some index on to lie inside the upper band, but this will never happen. As soon as a point (n, a_n) lies in the upper band, every alternate point starting with $(n + 1, a_{n+1})$ will lie in the lower band. Likewise, the sequence cannot converge to -1. On the other hand, because the terms of the sequence get increasingly close to 1 and -1 alternately, they never accumulate near any other value.

$a_6\ a_4\ a_2 \quad a_1 \quad a_3\ a_5$

$-1 \quad 0 \quad 1$

$$a_n = (-1)^{n+1}\left(1 - \frac{1}{n}\right)$$

Neither the ϵ interval about 1 nor the ϵ interval about -1 contains a complete tail of the sequence.

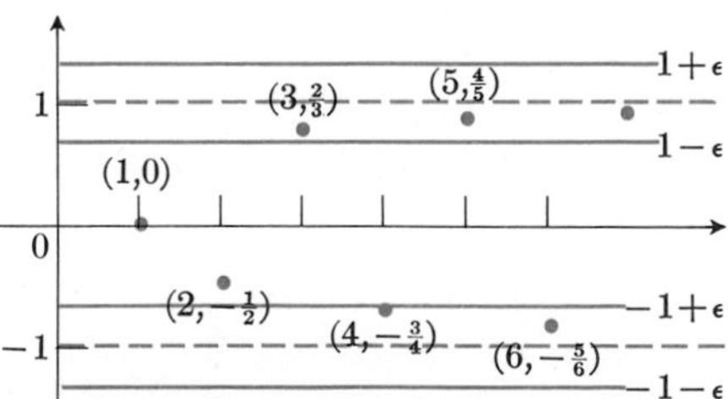

Neither of the ϵ bands shown here contains all the points (n,a_n) from some index onward.

16–3 The sequence $\{(-1)^{n+1}[1 - (1/n)]\}$ diverges.

REMARK 1. A *tail* of a sequence $\{a_n\}$ is the collection of all the terms whose indices are greater than some index N; in other words, one of the sets $\{a_n \mid n > N\}$. Another way to say $a_n \to L$ is to say that every ϵ-interval about L contains a tail. As Example 4 suggests, a sequence cannot have more than one limit. There cannot be two different numbers with the property that every ϵ-interval about each one contains a complete tail.

REMARK 2. The behavior of the sequence $\{(-1)^{n+1}(1 - 1/n)\}$ is qualitatively different from that of $\{n - 1\}$, which diverges because it outgrows every real number L. We describe the behavior of $\{n - 1\}$ by writing

$$\lim_{n \to \infty} (n - 1) = \infty.$$

In speaking of infinity as a limit of a sequence $\{a_n\}$, we do not mean that the difference between a_n and infinity becomes small as n increases. We mean that a_n becomes numerically large as n increases.

REMARK 3. Some sequences are defined *iteratively*, by giving a rule for computing the nth term from earlier terms in the sequence, and stating how to start the sequence. For example, Newton's method for finding a solution of an equation $f(x) = 0$ is to guess a first approximation x_1 and then to use the formula

$$x_{n+1} = x_n - \frac{f(x_n)}{f'(x_n)}$$

to generate, by iteration, a sequence $\{x_n\}$. In favorable circumstances, the sequence converges to a number L which satisfies the equation $f(L) = 0$. As a second example, setting

$$a_1 = 1, \qquad a_2 = 1,$$

and

$$a_n = a_{n-1} + a_{n-2} \qquad \text{for} \quad n \geq 3$$

defines a Fibonacci sequence:

$$1, \quad 1, \quad 2, \quad 3, \quad 5, \quad 8, \quad 13, \quad 21, \quad \ldots .$$

REMARK 4. Iteration is used as a method for solving many kinds of problems by computer. The technique is to start with a first approximation, use that to compute a second approximation, use the second to get a third, and so on. The idea is to generate a sequence whose terms approximate the solution with increasing accuracy.

The study of limits of sequences would be a cumbersome business if every question about convergence had to be answered by applying Definition 2 directly, as we have had to do so far. Fortunately there are three theorems that will make this process largely unnecessary from now on. The first two are the ones with which we began the study of limits of functions in Chapter 1. We restate them here in the notation of sequences.

Theorem 1. *If* $A = \lim_{n\to\infty} a_n$ *and* $B = \lim_{n\to\infty} b_n$ *both exist and are finite, then*

i) $\lim \{a_n + b_n\} = A + B$,

ii) $\lim \{ka_n\} = kA$ (*k any number*),

iii) $\lim \{a_n \cdot b_n\} = A \cdot B$,

iv) $\lim \left\{\frac{a_n}{b_n}\right\} = \frac{A}{B}$, *provided* $B \neq 0$ *and* b_n *is never* 0,

it being understood that all of the limits are to be taken as $n \to \infty$.

By combining Theorem 1 with Examples 2 and 3, we can proceed immediately to

$$\lim_{n\to\infty} -\frac{1}{n} = -1 \cdot \lim_{n\to\infty} \frac{1}{n} = -1 \cdot 0 = 0,$$

$$\lim_{n\to\infty} \left(1 - \frac{1}{n}\right) = \lim_{n\to\infty} 1 - \lim_{n\to\infty} \frac{1}{n} = 1 - 0 = 1,$$

$$\lim_{n\to\infty} \frac{5}{n^2} = 5 \cdot \lim_{n\to\infty} \frac{1}{n} \cdot \lim_{n\to\infty} \frac{1}{n} = 5 \cdot 0 \cdot 0 = 0,$$

$$\lim_{n\to\infty} \frac{4 - 7n^6}{n^6 + 3} = \lim_{n\to\infty} \frac{(4/n^6) - 7}{1 + (3/n^6)} = \frac{0 - 7}{1 + 0} = -7.$$

A corollary of Theorem 1 that will be useful later on is that every nonzero multiple of a divergent sequence is divergent.

Corollary. *If the sequence* $\{a_n\}$ *diverges, and if c is any number different from* 0, *then the sequence* $\{ca_n\}$ *diverges.*

Proof of the corollary. Suppose, on the contrary, that $\{ca_n\}$ converges. Then, by taking $k = 1/c$ in part (ii) of Theorem 1, we see that the sequence

$$\left\{\frac{1}{c} \cdot ca_n\right\} = \{a_n\}$$

converges. Thus $\{ca_n\}$ cannot converge unless $\{a_n\}$ converges. If $\{a_n\}$ does not converge, then $\{ca_n\}$ does not converge. Q.E.D.

The next theorem is the sequence version of the *Sandwich Theorem* of Article 1–10.

Theorem 2. *If* $a_n \leq b_n \leq c_n$ *for all n beyond some index N, and if* $\lim a_n = \lim c_n = L$, *then* $\lim b_n = L$ *also.*

An immediate consequence of Theorem 2 is that, if $|b_n| \leq c_n$ and $c_n \to 0$, then $b_n \to 0$ because $-c_n \leq b_n \leq c_n$. We use this fact in the next example.

EXAMPLE 5

$$\frac{\cos n}{n} \to 0 \quad \text{because} \quad 0 \leq \left|\frac{\cos n}{n}\right| = \frac{|\cos n|}{n} \leq \frac{1}{n}.$$

EXAMPLE 6

$$\frac{1}{2^n} \to 0 \qquad \text{because} \quad 0 \le \frac{1}{2^n} \le \frac{1}{n}.$$

EXAMPLE 7

$$(-1)^n \frac{1}{n} \to 0 \qquad \text{because} \quad 0 \le \left|(-1)^n \frac{1}{n}\right| \le \frac{1}{n}.$$

The application of Theorems 1 and 2 is broadened by a theorem that says that the result of applying a continuous function to a convergent sequence is again a convergent sequence. We state the theorem without proof.

Theorem 3. *If $a_n \to L$ and if f is a function that is continuous at L and defined at all the a_n's, then $f(a_n) \to f(L)$.*

EXAMPLE 8. Because $\sqrt{x}$ is continuous at 1 and $(n + 1)/n \to 1$,

$$\sqrt{\frac{n+1}{n}} \to \sqrt{1} = 1.$$

EXAMPLE 9. Because 2^x is continuous at 0 and $1/n \to 0$,

$$\sqrt[n]{2} = 2^{1/n} \to 2^0 = 1.$$

L'Hôpital's rule can be used to determine the limits of some sequences. The next example shows how.

EXAMPLE 10. Find $\lim_{n\to\infty} (\ln n)/n$.

Solution. The function $(\ln x)/x$ is defined for all $x \ge 1$ and agrees with the given sequence on the positive integers. Therefore $\lim_{n\to\infty} (\ln n)/n$ will equal $\lim_{x\to\infty} (\ln x)/x$ if the latter exists. A single application of l'Hôpital's rule shows that

$$\lim_{x\to\infty} \frac{\ln x}{x} = \lim_{x\to\infty} \frac{1/x}{1} = \frac{0}{1} = 0.$$

We conclude that $\lim_{n\to\infty} (\ln n)/n = 0$.

When we use l'Hôpital's rule to find the limit of a sequence, we often treat n as a continuous real variable, and differentiate directly with respect to n. This saves us from having to rewrite the formula for a_n as we did in Example 10.

EXAMPLE 11. Find $\lim_{n\to\infty} (2^n/5n)$.

Solution. By l'Hôpital's rule,

$$\lim_{n\to\infty} \frac{2^n}{5n} = \lim_{n\to\infty} \frac{2^n \cdot \ln 2}{5} = \infty.$$

PROBLEMS

Write a_1, a_2, a_3, and a_4 for each of the following sequences $\{a_n\}$. Determine which of the sequences converge and which diverge. Find the limit of each sequence that converges.

1. $a_n = \dfrac{1-n}{n^2}$
2. $a_n = \dfrac{n}{2^n}$
3. $a_n = \left(\dfrac{1}{3}\right)^n$
4. $a_n = \dfrac{1}{n!}$
5. $a_n = \dfrac{(-1)^{n+1}}{2n-1}$
6. $a_n = 2 + (-1)^n$
7. $a_n = \cos \dfrac{n\pi}{2}$
8. $a_n = 8^{1/n}$
9. $a_n = \dfrac{(-1)^{n-1}}{\sqrt{n}}$
10. $a_n = \sin^2 \dfrac{1}{n} + \cos^2 \dfrac{1}{n}$

Determine which of the following sequences $\{a_n\}$ converge and which diverge. Find the limit of each sequence that converges.

11. $a_n = \dfrac{1}{10n}$
12. $a_n = \dfrac{n}{10}$
13. $a_n = 1 + \dfrac{(-1)^n}{n}$
14. $a_n = \dfrac{1 + (-1)^n}{n}$
15. $a_n = (-1)^n\left(1 - \dfrac{1}{n}\right)$
16. $a_n = 1 + (-1)^n$
17. $a_n = \dfrac{2n+1}{1-3n}$
18. $a_n = \dfrac{n^2 - n}{2n^2 + n}$
19. $a_n = \sqrt{\dfrac{2n}{n+1}}$
20. $a_n = \dfrac{\sin n}{n}$
21. $a_n = \sin \pi n$
22. $a_n = \sin\left(\dfrac{\pi}{2} + \dfrac{1}{n}\right)$
23. $a_n = n\pi \cos n\pi$
24. $a_n = \dfrac{\sin^2 n}{2^n}$
25. $a_n = \dfrac{n^2}{(n+1)^2}$
26. $a_n = \dfrac{\sqrt{n-1}}{\sqrt{n}}$
27. $a_n = \dfrac{1 - 5n^4}{n^4 + 8n^3}$
28. $a_n = \sqrt[n]{3^{2n+1}}$
29. $a_n = \tanh n$
30. $a_n = \dfrac{\ln n}{\sqrt{n}}$
31. $a_n = \dfrac{2(n+1)+1}{2n+1}$
32. $a_n = \dfrac{(n+1)!}{n!}$
33. $a_n = 5$
34. $a_n = 5^n$
35. $a_n = (0.5)^n$
36. $a_n = \dfrac{10^{n+1}}{10^n}$
37. $a_n = \dfrac{n^n}{(n+1)^{n+1}}$
38. $a_n = (0.03)^{1/n}$
39. $a_n = \sqrt{2 - \dfrac{1}{n}}$
40. $a_n = 2 + (0.1)^n$
41. $a_n = \dfrac{3^n}{n^3}$
42. $a_n = \dfrac{\ln (n+1)}{n+1}$
43. $a_n = \ln n - \ln (n+1)$
44. $a_n = \dfrac{1 - 2^n}{2^n}$
45. $a_n = \dfrac{n^2 - 2n + 1}{n-1}$
46. $a_n = \dfrac{n + (-1)^n}{n}$
47. $a_n = \left(-\dfrac{1}{2}\right)^n$
48. $a_n = \dfrac{\ln n}{\ln 2n}$
49. $a_n = \tan^{-1} n$
50. $a_n = \sinh (\ln n)$
51. $a_n = n \sin \dfrac{1}{n}$
52. $a_n = \dfrac{2n + \sin n}{n + \cos 5n}$
53. $a_n = \dfrac{n^2}{2n-1} \sin \dfrac{1}{n}$
54. $a_n = n\left(1 - \cos \dfrac{1}{n}\right)$

55. Show that $\lim_{n\to\infty} (n!/n^n) = 0$.

[*Hint.* Expand the numerator and denominator and compare the quotient with $1/n$.]

56. (*Calculator*) The formula $x_{n+1} = (x_n + a/x_n)/2$ is the one produced by Newton's method to generate a sequence of approximations to the positive solution of $x^2 - a = 0$, $a > 0$. Starting with $x_1 = 1$ and $a = 3$, use the formula to calculate successive terms of the sequence until you have approximated $\sqrt{3}$ as accurately as your calculator permits.

57. (*Calculator*) If your calculator has a square-root key, enter $x = 10$ and take successive square roots to approximate the terms of the sequence $10^{1/2}, 10^{1/4}, 10^{1/8}, \ldots$, continuing as far as your calculator permits. Repeat, with $x = 0.1$. Try other positive numbers above and below 1. When you have enough evidence, guess the answers to these questions: Does $\lim_{n\to\infty} x^{1/n}$ exist when $x > 0$? Does it matter what x is?

58. (*Calculator*) If you start with a reasonable value of x_1, then the rule $x_{n+1} = x_n + \cos x_n$ will generate a sequence that converges to $\pi/2$. Figure 16–4 shows why. The convergence is rapid. With $x_1 = 1$, calculate x_2, x_3, and x_4. Find out what happens when you start with $x_1 = 5$. Remember to use radians.

59. Suppose that $f(x)$ is defined for all $0 \le x \le 1$, that f is differentiable at $x = 0$, and that $f(0) = 0$. Define a sequence $\{a_n\}$ by the rule $a_n = nf(1/n)$. Show that $\lim a_n = f'(0)$.

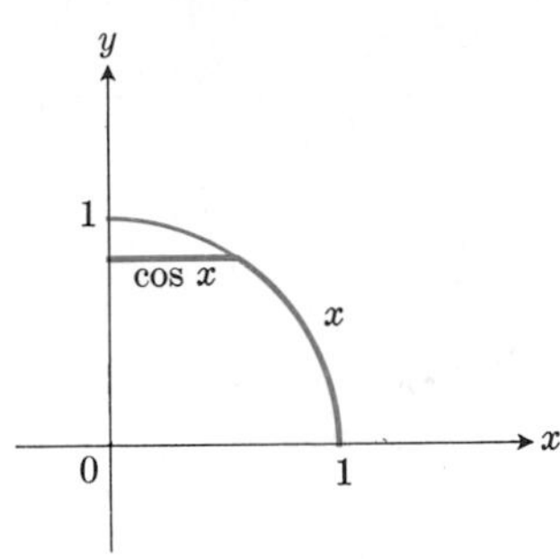

16–4 The length $\pi/2$ of the circular arc is approximated by $x + \cos x$.

Use the result of Problem 59 to find the limits of the sequences in Problems 60 and 61.

60. $a_n = n \tan^{-1} \dfrac{1}{n}$ **61.** $a_n = n(e^{1/n} - 1)$

62. Prove that a sequence $\{a_n\}$ cannot have two different limits L and L'. [*Hint*. Take $\epsilon = \frac{1}{2}|L - L'|$ in Eq. (4).]

63. Prove that, if f is a function that is defined for $x > 0$, and if $\lim_{x\to\infty} f(x) = L$, then $\lim_{n\to\infty} f(n) = L$. [*Hint*. If $|f(x) - L| < \epsilon$ for all x beyond some x_0, then $|f(x) - L| < \epsilon$ for all x beyond some integer $N > x_0$.]

64. Prove Theorem 2.

65. Prove Theorem 3.

16–3 LIMITS THAT ARISE FREQUENTLY

Some limits arise so frequently that they are worth special attention. In this article we investigate these limits and look at examples in which they occur.

1. $\displaystyle\lim_{n\to\infty} \frac{\ln n}{n} = 0$ **2.** $\displaystyle\lim_{n\to\infty} \sqrt[n]{n} = 1$

3. $\displaystyle\lim_{n\to\infty} x^{1/n} = 1 \quad (x > 0)$ **4.** $\displaystyle\lim_{n\to\infty} x^n = 0 \quad (|x| < 1)$

5. $\displaystyle\lim_{n\to\infty} \left(1 + \frac{x}{n}\right)^n = e^x \quad (\text{any } x)$ **6.** $\displaystyle\lim_{n\to\infty} \frac{x^n}{n!} = 0 \quad (\text{any } x)$

Calculation of the Limits

1. $\displaystyle\lim_{n\to\infty} \frac{\ln n}{n} = 0$

This limit was calculated in Example 10 of Article 16–2.

2. $\displaystyle\lim_{n\to\infty} \sqrt[n]{n} = 1$

Let $a_n = n^{1/n}$. Then

$$\ln a_n = \ln n^{1/n} = \frac{1}{n} \ln n \to 0, \tag{1}$$

so that, by applying Theorem 3 of Article 16–2 to $f(x) = e^x$, we have

$$a_n = n^{1/n} = e^{\ln a_n} \to e^0 = 1. \tag{2}$$

3. $\displaystyle\lim_{n\to\infty} x^{1/n} = 1$, **if** $x > 0$

Let $a_n = x^{1/n}$. Then

$$\ln a_n = \ln x^{1/n} = \frac{1}{n} \ln x \to 0, \tag{3}$$

because x remains fixed while n gets large. Thus, again by Theorem 3, with $f(x) = e^x$,

$$a_n = x^{1/n} = e^{\ln a_n} \to e^0 = 1. \tag{4}$$

4. $\lim_{n\to\infty} x^n = 0$, **if** $|x| < 1$

Our scheme here is to show that the criteria of Definition 2 of Article 16–2 are satisfied, with $L = 0$. That is, we will show that to each $\epsilon > 0$ there corresponds an index N so large that

$$|x^n| < \epsilon \qquad \text{for} \quad n > N. \tag{5}$$

Since $\epsilon^{1/n} \to 1$, while $|x| < 1$, there is an index N for which

$$|x| < \epsilon^{1/N}. \tag{6}$$

In other words,

$$|x^N| = |x|^N < \epsilon. \tag{7}$$

This is the index we seek, because

$$|x^n| < |x^N| \qquad \text{for} \quad n > N. \tag{8}$$

Combining (7) and (8) produces

$$|x^n| < |x^N| < \epsilon \qquad \text{for} \quad n > N, \tag{9}$$

which is just what we needed to show.

5. $\lim_{n\to\infty} \left(1 + \frac{x}{n}\right)^n = e^x$ **(any x)**

Let

$$a_n = \left(1 + \frac{x}{n}\right)^n.$$

Then

$$\ln a_n = \ln \left(1 + \frac{x}{n}\right)^n = n \ln \left(1 + \frac{x}{n}\right) \to x,$$

as we can see by the following application of l'Hôpital's rule, in which we differentiate with respect to n:

$$\begin{aligned}\lim_{n\to\infty} n \ln \left(1 + \frac{x}{n}\right) &= \lim_{n\to\infty} \frac{\ln (1 + x/n)}{1/n} \\ &= \lim_{n\to\infty} \frac{\left(\dfrac{1}{1 + x/n}\right) \cdot \left(-\dfrac{x}{n^2}\right)}{-1/n^2} \\ &= \lim_{n\to\infty} \frac{x}{1 + x/n} = x.\end{aligned}$$

Thus,

$$a_n = \left(1 + \frac{x}{n}\right)^n = e^{\ln a_n} \to e^x.$$

6. $\lim\limits_{n\to\infty} \dfrac{x^n}{n!} = 0$ **(any x)**

Since

$$-\frac{|x|^n}{n!} \le \frac{x^n}{n!} \le \frac{|x|^n}{n!},$$

all we really need to show is that $|x|^n/n! \to 0$. The first step is to choose an integer $M > |x|$, so that

$$\frac{|x|}{M} < 1 \qquad \text{and} \qquad \left(\frac{|x|}{M}\right)^n \to 0.$$

We then restrict our attention to values of $n > M$. For these values of n, we can write

$$\frac{|x|^n}{n!} = \frac{|x|^n}{1\cdot 2\cdots M\cdot \underbrace{(M+1)(M+2)\cdots n}_{(n-M)\text{ factors}}}$$

$$\le \frac{|x|^n}{M!\,M^{n-M}} = \frac{|x|^n M^M}{M!\,M^n} = \frac{M^M}{M!}\left(\frac{|x|}{M}\right)^n.$$

Thus,

$$0 \le \frac{|x|^n}{n!} \le \frac{M^M}{M!}\left(\frac{|x|}{M}\right)^n.$$

Now, the constant $M^M/M!$ does not change with n. Thus the Sandwich Theorem tells us that

$$\frac{|x|^n}{n!} \to 0 \qquad \text{because} \qquad \left(\frac{|x|}{M}\right)^n \to 0. \qquad \text{Q.E.D.}$$

A large number of limits can be found directly from the six limits we have just calculated.

EXAMPLES

1. If $|x| < 1$, then $x^{n+4} = x^4 \cdot x^n \to x^4 \cdot 0 = 0$.

2. $\sqrt[n]{2n} = \sqrt[n]{2}\,\sqrt[n]{n} \to 1 \cdot 1 = 1$.

3. $\left(1 + \dfrac{1}{n}\right)^{2n} = \left[\left(1 + \dfrac{1}{n}\right)^n\right]^2 \to e^2$.

4. $\dfrac{100^n}{n!} \to 0$

5. $\dfrac{x^{n+1}}{(n+1)!} = \dfrac{x}{(n+1)} \cdot \dfrac{x^n}{n!} \to 0 \cdot 0 = 0.$

Still other limits can be calculated by using logarithms or l'Hôpital's rule, as in the calculations of limits (2), (3), and (5) at the beginning of this article.

EXAMPLE 6. Find $\lim_{n\to\infty} (\ln(3n+5))/n$.

Solution. By l'Hôpital's rule,

$$\lim_{n\to\infty} \frac{\ln(3n+5)}{n} = \lim_{n\to\infty} \frac{3/(3n+5)}{1} = 0.$$

EXAMPLE 7. Find $\lim_{n\to\infty} \sqrt[n]{3n+5}$.

Solution. Let

$$a_n = \sqrt[n]{3n+5} = (3n+5)^{1/n}.$$

Then,

$$\ln a_n = \ln(3n+5)^{1/n} = \frac{\ln(3n+5)}{n} \to 0,$$

as in Example 6. Therefore,

$$a_n = e^{\ln a_n} \to e^0 = 1,$$

by Theorem 3 of Article 16–2.

PROBLEMS

Determine which of the following sequences $\{a_n\}$ converge and which diverge. Find the limit of each sequence that converges.

1. $a_n = \dfrac{1+\ln n}{n}$
2. $a_n = \dfrac{\ln n}{3n}$
3. $a_n = \dfrac{(-4)^n}{n!}$
4. $a_n = \sqrt[n]{10n}$
5. $a_n = (0.5)^n$
6. $a_n = \dfrac{1}{(0.9)^n}$
7. $a_n = \left(1 + \dfrac{7}{n}\right)^n$
8. $a_n = \left(\dfrac{n+5}{n}\right)^n$
9. $a_n = \dfrac{\ln(n+1)}{n}$
10. $a_n = \sqrt[n]{n+1}$
11. $a_n = \dfrac{n!}{10^{6n}}$
12. $a_n = \dfrac{1}{\sqrt{2^n}}$
13. $a_n = \sqrt[2n]{n}$
14. $a_n = (n+4)^{1/(n+4)}$
15. $a_n = \dfrac{1}{3^{2n-1}}$
16. $a_n = \ln\left(1 + \dfrac{1}{n}\right)^n$
17. $a_n = \left(\dfrac{n}{n+1}\right)^n$
18. $a_n = \left(1 + \dfrac{1}{n}\right)^{-n}$
19. $a_n = \dfrac{\ln(2n+1)}{n}$
20. $a_n = \sqrt[n]{2n+1}$
21. $a_n = \sqrt[n]{\dfrac{x^n}{2n+1}}, \quad x > 0$
22. $a_n = \sqrt[n]{n^2}$
23. $a_n = \sqrt[n]{n^2+n}$
24. $a_n = \dfrac{3^n \cdot 6^n}{2^{-n} \cdot n!}$
25. $a_n = \left(\dfrac{3}{n}\right)^{1/n}$
26. $a_n = \sqrt[n]{4^n n}$
27. $a_n = \left(1 - \dfrac{1}{n}\right)^n$
28. $a_n = \left(1 - \dfrac{1}{n^2}\right)^n$

29. $a_n = \frac{1}{n}\int_1^n \frac{1}{x}\,dx$

30. $a_n = \int_1^n \frac{1}{x^p}\,dx, \quad p > 1$

(*Calculator*) In Problems 31–33, use a calculator to find a value of N such that the given inequality is satisfied for $n \geq N$.

31. $|\sqrt[n]{0.5} - 1| < 10^{-3}$

32. $|\sqrt[n]{n} - 1| < 10^{-3}$

33. $\frac{2^n}{n!} < 10^{-9}$

[*Hint.* If you do not have a factorial key, then write

$$\frac{2^n}{n!} = \left(\frac{2}{1}\right)\left(\frac{2}{2}\right)\cdots\left(\frac{2}{n}\right).$$

That is, calculate successive terms by multiplying by 2 and dividing by the next value of n.]

16–4 INFINITE SERIES

Infinite series are sequences of a special kind.

Definition

1. *If $\{a_n\}$ is a sequence, and*

$$s_n = a_1 + a_2 + \cdots + a_n,$$

then the sequence $\{s_n\}$ is called an ***infinite series.***

2. *Instead of $\{s_n\}$ we usually use the notation*

$$\sum_{n=1}^{\infty} a_n$$

for the series, because it shows how the sums s_n are to be constructed.

3. *The number a_n is called the nth* term *of the series (it is still the nth term of the sequence $\{a_n\}$) and the number s_n is the nth* ***partial sum*** *of the series.*

4. *If the sequence $\{s_n\}$ of partial sums converges to a finite limit L, we say that the series $\sum_{n=1}^{\infty} a_n$* ***converges*** *to L or that its* ***sum*** *is L, and we write*

$$\sum_{n=1}^{\infty} a_n = L \quad \text{or} \quad a_1 + a_2 + \cdots + a_n + \cdots = L.$$

If no such limit exists, that is if $\{s_n\}$ diverges, we say that the series $\sum_{n=1}^{\infty} a_n$ ***diverges.***

We shall illustrate the method of finding the sum of an infinite series with the repeating decimal

$$0.3333\ldots = \frac{3}{10} + \frac{3}{100} + \frac{3}{1000} + \frac{3}{10{,}000} + \cdots$$

$$s_1 = \frac{3}{10},$$

$$s_2 = \frac{3}{10} + \frac{3}{10^2},$$

$$\vdots$$

$$s_n = \frac{3}{10} + \frac{3}{10^2} + \cdots + \frac{3}{10^n}.$$

We can obtain a simple expression for s_n in closed form as follows: We multiply both sides of the equation for s_n by $\frac{1}{10}$ and obtain

$$\frac{1}{10}s_n = \frac{3}{10^2} + \frac{3}{10^3} + \cdots + \frac{3}{10^n} + \frac{3}{10^{n+1}}.$$

When we subtract this from s_n, we have

$$s_n - \frac{1}{10}s_n = \frac{3}{10} - \frac{3}{10^{n+1}} = \frac{3}{10}\left(1 - \frac{3}{10^n}\right).$$

Therefore,

$$\frac{9}{10}s_n = \frac{3}{10}\left(1 - \frac{1}{10^n}\right),$$

$$s_n = \frac{3}{9}\left(1 - \frac{1}{10^n}\right).$$

As $n \to \infty$, $(\frac{1}{10})^n \to 0$ and

$$\lim_{n\to\infty} s_n = \frac{3}{9} = \frac{1}{3}.$$

We therefore say that the sum of the infinite series

$$\frac{3}{10^1} + \frac{3}{10^2} + \frac{3}{10^3} + \cdots + \frac{3}{10^n} + \cdots$$

is $\frac{1}{3}$, and we write

$$\sum_{n=1}^{\infty} \frac{3}{10^n} = \frac{1}{3}.$$

A repeating decimal is a special kind of *geometric series.*

Definition. *A series of the form*

$$a + ar + ar^2 + ar^3 + \cdots + ar^{n-1} + \cdots \tag{1}$$

is called a ***geometric series****. The ratio of any term to the one before it is r.*

The ratio r can be positive, as in

$$1 + \frac{1}{2} + \frac{1}{4} + \cdots + \frac{1}{2^{n-1}} + \cdots, \tag{2}$$

or negative, as in

$$1 - \frac{1}{3} + \frac{1}{9} - \cdots + (-1)^n\frac{1}{3^{n-1}} + \cdots. \tag{3}$$

The sum of the first n terms of (1) is

$$s_n = a + ar + ar^2 + \cdots + ar^{n-1}. \tag{4}$$

Multiplying both sides of (4) by r gives

$$rs_n = ar + ar^2 + \cdots + ar^{n-1} + ar^n. \tag{5}$$

When we subtract (5) from (4), nearly all the terms cancel on the right side, leaving

$$s_n - rs_n = a - ar^n,$$

or

$$(1 - r)s_n = a(1 - r^n). \qquad \textbf{(6)}$$

If $r \neq 1$, we may divide (6) by $(1 - r)$ to obtain

$$s_n = \frac{a(1 - r^n)}{1 - r}, \qquad r \neq 1. \qquad \textbf{(7a)}$$

On the other hand, if $r = 1$ in (4), we get

$$s_n = na, \qquad r = 1. \qquad \textbf{(7b)}$$

We are interested in the limit as $n \to \infty$ in Eqs. (7a) and (7b). Clearly, (7b) has no finite limit if $a \neq 0$. If $a = 0$, the series (1) is just

$$0 + 0 + 0 + \cdots,$$

which converges to the sum zero.

If $r \neq 1$, we use (7a). In the right side of (7a), n appears only in the expression r^n. This approaches zero as $n \to \infty$ if $|r| < 1$. Therefore,

$$\lim_{n\to\infty} s_n = \lim_{n\to\infty} \frac{a(1 - r^n)}{1 - r}$$

$$= \frac{a}{1 - r}, \qquad \text{if} \quad |r| < 1. \qquad \textbf{(8)}$$

If $|r| > 1$, then $|r^n| \to \infty$, and (1) diverges.

The remaining case is where $r = -1$. Then $s_1 = a$, $s_2 = a - a = 0$, $s_3 = a$, $s_4 = 0$, and so on. If $a \neq 0$, this sequence of partial sums has no limit as $n \to \infty$, and the series (1) diverges.

We have thus proved the following theorem.

Theorem 1. The geometric series theorem. *If $|r| < 1$, the geometric series*

$$a + ar + ar^2 + \cdots + ar^{n-1} + \cdots$$

converges to $a/(1 - r)$. If $|r| \geq 1$, the series diverges unless $a = 0$. If $a = 0$, the series converges to 0.

EXAMPLE 1. A ball is dropped from a meters above a flat surface. Each time the ball hits after falling a distance h, it rebounds a distance rh, where r is a positive number less than one. Find the total distance the ball travels up and down.

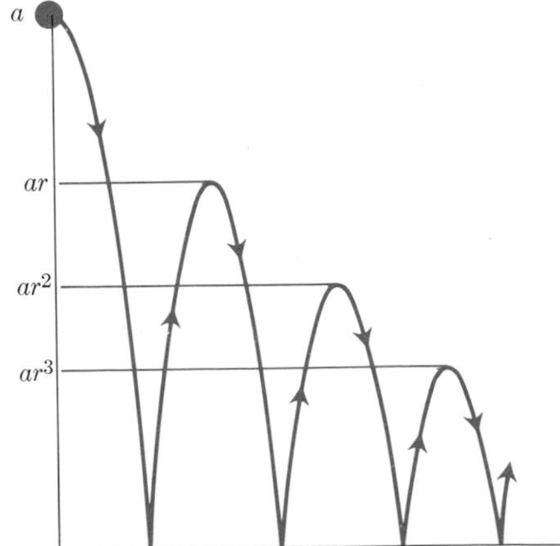

16–5 The height of each rebound is reduced by the factor r.

Solution. (See Fig. 16–5.) The distance is given by the series

$$s = a + 2ar + 2ar^2 + 2ar^3 + \cdots$$

The terms following the first term form a geometric series of sum $2ar/(1 - r)$.

Hence the distance is

$$s = a + \frac{2ar}{1-r} = a\frac{1+r}{1-r}.$$

For instance, if a is 6 meters and $r = \frac{2}{3}$, the distance is

$$s = 6\frac{1+\frac{2}{3}}{1-\frac{2}{3}} = 30 \text{ m}.$$

EXAMPLE 2. If we take $a = 1$ and $r = x$ in the geometric series theorem, we obtain

$$\frac{1}{1-x} = 1 + x + x^2 + \cdots + x^{n-1} + \cdots, \qquad |x| < 1, \tag{9}$$

which is the result we sought in Article 16–1.

To find the sum of the geometric series of Theorem 1, we first found a closed expression for s_n and then used our experience with sequences to find $\lim_{n\to\infty} s_n$. We use the same procedure in the next example.

EXAMPLE 3. Determine whether $\sum_{n=1}^{\infty} [1/(n(n+1))]$ converges. If it does, find the sum.

Solution. We begin by looking for a pattern in the sequence of partial sums that might lead us to a closed expression for s_k. The key to success here, as in the integration

$$\int \frac{dx}{x(x+1)} = \int \frac{dx}{x} - \int \frac{dx}{x+1},$$

is the use of partial fractions:

$$\frac{1}{k(k+1)} = \frac{1}{k} - \frac{1}{k+1}.$$

This permits us to write the partial sum

$$\sum_{n=1}^{k} \frac{1}{n(n+1)} = \frac{1}{1\cdot 2} + \frac{1}{2\cdot 3} + \cdots + \frac{1}{k\cdot(k+1)}$$

as

$$s_k = \left(\frac{1}{1} - \frac{1}{2}\right) + \left(\frac{1}{2} - \frac{1}{3}\right) + \cdots + \left(\frac{1}{k} - \frac{1}{k+1}\right).$$

By removing parentheses on the right, and combining terms, we find that

$$s_k = 1 - \frac{1}{k+1} = \frac{k}{k+1}. \tag{12}$$

From this formulation of s_k, we see immediately that $s_k \to 1$. Therefore the series does converge, and

$$\sum_{n=1}^{\infty} \frac{1}{n(n+1)} = 1. \tag{13}$$

There are, of course, other series that diverge besides geometric series with $|r| \geq 1$.

EXAMPLE 4

$$\sum_{n=1}^{\infty} n^2 = 1 + 4 + 9 + \cdots + n^2 + \cdots$$

diverges because the partial sums grow beyond every number L. The number $s_n = 1 + 4 + 9 + \cdots + n^2$ is greater than or equal to n^2 at each stage.

EXAMPLE 5

$$\sum_{n=1}^{\infty} \frac{n+1}{n} = \frac{2}{1} + \frac{3}{2} + \frac{4}{3} + \cdots + \frac{n+1}{n} + \cdots$$

The sequence of partial sums eventually outgrows every preassigned number: each term is greater than 1, so the sum of n terms is greater than n.

A series can diverge without having its partial sums become large. For instance, the partial sums may oscillate between two extremes, as they do in the next example.

EXAMPLE 6. $\sum_{n=1}^{\infty} (-1)^{n+1}$ diverges because its partial sums alternate between 1 and 0:

$$\begin{aligned} s_1 &= (-1)^2 = 1, \\ s_2 &= (-1)^2 + (-1)^3 = 1 - 1 = 0, \\ s_3 &= (-1)^2 + (-1)^3 + (-1)^4 = 1 - 1 + 1 = 1, \end{aligned}$$

and so on.

The next theorem provides a quick way to detect the kind of divergence that occurred in Examples 4, 5, and 6.

***Theorem 2.* The *n*th-term test for divergence.** *If* $\lim_{n\to\infty} a_n \neq 0$, *or if* $\lim_{n\to\infty} a_n$ *fails to exist, then* $\sum_{n=1}^{\infty} a_n$ *diverges.*

When we apply Theorem 2 to the series in Examples 4, 5, and 6, we find that:

$\sum_{n=1}^{\infty} n^2$ diverges because $n^2 \to \infty$;

$\sum_{n=1}^{\infty} \frac{n+1}{n}$ diverges because $\frac{n+1}{n} \to 1 \neq 0$;

$\sum_{n=1}^{\infty} (-1)^{n+1}$ diverges because $\lim_{n\to\infty} (-1)^{n+1}$ does not exist.

Proof of the theorem. We prove Theorem 2 by showing that if $\sum a_n$ converges, then $\lim_{n\to\infty} a_n = 0$. Let

$$s_n = a_1 + a_2 + \cdots + a_n,$$

and suppose that $\sum a_n$ converges to S; that is

$$s_n \to S.$$

Then, corresponding to any preassigned number $\epsilon > 0$, there is an index N such that all the terms of the sequence $\{s_n\}$ after the Nth one lie between $S - (\epsilon/2)$ and $S + (\epsilon/2)$. Hence, no two of them may differ by as much as ϵ. That is, if m and n are both greater than N, then

$$|s_n - s_m| < \epsilon.$$

In particular, this inequality holds if $m = n - 1$ and $n > N + 1$, so that

$$|s_n - s_{n-1}| = |a_n| < \epsilon \qquad \text{when} \quad n > N + 1.$$

Since ϵ was any positive number whatsoever, this means that

$$\lim_{n\to\infty} a_n = 0. \qquad \text{Q.E.D.}$$

Because of how it is proved, Theorem 2 is often stated in the following shorter way.

Theorem 3. *If $\sum_{n=1}^{\infty} a_n$ converges, then $a_n \to 0$.*

A word of caution. Theorem 3 does *not* say that if $a_n \to 0$ then $\sum a_n$ converges. The series $\sum a_n$ may diverge even though $a_n \to 0$. Thus, $\lim a_n = 0$ is a necessary, but not a sufficient condition for the series $\sum a_n$ to converge.

EXAMPLE 7. The series

$$1 + \underbrace{\frac{1}{2} + \frac{1}{2}}_{2\text{ terms}} + \underbrace{\frac{1}{4} + \frac{1}{4} + \frac{1}{4} + \frac{1}{4}}_{4\text{ terms}} + \underbrace{\frac{1}{8} + \frac{1}{8} + \cdots + \frac{1}{8}}_{8\text{ terms}} + \cdots + \underbrace{\frac{1}{2^n} + \frac{1}{2^n} + \cdots + \frac{1}{2^n}}_{2^n\text{ terms}} + \cdots$$

diverges even though its terms form a sequence that converges to 0.

Whenever we have two convergent series we can add them, subtract them, and multiply them by constants, to make other convergent series. The next theorem gives the details.

Theorem 4. *If $A = \sum_{n=1}^{\infty} a_n$ and $B = \sum_{n=1}^{\infty} b_n$ both exist and are finite, then*

i) $\sum_{n=1}^{\infty} (a_n + b_n) = A + B$;

ii) $\sum_{n=1}^{\infty} ka_n = k \sum_{n=1}^{\infty} a_n = kA$ (*k any number*).

Proof of the theorem. Let

$$A_n = a_1 + a_2 + \cdots + a_n, \qquad B_n = b_1 + b_2 + \cdots + b_n.$$

Then the partial sums of $\sum_{n=1}^{\infty} (a_n + b_n)$ are:

$$\begin{aligned} S_n &= (a_1 + b_1) + (a_2 + b_2) + \cdots + (a_n + b_n) \\ &= (a_1 + \cdots + a_n) + (b_1 + \cdots + b_n) \\ &= A_n + B_n. \end{aligned}$$

Since $A_n \to A$ and $B_n \to B$, we have $S_n \to A + B$. The partial sums of $\sum_{n=1}^{\infty} (ka_n)$ are:

$$\begin{aligned} S_n &= ka_1 + ka_2 + \cdots + ka_n \\ &= k(a_1 + a_2 + \cdots + a_n) \\ &= kA_n, \end{aligned}$$

which converge to kA. Q.E.D.

REMARK 1. If you think there should be two more parts of Theorem 4 to match those of Theorem 1, Article 16–2, see Problems 44–46. Also, see Problem 41, Article 16–5, and Problem 39, Article 16–7.

Part (ii) of Theorem 4 says that every multiple of a convergent series converges. A companion to this is the next corollary, which says that every *nonzero* multiple of a divergent series diverges.

Corollary. *If $\sum_{n=1}^{\infty} a_n$ diverges, and if c is any number different from* 0, *then the series of multiples $\sum_{n=1}^{\infty} ca_n$ diverges.*

Proof of the corollary. Suppose, to the contrary, that $\sum_{n=1}^{\infty} ca_n$ actually converges. Then, when we take $k = 1/c$ in part (ii) of Theorem 4 we find that

$$\frac{1}{c} \cdot \sum_{n=1}^{\infty} ca_n = \sum_{n=1}^{\infty} \frac{1}{c} \cdot ca_n = \sum_{n=1}^{\infty} a_n$$

converges. That is, $\sum_{n=1}^{\infty} ca_n$ cannot converge unless $\sum_{n=1}^{\infty} a_n$ also converges. Thus, if $\sum_{n=1}^{\infty} a_n$ diverges, then $\sum_{n=1}^{\infty} ca_n$ must diverge. Q.E.D.

REMARK 2. An immediate consequence of Theorem 4 is that, if $A = \sum_{n=1}^{\infty} a_n$ and $B = \sum_{n=1}^{\infty} b_n$, then

$$\sum (a_n - b_n) = \sum a_n + \sum (-1)b_n = \sum a_n - \sum b_n = A - B. \tag{14}$$

The series $\sum_{n=1}^{\infty} (a_n - b_n)$ is called the *difference* of $\sum_{n=1}^{\infty} a_n$ and $\sum_{n=1}^{\infty} b_n$, while $\sum_{n=1}^{\infty} (a_n + b_n)$ is called their *sum*.

EXAMPLE 8

a) $\displaystyle\sum_{n=1}^{\infty} \frac{4}{2^{n-1}} = 4 \sum_{n=1}^{\infty} \frac{1}{2^{n-1}} = 4 \frac{1}{1 - \frac{1}{2}} = 8;$

b)
$$\begin{aligned}\sum_{n=0}^{\infty} \frac{3^n - 2^n}{6^n} &= \sum_{n=0}^{\infty} \left(\frac{1}{2^n} - \frac{1}{3^n}\right)\\ &= \sum_{n=0}^{\infty} \frac{1}{2^n} - \sum_{n=0}^{\infty} \frac{1}{3^n}\\ &= \frac{1}{1 - \frac{1}{2}} - \frac{1}{1 - \frac{1}{3}}\\ &= 2 - \tfrac{3}{2}\\ &= \tfrac{1}{2}.\end{aligned}$$

REMARK 3. A finite number of terms can always be deleted from or added to a series without altering its convergence or divergence. If $\sum_{n=1}^{\infty} a_n$ converges and k is an index greater than 1, then $\sum_{n=k}^{\infty} a_n$ converges, and

$$\sum_{n=1}^{\infty} a_n = a_1 + a_2 + \cdots + a_{k-1} + \sum_{n=k}^{\infty} a_n. \tag{15}$$

Conversely, if $\sum_{n=k}^{\infty} a_n$ converges for any $k > 1$, then $\sum_{n=1}^{\infty} a_n$ converges and the sums continue to be related as in Eq. (15). Thus, for example,

$$\sum_{n=1}^{\infty} \frac{1}{5^n} = \frac{1}{5} + \frac{1}{25} + \frac{1}{125} + \sum_{n=4}^{\infty} \frac{1}{5^n} \tag{16}$$

and

$$\sum_{n=4}^{\infty} \frac{1}{5^n} = \sum_{n=1}^{\infty} \frac{1}{5^n} - \frac{1}{5} - \frac{1}{25} - \frac{1}{125}. \tag{17}$$

Note that while the addition or removal of a finite number of terms from a series has no effect on the convergence or divergence of the series, these operations can change the *sum* of a convergent series.

REMARK 4. The indexing of the terms of a series can be changed without altering convergence of the series. For example, the geometric series that starts with

$$1 + \frac{1}{2} + \frac{1}{4} + \cdots$$

can be described as

$$\sum_{n=0}^{\infty} \frac{1}{2^n} \quad \text{or} \quad \sum_{n=-4}^{\infty} \frac{1}{2^{n+4}} \quad \text{or} \quad \sum_{n=5}^{\infty} \frac{1}{2^{n-5}}. \tag{18}$$

The partial sums remain the same no matter what indexing is chosen, so that we are free to start indexing with whatever integer we want. Preference is usually given to an indexing that leads to a simple expression. In Example 8(b) we chose to start with $n = 0$ instead of $n = 1$, because this allowed us to describe the series we had in mind as:

$$\sum_{n=0}^{\infty} \frac{3^n - 2^n}{6^n} \quad \text{instead of} \quad \sum_{n=1}^{\infty} \frac{3^{n-1} - 2^{n-1}}{6^{n-1}}. \tag{19}$$

PROBLEMS

In Problems 1 through 8, find a closed expression for the sum s_n of the first n terms of each series. Then compute the sum of the series if the series converges.

1. $\frac{1}{2 \cdot 3} + \frac{1}{3 \cdot 4} + \frac{1}{4 \cdot 5} + \cdots + \frac{1}{(n+1)(n+2)} + \cdots$

2. $\ln \frac{1}{2} + \ln \frac{2}{3} + \ln \frac{3}{4} + \cdots + \ln \frac{n}{n+1} + \cdots$

3. $1 + e^{-1} + e^{-2} + \cdots + e^{-(n-1)} + \cdots$

4. $1 - \frac{1}{2} + \frac{1}{4} - \frac{1}{8} + \cdots + (-1)^{n-1} \frac{1}{2^{n-1}} + \cdots$

5. $1 - 2 + 4 - 8 + \cdots + (-1)^{n-1} 2^{n-1} + \cdots$

6. $2 + \frac{2}{3} + \frac{2}{9} + \frac{2}{27} + \cdots + \frac{2}{3^{n-1}} + \cdots$

7. $\frac{9}{100} + \frac{9}{100^2} + \frac{9}{100^3} + \cdots + \frac{9}{100^n} + \cdots$

8. $1 + 2 + 3 + \cdots + n + \cdots$

9. The series in Problem 1 can be described as

$$\sum_{n=1}^{\infty} \frac{1}{(n+1)(n+2)}.$$

It can also be described as a summation beginning with $n = -1$:

$$\sum_{n=-1}^{\infty} \frac{1}{(n+3)(n+4)}.$$

Describe the series as a summation beginning with

a) $n = -2$ **b)** $n = 0$ **c)** $n = 5$.

10. A ball is dropped from a height of 4 m. Each time it strikes the pavement after falling from a height of h meters, it rebounds to a height of $0.75h$ meters. Find the total distance traveled up and down by the ball.

In Problems 11 through 14, write out the fourth partial sum of each series. Then find the sum of the series.

11. $\sum_{n=0}^{\infty} \frac{1}{4^n}$ **12.** $\sum_{n=2}^{\infty} \frac{1}{4^n}$

13. $\sum_{n=1}^{\infty} \frac{7}{4^n}$ **14.** $\sum_{n=0}^{\infty} (-1)^n \frac{5}{4^n}$

Find the sum of each series.

15. $\sum_{n=0}^{\infty} \left(\frac{5}{2^n} + \frac{1}{3^n}\right)$ **16.** $\sum_{n=0}^{\infty} \left(\frac{5}{2^n} - \frac{1}{3^n}\right)$

17. $\sum_{n=0}^{\infty} \left(\frac{2^n}{5^n}\right)$ **18.** $\sum_{n=0}^{\infty} \left(\frac{2^{n+1}}{5^n}\right)$

Use partial fractions to find the sum of each series.

19. $\sum_{n=1}^{\infty} \frac{4}{(4n-3)(4n+1)}$ **20.** $\sum_{n=1}^{\infty} \frac{1}{(4n-3)(4n+1)}$

21. $\sum_{n=3}^{\infty} \frac{4}{(4n-3)(4n+1)}$ **22.** $\sum_{n=1}^{\infty} \frac{2n+1}{n^2(n+1)^2}$

23. a) Express the repeating decimal

$$0.234\ 234\ 234 \ldots$$

as an infinite series, and give the sum as a ratio p/q of two integers.

b) Is it true that *every* repeating decimal is a rational number p/q? Give a reason for your answer.

24. Express the decimal number

$$1.24\ 123\ 123\ 123 \ldots,$$

which begins to repeat after the first three figures, as a rational number p/q.

In Problems 25 through 38, determine whether each series converges or diverges. If it converges, find the sum.

25. $\sum_{n=0}^{\infty} \left(\frac{1}{\sqrt{2}}\right)^n$

26. $\sum_{n=1}^{\infty} \ln \frac{1}{n}$

27. $\sum_{n=1}^{\infty} (-1)^{n+1} \frac{3}{2^n}$

28. $\sum_{n=1}^{\infty} (\sqrt{2})^n$

29. $\sum_{n=0}^{\infty} \cos n\pi$

30. $\sum_{n=0}^{\infty} \frac{\cos n\pi}{5^n}$

31. $\sum_{n=0}^{\infty} e^{-2n}$

32. $\sum_{n=1}^{\infty} \frac{n^2+1}{n}$

33. $\sum_{n=1}^{\infty} (-1)^{n+1} n$

34. $\sum_{n=1}^{\infty} \frac{2}{10^n}$

35. $\sum_{n=0}^{\infty} \frac{2^n - 1}{3^n}$

36. $\sum_{n=1}^{\infty} \left(1 - \frac{1}{n}\right)^n$

37. $\sum_{n=0}^{\infty} \frac{n!}{1000^n}$

38. $\sum_{n=0}^{\infty} \frac{1}{x^n}, \quad |x| > 1$

In Problems 39 and 40, the equalities are instances of Theorem 1. Give the value of a and of r in each case.

39. $\frac{1}{1+x} = \sum_{n=0}^{\infty} (-1)^n x^n, \quad |x| < 1$

40. $\frac{1}{1+x^2} = \sum_{n=0}^{\infty} (-1)^n x^{2n}, \quad |x| < 1$

41. Figure 16–6 shows the first five of an infinite series of squares. The outermost square has an area of 4, and each of the other squares is obtained by joining the midpoints of the sides of the square before it. Find the sum of the areas of all the squares.

42. Find a closed-form expression for the nth partial sum of the series $\sum_{n=1}^{\infty} (-1)^{n+1}$.

43. Show by example that the term-by-term sum of two divergent series may converge.

44. Find convergent geometric series $A = \sum_{n=1}^{\infty} a_n$ and $B = \sum_{n=1}^{\infty} b_n$ that illustrate the fact that $\sum_{n=1}^{\infty} a_n \cdot b_n$ may converge without being equal to $A \cdot B$.

45. Show by example that $\sum_{n=1}^{\infty} (a_n/b_n)$ may diverge even though $\sum_{n=1}^{\infty} a_n$ and $\sum_{n=1}^{\infty} b_n$ converge and no $b_n = 0$.

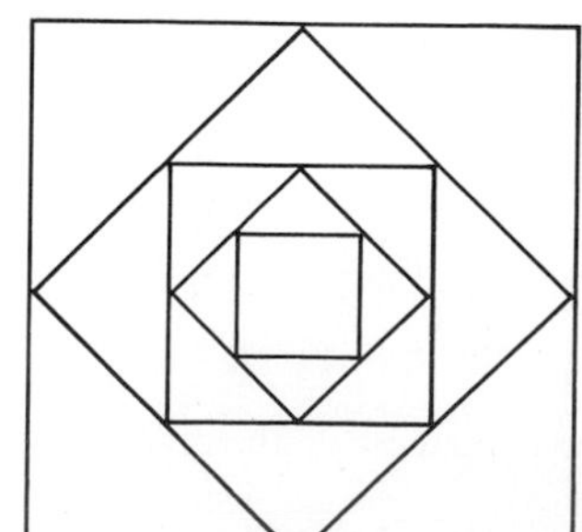

Figure 16–6

46. Show by example that $\sum_{n=1}^{\infty} (a_n/b_n)$ may converge to something other than A/B even when $A = \sum_{n=1}^{\infty} a_n$, $B = \sum_{n=1}^{\infty} b_n \neq 0$, and no $b_n = 0$.

47. Show that if $\sum_{n=1}^{\infty} a_n$ converges, and $a_n \neq 0$ for all n, then $\sum_{n=1}^{\infty} (1/a_n)$ diverges.

48. a) Verify by long division that

$$\frac{1}{1+t} = 1 - t + t^2 - t^3 + \cdots + (-1)^n t^n + \frac{(-1)^{n+1} t^{n+1}}{1+t}.$$

b) By integrating both sides of the equation in part (a) with respect to t, from 0 to x, show that

$$\ln(1+x) = x - \frac{x^2}{2} + \frac{x^3}{3} - \frac{x^4}{4} + \cdots + (-1)^n \frac{x^{n+1}}{n+1} + R,$$

where

$$R = (-1)^{n+1} \int_0^x \frac{t^{n+1}}{1+t}\, dt.$$

c) If $x > 0$, show that

$$|R| \leq \int_0^x t^{n+1}\, dt = \frac{x^{n+2}}{n+2}.$$

[*Hint.* As t varies from 0 to x, $1 + t \geq 1$.]

d) If $x = \frac{1}{2}$, how large should n be in part (c) above if we want to be able to guarantee that $|R| < 0.001$? Write a polynomial that approximates $\ln(1+x)$ to this degree of accuracy for $0 \leq x \leq \frac{1}{2}$.

e) If $x = 1$, how large should n be in part (c) above if we want to be able to guarantee that $|R| < 0.001$?

49. (*Calculator*) The concentration in the blood resulting from a single dose of a drug normally decreases with time as the drug is eliminated from the body. Doses may therefore be repeated to maintain the concentration. One model for the effect of repeated doses gives the residual concentration just before the $(n+1)$st dose as:

$$R_n = C_0 e^{-kt_0} + C_0 e^{-2kt_0} + \cdots + C_0 e^{-nkt_0},$$

where C_0 = concentration achievable by a single dose (mg/ml), k = the *elimination constant* (hr^{-1}), and t_0 = time between doses (hr). See Fig. 16–7.

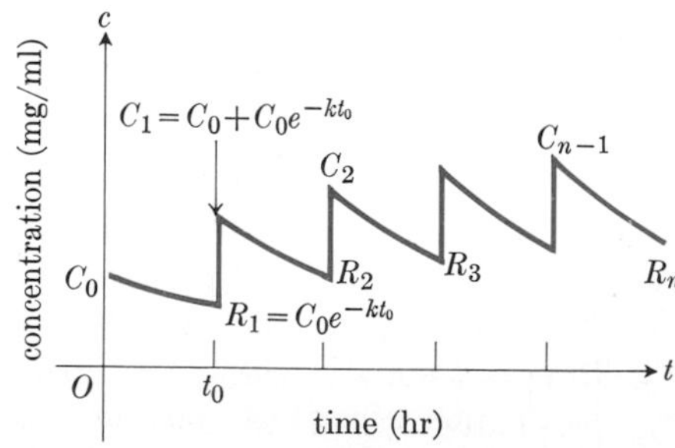

16–7 One possible effect of repeated doses on the concentration of a drug in the bloodstream.

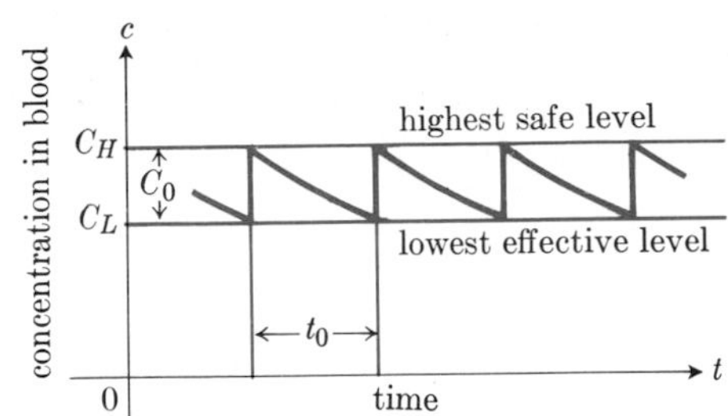

16–8 Safe and effective concentrations of a drug. C_0 is the change in concentration produced by one dose; t_0 is the time between doses.

a) Write R_n in closed form, and find $R = \lim_{n\to\infty} R_n$.

b) Calculate R_1 and R_{10} for $C_0 = 1$ mg/ml, $k = 0.1\ \text{hr}^{-1}$, and $t_0 = 10$ hr. How good an estimate of R is R_{10}?

c) If $k = 0.01\ \text{hr}^{-1}$ and $t_0 = 10$ hr, find the smallest n such that $R_n > \frac{1}{2}R$.

d) If a drug is known to be ineffective below a concentration C_L and harmful above some higher concentration C_H, one needs to find values of C_0 and t_0 that will produce a concentration that is safe (not above C_H) but effective (not below C_L). See Fig. 16–8. We therefore want to find values of C_0 and t_0 for which

$$R = C_L \quad \text{and} \quad C_0 + R = C_H.$$

Thus $C_0 = C_H - C_L$. Show that, when these values are substituted in the equation for R obtained in (a), the resulting equation simplifies to:

$$t_0 = \frac{1}{k} \ln \frac{C_H}{C_L}.$$

To reach an effective level rapidly, one might administer a "loading" dose that would produce a concentration of C_H mg/ml. This could be followed every t_0 hours by a dose that raises the concentration by $C_0 = C_H - C_L$ mg/ml.

e) If $k = 0.05\ \text{hr}^{-1}$ and the highest safe concentration is e times the lowest effective concentration, find the length of time between doses that will assure safe and effective concentrations.

f) Given $C_H = 2$ mg/ml, $C_L = 0.5$ mg/ml, and $k = 0.02\ \text{hr}^{-1}$, determine a scheme for administering the drug.

g) Suppose that $k = 0.2\ \text{hr}^{-1}$ and that the smallest effective concentration is 0.03 mg/ml. A single dose that produces a concentration of 0.1 mg/ml is administered. About how long will the drug remain effective?

(This problem was adapted from Horelick and Koont's *Prescribing Safe and Effective Dosage*, Project UMAP, Education Development Center, Newton, MA, 1977.)

16–5

TESTS FOR CONVERGENCE OF SERIES WITH NONNEGATIVE TERMS

In this article we will study series that do not have negative terms. The reason for this restriction is that the partial sums of these series always form increasing sequences, and increasing sequences that are bounded above always converge, as we will see. Thus, to show that a series of nonnegative terms converges, we need only show that there is some number beyond which the partial sums never go.

It may at first seem to be a drawback that this approach establishes the fact of convergence without actually producing the sum of the series in question. Surely it would be better to compute sums of series directly from nice formulas for their partial sums. But in most cases such formulas are not available, and in their absence we have to turn instead to a two-step procedure of first establishing convergence and then approximating the sum. In this article and the next, we focus on the first of these two steps.

Surprisingly enough it is not a severe restriction to begin our study of convergence with the temporary exclusion of series that have one or more negative terms, for it is a fact, as we shall see in the next article, that a series $\sum_{n=1}^{\infty} a_n$ will converge whenever the corresponding series of absolute values $\sum_{n=1}^{\infty} |a_n|$ converges. Thus, once we know that

$$\sum_{n=1}^{\infty} \frac{1}{n^2} = 1 + \frac{1}{4} + \frac{1}{9} + \frac{1}{16} + \frac{1}{25} + \cdots \qquad (1)$$

converges, we will know that *all* of the series like

$$1 - \frac{1}{4} + \frac{1}{9} - \frac{1}{16} + \frac{1}{25} + \cdots \tag{2}$$

and

$$-1 - \frac{1}{4} + \frac{1}{9} + \frac{1}{16} - \frac{1}{25} - \cdots, \tag{3}$$

that can be obtained from (1) by changing the sign of one or more terms, also converge! We might not know at first what they converge to, but at least we know they converge, and that is a first and necessary step towards estimating their sums.

Suppose now that $\sum_{n=1}^{\infty} a_n$ is an infinite series that has no negative terms. That is, $a_n \geq 0$ for every n. Then, when we calculate the partial sums s_1, s_2, s_3, and so on, we see that each one is greater than or equal to its predecessor because $s_{n+1} = s_n + a_n$. That is,

$$s_1 \leq s_2 \leq s_3 \leq \cdots \leq s_n \leq s_{n+1} \leq \cdots. \tag{4}$$

A sequence $\{s_n\}$ like the one in (4), with the property that $s_n \leq s_{n+1}$ for every n, is called an *increasing* sequence. The cardinal principle governing increasing sequences is contained in the following theorem.

Theorem 1. *Let $s_1, s_2, s_3, \ldots$ be an increasing sequence of real numbers. Then one or the other of the following alternatives must hold:*

A. *The terms of the sequence are all less than or equal to some finite constant M. In this case, the sequence has a finite limit L which is also less than or equal to M.*

B. *The sequence diverges to plus infinity; that is, the numbers in the sequence $\{s_n\}$ ultimately exceed every preassigned number, no matter how large.*

When all of the terms of a sequence $\{s_n\}$ are less than or equal to some finite constant M, we say that the sequence is *bounded from above*, and we call the number M an *upper bound* for the sequence. In these terms, Theorem 1 says:

A. Every increasing sequence that is bounded from above converges.

B. Every increasing sequence that is *not* bounded from above becomes infinite.

Note that the theorem does not tell us how to find the limit L when it exists.

We shall not prove Theorem 1, but we may gain an intuitive appreciation of the result by plotting the points $(1, s_1)$, $(2, s_2)$, $\ldots$, (n, s_n), $\ldots$, in the xy-plane (Fig. 16–9). Then if there is a line $y = M$ such that *none* of the points (n, s_n) lies above this line, it is intuitively clear that there is a *lowest* such line. That is, there is a line

$$y = L$$

such that none of the points lies above it but such that there are points (n, s_n) that lie above any *lower* line

$$y = L - \epsilon,$$

where ϵ is any positive number. Analytically, this means that the number L

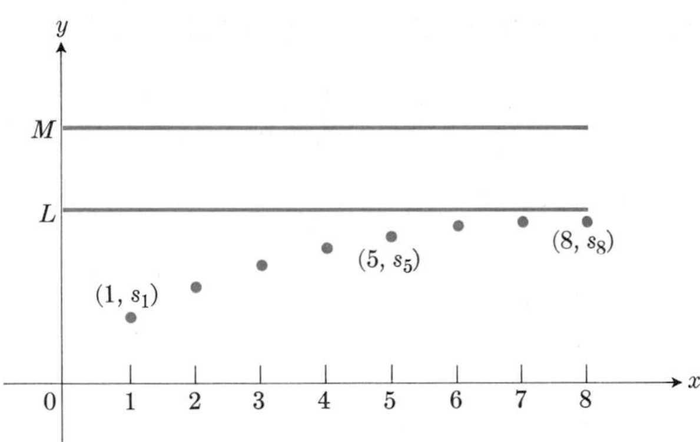

16–9 When the terms of an increasing sequence have an upper bound M, they have a limit $L \leq M$.

has the properties (a) $s_n \leq L$ for *all* values of n, (b) given any $\epsilon > 0$, there exists at least one integer N such that

$$s_N > L - \epsilon.$$

Then the fact that $\{s_n\}$ is an increasing sequence tells us further that

$$s_n \geq s_N > L - \epsilon \qquad \text{for all} \quad n \geq N.$$

This means that *all* the numbers s_n, beyond the Nth one in the sequence, lie within ϵ distance of L. This is precisely the condition for L to be the limit of the sequence s_n,

$$L = \lim_{n \to \infty} s_n.$$

Alternative B of the theorem is what happens when there are points (n, s_n) above any given line $y = M$, no matter how large M may be.

Let us now apply Theorem 1 to the convergence of infinite series of nonnegative numbers. If $\sum a_n$ is such a series, its sequence of partial sums $\{s_n\}$ is an increasing sequence. Therefore, $\{s_n\}$, and hence $\sum a_n$, will converge if and only if the numbers s_n have an upper bound. The question is how to find out in any particular instance whether the s_n's do have an upper bound.

Sometimes we can show that the s_n's are bounded above by showing that each one is less than or equal to the corresponding partial sum of a series that is already known to converge. The next example shows how this can happen.

EXAMPLE 1

$$\sum_{n=0}^{\infty} \frac{1}{n!} = 1 + \frac{1}{1!} + \frac{1}{2!} + \frac{1}{3!} + \cdots \tag{5}$$

converges because its terms are all positive and less than or equal to the corresponding terms of

$$1 + \sum_{n=0}^{\infty} \frac{1}{2^n} = 1 + 1 + \frac{1}{2} + \frac{1}{2^2} + \cdots. \tag{6}$$

To see how this relationship between these two series leads to an upper bound for the partial sums of $\sum_{n=0}^{\infty}(1/n!)$, let

$$s_n = 1 + \frac{1}{1!} + \frac{1}{2!} + \cdots + \frac{1}{n!},$$

and observe that, for each n,

$$s_n \leq 1 + 1 + \frac{1}{2} + \frac{1}{2^2} + \cdots + \frac{1}{2^n} < 1 + \sum_{n=0}^{\infty} \frac{1}{2^n} = 1 + \frac{1}{1-\frac{1}{2}} = 3. \tag{7}$$

Thus the partial sums of $\sum_{n=0}^{\infty}(1/n!)$ are all less than 3. Therefore, $\sum_{n=0}^{\infty}(1/n!)$ converges.

Just because 3 is an upper bound for the partial sums of $\sum_{n=0}^{\infty}(1/n!)$ we cannot conclude that the series converges to 3. The series actually converges to $e = 2.71828\ldots.$

We established the convergence of the series in Example 1 by comparing it with a series that was already known to converge. This kind of comparison is typical of a procedure called the *comparison test* for convergence of series of nonnegative terms.

Comparison Test for Series of Nonnegative Terms

Let $\sum_{n=1}^{\infty} a_n$ be a series that has no negative terms.

A. *Test for* ***convergence*** *of $\sum a_n$. The series $\sum a_n$ converges if there is a convergent series of nonnegative terms $\sum c_n$ with $a_n \leq c_n$ for all n.*

B. *Test for* ***divergence*** *of $\sum a_n$. The series $\sum a_n$ diverges if there is a divergent series of nonnegative terms $\sum d_n$ with $a_n \geq d_n$ for all n.*

To see why the test works, we need only observe that in (A) the partial sums of $\sum a_n$ are bounded above by $M = \sum c_n$, while in (B) the partial sums of $\sum a_n$, being greater than or equal to the corresponding partial sums of a divergent series of nonnegative terms, eventually exceed every preassigned number.

To apply the comparison test to a series, we do not have to include the early terms of the series. We can start the test with any index N, provided we include all the terms of the series being tested from there on.

EXAMPLE 2. The convergence of the series

$$5 + \frac{2}{3} + 1 + \frac{1}{7} + \frac{1}{2} + \frac{1}{3!} + \frac{1}{4!} + \cdots + \frac{1}{k!} + \cdots$$

can be established by ignoring the first four terms and comparing the remainder of the series from the fifth term on (the fifth term is $\frac{1}{2}$) with the convergent series

$$\sum_{n=1}^{\infty} \frac{1}{2^n} = \frac{1}{2} + \frac{1}{4} + \frac{1}{8} + \cdots$$

To apply the comparison test we need to have on hand a list of series that are known to converge and a list of series that are known to diverge. Our next example adds a divergent series to the list.

EXAMPLE 3. The *harmonic series*

$$\sum_{n=1}^{\infty} \frac{1}{n} = 1 + \frac{1}{2} + \frac{1}{3} + \frac{1}{4} + \cdots$$

diverges.

To see why, we represent the terms of the series as the areas of rectangles each of base unity and having altitudes $1, \frac{1}{2}, \frac{1}{3}, \ldots$, as in Fig. 16–10. The sum of the first n terms of the series,

$$s_n = 1 + \frac{1}{2} + \frac{1}{3} + \cdots + \frac{1}{n},$$

represents the sum of n rectangles each of which is somewhat greater than the area underneath the corresponding portion of the curve $y = 1/x$. Thus s_n is greater than the area under this curve between $x = 1$ and $x = n + 1$:

$$s_n > \int_1^{n+1} \frac{dx}{x} = \ln (n + 1).$$

Therefore $s_n \to +\infty$ because $\ln (n + 1) \to +\infty$. The series

$$1 + \frac{1}{2} + \frac{1}{3} + \cdots + \frac{1}{n} + \cdots$$

diverges to plus infinity.

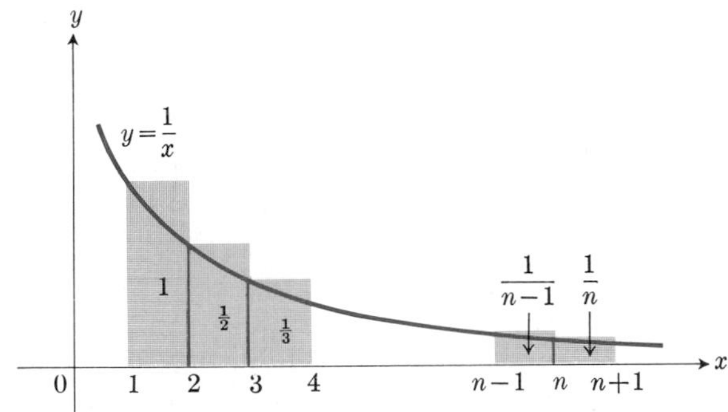

16–10 $1 + \frac{1}{2} + \frac{1}{3} + \cdots + \frac{1}{n} > \int_1^{n+1} \frac{1}{x}\, dx = \ln (n + 1).$

REMARK 1. The harmonic series $\sum_{n=1}^{\infty} (1/n)$ is another series whose divergence cannot be detected by the nth-term test for divergence. The series diverges in spite of the fact that $1/n \to 0$.

REMARK 2. We know that every nonzero multiple of a divergent series diverges (Corollary of Theorem 4 in the preceding article). Therefore, the divergence of the harmonic series implies the divergence of series like

$$\sum_{n=1}^{\infty} \frac{1}{2n} = \frac{1}{2} + \frac{1}{4} + \frac{1}{6} + \frac{1}{8} + \cdots$$

and

$$\sum_{n=1}^{\infty} \frac{1}{100n} = \frac{1}{100} + \frac{1}{200} + \frac{1}{300} + \frac{1}{400} + \cdots.$$

In Example 3 we deduced the divergence of the harmonic series by comparing its sequence of partial sums with a divergent sequence of integrals. This comparison is a special case of a general comparison process called the *integral test*, a test that gives criteria for convergence as well as for divergence of series whose terms are positive.

The Integral Test

Let the function $y = f(x)$, obtained by introducing the continuous variable x in place of the discrete variable n in the nth term of the positive series

$$\sum_{n=1}^{\infty} a_n,$$

be a decreasing function of x for $x \geq 1$. Then the series and the integral

$$\int_1^{\infty} f(x)\, dx$$

both converge or both diverge.

a)

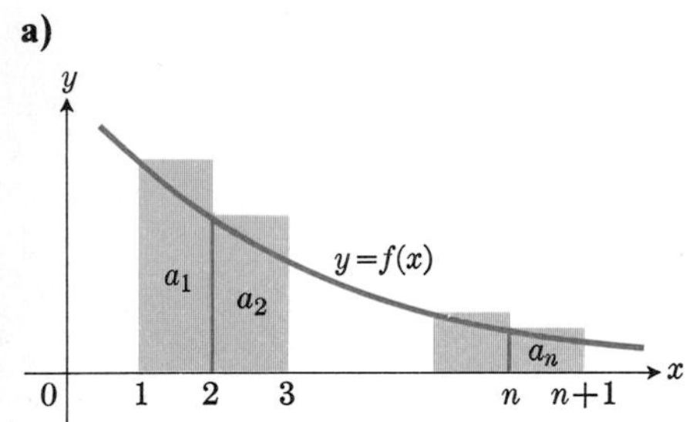

b)

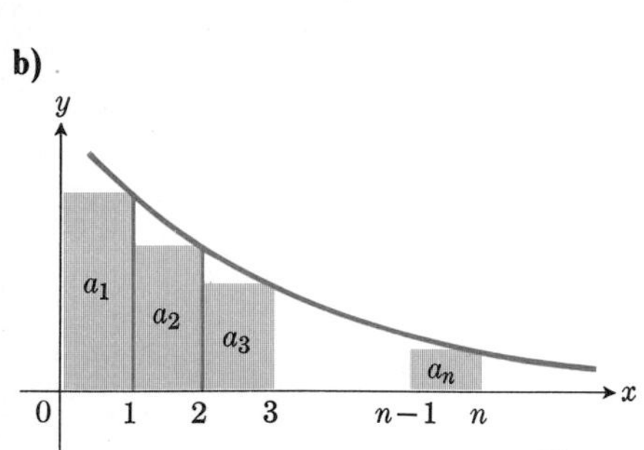

16–11 $\int_1^{n+1} f(x)\, dx \leq a_1 + a_2 + \cdots + a_n \leq a_1 + \int_1^n f(x)\, dx.$

Proof. We start with the assumption that f is a decreasing function with $f(n) = a_n$ for every n. This leads us to observe that the rectangles in Fig. 16–11(a), which have areas $a_1, a_2, \ldots, a_n$, collectively enclose more area than that under the curve $y = f(x)$ from $x = 1$ to $x = n + 1$. That is,

$$\int_1^{n+1} f(x)\, dx \leq a_1 + a_2 + \cdots + a_n.$$

In Fig. 16–11(b) the rectangles have been faced to the left instead of to the right. If we momentarily disregard the first rectangle, of area a_1, we see that

$$a_2 + a_3 + \cdots + a_n \leq \int_1^n f(x)\, dx.$$

If we include a_1, we have

$$a_1 + a_2 + \cdots + a_n \leq a_1 + \int_1^n f(x)\, dx.$$

Combining these results, we have

$$\int_1^{n+1} f(x)\, dx \leq a_1 + a_2 + \cdots + a_n \leq a_1 + \int_1^n f(x)\, dx. \tag{8}$$

If the integral $\int_1^{\infty} f(x)\, dx$ is finite, the righthand inequality shows that

$$\sum_{n=1}^{\infty} a_n$$

is also finite. But if $\int_1^\infty f(x)\,dx$ is infinite, then the lefthand inequality shows that the series is also infinite. Hence the series and the integral are both finite or both infinite.

EXAMPLE 4. ***The p-series.*** If p is a real constant, the series

$$\sum_{n=1}^{\infty} \frac{1}{n^p} = \frac{1}{1^p} + \frac{1}{2^p} + \frac{1}{3^p} + \cdots + \frac{1}{n^p} + \cdots$$

converges if $p > 1$ and diverges if $p \leq 1$. To prove this, let

$$f(x) = \frac{1}{x^p}.$$

Then, if $p > 1$, we have

$$\int_1^\infty x^{-p}\,dx = \lim_{b\to\infty} \left.\frac{x^{-p+1}}{-p+1}\right|_1^b = \frac{1}{p-1},$$

which is finite. Hence the p-series converges if p is greater than one.

If $p = 1$, we have

$$1 + \frac{1}{2} + \frac{1}{3} + \cdots + \frac{1}{n} + \cdots,$$

which we already know diverges. Or, by the integral test,

$$\int_1^\infty x^{-1}\,dx = \lim_{b\to\infty} \ln x \Big|_1^b = +\infty,$$

and, since the integral diverges, the series does likewise.

Finally, if $p < 1$, then the terms of the p-series are greater than the corresponding terms of the divergent harmonic series. Hence the p-series diverges, by the comparison test.

Thus, we have convergence for $p > 1$, but divergence for every other value of p.

Estimation of Remainders by Integrals

The difference $R_n = L - s_n$ between the sum of a convergent series and its nth partial sum is called a *remainder* or a *truncation error.* Since R_n itself is given as an infinite series, which, in principle, is as difficult to evaluate as the original series, you might think that there would be no advantage in singling out R_n for attention. But sometimes even a crude estimate for R_n can lead to an estimate of L that is closer to L than s_n is.

Suppose, for example, that we are interested in learning the numerical value of the series

$$\sum_{k=1}^{\infty} \frac{1}{k^2} = \frac{1}{1^2} + \frac{1}{2^2} + \frac{1}{3^2} + \cdots$$

This is a p-series with $p = 2$, and hence is known to converge. This means that the sequence of partial sums

$$s_n = \frac{1}{1^2} + \frac{1}{2^2} + \cdots + \frac{1}{n^2}$$

has a limit L. If we want to know L to a couple of decimal places, we might try to find an integer n such that the corresponding *finite* sum s_n differs from L by less, say, than 0.005. Then we would use this s_n in place of L, to two decimals. If we write

$$L = \sum_{k=1}^{\infty} \frac{1}{k^2} = \frac{1}{1^2} + \frac{1}{2^2} + \cdots + \frac{1}{n^2} + \frac{1}{(n+1)^2} + \cdots,$$

we see that

$$R_n = L - s_n = \frac{1}{(n+1)^2} + \cdots.$$

We estimate the error R_n by comparing it with the area under the curve

$$y = \frac{1}{x^2}$$

from $x = n$ to ∞.

From Fig. 16–12 we see that

$$R_n < \int_n^{\infty} \frac{1}{x^2}\,dx = \frac{1}{n},$$

which tells us that, by taking 200 terms of the series, we can be sure that the difference between the sum L of the entire series and the sum s_{200} of these 200 terms will be less than 0.005.

A somewhat closer estimate of R_n results from using the trapezoidal rule to approximate the area under the curve in Fig. 16–12. Let us write u_k for $1/k^2$ and consider the trapezoidal approximation

$$\begin{aligned} T_n &= \sum_{k=n}^{\infty} \tfrac{1}{2}(u_k + u_{k+1}) = \tfrac{1}{2}(u_n + u_{n+1}) + \tfrac{1}{2}(u_{n+1} + u_{n+2}) + \cdots \\ &= \tfrac{1}{2}u_n + u_{n+1} + u_{n+2} + \cdots = \tfrac{1}{2}u_n + R_n. \end{aligned}$$

Now since the curve $y = 1/x^2$ is concave upward,

$$T_n > \int_n^{\infty} \frac{1}{x^2}\,dx = \frac{1}{n},$$

and we have

$$R_n = T_n - \frac{1}{2}u_n > \frac{1}{n} - \frac{1}{2n^2}.$$

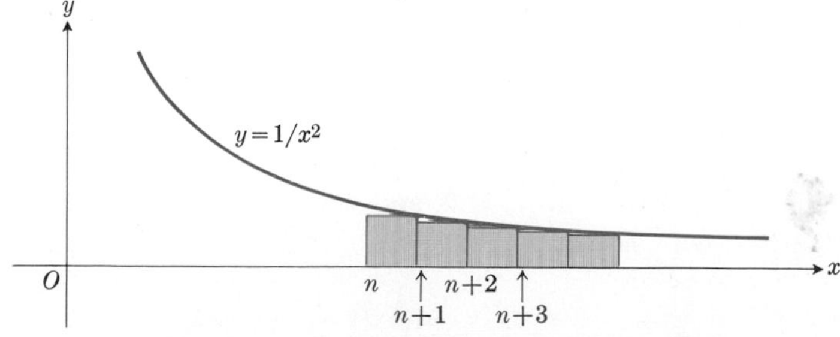

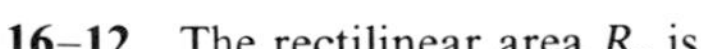

16–12 The rectilinear area R_n is

$$\frac{1}{(n+1)^2} + \frac{1}{(n+2)^2} + \frac{1}{(n+3)^2} + \cdots < \int_n^{\infty} \frac{dx}{x^2}.$$

We now know that

$$\frac{1}{n} > R_n > \frac{1}{n} - \frac{1}{2n^2},$$

and $L = s_n + R_n$ may be estimated as follows:

$$s_n + \frac{1}{n} > L > s_n + \frac{1}{n} - \frac{1}{2n^2}. \tag{9}$$

Thus, by using $s_n + 1/n$ in place of s_n to estimate L, we shall be making an error which is numerically less than $1/(2n^2)$. By taking $n \geq 10$, this error is then made less than 0.005. The difference in time required to compute the sum of 10 terms versus 200 terms is sufficiently great to make this sharper analysis of practical importance.

What we have done in the case of this specific example may be done in any case where the graph of the function $y = f(x)$ is concave upward as in Fig. 16–12. We find that when $\int_n^\infty f(x)\,dx$ exists,

$$u_1 + u_2 + \cdots + u_n + \int_n^\infty f(x)\,dx \tag{10}$$

tends to overestimate the value of the series, but by an amount that is less than $u_n/2$.

Ratio Test and Root Test

It is not always possible to tell whether a particular series converges by using the comparison test. We might not be able to find a series to compare it with. Nor is it always possible to use the integral test to answer whatever questions of convergence then remain unanswered. The terms of the series might not decrease as n increases, or we might not find a formula for the nth term that we can integrate. What we really need is an intrinsic test for convergence, one that can be applied to the series without outside help, so to speak. The next two tests are intrinsic in this sense. They are also easy to apply, and they succeed on a wide variety of series. The first of these is the *ratio test*, for series with positive terms.

The Ratio Test

Let $\sum a_n$ be a series with positive terms, and suppose that

$$\lim_{n\to\infty} \frac{a_{n+1}}{a_n} = \rho \qquad \text{(Greek letter rho).}$$

Then,

a) *the series **converges** if $\rho < 1$;*
b) *the series **diverges** if $\rho > 1$;*
c) *the series **may converge or it may diverge** if $\rho = 1$.*

Proof. **a)** Assume first that $\rho < 1$ and let r be a number between ρ and 1. Then the number

$$\epsilon = r - \rho$$

is positive. Since

$$\frac{a_{n+1}}{a_n} \to \rho,$$

a_{n+1}/a_n must lie within ϵ of ρ when n is large enough, say, for all $n \geq N$. In particular,

$$\frac{a_{n+1}}{a_n} < \rho + \epsilon = r, \qquad \text{when } n > N.$$

That is,

$$\begin{aligned} a_{N+1} &< r a_N, \\ a_{N+2} &< r a_{N+1} < r^2 a_N, \\ a_{N+3} &< r a_{N+2} < r^3 a_N, \\ &\vdots \\ a_{N+m} &< r a_{N+m-1} < r^m a_N, \end{aligned}$$

and

$$\begin{aligned} \sum_{n=1}^{\infty} a_n &= a_1 + a_2 + \cdots + a_{N-1} + a_N + a_{N+1} + \cdots \\ &< a_1 + a_2 + \cdots + a_{N-1} + a_N(1 + r + r^2 + \cdots). \end{aligned} \tag{11}$$

Since $|r|$ is less than one, the geometric series $1 + r + r^2 + \cdots$ converges and the right side of the inequality (11) is finite. Therefore the series on the left converges, by the comparison test.

b) Next, suppose $\rho > 1$. Then, from some index M on, we have

$$\frac{a_{n+1}}{a_n} > 1$$

or

$$a_M < a_{M+1} < a_{M+2} < \cdots.$$

Hence, the terms of the series do not approach 0 as n becomes infinite, and the series diverges, by the nth-term test.

c) Finally, the two series

$$\sum_{n=1}^{\infty} \frac{1}{n} \qquad \text{and} \qquad \sum_{n=1}^{\infty} \frac{1}{n^2}$$

show that, when $\rho = 1$, some other test for convergence must be used.

For $\sum_{n=1}^{\infty} \frac{1}{n}$: $\qquad \rho = \dfrac{1/(n+1)}{1/n} = \dfrac{n}{n+1} \to 1;$

For $\sum_{n=1}^{\infty} \frac{1}{n^2}$: $\qquad \rho = \dfrac{1/(n+1)^2}{1/n^2} = \left(\dfrac{n}{n+1}\right)^2 \to 1^2 = 1.$

In both cases $\rho = 1$, yet the first series diverges while the second converges. Q.E.D.

EXAMPLE 5. For the series $\sum_{n=0}^{\infty} (2^n + 5)/3^n$,

$$\frac{a_{n+1}}{a_n} = \frac{(2^{n+1} + 5)/3^{n+1}}{(2^n + 5)/3^n} = \frac{1}{3} \cdot \frac{2^{n+1} + 5}{2^n + 5} = \frac{1}{3} \cdot \left(\frac{2 + 5 \cdot 2^{-n}}{1 + 5 \cdot 2^{-n}}\right) \to \frac{1}{3} \cdot \frac{2}{1} = \frac{2}{3}.$$

The series converges because $\rho = \frac{2}{3}$ is less than 1.

This does *not* mean that $\frac{2}{3}$ is the sum of the series. In fact,

$$\sum_{n=0}^{\infty} \frac{2^n + 5}{3^n} = \sum_{n=0}^{\infty} \left(\frac{2}{3}\right)^n + \sum_{n=0}^{\infty} \frac{5}{3^n} = \frac{1}{1 - \frac{2}{3}} + \frac{5}{1 - \frac{1}{3}} = 10\tfrac{1}{2}.$$

EXAMPLE 6. For what values of x does the series

$$x + \frac{x^3}{3} + \frac{x^5}{5} + \frac{x^7}{7} + \cdots + \frac{x^{2n-1}}{2n - 1} + \cdots \tag{12}$$

converge?

Solution. The nth term of the series is

$$a_n = \frac{x^{2n-1}}{2n - 1}.$$

We consider first the case where x is positive. Then the series is a positive series and

$$\frac{a_{n+1}}{a_n} = \frac{(2n - 1)x^2}{(2n + 1)} \to x^2.$$

The ratio test therefore tells us that the series converges if x is positive and less than one and diverges if x is greater than one.

Since only odd powers of x occur in the series, we see that the series simply changes sign when x is replaced by $-x$. Therefore the series also converges for $-1 < x \le 0$ and diverges for $x < -1$. The series converges to zero when $x = 0$.

We know, thus far, that the series

$$\text{converges for } |x| < 1,$$

$$\text{diverges for } |x| > 1,$$

but we don't know what happens when $|x| = 1$. To test at $x = 1$, we apply the integral test to the series

$$1 + \frac{1}{3} + \frac{1}{5} + \frac{1}{7} + \cdots + \frac{1}{2n - 1} + \cdots,$$

which we get by taking $x = 1$ in the series (12). The companion integral is

$$\int_1^{\infty} \frac{dx}{2x - 1} = \frac{1}{2} \ln (2x - 1)\Big|_1^{\infty} = \infty.$$

Hence the series diverges to $+\infty$ when $x = 1$. It diverges to $-\infty$ when $x = -1$. Therefore the only values of x for which the given series converges are $-1 < x < 1$.

REMARK. When $\rho < 1$, the ratio test is also useful in estimating the truncation error that results from using

$$s_N = a_1 + a_2 + \cdots + a_N$$

as an approximation to the sum of a convergent series of positive terms

$$S = a_1 + a_2 + \cdots + a_N + (a_{N+1} + \cdots);$$

for, if we know that

$$r_1 \le \frac{a_{n+1}}{a_n} \le r_2 \qquad \text{for} \quad n \ge N, \tag{13}$$

where r_1 and r_2 are constants that are both less than one, then the inequalities

$$r_1 a_n \le a_{n+1} \le r_2 a_n \qquad (n = N, N + 1, N + 2, \ldots)$$

enable us to deduce that

$$a_N(r_1 + r_1^2 + r_1^3 + \cdots) \le \sum_{n=N+1}^{\infty} a_n \le a_N(r_2 + r_2^2 + r_2^3 + \cdots). \tag{14}$$

The two geometric series have sums

$$r_1 + r_1^2 + r_1^3 + \cdots = \frac{r_1}{1 - r_1},$$

$$r_2 + r_2^2 + r_2^3 + \cdots = \frac{r_2}{1 - r_2}.$$

Hence, the error

$$R_N = \sum_{n=N+1}^{\infty} a_n$$

lies between

$$a_N \frac{r_1}{1 - r_1} \qquad \text{and} \qquad a_N \frac{r_2}{1 - r_2}.$$

That is,

$$a_N \frac{r_1}{1 - r_1} \le S - s_n \le a_N \frac{r_2}{1 - r_2} \tag{15}$$

if

$$0 \le r_1 \le \frac{a_{n+1}}{a_n} \le r_2 < 1 \qquad \text{for} \quad n \ge N.$$

The second of the two intrinsic tests we referred to earlier is called the *root test.*

The Root Test

Let $\sum a_n$ *be a series with no negative terms, and suppose that*

$$\sqrt[n]{a_n} \to \rho.$$

Then,

a) *the series* ***converges*** *if* $\rho < 1$
b) *the series* ***diverges*** *if* $\rho > 1$
c) *the test is* ***not conclusive*** *if* $\rho = 1$.

Proof. **a)** Suppose that $\rho < 1$, and choose an $\epsilon > 0$ so small that $\rho + \epsilon < 1$ also. Since $\sqrt[n]{a_n} \to \rho$, the terms $\sqrt[n]{a_n}$ eventually get closer than ϵ to ρ. In other words,

$$\sqrt[n]{a_n} < \rho + \epsilon$$

for n sufficiently large, or

$$a_n < (\rho + \epsilon)^n \qquad \text{for} \quad n \geq N.$$

Now,

$$\sum_{n=N}^{\infty} (\rho + \epsilon)^n,$$

a geometric series with ratio $(\rho + \epsilon) < 1$, converges. By comparison,

$$\sum_{n=N}^{\infty} a_n$$

converges, from which it follows that

$$\sum_{n=1}^{\infty} a_n = a_1 + \cdots + a_{N-1} + \sum_{n=N}^{\infty} a_n$$

converges.

b) Suppose that $\rho > 1$. Then, for all indices beyond some index M, we have

$$\sqrt[n]{a_n} > 1,$$

so that

$$a_n > 1 \qquad \text{for} \quad n > M,$$

and the terms of the series do not converge to 0. The series therefore diverges by the nth-term test.

c) The series $\sum_{n=1}^{\infty} (1/n)$ and $\sum_{n=1}^{\infty} (1/n^2)$ show that the test is not conclusive when $\rho = 1$. The first series diverges and the second converges, but in both cases $\sqrt[n]{a_n} \to 1$. Q.E.D.

EXAMPLE 7. For the series $\sum_{n=1}^{\infty} (1/n^n)$,

$$\sqrt[n]{\frac{1}{n^n}} = \frac{1}{n} \to 0.$$

The series converges.

EXAMPLE 8. For the series $\sum_{n=1}^{\infty} (2^n/n^2)$,

$$\sqrt[n]{\frac{2^n}{n^2}} = \frac{2}{\sqrt[n]{n^2}} = \frac{2}{(\sqrt[n]{n})^2} \to \frac{2}{1^2} = 2.$$

The series diverges.

EXAMPLE 9. For the series $\sum_{n=1}^{\infty} (1 - 1/n)^n = 0 + \frac{1}{4} + \frac{8}{27} + \cdots$,

$$\sqrt[n]{\left(1 - \frac{1}{n}\right)^n} = \left(1 - \frac{1}{n}\right) \to 1.$$

Because $\rho = 1$, the root test is not conclusive. However, if we apply the nth-term test for divergence, we find that

$$\left(1 - \frac{1}{n}\right)^n = \left(1 + \frac{-1}{n}\right)^n \to e^{-1} = \frac{1}{e}.$$

The series diverges.

We now have five tests for divergence and convergence of infinite series:

1. The nth-term test for divergence (applies to all series).
2. **A)** The comparison test for convergence (nonnegative series);
   B) The comparison test for divergence (nonnegative series).
3. The integral test (positive decreasing series).
4. The ratio test (positive series).
5. The root test (nonnegative series).

These tests can be applied to settle questions about the convergence or divergence of series of nonpositive or negative terms. Just factor -1 from the series in question, and test the resulting series of nonnegative or positive terms.

EXAMPLE 10

$$\sum_{n=1}^{\infty} -\frac{1}{n} = -1 \cdot \sum_{n=1}^{\infty} \frac{1}{n} \qquad \text{diverges.}$$

EXAMPLE 11

$$\sum_{n=0}^{\infty} -\frac{1}{2^n} = -1 \cdot \sum_{n=0}^{\infty} \frac{1}{2^n} = -1 \cdot 2 = -2.$$

PROBLEMS

In each of the following problems, determine whether the given series converges or diverges. In each case, give a reason for your answer.

1. $\sum_{n=1}^{\infty} \frac{1}{10^n}$
2. $\sum_{n=1}^{\infty} \frac{n}{n+2}$
3. $\sum_{n=1}^{\infty} \frac{\sin^2 n}{2^n}$
4. $\sum_{n=1}^{\infty} \frac{5}{n}$
5. $\sum_{n=1}^{\infty} \frac{n^3}{2^n}$
6. $\sum_{n=1}^{\infty} -\frac{1}{8^n}$
7. $\sum_{n=1}^{\infty} \frac{\ln n}{n}$
8. $\sum_{n=1}^{\infty} \frac{1}{n\sqrt{n}}$
9. $\sum_{n=1}^{\infty} \frac{2^n}{3^n}$
10. $\sum_{n=0}^{\infty} \frac{-2}{n+1}$
11. $\sum_{n=1}^{\infty} \frac{1}{1 + \ln n}$
12. $\sum_{n=1}^{\infty} \frac{1}{\sqrt{n+1}}$
13. $\sum_{n=1}^{\infty} \frac{2^n}{n+1}$
14. $\sum_{n=1}^{\infty} \left(\frac{n}{3n+1}\right)^n$
15. $\sum_{n=1}^{\infty} -\frac{n^2}{2^n}$
16. $\sum_{n=1}^{\infty} \frac{1}{\sqrt{n}}$
17. $\sum_{n=1}^{\infty} \frac{1}{\sqrt{n^3+2}}$
18. $\sum_{n=1}^{\infty} \frac{1}{\sqrt[n]{2}}$

19. $\sum_{n=1}^{\infty} \frac{(n+1)(n+2)}{n!}$

20. $\sum_{n=1}^{\infty} \frac{\sqrt{n}}{n^2+1}$

21. $\sum_{n=1}^{\infty} \frac{n}{n^2+1}$

22. $\sum_{n=1}^{\infty} n^2 e^{-n}$

23. $\sum_{n=1}^{\infty} \left(1+\frac{1}{n}\right)^n$

24. $\sum_{n=1}^{\infty} \frac{1}{3^{n-1}+1}$

25. $\sum_{n=1}^{\infty} \frac{(n+3)!}{3!\,n!\,3^n}$

26. $\sum_{n=2}^{\infty} \frac{1}{n \ln n}$

27. $\sum_{n=1}^{\infty} \frac{1}{(2n+1)!}$

28. $\sum_{n=1}^{\infty} \frac{1}{(\ln 2)^n}$

29. $\sum_{n=1}^{\infty} \frac{n!}{n^n}$

30. $\sum_{n=1}^{\infty} \frac{1-n}{n \cdot 2^n}$

31. Show that the series

$$\sum_{n=1}^{\infty} \frac{1}{2n-1} = 1 + \frac{1}{3} + \frac{1}{5} + \cdots$$

diverges. [*Hint.* Compare the series with a multiple of the harmonic series.]

In Problems 32 through 34, find all values of x for which the given series converge. Begin with the ratio test or the root test, and then apply other tests as needed.

32. $\sum_{n=1}^{\infty} \left(\frac{x^2+1}{3}\right)^n$

33. $\sum_{n=1}^{\infty} \frac{x^{2n+1}}{n^2}$

34. $\sum_{n=1}^{\infty} \left(\frac{1}{|x|}\right)^n$

35. (*Calculator*) Use Inequality (9) of this article to estimate $\sum_{n=1}^{\infty} (1/n^2)$ with an error less than 0.005. Compare your result with the value given in Problem 36.

36. (*Calculator*) Euler discovered that

$$\sum_{n=1}^{\infty} \frac{1}{n^2} = \sum_{n=1}^{\infty} \frac{3[(n-1)!]^2}{(2n)!} = \frac{\pi^2}{6}.$$

Compute s_6 for each series. To 10 decimal places, $\pi^2/6 = 1.6449340668$.

37. (*Calculator*) Use the expression in (10) of this article to find the value of $\sum_{n=1}^{\infty} (1/n^4) = (\pi^4/90)$ with an error less than 10^{-6}.

38. (*Calculator*) To estimate partial sums of the divergent harmonic series, Inequality (8) with $f(x) = 1/x$ tells us that

$$\ln n < 1 + \frac{1}{2} + \cdots + \frac{1}{n} < 1 + \ln n.$$

Suppose that the summation started with $s_1 = 1$ thirteen billion years ago (one estimate of the age of the universe) and that a new term has been added every *second* since then. How large would you expect s_n to be today?

39. There are no values of x for which $\sum_{n=1}^{\infty} (1/nx)$ converges. Why?

40. Show that if $\sum_{n=1}^{\infty} a_n$ is a convergent series of nonnegative numbers then the series $\sum_{n=1}^{\infty} (a_n/n)$ converges.

41. Show that if $\sum a_n$ and $\sum b_n$ are convergent series with $a_n \geq 0$ and $b_n \geq 0$, then $\sum a_n b_n$ converges. [*Hint.* From some index on, $a_n b_n < a_n + b_n$.]

42. A sequence of numbers

$$s_1 \geq s_2 \geq \cdots \geq s_n \geq s_{n+1} \geq \cdots,$$

in which $s_n \geq s_{n+1}$ for every n, is called a *decreasing sequence*. A sequence $\{s_n\}$ is *bounded from below* if there is a finite constant M with $M \leq s_n$ for every n. Such a number M is called a *lower bound* for the sequence. Deduce from Theorem 1 that a decreasing sequence that is bounded from below converges, and that a decreasing sequence that is not bounded from below diverges.

43. The *Cauchy condensation test* says:

Let $\{a_n\}$ be a decreasing sequence ($a_n \geq a_{n+1}$, all n) of positive terms that converges to 0. Then,

$$\sum a_n \text{ converges} \quad \text{if and only if} \quad \sum 2^n a_{2^n} \text{ converges.}$$

For example, $\sum (1/n)$ diverges because $\sum 2^n \cdot (1/2^n) = \sum 1$. Show why the test works.

44. Use the Cauchy condensation test of Problem 43 to show that

a) $\sum_{n=2}^{\infty} \frac{1}{n \ln n}$ diverges.

b) $\sum_{n=1}^{\infty} \frac{1}{n^p}$ converges if $p > 1$ and diverges if $p \leq 1$.

45. Pictures like the one in Fig. 16–10 suggest that, as n increases, there is very little change in the difference between the sum

$$1 + \frac{1}{2} + \cdots + \frac{1}{n}$$

and the integral

$$\ln n = \int_1^n \frac{1}{x}\,dx.$$

To explore this idea, carry out the following steps.

a) By taking $f(x) = (1/x)$ in inequality (8), show that

$$\ln n < 1 + \frac{1}{2} + \cdots + \frac{1}{n} < 1 + \ln n$$

or

$$0 < 1 + \frac{1}{2} + \cdots + \frac{1}{n} - \ln n < 1.$$

Thus, the sequence

$$a_n = 1 + \frac{1}{2} + \cdots + \frac{1}{n} - \ln n$$

is bounded from below.

b) Show that

$$\frac{1}{n+1} < \int_n^{n+1} \frac{1}{x}\,dx = \ln(n+1) - \ln n,$$

so that the sequence $\{a_n\}$ in part (a) is decreasing.

Since a decreasing sequence that is bounded from below converges (Problem 42) the numbers a_n defined in (a) converge:

$$1 + \frac{1}{2} + \cdots + \frac{1}{n} - \ln n \to \gamma.$$

The number γ, whose value is 0.5772..., is called *Euler's constant*. In contrast to other special numbers like π and e, no other expression with a simple law of formulation has ever been found for γ.

16-6 ABSOLUTE CONVERGENCE

We now extend to series that have both positive and negative terms the techniques that we have developed for answering questions about the convergence of series of nonnegative numbers. The extension is made possible by a theorem that says that, if a series converges after all its negative terms have been made positive, then the unaltered series converges also.

Theorem. *If $\sum_{n=1}^{\infty} |a_n|$ converges, then $\sum_{n=1}^{\infty} a_n$ converges.*

Proof of the theorem. For each n,

$$-|a_n| \le a_n \le |a_n|,$$

so that

$$0 \le a_n + |a_n| \le 2|a_n|.$$

If $\sum_{n=1}^{\infty} |a_n|$ converges, then $\sum_{n=1}^{\infty} 2|a_n|$ converges and, by the comparison test, the nonnegative series

$$\sum_{n=1}^{\infty} (a_n + |a_n|)$$

converges. The equality $a_n = (a_n + |a_n|) - |a_n|$ now lets us express $\sum_{n=1}^{\infty} a_n$ as the difference of two convergent series:

$$\sum_{n=1}^{\infty} a_n = \sum_{n=1}^{\infty} (a_n + |a_n| - |a_n|) = \sum_{n=1}^{\infty} (a_n + |a_n|) - \sum_{n=1}^{\infty} |a_n|.$$

Therefore, $\sum_{n=1}^{\infty} a_n$ converges.

Definition. *A series $\sum_{n=1}^{\infty} a_n$ is said to* **converge absolutely** *if $\sum_{n=1}^{\infty} |a_n|$ converges.*

Our theorem can now be rephrased to say that *every absolutely convergent series converges.* We will see in the next article, however, that the converse of this statement is false. Many convergent series do not converge absolutely. That is, there are many series whose convergence depends on the presence of negative terms.

Here are some examples of how the theorem can and cannot be used to determine convergence.

EXAMPLE 1. For $\sum_{n=1}^{\infty} (-1)^{n+1} \frac{1}{n^2} = 1 - \frac{1}{4} + \frac{1}{9} - \frac{1}{16} + \cdots$,

the corresponding series of absolute values is

$$\sum_{n=1}^{\infty} \frac{1}{n^2} = 1 + \frac{1}{4} + \frac{1}{9} + \frac{1}{16} + \cdots,$$

which converges because it is a p-series with $p = 2 > 1$ (Article 16–5). Therefore

$$\sum_{n=1}^{\infty} (-1)^{n+1} \frac{1}{n^2}$$

converges absolutely. Therefore

$$\sum_{n=1}^{\infty} (-1)^{n+1} \frac{1}{n^2}$$

converges.

EXAMPLE 2. For $\sum_{n=1}^{\infty} \frac{\sin n}{n^2} = \frac{\sin 1}{1} + \frac{\sin 2}{4} + \frac{\sin 3}{9} + \cdots$,

the corresponding series of absolute values is

$$\sum_{n=1}^{\infty} \left| \frac{\sin n}{n^2} \right| = \frac{|\sin 1|}{1} + \frac{|\sin 2|}{4} + \cdots,$$

which converges by comparison with $\sum_{n=1}^{\infty} (1/n^2)$, because $|\sin n| \le 1$ for every n. The original series converges absolutely; therefore it converges.

EXAMPLE 3. For $\sum_{n=1}^{\infty} (-1)^{n+1} \frac{1}{n} = 1 - \frac{1}{2} + \frac{1}{3} - \frac{1}{4} + \cdots$,

the corresponding series of absolute values is

$$\sum_{n=1}^{\infty} \frac{1}{n} = 1 + \frac{1}{2} + \frac{1}{3} + \frac{1}{4} + \cdots,$$

which diverges. *We can draw no conclusion from this about the convergence or divergence of the original series.* Some other test must be found. In fact, the original series converges, but we will have to wait until the next article to see why.

* If the "absolute" series converges, the "original" series converges. If the "absolute" series diverges, no conclusion can be drawn.

EXAMPLE 4. The series

$$\sum_{n=1}^{\infty} (-1)^n \frac{n}{5n+1} = -\frac{1}{6} + \frac{2}{11} - \frac{3}{16} + \frac{4}{21} - \cdots$$

does not converge, by the nth term test. Therefore, the series does not converge absolutely.

nth term test: $a_n \neq 0$, Σa_n diverges

REMARK. We know that $\sum a_n$ converges if $\sum |a_n|$ converges, but the two series will generally not converge to the same sum. For example,

$$\sum_{n=0}^{\infty} \left| \frac{(-1)^n}{2^n} \right| = \sum_{n=0}^{\infty} \frac{1}{2^n} = \frac{1}{1 - \frac{1}{2}} = 2,$$

while

$$\sum_{n=0}^{\infty} \frac{(-1)^n}{2^n} = \frac{1}{1+\frac{1}{2}} = \frac{2}{3}.$$

In fact, when a series $\sum a_n$ converges absolutely, we can expect $\sum a_n$ to equal $\sum |a_n|$ only if none of the numbers a_n is negative.

PROBLEMS

Determine whether the following series converge absolutely. In each case give a reason for the convergence or divergence of the corresponding series of absolute values.

1. $\sum_{n=1}^{\infty} \frac{1}{n^2}$
2. $\sum_{n=1}^{\infty} \frac{1}{(-n)^3}$
3. $\sum_{n=1}^{\infty} \frac{1-n}{n^2}$
4. $\sum_{n=1}^{\infty} \left(-\frac{1}{5}\right)^n$
5. $\sum_{n=1}^{\infty} \frac{-1}{n^2+2n+1}$
6. $\sum_{n=1}^{\infty} \frac{(-1)^n}{2n}$
7. $\sum_{n=1}^{\infty} \frac{\cos n\pi}{n\sqrt{n}}$
8. $\sum_{n=1}^{\infty} \frac{-10}{n}$
9. $\sum_{n=0}^{\infty} \frac{(-1)^n}{(2n)!}$
10. $\sum_{n=0}^{\infty} \frac{(-1)^n}{(2n+1)!}$
11. $\sum_{n=2}^{\infty} (-1)^n \frac{n}{n+1}$
12. $\sum_{n=1}^{\infty} \frac{-n}{2^n}$
13. $\sum_{n=1}^{\infty} (5)^{-n}$
14. $\sum_{n=1}^{\infty} \left(\frac{1}{2^n} - 1\right)$
15. $\sum_{n=1}^{\infty} \frac{(-100)^n}{n!}$
16. $\sum_{n=2}^{\infty} (-1)^n \frac{\ln n}{\ln n^2}$
17. $\sum_{n=1}^{\infty} \frac{2-n}{n^3}$
18. $\sum_{n=1}^{\infty} \left(\frac{1}{2^n} - \frac{1}{3^n}\right)$
19. Show that if $\sum_{n=1}^{\infty} a_n$ diverges, then $\sum_{n=1}^{\infty} |a_n|$ diverges.
20. Show that if $\sum_{n=1}^{\infty} a_n$ converges absolutely, then

$$\left|\sum_{n=1}^{\infty} a_n\right| \le \sum_{n=1}^{\infty} |a_n|.$$

21. Show that if $\sum_{n=1}^{\infty} a_n$ and $\sum_{n=1}^{\infty} b_n$ both converge absolutely, then so does
   a) $\sum (a_n + b_n)$ b) $\sum (a_n - b_n)$
   c) $\sum ka_n$ (k any number)

16–7 ALTERNATING SERIES. CONDITIONAL CONVERGENCE

When some of the terms of a series $\sum a_n$ are positive and others are negative, the series converges if $\sum |a_n|$ converges. Thus we may apply any of our tests for convergence of nonnegative series, provided we apply them to the series of absolute values. But we do not know, when the series of absolute values *diverges*, whether the *original* series diverges or converges. If it converges, but not absolutely, we say that it *converges conditionally*.

We shall discuss one simple case of series with mixed signs, namely, series that take the form

$$a_1 - a_2 + a_3 - a_4 + \cdots (-1)^{n+1}a_n + \cdots, \tag{1}$$

with all a's > 0. Such series are called *alternating series* because successive terms have alternate signs. Examples of alternating series are:

$$1 - \tfrac{1}{2} + \tfrac{1}{3} - \tfrac{1}{4} + \tfrac{1}{5} - \tfrac{1}{6} + \cdots, \tag{2}$$

$$\frac{1}{\ln 2} - \frac{1}{\ln 3} + \frac{1}{\ln 4} - \frac{1}{\ln 5} + \cdots \tag{3}$$

$$1 - \sqrt{2} + \sqrt{3} - \sqrt{4} + \cdots. \tag{4}$$

The series

$$1 - \frac{1}{2} - \frac{1}{4} + \frac{1}{6} - \frac{1}{8} - \frac{1}{10} + \frac{1}{12} \cdots \tag{5}$$

is *not* an alternating series. The signs of its terms do not alternate.

Definition. *A sequence $\{a_n\}$ is called a* **decreasing sequence** *if $a_n \geq a_{n+1}$ for every n.*

Examples of decreasing sequences are

$$1, \quad \frac{1}{2}, \quad \frac{1}{3}, \quad \frac{1}{4}, \quad \ldots,$$

$$1, \quad 1, \quad 1, \quad 1, \quad \ldots.$$

The sequence

$$\frac{1}{3}, \quad \frac{1}{2}, \quad \frac{1}{6}, \quad \frac{1}{4}, \quad \ldots, \quad \frac{1}{3n}, \quad \frac{1}{2n}, \quad \ldots$$

is *not* a decreasing sequence even though it converges to 0 from above.

One reason for selecting alternating series for study is that every alternating series whose numbers a_n form a decreasing sequence with limit 0 converges. Another reason is that whenever an alternating series converges, it is easy to estimate its sum. This fortunate combination of assured convergence and easy estimation gives us an opportunity to see how a wide variety of series behave. We look first at the convergence.

Theorem 1. **Leibniz's Theorem.** *$\sum_{n=1}^{\infty} (-1)^{n+1} a_n$ converges if all three of the following conditions are satisfied:*

1. *The a_n's are all positive;*
2. *$a_n \geq a_{n+1}$ for every n;*
3. *$a_n \to 0$.*

Proof. If n is an even integer, say $n = 2m$, then the sum of the first n terms is

$$\begin{aligned} s_{2m} &= (a_1 - a_2) + (a_3 - a_4) + \cdots + (a_{2m-1} - a_{2m}) \\ &= a_1 - (a_2 - a_3) - (a_4 - a_5) - \cdots - (a_{2m-2} - a_{2m-1}) - a_{2m}. \end{aligned}$$

The first equality exhibits s_{2m} as the sum of m nonnegative terms, since each expression in parentheses is positive or zero. Hence $s_{2m+2} \geq s_{2m}$, and the sequence $\{s_{2m}\}$ is increasing. The second equality shows that $s_{2m} \leq a_1$. Since $\{s_{2m}\}$ is increasing and bounded from above it has a limit, say

$$\lim_{n \to \infty} s_{2m} = L. \tag{6}$$

If n is an odd integer, say $n = 2m + 1$, then the sum of the first n terms is

$$s_{2m+1} = s_{2m} + a_{2m+1}.$$

Since $a_n \to 0$,

$$\lim_{m \to \infty} a_{2m+1} = 0.$$

Hence, as $m \to \infty$,

$$s_{2m+1} = s_{2m} + a_{2m+1} \to L + 0 = L. \tag{7}$$

Finally, we may combine (6) and (7) and say simply

$$\lim_{n \to \infty} s_n = L. \qquad \text{Q.E.D.}$$

Here are some examples of what Theorem 1 can do.

EXAMPLE 1. The *alternating harmonic* series

$$\sum_{n=1}^{\infty} (-1)^{n+1} \frac{1}{n} = 1 - \frac{1}{2} + \frac{1}{3} - \frac{1}{4} + \cdots$$

satisfies the three requirements of the theorem; therefore it converges. It converges conditionally because the corresponding series of absolute values is the harmonic series, which diverges.

EXAMPLE 2

$$\sum_{n=1}^{\infty} (-1)^{n+1} \sqrt{n} = 1 - \sqrt{2} + \sqrt{3} - \sqrt{4} + \cdots$$

diverges by the nth-term test.

EXAMPLE 3. Theorem 1 gives no information about

$$\frac{2}{1} - \frac{1}{1} + \frac{2}{2} - \frac{1}{2} + \frac{2}{3} - \frac{1}{3} + \cdots + \frac{2}{n} - \frac{1}{n} + \cdots.$$

The sequence $\frac{2}{1}, \frac{1}{1}, \frac{2}{2}, \frac{1}{2}, \frac{2}{3}, \frac{1}{3}, \ldots$ is not a decreasing sequence. Some other test must be found. When we group the terms of the series in consecutive pairs

$$\left(\frac{2}{1} - \frac{1}{1}\right) + \left(\frac{2}{2} - \frac{1}{2}\right) + \left(\frac{2}{3} - \frac{1}{3}\right) + \cdots + \left(\frac{2}{n} - \frac{1}{n}\right) + \cdots,$$

we see that the $2n$th partial sum of the given series is the same number as the nth partial sum of the harmonic series. Thus the sequence of partial sums, and hence the series, diverges.

We use the following graphical interpretation of the partial sums to gain added insight into the way in which an alternating series converges to its limit L when the three conditions of the theorem are satisfied. Starting from the origin O on a scale of real numbers (Fig. 16–13), we lay off the positive distance

$$s_1 = a_1.$$

To find the point corresponding to

$$s_2 = a_1 - a_2$$

we must back up a distance equal to a_2. Since $a_2 \leq a_1$, we do not back up any farther than O at most. Next we go forward a distance a_3 and mark the point corresponding to

$$s_3 = a_1 - a_2 + a_3.$$

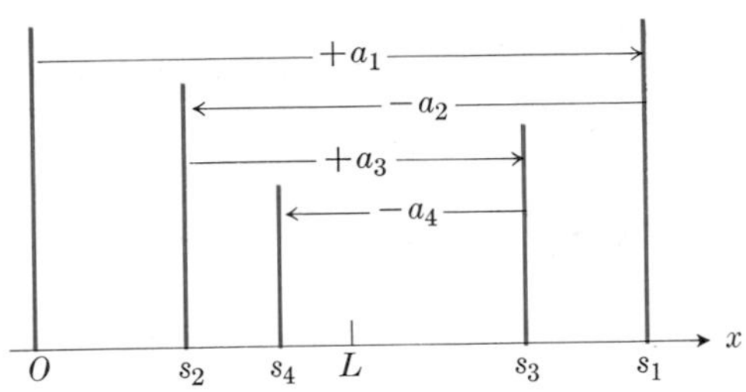

16–13 The partial sums of an alternating series that satisfies the hypotheses of Leibniz's theorem straddle their limit.

Since $a_3 \le a_2$, we go forward by an amount that is no greater than the previous backward step; that is, s_3 is less than or equal to s_1. We continue in this seesaw fashion, backing up or going forward as the signs in the series demand. But each forward or backward step is shorter than (or at most the same size as) the preceding step, because $a_{n+1} \le a_n$. And since the nth term approaches zero as n increases, the size of step we take forward or backward gets smaller and smaller. We thus oscillate across the limit L, but the amplitude of oscillation continually decreases and approaches zero as its limit. The even-numbered partial sums $s_2, s_4, s_6, \ldots, s_{2m}$ continually increase toward L, while the odd-numbered sums $s_1, s_3, s_5, \ldots, s_{2m+1}$ continually decrease toward L. The limit L is between any two successive sums s_n and s_{n+1} and hence differs from s_n by an amount less than a_{n+1}.

It is because

$$|L - s_n| < a_{n+1} \qquad \text{for every } n \tag{8}$$

that we can make useful estimates of the sums of convergent alternating series.

Theorem 2. **The Alternating Series Estimation Theorem.** *If*

$$\sum_{n=1}^{\infty} (-1)^{n+1} a_n$$

is an alternating series that satisfies the three conditions of Theorem 1, then

$$s_n = a_1 - a_2 + \cdots + (-1)^{n+1} a_n$$

approximates the sum L of the series with an error whose absolute value is less than a_{n+1}, the numerical value of the first unused term. Furthermore, the remainder, $L - s_n$, has the same sign as the first unused term.

We will leave the determination of the sign of the remainder as an exercise.

EXAMPLE 4. Let us first try the estimation theorem on an alternating series whose sum we already know, namely, the geometric series:

$$\sum_{n=0}^{\infty} (-1)^n \frac{1}{2^n} = 1 - \frac{1}{2} + \frac{1}{4} - \frac{1}{8} + \frac{1}{16} - \frac{1}{32} + \frac{1}{64} - \frac{1}{128} \Big| + \frac{1}{256} - \cdots$$

Theorem 2 says that, when we truncate the series after the eighth term, we throw away a total that is positive and less than $\frac{1}{256}$. A rapid calculation shows that the sum of the first eight terms is

$$0.6640625.$$

The sum of the series is

$$\frac{1}{1-(-\frac{1}{2})} = \frac{1}{3/2} = \frac{2}{3}. \tag{9}$$

The difference,

$$\frac{2}{3} - 0.6640625 = 0.0026041666\ldots,$$

is positive and less than

$$\tfrac{1}{256} = 0.00390625.$$

A series for computing $\ln(1 + x)$ when $|x| < 1$ is

$$\ln(1 + x) = x - \frac{x^2}{2} + \frac{x^3}{3} - \cdots + (-1)^{n+1}\frac{x^n}{n}\cdots. \tag{10}$$

For $0 < x < 1$, this series satisfies all three conditions of Theorem 1, and we may use the estimation theorem to see how good an approximation of $\ln(1 + x)$ we get from the first few terms of the series.

EXAMPLE 5. Calculate ln 1.1 with the approximation

$$\ln(1 + x) \approx x - \frac{x^2}{2}, \tag{11}$$

and estimate the error involved. Is $x - (x^2/2)$ too large, or too small in this case?

Solution

$$\ln(1.1) \approx (0.1) - \frac{(0.1)^2}{2} = 0.095.$$

This approximation differs from the exact value of ln 1.1 by less than

$$\frac{(0.1)^3}{3} = 0.000333\ldots.$$

Since the sign of this, the first unused term, is positive, the remainder is positive. That is, 0.095 underestimates ln 1.1.

EXAMPLE 6. How many terms of the series (10) do we need to use in order to be sure of calculating ln (1.2) with an error of less than 10^{-6}?

Solution

$$\ln(1.2) = (0.2) - \frac{(0.2)^2}{2} + \frac{(0.2)^3}{3} - \cdots$$

We find by trial that the eighth term

$$-\frac{(0.2)^8}{8} = -3.2 \times 10^{-7}$$

is the first term in the series whose absolute value is less than 10^{-6}. Therefore the sum of the first *seven* terms will give ln 1.2 with an error of less than 10^{-6}. The use of more terms would give an approximation that is even better, but seven terms are enough to guarantee the accuracy we wanted. Note also that we have not shown that six terms would *not* provide that accuracy.

PROBLEMS

In Problems 1 through 10, determine which of the following alternating series converge and which diverge.

1. $\sum_{n=1}^{\infty} (-1)^{n+1}\frac{1}{n^2}$

2. $\sum_{n=2}^{\infty} (-1)^{n+1}\frac{1}{\ln n}$

3. $\sum_{n=1}^{\infty} (-1)^{n+1}$

4. $\sum_{n=1}^{\infty} (-1)^{n+1}\frac{10^n}{n^{10}}$

5. $\sum_{n=1}^{\infty} (-1)^{n+1}\frac{\sqrt{n+1}}{n+1}$

6. $\sum_{n=1}^{\infty} (-1)^{n+1}\frac{\ln n}{n}$

7. $\sum_{n=1}^{\infty} (-1)^{n+1}\frac{1}{n^{3/2}}$

8. $\sum_{n=1}^{\infty} (-1)^{n+1}\frac{\ln n}{\ln n^2}$

9. $\sum_{n=1}^{\infty} (-1)^{n}\ln\left(1+\frac{1}{n}\right)$

10. $\sum_{n=1}^{\infty} (-1)^{n+1}\frac{3\sqrt{n+1}}{\sqrt{n}+1}$

In Problems 11 through 28, determine whether the following series are absolutely convergent, conditionally convergent, or divergent.

11. $\sum_{n=1}^{\infty} (-1)^{n+1}(0.1)^n$

12. $\sum_{n=1}^{\infty} (-1)^{n+1}\frac{1}{\sqrt{n}}$

13. $\sum_{n=1}^{\infty} (-1)^{n+1}\frac{n}{n^3+1}$

14. $\sum_{n=1}^{\infty} \frac{n!}{2^n}$

15. $\sum_{n=1}^{\infty} (-1)^{n}\frac{1}{n+3}$

16. $\sum_{n=1}^{\infty} (-1)^{n}\frac{\sin n}{n^2}$

17. $\sum_{n=1}^{\infty} (-1)^{n+1}\frac{3+n}{5+n}$

18. $\sum_{n=2}^{\infty} (-1)^{n}\frac{1}{\ln n^3}$

19. $\sum_{n=1}^{\infty} (-1)^{n+1}\frac{1+n}{n^2}$

20. $\sum_{n=1}^{\infty} \frac{(-2)^{n+1}}{n+5^n}$

21. $\sum_{n=1}^{\infty} n^2(\frac{2}{3})^n$

22. $\sum_{n=1}^{\infty} (-1)^{n+1}(\sqrt[n]{10})$

23. $\sum_{n=1}^{\infty} (-1)^{n}\frac{\tan^{-1} n}{n^2+1}$

24. $\sum_{n=2}^{\infty} (-1)^{n+1}\frac{1}{n\ln n}$

25. $\sum_{n=1}^{\infty} \left(\frac{1}{n}-\frac{1}{2n}\right)$

26. $\sum_{n=1}^{\infty} (-1)^{n+1}\frac{(0.1)^n}{n}$

27. $\sum_{n=1}^{\infty} (-1)^{n+1}(\sqrt{n+1}-\sqrt{n})$

28. $\sum_{n=1}^{\infty} \frac{(-1)^{n+1}(n!)^2}{(2n)!}$

In Problems 29 through 32, estimate the magnitude of the error if the first four terms are used to approximate the series.

29. $\sum_{n=1}^{\infty} (-1)^{n+1}\frac{1}{n}$

30. $\sum_{n=1}^{\infty} (-1)^{n+1}\frac{1}{10^n}$

31. $\ln(1.01) = \sum_{n=1}^{\infty} (-1)^{n+1}\frac{(0.01)^n}{n}$

32. $\frac{1}{1+t} = \sum_{n=0}^{\infty} (-1)^n t^n, \quad 0 < t < 1$

Approximate the following two sums to five decimal places (magnitude of the error less than 5×10^{-6}).

33. $\sum_{n=0}^{\infty} (-1)^n\frac{1}{(2n)!}$

(This is cos 1, the cosine of one radian.)

34. $\sum_{n=0}^{\infty} (-1)^n\frac{1}{n!}$ (This is $1/e$.)

35. **a)** The series

$$\frac{1}{3}-\frac{1}{2}+\frac{1}{9}-\frac{1}{4}+\frac{1}{27}-\frac{1}{8}+\cdots+\frac{1}{3^n}-\frac{1}{2^n}+\cdots$$

does not meet one of the conditions of Theorem 1. Which one?

b) Find the sum of the series in (a).

36. The limit L of an alternating series that satisfies the conditions of Theorem 1 lies between the values of any two consecutive partial sums. This suggests using the average

$$\frac{s_n + s_{n+1}}{2} = s_n + \frac{1}{2}a_{n+1}$$

to estimate L. Compute

$$s_{20} + \tfrac{1}{2}\cdot\tfrac{1}{21}$$

as an approximation to the sum of the alternating harmonic series. The exact sum is ln 2.

1.4

37. Show that whenever an alternating series is approximated by one of its partial sums, if the three conditions of Leibniz's theorem are satisfied, then the *remainder* (sum of the unused terms) has the same sign as the first unused term. [*Hint*. Group the terms of the remainder in consecutive pairs.]

38. Prove the "zipper" theorem for sequences: If $\{a_n\}$ and $\{b_n\}$ both converge to L, then the sequence

$$a_1, \quad b_1, \quad a_2, \quad b_2, \quad \ldots, \quad a_n, \quad b_n, \quad \ldots$$

also converges to L.

39. Show by example that $\sum_{n=1}^{\infty} a_n b_n$ may diverge even though $\sum_{n=1}^{\infty} a_n$ and $\sum_{n=1}^{\infty} b_n$ both converge.

16–8 POWER SERIES FOR FUNCTIONS

The rational operations of arithmetic are addition, subtraction, multiplication, and division. Using only these simple operations, we can evaluate any rational function of x. But other functions, such as $\sqrt{x}$, $\ln x$, $\cos x$, and so on, cannot be evaluated so simply. These functions occur so frequently, however, that their values have been printed in mathematical tables, and many calculators and computers have been programmed to produce them on demand. One may wonder where the values in the tables came from, and how a calculator produces the number it displays. By and large, these numbers come from calculating partial sums of power series.

Definition. *A **power series** is a series of the form*

$$\sum_{n=0}^{\infty} a_n x^n = a_0 + a_1 x + a_2 x^2 + \cdots.$$

In this article we shall show how a power series can arise when we seek to approximate a function

$$y = f(x) \tag{1}$$

by a sequence of polynomials $f_n(x)$ of the form

$$f_n(x) = a_0 + a_1 x + a_2 x^2 + \cdots + a_n x^n. \tag{2}$$

We shall be interested, at least at first, in making the approximation for values of x near 0, because we want the term $a_n x^n$ to decrease as n increases. Hence we focus our attention on a portion of the curve $y = f(x)$ near the point $A(0, f(0))$, as shown in Fig. 16–14.

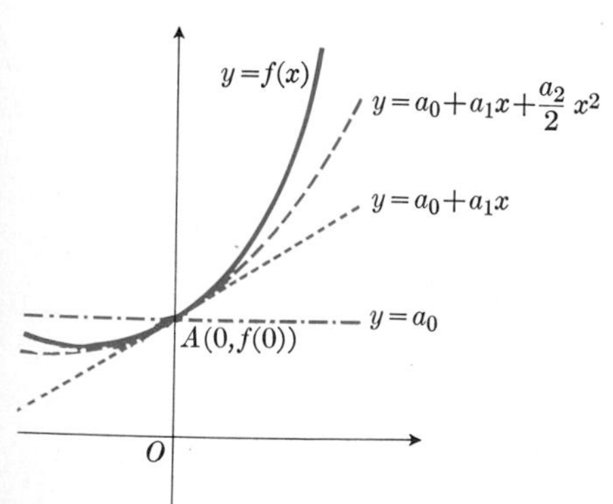

16–14 $f(x)$ is approximated near $x = 0$ by polynomials whose derivatives at $x = 0$ match the derivatives of f.

1. The graph of the polynomial $f_0(x) = a_0$ of degree zero will pass through $(0, f(0))$ if we take

$$a_0 = f(0).$$

2. The graph of the polynomial $f_1(x) = a_0 + a_1 x$ will pass through $(0, f(0))$ and have the same slope as the given curve at that point if we choose

$$a_0 = f(0) \quad \text{and} \quad a_1 = f'(0).$$

3. The graph of the polynomial $f_2(x) = a_0 + a_1 x + a_2 x^2$ will pass through $(0, f(0))$ and have the same slope and curvature as the given curve at that point if

$$a_0 = f(0), \quad a_1 = f'(0), \quad \text{and } a_2 = \frac{f''(0)}{2}.$$

4. In general, the polynomial $f_n(x) = a_0 + a_1 x + a_2 x^2 + \cdots + a_n x^n$, which we choose to approximate $y = f(x)$ near $x = 0$, is the one whose graph passes through $(0, f(0))$ and whose first n derivatives match the derivatives of $f(x)$ at $x = 0$. To match the derivatives of f_n to those of f at $x = 0$, we merely have to choose the coefficients a_0 through a_n properly. To see how this may be done, we write down the polynomial and its derivatives as follows:

$$\begin{aligned}
f_n(x) &= a_0 + a_1 x + a_2 x^2 + a_3 x^3 + \cdots + a_n x^n \\
f'_n(x) &= a_1 + 2a_2 x + 3a_3 x^2 + \cdots + na_n x^{n-1} \\
f''_n(x) &= 2a_2 + 3 \cdot 2a_3 x + \cdots + n(n-1)a_n x^{n-2} \\
&\vdots \\
f_n^{(n)}(x) &= (n!)a_n.
\end{aligned}$$

When we substitute 0 for x in the array above, we find that

$$a_0 = f(0), \qquad a_1 = f'(0), \qquad a_2 = \frac{f''(0)}{2!}, \qquad \ldots, \qquad a_n = \frac{f^{(n)}(0)}{n!}.$$

Thus,

$$f_n(x) = f(0) + f'(0)x + \frac{f''(0)}{2!}x^2 + \cdots + \frac{f^{(n)}(0)}{n!}x^n \tag{3}$$

is the polynomial we seek. Its graph passes through the point $(0, f(0))$, and its first n derivatives match the first n derivatives of $y = f(x)$ at $x = 0$. It is called the nth-degree *Taylor polynomial of f at $x = 0$*.

EXAMPLE 1. Find the Taylor polynomials $f_n(x)$ for the function $f(x) = e^x$.

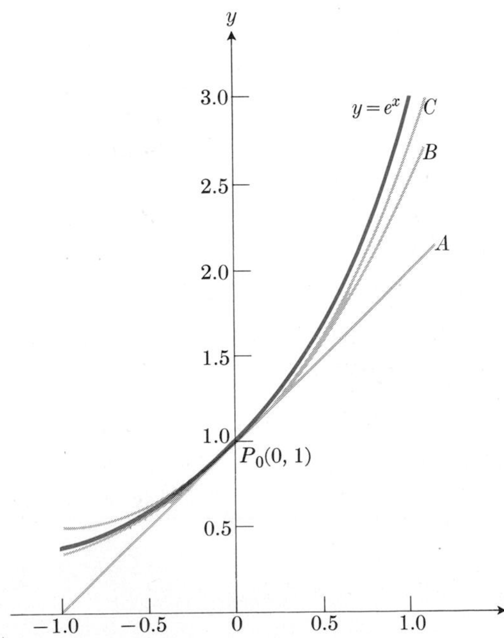

16–15 The graph of the function $y = e^x$, and graphs of three approximating polynomials, (A) a straight line, (B) a parabola, and (C) a cubic curve.

Solution. Expressed in terms of x, the given function and its derivatives are

$$f(x) = e^x, \quad f'(x) = e^x, \quad \ldots, \quad f^{(n)}(x) = e^x,$$

so that

$$f(0) = e^0 = 1, \quad f'(0) = 1, \quad \ldots, \quad f^{(n)}(0) = 1,$$

and

$$f_n(x) = 1 + x + \frac{x^2}{2!} + \frac{x^3}{3!} + \cdots + \frac{x^n}{n!}.$$

See Fig. 16–15.

EXAMPLE 2. Find the Taylor polynomials $f_n(x)$ for $f(x) = \cos x$.

Solution. The cosine and its derivatives are

$$\begin{aligned} f(x) &= \cos x, & f'(x) &= -\sin x, \\ f''(x) &= -\cos x, & f^{(3)}(x) &= \sin x, \\ &\vdots & &\vdots \\ f^{(2k)}(x) &= (-1)^k \cos x, & f^{(2k+1)}(x) &= (-1)^{k+1} \sin x. \end{aligned}$$

When $x = 0$, the cosines are 1 and the sines are 0, so that

$$f^{(2k)}(0) = (-1)^k, \quad f^{(2k+1)}(0) = 0.$$

The Taylor polynomials have only even-powered terms, and for $n = 2k$ we have

$$f_{2k}(x) = 1 - \frac{x^2}{2!} + \frac{x^4}{4!} - \cdots + (-1)^k \frac{x^{2k}}{(2k)!}. \tag{4}$$

Figure 16–16 shows how well these polynomials can be expected to approximate $y = \cos x$ near $x = 0$. Only the righthand portions of the graphs are shown because the graphs are symmetric about the y-axis.

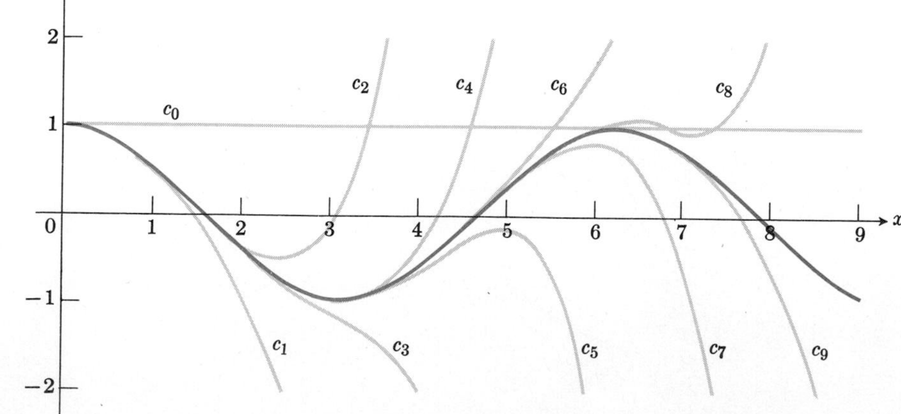

16–16 The polynomials $c_n(x) = \sum_{k=0}^{n} [(-1)^k x^{2k}/(2k)!]$ converge to $\cos x$ as $n \to \infty$. (Adapted from Helen M. Kammerer, *American Mathematical Monthly*, 43(1936), 293–294.)

The degrees of the Taylor polynomials of a given function are limited by the degree of differentiability of the function at $x = 0$. But if $f(x)$ has derivatives of all orders at the origin, it is natural to ask whether, for a fixed value of x, the values of these approximating polynomials converge to $f(x)$ as $n \to \infty$. Now, these polynomials are precisely the partial sums of a series known as the *Maclaurin series* for f:

The Maclaurin series for f

$$f(0) + f'(0)x + \frac{f''(0)}{2!}x^2 + \cdots + \frac{f^{(n)}(0)}{n!}x^n + \cdots. \tag{5}$$

Thus, the question just posed is equivalent to asking whether the Maclaurin series for f converges to $f(x)$ as a sum. It certainly has the correct value, $f(0)$, at $x = 0$, but how far away from $x = 0$ may we go and still have convergence? And if the series does converge away from $x = 0$, does it still converge to $f(x)$? The graphs in Figs. 16–15 and 16–16 are encouraging, and the next few articles will confirm that we can normally expect a Maclaurin series to converge to its function in an interval about the origin. For many functions, this interval is the entire x-axis.

If, instead of approximating the values of f near zero, we are concerned with values of x near some other point a, we write our approximating polynomials in powers of $(x - a)$:

$$f_n(x) = a_0 + a_1(x - a) + a_2(x - a)^2 + \cdots + a_n(x - a)^n. \tag{6}$$

When we now determine the coefficients $a_0, a_1, \ldots, a_n$, so that the polynomial and its first n derivatives agree with the given function and its derivatives at $x = a$, we are led to a series that is called the *Taylor series expansion of f about $x = a$*, or simply the *Taylor series for f at $x = a$*.

The Taylor series for f at $x = a$

$$f(a) + f'(a)(x - a) + \frac{f''(a)}{2!}(x - a)^2 + \cdots + \frac{f^{(n)}(a)}{n!}(x - a)^n + \cdots. \tag{7}$$

There are two things to notice here. The first is that Maclaurin series are Taylor series with $a = 0$. The second is that a function cannot have a Taylor series expansion about $x = a$ unless it has finite derivatives of all orders at $x = a$. For instance, $f(x) = \ln x$ does not have a Maclaurin series expansion, since the function itself, to say nothing of its derivatives, does not have a finite value at $x = 0$. On the other hand, it does have a Taylor series expansion in powers of $(x - 1)$, since $\ln x$ and all its derivatives are finite at $x = 1$.

Here are some examples of Taylor series.

EXAMPLE 3. From the formula derived for the Taylor polynomials of $\cos x$ in Example 2, it follows immediately that

$$\sum_{k=0}^{\infty} (-1)^k \frac{x^{2k}}{(2k)!} = 1 - \frac{x^2}{2!} + \frac{x^4}{4!} - \frac{x^6}{6!} + \cdots$$

is the Maclaurin series for $\cos x$.

EXAMPLE 4. Find the Taylor series expansion of $\cos x$ about the point $a = 2\pi$.

Solution. The values of $\cos x$ and its derivatives at $a = 2\pi$ are the same as their values at $a = 0$. Therefore,

$$f^{(2k)}(2\pi) = f^{(2k)}(0) = (-1)^k \quad \text{and} \quad f^{(2k+1)}(2\pi) = f^{(2k+1)}(0) = 0,$$

as in Example 2. The required series is

$$\sum_{k=0}^{\infty} (-1)^{2k} \frac{(x - 2\pi)^{2k}}{(2k)!} = 1 - \frac{(x - 2\pi)^2}{2!} + \frac{(x - 2\pi)^4}{4!} - \cdots.$$

REMARK. There is a convention about how formulas like

$$\frac{x^{2k}}{(2k)!} \quad \text{and} \quad \frac{(x - 2\pi)^{2k}}{(2k)!},$$

which arise in the power series of Examples 3 and 4, are to be evaluated when $k = 0$. Besides the usual agreement that $0! = 1$, we also assume that

$$\frac{x^0}{0!} = \frac{1}{1} = 1 \quad \text{and} \quad \frac{(x - 2\pi)^0}{0!} = \frac{1}{1} = 1,$$

even when $x = 0$ or 2π.

One of the most celebrated series of all times, the *binomial series*, is the Maclaurin series for the function $f(x) = (1 + x)^m$. Newton used it to estimate integrals (we will, in Article 16–13) and it can be used to give accurate estimates of roots. To derive the series, we first list the function and its derivatives:

$$\begin{aligned}
f(x) &= (1 + x)^m, \\
f'(x) &= m(1 + x)^{m-1}, \\
f''(x) &= m(m - 1)(1 + x)^{m-2}, \\
f'''(x) &= m(m - 1)(m - 2)(1 + x)^{m-3}, \\
&\vdots \\
f^{(k)}(x) &= m(m - 1)(m - 2) \cdots (m - k + 1)(1 + x)^{m-k}.
\end{aligned}$$

We then substitute the values of these at $x = 0$ in the basic Maclaurin series (5) to obtain

$$1 + mx + \frac{m(m - 1)}{2!} x^2 + \cdots + \frac{m(m - 1)(m - 2) \cdots (m - k + 1)}{k!} x^k + \cdots \quad \textbf{(8)}$$

If m is an integer, the series terminates after $(m + 1)$ terms, because the coefficients from $k = m + 1$ on are 0. But when k is not an integer, the series is infinite. (For a proof that the series converges to $(1 + x)^m$ when $|x| < 1$, see Courant and John's *Introduction to Calculus and Analysis*, Wiley-Interscience, 1974.)

EXAMPLE 5. Use the binomial series to estimate $\sqrt{1.25}$ with an error of less than 0.001.

Solution. We take $x = \frac{1}{4}$ and $m = \frac{1}{2}$ in (8) to obtain

$$(1 + \tfrac{1}{4})^{1/2} = 1 + \tfrac{1}{2}(\tfrac{1}{4}) + \frac{(\frac{1}{2})(-\frac{1}{2})}{2!}(\tfrac{1}{4})^2 + \frac{(\frac{1}{2})(-\frac{1}{2})(-\frac{3}{2})}{3!}(\tfrac{1}{4})^3 + \cdots$$

$$= 1 + \tfrac{1}{8} - \tfrac{1}{128} + \tfrac{1}{1024} - \tfrac{1}{32768} + \cdots$$

The series alternates after the first term, so that the approximation

$$\sqrt{1.25} \approx 1 + \tfrac{1}{8} - \tfrac{1}{128} \approx 1.117$$

is within $\frac{1}{1024}$ of the exact value and thus has the required accuracy.

PROBLEMS

In Problems 1 through 9, use Eq. (3) to write the Taylor polynomials $f_3(x)$ and $f_4(x)$ for each of the following functions $f(x)$. In each case, your first step should be to complete a table like the one shown below.

n	$f^{(n)}(x)$	$f^{(n)}(0)$
0		
1		
2		
3		
4		

1. e^{-x}
2. $\sin x$
3. $\cos x$
4. $\sin\left(x + \dfrac{\pi}{2}\right)$
5. $\sinh x$
6. $\cosh x$
7. $x^4 - 2x + 1$
8. $x^3 - 2x + 1$
9. $x^2 - 2x + 1$

In Problems 10 through 13, find the Maclaurin series for each function.

10. $\dfrac{1}{1+x}$
11. x^2
12. $(1 + x)^2$
13. $(1 + x)^{3/2}$
14. Find the Maclaurin series for $f(x) = 1/(1 - x)$. Show that the series diverges when $|x| \geq 1$ and converges when $|x| < 1$.

In Problems 15–20, use Eq. (7) to write the Taylor series expansion of the given function about the given point a.

15. $f(x) = e^x, \quad a = 10$
16. $f(x) = x^2, \quad a = \frac{1}{2}$
17. $f(x) = \ln x, \quad a = 1$
18. $f(x) = \sqrt{x}, \quad a = 4$
19. $f(x) = \dfrac{1}{x}, \quad a = -1$
20. $f(x) = \cos x, \quad a = -\dfrac{\pi}{4}$

In Problems 21 and 22, write the sum of the first three terms of the Taylor series for the given function about the given point a.

21. $f(x) = \tan x, \quad a = \dfrac{\pi}{4}$
22. $f(x) = \ln \cos x, \quad a = \dfrac{\pi}{3}$
23. Use the binomial theorem to estimate $\sqrt{1.02}$ with an error of less than 0.001.

16–9

TAYLOR'S THEOREM WITH REMAINDER: SINES, COSINES, AND e^x

In the previous article, we asked when a Taylor series for a function can be expected to converge to the function. In this article, we answer the question with a theorem named after the English mathematician Brook Taylor (1685–1731). Unfortunately, although several proofs of the theorem are known, none of them seems to have an obvious point of departure.

The path we shall follow starts with the simple formula

$$\int_a^b f'(t)\,dt = f(t)\Big|_a^b = f(b) - f(a), \tag{1}$$

which we rewrite in the form

$$f(b) = f(a) + \int_a^b f'(t)\, dt. \tag{2}$$

We then apply the integration-by-parts formula

$$\int u\, dv = uv - \int v\, du$$

with

$$u = f'(t) \qquad \text{and} \qquad v = t - b,$$

where, in determining v from $dv = dt$, we introduce the constant of integration $-b$ for future convenience. As a result,

$$\begin{aligned} f(b) &= f(a) + (t - b)f'(t)\Big|_a^b - \int_a^b (t - b)f''(t)\, dt \\ &= f(a) + (b - a)f'(a) + \int_a^b (b - t)f''(t)\, dt. \end{aligned}$$

A second integration by parts, with

$$u = f''(t), \qquad v = -\frac{(b - t)^2}{2},$$

leads to

$$\begin{aligned} f(b) &= f(a) + (b - a)f'(a) - \frac{(b - t)^2}{2} f''(t)\Big|_a^b + \int_a^b \frac{(b - t)^2}{2} f'''(t)\, dt \\ &= f(a) + (b - a)f'(a) + \frac{(b - a)^2}{2!} f''(a) + \int_a^b \frac{(b - t)^2}{2!} f'''(t)\, dt. \end{aligned}$$

By continuing in this fashion, we find that

$$\begin{aligned} f(b) = f(a) &+ (b - a)f'(a) + \frac{(b - a)^2}{2!} f''(a) + \cdots \\ &+ \frac{(b - a)^n}{n!} f^{(n)}(a) + \int_a^b \frac{(b - t)^n}{n!} f^{(n+1)}(t)\, dt. \end{aligned}$$

Finally, we replace b by x, to obtain the formula of Taylor's theorem.

Theorem 1. Taylor's Theorem. *Let f be a function that is continuous together with its first $n + 1$ derivatives on an interval containing a and x. Then the value of the function at x is given by*

$$\begin{aligned} f(x) = f(a) &+ f'(a) \cdot (x - a) + \frac{f''(a)}{2!}(x - a)^2 + \frac{f'''(a)}{3!}(x - a)^3 + \cdots \\ &+ \frac{f^{(n)}(a)}{n!}(x - a)^n + R_n(x, a), \end{aligned} \tag{3}$$

where

$$R_n(x, a) = \int_a^x \frac{(x - t)^n}{n!} f^{(n+1)}(t)\, dt.$$

Equation (3) is often referred to as *Taylor's formula*.

The application of integration by parts n times in succession requires that the integral in Eq. (3) exist at each stage. This will indeed be the case provided the $(n + 1)$st derivative of the function exists and is continuous in some closed interval that includes the domain of integration from a to x.

The term $R_n(x, a)$ is called the *remainder* in the Taylor-series expansion for $f(x)$. If the remainder is omitted in Eq. (3), the right side becomes the Taylor polynomial approximation to $f(x)$. The error in this approximation is what is measured by $R_n(x, a)$. Hence, we can pursue the question of whether the series converges to $f(x)$ by investigating this remainder. The series will converge to $f(x)$ provided

$$\lim_{n\to\infty} R_n(x, a) = 0. \tag{4}$$

In other words, when this limit is 0,

$$f(x) = \sum_{k=0}^{\infty} \frac{f^{(k)}(a)}{k!}(x - a)^k.$$

EXAMPLE 1. Let $f(x) = e^x$. This function and all its derivatives are continuous at every point, so Taylor's theorem may be applied with any convenient value of a. We take $a = 0$, since the values of f and its derivatives are easy to compute there. Taylor's theorem leads to

$$e^x = 1 + x + \frac{x^2}{2!} + \frac{x^3}{3!} + \cdots + \frac{x^n}{n!} + R_n(x, 0), \tag{5}$$

with

$$R_n(x, 0) = \int_0^x \frac{(x - t)^n}{n!} e^t\, dt. \tag{6}$$

When x is positive, we may *estimate* the remainder (6) by observing that the integrand is positive for $0 < t < x$, and that $e^t < e^x < 3^x$. Therefore,

$$|R_n(x, 0)| \le \int_0^x \frac{(x - t)^n}{n!} 3^x\, dt = 3^x \int_0^x \frac{(x - t)^n}{n!}\, dt = 3^x \frac{x^{n+1}}{(n + 1)!}, \qquad x > 0. \tag{7}$$

When x is negative, we merely replace x by $|x|$ on the right, and the inequality continues to hold. Therefore, for all real values of x, we have

$$|R_n(x, 0)| \le 3^{|x|} \frac{|x|^{n+1}}{(n + 1)!}, \tag{8}$$

and since

$$\lim_{n\to\infty} 3^{|x|} \frac{|x|^{n+1}}{(n + 1)!} = 3^{|x|} \lim_{n\to\infty} \frac{|x|^{n+1}}{(n + 1)!} = 3^{|x|} \cdot 0 = 0, \tag{9}$$

we know that

$$R_n(x, 0) \to 0.$$

Therefore, the Taylor series for e^x converges to e^x for every x:

$$e^x = \sum_{n=0}^{\infty} \frac{x^n}{n!} = 1 + x + \frac{x^2}{2!} + \frac{x^3}{3!} + \cdots.$$

Estimating the Remainder

It is often possible to estimate $R_n(x, a)$ as we did in Example 1 without having to evaluate the integral for it. The basis for such estimates is the following theorem, although the reason may not be immediately apparent upon reading the Theorem. We first state and prove the theorem. Then we state a corollary of the theorem (we will call the corollary Theorem 3) that is formulated specifically for estimating remainders.

Theorem 2. *Let $g(t)$ and $h(t)$ be continuous for $a \leq t \leq b$, and suppose that $h(t)$ does not change sign in this interval. Then there exists a number c between a and b such that*

$$\int_a^b g(t)h(t)\,dt = g(c)\int_a^b h(t)\,dt. \tag{10}$$

Proof. Let m and M be respectively the least and greatest values of $g(t)$ for $a \leq t \leq b$. Then

$$m \leq g(t_i) \leq M \tag{11}$$

for any t_i between a and b, inclusive. We form a subdivision

$$a = t_0 < t_1 < t_2 < \cdots < t_n = b$$

of the interval $a \leq t \leq b$ with

$$t_i - t_{i-1} = \Delta t = (b - a)/n, \qquad (i = 1, \ldots, n),$$

and multiply each term in the inequalities (11) by $h(t_i)\,\Delta t$. Since the sign of $h(t)$ does not change over the interval $a \leq t \leq b$, all the terms $h(t_i)\,\Delta t$ are of the same sign, say positive. [If they are all negative, replace $h(t)$ by $-h(t)$ in the argument that follows.] Then

$$mh(t_i)\,\Delta t \leq g(t_i)h(t_i)\,\Delta t \leq Mh(t_i)\,\Delta t,$$

and the order of inequality is preserved when we sum on i from 1 to n; that is,

$$\sum_{i=1}^{n} mh(t_i)\,\Delta t \leq \sum_{i=1}^{n} g(t_i)h(t_i)\,\Delta t \leq \sum_{i=1}^{n} Mh(t_i)\,\Delta t. \tag{12}$$

Finally, we let n increase indefinitely and recall that, because the functions involved are continuous on $[a, b]$, the sums converge to definite integrals:

$$m\int_a^b h(t)\,dt \leq \int_a^b g(t)h(t)\,dt \leq M\int_a^b h(t)\,dt,$$

or

$$m \leq \frac{\int_a^b g(t)h(t)\,dt}{\int_a^b h(t)\,dt} \leq M. \tag{13}$$

Since

$$Q = \frac{\int_a^b g(t)h(t)\,dt}{\int_a^b h(t)\,dt} \tag{14}$$

is a number between the least and greatest values taken on by $g(t)$ for $a \leq t \leq b$ and $g(t)$ is assumed to be continuous, there is a number c between

a and b such that

$$Q = g(c).$$

This leads at once to the result in Eq. (10) and completes the proof of the theorem. Q.E.D.

We now apply this theorem to the integral in Eq. (3) with

$$h(t) = \frac{(x-t)^n}{n!}, \qquad g(t) = f^{(n+1)}(t).$$

As t varies from a to x, $h(t)$ is continuous and does not change sign. Hence, if $f^{(n+1)}(t)$ is continuous, Eq. (10) applies, and we have

$$R_n(x, a) = f^{(n+1)}(c) \int_a^x \frac{(x-t)^n}{n!}\,dt$$

$$= f^{(n+1)}(c) \frac{(x-a)^{n+1}}{(n+1)!}.$$

This is known as *Lagrange's* form of the remainder:

Lagrange's Form of the Remainder

$$R_n(x, a) = f^{(n+1)}(c) \frac{(x-a)^{n+1}}{(n+1)!}, \qquad c \text{ between } a \text{ and } x.^* \tag{15}$$

In applying Lagrange's form we can, in general, only estimate $f^{(n+1)}(c)$ because we do not know c exactly. But we do know that if the values of $|f^{(n+1)}(t)|$ are bounded above by some constant M for all t between a and x, inclusive, then

$$|R_n(x, a)| = |f^{(n+1)}(c)| \frac{|x-a|^{n+1}}{(n+1)!} \le M \frac{|x-a|^{n+1}}{(n+1)!}. \tag{16}$$

This was the estimate used in Example 1 when e^t in Eq. (6) was replaced by $M = 3^{|x|}$ to produce the inequality in (7), although the work was done in several steps there.

This method of estimation is so convenient that we state it as a theorem for future reference.

Theorem 3. The Remainder Estimation Theorem. *If there is a positive constant M such that $|f^{(n+1)}(t)| \le M$ for all t between a and x, inclusive, then the remainder term $R_n(x, a)$ in Taylor's theorem satisfies the inequality*

$$|R_n(x, a)| \le M \frac{|x-a|^{n+1}}{(n+1)!}.$$

---

* Another proof of Taylor's theorem, leading directly to the Lagrange form of the remainder, is outlined in Problem 74 (Extended Mean Value Theorem), in the miscellaneous problems at the end of Chapter 3.

We are now ready to look at some examples of how the Remainder Estimation Theorem and Taylor's Theorem can be used together to settle questions of convergence. As you will see, they can also be used to determine the accuracy with which a function is approximated by one of its Taylor polynomials.

EXAMPLE 2. The Maclaurin series for $\sin x$ converges to $\sin x$ for all x.

Expressed in terms of x, the function and its derivatives are

$$\begin{aligned} f(x) &= \sin x, & f'(x) &= \cos x, \\ f''(x) &= -\sin x, & f'''(x) &= -\cos x, \\ &\vdots & &\vdots \\ f^{(2k)}(x) &= (-1)^k \sin x, & f^{(2k+1)}(x) &= (-1)^k \cos x, \end{aligned}$$

so that

$$f^{(2k)}(0) = 0 \quad \text{and} \quad f^{(2k+1)}(0) = (-1)^k.$$

The series has only odd-powered terms and, for $n = 2k + 1$, Taylor's formula gives

$$\sin x = x - \frac{x^3}{3!} + \frac{x^5}{5!} - \cdots + \frac{(-1)^k x^{2k+1}}{(2k+1)!} + R_{2k+1}(x, 0).$$

Now, since all the derivatives of $\sin x$ have absolute values less than or equal to 1, we can apply the Remainder Estimation Theorem with $M = 1$ to obtain

$$|R_{2k+1}(x, 0)| \leq 1 \cdot \frac{|x|^{2k+2}}{(2k+2)!}.$$

Since $[|x|^{2k+2}/(2k+2)!] \to 0$ as $k \to \infty$, whatever the value of x,

$$R_{2k+1}(x, 0) \to 0,$$

and the Maclaurin series for $\sin x$ converges to $\sin x$ for every x:

$$\sin x = \sum_{k=0}^{\infty} \frac{(-1)^k x^{2k+1}}{(2k+1)!} = x - \frac{x^3}{3!} + \frac{x^5}{5!} - \frac{x^7}{7!} + \cdots$$

EXAMPLE 3. The Maclaurin series for $\cos x$ converges to $\cos x$ for every value of x. We begin by adding the remainder term to the Taylor polynomial for $\cos x$ in Eq. (4) of the previous article, to obtain Taylor's formula for $\cos x$ with $n = 2k$:

$$\cos x = 1 - \frac{x^2}{2!} + \frac{x^4}{4!} - \cdots + (-1)^k \frac{x^{2k}}{(2k)!} + R_{2k}(x, 0).$$

Since the derivatives of the cosine have absolute value less than or equal to 1, we apply the Remainder Estimation Theorem with $M = 1$ to obtain

$$|R_{2k}(x, 0)| \leq 1 \cdot \frac{|x|^{2k+1}}{(2k+1)!}.$$

For every value of x, $R_{2k} \to 0$ as $k \to 0$. Therefore, the series converges to cos x for every value of x.

$$\cos x = \sum_{k=0}^{\infty} \frac{(-1)^k x^{2k}}{(2k)!} = 1 - \frac{x^2}{2!} + \frac{x^4}{4!} - \frac{x^6}{6!} + \cdots.$$

EXAMPLE 4. Find the Maclaurin series for cos $2x$ and show that it converges to cos $2x$ for every value of x.

Solution. The Maclaurin series for cos x converges to cos x for every value of x, and therefore converges for every value of $2x$:

$$\cos 2x = \sum_{k=0}^{\infty} \frac{(-1)^k (2x)^{2k}}{(2k)!} = 1 - \frac{(2x)^2}{2!} + \frac{(2x)^4}{4!} - \frac{(2x)^6}{6!} + \cdots$$

Taylor series can be added, subtracted, and multiplied by constants, just as other series can, and the results are once again Taylor series. The Taylor series for $f(x) + g(x)$ is the sum of the Taylor series for $f(x)$ and $g(x)$, because the nth derivative of $f(x) + g(x)$ is $f^{(n)}(x) + g^{(n)}(x)$, and so on. In the next example, we add the series for e^x and e^{-x} and divide by 2, to obtain the Taylor series for cosh x.

EXAMPLE 5. Find the Taylor series for cosh x.

Solution

$$e^x = 1 + x + \frac{x^2}{2!} + \frac{x^3}{3!} + \frac{x^4}{4!} + \frac{x^5}{5!} + \cdots,$$

$$e^{-x} = 1 - x + \frac{x^2}{2!} - \frac{x^3}{3!} + \frac{x^4}{4!} - \frac{x^5}{5!} + \cdots;$$

$$\cosh x = \frac{e^x + e^{-x}}{2} = 1 + \frac{x^2}{2!} + \frac{x^4}{4!} + \cdots = \sum_{k=0}^{\infty} \frac{x^{2k}}{(2k)!}.$$

Here are some examples of how to use the Remainder Estimation Theorem to estimate truncation error.

EXAMPLE 6. Calculate e with an error of less than 10^{-6}.

Solution. By Taylor's Theorem,

$$e = e^1 = 1 + 1 + \frac{1}{2!} + \frac{1}{3!} + \cdots + \frac{1}{n!} + R_n(x, 0),$$

where

$$R_n(x, 0) = \int_0^1 \frac{(x-t)^n}{n!} e^t \, dt.$$

The interval of integration is $0 \le t \le 1$. Since $|e^t| < 3$ when $0 \le t \le 1$, the Remainder Estimation Theorem, with $M = 3$ and $x = 1$, gives

$$|R_n| \le 3 \cdot \frac{|1|^{n+1}}{(n+1)!} = \frac{3}{(n+1)!}.$$

By trial we find that $3/9! > 10^{-6}$, while $3/10! < 10^{-6}$. Thus we should take $(n+1)$ to be at least 10, or n to be at least 9. With an error of less than 10^{-6},

$$e = 1 + 1 + \frac{1}{2} + \frac{1}{3!} + \cdots + \frac{1}{9!} \approx 2.718282.$$

EXAMPLE 7. For what values of x can $\sin x$ be replaced by $x - (x^3/3!)$ with an error of magnitude no greater than 3×10^{-4}?

Solution. Here we can take advantage of the fact that the Maclaurin series for $\sin x$ is an alternating series for every nonzero value of x. According to the Alternating Series Estimation Theorem in Article 16–7, the error in truncating

$$\sin x = x - \frac{x^3}{3!} + \frac{x^5}{5!} - \cdots$$

after $(x^3/3!)$ is no greater than

$$\left|\frac{x^5}{5!}\right| = \frac{|x|^5}{120}.$$

Therefore the error will be less than or equal to 3×10^{-4} if

$$\frac{|x|^5}{120} < 3 \times 10^{-4}$$

or

$$|x| < \sqrt[5]{360 \times 10^{-4}} \approx 0.514.$$

The Alternating Series Estimation Theorem tells us something that the Remainder Estimation Theorem does not: namely, that the estimate $x - (x^3/3!)$ for $\sin x$ is an underestimate when x is positive, because then $x^5/120$ is positive.

Figure 16–17 shows the graph of $\sin x$, along with the graphs of a number of its approximating Taylor polynomials. Note that the graph of $s_1 = x - (x^3/3!)$ is almost indistinguishable from the sine curve when $-1 \leq x \leq 1$. However, it crosses the x-axis at $\pm\sqrt{6} \approx \pm 2.45$, whereas the sine curve crosses the axis at $\pm\pi \approx \pm 3.14$.

One might wonder how the estimate given by the Remainder Estimation Theorem would compare with the one we just obtained from the Alternating Series Estimation Theorem. If we write

$$\sin x = x - \frac{x^3}{3!} + R_3,$$

then the Remainder Estimation Theorem gives

$$|R_3| \leq 1 \cdot \frac{|x|^4}{4!} = \frac{|x|^4}{24},$$

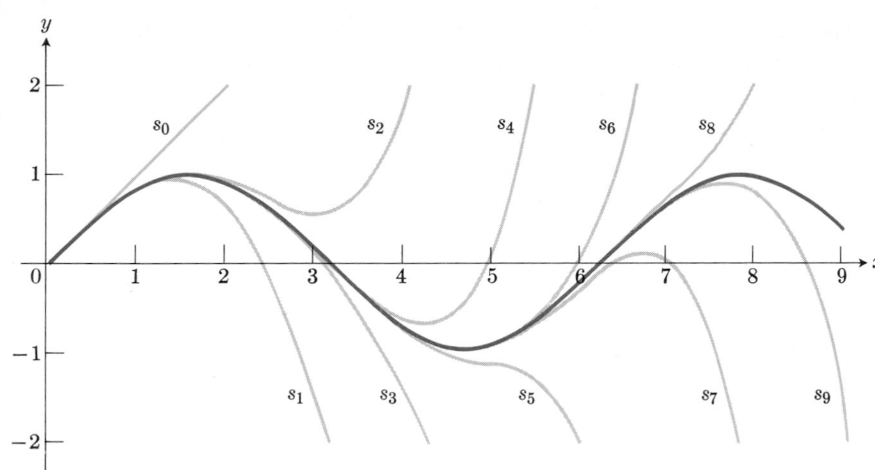

16–17 The polynomials $s_n(x) = \sum_{k=0}^{n} [(-1)^k x^{2k+1}/(2k+1)!]$ converge to $\sin x$ as $n \to \infty$. (Adapted from Helen M. Kammerer, *American Mathematical Monthly*, 43(1936), 293–294.)

which is not very good. But, if we are clever, and write

$$\sin x = x - \frac{x^3}{3!} + 0 + R_4,$$

then the Remainder Estimation Theorem gives

$$|R_4| \leq 1 \cdot \frac{|x|^5}{5!} = \frac{|x|^5}{120},$$

which is just what we had from the Alternating Series Estimation Theorem.

PROBLEMS

In Problems 1 through 6, write the Maclaurin series for each function.

1. $e^{x/2}$ **2.** $\sin 3x$

3. $5 \cos \frac{x}{\pi}$ **4.** $\sinh x$

5. $\frac{x^2}{2} - 1 + \cos x$ **6.** $\cos^2 2x = \frac{1 + \cos 2x}{2}$

7. Use series to verify that

a) $\cos(-x) = \cos x$ **b)** $\sin(-x) = -\sin x$

8. Show that

$$e^x = e^a \left[1 + (x - a) + \frac{(x-a)^2}{2!} + \cdots\right]$$

In Problems 9 through 11, write Taylor's formula (Eq. (3)), with $n = 2$ and $a = 0$, for the given function.

9. $\frac{1}{1+x}$ **10.** $\ln(1 + x)$ **11.** $\sqrt{1+x}$

12. Find the Taylor series for e^x at $a = 1$. Compare your series with the result in Problem 8.

13. For approximately what values of x can one replace $\sin x$ by $x - (x^3/6)$ with an error of magnitude no greater than 5×10^{-4}?

14. If $\cos x$ is replaced by $1 - (x^2/2)$ and $|x| < 0.5$, what estimate can be made of the error? Does $1 - (x^2/2)$ tend to be too large, or too small?

15. How close is the approximation $\sin x = x$ when $|x| < 10^{-3}$? For which of these values of x is $x < \sin x$?

16. The estimate $\sqrt{1+x} = 1 + (x/2)$ is used when $|x|$ is small. Estimate the error when $|x| < 0.01$.

17. The approximation $e^x = 1 + x + (x^2/2)$ is used when x is small. Use the Remainder Estimation Theorem to estimate the error when $|x| < 0.1$.

18. When $x < 0$, the series for e^x is an alternating series. Use the Alternating Series Estimation Theorem to estimate the error that results from replacing e^x by $1 + x + (x^2/2)$ when $-0.1 < x < 0$. Compare with Problem 17.

19. Estimate the error in the approximation $\sinh x = x + (x^3/3!)$ when $|x| < 0.5$. [*Hint.* Use R_4, not R_3.]

20. When $0 \le h \le 0.01$, show that e^h may be replaced by $1 + h$ with an error of magnitude no greater than six-tenths of one percent of h. Use $e^{0.1} = 1.105$.

21. Let $f(x)$ and $g(x)$ have derivatives of all orders at $a = 0$. Show that the Maclaurin series for $f + g$ is

$$\sum_{n=0}^{\infty} \frac{f^{(n)}(0) + g^{(n)}(0)}{n!} x^n.$$

22. Each of the following sums is the value of an elementary function at some point. Find the function and the point.

a) $(0.1) - \dfrac{(0.1)^3}{3!} + \dfrac{(0.1)^5}{5!} - \cdots + \dfrac{(-1)^k(0.1)^{2k+1}}{(2k+1)!} + \cdots$

b) $1 - \dfrac{\pi^2}{4^2 \cdot 2!} + \dfrac{\pi^4}{4^4 \cdot 4!} - \cdots + \dfrac{(-1)^k(\pi)^{2k}}{4^{2k} \cdot (2k)!} + \cdots$

c) $1 + \dfrac{1}{2!} + \dfrac{1}{4!} + \cdots + \dfrac{1}{(2k)!} + \cdots$

16-10 FURTHER COMPUTATIONS, LOGARITHMS, ARCTANGENTS, AND π

The Taylor-series expansion

$$f(x) = f(a) + f'(a)(x-a) + \frac{f''(a)}{2!}(x-a)^2 + \cdots + \frac{f^{(n)}(a)}{n!}(x-a)^n + R_n(x, a) \tag{1}$$

expresses the value of the function at x in terms of its value and the values of its derivatives at a, plus a remainder term, which we hope is so small that it may safely be omitted. In applying series to numerical computations, it is therefore *necessary* that a be chosen so that $f(a), f'(a), f''(a), \ldots$ are known. In dealing with the trigonometric functions, for example, one might take $a = 0, \pm\pi/6, \pm\pi/4, \pm\pi/3, \pm\pi/2$, and so on. It is also clear that it is *desirable* to choose the value of a near to the value of x for which the function is to be computed, in order to make $(x - a)$ small, so that the terms of the series decrease rapidly as n increases.

EXAMPLE 1. What value of a might one choose in the Taylor series (1) to compute sin 35°?

Solution. We could choose $a = 0$ and use the series

$$\sin x = x - \frac{x^3}{3!} + \frac{x^5}{5!} - \cdots + (-1)^n \frac{x^{2n+1}}{(2n+1)!} + 0 \cdot x^{2n+2} + R_{2n+2}(x, 0), \tag{2}$$

or we could choose $a = \pi/6$ (which corresponds to 30°) and use the series

$$\sin x = \sin\frac{\pi}{6} + \cos\frac{\pi}{6}\left(x - \frac{\pi}{6}\right) - \sin\frac{\pi}{6}\frac{(x-\pi/6)^2}{2!} - \cos\frac{\pi}{6}\frac{(x-\pi/6)^3}{3!} + \cdots + \sin\left(\frac{\pi}{6} + n\frac{\pi}{2}\right)\frac{(x-\pi/6)^n}{n!} + R_n\left(x, \frac{\pi}{6}\right).$$

The remainder in the series (2) satisfies the inequality

$$|R_{2n+2}(x, 0)| \le \frac{|x|^{2n+3}}{(2n+3)!}, \tag{3}$$

which tends to zero as n becomes infinite, no matter how large $|x|$ may be.

We could therefore calculate sin 35° by placing

$$x = \frac{35\pi}{180} = 0.61086\,52$$

in the approximation

$$\sin x \approx x - \frac{x^3}{6} + \frac{x^5}{120} - \frac{x^7}{5040},$$

with an error of magnitude no greater than 3.3×10^{-8}, since

$$\left| R_8\left(\frac{35\pi}{180}, 0\right) \right| < \frac{(0.611)^9}{9!} < 3.3 \times 10^{-8}.$$

By using the series with $a = \pi/6$, we could obtain equal accuracy with a smaller exponent n, but at the expense of introducing $\cos \pi/6 = \sqrt{3}/2$ as one of the coefficients. In this series, with $a = \pi/6$, we would take

$$x = \frac{35\pi}{180},$$

but the quantity that appears raised to the various powers is

$$x - \frac{\pi}{6} = \frac{5\pi}{180} = 0.08726\,65,$$

which decreases rapidly when raised to high powers.

As a matter of fact, various trigonometric identities may be used, such as

$$\sin\left(\frac{\pi}{2} - x\right) = \cos x,$$

to facilitate the calculation of the sine or cosine of any angle with the Maclaurin series of the two functions. This method of finding the sine or cosine of an angle is used in computers.

Computation of Logarithms

Natural logarithms may be computed from series. The starting point is the series for $\ln(1 + x)$ in powers of x:

$$\ln(1 + x) = x - \frac{x^2}{2} + \frac{x^3}{3} - \cdots + (-1)^{n-1}\frac{x^n}{n} + \cdots$$

This series may be found directly from the Taylor-series expansion, Eq. (1), with $a = 0$. It may also be obtained by integrating the geometric series for $1/(1 + t)$ from $t = 0$ to $t = x$:

$$\int_0^x \frac{dt}{1+t} = \int_0^x (1 - t + t^2 - t^3 + \cdots)\, dt,$$

$$\ln(1 + t)\Big]_0^x = t - \frac{t^2}{2} + \frac{t^3}{3} - \frac{t^4}{4} + \cdots\Big]_0^x,$$

$$\ln(1 + x) = x - \frac{x^2}{2} + \frac{x^3}{3} - \frac{x^4}{4} + \cdots \tag{4}$$

The expansion (4) is valid for $|x| < 1$, since then the remainder, $R_n(x, 0)$, approaches zero as $n \to \infty$, as we shall now see. The remainder is given by the integral of the remainder in the geometric series, that is,

$$R_n(x, 0) = \int_0^x \frac{(-1)^n t^n}{1+t}\, dt. \tag{5}$$

We now suppose that $|x| < 1$. For every t between 0 and x inclusive we have

$$|1 + t| \geq 1 - |x|$$

and

$$|(-1)^n t^n| = |t|^n,$$

so that

$$\left| \frac{(-1)^n t^n}{1+t} \right| \leq \frac{|t|^n}{1 - |x|}.$$

Therefore,

$$|R_n(x, 0)| \leq \int_0^{|x|} \frac{t^n}{1 - |x|}\, dt = \frac{1}{n+1} \cdot \frac{|x|^{n+1}}{1 - |x|}. \tag{6}$$

When $n \to \infty$, the right side of the inequality (6) approaches zero, and so must the left side. Thus (4) holds for $|x| < 1$.

If we replace x by $-x$, we obtain

$$\ln (1 - x) = -x - \frac{x^2}{2} - \frac{x^3}{3} - \cdots - \frac{x^n}{n} - \cdots, \tag{7}$$

which is also valid for $|x| < 1$. When we subtract (7) from (4), we get

$$\ln \frac{1+x}{1-x} = 2\left(x + \frac{x^3}{3} + \frac{x^5}{5} + \cdots + \frac{x^{2k-1}}{2k-1} + \cdots\right), \tag{8}$$

which is true for $|x| < 1$. Equation (8) may be used to compute the natural logarithm of any positive number y by taking

$$y = \frac{1+x}{1-x} \qquad \text{or} \qquad x = \frac{y-1}{y+1}.$$

But the series converges most rapidly for values of x near zero, or when $(1 + x)/(1 - x)$ is near one. For this reason, the logarithms of the numbers

$$\frac{2}{1}, \ \frac{3}{2}, \ \frac{4}{3}, \ \frac{5}{4}, \ \ldots, \ \frac{N+1}{N}$$

are ordinarily computed first in forming a table of natural logarithms of the integers. Then it is a matter of simple arithmetic to compute

$$\begin{aligned}
\ln 3 &= \ln \tfrac{2}{1} + \ln \tfrac{3}{2},\\
\ln 4 &= \ln 3 + \ln \tfrac{4}{3},\\
\ln 5 &= \ln 4 + \ln \tfrac{5}{4},\\
&\ \vdots\\
\ln (N + 1) &= \ln N + \ln \frac{N+1}{N}.
\end{aligned}$$

For this purpose, one may solve the equation

$$\frac{1+x}{1-x} = \frac{N+1}{N}$$

for

$$x = \frac{1}{2N+1}.$$

This may be substituted into Eq. (8), which becomes

$$\ln\frac{N+1}{N} = 2\left(\frac{1}{2N+1} + \frac{1}{3(2N+1)^3} + \frac{1}{5(2N+1)^5} + \cdots\right). \tag{9}$$

For example, to calculate ln 2, we take $N = 1$, $x = \frac{1}{3}$, and calculate

$$\begin{aligned}
x &= 0.33333 \quad 33,\\
\frac{x^3}{3} &= 0.01234 \quad 57,\\
\frac{x^5}{5} &= 0.00082 \quad 30,\\
\frac{x^7}{7} &= 0.00006 \quad 53,\\
\frac{x^9}{9} &= 0.00000 \quad 56,\\
\frac{x^{11}}{11} &= 0.00000 \quad 05,\\
\hline
\text{Sum} &= 0.34657 \quad 34, \qquad \ln 2 \approx 0.69314 \quad 68.
\end{aligned}$$

Computation of π

Archimedes (287–212 B.C.) gave the approximation

$$3\tfrac{1}{7} > \pi > 3\tfrac{10}{71},$$

in the third century B.C. A French mathematician, Viéta (1540–1603), gave the formula

$$\frac{2}{\pi} = \sqrt{\tfrac{1}{2}} \times \sqrt{\left(\tfrac{1}{2} + \tfrac{1}{2}\sqrt{\tfrac{1}{2}}\right)} \times \sqrt{\left(\tfrac{1}{2} + \tfrac{1}{2}\sqrt{\left(\tfrac{1}{2} + \tfrac{1}{2}\sqrt{\tfrac{1}{2}}\right)}\right)} \times \cdots,$$

which Turnbull* calls "the first actual formula for the time-honoured number π." Other interesting formulas for π include†

$$\frac{\pi}{4} = \cfrac{1}{1 + \cfrac{1^2}{2 + \cfrac{3^2}{2 + \cfrac{5^2}{2 + \cdots}}}},$$

* *World of Mathematics*, Vol. 1, p. 121.

† *Ibid.*, p. 138.

which is credited to Lord Brouncker, an Irish peer;

$$\frac{\pi}{4} = \frac{2 \times 4 \times 4 \times 6 \times 6 \times 8 \times \cdots}{3 \times 3 \times 5 \times 5 \times 7 \times 7 \times \cdots},$$

discovered by the English mathematician Wallis; and

$$\frac{\pi}{4} = 1 - \frac{1}{3} + \frac{1}{5} - \frac{1}{7} + \cdots,$$

known as Leibniz's formula.

All of these formulas involve limits. To derive Viéta's formula, for example, we may begin with the trigonometric half-angle formulas:

$$\begin{aligned} \sin x &= 2 \sin \frac{x}{2} \cos \frac{x}{2}, \\ \sin \frac{x}{2} &= 2 \sin \frac{x}{4} \cos \frac{x}{4}, \\ \sin \frac{x}{4} &= 2 \sin \frac{x}{8} \cos \frac{x}{8}, \\ &\vdots \end{aligned} \tag{10}$$

With these we write

$$\begin{aligned} \sin x &= 2 \sin \frac{x}{2} \cos \frac{x}{2} \\ &= 2^2 \sin \frac{x}{4} \cos \frac{x}{2} \cos \frac{x}{4} \\ &= 2^3 \sin \frac{x}{8} \cos \frac{x}{2} \cos \frac{x}{4} \cos \frac{x}{8} \\ &\vdots \end{aligned} \tag{11}$$

Then, by induction on n,

$$\sin x = 2^n \sin \left(\frac{x}{2^n}\right) \cos \frac{x}{2} \cos \frac{x}{4} \cdots \cos \left(\frac{x}{2^n}\right).$$

Hence,

$$\frac{\sin x}{x} = \frac{\sin (x/2^n)}{(x/2^n)} \cos \frac{x}{2} \cos \frac{x}{4} \cdots \cos \left(\frac{x}{2^n}\right). \tag{12}$$

When $n \to \infty$,

$$\frac{\sin (x/2^n)}{(x/2^n)} \to 1,$$

while the left side of Eq. (12) remains unchanged. Therefore,

$$\begin{aligned} \frac{\sin x}{x} &= \lim_{n \to \infty} \frac{\sin (x/2^n)}{(x/2^n)} \cos \frac{x}{2} \cos \frac{x}{4} \cdots \cos \frac{x}{2^n} \\ &= 1 \cdot \cos \frac{x}{2} \cos \frac{x}{4} \cos \frac{x}{8} \cos \frac{x}{16} \cdots \end{aligned} \tag{13}$$

Finally, substituting $x = \pi/2$ in Eq. (13) gives

$$\frac{2}{\pi} = \cos\frac{\pi}{4}\cos\frac{\pi}{8}\cos\frac{\pi}{16}\cos\frac{\pi}{32}\cdots \tag{14}$$

$$= \sqrt{\tfrac{1}{2}} \times \sqrt{\tfrac{1}{2}(1+\sqrt{\tfrac{1}{2}})} \times \sqrt{\tfrac{1}{2}(1+\sqrt{\tfrac{1}{2}(1+\sqrt{\tfrac{1}{2}})})} \times \cdots, \tag{15}$$

which is Viéta's formula. The law of formation on the right is

$$\cos\frac{\pi}{4} = \sqrt{\tfrac{1}{2}}, \qquad \cos\frac{\theta}{2} = \sqrt{\tfrac{1}{2}(1+\cos\theta)}.$$

Similarly, we could interpret the other formulas as expressing certain limits in terms of π. However, we now turn our attention to the series for $\tan^{-1} x$, since it leads to the Leibniz formula and others from which π has been computed to a great many decimal places.

Since

$$\tan^{-1} x = \int_0^x \frac{dt}{1+t^2},$$

we integrate the geometric series, with remainder,

$$\frac{1}{1+t^2} = 1 - t^2 + t^4 - t^6 + \cdots + (-1)^n t^{2n} + \frac{(-1)^{n+1}t^{2n+2}}{1+t^2}. \tag{16}$$

Thus

$$\tan^{-1} x = x - \frac{x^3}{3} + \frac{x^5}{5} - \frac{x^7}{7} + \cdots + (-1)^n \frac{x^{2n+1}}{2n+1} + R,$$

where

$$R = \int_0^x \frac{(-1)^{n+1}t^{2n+2}}{1+t^2}\,dt.$$

The denominator of the integrand is greater than or equal to 1; hence

$$|R| \le \int_0^{|x|} t^{2n+2}\,dt = \frac{|x|^{2n+3}}{2n+3}.$$

If $|x| \le 1$, the right side of this inequality approaches zero as $n \to \infty$. Therefore R also approaches zero and we have:

$$\tan^{-1} x = \sum_{n=0}^{\infty} \frac{(-1)^n x^{2n+1}}{2n+1},$$

or

$$\tan^{-1} x = x - \frac{x^3}{3} + \frac{x^5}{5} - \frac{x^7}{7} + \cdots, \quad |x| \le 1. \tag{17}$$

Various trigonometric identities are useful if one wishes to use Eq. (17) to calculate π. For example, if

$$\alpha = \tan^{-1}\tfrac{1}{2} \qquad \text{and} \qquad \beta = \tan^{-1}\tfrac{1}{3},$$

then

$$\tan(\alpha+\beta) = \frac{\tan\alpha + \tan\beta}{1 - \tan\alpha\tan\beta} = \frac{\tfrac{1}{2}+\tfrac{1}{3}}{1-\tfrac{1}{6}} = 1 = \tan\frac{\pi}{4}$$

and

$$\frac{\pi}{4} = \alpha + \beta = \tan^{-1} \tfrac{1}{2} + \tan^{-1} \tfrac{1}{3}. \tag{18}$$

Now Eq. (17) may be used with $x = \frac{1}{2}$ to evaluate $\tan^{-1} \frac{1}{2}$ and with $x = \frac{1}{3}$ to give $\tan^{-1} \frac{1}{3}$. The sum of these results, multiplied by 4, gives π.

In 1961, π was computed to more than 100,000 decimal places on an IBM 7090 computer. More recently, in 1973, Jean Guilloud and Martine Bouyer computed π to 1,000,000 decimal places on a CDC 7600 computer, by applying the arctangent series (17) to the formula

$$\pi = 48 \tan^{-1} \tfrac{1}{18} + 32 \tan^{-1} \tfrac{1}{57} - 20 \tan^{-1} \tfrac{1}{239}. \tag{19}$$

They checked their work with the formula

$$\pi = 24 \tan^{-1} \tfrac{1}{8} + 8 \tan^{-1} \tfrac{1}{57} + 4 \tan^{-1} \tfrac{1}{239}. \tag{20}$$

A number of current computations of π are being carried out with an algorithm discovered by Eugene Salamin (Problem 17). The algorithm produces sequences that converge to π even more rapidly than the sequence of partial sums of the arctangent series in Eqs. (19) and (20). [For a delightful account of attempts to compute, and even to *legislate*(*!*) the value of π, see Chapter 12 of David A. Smith's *Interface: Calculus and the Computer*, Houghton Mifflin Company, Boston, MA, 1976.]

REMARK. Two types of numerical error tend to occur in computing with series. One is the *truncation error*, which is the remainder $R_n(x, a)$ and consists of the sum of the infinite number of terms in the series that follow the term $(x - a)^n f^{(n)}(a)/n!$. This is the only error we have discussed so far.

The other is the *round-off error* that enters in calculating the sum of the finite number of terms

$$f(a) + f'(a)(x - a) + \cdots + \frac{f^{(n)}(a)(x - a)^n}{n!}$$

when we approximate each of these terms by a decimal number with only a finite number of decimal places. For example, taking 0.3333 in place of $\frac{1}{3}$ introduces a round-off error equal to $10^{-4}/3$. There are likely to be round-off errors associated with each term, some of these being positive and some negative. When the need for accuracy is paramount, it is important to control both the truncation error and the round-off errors. *Truncation* errors can be reduced by taking more terms of the series; *round-off* errors can be reduced by taking more decimal places.

PROBLEMS

In each of Problems 1 through 6, use a suitable series to calculate the indicated quantity to three decimal places. In each case, show that the remainder term does not exceed 5×10^{-4}.

1. $\cos 31°$

2. $\tan 46°$

3. $\sin 6.3$

4. $\cos 69$

5. $\ln 1.25$

6. $\tan^{-1} 1.02$

7. Find the Maclaurin series for $\ln(1 + 2x)$. For what values of x does the series converge?

8. For what values of x can one replace $\ln(1 + x)$ by x with an error of magnitude no greater than one percent of the absolute value of x?

Use series to evaluate the integrals in Problems 9 and 10 to three decimals.

9. $\int_0^{0.1} \frac{\sin x}{x}\,dx$ **10.** $\int_0^{0.1} e^{-x^2}\,dx$

11. Show that the ordinate of the catenary $y = a \cosh x/a$ deviates from the ordinate of the parabola $x^2 = 2a(y - a)$ by less than $0.003|a|$ over the range $|x/a| \le \frac{1}{3}$.

12. Construct a table of natural logarithms $\ln N$ for $N = 1, 2, 3, \ldots, 10$ by the method discussed in connection with Eq. (9), but taking advantage of the relationships

$$\ln 4 = 2 \ln 2, \qquad \ln 6 = \ln 2 + \ln 3, \qquad \ln 8 = 3 \ln 2,$$

$$\ln 9 = 2 \ln 3, \qquad \ln 10 = \ln 2 + \ln 5$$

to reduce the job to the calculation of relatively few logarithms by series. In fact, you may use ln 2 as given in the text and calculate $\ln \frac{3}{2}$, $\ln \frac{5}{4}$, and $\ln \frac{7}{6}$ by series, and then combine these in suitable ways to get the logarithms of numbers N from 1 to 10.

13. Find the sum of the series

$$\tfrac{1}{2} - \tfrac{1}{2}(\tfrac{1}{2})^2 + \tfrac{1}{3}(\tfrac{1}{2})^3 - \tfrac{1}{4}(\tfrac{1}{2})^4 + \cdots$$

14. How many terms of the series for $\tan^{-1} 1$ would you have to add for the Alternating Series Estimation Theorem to guarantee a calculation of $\pi/4$ to two decimals?

15. (*Calculator*) Equations (17) and (19) yield a series that converges to $\pi/4$ fairly rapidly. Estimate π to three decimal places with this series. In contrast, the convergence of $\sum_{n=1}^{\infty} (1/n^2)$ to $\pi^2/6$ is so slow that even fifty terms will not yield two-place accuracy.

16. (*Calculator*) (a) Find π to two decimals with the formulas of Lord Brouncker and Wallis. (b) If your calculator is programmable, use Viéta's formula, Eqs. (14) or (15), to calculate π to five decimal places.

17. (*Calculator*) A special case of Salamin's algorithm for estimating π begins with defining sequences $\{a_n\}$ and $\{b_n\}$ by the rules

$$a_0 = 1, \qquad b_0 = \frac{1}{\sqrt{2}},$$

$$a_{n+1} = \frac{(a_n + b_n)}{2}, \qquad b_{n+1} = \sqrt{a_n b_n}.$$

Then the sequence $\{c_n\}$ defined by

$$c_n = \frac{4a_n b_n}{1 - \sum_{j=1}^{n} 2^{j+1}(a_j^2 - b_j^2)}$$

converges to π. Calculate c_3. (E. Salamin, "Computation of π using arithmetic–geometric mean," *Mathematics of Computation*, **30**, July, 1976, pp. 565–570.)

18. Show that the series in Eq. (17) for $\tan^{-1} x$ diverges for $|x| > 1$.

19. Show that

$$\int_0^x \frac{dt}{1 - t^2} = \int_0^x \left(1 + t^2 + t^4 + \cdots + t^{2n} + \frac{t^{2n+2}}{1 - t^2}\right) dt$$

or, in other words, that

$$\tanh^{-1} x = x + \frac{x^3}{3} + \frac{x^5}{5} + \cdots + \frac{x^{2n+1}}{2n+1} + R,$$

where

$$R = \int_0^x \frac{t^{2n+2}}{1 - t^2}\,dt.$$

20. Show that R in Problem 19 is no greater than

$$\frac{1}{1 - x^2} \cdot \frac{|x|^{2n+3}}{2n+3}, \qquad \text{if } x^2 < 1.$$

21. a) Differentiate the identity

$$\frac{1}{1 - x} = 1 + x + x^2 + \cdots + x^n + \frac{x^{n+1}}{1 - x}$$

to obtain the expansion

$$\frac{1}{(1 - x)^2} = 1 + 2x + 3x^2 + \cdots + nx^{n-1} + R.$$

b) Prove that, if $|x| < 1$, then $R \to 0$ as $n \to \infty$.

c) In one throw of two dice, the probability of getting a score of 7 is $p = \frac{1}{6}$. If the dice are thrown repeatedly, the probability that a 7 will appear for the first time at the nth throw is $q^{n-1}p$, where $q = 1 - p = \frac{5}{6}$. The expected number of throws until a 7 first appears is $\sum_{n=1}^{\infty} nq^{n-1}p$. Evaluate this series numerically.

d) In applying statistical quality control to an industrial operation, an engineer inspects items taken at random from the assembly line. Each item sampled is classified as "good" or "bad." If the probability of a good item is p and of a bad item is $q = 1 - p$, the probability that the first bad item found is the nth inspected is $p^{n-1}q$. The average number inspected up to and including the first bad item found is $\sum_{n=1}^{\infty} np^{n-1}q$. Evaluate this series, assuming $0 < p < 1$.

22. In probability theory, a random variable X may assume the values $1, 2, 3, \ldots$, with probabilities $p_1, p_2, p_3, \ldots$, where p_k is the probability that X is equal to k $(k = 1, 2, \ldots)$. It is customary to assume $p_k \ge 0$ and $\sum_{k=1}^{\infty} p_k = 1$. The *expected value* of X denoted by $E(X)$ is defined as $\sum_{k=1}^{\infty} kp_k$, provided this series converges. In each of the following cases, show that $\sum p_k = 1$ and find $E(X)$, if it exists. [*Hint.* See Problem 21.]

a) $p_k = 2^{-k}$ **b)** $p_k = \frac{5^{k-1}}{6^k}$

c) $p_k = \frac{1}{k(k+1)} = \frac{1}{k} - \frac{1}{k+1}$

*16–11 A SECOND DERIVATIVE TEST FOR MAXIMA AND MINIMA OF FUNCTIONS OF TWO INDEPENDENT VARIABLES

In this article we apply Taylor's theorem to study the behavior of a function

$$w = f(x, y)$$

when the point (x, y) is close to a point (a, b) where the first-order partial derivatives vanish,

$$f_x(a, b) = f_y(a, b) = 0. \tag{1}$$

We shall assume that w and its first- and second-order partial derivatives are continuous throughout some neighborhood G of the point $P(a, b)$, Fig. 16–18. In the discussion that follows, a, b, h, and k are held fixed. In addition, h and k are to be small, so that the point $Q(a + h, b + k)$ together with all points

$$x = a + ht, \qquad y = b + kt, \qquad 0 \le t \le 1, \tag{2}$$

on the line PQ also lie in G. We consider the values of $w = f(x, y)$ along the line PQ of Eq. (2) as t varies from 0 to 1. Thus, if we let

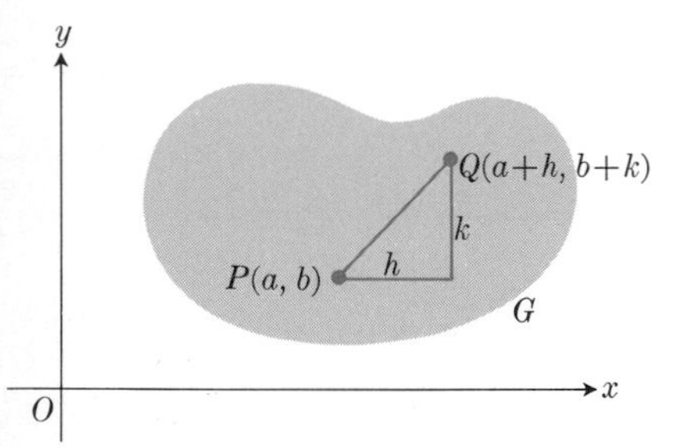

16–18 A neighborhood G of the point $P(a, b)$.

$$F(t) = f(a + ht, b + kt), \tag{3}$$

we have

$$F(0) = f(a, b) \qquad \text{when} \quad t = 0,$$
$$F(1) = f(a + h, b + k) \qquad \text{when} \quad t = 1.$$

Now, by Taylor's theorem, we have

$$F(t) = F(0) + tF'(0) + \frac{t^2}{2!}F''(t_1),$$

where t_1 is between 0 and t. In particular, taking $t = 1$,

$$F(1) = F(0) + F'(0) + \tfrac{1}{2}F''(t_1), \tag{4}$$

with $0 < t_1 < 1$.

The derivatives in Eq. (4) may be calculated from (3) by the chain rule for partial derivatives. First of all,

$$F'(t) = \frac{\partial f}{\partial x}\frac{dx}{dt} + \frac{\partial f}{\partial y}\frac{dy}{dt}.$$

Then, since

$$\frac{dx}{dt} = h, \qquad \frac{dy}{dt} = k,$$

from Eq. (2), we have

$$F'(t) = h\frac{\partial f}{\partial x} + k\frac{\partial f}{\partial y}. \tag{5}$$

The chain rule may be applied again to calculate

$$F''(t) = h\frac{\partial F'(t)}{\partial x} + k\frac{\partial F'(t)}{\partial y}, \tag{6}$$

where we have used the brackets to indicate the expression on the right side of Eq. (5); that is,

$$\frac{\partial F'(t)}{\partial x} = h\frac{\partial^2 f}{\partial x^2} + k\frac{\partial^2 f}{\partial x\,\partial y}, \tag{7}$$

$$\frac{\partial F'(t)}{\partial y} = h\frac{\partial^2 f}{\partial y\,\partial x} + k\frac{\partial^2 f}{\partial y^2}.$$

When we substitute from (7) into (6), and collect terms, we have

$$F''(t) = h^2\frac{\partial^2 f}{\partial x^2} + 2hk\frac{\partial^2 f}{\partial x\,\partial y} + k^2\frac{\partial^2 f}{\partial y^2}. \tag{8}$$

Equation (5) may be interpreted as saying that applying d/dt to $F(t)$ gives the same result as applying

$$\left(h\frac{\partial}{\partial x} + k\frac{\partial}{\partial y}\right)$$

to $f(x, y)$. Similarly, Eq. (8) says that applying d^2/dt^2 to $F(t)$ gives the same result as applying

$$\left(h\frac{\partial}{\partial x} + k\frac{\partial}{\partial y}\right)^2 = h^2\frac{\partial^2}{\partial x^2} + 2hk\frac{\partial^2}{\partial x\,\partial y} + k^2\frac{\partial^2}{\partial y^2}$$

to $f(x, y)$. These are the first two instances of a more general formula that says that

$$F^{(n)}(t) = \frac{d^n}{dt^n}F(t) = \left(h\frac{\partial}{\partial x} + k\frac{\partial}{\partial y}\right)^n f(x, y), \tag{9}$$

where the term in parentheses on the right is to be expanded by the binomial theorem and then applied term by term to $f(x, y)$.

If we now take $t = 0$ in Eq. (5) and $t = t_1$ in Eq. (8) and substitute the results into Eq. (4), we obtain

$$\begin{aligned} f(a + h, b + k) &= f(a, b) + (hf_x + kf_y)_{(a,b)} \\ &\quad + \tfrac{1}{2}(h^2 f_{xx} + 2hkf_{xy} + k^2 f_{yy})_{(a+t_1h,\,b+t_1k)}. \end{aligned} \tag{10}$$

If we extend the Maclaurin series for $F(t)$ to more terms,

$$F(t) = F(0) + F'(0)\cdot t + \frac{F''(0)}{2!}t^2 + \cdots + \frac{F^{(n)}(0)}{n!}t^n + \cdots,$$

and then take $t = 1$, we obtain

$$F(1) = F(0) + F'(0) + \frac{F''(0)}{2!} + \cdots + \frac{F^{(n)}(0)}{n!} + \cdots.$$

Finally, when we replace each derivative on the right of this last series by its equivalent expression from Eq. (9) evaluated at $t = 0$, and expand each term by the binomial theorem, we arrive at the following formula:

$$
\begin{aligned}
f(a+h, b+k) = f(a, b) &+ (hf_x + kf_y)_{(a,b)} \\
&+ \frac{1}{2!}(h^2 f_{xx} + 2hkf_{xy} + k^2 f_{yy})_{(a,b)} \\
&+ \frac{1}{3!}(h^3 f_{xxx} + 3h^2 k f_{xxy} + 3hk^2 f_{xyy} + k^3 f_{yyy})_{(a,b)} \\
&+ \cdots \\
&+ \frac{1}{n!}\left[\left(h\frac{\partial}{\partial x} + k\frac{\partial}{\partial y}\right)^n f\right]_{(a,b)} + \cdots
\end{aligned}
\tag{11}
$$

This expresses the value of the function $f(x, y)$ at $x = a + h$, $y = b + k$, in terms of the values of the function and its partial derivatives at (a, b), and powers of $h = x - a$ and $k = y - b$. This is the Taylor series expansion, about the point (a, b), of the function $f(x, y)$. Analogous formulas hold for functions of more independent variables.

Suppose, now, that we have found a point (a, b) where the first-order derivatives f_x and f_y are both zero, and we wish to determine whether the function $w = f(x, y)$ has a maximum or a minimum at (a, b). We may then rewrite Eq. (10) in the form

$$
\begin{aligned}
f(a+h, b+k) - f(a, b) &= \tfrac{1}{2}(h^2 f_{xx} + 2hkf_{xy} + k^2 f_{yy})_{(a+t_1h, b+t_1k)} \\
&= \phi(t_1).
\end{aligned}
$$

Since a maximum or minimum value of w at (a, b) is reflected in the sign of $\phi(t_1)$, we are led to a consideration of the sign of $\phi(t)$. The second-order derivatives that enter this expression are to be evaluated at a point on the line segment PQ (Fig. 16–18). This is not convenient for our purposes, since we do not know precisely where to take this point; that is, we do not know anything more about t_1 than that $0 \le t_1 \le 1$. However, since we are assuming that f_{xx}, f_{xy}, and f_{yy} are *continuous* throughout the region G, and since both h and k are assumed to be *small*, the values of these derivatives at $(a + t_1 h, b + t_1 k)$ are nearly the same as their values at (a, b). In particular, the *sign* of $\phi(t_1)$ is the same, for sufficiently small values of h and k, as the sign of

$$\phi(0) = h^2 f_{xx}(a, b) + 2hkf_{xy}(a, b) + k^2 f_{yy}(a, b). \tag{12}$$

We therefore have the following criteria:

Sufficient Conditions for Maxima, Minima, and Saddle Points

Let

$$\phi(0) = h^2 f_{xx}(a, b) + 2hkf_{xy}(a, b) + k^2 f_{yy}(a, b).$$

Then,

1. $f(x, y)$ has a relative *minimum* at (a, b) provided $f_x(a, b) = f_y(a, b) = 0$, and $\phi(0)$ is *positive* for all sufficiently small values of h and k (excluding, of course, the case where $h = k = 0$).

2. $f(x, y)$ has a relative *maximum* at (a, b) provided $f_x(a, b) = f_y(a, b) = 0$ and $\phi(0)$ is *negative* for all sufficiently small values of h and k (again excluding $h = k = 0$).

3. $f(x, y)$ has a *saddle point* at (a, b) provided $f_x(a, b) = f_y(a, b) = 0$, and every neighborhood of (a, b) contains points $(a + h, b + k)$ at which $\phi(0)$ is positive and points $(a + h, b + k)$ at which $\phi(0)$ is negative.

See Problems 1 and 9.

EXAMPLE. The function

$$f(x, y) = x^2 + xy + y^2 + x - 4y + 5$$

has partial derivatives

$$f_x = 2x + y + 1,$$
$$f_y = x + 2y - 4,$$

which vanish at $(-2, 3)$. The second partial derivatives are all constant:

$$f_{xx} = 2, \qquad f_{xy} = 1, \qquad f_{yy} = 2,$$

and the expression whose sign determines whether f has a maximum, a minimum, or a saddle point at $(-2, 3)$ is

$$2h^2 + 2hk + 2k^2.$$

If we multiply this by 2, we have

$$4h^2 + 4hk + 4k^2 = (2h + k)^2 + 3k^2,$$

which is the sum of two nonnegative terms and is zero only when $h = k = 0$. Hence, the function has a relative *minimum* at $(-2, 3)$. In fact, this is its absolute minimum, since

$$f(-2 + h, 3 + k) \geq f(-2, 3)$$

for *all* h and k.

PROBLEMS

1. a) Let $A = f_{xx}(a, b)$, $B = f_{xy}(a, b)$, $C = f_{yy}(a, b)$ and show that the expression for $\phi(0)$ in Eq. (12), when multiplied by A, becomes the same as

$$A\phi(0) = (Ah + Bk)^2 + (AC - B^2)k^2.$$

b) Suppose $f_x(a, b) = f_y(a, b) = 0$ and $A \neq 0$. Use the result of part (a), and the three conditions that follow Eq. (12), to show that $f(x, y)$ has at (a, b):

i) a relative minimum if $AC - B^2 > 0$ and $A > 0$,
ii) a relative maximum if $AC - B^2 > 0$ and $A < 0$,
iii) a saddle point if $AC - B^2 < 0$.

Test the following surfaces for maxima, minima, and saddle points.

2. $z = x^2 + y^2 - 2x + 4y + 6$

3. $z = x^2 - y^2 - 2x + 4y + 6$

4. $z = x^2 - 2xy + 2y^2 - 2x + 2y + 1$

5. $z = x^2 + 2xy$

6. $z = 3 + 2x + 2y - 2x^2 - 2xy - y^2$

7. $z = x^3 - y^3 - 2xy + 6$

8. $z = x^3 + y^3 + 3x^2 - 3y^2 - 8$

9. In Eq. (12), let

$$h = c \cos \alpha, \qquad k = c \sin \alpha, \qquad c > 0,$$

and show that $\phi(0) = c^2(d^2f/ds^2)$, where d^2f/ds^2 is the second-order directional derivative of f at (a, b) in the direction of the unit vector $\mathbf{u} = \mathbf{i} \cos \alpha + \mathbf{j} \sin \alpha$. Express the three criteria for maxima, minima, and saddle points at the end of Article 16–11 in terms of d^2f/ds^2. [Similar criteria also apply in higher-dimensional problems.]

10. (a) Taking $a + h = x$, $b + k = y$, and $a = b = 0$ in Eq. (11), obtain the series through the terms of second degree in x and y, for the function $f(x, y) = e^x \cos y$. (b) Obtain the series for part (a) more simply by multiplication of the series for e^x by the series for $\cos y$.

11. Write out explicitly, through the terms of second degree, the Taylor series for a function $f(x, y, z)$, in powers of

$$(x - a), \qquad (y - b), \qquad (z - c),$$

and the values of f and its partial derivatives at (a, b, c).

16–12 INDETERMINATE FORMS

In considering the ratio of two functions $f(x)$ and $g(x)$, we sometimes wish to know the value

$$\lim_{x \to a} \frac{f(x)}{g(x)} \tag{1}$$

at a point a where $f(x)$ and $g(x)$ are both zero. L'Hôpital's rule is often a help, but the differentiation involved can be time-consuming, especially if the rule has to be applied several times to reach a determinate form. In many instances, the limit in (1) can be calculated more quickly if the functions involved have power series expansions about $x = a$. In fact, the ease and reliability of the kind of calculation we are about to illustrate contributed to the early popularity of power series. The theoretical justification of the technique is too long to discuss here, but the formal manipulations are worth learning by themselves.

Suppose, then, that the functions f and g both have series expansions in powers of $x - a$,

$$f(x) = f(a) + f'(a) \cdot (x - a) + \frac{f''(a)}{2!}(x - a)^2 + \cdots, \tag{2a}$$

$$g(x) = g(a) + g'(a) \cdot (x - a) + \frac{g''(a)}{2!}(x - a)^2 + \cdots, \tag{2b}$$

that are known to us and that converge in some interval $|x - a| < \delta$. We then proceed to calculate the limit (1), provided the limit exists, in the manner shown by the following examples.

EXAMPLE 1. Evaluate $\lim_{x \to 1} [(\ln x)/(x - 1)]$.

Solution. Let $f(x) = \ln x$, $g(x) = x - 1$. The Taylor series for $f(x)$, with $a = 1$, is found as follows:

$$f(x) = \ln x, \qquad f(1) = \ln 1 = 0,$$

$$f'(x) = 1/x, \qquad f'(1) = 1,$$

$$f''(x) = -1/x^2, \qquad f''(1) = -1,$$

so that

$$\ln x = 0 + (x - 1) - \tfrac{1}{2}(x - 1)^2 + \cdots$$

Hence

$$\frac{\ln x}{x - 1} = 1 - \tfrac{1}{2}(x - 1) + \cdots$$

and

$$\lim_{x\to 1} \frac{\ln x}{x-1} = \lim_{x\to 1} [1 - \tfrac{1}{2}(x-1) + \cdots] = 1.$$

EXAMPLE 2. Evaluate $\lim_{x\to 0} [(\sin x - \tan x)/x^3]$.

Solution. The Maclaurin series for sin x and tan x, to terms in x^5, are

$$\sin x = x - \frac{x^3}{3!} + \frac{x^5}{5!} - \cdots,$$

$$\tan x = x + \frac{x^3}{3} + \frac{2x^5}{15} + \cdots$$

Hence

$$\sin x - \tan x = -\frac{x^3}{2} - \frac{x^5}{8} - \cdots$$

$$= x^3\left(-\frac{1}{2} - \frac{x^2}{8} - \cdots\right),$$

and

$$\lim_{x\to 0} \frac{\sin x - \tan x}{x^3} = \lim_{x\to 0} \left(-\frac{1}{2} - \frac{x^2}{8} - \cdots\right) = -\frac{1}{2}.$$

When we apply series to compute the limit $\lim_{x\to 0} (1/\sin x - 1/x)$ of Example 7, Article 3–9, we not only compute the limit successfully, but also discover a nice approximation formula for csc x.

EXAMPLE 3. Find

$$\lim_{x\to 0} \left(\frac{1}{\sin x} - \frac{1}{x}\right).$$

Solution

$$\frac{1}{\sin x} - \frac{1}{x} = \frac{x - \sin x}{x \sin x} = \frac{x - \left[x - \frac{x^3}{3!} + \frac{x^5}{5!} - \cdots\right]}{x \cdot \left[x - \frac{x^3}{3!} + \frac{x^5}{5!} - \cdots\right]}$$

$$= \frac{x^3\left[\frac{1}{3!} - \frac{x^2}{5!} + \cdots\right]}{x^2\left[1 - \frac{x^2}{3!} + \cdots\right]} = x\,\frac{\frac{1}{3!} - \frac{x^2}{5!} + \cdots}{1 - \frac{x^2}{3!} + \cdots}.$$

Therefore,

$$\lim_{x\to 0} \left(\frac{1}{\sin x} - \frac{1}{x}\right) = \lim_{x\to 0} \left[x\,\frac{\frac{1}{3!} - \frac{x^2}{5!} + \cdots}{1 - \frac{x^2}{3!} + \cdots}\right] = 0.$$

In fact, from the series expressions above we can see that if $|x|$ is small, then

$$\frac{1}{\sin x} - \frac{1}{x} \approx x \cdot \frac{1}{3!} = \frac{x}{6}$$

or

$$\csc x \approx \frac{1}{x} + \frac{x}{6}.$$

PROBLEMS

Use series to evaluate the limits in Problems 1 through 20.

1. $\lim_{h\to 0} \frac{\sin h}{h}$

2. $\lim_{x\to 0} \frac{e^x - (1+x)}{x^2}$

3. $\lim_{t\to 0} \frac{1-\cos t - \frac{1}{2}t^2}{t^4}$

4. $\lim_{x\to\infty} x \sin \frac{1}{x}$

5. $\lim_{x\to 0} \frac{x^2}{1-\cosh x}$

6. $\lim_{h\to 0} \frac{(\sin h)/h - \cos h}{h^2}$

7. $\lim_{x\to 0} \frac{1-\cos x}{\sin x}$

8. $\lim_{x\to 0} \frac{\sin x}{e^x - 1}$

9. $\lim_{z\to 0} \frac{\sin(z^2) - \sinh(z^2)}{z^6}$

10. $\lim_{t\to 0} \frac{\cos t - \cosh t}{t^2}$

11. $\lim_{x\to 0} \frac{\sin x - x + \frac{x^3}{6}}{x^5}$

12. $\lim_{x\to 0} \frac{e^x - e^{-x} - 2x}{x - \sin x}$

13. $\lim_{x\to 0} \frac{x - \tan^{-1} x}{x^3}$

14. $\lim_{x\to 0} \frac{\tan x - \sin x}{x^3 \cos x}$

15. $\lim_{x\to\infty} x^2(e^{-1/x^2} - 1)$

16. $\lim_{x\to 0} \frac{\ln(1+x^2)}{1-\cos x}$

17. $\lim_{x\to 0} \frac{\tan 3x}{x}$

18. $\lim_{x\to 1} \frac{\ln x^2}{x-1}$

19. $\lim_{x\to\infty} \frac{x^{100}}{e^x}$

20. $\lim_{x\to 0} \left(\frac{1}{2-2\cos x} - \frac{1}{x^2}\right)$

21. **a)** Prove that $\int_0^x e^{t^2}\,dt \to +\infty$ as $x \to +\infty$.
b) Find $\lim_{x\to\infty} x \int_0^x e^{t^2 - x^2}\,dt$

22. Find values of r and s such that

$$\lim_{x\to 0} (x^{-3} \sin 3x + rx^{-2} + s) = 0.$$

23. (*Calculator*) The approximation for csc x in Example 3 leads to the approximation $\sin x \approx 6x/(6+x^2)$. Evaluate both sides of this approximation for $x = \pm 1.0$, ± 0.1, and ± 0.01 radians. Try these values of x in the approximation $\sin x \approx x$. Which approximation appears to give better results?

16–13 CONVERGENCE OF POWER SERIES; INTEGRATION AND DIFFERENTIATION

We now know that some power series, like the Maclaurin series for $\sin x$, $\cos x$, and e^x, converge for all values of x, while others, like the series we derived for $\ln(1+x)$ and $\tan^{-1} x$, converge only on finite intervals. But we learned all this by analyzing remainder formulas, and we have yet to face the question of how to investigate the convergence of a power series when there is no remainder formula to analyze. Moreover, all of the power series we have worked with have been Taylor series of functions for which we already had expressions in closed forms. What about other power series? Are they Taylor series, too, of functions otherwise unknown?

The first step in answering these questions is to note that a power series $\sum_{n=0}^{\infty} a_n x^n$ defines a function whenever it converges, namely, the function f whose value at each x is the number

$$f(x) = \sum_{n=0}^{\infty} a_n x^n. \tag{1}$$

We can then ask what kind of domain f has, how f is to be differentiated and integrated (if at all), whether f has a Taylor series, and, if it has, how its Taylor series is related to the defining series $\sum_{n=0}^{\infty} a_n x^n$.

The questions of what domain f has, and for what values the series (1) may be expected to converge, are answered by Theorem 1 and the discussion that follows it. We will prove Theorem 1, and then, after looking at examples, will proceed to Theorems 2 and 3, which answer the questions of whether f *can* be differentiated and integrated and *how* to do so when it can be. Theorem 3 also solves a problem that arose many chapters ago but that has remained unsolved until now: that of finding convenient expressions for evaluating integrals like

$$\int_0^1 \sin x^2\, dx \qquad \text{and} \qquad \int_0^{0.5} \sqrt{1 + x^4}\, dx,$$

which frequently arise in applications. Finally, we will see that, in the interior of its domain of definition, the function f does have a Maclaurin series, and that this is none other than the defining series $\sum_{n=0}^{\infty} a_n x^n$.

Theorem 1. The convergence theorem for power series. *If a power series*

$$\sum_{n=0}^{\infty} a_n x^n = a_0 + a_1 x + a_2 x^2 + \cdots \tag{2}$$

converges for $x = c$ ($c \neq 0$), then it converges absolutely for all $|x| < |c|$. If the series diverges for $x = d$, then it diverges for all $|x| > |d|$.

Proof. Suppose the series

$$\sum_{n=0}^{\infty} a_n c^n \tag{3}$$

converges. Then

$$\lim_{n \to \infty} a_n c^n = 0.$$

Hence, there is an index N such that

$$|a_n c^n| < 1 \qquad \text{for all} \quad n \geq N.$$

That is,

$$|a_n| < \frac{1}{|c|^n} \qquad \text{for} \quad n \geq N. \tag{4}$$

Now take any x such that $|x| < |c|$ and consider

$$|a_0| + |a_1 x| + \cdots + |a_{N-1} x^{N-1}| + |a_N x^N| + |a_{N+1} x^{N+1}| + \cdots$$

There is only a finite number of terms prior to $|a_N x^N|$ and their sum is finite. Starting with $|a_N x^N|$ and beyond, the terms are less than

$$\left|\frac{x}{c}\right|^N + \left|\frac{x}{c}\right|^{N+1} + \left|\frac{x}{c}\right|^{N+2} + \cdots \tag{5}$$

by virtue of the inequality (4). But the series in (5) is a geometric series with ratio $r = |x/c|$, which is less than one, since $|x| < |c|$. Hence the series (5) converges, so that the original series (3) converges absolutely. This proves the first half of the theorem.

The second half of the theorem involves nothing new. For if the series diverges at $x = d$ and converges at a value x_0 with $|x_0| > |d|$, we may take $c = x_0$ in the first half of the theorem and conclude that the series converges absolutely at d. But the series cannot both converge absolutely and diverge at one and the same time. Hence, if it diverges at d, it diverges for all $|x| > |d|$. Q.E.D.

The significance of Theorem 1 is that a power series always behaves in exactly *one* of the following ways. (See Fig. 16–19.)

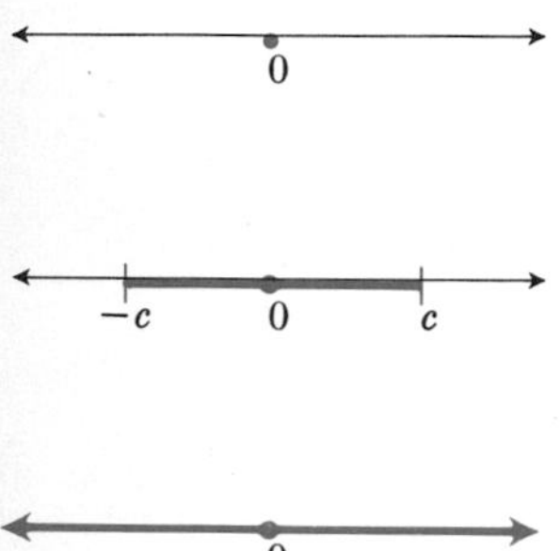

Figure 16–19

1. It converges at $x = 0$ and diverges everywhere else.

2. There is a positive number c such that the series diverges for $|x| > c$ but converges absolutely for $|x| < c$. It may or may not converge at either of the endpoints $x = c$ and $x = -c$.

3. It converges absolutely for every x.

In Case 2, the set of points at which the series converges is a finite interval. We know from past examples that this interval may be open, half open, or closed, depending on the series in question. But no matter which kind of interval it is, c is called the *radius of convergence* of the series, and the convergence is absolute at every point in the interior of the interval. The interval is called the *interval of convergence*. If a power series converges absolutely for all values of x, we say that its radius of convergence is infinite. If it converges only at $x = 0$, we say that its radius of convergence is 0.

As examples of power series whose radii of convergence are infinite, we have the Taylor series of $\sin x$, $\cos x$, and e^x. These series converge for every value of $c = 2x$, and therefore converge absolutely for every value of x.

As examples of series whose radii of convergence are finite we have:

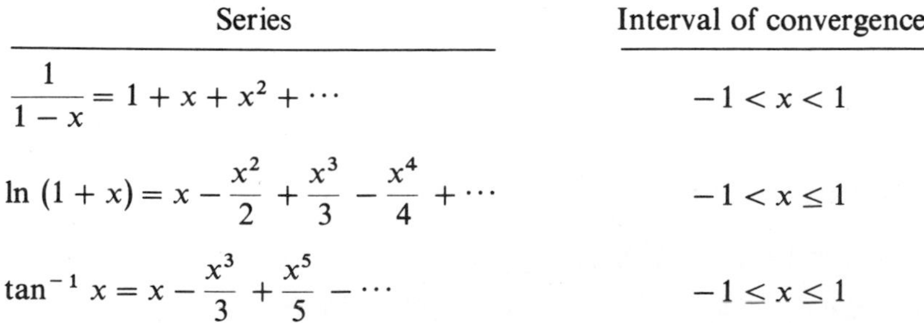

Series	Interval of convergence
$\dfrac{1}{1-x} = 1 + x + x^2 + \cdots$	$-1 < x < 1$
$\ln(1+x) = x - \dfrac{x^2}{2} + \dfrac{x^3}{3} - \dfrac{x^4}{4} + \cdots$	$-1 < x \leq 1$
$\tan^{-1} x = x - \dfrac{x^3}{3} + \dfrac{x^5}{5} - \cdots$	$-1 \leq x \leq 1$

The interval of convergence of a power series

$$\sum_{n=0}^{\infty} a_n x^n$$

can often be found by applying the ratio test or the root test to the series of absolute values,

$$\sum_{n=0}^{\infty} |a_n x^n|.$$

Thus, if

$$\rho = \lim_{n\to\infty} \left| \frac{a_{n+1}x^{n+1}}{a_n x^n} \right|$$

or if

$$\rho = \lim_{n\to\infty} \sqrt[n]{|a_n x^n|},$$

then,

a) $\sum |a_n x^n|$ converges at all values of x for which $\rho < 1$;

b) $\sum |a_n x^n|$ diverges at all values of x for which $\rho > 1$;

c) $\sum |a_n x^n|$ may either converge or diverge at a value of x for which $\rho = 1$.

How do these three alternatives translate into statements about the series $\sum a_n x^n$? Case (a) says that $\sum a_n x^n$ converges absolutely at all values of x for which $\rho < 1$. Case (c) does not tell us anything more about the series $\sum a_n x^n$ than it does about the series $\sum |a_n x^n|$. Either series might converge or diverge at a value of x for which $\rho = 1$. In Case (b), we can actually conclude that $\sum a_n x^n$ diverges at all values of x for which $\rho > 1$. The argument goes like this: As you may recall from the discussions in Article 16–5, the fact that ρ is greater than 1 means that either

$$0 < |a_n x^n| < |a_{n+1}x^{n+1}| < |a_{n+2}x^{n+2}| < \cdots$$

or

$$\sqrt[n]{|a_n x^n|} > 1$$

for n sufficiently large. Thus the terms of the series do not approach 0 as n becomes infinite, and the series diverges *with or without absolute values*, by the nth-term test.

Therefore, the ratio and root tests, when successfully applied to $\sum |a_n x^n|$, lead us to the following conclusions about $\sum a_n x^n$:

A) $\sum a_n x^n$ converges absolutely for all values of x for which $\rho < 1$;

B) $\sum a_n x^n$ diverges at all values of x for which $\rho > 1$;

C) $\sum a_n x^n$ may either converge or diverge at a value of x for which $\rho = 1$. Another test is needed.

EXAMPLE 1. Find the interval of convergence of

$$\sum_{n=1}^{\infty} \frac{x^n}{n}. \tag{6}$$

Solution. We apply the ratio test to the series of absolute values, and find

$$\rho = \lim_{n\to\infty} \left| \frac{x^{n+1}}{n+1} \cdot \frac{n}{x^n} \right| = |x|.$$

Therefore the original series converges absolutely if $|x| < 1$ and diverges if $|x| > 1$. When $x = +1$, the series becomes

$$1 + \tfrac{1}{2} + \tfrac{1}{3} + \tfrac{1}{4} + \cdots,$$

which diverges. When $x = -1$, the series becomes

$$-(1 - \tfrac{1}{2} + \tfrac{1}{3} - \tfrac{1}{4} + \cdots),$$

which converges, by Leibnitz's Theorem. Therefore the series (6) converges for $-1 \le x < 1$ and diverges for all other values of x.

EXAMPLE 2. For what values of x does the series

$$\sum_{n=1}^{\infty} \frac{(2x-5)^n}{n^2}$$

converge?

Solution. We treat the series as a power series in the variable $2x - 5$. An application of the root test to the series of absolute values yields

$$\rho = \lim_{n\to\infty} \sqrt[n]{\left|\frac{(2x-5)^n}{n^2}\right|} = \lim_{n\to\infty} \frac{|2x-5|}{\sqrt[n]{n^2}} = \frac{|2x-5|}{1} = |2x-5|.$$

The series converges absolutely for

$$|2x-5| < 1 \qquad \text{or} \qquad -1 < 2x - 5 < 1$$

or

$$4 < 2x < 6 \qquad \text{or} \qquad 2 < x < 3.$$

When $x = 2$, the series is $\sum_{n=1}^{\infty} [(-1)^n/n^2]$, which converges.

When $x = 3$, the series is $\sum_{n=1}^{\infty} [(1)^n/n^2]$, which converges. Therefore, the interval of convergence is $2 \le x \le 3$.

Sometimes the comparison test does as well as any.

EXAMPLE 3. For what values of x does

$$\sum_{n=1}^{\infty} \frac{\cos^n x}{n!}$$

converge?

Solution. For every value of x,

$$\left|\frac{\cos^n x}{n!}\right| \le \frac{1}{n!}.$$

The series converges for every value of x.

The next theorem says that a function defined by a power series has derivatives of all orders at every point in the interior of its interval of convergence. The derivatives can be obtained as power series by differentiating the terms of the original series. The first derivative is obtained by differentiating the terms of the original series once:

$$\frac{d}{dx}\sum_{n=0}^{\infty}(a_n x^n)=\sum_{n=0}^{\infty}\frac{d}{dx}(a_n x^n)=\sum_{n=0}^{\infty} n a_n x^{n-1}.$$

For the second derivative, the terms are differentiated again, and so on. We state the theorem without proof, and go directly to the examples.

***Theorem* 2.** The term-by-term differentiation theorem. *If* $f(x)=\sum_{n=0}^{\infty} a_n x^n$ *converges on the open interval* $(-c, c)$, *then,*

1. $\sum_{n=0}^{\infty} n a_n x^{n-1}$ *converges on* $(-c, c)$;
2. $f(x)$ *is differentiable on* $(-c, c)$; *and*
3. $f'(x)=\sum_{n=0}^{\infty} n a_n x^{n-1}$ *on* $(-c, c)$.

Ostensibly, Theorem 2 mentions only f and f'. But note that f' has the same radius of convergence that f has, so that the theorem applies equally well to f', saying that it has a derivative f'' on $(-c, c)$. This in turn implies that f'' is differentiable on $(-c, c)$, and so on. Thus, if $f(x)=\sum_{n=0}^{\infty} a_n x^n$ converges on $(-c, c)$, it has derivatives of all orders at every point of $(-c, c)$.

EXAMPLE 4. The relation $(d/dx)(\sin x)=\cos x$ is easily checked by differentiating the series for $\sin x$ term by term:

$$\sin x = x - \frac{x^3}{3!} + \frac{x^5}{5!} - \frac{x^7}{7!} + \cdots$$

$$\frac{d}{dx}(\sin x) = 1 - \frac{x^2}{2!} + \frac{x^4}{4!} - \frac{x^6}{6!} + \cdots$$

$$= \cos x.$$

Convergence at one or both endpoints of the interval of convergence of a power series may be lost in the process of differentiation. That is why Theorem 2 mentions only the *open* interval $(-c, c)$.

EXAMPLE 5. The series $f(x)=\sum_{n=1}^{\infty}(x^n/n)$ of Example 1 converges for $-1 \le x < 1$. The series of derivatives

$$f'(x)=\sum_{n=1}^{\infty} x^{n-1} = 1 + x + x^2 + x^3 + \cdots$$

is a geometric series that converges only for $-1 < x < 1$. The series diverges at the endpoint $x = -1$, as well as at the endpoint $x = 1$.

Example 5 shows, however, that when the terms of a series are integrated, the resulting series may converge at an endpoint that was not a point of convergence before. The justification for term-by-term integration of a series is the following theorem, which we also state without proof.

Theorem 3. The term-by-term integration theorem. *If* $f(x) = \sum_{n=0}^{\infty} a_n x^n$ *converges on the open interval* $(-c, c)$, *then,*

1. $\displaystyle\sum_{n=0}^{n=\infty} \frac{a_n x^{n+1}}{n+1}$ *converges on* $(-c, c)$;

2. $\int f(x)\,dx$ *exists for* x *in* $(-c, c)$;

3. $\displaystyle\int f(x)\,dx = \sum_{n=0}^{n=\infty} \frac{a_n x^{n+1}}{n+1} + C$ *on* $(-c, c)$.

EXAMPLE 6. The series

$$\frac{1}{1+t} = 1 - t + t^2 - t^3 \cdots$$

converges on the open interval $-1 < t < 1$. Therefore,

$$\ln(1+x) = \int_0^x \frac{1}{1+t}\,dt = t - \frac{t^2}{2} + \frac{t^3}{3} - \frac{t^4}{4} + \cdots\Big]_0^x, \qquad -1 < x < 1,$$

$$= x - \frac{x^2}{2} + \frac{x^3}{3} - \frac{x^4}{4} + \cdots$$

As you know, the latter series also converges at $x = 1$, but that was not guaranteed by the theorem.

EXAMPLE 7. By replacing t by t^2 in the series of Example 6, we obtain

$$\frac{1}{1+t^2} = 1 - t^2 + t^4 - t^6 + \cdots, \qquad -1 < t < 1.$$

Therefore

$$\tan^{-1} x = \int_0^x \frac{1}{1+t^2}\,dt = t - \frac{t^3}{3} + \frac{t^5}{5} - \frac{t^7}{7} + \cdots\Big]_0^x$$

$$= x - \frac{x^3}{3} + \frac{x^5}{5} - \frac{x^7}{7} + \cdots, \qquad -1 < x < 1.$$

This is not as refined a result as the one we obtained in Article 16–10, where we were able to show that the interval of convergence was $-1 \le x \le 1$ by analyzing a remainder. But the result here is obtained more quickly.

EXAMPLE 8. Express

$$\int \sin x^2\,dx$$

as a power series.

Solution. From the series for $\sin x$ we obtain

$$\sin x^2 = x^2 - \frac{x^6}{3!} + \frac{x^{10}}{5!} - \frac{x^{14}}{7!} + \cdots, \qquad -\infty < x < \infty.$$

Therefore,

$$\int \sin x^2\,dx = C + \frac{x^3}{3} - \frac{x^7}{7\cdot 3!} + \frac{x^{11}}{11\cdot 5!} - \frac{x^{15}}{15\cdot 7!} + \cdots, \qquad -\infty < x < \infty.$$

EXAMPLE 9. Estimate $\int_0^1 \sin x^2\,dx$ with an error of less than 0.001.

Solution. From the indefinite integral in Example 8,

$$\int_0^1 \sin x^2\,dx = \frac{1}{3} - \frac{1}{7\cdot 3!} + \frac{1}{11\cdot 5!} - \frac{1}{15\cdot 7!} + \frac{1}{19\cdot 9!} - \cdots$$

The series alternates, and we find by trial that

$$\frac{1}{11\cdot 5!} \approx 0.00076$$

is the first term to be numerically less than 0.001. The sum of the preceding two terms gives

$$\int_0^1 \sin x^2\,dx \approx \tfrac{1}{3} - \tfrac{1}{42} \approx 0.310.$$

With two more terms we could estimate

$$\int_0^1 \sin x^2\,dx \approx 0.310268$$

with an error of less than 10^{-6}; and with only one term beyond that we have

$$\int_0^1 \sin x^2\,dx \approx \tfrac{1}{3} - \tfrac{1}{42} + \tfrac{1}{1320} - \tfrac{1}{75600} + \tfrac{1}{6894720} \approx 0.310268303,$$

with an error of less than 10^{-9}. To guarantee this accuracy with the error formula for the trapezoid rule would require using about 13,000 subintervals.

EXAMPLE 10. Estimate $\int_0^{0.5} \sqrt{1+x^4}\,dx$ with an error of less than 10^{-4}.

Solution. The binomial expansion of $(1+x^4)^{1/2}$ is

$$(1+x^4)^{1/2} = 1 + \tfrac{1}{2}x^4 - \tfrac{1}{8}x^8 + \cdots,$$

a series whose terms alternate in sign after the second term. Therefore,

$$\begin{aligned}\int_0^{0.5} \sqrt{1+x^4}\,dx &= x + \frac{1}{2\cdot 5}x^5 - \frac{1}{8\cdot 9}x^9 + \cdots\Big]_0^{0.5}\\ &= 1 + 0.0031 - 0.00003 + \cdots\\ &\approx 1.0031,\end{aligned}$$

with an error of magnitude less than 0.00003.

At the beginning of this article we asked whether a function

$$f(x) = \sum_{n=0}^{\infty} a_n x^n$$

defined by a convergent power series has a Taylor series. We can now answer that a function defined by a power series with a radius of convergence $c > 0$ has a Maclaurin series that converges to the function at every point of $(-c, c)$. Why? Because the Maclaurin series for the function $f(x) = \sum_{n=0}^{\infty} a_n x^n$ is the series $\sum_{n=0}^{\infty} a_n x^n$ itself. To see this, we differentiate

$$f(x) = a_0 + a_1 x + a_2 x^2 + \cdots + a_n x^n + \cdots$$

term by term and substitute $x = 0$ in each derivative $f^{(n)}(x)$. This produces

$$f^{(n)}(0) = n!\, a_n \qquad \text{or} \qquad a_n = \frac{f^{(n)}(0)}{n!}$$

for every n. Thus,

$$f(x) = \sum_{n=0}^{\infty} a_n x^n = \sum_{n=0}^{\infty} \frac{f^{(n)}(0)}{n!} x^n, \qquad -c < x < c. \tag{7}$$

An immediate consequence of this is that series like

$$x \sin x = x^2 - \frac{x^4}{3!} + \frac{x^6}{5!} - \frac{x^8}{7!} + \cdots,$$

and

$$x^2 e^x = x^2 + x^3 + \frac{x^4}{2!} + \frac{x^5}{3!} + \cdots,$$

which are obtained by multiplying Maclaurin series by powers of x, as well as series obtained by integration and differentiation of power series, are themselves the Maclaurin series of the functions they represent.

Another consequence of (7) is that, if two power series $\sum_{n=0}^{\infty} a_n x^n$ and $\sum_{n=0}^{\infty} b_n x^n$ are equal for all values of x in an open interval that contains the origin $x = 0$, then $a_n = b_n$ for every n. For if

$$f(x) = \sum_{n=0}^{\infty} a_n x^n = \sum_{n=0}^{\infty} b_n x^n, \qquad -c < x < c,$$

then a_n and b_n are both equal to $f^{(n)}(0)/n!$.

PROBLEMS

In Problems 1–20, find the interval of absolute convergence. If the interval is finite, determine whether the series converges at each endpoint.

1. $\sum_{n=0}^{\infty} x^n$

2. $\sum_{n=0}^{\infty} n^2 x^n$

3. $\sum_{n=1}^{\infty} \frac{nx^n}{2^n}$

4. $\sum_{n=0}^{\infty} \frac{(2x)^n}{n!}$

5. $\sum_{n=0}^{\infty} \frac{(-1)^n x^{2n+1}}{(2n+1)!}$

6. $\sum_{n=1}^{\infty} (-1)^{n-1} \frac{(x-1)^n}{n}$

7. $\sum_{n=0}^{\infty} \frac{n^2}{2^n}(x+2)^n$

8. $\sum_{n=0}^{\infty} \frac{x^{2n+1}}{2n+1}$

9. $\sum_{n=0}^{\infty} (-1)^n \frac{x^{2n+1}}{2n+1}$

10. $\sum_{n=1}^{\infty} \frac{(x-2)^n}{n^2}$

11. $\sum_{n=0}^{\infty} \frac{\cos nx}{2^n}$

12. $\sum_{n=1}^{\infty} \frac{2^n x^n}{n^5}$

13. $\sum_{n=0}^{\infty} \frac{x^n e^n}{n+1}$

14. $\sum_{n=1}^{\infty} \frac{(\cos x)^n}{n^n}$

15. $\sum_{n=0}^{\infty} n^n x^n$

16. $\sum_{n=0}^{\infty} \frac{(3x+6)^n}{n!}$

17. $\sum_{n=1}^{\infty} (-2)^n (n+1)(x-1)^n$

18. $\sum_{n=1}^{\infty} \frac{(-1)^{n+1}(x-2)^n}{n \cdot 2^n}$

19. $\sum_{n=0}^{\infty} \left(\frac{x^2-1}{2}\right)^n$

20. $\sum_{n=1}^{\infty} \frac{(x+3)^{n-1}}{n}$

21. Find the sum of the series in Problem 16.

22. When the series of Problem 19 converges, to what does it converge?

23. Use series to verify that:

a) $\frac{d}{dx}(\cos x) = -\sin x$ **b)** $\int_0^x \cos t\, dt = \sin x$

c) $y = e^x$ is a solution of the equation $y' = y$.

24. Obtain the Maclaurin series for $1/(1 + x)^2$ from the series for $-1/(1 + x)$.

25. Use the Maclaurin series $1/(1 - x^2)$ to obtain a series for $2x/(1 - x^2)^2$.

26. Use the identity $\sin^2 x = (1 - \cos 2x)/2$ to obtain a series for $\sin^2 x$. Then differentiate this series to obtain a series for $2 \sin x \cos x$. Check that this is the series for $\sin 2x$.

(*Calculator*) In Problems 27 through 34, use series and a calculator to estimate each integral with an error of magnitude less than 0.001.

27. $\int_0^{0.2} \sin x^2\, dx$ **28.** $\int_0^{0.1} \tan^{-1} x\, dx$

29. $\int_0^{0.1} x^2 e^{-x^2}\, dx$ **30.** $\int_0^{0.1} \frac{\tan^{-1} x}{x}\, dx$

31. $\int_0^{0.4} \frac{1 - e^{-x}}{x}\, dx$ **32.** $\int_0^{0.1} \frac{\ln (1 + x)}{x}\, dx$

33. $\int_0^{0.1} \frac{1}{\sqrt{1 + x^4}}\, dx$ **34.** $\int_0^{0.25} \sqrt[3]{1 + x^2}\, dx$

35. (*Calculator*) **a)** Obtain a power series for

$$\sinh^{-1} x = \int_0^x \frac{dt}{\sqrt{1 + t^2}}.$$

b) Use the result of (a) to estimate $\sinh^{-1} 0.25$ to three decimal places.

36. (*Calculator*) Estimate $\int_0^1 \cos x^2\, dx$ with an error of less than one millionth.

37. Show by example that there are power series that converge only at $x = 0$.

38. Show by examples that the convergence of a series at an endpoint of its interval of convergence may be either conditional or absolute.

39. Let r be any positive number. Use Theorem 1 to show that if $\sum_{n=0}^{\infty} a_n x^n$ converges for $-r < x < r$, then it converges absolutely for $-r < x < r$.

40. Use the ratio test to show that the binomial series converges for $|x| < 1$. (This still does not show that the series converges to $(1 + x)^m$.)

REVIEW QUESTIONS AND EXERCISES

1. Define "sequence," "series," "sequence of partial sums of a series."

2. Define "convergence" (a) of a sequence, (b) of an infinite series.

3. Which of the following statements are true, and which are false?

a) If a sequence does not converge, then it diverges.

b) If a sequence $\{n, f(n)\}$ does not converge, then $f(n)$ tends to infinity as n does.

c) If a series does not converge, then its nth term does not approach zero as n tends to infinity.

d) If the nth term of a series does not approach zero as n tends to infinity, then the series diverges.

e) If a sequence $\{n, f(n)\}$ converges, then there is a number L such that $f(n)$ lies within 1 unit of L (i) for all values of n, (ii) for all but a finite number of values of n.

f) If all partial sums of a series are less than some constant L, then the series converges.

g) If a series converges, then its partial sums s_n are bounded (that is, $m \le s_n \le M$ for some constants m and M).

4. List three tests for convergence (or divergence) of an infinite series.

5. Under what circumstances do you know that a bounded sequence converges?

6. Define "absolute convergence" and "conditional convergence." Give examples of series that are (a) absolutely convergent, (b) conditionally convergent.

7. State Taylor's theorem, with remainder, giving two different expressions for the remainder.

8. It can be shown (though not very simply) that the function f defined by

$$f(x) = \begin{cases} 0 & \text{when } x = 0, \\ e^{-1/x^2} & \text{when } x \neq 0 \end{cases}$$

is everywhere continuous, together with its derivatives of all orders. At 0, the derivatives are all equal to 0.

a) Write the Taylor series expansion of f in powers of x.

b) What is the remainder $R_n(x, 0)$ for this function? Does the Taylor series for f converge to $f(x)$ at some value of x different from zero? Give a reason for your answer.

9. If a Taylor series in powers of $x - a$ is to be used for the numerical evaluation of a function, what is necessary or desirable in the choice of a?

10. Write the Taylor series in powers of $x - a$ and $y - b$ for a function f of two variables x and y, about the point (a, b).

11. Describe a method that may be useful in finding $\lim_{x \to a} f(x)/g(x)$ if $f(a) = g(a) = 0$. Illustrate.

12. What tests may be used to find the interval of convergence of a power series? Do they also work at the endpoints of the interval? Illustrate with examples.

13. What test is usually used to decide whether a given alternating series converges? Give examples of convergent and divergent alternating series.

MISCELLANEOUS PROBLEMS

1. Find explicitly the nth partial sum of the series $\sum_{n=2}^{\infty} \ln(1 - 1/n^2)$, and thereby determine whether the series converges.

2. Evaluate $\sum_{k=2}^{\infty} 1/(k^2 - 1)$ by finding the nth partial sum and taking the limit as n becomes infinite.

3. Prove that the sequence $\{x_n\}$ and the series $\sum_{k=1}^{\infty} (x_{k+1} - x_k)$ both converge or both diverge.

4. In an attempt to find a root of the equation $x = f(x)$, a first approximation x_1 is estimated from the graphs of $y = x$ and $y = f(x)$. Then $x_2, x_3, \ldots, x_n, \ldots$ are computed successively from the formula $x_n = f(x_{n-1})$. If the points $x_1, x_2, \ldots, x_n, \ldots$ all lie on an interval $a \le x \le b$ on which $f(x)$ has a derivative such that $|f'(x)| < M < 1$, show that the sequence $\{x_n\}$ converges to a root of the given equation.

5. Assuming $|x| > 1$, show that

$$\frac{1}{1-x} = -\frac{1}{x} - \frac{1}{x^2} - \frac{1}{x^3} - \cdots$$

6. (a) Find the expansion, in powers of x, of $x^2/(1 + x)$. (b) Does the series expansion of $x^2/(1 + x)$ in powers of x converge when $x = 2$? (Give a brief reason.)

7. Obtain the Maclaurin series expansion for $\sin^{-1} x$ by integrating the series for $(1 - t^2)^{-1/2}$ from 0 to x. Find the intervals of convergence of these series.

8. Obtain the Maclaurin series for $\ln(x + \sqrt{x^2 + 1}) = \sinh^{-1} x$ by integrating the series for $(1 + t^2)^{-1/2}$ from 0 to x. Find the intervals of convergence of these two series.

9. Obtain the first four terms in the Maclaurin series for $e^{\sin x}$ by substituting the series for $y = \sin x$ in the series for e^y.

10. Assuming $|x| > 1$, obtain the expansions

$$\tan^{-1} x = \frac{\pi}{2} - \frac{1}{x} + \frac{1}{3x^3} - \frac{1}{5x^5} + \cdots, \qquad x > 1,$$

$$\tan^{-1} x = -\frac{\pi}{2} - \frac{1}{x} + \frac{1}{3x^3} - \frac{1}{5x^5} + \cdots, \qquad x < -1,$$

by integrating the series

$$\frac{1}{1+t^2} = \frac{1}{t^2} \cdot \frac{1}{1 + (1/t^2)} = \frac{1}{t^2} - \frac{1}{t^4} + \frac{1}{t^6} - \frac{1}{t^8} + \cdots$$

from x (> 1) to $+\infty$ or from $-\infty$ to x (< -1).

11. (a) Obtain the Maclaurin series, through the term in x^6, for $\ln(\cos x)$ by substituting the series for $y = 1 - \cos x$ in the series for $\ln(1 - y)$. (b) Use the result of part (a) to estimate $\int_0^{0.1} \ln(\cos x)\, dx$ to five decimal places.

12. Compute $\int_0^1 [(\sin x)/x]\, dx$ to three decimal places.

13. Compute $\int_0^1 e^{-x^2}\, dx$ to three decimal places.

14. Expand the function $f(x) = \sqrt{1 + x^2}$ in powers of $(x - 1)$, obtaining three nonvanishing terms.

15. Expand the function $f(x) = 1/(1 - x)$ in powers of $(x - 2)$, and find the interval of convergence.

16. Find the first three nonvanishing terms of the Maclaurin series of $\tan x$.

17. Expand $f(x) = 1/(x + 1)$ in powers of $(x - 3)$.

18. Expand $\cos x$ in powers of $(x - \pi/3)$.

19. Find the first three terms of the Taylor series expansion of the function $1/x$ about the point π.

20. Let f and g be functions satisfying the following conditions: (a) $f(0) = 1$, (b) $f'(x) = g(x)$, $g'(x) = f(x)$, (c) $g(0) = 0$. Estimate $f(1)$ to three decimal places.

21. Suppose $f(x) = \sum_{n=0}^{\infty} a_n x^n$. Prove that (a) if $f(x)$ is an even function, then $a_1 = a_3 = a_5 = \cdots = 0$; (b) if $f(x)$ is an odd function, then $a_0 = a_2 = a_4 = \cdots = 0$.

22. Find the first four terms (up to x^3) of the Maclaurin series of $f(x) = e^{(e^x)}$.

23. Estimate the error involved in using $x - x^2/2$ as an approximation to $\ln(1 + x)$ for values of x between 0 and 0.2, inclusive.

24. If $(1 + x)^{1/3}$ is replaced by $1 + x/3$ and $0 \le x \le \frac{1}{10}$, what estimate can be given for the error?

25. Use series to find

$$\lim_{x \to 0} \frac{\ln(1 - x) - \sin x}{1 - \cos^2 x}.$$

26. Find $\lim_{x \to 0} [(\sin x)/x]^{1/x^2}$.

27. Does the series $\sum_{n=1}^{\infty} \operatorname{sech} n$ converge? Why?

28. Does $\sum_{n=1}^{\infty} (-1)^n \tanh n$ converge? Why?

Establish the convergence or divergence of the series whose nth terms are given in Problems 29–40.

29. $\dfrac{1}{\ln(n + 1)}$

30. $\dfrac{n}{2(n + 1)(n + 2)}$

31. $\dfrac{\sqrt{n + 1} - \sqrt{n}}{\sqrt{n}}$

32. $\dfrac{1}{n(\ln n)^2}, \quad n \ge 2$

33. $\dfrac{1 + (-2)^{n-1}}{2^n}$

34. $\dfrac{n}{1000n^2 + 1}$

35. $e^n/n!$

36. $\dfrac{1}{n\sqrt{n^2+1}}$

37. $\dfrac{1}{n^{1+1/n}}$

38. $\dfrac{1\cdot 3\cdot 5\cdots(2n-1)}{2\cdot 4\cdot 6\cdots(2n)}$

39. $\dfrac{n^2}{n^3+1}$

40. $\dfrac{n+1}{n!}$

41. Find the sum of the convergent series

$$\sum_{n=1}^{\infty}\frac{1}{(n+1)(n+2)}.$$

42. (a) Suppose $a_1, a_2, a_3, \ldots, a_n$ are positive numbers satisfying the following conditions:

i) $a_1 \geq a_2 \geq a_3 \geq \cdots$;
ii) the series $a_2 + a_4 + a_8 + a_{16} + \cdots$ diverges.

Show that the series

$$\frac{a_1}{1}+\frac{a_2}{2}+\frac{a_3}{3}+\cdots$$

diverges. (b) Use the result above to show that

$$\sum_{n=2}^{\infty}\frac{1}{n\ln n}$$

diverges.

43. Given $a_n \neq 1$, $a_n > 0$, $\sum a_n$ converges. (a) Show that $\sum a_n^2$ converges. (b) Does $\sum a_n/(1-a_n)$ converge? (c) Does $\sum \ln(1+a_n)$ converge? Explain.

44. Show that $\sum_{n=2}^{\infty} 1/[n(\ln n)^k]$ converges for $k > 1$.

In Problems 45–52, find the interval of convergence of each series. Test for convergence at the endpoints if the interval is finite.

45. $1+\dfrac{x+2}{3\cdot 1}+\dfrac{(x+2)^2}{3^2\cdot 2}+\cdots+\dfrac{(x+2)^n}{3^n\cdot n}+\cdots$

46. $1+\dfrac{(x-1)^2}{2!}+\dfrac{(x-1)^4}{4!}+\cdots+\dfrac{(x-1)^{2n-2}}{(2n-2)!}+\cdots$

47. $\displaystyle\sum_{n=1}^{\infty}\frac{x^n}{n^n}$

48. $\displaystyle\sum_{n=1}^{\infty}\frac{n!x^n}{n^n}$

49. $\displaystyle\sum_{n=0}^{\infty}\frac{n+1}{2n+1}\frac{(x-3)^n}{2^n}$

50. $\displaystyle\sum_{n=0}^{\infty}\frac{n+1}{2n+1}\frac{(x-2)^n}{3^n}$

51. $\displaystyle\sum_{n=1}^{\infty}\frac{(-1)^{n-1}(x-1)^n}{n^2}$

52. $\displaystyle\sum_{n=1}^{\infty}\frac{x^n}{n}$

Determine *all* the values of x for which the following series converge:

53. $\displaystyle\sum_{n=1}^{\infty}\frac{(x-2)^{3n}}{n!}$,

54. $\displaystyle\sum_{n=1}^{\infty}\frac{2^n(\sin x)^n}{n^2}$,

55. $\displaystyle\sum_{n=1}^{\infty}\frac{1}{n}\left(\frac{x-1}{x}\right)^n$.

56. A function is defined by the power series

$$y = 1+\frac{1}{6}x^3+\frac{1}{180}x^6+\cdots+\frac{1\cdot 4\cdot 7\cdots(3n-2)}{(3n)!}x^{3n}+\cdots$$

a) Find the interval of convergence of the series.
b) Show that there exist two constants a and b such that the function so defined satisfies a differential equation of the form $y'' = x^a y + b$.

57. If $a_n > 0$ and the series $\sum_{n=1}^{\infty} a_n$ converges, prove that $\sum_{n=1}^{\infty} a_n/(1+a_n)$ converges.

58. If $1 > a_n > 0$ and $\sum_{n=1}^{\infty} a_n$ converges, prove that $\sum_{n=1}^{\infty}\ln(1-a_n)$ converges. [*Hint.* First show that $|\ln(1-a_n)| \leq a_n/(1-a_n)$; then apply the answer to Problem 43(b).]

59. An infinite product, indicated by $\prod_{n=1}^{\infty}(1+a_n)$, is said to converge if the series $\sum_{n=1}^{\infty}\ln(1+a_n)$ converges. (The series is the natural logarithm of the product.) Prove that the product converges if every $a_n > -1$ and $\sum_{n=1}^{\infty}|a_n|$ converges. [*Hint.* Show that

$$|\ln(1+a_n)| \leq \frac{|a_n|}{1-|a_n|} < 2|a_n|$$

when $|a_n| < \frac{1}{2}$.]

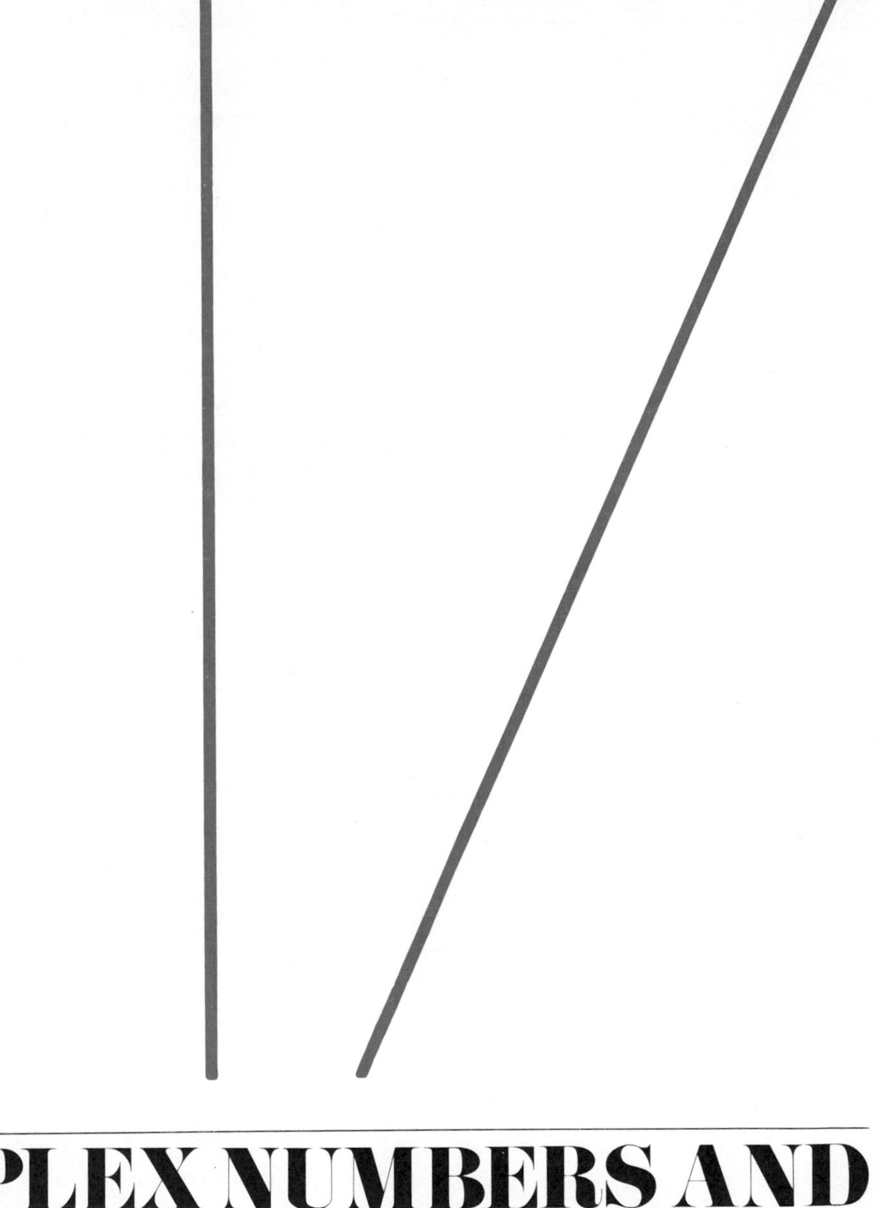

COMPLEX NUMBERS AND FUNCTIONS

17–1 INVENTED NUMBER SYSTEMS

In this chapter we shall discuss complex numbers. These are expressions of the form $a + ib$, where a and b are "real" numbers and i is a symbol for $\sqrt{-1}$. Unfortunately, the words "real" and "imaginary" have connotations that somehow place $\sqrt{-1}$ in a less favorable position than $\sqrt{2}$ in our minds. As a matter of fact, a good deal of imagination, in the sense of *inventiveness*, has been required to construct the *real* number system, which forms the basis of the calculus we have studied thus far. In this article we shall review the various stages of this invention. The further invention of a complex number system does not then seem to be so strange. It is fitting for us to study such a system, since modern engineering has found therein a convenient language for describing vibratory motion, harmonic oscillation, damped vibrations, alternating currents, and other wave phenomena.

The earliest stage of development of man's number consciousness was the recognition of the *counting numbers* 1, 2, 3, ..., which we now call the *natural numbers*, or the *positive integers*. Certain simple arithmetical operations can be performed with these numbers without getting outside the system. That is, the system of positive integers is *closed* with respect to the operations of *addition* and *multiplication*. By this we mean that, if m and n are any positive integers, then

$$m + n = p \qquad \text{and} \qquad mn = q \tag{1}$$

are also positive integers. Given the two positive integers on the *left side* of either equation in (1), we can find the corresponding positive integer on the right. More than this, we may sometimes specify the positive integers m and p and find a positive integer n such that $m + n = p$. For instance, $3 + n = 7$ can be *solved* when the only numbers we know are the positive integers. But the equation $7 + n = 3$ cannot be solved unless the number system is enlarged. Man therefore used *imagination* and invented the number concepts that we denote by zero and the *negative* integers. In a civilization that recognizes all the integers

$$\ldots, -3, -2, -1, 0, 1, 2, 3, \ldots, \tag{2}$$

an educated person may always find the missing integer that solves the equation $m + n = p$ when given the other two integers in the equation.

Suppose our educated people also know how to multiply any two integers of the set in (2). If, in Eq. (1), they are given m and q, they discover that sometimes they can find n and sometimes they can't. If their *imagination* is still in good working order, they may be inspired to invent still more numbers and introduce fractions, which are just ordered pairs m/n of integers m and n. The number zero has special properties that may bother them for a while, but they ultimately discover that it is handy to have all ratios of integers m/n, excluding only those having zero in the denominator. This system, called the set of *rational numbers*, is now rich enough for them to perform the so-called *rational operations* of:

1. a) addition **2. a)** multiplication
b) subtraction **b)** division

on any two numbers in the system, *except that they cannot divide by zero.*

The geometry of the unit square (Fig. 17–1) and the Pythagorean Theorem showed that they could construct a geometric line segment which, in terms of some basic unit of length, has length equal to $\sqrt{2}$. Thus they could solve the equation

$$x^2 = 2$$

by a geometric construction. But then they discovered that the line segment representing $\sqrt{2}$ and the line segment representing the unit of length 1 were incommensurable quantities. This means that the ratio $\sqrt{2}/1$ cannot be expressed as the ratio of two *integral* multiples of some other, presumably more fundamental, unit of length. That is, our educated people could not find a rational number solution of the equation $x^2 = 2$.

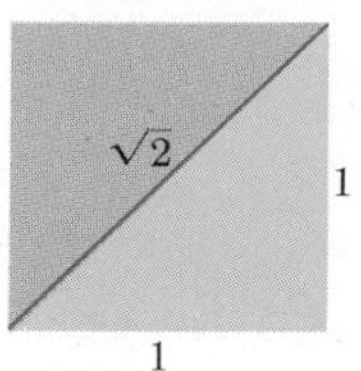

17–1 Segments of irrational length can be constructed with straightedge and compass.

There is a nice algebraic argument that there is no rational number whose square is 2. Suppose that there were such a rational number. Then we could find integers p and q with no common factor other than 1, and such that

$$p^2 = 2q^2. \tag{3}$$

Since p and q are integers, p must then be even, say $p = 2p_1$, where p_1 is an integer. This leads to $2p_1^2 = q^2$, which says that q must also be even, say $q = 2q_1$, where q_1 is also an integer. But this is contrary to our choice of p and q as integers having no common factor other than unity. Hence there is no rational number whose square is 2.

Our educated people *could*, however, get a *sequence* of rational numbers

$$\frac{1}{1}, \quad \frac{7}{5}, \quad \frac{41}{29}, \quad \frac{239}{169}, \quad \ldots, \tag{4}$$

whose squares form a sequence

$$\frac{1}{1}, \quad \frac{49}{25}, \quad \frac{1681}{841}, \quad \frac{57{,}121}{28{,}561}, \quad \ldots, \tag{5}$$

which converges to 2 as its *limit*. This time their *imagination* suggested that they needed the concept of a *limit of a sequence* of rational numbers. If we accept the fact that a monotone increasing sequence that is bounded always approaches a limit, and observe that the sequence in (4) has these properties, then we want it to have a limit L. This would also mean, from (5), that $L^2 = 2$, and hence L is *not* one of our rational numbers. If to the *rational* numbers we further add the *limits* of all bounded monotone increasing sequences, we arrive at the system of all "real" numbers. The word *real* is placed in quotes because there is nothing that is either "more real" or "less real" about this system than there is about any other well-defined mathematical system.

Imagination was called upon at many stages during the development of the real number system from the system of positive integers. In fact, the art of invention was needed at least three times in constructing the systems we have discussed so far:

1. The *first invented* system; the set of *all integers* as constructed from the counting numbers.

2. The *second invented* system; the set of *rational* numbers m/n as constructed from the integers.

3. The *third invented* system; the set of all "*real*" numbers x as constructed from the rational numbers.

These invented systems form a hierarchy in which each system contains the previous system. Each system is also richer than its predecessor in that it permits more operations to be performed without going outside the system. Expressed in algebraic terms, we may say that:

1. In the system of all integers, we can solve all equations of the form

$$x + a = 0, \tag{6}$$

where a may be any integer.

2. In the system of all rational numbers, we can solve all equations of the form

$$ax + b = 0 \tag{7}$$

provided a and b are rational numbers and $a \neq 0$.

3. In the system of all real numbers, we can solve all of the Eqs. (6) and (7) and, in addition, all quadratic equations

$$ax^2 + bx + c = 0 \qquad \text{having} \qquad a \neq 0 \quad \text{and} \quad b^2 - 4ac \geq 0. \tag{8}$$

Every student of algebra is familiar with the formula that gives the solutions of (8), namely,

$$x = \frac{-b \pm \sqrt{b^2 - 4ac}}{2a}, \tag{9}$$

and familiar with the further fact that when the discriminant, $d = b^2 - 4ac$, is *negative*, the solutions in (9) do *not* belong to any of the systems discussed above. In fact, the very simple quadratic equation

$$x^2 + 1 = 0 \tag{10}$$

is impossible to solve if the only number systems that can be used are the three invented systems mentioned so far.

Thus we come to the *fourth invented* system, the set of all complex numbers $a + ib$. We could, in fact, dispense entirely with the symbol i and use a notation like (a, b). We would then speak simply of a pair of real numbers a and b. Since, under algebraic operations, the numbers a and b are treated somewhat differently, it is essential to keep the *order* straight. We therefore might say that *the complex number system consists of the set of all ordered pairs of real numbers* (a, b), together with the rules by which they are to be equated, added, multiplied, and so on, listed below. We shall use both the (a, b) notation and the notation $a + ib$. We call a the "real part" and b the "imaginary part" of (a, b). We make the following definitions.

Equality

$a + ib = c + id$ if and only if $a = c$ and $b = d$.	Two complex numbers (a, b) and (c, d) are *equal* if and only if $a = c$ and $b = d$.

Addition

$(a + ib) + (c + id)$ $= (a + c) + i(b + d)$	The sum of the two complex numbers (a, b) and (c, d) is the complex number $(a + c, b + d)$.

Multiplication

$(a + ib)(c + id)$ $= (ac - bd) + i(ad + bc)$	The product of two complex numbers (a, b) and (c, d) is the complex number $(ac - bd, ad + bc)$.
$c(a + ib) = ac + i(bc)$	The product of a real number c and the complex number (a, b) is the complex number (ac, bc).

The set of all complex numbers (a, b) in which the second number is zero has all the properties of the set of ordinary "real" numbers a. For example, addition and multiplication of $(a, 0)$ and $(c, 0)$ give

$$(a, 0) + (c, 0) = (a + c, 0),$$

$$(a, 0) \cdot (c, 0) = (ac, 0),$$

which are numbers of the same type with "imaginary part" equal to zero. Also, if we multiply a "real number" $(a, 0)$ and the "complex number" (c, d), we get

$$(a, 0) \cdot (c, d) = (ac, ad) = a(c, d).$$

In particular, the complex number $(0, 0)$ plays the role of zero in the complex number system and the complex number $(1, 0)$ plays the role of unity.

The number pair $(0, 1)$, which has "real part" equal to zero and "imaginary part" equal to one has the property that its square,

$$(0, 1)(0, 1) = (-1, 0),$$

has "real part" equal to minus one and "imaginary part" equal to zero. Therefore, in the system of complex numbers (a, b), there is a number $x = (0, 1)$ whose square can be added to unity $= (1, 0)$ to produce zero $=$ $(0, 0)$; that is,

$$(0, 1)^2 + (1, 0) = (0, 0).$$

The equation

$$x^2 + 1 = 0$$

therefore has a solution $x = (0, 1)$ in this new number system.

You are probably more familiar with the $a + ib$ notation than you are with the notation (a, b). And since the laws of algebra for the ordered pairs enable us to write

$$(a, b) = (a, 0) + (0, b) = a(1, 0) + b(0, 1),$$

while $(1, 0)$ behaves like unity and $(0, 1)$ behaves like a square root of minus one, we need not hesitate to write $a + ib$ in place of (a, b). The i associated with b is like a tracer element that tags the "imaginary part" of $a + ib$. We can pass at will from the realm of ordered pairs (a, b) to the realm of expressions $a + ib$, and conversely. But there is nothing less "real" about the symbol $(0, 1) = i$ than there is about the symbol $(1, 0) = 1$, once we have learned the laws of algebra in the complex number system (a, b).

PROBLEMS

1. In the definition of multiplication of complex numbers as ordered pairs of real numbers, the product $(a, b) \cdot (c, d)$ can be found by writing a and b on one line, c and d beneath them, and then:

For the *real* part of the product, multiply the numbers a and c in the first column and from their product subtract the product of the numbers b and d in the second column.

For the *imaginary* part of the product, cross-multiply and add the products ad and bc.

Apply this method to find the following products:

a) $(2, 3) \cdot (4, -2)$ **b)** $(2, -1) \cdot (-2, 3)$
c) $(-1, -2) \cdot (2, 1)$

[*Note.* This is the way in which complex numbers are multiplied on modern computers.]

2. Solve the following equations for the real numbers x and y:

a) $(3 + 4i)^2 - 2(x - iy) = x + iy$

b) $\left(\frac{1+i}{1-i}\right)^2 + \frac{1}{x+iy} = 1 + i$

c) $(3 - 2i)(x + iy) = 2(x - 2iy) + 2i - 1$

17–2 THE ARGAND DIAGRAM

To reduce any rational combination of complex numbers to a single complex number, we need only apply the laws of elementary algebra, replacing i^2 wherever it appears by -1. Of course, we cannot divide by the complex number $(0, 0) = 0 + i0$. But if $a + ib \neq 0$, then we may carry out a division as follows:

$$\frac{c + id}{a + ib} = \frac{(c + id)(a - ib)}{(a + ib)(a - ib)} = \frac{(ac + bd) + i(ad - bc)}{a^2 + b^2}.$$

The result is a complex number $x + iy$ with

$$x = \frac{ac + bd}{a^2 + b^2}, \qquad y = \frac{ad - bc}{a^2 + b^2},$$

and $a^2 + b^2 \neq 0$, since $a + ib = (a, b) \neq (0, 0)$. The number $a - ib$ that is used as multiplier to clear the i out of the denominator is called the *complex conjugate* of $a + ib$. It is customary to use $\bar{z}$ (read "z bar") to denote the complex conjugate of z; thus

$$z = a + ib, \qquad \bar{z} = a - ib.$$

Thus, we multiplied the numerator and denominator of the complex fraction $(c + id)/(a + ib)$ by the complex conjugate of the denominator. This will always replace the denominator by a real number.

There are two geometric representations of the complex number $z = x + iy$:

a) as the point $P(x, y)$ in the xy-plane, or

b) as the vector $\overrightarrow{OP}$ from the origin to P.

In each representation, the x-axis is called the "axis of reals" and the y-axis is the "imaginary axis." Both representations are called *Argand diagrams* (Fig. 17–2).

In terms of the polar coordinates of x and y, we have

$$x = r \cos \theta, \qquad y = r \sin \theta,$$

and

$$z = x + iy = r(\cos \theta + i \sin \theta). \tag{1}$$

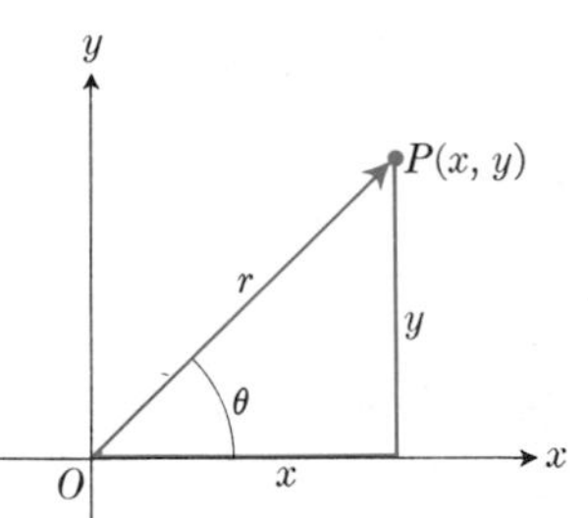

17–2 An Argand diagram representing $z = x + iy$ both as a point $P(x, y)$ and as a vector $\overrightarrow{OP}$.

We define the *absolute value* of a complex number $x + iy$ to be the length r of a vector $\overrightarrow{OP}$ from the origin to $P(x, y)$. We denote the absolute value by vertical bars, thus:

$$|x + iy| = \sqrt{x^2 + y^2}. \tag{2a}$$

Since we can always choose the polar coordinates r and θ so that $r \geq 0$, we have

$$r = |x + iy|. \tag{2b}$$

The polar angle θ is called the *argument* of z and written $\theta = \arg z$. Of course, any integral multiple of 2π may be added to θ to produce another appropriate angle. The *principal value* of the argument will, in this book, be taken to be that value of θ for which $-\pi < \theta \leq +\pi$.

The following equation gives a useful formula connecting a complex number z, its conjugate $\bar{z}$, and its absolute value $|z|$, namely,

$$z \cdot \bar{z} = |z|^2. \tag{2c}$$

We shall show in a later section how $\cos \theta + i \sin \theta$ can be expressed very conveniently as $e^{i\theta}$. But for the present, let us just introduce the abbreviation

$$\text{cis } \theta = \cos \theta + i \sin \theta. \tag{3}$$

Since cis θ is what we get from Eq. (1) by taking $r = 1$, we can say that cis θ is represented by a *unit* vector that makes an angle θ with the positive x-axis (Fig. 17–3).

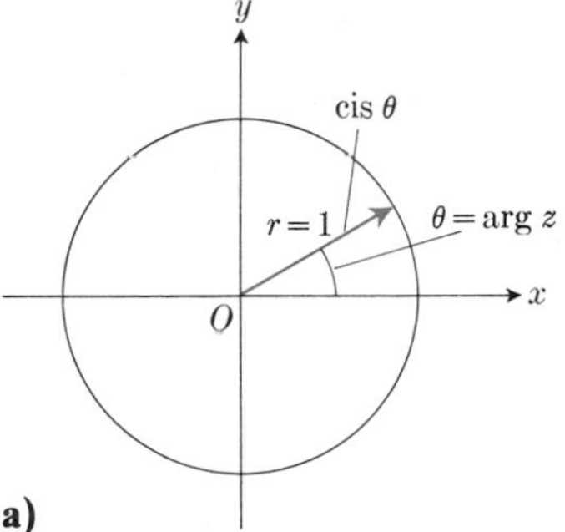

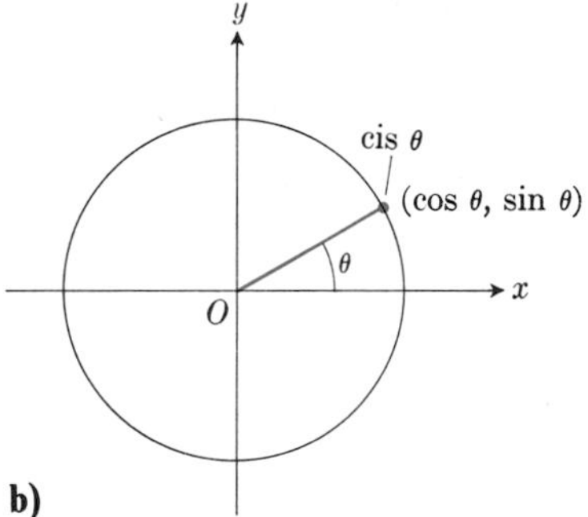

17–3 Argand diagrams for $\cos \theta + i \sin \theta$: (a) as a vector; (b) as a point.

EXAMPLE 1

$$\text{cis } 0 = \cos 0 + i \sin 0 = 1,$$

$$\text{cis } \frac{\pi}{4} = \cos \frac{\pi}{4} + i \sin \frac{\pi}{4} = \frac{1+i}{\sqrt{2}},$$

$$\text{cis } \frac{3\pi}{2} = \cos \frac{3\pi}{2} + i \sin \frac{3\pi}{2} = -i.$$

The complex-valued function cis θ has some interesting properties. For example, we shall show that

$$\text{cis } \theta_1 \cdot \text{cis } \theta_2 = \text{cis } (\theta_1 + \theta_2), \tag{4a}$$

$$(\text{cis } \theta)^{-1} = \text{cis } (-\theta), \tag{4b}$$

$$\frac{\text{cis } \theta_1}{\text{cis } \theta_2} = \text{cis } (\theta_1 - \theta_2). \tag{4c}$$

To prove the first of these, we simply multiply

$$\begin{aligned}\operatorname{cis}\theta_1\cdot\operatorname{cis}\theta_2 &= (\cos\theta_1 + i\sin\theta_1)(\cos\theta_2 + i\sin\theta_2)\\ &= (\cos\theta_1\cos\theta_2 - \sin\theta_1\sin\theta_2)\\ &\quad + i(\sin\theta_1\cos\theta_2 + \cos\theta_1\sin\theta_2).\end{aligned}$$

From trigonometry we recognize the expressions in parentheses to be

$$\begin{aligned}\cos(\theta_1+\theta_2) &= \cos\theta_1\cos\theta_2 - \sin\theta_1\sin\theta_2,\\ \sin(\theta_1+\theta_2) &= \sin\theta_1\cos\theta_2 + \cos\theta_1\sin\theta_2,\end{aligned}$$

which give us

$$\operatorname{cis}\theta_1\cdot\operatorname{cis}\theta_2 = \cos(\theta_1+\theta_2) + i\sin(\theta_1+\theta_2) = \operatorname{cis}(\theta_1+\theta_2),$$

and establish (4a). In particular,

$$\operatorname{cis}\theta\cdot\operatorname{cis}(-\theta) = \operatorname{cis}(\theta-\theta) = \operatorname{cis}0 = 1,$$

whence

$$\operatorname{cis}(-\theta) = \frac{1}{\operatorname{cis}\theta},$$

which establishes (4b). Finally, we may combine Eqs. (4a, b) and write

$$\frac{\operatorname{cis}\theta_1}{\operatorname{cis}\theta_2} = (\operatorname{cis}\theta_1)(\operatorname{cis}\theta_2)^{-1} = \operatorname{cis}\theta_1\cdot\operatorname{cis}(-\theta_2) = \operatorname{cis}(\theta_1-\theta_2).$$

These properties of cis θ lead to interesting geometrical interpretations of the product and quotient of two complex numbers in terms of the vectors that represent them.

Product

Let

$$z_1 = r_1\operatorname{cis}\theta_1, \qquad z_2 = r_2\operatorname{cis}\theta_2, \tag{5}$$

so that

$$|z_1| = r_1,\ \ \arg z_1 = \theta_1; \qquad |z_2| = r_2,\ \ \arg z_2 = \theta_2. \tag{6}$$

Then

$$z_1z_2 = r_1\operatorname{cis}\theta_1\cdot r_2\operatorname{cis}\theta_2 = r_1r_2\operatorname{cis}(\theta_1+\theta_2)$$

and hence

$$\begin{aligned}|z_1z_2| &= r_1r_2 = |z_1|\cdot|z_2|,\\ \arg(z_1z_2) &= \theta_1+\theta_2 = \arg z_1 + \arg z_2.\end{aligned} \tag{7}$$

Thus the product of two complex numbers is represented by a vector whose length is the product of the lengths of the two factors and whose argument is the sum of their arguments (Fig. 17–4). In particular, a vector may be rotated in the counterclockwise direction through an angle θ by simply multiplying it by cis θ. Multiplication by i rotates 90°, by -1 rotates 180°, by $-i$ rotates 270°, etc.

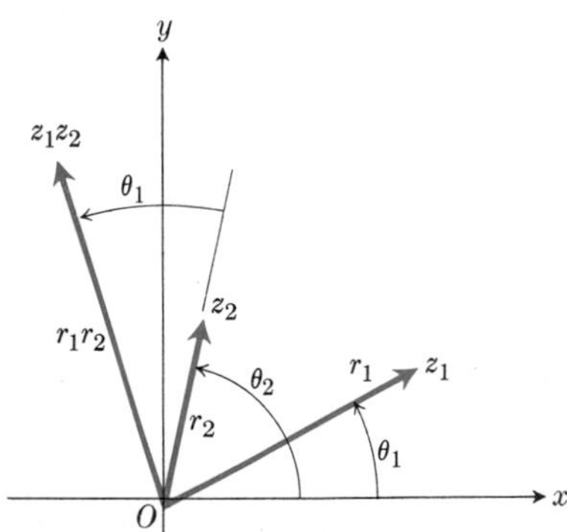

17–4 When z_1 and z_2 are multiplied, $z_1z_2 = r_1\cdot r_2$, and $\arg(z_1z_2) = \theta_1+\theta_2$.

EXAMPLE 2. Let

$$z_1 = 1 + i, \qquad z_2 = \sqrt{3} - i.$$

We plot these complex numbers in an Argand diagram (Fig. 17–5) from which we read off the polar representations

$$z_1 = \sqrt{2} \text{ cis } \frac{\pi}{4}, \qquad z_2 = 2 \text{ cis } \left(-\frac{\pi}{6}\right).$$

Then

$$\begin{aligned} z_1 z_2 &= 2\sqrt{2} \text{ cis } \left(\frac{\pi}{4} - \frac{\pi}{6}\right) \\ &= 2\sqrt{2} \text{ cis } \frac{\pi}{12} \\ &= 2\sqrt{2} (\cos 15° + i \sin 15°) \\ &\approx 2.73 + 0.73i. \end{aligned}$$

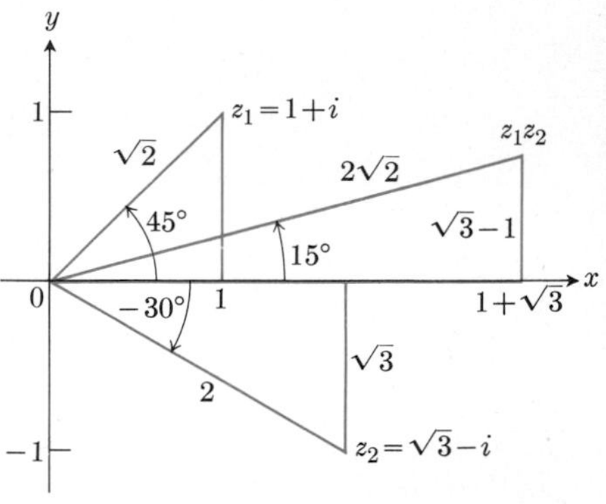

17–5 To multiply two complex numbers, one multiplies their absolute values, and adds their arguments.

Quotient

Suppose $r_2 \neq 0$ in Eq. (5). Then

$$\frac{z_1}{z_2} = \frac{r_1 \text{ cis } \theta_1}{r_2 \text{ cis } \theta_2} = \frac{r_1}{r_2} \text{cis } (\theta_1 - \theta_2).$$

Hence

$$\left|\frac{z_1}{z_2}\right| = \frac{r_1}{r_2} = \frac{|z_1|}{|z_2|},$$

$$\arg (z_1/z_2) = \theta_1 - \theta_2 = \arg z_1 - \arg z_2.$$

That is, we divide lengths and subtract angles.

EXAMPLE 3. Let $z_1 = 1 + i$ and $z_2 = \sqrt{3} - i$, as in Example 2. Then,

$$\begin{aligned} \frac{1+i}{\sqrt{3}-i} &= \frac{\sqrt{2} \text{ cis } \pi/4}{2 \text{ cis } (-\pi/6)} = \frac{\sqrt{2}}{2} \text{cis } (5\pi/12) \\ &\approx 0.707 (\cos 75° + i \sin 75°) \\ &\approx 0.183 + 0.683i. \end{aligned}$$

Powers

If n is a positive integer, we may apply the product formulas, Eq. (7), to find

$$z^n = z \cdot z \cdot z \cdots z \qquad (n \text{ factors})$$

when

$$z = r \text{ cis } \theta.$$

Doing so, we obtain

$$(r \text{ cis } \theta)^n = r^n \text{ cis } (\theta + \theta + \cdots + \theta) \qquad (n \text{ summands})$$
$$= r^n \text{ cis } n\theta. \tag{8}$$

In vector language, we see that the length, $r = |z|$, is raised to the nth power and the angle, $\theta = \arg z$, is multiplied by n.

In particular, if we place $r = 1$ in Eq. (8), we obtain *De Moivre's theorem*:

$$(\cos \theta + i \sin \theta)^n = \cos n\theta + i \sin n\theta. \tag{9}$$

If we expand the left side of this equation by the binomial theorem and reduce it to the standard form $a + ib$, we obtain formulas for $\cos n\theta$ and $\sin n\theta$ as polynomials of degree n in $\cos \theta$ and $\sin \theta$.

EXAMPLE 4. If we take $n = 3$ in Eq. (9), we have

$$(\cos \theta + i \sin \theta)^3 = \cos 3\theta + i \sin 3\theta.$$

The left side of this equation is

$$\cos^3 \theta + 3i \cos^2 \theta \sin \theta - 3 \cos \theta \sin^2 \theta - i \sin^3 \theta.$$

The real part of this must equal $\cos 3\theta$ and the imaginary part must equal $\sin 3\theta$; hence

$$\cos 3\theta = \cos^3 \theta - 3 \cos \theta \sin^2 \theta,$$
$$\sin 3\theta = 3 \cos^2 \theta \sin \theta - \sin^3 \theta.$$

Roots

If $z = r \text{ cis } \theta$ is a complex number different from zero and n is a positive integer, then there are precisely n different complex numbers $w_0, w_1, \ldots, w_{n-1}$, each of which is an nth root of z. Let $w = \rho \text{ cis } \alpha$ be an nth root of $z = r \text{ cis } \theta$, so that

$$w^n = z$$

or

$$\rho^n \text{ cis } n\alpha = r \text{ cis } \theta. \tag{10}$$

Then

$$\rho = \sqrt[n]{r} \tag{11}$$

is the real, positive, nth root of r. As regards the angle, although we cannot say that $n\alpha$ and θ must be equal, we can say that they may differ only by an integral multiple of 2π. That is,

$$n\alpha = \theta + 2k\pi, \qquad k = 0, \pm 1, \pm 2, \ldots \tag{12}$$

Therefore

$$\alpha = \frac{\theta}{n} + k\frac{2\pi}{n}.$$

Hence all nth roots of $z = r \text{ cis } \theta$ are given by

$$\sqrt[n]{r \text{ cis } \theta} = \sqrt[n]{r} \text{ cis}\left(\frac{\theta}{n} + k\frac{2\pi}{n}\right), \qquad k = 0, \pm 1, \pm 2, \ldots \tag{13}$$

REMARK. It might appear that there are infinitely many different answers corresponding to the infinitely many possible values of k. But one readily sees that $k = n + m$ gives the same answer as $k = m$ in Eq. (13). Thus we need only take n consecutive values for k to obtain all the different nth roots of z. For convenience, we may take

$$k = 0, 1, 2, \ldots, n - 1.$$

It is worth noting that all the nth roots of $r \text{ cis } \theta$ lie on a circle centered at the origin O and having radius equal to the real, positive nth root of r. One of them has argument $\alpha = \theta/n$. The others are uniformly spaced around the circumference of the circle, each being separated from its neighbors by an angle equal to $2\pi/n$. Figure 17–6 illustrates the placement of the three cube roots, w_0, w_1, w_2, of the complex number $z = r \text{ cis } \theta$.

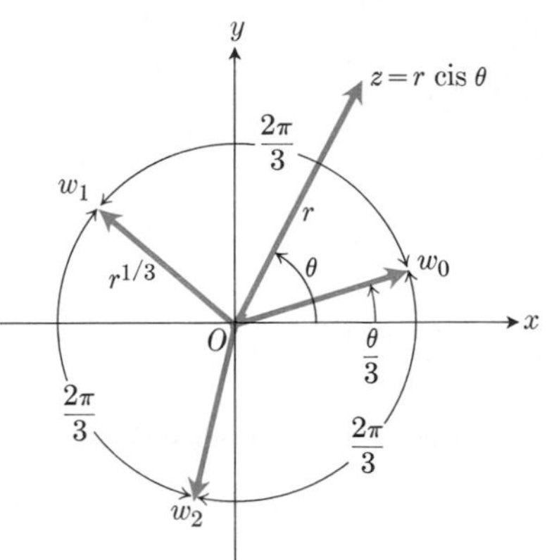

17–6 The three cube roots of $z = r \text{ cis } \theta$.

EXAMPLE 5. Find the four fourth roots of -16.

Solution. As our first step, we plot the given number in an Argand diagram (Fig. 17–7) and determine its polar representation $r \text{ cis } \theta$. Here,

$$z = -16, \qquad r = +16, \qquad \theta = \pi.$$

One of the fourth roots of $16 \text{ cis } \pi$ is $2 \text{ cis } (\pi/4)$. We obtain others by successive additions of $2\pi/4 = \pi/2$ to the argument of this first one. Hence

$$\sqrt[4]{16 \text{ cis } \pi} = 2 \text{ cis}\left(\frac{\pi}{4}, \frac{3\pi}{4}, \frac{5\pi}{4}, \frac{7\pi}{4}\right),$$

and the four roots are

$$w_0 = 2\left[\cos\frac{\pi}{4} + i \sin\frac{\pi}{4}\right] = \sqrt{2}(1 + i),$$

$$w_1 = 2\left[\cos\frac{3\pi}{4} + i \sin\frac{3\pi}{4}\right] = \sqrt{2}(-1 + i),$$

$$w_2 = 2\left[\cos\frac{5\pi}{4} + i \sin\frac{5\pi}{4}\right] = \sqrt{2}(-1 - i),$$

$$w_3 = 2\left[\cos\frac{7\pi}{4} + i \sin\frac{7\pi}{4}\right] = \sqrt{2}(1 - i).$$

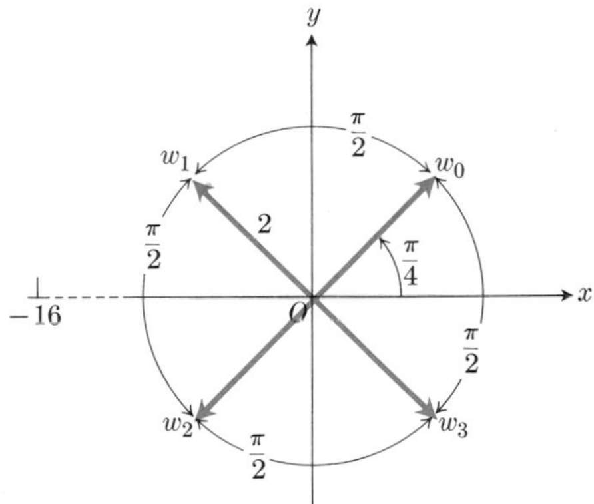

17–7 The four fourth roots of -16.

REMARK. One may well say that the invention of $\sqrt{-1}$ is all well and good and leads to a number system that is richer than the real number system alone; but where will this process end? Are we also going to invent still more systems so as to obtain $\sqrt[4]{-1}$, $\sqrt[6]{-1}$, and so on? By now it should be clear that this is not necessary. These numbers are already expressible in terms of the complex number system $a + ib$. In fact, the *Fundamental Theorem of*

Algebra (which is rather difficult to prove; we can only state it here) says that: Every polynomial equation of the form

$$a_0 z^n + a_1 z^{n-1} + a_2 z^{n-2} + \cdots + a_{n-1} z + a_n = 0,$$

in which the coefficients $a_0, a_1, \ldots, a_n$ are any complex numbers, whose degree n is greater than or equal to one, and whose leading coefficient a_0 is not zero, possesses precisely n roots in the complex number system, provided each multiple root of multiplicity m is counted as m roots.

PROBLEMS

1. Show with an Argand diagram that the law for addition of complex numbers is the same as the parallelogram law for adding vectors.

2. How may the following complex numbers be obtained from $z = x + iy$ geometrically? Sketch. (a) $\bar{z}$, (b) $\overline{(-z)}$, (c) $-z$, (d) $1/z$.

3. Show that the conjugate of the sum (product, or quotient) of two complex numbers z_1 and z_2 is the same as the sum (product, or quotient) of their conjugates.

4. (a) Extend the results of Problem 3 to show that

$$f(\bar{z}) = \overline{f(z)} \text{ if } f(z) = a_0 z^n + a_1 z^{n-1} + \cdots + a_{n-1} z + a_n$$

is a polynomial with real coefficients $a_0, a_1, \ldots, a_n$. (b) If z is a root of the equation $f(z) = 0$, where $f(z)$ is a polynomial with real coefficients as in part (a) above, show that the conjugate $\bar{z}$ is also a root of the equation. [*Hint.* Let $f(z) = u + iv = 0$; then both u and v are zero. Now use the fact that $f(\bar{z}) = \overline{f(z)} = u - iv$.]

5. Show that $|\bar{z}| = |z|$.

6. If z and $\bar{z}$ are equal, what can you say about the location of the point z in the complex plane?

7. Let $R(z)$, $I(z)$ denote respectively the real and imaginary parts of z. Show that:

a) $z + \bar{z} = 2R(z)$ **b)** $z - \bar{z} = 2iI(z)$

c) $|R(z)| \le |z|$

d) $|z_1 + z_2|^2 = |z_1|^2 + |z_2|^2 + 2R(z_1 \bar{z}_2)$

e) $|z_1 + z_2| \le |z_1| + |z_2|$

8. Show that the distance between the two points z_1 and z_2 in an Argand diagram is equal to $|z_1 - z_2|$.

In Problems 9–13, graph the points $z = x + iy$ that satisfy the given conditions:

9. a) $|z| = 2$ **b)** $|z| < 2$ **c)** $|z| > 2$

10. $|z - 1| = 2$ **11.** $|z + 1| = 1$

12. $|z + 1| = |z - 1|$ **13.** $|z + i| = |z - 1|$

Express the answer to each of the Problems 14–17 in the form r cis θ, with $r \ge 0$ and $-\pi < \theta \le \pi$. Sketch.

14. $(1 + \sqrt{-3})^2$ **15.** $\dfrac{1 + i}{1 - i}$

16. $\dfrac{1 + i\sqrt{3}}{1 - i\sqrt{3}}$ **17.** $(2 + 3i)(1 - 2i)$

18. Use De Moivre's theorem to express $\cos 4\theta$ and $\sin 4\theta$ as polynomials in $\cos \theta$ and $\sin \theta$.

19. Find the three cube roots of unity.

20. Find the two square roots of i.

21. Find the three cube roots of $-8i$.

22. Find the six sixth roots of 64.

23. Find the four roots of the equation $z^4 - 2z^2 + 4 = 0$.

24. Find the six roots of the equation $z^6 + 2z^3 + 2 = 0$.

25. Find all roots of the equation $x^4 + 4x^2 + 16 = 0$.

26. Solve: $x^4 + 1 = 0$.

17–3 COMPLEX VARIABLES

A set S of complex numbers $z = x + iy$ may be represented by points in an Argand diagram. For instance, S might be all complex z for which $|z| \le 1$. The corresponding points in the Argand diagram, or in the *z-plane* as it is called, then would be all points inside or on the circumference of a circle of radius 1 centered at O (Fig. 17–8). During a discussion, we might wish to consider the symbol z as representing any one of the complex numbers in the set S. We would then think of z as a variable whose domain is S. Or we may wish to consider a moving point that starts at time $t = 0$ from the point z_0 and moves continuously along some path in the z-plane as t increases to a second value, say $t = 1$. We would again consider the complex number z associated with this moving point (x, y) by the equation $z = x + iy$ to be a variable. This time it is a dependent variable, since its value depends upon the value of t.

The *distance* between two complex numbers $z_1 = x_1 + iy_1$ and $z_2 = x_2 + iy_2$ in the complex plane is

$$\sqrt{(x_1 - x_2)^2 + (y_1 - y_2)^2} = |z_1 - z_2|.$$

We say that the complex variable $z = x + iy$ approaches the *limit* $\alpha = a + ib$ if the distance between z and α approaches zero (Fig. 17–9). That is.

$$z \to \alpha \qquad \text{if and only if} \qquad |z - \alpha| \to 0. \tag{1}$$

If we imagine z to be a function of time, we would say, for example, that

$$\lim_{t \to 1} z = \alpha \tag{2}$$

provided it is true that

$$\lim_{t \to 1} |z - \alpha| = 0. \tag{3}$$

One way to interpret Eq. (3) is to say that if it holds, then one may prescribe as small a circle about α as center as one pleases, and the point $z = x + iy$ will be inside that circle for all values of t sufficiently close to 1. That is, $|z - \alpha|$ is small when $|t - 1|$ is small. Since

$$\begin{aligned} |z - \alpha| &= |(x + iy) - (a + ib)| \\ &= |(x - a) + i(y - b)| \\ &= \sqrt{(x - a)^2 + (y - b)^2} \le |x - a| + |y - b|, \end{aligned}$$

while both

$$|x - a| \qquad \text{and} \qquad |y - b| \qquad \text{are} \qquad \le |z - \alpha|,$$

we see that

$$z \to \alpha \qquad \text{if and only if} \qquad x \to a \quad \text{and} \quad y \to b. \tag{4}$$

Both $|x - a|$ and $|y - b|$ are small when $|z - \alpha|$ is small; and conversely, if both $|x - a|$ and $|y - b|$ are small, then $|z - \alpha|$ is also small.

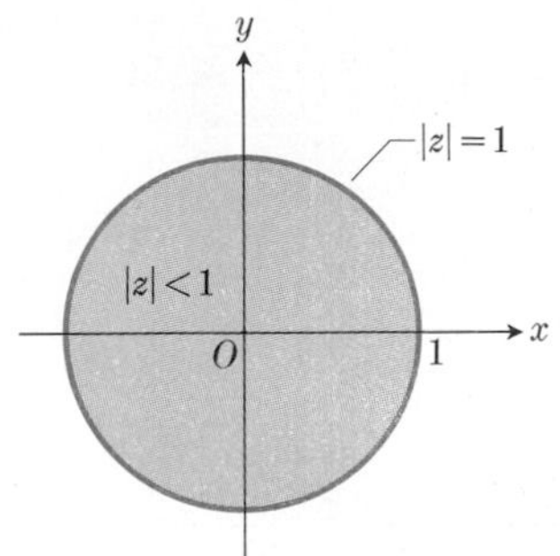

17–8 The unit circle $|z| = 1$ and its interior $|z| < 1$ in the z-plane.

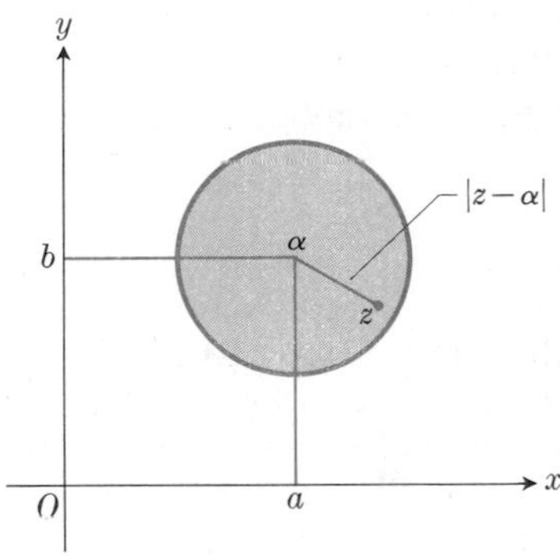

17–9 The distance between z and α in the z-plane is $|z - \alpha|$.

Function

We say that w is a function of z on a domain S and write

$$w = f(z), \qquad z \text{ in } S \tag{5}$$

if, to each z in the set S, there corresponds a complex number $w = u + iv$. For instance, S may be the set of all complex numbers and

$$w = z^2. \tag{6}$$

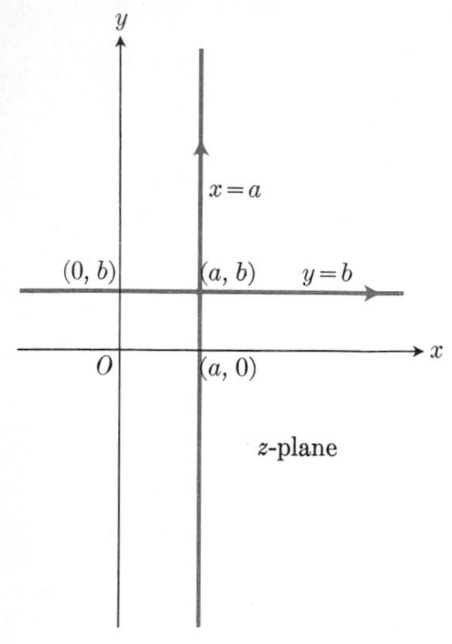

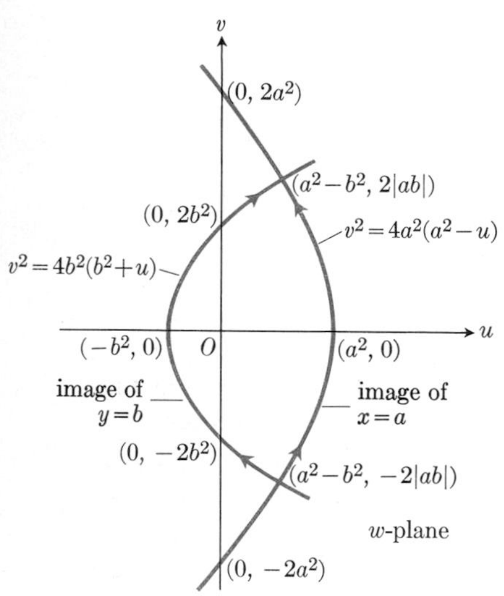

17–10 The function $w = z^2$ changes all but two of the horizontal and vertical lines of the z-plane into parabolas. The exceptions are the two axes of the z-plane, which are changed into rays instead (see Problem 1).

For each point $z = x + iy$ in the z-plane, Eq. (6) produces a complex number $w = u + iv$:

$$u + iv = (x + iy)^2 = x^2 + 2ixy + i^2y^2 = (x^2 - y^2) + i(2xy). \tag{7}$$

One way to represent such a function graphically is by a technique called "mapping." For example, we may use Eq. (7) to map a vertical line, $x = a$, into the w-plane. What does the image point w do as the z point traverses the line $x = a$ from $y = -\infty$ to $y = +\infty$? To find out, we separate the real and imaginary parts of Eq. (7) and obtain

$$u = x^2 - y^2 = a^2 - y^2, \qquad v = 2xy = 2ay. \tag{8a}$$

These equations are parametric equations (in the parameter y) of the parabola

$$v^2 = 4a^2(a^2 - u). \tag{8b}$$

When a is positive (Fig. 17–10), $v = 2ay$ has the same sign as y. Thus as the z point moves up along the line $x = a$ from $y = -\infty$ to $y = +\infty$, the w point moves upward along the parabola, (8b), in the direction indicated by the arrows in the figure.

Similarly, the image in the w-plane of the line $y = b$ has parametric equations

$$u = x^2 - b^2, \qquad v = 2bx, \qquad -\infty < x < +\infty, \tag{9a}$$

which represent the parabola

$$v^2 = 4b^2(b^2 + u). \tag{9b}$$

It is easily seen from (8a, b) that the line $x = -a$ maps onto the same parabola (8b) that the line $x = a$ does; but this time the parabola is traced in the opposite sense as y varies from $-\infty$ to $+\infty$. Similarly, the line $y = -b$ maps onto the same parabola as the line $y = b$. These phenomena are to be expected, since the point z and the point $-z$ both map into the same point $w = z^2 = (-z)^2$ in the w-plane.

Continuity

A function $w = f(z)$ that is defined throughout some neighborhood of the point $z = \alpha$ is said to be *continuous* at α if

$$|f(z) - f(\alpha)| \to 0 \quad \text{as} \quad |z - \alpha| \to 0. \tag{10}$$

Expressed in the language of mapping, the conditions in (10) say simply that the image of z is near the image of α when z is near α. Another way to say it is that for any circle C centered at $f(\alpha)$ in the w-plane, no matter how small, there is a circle C' centered at α in the z-plane with the property that whenever z is inside C', the image point w lies inside C. (See Fig. 17–11.)

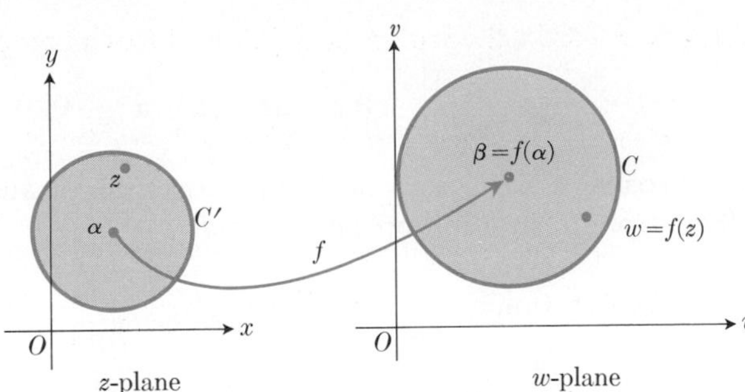

17–11 The continuity of $w=f(z)$ requires the image of z to be near the image of α whenever z is near α.

EXAMPLE. $f(z)=z^2$ is continuous at any point $z=\alpha$, for we have

$$|f(z)-f(\alpha)| = |z^2-\alpha^2| = |(z-\alpha)(z+\alpha)| = |z-\alpha|\cdot|z+\alpha|.$$

Now as $z \to \alpha$, we have

$$\lim_{z\to\alpha} (z+\alpha) = 2\alpha,$$

so that

$$\lim_{z\to\alpha} |f(z)-f(\alpha)| = \lim_{z\to\alpha} |(z-\alpha)|\cdot|(z+\alpha)|$$
$$= |2\alpha| \lim_{z\to\alpha} |z-\alpha| = 0,$$

so that condition (10) is satisfied.

PROBLEMS

1. In connection with the function $w=z^2$ discussed in the text, sketch the images in the w-plane of the following figures in the z-plane. [*Hint*. Use polar coordinates.]

a) $|z|=1,\quad 0\le \arg z\le \pi$

b) $|z|=2,\quad \pi/2\le \arg z\le \pi$

c) $\arg z=\pi/4$ **d)** $|z|<1,\quad -\pi<\arg z\le 0$

e) the x-axis **f)** the y-axis

2. Show that the two parabolas in the w-plane in Fig. 17–10 intersect orthogonally if neither a nor b is zero.

3. Show that the function $w=z^3$ maps the wedge $0\le\arg z\le\pi/3$ in the z-plane onto the upper half of the w-plane. Use polar coordinates and sketch.

4. Show that $f(z)=z^3$ is continuous at $z=\alpha$ for any α.

5. Show that $f(z)=1/z$ is continuous at $z=\alpha$ if $\alpha\ne 0$.

17–4 DERIVATIVES

The derivative of a function $w=f(z)$ is defined in the same way as the derivative of a real-valued function of the real variable x. Namely, the derivative at $z=\alpha$ is

$$f'(\alpha) = \lim_{z\to\alpha} \frac{f(z)-f(\alpha)}{z-\alpha}, \tag{1}$$

provided the limit exists. By saying that the limit in (1) exists, we mean, of course, that there is some complex number, which we have called $f'(\alpha)$, such that

$$\left| f'(\alpha) - \frac{f(z) - f(\alpha)}{z - \alpha} \right| \to 0 \quad \text{as} \quad |z - \alpha| \to 0. \tag{2}$$

Since z may approach α *along any path*, the existence of such a limit imposes a rather strong restriction on the function $w = f(z)$.

EXAMPLE 1. The function

$$w = \bar{z} = f(z), \tag{3}$$

where

$$z = x + iy, \qquad \bar{z} = x - iy$$

has no derivative at any point. For if we take $\alpha = a + ib$, then

$$\frac{f(z) - f(\alpha)}{z - \alpha} = \frac{\bar{z} - \bar{\alpha}}{z - \alpha} = \frac{(x - a) - i(y - b)}{(x - a) + i(y - b)}. \tag{4}$$

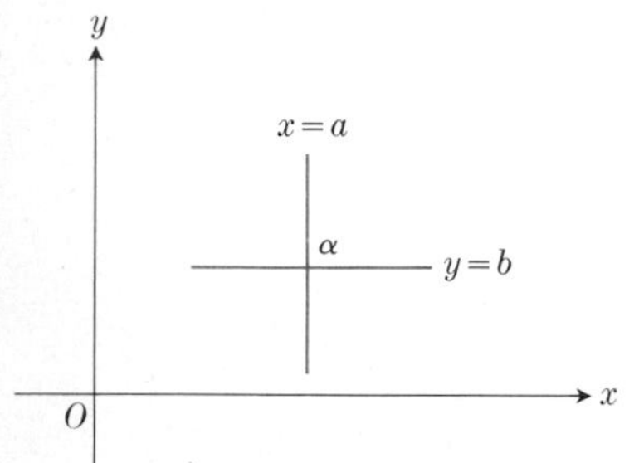

17–12 We know that the function $w = \bar{z}$ is not differentiable at any point α because the quotient $(\bar{z} - \bar{\alpha})/(z - \alpha)$ has different limits as z approaches α along the lines $x = a$ and $y = b$.

Now, from among the many different ways in which z might approach α, we shall single out for special attention the following two:

a) along the line $y = b$, and

b) along the line $x = a$. (See Fig. 17–12.)

In the first case, we therefore take $y = b$ and let $x \to a$. Then Eq. (4) becomes

$$y = b: \qquad \frac{f(z) - f(\alpha)}{z - \alpha} = \frac{x - a}{x - a} = +1,$$

so that

$$\lim_{\substack{x \to a \\ y = b}} \frac{f(z) - f(\alpha)}{z - \alpha} = +1. \tag{5a}$$

In the second case, we take $x = a$ and let $y \to b$. This time Eq. (4) becomes

$$x = a: \qquad \frac{f(z) - f(\alpha)}{z - \alpha} = \frac{-i(y - b)}{i(y - b)} = -1,$$

and hence

$$\lim_{\substack{x = a \\ y \to b}} \frac{f(z) - f(\alpha)}{z - \alpha} = -1. \tag{5b}$$

Since these two different paths along which z may approach α lead to two different limiting values of the difference quotient $(f(z) - f(\alpha))/(z - \alpha)$, there is no single complex number which we can call $f'(\alpha)$ in Eq. (1) or (2). That is, the function $w = \bar{z}$ does not have a derivative. *Question.* Is the function $w = \bar{z}$ *continuous* for some, none, or all values of z? Can you justify your answer?

In terms of the Δ-notation, we may call

$$z - \alpha = \Delta z, \qquad f(z) - f(\alpha) = \Delta w$$

and say that $w = f(z)$ has a derivative

$$\frac{dw}{dz} = \lim_{\Delta z \to 0} \frac{\Delta w}{\Delta z} \tag{6}$$

provided the limit exists and is independent of the manner in which $\Delta z \to 0$.

The formulas for differentiating sums, products, quotients, and powers are the same for complex variables as for real variables. In other words, if c is any complex constant, n is a positive integer, and if $f(z)$ and $g(z)$ are functions that have derivatives at $z = \alpha$, then at $z = \alpha$:

1. $\dfrac{dc}{dz} = 0,$

2. $\dfrac{dcf(z)}{dz} = c\dfrac{df(z)}{dz},$

3. $\dfrac{d[f(z) + g(z)]}{dz} = \dfrac{df(z)}{dz} + \dfrac{dg(z)}{dz},$

4. $\dfrac{d}{dz}[f(z)g(z)] = f(z)\dfrac{dg(z)}{dz} + g(z)\dfrac{df(z)}{dz},$

5. $\dfrac{d}{dz}\dfrac{f(z)}{g(z)} = \dfrac{g(z)\dfrac{df(z)}{dz} - f(z)\dfrac{dg(z)}{dz}}{[g(z)]^2}, \qquad g(z) \neq 0,$

6. a) $\dfrac{d}{dz}[f(z)]^n = n[f(z)]^{n-1}\dfrac{df(z)}{dz},$ **b)** $\dfrac{d(z^n)}{dz} = nz^{n-1}.$

These formulas may all be derived rather easily in the Δ-notation, provided one first proves that the limit of a sum, product, or quotient of two complex functions is the sum, product, or quotient of their limits (always, of course, excluding division by zero), whenever the individual limits exist. We shall omit these proofs and content ourselves here with a simple example.

EXAMPLE 2. Show that

$$\frac{d(z^3)}{dz} = 3z^2.$$

Solution. Let $w = z^3$. Then

$$w + \Delta w = z^3 + 3z^2\,\Delta z + 3z\,(\Delta z)^2 + (\Delta z)^3,$$

$$\frac{\Delta w}{\Delta z} = 3z^2 + 3z\,(\Delta z) + (\Delta z)^2,$$

and

$$\left| \frac{\Delta w}{\Delta z} - 3z^2 \right| = |3z + \Delta z| \cdot |\Delta z| \to 0 \quad \text{as} \quad \Delta z \to 0. \tag{7}$$

Therefore,

$$\lim_{\Delta z \to 0} \frac{\Delta w}{\Delta z} = 3z^2;$$

that is,

$$\frac{d(z^3)}{dz} = 3z^2.$$

Note that it makes no difference *how* Δz approaches zero in (7) above. When $|\Delta z|$ is small, the whole right side of the equation is small.

PROBLEMS

In Problems 1–3, find the derivative with respect to z of the given function at the given point z_0.

1. $\frac{z+1}{z-1}$, $z_0 = 1 + i$

2. $z^3 + 3z^2 + 3z + 2$, $z_0 = -1 + 2i$

3. $\sqrt{z^2+1}$, $z_0 = (1+i)/\sqrt{2}$. (Here we get *two* answers, depending upon our choice of the square root.)

4. Use the definition in Eq. (1) to find $f'(\alpha)$ if $f(z) = 1/z$ and $\alpha \neq 0$.

17–5 THE CAUCHY–RIEMANN EQUATIONS

If the complex function $w = u + iv = f(z)$ is differentiable (i.e., has a derivative) at the point $\alpha = a + ib$, then by making $z \to \alpha$, once along the line $y = b$ (i.e., take $\Delta y = 0$ and make $\Delta x \to 0$) and then along the line $x = a$ (i.e., take $\Delta x = 0$ and make $\Delta y \to 0$), we quickly learn that the equations

$$\frac{\partial u}{\partial x} = \frac{\partial v}{\partial y} \quad \text{and} \quad \frac{\partial v}{\partial x} = -\frac{\partial u}{\partial y} \tag{1}$$

must be satisfied at the point (a, b).

For, assuming that dw/dz does exist at $z = \alpha$, we have

$$f'(\alpha) = \lim_{\substack{\Delta y = 0 \\ \Delta x \to 0}} \frac{\Delta u + i\,\Delta v}{\Delta x + i\,\Delta y} = \lim_{\Delta x \to 0} \left(\frac{\Delta u}{\Delta x} + i\frac{\Delta v}{\Delta x}\right)$$

$$= \left(\frac{\partial u}{\partial x} + i\frac{\partial v}{\partial x}\right)_{z=\alpha} \tag{2a}$$

and also

$$f'(\alpha) = \lim_{\substack{\Delta x = 0 \\ \Delta y \to 0}} \frac{\Delta u + i\,\Delta v}{\Delta x + i\,\Delta y} = \lim_{\Delta y \to 0} \left(\frac{\Delta u}{i\,\Delta y} + \frac{\Delta v}{\Delta y}\right)$$

$$= \left(\frac{1}{i}\frac{\partial u}{\partial y} + \frac{\partial v}{\partial y}\right)_{z=\alpha}$$

$$= \left(-i\frac{\partial u}{\partial y} + \frac{\partial v}{\partial y}\right)_{z=\alpha}. \tag{2b}$$

We have now only to equate the real and imaginary parts of these two expressions for $f'(\alpha)$, Eq. (2a, b), in order to obtain the results in Eq. (1).

These relationships, which connect the four partial derivatives of u and v with respect to x and y, are known as the *Cauchy–Riemann* differential equations. We have just shown that they must be satisfied at any point where $w = f(z)$ has a derivative. Thus we cannot, in general, specify the functions $u = u(x, y)$ and $v = v(x, y)$ independently and expect the resulting function $w = u + iv$ to be differentiable with respect to $z = x + iy$. However, if we take functions that do satisfy the Cauchy–Riemann equations and, in addition, have *continuous* partial derivatives, u_x, u_y, v_x, v_y, then it is true (but we shall not prove it here) that the resulting function $w = u + iv$ is differentiable with respect to z. In a sense, this says that if the derivatives calculated along the *two* directions $x = a$ and $y = b$ are equal, and if the partial derivatives u_x, etc., are *continuous*, then one will also get the same answer for $f'(\alpha)$ along *all* directions.*

If a function $w = f(z)$ has a derivative at every point of some region G in the z-plane, then the function is said to be *analytic* in G. If a function fails to have a derivative at one point α but does have a derivative everywhere else in a region G, we still say that it is analytic in G *except* at α and say that α is a *singular* point of the function. Thus, for example, a rational function $f(z)/g(z)$, where $f(z)$ and $g(z)$ are polynomials, is analytic everywhere except at those points where the denominator is zero. For all points where $g(z) \neq 0$, the function has a derivative

$$\frac{g(z)f'(z) - f(z)g'(z)}{[g(z)]^2}.$$

EXAMPLE. Show that the real and imaginary parts of the function $w = 1/z$ satisfy the Cauchy–Riemann equations at all points where $z \neq 0$.

Solution. Let

$$w = u + iv = \frac{1}{x + iy} = \frac{x - iy}{x^2 + y^2},$$

so that

$$u = \frac{x}{x^2 + y^2}, \qquad v = \frac{-y}{x^2 + y^2}; \qquad x^2 + y^2 \neq 0.$$

Then we find, by calculating the partial derivatives, that

$$\frac{\partial u}{\partial x} = \frac{y^2 - x^2}{(x^2 + y^2)^2} = \frac{\partial v}{\partial y},$$

$$\frac{\partial v}{\partial x} = \frac{2xy}{(x^2 + y^2)^2} = -\frac{\partial u}{\partial y},$$

so that the Cauchy–Riemann equations are satisfied at all points where

$$x^2 + y^2 \neq 0; \qquad \text{that is,} \quad z \neq 0.$$

* For a discussion of conditions that, together with the Cauchy–Riemann equations, imply the differentiability of a function $w = f(z)$, see J. D. Gray and S. A. Morris, "When is a function that satisfies the Cauchy–Riemann equations analytic?" *Amer. Math. Monthly* **85** (1978), 4, pp. 246–254.

PROBLEMS

Find the real and imaginary parts of the functions $w = f(z)$, $w = u + iv$, $z = x + iy$, and show that they satisfy the Cauchy–Riemann equations

1. z^2 **2.** z^3 **3.** z^4 **4.** $1/z^2, \quad z \neq 0$

5. If the partial derivatives of first and second order of the real and imaginary parts $u = u(x, y)$, $v = v(x, y)$ of an analytic function $w = f(z)$ are continuous, show that

$$\frac{\partial^2 u}{\partial x^2} + \frac{\partial^2 u}{\partial y^2} = 0 \quad \text{and} \quad \frac{\partial^2 v}{\partial x^2} + \frac{\partial^2 v}{\partial y^2} = 0.$$

6. Verify that the equations in Problem 5 are satisfied by the real and imaginary parts of the functions (a) z, (b) z^2, (c) z^3.

COMPLEX SERIES

The simplest functions of the complex variable $z = x + iy$ are polynomials and rational functions (ratios of polynomials) in z. These have been briefly discussed above. We might now ask whether or not it is possible to make useful definitions of other elementary functions, such as $\sin z$, $\cos z$, e^z, $\cosh z$, and so on. It is hard for us to imagine $\sin(2 + 3i)$, for example, if we try to think of $2 + 3i$ as meaning an angle. In fact, we may have had trouble thinking of the meaning of the simpler expression sin 2. Of course, in the latter case, we ask "2 what?" and answer "2 radians," and look up sin 2 in a table. But how was the table itself constructed? Why, by means of the series

$$\sin x = x - \frac{x^3}{3!} + \frac{x^5}{5!} - \frac{x^7}{7!} + \cdots \tag{1}$$

To use the series to calculate sin 2, for example, we don't need to think of radians at all, but just take $x = 2$ as a pure number. To be sure, the trigonometric identities for $\sin(x + y)$, $\cos(x + y)$, and so on, are also used in constructing tables, but the series in Eq. (1) is the basic thing.

Now, we may ask ourselves, why can't we go ahead and define $\sin z = \sin(x + iy)$ by a series like (1) but having z in place of x? The answer is, of course, we can do this if we want to and if the series converges. We are therefore led to investigate power series in z, such as

$$\sin z = z - \frac{z^3}{3!} + \frac{z^5}{5!} - \frac{z^7}{7!} + \cdots \tag{2}$$

When y is zero, then $z = x + iy = x$ and the series in (2) is the same as the series in (1). Thus it would be consistent to use the series to extend the domain of definition of $\sin z$ from the real axis into the complex plane.

Convergence

We say that a power series

$$\sum_{n=0}^{\infty} a_n z^n = a_0 + a_1 z + a_2 z^2 + \cdots \tag{3}$$

converges at a point z if the sequence of partial sums

$$\begin{aligned} s_0 &= a_0, \\ s_1 &= a_0 + a_1 z, \\ &\vdots \\ s_n &= a_0 + a_1 z + \cdots + a_n z^n \end{aligned} \tag{4}$$

tends to a limit as n becomes infinite. If we separate s_n into its real and imaginary parts,

$$s_n = u_n(x, y) + iv_n(x, y), \tag{5}$$

then

$$s_n \to u + iv \qquad \text{if and only if} \qquad u_n \to u \quad \text{and} \quad v_n \to v. \tag{6}$$

This follows from the fact that

$$\begin{aligned} |s_n - (u + iv)| &= |(u_n - u) + i(v_n - v)| \\ &= \sqrt{(u_n - u)^2 + (v_n - v)^2} \end{aligned}$$

approaches zero if and only if $u_n - u \to 0$ and $v_n - v \to 0$.

We say that the series (3) *converges absolutely* if and only if the corresponding series of absolute values

$$\sum_{n=0}^{\infty} |a_n z^n| = |a_0| + |a_1 z| + |a_2 z^2| + \cdots \tag{7}$$

converges. Since this is a series of nonnegative real numbers, we already know tests (the comparison test, integral test, ratio test, root test) for determining whether it converges. Then, if (7) does converge, the following theorem tells us that (3) also converges.

Theorem. *If a series $\sum_{n=0}^{\infty} a_n z^n$ converges absolutely, then it converges.*

Proof. Separate each term of the series into its real and imaginary parts, say

$$a_k z^k = c_k + id_k, \qquad k = 0, 1, 2, \ldots, \tag{8}$$

where c_k and d_k are real. Then if the series (7) converges, we use the fact that

$$|c_k| \le \sqrt{c_k^2 + d_k^2} = |a_k z^k|, \qquad |d_k| \le \sqrt{c_k^2 + d_k^2} = |a_k z^k|,$$

and the comparison test for nonnegative real series, to show that

$$\sum |c_k| \qquad \text{and} \qquad \sum |d_k|$$

both converge. But from this we conclude that the series

$$\sum c_k \qquad \text{and} \qquad \sum d_k,$$

(without absolute value signs) both converge. Hence

$$\sum (c_k + id_k) = \sum c_k + i \sum d_k$$

also converges. Q.E.D.

EXAMPLE. The series for $\sin z$ in Eq. (2) converges for all complex numbers z, $|z| < \infty$.

Proof. We test (2) for *absolute convergence* by examining

$$\sum_{k=1}^{\infty} \left| \frac{(-1)^{k-1} z^{2k-1}}{(2k-1)!} \right|. \tag{9}$$

We apply the ratio test with

$$U_n = \left| \frac{(-1)^{n-1} z^{2n-1}}{(2n-1)!} \right|,$$

and calculate

$$\frac{U_{n+1}}{U_n} = \frac{|z^2|}{2n(2n+1)}.$$

For *any* fixed z such that $|z| < \infty$, we then find

$$\lim_{n\to\infty} \frac{U_{n+1}}{U_n} = \lim_{n\to\infty} \frac{|z^2|}{2n(2n+1)} = 0.$$

Since this limit is less than unity, series (9) converges. That is, series (2) converges *absolutely*. Hence, by our theorem, it also converges without the absolute value signs.

PROBLEMS

Write out the first four terms of the series in Problems 1–5, and find the region in the complex plane in which each series converges absolutely.

1. $\sum_{n=0}^{\infty} z^n$

2. $\sum_{n=1}^{\infty} (-1)^{n-1} n z^{n-1}$

3. $\sum_{n=1}^{\infty} (-1)^{n-1} \frac{(z-1)^n}{n}$

4. $\sum_{n=1}^{\infty} \frac{(z+i)^n}{n}$

5. $\sum_{n=0}^{\infty} (-1)^n \frac{(z+1)^n}{2^n}$

6. Show that $\sum z^k/k!$ converges absolutely for all $|z| < \infty$.

7. Show that $\sum (-1)^k z^{2k}/(2k)!$ converges absolutely for all $|z| < \infty$.

8. Show that $\sum (-1)^{k-1} z^k/k$ converges absolutely for $|z| < 1$.

17–7 ELEMENTARY FUNCTIONS

We may define other functions of a complex variable as we did the function $\sin z$, by extending formulas already developed for real valued functions. Formally, we just substitute z for x, to obtain such formulas as

$$e^z = 1 + z + \frac{z^2}{2!} + \frac{z^3}{3!} + \cdots = \sum_{k=0}^{\infty} \frac{z^k}{k!}, \tag{1}$$

$$\sin z = z - \frac{z^3}{3!} + \frac{z^5}{5!} - \frac{z^7}{7!} + \cdots = \sum_{k=1}^{\infty} \frac{(-1)^{k-1} z^{2k-1}}{(2k-1)!}, \tag{2}$$

$$\cos z = 1 - \frac{z^2}{2!} + \frac{z^4}{4!} - \frac{z^6}{6!} + \cdots = \sum_{k=0}^{\infty} \frac{(-1)^k z^{2k}}{(2k)!}, \tag{3}$$

$$\tan^{-1} z = z - \frac{z^3}{3} + \frac{z^5}{5} - \frac{z^7}{7} + \cdots = \sum_{k=1}^{\infty} \frac{(-1)^{k-1} z^{2k-1}}{2k-1}, \tag{4}$$

$$\ln (1+z) = z - \frac{z^2}{2} + \frac{z^3}{3} - \frac{z^4}{4} + \cdots = \sum_{k=1}^{\infty} (-1)^{k-1} \frac{z^k}{k}. \tag{5}$$

It is easy to show, by the ratio test, that the first three of these series converge absolutely for $|z| < \infty$. The last two converge absolutely if z is inside the unit circle $|z| < 1$, and diverge if $|z| > 1$. We realize that the inverse tangent function is multiple-valued, and the series in (4) gives the so-called *principal value* of $\tan^{-1} z$. We shall show that the logarithm of a complex number is also multiple-valued, and the series in (5) gives the principal value of $\ln(1 + z)$ when $|z| < 1$.

It is a basic theorem in the theory of functions of a complex variable that a power series $\sum a_k z^k$ either

a) converges only at $z = 0$, or
b) converges inside a circle $|z| < R$, or
c) converges for all z, $|z| < \infty$.

The second case occurs when the function represented by the power series is analytic everywhere inside the circle $|z| < R$, but has a singularity on the circle $|z| = R$. In this case, the theorem tells us that the *largest* circle inside which the series will converge has radius R equal to the distance from $z = 0$ to the nearest singular point of the function. Thus, for example,

$$\frac{1}{1+z^2} = 1 - z^2 + z^4 - z^6 + \cdots = \sum_{k=0}^{\infty} (-1)^k z^{2k} \tag{6}$$

converges inside a circle of radius $R = 1$, since the singularities of the function occur at $z = \pm i$, which are at distance $R = 1$ from the origin. We call the circle $|z| = 1$ the "circle of convergence," by which we mean that the series converges for all z *inside* this circle and diverges for any z *outside* it (Fig. 17–13). Behavior *on* the circle of convergence constitutes a difficult problem, which we are not prepared to discuss.

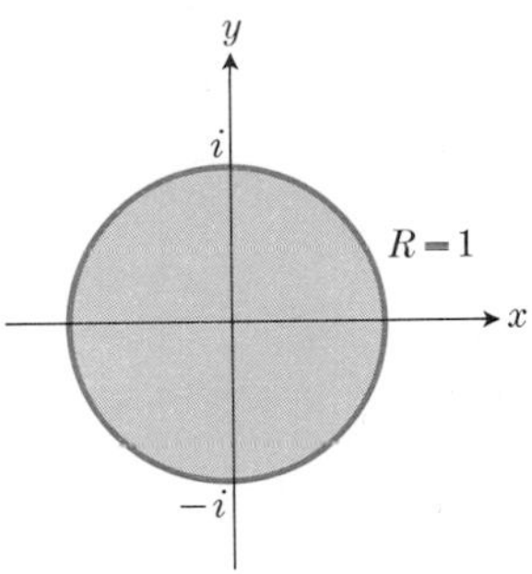

17–13 The circle of convergence of the series $\sum_{k=0}^{\infty} (-1)^k z^{2k}$.

Certain basic properties of the elementary functions can be shown to extend from the domain of real variables x to complex variables z by algebraic manipulation with series. For example, we can prove the following theorem by appealing to the series definition of e^z.

Theorem. $e^{z_1} \cdot e^{z_2} = e^{z_1 + z_2}$ **(7)**

Proof. We multiply the series for e^{z_1} by the series for e^{z_2} and collect terms of like degree. By the *degree* of a term

$$z_1^p z_2^q,$$

we mean simply the sum of the exponents $p + q$. We shall focus our attention on all those terms in the product that are of a certain degree, say n. Then we may safely ignore all powers

$$z_1^{n+1}, \quad z_1^{n+2}, \quad \ldots \qquad \text{and} \qquad z_2^{n+1}, \quad z_2^{n+2}, \quad \ldots,$$

since these would enter only in terms of degree greater than n. Now we want all terms of the form $z_1^k z_2^{n-k}$, with $k = 0, 1, 2, \ldots, n$. When we multiply

$$e^{z_1} = 1 + z_1 + \frac{z_1^2}{2!} + \frac{z_1^3}{3!} + \cdots + \frac{z_1^n}{n!} + \cdots$$

by

$$e^{z_2} = 1 + z_2 + \frac{z_2^2}{2!} + \frac{z_2^3}{3!} + \cdots + \frac{z_2^n}{n!} + \cdots,$$

the following terms are of degree n:

$$\frac{z_1^n}{n!} \cdot 1 + \frac{z_1^{n-1}}{(n-1)!} \cdot z_2 + \frac{z_1^{n-2}}{(n-2)!} \cdot \frac{z_2^2}{2!} + \cdots$$

$$+ \frac{z_1^{n-k}}{(n-k)!} \cdot \frac{z_2^k}{k!} + \cdots + 1 \cdot \frac{z_2^n}{n!} = \sum_{k=0}^{n} \frac{z_1^{n-k} z_2^k}{(n-k)!\, k!}. \tag{8}$$

On the other hand, the terms of degree n in the series for

$$e^{z_1+z_2} = 1 + (z_1 + z_2) + \frac{(z_1 + z_2)^2}{2!} + \cdots + \frac{(z_1 + z_2)^n}{n!} + \cdots$$

are in the one binomial expression

$$\frac{(z_1 + z_2)^n}{n!} = \frac{1}{n!} \left[z_1^n + n z_1^{n-1} z_2 + \frac{n(n-1)}{2!} z_1^{n-2} z_2^2 + \cdots \right.$$

$$\left. + \frac{n(n-1) \cdots (n-k+1)}{k!} z_1^{n-k} z_2^k + \cdots + z_2^n \right].$$

By noticing that

$$\frac{n(n-1) \cdots (n-k+1)}{k!} \cdot \frac{(n-k)!}{(n-k)!} = \frac{n!}{k!\,(n-k)!},$$

we may also write this in summation form as

$$\frac{(z_1 + z_2)^n}{n!} = \frac{1}{n!} \sum_{k=0}^{n} \frac{n!}{k!\,(n-k)!} z_1^{n-k} z_2^k = \sum_{k=0}^{n} \frac{z_1^{n-k} z_2^k}{(n-k)!\, k!}. \tag{9}$$

A comparison of Eqs. (8) and (9) shows us that we have precisely the same terms of degree n in the product of the two series for e^{z_1} and e^{z_2} that we have in the series for $e^{z_1+z_2}$. The argument above is valid for any positive integer n. For $n = 0$, the terms of degree zero are

$$z_1^0 \cdot z_2^0 = 1 \qquad \text{and} \qquad (z_1 + z_2)^0 = 1,$$

respectively, and these again are equal. Thus the terms of degree n ($n = 0, 1, 2, 3, \ldots$) are the same in the product of the series for e^{z_1} and e^{z_2} as they are in the series for $e^{z_1+z_2}$; that is,

$$(\text{the series for } e^{z_1}) \cdot (\text{the series for } e^{z_2}) = (\text{the series for } e^{z_1+z_2}).$$

Q.E.D.

REMARK. The sum of the series we get when we multiply two series together may depend on how the terms of the product series are arranged or grouped. The way we arranged the terms of the product $e^{z_1} \cdot e^{z_2}$ in the proof of the preceding theorem, for instance, is quite different from

$$1 \cdot \left(1 + z_2 + \frac{z_2^2}{2!} + \cdots\right) + z_1\left(1 + z_2 + \frac{z_2^2}{2!} + \cdots\right) + \cdots$$
$$+ \frac{z_1^n}{n!}\left(1 + z_2 + \frac{z_2^2}{2!} + \cdots\right) + \cdots,$$

where we agree to add all terms not containing z_1, then all terms containing only the first power of z_1, then all terms containing only the second power of z_1, and so on. This certainly isn't convenient to do if we are trying to show that the result is the same as

$$1 + (z_1 + z_2) + \frac{(z_1 + z_2)^2}{2!} + \frac{(z_1 + z_2)^3}{3!} + \cdots$$

And conceivably it might lead to a different answer. However, it is shown in more advanced courses in analysis that when both of the series in a product are *absolutely convergent*, then it is permissible to arrange the terms in any way one may wish, provided one ultimately takes all terms into account. The series for e^z does converge absolutely for all values of z. Hence the series for e^{z_1} and e^{z_2} satisfy the requirements of this theorem, and it is permissible to arrange the terms according to ascending degree, as we have done above.

By similar operations with power series, one can show that

$$\sin (z_1 + z_2) = \sin z_1 \cos z_2 + \cos z_1 \sin z_2,$$
$$\cos (z_1 + z_2) = \cos z_1 \cos z_2 - \sin z_1 \sin z_2,$$
$$\sin^2 z + \cos^2 z = 1.$$

One of the most famous results involving the elementary complex functions is the formula

$$e^{iz} = \cos z + i \sin z, \tag{10}$$

which is known as *Euler's formula*. To establish Eq. (10) we simply substitute iz in place of z in the series (1). The various powers of i that enter can all be reduced to one of the four numbers

$$i, \quad -1, \quad -i, \quad +1$$

by observing that

$$i^2 = -1, \qquad i^3 = i^2 \cdot i = -i,$$
$$i^4 = (i^2)^2 = (-1)^2 = +1, \qquad i^5 = i^4 \cdot i = i,$$

and so on. In fact, if n is any integer, then

$$i^{4n} = +1, \qquad i^{4n+1} = i, \qquad i^{4n+2} = -1, \qquad i^{4n+3} = -i.$$

Thus we have

$$e^{iz} = 1 + iz + \frac{(iz)^2}{2!} + \frac{(iz)^3}{3!} + \frac{(iz)^4}{4!} + \frac{(iz)^5}{5!} + \cdots$$
$$= \left(1 - \frac{z^2}{2!} + \frac{z^4}{4!} - \frac{z^6}{6!} + \cdots\right) + i\left(z - \frac{z^3}{3!} + \frac{z^5}{5!} - \frac{z^7}{7!} + \cdots\right)$$
$$= \cos z + i \sin z,$$

where we have recognized the series for sin z and cos z, Eqs. (2) and (3).

If we use Euler's formula (10) and the companion equation

$$e^{-iz} = \cos z - i \sin z, \tag{11}$$

which results from replacing z by $-z$ in (10), we may express the trigonometric functions of z in terms of exponentials. For example, if we add Eqs. (10) and (11) and then divide by two, we obtain

$$\cos z = \tfrac{1}{2}(e^{iz} + e^{-iz}). \tag{12a}$$

On the other hand, if we subtract (11) from (10) we may express sin z in the form

$$\sin z = \frac{1}{2i}(e^{iz} - e^{-iz}). \tag{12b}$$

The other trigonometric functions of z are defined in the usual way in terms of sin z and cos z.

Thus, for example,

$$\tan z = \frac{\sin z}{\cos z} = \frac{1}{i}\frac{e^{iz} - e^{-iz}}{e^{iz} + e^{-iz}}.$$

To establish the usual trigonometric identities, we may express the trigonometric functions as exponentials and use Eq. (7).

EXAMPLE. Show that

$$\cos^2 z + \sin^2 z = 1.$$

Solution. We square both sides of Eqs. (12a, b) and add:

$$\begin{aligned}\cos^2 z + \sin^2 z &= \tfrac{1}{4}(e^{2iz} + 2e^0 + e^{-2iz}) - \tfrac{1}{4}(e^{2iz} - 2e^0 + e^{-2iz})\\ &= \tfrac{1}{4}(4e^0) = 1.\end{aligned}$$

Equations (12a, b) show the very intimate relationship between the circular functions and the hyperbolic functions. For if we define, as in the real case,

$$\cosh z = \tfrac{1}{2}(e^z + e^{-z}) = 1 + \frac{z^2}{2!} + \frac{z^4}{4!} + \frac{z^6}{6!} + \cdots,$$

$$\sinh z = \tfrac{1}{2}(e^z - e^{-z}) = z + \frac{z^3}{3!} + \frac{z^5}{5!} + \frac{z^7}{7!} + \cdots,$$

then Eqs. (12a, b) say that

$$\cos z = \cosh iz, \tag{13a}$$

$$i \sin z = \sinh iz. \tag{13b}$$

These relationships explain the similarity in form between the identities of circular trigonometry, such as

$$\cos^2 z + \sin^2 z = 1, \tag{14a}$$

and the corresponding identities of hyperbolic trigonometry, such as

$$\cosh^2 u - \sinh^2 u = 1. \tag{14b}$$

In fact, any identity in circular functions produces a corresponding identity in hyperbolic functions, provided $\sin^2$ is replaced by $-\sinh^2$. The minus is a consequence of the i in Eq. (13b).

PROBLEMS

1. Take $z = (1 + i)/\sqrt{2}$ in Eq. (1), and calculate an approximation to $e^{(1+i)/\sqrt{2}}$ by using the first four terms of the series.

2. Express the sines and cosines in the following identity in terms of exponentials and thereby show that

$$\sin(A + B) = \sin A \cos B + \cos A \sin B$$

is a consequence of the exponential law $e^{z_1} \cdot e^{z_2} = e^{z_1 + z_2}$.

3. By differentiating the appropriate series, Eqs. (1)–(5), term by term, show that

a) $\dfrac{de^z}{dz} = e^z$ **b)** $\dfrac{d \sin z}{dz} = \cos z$

c) $\dfrac{d \cos z}{dz} = -\sin z$ **d)** $\dfrac{d \tan^{-1} z}{dz} = \dfrac{1}{1 + z^2}$

e) $\dfrac{d \ln(1 + z)}{dz} = \dfrac{1}{1 + z}$

4. a) Show that $y = e^{i\omega x}$ and $y = e^{-i\omega x}$ are solutions of the differential equation

$$\frac{d^2y}{dx^2} + \omega^2 y = 0.$$

b) Show that $y = e^{(a+ib)x}$ and $y = e^{(a-ib)x}$ are solutions of the differential equation

$$\frac{d^2y}{dx^2} - 2a\frac{dy}{dx} + (a^2 + b^2)y = 0.$$

c) Assuming that a and b are real in part 4(b) above, show that both

$$e^{ax} \cos bx = R(e^{(a+ib)x}) \quad \text{and} \quad e^{ax} \sin bx = I(e^{(a+ib)x})$$

are solutions of the given differential equation.

5. Find values of m such that $y = e^{mx}$ is a solution of the differential equation:

a) $\dfrac{d^2y}{dx^2} + 2\dfrac{dy}{dx} + 5y = 0$ **b)** $\dfrac{d^4y}{dx^4} + 4y = 0$

c) $\dfrac{d^3y}{dx^3} - 8y = 0.$

6. Show that the point (x, y) describes a unit circle with angular velocity ω if $z = x + iy = e^{i\omega t}$ and ω is a real constant.

7. If x and y are real, show that $|e^{x+iy}| = e^x$.

8. Show that the real and imaginary parts of $\omega = e^z$ satisfy the Cauchy–Riemann equations.

9. Show by reference to the appropriate series that (a) $\sin(iz) = i \sinh z$, (b) $\cos(iz) = \cosh z$.

10. Show, by reference to the results of Problems 2 and 9, that $\sin(x + iy) = \sin x \cosh y + i \cos x \sinh y$, and find a value of z such that $\sin z = 2$.

11. Show that the real and imaginary parts of $\omega = \sin z$, Problem 10, satisfy the Cauchy–Riemann equations.

12. Show that $|\sin(x + iy)| = \sqrt{\sin^2 x + \sinh^2 y}$ if x and y are real.

13. Let $z = x + iy$, $w = u + iv$, $w = \sin z$. Show that the line segment $y =$ constant, $-\pi < x \leq +\pi$, in the z-plane maps into the ellipse

$$\frac{u^2}{\cosh^2 y} + \frac{v^2}{\sinh^2 y} = 1$$

in the w-plane.

14. Show that the only complex roots $z = x + iy$ (x and y real) of the equation $\sin z = 0$ are at points on the real axis $(y = 0)$ at which $\sin x = 0$.

15. Show that

$$\cosh(x + iy) = \cosh x \cos y + i \sinh x \sin y.$$

16. Show that

$$|\cosh(x + iy)| = \sqrt{\cos^2 y + \sinh^2 x}$$

if x and y are real.

17. If x and y are real and $\cosh(x + iy) = 0$, show that $x = 0$ and $\cos y = 0$.

18. What is the image in the w-plane of a line $x =$ constant in the z-plane if (a) $w = e^z$, (b) $w = \sin z$? Sketch.

19. Integrate: $\int e^{(a+ib)x}\,dx$ and, by equating real and imaginary parts, obtain formulas for $\int e^{ax} \cos bx\,dx$ and $\int e^{ax} \sin bx\,dx$.

17–8 LOGARITHMS

In the previous article, we mentioned that the logarithm (as an inverse of the exponential) is a multiple-valued function of z. The multiple-valuedness is introduced by the polar angle θ. We see this when we write

$$z = r \text{ cis } \theta$$

or, as we may do in view of Euler's formula,

$$z = re^{i\theta}, \tag{1}$$

and ask that

$$\begin{aligned}\log_e z &= \log_e r + \log_e e^{i\theta}\\ &= \ln r + i\theta.\end{aligned} \tag{2}$$

Then the angle θ may be given its principal value θ_0, $-\pi < \theta_0 \le \pi$, which leads to the *principal value* of $\log z$,

$$\ln z = \ln r + i\theta_0, \qquad -\pi < \theta_0 \le \pi. \tag{3}$$

But many other values of θ will still give the same z in Eq. (1), namely,

$$\theta = \theta_0 + 2n\pi, \qquad n = 0, \pm 1, \pm 2, \ldots, \tag{4}$$

and each of these values of θ gives rise, in turn, to a value of $\log z$ (we shall omit writing the base e henceforth), namely,

$$\log z = \ln r + i(\theta_0 + 2n\pi). \tag{5a}$$

In terms of the principal value, we have

$$\log z = \ln z + 2n\pi i, \tag{5b}$$

so that all of the infinitely many different values of $\log z$ differ from the principal value by an integral multiple of $2\pi i$.

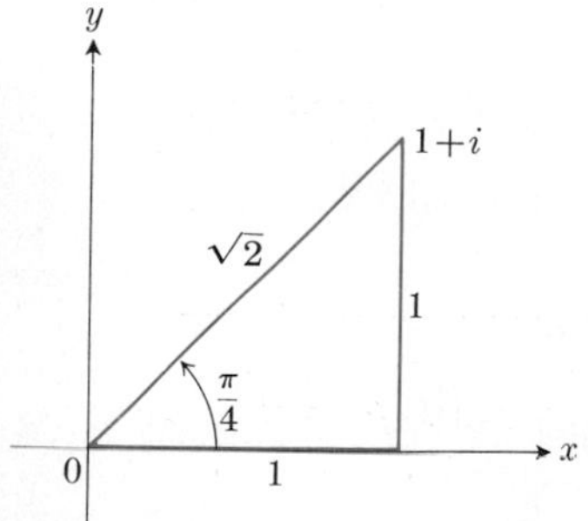

17–14 Argand diagram of $1 + i$.

EXAMPLE. Find all values of $\log(1 + i)$.

Solution. The complex number $1 + i$ is seen to have polar coordinates $r = \sqrt{2}$, $\theta_0 = \pi/4$ (Fig. 17–14). Hence

$$1 + i = \sqrt{2}\, e^{i(\pi/4 + 2n\pi)}$$

and

$$\log(1 + i) = \ln\sqrt{2} + i\left(\frac{\pi}{4} + 2n\pi\right),$$

$$n = 0, \pm 1, \pm 2, \ldots$$

PROBLEMS

1. Find the principal value of log z for each of the following complex numbers z:

a) $2 - 2i$, b) $\sqrt{3} + i$, c) -4,

d) $+4$, e) $2i$, f) $\dfrac{1+i}{1-i}$.

2. Find *all* values of log z for each of the following complex numbers z:

a) 2, b) -2, c) $2i$,

d) $-2i$, e) $i - \sqrt{3}$.

3. Express $w = \tan z$ in terms of exponentials; then solve for z in terms of w and thereby show that

$$\tan^{-1} w = \frac{1}{2i} \log \frac{1 + iw}{1 - iw}.$$

4. a) Show that

$$\sin^{-1} z = -i \log (iz + \sqrt{1 - z^2}).$$

b) Find $\sin^{-1} 3$.

5. Sketch the images in the w-plane of the following sets in the z-plane, under the mapping function $w = \ln z$:

a) $|z| =$ constant, $-\pi < \arg z \le +\pi$,

b) $\arg z =$ constant, $0 < |z| < +\infty$.

REVIEW QUESTIONS AND EXERCISES

1. Define the system of complex numbers.

2. Define, for complex numbers, the concepts of equality, addition, multiplication, and division.

3. Is the system of complex numbers closed under the operations of addition, subtraction, multiplication, division (by numbers $\neq 0$), and raising to powers (including complex exponents; see Article 6–9, Eq. (3))? [A system is said to be *closed* under an operation $\otimes$ if $a \otimes b$ is in the system whenever a and b are.]

4. How may the complex number $a + ib$ be represented graphically in an Argand diagram?

5. Illustrate, on an Argand diagram, how the absolute values and arguments of the product and quotient of two complex numbers z_1 and z_2 are related to the absolute values and the arguments of z_1 and z_2.

6. State De Moivre's theorem, and explain how it may be used to find expressions for $\cos n\theta$ and $\sin n\theta$ as polynomials in $\cos \theta$ and $\sin \theta$.

7. Prove that, if n is an even positive integer, then $\cos n\theta$ may be expressed as a polynomial, with integral coefficients, in $\cos^2 \theta$. [*Example*. $\cos 2\theta = 2 \cos^2 \theta - 1$.]

8. Using an Argand diagram, explain how to find the n complex nth roots of any complex number $a + ib$.

9. On an Argand diagram, illustrate how the conjugate and the reciprocal of a complex number $a + ib$ are related to that number.

10. If the conjugate of a complex number is equal to the number, what else can you conclude about the number?

11. If z is a complex number such that $z = -\bar{z}$, what more can you conclude about z?

12. What is the location of the complex variable z if:

a) $|z - \alpha| = k$ b) $|z - \alpha| < k$ c) $|z - \alpha| > k$,

when $\alpha = a + ib$ is a given complex number and k is a positive real constant?

13. Define the concept of continuity of a function of a complex variable, $w = f(z)$. Define the derivative of f at $\alpha = a + ib$.

14. What are the Cauchy–Riemann equations, and when are they known to be satisfied?

15. Define convergence of a series of complex numbers.

16. How do we define e^z, $\sin z$, $\cos z$, $\log z$, and $\tan z$ for complex $z = x + iy$?

17. How would you define z^α for complex z and α? Illustrate for $z = 1 + i$, $\alpha = 2i$.

MISCELLANEOUS PROBLEMS

1. Let $z = 2 - 2i$, $i = \sqrt{-1}$. (a) Plot the points z, $\bar{z}$, and z^2. (b) Plot the three complex cube roots of z^2 (that is, $z^{2/3}$).

2. Express each of the following complex numbers in the form $re^{i\theta}$ with $r \ge 0$ and $-\pi < \theta \le \pi$. Sketch.

a) $(1 + i)(1 - i\sqrt{3})^2$ b) $\sqrt[3]{2 - 2i}$ (three answers).

3. Express the following complex numbers in the form $a + bi$.

a) The four 4th roots of $-16i$

b) $\sin^{-1} (5)$.

4. (a) Solve the equation $z^4 + 16 = 0$, obtaining four dis-

tinct roots. (b) Express the five roots of the equation $z^5 + 32 = 0$ in polar form.

5. (a) Find all complex numbers z such that $z^4 + 1 + i\sqrt{3} = 0$. (b) Express the number $e^{2+\pi i/4}$ in the form $a + bi$.

6. Plot the complex number $2 - 2\sqrt{3}\,i$ in an Argand diagram and find (a) its two square roots, (b) the principal value of its logarithm.

7. Find values of r and θ such that $3 + 4i = re^{i\theta}$.

8. If $z = 3 - 3i$, find all values of $\log z$.

9. Find a complex number $a + ib$ that will satisfy the equation

$$e^{a+ib} = 1 - i\sqrt{3}.$$

10. Express the following in the form $a + bi$:

a) $(-1 - i)^{1/3}$ (write down all the roots),
b) $\ln (3 + i\sqrt{3})$,
c) $e^{2+\pi i}$.

11. Let $f(z) = \bar{z} =$ the conjugate of z. (a) Study the behavior of the quotient

$$\frac{f(z) - f(z_1)}{z - z_1}$$

when $z \to z_1$ along straight lines of slope m. (b) From the results of (a) what can you conclude about the derivative of $f(z)$?

12. If $f(z) = \sum_{n=0}^{\infty} a_n z^n$ and $f(\bar{z}) = \overline{f(z)}$, for $|z| < R$, show that the a_n are real.

13. If $f(z) = \sum_{n=0}^{\infty} a_n z^n$ and $f(\bar{z}) = f(z)$, for $|z| < R$, show that $f(z)$ is a constant.

14. Show that

$$\frac{d^n}{d\theta^n}(\cos \theta + i \sin \theta) = i^n(\cos \theta + i \sin \theta).$$

15. In each of the following, indicate graphically the locus of points $z = x + iy$ that satisfy the given condition:

a) $R(z) > 0$, **b)** $I(z - i) \le 0$, **c)** $\left|\frac{z - i}{z + i}\right| < 1$,
d) $|e^z| \ge 1$, **e)** $|\sin z| \le 1$.

16. If $u(x, y)$, $v(x, y)$ are the real and imaginary parts of an analytic function of $z = x + iy$, show that the family of curves $u =$ constant is orthogonal to the family $v =$ constant at every point of intersection where $f'(z) \ne 0$.

17. Let $u(x, y) + iv(x, y) = (x + iy)^2$. Sketch the curves $u(x, y) = a$, $v(x, y) = b$, for the cases $a = 1, 0, -1$, and $b = 1, 0, -1$. Show that the locus $u = 0$ is not orthogonal to the locus $v = 0$.

18. Verify that the real and imaginary parts of the following functions satisfy Laplace's equation $\phi_{xx} + \phi_{yy} = 0$:

a) $\sin z$ **b)** $\ln z$ $(z \ne 0)$
c) e^z **d)** $\cosh z$

19. Find all solutions of the following equations:

a) $z^5 = 32$ **b)** $e^z = -2$
c) $\cos z = 10$ **d)** $\tanh z = 2$
e) $z = i^i$ **f)** $z^3 + 3z^2 + 3z + 9 = 0$

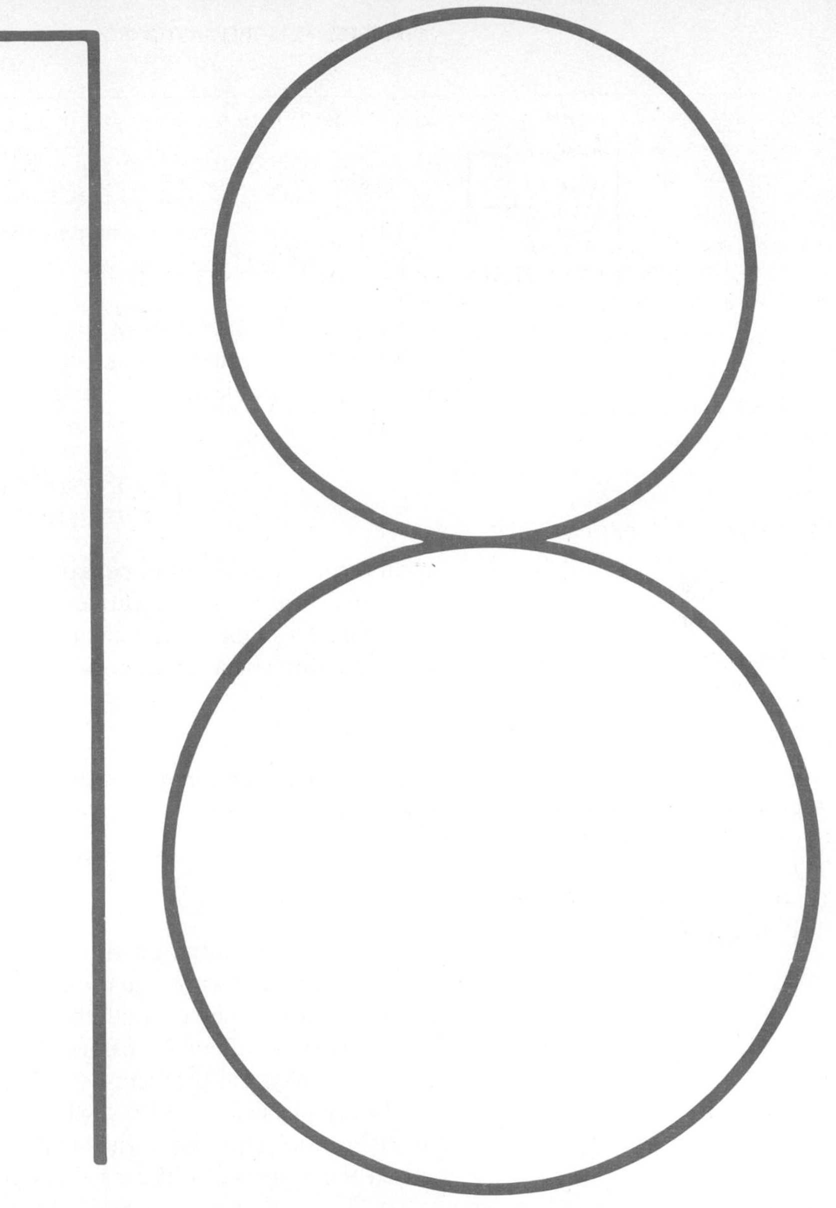

DIFFERENTIAL EQUATIONS

18–1 INTRODUCTION

A differential equation is an equation that involves one or more derivatives, or differentials. Differential equations are classified by

a) type (namely, *ordinary* or *partial*),

b) order (that of the highest order derivative that occurs in the equation), and

c) degree (the exponent of the highest power of the highest order derivative, after the equation has been cleared of fractions and radicals in the dependent variable and its derivatives).

For example,

$$\left(\frac{d^3y}{dx^3}\right)^2 + \left(\frac{d^2y}{dx^2}\right)^5 + \frac{y}{x^2+1} = e^x \tag{1}$$

is an ordinary differential equation, of order three and degree two.

Only "ordinary" derivatives occur when the dependent variable y is a function of a single independent variable x. On the other hand, if the dependent variable y is a function of two or more independent variables, say

$$y = f(x, t),$$

where x and t are independent variables, then partial derivatives of y may occur. For example,

$$\frac{\partial^2 y}{\partial t^2} = a^2 \frac{\partial^2 y}{\partial x^2} \tag{2}$$

is a partial differential equation, of order two and degree one. (It is the one-dimensional "wave equation." A systematic treatment of partial differential equations lies beyond the scope of this book. For a discussion of partial differential equations, including the wave equation, and solutions of associated physical problems, see Kaplan, *Advanced Calculus*, Chapter 10.)

Many physical problems, when formulated in mathematical terms, lead to differential equations. In Article 11–2, for example, we discussed and solved the system of differential equations

$$m\frac{d^2x}{dt^2} = 0, \qquad m\frac{d^2y}{dt^2} = -mg \tag{3}$$

which described the motion of a projectile (neglecting air resistance). Indeed, one of the chief sources of differential equations in mechanics is Newton's second law:

$$\mathbf{F} = \frac{d}{dt}(m\mathbf{v}), \tag{4}$$

where $\mathbf{F}$ is the resultant of the forces acting on a body of mass m and $\mathbf{v}$ is its velocity.

In the field of radiochemistry, the following situation is a typical simplification of what may happen. Suppose that, at time t, there are x, y, and z grams, respectively, of three radioactive substances A, B, and C, which have the following properties:

i) A, through radioactive decomposition, transforms into B at a rate proportional to the amount of A present.
ii) B, in turn, transforms into C at a rate proportional to the amount of B present.
iii) Finally, C is caused to transform back into A at a rate proportional to the amount of C present; see Fig. 18–1.

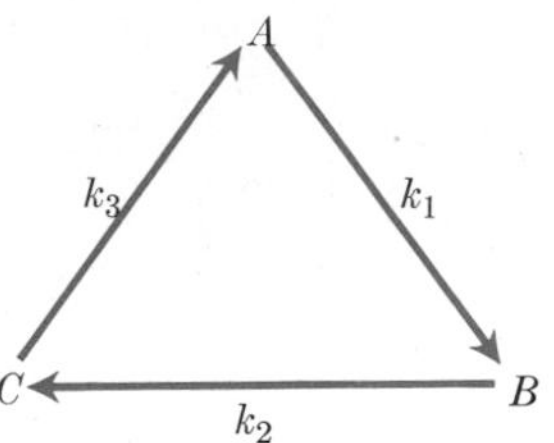

18–1 Three substances may transform in such a way that A changes into B, B into C, and C back into A.

If we call the proportionality factors k_1, k_2, and k_3, respectively, we have the following system of differential equations:

$$\frac{dx}{dt} = -k_1 x + k_3 z, \qquad \frac{dy}{dt} = k_1 x - k_2 y, \qquad \frac{dz}{dt} = k_2 y - k_3 z. \tag{5}$$

The first of these simply says that the amount of A present at time t, namely x, is decreasing at a rate $k_1 x$ through transformation into substance B, but is gaining at a rate $k_3 z$ from substance C. The other two equations have similar meanings. It is an immediate consequence of Eqs. (5) that

$$\frac{dx}{dt} + \frac{dy}{dt} + \frac{dz}{dt} = 0. \tag{6}$$

From Eq. (6), in turn, we readily deduce that

$$x + y + z = \text{constant}.$$

In other words, in the hypothetical case under consideration, the total amount of substances A, B, and C remains constant.

18–2 SOLUTIONS

A function

$$y = f(x)$$

is said to be a *solution* of a differential equation if the latter is satisfied when y and its derivatives are replaced throughout by $f(x)$ and its corresponding derivatives. For example, if C_1 and C_2 are any constants, then

$$y = C_1 \cos x + C_2 \sin x \tag{1a}$$

is a solution of the differential equation

$$\frac{d^2y}{dx^2} + y = 0. \tag{1b}$$

A physical problem that translates into a differential equation usually involves additional conditions not expressed by the differential equation itself. In mechanics, for example, the initial position and velocity of the moving body are usually prescribed, as well as the forces. The differential equation, or equations, of motion will usually have solutions in which certain arbitrary constants occur, as in (1a) above. Specific values are then assigned to these arbitrary constants to meet the prescribed initial conditions. (See the examples worked out in Articles 6–11 and 11–2.)

A differential equation of order n will generally have a solution involving n arbitrary constants. (There is a more precise mathematical theorem, which we shall neither state nor prove.) This solution is called the *general* solution. Once this general solution is known, it is only a matter of algebra to determine specific values of the constants if initial conditions are also prescribed. Hence we shall devote our attention to the problem of finding the general solutions of certain types of differential equations.

The subject of differential equations is complex, and there are many textbooks on differential equations and advanced calculus where you can find a more extensive treatment than we shall present here. The field is also the subject of a great deal of current research; and, with the widespread availability of computers, numerical methods for solving differential equations play an important role.

In the remainder of this chapter, the following topics will be treated. Throughout, only *ordinary* differential equations will be considered.

1. First order.
   - **a)** Variables separable.
   - **b)** Homogeneous.
   - **c)** Linear.
   - **d)** Exact differentials.
2. Special types of second order.
3. Linear equations with constant coefficients.
   - **a)** Homogeneous.
   - **b)** Nonhomogeneous.

Several new terms occur in this list, and they will be defined in the appropriate places.

PROBLEMS

Show that each function is a solution of the accompanying differential equation.

1. $xy'' - y' = 0;$
a) $y = x^2 + 3;$ **b)** $y = C_1x^2 + C_2$

2. $x^3y''' + 4x^2y'' + xy' + y = x;\quad y = \frac{1}{2}x$

3. $yy'' = 2(y')^2 - 2y';$
a) $y = C;$ **b)** $C_1y = \tan(C_1x + C_2)$

4. $y' + \frac{1}{x}y = 1;\quad y = \frac{C}{x} + \frac{x}{2}$

5. $2y' + 3y = e^{-x};\quad y = e^{-x} + Ce^{-(3/2)x}$

6. $(x \sin x)y' + (\sin x + x \cos x)y = e^x/x;$

$$y = \frac{1}{x \sin x}\int_{-1/2}^{x} \frac{e^t}{t}\,dt$$

18–3 FIRST ORDER: VARIABLES SEPARABLE

A first order differential equation can be solved by integration if it is possible to collect all y terms with dy and all x terms with dx. That is, if it is possible to write the equation in the form

$$f(y)\,dy + g(x)\,dx = 0,$$

then the general solution is

$$\int f(y)\,dy + \int g(x)\,dx = C,$$

where C is an arbitrary constant.

EXAMPLE. Solve the equation

$$(x+1)\frac{dy}{dx} = x(y^2+1).$$

Solution. We change to differential form, separate the variables, and integrate:

$$(x+1)\,dy = x(y^2+1)\,dx,$$

$$\frac{dy}{y^2+1} = \frac{x\,dx}{x+1},$$

$$\tan^{-1} y = x - \ln|x+1| + C.$$

Some models of population growth assume that the rate of change of the population at time t is proportional to the number y of individuals present at that time. This leads to the equation

$$\frac{dy}{dt} = ky, \tag{1}$$

where k is a constant that is positive if the population is increasing and negative if it is decreasing. To solve Eq. (1), we separate variables and integrate, to obtain

$$\int \frac{dy}{y} = \int k\,dt,$$

or

$$\ln y = kt + C_1$$

(remember that y is positive). It follows that

$$y = e^{kt+C_1}$$
$$= Ce^{kt},$$

where $C = e^{C_1}$. If y_0 denotes the population when $t = 0$, then $C = y_0$ and

$$y = y_0 e^{kt}. \tag{2}$$

This equation is called the *law of exponential growth.*

PROBLEMS

Separate the variables and solve the following differential equations.

1. $x(2y-3)\,dx + (x^2+1)\,dy = 0$
2. $x^2(y^2+1)\,dx + y\sqrt{x^3+1}\,dy = 0$
3. $\dfrac{dy}{dx} = e^{x-y}$
4. $\sqrt{2xy}\dfrac{dy}{dx} = 1$
5. $\sin x\dfrac{dx}{dy} + \cosh 2y = 0$
6. $\ln x\dfrac{dx}{dy} = \dfrac{x}{y}$
7. $xe^y\,dy + \dfrac{x^2+1}{y}\,dx = 0$
8. $y\sqrt{2x^2+3}\,dy + x\sqrt{4-y^2}\,dx = 0$
9. $\sqrt{1+x^2}\,dy + \sqrt{y^2-1}\,dx = 0$
10. $x^2y\dfrac{dy}{dx} = (1+x)\csc y$
11. *Growth of bacteria.* Suppose that the bacteria in a colony can grow unchecked, by the law of exponential

growth. The colony starts with one bacterium, and doubles every half hour. How many bacteria will the colony contain at the end of 24 hours? (Under favorable laboratory conditions, the number of cholera bacteria can double every 30 minutes. Of course, in an infected person, many of the bacteria are destroyed, but this example helps to explain why a person who feels well in the morning may be dangerously ill by evening.)

12. *Discharging capacitor.* As a result of leakage, an electrical capacitor discharges at a rate proportional to the charge. If the charge Q has the value Q_0 at the time $t = 0$, find Q as a function of t.

13. *Electric current.* Ohm's law, $E = Ri$, requires modification in a circuit containing self-inductance, as in a coil. The modified form is

$$L\frac{di}{dt} + Ri = E$$

for the series circuit shown in Fig. 18–2. Here R denotes the resistance of the circuit in ohms, L is the inductance in henries, E is the impressed electromotive force in volts, i is the current in amperes, and t is the time in seconds. (See Sears, Zemansky, Young, *University Physics* (Fifth ed., 1976), Chapter 28.) (a) Solve the differential equation under the assumption that E is constant, and that $i = 0$ when $t = 0$. (b) Find the steady-state current $i_{ss} = \lim_{t\to\infty} i$. (See Fig. 18–3.)

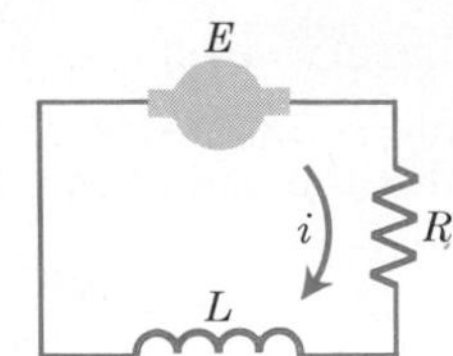

18–2 A simple series circuit.

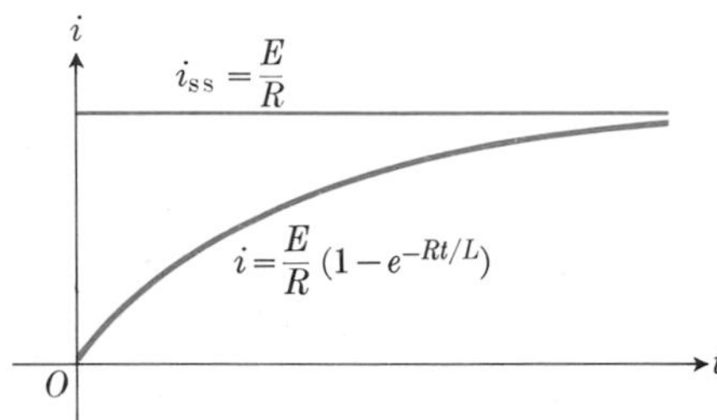

18–3 The current i in the circuit shown in Fig. 18–2 increases toward the steady state value E/R.

14. The decay of a radioactive element can be described by Eq. (2), because the rate of decay is proportional to the number of radioactive nuclei present. The *half-life* of a radioactive element is the time required for half of the radioactive nuclei originally present in any sample to decay. Show that the half-life of a radioactive element is a constant that does not depend on the number of radioactive nuclei initially present in the sample.

15. *Carbon-14 dating.* The half-lives of radioactive elements (see Problem 14) can sometimes be used to date events from the earth's past. The ages of rocks more than 2 billion years old have been measured by the extent of the radioactive decay of uranium (half-life 4.5 billion years!). In a living organism, the ratio of radioactive carbon, carbon-14, to ordinary carbon stays fairly constant during the lifetime of the organism, being approximately equal to the ratio in the organism's surroundings at the time. After the organism's death, however, no new carbon is ingested, and the proportion of carbon-14 in the organism's remains decreases as the carbon-14 decays. Since the half-life of carbon-14 is known to be about 5700 years, it is possible to estimate the age of organic remains by comparing the proportion of carbon-14 they contain with the proportion assumed to have been in the organism's environment at the time it lived. Archeologists have dated shells (which contain $CaCO_3$), seeds, and wooden artifacts this way. The estimate of 15,500 years for the age of the cave paintings at Lascaux, France, is based on carbon-14 dating.

a) Find k in Eq. (2) for carbon-14.

b) What is the age of a sample of charcoal in which 90 percent of the carbon-14 has decayed?

c) The charcoal from a tree killed in the volcanic eruption that formed Crater Lake in Oregon contained $44\frac{1}{2}$ percent of the carbon-14 found in living matter. About how old is Crater Lake?

18–4

FIRST ORDER: HOMOGENEOUS

Occasionally a differential equation whose variables cannot be separated can be transformed by a change of variable into an equation whose variables can be separated. This is the case with any equation that can be put into the form

$$\frac{dy}{dx} = F\left(\frac{y}{x}\right). \tag{1}$$

Such an equation is called *homogeneous.*

To transform Eq. (1) into an equation whose variables may be separated, we introduce the new independent variable

$$v = \frac{y}{x}. \tag{2}$$

Then

$$y = vx, \qquad \frac{dy}{dx} = v + x\frac{dv}{dx},$$

and (1) becomes

$$v + x\frac{dv}{dx} = F(v). \tag{3}$$

Equation (3) can be solved by separation of variables:

$$\frac{dx}{x} + \frac{dv}{v - F(v)} = 0. \tag{4}$$

After (4) is solved, the solution of the original equation is obtained when we replace v by y/x.

EXAMPLE. Show that the equation

$$(x^2 + y^2)\,dx + 2xy\,dy = 0$$

is homogeneous, and solve it.

Solution. From the given equation, we have

$$\frac{dy}{dx} = -\frac{x^2 + y^2}{2xy} = -\frac{1 + (y/x)^2}{2(y/x)}.$$

This has the form of Eq. (1), with

$$F(v) = -\frac{1 + v^2}{2v}, \qquad \text{where} \quad v = \frac{y}{x}.$$

Then Eq. (4) becomes

$$\frac{dx}{x} + \frac{dv}{v + \dfrac{1 + v^2}{2v}} = 0,$$

or

$$\frac{dx}{x} + \frac{2v\,dv}{1 + 3v^2} = 0.$$

The solution of this is

$$\ln|x| + \tfrac{1}{3}\ln(1 + 3v^2) = \tfrac{1}{3}\ln C,$$

so that

$$x^3(1 + 3v^2) = \pm C.$$

In terms of y and x, the solution is

$$x(x^2 + 3y^2) = C.$$

PROBLEMS

Show that the following equations are homogeneous, and solve.

1. $(x^2 + y^2)\,dx + xy\,dy = 0$
2. $x^2\,dy + (y^2 - xy)\,dx = 0$
3. $(xe^{y/x} + y)\,dx - x\,dy = 0$
4. $(x + y)\,dy + (x - y)\,dx = 0$
5. $y' = \dfrac{y}{x} + \cos\dfrac{y - x}{x}$
6. $\left(x \sin\dfrac{y}{x} - y\cos\dfrac{y}{x}\right)dx + x\cos\dfrac{y}{x}\,dy = 0$
7. Solve the equation

$$(x + y + 1)\,dx + (y - x - 3)\,dy = 0$$

by making a change of variable of the form

$$x = r + a, \qquad y = s + b,$$

and choosing the constants a and b so that the resulting equation is

$$(r + s)\,dr + (r - s)\,ds = 0.$$

Then solve this equation and express its solution in terms of x and y.

8. Use the substitution $u = x + y$ to solve the equation $y' = (x + y)^2$.

If every member of a family of curves is a solution of the differential equation

$$M(x, y)\,dx + N(x, y)\,dy = 0,$$

while every member of a second family of curves is a solution of the related equation

$$N(x, y)\,dx - M(x, y)\,dy = 0,$$

then each curve of the one family is orthogonal to every curve of the other family. Each family is said to be a family of *orthogonal trajectories* of the other. In Problems 9 and 10, find the family of solutions of the given differential equation and the family of orthogonal trajectories. Sketch both families.

9. $x\,dy - 2y\,dx = 0$
10. $2xy\,dy + (x^2 - y^2)\,dx = 0$
11. Find the orthogonal trajectories of the family of curves $xy = c$.

18–5 FIRST ORDER: LINEAR

The complexity of a differential equation depends primarily upon the way in which the *dependent* variable and its derivatives occur. Of particular importance are those equations that are linear. In a linear differential equation, each term of the equation is of degree one or zero, where, in computing the degree of a term, we add the exponents of the dependent variable and of any of its derivatives that occur. Thus, for example, (d^2y/dx^2) is of the first degree, while $y(dy/dx)$ is of the second degree because we must add 1 for the exponent of y, and 1 for the exponent of dy/dx.

A differential equation of first order, which is also linear, can always be put into the standard form

$$\frac{dy}{dx} + Py = Q, \tag{1}$$

where P and Q are functions of x.

One method for solving Eq. (1) is to find a function $\rho = \rho(x)$ such that if the equation is multiplied by ρ, the left side becomes the derivative of the product ρy. That is, we multiply (1) by ρ,

$$\rho\frac{dy}{dx} + \rho P y = \rho Q, \tag{1$'$}$$

and then try to impose upon ρ the condition that

$$\rho \frac{dy}{dx} + \rho P y = \frac{d}{dx}(\rho y). \tag{2}$$

When we expand the right side of (2) and cancel terms, we obtain, as the condition to be satisfied by ρ,

$$\frac{d\rho}{dx} = \rho P. \tag{3}$$

In Eq. (3), $P = P(x)$ is a known function, so we can separate the variables and solve for ρ:

$$\frac{d\rho}{\rho} = P\,dx, \qquad \ln|\rho| = \int P\,dx + \ln C,$$

$$\rho = \pm C e^{\int P\,dx}. \tag{4}$$

Since we do not require the most general function ρ, we may take $\pm C = 1$ in (4) and use

$$\rho = e^{\int P\,dx}. \tag{5}$$

This function is called an *integrating factor* for Eq. (1). With its help, (1′) becomes

$$\frac{d}{dx}(\rho y) = \rho Q,$$

whose solution is

$$\rho y = \int \rho Q\,dx + C. \tag{6}$$

Since ρ is given by (5), while P and Q are known from the given differential equation (1), we have, in Eqs. (5) and (6), a summary of all that is required to solve (1).

EXAMPLE 1. Solve the equation

$$\frac{dy}{dx} + y = e^x.$$

Solution

$$P = 1, \qquad Q = e^x,$$

$$\rho = e^{\int dx} = e^x,$$

$$e^x y = \int e^{2x}\,dx + C = \tfrac{1}{2}e^{2x} + C,$$

$$y = \tfrac{1}{2}e^x + Ce^{-x}.$$

EXAMPLE 2. Solve the equation

$$x\frac{dy}{dx} - 3y = x^2.$$

Solution. We put the equation in standard form,

$$\frac{dy}{dx} - \frac{3}{x}y = x,$$

and then read off

$$P = -\frac{3}{x}, \qquad Q = x.$$

Hence

$$\rho = e^{\int -(3/x)\,dx} = e^{-3\ln x} = \frac{1}{e^{3\ln x}} = \frac{1}{x^3},$$

and

$$\frac{1}{x^3}y = \int \frac{x}{x^3}\,dx + C = -\frac{1}{x} + C,$$

$$y = -x^2 + Cx^3.$$

REMARKS. Note that whenever $\int P\,dx$ involves logarithms, as in Example 2, it is profitable to simplify the expression for $e^{\int P\,dx}$ before substituting into Eq. (6). To simplify the expression, we use the properties of the logarithmic and exponential functions:

$$e^{\ln A} = A, \qquad e^{m\ln A} = A^m, \qquad e^{n+m\ln A} = A^m e^n.$$

A differential equation that is linear in y and dy/dx may also be separable, or homogeneous. In such cases, we have a choice of methods of solution. Observe also that an equation that is linear in x and dx/dy can be solved by the technique of this article; one need only interchange the roles of x and y in Eqs. (1), (5), and (6).

PROBLEMS

Solve:

1. $\dfrac{dy}{dx} + 2y = e^{-x}$

2. $2\dfrac{dy}{dx} - y = e^{x/2}$

3. $x\dfrac{dy}{dx} + 3y = \dfrac{\sin x}{x^2}$

4. $x\,dy + y\,dx = \sin x\,dx$

5. $x\,dy + y\,dx = y\,dy$

6. $(x-1)^3\dfrac{dy}{dx} + 4(x-1)^2y = x + 1$

7. $\cosh x\,dy + (y\sinh x + e^x)\,dx = 0$

8. $e^{2y}\,dx + 2(xe^{2y} - y)\,dy = 0$

9. $(x - 2y)\,dy + y\,dx = 0$

10. $(y^2 + 1)\,dx + (2xy + 1)\,dy = 0$

11. If glucose is fed intravenously at a constant rate, the change in the overall concentration $c(t)$ of glucose in the blood with respect to time may be described by the differential equation

$$\frac{dc}{dt} = \frac{G}{100V} - kc.$$

In this equation, G, V, and k are positive constants, G being the rate at which glucose is admitted, in milligrams per minute, and V the volume of blood in the body, in liters (around 5 liters for an adult). The concentration $c(t)$ is measured in milligrams per centiliter. The term $-kc$ is included because the glucose is assumed to be changing continually into other molecules at a rate proportional to its concentration. (a) Solve the equation for $c(t)$, using c_0 to denote $c(0)$. (b) Find the steady state concentration, $\lim_{t\to\infty} c(t)$.

18–6
FIRST ORDER: EXACT

An equation that can be written in the form

$$M(x, y)\, dx + N(x, y)\, dy = 0, \tag{1}$$

and having the property that

$$\frac{\partial M}{\partial y} = \frac{\partial N}{\partial x}, \tag{2}$$

is said to be *exact*, because its left side is an exact differential. The technique of solving an exact equation consists in finding a function $f(x, y)$ such that

$$df = M\, dx + N\, dy. \tag{3}$$

Then (1) becomes

$$df = 0$$

and the solution is

$$f(x, y) = C,$$

where C is an arbitrary constant. The method of finding $f(x, y)$ to satisfy (3) is discussed and illustrated in Article 13–13.

It can be proved that every first-order differential equation

$$P(x, y)\, dx + Q(x, y)\, dy = 0$$

can be made exact by multiplication by a suitable *integrating factor* $\rho(x, y)$. Such an integrating factor has the property that

$$\frac{\partial}{\partial y}[\rho(x, y)P(x, y)] = \frac{\partial}{\partial x}[\rho(x, y)Q(x, y)].$$

Unfortunately, it is not easy to determine ρ from this equation. In fact, there is no general technique by which even a single integrating factor can be produced for an arbitrary differential equation, and the search for one can be a frustrating experience. However, one can often recognize certain combinations of differentials that can be made exact by the use of "ingenious devices."

EXAMPLE. Solve the equation

$$x\, dy - y\, dx = xy^2\, dx.$$

Solution. The combination $x\, dy - y\, dx$ may ring a bell in our memories and cause us to recall the formula

$$d\left(\frac{u}{v}\right) = \frac{v\, du - u\, dv}{v^2} = -\left[\frac{u\, dv - v\, du}{v^2}\right].$$

Therefore we might divide the given equation by x^2, or change signs and divide by y^2. Clearly, the latter approach will be more profitable, so we proceed as follows:

$$x\,dy - y\,dx = xy^2\,dx, \qquad \frac{y\,dx - x\,dy}{y^2} = -x\,dx,$$

$$d\left(\frac{x}{y}\right) + x\,dx = 0, \qquad \frac{x}{y} + \frac{x^2}{2} = C.$$

The same result would be obtained if we wrote our equation in the form

$$(xy^2 + y)\,dx - x\,dy = 0$$

and multiplied by the integrating factor $1/y^2$. This would give

$$\left(x + \frac{1}{y}\right)dx - \left(\frac{x}{y^2}\right)dy = 0,$$

which is exact, since

$$\frac{\partial}{\partial y}\left(x + \frac{1}{y}\right) = \frac{\partial}{\partial x}\left(-\frac{x}{y^2}\right).$$

PROBLEMS

In Problems 1–3, use the given integrating factors to make differential equations exact. Then solve the equations.

1. $(x + 2y)\,dx - x\,dy = 0;\quad 1/x^3$

2. $y\,dx + x\,dy = 0;$

a) $\dfrac{1}{xy}$ **b)** $\dfrac{1}{(xy)^2}$

3. $y\,dx - x\,dy = 0;$

a) $\dfrac{1}{y^2}$ **b)** $\dfrac{1}{x^2}$

c) $\dfrac{1}{xy}$ **d)** $\dfrac{1}{x^2 + y^2}$

Solve:

4. $(x + y)\,dx + (x + y^2)\,dy = 0$

5. $(2xe^y + e^x)\,dx + (x^2 + 1)e^y\,dy = 0$

6. $(2xy + y^2)\,dx + (x^2 + 2xy - y)\,dy = 0$

7. $(x + \sqrt{y^2 + 1})\,dx - \left(y - \dfrac{xy}{\sqrt{y^2 + 1}}\right)dy = 0$

8. $x\,dy - y\,dx + x^3\,dx = 0$

9. $x\,dy - y\,dx = (x^2 + y^2)\,dx$

10. $(x^2 + x - y)\,dx + x\,dy = 0$

11. $\left(e^x + \ln y + \dfrac{y}{x}\right)dx + \left(\dfrac{x}{y} + \ln x + \sin y\right)dy = 0$

12. $\left(\dfrac{y^2}{1 + x^2} - 2y\right)dx + (2y \tan^{-1} x - 2x + \sinh y)\,dy = 0$

13. $dy + \dfrac{y - \sin x}{x}\,dx = 0$

18–7 SPECIAL TYPES OF SECOND ORDER EQUATIONS

Certain types of second order differential equations, of which the general form is

$$F\left(x, y, \frac{dy}{dx}, \frac{d^2y}{dx^2}\right) = 0, \tag{1}$$

can be reduced to first order equations by a suitable change of variables.

Type 1. *Equations with dependent variable missing.* When Eq. (1) has the special form

$$F\left(x, \frac{dy}{dx}, \frac{d^2y}{dx^2}\right) = 0, \tag{2}$$

we can reduce it to a first order equation by substituting

$$p = \frac{dy}{dx}, \qquad \frac{d^2y}{dx^2} = \frac{dp}{dx}.$$

Then Eq. (2) takes the form

$$F\left(x, p, \frac{dp}{dx}\right) = 0,$$

which is of the first order in p. If this can be solved for p as a function of x, say

$$p = \phi(x, C_1);$$

then we can find y by one additional integration:

$$y = \int (dy/dx)\, dx = \int p\, dx = \int \phi(x, C_1)\, dx + C_2.$$

The differential equation

$$\frac{d^2y}{dx^2} = \frac{w}{H}\sqrt{1 + \left(\frac{dy}{dx}\right)^2}$$

was solved by this technique in Article 9–6.

Type 2. *Equations with independent variable missing.* When Eq. (1) does not contain x explicitly but has the form

$$F\left(y, \frac{dy}{dx}, \frac{d^2y}{dx^2}\right) = 0, \tag{3}$$

the substitutions to use are

$$p = \frac{dy}{dx} \quad \text{and} \quad \frac{d^2y}{dx^2} = p\frac{dp}{dy}.$$

Then Eq. (3) takes the form

$$F\left(y, p, p\frac{dp}{dy}\right) = 0,$$

which is of the first order in p. Its solution gives p in terms of y, and then a further integration gives the solution of Eq. (3).

EXAMPLE. Solve the equation

$$\frac{d^2y}{dx^2} + y = 0.$$

Solution. Let

$$\frac{dy}{dx} = p, \qquad \frac{d^2y}{dx^2} = \frac{dp}{dx} = \frac{dp}{dy}\frac{dy}{dx} = \frac{dp}{dy}p.$$

Then we proceed as follows:

$$p\frac{dp}{dy} + y = 0, \qquad p\,dp + y\,dy = 0,$$

$$\frac{p^2}{2} + \frac{y^2}{2} = \frac{C_1^2}{2}, \qquad p = \frac{dy}{dx} = \pm\sqrt{C_1^2 - y^2},$$

$$\frac{dy}{\sqrt{C_1^2 - y^2}} = \pm dx, \qquad \sin^{-1}\frac{y}{C_1} = \pm(x + C_2),$$

$$y = C_1 \sin[\pm(x + C_2)] = \pm C_1 \sin(x + C_2).$$

Since C_1 is arbitrary, there is no need for the $\pm$ sign, and we have

$$y = C_1 \sin(x + C_2)$$

as the general solution.

PROBLEMS

Solve:

1. $\frac{d^2y}{dx^2} + \frac{dy}{dx} = 0$

2. $\frac{d^2y}{dx^2} + y\frac{dy}{dx} = 0$

3. $\frac{d^2y}{dx^2} + x\frac{dy}{dx} = 0$

4. $x\frac{d^2y}{dx^2} + \frac{dy}{dx} = 0$

5. $\frac{d^2y}{dx^2} - y = 0$

6. $\frac{d^2y}{dx^2} + \omega^2 y = 0 \quad (\omega = \text{constant} \neq 0)$

7. $xy'''' - 2y'' = 0$. [*Hint.* Substitute $y'' = q$.]

8. $2y'' - (y')^2 + 1 = 0$

9. A mass m is suspended from one end of a vertical spring whose other end is attached to a rigid support. The body is allowed to come to rest, and is then pulled down an additional slight amount A and released. Find its motion. [*Hint.* Assume Newton's second law of motion and Hooke's law, which says that the tension in the spring is proportional to the amount it is stretched. Let x denote the displacement of the body at time t, measured from the equilibrium position. Then $m(d^2x/dt^2) = -kx$, where k, the "spring constant," is the proportionality factor in Hooke's law.]

10. A man suspended from a parachute falls through space under the pull of gravity. If air resistance produces a retarding force proportional to the man's velocity and he starts from rest at time $t = 0$, find the distance he falls in time t.

18–8 LINEAR EQUATIONS WITH CONSTANT COEFFICIENTS

An equation of the form

$$\frac{d^ny}{dx^n} + a_1\frac{d^{n-1}y}{dx^{n-1}} + a_2\frac{d^{n-2}y}{dx^{n-2}} + \cdots + a_{n-1}\frac{dy}{dx} + a_n y = F(x), \tag{1}$$

which is linear in y and its derivatives, is called a *linear* equation of order n. If $F(x)$ is identically zero, the equation is said to be *homogeneous*; otherwise it is called *nonhomogeneous.* The equation is called linear even when the coefficients $a_1, a_2, \ldots, a_n$ are functions of x. However, we shall consider only the case where these coefficients are *constants.*

It is convenient to introduce the symbol D to represent the operation of differentiation with respect to x. That is, we write $Df(x)$ to mean $(d/dx)f(x)$.

Furthermore, we define powers of D to mean taking successive derivatives:

$$D^2 f(x) = D\{Df(x)\} = \frac{d^2 f(x)}{dx^2},$$

$$D^3 f(x) = D\{D^2 f(x)\} = \frac{d^3 f(x)}{dx^3},$$

and so on. A polynomial in D is to be interpreted as an operator which, when applied to $f(x)$, produces a linear combination of f and its successive derivatives. For example,

$$(D^2 + D - 2)f(x) = D^2 f(x) + Df(x) - 2f(x)$$
$$= \frac{d^2 f(x)}{dx^2} + \frac{df(x)}{dx} - 2f(x).$$

Such a polynomial in D is called a *linear differential operator* and may be denoted by the single letter L. If L_1 and L_2 are two such linear operators, their sum and product are defined by the equations

$$(L_1 + L_2)f(x) = L_1 f(x) + L_2 f(x),$$
$$L_1 L_2 f(x) = L_1(L_2 f(x)).$$

Linear differential operators that are polynomials in D with constant coefficients satisfy basic algebraic laws that make it possible to treat them like ordinary polynomials so far as addition, multiplication, and factoring are concerned. Thus,

$$(D^2 + D - 2)f(x) = (D + 2)(D - 1)f(x)$$
$$= (D - 1)(D + 2)f(x). \tag{2}$$

Since Eq. (2) holds for any twice-differentiable function f, we also write the equality between operators:

$$D^2 + D - 2 = (D + 2)(D - 1) = (D - 1)(D + 2). \tag{3}$$

18–9 LINEAR, SECOND ORDER, HOMOGENEOUS EQUATIONS WITH CONSTANT COEFFICIENTS

Suppose, now, we wish to solve a differential equation of order two, say

$$\frac{d^2 y}{dx^2} + 2a\frac{dy}{dx} + by = 0, \tag{1}$$

where a and b are constants. In operator notation, this becomes

$$(D^2 + 2aD + b)y = 0. \tag{1$'$}$$

Associated with this differential equation is the algebraic equation

$$r^2 + 2ar + b = 0, \tag{1$''$}$$

which we get by replacing D by r and suppressing y. This is called the *characteristic equation* of the differential equation. Suppose the roots of (1″)

are r_1 and r_2. Then

$$r^2 + 2ar + b = (r - r_1)(r - r_2)$$

and

$$D^2 + 2aD + b = (D - r_1)(D - r_2).$$

Hence Eq. (1′) is equivalent to

$$(D - r_1)(D - r_2)y = 0. \tag{2}$$

If we now let

$$(D - r_2)y = u \tag{3a}$$

and

$$(D - r_1)u = 0, \tag{3b}$$

we can solve Eq. (1′) in two steps. From Eq. (3b), which is separable, we find

$$u = C_1 e^{r_1 x}.$$

We substitute this into (3a), which becomes

$$(D - r_2)y = C_1 e^{r_1 x}$$

or

$$\frac{dy}{dx} - r_2 y = C_1 e^{r_1 x}.$$

This equation is linear. Its integrating factor is

$$\rho = e^{-r_2 x},$$

(see Article 18–5), and its solution is

$$e^{-r_2 x} y = C_1 \int e^{(r_1 - r_2)x}\, dx + C_2. \tag{4}$$

How we proceed at this point depends on whether r_1 and r_2 are equal.

CASE 1. If $r_1 \neq r_2$, the evaluation of the integral in Eq. (4) leads to

$$e^{-r_2 x} y = \frac{C_1}{r_1 - r_2} e^{(r_1 - r_2)x} + C_2$$

or

$$y = \frac{C_1}{r_1 - r_2} e^{r_1 x} + C_2 e^{r_2 x}.$$

Since C_1 is an arbitrary constant, so is $C_1/(r_1 - r_2)$, and the solution of Eq. (2) can be written simply as

$$y = C_1 e^{r_1 x} + C_2 e^{r_2 x}, \qquad \text{if} \quad r_1 \neq r_2. \tag{5}$$

CASE 2. If $r_1 = r_2$, then $e^{(r_1 - r_2)x} = e^0 = 1$, and Eq. (4) reduces to

$$e^{-r_2 x} y = C_1 x + C_2$$

or

$$y = (C_1 x + C_2)e^{r_2 x}, \qquad \text{if} \quad r_1 = r_2. \tag{6}$$

EXAMPLE 1. Solve the equation

$$\frac{d^2y}{dx^2} + \frac{dy}{dx} - 2y = 0.$$

Solution. $r^2 + r - 2 = 0$ has roots $r_1 = 1$, $r_2 = -2$. Hence, by Eq. (5), the solution of the differential equation is

$$y = C_1 e^x + C_2 e^{-2x}.$$

EXAMPLE 2. Solve the equation

$$\frac{d^2y}{dx^2} + 4\frac{dy}{dx} + 4y = 0.$$

Solution

$$r^2 + 4r + 4 = (r + 2)^2,$$

$$r_1 = r_2 = -2,$$

$$y = (C_1 x + C_2)e^{-2x}.$$

Imaginary Roots

If the coefficients a and b in Eq. (1) are real, the roots of the characteristic Eq. (1″) either will be real, or will be a pair of complex conjugate numbers:

$$r_1 = \alpha + i\beta, \qquad r_2 = \alpha - i\beta. \tag{7}$$

If $\beta \neq 0$, Eq. (5) applies, with the result

$$\begin{aligned} y &= c_1 e^{(\alpha + i\beta)x} + c_2 e^{(\alpha - i\beta)x} \\ &= e^{\alpha x}[c_1 e^{i\beta x} + c_2 e^{-i\beta x}]. \end{aligned} \tag{8}$$

By Euler's formula, Eq. (10) of Article 17–7,

$$e^{i\beta x} = \cos \beta x + i \sin \beta x,$$

$$e^{-i\beta x} = \cos \beta x - i \sin \beta x.$$

Hence, Eq. (8) may be replaced by

$$y = e^{\alpha x}[(c_1 + c_2) \cos \beta x + i(c_1 - c_2) \sin \beta x]. \tag{9}$$

Finally, if we introduce new arbitrary constants

$$C_1 = c_1 + c_2, \qquad C_2 = i(c_1 - c_2),$$

Eq. (9) takes the form

$$y = e^{\alpha x}[C_1 \cos \beta x + C_2 \sin \beta x]. \tag{9′}$$

The arbitrary constants C_1 and C_2 in (9′) will be real provided the constants c_1 and c_2 in (9) are complex conjugates:

$$c_1 = \tfrac{1}{2}(C_1 - iC_2), \qquad c_2 = \tfrac{1}{2}(C_1 + iC_2).$$

To solve a problem where the roots of the characteristic equation are complex conjugates, we simply write down the appropriate version of Eq. (9′).

EXAMPLE 3. Solve the equation

$$\frac{d^2y}{dx^2} + 2\frac{dy}{dx} + 2y = 0.$$

Solution. $r^2 + 2r + 2 = 0$ has roots $r_1 = -1 + i$, $r_2 = -1 - i$. Hence, in Eq. (9′), we take

$$\alpha = -1, \qquad \beta = 1,$$

and obtain

$$y = e^{-x}[C_1 \cos x + C_2 \sin x].$$

EXAMPLE 4. Solve the equation

$$\frac{d^2y}{dx^2} + \omega^2 y = 0, \qquad \omega \neq 0.$$

Solution. $r^2 + \omega^2 = 0$ has roots $r_1 = i\omega$, $r_2 = -i\omega$. Hence we take $\alpha = 0$, $\beta = \omega$ in Eq. (9′), and

$$y = C_1 \cos \omega x + C_2 \sin \omega x.$$

PROBLEMS

Solve:

1. $\frac{d^2y}{dx^2} + 2\frac{dy}{dx} = 0$
2. $\frac{d^2y}{dx^2} + 5\frac{dy}{dx} + 6y = 0$
3. $\frac{d^2y}{dx^2} + 6\frac{dy}{dx} + 5y = 0$
4. $\frac{d^2y}{dx^2} - 2\frac{dy}{dx} - 3y = 0$
5. $\frac{d^2y}{dx^2} + \frac{dy}{dx} + y = 0$
6. $\frac{d^2y}{dx^2} - 4\frac{dy}{dx} + 4y = 0$
7. $\frac{d^2y}{dx^2} + 6\frac{dy}{dx} + 9y = 0$
8. $\frac{d^2y}{dx^2} - 6\frac{dy}{dx} + 10y = 0$
9. $\frac{d^2y}{dx^2} - 2\frac{dy}{dx} + 4y = 0$
10. $\frac{d^2y}{dx^2} - 10\frac{dy}{dx} + 16y = 0$

18–10

LINEAR, SECOND ORDER, NONHOMOGENEOUS EQUATIONS WITH CONSTANT COEFFICIENTS

In Article 18–9, we learned how to solve the homogeneous equation

$$\frac{d^2y}{dx^2} + 2a\frac{dy}{dx} + by = 0. \tag{1}$$

We can now describe a method for solving the nonhomogeneous equation

$$\frac{d^2y}{dx^2} + 2a\frac{dy}{dx} + by = F(x). \tag{2}$$

To solve Eq. (2), we first obtain the general solution of the related homogeneous Eq. (1) obtained by replacing $F(x)$ by zero. Denote this solution by

$$y_h = C_1 u_1(x) + C_2 u_2(x), \tag{3}$$

where C_1 and C_2 are arbitrary constants and $u_1(x)$, $u_2(x)$ are functions of one or more of the following forms:

$$e^{rx}, \quad xe^{rx}, \quad e^{\alpha x}\cos\beta x, \quad e^{\alpha x}\sin\beta x.$$

Now we might, by inspection or by inspired guesswork, be able to discover *one* particular function $y = y_p(x)$ that satisfies Eq. (2). In this case, we would be able to solve Eq. (2) completely, as

$$y = y_h(x) + y_p(x).$$

EXAMPLE 1. Solve the equation

$$\frac{d^2y}{dx^2} + 2\frac{dy}{dx} - 3y = 6.$$

Solution. y_h satisfies

$$\frac{d^2y_h}{dx^2} + 2\frac{dy_h}{dx} - 3y_h = 0.$$

The characteristic equation is

$$r^2 + 2r - 3 = 0,$$

and its roots are

$$r_1 = -3, \qquad r_2 = 1.$$

Hence

$$y_h = C_1e^{-3x} + C_2e^x.$$

Now, to find a particular solution of the original equation, observe that $y =$ constant would do, provided $-3y = 6$. Hence,

$$y_p = -2$$

is one particular solution. The complete solution is

$$y = y_p + y_h = -2 + C_1e^{-3x} + C_2e^x.$$

Variation of Parameters

Fortunately, there is a general method for finding the solution of the nonhomogeneous Eq. (2) once the general solution of the corresponding homogeneous equation is known. The method is known as the method of *variation of parameters*. It consists in replacing the constants C_1 and C_2 in Eq. (3) by functions $v_1 = v_1(x)$ and $v_2 = v_2(x)$, and requiring (in a way to be explained) that the resulting expression satisfy Eq. (2). There are two functions to be determined, and requiring that Eq. (2) be satisfied is only one condition. As a second condition, we also require that

$$v_1'u_1 + v_2'u_2 = 0. \tag{4}$$

Then we have

$$y = v_1 u_1 + v_2 u_2,$$

$$\frac{dy}{dx} = v_1 u_1' + v_2 u_2',$$

$$\frac{d^2y}{dx^2} = v_1 u_1'' + v_2 u_2'' + v_1' u_1' + v_2' u_2'.$$

If we substitute these expressions into the left side of Eq. (2), we obtain

$$v_1\left[\frac{d^2u_1}{dx^2} + 2a\frac{du_1}{dx} + bu_1\right] + v_2\left[\frac{d^2u_2}{dx^2} + 2a\frac{du_2}{dx} + bu_2\right] + v_1' u_1' + v_2' u_2' = F(x).$$

The two bracketed terms are zero, since u_1 and u_2 are solutions of the homogeneous Eq. (1). Hence Eq. (2) is satisfied if, in addition to Eq. (4), we require that

$$v_1' u_1' + v_2' u_2' = F(x). \tag{5}$$

Equations (4) and (5) together may be solved for the unknown functions v_1' and v_2'. Then v_1 and v_2 can be found by integration. In applying the method, we can work directly from Eqs. (4) and (5); it is not necessary to rederive them.

EXAMPLE 2. Solve the equation

$$\frac{d^2y}{dx^2} + 2\frac{dy}{dx} - 3y = 6$$

of Example 1 by variation of parameters.

Solution. We first solve the associated homogeneous equation to find

$$u_1(x) = e^{-3x}, \qquad u_2(x) = e^x.$$

We then have

$$v_1' e^{-3x} + v_2' e^x = 0,$$

$$v_1'(-3e^{-3x}) + v_2' e^x = 6.$$

By Cramer's rule:

$$v_1' = \frac{\begin{vmatrix} 0 & e^x \\ 6 & e^x \end{vmatrix}}{\begin{vmatrix} e^{-3x} & e^x \\ -3e^{-3x} & e^x \end{vmatrix}} = -\frac{3}{2}e^{3x}, \qquad v_2' = \frac{\begin{vmatrix} e^{-3x} & 0 \\ -3e^{-3x} & 6 \end{vmatrix}}{\begin{vmatrix} e^{-3x} & e^x \\ -3e^{-3x} & e^x \end{vmatrix}} = \frac{3}{2}e^{-x}.$$

Hence

$$v_1 = \int -\tfrac{3}{2}e^{3x}\,dx = -\tfrac{1}{2}e^{3x} + C_1,$$

$$v_2 = \int \tfrac{3}{2}e^{-x}\,dx = -\tfrac{3}{2}e^{-x} + C_2,$$

and

$$\begin{aligned} y &= v_1 u_1 + v_2 u_2 \\ &= (-\tfrac{1}{2}e^{3x} + C_1)e^{-3x} + (-\tfrac{3}{2}e^{-x} + C_2)e^x \\ &= -2 + C_1 e^{-3x} + C_2 e^x. \end{aligned}$$

PROBLEMS

Solve:

1. $\dfrac{d^2y}{dx^2} + \dfrac{dy}{dx} = x$

2. $\dfrac{d^2y}{dx^2} + y = \tan x$

3. $\dfrac{d^2y}{dx^2} + y = \sin x$

4. $\dfrac{d^2y}{dx^2} + 2\dfrac{dy}{dx} + y = e^x$

5. $\dfrac{d^2y}{dx^2} + 2\dfrac{dy}{dx} + y = e^{-x}$

6. $\dfrac{d^2y}{dx^2} - y = x$

7. $\dfrac{d^2y}{dx^2} - y = e^x$

8. $\dfrac{d^2y}{dx^2} - y = \sin x$

9. $\dfrac{d^2y}{dx^2} + 4\dfrac{dy}{dx} + 5y = 10$

10. $\dfrac{d^2y}{dx^2} + 4\dfrac{dy}{dx} + 5y = x + 2$

11. Solve the integral equation

$$y(x) + \int_0^x y(t)\, dt = x.$$

[*Hint*. Differentiate.]

12. *Bernouilli's equation of order* 2. Solve the equation

$$\frac{dy}{dx} + y = (xy)^2$$

by carrying out the following steps: (1) divide both sides of the equation by y^2; (2) make the change of variable $u = y^{-1}$; (3) solve the resulting equation for u in terms of x; (4) let $y = u^{-1}$.

18–11 HIGHER ORDER LINEAR EQUATIONS WITH CONSTANT COEFFICIENTS

The methods of Articles 18–9 and 18–10 can be extended to equations of higher order. The characteristic algebraic equation associated with the differential equation

$$(D^n + a_1 D^{n-1} + \cdots + a_{n-1} D + a_n)y = F(x) \tag{1}$$

is

$$r^n + a_1 r^{n-1} + \cdots + a_{n-1} r + a_n = 0. \tag{2}$$

If its roots $r_1, r_2, \ldots, r_n$ are all distinct, the solution of the homogeneous equation obtained by replacing $F(x)$ by 0 in Eq. (1) is

$$y_h = c_1 e^{r_1 x} + c_2 e^{r_2 x} + \cdots + c_n e^{r_n x}.$$

Pairs of complex conjugate roots $\alpha \pm i\beta$ can be grouped together, and the corresponding part of y_h can be written in terms of the functions

$$e^{\alpha x} \cos \beta x \qquad \text{and} \qquad e^{\alpha x} \sin \beta x.$$

In case the roots of Eq. (2) are not all distinct, the portion of y_h which corresponds to a root r of multiplicity m is to be replaced by

$$(C_1 x^{m-1} + C_2 x^{m-2} + \cdots + C_m)e^{rx}.$$

Note that the polynomial in parentheses contains m arbitrary constants.

EXAMPLE. Solve the equation

$$\frac{d^4y}{dx^4} - 3\frac{d^3y}{dx^3} + 3\frac{d^2y}{dx^2} - \frac{dy}{dx} = 0.$$

Solution. $r^4 - 3r^3 + 3r^2 - r = r(r-1)^3$. The roots of the characteristic equation are

$$r_1 = 0, \qquad r_2 = r_3 = r_4 = 1.$$

The solution is

$$y = C_1 + (C_2x^2 + C_3x + C_4)e^x.$$

Variation of Parameters

If the general solution of the homogeneous equation is

$$y_h = C_1u_1 + C_2u_2 + \cdots + C_nu_n,$$

then

$$y = v_1u_1 + v_2u_2 + \cdots + v_nu_n$$

will be a solution of the nonhomogeneous Eq. (1), provided

$$\begin{aligned}
v_1'u_1 + v_2'u_2 &+ \cdots + v_n'u_n = 0,\\
v_1'u_1' + v_2'u_2' &+ \cdots + v_n'u_n' = 0,\\
&\vdots\\
v_1'u_1^{(n-2)} + v_2'u_2^{(n-2)} &+ \cdots + v_n'u_n^{(n-2)} = 0,\\
v_1'u_1^{(n-1)} + v_2'u_2^{(n-1)} &+ \cdots + v_n'u_n^{(n-1)} = F(x).
\end{aligned}$$

These equations may be solved for $v_1', v_2', \ldots, v_n'$ by Cramer's rule, and the results integrated to give $v_1, v_2, \ldots, v_n$.

PROBLEMS

Solve:

1. $\dfrac{d^3y}{dx^3} - 3\dfrac{d^2y}{dx^2} + 2\dfrac{dy}{dx} = 0$
2. $\dfrac{d^3y}{dx^3} - y = 0$
3. $\dfrac{d^4y}{dx^4} - 4\dfrac{d^2y}{dx^2} + 4y = 0$
4. $\dfrac{d^4y}{dx^4} - 16y = 0$
5. $\dfrac{d^4y}{dx^4} + 16y = 0$
6. $\dfrac{d^3y}{dx^3} - 3\dfrac{dy}{dx} + 2y = e^x$
7. $\dfrac{d^4y}{dx^4} - 4\dfrac{d^3y}{dx^3} + 6\dfrac{d^2y}{dx^2} - 4\dfrac{dy}{dx} + y = 7$
8. $\dfrac{d^4y}{dx^4} + y = x + 1$

18–12 VIBRATIONS

A spring of natural length L has its upper end fastened to a rigid support at A (Fig. 18–4). A weight W, of mass m, is suspended from the spring. The weight stretches the spring to a length $L + s$ when the system is allowed to come to rest in a new equilibrium position. By Hooke's law, the tension in the spring is ks, where k is the so-called spring constant. The force of gravity pulling down on the weight is $W = mg$. Equilibrium requires

$$ks = mg. \tag{1}$$

Suppose now that the weight is pulled down an additional amount a beyond the equilibrium position, and released. We shall discuss its motion.

Let x, positive direction downward, denote the displacement of the weight away from equilibrium at any time t after the motion has started. Then the forces acting upon the weight are

$+mg$, due to gravity,

$-k(s + x)$, due to the spring tension.

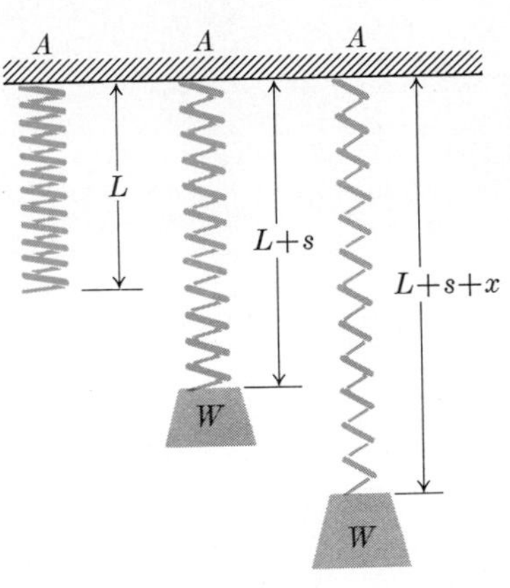

18–4 A spring stretched beyond its natural length by a weight.

The resultant of these forces is, by Newton's second law, also equal to

$$m \frac{d^2x}{dt^2}.$$

Therefore

$$m \frac{d^2x}{dt^2} = mg - ks - kx. \tag{2}$$

By Eq. (1), $mg - ks = 0$, so that (2) becomes

$$m \frac{d^2x}{dt^2} + kx = 0. \tag{3}$$

In addition to the differential equation (3), the motion satisfies the initial conditions:

$$\text{At } t = 0: \quad x = a \quad \text{and} \quad \frac{dx}{dt} = 0. \tag{4}$$

Let $\omega = \sqrt{k/m}$. Then Eq. (3) becomes

$$\frac{d^2x}{dt^2} + \omega^2 x = 0$$

or

$$(D^2 + \omega^2)x = 0,$$

where

$$D = \frac{d}{dt}.$$

The roots of the characteristic equation

$$r^2 + \omega^2 = 0$$

are complex conjugates

$$r = \pm \omega i.$$

Hence

$$x = c_1 \cos \omega t + c_2 \sin \omega t \tag{5}$$

is the general solution of the differential equation. To fit the initial conditions, we also compute

$$\frac{dx}{dt} = -c_1 \omega \sin \omega t + c_2 \omega \cos \omega t,$$

and then substitute from (4). This yields

$$a = c_1, \qquad 0 = c_2 \omega.$$

Therefore

$$c_1 = a, \qquad c_2 = 0,$$

and

$$x = a \cos \omega t \tag{6}$$

describes the motion of the weight. Equation (6) represents simple harmonic motion of amplitude a and period $T = 2\pi/\omega$.

The two terms on the right side of Eq. (5) can be combined into a single term by using the trigonometric identity

$$\sin(\omega t + \phi) = \cos \omega t \sin \phi + \sin \omega t \cos \phi.$$

To apply the identity, we take

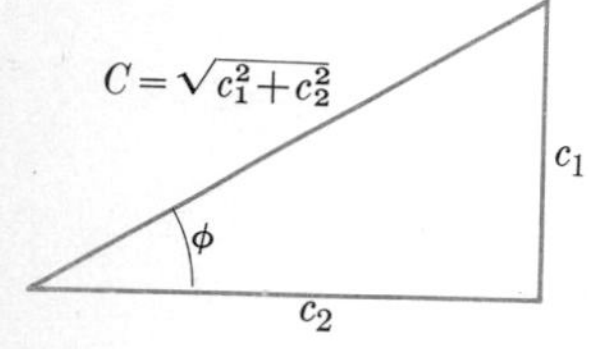

18–5 $c_1 = C \sin \phi$ and $c_2 = C \cos \phi$.

$$c_1 = C \sin \phi, \qquad c_2 = C \cos \phi, \tag{7a}$$

where

$$C = \sqrt{c_1^2 + c_2^2}, \qquad \phi = \tan^{-1} \frac{c_1}{c_2}, \tag{7b}$$

as in Fig. 18–5. Then Eq. (5) can be written in the alternative form

$$x = C \sin(\omega t + \phi). \tag{8}$$

Here C and ϕ may be taken as two new arbitrary constants, replacing the two constants c_1 and c_2 of Eq. (5). Equation (8) represents simple harmonic motion of amplitude C and period $T = 2\pi/\omega$. The angle $\omega t + \phi$ is called the *phase angle*, and ϕ may be interpreted as the initial value of the phase angle. A graph of Eq. (8) is given in Fig. 18–6.

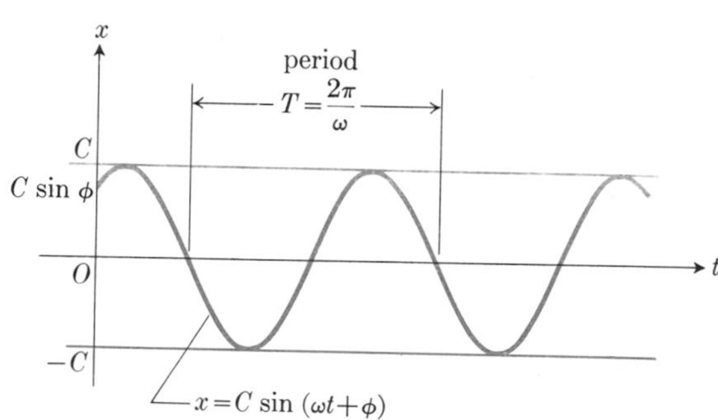

18–6 Undamped vibration.

Equation (3) assumes that there is no friction in the system. Next, consider the case where the motion of the weight is retarded by a friction force $c(dx/dt)$ proportional to the velocity, where c is a positive constant. Then the differential equation is

$$m \frac{d^2x}{dt^2} = -kx - c \frac{dx}{dt},$$

or

$$\frac{d^2x}{dt^2} + 2b \frac{dx}{dt} + \omega^2 x = 0, \tag{9}$$

where

$$2b = \frac{c}{m} \quad \text{and} \quad \omega = \sqrt{\frac{k}{m}}.$$

If we introduce the operator $D = d/dt$, Eq. (9) becomes

$$(D^2 + 2bD + \omega^2)x = 0.$$

The characteristic equation is

$$r^2 + 2br + \omega^2 = 0$$

with roots

$$r = -b \pm \sqrt{b^2 - \omega^2}. \tag{10}$$

Three cases now present themselves, depending upon the relative sizes of b and ω.

CASE 1. If $b = \omega$, the two roots in Eq. (10) are equal, and the solution of (9) is

$$x = (c_1 + c_2 t)e^{-\omega t}. \tag{11}$$

As time goes on, x approaches zero. The motion is not oscillatory.

CASE 2. If $b > \omega$, then the roots (10) are both real but unequal, and

$$x = c_1 e^{r_1 t} + c_2 e^{r_2 t}, \tag{12}$$

where

$$r_1 = -b + \sqrt{b^2 - \omega^2} \quad \text{and} \quad r_2 = -b - \sqrt{b^2 - \omega^2}.$$

Here again the motion is not oscillatory. Both r_1 and r_2 are negative, and x approaches zero as time goes on.

CASE 3. If $b < \omega$, let

$$\omega^2 - b^2 = \alpha^2.$$

Then

$$r_1 = -b + \alpha i, \qquad r_2 = -b - \alpha i$$

and

$$x = e^{-bt}[c_1 \cos \alpha t + c_2 \sin \alpha t]. \tag{13a}$$

If we introduce the substitutions (7), we may also write Eq. (13a) in the equivalent form

$$x = Ce^{-bt} \sin (\alpha t + \phi). \tag{13b}$$

This equation represents damped vibratory motion. It is analogous to simple harmonic motion, of period $T = 2\pi/\alpha$, except that the amplitude is not constant but is given by Ce^{-bt}. Since this tends to zero as t increases, the vibrations tend to die out as time goes on. Observe, however, that Eq. (13b) reduces to Eq. (8) in the absence of friction. The effect of friction is twofold:

1. $b = c/(2m)$ appears as a coefficient in the exponential *damping factor* e^{-bt}. The larger b is, the more quickly do the vibrations tend to become unnoticeable.

2. The period $T = 2\pi/\alpha = 2\pi/\sqrt{\omega^2 - b^2}$ is greater than the period $T_0 = 2\pi/\omega$ in the friction-free system.

Curves representing solutions of Eq. (9) in typical cases are shown in Figs. 18–6 and 18–7. The size of b, relative to ω, determines the kind of solution, and b also determines the rate of damping. It is therefore customary to say that there is

a) critical damping if $b = \omega$;
b) overcritical damping if $b > \omega$;
c) undercritical damping if $0 < b < \omega$;
d) no damping if $b = 0$.

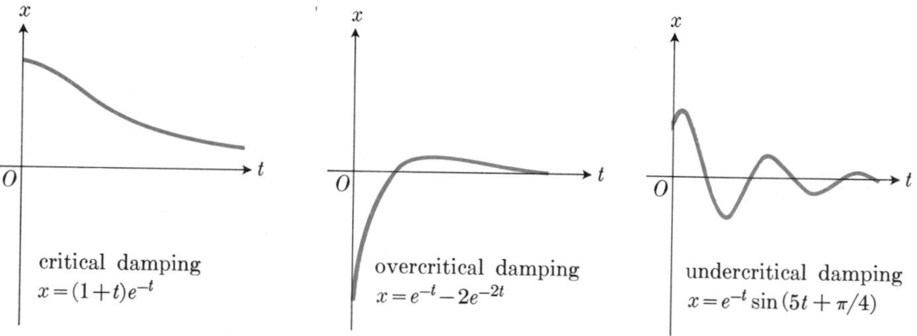

18–7 Three kinds of damping of vibration.

PROBLEMS

1. Suppose the motion of the weight in Fig. 18–4 is described by the differential equation (3). Find the motion if $x = x_0$ and $dx/dt = v_0$ at $t = 0$. Express the answer in two equivalent forms [Eqs. (5) and (8)].

2. A 5-lb weight is suspended from the lower end of a spring whose upper end is attached to a rigid support. The weight extends the spring by 2 in. If, after the weight has come to rest in its new equilibrium position, it is struck a sharp blow that starts it downward with a velocity of 4 ft/sec, find its subsequent motion, assuming there is no friction.

3. A simple electrical circuit shown in Fig. 18–8 contains a capacitor of capacitance C farads, a coil of inductance L henrys, a resistance of R ohms, and a generator which produces an electromotive force E volts, in series. If the current intensity at time t at some point of the circuit is I amperes, the differential equation describing the current I is

$$L\frac{d^2I}{dt^2} + R\frac{dI}{dt} + \frac{1}{C}I = \frac{dE}{dt}.$$

Find I as a function of t if

a) $R = 0$, $1/(LC) = \omega^2$, $E =$ constant,
b) $R = 0$, $1/(LC) = \omega^2$, $E = A \sin \alpha t$; $\alpha =$ constant $\neq \omega$,
c) $R = 0$, $1/(LC) = \omega^2$, $E = A \sin \omega t$,
d) $R = 50$, $L = 5$, $C = 9 \times 10^{-6}$, $E =$ constant.

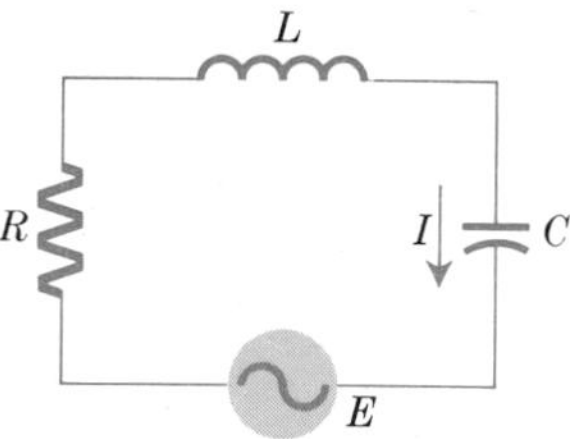

18–8 A simple electrical circuit.

4. A simple pendulum of length l makes an angle θ with the vertical. As it swings back and forth, its motion, neglecting friction, is described by the differential equation

$$\frac{d^2\theta}{dt^2} = -\frac{g}{l}\sin\theta,$$

where g (the acceleration due to gravity, $g \approx 32$ ft/sec^2) is a constant. Solve the differential equation of motion, under the assumption that θ is so small that $\sin\theta$ may be replaced by θ without appreciable error. Assume that $\theta = \theta_0$ and $d\theta/dt = 0$ when $t = 0$.

5. A circular disk of mass m and radius r is suspended by a thin wire attached to the center of one of its flat faces. If the disk is twisted through an angle θ, torsion in the wire tends to turn the disk back in the opposite direction. The differential equation for the motion is

$$\tfrac{1}{2}mr^2 \frac{d^2\theta}{dt^2} = -k\theta,$$

where k is the coefficient of torsion of the wire. Find the motion if $\theta = \theta_0$ and $d\theta/dt = v_0$ at $t = 0$.

6. A cylindrical spar buoy, diameter 1 foot, weight 100 lb, floats, partially submerged, in an upright position. When it is depressed slightly from its equilibrium position and released, it bobs up and down according to the differential equation

$$\frac{100}{g}\frac{d^2x}{dt^2} = -16\pi x - c\frac{dx}{dt}.$$

Here $c\,(dx/dt)$ is the frictional resistance of the water. Find c if the period of oscillation is observed to be 1.6 sec. (Take $g = 32$ ft/sec^2.)

7. Suppose the upper end of the spring in Fig. 18–4 is attached, not to a rigid support at A, but to a member which itself undergoes up and down motion given by a function of the time t, say $y = f(t)$. If the positive direction of y is downward, the differential equation of motion is

$$m\frac{d^2x}{dt^2} + kx = kf(t).$$

Let $x = x_0$ and $dx/dt = 0$ when $t = 0$, and solve for x:

a) if $f(t) = A \sin \alpha t$ and $\alpha \neq \sqrt{k/m}$,
b) if $f(t) = A \sin \alpha t$ and $\alpha = \sqrt{k/m}$.

18–13 POISSON PROBABILITY DISTRIBUTION

In the study of emission of particles from a radioactive substance, it is found that the number X of particles emitted during a fixed time interval is not precisely predictable. In fact X is a variable that can assume only the values 0, 1, 2, ... Some of these values are more likely to be observed than others. It is useful to introduce the symbol $P_n(t)$ to denote the *probability* that n particles will be emitted in a t-second interval. It is possible to arrive at a formula for $P_n(t)$ if we make the following assumptions:

1. The number of particles emitted in any time interval is independent of the number emitted in any other nonoverlapping time interval.

2. The probability that a single particle is emitted in an interval $(t, t + h)$ is $\lambda \cdot h + o(h)$, where λ is a constant (for a particular substance) and $o(h)$, read "small oh of h," denotes a function having the property

$$\lim_{h\to 0} \frac{o(h)}{h} = 0. \qquad \textbf{(1)}$$

3. The probability that more than one particle will be emitted in $(t, t + h)$ is $o(h)$.

A variable that satisfies these three postulates will be called a *Poisson random variable*. The significance of the postulates is as follows:

1. Independence of numbers of particles emitted in nonoverlapping time intervals means that the probability of r particles in one interval and s in another is the product of the respective probabilities:

(Probability of r particles in 1st time interval)

times

(Probability of s particles in 2nd time interval).

2. (Probability of particle in interval $t, t + h) = \lambda \cdot h + o(h)$ means that the probability is approximately proportional to the length h of the time interval. The approximation λh is better the smaller h is, the error $o(h)$ being composed of terms (like h^2 or $h \sin h$, for instance) which are themselves small compared to h, since $(o(h)/h) \to 0$ as $h \to 0$.

3. The probability that more than one particle is emitted in a very short time interval $(t, t+h)$ is $o(h)$, and is small compared to h.

From postulates 2 and 3 it follows that the probability of one *or more* particles in the interval $[t, t+h]$ is also $\lambda h + o(h)$, because

$$P(1 \text{ or more particles})^* = P(1 \text{ particle}) + P(\text{more than 1 particle})$$

and

$$P(1 \text{ particle}) = \lambda h + o_1(h), \qquad P(\text{more than 1 particle}) = o_2(h).$$

Hence

$$\begin{aligned} P(1 \text{ or more particles}) &= \lambda h + o_1(h) + o_2(h) \\ &= \lambda h + o(h), \end{aligned} \tag{2}$$

since the sum of two functions $o_1(h)$ and $o_2(h)$, having the property that

$$\lim_{h \to 0} \frac{o_1(h)}{h} = 0, \qquad \lim_{h \to 0} \frac{o_2(h)}{h} = 0,$$

is a function having the same property:

$$\lim_{h \to 0} \frac{o_1(h) + o_2(h)}{h} = \lim_{h \to 0} \frac{o_1(h)}{h} + \lim_{h \to 0} \frac{o_2(h)}{h} = 0.$$

From the postulates for a Poisson random variable, we may deduce the following system of differential equations:

$$\frac{dP_0(t)}{dt} = -\lambda P_0(t), \tag{3a}$$

$$\frac{dP_n(t)}{dt} = -\lambda P_n(t) + \lambda P_{n-1}(t), \qquad n = 1, 2, 3, \ldots \tag{3b}$$

Demonstration

We first establish (3a). Consider

$$\begin{aligned} P_0(t+h) &= P(0 \text{ emissions in time } t+h) \\ &= P(0 \text{ in time } t) \times P(0 \text{ in time } [t, t+h]) \\ &= P_0(t) \cdot \{1 - P(1 \text{ or more in } [t, t+h])\} \\ &= P_0(t) \cdot [1 - \lambda h - o(h)]. \end{aligned}$$

---

* The notation P(1 or more particles) is an abbreviation for "probability that 1 or more particles are emitted."

Therefore

$$P_0(t+h) - P_0(t) = -P_0(t) \cdot [\lambda h + o(h)],$$

$$\frac{P_0(t+h) - P_0(t)}{h} = -P_0(t) \cdot \left[\lambda + \frac{o(h)}{h}\right],$$

$$\frac{dP_0(t)}{dt} = \lim_{h \to 0} \frac{P_0(t+h) - P_0(t)}{h} = -P_0(t) \cdot [\lambda + 0] = -\lambda P_0(t).$$

Thus (3a) holds.

To establish (3b), consider the probability of n emissions in a time $(0, t+h)$, where n is a positive integer. Consider the nonoverlapping intervals of time $(0, t)$ and $(t, t+h)$. The only possibilities for n particles in $(0, t+h)$ are:

a) n particles in $(0, t)$ and 0 in $(t, t+h)$,
b) $(n-1)$ particles in $(0, t)$ and 1 in $(t, t+h)$,
c) $(n-2)$ particles in $(0, t)$ and 2 in $(t, t+h)$,
d) $(n-3)$ particles in $(0, t)$ and 3 in $(t, t+h)$, and so on.

Since these are mutually exclusive events, their probabilities add, and

$$P_n(t+h) = P_n(t) \cdot P_0(h) + P_{n-1}(t) \cdot P_1(h) + P_{n-2}(t) \cdot P_2(h) + \cdots + P_0(t) \cdot P_n(h). \tag{4}$$

Now for any $t \geq 0$,

$$P_0(t) + P_1(t) + P_2(t) + \cdots = 1, \tag{5}$$

since it is certain (that is, the probability = 1) that the number of particles emitted in time t is one of the integers 0, or 1, or 2, or 3, ..., and these possibilities are mutually exclusive so their probabilities add. Hence, in particular, if $t = h$ is small, we may replace t by h in (5) and use the fact, Eq. (2), that

$$P(1 \text{ or more particles}) = P_1(h) + P_2(h) + \cdots = \lambda h + o(h)$$

to obtain

$$P_0(h) = 1 - \lambda h - o(h). \tag{6}$$

Hence Eq. (4) becomes

$$P_n(t+h) = P_n(t) \cdot [1 - \lambda h - o(h)] + P_{n-1}(t) \cdot [\lambda h + o_1(h)] + o_2(h), \tag{7}$$

sincc

$$P_{n-2}(t) \cdot P_2(h) + P_{n-3}(t) \cdot P_3(h) + \cdots + P_0(t) \cdot P_n(h) \leq 1 \cdot P_2(h) + 1 \cdot P_3(h) + \cdots + 1 \cdot P_n(h) = o(h).$$

Therefore, from Eq. (7),

$$P_n(t+h) - P_n(t) = -P_n(t) \cdot [\lambda h + o(h)] + P_{n-1}(t) \cdot [\lambda h + o_1(h)] + o_2(h),$$

and

$$\begin{aligned}\frac{dP_n}{dt} &= \lim_{h\to 0} \frac{P_n(t+h) - P_n(t)}{h} \\ &= \lim_{h\to 0} \left[-P_n(t)\cdot\left(\lambda + \frac{o(h)}{h}\right) + P_{n-1}(t)\cdot\left(\lambda + \frac{o_1(h)}{h}\right) + \frac{o_2(h)}{h}\right] \\ &= -\lambda P_n(t) + \lambda P_{n-1}(t).\end{aligned}$$

Q.E.D.

The probabilities $P_0(t)$, $P_1(t)$, ... satisfy the system of differential equations (3a, b) and the initial conditions:

$$P_0(0) = 1, \qquad P_1(0) = P_2(0) = \cdots P_n(0) = 0, \qquad n > 1. \tag{8}$$

That is, the number of particles emitted in 0 time is 0, with probability 1. The solution of Eq. (3a), with $P_0(0) = 1$, is

$$P_0(t) = e^{-\lambda t}.$$

If we substitute this into Eq. (3b), with $n = 1$, we have

$$\frac{dP_1(t)}{dt} = -\lambda P_1(t) + e^{-\lambda t},$$

or

$$\frac{dP_1(t)}{dt} + \lambda P_1(t) = e^{-\lambda t}.$$

This equation is linear in $P_1(t)$, with integrating factor $e^{\lambda t}$. It is equivalent to

$$\frac{d}{dt}[e^{\lambda t}P_1(t)] = \lambda.$$

Hence

$$e^{\lambda t}P_1(t) = \lambda t + C_1.$$

But when $t = 0$, $P_1(0) = 0$, so

$$C_1 = 0.$$

Therefore

$$P_1(t) = \lambda t e^{-\lambda t}.$$

We can now substitute this into (3b) with $n = 2$ and have

$$\frac{dP_2(t)}{dt} + \lambda P_2(t) = \lambda(\lambda t)e^{-\lambda t}.$$

Again the equation is linear, with integrating factor $e^{\lambda t}$, and

$$\begin{aligned}\frac{d}{dt}[e^{\lambda t}P_2(t)] &= e^{\lambda t}\cdot\lambda(\lambda t)e^{-\lambda t} \\ &= \lambda^2 t.\end{aligned}$$

Hence

$$e^{\lambda t}P_2(t) = \frac{\lambda^2 t^2}{2} + C_2,$$

but $P_2(0) = 0$, so

$$C_2 = 0.$$

Therefore

$$P_2(t) = \frac{(\lambda t)^2}{2!} e^{-\lambda t}.$$

Proceeding in this fashion, one discovers that

$$P_3(t) = \frac{(\lambda t)^3}{3!} e^{-\lambda t},$$

$$P_4(t) = \frac{(\lambda t)^4}{4!} e^{-\lambda t},$$

and so on. The general term is

$$P_n(t) = e^{-\lambda t} \frac{(\lambda t)^n}{n!}, \qquad n = 0, 1, 2, \ldots \tag{9}$$

The set of numbers 0, 1, 2, 3, ..., with corresponding probabilities given by Eq. (9), is called a *Poisson probability distribution.* Figure 18–9 shows the graph of a Poisson distribution with $\lambda t = 2$. The viewpoint to adopt when considering a Poisson distribution is, in most instances, to imagine λt as fixed, and then Eq. (9) gives the probability of observing n occurrences of the event in question, for all possible different values of n.

The probability of 0 emissions is $P_0(t) = e^{-\lambda t}$. Observe that this probability tends to 0 as t increases: It becomes very improbable that *no* emissions occur over a very long interval of time.

Do the probabilities found in Eq. (9) add up to 1, as Eq. (4) requires? Let's try it and see:

$$\begin{aligned} P_0(t) + P_1(t) + \cdots &= e^{-\lambda t}\left[1 + \frac{\lambda t}{1!} + \frac{(\lambda t)^2}{2!} + \cdots\right] \\ &= e^{-\lambda t} \sum_{n=0}^{\infty} \frac{(\lambda t)^n}{n!} \\ &= e^{-\lambda t} \cdot e^{\lambda t} \\ &= e^0 = 1. \end{aligned}$$

Q.E.D.

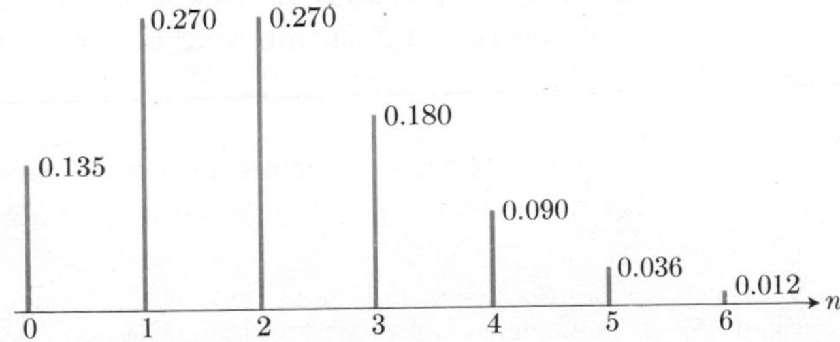

18–9 Poisson distribution with $\lambda t = 2$.

Interpretation of λ

The *mean* value of a random variable X is obtained by taking the weighted average of the possible values X may assume, each weighted according to its probability of occurring. Equations (9) give these probabilities for a Poisson random variable, shown in Table 18–1.

Table 18–1. Probabilities for a Poisson random variable

Possible values of X	Probabilities of these possibilities	(Possible values) × (probability)
0	$e^{-\lambda t}$	$0 \cdot e^{-\lambda t}$
1	$e^{-\lambda t} \cdot (\lambda t)$	$1 \cdot e^{-\lambda t} \cdot (\lambda t)$
2	$e^{-\lambda t} \cdot (\lambda t)^2/2!$	$2 \cdot e^{-\lambda t} \cdot (\lambda t)^2/2!$
3	$e^{-\lambda t} \cdot (\lambda t)^3/3!$	$3 \cdot e^{-\lambda t} \cdot (\lambda t)^3/3!$
$\vdots$	$\vdots$	$\vdots$
n	$e^{-\lambda t} \cdot (\lambda t)^n/n!$	$n \cdot e^{-\lambda t} \cdot (\lambda t)^n/n!$
$\vdots$	$\vdots$	$\vdots$

Thus, the mean value of the Poisson random variable is

$$\begin{aligned}
&e^{-\lambda t}[0 + 1 \cdot (\lambda t) + 2 \cdot (\lambda t)^2/2! + 3 \cdot (\lambda t)^3/3! + \cdots + n \cdot (\lambda t)^n/n! + \cdots] \\
&\qquad = e^{-\lambda t} \cdot (\lambda t) \cdot [1 + (\lambda t) + (\lambda t)^2/2! + \cdots + (\lambda t)^{n-1}/(n-1)! + \cdots] \\
&\qquad = e^{-\lambda t} \cdot (\lambda t) \cdot e^{\lambda t} = \lambda t.
\end{aligned}$$

Therefore λt is the *mean* number of particles emitted in time $(0, t)$. In particular, the mean number emitted in unit time, $t = 1$, is λ. In 2 units of time, it is 2λ, and so on. The mean number in t units of time is proportional to t, and λ is the proportionality factor.

REMARKS. Many phenomena have been found that satisfy the postulates for a Poisson random variable, or nearly do.* Among these are: the number of telephone calls coming into a central office during a particular hour of the day, the number of splices in a certain manufactured tape (per linear foot), the number of surface flaws (per square foot) in plating sheets of metal, the number of failures of electron tubes (per hour) in a given airborne instrumentation device, the number of flying bomb hits in the south of London during World War II (on regions of area $= \frac{1}{4}$ square kilometer). In some of these cases, the "t" in Eqs. (9) should be interpreted as so many units of length, or of area, rather than of time; but the formulas are correct with such interpretations and with λ equal to the mean number of occurrences of the event in question per unit of t.

EXAMPLE 1. Suppose there are 500 misprints in a book of 750 pages. Assuming that the number of misprints per page is (approximately) a Pois-

* *References.* W. Feller, *An Introduction to Probability Theory and Its Applications*, 3rd edition, Wiley, 1968, p. 159. B. W. Lindgren and G. W. McElrath, *Introduction to Probability and Statistics*, Macmillan, 1959, pp. 54–59.

son random variable, find:

a) the probability that a page selected at random has no misprints,
b) the probability of more than one misprint on a given page.

Solution. Let one page be the unit, $t = 1$. The mean number of misprints, per page, is $500/750 = \frac{2}{3}$. So we apply (9) with $\lambda = \frac{2}{3}$:

$$P_n(t) = \text{probability of } n \text{ misprints on } t \text{ pages}$$
$$= e^{-(2/3)t}\frac{(\frac{2}{3}t)^n}{n!}, \qquad n = 0, 1, 2, \ldots$$

a) The probability of no misprints on a single page is $P_n(t)$ with $n = 0$, $t = 1$, or

$$P_0(1) = e^{-2/3} \approx 0.514.$$

b) The probability of more than one misprint on a single page is $\sum_{n=2}^{\infty} P_n(t)$ with $t = 1$. This is also equal to $1 - P_0(t) - P_1(t)$, or

$$1 - e^{-2/3}[1 + \tfrac{2}{3}] \approx 0.143.$$

PROBLEMS

1. Substitute $n = 3$ and $P_2(t) = e^{-\lambda t}(\lambda t)^2/2!$ into Eq. (3b) and solve for $P_3(t)$, subject to the appropriate initial condition.

2. Assuming that Eq. (9) is correct for some integer $n - 1$, so that $P_{n-1}(t) = e^{-\lambda t}(\lambda t)^{n-1}/(n-1)!$, solve Eq. (3b) for $P_n(t)$, subject to the appropriate initial condition. [In other words, show that Eq. (9) is valid for all integers $n \geq 0$ by the method of mathematical induction.]

3. Sketch the graph of $y = P_n(t)$ as a function of t, $t \geq 0$, for $n = 2$ and $\lambda = 2$, 1, and $\frac{1}{2}$. Find the maximum, minimum, and inflection points.

4. Prove directly that $e^{-\lambda t}(\lambda t)^n/n!$ is never greater than 1 if $\lambda > 0$, $t \geq 0$, and n is an integer ≥ 0. This result must be true, of course, since $P_n(t)$ is a probability and hence is never greater than 1.

5. In the example of the book of 750 pages and 500 misprints, what is the probability:

a) that a chapter of 15 pages has no misprints?
b) that a section of 6 pages has 1 or more misprints?

6. A company that makes automobile radiators found that the number of minor defects in its radiators is (approximately) a Poisson random variable with mean equal to 0.02. If 20 radiators are selected at random from the production line, what is the probability that there will be:

a) no minor defects in the entire group of 20 radiators?
b) one or more minor defects in the group of 20 radiators?
c) no minor defects in the first radiator of the 20?

7. A bakery finds that the number of raisins, per loaf, in its raisin bread is (approximately) a Poisson random variable with mean equal to 200 raisins per loaf. Suppose that each loaf is sliced into 20 slices of uniform size.

a) What is the mean number of raisins per slice?
b) What is the probability of getting 5 or fewer raisins in a slice?

8. The first term of a certain Poisson probability distribution is $P_0(t) = 0.135$. Find (a) $P_1(t)$, (b) $P_3(t)$, (c) $P_0(t/2)$, (d) $P_1(2t)$.

9. Assume that the number of α-particles registered by a Geiger counter in a certain experiment is a Poisson random variable. Suppose that the mean number registered per ten-second interval of time is eight. What is the probability that there will be exactly four registered in a given interval of five seconds?

10. Let $Q_n(t, t + h)$ be the probability that the nth particle is emitted between times t and $t + h$. Then, explain why it is true that if $t + h > t > 0$,

$$Q_n(t, t+h) = P_{n-1}(t) \cdot P_1(h) + P_{n-2}(t) \cdot P_2(h) + \cdots + P_0(t) \cdot P_n(h);$$

and from this show that

$$Q_n(t, t+h) = he^{-\lambda t}\lambda^n t^{n-1}/(n-1)! + o(h).$$

11. Using the result in Problem 10, show that

$$Q_n(a, b) = \int_a^b \frac{e^{-\lambda t}\lambda^n t^{n-1}}{(n-1)!}\,dt, \qquad b > a > 0.$$

[*Hint.* Let p be a positive integer, $\Delta t = h = (b-a)/p$, and

$$\begin{aligned} Q_n(a, b) &= Q_n(a, a+h) + Q_n(a+h, a+2h) + \cdots + Q_n(b-h, b) \\ &= \sum_{i=1}^{p} f(t_i)\,\Delta t + \frac{b-a}{h}\,o(h), \end{aligned}$$

with $f(t) = e^{-\lambda t}\lambda^n t^{n-1}/(n-1)!$ and $t_i = a + (i-1)h$. Then let $p \to \infty$.]

12. Let $F(n) = \int_0^\infty e^{-\lambda t}\lambda^n t^{n-1}\,dt = \int_0^\infty e^{-u}u^{n-1}\,du$.

a) Integrate by parts and show that $F(n) = (n-1)F(n-1)$.

b) Show directly that $F(1) = 1$.

c) From (a) and (b), show that $F(2) = 1$, $F(3) = 2F(2) = 2!$, and in general $F(n) = (n-1)!$.

d) Using the result of part (c) above, and of Problem 11, show that $Q_n(0, \infty) = 1$, for any integer $n \geq 1$. What does this mean in terms of probability?

REVIEW QUESTIONS AND EXERCISES

1. List some differential equations (having physical interpretations) that you have come across in your courses in chemistry, physics, engineering, or life and social sciences; or look for some in the articles on differential equations, dynamics, electromagnetic waves, hydromechanics, quantum mechanics, or thermodynamics, in the *Encyclopaedia Britannica*.

2. How are differential equations classified?

3. What is meant by a "solution" of a differential equation?

4. Review methods for solving ordinary, first-order, and first-degree differential equations:

a) when the variables are separable,
b) when the equation is homogeneous,
c) when the equation is linear in one variable,
d) when the equation is exact.

Illustrate each with an example.

5. Review methods of solving second order equations:

a) with dependent variable missing,
b) with independent variable missing.

Illustrate each with an example.

6. Review methods for solving linear differential equations with constant coefficients:

a) in the homogeneous case,
b) in the nonhomogeneous case.

Illustrate each with an example.

7. If an external force F acts upon a system whose mass varies with time, Newton's law of motion is

$$\frac{d(mv)}{dt} = F + (v+u)\frac{dm}{dt}.$$

In this equation, m is the mass of the system at time t, v its velocity, and $v + u$ is the velocity of the mass that is entering (or leaving) the system at the rate dm/dt. Suppose that a rocket of initial mass m_0 starts from rest, but is driven upward by firing some of its mass directly backward at the constant rate of $dm/dt = -b$ units per second and at constant speed relative to the rocket $u = -c$. The only external force acting on the rocket is $F = -mg$ due to gravity. Under these assumptions, show that the height of the rocket above the ground at the end of t seconds (t small compared to m_0/b) is

$$y = c\left[t + \frac{m_0 - bt}{b}\ln\frac{m_0 - bt}{m_0}\right] - \frac{1}{2}gt^2.$$

(See Martin and Reissner, *Elementary Differential Equations*, 2nd edition, Addison-Wesley, 1961, pp. 26 ff.)

MISCELLANEOUS PROBLEMS

Solve the following differential equations:

1. $y \ln y\,dx + (1 + x^2)\,dy = 0$ **2.** $\dfrac{dy}{dx} = \dfrac{y^2 - y - 2}{x^2 + x}$

3. $e^{x+2y}\,dy - e^{y-2x}\,dx = 0$ **4.** $\sqrt{1 + \left(\dfrac{dy}{dx}\right)^2} = ky$

5. $y\,dy = \sqrt{1 + y^4}\,dx$ **6.** $(2x + y)\,dx + (x - 2y)\,dy = 0$

7. $\dfrac{dy}{dx} = \dfrac{x^2 + y^2}{2xy}$ **8.** $x\dfrac{dy}{dx} = y + \sqrt{x^2 + y^2}$

9. $x\,dy = \left(y + x\cos^2\dfrac{y}{x}\right)dx$

10. $x(\ln y - \ln x)\,dy = y(1 + \ln y - \ln x)\,dx$

11. $x\,dy + (2y - x^2 - 1)\,dx = 0$

12. $\cos y\,dx + (x \sin y - \cos^2 y)\,dy = 0$

13. $\cosh x\,dy - (y + \cosh x) \sinh x\,dx = 0$

14. $(x + 1)\,dy + (2y - x)\,dx = 0$

15. $(1 + y^2)\,dx + (2xy + y^2 + 1)\,dy = 0$

16. $(x^2 + y)\,dx + (e^y + x)\,dy = 0$

17. $(x^2 + y^2)\,dx + (2xy + \cosh y)\,dy = 0$

18. $(e^x + \ln y)\,dx + \dfrac{x + y}{y}\,dy = 0$

19. $x(1 + e^y)\,dx + \frac{1}{2}(x^2 + y^2)e^y\,dy = 0$

20. $\left(\sin x + \tan^{-1} \dfrac{y}{x}\right) dx - (y - \ln \sqrt{x^2 + y^2})\,dy = 0$

21. $\dfrac{d^2y}{dx^2} - 2y\dfrac{dy}{dx} = 0$

22. $\dfrac{d^2x}{dy^2} + 4x = 0$

23. $\dfrac{d^2y}{dx^2} = 1 + \left(\dfrac{dy}{dx}\right)^2$

24. $\dfrac{d^2x}{dy^2} = 1 - \left(\dfrac{dx}{dy}\right)^2$

25. $x^2\dfrac{d^2y}{dx^2} + x\dfrac{dy}{dx} = 1$

26. $\dfrac{d^2y}{dx^2} - 4\dfrac{dy}{dx} + 3y = 0$

27. $\dfrac{d^3y}{dx^3} - 2\dfrac{d^2y}{dx^2} + \dfrac{dy}{dx} = 0$

28. $\dfrac{d^2y}{dx^2} + 4y = \sec 2x$

29. $\dfrac{d^2y}{dx^2} - \dfrac{dy}{dx} - 2y = e^{2x}$

30. $\dfrac{d^2y}{dx^2} - 2\dfrac{dy}{dx} + 5y = e^{-x}$

31. Find the *general solution* of the differential equation $4x^2y'' + 4xy' - y = 0$, given that there is a particular solution of the form $y = x^c$ for some constant c.

32. Show that the only plane curves that have constant curvature are circles and straight lines. (Assume that the appropriate derivatives exist and are continuous.)

33. Find the orthogonal trajectories of the family of curves $x^2 = Cy^3$. [*Caution.* The differential equation should not contain the arbitrary constant C.]

34. Find the orthogonal trajectories of the family of circles $(x - C)^2 + y^2 = C^2$.

35. Find the orthogonal trajectories of the family of parabolas $y^2 = 4C(C - x)$.

36. The equation $d^2y/dt^2 + 100y = 0$ represents a simple harmonic motion. Find the general solution of the equation and determine the constants of integration if $y = 10$, $dy/dt = 50$, when $t = 0$. Find the period and the amplitude of the motion.

APPENDIX A

MATRICES AND DETERMINANTS

MATRICES

A *matrix* is a rectangular array of numbers. For example,

$$A = \begin{bmatrix} 2 & 1 & 3 \\ 1 & 0 & -2 \end{bmatrix} \tag{1}$$

is a matrix with two rows and three columns. We call A a "2 by 3" matrix. More generally, an "m by n" matrix is one that has m rows and n columns.

The element in the ith row and jth column of a matrix can be represented by a_{ij}. In the example above, we have

$$a_{11} = 2, \quad a_{12} = 1, \quad a_{13} = 3,$$
$$a_{21} = 1, \quad a_{22} = 0, \quad a_{23} = -2.$$

Two matrices A and B are *equal* if and only if they have the same elements in the same positions. That is, $A = B$ if and only if A and B have the same number of rows, say m, and the same number of columns, say n, and

$$a_{ij} = b_{ij} \quad \text{for} \quad i = 1, 2, \ldots, m \quad \text{and} \quad j = 1, 2, \ldots, n.$$

For example, if

$$B = \begin{bmatrix} b_{11} & b_{12} & b_{13} \\ b_{21} & b_{22} & b_{23} \end{bmatrix} \tag{2}$$

and $B = A$, with A given by Eq. (1), then

$$b_{11} = 2, \quad b_{12} = 1, \quad b_{13} = 3,$$
$$b_{21} = 1, \quad b_{22} = 0, \quad b_{23} = -2.$$

Two matrices A and B can be added if and only if they have the same number of rows and the same number of columns. Their sum, $A + B$, is the matrix we get by adding corresponding elements in the two matrices. For example,

$$\begin{bmatrix} 2 & 1 & 3 \\ 1 & 0 & -2 \end{bmatrix} + \begin{bmatrix} 1 & -2 & 2 \\ 2 & 3 & -1 \end{bmatrix} = \begin{bmatrix} 3 & -1 & 5 \\ 3 & 3 & -3 \end{bmatrix}.$$

To multiply a matrix by a number c, we multiply each element by c. For example,

$$7\begin{bmatrix} 2 & 1 & 3 \\ 1 & 0 & -2 \end{bmatrix} = \begin{bmatrix} 14 & 7 & 21 \\ 7 & 0 & -14 \end{bmatrix}. \tag{3}$$

A system of simultaneous linear equations

$$\begin{aligned} a_{11}x + a_{12}y + a_{13}z &= b_1, \\ a_{21}x + a_{22}y + a_{23}z &= b_2, \end{aligned} \tag{4a}$$

can be written in matrix form as

$$\begin{bmatrix} a_{11} & a_{12} & a_{13} \\ a_{21} & a_{22} & a_{23} \end{bmatrix} \begin{bmatrix} x \\ y \\ z \end{bmatrix} = \begin{bmatrix} b_1 \\ b_2 \end{bmatrix}, \tag{4b}$$

or, more compactly, as

$$AX = B, \tag{4c}$$

where

$$A = \begin{bmatrix} a_{11} & a_{12} & a_{13} \\ a_{21} & a_{22} & a_{23} \end{bmatrix}, \quad X = \begin{bmatrix} x \\ y \\ z \end{bmatrix}, \quad B = \begin{bmatrix} b_1 \\ b_2 \end{bmatrix}. \tag{4d}$$

To form the product indicated by AX in Eq. (4c), we take the elements of the first row of A in order from left to right and multiply by the corresponding elements of X from the top down, and add these products. The result is the left side of the first equation in Eqs. (4a) and we set it equal to b_1, the element in the first row of B. Then we repeat the process using the second row of A: Multiply its individual elements by the corresponding elements in X, add the products, and set the result equal to b_2, the element in the second row of B.

More generally, a matrix A that has m rows and n columns can multiply a matrix B that has n rows and p columns to give a matrix $C = AB$ that has m rows and p columns. The element in the ith row and jth column of AB is the sum

$$c_{ij} = a_{i1}b_{1j} + a_{i2}b_{2j} + \cdots + a_{in}b_{nj} = \sum_{k=1}^{n} a_{ik}b_{kj}, \tag{5}$$

$$i = 1, 2, \ldots, m \quad \text{and} \quad j = 1, 2, \ldots, p.$$

For example:

$$\begin{bmatrix} 2 & -1 & 3 \\ 3 & 2 & 2 \end{bmatrix} \begin{bmatrix} a & b & c \\ d & e & f \\ u & v & w \end{bmatrix}$$

$$= \begin{bmatrix} 2a - d + 3u & 2b - e + 3v & 2c - f + 3w \\ 3a + 2d + 2u & 3b + 2e + 2v & 3c + 2f + 2w \end{bmatrix}.$$

There are two rows in the answer on the right, one for each row in the first factor on the left. There are three columns in the product AB, one for each column in B. In words, Eq. (5) is saying "to get the element in the ith row and jth column of AB, multiply the individual entries in the ith row of A, one after the other from left to right, by the corresponding entries in the jth column of B from top to bottom, and add these products: their sum is a single number c_{ij}."

PROBLEMS

1. Write the following system of linear equations in matrix form $AX = B$:

$$2x - 3y + 4z = -19,$$
$$6x + 4y - 2z = 8,$$
$$x + 5y + 4z = 23.$$

2. Let A be an arbitrary matrix with 3 rows and 3 columns and let I be the 3 by 3 matrix that has 1's on the main diagonal and zeros elsewhere:

$$I = \begin{bmatrix} 1 & 0 & 0 \\ 0 & 1 & 0 \\ 0 & 0 & 1 \end{bmatrix}.$$

Show that $IA = A$ and also that $AI = A$. For this reason, I is called the 3 by 3 identity matrix: It is the multiplicative identity matrix for all 3 by 3 matrices.

3. Let A be an arbitrary 3 by 3 matrix and let R_{12} be the matrix that is obtained from the 3-by-3 identity matrix by interchanging rows 1 and 2:

$$R_{12} = \begin{bmatrix} 0 & 1 & 0 \\ 1 & 0 & 0 \\ 0 & 0 & 1 \end{bmatrix}.$$

Compute $R_{12}A$ and show that you would get the same result by interchanging rows 1 and 2 of A.

4. Let A and R_{12} be as in Problem 3 above. Compute AR_{12} and show that the result is what you would get by interchanging columns 1 and 2 of A. (Note that R_{12} is also the result of interchanging columns 1 and 2 of the 3 by 3 identity matrix I.)

A–2 ELEMENTARY ROW OPERATIONS AND ROW REDUCTION

Two systems of linear equations are called *equivalent* if they have the same set of solutions. To solve a system of linear equations it is often possible to transform it step by step into an equivalent system of equations that is so simple it can be solved by inspection. We shall illustrate such a sequence of steps by transforming the system of equations

$$\begin{aligned} 2x + 3y - 4z &= -3, \\ x + 2y + 3z &= 3, \\ 3x - y - z &= 6, \end{aligned} \tag{1}$$

into the equivalent system of equations

$$\begin{aligned} x &= 2, \\ y &= -1, \\ z &= 1. \end{aligned} \tag{2}$$

EXAMPLE. Solve the system of equations (1).

Solution. The system (1) is the same as

$$AX = B, \qquad A = \begin{bmatrix} 2 & 3 & -4 \\ 1 & 2 & 3 \\ 3 & -1 & -1 \end{bmatrix}, \qquad B = \begin{bmatrix} -3 \\ 3 \\ 6 \end{bmatrix}. \tag{3}$$

We start with the 3 by 4 matrix $[A \,\vdots\, B]$ whose first three columns are the columns of A, and whose fourth column is B. That is,

$$[A \,\vdots\, B] = \left[\begin{array}{ccc:c} 2 & 3 & -4 & -3 \\ 1 & 2 & 3 & 3 \\ 3 & -1 & -1 & 6 \end{array}\right]. \tag{4}$$

We are going to transform this augmented matrix with a sequence of so-called *elementary row operations*. These operations, which are to be performed on the rows of the matrix, are of three kinds:

1. Multiply any row by a constant different from 0.
2. Add a constant multiple of any row to another row.
3. Interchange two rows.

Our goal is to replace the matrix $[A \mid B]$ by the matrix $[I \mid S]$, where

$$I = \begin{bmatrix} 1 & 0 & 0 \\ 0 & 1 & 0 \\ 0 & 0 & 1 \end{bmatrix} \quad \text{and} \quad S = \begin{bmatrix} s_1 \\ s_2 \\ s_3 \end{bmatrix}. \tag{5}$$

If we succeed, the matrix $[I \mid S]$ will be the matrix of the system

$$\begin{aligned} x \qquad\qquad &= s_1, \\ y \qquad &= s_2, \\ z &= s_3. \end{aligned} \tag{6}$$

The virtue of this system is that its solution, $x = s_1$, $y = s_2$, $z = s_3$, is the same as the solution of (1).

Our systematic approach will be to get a 1 in the upper left corner and use Type 2 operations to get zeros elsewhere in the first column. That will make the first column the same as the first column of I. Then we will use Type 1 or Type 3 operations to get a 1 in the second position in the second row, and follow that by Type 2 operations to get the second column to be what we want: namely, like the second column of I. Then we will work on the third column.

STEP 1. Interchange rows 1 and 2 and get

$$\left[\begin{array}{ccc|c} 1 & 2 & 3 & 3 \\ 2 & 3 & -4 & -3 \\ 3 & -1 & -1 & 6 \end{array}\right]. \tag{7}$$

STEP 2. Add -2 times row 1 to row 2.

STEP 3. Add -3 times row 1 to row 3.

The result of steps 2 and 3 is

$$\left[\begin{array}{ccc|c} 1 & 2 & 3 & 3 \\ 0 & -1 & -10 & -9 \\ 0 & -7 & -10 & -3 \end{array}\right]. \tag{8}$$

STEP 4. Multiply row 2 by -1; then

STEP 5. Add -2 times row 2 to row 1, and

STEP 6. Add 7 times row 2 to row 3.

The combined result of these steps is

$$\left[\begin{array}{ccc|c} 1 & 0 & -17 & -15 \\ 0 & 1 & 10 & 9 \\ 0 & 0 & 60 & 60 \end{array}\right]. \tag{9}$$

STEP 7. Multiply row 3 by 1/60.

STEP 8. Add 17 times row 3 to row 1.

STEP 9. Add -10 times row 3 to row 2.

The final result is

$$[I \,\vdots\, S] = \begin{bmatrix} 1 & 0 & 0 & \vdots & 2 \\ 0 & 1 & 0 & \vdots & -1 \\ 0 & 0 & 1 & \vdots & 1 \end{bmatrix}. \tag{10}$$

This represents the system (2). The solution of this system, and therefore of the system (1), is $x = 2$, $y = -1$, $z = 1$. To check the solution, we substitute these values in (1) and find that

$$\begin{aligned} 2(2) + 3(-1) - 4(1) &= -3, \\ (2) + 2(-1) + 3(1) &= 3, \\ 3(2) - (-1) - (1) &= 6. \end{aligned} \tag{11}$$

The method of using elementary row operations to reduce the augmented matrix of a system of linear equations to a simpler form is sometimes called the *method of row reduction.* It works because at each step the system of equations represented by the transformed matrix is equivalent to the original system. Thus, in the Example, when we finally arrived at the matrix (10), which represented the system (2) whose solution could be found by inspection, we knew that this solution was also the solution of (1). Note that we checked the solution anyhow. It is always a good idea to do that.

The matrix I in Eq. (5) is the multiplicative identity for all 3 by 3 matrices. That is, if M is any 3 by 3 matrix, then

$$IM = MI = M. \tag{12}$$

If P is a matrix with the property that

$$PM = I,$$

then we call P the *inverse* of M, and use the alternative notation

$$P = M^{-1},$$

pronounced "M inverse."

The sequence of row operations that we used in the Example to find the solution of the system $AX = B$ can be used to find the inverse of the matrix A. We start with the 3 by 6 matrix $[A \,\vdots\, I]$ whose first three columns are the columns of A and whose last three columns are the columns of I, namely

$$[A \,\vdots\, I] = \begin{bmatrix} 2 & 3 & -4 & \vdots & 1 & 0 & 0 \\ 1 & 2 & 3 & \vdots & 0 & 1 & 0 \\ 3 & -1 & -1 & \vdots & 0 & 0 & 1 \end{bmatrix}. \tag{13}$$

We then carry out Steps 1 through 9 of the Example on the augmented matrix $[A \,\vdots\, I]$. The final result is

$$[A \,\vdots\, A^{-1}] = \begin{bmatrix} 1 & 0 & 0 & \vdots & \frac{1}{60} & \frac{7}{60} & \frac{17}{60} \\ 0 & 1 & 0 & \vdots & \frac{10}{60} & \frac{10}{60} & -\frac{10}{60} \\ 0 & 0 & 1 & \vdots & -\frac{7}{60} & \frac{11}{60} & \frac{1}{60} \end{bmatrix}. \tag{14}$$

The 3-by-3 matrix in the last 3 columns is

$$A^{-1} = \frac{1}{60}\begin{bmatrix} 1 & 7 & 17 \\ 10 & 10 & -10 \\ -7 & 11 & 1 \end{bmatrix}. \tag{15}$$

By direct matrix multiplication, we verify our answer:

$$\begin{aligned} A^{-1}A &= \frac{1}{60}\begin{bmatrix} 1 & 7 & 17 \\ 10 & 10 & -10 \\ -7 & 11 & 1 \end{bmatrix}\begin{bmatrix} 2 & 3 & -4 \\ 1 & 2 & 3 \\ 3 & -1 & -1 \end{bmatrix} \\ &= \frac{1}{60}\begin{bmatrix} 2+7+51 & 3+14-17 & -4+21-17 \\ 20+10-30 & 30+20+10 & -40+30+10 \\ -14+11+3 & -21+22-1 & 28+33-1 \end{bmatrix} \\ &= \frac{1}{60}\begin{bmatrix} 60 & 0 & 0 \\ 0 & 60 & 0 \\ 0 & 0 & 60 \end{bmatrix} = \begin{bmatrix} 1 & 0 & 0 \\ 0 & 1 & 0 \\ 0 & 0 & 1 \end{bmatrix}. \end{aligned} \tag{16}$$

Knowing A^{-1} provides a second way to solve the system of equations with which this article began. We write the system in the form given in (3), and then multiply B on the left by A^{-1} to find the solution matrix X. Thus,

$$\begin{aligned} X = IX = (A^{-1}A)X = A^{-1}(AX) = A^{-1}B &= \frac{1}{60}\begin{bmatrix} 1 & 7 & 17 \\ 10 & 10 & -10 \\ -7 & 11 & 1 \end{bmatrix}\begin{bmatrix} -3 \\ 3 \\ 6 \end{bmatrix} \\ &= \frac{1}{60}\begin{bmatrix} 120 \\ -60 \\ 60 \end{bmatrix} = \begin{bmatrix} 2 \\ -1 \\ 1 \end{bmatrix}. \end{aligned} \tag{17}$$

REMARK 1. Only square matrices can have inverses. If an n by n matrix A has an inverse, the method shown above for $n = 3$ will give it: Put the n by n identity matrix alongside A and use the row operations to get an n by n identity matrix in place of A. The n by n matrix that is now beside that is A^{-1}.

REMARK 2. Not every n by n matrix has an inverse. For example, the 2 by 2 matrix

$$\begin{bmatrix} 1 & 1 \\ a & a \end{bmatrix}$$

has no inverse. The method we outlined above would reduce this to

$$\begin{bmatrix} 1 & 1 \\ 0 & 0 \end{bmatrix},$$

which cannot be further changed by elementary row operations into the 2 by 2 identity matrix. We shall have more to say about inverses in the next article.

REMARK 3. A system of m equations in n unknowns may have no solutions, only one solution, or infinitely many solutions. If there are any solutions, they can be found by the method of successive elimination, which is like the elementary row operations we used above.

PROBLEMS

1. Use the method of row operations to find the inverse of each of the following matrices:

a) $A = \begin{bmatrix} 1 & 2 \\ 2 & 3 \end{bmatrix}$ **b)** $A = \begin{bmatrix} 1 & 2 & 3 \\ 0 & 2 & 4 \\ 0 & 0 & 3 \end{bmatrix}$

2. Define the determinant of the 2 by 2 matrix

$$A = \begin{bmatrix} a & b \\ c & d \end{bmatrix} \quad \text{by} \quad \det A = ad - bc.$$

If $ad - bc \neq 0$, verify that the matrix

$$P = \frac{1}{ad - bc}\begin{bmatrix} d & -b \\ -c & a \end{bmatrix}$$

is the inverse of A; that is, show that

$$AP = PA = I_2 = \begin{bmatrix} 1 & 0 \\ 0 & 1 \end{bmatrix}.$$

3. Use the result of Problem 2 to write down by inspection the inverses of the following matrices:

a) $A = \begin{bmatrix} 2 & -1 \\ 3 & 1 \end{bmatrix}$ **b)** $B = \begin{bmatrix} 2 & 3 \\ -1 & 1 \end{bmatrix}$

(In this example, B is the transpose of A. Is B^{-1} also the transpose of A^{-1}? *Note.* "Transpose" means to write the rows of a matrix as columns.)

4. Solve the system of equations in Problem 1, Article A–1.

5. Solve the equations for x and y in terms of z:

$$\begin{aligned} 2x - y + 2z &= 5 \\ 3x + y - 3z &= 7 \end{aligned} \quad \text{or} \quad \begin{bmatrix} 2 & -1 \\ 3 & 1 \end{bmatrix}\begin{bmatrix} x \\ y \end{bmatrix} = \begin{bmatrix} 5 - 2z \\ 7 + 3z \end{bmatrix}.$$

You can use the result of Problem 3(a) above if you want to. (Each equation represents a plane. In how many points do the planes intersect?)

6. Apply the nine steps of the Example to the matrix in (13), to obtain the matrix in (14).

A–3 DETERMINANTS

An n by n square matrix is called a *matrix of order n*, for short. With such a matrix we associate a number called the *determinant* of A and written sometimes det A and sometimes $|a_{ij}|$ with vertical bars (which do not mean absolute value). For $n = 1$ and $n = 2$ we have these definitions:

$$\det [a] = a, \qquad \det \begin{bmatrix} a & b \\ c & d \end{bmatrix} = ad - bc. \tag{1}$$

For a matrix of order 3, we define

$$\det \begin{bmatrix} a_{11} & a_{12} & a_{13} \\ a_{21} & a_{22} & a_{23} \\ a_{31} & a_{32} & a_{33} \end{bmatrix} = \begin{matrix} \text{Sum of all signed products} \\ \text{of the form } \pm a_{1i}a_{2j}a_{3k}, \end{matrix}$$

where i, j, k is a permutation of 1, 2, 3 in some order. There are $3! = 6$ such permutations, so there are six terms in the sum. Half of these have plus signs and the other half have minus signs, according to the index of the permutation, where the index is a number we next define.

Index of a permutation. *Given any permutation of the numbers* $1, 2, 3, \ldots, n$, *denote the permutation by* $i_1, i_2, i_3, \ldots, i_n$. *In this arrangement, some of the* *numbers following i_1 may be less than i_1, and however many of these there are is called the* ***number of inversions*** *in the arrangement pertaining to i_1. Likewise, there is a number of inversions pertaining to each of the other i's; it is the number of indices that come after that particular one in the arrangement and are less than it. The* ***index*** *of the permutation is the sum of all of the numbers of inversions pertaining to the separate indices.*

EXAMPLE 1. For $n = 5$, the permutation

$$5\ 3\ 1\ 2\ 4$$

has

4 inversions pertaining to the first element, 5,

2 inversions pertaining to the second element, 3,

and no further inversions, so the index is $4 + 2 = 6$.

The following table shows the permutations of 1, 2, 3 and the index of each permutation. The signed product in the determinant of Eq. (2) is also shown.

Permutation	*Index*	*Signed product*
1 2 3	0	$+a_{11}a_{22}a_{33}$
1 3 2	1	$-a_{11}a_{23}a_{32}$
2 1 3	1	$-a_{12}a_{21}a_{33}$
2 3 1	2	$+a_{12}a_{23}a_{31}$
3 1 2	2	$+a_{13}a_{21}a_{32}$
3 2 1	3	$-a_{13}a_{22}a_{31}$

The sum of the six signed products is:

$$a_{11}(a_{22}a_{33} - a_{23}a_{32}) - a_{12}(a_{21}a_{33} - a_{23}a_{31}) + a_{13}(a_{21}a_{32} - a_{22}a_{31})$$

$$= a_{11}\begin{vmatrix} a_{22} & a_{23} \\ a_{32} & a_{33} \end{vmatrix} - a_{12}\begin{vmatrix} a_{21} & a_{23} \\ a_{31} & a_{33} \end{vmatrix} + a_{13}\begin{vmatrix} a_{21} & a_{22} \\ a_{31} & a_{32} \end{vmatrix}$$

$$= \begin{vmatrix} a_{11} & a_{12} & a_{13} \\ a_{21} & a_{22} & a_{23} \\ a_{31} & a_{32} & a_{33} \end{vmatrix}. \qquad (2)$$

Minors and Cofactors

In Eq. (2) there are some second order determinants. There are other ways in which the six terms in the expansion of the third order determinant could be written. We have chosen to write it as the sum of the products of the elements of the first row of the matrix A, each multiplied by its *cofactor*. In order to define the cofactor of an element in a matrix, we first define the *minor* of that element, which is the determinant of the matrix that remains when the row and column that contain the given element are deleted. Thus the *minor* of the element in the ith row and jth column is the determinant of the $(n-1)$ by $(n-1)$ matrix that remains when row i and column j are deleted. The *cofactor* of a_{ij} is denoted by A_{ij} and it is $(-1)^{i+j}$ times the minor of a_{ij}.

EXAMPLE 2. Find the cofactors of the matrix

$$A = \begin{bmatrix} 2 & 1 & 3 \\ 3 & -1 & -2 \\ 2 & 3 & 1 \end{bmatrix},$$

and evaluate det (A).

Solution. The cofactors are

$$A_{11} = (-1)^{1+1}\begin{vmatrix} -1 & -2 \\ 3 & 1 \end{vmatrix}, \qquad A_{12} = (-1)^{1+2}\begin{vmatrix} 3 & -2 \\ 2 & 1 \end{vmatrix},$$

$$A_{13} = (-1)^{1+3}\begin{vmatrix} 3 & -1 \\ 2 & 3 \end{vmatrix}.$$

To find det (A), we multiply each element of the first row of A by its cofactor and add:

$$\begin{aligned} \det(A) &= 2\begin{vmatrix} -1 & -2 \\ 3 & 1 \end{vmatrix} + (-1)\begin{vmatrix} 3 & -2 \\ 2 & 1 \end{vmatrix} + 3\begin{vmatrix} 3 & -1 \\ 2 & 3 \end{vmatrix} \\ &= 2(-1+6) - 1(3+4) + 3(9+2) = 10 - 7 + 33 = 36. \end{aligned}$$

Note. There is a simple checkerboard pattern for remembering the signs that correspond to $(-1)^{i+j}$ and that can be applied to convert the *minor* of an element in a matrix to the *cofactor* of the element. For a third order determinant the sign pattern is

$$\begin{matrix} + & - & + \\ - & + & - \\ + & - & + \end{matrix}$$

In the upper left corner, $i = 1, j = 1$ and $(-1)^{1+1} = +1$. In going from any cell to an adjacent cell in the same row or column, we change i by 1 or j by 1, but not both, so we change the exponent from even to odd or from odd to even, which changes the sign from $+$ to $-$ or from $-$ to $+$.

If we were to expand the determinant in Example 2 by cofactors according to elements of its third column, say, we would get

$$\begin{aligned} &+3\begin{vmatrix} 3 & -1 \\ 2 & 3 \end{vmatrix} - (-2)\begin{vmatrix} 2 & 1 \\ 2 & 3 \end{vmatrix} + 1\begin{vmatrix} 2 & 1 \\ 3 & -1 \end{vmatrix} \\ &= 3(9+2) + 2(6-2) + 1(-2-3) = 33 + 8 - 5 = 36. \end{aligned}$$

It is no accident that the answer is the same. If we were to multiply the elements of any row (or column) by the cofactors of the corresponding elements and add the products, we would get the same answer: the value of the determinant.

PROBLEM

Evaluate the following third order determinant by expanding according to cofactors of (a) the first row, and (b) the second column:

$$\begin{vmatrix} 2 & -1 & 2 \\ 1 & 0 & 3 \\ 0 & 2 & 1 \end{vmatrix}.$$

A–4

PROPERTIES OF DETERMINANTS

We now state some facts about determinants. You should know and be able to use these facts, but we omit the proofs.

FACT 1. If two rows of a matrix are identical, the determinant is zero.

FACT 2. If two rows of a matrix are interchanged, the determinant just changes its sign.

FACT 3. The determinant of a matrix is the sum of the products of the elements of the ith row (or column) by their cofactors, for any i.

FACT 4. The determinant of the transpose of a matrix is equal to the original determinant.

FACT 5. If each element of some row (or column) of a matrix is multiplied by a constant c, the determinant is multiplied by c.

FACT 6. If all elements of a matrix above the principal diagonal (or all below it) are zero, the determinant of the matrix is the product of the elements on the main diagonal.

EXAMPLE 1

$$\begin{vmatrix} 3 & 4 & 7 \\ 0 & -2 & 5 \\ 0 & 0 & 5 \end{vmatrix} = (3)(-2)(5) = -30.$$

FACT 7. If the elements of any row of a matrix are multiplied by the cofactors of the corresponding elements of a different row and these products are summed, the sum is zero.

EXAMPLE 2. If A_{11}, A_{12}, A_{13} are the cofactors of the elements of the first row of $A = a_{ij}$, then the sums

$$a_{21}A_{11} + a_{22}A_{12} + a_{23}A_{13}$$

(elements of second row times cofactors of elements of first row)

and

$$a_{31}A_{11} + a_{32}A_{12} + a_{33}A_{13}$$

are both zero. A similar result holds for columns.

FACT 8. If the elements of any column of a matrix are multiplied by the cofactors of the corresponding elements of a different column and these products are summed, the sum is zero.

FACT 9. If each element of a row of a matrix is multiplied by a constant c and the results are added to a different row, the determinant is not changed.

EXAMPLE 3. Evaluate the fourth order determinant

$$\begin{vmatrix} 1 & -2 & 3 & 1 \\ 2 & 1 & 0 & 2 \\ -1 & 2 & 1 & -2 \\ 0 & 1 & 2 & 1 \end{vmatrix}.$$

Solution. By adding appropriate multiples of row 1 to rows 2 and 3, we can get the equal determinant

$$\begin{vmatrix} 1 & -2 & 3 & 1 \\ 0 & 5 & -6 & 0 \\ 0 & 0 & 4 & -1 \\ 0 & 1 & 2 & 1 \end{vmatrix}.$$

We could further reduce this to a triangular matrix (one with zeros below the main diagonal), or expand it by cofactors of its first column. By multiplying the elements of the first column by their respective cofactors, we get the third order determinant

$$\begin{vmatrix} 5 & -6 & 0 \\ 0 & 4 & -1 \\ 1 & 2 & 1 \end{vmatrix} = 5(4 + 2) - (-6)(0 + 1) + 0 = 36.$$

PROBLEMS

Evaluate the following determinants.

1. $\begin{vmatrix} 2 & 3 & 1 \\ 4 & 5 & 2 \\ 1 & 2 & 3 \end{vmatrix}$

2. $\begin{vmatrix} 2 & -1 & -2 \\ -1 & 2 & 1 \\ 3 & 0 & -3 \end{vmatrix}$

3. $\begin{vmatrix} 1 & 2 & 3 & 4 \\ 0 & 1 & 2 & 3 \\ 0 & 0 & 2 & 1 \\ 0 & 0 & 3 & 2 \end{vmatrix}$

4. $\begin{vmatrix} 1 & -1 & 2 & 3 \\ 2 & 1 & 2 & 6 \\ 1 & 0 & 2 & 3 \\ -2 & 2 & 0 & -5 \end{vmatrix}$

A–5

DETERMINANTS AND THE INVERSE OF A MATRIX

Here is another way to find the inverse of a square matrix A (assuming that A has one). It depends on the fact that square matrix A has an inverse if and only if $\det(A) \neq 0$. First we describe the method. Then we do an example. Finally, we indicate why the method works.

THE METHOD. Given the matrix A, construct, in order,

i) the matrix of minors of elements of A;
ii) by appropriate sign changes, the matrix of cofactors of the elements of A;
iii) The transposed matrix of cofactors. This matrix is called the *adjoint* of A:

$$\text{adj } A = \text{transposed matrix of cofactors.}$$

iv) Then,

$$A^{-1} = \frac{1}{\det A} \text{adj } A.$$

EXAMPLE. Let us take the same matrix A that we used in illustrating the method of elementary row operations:

$$A = \begin{bmatrix} 2 & 3 & -4 \\ 1 & 2 & 3 \\ 3 & -1 & -1 \end{bmatrix}.$$

You can verify that the matrix of minors is

$$\begin{bmatrix} 1 & -10 & -7 \\ -7 & 10 & -11 \\ 17 & 10 & 1 \end{bmatrix}.$$

We next apply the sign corrections according to the checkerboard pattern $(-1)^{i+j}$ to get the matrix of cofactors

$$\begin{bmatrix} 1 & 10 & -7 \\ 7 & 10 & 11 \\ 17 & -10 & 1 \end{bmatrix}.$$

The adjoint of A is the transposed cofactor matrix

$$\text{adj } A = \begin{bmatrix} 1 & 7 & 17 \\ 10 & 10 & -10 \\ -7 & 11 & 1 \end{bmatrix}.$$

We get the determinant of A by multiplying the first row of A and the first column of adj A (which is the first row of the matrix of cofactors, so we are multiplying the elements of the first row of A by their own cofactors):

$$\det A = 2(1) + 3(10) + (-4)(-7) = 2 + 30 + 28 = 60.$$

Therefore, when we divide adj A by det A, we get

$$A^{-1} = \frac{1}{60}\begin{bmatrix} 1 & 7 & 17 \\ 10 & 10 & -10 \\ -7 & 11 & 1 \end{bmatrix},$$

which agrees with our previous work.

Why does the method work? Let us take a closer look at the products A adj A and (adj A) A for $n = 3$. Because adj A is the transposed cofactor matrix, we get:

$$A\,(\text{adj } A) = \begin{bmatrix} a_{11} & a_{12} & a_{13} \\ a_{21} & a_{22} & a_{23} \\ a_{31} & a_{32} & a_{33} \end{bmatrix}\begin{bmatrix} A_{11} & A_{21} & A_{31} \\ A_{12} & A_{22} & A_{32} \\ A_{13} & A_{23} & A_{33} \end{bmatrix} = \begin{bmatrix} \det A & 0 & 0 \\ 0 & \det A & 0 \\ 0 & 0 & \det A \end{bmatrix};$$

(here A_{ij} = cofactor of a_{ij}).

An element on the main diagonal in the final product is the product of a row of A and the corresponding column of adj A. This is the same as the sum of the products of the elements of a row of A and the cofactors of the same row, which is just det A. For those elements not on the main diagonal in the product, we are adding products of elements of some row of A by the cofactors of the corresponding elements of a different row of A, and that sum is zero.

If we were to multiply in the other order, (adj A) A, we would again get

$$(\text{adj } A)\,A = \begin{bmatrix} \det A & 0 & 0 \\ 0 & \det A & 0 \\ 0 & 0 & \det A \end{bmatrix},$$

because we are multiplying the elements of the jth column of A, say, by the cofactors of the corresponding elements of the ith column, in order to get the entry in the ith row and jth column in the product. The result is det A when $i = j$ and is 0 when $i \neq j$.

PROBLEMS

Use the method of cofactors and adjoint matrices to find A^{-1} in each case where det $A \neq 0$. Check your work by computing A (adj A).

1. $A = \begin{bmatrix} 1 & 2 \\ 2 & 3 \end{bmatrix}$

2. $A = \begin{bmatrix} -1 & 2 & 1 \\ 2 & 2 & 1 \\ 1 & 0 & 2 \end{bmatrix}$

3. $A = \begin{bmatrix} 2 & 1 & 1 & 1 \\ 0 & 2 & 1 & 1 \\ 0 & 0 & 2 & 1 \\ 0 & 0 & 0 & 2 \end{bmatrix}$

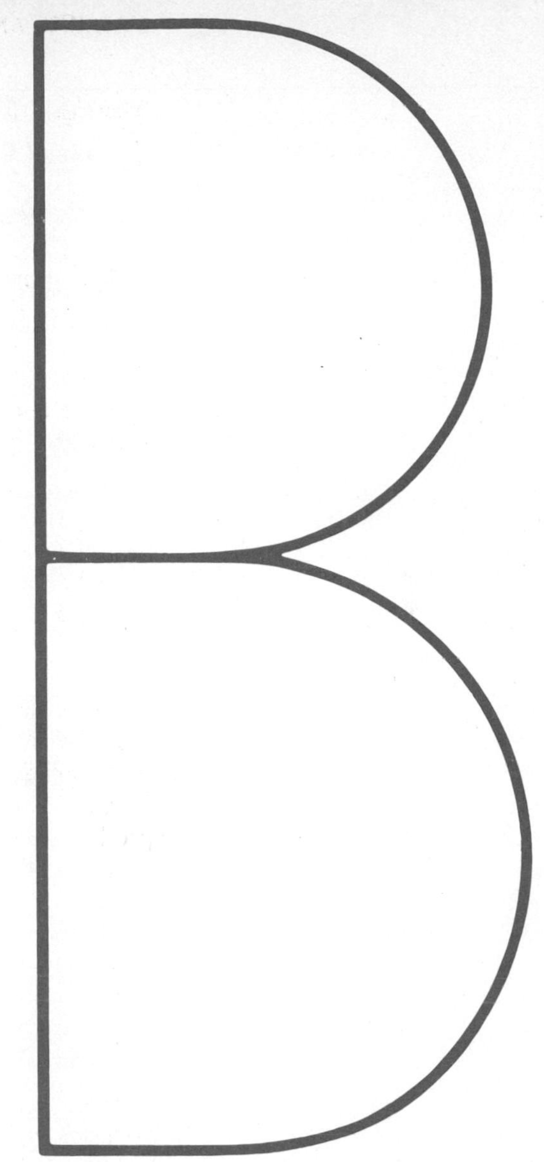

APPENDIX B

FORMULAS FROM ELEMENTARY MATHEMATICS

ALGEBRA

1. Laws of Exponents

$$a^m a^n = a^{m+n}, \quad (ab)^m = a^m b^m, \quad (a^m)^n = a^{mn}, \quad a^{m/n} = \sqrt[n]{a^m}.$$

If $a \neq 0$,

$$\frac{a^m}{a^n} = a^{m-n}, \quad a^0 = 1, \quad a^{-m} = \frac{1}{a^m}.$$

2. Zero

$$a \cdot 0 = 0 \cdot a = 0 \text{ for any finite number } a.$$

If $a \neq 0$,

$$\frac{0}{a} = 0, \quad 0^a = 0, \quad a^0 = 1.$$

Division by zero is not defined.

3. Fractions

$$\frac{a}{b} + \frac{c}{d} = \frac{ad + bc}{bd}, \quad \frac{a}{b} \cdot \frac{c}{d} = \frac{ac}{bd}, \quad \frac{a/b}{c/d} = \frac{a}{b} \cdot \frac{d}{c}, \quad \frac{-a}{b} = -\frac{a}{b} = \frac{a}{-b}.$$

$$\frac{(a/b) + (c/d)}{(e/f) + (g/h)} = \frac{(a/b) + (c/d)}{(e/f) + (g/h)} \cdot \frac{bdfh}{bdfh} = \frac{(ad + bc)fh}{(eh + fg)bd}.$$

4. Binomial Theorem, for n = positive integer

$$(a + b)^n = a^n + na^{n-1}b + \frac{n(n-1)}{1 \cdot 2} a^{n-2}b^2 + \frac{n(n-1)(n-2)}{1 \cdot 2 \cdot 3} a^{n-3}b^3 + \cdots + nab^{n-1} + b^n.$$

5. Proportionality Factor

If y is proportional to x, or y varies directly as x, then $y = kx$ for some constant k, called the *proportionality factor.* If $y = k/x$, we say that y is *inversely proportional* to x, or that y *varies inversely* as x.

6. Remainder Theorem and Factor Theorem

If the polynomial $f(x)$ is divided by $x - r$ until a remainder R independent of x is obtained, then $R = f(r)$. In particular, $x - r$ is a *factor* of $f(x)$ if and only if r is a *root* of the equation $f(x) = 0$.

7. Quadratic Formula

If $a \neq 0$, the roots of the equation $ax^2 + bx + c = 0$ are given by the formula

$$x = \frac{-b \pm \sqrt{b^2 - 4ac}}{2a}.$$

GEOMETRY

(A = area, B = area of base, C = circumference, S = lateral area or surface area, V = volume.)

1. Triangle

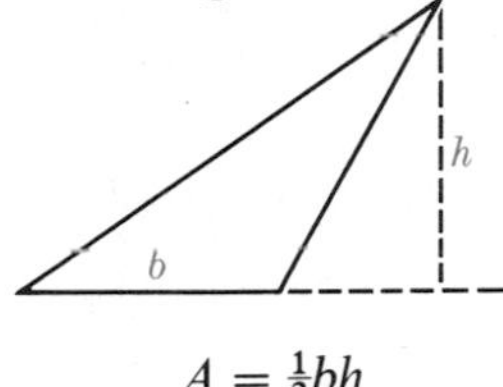

$$A = \tfrac{1}{2}bh.$$

2. Similar Triangles

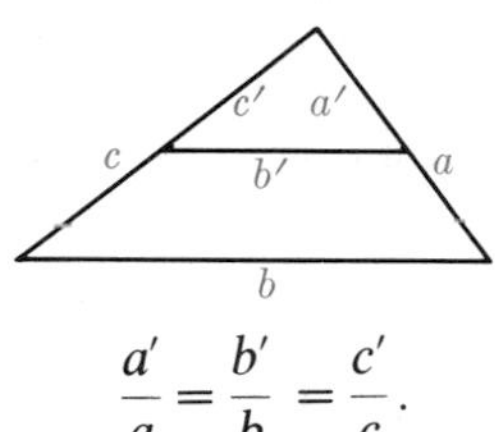

$$\frac{a'}{a} = \frac{b'}{b} = \frac{c'}{c}.$$

3. Theorem of Pythagoras

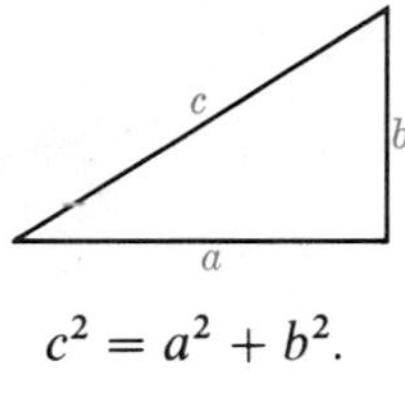

$$c^2 = a^2 + b^2.$$

4. Parallelogram

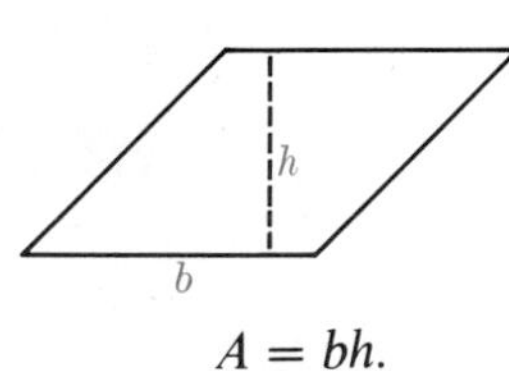

$$A = bh.$$

5. Trapezoid

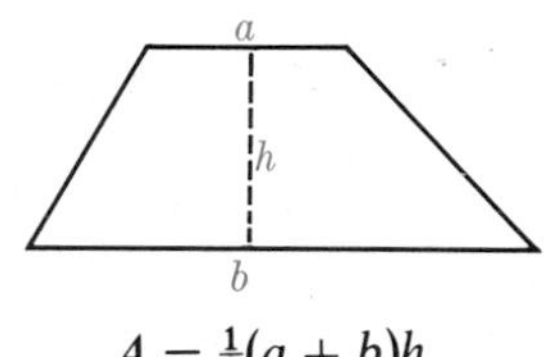

$$A = \tfrac{1}{2}(a + b)h.$$

6. Circle

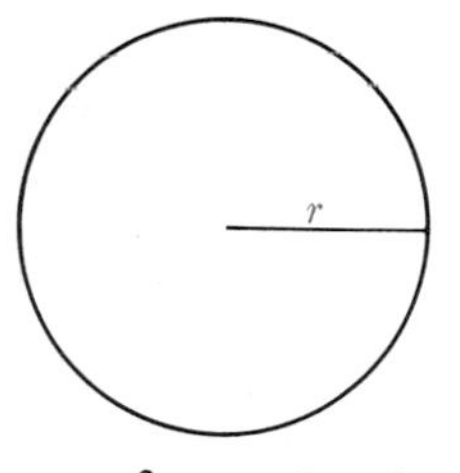

$$A = \pi r^2, \qquad C = 2\pi r.$$

7. Any Cylinder or Prism with Parallel Bases

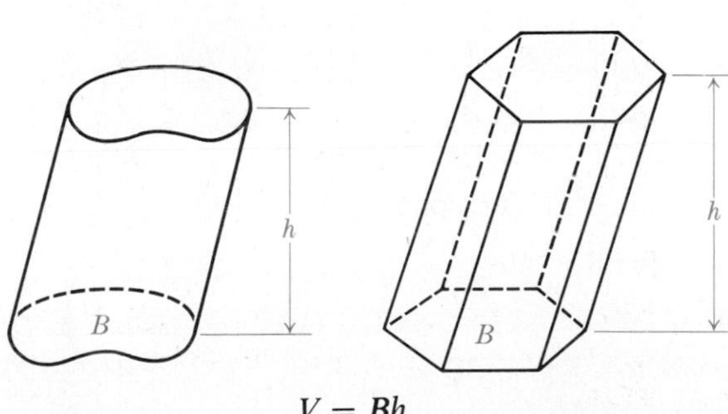

$$V = Bh.$$

8. Right Circular Cylinder

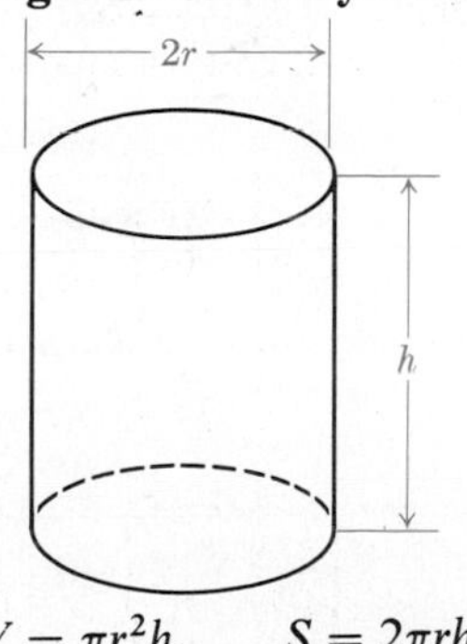

$$V = \pi r^2 h, \qquad S = 2\pi rh.$$

9. Any Cone or Pyramid

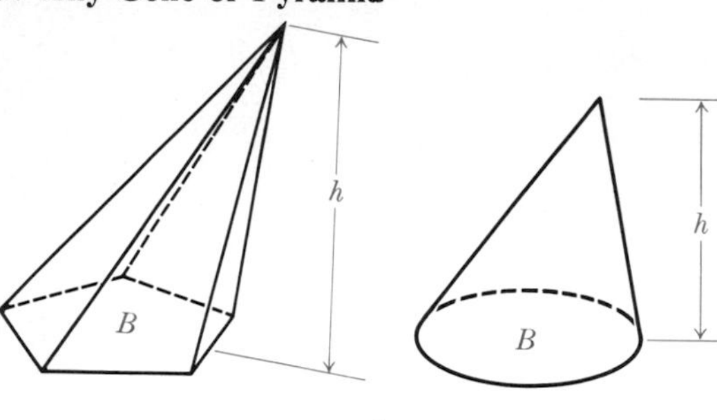

$V = \frac{1}{3}Bh.$

10. Right Circular Cone

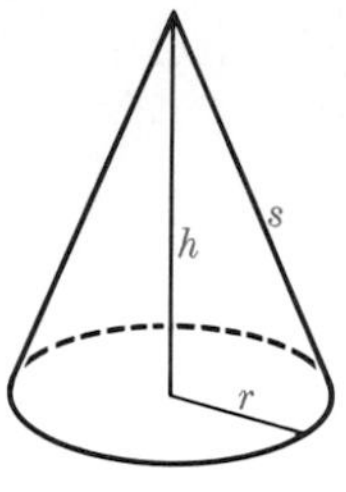

$V = \frac{1}{3}\pi r^2 h, \qquad S = \pi r s.$

11. Sphere

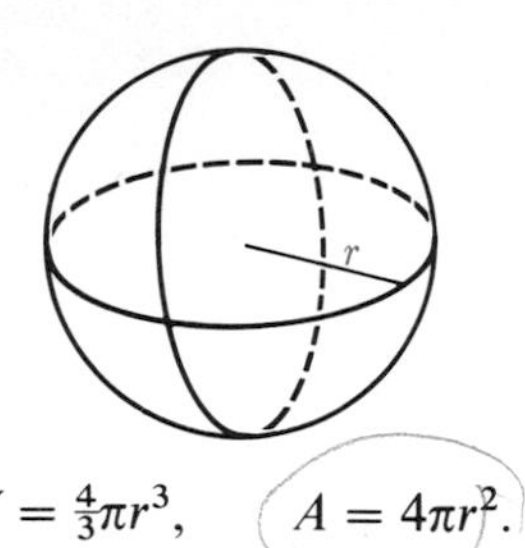

$V = \frac{4}{3}\pi r^3, \qquad A = 4\pi r^2.$

C

TRIGONOMETRY

1. Definitions and Fundamental Identities

$$\sin \theta = \frac{y}{r} = \frac{1}{\csc \theta}.$$

$$\cos \theta = \frac{x}{r} = \frac{1}{\sec \theta}.$$

$$\tan \theta = \frac{y}{x} = \frac{1}{\cot \theta}.$$

$$\sin(-\theta) = -\sin \theta, \qquad \cos(-\theta) = \cos \theta.$$

$$\sin^2 \theta + \cos^2 \theta = 1.$$

$$\sin 2\theta = 2 \sin \theta \cos \theta, \qquad \cos 2\theta = \cos^2 \theta - \sin^2 \theta.$$

$$\sin^2 \frac{\theta}{2} = \frac{1 - \cos \theta}{2}, \qquad \cos^2 \frac{\theta}{2} = \frac{1 + \cos \theta}{2}.$$

$$\sin(\alpha + \beta) = \sin \alpha \cos \beta + \cos \alpha \sin \beta.$$

$$\cos(\alpha + \beta) = \cos \alpha \cos \beta - \sin \alpha \sin \beta.$$

$$\tan(\alpha + \beta) = \frac{\tan \alpha + \tan \beta}{1 - \tan \alpha \tan \beta}.$$

2. Angles and Sides of a Triangle

Law of cosines: $a^2 = b^2 + c^2 - 2bc \cos A.$

Law of sines: $\dfrac{\sin A}{a} = \dfrac{\sin B}{b} = \dfrac{\sin C}{c}.$

Area $= \frac{1}{2}bc \sin A = \frac{1}{2}ac \sin B = \frac{1}{2}ab \sin C.$

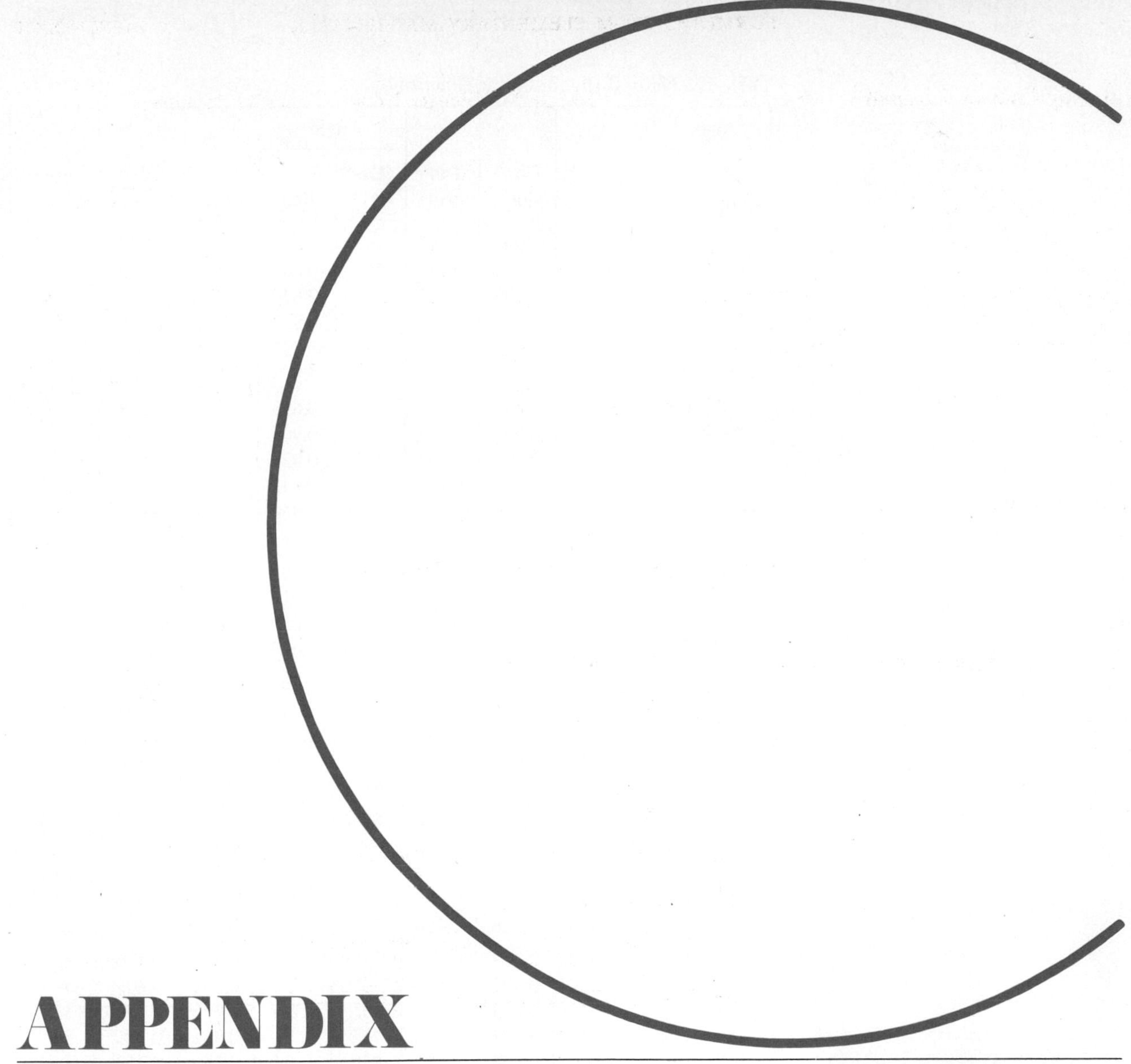

APPENDIX C

TABLES

Table 1. Natural trigonometric functions

Angle					Angle				
Degree	Radian	Sine	Cosine	Tangent	Degree	Radian	Sine	Cosine	Tangent
0°	0.000	0.000	1.000	0.000					
1°	0.017	0.017	1.000	0.017	46°	0.803	0.719	0.695	1.036
2°	0.035	0.035	0.999	0.035	47°	0.820	0.731	0.682	1.072
3°	0.052	0.052	0.999	0.052	48°	0.838	0.743	0.669	1.111
4°	0.070	0.070	0.998	0.070	49°	0.855	0.755	0.656	1.150
5°	0.087	0.087	0.996	0.087	50°	0.873	0.766	0.643	1.192
6°	0.105	0.105	0.995	0.105	51°	0.890	0.777	0.629	1.235
7°	0.122	0.122	0.993	0.123	52°	0.908	0.788	0.616	1.280
8°	0.140	0.139	0.990	0.141	53°	0.925	0.799	0.602	1.327
9°	0.157	0.156	0.988	0.158	54°	0.942	0.809	0.588	1.376
10°	0.175	0.174	0.985	0.176	55°	0.960	0.819	0.574	1.428
11°	0.192	0.191	0.982	0.194	56°	0.977	0.829	0.559	1.483
12°	0.209	0.208	0.978	0.213	57°	0.995	0.839	0.545	1.540
13°	0.227	0.225	0.974	0.231	58°	1.012	0.848	0.530	1.600
14°	0.244	0.242	0.970	0.249	59°	1.030	0.857	0.515	1.664
15°	0.262	0.259	0.966	0.268	60°	1.047	0.866	0.500	1.732
16°	0.279	0.276	0.961	0.287	61°	1.065	0.875	0.485	1.804
17°	0.297	0.292	0.956	0.306	62°	1.082	0.883	0.469	1.881
18°	0.314	0.309	0.951	0.325	63°	1.100	0.891	0.454	1.963
19°	0.332	0.326	0.946	0.344	64°	1.117	0.899	0.438	2.050
20°	0.349	0.342	0.940	0.364	65°	1.134	0.906	0.423	2.145
21°	0.367	0.358	0.934	0.384	66°	1.152	0.914	0.407	2.246
22°	0.384	0.375	0.927	0.404	67°	1.169	0.921	0.391	2.356
23°	0.401	0.391	0.921	0.424	68°	1.187	0.927	0.375	2.475
24°	0.419	0.407	0.914	0.445	69°	1.204	0.934	0.358	2.605
25°	0.436	0.423	0.906	0.466	70°	1.222	0.940	0.342	2.748
26°	0.454	0.438	0.899	0.488	71°	1.239	0.946	0.326	2.904
27°	0.471	0.454	0.891	0.510	72°	1.257	0.951	0.309	3.078
28°	0.489	0.469	0.883	0.532	73°	1.274	0.956	0.292	3.271
29°	0.506	0.485	0.875	0.554	74°	1.292	0.961	0.276	3.487
30°	0.524	0.500	0.866	0.577	75°	1.309	0.966	0.259	3.732
31°	0.541	0.515	0.857	0.601	76°	1.326	0.970	0.242	4.011
32°	0.559	0.530	0.848	0.625	77°	1.344	0.974	0.225	4.332
33°	0.576	0.545	0.839	0.649	78°	1.361	0.978	0.208	4.705
34°	0.593	0.559	0.829	0.675	79°	1.379	0.982	0.191	5.145
35°	0.611	0.574	0.819	0.700	80°	1.396	0.985	0.174	5.671
36°	0.628	0.588	0.809	0.727	81°	1.414	0.988	0.156	6.314
37°	0.646	0.602	0.799	0.754	82°	1.431	0.990	0.139	7.115
38°	0.663	0.616	0.788	0.781	83°	1.449	0.993	0.122	8.144
39°	0.681	0.629	0.777	0.810	84°	1.466	0.995	0.105	9.514
40°	0.698	0.643	0.766	0.839	85°	1.484	0.996	0.087	11.43
41°	0.716	0.656	0.755	0.869	86°	1.501	0.998	0.070	14.30
42°	0.733	0.669	0.743	0.900	87°	1.518	0.999	0.052	19.08
43°	0.750	0.682	0.731	0.933	88°	1.536	0.999	0.035	28.64
44°	0.768	0.695	0.719	0.966	89°	1.553	1.000	0.017	57.29
45°	0.785	0.707	0.707	1.000	90°	1.571	1.000	0.000	

Table 2. Exponential functions

x	e^x	e^{-x}	x	e^x	e^{-x}
0.00	1.0000	1.0000	2.5	12.182	0.0821
0.05	1.0513	0.9512	2.6	13.464	0.0743
0.10	1.1052	0.9048	2.7	14.880	0.0672
0.15	1.1618	0.8607	2.8	16.445	0.0608
0.20	1.2214	0.8187	2.9	18.174	0.0550
0.25	1.2840	0.7788	3.0	20.086	0.0498
0.30	1.3499	0.7408	3.1	22.198	0.0450
0.35	1.4191	0.7047	3.2	24.533	0.0408
0.40	1.4918	0.6703	3.3	27.113	0.0369
0.45	1.5683	0.6376	3.4	29.964	0.0334
0.50	1.6487	0.6065	3.5	33.115	0.0302
0.55	1.7333	0.5769	3.6	36.598	0.0273
0.60	1.8221	0.5488	3.7	40.447	0.0247
0.65	1.9155	0.5220	3.8	44.701	0.0224
0.70	2.0138	0.4966	3.9	49.402	0.0202
0.75	2.1170	0.4724	4.0	54.598	0.0183
0.80	2.2255	0.4493	4.1	60.340	0.0166
0.85	2.3396	0.4274	4.2	66.686	0.0150
0.90	2.4596	0.4066	4.3	73.700	0.0136
0.95	2.5857	0.3867	4.4	81.451	0.0123
1.0	2.7183	0.3679	4.5	90.017	0.0111
1.1	3.0042	0.3329	4.6	99.484	0.0101
1.2	3.3201	0.3012	4.7	109.95	0.0091
1.3	3.6693	0.2725	4.8	121.51	0.0082
1.4	4.0552	0.2466	4.9	134.29	0.0074
1.5	4.4817	0.2231	5	148.41	0.0067
1.6	4.9530	0.2019	6	403.43	0.0025
1.7	5.4739	0.1827	7	1096.6	0.0009
1.8	6.0496	0.1653	8	2981.0	0.0003
1.9	6.6859	0.1496	9	8103.1	0.0001
2.0	7.3891	0.1353	10	22026	0.00005
2.1	8.1662	0.1225			
2.2	9.0250	0.1108			
2.3	9.9742	0.1003			
2.4	11.023	0.0907			

Table 3. Natural logarithms of numbers

n	$\log_e n$	n	$\log_e n$	n	$\log_e n$
0.0	*	4.5	1.5041	9.0	2.1972
0.1	7.6974	4.6	1.5261	9.1	2.2083
0.2	8.3906	4.7	1.5476	9.2	2.2192
0.3	8.7960	4.8	1.5686	9.3	2.2300
0.4	9.0837	4.9	1.5892	9.4	2.2407
0.5	9.3069	5.0	1.6094	9.5	2.2513
0.6	9.4892	5.1	1.6292	9.6	2.2618
0.7	9.6433	5.2	1.6487	9.7	2.2721
0.8	9.7769	5.3	1.6677	9.8	2.2824
0.9	9.8946	5.4	1.6864	9.9	2.2925
1.0	0.0000	5.5	1.7047	10	2.3026
1.1	0.0953	5.6	1.7228	11	2.3979
1.2	0.1823	5.7	1.7405	12	2.4849
1.3	0.2624	5.8	1.7579	13	2.5649
1.4	0.3365	5.9	1.7750	14	2.6391
1.5	0.4055	6.0	1.7918	15	2.7081
1.6	0.4700	6.1	1.8083	16	2.7726
1.7	0.5306	6.2	1.8245	17	2.8332
1.8	0.5878	6.3	1.8405	18	2.8904
1.9	0.6419	6.4	1.8563	19	2.9444
2.0	0.6931	6.5	1.8718	20	2.9957
2.1	0.7419	6.6	1.8871	25	3.2189
2.2	0.7885	6.7	1.9021	30	3.4012
2.3	0.8329	6.8	1.9169	35	3.5553
2.4	0.8755	6.9	1.9315	40	3.6889
2.5	0.9163	7.0	1.9459	45	3.8067
2.6	0.9555	7.1	1.9601	50	3.9120
2.7	0.9933	7.2	1.9741	55	4.0073
2.8	1.0296	7.3	1.9879	60	4.0943
2.9	1.0647	7.4	2.0015	65	4.1744
3.0	1.0986	7.5	2.0149	70	4.2485
3.1	1.1314	7.6	2.0281	75	4.3175
3.2	1.1632	7.7	2.0412	80	4.3820
3.3	1.1939	7.8	2.0541	85	4.4427
3.4	1.2238	7.9	2.0669	90	4.4998
3.5	1.2528	8.0	2.0794	95	4.5539
3.6	1.2809	8.1	2.0919	100	4.6052
3.7	1.3083	8.2	2.1041		
3.8	1.3350	8.3	2.1163		
3.9	1.3610	8.4	2.1282		
4.0	1.3863	8.5	2.1401		
4.1	1.4110	8.6	2.1518		
4.2	1.4351	8.7	2.1633		
4.3	1.4586	8.8	2.1748		
4.4	1.4816	8.9	2.1861		

* Subtract 10 from $\log_e n$ entries for $n < 1.0$.

ANSWERS

CHAPTER 1

Article 1–2, pp. 4–5

1 to 13. If P is the point (x, y), then the other points are: $Q(x, -y)$, $R(-x, y)$, $S(-x, -y)$, $T(y, x)$. **14.** 45°
15. Missing vertices: $(-1, 4)$, $(-1, -2)$, $(5, 2)$. See figure. **16. a)** $(-3, 0)$ **b)** $(-3, 3)$ **17.** $b = 2$

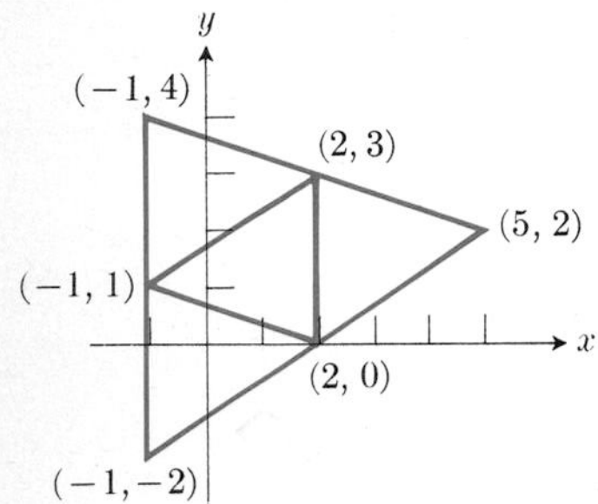

Article 1–3, p. 7

1. $(1, 1)$; 2; 1; $\sqrt{5}$ **2.** $(-1, 2)$; -2; -3; $\sqrt{13}$ **3.** $(-1, 2)$; 2; -4; $2\sqrt{5}$ **4.** $(-3, -2)$; -2; 4; $2\sqrt{5}$ **5.** $(-8, 1)$; -5; 0; 5
6. $(0, 4)$; 0; -6; 6 **7.** $x^2 + y^2 = 25$ **8.** $x^2 + y^2 - 10x = 0$ **9.** $x^2 + y^2 + 6x - 8y = 0$ **10.** $(x - h)^2 + (y - k)^2 = 25$
11. $B(3, -3)$ **12.** $(-2, -9)$ **13.** $A(u - h, v - k)$ **14.** $B(0, 11)$
15. $B(x, y) = B(x, x^2)$; $\Delta y = x^2 - 1 = (x - 1)(x + 1)$; $\Delta x = x - 1$; $\Delta y/\Delta x = x + 1$ if $x \neq 1$ (or $\Delta x \neq 0$)

Article 1–4, p. 10

1. 3; $-\frac{1}{3}$ **2.** $-\frac{1}{3}$; 3 **3.** -1; 1 **4.** 0; ∞ (vertical) **5.** 0; ∞ (vertical) **6.** ∞ (vertical); 0 **7.** 2; $-\frac{1}{2}$ **8.** $\frac{2}{3}$; $-\frac{3}{2}$
9. y/x; $-(x/y)$ **10.** 0; ∞ (vertical) **11.** ∞ (vertical); 0 **12.** $-(b/a)$; a/b **13.** Rectangle **14.** Rectangle **15.** No **16.** No
17. a) $-1/0.35 \approx -2.9$ **b)** $(9 - 68)/(4 - 0.4) \approx -16.4$ **c)** $(4 - 9)/(4.7 - 4) \approx -7.1$
18. Fiber glass is the best insulator (slope has greatest absolute value); gypsum wallboard is the poorest insulator (slope has least absolute value). **19.** $(1, 2)$ **20.** If $P(x, y)$ lies on L, then $(y - 0)/(x - 0) = -\frac{1}{2}$ or $y = -(x/2)$. **21.** Yes **22.** No
23. No **24.** $[(x_1 + x_2)/2, (y_1 + y_2)/2]$

Article 1–5, pp. 14–15

1. $2y = 3x$ **2.** $y = 1$ **3.** $x = 1$ **4.** $3x + 4y + 2 = 0$ **5.** $x = -2$ **6.** $x + y = 4$ **7.** $x/a + y/b = 1$ **8.** $y = 0$ **9.** $x = 0$
10. $x + y = 1$ **11.** Slope: 3; x-intercept: $(-\frac{5}{3}, 0)$; y-intercept: $(0, 5)$ **12.** $\frac{3}{2}$; $(-\frac{5}{3}, 0)$; $(0, \frac{5}{2})$ **13.** -1; $(2, 0)$; $(0, 2)$
14. 2; $(2, 0)$; $(0, -4)$ **15.** $\frac{1}{2}$; $(4, 0)$; $(0, -2)$ **16.** $-\frac{3}{4}$; $(4, 0)$; $(0, 3)$ **17.** $\frac{4}{3}$; $(3, 0)$; $(0, -4)$ **18.** $\frac{1}{2}$; $(-5, 0)$; $(0, \frac{5}{2})$
19. a) $x/20 + p/(10/3) = 1$ **b)** $\frac{10}{3}$ dollars/pound; 20 pounds/person **c)** 1.2 dollars/pound **d)** 12.2 pounds/person
20. $x + 2y = 5$ **21. a)** $x - 2y + 6 = 0$ **b)** $(\frac{2}{5}, \frac{16}{5})$ **c)** $6\sqrt{5}/5$ **22.** $y - 4 = \sqrt{3}(x - 1)$ **23.** $180° - \tan^{-1}(2) \approx 116° 34'$
24. a) $p = 0.1042d$ **b)** 5.21 atmospheres **25.** $y = x - 1, x \geq 1$ **26.** $70\ell - 0.16t = 2439.6$ (ℓ in feet, t in degrees F)

Article 1–6, pp. 27–28

1. $x \geq -4$, $y \geq 0$ **2.** $0 \leq x \leq 1, 0 \leq y \leq 1$ **3.** $-\infty < x < \infty, 0 \leq y < 1$ **4.** $x < -1$ or $x \geq 0$; $y \geq 0$, $y \neq 1$
5. $x \neq 0$, $-\infty < y < \infty$ **6.** $x \geq 0$, $y \geq 0$

7.

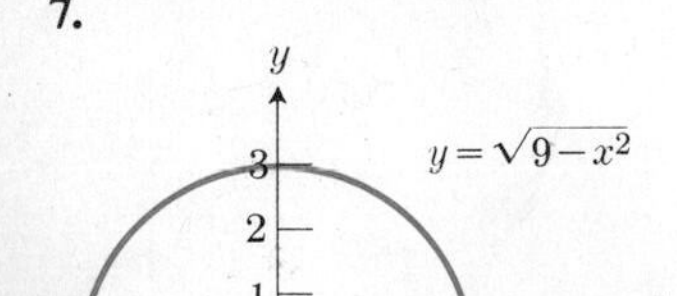

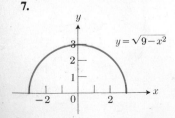

8.

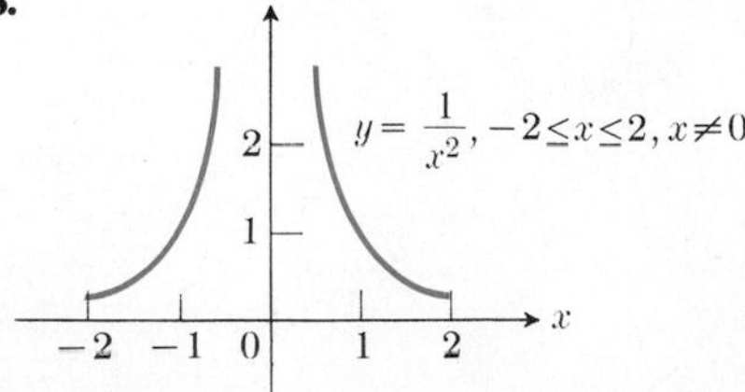

9.

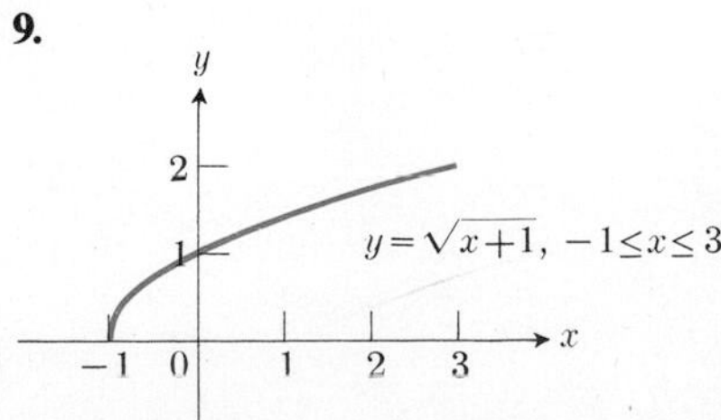

10. (a), because value of y at $x = 0$ must be negative. **11.** (d), because value of y at $x = 1$ must be 0.

12. $y = \pm\sqrt{1 - x^2}$

$y=\sqrt{1-x^2}$

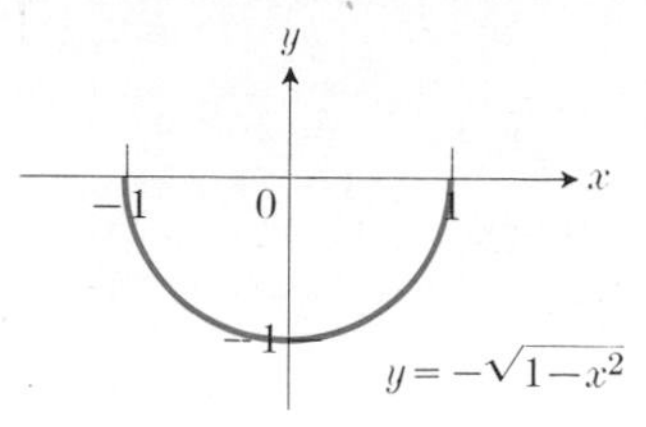

13.

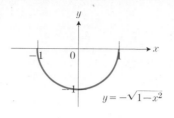

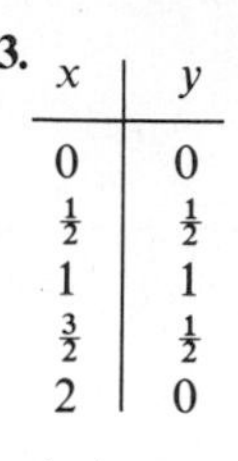

x	y
0	0
$\frac{1}{2}$	$\frac{1}{2}$
1	1
$\frac{3}{2}$	$\frac{1}{2}$
2	0

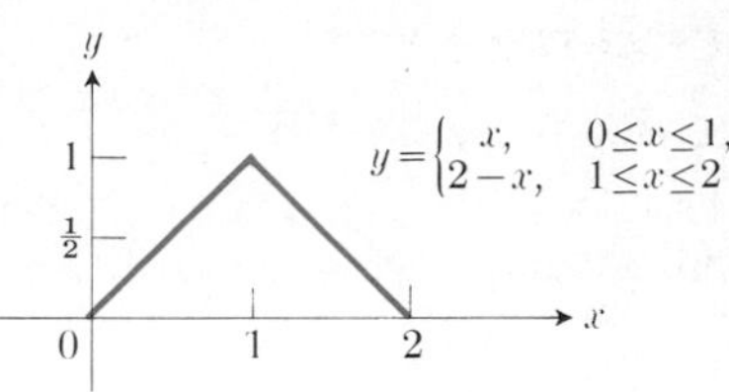

14. $-2 < x < 2$ **15.** $x \le -2$ or $x \ge 2$ **16.** $-4 \le x \le 6$ **17.** $0 \le x \le 4$ **18.** $|x| \le 8$ **19.** $|x - 1| < 4$ **20.** $|x + 3| < 2$
21. $|1 - x| = 1 - x$ when $x \le 1$; $|1 - x| = x - 1$ when $x \ge 1$.

22.

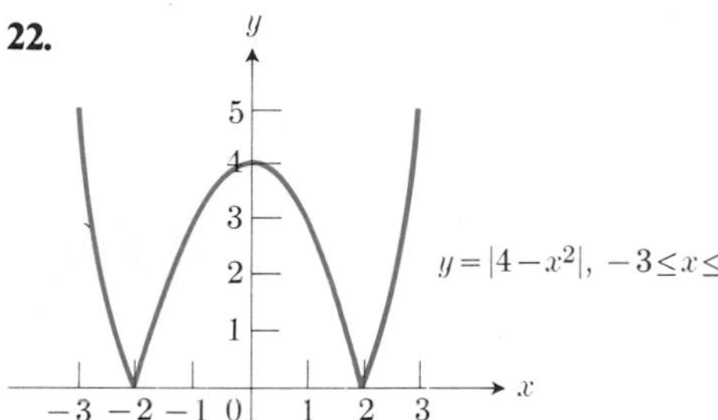

23.

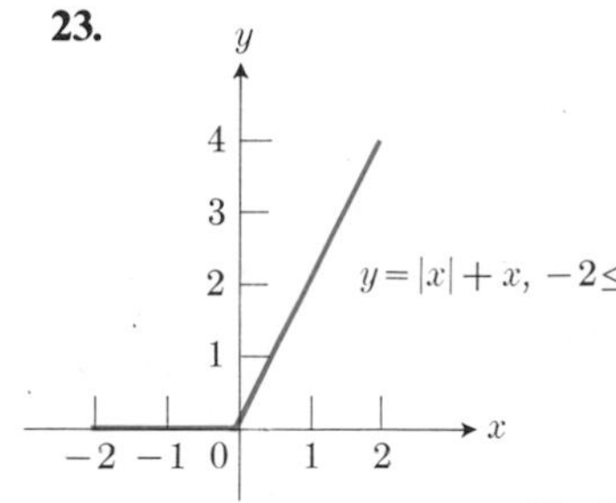

24. $\pi/4$ **25.** $-(\pi/3)$ **26.** $\pi/2$
27. $2\pi/3$ **28.** $-(\pi/6)$ **29.** $-(3\pi/4)$
30. 60° **31.** −30° **32.** 45°
33. 120° **34.** 270° **35.** −90°
36. Odd **37.** Even **38.** Even
39. Odd **40.** Even **41.** Odd
42. $\frac{1}{2}$; $1/(x + 2)$; $-x/(4x + 8)$ **43.** 4
44. $\sqrt{x - 7}$ **45.** $3x + 6$ **46.** $\sqrt{x}$
47. x^2 **48.** 20,000 years

49. 21 mowers **50.** $\sqrt{2}$; 4 **51.** No closer than ≈ 52.02 km **52.** $[x] = \begin{cases} x \text{ if } x \text{ is an integer } < 0 \\ \text{integer part of decimal form } \textit{less one} \\ \text{if } x < 0 \text{ is not an integer.} \end{cases}$

53.

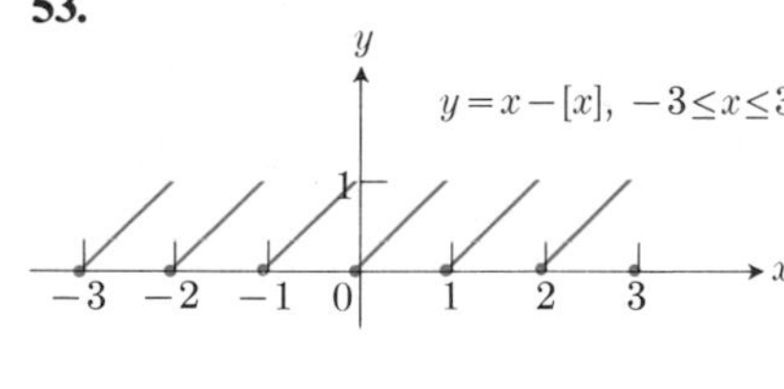

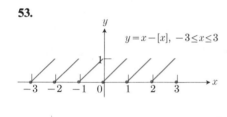

54.

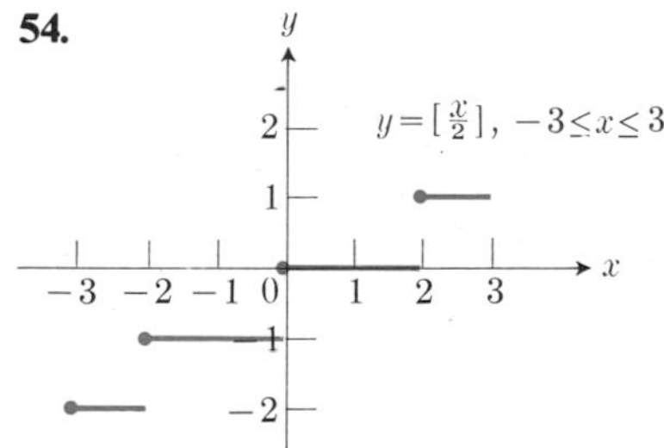

Article 1–7, p. 30

1. $2x - 2$ **2.** $4x - 1$ **3.** $-2x$ **4.** $2x - 4$ **5.** $2x - 4$ **6.** $2x + 4$ **7.** $1 - 2x$ **8.** $5 - 2x$ **9.** $2x + 3$ **10.** $-1 - 2x$
11. $6x^2 + 6x - 12$ **12.** $3x^2 - 3$ **13.** $3x^2 - 12$ **14.** $12x^2 + 6x$ **15.** $3x^2 - 6x$ **16.** ~ 18 flies.

Article 1–8, p. 37

1. $2x$, 6, $y = 6x - 9$ **2.** $3x^2$, 27, $y = 27x - 54$ **3.** 2, 2, $y = 2x + 3$ **4.** $2x - 1$, 5, $y = 5x - 8$ **5.** $-(1/x^2)$, $-\frac{1}{9}$, $x + 9y = 6$
6. $-(2/x^3)$, $-\frac{2}{27}$, $2x + 27y = 9$ **7.** $-2/(2x + 1)^2$, $-\frac{2}{49}$, $2x + 49y = 13$ **8.** $+1/(x + 1)^2$, $\frac{1}{16}$, $x - 16y + 9 = 0$
9. $4x - 1$, 11, $y = 11x - 13$ **10.** $3x^2 - 12$, 15, $y = 15x - 43$ **11.** $4x^3$, 108, $y = 108x - 243$
12. $2ax + b$, $6a + b$, $y = (6a + b)x - 9a + c$ **13.** $1 + (1/x^2)$, $1\frac{1}{9}$, $10x - 9y = 6$ **14.** $a - (b/x^2)$, $a - (b/9)$, $9y = (9a - b)x + 6b$
15. $1/\sqrt{2x}$, $1/\sqrt{6}$, $\sqrt{6}\,y = x + 3$ **16.** $1/(2\sqrt{x + 1})$, $\frac{1}{4}$, $x - 4y + 5 = 0$ **17.** $1/\sqrt{2x + 3}$, $\frac{1}{3}$, $y = (x/3) + 2$
18. $-1/(2x\sqrt{x})$, $-1/6\sqrt{3}$, $x + 6\sqrt{3}\,y = 9$ **19.** $-1/(2x + 3)^{3/2}$, $-\frac{1}{27}$, $x + 27y = 12$
20. $x/\sqrt{x^2 + 1}$, $3/\sqrt{10}$, $y = (3x/\sqrt{10}) + (1/\sqrt{10})$
21. **22.** 0, 0 **23.** 1700, 1250

$y=|x|$

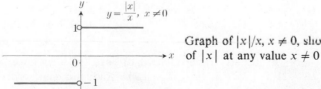

$y=\frac{|x|}{x}, x\ne 0$

Graph of $|x|/x$, $x \ne 0$, shows slope of $|x|$ at any value $x \ne 0$

Article 1–9, p. 41–42

2. $4t + 5$ **3.** $gt + v_0$ **4.** 4 **5.** $2t - 3$ **6.** $-2 - 2t$ **7.** $8t + 12$ **8.** $2t - 4$ **9.** $-4t$ **10.** $64 - 32t$

11.

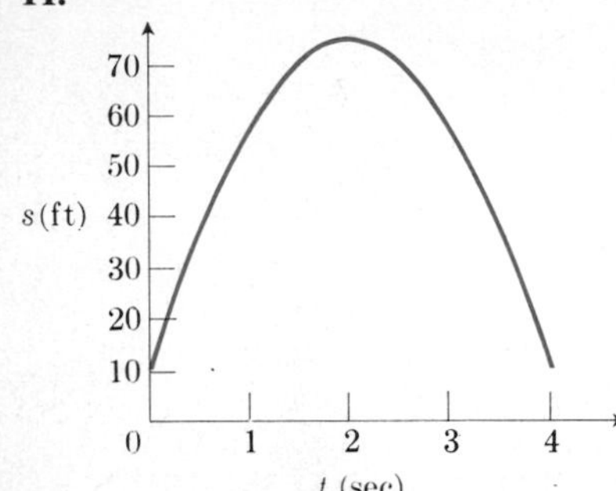

The data satisfy
$s = -16t^2 + 64t + 10$ ft
a) 32 ft/sec
b) -16 ft/sec
c) 0 ft/sec

12. a) 1.23 mole/min **b)** Rate $\approx$ 1.15 mole/min

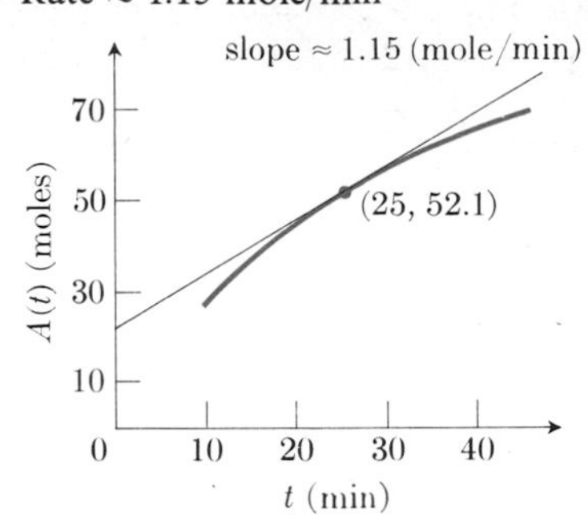

13. 190 ft/sec **14.** 2 sec **15.** After 8 seconds; velocity was 0 ft/sec **16.** At about $t = 11$ sec; falling at 95 ft/sec **17.** 3 sec **18. a)** 110 dollars/machine **b)** 80 dollars/machine **c)** (i) $f(101) - f(100) = 79.9$ dollars **19. a)** 10^4 **b)** 0 **c)** -10^4 (Units are bacteria/hr) **d)** $5(1 + \sqrt{41})$ hrs (≈ 37.02 hrs) **20.** 8000 gal/min; 10,000 gal/min **21. a)** $2\pi r + \pi\,\Delta r$ **b)** $2\pi r$ **22.** $4\pi r^2$ **23.** πh^2

Article 1–10, pp. 51–52

1. $\frac{5}{4}$ **2.** 2 **3.** 5 **4.** -1 **5.** -2 **6.** $\frac{1}{7}$ **7.** 0 **8.** $\frac{1}{2}$ **9. a)** $0 < x < 1$, $1 < x < 2$ (that is, $x \neq 0, 1, 2$) **b)** $x = 2$ **c)** $x = 0$

10.

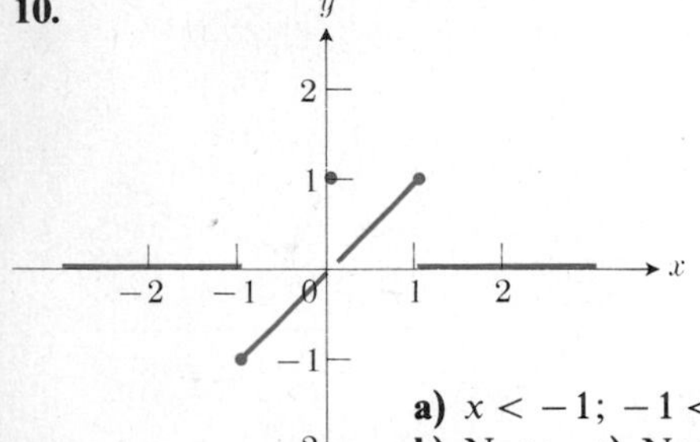

a) $x < -1$; $-1 < x < 1$; $x > 1$
b) None **c)** None

11. $\lim_{\Delta x \to 0^+} (|\Delta x|/\Delta x) = 1$; $\lim_{\Delta x \to 0^-} (|\Delta x|/\Delta x) = -1$ **12. a)** $|t - 3| < \frac{1}{80}$ will work **b)** $|t - 3| < \frac{1}{800}$ will work **c)** $|t - 3| \leq \min\{1, \epsilon/8\}$ **13.** $1/x^2$ increases most rapidly; $1/\sqrt{x}$ increases least rapidly. **14.** n **15.** $\frac{1}{4}$ **16.** 1 **17.** 0 **18.** 0 **19.** $\sqrt{4 + x}$; $\sin x$ **20.** $f(x) = x^2$ at $x = 1$, or $f(x) = (x + 1)^2$ at $x = 0$ **21.** $f(x) = |x|$ at $x = -1$, or $f(x) = |x - 1|$ at $x = 0$ **22.** 1

Article 1–11, p. 55

1. a) $\lim_{t \to c} t = c$. [*Proof.* Given $\epsilon > 0$, let $\delta = \epsilon$. Then $|t - c| < \epsilon$ when $|t - c| < \delta$.] **b)** $\lim_{t \to c} k = k$, k constant. [*Proof.* Given $\epsilon > 0$, let δ be anything greater than 0. Then $0 = |k - k| < \epsilon$ when $|t - c| < \delta$.] **2.** Apply Theorem 1, part (i), to F_1, F_2. Then apply again to $(F_1 + F_2)$, F_3. In general, use induction argument. **3.** Use an induction argument, applying Theorem 1, part (iii). **4.** $\lim_{t \to c} t^n = (\lim_{t \to c} t)^n = c^n$, for n a positive integer. **5.** $\lim_{t \to c} a_i t^{n-i} = a_i \lim_{t \to c} t^{n-i} = a_i c^{n-i}$, by Problems 1(b), 4, 1(a). Then $\lim_{t \to c} (a_0 t^n + a_1 t^{n-1} + \cdots + a_n) = a_0 c^n + a_1 c^{n-1} + \cdots + a_n$, by Problem 2. So $\lim_{t \to c} f(t) = f(c)$ for polynomial functions $f(x)$. **6.** $\lim_{t \to c} f(t) = f(c)$; $\lim_{t \to c} g(t) = g(c)$. If $g(c) \neq 0$, Theorem 1, part (iv) implies $\lim_{t \to c} (f(t)/g(t)) = (f(c)/g(c))$.

Miscellaneous Problems Chapter 1, pp. 56–58

1. b) $-\frac{3}{2}, \frac{2}{3}, -\frac{3}{2}, \frac{2}{3}, 0, \infty$ **c)** $ABCD$ is a parallelogram (its opposite sides are parallel). **d)** Yes, AEB **e)** Yes, CD **f)** $3x + 2y = 26$; $3x + 2y = 0$; $-2x + 3y = -13$; $y = 6$; $x = 2$

g)

L	AB	CD	AD	CE	BD
y-intercept	13	0	$-\frac{13}{3}$	6	None
x-intercept	$\frac{26}{3}$	0	$\frac{13}{2}$	None	2

2. a) $2x + 3y = -7$ **b)** $\sqrt{13}$
3. a) No **b)** No **c)** Outside **d)** $(-2, -\frac{9}{7})$
4. $3x + 4y = 0$; $x = 0$

5. $[(x_1 + x_2)/2, (y_1 + y_2)/2]$ **7. a)** $-(a/b)$ **b)** $(0, -(c/b))$ **c)** $(-(c/a), 0)$ **d)** $-bx + ay = 0$ **9.** Four; centers $(0, \sqrt{5} - 2)$, $(0, -\sqrt{5} - 2)$, $(-\sqrt{5} - 1, 1)$, $(\sqrt{5} - 1, 1)$. Radii (in same order): $(3\sqrt{2} - \sqrt{10})/2$, $(3\sqrt{2} + \sqrt{10})/2$, $(\sqrt{10} + \sqrt{2})/2$, $(\sqrt{10} - \sqrt{2})/2$. **10.** $|b' - b|/\sqrt{1 + m^2}$

11. Straight line through point of intersection of the two given lines. **12.** $(\frac{17}{18}, \frac{23}{6})$ **13.** $x + 5y = \pm 5\sqrt{2}$
14. $x = \sqrt{(y+2)/(y-1)}$; $y \le -2$, $y > 1$ **15.** $A = \pi r^2$, $C = 2\pi r$, $A = C^2/4\pi$
16. a) $x < -1, x > -1$; $y < 0, y > 0$ **b)** All x; $0 < y \le 1$ **c)** $x \ge 0, 0 < y \le 1$ **17.** $-5 < x < 3$
18. For $y \le 4$, $x = y - 2$; for $y \ge 4$, $x = (y+2)/3$. **19.** $y > 2$, $x = (y+2)/2$ **20.** $x = (y \pm \sqrt{y^2 - 4})/2$, $|y| \ge 2$
21. a) $f(-2) = -3$, $f(-1) = -4$, $f(x_1) = x_1^2 + 2x_1 - 3$, $f(x_1 + \Delta x) = x_1^2 + 2x_1\,\Delta x + (\Delta x)^2 + 2x_1 + 2\,\Delta x - 3$
22. c) $(\frac{1}{2}, -\frac{3}{4})$
23. Range: $-2 \le y \le 6$

y; $(2, 6)$; $y = |x+2| + x$, $-5 \le x \le 2$; $(-5, -2)$; $(-2, -2)$; x; -5 -4 -3 -2 -1 0 1 2

24. $m(a, b) = (a + b - |a - b|)/2$ **26.** Take $\phi_k(x) = g_k(x)/g_k(x_k)$ where $g_k(x)$ is the product $(x - x_1)(x - x_2) \cdots (x - x_n)$ with the factor $(x - x_k)$ deleted.
27. $f(d) = g(b)$ **29. a)** $1/(1-x)$ **b)** $x/(x+1)$ **c)** x **d)** $1 - x$
30. a) $2/(x+1)^2$ **b)** $3\sqrt{x}/2$ **c)** $\frac{1}{3}x^{-(2/3)}$ **31. a)** $2x - 3$ **b)** $-1/(3x^2) + 2$ **c)** $1/(2\sqrt{t-4})$ **32. a)** 6 **b)** (0, 2) **33. a)** $f(0) = 0, f(-1) = 1, f(1/x) = 2/(1-x)$ **b)** $-2/(x-1)(x + \Delta x - 1)$ **c)** $-2/(x-1)^2$ **34.** $P(\frac{45}{8}, \frac{2025}{4})$
35. $v = 180 - 32t$, $t = \frac{45}{8}$ **36.** $t = 1$ sec, $s = 16$ ft **37. a)** $-1/(v(v + \Delta v))$ **b)** $-\frac{1}{4}$
38. 28 in^3/sec **39. a)** 0 **b)** $-\frac{1}{3}$ **c)** $f(-(1/x)) = -x(x+1)/(5x^2 + 7x + 2)$, $f(0) = -\frac{1}{5}$, $1/f(x) = 2x - 5$ **40.** $((c+1)/(3c+2), -1/(5(3c+2)))$, $(\frac{2}{5}, -\frac{1}{25})$
41. a) 0 **b)** $\frac{1}{2}$ **42.** δ less than or equal to min $\{1, \epsilon^2/3\}$ **43.** $M = 1 + (1/\epsilon)$

48. a) $a^2 = |a|^2$, $b^2 = |b|^2$; $a^2, b^2 \ge 0$. For nonnegative numbers, $f(x) = x^2$ and $g(x) = x^{1/2}$ are increasing functions (look at derivatives). **b)** $2ab \le 2|a||b|$, $a^2 + b^2 = |a|^2 + |b|^2$. So $a^2 + 2ab + b^2 \le |a|^2 + 2|a||b| + |b|^2$, $(a+b)^2 \le (|a| + |b|)^2$ and $(a + b) \le |a| + |b|$, by part (a). **c)** $|a| = |a - b + b| \le |a - b| + |b|$, so $|a - b| \ge |a| - |b|$; $|b| = |b - a + a| \le |b - a| + |a|$, so $|a - b| \ge |b| - |a|$. Hence, $|a - b| \ge ||a| - |b||$
d) True for $n = 2$ by part (b). Assume for $n - 1$. $|a_1 + a_2 + \cdots + a_{n-1} + a_n| \le |a_1 + \cdots + a_{n-1}| + |a_n|$ by part (b); $\le |a_1| + \cdots + |a_{n-1}| + |a_n|$ by induction hypothesis. **e)** $|a_1| = |a_1 + \cdots + a_n - a_2 - \cdots - a_n| \le |a_1 + \cdots + a_n| + |a_2| + \cdots + |a_n|$ by (d). So $|a_1 + \cdots + a_n| \ge |a_1| - |a_2| - \cdots - |a_n|$.

49.

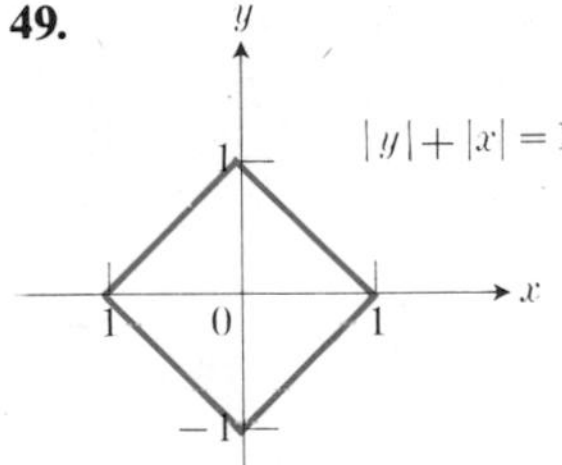

I: $y = -x + 1, 0 \le x \le 1$;
II: $y = x + 1, -1 \le x \le 0$;
III: $y = -x - 1, -1 \le x \le 0$;
IV: $y = x - 1, 0 \le x \le 1$.

50.

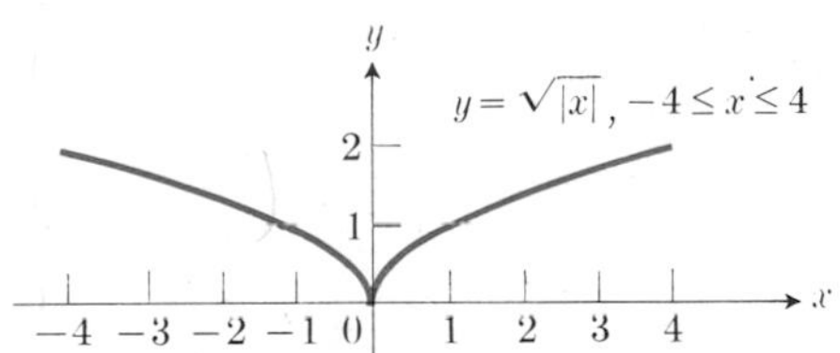

CHAPTER 2

Article 2–2, p. 67

1. $v = 2t - 4$, $a = 2$ **2.** $v = 6t^2 - 10t + 4$, $a = 12t - 10$ **3.** $v = gt + v_0$, $a = g$ **4.** $v = 4 - 2t$, $a = -2$
5. $v = 8t + 12$, $a = 8$ **6.** $y' = 4x^3 - 21x^2 + 4x$; $y'' = 12x^2 - 42x + 4$ **7.** $y' = 15(x^2 - x^4)$; $y'' = 30(x - 2x^3)$
8. $y' = 8(x - 1)$; $y'' = 8$ **9.** $y' = x^3 - x^2 + x - 1$; $y'' = 3x^2 - 2x + 1$ **10.** $y' = 8(x^3 - x)$; $y'' = 8(3x^2 - 1)$
11. $y' = 2x^3 - 3x - 1$; $y'' = 6x^2 - 3$ **12.** $y' = 21(x^6 - x^2 + 2x)$; $y'' = 42(3x^5 - x + 1)$
13. $y' = 5x^4 - 2x$; $y'' = 20x^3 - 2$ **14.** $y' = 2x + 1$; $y'' = 2$ **15.** $y' = 12x + 13$; $y'' = 12$ **16. a)** 400 ft **b)** 96 ft/sec
17. $y = 8x - 5$ **18.** $y = 4x \pm 2$. Least slope is $+1$ at (0, 0). **19.** $(-1, 27)$, $(2, 0)$ **20.** Slope of $TP = 2x =$ slope of tangent at P. **21.** $t = ((n-1)/n)x_1 = x_1 - (x_1/n)$. Construct line L through $(0, n)$ and $(x_1, 0)$ and L' through $(0, n-1)$ parallel to L. Then L' intersects the x-axis at T. Draw TP. **22.** x-intercept: $-\frac{4}{3}$; y-intercept: 16 **23.** (2, 6)
24. a) 2 **b)** $2\sqrt{5}/25 = 2/(5\sqrt{5})$ **c)** 0 **25.** $a = b = 1$, $c = 0$ **26.** $a = -3$, $b = 2$, $c = 1$ **27.** $c = \frac{1}{4}$

Article 2–3, p. 75

1. $x^2 - x + 1$ **2.** $(x-1)^2(x+2)^3(7x+2)$ **3.** $10x(x^2+1)^4$ **4.** $12(x^2 - 1)(x^3 - 3x)^3$ **5.** $-2(2x^2 + 3x - 1)(x+1)(x^2+1)^{-4}$
6. $-2(x^2 + x + 1)/(x^2 - 1)^2$ **7.** $-19/(3x - 2)^2$ **8.** $-4(x+1)(x-1)^{-3}$ **9.** $(1 - t^2)/(t^2 + 1)^2$ **10.** $6(2t + 3)^2$
11. $-2(2t - 1)(t^2 - t)^{-3}$ **12.** $(t^2 + 2t)(t + 1)^{-2}$ **13.** $(2 - 6t^2)/(3t^2 + 1)^2$ **14.** $2(t - t^{-3})$ **15.** $3(2t + 3)(t^2 + 3t)^2$
19. Increasing at 1%. **21.** $a_0 = f(1) = 2$, $a_1 = f'(1) = 1$, $a_2 = f''(1)/2 = 3$, $a_3 = f'''(1)/6 = 1$. Error is approximately $a_2(x-1)^2 = 3(x-1)^2$. $\lim_{x \to 1} (f(x) - L_1(x))/(x-1)^2 = a_2 = 3$.

Article 2–4, p. 79

1. $g(x) = \frac{1}{2}(x - 3); g'(x) = \frac{1}{2} = 1/f'(x)$. **2.** $\frac{1}{3}(x - 1)^{-(2/3)}$ **3.** Slope at $P(a, 1/a)$: $-(1/a^2)$; slope at $P'(1/a, a)$: $-a^2$. They satisfy Rule 10 when $a \neq 0$. **4.** $db/da = (\frac{2}{3})a^{-(1/3)}$; $a \neq 0$. **5.** x-intercept: -4; y-intercept: 1.
6. $C_0 = \frac{5}{2}$; $C_1 = \frac{3}{16}$; $C_2 = -\frac{1}{256}$. Error estimate: $-(x - 4)^2/256$. At $x = 4.41$, estimate is: -0.00065664. Actual error is: -0.000684524. **7. b)** $y = x^{1/3}$ fails to have a derivative at $x = 0$. Slope of $y = x^3$ at $x = 0$ is 0. The y-axis is tangent to $y = x^{1/3}$ at $x = 0$. The x-axis is tangent to $y = x^3$ at $x = 0$.

Article 2–5, pp. 83–84

1. $-(x/y)$ **2.** $1/(y(x + 1)^2)$ **3.** $-(2x + y)/x$ **4.** $-(2xy + y^2)/(x^2 + 2xy)$ **5.** $3x^2/2y$ **6.** $-(y/x)^{1/3}$ **7.** $-(y/x)^{1/2}$
8. $(y - 3x^2)/(3y^2 - x)$ **9.** $(y/x) - (x + y)^2$ **10.** $(x^2 + 1)^{-(3/2)}$ **11.** $(2x^2 + 1)(x^2 + 1)^{-(1/2)}$ **12.** $(x^4 - 1)/x^3y$
13. $(1 - 2y)/(2x + 2y - 1)$ **14.** $\frac{1}{2}x^{-(1/2)} + \frac{1}{3}x^{-(2/3)} + \frac{1}{4}x^{-(3/4)}$ **15.** $2x/(y(x^2 + 1)^2)$ **16.** $(2x^3 - 3x^2 - 3y^2)/(6xy - 2y^3)$
17. $5(3x + 7)^4/(2y^2)$ **18.** $(10x^2 + 30x - 8)(x + 5)^3(x^2 - 2)^2$ **19.** $-(y^2/x^2)$ **20.** $(6x + 15)(x^2 + 5x)^2$ **21.** $(2x - 1)/(2y)$
22. $x(y^2 - 1)/y(1 - x^2)$ **23.** $-(x^2 + 9)/[3x^2(x^2 + 3)^{2/3}]$ **25. a)** $-(x/y)$ **b)** $-(1/y^3)$ **26. a)** $-(x^2/y^2)$ **b)** $-(2x/y^5)$
27. a) $-x^{-(1/3)}y^{1/3}$ **b)** $\frac{1}{3}x^{-(4/3)}y^{-(1/3)}$ **28. a)** $-y(x + 2y)^{-1}$ **b)** $2(x + 2y)^{-3}$ **30. a)** $7x - 4y = 2$ **b)** $4x + 7y = 29$
31. a) $3x - 4y = 25$, $4x + 3y = 0$ **32. a)** $y = 3x + 6$ **b)** $x + 3y = 8$ **33. a)** $x = 3y$ **b)** $3x + y = 10$
34. a) $3x - 4y = 10$ **b)** $4x + 3y = 30$ **35.** x-intercepts: $x = \pm\sqrt{7}$. Slope of tangents: -2
36. a) $x = \pm\sqrt{\frac{7}{3}}$, $y = -2x$ **b)** $y = \pm\sqrt{\frac{7}{3}}$, $x = -2y$. At these points, $dx/dy = 0$. **37.** $y = (-x \pm (-3x^2 + 28)^{1/2})/2$; $-\frac{4}{5}$

Article 2–6, p. 85

1. a) $(2x + 2)\,\Delta x + (\Delta x)^2$ **b)** $(2x + 2)\,\Delta x$ **c)** $(\Delta x)^2$ **2. a)** $(4x + 4)\,\Delta x + 2(\Delta x)^2$ **b)** $(4x + 4)\,\Delta x$ **c)** $2(\Delta x)^2$
3. a) $(3x^2 - 1)\,\Delta x + 3x(\Delta x)^2 + (\Delta x)^3$ **b)** $(3x^2 - 1)\,\Delta x$ **c)** $3x(\Delta x)^2 + (\Delta x)^3$
4. a) $4x^3\,\Delta x + 6x^2(\Delta x)^2 + 4x(\Delta x)^3 + (\Delta x)^4$ **b)** $4x^3\,\Delta x$ **c)** $6x^2(\Delta x)^2 + 4x(\Delta x)^3 + (\Delta x)^4$
5. a) $-\Delta x/[x(x + \Delta x)]$ **b)** $-(\Delta x/x^2)$ **c)** $(\Delta x)^2/[x^2(x + \Delta x)]$ **6.** 2.13 **7.** 1.96 **8.** 0.48 **9.** 5.16 **10.** 0.58

Article 2–7, p. 88

1. 0.618 **2.** 0.682 **3.** 1.165 **4.** 1.189 **5.** -1.189 **6.** 3 **7.** $x_1 = x_2 = x_3$, etc. **8.** $m_1 = (q - 1)/q$, $m_2 = 1/q$
10. Yes, they may get worse.

Article 2–8, p. 93

1. $9y = (x - 1)^2$ **2.** $y^2 = x^3$ **3.** $y = (x/(1 + x))^2$ **4.** $y = x^2/(1 - x)$ **5.** -3 **6.** $8x + 10$ **7.** $1/2(x + 1)^2$
8. $4x/3(x^2 + 1)^{1/3}$ **9.** $18x + (1/3x^2)$ **10.** $12((3x + 2)^4 - 1)/(3x + 2)^3$

Article 2–9, pp. 100–101

1.

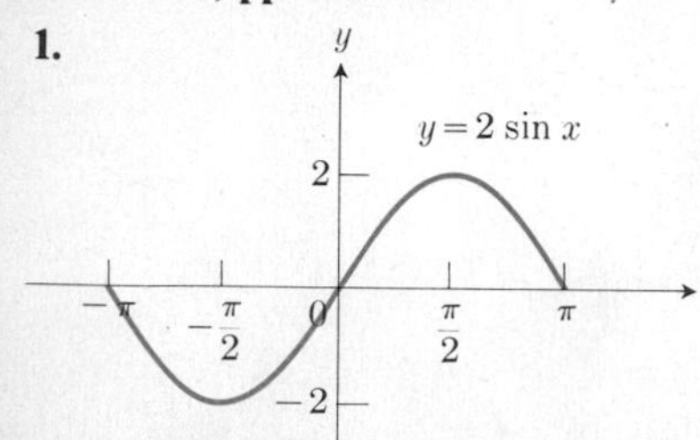

2.

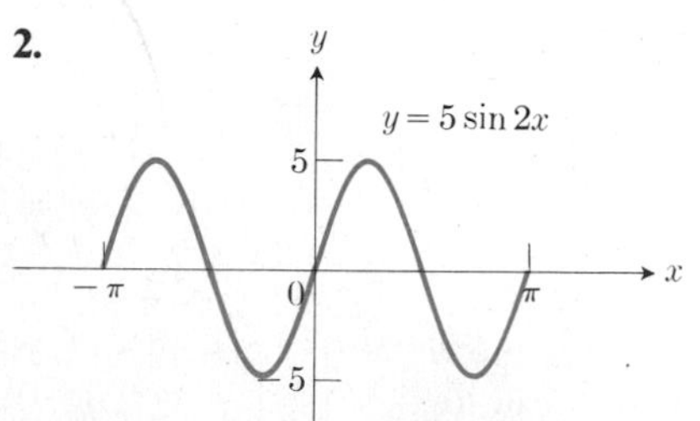

3.

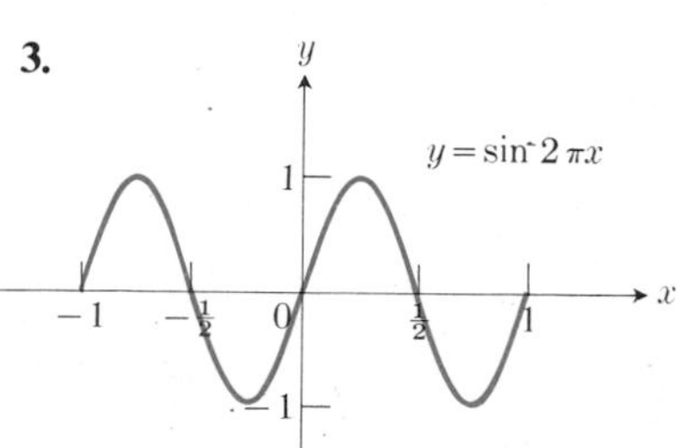

4.

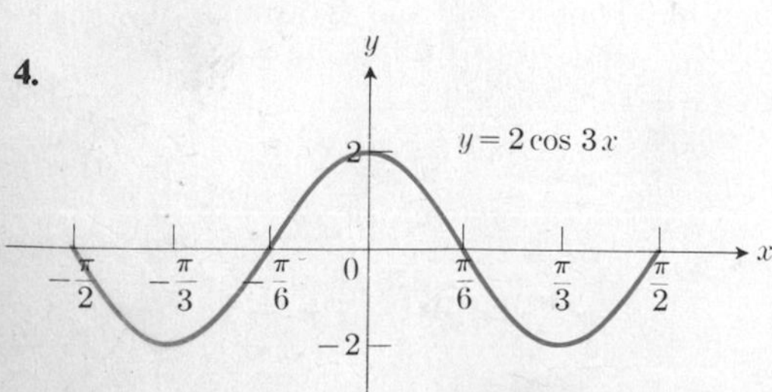

5.

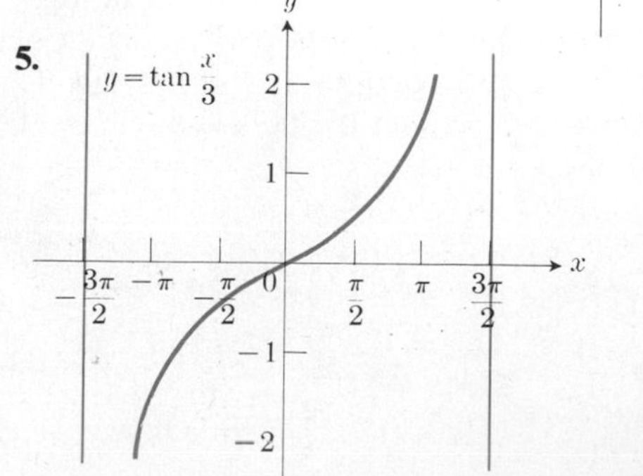

6.

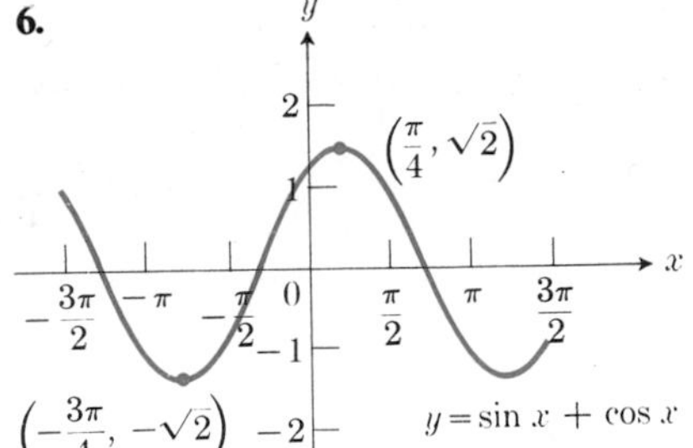

7.

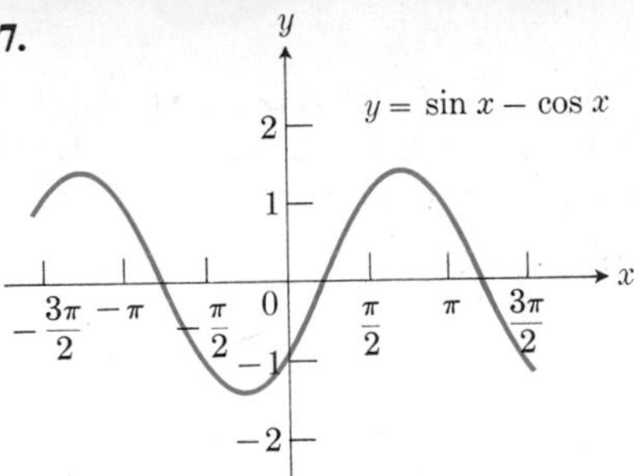

8.

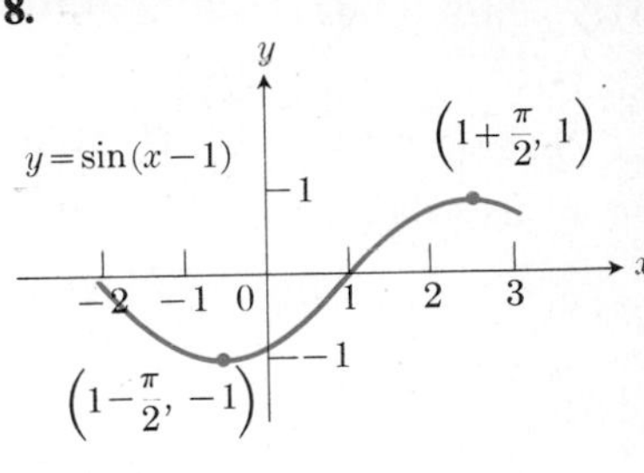

9.

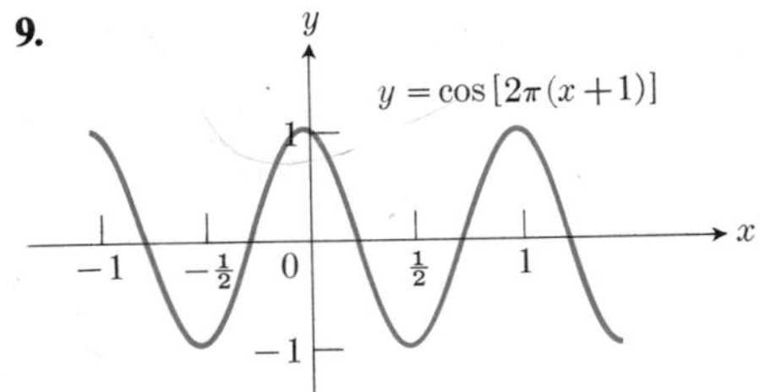

10. 37, 365, 101, 25 **11. a)** 62°, 193rd day **b)** $-12°$, 10th day **c)** 25°; average of $y = \sin x$ is zero, and shift is upward 25°. **14.** $\cos^2 A + \sin^2 A = \cos 0 = 1$ **15.** $\sin 0 = 0$ **16.** $\tan(A - B) = (\tan A - \tan B)/(1 + \tan A \tan B)$ **17.** $\tan(A + B) = (\tan A + \tan B)/(1 - \tan A \tan B)$ **19.** Cosine and secant are even. Sine, tangent, cotangent, cosecant are odd. **20.** $\cos 2A = \cos^2 A - \sin^2 A$, $\sin 2A = 2 \sin A \cos A$ **26.** $4n\pi \le \theta \le (4n + 2)\pi$, n integer **27.** $(4n - 1)\pi \le \theta \le (4n + 1)\pi$, n integer

Article 2–10, p. 107

1. 1 **2.** 1 **3.** 2 **4.** $\frac{1}{3}$ **5.** 1 **6.** $\frac{1}{3}$ **7.** $\frac{5}{3}$ **8.** $\frac{1}{2}$ **9.** 0 **10.** 0 **11.** $\frac{1}{2}$ **12.** $\frac{2}{3}$ **13.** $\frac{3}{5}$ **14.** 1 **15.** 2π **16.** -2 **17.** $\frac{1}{2}$ **18.** 1 **19.** 2 **20.** $\cos a$ **21.** $-\sin a$ **22.** $\pi/4$ **23.** $3\cos(3x + 4)$ **24.** $x \cos x + \sin x$ **25.** $(x \cos x - \sin x)/x^2$ **26.** $-5 \sin 5x$ **27.** $3x^2 \cos 3x + 2x \sin 3x$ **28.** $-\sin 2x/(2 + \cos 2x)^{1/2}$ **29.** 0 **30.** $6 \sin 3x/\cos^2 3x$ **31.** $6 \cos 2x + 8 \sin 2x$ **32.** $-24 \sin 2x \cos 2x$ or $-12 \sin 4x$ **33.** $2(\cos^2 x - \sin^2 x)$ or $2 \cos 2x$ **34.** $-\cos x/\sin^2 x$ **35.** $-3 \sin 6x$ **36.** $-1/\sin^2 x$ **37.** $4x \sin(x^2)\cos(x^2) = 2x \sin(2x^2)$ **38.** $(-x/\sqrt{x^2 + 1})[\sin(\sin\sqrt{x^2 + 1})][\cos\sqrt{x^2 + 1}]$ **39.** $(\sin 2y + 2y \sin 2x)/(\cos 2x - 2x \cos 2y)$ **40.** $-(\sin 8x)/y$ **41.** $y = mx$

Article 2–11, p. 117

1. b) Take δ less than or equal to the smaller of the two numbers 1 and $\epsilon/91$. Then $|x^2 + 5x + 25| < 91$ and $|x^3 - 5^3| < \epsilon$ when $|x - 5| < \delta$. **2. a)** $x = -1$ **b)** $x = 1$ or 3 **3.** Continuous **4.** Take $\delta \le \epsilon$ **5.** max = 1, min = 0 **6.** Neither a maximum nor a minimum since $f(x_2) > f(x_1)$ if $0 < x_1 < x_2 < 1$. Hence we can always find x_2 such that $f(x_2) > f(x_1)$, so $f(x_1)$ is *not* the maximum. This is true for any x_1 in the given domain. The same argument shows that no x_2 in the domain can give a minimum. **7.** Take $a = 0$, $b = 1$, and $N = 0$ in Theorem 4. **8.** Continuous but not differentiable. **10.** 7.

Article 2–13, p. 121

1. $(3x^2 - 6x + 5)\,dx$ **2.** $(9x/2y)(3x^2 + 1)^{1/2}\,dx$ **3.** $-[(2xy + y^2)/(2xy + x^2)]\,dx$ **4.** $2(1 - x^2)(1 + x^2)^{-2}\,dx$ **5.** $[(1 - 2x^2)/\sqrt{1 - x^2}]\,dx$ **6.** $(6 - 2x - x^2)(x^2 - 2x + 4)^{-2}\,dx$ **7.** $3(1 - x)^2(2x - 1)(2 - 3x)^{-2}\,dx$ **8.** $(2 - 2x + x^2)(1 - x)^{-2}\,dx$ **9.** 12.04 **10.** 9.2 **11.** 2.03 **12.** 0.5013 **13.** 79.69 **14. c)** $5x - 3y = 8$ **15. c)** $15x - y = 20$ **16. c)** $11y = x + 16$ **17. c)** $9x + y = 6$ **18. c)** $4x + 2y = 9$ **19.** $-4t^3(t^2 - 1)^{-3}$ **20.** $2(t + 1)^3(t - 1)^{-3}$ **22.** If a changes by $m\%$ and b changes by $n\%$, then $A = ab$ changes by approximately $(m + n)\%$ (assuming m, n are small).

Miscellaneous Problems Chapter 2, pp. 123–124

1. $-4(x^2 - 4)^{-(3/2)}$ **2.** $(5 - 2x - y)/(x + 2y)$ **3.** $-y/(x + 2y)$ **4.** $(3x^2 + 4y)/(9y^2 - 4x)$ **5.** $-y(2x + y)/(x(2y + x))$ **6.** $-2(x + 1)(x^2 + 2x + 2)/(x^3(x + 2)^3)$ **7.** $2 \sin(1 - 2x)$ **8.** $-1/\sin^2 x$ **9.** $(x + 1)^{-2}$ **10.** $(2x + 1)^{-(1/2)}$ **11.** $(3x^3 - 2a^2x)/\sqrt{x^2 - a^2}$ **12.** $-4(2x - 1)^{-2}$ **13.** $2x(1 - x^2)^{-2}$ **14.** $3(x^2 + x + 1)^2(2x + 1)$ **15.** $10 \sin(5x)/\cos^3(5x)$ **16.** $(\sin^2 x \cos x - \cos^2 x \sin x)/(\sin^3 x + \cos^3 x)^{2/3}$ **17.** $[(4x + 5)/2]\sqrt{2x^2 + 5x}$ **18.** $-(9/2)(4x + 5)(2x^2 + 5x)^{-(5/2)}$ **19.** $-(y/x)[(2y\sqrt{xy} + 1)/(4y\sqrt{xy} + 1)]$ **20.** $(2x - y)/(x + 2y)$ **21.** $-(y/x)^{1/3}$ **22.** $-\sqrt{y/x}$ **23.** $-(y/x)$ **24.** $-(y/x)$ **25.** $-\frac{1}{2}[(x + 2y + y^2)/(x + 2y + xy)]$ **26.** $(x^2 - 2x - 1)/(2(1 - x)^{1/2}(1 + x^2)^{3/2})$ **27.** $1/(2y(x + 1)^2)$ or $(x + 1)^{-2}/(2y)$ **28.** $(12x - 2xy - y^2)/(x^2 + 2xy - 12y)$ **29.** $-(y + 2)/(x + 3)$ **30.** 1 **31.** $(4x + 8)/\sqrt{4x^2 + 16x + 15}$ **32.** $2t(1 + t^2)^2/(1 - t^2)$ **33.** $2x[1 + ((1 - x^2)/(1 + x^2)^3)]$ **34.** $m = 1$, $y = x$ **35.** $2x + y = 6$ **36.** $c = 4$ **37.** $m = 2$, $y - 2x = -5$ **38.** $(2, 0)$ and $(-1, 27)$ **39. a)** $10(x^2 + 2x)^4(x + 1)$ **b)** $(3t - 1)/\sqrt{3t^2 - 2t}$ **c)** $r[(r^2 + 5)^{-(1/2)} + (r^2 - 5)^{-(1/2)}]$ **d)** $4x/(x^2 + 1)^2$ **40.** $x + 27y = 28$

41. $x + y = 3$ **42.** $(2x + 3)^{-(1/2)}$ **43.** $-6(2 - 3x), f(x) = (2 - 3x)^2$ **44.** $-\frac{8}{5}$
45. $6\pi(\Delta r)^2$; a shell around the can with thickness Δr. **46.** $\pi x(20 - x)$ **47.** $x_1 = 40$, $p = 4$ (= 20¢) **49.** $(x - 1)(2x - 1)$
50. $(2x + 1)/9$ **51.** 56 ft/sec **52.** $-\frac{12}{5}$ **53. a)** $h + 2k = 5$ **b)** $h = -4$, $k = \frac{9}{2}$, $r = 5\sqrt{5}/2$ **54.** $2\sqrt{x^2 + 1}$
55. $2/[3(2y + 1)(2x + 1)\sqrt{x^2 + x}]$ **56.** $2x\sqrt{3x^4 - 1}$ **57.** $(3/(x + 1)^2) \sin [((2x - 1)/(x + 1))^2]$
58. $dy/du = (dy/dx)(dx/du) = 12u \cos (2u^2 + 2\pi)$. At $u = 0$, $dy/du = 0$. **60.** $3(x - 2)/(2x - 3)^{3/2})$ **61.** $-\frac{3}{32}$ **62.** $y' = 2$, $y'' = -2$ **64. a)** $3(2x - 1)^{-(5/2)}$ **b)** $-162(3x + 2)^{-4}$ **c)** $6a$ **66.** $\Delta y = 0.92$, principal part = 0.9
67. a) Length of each side = $2r \sin (\pi/n)$ **b)** $2\pi r$; yes. **68.** $dy/dx = -2x$; $d^2y/dx^2 = -2$ **69.** 14 ± 0.044 ft
70. a) $(x(x + 2)/(x + 1)^2)\, dx$ **b)** $(x/y)\, dx$ **c)** $(-y/(x + 2y))\, dx$
72. $\delta = \epsilon/4$; the function is uniformly continuous for $-2 \le x \le 2$. **75.** $m = \frac{1}{2}$, $c = \sqrt{2}$

CHAPTER 3

Article 3–1, p. 127

1. Falling $x < \frac{1}{2}$, rising $x > \frac{1}{2}$. Low point at $(\frac{1}{2}, \frac{3}{4})$. **2.** Rising $x < -1$, falling $-1 < x < 2$, rising $x > 2$. High point at $(-1, \frac{3}{2})$, low at $(2, -3)$. **3.** Rising $x < 0$, falling $0 < x < 1$, rising $x > 1$. High at $(0, 3)$, low at $(1, 2)$. **4.** Rising $x < -3$, falling $-3 < x < 3$, rising $x > 3$. High at $(-3, 90)$, low at $(3, -18)$. **5.** Falling $x < -2$, rising $-2 < x < 0$, falling $0 < x < 2$, rising $x > 2$. Low points $(\pm 2, 0)$, high $(0, 16)$. **6.** Defined on $x \neq 0$. Falling $x < 0$. Discontinuity at $x = 0$. Falling $x > 0$. **7.** Rising $-(\pi/2) + 2\pi k < x < (\pi/2) + 2\pi k$. Falling $(\pi/2) + 2\pi k < x < (3\pi/2) + 2\pi k$. High points $((\pi/2) + 2\pi k, 1)$. Low points $((3\pi/2) + 2\pi k, -1)$. (k can be any integer.) **8.** Discontinuous at $x = (\pi/2) + \pi k$. Rising $-(\pi/2) + \pi k < x < (\pi/2) + \pi k$. ($k$ can be any integer.) **9.** Rising all x.

Article 3–2, pp. 131–132

1. $(dA/dt) = 2\pi r(dr/dt)$ **2.** $(dV/dt) = 4\pi r^2(dr/dt)$ **3.** $(8/5\pi)$ ft/min **5.** $(ax + by)/\sqrt{x^2 + y^2}$ ft/sec **6.** $(25/9\pi)$ ft/min **7.** $10/\sqrt{21} \approx 2.2$ ft/sec **8.** Increasing 33.7 ft/sec **9.** $(125/144\pi)$ ft/min **10.** $(dy/dt) = -x$. Clockwise. **11.** 8 ft/sec toward the lamp post. Decreasing 3 ft/sec **12.** Increasing 8.75 psi/sec **13.** 1500 ft/sec **14.** 20 ft/sec **15.** Thickness decreasing at the rate of $(5/72\pi)$ in/min. Area decreasing at the rate of $(10/3)$ in^2/min. **16.** $260/\sqrt{37}$ mi/hr.

Article 3–4, pp. 137–138

1. a) $x > 2$ **b)** $x < 2$ **c)** Always **d)** Never $m(2, -1)$ **2. a)** Always **b)** Never **c)** $x < -1$ **d)** $x > -1$ **3. a)** $-1 < x < 1$ **b)** $x < -1, x > 1$ **c)** $x < 0$ **d)** $x > 0$ $M(1, 6)$; $m(-1, 2)$; $I(0, 4)$ **4. a)** $x < -2, x > 3$ **b)** $-2 < x < 3$ **c)** $x > \frac{1}{2}$ **d)** $x < \frac{1}{2}$ $M(-2, \frac{22}{3})$; $m(3, -\frac{27}{2})$; $I(\frac{1}{2}, -\frac{37}{12})$ **5. a)** $x < -2, x > 2$ **b)** $-2 < x < 2, x \neq 0$ **c)** $x > 0$ **d)** $x < 0$, $M(-2, -4)$; $m(2, 4)$ **6. a)** $-\pi + 2\pi k < x < 2\pi k$ **b)** $2\pi k < x < \pi + 2\pi k$ **c)** $(\pi/2) + 2\pi k < x < (3\pi/2) + 2\pi k$ **d)** $-(\pi/2) + 2\pi k < x < (\pi/2) + 2\pi k$; $M(2\pi k, 1)$; $m(\pi + 2\pi k, -1)$; $I((\pi/2) + \pi k, 0)$; k any integer **9.** $M(-1, 7)$ **10.** $m(1, 1)$
11. $M(-2, 28)$; $m(2, -4)$; $I(0, 12)$ **12.** $M(0, 2)$; $m(2, -2)$; $I(1, 0)$
13. $M(0, 0)$ **14.** $m(2, 0)$ **15.** $(1, -1)$ **16.** $(16, -3)$, $(-16, 1)$
17. $(2, 0)$, $(1, \pm 1)$ **18.** $(3, 1)$ **21.** Concave downward because $f''(x) = -(1/x^2)$ is negative. **23. a)** 3 times; near $x = -1.2, -0.4, +0.8$ **b)** Once; near $x = -1.8$ **c)** Once; near $x = 1.2$

24. $dy/dx = 1 + \cos x = 0$ at $x = \pi + 2\pi k$; elsewhere the slope is positive and the graph is rising.

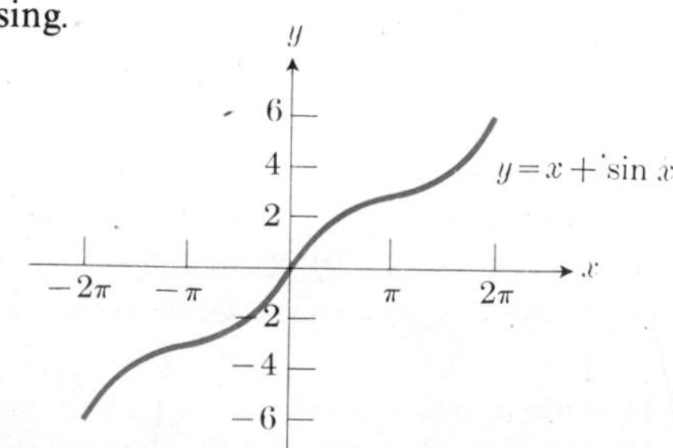

Article 3–6, pp. 151–153

2. $(r\sqrt{2}) \times (r/\sqrt{2})$ **3.** 32 **4.** $\frac{5}{3} \times \frac{14}{3} \times \frac{35}{3}$ (inches) **5.** Use one-half of the fence parallel to the river.
6. $\sqrt{A/3} \times \sqrt{A/3} \times \frac{1}{2}\sqrt{A/3}$, where A = given amount of material. **7.** 4″ × 4″ × 2″ **8.** 4 **9.** 9 inches wide and 18 inches high
10. $V_{max} = 2\pi h^3/(9\sqrt{3})$, h = given hypotenuse **11.** $(100 + c)/2$ **12.** $0.58L$
13. a) 16 **b)** -54 **c)** -1 **d)** $f'(x) = 0$ when $2x^3 = a$ and then $f''(x) = +6$ or $+2$, according as $a \neq 0$ or $a = 0$.

14. a) $a = -3, b = -9$ **b)** $a = -3, b = -24$ **15. a)** $4L/(4 + 3\sqrt{3})$ for the square, $3\sqrt{3}\,L/(4 + 3\sqrt{3})$ for the triangle **b)** Use it all for the square **16.** $(\frac{1}{2}, -\frac{1}{2})$ and $(-\frac{1}{2}, \frac{1}{2})$ **17. a)** $(c - \frac{1}{2}, \sqrt{c - \frac{1}{2}})$ **b)** (0, 0) **18.** $\frac{32}{81}\pi r^3$ **19.** $\frac{4}{9}\pi r^3\sqrt{3}$
21. Width $= 2r/\sqrt{3}$, depth $= 2r\sqrt{\frac{2}{3}}$ **22.** Width of beam = radius of log. **23.** $x/(c - x) = \sqrt[3]{a/b}$, where x is the distance from the source of strength a. **24.** Height of rectangle $= (4 + \pi)/8$ times diameter of semicircle **25.** $4/\pi$ **26.** Diameter = altitude of cylinder $= \sqrt[3]{3V/\pi}$, V = total volume **27. a)** Unity **b)** Zero **31.** Before tax: Production = 7,500; price = \$1.25; profit = \$5,425. After tax: Production = 7,000; price = \$1.30; profit = \$4,700. To maximize profit the company should absorb 5¢ of the tax and add 5¢ to the price. **32.** Still $Q = \sqrt{2KM/h}$. Of course the average weekly cost increases if $p > 0$. **35.** Maxima: $x = (\pi/4) + 2\pi k$, k any integer, $y = \sqrt{2}$. Minima: $x = (5\pi/4) + 2\pi k$, k any integer, $y = -\sqrt{2}$. [*Note.* $\sin x + \cos x = \sqrt{2}\sin[x + (\pi/4)]$.]

Article 3–7, p. 155

6. The function is not continuous on the closed interval $0 \le x \le 1$.

Article 3–8, pp. 159–160

1. $\frac{1}{2}$ **2.** $\sqrt{3}$ **3.** $\frac{8}{27}$ **4.** 1 **5.** $\frac{3}{2}$ **7. a)** $3\frac{1}{6}$ **b)** 4.012 **c)** 0.0101

Article 3–9, p. 165

1. $\frac{1}{4}$ **2.** 2 **3.** $\frac{5}{7}$ **4.** $\frac{3}{11}$ **5.** 0 **6.** -2 **7.** 5 **8.** $-\frac{1}{2}$ **9.** 1 **10.** $\frac{1}{4}$ **11.** $\frac{1}{6}$ **12.** $\frac{1}{2}$ **13.** $+\infty$ **14.** 3 **15.** $\cos a$ **16.** an **17.** $+\infty$ **18.** $-\frac{1}{2}$ **19.** (b) is correct. L'Hôpital's rule does not apply because the limit of the denominator is finite and nonzero. **20.** -1 **21.** $(a + b)/2$ **22.** $(-1 + \sqrt{37})/3 \approx 1.694$

Miscellaneous Problems Chapter 3, pp. 171–174

1. a) $x < \frac{9}{2}$ **b)** $x > \frac{9}{2}$ **c)** No values **d)** All values **2. a)** $x > 3, x < \frac{1}{3}$ **b)** $\frac{1}{3} < x < 3$ **c)** $x > \frac{5}{3}$ **d)** $x < \frac{5}{3}$
3. a) $x < 3$ **b)** $x > 3$ **c)** $0 < x < 2$ **d)** $x < 0, x > 2$ **4. a)** $|x| > \frac{1}{2}$ **b)** $|x| < \frac{1}{2}$ **c)** $x > 0$ **d)** $x < 0$
5. a) $x > \sqrt[3]{2}$ **b)** $x < \sqrt[3]{2}$ **c)** $x > 0, x < -\sqrt[3]{4}$ **d)** $-\sqrt[3]{4} < x < 0$ **6. a)** $x < 0, x > 2$ **b)** $0 < x < 2$ **c)** $x \neq 0$ **d)** Never
7. a) $x < 0$ **b)** $x > 0$ **c)** $x \neq 0$ **d)** Never **8. a)** $x \neq -1$ **b)** Never **c)** $x < -1$ **d)** $x > -1$ **9. a)** $x \neq 0$ **b)** Never **c)** $x < 0$ **d)** $x > 0$ **10. a)** $-1 < x < 0, x > 1$ **b)** $x < -1, 0 < x < 1$ **c)** $x < -1/\sqrt{3}, x > 1/\sqrt{3}$ **d)** $|x| < 1/\sqrt{3}$
11. a) $x < -2b/a, x > 0$ **b)** $-2b/a < x < 0$ **c)** $x > -b/a$ **d)** $x < -b/a$
12. a) $x < 1, x > 2$ **b)** $1 < x < 2$ **c)** $x > \frac{3}{2}$ **d)** $x < \frac{3}{2}$ **13. a)** $x < -1, x > \frac{1}{3}$ **b)** $-1 < x < \frac{1}{3}$ **c)** $x > -\frac{1}{3}$ **d)** $x < -\frac{1}{3}$
14. a) $0 < x < 4$ **b)** $x < 0, x > 4$ **c)** $x < 2$ **d)** $x > 2$
15. a) At $x = 1$; because y' goes from + to −. **b)** At $x = 3$; because y' goes from − to +.
17. If $v = k/\sqrt{s}$, then $dv/dt = -k^2/2s^2$ **18.** $k^2/2$ **19.** $\frac{1}{4}$ in/min **20.** $(3/400\pi)$ ft/min
21. $dr/dt = -(3/400)$ ft/min. $dA/dt = -\frac{6}{5}\pi$ ft²/min. $\Delta r \approx -(3/4000)$ ft; $\Delta A \approx -(3\pi/25)$ ft²
22. a) Approx. 606 mi/hr **b)** Approx. 0.83 mi **23.** $\frac{1}{2}\sqrt{3}$ **24.** $-480\sqrt{2}/7$ **25.** Yes, it will fill, because $dy/dt > 0.007$ for $y \le 10$.
26. $a = -gR^2/s^2$ **28.** $(\sqrt{3}/30)r$, increasing **29.** ≈ 18 mi/hr **30.** $(8/9\pi)$ ft/min **31.** $\frac{20}{3}$ and $\frac{40}{3}$ **32.** 10 **33.** 18 and 18. No.
34. $a = 1$; $b = -3$; $c = -9$; $d = 5$ **35.** $\frac{1}{2}$ **36.** $r = 25$ ft **37.** $t = 1, s = 16$ **38.** $r = 4, h = 4$ **39.** Diameter = height = 4 in
40. $4\sqrt{3}$ **41.** 276 (approx.) **42. a)** $(2, \pm\sqrt{3})$ **b)** and **c)** (1, 0) **43. a)** $2\frac{1}{12}$ mi from A; **b)** $2\frac{1}{12}$ mi from A; **c)** at B
44. a) True **b)** False **c)** True **d)** False **45.** Each $= (P - b)/2$ **46.** Each $= \tan^{-1}(4k/b^2)$ **48.** $m = \frac{1}{4}$
50. Sides 100 m; radius of semicircular ends $100/\pi$ m **57.** 6 × 18 ft **58.** Approx. 16.4 in. **59.** $(h^{2/3} + w^{2/3})^{3/2}$ m
60. $v = \sqrt[n]{a/((n - 1)b)}$ **61.** $r = \sqrt{A}$, $\theta = 2$ rad **62.** Approx. 1.94 gal **63. a)** A decreasing 0.04π cm²/sec **b)** $t = (5b - 3a)/(a^2 - b^2)$ **64.** $t = (R - cr)/(ca - b)$, where $c = \sqrt{a/b}$ **66. a)** True **b)** Not necessarily true: $f(x) = g(x) = 5 + x + x^3$ for $|x| \le 1$, $a = 0$. **67.** $x = (1/n)\sum_{i=1}^{n} c_i$ **68.** $m = \frac{5}{7}$ **70.** Doesn't apply; derivative doesn't exist at $x = 0$. **72.** $c = \pm((b^{2/3} + a^{1/3}b^{1/3} + a^{2/3})/3)^{3/2}$ **73.** Root -0.67 **75. a)** $x = (c - b)/(2e)$ **b)** $P = \frac{1}{2}(b + c)$ **c)** $-a + (c - b)^2/(4e)$ **d)** $P = \frac{1}{2}(b + t + c)$; that is, it adds $\frac{1}{2}t$ to its previous price. **76. a)** $\frac{10}{3}$ **b)** $\frac{5}{3}$ **c)** $\frac{1}{2}$ **d)** 0

CHAPTER 4

Article 4–2, p. 181

1. $y = (x^3/3) + x + C$ **2.** $y = -(1/x) + (x^2/2) + C$ **3.** $y^2 = x^2 + C$ **4.** $3y^{1/2} = x^{3/2} + C$ **5.** $y^{2/3} = x^{2/3} + C$ **6.** $-(1/y) = x^2 + C$ **7.** $y = x^3 - x^2 + 5x + C$ **8.** $s = t^3 + 2t^2 - 6t + C$ **9.** $r = (2z + 1)^4/8 + C$ **10.** $-u^{-1} = 2v^4 - 4v^{-2} + C$
11. $x^{1/2} = 4t + C$ **12.** $y = 4t^3/3 + 4t - t^{-1} + C$ **13.** $y = z^3/3 - z^{-1} + C$ **14.** $x^2 + 3x + C$ **15.** $(x^3/3) - (2x^{3/2}/3) + C$

16. $(3x-1)^{235}/705 + C$ **17.** $-3(2-7t)^{5/3}/35 + C$ **18.** $2(2+5y)^{3/2}/15 + C$ **19.** $-1/(9x+6) + C$ **20.** $-3\sqrt{1-r^2} + C$ **21.** $(2x^2+1)^{3/2}/6 + C$ **22.** $\frac{1}{2}(1+2t^3)^{1/3} + C$ **23.** $\frac{1}{2}\sqrt{2y^2+1} + C$ **24.** $\frac{2}{3}x^{3/2} + 2x^{1/2} + C$ **25.** $\frac{3}{4}(z^2+2z+2)^{2/3} + C$

Article 4–3, p. 184

1. $s = t^3 + s_0$ **2.** $s = t^2 + t + s_0$ **3.** $s = \frac{1}{3}(t+1)^3 - \frac{1}{3} + s_0$ **4.** $s = \frac{1}{5}t^5 + \frac{2}{3}t^3 + t + s_0$ **5.** $s = -(t+1)^{-1} + 1 + s_0$ **6.** $s = s_0 + t\sqrt{2gs_0} + \frac{1}{2}gt^2$ **7.** $v = gt + v_0$; $s = \frac{1}{2}gt^2 + v_0 t + s_0$ **8.** $v = \frac{1}{2}t^2 + v_0$; $s = \frac{1}{6}t^3 + v_0 t + s_0$ **9.** $v = \frac{3}{8}(2t+1)^{4/3} + v_0 - \frac{3}{8}$; $s = \frac{9}{112}(2t+1)^{7/3} + (v_0 - \frac{3}{8})t + s_0 - \frac{9}{112}$ **10.** $v = -\frac{1}{4}(2t+1)^{-2} + v_0 + \frac{1}{4}$; $s = \frac{1}{8}(2t+1)^{-1} + (v_0 + \frac{1}{4})t + s_0 - \frac{1}{8}$ **11.** $v = \frac{1}{5}t^5 + \frac{2}{3}t^3 + t + v_0$; $s = \frac{1}{30}t^6 + \frac{1}{6}t^4 + \frac{1}{2}t^2 + v_0 t + s_0$ **13.** $y = 3x^3 - 2x^2 + 5x + 10$ **14.** $y = (x-7)^4 + 9$ **15.** $y = \frac{2}{3}x^{3/2} + \frac{4}{5}x^{5/4} - 2$ **16.** $y = x - (1/x) + 1$ **17.** $4\sqrt{y} = x^2 + 4$ **18.** $-y^{-1} = x^2 - 2$ **19.** $(3y+10)^2 = (1+x^2)^3$ **20.** $(1+y^2)^{-(1/2)} = (1/\sqrt{2}) - 4x$ **21. a)** $R(x) = 250\sqrt{x} + (100/x) - 101$ **b)** \$1,035.03

Article 4–4, pp. 187–188

1. $-\frac{1}{3}\cos 3x + C$ **2.** $\frac{1}{2}\sin(2x+4) + C$ **3.** $-\frac{1}{4}\cos(2x^2) + C$ **4.** $2\sin\sqrt{x} + C$ **5.** $-\frac{1}{2}\cos 2t + C$ **6.** $\frac{1}{3}\sin(3\theta - 1) + C$ **7.** $\frac{4}{3}\sin 3y + C$ **8.** $\sin^2 z + C$ **9.** $\frac{1}{3}\sin^3 x + C$ **10.** $-\frac{1}{6}\cos^3 2y + C$ **11.** $\frac{1}{3}\sin 3t - \frac{1}{9}\sin^3 3t + C$ **12.** $(1/\cos x) + C$ **13.** $-(1/\sin x) + C$ **14.** $\frac{2}{9}(2 + \sin 3t)^{3/2} + C$ **15.** $\sqrt{2 - \cos 2t} + C$ **16.** $\frac{1}{2}\sin^4(y/2) + C$ **17.** $3\sec[(z-1)/3] + C$ **18.** $-\frac{1}{2}\cos^3(2x/3) + C$ **19.** $\frac{1}{5}(1 + \sin 2t)^{5/2} + C$ **20.** $-\frac{3}{2}\cos 2x + \frac{4}{3}\sin 3x + C$ **21.** $\frac{1}{3}(\sin^3 t - \cos^3 t) + C$ **22.** $x\sin x + C$ **23.** $y^2 = (5x^2/2) + 3\cos x - 3$ **24.** $y^{3/2} = \frac{3}{2}\sin \pi x - \frac{1}{2}$ **25.** Yes; from the identities $\cos^2 x + \sin^2 x = 1$, $\cos 2x = \cos^2 x - \sin^2 x$, we find that the constants have to satisfy the relations: $C_2 = C_1 + 1$, $C_3 = C_1 + \frac{1}{2}$.

Article 4–5, p. 191

1. 1.75, 2.25 **2.** 0.25, 1.25 **3.** $\pi/(2\sqrt{2}) \approx 1.12$, $(\pi/2)(1 + (1/\sqrt{2})) \approx 2.68$ **4.** 0.6345, 0.7595 **5.** 4.146, 6.146 **6.** $\sum_{k=1}^{5}(1/k) = \frac{1}{1} + \frac{1}{2} + \frac{1}{3} + \frac{1}{4} + \frac{1}{5}$ **7.** $\sum_{i=-1}^{3} 2^i = 2^{-1} + 2^0 + 2^1 + 2^2 + 2^3 = \frac{1}{2} + 1 + 2 + 4 + 8$ **8.** $\sum_{n=1}^{4}\cos n\pi x = \cos \pi x + \cos 2\pi x + \cos 3\pi x + \cos 4\pi x$ **9.** $\frac{5}{2}$ **10.** $\frac{7}{6}$ **11.** 1

Article 4–7, p. 200

1. 12 **2.** 4 **3.** $8\frac{2}{3}$ **4.** 2 **5.** $\frac{1}{15}$ **6.** $57\frac{1}{3}$ **7.** 10 **8.** $4\frac{1}{3}$ **9.** 1 **10.** $\frac{2}{9}$ **11.** $\frac{1}{2}$ **12.** $10\frac{2}{3}$ **13.** 2 **14.** $\frac{2}{3}$ **15.** $\frac{4}{3}$ **16.** $\frac{2}{3}$ **17.** $\pi/6$ **18. b)** $\pi a^2/4$

Article 4–8, pp. 209–210

1. a) $c_k = \frac{1}{2}(x_k + x_{k-1})$ **b)** $c_k = \pm\sqrt{(x_{k-1}^2 + x_{k-1}x_k + x_k^2)/3}$, the sign being determined by the interval (x_{k-1}, x_k) **c)** $c_k = \sqrt[3]{(x_{k-1}^3 + x_{k-1}^2 x_k + x_{k-1}x_k^2 + x_k^3)/4}$ **d)** $c_k = ((\sqrt{x_{k-1}} + \sqrt{x_k})/2)^2$ **4.** $S_n = b^4/4$ **5.** $S_n = 2(\sqrt{b} - 1)$ **6.** 8 **7.** $\frac{7}{3}$ **8.** $\frac{8}{3}$ **9.** $\frac{13}{3}$ **10.** 2 **11.** 0 **12.** $\sqrt{2} - 1$ **13.** $\frac{1}{2}$ **14.** $\pi/2$ **15.** π/w **16.** $\frac{2}{9}$ **17. a)** $A = \lim_{n\to\infty}\sum_{k=1}^{n}(18 - 2x_k^2)\,\Delta x_k$, $(x_1 = -3, x_{n+1} = 3)$ **b)** $A = \int_{-3}^{3}(18 - 2x^2)\,dx = 72$ **18.** $\sqrt{1+x^2}$ **19.** $1/x$ **20.** $-\sqrt{1-x^2}$ **21.** $1/(1+x^2)$ **22.** $2\cos(4x^2)$ **23.** $2x/(1 + \sqrt{1-x^2})$ **24.** $-\cos x/(2 + \sin x)$

Article 4–9, pp. 218–219

1. $\int_a^b f(x)\,dx = T - [(b-a)/12]f''(e)h^2$ **a)** Concave upward over $a < x < b$, then $f''(e) > 0$, $T > \int_a^b f(x)\,dx$ **b)** Concave downward over $a < x < b$, then $f''(e) < 0$, $T < \int_a^b f(x)\,dx$ **2. a)** 2 **b)** 2 **c)** 2 **d)** 1 (smallest possible for trapezoidal method) **e)** 2 (smallest possible for Simpson's method) **3. a)** $\frac{11}{4}$ **b)** $\frac{8}{3}$ **c)** $\frac{8}{3}$ **d)** 366 **e)** 2 **4. a)** $\frac{17}{4}$ **b)** 4 **c)** 4 **d)** 895 **e)** 2 **5. a)** ≈ 0.50899 **b)** ≈ 0.50042 **c)** $\frac{1}{2}$ (or 0.5) **d)** 224 **e)** 18 (must be even) **6. a)** ≈ 4.65509 **b)** ≈ 4.66622 **c)** $\frac{14}{3}$ (≈ 4.66667) **d)** 238 **e)** 20 **7. a)** ≈ 1.89612 $((\pi/4)(1 + \sqrt{2}))$ **b)** ≈ 2.00456 $((\pi/6)(1 + 2\sqrt{2}))$ **c)** 2 **d)** 509 **e)** 22 **8. a)** $\frac{1}{4800} \le |E_T| \le \frac{1}{600}$ **b)** $4.1\overline{6} \times 10^{-6} \le |E_S| \le 1.\overline{3} \times 10^{-5}$ **9.** $n \ge 8$ (With $n = 8$, one gets ≈ 0.69315453. Compare with: $\ln 2 \approx 0.69314718$.) **10.** milligram-seconds/liter **12. a)** 40.25 lumen-milliseconds **b)** 55.50 lumen-milliseconds

Article 4–10, p. 223

1. $\int_a^b f(t)\,dt = -\int_b^a f(t)\,dt$; $\int_a^c f(t)\,dt = \int_a^b f(t)\,dt + \int_b^c f(t)\,dt$; $(d/dx)\int_a^x f(t)\,dt = f(x)$; $\int_a^b f(t)\,dt = f(c)\cdot(b-a)$; $\int_a^b f(t)\,dt = F(b) - F(a)$. **2. a)** $(\pi - 4)/2\pi$ **b)** $\frac{55}{42}$ **3. a)** $\frac{1}{2}, -1$ **b)** $\sqrt{\frac{1}{2}}, (\frac{9}{2})^{-(1/3)}$ **c)** $\frac{2}{3}, -\frac{2}{5}$

Miscellaneous Problems Chapter 4, pp. 224–225

1. $x^2 y + 2 = cy$ **2.** $3\sqrt{y+1} = (1+x)^{3/2} + C$ **3.** $y^3 + 3y = x^3 - 3x + C$ **4.** $3(x^2 - y^2) + 4(x^{3/2} + y^{3/2}) = C$

5. $(2+x)^{-1} = -(3-y)^{-1} + C$ **6. a)** $y = \frac{1}{3}(x^2-4)^{3/2} + 3$ **b)** $y^2(1-x^2) = 1$ **7.** Yes; $y = x$ is such a curve.
8. $y = x^3 + 2x - 4$ **9.** $(2\sqrt{2}/3)b^{3/4}$ **10. a)** $v = \frac{2}{3}t^{3/2} - 2\sqrt{t} + \frac{4}{3}$ **b)** $s = \frac{4}{15}t^{5/2} - \frac{4}{3}t^{3/2} + \frac{4}{3}t - \frac{4}{15}$
11. $v = t^2 + 3t + 4$, $\Delta s = 61\frac{1}{3}$ **12.** -8 ft/sec [*Note.* $d^2x/dt^2 = v(dv/dx)$, where $v = dx/dt$.] **13.** $h(10) = h(0) = 5$
14. $(1+y')(1+y'^2) + y''(y-x) = 0$ **15. a)** $k = 38.72$ ft/sec^2 **b)** 25 ft **16.** $3y = (1+x^2)^{3/2} - 7$ **17.** $h = 96t - 16t^2$; 144 ft
19. a) ≈ 1.76 **b)** ≈ 1.73 **20. a)** 4 ft/sec **b)** $\frac{64}{3}$ ft **21.** $(x^2/2) - x^{-1} + C$ **22.** $\frac{1}{3}(y^2+1)^{3/2} + C$ **23.** $-\frac{1}{8}(1+t^{4/3})^{-6} + C$
24. $\frac{4}{3}(1+\sqrt{u})^{3/2} + C$ **25.** $-\frac{3}{5}(7-5r)^{1/3} + C$ **26.** $\frac{1}{4}\sin 4x + C$ **27.** $\frac{1}{9}\sin^3 3x + C$ **28.** $2\sqrt{\sin x} + C$ **29.** $\frac{1}{2}\sin(2x-1) + C$
30. $-\frac{1}{4}\sqrt{25-4y^2} + C$ **31.** $-\sqrt{2/t} + C$ **32.** $\frac{1}{3}(x^3 - 2x^{3/2}) + C$ **33.** $\frac{1}{3}(2-3x)^{-1} + C$ **35.** $r\sqrt{2}/2$ ft **37.** $|a|$
38. Yes; no; applies to identities, but not to equations. **39.** 480π mi/hr **40.** $|3a\omega \sin\theta \cos\theta|$ **41.** $f(x) = x/\sqrt{x^2+1}$
42. $\int_0^1 f(x)\,dx$ **43. a)** $\frac{1}{16}$ **b)** $\frac{2}{3}$ **c)** $2/\pi$ **d)** $\sqrt{1+x^2} - x$ **e)** $x_1 f(x_1)$ **44.** $d^2y/dx^2 = 4y$

CHAPTER 5

Article 5–2, p. 230

1. a) $\lim_{\Delta y \to 0} \sum_a^b (f(y) - g(y))\,\Delta y$ **b)** $\int_a^b (f(y) - g(y))\,dy$ **2.** $\frac{4}{3}$ **3.** $\frac{1}{12}$ **4.** $\frac{32}{3}$ **5.** $\frac{32}{3}$ **6.** $\frac{1}{6}$ **7.** $\frac{4}{3}$ **8.** $\frac{128}{15}$ **9.** $\sqrt{2} - 1$
10. $\sqrt[3]{16} \approx 2.52$ **11.** $\frac{1}{6}$ **12.** $A \approx 3.141591$ (Actual area $= \pi$)

Article 5–3, pp. 233–234

1. 6 ft **2.** $5\frac{1}{6}$ ft **3.** $3\frac{2}{3}$ ft **4.** 1 ft **5.** 6 ft **6.** 8 ft **7.** $2\sqrt{2}$ ft **8.** $2\frac{2}{3}$ ft **9.** $6 - \sin 2 \approx 5.09$ ft **10.** $1 + \cos 2 \approx 0.58$ ft
11. $2g$ **12.** $4\frac{29}{30}$ ft **13.** $3\frac{1}{6}$ ft **15.** 1.56 miles (using Simpson's rule with $n = 12$)

Article 5–4, p. 239

1. $8\pi/3$ **2.** $\pi^2/2$ **3.** $\pi/30$ **4.** $81\pi/10$ **5.** $16\pi/15$ **6.** $128\pi/7$ **7.** $\pi/9$ **8.** π **9. a)** $32\pi/5$ **b)** $8\pi/3$
10. a) $\pi r^2 h/3$ **b)** $2\pi h^2 r/3$ **11. a)** $\pi h^2(a - h/3)$ **b)** $0.1/12\pi$ ft/sec $= 6/\pi$ in/min **12.** $\frac{4}{3}\pi ab^2$ **13.** $512\pi/15$ **14.** $16a^3/3$
15. $8a^3/3$ **16.** $8a^3/3$ **17.** $\pi\sqrt{3}/16$ **18.** 15,990 ft^3

Article 5–5, pp. 245–246

1. $8\pi/3$ **2.** $8\pi/3$ **3.** $56\pi/15$ **4.** $2\pi/3$ **5.** $256\pi/5$ **6.** $48\pi/5$ **7.** $117\pi/5$ **8.** $108\pi/5$ **9.** $\pi/3$ **10.** $64\pi/5$ **11. a)** $5\pi/3$ **b)** $4\pi/3$
12. $4\pi/15$ **13. a)** 8π **b)** $224\pi/15$ **14.** $\pi/2$ **15.** $4\pi/5$ **16.** $32\pi/3$ **17.** $2\pi^2$
18. a) 8π **b)** $512\pi/15$ **c)** $256\pi/5$ **d)** $1088\pi/15$ **e)** $128\pi/3$ **19.** $2\pi^2 a^2 b$

Article 5–7, pp. 254–255

1. 12 **2.** $\frac{8}{27}(10\sqrt{10} - 1)$ **3.** $\frac{14}{3}$ **4.** $\frac{53}{6}$ **5.** $\frac{123}{32}$ **6.** $\frac{4}{27}(10\sqrt{10} - 1)$ **7.** $a\pi^2/8$ **8.** 8 **9.** 12 **10.** $\frac{21}{2}$ **11.** 3.8202824

Article 5–8, p. 260

1. $99\pi/2$ **2.** $(\pi/27)(10\sqrt{10} - 1)$ **3.** $(\pi/6)(17\sqrt{17} - 1)$ **4.** $1823\pi/18$ **5.** $253\pi/20$ **6.** $(2\pi/3)(2\sqrt{2} - 1)$ **7.** $(\pi/6)(5\sqrt{5} - 1)$
8. $12\pi a^2/5$ **9.** $(2\pi/3)(26\sqrt{26} - 2\sqrt{2})$ **10.** $56\pi\sqrt{3}/5$

Article 5–9, pp. 263–264

1. a) $2/\pi$ **b)** 0 **2. a)** $\frac{1}{2}$ **b)** $\frac{1}{2}$ **3.** $\frac{49}{12}$ **4.** $\frac{1}{2}$ **5.** $\alpha((a+b)/2) + \beta$ **6.** $I_{av} = 300$; 6 dollars/day
7. $I_{av} = 200$; 1 dollar/day **8.** 25°F **9. a)** Average $= 67.25/60.00 \approx 1.12$ millions of lumens/millisecond **b)** $t \approx 87.91$ seconds
10. $\pi a/2$ **11.** $4a/\pi$ **12.** $8a^2/3$ **13.** $2a^2$

Article 5–10, p. 270

1. $(4a/3\pi, 4a/3\pi)$ **2.** $(0, \frac{2}{5}h^2)$ **3.** $(2a/(3(4-\pi)), 2a/(3(4-\pi)))$ **4.** $(\pi/2, \pi/8)$ **5.** $(\frac{2}{5}, 1)$ **6.** $\frac{3}{7}h$ **7.** $\frac{3}{5}h$
8. On the axis, $(3h/4)$ from the vertex. **9.** On the axis, $(3h/5)$ from the vertex. **10.** On the axis, $(h/2)$ from the vertex. **11.** $(0, \pi r/4)$

Article 5–11, pp. 273–274

1. $(0, 2c^2/5)$ **2.** $(\frac{16}{105}, \frac{8}{15})$ **3.** $(0, \frac{12}{5})$ **4.** $(1, -\frac{3}{5})$ **5.** $(\frac{3}{5}, 1)$ **6.** On the axis, $(3h/4)$ from the vertex. **7.** $(0, \frac{8}{3})$ **8.** $(\frac{4}{5}, 0)$
9. On the axis, $(2h/3)$ from the vertex. **10.** $(-r, 3r/(2+\pi))$ **11.** $(17\sqrt{17} - 1)/12$ **12.** $(2r/\pi, 2r/\pi)$

Article 5–12, pp. 276–277

2. $(0, 2r/\pi)$ **3.** $2\pi(\pi - 2)r^2$ **4.** $[(3\pi + 4)/3]\pi r^3$ **5.** $[(3\pi + 4)/3(\pi r^3/\sqrt{2})]$ **6.** $\pi\sqrt{2}(\pi + 2)r^2$ **7.** $2r^3/3$ **8.** $(4 + 3\pi)r^3/6$ **9.** $(4 + 3\pi)r^3/(6\sqrt{2})$

Article 5–13, p. 280

1. 375 lb **2.** $111\frac{1}{9}$ lb **3.** $1666\frac{2}{3}$ lb **4.** $116\frac{2}{3}$ lb **5.** $41\frac{2}{3}$ lb **6.** 975 tons **7.** 8450 ton-ft

Article 5–14, pp. 284–285

1. $c = 5$ lb/in; 80 inch-lb **2. a)** $c = 200$ lb/in **b)** 400 inch-lb **c)** 8 inches **3. a)** 1250 inch-lb **b)** 3750 inch-lb **4. a)** $\frac{5}{2}$ ft-lb **b)** 12 ft **5.** $18\frac{3}{4}$ inch-lb; 300 lb **6.** $c = (10/\sin 10°)$ lb; 78.5 inch-lb **7.** $\frac{1}{2}k$, where k is the proportionality factor **8.** $\frac{1}{3}k$, k as above **9.** $\frac{1}{2}mgR$ **10.** 1944 ft-lb **12.** (Work done *on* the gas) = −(Work done by the gas) = $3164\frac{1}{16}$ ft-lb **13.** $(200\pi/3)$ ft-tons **14.** 27.2 ft-tons

Miscellaneous Problems Chapter 5, pp. 285–287

1. $\frac{9}{2}$ **2.** $6\frac{3}{4}$ **3.** 1 **4.** $(7 - 4\sqrt{2})/2$ **5.** $\frac{9}{2}$ **6.** $\frac{32}{3}$ **7.** 18 **8.** $3^5/2^3$ **9.** $a^2/6$ **10.** $1 - \cos x_0 - (\sqrt{2}/4)x_0^2 \approx 0.137087$, where $x_0 \approx 1.391557$ is the root of $\sin x = x/\sqrt{2}$, $x > 0$. **11.** 8 **12.** $(\pi^2/32) + ((\sqrt{2}/2) - 1) \approx 0.015532$ **13.** $\frac{13}{3}$ **14.** $\frac{9}{8}$ **15.** $\frac{64}{3}$ **16. a)** $0 \le x < 2$ **b)** $2 < x < 3$ **c)** $\frac{29}{2}$ ft **17. a)** $\frac{3}{7}$ **b)** $\frac{3}{8}$ **c)** $y = 3/(2\sqrt{1 + 3x})$ **d)** $\frac{3}{7}$ **18.** $f(x) = \sqrt{(2x - a)/\pi}$ **19. a)** $3^5\pi/5$ **b)** $189\pi/2$ **c)** $81\pi/2$ **d)** $2^9\pi/15$ **e)** $2^7\pi/3$ **20.** $f(x) = \pm\sqrt{(2x + 1)/\pi}$ **21.** $32\pi/3$ **22. a)** $2\pi a^3$ **b)** $(\frac{16}{15})\pi a^3$ **c)** $(\frac{8}{5})\pi a^3$ **23.** $V = 2\pi \int_0^2 x^2/\sqrt{x^3 + 8}\, dx = (8\pi/3)(2 - \sqrt{2})$ **24.** $(\pi/15)(88\sqrt{2} + 107)$ **25.** $112\pi a^3/15$ **26.** $V = hs^2$ **27.** $(\frac{8}{3})r^3$ **28.** $\pi^2/4$ **29.** $28\pi/3$ **30.** $72\pi/35$ **31.** $2\sqrt{3}\,a^3$ **32.** $\frac{19}{3}$ **33.** $424\pi/15$ **34.** $\frac{27}{20}$ **35.** $153\pi/40$ **36.** $(a/3)(3\sqrt{3} - 1)$ **37. a)** $\frac{2}{3}b^2$ **b)** $\frac{2}{3}b$ **38. a)** $f(x) = a \pm x\sqrt{A^2 - 1}$, $|A| \ge 1$ **b)** No **39. a)** $\bar{v} = 72$ **b)** $82\frac{2}{3}$ **40.** Volume 401π; average area 40.1π **41.** $(\frac{9}{10}, \frac{9}{5})$ **42.** $(\frac{3}{2}, \frac{12}{5})$ **43.** $(1, \frac{12}{5})$ **44.** $(\frac{3}{4}, \frac{3}{10})$ **46. a)** $(5a/7, 0)$ **b)** $(2a/3, 0)$ **47. a)** $\bar{x} = \bar{y} = 4(a^2 + ab + b^2)/(3\pi(a + b))$ **b)** $(2a/\pi, 2a/\pi)$ **48. a)** $(2a/5, 2a/5)$ **b)** $(0, 15\pi a/256)$ **49.** 5 in., $7\frac{1}{9}$ in., $4\frac{8}{9}$ in. **50.** 7000/3 lb **51.** $5 \times 10^6/3$ lb **52. a)** $2h/3$ below surface **b)** $(a + h(4a + 3h))/(6a + 4h)$ below surface **53.** $504d_1 + 72d_2$ **54.** $Mah + (h^2/a)$ **55.** $k(b - a)/ab$ **56.** $wr[1 - (r/2R)]$ ft-lb, R = radius of earth in feet **57.** $(320w/3)(15\pi + 8)$ ft-lb

CHAPTER 6

Article 6–1, p. 294

13. $6x \sec^2(3x^2)$ **14.** $-2 \sin x \tan(\cos x) \sec^2(\cos x)$ **15.** $-3 \csc^2(3x + 5)$ **16.** $-\frac{1}{2}(\cot x)^{-(1/2)} \csc^2 x$ **17.** 0 **18.** $\sec^3 x \tan x$ **19.** $3(1 + \sec^2 3x)$ **20.** $6 \sec^2 2x$ **21.** $-\tan^2 x$ **22.** $4 \sec^2 x \tan x$ **23.** $-2 \csc x(\csc x + \cot x)^2$ **24.** $12 \sin 3x \cos 3x$, or $6 \sin 6x$ **25.** $\frac{1}{2}(1 - \cos 2x)$, or $\sin^2 x$ **26.** $\frac{1}{2}(1 + \cos 2x)$, or $\cos^2 x$ **27.** $-\cos^3(x/3)$ **28.** $-3 \cos(x/2) \sin(x/2)$, or $-\frac{3}{2} \sin x$ **29.** $(x/2) \sin(x/2)$ **30.** $2x/(\cos y + 2 \cos 2y)$ **31.** $3(\sin^2 x \cos x - \cos 3x)$ **32.** $-5 \cos^3 5x$ **33.** $-(\cos^2(xy) + y)/x$ **34.** 10 when $x = -\sin^{-1}(\frac{4}{5})$ **35.** max $y = \frac{3}{2}$ when $x = \pi/6$; min $y = 1$ when $x = 0$ or $\pi/2$. **36.** 61° **38.** 1.6π mi/sec **39.** 120° **40.** $-\frac{1}{3} \cos 3t + C$ **41.** $\frac{1}{2} \tan 2\theta + C$ **42.** $\frac{1}{4} \tan^4 x + C$ **43.** $\frac{1}{3} \sec^3 x + C$ **44.** $2 \sec(x/2) + C$ **45.** $\frac{1}{2}y + \frac{1}{4} \sin 2y + C$ **46.** $\tan \theta + C$ **47.** $-3 \cot(\theta/3) + C$ **48.** $\frac{3}{2}$ **49.** $(\pi/4)(4 - \pi)$ **50.** $\frac{1}{3}$ **51.** $\frac{1}{2}$ **52.** 2 **53.** $\frac{1}{6}$

54.

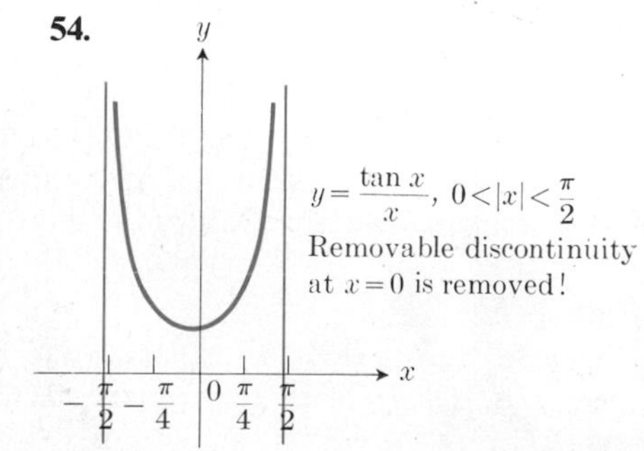

Article 6–2, p. 299

1. $\sqrt{3}/2$, $\sqrt{3}/3$, $2\sqrt{3}/3$, 2 **2.** $\sqrt{3}/2$, $-\sqrt{3}$, -2, $2\sqrt{3}/3$ **3.** π **4.** $\pi/2$ **5.** $-\pi/3$ **8. a)** 0.735 **b)** 0.6 **c)** 0.96 **d)** $\pi/3$ **e)** $2\pi/3$ **f)** $\pi/6$ **9. a)** $\theta_2 = \sin^{-1}((\sin \theta_1)/n_{12})$ **b)** If $n_{12} \le 1$, max $\theta_1 = \sin^{-1} n_{12}$. If $n_{12} > 1$, then $0 \le \theta_1 < (\pi/2)$. **10.** $c = \pi/4$

Article 6–3, pp. 302–303

5. $1/\sqrt{4-x^2}$ **6.** $1/(9+x^2)$ **7.** $1/(|x|\sqrt{25x^2-1})$ **8.** $-2/\sqrt{1-4x^2}$ **9.** $4/(4+x^2)$ **10.** $1/((x+1)\sqrt{x})$ **11.** $1/(x^2+1)$ **12.** $\sin^{-1} x$ **13.** $(\sin^{-1} x)^2$ **14.** $\cos^{-1} 2x$ **15.** $\sqrt{b(a+b)}$ ft **16.** $\pi/6$ **17.** $\pi/2$ **18.** $\pi/12$ **19.** $-\pi/12$ **20.** $\frac{1}{2}\sin^{-1} 2x + C$ **21.** $\pi/6$ **22.** $y = \begin{cases} \sec^{-1}(2x) + 2 - (\pi/3), & x > \frac{1}{2} \\ -\sec^{-1}(2x) + ((2\pi/3) - 1), & x < -\frac{1}{2} \end{cases}$ **23. a)** 2 **b)** $\frac{6}{5}$ **c)** $\frac{1}{6}$ **d)** $-\frac{1}{3}$ **24.** $A_S = (7\pi/36) \approx 0.6109$; $A_T = (5\pi/24) \approx 0.6545$ **25.** $(\pi/2) - 1$

Article 6–4, pp. 304–305

1. 0.1826 **2.** 0.3369 **3.** 0.6938 **4.** -0.6956 **5. a)** Circumscribed **b)** Inscribed **6. a)** 0.0392 **b)** -0.0408 **7.** $\pi \ln 2 \approx 2.1776$ **8.** $0.18226 < \ln 1.2 < 0.18267$

Article 6–5, p. 307

1. $(2x+2)/(x^2+2x)$ **2.** $(3/x)(\ln x)^2$ **3.** $-\tan x$ **4.** $\sec x$ **5.** $(1/x) + x/(x^2+1)$ **6.** $(1/x) + 1/(2(x+2))$ **7.** $\ln x$ **8.** $3x^2 \ln(2x) + x^2$ **9.** $1/(1-x^2)$ **10.** $1/(x(1+x^3))$ **11.** $2/(x(2+3x))$ **12.** $-\tan^{-1}(x/2)$ **13.** $(\tan^{-1} x)/x^2$ **14.** $3(\ln x)^2 + (\ln x)^3$ **15.** $2\cos(\ln x)$ **16.** $\sec^{-1} x$ **17.** $\ln(a^2+x^2)$ **18.** $1/(x \ln x)$ **19.** $\frac{1}{2}\ln|2x+3| + C$ **20.** $-\frac{1}{3}\ln|2-3x| + C$ **21.** $\frac{1}{8}\ln(4x^2+1) + C$ **22.** $\ln(2-\cos x) + C$ **23.** $\ln|\sin x| + C$ **24.** $2x - 5\ln|x| + C$ **25.** $x - \ln|x+1| + C$ **26.** $-\frac{1}{3}\ln|4-x^3| + C$ **27.** $-\frac{1}{2}\ln|1-x^2| + C$ **28.** $2\ln(1+\sqrt{x}) + C$ **29.** $\frac{1}{3}(\ln x)^3 + C$ **30.** $-1/(4x+6) + C$ **31.** $-\ln|\cos x| + C$ **32.** $\ln|\ln x| + C$ **33.** $\frac{1}{2}(\ln x)^2 + C$ **34. a)** -2 **b)** 0 **c)** 0 **d)** 0 **35.** $\ln(1+\sqrt{2})$

Article 6–6, p. 309

1. $4a$ **2.** $2b/3$ **3.** $3a/2$ **4.** $-2a$ **5.** $2a - 2b$ **6.** $2a + b$ **7.** $2b - 3a$ **8.** $2a + 2b$ **9.** $2b - a$ **10.** $(3b - a)/2$

Article 6–7, p. 311

2. No inflection point since $y'' = 1/x$ is positive because x is positive. **3.** Slope at $(x, y) = y$. Concave up because $y'' = y' = y$ is positive. **7.** $\log_{10} N = (\ln N)/(\ln 10)$; 0.30103

Article 6–8, pp. 315–316

1. a) x **b)** x **c)** x^{-2} **d)** $-x^2$ **e)** $1/x$ **f)** $-x$ **g)** $1/x$ **h)** x **i)** $2x$ **j)** x^2 **k)** $x - x^2$ **l)** $-2x + 2\ln x$ **m)** xe^x **n)** x/y^2 **2.** $(x^2+2x)e^x$ **3.** $13e^{2x}\cos 3x$ **4.** $1/(1+e^x)$ **5.** $\frac{1}{2}(e^x + e^{-x})$ **6.** $\frac{1}{2}(e^x - e^{-x})$ **7.** $4/(e^x + e^{-x})^2$ **8.** $e^{\sin^{-1} x}/\sqrt{1-x^2}$ **9.** $-4xe^{-2x}$ **10.** $27x^2e^{3x}$ **11.** xe^{ax} **12.** $-2xe^{-x^2}$ **13.** $2e^{-x^2}(x - x^3)$ **14.** $e^x(\ln x + (1/x))$ **15.** $e^x/(1+e^{2x})$ **16.** $2/\sqrt{e^{4x}-1}$ **17.** $\frac{2}{3}e^{2x}\sec(x+3y) - \frac{1}{3}$ **18.** $-e^{1/x}/x^2$ **19.** $(\cos^2 y)(e^x + (1/x))$ **20. b)** $y = 3e^{-2t}$ **21. a)** $\frac{1}{2}$ **b)** ∞ **22.** $\frac{1}{2}e^{2x} + C$ **23.** $\frac{1}{2}e^{x^2} + C$ **24.** $e^{\sin x} + C$ **25.** $3e^{x/3} + C$ **26.** $(-4/3)e^{-3x} + C$ **27.** $\frac{1}{2}\ln|1+2e^x| + C$ **28.** $\ln 2$ **29.** $\ln|e^x + e^{-x}| + C$ **30.** $xe^x - e^x + C$ **32.** $M(e, 0.36788)$; $I(4.48, 0.335)$ **33.** $M(0, 1)$; $I(1, 0.736)$ **34.** Relative max $(7\pi/4, 0.003)$; $I(\pi, 0.0432)$; relative min $(3\pi/4, -0.067)$ **35.** $(\pi/2)(e^{-2} - 0.01) \approx 0.1969$ **36.** $\sqrt{2}(e^{\pi} - 1) \approx 31.312$

Article 6–9, pp. 320–321

1. $(y(2x+1)/(2x(x+1))$ **2.** $-2y/(3(x^2-1))$ **3.** $(y(4x^3+6x^2+x+3))/(3x(x+1)(x^2+1))$ **4.** $(y/3)[(1/x) + [1/(x+1)] + [1/(x-2)] - [2x/(x^2+1)] - [2/(2x+3)]]$ **5.** $y[(\sin x)/x + \cos x \cdot \ln x]$ **6.** $y[1 + \sec^2 x \cdot \ln(\sin x)]$ **7.** $y(\sec x \tan x)\ln 2$ **8.** $(2y \ln x)/x$ **11.** $\frac{3}{8}$ **12.** $(3^{1.2} - 1)/\ln 3 \approx 2.49$ **13.** $(4\ln 4)^{-1} \approx 0.180$ **14.** $24/(50\ln 5) \approx 0.298$ **15.** $(2\ln 4)^{-1} \approx 0.360$ **18. c)** 0.485, 3.2124 **19.** 1, 2

Article 6–10, p. 323

1. a) 2 **b)** $\frac{5}{3}$ **c)** -2 **d)** -2 **2. a)** 2 **b)** $\frac{1}{2}$ **c)** $\frac{4}{3}$ **d)** $\frac{2}{5}$ **3.** $\log_{1.5} 2 = (\ln 2)/(\ln 1.5)$ **4.** 12 **6. a)** 1.30103, 2.30103; 9.30103 − 10, 8.30103 − 10 **b)** 2.99574, 5.29833; 8.39056 − 10, 6.08797 − 10 **7.** f_2 **8.** $m = 1/(\ln 10) \approx 0.43429$ **9. a)** $3^{\tan x}\sec^2 x \ln 3$ **b)** $y[(1/x)\ln(x^2+1) + [2x/(x^2+1)]\ln x]$ **c)** $-2t(\ln 2)2^{-t^2}$ **d)** $e^{-2\theta}(1 - 2\theta)$

Article 6–11, pp. 327–328

1. 17.67 years **2.** 4.875% **4.** $(mv_0/k)[1 - e^{-kt/m}]$ where k is a constant of proportionality. **5.** $Q_0 e^{-kt}$ **6.** $N_0 e^{kt}$ **7.** 1, 3 **8.** $-1, 2$ **9.** $-5, -1$ **10.** $\pm 3, \pm 2$

Miscellaneous Problems Chapter 6, pp. 328–330

1. $2\cos 2x$ **2.** $-8\sin(2x+(\pi/4))$ **3.** $2\cos x+2\cos 2x$ **4.** $(1+\cos x)^{-1}$ **5.** $-\csc y$ **6.** $\cos^2 y$ **7.** $-2\cos(x/2)$ **8.** $-\cos x$ **9.** $1-\cos x$ **10.** $[(x\cos x-\sin x)/x^2]$ where $y\to 1$ as $x\to 0$ and $y\to 0$ as $x\to\infty$. **11.** $[(x\cos x-2\sin x)/x^3]$ where $y\to\infty$ as $x\to 0$ and $y\to 0$ as $x\to\infty$. **12.** $\sin(1/x)-(1/x)\cos(1/x)$ where $y\to 0$ as $x\to 0$ and $y\to 1$ as $x\to\infty$. **13.** $2x\sin(1/x)-\cos(1/x)$ where $y\to 0$ as $x\to 0$ and $y\to\infty$ as $x\to\infty$. **14.** $(2/\pi)\cos^2(\pi y/2)$ **15. a)** $\frac{1}{2}(e^x-e^{-x})$ **b)** $\frac{1}{2}(e^x+e^{-x})$ **c)** $4(e^x+e^{-x})^{-2}$ **16.** $e^{-x}(1-x)$ **17. a)** $1+\ln x$ **b)** $\frac{1}{2}x^{-(1/2)}(2+\ln x)$ **18. a)** $x^{-2}(1-\ln x)$ **b)** $\frac{1}{2}x^{-(3/2)}(2-\ln x)$ **c)** $x^{-3}(1-2\ln x)$ **19.** $e^{-x}(2\cos 2x-\sin 2x)$ **20. a)** $2-e^{2x}$ **b)** $(2-e^{2x})e^{(2x-(1/2)e^{2x})}$ **21. a)** $1-e^x$ **b)** $(1-e^x)e^{(x-e^x)}$ **22.** $(1+x^2)^{-(1/2)}$ **23.** $(1-x^2)^{-1}$ **24.** $2x/(x^2+4)$ **25.** $\tan^{-1}(x/2)+2x/(x^2+4)$ **26.** $8(e^{2x}+e^{-2x})^{-2}$ **27.** $2\sec x$ **28.** $xe^{2x}(3x\cos 3x+2x\sin 3x+2\sin 3x)$ **29.** $2x(1-x^4)^{-(1/2)}-(2x^2+1)e^{x^2}$ **30.** $(4+x^3)/(x(1+x^3))+\frac{2}{3}x^{-(1/3)}7^{x^{2/3}}\ln 7$ **31.** $2x(2-x)(x^2+2)^{1-x}-(x^2+2)^{2-x}\ln(x^2+2)$ **32.** $x^{-1}e^{-x}(1-x\ln x)$ **33.** $1/(x(x^2+1))$ **34.** $3/(3x-4)$ **35.** $(6x+4)/(3x^2+4x)$ **36.** $(\ln x)^2(\ln x+3)$ **37.** $3(1+\ln x)$ **38.** $x^2(1+3\ln x)$ **39.** 1 **40.** $(x^2+2x)e^x$ **41.** e^x **42.** $1/(x\ln x)$ **43. a)** $(1-x^2)/((1+x^2)^2)$ **b)** $\frac{2}{3}(x^2+x-1)x^{-(2/3)}(x-2)^{-(2/3)}(x^2+1)^{-(4/3)}$ **44.** $f(0)=1; f'(0)=5; f(0.01)\approx 1.05$ **45. a)** $a^{x^2-x}(2x-1)\ln a$ **b)** $(1+e^x)^{-1}$ **c)** $\ln x$ **d)** $x^{(1-2x)/x}(1-\ln x)$ **48.** $x=1+\sqrt{2}$ **49.** $(d^2y/dx^2)=4(e^x+e^{-x})^{-2}$; $y=\ln(e^x+e^{-x})+C$ **50.** $y=\ln|2x-9|$ **52.** 0.88 **53.** $E=E_0e^{-t/40}$, $t=92.1$ sec **54.** $y/y_1=(x/x_1)^2$ **55.** $y=1-\frac{1}{2}(e^x+e^{-x})$ **56.** $t(\frac{1}{4})=1/\pi$; it will not reach $x=\frac{1}{2}$, because $t=(1/\pi)\tan(\pi x)$. **57.** $1+4\ln\frac{3}{2}\approx 2.62$ **58.** $2\sqrt{2}$ **59.** $y=2e^x/(2-e^x)$ **60.** $N=N_0e^{0.02t}$, $t=34.7$ yr **62.** $(\pm a/\sqrt{2}, e^{-(1/2)})$ **63.** $\pi\sqrt{3}$ **64.** $(64a^2+b^2\ln 3)/8a$ **65.** $\pi(e^4-1)/2\approx 84.2$ **66.** $(e-e^{-1})a^2\approx 2.35a^2$ **67.** $y^2=4x$ **68.** $-\frac{1}{3}\ln|4-3x|+C$ **69.** $5\ln|x-3|+C$ **70.** $\frac{1}{2}\ln 3\approx 0.550$ **71.** $\frac{1}{6}$ **72.** $x+\ln x+C$ **73.** $-\frac{1}{4}\ln|2x+1|+(x/2)+C$ **74.** $\frac{1}{3}\ln 2\approx 0.23$ **75.** $\frac{1}{2}(e^8-e^{-1})\approx 1490$ **76.** $\ln 3\approx 1.10$ **77.** $\frac{1}{2}\ln 26\approx 1.63$ **78.** e **79.** 585 lb **80.** $2000\pi(\frac{9}{10})^t$ ft^3 **82. a)** No, x could be 4. **b)** Yes; consider the graph of $y=(\ln x)/x$ for $x>0$. **88.** $e-1$

CHAPTER 7

Article 7–1, pp. 335–336

1. $\frac{1}{3}(2x+3)^{3/2}+C$ **2.** $\frac{1}{3}\ln|3x+5|+C$ **3.** $-1/(4x-14)+C$ **4.** $\frac{1}{2}\ln|x^2+2x+3|+C$ **5.** $-\ln|2+\cos x|+C$ **6.** $\frac{1}{8}\tan^4 2x+C$ **7.** $-\frac{1}{4}\sqrt{1-4x^2}+C$ **8.** $\frac{1}{2}(x^{4/3}-1)^{3/2}+C$ **9.** $\sin^{-1}(2x)+C$ **10.** $\sin^{-1}(v^2)+C$ **11.** $-1/(12(3x^2+4)^2)+C$ **12.** $\frac{2}{9}(x^3+5)^{3/2}+C$ **13.** $\frac{2}{3}(x^3+5)^{1/2}+C$ **14.** $\frac{1}{8}\ln(4x^2+1)+C$ **15.** $\frac{1}{2}e^{2x}+C$ **16.** $-e^{\cos x}+C$ **17.** $-\frac{1}{3}e^{-3x}+C$ **18.** $2e^{\sqrt{x+1}}+C$ **19.** $\tan^{-1}(e^x)+C$ **20.** $\frac{1}{3}\tan^{-1}(3t)+C$ **21.** $-\frac{1}{3}\cos^3 x+C$ **22.** $-\frac{1}{2}\csc^2 x+C$ **23.** $-\frac{1}{4}\cot^4 x+C$ **24.** $\frac{1}{6}\tan^2 3x+C$ **25.** $\frac{1}{2}\ln|e^{2x}-e^{-2x}|+C$ **26.** $-\frac{1}{6}\cos^3 2x+C$ **27.** $-\frac{1}{4}(1+\cos\theta)^4+C$ **28.** $-\frac{1}{2}e^{-t^2}+C$ **29.** $\sec^{-1}|2t|+C$ **30.** $\sec^{-1}|e^x|+C$ **31.** $\ln|\sin x|+C$ **32.** $\ln|1+\sin x|+C$ **33.** $\frac{1}{3}\sec^3 x+C$ **34.** $-2\sqrt{1+\cos\theta}+C$ **35.** $\frac{1}{3}e^{\tan 3x}+C$ **36.** $-\frac{1}{3}(4-\sin 2t)^{3/2}+C$ **37.** $-\frac{1}{2}(\csc 2x+\cot 2x)+C$ **38.** $x-\frac{1}{2}\sin 2x+C$ **39.** $-\sqrt{1-\cot 2t}+C$ **40.** $\frac{1}{3}e^{3x}+C$ **41.** $\frac{1}{2}e^{\tan^{-1}2t}+C$ **42.** $-\frac{1}{2}e^{-x^2}+C$ **43.** $3^x/(\ln 3)+C$ **44.** $10^{2x}/(2\ln 10)+C$ **45.** Yes. Constants C differ; $\cos^{-1}(-x)=(\pi/2)+\sin^{-1}x$ **46. a)** $\pi/2$ **b)** $\pi/2$ **47. a)** -1; $\frac{1}{2}(\ln x)^2+C$ **b)** 2; $\frac{1}{3}e^{x^3}+C$ **c)** $-\frac{1}{2}$; $-2\cos\sqrt{x}+C$

Article 7–2, pp. 342–343

1. $\frac{2}{5}(\sin x)^{5/2}+C$ **2.** $-\frac{2}{3}(\cos x)^{3/2}+C$ **3.** $-\frac{2}{3}(1+\cos t)^{3/2}+C$ **4.** $\ln|2-\cos\theta|+C$ **5.** $\frac{1}{2}\ln|1+\tan 2x|+C$ **6.** $-\frac{1}{3}\ln|\cos 3x|+C$ **7.** $\sin x-\frac{1}{3}\sin^3 x+C$ **8.** $\frac{1}{4}\tan 4\theta-\theta+C$ **9. a)** $\frac{1}{5}\cos^5 x-\frac{1}{3}\cos^3 x+C$ **b)** $\cos x+\sec x+C$ **10.** $((\sec^n x)/n)+C$ if $n\neq 0$; $\ln|\sec x|+C$ if $n=0$ **11.** $[(\tan^{n+1}x)/(n+1)]+C$ if $n\neq -1$; $\ln|\tan x|+C$ if $n=-1$ **12.** $[(\sin^{n+1}x)/(n+1)]+C$ if $n\neq -1$; $\ln|\sin x|+C$ if $n=-1$ **13.** $[(-\cos^{n+1}x)/(n+1)]+C$ if $n\neq -1$; $-\ln|\cos x|+C$ if $n=-1$ **14.** $\frac{1}{9}\sin^3 3x+C$ **15.** $-\frac{1}{8}\cos^4 2x+C$ **16.** $\frac{1}{12}\sec^4 3x+C$ **17.** $\frac{1}{9}\tan^3 3x+\frac{1}{3}\tan 3x+C$ **18.** $\frac{1}{2}\sin 2x-\frac{1}{6}\sin^3 2x+C$ **19.** $\frac{1}{4}\tan^2 2x+\frac{1}{2}\ln|\cos 2x|+C$ **20.** $\frac{1}{3}\sec^3 x-\sec x+C$ **21.** $\frac{1}{3}\cos^3 x-\cos x+C$ **22.** $-1/(1+\sin x)+C$ **23.** $\ln|2+\tan x|+C$ **24.** $-\sin t-\csc t+C$ **25.** $\ln|1+e^x|+C$ **26.** $[(\ln ax)^{n+1}/(n+1)]+C$ if $n\neq -1$; $\ln|\ln ax|+C$ if $n=-1$ **27.** $\ln|\ln 3x|+C$ **28.** $-\ln|\sin x|-\frac{1}{2}\cot^2 x+C$ **29.** $-\frac{1}{6}\csc^3 2t+C$ **30.** $-\cot x-\frac{1}{3}\cot^3 x+C$ **31.** $\ln|\sec x+\tan x|+C$ **32.** $\ln|1+\sqrt{2}|\approx 0.8814$ **33.** $-\ln|\csc\theta+\cot\theta|+C$ **34. a)** $25\ln((\sqrt{3}+\sqrt{6})/3)\approx 8.302$ cm **b)** $25\ln((2+\sqrt{3})/(1+\sqrt{2}))\approx 10.890$ cm **35.** $(2\pi/27)[(1+9\sqrt[3]{4})^{3/2}-1]\approx 13.676$ **36.** $-(\cot^{n-1}(ax))/((n-1)a)-\int\cot^{n-2}(ax)\,dx$; $-[(\cot^3 3x)/9]+[(\cot 3x)/3]+x+C$ **37.** $\ln(2+\sqrt{3})\approx 1.317$

Article 7–3, p. 345

1. $(x/8)-[(\sin 4x)/32]+C$ **2.** $(y/16)-[(\sin 4y)/64]-[(\sin^3 2y)/48]+C$ **3.** $(t/2)-\frac{1}{8}\sin 4t+C$ **4.** $(\theta/2)+\frac{1}{12}\sin 6\theta+C$ **5.** $\frac{3}{8}x-(1/4a)\sin 2ax+(1/32a)\sin 4ax+C$ **6.** $\tan x-\frac{3}{2}x+[(\sin 2x)/4]+C$ **7.** $\tan x+C$ **8.** $-\frac{1}{3}\cot^3 x-\cot x+C$

9. $-\frac{1}{6}\csc^3 2t + C$ **10.** $\frac{5}{16}x - \frac{1}{4}\sin 2x + \frac{3}{64}\sin 4x + \frac{1}{48}\sin^3 2x + C$ **11.** 4 **12.** $2\sqrt{2}$ **13.** 2/5 **14.** 8 **15.** $64\pi/3$ **16.** $\pi^2/2$

Article 7–4, p. 352

1. $0.2a$ **2.** $\frac{1}{2}\sin^{-1} 2x + C$ **3.** $\pi a^2/4$ **4.** $\sin^{-1}((x-1)/2) + C$ **5.** $\frac{1}{2}\ln|\sec 2t + \tan 2t| + C$ **6.** $\ln(1+\sqrt{2}) \approx 0.88$ **7.** $\pi/6$ **8.** $\sqrt{4+x^2} + C$ **9.** $\frac{1}{2}\ln 2$ **10.** $\pi/8$ **11.** $\frac{1}{4}\ln 3 = 0.2747$ **12.** $(2-\sqrt{2})/3$ **13.** $(1/a)\ln|x/(a+\sqrt{a^2+x^2})| + C$ **14.** $-\sqrt{4-x^2} + \sin^{-1}(x/2) + C$ **15.** $(1/\sqrt{5})\sin^{-1}(x\sqrt{\frac{5}{3}}) + C$ **16.** $\cos^{-1}((\cos\theta)/\sqrt{2}) + C$ **17.** $(1/|a|)\sec^{-1}|x/a| + C$ **18.** $(1/a)\ln|x/(a+\sqrt{a^2-x^2})| + C$ **19.** $(1/a^2)(x/\sqrt{a^2-x^2}) + C$ **20.** $(1/2a^3)(\tan^{-1}(x/a) + ax/(a^2+x^2)) + C$ **21.** $3\pi/4$ **22.** $2\sqrt{2}$ **23.** $\cos\theta = \sqrt{1-(u^2/4)} = \frac{1}{2}\sqrt{4-u^2}$; $\tan\theta = u/\sqrt{4-u^2}$ **24. a)** $u/\sqrt{a^2+u^2}$ **b)** a/u

Article 7–5, p. 355

1. $\pi/8$ **2.** $\sqrt{x^2-2x+5} + \ln|x-1+\sqrt{x^2-2x+5}| + C$ **3.** $2\sin^{-1}(x-1) - \sqrt{2x-x^2} + C$ **4.** $\sqrt{x^2-4x+3} + \ln|x-2+\sqrt{x^2-4x+3}| + C$ **5.** $2\sin^{-1}[(x-2)/3] - \sqrt{5+4x-x^2} + C$ **6.** $\ln|x-1+\sqrt{x^2-2x-8}| + C$ **7.** $\sqrt{8+2x-x^2} + C$ **8.** $\sqrt{x^2+4x+5} - 2\ln|x+2+\sqrt{x^2+4x+5}| + C$ **9.** $\frac{1}{2}\ln(x^2+4x+5) - 2\tan^{-1}(x+2) + C$ **10.** $\frac{1}{4}\ln(4x^2+4x+5) + \frac{1}{2}\tan^{-1}(x+\frac{1}{2}) + C$

Article 7–6, pp. 362–363

1. $\frac{1}{2}\ln|(x+1)/(x-1)| + C$ **2.** $-[(\ln|\theta|)/2] + [(\ln|\theta+2|)/6] + [(\ln|\theta-1|)/3] + C$ **3.** $\frac{1}{6}\ln|(x+5)^5(x-1)| + C$ **4.** $\frac{3}{4}\ln|x-3| + \frac{1}{4}\ln|x+1| + C$ **5.** $\frac{2}{3}\ln|x+5| + \frac{1}{3}\ln|x-1| + C$ **6.** $x - 2\ln|x+1| - [1/(x+1)] + C$ **7.** $\ln|x/(x+1)| + [1/(x+1)] + C$ **8.** $\frac{1}{4}\ln[(x+1)^2/(x^2+1)] + \frac{1}{2}\tan^{-1}x + C$ **9.** $-\frac{3}{8}\ln|x| + \frac{1}{16}\ln|x+2| + \frac{5}{16}\ln|x-2| + C$ **10.** $-\frac{1}{5}\ln|\sin x + 3| + \frac{1}{5}\ln|\sin x - 2| + C$ **11.** $5x - 5\tan^{-1}x + C$ **12.** $(x^2/2) + 2x + 3\ln|x-1| - [1/(x-1)] + C$ **13.** $\frac{1}{2}\ln[x^2/(x^2+x+1)] - (1/\sqrt{3})\tan^{-1}((2x+1)/\sqrt{3}) + C$ **14.** $\frac{1}{3}\ln[(2+\cos\theta)/(1-\cos\theta)] + C$ **15.** $\ln[(1+e^t)/(2+e^t)] + C$ **16.** $\frac{1}{2}(\tan^{-1}x + [x/(1+x^2)]) + C$ **17.** $x - \frac{3}{2}\tan^{-1}x + \frac{1}{2}[x/(1+x^2)] + C$ **18.** $\ln|x+1| + \ln|x-1| + \ln|x-3| + \ln|x+3| + C$ **19.** Using first method, there is no equation for the coefficient of x^2. Using Heaviside method, one gets $A = \frac{1}{2}$, $B = -\frac{1}{2}$, yet result is not equivalent to $x^2/(x^2-1)$. **20.** If $a = b$: $x = a - (a-x_0)/[1+kt(a-x_0)]$. If $a \neq b$: $\ln|(a-x)/(b-x)| = (a-b)kt + \ln|(a-x_0)/(b-x_0)|$.

Article 7–7, pp. 367–368

1. $(x^2/2)\ln x - (x^2/4) + C$ **2.** $[x^{n+1}/(n+1)]\ln ax - [x^{n+1}/((n+1)^2)] + C$ **3.** $[(x^2+1)/2]\tan^{-1}x - (x/2) + C$ **4.** $x\sin^{-1}ax + (1/a)\sqrt{1-a^2x^2} + C$ **5.** $(1/a^2)\sin ax - (1/a)x\cos ax + C$ **6.** $(2x/a^2)\cos ax - (2/a^3)\sin ax + (x^2/a)\sin ax + C$ **7.** $(x/a)\tan ax - (1/a^2)\ln|\sec ax| + C$ **8.** $[e^{ax}/(a^2+b^2)](a\sin bx - b\cos bx) + C$ **9.** $(x/2)[\sin(\ln x) - \cos(\ln x)] + C$ **10.** $(x/2)[\sin(\ln x) + \cos(\ln x)] + C$ **11.** $x\ln(a^2+x^2) - 2x + 2a\tan^{-1}(x/a) + C$ **12.** $(x/2)\sin(2x+1) + \frac{1}{4}\cos(2x+1) + C$ **13.** $((x^2/2) - \frac{1}{4})\sin^{-1}x + (x/4)\sqrt{1-x^2} + C$ **14.** $(4\pi - 3\sqrt{3})/6$ **15.** $(4\pi - 3\sqrt{3})/3$ **16.** $(x^3/3)\tan^{-1}x - (x^2/6) + \frac{1}{6}\ln(x^2+1) + C$ **17. b)** $(x^4/32)[8(\ln x)^2 - 4\ln x + 1] + C$ **18. b)** $\pi/16$ **19. b)** $(x^3 - 3x^2 + 6x - 6)e^x + C$ **20. b)** $\frac{1}{2}(\sec x\tan x + \ln|\sec x + \tan x|) + C$ **c)** $\frac{1}{2}(x\sqrt{x^2+a^2} + a^2\ln|x+\sqrt{x^2+a^2}|) + C$ **21.** $P(x) = 1 - 3x^2$ **22.** $\pi^2 - 2\pi$ **23.** $\bar{x} = (-2e+6)/(e-2)$; $\bar{y} = (e^2-3)/[8(e-2)]$ **24.** $\bar{x} = (e^2-3)/4(e-2) \approx 1.53$; $\bar{y} = 1/2(e-2) \approx 0.696$ **25.** 2

Article 7–8, p. 371

1. 2 **2.** 1 **3.** $\tan x + \sec x + C$ **4.** $\pi/3\sqrt{3}$ **5.** $(4/\sqrt{3})\tan^{-1}(\sqrt{3}\tan(x/2)) - x + C$ **6.** $-\frac{2}{5}$ **7.** 0 **8.** π

Article 7–9, p. 374

1. $-x + 4\sqrt{x} - 4\ln|1+\sqrt{x}| + C$ **2.** $(2\sqrt{x}/b) - (2a/b^2)\ln|a+b\sqrt{x}| + C$ **3.** $[2(x+a)^{3/2}/105](15x^2 - 12ax + 8a^2) + C$ **4.** $2\sqrt{x-a} - 2\sqrt{b-a}\tan^{-1}\sqrt{(x-a)(b-a)} + C$ **5.** $[(b-a)/2](\ln|(u-1)/(u+1)| - 2u/(u^2-1)) + C$, where $u = \sqrt{(a+x)/(b+x)}$ **6.** $\frac{1}{2}\ln|x+\sqrt{x^2+a^2}| + [(x\sqrt{a^2+x^2} - x^2)/2a^2] + C$ **7.** $(3\sqrt{2} - 4)/2$ **8.** $(1/nc)\ln|x^n/(ax^n+c)| + C$ **9.** $2 + 2\ln(\frac{3}{2})$ **10.** $3\ln|\sqrt[3]{x} - 1| + C$ **11.** $-1 + 4\ln(\frac{3}{2})$ **12.** $4\ln|\sqrt[4]{x}/(1-\sqrt[4]{x})| + C$ **13.** $\frac{3}{2}y^{2/3} + \ln|1+y^{1/3}| - \frac{1}{2}\ln|y^{2/3} - y^{1/3} + 1| - \sqrt{3}\tan^{-1}((2y^{1/3}-1)/\sqrt{3}) + C$ **14.** $\frac{2}{9}(z^3-2)\sqrt{z^3+1} + C$ **15.** $\frac{2}{3}(\sqrt{t^3-1} - \tan^{-1}\sqrt{t^3-1}) + C$ **16.** $\ln(\frac{4}{3})$ **17.** $2 + 4\ln(\frac{2}{3})$ **18.** $-\frac{1}{2}\ln|\sin x + \cos^2 x| - [1/(2\sqrt{5})]\ln|(2\sin x - 1 - \sqrt{5})/(2\sin x - 1 + \sqrt{5})| + C$ **19.** $\frac{1}{3}\ln|x+1| - \frac{1}{6}\ln|x^2-x+1| + (1/\sqrt{3})\tan^{-1}((2x-1)/\sqrt{3}) + C$ **20.** $-2y^{1/2} - 3y^{1/3} - 6y^{1/6} - 6\ln|y^{1/6} - 1| + C$

Article 7–10, p. 382

1. $\pi/2$ **2.** 2 **3.** 6 **4.** 1000 **5.** 4 **6.** $\pi/2$ **7.** $\frac{1}{2}$ **8.** 1000 **9.** Diverges **10.** Converges **11.** Converges **12.** Diverges **13.** Converges **14.** Converges **15.** Diverges **16.** Diverges **17.** Converges **18.** Diverges **19.** Converges **20.** 0.88617 **21.** π **23.** 5000 dollars **24.** $r = [(\ln(\frac{4}{3}))/5]$ ($\approx 5.75\%$) **25. a)** $100/(0.05 - \ln 0.95)$ (≈ 987.23) dollars **b)** 2000 dollars

Miscellaneous Problems Chapter 7, pp. 383–386

1. $2\sqrt{1+\sin x} + C$ **2.** $(\sin^{-1} x)^2/2 + C$ **3.** $(\tan^2 x)/2 + C$ **4.** $\tan x + \sec x + C$ **5.** $(2x^{3/2})/3 + C$ **6.** $2 \sin \sqrt{x} + C$ **7.** $\ln|x + 1 + \sqrt{x^2+2x+2}| + C$ **8.** $\ln|(x-2)(x-3)/(x-1)^2| + C$ **9.** $(x^2 - 2x + 2)e^x + C$ **10.** $\frac{1}{2}(\ln|x + \sqrt{x^2+1}| + x\sqrt{1+x^2}) + C$ **11.** $\tan^{-1}(e^t) + C$ **12.** $\tan^{-1}(e^x) + C$ **13.** $2\sqrt{x} - 2\ln(1+\sqrt{x}) + C$ **14.** $\frac{4}{3}(\sqrt{x}-2)\sqrt{1+\sqrt{x}} + C$ **15.** $\frac{9}{25}(t^{5/3}+1)^{5/3} + C$ **16.** $\ln|\ln \sin x| + C$ **17.** $\ln[(\sqrt{1+e^t}-1)/(\sqrt{1+e^t}+1)] + C$ **18.** $t + 2\ln(1 + \sqrt{1-e^{-t}}) + C$ **19.** $e^{\sec x} + C$ **20.** $\tan^{-1}(\sin x) + C$ **21.** $\sin^{-1}(x-1) + C$ **22.** $\cot^{-1}(\cos x) + C$ **23.** $\frac{1}{2}\ln|1 + \sin 2t| + C$ **24.** $\ln|\tan x| + C$ **25.** $(-2\cos x)/\sqrt{1+\sin x} + C$ **26.** $(2\cos x)/\sqrt{1-\sin x} + C$ **27.** $x/(a^2\sqrt{a^2-x^2}) + C$ **28.** $x/(a^2\sqrt{a^2+x^2}) + C$ **29.** $\frac{1}{3}\ln[(1-\cos x)/(4-\cos x)] + C$ **30.** $\frac{3}{10}(2e^x - 3)(1+e^x)^{2/3} + C$ **31.** $\sum_{k=0}^{m} [(-1)^k/(k!\,(m-k)!)] \ln|x+k| + C$ **32.** $\frac{1}{12}\ln[(x-1)^2(x^2-x+1)/((x+1)^2(x^2+x+1))] - (\sqrt{3}/6)\tan^{-1}(x\sqrt{3}/(1-x^2)) + C$ **33.** $\frac{1}{3}[(2y^3+1)^{-1} + \ln|2y^3/(2y^3+1)|] + C$ **34.** $\frac{2}{3}x^{3/2} - x + 2x^{1/2} - 2\ln(1+x^{1/2}) + C$ **35.** $\frac{1}{2}[\ln x^2 - \ln(1+x^2) - x^2(1+x^2)^{-1}] + C$ **36.** $(x-1)\ln\sqrt{x-1} - (x/2) + C$ **37.** $\ln|e^x - 1| - x + C$ **38.** $\frac{1}{4}\ln|(1+\tan\theta)/(1-\tan\theta)| + \frac{1}{2}\theta + C$ **39.** $x^{-1} + 2\ln|1 - x^{-1}| + C$ **40.** $\frac{1}{2}\ln|(x+3)^3(x+1)^{-1}| + C$ **41.** $-\frac{1}{2}[1/(e^{2u}-1)] + C$ **42.** $\ln|x/\sqrt{x^2+4}| + C$ **43.** $\frac{1}{3}\tan^{-1}[(5x+4)/3] + C$ **44.** $\sqrt{x^2-a^2} - a\tan^{-1}(\sqrt{x^2-a^2}/a) + C$ **45.** $e^x(\cos 2x + 2\sin 2x)/5 + C$ **46.** $\ln x - 2\ln(1+3\sqrt{x}) + C$ **47.** $\ln|x| - 3\ln|1+\sqrt[3]{x}| + C$ **48.** $\ln|\sin\theta| - \frac{1}{2}\ln(1+\sin^2\theta) + C$ **49.** $\frac{1}{15}(8 - 4z^2 + 3z^4)(1+z^2)^{1/2} + C$ **50.** $\frac{3}{8}(e^{2t} - 3) \times (1+e^{2t})^{1/3} + C$ **51.** $\frac{5}{2}(1+x^{4/5})^{1/2} + C$ **52.** $x\tan x + \ln|\cos x| + C$ **53.** $\frac{1}{4}[(2x^2-1)\sin^{-1} x + x\sqrt{1-x^2}] + C$ **54.** $(x^2/2) + \frac{4}{3}\ln|x+2| + \frac{2}{3}\ln|x-1| + C$ **55.** $x + \ln|(x-1)/x| + C$ **56.** $\ln|x-1| - (x-1)^{-1} + C$ **57.** $\frac{2}{3}(3e^{2x} - 6e^x - 1)^{1/2} + (1/\sqrt{3})\ln|e^x - 1 + \sqrt{e^{2x} - 2e^x - \frac{1}{3}}| + C$ **58.** $\frac{3}{2}(x^2+2x-3)^{1/3} + C$ **59.** $\tan^{-1}(2\sqrt{y^2+y}) + C$ **60.** $-\sqrt{a^2-x^2}/a^2x + C$ **61.** $\frac{3}{8}\sin^{-1} x + \frac{1}{8}(5x - 2x^3)\sqrt{1-x^2} + C$ **62.** $x\ln(x + \sqrt{1+x^2}) - \sqrt{1+x^2} + C$ **63.** $x\tan x - (x^2/2) + \ln|\cos x| + C$ **64.** $-(\tan^{-1} x)/x + \ln|x| - \ln\sqrt{1+x^2} + C$ **65.** $(x^2/4) + [(x\sin 2x)/4] + [(\cos 2x)/8] + C$ **66.** $-x^2\cos x + 2x\sin x + 2\cos x + C$ **67.** $(x^2/4) - [(x\sin 2x)/4] - [(\cos 2x)/8] + C$ **68.** $\frac{1}{2}\tan^{-1} t - [1/(2\sqrt{3})]\tan^{-1}(t/\sqrt{3}) + C$ **69.** $\frac{1}{12}[4u - 3\ln(1+e^{2u}) + \ln(3+e^{2u})] + C$ **70.** $\frac{1}{4}(x^2-4)\ln(x+2) - x^2/8 + x/2 + C$ **71.** $(x^2+1)e^x + C$ **72.** $x\sec^{-1} x - \ln(|x| + \sqrt{x^2-1}) + C$ **73.** $-2x^{-2} + 2x^{-1} + \ln|x/(x+2)| + C$ **74.** $\frac{1}{16}\ln|(x^2-4)/(x^2+4)| + C$ **75.** $2 - \sqrt{2}\ln(1+\sqrt{2})$ **76.** $\ln|\cot x| + C$ **77.** $-\frac{1}{2}[1/(e^{2u}+1)] + C$ **78.** $x - 2\sqrt{x} + (4/\sqrt{3})\tan^{-1}((1+2\sqrt{x})/\sqrt{3}) + C$ **79.** $\ln|\tan t - 2| - \ln|\tan t - 1| + C$ **80.** $-t + \sqrt{2}\tan^{-1}(\sqrt{2}\tan t) + C$ **81.** $(1/\sqrt{2})\tan^{-1}((\tan x)/\sqrt{2}) + C$ **82.** $e^t\sin(e^t) + \cos(e^t) + C$ **83.** $x\ln\sqrt{x^2+1} - x + \tan^{-1} x + C$ **84.** $\frac{1}{2}x^2\ln(x^3+x) - \frac{3}{4}x^2 + \frac{1}{2}\ln(x^2+1) + C$ **85.** $\frac{1}{2}(x^2-1)e^{x^2} + C$ **86.** $\ln|\sin x + \sqrt{3+\sin^2 x}| + C$ **87.** $\sin^{-1}(3^{-(1/2)}\tan x) + C$ **88.** $(x^2-2)\cos(1-x) + 2x\sin(1-x) + C$ **89.** $\tan x - \sec x + C$ **90.** $3^{-(1/2)}[\ln|1 + 2\sin x| - \ln|2 + \sin x + \sqrt{3}\cos x|] + C$ **91.** $-\frac{1}{2}\cot x\csc x + \frac{1}{4}\ln[(1-\cos x)/(1+\cos x)] + C$ **92.** $\frac{1}{2}\tan^2 x + \ln|\cos x| + C$ **93.** $x(\sin^{-1} x)^2 - 2x + 2\sqrt{1-x^2} \times \sin^{-1} x + C$ **94.** $\frac{1}{54}(9x^2-1)\ln|3x+1| - x^2/12 + x/18 + C$ **95.** $\frac{1}{2}\ln(x^2+1) + \frac{1}{2}(x^2+1)^{-1} + C$ **96.** $-\frac{2}{3}(x+2) \times \sqrt{1-x} + C$ **97.** $\frac{1}{15}(3x-1)(2x+1)^{3/2} + C$ **98.** $x\ln(x + \sqrt{x^2-1}) - \sqrt{x^2-1} + C$ **99.** $x\ln(x - \sqrt{x^2-1}) + \sqrt{x^2-1} + C$ **100.** $\frac{1}{2}\ln|t - \sqrt{1-t^2}| - \frac{1}{2}\sin^{-1} t + C$ **101.** $x - e^{-x}\tan^{-1}(e^x) - \frac{1}{2}\ln(1+e^{2x}) + C$ **102.** $\frac{1}{2}(x-x^2)^{1/2} - \frac{1}{4}(1-2x)\sin^{-1}\sqrt{x} + C$ **103.** $x\ln(x+\sqrt{x}) - x + \sqrt{x} - \ln(1+\sqrt{x}) + C$ **104.** $(x+1)\tan^{-1}\sqrt{x} - \sqrt{x} + C$ **105.** $x\ln(x^2+x) + \ln(x+1) - 2x + C$ **106.** $(x+\frac{1}{2})\ln(\sqrt{x} + \sqrt{1+x}) - \frac{1}{2}\sqrt{x^2+x} + C$ **107.** $2\sqrt{x}\sin\sqrt{x} + 2\cos\sqrt{x} + C$ **108.** $-2\sqrt{x}\cos\sqrt{x} + 2\sin\sqrt{x} + C$ **109.** $(x+2)\tan^{-1}\sqrt{x+1} - \sqrt{x+1} + C$ **110.** $\frac{1}{4}(\sin^{-1} x)^2 + \frac{1}{2}x\sqrt{1-x^2}\sin^{-1} x - x^2/4 + C$ **111.** $\frac{1}{4}x^2 - \frac{1}{8}x\sin 4x - \frac{1}{32}\cos 4x + C$ **112.** $\sec x - \tan x + x + C$ **113.** $\ln(\sqrt{e^{2t}+1} - 1) - t + C$ **114.** $\ln[(1-\sin x)^{1/2}(1+\sin x)^{-(1/18)}(2-\sin x)^{-(4/9)}] + 1/(6 - 3\sin x) + C$ **115.** $(1/ac)\ln|e^{ct}/(a+be^{ct})| + C$ **116.** $-2\sin^{-1}[(\cos(x/2))/(\cos(\alpha/2))] + C$ **117.** $(1/\sqrt{2})\ln|\csc(x - (\pi/4)) - \cot(x - (\pi/4))| + C$ **118.** $x\ln\sqrt{1+x^2} - x + \tan^{-1} x + C$ **119.** $x\ln(2x^2+4) + 2\sqrt{2}\tan^{-1}(x/\sqrt{2}) - 2x + C$ **120.** $-\frac{1}{3}(1-x^2)^{1/2}(2+x^2) + C$ **121.** $\ln|2 + \ln x| + C$ **122.** $x - \tan x + C$ **123.** $\frac{1}{3}\ln|x+1| - \frac{1}{6}\ln(x^2-x+1) + (1/\sqrt{3})\tan^{-1}[(2x-1)/\sqrt{3}] + C$ **124.** $\frac{4}{21}(e^x+1)^{3/4}(3e^x-4) + C$ **125.** $\tan^{-1}(e^x) + C$ **126.** $2e^{\sqrt{t}}(\sqrt{t}-1) + C$ **127.** $-2\sqrt{x+1}\cos\sqrt{x+1} + 2\sin\sqrt{x+1} + C$ **128.** $-2\sqrt{1-x}\sin\sqrt{1-x} - 2\cos\sqrt{1-x} + C$ **129.** $\ln 2$ **130.** $2\sqrt{2} - 2$ **131.** $2/\pi$ **132.** $e - 1$ **133.** $\pi/4$ **134.** $2\ln 2 - 1$ **135.** $\pi/2$ **136.** $\frac{1}{2}$ **137.** -1 **139.** e^{-4} **140.** $4p^2(2\sqrt{2}-1)/3$ **141.** Area $(\pi - 2)r^2/4$; centroid $2r\sqrt{2}/(3\pi - 6)$ from center. **142.** $(1/(2e-4), (e^2-3)/(4e-8)) \approx (0.7, 1.5)$ **143.** $2\pi^2kr^2$ **144.** $w(3e^8 - 20e^4 + 9)/4 \approx$ 123,000 lb **145.** Integrals for A, V, and S converge. $A = 1$, $V = \pi/2$, $S = \pi[\sqrt{2} + \ln(1+\sqrt{2})]$. **146.** About 2

147. About 23 **148.** About 6.8 **149.** About 175 **150.** $2\pi[\sqrt{2} + \ln(1 + \sqrt{2})] \approx 14.4$ **151.** 1.9100989
152. (0, 0.6) for arch $|x| \leq \pi/2$ **153.** 2π **154.** $6a$ **155.** $12\pi a^2/5$ **156.** $(2a/5, 2a/5)$ for first-quadrant arch **157.** Converges, compare with $\int_1^\infty x^{-(3/2)}\,dx$ **158. c)** $1 - e^{-e^b}$ **d)** 1 **160.** Converges **161.** $x = a \cos kt$ **162.** $\frac{1}{2}$

CHAPTER 8

Article 8–1, p. 394

1.

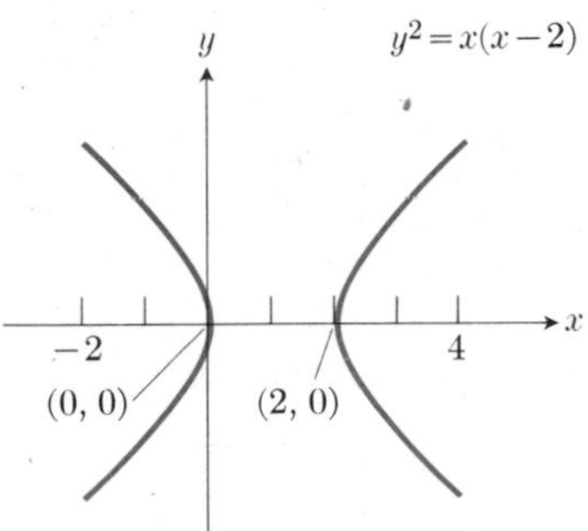

a) About the x-axis **b)** No curve for $0 < x < 2$ **c)** (0, 0), (2, 0) **e)** ∞

2.

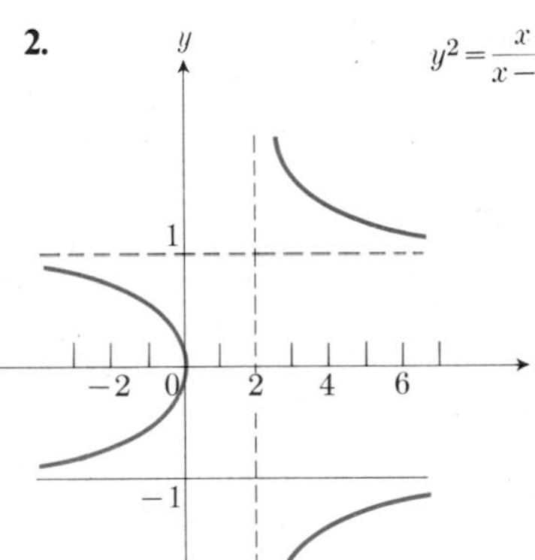

a) About the x-axis **b)** No curve for $0 < x \leq 2$ **c)** (0, 0) **d)** $y = \pm 1$; $x = 2$ **e)** ∞

3.

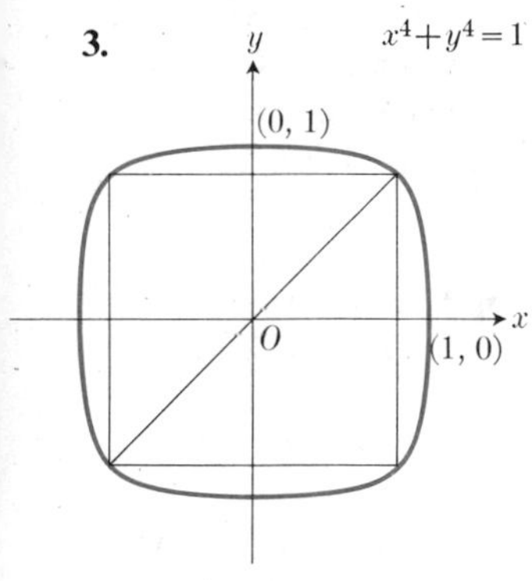

a) About both axes, the origin and the line $y = x$ **b)** Curve is inside the square $|x| \leq 1$, $|y| \leq 1$ **c)** $(0, \pm 1)$, $(\pm 1, 0)$ **e)** Slope is 0 at $(0, \pm 1)$, ∞ at $(\pm 1, 0)$

4.

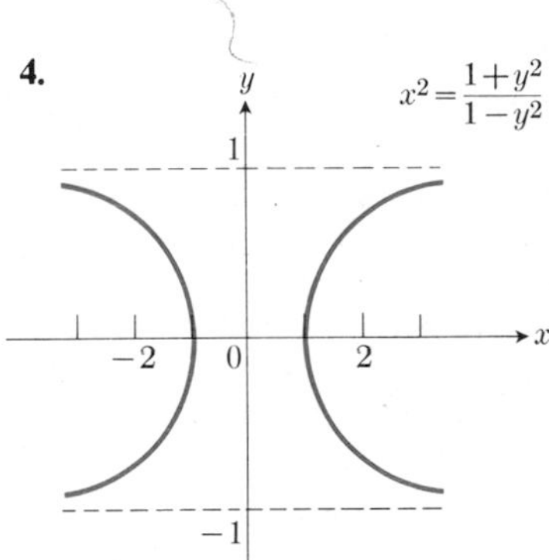

a) About both axes, and the origin. **b)** No curve for $|y| \geq 1$. No curve for $|x| < 1$ **c)** $(\pm 1, 0)$ **d)** $y = \pm 1$ **e)** ∞

5.

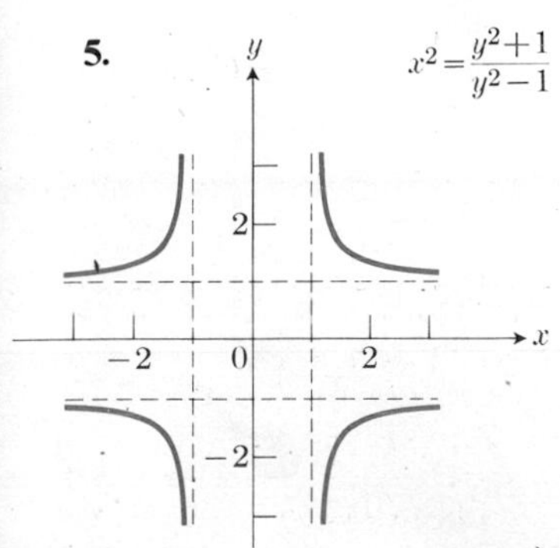

a) About both axes and the origin and $y = x$ **b)** No curve for $|y| \leq 1$. No curve for $|x| \leq 1$ **c)** No intercepts **d)** $x = \pm 1$; $y = \pm 1$

6.

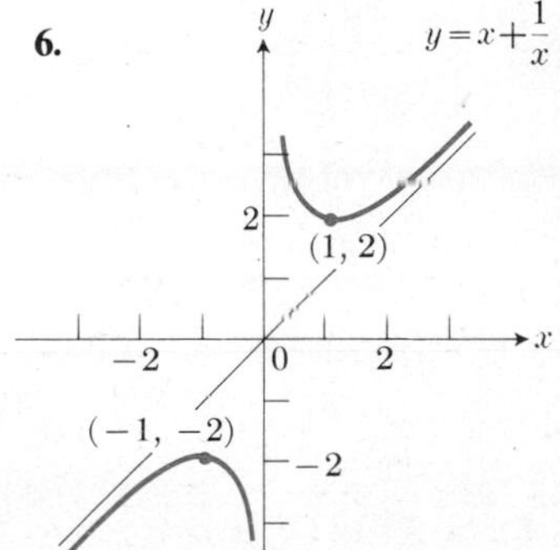

a) About the origin **b)** No curve for $|y| < 2$ **c)** No intercepts **d)** $x = 0$; $y = x$ is also an asymptote **e)** Low point at (1, 2); high point at $(-1, -2)$

7.

a) About the y-axis
b) Curve is confined to $y \geq 1$
c) $(0, 1)$
e) 0

8.

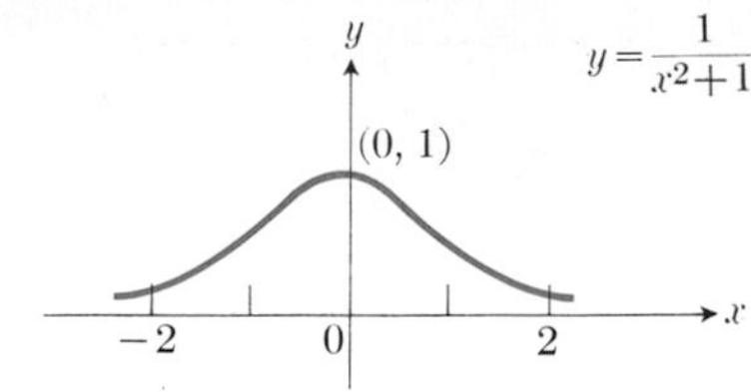

a) About the y-axis
b) $0 < y \leq 1$
c) $(0, 1)$
d) $y = 0$
e) 0

9.

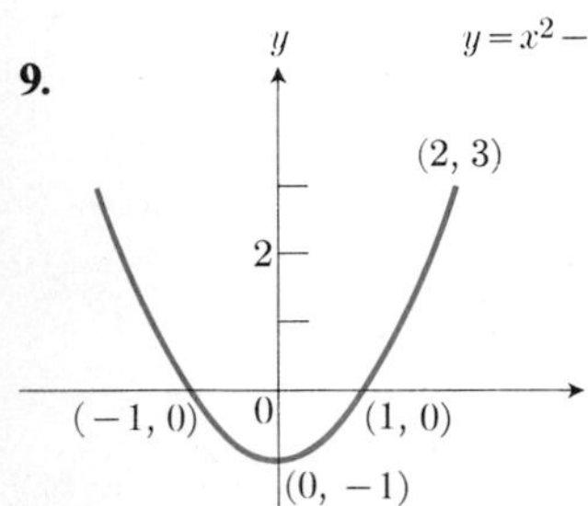

a) About the y-axis
b) $y \geq -1$
c) $(0, -1)$; $(\pm 1, 0)$
e) 0; ± 2

10.

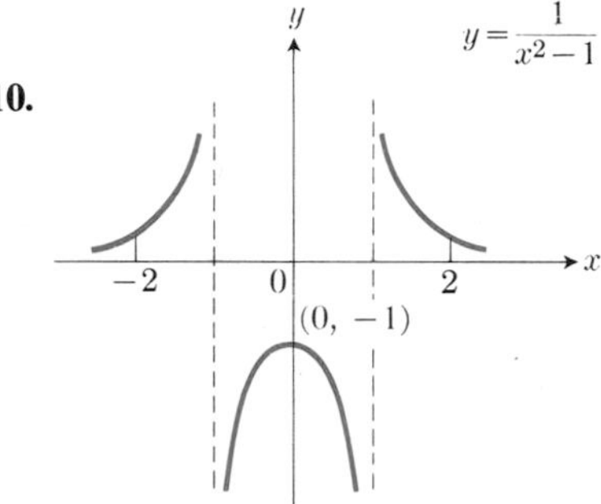

a) About the y-axis
b) No curve for $-1 < y \leq 0$ c) $(0, -1)$ d) $x = \pm 1$; $y = 0$ e) 0

Article 8–2, pp. 398–399

1. $x + y + 1 = 0$ **2.** $x + 2y = 7$ **3.** $6x - y = 14$; $y - 6x = 18$ **4.** $2x + y = \pm 3$ **5.** Lines are: $y = 2x - 3$, $y = -\frac{1}{2}x + \frac{3}{4}$ **7.** Yes, $(-2, -8)$ **8.** $(-1, -1)$. No, because $2x_1^3 - 3x_1^2 + 5 = 0$ and this equation has only one real root. **9.** $2x + 3y = \pm 12$ **10.** $x + y = 1$; $4x + y = -2$ **11.** $(-\frac{13}{4}, \frac{17}{16})$ **15.** ± 16 **16.** $\pm 1/\sqrt{3}$ **17.** $A = \tan^{-1}(\frac{5}{3})$, $B = \tan^{-1} 5$, $C = \tan^{-1}(\frac{10}{11})$ **18.** $(-5 + \sqrt{221})/14 \approx 0.705$ **20.** $\tan A = 7$, $\tan B = \frac{7}{9}$, $\tan C = \frac{7}{4}$ **21.** **a)** $45°$ **b)** $\tan^{-1} 3$ **c)** $\tan^{-1}(5/\sqrt{3})$ **d)** $\tan^{-1}(\frac{14}{3})$

Article 8–3, p. 400

1. $x - y = 1$ **2.** $x^2 + y^2 - 6x + 5 = 0$ **3.** $(x^2 + y^2)^2 + 8(y^2 - x^2) = 0$ **4.** $3x^2 + 3y^2 + 2xy - 4x - 4y = 0$ **5.** $3x^2 + 4y^2 - 20x + 12 = 0$ **6.** $5x^2 - 4y^2 = 20$ (right half only) **7.** $x^2 = 10 - 2y + 6|y - 1|$; or $x^2 = 4y + 4$ when $y \geq 1$, and $x^2 = 16 - 8y$ when $y < 1$. **8.** $x^2 + y^2 - 4x - 6y + 4 = 0$ **9.** $(2, 2)$; $\sqrt{5}$ **10.** $|Ax_1 + By_1 + C|/\sqrt{A^2 + B^2}$

Article 8–4, p. 404

1. $x^2 + y^2 - 4y = 0$ **2.** $x^2 + y^2 + 4x = 5$ **3.** $x^2 + y^2 - 6x + 8y = 0$ **4.** $x^2 + y^2 - 2x - 2y = 0$ **5.** $x^2 + y^2 + 4x + 2y < 1$ **6.** $x^2 + y^2 + 8x - 4y > -4$ **7.** $(0, 1)$; 2 **8.** $(-1, 0)$; 3 **9.** $(-1, 0)$; $2/\sqrt{3}$ **10.** $(-\frac{1}{4}, -\frac{1}{4})$; $1/(2\sqrt{2})$ **11.** $(-1, 2)$ **12.** All points in cartesian plane. **13.** $x^2 + y^2 - 4x - 4y = 5$ **14.** $5x^2 + 5y^2 + 10x - 10y + 1 = 0$ **15.** $(x - 0.7)^2 + (y - 1.3)^2 = 12.58$ **17.** $x^2 + y^2 + 2x + 2y - 23 = 0$ **18.** Circle, with center $(-2, 3)$, and radius 4. **19.** Center of circle is $(1, 2)$; radius $\sqrt{2}$. Distance of $(0.1, 3.1)$ from center is $\sqrt{2.02}$. Point is outside the circle. **20.** Center $(-2, 4)$, radius $2\sqrt{5}$. **21.** Center $(-1, 1)$, radius 5. **24.** **a)** $C_1 = -2h$, $C_2 = -2k$, $C_3 = h^2 + k^2 - r^2$ **b)** $h = -C_1/2$, $k = -C_2/2$, $r = \sqrt{(C_1^2 + C_2^2 - 4C_3)/4}$

Article 8–5, pp. 410–411

1. $x^2 = 8y$; $y = -2$ **2.** $y^2 = -8x$; $x = 2$ **3.** $(x + 2)^2 = 4(y - 3)$; $y = 2$ **4.** $(y - 3)^2 = -4x$; $x = 1$ **5.** $(y - 1)^2 = 12(x + 3)$; $x = -6$ **6.** $(x - 1)^2 = 12(y + 3)$; $y = -6$ **7.** $y^2 = 8(x - 2)$; $F(4, 0)$ **8.** $(x - 1)^2 = -8(y + 2)$; $F(1, -4)$ **9.** $(y - 1)^2 = -16(x + 3)$; $F(-7, 1)$ **10.** $(x + 2)^2 = 4(y + 2)$; $F(-2, -1)$ **11.** $(y - 1)^2 = 4x$; $F(1, 1)$ **12.** $x^2 = -4(y - 1)$; $F(0, 0)$ **13.** $V(1, 1)$; $x = 1$; $F(1, -1)$; $y = 3$ **14.** $V(-4, -3)$; $x = -4$; $F(-4, -\frac{5}{2})$; $y = -\frac{7}{2}$ **15.** $V(2, 0)$; $y = 0$; $F(1, 0)$; $x = 3$ **16.** $V(0, -\frac{1}{2})$; $x = 0$; $F(0, \frac{3}{2})$; $y = -\frac{5}{2}$ **17.** $V(-1, -1)$; $x = -1$; $F(-1, 0)$; $y = -2$ **18.** $V(\frac{1}{4}, -\frac{1}{2})$; $y = -\frac{1}{2}$; $F(0, -\frac{1}{2})$; $x = \frac{1}{2}$ **19.** $V(2, 1)$; $y = 1$; $F(\frac{29}{16}, 1)$; $x = \frac{35}{16}$ **20.** $V(2, -3)$; $y = -3$; $F(\frac{3}{2}, -3)$; $x = \frac{5}{2}$ **21.** $V(2, -2)$; $x = 2$; $F(2, -\frac{4}{3})$; $y = -\frac{8}{3}$

22. $V(-3, -1)$; $y = -1$; $F(-\frac{21}{8}, -1)$; $x = -\frac{27}{8}$ **23.** Points above parabola $x^2 = 8y$ **24. b)** $\frac{5}{3}$ dollars/lb; 10 lbs/person
25. a) $x = 125 - \frac{1}{5}p^2$
b) \$14.43

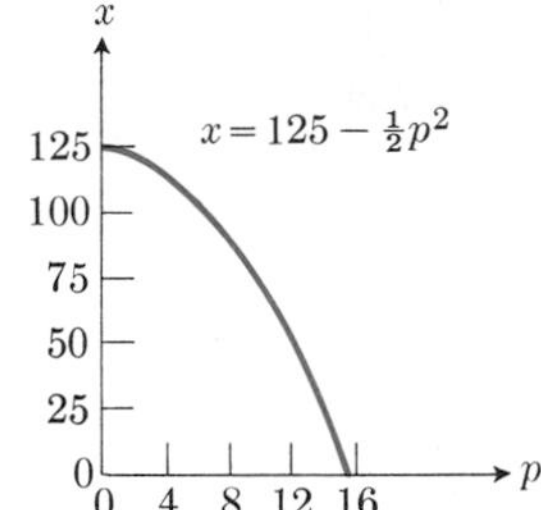

26. $4p$ **27.** $b^2y = 4hx(b - x)$ **28. a)** $7y^2 - 3y + 6x - 16 = 0$ **b)** $7x^2 - 9x - 6y - 4 = 0$
30. The points of the line $2x + y - 3 = 0$, the circle $x^2 + y^2 - 4 = 0$, and the parabola $x^2 - 8y = 0$. The product is zero if and only if at least one factor is zero.
37.

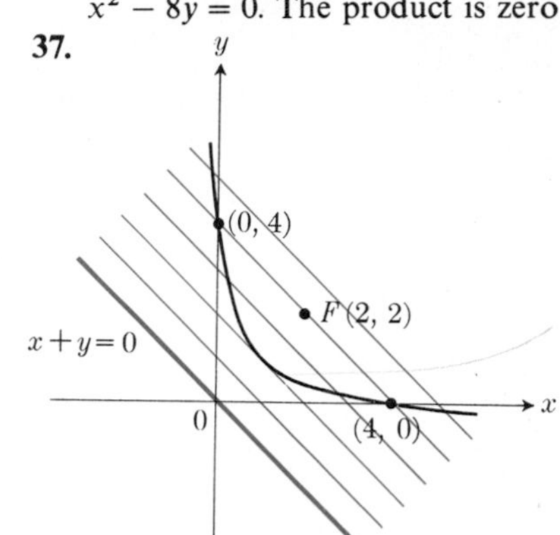

38. $x^2 + y^2 - 8x - 8y - 2xy + 16 = 0$

Article 8–6, pp. 417–418

1. $(x^2/12) + (y^2/16) = 1$; $e = \frac{1}{2}$ **2.** $(x^2/25) + (y^2/16) = 1$; $e = \frac{3}{5}$ **3.** $9x^2 + 5(y - 2)^2 = 45$; $e = \frac{2}{3}$ **4.** $[(x + 3)^2/12] + (y^2/16) = 1$; $e = \frac{1}{2}$ **5.** $(x - 2)^2 + 10(y - 2)^2 = 10$; $e = 3/\sqrt{10}$ **6.** $9(x - 1)^2 + 4(y - 4)^2 = 36$; $F(1, 4 \pm \sqrt{5})$ **7.** $(2, -3)$; $(2, 2)$, $(2, -8)$; $(2, 1)$, $(2, -7)$ **9.** $x^2 + 2y^2 - 4y = 0$ **10.** $e = \frac{3}{4}$; $y = \pm\frac{16}{3}$ **11.** $\frac{4}{3}\pi ab^2$ **12. a)** $\int_0^a \sqrt{a^2 - x^2}\,dx$ ($= \frac{1}{4}\pi a^2$ for $\frac{1}{4}$ of a circle) **b)** $(b/a)\int_0^a \sqrt{a^2 - x^2}\,dx$. Area of ellipse $= \pi ab$. **14.** $2b^2/a$ **15.** $5x^2 + 9y^2 = 180$ **16.** $A = C = 0$, $B = -4$

18. Interior of ellipse $9x^2 + 16y^2 = 144$ **19.** Graph consists of parabola $x^2 + 4y = 0$, straight line $2x - y - 3 = 0$, circle $x^2 + y^2 - 25 = 0$, ellipse $x^2 + 4y^2 - 4 = 0$. **20.** One factor must be positive, the other negative. Graph consists of region between circle $x^2 + y^2 = 1$ and ellipse $9x^2 + 4y^2 = 36$.

21.

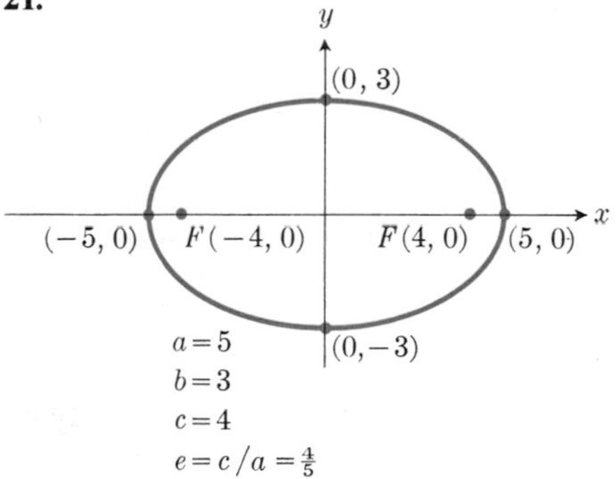

22.

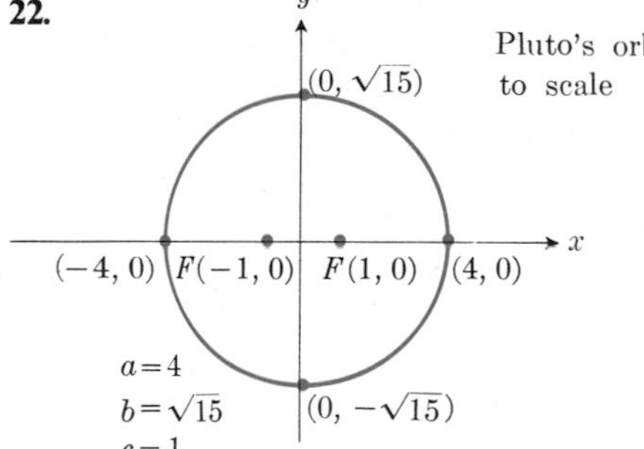

23. $e \approx 0.968$ **24. c)** $L \approx 5.8698$ by trapezoidal approximation. $L \approx 5.8700$ from tables of elliptic integrals. **d)** Estimated $|E_T| < 0.013$ for full ellipse. Actual error ≈ 0.0002. **25. a)** Distances to the two pegs along taut rope sum to a constant. **b)** The height of the weight is minimized when the ring is in the symmetric position.

Article 8–7, pp. 425–426

2. $C(2, -3)$; $V(2 \pm 2, -3)$; $F(2 \pm \sqrt{13}, -3)$; A: $3(x - 2) = \pm 2(y + 3)$ **3.** $C(2, -3)$; $V(2 \pm 3, -3)$; $F(2 \pm \sqrt{13}, -3)$; A: $2(x - 2) = \pm 3(y + 3)$ **4.** $C(2, -3)$; $V(2, -3 + \frac{1}{3})$; $F(2, -3 + \sqrt{13}/6)$; A: $2(y + 3) = +3(x - 2)$ **5.** $C(-2, 1)$; $V(-2 \pm 2, 1)$; $F(-2 \pm 3, 1)$; A: $\sqrt{5}(x + 2) = \pm 2(y - 1)$ **6.** $C(0, 2)$; $V(\pm 1, 2)$; $F(\pm\sqrt{5}, 2)$; A: $2x = \pm(y - 2)$
7. $C(2, 0)$; $V(2 \pm 2, 0)$, $F(2 \pm \sqrt{5}, 0)$; A: $x - 2 = \pm 2y$ **8.** $C(2, 1)$; $V(2, 1 \pm 2)$, $F(2, 1 \pm 3)$; A: $2(x - 2) = \pm\sqrt{5}(y - 1)$
10. $\frac{4}{3}\pi(b^4/a)$ **12.** $x^2 - 3y^2 + 12y = 9$ **13.** $4x^2 - 5y^2 - 8x + 60y + 4 = 0$ **15. a)** It lies on the branch nearest A of the hyperbola with foci at A, B and with $a = 6.86 \times 10^5$ ft.

Article 8–8, pp. 429–430

1. $(x')^2 - (y')^2 = 4$ **2.** $3(x')^2 + (y')^2 = 2$ **3.** $(\frac{1}{2} - \sqrt{3})(x')^2 + (\frac{1}{2} + \sqrt{3})(y')^2 = 2$ or $-1.232(x')^2 + 2.232(y')^2 = 2$

4. $4(x')^2 + 2(y')^2 = 19$ **5.** $5(y')^2 - (x')^2 = 10$ **6.** $5(x')^2 - 3(y')^2 = 7$ **7.** $15x^2 + 13y^2 - 2\sqrt{3}xy - 14\sqrt{3}y + 18x = 33$, $\alpha = 60°$ **12.** $2(y')^2 = 1$

Article 8–9, p. 432

1. Ellipse **2.** Hyperbola **3.** Parabola **4.** Circle **5.** Hyperbola **6.** Parabola **7.** Hyperbola **8.** Ellipse **9.** Ellipse **12.** If $C = -A$, then $A + C = A' + C' = 0$, and $C' = -A'$. Hence $A' = C' = 0$ if $\tan 2\alpha = -2A/B$ by Eqs. (6), Article 8–8

Article 8–10, p. 434

3. Line L and the point D do not exist. **4.** $(1 - e^2)x^2 + y^2 - 2pe^2x - p^2e^2 = 0$.

Miscellaneous Problems Chapter 8, pp. 435–438

1. a) A. Symmetric about the x-axis B. $0 \le x \le 4$, $-2 \le y \le 2$ C. (0, 0), (4, 0) D. None E. ∞ at both intercepts **b)** A. Symmetric about the x-axis B. $x \le 0$, $x \ge 4$, all y C. (0, 0), (4, 0) D. Asymptotic to $y = \pm(x - 2)$ E. ∞ at both intercepts **c)** A. Symmetric about the x-axis B. $0 \le x < 4$, all y C. (0, 0) D. Asymptotic to $x = 4$ E. ∞ at (0, 0)
2. a) A. None B. All y, $|x| > 0$ C. $(-1, 0)$ D. $y = x$, $x = 0$ E. 3 **b)** A. Symmetric about the x-axis B. All y; $-1 \le x < 0$, $x > 0$ C. $(-1, 0)$ D. $x = 0$ E. ∞ **c)** A. None B. All y, $|x| > 0$ C. $(-1, 0)$ D. $x = 0$ E. -3
3. a) A. None B. All y, all x C. (0, 0), $(-1, 0)$, (2, 0) D. None E. -2 at (0, 0), 3 at $(-1, 0)$, 6 at (2, 0) **b)** A. Symmetric about the x-axis B. All y, $-1 \le x \le 0$, $x \ge 2$ C. (0, 0), $(-1, 0)$, (2, 0) D. None E. ∞ at all intercepts
4. a) A. Symmetric about the y-axis B. All x, $0 < y \le 2$ C. (0, 2) D. $y = 0$ E. 0 **b)** A. Symmetric about the y-axis B. $y < 0$, $y \ge 2$; $x^2 \ne 4$ C. (0, 2) D. $y = 0$, $x = \pm 2$ E. 0 **c)** A. Symmetric about the origin B. $|y| \le 2$, all x C. (0, 0) D. $y = 0$ E. 2
5. a) A. Symmetric about the origin B. $|y| \ge 2$, $|x| > 0$ C. None D. $y = x$, $x = 0$ E. —— **b)** A. About (1, 2) B. $y \le 0$, $y \ge 4$; $x \ne 1$ C. (0, 0) D. $x = 1$, $y = x + 1$ E. 0. *Remark.* Translate axes to new origin at (1, 2); becomes same as 5(a).
6. a) A. Symmetric about both axes and the origin B. All y, $|x| \ge 1$ and $x = 0$ C. (0, 0), $(-1, 0)$, (1, 0) D. None E. ∞ at $(\pm 1, 0)$; no derivative exists at the isolated point (0, 0) **b)** A. Symmetric about the x-axis B. $x \le 1$, $x > 2$; $y^2 \ne 1$ C. $(0, \pm\sqrt{2}/2)$, (1, 0) D. $y = \pm 1$, $x = 2$ E. $\mp\sqrt{2}/8$ at $(0, \pm\sqrt{2}/2)$, ∞ at (1, 0)
7. A. None B. $y \le 4 - 2\sqrt{3}$, $y \ge 4 + 2\sqrt{3}$; $x^2 \ne 1$ C. (0, 8), (2, 0) D. $x = \pm 1$, $y = 0$ E. -4 at (0, 8), $\frac{4}{3}$ at (2, 0)
8. A. Symmetric about the y-axis B. $y \le -1$, $y > 1$; $x^2 \ne 1$ C. $(0, -1)$ D. $x = \pm 1$, $y = 1$ E. 0 **9.** A. Symmetric about the origin B. $|x| \le 2$, $|y| \le 2$ C. $(0, \pm\sqrt{3})$, $(\pm\sqrt{3}, 0)$ D. None E. $-\frac{1}{2}$ at $(0, \pm\sqrt{3})$; -2 at $(\pm\sqrt{3}, 0)$
10. $x^2 + xy + y^2 = 3k^2$ **12.** $a = c = d = e = 1$; $b = f = g = 0$ **14.** $y + 2x = 6$ **16.** $y = 6x - 14$; $y = 6x + 18$ **18. b)** 1:1
21. $5x^2 + 5y^2 = 4x + 8y$ **23.** $x = 2pm$ **24.** $Q(4p^3/y_1^2, -4p^2/y_1)$ **25.** $(\pm\frac{8}{9}\sqrt{3}, \frac{4}{3})$ **27.** $(-2, 1)$, $(2, -1)$
28. $27x - 3y + 56 = 0$, $27x - 3y - 104 = 0$ **30.** $r = 2.56$, center (4, 1.61); results are approximate and are based on 1.55 as positive root of $x^4 + 4x - 12 = 0$. **31.** $(-\frac{16}{5}, \frac{53}{10})$
32. a) A conic passing through the points of intersection of the three lines, and tangent to the lines $L_1 + hL_3 = 0$, $L_2 + kL_3 = 0$, $hL_2 + kL_1 = 0$. **b)** $3x^2 + 3y^2 - 8x - 16y + 20 = 0$ **c)** $2y = 3x^2 - 4x + 4$ **33.** 10^7 mi **34.** $\pi/2$
35. $y^2 = 2x - 7$ **36.** $(5, 10\sqrt{10/3})$ **38.** $3x^2 + 3y^2 - 16y + 16 = 0$, circle **40.** Curves consist of circle $x^2 + y^2 = 9$ and hyperbola $y^2 - x^2 = 9$. **41.** No; for points inside the circle, $x^2 + (y^2 - 9)$ is negative while $x^2 - (y^2 - 9)$ is positive, so their product cannot equal 1. **43.** $5x^2 + 9y^2 - 30x = 0$
44. a) $F_1P = 5$, $F_2P = \sqrt{5}$ **b)** Outside, since $OF_1 + OF_2 = 8 > F_1P + F_2P = 5 + \sqrt{5}$ **45.** $2ab$ **47.** $x^2 + 4xy + 5y^2 = 1$
48. $(x + 3)^2/36 + (y - 1)^2/20 = 1$ **50.** $x^2 - y^2 = 4$ **51.** Center at $(\frac{1}{2}\sqrt{2}, 0)$, $e = \sqrt{2}$
52. [*Hint.* Eliminate λ^2 and obtain the differential equation $xy(y')^2 + (x^2 - y^2 - c^2)y' - xy = 0$ for both families. The product of the roots $y' = m_1$ and $y' = m_2$ is $m_1 m_2 = -1$.] **53.** Square, area = 2
55. a) Center $(2, -1)$, foci $((4 \pm 3\sqrt{3})/2, -1)$, major axis 6, minor axis 3, $e = \sqrt{3}/2$ **b)** Center $(-2, -\frac{3}{2})$, foci $(-2 \pm \sqrt{13}, -\frac{3}{2})$, major axis $= \sqrt{13}$, conjugate axis $= \sqrt{39}$, $e = 2$, asymptotes: $2y \pm 2\sqrt{3}x + (3 \pm 4\sqrt{3}) = 0$ **57. b)** Bounded; both $9x^2 + 4y^2 - 36$ and $4x^2 + 9y^2 - 36$ exceed one when $4(x^2 + y^2) > 37$
58. Foci: $(\pm\sqrt{p - q}, 0)$ **59.** $\sqrt{2}$ **60.** On a branch of a hyperbola with the rifle and target at its foci
62. Center $(1, -2)$; foci $(1, -2 \pm \sqrt{13})$; asymptotes: $2(y + 2) = \pm 3(x - 1)$ **63.** $9x^2 - y^2 = 9$ or $9y^2 - x^2 = 9$
65. a) Center (3, 2); $e = \sqrt{\frac{11}{12}}$ **b)** (3, 0) **66.** $x^2 + y^2 - 6x - 15y + 9 = 0$ **67.** With $A(0, 0)$ and $B(c, 0)$, curve is left branch of hyperbola $3x^2 - y^2 - 4cx + c^2 = 0$. **68.** $2y'^2 - 2a\sqrt{2}x' + a^2 = 0$

CHAPTER 9

Article 9–2, p. 443

	sinh u	cosh u	tanh u	coth u	sech u	csch u
6. a)	$-\frac{3}{4}$	$\frac{5}{4}$	$-\frac{3}{5}$	$-\frac{5}{3}$	$\frac{4}{5}$	$-\frac{4}{3}$
b)	$\pm\frac{8}{15}$	$\frac{17}{5}$	$\pm\frac{8}{17}$	$\pm\frac{17}{8}$	$\frac{15}{17}$	$\pm\frac{15}{8}$
c)	$-\frac{7}{24}$	$\frac{25}{24}$	$-\frac{7}{25}$	$-\frac{25}{7}$	$\frac{24}{25}$	$-\frac{24}{7}$
d)	$\frac{12}{5}$	$\frac{13}{5}$	$\frac{12}{13}$	$\frac{13}{12}$	$\frac{5}{13}$	$\frac{5}{12}$
e)	$\pm\frac{4}{3}$	$\frac{5}{3}$	$\pm\frac{4}{5}$	$\pm\frac{5}{4}$	$\frac{3}{5}$	$\pm\frac{3}{4}$
f)	$\frac{12}{5}$	$\frac{13}{5}$	$\frac{12}{13}$	$\frac{13}{12}$	$\frac{5}{13}$	$\frac{5}{12}$

Article 9–3, p. 447

2. $3 \cosh 3x$ **3.** $10 \cosh 5x \sinh 5x = 5 \sinh 10x$ **4.** 0 **5.** $2 \operatorname{sech}^2 2x$ **6.** $-\sec^2 x \operatorname{csch}^2 (\tan x)$ **7.** $-3 \operatorname{sech}^3 x \tanh x$ **8.** $-\operatorname{csch} (x/4) \coth (x/4)$ **9.** $\sec^2 x \operatorname{sech} y$ **10.** $\frac{1}{2} \sinh (2x + 1) + C$ **11.** $\ln \cosh x + C$ **12.** $-\frac{1}{3} \operatorname{sech}^3 x + C$ **13.** $\tanh x + C$ **14.** $\ln \cosh x + C$ **15.** $x - \tanh x + C$ **16.** $2 \cosh \sqrt{x} + C$ **17.** $\frac{1}{2}x + \frac{1}{12} \sinh 6x + C$ **18.** $2\sqrt{2} \cosh (x/2) + C$ **19.** $u/2$ **20.** $\frac{1}{2}(e - (1/e)) = \sinh 1 \approx 1.1752$ **22. a)** 115 ft **b)** 16 lb

Article 9–5, p. 454

2. $\cosh^{-1} x = \ln (x + \sqrt{x^2 - 1})$ **6.** $2/\sqrt{1 + 4x^2}$ **7.** $-\csc x$ **8.** $\sec x$ if $\tan x > 0$, $-\sec x$ if $\tan x < 0$ **9.** $-\csc x$ **10.** $-2 \csc 2x$ if $\cos 2x > 0$, $2 \csc 2x$ if $\cos 2x < 0$ **11.** $\frac{1}{2} \sinh^{-1} 2x + C$ **12.** $\sinh^{-1} (x/2) + C$ **13.** 0.5493 **14.** -0.5493 **15.** $-\frac{1}{2} \operatorname{csch}^{-1} (|x|/2) + C = -\frac{1}{2} \sinh^{-1} (2/|x|) + C$

Article 9–6, pp. 456–457

1. $a \sinh (x_1/a)$ **3.** $(\pi a/2)(2x_1 + a \sinh (2x_1/a))$ **4.** $\bar{x} = 0, \bar{y} = \frac{1}{2}y_1 + (x_1/2) \operatorname{csch} (x_1/a)$ **5.** $(\pi a^2/4)(2x_1 + a \sinh (2x_1/a))$ **6. b)** $dx/ds = a/\sqrt{s^2 + a^2}$, $dy/ds = s/\sqrt{a^2 + s^2}$ **7. c)** $a = 25$ ft, dip ≈ 4.6 ft **d)** $H = 50$ lb

Miscellaneous Problems Chapter 9, pp. 457–458

3. $\lim PQ = 0$ **4.** $\sinh x = \pm\frac{3}{4}$, $\tanh x = \pm\frac{3}{5}$ **5.** $\cosh x = \frac{41}{9}$, $\tanh x = -\frac{40}{41}$ **9.** $y = 1$ **12.** $3 \sinh 6x$ **13.** $\sec^2 x/(2 \tanh y \operatorname{sech}^2 y)$ **14.** $-(\cosh y \coth y)/\sqrt{1 - x^2}$ **15.** $\tanh y \tan x$ **16.** $(1 + y^2)/(1 - x^2)$ **17.** $x^{-1} \operatorname{sech}^2 (\ln x) = 4x(x^2 + 1)^{-2}$ **18.** $y \operatorname{csch} (\ln y)$ **19.** $3e^{3x} \cosh (\tan^{-1} e^{3x})/(1 + e^{6x})$ **20.** $|\sec x|$ **21.** $-(\cosh y + \sinh 2x)/(2y + x \sinh y)$ **22.** $-e^{-\theta} + C$ **23.** $(2\theta - e^{-2\theta})/4$ **24.** $(\cosh^3 x - 3 \cosh x)/3 + C$ **25.** $(e^{3x} + 3e^{-x})/6 + C$ **26.** $\ln (\cosh x) + C$ **27.** $\frac{1}{2} \tanh^{-1} (\frac{1}{2})$ **28.** $\frac{1}{2}(\coth^{-1} \frac{5}{2} - \coth^{-1} \frac{3}{2})$ **29.** $\sinh^{-1} (e^t) + C$ **30.** $-\tanh^{-1} (\cos x) + C$ **31.** $\cosh^{-1} (\tan \theta) + C$ **36. a)** $\lim v = \sqrt{mg/k}$ where k = resistance proportionality factor; m = mass of body; g = acceleration due to gravity. **b)** $s = (m/k) \ln \cosh (t\sqrt{gk/m})$ **37.** ln 2 **38.** $\ln [2/(1 + \sqrt{2})]$

CHAPTER 10

Article 10–1, pp. 463–464

1. a) $(3, (\pi/4) + 2n\pi)$, $(-3, -(3\pi/4) + 2n\pi)$, n any integer. **b)** $(-3, (\pi/4) + 2n\pi)$, $(3, -(3\pi/4) + 2n\pi)$, n any integer. **c)** $(3, -(\pi/4) + 2n\pi)$, $(-3, (3\pi/4) + 2n\pi)$, n any integer. **d)** $(-3, -(\pi/4) + 2n\pi)$, $(3, (3\pi/4) + 2n\pi)$, n any integer.

2.

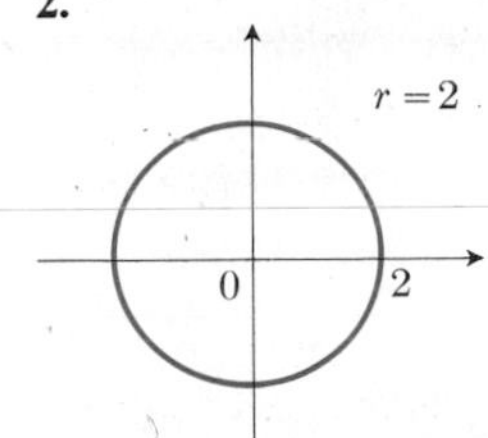

3.

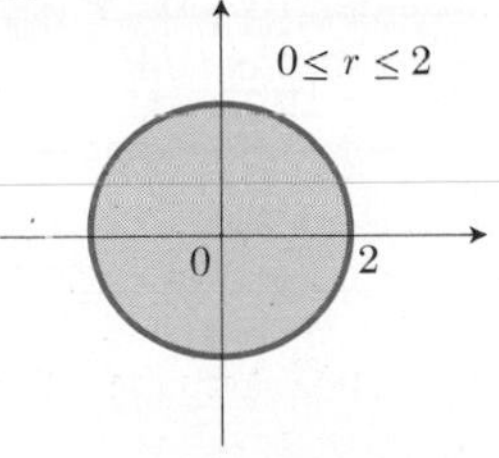

4.

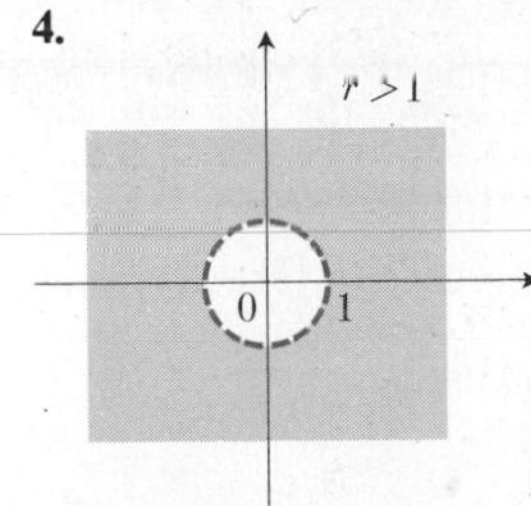

5.

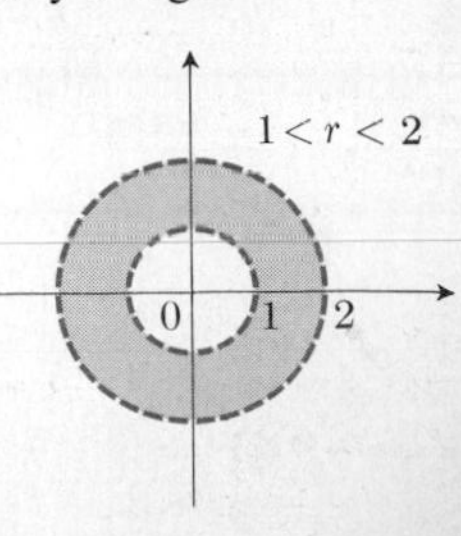

6.
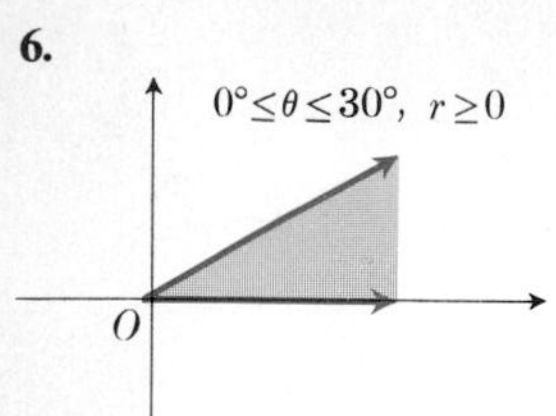

7.
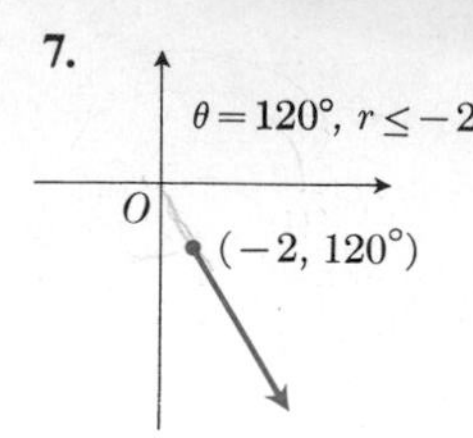

8.
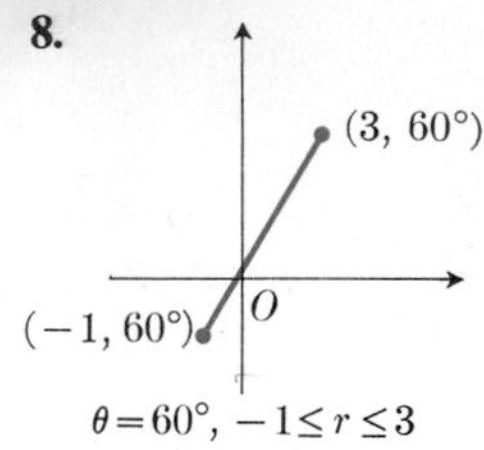

9.
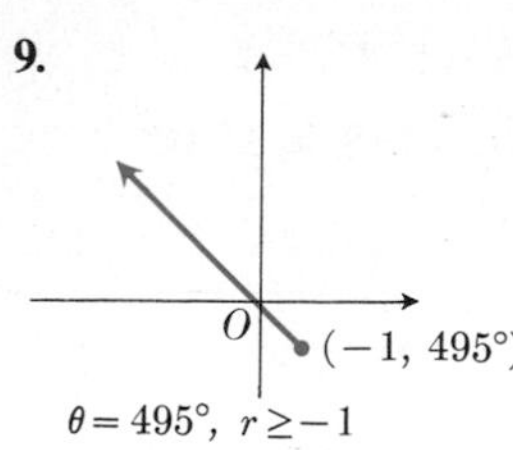

10. a) $(3/\sqrt{2}, 3/\sqrt{2})$ **b)** $(-3/\sqrt{2}, -3/\sqrt{2})$ **c)** $(3/\sqrt{2}, -3/\sqrt{2})$ **d)** $(-3/\sqrt{2}, 3/\sqrt{2})$ **11.** $x = 2$ **12.** $y = -1$
13. $x + y = 1$ **14.** $y = x$ **15.** $x + \sqrt{3}\,y = 6$ **16.** $\sqrt{2}\,x + \sqrt{2}\,y = 8$ **17.** $x - y = 2$ **18.** $\sqrt{3}\,x + y = 0$
19. $(2, \frac{3}{4}\pi)$ is the same as $(-2, -(\pi/4))$ and $2 \sin(-(\pi/2)) = -2$ **20.** $(\frac{1}{2}, \frac{3}{2}\pi) = (-\frac{1}{2}, (\pi/2))$ and $-\sin(\pi/6) = -\frac{1}{2}$
21. If (r_1, θ_1) satisfies $r_1 = \cos\theta_1 + 1$, then the same point has coordinates $(-r_1, \theta_1 + \pi)$ which satisfy the second equation. Also, if (r_2, θ_2) satisfies the second equation, the coordinates $(-r_2, \theta_2 + \pi)$ of the same point satisfy the first equation.
22. $(\pm a, 15°)$, $(\pm a, 75°)$ **23.** The origin and $(a/\sqrt{2}, 45°)$ **24.** The origin and $(a + (a/\sqrt{2}), -(\pi/4))$, $(a - (a/\sqrt{2}), (3\pi/4))$
25. The origin and $(\frac{8}{5}a, \sin^{-1}\frac{3}{5})$ **26.** The origin, $(a, \pm(\pi/2))$, $(a/2, \pm(2\pi/3))$, $(0.22a, \pm 141.3°)$

Article 10–2, p. 467

1. $r[3\cos\theta + 4\sin\theta] = 5$ **2.** $x^2 + y^2 = 2ax$ **11. a)** $(\frac{3}{2}a, \pm 60°)$, $(0, 180°)$ **b)** $(2a, 0°)$, $(\frac{1}{2}a, \pm 120°)$ **12.** 30°
13. Symmetry about the y-axis

Article 10–3, pp. 471–472

1. $r = a \sin 2\theta$; rose of 4 leaves. **2.** $r = 2a \sin\theta \tan\theta$, $x = r\cos\theta = 2a\sin^2\theta \to 2a$ as $\theta \to \pi/2$ **3.** $r = 2a \sin\theta$
4. $r = a(1 - \cos\theta)$, $r = -a(1 + \cos\theta)$ (Both equations represent the same curve.) **5.** $r\cos(\theta - \alpha) = p$
6. $r(1 - \cos\theta) = 2a$, $r(1 + \cos\theta) = -2a$ (Both equations represent the same curve.) **7.** $r^2 = \cos 2\theta$ **8.** $x^2 + y^2 = 4x$
9. $x^2 + y^2 = 6y$ **10.** $(x^2 + y^2)^3 = 4x^2y^2$ **11.** $(x^2 + y^2)^2 = 2a^2(x^2 - y^2)$ **12.** $3x^2 - y^2 + 32x + 64 = 0$
13. $x^2 + y^2 - ay = a\sqrt{x^2 + y^2}$ **15.** d **16.** e **17.** l **18.** f **19.** k **20.** h **21.** i **22.** j
23. a) $p = |c|/\sqrt{a^2 + b^2}$, $\cos\beta = a/\sqrt{a^2 + b^2}$, $\sin\beta = b/\sqrt{a^2 + b^2}$ **b)** $p = 3$, $\beta = 30°$ **24.** $r = 4/(1 - \cos\theta)$
25. $(50, 0°)$, $r = 45/(4 + 5\cos\theta)$ **26.** $(-\frac{16}{15}, 0°)$, $r = 8/(4 + \cos\theta)$ **27. a)** max $= \sqrt{a^2 + b^2}$, min $= \sqrt{|a^2 - b^2|}$
b) max $= a\sqrt{5}$, min $= a\sqrt{3}$; max $= a\sqrt{2}$, min $= 0$; max $= a\sqrt{5}/2$, min $= a\sqrt{3}/2$
28. ± 1 **29.** $(\frac{2}{3}, 0°)$ **30.** $\pm\sqrt{e^2 - 1}$

Article 10–4, p. 477

2. When $\tan\psi_2 = -1/\tan\psi_1$. **3.** $(2, \pm 60°)$; 90° **4.** $(\frac{3}{2}a, \pm 60°)$, $(0, 180°)$ **5.** $8a$ **6.** $(\frac{4}{5}a, 0)$ **7.** $4\pi a^2(2 - \sqrt{2})$
8. $2a$. The curve is the cardioid $r = (a/2)(1 - \cos\theta)$ **9.** $(a/3)[(4 + \pi^2)^{3/2} - 8]$ **10.** $(a/8)(4\pi - 3\sqrt{3})$ **11.** $4\pi^2a^2$

Article 10–5, p. 479

1. $\frac{3}{2}\pi a^2$ **2.** πa^2 **3.** $2a^2$ **4.** $(a^2/3)(3\sqrt{3} - \pi)$ **5.** $\frac{9}{2}\pi a^2$ **6.** $(a^2/2)(\pi - 2)$ **7.** πa^2 **9.** $(\frac{5}{6}a, 0)$ **10.** $(4a/3\pi)$ from center

Miscellaneous Problems Chapter 10, pp. 480–481

15. $\pi/3$ at $(a, \pi/6)$ and $(a, 5\pi/6)$ **16.** $\pi/4$ at $(a, 0)$ and (a, π) **17.** 0 at $(a\sqrt{2}, \pi/4)$ **18.** $\pi/2$ at $r = 0$ **19.** $\pi/4$ at $r = 0$; $2\tan^{-1}(\sqrt{3}/6)$ at $(a/2, \theta_i)$ where $\theta_i = \pm\pi/3, \pm 2\pi/3$ **20.** $\pi/3$ at $(\sqrt{2}, \pm\pi/6)$ and $(\sqrt{2}, \pm 5\pi/6)$ **21.** $r = 2/(1 + \cos\theta)$
22. $r(b\cos\theta + a\sin\theta) = ab$ **23.** $r = -2a\cos\theta$ **24.** $r[1 + \cos(\theta - \pi/4)] = 2a$ **25.** $r = 8/(3 - \cos\theta)$ **26.** $r = 3/(1 + 2\sin\theta)$
27. $(0.75a, -3.44°)$, approx. **29.** $\pi/4$ **30.** $\pi/2$ **31.** -1 **32.** $\pi/2$ **33. b)** $xy = 1$ **c)** $\pi/2$ **34. a)** $(1/4)\tan\alpha$ **b)** $\sec\alpha$
35. a) $32\pi a^2/5$ **b)** $\bar{y} = 0$; $\bar{x} = 5a\int_0^\pi \sin^6(\theta/2)\cos(\theta/2)\cos\theta\, d\theta$ **c)** $\bar{x} = -50a/63$ **38.** $P = 3\pi a/2$ **39.** $2a^2$ **40.** $(3\pi - 8)a^2/2$
41. a^2 **42.** $9a^2\pi/2$ **43.** $3\pi a^2/2$ **44.** πa^2 **45.** πa^2 **46.** $4a^2$ **47.** $a^2(\pi + 2)$ **48.** $5\pi a^2/4$

CHAPTER 11

Article 11–1, p. 487

1. $\mathbf{i} - 4\mathbf{j}$ **2.** $-\mathbf{i} + \mathbf{j}$ **3.** $-2\mathbf{i} - 3\mathbf{j}$ **4.** 0 **5.** $\frac{1}{2}\sqrt{3}\,\mathbf{i} + \frac{1}{2}\mathbf{j}$ **6.** $\frac{1}{2}\sqrt{3}\,\mathbf{i} - \frac{1}{2}\mathbf{j}$ **7.** $\frac{3}{5}\mathbf{i} - \frac{4}{5}\mathbf{j}$ **8.** $(\mathbf{i} + 4\mathbf{j})/\sqrt{17}$ **9.** $(-4\mathbf{i} + \mathbf{j})/\sqrt{17}$ **10.** $-y\mathbf{i} + x\mathbf{j}$ or $y\mathbf{i} - x\mathbf{j}$ **11.** $\sqrt{2}$, 45° **12.** $\sqrt{13}$, $\tan^{-1}(-1.5) = -56.3°$ **13.** 2, 30° **14.** $\sqrt{13}$, $180° - \tan^{-1}(1.5) = 123.7°$ **15.** 13, $\tan^{-1}\frac{12}{5} = 67.4°$ **16.** 13, $180° + \tan^{-1}\frac{12}{5} = 247.4°$

Article 11–2, pp. 490–491

1. $\alpha_1 = \frac{1}{2}\sin^{-1} 0.8 = 26°34'$, $\alpha_2 = 90° - \alpha_1 = 63°26'$ **5.** $x = e^t$, $y = -(7 + e^{2t})/2$ **6.** $y = (1-t)^{-1}$, $x = -\ln|1-t|$ **7.** $x = \sin t$, $y = 1 + (t - \sin t \cos t)/2$, for $0 \le t \le \pi/2$; $x = 1$, $y = t + 1 - \pi/4$, for $t > \pi/2$

Article 11–3, pp. 496–497

1. $x^2 + y^2 = 1$ **2.** $x = 1 - 2y^2$; $|y| \le 1$ **3.** $x^2 - y^2 = 1$; $x > 0$ **4.** $[(x-2)^2/16] + [(y-3)^2/4] = 1$ **5.** $y = x^2 - 6x$ **6.** $4x^2 - y^2 = 4$; $x \ge 1$, $y \ge 0$ **7.** $(x-2)(y-2) + 1 = 0$; $x > 2$, $y < 2$ **8.** $y = x^2 - 2x + 5$; $x \ge 1$ **9.** $2(x+y) = (x-y)^2$ **10.** $[(x-3)^2/4] + [(y-4)^2/9] = 1$; $x > 3$ **11.** $x = -at/\sqrt{t^2+1}$, $y = a/\sqrt{t^2+1}$ **12.** $x = a \tanh\theta$, $y = a\,\text{sech}\,\theta$ **13.** $x = a\cos(s/a)$, $y = a\sin(s/a)$ **14.** $x = a\sinh^{-1}(s/a)$, $y = \sqrt{a^2+s^2}$ **15.** $x = a\cos\phi + a\phi\sin\phi$, $y = a\sin\phi - a\phi\cos\phi$ **16.** $x = (a+b)\cos\theta - b\cos([(a+b)/b]\theta)$, $y = (a+b)\sin\theta - b\sin([(a+b)/b]\theta)$ **17.** $x = (a-b)\cos\theta + b\cos([(a-b)/b]\theta)$, $y = (a-b)\sin\theta - b\sin([(a-b)/b]\theta)$ **18.** $8a$ **21. a)** $x = 2a\cot\theta$, $y = 2a\sin^2\theta$ **b)** $y = 8a^3/(x^2 + 4a^2)$ **22.** 6723 ft

Article 11–4, p. 500

1. Straight line parallel to z-axis. **2.** Straight line, 5 units above and parallel to the line $y = x$ in the xy-plane. **3.** Circle in the plane $z = -2$, center $(0, 0, -2)$, radius 2. **4.** Ellipse in the yz-plane, center (0, 0, 0), semi-axes a and b. **5.** Circle in the plane $z = 3$, radius 2, center (0, 0, 3). **6.** Straight line in the plane $\theta = \pi/6$, making an angle of 45° with the plane $z = 0$. **7.** A right circular helix wound on a cylinder of radius 3. **8.** A right conical helix wound on a right circular cone. **9.** A semicircle of radius 5, center at the origin, lying in the plane $\theta = \pi/4$. **10.** The intersection of the sphere $\rho = 5$ and the cone $\phi = \pi/4$ is a circle of radius $\rho\sin\phi = 5/\sqrt{2}$. **11.** The plane $\theta = \pi/4$ and the cone $\phi = \pi/4$ intersect in a straight line through the origin. **12.** A semicircle in the yz-plane, center at (0, 0, 2) on the z-axis, radius 2. **13.** $\rho = 2$; $r^2 + z^2 = 4$. **14.** $\rho = 4\cos\phi$; $r^2 + z^2 = 4z$. **15.** $z^2 = x^2 + y^2$; $\phi = \pi/4$, $\phi = 3\pi/4$. **16.** $x^2 + y^2 + z^2 = 6z$; $r^2 + z^2 = 6z$ **17.** Plane $x = 0$ and half-space where $x > 0$. **18.** Spheres $\rho = 3$, $\rho = 5$, and shell between them. **19.** On or inside sphere $\rho = 5$ but outside or on cylinder $r = 2$. **20.** Wedge with two intersecting plane boundaries $\theta = 0$, $\theta = \pi/4$, and curved boundary part of cone $\phi = \pi/4$. **21.** Interior and boundary of elliptic cylinder $4x^2 + 9y^2 = 36$.

Article 11–5, p. 502

1. $(-2, 0, 2)$, $\sqrt{8}$ **2.** $(-\frac{1}{4}, -\frac{1}{4}, -\frac{1}{4})$, $\sqrt{75}/4$ **3.** $(0, 0, a)$, $|a|$ **4.** $(0, -\frac{1}{3}, \frac{1}{3})$, $\sqrt{29}/3$ **5. a)** $\sqrt{y^2+z^2}$ **b)** $\sqrt{z^2+x^2}$ **c)** $\sqrt{x^2+y^2}$ **d)** $|z|$ **6. a)** $x^2 + y^2 + (z-4)^2 = 4$ **b)** $4x^2 + 4y^2 + 3(z - \frac{3}{2})^2 = 27$ **c)** $5(z - \frac{3}{2})^2 - 4x^2 - 4y^2 = 5$ **7.** 3 **8.** 7 **9.** 9 **10.** 11 **11.** $(4\mathbf{i} + 3\mathbf{j} + 12\mathbf{k})/13$ **12.** $(2\mathbf{i} + 2\mathbf{j} + 4\mathbf{k})/3$

Article 11–6, p. 507

1. No; we cannot conclude that $\mathbf{B}_1 = \mathbf{B}_2$. All we can say is that $\mathbf{B}_1$ and $\mathbf{B}_2$ have the same projection on $\mathbf{A}$ when all three vectors start from the same initial point. **2. a)** $(\mathbf{A}\cdot\mathbf{B}/\mathbf{A}\cdot\mathbf{A})\mathbf{A}$ **b)** $\frac{7}{45}\mathbf{A}$ **3.** $\angle A = \angle C = 71.1°$, $\angle B = 37.8°$ **4.** (3, 3, 0) **5.** $\frac{13}{15}$ **6.** $\cos^{-1}(1/\sqrt{3}) = 54.7°$ **7.** $\cos^{-1}(\sqrt{6}/3) = 35.3°$ **8.** $\cos^{-1}(\frac{13}{45}) = 73.2°$ **9.** Two: 45°, 135° **12.** $z = \sqrt{x^2+y^2}$ **13.** $w(z_1 - z_2)$ **18.** If $|\mathbf{v}_1| = |\mathbf{v}_2|$, then $(\mathbf{v}_1 + \mathbf{v}_2)$ and $(\mathbf{v}_1 - \mathbf{v}_2)$ are orthogonal.

Article 11–7, p. 512

1. $-\mathbf{i} - 3\mathbf{j} + 4\mathbf{k}$ **2.** $c(2\mathbf{i} + \mathbf{j} + \mathbf{k})$, c = scalar **3.** $2\sqrt{6}$ **4.** $\sqrt{6}/2$ **5.** $c(\mathbf{i} - \mathbf{j})$, c = scalar **6.** $\pm[4/(3\sqrt{2}), 1/(3\sqrt{2}), 1/(3\sqrt{2})]$ **7.** $11/\sqrt{107}$ **8. a)** 60.6° **b)** Yes, because the angle between the two planes is equal to the angle between their normals and this angle is neither 0° nor 180°. **c)** $\mathbf{j} + \mathbf{k}$

Article 11–8, pp. 517–518

1. $(9, -5, 12)$ **2.** $x = 1 + t$, $y = 2 + t$, $z = -1 - t$; $x - 1 = y - 2 = -(z + 1)$ **4. a)** The complement of the angle between the line and a normal to the plane. **b)** 22.4° **5.** $3x + y + z = 5$ **6.** $|D_2 - D_1|/7$ **8.** $7x - 5y - 4z = 6$

9. Plane through the three points. **10.** $x - 2y + z = 6$ **11.** $x - y + z = 0$ **12.** $x + 6y + z = 16$ **13.** 3 **14. b)** Yes **16.** $17x - 26y + 11z = -40$ **17.** $2x - y + z = 5$ **18.** $1/\sqrt{75}, 5/\sqrt{75}, 7/\sqrt{75}$ **19.** The set of points in the half-space that lies on the side of the plane toward which **N** points. **20.** $(\cos\alpha)(x - x_0) + (\cos\beta)(y - y_0) + (\cos\gamma)(z - z_0) = 0$

Article 11–9, p. 523

1. $-2\mathbf{C} = -6\mathbf{i} + 8\mathbf{j} - 24\mathbf{k}$; $-22\mathbf{A} = -88\mathbf{i} + 176\mathbf{j} - 22\mathbf{k}$ **2.** 245 **3. a)** $\mathbf{A} \times \mathbf{B} = 15\mathbf{i} + 10\mathbf{j} + 20\mathbf{k}$; $(\mathbf{A} \times \mathbf{B}) \times \mathbf{C} = 200\mathbf{i} - 120\mathbf{j} - 90\mathbf{k}$ **b)** $(\mathbf{A} \cdot \mathbf{C})\mathbf{B} - (\mathbf{B} \cdot \mathbf{C})\mathbf{A} = 56\mathbf{B} + 22\mathbf{A} = 200\mathbf{i} - 120\mathbf{j} - 90\mathbf{k}$ **5.** $a = (\mathbf{A} \times \mathbf{B}) \cdot \mathbf{D}$, $b = -(\mathbf{A} \times \mathbf{B}) \cdot \mathbf{C}$ **6.** $\frac{2}{3}$ **10.** $7 - x = (3y - 19)/12 = (4 - 3z)/30$ **11. a)** $S(0, 9, -3)$ **b)** Area $PQRS = |-29\mathbf{i} - \mathbf{j} + 11\mathbf{k}| = \sqrt{963} \approx 31.03$ **c)** 11; 29; 1

Article 11–10, p. 526

1. Right circular cylinder of radius 1, elements parallel to y-axis, axis along y-axis. **2.** Parabolic cylinder, with one element being the y-axis. **3.** Parabolic cylinder, one element being the z-axis. **4.** Elliptic cylinder, axis along the z-axis. **5.** Plane, with one element being the x-axis. **6.** Hyperbolic cylinder, axis along the z-axis. **7.** Hyperbolic cylinder, axis along the y-axis. **8.** Hyperbolic cylinder, axis along the x-axis. **9.** Right circular cylinder of radius 4, axis along the z-axis. **10.** Right circular cylinder of radius $\frac{1}{2}$; axis is the line $x = 0$, $y = \frac{1}{2}$. **11.** Right circular cylinder, radius $\frac{1}{2}$; axis is the line $x = \frac{1}{2}$, $y = 0$. **12.** Cylinder with elements parallel to z-axis. Cross sections are cardioids. **13.** Right circular cylinder, radius a, axis along z-axis. **14.** Right circular cylinder, radius 2; axis is the line $y = 0$, $z = 2$. The x-axis is one element. **15.** Elliptic cylinder; axis is the line $x = 0$, $z = \frac{1}{2}$. The y-axis is one element.

Article 11–11, pp. 531–532

1. Paraboloid of revolution, vertex (0, 0, 1), opening upward. **2.** Sphere of radius 4, center $(-2, 3, 0)$. **3.** Ellipsoid, center (0, 0, 0), semiaxes $a = 2$, $b = 1$, $c = 2$. **4.** Ellipsoid, center (0, 1, 0), semiaxes $a = 2$, $b = 1$, $c = 2$. **5.** Sphere, center (0, 1, 0), radius 1. **6.** One-sheeted hyperboloid of revolution, axis of symmetry parallel to Oy, center $(-2, -3, 0)$. **7.** Two-sheeted hyperboloid of revolution, axis parallel to Ox, center $(-2, -3, 0)$. **8.** Parabolic cylinder, one element being Oy. **9.** Rotate the xy-axes through 45° and have $z^2 + 2y'^2 = 2x'^2$; elliptic cone with vertex O, axis along Ox'. **10.** Rotate xy-axes 45°; $z = 2(x'^2 - y'^2)$, hyperbolic paraboloid ("saddle"). **11.** Paraboloid of revolution obtained by rotating the parabola $z = x^2$ about the z-axis. **12.** Rotate the line $z = x$ about the z-axis; right circular cone. **13.** Rotate $z^2 = x$ about the z-axis. **14.** Elliptic cone, vertex O, axis Oz. **15.** Elliptic cone, vertex O, axis Ox. **16.** Right circular cone, vertex O, axis Oy. **17.** $(x - 1)^2 + 4(y + 1)^2 - (z - 2)^2 = 1$. One-sheeted hyperboloid, center $(1, -1, 2)$, axis $x - 1 = y + 1 = 0$. **18.** $(z - 2)^2 = (x - 1)^2 + 4(y + 1)^2$. Elliptic cone, vertex $(1, -1, 2)$, axis $x - 1 = y + 1 = 0$. **19.** Elliptic cylinder, axis along Oy. **20.** Elliptic paraboloid, vertex (1, 0, 0), axis along Ox. **21.** Plane, $z = x$. **22.** Plane, $z = y$. **23.** Ruled surface generated by rotating about Oz a line parallel to the xy-plane and passing through Oz, whose distance above the xy-plane is $z = \sin\theta$. **24.** Ruled surface generated by rotating about Oz a line, parallel to the xy-plane and passing through Oz, whose distance above the xy-plane is $z = \cosh\theta$. **25. a)** $A(z_1) = \pi ab(1 - (z_1^2/c^2))$ **b)** $V = \frac{4}{3}\pi abc$ **27. a)** $\pi abh(1 + (h^2/3c^2))$ **b)** $A_0 = \pi ab$, $A_h = \pi ab(1 + (h^2/c^2))$, $V = (h/3)(2A_0 + A_h)$ **28.** Vertex $(0, y_1, (cy_1^2/b^2))$, focus $(0, y_1, (cy_1^2/b^2) - (a^2/4c))$ **29.** In any plane $\theta =$ constant, the equation $\rho = F(\phi)$ may be considered as the polar equation of a plane curve C having polar coordinates ρ and ϕ. Since the space equation is independent of θ, the surface is generated by rotating the curve C around the z-axis. **30.** A sphere, center $\rho = (a/2)$, $\phi = 0$, $\theta = 0$ and radius $(a/2)$. **31.** A cardioid of revolution.

Miscellaneous Problems Chapter 11, pp. 532–535

1. $x = (1 - t)^{-1}$, $y = 1 - \ln(1 - t)$, $t < 1$ **2.** $x = \tan^{-1}(t + 1)$, $y = (t + 1)\tan^{-1}(t + 1) - \frac{1}{4}\pi - \frac{1}{2}\ln(1 + t + \frac{1}{2}t^2)$ **3.** $x = e^t$, $y = e^{e^t} - e$ **4.** $x = 3 - 3\cos 2t$, $y = 4 + 2\sin 2t$ **5.** $x = t - \sin t$, $y = 1 - \cos t$ **6.** $y = e^t$, $x = 2\sqrt{1 + e^t} - 2\sqrt{2} - 2\coth^{-1}\sqrt{1 + e^t} + 2\coth^{-1}\sqrt{2}$ **7.** $x = \sinh^{-1} t$, $y = t\sinh^{-1} t - \sqrt{1 + t^2} + 1$ **8.** $x = 2 + 2\sinh(t/2)$, $y = 2t - 4 + 4\cosh(t/2)$ **9.** $x = 4\sin t$, $y = 4\cos t$ **10.** $x = 2 - e^{-t}$, $y = 2t + e^{-t}$ **12.** $x = 8t - 2\sin 2t$, $y = 4 - 2\cos 2t$ **13.** $x = 2a\sin^2\theta\tan\theta$, $y = 2a\sin^2\theta$ **14.** $x = \cot\theta \pm a\cos\theta$, $y = \pm a\sin\theta$ **15. a)** $3\pi a^2$ **b)** $8a$ **c)** $64\pi a^2/3$ **d)** $(\pi a, 5a/6)$ **17.** 0 **24.** $\frac{3}{11}(3\mathbf{i} - \mathbf{j} + \mathbf{k})$ **25.** $-\frac{1}{10}$ **26.** $\mathbf{C} = [(\mathbf{A} \cdot \mathbf{B})/(\mathbf{B} \cdot \mathbf{B})]\mathbf{B}$, $\mathbf{D} = [(\mathbf{B} \cdot \mathbf{B})\mathbf{A} - (\mathbf{A} \cdot \mathbf{B})\mathbf{B}]/(\mathbf{B} \cdot \mathbf{B})$ **27.** $7\sqrt{2}/10$ **29.** $\mathbf{j} - \mathbf{k}$ **30.** $5\mathbf{i} + 7\mathbf{j} + \mathbf{k}$ **31.** $(\mathbf{j} + \mathbf{k})/\sqrt{2}$ **33.** $(10\mathbf{i} - 2\mathbf{j} - 6\mathbf{k})/\sqrt{35}$ **35.** $\cos^{-1}(3/\sqrt{35})$ **36.** $\mathbf{B} = (1/|\mathbf{A}|^2)(d\mathbf{A} + \mathbf{C} \times \mathbf{A})$ **38.** $z = 3$, $x - \sqrt{3}y + 2\sqrt{3} - 1 = 0$ **39.** $(1, -2, -1)$, $(x - 1)/-5 = (y + 2)/3 = (z + 1)/4$ **40.** $25/\sqrt{38}$ **42.** $(\frac{11}{9}, \frac{26}{9}, -\frac{7}{9})$ **43.** $\frac{1}{3}\sqrt{78}$ **44.** $2x - y + 2z - 8 = 0$

45. a) $2x + 7y + 2z + 10 = 0$ **b)** $9/(5\sqrt{57})$ **46.** $2x + 2y + z = 5$ **49. a)** 1 **b)** $-10\mathbf{i} - 2\mathbf{j} - 12\mathbf{k}$ **50.** $\frac{1}{3}$, $\cos\theta = -\sqrt{2}/3$
56. Hyperboloid of two sheets, center $(2, -1, -1)$ **57.** $(x-1)^2 + (y-2)^2 + (z-3)^2 = 3$ **58.** $z^6 - y = 0$, $y = (x^2 + z^2)^3$

CHAPTER 12

Article 12–1, p. 542

1. $\mathbf{i}2e^{2t} + \mathbf{j}(1-t)e^{-t}$, $-\infty < t < \infty$ **2.** $\mathbf{i}[1/(2(1+t))] - \mathbf{j}[t/\sqrt{1-t^2}]$, $-1 < t < 1$
3. $\mathbf{i}(2/\sqrt{1-4t^2}) + \mathbf{j}(3\sec^2 3t) - \mathbf{k}(1/t^2)$, $-\frac{1}{2} < t < \frac{1}{2}$, $t \neq 0$.
4. $\mathbf{i}(1/(|x|\sqrt{9x^2-1})) + \mathbf{j}(2\sinh 2x) + \mathbf{k}(4\operatorname{sech}^2 4x)$, $|x| > \frac{1}{3}$ **5.** $\mathbf{i}[4/(2t+1)^2] - \mathbf{j}(8t/(1-4t^2))$, $-\frac{1}{2} < t < \frac{1}{2}$

Article 12–2, p. 546

1. $\mathbf{v} = -(a\omega\sin\omega t)\mathbf{i} + (a\omega\cos\omega t)\mathbf{j}$, $\mathbf{a} = -(a\omega^2\cos\omega t)\mathbf{i} - (a\omega^2\sin\omega t)\mathbf{j} = -\omega^2\mathbf{R}$;
when $\omega t = \pi/3$, $\mathbf{v} = a\omega(-\frac{1}{2}\sqrt{3}\,\mathbf{i} + \frac{1}{2}\mathbf{j})$, speed $= a\omega$, $\mathbf{a} = -a\omega^2(\frac{1}{2}\mathbf{i} + \frac{1}{2}\sqrt{3}\,\mathbf{j})$.
2. $\mathbf{v} = -(2\sin t)\mathbf{i} + (3\cos t)\mathbf{j}$, $\mathbf{a} = -(2\cos t)\mathbf{i} - (3\sin t)\mathbf{j}$;
at $t = \pi/4$, $\mathbf{v} = -\sqrt{2}\,\mathbf{i} + \frac{3}{2}\sqrt{2}\,\mathbf{j}$, speed $= \sqrt{6.5}$, $\mathbf{a} = -\sqrt{2}\,\mathbf{i} - \frac{3}{2}\sqrt{2}\,\mathbf{j}$.
3. $\mathbf{v} = \mathbf{i} + 2t\mathbf{j}$, $\mathbf{a} = 2\mathbf{j}$; at $t = 2$, $\mathbf{v} = \mathbf{i} + 4\mathbf{j}$, $\mathbf{a} = 2\mathbf{j}$, speed $= \sqrt{17}$.
4. $\mathbf{v} = -(2\sin 2t)\mathbf{i} + (2\cos t)\mathbf{j}$, $\mathbf{a} = -(4\cos 2t)\mathbf{i} - (2\sin t)\mathbf{j}$; at $t = 0$, $\mathbf{v} = 2\mathbf{j}$, $a = -4\mathbf{i}$, speed $= 2$.
5. $\mathbf{v} = e^t\mathbf{i} - 2e^{-2t}\mathbf{j}$, $\mathbf{a} = e^t\mathbf{i} + 4e^{-2t}\mathbf{j}$; at $t = \ln 3$, $\mathbf{v} = 3\mathbf{i} - \frac{2}{9}\mathbf{j}$, $\mathbf{a} = 3\mathbf{i} + \frac{4}{9}\mathbf{j}$, speed $= \frac{1}{9}\sqrt{733}$.
6. $\mathbf{v} = (\sec t\tan t)\mathbf{i} + (\sec^2 t)\mathbf{j}$, $\mathbf{a} = (\sec^3 t + \sec t\tan^2 t)\mathbf{i} + (2\sec^2 t\tan t)\mathbf{j}$;
at $t = \pi/6$, $\mathbf{v} = \frac{2}{3}\mathbf{i} + \frac{4}{3}\mathbf{j}$, $\mathbf{a} = (10\mathbf{i} + 8\mathbf{j})/(3\sqrt{3})$, speed $= \frac{1}{3}\sqrt{20}$.
7. $\mathbf{v} = (3\sinh 3t)\mathbf{i} + (2\cosh t)\mathbf{j}$, $\mathbf{a} = (9\cosh 3t)\mathbf{i} + (2\sinh t)\mathbf{j}$; at $t = 0$, $\mathbf{v} = 2\mathbf{j}$, $\mathbf{a} = 9\mathbf{i}$, speed $= 2$.
8. $\mathbf{v} = [\mathbf{i}/(t+1)] + 2t\mathbf{j}$, $\mathbf{a} = [-\mathbf{i}/(t+1)^2] + 2\mathbf{j}$; at $t = 1$, $\mathbf{v} = \frac{1}{2}\mathbf{i} + 2\mathbf{j}$, $\mathbf{a} = -\frac{1}{4}\mathbf{i} + 2\mathbf{j}$, speed $= \frac{1}{2}\sqrt{17}$.
9. $\mathbf{R} = -\frac{1}{2}gt^2\mathbf{j} + \mathbf{v}_0 t = (tv_0\cos\alpha)\mathbf{i} + (tv_0\sin\alpha - \frac{1}{2}gt^2)\mathbf{j}$.
11. $\mathbf{v} = e^t[\mathbf{i} + \mathbf{j}(\cos t + \sin t) + \mathbf{k}(\cos t - \sin t)]$, $\mathbf{a} = e^t[\mathbf{i} + 2\mathbf{j}\cos t - 2\mathbf{k}\sin t]$, $\theta = \cos^{-1}(\sqrt{15}/5) = 39.2°$.
12. $\mathbf{v} = \mathbf{i}\sec^2 t + 2\mathbf{j}\cosh 2t - 3\mathbf{k}\operatorname{sech} 3t\tanh 3t$, $\mathbf{a} = 2\mathbf{i}\sec^2 t\tan t + 4\mathbf{j}\sinh 2t + 9\mathbf{k}\operatorname{sech} 3t(\tanh^2 3t - \operatorname{sech}^2 3t)$, $\theta = 90°$.
13. $\mathbf{v} = [2t/(t^2+1)]\mathbf{i} + [1/(t^2+1)]\mathbf{j} + (t/\sqrt{t^2+1})\mathbf{k}$, $\mathbf{a} = [2(1-t^2)/(1+t^2)^2]\mathbf{i} - [2t/(1+t^2)^2]\mathbf{j} + [\mathbf{k}/(t^2+1)^{3/2}]$, $\theta = 90°$.
14. $\mathbf{R} = (3\cos\theta)\mathbf{i} + (3\sin\theta)\mathbf{j} + (6\cos\theta + 9\sin\theta)\mathbf{k}$, $\mathbf{v} = -3\omega(\sin\theta)\mathbf{i} + 3\omega(\cos\theta)\mathbf{j} + 3\omega(3\cos\theta - 2\sin\theta)\mathbf{k}$, $\mathbf{a} = -\omega^2\mathbf{R}$.

Article 12–3, p. 551

1. $-\mathbf{i}\sin t + \mathbf{j}\cos t$ **2.** $(e^t\mathbf{i} + 2t\mathbf{j})/\sqrt{e^{2t} + 4t^2}$ **3.** $-\mathbf{i}\cos t + \mathbf{j}\sin t$ **4.** $(\mathbf{i} + 2x\mathbf{j})/\sqrt{1+4x^2}$ **5.** $-(2\mathbf{i}\cos t + \mathbf{j})|\sqrt{1 + 4\cos^2 t}$
6. $(\mathbf{i}t + \mathbf{j})/\sqrt{1+t^2}$ **7.** $[(\cos t - \sin t)/\sqrt{2}]\mathbf{i} + [(\cos t + \sin t)/\sqrt{2}]\mathbf{j}$ **8.** $(\tanh t)\mathbf{i} + (\operatorname{sech} t)\mathbf{j}$.
9. $\frac{1}{13}((12\cos 2t)\mathbf{i} - (12\sin 2t)\mathbf{j} + 5\mathbf{k})$ **10.** $\sqrt{\frac{1}{3}}[(\cos t - \sin t)\mathbf{i} + (\cos t + \sin t)\mathbf{j} + \mathbf{k}]$ **11.** $(\mathbf{i}\tanh 2t + \mathbf{j} + \mathbf{k}\operatorname{sech} 2t)/\sqrt{2}$
12. $(9t^2 + 25)^{-(1/2)}[3(\cos t - t\sin t)\mathbf{i} + 3(\sin t + t\cos t)\mathbf{j} + 4\mathbf{k}]$ **13.** 13π **14.** $\sqrt{3}(e^\pi - 1)$ **15.** $3\sqrt{2}\sinh 2\pi$
16. $\pi\sqrt{9\pi^2 + 25}/2 + (25/6)\sinh^{-1}(3\pi/5)$

Article 12–4, p. 557

1. $(1/a)\operatorname{sech}^2(x/a)$ **2.** $|\cos x|$ **3.** $4e^{2x}/(1 + 4e^{4x})^{3/2}|$ **4.** $1/(3a|\sin t\cos t|)$ **5.** $1/|a\theta|$ **6.** $(1/4a)|\csc(\theta/2)|$ **7.** $|\cos y|$
8. $2/[\sqrt{y^2+2}(y^2+1)^2]$ **9.** $48y^5/[(4y^6+1)^2]$ **10.** $1/[2(1+t^2)^{3/2}]$ **11.** $1/[|t|(1+t^2)^{3/2}]$ **12.** $e^{-t}/\sqrt{2}$
13. $(x+2)^2 + (y-3)^2 = 8$. For the circle: $y' = -(x+2)/(y-3)$, $y'' = -8/(y-3)^3$. Both of these $= +1$ at $(0, 1)$.
15. $\mathbf{N} = -\mathbf{i}\sin 2t - \mathbf{j}\cos 2t$, $\kappa = \frac{24}{169}$, $\mathbf{B} = \frac{1}{13}((5\cos 2t)\mathbf{i} - (5\sin 2t)\mathbf{j} - 12\mathbf{k})$.
16. $\mathbf{N} = -(\mathbf{i}/\sqrt{2})(\sin t + \cos t) + (\mathbf{j}/\sqrt{2})(\cos t - \sin t)$, $\kappa = \sqrt{2}e^{-t}/3$, $\mathbf{B} = [\mathbf{i}(\sin t - \cos t) - \mathbf{j}(\sin t + \cos t) + 2\mathbf{k}]/\sqrt{6}$
17. $\mathbf{N} = \mathbf{i}\operatorname{sech} 2t - \mathbf{k}\tanh 2t$, $\kappa = \frac{1}{6}\operatorname{sech}^2 2t$, $\mathbf{B} = (-\mathbf{i}\tanh 2t + \mathbf{j} - \mathbf{k}\operatorname{sech} 2t)/\sqrt{2}$
18. $d\mathbf{R}/dt = \mathbf{T}(ds/dt)$, $d^2\mathbf{R}/dt^2 = \mathbf{T}(d^2s/dt^2) + \mathbf{N}\kappa(ds/dt)^2$

Article 12–5, pp. 563–564

5. $\mathbf{v} = 2\mathbf{i}\sinh 2t + 2\mathbf{j}\cosh 2t$, $\mathbf{a} = 4\mathbf{i}\cosh 2t + 4\mathbf{j}\sinh 2t$, $ds/dt = |\mathbf{v}| = 2\sqrt{\cosh 4t}$; $a_{\mathbf{T}} = d^2s/dt^2 = (4\sinh 4t)/\sqrt{\cosh 4t}$,
$a_{\mathbf{N}} = \sqrt{|\mathbf{a}|^2 - a_{\mathbf{T}}^2} = 4\sqrt{\operatorname{sech} 4t}$ **6.** $a_{\mathbf{T}} = 2t/\sqrt{1+t^2}$, $a_{\mathbf{N}} = 2/\sqrt{1+t^2}$ **7.** $a_{\mathbf{T}} = 0$, $a_{\mathbf{N}} = \omega^2 a$ **8.** $a_{\mathbf{T}} = 0$, $a_{\mathbf{N}} = 2/(t^2+1)$
9. $a_{\mathbf{T}} = \sqrt{2}\,e^t$, $a_{\mathbf{N}} = \sqrt{2}\,e^t$ **14.** $\frac{1}{2}$

Article 12–6, p. 566

2. $\mathbf{v} = 3a \sin \theta \mathbf{u}_r + 3a(1 - \cos \theta)\mathbf{u}_\theta$, $\mathbf{a} = 9a(2 \cos \theta - 1)\mathbf{u}_r + 18a \sin \theta \mathbf{u}_\theta$. **3.** $\mathbf{v} = 4at \cos 2\theta \mathbf{u}_r + 2at \sin 2\theta \mathbf{u}_\theta$, $\mathbf{a} = (4a \cos 2\theta - 20at^2 \sin 2\theta)\mathbf{u}_r + (2a \sin 2\theta + 16at^2 \cos 2\theta)\mathbf{u}_\theta$. **4.** $\mathbf{v} = 2ae^{a\theta}\mathbf{u}_r + 2e^{a\theta}\mathbf{u}_\theta$, $\mathbf{a} = 4e^{a\theta}(a^2 - 1)\mathbf{u}_r + 8ae^{a\theta}\mathbf{u}_\theta$.
5. $\mathbf{v} = (a \cos t)\mathbf{u}_r + ae^{-t}(1 + \sin t)\mathbf{u}_\theta$, $\mathbf{a} = -a[\sin t + e^{-2t}(1 + \sin t)]\mathbf{u}_r + ae^{-t}[2 \cos t - 1 - \sin t]\mathbf{u}_\theta$.
6. $\mathbf{v} = -(8 \sin 4t)\mathbf{u}_r + (4 \cos 4t)\mathbf{u}_\theta$, $\mathbf{a} = -(40 \cos 4t)\mathbf{u}_r - (32 \sin 4t)\mathbf{u}_\theta$

Miscellaneous Problems Chapter 12, pp. 567–569

1. a) $\mathbf{v} = 2^{-(3/2)}(-\mathbf{i} + \mathbf{j})$, $\mathbf{a} = 2^{-(5/2)}(\mathbf{i} - 3\mathbf{j})$ **b)** $t = 0$ **2. a)** $\mathbf{v} = \pi(\mathbf{i}(1 - \cos \pi t) + \mathbf{j} \sin \pi t)$, $\mathbf{a} = \pi^2(\mathbf{i} \sin \pi t + \mathbf{j} \cos \pi t)$ **b)** Slope of $PC = \cot \pi t$, slope of $PQ = \csc \pi t + \cot \pi t$ **c)** Slope of $\mathbf{v}$ = slope of PQ, slope of $\mathbf{a}$ = slope of PC
3. Speed $= a\sqrt{1 + t^2}$, $a_T = at/\sqrt{1 + t^2}$, $a_N = a(t^2 + 2)/\sqrt{1 + t^2}$ **5. b)** $\pi/2$ **6.** $|ad - bc|(a^2 + b^2)^{-(3/2)}$, provided $a^2 + b^2 \neq 0$ **7.** $x = a\theta + a \sin \theta$, $y = -a(1 - \cos \theta)$ **8.** $(-\frac{1}{2} \ln 2, 1/\sqrt{2})$ **9. b)** πab, πa^2 **10.** $\kappa = \pi s$
11. $y = \pm\sqrt{1 - x^2} \pm \ln((1 - \sqrt{1 - x^2})/x) + C$. Set $C = 0$. Then $x = e^{-s}$ [$s = -\ln x$, measured from (1, 0)]; $y = \pm\sqrt{1 - e^{-2s}} \pm \ln(e^s - \sqrt{e^{2s} - 1})$. **12.** $s = s_0 + 2\pi p$, $A = A_0 + s_0 p + \pi p^2$, $R = R_0 + p$, where s_0, A_0, R_0 are the length of arc, area, and radius of curvature of the original curve. **13. a)** $320\sqrt{10}$ **b)** $16[\sqrt{2} + \ln(\sqrt{2} + 1)]$
14. $\mathbf{v} = (3 \cos t)\mathbf{i} - (2 \sin t)\mathbf{j}$, $\mathbf{a} = -(3 \sin t)\mathbf{i} - (2 \cos t)\mathbf{j}$, speed $= (4 + 5 \cos^2 t)^{1/2}$, $a_T = -5 \sin t \cos t(4 + 5 \cos^2 t)^{-(1/2)}$, $a_N = 6(4 + 5 \cos^2 t)^{-(1/2)}$ **15. a)** $a_T = 0, a_N = 4$ **b)** 1 **c)** $r = 2 \cos \theta$
16. $\mathbf{v} = (\cos t - t \sin t)\mathbf{i} + (\sin t + t \cos t)\mathbf{j}$, $\mathbf{a} = -(t \cos t + 2 \sin t)\mathbf{i} - (t \sin t - 2 \cos t)\mathbf{j}$, $\kappa = (t^2 + 2)/(t^2 + 1)^{3/2}$
17. $\kappa = |f^2 + 2f'^2 - ff''|/(f^2 + f'^2)^{3/2}$ **18. a)** $r = e^{2\theta}$ **b)** $\frac{1}{2}\sqrt{5}(e^{4\pi} - 1)$ **19.** $\sqrt{2}\,\mathbf{u}_r$ **20.** $2(\omega^2 - 1)\mathbf{i}$
21. a) $\mathbf{v} = -\mathbf{u}_r + 3\mathbf{u}_\theta$, $\mathbf{a} = -9\mathbf{u}_r - 6\mathbf{u}_\theta$ **b)** $\sqrt{37} + \frac{1}{6} \ln(6 + \sqrt{37})$ **22.** $r = a \cosh \omega t$ **23.** $\mathbf{R} = r\mathbf{u}_r + z\mathbf{k}$
24. $\mathbf{v} = \mathbf{u}_r(dr/dt) + \mathbf{u}_\theta(r\, d\theta/dt) + \mathbf{k}(dz/dt)$, $\mathbf{a} = \mathbf{u}_r[(d_r^2/dt^2) - r(d\theta/dt)^2] + \mathbf{u}_\theta[r(d^2\theta/dt^2) + 2(dr/dt)(d\theta/dt)] + \mathbf{k}(d^2z/dt^2)$
25. a) $2\sqrt{\pi bg/(a^2 + b^2)}$ **b)** $\theta = [b/(a^2 + b^2)](\frac{1}{2}gt^2)$, $z = [b^2/(a^2 + b^2)](\frac{1}{2}gt^2)$
c) $d\mathbf{R}/dt = gt[b/\sqrt{a^2 + b^2}]\mathbf{T}$, $d^2\mathbf{R}/dt^2 = g[b/\sqrt{a^2 + b^2}]\mathbf{T} + (gt)^2[ab^2/(a^2 + b^2)^2]\mathbf{N}$.
There is never any component of acceleration in the direction of the binormal.
26. a) $d\theta/dt = \sqrt{2gb\theta/(a^2 + b^2 + a^2\theta^2)}$ **b)** $\frac{1}{2}\{\theta\sqrt{a^2 + b^2 + a^2\theta^2} + [(a^2 + b^2)/a] \sinh^{-1}(a\theta)/\sqrt{a^2 + b^2}\}$
27. a) $\mathbf{u}_\rho = \mathbf{i} \sin \phi \cos \theta + \mathbf{j} \sin \phi \sin \theta + \mathbf{k} \cos \phi$, $\mathbf{u}_\phi = \mathbf{i} \cos \phi \cos \theta + \mathbf{j} \cos \phi \sin \theta - \mathbf{k} \sin \phi$, $\mathbf{u}_\theta = -\mathbf{i} \sin \theta + \mathbf{j} \cos \theta$.
d) Yes, they form a right-handed system of mutually orthogonal vectors because of (b) and (c).
28. $\mathbf{R} = \rho\mathbf{u}_\rho$, $(d\mathbf{R}/dt) = \mathbf{u}_\rho(d\rho/dt) + \mathbf{u}_\phi \rho(d\phi/dt) + \mathbf{u}_\theta \rho \sin \phi(d\theta/dt)$
29. a) $ds^2 = dr^2 + r^2\, d\theta^2 + dz^2$ **b)** $ds^2 = d\rho^2 + \rho^2\, d\phi^2 + \rho^2 \sin^2 \phi\, d\theta^2$
30. a) $7\sqrt{3}a$ **b)** $7\sqrt{5}$ **31.** $x = (a \cos \theta)/\sqrt{1 + \sin^2 \theta}$, $y = (a \sin \theta)/\sqrt{1 + \sin^2 \theta}$, $z = -(a \sin \theta)/\sqrt{1 + \sin^2 \theta}$; $L = 2\pi a$
32. a) $dx/dt = \cos \theta(dr/dt) - \sin \theta(r\, d\theta/dt)$, $dy/dt = \sin \theta(dr/dt) + \cos \theta(r\, d\theta/dt)$
b) $dr/dt = \cos \theta(dx/dt) + \sin \theta(dy/dt)$, $r\, d\theta/dt = -\sin \theta(dx/dt) + \cos \theta(dy/dt)$ **33.** $2\sqrt{3}(\mathbf{i} + \mathbf{j} - 2\mathbf{k})$
34. $3x + 3y + 3z - 8 = 0$ **35. a)** $\mathbf{T}(\frac{2}{3}, \frac{1}{3}, \frac{2}{3})$, $\mathbf{N}(1/\sqrt{5}, -2/\sqrt{5}, 0)$, $\mathbf{B}(4/3\sqrt{5}, 2/3\sqrt{5}, -5/3\sqrt{5})$ **b)** $2\sqrt{5}/9$
36. a) $x + 2y + 3z = 6$ **b)** $3x - 3y + z = 1$ **37.** $\frac{1}{3}(t^2 + 1)^{-2}$ **39.** $x^2/4 + y^2/9 + z^2/1 = 1$, an ellipsoid
40. $1/r = \gamma M/v_0^2 r_0^2 + ((1/r_0) - (\gamma M/v_0^2 r_0^2)) \cos \theta$.

CHAPTER 13

Article 13–1, p. 573

1. Let $r = \sqrt{x^2 + y^2}$. **a)** $r < 0.1$ **b)** $r < 0.001$ **2. a)** Let $\rho = \sqrt{x^2 + y^2 + z^2}$; $\rho < 0.1$, $\rho < 0.2\sqrt{3}$ **b)** Yes, because $|f(x, y, z) - f(0, 0, 0)| = x^2 + y^2 + z^2 = \rho^2$ is less than any positive ϵ if $\rho < \sqrt{\epsilon}$.
3. a) Along line $x = 1$, $f(x, y) = f(1, y) \to 1$; along line $y = -1$, $f(x, y) = f(x, -1) \to \frac{1}{2}$. **b)** No, because different limits are approached as $(x, y) \to (1, -1)$ in different ways. [See answer to part (a) above.]
4. $g = r \cos^2 \theta \sin \theta$, $\lim_{(x,y)\to(0,0)} g(x, y) = 0$.
5. $h = \cos^2 \theta$. No limit as $(x, y) \to (0, 0)$. Takes on all values between 0 and 1, arbitrarily close to (0, 0).
6. $w = \cos 2\theta$. No limit as $(x, y) \to (0, 0)$. Takes on values between -1 and 1, arbitrarily close to (0, 0).
7. $z = \frac{1}{2}r \sin 2\theta$, $\lim_{(x,y)\to(0,0)} z(x, y) = 0$. **8.** 5 **9.** 1 **10.** The xy-plane $(-\infty < x, y < \infty)$
11. The xy-plane with the point (0, 0) excluded $((x, y) \neq (0, 0))$. **12.** The xy-plane with the axes excluded; $x \neq 0$, $y \neq 0$. **13.** The open upper half-plane $(-\infty < x < \infty; y > 0)$.

Article 13–2, pp. 580–581

6. $\partial w/\partial x = e^x \cos y$, $\partial w/\partial y = -e^x \sin y$ **7.** $\partial w/\partial x = e^x \sin y$; $\partial w/\partial y = e^x \cos y$
8. $\partial w/\partial x = -y/(x^2 + y^2)$; $\partial w/\partial y = x/(x^2 + y^2)$ **9.** $\partial w/\partial x = x/(x^2 + y^2)$; $\partial w/\partial y = y/(x^2 + y^2)$

10. $\partial w/\partial x = -(y/x^2)\sinh(y/x)$; $\partial w/\partial y = (1/x)\sinh(y/x)$
11. $f_x = 2xe^{2y+3z}\cos(4w)$; $f_y = 2f$; $f_z = 3f$; $f_w = -4x^2e^{2y+3z}\sin(4w)$
12. $f_x = -yz/\sqrt{x^4 - x^2y^2}$; $f_y = |x|z/(x\sqrt{x^2 - y^2})$; $f_z = \sin^{-1}(y/x)$
13. $f_u = 2u/(v^2 + w^2)$; $f_v = -2v(u^2 + w^2)/(v^2 + w^2)^2$; $f_w = -2w(u^2 - v^2)/(v^2 + w^2)^2$
14. $f_r = (z^2 - r^2)(2 - \cos 2\theta)/(r^2 + z^2)^2$; $f_\theta = 2r\sin 2\theta/(r^2 + z^2)$; $f_z = -2rz(2 - \cos 2\theta)/(r^2 + z^2)^2$
15. $f_x = 2x/(u^2 + v^2)$; $f_y = 2y/(u^2 + v^2)$; $f_u = -2u(x^2 + y^2)/(u^2 + v^2)^2$; $f_v = -2v(x^2 + y^2)/(u^2 + v^2)^2$
16. $f_x = 2\cos 2x\cosh 3r$, $f_y = 3\cosh 3y\cos 4s$, $f_r = 3\sin 2x\sinh 3r$, $f_s = -4\sinh 3y\sin 4s$
17. By the law of cosines, $\cos A = (b^2 + c^2 - a^2)/(2bc)$. $\partial A/\partial a = a/(bc\sin A)$, $\partial A/\partial b = (c^2 - a^2 - b^2)/(2b^2c\sin A)$
18. By the law of sines, $a = b\sin A\csc B$. $\partial a/\partial A = b\cos A\csc B$, $\partial a/\partial B = -b\sin A\csc B\cot B$
19. $x/\rho = x/\sqrt{x^2 + y^2 + z^2}$ **20.** $-(x^2 + y^2)/(\rho^3\sin\phi) = -\sqrt{x^2 + y^2}/(x^2 + y^2 + z^2)$ **21.** $x/(x^2 + y^2)$ **22.** 0
23. $xz/(\rho^3\sin\phi) = xz/[(x^2 + y^2 + z^2)\sqrt{x^2 + y^2}]$ **24.** $-y/(x^2 + y^2)$ **25.** $\mathbf{i}\sin\phi\cos\theta + \mathbf{j}\sin\phi\sin\theta + \mathbf{k}\cos\phi$
26. $\rho\cos\phi(\mathbf{i}\cos\theta + \mathbf{j}\sin\theta) - \mathbf{k}\rho\sin\phi$ **27.** $\rho\sin\phi(-\mathbf{i}\sin\theta + \mathbf{j}\cos\theta)$ **28.** $\partial\mathbf{R}/\partial\rho = \mathbf{u}_\rho$; $\partial\mathbf{R}/\partial\phi = \rho\mathbf{u}_\phi$; $\partial\mathbf{R}/\partial\theta = \rho\sin\phi\mathbf{u}_\theta$
29. **a)** $\partial\mathbf{R}/\partial x$ is tangent to the curve in which the surface $w = f(x, y)$ and the plane $y = y_0$ intersect. **b)** $\partial\mathbf{R}/\partial y$ is tangent to the curve in which the surface $w = f(x, y)$ and the plane $x = x_0$ intersect. **c)** $\mathbf{v} = -\mathbf{i}f_x(x_0, y_0) - \mathbf{j}f_y(x_0, y_0) + \mathbf{k}$ is normal to the surface at (x_0, y_0, w_0).

Article 13–3, p. 583

1. $6x + 8y = z + 25$, $(x - 3)/6 = (y - 4)/8 = (z - 25)/-1$ **2.** $x - 2y + 2z = 9$, $2x = -y = z$
3. $x - 3y = z - 1$, $x - 1 = (1 - y)/3 = -z - 1$ **4.** $x - y + 2z = \pi/2$, $x - 1 = 1 - y = \frac{1}{2}(z - (\pi/4))$
5. $16x + 12y = 125z - 75$, $(x - 3)/16 = (y + 4)/12 = (3 - 5z)/625$
6. **a)** $\mathbf{N} = C(-\mathbf{i} + \mathbf{j}f_y + \mathbf{k}f_z)$, C = scalar **b)** $x - 2y + z = 1$, $2x = 3 - y = 2(z - 1)$
7. Line: $z = -11x/6 = -22y/7$; plane: $12x + 14y + 11z = 0$ **8.** Vertex: $(0, 0, z_0 + \frac{1}{2})$ **9.** $\begin{vmatrix} \mathbf{i} & \mathbf{j} & \mathbf{k} \\ f_x & f_y & -1 \\ g_x & g_y & -1 \end{vmatrix}$
10. $\pm\sqrt{3/1105}[3\mathbf{i} + 14\mathbf{j} - 30\mathbf{k}]$

Article 13–4, p. 592

1. $\Delta w_{\tan} = 0.14$, $\Delta w = 0.1407$ **2.** $\Delta w = (2x + y)\,\Delta x + x\,\Delta y + (\Delta x)^2 + \Delta x\,\Delta y$; $\Delta w_{\tan} = (2x + y)\,\Delta x + x\,\Delta y$; $\epsilon_1 = \Delta x$, $\epsilon_2 = \Delta x$ **3.** $|x - y| < 0.0224$ **4.** **a)** $\frac{1}{2}, \frac{1}{2}$ **b)** 0.4545, 0.45 **5.** **a)** x **b)** y **c)** $(x + y)/\sqrt{2}$ **6.** **a)** $2 - y$ **b)** x
7. **a)** $x + 1$ **b)** $-y + \pi/2$ **8.** $r = 2h$ **9.** **a)** $S_0[(\Delta p/100) + \Delta\ell - 5\,\Delta w - 30\,\Delta h]$ **b)** 1 cm increase in height decreases sag 6 times as much as 1 cm increase in width. **10.** 6% **11.** **a)** $\Delta Q \approx 10\,\Delta K + \Delta M - 400\,\Delta h$ **b)** Most sensitive to change in h; least sensitive to change in M. **12.** (13 ± 0.03) in.

Article 13–5, p. 596

1. $\frac{2}{3}$ **2.** $\frac{9}{1183}$ **3.** $4\sqrt{3}$ **4.** $\frac{43}{15}$ **5.** In the direction of $3\mathbf{i} - \mathbf{j}$ **6.** $-7/\sqrt{5}$ **8.** $(\pi - 3)/(2\sqrt{5}) \approx 0.032$ **9.** $\pm(\mathbf{i} + \mathbf{j})$

Article 13–6, pp. 599–600

1. $-2\mathbf{i} - 2\mathbf{j} + 4\mathbf{k}$ **2.** $6\mathbf{i} + 6\mathbf{j}$ **3.** $2\mathbf{i}$ **4.** $(-3\mathbf{i} - 4\mathbf{j})/25$ **5.** $(\mathbf{i} + 2\mathbf{j} - 2\mathbf{k})/27$ **6.** $(3\sqrt{3}\,\mathbf{i} + 4\sqrt{3}\,\mathbf{j} + 5\mathbf{k})/2$ **7.** $5\mathbf{k}$
8. $(x - 3)/3 = (y - 4)/4 = (z + 5)/5$
9. **a)** $x = y = z$; $-x = -y = z$; $x = y = 0$
b) (1, 1, 1) and (−2, −2, −2); (2, 2, −2) and (−1, −1, 1); (0, 0, 2)
10. Two lines; $x = z = -y \pm 4$ **11.** Tangent plane: $3x + 5y + 4z = 18$; normal line: $(x - 3)/3 = (y - 5)/5 = (z + 4)/4$
12. In the direction of grad $f = 10\mathbf{i} + 4\mathbf{j} + 10\mathbf{k}$. Max $(df/ds) = |\text{grad } f| = \sqrt{216} = 6\sqrt{6}$
14. grad $w = \mathbf{u}_\rho(\partial w/\partial\rho) + \mathbf{u}_\phi(1/\rho)(\partial w/\partial\phi) + \mathbf{u}_\theta[1/(\rho\sin\phi)](\partial w/\partial\theta)$
15. **a)** $\mathbf{i}(\partial f/\partial x) + \mathbf{j}(\partial f/\partial y)$ **b)** In the direction given by the vector grad $f = -\mathbf{i} + \mathbf{j}$; $|dw/ds| = \sqrt{2}$ in this direction.
23. $h = f_0/(f_x^2 + f_y^2 + f_z^2)_0$ (Smaller values of h should probably be used in calculations.) For the three equations given, we might use $h = 0.001$. One approximate solution is $(x, y, z) = (1.059, 1.944, 3.886)$. For any solution (x, y, z), there are five other solutions: (z, y, x), $(-y, -x, z)$, $(z, -x, -y)$, $(x, -z, -y)$, and $(-y, -z, x)$.

Article 13–7, pp. 604–605

1. $2e^t[x(\cos t - \sin t) + y(\sin t + \cos t) + z] = 4e^{2t}$ **2.** $(y(y^2 - x^2)\sinh t + x(x^2 - y^2)\cosh t)/(x^2 + y^2)^2 = \text{sech}^2\, 2t$
3. $e^{2x+3y}((8t^2 + 2)\cos 4z/(t(t^2 + 1)) - 4\sin 4z) = 2t(t^2 + 1)^2[(4t^2 + 1)\cos 4t - 2t(t^2 + 1)\sin 4t]$
4. $\partial w/\partial r = e^{2r}/\sqrt{e^{2r} + e^{2s}}$; $\partial w/\partial s = e^{2s}/\sqrt{e^{2r} + e^{2s}}$ **5.** $\partial w/\partial r = \partial w/\partial s = 2/(r + s)$
13. $f_x = (\partial w/\partial r)\cos\theta - (1/r)(\partial w/\partial\theta)\sin\theta$; $f_y = (\partial w/\partial r)\sin\theta + (1/r)(\partial w/\partial\theta)\cos\theta$

Article 13–8, p. 609

2. $\frac{47}{24}$ ft^3 **3.** Approx. 340 ft^2 **4. a)** $dx = \cos\theta\, dr - r\sin\theta\, d\theta$, $dy = \sin\theta\, dr + r\cos\theta\, d\theta$ **b)** $dr = \cos\theta\, dx + \sin\theta\, dy$, $d\theta = -(\sin\theta/r)\,dx + (\cos\theta/r)\,dy$ **c)** $\partial r/\partial x = \cos\theta = x/r$, $\partial r/\partial y = \sin\theta = y/r$

5. a) $dx = f_u\,du + f_v\,dv$, $dy = g_u\,du + g_v\,dv$

b) $du = \begin{vmatrix} dx & f_v \\ dy & g_v \end{vmatrix} \Big/ \begin{vmatrix} f_u & f_v \\ g_u & g_v \end{vmatrix}$, $dv = \begin{vmatrix} f_u & dx \\ g_u & dy \end{vmatrix} \Big/ \begin{vmatrix} f_u & f_v \\ g_u & g_v \end{vmatrix}$

6. a) $dx = \sin\phi\cos\theta\, d\rho + \rho\cos\phi\cos\theta\, d\phi - \rho\sin\phi\sin\theta\, d\theta$
$dy = \sin\phi\sin\theta\, d\rho + \rho\cos\phi\sin\theta\, d\phi + \rho\sin\phi\cos\theta\, d\theta$
$dz = \cos\phi\, d\rho - \rho\sin\phi\, d\phi$

b) $d\rho = \begin{vmatrix} dx & \rho\cos\phi\cos\theta & -\rho\sin\phi\sin\theta \\ dy & \rho\cos\phi\sin\theta & \rho\sin\phi\cos\theta \\ dz & -\rho\sin\phi & 0 \end{vmatrix} \Bigg/ \begin{vmatrix} \sin\phi\cos\theta & \rho\cos\phi\cos\theta & -\rho\sin\phi\sin\theta \\ \sin\phi\sin\theta & \rho\cos\phi\sin\theta & \rho\sin\phi\cos\theta \\ \cos\phi & -\rho\sin\phi & 0 \end{vmatrix}$

c) $\partial\rho/\partial x = \sin\phi\cos\theta = x/\rho$

7. $df = -u_0$ and $dg = -v_0$ provided $dx = ((vf_y - ug_y)/(f_x g_y - g_x f_y))_0$ and $dy = ((ug_x - vf_x)/(f_x g_y - g_x f_y))_0$

8. $dx = -\begin{vmatrix} u_0 & f_y & f_z \\ v_0 & g_y & g_z \\ w_0 & h_y & h_z \end{vmatrix} \Bigg/ \begin{vmatrix} f_x & f_y & f_z \\ g_x & g_y & g_z \\ h_x & h_y & h_z \end{vmatrix}$, with similar expressions for dy and dx

Article 13–9, p. 612

1. Low: $(-3, 3, -5)$ **2.** Low: $(15, -8, -63)$ **3.** High: $(-8, -23, 59)$ **4.** High: $(\frac{2}{3}, \frac{4}{3}, 0)$ **5.** $(-2, 1, 3)$ is a saddle point **6.** $(-2, 2, 2)$ is a saddle point **7.** Low: $(0, 0, 0)$; high: $(\pm 1, \pm 1, \sqrt{2})$. The partial derivatives do not exist at $(0, 0)$. They exist but are not zero at $(\pm 1, \pm 1)$.

Article 13–10, pp. 615–616

1. b) $m = \begin{vmatrix} \sum y_i & n \\ \sum x_i y_i & \sum x_i \end{vmatrix} \Big/ D$, $b = \begin{vmatrix} \sum x_i & \sum y_i \\ \sum x_i^2 & \sum x_i y_i \end{vmatrix} \Big/ D$, where $D = \begin{vmatrix} \sum x_i & n \\ \sum x_i^2 & \sum x_i \end{vmatrix}$

2. $26y + 19x = 30$ **3.** $12y = 9x + 20$ **4.** $6y = 9x + 1$ **5. a)** $y = -0.369x$ **b)** $I/I_0 = e^{-0.369x}$

6. $y = 0.123x + 3.580$ **7.** $H \approx 17$ **8.** $F = 55{,}096(1/D^2) - 2.826$

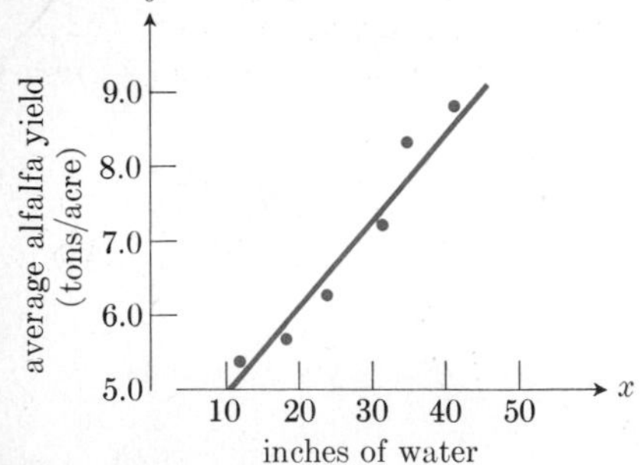

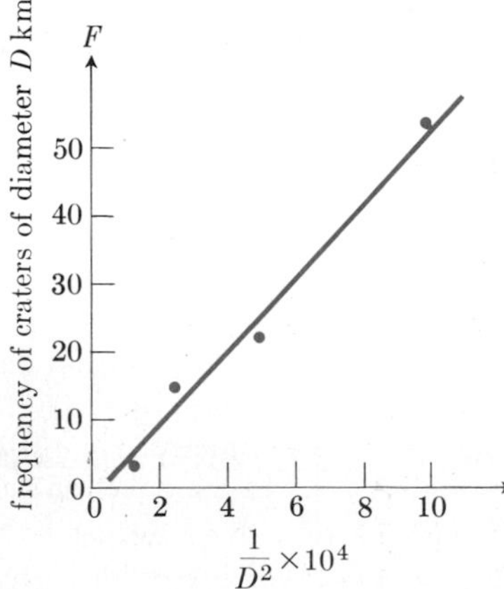

Article 13–11, pp. 627–628

1. Max is 5 at $(\sqrt{5}, \sqrt{5})$, $(-\sqrt{5}, -\sqrt{5})$; min is -5 at $(-\sqrt{5}, \sqrt{5})$, $(\sqrt{5}, -\sqrt{5})$

2. a) No point at which minimum occurs; decreases without bound. Local minimum at $(4, 4)$. **b)** Max is 64 at $(8, 8)$.

3. 5.4 **4.** $(0, 0, 1)$ **5.** Square bottom 8 in. by 8 in., 4 in. deep

6. Square bottom $\sqrt[3]{V/2}$ by $\sqrt[3]{V/2}$, depth $\sqrt[3]{4V}$, where V is the given volume. **7.** $x + 2y + 2z = 6$

8. h = altitude of triangle = $\sqrt{A/(6 + 3\sqrt{3})}$; $2x$ = width of rectangle = $(2\sqrt{3})h$; y = altitude of rectangle = $(1 + \sqrt{3})h$

9. $z = -\frac{1}{2}x + \frac{3}{2}y - \frac{1}{4}$ **10. a)** Spheres, center at origin **b)** No **c)** Circle or point of tangency. Yes. In a circle. **d)** Yes

11. $(-3.621, 1.5)$ and $(3.621, -1.5)$ for maximum, $(0.621, 1.5)$ and $(-0.621, -1.5)$ for minimum
12. a) $(-5/\sqrt{14}, -10/\sqrt{14}, -15/\sqrt{14}), f = -5\sqrt{14}$ **b)** $(5/\sqrt{14}, 10\sqrt{14}, 15/\sqrt{14}), f = 5\sqrt{14}$.
Geometric interpretation: Planes $f =$ constant are tangent to the sphere for $f = \pm 5\sqrt{14}$.
13. Cone $|z| = r$, plane $z = 1 + r(\cos\theta + \sin\theta) = 1 + r\sqrt{2}\sin(\theta + \pi/4)$; curve of intersection lies on the hyperbolic cylinder $r = g(\theta) = 1/[\pm 1 - \sqrt{2}\sin(\theta + \pi/4)]$, $|\overrightarrow{OP}| = \sqrt{2}\,r$ with $r = g(\theta)$. The minimum value of $|g(\theta)|$ is $1/(1 + \sqrt{2}) = \sqrt{2} - 1$, and $|\overrightarrow{OB}| = \sqrt{2}(\sqrt{2} - 1) = 2 - \sqrt{2} = \sqrt{(6 - 4\sqrt{2})}$. B is the point on the cone nearest the origin; A is the point nearest the origin on the other branch of the hyperbola; there is no point farthest from the origin. **14.** If $y = x$, $z = 1 + 2x$, and $z^2 = x^2 + y^2$, then $(1 + 2x)^2 = 2x^2$ and $x = -1 \pm \sqrt{\tfrac{1}{2}}$, so x is not an *independent variable*. (We have no right to differentiate with respect to x if x is restricted to the set $\{-1 + \sqrt{\tfrac{1}{2}}, -1 - \sqrt{\tfrac{1}{2}}\}$.)
15. a) $2xy + 2x + 2y + 1 = 0$ is the hyperbola $2(x + 1)(y + 1) = 1$ in the xy-plane. **b)** In space, $\{(x, y, z)\colon 2xy + 2x + 2y + 1 = 0\}$ is a hyperbolic cylinder. Minimum for $y = x = -1 + \sqrt{\tfrac{1}{2}}$; no maximum.

Article 13–12, p. 632

14. $e^x \cosh y + 6\cos(2x - 3y)$ **15.** $-6/(2x + 3y)^2$ **16.** $(y^2 - x^2)(x^2 + y^2)^{-2}$ **17.** $2y + 6xy^2 + 12x^2y^3$
18. a) $F(x) = (2bk + k^2)x^3$ **b)** $c_1 = \pm\sqrt{a^2 + ah + \tfrac{1}{3}h^2}$ ($\pm$ sign to be chosen depending upon the signs of a and $(a + h)$)
c) $g(y) = 3c_1^2y^2 = (3a^2 + 3ah + h^2)y^2$ **d)** $d_1 = b + (k/2)$
19. $d_2 = b + (k/2)$, $c_2 = \pm\sqrt{a^2 + ah + \tfrac{1}{3}h^2}$ (with the $\pm$ sign depending upon the signs of a and $(a + h)$)

Article 13–13, p. 637

1. Exact, $f = (2x^5 + 5x^2y^3 + 3y^5)/5 + C$ **2.** Not exact **3.** Exact, $f = x^2 + xy + y^2 + C$
4. Exact, $f = x\cosh y + y\sinh x + C$ **5.** Not exact **6.** Exact, $f = e^x(y - x + 1) + y + C$ **7.** Not exact

Article 13–14, p. 639

1. $1/x$ **2.** $-1/(2x^2)$ **3.** $(4 - x)/(2x^3)$ **4.** $x/(\sqrt{1 - x^2}\sin^{-1}x)$ **5.** $(4x - 1)\ln x$ **7.** $2xe^{x^2}$ **8.** $y(x^2\tanh x + 2x\ln\cosh x)$
9. $y(2/(x^2 + 1) - [\ln(x^2 + 1)]/x^2)$ **10.** $y([(8x + 4)/(4x^2 + 4x + 3)]\int_x^{x^2}\ln t\,dt + (4x - 1)\ln x\ln(4x^2 + 4x + 3))$

Miscellaneous Problems Chapter 13, pp. 640–645

1. No, $\lim_{x\to 0} f(x, 0) = 1$, $\lim_{x\to 0} f(x, x) = 0$ **2.** Yes
4. If f is constant, then f has the same value for all points and there is nothing more to prove. Next, suppose f is not constant. Then there are points Q_1 and Q_2 such that $f(Q_1) \neq f(Q_2)$. Let m be any number between $f(Q_1)$ and $f(Q_2)$. Let C be a circular arc joining Q_1 and Q_2. Since f is continuous along this arc it takes all values between $f(Q_1)$ and $f(Q_2)$. Hence there is a point P_1 on C such that $f(P_1) = m$. Repeat the argument with a different circular arc; there is a point P_2 on it such that $f(P_2) = f(P_1) = m$. There are infinitely many circular arcs joining Q_1 and Q_2, and on each of them is a point P such that $f(P) = m$.
5. $\partial/\partial x(\sin xy)^2 = y\sin 2xy$, $\partial/\partial y(\sin xy)^2 = x\sin 2xy$ $\partial/\partial x\sin(xy)^2 = 2xy^2\cos(xy)^2$, $\partial/\partial y\sin(xy)^2 = 2x^2y\cos(xy)^2$
6. $-2/\sqrt{3}$ **8.** $54(x - 3) + 2y - 27(z + 2) = 0$; $(x - 3)/54 = y/2 = -(z + 2)/27$; $(54/\sqrt{3649}, 2/\sqrt{3649}, -27/\sqrt{3649})$
9. a) Hyperboloid of one sheet **b)** $2\mathbf{i} + 3\mathbf{j} + 3\mathbf{k}$ **c)** $2(x - 2) + 3(y + 3) + 3(z - 3) = 0$, $(x - 2)/2 = (y + 3)/3 = (z - 3)/3$
10. a) $13(x + 2) - (y - 1) + 12(z - 2) = 0$, **b)** $(x + 2)/13 = 1 - y = (z - 2)/12$
11. $\partial f/\partial x = 1$, $\partial f/\partial y = 3$, $dw/ds = 3$ **14. a)** $D_u f = f_x u_1 + f_y u_2 + f_z u_3$
b) $D_v(D_u f) = f_{xx}u_1v_1 + f_{yy}u_2v_2 + f_{zz}u_3v_3 + f_{xy}(u_1v_2 + u_2v_1) + f_{xz}(u_1v_3 + u_3v_1) + f_{yz}(u_2v_3 + u_3v_2)$
15. $dw/ds = \sqrt{3}$, maximum $= \sqrt{3}$ **16.** $(f_x = f_y = 2)$ $df/ds = \tfrac{14}{5}$ **17.** 7 **18.** $-14/\sqrt{6}$ **19.** $-\sqrt{\tfrac{2}{3}}$
21. a) $\mathbf{N}(x, y, z) = (x^2 + y^2)^{-(1/2)}[x(1 + 3x^2 + 3y^2)\mathbf{i} + y(1 + 3x^2 + 3y^2)\mathbf{j} - \sqrt{x^2 + y^2}\,\mathbf{k}]$
b) $[(1 + 3x^2 + 3y^2)^2 + 1]^{-(1/2)}$, $1/\sqrt{2}$
22. $a^2 + b^2 + c^2 = 2$ **23. a)** $4\mathbf{j} + 6\mathbf{k}$ **b)** $4(y + 1) + 6(z - 3) = 0$ **24.** $(2\mathbf{i} + 6\mathbf{j} - 3\mathbf{k})/7$ **26.** $\pm\sqrt{3}$
28. $\nabla f = \mathbf{u}_r(\partial f/\partial r) + \mathbf{u}_\theta(1/r)(\partial f/\partial\theta)$ **30. c)** $(x^2 + y^2 + z^2)/2$ **31.** $\theta + (\pi/2)$, $1/r$
34. a) $f = \phi(bx - ay)$ **b)** $f = \phi(x^2 + y^2)$, ϕ arbitrary in each case **35.** $h'(x) = f_x(x, y) + f_y(x, y)[-g_x(x, y)/g_y(x, y)]$
36. $\partial g/\partial z = 1/(\partial f/\partial x)$ **37.** $dx/dz = (\sin y + \sin z - 2y^2\cos z)(\sin y + \sin z)^{-1}(\sin x + x\cos x)^{-1}$
39. $\partial F/\partial x = \tfrac{1}{2}(\partial f/\partial u + \partial f/\partial v)$, $\partial F/\partial y = \tfrac{1}{2}(\partial f/\partial v - \partial f/\partial u)$ **42.** $\partial^2 f/\partial u^2 + (y^2 + 2xy)(\partial^2 f/\partial u\,\partial v) + 2xy^3(\partial^2 f/\partial v^2) + 2y(\partial f/\partial v)$
43. $a = b = 1$ **44.** 2 **47.** $d^2y/dx^2 = -(1/f_y^3)(f_{xx}f_y^2 - 2f_{xy}f_xf_y + f_{yy}f_x^2)$ **49.** $dz/dx = (f_y - f_x)/(f_y + f_z)$
50. $x_t = x - v + ax_{vv}/x_v^2$, $0 \le v \le 1$, $t \ge 0$, $x(0, t) = 0$, $x(1, t) = 1$ **55.** 60.44 **56.** Minimum $(\tfrac{1}{2}, 0)$, $T = -\tfrac{1}{4}$. Maximum $(-\tfrac{1}{2}, \pm\sqrt{3}/2)$, $T = 2\tfrac{1}{4}$. **57.** 50 **58. a)** Max $z = \sqrt{3}$ at $(0, 0)$, min $z = -\sqrt{3}$ at $(0, 0)$ **b)** Min $z = 0$ at $(0, 0)$ **c)** None

59. (1, 1, 1); (1, −1, −1); (−1, 1, −1); (−1, −1, 1) **60.** Length = $(c^2V/ab)^{1/3}$, depth = $(b^2V/ca)^{1/3}$, height = $(a^2V/bc)^{1/3}$
61. $e^{-2}/6$ **62.** Minimum **63.** $(\sum_{i=1}^{n} a_i^2)^{1/2}$ **64.** $(\sqrt{3}/2)abc$
66. $\partial^2 z/\partial x\,\partial y = \cos^{-3}(y+z)[\cos^2(y+z)\sin(x+y) + \sin(y+z)\cos^2(x+y)]$ **67.** y^2 **68.** 0
70. $f_{yx}(0, 0) = -1, f_{xy}(0, 0) = 1$ **71.** $f(x, y) = \frac{1}{5}(2x^5 + 5x^2y^3 + 3y^5) + C$ **72.** $f(x, y) = y \ln x + xe^y + y^2 + C$
73. $w = f(x, y) = x + e^x \cos y + y^2 + C$ **75. a)** 1 **b)** 0 **c)** 0

CHAPTER 14

Article 14–1, p. 652

1. $(4 + \pi^2)/2$

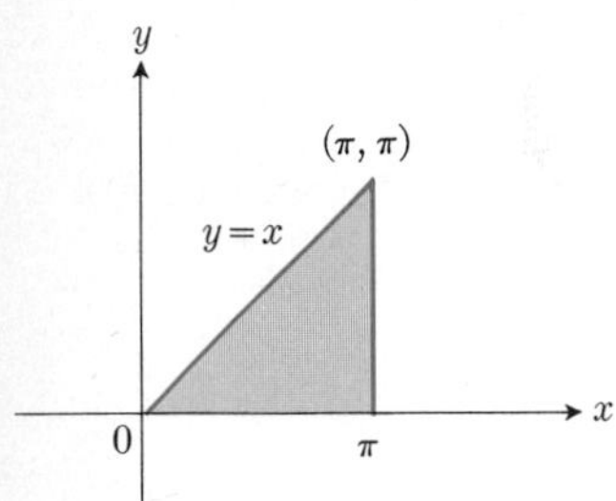

2. $8 \ln 8 - 16 + e$

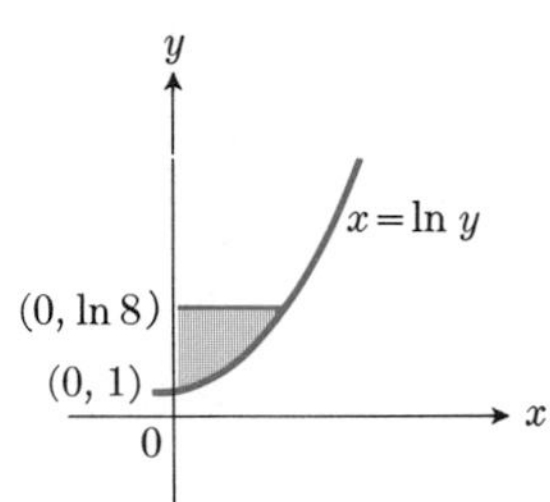

3. $\pi/4$

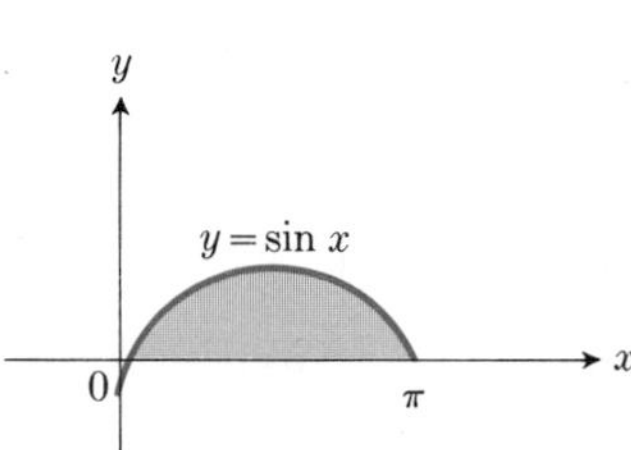

4. $\frac{5}{6}$

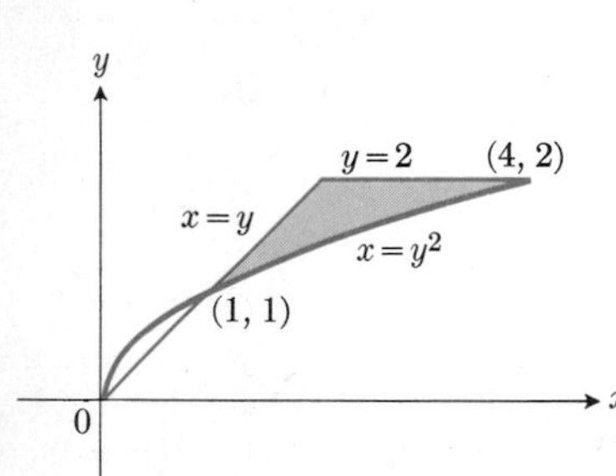

5. $\int_1^{e^2}\int_{\ln y}^{2} dx\,dy = e^2 - 3$

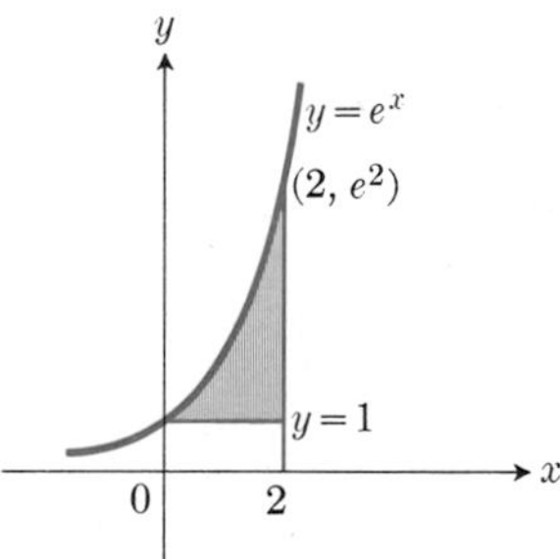

6. $\int_0^1\int_0^{x^2} dy\,dx = \frac{1}{3}$

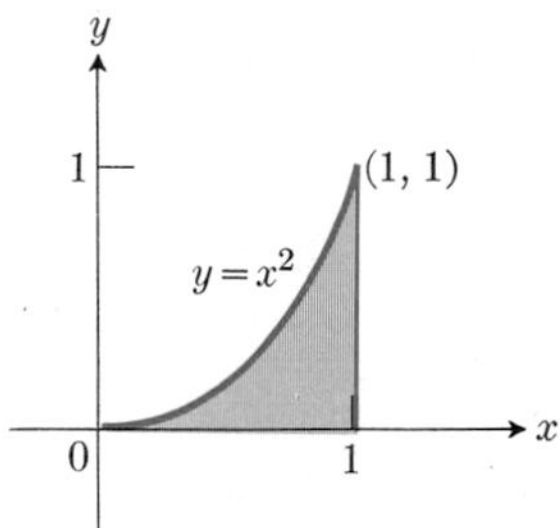

7. $\int_{-2}^{2}\int_0^{\sqrt{(4-x^2)/2}} y\,dy\,dx = \frac{8}{3}$

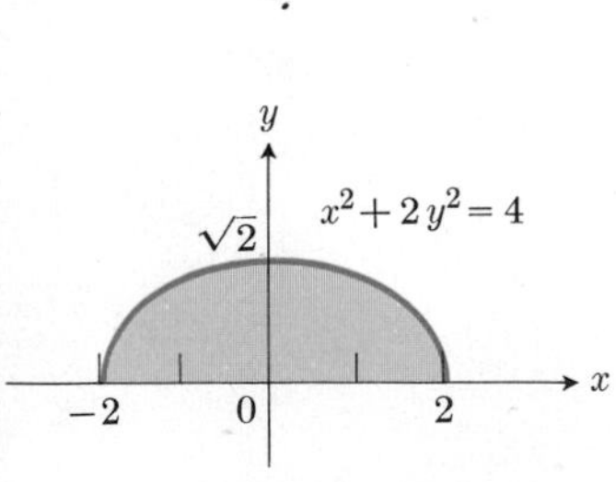

8. $\int_{-4}^{5}\int_{(y-2)/3}^{-2+\sqrt{y+4}} dx\,dy = \frac{9}{2}$

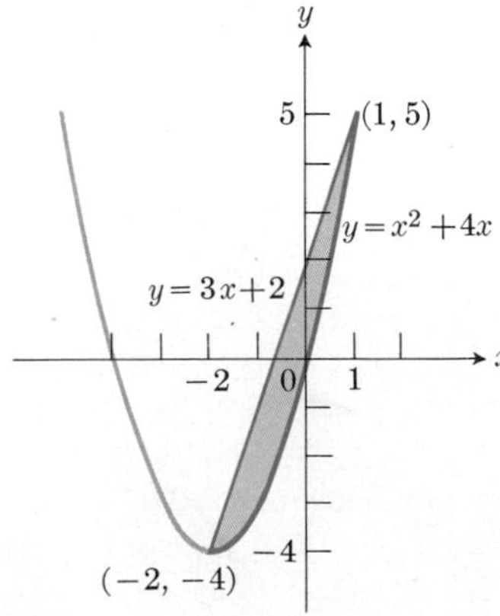

9. $\int_{-4}^{1}\int_{3x}^{4-x^2} (x + 4)\,dy\,dx = \frac{625}{12}$ **10.** $4\int_0^a\int_0^{\sqrt{a^2-x^2}} [(x^2 + y^2)/a]\,dy\,dx = \pi a^3/2$

Article 14–2, p. 654

1. $a^2/2$ **2.** $e - 1$ **3.** 4 **4.** $\frac{9}{2}$ **5.** $\frac{1}{3}$ **6.** $a^2(\pi + 4)/2$ **7.** $\frac{4}{3}$

8.

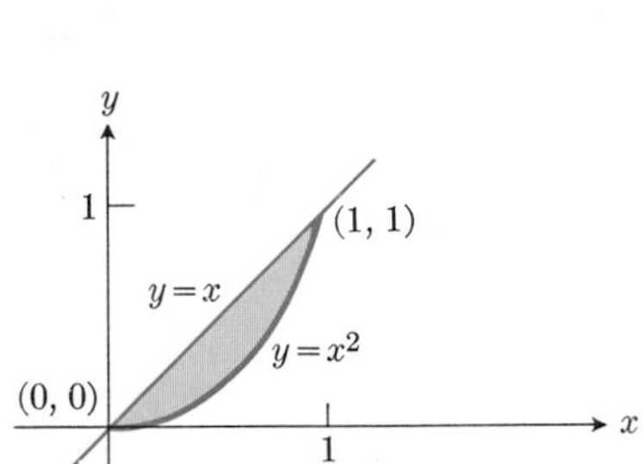

9.

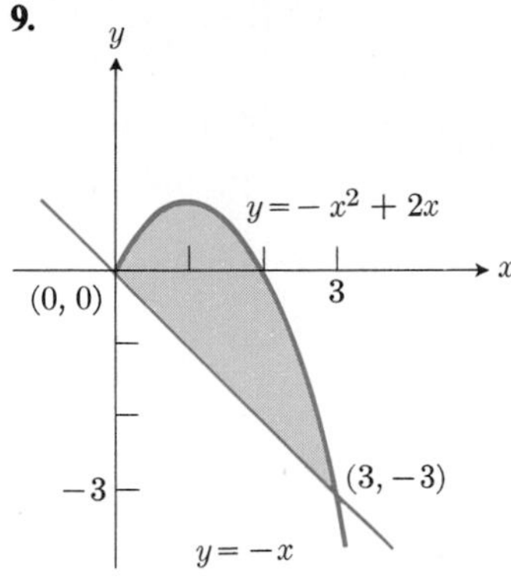

10.

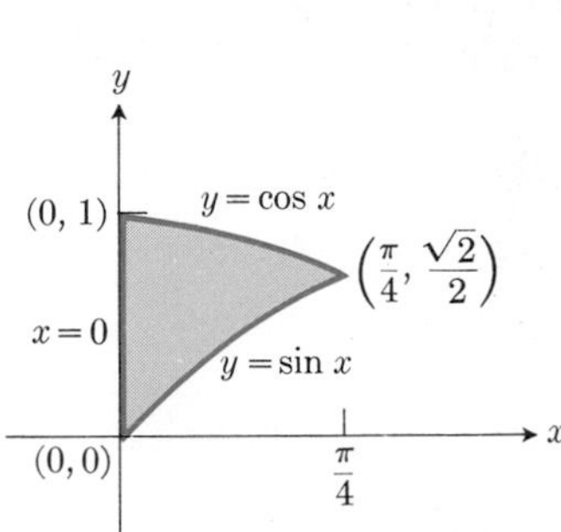

11.

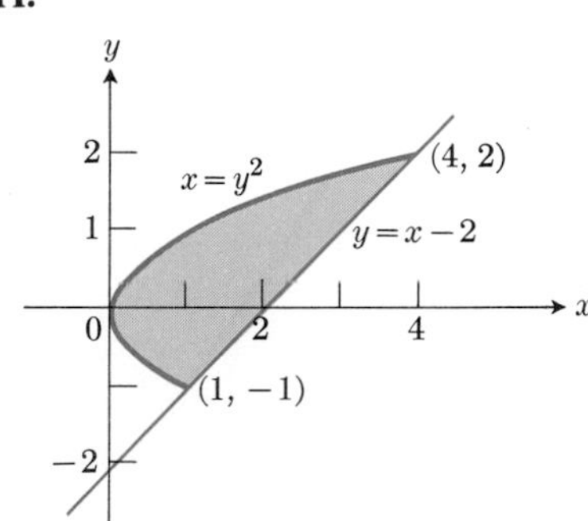

12.

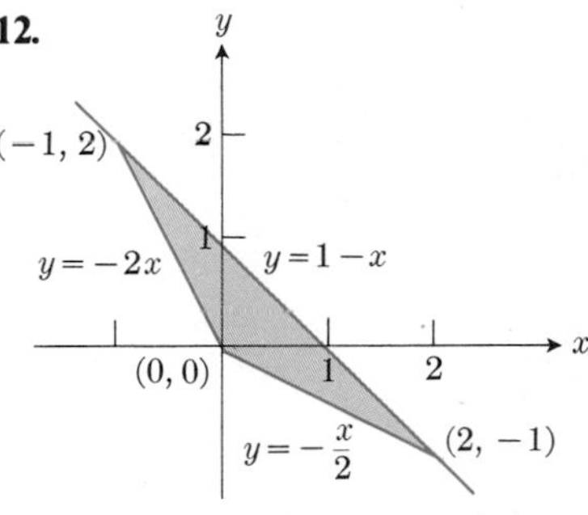

Article 14–3, p. 658

1. $(a/3, a/3)$ **2.** $I_x = (e^3 - 1)/9$ **3.** $\frac{104}{3}$ **4.** $(-\frac{8}{5}, -\frac{1}{2})$ **5.** $\frac{1}{6}$ **6.** $(0, a(8 + 3\pi)/(40 + 12\pi))$ **7.** $\frac{64}{105}$

Article 14–4, p. 663

1. $\int_0^{2\pi} \int_0^a r\,dr\,d\theta = \pi a^2$ **2.** $\int_0^{\pi/2} \int_0^a r^3\,dr\,d\theta = \pi a^4/8$ **3.** $\int_0^{\pi/4} \int_0^a r^2 \cos\theta\,dr\,d\theta = a^3\sqrt{2}/6$ **4.** $\int_0^{\pi/2} \int_0^\infty e^{-r^2} r\,dr\,d\theta = \pi/4$
5. $\int_0^{\pi/4} \int_0^{2\sec\theta} r^2 \sin\theta\,dr\,d\theta = 4/3$ **6.** $\int_0^{\pi/2} \int_0^{2a\cos\theta} r^3 \cos^2\theta\,dr\,d\theta = 5\pi a^4/8$ **7.** $a^2(8 + \pi)/4$ **8.** $\bar{x} = a(32 + 15\pi)/(48 + 6\pi)$, $\bar{y} = 0$ **9.** $I_0 = a^4(320 + 81\pi)/96$ **10.** $a^3(15\pi + 32)/24$ **11.** $2a^2$ **12.** $(3\pi + 20 - 16\sqrt{2})2\sqrt{2}\,a^3/9$

Article 14–5, p. 666

1. $\frac{1}{6}|abc|$ **2.** $\frac{2}{3}$ **3.** $\frac{1}{3}$ **4.** 4 **5.** $\frac{20}{3}$ **6.** 32π **7.** 4π **8.** $16a^3/3$ **9.** 27π **10.** $\frac{4}{3}\pi abc$

Article 14–6, p. 667

1. $5\pi/2$ **2.** 32π **3.** $4\pi a^3(8 - 3\sqrt{3})/3$ **4.** $\pi/2$ **5.** $(8\sqrt{2} - 7)\pi a^3/6$ **6.** $a^3/3$

Article 14–7, p. 669

1. $64\pi a^5(\frac{4}{15} - (17\sqrt{3}/160)) \approx 16.6a^5$ **2.** $2\pi/3$ **3.** $\bar{x} = \frac{1}{2}$ **4.** $\bar{x} = \bar{y} = 0$, $\bar{z} = 7a/(2(8\sqrt{2} - 7))$ **5.** $\frac{2}{5}Ma^2$ **6.** $8\pi a^3/3$
7. $64\pi a^5/35$ **8.** $\frac{3}{20}(a^2 + 4h^2)M$ **9.** $\frac{7}{5}Ma^2$ **10.** $\bar{y} = \bar{z} = 0$, $\bar{x} = (3\sqrt{2}/8)a$ **11.** $M(3a^2 + 4b^2)/4$

Article 14–8, p. 670

1. $(16 - 10\sqrt{2})\pi/3$ **2.** $\bar{x} = \bar{y} = 0$, $\bar{z} = 3a/[16(2 - \sqrt{3})] \approx 0.7a$ **3.** $8\pi a^3/3$ **4.** $a\sqrt{1270/651} \approx 1.4a$

5.

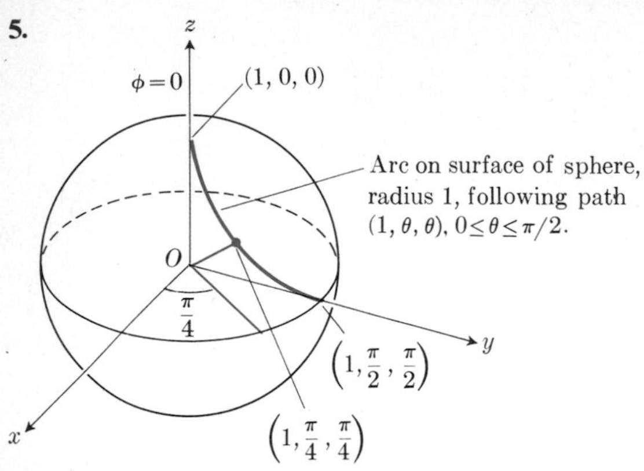

Article 14–9, p. 675

2. $\frac{1}{2}\sqrt{b^2c^2 + a^2c^2 + a^2b^2}$ **3.** $\pi a^2/2$ **4.** $8a^2(\pi - 2)$ **5.** $(\pi/6)(37\sqrt{37} - 5\sqrt{5})$ **6.** $2\pi a^2(2 - \sqrt{2})$ **7.** $\pi a^2\sqrt{1 + c^2}$
8. $2\pi a^2/3$ **9.** $(5\sqrt{5} - 1)\pi a^2/6$ **10.** $16a^2$

Miscellaneous Problems Chapter 14, pp. 675–678

1. $\int_{-2}^{0} \int_{2x+4}^{4-x^2} dy\, dx = \frac{4}{3}$ **2.** $\frac{1}{5}$ **3.** $\int_0^1 \int_{-\sqrt{y}}^{\sqrt{y}} dx\, dy$ **4.** 31.25 **5.** $\int_0^1 \int_x^{2-x} (x^2 + y^2)\, dy\, dx = \frac{4}{3}$
6. a) $(a^2 + m^2)^{-2}\{(m^2 - a^2) \cos ax - 2am \sin ax + [(a^2 - m^2) + mx(a^2 + m^2)]e^{mx}\}$
b) $(a^2 + m^2)^{-3}\{m(3a^2 - m^2) \cos ax + a(3m^2 - a^2) \sin ax + [(m/2)(a^2 + m^2)^2x^2 + (a^4 - m^4)x + m(m^2 - 3a^2)]e^{mx}\}$
8. $\ln (b/a)$ **9.** $(4a/3\pi, 4a/3\pi)$ **10.** $(2a \sin \alpha/3\alpha, 0)$
11. $(28\sqrt{2}/9\pi, 28\sqrt{2}(\sqrt{2} - 1)/9\pi)$ (cartesian coordinates) **12.** $(-\frac{12}{5}, 2)$ **14. a)** $\frac{1}{3}(a^3t + at^3 - t^4)$ **b)** 0
16. $A = a^2 \cos^{-1} (b/a) - b\sqrt{a^2 - b^2}$; $I_0 = (a^4/2) \cos^{-1} (b/a) - b\sqrt{a^2 - b^2}(a^2 + 2b^2)/6$
17. $b\sqrt{2/5}$ **18. a)** $(a/2)\sqrt{\pi/4 - \frac{2}{3}}$ **b)** $(a/2)\sqrt{\pi/4 + \frac{2}{3}}$
21. $\int_{-\pi/2}^{\pi/2} \int_0^a r^2 \cos \theta\, dr\, d\theta$ **24.** $a > 0, c > 0, ac - b^2 = \pi^2$
25. $A = 2a^2$, $I_y = (3\pi + 8)a^4/12$ **26. a)** $(\pi - 2)/4$ **b)** $(\sqrt{3}/4) \tan^{-1} \frac{4}{3}$
27. $K(a) = \int_0^{a \cos \beta} dx \int_0^{x \tan \beta} \ln (x^2 + y^2)\, dy + \int_{a \cos \beta}^{a} dx \int_0^{\sqrt{a^2 - x^2}} \ln (x^2 + y^2)\, dy$
28. $\pi/8$ **29.** $(0, 0, \frac{1}{4})$ **30.** $(4\pi a^3/3)(\sqrt{2} - \frac{7}{8})$ **31.** $\pi/4$ **32.** $\pi/\sqrt{2}$ **33.** $49\pi a^5/15$ **34.** $\frac{4}{3}\pi abc$ **35.** $a^2b^2c^2/6$ **36.** $16a^3/3$
37. $x^2 + y^2 + z^2 = 4$; $x^2 + y^2 = 2x$; $y = 0$; $\int_0^{\pi/2} \int_0^{2 \cos \theta} \int_{-\sqrt{4-r^2}}^{\sqrt{4-r^2}} dz\, r\, dr\, d\theta$
38. $4\pi a^3/3 + (16/3)[(b/2)(3a^2 - b^2) \sin^{-1} (b/\sqrt{a^2 - b^2}) + (b^2/2)\sqrt{a^2 - 2b^2} - a^3 \tan^{-1} (a/\sqrt{a^2 - 2b^2})]$
39. a) Radius of sphere = 2, of hole = 1 **b)** $4\pi\sqrt{3}$
40. $\int_0^1 \int_{\sqrt{1-x^2}}^{\sqrt{3-x^2}} \int_1^{\sqrt{4-x^2-y^2}} xyz^2\, dz\, dy\, dx + \int_1^{\sqrt{3}} \int_0^{\sqrt{3-x^2}} \int_1^{\sqrt{4-x^2-y^2}} xyz^2\, dz\, dy\, dx$
41. $3\pi a^3/4$ **42.** $2a^3(3\pi - 4)/9$ **43.** $\pi a^5/12$ **44.** $\pi^2a^3/4$ **45.** $8\pi\delta(b^5 - a^5)/15$ **47.** $\rho_0(1 - \frac{1}{2}\epsilon^2)$ **48.** $2\pi(\sqrt{3} - 1)$
49. $\pi\sqrt{3}$ **50.** $\pi\sqrt{2}\,a^2$ **51.** $2a^2(\pi - 2)$ **52.** $\pi\sqrt{2}$ **53. a)** 144π **b)** -16π **c)** 128π
54. $4 \int_0^a \sqrt{a^2 - y^2}\, \sqrt{4y^2 + 1}\, dy$ **55.** $16\pi(\sqrt{2} - 1)$ **56.** $8\pi^2$ **57.** $\pi^2/2$
58. $8r^2$ **60.** $(6M/a^2)(1 - h/\sqrt{a^2 + h^2})$ **62.** $z = 1$ **63.** $4a/3$

CHAPTER 15

Article 15–1, p. 684

1. a) $x = 0, y = 0$ **b)** $x^2 + y^2 = a^2$ **2.** $\delta\pi a^4/2$ **4.** Helix
5. Replace x, y, z by $x - x_0, y - y_0, z - z_0$. **6.** $\mathbf{F}(x, y, z) = \exp (2y + 3z)[2x\mathbf{i} + 2x^2\mathbf{j} + 3x^2\mathbf{k}]$
7. $\mathbf{F}(x, y, z) = 2(x^2 + y^2 + z^2)^{-1}[x\mathbf{i} + y\mathbf{j} + z\mathbf{k}]$ **8.** $\mathbf{F}(x, y, z) = (z^2 + x^2y^2)^{-1}[yz\mathbf{i} + xz\mathbf{j} - xy\mathbf{k}]$
9. $\mathbf{F}(x, y, z) = 2\mathbf{i} - 3\mathbf{j} + 5\mathbf{k}$ **10.** $\mathbf{F}(x, y, z) = n(x^2 + y^2 + z^2)^{(n-2)/2}[x\mathbf{i} + y\mathbf{j} + z\mathbf{k}]$

Article 15–2, p. 690

4. πa^3 **5.** $\frac{28}{3}\sqrt{14}$ **6.** $\frac{28}{3}\sqrt{14}$ **7.** $\pi a^2/2$ **8.** 0 **9.** $\pi a^3/6$ **10.** $\pi a^3/3$

Article 15–3, pp. 701–703

1. $\frac{5}{6}\sqrt{2}$ **3.** π **4.** 0 **5. a)** 0 **b)** $-\frac{1}{3}$ **8.** $n = -1$ **9. a)** $\frac{9}{2}$ **b)** $\frac{9}{2}$ **c)** $\frac{9}{2}$ **10. a)** 2.143 **b)** 2.538 **c)** $2 + \sin 1$
11. a) 3 **b)** 3 **c)** 3 **12. a)** e^3 **b)** e^3 **c)** e^3 **13. a)** $\sin 1 = 0.8415$ **b)** 0.8415 **c)** 0.8415
14. $f(x, y, z) = x^2 + \frac{3}{2}y^2 + 2z^2 + C$ **15.** $f(x, y, z) = xy + yz + zx + C$ **16.** $f(x, y, z) = xe^{y+2z} + C$
17. $f(x, y, z) = xy \sin z + C$ **19.** 8 **20.** 24 **21.** $-e^{-2\pi} + 1$ **25. b)** $\nabla \times \mathbf{F} = \mathbf{0}$

Article 15–4, p. 709

2. $\pi/2$ **3.** $2\pi\delta$ **5. a)** 0 **b)** 4π **6. a)** 0 **b)** 4π

Article 15–5, p. 718

3. 0 **4.** 0 **5.** $\pi a^4/2$ **6.** 0 **7.** $-\pi a^2$ **11.** 0 **12.** -2 **13.** $\int_C M(x, y)\, dy - N(x, y)\, dx = \iint_R (\partial M/\partial x + \partial N/\partial y)\, dx\, dy$

Article 15–6, pp. 725–726

1. 0 **2.** 24 **3.** 0 **4.** 16 **5.** 0 **6.** 24π **7.** 48π **8.** 135π **9.** $4\pi a^3$ **10.** 24

Article 15–7, p. 734

1. 0 **2.** 0 **3.** $-\pi/4$ **4.** 0 **5.** Zero, because curl grad $\phi = \mathbf{0}$.

Miscellaneous Problems Chapter 15, pp. 735–737

5. 0 **6.** $\sqrt{3}\,\pi$ **7.** $(\pi/60)(17^{5/2} - 41)$ **8.** $4\pi a^4/3$ **9.** $8\pi a^3$ **10.** $-8\pi a$ **11.** $-\frac{25}{3}$ **12.** $\pi a/2$ **13.** 0 **14.** 2π **15.** 2π **16.** 0
17. 0 **18.** 0 **19.** 0 **20.** -3 **31. a)** $C_1 = -100, C_2 = 200$ **b)** $C_1 = 100, C_2 = 0$

CHAPTER 16

Article 16–2, pp. 748–749

1. $0, -\frac{1}{4}, -\frac{2}{9}, -\frac{3}{16}$; converges to 0 **2.** $\frac{1}{2}, \frac{1}{2}, \frac{3}{8}, \frac{1}{4}$; converges to 0 **3.** $\frac{1}{3}, \frac{1}{9}, \frac{1}{27}, \frac{1}{81}$; converges to 0 **4.** $1, \frac{1}{2}, \frac{1}{6}, \frac{1}{24}$; converges to 0
5. $1, -\frac{1}{3}, \frac{1}{5}, -\frac{1}{7}$; converges to 0 **6.** 1, 3, 1, 3; diverges **7.** 0, −1, 0, 1; diverges
8. $8, 8^{1/2}, 8^{1/3}, 8^{1/4}$; converges to 1 **9.** $1, -1/\sqrt{2}, 1/\sqrt{3}, -\frac{1}{2}$; converges to 0
10. 1, 1, 1, 1; converges to 1 **11.** Converges to 0 **12.** Diverges **13.** Converges to 1 **14.** Converges to 0 **15.** Diverges
16. Diverges **17.** Converges to $-\frac{2}{3}$ **18.** Converges to $\frac{1}{2}$ **19.** Converges to $\sqrt{2}$ **20.** Converges to 0
21. Diverges **22.** Converges to 1 **23.** Diverges **24.** Converges to 0 **25.** Converges to 1
26. Converges to 1 **27.** Converges to −5 **28.** Converges to 9 **29.** Converges to 1 **30.** Converges to 0
31. Converges to 1 **32.** Diverges **33.** Converges to 5 **34.** Diverges **35.** Converges to 0
36. Converges to 10 **37.** Converges to 0 **38.** Converges to 1 **39.** Converges to $\sqrt{2}$ **40.** Converges to 2
41. Diverges **42.** Converges to 0 **43.** Converges to 0 **44.** Converges to −1 **45.** Diverges
46. Converges to 1 **47.** Converges to 0 **48.** Converges to 1 **49.** Converges to $\pi/2$ **50.** Diverges
51. Converges to 1 **52.** Converges to 2 **53.** Converges to $\frac{1}{2}$ **54.** Converges to 0 **55.** Use $0 < n!/n^n \le 1/n$
56. $x_7 = 1.732050808 = x_6$ **57.** Yes. No; the limit is 1 for any $x > 0$.
58. a) $x_1 = 1, x_2 = 1.54\ldots, x_3 = 1.57\ldots, x_4 = 1.570796327$ **b)** $x_1 = 5, \ldots, x_8 = x_9 = 7.853981634\ (\approx 5\pi/2)$ **60.** 1 **61.** 1

Article 16–3, pp. 752–753

1. Converges; $L = 0$ **2.** Converges; $L = 0$ **3.** Converges; $L = 0$ **4.** Converges; $L = 1$ **5.** Converges; $L = 0$
6. Diverges **7.** Converges; $L = e^7$ **8.** Converges; $L = e^5$ **9.** Converges; $L = 0$ **10.** Converges; $L = 1$
11. Diverges **12.** Converges; $L = 0$ **13.** Converges; $L = 1$ **14.** Converges; $L = 1$ **15.** Converges; $L = 0$
16. Converges; $L = 1$ **17.** Converges; $L = 1/e$ **18.** Converges; $L = 1/e$ **19.** Converges; $L = 0$ **20.** Converges; $L = 1$
21. Converges; $L = x$ **22.** Converges; $L = 1$ **23.** Converges; $L = 1$ **24.** Converges; $L = 0$ **25.** Converges; $L = 1$
26. Converges; $L = 4$ **27.** Converges; $L = 1/e$ **28.** Converges; $L = 1$ **29.** Converges; $L = 0$ **30.** Converges; $L = 1/(p - 1)$
31. $N \ge 693$ **32.** $N \ge 9124$ **33.** $N \ge 17$

Article 16–4, pp. 761–763

1. $s_n = \frac{1}{2} - (1/n+2)$, $\lim_{n\to\infty} s_n = \frac{1}{2}$ **2.** $s_n = -\ln(n+1)$, diverges **3.** $s_n = (1-(1/e)^n)/(1-(1/e))$, $\lim_{n\to\infty} s_n = e/(e-1)$
4. $s_n = \frac{2}{3}(1-(-1/2)^n)$, $\lim_{n\to\infty} s_n = \frac{2}{3}$ **5.** $s_n = \frac{1}{3}(1-(-2)^n)$, diverges **6.** $s_n = 3(1-(\frac{1}{3})^n)$, $\lim_{n\to\infty} s_n = 3$
7. $s_n = \frac{1}{11}(1-(\frac{1}{100})^n)$, $\lim_{n\to\infty} s_n = \frac{1}{11}$ **8.** $s_n = n(n+1)/2$, diverges
9. a) $\sum_{n=-2}^{\infty} 1/[(n+4)(n+5)]$ **b)** $\sum_{n=0}^{\infty} 1/[(n+2)(n+3)]$ **c)** $\sum_{n=5}^{\infty} 1/[(n-3)(n-2)]$ **10.** $28m$
11. $1+\frac{1}{4}+\frac{1}{16}+\frac{1}{64}$; $\frac{4}{3}$ **12.** $\frac{1}{16}+\frac{1}{64}+\frac{1}{256}+\frac{1}{1024}$; $\frac{1}{12}$ **13.** $\frac{7}{4}+\frac{7}{16}+\frac{7}{64}+\frac{7}{256}$; $\frac{7}{3}$
14. $5-\frac{5}{4}+\frac{5}{16}-\frac{5}{64}$; 4 **15.** 11.5 **16.** 8.5 **17.** 5/3 **18.** 10/3 **19.** 1 **20.** $\frac{1}{4}$ **21.** $\frac{1}{9}$ **22.** 1
23. a) 234/999 **b)** Yes; if $x = 0.a_1 a_2 \cdots a_n \overline{a_1 a_2 \cdots a_n}$, then $(10^n - 1)x = a_1 a_2 \cdots a_n = p$ is an integer and $x = p/q$ with $q = 10^n - 1$. **24.** 123999/99900 **25.** $2+\sqrt{2}$ **26.** Diverges **27.** 1 **28.** Diverges **29.** Diverges **30.** 5/6 **31.** $e^2/(e^2-1)$
32. Diverges **33.** Diverges **34.** 2/9 **35.** 3/2 **36.** Diverges **37.** Diverges **38.** $x/(x-1)$ **39.** $a=1, r=-x$
40. $a=1, r=-x^2$ **41.** 8 **42.** $s_n = (1+(-1)^{n+1})/2$ **48. d)** $n \geq 6$ **e)** $n \geq 999$
49. a) $R_n = C_0 e^{-kt_0}(1-e^{-nkt_0})/(1-e^{-kt_0})$, $R = C_0(e^{-kt_0})/(1-e^{-kt_0}) = C_0/(e^{kt_0}-1)$
b) $R_1 = 1/e \approx 0.368$, $R_{10} = R(1-e^{-10}) \approx R(0.9999546) \approx 0.58195$; $R \approx 0.58198$; $0 < (R-R_{10})/R < 0.0001$.
c) 7 **e)** 20 hr **f)** Give initial dose that produces a concentration of 2 mg/ml, followed every 100 ln 2 ≈ 69.31 hr by dose that raises concentration by 1.5 mg/ml **g)** $5 \ln(10/3) \approx 6$ (hr)

Article 16–5, pp. 776–778

[*Note.* The tests mentioned in Problems 1–30 may not be the only ones that apply.]

1. Converges; ratio test; geometric series, $r < 1$. **2.** Diverges; $\lim_{n\to\infty} a_n = 1$ **3.** Converges; compare with $\sum (1/2^n)$
4. Diverges; multiple of $\sum (1/n)$ **5.** Converges; ratio test **6.** Converges; ratio test **7.** Diverges; compare with $\sum (1/n)$
8. Converges; p-series, $p > 1$ **9.** Converges; ratio test **10.** Diverges; integral test; multiple of $\sum_{n=1}^{\infty} (1/n)$
11. Diverges; compare with $\sum (1/n)$ **12.** Diverges; p-series, $p < 1$; integral test **13.** Diverges; ratio test
14. Converges; compare with $\sum (\frac{1}{3})^n$; root test **15.** Converges; ratio test (or root test) **16.** Diverges; p-series, $p < 1$
17. Converges; comparison with $\sum (1/n^{3/2})$ **18.** Diverges; nth-term test **19.** Converges; ratio test **20.** Converges; compare with $\sum (1/n^{3/2})$ **21.** Diverges; integral test **22.** Converges; ratio test (or root test) **23.** Diverges; nth-term test, $a_n \to e$
24. Converges; compare with $\sum (1/3^n)$ **25.** Converges; ratio test **26.** Diverges; integral test **27.** Converges; ratio test or comparison with $\sum (1/n!)$ **28.** Diverges; root test
29. Converges; ratio test **30.** Converges; ratio test; comparison to $\sum (1/2^n)$ **32.** $x^2 < 2$ **33.** $x^2 \leq 1$
34. $|x| > 1$ **35.** 1.649767731 **36.** $\sum_{n=1}^{6} (1/n^2) = 1.49138$, $\sum_{n=1}^{6} [3[(n-1)!]^2/(2n)!] = 1.644911616$
37. $n = 27$, $s_n + n^{-3}/3 = 1.082324151$; $\pi^4/90 = 1.082323234$; difference $\approx 0.9 \times 10^{-6}$
38. $40.5548555 < s_n < 41.5548555$ **39.** $\sum (1/n)$ is divergent, as is any nonzero multiple of this series.

Article 16–6, p. 780

[*Note.* In the answers provided for this article, "Yes" means that the series converges absolutely. "No" means that the series does *not* converge absolutely. The reasons given for the convergence or divergence of the series of absolute values may not be the only appropriate ones.]

1. Yes; p-series, $p = 2$ **2.** Yes; p-series, $p = 3$ **3.** No; harmonic series divergence **4.** Yes; geometric series; $r < 1$
5. Yes; comparison to p-series, $p = 2$ **6.** No; multiple of harmonic series **7.** Yes: comparison to p-series, $p = \frac{3}{2}$ **8.** No; multiple of harmonic series **9.** Yes; comparison test **10.** Yes; comparison test **11.** No; nth-term test
12. Yes; root test or ratio test **13.** Yes; geometric series, $r < 1$ **14.** No; nth-term test **15.** Yes; ratio test
16. No; nth-term test **17.** Yes; compare with $(2+n)/n^3$ **18.** Yes; compare with $(1/2^n) + (1/3^n)$

Article 16–7, pp. 785–786

1. Converges **2.** Converges **3.** Diverges **4.** Diverges **5.** Converges **6.** Converges **7.** Converges **8.** Diverges
9. Converges **10.** Diverges **11.** Absolutely convergent **12.** Conditionally convergent **13.** Absolutely convergent
14. Divergent **15.** Conditionally convergent **16.** Absolutely convergent **17.** Divergent **18.** Conditionally convergent
19. Conditionally convergent **20.** Absolutely convergent **21.** Absolutely convergent **22.** Divergent
23. Absolutely convergent **24.** Conditionally convergent **25.** Divergent **26.** Absolutely convergent **27.** Conditionally convergent **28.** Absolutely convergent **29.** $\frac{1}{5} = 0.2$ **30.** 10^{-5} **31.** $(0.01)^5/5 = 2 \times 10^{-11}$ **32.** t^4
33. 0.54030 (actual: cos 1 = 0.540302306) **34.** 0.36788 (actual: $1/e = 0.367879441$)
35. a) It is not decreasing (condition 2) **b)** $-\frac{1}{2}$ **36.** $s_{20} + \frac{1}{2} \cdot \frac{1}{21} = 0.692580927$, ln 2 = 0.693147181
39. $\sum_{n=1}^{\infty} a_n = \sum_{n=1}^{\infty} (-1)^n (1/\sqrt{n})$, $\sum_{n=1}^{\infty} b_n = \sum_{n=1}^{\infty} (-1)^n (1/\sqrt{n})$, $\sum_{n=1}^{\infty} a_n b_n = \sum_{n=1}^{\infty} (1/n)$

Article 16–8, p. 791

1. $1 - x + (x^2/2!) - (x^3/3!)$; $1 - x + (x^2/2!) - (x^3/3!) + (x^4/4!)$ **2.** $x - (x^3/3!)$; $x - (x^3/3!)$
3. $1 - (x^2/2!)$; $1 - (x^2/2!) + (x^4/4!)$ **4.** $1 - (x^2/2!)$; $1 - (x^2/2!) + (x^4/4!)$
5. $x + (x^3/3!)$; $x + (x^3/3!)$ **6.** $1 + (x^2/2!)$; $1 + (x^2/2!) + (x^4/4!)$ **7.** $-2x + 1$; $x^4 - 2x + 1$
8. $x^3 - 2x + 1$; $x^3 - 2x + 1$ **9.** $x^2 - 2x + 1$; $x^2 - 2x + 1$ **10.** $\sum_{n=0}^{\infty} (-1)^n x^n = 1 - x + x^2 - \cdots$ **11.** x^2 **12.** $x^2 + 2x + 1$
13. $1 + (3x/2) + (3/2 \cdot 4)x^2 - [3/(8 \cdot 3!)]x^3 + [9/(16 \cdot 4!)]x^4 - [45/(32 \cdot 5!)]x^5 + \cdots = \sum_{n=0}^{\infty} (3/n^2)x^n$
14. $1 + x + x^2 + x^3 + \cdots$; geometric series with $r = x$
15. $e^{10} + e^{10}(x - 10) + (e^{10}/2!)(x - 10)^2 + (e^{10}/3!)(x - 10)^3 + \cdots$ **16.** $\frac{1}{4} + (x - \frac{1}{2}) + (x - \frac{1}{2})^2$
17. $(x - 1) - [(x - 1)^2/2] + [(x - 1)^3/3] - [(x - 1)^4/4] + \cdots$
18. $2 + \frac{1}{2}(x - 4)/2 - [1/(2 \cdot 4)][(x - 4)^2/2^3] + [(1 \cdot 3)/(2 \cdot 4 \cdot 6)][(x - 4)^3/2^5] - [(1 \cdot 3 \cdot 5)/(2 \cdot 4 \cdot 6 \cdot 8)][(x - 4)^4/2^7]$
19. $-1 - (x + 1) - (x + 1)^2 - (x + 1)^3 - \cdots$ **20.** $(\sqrt{2}/2)[1 + (x + (\pi/4)) - [(x + (\pi/4))^2/2!] - [(x + (\pi/4))^3/3!] + \cdots]$
21. $1 + 2(x - (\pi/4)) + 2(x - (\pi/4))^2$ **22.** $\ln (0.5) - \sqrt{3}(x - (\pi/3)) - 2(x - (\pi/3))^2$
23. 1.0100 with error less than 0.0001 (use 2 terms)

Article 16–9, pp. 799–800

1. $1 + \frac{1}{2}x + \frac{1}{4}(x^2/2!) + \frac{1}{8}(x^3/3!) + \frac{1}{16}(x^4/4!) + \cdots$ **2.** $3x - 3^3(x^3/3!) + 3^5(x^5/5!) - 3^7(x^7/7!) + \cdots$
3. $5 - (5/\pi^2)(x^2/2!) + (5/\pi^4)(x^4/4!) - (5/\pi^6)(x^6/6!) + \cdots$ **4.** $x + (x^3/3!) + (x^5/5!) + (x^7/7!) + \cdots$
5. $(x^4/4!) - (x^6/6!) + (x^8/8!) - (x^{10}/10!) + \cdots$ **6.** $1 - x^2 + (8x^4/4!) - (32x^6/6!) + (128x^8/8!) - \cdots$
9. $1 - x + x^2 - 3 \int_0^x (x - t)^2(1 + t)^{-11}\, dt$ **10.** $x - (x^2/2) + \int_0^x (x - t)^2(1 + t)^{-3}\, dt$
11. $1 + (x/2) - \frac{1}{8}x^2 + \frac{3}{16} \int_0^x (x - t)^2(1 + t)^{-(5/2)}\, dt$ **12.** $e[1 + (x - 1) + [(x - 1)^2/2!] + [(x - 1)^3/3!] + \cdots]$
13. $|x| < \sqrt[5]{0.06} \approx 0.57$ **14.** $|R| < 0.00261$. Too small. **15.** $|R| < (10^{-9}/6)$; $x < \sin x$ for $x < 0$.
16. $|R| < 1.3 \times 10^{-5}$ **17.** $|R| < e^{0.1}/6{,}000 \approx 1.84 \times 10^{-4}$ **18.** $1.\bar{6} \times 10^{-4}$
19. $R_4(x, 0) < 0.0003$ **22. a)** $\sin 0.1$ **b)** $\cos (\pi/4)$ **c)** $\cosh 1$

Article 16–10, pp. 806–807

1. Use $\cos x \approx (\sqrt{3}/2) - \frac{1}{2}(x - (\pi/6))$. $\cos 31° \approx 0.857\,299$. Actual: $\cos 31° = 0.857\,167$.
2. Use $\tan x \approx 1 + 2(x - (\pi/4)) + 4[(x - (\pi/4))^2/2!]$. $\tan 46° \approx 1.035\,516$. Actual: $\tan 46° = 1.035\,530$.
3. Use $\sin x \approx (x - 2\pi)$. $\sin (6.3) \approx 0.0168\,147$. Actual: $\sin (6.3) = 0.0168\,139$.
4. Use $\cos x \approx 1 - [(x - 22\pi)^2/2!]$. $\cos 69 \approx 0.993\,383$. Actual: $\cos 69 = 0.993\,390$.
5. Use $\ln x \approx (x - 1) - [(x - 1)^2/2] + [(x - 1)^3/3] - [(x - 1)^4/4]$. $\ln 1.25 \approx 0.222\,982$. Actual: $\ln 1.25 = 0.223\,144$.
6. Use $\tan^{-1} x \approx (\pi/4) + \frac{1}{2}(x - 1)$. $\tan^{-1} 1.02 \approx 0.795\,398$. Actual: $\tan^{-1} 1.02 = 0.795\,299$.
7. $\ln (1 + 2x) = 2x - [(2x)^2/2] + [(2x)^3/3] - [(2x)^4/4] + \cdots = \sum_{n=1}^{\infty} (-1)^{n+1}[(2x)^n/n]$; converges for $|x| < \frac{1}{2}$.
8. $|x| < 0.0197$ **9.** $\int_0^{0.1} [(\sin x)/x]\, dx \approx x - (x^3/18)]_0^{0.1} \approx 0.09994$
10. $\int_0^{0.1} e^{-x^2}\, dx \approx x - (x^3/3)]_0^{0.1} = 0.09967$ **13.** $\ln 1.5 \approx 0.405\,465$ **14.** 50 terms (through $\frac{1}{99}$)
17. $c_3 = 3.141592665$ **21. c)** 6 **d)** $1/q$ **22. a)** $E(x) = 2$ **b)** $E(x) = 6$ **c)** The series for $E(x)$ diverges.

Article 16–11, pp. 811–812

2. Minimum at $x = 1$, $y = -2$ **3.** Saddle point at $x = 1$, $y = 2$ **4.** Minimum at $x = 1$, $y = 0$
5. Saddle point at $x = 0$, $y = 0$ **6.** Maximum at $x = 0$, $y = 1$ **7.** Saddle point $(0, 0, 6)$; relative max $(-\frac{2}{3}, \frac{2}{3}, 6 + \frac{8}{27})$
8. Saddle points $(0, 0, -8)$, $(-2, 2, -8)$; relative max $(-2, 0, -4)$; relative min $(0, 2, -12)$
9. If $f_x(a, b) = f_y(a, b) = 0$, then $f(x, y)$ has, at the point $x = a$, $y = b$, **a)** a relative minimum if d^2f/ds^2 is positive in all directions emanating from (a, b); **b)** a relative maximum if d^2f/ds^2 is negative in all directions emanating from (a, b); and **c)** a saddle point if d^2f/ds^2 is positive in some directions and negative in other directions emanating from (a, b). **10.** $1 + x + [(x^2 - y^2)/2!] +$
11. $f(x, y, z) = f(a, b, c) + f_x(a, b, c) \cdot (x - a) + f_y(a, b, c) \cdot (y - b) + f_z(a, b, c) \cdot (z - c) + (1/2!)[f_{xx}(a, b, c) \cdot (x - a)^2$
$+ f_{yy}(a, b, c) \cdot (y - b)^2 + f_{zz}(a, b, c) \cdot (z - c)^2$
$+ 2f_{xy}(a, b, c) \cdot (x - a)(y - b) + 2f_{xz}(a, b, c) \cdot (x - a)(z - c) + 2f_{yz}(a, b, c) \cdot (y - b)(z - c)] + \cdots$

Article 16–12, p. 814

1. 1 **2.** $\frac{1}{2}$ **3.** $-\frac{1}{24}$ **4.** 1 **5.** -2 **6.** $\frac{1}{3}$ **7.** 0 **8.** 1 **9.** $-\frac{1}{3}$ **10.** -1 **11.** $\frac{1}{120}$ **12.** 2 **13.** $\frac{1}{3}$
14. $\frac{1}{2}$ **15.** -1 **16.** 2 **17.** 3 **18.** 2 **19.** 0 **20.** $\frac{1}{12}$ **21. b)** $\frac{1}{2}$ **22.** $r = -3$, $s = \frac{9}{2}$

23. This approximation gives better results than the approximation $\sin x \approx x$. See table.

x	± 1.0	± 0.1	± 0.01
$6x/(6 + x^2)$	± 0.857142857	± 0.099833611	± 0.009999833
$\sin x$	± 0.841470985	± 0.099833417	± 0.009999833

Article 16–13, pp. 822–823

1. $|x| < 1$. Diverges at $x = \pm 1$ **2.** $|x| < 1$. Diverges at $x = \pm 1$ **3.** $|x| < 2$. Diverges at $x = \pm 2$

4. $-\infty < x < \infty$ **5.** $-\infty < x < \infty$ **6.** $0 < x < 2$. Converges at $x = 2$; diverges at 0

7. $-4 < x < 0$. Diverges at $x = 0, -4$ **8.** $|x| < 1$. Diverges at $x = \pm 1$ **9.** $|x| < 1$. Converges at $x = \pm 1$

10. $1 \le x \le 3$ **11.** $|x| < \infty$ **12.** $|x| \le \frac{1}{2}$ **13.** $|x| < (1/e)$. Converges at $x = -(1/e)$; diverges at $(1/e)$

14. $|x| < \infty$ **15.** $x = 0$ **16.** $|x| < \infty$ **17.** $\frac{1}{2} < x < \frac{3}{2}$. Diverges at $x = \frac{1}{2}, \frac{3}{2}$

18. $0 < x < 4$. Converges at $x = 4$; diverges at 0 **19.** $|x| < \sqrt{3}$. Diverges at $x = \pm\sqrt{3}$

20. $-4 < x < -2$. Converges at $x = -4$; diverges at -2 **21.** e^{3x+6} **22.** $2/(3 - x^2)$

24. $1 - 2x + 3x^2 - 4x^3 + \cdots = \sum_{n=0}^{\infty} (-1)^n(n + 1)x^n$ **25.** $\sum_{n=1}^{\infty} 2nx^{2n-1}$

26. $\sin^2 x = \frac{1}{2}([(2x)^2/2!] - [(2x)^4/4!] + \cdots)$, $(d/dx)(\sin^2 x) = 2 \sin x \cos x = (2x/1!) - [(2x)^3/3!] + \cdots = \sin 2x$

27. 0.002666 **28.** 0.004992 **29.** 0.000331 **30.** 0.099889 **31.** 0.363305 **32.** 0.097605 **33.** 0.099999 **34.** 0.251715

35. a) $\sinh^{-1} x = x - \frac{1}{2}(x^3/3) + [(1 \cdot 3)/(2 \cdot 4)](x^5/5) - [(1 \cdot 3 \cdot 5)/(2 \cdot 4 \cdot 6)](x^7/7) + \cdots$
b) $\sinh^{-1} 0.25 \approx 0.247$ (Actual: $\sinh^{-1} 0.25 = \ln (0.25 + \sqrt{(0.25)^2 + 1}) \approx 0.24746646$)

36. 0.904531532 **37.** $\sum_{n=1}^{\infty} n^n x^n$ **38.** $\sum_{n=1}^{\infty} (x^n/n)$; conditional at $x = -1$; $\sum_{n=1}^{\infty} (x^n/n^2)$; absolute at $x = \pm 1$

39. By the theorem, the series converges absolutely for $|x| < d$, for all positive $d < r$. This means it converges absolutely for all $|x| < r$. [Take $d = \frac{1}{2}(r + |x|)$.]

40. $|a_{n+1}/a_n| = |x_{m-n}/n|$; $\lim_{n\to\infty} |a_{n+1}/a_n| = |x|$. So the series converges for $|x| < 1$.

Miscellaneous Problems Chapter 16, pp. 824–825

1. $s_n = \ln [(n + 1)/(2n)]$; series converges to $-\ln 2$ **2.** $s_n = \frac{1}{2}[\frac{3}{2} - 1/(n + 1)]$; limit $= \frac{3}{4}$

6. a) $\sum_{n=2}^{\infty} (-1)^n x^n$ **b)** No, because it will converge in an interval symmetric about $x = 0$, and it cannot converge when $x = -1$.

7. $(1 - t^2)^{-(1/2)} = \sum_{k=0}^{\infty} 2^{-2k}(k!)^{-2}(2k)!\, t^{2k}$, $-1 < t < 1$, $\sin^{-1} x = \sum_{k=0}^{\infty} 2^{-2k}(k!)^{-2}(2k)!\, x^{2k+1}/(2k + 1)$, $-1 \le x \le 1$

8. $(1 + t^2)^{-(1/2)} = \sum_{k=0}^{\infty} (-1)^k 2^{-2k}(k!)^{-2}(2k)!\, t^{2k}$, $-1 \le t \le 1$,
$\sinh^{-1} x = \sum_{k=0}^{\infty} (-1)^k 2^{-2k}(k!)^{-2}(2k)!\, x^{2k+1}/(2k + 1)$, $-1 \le x \le 1$

9. $e^{\sin x} = 1 + x + x^2/2! - 3x^4/4! - \cdots$ **11. a)** $\ln \cos x = -(x^2/2) - (x^4/12) - (x^6/45) - \cdots$ **b)** -0.00017 **12.** 0.946

13. 0.747 **14.** $\sqrt{2}[1 + (x - 1)/2 + (x - 1)^2/8 + \cdots]$ **15.** $\sum_{n=0}^{\infty} (-1)^{n+1}(x - 2)^n$, $1 < x < 3$

16. $\tan x = x + x^3/3 + 2x^5/15 + \cdots$ **17.** $\sum_{n=0}^{\infty} [(-1)^n(x - 3)^n/4^{n+1}]$

18. $\cos x = \frac{1}{2} \sum_{n=0}^{\infty} (-1)^n[1/(2n)!\, (x - (\pi/3))^{2n} + \sqrt{3}/(2n + 1)!\, (x - (\pi/3))^{2n+1}]$ **19.** $\sum_{n=0}^{\infty} (-1)^n(x - \pi)^n/\pi^{n+1}$ **20.** 1.543

22. $e^{e^x} = e(1 + x + 2x^2/2! + 5x^3/3! + \cdots$ **23.** 0.0027 **24.** -0.0011 **25.** $-\infty$ **26.** $e^{-(1/6)}$

27. Converges; by integral test **28.** Diverges, since nth term doesn't approach zero

29. Diverges **30.** Diverges **31.** Diverges **32.** Converges **33.** Diverges **34.** Diverges **35.** Converges **36.** Converges

37. Diverges **38.** Diverges **39.** Diverges **40.** Converges **41.** $\frac{1}{2}$

43. b) Converges **c)** Converges, by comparison test **45.** $-5 \le x < 1$ **46.** $-\infty < x < \infty$ **47.** $-\infty < x < \infty$

48. $-e < x < e$ **49.** $1 < x < 5$ **50.** $-1 < x < 5$ **51.** $0 \le x \le 2$ **52.** $-1 \le x < 1$ **53.** $-\infty < x < \infty$

54. $(6n - 1)\pi/6 \le x \le (6n + 1)\pi/6$ $(n = 0, \pm 1, \pm 2, \ldots)$ **55.** $x \ge \frac{1}{2}$ **56. a)** $-\infty < x < \infty$ **b)** $y'' = xy$ $(a = 1, b = 0)$

CHAPTER 17

Article 17–1, p. 832

1. a) (14, 8) **b)** $(-1, 8)$ **c)** $(0, -5)$ **2. a)** $(-\frac{7}{3}, -24)$ **b)** $(\frac{2}{5}, -\frac{1}{5})$ **c)** $(-1, 0)$

Article 17–2, p. 838

2. a) By reflecting z across the real axis **b)** By reflecting z across the imaginary axis **c)** By reflecting z in the origin
d) By reflecting z in the real axis and then multiplying the length of the vector by $1/|z|^2$ **6.** On the real axis

9. a) Points on the circle $x^2 + y^2 = 4$ **b)** Points inside the circle $x^2 + y^2 = 4$ **c)** Points outside the circle $x^2 + y^2 = 4$
10. Points on a circle of radius 2, center (1, 0) **11.** Points on a circle of radius 1, center (−1, 0)
12. Points on the y-axis **13.** Points on the line $y = -x$ **14.** $4 \text{ cis } (2\pi/3)$ **15.** $1 \text{ cis } (\pi/2)$ **16.** $1 \text{ cis } (2\pi/3)$
17. $\sqrt{65} \text{ cis } (-\tan^{-1} 0.125) = \sqrt{65} \text{ cis } (-7°7.5')$
18. $\cos 4\theta = \cos^4 \theta - 6 \cos^2 \theta \sin^2 \theta + \sin^4 \theta, \quad \sin 4\theta = 4 \sin \theta \cos \theta(\cos^2 \theta - \sin^2 \theta)$
19. $1, \text{cis } (2\pi/3) = (-1 + i\sqrt{3})/2, \text{cis } (-2\pi/3) = (-1 - i\sqrt{3})/2$ **20.** $\text{cis } (\pi/4, 5\pi/4) = \pm\text{cis } (\pi/4) = \pm(1 + i)/\sqrt{2}$
21. $2i, 2 \text{ cis } (-5\pi/6) = -\sqrt{3} - i, 2 \text{ cis } (-\pi/6) = \sqrt{3} - i$
22. $2 \text{ cis } (0°, 60°, 120°, 180°, 240°, 300°)$; that is, $2, 1 + i\sqrt{3}, -1 + i\sqrt{3}, -2, -1 - i\sqrt{3}, 1 - i\sqrt{3}$
23. $\pm\sqrt{2} \text{ cis } (\pm 30°)$; that is, $(\sqrt{3} + i)/\sqrt{2}, -(\sqrt{3} + i)/\sqrt{2}, (\sqrt{3} - i)/\sqrt{2}, (-\sqrt{3} + i)/\sqrt{2}$
24. $\sqrt[6]{2} \text{ cis } (45°, 165°, 285°, 75°, 195°, 315°)$ **25.** $2 \text{ cis } (60°, 120°, 240°, 300°)$; or $1 \pm i\sqrt{3}, -1 \pm i\sqrt{3}$
26. $\text{cis } (45°, 135°, 225°, 315°)$; or $(1 \pm i)/\sqrt{2}, (-1 \pm i)/\sqrt{2}$

Article 17–3, p. 841

1. a) $|w| = 1, 0 \leq \arg w \leq 2\pi$ **b)** $|w| = 4, \pi \leq \arg w \leq 2\pi$ **c)** $\arg w = \pi/2$ **d)** $|w| < 1, -2\pi < \arg w \leq 0$
e) The u-axis, $u \geq 0$ **f)** The u-axis, $u \leq 0$

Article 17–4, p. 844

1. $-2/(z_0 - 1)^2 = +2$ **2.** $3(z_0 + 1)^2 = -12$ **3.** $z_0/\sqrt{z_0^2 + 1} = 2^{-(1/4)} \text{ cis } (\pi/8, 9\pi/8)$ **4.** $-1/\alpha^2$

Article 17–5, p. 846

1. $u = x^2 - y^2, v = 2xy$ **2.** $u = x^3 - 3xy^2, v = 3x^2y - y^3$ **3.** $u = x^4 - 6x^2y^2 + y^4, v = 4x^3y - 4xy^3$
4. $u = (x^2 - y^2)/(x^2 + y^2)^2, v = -2xy/(x^2 + y^2)^2$

Article 17–6, p. 848

1. $1 + z + z^2 + z^3 + \cdots, |z| < 1$ **2.** $1 - 2z + 3z^2 - 4z^3 + \cdots, |z| < 1$
3. $(z - 1) - [(z - 1)^2/2] + [(z - 1)^3/3] - [(z - 1)^4/4] + \cdots, |z - 1| < 1$
4. $(z + i) + [(z + i)^2/2] + [(z + i)^3/3] + [(z + i)^4/4] + \cdots, |z + i| < 1$
5. $1 - [(z + 1)/2] + [(z + 1)^2/4] - [(z + 1)^3/8] + [(z + 1)^4/16] - \cdots, |z + 1| < 2$

Article 17–7, p. 853

1. $1.59 + 1.32i$ **5. a)** $-1 \pm 2i$ **b)** $1 \pm i, -1 \pm i$ **c)** $2, -1 \pm i\sqrt{3}$
18. a) The circle $u^2 + v^2 = e^{2x}$, described once in the counterclockwise direction each time y increases through a 2π interval of values; for instance, $-\pi < y \leq \pi$, etc. **b)** The branch of the hyperbola $[u^2/(\sin^2 x)] - [v^2/(\cos^2 x)] = 1$ (x not an integer multiple of $\pi/2$) on which u and $\sin x$ have the same sign. The lines $x = n\pi (n = 0, \pm 1, \ldots)$ map into the v-axis. The lines $x = \pi/2 + 2n\pi (n = 0, \pm 1, \ldots)$ map into the u-axis, $u \geq 1$. The lines $x = -\pi/2 + 2n\pi (n = 0, \pm 1, \ldots)$ map into the u-axis, $u \leq -1$.
19. $\int e^{ax} \cos bx\, dx = [e^{ax}/(a^2 + b^2)](a \cos bx + b \sin bx) + C, \quad \int e^{ax} \sin bx\, dx = [e^{ax}/(a^2 + b^2)](a \sin bx - b \cos bx) + C$

Article 17–8, p. 855

1. a) $\ln (2^{3/2}) - i(\pi/4)$ **b)** $\ln 2 + i(\pi/6)$ **c)** $\ln 4 + i\pi$ **d)** $\ln 4$ **e)** $\ln 2 + i(\pi/2)$ **f)** $i(\pi/2)$
2. a) $\ln 2 + 2n\pi i$ **b)** $\ln 2 + (2n + 1)\pi i$ **c)** $\ln 2 + (2n + \frac{1}{2})\pi i$ **d)** $\ln 2 + (2n - \frac{1}{2})\pi i$ **e)** $\ln 2 + (2n + \frac{5}{6})\pi i$ $(n = 0, \pm 1, \pm 2, \ldots)$
4. b) $((\pi/2) + 2n\pi) - i \ln (3 + 2\sqrt{2})$
5. a) The image is a straight line segment joining the points $(\ln |z|, -\pi)$ and $(\ln |z|, +\pi)$. **b)** The image is the line $v = \arg z$, parallel to the real axis.

Miscellaneous Problems Chapter 17, pp. 855–856

1. $z = 2 - 2i, \bar{z} = 2 + 2i, z^2 = -8i$; $2 \text{ cis } (-\pi/6), 2 \text{ cis } (\pi/2), 2 \text{ cis } (7\pi/6)$
2. a) $r = 4\sqrt{2}, \theta = -\tan^{-1} (2 + \sqrt{3})$ **b)** $r = \sqrt{2}, \theta = -\pi/12, 7\pi/12, 15\pi/12$
3. a) $\pm(\sqrt{2 + \sqrt{2}} - i\sqrt{2 - \sqrt{2}}), \pm(\sqrt{2 - \sqrt{2}} + i\sqrt{2 + \sqrt{2}})$ **b)** $\sin^{-1} 5 = 2n\pi + \pi/2 - i \ln (5 + \sqrt{24}), (n = 0, \pm 1, \pm 2, \ldots)$
4. a) $\pm\sqrt{2}(1 + i), \pm\sqrt{2}(1 - i)$ **b)** $2e^{i(2n\pi + \pi)/5}$ $(n = 0, 1, 2, 3, 4)$
5. a) $2^{1/4}e^{i\pi(2 + 3n)/6}$ $(n = 0, 1, 2, 3)$ **b)** $e^2/\sqrt{2} + i(e^2/\sqrt{2})$ **6. a)** $\pm(\sqrt{3} - i)$ **b)** $\ln 4 - i\pi/3$ **7.** $r = 5, \theta = \tan^{-1} \frac{4}{3}$
8. $\ln (3\sqrt{2}) + i(2n\pi - \pi/4)$ (n any integer) **9.** $\ln 2 - i\pi/3$

10. a) $2^{1/3}(-1-i)$, $2^{5/6}(\sqrt{2+\sqrt{3}}-i\sqrt{2-\sqrt{3}})$, $2^{-(5/6)}(-\sqrt{2-\sqrt{3}}+i\sqrt{2+\sqrt{3}})$
b) $\ln(3\sqrt{2})+i(2n\pi+\pi/4)$ (n any integer) **c)** $-e^2$ **11. b)** Derivative doesn't exist.
19. a) $2e^{i2n\pi/5}$ ($n=0, 1, 2, 3, 4$) **b)** $\ln 2+(2n+1)\pi i$ (n any integer)
c) $2n\pi \pm i\cosh^{-1}(10)$, or $2n\pi+i\ln(10\pm 3\sqrt{11})$ (n any integer) **d)** $\ln\sqrt{3}+(2n+1)\pi i/2$ (n any integer)
e) $e^{-(4n+1)\pi/2}$ (n any integer) **f)** -3, $\pm i\sqrt{3}$

CHAPTER 18

Article 18–3, pp. 861–862

1. $(x^2+1)(2y-3)=C$ **2.** $2/3\sqrt{x^3+1}+\frac{1}{2}\ln(y^2+1)=C$ **3.** $e^y=e^x+C$ **4.** $y^{3/2}=3\sqrt{x/2}+C$
5. $\sinh 2y-2\cos x=C$ **6.** $\frac{1}{2}(\ln|x|)^2=\ln|y|+C$ **7.** $(y-1)e^y+(x^2/2)+\ln|x|=C$ **8.** $\sqrt{2x^2+3}-2\sqrt{4-y^2}=C$
9. $\cosh^{-1}y+\sinh^{-1}x=C$ **10.** $-y\cos y+\sin y=-x^{-1}+\ln|x|+C$ **11.** $2^{48}\approx 2.815\times 10^{14}$ **12.** $Q=Q_0e^{kt}$
13. $i=(E/R)(1-e^{-Rt/L})$, E/R **15. a)** $(\ln 2)/5700\approx 1.216\times 10^{-4}$ **b)** 18,935 years **c)** 6,658 years

Article 18–4, p. 864

1. $x^2(x^2+2y^2)=C$ **2.** $x/y=\ln|x|+C$ **3.** $\ln|x|+e^{-(y/x)}=C$ **4.** $2\tan^{-1}(y/x)+\ln(x^2+y^2)=C$
5. $\ln|x|-\ln|\sec((y/x)-1)+\tan((y/x)-1)|=C$ **6.** $x\sin(y/x)=C$
7. $\ln((x+2)^2+(y-1)^2)+2\tan^{-1}((x+2)/(y-1))=C$, $a=-2$, $b=1$ **8.** $\tan^{-1}(x+y)=x+C$
9. a) $x^2=yC$ **b)** $x^2+2y^2=C$ **10. a)** $x^2+y^2=Cx$ **b)** $x^2+y^2=Cy$ **11.** $x^2-y^2=C$

Article 18–5, p. 866

1. $y=e^{-x}+Ce^{-2x}$ **2.** $y=\frac{1}{2}(x+C)e^{x/2}$ **3.** $x^3y=C-\cos x$ **4.** $xy=C-\cos x$ **5.** $x=(y/2)+(C/y)$
6. $(x-1)^4y=(x^3/3)-x+C$ **7.** $y\cosh x=C-e^x$ **8.** $xe^{2y}=y^2+C$ **9.** $xy=y^2+C$ **10.** $x=(C-y)/(1+y^2)$
11. a) $C=G/100kV+(C_0-G/100kV)e^{-kt}$ **b)** $G/100kV$

Article 18–6, p. 868

1. $y=Cx^2-x$ **2.** $xy=C$ **3.** $y=Cx$ **4.** $(x^2/2)+xy+(y^3/3)=C$ **5.** $e^x+e^y(x^2+1)=C$ **6.** $x^2y+xy^2-(y^2/2)=C$
7. $x^2+2x\sqrt{y^2+1}-y^2=C$ **8.** $2y+x^3=Cx$ **9.** $y=x\tan(x+C)$ **10.** $y=x(C-x-\ln|x|)$
11. $e^x+x\ln y+y\ln x-\cos y=C$ **12.** $y^2\tan^{-1}x-2xy+\cosh y=C$ **13.** $xy+\cos x=C$

Article 18–7, p. 870

1. $y=C_1e^{-x}+C_2$ **2.** $y=C$, or $y=-2a\tan(ax+C)$, or $y=2a\tanh(ax+C)$, or $y=2/(x+C)$
3. $y=C_1\int e^{-x^2/2}\,dx+C_2$. Note that the integral appearing here could be evaluated as an infinite series, giving
$y=C_1[x-[x^3/(2\cdot 3)]+[x^5/(2\cdot 4\cdot 5)]-[x^7/(2\cdot 4\cdot 6\cdot 7)]+\cdots]+C_2$
4. $y=C_1\ln|x|+C_2$ **5.** $y=C_1\sinh(x+C_2)$ **6.** $y=C_1\sin(\omega x+C_2)$ **7.** $y=C_1x^4+C_2x+C_3$
8. $y=-2\ln|e^{-x/2}-C_1e^{x/2}|+C_2$; or $x=\pm\ln|(u-1)/(u+1)|+C_2$, where $u=(1+C_1e^y)^{1/2}$
9. $x=A\sin(\sqrt{k/m}\,t+(\pi/2))=A\cos(\sqrt{k/m}\,t)$
10. $s=(m^2g/k^2)[(kt/m)+e^{-kt/m}-1]$, where m is the man's mass, g is the acceleration due to gravity, and k is the factor of proportionality in the air resistance $-kv$ (v being velocity).

Article 18–9, p. 874

1. $y=C_1+C_2e^{-2x}$ **2.** $y=C_1e^{-2x}+C_2e^{-3x}$ **3.** $y=C_1e^{-x}+C_2e^{-5x}$ **4.** $y=C_1e^{3x}+C_2e^{-x}$
5. $y=e^{-x/2}[C_1\cos(x\sqrt{3}/2)+C_2\sin(x\sqrt{3}/2)]$ **6.** $y=(C_1+C_2x)e^{2x}$ **7.** $y=(C_1+C_2x)e^{-3x}$
8. $y=e^{3x}(C_1\cos x+C_2\sin x)$ **9.** $y=e^x(C_1\cos\sqrt{3}x+C_2\sin\sqrt{3}x)$ **10.** $y=C_1e^{2x}+C_2e^{8x}$

Article 18–10, p. 877

1. $y=(x^2/2)-x+C_1+C_2e^{-x}$ **2.** $y=-\cos x\sinh^{-1}(\tan x)+C_1\cos x+C_2\sin x$
3. $y=-\frac{1}{2}x\cos x+C_1\cos x+C_2\sin x$
4. $y=\frac{1}{4}e^x+e^{-x}(C_1+C_2x)$ **5.** $y=e^{-x}(C_1+C_2x+\frac{1}{2}x^2)$ **6.** $y=C_1e^x+C_2e^{-x}-x$ **7.** $y=C_1e^x+C_2e^{-x}+(x/2)e^x$
8. $y=C_1e^x+C_2e^{-x}-\frac{1}{2}\sin x$ **9.** $y=e^{-2x}(C_1\cos x+C_2\sin x)+2$ **10.** $y=e^{-2x}(C_1\cos x+C_2\sin x)+\frac{1}{5}x+\frac{6}{25}$
11. $y=1-e^{-x}$ **12.** $y=[x^2+2x+2+Ce^x]^{-1}$

Article 18–11, p. 878

1. $y = C_1 + C_2 e^x + C_3 e^{2x}$ **2.** $y = C_1 e^x + e^{-x/2}[C_2 \cos(x\sqrt{3}/2) + C_3 \sin(x\sqrt{3}/2)]$
3. $y = (C_1 + C_2 x)e^{\sqrt{2}x} + (C_3 + C_4 x)e^{-\sqrt{2}x}$ **4.** $y = C_1 e^{2x} + C_2 e^{-2x} + C_3 \cos 2x + C_4 \sin 2x$
5. $y = e^{\sqrt{2}x}(C_1 \cos\sqrt{2}x + C_2 \sin\sqrt{2}x) + e^{-\sqrt{2}x}(C_3 \cos\sqrt{2}x + C_4 \sin\sqrt{2}x)$
6. $y = e^x((x^2/6) + C_1 x + C_2) + C_3 e^{-2x}$ **7.** $y = (C_1 + C_2 x + C_3 x^2 + C_4 x^3)e^x + 7$
8. $y = e^{x/\sqrt{2}}(C_1 \cos(x/\sqrt{2}) + C_2 \sin(x/\sqrt{2})) + e^{-x/\sqrt{2}}(C_3 \cos(x/\sqrt{2}) + C_4 \sin(x/\sqrt{2})) + x + 1$

Article 18–12, pp. 882–883

1. $x = x_0 \cos\omega t + (v_0/\omega)\sin\omega t = \sqrt{x_0^2 + (v_0^2/\omega^2)}\sin(\omega t + \phi)$, where $\omega = \sqrt{k/m}$, $\phi = \tan^{-1}(\omega x_0/v_0)$
2. $x = 0.288 \sin(13.9t)$; x in feet, t in sec
3. a) $I = C_1 \cos\omega t + C_2 \sin\omega t$ **b)** $I = C_1 \cos\omega t + C_2 \sin\omega t + (A\alpha/L(\omega^2 - \alpha^2))\cos\alpha t$
c) $I = C_1 \cos\omega t + C_2 \sin\omega t + (A/2L)t \sin\omega t$ **d)** $I = e^{-5t}(C_1 \cos 149t + C_2 \sin 149t)$
4. $\theta = \theta_0 \cos(\sqrt{g/\ell}\,t)$ **5.** $\theta = \theta_0 \cos\omega t + (v_0/\omega)\sin\omega t$, where $\omega = \sqrt{2k/mr^2}$ **6.** $C = 5.1$ lb sec/ft.
7. a) $x = C_1 \cos\omega t + C_2 \sin\omega t + (\omega^2 A/(\omega^2 - \alpha^2))\sin\alpha t$, where $\omega = \sqrt{k/m}$
b) $x = C_1 \cos\omega t + C_2 \sin\omega t - (\omega A/2)t\cos\omega t$, with $\omega = \sqrt{k/m}$

Article 18–13, pp. 889–890

3. Min at $t = 0$; max at $\lambda t = 2$; inflection points at $\lambda t = 2 - \sqrt{2}, 2 + \sqrt{2}$. **5. a)** $e^{-10} = 0.000045$ **b)** $1 - e^{-4} = 0.9817$
6. a) 0.67 **b)** 0.33 **c)** 0.98 **7. a)** 10 **b)** $e^{-10}\sum_{n=0}^{5}[(10)^n/n!] \approx 0.067$
8. a) 0.270 **b)** 0.180 **c)** 0.368 **d)** 0.073 **9.** 0.195

Miscellaneous Problems Chapter 18, pp. 890–891

1. $\ln(C\ln y) = -\tan^{-1}x$ **2.** $y = [Cx^3 + 2(x+1)^3][(x+1)^3 - Cx^3]^{-1}$ **3.** $y = \ln(C - \frac{1}{3}e^{-3x})$ **4.** $ky + \sqrt{k^2y^2 - 1} = Ce^{kx}$
5. $y^2 + \sqrt{y^4 + 1} = Ce^{2x}$ **6.** $x^2 + xy - y^2 = C$ **7.** $y^2 = x^2 + Cx$ **8.** $y + \sqrt{x^2 + y^2} = Cx^2$ **9.** $y = x\tan^{-1}(\ln Cx)$
10. $y = xe^{\sqrt{2\ln Cx}}$ **11.** $y = (x^2 + 2)/4 + Cx^{-2}$ **12.** $y - x\sec y = C$ **13.** $y = \cosh x \ln(C\cosh x)$
14. $y = \frac{1}{6}(2x^3 + 3x^2 + C)(x+1)^{-2}$ **15.** $y^3 + 3xy^2 + 3(x + y) = C$ **16.** $x^3 + 3xy + 3e^y = C$ **17.** $x^3 + 3xy^2 + 3\sinh y = C$
18. $e^x + x\ln y + y = C$ **19.** $x^2 + e^y(x^2 + y^2 - 2y + 2) = C$ **20.** $2x\tan^{-1}(y/x) + y\ln(x^2 + y^2) - 2\cos x - (y+1)^2 = C$
21. $y = C$, or $y = a\tan(ax + C)$, or $y = -a\tanh(ax + C)$, or $y = -1/(x + C)$ **22.** $x = C_1\cos 2y + C_2 \sin 2y$
23. $y = -\ln|\cos(x + C)| + D$ **24.** $x = \pm(y + C)$, or $x + C_2 = \ln\cosh(y + C_1)$, or $x + C_2 = \ln\sinh(y + C_1)$
25. $y = \frac{1}{2}(\ln Cx)^2 + D$ **26.** $y = C_1e^x + C_2e^{3x}$ **27.** $y = C_1 + (C_2x + C_3)e^x$ **28.** $y = C_1\sin 2x + C_2\cos 2x + (x/2)\sin 2x + \frac{1}{4}\cos 2x \ln\cos 2x$ **29.** $y = C_1e^{-x} + (C_2 + x/3)e^{2x}$ **30.** $y = e^x(C_1\cos 2x + C_2\sin 2x) + \frac{1}{8}e^{-x}$ **31.** $y = C_1\sqrt{x} + C_2/\sqrt{x}$
33. $\frac{3}{2}x^2 + y^2 = D$ **34.** $x^2 + (y - D)^2 = D^2$ **35.** $y^2 = D^2 + 2Dx$ **36.** $y = 10\cos 10t + 5\sin 10t$

APPENDIX

Article A–1, pp. A–3 to A–4

1. $\begin{bmatrix} 2 & -3 & 4 \\ 6 & 4 & -2 \\ 1 & 5 & 4 \end{bmatrix}\begin{bmatrix} x \\ y \\ z \end{bmatrix} = \begin{bmatrix} -19 \\ 8 \\ 23 \end{bmatrix}$ **3.** $\begin{bmatrix} a_{21} & a_{22} & a_{23} \\ a_{11} & a_{12} & a_{13} \\ a_{31} & a_{32} & a_{33} \end{bmatrix}$ **4.** $\begin{bmatrix} a_{12} & a_{11} & a_{13} \\ a_{22} & a_{21} & a_{23} \\ a_{32} & a_{31} & a_{33} \end{bmatrix}$

Article A–2, p. A–8

1. a) $\begin{bmatrix} -3 & 2 \\ 2 & -1 \end{bmatrix}$ **b)** $\begin{bmatrix} 1 & -1 & \frac{1}{3} \\ 0 & \frac{1}{2} & -\frac{2}{3} \\ 0 & 0 & \frac{1}{3} \end{bmatrix}$ **3. a)** $\begin{bmatrix} \frac{1}{5} & \frac{1}{5} \\ -\frac{3}{5} & \frac{2}{5} \end{bmatrix}$ **b)** $\begin{bmatrix} \frac{1}{5} & -\frac{3}{5} \\ \frac{1}{5} & \frac{2}{5} \end{bmatrix}$. Yes.

4. $x = -2, y = 5, z = 0$ **5.** $x = \frac{12}{5} + \frac{1}{5}z$, $y = -\frac{1}{5} + \frac{12}{5}z$

Article A–3, p. A–11

1. a) $2 \cdot \begin{vmatrix} 0 & 3 \\ 2 & 1 \end{vmatrix} + 1 \cdot \begin{vmatrix} 1 & 3 \\ 0 & 1 \end{vmatrix} + 2 \cdot \begin{vmatrix} 1 & 0 \\ 0 & 2 \end{vmatrix} = -7$ **b)** $1 \cdot \begin{vmatrix} 1 & 3 \\ 0 & 1 \end{vmatrix} + 0 \cdot \begin{vmatrix} 2 & 2 \\ 0 & 1 \end{vmatrix} - 2 \cdot \begin{vmatrix} 2 & 2 \\ 1 & 3 \end{vmatrix} = -7$

Article A–4, p. A–12

1. -5 **2.** 0 **3.** 1 **4.** 2

Article A–5, p. A–14

1. $\begin{bmatrix} -3 & 2 \\ 2 & -1 \end{bmatrix}$ **2.** $\begin{bmatrix} -\frac{1}{3} & \frac{1}{3} & 0 \\ \frac{1}{4} & \frac{1}{4} & -\frac{1}{4} \\ \frac{1}{6} & -\frac{1}{6} & \frac{1}{2} \end{bmatrix}$ **3.** $\begin{bmatrix} \frac{1}{2} & -\frac{1}{4} & -\frac{1}{8} & -\frac{1}{16} \\ 0 & \frac{1}{2} & -\frac{1}{4} & -\frac{1}{8} \\ 0 & 0 & \frac{1}{2} & -\frac{1}{4} \\ 0 & 0 & 0 & \frac{1}{2} \end{bmatrix}$

INDEX

Note. Numbers in parentheses refer to exercises on the pages indicated.

65. $\displaystyle\int \frac{\cos ax}{\sin ax}\,dx = \frac{1}{a}\ln|\sin ax| + C$

66. $\displaystyle\int \cos^n ax \sin ax\,dx = -\frac{\cos^{n+1} ax}{(n+1)a} + C, \qquad n \neq -1$

67. $\displaystyle\int \frac{\sin ax}{\cos ax}\,dx = -\frac{1}{a}\ln|\cos ax| + C$

68. $\displaystyle\int \sin^n ax \cos^m ax\,dx = -\frac{\sin^{n-1} ax \cos^{m+1} ax}{a(m+n)} + \frac{n-1}{m+n}\int \sin^{n-2} ax \cos^m ax\,dx,$

$n \neq -m \qquad$ (If $n = -m$, use No. 86.)

69. $\displaystyle\int \sin^n ax \cos^m ax\,dx = \frac{\sin^{n+1} ax \cos^{m-1} ax}{a(m+n)} + \frac{m-1}{m+n}\int \sin^n ax \cos^{m-2} ax\,dx;$

$m \neq -n \qquad$ (If $m = -n$, use No. 87.)

70. $\displaystyle\int \frac{dx}{b + c\sin ax} = \frac{-2}{a\sqrt{b^2 - c^2}}\tan^{-1}\left[\sqrt{\frac{b-c}{b+c}}\tan\left(\frac{\pi}{4} - \frac{ax}{2}\right)\right] + C, \qquad b^2 > c^2$

71. $\displaystyle\int \frac{dx}{b + c\sin ax} = \frac{-1}{a\sqrt{c^2 - b^2}}\ln\left|\frac{c + b\sin ax + \sqrt{c^2 - b^2}\cos ax}{b + c\sin ax}\right| + C, \qquad b^2 < c^2$

72. $\displaystyle\int \frac{dx}{1 + \sin ax} = -\frac{1}{a}\tan\left(\frac{\pi}{4} - \frac{ax}{2}\right) + C$

73. $\displaystyle\int \frac{dx}{1 - \sin ax} = \frac{1}{a}\tan\left(\frac{\pi}{4} + \frac{ax}{2}\right) + C$

74. $\displaystyle\int \frac{dx}{b + c\cos ax} = \frac{2}{a\sqrt{b^2 - c^2}}\tan^{-1}\left[\sqrt{\frac{b-c}{b+c}}\tan\frac{ax}{2}\right] + C, \qquad b^2 > c^2$

75. $\displaystyle\int \frac{dx}{b + c\cos ax} = \frac{1}{a\sqrt{c^2 - b^2}}\ln\left|\frac{c + b\cos ax + \sqrt{c^2 - b^2}\sin ax}{b + c\cos ax}\right| + C, \qquad b^2 < c^2$

76. $\displaystyle\int \frac{dx}{1 + \cos ax} = \frac{1}{a}\tan\frac{ax}{2} + C$

77. $\displaystyle\int \frac{dx}{1 - \cos ax} = -\frac{1}{a}\cot\frac{ax}{2} + C$

78. $\displaystyle\int x\sin ax\,dx = \frac{1}{a^2}\sin ax - \frac{x}{a}\cos ax + C$

79. $\displaystyle\int x\cos ax\,dx = \frac{1}{a^2}\cos ax + \frac{x}{a}\sin ax + C$

80. $\displaystyle\int x^n \sin ax\,dx = -\frac{x^n}{a}\cos ax + \frac{n}{a}\int x^{n-1}\cos ax\,dx$

81. $\displaystyle\int x^n \cos ax\,dx = \frac{x^n}{a}\sin ax - \frac{n}{a}\int x^{n-1}\sin ax\,dx$

82. $\displaystyle\int \tan ax\,dx = -\frac{1}{a}\ln|\cos ax| + C$

83. $\displaystyle\int \cot ax\,dx = \frac{1}{a}\ln|\sin ax| + C$

84. $\displaystyle\int \tan^2 ax\,dx = \frac{1}{a}\tan ax - x + C$

85. $\displaystyle\int \cot^2 ax\,dx = -\frac{1}{a}\cot ax - x + C$

86. $\displaystyle\int \tan^n ax\,dx = \frac{\tan^{n-1} ax}{a(n-1)} - \int \tan^{n-2} ax\,dx, \qquad n \neq 1$

87. $\displaystyle\int \cot^n ax\,dx = -\frac{\cot^{n-1} ax}{a(n-1)} - \int \cot^{n-2} ax\,dx, \qquad n \neq 1$

88. $\displaystyle\int \sec ax\,dx = \frac{1}{a}\ln|\sec ax + \tan ax| + C$

89. $\displaystyle\int \csc ax\,dx = -\frac{1}{a}\ln|\csc ax + \cot ax| + C$

Continued overleaf.

90. $\int \sec^2 ax\,dx = \frac{1}{a}\tan ax + C$

91. $\int \csc^2 ax\,dx = -\frac{1}{a}\cot ax + C$

92. $\int \sec^n ax\,dx = \frac{\sec^{n-2} ax \tan ax}{a(n-1)} + \frac{n-2}{n-1}\int \sec^{n-2} ax\,dx, \qquad n \neq 1$

93. $\int \csc^n ax\,dx = -\frac{\csc^{n-2} ax \cot ax}{a(n-1)} + \frac{n-2}{n-1}\int \csc^{n-2} ax\,dx, \qquad n \neq 1$

94. $\int \sec^n ax \tan ax\,dx = \frac{\sec^n ax}{na} + C, \qquad n \neq 0$

95. $\int \csc^n ax \cot ax\,dx = -\frac{\csc^n ax}{na} + C, \qquad n \neq 0$

96. $\int \sin^{-1} ax\,dx = x\sin^{-1} ax + \frac{1}{a}\sqrt{1-a^2x^2} + C$

97. $\int \cos^{-1} ax\,dx = x\cos^{-1} ax - \frac{1}{a}\sqrt{1-a^2x^2} + C$

98. $\int \tan^{-1} ax\,dx = x\tan^{-1} ax - \frac{1}{2a}\ln(1+a^2x^2) + C$

99. $\int x^n \sin^{-1} ax\,dx = \frac{x^{n+1}}{n+1}\sin^{-1} ax - \frac{a}{n+1}\int \frac{x^{n+1}\,dx}{\sqrt{1-a^2x^2}}, \qquad n \neq -1$

100. $\int x^n \cos^{-1} ax\,dx = \frac{x^{n+1}}{n+1}\cos^{-1} ax + \frac{a}{n+1}\int \frac{x^{n+1}\,dx}{\sqrt{1-a^2x^2}}, \qquad n \neq -1$

101. $\int x^n \tan^{-1} ax\,dx = \frac{x^{n+1}}{n+1}\tan^{-1} ax - \frac{a}{n+1}\int \frac{x^{n+1}\,dx}{1+a^2x^2}, \qquad n \neq -1$

102. $\int e^{ax}\,dx = \frac{1}{a}e^{ax} + C$

103. $\int b^{ax}\,dx = \frac{1}{a}\frac{b^{ax}}{\ln b} + C, \qquad b > 0, \quad b \neq 1$

104. $\int xe^{ax}\,dx = \frac{e^{ax}}{a^2}(ax-1) + C$

105. $\int x^n e^{ax}\,dx = \frac{1}{a}x^n e^{ax} - \frac{n}{a}\int x^{n-1}e^{ax}\,dx$

106. $\int x^n b^{ax}\,dx = \frac{x^n b^{ax}}{a\ln b} - \frac{n}{a\ln b}\int x^{n-1}b^{ax}\,dx, \qquad b > 0, \quad b \neq 1$

107. $\int e^{ax}\sin bx\,dx = \frac{e^{ax}}{a^2+b^2}(a\sin bx - b\cos bx) + C$

108. $\int e^{ax}\cos bx\,dx = \frac{e^{ax}}{a^2+b^2}(a\cos bx + b\sin bx) + C$

109. $\int \ln ax\,dx = x\ln ax - x + C$

110. $\int x^n \ln ax\,dx = \frac{x^{n+1}}{n+1}\ln ax - \frac{x^{n+1}}{(n+1)^2} + C, \qquad n \neq -1$

111. $\int x^{-1}\ln ax\,dx = \frac{1}{2}(\ln ax)^2 + C$

112. $\int \frac{dx}{x\ln ax} = \ln|\ln ax| + C$

113. $\int \sinh ax\,dx = \frac{1}{a}\cosh ax + C$

114. $\int \cosh ax\,dx = \frac{1}{a}\sinh ax + C$

115. $\int \sinh^2 ax\,dx = \frac{\sinh 2ax}{4a} - \frac{x}{2} + C$

116. $\int \cosh^2 ax\,dx = \frac{\sinh 2ax}{4a} + \frac{x}{2} + C$

117. $\int \sinh^n ax\,dx = \frac{\sinh^{n-1} ax \cosh ax}{na} - \frac{n-1}{n}\int \sinh^{n-2} ax\,dx, \qquad n \neq 0$